HAR
and HOLBORN

Sociology

Themes and
Perspectives

COLLINS

fifth edition

Published by HarperCollins *Publishers* Limited
77–85 Fulham Palace Road
Hammersmith
London W6 8JB

www.CollinsEducation.com
On-line Support for Schools and Colleges

First Edition published in 1980 by University Tutorial Press
Second Edition published in 1985 by University Tutorial Press
Third Edition published in 1990 by Unwin Hyman Ltd
Fourth Edition published in 1995 by Collins Educational

British Library Cataloguing in Publication Data
A catalogue record for this publication
is available from the British Library.

ISBN 000 327507 8

Commissioned by Emma Dunlop
Edited by Sarah Pearsall
Text and cover design by Patricia Briggs
Typesetting and artwork by Hardlines Illustration and Design
Picture research by Ginny Stroud-Lewis and Helen Desmond
Printed and bound by Scotprint, Musselburgh

Picture credits: Skyscan Balloon Photography (p. 1); Bob Watkins/Photofusion
(p. 22); David Montford/Photofusion (p. 126); Ian Waldie/Popperfoto (p. 198);
Benetton/Colors (pp. 248 and 249); Stefen Schmidt/Popperfoto (p. 290);
ACE Photo Agency (p. 347); Lee Jae-Won/Popperfoto (p. 430); Tim Dub/
Photofusion (p. 502); Mark Campbell/Photofusion (p. 587); Gary L. Benson/
Tony Stone Images (p. 684); Joanne O'Brien/Format (p. 773); Ian Waldie/
Popperfoto (p. 883); The Bridgeman Art Library (pp. 893 and 894 (×2));
T&J Florian/ACE photo agency (p. 934); Andy Sacks/Tony Stone Images (p. 964);
Thomas Brase/Tony Stone Images (p. 1031).

You might also like to visit:

www.fireandwater.com
The book lover's website

Contents

Preface to the fifth edition

Sociology: Themes and Perspectives was first published in 1980 and aimed to provide a systematic introduction to sociology for UK A level students, undergraduates and the general reader. Since then, in its various editions, it has sold around one million copies worldwide. This edition aims to build on the success of previous editions and it has been improved in a number of ways. There are two entirely new chapters on Culture and identity and Communication and the media, as well as extensive updates of existing chapters. This edition takes full account of theoretical and empirical developments in the subject, with substantial coverage of what has been called the 'cultural turn' in sociology and issues such as postmodernism and globalization. For the first time the book is published in two colours and the referencing has been much improved.

The division of labour for the writing of the various editions was as follows. Mike Haralambos wrote the first two editions, with Robin Heald as the co-author of the Organizations and bureaucracy chapter (no longer a separate chapter in the fifth edition). Martin Holborn wrote all the new material for the third, fourth and fifth editions, with the exception of the chapter on Communication and the media in the latest edition, which was written by Paul Trowler. Many thanks to Paul Trowler for contributing an excellent media chapter at such short notice.

A̲p̲a̲r̲t̲ ̲f̲r̲om the authors, many people contribute to t̲h̲e̲ ̲p̲r̲o̲d̲u̲c̲t̲i̲on of a book. The authors would like to t̲h̲a̲n̲k̲ ̲f̲r̲i̲ends and colleagues whose encouragement and enthusiasm have contributed a great deal to the different editions. Thanks to Jim O'Gorman, Liz Ronayne, Morag Campbell, Lata Patel, Joan Blake, Linda Barton, Alison Robinson, Frances Smith, Christine Robinson, Peter Adamson, Dave Beddow, Maurice Gavan, Vincent Farrell, Pauline Cowburn

and Terry Richards. Many thanks also to those who provided skilful editorial support for previous editions: Chris Kingston, Simon Boyd, Josephine Warrior, Pat McNeill and Emma Dunlop. For this edition Emma Dunlop initiated the project and Patricia Briggs played an invaluable role in coordinating it. Pat McNeill provided very useful and perceptive editorial comments, and Sarah Pearsall edited the manuscript with great precision and a tremendous eye for detail. The authors would also like to thank the academic experts who commented on particular chapters and made suggestions for changes.

Mike Haralambos would like to thank Pauline for her unwavering support and encouragement over the four years that it took to write the original manuscript. She took over the many responsibilities and remained cheerful and optimistic when it seemed as though the book would never be completed. He would also like to thank Barbara Grimshaw and Jean Buckley for typing the original manuscript.

Martin Holborn would like to thank Emma Holborn for her love and support during the writing of the fourth and fifth editions. Writing the fifth edition was only possible because she took so much of the responsibility for looking after our boys, Henry and Ted. Thanks to Emma, Henry and Ted for cheering me up when the burden of writing was getting me down.

Finally, thanks again to everybody who has read the book over the last twenty years. We hope it will continue to encourage people to study this fascinating subject further for some time to come.

Martin Holborn
Mike Haralambos
January 2000

Sociological perspectives

Sociological perspectives

Introduction

'Human beings learn their behaviour and use their intelligence whereas animals simply act on instinct.' Like most commonsense notions, this idea has an element of truth, but reality is far more complex.

The regimented society of social insects such as ants and bees is an object lesson in order and organization. Every member has clearly defined tasks in a cooperative enterprise. Thus in a beehive the worker bees, depending on their age, will either feed the young, stand guard and repel strangers, forage for food, or ventilate the hive by beating their wings. The behaviour of insects is largely 'instinctive', it is based on programmes contained in the genes which direct their actions. However, it would be a mistake to assume that the behaviour of insects is based *solely* on instinct. Experiments have indicated that at least some have the ability to learn. For example, ants are able to memorize the path through a maze and are capable of applying this learning to other mazes.

Moving on from insects to reptiles, and on again to mammals, the importance of learned, as opposed to genetically determined, behaviour gradually increases. Studies of macaque monkeys on islands in northern Japan provide some indication of the importance of learned behaviour. On one island the macaques were living in the forested interior. Japanese scientists attempted to discover whether they could change the behaviour patterns of the troupe. They began by dumping potatoes in a clearing in the forest. Gradually the macaques changed their eating habits until they became largely dependent on potatoes – a food previously unknown to them – as their staple diet. The scientists slowly moved the food dumps towards the shoreline and the troupe followed. The potatoes were then regularly placed on the beach, which now became the normal habitat for the macaques.

In the following months, without any encouragement from the scientists, a number of new behaviour patterns emerged in the troupe. First, some members began washing the potatoes in the sea before eating them. Others followed suit until it became standard practice in the group. Then some of the younger macaques began paddling in the sea and eventually took the plunge and learned how to swim. They were imitated by their elders and, again, the novel behaviour of the few became the accepted behaviour of the group. Finally, some adventurous youngsters began diving off low rocky outcroppings on the shoreline, a practice which was copied by other members of the troupe.

The Japanese macaques had learned new behaviour patterns and these patterns were shared by members of the group. The simple generalization that animal behaviour is genetically determined whereas the behaviour of humans is learned is clearly incorrect. However, the range and complexity of learned behaviour in humans are far greater than in any other species. This is shown by experiments with humanity's nearest living relative, the chimpanzee. When chimpanzees are raised in human households, for the first few years they learn at the same rate as human infants of the same age, but they soon reach the limit of their ability and are rapidly overtaken by human youngsters. Compared to mammals other than humans, chimpanzees have a considerable learning capacity. They can solve simple problems in order to obtain food, they can learn a basic sign language to communicate with humans, and they can even ape their more intelligent cousins in the famous chimpanzee tea party. Yet, despite this capacity to learn, the behavioural repertoire of chimpanzees is rudimentary and limited compared to the behaviour of people.

More than any other species, humans rely for their survival on behaviour patterns that are learned. Humans have no instincts, that is they have no genetically programmed directives to behave in particular ways. An instinct involves not only the impulse to do something, but also specific instructions on how to do it. Birds have an instinct to build nests. They have an impulse for nest building and all members of a particular species are programmed to build nests in the same way.

If we look at the range and variety of dwellings constructed by humans we can see that there are no directives based on instinct. The following examples from nineteenth-century North America provide an illustration. In the Arctic, the Eskimos constructed igloos from rectangular blocks cut from closely compacted snow. On the north-west coast of the USA and the west coast of Canada, tribes such as the Nootka built oblong houses with a framework of cedar logs, walled and roofed with planks. On the opposite side of the subcontinent, in the eastern woodlands, the Iroquois also lived in oblong dwellings, known as 'long houses', but they substituted birch bark for planks. On the prairies, the easily transportable conical tipi made from long saplings covered in buffalo hides provided shelter for tribes such as the Sioux and Cheyenne. Further south, the Apache of Arizona and New Mexico lived in domed wickiups made from brushwood and scrub. In the same area, tribes such as the Zuñi and the Hopi built the first apartment houses in the USA. Even today many members of these tribes live in multi-occupation dwellings made from sun-dried mud bricks known as adobe. These examples show clearly that the human genetic code does not contain specific instructions to behave in a particular way – at least as far as housebuilding is concerned.

Culture and society

To all intents and purposes a newborn human baby is helpless. Not only is it physically dependent on older members of the species but it also lacks the behaviour patterns necessary for living in human society. It relies primarily on certain biological drives, such as hunger, and on the charity of its elders to satisfy those drives. The infant has a lot to learn. In order to survive, it must learn the skills, knowledge and accepted ways of behaving of the society into which it is born. It must learn a way of life; in sociological terminology, it must learn the culture of its society.

Ralph Linton states that 'The culture of a society is the way of life of its members; the collection of ideas and habits which they learn, share and transmit from generation to generation.' In Clyde Kluckhohn's elegant phrase, culture is a 'design for living' held by members of a particular society. Since humans have no instincts to direct their actions, their behaviour must be based on guidelines that are learned. In order for a society to operate effectively, these guidelines must be shared by its members. Without a shared culture, members of society would be unable to communicate and cooperate, and confusion and disorder would result. Culture therefore has two essential qualities: first, it is learned, second, it is shared. Without it there would be no human society.

Culture and behaviour

To a large degree culture determines how members of society think and feel: it directs their actions and defines their outlook on life. Members of society usually take their culture for granted. It has become so much a part of them that they are often unaware of its existence. The following example given by Edward T. Hall (1973) provides an illustration. Two individuals, one from North America, the other from South America, are conversing in a hall 40 feet long. They begin at one end of the hall and finish at the other end, the North American steadily retreating, the South American relentlessly advancing. Each is trying to establish the 'accustomed conversation distance' defined by their own culture. To the North American, the South American comes too close for comfort, whereas the South American feels uneasy conversing at the distance the North American demands. Often it takes meetings such as this to reveal the pervasive nature of culturally determined behaviour.

Culture defines accepted ways of behaving for members of a particular society. Such definitions vary from society to society. This can lead to considerable misunderstanding between members of different societies, as the following example provided by Otto Klineberg shows (Klineberg, 1971). Amongst the Sioux Indians of South Dakota, it is regarded as incorrect to answer a question in the presence of others who do not know the answer. Such behaviour would be regarded as boastful and arrogant, and, since it reveals the ignorance of others, it would be interpreted as an attempt to undermine their confidence and shame them. In addition, the Sioux regard it as wrong to answer a question unless they are absolutely sure of the correct answer. Faced with a classroom of Sioux children, a white American teacher, who is unaware of their culture, might easily interpret their behaviour as a reflection of ignorance, stupidity or hostility.

Every society has certain common problems to deal with: for example the problem of dependent members such as the very young and the very old. However, solutions to such problems are culturally determined: they vary from society to society. The solutions provided in one society may well be regarded as unacceptable by members of other societies.

Under certain circumstances, infanticide (the killing of infants) and geronticide (the killing of old people) have been practised by particular groups of Australian aborigines, Eskimos and Caribou Indians. Particularly in the more arid parts of Australia, female infanticide was practised to reduce the population in times of famine, and occasionally the baby was eaten. In Tasmania aborigine hunters led a nomadic life to take advantage of the seasonal food supply in different regions. The old and infirm who were too feeble to keep up with the band were left behind to die. The Caribou Indians, who lived to the west of Hudson Bay in Canada, were dependent for their food supply on the caribou herds. Sometimes, in winter, the herds failed to appear. To prevent the starvation of the whole community, the following priorities were established. First, the active male adults were fed, because if they were too weak to hunt, nobody would eat. Next, their wives were fed, since they could bear more children. Male infants were considered more important than female because they would grow up to become hunters. Old people were the most expendable and in times of famine they committed suicide by walking naked into the snow. If there were no old people left, girl babies would be killed. The practices of infanticide and geronticide described here are culturally defined behaviour patterns designed to ensure the survival of the group in times of extreme food shortages. Like many of the customs of non-Western societies, they appear strange and even heartless to Westerners, but, in the context of the particular society, they are sensible, rational and an accepted part of life.

The above examples of culturally defined behaviour have been selected because they differ considerably from behaviour patterns in Western society. By looking at examples that appear strange to us as Westerners, it is easier to appreciate the idea that human behaviour is largely determined by culture.

Socialization

The process by which individuals learn the culture of their society is known as socialization. Primary socialization, probably the most important aspect of the socialization process, takes place during infancy, usually within the family. By responding to the approval and disapproval of its parents and copying their example, the child learns the language and many of the basic behaviour patterns of its society. In Western society, other important agencies of social-ization include the educational system, the occupa-

tional group and the peer group (a group whose members share similar circumstances and are often of a similar age). Within its peer group, the young child, by interacting with others and playing childhood games, learns to conform to the accepted ways of a social group and to appreciate the fact that social life is based on rules.

Socialization is not, however, confined to childhood. It is a lifelong process. At the beginning of their working lives, the young bricklayer, teacher and accountant soon learn the rules of the game and the tricks of the trade. Should they change jobs in later life, they will join a different occupational group and may well have to learn new skills and adopt different mannerisms and styles of dress.

Without socialization, an individual would bear little resemblance to any human being defined as normal by the standards of his or her society. The following examples, though they lack the reliability demanded by today's standards of reporting, nevertheless provide some indication of the importance of socialization.

It is reported that Akbar, who was an emperor in India from 1542 to 1602, ordered that a group of children be brought up without any instruction in language, to test the belief that they would eventu-ally speak Hebrew, the language of God. The children were raised by deaf mutes. They developed no spoken language and communicated solely by gestures.

There is also an extensive, though somewhat unreliable, literature on children raised by animals. One of the best-documented cases concerns the so-called 'wolf-children of Midnapore'. Two females, aged 2 and 8, were reportedly found in a wolf den in Bengal in 1920. They walked on all fours, preferred a diet of raw meat, they howled like wolves and lacked any form of speech. Whether these children had been raised by wolves or simply abandoned and left to their own devices in the forest is unclear. However, such examples indicate that socialization involving prolonged interaction with adults is essential not only for fitting new members into society but also to the process of actually becoming human.

Norms and values

Norms

Every culture contains a large number of guidelines that direct conduct in particular situations. Such guidelines are known as norms. A norm is a specific guide to action which defines acceptable and appropriate behaviour in particular situations. For example, in all societies, there are norms governing dress. Members of society generally share norms which define acceptable male and female apparel and appropriate dress for different age groups: for example, in British society, a 70-year-old grandmother dressed as a teenager would contravene the norms for her age group. Norms of dress provide guidelines on what to wear on particular occasions. A formal dance, a funeral, a day out on the beach, a working day in the bank, on the building site or in the hospital – all these situations are governed by norms which specify appropriate attire for the occasion.

Norms of dress vary from society to society. For example, take the case of the male missionary who was presented with bare-breasted African females in his congregation. Flushed with embarrassment, he ordered a consignment of brassières. The women could make little sense of them in terms of their norms of dress. From their point of view, the most reasonable way to interpret these strange articles was to regard them as headgear. Much to the dismay of the missionary, they placed the two cups on the top of their heads and fastened the straps under their chins.

Norms are enforced by positive and negative sanctions, that is rewards and punishments. Sanctions can be informal, such as an approving or disapproving glance, or formal, such as a reward or a fine given by an official body. Continuing the example of norms of dress, an embarrassed silence, a hoot of derision or a contemptuous stare will make most members of society who have broken norms of dress change into more conventional attire. Usually the threat of negative sanctions is sufficient to enforce normal behaviour. Conversely, an admiring glance, a word of praise or an encouraging smile provide rewards for conformity to social norms. Certain norms are formalized by translation into laws which are enforced by official sanctions. In terms of laws governing dress, the nude bather on a public beach, the 'streaker' at a sporting event, and the 'flasher' who exposes himself or herself to an unsuspecting individual are all subject to official punishments of varying severity. Like informal sanctions, formal sanctions may be positive or negative. In terms of norms associated with dress, awards are made by official bodies such as tailors' organizations to the best-dressed men in Britain.

To summarize, norms define appropriate and acceptable behaviour in specific situations. They are enforced by positive and negative sanctions which may be formal or informal. The sanctions that enforce norms are a major part of the mechanisms of social control which are concerned with maintaining order in society.

Values

Unlike norms, which provide specific directives for conduct, values provide more general guidelines. A value is a belief that something is good and desirable. It defines what is important, worthwhile and worth striving for. It has often been suggested that individual achievement and materialism are major values in Western industrial society. Thus individuals believe it is important and desirable to come top of the class, to win a race or to reach the top of their chosen profession. Individual achievement is often symbolized and measured by the quality and quantity of material possessions that a person can accumulate. In the West, the value of materialism motivates individuals to invest time and energy producing and acquiring material possessions.

Like norms, values vary from society to society. The Sioux Indians placed a high value on generosity. In terms of Sioux values, the acquisitive individual of Western society would at best be regarded as peculiar and more probably would be condemned as grasping, self-seeking and anti-social.

Many norms can be seen as reflections of values. A variety of norms can be seen as expressions of a single value. In Western society the value placed on human life is expressed in terms of the following norms: the norms associated with hygiene in the home and in public places; the norms defining acceptable ways for settling an argument or dispute, which usually exclude physical violence and manslaughter; the array of rules and regulations dealing with transport and behaviour on the highway, which are concerned with protecting life and limb; and similar standards that apply to safety regulations in the workplace, particularly in mining and manufacturing industries. All of these norms concerned with the health and safety of members of society can be seen as expressions of the value placed on human life.

Many sociologists maintain that shared norms and values are essential for the operation of human society. Since humans have no instincts, their behaviour must be guided and regulated by norms. Without shared norms, members of society would be unable to cooperate or even comprehend the behaviour of others. Similar arguments apply to values. Without shared values, members of society would be unlikely to cooperate and work together. With differing or conflicting values they would often be pulling in different directions and pursuing incompatible goals. Disorder and disruption might well result. Thus an ordered and stable society requires shared norms and values. This viewpoint will be considered in greater detail in a later section.

Status and role

All members of society occupy a number of social positions known as statuses. In Western society, an individual will usually have an occupational status such as bus driver, secretary or solicitor; a family status such as son or daughter, father or mother; and a gender status such as male or female. Statuses are culturally defined, despite the fact that they may be based on biological factors such as sex or race. For example, skin colour assigns individuals to racial statuses such as black and white, but this merely reflects the conventions of particular societies. Other biological characteristics such as hair colour have no connection with an individual's status, and in future societies skin colour may be equally insignificant.

Some statuses are relatively fixed and there is little individuals can do to change their assignment to particular social positions. Examples of such fixed or ascribed statuses include gender and aristocratic titles. On rare occasions, however, ascribed statuses can be changed. Edward VIII was forced to abdicate for insisting on marrying an American divorcée. Revolutions in America and Russia abolished the ascribed status of members of the aristocracy. Ascribed statuses are usually fixed at birth. In many societies occupational status has been or still is transmitted from father to son and from mother to daughter. Thus in the traditional Indian caste system, a son automatically entered the occupation of his father.

Statuses that are not fixed by inheritance, biological characteristics, or other factors over which the individual has no control, are known as achieved statuses. An achieved status is entered as a result of some degree of purposive action and choice. In Western society an individual's marital status and occupational status are achieved. However, as Chapter 2 on social stratification will indicate, the distinction between ascribed and achieved status is less clearcut than has so far been suggested.

Each status in society is accompanied by a number of norms that define how an individual occupying a particular status is expected to act. This group of norms is known as a role. Thus the status of husband is accompanied by the role of husband, the status of solicitor by the role of solicitor and so on. As an example, solicitors are expected to possess a detailed knowledge of certain aspects of the law, to support their client's interests and respect the

confidentiality of their business. Solicitors' attire is expected to be sober, their manner restrained and confident yet understanding, their standing in the community beyond reproach. Playing or performing roles involves social relationships in the sense that an individual plays a role in relation to other roles. Thus the role of doctor is played in relation to the role of patient, the role of husband in relation to the role of wife. Individuals therefore interact in terms of roles.

Social roles regulate and organize behaviour. In particular, they provide the means for accomplishing certain tasks. It can be argued, for example, that teaching can be accomplished more effectively if teacher and student adopt their appropriate roles. This involves the exclusion of other areas of their lives in order to concentrate on the matter in hand. Roles provide social life with order and predictability. Interacting in terms of their respective roles, teacher and student know what to do and how to do it. With a knowledge of each other's roles they are able to predict and comprehend the actions of the other. As an aspect of culture, roles provide an important part of the guidelines and directives necessary for an ordered society.

This section has introduced some of the basic concepts used by many sociologists. In doing so, however, it has presented a somewhat one-sided view of human society. Individuals have been pictured rather like automatons who simply respond to the dictates of their culture. All members of a particular society appear to be produced from the same mould. They are all efficiently socialized in terms of a common culture. They share the same values, follow the same norms and play a variety of roles, adopting the appropriate behaviour for each. Clearly this picture of conformity has been overstated and the pervasive and constraining influence of culture has been exaggerated. There are two reasons for this. First, overstatement has been used to make the point. Second, many of the ideas presented so far derive from a particular perspective in sociology which has been subject to the criticisms noted above. This perspective, known as functionalism, will be examined later in this chapter (see pp. 9–11).

The development of human societies

Some sociologists believe that human societies have passed through certain broad phases of development. Many sociologists distinguish between premodern and modern societies. The distinction is a very general one and can neglect differences between the

societies of each type. Nevertheless, the distinction is both influential and useful. It is useful because it has allowed sociologists to identify some of the key changes that have taken place in human history. They have then been able to discuss the significance of these changes. Some sociologists, though by no means all, argue that a new type of society, the postmodern society, has recently developed or is developing.

In this section we will briefly introduce some of the main ideas associated with the distinctions between premodern, modern and postmodern societies. These concepts have a very important role in the development of sociological thinking and will be developed in detail throughout the book.

Premodern societies

Premodern societies took a number of forms. Anthony Giddens distinguishes between three main types, hunting and gathering societies, pastoral and agrarian societies and non-industrial civilizations (Giddens, 1997).

Hunting and gathering societies

The earliest human societies survived by gathering fruit, nuts and vegetables and by hunting or trapping animals for food. They usually consisted of small tribal groups often numbering fewer than fifty people. Such societies tended to have few possessions and little material wealth. What possessions they did have were shared. According to Giddens, they had relatively little inequality, although elder members of the tribe may have had more status and influence than younger ones. Hunting and gathering societies have largely disappeared, but Giddens calculates that some 250,000 people (just 0.0001 per cent of the world's population) still survive largely through hunting and gathering. Hunters and gatherers still exist in regions of Africa, New Guinea and Brazil, but few have remained untouched by the spread of Western culture.

Pastoral and agrarian societies

According to Giddens, these first emerged some 20,000 years ago. Pastoral societies may hunt and gather but they also keep and herd animals (for example cattle, camels or horses). Animal herds provide supplies of milk and meat and the animals may also be used as a means of transport. Unlike hunting and gathering societies, pastoral societies make it possible for individuals to accumulate wealth in the form of their animals. They therefore tend to have more inequality than hunting and gathering bands. They also tend to be nomadic, since they have to move around to find pasture for their animals. Because of this they are likely to come into contact with other groups. The individual societies have tended to be larger than hunting and gathering bands and in all may number as many as 250,000. There are still some pastoral societies in parts of the Middle East, Africa and Asia.

Agrarian societies rely largely upon the cultivation of crops to feed themselves. Like the herding of animals, this provides a more reliable and predictable source of food than hunting and gathering and it can therefore support much larger populations. Such societies are not likely to be nomadic. Food such as grain is often stored and it is possible for individuals to accumulate substantial personal wealth. Agrarian societies can therefore have considerable inequality. Agriculture remains the main way of earning a living in many parts of the world today. Giddens quotes 1990 figures which showed that over 90 per cent of the population of Nepal and Rwanda, over 80 per cent of the population of Uganda, and nearly 70 per cent of the Bangladeshi population worked in agriculture. However, the culture of contemporary agrarian societies has not remained entirely traditional. Most have been influenced by the culture of modern, industrial societies.

Non-industrial civilizations

These types of society first developed around 6000 BC. According to Giddens, they 'were based on the development of cities, showed very pronounced inequalities of wealth and power, and were associated with the rule of kings and emperors'. Compared to the hunting and gathering and early pastoral and agrarian societies, they were more developed in the areas of art and science and had more institutionalized and centralized systems of government. Non-industrial civilizations also invented writing. Some of these civilizations expanded across wide areas and developed their own empires. Examples of non-industrial civilizations include the Aztecs, the Maya and the Incas in South and Central America; Ancient Greece and the Roman Empire in Europe; Ancient Egypt in Africa; and Indian and Chinese civilizations in Asia. Most of them had substantial armed forces, and some, such as the Romans, managed major military conquests. None of these civilizations survived indefinitely and none exist today. Despite their importance, none has had as big an impact on the development of human society as modern industrial societies. These first emerged in the eighteenth and nineteenth centuries.

Modern industrial societies

According to Lee and Newby, in the early nineteenth century 'there was widespread agreement among observers and commentators at this time that Northern Europe and North America were passing through the most profound transformation of society in the history of mankind' (Lee and Newby, 1983).

Lee and Newby identify four main transformations that took place:

1 Industrialism. The industrial revolution, which started in the late eighteenth century, transformed Britain, and later other societies, from economies based largely on agriculture to economies based largely on manufacturing. New technology led to massive increases in productivity, first in the cotton industry and then in other industries. An increasingly specialized division of labour developed, that is people had more specialist jobs. Social life was no longer governed by the rhythms of the seasons and of night and day; instead people's lives were based on the clock. Instead of working when the requirements of agriculture demanded, people started working long shifts of fixed periods (often twelve hours) in the new factories.

2 Capitalism. Closely connected to the development of industrialism was the development of capitalism. Capitalism involves wage labour and businesses run for the purpose of making a profit. Before the advent of capitalism many peasants worked for themselves, living off the produce they could get from their own land. Increasingly, peasants lost their land and had to rely upon earning a wage either as agricultural labourers or as workers in the developing factories. Capitalist businesses were developed with the aim of making a profit year after year. New classes emerged – principally a class of entrepreneurs who made their living by setting up and running capitalist businesses, and a working class of wage labourers employed in the entrepreneurs' factories.

3 Urbanism. The development of industry was accompanied by a massive movement from rural to urban areas. In Britain in 1750, before the industrial revolution, only two cities had populations of over 50,000 (London and Edinburgh). By 1851, 29 British cities had a population of more than 50,000. The population no longer needed to be thinly spread across agricultural land, and was increasingly concentrated in the centres of capitalist industry. Urbanism – the growth of towns and cities – brought with it numerous social problems such as crime, riots, and health problems caused by overcrowding and lack of sanitation. To many commentators the new towns and cities also destroyed the traditional sense of community that they associated with the rural villages. They believed that urbanism undermined the informal mechanisms of social control (such as gossip), which operated in close-knit communities, but which became ineffective in the anonymity of urban life.

4 Liberal democracy. Before the changes of the eighteenth and nineteenth centuries the right of kings and queens to rule was rarely questioned (an exception being the English Civil War of the seventeenth century). The monarch was accepted as God's representative on earth, and their authority

was not therefore open to question. However, in the French Revolution of 1789 the French monarchy was overthrown. Similarly British monarchical rule in America was overthrown by the American War of Independence (1775–1783). In both cases there was a new emphasis on the citizenship rights of individuals – individuals were now to have a say in how their countries were ruled rather than accepting what they were told by monarchs. This opened the way for the development of political parties and new perspectives on society. How society was to be run became more a matter for debate than it had ever been before.

Modernity

Taken together, the changes described above are often seen as characterizing modern societies, or as constituting an era of modernity. Modernity involves the following concepts: a belief in the possibility of human progress; rational planning to achieve objectives; a belief in the superiority of rational thought compared to emotion; faith in the ability of technology and science to solve human problems; a belief in the ability and rights of humans to shape their own lives; and a reliance upon manufacturing industry to improve living standards. Sociology developed alongside modernity and, not surprisingly, it has tended to be based upon similar foundations. Thus early sociological theories tended to believe that societies could and would progress, that scientific principles could be used to understand society, and that rational thought could be employed to ensure that society was organized to meet human needs. For most of its history, sociological thinking has been dominated by such approaches. However, some thinkers, including some sociologists, believe that modernity is being, or has been, replaced by an era of postmodernity.

Postmodernity

Some sociologists believe that in recent years fundamental changes have taken place in Western societies. These changes have led to, or are in the process of leading to, a major break with the old concept of modernity. They suggest that people have begun to lose their faith in science and technology. They have become aware, for example, of the damaging effects of pollution, the dangers of nuclear war and the risks of genetic engineering. People have become more sceptical about the benefits of rational planning. For example, many people doubt that large, rational, bureaucratic organizations (such as big companies or the British National Heath Service) can meet human needs. They have lost faith in political beliefs and grand theories that claim to be able to improve society. Furthermore, few people now believe that communism can lead to a perfect society. The modern belief in progress has therefore been undermined and there has been a movement away from science and rationalism. Some people have turned to non-rational beliefs such as New Age philosophies (see Chapter 7) and religious cults as a reaction against scientific rationalism.

According to some postmodernists, these changes are linked to changes in the economy. Industrial society has been superseded by post-industrial society. Relatively few people in Western societies now work in manufacturing industry. More and more are employed in services and particularly in jobs concerned with communications and information technology. Computer technology has meant that fewer and fewer people are needed to work in manufacturing, and communications have become

th
it i
as th
people
labels.
in people

Althoug
edly taken
that the chan
to justify the
modern to post
that *societies* hav
theories of society
examined after we
longer-established so

Theories of society

In this section we will examine some of the most influential theories of society. A theory is a set of ideas which claims to explain how something works. A sociological theory is therefore a set of ideas which claims to explain how society or aspects of society work. The theories in this section represent only a selection from the range of modern sociological theories. They have been simplified and condensed to provide a basic introduction. Since they are applied to various topics throughout the text, an initial awareness is essential. Criticism of the theories has been omitted from this chapter for the sake of simplicity, but it will be dealt with throughout the text and in detail in the final chapter.

There are many variations on the basic theories examined in this chapter. Again, for simplicity, most of these variations will not be mentioned at this stage, but will be introduced when they become relevant to particular topics.

Functionalism

Functionalism first emerged in nineteenth-century Europe. The French sociologist Emile Durkheim was the most influential of the early functionalists. The theory was developed by American sociologists such as Talcott Parsons in the twentieth century, and it became the dominant theoretical perspective in sociology during the 1940s and 1950s, particularly in the USA. From the mid-1960s onwards its popularity steadily declined, due partly to damaging criticism, partly to competing perspectives which appeared to provide superior explanations, and partly to changes

in fashion. The key points of the functionalist perspective may be summarized by a comparison drawn from biology. If biologists wanted to know how an organism such as the human body worked, they might begin by examining the various parts such as the brain, lungs, heart and liver. However, if they simply analysed the parts in isolation from each other, they would be unable to explain how life was maintained. To do this, they would have to examine the parts in relation to each other, since they work together to maintain the organism. Therefore they would analyse the relationships between the heart, lungs, brain and so on to understand how they operated and appreciate their importance. In other words, any part of the organism must be seen in terms of the organism as a whole.

Functionalism adopts a similar perspective. The various parts of society are seen to be interrelated and, taken together, they form a complete system. To understand any part of society, such as the family or religion, the part must be seen in relation to society as a whole. Thus where a biologist will examine a part of the body, such as the heart, in terms of its contribution to the maintenance of the human organism, the functionalist will examine a part of society, such as the family, in terms of its contribution to the maintenance of the social system.

Structure

Functionalism begins with the observation that behaviour in society is structured. This means that relationships between members of society are organized in terms of rules. Social relationships are

...provide
...they are
...ctives in terms of
...re of society can be seen
...native behaviour – the sum
...ionships, which are governed by
...ain parts of society, its institutions –
...e family, the economy, and the
...cational and political systems – are major aspects
of the social structure. Thus an institution can be
seen as a structure made up of interconnected roles
or interrelated norms. For example, the family is
made up of the interconnected roles of husband,
father, wife, mother, son and daughter. Social
relationships within the family are structured in terms
of a set of related norms.

Function

Having established the existence of a social structure,
functionalist analysis turns to a consideration of how
that structure functions. This involves an examination
of the relationship between the different parts of the
structure and their relationship to society as a whole.
This examination reveals the functions of institutions.
At its simplest, function means effect. Thus the
function of the family is the effect it has on other
parts of the social structure and on society as a whole.
In practice, the term function is usually used to
indicate the contribution an institution makes to the
maintenance and survival of the social system. For
example, a major function of the family is the socialization of new members of society. This represents an
important contribution to the maintenance of society,
since order, stability and cooperation largely depend
on learned, shared norms and values.

Functional prerequisites

In determining the functions of various parts of the
social structure, functionalists are guided by the
following ideas. Societies have certain basic needs or
requirements that must be met if they are to survive.
These requirements are sometimes known as
functional prerequisites. For example, a means of
producing food and shelter may be seen as a
functional prerequisite, since without food and
shelter members of society could not survive. A
system for socializing new members of society may
also be regarded as a functional prerequisite, since,
without culture, social life would not be possible.
Having assumed a number of basic requirements for
the survival of society, the next step is to look at the
parts of the social structure to see how they meet
such functional prerequisites. Thus a major function
of the economic system is the production of food and
shelter. An important function of the family is the
socialization of new members of society.

Value consensus

From a functionalist perspective, society is regarded
as a system. A system is an entity made up of
interconnected and interrelated parts. From this
viewpoint, it follows that each part will in some way
affect every other part and the system as a whole. It
also follows that, if the system is to survive, its
various parts must have some degree of fit or
compatibility. Thus a functional prerequisite of
society involves at least a minimal degree of integration between the parts. Many functionalists argue
that this integration is based largely on value
consensus, that is on agreement about values by
members of society. Thus if the major values of
society are expressed in the various parts of the
social structure, those parts will be integrated. For
example, it can be argued that the value of materialism integrates many parts of the social structure in
Western industrial society. The economic system
produces a large range of goods, and ever-increasing
productivity is regarded as an important goal. The
educational system is partly concerned with
producing the skills and expertise to expand production and increase its efficiency. The family is an
important unit of consumption with its steadily rising
demand for consumer durables such as washing
machines, videos and microwaves. The political
system is partly concerned with improving material
living standards and raising productivity. To the
extent that these parts of the social structure are
based on the same values, they may be said to be
integrated.

Social order

One of the main concerns of functionalist theory is to
explain how social life is possible. The theory
assumes that a certain degree of order and stability is
essential for the survival of social systems.
Functionalism is therefore concerned with explaining
the origin and maintenance of order and stability in
society. Many functionalists see shared values as the
key to this explanation: value consensus integrates
the various parts of society. It forms the basis of
social unity or social solidarity since individuals will
tend to identify and feel kinship with those who
share the same values as themselves. Value consensus
provides the foundation for cooperation since
common values produce common goals. Members of
society will tend to cooperate in pursuit of goals that
they share.

Having attributed such importance to value
consensus, many functionalists then focus on the
question of how this consensus is maintained. Indeed
the American sociologist Talcott Parsons has stated
that the main task of sociology is to examine 'the
institutionalization of patterns of value orientation in

the social system'. Emphasis is therefore placed on the process of socialization whereby values are internalized and transmitted from one generation to the next. In this respect, the family is regarded as a vital part of the social structure. Once learned, values must be maintained. In particular those who deviate from society's values must be brought back into line. Thus the mechanisms of social control discussed earlier in the chapter are seen as essential to the maintenance of social order.

In summary, society, from a functionalist perspective, is a system made up of interrelated parts. The social system has certain basic needs that must be met if it is to survive. These needs are known as functional prerequisites. The function of any part of society is its contribution to the maintenance of society. The major functions of social institutions are those that help to meet the functional prerequisites of society. Since society is a system, there must be some degree of integration between its parts. A minimal degree of integration is therefore a functional prerequisite of society. The progress of society is best achieved through maintaining order and then allowing society to evolve naturally without too much planning. Many functionalists maintain that the order and stability they see as essential for the maintenance of the social system are largely provided by value consensus. This means that an investigation of the source of value consensus is a major concern of functionalist analysis.

Conflict perspectives

Although functionalists emphasize the importance of value consensus in society, they do recognize that conflict can occur. However, they see conflict as being the result of temporary disturbances in the social system. These disturbances are usually quickly corrected as society evolves. Functionalists accept that social groups can have differences of interest, but these are of minor importance compared to the interests that all social groups share in common. They believe that all social groups benefit if their society runs smoothly and prospers.

Conflict theories differ from functionalism in that they hold that there are fundamental differences of interest between social groups. These differences result in conflict being a common and persistent feature of society, and not a temporary aberration.

There are a number of different conflict perspectives and their supporters tend to disagree about the precise nature, causes and extent of conflict. For the sake of simplicity, in this introductory chapter we will concentrate upon two conflict theories: Marxism and feminism. Other conflict theories will be introduced later in the book. (For example, the

influential conflict theory of Max Weber is dealt with in Chapter 2, pp. 36–8.)

Marxism

Marxist theory offers a radical alternative to functionalism. It became increasingly influential in sociology during the 1970s, partly because of the decline of functionalism, partly because it promised to provide answers that functionalism failed to provide, and partly because it was more in keeping with the tenor and mood of the times. 'Marxism' takes its name from its founder, the German-born philosopher, economist and sociologist, Karl Marx (1818–83). The following account is a simplified version of Marxist theory. It must also be seen as one interpretation of that theory: Marx's extensive writings have been variously interpreted and, since his death, several schools of Marxism have developed. (See Marx and Engels, 1949, 1950 for extracts from Marx's most important writings.)

Contradiction and conflict

Marxist theory begins with the simple observation that, in order to survive, humans must produce food and material objects. In doing so they enter into social relationships with other people. From the simple hunting band to the complex industrial state, production is a social enterprise. Production also involves a technical component known as the forces of production, which includes the technology, raw materials and scientific knowledge employed in the process of production. Each major stage in the development of the forces of production will correspond with a particular form of the social relationships of production. This means that the forces of production in a hunting economy will correspond with a particular set of social relationships.

Taken together, the forces of production and the social relationships of production form the economic basis or infrastructure of society. The other aspects of society, known as the superstructure, are largely shaped by the infrastructure. Thus the political, legal and educational institutions and the belief and value systems are primarily determined by economic factors. A major change in the infrastructure will therefore produce a corresponding change in the superstructure.

Marx maintained that, with the possible exception of the societies of prehistory, all historical societies contain basic contradictions, which means that they cannot survive forever in their existing form. These contradictions involve the exploitation of one social group by another: in feudal society, lords exploit their serfs; in capitalist society, employers exploit their employees. This creates a fundamental conflict of interest between social groups since one gains at the expense of another. This conflict of interest must ultimately be resolved since a social system containing such contradictions cannot survive unchanged.

We will now examine the points raised in this brief summary of Marxist theory in greater detail. The major contradictions in society are between the forces and relations of production. The forces of production include land, raw materials, tools and machinery, the technical and scientific knowledge used in production, the technical organization of the production process, and the labour power of the workers. The 'relations of production' are the social relationships which people enter into in order to produce goods. Thus in feudal society they include the relationship between the lord and vassal, and the set of rights, duties and obligations which make up that relationship. In capitalist industrial society they include the relationship between employer and employee and the various rights of the two parties. The relations of production also involve the relationship of social groups to the means and forces of production.

The means of production consist of those parts of the forces of production that can be legally owned. They therefore include land, raw materials, machinery, buildings and tools, but not technical knowledge or the organization of the production process. Under capitalism, labour power is not one of the means of production since the workers are free to sell their labour. In slave societies, though, labour power is one of the means of production since the workforce is actually owned by the social group in power. In feudal society, land, the major means of production, is owned by the lord, whereas the serf has the right to use land in return for services or payment to the lord. In Western industrial society, the capitalists own the means of production, whereas the workers own only their labour, which they hire to the employer in return for wages.

Exploitation and oppression

The idea of contradiction between the forces and relations of production may be illustrated in terms of the infrastructure of capitalist industrial society. Marx maintained that only labour produces wealth. Thus wealth in capitalist society is produced by the labour power of the workers. However, much of this wealth is appropriated in the form of profits by the capitalists, the owners of the means of production. The wages of the workers are well below the value of the wealth they produce. There is thus a contradiction between the forces of production, in particular the labour power of the workers which produces wealth, and the relations of production which

involve the appropriation of much of that wealth by the capitalists.

A related contradiction involves the technical organization of labour and the nature of ownership. In capitalist society, the forces of production include the collective production of goods by large numbers of workers in factories. Yet the means of production are privately owned, and the profits are appropriated by individuals. The contradiction between the forces and relations of production lies in the social and collective nature of production and the private and individual nature of ownership. Marx believed that these and other contradictions would eventually lead to the downfall of the capitalist system. He maintained that, by its very nature, capitalism involves the exploitation and oppression of the worker. He believed that the conflict of interest between capital and labour, which involves one group gaining at the expense of the other, could not be resolved within the framework of a capitalist economy.

Contradiction and change

Marx saw history as divided into a number of time periods or epochs, each being characterized by a particular mode of production. Major changes in history are the result of new forces of production. Thus the change from feudal to capitalist society stemmed from the emergence, during the feudal epoch, of the forces of production of industrial society. This resulted in a contradiction between the new forces of production and the old feudal relations of production. Capitalist industrial society required relations of production based on wage labour rather than the traditional ties of lord and vassal. When they reach a certain point in their development, the new forces of production will lead to the creation of a new set of relations of production. Then, a new epoch of history will be born which will sweep away the social relationships of the old order.

However, the final epoch of history, the communist or socialist society that Marx believed would eventually supplant capitalism, will not result from a new force of production. Rather it will develop from a resolution of the contradictions contained within the capitalist system. Collective production will remain but the relations of production will be transformed. Ownership of the means of production will be collective rather than individual, and members of society will share the wealth that their labour produces. No longer will one social group exploit and oppress another. This will produce an infrastructure without contradiction and conflict. In Marx's view this would mean the end of history since communist society would no longer contain the contradictions which generate change.

Ideology and false consciousness

In view of the contradictions that beset historical societies, it appears difficult to explain their survival. Despite its internal contradictions, capitalism has continued in the West for over 200 years. This continuity can be explained in large part by the nature of the superstructure. In all societies the superstructure is largely shaped by the infrastructure. In particular, the relations of production are reflected and reproduced in the various institutions, values and beliefs that make up the superstructure. Thus the relationships of domination and subordination found in the infrastructure will also be found in social institutions. The dominant social group or ruling class, that is the group which owns and controls the means of production, will largely monopolize political power, and its position will be supported by laws which are framed to protect and further its interests.

In the same way, beliefs and values will reflect and legitimate the relations of production. Members of the ruling class produce the dominant ideas in society. These ideas justify their power and privilege and conceal from all members of society the basis of exploitation and oppression on which their dominance rests. Thus, under feudalism, honour and loyalty were 'dominant concepts' of the age. Vassals owed loyalty to their lords and were bound by an oath of allegiance that encouraged the acceptance of their status. In terms of the dominant concepts of the age, feudalism appeared as the natural order of things. Under capitalism, exploitation is disguised by the ideas of equality and freedom. The relationship between capitalist and wage labourer is defined as an equal exchange. The capitalist buys the labour power that the worker offers for hire. The worker is defined as a free agent since he or she has the freedom to choose his or her employer. In reality, equality and freedom are illusions: the employer–employee relationship is not equal. It is an exploitative relationship. Workers are not free since they are forced to work for the capitalist in order to survive. All they can do is exchange one form of 'wage slavery' for another.

Marx refers to the dominant ideas of each epoch as ruling class ideology. Ideology is a distortion of reality, a false picture of society. It blinds members of society to the contradictions and conflicts of interest that are built into their relationships. As a result they tend to accept their situation as normal and natural, right and proper. In this way a false consciousness of reality is produced which helps to maintain the system. However, Marx believed that ruling class ideology could only slow down the disintegration of the system. The contradictions embedded in the structure of society must eventually find expression.

In summary, the key to understanding society from a Marxist perspective involves an analysis of the infrastructure. In all historical societies there are basic contradictions between the forces and relations of production, and there are fundamental conflicts of interest between the social groups involved in the production process. In particular, the relationship between the major social groups is one of exploitation and oppression. The superstructure derives largely from the infrastructure and therefore reproduces the social relationships of production. It will thus reflect the interests of the dominant group in the relations of production. Ruling class ideology distorts the true nature of society and serves to legitimate and justify the status quo. However the contradictions in the infrastructure will eventually lead to a disintegration of the system and the creation of a new society in which there is no exploitation and oppression.

Although highly critical of capitalism, Marx did see it as a stepping stone on the way towards a communist society. Capitalism would help to develop technology that would free people from material need; there would be more than enough goods to feed and clothe the population. In these circumstances it would be possible to establish successful communist societies in which the needs of all their members were met. Despite its pessimistic tone, Marxism shares with functionalism the modern belief that human societies will improve, and that rational, scientific thinking can be used to ensure progress.

Feminism

There are several different versions of feminism but most share a number of features in common. Like Marxists, feminists tend to see society as divided into different social groups. Unlike Marxists, they see the major division as being between men and women rather than between different classes. Like Marxists, they tend to see society as characterized by exploitation. Unlike Marxists, they see the exploitation of women by men as the most important source of exploitation, rather than that of the working class by the ruling class. Many feminists characterize contemporary societies as patriarchal, that is they are dominated by men. For example, feminists have argued that men have most of the power in families, that they tend to be employed in better-paid and higher-status jobs than women, and that they tend to monopolize positions of political power. The ultimate aim of these types of feminism is to end men's domination and to rid society of the exploitation of women. Such feminists advance a range of explanations for, and solutions to, the exploitation of women. However, they all believe that the development of society can be explained and that progress towards an improved future is possible.

Some feminist writers (sometimes called difference feminists) disagree that all women are equally oppressed and disadvantaged in contemporary societies. They believe that it is important to recognize the different experiences and problems faced by various groups of women. For example, they do not believe that all husbands oppress their wives, that women are equally disadvantaged in all types of work, or that looking after children is necessarily oppressive to women. They emphasize the differences between women of different ages, class backgrounds and ethnic groups. Like other feminists, they believe that the oppression of women exists, but they do not see it as affecting all women to the same extent and in the same way. For example, a wealthy white woman in a rich capitalist country is in a very different position to a poor black woman living in an impoverished part of Africa. Since their problems are different, they would require very different solutions.

Despite their disagreements, feminists tend to agree that, at least until recently, sociology has neglected women. Certainly until the 1970s sociology was largely written by men about men. There were relatively few studies of women, and issues of particular concern to women (such as housework and women's health) were rarely studied. A number of feminists criticize what they call malestream sociology. By this they mean mainstream, male-dominated sociology. They have attacked not just what male sociologists study, but also how they carry out their studies. For example, they have suggested that feminist sociology should get away from rigid 'scientific' methods and should adopt more sympathetic approaches. These can involve working in partnership with those being studied rather than treating them as simply the passive providers of data (see Chapter 4).

As feminist scholarship has developed it has started to examine numerous aspects of social life from feminist viewpoints. Many of the resulting studies will be examined in later chapters. (Feminist perspectives are discussed in detail in Chapter 3.)

Interactionism

Functionalism and Marxism have a number of other characteristics in common. First, they offer a general explanation of society as a whole, and as a result are sometimes known as macro-theories. Second, they regard society as a system, hence they are sometimes referred to as system theories. Third, they tend to see human behaviour as shaped by the system. In terms of Talcott Parsons's version of functionalism, behaviour is largely directed by the norms and values of the social system. From a Marxist viewpoint, behaviour is ultimately determined by the economic infrastructure. Some versions of feminism have similar characteristics in that they explain how society works in terms of the existence of a patriarchal system and explain the behaviour of males and females in terms of that system. (Other feminist theories are very different and share some features in common with interactionism.)

Interactionism differs from functionalism, Marxism and most feminist theories in that it focuses on small-scale interaction rather than society as a whole. It usually rejects the notion of a social system. As a result it does not regard human action as a response or reaction to the system. Interactionists believe that it is possible to analyse society systematically and that it is possible to improve society. However, improvements have to be made on a smaller scale and in a more piecemeal way than those implied by macro or system theories.

Meaning and interpretation

As its name suggests, interactionism is concerned with interaction, which means action between individuals. The interactionist perspective seeks to understand this process. It begins from the assumption that action is meaningful to those involved. It therefore follows that an understanding of action requires an interpretation of the meanings that the actors give to their activities. Picture a man and a woman in a room and the man lighting a candle. This action is open to a number of interpretations. The couple may simply require light because a fuse has blown or a power cut has occurred. Or, they may be involved in some form of ritual in which the lighted candle has a religious significance. Alternatively, the man or woman may be trying to create a more intimate atmosphere as a prelude to a sexual encounter. Finally, the couple may be celebrating a birthday, a wedding anniversary or some other red-letter day. In each case a different meaning is attached to the act of lighting a candle. To understand the act, it is therefore necessary to discover the meaning held by the actors.

Meanings are not fixed entities. As the above example shows, they depend in part on the context of the interaction. Meanings are also created, developed, modified and changed within the actual process of interaction. A pupil entering a new class may initially define the situation as threatening and even hostile. This definition may be confirmed, modified or changed depending on the pupil's perception of the interaction that takes place in the classroom. The pupil may come to perceive the teacher and fellow pupils as friendly and understanding and so change his or her assessment of the situation. The way in which actors define situations has important consequences. It represents their reality in terms of which they structure their actions. For example, if the pupil maintains a definition of the classroom as threatening and hostile, they may say little and speak only when spoken to. Conversely if the definition changed, there would probably be a corresponding change in the pupil's actions in that context.

Self-concepts

The actions of the pupil in the above example will depend in part on their interpretation of the way others see them. For this reason many interactionists place particular emphasis on the idea of the self. They suggest that individuals develop a self-concept, a picture of themselves, which has an important influence on their actions. A self-concept develops from interaction processes, since it is in large part a reflection of the reactions of others towards the individual: hence the term looking glass self coined by Charles Cooley (1864–1929) (discussed in Coser, 1977). Actors tend to act in terms of their self-concept. Thus if they are consistently defined as disreputable or respectable, servile or arrogant, they will tend to see themselves in this light and act accordingly.

The construction of meaning

Since interactionists are concerned with definitions of situation and self, they are also concerned with the process by which those definitions are constructed. For example, how does an individual come to be defined in a certain way? The answer to this question involves an investigation of the construction of meaning in interaction processes. This requires an analysis of the way actors interpret the language, gestures, appearance and manner of others and their interpretation of the context in which the interaction takes place.

The definition of an individual as a delinquent is an example. Research has indicated that police are more likely to perceive an act as delinquent if it occurs in a low-income inner city area. The context will influence the action of the police since they typically define the inner city as a 'bad area'. Once arrested, a male youth is more likely to be defined as a juvenile delinquent if his manner is interpreted as aggressive and uncooperative, if his appearance is seen as unconventional or slovenly, if his speech is defined as ungrammatical or slang, and if his posture gives the impression of disrespect for authority, or arrogance. Thus the black American youth from the inner city ghetto with his cool, arrogant manner and colourful clothes is more likely to be defined as a

delinquent than the white 'all-American girl' from the tree-lined suburbs.

Definitions of individuals as certain kinds of persons are not, however, simply based on preconceptions which actors bring to interaction situations. For example, the police will not automatically define black juveniles involved in a fight as delinquent and white juveniles involved in a similar activity as non-delinquent. A process of negotiation occurs from which the definition emerges. Often negotiations will reinforce preconceptions, but not necessarily. The young blacks may be able to convince the police officer that the fight was a friendly brawl which did not involve intent to injure or steal. In this way they may successfully promote images of themselves as high-spirited teenagers rather than as malicious delinquents. Definitions and meanings are therefore constructed in interaction situations by a process of negotiation.

Negotiation and roles

The idea of negotiation is also applied to the concept of role. Like functionalists, the interactionists employ the concept of role but they adopt a somewhat different perspective. Functionalists imply that roles are provided by the social system, and individuals enact their roles as if they were reading off a script that contains explicit directions for their behaviour. Interactionists argue that roles are often unclear, ambiguous and vague. This lack of clarity provides actors with considerable room for negotiation, manoeuvre, improvisation and creative action. At most, roles provide very general guidelines for action. What matters is how they are employed in interaction situations.

For example, two individuals enter marriage with a vague idea about the roles of husband and wife. Their interaction will not be constrained by these roles. Their definition of what constitutes a husband, a wife, and a marital relationship will be negotiated and continually renegotiated. It will be fluid rather than fixed, changeable rather than static. Thus, from an interactionist perspective, roles, like meanings and definitions of the situation, are negotiated in interaction processes.

In summary, interactionism focuses on the process of interaction in particular contexts. Since all action is meaningful, it can only be understood by discovering the meanings that actors assign to their activities. Meanings both direct action and derive from action. They are not fixed but constructed and negotiated in interaction situations. From their interaction with others, actors develop a self-concept. This has important consequences since individuals tend to act in terms of their definition of self. Understanding the construction of meanings and self-concepts involves an appreciation of the way actors interpret the process of interaction. This requires an investigation of the way in which they perceive the context of the interaction and the manner, appearance and actions of others.

While interactionists admit the existence of roles, they regard them as vague and imprecise and therefore as open to negotiation. From an interactionist perspective, action proceeds from negotiated meanings that are constructed in ongoing interaction situations.

Postmodernism

The challenge to modernism

Since the 1980s, postmodern perspectives have become increasingly influential in sociology. These perspectives take a number of forms, and the more radical of these represent a major challenge to the perspectives examined so far.

Some postmodern theorists content themselves with describing and explaining what they see as the crucial changes in society. They retain elements of conventional approaches in sociology. For example, they still believe that it is possible to explain both human behaviour and the ways in which societies are changing. They no longer assume that the changes are progressive, but they stick to a belief that they can be explained through developing sociological theories. Some postmodernists go much further than this. They argue that conventional, modern approaches in sociology, which grew out of modern society, must be abandoned. While approaches such as Marxism, functionalism, feminism and interactionism might have explained how the social world worked in previous eras, they are no longer useful. New theories are needed for the postmodern age. They support this claim in two main ways.

First, some postmodernists argue that social behaviour is no longer shaped as it used to be by people's background and their socialization. They argue that factors such as class, ethnic group and whether people are male or female influence people a great deal less than they used to. Instead, people are much freer to choose their own identity and lifestyle. Thus, for example, people can choose whether to be heterosexual or homosexual, they have more choice about where they live and where they travel to, what sort of people they mix with and what clothes they wear. The boundaries between social groups are breaking down and you can no longer predict the sorts of lifestyles that people will adopt. If so much choice exists, then many of the aspects of social life studied by modern sociologists are no longer important and their studies are no longer useful.

Second, some postmodernists question the belief that there is any solid foundation for producing knowledge about society. They argue that modern sociologists were quite wrong to believe that sociology could discover the truth by adopting the methods of physical sciences. From their perspective, all knowledge is based upon the use of language. Language can never describe the external world perfectly. Knowledge is essentially subjective – it expresses personal viewpoints which can never be proved to be correct. Postmodernists such as Jean Baudrillard argue that it has become increasingly difficult to separate media images from anything even approximating to reality (see Chapter 15). Society has become so saturated with media images that people now confuse, for example, media characters with real life. An example of this occurred when some viewers launched a campaign to free Deirdre Rashid (a character in the British soap opera *Coronation Street*) from prison.

Postmodernists such as Jean François Lyotard (see Chapter 15) are particularly critical of any attempt to produce a general theory of how society works (for example Marxism or functionalism). Lyotard believes that all attempts to produce such theories are doomed to failure. They cannot truly explain something as complex as the social world. Generally such theories are simply used by groups of people to try to impose their ideas on other people, for example in communist or fascist societies. General theories are therefore dangerous and should always be rejected. In Lyotard's view, modern sociological theories fall into this category and should be rejected.

Difference

Many writers who adopt some of the stronger claims of postmodernism emphasize differences between people rather than similarities between members of social groups. They believe that it is the job of the researcher to uncover and describe these differences rather than to make generalizations about whole social groups. This involves acknowledging that there are many different viewpoints on society and that you should not judge between them. All viewpoints are seen as being equally valid; none is superior to any other. Sociologists should not try to impose their views on others, but should merely enable the voices of different people to be heard. This is very different from the goals of other sociologists (such as Marxists and functionalists) who set out to produce scientific explanations of how society works and how social groups behave.

Postmodern perspectives will be examined and evaluated in more detail later in relation to particular topics. The theory of postmodernism will be discussed in detail in Chapter 15.

Views of human behaviour

The last section looked briefly at five theoretical perspectives in sociology. This section deals with philosophical views of human behaviour. These views have influenced both the type of data sociologists have collected and the methods they have employed to collect the data.

Views of human behaviour can be roughly divided into those that emphasize external factors and those that stress internal factors. The former approach sees behaviour as being influenced by the structure of society. The latter approach places more emphasis upon the subjective states of individuals: their feelings, the meanings they attach to events, and the motives they have for behaving in particular ways. The use of this 'dichotomy' (sharply defined division) is somewhat artificial. In practice most sociologists make use of the insights provided by both approaches when carrying out research and interpreting the results. There are also a number of variations on each approach. For example, as a later section will show, phenomenologists differ in their approach from other sociologists who emphasize the importance of internal influences upon human behaviour.

Positivism

Many of the founders of sociology believed it would be possible to create a science of society based upon the same principles and procedures as the natural sciences such as chemistry and biology, even though the natural sciences often deal with inanimate matter and so are not concerned with feeling, emotions and other subjective states. The most influential attempt to apply natural science methodology to sociology is known as positivism.

Auguste Comte (1798–1857), who is credited with inventing the term sociology and regarded as one of the founders of the discipline, maintained that the application of the methods and assumptions of the natural sciences would produce a 'positive science of society'. He believed that this would reveal that the evolution of society followed 'invariable laws'. It would show that the behaviour of humans was governed by principles of cause and effect that were just as invariable as the behaviour of matter, the subject of the natural sciences.

In terms of sociology, the positivist approach makes the following assumptions. The behaviour of humans, like the behaviour of matter, can be objectively measured. Just as the behaviour of matter can be quantified by measures such as weight, temperature and pressure, methods of objective measurement can be devised for human behaviour. Such measurement is essential to explain behaviour.

For example, in order to explain the reaction of a particular chemical to heat, it is necessary to provide exact measurements of temperature, weight and so on. With the aid of such measurements it will be possible to observe accurately the behaviour of matter and produce a statement of cause and effect. This statement might read $A \times B = C$ where A is a quantity of matter, B a degree of heat and C a volume of gas. Once it has been shown that the matter in question always reacts in the same way under fixed conditions, a theory can be devised to explain its behaviour.

From a positivist viewpoint such methods and assumptions are applicable to human behaviour. Observations of behaviour based on objective measurement will make it possible to produce statements of cause and effect. Theories may then be devised to explain observed behaviour.

The positivist approach in sociology places particular emphasis on behaviour that can be directly observed. It argues that factors that are not directly observable – such as meanings, feelings and purposes – are not particularly important and can be misleading. For example, if the majority of adult members of society enter into marriage and produce children, these facts can be observed and quantified. They therefore form reliable data. However, the range of meanings that members of society give to these activities – their reasons for marriage and procreation – are not directly observable. Even if they could be accurately measured, they might well divert attention from the real cause of behaviour. One person might believe they entered marriage because they were lonely, another because they were in love, a third because it was the 'thing to do', and a fourth because they wished to have children. Reliance on this type of data for explanation assumes that individuals know the reasons for marriage. This can obscure the real cause of their behaviour.

The positivists' emphasis on observable 'facts' is due largely to the belief that human behaviour can be explained in much the same way as the behaviour of matter. Natural scientists do not inquire into the meanings and purposes of matter. Atoms and molecules do not act in terms of meanings, they simply react to external stimuli. Thus if heat, an external stimulus, is applied to matter, that matter will react. The job of the natural scientist is to observe, measure, and then explain that reaction.

The positivist approach to human behaviour applies a similar logic. People react to external stimuli and their behaviour can be explained in terms of this reaction. They enter into marriage and produce children in response to the demands of society: society requires such behaviour for its survival and its members simply respond to this requirement. The meanings and purposes they attach to this behaviour are largely inconsequential.

It has often been argued that systems theory in sociology adopts a positivist approach. Once behaviour is seen as a response to some external stimulus (such as economic forces or the require-ments of the social system), the methods and assumptions of the natural sciences appear appropriate to the study of humans. Marxism has sometimes been regarded as a positivist approach, since it can be argued that it sees human behaviour as a reaction to the stimulus of the economic infrastructure. Functionalism has been viewed in a similar light. The behaviour of members of society can be seen as a response to the functional prerequi-sites of the social system. These views of systems theory represent a considerable oversimplification. However, it is probably fair to say that systems theory is closer to a positivist approach than the views that will now be considered.

Social action perspectives

Advocates of social action perspectives argue that the subject matter of the social and natural sciences is fundamentally different. As a result, the methods and assumptions of the natural sciences are inappropriate to the study of humans. The natural sciences deal with matter. To understand and explain the behaviour of matter it is sufficient to observe it from the outside. Atoms and molecules do not have conscious-ness: they do not have meanings and purposes that direct their behaviour. Matter simply reacts unconsciously to external stimuli; in scientific language, it 'behaves'. As a result, the natural scientist is able to observe, measure, and impose an external logic on that behaviour in order to explain it. Scientists have no need to explore the internal logic of the consciousness of matter simply because it does not exist.

Unlike matter, humans have consciousness – thoughts, feelings, meanings, intentions and an awareness of being. Because of this, humans' actions are meaningful: they define situations and give meaning to their actions and those of others. As a result, they do not just react to external stimuli, they do not merely behave – they act.

Imagine the response of early humans to fire caused by volcanoes or spontaneous combustion.

They did not simply react in a uniform manner to the experience of heat. They attached a range of meanings to it and these meanings directed their actions. They defined fire as a means of warmth and used it to heat their dwellings; they saw it as a means of defence and used it to ward off wild animals; and they saw it as a means of transforming substances and employed it for cooking and hardening the points of wooden spears. Humans do not just react to fire, they act upon it in terms of the meanings they give to it.

If action stems from subjective meanings, it follows that the sociologist must discover those meanings in order to understand action. Sociologists cannot simply observe action from the outside and impose an external logic upon it. They must interpret the internal logic that directs the actions of the actor.

Max Weber (1864–1920) was one of the first sociologists to outline this perspective in detail. He argued that sociological explanations of action should begin with observing and interpreting the subjective 'states of minds' of people. As the previous section indicated, interactionism adopts a similar approach, with particular emphasis on the process of interaction. Where positivists emphasize facts and cause-and-effect relationships, interactionists emphasize insight and understanding. Since it is not possible to get inside the heads of actors, the discovery of meaning must be based on interpreta-tion and intuition. For this reason, objective measure-ment is not possible and the exactitude of the natural sciences cannot be duplicated. Since meanings are constantly negotiated in ongoing interaction processes, it is not possible to establish simple cause-and-effect relationships. Thus some sociologists argue that sociology is limited to an interpretation of social action.

Nevertheless, both Weber and the interactionists did think it was possible to produce causal explana-tions of human behaviour, so long as an understanding of meanings formed part of those explanations. Some sociologists, particularly phenomenologists, take the argument further and claim that it is impossible for sociologists to find the causes of human action.

Phenomenology

To phenomenologists, it is impossible to measure objectively any aspect of human behaviour. Humans make sense of the world by categorizing it. Through language they distinguish between different types of objects, events, actions and people. For instance, some actions are defined as criminal and others are not; similarly some people are defined as criminals while others are seen as law-abiding. The process of categorization is subjective: it depends upon the opinions of the observer. Statistics are simply the product of the opinions of those who produce them. Thus crime statistics are produced by the police and the courts, and they represent no more than the opinions of the individuals involved. If sociologists produce their own statistics, these too are the result of subjective opinions – in this case the opinions of sociologists.

Phenomenologists believe that it is impossible to produce factual data and that it is therefore impossible to produce and check causal explanations. The most that sociologists can hope to do is to understand the meaning that individuals give to particular phenomena. Phenomenologists do not try to establish what causes crime; instead they try to discover how certain events come to be defined as crimes and how certain people come to be defined as criminal. Phenomenologists therefore examine the way that police officers reach decisions about whether to arrest and charge suspects. In doing so, they hope to establish the meanings attached to the words 'crime' and 'criminal' by the police. The end product of phenomenological research is an understanding of the meanings employed by members of society in their everyday life.

Although there are differences between those who support social action and phenomenological views, they all agree that the positivist approach has produced a distorted picture of social life.

Peter Berger argues that society has often been viewed as a puppet theatre with its members portrayed as 'little puppets jumping about on the ends of their invisible strings, cheerfully acting out the parts that have been assigned to them' (Berger, 1966). Society instils values, norms and roles, and humans dutifully respond like Berger's puppets. However, interactionists and phenomenologists believe that humans do not react and respond passively to an external society. They see humans as actively creating their own meanings and their own society in interaction with each other. In this respect they have similarities with some of the postmodern approaches discussed earlier (see p. 16).

Sociology and values

The positivist approach assumes that a science of society is possible. It therefore follows that objective observation and analysis of social life are possible. An objective view is free from the values, moral judgements and ideology of the observer: it provides facts and explanatory frameworks which are uncoloured by the observer's feelings and opinions.

An increasing number of sociologists argue that a value-free science of society is not possible. They maintain that the values of sociologists directly influence every aspect of their research. They argue that the various theories of society are based, at least in part, on value judgements and ideological positions. They suggest that sociological perspectives are shaped more by historical circumstances than by objective views of the reality of social life.

Those who argue that an objective science of society is not possible maintain that sociology can never be free from ideology. The term ideology refers to a set of ideas which present only a partial view of reality. An ideological viewpoint also includes values. It involves not only a judgement about the way things are, but also about the way things ought to be. Thus ideology is a set of beliefs and values that provides a way of seeing and interpreting the world, which results in a partial view of reality. The term ideology is often used to suggest a distortion, a false picture of reality. However there is considerable doubt about whether reality and ideology can be separated. As Nigel Harris suggests, 'Our reality is the next man's ideology and vice versa' (Harris, 1971).

Ideology can be seen as a set of beliefs and values that express the interests of a particular social group. Marxists use the term in this way when they talk about the ideology of the ruling class. In this sense, ideology is a viewpoint that distorts reality and justifies and legitimates the position of a social group. Karl Mannheim (Mannheim, 1948) uses the term in a similar way. He states that ideology consists of the beliefs and values of a ruling group which 'obscures the real condition of society both to itself and others and thereby stabilizes it'. Mannheim distinguishes this form of ideology from what he calls utopian ideology. Rather than supporting the status quo – the way things are – utopian ideologies advocate a complete change in the structure of society. Mannheim argues that such ideologies are usually found in oppressed groups whose members want radical change. As their name suggests, utopian ideologies are based on a vision of an ideal society, a perfect social system. Mannheim refers to them as 'wish-images' for a future social order. Like the ideologies of ruling groups, he argues that utopian ideologies are a way of seeing the world which prevents true insight and obscures reality.

Mannheim's ideas will now be applied to two of the major theoretical perspectives in sociology: Marxism and functionalism. It has often been argued that Marxism is largely based on a utopian ideology, and functionalism on a ruling class ideology. Marxism contains a vision and a promise of a future ideal society – the communist utopia. In this society the means of production are communally owned and, as a result, oppression and exploitation disappear.

The communist utopia provides a standard of comparison for present and past societies. Since they inevitably fall far short of this ideal, their social arrangements will be condemned. It has been argued that the communist utopia is not a scientific prediction but merely a projection of the 'wish-images' of those who adopt a Marxist position. Utopian ideology has therefore been seen as the basis of Marxist theory.

By comparison, functionalism has often been interpreted as a form of ruling class ideology. Where Marxism is seen to advocate radical change, functionalism is seen to justify and legitimate the status quo. With its emphasis on order and stability, consensus and integration, functionalism appears to adopt a conservative stance. Rapid social change is not recommended since it will disrupt social order. The major institutions of society are justified by the belief that they are meeting the functional prerequisites of the social system. Although functionalists have introduced the concept of dysfunction to cover the harmful effects of parts of the system on society as a whole, the concept is rarely employed. In practice, functionalists appear preoccupied with discovering the positive functions and the beneficial effects of social institutions. As a result, the term function is associated with the idea of useful and good. This interpretation of society tends to legitimate the way things are. Ruling class ideology has therefore been seen as the basis of functionalist theory.

It is important to note that the above interpretation of the ideological bases of Marxism and functionalism is debatable. However, a case can be made to support the view that both perspectives are ideologically based.

The view that Marxism and functionalism are ideologically based would certainly be supported by postmodernists. Postmodernists do not just reject these particular perspectives – they reject any attempt to produce a theory of society as a whole. They see such theories as dangerous. This is because they can lead to one group trying to impose its will on others. From this viewpoint it is neither possible nor desirable to try to remove values from sociology. Instead, a range of different values should be accepted and tolerated. People have a right to be different from one another and to hold different views. It is not the job of the sociologist to arbitrate between these differences and say which is better.

Some sociologists reject this standpoint. Critical social scientists (whose ideas are examined in Chapter 14) do not deny that values must inevitably enter into sociology. However, they do not believe that sociologists should just accept the range of different values present in society. Rather, it is the duty of social scientists to try to improve society. If, like postmodernists, they were simply to accept the range of different values that exists, they would be shirking their responsibility. By refusing to make any judgement about whose values are better, they would be accepting the way society is. Taken to extremes, this would mean, for example, that the values of the rapist are no worse than those of the rape victim; the values of racists are no worse than those of people who campaign against racism; and the values of capitalists who exploit their workers are no worse than those of people who try to help the poor. Critical social scientists argue that sociologists should take sides and they should try to use their work to fight injustice and improve society.

This section has provided a brief introduction to the question of the relationship between sociology and values. The relationship will be considered in detail throughout the text. Each chapter in the main section of the book will conclude with an interpretation of the values involved in the views that are discussed.

The sociological imagination

Although sociologists vary in their perspectives, methods and values, they all (with the exception of some versions of postmodernism) share the aim of understanding and explaining the social world. Combining the insights offered by different approaches might be the best way of achieving this goal.

Structural theories of society, such as functionalism and Marxism, emphasize the importance of society in shaping human behaviour. On the other hand, approaches such as interactionism emphasize the importance of human behaviour in shaping society. Many sociologists today believe that good sociology must examine both the structure of society and social interaction. They believe that it is only by combining the study of the major changes in society and individual lives that sociologists can develop their understanding of social life.

This idea is not new. It was supported by the very influential German sociologist Max Weber (1864–1920) (see Chapter 15), and more recently has been examined in depth by the British sociologist

Anthony Giddens (see Chapter 15). However, perhaps the clearest exposition of this view was put forward by the American sociologist C. Wright Mills.

Mills called the ability to study the structure of society at the same time as individuals' lives the 'sociological imagination' (Mills, 1959). Mills argued that the sociological imagination allowed people to understand their 'private troubles' in terms of 'public issues'. Unemployment, war and marital breakdown are all experienced by people in terms of the problems they produce in their personal lives. They react to them as individuals, and their reactions have consequences for society as a whole. However, to Mills, these issues can only be fully understood in the context of wider social forces. For example, very specific circumstances might lead to one person becoming unemployed, but when unemployment rates in society as a whole rise, it becomes a public issue that needs to be explained. The sociologist has to consider 'the economic and political institutions of the society, and not merely the personal situation and character of a scatter of individuals'.

According to Mills, then, sociology should be about examining the biography of individuals in the context of the history of societies. The sociological imagination is not just of use to sociologists, it is important to all members of society if they wish to understand, change and improve their lives. Perhaps sociology can be seen as succeeding when it allows people to achieve this imagination, and the theories and studies examined in the rest of the book can be judged in these terms.

Chapter 2

Social stratification

Social stratification

Introduction

Egalitarianism

People have long dreamed of an egalitarian society, a society in which all members are equal. In such a society people will no longer be ranked in terms of prestige: no one will experience the satisfaction of occupying a high social status; no one will suffer the indignity of being put in a position that commands little respect. No longer will high status provoke deference and admiration or envy and resentment from those in less 'worthy' positions. Wealth will be distributed equally among the population: the rich and poor, haves and have-nots will be a thing of the past. Words such as 'privilege' and 'poverty' will either change their meaning or disappear from the vocabulary.

In an egalitarian society, the phrase 'power to the people' will become a reality. There will be an end to some people having power over others: positions of authority and the obedience they command will disappear. Exploitation and oppression will be concepts of history which have no place in the description of contemporary social reality. People will be equal both in the sight of God and in the eyes of their fellow people.

Clearly the egalitarian society remains a dream. All human societies from the simplest to the most complex have some form of social inequality. In particular, power and prestige are unequally distributed between individuals and social groups and in many societies there are also marked differences in the distribution of wealth.

1 Power refers to the degree to which individuals or groups can impose their will on others, with or without the consent of those others.

2 Prestige relates to the amount of esteem or honour associated with social positions, qualities of individuals and styles of life.

3 Wealth refers to material possessions defined as valuable in particular societies. It may include land, livestock, buildings, money and many other forms of property owned by individuals or social groups.

In this chapter we are going to study the unequal distribution of power, prestige and wealth in society.

Social inequality and social stratification

It is important at the outset to make a distinction between social inequality and social stratification. The term social inequality simply refers to the existence of socially created inequalities. Social stratification is a particular form of social inequality. It refers to the presence of distinct social groups which are ranked one above the other in terms of factors such as prestige and wealth. Those who belong to a particular group or stratum will have some awareness of common interests and a common identity. They will share a similar lifestyle which, to some degree, will distinguish them from members of other social strata. The Indian caste system provides one example of a social stratification system.

In traditional India, Hindu society was divided into five main strata: four *varnas* or castes, and a fifth group, the outcaste, whose members were known as untouchables. Each caste was subdivided into *jatis* or subcastes, which in total numbered many thousands. *Jatis* were occupational groups – there were carpenter *jatis*, goldsmith *jatis*, potter *jatis*, and so on.

Castes were ranked in terms of ritual purity. The Brahmins, or priests, members of the highest caste, personified purity, sanctity and holiness. They were the source of learning, wisdom and truth. They alone performed the most important religious ceremonies.

At the other extreme, untouchables were defined as unclean, base and impure, a status that affected all their social relationships. They had to perform unclean and degrading tasks such as the disposal of dead animals. They were segregated from members of the caste system and lived on the outskirts of villages or in their own communities. Their presence polluted to the extent that even if the shadow of an untouchable fell across the food of a Brahmin it would render it unclean.

In general, the hierarchy of prestige based on notions of ritual purity was mirrored by the hierarchy of power. The Brahmins were custodians of the law, and the legal system they administered was based largely on their pronouncements. Inequalities of wealth were usually linked to those of prestige and power. In a largely rural economy, the Brahmins tended to be the largest landowners and the control of land was monopolized by members of the two highest castes. Although the caste system has been made illegal in modern India, it still exercises an influence, particularly in rural areas.

As shown by the caste system, social stratification involves a hierarchy of social groups. Members of a particular stratum have a common identity, similar interests and a similar lifestyle. They enjoy or suffer the unequal distribution of rewards in society as members of different social groups.

Social stratification, however, is only one form of social inequality. It is possible for social inequality to exist without social strata. For example, some sociologists have argued that it is no longer correct to regard Western industrial society, particularly the USA, as being stratified in terms of a class system. They suggest that social classes have been replaced by a continuous hierarchy of unequal positions. Where there were once classes, whose members had a consciousness of kind, a common way of life and shared interests, there is now an unbroken continuum of occupational statuses which command varying degrees of prestige and economic reward. Thus it is suggested that a hierarchy of social groups has been replaced by a hierarchy of individuals.

Although many sociologists use the terms social inequality and social stratification interchangeably, the importance of seeing social stratification as a specific form of social inequality will become apparent as this chapter develops.

Strata subcultures

Before looking at some of the major issues raised in the study of social stratification, it is necessary to examine certain aspects of stratification systems. There is a tendency for members of each stratum to develop their own subculture, that is certain norms, attitudes and values which are distinctive to them as a social group. When some members of society experience similar circumstances and problems that are not common to all members, a subculture tends to develop.

For example, it has often been suggested that distinctive working-class and middle-class subcultures exist in Western industrial societies. Similar circumstances and problems often produce similar responses. Members of the lowest stratum in stratification systems that provide little opportunity for improvement of status tend to have a fatalistic attitude towards life. This attitude becomes part of their subculture and is transmitted from generation to generation. It sees circumstances as largely unchangeable; it regards luck and fate rather than individual effort as shaping life, and therefore tends to encourage acceptance of the situation. An attitude of fatalism may be seen in typical phrases from traditional low-income black American subculture such as 'I've been down so long that down don't bother me', 'I was born under a bad sign' and 'It's an uphill climb to the bottom.'

Members of a social group who share similar circumstances and a common subculture are likely to develop a group identity. They tend to have a feeling of kinship with other group members. They will therefore tend to identify with their particular stratum and regard themselves, for example, as middle or working class.

Social mobility

Strata subcultures tend to be particularly distinctive when there is little opportunity to move from one stratum to another. This movement is known as social mobility. Social mobility can be upward, for example moving from the working to the middle class, or downward.

Stratification systems which provide little opportunity for social mobility may be described as closed; those with a relatively high rate of social mobility as open. In closed systems an individual's position is largely ascribed: often it is fixed at birth and there is little he or she can do to change status. Caste provides a good example of a closed stratification system: individuals automatically belonged to the caste of their parents and, except in rare instances, spent the rest of their life in that status.

By comparison, social class, the system of stratification in capitalist industrial society, provides an example of an open system. Some sociologists claim that an individual's class position is largely achieved: it results from their personal qualities and abilities and the use they make of them rather than ascribed characteristics such as the status of their parents or the colour of their skin. By comparison with the caste system, the rate of social mobility in class systems is high.

Life chances

A person's position in a stratification system may have important effects on many areas of life. It may enhance or reduce life chances, that is their chances of obtaining those things defined as desirable and avoiding those things defined as undesirable in their society. Gerth and Mills, referring to Western society, state that life chances include:

Everything from the chance to stay alive during the first year after birth to the chance to view fine arts, the chance to remain healthy and grow tall, and if sick to get well again quickly, the chance to avoid becoming a juvenile delinquent and very crucially, the chance to complete an intermediary or higher educational grade

Gerth and Mills, 1954, p. 313

Social versus natural inequalities

Biology and inequality

Many stratification systems are accompanied by beliefs which state that social inequalities are biologically based. Such beliefs are often found in systems of racial stratification where, for example, whites might claim biological superiority over blacks, and see this as the basis for their dominance.

The question of the relationship between biologically based and socially created inequality has proved extremely difficult to answer. The eighteenth-century French philosopher Jean-Jacques Rousseau (1712–78) provided one of the earliest examinations of this question. He refers to biologically based inequality as: 'natural or physical, because it is established by nature, and consists in a difference of age, health, bodily strength, and the qualities of the mind or the soul'. By comparison, socially created inequality: 'consists of the different privileges which some men enjoy to the prejudice of others, such as that of being more rich, more honoured, more powerful, or even in a position to exact obedience'.

Rousseau believed that biologically based inequalities between people were small and relatively unimportant whereas socially created inequalities provide the major basis for systems of social stratification. Most sociologists would support this view.

However, it could still be argued that biological inequalities, no matter how small, provide the foundation upon which structures of social inequality are built. This position is difficult to defend in the case of certain forms of stratification. In the caste system, an individual's status was fixed by birth. People belonged to their parents' *jati* and automatically followed the occupation of the *jati* into which they were born. Thus, no matter what the biologically based aptitudes and capacities of an untouchable, there was no way he or she could become a Brahmin. Unless it is assumed that superior genes are permanently located in the Brahmin caste (and there is no evidence that this is the case) then there is probably no relationship between genetically based and socially created inequality in traditional Hindu society.

A similar argument can be advanced in connection with the feudal or estate system of medieval Europe. Stratification in the feudal system was based on landholding. The more land an individual controlled, the greater his or her wealth, power and prestige. The position of the dominant stratum, the feudal nobility, was based on large grants of land from the monarch. Their status was hereditary, land and titles being passed on from parent to child. It is difficult to sustain the argument that feudal lords ultimately owed their position to biological superiority when their children, no matter what their biological make-up, inherited the status of their parents.

Natural and cultural inequality

So far we have not answered the question of what exactly constitutes biological inequality. It can be argued that biological differences become biological inequalities when people define them as such. Biological factors assume importance in many stratification systems because of the meanings assigned to them by different cultures. For example, old age has very different meanings in different societies. In traditional aborigine societies in Australia it brought high prestige and power since the elders directed the affairs of the tribe, but in Western societies, the elderly are usually pensioned off, and old age assumes a very different meaning. Even with a change of name to 'senior citizen', the status of old age pensioner commands little power or prestige.

So-called racial characteristics are evaluated on the basis of similar principles, that is values which are relative to time and place. The physical characteristics of blacks in America were traditionally defined as undesirable and associated with a range of negative qualities. However, with the rise of Black Power during the late 1960s, this evaluation was slowly changed with slogans such as 'Black is beautiful.' In South Africa, such negative stereotypes among white South Africans began to be undermined when the apartheid regime, which treated black people as inferior, came to an end in 1992. The widespread respect for the first black leader of the country, Nelson Mandela, made it more difficult for the extreme racism of apartheid to be sustained.

Biological differences form a component of some social stratification systems simply because members of those systems select certain characteristics and evaluate them in a particular way. Differences therefore become inequalities only because they are defined as such. André Béteille argues that the search for a biological basis for social stratification is bound to end in failure since the 'qualities are not just there, so to say, in nature: they are as human beings have defined them, in different societies, in different historical epochs' (Béteille, 1977).

Beliefs which state that systems of social stratification are based on biological inequalities can be seen as rationalizations for those systems. Such beliefs serve to explain the system to its members: they make social inequality appear rational and reasonable. They therefore justify and legitimate the system by appeals to nature. In this way a social contrivance appears to be founded on the natural order of things.

Inequalities between men and women and between different 'racial' groups are sometimes seen as being based on biological differences. We will discuss sociologists' views of whether this is justified in later chapters. (See Chapter 3 on sex and gender and Chapter 4 on 'race'.)

Having considered social stratification in general terms, we will now look at this subject from the various sociological perspectives.

Social stratification – a functionalist perspective

Functionalist theories of stratification must be seen in the context of functionalist theories of society. When functionalists attempt to explain systems of social stratification, they set their explanations in the framework of larger theories which seek to explain the operation of society as a whole. They assume that society has certain basic needs or functional prerequisites that must be met if it is to survive. They therefore look to social stratification to see how far it meets these functional prerequisites.

Functionalists assume that the parts of society form an integrated whole and thus they examine the ways in which the social stratification system is integrated with other parts of society. They maintain that a certain degree of order and stability is essential for the operation of social systems. They will therefore consider how stratification systems help to maintain order and stability in society. In summary, functionalists are primarily concerned with the function of social stratification: with its contribution to the maintenance and well-being of society.

Talcott Parsons – stratification and values

Like many functionalists, Talcott Parsons believed that order, stability and cooperation in society are based on value consensus – a general agreement by members of society concerning what is good and worthwhile. Parsons argued that stratification systems derive from common values. If values exist, then it follows that individuals will be evaluated and placed in some form of rank order. In Parsons's words, 'stratification, in its valuational aspect, then, is the ranking of units in a social system in accordance with the common value system'.

In other words, those who perform successfully in terms of society's values will be ranked highly and they will be likely to receive a variety of rewards. At a minimum they will be accorded high prestige because they exemplify and personify common values.

For example, if a society places a high value on bravery and generosity, as was the case of the Sioux Indians in North America, those who excel in terms of these qualities will receive a high rank in the stratification system. The Sioux warrior who successfully raided the Crow and Pawnee – the traditional enemies of his tribe – captured their horses and distributed them to others, could have received a variety of rewards. He may have been given a seat on the tribal council, a position of power and prestige. His deeds would be recounted in the warrior societies and the women would sing of his exploits. Other warriors would follow him in raids against neighbouring tribes and the success of these expeditions might have led to his appointment as a war chief. In this way, excellence in terms of Sioux values was rewarded by power and prestige.

Because different societies have different value systems, the ways of attaining a high position will vary from society to society. Parsons argued that American society values individual achievement, efficiency and 'puts primary emphasis on productive activity within the economy'. Thus, successful business executives who have achieved their position through their own initiative, ability and ambition, and run efficient and productive businesses, will receive high rewards.

Parsons's argument suggests that stratification is an inevitable part of all human societies. If value consensus is an essential component of all societies, then it follows that some form of stratification will result from the ranking of individuals in terms of common values. It also follows from Parsons's argument that there is a general belief that stratification systems are just, right and proper, because they are basically an expression of shared values. Thus American business executives are seen to deserve their rewards because members of society place a high value on their skills and achievements.

This is not to say there is no conflict between the haves and have-nots, the highly rewarded and those with little reward. Parsons recognized that in Western industrial society there will be 'certain tendencies to arrogance on the part of some winners and to resentment and to a "sour grapes" attitude on the part of some losers'. However, he believed that this conflict is kept in check by the common value system which justifies the unequal distribution of rewards.

Organization and planning

Functionalists tend to see the relationship between social groups in society as one of cooperation and interdependence. In complex industrial societies, different groups specialize in particular activities. As no one group is self-sufficient, it alone cannot meet the needs of its members. It must, therefore, exchange goods and services with other groups, and so the relationship between social groups is one of reciprocity (mutual give and take).

This relationship extends to the strata in a stratification system. An oversimplified example is the argument that many occupational groups within the middle class in Western society plan, organize and coordinate the activities of the working class. Each class needs and cooperates with the other, since any large-scale task requires both organization and execution. In societies with a highly specialized division of labour, such as industrial societies, some members will specialize in organization and planning while others will follow their directives. Parsons argued that this inevitably leads to inequality in terms of power and prestige. Referring to Western society:

> Organization on an ever increasing scale is a fundamental feature of such a system. Such organization naturally involves centralization and differentiation of leadership and authority; so that those who take responsibility for coordinating the actions of many others must have a different status in important respects from those who are essentially in the role of carrying out specifications laid down by others.
>
> Parsons, 1964, p. 327

Thus those with the power to organize and coordinate the activities of others will have a higher social status than those they direct.

Power

As with prestige differentials, Parsons argued that inequalities of power are based on shared values. Power is legitimate authority in that it is generally accepted as just and proper by members of society as a whole. It is accepted as such because those in positions of authority use their power to pursue collective goals which derive from society's central values. Thus the power of the American business executive is seen as legitimate authority because it is used to further productivity, a goal shared by all members of society. This use of power therefore serves the interests of society as a whole.

Summary and evaluation

Parsons saw social stratification as both inevitable and functional for society.

1 It is inevitable because it derives from shared values which are a necessary part of all social systems.
2 It is functional because it serves to integrate various groups in society.

Power and prestige differentials are essential for the coordination and integration of a specialized division of labour. Without social inequality, Parsons found it difficult to see how members of society could effectively cooperate and work together. Finally, inequalities of power and prestige benefit all members of society since they serve to further collective goals which are based on shared values.

Parsons has been strongly criticized on all these points. Other sociologists have seen stratification as a divisive rather than an integrating force. They have regarded it as an arrangement whereby some gain at the expense of others, and questioned the view that stratification systems derive ultimately from shared values. We will examine these criticisms in detail in later sections.

Kingsley Davis and Wilbert E. Moore – role allocation and performance

The most famous functionalist theory of stratification was first presented in 1945, in an article by the American sociologists Davis and Moore entitled *Some Principles of Stratification*.

Effective role allocation and performance

Davis and Moore began with the observation that stratification exists in every known human society. They attempted to explain 'in functional terms, the universal necessity which calls forth stratification in any social system'. They argued that all social systems share certain functional prerequisites which must be met if the system is to survive and operate efficiently. One such functional prerequisite is effective role allocation and performance. This means that:

1 all roles must be filled
2 they must be filled by those best able to perform them
3 the necessary training for them must be undertaken
4 the roles must be performed conscientiously.

Davis and Moore argued that all societies need some 'mechanism' for ensuring effective role allocation and performance. This mechanism is social stratification, which they saw as a system that attaches unequal rewards and privileges to the different positions in society.

If the people and positions that make up society did not differ in important respects there would be no need for stratification. However, people differ in terms of their innate ability and talent, and positions differ in terms of their importance for the survival and maintenance of society. Certain positions are more functionally important than others. These require special skills for their effective performance and the number of individuals with the necessary ability to acquire such skills is limited.

A major function of stratification is to match the most able people with the functionally most important positions. It does this by attaching high rewards to those positions. The desire for such rewards motivates people to compete for them, and in theory the most talented will win through. Such positions usually require long periods of training that involve certain sacrifices, such as loss of income. The promise of high rewards is necessary to provide an incentive to encourage people to undergo this training and to compensate them for the sacrifice involved. It is essential for the well-being of society that those who hold the functionally most important positions perform their roles diligently and conscientiously. The high rewards built into these positions provide the necessary inducement and generate the required motivation for such performance. Davis and Moore therefore concluded that social stratification is a 'device by which societies ensure that the most important positions are conscientiously filled by the most qualified persons'.

Functional importance

Davis and Moore realized that one difficulty with their theory was showing clearly which positions are functionally most important. A position may be highly rewarded without necessarily being functionally important. They suggested that the importance of a position can be measured in two ways.

1 It can be measured by the 'degree to which a position is functionally unique, there being no other positions that can perform the same function satisfactorily'. Thus it could be argued that doctors are functionally more important than nurses since their position carries with it many of the skills necessary to perform a nurse's role but not vice versa.

2 The second measure of importance is the 'degree to which other positions are dependent on the one in question'. Thus it may be argued that managers are

more important than routine office staff since the latter are dependent on direction and organization from management.

To summarize, Davis and Moore regarded social stratification as a functional necessity for all societies. They saw it as a solution to a problem faced by all social systems, that of 'placing and motivating individuals in the social structure'. They offered no other means of solving this problem and implied that social inequality is an inevitable feature of human society. They concluded that differential rewards are functional for society, because they contribute to the maintenance and well-being of social systems.

Melvin M. Tumin – a critique of Davis and Moore

Davis and Moore's theory provoked a lengthy debate. Melvin Tumin, their most famous opponent, produced a comprehensive criticism of their ideas.

Functional importance

Tumin began by questioning the adequacy of their measurement of the functional importance of positions. Davis and Moore tended to assume that the most highly rewarded positions are indeed the most important. Many occupations, however, which afford little prestige or economic reward, can be seen as vital to society. Tumin therefore argued that 'some labour force of unskilled workmen is as important and as indispensable to the factory as some labour force of engineers'.

In fact, a number of sociologists have argued that there is no objective way of measuring the functional importance of positions. Whether lawyers and doctors are considered as more important than farm labourers and refuse collectors is simply a matter of opinion.

Power and rewards

Tumin argued that Davis and Moore ignored the influence of power on the unequal distribution of rewards. Differences in pay and prestige between occupational groups may be due to differences in their power rather than their functional importance. For example, the difference between the wages of farm labourers and coal miners can be interpreted as a result of the relative bargaining power of the two groups. We will examine this point in detail in later sections.

The pool of talent

Davis and Moore assumed that only a limited number of individuals have the talent to acquire the skills necessary for the functionally most important positions. Tumin regarded this as a very questionable assumption for three reasons:

1 An effective method of measuring talent and ability has yet to be devised (as the chapter on education in this book indicates).
2 There is no proof that exceptional talents are required for those positions which Davis and Moore considered important.
3 The pool of talent in society may be considerably larger than Davis and Moore assumed (as the chapter on education suggests). As a result, unequal rewards may not be necessary to harness it.

Training

Tumin also questioned the view that the training required for important positions should be regarded as a sacrifice and therefore in need of compensation. He pointed to the rewards of being a student - leisure, freedom and the opportunity for self-development. He noted that any loss of earnings can usually be made up during the first ten years of work. Differential rewards during this period may be justified. However, Tumin saw no reason for continuing this compensation for the rest of an individual's working life.

Motivation

The major function of unequal rewards, according to Davis and Moore, is to motivate talented individuals and allocate them to the functionally most important positions. Tumin rejected this view. He argued that social stratification can, and often does, act as a barrier to the motivation and recruitment of talent.

This is readily apparent in closed systems such as caste and racial stratification: the ascribed status of untouchables prevented even the most talented from becoming Brahmins. Until recently, the ascribed status of blacks in South Africa blocked them from achieving political office and entering highly rewarded occupations. Thus closed stratification systems operate in exactly the opposite way to Davis and Moore's theory.

Tumin suggested, however, that even relatively open systems of stratification erect barriers to the motivation and recruitment of talent. As Chapter 12 on education shows, there is considerable evidence to indicate that the class system in Western industrial society limits the possibilities of the discovery and utilization of talent. In general, the lower an individual's class position, the more likely he or she is to leave school at the minimum leaving age and the less likely to aspire and strive for a highly rewarded position. Thus the motivation to succeed is unequally distributed throughout the class system. As a result, social class can act as an obstacle to the motivation of talent.

In addition, Tumin argued that Davis and Moore failed to consider the possibility that those who occupy highly rewarded positions erect barriers to recruitment. Occupational groups often use their power to restrict access to their positions, so creating a high demand for their services and increasing the rewards they receive.

Tumin used the American Medical Association as an example. By controlling entry into the profession, it has maintained a shortage of doctors and so ensured high rewards for medical services. In this way the self-interested use of power can restrict the recruitment of talented individuals.

Inequality of opportunity

Tumin concluded that stratification, by its very nature, can never adequately perform the functions which Davis and Moore assigned to it. He argued that those born into the lower strata can never have the same opportunities for realizing their talents as those born into the higher strata. Tumin maintained:

> It is only when there is a genuinely equal access to recruitment and training for all potentially talented persons that differential rewards can conceivably be justified as functional. And stratification systems are apparently inherently antagonistic to the development of such full equality of opportunity.
>
> Tumin, 1953, in Bendix and Lipset, 1967, p. 55

Social divisions

Finally, Tumin questioned the view that social stratification functions to integrate the social system. He argued that differential rewards can 'encourage hostility, suspicion and distrust among the various segments of a society'. From this viewpoint, stratification is a divisive rather than an integrating force.

Stratification can also weaken social integration by giving members of the lower strata a feeling of being excluded from participation in the larger society. This is particularly apparent in systems of racial stratification. By tending to exclude certain groups from full participation in society, stratification 'serves to distribute loyalty unequally in the population', and therefore reduces the potential for social solidarity.

Tumin concluded that in their enthusiastic search for the positive functions of stratification, functionalists have tended to ignore or play down its many dysfunctions.

The debate between Davis and Moore and Tumin took place in the 1940s and 1950s. Interest in the issues raised by this debate has recently been revived with the development of 'New Right' perspectives in sociology. In the next section we will analyse the New Right theories of social stratification.

Social stratification – a New Right perspective

Introduction

The ideas of the 'New Right' became influential in the 1980s. In politics, they were closely associated with the British prime minister Margaret Thatcher and the American president Ronald Reagan. The American economist Milton Friedman and the Austrian academic Friedrich Hayek contributed much to the development of New Right thinking (see for example Friedman, 1962 and Hayek, 1944). In British sociology, Peter Saunders and David Marsland have been perhaps the most prominent advocates of this perspective. Marsland's views on poverty will be examined in Chapter 5 (pp. 318–19) and Peter Saunders's theory of stratification is discussed below.

The New Right bases its theories on nineteenth-century liberalism. This regarded the free market in capitalist economies as the best basis for organizing society. Market forces encourage competition, which stimulates innovation and efficiency. Businesses have to make products that are cheaper or better than those of their competitors in order to survive. Free market economies are based upon the choices made by individuals when spending their money, selling their labour or purchasing other people's labour. They therefore promote individual liberty.

Like their nineteenth-century liberal counterparts, the New Right sociologists believe that excessive state intervention in the economy must be avoided. The state should not act to redistribute resources and interfere with the workings of the free market. If it tries to do so it will undermine economic efficiency. Inefficient concerns propped up by the government needlessly use up resources. State intervention may take away the motivation for people to work hard. There is little incentive to strive for success if individuals know that the state will help them no matter how little effort they make. Government interference may also create injustice, taking from those who have earned their rewards and giving to those who are undeserving. Furthermore, as the state becomes stronger, the freedom of individuals may be suppressed. For all these reasons the New Right is strongly opposed to Marxism and socialism.

Peter Saunders – stratification and freedom

Saunders (1990) is generally sympathetic to Davis and Moore's theory of stratification: he is certainly much less critical than Melvin Tumin. He points out that even critics like Tumin accepted that all societies have been stratified – there has never been a completely egalitarian society. Furthermore, he suggests that systems which reward different positions unequally can be shown to have beneficial effects, such as motivating people to work hard.

However, Saunders does not argue that unequal rewards are the only way that a society could fill the important positions with capable people. He says that 'it is possible to imagine a society where all positions are rewarded equally in terms of material resources and formal status'. Such a society would have serious problems, however. Some people would not be happy to do the jobs they were allocated and others would not put in the effort needed to do their jobs properly. Saunders believes:

> In the absence of economic rewards and penalties, the only sanctions available would be those involving the threat or use of physical force. Such people, in other words would have to be jailed, or forcibly set to work in supervised colonies, or even executed as an example to others.
>
> Saunders, 1990, p. 65

This would be necessary because allowing people to get away with doing less than their fair share of work would undermine the whole system because it would reduce the commitment of others.

Saunders does not therefore accept the functionalist claim that stratification systems based upon economic differences are inevitable. However, he certainly agrees with functionalists that they are desirable. He admits that capitalist societies tend to create more inequality than socialist societies. He also argues that socialist societies are bound to be more repressive than capitalist ones in making people perform their roles. In the absence of adequate economic rewards, force must be used. Saunders even predicts that as countries such as China and the states of the former Soviet Union move towards market-based economies 'state coercion may be expected to decline'.

Equality and justice

In developing his own theory of stratification, Saunders distinguishes three types of equality:

1   Formal or legal equality involves all members of society being subject to the same laws or rules. Individuals are judged according to what they do, for example whether they break the law, and not according to who they are. Sanders sees this type of equality as being an integral part of Western capitalist societies, although he admits that 'in practice it is not always as rigorously applied as it

might be'. Legal equality does not imply that everybody ends up in the same position.

2   The second type of equality, equality of opportunity, means that people have an equal chance to become unequal. Individuals compete for success and those with greater merit achieve more. Merit might involve the ability to work harder or the possession of attributes or characteristics which are valued in a society. A society based on this type of equality is often called a meritocracy.

3   Equality of outcome goes further than the idea of equality of opportunity. Saunders explains:

> If a meritocracy is like a race where everybody lines up together at the start, a fully-fledged egalitarian society would be like a perfectly handicapped race where everyone passes the finishing tape at the same time no matter how hard and fast they have tried to run.
>
> Saunders, 1990, p. 44

Broadly, Saunders accepts the principles behind the first two conceptions of equality but rejects the third. Following the ideas of Hayek, he argues that attempts to create equality of outcome undermine equality of opportunity and legal equality. To obtain equality of outcome you have to treat people differently. For example, 'affirmative action' programmes or 'positive discrimination', designed to equalize the achievements of men and women or blacks and whites, result in discrimination. Whites and males are discriminated against while blacks and females enjoy discrimination in their favour.

Saunders uses an example put forward by another New Right writer, Robert Nozick (1974), to show how pursuing equality of outcome leads to injustice. A group of students could agree before an exam that they should all be given a mark of 50 per cent. All would pass and none would have to fear failure, but the result would not be just. Some individuals would feel rightly aggrieved if they were stripped of 30 per cent of the marks they would normally have gained and which they had earned through their own efforts.

Saunders and Nozick therefore adopt a conception of equality based on legal equality and the idea of entitlement. Social justice is served when people are allowed to keep those things to which they are entitled. So long as people have earned the resources or money they possess legally through their own work or 'uncoerced exchanges with others', then there should be no question of them being robbed of their possessions. If people pass their wealth on to others then the recipients become entitled to keep it.

Saunders does, however, admit that there is one flaw in this argument. In a society such as Britain, it is not clear that all of the wealthy are actually entitled to what they own. Some of the land in private hands has been passed down to the descendants of Norman warlords who helped William the Conqueror conquer England. Saunders does not want to see the wealth of landowners such as the Duke of Westminster or the Queen taken from them. To do so would undermine 'the whole basis of modern-day property ownership'. He therefore turns to a second justification for inequality which comes from the work of Hayek.

Both Saunders and Hayek believe that inequality is justified because it promotes economic growth. By allowing and encouraging people to pursue their own self-interest, the interests of society as a whole are promoted. Some entrepreneurs who set up businesses fail. When this happens they bear the costs of their own failure. When they succeed they may, as Saunders says, 'accumulate a fortune, but in doing so they will have added to the productive power and wealth of the society as a whole'.

Competition ensures that goods or services increase in quality and fall in price, making them available to a wider section of the population. Not everyone will be able to afford consumer products initially, or indeed in the end, but living standards will constantly increase. The efforts of entrepreneurs make some of them rich, but at the same time 'the rest of society grows more affluent as it gains by their efforts'.

Saunders cites cars, air travel, ballpoint pens, colour televisions, home computers and central heating as examples of things that have become affordable for ordinary people.

Opportunity and inequality

Saunders clearly believes that competition in capitalist societies benefits the population. In his recent work, he has argued that Britain is close to being a meritocracy (Saunders, 1996). Although he does not claim that Britain or similar societies are perfect meritocracies, in which everyone has genuinely equal opportunities to use their talents to achieve success, he does believe that the distribution of economic rewards is closely related to merit.

He argues that much of the apparent inequality of opportunity between classes in capitalist societies may be due to the unequal distribution of ability and effort. In other words, the children of middle-class parents may deserve to be more successful than those from working-class backgrounds because they tend to have greater genetically inherited ability and because they work harder.

If this is the case, then it is not surprising if the children of the middle class get better jobs and higher pay than the children of the working class. Nor is this evidence of inequality of opportunity as the differences of outcome may well be based on merit. Saunders's claim that Britain is close to being a meritocracy is highly controversial. It will be discussed in detail later in the chapter in the light of studies of social mobility (see pp. 105–8).

Saunders also emphasizes the increasing opportunities for people from all backgrounds as the proportion of well-paid, middle-class jobs in the occupational structure has steadily increased.

In societies such as Britain and the USA there are fewer people who are unsuccessful than there were in the past. Whatever the relative chances of people from different classes getting a higher-class job, the absolute chances have increased for everybody. Capitalism creates more well-paid, skilled and white-collar jobs for which people from all backgrounds can compete. Saunders concludes:

> *Capitalism is dynamic because it is unequal, and any attempt to equalise wealth and income will succeed only at the expense of stifling initiative, innovation and social and economic development.*
>
> Saunders, 1990, p. 53

A critique of the New Right perspective

The New Right perspective on stratification is open to a number of criticisms. Some of Tumin's criticisms of Davis and Moore are also relevant to New Right theories. For example, the New Right can be accused of playing down the possible harmful effects of stratification in undermining social cohesion and integration. Saunders's view that socialist societies are inevitably more repressive than free-market capitalist ones could be seen as an unjustified, sweeping generalization. For example:

1 Early capitalism was partly based upon the use of slave labour.

2 In South Africa, until relatively recently, a capitalist-free market economy went hand-in-hand with the apartheid system that separated 'races' and gave black South Africans very few opportunities.

3 In Chile, a democratically elected socialist government under the leadership of President Allende was overthrown in the 1970s in a coup led by General Pinochet. Pinochet followed free market economic policies and his seizure of power was partly engineered by the USA. Yet his regime was far more repressive than that of his predecessor. One of the Pinochet regime's first actions was to round up thousands of potential opponents and take them to the national football stadium where many were executed.

Examples such as these suggest that the free market and freedom do not inevitably go hand-in-hand.

Gordon Marshall and Adam Swift – social class and social justice

Marshall and Swift (1993) have made the most detailed evaluation of Saunders's views on stratification. They criticize him for trying to argue in favour of both equality of opportunity and formal or legal equality. These two principles may sometimes coincide, but often they do not. For example, Marshall and Swift argue:

> *If a millionaire chooses to bequeath his money to an untalented layabout then justice as entitlement demands that he be permitted to do so, and forbids taxation of the inheritance despite the fact that any normal conception of justice as desert or merit is here clearly violated.*
>
> Marshall and Swift, 1993, p. 191

Marshall and Swift then go on to examine the meritocracy thesis. They question the view that market forces necessarily reward merit. Success in business, for example, may depend as much on luck as on the hard work or personal attributes of the entrepreneur.

Furthermore, Marshall and Swift provide evidence which they claim shows that capitalist societies are not genuinely meritocratic. They use data from a study conducted by Gordon Marshall, Howard Newby, David Rose and Carolyn Vogler (1988). This study found that patterns of social mobility were influenced by class even when educational attainment was taken into account. People from working-class backgrounds had less chance than those from higher-class backgrounds of obtaining a position in one of the top classes even when they had the same level of educational qualifications.

This undermines Saunders's claim that inequalities between classes could be the result of genetic differences. Working-class people with, for example, the ability to get a degree, were still disadvantaged because of their class background. As Marshall and Swift say:

> *If people find their place in the occupational order according to meritocratic principles, then the impact of class background should not be apparent in class destinations, except as this is mediated by educational achievements.*
>
> Marshall and Swift, 1993, p. 202

The free market does not guarantee that merit is equally rewarded for all social groups. Social justice may therefore be promoted if the state intervenes to try to make job allocation meritocratic. (For more details of the study by Marshall *et al.* see pp. 102–5. For a fuller discussion of Saunders on Britain being a meritocracy see pp. 105–8.)

Social stratification – a Marxist perspective

Marxist perspectives provide a radical alternative to functionalist views of the nature of social stratification. They regard stratification as a divisive rather than an integrative structure. They see it as a mechanism whereby some exploit others, rather than as a means of furthering collective goals.

Marxists focus on social strata rather than social inequality in general. Functionalists, such as Parsons and Davis and Moore, say little about social stratification in the sense of clearly defined social strata whose members have shared interests. However, this view of social stratification is central to Marxist theory.

Marx's views will first be briefly summarized and then examined in more detail. For details of Marx's theory of stratification, see Marx 1970 (1867), 1974 (1909), Marx and Engels 1848, and Bottomore and Rubel 1963.

Classes

1 In all stratified societies, there are two major social groups: a ruling class and a subject class.

2 The power of the ruling class comes from its ownership and control of the means of production (land, capital, labour power, buildings and machinery).

3 The ruling class exploits and oppresses the subject class.

4 As a result, there is a basic conflict of interest between the two classes.

5 The various institutions of society, such as the legal and political systems, are instruments of ruling-class domination and serve to further its interests.

6 Only when the means of production are communally owned will classes disappear, thereby bringing an end to the exploitation and oppression of some by others.

From a Marxist perspective, systems of stratification derive from the relationships of social groups to the means of production. Marx used the term 'class' to refer to the main strata in all stratification systems, although most modern sociologists would reserve the term for strata in capitalist society. From a Marxist viewpoint, a class is a social group whose members share the same relationship to the means of production.

For example, in a feudal epoch, there are two main classes distinguished by their relationship to land (the crucial part of the means of production in an agricultural society). They are the feudal nobility who own the land, and the landless serfs who work the land. Similarly, in a capitalist era, there are two main classes: the bourgeoisie or capitalist class, which owns the means of production, and the proletariat or working class, whose members own only their labour which they hire to the bourgeoisie in return for wages.

Classes and historical epochs

Marx believed that Western society had developed through four main epochs:

1 primitive communism
2 ancient society
3 feudal society
4 capitalist society.

Primitive communism is represented by the societies of prehistory and provides the only example of a classless society. From then on, all societies are divided into two major classes: masters and slaves in ancient society, lords and serfs in feudal society and capitalists and wage labourers in capitalist society.

During each historical epoch, the labour power required for production was supplied by the subject class, that is by slaves, serfs and wage labourers respectively. The subject class is made up of the majority of the population whereas the ruling or dominant class forms a minority. The relationship between the two major classes will be discussed shortly.

Classes did not exist during the era of primitive communism when societies were based on a socialist mode of production. In a hunting and gathering band, the earliest form of human society, the land and its products were communally owned. The men hunted and the women gathered plant food, and the produce was shared by members of the band. Classes did not exist since all members of society shared the same relationship to the means of production. Every member was both producer and owner, all provided labour power and shared the products of their labour. Hunting and gathering is a subsistence economy which means that production only meets basic survival needs.

Classes emerge when the productive capacity of society expands beyond the level required for subsistence. This occurs when agriculture becomes the dominant mode of production. In an agricultural economy, only a section of society is needed to produce the food requirements of the whole society. Many individuals are thus freed from food production and are able to specialize in other tasks. The rudimentary division of labour of the hunting and gathering band is replaced by an increasingly more complex and specialized division.

For example, in the early agricultural villages, some individuals became full-time producers of pottery, clothing and agricultural implements. As agriculture developed, surplus wealth – that is goods above the basic subsistence needs of the community – was produced. This led to an exchange of goods, and trading developed rapidly both within and between communities. This was accompanied by the development of a system of private property. Goods were increasingly seen as commodities or articles of trade to which the individual rather than the community had right of ownership.

Private property, and the accumulation of surplus wealth, form the basis for the development of class societies. In particular, they provide the preconditions for the emergence of a class of producers and a class of non-producers. Some people are able to acquire the means of production, and others are therefore obliged to work for them. The result is a class of non-producers which owns the means of production, and a class of producers which owns only its labour.

Dependency and conflict

From a Marxist perspective, the relationship between the major social classes is one of mutual dependence and conflict. Thus, in capitalist society, the bourgeoisie and proletariat are dependent upon each other. Wage labourers must sell their labour power in order to survive, as they do not own a part of the means of production and lack the means to produce goods independently. They are, therefore, dependent for their livelihood on the capitalists and the wages they offer. The capitalists, as non-producers, are dependent on the labour power of wage labourers, since, without it, there would be no production.

However, the mutual dependency of the two classes is not a relationship of equal or symmetrical reciprocity. Instead, it is a relationship of exploiter and exploited, oppressor and oppressed. In particular, the ruling class gains at the expense of the subject class and there is therefore a conflict of interest between them.

This may be illustrated by Marx's view of the nature of ownership and production in capitalist society.

The capitalist economy and exploitation

The basic characteristics of a capitalist economy may be summarized as follows:

1   Capital may be defined as money used to finance the production of commodities for private gain.

2   In a capitalist economy, goods and the labour power, raw materials and machinery used to produce them, are given a monetary value.

3   The capitalists invest their capital in the production of goods.

4   Capital is accumulated by selling those goods at a value greater than their cost of production.

Capitalism therefore involves the investment of capital in the production of commodities with the aim of maximizing profit in order to accumulate more capital. Money is converted into commodities by financing production, those commodities are then sold and converted back into money at such a price that the capitalists end up with more money than they started with.

Capital is privately owned by a minority, the capitalist class. In Marx's view, however, this capital is gained from the exploitation of the mass of the population, the working class. Marx argued that capital, as such, produces nothing. Only labour produces wealth. Yet the wages paid to the workers for their labour are well below the value of the goods they produce.

The difference between the value of wages and commodities is known as surplus value. This surplus value is appropriated in the form of profit by the capitalists. Because they are non-producers, the bourgeoisie are therefore exploiting the proletariat, the real producers of wealth.

Marx maintained that in all class societies, the ruling class exploits and oppresses the subject class.

Power and the superstructure

Political power, in Marxist theory, comes from economic power. The power of the ruling class therefore stems from its ownership and control of the means of production. As the superstructure of society – the major institutions, values and belief systems – is seen to be largely shaped by the economic infrastructure, the relations of production will be reproduced in the superstructure. Therefore, the dominance of the ruling class in the relations of production will be reflected in the superstructure. In particular, the political and legal systems will reflect ruling-class interests since, in Marx's words, 'the existing relations of production between individuals must necessarily express themselves also as political and legal relations'.

For instance, the various ownership rights of the capitalist class will be enshrined in and protected by the laws of the land. Thus the various parts of the superstructure can be seen as instruments of ruling-class domination and as mechanisms for the oppression of the subject class.

In the same way, the position of the dominant class is supported by beliefs and values which are systematically generated by the infrastructure. As noted on page 13, Marx referred to the dominant concepts of class societies as ruling-class ideology since they justify and legitimate ruling-class domination and project a distorted picture of reality. For example, the emphasis on freedom in capitalist society, illustrated by phrases such as 'the free market', 'free democratic societies' and 'the free world', is an illusion that disguises the wage slavery of the proletariat.

Ruling-class ideology produces false class consciousness, a false picture of the nature of the relationship between social classes. Members of both classes tend to accept the status quo as normal and natural and are largely unaware of the true nature of exploitation and oppression. In this way, the conflict of interest between the classes is disguised and a degree of social stability produced, but the basic contradictions and conflicts of class societies remain unresolved.

Class and social change

Class struggle

Marx believed that the class struggle was the driving force of social change. He stated that 'the history of all societies up to the present is the history of the class struggle'.

A new historical epoch is created by the development of superior forces of production by a new social group. These developments take place within the framework of the previous era. The merchants and industrialists who spearheaded the rise of capitalism emerged during the feudal era. They accumulated capital, laid the foundations for industrial manufacture, factory production and the system of wage labour, all of which were essential components of capitalism. The superiority of the capitalist mode of production led to a rapid transformation of the structure of society. The capitalist class became dominant, and although the feudal aristocracy maintained aspects of its power well into the nineteenth century, it was fighting a losing battle.

The class struggles of history have been between minorities. Capitalism, for instance, developed from the struggle between the feudal aristocracy and the emerging capitalist class, both groups in numerical terms forming a minority of the population. Major changes in history have involved the replacement of one form of private property by another, and of one type of production technique by another: capitalism involved the replacement of privately owned land and an agricultural economy by privately owned capital and an industrial economy.

Marx believed that the class struggle that would transform capitalist society would involve none of these processes. The protagonists would be the bourgeoisie and the proletariat, a minority versus a majority. Private property would be replaced by communally owned property. Industrial manufacture

would remain as the basic technique of production in the new society.

Marx believed that the basic contradictions contained in a capitalist economic system would lead to its eventual destruction. The proletariat would overthrow the bourgeoisie and seize the means of production, the source of power. Property would be communally owned and, since all members of society would now share the same relationship to the means of production, a classless society would result. Since history is the history of the class struggle, history would now end. The communist society which would replace capitalism would contain no contradictions, no conflicts of interest, and would therefore be unchanging. However, certain changes were necessary before the dawning of this utopia.

Class consciousness

Marx distinguished between a 'class in itself' and a 'class for itself'. A class in itself is simply a social group whose members share the same relationship to the means of production. Marx argued that a social group only fully becomes a class when it becomes a class for itself. At this stage, its members have class consciousness and class solidarity. Class consciousness means that false class consciousness has been replaced by a full awareness of the true situation, by a realization of the nature of exploitation. Members of a class then develop a common identity, recognize their shared interests and unite, so creating class solidarity. The final stage of class consciousness and class solidarity is reached when members realize that only by collective action can they overthrow the ruling class, and take positive steps to do so.

Marx believed that the following aspects of capitalist society would eventually lead to the proletariat developing into a 'class for itself'.

1 Capitalist society is by its very nature unstable. It is based on contradictions and antagonisms which can only be resolved by its transformation. In particular, the conflict of interest between the bourgeoisie and the proletariat cannot be resolved within the framework of a capitalist economy. The basic conflict of interest involves the exploitation of workers by the capitalists.

2 Marx believed that this first contradiction would be highlighted by a second: the contradiction between social production and individual ownership. As capitalism developed, the workforce was increasingly concentrated in large factories where production was a social enterprise. Social production juxtaposed with individual ownership illuminates the exploitation of the proletariat. Social production also makes it easier for workers to organize themselves against the capitalists. It facilitates communication and encourages a recognition of common circumstances and interests.

Polarization of the classes

Apart from the basic contradictions of capitalist society, Marx believed that certain factors in the natural development of a capitalist economy would hasten its downfall. These factors would result in the polarization of the two main classes: the gap between the proletariat and the bourgeoisie will become greater and the contrast between the two groups will become more stark. Such factors include:

1 First, the increasing use of machinery will result in a homogeneous working class. Since 'machinery obliterates the differences in labour', members of the proletariat will become increasingly similar. The differences between skilled, semi-skilled and unskilled workers will tend to disappear as machines remove the skill required in the production of commodities.

2 Second, the difference in wealth between the bourgeoisie and the proletariat will increase as the accumulation of capital proceeds. Even though the real wages and living standards of the proletariat may rise, its members will become poorer in relation to the bourgeoisie. This process is known as pauperization.

3 Third, the competitive nature of capitalism means that only the largest and most wealthy companies will survive and prosper. Competition will depress the intermediate strata – those groups lying between the two main classes – into the proletariat. Thus the petty bourgeoisie, the owners of small businesses, will sink into the proletariat. At the same time the surviving companies will grow larger and capital will be concentrated into fewer hands.

These three processes – the obliteration of the differences in labour, the pauperization of the working class, and the depression of the intermediate strata into the proletariat – will result in the polarization of the two major classes.

Marx believed he could see the process of polarization in nineteenth-century Britain. He wrote that 'society as a whole is more and more splitting into two great hostile camps ... bourgeoisie and proletariat'. The battle lines were now clearly drawn: Marx hoped that the proletarian revolution would shortly follow and the communist utopia of his dreams would finally become a reality.

Marx's work on class has been examined in detail for the following reasons:

1 Many sociologists claim that his theory still provides the best explanation of the nature of class in capitalist society.

2 Much of the research on class has been inspired by ideas and questions raised by Marx.

3 Many of the concepts of class analysis introduced by Marx have proved useful to Marxists and non-Marxists alike.

Social stratification – a Weberian perspective

The work of the German sociologist Max Weber (1864–1920) represents one of the most important developments in stratification theory since Marx. Weber believed that social stratification results from a struggle for scarce resources in society. Although he saw this struggle as being primarily concerned with economic resources, it can also involve struggles for prestige and for political power.

Market situation

Like Marx, Weber saw class in economic terms (Weber, 1947). He argued that classes develop in market economies in which individuals compete for economic gain. He defined a class as a group of individuals who share a similar position in a market economy, and by virtue of that fact receive similar economic rewards. Thus, in Weber's terminology, a person's 'class situation' is basically their 'market situation'. Those who share a similar class situation also share similar life chances. Their economic position will directly affect their chances of obtaining those things defined as desirable in their society, for example access to higher education and good quality housing.

Like Marx, Weber argued that the major class division is between those who own the forces of production and those who do not. Thus those who have substantial property holdings will receive the highest economic rewards and enjoy superior life chances. However, Weber saw important differences in the market situation of the propertyless groups in society. In particular, the various skills and services offered by different occupations have differing market values. For instance, in capitalist society, managers, administrators and professionals receive relatively high salaries because of the demand for their services. Weber distinguished the following class groupings in capitalist society:

1 the propertied upper class

2 the propertyless white-collar workers

3 the petty bourgeoisie

4 the manual working class.

In his analysis of class, Weber disagreed with Marx on a number of important issues:

1 Factors other than the ownership or non-ownership of property are significant in the formation of classes. In particular, the market value of the skills of the propertyless groups varies and the resulting differences in economic return are sufficient to produce different social classes.

2 Weber saw no evidence to support the idea of the polarization of classes. Although he saw some decline in the numbers of the petty bourgeoisie (the small property owners) due to competition from large companies, he argued that they enter white-collar or skilled manual trades rather than being depressed into the ranks of unskilled manual workers. More importantly, Weber argued that the white-collar 'middle class' expands rather than contracts as capitalism develops. He maintained that capitalist enterprises and the modern nation state require a 'rational' bureaucratic administration which involves large numbers of administrators and clerical staff. Thus Weber saw a diversification of classes and an expansion of the white-collar middle class, rather than a polarization.

3 Weber rejected the view, held by some Marxists, of the inevitability of the proletarian revolution. He saw no reason why those sharing a similar class situation should necessarily develop a common identity, recognize shared interests and take collective action to further those interests. For example, Weber suggested that individual manual workers who are dissatisfied with their class situation may respond in a variety of ways. They may grumble, work to rule, sabotage industrial machinery, take strike action, or attempt to organize other members of their class in an effort to overthrow capitalism. Weber admitted that a common market situation might provide a basis for collective class action but he saw this only as a possibility.

4 Weber rejected the Marxist view that political power necessarily derives from economic power. He argued that class forms only one possible basis for power and that the distribution of power in society is not necessarily linked to the distribution of class inequalities.

Status situation

While class forms one possible basis for group formation, collective action and the acquisition of political power, Weber argued that there are other bases for these activities. In particular, groups form because their members share a similar status situation. Whereas class refers to the unequal distribution of economic rewards, status refers to the unequal distribution of 'social honour'.

Occupations, ethnic and religious groups, and, most importantly, lifestyles, are accorded differing degrees of prestige or esteem by members of society. A status group is made up of individuals who are awarded a similar amount of social honour and therefore share the same status situation. Unlike classes, members of status groups are almost always aware of their common status situation. They share a similar lifestyle, identify with and feel they belong to their status group, and often place restrictions on the ways in which outsiders may interact with them.

Weber argued that status groups reach their most developed form in the caste system of traditional Hindu society in India. Castes and sub-castes were formed and distinguished largely in terms of social honour; lifestyles were sharply differentiated and accorded varying degrees of prestige.

Social closure

Castes also provide a good example of the process described by Weber as social closure. Social closure involves the exclusion of some people from member-ship of a status group. In the caste system social closure is achieved through prohibitions which prevent members of a caste from marrying outside their caste. The caste system is an extreme example of social closure since the exclusion of outsiders from the status group is so complete. Another example was the apartheid system in South Africa which lasted from the 1940s until 1992. The population was divided into whites, Asians, black Africans, and 'coloured' people descended from more than one 'race'. These different groups were kept apart in public places (for example they were required to use different public toilets), they had to live in different neighbourhoods and they were prohibited from marrying someone from a different group. Not surprisingly the better facilities and neighbourhoods were reserved for the dominant white population.

Other status groups erect less formidable barriers to entry. In modern Britain, studies of elite self-recruitment suggest that certain types of job, such as senior positions in the Civil Service, are usually filled by those who have attended public school. Although individuals who went to state schools have some chance of entering these jobs, public school educated elites largely reserve such positions for themselves and their children's group. (For details of elite self-recruitment see Chapter 9.)

Class and status groups

In many societies, class and status situations are closely linked. Weber noted that 'property as such is not always recognized as a status qualification, but in the long run it is, and with extraordinary regularity'. However, those who share the same class situation will not necessarily belong to the same status group. For example, the *nouveaux riches* (the newly rich) are sometimes excluded from the status groups of the privileged because their tastes, manners and dress are defined as vulgar.

Status groups may create divisions within classes. In a study of Banbury, in Oxfordshire, conducted in the 1950s, Margaret Stacey (1960) found that members of the manual working class distinguished three status groups within that class: the 'respectable working class', the 'ordinary working class' and the 'rough working class'.

Economic factors influenced the formation of these groups – for example, the 'roughs' were often in the lowest income bracket – but they did not determine status since the income of many 'roughs' was similar to that of members of other status groups.

Status groups can also cut across class divisions. For example, homosexuals from different class backgrounds are involved in Gay Rights organizations and events such as the annual Gay Pride celebration in Britain.

Weber's observations on status groups are important because they suggest that in certain situations status rather than class provides the basis for the formation of social groups. In addition, the presence of different status groups within a single class and of status groups which cut across class divisions can weaken class solidarity and reduce the potential for class consciousness. These points are illustrated by Weber's analysis of 'parties'.

Parties

Weber defined parties as groups which are specifically concerned with influencing policies and making decisions in the interests of their membership. In Weber's words, parties are concerned with 'the acquisition of social "power"'.

Parties include a variety of associations, from the mass political parties of Western democracies to the whole range of pressure or interest groups which include professional associations, trades unions, the Automobile Association and the RSPCA. Parties often, but not necessarily, represent the interests of classes or status groups. In Weber's words, 'Parties may represent interests determined through "class situation" or "status situation" .... In most cases they

are partly class parties and partly status parties, but sometimes they are neither.'

The combination of class and status interests can be seen in a group such as the Nation of Islam in the USA. As well as being a religious group it is also active in trying to achieve political change. It represents a status group but it also represents class interests – the majority of its members are working class.

Weber's view of parties suggests that the relationship between political groups and class and status groups is far from clearcut. Just as status groups can both divide classes and cut across class boundaries, so parties can divide and cut across both classes and status groups. Weber's analysis of classes, status groups and parties suggests that no single theory can pinpoint and explain their relationship. The interplay of class, status and party in the formation of social groups is complex and variable and must be examined in particular societies during particular time periods.

Marx attempted to reduce all forms of inequality to social class and argued that classes formed the only significant social groups in society. Weber argues that the evidence provides a more complex and diversified picture of social stratification.

Modern theories of stratification

Most contemporary studies of stratification are based either upon a Marxist or a Weberian perspective. Some modern sociologists have remained close to the original theories of Marx and Weber. Others have drawn their inspiration from one or other of these classic sociologists, but have made significant alterations to their original theories in an attempt to describe and explain the class structures of capitalist industrial societies. Such sociologists can be referred to as new, or neo-Marxists and neo-Weberians.

There has been a long-standing debate between those who draw their inspiration from Marx, and those who follow Weber, as to which approach is more useful as a way of developing a sociological understanding of class. We will analyse this debate in later sections of this chapter when we deal with the different classes in contemporary capitalism. Contemporary neo-Marxist and neo-Weberian theories of the class structure as a whole will also be examined towards the end of the chapter. In the next section, however, we will consider how the stratification system has changed over time in British society.

Changes in the British stratification system

As we discovered in the previous section, most contemporary theories of stratification have been influenced by the pioneering work of Marx or Weber. Despite the differences between these sociologists, both gave primary importance to material inequalities. Marx saw the most important divisions in any system of stratification as stemming from differences in the ownership of wealth, and specifically ownership of the means of production. Weber also saw ownership of wealth as an important criterion for distinguishing classes. Weber, however, placed more emphasis than Marx on divisions within the propertyless class – the class whose members did not own sufficient property to support themselves without working. Income levels and other life chances for this group depended largely upon the market situation of the occupational group to which the individuals belonged.

No system of class stratification is fixed and static. The distribution of resources within the class system constantly changes, and the size and market situation of occupational groups also alters over time. The next sections will describe some of the broad patterns of change in the composition of the occupational structure and the distribution of income and wealth in Britain in the twentieth century. Later sections will examine the changing position of particular classes in more detail.

Changes in the occupational structure

Sociologists from Marx and Weber onwards have debated how best to define social classes. Many, though not all, now base their class categories, at least partly, upon occupational groupings. Official government statistics distinguish between socio-economic groups, which, it is claimed, bring together people with jobs of similar social and economic status.

Although there are disagreements about where the boundary between the middle and working classes should be placed, it has often been the case that manual workers are regarded as being working class, and non-manual workers as middle class. In official publications, types of manual job are usually distinguished according to levels of skill, with separate categories being used for the unskilled, semi-skilled and skilled manual worker. Non-manual jobs are also usually divided into three categories: routine non-manual jobs, which include clerical and secretarial work; intermediate non-manual jobs such as teachers, nurses, librarians and some managers;

Table 2.1 Occupational class and industrial status of the gainfully occupied population in Great Britain, 1911, 1921, 1931, 1951, 1971: numbers in thousands

	All					Males					Females				
	1911	1921	1931	1951	1971	1911	1921	1931	1951	1971	1911	1921	1931	1951	1971
1 Professional															
(a) Higher															
Employers	–	25	38	34	79	–	25	37	33	75	–	–	–	1	4
Own account	–	36	44	44	59	–	35	41	40	53	–	2	3	4	7
Employees	–	134	158	356	687	–	126	144	326	646	–	8	15	31	40
All	184	195	240	434	824	173	186	222	399	774	11	10	18	36	50
%	1.00	1.01	1.14	1.93	3.29	1.34	1.36	1.50	2.56	4.87	0.20	0.18	0.29	0.52	0.55
(b) Lower															
Employers	–	18	15	10	25	–	14	8	7	17	–	4	7	3	7
Own account	–	62	70	42	59	–	20	22	22	37	–	42	48	20	22
Employees	–	600	643	1,007	1,863	–	242	270	463	892	–	357	373	544	971
All	560	680	728	1,059	1,946	208	276	300	492	946	352	403	428	567	1,000
%	3.05	3.52	3.46	4.70	7.78	1.61	2.02	2.03	3.16	5.95	6.49	7.07	6.83	8.18	10.95

continued ...

	All					Males					Females				
	1911	1921	1931	1951	1971	1911	1921	1931	1951	1971	1911	1921	1931	1951	1971
2 Employers, administrators, managers															
(a) Employers and proprietors															
Employers	763	692	727	457	621	661	613	646	400	485	102	79	82	56	136
Own account	469	626	682	661	435	339	435	483	494	320	130	191	196	167	115
All	1,232	1,318	1,409	1,118	1,056	1,000	1,048	1,129	894	805	232	270	278	223	251
%	6.71	6.82	6.70	4.97	4.22	7.74	7.69	7.65	5.74	5.07	4.28	4.74	4.44	3.22	2.75
(b) Managers and administrators															
Own account	21	29	30	31	46	20	27	28	27	35	2	2	2	2	11
Employees	608	675	740	1,215	2,008	486	557	642	1,029	1,698	123	118	98	186	310
All	629	704	770	1,246	2,054	506	584	670	1,056	1,733	125	120	100	189	321
%	3.43	3.64	3.66	5.53	8.21	3.91	4.28	4.54	6.78	10.91	2.30	2.11	1.60	2.73	3.51
3 Clerical workers															
Own account	–	1	2	3	22	–	1	2	2	5		–	–	1	17
Employees	887	1,299	1,463	2,401	3,457	708	735	815	988	1,008	179	564	648	1,413	2,449
All	887	1,300	1,465	2,404	3,479	708	736	817	990	1,013	179	564	648	1,414	2,466
%	4.84	6.72	6.97	10.68	13.90	5.48	5.40	5.53	6.35	6.38	3.30	9.90	10.34	20.41	27.00
4 Foremen, inspectors, supervisors															
Employees	236	279	323	590	968	227	261	295	511	801	10	18	28	79	168
%	1..29	1.44	1.54	2.62	3.87	1.75	1.91	2.00	3.28	5.04	0.18	0.32	0.45	1.14	1.84
5 Skilled manual															
Own account	329	293	268	251	349	170	205	200	214	324	159	88	68	37	25
Employees	5,279	5,280	5,351	5,365	5,045	4,094	4,200	4,223	4,519	4,295	1,185	1,080	1,128	847	750
All	5,608	5,573	5,619	5,616	5,394	4,264	4,405	4,423	4,733	4,619	1,344	1,168	1,196	884	775
%	30.56	28.83	26.72	24.95	21.56	32.99	32.30	29.96	30.36	29.08	24.78	20.50	19.09	12.75	8.48
6 Semi-skilled manual															
Own account	71	98	96	82	53	41	70	78	73	35	30	28	17	10	18
Employees	7,173	6,446	7,264	7,256	6,258	4,305	3,789	4,181	4,279	3,272	2,868	2,656	3,084	2,978	2,986
All	7,244	6,544	7,360	7,338	6,312	4,346	3,859	4,259	4,352	3,307	2,898	2,684	3,101	2,988	3,005
%	39.48	33.85	35.00	32.60	25.23	33.63	28.30	28.85	27.92	20.82	53.42	47.11	49.51	43.12	32.90
7 Unskilled manual															
Own account	47	62	78	33	92	38	48	65	29	86	9	14	13	3	6
Employees	1,720	2,678	3,034	2,676	2,895	1,455	2,232	2,580	2,129	1,803	265	446	454	547	1,092
All	1,767	2,740	3,115	2,709	2,987	1,493	2,280	2,645	2,158	1,889	274	460	467	550	1,098
%	9.63	14.17	14.81	12.03	11.94	11.55	16.72	17.92	13.84	11.89	5.05	8.07	7.45	7.94	12.02
All	18,347	19,333	21,029	22,514	25,021	12,925	13,636	14,761	15,584	15,884	5,425	5,697	6,264	6,930	9,138
%	100.00	100.00	100.00	100.00	100.00	100.00	100.00	100.00	100.00	100.00	100.00	100.00	100.00	100.00	100.00

Note: Because numbers are rounded to the nearest thousand, totals may not equal the sum of thier parts.
Source: G. Routh (1980) *Occupation and Pay in Great Britain 1906–79*, Macmillan, London, pp. 6-7.

Table 2.2 Socio-economic group by sex: 1975 to 1994

All persons aged 16 and over (%) Socio-economic group*	1975	1979	1981	1983	1985	1987	1989	1991	1993	1994
Men										
Professional	5	6	4	5	6	7	7	7	7	7
Employers and managers	15	15	15	17	19	19	20	19	20	21
Intermediate and junior non-manual	17	17	17	15	17	16	16	17	17	17
Skilled manual and self-employed	41	40	41	39	37	37	38	38	37	35
Semi-skilled manual and personal service	17	17	18	18	16	15	15	14	14	14
Unskilled manual	5	5	5	5	5	5	5	5	4	5
Base = 100%	10,902	10,280	10,880	8,886	8,787	9,190	8,815	8,596	8,089	7,948
Women										
Professional	1	1	1	1	1	1	1	1	2	2
Employers and managers	4	5	5	6	7	8	9	9	10	11
Intermediate and junior non-manual	46	45	46	46	48	47	47	48	49	48
Skilled manual and self-employed	9	9	9	9	9	9	9	9	8	8
Semi-skilled manual and personal service	31	30	29	30	27	26	25	22	22	22
Unskilled manual	9	10	10	9	7	9	8	11	10	9
Base = 100%	11,799	11,102	11,743	9,754	9,439	9,976	9,600	9,254	9,009	8,698
Total										
Professional	3	3	2	3	3	4	4	4	4	4
Employers and managers	9	10	9	11	13	14	14	14	15	16
Intermediate and junior non-manual	32	32	32	31	33	32	32	33	34	33
Skilled manual and self-employed	24	24	24	24	23	23	23	23	22	21
Semi-skilled manual and personal service	24	24	24	24	22	21	20	18	18	18
Unskilled manual	7	8	8	7	6	7	7	8	7	7
Base = 100%	22,701	21,382	22,623	18,640	18,226	19,166	18,415	17,850	17,098	16,646

* The socio-economic group shown is based on the informant's own job (or last job if not in employment). Excludes those in the armed forces and any who have never worked.

Source: N. Bennett, L. Jarvis, O. Rowlands, N. Singleton and L. Haselden (1996) *Living in Britain: Results from the 1994 General Household Survey*, HMSO, London, p. 195

and the highest class in this scheme, which includes professionals, such as doctors and accountants, as well as senior managers.

Although calculated in different ways, Tables 2.1 and 2.2 are both based upon the idea of socio-economic grouping. Table 2.1 shows changes in the occupational structure between 1911 and 1971. Table 2.2 is calculated on a different basis but shows changes between 1975 and 1994. (Table 2.2 includes personal service workers in the same category as semi-skilled manual and so includes a wider range of workers in the lower classes than Table 2.1.)

The shift to non-manual employment

The information contained in Tables 2.1 and 2.2 shows that there has been a long-term trend during the twentieth century for the proportion of non-manual jobs to increase, and of manual jobs to decrease. Less than half of all employees now have manual jobs, whereas in 1911, according to Routh, 79 per cent of jobs were manual. According to the *General Household Survey*, the proportion of manual and personal service workers declined from 55 per cent to 46 per cent between 1975 and 1994. There have been marked increases in professional, managerial, and routine non-manual work.

Over the course of the twentieth century various factors contributed to the shift towards non-manual employment. Manufacturing industry declined, while service industries, which employ a lower proportion of manual workers, expanded.

Between 1983 and June 1997, employment in all production and construction industries fell from 5,644,000 to 4,245,000. Employment in service industries over the same period rose from 13,541,000 to 16,865,000 (*Labour Market Trends*, 1997).

For much of the period since the Second World War, increasing numbers of people have been employed in jobs connected to the welfare state, particularly in the National Health Service (NHS), education and the welfare services. Employment has also expanded in local and national government. However, government policies since the late 1980s have reduced employment in local government and the civil service as a number of government functions have been privatized. Employment in

public administration, defence and compulsory social security fell from 1,468,000 in 1983 to 1,308,000 in June 1997. Over the same period employment in hotels and restaurants rose from 917,000 to 1,249,000, and in renting, research, computer and other business activities from 1,562,000 to 2,617,000 (*Labour Market Trends*, 1997). Most of the increases in service sector employment have therefore come from the private sector.

Gender, full-time and part-time work

Women, particularly married women, increasingly started taking paid employment during the twentieth century, but they are not equally distributed throughout the occupational structure. Although women are more likely to have non-manual jobs than men, most female non-manual workers are concentrated in the lowest-paid sectors of non-manual work, and have routine non-manual jobs. As Table 2.2 shows, 48 per cent of female employees were in intermediate and junior non-manual jobs in 1994. Most of the remaining female employees (31 per cent) were in semi-skilled or unskilled manual work or personal service jobs.

Table 2.3, showing full- and part-time employment by gender, reveals a number of significant

Table 2.3   Full and part-time employment[1]: by gender

	Males (thousands)			Females (thousands)		
	Full-time	Part-time	All in employment[2]	Full-time	Part-time	All in employment[2]
1984	13,408	610	14,083	5,543	4,356	9,936
1985	15,537	670	14,217	5,697	4,465	10,173
1986	13,450	707	14,174	5,834	4,523	10,371
1987	13,488	798	14,309	5,953	4,651	10,621
1988	13,941	852	14,824	6,276	4,739	11,036
1989	14,347	846	15,219	6,493	4,964	11,470
1990	14,387	920	15,318	6,643	4,968	11,617
1991	13,958	919	14,887	6,541	4,966	11,512
1992	13,304	1,009	14,321	6,445	5,040	11,491
1993	12,990	1,037	14,035	6,383	5,085	11,476
1994	13,050	1,115	14,171	6,354	5,163	11,526
1995	13,200	1,171	14,374	6,440	5,153	11,599
1996	13,197	1,244	14,446	6,464	5,305	11,773
1997	13,386	1,328	14,720	6,592	5,367	11,962

1 At spring each year, includes employees, self-employed, those on government employment and training schemes and, from 1992, unpaid family workers. Full/part-time is based on respondents' self-assessment.
2 Includes those who did not state whether they worked full-time or part-time.

Source: (1998) *Social Trends*, HMSO, London, p. 80.

trends. Male full-time employment declined slightly between 1984 and 1997, but part-time employment for men increased considerably, while female full-time and part-time employment both increased significantly. The traditional male 'breadwinner' with a full-time job is part of a declining group in the workforce. Women make up a growing proportion of the workforce and are rapidly catching up with men. Traditionally studies of class have concentrated on male full-time workers. The changes outlined here indicate that this is becoming less and less justifiable.

The changing distribution of income

The importance of income

Some sociologists have argued that inequalities in industrial societies are being progressively reduced; others go further and claim that class divisions are disappearing. Income has an important effect upon your life chances: for example on the chances of owning your own home, and on your life expectancy. If income inequalities were gradually disappearing this would be strong evidence that class divisions were weakening.

Some government policies seem designed to achieve greater income equality by redistributing income from more affluent to poorer groups. However, as we will see in the following sections, income can be measured in various ways and official statistics should be used with caution. In addition, it should not be assumed that long-term trends in income distribution continue forever: there is evidence that there have been significant changes in these trends in Britain in recent years. In particular, a long-term trend towards a more equitable distribution of income has been reversed.

The measurement of income distribution

Official statistics measure income in a variety of ways:

1 Original income refers to income from sources such as employment, occupational pensions, gifts, alimony payments, and investment. Figures on original income do not include benefits such as state pensions, family credit, and income support, which are paid by the state.

2 Gross income is a measure of all sources of income. Most individuals are not, however, free to spend all of their gross income, for some is deducted to pay income tax and national insurance contributions.

3 Disposable income is a measure of gross income less the above deductions.

4 Some taxes (indirect taxes) are not paid directly out of income, but are paid by consumers as part of the purchase price of goods. For example, value added

tax (VAT) is payable on most categories of goods in the UK. Duties are also payable on products such as petrol, tobacco and alcohol. Post-tax income is the measure of income after the above taxes, and taxes such as the Council Tax, are deducted.

5 Final income adds on to income after taxes the value of benefits provided by the state which are not given in cash, for example medical care and education.

By examining these different measures it is possible to discover the effects of government policy on the distribution of income. Table 2.4 gives figures for 1995–6, based upon the *Family Expenditure Survey*.

The effects of taxation and benefits

Table 2.4 demonstrates that even after taxation and benefits are taken into account, considerable income inequalities remain. In 1995–6, the poorest 20 per cent of households received little more than half the average final income, whilst the richest 20 per cent received nearly twice the national average. However, it is clear that benefits help to reduce income inequality. In particular, benefits boost the very low original income of the poorest 20 per cent of households. Overall taxation and benefits also reduce the final income of richer groups in the population, although less than the higher rates of income tax for high earners would suggest. This is partly because poorer groups in the population tend to pay a higher proportion of their income in indirect taxes than richer ones.

The official government figures need to be treated with some caution. Only about 70 per cent of households approached agreed to participate in the *Family Expenditure Survey*. Furthermore, there is no guarantee that the information obtained is entirely reliable. Individuals may not declare all their income, particularly if they have not been truthful to the Inland Revenue or the DSS. The figures may be particularly prone to underestimating the income of the highest earners, who have more opportunities to hide substantial amounts of income than middle- and lower-income groups.

Sources of income

Income comes from a number of sources. According to British government statistics, wages and salaries are the most important source of income in the United Kingdom. In 1995, 56 per cent of all household income came from this source, 13 per cent from social security benefits, 11 per cent from private pensions and annuities, etc., 10 per cent from self-employment, 7 per cent from rent, dividends and interest, and 3 per cent from other current transfers (such as payments from abroad, from charities and government grants) (*Social Trends*, 1997).

Table 2.4   Redistribution of income through taxes and benefits, 1995–6

	Quintile group of households (£ per year)					
	Bottom fifth	Next fifth	Middle fifth	Next fifth	Top fifth	All
Average per household						
Wages and salaries	1,390	4,050	10,390	17,610	29,810	12,650
Imputed income from benefits in kind	30	30	100	290	890	270
Self-employment income	370	570	1,250	1,670	5,050	1,780
Occupational pensions, annuities	290	950	1,310	1,790	2,410	1,350
Investment income	200	340	580	830	2,640	920
Other income	150	160	170	250	460	240
Total original income	2,430	6,090	13,790	22,450	41,260	17,200
plus Benefits in cash						
Contributory	1,860	2,280	1,710	1,180	770	1,560
Non-contributory	3,050	2,380	1,650	950	430	1,690
Gross income	7,340	10,750	17,150	24,580	42,450	20,450
less Income tax and NIC	540	930	2,480	4,470	9,660	3,610
less Local taxes (gross)	590	590	650	710	820	670
Disposable income	6,210	9,230	14,020	19,400	31,980	16,170
less Indirect taxes	1,930	2,340	3,290	4,090	5,090	3,350
Post-tax income	4,280	6,890	10,730	15,310	26,890	12,820
plus Benefits in kind						
Education	1,810	1,300	1,420	1,070	830	1,290
National Health Service	1,890	1,830	1,730	1,520	1,330	1,660
Housing subsidy	90	80	40	20	10	50
Travel subsidies	50	70	60	60	140	70
School meals and welfare milk	100	30	10	–	—	30
Final income	8,230	10,200	13,990	17,980	29,200	15,920

Source: (1998) *Social Trends*, HMSO, London, p. 101.

Alissa Goodman, Paul Johnson and Steven Webb have conducted a study of household income inequality between 1961 and 1993 in Britain, based on data from the *Family Expenditure Survey* (Goodman, Johnson and Webb, 1997). They found that over this period the proportion of income received from wages declined from over three-quarters of all income to around 60 per cent, whereas social security payments doubled from around 10 per cent of all income to around 20 per cent. One of the main reasons for this change was the rising numbers of unemployed, pensioners, single parents, sick and disabled who are entitled to benefit. The sources of income vary considerably for households at different income levels. For example, Goodman, Johnson and Webb found that, in 1992–3, the richest fifth of the population received 61 per cent of all income from investments, compared to the poorest fifth who received just 3 per cent of income from this source. In comparison, 29 per cent of social security payments went to the poorest fifth of the population compared to 8 per cent going to the richest fifth.

Trends in income distribution 1949–79

Despite the limitations of the official figures, they do at least provide some indication of the overall historical trends in the distribution of income. In 1979, the Royal Commission on the Distribution of Income and Wealth published a report examining the changes in the distribution of income and wealth between 1949 and 1978–9. The results relating to income are summarized in Table 2.5.

Table 2.5 demonstrates that in the period covered there was some income redistribution, but mainly towards middle-income groups rather than those on the lowest levels. The top 10 per cent of income earners reduced their share of total income by 3.7 per cent, but the bottom 30 per cent also had their share reduced, in this case by 2.5 per cent. Although there was a slight shift in income distribution – from the top half of income earners to the bottom half – the poorest were not the beneficiaries.

Changes in taxation

The Royal Commission report was published in 1979, the same year as Margaret Thatcher's Conservative government came to power. Successive Conservative governments implemented policies that reversed the slight trend for income redistribution to poorer groups. The policies that had the most direct impact concerned income tax.

Income tax is a progressive tax because higher earners pay a higher proportion of their income in this tax than lower earners. If overall levels of income tax are cut, and if the higher rates in particular are reduced, the redistributive effects of taxation become smaller. Between 1979 and 1997, the basic rate of income tax was reduced from 33 to 23 per cent, while the highest rate fell from 80 to 40 per cent. In 1992, a lower-rate band of 20 per cent was introduced on the first £2,000 of taxable income; this was widened to £4,100 by April 1997. By the early 1990s the government was running into problems financing government spending and was forced to raise extra taxes. Although most of the extra revenue needed was raised through increases in indirect tax, there was an increase in national insurance contributions of 1 per cent in 1994. National Insurance contributions are effectively a form of direct tax. In 1997, a new Labour government was elected in Britain, the first Labour government for 18 years. Although traditionally committed to a redistributive tax system, the incoming government pledged not to increase income tax rates and to stick to Conservative spending limits in its early years in government.

Since 1979 there has been a distinct shift towards indirect taxation, which tends to take a greater proportion of the income of lower income groups than it takes from those on higher incomes. Government statistics show that the 20 per cent of households with the highest disposable income paid much less than 20 per cent of their disposable income in indirect taxes, compared to the poorest 20 per cent, who paid nearly 30 per cent of their income in this way (*Social Trends*, 1997). In 1979, the twin VAT rates of 8 and 12.5 per cent were replaced with a single rate of 15 per cent. This was raised again to 17.5 per cent in 1991.

In March 1993, it was announced that VAT would be extended to include domestic fuel and would be charged at 8 per cent. In 1997, the new Labour government cut the VAT rate on domestic fuel from 8 to 5 per cent. Other important types of indirect tax are the duties levied on petrol, alcohol and tobacco.

There have also been important changes in the local taxes used to finance local government. In 1990

Table 2.5	Distribution of income in the UK before and after tax, 1949–78/9					
	Percentage share of total income					
	Before tax			After tax		
	Top 10%	Next 60%	Bottom 30%	Top 10%	Next 60%	Bottom 30%
1949	33.2	54.1	12.7	27.1	58.3	14.6
1954	29.8	59.3	10.9	24.8	63.1	12.1
1959	29.4	60.9	9.7	25.2	63.5	11.2
1964	29.0	61.2	9.6	25.1	64.1	10.8
1967	28.0	61.6	10.4	24.3	63.7	12.0
1973–74	26.8	62.3	10.9	23.6	63.6	12.8
1978–79	26.1	63.5	10.4	23.4	64.5	12.1

Source: A.B. Atkinson (1983) *The Economics of Inequality*, Oxford University Press, Oxford, p. 63.

the community charge, or 'poll tax', replaced a system based on property values called 'rates'. This meant that the taxation system in Britain became more regressive. Regressive taxes take a higher proportion of the income of those with low incomes than of those with high incomes. Under the poll tax, all those living in particular areas were charged the same, regardless of their ability to pay. Even though there were rebates on this tax of up to 80 per cent for the poorest, under the old rates system the worst-off had been able to claim a full 100 per cent rebate. The new tax proved extremely unpopular and in 1993 it was replaced by the rather less regressive council tax. This went back to the principle of basing local taxes on the value of property.

Figure 2.1 shows the results of a study by Christopher Giles and Paul Johnson into the effects of tax changes on the proportions of their income paid in tax by different groups in the population (Giles and Johnson, 1994). The population is divided into ten groups ranked according to level of income. Decile 1 represents the 10 per cent of the population with the lowest income; decile 10 the 10 per cent with the highest. The figure shows that between 1985 and 1995 taxation changes continued to favour the better off. The poorest 50 per cent of the population of Britain saw its taxes rise, while the richest 50 per cent saw its taxes cut.

Recent changes in the distribution of income

The study of household income inequality by Goodman, Johnson and Webb introduced above (see p. 44) clearly shows that any long-term trend towards more equitable income distribution has been reversed in the UK.

Table 2.6 shows that the poorest tenth and the poorest 50 per cent of the population both saw a fall in the proportion of national income they received between 1981–3 and 1991–3. This was particularly pronounced in the poorest tenth of the population whose share fell from 4.1 to 2.9 per cent. On the other hand, the richest 10 per cent of the population saw a rise from 21.3 to 26.2 per cent over the same period.

Goodman, Johnson and Webb found a number of reasons for these trends. One was a rise in inequalities in pay for male workers during the 1980s. Unemployment among males rose particularly fast in households where nobody else was working, making those households completely reliant upon benefits. Technological changes and government policies led to a reduction in the demand for unskilled labour and increasing unemployment and falling wages for unskilled workers. More people became reliant upon self-employment as their main source of income. The self-employed are disproportionately found among both the highest-earning and the lowest-earning groups, further widening income inequalities.

Although income inequalities have been reduced in Britain this century, this reduction has not been sufficient to justify the claim that class divisions are disappearing. The figures suggest that both an increase in income inequality and a strengthening of class divisions occurred during the 1980s and the first half of the 1990s.

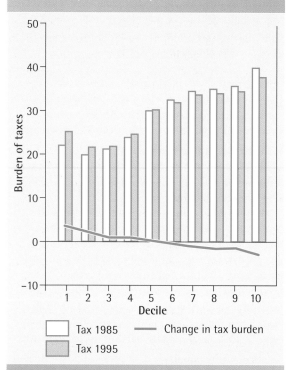

Figure 2.1   Proportions of income taken in personal tax, by decile

Tax 1985 — Change in tax burden
Tax 1995

Source: C. Giles and P. Johnson (1994) *Taxes Down, Taxes Up: The Effects of a Decade of Tax Changes*, The Institute for Fiscal Studies, London, p. 20.

Table 2.6 Percentage income shares

	1961–63	1971–73	1981–83	1991–93
Bottom tenth	3.7	3.9	4.1	2.9
Bottom half	32.6	32.2	32.1	27.1
Top tenth	21.2	21.4	21.3	26.2

Source: A. Goodman, P. Johnson and S. Webb (1997) *Inequality in the UK*, Oxford University Press, Oxford, p. 92.

The changing distribution of wealth?

The importance of wealth

Inequalities in the distribution of wealth, like inequalities in the distribution of income, are an important indicator of class divisions and class inequality. A particular form of wealth – the means of production – is especially important to Marxist sociologists. Like income, wealth can affect life chances, but to Marxists, ownership of the means of production also gives power. (Today ownership of the means of production usually takes the form of share ownership.) Wealth is also important in Weberian theories of stratification, although it is given less emphasis than in Marxist theories.

If it could be shown that over the years there had been a major redistribution of wealth from the rich to the poor, this would indicate a reduction in class inequalities. However, wealth is perhaps even more difficult to measure than income and reliable data prove elusive.

Measuring wealth

The definition and measurement of wealth, like income, are not straightforward. One problem is that the government does not collect information on wealth for tax purposes.

There is no wealth tax on the living, but taxes do have to be paid on the estates of those who have died. Figures on the value of estates left by the deceased are sometimes used to calculate the overall distribution of wealth. However, they may not be a reliable guide to the distribution of wealth among the living: for instance individuals may transfer some of their wealth to other family members before they die. Moreover, those who die tend to be older than other members of the population, and wealth is not equally distributed between age groups.

Another method of collecting information on wealth distribution is to use survey research, but this too has its drawbacks. Those who refuse to cooperate with the research may be untypical of the population as a whole, and their failure to take part may distort the findings. Those who do cooperate may not be entirely honest, and the richest members of society may be particularly prone to underestimating their wealth.

Defining wealth

Not only is wealth difficult to measure, but defining it is also problematic. Official statistics distinguish between marketable wealth and non-marketable wealth:

1 Marketable wealth includes any type of asset that can be sold and its value realized. It therefore includes land, shares, savings in bank, building society or other accounts, homes (minus any outstanding mortgage debts), and personal possessions such as cars, works of art, and household appliances. The figures on marketable wealth exclude the value of occupational pensions which cannot normally be sold. If such pensions are included in the figures, the statistics show wealth as being more equally distributed than is otherwise the case.

2 Non-marketable wealth includes items such as salaries and non-transferable pensions.

From a sociological point of view, the official figures on wealth are not ideal. They fail to distinguish between wealth used to finance production and wealth used to finance consumption. Wealth used for production (for example shares) is of particular interest to Marxist sociologists because they believe that power largely derives from ownership of the means of production. The distribution of wealth used for consumption is of less interest to Marxists, though its distribution does give some indication of lifestyle. Such figures are also useful for indicating the distribution of various life chances, for instance the chance that different social groups have of owning their own home.

Trends in wealth distribution

Despite the limitations of the available figures, it is possible to discern overall trends in wealth distribution over the twentieth century. Table 2.7 shows trends between 1911 and 1960. Table 2.8 shows trends between 1976 and 1994. The figures in the two tables are not strictly comparable since they are calculated on a different basis. The figures in Table 2.7 include an estimate for hidden wealth; those in Table 2.8 do not. The later figures may therefore underestimate the extent to which wealth is concentrated.

Table 2.7 suggests that there has been a considerable reduction in the degree of wealth inequality this century. The changes have been more marked than the changes in the distribution of income.

Table 2.8 shows that the trend towards greater equality of wealth distribution continued until the early 1990s, when it went into reverse. Although the long-term trend was towards greater equality, this is no longer the case, and most wealth still remains concentrated in the hands of a small minority. Thus in 1994 the wealthiest 1 per cent of the population still owned 19 per cent of all marketable wealth, and the wealthiest 10 per cent owned 51 per cent, leaving the other 90 per cent of the population to share the remaining 49 per cent between them.

A number of factors have contributed to the trends noted above. Westergaard and Resler (who produced the figures for the period up to 1960 in

Table 2.7   The distribution of private property, from 1911 to 1960

Groups within adult population (aged 25+) owning stated proportions of aggregate personal wealth	Estimated proportion of aggregate personal wealth Period 1911–60 (common basis)				
	1911–13 %	1924–30 %	1936–38 %	1954 %	1960 %
Richest 1% owned	69	62	56	43	42
Richest 5% owned	87	84	79	71	75
Richest 10% owned	92	91	88	79	83
Hence:					
Richest 1% owned	69	62	56	43	42
Next 2–5% owned	18	22	23	28	33
Next 6–10% owned	5	7	9	8	8
95% owned only	13	16	21	29	25
90% owned only	8	9	12	21	17

Source: J. Westergaard and H. Resler (1976) *Class in a Capitalist Society*, Penguin, Harmondsworth, p. 112

Table 2.8   The distribution of wealth, 1976 to 1994

	1976	1981	1986	1991	1994
Marketable wealth					
Percentage of wealth owned by:					
Most wealthy 1%	21	18	18	17	19
Most wealthy 5%	38	36	36	35	38
Most wealthy 10%	50	50	50	47	51
Most wealthy 25%	71	73	73	71	73
Most wealthy 50%	92	92	90	92	93
Total marketable wealth (£ billion)	280	565	955	1,711	1,955
Marketable wealth less value of dwellings					
Percentage of wealth owned by:					
Most wealthy 1%	29	26	25	29	28
Most wealthy 5%	47	45	46	51	52
Most wealthy 10%	57	56	58	64	65
Most wealthy 25%	73	74	75	80	82
Most wealthy 50%	88	87	89	93	94

Source: (1998) *Social Trends*, HMSO, London, p. 104

Table 2.6) suggest that the most significant redistribution was within the wealthiest groups, rather than between them and the less well-off. A major reason for this was the transfer of assets from wealthy individuals to friends and other family members in order to avoid death duties.

In recent decades the most important factor has probably been the increasing number of home owners, although the slump in house prices in the early 1990s temporarily reduced the significance of home ownership. Wealth is less unequally distributed when non-marketable wealth is included in the calculations. This is mainly because of the value of occupational pensions, which have become an increasingly important component of all wealth holdings in Britain. However, few of the poor have substantial pension rights.

Share ownership

Shares are a particularly important type of wealth, used to finance production. In Britain there has certainly been an increase in recent years in the percentage of the population who own shares. Westergaard and Resler estimated that in 1970 only 7 per cent of adults over the age of 25 owned shares. In 1995–6, according to the *Family Resources Survey*, around 16 per cent of adults in the UK owned shares.

Much of the increase in share ownership was due to the Conservative government's privatization programme, which encouraged small investors to buy shares in companies such as British Telecom and British Gas. In the 1990s share ownership was increased by the demutualization of building societies, such as the Halifax, Alliance & Leicester and Cheltenham & Gloucester, and the flotation of insurance companies such as Norwich Union. For example, around nine million people were entitled to shares as a result of the flotation of the Halifax in 1997. However, many of the new shareholders created by these flotations sold their shares very quickly. Furthermore, most new shareholders have only a very small stake in the companies in which they have invested, and in reality they may have little influence upon the way that the companies are run.

Most privately owned shares remain in the hands of a small minority of the population. Furthermore, the importance of privately held shares has declined. In 1971, 23 per cent of personal wealth was held in stocks, shares and unit trusts. This had declined to 15 per cent in 1995. On the other hand, the proportion of personal wealth held in life assurance and pension funds had increased from 15 to 34 per cent over the same period (*Social Trends*, 1997). Arguably, those who have wealth in life assurance and pension funds have even less control over how those assets are used than those who hold shares in individual companies.

Wealth taxes

Successive governments in Britain have made much less attempt to tax wealth than income. Before 1974 the main tax on wealth was estate duty, paid on the estate of someone who had died. It was easy to avoid this tax by transferring assets before death. In 1974, the Labour government introduced capital transfer tax which taxed certain gifts given by people who were alive. In 1981, the Conservative government abolished capital transfer tax and replaced it with inheritance tax. This raised the limits before which tax on wealth transfers were paid, and abolished taxes on gifts made ten years or more before someone died.

In 1986, this period was reduced to seven years and a sliding scale was introduced to determine the amount of tax paid. The longer people survived after giving assets to someone, the less tax they paid on the gift. These changes have considerably reduced the burden of taxation on the wealthy.

Classes in capitalist societies

We will now examine the changing position of particular classes within the class structure of capitalist societies, using British and American data. Three main classes – the upper class, the middle class and the working class – will be considered in turn,

though as we will show, the location of the boundaries between these classes is disputed.

Most of the views dealt with in the following sections have been influenced by Marxist or Weberian theories of stratification.

The upper class

John Westergaard and Henrietta Resler – a Marxist view of the ruling class

Class divisions

In a study first published in 1975, John Westergaard and Henrietta Resler argue, essentially from a Marxist

perspective, that Britain is dominated by a ruling class. They claim that the private ownership of capital provides the key to explaining class divisions.

Westergaard and Resler argue that in detail the class system is complex, but in essence it is simple: the major division is still between capital and labour. Sociologists who focus on the details of class – for example, the differences between manual and routine white-collar workers – merely obscure the overall simplicity of the system. Such differences are insignificant compared to the wide gulf that separates the ruling class from the bulk of the wage- and salary-earning population.

Distribution of wealth

To support their argument, Westergaard and Resler point to the concentration of wealth in the hands of a small minority, the richest 5 per cent of the population. Although there has been some change in the distribution of wealth in Britain this century, this has largely taken place within the richest 10 per cent. Some members of the ruling class have transferred property to relatives and friends to avoid death duties. The spread of home ownership has spread wealth a little more widely, but the ownership of capital in private industry has remained highly concentrated.

In 1970, as we have seen (see p. 49), only about 7 per cent of adults over 25 owned any shares, and most of those who did own shares were 'smallholders', with stock worth less than £1,000.

Ruling-class power

Westergaard and Resler argue that the maintenance of inequalities of wealth is due to the power of the ruling class. They maintain:

> *The favoured group enjoys effective power, even when its members take no active steps to exercise power. They do not need to do so – for much of the time at least – simply because things work that way in any case.*
>
> Westergaard and Resler, 1976, p. 143

It is generally taken for granted (by members of society and governments alike) that investments should bring profit and that the living standards of the propertyless should be based on the demands of the market for their skills. In general, governments have favoured the interests of capital, assuming that the well-being of the nation is largely dependent upon the prosperity of private industry.

Composition of the ruling class

Westergaard and Resler believe that the ruling class is made up of perhaps 5 per cent, and at most 10 per cent of the population. It includes the major owners of the means of production, company directors, top managers, higher professionals and senior civil servants, many of whom are large shareholders in private industry. The subordinate classes consist of the bulk of the wage- and salary-earning population.

Westergaard and Resler reject the view that the so-called separation of ownership and control in the joint stock company results in the rise of salaried

managers who should properly be placed in a middle class. They argue that 'directors in general are themselves large owners of share capital' and they make the crucial decisions for companies. Like the 'absentee owners', their main concern is the maximization of profit. As such, the interests of owners and controllers are largely similar.

Westergaard and Resler put forward what is essentially a conventional Marxist view of the ruling class. They assume that the ruling class continues to exist. They claim that it is a united group which continues to dominate British society, and argue that social changes have not significantly redistributed wealth and power. These views have been challenged by New Right theorists.

Peter Saunders – a New Right view of higher classes

An influential economic elite

Peter Saunders (1990) does not deny that there is a small group of people in British society who have considerable wealth and more power than other members of society. He accepts that many directors and top managers own shares in their own and other companies, and he also accepts that there is 'an interlocking network at the top of British industry and finance in which the same names and faces keep cropping up with different hats on'. He notes that the hundred largest companies produce more than half of Britain's manufacturing output, and therefore:

> *a few thousand individuals at most are today responsible for taking the bulk of the key financial and administrative decisions which shape the future development of British industry and banking.*
>
> Saunders, 1990, p. 88

However, Saunders rejects the Marxist view that such people constitute a capitalist ruling class. He sees them as merely 'an influential economic elite'.

Wealth, ownership and the capitalist class

Saunders identifies some groups who might be seen as a capitalist class. These consist of families who continue to own majority shareholdings in established large companies, entrepreneurs who have built up and still own big businesses, and large landowners.

Such people, however, control only a small fraction of the British economy. Most businesses are run by directors and managers whose income and power derive principally from their jobs and not from their ownership of wealth. Saunders claims that less than 25 per cent of the top 250 British companies are run by managers and directors who own 5 per cent or more of the company's shares. Such people are part of the 'economic elite', but they do not own substantial parts of the means of production, so they cannot be seen as part of the capitalist class.

Furthermore, Saunders argues that 'it has become much more difficult than it once was to identify a distinctive capitalist class'. Although few people are very rich, many people have a direct stake in owning British enterprises. During the course of the twentieth century the proportion of shares owned by individuals has declined. Most shares, and a large proportion of commercial land, are owned by banks, unit trusts, building societies and pension funds. Millions of ordinary people therefore have investments tied up in the capitalist economy by virtue of their pension schemes, endowment mortgages, life insurance policies and savings in banks and building societies. In addition, the privatization programme has widened direct share ownership. Saunders therefore claims that the capitalist class 'has fragmented into millions of tiny pieces', and says 'To see these pieces look around you.'

The ruling class

From Saunders's point of view, then, directors and managers lack the wealth to be seen as a capitalist class. He further argues that they lack the power to be a ruling class. Although they make many important investment decisions, they do not monopolize power and they frequently fail to get their own way. There are many areas of society that they do not control. These include the government, the mass media and the education system. Indeed, members of the economic elite are 'sometimes dismayed' when politicians, editors and educationalists fail 'to defer to their wishes and interests'.

Saunders believes that the class divisions of previous centuries have been weakened by the development of capitalism. Inequality is essential if a society is to be just and successful, but the success of capitalism spreads wealth and power more widely. In doing so it ensures that the most wealthy do not rule society.

John Scott – *Who Rules Britain?*

John Scott (1982, 1991) has provided the most comprehensive description and analysis of the development of the upper classes in Britain. His analysis suggests that there have been important changes within higher classes in British society, but he does not believe the upper class has disappeared. He discusses many of the trends mentioned by Saunders but denies that they show the death or fragmentation of the ruling class. Scott uses Weberian concepts and borrows some elements of elite theory. (Elite theory is examined in Chapter 9.)

In the end, however, he supports the Marxist view that Britain retains a ruling class

The historical development of the upper classes

Scott sees classes as consisting of 'clusters of households which stand in a similar position with respect to the distribution of income and wealth and the overall distribution of life chances'. These clusters of households, particularly those in higher classes, may well have groups of intermarrying and interconnected families.

The composition of the classes at the top of the British stratification system has changed since pre-industrial times. Before the Industrial Revolution, the landed aristocracy and the gentry were the dominant groupings in British society. Family contacts were important in uniting the upper classes and achieving a high degree of social closure (the exclusion of outsiders).

The development of British industry during the eighteenth and nineteenth centuries opened up new avenues for achieving success and becoming part of the upper class. Most successful entrepreneurial business people made use of social assets based on kinship, friendship and other social contacts. Most early industrial enterprises were owned and controlled by groups of individuals united by kinship. It was common for families which were linked through a business partnership to become linked by marriage as well, and vice versa.

Divisions in the upper classes

Scott claims that during the nineteenth century there were three overlapping, but not united, sections of the upper class: landowners, manufacturers and financiers (mainly in the City of London).

As the nineteenth century progressed these three groups moved closer together. For example, some landowners invested money in manufacturing or industries such as mining, and some manufacturers bought large estates in an attempt to gain the social acceptance enjoyed by the aristocracy.

However, the most distinctive group remained the financiers, merchants and bankers, such as the Rothschilds and the Barings. Scott argues that these financiers formed a well-integrated group involved in a variety of overlapping business activities. Most were based in close physical proximity to each other in the City of London; they were often related or united by ties of friendship, and had ample opportunity to meet one another informally in coffee houses or elsewhere. Despite their distinctiveness, they had much in common with the other upper-class groups; and they were an important source of loans for the growing group of entrepreneurs.

The growth of joint stock companies

The development of the industrial and financial bourgeoisie during industrialization ended the dominance of landowners. The potential for conflict between these groups was reduced by kinship and friendship ties, and by involvement together in common enterprises. The opportunities for common involvement in enterprise were, however, limited by the fact that most companies remained family owned. As the nineteenth century gave way to the twentieth, two related changes began to alter the relationship between the upper classes and the ownership of the means of production:

1 First, companies became larger and larger as wealth became concentrated in the hands of a small number of firms.
2 Second, family ownership began to be replaced by the joint stock company in which shares could be bought and sold in the open market.

As late as 1880, the top hundred industrial firms controlled only 10 per cent of the total market for goods. However, legislation in the middle of the nineteenth century had begun to make it easier for partnerships and individually owned firms to issue shares. This allowed them to take advantage of limited liability: the owners of the shares were not liable for repaying the firm's debts. Joint stock companies found it possible to grow larger by issuing new shares to increase their capital, and the average size of firms grew through mergers and takeovers. According to Scott, by 1909 the top hundred manufacturing companies were producing 15 per cent of total output, and 26 per cent by 1930. He believes that during the inter-war years the three sections of the upper class virtually fused together as they all became increasingly involved in the growing industrial enterprises.

As the twentieth century progressed, the family-owned firm became less and less important in British capitalism. From the Second World War onwards, the top hundred firms became even more dominant: by 1970 they produced 45 per cent of total output. Many of the major firms became too large to be owned by an individual or single family, and the number of shareholders in each firm increased. At the same time, the proportion of shares held by individuals began to decline. Increasingly, institutions such as pension funds, insurance companies, and unit and investment trusts, held the majority of shares.

Table 2.9 shows that by 1988 only 27 of Britain's top 250 companies were controlled by individual entrepreneurs or families. Nevertheless, this group included important companies, such as J. Sainsbury, the supermarket chain, Lonrho, and the merchant bank N. M. Rothschild.

Table 2.9 Control of large companies, 1988

	Top 250 companies of 1988 (no.)		
	Industrial	Financial	Total
Controlled by entrepreneurs	21	6	27
Controlled by institutions	96	17	113
Foreign, state, and other control	83	27	110
Totals	200	50	250

Source: J. Scott (1991) *Who Rules Britain?* Polity Press, Cambridge, p. 78

The 'managerial revolution'

Commentators such as Saunders have suggested that a decline in the family ownership of companies has meant that a ruling class based on the ownership of the means of production no longer exists. According to their arguments, shareholdings have become too fragmented for individuals to exercise control over the companies in which they have a stake. A managerial revolution has taken place that has resulted in effective control over industry passing from owners to managers.

The increasing percentage of shares owned by pension funds, insurance companies, and the like, also implies that the ruling class has lost power. Many of the funds held by such institutions come from investments made by ordinary employees, rather than from the most wealthy members of society.

The persistence of the capitalist class

John Scott rejects the view that the changes described above have led to the disappearance of a capitalist class. He says unequivocally that 'there is in Britain today a capitalist class whose members owe their advantaged life chances to the occupancy of capitalist economic locations' (Scott, 1991). Legal and financial developments have certainly changed this class but, according to Scott, 'it remains a centrally important feature of contemporary British society'.

During the twentieth century certain types of property became more widely owned. More people now own their own houses and possess consumer goods and cars. Such possessions, however, are property for use. They are important for the lifestyle and life chances of individuals and families, but they do not place individuals in a capitalist class. Capitalists own property for power. This consists of capital invested in land, shares and commercial enterprises in general. True capitalists own considerable amounts of capital and not just, for example, a few hundred shares in one company. Scott notes that the proportion of the population owning any shares increased from 6 per cent in 1984 to 20 per cent in 1988, but most of these shareholdings were very small. It has not resulted in an increase in the numbers of people with large personal shareholdings.

Scott says that property, and the income it can generate, are the primary basis for the privileges of the capitalist class, but that the property does not necessarily have to be personal property. Table 2.10 shows the highest-paid company directors in 1990. Clearly, the income of directors like these is such that they can accumulate sufficient wealth to become members of the capitalist class. Scott argues:

> *Those who hold directorships in large enterprises occupy capitalist locations, and if the income from employment is substantial they may be able to sustain a relatively secure foothold in the capitalist class.*
>
> Scott, 1991, p. 85

He admits that directors who achieve their positions late in their careers may not have time to accumulate sufficient wealth to become members of the capitalist class and he says 'the dividing line between the capitalist class and the service class is difficult to draw with any precision'. Nevertheless, he rejects the view that there has been a managerial revolution which has undermined the power of a capitalist class. A considerable number of top managers and directors are able to join the capitalist class themselves. The rest are only likely to retain their jobs if their actions favour the capitalist class.

Scott also attacks the idea that institutional control over many large companies has led to the disappearance of a capitalist class. Even if in theory the assets of pension schemes, banks, insurance companies and similar institutions are owned by a multitude of small investors, in practice they are controlled by a few key members of the capitalist class. The policies of these institutions are largely determined by their directors who themselves are often members of the capitalist class in their own right. It is these finance capitalists who make the key investment decisions that affect the lives of millions.

Within this group is an inner core who sit on the boards of more than one company. Scott calculates that in 1988 there were 290 individuals (only five of them women) who held directorships on the boards of two or more of the top 250 companies. This group is in a strong position to coordinate the activities of the capitalist class as a whole because they have connections with a number of capitalist concerns, perhaps involved in different sectors of the economy. Far from leading to the death of the capitalist class, institutional control improves coordination and cooperation within it.

The composition of the capitalist class

The capitalist class then, includes many of the directors of the largest companies, especially those with multiple directorships, successful entrepreneurs and those who have inherited substantial amounts of wealth. Scott claims that in Britain this means about 0.1 per cent of the adult population, around 43,500 people. Members of this group owned about 7 per cent of the nation's wealth between them in 1986. At that time each was worth a minimum of £740,000. Within this group the richest 200 families all had more than £50 million in assets. Table 2.11 shows the richest families of all in 1990, according to research carried out by the *Sunday Times*.

According to Scott, 104 of the richest 200 families in 1990 owed most of their wealth to inheritance. There are a number of entrepreneurs among the most wealthy, but the majority started their lives with advantages over much of the population. Scott says:

> *Inheriting from their own parents in the entrepreneurial middle class or marrying a woman who had inherited wealth from her parents was the way in which many men secured the funds to invest in the ventures which subsequently made their fortunes.*
>
> Scott, 1991, p. 85

Some of those who have made recent fortunes have a less secure position than those who possess 'old money' invested in land. Robert Maxwell, whose publishing empire collapsed in debt after his death in 1991, is a case in point.

Table 2.10 Britain's highest-paid directors, 1990		
	Company	Annual salary (£)
Lord Hanson	Hanson Trust	1,530,000
Tiny Rowland	Lonrho	1,310,000
Dick Giordano	BOC	937,000
Sir Ralph Halpern	Burton Group	899,000
Sir Kit McMahon	Midland Bank	725,844
Sir Peter Walters	BP	708,722
Geoff Mulcahy	Kingfisher	701,000
Cyril Stein	Ladbroke	603,000
Sir Paul Girolami	Glaxo	598,081
Sir Denys Henderson	ICI	514,000
Allen Sheppard	Grand Metropolitan	506,438

Source: *The Guardian*, 3 May 1990, p. 3.

Table 2.11 Britain's richest families, 1990

	Family	Estimated wealth(£m)	Main source of wealth
1	The Royal Family	6,700	Land and urban property
2	Grosvenor (Duke of Westminster)	4,200	Land and urban property
3	Rausing	2,040	Food packaging
4	Sainsbury	1,777	Food retailing
5	Weston	1,674	Food production and retailing
6	Moores	1,670	Football pools, retailing
7	Vestey	1,420	Food production
8	Getty	1,350	Oil
9	Maxwell	1,100	Publishing
10	Feeney	1,020	Retailing
11	Hinduja	1,000	Trading
12	Livanos	930	Shipping
13	Goldsmith	750	Retailing and finance
14	Swire	692	Shipping and aviation
15	Ronson	548	Urban property, petrol distribution
16	Barclay	500	Hotels and urban property
17	Branson	488	Music and aviation
18	Cadogan (Earl Cadogan)	450	Land and urban property
19	Jerwood	400	Trading
20	Portman (Viscount Portman)	400	Land and urban property
21	Thompson	400	Food processing, property

Source: J. Scott (1991) *Who Rules Britain?* Polity Press, Cambridge, p. 83.

The ruling class

Having claimed to have established that a capitalist class still exists, Scott goes on to try to show that it remains a ruling class. He says that a ruling class exists when 'there is both political domination and political rule by a capitalist class'. He goes on to argue:

> *This requires that there be a power bloc dominated by a capitalist class, a power elite recruited from this power bloc, in which the capitalist class is disproportionately represented, and there are mechanisms which ensure that the state operates in the interests of the capitalist class and the reproduction of capital.*
>
> Scott, 1991, p. 124

By a power bloc, Scott means a group of people who can monopolize political power over a country for some time. The power elite are those people from the power bloc who occupy key positions in the state. In Britain these positions include those held by the prime minister, members of the Cabinet, MPs, senior judges and top civil servants.

Scott argues that capitalist interests have dominated state policy over recent decades. A power bloc, based around the Conservative Party, has incorporated many managers and members of the professional middle classes. It has been sustained in office by an even wider electoral bloc incorporating some members of the working class, but it remains dominated by capitalists. Many Cabinet members, for example, come from public schools. Only two members of the 1990 Cabinet had not been to a fee-paying school and 16 had been to either Oxford or Cambridge university.

Scott also quotes figures showing that top civil servants and others in elite positions continue to be predominantly recruited from public school backgrounds. (Figures on elite self-recruitment are discussed in Chapter 9.) Elite positions are not completely monopolized by members of the capitalist class, but they are disproportionately represented.

Scott concludes that the evidence on self-recruitment shows that a power bloc continues to exist and is dominated by members of the capitalist class.

Periods of Labour government have not, in Scott's view, made any significant difference. While the power bloc has had to give up some of the positions it usually occupies, its supporters have continued to hold most of the non-elected posts. The Labour Party has therefore 'governed, but it has not ruled'. The state's policies have not only benefited the capitalist class, but the latter's dominance ensures that its interests are never seriously challenged, even by Labour governments. Scott says:

> When the state's activities advantage several classes rather than simply the dominant class, it is still possible to speak of a ruling class, so long as these activities do not undermine the existing relations of production and continue, in the long term, to reinforce them.
>
> Scott, 1991, p.140

The policies of British governments have done just that. According to Scott, British governments have become increasingly constrained in their economic policies. They have to pay close attention to the financial markets if they are going to borrow money, maintain the exchange rate of the currency and attract investment into the country. They cannot afford to ignore the interests of capitalists.

In particular, government policy is strongly influenced by an inner core of finance capitalists in the City of London. The 'City point of view', advocated by this group, is 'rooted in short-term commercialism' and 'involves a commitment to free international capital flows, stable sterling exchange rates, and tight monetary controls'. It has used informal contacts with the government, lobbying, contributions to Conservative Party funds, and sometimes direct participation in government itself to ensure that its views have prevailed.

Changes in the ruling class

Scott certainly believes that there have been changes in the ruling class. At the beginning of the century it was based around an 'upper circle of status superiors', many of whom had connections to the aristocracy. Social events such as the Henley Regatta, Wimbledon fortnight, the monarch's garden parties and society balls used to be far more important. Nevertheless, public schools, particularly top schools like Eton, continue to be important for developing contacts among members of the ruling class. The 'old boy network' is used to fill many jobs in the City of London. Gentlemen's clubs are still used by members of the capitalist class to exchange information and maintain contacts, although the best London restaurants are also becoming important venues for these activities.

While some of the changes that have taken place in the twentieth century have affected the character of the ruling class, according to Scott its survival and continued domination of British society have never been in question.

Leslie Sklair – the global system and the transnational capitalist class

So far the idea of an upper or ruling class has been examined from the viewpoint of individual societies, in particular Great Britain. Advocates of the theory of globalization argue, however, that it is misleading to study individual nation-states as independent entities. They believe that national boundaries are becoming less important and power is increasingly exercised in transnational relationships, relationships that cut across state boundaries. Thus, rather than looking for or studying a class that might be dominant in a particular nation, it is necessary to consider the possibility that a single class might exercise power across many nations.

According to Leslie Sklair (1995) the contemporary world is a global system in which nation-states are only one set of actors. The global system is made up of a number of transnational practices. He identifies a wide range of transnational or global phenomena including travel, tourism, finance, and products which are sold worldwide, but he focuses on three main transnational practices. He defines transnational practices as 'practices that originate with non-state actors and cross state borders' and identifies three spheres in which they operate, the economic, the political and the cultural-ideological. These correspond to the transnational practices of the transnational corporation (TNC), the transnational capitalist class and the culture-ideology of consumerism.

Sklair sees the capitalist economy as the foundation of the global system and the source of the increasing power of the transnational capitalist class. World production is increasingly dominated by incredibly wealthy corporations. Individual states bend over backwards to attract inward investment from such corporations, while vast numbers of people throughout the world are persuaded to buy the products of these same corporations through advertising.

Thus, for example, corporations such as McDonalds, General Motors, Sony, Ford, and Coca Cola can exercise as much power as many nation-states. Their products, and the ideology which encourages people to consume those products, are increasingly penetrating the 'third world' of poorer nations, the former communist countries and even the more urbanized parts of China

The transnational capitalist class

The most powerful class in a global system consists of those groups that exercise power across nation-states as well as within them. The transnational capitalist class, the 'driver' of global capitalism, comprises the executives of TNCs and their local affiliates, 'globalizing state bureaucrats', 'capitalist-inspired politicians and professionals' and 'consumerist elites (merchants, media)'.

This class is seen as making system-wide decisions that affect the whole of the global system as it seeks to maintain that system in order to further its interests. It opposes protectionism – through which countries erect tariff barriers to make it difficult for imports to compete with domestic industry. It supports free trade because that offers the best possibilities for corporations to make global profits. The transnational capitalist class also tries to deal with the threat posed by 'anti-capitalist global system movements', particularly the green movement.

Although Sklair does not claim that ruling classes within individual countries have lost all power, he does say that 'as the transnational practices of the global capitalist system become increasingly powerful, only those domestic (i.e. non-transnational) practices that do not threaten the global capitalist project are tolerated'. Politicians, for example, who try to put domestic interests before those of global capitalism, will soon find that investment flows out of the country leaving them little choice but to change tack. (An example might be the French socialist President Mitterrand who had to moderate the more radical policies he tried to follow when he first came to office.)

An evaluation of Sklair

Given the enormous influence of world capitalism, Sklair is undoubtedly right to point to the existence of a powerful capitalist class whose activities are not confined to individual nation-states. Theories of upper and ruling classes need to pay more attention to their relationship to non-nationals who exercise power from outside countries.

However, Sklair's analysis of the transnational capitalist class tends to underplay the differences of interest which might exist between different groups of capitalists (between finance capitalists and those involved in manufacturing, for example). Indeed, the whole analysis of capitalism tends to focus on production through the activities of TNCs to the neglect of finance. Sklair has relatively little to say about the power of, for example, bankers in the global system.

Furthermore, nation-states do retain considerable bargaining power in their relations with transnational corporations. As such it can be argued that both domestic and transnational ruling or upper classes have considerable power and neither should be ignored in the analysis of ruling classes. (See Chapter 9 for a discussion of globalization, power and the nation-state.)

Other views

1 Elite theories accept that power is concentrated in the hands of a few, but deny that the power comes from wealth. Instead, they see power deriving from the occupation of top jobs in society (see Chapter 9 for further details).
2 Pluralists deny that higher social classes monopolize power and believe that in liberal democracies the wishes of the people determine government policy. According to this view, power is dispersed and not concentrated in the hands of the upper classes (see Chapter 9 for details).

Chapter 9 will examine these quite different views about the 'top' of the stratification system.

The middle classes

Marx and the middle class

The most usual way of defining the middle class is to see it as consisting of those individuals who have non-manual occupations, that is occupations which involve, in some sense, an intellectual element. If the distinction between manual and non-manual labour is used to distinguish the middle class, then, as we indicated earlier (see pp. 41–2), it is a growing sector of capitalist industrial societies such as Britain.

The attempt to analyse the position of the middle class in the class structure has been a major preoccupation of sociologists of stratification. This has been the case particularly for Marxist and neo-

Marxist sociologists, since the growth of the middle class has often been cited as evidence against Marx's theory of class.

According to many interpretations of his work, Marx saw capitalist society as divided into only two classes of any importance: the bourgeoisie and the proletariat. This leaves no room for a middle class. In reality, though, Marx recognized the existence of intermediate classes (for example, members of the petty bourgeoisie, such as shopkeepers and small business people). Moreover, the growth of what is usually called the middle class has largely been the result of the increasing amount of white-collar work. In Volume 3 of *Capital*, Marx noted this trend when he argued that the increasing size of enterprises made it impossible for them to be run by a single person. In these circumstances there was a need for 'the employment of commercial wage-workers who make up the actual office staff'.

Although he identified the trend towards more non-manual workers, Marx made no detailed attempt to explain how they fitted into his theory of stratifica-tion. On the surface, at least, as non-owners of the means of production, they can hardly be considered as part of the bourgeoisie. Nor, it is often argued, can they be seen as part of the proletariat. Many commentators suggest that non-manual workers enjoy considerable advantages in employment over their manual counterparts: they tend to enjoy greater job security, shorter working hours, have longer holidays, more fringe benefits, and greater promotion prospects.

Life chances

A variety of studies have also shown that non-manual workers enjoy advantages over manual workers in terms of their life chances. They are likely to enjoy higher standards of health, and to live longer; they are less likely to be convicted of a criminal offence; they are more likely to own their own house and a variety of consumer goods.

Many of these relative advantages for the middle class may be related to their most obvious material advantage: a higher income. As Table 2.12 shows (see below), there has been a consistent gap between the earnings of the two groups among both men and women. This gap in earnings has existed throughout the twentieth century. Westergaard and Resler calculated that in 1913–14 men in full-time non-manual employment earned 142 per cent of the average male wage, male manual workers 88 per cent (Westergaard and Resler, 1976). The situation had changed little by 1960 when the figures were 145 per cent and 82 per cent respectively.

Conflicting perspectives on the middle class

In Weberian terms, the sort of evidence outlined above can be used to suggest that there is a middle class in Britain, distinguished from the working class through its superior market situation and life chances. From this point of view, the middle class is held to consist of non-manual workers. However, this relatively simple and straightforward view has, for a variety of reasons, been rejected by many sociologists:

Table 2.12 Gross weekly and hourly earnings of full-time adult employees in Great Britain

	Manual men	Median gross weekly earnings (£) Non-manual men	Manual women	Non-manual women
1986	163.4	219.4	101.1	131.5
1987	173.9	235.7	108.2	142.2
1988	188.0	259.7	115.6	157.1
1989	203.9	285.7	125.9	173.5
1990	221.3	312.1	137.3	191.8
1990*	223.1	305.4	136.2	190.7
1991	235.4	332.2	147.4	211.1
1992	250.7	353.4	156.6	227.6
1994	280.7	428.2	181.9	278.4
1995	291.3	443.3	188.1	288.1
1996	301.3	464.5	195.2	302.4
1997	312.6	484.9	203.0	317.3

*Two sets of figures are given for 1990 due to a change in the collection of statistical data

Source: (1997) *Annual Abstract of Statistics*, HMSO, London, p.143 and *Labour Market Trends*, August 1997, p. 293

1 First, the distinction between manual and non-manual work is not seen by some as an adequate way of distinguishing between classes. Often Marxist and neo-Marxist sociologists try to distinguish classes according to their role within the economic system, while Weberians are more likely to analyse class in terms of the market situation of particular occupational groups.

2 Second, on the face of it, the middle class contains an extremely diverse group of workers ranging from secretaries to accountants, shop-assistants to managers, shopkeepers to social workers.

3 Third, the position of particular occupational groups – their wages, conditions of employment and responsibilities – has changed during the course of the twentieth century, and these changes may in turn have affected the class structure as a whole.

These complications have led to a whole variety of views as to the composition of the middle class and its place in the social structure. Some have argued that there is a distinctive and relatively homogeneous middle class; others that the middle class as such does not exist. Some of those who accept the existence of a middle class believe that it is divided into many different strata; others that it is divided, but only into two main groupings.

The precise location of the boundaries between the middle class and the classes above and below it has also been the subject of dispute. Before we examine the place of the middle class as a whole in the class structure, we will examine the main strata of the middle class in detail.

The upper middle class

For the sake of convenience, different parts of the middle class will be examined in two main sections. In this first section we will consider the position of the more highly rewarded groups, including professionals, senior managers and administrators, and more successful small business people.

In the early twentieth century, small business people (the self-employed and shopkeepers) made up a greater proportion of the working population than they did in 1971. As the size of many businesses grew, the number of employers was reduced. Guy Routh found that the number of employers in Britain declined from 763,000 in 1911 to 621,000 in 1971. The number of self-employed also fell by 24,000 over the same period (Routh, 1980).

Obviously larger employers might be considered part of the upper class, but the others are often seen as part of the 'old' middle class. Marx predicted that this group, which he referred to as the petty (or *petit*) bourgeoisie, would be progressively squeezed into the proletariat. They would be unable to compete with larger companies that could buy and sell in bulk, and take advantage of advanced technology (Marx and Engels, 1848).

Although up to 1971 the trends provided support for Marx's view on the likely fate of the petty bourgeoisie, data since the 1980s indicate a reversal of previous trends. According to official figures, the numbers of self-employed and small proprietors rose from 1,954,000 in December 1971, to 2,902,000 in June 1993. From 1993 to 1997 there was a further rise in the number of self-employed in Great Britain from 3,196,000 to 3,325,000 (*Labour Market Trends*, 1997). Nevertheless, most of the expansion of the

upper middle class is accounted for by the growth of white-collar employment.

Some sociologists distinguish between different strata of the upper middle class, identifying, for example, higher professionals, lower professionals, and managers as separate groups. Others see the upper middle class as being more homogeneous. In the following section we will examine the position of one stratum of the upper middle class – the professions – in the class structure.

The professions in the class structure

The growth of the professions

The professions were one of the fastest growing sectors of the occupational structure during the twentieth century. According to Guy Routh, the professions rose from 4 per cent of the employed population in 1911 to 11 per cent in 1971 (Routh, 1980). Using a slightly different definition of the professions, the government's *Labour Force Survey* calculated a rise in the proportion of employees in the UK in professional work between 1991 and 1996 from 10 to 12 per cent among men and from 8 to 10 per cent among women (quoted in *Social Trends*, 1997). Similar trends are evident in all Western industrial capitalist societies.

Several reasons have been given for the rapid growth of the professions. The increasing complexity of business demands financial and legal experts such as accountants and lawyers. The development of industry requires more specialized scientific and technical knowledge which results in the development of professions such as science and engineering. The creation of the welfare state and the expansion of local and national government have produced a range of 'welfare professions', and have led to the growth of the medical and teaching professions, as well as the greater employment of professionals in government bureaucracies. From another viewpoint, the growth of the professions may also be associated with the attempts of more and more groups of workers to get their jobs accepted as 'professional'.

Higher and lower professionals

In terms of their market situation, the professionals can be divided into two groups: the higher and lower professionals.

1 The higher professionals include judges, barristers, solicitors, architects, planners, doctors, dentists, university lecturers, accountants, scientists and engineers.

2 The lower professionals include school teachers, nurses, social workers and librarians.

Guy Routh's research suggests there have long been significant differences in earnings between the two groups. He found that in 1913–14 higher professional men earned 230 per cent of average male pay and 159 per cent of the average in 1978. The equivalent figures for male lower professionals were 109 per cent and 104 per cent. More recent figures show that significant differences continue. Savage, Barlow, Dickens and Fielding (1992) use a distinction between professions and welfare professions. This

Table 2.13 Middle-class earnings, broken down by occupational group, 1973–89

Occupational group	1973 weekly earnings (£)	Increase 1973–79 (%)	Increase 1979–89 (%)	1989 weekly earnings (£)
Men employed full-time				
1 Top managerial	91.80	+87	–	–
2 Professional	58.30	+121	+213	404.20
3 Professional: welfare	50.90	+122	+181	317.80
4 Literary	50.30	+128	+190	331.80
5 Professional: services	50.60	+136	+172	324.30
6 Managerial	49.70	+130	+177	317.00
7 Clerical	35.10	+138	+153	211.90
8 Selling	38.20	+147	+156	241.50
9 Security	45.20	+131	+164	275.50
All non-manual	48.10	+135	+186	323.60
All occupations	41.90	+142	+166	269.50
Women employed full-time				
2 Professional	–	–	+220	302.80
3 Professional: welfare	31.40	+155	+195	236.20
4 Literary	27.30	+197	+202	244.90
5 Professional: services	–	–	+193	220.40
6 Managerial	–	–	+210	218.90
7 Clerical	22.40	+167	+174	164.60
8 Selling	–	–	+201	142.30
9 Security	–	–	+201	246.90
All non-manual	34.70	+167	+195	195.00
All occupations	23.10	+167	+189	182.30

Note: Earnings are gross weekly earnings. Dash indicates no information because of insufficient numbers
Source: Mike Savage, James Barlow, Peter Dickens and Tony Fielding (1992): *Property, Bureaucracy and Culture: Middle-Class Formation in Contemporary Britain*, Routledge, London, p. 77

distinction is not exactly the same as that between higher and lower professions, but most lower professionals are employed in welfare state jobs. As Table 2.13 shows, using data from the *New Earnings Survey*, they found that in 1989 professional men earned £404.20 per week and professional women £302.80. Men in the welfare professions earned just £317.80 and females a mere £236.20. The table also reveals that gender has a major impact on earnings as well as status.

Measured in terms of earnings, the market situation of lower professionals is not substantially superior to that of most non-manual workers. However, compared to manual workers, lower professionals have a number of market advantages, including greater security of employment, wider promotion opportunities, annual salary increments, and more valuable fringe benefits.

The functionalist perspective on professions

Various explanations have been advanced to account for the occupational rewards of professionals. These explanations are influenced by the individual sociologist's theoretical perspective and his or her evaluation of the services provided by professionals.

Bernard Barber (1963) offers a functionalist view of the role and rewards of higher professionals. He argues that professionalism involves 'four essential attributes':

1 Professionalism requires a body of systematic and generalized knowledge that can be applied to a variety of problems. For instance, doctors have a body of medical knowledge which they apply to diagnose and treat a range of illnesses.

2 Professionalism involves a concern for the interests of the community rather than self-interest. Thus the primary motivation of professionals is public service rather than personal gain: doctors are concerned primarily with the health of their patients rather than with lining their own pockets.

3 The behaviour of professionals is strictly controlled by a code of ethics which is established and maintained by professional associations and learned as part of the training required to qualify as a professional. For example, doctors take the Hippocratic Oath which lays down the obligations and proper conduct of their profession. Should they break this code of conduct, their association can strike them from the register and ban them from practising medicine.

4 The high rewards received by professionals, which include the prestige accorded to professional status as well as earnings, are symbols of their achievements. They denote the high regard in which professionals are held and reflect the value of their contribution to society.

Barber argues that the knowledge and skills of professionals provide them with considerable power, and it is therefore essential for the well-being of society that this power is used for the benefit of all. He accepts the view that professionals are primarily concerned with service to the community, and believes they use their expertise for public benefit. He claims that professionals make important contributions to the functional well-being of society and, in addition, their services are highly regarded in terms of society's values. Professionals are highly rewarded as a result.

Criticisms of functionalism

Functionalist explanations of the role and rewards of professionals have been strongly criticized on the grounds that they make the following assumptions, all of which are questionable:

1 First, professionals make important contributions to the well-being of society as a whole.

2 Second, they serve all members of society rather than particular groups.

3 Third, they are concerned with service to the community rather than with self-interest.

In recent years, there has been increasing criticism of the view that professionals provide valuable services to society. Prince Charles has denounced architects for defacing British cities; Margaret Thatcher's governments challenged the monopolies enjoyed by opticians and the legal profession; planners have been condemned for producing urban chaos; teachers have been attacked for allowing children to underachieve; and lawyers have been accused of mystifying the legal system to the point where the layperson finds it largely unintelligible, and of sometimes helping the guilty to go free while the innocent are convicted.

In *Medical Nemesis* (Illich, 1975), a savage attack on the medical profession, Ivan Illich provides an example of this type of criticism. He claims that medicine can actually be damaging to health. Contrary to the view promoted by the medical profession, Illich argues that the environment – in particular food, working conditions, housing and hygiene – rather than medical provision, is the main determinant of the health of a population. He notes that the incidence of diseases such as tl. He attributes this decline to changes in the environuberculosis, cholera, dysentery, typhoid and scarlet fever was in rapid decline long before medical controment rather than to antibiotics and widespread immunization.

In the same way, Illich argues that much of the illness in contemporary society is due to the environment. He claims that industrial society is characterized by boring and monotonous work, lack of freedom for the individual to control his or her own life, and a compulsion to acquire material possessions, inspired by the mistaken belief that they bring happiness and fulfilment. These 'ills' of industrial society are responsible for much of the illness experienced by its members.

In claiming to diagnose and treat this illness, doctors can do more harm than good. In Illich's view, such treatment 'is but a device to convince those who are sick and tired of society that it is they who are ill, impotent and in need of repair'. By claiming exclusive rights to the diagnosis of illness, doctors obscure its real source. By treating the individual rather than the environment, doctors not only do little to prevent illness but also direct attention away from measures which could prove more effective.

Space prevents us from giving a full summary of Illich's closely reasoned attack on the medical profession, but his views suggest that the functionalist argument that the higher professions confer positive benefits on society is at least questionable. (See Chapter 11 for Illich's criticisms of the teaching profession.)

The Weberian perspective on professions

From a Weberian point of view, the professions can be seen as occupational groups that have succeeded in controlling and manipulating the labour market in such a way that they can maximize their rewards. Thus Noel and José Parry define professionalism as 'a strategy for controlling an occupation in which colleagues set up a system of self-government' (Parry and Parry, 1976). The occupation is controlled primarily in the interests of its members. From this perspective, professionalism can be said to involve the following factors:

1 There is restricted entry into the occupation, provided by the profession's control of the training and qualifications required for membership and the numbers deemed necessary to provide an adequate service. By controlling supply, professionals can maintain a high demand for their services and so gain high rewards.

2 Professionalism involves an association that controls the conduct of its members 'in respects which are defined as relevant to the collective interests of the profession' (Parry and Parry, 1976). In particular, professional associations are concerned with promoting the view that professional conduct is above reproach and that professionals are committed to public service. This serves to justify high occupational rewards. By claiming the right to discipline their own members, professional associations largely prevent public scrutiny of their affairs and so maintain the image which they project of themselves.

3 Professionalism involves a successful claim that only members are qualified to provide particular services. This claim is often reinforced by law. Thus in Britain, for example, a series of laws have guaranteed solicitors a monopoly on particular services. These monopolies are jealously guarded: the Law Society has prosecuted unqualified individuals for performing services which are defined as a legal monopoly of the law profession.

In these ways, professions can control rival occupational groups which might threaten their dominance of a section of the market. Parry and Parry conclude that, by adopting the strategy of professionalism, certain occupational groups are able to extract high rewards from the market.

Viewing professionalism as a market strategy provides an explanation for the differing rewards of various so-called professions. Some of the occupational groups that claim professional status lack many of the attributes of professionalism. In terms of Parry and Parry's definition, they are professions in name only. They have little control over their market situation and, as a result, receive lower rewards than occupational groups that are more fully professionalized.

Parry and Parry illustrate this point by a comparison of doctors and teachers. They claim that doctors receive higher rewards than teachers because they are more fully professionalized. This is due largely to the fact that doctors were able to organize themselves into a professional group before the state intervened in medicine and became a major employer of medical practitioners.

The British Medical Association was founded in 1832, and the Medical Registration Act of 1858 granted doctors a monopoly on the practice of medicine and gave them important powers of self-government. Once established as a professional body, doctors had considerable control over their market situation.

Teachers, by contrast, failed to achieve professionalism before state intervention in education. Because the state was largely responsible for initiating and paying for mass education, it was able to establish greater control over teachers. In particular, the state controlled both the supply of teachers and standards for entry into the occupation. Because they lack the market control which professionalism provides, teachers have turned to trade unionism to improve their market situation. Parry and Parry conclude that the differences in occupational reward between doctors and teachers are attributable to the degree of professionalization of the two groups.

Keith Macdonald – the professional project

Drawing on a range of theoretical approaches to the professions, particularly the Weberian approach, Keith

Macdonald argues that the professional project – the attempt to establish an occupational group as an accepted profession – is a complex and continuous process (Macdonald, 1997).

Occupational groups do not suddenly achieve professional status at a particular point in their development – they continually struggle to enhance their status as the profession develops. To Macdonald, the professional project aims to establish a 'monopoly in the market for services based on their expertise, and for status in the social order'. This is particularly important for professions because what they sell is intangible since it takes the form of 'services which cannot be seen in advance in the shop-window, as it were, but which also require the customer to trust the practitioner with their lives, their health, their money, their property and even their immortal souls'. Achieving the appropriate status is vital to gaining the necessary trust.

Macdonald discusses how professions try to establish their position. First they need to develop a strategy of social closure, that is they exclude others from practising their profession. Second, they have to establish their own jurisdiction, and define the area over which they have expertise to claim a right to practice. Third, they have to produce the producers, that is train the members of their profession. Fourth, they have to try to monopolize their professional expertise to make sure that others cannot make claims on their area of jurisdiction. Fifth, they need to attain respectability.

In pursuing these objectives professions will have to deal with competing occupational groups, and enter into relationships with the state and with educational institutions which will be involved in the training of practitioners.

Using the example of the accountancy profession in Britain, Macdonald shows how these processes take place. Today, professional accountants in Britain are either Chartered Accountants or Certified Public Accountants. In the mid-nineteenth century, however, when the accountancy profession was developing, similar work was often undertaken by clerical workers using fairly basic book-keeping skills. Accountancy developed as a distinguishable profession through the passing of legislation governing various aspects of business law. Thus the Bankruptcy Act of 1831 probably made the first mention of accountants in English law. The Companies Act of 1867 increased demand for accountancy services, although it was still assumed that any competent business person without special qualifications could carry out the necessary work. In 1880, English accountants formed the first national accountancy organization and managed to obtain a Royal Charter. They developed their own training programme where trainees were 'articled' to receive on-the-job training from an established accountant. By demanding fairly high educational qualifications for entry to the profession, and by charging substantial fees for training, they ensured that only those of quite high social status could train, and thereby enhanced the prestige of the profession. They also tried to gain status by erecting a prestigious building in the City of London as the head office of the Institute of Chartered and Public Accountants.

By the end of the nineteenth century accountancy had established itself as a distinctive profession in England, but unlike some professions had not achieved a monopoly over the practice of its professional work. While it has never achieved an absolute monopoly over this type of work, the accountancy profession has persuaded parliament to pass Acts that require certain types of work to be undertaken by chartered accountants. For example, it is a legal requirement for the accounts of local authorities and public utilities to be audited by a chartered accountant. Indeed accountants now have a monopoly of all auditing if not of all accountancy work.

Accountants continue to try to strengthen the position of their profession. Since the 1960s the profession has been almost completely confined to graduates and 'the increase in the complexity and the volume of the legislation that governs the accountants' jurisdiction has increased and the exams required to test this knowledge have become correspondingly difficult'.

The tactics described by Macdonald in the 'professional project' of British accountants have certainly proved successful. While accountancy may not have acquired perhaps the same kudos as medicine and the law, accountants have succeeded in putting themselves in a position where they are among the highest-paid and most influential of professions in the running of the British economy.

Professions as servants of the powerful

The Weberian claim that the professions are able to act primarily in their own interests has been called into question. It has been argued that the higher professionals primarily serve the interests of the wealthy and powerful. Accountants and lawyers are employed in the service of capital, architects build for the wealthy, and doctors and psychiatrists in private practice care for the physical and mental needs of the rich.

The American sociologist C. Wright Mills (1951) made the following observations on the law profession in the USA. Rather than being guardians of the law for the benefit of all, lawyers have increasingly become the servants of the large corporation. They are busily employed 'teaching the financiers how to do what they want within the law, advising on the chances they are taking and how to best cover themselves'. Lawyers draw up contracts, minimize taxation, advise on business deals and liaise between banks, commercial and industrial enterprises. In the service of the corporation, the 'leading lawyer is selected for skill in the sure fix and the easy out-of-court settlement'.

The lucrative business open to members of the legal profession means that members of low-income groups are largely unable to afford their services. Mills suggested that the rewards of the professionals are directly related to the demand for their services by the rich and powerful. Since lawyers increasingly serve 'a thin upper crust and financial interests', they are highly rewarded.

C. Wright Mills saw professionals as increasingly becoming the servants of the wealthy and influential, but he did not believe that the individual professionals themselves are losing their power and influence. Although they act more as employees than as members of a profession, they have important positions within the companies for which they work. Indeed, Mills saw some professionals as members of the 'power elite' that dominates American society. For example, he argued that the corporate lawyer acts as a key go-between in the affairs of business, political and military elites.

The deskilling of professions

A number of sociologists have followed Mills in arguing that professionals are increasingly employed in large organizations, and in this situation are less able to pursue the interests of their profession. However, unlike Mills, such sociologists see professional groups as losing their power and influence rather than as joining the power elite. This view has been inspired by the work of the American Marxist Harry Braverman.

Braverman (1974) claims that deskilling has taken place in many white-collar jobs. As the skill content of the work has been reduced, so some white-collar workers have lost the advantages they previously enjoyed over manual employees. They have become proletarianized.

Although primarily concerned with routine white-collar work, Braverman does believe that some professional jobs have also become deskilled. The people who do these jobs lose the power they once had, their work is closely regulated, and they are made aware of their subordination. Examples, according to Braverman, include draughtsmen, technicians, engineers, accountants, nurses and teachers. Such groups find that their work becomes more and more routine as it is divided into specialist tasks. Their pay levels are threatened as they become unable to control the supply of labour

into their profession: there is always a 'reserve army' of suitably qualified workers ready to step into their jobs.

The declining independence of the professions

Braverman's views are rather general, but other sociologists have suggested ways in which the position of specific professional groups in the class structure have deteriorated. Geoff Esland (1980) points out that since the 1946 National Health Service Act levels of pay and conditions of work in the medical profession, and spending on medical research, have been largely determined by central government. He points to the growth of unionism among junior doctors as evidence of their need to move beyond professionalism as a market strategy for protecting their interests.

Similarly, Martin Oppenheimer (1973) claims that many professionals employed in the public sector find that their jobs are 'related to the oppressive functions of government – keeping welfare clients quiet, policing, regulating'. Their jobs become more and more difficult, their independence is eroded, and their wages are threatened by government attempts to cut spending.

Other writers have made similar claims about professionals employed in private companies. Kumar (1978) has tried to show how engineers in private industry have had their work increasingly fragmented and broken down into a series of simple individual steps. Computerized systems have reduced the amount of skill required by many engineers and their performance is closely regulated.

Terence Johnson (1972) has pointed to the limits that can be placed on some professions by their clients or employers. In the accountancy profession most practitioners are employed by companies and are not independent advisors. Accountants are expected to be loyal first and foremost to their company, and not to their profession. Some of their skills and knowledge are specific to the company for which they work, and would be of less value to another company. Consequently accountants are in a highly dependent position compared to most professions; it is difficult for them to use professionalism as a market strategy. However, as Macdonald has shown (see p. 62), they have had some success in overcoming these problems.

It may be true that during the course of the last century some groups of professionals increasingly became employees, rather than being employers or self-employed; and it may also be true that some professional groups have had their independence and autonomy reduced. However, it is certainly an exaggeration to claim that they have been proletarianized. Higher professionals in particular continue to enjoy many advantages over manual workers, and, for that matter, routine non-manual workers. They also have much more power than either group.

Barbara and John Ehrenreich – the professional-managerial class

Although many sociologists see professionals as a distinctive part of the upper middle class, others have argued that they have much in common with managers. Barbara and John Ehrenreich (1979), arguing from a neo-Marxist point of view, claim that there is a distinctive professional-managerial class, which consists of 'salaried mental workers who do not own the means of production and whose major function in the social division of labor may be described broadly as the reproduction of capitalist culture and capitalist class relations'.

The Ehrenreichs estimate that 20–25 per cent of the population in the USA are members of the professional-managerial class. Members of this class include teachers, social workers, psychologists, entertainers, writers of advertising copy, and middle-level administrators, managers and engineers.

Origins and functions

In identifying this class the Ehrenreichs diverge from more conventional Marxist accounts of class in capitalist societies. Unlike some other Marxists, the Ehrenreichs believe that there are three main classes in capitalist society rather than two.

According to their account, the professional-managerial class started to develop towards the end of the nineteenth century, as a class which specialized in the 'reproduction of capitalist class relations' became necessary.

1 The first function of the new class was to organize the process of production. Some scientists and engineers are directly involved in developing productive technology for the benefit of the ruling class, while many managers are involved in applying the principle of 'scientific management' to the workforce (see Chapter 10 for a description and discussion of scientific management).

2 The second function of the professional-managerial class is to exercise social control over children and the working class. Thus teachers and social workers exercise social control over children and 'problem' members of society.

3 A third function is to propagate ruling-class ideology. This is carried out by groups such as entertainers, teachers and advertising copy writers.

4 The final function that the professional-managerial class performs for the ruling class is helping to develop the consumer goods market, ensuring that the working class consume new products produced by capitalism.

The overall role of the professional-managerial class then is to reproduce the relationship of domination and subordination between the ruling and subject classes.

Evidence of reproduction

Although the Ehrenreichs define the professional-managerial class in terms of the functions it performs for capitalism, they also advance empirical evidence to show that it is a distinct grouping within the stratification system. For example, they claim that children of professional-managerial class parents are more than twice as likely to enter the professional-managerial class themselves, than the children of working-class parents. Entry to the professional-managerial class depends largely upon educational qualifications, and the class helps to reproduce itself by devoting considerable effort to ensuring the educational success of its children. In addition, members of the class usually find marriage partners from the same class.

Interests

The Ehrenreichs believe that the professional-managerial class has quite different interests from the working class, even though both groups consist of wage labourers. The professional-managerial class is paid out of the surplus produced by the working class. In the course of their work, members of the professional-managerial class develop techniques to control the working class. They also encourage the development of false class consciousness. These differences of interest are reflected in the tension, distrust and conflict which are often evident between social workers and clients, managers and workers, and teachers and students.

The professional-managerial class also has different interests from the ruling class. Both groups have an interest in maintaining the capitalist system, but the professional-managerial class has an interest in maximizing its own independence or autonomy; the ruling class, on the other hand, tries to restrict it as far as possible.

Managers and professionals justify or legitimate their position in terms of their technical expertise, objectivity and rationality. In these circumstances they cannot be seen to be sacrificing their independence, for that would undermine their claims to being objective in taking decisions at work. From this point of view, members of the professional-managerial class are likely to try to maintain their position by forming themselves into professions. Some groups of workers are more successful than others in achieving this. The Ehrenreichs suggest that in the USA between 1880 and 1920, medicine, law, social work and teaching established themselves as professions, whilst, for example, engineering did not.

The Ehrenreichs accept some degree of division within the professional-managerial class. Some members of the class, including some managers, administrators and engineers, work directly for industry and may aspire to joining the ruling class. Others are not employed directly by the ruling class and work in the liberal arts and service professions. Although there may have been some 'suspicion and contempt' between the two sections of the professional-managerial class, the Ehrenreichs stress that the division should not be exaggerated and that it has progressively narrowed. Professionals in academic institutions often have an administrative and managerial role within the institution; and over 80 per cent of managers have had a college education, half of them studying liberal arts subjects. Such divisions that exist are no greater than those within the working class.

Class conflict

Having discussed the place of the professional-managerial class in the stratification system, the Ehrenreichs go on to consider the role that it has played in class conflict in the USA over recent decades. They argue that during the 1960s the USA possessed a growing and increasingly confident professional-managerial class which came into conflict with the ruling class. Students in particular began to demand greater independence, and claimed the right to run society more in their own interests than those of the ruling class.

The Vietnam War was particularly important in stimulating the rise of the New Left. The American capitalist state looked to universities to help it in its war effort, enlisting the help of scientists, engineers, psychologists and sociologists. The Ehrenreichs claim that, partly as a reaction against the actions of the government, 'large numbers of young people pushed professional-managerial class radicalism to its limits and found themselves, ultimately, at odds with their own class'. Students turned against their universities, and universities are the most important institutions for the professional-managerial class.

The growing radicalism was partly a consequence of the increasing recruitment of working-class students who were needed to fill the rising number of professional-managerial class jobs. One section of the New Left allied itself to the black working class, demanding civil rights, and so acted against the narrow interests of the professional-managerial class. These developments led to a split within the professional-managerial class in the 1970s. One group distanced itself from the class and adopted a communist ideology, advocating the overthrow of

capitalism by the working class. The more moderate group of radicals continued the traditions of the New Left by trying to work within the professions to improve society.

Criticisms of the Ehrenreichs

The Ehrenreichs provide an interesting attempt to analyse the position of one part of the middle class within a neo-Marxist framework. However, they have been criticized by Marxists and non-Marxists alike.

Nicholas Abercrombie and John Urry (1983) accuse them of failing to take account of 'proletarianizing tendencies' within the professional-managerial class. After 1971 there was a reduction in demand for professional and managerial workers in the USA. This led to a surplus of qualified workers and made it possible for their work and pay to be devalued. Abercrombie and Urry also claim that the professional-managerial class is 'proportionately and politically stronger' in the USA than in other capitalist countries. They therefore question the degree to which the views of the Ehrenreichs are applicable to Europe.

The American neo-Marxist Erik Olin Wright (1978) does not accept that there is a unified professional-managerial class. He argues that capitalist societies remain polarized between two main classes: the ruling class and the working class. He does not deny that there are groups of workers who are intermediate between these two classes, but he argues that they do not constitute a fully developed class. Instead he sees them as occupying a number of strata which are in 'contradictory class locations'. Some of their interests coincide with those of the working class, and some with those of the ruling class, but they do not have a coherent set of interests of their own.

Weberian theories

Weberian and neo-Weberian sociologists generally reject the approach to defining and distinguishing classes adopted by the Ehrenreichs. They deny that classes can be defined in terms of their functions for capitalism, and instead stress the importance of the market situation of those in particular occupations.

This has led to one Weberian sociologist, Anthony Giddens (1973), identifying a larger middle class than the professional-managerial class discussed by the Ehrenreichs. From Giddens's point of view, the middle class should also include lower-level white-collar workers (for further details see pp. 69-70).

We will consider the implications of these various views for the analysis of the middle class as a whole after we have discussed the lower middle class in the next section.

Mobility between professions and management

Some research on the upper middle class in Britain has examined the degree of mobility between professional and managerial jobs. The greater the degree of mobility the easier it is to argue that the professions and management have become one class, in line with the views of the Ehrenreichs. If there is little mobility between the two groups, however, then this suggests they should be seen as separate classes.

Colin Mills (1995) used data from two surveys (a *Government Social Survey* conducted in 1949 and the Economic and Social Research Council's *Social Change and Economic Life Survey* of 1986) to discover the amount of movement between professions and management. The surveys suggested increasing

movement between these two groups, with a consequent blurring of the distinction between them.

Tony Fielding (1995) uses data from an Office of Population Censuses and Surveys longitudinal study of a 1 per cent sample of the population of England and Wales. This data allowed Fielding to determine how much movement between jobs these people had experienced between 1981 and 1991. He found that managers and professionals were more likely to stay in the same occupational grouping than any other groups of workers. Some 52 per cent of professionals in 1981 were still professionals in 1991, 17 per cent had retired and just 10 per cent had moved into management. Over the same period, 36 per cent of managers remained managers, 21 per cent had retired and just 10 per cent became professionals.

The lower middle class

Routine white-collar workers include such groups as clerks, secretaries and shop-assistants. The growth in their numbers during the twentieth century has led to a long-standing debate about their position in the class structure.

1 Some sociologists argue that they have become proletarianized, that is they have effectively become members of the working class.

2 Others claim that routine white-collar workers still belong to the middle class.

3 A third viewpoint suggests that they form an intermediate group between the middle and working classes.

Proletarianization

The theory of proletarianization suggests that routine white-collar workers have become part of the proletariat and so can no longer be considered middle class. This viewpoint has most usually been associated with Marxist sociologists who have questioned the assumption that the working class is a rapidly declining section of the population in capitalist societies. They see routine non-manual workers as little different from manual workers: they neither own the means of production nor do they perform important social control functions for capitalists.

For example, the British Marxists Westergaard and Resler (1976) estimated that in 1913–14 male clerks earned 122 per cent of the average manual wage, but by 1971 this had fallen to just 96 per cent. They argued that, at least with respect to

earnings, 'male clerks and shopworkers are now firmly among the broad mass of ordinary labour; and indeed often well down towards the bottom of the pile'.

Harry Braverman – the deskilling of clerical work

The American Marxist Harry Braverman (1974) supports the proletarianization thesis on the grounds that many routine non-manual jobs have become deskilled. He argues that over the last century or so the number of white-collar jobs has increased rapidly, but at the same time the skill required to do the jobs has been reduced. He calculates that in 1870 0.6 per cent of the population of the USA were engaged in clerical work; by 1970 it had reached 18 per cent. At the same time, however, the wages of clerical workers fell in relation to other occupational groups. By 1970 they earned less on average than any category of manual worker in the USA.

According to Braverman, clerical workers in 1870 shared many similarities with manual craft workers: both had wide-ranging responsibilities and had plenty of opportunity to use their initiative and develop their skills. Each company would employ a small number of clerical workers who would take care of all the dealings the organization had with the outside world. Each clerk would have the knowledge and experience to deal with many different tasks, and would be a valued member of the workforce.

As companies grew larger and their clerical workforce expanded, clerical work was reorganized so that each worker specialized in particular tasks.

As a result the skills required became minimal. As tasks were broken down, the office became like a production line for mental work. Clerical workers lost the opportunity to use their initiative and instead their work became highly regulated. The nature of the workforce changed at the same time as the work. Clerical work was increasingly feminized: by 1970, 75 per cent of clerical workers in the USA were women.

Braverman also claims that most 'service workers' have been deskilled. He says:

> the demand for the all-round grocery clerk, fruiterer and vegetable dealer, dairyman, butcher, and so forth, has long ago been replaced by a labor configuration in the supermarkets which calls for truck unloaders, shelf stockers, checkout clerks, meat wrappers, and meat cutters; of these only the last retain any semblance of skill, and none require any general knowledge of retail trade.
>
> Braverman, 1974, p. 371

Computerization has further reduced the skill required of checkout assistants, and the control of stock and the keeping of accounts have also become largely automated.

Braverman believes that, as a consequence of the changes outlined above, the skills required of most routine white-collar workers are now minimal. Basic numeracy and literacy are often all that are needed. With the advent of mass compulsory education, the vast majority of the population now have the necessary skills to undertake this type of work. As a result the bargaining position of these workers when they try to find work or gain promotion is little better than that of manual workers.

David Lockwood – a Weberian perspective

According to many Marxists then, the positions in the class structure occupied by most routine non-manual workers have been proletarianized. In an early study of clerks from a neo-Weberian point of view, however, David Lockwood denied that clerks had been proletarianized (Lockwood, 1958). Lockwood did not follow Weber in identifying an upper class based on the ownership of property; he did, though, use a Weberian approach to distinguish between different groups of employees. He suggested that there were three aspects of class situation. These were market situation, work situation and status situation.

1 By market situation he was referring to such factors as wages, job security and promotion prospects.
2 By work situation he meant social relationships at work between employers and managers and more junior staff; this involved consideration of how closely work was supervised.

3 By status situation he meant the degree of prestige enjoyed by particular groups of workers in society.

In terms of market situation Lockwood admitted that the wages of clerical workers began to drop below the average for skilled manual workers from the 1930s onwards. However, he claimed that in other respects clerks had retained distinct market advantages over manual workers. They had greater job security and were less likely to be laid off or made redundant. They also worked shorter hours, had more chance of being promoted to supervisory and managerial positions, and they were more likely to be given fringe benefits such as membership of a pension scheme. Some manual workers had only overtaken clerical workers in terms of pay because of the overtime they worked.

Lockwood reached similar conclusions with regard to work situation. He accepted that there had been changes – in particular the offices had grown in size – but he denied that this had led to clerical workers becoming proletarian. Compared to manual workers at that time, clerks still worked in relatively small units; they did not work on huge factory floors. Lockwood accepted that clerical work was often divided up into separate departments, but he did not believe that this had led to deskilling. He believed that the division of the clerical workforce into smaller groups with specialized roles led to closer contacts and greater cooperation between them and management. Furthermore, he claimed that attempts to make clerical work more routine had had a limited impact because clerical skills and qualifications had not been standardized. The job of each clerical worker therefore had unique elements. It was not as easy to switch clerical workers around or to replace them as it was with manual workers.

Finally, in terms of status situation Lockwood was more willing to concede a deterioration in the position of the clerical workforce. He attributed this to the rise of the modern office, mass literacy, the recruitment of growing numbers of clerical workers from manual backgrounds, and the increasing employment of female labour in these jobs. Nevertheless, he did not believe that clerical workers had an identical status to the working class. Nor did they have the same status as managers. Lockwood believed that clerks were in a position of status ambiguity which fell somewhere between the degree of status enjoyed by the middle and working classes.

Lockwood's work is now dated and it is debatable how far his claims apply to contemporary clerical work. Nevertheless, it was an important study since it established many of the issues that were to occupy later sociologists who studied clerical work.

John H. Goldthorpe – clerks as an intermediate stratum

John H. Goldthorpe *et al.* (1968) also maintained that clerical workers fell between the working class and the middle class. Like Lockwood they based their analysis on market and work situations, but they did not take account of status situation. They believed that there was an intermediate stratum sandwiched between what they referred to as the working and service classes. This intermediate stratum also included such groups as personal service workers, the self-employed, and supervisors of manual workers. The intermediate group lacked any strong class identity because of the range of occupations within it, and because many of its members become socially mobile and moved into a different class.

A. Stewart, K. Prandy and R. M. Blackburn – clerks and social mobility

Other sociologists have supported Lockwood and Goldthorpe in denying that clerical workers have become proletarian, but they have attacked the proletarianization thesis in a different way.

In a study based on a sample of male white-collar workers in firms employing over 500 people, Stewart, Prandy and Blackburn argue that individual workers in the stratification system should be distinguished from the positions that they occupy (Stewart, Prandy and Blackburn, 1980). To them, whether or not routine white-collar work has become deskilled is largely irrelevant in discussing whether the workers in these jobs have become proletarian. This is because most male clerks do not stay as clerks for all their working lives.

Stewart *et al.*'s figures indicate that only 19 per cent of those who start work as clerks are still employed in clerical work by the time that they are 30. By that age, 51 per cent have been promoted out of clerical work. For them it is merely a stepping-stone to a higher-status non-manual job. The remaining 30 per cent leave clerical work before they are 30. Stewart *et al.* claim that many of those who are promoted before they are 30 embark upon successful management careers and end up in unambiguously middle-class jobs.

According to this study, clerical work is merely an occupational category through which men pass. Stewart *et al.* argue that clerks can have varied relationships to the labour market. Young men who take clerical work as the first step in a management career can be considered middle class. Older men who change from manual work to non-manual clerical work late in their careers can more reasonably be regarded as proletarian. However, as Stewart *et al.* point out, as the latter have always been proletarian, it is senseless to see them as being proletarianized.

R. Crompton and G. Jones – a defence of the proletarianization thesis

Rosemary Crompton and Gareth Jones have strongly attacked the work of Stewart *et al.* (Crompton and Jones, 1984). Crompton and Jones studied 887 white-collar employees in three large bureaucracies: a local authority, a life assurance company, and a major bank. They advance four main arguments to undermine the conclusions of Stewart *et al.*:

1 They point out that the study by Stewart *et al.* ignored female white-collar workers. In their own sample, a large majority of clerical workers – 70 per cent – were female. Furthermore, they found that female clerical workers were much less likely to achieve promotion than their male counterparts. Crompton and Jones found that 82 per cent of female white-collar workers in their sample were on clerical grades, compared to 30 per cent of men. Only 12 per cent of female workers had reached supervisory level and 1 per cent managerial positions, while the equivalent figures for men were 36 per cent and 34 per cent. Thus, the high rates of male upward social mobility out of clerical work were at the expense of the large number of female workers who were left behind. They argue that even if male clerical workers cannot be considered proletarian because of their upward mobility, this is not true of female clerks.

2 Crompton and Jones point out that the high rates of upward mobility for men in the study by Stewart *et al.* depended not only on the immobility of women, but also on the 30 per cent of male clerks who left this type of employment. Crompton and Jones suggest that in the future it will not necessarily be the case that male clerks will be able to enjoy so much upward mobility. If the number of managerial jobs does not continue expanding, more and more men may become trapped in the way that female clerks already are.

3 Crompton and Jones question the view that promotion to managerial and administrative jobs necessarily represents genuine upward mobility. On the basis of their own study they claim that many managerial and administrative jobs have become increasingly routine and require little use of initiative. They claim that employers use the grade structure to encourage loyalty and dedication from employees, but in reality many of the lower-level management and administrative jobs are little different from clerical work. Promotion might not necessarily represent a change in class position for all white-collar workers.

4 Crompton and Jones suggest that Stewart *et al.* ignored one of the central issues in the proletarianization debate, that is, whether clerical work had actually been deskilled. Crompton and Jones disagree that class consists only of people, and has nothing to do with places in the stratification

system. They say 'classes can be conceived of as sets of places within the social division of labour'. If the places occupied by clerical workers have lost their advantages over working-class jobs, then clerks can be considered proletarian.

Crompton and Jones carried out detailed investigations of the three institutions they studied and found strong evidence that proletarianization had taken place. Some 91 per cent of their sample of clerical workers did not exercise any control over how they worked: they simply followed a set of routines without using their initiative. As a result their work required very little skill. Deskilling appeared to be closely linked to computerization: least skill was required by the clerks at the most computerized of the institutions, the local authority.

Crompton and Jones concluded that clerical workers were a white-collar proletariat, and that female clerical workers in particular have little chance of promotion to what could be called middle-class or service-class jobs.

G. Marshall, H. Newby, D. Rose and C. Vogler – clerks and personal service workers

In a more recent contribution to the debate, Gordon Marshall, Howard Newby, David Rose and Carolyn Vogler (1988; see also Marshall, 1997) have rejected Crompton and Jones's view that clerical work has been deskilled. Marshall *et al.* do accept, though, that personal service workers such as shop-assistants, check-out and wrap operators, and receptionists are little different from the working class. Their evidence is based on structured interviews carried out with a sample of 1,770 British men and women.

In one of their questions they asked respondents whether their job required more, less or the same skill as when they had started work. Overall only 4 per cent claimed that their jobs required less skill, and only 4 per cent of women in lower-grade white-collar jobs claimed to have been deskilled. No men in the latter type of job claimed that skill requirements had gone down. Workers were also questioned about such issues as whether they could design and plan important parts of their work, decide on day-to-day tasks, and decide the amount and pace of their work.

From this evidence Marshall *et al.* also conclude that clerical work has not been proletarianized. They support the views of Goldthorpe and Lockwood that clerical workers are in an intermediate class between the working and service classes.

They did, however, find that personal service workers tended to give different answers to the questions about autonomy at work. For example, 80 per cent of female personal service workers said they could not design and plan important parts of their work; 96 per cent said they could not decide their starting and finishing times; and 63 per cent said they could not initiate new tasks during their work. Marshall *et al.* conclude that personal service workers are 'more or less indistinguishable' from the working class.

The work of Marshall *et al.* draws attention to the position of personal service workers in the stratification system. Compared to clerical workers, they have been a somewhat neglected part of the workforce in stratification research. Certainly it is hard to see how it is possible to regard, for example, check-out assistants as middle class given their low wages, working conditions, and lack of autonomy.

Marshall *et al.*'s rejection of the proletarianization theory for clerical workers must, however, be regarded with some caution. In particular, the significance of the small number who say their work has been deskilled is open to question. The deskilling argument as advanced by Braverman refers to a time-span of a century or more, stretching back far earlier than the experience of those currently employed in such jobs. Indeed, Marshall *et al.* themselves admit that 'a definitive answer to the question of job techniques and job autonomy could be provided only by systematic and direct observation over a prolonged period of time'.

Middle class, or middle classes?

As we have seen, there is no agreement among sociologists about the position of the middle class, or classes, in the stratification system. They are divided about which non-manual workers should be placed in the middle class, and disagree about whether the middle class is a united and homogeneous, or divided and heterogeneous group.

Anthony Giddens – the middle class

The simplest position is taken by Anthony Giddens (1973). He argues that there is a single middle class, based on the possession of 'recognised skills – including educational qualifications'. Unlike the members of the working class, who can sell only their manual labour power, members of the middle class can also sell their mental labour power. Giddens distinguishes the middle class from the upper class because the middle class does not own 'property in the means of production' and so has to work for others to earn a living.

John H. Goldthorpe – the service and intermediate classes

Giddens follows Weber's views quite closely, but other neo-Weberians do not agree that there is a single middle class. John Goldthorpe, in his early work (Goldthorpe, 1980, and Goldthorpe, Llewellyn and Payne, 1987), defines class in terms of market and work situation, but in his research does not follow Weber in distinguishing the propertied from the propertyless. Goldthorpe does not therefore clearly distinguish an upper class, nor does he claim that there is a united middle class. As Figure 2.6 (on p. 115) shows, Goldthorpe sees the highest class as the service class, and this includes large proprietors as well as administrators, managers and professionals. This class itself is internally divided between those in upper and lower positions. However, he sees no significant division between managers and professionals within the service class.

Goldthorpe's class in the middle is not called the middle class, but the intermediate class. It includes clerical workers, personal service workers, small proprietors and lower-grade technicians. To Goldthorpe these workers have poorer market and work situations than the service class. In his scheme this class is also seen as being internally divided, but nevertheless at the most basic level he sees what is normally regarded as the middle class as being split in two. (For further details of Goldthorpe's views see pp. 114–15.)

In his later work, Goldthorpe (1995) has changed tack and argues that there is a primary division between different sections of the middle class based on employment status. That is, the employed, employees and the self-employed are in different positions. Beyond that, there are secondary divisions based on different employee relationships and it is these, rather than the nature of the work tasks that they do, that distinguishes classes. What makes the service class distinctive is that it not only receives a salary but is also provided with increments, pension rights, and career development opportunities.

Goldthorpe's views are controversial. In particular, many sociologists argue, in contradiction to both of Goldthorpe's approaches, that there is a significant division between professionals and managers in Goldthorpe's service class (for example, Savage, Barlow, Dickens and Fielding, 1992). A further problem is that Goldthorpe himself admits that, strictly speaking, large employers should be seen as a separate category from the service class employees. However, in his social mobility research, for example, he incorporates large employers into his category of the service class because the group is so small. He accepts that this 'means introducing some, though in all probability only a quite small, degree of error'.

K. Roberts, F. G. Cook, S. C. Clark and E. Semeonoff – the fragmented middle class

Some sociologists see the middle class as being even more divided than Goldthorpe does.

From a study of images of class, Roberts, Cook, Clark and Semeonoff claim that 'the middle classes are being splintered' (Roberts *et al.*, 1977). They argue that the middle class is becoming increasingly divided into a number of different strata, each with a distinctive view of its place in the stratification system. Roberts *et al.* base these observations on a survey conducted in 1972, of the class images of a sample of 243 male white-collar workers. They found a number of different images of class. Below are the four most common:

1 Some 27 per cent of the white-collar sample had a middle-mass image of society. They saw themselves as part of a middle class made up of the bulk of the working population. This middle mass lay between a small, rich and powerful upper class and a small, relatively impoverished, lower class. No division was drawn between most manual and non-manual workers, and within the large central class 'no basic ideological cleavages, divisions of interest or contrasts in life-styles' were recognized. Those who held a middle-mass image of society were likely to be in the middle-range income bracket for white-collar workers.

2 The second most common image, held by 19 per cent of the sample, was that of a compressed middle class. Those who subscribed to this view saw themselves as members of a narrow stratum squeezed between two increasingly powerful classes. Below them, the bulk of the population formed a working class and above them was a small upper class. Small business people typically held this compressed middle-class image. They felt threatened by what they saw as an increasingly powerful and organized working class, and by government and big business which showed little inclination to support them.

3 A third group of white-collar workers saw society in terms of a finely graded ladder containing four or more strata. Although this is assumed to be the typical middle-class image of society, it was subscribed to by only 15 per cent of the sample. Those who saw society in these terms tended to be well educated, with professional qualifications, and relatively highly paid. Though they described

themselves as middle class, they indicated no apparent class loyalty and often rejected the whole principle of social class.

4 Finally, 14 per cent of the white-collar sample held a proletarian image of society. They defined themselves as working class and located themselves in what they saw as the largest class at the base of the stratification system. They saw themselves as having more in common with manual workers than with top management and higher professionals. Those who held a proletarian image were usually employed in routine white-collar occupations with few promotion prospects and relatively low wages.

The wide variation in white-collar class imagery leads Roberts et al. to conclude that not only is the middle class fragmented but social trends will make it even more so in the future. The middle classes will come to form separate and distinctive strata in the stratification system.

The diversity of class images, market situations, market strategies and interests within the white-collar group suggests that the middle class is becoming increasingly fragmented. Indeed, the proposition that white-collar groups form a single social class is debatable.

Criticisms of Roberts et al.

The work of Roberts et al. can be criticized for relying on subjective class images. Neo-Weberians such as Goldthorpe (Goldthorpe et al., 1987) prefer to analyse class in terms of market and work situation, while neo-Marxists such as the Ehrenreichs (1979) advocate a discussion of the function that different strata perform for capitalism. For most Marxists it is the places in the stratification system (which are produced by the economic system) that are important in defining class, and not the individuals who occupy those places. For some Marxists this leads to the conclusion that the middle class is split in two.

Writers such as Crompton and Jones (1984) Braverman (1974) and the Ehrenreichs (1979) all agree that routine white-collar work has been deskilled and proletarianized. These workers do not have any stake in owning the means of production; they have little autonomy or responsibility at work; and they have lower wages than many members of the working class.

The upper reaches of what is usually referred to as the middle class, are, however, much closer to the bourgeoisie. They are unproductive labourers who do not produce wealth, but carry out important functions for capitalists. For example, managers play a vital role in controlling the workforce. Marxists and neo-Marxists disagree about the extent of their independence from the bourgeoisie. Braverman believes that they have little independence, while the Ehrenreichs claim that the professional-managerial class has increasingly come to defend its own interests rather than those of the ruling class.

N. Abercrombie and J. Urry – the polarizing middle class

In a review of debates about the middle class, Nicholas Abercrombie and John Urry argue that both Marxist and Weberian theories of stratification are useful, and that the two approaches can be combined (Abercrombie and Urry 1983). To Abercrombie and Urry, classes consist both of individuals, or people, and the places that they occupy.

They disagree with Marxists who argue that the capitalist economic system automatically produces certain types of job with particular functions, since they point out that groups of workers can organize to try to protect their work. Professional workers have thus been quite successful in retaining their independence and work responsibilities, whereas clerical workers have not. The result has been to split the middle class in two.

In terms of the Marxist concept of functions performed, and also in terms of the Weberian concepts of market and work situations, there is a major division between managers and professionals on the one hand, and routine white-collar workers on the other. According to Abercrombie and Urry, whether a Marxist or a Weberian theory of class is used, one section of the middle class has moved closer to the upper class, while the other has more or less become proletarian. In between, the so-called 'middle class' is hard to find.

Mike Savage, James Barlow, Peter Dickens and Tony Fielding – Property, Bureaucracy and Culture

Savage, Barlow, Dickens and Fielding (1992) follow many other theories by claiming that the middle class is not a united group. However, they do not argue that this lack of unity is inevitable, nor that the divisions within the middle class always stay the same. For example, they believe that France has tended to have a more united service class (of managers and professionals) than Britain. Furthermore, they believe that the nature of divisions in the British middle class may have been changing in recent times.

Savage et al. distinguish groups in the middle class according to the types of assets that they possess, rather than in terms of a hierarchy according to their seniority in the class structure. The importance of these different groups can change over time and is affected by the particular circumstances in which classes are formed. Thus, for example, in one set of circumstances, professionals might form a more cohesive and influential class than managers; at another time in another place the reverse might be true.

Social classes

Savage *et al.* see social classes as 'social collectivities rooted in particular types of exploitative relationships'. These social collectivities are 'groups of people with shared levels of income and remuneration, lifestyles, cultures, political orientations and so forth'. As collectivities they may engage in social action that will affect how societies develop. However, to do this they have to actively form themselves into classes. Class formation does not automatically follow from social divisions. Savage *et al.* therefore examine how class formation has developed in the middle classes.

They point out, though, that there are many social collectivities with, for example, a shared lifestyle. What makes class distinctive is that it is based around exploitative relationships in which some people become better off at the expense of others. These may take place through wage labour (as in Marxist theory), but exploitation can also be found outside the workplace. One example is where a person's contribution to an activity is neither recognized nor rewarded. They illustrate this with the case of a male academic who relies on his wife to type his manuscript or do the housework so that he can get on with writing. He gives her no share of the royalties and no acknowledgement as a co-author. Savage *et al.* say, 'her labour has been "deleted"'.

Classes and types of asset

The three types of asset which give the middle classes their advantaged life chances are: property assets, organizational assets and cultural assets. Individuals may have some combination of these three types of asset, but distinctive middle classes can develop based on each type. Different types of asset have different qualities and provide different possibilities for exploitation.

1   The propertied middle class are those who have property assets. This group consists of the 'petit bourgeoisie', which includes the self-employed and small employers. Their property assets are not as great as those of the 'dominant class' made up of landowners, financiers and capitalists. Property assets are most easily passed down from generation to generation. They can be stored in the form of various types of capital or in other possessions such as property. Property assets are the most 'robust in conveying exploitative potential'. As Marxist theory claims, you can use capital to hire and exploit the labour of others by not giving them the full value of their labour.

2   Organizational assets stem from holding positions in large bureaucratic organizations. These assets are held by managers. In the past a considerable number of people gained organizational assets by working their way up a bureaucratic hierarchy in a company without necessarily having high educational qualifications. Organizational assets are the most fragile type of asset. They cannot be stored and it may be very difficult to pass them down to the next generation. Certainly, today, managers are unlikely to be able to ensure that their children also obtain jobs as managers. In some cases, the assets are specific to a single organization and cannot readily be transferred to another company if the employee tries to move job. On the other hand, employment in organizations does provide opportunities for exploiting the labour of others.

3   Cultural assets derive partly from educational attainment and credentials. These sorts of cultural asset are particularly important to professional workers. However, they can also take the form of class taste. They can be found in 'what Bourdieu calls the habitus, or set of internalised dispositions which govern people's behaviour. Cultural assets are stored physically in people's bodies and minds: the body itself materialises class tastes. They can be reproduced through the passing on of cultural tastes to offspring.'

Class taste can be important in gaining educational qualifications (see the discussion of Bourdieu's concept of 'cultural capital', in Chapter 11). Women play a key role here because of their prevalence in the teaching profession and their importance in the provision of childcare. Cultural assets, however, cannot be used to directly exploit the labour of others. For this to happen they have to be used to accumulate property assets or to achieve positions which bring with them organizational assets.

Different sections of the middle class will tend to try to use their assets to gain other assets that will make their position secure, and enable them to exploit other workers and pass down their advantages to their children. So, for example, the cultured will try to obtain good jobs or use their cultural assets to start their own businesses. Managers who have worked their way up in a company may try to gain educational qualifications so they have the option of applying for jobs in other companies. Owners of successful small businesses may pay for a private education for their children in the hope that they will acquire cultural assets.

Historical middle-class formation in Britain

According to Savage *et al.*, these three sections of the middle class in Britain have all enjoyed different degrees of success at different times.

The *petit bourgeoisie* were of little importance in rural parts of Britain after the enclosure of land and the Industrial Revolution. Most of the land was owned by big landowners, with others reduced to landless labourers. In the towns, however, the *petit bourgeoisie* were more important, with shopkeepers and private landlords being particularly prominent. They were distinctive in their attitudes and lifestyles, partly because they tended to oppose the kinds of government expenditure that were welcomed by the professional middle class. Because of the nature of their assets it was relatively easy for them to pass them on to their children.

The professions have been a particularly successful group in the development of British society. The state played a crucial role in establishing an education system that formalized qualifications, from quite early on. It has also employed many professionals or defined the terms under which they could operate.

Professional associations have tended to link membership of professions closely with cultural assets by ensuring that a general liberal education was a prerequisite for a professional training. The professions have therefore had a high level of self-recruitment, with most new professionals coming from professional backgrounds.

In Britain the distinction between professionals and managers has been quite strong. Managers have generally been in a weaker position than professionals. Although their pay has been quite high, they have, until recently, relied very much on internal promotions within companies and have had little chance to switch between employers to further their careers. Levels of self-recruitment have not been so high and managers have not formed as cohesive a class as professionals.

Contemporary class formation in the British middle class

Savage *et al.* claim to have detected some significant changes in the middle class in contemporary Britain. The emphasis on controlling or reducing public expenditure by successive governments, and the increased stress on market forces, have tended to weaken the position of public sector professionals. There have also been important changes in industry. Savage *et al.* support the view that industry has moved in the direction of becoming post-Fordist. This involves moving away from mass production in very large hierarchical firms and instead producing smaller batches of more specialized products in less hierarchical and more flexible firms. (See Chapter 10 for a discussion of post-Fordism.) In the process, firms have come to rely more upon self-employed consultants of various types.

Particularly important are professionals and others working in areas such as advertising and marketing. They play an important role in 'defining and perpetuating consumer cultures associated with private commodity production'. Their cultural capital is not legitimated so much by qualifications and by employment by the state, as by their ability to make money by tapping into consumer tastes. Managers have become even less of a cohesive grouping than they once were. The internal labour markets of companies have become less important for promotion prospects. Managers have tried to cement their position by gaining greater cultural assets such as educational qualifications. These make them less reliant on single companies.

Savage *et al.* claim, on the basis of such arguments, that there is a new division in the British middle classes between:

> *a public sector, professional, increasingly female, middle class on the one hand, opposed to an entrepreneurial, private sector, propertied middle class on the other. This latter group might include the self-employed, some managerial groupings and the private sector professionals.*

> *Historically, we have argued, the professional middle class lorded over the rest: today managerial and private sector professionals may be shifting from its sphere of influence and may be joining the previously marginalised petit bourgeoisie in a more amorphous and increasingly influential private sector middle class.*

Savage, Barlow, Dickens and Fielding, 1992, p. 218

The culture and lifestyles of the middle classes

Using data from 1988 survey research from the British Market Research Bureau, Savage *et al.* claim to have detected cultural differences between these new middle-class groupings. However, they distinguish three lifestyle groups rather than two. The public sector professionals – such as those working in health and education and social workers, who are described as 'people with cultural asset, but not much money' – were found to have 'an ascetic lifestyle founded on health and exercise'. They drank less alcohol than the middle class as a whole and were heavily involved in sports such as hiking, skating and climbing.

On the other hand, the rather better paid 'private sector professionals and specialists' had a 'postmodern' lifestyle. This involved an appreciation of high art and of pop culture, and a combination of extravagance and concern for health and fitness. Thus 'appreciation of high cultural forms of art such as opera and classical music exists cheek by jowl with an interest in disco dancing or stock car racing ... a binge in an expensive restaurant one day might be followed by a diet the next'. This lifestyle was 'post-modern' because it rejected traditional cultural values about the worthiness of different types of art, and because it drew on consumer culture and its willingness to combine a wide variety of images and lifestyles (see pp. 119–22 for a discussion of post-modernism). A third group, consisting largely of managers and civil servants, is described as having an undistinctive lifestyle.

If Savage *et al.* are right, then the middle classes remain divided, but the nature of those divisions has changed significantly over recent decades. These changes have been influenced by the policies of the British state, and the middle classes have also exercised greater choice in deciding to adopt different lifestyles.

Evaluation

The work of Savage *et al.* does highlight some important divisions within the middle class. It provides a useful analysis of the basis of middle-class life chances. It does not fall into the trap of assuming that class divisions are static, and rightly emphasizes the active role of groups in developing their own class identities. It does concentrate, however, on the higher reaches of the middle class – their theory does not explain the position of routine white-collar workers.

Furthermore, it could be argued that their analysis of contemporary divisions in the middle class is not entirely convincing. Senior managers could be seen as forming an increasingly powerful and influential group in Britain, who may have combined the acquisition of qualifications with gaining increased opportunities for movement between companies. For example, those with MBA (Master of Business Administration) qualifications, particularly from the most prestigious business schools, may find it easier to gain and move between powerful and highly paid jobs. In a later work, Savage and Butler (1995) do admit that some senior managerial groups may have benefited from recent changes. They say 'it seems likely that the most senior managers of large organizations actually have enhanced powers. Such senior managers are also increasingly likely to be significant property owners of their organizations, through devices such as share options.' They speculate that such managers may have professional backgrounds and they are increasingly forming 'a small cadre who can mobilize organization, property and cultural assets simultaneously'.

The characterization of the lifestyle of different groups does seem to be based on rather simplified generalizations. For example, there are plenty of teachers and doctors who drink large amounts of alcohol and who are interested in popular culture. There are also plenty of private sector professionals who have a particular interest in health and fitness. If some theorists of postmodernism are correct, lifestyles are becoming less associated with particular class groupings in any case.

The working class

The market situation of manual workers

In official statistics based upon the Registrar-General's scale, and in most occupational classifications, the working class is usually regarded as consisting of manual workers. As we saw previously (see p. 57), there are important differences between manual and non-manual workers:

1 Non-manual workers, on average, receive higher wages than their manual counterparts.
2 A second market advantage of white-collar workers concerns the differences in income careers between manual and non-manual employees. The wages of manual workers typically rise gradually during their twenties, peak in their early thirties, and then slowly but steadily fall. By comparison, the earnings of many white-collar workers continue to rise during most of their working lives. Manual workers have

relatively few opportunities for promotion and their pay structure is unlikely to include incremental increases.
3 A third white-collar market advantage involves security of earnings and employment: compared to non-manual workers, manual workers have a greater risk of redundancy, unemployment, lay-offs, and short-time working.
4 Finally, the gross weekly earnings of white- and blue-collar workers do not reveal the economic value of fringe benefits. Such benefits include company pension schemes, paid sick leave, the use of company cars, and meals and entertainment which are paid for in part or in total by the employer.

Life chances

The inferior market situation of manual workers is also reflected in their inferior life chances. A variety of studies show that, compared with non-manual workers, they die younger and are more likely to suffer from poor health; they are less likely to own their own homes and a variety of consumer goods; they are more likely to be convicted of a criminal offence; and their children are less likely to stay on at school after the age of 16 to achieve educational qualifications, or to go on to higher education. In short, compared to non-manual workers, manual workers have less chance of experiencing those things defined as desirable in Western societies, but more chance of experiencing undesirable things.

Class and lifestyle

The above evidence suggests that manual workers form at least part of the working class in Britain. As previous sections have indicated, some sociologists – particularly those influenced by Marxism – would also include routine non-manual workers in the working class. However, many sociologists argue that social class involves more than a similar market situation and similar life chances.

In order to become a social class, a collection of similarly placed individuals must, to some degree, form a social group. This involves at least a minimal awareness of group identity, and some appreciation of and commitment to common interests. It also involves some similarity of lifestyle. Members of a social group usually share certain norms, values and attitudes that distinguish them from other members of society. Finally, belonging to a social group usually means that a member will interact primarily with other members of that group.

We will now analyse manual workers in terms of these criteria for class formation.

Class identity

A number of studies conducted in Britain over the past 30 years have revealed that the vast majority of the population believes that society is divided into social classes. These studies show that most manual workers describe themselves as working class, and most white-collar workers see themselves as middle class. For example, in a study by Marshall, Newby, Rose and Vogler (1988), 60 per cent of respondents said they thought of themselves as belonging to a particular class, and 90 per cent could assign themselves to a class category (see pp. 84–5 for further details of this study).

However, there are a number of problems with this type of evidence. Because people identify with a class does not necessarily mean that they will act in ways consistent with that identification. In addition, the labels 'middle and working class' may mean different things to different people.

In a survey conducted in 1950, F. M. Martin (1954) found that 70 per cent of manual workers regarded themselves as working class. The remaining 30 per cent, who defined themselves as middle class, did so partly because of the meanings they attached to the term working class. They saw the working class as a group bordering on poverty and defined its members as lazy and irresponsible; hence their desire to dissociate themselves from this classification.

However, despite the above problems, the fact that most manual workers define themselves as working class indicates at least a minimal awareness of class identity.

Class subcultures

From his observations of the working class in nineteenth-century England, Freidrich Engels wrote: 'the workers speak other dialects, have other thoughts and ideals, other customs and moral principles, a different religion and other politics than those of the bourgeoisie. Thus they are two radically dissimilar nations.'

Few, if any, sociologists would suggest that the gulf between the classes is as great today. Many, though, would argue that the norms, values and attitudes of the working and middle classes differ to some degree. They would therefore feel justified in talking about working-class subculture and middle-class subculture. As a result it has been argued that manual and non-manual workers form social groups distinguished by relatively distinct subcultures.

The proletarian traditionalist

Sociologists have long been aware of variations in working-class subcultures. Members of the working class have never had identical lifestyles. Nevertheless, a number of sociologists have identified characteristics that have been seen as typical of the traditional working class. Basing his ideas on classic studies of working-class communities, David Lockwood (1966) described the subculture of one working-class group, the proletarian traditionalists. When sociologists try to determine the extent to which the working class might have changed, they tend to make comparisons with the proletarian traditionalist.

The proletarian traditionalist lives in close-knit working-class communities and is employed in long-established industries such as mining, docking and shipbuilding. Such industries tend to concentrate workers together in communities dominated by a single occupational group. These communities are relatively isolated from the wider society. Consequently, they tend to produce a strong sense of belonging and solidarity. The workers are very loyal to their workmates and 'a strong sense of shared occupational experiences make for feelings of fraternity and comradeship'.

Friendship with workmates extends into leisure activities. Workmates are often neighbours and relatives as well. They spend much of their leisure time together in pubs and working men's clubs. There is little geographical and social mobility, so the sense of belonging to a community is reinforced. The strong social networks 'emphasise mutual aid in everyday life and the obligation to join in the gregarious pattern of leisure'.

The proletarian traditionalist is not an individualist. Lockwood describes 'a public and present-oriented conviviality' which 'eschews individual striving "to be different"'. Unlike the middle class, proletarian traditionalists do not pursue individual achievement by trying to gain promotion at work or success in running their own businesses. Instead they identify strongly with the pursuit of collective goals. This is often expressed through strong loyalty to a trades union. This loyalty comes from an emotional attachment to the organization rather than from a calculation of the benefits that union membership might bring.

The proletarian traditionalist's attitude to life tends to be fatalistic. From this perspective there is little individuals can do to alter their situation, and changes or improvements in their circumstances are largely due to luck or fate. In view of this, life must be accepted as it comes. Since there is little chance of individual effort changing the future, long-term planning is discouraged in favour of present-time orientation. There is a tendency to live from day to day and planning is limited to the near future. As a result, there is an emphasis on immediate gratification. There is little pressure to sacrifice pleasures of the moment for future rewards; desires are to be gratified in the present rather than at a later date. This attitude to life may be summarized by the following everyday phrases: 'what will be will be', 'take life as it comes', 'make the best of it', 'live for today because tomorrow may never come.'

By comparison, middle-class subculture is characterized by a purposive approach to life; humanity has control over its destiny and, with ability, determination and ambition, can change and improve its situation. Associated with this attitude is an emphasis on future-time orientation and deferred gratification. Long-term planning and deferring or putting off present pleasures for future rewards are regarded as worthwhile. Thus individuals are encouraged to sacrifice money and/or leisure at certain stages of their lives to improve career prospects.

Images and models of class

In addition to particular values and attitudes, members of society usually have a general image or picture of the social structure and the class system.

These pictures are known as images of society or, more particularly, images of class.

The proletarian traditionalist tends to perceive the social order as sharply divided into 'us' and 'them'. On one side are the bosses, managers and white-collar workers who have power, and on the other, the relatively powerless manual workers. There is seen to be little opportunity for individual members of the working class to cross the divide separating them from the rest of society.

This view of society is referred to as a power model. Research has indicated that traditional workers may hold other images of society and their perceptions of the social order are not as simple and clearcut as the above description suggests. However, the power model appears to be the nearest thing to a consistent image of society held by a significant number of traditional workers.

By comparison, the middle-class image of society resembles a ladder. There are various strata or levels differentiated in terms of occupational status and lifestyles of varying prestige. Given ability and ambition, opportunities are available for individuals to rise in the social hierarchy. This view of the social order is known as a status or prestige model.

The above account of proletarian traditionalists is largely based on a description of men. Working-class communities have usually been seen as having strongly segregated gender roles. Husbands have been regarded as the main breadwinners while wives have retained responsibility for childcare and housework. Husbands and wives tend to spend leisure time apart. While the men mix with their work colleagues, women associate more with female relatives. The bond between mother and daughter is particularly strong. (For an example of a detailed description of gender roles in a traditional working-class community see Chapter 8.)

The description is also one which has been applied largely to white men rather than to members of ethnic minorities.

Marxism and the working class

Marxist sociologists have tended to support the view that there is a distinctive working class which is distinguished by its non-ownership of the means of production and its role in providing manual labour power for the ruling class. Marxists also tend to see the working class as a social group with a distinctive subculture and at least some degree of class consciousness.

Marx himself predicted that the working class would become increasingly homogeneous: its members would become more and more similar to one another. He assumed that technical developments in industry would remove the need for manual skills.

As a result craftspeople and tradespeople would steadily disappear and the bulk of the working class would become unskilled machine minders. The growing similarity of wages and circumstances would increase working-class solidarity. Marx argued:

The interests and life situations of the proletariat are more and more equalized, since the machinery increasingly obliterates the differences of labour and depresses the wage almost everywhere to an equally low level.

Marx and Engels, 1950, p. 40

Marx thought that, as a consequence, members of the working class would be drawn closer together and would eventually form a revolutionary force which would overthrow capitalism and replace it with communism. There have been several revolutionary movements in capitalist industrial societies, but none have come close to success.

Changes in the working class

Some sociologists now believe that the working class has undergone changes during the twentieth century that have weakened and divided it, reducing its distinctiveness from the middle class, and removing the potential for the development of class consciousness. One of the most obvious changes is the shrinking size of the working class if it is defined as consisting of manual workers. According to Routh, manual workers declined from 79 per cent of those in employment in 1911, to just under half in 1971 (Routh, 1980).

A somewhat different impression is provided by the *General Household Survey*, a survey carried out regularly by the British government. This uses slightly different categories from the manual/non-manual division, including personal service workers and self-employed non-professional workers with manual workers. On this basis 47 per cent of the population were found to be in the working class in 1994, compared to 55 per cent in 1975 (see Table 2.2, p. 41).

In part, this decline has been due to de-industrialization as manufacturing industry employs a decreasing percentage of the workforce. Between 1966 and 1997, the number of people employed in manufacturing in Great Britain fell from 8.6 to 4 million. In 1997, only around 18 per cent of those in employment had jobs in manufacturing. If all jobs in construction and production are combined, they still only represented about 23 per cent of those employed in 1997 (*Labour Market Trends*, 1997).

Employment has fallen particularly rapidly in those jobs most likely to produce the subculture of the traditional proletarian worker. Heavy industries such as coalmining, shipbuilding and the steel industry, in which employees tend to live close together in occupational communities, have declined. In 1947 there were 740,000 British miners; by 1997 just 56,500 were employed in the mining and quarrying of all energy-producing materials, and the numbers have fallen since then (Beynon, 1992 and *Labour Market Trends*, 1997).

Recent declines in manufacturing employment have gone beyond the traditional heavy industries. As Huw Beynon points out, 'the car workers, it seems have gone the way of miners; as have the shipyard workers, the steel workers and those men ... who in mechanical engineering factories supplied components for the consumer industries'. In 1992 there were more people employed in hotel and catering than in steel, shipyards, cars, mechanical engineering and coal combined.

The new industrial jobs tend to be concentrated in the electronics industries located in such areas as 'silicon glen' in Scotland, East Anglia, the M4 corridor and South Wales. These changes have been accompanied by a major shift in the proportions of men and women employed in manufacturing. Beynon describes the 'rise of industries based upon information technology, in which women play a central part: they manufacture the microchip in factories in the Far East and they assemble the computer boards in the lowlands of Scotland'.

The end of the industrial worker?

Although he accepts that industrial work has changed a great deal and declined significantly, Beynon argues that we are far from witnessing the 'end of the industrial worker' or the demise of the working class. He argues that the decline of industrial work may be exaggerated, for a number of reasons:

1   Many manufacturing jobs have not disappeared, they have simply been moved abroad to take advantage of cheaper labour costs. In countries such as Brazil, Mexico, Malaysia, South Korea and China, manufacturing employment has risen rapidly since the war. Manufacturing employment in Britain is also low compared to most other advanced industrial capitalist countries because of 'a competitively weak industrial structure and the economic policies followed in the UK in the 1980s'.

2   Many jobs which are classified as being in the service sector are involved in producing things, and the distinction between manufacturing and services is therefore somewhat artificial. For example, workers at McDonald's are mainly involved in 'distinctly manual, repetitive and unpleasant work'. Cooking beefburgers is as much a manual task as assembling motor cars, yet it is not classified as such.

3   Some jobs have been redefined as belonging to the service sector because of changes in who employs

the workers rather than changes in the nature of the work. For example, at companies like Nissan, jobs such as cleaning have been subcontracted out to independent companies. As a result they are no longer defined as manufacturing jobs.

Beynon concludes that there are still very substantial numbers of workers involved in manufacturing and it cannot be argued that the industrial worker is disappearing.

Living standards and splits in the working class

Although the number of manual workers has declined, average living standards for manual workers in regular employment have improved. According to government figures, net income after housing costs for individuals rose by about 80 per cent between 1971 and 1990, and, while economic growth has levelled off in most years since then, there was a record growth of 2.2 per cent in 1995 (*Social Trends*, 1997). The better-paid groups of manual workers were among the beneficiaries of this general rise in living standards.

As early as the 1960s, some commentators were arguing that rising living standards were creating a new group of affluent members of the working class who had started acting like members of the middle class. Affluent manual workers were seen as developing a privatized home-based lifestyle and as becoming more concerned with purchasing consumer goods than with showing solidarity with their workmates. A recent variation on this theme suggests that home ownership, particularly among former council house tenants, has transformed the attitudes and values of some sections of the working class.

Some sociologists do not accept that affluent manual workers have become middle class, nor that they have developed a more privatized lifestyle, but they do believe that the working class is increasingly split into different groups. Workers with different degrees of skill, and those belonging to particular trades, are more concerned with protecting their own interests than they are with making common cause with the working class as a whole. To some, members of the working class have become interested primarily in the size of their wage packets, and they have little potential for developing class consciousness. We will now examine these views in more detail.

Embourgeoisement

Writing in the nineteenth century, Marx predicted that the intermediate stratum would be depressed into the proletariat. During the 1950s and early 1960s, a number of sociologists suggested that just the opposite was happening. They claimed that a process of embourgeoisement was occurring whereby increasing numbers of manual workers were entering the middle stratum and becoming middle class.

During the 1950s there was a general increase in prosperity in advanced industrial societies and, in particular, among a growing number of manual workers whose earnings now fell within the white-collar range. These highly-paid, affluent workers were seen as increasingly typical of manual workers.

This development, coupled with studies that suggested that poverty was rapidly disappearing, led to the belief that the shape of the stratification system was being transformed. From the triangle or pyramid shape of the nineteenth century (with a large and relatively impoverished working class at the bottom and a small wealthy group at the top), many now argued that the stratification system was changing to a diamond or pentagon shape, with an increasing proportion of the population falling into the middle range. In this middle-mass society, the mass of the population was middle- rather than working-class.

Economic determinism

The theory used to explain this presumed development was a version of economic determinism. It was argued that the demands of modern technology and an advanced industrial economy determined the shape of the stratification system.

For instance, the American sociologist Clark Kerr (Kerr *et al.* 1962) claimed that advanced industrialism requires an increasingly highly educated, trained and skilled workforce which, in turn, leads to higher pay and higher status occupations. In particular, skilled technicians are rapidly replacing unskilled machine minders.

Jessie Bernard (1957) argued that working-class affluence is related to the needs of an industrial economy for a mass market. In order to expand, industry requires a large market for its products. Mass consumption has been made possible by high wages which, in turn, have been made possible because large sectors of modern industry have relatively low labour costs and high productivity. Bernard claimed that there is a rapidly growing middle market which reflects the increased purchasing power of affluent manual workers. Home ownership and consumer durables such as washing machines, refrigerators, televisions and cars are no longer the preserve of white-collar workers. With reference to the class system, Bernard states:

> The 'proletariat' has not absorbed the middle class but rather the other way round. In the sense that the class structure here described reflects modern technology, it vindicates the Marxist thesis that social organization is 'determined' by technological forces.

Quoted in Goldthorpe and Lockwood 1969, p. 9.

Thus Bernard suggests that Marx was correct in emphasizing the importance of economic factors but wrong in his prediction of the direction of social change.

The supporters of embourgeoisement argued that middle-range incomes led to middle-class lifestyles. It was assumed that the affluent worker was adopting middle-class norms, values and attitudes. For example, in Britain, it was believed that affluence eroded traditional political party loyalties and that increasing numbers of manual workers were now supporting the Conservative Party.

The process of embourgeoisement was seen to be accelerated by the demands of modern industry for a mobile labour force. This tended to break up traditional close-knit working-class communities found in the older industrial areas. The geographically mobile, affluent workers moved to newer, suburban areas where they were largely indistinguishable from their white-collar neighbours.

J. Goldthorpe, D. Lockwood, F. Bechhofer and J. Platt – *The Affluent Worker in the Class Structure*

Despite the strong support for embourgeoisement, the evidence on which it was based was largely impressionistic. As such, embourgeoisement remained a hypothesis, a process that was assumed to be occurring but which had not been adequately tested.

In a famous study entitled *The Affluent Worker in the Class Structure*, conducted in the 1960s, Goldthorpe, Lockwood, Bechhofer and Platt (1968a, 1968b, 1969) presented the results of research designed to test the embourgeoisement hypothesis. They tried to find as favourable a setting as possible for the confirmation of the hypothesis. If embourgeoisement were not taking place in a context that offered every opportunity, then it would probably not be occurring in less favourable contexts.

Goldthorpe *et al.* chose Luton, then a prosperous area in south-east England with expanding industries. A sample of 229 manual workers was selected, plus a comparative group of 54 white-collar workers drawn from various grades of clerks. The study was conducted from 1963 to 1964 and examined workers from Vauxhall Motors, Skefko Ball Bearing Company and Laporte Chemicals. Nearly half the manual workers in the survey had come from outside the south-east area in search of stable, well-paid jobs. All were married and 57 per cent were home owners or buyers. They were highly paid relative to other manual workers and their wages compared favourably with those of many white-collar workers.

Although the Luton study was not primarily concerned with economic aspects of class, Goldthorpe, *et al.* argue, like many of the opponents of the embourgeoisement thesis, that similarity of earnings is not the same thing as similarity of market situation. White-collar workers retained many of their market advantages such as fringe benefits and promotion chances.

The Luton study tested the embourgeoisement hypothesis in four main areas:

1 attitudes to work
2 interaction patterns in the community
3 aspirations and social perspectives
4 political views.

If affluent workers were becoming middle class they should be largely indistinguishable from white-collar workers in these areas.

Instrumental orientation to work

The affluent workers defined their work in instrumental terms, as a means to an end rather than an end in itself. Work was simply a means of earning money to raise living standards. Largely because of this instrumental orientation they derived little satisfaction from work. They had few close friends at work and participated little in the social clubs provided by their firms.

Most affluent workers accepted their position as manual wage earners as more or less permanent. They felt that there was little chance for promotion. They were concerned with making a 'good living' from their firms rather than a 'good career' within their company.

Like the traditional worker, affluent workers saw improvements in terms of wages and working conditions as resulting from collective action in trade unions rather than individual achievement. However, their attitude to unions differed from traditional working-class collectivism which was based largely on class solidarity, on strong union loyalty and the belief that members of the working class ought to stick together. The affluent workers joined with their workmates as self-interested individuals to improve their wages and working conditions. Thus the solidaristic collectivism of the traditional worker had largely been replaced by the instrumental collectivism of the affluent worker.

By contrast, white-collar workers did not define work in purely instrumental terms. They expected and experienced a higher level of job satisfaction. They made friends at work, became involved in social clubs and actively sought promotion. However, because promotion prospects were increasingly slim for many lower-grade white-collar workers, they were adopting a strategy of instrumental collectivism and joining trades unions in order to improve their market situation.

In general, though, Goldthorpe et al. concluded that, in the area of work, there were significant differences between affluent manual workers and white-collar workers.

Friendship, lifestyle and norms

Supporters of the embourgeoisement thesis argued that once the affluent workers left the factory gates, they adopted a middle-class lifestyle.

Goldthorpe *et al.* found little support for this view. Affluent workers drew their friends and companions from predominantly working-class kin and neighbours and in this respect they followed traditional working-class norms. By comparison, white-collar workers mixed more with friends made at work and with people who were neither kin nor neighbours. The affluent workers showed no desire to mix with members of the middle class and there was no evidence that they either valued or sought middle-class status.

In one respect there was a convergence between the lifestyles of the affluent worker and the lower middle class. Both tended to lead a privatized and home-centred existence. The affluent workers' social relationships were centred on and largely restricted to the home. Their time was spent watching television, gardening, doing jobs around the house and socializing with their immediate family. There was no evidence of the communal sociability of the traditional working class. However, apart from the similarity of the privatized and family-centred life of affluent workers and the lower middle class, Goldthorpe *et al.* argued that the affluent workers had not adopted middle-class patterns of sociability.

Images of society

In terms of their general outlook on life, affluent workers differed in important respects from the traditional workers. Many had migrated to Luton in order to improve their living standards rather than simply accepting life in their towns of origin. In this respect, they had a purposive rather than a fatalistic attitude. As we noted previously, however, the means they adopted to realize their goals – instrumental collectivism – was not typical of the middle class as a whole. In addition, their goals were distinct from those of the middle class in that they focused simply on material benefits rather than a concern with advancement in the prestige hierarchy.

This emphasis on materialism was reflected in the affluent workers', images of society. Few saw society in terms of either the power model, based on the idea of 'us and them' which was characteristic of the traditional workers, or the prestige model which was typical of the middle class. The largest group (56 per cent) saw money as the basis of class divisions. In terms of this money, or pecuniary model, they saw a large central class made up of the majority of the working population.

Although differing from the traditional workers, the affluent workers' outlook on life and their image of society did not appear to be developing in a middle-class direction.

Political attitudes

Finally, Goldthorpe *et al.* found little support for the view that affluence leads manual workers to vote for the Conservative Party. In the 1959 election, 80 per cent of the affluent worker sample voted Labour, a higher proportion than for the manual working class as a whole. However, support for the Labour Party, like support for trade unions, was often of an instrumental kind. There was little indication of the strong loyalty to Labour that is assumed to be typical of the traditional worker.

The 'new working class'

Goldthorpe *et al.* tested the embourgeoisement hypothesis under conditions favourable to its confirmation, but found it was not confirmed. They concluded that it was therefore unlikely that large numbers of manual workers were becoming middle class. Even so, the Luton workers differed in significant respects from the traditional working class. In view of this, Goldthorpe *et al.* suggested that they may have formed the vanguard of an emerging new working class. While the new working class was not being assimilated into the middle class, there were two points of normative convergence between the classes: privatization and instrumental collectivism.

Finally, Goldthorpe *et al.* argued that the results of their study represented a rejection of economic determinism. The affluent worker had not simply been shaped by economic forces. Instead, the lifestyle and outlook of the affluent worker were due in large part to the adaptation of traditional working-class norms to a new situation; they were not simply shaped by that situation.

Embourgeoisement and the privatized worker

David Lockwood (1966) believed that the privatized instrumentalist revealed by the affluent worker study would gradually replace the proletarian traditionalist. John Goldthorpe (1978) went further, claiming that working-class instrumentalism was a major factor in causing inflation in the 1970s. As groups of workers pushed for higher wages and tried to keep ahead of other manual workers in the earnings league, industrial costs went up, and with them prices. As prices rose, workers demanded even higher wages.

Stephen Hill – London dockers

A study of London dockers conducted in the 1970s by Stephen Hill (1976) provided some support for the view that the privatized instrumental worker was becoming more common. However, the study also raised doubts about the extent to which workers had ever conformed to the image of the proletarian traditionalist.

Stephen Hill suggests that the new working class might not be as new as Goldthorpe *et al.* believed. The 139 dock labourers in Hill's survey were remarkably similar to the Luton workers. Judging from past studies, the docks are one of the heartlands of proletarian traditionalism. Strong working-class solidarity, long-standing loyalties to unions and the Labour Party, close bonds between workmates, communal leisure activities, an emphasis on mutual aid, and a power model of society have all been seen as characteristic of dock workers. Either this picture has been exaggerated, or there have been important changes in dockland life.

There is probably some truth in both these viewpoints. The system of casual labour in the docks was abolished in 1967 and replaced by permanent employment. The constant threat of underemployment entailed in the casual labour system tended to unite dock workers. The change to permanent employment may have reduced the traditional solidarity of dockland life.

Like the Luton workers, the dockers in Hill's study defined their work primarily in instrumental terms. Their main priority was to increase their living standards. Only a minority made close friends at work, and only 23 per cent reported seeing something of their workmates outside work. Most dockers lived a privatized lifestyle and leisure activities were mainly home- and family-centred.

Like the Luton workers, the dockers regarded collective action in trade unions as essential for economic improvement. Over 80 per cent of dockers voted Labour, the most common reason for this being an identification with Labour as the party of the working class. Again these findings are very similar to those of the Luton study.

In terms of their views of society, the dockers belied their proletarian traditionalist image. Only 14 per cent saw the class structure in terms of a power model, whereas 47 per cent – the largest group subscribing to one particular view – saw society in terms of a money model. In this respect they are again similar to the Luton workers. Hill concludes that the working class is a relatively homogeneous group and the argument that there is a division between an old and new working class has been exaggerated.

Fiona Devine – *Affluent Workers Revisited*

Fiona Devine (1992) has directly tested Lockwood's claim that the privatized instrumentalist would become the typical member of the working class. While Hill had examined a traditional proletarian group and found evidence to support Lockwood, Devine went back to studying 'affluent workers'.

Between July 1986 and July 1987 she conducted in-depth interviews with a sample of 62 people from Luton. The sample consisted of 30 male manual workers employed on the shop floor at the Vauxhall car plant, their wives, and two further wives of Vauxhall workers whose husbands refused to participate. By returning to Luton, Devine was able to make direct comparisons between her own findings in the 1980s and those of Goldthorpe *et al.* in the 1960s.

Geographical mobility

Like the earlier study, Devine's found high levels of geographical mobility. Some 30 per cent of the sample had grown up away from Luton. However, unlike Goldthorpe *et al.*, she did not find that they had moved to Luton in search of higher living standards. With high levels of unemployment in the 1980s many had gone to Luton in search of greater job security. Some of those who had moved from London had done so in order to find more affordable housing.

Orientation to work

Devine found that her sample was interested in using work as a means of improving their living standards. However, they were 'faced with the threat of redundancy and unemployment which hung over their daily lives'. Thus, while they wanted to 'better themselves', they were more concerned with attaining greater security. They expected no more than 'small, cumulative gains' in their living standards. Their consumer aspirations were more limited than those of their 1960s counterparts, though they were still rather greater than those supposed to be possessed by the 'traditional' working class.

The 1980s sample continued to belong to and support trades unions. Furthermore, they saw unions as a 'collective means of securing working class interests'. Money was not their only concern, and other issues led to feelings of solidarity with fellow workers. Devine says that 'their poor conditions of work, for example, were often shared with fellow workers, and this was recognised to be the case'. They were also concerned about the distribution of power at work, and were interested in securing humane and fair treatment for their colleagues and themselves in their working lives. Many of them were critical of unions, but these criticisms were directed at union tactics and not at the principle of having unions to defend working-class interests.

Overall, Devine follows Goldthorpe *et al.* in describing the workers' orientation to work as instrumental collectivism, but she found more evidence of collectivism in the 1980s than had appeared to be present in the 1960s. The concern with money and living standards did not prevent them from feeling a sense of solidarity with fellow workers.

Friendship, lifestyle and norms

Like Goldthorpe *et al.*, Devine did not find that Vauxhall manual workers were befriending members of the middle class. In some respects they had traditional working-class friendship patterns: men had friends from work and many of their wives retained close contacts with relatives. Men still enjoyed leisure outside the home with other men, particularly playing sports or going to the pub. Traditional gender roles were also in evidence; although many wives had paid employment they still had primary responsibility for domestic chores. This reduced their freedom to engage in leisure outside the home.

Nevertheless, Devine did find important differences between her sample and the supposed characteristics of traditional workers. She says that they 'were not engaged in extensive sociability in pubs, clubs or whatever', and they did not have a communal existence based on their neighbourhood. Their lifestyles 'did not totally revolve around the immediate family in the home' but at particular stages in the life cycle the home was very important. Families with young children had restricted opportunities for leisure in the community. Men were often working overtime to help provide materially for the

family, and women had most of the responsibility for childcare. In short, their lifestyle was neither as communal as that of the proletarian traditionalist, nor as home-centred and privatized as Goldthorpe *et al.*'s affluent workers.

Images of society

The images of society held by Devine's sample were found to be very similar to those in the earlier study. They had a 'pecuniary model of the class structure.' Most saw themselves as belonging to a 'mass working/middle class' in between the very rich and the very poor. This did not, though, prevent them from sharing certain values with the traditional working class. Many felt resentment at those who had inherited money and a sense of injustice at the existence of extreme class inequalities. One said 'I disagree with a silver spoon. People should work for their money, not inherit it.' They wanted some redistribution of wealth away from the very rich and, with it, the creation of a somewhat more egalitarian society.

Political attitudes

Devine did find evidence of declining support for the Labour Party. As Table 2.14 shows, only 24 of the 62 in the sample had voted Labour in the 1979 or 1983 elections. On the surface this would seem to support the view that affluent workers were increasingly voting for individualistic and instrumental reasons. However, Devine did not find that disillusioned Labour Party supporters had abandoned their belief in the values traditionally associated with voting Labour. Instead, they had withdrawn their allegiance, perhaps only temporarily, because of the party's political failings. They were highly critical of the 'Winter of Discontent' in 1978–9 when a Labour government had presided over widespread strikes. They were also unhappy about the breakdown in relations between the party and the unions, and critical of the party's performance in running the economy during the 1970s, and of internal divisions during the 1980s.

Table 2.14	Political allegiances of the interviewees in Devine's study
Political allegiance	**Number of interviewees**
Labour Party supporters	24
Disillusioned Labour Party supporters	24
Non-Labour Party supporters	14
Total	62

Source: F. Devine (1992) *Affluent Workers Revisited*, Edinburgh University Press, Edinburgh, p. 189

A number of the disillusioned voters felt fatalistic about politics. While they still felt that theoretically the Labour Party represented working-class interests, they doubted its ability to deliver economic prosperity or low unemployment. Nine of the disillusioned Labour voters said they intended to vote Conservative at the next election. Yet they hardly embraced the Conservative Party with wholehearted enthusiasm: for them, 'the only positive attraction of the Conservatives was their policy of selling council houses which was seen as "giving people the chance to better themselves".

Conclusion

Devine's findings are rather different from those of Goldthorpe *et al.* some three decades earlier. She did not find that her sample had become the increasingly instrumental privatized workers predicted. She says:

> *The interviewees were not singularly instrumental in their motives for mobility or in their orientations to work. Nor did they lead exclusively privatised styles of life. Their aspirations and social perspectives were not entirely individualistic. Lastly, the interviewees were critical of the trades unions and the Labour Party, but not for the reasons identified by the Luton team [i.e. Goldthorpe* et al.]*

Devine, 1994, p. 9.

Devine rejects the idea of a 'new' working class and denies that the affluent workers have been persuaded to accept capitalist society uncritically. They have aspirations as consumers and their living standards have risen, but they would still like to see a more egalitarian society. They have lost faith in the ability of unions and the Labour Party to deliver this objective, but they have not fundamentally changed their values.

G. Marshall, H. Newby, D. Rose and C. Vogler – continuities in the working class

There is considerable support for Devine's findings in a study of the British stratification system carried out by Gordon Marshall, Howard Newby, David Rose and Carolyn Vogler (1988). Based on a national sample of 1,770 adults, the study found that 'sectionalism, instrumentalism, and privatism among the British working class are not characteristics somehow peculiar to the recent years of economic recession'.

Marshall *et al.* claim that historical studies show that there were artisans who put primary emphasis on their home life, and who had an instrumental attitude to work, well back into the nineteenth century. Furthermore, their data on contemporary workers

suggest that they retain some commitment to their work and do not follow completely privatized lifestyles. For example, 73 per cent of their sample thought that their work was at least as important as any non-work activity, and over half numbered one or more workmates among their friends. They concluded that there was no evidence of a significant shift towards instrumentalism and privatism.

Divisions in the working class

Marxism and the homogeneous working class

Marx and Engels (1848) predicted that members of the working class would become increasingly homogeneous, or alike. The American Marxist Harry Braverman (1974) agrees with Marx. He claims that the pursuit of profit has led to more and more automation in factories. This in turn has reduced the need for skilled workers and has led to an increasingly undifferentiated and unskilled working class.

Ralf Dahrendorf – the disintegration of the working class

Official employment figures directly contradict this picture, and suggest that during the course of the twentieth century the number of skilled manual workers increased, while the number of unskilled manual workers fell. Such statistics seem to support the views of the German sociologist Ralf Dahrendorf (1959), rather than those of Marx and Braverman.

Dahrendorf argued that, contrary to Marx's prediction, the manual working class has become increasingly heterogeneous, or dissimilar. He saw this as resulting from changes in technology, arguing that 'increasingly complex machines require increasingly qualified designers, builders, maintenance and repair men and even minders'.

Dahrendorf claimed that the working class is now divided into three distinct levels: unskilled, semi-skilled and skilled manual workers. Differences in economic and prestige rewards are linked to this hierarchy of skill. Thus skilled craftspeople enjoy higher wages, more valuable fringe benefits, greater job security and higher prestige than semi-skilled and unskilled workers.

Dahrendorf argued that in place of a homogeneous proletariat 'we find a plurality of status and skill groups whose interests often diverge'. For example, craftspeople jealously guard their wage differentials against claims for pay increases by the less skilled.

In view of the differences in skill, economic and status rewards and interests within the ranks of manual workers, Dahrendorf claimed that 'it has become doubtful whether speaking of the working class still makes much sense'. He believed that during the twentieth century there has been a 'decomposition of labour', a disintegration of the manual working class.

Roger Penn – historical divisions in the working class

Roger Penn (1983) agrees with Dahrendorf that the British working class is divided between different levels of skill; however, he does not believe that these divisions are anything new. Penn's views are based upon a study of workers in the cotton and engineering industries in Rochdale between 1856 and 1964.

He found that over the whole of that period the working class was sectionally organized in unions that represented specific groups of workers. The unions of skilled workers used social closure – they attempted to limit the recruitment and training of workers in skilled jobs – in order to maintain or improve the bargaining position of their members.

Penn found that unions were fairly successful over long periods of time in maintaining relatively high levels of pay for skilled and semi-skilled workers. Not surprisingly this tended to create competing groups within the working class and to weaken the extent to which members of different segments of the working class could act together.

However, if this has been the case for a century or more, it implies that Dahrendorf was wrong to see the working class as being more divided in the twentieth century than it was in the nineteenth.

Ivor Crewe – the 'new working class'

A second argument relating to divisions within the working class originates from studies of voting, and has been used to explain the failure of the Labour Party to retain working-class loyalty in the late 1970s and 1980s in UK elections. On the basis of his studies of British voting patterns, Ivor Crewe (1983) claims that the working class is divided, but not according to levels of skill but rather according to more specific factors.

Crewe believes that there is a new working class whose members possess one or more of the following characteristics:

1 they live in the south
2 they are union members
3 they work in private industry
4 they own their own homes.

They can be distinguished from the diminishing numbers of old working class who live in the north, belong to unions, work directly or indirectly for the government, and live in council houses. Crewe uses figures such as those in Table 2.15 to suggest that the new working class are deserting the Labour Party in large numbers, and abandoning the traditional proletarian socialist collectivism.

Crewe accepts that traditional proletarian collectivist views continue to exist, but believes that they are held by an ever-decreasing segment of the population. (For further details and evaluation of Crewe's work see Chapter 9.)

G. Marshall, H. Newby, D. Rose and C. Vogler – skill and sectional divisions

Gordon Marshall, Howard Newby, David Rose and Carolyn Vogler (1988) have used data from their study of the British stratification system to evaluate the claim that the working class is divided. In general terms, they support the view that the working class is divided into strata according to the level of skill involved in their work, but deny that the types of sectoral divisions identified by Crewe are significant.

Like Roger Penn, Marshall et al. believe that competition between different sections of the working class has created divisions lasting from the nineteenth century until the present day. In the nineteenth century, for example, the 'labour aristocracy' of skilled artisans caused splits in the working class. However, Marshall et al. do not claim that such divisions automatically prevent the working class acting as a group. They say:

Table 2.15 The two working classes: percentage of three-party vote 1983						
	New working class			Old working class		
	Owner-occupiers	Works in private sector	Lives in south	Council tenants	Works in public sector	Lives in Scotland/north
	%	%	%	%	%	%
Conservative	47	36	42	19	29	32
Labour	25	37	26	57	46	42
Liberal/SDP	28	27	32	24	25	26

Source: I. Crewe, *The Guardian*, 13 June 1983.

The 'working class' has always been stratified according to industry, locality, grade and occupation, and was so long before the emergence of Labour as a political force. Yet this prevented neither the emergence of a specifically working class party on the political stage nor the subsequent structuring of politics along class lines.

Marshall *et al.*, 1988, pp. 253–4

According to Marshall *et al.*, these class divisions are, nevertheless, much more important than sectoral cleavages. They measured the voting intentions of their sample and compared different classes, home owners and tenants, and public and private sector workers. Class was most closely connected with voting behaviour while there was no significant difference between the voting intentions of those in public or private sector employment. Council tenants were more likely to vote Labour whatever their social class, but an overwhelming majority of council tenants were working-class anyway.

Dennis Warwick and Gary Littlejohn – divisions in mining communities

Warwick and Littlejohn (1992) studied four communities in a mining area of West Yorkshire, surveying a total of 324 households in 1986 and 1987. They found evidence which appeared to contradict Marshall *et al.*'s views on the insignificance of sectoral cleavages. There was a 'strong element of anti-Thatcherism' among owner-occupiers and council tenants alike. For example, a majority in both groups opposed government support for private health and private education, and wanted higher taxes for the rich and reduced spending on defence. But there were significant differences in their politics. Some 65 per cent of tenants and 65 per cent of owner-occupiers claimed their parents had voted Labour. However, among males, 83 per cent of tenants now supported Labour compared to 57 per cent of those who owned or were buying their own homes.

Warwick and Littlejohn do not follow Crewe in claiming that housing tenure itself is the cause of increased divisions within the working class. Instead, they argue that housing tenure reflects a polarization between the relatively economically secure who have regular employment, and the rest. For the less well-off members of the working class, insecure employment, low income and poor health and residence in council housing tended to go together. Rising unemployment in the economic recessions, combined with the sale of council houses to the better-off, had led to a 'cleavage between citizens who still have clear means of participating in democracy, and those who are being pushed into what some call an "underclass"'.

From this point of view then, the major division in the working class is based on economic differences rather than level of skill. While there are sectoral cleavages, these derive from economic inequalities. Warwick and Littlejohn use the concept of an underclass very tentatively. This is not surprising since this concept is highly controversial. We will discuss it in detail later in the chapter (see pp. 89–96).

Class consciousness

Many Marxist sociologists argue that the contradictions of capitalism will eventually lead to a class-conscious proletariat. Class consciousness involves a full awareness by members of the working class of the reality of their exploitation, a recognition of common interests, the identification of an opposing group with whom their interests are in conflict, and a realization that only by collective class action can that opponent be overthrown. When practical steps are taken in pursuit of this goal, the working class becomes a 'class for itself'. Evidence from a variety of studies suggests that the working class is a long way from becoming a class for itself.

The limits to class consciousness

It has often been argued that the image of society held by proletarian traditionalists contains certain elements of class consciousness. The power model, with its emphasis on 'us and them', implies some recognition of common class interests, an indication of class solidarity, and at least a vague awareness of an opponent with whom the workers are in conflict.

The money model, on the other hand – which, judging from the studies of Goldthorpe *et al.* (1968a, 1968b, 1969), and Hill (1976), is the dominant image of society held by workers in Britain – suggests that the working class is becoming less rather than more class-conscious.

Further evidence from these studies supports this view. Nearly 70 per cent of the Luton workers believed that the inequalities portrayed in their images of society were a necessary and inevitable feature of industrial society. They were concerned with improving their position in the existing society rather than trying to create a new social order. Given the fact that they had improved their economic position, they had some commitment to the existing order. More recent evidence of the persistence of such attitudes can be found in a study conducted for the International Social Attitudes Report (Evans, 1993). This survey, based on a sample of nearly 2,500 people in Britain in 1987, found that 66 per cent of the working class and 62 per cent of skilled manual workers agreed that large differences in pay are necessary.

Marxists have often argued that the road to revolution involves an alliance between the trade union movement and a radical political party. Workers must see the politics of the workplace and society as one and the same. The Luton workers typically saw the union as an organization limited to advancing their economic interests in the workplace. In fact 54 per cent of the Luton trade unionists expressed clearcut disapproval of the link between trade unions and the Labour Party.

In general the Luton workers saw little opposition between themselves and their employer, 67 per cent agreeing with the statement that at work 'teamwork means success and is to everyone's advantage'. They were largely indifferent to 'exploitation' at work, home and family being their central life interest.

This picture of harmony must not be overdrawn. As Goldthorpe and Lockwood et al. state (Goldthorpe and Lockwood, 1968a, 1968b, 1969), the employer–employee relationship is not free from 'basic opposi-tions of interest'. Workers are concerned with maxim-izing wages, employers with maximizing profits. The teamwork image of industrial relations held by the majority of workers did not prevent a bitter strike in 1966 at the Luton branch of Vauxhall Motors.

Despite the apparent acceptance of the social order by the Luton workers, their responses to a number of questions indicate some resentment about social inequality: 75 per cent agreed with the statement that there is 'one law for the rich and another for the poor' and 60 per cent agreed that big business has 'too much power'.

The dock labourers in Stephen Hill's study (1976) expressed similar attitudes to those of the Luton workers. They showed no great hostility to employers or management, the majority being 'fairly indifferent' towards them. Most were opposed to the link between trades unions and the Labour Party. Hill states:

> *The dock workers I interviewed were certainly hostile to the traditional alliance between unionism and Labour, refusing to accept the view that these formed the industrial and political wings of an integrated labour movement.*
>
> Hill, 1976, p. 140

However, despite the lack of radicalism in the workers' views of employers and of the link between trade unions and political parties, Hill did find evidence of left-wing opinions. Over 80 per cent of the dockers agreed with the statements that there is 'one law for the rich and another for the poor' and 'big business has too much power', and nearly 75 per cent agreed that 'the upper classes prevent fair shares'. Thus, like the Luton workers, the dockers

appear to hold apparently conflicting radical and conservative views. We will discuss possible reasons for this shortly.

The potential for class consciousness

The studies by Hill, and Goldthorpe et al. may be interpreted as indicating a reduction of the potential for class consciousness. It appears that the proletarian traditionalist has been replaced by the privatized worker who is preoccupied with home and family and largely indifferent to wider political issues. John Westergaard, however, takes a rather different view (Westergaard, 1975):

1 First, he argues that the relatively self-contained working-class communities of the proletarian traditionalist encouraged a parochial outlook. Workers tended to have a narrow identification with their occupational group rather than with the working class as a whole. Westergaard argues that the break-up of traditional working-class communities may be necessary to provide 'a recognition of common interests with workers in other situations, outside the immediate locality'.

2 Second, since privatized workers define their work in instrumental terms, their sole attachment to work is the cash-nexus or money connection. As such, their attachment to work is single-stranded. It is not strengthened by pride in work, friendships at work or loyalty to the employer. A single-stranded connection is brittle: it can easily snap. If the privatized workers' demands for high wages and rising living standards are not met (for example in times of economic depression) the cash-nexus may well snap and there will be nothing else to hold them to their jobs and make them accept the situation. In such circumstances, privatized workers may become increasingly radical and recognize that their interests lie in collective class action.

3 Third, Westergaard argues that the seeds of class consciousness are already present even in the apparently conservative Luton workers. He sees evidence of this from their views on the power of big business and the workings of the legal system, views echoed by the London dockers. Westergaard claims that this demonstrates that the working class have at least a basic grasp of their class interests and of the conflict in interests between themselves and the ruling class.

The persistence of class consciousness

Westergaard's view that the seeds of class conscious-ness remain within the working class has been supported by Fiona Devine (1992, 1994). Her study of affluent workers in Luton during the 1980s (see pp. 81–3 for further details) found considerable evidence of the persistence of class consciousness. The workers wanted to improve their living standards and those of their families, but that did not prevent them from perceiving society as unjust or from desiring change. They shared with other workers a similar living standard and a desire to improve it and gain increased security.

According to Devine, these shared experiences and desires were a basis for class solidarity. The affluent workers' sense of injustice focused on the very rich. Many resented the fact that, unlike ordinary members of society, the very rich did not have to work for a living. This led the affluent workers to hope for:

> a more equitable distribution of resources in society as it stood, and, by implication, a more equal, free and democratic society in which people would be more justly and fairly rewarded than at present.
>
> Devine, 1994, p. 8.

Trade unions and the Labour Party were still regarded as 'collective means of securing both individual and collective ends'. However, support for them had declined because some of Devine's sample thought they had failed in delivering improvements for the working class.

While there was a strong awareness of a class division between the very rich and ordinary workers, there was less consciousness of a split between the working class and the middle class. Most of the sample thought that class divisions had declined in significance and saw themselves as belonging to a large class of 'ordinary' working people. Nevertheless, those who were employed at the Vauxhall plant still experienced a strong sense of class division at work:

> Manual workers at the car plant were aware of a sense of superiority and separateness held by the foremen and white-collar workers which placed them in an inferior position. The status aspects of the organisation of the workplace and people's attitudes of social superiority were a considerable source of grievance.
>
> Devine, 1994

The affluent workers of the 1980s were more pessimistic about the prospects for changing society but they had not lost the desire for change nor their sense of class inequality. To Devine, they retained a considerable amount of class consciousness.

Inconsistencies in class consciousness

There is a tendency in many studies of class consciousness to assume that workers hold a clear, consistent and coherent image of society, and to mould data into neat, tidy categories.

For example, the Luton workers of the 1960s are usually discussed in terms of their money model of society, yet only 54 per cent held that model, while 26 per cent had images which fitted neither power,

prestige nor money models, and 7 per cent had 'no communicable image' (Goldthorpe *et al.* 1969). Hill's study revealed that only 47 per cent of dockers held a money model and he was impressed with 'the range of different images which people within one group can embrace' (Hill, 1976). More emphasis might well be given to the variety and diversity of workers' images of society.

In addition, many workers do not hold clear and consistent views on society. Hill found that the dockers' fairly radical opinions on the power of big business, the workings of the law and the maintenance of inequality by the upper classes were inconsistent with their relatively conservative views on the role of trade unions and the nature of employment. He notes that they 'appeared to have their views fairly well compartmentalized'. As a result, the dockers seemed to have no problem with holding apparently contradictory views.

Similar findings were produced from a study of the ideology of 951 unskilled manual workers in Peterborough, conducted in 1970–1 by R. M. Blackburn and Michael Mann (1975). They found that both right- and left-wing views co-existed in the workers' ideology. Blackburn and Mann concluded that the workers did not possess consistent images of society.

In fact, Blackburn and Mann suggest that there is every reason to expect that this should be the case. The workers' experience of subordination and exploitation in the workplace tends to produce a power model of society and radical attitudes that demand a change in the status quo. However, the workers are also exposed to the ideology of the dominant class broadcast by the mass media and transmitted by the educational system and various other institutions. This ideology is conservative: it supports the existing social arrangements and states that the relationship between capital and labour is right, natural and inevitable. As a result, workers 'remain confused by the clash between conservatism and proletarianism, but touched by both'.

Beliefs and actions

On the basis of questionnaire research with a national sample of British adults, David Marshall, Howard Newby, David Rose and Carolyn Vogler (1988) reached somewhat similar conclusions to Blackburn and Mann. They claimed that class consciousness often did not produce a coherent view of the world. Respondents quite frequently gave inconsistent answers. For example:

1 Only 30 per cent of those who rejected leaving the economy to market forces to produce economic revival, also supported using government intervention for this purpose.

2 Some 19 per cent of those who wanted increased taxation to expand the welfare state, were themselves unwilling to pay more tax for this purpose.

3 A mere 25 per cent of those who supported the use of an incomes policy to reduce wage differentials, were themselves willing to accept pay restraint to achieve it.

The last two examples suggest that beliefs and actions will not always coincide, so class consciousness does not necessarily lead to class-based actions.

The continuing relevance of class

Nevertheless, Marshall *et al.* emphasize the continuing relevance and importance of class for the British population. Rose and Marshall summarize some of their findings in the following way:

over 90 per cent of our respondents could place themselves in one of the conventionally defined class categories; 73 per cent viewed class as an inevitable feature of British society; and 52 per cent recognised the existence of class conflicts over important social issues in Britain.

Rose and Marshall, 1988 p. 23

Furthermore, half of the sample believed there was a dominant class that possessed economic and political power, and a lower class that had no economic and political power.

Marshall *et al.* found a surprisingly widespread sense of injustice about the distribution of income and wealth in British society. Table 2.16 shows the percentage of the population who believed the distribution of income in Britain was unfair, and the reasons they gave for this belief. The class categories

Table 2.16 Attitudes to distributional justice by Goldthorpe class

A 'Is distribution of wealth and income fair?'					Class				
	I	II	III	IV	V	VI	VII	All	Total
Yes	31	34	28	44	24	25	22	29	(368)
No	69	66	72	56	76	75	78	71	(914)

B 'Why not?'	I	II	III	IV	V	VI	VII
Distribution favours those at the top							
Gap between haves and have-nots is too wide	57	59	63	64	55	63	63
Pay differentials are too wide	21	19	19	19	26	21	19
Too much poverty, wages too low, too many reduced to welfare	13	17	20	16	13	17	18
Some people acquire wealth too easily (unearned income, etc.)	31	16	13	13	20	10	9
The higher paid are not taxed severely enough	9	15	11	9	12	20	16
Welfare benefits are too low	6	5	6	2	8	9	6
The lower paid or working class are taxed too severely	2	3	3	5	3	0	2
Inequalities of opportunity (in education, for jobs, etc.)	2	2	2	0	0	1	2
Unequal regional distribution (of jobs, income, etc.)	4	3	3	0	2	1	2
Distribution favours those at the bottom							
There are too many scroungers around	6	5	12	9	15	8	10
Pay differentials are too narrow	5	4	1	3	4	4	4
The higher paid are taxed too severely	4	2	3	8	3	3	3
Other reasons							
Inequality of wealth and income inevitable	1	4	4	2	7	2	2
Key groups of workers can hold the country to ransom	1	1	0	0	0	0	0

Note: Percentages in the 'Why not?' columns are based on respondents. Valid cases = 899
Source: G. Marshall, H. Newby, D. Rose and C. Vogler (1988) *Social Class in Modern Britain*, Hutchinson, London, p. 186.

used are based upon John Goldthorpe's classifications (see pp. 114–16 for further details). They show that a majority of all social classes believed that the existing distribution of income and wealth was unfair, and, although lower classes were more likely to believe this, the percentage difference between them and higher classes was not particularly great.

Marshall *et al.* do not claim that there is widespread support for radical changes in the social structure, but they do believe that there is support for reforms that would lead to a more equitable society. They found little optimism, though, that such reforms were likely, or even possible.

Rose and Marshall claim:

> At the risk of oversimplifying, it would appear that while most people disapprove of social injustice, they do not think that they can do anything to change the system. Nor do they think that our elected leaders will do anything either.
>
> Rose and Marshall, 1988, p. 24.

Marshall *et al.* do not believe that class consciousness is automatically produced by the existence of class divisions. Rose and Marshall say:

> class consciousness is not simply a matter of individual beliefs, attitudes and values, which can be explained by reference to social locations and can be tapped by questions in a survey. To be sure, individuals have beliefs and experiences which reflect their social location. But for such beliefs to have effectiveness, for them to produce class consciousness rather than class awareness, requires that they be given explanation and direction. That is, they require organising.
>
> Rose and Marshall, 1988, p. 25

Despite the potential for class consciousness, the British population has not been mobilized in support of a programme that would tackle the sources of their sense of injustice. In this respect, Rose and Marshall point their fingers at the Labour Party for having failed to tap the reservoir of potential support for change.

Many Marxists believe that class consciousness will eventually be generated by the contradictions of capitalism. Many non-Marxists would regard this as a possibility, but an unlikely one: they would tend to agree with Ken Roberts *et al.* (1997) that 'the working class remains an unstable and continuing challenge but not a revolutionary threat'.

The lower strata

Although some sociologists see the working class as the lowest stratum in capitalist societies, others argue that there is a group beneath it. The most disadvantaged sections of capitalist society have been described in many ways. Kirk Mann says:

> Terms such as 'the underclass', 'marginalized groups/stratum', 'excluded groups', 'reserve army of labour', 'housing classes', 'the pauper class', 'the residuum', 'relative stagnant population' and, more obviously, the poor, have all been used to describe a section of society which is seen to exist within and yet at the base of the working class.
>
> Mann, 1992, p. 2.

Of these terms, underclass is the one that has enjoyed the widest currency in recent years. Those sociologists who have identified a group of people at the bottom of the stratification system have seen them as having various distinguishing characteristics. These have included being poor, unemployed or dependent on benefits. In some cases they have been defined as a group whose behaviour contravenes the norms and values of society. Thus some sociologists have emphasized the economic distinctiveness of the lower strata while others have concentrated on their supposed cultural or behavioural differences from the rest of the population.

In the latter case, the lower strata have been seen as constituting a social problem that poses a threat to society. They can also, however, be seen as a sociological problem for theories of stratification. Some theories of stratification have been based upon occupations, leaving the unemployed as a group who are difficult to categorize. In this chapter we will focus on the implications of the existence of lower strata for theories of stratification. Later chapters will discuss the relationship between the underclass and poverty (see pp. 323–33), and the underclass and ethnicity (see pp. 283–5).

Marx's view of the lower strata

The lumpenproletariat

In recent years, sociologists, journalists and politicians have all paid considerable attention to the 'problem' of the lower strata, but this interest is nothing new. In the nineteenth century Karl Marx was among those who expressed views on these groups. He used a number of different terms to describe those at the bottom of the stratification system of capitalist societies.

He used the word 'lumpenproletariat' to describe the lowest group of all. The picture he paints of them is less than flattering. They are variously seen as:

> *This scum of the depraved elements of all classes ... decayed roués, vagabonds, discharged soldiers, discharged jailbirds, escaped galley slaves, swindlers, mountebanks, lazzaroni, pickpockets, tricksters, gamblers, brothel keepers, tinkers, beggars, the dangerous class, the social scum, that passively rotting mass thrown off by the lowest layers of the old society.*
>
> Marx and Engels, 1950, p. 267

It is unclear from Marx's writing whether he regarded this group as a class or not.

Lydia Morris points out that his usage of the term is inconsistent and it may 'variously refer to an historical remnant from an earlier society, a group of individual social degenerates, or a category located outside of the economic system of industrial capitalism'.

Although, at times, Marx did refer to these people as a class, at other times he dismissed the idea that they can form a class because he saw them as having little potential for developing class consciousness or taking collective action.

The reserve army of labour

The term lumpenproletariat has not been widely used by contemporary sociologists, but the idea of a reserve army of labour has been more influential. It exists because of the way the capitalist economy works. According to Marx, there are inevitably periods of boom, during which more workers are taken on, and periods of slump when many workers lose their jobs. The reserve army of labour consists of those who are employed as substitute workers and who are only needed during the booms.

To Marx, they perform important functions in capitalist societies. In *Capital* he says: 'the industrial reserve army, during periods of stagnation and average prosperity, weighs down the active army of workers; during the periods of over-production and feverish activity, it puts a curb on their pretensions'. It helps to drive down wage costs for capitalist employers by providing a flexible group of workers who are desperate for jobs and are willing to undercut the wages demanded by other workers. They will take the places of those who are sacked or made redundant. When the profitability of a company falls, threatening its survival, the employer may be forced to recruit cheaper workers from the reserve army of labour.

The existence of a reserve army of labour makes it more difficult for the employed workforce to be radical and to resist, for example, the introduction of new machinery or more intensive work practices.

The relative surplus population

Rather confusingly, Marx also used a third term, the relative surplus population, to refer to those at the bottom of the stratification system. This includes members of the reserve army of labour, but it also embraces groups which at other times he defined as members of the lumpenproletariat.

The relative surplus population is divided into four:

1 The floating surplus population consists of workers who are employed until they reach adulthood but are then dismissed, because adults are paid higher wages. (In contemporary Britain those young people on government training programmes who are used as a cheap labour force and are not offered a job on completion of their training could be seen as part of this group.)

2 The latent surplus population is made up of agricultural workers who are no longer needed and who are on the point of seeking work in urban areas.

3 The stagnant surplus population is part of the active labour force 'but with extremely irregular employment'. It is part of 'an inexhaustible reservoir of disposable labour-power', and it has living standards that are lower than average for the working class. Workers who have been made redundant and whose jobs have been lost as a result of new technology are likely to be in this group. Marx claimed that members of the stagnant surplus population tend to have large families – indeed the lower the workers' wages, the more children they have.

4 At the bottom of the relative surplus population 'dwells the sphere of pauperism'. Pauperism is itself divided into four groups: first, 'criminals, vagabonds, prostitutes, in short the actual lumpenproletariat'; second, paupers who are capable of working but who simply cannot find jobs; third, 'orphans and pauper children' who are likely to be recruited to the reserve army of labour in prosperous years; and fourth, 'the demoralized, the ragged and those unable to work'. This includes the elderly, victims of industrial accidents, 'the mutilated, the sickly, the widows, etc.'

Evaluation and criticisms of Marx

Some aspects of Marx's work on the lower strata have been quite influential. For example, the concept of a reserve army of labour has been applied by some feminist sociologists to the position of women in modern capitalist societies (see pp. 170–1). However, his views have also been heavily criticized.

Kirk Mann argues that Marx uses a wide range of criteria to distinguish the lower strata from the rest of the working class. He says 'Marx links economic, social and psychological issues to the pathology of individuals and social groups'. He does not stick to using the purely economic definition of class which characterizes his work on other classes. Furthermore, many of Marx's views are so critical of the lower strata they seem to represent little more than personal prejudice. Mann argues:

Even allowing for the late Victorian period, the terms 'stagnant', 'floating', 'latent' and 'lowest sediment' suggest an unsympathetic stance. When he asserts that certain sections of the reserve army of labour breed more rapidly, and 'succumb to their incapacity for adaptation', while others are part of some criminal class, Marx reproduces the prejudices of the Victorian middle classes.

Mann, 1992, p. 139

One reason perhaps why Marx was so critical of the relative surplus population was that he did not see them as having the potential to develop class consciousness. Mann questions this view, suggesting, for example, that urban riots and the existence of Claimants' Unions (organizations for those drawing benefits) show that the 'surplus population' is no more conservative than the working class.

Although Marx's writings on these particular groups seem rather dated, they do reflect problems that more contemporary sociologists have faced in trying to distinguish a group below the working class. Some have emphasized the cultural distinctiveness of such a group, while others have looked for a definition based upon economic differences. Both these elements are contained in Marx's work. Unlike Marx, most contemporary sociologists have used the term underclass to describe the groups at the bottom of the stratification system.

Charles Murray – the underclass in America and Britain

The underclass in America

Although not the first writer in recent times to use the term underclass, the American sociologist Charles Murray has probably done more than anyone else to popularize its usage. In *Losing Ground*, published in 1984, Murray argues that the USA has a growing underclass which poses a serious threat to American society. Murray argues that government policies are encouraging increasing numbers of Americans to become dependent on benefits. During the 1960s, welfare reforms led to an increase in the numbers of never-married black single parents, and to many black youths losing interest in getting a job. Increases in the level of benefits and changes in the rules governing them discouraged self-sufficiency. Murray argues that the growing size of the underclass is a

threat to the social and economic well-being of the country because its members are responsible for a rising crime rate and the benefits paid to them are costly to taxpayers.

The underclass in Britain

Charles Murray visited Britain in 1989 and wrote an article for the *Sunday Times*. In it he argues that Britain too has a developing underclass, although unlike America it is neither firmly established nor is it mainly composed of ethnic minorities. Murray defines the underclass in terms of behaviour. He says 'the "underclass" does not refer to a degree of poverty, but to a type of poverty'. These types of poor people were known to him in his youth and:

They were defined by their behaviour. Their homes were littered and unkempt. The men in the family were unable to hold a job for more than a few weeks at a time. Drunkenness was common. The children grew up ill-schooled and ill-behaved and contributed a disproportionate share to the local juvenile delinquents.

Murray, 1989. p. 26

Describing himself as 'a visitor from a plague area come to see if the disease is spreading', he finds signs that Britain too is being infected. These signs consist of figures showing rising rates of illegitimacy, a rising crime rate and an alleged unwillingness among many of Britain's youth to take jobs. In certain neighbourhoods, traditional values such as beliefs in honesty, family life and hard work have been seriously undermined. As a consequence, increasing numbers of children are being raised in a situation where they are likely to take on the underclass values of their parents.

Evaluation of Murray

Murray's views on the underclass add little to theories of stratification. By insisting on using a cultural definition of the underclass he neglects any economic divisions that contribute to the creation of any such class: in many ways his work is better seen as a theory of poverty than as a theory of stratification. We will therefore evaluate his work in more detail in Chapter 5 on poverty and social exclusion (see pp. 323–8), where we will show that in America much of the evidence suggests that the benefits system does not have the effects he claims. The evidence he uses to make out the case for an underclass in Britain is flimsy and sometimes contradictory.

Murray blames the underclass for its predicament, explaining the situation in terms of its own aberrant behaviour. To quote Kirk Mann, he sees the British underclass as 'criminally violent bastards who refuse to work'. Most sociologists view the so-called underclass rather more sympathetically. Unlike behavioural and cultural accounts of the underclass, structural accounts tend to see the lowest strata in society as the victims of inequality. They therefore tend to make more explicit connections between the underclass and the stratification system of society as a whole.

Ralf Dahrendorf – the underclass and the erosion of citizenship

The culture of the underclass

Dahrendorf's characterization of the underclass has some similarities with that of Murray. Dahrendorf also sees the underclass as a type of social illness, calling it 'a cancer which eats away at the texture of societies'. He believes that an underclass exists both in America and in Britain, and he sees it as having undesirable cultural characteristics. Its culture:

> includes a lifestyle of laid-back sloppiness, association in changing groups of gangs, congregation around discos or the like, hostility to middle class society, peculiar habits of dress, of hairstyle, often drugs or at least alcohol – a style in other words which has little in common with the values of the work society around.
>
> Dahrendorf, 1992 p. 13

Although this is very similar in tone to Murray's argument, Dahrendorf parts company from him in explaining how the underclass came about.

Changes in work

Dahrendorf claims that the development of an underclass has been caused by changes in work. Technological innovation has made it possible to produce far more with far fewer workers. He says 'we can produce mountains of goods while reducing the number of producers', and claims that current levels of output could be achieved with 20 per cent fewer workers.

Some have argued that jobs in services will replace jobs in manufacturing, but Dahrendorf does not believe this will eliminate the problem. Wage costs are high in much of Europe and this makes many services too expensive for consumers to afford. The consequence is that they generate little extra employment and they do not prevent the growth of an underclass of the unemployed. In the USA, on the other hand, wages are more flexible and it is more common to employ workers at very low wage rates to provide services. The problem is that these wages are so low that those receiving them cannot escape membership of the underclass.

Even those who have relatively well-paid employment are increasingly employed part-time or on short-term contracts. Many worry about their job security and 'such doubts are one of the reasons why they tend to close doors behind them'. The successful majority who have adequate sources of income make sure that their position is protected. Trade unions, companies and educational establishments all tend to exclude the underclass from the institutions that could bring them success. Unions protect their members' wages at the expense of creating unemployment for others; companies employ the well-qualified; and the education system does not give members of the underclass adequate opportunities to gain the qualifications they need. Dahrendorf says 'Those who are in, by and large, stay in, but those who are not, stay outside.'

The underclass and citizenship

Dahrendorf argues that citizenship involves the existence of entitlements which everybody shares. Members of the underclass are not full citizens because they do not have an economic stake in society, and society provides them with little security. They include many immigrants and young people who have not had a chance to become full members of society, while some of the elderly and 'those who have suffered mishaps of one kind or another' have lost their place in society.

Those who lack a stake in society have no reason to conform to society's norms. They develop their own norms. These are sometimes antagonistic to mainstream society and are passed down from generation to generation. The underclass then comes to pose a threat to other members of society. Although it is not a revolutionary force, the frustrations of the underclass do lead to rioting and violent crime. It therefore threatens the well-being of those who are full citizens.

Dahrendorf sees no easy solution to the problem of the underclass. He doubts that full employment can ever be achieved again but he does believe that there is something to be gained by a more equitable distribution of work. Job sharing and similar measures will allow more members of society to become full citizens. He also calls for 'a hundred if not a thousand local initiatives' by charismatic individuals who can help the underclass escape from its position by promoting community development.

Evaluation

Dahrendorf provides a rather more convincing explanation of the development of the underclass than Murray, but he too resorts to rather stereotypical descriptions of its behaviour. He includes a wide variety of groups in his underclass: the elderly, those who have suffered 'misfortune', the unemployed, the low-paid, the young and immigrants who have not gained a foothold in society. It is unclear exactly what these groups have in common. While they are all held to lack citizenship rights, Dahrendorf fails to provide a precise definition of those rights.

Furthermore, in his original article (1987) he is unclear about whether the underclass should be seen as a class or not. He says that 'one may wonder whether the word class is as yet appropriate'. The lack of precision in his argument makes it difficult to determine whether the use of the term underclass is appropriate or not. In a later article he says that 'it is precisely not a class', arguing that the underclass is simply a group of people who are not needed by society and who represent a challenge to dominant values.

If Dahrendorf's view that the underclass is not a class is accepted, then, as in the case of Murray, his work seems to add little to theories of stratification.

Anthony Giddens – the underclass and the dual labour market

The middle class, working class and underclass

Giddens (1973) is more confident than Dahrendorf that an underclass exists. He also integrates his theory of the underclass more fully into a theory of stratification, and he defines the underclass more precisely. As mentioned earlier in the chapter (see pp. 69–70), Giddens sees the middle class as those who possess educational or technical qualifications. This gives them an advantage in the labour market over the working class who have only their manual labour power to sell. Members of the underclass also have to rely upon selling their manual labour power, but, compared to the working class, they are at a disadvantage when trying to do so. As a result, they tend to secure employment in the least desirable and most insecure jobs.

The dual labour market

Giddens argues that contemporary capitalist societies have a dual labour market. Jobs in the primary labour market have 'high and stable or progressive levels of economic returns, security of employment and some chance of career mobility'. Jobs in the secondary labour market have 'a low rate of economic return, poor job security, and low chances of career advancement'. Employers need to plan ahead, and to be able to do so they need a reliable and committed group of workers in key positions. High and secure rewards are necessary to ensure the loyalty of these workers. This inevitably raises labour costs. In order to reduce overall costs, workers who

are in less important positions and who are more easily replaced are paid much lower wages and are offered less job security. It is these secondary sector workers who come to make up the underclass.

The composition of the underclass

Giddens argues that women and ethnic minorities are particularly likely to be found in the underclass. Employers recruit women to underclass jobs partly because of 'social prejudice', but also because they are likely to interrupt their careers as a result of marriage and childbirth. Ethnic minorities are also the victims of discrimination and prejudice. In the USA, blacks and Hispanics form the main members of the underclass. Indeed, at one point Giddens defines the underclass in terms of its ethnicity. He says:

> Where ethnic differences serve as a 'disqualifying' market capacity, such that those in the category are heavily concentrated in the lowest paid occupations, or are chronically unemployed or semi-employed, we may speak of the existence of an underclass.
>
> Giddens, 1973, p. 112.

Giddens sees the American underclass as the most developed, but also sees West Indians and Asians in Britain, and Algerians in France as constituting underclasses. He notes that migrant workers often become members of the underclass. Many black Americans in the underclass migrated to the cities from rural areas. He claims that 'in many contemporary European societies the lack of an indigenous ethnic minority leads to a 'transient underclass' (which turns out not to be so transient after all) being imported from the outside'.

The underclass and class conflict

Giddens argues that there is a basic difference of interest between the underclass and the working class. The underclass are radicalized by their experience of deprivation. On the other hand, members of the working class, with relatively secure jobs and comfortable living standards, have more conservative attitudes. They are likely to be hostile to calls for radical social change emanating from the underclass.

Evaluation of Giddens

Although Giddens's argument is more coherent than Dahrendorf's, it has also come in for strong criticism.

Kirk Mann has raised serious questions about the concept at the heart of Giddens's theory, that of the dual labour market. He argues that there is no clear dividing line between a primary and a secondary labour market. For example, some jobs are well paid but with little job security; others are poorly paid but relatively secure. It is unclear from the dual labour market theory whether such jobs should be seen as primary or secondary jobs.

Mann also questions the claim that dual labour markets, if they exist, result from the tactics used by employers to recruit suitable workers and keep their labour costs down. He gives an example saying:

> The miners in the mid-1970s were able to gain large wage increases and considerable improvements in their pension and other occupational welfare packages, but these were not offered by the National Coal Board (NCB). On the contrary, they were fought for and squeezed from the NCB at a time when the NCB was trying to shed labour.
>
> Mann, 1992, p. 122.

The labour market is influenced by the actions of workers as well as the wishes of employers.

Perhaps Mann's strongest criticism concerns the theory's attempt to explain why certain groups of workers end up in the dual labour market. According to Mann there is no real explanation of why particular groups are the victims of discrimination. The dual labour market theory fails to provide an account of the 'racist and sexist ideologies' that lead to the exclusion of women and ethnic minorities from many of the better jobs. Furthermore, Giddens and other dual labour market theorists ignore the role of workers and union organizations in excluding women and ethnic minorities.

The relationships between ethnicity and the underclass and between gender and poverty have both been the subject of considerable sociological controversy. We analyse these controversies in later chapters (see pp. 283–5 on ethnicity and the underclass and pp. 311–13 on gender and poverty). Some sociologists have also questioned Giddens's view that the underemployed or semi-employed should be included as part of the underclass. These views will be dealt with later in this section.

Duncan Gallie – the heterogeneity of the underclass

Labour market inequalities

Duncan Gallie (1988, 1994) has questioned both conservative views of the underclass (such as those of Murray) and radical ones (such as those of Giddens). He denies that the so-called underclass has a distinctive culture. Like Mann, he rejects the idea of a dual labour market, suggesting that there is little empirical evidence that it exists. However, he follows Giddens in arguing that there are substantial and increasing numbers of people in a very weak position in the labour market. He says:

> A significant sector of the employed population receives pay close to or below the official poverty line and there are marked inequalities of pay by race and gender. There has been a substantial increase in the proportion of part-time rather than full-time work. Perhaps most important of all, there has been a substantial increase in the 1980s of the most severe type of labour market disadvantage, the experience of unemployment.
>
> Gallie, 1988

All of this does seem to point to a growing underclass, but what Gallie questions is whether the groups involved can be seen as forming a class in either cultural or other terms.

The culture of the underclass

Gallie uses data from the Economic and Social Research Council's Social Change and Economic Life Initiative to evaluate different claims about the underclass (Gallie, 1994). This research used interviews carried out in 1986 to examine the labour market in six areas: Swindon, Aberdeen, Northampton, Coventry, Rochdale and Kircaldy. It found no evidence to support Murray's claim that the unemployed lacked the attitudes and commitment necessary to hold down employment. Both the employed and the unemployed had had an average of six jobs during their work careers.

Looking at the average length of the longest job ever held by different groups again revealed little variation. For the employed the average was 76 months, for the unemployed 74 months, and for the long-term unemployed 73 months. The unemployed, it seemed, had, in the past at least, been able to keep jobs for a substantial period, suggesting they were by no means unemployable. Furthermore, the unemployed were more committed to working than the employed: 77 per cent of the unemployed said they would want to work even if they had enough money to retire in comfort, compared to 66 per cent of the employed and self-employed.

Nor was there any evidence that the long-term unemployed became apathetic and resigned to being without work. Those who had been unemployed for long periods felt a greater sense of deprivation at being without work than those who had been without work for only a short time.

Divisions in the underclass

Gallie's research did find that the unemployed were materially deprived, and tended to be considerably worse off than those in employment. Nevertheless, he did not accept the view of some radical writers that this had led to them forming a distinctive group below the working class. To Gallie, there was little chance of, or evidence for, either the unemployed, or more generally the most disadvantaged in society, forming a united, class-conscious group.

Ethnic minorities are disadvantaged in the labour market, but there is considerable variation in individual situations. Some members of ethnic minorities are very successful.

The same applies to women, and in any case women are less likely to be unemployed than men. Although many women leave the labour market when they have young children, most women appear to regard this as 'basically legitimate'. They have little sense of grievance that would lead them to make common cause with other people who have no paid employment. Women are more likely to be employed in part-time work than men, 'but the evidence suggests that women involved in such work have high levels of satisfaction with their employment situation'.

Gallie sees the unemployed as the group most likely to develop some sort of distinctive underclass culture. Even so, many of the unemployed quickly find work and 'there are huge flows into and out of the stock of the unemployed each month'. This does not disguise the existence of a large and growing group of long-term unemployed. Yet even this group is unlikely to develop any sort of underclass consciousness.

The long-term unemployed are quite hetero-geneous. Men and women in this group are often in different personal circumstances, and individuals suffering long-term unemployment may be at very different stages in the life cycle. For example, an unemployed female school leaver may feel she has little in common with an unemployed man of 55.

The underclass and the working class

Gallie also found little evidence of a political split between the working class and the underclass. Members of the working class who had kept their jobs did not blame unemployment on the laziness or personal inadequacy of those without jobs. There is no evidence of a 'conservative backlash'.

In his later research (1994), Gallie found that the unemployed tended to have traditional working-class political views. Very few of them had engaged in non-conventional political protests, such as going on demonstrations and marches or undertaking direct action. On the other hand, they were more likely to express support for government spending on the welfare state than members of the working class. They were also more likely to support the Labour Party: 54 per cent of employed unskilled manual workers said they would vote Labour, compared to 67 per cent of the short-term unemployed, 78 per cent of the medium-term, and 78 per cent of the long-term unemployed who had previously had unskilled

manual work. Gallie concludes that 'unemployment neither leads to a propensity to direct action nor to political passivity. Rather the resentments of the unemployed are channelled into increased support for the traditional party of the working class – the Labour Party.'

Despite all his arguments, Gallie does not dismiss the idea of an underclass out of hand. He does say:

> *The one case where the concept of an underclass would appear to have some relevance is that of the long-term unemployed. Their deprivations are distinctive from those generated directly by the employment relationship and they have the type of stability over time that is assumed by underclass theory.*
>
> Gallie, 1988

Even this tentative use of the term is qualified. Gallie points out that the long-term unemployed have close connections with the working class: most were formerly manual workers or came from working-class backgrounds.

Evaluation

While Gallie successfully shows that the supposed underclass, particularly the unemployed, may not form a particularly cohesive group, some writers question whether this invalidates the idea of the underclass altogether. Ken Roberts (1997) argues that the underclass includes a wide variety of groups with different lifestyles, but it may still be a useful concept.

Similarly 'hustlers, the homeless, and young single mothers do not share a common way of life. Welfare dependants who need to know their rights develop quite different skill repertoires to drug dealers.' Nevertheless, they all have certain characteristics in common. They are all more deprived than the working class, their deprivation may persist over considerable periods of time, and they may have lifestyles and social networks which are distinct from those in employment.

While Roberts is not sure that an underclass exists yet, in contrast to Gallie he does believe it is quite likely that one is being formed and that it will become well established in the future. (See pp. 330–3 for ethnographic studies relating to the underclass debate.)

W.G. Runciman – the underclass as claimants

The underclass and the class structure

Runciman has devised a seven-class model of the British class structure based upon differences in control, ownership and marketability (Runciman,

1990). We will examine this model in detail later in this chapter (see pp. 117–18). Runciman identifies an underclass at the bottom of his class structure. He explicitly rejects Giddens's view that it should be defined as 'a category of workers systematically disadvantaged in the labour market'. Runciman mentions Gallie's work in suggesting that a different definition of the underclass is needed.

Runciman defines the underclass as: 'those members of British society whose roles place them more or less permanently at the economic level where benefits are paid by the state to those unable to participate in the labour market at all'.

Many are from ethnic minority backgrounds, and many are women, particularly single mothers, but it is their reliance upon state benefits that places them in the underclass, not their gender or ethnicity. (A similar view which also sees the underclass as consisting of claimants has been put forward by Frank Field. It is discussed on pp. 328–30.)

Criticisms of Runciman

Runciman appears to offer a straightforward and plausible definition of the underclass. However, Hartley Dean and Peter Taylor-Gooby (1992) have attacked his views. They point out that Runciman stresses the importance of 'career' in class analysis: that is, the future prospects and past history of individuals in the class system must be examined before allocating them to a class. Yet Runciman fails to take this into account when considering the underclass.

For example, figures suggest that on average lone parents stay as lone parents for a mere 35 months. Similarly, most of the long-term unemployed have had jobs in the past. They are unstable members of the working class rather than members of a stable underclass. To Dean and Taylor-Gooby the so-called underclass is simply too unstable and impermanent to be seen as a class.

They also attack Runciman for basing his defini-tion of the underclass on quite different criteria to those used in his definitions of other classes. Members of the underclass are not defined in terms of their relationship to the market but in 'purely institutional terms'. They exist in a relationship with the state, not the economic system. In terms of Runciman's definition, their existence depends upon the existence of state benefits. Nevertheless, in comparing his class scheme with classes in Britain in 1910, Runciman equates the underclass with a 'loafer

class' described by an Edwardian commentator called D'Aeth. Dean and Taylor-Gooby say:

> *The implication would seem to do Runciman's argument no good at all, because without an institutional relationship to the post-war welfare state, the roles assigned to the underclass are defined in terms of behaviour – the intermittence of their labour and their drinking habits.*
>
> Dean and Taylor-Gooby, 1992, pp. 40–1

Conclusion

Dean and Taylor-Gooby's latter criticism is not particularly strong. However Runciman defines the Edwardian underclass, it is clear that the contempo-rary underclass is defined in terms of its dependence on benefits and not in terms of behaviour. This dependence can be seen as a consequence of the lack of control, power and particularly marketability possessed by the underclass.

However, Dean and Taylor-Gooby do have a point when they suggest that there is a constant danger of the term underclass being misused. They say that 'underclass is a symbolic term with no single meaning, but a great many applications. It represents, not a useful concept, but a potent symbol.' It has become a symbol of 'socially constituted definitions of failure'. However it is used by sociologists, in society in general it is used to lay the blame on the disadvantaged for the social problems of which they are the victims.

Dean suggests that the term underclass should be abandoned. Not only is it misused, but in his view no underclass as such exists. He says that it 'does not usefully define a real or tangible phenomenon'. He believes that the debate about the underclass has touched on important issues though. He therefore concludes:

> *Recent structural and cultural changes have intersected, not to produce an 'underclass', but to shift the boundaries between core workers, peripheral workers and non-workers; between the individual and the family; and between the citizen and the welfare state. Such changes have also exacerbated regional inequalities and inner-city decay and, some would argue, may have contributed to rising levels of crime. We should not go in search of the underclass, but strive for a better understanding of structural and cultural changes and their complex interrelationships and effects.*
>
> Dean, 1991

Social mobility in capitalist society

Having looked at the different classes, we will now consider the amount of movement from one class to another within capitalist society.

Ascription and achievement

This section examines the nature of social mobility in capitalist society. It is generally agreed that the rate of social mobility – the amount of movement from one stratum to another – is significantly higher in industrial societies than in pre-industrial societies. Industrial societies are therefore sometimes described as open. In other words, they have a relatively low degree of closure.

In particular, it is argued that status in pre-industrial societies is largely ascribed, whereas in industrial societies it is increasingly achieved. As a result, ascribed characteristics such as class of origin, sex, race and kinship relationships have less and less influence on an individual's social status. Status is seen to be increasingly achieved on the basis of merit: talent, ability, ambition and hard work are steadily replacing ascribed characteristics as the criteria for determining a person's position in the class system. Indeed, a number of sociologists have suggested that this mechanism of social selection is built into the values of industrial society. Thus Talcott Parsons (1964) argues that achievement is one of the major values of American society. Individuals are judged and accorded prestige in terms of their occupational status, which is seen to be largely achieved by their own effort and ability.

The importance of social mobility

Sociologists are interested in social mobility for a number of reasons:

1 The rate of social mobility may have an important effect on class formation. For example, Anthony Giddens (1973) suggests that if the rate of social mobility is low, class solidarity and cohesion will be high. Most individuals will remain in their class of origin and this will 'provide for the reproduction of common life experiences over the generations'. As a result, distinctive class subcultures and strong class identifications will tend to develop.

2 A study of social mobility can provide an indication of the life chances of members of society. For example, it can show the degree to which a person's class of origin influences his or her chances of obtaining a high status occupation.

3 It is important to know how people respond to the experience of social mobility. For example, do the downwardly mobile resent their misfortune and

form a pool of dissatisfaction which might threaten the stability of society?

Before considering these issues, it is necessary to examine the nature and extent of social mobility in capitalist society.

Types of social mobility

Sociologists have identified two main types of social mobility:

1 The first, intragenerational mobility, refers to social mobility within a single generation. It is measured by comparing the occupational status of an individual at two or more points in time. Thus, if a person begins their working life as an unskilled manual worker and ten years later is employed as an accountant, they are socially mobile in terms of intragenerational mobility.

2 The second type, intergenerational mobility, refers to social mobility between generations. It is measured by comparing the occupational status of sons with that of their fathers (and only rarely the occupational status of fathers or mothers with that of their daughters). Thus, if the son of an unskilled manual worker becomes an accountant, he is socially mobile in terms of intergenerational mobility.

This section will focus mainly on intergenerational mobility, the type of social mobility most frequently studied by sociologists.

Problems of measurement

There are many problems associated with the study of social mobility:

1 Occupation is used as an indicator of social class and researchers use different criteria for ranking occupations. Many researchers classify occupations in terms of the prestige associated with them; others place more emphasis on the economic rewards attached to them. As a result, occupational classifications differ and the results of various studies are not strictly comparable.

2 A further problem arises from the fact that it is not possible to identify many members of the bourgeoisie on the basis of their occupations: a person's occupation does not necessarily say anything about the extent of their investments in private industry.

3 Furthermore, many studies of social mobility have not included data on women's mobility, and patterns of female mobility tend to be rather different from men's. This is largely because women tend to be concentrated in particular parts of the occupational structure.

4 The findings of studies can be expressed in different ways; for example in simple percentages or in odds ratios, and odds ratios themselves can be calculated in different ways (see below, p. 103). There is controversy about which types of data best represent the structure of opportunity in society. Similar controversies surround the use of absolute and relative mobility rates (see below for details).

In view of these and other problems, the findings of social mobility studies must be regarded with caution.

David Glass – social mobility before 1949

The first major study of intergenerational mobility in England and Wales was conducted by David Glass and his associates in 1949 (Glass (ed.), 1954). The main findings of this study are summarized in Table 2.17.

The percentages in the horizontal rows (in the top right-hand corner of each cell) compare the status of sons with the status of their fathers. Thus, taking all the sons whose fathers were in the status category 1, 38.8 per cent of these sons are themselves in category 1, 14.6 per cent are in category 2 and so on through to category 7 in which only 1.5 per cent of sons born into category 1 are located. The figures in bold print, going diagonally across the table, indicate the extent to which sons share the same status as their fathers. For example, 27.4 per cent of all sons whose fathers were in category 7 are themselves in that same category in 1949.

The percentages in the vertical columns (in the bottom left-hand corner of each cell) refer to the parental status of the men found in each category in 1949. For example, of all the men in status category 1 in 1949, 48.5 per cent have fathers who were in that category, 15.5 per cent have

fathers who were in category 2 and so on. The bold figures show the percentage of men in each category who have the same status as their fathers. For example, 25 per cent of all the men in category 7 are the sons of fathers from that category.

Overall, the table indicates a fairly high level of intergenerational mobility. Nearly two-thirds of the men interviewed in the 1949 study were in a different status category from that of their fathers. Roughly one-third moved upward and one-third downward. However, for the most part, the change in status is not very great. Most mobility is short range: sons generally moving to a category either adjacent or close to that of their fathers. There is little long-range mobility either from top to bottom or vice versa.

In the higher-status categories there is a considerable degree of self-recruitment – a process by which members of a stratum are recruited from the sons of

Table 2.17 Social mobility in England and Wales before 1949

Sons' status category in 1949

		1	2	3	4	5	6	7	Total
	1	**38.8** / 48.5	14.6 / 11.9	20.2 / 7.9	6.2 / 1.7	14.0 / 1.3	4.7 / 1.0	1.5 / 0.5	100.0 / (129)
	2	10.7 / 15.5	**26.7** / **25.2**	22.7 / 10.3	12.0 / 3.9	20.6 / 2.2	5.3 / 1.4	2.0 / 0.7	100.0 / (150)
Fathers' status category	3	3.5 / 11.7	10.1 / 22.0	**18.8** / **19.7**	19.1 / 14.4	35.7 / 8.6	6.7 / 3.9	6.1 / 5.0	100.0 / (345)
	4	2.1 / 10.7	3.9 / 12.6	11.2 / 17.6	**21.2** / **24.0**	43.0 / 15.6	12.4 / 10.8	6.2 / 7.5	100.0 / (518)
	5	0.9 / 13.6	2.4 / 22.6	7.5 / 34.5	12.3 / 40.3	**47.3** / **50.0**	17.1 / 43.5	12.5 / 44.6	100.0 / (1,510)
	6	0.0 / 0.0	1.3 / 3.8	4.1 / 5.8	8.8 / 8.7	39.1 / 12.5	**31.2** / **24.1**	15.5 / 16.7	100.0 / (458)
	7	0.0 / 0.0	0.8 / 1.9	3.6 / 4.2	8.3 / 7.0	36.4 / 9.8	23.5 / 15.3	**27.4** / **25.0**	100.0 / (387)
Total		100.0 / (103)	100.0 / (159)	100.0 / (330)	100.0 / (459)	100.0 / (1,429)	100.0 / (593)	100.0 / (424)	(3,497)

Status categories
No. Description
1 Professional and high administrative
2 Managerial and executive
3 Inspectional, supervisory and other non-manual (higher grade)
4 Inspectional, supervisory and other non-manual (lower grade)
5 Skilled manual and routine grades of non-manual
6 Semi-skilled manual
7 Unskilled manual

Source: D. V. Glass (ed.) (1954) *Social Mobility in Britain*, Routledge & Kegan Paul, London p. 183

those who already belong to that stratum. The way the figures are presented tends to disguise the degree of self-recruitment. From the table it appears that the highest level of self-recruitment is in category 5: in 1949, 50 per cent of the members of category 5 are the sons of fathers who were in that same category. However, since category 5 is by far the largest group, a relatively high degree of self-recruitment is to be expected. By comparison, category 1 is a very small group made up of just over 3.5 per cent of the sample. Yet in 1949, 48.5 per cent of the members of category 1 are the sons of fathers who were in that same category. This is over 13 times greater than would be expected by chance. If parental occupation had no influence on a person's status, only some 3.5 per cent of the sons in category 1 would have fathers in that category.

Family background appears to have an important influence on life chances. The higher the occupational status of the father, the more likely the son is to obtain a high-status position. Most men are likely to stay at roughly the same level as their fathers and this is particularly true at the top end of the scale. Glass's study therefore reveals a significant degree of inequality of opportunity.

Criticisms of Glass

Any conclusions drawn from this study must, however, be tentative. Not only is the data now very dated, but the research methodology has been the subject of lengthy criticism. In particular, it has been argued that Glass's findings do not reflect changes in the occupational structure before 1949. For example, a comparison of the actual numbers of sons born into the first four status categories (shown in the right-hand vertical column of the table) with the number found in those categories in 1949 (shown in the horizontal row across the bottom) suggests a contraction of white-collar occupations. However, as Payne, Ford and Robertson note (1977) there was a 16 per cent expansion of these occupations during the 30 years preceding 1949. This throws doubt on the validity of Glass's sample. It suggests that his findings may seriously underestimate the rate of social mobility and in particular the degree of long-range upward mobility. (For a detailed criticism of Glass's methodology see Payne, Ford and Robertson, 1977.)

The Oxford Mobility Study

After 1949, the next major study of social mobility in England and Wales was conducted in 1972 and published in 1980, with an updated version published in 1987 (Goldthorpe, 1980, Goldthorpe *et al.*, 1987). Known as the Oxford Mobility Study, it was undertaken by a group of sociologists at Nuffield College, Oxford. The results cannot be compared in detail with those of the 1949 study since different criteria were used as a basis for constructing the various strata. Where Glass used a classification based on occupational prestige, the Oxford study categorized occupations largely in terms of their market rewards. These categories are based on John Goldthorpe's original seven-class scheme, which was introduced earlier in the chapter (see p. 70) and will be discussed later (see pp. 114–15).

Table 2.18 summarizes the main findings on intergenerational mobility from the Oxford survey.

Absolute mobility

The 1972 study revealed higher rates of long-range mobility than the 1949 study. For example, Table 2.18 shows that 7.1 per cent of sons of class 7 fathers were in class 1 in 1972. In addition, the table suggests that there are high rates of absolute mobility (the total amount of social mobility); in no social class did more than 50 per cent of the sample originate from the same social class. The Oxford Mobility Study found high rates of social mobility, and more was upward than downward. It also found that the chances of those from working-class backgrounds reaching a higher social class had improved during the course of the century.

Relative mobility

On the surface, these findings seem to support the claim that British society is becoming more open. However, the study found that relative mobility chances varied greatly between the classes, and the relative chances had changed little during the course of the century.

The concept of relative mobility refers not to the total amount of social mobility, but to the comparative chances of those from various class backgrounds of reaching particular positions in the social structure. Thus 45.7 per cent of sons with class 1 fathers – but just 7.1 per cent of those with class 7 fathers – ended up in class 1.

By comparing the relative mobility chances of different generations it is possible to determine whether the class structure has become more open. In Figure 2.2 those born in 1908–17 are compared with those born in 1938–47. The seven-class scheme usually used by Goldthorpe is simplified by amalgamating classes to reduce the number of classes to three. (The service class consists of classes 1 and 2, the intermediate class of classes 3, 4 and 5, and the working class of classes 6 and 7.)

Figure 2.2 shows that the chances of members of all social classes attaining service-class jobs increased over the period studied. However, this was largely the result of changes in the occupational structure: service-class jobs as a proportion of male employment rose from 13 to 25 per cent, while intermediate jobs declined from 33 to 30 per cent, and working-class jobs from 54 to 45 per cent. The relative chances of the sons of those from different classes taking advantage of the increasing room at the top of the stratification system changed little.

This has been neatly summarized by Kellner and Wilby (1980) as the 1:2:4 rule of relative hope. This rule suggests that over the period covered, as a rough estimate, whatever the chances of a working-class boy reaching the service class, they were twice as great for intermediate-class boys, and four times as great for service-class boys. In other words, there has been no significant increase in the openness of the British stratification system.

Trends since the Oxford Mobility Study

In a follow-up study Goldthorpe and Payne (1986) brought figures on social mobility more up-to-date by examining data from the 1983 British Election Survey. They wanted to discover whether economic recession in the period 1972–83 had produced different patterns of mobility to those found in the Oxford study, carried out during a period of economic expansion.

Overall, they found few differences between the results of the two studies. Service-class jobs continued to expand as a proportion of all male jobs; absolute mobility continued to increase, but relative mobility stayed about the same.

However, they did find that unemployment had affected the position of all classes, and the working class in particular. There were still opportunities for upward mobility from the working class, but members of the working class were more likely to become unemployed than members of the higher classes.

Elite self-recruitment

The Oxford Mobility Study and Goldthorpe's later work suggest that there is not a high degree of social closure at the top of the British stratification system, but Goldthorpe can be criticized for ignoring the existence of small elites or, in Marxist terms, a ruling class. Goldthorpe's class 1 is a relatively large grouping, containing 10–15 per cent of the male working population. Studies that concentrate on small elite groups within class 1 reveal a much higher degree of closure.

The process by which members of wealthy and powerful groups are drawn from the children of those who already belong to such groups is known as elite self-recruitment. A number of studies have indicated the degree of elite self-recruitment in Britain. For example, a survey by Stanworth and

Table 2.18 The Oxford study of mobility

Fathers' class	Sons' class in 1972							
	1	2	3	4	5	6	7	Total
1	**45.7**	19.1	11.6	6.8	4.9	5.4	6.5	100.0
	25.3	12.4	9.6	6.7	3.2	2.0	2.4	(680)
2	29.4	**23.3**	12.1	6.0	9.7	10.8	8.6	100.0
	13.1	**12.2**	8.0	4.8	5.2	3.1	2.5	(547)
3	18.6	15.9	**13.0**	7.4	13.0	15.7	16.4	100.0
	10.4	10.4	**10.8**	7.4	8.7	5.7	6.0	(687)
4	14.0	14.4	9.1	**21.1**	9.9	15.1	16.3	100.0
	10.1	12.2	9.8	**27.2**	8.6	7.1	7.7	(886)
5	14.4	13.7	10.2	7.7	**15.9**	21.4	16.8	100.0
	12.5	14.0	13.2	12.1	**16.6**	12.2	9.6	(1,072)
6	7.8	8.8	8.4	6.4	12.4	**30.6**	25.6	100.0
	16.4	21.7	26.1	24.0	31.0	**41.8**	35.2	(2,577)
7	7.1	8.5	8.8	5.7	12.9	24.8	**32.2**	100.0
	12.1	17.1	22.6	17.8	26.7	28.0	**35.6**	(2,126)
Total	100.0	100.0	100.0	100.0	100.0	100.0	100.0	
	(1,230)	(1,050)	(827)	(687)	(1,026)	(1,883)	(1,872)	(8,575)

Classes
No. Description
1 Higher professionals, higher grade administrators, managers in large industrial concerns and large proprietors
2 Lower professionals, higher grade technicians, lower grade administrators, managers in small businesses and supervisors of non-manual employees
3 Routine non-manual – mainly clerical and sales personnel
4 Small proprietors and self-employed artisans .
5 Lower grade technicians and supervisors of manual workers
6 Skilled manual workers
7 Semi-skilled and unskilled manual workers

Source: J. Goldthorpe (1980) Social Mobility and Class Structure in Modern Britain, Clarendon Press, Oxford, pp. 44, 48.

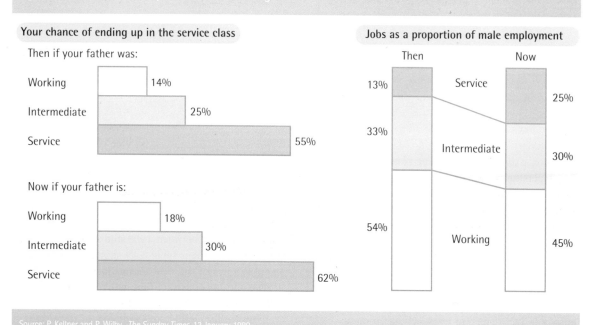

Figure 2.2 Relative mobility chances of different generations

Your chance of ending up in the service class

Then if your father was:

Working — 14%
Intermediate — 25%
Service — 55%

Now if your father is:

Working — 18%
Intermediate — 30%
Service — 62%

Jobs as a proportion of male employment

Then   Now

13% Service 25%

33% Intermediate 30%

54% Working 45%

Source: P. Kellner and P. Wilby, *The Sunday Times*, 13 January 1980.

Giddens (1974), designed to investigate the social origins of company chairmen, revealed a high degree of elite self-recruitment. Out of 460 company chairmen in 1971, only 1 per cent had manual working-class origins, 10 per cent had middle-class backgrounds, and 66 per cent came from the upper class, which was defined as 'industrialists, landowners, (and) others who possess substantial property and wealth'. (There were insufficient data to classify the remaining 23 per cent.) (See Chapter 9 for further studies of elite self-recruitment.)

Thus the Oxford study, while showing a relatively high rate of mobility into class 1, does not indicate the degree of elite self-recruitment. Though class 1 as a whole appears fairly open, elite groups within that class are relatively closed.

Gender and mobility

J. H. Goldthorpe and C. Payne's views on gender and social mobility

A second major problem with the Oxford Mobility Study is the fact that it ignores women. Goldthorpe believes that the unit of stratification in industrial societies is the family. The class position of the family is given according to the occupation of the main breadwinner, which is usually a man. Other sociologists hotly dispute this view. (For details of the debate on gender and stratification see pp. 109–11.)

With specific reference to gender and social mobility, Goldthorpe and Payne have examined data

from the 1983 *British Election Survey* to determine what difference it makes to the results of studies of social mobility if three different approaches are adopted to including women in the data (Goldthorpe and Payne, 1986):

1   In the first approach, women are included but their class is determined by their husband's occupation. Goldthorpe and Payne found this made little difference to either the absolute or relative rates of intergenerational social mobility found in studies using an all-male sample.

2   In the second approach, the occupation of the partner in full-time employment with the highest class position is used to determine the class of both partners. Single women are included on the basis of their own job. This approach also made little difference to relative mobility rates although Goldthorpe and Payne conceded that it does at least allow information on women who are unattached, or who are household heads, to be included.

3   In the third approach, individuals are allocated to classes on the basis of their own jobs. This did show that absolute mobility rates for women and men were very different. This was largely due to the fact that women are distributed differently from men in the occupational structure (see later sections). However, once again this method of including women in the data made little difference to the intergenerational, relative mobility rates of different classes. In other words, the mobility chances of women compared to other women from different classes were as unequal as the social mobility chances of men compared to men from other classes.

| | | Mobility (%) | | % Upwardly mobile found in | |
Gender	Upward	Static	Downward	Classes I or III	Classes II or IV
Men	42.5	27.4	30.4	44	29
Women	32.2	19.9	48.8	6	67

Table 2.19 Gross mobility rates by gender in the Scottish Mobility Study in 1974–5

Source: P. Abbott and G. Payne, 'Women's social mobility reconsidered' in G. Payne and P. Abbott (eds) (1990) *The Social Mobility of Women*, Falmer Press, Basingstoke, p. 18

Goldthorpe and Payne therefore concluded that the non-inclusion of women in earlier studies of social mobility was not important since it made little difference to the overall results, at least in terms of determining the openness of the stratification system.

Alternative views

Michelle Stanworth (1984) is highly critical of Goldthorpe for insisting on categorizing women in social mobility studies according to the class of their husband. She prefers an approach based upon individuals being allocated to a class according to their own job.

Some research seems to support Stanworth's view in that it shows important differences in the social mobility of men and women. Anthony Heath has used data from the 1972 and 1975 *General Household Surveys* to examine the intergenerational mobility of women (Heath, 1981). He compared women's social class with their father's class (though not their mother's), and reached the following conclusions:

1 Women of class 1 and 2 origins were much more likely to be downwardly mobile than men of the same class origin. This was largely because of the preponderance of females in class 3 (routine non-manual jobs).

2 Women from higher social classes were less likely to follow in their father's footsteps than men from the same classes.

3 On the other hand, women of class 5, 6 or 7 origins were far more likely to be upwardly mobile to class 3 than their male counterparts, although Heath points out that whether this movement can be considered 'upward mobility' is a moot point. As indicated earlier, some sociologists do not believe that routine non-manual workers have any significant advantages over most manual workers (see pp. 66–7, 68–9).

Heath argues that the disadvantages suffered by the daughters of fathers in the higher classes are greater than the advantages experienced by the daughters of fathers from lower classes. If Heath is to be believed, then the British stratification system is less open than studies based on males would suggest.

Rather similar conclusions have been reached by Pamela Abbott and Geoff Payne (1990). They used data from a study of social mobility in Scotland to compare men and women. This study was carried out by Geoff Payne in 1974–5 and used a sample of 5,000 men born between 1909 and 1955 and 3,500 wives of these men. Table 2.19 shows the gross mobility rates of the men and women in the sample.

The data demonstrate that many more women than men were downwardly mobile, fewer women were upwardly mobile, and very few of the women who did manage to be upwardly mobile ended up in the top two classes. Once again they suggest that the omission of women from data can give a misleading impression of absolute mobility rates.

The Essex study of mobility

As part of their study of social class in Britain, Gordon Marshall, David Rose, Howard Newby and Carolyn Vogler (1988) collected data on social mobility (details of the study can be found on p. 83). Since the study collected data on male and female mobility rates it allows some evaluation of the controversies about female mobility. It also provides more recent data than the Oxford Mobility Study as it was carried out in 1984. The study collected information on both intergenerational and intragenerational mobility.

Table 2.20 shows Marshall *et al.*'s results on intergenerational mobility. These are based on a comparison between the respondent and the person who was their 'chief childhood supporter' at the same age as the respondent. It uses Goldthorpe's original seven-class model (see pp. 114–15 for details of this model).

Like earlier studies the Essex study found there had been an expansion of white-collar jobs and consequently there were high absolute rates of upward mobility. The results for men are fairly similar to those in the Oxford study, but the results for women show different patterns of social mobility. They confirm the findings of Heath, and Abbott and Payne that women's mobility patterns are affected a great deal by the concentration of

Table 2.20   Class distribution of respondents by sex and class of chief childhood supporter at same age as respondent – Goldthorpe class categories

					Class of respondent					
		I	II	III	IV	V	VI	VII	Total	
Males (n = 632)										
	I	27.7	31.9	12.8	6.4	4.3	10.6	6.4	100.0	(47)
	II	20.8	39.6	3.8	11.3	1.9	13.2	9.4	100.0	(53)
Class of chief	III	25.0	21.9	0.0	6.3	9.4	31.3	6.3	100.0	(32)
childhood	IV	14.4	15.6	5.6	28.9	10.0	11.1	14.4	100.0	(90)
supporter	V	14.4	18.9	4.5	7.2	13.5	13.5	27.9	100.0	(111)
	VI	8.0	12.4	9.5	6.6	14.6	23.4	25.5	100.0	(139)
	VII	11.9	8.1	4.4	11.9	10.0	18.8	35.0	100.0	(160)
Females (n = 425)										
	I	13.8	27.6	48.3	3.4	0.0	0.0	6.9	100.0	(29)
	II	14.3	42.9	32.1	0.0	0.0	0.0	10.7	100.0	(28)
Class of chief	III	4.2	37.5	37.5	4.2	0.0	4.2	12.5	100.0	(24)
childhood	IV	9.1	25.5	30.9	9.1	3.6	1.8	20.0	100.0	(55)
supporter	V	0.0	27.5	42.5	6.3	1.3	6.3	16.3	100.0	(80)
	VI	3.6	15.3	44.1	2.7	5.4	8.1	20.7	100.0	(111)
	VII	2.0	8.2	30.6	8.2	6.1	5.1	39.8	100.0	(98)

Source: G. Marshall, D. Rose, H. Newby and C. Vogler (1988) *Social Class in Modern Britain*, Unwin Hyman, London, p. 77.

women in routine non-manual jobs. Large numbers of women were both upwardly and downwardly mobile into class III.

Odds ratios

The Essex study also expressed the data collected in terms of odds ratio tables measuring relative mobility chances. These compare the chances of people competing for places in classes. For example, they measure the chances of service-class children ending up in the working class compared to the chances of working-class children ending up in the service class. As Marshall *et al.* put it, they 'are an indication of the relative chances of getting to alternative class destinations. They are the outcomes, as it were, of a competition between individuals of different class origins to achieve or avoid one rather than another destination in the class structure.' Tables 2.21, 2.22 and 2.23 use this type of data:

1 Table 2.21 compares the class of a person's chief childhood supporter with that person's first job.

2 Table 2.22 compares the class of a person's chief childhood supporter with that person's current job.

3 Table 2.23 compares a person's class in their first job with their current class.

The tables are based upon a simplified three-class version of Goldthorpe's scheme (i.e. service class, intermediate class and working class). For example, Table 2.21 shows that when men from service- and working-class backgrounds compete for service-class rather than working-class destinations, those from service-class backgrounds are 7.76 times as successful. For women the equivalent figure is 14.07.

According to the authors, the tables support Goldthorpe's contention that relative intergenerational mobility rates for women are influenced by class in a similar way and to a similar extent to those of men. Marshall *et al.* say 'Overall patterns among women and men are not dissimilar although there are differences in the relative odds pertaining to particular transitions.' According to this view, class background influences women's mobility as much as it does men's, although the absolute patterns of mobility are different for the sexes because women are more highly concentrated in certain parts of the stratification system than men.

Table 2.21   Relative mobility chances in terms of odds ratios, by Goldthorpe class and sex. Transition from class of origin to class position on entry into employment

| Pairs of origin classes 'in competition' | Pairs of destination classes 'competed for' | | | | | |
| | Men | | | Women | | |
	S vs I	S vs W	I vs W	S vs I	S vs W	I vs W
S vs I	2.02	4.13	2.05	2.43	4.63	1.90
S vs W	1.95	7.76	4.09	3.84	14.07	3.63
I vs W	0.96	1.88	2.00	1.58	3.04	1.91

Table 2.22   Relative mobility chances in terms of odds ratios, by Goldthorpe class and sex. Transition from class of origin to present class position

| Pairs of origin classes 'in competition' | Pairs of destination classes 'competed for' | | | | | |
| | Men | | | Women | | |
	S vs I	S vs W	I vs W	S vs I	S vs W	I vs W
S vs I	2.75	3.09	1.12	1.67	3.75	2.23
S vs W	4.00	7.35	1.82	3.77	12.95	3.43
I vs W	1.47	2.37	1.62	2.23	3.45	1.54

Table 2.23   Relative mobility chances in terms of odds ratios, by Goldthorpe class and sex. Transition from class on entry into employment to present class position

| Pairs of origin classes 'in competition' | Pairs of destination classes 'competed for' | | | | | |
| | Men | | | Women | | |
	S vs I	S vs W	I vs W	S vs I	S vs W	I vs W
S vs I	2.39	8.71	3.64	4.31	10.96	2.51
S vs W	6.08	41.68	7.01	6.04	50.00	8.15
I vs W	2.54	4.79	1.93	1.40	4.56	3.25

Key :   S = Service (classes I and II)
          I = Intermediate (classes III, IV and V)
          W = Working (classes VI and VII)

Source: G. Marshall, D. Rose, H. Newby, and C. Vogler (1988) *Social Class in Modern Britain*, Unwin Hyman, London, p. 105.

Sex, class, intergenerational and intragenerational mobility

The Essex study also examined the relationship between sex, class of origin and class at entry into employment and present class. Figure 2.3 illustrates its findings. The number of heads in the arrow indicates the strength of the effects involved. Thus the data suggests that sex has a particularly strong influence on first jobs but a rather weaker effect upon current class. Class of origin has a strong effect upon present class, and the first job also affects the class people end up in.

The data include some interesting findings on intragenerational mobility. Some 84 per cent of men who started their careers in service-class jobs and

Figure 2.3   Relationship between class of origin, class destination and sex

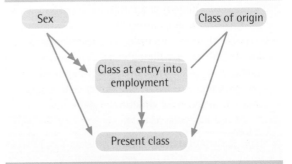

Source: G. Marshall, D. Rose, H. Newby, and C. Vogler (1988) *Social Class in Modern Britain*, Unwin Hyman, London, p. 110

who came from service-class backgrounds were still in the service class when they were interviewed. However only 64 per cent of men who started work in the service class but came from working-class backgrounds were still in the service class. (For women the corresponding figures were 77 per cent and 43 per cent.) Thus even when individuals start their careers in the upper part of the stratification system, class background still exercises a strong influence on their chances in life, dragging down a considerable proportion of those from working-class backgrounds.

As we shall see, though, some aspects of the Essex study have been attacked by Peter Saunders.

Is Britain a meritocracy?

Peter Saunders – *Unequal but Fair?*

All the evidence examined so far would suggest that Britain is not a meritocracy: success and failure in the labour market do not depend on ability and effort. Peter Saunders, however, whose New Right theory of stratification was outlined earlier (see pp. 30–2), challenges the view that studies of social mobility demonstrate a high degree of inequality of opportunity. In *Unequal but Fair?* (1996), Saunders seeks 'to demonstrate, against the popular myth and the received sociological wisdom, that occupational selection and recruitment is much more meritocratic than most of us realise or care to believe'. Although he does not claim that Britain is a perfect meritocracy, he does believe that merit is the most important factor determining the sort of jobs that people get. He advances a number of arguments to support this claim:

1 Many studies which deny Britain is meritocratic nevertheless find considerable upward mobility from the working class. Thus the Essex study found that one-third of those in the service class were from working-class backgrounds.

2 Studies of social mobility tend to stress relative mobility rates and fail to emphasize the degree of openness that is demonstrated by the very high rates of absolute mobility. He compares the position to a one-metre dwarf and a three-metre giant in a hot air balloon. As they rise into the sky in the balloon, 'both clearly benefit from an enhanced view but the dwarf never gets his or her head to the level enjoyed by the giant'. Relying on relative mobility rates stresses the remaining difference in their viewpoints, whereas in reality both are much better off.

3 Saunders argues that relative inequality is further exaggerated by the odds ratios used in the Essex study to measure inequality of opportunity. To Saunders, 'odds ratios are extreme measures which combine success and failure chances in a single statistic and which therefore multiply up any apparent class advantages or disadvantages enjoyed by one group relative to another'. Thus, for example, they compare the chances of service-class children ending up in the working class with the chances of working-class children moving in the opposite direction. Because these two sets of odds are multiplied together it results in what appear to be very unequal opportunities in the statistics. Saunders thinks it is far better to use what he calls disparity ratios. These simply compare the odds on children from different origins ending up in the same class. For example, they might compare the chances of working-class and service-class children ending up in the service class. When calculated in this way they show much less extreme differences in mobility patterns.

4 According to Saunders, the relatively small inequalities discovered in such studies of social mobility might be largely explicable in terms of inherited intelligence, talent and motivation. Saunders says, 'what if the sons and daughters of doctors are on average, more talented or more motivated that the sons and daughters of dockers? If this were the case, evidence on relative mobility rates would of itself tell us nothing about the fairness of the system, for we would then expect children from certain origins to perform better than those from others.' Saunders then carries out a statistical study to try to demonstrate that middle-class children might do better than working-class ones simply because they are cleverer and work harder.

Evidence of meritocracy

In order to test his claims, Saunders uses evidence from the *National Child Development Survey*: a panel study or longitudinal study that has collected a wide range of information on (as far as possible) all children born between the 3rd and 9th of March 1958. The study used an initial panel of 17,414 children, and by 1991 the researchers were still succeeding in collecting data from 11,397 of the original panel.

In 1991, 6,795 individuals in the study were in full-time employment, and these were allocated to three classes on the basis of British government classifications. Saunders calls these the middle class, the intermediate class and the lower working class. Some 52 per cent had experienced intergenerational mobility, and those with middle-class fathers were twice as likely as those with lower working-class fathers to end up as middle-class. This is a less marked difference than that found in most previous studies. The difference was somewhat greater when women were excluded from the analysis (as they were in the Oxford Mobility Study), with men from middle-class backgrounds having 2.6 times the chance of being in middle-class jobs compared with those from lower working-class backgrounds.

More importantly, from Saunders's point of view, the data provided a chance to try to test the significance of ability in determining people's class destinations. All children took tests of their verbal and non-verbal abilities at ages 7, 11, and 16. Although there was a statistical relationship with their class of origin (with middle-class children doing better than those from the other classes), there was a stronger relationship with the class they ended up in. Their abilities as children could have been related to inherited ability or to social and economic factors, but to Saunders it was highly significant that ability was closely linked to the sort of job they ended up with. This suggested that occupational status was closely linked to merit.

Saunders did also find, however, that substantial numbers of low-ability children (as measured in tests) ended up in the middle class. If occupation were entirely determined by ability, then only those who scored 49 or more in their general ability tests as children would have gained middle-class jobs. In fact, 38 per cent of those who gained middle-class jobs had scores lower than 49. Furthermore, the majority of them came from middle-class backgrounds: 32 per cent of this group were of middle-class origin, compared to just 17 per cent from lower working-class origins.

This might seem to undermine Saunders's claim that Britain is meritocratic, since it appears that class background as well as ability has an important influence on your chances. However, he goes on to point out that the idea of meritocracy also involves effort, and the differences in opportunity that were not explained by differences in ability might be explicable in terms of differences in effort. In short, they could result from middle-class children and young adults working harder.

The *Child Development Survey* included data on a number of factors that could be used to measure the amount of effort children were prepared to put into achieving success. Saunders uses three types of information to measure 'effort':

1 A motivation scale derived from questions put to the sample when 16 years old.
2 A measure of absenteeism from school based on truancy records and 'reports of trivial absences'.

3 A measure of 'job commitment' based on answers to attitude questionnaires the sample were given when they were 33 years old.

Saunders also examined data that could be used to measure the extent of social and economic deprivation. These included how often parents read to their children, the parents' educational qualifications, overcrowding in the childhood home, and so on. Saunders found that most of these factors made no difference to the class the children ended up in. Ability test scores remained the most powerful predictor, while measures of motivation were the second best predictor.

Saunders reaches three key conclusions on the basis of such evidence. First, he argues that 'ability correlates more strongly with class of destination than class of origin'. Second, 'ability and motivation are the key predictors of lower-working-class success and of middle-class failure'. Third, in view of the first two findings, he feels confident in claiming that 'class destinations reflect individual merit (ability and motivation) much more than class background'.

Criticisms of Saunders

If Saunders were correct, it would mean that sociologists had greatly exaggerated the inequality of opportunity in Britain and that little needs to change to make Britain a genuine meritocracy. However, there are a number of flaws in Saunders's arguments and his interpretation of the research. First, Saunders excludes the unemployed and those in part-time employment from his analysis. These might be the very groups most disadvantaged by virtue of their class background.

Second, a number of the measures of ability and effort might themselves reflect class differences as much as real differences in the 'merit' of individuals. As Saunders himself notes, there is the possibility of class bias in ability tests. Measures of absenteeism and trivial absences might reflect the labelling and stereotypes of teachers (see Chapter 11 for details of labelling theory and education) as much as a real lack of motivation on the part of working-class pupils. Furthermore, factors such as ill-health and unsympathetic teachers might encourage children to be absent from school, and these factors in turn may be related to children's backgrounds.

It is not surprising if those from working-class backgrounds who have gained middle-class jobs appear more motivated in their work than those from middle-class backgrounds, since the former have all had substantial upward mobility and are likely to have experienced significant improvements in their living standards. Thus many of the measures used by Saunders may reflect social class differences rather than showing that non-class differences are especially significant.

Gordon Marshall and Adam Swift have replied to some of Saunders's criticisms (Marshall and Swift, 1996). They point out that measures of absolute mobility do not reveal anything about social justice and meritocracy as such. Whatever the structural changes in the availability of different types of employment, only relative mobility rates reveal anything about whether or not there is inequality of opportunity.

They say, 'the concept of equality is inherently comparative: it necessarily invites us to examine the advantages of different groups or different individuals and to assess these advantages relative to one another'.

Marshall and Swift accept that different figures are produced by using disparity ratios compared to odds ratios. However, they claim that they make no significant differences to the results:

We could state our mobility findings in terms of disparity ratios if that is what he would prefer. We would then report that (say) men who were the sons of service-class fathers were almost four times more likely to be found in service-class positions than were men who were the sons of working-class fathers.

Marshall and Swift, 1996, pp. 376–7

All methods of calculating figures suggest that significant class inequalities of opportunity remain even when meritocratic factors are taken into account. As discussed earlier in the chapter (see p. 32), Marshall and Swift (1993), using data from the Essex study, found that there were class differences in social mobility even allowing for differences in educational attainment. Thus they found that 'at the lowest educational level, 23 per cent of those from service-class backgrounds have arrived at service-class destinations – as compared with only 7 per cent of men and women from working-class backgrounds'.

Mike Savage and Muriel Egerton – social mobility and individual ability

Support for the claims of critics of Saunders can also be found in the work of Savage and Egerton (1997). They followed Saunders in using data from the *National Child Development Survey*, but they analysed the data somewhat differently and reached very different conclusions.

Unlike other studies of social mobility they distinguished between professional and managerial workers on the grounds that these groups might have

different types of assets that might affect the patterns of social mobility passed on to their children (see pp. 71–4 for details of this approach to the middle class). Like Saunders they used details from ability tests taken at age 11 as a measure of ability. (Children were divided into high, average and low ability groups based on these tests.) However, unlike Saunders, they fully recognized that such tests are as much a measure of the social advantages and disadvantages of different types of upbringing as they are of inherent intelligence. The relationship between such test results and social mobility is therefore a measure of the effects of class early in life rather than later. They say,

Thus, if we find that once 'ability' is taken into account there are few class differences in mobility chances, this would suggest that all salient class advantages come early in life and are mediated through the construction of ability in children.

Savage and Egerton, 1997, p. 652.

Savage and Egerton found quite high rates of upward mobility compared to other studies. About 40 per cent of sons from intermediate backgrounds and 25 per cent of sons from working-class backgrounds had moved into the service classes by the time they were 33. In line with other studies, large numbers of women were found to be both upwardly and downwardly mobile to the intermediate class.

When 'ability' was taken into account significant class differences remained. For example, even among low-ability sons with managerial fathers, more stayed in the service classes than slipped down to the working class. Among high-ability sons from professional backgrounds, 75.5 per cent ended up with service-class jobs, compared to 45 per cent of high-ability sons from unskilled working-class backgrounds. There were also great disparities among daughters: 67.7 per cent of high-ability daughters and 25 per cent of low-ability daughters ended up in service-class jobs. In comparison, the equivalent figures for daughters from unskilled manual backgrounds were 28.3 per cent for those of high ability, and just 11.3 per cent for those of low ability.

With the exception of daughters with professional fathers (who were particularly advantaged by their class background), the class differences in opportunity for daughters were somewhat less than those for sons. Ability therefore seemed more important for daughters. Savage and Egerton suggest 'that the transmission of class advantages to girls depends more exclusively on endowing them with the appropriate "ability" to do well in the educational system than is the case with boys. Boys seem to have more potential to tap other resources than those based on "ability" alone.'

While Savage and Egerton did find differences in occupational achievement to be related to measured 'ability', they argue that differences in 'ability' are largely the result of different classes possessing different amounts of cultural capital rather than natural ability (see Chapter 11 for a discussion of cultural capital). In other words, class had a strong influence on 'ability'. Furthermore, discussing professionals in particular they say, 'the important point to note is that the advantages remain even after controlling for ability tests, suggesting that they may have as much to do with the material advantages, social networks, etc., of professionals as with issues of cultural capital'.

The evidence of other researchers would thus suggest that Britain is nowhere near being a meritocracy. While 'ability' and effort might play some role in patterns of social mobility, there is no doubt that class continues to be important, both through the way it affects ability and effort, and independently.

Explanations of mobility rates

The following reasons have been given to account for the rate of social mobility in industrial society:

1   There is considerable change in the occupational structure. For example, in Britain, the proportion of manual workers in the male labour force declined substantially in the twentieth century, so for each succeeding generation, there were more white-collar and fewer blue-collar jobs available. This helps account for the finding of the Oxford study that upward mobility considerably exceeds downward mobility.

2   Manual and non-manual fertility rates differ. In particular, working-class fathers generally have had more children than middle-class fathers. This differential fertility can also be seen as a reason for the relatively high rate of upward mobility. As the Oxford study indicated, class 1 fathers did not produce sufficient sons to fill the rapidly growing numbers of class 1 occupations. As a result, recruitment from lower strata was essential to fill those positions.

3   Some sociologists have argued that occupational status in industrial society is increasingly achieved on the basis of merit. Jobs are allocated in terms of talent and ability, rather than through family and friendship connections. Education is seen to play a key part in this process. The educational system grades people in terms of ability, and educational qualifications have a growing influence on occupational status and reward. Since educational opportunities are increasingly available to all young people, no matter what their social background, the result is a more open society and a higher rate of social mobility. There will be a further discussion of the issues involved in Chapter 11.

Class formation and class conflict

The nature and extent of social mobility in Western industrial societies pose a number of questions concerning class formation and class conflict.

Marx believed that a high rate of social mobility would tend to weaken class solidarity: classes would become increasingly heterogeneous as their members ceased to share similar backgrounds. Distinctive class subcultures would tend to disintegrate since norms, attitudes and values would no longer be passed from generation to generation within a single stratum. Class identification and loyalty would weaken, as it would be difficult for mobile individuals to feel a strong consciousness of kind with other members of the class in which they found themselves. As a result, the intensity of class conflict and the potential for class consciousness would be reduced.

Ralf Dahrendorf (1959) believed that this situation had arrived in modern Western societies. He argued that, as a result of the high rate of social mobility, the nature of conflict had changed. In an open society, there are considerable opportunities for individual advancement. There is therefore less need for people to join together as members of a social class in order to improve their situation. In Dahrendorf's words 'instead of advancing their claims as members of homogeneous groups, people are more likely to compete with each other as individuals for a place in the sun'. As a result, class solidarity and the intensity of specifically class conflict will be reduced.

Dahrendorf then went a step further and questioned whether the rather loose strata of mobile individuals could still be called social classes. However, he stopped short of rejecting the concept of class, arguing that 'although mobility diminishes the coherence of groups as well as the intensity of class conflict, it does not eliminate either'.

In an article based on the Oxford Mobility Study, John H. Goldthorpe and Catriona Llewellyn (1977b) make the following observations on the relationship between social mobility and class formation:

1   The findings of the Oxford study indicate that the highest degree of homogeneity in terms of social background is found in the manual working class: in 1972, around 70 per cent of its members were the sons of manual workers.

2   If present trends continue, this level of self-recruitment will increase.

Goldthorpe and Llewellyn claim that this makes increased working-class solidarity likely. The similarity of origins and experience of the majority of manual workers provides a basis for collective action in pursuit of common interests.

The Oxford study indicates a high rate of mobility out of the working class. As Dahrendorf suggests, this might encourage individual rather than collective strategies. However, since upward mobility is substantially greater than downward mobility, relatively few people move down into the working class. Again this will tend to increase the homogeneity of the class.

By comparison, the middle class is increasingly heterogeneous in terms of the social background of its members: in Goldthorpe's words, it is 'a class of low classness'. It lacks coherence and class solidarity, an observation which matches Kenneth Roberts's picture of a 'fragmentary' middle class.

Mobility and social order

A number of sociologists have attempted to assess the effects of mobility on social order. Frank Parkin (1972) saw the relatively high rate of upward mobility as a 'political safety-valve'. It provides opportunities for many able and ambitious members of the working class to improve their situation. As a result, the frustration that might result (if opportunities for upward mobility were absent) is prevented from developing.

To some degree this will weaken the working class. The upwardly mobile have found individual solutions to the problems of low status and low pay; if they remained within the working class, they might well join with other members in collectivist strategies that might benefit the class as a whole.

In addition, those who move out of the working class show little desire to improve the lot of their class of origin. Research from a number of Western societies indicates that upwardly mobile individuals tend to take on the social and political outlooks of the class into which they move. American studies in particular suggest that those who move upward into the middle class often become more conservative than those born into it. Thus the upwardly mobile pose no threat to social stability: indeed, they can be seen to reinforce it.

Similar conclusions have been drawn from studies of downward mobility. American sociologists Harold Wilensky and Hugh Edwards (1974) examined the response of 'skidders' – persons moving down into the working class – to the experience of social demotion. They found that the downwardly mobile tended to be more politically conservative than those born into and remaining within the working class. The experience of downward mobility did not lead them to reject the social order and so threaten the stability of society. Instead they clung to middle-class values, anticipating upward mobility and a restoration of their former status. Their presence in the working class tends to weaken that class since they are not really a part of it. Wilensky and Edwards state:

> Skidders, along with other workers who escape from working-class culture psychologically or actually, function to reduce working-class solidarity and social criticism from below – and therefore slow down the push towards equality.
>
> Wilensky and Edwards, 1974, p. 561

Thus, both upward and downward mobility tend to reinforce the status quo: both introduce conservative elements into social strata; both appear to weaken working-class solidarity and therefore reduce the intensity of class conflict.

Gender and social class

The issue of social mobility illustrates how gender was neglected in many early studies. When men were the main breadwinners in most families and comparatively few married women worked, women seemed of little importance in theories of class to the predominantly male sociologists carrying out research. However, as women have increasingly combined paid work with domestic tasks and have become as numerous as men in the labour force, it has become impossible to construct theories of stratification without considering the position of women. The inclusion of women poses a number of theoretical problems for theories of stratification, because women are more likely to work part-time than men, some women are housewives, and male and female partners may have jobs in different classes.

On the one hand, women might be seen as a part of the class structure without in any way forming a distinctive group within it. In other words, individual men and women are first and foremost members of a class rather than members of the gender groups 'male' and 'female'. This suggests that a working-class woman has more in common with a working-class man than with a middle-class woman.

Alternatively, gender groupings might be seen to cut across social class, and perhaps even be more important than class. This view implies that a working-class woman would have more in common with a middle-class woman than with a working-class man.

There are numerous variations on these points of view. In the following sections we demonstrate different ways in which sociologists have struggled to resolve the problem of the relationship between class and gender.

The household as the unit of class analysis

The first and simplest way to deal with the relationship between gender and class is to more or less ignore it. In official statistics in Great Britain a person's class is determined by the occupation of the 'head' of their household.

Before the 1981 census males were always considered to be the heads of households in which women also lived. Thus all the women in such a household were deemed to have the same class as the male 'head'. In the 1981 census the possibility of having a female 'head' of the household was first accepted, but in practice the class of the household was still very likely to be determined by the occupation of the husband. Single women and those in all-female households make up the vast majority of women whose class is measured in terms of their own occupation.

Ann and Robin Oakley (1979) point out that many sociological studies have followed this procedure. The family has been taken as the unit of stratification, and the family's class has been derived from the occupation of the family's head.

One supporter of this approach is Frank Parkin (1972). He argues that the social and economic rewards of women are largely determined by their marital and family relationships and, in particular, by the status of the male breadwinner. Parkin states:

> *If the wives and daughters of unskilled labourers*
> *have some things in common with the wives and*
> *daughters of wealthy landowners, there can be no*
> *doubt that the differences in their overall*
> *situation are far more striking and significant.*
>
> Parkin, 1972, p. 15

In other words, the inequalities of sexual status are insignificant compared to the inequalities of class status. However, Nicky Britten and Anthony Heath (1983) point to an obvious problem with this approach. In some families, which they term cross-class families, it is the woman who has the higher-class occupation on the Registrar-General's scale: for example, a male manual worker married to a female non-manual worker. From an analysis of the data from *The Child Health and Education Study* of 1980, Britten and Heath found significant differences between these families and those in which both husband and wife had a manual job. For example, over 79 per cent of cross-class families had an income of over £99 per week, compared to 67 per cent of families with two manual workers. This might indicate that in cross-class families the wife's occupa-

tion is the best indicator of the family's class position.

Nevertheless, some sociologists maintain, with only slight reservations, that a woman's social class should still usually be determined with reference to her husband's occupation. For instance, Westergaard and Resler (1976) assert that the life chances of households are still largely shaped by men's positions in the labour market rather than the position of their female partners. In other words, Westergaard and Resler would claim that they are not being sexist, they are simply taking account of the 'facts': the class position and life chances of a family – indeed the type of employment done by the wife – are all largely dependent on the husband's job.

John Goldthorpe – husbands, wives and class positions

John Goldthorpe (1983) further defends this position. He agrees with Parkin, and Westergaard and Resler, that the family is the unit of stratification. Furthermore, he relates class to a family's position in the labour market. He does not believe, though, that a male, where present, should automatically be considered head of a household. The head should be defined as 'the family member who has the greatest commitment to, and continuity in, the labour market'.

In theory this position might pose problems for existing methods of measuring class. If it were found that many wives had a greater involvement in, and commitment to, the labour market than their husbands, then the class position of many families might have been mistakenly defined in the past.

Furthermore, if there were many families in which it was unclear whether the husband or the wife had the greater involvement in the labour market, and their jobs placed them in different classes, it would be difficult to determine in which class to place many families. According to Goldthorpe these problems do not arise for the following reasons:

1   First, by using data from the Oxford Mobility Study (for further details of this study see pp. 99–100), Goldthorpe claims that the vast majority of working wives withdraw from work once or more during their working life. Thus it is their husbands who have a greater commitment to paid work and therefore it is on the basis of the husband's work that the class of the family should be calculated.

2   Second, Goldthorpe denies that there are a large number of cross-class families in which the wife has a higher social class than the husband. He argues that many families only appear to be cross-class families because the class of the wife has been determined in an inappropriate manner. Most female non-manual workers have routine or unskilled white-collar jobs. Goldthorpe claims that these women have a much less favourable market

situation than their male counterparts in lower-level non-manual jobs. The female workers tend to receive lower pay, fewer fringe benefits and enjoy less job security. In these circumstances it makes little sense to attribute such families to the middle class: the woman's job does not provide the family with middle-class life chances, and the husband's job is still the best measure of the family's class.

Criticisms of Goldthorpe

In a reply to Goldthorpe, Anthony Heath and Nicky Britten insist that 'women's jobs do make a difference', although they accept some of Goldthorpe's criticisms of the concept of cross-class families.

They admit that some non-manual jobs for women offer little significant advantage over male manual jobs. They accept that women working in sales (for example, shop-assistants), and in personal services (for example, hairdressing), do not have what could reasonably be called middle-class jobs. However, those in professional, supervisory and managerial occupations clearly have a superior market situation to husbands in manual jobs. Furthermore, female junior office workers also have advantages over male manual workers.

Heath and Britten therefore conclude that most families with female non-manual workers must still be regarded as cross-class families.

Stronger criticisms of Goldthorpe are advanced by Michelle Stanworth (1984). She argues quite simply that husbands and wives should be allocated to classes as individuals rather than as part of a family unit. Using data from the *General Household Survey* of 1979, she found that only 19 per cent of working men were the sole providers of financial support for their wives. Furthermore, she also suggests that the

material situations of husband and wife are not necessarily the same. There may be inequalities within the family – for example, if the husband has more money to spend on personal consumption than the wife.

Individuals and families as units of stratification

David Rose and Gordon Marshall (1988) agree to some extent with both Goldthorpe and Stanworth. Their research into social class in Britain conducted in 1984 (see pp. 83, 102–5 for further details) found that some class actions taken by women seemed to be affected more by the class of their family than by their own class. For example, the voting intentions of wives were better predicted by the class of their husbands than by their own class.

On the other hand, Rose and Marshall found that class fates were affected more by the class of individuals than by the class of their families. Women had less chance of upward social mobility than men, regardless of their husband's occupation.

Rose and Marshall concluded:

> an approach to class analysis which takes the individual as the unit of analysis is as legitimate as one which takes families as the basic unit. Indeed, we believe that both approaches are important because social classes are made up of neither individuals nor families but of individuals in families.
>
> Rose and Marshall, 1988, p. 18

None of the approaches that we have discussed so far considers the possibility that women and men should be seen as constituting distinctive strata in the stratification system. This idea is discussed on pp. 179-81.

Contemporary theories of stratification

As we indicated earlier in the chapter, most contemporary approaches to stratification take their inspiration from either Marx's or Weber's writings on class. In this section we will examine the work of a leading neo-Marxist theorist, Erik Olin Wright, and a leading neo-Weberian, John Goldthorpe. Their work represents perhaps the best-known attempts to update the work of Marx and Weber on class by applying it to contemporary societies. We have already mentioned both theorists – and particularly Goldthorpe – in earlier parts of this chapter. Here their models of the class structure as a whole will be compared and evaluated. We will end this section with an analysis of the work of W. G. Runciman, who draws on the work of both Marxists and Weberians

in producing an alternative view of class in contemporary Britain.

Erik Olin Wright – a neo-Marxist theory of class

The American neo-Marxist Erik Olin Wright (1978, 1985, 1989) has been developing theoretical approaches to class since the 1970s. His work has undergone a number of changes and his early work will be examined first.

One of the biggest problems for Marxist theories of class in the twentieth century was the growth of a middle class of salaried employees. Unlike the bourgeoisie they are not owners of the means of production, yet compared with the proletariat they can command relatively high wages and enjoy a reasonable level of job security. In developing a neo-Marxist approach to class, Wright was concerned to develop a framework that could explain the position of this group without resorting to Weberian concepts.

Marxist approaches emphasize that classes are antagonistic groups with different interests and that they are differentiated by their role in production. Weberians emphasize relationships in the market, for example in buying and selling labour power, rather than relationships in production. Wright's first solution to this problem was to use the concept of contradictory class locations.

The early theory – basic classes

In his early theory, Wright (1978) starts off by distinguishing three classes. Within the capitalist mode of production the bourgeoisie is distinguished from the proletariat. The former group has control over the means of production, control over labour power and control over investments and accumulation. The proletariat has none of these types of control.

The third class, the petty bourgeoisie, is involved in a different mode of production, simple commodity production. Wright comments that 'real capitalist societies always contain subordinate modes of production other than the capitalist mode of production itself'. Simple commodity production is not based upon the exploitation of wage labour by employers but is 'production organized for the market by independent self-employed producers who employ no workers'. The petty bourgeoisie has control over the means of production and some control over investments and the accumulation process, but no control over labour power as its members employ no workers.

Contradictory class locations

This leaves some workers who are in 'contradictory locations within class relations', because they have some characteristics in common with two classes, rather than being pure members of one. Managers, supervisors, technocrats and 'foremen' are in a contradictory location between the bourgeoisie and the proletariat. They have some degree of control but not as much as the bourgeoisie nor as little as the proletariat. For example, top managers have control over the means of production and the labour power of others, but only partial control over investments. 'Foremen' do not have control over the means of production or over investment, but they do have minimal control over the labour power of others.

Between the petty bourgeoisie and the bourgeoisie are small employers. Wright defines this group as consisting of those who employ other workers but more than half the profit their business makes comes from their own labour or that of other family members.

Semi-autonomous wage-earners are situated between the proletariat and the petty bourgeoisie. They have some control over how they work and what they produce and therefore have minimal control over the means of production. Wright cites laboratory researchers, professors in elite universities, and some very skilled craft workers as examples.

Wright estimated that in the USA in 1969 the bourgeoisie made up 1–2 per cent of the population, the petty bourgeoisie 4–5 per cent, the proletariat 41–54 per cent, small employers 6–7 per cent, semi-autonomous employees 5–11 per cent, and managers and supervisors 30–35 per cent. His illustration of the class system is reproduced in Figure 2.4.

Revising the theory

In the 1980s Wright became concerned with some aspects of his original theory. He was particularly troubled by the category 'semi-autonomous employees', which had proved 'impossible to operationalize in a rigorous manner'. Furthermore, his whole scheme was based on degrees of control or domination of one class by another. He decided that exploitation rather than domination should be central to any Marxist theory of class. After trying unsuccessfully to resolve these and other problems by modifying the original theory, he chose to abandon it in favour of a new one.

Exploitation

In line with his thinking, Wright set about producing a new Marxist set of class categories based on exploitation. After considering various alternatives, he decided that exploitation involves 'the appropriation of the fruits of labour of one class by another'. This always involves a situation where the class doing the exploiting would be harmed if the exploited class stopped working.

Exploitation results from the unequal distribution of a particular asset, but in different economic systems the crucial asset that is unequally distributed varies:

1   In feudalism, it is labour power which is unequally distributed when the feudal aristocracy coercively extracts the surplus labour of the serfs.

2   In capitalism, the means of production are unequally distributed as capitalists exploit workers through buying and selling labour power and commodities.

3   In statism (by which Wright means communist societies with a strong central state such as the former USSR), organizational assets are unequally distributed. With private ownership of the means of production virtually abolished, those who hold senior

Figure 2.4   The relationship of contradictory class positions to class forces in capitalist society

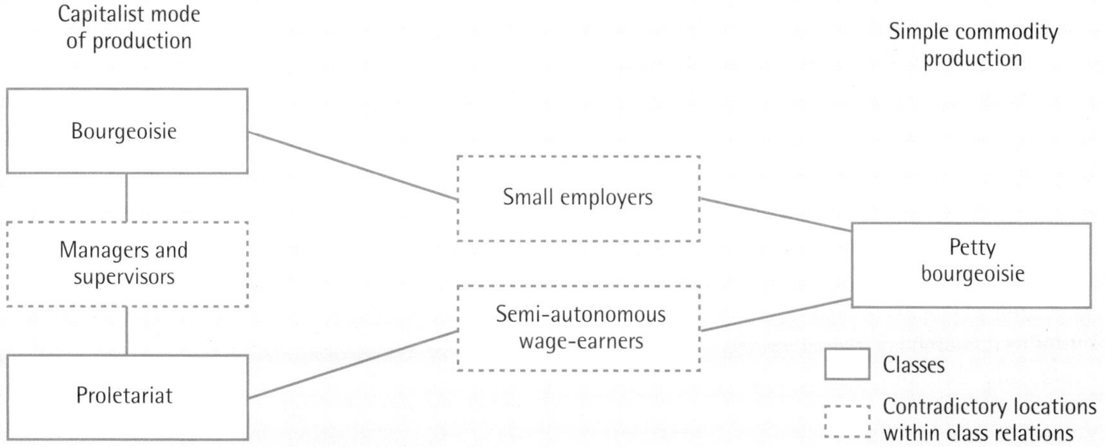

Source: E. O. Wright (1983) *Class, Crisis and the State*, Verso, London, p. 63

positions in the organizations which control production use their position to exploit others. Wright describes this exploitation by bureaucrats, managers and party officials as 'planned appropriation and distribution of surplus based on hierarchy'.

4 Finally, Wright distinguishes exploitation based on skills. This would be characteristic of a future socialist society when democratization had taken place and in which society was no longer organized on hierarchical principles. Despite the considerable equality in such a society, those with particular skills might be able to use them to procure more of the surplus for themselves than went to ordinary workers.

A new typology of class locations

Wright goes on to observe, as he did in his earlier work, that societies are rarely characterized by a single mode of production. This enables him to develop a typology of classes in capitalist society based upon the ownership or non-ownership of different assets which can form the basis for exploitation.

First he divides the class structure into the owners and non-owners of the means of production. Among the owners he distinguishes those who own enough to hire workers and do not have to work themselves, those who hire workers but also have to work themselves, and the petty bourgeoisie who work for themselves and don't employ other workers.

Wage labourers are then distinguished according to whether they have above average, about average or below average skill/credential (or qualification) assets and organizational assets. This leads to nine categories of wage labourers, ranging from the skilled, well-qualified expert managers with powerful

positions in organizations to the proletarians who lack skill, qualifications or positions of power. His typology is illustrated in Figure 2.5.

Wright concludes from his new typology that class conflict and class struggle are considerably more complex than it would seem in the traditional Marxist theory, with its emphasis on the division between just two classes: the bourgeoisie and the proletariat. He goes as far as to suggest there might be alternatives to the proletariat ushering in changes in capitalism. Bureaucratic managers are seen as 'having the potential to propose state socialism as an alternative to capitalism'.

Criticisms of Wright

Wright's theory of class has come in for extensive criticism. Stephen Edgell (1993) makes some of the most damaging points. He argues that Wright has abandoned the distinctive features of a Marxist approach to class. For example, Marxists see class in relational terms. That is, classes are distinct entities which have particular roles in the economic system (such as employer and employees, slave and slave owner). They are not distinguished in gradational terms, that is by placing individuals on a continuum according to, say, how much they earn or how much money they have. Yet Wright's theory ends up being gradational by categorizing people according to their level of organizational and skill/credential assets.

Edgell also argues that it is not clear why the possession of skill or the lack of it should lead to the exploitation of one group by another. It might lead to different wage levels but that in itself does not constitute exploitation.

Edgell concludes that the inclusion of organizational and skill/credential assets means that Wright's

Figure 2.5   Wright's second class map

Production assets

Owners of means of production		Non-owners (wage labourers)				
Own sufficient capital to hire workers and not work	1 Bourgeoisie	4 Expert managers	7 Semi-credentialled managers	10 Uncredentialled managers	+	
Own sufficient capital to hire workers but must work	2 Small employers	5 Expert supervisors	8 Semi-credentialled workers	11 Uncredentialled supervisors	0	Organization assets
Own sufficient capital to work for self but not to hire workers	3 Petty bourgeoisie	6 Expert non-managers	9 Semi-credentialled supervisors	12 Proletariat	–	
		+	0	–		

Skill/credential assets

position has become almost identical to Weber's. In effect Wright is doing no more than distinguishing different market and work situations, which, can be better understood from a Weberian perspective.

In the Essex study of class in Britain, Gordon Marshall *et al.* (1988) set out to test Wright's theory and compare it with Goldthorpe's (which will be discussed next). They came down firmly against Wright. Like Edgell they believe that Wright's new scheme 'closely resembles' Weberian conceptions of class. Their strongest attack, though, is based upon putting Wright's class categories into operation.

The Essex study tried using both Wright's earlier and later class schemes. Using the earlier scheme they found, as Wright himself had suspected, that the category 'semi-autonomous employee' caused confusion. Using Wright's own criteria for allocating occupations to categories, this class included some teachers, computer programmers, social workers, coal miners, motor mechanics and process workers. This unlikely combination of people was put together simply because they were not capitalists or managers and they all claimed they had autonomy at work. When Marshall *et al.* tried using Wright's new class scheme they also found many apparent discrepancies. For example, the 'proletarians' included a buying and purchasing supervisor, an investment broker, a secretarial supervisor and a hospital matron. On the other hand, a skilled machinist is among those seen as belonging to a higher class on the grounds that he has an apprentice working under him.

Wright himself (1989) has tried to defend his theories from this type of criticism. He accepts that there are such anomalies but argues that they stem simply from operational choices involved in applying the scheme. Although the procedures for allocating people to classes might need to be altered, in his view this does not undermine the overall conceptual framework.

John Goldthorpe – a neo-Weberian theory of class

Goldthorpe's approach to class has been highly influential and widely used in British sociology (Goldthorpe, 1967, 1980, 1983, Goldthorpe *et al.*, 1987). While Wright has concentrated on the theoretical development of a Marxist approach, Goldthorpe has been more concerned with the practical application of Weberian ideas. Goldthorpe's class scheme was originally developed for the particular purpose of studying social mobility, and was the basis for the Oxford Mobility Study (see pp. 99–100).

The basis of Goldthorpe's scheme

Goldthorpe's class scheme is based on Lockwood's distinction between market and work situations which was originally used in his study of clerical work (see p. 68).

However, the procedure Goldthorpe adopted for determining market and work situations was much simpler than that used by Lockwood. Instead of using questionnaire or interview data to determine, for example, autonomy at work, he uses just two types of information: a job title and information about whether the person was self-employed, an employer or an employee. Each individual is then given an employment status (e.g. large proprietor or self-employed without employees) and is placed in an occupational group according to the type of work he or she does. The former information is held to be a measure of work situation; the latter of market situation. Individuals are then allocated to pre-determined class categories according to a combination of their work and market situations.

This procedure led to Goldthorpe identifying seven classes as illustrated in Figure 2.6. Each class was said to combine:

> *occupational categories whose members would appear to be typically comparable, on the one hand, in terms of their sources and levels of income, their degree of economic security and chances of advancement; and, on the other, in their location within systems of authority and control governing the process of production in which they are engaged, and hence their degree of autonomy in performing their work-tasks and roles.*
>
> Goldthorpe, 1980, p. 39

The seven classes are sometimes condensed into three, as shown. The service class contains only white-collar occupations and includes both employers and employees. The intermediate class is made up of a mixture of white- and blue-collar workers and includes small proprietors and the self-employed as well as employees. The working class is made up of employed blue-collar workers.

As we discussed in a previous section (see pp. 110–11), Goldthorpe allocates individuals to a class according to the position of the male head of household, where there is one. This scheme was originally devised to study male mobility patterns but Goldthorpe insists that class position stems from the position of the family, not the individual, and in practice the position of the family is determined by the position of the male breadwinner.

Modifications to the scheme

Goldthorpe has undertaken one major revision to his class scheme (Goldthorpe *et al.*, 1987). This is illustrated in Figure 2.7. The modification was carried out for use in an international study of male mobility. The following changes were made:

1 The top two classes were merged since, Goldthorpe claimed, it would be difficult to distinguish clearly between them in all countries in a cross-national study.

2 Classes 5 and 6 were merged for the same reason, to form an enlarged working class. Lower-grade technicians and supervisors of manual workers were effectively demoted from the intermediate class to the working class. Goldthorpe has described this group as a 'marginal case' but has not fully explained the reason for the change.

3 Separate classes of farmers and agricultural workers were added to the scheme to take account of the importance of agriculture in some societies.

Criticisms of Goldthorpe

Not surprisingly Goldthorpe has been criticized by supporters of Wright's neo-Marxist class scheme. Goran Ahrne (1990), a Swedish sociologist who has applied Wright's class scheme in his own country, is one example. Ahrne notes that Goldthorpe makes very little attempt to explain the theoretical thinking behind his scheme. He says: 'the theoretical basis of the model is not clearly elaborated and, moreover, it is neither very logical nor theoretically consistent. At best it may be regarded as a well-made commonsensical classification of occupations.'

According to Ahrne, Goldthorpe's criteria for distinguishing different market and work situations are inadequate. The approach adopted to market situations contains no discussion of supply and demand for labour power, and the approach to work

Figure 2.6 Goldthorpe's class scheme

Classes	No.	Description
Service class	1	Higher professionals, higher-grade administrators, managers in large industrial concerns and large proprietors
	2	Lower professionals, higher-grade technicians, lower-grade administrators, managers in small businesses and supervisors of non-manual employees
Intermediate class	3	Routine non-manual – mainly clerical and sales personnel
	4	Small proprietors and self-employed artisans
	5	Lower-grade technicians and supervisors of manual workers
Working class	6	Skilled manual workers
	7	Semi-skilled and unskilled manual workers

Source: J. H. Goldthorpe (1980) *Social Mobility and Class Structure in Modern Britain*, Clarendon Press, Oxford, pp. 44 and 48.

situations contains no way of measuring autonomy and control at work.

Ahrne also argues that the ranking of classes is arbitrary: Goldthorpe does not explain why the petty bourgeoisie are allocated to class 4 (in the original scheme) while routine non-manual workers are in class 3. Nor does Goldthorpe explain why particular types of worker who seem to have much in common are placed in different classes. For example, a self-employed electrician is placed in the intermediate class, while a self-employed engineer is placed in the service class.

The muddled theoretical thinking continues in the descriptions of the classes. Ahrne notes that 'two additional grounds for classification are introduced which are neither explained nor discussed'. These are the distinctions between higher-grade and lower-grade and between manual and non-manual work. Ahrne concludes:

> the class model as a whole does not contain any rigorous theoretical logic. It seems to be a mixture of practical and commonsensical considerations that may work for certain mobility studies, but whose application gives very little theoretical insight into the relationship between structurally derived power relations and everyday class realities.
>
> Ahrne, 1990. p. 69

In an early critique, Roger Penn (1981) raised what he saw as problems with Goldthorpe's concepts of the service and intermediate classes. By merging large proprietors and managerial and professional workers into a service class, Goldthorpe seemed to be denying the existence of a separate ruling or upper class. Penn also argued that the intermediate class included a diverse range of groups. Some small proprietors, for

example, are in a highly advantageous position compared to most workers in the intermediate class.

Goldthorpe has also been strongly attacked by feminist sociologists. As we discovered earlier in the chapter, such sociologists argue that using the occupation of the male head of household to determine the position of women in the class structure is inappropriate. Others go further and argue that the whole class scheme is based on the characteristics of men's jobs and therefore gives a misleading impression of the social structure. For example, S. Arber, A. Dale and N. Gilbert (1986) have constructed an alternative class scheme which includes some classes that are made up largely of female workers. Sometimes known as the Surrey occupational class scale, it adopts a nine-class model and includes secretarial and clerical workers as class 4, and shop and personal service workers as class 6.

A defence of Goldthorpe

In the Essex study of class carried out by Gordon Marshall et al. (1988), Goldthorpe's class scale was tested and was generally supported by the data. According to Marshall et al., his class categories work much better than Wright's when used to collect data. People placed together in a particular class were found to have more in common with each other than was the case when Wright's categories were used.

Marshall et al. argue that Goldthorpe is justified in putting employers and top managers together in the service class. There are so few members of the bourgeoisie that they are unlikely to crop up in significant numbers in a mobility study. In any case, the distinction between the two groups has become blurred as family or individual ownership of firms has declined. Marshall et al. cite the example of one

Figure 2.7	Goldthorpe's class scheme (revised version)	
1	Classes I and II	All professionals, administrators and managers (including large proprietors), higher-grade technicians and supervisors of non-manual workers
2	Class III	Routine non-manual employees in administration and commerce, sales personnel, other rank-and-file service workers
3	Class IVab	Small proprietors, self-employed artisans and other 'own-account' workers with or without employees (other than in primary production)
4	Class IVc	Farmers and smallholders and other self-employed workers in primary production
5	Classes V and VI	Lower-grade technicians; supervisors of manual workers and skilled manual workers
6	Class VIIa	Semi- and unskilled manual workers (other than in primary production)
7	Class VIIb	Agricultural and other workers in primary production

Source: J. H. Goldthorpe (revised edition 1987) *Social Mobility and Class Structure in Modern Britain*, Clarendon Press, Oxford, p. 305.

individual in their study, an engineer who had bought a partnership in his firm with his savings after working his way up from the shop floor. They argue that his situation is little different from that of top managers who earn enough to put some money aside to invest.

Marshall *et al.* do, however, criticize Goldthorpe's approach to gender and stratification. They point out, for example, that men's social mobility cannot be understood or explained adequately if women are allocated to the same class as their husbands. Men and women have to compete with each other for jobs, and, as women form an increasing proportion of the labour force, the mobility chances of men are heavily influenced by the jobs held by women. Mobility patterns cannot be understood while half the workers are ignored.

W. G. Runciman – the class structure, roles and power

In an attempt to determine the number of classes in British society, W. G. Runciman has developed a new approach to analysing the stratification system (Runciman, 1990). This approach uses both Marxist concepts, such as 'the means of production', and Weberian ones, such as 'marketability'.

Roles and classes

Runciman starts by arguing that the class structure consists of sets of roles. A role is defined as a position 'embodying consistently recurring patterns of institutional behaviour informed by mutually shared beliefs about their incumbents' capacity directly or indirectly to influence the behaviour of each other'. Occupational roles are the most important, but not everyone has an occupational role. Those without jobs should also be assigned roles according to the 'economic power attaching to whatever different roles they occupy'. A person married to someone with a job should be seen as having the same role as their spouse, assuming they share the economic power of their spouse. Where partners have different jobs, then both should be given the class of the one with the highest ranking role, again assuming that they share their economic power. Whether power is shared cannot be determined theoretically but needs to be determined from the evidence in each case.

For those with jobs, classes should be determined using the concept of a career. In other words, it is necessary to take account of promotion prospects as well as current position. Some male white-collar workers, for example, might be seen as being in a higher class than some female white-collar workers who have similar jobs but much less chance of moving into management. Where individuals have more than one role (for example if they have two jobs), the highest ranking role should again be used to determine a person's class.

Classes and power

Runciman then goes on to explain how roles should be allocated to classes. He defines classes as: 'sets of roles whose common location in social space is a function of the nature and degree of economic power (or lack of it) attaching to them through their relation to the institutional processes of production, distribution and exchange'.

Economic power can come from three sources:

1 Ownership, or 'legal title to some part of the means of production'.

2 Control, or 'a contractual right to direct the application to the process of production of some part of the means of production, whether fixed or financial assets or labour'. Managers and supervisors are examples of people who possess control by virtue of their jobs.

3 Marketability, or the possession of an 'attribute or capacity' which can be sold to employers. In other words this refers to the skills, qualifications and the ability to carry out physical labour possessed by individual workers.

The class an individual belongs to is determined by examining a combination of these three types of economic power. People can end up in a higher class by having ownership, control or marketability, or indeed any combination of the three.

Runciman illustrates this approach with the example of three engineers. Engineer A is an employee who earns £40,000 per year and has a good pension scheme. Engineer B owns a small engineering business which he has been able to buy through mortgaging his house. After paying interest, he makes £10,000 per year profit. Engineer C is a self-employed freelance engineer who employs his wife as his secretary and earns between £10,000 and £40,000 depending on how successful the year was.

All three of these people should be placed in the same class according to Runciman. They have different sorts of power. The first derives most of his power from control, the second from ownership, and the third from marketability, but each has about the same amount of power.

Those towards the bottom of the stratification system have little or no control over production, they have very little wealth, and little or nothing in the way of marketable skills or capacities.

The seven classes

Runciman identifies seven classes based upon the possession of different amounts of ownership, control and marketability. These are detailed in Table 2.24

Table 2.24 The Runciman classes

Class	Size in 1990
Upper class	0.1–0.2%
Upper middle class	<10%
Middle middle class	15%
Lower middle class	20%
Skilled working class	20%
Unskilled working class	30%
Underclass	5%

Source: W. G. Runciman (1990) 'How many classes are there in contemporary British society?' *Sociology*, vol. 24, no. 3, pp. 377–96.

with Runciman's estimate of the percentage of the British population in each class.

The highest class, which he calls the upper class, contains between a tenth and a fifth of 1 per cent of the population. It is made up of the owners of the means of production, the most senior managers, and those with absolutely exceptional marketability. He cites examples of each of these three types: the Duke of Northumberland who qualifies in terms of ownership; the chief executive of Shell who has control; and 'the senior partners of the biggest firms of City accountants' who have marketability. Runciman specifically excludes very highly-paid entertainers because their role is 'irrelevant' to 'the institutional processes of production, distribution and exchange'.

Runciman chooses to divide the middle class into three groups. The higher-grade professionals, senior civil servants and managers are placed in the highest of these three classes, and routine white-collar workers in 'more or less "deskilled"' jobs are placed in the lowest of them. He argues that there is sufficient gap between the economic power of these two extremes in the middle class to justify the inclusion of a third group in between. This middle middle class includes lower professions and middle managers. Proprietors who are not in the upper class are allocated to one of the middle classes according to what 'the scale and kind of their property makes appropriate'. Runciman argues that workers such as shop-assistants, checkout operators and copy- and audio-typists have insufficient economic power in terms of the marketability of their skills to be placed in the middle class. Instead, they are seen as part of the working class.

The working class itself is divided in two: an upper or skilled working class, and a lower or unskilled working class. Semi-skilled workers are seen as belonging to the lower working class since,

according to Runciman, it has become common for workers with minimal skills to be defined as semi-skilled. When he uses the terms skilled, semi-skilled and unskilled, Runciman is not referring to some abstract measure of technical knowledge which is required to carry out jobs. He is thinking instead of the different degrees of marketability, control and ownership that individual workers possess. Thus a worker might be placed in the upper working class on the grounds of ownership if they own their own tools, on the grounds of control if they have control over the operation of machinery, or on the grounds of marketability if their skills are in demand.

Unlike Wright or Goldthorpe, Runciman distinguishes an underclass at the bottom of the stratification system. It consists of those 'whose roles place them more or less permanently at the economic level where benefits are paid by the state to those unable to participate in the labour market at all'.

In effect, members of the underclass have no control, ownership or marketability. (We described and evaluated Runciman's views on the underclass in more detail earlier in the chapter, see pp. 95–6.)

Operationalizing the class scheme

Runciman made no attempt to use his class scheme for research, but he did suggest how that might be done. It would be necessary to determine individuals' jobs, the amount and source of their income, their 'actual and prospective capital resources', and their economic position within the household. These different types of information could then be combined to determine a person's class.

Evaluation of Runciman

There are a number of problems with Runciman's class scheme. It would be extremely difficult to use in research since it means gathering a wide range of data on individuals and the households in which they live. Many respondents to a survey might be unwilling or unable to give precise details of, for example, their wealth.

Runciman also offers no clear dividing lines between the classes: it is unclear how much marketability, power or control a person needs for them to be placed in a particular class. His view that groups such as the self-employed or small proprietors should not be seen as constituting separate classes is somewhat controversial. Runciman himself admits that such groups might be distinctive in terms of 'intergenerational mobility rates' and 'socio-political attitudes', but he is still unwilling to allocate them to a separate class because they do not necessarily have similar amounts of economic power to one another.

In addition, because Runciman uses a gradational approach to class, where the differences between classes are a matter of degree rather than kind, his decision to settle on seven classes seems rather arbitrary. He could just as easily have settled on a six- or an eight-class model.

Rosemary Crompton (1993), however, argues that Runciman's scheme is one of the few approaches to the class structure that has had some success in coming to terms with the social changes that have taken place in Britain since the Second World War. She argues that these changes include:

> a move away from the conventionally established 'class' boundary between manual and non-manual work following the expansion of the service sector and the routinization and feminization of much lower-level white-collar employment; an emphasis on the diversity of middle class locations, and the identification of the poorest and most deprived as an 'underclass' – this identification being linked, to varying degrees, with the condition of state dependency. A major element of continuity, however, lies in the persisting concentration of economic, organizational and political power within an 'upper' class which comprises only a small minority of the population.
>
> Crompton, 1993, pp. 191–2

Her description of changes in the class structure provides a succinct summary of some of the main social trends discussed in this chapter.

The death of class?

There have long been claims that class is becoming less significant, that class analysis is no longer useful for sociologists, or even that social class is dying. Thus, according to David Lee and Bryan Turner (1997), as early as at the end of the nineteenth century the German Eduard Benstein argued that improvements in the conditions of the masses were making class-based politics outdated. More recently, theories such as those of embourgeoisement (see above pp. 78–9) and the claims of Peter Saunders that Britain might be meritocratic (see above pp. 105–7) have been used to suggest that class has lost its significance. Some versions of the underclass theory (for example, Murray, 1989) also imply that economic class is becoming less significant and it is only a deficient culture that keeps some people at the bottom of the stratification system. However, perhaps the strongest claims of all that class is dying have been put forward by some postmodern theorists, whose work will now be examined.

Jan Pakulski and Malcolm Waters – postmodernism and the death of class

Class and other social divisions

In their book, *The Death of Class* (1996), the Australian sociologists Pakulski and Waters claim that 'like beads and Ché Guevara berets, class is passé, especially among advocates of the post-modernist avant-garde and practitioners of the new gender-, eco- and ethno-centred politics'. In other words, they believe that it is unfashionable to consider class important. While they admit that fashion alone should not dictate how sociologists see the world, they go on to say that 'arguments about the salience of class can no longer be dismissed as symptoms of ideological bias, intellectual weakness or moral corruption'. This is because, they claim, there is growing empirical evidence that class is losing its significance.

According to Pakulski and Waters, classes only exist if there is a 'minimum level of clustering or groupness' and such clusterings or groupness are no longer evident. People no longer feel they belong to class groupings, and members of supposed classes include a wide variety of very different people. Pakulski and Waters do not claim that social inequality is disappearing, but they do argue that there are new 'cleavages that are emerging in post-class society' which overshadow class differences. If people do not act as members of classes and do not see class-based issues as of special significance, then sociologists should not give special importance to class. To Pakulski and Waters, class can be seen as just one, not very important, division in society along with 'race', ethnicity, gender, age, etc.

Types of society

Pakulski and Waters argue that the stratification systems of capitalist societies have gone through three phases.

In economic-class society, which existed in the nineteenth century, society was divided into property owners and workers. The property-owning class controlled the state, and culture was divided into 'dominant and subordinate ideologies and into high and low cultures'.

Organized-class society existed during roughly the first 75 years of the twentieth century. The state became the dominant force in society and it was 'typically ruled by a single unified bloc, a political-bureaucratic elite, that exercises power over subordinated masses'. The state elite exercised a strong control over the economy and may have followed policies of redistribution or state ownership of some industries. With this type of government in office the mass of the population tried to influence the state through political parties rather than through conflicts within industry.

In the last quarter of the twentieth century capitalist societies developed into status-conventional societies. In this phase stratification has become based on cultural rather than economic differences. Pakulski and Waters say 'the strata are lifestyle- and/or value-based status configurations. They can form around differentiated patterns of value consumption, identity, belief, symbolic meaning, taste, opinion or consumption.' People can choose their lifestyles and values and are therefore not restricted in the groups they can join by their background or job. Because people's tastes and identities can change rapidly the stratification system 'appears as a shifting mosaic'. There are many different groupings within society based on these cultural differences and status depends on the values of these groupings.

Economic inequalities become much less important in shaping status differences. 'Symbolic values', the value of different images, become the crucial factor shaping stratification, and the conventions which establish these values form the basis of hierarchies in status-conventional societies. For example, how fashionable the decor of your house is becomes more important than the value of your house. Similarly, low-paid but desirable jobs in the media might give you more status than less well-paid but unfashionable jobs in manufacturing industry.

Pakulski and Waters distinguish four key features of the change in the stratification system in status-conventional societies:

1 Culturalism. Stratification is based on lifestyles, aesthetics and information flows. 'Material and power phenomena are reducible to these symbolically manifested lifestyle and value phenomena.'

2 Fragmentation. In this new type of society people have many different statuses based on their membership of different groups and different patterns of consumption. There is a 'virtually infinite overlap of associations and identifications that are shifting and unstable'.

3 Autonomization. Individuals become more autonomous or independent in their values and behaviour. People choose how to act and what to believe and you can no longer predict these things from their class background or other characteristics.

4 Resignification. People can change their preferences and identifications, leading to great fluidity and unpredictability in the status system of society. People constantly change what they see as especially significant.

In arguing for this change in the nature of stratification, Pakulski and Waters are highly critical of those theorists who, as they see it, cling on to outdated notions about the centrality of class.

They say that sociology is still failing:

> to recognize that oppression, exploitation, and conflict are being socially constructed around transcendent conceptions of individual human rights and global values that identify and empower struggles around such diverse focuses as postcolonial racism, sexual preferences, gender discrimination, environmental degradation, citizen participation, religious commitments and ethnic self-determination. These issues have little to do with class. In the contemporary period of history, the class paradigm is intellectually and morally bankrupt.
>
> Pakulski and Waters, 1996

To Pakulski and Waters, class politics is dead and issues to do with ethnicity, gender, religion and cultural differences and preferences are far more important. People have become more interested in saving the environment than fighting for class interests, and a much wider variety of issues has become politically important.

Reasons for the death of class

Pakulski and Waters offer a number of explanations for the death of class. Class divisions in earlier years of the twentieth century were first undermined by the growth of increasingly interventionist states. The most interventionist states of all were fascist (e.g. Nazi Germany) or communist (e.g. the USSR). In other societies, the development of welfare states and consensus between governments, business and unions reduced the direct impact of class relationships.

More recently there has been a shift towards 'market-meritocratic' relationships, where the state intervenes less in the economy and society. Alongside this, the division of labour has become more complex, and educational qualifications and professional skills have become more important than class background in shaping job opportunities.

Property has increasingly moved from private hands to being owned by organizations. Fewer large businesses are owned by individuals or families. Property ownership has also become more dispersed making property 'a decreasing source of power'. Many people own their own homes and have some savings. Pakulski and Waters argue that in capitalist societies wealth became progressively more equally distributed during the twentieth century.

Pakulski and Waters do accept that there is some evidence that in recent years class inequalities have started to grow in countries like the USA, Australia and the UK. However, they argue that the changes are small, the trends inconsistent and any overall effect unimportant. In any case, 'short-term fluctuations are probably influenced more by the changing cash value of assets than by the redistribution of ownership'. For example, changes in house prices and share values affect the overall distribution of wealth as much as houses and shares changing hands.

With wider distribution of wealth more people are able to consume products well in excess of what they need for physical survival. As a result, there is much more opportunity for individuals to demonstrate taste and to choose products that match their identities. Similarly they can judge others in terms of what they consume. Thus the ecologically aware might judge those who have more money but who consume ecologically damaging products to be inferior.

Consumption, according to Pakulski and Waters:

> is becoming the standard by which individuals judge others and themselves. Consumer goods become signs of association and lifestyle. They are consumed for the images they convey, rather than because of utility or aesthetics, much less out of necessity. Few consumers would seriously believe, for example, that they can make a difference to the environment, much less to a clean domestic environment, by using 'green' household cleaning materials, but they can, by consuming them, indicate a commitment to environmentalist values.
>
> Pakulski and Waters, 1996

Globalization of the world economy has meant that class inequalities within individual countries have become less important (see Chapter 9 for a discussion of globalization). Since exploitation now stretches beyond nations there is much less common ground for class conflict developing within particular societies. Partly as a consequence of this, voting and party-allegiance become less based on class and there is a 'decline in the use of class imagery and consciousness in politics'. For example, Pakulski and Waters quote studies of voting in Britain, France, Germany, Sweden and the USA which suggest that there has been a decline in the strength of the relationship between manual workers voting for left-wing parties and non-manual workers voting for right-wing parties. In its place 'new politics' based on non-class issues has grown in significance. They say 'class simply does not fit the wars and conflicts of the Middle East, the rise of Islamic fundamentalism, the Bosnian conflict, or the religious and ethnic conflicts of the Indian subcontinent. National, religious, regional, ethnic, gender, racial and sexual preference identities are much more important.'

Although these various identities and non-class sources of conflict have always existed, they used to be overshadowed by class issues. Now, *they* overshadow class issues. Pakulski and Waters thus conclude that 'the intellectual armoury of class theory is about as useful for the contemporary social scene as a cavalry brigade in a tank battle'.

Even apparently new classes, such as the 'underclass', cannot be seen in conventional class terms. According to Pakulski and Waters, 'membership of the underclass is a function not of its members' exploitation but of their incapacity to consume. An earlier generation of social scientists wrote of poverty as a culture. Perhaps it is time to do so once again.'

Criticisms of Pakulski and Waters

Although Pakulski and Waters identify some important changes in capitalist societies, not surprisingly their claim that class is dying has attracted strong criticism.

First, some writers have criticized Pakulski and Waters for using inconsistent and confused definitions of class. Harriet Bradley (1997) points out that at some points they use primarily economic definitions of class but at others they 'measure the existence of class in terms of its presence or absence in political discourse'. However, whether politicians talk in class terms is not crucial to whether class in economic terms exists. Bradley argues that 'such definitional sleight of hand serves to write class altogether out of the script, where a more balanced assessment might suggest that class is legitimately seen as one of many aspects of social inequality and political identification'. Indeed, as earlier parts of this chapter have indicated, in Britain at least, people continue to believe that classes exist and see themselves as belonging to particular classes (see pp. 87–9).

Second, by claiming that consumption patterns and differences in lifestyle have become more significant than class differences, Pakulski and Waters neglect the obvious point that class differences influence the types of lifestyle that different groups can afford. It seems strange that they appear to think that the underclass *choose* a poverty-stricken lifestyle rather than that they adopt such a lifestyle due to lack of money. The culture of poverty theory, which Pakulski and Waters mention approvingly, has come in for sustained and highly damaging criticism (see pp. 319–21). Of course, people with similar levels of income can make different decisions about their lifestyles and and consumption patterns, but those with few resources are inevitably excluded from the many choices that are only available to those with sufficient income or wealth. As John Westergaard puts it, 'consumer power, after all, is money power: quite simply, the rich and the comfortably off have much more of it than ordinary wage-earners, let alone the poor who are out of wage work' (Westergaard, 1997).

Third, Pakulski and Waters have been criticized for making unsubstantiated generalizations. For example, Bradley (1997) points out that Pakulski and Waters claim that patriarchy is dying because new technology is freeing women from housework and the demands of child-bearing. No real evidence is used to back up this claim which contradicts a sizeable amount of feminist research. Furthermore, Bradley asks 'what is one to make of wildly overstated generalisations like this: "the family is more or less entirely losing its function of social and cultural reproduction"'. Bradley accuses much of *The Death of Class* as being 'a rehashing of the usual postmodern truisms about change, invoking consumerism, fragmentation and destabilisation with insufficient empirical backing'. To other critics, this lack of empirical backing – the lack of adequate evidence – is also true of their claims about class.

Gordon Marshall (1997) argues that their work 'misrepresents the evidence in order to substantiate their arguments'. Pakulski and Waters quote work by Peter Saunders which argues that the consumption of housing might lead to a division between home owners and those in rented housing, without acknowledging Saunders's own admission that class remains the key factor shaping voting patterns in Britain.

Pakulski and Waters also claim that height differences between the classes are being reduced and ignore evidence that middle-class people in Britain are still, on average, about two inches taller than working-class people. Marshall concludes that 'these illustrations confirm that the postmodernist critique of class analysis has largely detached itself from empirical reality'.

John H. Westergaard – the hardening of class inequality

John Westergaard (1995, 1997) takes a very different approach to that of Pakulski and Waters. He argues that, far from dying, class differences became stronger in the late twentieth century, particularly in Britain. While the claims of postmodernists and politicians' rhetoric might suggest that class is less important, the objective reality is that class divisions are becoming more important not less.

Westergaard broadly follows Weberian and Marxist approaches to class, saying that 'class structure is first of all a matter of people's circumstances in life as set by their unequal places in the economic order'. He goes on to state unequivocally, 'in that sense, class structure has recently hardened

in Britain'. He tries to substantiate this claim with a range of empirical evidence.

Evidence of the hardening of class structure
Westergaard (1997) quotes a variety of statistics from British government sources to back up his claim.

First, between 1980 and 1990, the earnings of the highest-paid tenth of white-collar workers rose by approximately 40 per cent in real terms, while the poorest-paid tenth of blue-collar workers saw virtually no rise in their real incomes.

Second, the share of total household income going to the poorest 20 per cent of households fell from 10 per cent in the late 1970s to 7 per cent by the late 1980s, while the share of the richest 20 per cent grew from 37 to 44 per cent.

Third, private ownership of property has become more concentrated. Thus the share of marketable wealth owned by the richest 5 per cent of the British population rose from 36 per cent at the start of the 1980s to 38 per cent at the end of that decade.

Westergaard also argues that the power of the highest social classes, and of big business, has also been growing. He says that:

> the power of private business has grown, of course, as free market policies intended. To take just one instance, business representation in the governance of public education and health has been consistently stepped up; and, more generally, business-style prescriptions for 'cost-efficiency' have spread widely in the conduct of public-sector affairs.

Westergaard, 1997

The denationalization of public enterprises (such as British Steel and British Airways) has concentrated more power in the hands of private businesses. Changes in the City of London have increased the power of finance capitalists, while the influence of trade unions has declined. According to Westergaard, 'a small network of top people from top corporations and institutions' including 'insurance companies and pension funds' wields enormous power which 'comes from the mass of corporate assets whose strategic deployment they lead'. The top class comprises less than 1 per cent of the total population but, from this viewpoint, its power steadily increased from 1979 to the late 1990s.

Reasons for the hardening of class inequality
The main reasons for these changes, according to Westergaard, are economic and political. Economic growth has become more varied and the North American and western European economies have faced growing competition from Asia. Transnational

corporations have developed faster than nationally based companies.

British government policies changed from 1979 onwards in response to these developments. What Westergaard calls the 'class compromise' of the 1940s involved redistributive taxation and a commitment to the welfare state and state ownership of some industries. Conservative governments strengthened the importance of market relationships in the economy and reduced the progressive elements in taxation. There were increased inequalities in earnings as the market value of unskilled labour declined and some types of skilled labour increased. The government accepted, even encouraged, the growth of these inequalities as necessary in a competitive market economy.

Class and other divisions

Westergaard accepts the point made by postmodernists such as Pakulski and Waters that there are important divisions other than class. However, he does not accept that these divisions have superseded class. As suggested above, divisions along consumption lines reflect differences in income to a considerable extent. He accepts that gender divisions are an important aspect of inequality. However, class and gender divisions 'twine together, to reinforce the effects of class rather than go against them'. For example, most women with white-collar jobs are married to men with white-collar jobs, and working-class women are largely married to working-class men. Many families therefore enjoy the material benefits of two white-collar salaries whereas few households have the income from one blue-collar wage boosted by a partner's higher professional or managerial salary. Women suffer the same sorts of class disadvantages as men. The main difference is that, typically, they are worse off than men.

Similarly, ethnic divisions are an important source of disadvantage, but again they tend to reinforce rather than contradict class divisions. Westergaard argues that 'racial division – on this score much like gender division – come to expres-

sion in good part as low placement of its victims precisely in the economic order of production and distribution: that is in the structure of class'. Nor does Westergaard see a sharp division between an underclass and the rest of the class structure. Those who are usually seen as part of the underclass tend to be those from working-class backgrounds who have retired or cannot find work. The unemployed or retired middle class tend to have savings or pensions which mean they are not as disadvantaged as those held to be in the underclass.

Class 'in itself' and 'class for itself'

Westergaard comments, in concluding his argument, that 'we are still left with a puzzle: when class division "in itself" has sharpened, why does class division "for itself" seem to have faded?' If the inequalities between classes are greater, why does there appear to be less class consciousness? He argues that, in Britain at least, the Labour Party may be largely responsible. As the party which traditionally represents the interests of the disadvantaged, it is important in expressing and mobilizing class consciousness in the working class. However, factors such as internal party disputes and the widespread strikes in the late 1970s, under a Labour government, led to disillusionment with the party. In order to regain support it abandoned many of its traditional policies which were in favour of redistribution to the less well-off. This left no major party to articulate the interests of a class-conscious working class.

Nevertheless, Westergaard maintains that there is the potential for the revival of class consciousness and left-wing policies. Reviewing opinion poll evidence he says, 'Many people, then, appear to want to see "fairer shares". And although many are sceptical about the means to that end, popular conceptions are nevertheless quite out of line with fashionable social theory and right-wing ideology.' Like Marshall et al. (see above pp. 87–9), and many other sociologists, he thinks that class is far from dead – indeed in some respects it is not only alive but kicking the disadvantaged in society harder than for many decades.

Sociology, values and social stratification

It is evident from this chapter that sociologists are not neutral, dispassionate observers of the social scene. Like everybody else, they see the world in terms of their values and attitudes. To some degree this will affect their analysis of society. Their commitment to a particular set of values will influence what they see, what they look for, what they consider important,

what they find and how they interpret their findings. Some sociologists have carried this argument a stage further and claimed that not only are the views of particular sociologists value-based, but so also are the major theoretical perspectives within the discipline. Thus, as the previous chapter indicated, functionalism and Marxism have been seen as ideologically based, with functionalism founded on a conservative ideology, and Marxism on a radical ideology. This argument can be illustrated from theories of social stratification.

At first sight, functionalist views on stratification appear value-free. The language of the functionalists is sober and restrained and their analyses have a scientific ring to them. However, functionalist theories of stratification have been strongly attacked for what many see as their right-wing, conservative bias.

For example, Alvin Gouldner (1971) criticizes Davis and Moore's (1967) assertion that social stratification is inevitable in all human societies. Gouldner claims that this statement is little more than an article of faith. He sees it as based ultimately on the conservative doctrine that 'the social world is for all time divided into rulers and ruled'. This implies that attempts to change fundamentally or eradicate systems of social stratification will be harmful to society. As a result, it can be argued that functionalist views provide support and justification for social inequality.

Gouldner claims that the logical conclusion of functionalist theories is that 'equality is a dream'. By suggesting that an egalitarian society is an illusion, the functionalists direct research away from alternatives to social stratification. This again encourages acceptance of the status quo rather than demands for radical change.

Finally, Gouldner argues that the basic assumptions of functionalist theory are essentially conservative. Functionalism is concerned with explaining the basis of social order. In pursuit of this aim, it focuses on the contributions of the various parts of society to the maintenance of order. Since stratified societies often provide evidence of order and stability, functionalism leads sociologists to assume that social stratification contributes to this situation. Since order and stability are assumed to be 'good' for society, any attempts to dismantle systems of social stratification will be seen as harmful to society. In Gouldner's words, the functionalist position implies that 'only "evil" – social disorder, tension or conflict – can come from efforts to remove the domination of man by man or to make fundamental changes in the character of authority'. In this way Gouldner claims that functionalism advocates the maintenance of the status quo.

By comparison, Marxist theories are openly radical. They advocate fundamental social change in many contemporary societies. They begin from the value judgement that some form of communist system is the only just and fair social arrangement. From this standpoint they evaluate various forms of social stratification. This often results in a passionate condemnation of social inequality, particularly of class systems in capitalist society.

The ideological basis of Marxist theory is clearly revealed in the use of value-laden terms such as 'exploitation' and 'oppression'. Indeed, Marxists usually make no secret of their political views. For example, the British sociologist John Westergaard openly condemns the concentration of power and wealth in capitalist society. Writing with Henrietta Resler in the 1970s (Westergaard and Resler, 1976), he argued that private property is increasingly threatened in Britain and added 'We ourselves hope that this threat will become a reality.'

It has often been argued that Marxist views of the contours of the class system are ideologically based. Starting from the judgement that capitalist society is divided into exploiters and exploited leads to the idea of a two-class system. Many non-Marxists argue that this view ignores other important divisions in society.

Thus David Lockwood (1958) attacked those Marxists who dismiss the clerks' middle-class identification as false class consciousness. Lockwood argued that this identification is based on real differences between the position of clerks and manual workers. He claimed that Marxists who dismiss these differences as insignificant are allowing their political views to influence their judgement.

Marxists often respond in the same vein. They accuse sociologists who focus on divisions within and between the so-called middle and manual working classes of a conservative bias. They claim that this directs attention away from the concentration of wealth and power at the top and, in doing so, protects privilege.

New Right theorists tend to be critical of Marxist and Weberian theories of stratification and to accuse them of ideological bias. For example, Peter Saunders accuses them of ignoring the degree of opportunity and mobility in capitalist societies and the benefits that flow from inequality. He says:

> *It is often thought that the British class system is closed and rigid, but we have seen that this is not the case. . . . It is also often thought that class inequality is self-evidently a 'bad thing' and that government should act more positively to reduce the economic differences between the classes. Again, however, we can see that such a view can be challenged, both on the grounds that inequality is the price to be paid for future growth from which all can benefit, and because moral and political philosophy shows us that 'social justice' has as much to do with how people came by what they have got as with how much or how little they end up with.*
>
> Saunders, 1990, p. 130

Sociologists such as John Westergaard (1992, 1997) regard such views as ideological. He claims that 'social climate' influences fashions in sociology, and the social climate of the 1980s and 1990s favoured New Right thinking. He believes that 'disillusionment with politics and politicians' has led to people accepting that nothing can be done about class inequalities, and this has allowed the 'radical right' to pursue 'its own brand of class politics with much vigour, to the effect of economic polarisation'. The denial of the importance of class has been used as an ideological justification which has widened class inequalities, and in reality class has become more important than ever. Westergaard's own views are, however, clearly influenced by his commitment to reducing inequality; a commitment which has influenced his writings for over a quarter of a century.

In this section we have shown that it is possible to argue that theories of stratification are based ultimately on ideology. Indeed, many sociologists accept this view and make no secret of their commitment to particular values. For example, Dahrendorf's position is clear when he approvingly quotes Kant to the effect that social inequality is 'a rich source of much that is evil, but also of everything that is good'. From the authors' viewpoint, however, there is much more to applaud in Melvin Tumin's statement that:

The evidence regarding the mixed outcomes of stratification strongly suggests the examination of alternatives. The evidence regarding the possibilities of social growth under conditions of more equal rewarding are such that the exploration of alternatives seems eminently worthwhile.

Tumin, 1967 p. 111

It may be that only a commitment to a more egalitarian society will lead to the kind of research that Tumin advocates.

Chapter 3

Sex and gender

Sex and gender

Introduction

In the Bible, Original Sin in the Garden of Eden was woman's. She tasted the forbidden fruit, tempted Adam, and has been paying for it ever since. In the Book of Genesis, the Lord said:

> *I will greatly multiply thy sorrow and thy conception; in sorrow thou shalt bring forth children; and thy desire shall be to thy husband, and he shall rule over thee.*

Genesis 3:16

Sociologists would regard the above quotation as a mythological justification for the position of women in society. Many women might see the summary it contains of their relationship with their spouses as an accurate description of their status through the ages, that is:

1 women produce children

2 women are mothers and wives

3 women do the cooking, cleaning, sewing and washing

4 they take care of men and are subordinate to male authority

5 they are largely excluded from high-status occupations and from positions of power.

These generalizations apply to practically every known human society. Some sociologists and anthropologists believe that there is not, and never has been, a society in which women do not have an inferior status to that of men. In recent decades, particularly with the development of feminist (and post-feminist) ideas, the explanation for such differences has been hotly debated.

Feminists have argued, with a good deal of justification, that prior to the 1970s nearly all sociology was written by men, about men and for men. There were relatively few female sociologists, nearly all sociological research used male samples, and aspects of society of particular relevance to women (such as housework and female crime) were rarely studied. Sociology largely ignored women. A number of writers now use the term 'malestream sociology' to

describe mainstream, male-dominated sociology. Since the early 1970s, however, sociological studies by and about women have proliferated.

Nearly all the early research and theoretical debate specifically concerned with the sociology of gender focused on women and femininity. In recent years, this emphasis has changed and it has been recognized that a more complete understanding of gender can be developed by also studying men and masculinity.

Sex and gender

Many writers use the distinction between sex and gender as the starting point for their analysis. The first person to make this distinction was the American psychoanalyst Dr Robert Stoller (1968). Stoller made the commonsense observation that the vast majority of the population can clearly be categorized as male or female according to their physical characteristics: 'external genitalia, internal genitalia, gonads (the organs which produce sex cells), hormonal states and secondary sex characteristics'. Because of these differences, women are capable of bearing and suckling children, whereas men are not. In addition, differences in physique between men and women usually mean that men are stronger and more muscular.

Biological differences are widely believed to be responsible for the differences in both the behaviour of men and women and the roles that they play in society. Stoller cautioned, though, against such an assumption. He said:

> *Gender is a term that has psychological and cultural connotations, if the proper terms for sex are 'male' and 'female', the corresponding terms for gender are 'masculine' and 'feminine'; these latter might be quite independent of (biological) sex.*

Stoller, 1968, p. 9

In other words, it does not necessarily follow that being a woman means being 'feminine', nor that being a man means behaving in a 'masculine' way: girls are not necessarily caring and compassionate; boys do not have to be aggressive and competitive.

Sociologists such as Ann Oakley (1972) take this argument a stage further, claiming that feminine social roles, such as those of housewives and mothers who care for their children, are not an inevitable product of female biology. Nor does Oakley believe that being a man makes it inevitable that men will be breadwinners. To Stoller and Oakley, it is the culture of a society that determines the behaviour of the sexes within it.

Most, though not all, sociologists of gender and feminists support this position. However, it is not immediately obvious how their claims can be justified. The belief that it is 'natural' for men and women to behave differently is widespread, and is supported by many scientists and some psychologists and sociologists.

We will now examine the relationship between sex and gender in detail. We will begin with those sociologists who believe that gender roles are biologically determined, and then consider those sociologists who argue that gender roles are culturally determined.

Sex and gender differences

Hormones and the brain

Some scientists believe that variations in the behaviour and social roles of men and women can be explained in terms of hormones and brain differences. Hormones are bodily secretions whose functions include the regulation of the development of male and female bodies so that they become capable of reproduction. The production and release of hormones are controlled by the hypothalamus in the brain. Both sexes produce a full range of sex hormones from a variety of glands (including the ovaries and testes). Normally women produce greater amounts of progesterone and oestrogen, while men produce more testosterone and other androgens. The higher levels of androgens in the male stop the hypothalamus from regulating hormonal production cyclically, which it does in the female menstruation and ovulation cycle. The activity of a wide range of hormones is closely integrated with the activity of the nervous system, and so hormones can influence behaviour, personality and emotional disposition.

Animal experiments might seem to provide some evidence for a link between androgens and aggressive behaviour:

1 Castrated male rats tend to fight less, while female rats given extra androgens after birth are more aggressive in adult life than other female rats.

2 Goy and Phoenix (1971) claim that female rhesus monkeys given extra androgens display more 'rough and tumble play' than other females.

3 Some studies seem to show a direct link between testosterone levels in human males and aggression, using supposed measures of aggression such as being in jail.

4 Ehrhardt (1969) has studied the development and behaviour of girls exposed as foetuses to high levels of androgens. He claims that such girls are more likely to exhibit 'tomboy' characteristics than their sisters or other girls of the same age, IQ, and who had fathers of the same occupation. For example, they were likely to choose boys for playmates, enjoy outdoor play and athletics, but showed little interest in dolls and infant care. Ehrhardt explained these differences in behaviour as the product of the 'masculinization' of the girls' brains due to their exposure to high androgen levels.

Criticisms of hormonal explanations

All these studies are, however, suspect as methods of showing that male and female human behaviour is governed by hormones. Ruth Bleier (1984) points to a number of flaws in using animal behaviour to explain human behavioural differences. In general, she observes that it is dangerous to assume that the same hormonal changes would result in the same changes in behaviour in humans as they had in animals. She does not accept that such experiments are conclusive.

The experiments with rats defined aggression simply in terms of fighting behaviour, yet these same experiments have been used to explain the supposed dominance and aggression of human males in all spheres of social life. Furthermore, the experiments were carried out in unnatural laboratory conditions, and fighting might not have increased if the rats had been in their normal environment.

The rhesus monkey experiments failed to take account of the fact that the androgens produced masculinized genitalia in the female monkeys. Bleier refers to studies which show that rhesus mothers treat their offspring differently from an early age according to their sex. The behaviour of the monkeys could therefore have resulted from them being treated as males because of their appearance. Oakley (1981) accepts that dominant males in monkey groups have higher testosterone levels than low dominance monkeys. However, she argues that social context affects hormone levels. Experiments show that when low dominance monkeys are caged with females only, their testosterone levels rise. Dominance, or lack of it, might affect testosterone levels, as well as vice versa.

In Ehrhardt's studies, the baby girls were born with what appeared to be masculine genitalia, and in all but one case they were initially treated as boys. It is therefore possible that their 'tomboy' behaviour was entirely a product of their early socialization. Oakley refers to one case studied by Ehrhardt in which the child, who was originally treated as a boy, underwent an operation at 7 months so that she took on the appearance of a girl. From 17 months old her name was changed from a boy's to a girl's, she was treated as a girl and dressed in girl's clothing. Later the mother commented on how 'feminine' the girl had become. This strongly suggests that it was environmental influences and not changes in the brain produced by hormones that had led to the 'tomboy' behaviour.

Brain lateralization

There are claims that hormones have indirect effects on male and female brain development, as well as the direct effects discussed above. One area of research has concentrated on the issue of brain lateralization. According to John Nicholson (1993) and others, the right and left hemispheres of the brain specialize in different tasks. Nicholson argues that in about 95 per cent of the population the left hemisphere specializes in verbal and language skills, while the right is mainly responsible for visuo-spatial abilities, which relate to the 'ability to locate objects in space'.

J.A. Gray and A.W.H. Buffery (1971) believe that the left hemisphere of the brain is more dominant in girls after the age of 2, and that boys have greater abilities in those functions concentrated in the right hemisphere. According to Gray and Buffery, this difference is due to hormonal influences on the brain, and accounts for the results of some tests which appear to show that girls have greater verbal ability than boys, but that boys perform better in spatial and mathematical tests.

This explanation of sex differences is, however, as suspect as those that relate to hormones and aggression. Ruth Bleier (1984) has noted the contradictory findings of studies in this area. For example, some studies claim that girls' brains are less lateralized than boys; some claim the reverse to be true; and some find no difference between boys and girls.

Bleier also raises doubts about the results of verbal and visuo-spatial tests. On average, girls do score slightly higher than boys in verbal tests and slightly lower in visuo-spatial tests. Nevertheless, she says:

There are no clearcut sex differences in either verbal or visuo-spatial abilities. All females do not score better than all males in verbal tests, nor do all males score better than all females in visuo-spatial tests, nor do the majority of either sex perform better than the majority of the other ... Comparable populations of males and females have the same range of test scores, the same range of abilities, and in some test situations the mean or average test scores may not differ at all, or, differ by only a few percentage points.

Bleier, 1984, p. 93

What small differences there are could well result from differences in socialization rather than from brain lateralization.

John Nicholson (1993) is willing to accept differences in the development of male and female brains and that testosterone may be linked to visuo-spatial abilities. However, men with very high testosterone levels in childhood actually do less well in visuo-spatial tests than men with very low levels. This suggests that a balance between male and female hormones is necessary to develop the highest levels of visuo-spatial abilities. Nicholson also points out that both verbal and visuo-spatial abilities are affected by and can be improved by training. Echoing Bleier's argument on lateralization and different aptitudes, he says that 'gender differences, where noted, are small, and are almost certainly exacerbated by social factors'.

Sociobiology – the evolution of human behaviour

There have been a number of attempts to relate sex differences to differences in the behaviour of men and women by using evolutionary ideas. Of these, perhaps the most influential today is sociobiology.

Sociobiology was first developed by E.O. Wilson (1975) and has been applied to sex and gender by

David Barash (1979). It is based in part on Charles Darwin's theory of evolution, but it goes well beyond Darwin's original theory.

Like Darwin, sociobiologists believe that humans and other species develop and change through a process of natural selection. Individuals of a species vary in their physical characteristics, and from this point of view, those which are best adapted to their environment are most likely to survive and reproduce. Since offspring tend to have characteristics similar to those of their parents due to genetic inheritance, the characteristics of a species can change as the fittest survive.

Thus, to use a simple example, giraffes have gradually evolved long necks because members of the species with longer necks had better access to food supplies in the upper levels of trees than their shorter-necked counterparts. As longer-necked giraffes and their offspring survived more frequently, a long neck became encoded in the genetic make-up of the species.

Sociobiologists go beyond Darwin in two main ways:

1 They argue that it is not just physical characteristics that evolve, but also behaviour.

2 They believe that behaviour in animals and humans is governed by a genetic instruction to maximize the chances of passing on their genes to future generations by breeding – that is, they try to ensure that they have offspring which survive. At the heart of sociobiology's attempt to explain sex differences in the behaviour of female and male humans is the claim that the two sexes employ different strategies to maximize their chances of passing on their genes.

Barash points out that human males produce millions of sperm during their lifetime, while females usually produce only one egg at a time, and about 400 in total during their lifetime. Furthermore, the female gestates the foetus in her body. The male therefore has an interest in making as many females as possible pregnant to produce the maximum number of offspring who will carry his genes. However, the female invests so much time and energy in each offspring that she must go for quality in her mates, so that each offspring has a good chance of ultimate survival. She therefore selects only the most genetically suitable male partners.

Wilson and Barash go on to assert that different reproductive strategies produce different behaviour in males and females and also lead them to occupy different social roles. In terms of sexual behaviour, men are likely to be more promiscuous, while women will be more circumspect in their pursuit of the best possible genetic partner. Wilson says that 'it pays males to be aggressive, hasty, fickle and undiscriminating. In theory, it is more profitable for women to be coy, to hold back until they can identify males with the best possible genes.'

Barash talks about there being advantages for men in 'playing fast and loose', and having a 'love 'em and leave 'em' attitude. Wilson claims that rape by males can be explained in this way.

Sociobiologists believe that women can tolerate infidelity by their partners more readily than men. Infidelity by men has little cost for women, but if the woman is unfaithful, the man may devote energy to raising someone else's child.

To Wilson and Barash, these differences have wider implications. Because a woman is always certain whether a child is genetically hers, she will be more willing to devote attention to childcare, and in a modern society may therefore be more willing to become a housewife. In addition, women's search for the best male to father their children leads to them seeking to marry males of a higher social status than themselves. Because women can produce so 'few' children, men must compete for access to the comparatively scarce reproductive capacities of females. The larger and more aggressive males will be more successful. Females do not need to compete for mates in this way, and ultimately this leads to the dominance of males over females.

One way in which men tried to attract females in early societies was through showing that as successful hunters they were the best providers. To sociobiologists, the roots of war and territoriality are to be found in the aggressive male's attempts to secure and retain access to his own females by preventing their access to other males.

Sociobiologists back up these sweeping claims largely with animal studies. They provide examples of ape species in which dominant males are more successful in mating, and of the male lions' domination of female prides. Wilson even claims there are examples of 'gang rape' by mallard ducks.

However, Barash denies that any of the views held by sociobiologists are sexist. He sees males and females as simply biologically different, each pursuing the maintenance of their genes in their own way.

Wilson admits that human males and females are not compelled to behave in the ways described above; they may choose different types of behaviour. But if they do, it goes against their biological predispositions and makes them less efficient at maintaining the species.

Criticisms of sociobiology

Sociobiologists assume a direct link between patterns of genetic inheritance and behaviour in humans. However, there is no scientific evidence that such a link exists.

In contrast to animals, human behaviour is shaped by environment rather than instinct. Steven Rose, Leon Kamin, and R.C. Lewontin (1984) note that, unlike most animals:

*the human infant is born with relatively few of
its neural pathways already committed. During
its long infancy connections between nerve
cells are formed not merely on the basis of
specific epigenetic programming but in the
light of experience .*

Rose *et al.*, 1984, p. 145

Bleier (1984) is dismissive of sociobiology. She
accuses it of being ethnocentric: of assuming that all
human behaviour corresponds to that in the white
capitalist world. For example, sociobiologists merely
assert that females are 'coy' and males 'aggressive'
without examining other societies.

Oakley (1972) points out that there are many
societies in which women are far from 'coy'. She
claims that 'amongst the Trobrianders, as also among
the Lesu, Kurtatchi, Lepcha, Kwoma, and Mataco,
women frequently take the initiative in sexual
relationships'.

According to the critics, then, sociobiology tries to
explain 'universal' human behaviour which is not
universal at all. Furthermore, the evidence sociobiologists use from the animal world to support their case
is selective. It ignores all the examples of animal
species where males are not aggressive and
dominant. Bleier notes that in some species of ape
and monkey there are no dominance hierarchies at
all. In others, such as Japanese macaques, the rank of
a male within the troop depends on the rank of his
mother. Bleier points out that recent studies have
revealed a wide variety of behaviour patterns in apes.
There are examples of female apes who 'protect
territory, fight for their own or other mothers' young,
take food from males, and bond with other females to
fight aggressive males'. In short, sociobiologists

simply ignore the evidence which contradicts their
view.

For this reason, many feminists regard sociobiology as a spurious attempt to provide 'scientific'
justification for male power.

John Nicholson (1993) argues that sociobiology is
based upon the naturalistic fallacy. Gender is seen as
being natural and inevitable. The way men and
women behave cannot be changed and should
therefore be left well alone. Nicholson believes that
this is untrue. Gender differences are not natural and
can be changed. The naturalistic fallacy gives sociobiology an inherently conservative bias: it opposes
changes in the status quo. This is despite the fact that
it is possible to argue that gender divisions are far
from ideal and may have negative consequences.

Nicholson points out that even in terms of the
logic of sociobiology, with its emphasis on passing
on genes, it may be better for men to play a greater
part in child rearing. We might, for example, argue
that it would have been counterproductive for men in
hunter-gatherer societies to sire large numbers of
children, because they would have been unable to
provide food and protection for all their mothers. As
a result, many of them would have died. Prolific
fathers would also not have been available to stand
in for their children's mothers when they became ill.

We could therefore make a perfectly respectable
case for saying that it would actually have been the
'stay-at-home man who had the best chance of being
survived by children carrying his genes'.

Another problem with sociobiology is that it has
great difficulty in explaining behaviour such as
homosexuality or voluntary celibacy that preclude
the possibility of passing on genes to offspring.

Biology and the sexual division of labour

Biologically based explanations of the behaviour of
men and women have not been confined to those who
have located these differences in the hormones, brains,
or genes of the two sexes. Other writers, including
anthropologists, have focused on more obvious
physical differences between males and females, and
related these to the allocation of social roles.

George Peter Murdock – biology and practicality

George Peter Murdock is an anthropologist who
argued that biological differences between men and
women are the basis of the sexual division of labour

in society (Murdock, 1949). However, he did not
suggest that men and women are directed by genetically based predispositions or characteristics to adopt
their particular roles. Instead, he simply suggested
that biological differences, such as the greater
physical strength of men and the fact that women
bear children, lead to gender roles out of sheer practicality. Given the biological differences between men
and women, a sexual division of labour is the most
efficient way of organizing society.

In a cross-cultural survey of 224 societies, ranging
from hunting and gathering bands to modern nation-
states, Murdock examined the activities assigned to
men and women. He found tasks such as hunting,
lumbering and mining to be predominantly male

roles, and cooking, gathering wild vegetable products, water-carrying and making and repairing clothes to be largely female roles. He stated that:

Man with his superior physical strength can better undertake the more strenuous tasks, such as lumbering, mining, quarrying, land clearance and housebuilding. Not handicapped, as is woman by the physiological burdens of pregnancy and nursing, he can range farther afield to hunt, to fish, to herd and to trade. Woman is at no disadvantage, however, in lighter tasks which can be performed in or near the home, e.g. the gathering of vegetable products, the fetching of water, the preparation of food, and the manufacture of clothing and utensils.

Murdock, 1949, p. 7

Thus, because of her biological function of childbearing and nursing, woman is tied to the home; because of her physique she is limited to less strenuous tasks.

Murdock found that the sexual division of labour was present in all of the societies in his sample and concluded that 'the advantages inherent in a division of labour by sex presumably account for its universality'.

Talcott Parsons – biology and the 'expressive' female

Similar arguments are advanced to account for the role of women in industrial society. As we will see in Chapter 8, Talcott Parsons (1955a) saw the isolated nuclear family in modern industrial society as specializing in two basic functions:

1 the socialization of the young
2 the stabilization of adult personalities.

For socialization to be effective, a close, warm and supportive group was essential. The family met this requirement and, within the family, the woman was primarily responsible for socializing the young.

Parsons turned to biology for his explanation of this fact. He stated:

In our opinion the fundamental explanation of the allocation of roles between the biological sexes lies in the fact that the bearing and early nursing of children establish a strong presumptive primacy of the relation of mother to the small child.

Parsons, 1955a, p. 23

Thus, because mothers bore and nursed children, they had a closer and stronger relationship with them. This was particularly so in modern industrial society where the isolation of the nuclear family:

focuses the responsibility of the mother role more sharply on one adult woman. Furthermore the absence of the husband father from the home premises so much of the time means that she has to take the primary responsibility for the children.

Parsons, 1955a, p. 23

Parsons characterized the woman's role in the family as expressive, which meant she provided warmth, security and emotional support. This was essential for the effective socialization of the young.

It was only a short step from applying these expressive qualities to her children to applying them also to her husband. This was her major contribution to the second function of the isolated nuclear family: the stabilization of adult personalities. The male breadwinner spent his working day competing in an achievement-oriented society. This instrumental role led to stress and anxiety. The expressive female relieved this tension by providing the weary breadwinner with love, consideration and understanding.

Parsons argued that there had to be a clearcut sexual division of labour for the family to operate efficiently as a social system. In this sense, the instrumental and expressive roles complemented each other. Like a button and a buttonhole, they locked together to promote family solidarity.

Although Parsons moved a long way from biology, it formed his starting point. Biological differences between the sexes provided the foundation on which the sexual division of labour was based.

John Bowlby – the mother–child bond

John Bowlby (1953) examined the role of women and, in particular, their role as mothers, from a psychological perspective. Like Parsons, he argued that a mother's place was in the home, caring for her children, especially during their early years.

Bowlby conducted a number of studies of juvenile delinquents and found that the most psychologically disturbed had experienced separation from their mothers at an early age. Many had been raised in orphanages, and as a result had been deprived of maternal love. They appeared unable to give or receive love and seemed compelled to adopt a career of destructive and anti-social relationships.

Bowlby concluded that it was essential for mental health that 'the infant and young child should experience a warm, intimate and continuous relationship with his mother'. Bowlby's arguments imply that there is a genetically based psychological need for a close and intimate mother–child relationship. Thus the mother role is firmly attached to the female. (For further details of Bowlby's views and related research, see Chapter 6.)

In this section we have examined some of the arguments which base the sexual division of labour on biological differences between the sexes. Although all the arguments allow some variation in the way gender roles are played, none holds out much hope for those who seek to abolish them.

Ann Oakley – the cultural division of labour

Ann Oakley (1974) explicitly rejects the views of Murdock, Parsons, and Bowlby. She does not accept that there is any natural or inevitable division of labour or allocation of social roles on the basis of sex. She says:

> Not only is the division of labour by sex not universal, but there is no reason why it should be. Human cultures are diverse and endlessly variable. They owe their creation to human inventiveness rather than invincible biological forces.
>
> Oakley, 1974

Oakley first takes George Peter Murdock to task, arguing that the sexual division of labour is not universal nor are certain tasks always performed by men, others by women. She maintains that Murdock's interpretation of his data is biased because he looks at other cultures through both Western and male eyes. In particular, she claims that he prejudges the role of women in terms of the Western housewife-mother role.

Culture and gender roles

Oakley finds plenty of evidence from Murdock's own data to attack the assumption that biology largely determines the sexual division of labour. There are 14 societies in Murdock's sample of 224 in which lumbering is done either exclusively by women or shared by both sexes, 36 societies in which women are solely responsible for land clearance, and 38 in which cooking is a shared activity.

Oakley then examines a number of societies in which biology appears to have little or no influence on women's roles:

1 The Mbuti Pygmies, a hunting and gathering society who live in the Congo rain forests, have no specific rules for the division of labour by sex. Men and women hunt together. The roles of father and mother are not sharply differentiated, both sexes sharing responsibility for the care of children.

2 Among the Australian Aborigines of Tasmania, women were responsible for seal hunting, fishing and catching opossums (tree-dwelling mammals).

3 Turning to present-day societies, Oakley notes that women form an important part of many armed forces, particularly those of China, the former USSR, Cuba and Israel. In India, women work on building sites, and in some Asian and Latin American countries they have worked in mines.

Culture and the mother–housewife role

Oakley also attacks the arguments of Parsons and Bowlby. Using the example of Alor, an island in .Indonesia, Oakley shows how in this and other small-scale horticultural societies, women are not tied to their offspring, and this does not appear to have any harmful effects on the children.

In traditional Alorese society, women were largely responsible for the cultivation and collection of vegetable produce. This involved them spending considerable time away from the village. Within a fortnight of the birth of their child, women returned to the fields leaving the infant in the care of a sibling, the father or a grandparent.

Turning to Western society, Oakley dismisses Bowlby's claim that an 'intimate and continuous' relationship between mother and child is essential for the child's well-being. She notes that a large body of research shows that the employment of the mother has no detrimental effects on the child's development. Some studies indicate that the children of working mothers are less likely to be delinquent than those of mothers who stay at home. In fact, Oakley claims that 'working mothers enjoy their children more and are less irritable with them than full-time mothers'.

Oakley is particularly scathing in her attack on Parsons's view of the family and the role of the 'expressive' female within it. She accuses him of basing his analysis on the beliefs and values of his own culture and, in particular, on the myths of male superiority and of the sanctity of marriage and the family. Oakley argues that the expressive housewife–mother role is not necessary for the functioning of the family unit – it merely exists for the convenience of men. She claims that Parsons's explanation of gender roles is simply a validating myth for the 'domestic oppression of women'.

Oakley draws the following conclusions:

1 Gender roles are culturally rather than biologically determined.

2 Evidence from a number of different societies shows that there are no tasks (apart from childbearing) which are performed exclusively by females.

3 Biological characteristics do not bar women from particular occupations.

4 The mother role is a cultural construction. Evidence from several societies indicates that children do not require a close, intimate and continuous relationship with a female mother figure.

The social construction of gender roles

Oakley believes that gender roles are culturally rather than biologically produced. In other words, humans learn the behaviour that is expected of males and females within their society. This behaviour is not produced by innate characteristics: studies of a number of societies show that gender roles can vary considerably. Whatever the biological differences between males and females, it is the culture of a society that exerts most influence in the creation of masculine and feminine behaviour. If there are biological tendencies for men and women to behave in different ways, these can be overridden by cultural factors.

Socialization and gender roles

Oakley (1974) outlines how socialization in modern industrial societies shapes the behaviour of girls and boys from an early age. Basing her work on the findings of Ruth Hartley, Oakley discusses four main ways in which socialization into gender roles takes place:

1 The child's self-concept is affected by manipulation. For example, mothers tend to pay more attention to girls' hair and to dress them in 'feminine' clothes.

2 Differences are achieved through canalization involving the direction of boys and girls towards different objects. This is particularly obvious in the provision of toys for girls which encourage them to rehearse their expected adult roles as mothers and housewives. Girls are given dolls, soft toys, and miniature domestic objects and appliances to play with. Boys, on the other hand, are given toys which encourage more practical, logical, and aggressive behaviour, for example bricks and guns.

3 Another aspect of socialization is the use of verbal appellations, such as 'You're a naughty boy', or 'That's a good girl'. This leads young children to identify with their gender and to imitate adults of the same gender.

4 Male and female children are exposed to different activities. For example, girls are particularly encouraged to become involved with domestic tasks. In addition, numerous studies have documented how stereotypes of masculinity and femininity are further reinforced throughout childhood, and indeed adult life. The media have been particularly strongly attacked by feminists for tending to portray men and women in their traditional social roles.

Gender attribution

From the viewpoint described above, gender is socially constructed in the sense that differences in the behaviour of males and females are learned rather than being the inevitable result of biology. The ethnomethodologists Suzanne J. Kessler and Wendy McKenna (1978) go a stage further. As ethnomethodologists they are interested in the ways that members of society categorize the world around them. From their perspective, gender attribution – the decision to regard another person as male or female – is socially produced in much the same way as gender roles.

For most people, it seems obvious whether someone is male or female, and it is taken for granted that a decision about the sex of another will coincide with the biological 'facts'. Kessler and McKenna disagree; they deny that there is any clearcut way of differentiating between men and women.

Two or more sexes?

This startling claim is backed up by a range of arguments and evidence. Kessler and McKenna try to demonstrate that there are exceptions to every rule which is supposed to distinguish the sexes.

The full range of hormones is present in both men and women, thus hormones do not provide a clear dividing line between the sexes. Some women have high androgen levels, while some men have comparatively low levels of this hormone.

Some individuals have male chromosomes (XY), but are insensitive to the effects of androgen and thus appear to be physically female. Despite their male genetic make-up, they are invariably identified as females.

Other individuals have a condition known as Turner's Syndrome. They have neither XY chromosomes, nor the normal female pairing of XX. Instead, they have a single X chromosome, normally indicated by the figures XO. A small number of people with this condition do have a few XYY chromosomes as well as the predominant XO. They have a female appearance but can fail 'sex tests' for women's athletics competitions.

Kessler and McKenna argue that the main way of determining gender at birth is through an inspection of the genitals. However, even this may produce ambiguous evidence. Some babies and adults have both male and female genitals, a condition known as hermaphroditism

Kessler and McKenna note that, despite these anomalies, both the public and scientists tend to see males and females as opposites, refusing to recognize the possibility of an intermediate state. However, this has not always been the case. Some societies have recognized a third gender role: the *berdache*. A number of North American Indian tribes contained *berdache*. They were usually 'men' who dressed and in some ways acted like women. In some societies they had a high status, in others a low one, but in all cases they were treated as a distinct gender. In Western industrial society, hermaphrodites are almost always categorized as male or female. In tribes such as the Potock of East Africa they would be more likely to be allocated to a third category.

Allocation to sexes

Having questioned the most basic assumption (that there are just two sexes), Kessler and McKenna go on to discuss how individuals are allocated to sexes by others. This process was studied by interviewing transsexuals, people who seem biologically normal but who feel themselves to be members of the 'opposite' sex. Some, but not all, transsexuals undergo operations to alter their genitals, usually changing from male to female.

Normally gender and genitals are equated with each other: the connection between them is taken for granted. However, people are not expected to ask others whom they have just met to remove their clothes so that they can determine which sex they are. Various types of evidence are pieced together so that a gender attribution can be made by the observer. Someone with the appearance and behaviour of a female or male will simply be assumed to have the appropriate genitals. The existence of transsexuals means that this assumption is not always accurate. Biological males sometimes live as, and are accepted as, females.

How then do people decide what gender another person is? According to Kessler and McKenna there are four main processes involved:

1 The content and manner of the speech of others are taken into account. Some male to female transsexuals have trained themselves to appear to be women by putting more inflection in their voice and by having more mobile facial movements when talking. Others introduce themselves as 'Miss' to settle any doubt there might be in an observer's mind.

2 Another important factor in gender attribution is public physical appearance. For example, female to male transsexuals may disguise their breasts by wearing baggy clothing or by using strapping.

3 The information people provide about their past life helps to determine gender attribution. Again,

transsexuals have to be careful to avoid suspicion. They may need a cover story. In one case a female to male transsexual attributed pierced ears to belonging to a tough street gang.

4 The final important factor is the private body. Usually there is little problem in keeping the body covered, but transsexuals may need to avoid certain situations (such as visiting beaches or sharing rooms with others) if they have not undergone the appropriate operations to change their sex physically.

Taking on the identity of a sex to which they do not belong biologically is difficult and demanding for the transsexual. For most people, hormones, chromosomes, genitals and the gender attributed to them will all coincide. Nevertheless, the exceptions studied by Kessler and McKenna demonstrate that even the most basic division – that between male and female – can be seen as being at least in part a social construct.

Sex and gender differences– conclusion

Some sociologists have tried to move beyond the debate on whether sex or gender shapes the behaviour of men and women. Both David Morgan (1986) and Linda Birke (1986) argue that sex and gender interact. Sex differences influence gender differences and vice versa. Linda Birke argues that 'women's biology actually and materially affects their lives'. She suggests that feminists cannot ignore biological facts, for example that women menstruate and can give birth.

However, both Morgan and Birke also argue that the cultural interpretation placed on biological differences is very important. Thus David Morgan says:

if certain distinctions between men and women come to be seen as crucial, this itself is a cultural fact and has its consequences, although this is the outcome of a complex interaction between the biological and the cultural rather than the primary assertion of the former.

Morgan, 1986, p. 35

In the nineteenth century, for example, some people believed that men and women had fixed amounts of energy. Unlike men, women were believed to use up much of this energy in menstruation, pregnancy and the menopause.

Today, many people believe that hormonal differences play a major part in shaping the behaviour of men and women. Birke points out that this belief is held despite the fact that 'there simply is no one hormone or even class of hormone, that belongs uniquely to one gender or the other'. What matters most is the meaning attached to differences, real or imagined, in a society. For a different view of the relationship between sex and gender differences, see the discussion of Connell's work on masculinity (pp. 191–6).

In recent years, there has been an increased theoretical emphasis upon the differences among women, and the differences among men. It has been recognized that there are a variety of ways to be feminine and a variety of ways to be masculine. There has been less emphasis on the sex/gender differences between men in general and women in general. These new approaches will be discussed later in the chapter (see pp. 157–63 and 191–6).

Gender inequality

So far in this chapter we have examined explanations for differences between men and women. These differences have sometimes been seen as the basis for inequalities between them, and we will now look at those inequalities in more detail.

The development of feminism has led to attention being focused on the subordinate position of women in many societies. Feminist sociologists have been mainly responsible for developing theories of gender inequality, yet there is little agreement about the causes of this inequality, nor about what actions should be taken to reduce or end it. More recently, the focus has changed from an emphasis on inequality to one on difference.

Several feminist approaches can be broadly distinguished:

1 radical feminism
2 Marxist and socialist feminism
3 liberal feminism
4 Black feminism
5 postmodern feminism.

There is considerable overlap between these approaches, and each contains feminists with a variety of views. Nevertheless, the distinction between these perspectives is important. It helps to clarify some of the major disputes within feminism, and feminists often attribute themselves to one of these categories.

We will briefly outline each perspective before considering a more detailed examination of how they have been applied to particular aspects of gender inequality.

Radical feminism

Radical feminism blames the exploitation of women on men. To a radical feminist, it is primarily men who have benefited from the subordination of women. Women are seen to be exploited because they undertake unpaid labour for men by carrying out childcare and housework, and because they are denied access to positions of power.

Radical feminists see society as patriarchal – it is dominated and ruled by men. From this point of view, men are the ruling class, and women the subject class. The family is often seen by radical feminists as the key institution oppressing women in modern societies. The family is certainly given more prominence than in Marxist sociology, where, as part of the superstructure, it is given only secondary importance.

Radical feminists tend to believe that women have always been exploited and that only revolutionary change can offer the possibility of their liberation. However, there are disagreements within this group about both the origins of women's oppression and the possible solutions to it. Some radical feminists, such as Shulamith Firestone (1972), believe women's oppression originated in their biology, particularly in the fact that they give birth. Others do not see biology as so important; they see male rule as largely a product of culture. Some stress rape and male violence towards women as the methods through which men have secured and maintained their power.

Because men are seen as the enemies of women's liberation, many radical feminists reject any assistance from the male sex in their struggle to achieve the rights they seek. Separatist feminists argue that women should organize independently of men outside the male-dominated society. A few, like The Leeds Revolutionary Feminist Group (1982), argue that only lesbians can be true feminists, since only they can be fully independent of men.

A particularly radical group, female supremacists, argue that women are not just equal but are actually morally superior to men. They wish to see patriarchy replaced by matriarchy (male rule replaced by female rule). From such perspectives, men are responsible not only for the exploitation of women, but also for many other problems. These may include conflict, war, destruction of the environment, the abuse of science so that it fails to meet human needs, and so on.

Rosemarie Tong distinguishes between two groups of radical feminists (Tong, 1998). Radical-libertarian feminists believe that it is both possible and desirable for gender differences to be eradicated or at least greatly reduced. They therefore aim for a state of androgyny in which men and women are not significantly different. The ideal state is one in which women and men take on the more desirable characteristics of one another. They believe that differences between the masculine and feminine are socially constructed. If they are removed then equality between men and women can follow.

The second group, radical-cultural feminists, believe in the superiority of the feminine. As Tong puts it:

> far from believing that the liberated woman must exhibit both masculine and feminine traits and behaviour, these radical-cultural feminists expressed the view that it is better to be female/feminine than it is to be male/masculine. Thus women should not try to be like men.
>
> Tong, 1998

According to Tong, they celebrate characteristics associated with femininity such as 'interdependence, community, connection, sharing, emotion, body, trust, absence of hierarchy, nature, immanence, process, joy, peace and life'. On the other hand, they are hostile to characteristics associated with masculinity, such as 'independence, autonomy, intellect, will, wariness, hierarchy, domination, culture, transcendence, product, asceticism, war and death'.

Tong accepts that a distinction between radical-libertarian feminists and radical-cultural feminists can be overstated, but believes that it does reflect real and significant differences.

Marxist and socialist feminism

Marxist and socialist feminists do not attribute women's exploitation entirely to men. They see capitalism rather than patriarchy as being the principal source of women's oppression, and capitalists as the main beneficiaries. Like radical feminists, they see women's unpaid work as housewives and mothers as one of the main ways in which women are exploited. Although men in general benefit, it is primarily capitalists who gain from women's unpaid work since new generations of workers are reproduced at no cost to the capitalist. (For a discussion of this issue see Chapter 8.)

Thus Marxist and socialist feminists relate women's oppression to the production of wealth, while radical feminists attribute greater importance to childbearing. Marxist feminists also place much greater stress on the exploitation of women in paid employment. The disadvantaged position of women is held to be a consequence of the emergence of private property and subsequently their lack of ownership of the means of production, which in turn deprives them of power.

Although Marxist and socialist feminists agree with radical feminists that women as a group are exploited, particularly since the advent of capitalism, they are more sensitive to the differences between women who belong to the ruling class and proletarian families. In this respect, women have interests in common with the working class, and Marxist and socialist feminists see greater scope for cooperation between women and working-class men than do radical feminists.

Marxist feminists share with radical feminists a desire for revolutionary change; however, they seek the establishment of a communist society. In such a society (where the means of production will be communally owned) they believe gender inequalities will disappear. This view is not shared by radical feminists who believe that women's oppression has different origins and causes, and therefore requires a different solution.

There is no clearcut division between Marxist and socialist feminists; they share much in common. Marxist feminists, though, tend to seek more sweeping changes than socialist feminists. Socialist feminists tend to give more credence to the possibility of capitalist societies gradually moving towards female equality. They see more prospect for change within the democratic system.

Liberal feminism

Liberal feminism does not have such clearly developed theories of gender inequalities as radical and Marxist and socialist feminism. Nevertheless, liberal feminism probably enjoys greater popular support than the other perspectives. This is largely because its aims are more moderate and its views pose less of a challenge to existing values. Liberal feminists aim for gradual change in the political, economic and social systems of Western societies.

To the liberal feminist, nobody benefits from existing gender inequalities; both men and women are harmed because the potential of females and males alike is suppressed. For example, many women with the potential to be successful and skilled members of the workforce do not get the opportunity to develop their talents, while men are denied some of the pleasures of having a close relationship with their children. The explanation of this situation, according to liberal feminists, lies not so much in the structures and institutions of society, but in its culture and the attitudes of individuals.

Socialization into gender roles has the consequence of producing rigid, inflexible expectations of men and women. Discrimination prevents women from having equal opportunities.

The creation of equal opportunities, particularly in education and work, is the main aim of liberal feminists. They pursue this aim through the introduction of legislation and by attempting to change attitudes. In Britain, they supported such measures as the Sex Discrimination Act (1975) and the Equal Pay Act (1970) in the hope that these laws would help to end discrimination. They try to eradicate sexism and stereotypical views of women and men from children's books and the mass media. They do not seek revolutionary changes in society: they want reforms that take place within the existing social structure, and they work through the democratic system. Since they believe that existing gender inequalities benefit nobody (although they are particularly harmful to women), liberal feminists are willing to work with any members of society who support their beliefs and aims.

Although the least radical of feminist perspectives, the liberal view could still lead to considerable social change. At the very least, the changes it supports could lead to women having the same access as men to high-status jobs.

Black feminism

Black feminism has developed out of dissatisfaction with other types of feminism. Black feminists such as Bell Hooks (1981) have argued that other feminists, as well as male anti-racists, have not addressed the particular problems faced by black women. Writing in 1981, Hooks claimed that black women in the USA had not joined:

> together to fight for women's rights because we did not see 'womanhood' as an important aspect of our identity. Racist, sexist socialization had conditioned us to devalue our femaleness and to regard race as the only relevant label of identification.
>
> Hooks, 1981

Black women had joined in the fight for civil rights, but the organizations were dominated by men, and women's issues received no consideration.

Hooks argued that contemporary black women could learn a lot from some of their nineteenth-century counterparts who had pioneered a distinctive Black feminism. Hooks describes the views of Sojourner Truth, a black American woman who had campaigned for black women to gain the right to vote along with black men. Truth had said that if black women failed in their campaign for voting

rights, but black men succeeded, then 'the coloured men will be masters over the women, and it will be just as bad as it was before' (quoted in Hooks, 1981). At a convention of the women's rights movement in Ohio in 1852, white males argued that women should not have equal rights to men because they were physically inferior to men and were unsuited to heavy manual labour. Sojourner Truth countered this argument in a passionate speech saying:

> Look at me! look at my arm! ... I have plowed and planted, and gathered into barns, and no man could head me – and ain't I a woman? I could work as much as any man (when I could get it), and bear de lash as well – and ain't I a woman?
>
> Hooks, 1981, p. 160

Truth's speech highlighted the differences in the experiences of black women and white women. For some Black feminists these differences are the legacy of slavery. Patricia Hill Collins (1990) says that slavery 'shaped all subsequent relationships that black women had within African-American families and communities, with employers, and among each other, and created the political context for women's intellectual work'. To Collins, writing in 1990, most feminist theory has 'suppressed Black women's ideas' and has concentrated on the experiences and grievances of white and usually middle-class women. For example, feminist critiques of family life tended to examine the situation of middle-class wives who were in a very different position from most black women. There was a 'masculinist bias in Black social and political thought' and a 'racist bias in feminist theory'.

Black feminism could correct that bias by drawing on black women's experiences. Many black women had been employed as domestic servants in white families. From this position they could see 'white power demystified'. They could see whites as they really were, yet they remained economically exploited outsiders. Thus Black feminists could draw upon the 'outsider-within perspective generated by black women's location in the labour market' and could develop a 'distinct view of the contradictions between the dominant groups' actions and ideologies'.

Like Hooks, Collins draws inspiration from the insights of Sojourner Truth to show how black women can attack patriarchal ideology. For example, they could attack the belief that women are fragile and weak by drawing on their own experience of physically demanding labour.

Rose M. Brewer (1993) sees the basis of Black feminist theory as an 'understanding of race, class and gender as simultaneous forces'. Black women suffer from disadvantages because they are black, because they are women, and because they are working-class, but their problems are more than the sum of these parts: each inequality reinforces and multiplies each of the other inequalities. Thus black women's problems can be represented as stemming from 'race × class × gender' rather than 'race + class + gender'. The distinctive feature of Black feminism to Brewer is that it studies the 'interplay' of race, class and gender in shaping the lives and restricting the life chances of black women.

Heidi Safia Mirza (1997) argues that there is a need for a distinctive Black British feminism. She does not claim that black British women have a unique insight into what is true and what is not, but she docs believe that this group can make an important contribution to the development of feminist and other knowledge. They can challenge the distorted assumptions of dominant groups by drawing on their own experiences. They offer 'other ways of knowing' and can 'invoke some measure of critical race/gender reflexivity into mainstream academic thinking'.

In particular, Black British feminists can challenge the predominant image of black British women as passive victims of racism, patriarchy and class inequality. They can undermine the image of 'the dutiful wife and daughter, the hard (but happy and grateful!) worker, the sexually available exotic other, the controlling asexual mother, or simply homogenized as the "third world" woman'. Instead, Black British feminists have been able to show how black British women have been 'brave, proud and strong'. They have struggled against domestic violence; tried to overcome sexism and racism in school; developed alternative family forms in which women have autonomy, and challenged the activities of the police and immigration authorities. They have made their own voice heard rather than relying on others to tell their story.

Black feminist thought has had some influence upon postmodern feminism. This will be discussed on pp. 157–63.

The origins of gender inequalities – feminist views

Although many feminists clearly align themselves to one of the perspectives that we have just outlined, others do not. Thus, in the subsequent sections, not all the explanations for gender inequalities that we will discuss can be 'neatly' attributed to one perspective.

Feminists do not agree about the origins of inequality between men and women. Some believe that women have always had a subordinate position in all societies; others argue that the origins of gender inequalities can be traced back to particular historical events.

Shulamith Firestone – a radical feminist view

In her book, *The Dialectics of Sex*, published in 1970, Firestone was the first to outline a radical feminist explanation of female inequality. To Firestone, sexual oppression was the first and most fundamental form of oppression. Unlike Marxists, Firestone does not attach primary importance to economic differences in the explanation of inequality. Although she acknowledges the importance of the work of Marx and Engels, she criticizes them for confining their studies to economic production. In her view, they ignored an important part of the material world: 'reproduction'.

Firestone believes that what she calls the sexual class system was the first form of stratification. It predated the class system and provided the basis from which other forms of stratification evolved. She

provides a very clear explanation for its origins. She says 'men and women were created different and not equally privileged'. Inequalities and the division of labour between men and women arose directly from biology. Biological differences produced a form of social organization she calls the biological family. Although societies vary in the roles of men and women and the form the family takes, all societies share the biological family, which has four key characteristics:

The biological family

1 Women are disadvantaged by their biology. Menstruation, the menopause and childbirth are all physical burdens for women, but pregnancy and breastfeeding have the most serious social consequences. At these times, when women are pregnant or looking after infants, they are 'dependent on males (whether brother, father, husband, lover or clan, government, community-at-large) for physical survival'.

2 Women's dependence on men is increased by the long periods during which human infants are dependent, compared to the infants of other species.

3 The interdependence between mother and child, and in turn their dependence on men, has been found in every society, and it has influenced the psychology of every human being. Dependence on men produced unequal power relationships and power psychology.

4   The final characteristic of the biological family is
    that it provides the foundations for all types of
    inequality and stratification. Men derived pleasure
    from their power over women and wished to extend
    their power to the domination of men. The sexual
    class system provided the blueprint and prototype
    for the economic class system. The economic class
    system provided the means through which some
    men came to dominate other men. Because the
    sexual class system is the basis for other class
    systems, Firestone believes that it must be destroyed
    before any serious progress can be made towards
    equality. She says 'the sexual class system is the
    model for all other exploitative systems and thus
    the tapeworm that must be eliminated first by any
    true revolution'.

Biology and equality

Because sexual class has a biological origin,
biological equality is the only effective starting point
for securing its elimination. Firestone believes that
effective birth control techniques have helped to
loosen the chains of women's slavery by giving them
more control over whether they become pregnant.
Even so, the pill and other contraceptives have not
freed women from pregnancy altogether; this would
only be possible when babies could be conceived and
developed outside the womb. Once this occurred,
women would no longer be forced into dependence
on men for part of their lives.

Yet even this would only be the first step towards
a complete revolution. In addition to the biological
changes, the economic class system and the cultural
superstructure would also have to be destroyed.
Economic equality would have to follow biological
equality, and power psychology would need to be
overcome.

The strength of Firestone's argument lies in its
ability to explain all forms of stratification, but this
radical feminist perspective on inequality has been
subject to criticism. Firestone does not explain
variations in women's status in different societies at
different times. For example, in some societies women
do not have primary responsibility for childcare and
women's biology does not seem to make them
dependent on men for long periods (as we saw in
Oakley's discussion on the cultural division of labour,
p. 133). If this is the case, then it may not be biology
alone that explains gender inequalities.

Sherry B. Ortner – culture and the devaluation of women

Sherry B. Ortner (1974) agrees with Firestone that
women are universally oppressed and devalued.
However, she claims that it is not biology as such
that ascribes women to their status in society, but the
way in which every culture defines and evaluates
female biology. Thus, if this universal evaluation
changed, then the basis for female subordination
would be removed.

Ortner argues that in every society, a higher value
is placed on culture than on nature. Culture is the
means by which humanity controls and regulates
nature. By inventing weapons and hunting
techniques, humans can capture and kill animals; by
inventing religion and rituals, humans can call upon
supernatural forces to produce a successful hunt or a
bountiful harvest. By the use of culture, humans do
not have to passively submit to nature: they can
regulate and control it. Thus humanity's ideas and
technology (that is, its culture), have power over
nature and are therefore seen as superior to it.

Women and nature

This universal evaluation of culture as superior to
nature is the basic reason for the devaluation of
women. Women are seen as closer to nature than
men, and therefore as inferior to men.

1   Ortner argues that women are universally defined as
    closer to nature because their bodies and
    physiological functions are more concerned with 'the
    natural processes surrounding the reproduction of
    the species'. These natural processes include
    menstruation, pregnancy, childbirth and lactation,
    processes for which the female body is 'naturally'
    equipped.
2   Women's social role as mothers is also seen as closer
    to nature. They are primarily responsible for the
    socialization of the young. Infants and young
    children are seen as 'barely human', as one step
    away from nature because their cultural repertoire is
    small compared to that of adults. Women's close
    relationships with young children further associate
    them with nature.
3   Since the mother role is linked to the family, the
    family itself is regarded as closer to nature compared
    to activities and institutions outside the family. Thus
    activities such as politics, warfare and religion are
    seen as more removed from nature, as superior to
    domestic tasks, and therefore as the province of men.
4   Finally, Ortner argues that woman's psyche, her
    psychological make-up, is defined as closer to nature.
    Because women are concerned with childcare and
    primary socialization, they develop more personal,
    intimate and particular relationships with others,
    especially their children. By comparison, men, by
    engaging in politics, warfare and religion, have a
    wider range of contacts and less personal and
    particular relationships. Thus men are seen as being
    more objective and less emotional: their thought
    processes are defined as more abstract and general,
    and less personal and particular. Ortner argues that
    culture is, in one sense, 'the transcendence, by means
    of systems of thought and technology, of the natural

givens of existence'. Thus men are seen as closer to culture since their thought processes are defined as more abstract and objective than those of women. Since culture is seen as superior to nature, woman's psyche is devalued and once again, men come out on top.

Ortner concludes that in terms of her biology, physiological processes, social roles and psychology, woman 'appears as something intermediate between culture and nature'.

Criticisms of Ortner

Ortner fails to show conclusively that in all societies culture is valued more highly than nature. Although many societies have rituals that attempt to control nature, it is not clear that nature is necessarily devalued in comparison to culture. Indeed it could be argued that the very existence of such rituals points to the superior power of nature.

Stephanie Coontz and Peta Henderson (1986) provide some examples to contradict Ortner. Among the Sherbo of West Africa, children are seen as close to nature, but adults of both sexes are seen as close to culture. Coontz and Henderson also claim that not all societies devalue nature. The Haganers of Papua and New Guinea distinguish culture and nature, but do not rank one above the other.

Michelle Z. Rosaldo – the public and the domestic

The anthropologist Michelle Zimbalist Rosaldo (1974) was the first to argue that women's subordination was the consequence of a division between the public and the private (or domestic) world.

She argues that there are two distinctive areas of social life:

1 She defines the domestic as 'institutions and modes of activity that are organized immediately around one or more mothers and their children'. As her use of the word 'mother' implies, she believes that it is usually women who are associated with this sphere.

2 In contrast, the public sphere is seen as being primarily the province of men. She defines the public as, 'activities institutions and forms of association that link, rank, organize, or subsume particular mother child groups'.

Thus the domestic sphere includes the family and life in the place of residence of the family, while the public sphere includes the activities and institutions associated with rituals and religion, politics and the economy.

Like Firestone and Ortner, Rosaldo argues that women have been disadvantaged in every known society – 'women everywhere lack generally

recognized and culturally valued authority'. Although she accepts that biology is the basis of women's oppression, she argues, like Ortner, that the link between the two is indirect. It is the *interpretation* given to women's biology that leads to their disadvantages, not the biology itself. This interpretation ties them to the rearing of children and the domestic sphere.

Men, on the other hand, are better able to keep their distance from domestic life. As a result, they do not need the same personal commitment to other humans as that required from mothers. Men are associated more with abstract authority, and with the political life of society as a whole. Men's separation from the domestic sphere sets them apart from the intimacy of the domestic world, and makes them more suitable for involvement in religious rituals. Rosaldo argues that as a consequence of men's involvement in religious and political life, they can exercise power over the domestic units which are the focus of women's lives.

Although Rosaldo argues that women have less power than men in all societies, she does believe that inequalities between the sexes are greater in some societies than in others. Even though she does not appear to accept that there is any prospect of a totally egalitarian society, she does believe that women can come closer to equality if men become more involved in domestic life.

Rosaldo justifies this claim with reference to societies in which men have an important domestic role. Thus the Mbuti Pygmies of Africa have a relatively egalitarian society because men and women cooperate in both domestic and economic life. Yet even here men retain some independence from the domestic sphere by having separate and secret flute cults.

Criticisms of Rosaldo

Undoubtedly the distinction between the domestic or private sphere and the public sphere provides a useful way of analysing and explaining the relative powerlessness of women in many societies. If women are largely excluded from the institutions that exercise power in society, then it is hardly surprising that men possess more power than women. Furthermore, this distinction helps to explain how the position of men and women in society has changed (see, for example, the section on 'Gender and industrialization', pp. 144–5).

However, there are difficulties involved in Rosaldo's theory and in the use of the terms 'public' and 'domestic'. Janet Siltanen and Michelle Stanworth (1984) point out that there are many ways in which public and private lives overlap. For example, in modern industrial societies it is women's labour in the home that makes it possible for men to devote themselves to work in the public sphere.

Linda Imray and Audrey Middleton (1983) argue that women's activities tend to be devalued even when they take place in the public sphere. When women take paid employment outside the home, the jobs they do are often regarded as being of less importance than those of men. From this point of view, the devaluation of women must have deeper roots than their association with domestic life. Certainly, as we will demonstrate in later sections, the increasing employment of women outside the private home has not produced equality for women within work.

Firestone, Ortner and Rosaldo all agree that women's subordination to men is universal. They all to some extent agree that the ultimate source of inequality between the sexes is biology, or the interpretation placed on biology. These views are not accepted by all sociologists. Marxist and socialist feminists question the view that women's subordination has always been universal. They claim that it is necessary to examine history to find out how and why inequality between the sexes came about. As Stephanie Coontz and Peta Henderson put it:

a number of scholars have begun to address the issue of male dominance as a historical phenomenon, grounded in a particular set of circumstances rather than flowing from some universal aspect of human nature or culture.

Coontz and Henderson, 1986, p. 1

We will examine some of these viewpoints next.

The origins of gender inequality – Marxist and socialist perspectives

Marx's associate, Freidrich Engels, devoted more attention to the sociology of gender than Marx himself. In *The Origins of the Family, Private Property and the State* (Engels, 1972), Engels outlined his theory of how human societies developed.

Engels – inequality and private property

In the earliest phases of societal development (which Engels called savagery and barbarism), gender inequalities favoured women rather than men. There was a division of labour by sex, with men mainly responsible for procuring food and women mainly responsible for the domestic sphere, but women were not subordinate to men. Private property existed in only a rudimentary form and consisted mainly of simple tools, utensils and weapons. What private property there was passed down through the female, not the male, line. This was because monogamous marriage did not exist. Both men and women could have sex with as many partners as they chose. Consequently, men could never be sure about who their children were. In contrast, as women give birth there is no such doubt about their offspring, and so the property was passed on to their children by the women.

According to Engels, it was during the period of barbarism that women suffered a 'world-historic' defeat. Men gained the upper hand when animals were domesticated and herded and became an important form of private property. Then meat and other animal products became crucial parts of the economy of early societies. Men gained the responsibility for owning and controlling livestock, and were unwilling to allow this important property to be passed down the female line; through owning livestock men overthrew the dominance of women in the household. In Engels's words, 'the man seized the reins in the house also, the woman was degraded, enthralled, the slave of the man's lust, a mere instrument for breeding children'.

In order to ensure that they could identify their own children, men increasingly put restrictions on women's choice of sexual partners. Eventually, during the period Engels calls civilization, monogamous marriage was established. By this stage, men had gained control over what was now the patriarchal family.

Criticisms of Engels

Unfortunately, Engels's theory was based upon unreliable anthropological evidence. His history of early societies no longer seems plausible in the light of more recent research into simple societies (which we discuss later in this chapter). Nevertheless, Engels's pioneering Marxist theory of the origins of gender inequalities laid the foundations upon which later Marxist and socialist feminists have built. Engels suggested that particular historical conditions led to the subordination of women, and he directed attention towards the material, economic reasons that could account for this.

Stephanie Coontz and Peta Henderson – women's work, men's property

Stephanie Coontz and Peta Henderson (1986) provide an example of an attempt to explain women's subordination from a Marxist/socialist perspective. They agree with Engels on a number of important points. Like him, they reject the view that women's subordination has always been a universal feature of human society, and they believe that the roots of women's oppression today are to be found in social causes. They emphasize that it was the difference between the roles of men and women in the production of goods that resulted in gender inequality, and not the difference between the contribution each makes to the reproduction of the species. In all these ways, Coontz and Henderson reject the radical feminism of Firestone.

However, they also disagree with Engels over some issues. For example, they deny that history started with a period of female dominance. On the basis of anthropological evidence, Coontz and Henderson argue that most early societies began with equality between the sexes. They accept that, from earliest times, there was a division of labour by sex, but this in itself did not make inequality inevitable. In most (though not all) societies, some women were excluded from hunting and risky tasks, such as trading and warfare, that could involve travel over long distances. However, it was only pregnant women and nursing mothers who had these restrictions placed on them. It was a matter of social convenience, rather than biological necessity, that led to an early division of labour. For example, it was difficult for women nursing children to combine this activity with warfare as young babies could prove a considerable inconvenience in battle. Women did, nevertheless, become successful warriors in some societies, for example, Dahomey in West Africa.

The existence of a sexual division of labour did not in itself lead to inequality. According to Coontz and Henderson, the earliest societies were communal – the resources produced by men and women alike were shared by everyone. Meat from the hunt and gathered vegetables were given both to the kin and the non-kin of those who produced the food. Even strangers would usually be fed. In these circumstances, it was not important to identify the father of a specific child since the offspring of particular individuals had no special rights to food.

Property and gender inequality

Like Engels, Coontz and Henderson believe that social inequalities developed as a result of changes in property ownership. They follow Engels in arguing that the introduction of herding and agriculture laid the foundations for gender inequalities. These new modes of production made it more likely that a surplus would be produced which could be accumulated or distributed. However, they suggest that some societies, including some North American Indian tribes, produced a surplus in favourable environmental conditions without developing herding or agriculture.

The most important factor in the transition to a society with gender stratification was the appearance of a form of communal property to which a group of kin had exclusive rights. Kin corporate property, as Coontz and Henderson describe it, meant that for the first time non-kin and strangers lost their right to share food and other resources. In these circumstances, parenthood and kinship relationships became important, and senior members of kinship groups gained control over property. Age and seniority began to provide greater economic power, as well as higher status.

Patrilocality and gender inequality

So far, Coontz and Henderson have tried to account for the origins of inequality, but have not explained why men became the dominant group. According to their theory, the key to this development lay in marriage arrangements. Some societies had a system of patrilocality, in other words wives went to live with their husband's kin. Women, as gatherers, continued to act as producers, but they lost control over the products of their labour. What they produced no longer belonged to their own kin corporate group but to that of their husband.

Not all societies had a system of patrilocality, some were matrilocal: husbands moved to live with their wife's kin group. Coontz and Henderson claim that such societies were more egalitarian; women retained greater power. Not only did the food they produced stay with their own kin group, but husbands had to share what they produced with their sister's household as well as their wife's. There was less opportunity for men to concentrate property in their own hands.

However, for a number of reasons matrilocal societies tended to be less successful. For example, patrilocal societies had more chance of producing a surplus. More successful kin groups could expand by the practice of polygamy (men could marry a number of women) and, in doing so, increase the labour force. The extra wives could gather and process more food. Patrilocal societies therefore expanded at the expense of matrilocal ones so that societies in which women were subordinate became more common than those in which they enjoyed greater equality.

To Coontz and Henderson, then, women's subordination arose out of a complex process in which kin corporate property made inequality possible, and patrilocal residence rules for those who married led to men's dominance. According to Coontz and Henderson, gender and class inequalities were closely linked: women lost power in the same process that led to some kin groups accumulating more property than others. Ultimately, property became largely owned by individuals rather than collective groups, and wealthy men came to dominate other men as well as women.

This theory of the development of gender inequalities is perhaps more sophisticated than Engels's, and rests upon sounder anthropological evidence. Despite its claims to provide an entirely social explanation, though, it still uses a biological starting-point. It assumes that women's capacities to give birth and suckle children tended to result in a division of labour in which women were largely responsible for cooking and gathering, and men for hunting.

Gender and industrialization

No blanket statements can be made about the position of women in industrializing societies. In different pre-industrial nations the position of women has varied, and has altered in several ways during industrialization. Nevertheless, Britain, as the first nation to industrialize, provides some indication of the effects of industrialization on women in Western industrial societies.

Women and industrialization – a historical perspective

Ann Oakley (1981) has traced the changing status of women in British society from the eve of the Industrial Revolution to the 1970s. She claims that 'the most important and enduring consequence of industrialization for women has been the emergence of the modern role of housewife as "the dominant mature feminine role"'. In this section, we summarize Oakley's view of the emergence of the housewife role.

The family as the unit of production

In pre-industrial Britain, the family was the basic unit of production. Marriage and the family were essential to individuals for economic reasons since all members of the family were involved in production. Agriculture and textiles were the main industries, and women were indispensable to both. In the production of cloth, the husband did the weaving while his wife spun and dyed the yarn. On the farm, women were in charge of dairy produce. Most of the housework – cooking, cleaning, washing, mending and childcare – was performed by unmarried offspring. The housewife role (which involved the domesticity of women and their economic dependence on men) had yet to arrive. Public life concerned with economic activity, and the private life of the family, were not as distinct as they are today.

The factory as the unit of production

During the early stages of industrialization (which Oakley dates from 1750 to 1841), the factory steadily replaced the family as the unit of production. Women were employed in factories where they often continued their traditional work in textiles.

The first major change that affected their status as wage earners was the Factory Acts, beginning in 1819, which gradually restricted child labour. Children became increasingly dependent upon their parents and required care and supervision, a role that fell to women. Oakley argues that 'the increased differentiation of child and adult roles, with the child's growing dependence, heralded the dependence of women in marriage and their restriction to the home'.

Restrictions on women's employment

From 1841 until the outbreak of the First World War in 1914, a combination of pressure from male workers and philanthropic reformers restricted female employment in industry. Women were seen by many male factory workers as a threat to their employment. As early as 1841, committees of male factory workers called for the 'gradual withdrawal of all female labour from the factory'. In 1842, the Mines Act banned the employment of women as miners. In 1851, one in four married women were employed; by 1911 this figure was reduced to one in ten.

Helen Hacker states that with the employment of women as wage earners:

Men were quick to perceive them as a rival group and make use of economic, legal and ideological weapons to eliminate or reduce their competition. They excluded women from the trade unions, made contracts with employers to prevent their hiring women, passed laws restricting the employment of

*married women, caricatured the working woman,
and carried on ceaseless propaganda to return
women to the home and keep them there.*

Hacker, 1972

Victorian ideology, particularly the versions of the
upper and middle classes, stated that a woman's
place was in the home. No less a figure than Queen
Victoria announced: 'Let woman be what God
intended, a helpmate for man, but with totally
different duties and vocations' (quoted in Hudson,
1970). The following quotations from articles in the
Saturday Review illustrate the ideal of womanhood in
mid-Victorian times. In 1859:

*Married life is a woman's profession, and to
this life her training – that of dependence –
is modelled.*

And in 1865:

*No woman can or ought to know very much of the
mass of meanness and wickedness and misery
that is loose in the wide world. She could not
learn it without losing the bloom and freshness
which it is her mission in life to preserve.*

Quoted in Hudson, 1970, pp. 53–4

Oakley claims that during the second half of the
nineteenth century these attitudes began to filter
down to the working class. Thus a combination of
factors which included ideology, the banning of child
labour, and restrictions on the employment of
women, locked the majority of married women into
the mother–housewife role.

The return to paid employment

Oakley states that from 1914 to 1950, there was a
'tendency towards the growing employment of
women coupled with a retention of housewifery as
the primary role expected of all women'. During these
years, women received many legal and political rights
(for example, the vote in 1928) but these had little
effect on the central fact of their lives: the
mother–housewife role.

Oakley concludes that industrialization has had
the following effects on the role of women:

1 the 'separation of men from the daily routines of
domestic life'
2 the 'economic dependence of women and children
on men'
3 the 'isolation of housework and childcare from
other work'.

In twentieth-century British society, the role of
housewife–mother became institutionalized as 'the
primary role for all women'.

These generalizations perhaps became less valid
as the twentieth century progressed. Subsequent
sections will suggest that women have made gains in
terms of increasing their economic independence.
Furthermore, although the housewife-mother role
may continue to be the primary role for many
women, it is not the case for all. The increase in
homeworking and male unemployment may have
had a small effect in reducing the separation of
men from domestic life. Even so, the changes
produced by the Industrial Revolution still exert a
powerful influence.

Gender in contemporary societies – radical feminist perspectives

For radical feminists, patriarchy is the most
important concept for explaining gender inequalities.
Although literally it means 'rule by the father',
radical feminists have used it more broadly to refer
to male dominance in society. From this point of
view, patriarchy consists of the exercise of power by
men over women. Kate Millett was one of the first
radical feminists to use the term and to provide a
detailed explanation of women's exploitation by men.

Kate Millett – radical feminism and sexual politics

In her book, *Sexual Politics*, Kate Millett (1970)
argues that politics is not just an activity confined to
political parties and parliaments, but one which

exists in any 'power-structured relationships,
arrangements whereby one group of persons is
controlled by another'. Such relationships of domination and subordination can exist at work where a
man instructs his female secretary to make a cup of
tea, or in the family when a husband's meal is
cooked by his wife. Political relationships between
men and women exist in all aspects of everyday life.

According to Millett, such relationships are
organized on the basis of patriarchy, a system in
which 'male shall dominate female'. She believes that
patriarchy is 'the most pervasive ideology of our
culture, its most fundamental concept of power'. It is
'more rigorous than class stratification, more
uniform, certainly more enduring'.

Like other radical feminists, Millett suggests that
gender is the primary source of identity for individ-

uals in modern societies. People react to others first and foremost as men and women, rather than in terms of their class membership. It is a rigid system of stratification: sex is ascribed and almost impossible to change.

The basis of patriarchy

Millett identifies no fewer than eight factors which explain the existence of patriarchy:

1 First, she considers the role of biology. Although she admits that it is difficult to be certain about the origins of patriarchy, she attributes some importance to superior male strength. She suggests that this on its own cannot explain female subordination, claiming that there may have been 'pre-patriarchal' societies in which men were not dominant. Furthermore, she points out that in contemporary, technologically advanced societies, strength is itself of little significance. Despite this, she speculates that at some point in history strength may have assumed a degree of importance which accounts for the origins of patriarchy.

To Millett though, it is more significant that in early socialization males are encouraged to be aggressive and females to be passive. Males and females are taught to behave and think in ways which reinforce the biological differences that exist.

2 Millett points to ideological factors in her search for the roots of patriarchy. Again, she attaches importance to socialization. Men are socialized to have a dominant temperament. This provides men with a higher social status, which in turn leads to them filling social roles in which they can exercise mastery over women.

3 Millett also considers sociological factors to be important. She claims that the family is the main institution of patriarchy, although men also exercise power in the wider society and through the state. Within the family it is the need for children to be legitimate, to have a socially recognized father, that gives men a particularly dominant position. Mothers and children come to rely for their social status on the position of husbands and fathers in society.

The family therefore plays an important part in maintaining patriarchy across generations, socializing children into having different temperaments and leading them to expect and accept different roles in later life.

4 Millett discusses the relationship between class and subordination. She believes that women have a caste-like status that operates independently of social class. Even women from higher-class backgrounds are subordinate to men. She believes that the economic dependency of women on men almost places them outside the class system. Romantic love appears to place males and females on an equal footing but in truth it merely 'obscures the realities of female status, and the burden of

economic dependency'. Women's inferior status is reinforced and underlined by the ability of men to gain psychological ascendancy through the use of physical or verbal bullying and obscene or hostile remarks.

5 Millett discusses the educational factors which handicap women and she expands upon the question of women's economic dependency. In traditional patriarchies, women lacked legal standing and were not able to own property or to earn their own living. In today's society, Millett accepts that women can and do take paid work, but believes that their work is usually menial, badly paid and lacking in status.

Furthermore, in societies in which women retain their roles as mothers and housewives, much of that work is unpaid. She sees women as being essentially a reserve labour force who are made use of when they are needed (for example, in wartime) but are discarded when not required.

Economic inequalities are reinforced by educational ones. Women tend to study the humanities which, according to Millett, have a lower status than sciences. As a result, women lack knowledge and this restricts their power. For example, women often do not understand technology so they cannot compete on equal terms with men to earn a living.

6 Millett argues that men also retain patriarchal power through myth and religion. Religion is used as a way of legitimating masculine dominance. As Millett puts it, 'patriarchy has God on its side'. To illustrate this point she notes that the Christian religion portrays Eve as an afterthought produced from Adam's spare rib, while the origins of human suffering are held to have their source in her actions.

7 An additional source of men's power is psychology. Patriarchal ideology is 'interiorized' by women because of all the above factors. Women develop a passive temperament and a sense of inferiority. This is further reinforced by sexist European languages which use words such as 'mankind' to refer to humanity. Media images of women also play their part, but to Millett the greatest psychological weapon available to men is the length of time they have enjoyed worldwide dominance. Women have simply come to take men's dominance for granted.

8 Millett identifies physical force as the final source of male domination. Despite the extent of men's ideological power, Millett believes that patriarchy is ultimately backed up by force. She points to many examples of the use of violence against women, such as the stoning to death of adulteresses in Muslim countries, and 'the crippling deformity of footbinding in China, the lifelong ignomiy of the Veil in Islam'. In modern Western societies, women are also the victims of violence. Millett does not admit that women are inevitably physically weaker, but 'physical and emotional training' make it very difficult for women to resist the force used against

them by individual men. Rape and other forms of sexual violence are ever-present possibilities and ways in which all women are intimidated by all men.

Criticisms of Millett

Millett made an important contribution towards explaining the disadvantaged position of women within society. However, her work has been criticized by socialist and Marxist feminists. They have identified three main weaknesses in her theory of sexual politics:

1 Sheila Rowbotham (1979) argues that patriarchy is too sweeping a category. Because Millett regards all societies as patriarchal, she fails to explain the particular circumstances which have produced male domination in its current forms. According to Rowbotham, describing all societies as patriarchal implies that male domination has some universal cause which stems from the biology of women and the fact that they bear and rear children. In Rowbotham's words, it 'ignores the multiplicity of ways in which societies have defined gender'.

2 Rowbotham questions the assumption implied in the use of the term 'patriarchy' – that all men exploit all women. She says that 'patriarchy cannot explain why genuine feelings of love and friendship are possible between men and women, and boys and girls, or why people have acted together in popular movements'.

3 Another criticism of Millett, and radical feminists in general, is that they ignore the material basis of much of the oppression of women. Robert McDonough and Rachel Harrison (1978) criticize Millett for ignoring the possibility that women's lack of wealth and economic power is the most important factor determining their disadvantages. To Marxist and socialist feminists, it is capitalism rather than patriarchy that explains women's oppression in modern societies.

Gender in contemporary societies – Marxist and socialist perspectives

Marx and Engels and women under communism

Apart from explaining the origins of inequality between men and women, Engels also tried to foresee how women's position in society would change as capitalism developed (Engels, 1972). Engels believed that economic factors caused women's subservience to men, and only economic changes could lead to their liberation. He stated that 'the predominance of the man in marriage is simply a consequence of his economic predominance and will vanish with it automatically'. Men enjoyed greater power than women because it was men who owned the means of production, or who earned a wage outside the home.

However, Marx and Engels believed that capitalism would eventually lead to some reduction in inequalities between men and women. They argued that the demand for female wage labour would raise the status and power of proletarian women within the family.

Marx believed that, despite its many evils, capitalist industry 'creates a new economic foundation for a higher form of the family and of relations between the sexes'. Female employment would largely free women from economic dependence upon their husbands and so from male dominance within the family. Engels took a similar view maintaining that with female wage labour:

the last remnants of male domination in the proletarian home have lost all foundation – except, perhaps, for some of the brutality towards women which became firmly rooted with the establishment of monogamy.

Engels, 1972

However, the bourgeois wife in capitalist society was still required to produce heirs and so forced to submit to male control.

Although women entered the labour force in increasing numbers in the twentieth century, many contemporary Marxist and socialist feminists deny that this led to the changes anticipated by Marx and Engels. As we will indicate in a later section, women continue to be financially disadvantaged compared to men, even when they take paid employment. They tend to get lower wages and lower-status jobs than men (see pp. 163–8). Furthermore, they still seem to have less power than men within the family. (Further details can be found in Chapter 8.)

Gender under communism

Engels believed that true equality between men and women would arrive with the establishment of communism when the means of production would be communally owned. Engels predicted that the communal ownership of the means of production would be accompanied by the socialization of housework and childcare. Sexual inequality would end. Gender roles would disappear.

Evidence from former communist countries suggests that Engels was wrong. In a review of studies of the USSR, Nickie Charles (1993) found that women did make significant progress under communism. In 1991, just before the USSR broke up with the collapse of communism, women made up a majority of the Soviet workforce – 51 per cent. Under communism women were guaranteed the right to work, and laws gave them the right to equal pay for equal work. Women also had the right to paid maternity leave and breaks during working hours to feed their babies.

However, although Charles believes that women made significant gains under communism, she does not think that they achieved full equality. In 1991, average wages for women were only about two-thirds of those for men. Laws made it easier for women to work and have children, but this also meant that 'childcare was viewed as a purely female concern'. As in Western capitalist societies, women continued to have most of the responsibility for childcare and housework even when they had full-time employment outside the home.

If women's progress under communism in the USSR was limited, early evidence suggests that the move towards a market economy and a Western-style democracy has undermined some of the gains that were made. Charles found that in 1992 after the withdrawal of the right to employment, women had twice the redundancy rate of men. In the light of rising unemployment, Charles thought it likely that women would 'be encouraged to return to the home either full or part-time' and state childcare services would be withdrawn.

Nickie Charles found that by the late 1980s women had high rates of participation in the East European labour market. Women made up 50 per cent of the workforce in East Germany and nearly 50 per cent in Czechoslovakia. In Poland and Hungary they made up about 44 per cent of the workforce. Charles argues that despite these figures women remained disadvantaged because of the persistence of a familial ideology 'which defined women primarily as wives and mothers'.

Such examples suggest that societies claiming to be communist had made inroads into reducing gender inequality, but did not succeed in coming anywhere near to eradicating it. Nickie Charles argues that communist states have made much more effort than capitalist states to reduce the burden of childcare and housework on women, but 'in both types of society women are to be found in the lowest paid and least skilled jobs'. This suggests that factors other than the economic system are at least partly responsible for gender inequalities.

Contemporary Marxist feminism

Some Marxist feminists have argued that women's position in society primarily benefits capitalism and capitalists rather than men. Margaret Benston (1972) argues that capitalism benefits from a large reserve labour force of women 'to keep wages down and profits up'. (For a discussion of the reserve army of labour theory see pp. 170–1.) In their roles as secondary breadwinners, married women provide a source of cheap and easily exploitable labour. Because women have been socialized to comply and submit, they form a docile labour force that can be readily manipulated and easily fired when not required.

Compared to male workers, women are less likely to join unions, to go on strike or take other forms of militant action against employers. Even when women join unions, they often find themselves in male-dominated organizations where, according to Barron and Norris (1976), men 'often do not share the interests or outlook of their fellow female unionists'. To some degree, sexist ideology splits the working class and in doing so serves the interests of capital. It divides workers along sex lines and thereby makes them easier to control.

Some Marxists also believe that women benefit capitalists and the capitalist system in their capacities as mothers and housewives by reproducing labour power at no cost to employers. (We discuss this in more detail in Chapter 8.)

Criticisms of Marxist feminism

There are a number of difficulties with Marxist approaches that explain gender inequalities in terms of how they benefit capitalism. Some Marxist feminists claim that such explanations ignore many of the questions raised by feminists. In terms of the Marxist theory, women appear insignificant: they sit on the sidelines of the grand struggle between capital and labour. Marxists may explain capitalism, but this does not explain patriarchy.

Heidi Hartmann (1981) compares the situation to a marriage in which the husband represents Marxism, the wife represents feminism, and it is the husband who has all the power. She says: 'the "marriage" of Marxism and feminism has been like the marriage of husband and wife depicted in English common law: Marxism and feminism are one, and that one is Marxism'.

She does not believe that Marxism on its own can explain gender inequalities because it is 'sex-blind'. In other words, Marxism can explain why capitalists exploit workers, but not why men exploit women. For example, it might be possible to explain in Marxist terms how it benefits capitalism for housework and childcare to be carried out free of charge, but not why women in particular should be responsible for these tasks. Capitalism would benefit as much from househusbands as housewives.

Michelle Barrett (1980, 1984) also attacks Marxist theories which see capitalism alone benefiting from the exploitation of women. She points out that working-class men can benefit from the labour of their wives as well as capitalists. Furthermore, there may be cheaper alternative ways of reproducing labour power than the use of the nuclear family unit with unpaid housewives. It might be less expensive for capitalist countries to use migrant workers. They could be accommodated in cheap barracks. Furthermore, their early socialization has already been carried out in another country at no cost to capitalists.

Both Hartmann and Barrett accept that Marxism can play an important part in explaining gender inequalities; however, they believe that feminism must be fully incorporated into any adequate theory. Both these writers attempt to cement a 'marriage' between Marxist and feminist theory.

The 'marriage' of Marxism and feminism

In her article 'The unhappy marriage of Marxism and feminism', Heidi Hartmann (1981) claims that Marxism makes an important contribution to explaining Western industrial societies, including 'the structure of production, the generation of a particular occupational structure, and the nature of the dominant ideology'. It explains the creation of particular jobs, but to Hartmann it is 'indifferent' to who fills them. Thus it does not explain why women have lower-paid and lower-status employment outside the home, nor why they continue to carry the main burden of domestic responsibilities, even when they are working as well.

Following radical feminists, Hartmann argues that patriarchy provides the key to explaining the sexual division of labour. Unlike radical feminists though, she believes that patriarchy has a 'material' base which is not directly related to biological differences between men and women. Men maintain their material control over women by controlling women's labour power. They largely deny access for working women to jobs that pay a living wage. They force women into financial dependence on husbands and thereby control the labour of women in their capacities as housewives and mothers. Because of men's dominance within the family they also control women's bodies and sexuality. Women who are married become almost their husbands' property.

Hartmann believes that capitalism and patriarchy are very closely connected – she describes them as 'intertwined' – but she does not believe that the interests of men as a group and capitalists as a group are identical. For example, ruling-class men may benefit from increasing numbers of women entering the labour force, whereas working-class men may prefer their wives to stay at home to perform personal services for them.

Furthermore, Hartmann denies that capitalism is all-powerful: the capitalist system has to be flexible, and the need for social control may sometimes become more important than the need to produce the maximum possible profit. In this context, Hartmann claims that historically there has been an accommodation between patriarchy and capitalism. They have learned to co-exist in a partnership that fundamentally damages neither partner.

Hartmann believes that in the nineteenth century capitalism gave way to pressure from men about female employment. Male-dominated trade unions in Britain persuaded the state to pass legislation limiting the degree to which women were permitted to participate in paid employment. Although capitalists may not have accepted this situation as ideal, it did have certain advantages for them. The family wage, paid to men and sufficiently large for them to be able to support their wives and children, led to some increase in the wage bill, but ensured that when women did work they could be paid very low wages. It also placated men since their power over women was maintained, and as such it reduced the likelihood of class-conscious action by male workers.

Hartmann accepts that the increasing participation of women in work today has made them slightly less dependent on men. There are more opportunities for women to become independent. Nevertheless, she believes that the persistence of relatively low wage levels for women prevents patriarchy from becoming seriously undermined. She claims 'women's wages allow very few women to support themselves independently and adequately'.

In *Women's Oppression Today*, Michelle Barrett (1980) adopts a similar approach. Although she considers herself a Marxist she believes that it is necessary to go beyond Marxism in order to explain women's oppression. Like Hartmann, she sees the origins of women's oppression today as lying in the nineteenth century, and she argues that a coalition of men and capitalists led to women being excluded from work and being forced to take on a primarily domestic role.

In this process women's oppression became lodged in what she calls the family-household system: members of the household came to rely on the wages of a few adults (primarily men) while all family members relied on the unpaid housework mainly carried out by women. In the process an ideology was developed in which this division of labour in the family came to be accepted as normal and natural.

In the twentieth century, the family-household system became an entrenched part of capitalism. Although there is no inevitable reason why capitalism needs women (as opposed to men, for example) to do the unpaid housework, the capitalist class does benefit politically from this division of labour. According to Barrett, the working class is divided by the family-household system; husbands and wives, men and women, fight each other instead of uniting to fight capitalism.

Biology, capitalism and the oppression of women

Both Hartmann and Barrett move away from seeing gender inequalities as being an inevitable product of capitalism. Both accept that an extra dimension needs to be added to Marxist analysis since Marxism is sex-blind. However, according to some critics, neither has succeeded in unifying Marxism and feminism.

Johanna Brenner and Maria Ramas (1984) believe that Barrett has adopted a dual-system approach, in which class inequalities are explained in terms of capitalism, and gender inequalities are explained in terms of patriarchal ideology, but the two approaches are not combined. They do not believe that Barrett has demonstrated a material need for men and women to have different roles within capitalism. According to Brenner and Ramas, there is a material basis for women's oppression under capitalism, and it is to be found in women's biology.

In pre-capitalist times women were able to combine the demands of childbirth, breastfeeding, and childcare with work, because work was largely based around the home. Furthermore, families could be flexible about when they carried out their work.

With the introduction of factory production, though, work and home became separated, and it also became uneconomic to allow breaks from work to allow women to breastfeed their children. This would have entailed interruptions in production which would have meant that expensive machinery was not fully used.

Furthermore, capitalists were unwilling to provide for expensive maternity leave or childcare facilities at work. With the long hours of work demanded in early factories, the high costs of any domestic help, and the lack of sterilization techniques which would have made bottlefeeding a viable proposition, there was little option but for mothers to withdraw from work.

Brenner and Ramas admit that many of the conditions that originally forced mothers into domestic roles have now changed. Bottlefeeding is now a safe option for babies; there is some provision for maternity leave; hours of work are shorter; it is easier to afford help with childcare; and in any case women are on average having fewer children. However, most women still get paid lower wages than most men, and for most working-class families there are likely to be real financial benefits if the woman rather than the man withdraws from work.

To Brenner and Ramas the sexual division of labour was at least in part produced by the rational choices taken by members of the working class. Because, however, the situation has now changed, there is considerable potential for greater gender equality. If that potential is to be realized, though, it will require a political struggle in which more state nurseries are demanded. It is still cheaper for capitalism if the family rather than the state pays for childcare.

Michelle Barrett (1984) remains unconvinced by the arguments of Brenner and Ramas. She believes that ideology played a greater role in producing the family-household system than biology.

Marxist feminists continue to disagree amongst themselves as well as with other feminists, and they have yet to provide a conclusive explanation for gender inequalities. Marxism and feminism remain something of an unhappy marriage, but the writers in this section have begun to explore how best to avoid separation, or even divorce, of the two perspectives.

Sylvia Walby – *Theorizing Patriarchy*

Sylvia Walby has developed an approach to understanding gender in contemporary societies which does not fit into any of the types of feminism described in earlier sections. Indeed, she starts her 1990 book, *Theorizing Patriarchy* (1990), by pointing out the main criticisms that have been made of other approaches.

Criticisms of existing perspectives

1 Radical feminism has been criticized for 'a false universalism which cannot understand historical change or take sufficient account of divisions between women based on ethnicity and class'.

2 Marxist feminism has been criticized for concentrating on gender inequalities under

capitalism and therefore being unable to explain the exploitation of women in non-capitalist societies.

3 Liberal feminism has been seen as lacking 'an account of the overall social structuring of gender inequality'. Its approach can provide no more than partial explanations. For example, it offers no explanation of how gender inequalities first developed.

4 Walby also criticizes what she calls dual-systems theory. By this she means approaches such as that of Hartmann (see pp. 149–50) which explain women's exploitation in terms of two separate systems of capitalism and patriarchy. Walby criticizes Hartmann for underestimating the amount of tension between capitalism and patriarchy and for failing to take account of aspects of patriarchy such as violence and sexuality.

Walby tries to improve on other perspectives by incorporating their strengths into her own theory while avoiding their weaknesses.

Patriarchy

To Walby, the concept of patriarchy must remain central to a feminist understanding of society. She says that '"patriarchy" is indispensable for an analysis of gender inequality' (Walby, 1990). However, her definition of patriarchy is different from that of other feminists. She argues that there are six patriarchal structures which restrict women and help to maintain male domination. These are:

1 paid work
2 patriarchal relations within the household
3 patriarchal culture
4 sexuality
5 male violence towards women
6 the state.

Each of these structures has some independence from the others, but they can also affect one another, reinforcing or weakening patriarchy in a different structure. Each structure is reproduced or changed by the actions of men and women, but the existence of the structure also restricts the choices that humans, particularly women, can make.

Walby claims that patriarchy is not a fixed and unchanging feature of society (as some radical feminists seem to imply) but both its strength and its form change over time. For example, she believes that patriarchy in Britain during the last two centuries has become slightly less strong and has changed from private patriarchy to public patriarchy. (We will examine the idea of a shift from private to public patriarchy at the end of this section.)

Walby's concept of patriarchy does not regard relations between males and females as the only source of inequality. She acknowledges that there are also 'divisions between women based on ethnicity and class', and she discusses the ways that patriarchy, racism and capitalism interact.

We will now examine in detail how Walby uses her concept of patriarchy to explain gender inequalities.

The structures of patriarchy

As we saw earlier, Walby identifies six structures of patriarchy. We will examine each of these in turn before looking at Walby's overall conclusions about changes in patriarchy.

Paid employment

Walby believes that paid employment has been and remains a key structure in creating disadvantages for women. In nineteenth-century Britain, regulations excluded women from whole areas of work altogether. Male-dominated trade unions and the state ensured that women's opportunities were severely restricted. In the twentieth century, women, and particularly married women, were able to take employment, but not on equal terms with men. In recent years, 'the degree of inequality between men and women in terms of pay, conditions, and access to well-rewarded occupations has declined only very slightly'. The gap between men's and women's wages has only been reduced a little and women continue to predominate in low-paid, part-time employment. In theory, the state has supported greater equality between men and women in the labour market by passing the Equal Pay (1970) and Sex Discrimination (1975) Acts, but in practice such policies are not 'pursued with vigour'.

Walby believes that the labour market has more influence than the family on women's decisions about whether to take paid employment. When women decide not to seek paid work they do so more because of the restricted opportunities open to them than because of cultural values that suggest that mothers and wives should stay at home. According to Walby, when opportunities have been presented to women in the labour market, they have taken advantage of them. For example, the removal of the bar on married women working in some occupations during the Second World War led to a big increase in the numbers of married women in paid work. Feminist struggles and capitalism's demands for cheap labour have created a big increase in women's employment but have failed to prevent exploitation at work. Some women continue to stay at home because the wages they are likely to earn are too low to make paid work worthwhile.

Household production

According to Walby, households sometimes involve distinctive patriarchal relations of production. Individual men directly exploit women by gaining benefits from women's unpaid labour, for example in the home. In the nineteenth century, many women were forced into patriarchal relations of production through their exclusion from the labour market. In the twentieth century, exploitation within this structure was reduced, at least for some women. Women now spend more time in paid work, and the relaxation of divorce laws means that women 'are no longer necessarily bound to an individual husband who expropriates their labour till death does them part'.

For some groups of women, life within households may seem like an escape from exploitation. For example, Walby points out that some Black feminists believe that the family can be 'a site of resistance to racism', and life within the family may be less exploitative for black women than life in the labour market where they tend to receive the least desirable jobs.

However, Walby does not see exploitation of women in the household as having disappeared. Women who are housewives spend as many hours on domestic labour as they did decades ago. Women with children who leave their husbands are disadvantaged in a 'patriarchally structured labour market'. They are unlikely to find a job with reasonable pay so that '"Liberation" from marriage is then usually a movement into poverty.' Some women continue to allow themselves to be exploited by their husbands because the alternatives are so unappealing. Marriage may offer personal survival and greater material comfort for many women when most women have such poorly paid work, but the short-term benefits of marriage for particular women undermine women's 'long-term interests in the eradication of the oppression which exists within the family'. This oppression is sometimes manifested in terms of violence and sexuality, which we will examine shortly.

Culture

Walby believes that the culture of Western societies has consistently distinguished between men and women and has expected different types of behaviour from them. She says that 'while variable across class, ethnicity and age in particular, femininity is consistently differentiated from masculinity over the last century and a half'. However, although the differentiation has remained strong, the characteristics which are seen as making a woman feminine have changed significantly.

In the nineteenth century, women were thought more feminine if they confined their activities to the domestic sphere and did not take paid work. Walby claims that 'the key sign of femininity today ... is sexual attractiveness to men'. Furthermore, 'it is no longer merely the femininity of young single women that is defined in this way, but increasingly that of older women as well'. Sexual attractiveness was also important in Victorian times, but less important than today. It was also 'relatively undercover' compared to contemporary culture.

Escaping from the confinement of domesticity has created greater freedom for women, but the new emphasis on sexuality is not without its costs. Pornography, in particular, increases the freedom of men while threatening the freedom of women. To Walby, 'the male gaze, not that of women, is the viewpoint of pornography', and pornography encourages the degradation of women by men and sometimes promotes sexual violence.

Sexuality

Walby argues that 'heterosexuality constitutes a patriarchal structure'. However, she accepts that the nature of this patriarchal structure has undergone important changes.

In the nineteenth century, women's sexuality was subject to strict control and was largely confined by a 'plethora of practices' to sex within marriage. Women's sexuality was therefore 'directed to one patriarchal agent for a lifetime', although the result was to reduce women's 'sexual interest in anything, including marriage'.

In the twentieth century it became easier for women to be sexually active. Improved contraception reduced the risk of unwanted pregnancy, and the increasing availability of divorce created the possibility of exchanging 'an inadequate husband for a new one'. Walby refers to a study by Lawson and Sampson conducted in 1988 which found that of women marrying in the 1960s, 75 per cent had remained faithful to their husbands during the first ten years of marriage whereas only 46 per cent of those who had married since the 1970s had done so. The study also found that for those married in the earlier period men had been more likely to be unfaithful, whereas for those married in the later period more women had had affairs.

Women themselves played an important part in fighting for greater sexual freedom in campaigning for birth control, abortion and easier divorce, but sexual liberalization has not worked to their advantage in every respect. For example, Walby says 'the sexual double standard is still alive and well'. Young women who are sexually active are condemned by males as 'slags'; those who are not are seen as 'drags'. On the other hand, males with many sexual conquests are admired for their supposed virility.

There is more pressure on women today to be heterosexually active and to 'service' males by marrying or cohabiting with them. Thus heterosexuality remains patriarchal, even though women have made some genuine gains.

Violence

Walby starts her discussion of violence by noting that 'male violence against women includes rape, sexual assault, wife beating, workplace sexual harassment and child sexual abuse'. Like other feminists, she sees violence as a form of power over women. The use of violence, or the threat of violence, helps to keep women in their place and discourages them from challenging patriarchy.

According to Walby, the lack of reliable evidence from the past makes it impossible to determine whether the amount of violence against women by men has increased or decreased. She does believe, however, that it is possible to detect changes in the response to male violence. The state, and in particular the police, have become more willing to take action against the worst offenders. Nevertheless, action against violent husbands is still infrequent and some women continue to be subject to male violence while other women continue to fear it.

The state

State policies relating to gender have changed considerably since the nineteenth century. For example there has been:

> the cessation of legal backing to exclusionary practices in employment; the increased ease of divorce and financial provision for non-wage earners; the ending of state backing to exclusionary practices in education and the removal of most forms of censorship of pornography; the decriminalization of contraception and abortion under most circumstances; and minor changes in the law making it marginally easier for a woman to leave a violent man.
>
> Walby, 1990

Most of these changes have been gains for women but, to Walby, 'the state is still patriarchal as well as capitalist and racist'. State policies are no longer directed at confining women to the private sphere of the home, yet there has been little real attempt to improve women's position in the public sphere. Women still receive lower wages than men, and equal opportunities legislation is not often enforced. Women in one-parent families receive little state benefit and women have been harmed by the greater availability of pornography. While the state itself is not so obviously as patriarchal as it used to be, it still does little to protect women from patriarchal power in society.

From private to public patriarchy

As we have seen in each of the preceding sections on the different structures of patriarchy, Walby recognizes that important changes have taken place in every aspect of gender relations. Liberal feminists tend to see these changes as progress. Radical feminists tend to argue that little has changed and patriarchal domination remains firmly intact. Marxists usually claim that industrialization and the advent of capitalism led to a deterioration in the position of women and since the Industrial Revolution little has improved.

Walby does not accept any of these general views, arguing instead that the nature of patriarchy has changed. To her, different aspects of patriarchy are interrelated and together they produce a system of patriarchy and it is this system which has changed.

In the nineteenth century, patriarchy was predominantly private; in the twentieth century, it became public. Table 3.1 summarizes how Walby characterizes this change.

Private patriarchy

In private patriarchy an individual patriarch, the male head of household, controls women 'individually and directly in the relatively private sphere of the home'. It is 'the man in his position as husband or father who is the direct oppressor and beneficiary, individually and directly, of the subordination of women'. Women remain oppressed because they are prevented from entering the public sphere in areas such as employment and politics.

Although household production was the most important structure of private patriarchy, it was backed up by the other patriarchal structures which excluded women.

The shift away from private patriarchy

The shift away from private patriarchy was in part a consequence of first wave feminism. Between 1850 and 1930, women in the USA and Britain campaigned for much more than just voting rights. They also sought:

> the containment of predatory male sexual behaviour (Christabel Pankhurst's slogan was 'Votes for women, chastity for men'), access to employment, training and education, reform of the legal status of married women so they could own property, for divorce and legal separation at the woman's behest as well as that of the husband ... for the collective rather than private organization of meal preparation.
>
> Walby, 1990

These campaigns took place 'against the background of an expanding capitalist economy' and capitalists

Table 3.1	Private and public patriarchy		
Form of patriarchy		**Private**	**Public**
Dominant structure		Household production	Employment/State
Wider patriarchal structures		Employment	Household production
		State	Sexuality
		Sexuality	Violence
		Violence	Culture
		Culture	
Period		Nineteenth century	Twentieth century
Mode of expropriation		Individual	Collective
Patriarchal strategy		Exclusionary	Segregationist

Source: S. Walby (1990) *Theorizing Patriarchy*, Blackwell, Oxford, p. 24

requiring a larger workforce. There was pressure from male trade unionists to continue to exclude women from employment so that they could not compete for men's jobs.

The result was a series of compromises in which women gained greater access to the public sphere, capitalists were able to employ more women in their enterprises, and male workers ensured that women were restricted in the employment opportunities open to them. (We will discuss Walby's ideas on male trade unionism and female employment later in the chapter. See pp. 172–3 for further details.) These compromises led to the emergence of a new public form of patriarchy.

Public patriarchy 'is a form in which women have access to both public and private arenas. They are not barred from the public arenas, but are nonetheless subordinated within them'. In the public sphere, women tend to be segregated into certain jobs which are lower-paid and are given a lower status than men's jobs. The state and employment become the dominant structures of patriarchy but the other structures remain important. Women are no longer exploited so much by individual patriarchs but instead are exploited collectively by men in general through their subordination in public arenas. As Walby puts it, 'women are no longer restricted to the domestic hearth, but have the whole society in which to roam and be exploited'.

Variations in patriarchy

Walby believes that there has been some reduction in patriarchal exploitation in certain areas as a consequence of the change from private to public patriarchy. The extent of any such reduction varies between groups of women, however, as does the balance between public and private elements of

patriarchy. For example, Walby believes that Muslim women are more restricted by family structures than other women, and are therefore more subject to private patriarchy than other groups. Afro-Caribbean women, on the other hand, are more likely to have paid employment and to head their own families than other ethnic groups, and are therefore more subject to public patriarchy.

Walby's arguments are largely confined to an examination of Britain and the USA, but she does give some indications of how these compare to other countries. She suggests that the state has played a more important role in public patriarchy in some countries, whereas in others the labour market has been more important. In the former communist countries of Eastern Europe, for instance, it was the state which was predominant. In the USA, the most capitalist and free-market of Western countries, employment has been of greatest importance. In Western Europe, with more developed welfare states, the state and employment have played a more equal role in public patriarchy.

Gender Transformations

In *Gender Transformations* (1997), Walby reviews changes in patriarchy in the 1990s. Although she discovers plenty of evidence that patriarchal structures remain in place in Britain, she also finds evidence of important changes. In particular, she claims that there is evidence of a generational difference between older and younger women. Older women tend to be restricted by the constraints of private patriarchy, which was the dominant form of patriarchy in their early lives. They are likely to have few qualifications and therefore have limited opportunities in the labour market. They are more likely than younger women to be dependent upon a male partner for their material well-being. They are particularly vulnerable with the increasing divorce rate which makes reliance upon a male partner problematic.

Younger women, on the other hand, have benefited from some of the changes that have taken place. Using official figures, Walby notes that women made up 49.6 per cent of employees in Britain in 1995. She also points out that female school leavers now have more qualifications than their male counterparts. Women are also catching up male peers in higher education. In other areas, women of all generations have made some gains, although the biggest beneficiaries have mostly been younger women. For example, the police have become more willing to intervene in dealing with male violence against women. There is more awareness of sexual harassment at work, and increasingly employers have policies to deal with it. Furthermore, 'there has been a decline in the discourse and practice of confining sexuality to marriage and an increase in its public presence'. Subjects such as AIDS and the affairs of the royal family have made the discussion of sexuality more open and, according to research, women are becoming more likely to engage in extra-marital sexual relationships. Women are also increasingly entering the public sphere by taking part in political and social movements such as environmental movements, the refuge movement for victims of domestic violence, and protest movements such as that against the poll tax in spring 1990.

However, the impact of such gains is tempered both by a polarization between different groups of women and by areas in which women have made little progress. Well-qualified young women have generally been able to take advantage of new opportunities in the labour market. The same is not true of most of those with few qualifications. The move towards a post-Fordist (see Chapter 10 for a discussion of post-Fordism) and 'flexible' labour market in Britain has relied upon the employment of large numbers of young women in low-paid and insecure jobs. Women have become more independent of men (74 per cent of women in Britain were married in 1979, but just 57 per cent in 1994), but conversely this has made some low-paid women poorer. The increasing number of female single-parents are particularly disadvantaged because childcare responsibilities greatly restrict their opportunities to do paid work.

In most of the most powerful positions in public life, women continue to be seriously under-represented. Walby notes that in 1992 only 9.2 per cent of MPs were women, there were no women Chief Constables until the 1990s, and in 1994 only

one in 25 High Court judges was a woman. In 1996, there was only one woman among 50 British ambassadors or heads of overseas missions. There are very few women heading major corporations or public bodies.

For these reasons, Walby argues that a 'system of patriarchy' continues to exist, although 'gender regimes' affect groups of women differently. She argues that:

> different forms of gender regime coexist as a result of the diversity in gender relations consequent upon age, class, ethnicity and region. As a result of the recent changes, older women will be more likely than younger women to be involved in a more domestic gender regime. Women whose own occupations place them in higher socio-economic groups are more likely to be involved in a more public form of patriarchy. Women of Pakistani and Bangladeshi descent are more likely to be in a domestic form and Black Caribbean women more likely to be in a more private form than white women. There are complex interactions between these different forms of gender regime, as well as between gender, ethnicity and class.
>
> Walby, 1997, p. 6

Evaluation of Walby

Walby's theory of patriarchy incorporates the insights of many different feminists. Like Marxist and socialist feminists, she acknowledges the importance of economic inequality. Like many radical feminists, she discusses how factors such as violence, sexuality and culture can maintain patriarchy. Like liberal feminists, she attaches some importance to changes in the law and accepts that in some respects women's campaigns have won important citizenship rights. Walby recognizes that patriarchy has undergone significant changes and she attempts to explain and understand these changes through the use of the concepts of private and public patriarchy.

Nevertheless, her work has been criticized. Floya Anthias and Nira Yuval-Davis (1992) criticize her for using what they see as a three-systems approach. According to them, Walby treats gender, 'race' and class as separate systems which interact with one another. Anthias and Yuval-Davis believe that patriarchy, capitalism and racism are all part of one system which advantages some groups and disadvantages others.

Jackie Stacey (1993) praises Walby for 'an all-encompassing account of the systematic oppression of women in society' and for showing an awareness of historical changes in the position of women. However, she criticizes her for her use of the concept of structure. Stacey says that 'some structures are more clearly conceptualised than others (for example, paid employment and culture)'. In the case of some other structures, Walby does not make such a good case for the existence of relatively fixed relationships which contain women. Stacey believes that Walby neglects 'any consideration of identity and lived experience' by focusing on a structuralist analysis which 'fails to explain how people negotiate such a system'.

To Stacey, good feminist sociology pays more attention to the subjective states of women and to how women come to terms with or resist the oppression of which they are a victim. Similar reservations are expressed by Anna Pollert (1996) who questions the usefulness of the whole concept of patriarchy

Anna Pollert – *The Poverty of Patriarchy*

Anna Pollert (1996) has criticized the use of the term patriarchy by feminists in general, and by Sylvia Walby in particular. She notes that feminists have attacked the use of male 'grand narratives', such as the Marxist analysis of capitalism and the whole idea of progress, but have stubbornly stuck to using the idea of patriarchy. Pollert, on the other hand, believes that the concept is of little use and tends to hold back feminist analysis rather than helping it to develop.

Pollert's central point is that the idea of patriarchy often involves the use of a circular argument. Patriarchy is used both as a description of inequalities between men and women and as an explanation of those inequalities. She uses the example of Heidi Hartmann's work (see pp. 149–50). According to Pollert, Hartmann sees patriarchy as based upon male control over female labour power. In doing so, she fails to explain how men come to control women's labour power in the first place. Hartmann argues that the control comes from the exclusion of women from independent work and control over their work, but this can only be explained in terms of the control over women's labour power which it is supposed to be explaining. Thus Pollert believes that Hartmann is arguing, in effect, that men have control over women because men have control over women. Such circular arguments are typical of most theories that employ the concept of patriarchy.

Other theories, such as that of Walby, can be criticized because they claim, but fail to establish, that patriarchy is a system which forms part of society. Thus Walby sees patriarchy as a system which is sustained by sub-structures such as violence, sexuality, culture, and so on. Pollert does not believe that patriarchy is a system or a structure in the same sense as capitalism. She says that 'there is no intrinsic motor or dynamic within "patriarchy" which can explain its self-perpetuation. Capitalism, on the other hand, does have such an internal dynamic: the self-expansion of capital – profit - which drives the system.' Capitalists are constrained to pursue profit. If they fail to do so, they will go out of business. Gender systems are not constrained in the same way. Men and women can treat each other differently, or even change sex, 'without social production grinding to a halt, or abolishing all gender relations between men and women'.

Pollert believes that theories such as those of Walby lose sight of 'agency'. That is, they neglect the choices made by individual actors as they reproduce or resist existing sets of social relationships. She describes Walby's division of patriarchy into six structures as 'an arbitrary exercise' which 'leads to the static perspective of arbitrating parts in which agency is even more absent than before.

Pollert believes that Walby has not succeeded in breaking free from dual systems theory, seeing capitalism and patriarchy as two separate if linked systems. Pollert argues they are not separate at all. She says 'class relations are infused with gender, race and other modes of social differentiation from the start'. Because class and gender are intertwined it is inappropriate to use structural analysis to understand how they relate to one another. Instead, it is necessary to carry out detailed empirical studies of how they and other social differences relate to each other in particular contexts.

Pollert is in favour of using a materialist analysis which stresses economic inequalities and favours detailed qualitative research. She herself has conducted research of this type with women working in a hosiery factory (Pollert, 1981). However, as Pollert acknowledges, this is not the only way in which sociologists have reacted to criticisms of structural concepts such as patriarchy. Postmodernists too have tended to reject any overarching theory of gender in favour of describing the viewpoints of different women. Pollert rejects postmodernism because it uses obscure language which is hard for ordinary people to understand. It is also relativistic, that is it records the viewpoints of different women but is unwilling to say that any viewpoint is stronger than any other. It therefore loses any sense of trying to change and improve the lives of women.

Notwithstanding Pollert's criticisms, postmodernism has become a major influence on the theories of gender which we will now consider.

Postmodernism, sex and gender

Barrett and Phillips –
Destabilizing Theory

Pollert notes that some sociologists who have rejected structural concepts such as patriarchy have turned to postmodernism as an alternative to detailed empirical studies (Pollert, 1996). As we have seen (p. 156), Pollert herself rejects postmodernism, but in recent years it has become an increasingly influential approach to the study of sex and gender.

Michèlle Barrett and Anne Phillips (1992) argue that new feminisms have developed because of a dissatisfaction with the general theories characteristic of traditional male-dominated social science. Feminism has always been suspicious of theories developed by men, but in the past liberal and socialist feminists have embraced aspects of male theories. Recently, however, there has been, 'a sweeping attack on the falsely universalizing, over-generalizing and over-ambitious models of liberalism, humanism, and Marxism. Many feminists have joined sympathies with post-structuralist and postmodernist critical projects' (Barrett and Phillips, 1992). They describe this attack as a process of 'destabilizing theory'. The apparent certainties offered by the liberal, Marxist/socialist and radical feminisms developed in earlier decades are no longer uncritically accepted. Despite the differences between different types of feminism, they were united in seeking to find the causes of women's oppression in inequalities in society. That consensus has now broken down.

Barrett and Phillips argue that this change was stimulated by three main factors:

1 The development of Black feminism. Dual systems theories (see p. 151) could not readily accommodate a third system.

2 Increased suspicion of the distinction between sex and gender. Both psychoanalysis and the belief that some aspects of femininity (such as mothering) were positively superior to masculinity, led some feminists to question the idea that men and women could be both equal and alike. Female difference came to be seen in a more positive light.

3 Postmodern ideas were having an increasingly influential role in social science generally.

Tensions and affinities between postmodernism and feminism

Susan Hekman (1990) argues that there are both affinities and tensions between postmodernism and feminism. She says that:

> despite the similarities between the two movements, however, there is at best an uneasy relationship between postmodernists and feminists. Few feminists are willing to label themselves postmodernists and, similarly, many postmodernists are profoundly sceptical of the feminist movement.
>
> Hekman, 1990

This tension exists because feminism could, in certain respects, be seen as a modern social theory. It is modern in the sense that it offers a general theory of how society works and it seeks to find ways to ensure progress towards a better society. Postmodernists reject the possibility both of a general theory and of a recipe for improving society.

However, there are important affinities between postmodernism and feminism. Hekman points out that both question conventional scientific models of knowledge. Feminists, for example, argue that knowledge can come from women's experiences rather than from positivist data produced by methods such as questionnaires (see Chapter 14). Both feminists and postmodernists question Enlightenment thinking (see Chapter 15 for a discussion of Enlightenment thinking) in the sense that neither believe that male rationality is adequate for understanding the social world. Furthermore, both question what Hekman calls the 'fundamental dichotomies of Enlightenment thought, dichotomies such as rational/irrational and subject/object' (see pp. 159–60).

Hekman believes that the affinities between feminism and postmodernism are sufficiently great for them to be able to combine into a postmodern feminism. Certainly, such an approach has become increasingly popular and has posed an important challenge to more conventional feminisms.

The main features of postmodern feminism

Postmodern feminism has some similarities with aspects of Black feminism. Postmodern feminism tends to reject the claim that there is a single theory that can explain the position of women in society. It encourages the acceptance of many different points of view as equally valid. In particular, it tends to deny that there is any single, unitary essence to the concept 'woman'. Different groups of women (for example, black women, lesbian women, white middle-class women) and individual women are different. Furthermore, groups of women and individual women change constantly and are therefore impossible to pin down to some essence or core. Pamela Abbott and Claire Wallace argue that 'central to postmodern theory is the recognition of difference – race, sex, age – and deconstruction – a multiply divided subject in a multiply divided society'. By rejecting the idea of a central core constituting the person, postmodernism shifts attention away from the subject as a manifestation of her 'essence' to 'the subject in process' – never unitary and never complete (Abbott and Wallace, 1997).

Postmodernism tends therefore to celebrate differences and to attack the idea that some characteristics are to be preferred to others. For this reason, postmodern feminists sometimes reject the idea that women can progress by taking on the characteristics and gaining the social positions traditionally reserved for men. Many postmodern theories reject the idea of progress altogether. Postmodern feminists see the whole idea of progress as a product of a dominant, male rationality. Some see ideas such as 'justice' and 'equality' as concepts associated with male reason, which seeks to manipulate and control the world. They reject these sorts of aims, which they see as the product of masculine styles of thinking. Rosemarie Tong says that:

> they view with suspicion any mode of feminist thought that aims to provide the explanation for why woman is oppressed or the ten steps all women must take to achieve liberation. Some postmodern feminists are so suspicious of traditional feminist thought that they reject it altogether.
>
> Tong, 1998

Nevertheless, postmodern feminists have suggested ways in which the interests of women in general can be pursued. Unlike more conventional feminisms, though, these have more to do with the use of language than with such things as improving job opportunities, freeing women from biological constraints or getting men to do more housework.

Such approaches see their principal aim as to deconstruct male language and a masculine view of the world. According to them, males see the world in term of pairs of opposites (for example, male/female, good/evil, true/false, beautiful/ugly). They take the male as normal and the female as a deviation from the norm. For example, Sigmund Freud saw women as men who lacked a penis and who envied males for possessing one (penis envy). Deconstruction involves attacking linguistic concepts typically regarded in a positive way and reinterpreting their opposites in a positive light. Deconstructionists thus turn conventional thinking on its head. For example, they might regard femininity, evil, falsehood and ugliness as desirable characteristics.

In fact, postmodern feminists go further than this, questioning the whole idea of truth by claiming that language cannot represent some external reality. Not only should the binary opposition projected by male thought be rejected, but language itself fails to represent a feminine understanding of the world. Language is the ally of male rationality. It is used to impose an artificial order on the world, and to express the masculine desire to manipulate and control, to plan and achieve objectives. Languages that have been developed primarily by men are less useful for understanding the ways in which women understand and experience the world.

To postmodernists, woman is the 'other', that which is not man. However, as Tong puts it, 'otherness, for all its associations with oppression and inferiority, is much more than an oppressed, inferior condition. It is also a way of being, thinking, and speaking allowing for openness, plurality, diversity and difference.' By making the voices of different women heard and taken seriously, it becomes possible to escape from the straitjacket of male thought and male, modern language. Such ideas have their origins in the work of French social theorists such as Jacques Lacan and Jacques Derrida. Their ideas on sex and gender will now be examined.

Influences on postmodern feminism

Jacques Lacan

Jacques Lacan (1977) argues that society consists of a symbolic order. Rosemarie Tong describes this as made up of 'a series of interrelated signs, roles, and rituals' (Tong, 1998). Language plays a key role in the symbolic order. Indeed, it is only through language that people become human.

Much of Lacan's work was influenced by (though different from) the psychoanalytic theories of Sigmund Freud. Following Freud, Lacan discusses how children develop from birth. An important part of their development is the way they internalize the symbolic order. However, this process affects males and females differently.

According to Lacan, in the first stage of development, the imaginary phase, the baby has no awareness of itself as an individual. It cannot differentiate between its mother and itself.

In the second stage, the mirror phase, the child begins to distinguish itself from its mother. When the child sees itself and an adult in the mirror for the first time, it fails to see the adult as a separate person. Later, however, the child begins to realize that the image is not real and finally recognizes that there is an image of itself which is separate from the adult. The child now enters the mirror stage in which she or he has a conception of his or herself as separate from the Other, in particular the mother.

In the third stage, the Oedipal phase, there is a growing divide between the child and the mother. Initially, Lacan claims, the child does not want to be close to the mother, he or she wants to provide the mother with what she is lacking, a penis or phallus. The child comes to realize that they have to communicate with the mother to express their wishes. However, the child becomes aware that the Other can only know them through the imperfect mechanism of language. The Other cannot enter the child's head and see the world as they do. They can therefore only understand and meet the child's needs imperfectly. The intervention of the father increases the child's sense of separation from the mother. As Madan Sarup describes it, 'there is, then, a symbolic castration: the father castrates the child by separating it from its mother' (Sarup, 1988).

Both males and females have to submit to what Lacan calls the law of the father. The forced symbolic separation of the child from their mother is imposed by the father who represents and imposes the rule of the symbolic.

During this phase, boys identify more with the father. Unlike the mother, the father was not originally seen by the child as an extension of himself or herself. Thus the father is seen as part of the symbolic order of language. Girls cannot identify with the father to the same extent as boys because the father is physically different from them. It is therefore harder for the girl to accept fully the symbolic order with its male connections. For this reason, boys and girls view the world from different perspectives. Male and female are not alike but different. Language is essentially a male phenomenon. Women have to use male language but cannot fully express themselves through it because women's feelings cannot be represented through male language. According to Tong, Lacan speculated that were men to try to do the impossible – to know women – they would have to begin their inquiry at the level of feminine sexual pleasure (*jouissance*). But like women, *jouissance* cannot be known because 'it can be neither thought nor spoken in the phallic language of the fathers' (Tong, 1998).

Lacan's ideas on the masculine nature of language have influenced some postmodern feminists, as has his emphasis on the differences in male and female perspectives. The idea of the law of the father has affinities with the concept of patriarchy. However,

Lacan's theories do make male dominance sound inevitable and neither postmodern nor other feminists are willing to accept this.

Jacques Derrida

Jacques Derrida is another French post-structuralist (see Chapter 12 for a discussion of post-structuralism) writer who, if anything, has had even more influence on postmodern feminism than Lacan (see Kamuf, 1991, for extracts from Derrida).

Derrida's ideas are developed primarily from linguistics - the analysis of language - rather than from psychoanalysis. By questioning the nature of language, Derrida opens up a whole range of implications for the study of society in general, and sex and gender in particular. The Swiss linguistic theorist Saussure first distinguished between the signifier, a word, and the signified, the thing to which it refers. Thus the word 'dog' is a signifier that refers to the signified, the actual animal. Saussure argued that signifiers were arbitrary. For example, there was no necessary connection between the word 'dog' and the animal to which it referred. Any other word would serve just as well as the signifier. However, Derrida went much further in questioning the nature of language and in doing so opened up questions of sex and gender.

Derrida argued that language was a self-contained system of signifiers. Signifiers referred not to some independent reality but to other signifiers. Thus the word 'dog' can only be understood with reference to other words or signifiers such as 'animal', 'bark' and so on. There is an unbridgeable gap between objects and the way we describe them. The objects are physically separate from those people who describe them and separated in time. We use the term 'dog' as an alternative to producing an actual dog to illustrate what we are talking about. Using the sign or signifier 'dog' is therefore based on the absence of a dog itself. Derrida uses the French word *differance* to indicate how the signifier is unlike the signified. *Differance* has two meanings in French: being unlike or dissimilar, and being delayed. *Differance* indicates therefore that words are fundamentally different to the things to which they refer and are postponed or delayed representations of things which are not present.

This abstract analysis of language leads Derrida to be highly suspicious of any claims to have established the truth. Since language cannot truly represent an objective reality, claims to absolute truth cannot be accepted. Attempts have been made to find a sign on which all other concepts can be based. Examples include God, and matter, but none have removed the distance between the subject and object, the human being and what they are describing.

Derrida argues that existing belief systems are based upon the use of binary oppositions. That is, they are based upon a belief in pairs of opposites. Sarup notes that some key oppositions according to Derrida are 'signifier/signified, sensible/intelligible, speech/writing ... space/time, passivity/activity' (Sarup, 1988). Usually, however, one of the pair is suppressed, the other is brought to the fore and regarded as superior. Thus good is seen as superior to evil, activity as superior to passivity, and so on. Such binary oppositions are closely connected to ideologies which make strong distinctions between what is desirable and what is not. It is possible to undermine these binary oppositions, and therefore the ideologies on which they are based, by the process of deconstruction. Deconstruction involves showing how the favoured term only has a meaning in contrast with its opposite. Thus good has no meaning unless its opposite, evil, exists. Furthermore, Derrida tries to show that there is really no reason for privileging one term at the expense of its opposite. Good is no better than evil, and evil no worse than good. By turning pairs of opposites against one another, he tries to undermine the whole idea that binary opposition should form the basis for thinking about the world.

Derrida's work tends to support relativism, that is denying that any one truth can be found. Any particular text can be taken apart and be shown to have contradictions within it. (By text he means any written or visual document that can be interpreted. Examples would include books, articles, films, paintings and so on.) By showing these contradictions it is possible to show that a text can have different meanings, with no one interpretation able to stand as superior to the others. The meaning of texts is also relative because of intertextuality. By this Derrida implies that texts are given their meaning by referring to meanings in other texts. However, these texts in turn only derive their meaning from further texts, so the meaning of any single text can never stand alone or be finally determined.

At times, Derrida's work touched directly on issues to do with gender. He regarded male–female and nature–culture as unacceptable dualisms in Western thought. He was also critical of phallocentric (or penis-centered) language which, according to Tong, 'connotes a unitary drive towards a single supposedly reachable goal' (Tong, 1998). Just as male sexuality involves the aim of orgasm and ejaculation, so male language is based upon achieving an identified objective. It puts little emphasis on the enjoyment of experience rather than the achievement of goals.

We will now examine the views of some postmodern feminists who have been influenced by Lacan and/or Derrida.

Postmodern feminists

Hélène Cixous

Hélène Cixous is a French novelist and feminist writer who sees language as a key part of gender difference. She says:

> everything is word, everything is only word ... we must grab culture by the word, as it seizes us in its word, in its language ... Indeed, as soon as we are, we are born into language and language speaks to us, language dictates its law, which is a law of death ... you will thus understand why I believe that political thought cannot do without language, work on language.
>
> Cixous, quoted in Haste, 1993

Cixous believes that language is male-dominated, or as she terms it, phallocentric. Its form is masculine. Both how things are said and what is said (and written) reflect masculinity and particularly male sexuality. Like Derrida, Cixous believes that male thought and language can be seen as phallic. She complains of 'the woman who still allows herself to be threatened by the big dick, who's still impressed by the commotion of the phallic stance' (Cixous, 1981a).

Male sexuality, the sexuality of the phallus, has a single focus, the penis, and is directed towards particular goals such as penetration and orgasm. Men have tended to define women in terms of a lack of a penis. Most men are afraid of women because they fear castration, and women, lacking a penis, are seen as being like castrated men. However, Cixous believes that in reality, female sexuality, which like Lacan she calls *jouissance*, is much more subtle and varied than male sexuality. Women can find pleasure in different parts of their bodies and can achieve greater pleasure than that offered by the phallus. Women's sexuality, and indeed the whole feminine perspective on the world, has been repressed and needs to escape from this repression and express itself openly.

In 'Castration or decapitation', Cixous illustrates her ideas by using a Chinese story (Cixous, 1981b). In the story, the king told his general, Sun Tse, to train his 180 wives to be warriors. The general agreed and proceeded to try to teach the king's wives to march in time. However, the wives ignored the instructions and instead talked and laughed among themselves. Sun Tse regarded this as mutiny and persuaded the king that his wives should be executed for their actions. The king agreed and started by beheading two of them. The rest of the wives now started following instructions and duly marched to order as required.

To Cixous this is an example of the 'masculine economy' which:

> *is governed by a rule that keeps time with two beats, three beats, four beats, with pipe and drum, exactly as it should be. An education that tries to make a soldier of the feminine by force, the force history keeps reserved for woman ... Women can keep their heads only on condition that they accept complete silence, turned into automatons.*
>
> Cixous, 1981b

Cixous then explains how women can begin to counter male force. She says that women and femininity should:

> *start speaking, stop saying that she has nothing to say! Stop learning in school that women are created to listen, to believe, to make no discoveries. Dare to speak her piece about giving ... Speak of her pleasure and, God knows, she has something to say about that, so that she gets to unblock a sexuality that's just as much feminine as masculine, 'de-phallocentralise' the body, relieve man of his phallus, return him to an erogenous field and a libido that isn't stupidly organized round that monument, but appears shifting, diffused, taking on all the others of oneself.*
>
> Cixous, 1981b

Such a change would not be easy. Current male-dominated language is incapable of expressing feminine sexual pleasure.

Cixous goes into further detail about the aspects of male language that need to be countered. Following Derrida, she claims that phallocentric language is based around dualisms, or pairs of opposites. These are all related to 'the couple man/woman' (Cixous, 1981a). Examples include:

Activity/Passivity
Sun/Moon
Culture/Nature
Day/Night
Father/Mother
Head/Heart
Intelligible/Sensitive
Logos/Pathos
Man/Woman.

The oppositions are hierarchical, with the masculine ranked higher than the feminine.

Despite the strength of phallocentrism in culture and language, Cixous does believe that change is possible. Furthermore, men could benefit from the change as well as women. Nor does she think that there is an absolute difference between men and women. Femininity and masculinity can be present in both sexes. If women can develop ways of expressing the joy of femininity and can succeed in speaking out, more men as well as women can benefit from the revelation of the feminine.

Helen Haste – *The Sexual Metaphor*

Like Cixous, Helen Haste (1993) also attaches great importance to the role of language and to the existence of dualisms. However, Haste puts particular emphasis on the role of metaphors in language. Metaphors are not merely comparisons between one thing and another, they also shape the way that people see the world and how they act. Gender differences go deeper than patriarchy or capitalism, they are enshrined in language. Different metaphors are used to understand the lives of men and those of women. She says, 'the lives of modern industrial men can be metaphorically constructed in terms of finite, achievable tasks'.

Women, however, experience their lives differently, in terms of cycles, rather than in terms of tasks which are completed and followed by another task. Haste says that 'women's lives are experienced, in so many areas as cycles - physical and biological cycles, diurnal cycles of nurturance and preparation of food, cycles of caring, cleansing, and the annual cycles of family life'. Only men working in agriculture have such close involvement with cycles.

Like Cixous, Haste believes that it is difficult to express and understand female experiences through a language dominated by men, and particularly by male metaphors. One such metaphor is the idea of 'Man the Hunter'. This has been used to reinforce dualisms such as public and private. Men should go out into the public sphere and do the literal or metaphorical hunting, while women should be confined to the private sphere. Haste says:

> *Man the Hunter illustrates some key points of my argument. The image implies a scenario or script for certain aspects of male behaviour. It contains a set of rules for behaviour, motives, skills and - most importantly - relations with others. The scenario is understood by all members of the culture. It gives meaning and symbolism beyond the literal context - the commercial entrepreneur is perceived as a metaphoric hunter, and his actions are construed in terms of a hunter's performance, skilfully pursuing prey, seeking spoils and returning to the female for approval.*
>
> Haste, 1993, p. 29

Such metaphors maintain dualistic thinking. Since the Enlightenment, the contrast between masculine rationality and female emotion has been a central dualism. Haste is critical of feminists who accept the male conception of rationality and simply assert that females can be as rational as men. Haste argues that there are distinctive and equally valid feminine ways of looking at the world. Male conceptions of truth see truth as something to be arrived at through the detached, impersonal use of logic. Female conceptions of truth see it as linked more to experience and negotiation with others. Thus she argues that:

> *one cannot know, either simply through detachment and objectification; one must gain knowledge through participation. Language and communication are vitally important, because our concepts depend on the language available to us. Persuasion - the recognition of the other person's point of view and the accommodation of one's arguments to that point of view - is essential for comprehension and the development of ideas.*
>
> Haste, 1993, p. 33

For women, who in contemporary cultures are defined as the 'Other' – that which is not male – the search for truth is the search for authenticity. They need to find out who they really are and move beyond being defined and defining themselves as simply the non-masculine.

Haste acknowledges that there have been significant changes in recent decades. For example, she points out that the most significant 'is the growing recognition that women are sexually autonomous beings who have their own sexual needs and their own sexual desires'. This change has also benefited men because it has led to their 'liberation from the need to pursue and to perform Olympically, and freedom to seek mutual sexual enjoyment and a more fulfilling and satisfying sexual egalitarianism'. But while Haste wants greater equality between the sexes, she does not want the sexes to become alike. She does not want males and females to become interchangeable in an androgynous world. The masculine view of the world should no longer be accepted as the only view. Women should no longer be seen as the Other to the male. What is needed is an acceptance of different viewpoints. She concludes that:

> *the metaphor of the two-way mirror in which both perspectives are possible is, in my view, the only one which can resolve this - just as recognising pluralism is the only way to resolve the debates that pit monolithic rationality against the chaos of relativism.*
>
> Haste, 1993

Postmodern feminism – an evaluation

Rosemarie Tong (1998) is among those who are generally supportive of postmodern feminism. She argues that it encourages an awareness and an acceptance of differences, differences between men and women, the masculine and the feminine, and between different types of masculinity and femininity. It supports an acceptance of the validity of the points of view of the 'excluded, ostracized, and alienated so-called abnormal, deviant, and marginal people'.

However, some critics accuse postmodern feminism of doing almost the opposite, of losing sight of inequality and oppression and mistakenly reducing them to differences in the use of language. Thus Sylvia Walby (1992) argues that the emphasis on difference rather than inequality leads postmodernists to 'conceptualize power as highly dispersed rather than concentrated in identifiable places or groups. In the face of the complexity of the social world the post-modernists' response is to deny the possibility of causality and macro-social concepts'. Walby is very much opposed to such tendencies. She admits that there are significant differences between groups of women, yet still thinks that concepts such as 'patriarchy' are valid. This becomes particularly obvious according to Walby when you examine the work of writers such as Mies (1986). Mies claims to show that women are disadvantaged throughout the world in rich and poor countries alike. If the exploitation is worldwide, the concept of patriarchy is valid and what unites women is as important as what makes them different from one another.

While Walby criticizes postmodernists for arguing that women are fragmented into many different groups, others have accused postmodern feminism of the opposite, of treating women as all alike. Writers such as Cixous can be seen as arguing that there is an essential difference between men and women. The way they see and experience the world is fundamentally different. Rosemarie Tong says that 'difference feminists, especially postmodern feminists, celebrated women's bodies, reproductive rhythms, and sexual organs ... critics of postmodern feminism claim that if the truth be told, difference feminists use the term difference in an "essentialist" way' (Tong, 1998). That is, they have reacted against the view of some conventional feminists who claim that there is no real difference between men and women, by going to the opposite extreme. They have returned to what might be seen as discredited arguments that men and women are fundamentally different. Tong rejects this criticism. She believes that writers such as Cixous distinguish between femininity and masculinity as ways of understanding the world, but do not make absolute distinctions between men and women. Men can have feminine perspectives and women masculine ones. However, this line of criticism does show that there are significant differences between postmodern feminists.

Some seem to celebrate the diversity of femininity while others concentrate more on the distinctiveness of femininity. Like most other broad perspectives within the social sciences, there are significant differences within each school of thought which can make generalizations about their strengths and weaknesses dangerous. Nevertheless, postmodern feminists do seem to be united in their emphasis on the importance of language. Language may well have been neglected by other social theories, but their emphasis on language does lead to a neglect of other sources of inequality and difference. For example, postmodern feminists say little about the use of physical force by males, or inequalities of wealth and income, which might play an important role in maintaining gender inequalities in general. They also say little about gender inequalities in paid employment, the subject of the next section.

Gender and paid employment

Gender inequalities at work

Most feminists believe that the position of women in the labour market is an important source of female disadvantage. (As we saw in a previous section, the radical feminist Firestone is an exception since she sees women's oppression as biological in origin.) Some radical feminists (Kate Millett, for example) see lack of employment opportunities as one – but only one – of many sources of gender inequalities. Marxist feminists, with their greater stress upon material, economic factors, generally attach rather more importance to employment opportunities. However, it is usually liberal feminists who have placed most emphasis on paid employment outside the home. They have sought the introduction of equal opportunities in the labour market through new legislation and through changing attitudes.

In the UK, a legislation has secured a number of important gains for women. In terms of attitudes, the election in 1979 of the first British woman prime minister, Margaret Thatcher, might possibly have heralded an era in which women were accepted in any job in society.

Equal opportunity legislation

In 1970, the Equal Pay Act was passed. This specified that women were entitled to equal pay to men if they were doing the same or broadly similar work, or if their work was shown through a job evaluation scheme to be of the same value as that carried out by men. A five-year period was allowed for the implementation of the Act.

In 1982, however, the European Court decided that the Equal Pay Act was not consistent with EC legislation and it was strengthened. A 1984 amendment allowed women to claim equal pay for work of equal value if they could show that their job made demands as great as the work carried out by male employees in the same organizations in terms of factors such as skill, effort and decision making.

The 1975 Sex Discrimination Act barred discrimination on the grounds of sex in employment, education, and the provision of goods, services and premises. In employment, women were to be given equal access to jobs, and equal chances for promotion. Some types of job (for example, being an attendant in a female public toilet) were excluded from the provisions of the Act, where there was considered to be 'a genuine occupational qualification by sex'.

Gender and the labour force

There have been considerable increases in recent years in the proportion of women who work. Figure 3.1 shows that, between 1971 and 1997, the gap between the percentage of males and females in the labour force has narrowed considerably. While the percentage of economically active men has fallen slightly, the main reason for the reduction is the rise in the percentage of economically active women. By 1997, there were 14.5 million men in employment and 11.4 million women (*Social Trends*, 1998). In

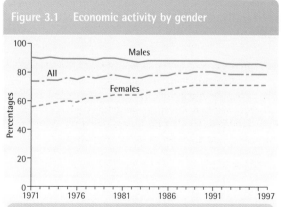

Figure 3.1 Economic activity by gender

Note: The figures include males aged 16 to 64, females aged 16 to 59, and show the percentage of the population that is in the labour force. The definition of the labour force changed in 1984 when the former Great Britain civilian labour force definition was replaced by the ILO definition which excludes members of the armed forces.

Source: Office for National Statistics *Labour Force Survey* (1998)

1961, women made up 32.3 per cent of the labour force, and 39.5 per cent in 1981. By 1997, according to *Social Trends*, women accounted for 45.7 per cent of those in employment and 43.3 per cent of the economically active. (The economically active includes the unemployed seeking work.) In spring 1997, there were about the same number of men working full-time as there had been in 1984, whereas the number of women working full-time had risen by nearly 20 per cent. Over the same period, though, part-time male workers had nearly doubled in number while part-time female workers had increased by just less than a quarter. Nevertheless, part-time work is still dominated by females. In 1997, there were 4.4 million women working part-time but just 0.9 million men (*Social Trends*, 1998).

Most of this rise in female employment has been due to the growing numbers of married mothers who work. In 1996-7, over 60 per cent of married couples with children had two earners, compared with about 50 per cent at the beginning of the 1980s. Over the same period, the proportion of such families where the husband alone was working fell from about 40 per cent to around 25 per cent (*Social Trends*, 1998). On the other hand, lone mothers have become less likely to have paid employment. In 1996, only 51 per cent of lone mothers were economically active (EOC Briefings, *Work and Parenting*, 1997).

Gender and earnings

In 1970, women working as full-time employees earned about 63 per cent of the average male full-time employees' wage per hour. Table 3.2 shows that in 1975 the figure was substantially higher at 71 per cent. There was then little further rise until the 1990s. In 1996, the figure stood at 80 per cent (EOC Briefings, *Pay*, 1997).

As Figures 3.3 and 3.4 indicate, significant differences in the pay of men and women remain even when they are carrying out similar types of work. Despite the legislation of the 1970s, women in all types of occupation are paid less than men, with female craft, sales, managerial and administrative workers doing particularly poorly.

Again, although women make up an increasing proportion of the labour force, they are not equally represented throughout the occupational structure. There is both horizontal and vertical segregation in men's and women's jobs:

1 Horizontal segregation refers to the extent to which men and women do different jobs.
2 Vertical segregation refers to the extent to which men have higher-status and higher-paid jobs than women.

Table 3.3 gives an indication of the extent of horizontal segregation by industry. It shows that males dominate in areas such as agriculture and fishing, energy and water supply, manufacturing, construction, and transport and communications. Women form a majority of the workforce in distribution, hotels and restaurants, public administration and other services. In banking, finance and insurance there is little difference in the numbers of male and female employees. In all industries, however, there are more part-time female workers than male, and these general figures hide significant variations in the specific types of job held by men and women.

Table 3.4 gives an indication of the extent of both horizontal and vertical segregation. Men dominate most areas of management and most higher-status professions such as medicine. When women have professional jobs they are more likely to be in lower-

Table 3.2	Average gross hourly earnings, excluding the effects of overtime, full-time employees on adult rates			
	Pence per hour			
	1975	1983	1993	1996
Females	98	288	668	750
Males	139	398	847	939
Differential	41	111	179	189
Female earnings as a percentage of male	71	72	79	80

Sources: Equal Opportunities Commission (1994 and 1997) *Some Facts About Women*, and EOC Briefings on Women and Men in Britain, *Pay* (1997)

Figure 3.2   Trends in the pay gap, 1975–96

Source: *New Earnings Surveys*, 1975–96, Volume A

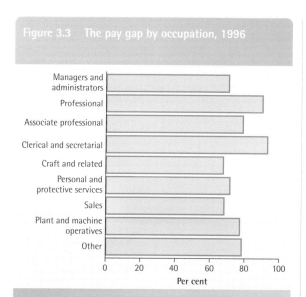

Figure 3.3   The pay gap by occupation, 1996

Source: *New Earnings Survey*, 1996, Volume A

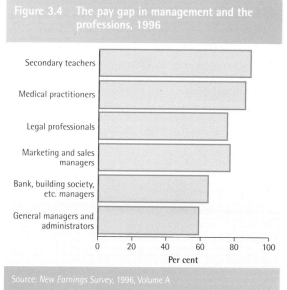

Figure 3.4   The pay gap in management and the professions, 1996

Source: *New Earnings Survey*, 1996, Volume A

Table 3.3   Gender and employment by industry, 1996

Employees aged 16 and over	Females (thousands)		Males (thousands)	
	Full-time	Part-time	Full-time	Part-time
Industrial sector				
Agriculture and fishing	31	35	143	10
Agriculture, hunting and forestry	31	35	140	10
Energy and water supply	43	10	226	–
Mining and quarrying	10	–	89	–
Electricity, gas and water supply	33	–	137	–
Manufacturing	1,000	277	3,312	76
Construction	86	66	791	17
Distribution, hotels and restaurants	869	1,540	1,590	416
Wholesale, retail and motor trade	671	1,222	1,356	279
Hotels and restaurants	197	419	234	137
Transport, storage and communication	238	102	1,007	48
Banking, finance and insurance, etc.	1,027	462	1,435	83
Real estate, renting and business activities	596	317	963	69
Public administration, education and health	2,210	1,844	1,685	154
Public administration and defence	470	167	798	28
Education	695	625	488	71
Health and social work	1,045	1,052	399	54
Other services	309	346	423	83
Other community, social and personal services	273	301	403	77
Total services	4,652	4,294	6,139	784
All industries and services*	5,817	4,688	10,623	889

* includes those not stating industry
– less than 10,000

Source: Office for National Statistics, *Labour Force Survey*, spring 1996.

Table 3.4	Gender and employment by occupation, 1996			
Employees aged 16 and over (thousands)	Females	% of group	Males	% of group
Occupational group				
Managers and administrators	1,318	33	2,700	67
Bank, building society and post office managers	30	29	72	71
Company secretaries	52	76	17	24
Professional	1,088	40	1,633	60
Medical practitioners	44	31	97	69
Primary and nursery school teachers	296	85	52	15
Associate professional and technical	1,227	50	1,215	50
Computer analysts/programmers	36	18	162	82
Nurses	445	88	58	12
Clerical and secretarial	2,782	75	933	25
Storekeepers and warehousepersons	45	13	289	87
Computer and office machine operators	80	63	46	37
Craft and related	299	10	2,806	90
Textiles, garments and related trades	159	69	72	31
Electrical/electronic trades	11	2	457	98
Personal and protective services	1,764	66	920	34
Police officers (Sgt and below)	19	13	123	87
Care assistants and attendants	391	92	35	8
Sales	1,282	64	721	36
Technical and wholesale sales reps	40	18	187	82
Retail cash-desk and checkout operators	188	86	30	14
Plant and machine operatives	494	20	1,948	80
Drivers of road goods vehicles	10	2	454	98
Assemblers/lineworkers of electrical goods	68	59	47	41
Other occupations	1,048	51	1,011	49
Postal workers, mail sorters	23	15	128	85
Counterhands, catering assistants	176	84	34	16
All occupations*	11,320	45	13,905	55

* includes those not stating occupation

Source: Office for National Statistics, *Labour Force Survey*, spring 1996.

status and less well-paid professions such as primary and nursery school teaching, and nursing. Routine white-collar jobs such as clerical and secretarial work are overwhelmingly carried out by women. In retailing, over 80 per cent of sales representatives are men but 86 per cent of cash-desk and checkout operators are women. In manual jobs, women are likely to have semi-skilled work such as assembling electrical goods, whereas most skilled craft jobs are done by men.

Veronica Beechey (1986) claims that vertical segregation actually increased in Britain during the twentieth century. Although women have made small gains in some areas (for example, they have made some inroads into management), they now make up a much greater proportion of clerical workers than they used to.

Within particular occupations women are usually concentrated in the lowest reaches of the occupational structure. For example, Table 3.5 shows how,

Table 3.5	Females and males in the legal profession in England and Wales, 1996			
	Females	% females	Males	% males
The judiciary				
Lords of Appeal in Ordinary	0	0	11	100
Heads of Divisions	0	0	5	100
Lord Justices of Appeal	1	3	34	97
High Court judges	7	7	89	93
Circuit judges	28	5	526	95
Recorders	64	7	839	93
Assistant recorders	57	16	293	84
District judges	36	11	300	89
Deputy district judges	79	12	601	88
Metropolitan stipendiary magistrates	11	21	41	79
Provincial stipendiary magistrates	4	10	36	90
Assistant recorders in training	10	16	51	84
Total	297	10	2,826	90
Barristers				
Barristers in independent practice	2,115	24	6,820	76
Queens Counsel in independent practice	60	6	865	94
Total	2,175	22	7,685	78
Solicitors				
Partners	4,115	15	22,436	85
Sole practitioners	794	17	3,808	83
Associate solicitors	456	43	597	57
Assistant solicitors	10,530	50	10,390	50
Consultants	255	11	2,110	89
Other private practice	89	49	93	51
All solicitors on the roll of The Law Society	16,239	29	39,434	71

Sources: Lord Chancellor's Department, The General Council of the Bar, The Law Society

in the legal profession, women made up 50 per cent of assistant solicitors in 1996, 24 per cent of barristers in independent practice, 6 per cent of Queen's Counsels, 5 per cent of circuit judges, and 3 per cent of Lords Justices of Appeal.

Although women have had some success in challenging the bastions of male dominance, it continues to be the case that few women occupy elite positions in society. In 1996, only 23 per cent of the board members of British government executive bodies and 11 per cent of board members of nationalized industries were women (EOC, *Some Facts about Women and Men in Great Britain*, 1997). In politics,

there has been a substantial rise in the proportion of female MPs, particularly after the election of numerous female Labour MPs in 1997. After the 1997 election there were 120 female MPs, nearly double the number there had been in the previous parliament, but still representing only 18 per cent of the total (Puwar, 1997).

Even in occupations in which women predominate (such as primary school teaching) they tend to miss out on the senior jobs. In 1994–5 in England there were more male than female headteachers in primary schools, although about 80 per cent of all primary school teachers were women. At higher levels in the education system, men comprised 72 per cent of academic staff in UK higher education institutions in 1994–5 and 93 per cent of the professors (EOC Briefing, *Women and the Professions*, 1997).

Explanations for gender inequalities in employment

As we have seen in the previous sections, women face a number of disadvantages in paid work:

1 They tend to be paid less than men.
2 They are more likely to be in part-time work.
3 They tend to be concentrated in the lower reaches of the occupations in which they work.
4 They tend to do particular types of jobs, usually those with a low status.

Some explanations for these inequalities concentrate on the characteristics of women and men. They generally see the inequalities in the labour market as stemming from women's role in the family. Other approaches concentrate on the labour market and the way in which it can restrict the opportunities open to women.

Functionalism and human capital theory

As we discussed earlier in the chapter (see p. 132), the functionalist Talcott Parsons argued that women are naturally suited to the 'expressive' role of childcare whereas men are more suited to the 'instrumental' role of competing in the labour market. This implies that women with children will give up or interrupt their careers in order to care for their children.

Human capital theory, which is advocated by some economists, argues that women's lack of commitment to paid employment is the cause of the disadvantages they suffer in the labour market. Because they are likely to abandon or interrupt their careers at an early age, women have less incentive to invest their time in undertaking lengthy programmes of training or education. They are therefore of less value to employers than their more highly-trained and more skilled male counterparts.

Similarly, on average, women will have less experience of their jobs than men because they are less likely than men to be in continuous employment for so many years. This makes it difficult for women to be promoted to higher-status and better-paid jobs. Once again, women are paid less than men because they are worth less to the employer. Their lack of training, qualifications and experience, which all result from the demands of childcare, create disadvantages for them in the labour market.

Anne Witz (1993) is among the many critics of functionalist and human capital approaches. She argues that even when women do work continuously without taking career breaks they still tend to end up in the lower-paid and lower-status jobs. Teresa Rees (1992) points out that American research designed to test the theory has found that only about half the pay differentials between men and women can be explained in terms of human capital theory.

Peter Sloane has investigated human capital theory using data collected for the Social Change and Economic Life Initiative, which investigated the labour markets of Rochdale, Swindon, Aberdeen, Coventry, Kirkcaldy and Northampton between 1985 and 1988 (Sloane, 1994). This found that professional qualifications had a big impact on pay, raising pay by 30 per cent compared to non-qualified groups. However, he also found that gender was an important variable, even when controlling for factors such as education, experience and training which are seen as important by human capital theory. Males still enjoyed a 29 per cent earnings advantage over females which could not be explained in human capital terms.

Human capital theory also ignores causes of inequality between male and female employees located within the structure of the labour market. These are the focus of the next theories we will look at.

The dual labour market theory

R.D. Barron and G.M. Norris (1976) were among the first British sociologists to apply dual labour market theory to gender inequalities. From this point of view, there are two, not one, labour markets.

1 The primary labour market is characterized by high pay, job security, good working conditions and favourable promotion prospects.
2 The secondary labour market consists of lower-paid jobs with less job security, inferior working conditions and few opportunities for promotion.

Primary and secondary labour markets often exist side-by-side within a company, but transfer from the secondary to the primary is difficult, perhaps impossible. Primary sector workers in a firm would include professional and managerial staff and highly skilled manual workers. Secondary sector workers include those doing unskilled or semi-skilled manual or non-manual jobs.

According to Barron and Norris, dual labour markets result from the tactics used by employers to obtain the types of labour they require. They are prepared to offer relatively high rewards to retain primary sector workers with the necessary skills and experience, but they regard secondary sector workers as more dispensable. Secondary sector workers can be easily replaced, and there is therefore little incentive to offer them high wages, job security or promotion prospects.

Both men and women can be found in the secondary sector, but Barron and Norris believe that women are more likely to have jobs in this sector. Employers tend to ascribe characteristics to women which make them particularly suited to these types of job: they are seen as easy to replace, as having less interest in gaining additional skills, and as less concerned than men with the size of their wage packets (since men are expected to be the main breadwinners within families).

The relatively low status of women in society and their tendency not to belong to unions weaken their position further and make it especially difficult for them to get a foothold in primary sector employment. Once recruited to the secondary sector, women are likely to remain captives within it for the rest of their working lives.

Dual labour market theory moves well away from looking at family life to explain the position of women in the labour market. It avoids concentrating on individual cases of discrimination and stresses the structures limiting women's employment opportunities. However, Veronica Beechey (1986) identifies a number of limitations to the theory:

1 Some women in skilled manual jobs (for example, in the textile industry) still receive low pay although their work is very similar to primary sector men's jobs.

2 Many women do have jobs in the primary sector, but not in industry: for example, nurses, teachers and social workers. The dual labour market theory is not particularly good at explaining the position of women outside manufacturing industry.

3 The dual labour market theory cannot explain why women gain promotion less often than men, even when they are doing the same jobs.

Gender and labour market segmentation

A more sophisticated analysis of divisions in the labour market is provided by Brendan Burchell and Jill Rubery (1994). This is based upon an analysis of data on work attitudes and work histories in Northampton in the mid-1980s, also collected for the Social Change and Economic Life Initiative (Scott (ed.), 1994). This found no simple division between a primary and secondary labour market, but instead claimed to discover five clusters of workers who had similar career and work attitudes:

1 The primary segment in the most advantaged jobs. Some 78 per cent of this group were men and nearly all had only left previous jobs to get a better one; 40 per cent of the sample were in the primary segment.

2 Stickers. This group, making up 31 per cent of the sample, was largely female; 62 per cent were women. They were relatively satisfied with their jobs and were not seeking to move employers to improve their prospects, although some were interested in gaining internal promotions.

3 Female descenders. This cluster made up just 13 per cent of the sample, but 96 per cent of the group were women. They received the lowest pay of any group and many had had falling incomes after changing jobs. They tended to have unstable work histories with frequent job changes and periods away from work. The main factor causing this downward career path appeared to be domestic responsibilities, particularly the need to combine childcare with work.

4 Young and mobile. Some 80 per cent of this group were male. Their average age was 30 and they were seeking to move around from employer to employer in search of better pay and improved prospects.

5 Labour market descenders. This was the smallest group, at just 4 per cent of the sample. Most (83 per cent) were men and they had all lost previous jobs, had periods of unemployment or had to move to jobs of a lower social status.

Unlike dual labour market theory, this study did not find a perfect fit between being male and in the most advantaged clusters, and being female and in the most disadvantaged. Nevertheless, it did find that there were more females than males in disadvantaged clusters and that men were more numerous in the more advantaged ones. They attributed the gender differences to a combination of past work histories, attitudes, future expectations and current job position.

Compared to other women, women in the primary segment were likely to be better-educated, more likely to have had training, and more likely to see their job as a career and to believe that they had promotion prospects. Women outside the primary segment were more likely to have worked part-time, and to have given up a job for domestic reasons at some time. Women who at some time had accepted some deterioration in the pay or status of their jobs seemed to be caught on a downward path, and found it difficult to start improving their careers again.

Burchell and Rubery concluded that female workers were very much divided into different groups, and they were not all concentrated in the secondary labour market. Indeed, younger women were particularly divided between the primary cluster and the female descenders cluster, whereas there were more older women among the stickers. This suggested, if anything, an increasing polarization between women with successful careers and those without.

Burchell and Rubery therefore argue that 'with the partial exception of women's domestic interference to their labour market participation, there is little evidence that gender can be treated as a meaningful unifying category of experiences' (Burchell and Rubery, 1994).

Deskilling and the labour process

Marxists and Marxist feminists tend to dismiss the sorts of approaches that have been discussed so far on the grounds that they fail to relate the position of women to the workings of the capitalist economy as a whole. The American Marxist Harry Braverman (1974) devoted part of his analysis of the labour process in capitalism to the role of women. (For a full discussion of Braverman's theory see Chapter 10.)

Braverman suggested that monopoly capitalism produced a progressive deskilling of work including clerical work, service sector work and retailing. According to Braverman, women have been drawn into these areas of work as the service sector has expanded, while the mainly male manufacturing sector has declined. He explained women's entry into such work in the following way:

1   Women were no longer needed to produce commodities such as food and clothing for their families since these items became easier for people to purchase.

2   Women were able to move quite easily from providing services for their family to providing them for other members of the community in return for a wage packet.

3   Women have had to become an increasingly important source of labour as the reserve supply of other types of labour (such as migrants from rural areas) has dried up.

4   Women are a particularly suitable source of labour in an economic system that increasingly wants to employ unskilled workers. Braverman believes that women have been used to replace skilled male workers and so have helped employers to deskill their labour force.

As we will discover in a later section of the book (see Chapter 10), a major problem with Braverman's views is his exclusive emphasis on deskilling. Not all jobs have been deskilled, nor for that matter do all women work in unskilled jobs. Furthermore, as Beechey (1983) points out, it is possible that some jobs attract low pay not because they require little skill, but simply because they are seen as women's jobs. Thus nurses receive comparatively low wages despite the professional skills and training required in that occupation.

Women as a reserve army of labour

Veronica Beechey (1986) has developed a second strand of Marxist thought in order to explain the position of women in the labour market.

Marx argued that capitalism required a reserve army of labour, that is a spare pool of potential recruits to the labour force. According to Marx, because of their in-built contradictions, capitalist economies went through cycles of slump and boom, and it was essential to be able to hire workers during the booms, and fire them during the slumps. Furthermore, in their pursuit of surplus value, capitalists tried constantly to improve the efficiency of their machinery. This reduced the workforce needed to produce existing products, but new products were constantly introduced. Again, a reserve army provided the necessary flexibility to deal with these changes.

One of the main functions of the reserve army is to reduce the wages of all members of the labour force. A group of unemployed people looking for work creates competition in the workforce. This gives employers an advantage and allows them to reduce wages and increase the rate of exploitation.

Beechey identifies a number of ways in which women in modern Britain are particularly suited to form part of this reserve army:

1   They are less likely to be unionized and so are less able to resist redundancy than men.

2   Women's jobs are least likely to be covered by redundancy legislation, so it is cheaper to make them redundant rather than men.

3   Unemployed married women may not be eligible to receive state benefits if their husbands are working, and for this reason they might not appear in unemployment statistics. Beechey says that 'women who are made redundant are able to disappear virtually without trace back into the family.'

4   Because of their position within the family and the primary importance placed on their domestic role, women are likely to provide a particularly flexible reserve labour force. They are more likely to accept part-time work and variations in their hours of work.

5   Women are often prepared to work for less than men because they can rely on their husbands' wages as the main source of income for the family.

The reserve army of labour theory certainly seems to explain some of the changes that took place in the proportions of women working in Britain during the twentieth century. For example, it would appear to account for the increased employment of women during the two world wars.

However, like the other theories examined in this section, it has serious drawbacks. For example, Beechey herself admits that it cannot explain horizontal segregation in the labour market (why women are largely confined to certain types of job).

More seriously, the theory has been challenged by Irene Bruegel (1979), who questions the assumption that the interests of capital must be served if women are used as a reserve army of labour. She points out that women can also benefit capitalism by producing use values in the home, since this reduces the amount that needs to be paid to male workers.

From a rather different point of view – the substitution theory – Gardiner (1975) claims that it benefits capital more if women are allowed to retain their jobs in a time of recession and rising unemployment since they can act as a comparatively cheap substitute for male workers.

Clearly the best way to test these theories is to examine what happens to women's employment when unemployment generally is rising. Veronica Beechey (1986) herself quotes figures which appear to support Gardiner's theory. According to the *Equal Opportunities Commission Report* of 1983, in the period of recession from 1971 to 1983, male employment declined from 13 million to 11.5 million, but female employment actually increased from 8.2 to 8.8 million. This increase was largely due to more women working part-time, thus confirming that women do form a relatively flexible labour force.

More recently, female part-time and full-time employment has continued to grow, suggesting that it is increasingly difficult to see women's participation in the labour market as a temporary phenomenon. High levels of female employment have continued through both booms and slumps, while unemployment has risen most among men. Thus, while women continue to have more flexible patterns of work than men, they cannot be seen as a reserve army of labour as such.

Linda McDowell – gender and post-Fordism

Linda McDowell (1992) argues that fundamental changes have taken place in the labour market since the late 1960s and these have had important effects on gender and employment. McDowell uses the theory of post-Fordism to understand changes in the labour market. As we will see in Chapter 10, this theory argues that businesses have moved away from mass production towards the flexible production of small batches of specialized products. In doing so, they employ a core of highly skilled workers who are capable of using their skills to produce a wide variety of products. Other work is carried out by part-time workers, or workers on short-term contracts, or is contracted out to other firms.

McDowell argues that these changes are reflected in the increased use of part-time female labour and the reduction in the employment of males in full-time permanent jobs. She points out that between 1971 and 1988 male employment fell by almost 1.8 million, whereas female employment rose by about 1.7 million. Women have been used to fill the increasing proportion of jobs in parts of the growing

service sector. These types of job have traditionally been done by women. Part-time workers are cheaper to employ because they do not have the same rights to unemployment and sick pay as full-time workers; their wages tend to be lower than those of full-time workers; and they are easier to dismiss because they do not have the same legal protections under employment legislation. In most areas of business, employers have been determined to cut costs and to have a more flexible labour force to cope with repeated recessions and increased competition.

Some women have benefited from these changes. A few have found secure and well-paid employment as core workers and have 'captured the labour market opportunities and rewards traditionally reserved for male workers'. Most, however, have not fared so well.

The majority of new jobs have been part-time. McDowell says:

> Part-time, 'flexible' work has not been created in response to 'demand' on the part of workers, whether men or women. Rather, many have had part-time or temporary jobs imposed on them or have taken them for want of alternatives while continuing to seek full-time and stable work.
>
> McDowell, 1992

McDowell points out that, according to the *New Earnings Survey*, pay per hour for female part-time workers fell from 81 per cent of that for female full-time workers in 1980 to 75 per cent in 1989. With the decline in the availability of well-paid and secure work for working-class men, this has left many working-class women considerably worse off.

John Lovering has conducted an investigation into how restructuring or reorganization within businesses has affected gender divisions in employment (Lovering, 1994). He examined the following employers in Swindon: an engineering company, a food manufacturing company, a pharmaceutical company, an electronic assembly company, a small hospital, a government department's customer service unit, a motorway service station, a shop which is part of a retail chain, and a high-technology research company.

He found significant differences between employers, but many had very traditional patterns of male and female employment. The longest-established manufacturing and public service industries tended to retain the strongest and most conventional division of labour, with more men in the high-status and full-time jobs. Men and women tended to apply for jobs traditionally associated with their sex, and employers were generally unlikely to do anything to change this aspect of employment.

Lovering did detect some evidence of change within the companies that came closest to being post-Fordist. Restructuring manufacturing companies and newly developing service employers tended to have more flexible ways of operating. He says, 'some new jobs were being created, and this was associated with attempts to reduce or modify the sex-typing of employment' (1994). New opportunities were opening up for internal promotion, with meritocratic considerations gaining in importance over gender stereotyping. Both the service station and the retailer offered some internal promotion opportunities that women were able to take advantage of. Nevertheless, even in such businesses, there was still little likelihood of women getting right to the top.

Lovering's research suggests that a move towards post-Fordism is characteristic of only some employers. Where it has happened, there might be some increase in opportunities for women. He further points out that women will only be able to take advantage of these limited increases in opportunities if they can gain the qualifications and experiences which will allow them to apply for the new jobs.

While it is clearly important to take account of changes in the labour market and the economy as a whole in order to understand changing patterns of gender inequality, it is necessary to be cautious about basing an analysis on the theory of post-Fordism. This theory has been heavily criticized on a number of grounds, and the work of Lovering and others suggests that post-Fordism cannot be seen as a general trend which has affected all employers. (See Chapter 10 for detailed criticisms of post-Fordism.)

Men, trade unions and women in the labour market

Marxist feminist approaches to women and employment (such as the theory of the reserve army of labour) stress the relationship between the economic system and women's work. From a radical feminist perspective, however, such approaches tend to ignore the role of men – and particularly male workers – in restricting women's employment opportunities.

Some feminists have tried to combine the insights of Marxist feminism with those of radical feminists to explain the disadvantages experienced by women in the labour market. They argue that these disadvantages are a consequence of both the operation of the capitalist economy and the attempts of men to maintain patriarchal control.

In an article critical of both dual labour market and Marxist theories, Jill Rubery (1980) has drawn attention to the activities of trade unions as a factor affecting gender divisions in employment. Like Braverman (1974), she notes that many areas of work have been deskilled, but she also points to reskilling in some occupations. Changes in technology and labour processes have been accompanied by struggles

in which workers, through their unions, have tried to retain the definition of their work as skilled even when such a definition is no longer justified. For example, before the 1980s, printing unions tried with some success to maintain the craft status of their work, along with high wages, despite the threats posed by the introduction of new technology.

To male workers who wish to maintain a strong position in the labour market, women workers may pose as great a threat as new technology. Women may undercut male wages, depress wage levels generally, and increase unemployment. If there is an influx of women into a particular occupation, it may make it easier for the employer to define that occupation as requiring little skill.

Rubery maintains that, in response to these threats, trade unions have played a crucial part in restricting opportunities for female employees.

Like Rubery, Sylvia Walby (1986) argues that unions have been an important factor in producing female disadvantage in employment. From a study of engineering, clerical work and textiles in Britain, she claims that two main strategies have been used by males in these industries – the exclusion of women altogether, or the confinement of women to the lower grades of work.

In many parts of the engineering industry, exclusion was the main tactic used (at least until 1943), while in clerical and textile work male unionists used grading more effectively. In the weaving industry, for example, men were successful in allowing only a few women to be promoted to overlookers. In recent years, male unionists have resorted to tactics mainly involving grading, as legislation has made it difficult to exclude women from whole areas of employment.

Although Walby follows Marxists in describing modern societies as capitalist, she puts particular stress on the concept of patriarchy in trying to explain gender inequalities in employment. She sees unions as patriarchal institutions. Her own research suggests that they are usually dominated by men, and they tend to act in the interests of male employees, even when women are a majority of the union's membership. Nevertheless, she accepts that women have made some gains in the union movement in recent years, and they have had some success in persuading unions to take gender equality more seriously.

Walby takes a different view to conventional sociological theories which see the origins of female disadvantage in the workplace as stemming from the home. Walby believes that work is a major factor shaping domestic relationships. Women suffer such disadvantages in the labour market that they become only too willing to accept the main responsibility for domestic tasks. As she puts it, 'housework is as good as anything else a woman is likely to get'.

Heidi Hartmann (1976, 1981) takes a similar view to Walby. She too believes unions play a major role in disadvantaging women, and she also uses the concept of patriarchy. Hartmann is perhaps even more critical of the way patriarchal power has been used. She claims that men have deliberately used job segregation as a way of reinforcing their dominance over women in the domestic sphere. Women have come to rely on their husbands' wages for financial support. Men have managed to maintain a patriarchal society despite the increased use of female labour by capitalists. A vicious circle has been created for women in which low-paid work strengthens women's dependence on men in the home, and their domestic dependence makes it easy to recruit women to low-paid and low-status jobs.

Radical feminism and female employment

Radical feminists believe that women's disadvantages in the labour market stem from the exploitation of women by men and have little to do with the operations of capitalism. They concentrate in particular on how men exercise power over women at work and protect their own interests by intimidating women and excluding women from senior positions. Radical feminists claim that one way that men do this is through the use of sexual harassment.

Elizabeth A. Stanko (1988) defines sexual harassment as:

> unwanted sexual attention. Its behavioural forms are many and include visual (leering); verbal (sexual teasing, jokes, comments or questions); unwanted pressures for sexual favours or dates; unwanted touching or pinching; unwanted pressures for sexual favours with implied threats of job-related consequences for non-co-operation; physical assault; sexual assault; rape.
>
> Stanko, 1988, p. 91

Men back up these types of harassment with their power within organizations. They are usually in a position to hire or fire women and may take action against them if they complain. According to Stanko, sexual harassment is a common occurrence at work. She refers to a number of British studies which found that over half of the women questioned had experienced sexual harassment.

Stanko believes that men use sexual harassment to intimidate women who seek to enter areas of traditionally male employment. In such jobs, 'men's working environments become part of men's territories'. The men talk about sport and about women. They may have pin-ups of nude females in the workplace and they resent any challenge to the

assumption that they can maintain a working environment which is male-dominated. Stanko says:

> Sexual jokes, comments, teasing or touching of women are part of the building and sustaining of male solidarity ... Women, it is commonly assumed, by entering into men's territory, must expect and accept these displays of male heterosexuality.
>
> Stanko, 1988, p. 97

In jobs predominantly done by women, the situation is somewhat different. Here, 'sexualising women who work in traditional occupations serves to eroticise women's subordination'. Waitresses and barmaids, for example, are expected to be sexually attractive and to accept that during their work they may be the recipients of unwanted attention from males. Secretaries 'to some extent become office wives'. Some leave their jobs if their male boss seeks to start an affair.

Another radical feminist, Rosemary Pringle (1992), argues that the work of female secretaries is largely governed by patriarchal images of the job. It is difficult for secretaries to be taken seriously or to have their work valued because of those images. Secretaries rarely have a clear job description and instead their work is viewed largely in terms of ideas about femininity.

Pringle claims that if 'secretaries are represented as women, they are represented almost exclusively in familial or sexual terms: as wives, mothers, spinster aunts, mistresses and femmes fatales'. At every place of work where she conducted her study, at least one person assumed that because Pringle was studying secretaries she must be investigating sexual scandals. Pringle argues that 'the emphasis on the sexual has made it easy to treat the work as trivial or invisible'. Secretaries are sometimes seen as doing little but sitting around and gossiping 'filing their nails or doing their knitting'. A secretary is often viewed as 'the extension of her boss, loyal, trustworthy and devoted'. The dominant images of secretaries make it very difficult for them to be regarded as skilled workers or considered as possible candidates for promotion into management.

Lisa Adkins - the sexualization of women's work

Lisa Adkins (1995) goes even further in seeing the gendering, and particularly the sexualization of work, as essential features of the labour market. Although generally supportive of the kinds of view advocated by Stanko and Pringle, Adkins believes that they still 'assume that capital produces jobs (the places in a hierarchy of waged-workers within the labour market), while (on top of this) the patriarchal control of women's labour limits women's access to those jobs'. To Adkins, though, the places in the labour market can have a gendered character – there are jobs for men or jobs for women, and not jobs that can be filled by either sex. Furthermore, what she calls sexual work is integral to many of the women's jobs. Sexuality does not just permeate the workplace for women, it is also linked to the 'production of men's economic and other advantages in the labour market'.

Adkins bases her arguments largely on research conducted by her into women's work in hotels and pubs and at a leisure park. Adkins found that many pub and hotel chains had a deliberate policy of employing married couples. Typically, they employ the husband as the manager but specify in the contract that the wife must contribute to the running of the hotel or pub. Couples in this sort of contract are usually paid about 25 per cent more than a single man. The wife, however, is not paid a salary in her own right, as the husband simply receives a higher salary. Breweries and hotel chains prefer married couples for a number of reasons. First, they get cheap labour, effectively paying only about a quarter of the salary they would need to employ a second manager. Second, they believe that married couples will be more reliable and harder-working than single men. Third, 'companies regard wives as "sexual attractions" who will boost sales. Wives being present encourages men to use the establishments.' The wives studied by Pringle were usually subject to direct control by their husbands. The husbands chose which jobs were done by which partner, often handpicking the most interesting or easiest work for themselves. Women's jobs usually included a combination of serving customers and doing the accounts.

Adkins thinks these arrangements are important because they show that family-based systems of production are alive and well in contemporary capitalist and patriarchal societies. Such arrangements did not die out during the Industrial Revolution but continue today. They allow companies to 'gain access into patriarchal family hierarchies, within which husbands ... appropriate wives' labour'. Some of that labour amounts to the provision of sexualized services for men, a theme which Adkins develops in her detailed research into a large hotel (which she calls 'Global Hotel') and an amusement park ('Fun Land').

There was strong horizontal segregation at both Global Hotel and Fun Land. At Fun Land operatives of high-speed rides were exclusively young and male, while most catering assistants were female. Operatives of children's rides were a mixture of women and men. Adkins found that the criteria for selecting female catering assistants (whose jobs included serving food and working in bars) included

looking attractive. No such criteria were applied to men. Two young women who looked 'too butch' to be catering assistants were given jobs as operatives of the children's rides. These operatives had little contact with male customers. Adkins found that the female employees were subject to continual sexual harassment from customers and from male operatives. While some senior staff frowned on the behaviour of the male operatives, they did nothing to prevent it. As far as customers were concerned, it was made clear to the young women that they were expected to cope with the attentions of male customers and they were prohibited from responding to them aggressively. Making the male customers feel good by smiling and making light of their sexual innuendos and other sexualized behaviour, was seen as part of their job.

This type of sexual servicing was essentially part of the product being offered by Fun Land. Women who were unable or unwilling to provide it, by not being young or attractive enough or by complaining about harassment, were not employed, were employed on children's rides, or in some cases dismissed. For example, the one woman who had the nerve to complain about sexual harassment was sacked for being 'too domineering'.

At Global Hotel, similar patterns were repeated. The chefs, cooks and bar staff were predominantly male while the waiters/waitresses were predominantly female. The company had personnel specifications to help managers appoint appropriate people to particular jobs. One criterion which was common to all the predominantly female jobs was 'being attractive'. No necessity to 'be attractive' was specified for the male-dominated jobs. Adkins therefore argued that such jobs 'shared the requirement to be "attractive" precisely because these occupations were filled either exclusively or primarily by women'. Furthermore, Global Hotel's manuals specified that women were required to 'look attractive, clean and fresh' while working, whereas men were not. Like their counterparts at Fun Land, female workers at Global Hotel were expected to make the male customers who harassed them feel good rather than complain about their behaviour.

Adkins concludes that, in many service sector jobs, being sexually attractive and engaging in sexual servicing are integral parts of women's work. Their job is as much about sexuality as it is about serving food or drinks or otherwise dealing with customers' practical needs. A consequence of this is that the 'compulsion on women to carry out sexual work locates men as a more powerful group of workers' and therefore helps to produce patriarchal relationships.

Approaches such as those developed by Stanko and Pringle illustrate how men may use intimidation and ideological power to maintain their domination at work. Adkins's work suggests how sexuality may be integral to much service sector work undertaken by women. These studies add extra dimensions to an understanding of gender inequalities and gender differences at work but, like all the approaches examined so far, they are somewhat limited in scope. They emphasize the importance of some sources of gender inequality at work while neglecting others. For example, Stanko pays little attention to the operation of the labour market as a whole.

The next study we examine attempts to overcome the limitations of previous approaches by trying to incorporate a wide range of factors into its explanations of gender differences in the labour market.

Rosemary Crompton and Kay Sanderson – *Gendered Jobs and Social Change*

Structuration

In their study of gender and work published in 1990, Rosemary Crompton and Kay Sanderson argue that gender inequalities in the labour market must be explained in different ways in different types of job (Crompton and Sanderson, 1990). Structural features of the labour market interact with the actions taken by individuals making individual decisions about their working lives. Crompton and Sanderson follow Anthony Giddens in using the concept of structuration. According to this view, 'what people do always presupposes some kind of structure (rules of behaviour, resources, etc.) but in what they do people simultaneously create the structure anew'. Thus, for example, men who choose to follow traditional masculine careers and women who choose to follow traditional feminine careers reinforce the structural features of the labour market that create gender differences. They help to make it difficult for other individuals to pursue careers which are not normally thought appropriate for their gender.

The structure of the labour market shapes people's choices but does not entirely determine them. Individuals can and do choose non-conventional career paths and employers sometimes choose to fill jobs with people who are not normally recruited to them. The actions of individuals may, then, help to transform the labour market over a period of time so that structural limitations on actions are weakened or the structure of the labour market changes. Thus Crompton and Sanderson believe that the 'occupational structure is at the same time a social "product" as it sets limits on, and creates opportunities for, the people with (and without) "jobs" who are producing

it'. (We discuss Giddens's concept of structuration in detail in Chapter 15.)

A model of the occupational structure

In their analysis, Crompton and Sanderson make use of a wide range of theories and concepts. Their overall model of the labour market is shown in Figure 3.5. The left axis (A/B) refers to the characteristics of employees and in particular how qualified they are. In line with human capital theory, Crompton and Sanderson believe that the labour market and the position of individuals within it are partly shaped by the qualifications held by the members of the workforce. However, they are aware that the value of qualifications is not fixed. They note that occupational groups can try to increase the value of the qualifications they hold by restricting access to their profession so that a shortage of qualified workers can lead to the market value of their work increasing. (This is similar to the Weberian perspective on the professions: see p. 61 for further details.)

The C/D axis in Figure 3.5 refers to the characteristics of the labour market, rather than those of the individual participants in it. Crompton and Sanderson see a division between occupational and organizational labour markets. Occupational labour markets have 'extensive (voluntary and involuntary) mobility' whereas organizational labour markets 'are restricted to and controlled by firms or organizations'. In this aspect of their theory, Crompton and Sanderson make use of the dual labour market theory, and indicate that workers with few skills in the occupational labour market tend to end up in secondary labour market jobs with few prospects.

Among more skilled workers, those in the occupational labour market are able to 'move between jobs without incurring any employer penalty'. They may be self-employed or may be highly-skilled professionals or craft workers whose skills are in demand. They are not tied to the internal labour market of a particular organization and therefore are not so restricted in their efforts to improve their pay or secure promotion.

Occupational internal labour markets often include workers similar to those in the occupational labour market, but in this case the status and rewards of workers depend partly upon their skills and partly upon their position within the organization for which they work. Company lawyers and accountants are typical of workers in occupational internal labour markets.

People in firm internal labour markets depend much more on their position in a particular firm for their status and rewards. There may be some opportunity to move from one organization to another, but

Figure 3.5   A preliminary model of the occupational structure

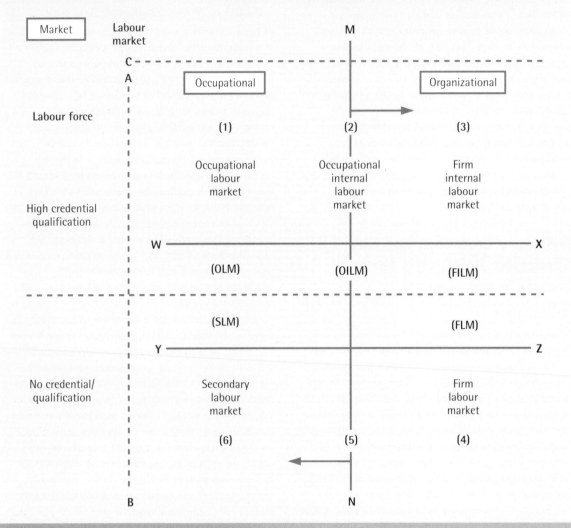

Source: R. Crompton and K. Sanderson (1990) *Gendered Jobs and Social Change*, Unwin Hyman, London, p. 39.

only if the organizations are very similar. For example, senior workers in a local authority may be able to move to do a similar job in another local authority, but they are unlikely to find employment in any other type of organization. In firm internal labour markets an employee is typically a 'highly trained generalist rather than the mobile specialist' of occupational or occupational internal labour markets.

Gender and the labour market

The characteristics and actions of individual workers and those seeking work interact with the characteristics of the labour market to give overall shape to patterns of employment. However, specific factors work within this overall framework to influence gender differences in employment. Crompton and Sanderson use the feminist concept of patriarchy,

although they see patriarchy as 'a particular aspect of gender relations' rather than as 'a universal system'. To them gender segregation is:

> *a product of the past sex-typing of occupations and conventional assumptions relating to the domestic roles of women, formal and informal exclusionary practices, and fluctuations in both the demand for labour and the nature of female labour available.*

Crompton and Sanderson, 1990

Conventional expectations and exclusionary practices can be overcome in some circumstances so that women can break into parts of the labour market to which they could not previously gain access. For example, they could use the 'qualifications lever' of high educational attainment to force their way into previously all-male domains. Whether this happens or not depends on the particular circumstances in different types of job.

Having outlined their theory, Crompton and Sanderson go on to support and illustrate it by researching four areas of employment: pharmacy, accountancy, building societies and cooking and serving.

Pharmacy

The Pharmaceutical Society of Great Britain was founded in 1841, but the first woman was not admitted to the profession until 1879. By 1941, women still made up only about 10 per cent of pharmacists. Female membership of the profession increased by around 5 per cent per decade during the 1940s and 1950s, but at around twice that rate during the 1970s and 1980s. By 1983, the majority of undergraduates studying pharmacy were women.

Crompton and Sanderson argue that 'as an occupation, pharmacy has not been sex typed'. Although it involves high levels of scientific training, usually associated with mainly male professions, it also offers flexible patterns of employment usually associated with predominantly female professions. Furthermore, men were unable to exclude females from the profession during the nineteenth century because, unlike accountancy, the constitution of the professional organization running the profession did not specify that the membership should be male. Women therefore became established in the profession relatively early in its development.

Regulations mean that a pharmacist has to be present if drugs are to be dispensed. This has led to the creation of considerable amounts of part-time work to cover for periods when full-time workers are not available. Women are attracted to such work because of the possibility of combining work with caring for their children.

Although women have come to form a high proportion of practising pharmacists, they tend to be concentrated towards the lower levels of the profession. Until the 1980s, part-time pharmacists in the NHS could not achieve promotion. In companies such as Boots, pharmacists are required to be geographically mobile to gain promotion, and women in the profession have been less geographically mobile than men. Thus, although women have been able to enter the occupational labour market in pharmacy, they have had limited success in gaining promotion within it.

Accountancy

Women entered accountancy in large numbers much later than they entered pharmacy. The oldest professional association in accountancy, the Institute of

Chartered Accountants of England and Wales, only started admitting women to its ranks in 1920. As late as the mid-1960s, less than 1 per cent of accountants were women, although by 1986 women made up 36 per cent of people training to be accountants.

Unlike pharmacy, there are a number of different recognized accountancy qualifications and the careers of some accountants are closely bound up with the firm internal labour market of particular organizations. Other accountants are self-employed or work in small independent accountancy practices. These accountants have occupational careers rather than ones based on organizations.

Crompton and Sanderson carried out in-depth interviews with six female qualified accountants. They found that those who worked in large organizations were often subject to discrimination by their male bosses and this tended to block promotion prospects. One woman reported how her boss had openly stated that 'I just think that that's where women are most fulfilled, at home having a family.' There were also few opportunities for accountants in large organizations to work part-time. Women who had young children therefore faced a clear choice between their careers or being at home with their children.

Building societies

Unlike accountancy, the majority of building society workers are female. Crompton and Sanderson note that in the late 1980s, over 70 per cent of building society workers were women. They attribute this partly to the very rapid expansion of employment in these organizations during the 1970s, a time when many married women were deciding to seek employment or to continue in work despite having children. Building societies recruited from this large pool of female labour.

Despite the predominance of women in this sector, they are concentrated towards the bottom of the hierarchies. Most of the clerical work is done by women but senior managers are almost exclusively male.

Crompton and Sanderson see building societies as examples of firm internal labour markets: prospects are largely tied to the chances of internal promotion. Men have been dominant in these labour markets and they have used their dominance largely to exclude women. Women tend to lack the formal qualifications, the willingness to do irregular overtime and the ability to be geographically mobile, all of which are necessary to give an employee of a building society a good chance of promotion.

There are also unofficial practices which block women's promotions. Senior managers sometimes act as 'sponsors' or as 'mentors' for aspiring junior staff, helping them with their careers. The senior staff, who are almost always male, nearly always sponsor other males. Women also lack access to male-dominated informal networks and clubs, which can be important ways of getting in with the right people to further their career.

In 1977, the Equal Opportunities Commission investigated alleged discrimination against women in the Leeds Building Society. It found that this building society tended to recruit men to its management training programmes even when women candidates were younger, better-qualified and had more relevant work experience. The findings of the Equal Opportunities Commission persuaded a number of building societies to examine their recruitment policies.

Crompton and Sanderson themselves conducted studies at three building societies of different sizes, interviewing a total of 8 managers and 24 clerical and supervisory workers. They found ample evidence of exclusionary practices by males. At one of the societies they studied (the 'Cloister Building Society'), though, they did find that the majority of manage- ment trainees since 1980 had been female. This suggested that male dominance was beginning to be challenged.

Cooking and serving

Work in catering and hotels has usually been consid- ered 'women's work' because of its similarity to unpaid domestic work. It is generally low-paid and low-status, although in some areas there are career prospects. Crompton and Sanderson conducted case study research on the school meals service of one education authority, and at two hotels.

Not surprisingly they found that school meal workers are almost all women. Since the school meals service is widely regarded as women's work and is seen as unskilled, there is little competition from men for the jobs. Women are attracted to the job because of the availability of part-time employ- ment during school hours, making it relatively easy to combine work with looking after school-age children.

In hotels the situation is different. Although most employees are women, there are areas where men predominate. For example, most porters and many of the most senior and well-paid chefs are men. Management is fairly evenly split between males and females but 'women predominate in housekeeping and personnel, as managers within institutional catering and as proprietors of small establishments'. At lower levels in the hotel job hierarchy, 'women are employed as counter and kitchen hands, waitresses, chambermaids, etc.'

Increasingly such workers are employed part-time and often on a casual basis. The hotel trade is highly competitive and employers are using more casual labour which can be laid off during slack times to cut costs. Male employees therefore tend to have more job security than female employees. Indeed this is a classic example of women at the lower levels in the profession being stuck in a secondary labour market with little security and few prospects.

Conclusion

Crompton and Sanderson believe that women continue to suffer considerable disadvantages within the labour market. However, the precise reasons for these disadvantages and the degree of inequality between men and women vary from industry to industry. Different factors are important in different parts of the labour market with diverse consequences. Overall though, Crompton and Sanderson do see some evidence of a reduction in gender divisions in employment. They say:

> The decline in manual occupations, and the intensification of competition between different types of disadvantaged labour at the lower levels of service employment, might be expected to result in a decline in sex-typed occupations in the structure as a whole.
>
> Crompton and Sanderson, 1990, p. 165

At higher levels, more women have been using their educational success and the 'qualifications lever' to force their way into male strongholds. However, Crompton and Sanderson also note that women are increasingly employed in part-time work. They conclude that while gender differences might become 'less oppressive and inegalitarian' they 'will be a persisting feature within work and employment' for the foreseeable future.

Evaluation

Dawn Burton (1994) has praised certain aspects of Crompton and Sanderson's study. She says:

> Gendered Jobs and Social Change provides a useful contribution to existing explanations of occupational segregation in Britain. The strength of Crompton and Sanderson's argument is that they point to a range of social, cultural and political processes which shape the division of labour between men and women in particular occupations.
>
> Burton, 1994

Burton welcomes the lack of reliance upon a single theoretical framework to explain gender differences in all types of employment. She is less complimen- tary, however, about their research methods. She points out that it is dangerous to generalize from case study research since the case studies selected may be unrepresentative of the phenomenon being studied. The findings of case study research become more reliable if a number of different case studies are examined, but Crompton and Sanderson only did this with building societies. Furthermore, they were sometimes vague about the research methods used. Burton says:

> In some cases the reader does not know how many people were interviewed, how these individuals were selected, where they were interviewed, or whether they were representative of others working in the occupation concerned.
>
> Burton, 1994

More fundamental objections to the study are raised by Lisa Adkins and Celia Lury (1992). They see the reliance upon a wide range of factors for explaining gender inequalities as a weakness rather than a strength. They say that:

> pluralistic conceptualization does little to move beyond previous understandings of the gendered dynamics of the labour market, and, indeed, in many ways, marks a regression in that such pluralism understates the significance of gender in the formation of occupations, occupational segregation, and forms of gendered inequality and exploitation.
>
> Adkins and Lury, 1992, p. 176

In particular, Adkins and Lury believe that Crompton and Sanderson see women as having more choices open to them than they really have. By applying Giddens's concept of structuration to men and women in the same way, the study fails to acknowledge that women's choices are strongly restricted by 'the actions of male workers'. Men shape the structure of the labour market much more than women.

Gender and stratification

In the previous section we showed how women tend to receive lower wages, have different types of job, and spend fewer years of their lives working in paid employment than men. Some women work exclusively as housewives, but increasingly women combine domestic tasks with paid work outside the home.

These points raise serious problems for those who wish to identify the position of women in the stratification systems of contemporary Western societies.

The problem of gender and class

Some approaches to this problem try to integrate women into theories of class alongside men; we analysed these in Chapter 2 (see pp. 109–11). However, many feminist writers, and particularly radical feminists, argue that women should be seen as a distinct group in their own right and that gender differences are at least as important as those between different occupations.

As we indicated in an earlier section, the radical feminist Shulamith Firestone (1972) argued that women formed a sex class based upon their biological differences to men. Margaret Eichler (1980) criticizes this approach for being 'non- or pre-sociological, for it assumes a direct relationship between a biological and social difference'. Obviously men and women form fairly distinct biological groupings, but it may be difficult to see each as a different 'class', in the usual sense of the word. Some women are wealthy and a few have occupations of

high status that attract high rewards; there is therefore no clear economic dividing line between men and women.

Some writers have therefore turned to non-class forms of stratification for models with which to describe and explain gender inequalities.

Gender and caste

Kate Millett (1970) suggests in passing that women have a caste-like status, and Eichler (1980) notes some similarities between the position of castes and those of gender groupings:

1 Membership of a caste and of a gender are both ascribed at birth. This ascribed status provides the basis for the different groups having different cultures.

2 Social mobility between the groups is more or less impossible.

3 Different groups receive different levels of reward.

However, as Eichler points out, there are also important differences between caste and gender stratification:

1 In the caste system, all members of the highest castes are clearly in an advantaged position over all members of lower castes: a Brahmin is always socially superior to an untouchable. Eichler suggests that the relationship between males and females in modern industrial societies is not so hierarchical. She says 'there are many women whose rank, by whatever criterion is higher than that of many men.'

2 Furthermore, caste systems are based upon endogamy, that is individuals can only marry members of the same caste. Men and women on the other hand are expected to intermarry. Gender-based stratification is therefore exogamous: individuals must take a marriage partner from outside the group to which they belong.

Gender and minority groups

An alternative to defining women as a caste is to see them as a minority group. This approach is taken by Helen Mayer Hacker (1972). She adopts Louis Wirth's definition of a minority group which reads:

> A minority group is any group of people who because of their physical or cultural characteristics, are singled out from others in the society in which they live for differential and unequal treatment, and who therefore regard themselves as objects of collective discrimination.
>
> Hacker, 1972

By comparing the situations of American blacks and women, Hacker indicates some of the advantages of classifying women as a minority group:

1 Both groups have high social visibility: blacks in terms of their 'racial' characteristics and to some extent their styles of dress; women in terms of their sexual characteristics and feminine clothes.

2 Both groups have similar ascribed attributes, that is attributes which are assigned to them by the majority group simply on the grounds of their minority group membership. Blacks have been characterized as emotional, 'primitive' and childlike; women as irresponsible, inconsistent and emotionally unstable. Both groups, to some degree, have been or are regarded as having a low intelligence. Compared to whites, blacks have been labelled 'inferior'; compared to men, women have been labelled as 'weaker'.

3 The status of both blacks and women is rationalized in similar ways by the majority group. Their position is seen as a reflection of their ascribed characteristics: 'Blacks are all right in their place and contented with their lot'. The same applies to women: 'Their place is in the home and they find happiness and fulfilment in their roles as wives and mothers'.

4 Both groups adopt accommodating behaviour in adapting to their situation. Both are deferential and flattering to the majority group. Relative powerlessness forces both to adopt devious methods in their dealings with members of the majority group. Blacks have various strategies for outwitting whites; women use so-called 'feminine wiles' for getting their own way.

5 Both groups suffer from similar discriminatory practices: their education is limited to fit them for

their ascribed status, and barriers are erected to prevent them from entering the political arena. In the labour market, blacks are largely confined to 'Black jobs', women to 'women's jobs'. These jobs have certain factors in common – low skill, low status and low pay.

Eichler criticizes minority group theory by saying:

> as a stratification concept it is very limited: it focuses solely on the consequences of belonging to a minority group but does not tell us anything about the power relationship as such, its variations, limitations, different manifestations, etc.
>
> Eichler, 1980

Sex stratification

The most promising approaches to gender and stratification have tried to bridge the gap between those theories that see gender as unimportant compared to class stratification, and those which ignore class and emphasize the distinction between the position of men and women in society.

Eichler (1980) has sketched the outlines of how such a theory could be developed. She states that 'Social stratification on bases other than sex is real, but so is sex stratification.' She argues that the basic problem is that much of the exploitation of women takes place outside the economy. It cannot therefore be discussed in terms of conventional Marxist notions of class, since it occurs within the context of the family.

If women are housewives and do not have paid employment, they cannot be categorized according to their own occupation, yet Eichler does not accept that their position should simply be related to their husband's. Personal dependency of wives on husbands cuts across class divisions: a working-class and a middle-class woman might both be refused credit unless they gained the agreement of their husband. Both might rely on their husband for any income they receive. Even in a family where husband and wife both work in paid employment, the wife might still be dependent if the husband makes most of the important decisions about family spending.

In conventional Marxist terms, non-working wives cannot be considered part of the class system. They do not produce exchange values through producing commodities which are sold in the market; they do not produce a profit or surplus value for employers. The products of housewives' labour are consumed by members of the family and are not sold.

Eichler argues that none of the above facts mean that women are not exploited. In effect, what housewives do is no different from what many paid workers do. For example, a housewife might transform the raw materials – eggs, flour, milk and spices – into a cake. The cake is consumed in the family, and the husband probably eats part of it. A baker could perform exactly the same tasks which produce a commodity that is sold and creates surplus value for an employer. In effect the exchange value created by housewives is 'stolen': the services she provides and the commodities she produces are consumed but cannot be sold. She produces use values but not exchange values.

In a family in which both spouses work outside the home, the wife can be seen as doubly or even triply exploited. Like other employees, she is exploited by employers who extract surplus value from her labour. Within the family, she may lose control over part of all the wages she has earned if the husband retains control over important financial decisions. Furthermore, it is usual for the wife to continue to do most of the housework, and the husband will receive some of the benefits from the use values she creates in the home.

According to Eichler, the reason a woman's position cannot be seen entirely in terms of the husband's social class is that the family is not a capitalist institution. The relationships within the family are not the same as purely economic relationships. A housewife might continue to produce use values, for example by cooking and cleaning, but be refused economic rewards for her efforts. Eichler uses the example of a housewife who continues to perform domestic duties conscientiously, but she is refused money by her husband because he knows she wishes to spend it on presents for her lover.

Eichler describes the family as a quasi-feudal institution. The husband provides money for food, shelter, clothing and protection in return for personal services. The situation of a wife has some similarities to that of a serf.

Eichler makes some interesting points about the situation of women, but fails to provide a clear analysis which can be applied to all women. She regards single working women as having a class position derived entirely from their work. From her point of view, such a woman shares nothing in common with a housewife in terms of their positions in the stratification system. However, it can be argued that both might suffer the same types of discrimination, have a sense of common grievance, identify with each other as 'sisters' (if they are feminists), and have an inferior social status to men. Radical feminists would deny that it is only married women who form a distinctive grouping within society's stratification systems.

Eichler is also unclear about the causes of women's disadvantages. In part they seem to be based upon economic inequalities, but to some extent they are also based upon personal relationships between husbands and wives. Eichler tends to assume, without advancing any evidence, that husbands are dominant within marriage and that women still have primary responsibility for domestic tasks.

Women's liberation – proposals and prospects

From the 1960s onwards, a vast literature in support of women's liberation has poured from the presses. Many suggestions have been made by feminist writers as to how women's position in society can be improved. There has, however, been no agreement about the ultimate aims of women's liberation, or how those aims are to be achieved.

David Bouchier (1983) distinguishes three objectives that have been advanced by feminists:

> *an integrated or egalitarian society where sex differences no longer count; an androgynous society where sex differences no longer exist; and a separatist society where men and women no longer share the same social world.*
>
> Bouchier, 1983

The first objective for an egalitarian society is generally supported by Marxist and socialist feminists. Liberal feminists also tend to have some sympathy with this aim, although they stop short of advocating a totally egalitarian society. Instead, they support a society in which there is equality of opportunity. Many believe that since men and women have equal abilities this will lead to the gradual disappearance of significant inequalities between the sexes.

The second and third objectives for androgyny and separatism are generally supported by radical feminists. Shulamith Firestone (1972) expresses the strongest support for androgyny in her suggestion that babies should be conceived and developed outside the womb. Separatist feminists do not necessarily believe that women's liberation should lead to equality. Supremacists believe that women would be dominant in a future feminist paradise. Most feminists, however, do not regard a separatist society as either desirable or practicable.

In recent years, feminist and anti-feminist ideas have developed in different ways. There has been something of a backlash against feminism from those who believe that the movement has either gone too far or that it has already substantially achieved its objectives. Within feminism there has been a degree of fragmentation, with specific groups (such as Black feminists, lesbian feminists and eco-feminists (who combine feminist and ecological beliefs) representing different strands of feminist thought. To some extent, this reflects a postfeminist view that it might be impossible or undesirable to develop a single, all-embracing feminist project for transforming society. There is now increased emphasis on the differences between groups of women, rather than inequality between women and men. With the development of the study of masculinity, men's proposals for changing gender inequalities and differences have been added to the growing list of voices commenting on the issues raised by feminism. We will now consider more specific proposals to improve the position of women.

The abolition of gender roles

Many feminist writers have advocated the abolition of gender roles, with the mother–housewife role being selected as the prime target. Ann Oakley (1974) argues that the following steps must be taken to liberate women:

1   The housewife role must be abolished. Oakley rejects less radical solutions such as payment for housework, which, she argues, will simply reinforce the woman equals housewife equation.

2   The family, as it now stands, must be abolished. This proposal follows from the first since the housewife and mother roles are part and parcel of the same thing. Abolishing the family will also serve to break the circle of the daughter learning her role from the mother, the son learning his role from the father.

3   The sexual division of labour must be eradicated in all areas of social life.

Oakley argues that 'we need an ideological revolution, a revolution in the ideology of gender roles current in our culture, a revolution in concepts of gender identity'. Thus, men and women must be seen as people, not as males and females.

Kate Millett (1970), a radical feminist writer, argues that in a society without culturally defined gender roles, each individual will be free to 'develop an entire – rather than a partial, limited, and conformist – personality'. Thus females may develop so-called male traits, and vice versa. This would involve complete tolerance of homosexual and lesbian relationships, 'so that the sex act ceases to be arbitrarily polarized into male and female'. Thus, those who are biologically male and female may

develop their personality and behaviour along lines best suited to themselves, rather than being cramped and confined by the culturally defined labels, male and female.

Modifications and alternatives to the family

The continuing debate on the role of women in society has produced a whole spectrum of modifications and alternatives to the housewife–mother role and the family. They range from Oakley's radical demands to abolish both, to more moderate suggestions which, in many cases, largely maintain the status quo with proposals to lighten the burdens of housework and motherhood. Ideas which fall into the latter category include payment for housework, the provision of crèches by employers, a free system of childcare provided as of right by the state for every mother who requires it, and maternity leave plus maternity benefits paid by employers or government, with the mother's job being held open should she wish to return to work.

Many radical feminists argue that such measures will not necessarily alter the position of women in the home. There, despite the fact that her burdens might be eased, she may still be relegated to the role of housewife and mother.

One of the simplest solutions to this problem has been put forward by Susan Brownmiller (1970). She suggests that husband and wife should split their traditional roles down the middle. Each should work for half a day and spend the rest of the time taking care of the children. Jessie Bernard supports this idea, arguing that 'with one stroke, it alleviates one of the major responsibilities of men (sole responsibility for the provider role) and of women (exclusive responsibility for housework and childcare)' (Bernard, 1976).

Many writers foresee a range of alternatives for the family's future. The socialist feminist Juliet Mitchell (1971) advocates various experiments in communal living to suit the personalities and circumstances of the individuals involved. She supports a 'range of institutions which match the free invention and variety of men and women'. Jessie Bernard takes a similar view. She looks forward to 'a future of marital options' hoping that 'people will be able to tailor their relationships to their circumstances and preferences'.

Two main themes dominate much of the writing on the future of the role of women in relation to the family. The first demands equality between the sexes; the second advocates freedom of choice with tolerance by all of the range of 'family life' that will emerge as a result. As Chapter 8 will show, family life in Britain and some other countries has become increasingly diverse; no one form of family is now dominant. However, this diversity has not always benefited women. For example, women are far more likely to end up as single parents than men, and single parenthood is often accompanied by poverty. Furthermore, while there has been some reduction in inequality in areas such as housework in two-parent families, evidence suggests that women still do more than their fair share (see Chapter 8).

Women and the labour market

Proposals to end discrimination against women in the labour market involve many of the suggested changes outlined above. Women must be freed from domestic burdens or share them equally with men if they are to compete for jobs on equal terms. An end to discrimination in the labour market would also involve the abolition of the sexual division of labour – the removal of distinctions between 'men's jobs' and 'women's jobs'.

The failure of women's entry into the labour market to end the sexual division of labour has led some writers to suggest that women as a group must gain control over a significant part of the forces of production in order to remove discrimination. Juliet Mitchell (1971) argues on these lines when she states that 'their entry into the labour force is not enough: they must enter in their own right with their own independent economic interest'.

Many feminist writers reject women's capitalism as a goal in itself. They argue that it will simply result in equality of exploitation; most men and most women will be equally exploited. However, as Mitchell suggests, it could provide a power base from which to move towards socialism and equality for all people.

Raising consciousness and creating solidarity

D.H.J. Morgan (1986) has applied the Marxist concepts of ideology, class consciousness and class solidarity to the position of women in society. Just as the class system is justified and legitimated by ruling-class ideology, so the position of women is justified and legitimated by what may be termed male ideology. This ideology defines a woman's place, how she should act, think and feel as a woman, and so maintains her subordination and justifies her exploitation.

Just as ruling-class ideology creates false class consciousness, so male ideology produces what can be seen as false gender consciousness. From a Marxist perspective, class consciousness and class solidarity are essential before the subject class can overthrow its oppressors. In terms of the Marxist analogy, gender consciousness and female solidarity are necessary for women's liberation.

Arguably, it is in this area that the Women's Liberation Movement has had most success. Feminists of every variety agree that women must become aware of their exploitation by men before they will be willing or able to change their position in society. Without some degree of female solidarity it seems unlikely that women will be able to achieve any of the aims of feminism. Most feminists also accept, though, that raising women's consciousness cannot on its own secure women's liberation. For this to occur, either women will need to have greater power, or the ideology of male supremacy will have to be seriously challenged among men as well as among women.

The Women's Liberation Movement

Support for the Women's Liberation Movement is nothing new. As early as 1869, John Stuart Mill and Harriet Taylor wrote:

> If the principle [of democracy] is true, we ought to act as if we believed it, and not to ordain that to be born a girl instead of a boy, any more than to be born black instead of white, or a commoner instead of a nobleman, shall decide the person's position throughout life.
>
> Mill and Taylor, 1974, first pub. 1869, p. 33

In the early years of the twentieth century, suffragettes mounted a campaign to secure the vote for women. As Sylvia Walby has pointed out, the 'first-wave' of feminism in the nineteenth and early twentieth centuries went well beyond a campaign for voting rights for women (Walby, 1990). There were also campaigns to make it easier for women to get divorced, for better education and training opportunities, and for married women to have the legal right to own property.

For most of the twentieth century feminists fought for civil rights, that is legal equality for all adults regardless of sex. However, it was only in the 1960s that a women's movement with much broader aims emerged.

The USA

Juliet Mitchell (1971) argues that the Women's Liberation Movement in the USA was partly triggered by the radical movements of the middle and late 1960s. She points to the various civil rights organizations which campaigned for the rights of ethnic minority groups:

1 The Black Power Movement, which spearheaded the demands of more militant blacks.
2 The Youth Movement, represented by organizations such as Students for a Democratic Society.
3 The Peace Movement, which coordinated protest against the war in Vietnam and later in Cambodia.

These movements preceded and paralleled the Women's Liberation Movement in the USA. They emphasized freedom, questioned established truths and attacked what they saw as oppression and exploitation.

Mitchell argues that such movements provided part of the impetus and philosophy for the Women's Liberation Movement. Women increasingly realized that they needed a movement of their own, since even as members of other radical movements they were often treated in terms of their traditional stereotypes. For example, when Stokely Carmichael, then leader of the SNCC (Student Nonviolent Coordinating Committee), a Black civil rights organization of the mid-1960s, was asked about the role of women in the organization, he replied, 'the only position for women in SNCC is prone'.

Barbara Deckard (1975) summarizes the results of women's participation in civil rights movements during the early and mid-1960s. She states:

> *Here many young women learned both the rhetoric and the organization of protest. Not surprisingly, as they become more sensitive to the blacks' second-class status, they became more aware of their own.*
>
> Deckard, 1975

The result was the Women's Liberation Movement.

Britain and the USA compared

In Britain, the Women's Liberation Movement was, according to David Bouchier (1983), more influenced by the labour movement. In 1968, working-class women trade unionists went on strike at the Ford motor plant at Dagenham. This, in turn, prompted the union movement as a whole to take a more active interest in women's issues. The International Marxist Group was the first left-wing political organization actively to promote the Women's Liberation Movement. Whereas in the USA radical oppression helped to stimulate the Women's Liberation Movement, in Britain class was more important. Women began to insist that their own disadvantages were at least as important as those suffered by the working class.

Because of these different origins, the Women's Liberation Movement has tended to develop in different ways in Britain and the USA. In the USA, the more moderate part of the movement has consisted of liberal feminists. The largest and most influential women's group in America is the liberal National Organization of Women. Alongside this liberal feminist tradition, radical feminism has also had some support. It is significant that two of the USA's leading feminists (Kate Millett and Shulamith Firestone) are both radicals.

In Britain, the Women's Liberation Movement has tended to be more socialist and Marxist in character, although there is some support for radical feminism. David Bouchier estimated that in 1983 there were some 300 separate feminist organizations in Britain, although many feminists choose to work through existing left-wing political organizations. Many feminist groups are locally based: British feminists have been less successful than the Americans in creating their own independent national organizations.

There have, though, been attempts to develop organizations at a national level. Nickie Charles (1993) notes that between 1970 and 1978 the National Women's Coordinating Committee held national conferences for the women's movement. Between 1971 and 1978 the conference passed resolutions demanding seven rights for women. In 1971 these were:

1 equal pay
2 equal education and job opportunities
3 abortion on demand and free contraception
4 free nurseries 24 hours a day.

In 1975:

5 legal and financial independence for women
6 the ending of discrimination against lesbians.

And in 1978:

7 freedom for women from the use or threat of physical or sexual violence by men.

The last issue caused a split in the national movement and led to the 1978 conference being the last. Radical feminists saw male violence as vital to understanding women's oppression, whereas socialist feminists placed greater emphasis on economic factors.

However, the demise of the national movement did not prevent women's groups from making significant gains for women in Britain.

Nickie Charles suggests that one important feature of feminism in Britain has been the establishment of services run by women for the benefit of women. These have included refuges for the victims of domestic violence, women's advice centres and pregnancy testing services. Women have also had some success in running national campaigns over individual issues: for example, in persuading the government to retain child allowances, and in protecting the facility for women to have abortions.

Despite the successes, Charles believes that by the end of the 1970s the splits in the movement were beginning to weaken it. Radical, liberal and socialist feminists fought with each other to have their own analyses of, and solutions to, women's oppression accepted. There was also increasing recognition that women of different ages, classes and ethnic groups might have different interests. White, middle-class feminists had paid little attention to the way gender inequalities could be compounded by a 'racist and class-divided society', alienating many Black and working-class women from the movement. These differences anticipated the development of postfeminisms in the 1990s, which will be discussed below.

Charles believes that the Women's Liberation Movement in Britain has achieved some important reforms but has not succeeded in achieving a radical transformation for women. She argues that there has been 'restructuring' of the gender division of labour and that:

> This restructuring has changed the distribution of women and men within the workforce and has made it more acceptable for men to be seen pushing prams and hanging out the washing; but it has not resulted in the elimination of women's subordination and it may have contributed to the fragmentation of the working class and the undermining of its resistance to capitalist exploitation.
>
> Charles, 1993

Susan Faludi – *Backlash*

In her 1992 book, *Backlash: The Undeclared War Against Women*, Susan Faludi argues that the Women's Liberation Movement has run into increased opposition. Women have been told by politicians, business leaders and advertisers, among others, that women have won the war for women's rights, and now enjoy equality with men. However, they are warned at the same time that the rights they have won have been at considerable cost. Faludi says:

> Behind this celebration of women's victory, behind the news cheerfully and endlessly repeated, that the struggle for women's rights is won, another message flashes. You may be free and equal now, it says to women, but you have never been more miserable.
>
> Faludi, 1992

In America, for example, magazines and newspapers have claimed that professional career women are prone to infertility and health problems such as alcoholism and hair loss, while women without children and women who do not get married are prone to depression or hysteria. Feminism is portrayed as the root cause of these problems.

Faludi denies that women have attained equality. For example, despite some newspaper reports that the pay differential between men and women was narrowing, in 1986 women in the USA working full-time still earned only 64 per cent of the male full-time worker's wage. The figures were exactly the same as they had been over three decades earlier in 1955. In Britain, female workers had increased their earnings compared to men, but by 1991 female full-time workers still earned less than 80 per cent of male full-time workers.

Faludi is also critical of many of the claims about the supposedly harmful effects of women's liberation. She quotes numerous studies which have found that single women and women with careers tend to have more healthy and fulfilling lives than married housewives. Faludi found that:

> The psychological indicators are numerous and they all point in the same direction. Married women in these studies report about 20 per cent more depression than single women and three times the rate of severe neurosis. Married women have more nervous breakdowns, nervousness, heart palpitations and inertia. Still other afflictions disproportionately plague married women: insomnia, trembling hands, dizzy spells, nightmares, hypochondria, passivity, agoraphobia and other phobias, unhappiness with their physical appearance and overwhelming feelings of guilt and shame.
>
> Faludi, 1992

To Faludi then, the backlash is not a genuine attempt to improve the lives of women, but rather represents an attempt by men to reassert their dominance. Even so, Faludi is generally optimistic that this attempt will not succeed. She claimed that there was 'no good reason, why the 1990s cannot be women's decade', and she concludes:

> whatever new obstacles are mounted against the future march towards equality, whatever new myths invented, penalties levied, opportunities rescinded or degradations imposed, no one can ever take from women the justness of their cause.
>
> Faludi, 1992

Postfeminism

The backlash described by Faludi has been termed postfeminism in some circles. However, this term has also been applied to more theoretical developments that have had consequences for the women's movement. Under the influence of postmodernism (see pp. 157–63), some women have begun to question the idea that there can ever be a single project to liberate women. This view argues that women are a highly diverse group and no one group of feminists can claim to speak for all women.

Furthermore, any set of solutions to the general problems of gender inequality is unlikely to be suitable for all groups of women. Like postmodernists, postfeminists of this sort reject the idea of a single 'metanarrative', or big story, which claims to offer a single design for improving the world. This change has entailed a focus on the differences between women rather than the inequalities between men and women. Thus Ann Brooks says, 'postfeminism as understood from this perspective is about the conceptual shift within feminism from debates around equality to a focus on debates around difference. It is fundamentally about, not a depoliticisation of feminism, but a political shift in feminism's conceptual and theoretical agenda' (Brooks, 1997). As part of this shift, the usefulness of terms such as 'patriarchy' and 'women' have been questioned. Postfeminists argue that such terms are over-generalized and falsely assume that oppression is the same for all women and that all women are fundamentally the same.

Brooks attributes this shift to the 'political impact of women of colour's critique of the racist and ethnocentric assumptions of a largely white, middle-class feminism', and to an increasing interest in sexual differences between women (for example heterosexual women and lesbians).

Writers such as Brooks see this change as progressive, and others agree that diverse feminisms have played an important part in the women's movement. Thus, for example, Imelda Whelehan says, 'an important function of black feminism has been to keep alive the vitality of the social and political environment from which it emerged' (Whelehan, 1995).

As socialist and Marxist feminism lost popularity and influence in Britain, the new feminisms kept women's issues in the public eye. Yet Whelehan warns against abandoning the ideas and language of the earlier era. She says that it 'is important not to lose sight of of the early aims of second wave feminism. No matter how simplistic some of their constructions seem today, early critiques made those important steps towards forging a language specific to the experiences of women.' Terms such as patriarchy may indeed be over-generalized but they have helped to unite women in trying to understand their common experiences and therefore have created a basis for political action to improve the position of all women.

Masculinity

In the earlier parts of this chapter we have seen how feminists have succeeded in putting the sociology of gender – and of women in particular – on the sociological map. Before 1970, few sociological studies were conducted about women and women's lives. Yet, paradoxically, some male sociologists have argued that men have also in some senses been 'invisible' in much sociology. While most studies have been conducted by men and the subjects of the research have been men, few have been about masculinity. Thus Jeff Hearn and David Morgan argue:

> *Studies which are routinely about men, in that men constitute the acknowledged or unacknowledged subjects, are not necessarily about men in a more complex, more problematized, sociological sense. They tend to be resource rather than topic. Studies of social mobility, for example, may be about men for methodological reasons or administrative convenience but they are rarely, if ever, about men in the sense that researchers believe that such studies might make any contribution to the sociology of gender or the critical understanding of men and masculinities.*
>
> Hearn and Morgan, 1990, p. 7

Men are simply taken for granted in studies; they are assumed to be the norm and their behaviour is not explained in terms of gender or compared to that of women.

Similarly, Michael Kimmel argues that sociology 'was, in part, responsible for the reproduction of gender relations that kept masculinity invisible and rendered femininity problematic' (Kimmel, 1990). Women were seen as a deviation from the norm (men) and their behaviour was therefore worthy of explanation in terms of their gender. Since the masculine gender was taken as the norm it did not need to be researched.

Kimmel argues that this situation could act in the interests of men. He says:

> *Men benefit from the inherited biological or sex-role definitions of masculinity, which imply activity, mastery, rationality, competence. If gender relations are encoded in our genes or culturally mandated, then the extent to which these definitions are based upon men's power over women is obscured.*
>
> Kimmel, 1990

It becomes unnecessary, for instance, to study how men use physical and sexual violence to control women or how men might help each other to exclude women from parts of society which they wish to reserve for themselves.

In this section we will examine some of the recent attempts that have been made to put right this 'neglect' of masculinity and to examine how masculinity shapes the lives of men and the social world in general.

David D. Gilmore – *Cultural Concepts of Masculinity*

Masculinity, sex and gender

In his 1990 book, *Manhood in the Making: Cultural Concepts of Masculinity*, the anthropologist David D. Gilmore discusses the way masculinity is defined in a wide range of societies. Gilmore describes masculinity as 'the approved way of being an adult male in any given society', and his study is an attempt to discover the extent to which this varies from place to place. He uses both his own field data from ethnographic research and the findings of other anthropological studies. He includes examples from all continents and 'from warrior and pacifist societies, from egalitarian and stratified ones' and from 'hunting-gathering bands, horticultural and pastoral tribes, peasants and postindustrial civilizations' (Gilmore, 1990).

Gilmore does not see masculinity as a set of characteristics which are entirely determined by biology. He says that feminists 'have convincingly demonstrated that the conventional bipolar model based on biology is invalid and that sex (biological inheritance) and gender (cultural norms) are distinct categories'. He also says that 'the answer to the manhood puzzle must lie in culture', but nevertheless he does not believe that biology is unimportant. He claims that 'culture uses or exaggerates biological potential in specific ways'. Nearly always this involves making a very clear distinction between masculinity and femininity.

In the vast majority of societies masculinity is defined in fairly similar ways, suggesting that biological differences do play some part in influencing the cultural definitions which are adopted.

The typical features of masculinity

Gilmore suggests that there are three typical features of masculinity found in most societies:

1   Man the impregnator. Men are expected to impregnate women. To do this they are normally required to take the initiative in courtship and sexual encounters. They are expected to compete with other men for access to women. For example, in Sicily 'masculine honour is always bound up with aggression and potency. A real man in Sicily is "a

man with big testicles"'. In Italy it is particularly important that men are seen to be able to reproduce by making their wife pregnant.

Similarly in the Truk Islands in the South Pacific, 'the Trukese man must be the initiator, totally in command'. He must be 'potent, having many lovers, bringing his partners to orgasm time and again'. If he fails the woman laughs at him and the man is shamed.

Unlike the aggressive and war-like Trukese, the Mehinaku Indians of the rain forests of central Brazil are a peaceful tribe and the men have never been warriors. Like the Trukese, though, the men are very concerned about their manly image and sex is important in producing and maintaining that image. Gilmore says of Mehinaku men that 'a man who fails to bring his wife or lover to orgasm, fails to satisfy his partner, fails to beget children, is ridiculed and publicly shamed'. Knowledge of his failure soon spreads around the village and he can become an outcast. Not surprisingly then, the men have developed 'an elaborate system of magical therapy' to help men avoid this predicament.

2   Man the provider. Having impregnated women, in most societies men are then expected to provide for them and their offspring.

According to Gilmore, in the Mediterranean 'the emphasis on male honour as a domestic duty is widespread'. In the traditional Greek peasant village, the honour of fathers rests upon their ability to provide their daughters with large dowries. In southern Italy, the honour associated with being a good man partly rests upon a husband's ability to support his wife and children, while Spanish men pursue 'the breadwinning role as a measure of their manhood'.

Men of the Sambia in New Guinea have their manhood measured partly through their competence in hunting. Women are not allowed to hunt – it is an entirely male preserve. Although hunting produces only a small proportion of the food needed by the Sambia, it has an important symbolic value. It provides the feathers and skins used in rituals. Men who fail in hunting are subject to ridicule and may have difficulty in finding a wife.

3   Man the protector. The third way in which most cultures define masculinity is in terms of men's role as protectors. Men must not simply impregnate women and provide for them and their children, they must also protect them from other men and any threats which might arise.

The Sikh Jats of the Punjab adhere strongly to the concept of izzat which is 'a philosophy of life which reflects their paramount concern for male power, in which "a man's duty is to be stalwart in the defence of his family". If anyone threatens a man's family he must, at the very least, threaten them back, and he must not be intimidated.' Gilmore says 'in this Sikh society, a man's first duty is to take risks in the service of his family'.

The Spanish in Andalusia use the concept of *hombria* to designate manliness. *Hombria* is 'physical and moral courage' in defending a man's own honour and that of his family. Men should always show courage and be stoical in the face of any threat.

In the East African Samburu tribe, males have to demonstrate their bravery during *moranhood*. This starts at around the age of 14 or 15 and lasts about 12 years. The first test is a circumcision ritual which is performed without anaesthetic. The boy must not flinch, despite the pain as his foreskin is cut off, or 'he is forever shamed as a coward'. Later in *moranhood*, the male proves himself by rustling cattle from other tribes. This runs the risk of being caught and beaten or even killed by the victims of the rustling. However, it confirms that the male has become manly, it makes him attractive to females, and shows that he will be able to take care of a family.

Masculinity and society

Gilmore argues that the roles of impregnator, protector and provider have some features in common. They are all dangerous or competitive and failure in any of the roles carries high costs. 'They place men at risk on the battlefield, in the hunt, or in confrontation with their fellows.' Men are expected to overcome the fear felt by all humans when they are placed at risk.

Gilmore suggests that this feature of masculinity may have benefits for society. Men are persuaded to do things which are necessary for society's survival which they would not otherwise do because of their desire for self-preservation. He says 'we may regard "real manhood" as an inducement for high performance in the social struggle for scarce resources, a code of conduct that advances collective interests by overcoming inner inhibitions'.

In putting forward these claims, Gilmore uses a functionalist approach. He explains the existence of ideals of masculinity in terms of the functions they perform for society. However, Gilmore is critical of some aspects of functionalism. He does not see the type of masculinity described above as an inevitable feature of all societies. Rather, it is one of a number of strategies of adaptation which can reconcile 'individual and social needs' through rewards and punishments. The societies described above all reward masculine men with high status and punish unmasculine men through ridicule and other negative sanctions, and in doing so persuade men to take physical and psychological risks they might otherwise avoid.

In a few societies, though, masculinity has a very different meaning. Societies can work with a wide variety of definitions of masculinity.

Men in Tahiti and Semai

Tahiti, one of the Society Islands in Polynesia, has a much less marked differentiation between masculinity and femininity than most societies. Furthermore, the Tahitian concept of masculinity does not require men to act as providers and protectors. There is little need for men to take physical risks since there is no warfare, and there are few dangerous occupations. The lagoon offers a plentiful supply of fish, so risky deep-sea fishing is not necessary. Families cooperate together in economic activities and there is no social pressure to be economically successful. Indeed, traditional Tahitian culture encourages a 'laconic attitude towards work'. It also encourages men to be timid and passive. They are expected to ignore insults and they very rarely fight one another.

Tahitian men are neither protective of their women nor possessive towards them. When an English ship, the *Dolphin*, arrived at Tahiti in 1767, the ship's captain reported that the Tahitian women 'came down and stripped themselves naked and made all the alluring gestures they could to entice them onshore' (quoted in Gilmore, 1990). The Tahitian men actually encouraged the women to do this and a later French explorer found that Tahitian men were extremely hospitable and even offered him their daughters.

The Semai people live in central Malaysia. Both men and women are strongly opposed to violence and aggression. Aggression is denoted by the word *punan* which also means taboo. The Semai try to avoid doing anything that frustrates another person and goes against their wishes. As a consequence, both men and women are usually expected to agree to a request for sex, even if they are married and the person requesting sex is not their spouse. However, it is also considered *punan* if a person repeatedly pesters another person for sex. There is very little jealousy and Semai men and women tolerate the extra-marital affairs of their spouses as being no more than a loan.

The Semai do not engage in competitive sport and are not materialistic. Men do not have to compete with each other because farming is cooperative and, if one man has too little land to get by, he simply asks another man for some of his. It is *punan* to refuse. Although the Semai do hunt, and hunting is reserved exclusively for males, the hunting is not dangerous or difficult. They hunt nothing larger or more dangerous than small pigs, they stop hunting before noon when it gets too hot, and 'if they encounter danger, they run away and hide without any shame or hesitation'.

There are some differences between men and women in both Tahitian and Semai society (although among the Semai they are not particularly pronounced), but neither has a cultural image of 'the real man'. Gilmore suggests that the unusual characteristics of masculinity in these societies may result from the material circumstances in which the societies exist.

Animals confronted with danger produce adrenalin which makes them more able to flee or to stay and fight the source of the danger. In humans, the choice between fight or flight is shaped by cultural conditioning. Most cultures seem to have put more emphasis on men fighting than fleeing but the Tahitians and Semai are exceptions. This may be due to the plentiful supply of food and other resources in both societies and the lack of 'serious hazards' in their environments such as dangerous animals or aggressive neighbours.

Gilmore admits that it is impossible to show conclusively that the ideology of passivity was caused by the material context. It could be that the culture creates the situation where the people have little material ambition and are content with what they have. Therefore they have no need to be competitive. He suggests that there might be a 'feedback relationship in which the ideology, once formed, assists in and intensifies a matching adaptation to the environment'.

Whatever the factors giving rise to these cultures, it is clear that the ideology of 'Man-the-Impregnator-Protector-Provider' is not universal.

Evaluation

Gilmore's work can be criticized for using functionalist analysis, which has been the subject of very strong criticism. Many feminists could criticize Gilmore for his apparent claims that men usually protect and provide for women. As we have seen in earlier sections of this chapter, it is often women who work harder than men and, far from protecting their wives, some men abuse and attack them. However, Gilmore's work does succeed in showing that culture has a very strong influence on ideologies of masculinity and that masculinity can therefore assume very different forms.

Victor J. Seidler – rationality and masculinity

Although Gilmore does use some examples from technologically advanced industrial or post-industrial societies, he relies mainly on examples from more traditional agricultural societies. Victor J. Seidler concentrates instead on men in Western societies (Seidler, 1989, 1994).

The Enlightenment

According to Seidler, ideas of masculinity in Western societies are closely connected with the thinking and beliefs associated with the Enlightenment. The Enlightenment is the name given to a range of interconnected philosophical, scientific and social beliefs which developed in Western Europe in the seventeenth and eighteenth centuries. Enlightenment thinking rejected emotion, superstition and belief in the supernatural as ways of understanding the world. It argued that the natural world could only be understood through objective, detached, unemotional science. Knowledge could only come from reason and rationality. Reason was contrasted with nature. As Seidler puts it, 'Nature is real but is bereft of consciousness and of value. It exists as separate and independent of the consciousness that is attempting to grasp it.' To understand the physical world humans had to detach themselves from it.

To Seidler and many other writers, Enlightenment thinking is the foundation of modernity. Modernity is a phase in human history in which it is believed that humans can use scientific knowledge to ensure progress. Science allows nature to be conquered and controlled for the benefit of people. (We discuss these ideas in more detail in Chapter 15.)

Masculinity, femininity and modernity

In modernity, science came to be associated with masculinity. For example the late sixteenth- and early seventeenth-century British philosopher Francis Bacon talked 'quite unashamedly about the new sciences as a masculinist philosophy'. In *The Protestant Ethic and the Spirit of Capitalism*, Max Weber described how the rational pursuit of profit encouraged by certain forms of Protestantism helped to produce the rationalization of the modern world (see Chapters 7 and 15 for a discussion of Weber). Not all humans, however, were seen as capable of understanding and controlling nature through reason. That privilege was reserved for men.

Women were seen as being closer to nature than men. As such they were regarded as being more emotional, less able to be detached, impersonal and rational. Emotions were valued less than reason. Seidler says 'emotions and feelings cannot be legitimated as sources of knowledge; rather, they reflect an interference or breakdown in the cool and autonomous logic of pure reason.' Men fear the consequences of being emotional. Emotions have no place, particularly in public arenas such as work, and so men suppress them. Seidler says that 'it is as if we do not have emotional needs of our own as men, for needs are a sign of weakness'.

Seidler sees the association of men with reason and rationality, and of women with nature and emotion as harmful and destructive. It damages personal relationships, making it difficult for men to build strong relationships with women. He says that 'self-sufficiency can make it difficult in relationships, for it creates its own forms of inequality as women are often left feeling that they alone have emotional needs and demands'.

The association of men with reason contributes to the creation and maintenance of male, patriarchal power at every level. Men are liable to tell their female partners in arguments that they are being irrational and emotional and to refuse to discuss matters further until the woman 'calms down'. Indeed, Seidler believes that men have become so accustomed to expecting to be in control of nature and their own emotions, that they scarcely notice that they have power over women. Men are 'constantly talking for others, while presenting themselves as the neutral voice of reason'.

Evaluation

Seidler's argument provides some interesting insights into the nature of masculinity in Western societies. However, it is somewhat abstract and is not based upon detailed empirical evidence. He admits that it may not be possible to generalize his claims about masculinity, saying 'I am talking from a particular experience of white, middle-class Jewish masculinity.' He also admits that it is not possible to identify one dominant form of masculinity in Western society.

Feminism and an increasing distrust of science have both contributed to the creation of a wider variety of masculinities in contemporary Western societies. We will examine some of these in the next section.

Jonathan Rutherford – 'Who's that man?'

Threats to traditional masculinity

Like Seidler, Rutherford links masculinity to ideas about reason. He says that a 'history of masculinity is a struggle to tame and subdue the emotional and sexual self and to recognise the ascendant and superior nature of reason and thought' (Rutherford, 1988). However, Rutherford believes that traditional conceptions of masculinity are under increasing threat. Men's definitions of themselves and of masculinity have begun to change. They have become more ambiguous, uncertain and varied.

Rutherford believes that 'the reality of men's heterosexual identities is that their endurance is contingent upon an array of structures and institutions'. If these structures are threatened or weakened then masculine identities can be threatened or weakened. A number of changes have undermined male dominance of certain structures and institutions:

1 Working-class masculinities have been threatened by the decline of manual heavy industry. Throughout the class structure, male unemployment has risen while female employment, particularly in part-time jobs, has increased.

2 In the domestic sphere, violent and sexual abuse of women and children by men has become better publicized and less tolerated.

3 The value of men's roles within the family has been questioned. Divorce laws 'far from being the Casanova's charter predicted by the popular press, have been predominantly used by women leaving their husbands'.

4 The women's movement has brought masculinity into question. It has exposed patriarchal power and portrayed men as self-interested abusers of that power rather than as the heroic conquerors of nature.

5 Furthermore, 'radical gay politics and black politics have produced new definitions of the world that are not attributed to the grand narrative of White Man'.

According to Rutherford, modern, white heterosexual men have long feared women, homosexuals and black men for the threats they can pose to their masculinity. The 'huge penis of the black man, the devouring female and the plague-like seduction of the homosexual' have, in heterosexual white men's minds, had the potential for challenging their masculine sexuality, their independence and their cool reason and calm rationality. As accounts of masculinity from the viewpoint of women, gay men and black men have gained in prominence, white heterosexual men have been forced to examine what masculinity means to them, and in some cases to change their beliefs.

Retributive man and new man

Rutherford recognizes that there have been numerous different responses to the changes outlined above. He says that 'the marketplace has produced a plurality of masculine identities; different models of fatherhood, sexualised images of men and new sensibilities.' However, he argues that, at its simplest, the responses can be divided into two groups: those of 'retributive men', and those of 'new men'.

Retributive men try to reassert traditional images of masculinity. They attack those who challenge their long-established and strongly-held view of what it means to be a real man. They have the 'notion of traitors: cowardly men who have abrogated their right to masculinity, and consequently to citizenship'.

The archetypal retributive man in contemporary popular culture is Rambo in films like *First Blood*.

Rambo 'confronts a world gone soft, pacified by traitors and cowards, dishonourable feminised men'. Retributive man in the form of Rambo responds with violence, trying to destroy all that threatens his concept of masculine honour.

However, retributive man is less problematic on screen than in real life. Rutherford suggests that the image of retributive man is undermined by the example of people such as Michael Ryan who try to mirror screen images in their own behaviour. Ryan went on the rampage in Hungerford in England in August 1987, indiscriminately shooting passers-by with his arsenal of firearms before shooting himself. The popular press portrayed Ryan in a less than flattering way as 'a lonely inadequate who employed a fantasy world to shore up his fragile masculinity'.

The alternative to the retributive man is the new man. The new man:

> is an expression of the repressed body of masculinity. It is a fraught and uneven attempt to express masculine emotional and sexual life. It is a response to the structural changes of the past decade and specifically to the assertiveness and feminism of women.
>
> Rutherford, 1988

For example, new men are liable to take fatherhood more seriously than traditional men. In films like *Kramer versus Kramer* (about the life of a lone father), men are portrayed as struggling with their new roles and trying to come to terms with having to acknowledge their own emotions. The high-street store, Mothercare, have started featuring fathers in the photographs in their catalogues and there is a 'new liberalised image of men pushing buggies, attending births and cuddling babies in public without fear of shame and ridicule'.

Men's bodies have increasingly featured in adverts such as the advert for Levis 501s where a man undresses in a launderette. In such contexts men have now become sex objects in a way that was once the sole prerogative of women. Rutherford argues that:

> For men to put their bodies on display contradicts the code of who looks and who is looked at. It pacifies us. Men have held the power of the look, the symbolic owning of women's bodies. Reversing the gaze offers the symbol of men's bodies on offer to women.
>
> Rutherford, 1988

The future of masculinity

Having described new men, Rutherford admits that they may be, at least partly, a media myth. He notes that research suggests that the division of labour between men and women in the home has not significantly changed. Women are still disadvantaged in the labour market to the extent that few families can afford to rely upon the wages of the woman while the man adopts the role of 'househusband'. Furthermore, the 'men's movement' has scarcely developed. In the 1970s there was some attempt to establish such a movement. Rutherford says that 'its main form was the consciousness raising "men's group", where men could explore areas of our lives such as sexuality and relationships, that had previously been taboo subjects in male company'. Yet most of the groups did not last long.

Most men have been left somewhat confused about what it means to be masculine. They can either try to defend the past by being retributive man, or embrace the future as new man. To Rutherford, the choice is between 'change or violence'. He comes down firmly in favour of the former, arguing that men should 'learn to live our differences without resort to oppression'.

Evaluation

Rutherford's work is rather journalistic and relies on anecdotal rather than systematic evidence. However, it does illustrate that the concept of masculinity has become increasingly complex. It raises interesting questions about how masculinity is changing, questions that have been taken up by the Australian sociologist Bob Connell.

R.W. Connell – *Masculinities*

Bob Connell (1995) follows writers such as Rutherford in arguing that there are many different types of masculinity in contemporary society. However, he goes much further than Rutherford in examining the relationships between different types of masculinity, theoretical issues relating to gender and masculinity and the historical changes in masculinity. Furthermore, he uses detailed empirical evidence to back up his arguments. For these reasons Connell's work makes a significant contribution to the development of theories of gender in general as well as of masculinity in particular.

The nature of gender

Connell's arguments are based upon a rejection of conventional approaches to the analysis of gender. He identifies three conventional approaches to this issue:

1 Those which see biological differences between male and female bodies as the cause of differences between women and men.

2 Those which believe that culture determines gender differences so that 'the body is a more or less

neutral surface or landscape on which a social symbolism is imprinted'.

3 Those which see gender as a product of a combination of biological and cultural factors.

An earlier section of this chapter examined these three approaches (see pp. 128–36).

Connell, however, sees all three as inadequate. He believes there is plenty of evidence that behaviour is not determined by biology. For example, there are cultures in which it is normal for men to engage in homosexuality at some points in the life cycle, and there have been cultures where rape did not exist, or was extremely rare. To Connell, biological arguments are based upon a powerful and influential metaphor of the body as a machine, a metaphor which is very misleading. However, he also rejects cultural determinism, the idea that behaviour is entirely shaped by culture. This is because bodies cannot be conceived as blank canvasses on which culture can create any type of behaviour. He says that 'bodies, in their own right as bodies, do matter. They age, get sick, enjoy, engender, give birth. There is an irreducible bodily dimension in experience and practice; the sweat cannot be excluded.'

Connell does not conclude, though, that biological and cultural factors can be seen as separate but interacting aspects of gender. Rather, the two need to be fused together by seeing the body as an active agent in social processes. The body acts within social institutions and social relationships, for example the institutions surrounding professional, masculine sport. But sport is also a bodily activity. Thus 'running, throwing, jumping or hitting' are 'symbolic and kinetic, social and bodily, at one and the same time, and these aspects depend on each other'. Bodily performance is part of being masculine or feminine. It can enable people to act in gendered ways, prevent people from acting in gendered ways, or persuade people to reinterpret their own gender.

He uses some examples from his own field research to illustrate this. One man he interviewed, Hugh Trelawney, describes how at university he became a 'legend', the 'animal of the year' through using his body for excessive drinking, drug-taking and having sex with many different women. Later in life, however, he found himself unable to sustain these activities through which he defined and established his own masculinity. After years of abuse, his body began to let him down. He became quite ill and had to undergo alcohol detoxification.

In another example, Connell describes how physical experiences led another interviewee to change his conception of his own sexuality. Don Merideth described how he got pleasure from the stimulation of his anus while having sex with a woman. This physical sensation led him to believe

that he should have homosexual relationships. The body led him towards a different set of social and physical practices. Connell therefore sees bodies as 'both objects and agents of practice', and the practices of bodies are involved in 'forming the structures within which bodies are appropriated and defined'. Bodies, whether male or female, are an active and integral part of social action and of the construction of gender, and are not separable from the societies in which they live.

Types of masculinity

Having established a foundation for the study of masculinities, Connell then discusses the different forms masculinity can take. Like writers such as Rutherford, he believes that masculinity can take more than one form. Masculinities constantly change, new forms can emerge and old forms decline, but in any particular era a broad distinction can be made between hegemonic and other types of masculinity.

Hegemonic masculinity is the form of masculinity that claims and tries to maintain a dominant influence over social life. Connell says, '"Hegemonic masculinity" is not a fixed character type, always and everywhere the same. It is, rather, the masculinity that occupies the hegemonic position in a given pattern of gender relations, a position always contestable.' The dominance of any one masculinity can be challenged by women and also by other masculinities. Thus white, heterosexual and middle-class masculinity might be dominant in contemporary western societies, but black, homosexual and working-class masculinities also exist and sometimes challenge hegemonic masculinity. Hegemonic masculinity may try to maintain its dominance through control over institutional structures. It can also be maintained through a 'rich vocabulary of abuse'. For example, the masculinity of heterosexual males can be put down through words such as 'wimp, milksop, nerd, turkey, sissy, lily liver, jellyfish, yellowbelly, candy ass, ladyfinger, pushover, cookie pusher, cream puff, motherfucker, pantywaist, mother's boy, four-eyes, ear-'ole, dweeb, geek, Milquetoast, Cedric, and so on. Here too the symbolic blurring with femininity is obvious.'

With some masculinities, hegemonic masculinity tries to maintain a situation of dominance and subordination. Thus heterosexual masculinity generally tries to keep homosexual masculinity subordinate. Many men are not subordinate to hegemonic masculinity but engage in relationships of complicity with it. That is they go along with aspects of hegemonic masculinity and try to gain by sharing in hegemonic masculinity's power over women and subordinate masculinities. However, they may be unable or unwilling to live up to the ideals of masculinity held up by the hegemonic type. Connell says, 'marriage, fatherhood and community life often involve extensive compromises with women rather than naked domination or an uncontested display of authority'. Within sets of gender relations, particular masculinities (or femininities) may be marginalized. Without necessarily being rejected outright, they are not acknowledged and accepted as legitimate. Thus in contemporary European societies the achievements of black sportsmen might be celebrated, but black masculinity in general is far from being fully accepted.

Each society, at a particular stage in its development, possesses a set of gender practices, or different ways of being male and female. It also possesses sets of relationships between masculinities ahd femininities, relationships of domination, subordination, complicity and marginalization. Together these practices and relationships create a gender order characteristic of the society. However, the gender order can always change and sometimes undergoes periods of crisis.

The changing gender order

Connell believes that between about 1450 and 1650 the modern capitalist economy was established and with it came the development of new masculinities. Capitalism encouraged individualism and the idea of the autonomous self. It was also linked to a growing emphasis on the relationship between husbands and wives in households. This was linked to the establishment of overseas empires by the European powers. Empires were gendered and empire-building was dominated by male soldiers and seafarers. There was little role for women. Empire builders, such as the Spanish conquistadors, were expected to display a violent and dominant masculinity as they fought for control in the conquest of lands to be colonized.

New forms of masculinity also related to the development of cities where more subtle masculinities were required than those on the frontier of empire. Connell calls the hegemonic type of masculinity that developed out of such changes gentry masculinity. The gentry, who were the dominant landowning class throughout Europe, developed a masculinity which was 'emphatic and violent'. The gentry had key roles in the military and in the enforcement of justice and were used to exercising force to control others. Under this form of masculinity, men had domestic authority over women and were largely free to pursue affairs with women other than their wife.

There were other masculinities which challenged this gender order. For example, in London, effeminate men met in 'molly houses' (often taverns) in which they cross-dressed, danced together and had homosexual sex. There were also the Quakers who

posed a rather different challenge by advocating equality between males and females.

According to Connell, the gender order of gentry masculinity has gradually been replaced over the last two hundred years by 'new hegemonic forms and the emergence of an array of subordinated and marginalized masculinities'. These changes were caused by a combination of factors. These included challenges from women to hegemonic masculinity, changes in industrial capitalism, and the end of empire with decolonization.

A key change was a move from the outright use of violence to achieve domination to a greater emphasis on the use of bureaucratic rationality in organizations. The importance of the gentry declined and hegemonic masculinity became split between managers, who dominated through holding positions of authority, and professionals whose dominance came from the possession of technical expertise.

The use of violence increasingly shifted to the colonies and away from the colonial powers. However, traces of the masculine ideology of the empire builders remained important. Thus Connell argues that 'wilderness, hunting and bushcraft were welded into a distinct ideology of manhood by figures such as Robert Baden-Powell, the founder of the scouting movement'.

In the late nineteenth century, hegemonic masculinity succeeded in defining homosexuality as a deviant and subordinate form of masculinity. Homosexual conduct was criminalized and began to be seen as males engaging in feminized or bestial behaviour. The expulsion of women from work in heavy industry created the ideology of separate spheres, with women's sphere confined to the private arena of domestic life. Among some of the working class there was the development of 'rough, disorderly masculinities among the marginalised "dangerous classes"'.

As the twentieth century progressed, the split between professional and managerial masculinity became more significant. The challenge to hegemonic masculinity from women increased. Some men began to take notice of feminist critiques of masculinity and tried to develop alternatives. Homosexual masculinity established itself as an alternative to hegemonic masculinity. Migration from former colonies to Europe, North America and elsewhere led to the masculinity of ethnic minorities adding to the diversity of masculinities in the richer capitalist nations. The hegemonic masculinities of such countries (Connell refers to them as metropolitan countries) have seen their influence spread throughout most of the world. Globalization (see Chapter 9 for a discussion of globalization) has allowed the mass media to spread the ideology of this type of masculinity worldwide. The image of masculinity produced by commercial sport has become influential, as has the association of masculinity with 'fast cars and powerful trucks'.

Despite the enormous wealth, power and influence of hegemonic masculinity in the metropolitan countries, it faces unprecedented challenges from the increasing variety of femininities and masculinities in the metropolitan countries themselves. Thus Connell says, 'the meaning of masculinity, the variety of masculinities, the difficulty of reproducing masculinity, the nature of gender and the extent of gender inequality all come into question and are furiously debated'.

Research into masculinities

As part of his research, Connell conducted detailed research into four distinctive groups of Australian men. He traced the life history of each of these men through the use of in-depth tape-recorded interviews. On the basis of these interviews, he claimed to have found evidence of 'crisis tendencies' in the contemporary gender order. According to Connell, hegemonic masculinity is increasingly challenged, making it difficult for people to agree about what it should mean to be masculine. In his research, Connell picked out four particular groups of men in which 'the construction or integration of masculinity was under pressure':

1 He described the first group as those who wish to, 'live fast die young'. This group of interviewees consisted of five, working-class men aged between 17 and 29. All of them had experienced long periods of unemployment, had little in the way of educational qualifications, and one was illiterate. They had all grown up in working-class households, some of which were very poor.

   In many ways these young men engaged in a form of exaggerated masculinity in which violence played an important part. Although they were divided about whether they should use violence towards women, they were all willing to use violence against other men if the occasion demanded it. All were subject to 'compulsory heterosexuality' (a phrase Connell borrows from Adrienne Rich). They felt obliged both to be heterosexual and to make the heterosexuality clear to others. One gave up masturbating because he believed it might lead to him getting too little pleasure out of sexual intercourse with women. Some of them had deliberately attacked gay men. At least part of the time the men demonstrated a 'thin, contemptuous misogyny, in which women are treated basically as disposable receptacles for semen'. Some of them rode motorbikes and engaged in showy displays of their masculine toughness.

   Connell believes that this group of men were demonstrating a form of 'protest masculinity', a

'marginalized masculinity, which picks up themes of hegemonic masculinity in the society at large but reworks them in the context of poverty'. Because of their class background and failure to gain educational qualifications, they 'have lost most of the patriarchal dividend. For instance, they have missed out on the economic gain over women that accrues to men in employment.' They try to make up for this through aggressive public displays of how tough and masculine they are. They try to maintain a strong 'front'.

However, Connell does not believe that 'protest masculinity' is a straightforward exaggeration of conventional masculinity. In a number of ways these men had contradictory and non-conventional ideas on masculinity. Many of them had been brought up in households where their mother was the only or main breadwinner. They did not see it as normal for a man to be the breadwinner and had no problem with women earning the money needed to care for children. A number of them wanted children and were positive about taking some responsibility for childcare themselves. Alongside their apparent hatred of women they also had 'a much more respectful, even admiring view of women's strengths'. Some even claimed to believe in 'equal rights' for women. Connell interprets these contradictions as showing that the focus of their ideas on gender differences was the body. He says that 'difference is confined to sexuality and violence, both being immediate functions of the body'. They had far less rigid views on social roles which were not directly bodily.

Connell also interviewed four working-class men who had had more success in education and employment. Despite coming from similar backgrounds to those who wanted to 'live fast and die young', they had developed different conceptions of themselves as masculine. One of the four had developed, in Connell's terms, a complicit masculinity in which he rejected the extreme and violent masculinity of some of his working-class counterparts, but accepted many aspects of hegemonic masculinity. Males such as this were 'distancing themselves from from the direct display of power but accepting the privilege of their gender'. The other three had gone much further in rejecting hegemonic rationality. One had started dressing and trying to live as a woman, another was scathing about male 'yobbos' and was not antagonistic to gay men. The third had become involved in 'green politics' (see below). These examples illustrate the very different types of masculinity that can develop even among people from similar backgrounds. These differences are explored further when Connell discusses other masculinities.

2 The second group consisted of six men involved in the environmental movement. (One of them was also among the working-class men discussed above.) All were heterosexual and all had been primarily

looked after by their mother in childhood. Each of these six men had largely embraced hegemonic masculinity in their early life, but each had distanced themselves from it as they got older. They followed very different paths towards the environmental movement, but for all of them this movement challenged hegemonic masculinity. There were several main themes in the movement which had this effect. These included, 'a practice and ideology of equality … emphasis on collectivity and solidarity', 'a practice and ideology of personal growth' and 'an ideology of organic wholeness'. The environmental movement questions the hierarchical dominance characteristic of hegemonic masculinity. It encourages group cooperation rather than individual competitiveness. It emphasizes developing as a person rather than achieving material success and encourages a connection with nature rather than an acceptance of the alienation of rationalization. All of the men had become familiar with feminist thinking, five of them as a direct consequence of involvement in environmentalism. Connell suggests that there was a certain degree of tension in the personalities of these men between identifying with their father (and brothers) or identifying with their mother who had mainly been responsible for looking after them. From childhood they had experienced the strength and resourcefulness of women and as a consequence they were open to taking feminist ideas seriously. Many of them experienced considerable guilt about the way men can treat women and had made a conscious decision to be different to the sort of men who accept hegemonic masculinity.

3 The third group Connell studied were what he calls 'very straight gays'. This group of eight men, aged in their twenties, thirties and forties, were all homosexual (though most had also had heterosexual relationships) and all lived in Sydney. All had grown up in fairly conventional families with employed fathers and mothers doing most of the parenting. They all maintained a fairly conventional masculine outward appearance. Some were critical of gay men who were effeminate and of those who were 'hyper masculine', dressing in leather. In these ways they had fairly conventional definitions of masculinity despite rejecting the 'compulsory heterosexuality' usually associated with it. Connell says 'the choice of a man as sexual object is not not just the choice of a body-with-penis, it is the choice of embodied-masculinity. The cultural meanings of masculinity are, generally, part of the package.'

Connell argues that 'young people's sexuality is a field of possibilities, not a deterministic system'. He does not believe that some men are predestined to be homosexual and others heterosexual. Both types of sexuality are 'produced by specific practices'. They come from the bodily experience of sex which develops into a 'sexual closure' in which one type of sexuality is chosen above the other. These choices, though, are not just personal and physical, because

they take place within the 'large-scale structure of gender'. They are also social in that there is now a well-established gay community in cities such as Sydney with its own infrastructure of shops, bars, organizations and so on. Therefore 'coming out' can 'also mean coming in to an already constituted gay milieu'.

All the men in Connell's study had first been brought up with the values and practices of hegemonic masculinity but had defined their own sexuality in homosexual terms and had then become involved with the gay community. In some respects, they remained conventional and were influenced by hegemonic ideas on what masculinity was. However, in their personal relationships with other men, they tended to have a more egalitarian outlook than is typical of hegemonic male/female relationships. Furthermore, simply by having an established alternative to hegemonic masculinity they show that different types of masculinity are possible.

4 The final group, 'men of reason', were part of hegemonic masculinity. These nine men, aged from the mid-twenties to the mid-forties, were all working in professional jobs and were all heterosexual. They all had post-school education. Their conception of masculinity was largely based upon the idea that men, unlike women, were rational. Unlike some working-class men, they did not associate masculinity so strongly with violence. Many were hostile to unconventional masculinities such as that of gay men.

Despite the apparently conventional and coherent nature of their masculinity, Connell did find some evidence of tensions within it. Although their masculinity encouraged them to embrace rationality, this was 'incompatible with men's categorical authority over women'. In principle, they accepted the logic of equal rights for men and women at work, but in practice they could find it hard to accept a female boss. Thus one man, Greg, had an emotional crisis, because he worked for his sister's company, and she was unwilling to give him much say in how the company was run.

Connell argues that the 'instrumental rationality of the marketplace has a power to disrupt gender' and this creates a certain tension in the professional part of hegemonic rationality. One of the interviewees, Hugh, was beginning to have doubts about conventional or hegemonic masculinity and was starting to question his competitive ethos and his sense of superiority to women.

Conclusions

Connell's study shows that there are many different masculinities, even among individuals from similar backgrounds, and that these masculinities can constantly change. Most masculinities are somewhat contradictory and there are elements within them that contradict or question the conventional gender order. Most men continue to benefit from hegemonic masculinity. According to Connell, men still remain dominant in social life. He argues that 'the material and institutional structures of patriarchy' have not been destroyed. However, he says that 'what has crumbled, in the industrial countries, is the legitimation of patriarchy'. Male dominance is no longer automatically accepted. It is questioned not just by feminists, but also by many men. Even men who are part of hegemonic masculinity have some reservations about it.

That does not mean that Connell is particularly optimistic about the immediate prospects for changing masculinity. He says 'taking a cool look around the political scenery of the industrial capitalist world, we must conclude that the project of transforming masculinity has almost no political weight at all'. Furthermore, globalization has actually spread conceptions of masculinity in these countries more widely. Nevertheless, he does believe that divisions between masculinities make change possible. He does think there are areas in which positive steps can be taken. These include 'the politics of the curriculum, work around AIDS/HIV and anti-racist politics'.

He believes that men are most likely to produce positive changes by working with other groups (such as the women's movement, the gay liberation movement and the green movement) rather than through concentrating on introspective 'men's groups' alone. While he is strongly in favour of overthrowing hegemonic masculinity, he does not deny that there are some aspects of it which are worth preserving. He says that:

> *abolishing hegemonic masculinity risks abolishing along with violence and hatred, the positive culture produced around hegemonic masculinity. This includes hero stories from the Ramayana to the Twilight of the Gods; participatory pleasures such as neighbourhood baseball; abstract beauty in fields such as pure mathematics; ethics of sacrifice on behalf of others. That is a heritage worth having, for girls and women as well as boys and men (as the rich heritage of feminine culture is worth having, for boys and men as well as girls and women).*
>
> Connell, 1995

Sociology, values and gender

Defining a situation as a problem involves a value judgement: it means that things are not as they ought to be. A large body of research in sociology has been directed by value judgements which state that particular social arrangements and circumstances are morally wrong. For example, alienating work, poverty and ruling elites are immoral. Such judgements draw attention to a subject, define it as worthy of study, commit sociologists to their research topic and give them the feeling that the questions they ask are of vital importance to the well-being of humanity.

Traditionally, men have defined problems in sociology. They have defined them in terms of male concerns and on the basis of male prejudice. As a result, sociology has, in many respects, been the sociology of men. For example, in the past, standard textbooks on the sociology of work have scarcely mentioned women. They could, with some justification, be retitled as 'the sociology of men's work'. It was with some justification that feminist sociologists started scathingly describing such work as 'malestream' sociology.

No sociologist wants to study something she or he considers insignificant. Given the prevailing perceptions of women in Western society and the fact that most sociologists used to be men, it was not surprising that there were so few serious studies of women before the 1970s. It took a woman, Ann Oakley (1974), to produce the first detailed study of housework. In terms of cultural definitions of housework as relatively unimportant work – as somehow not 'real work' – it is not surprising that male sociologists avoided this area of research. Indeed, when Oakley first proposed housework as a research topic her supervisor told her to go away and think of a proper topic!

The sociology of gender developed alongside the women's movement. Feminist sociologists were quick to attack the views of some of their male counterparts which they regarded as sexist and ideologically based. Thus they rejected the claims of writers such as Murdock and Parsons that male dominance was inevitable. However, feminist views themselves were undoubtedly influenced by different ideologies. Socialist and Marxist feminism was influenced by left-wing ideologies and liberal feminism by the ideology of liberals. Radical feminism at least seemed to be based on a new ideology, one that served the interests of women to the exclusion of other groups. However, because perspectives are ideologically based does not mean that they should be dismissed.

Feminist perspectives have not just opened up new topics for research, they have facilitated whole new ways of looking at and thinking about the social world.

The most recent forms of feminism, particularly postmodern feminisms, have questioned the male logic on which most social science is based. They have encouraged researchers to try to understand the social world from the viewpoint of a plurality of different groups such as black women, lesbian women and so on. They have rejected the approach that there is only *one reality* that can be discovered, *one theory* that can be used to understand the social world. This has allowed new insights to be developed and has even made space for a new branch of sociology, the sociology of masculinity. It is no mean achievement that feminist sociologists have succeeded in encouraging some male sociologists

(such as Bob Connell) to become critical of their own sex. Although there is a danger that such an approach to social science may simply be repeating the ideological viewpoint of many different groups, it does ensure that the views of the most powerful groups are not the only ones to be heard. It ensures that no set of values is likely to go unchallenged.

As Susan Faludi (1992) has documented, since the early 1990s feminist ideas themselves have come under renewed attack from a 'backlash'. This backlash encourages feminists to recognize that the social world is changing, and that women may not be as disadvantaged as they were several decades ago. Nevertheless, the evidence reviewed in this chapter and in other parts of the book suggests that there are not just gender differences that need understanding, there are also still important gender inequalities that need addressing.

Race, ethnicity and nationality

'Race', ethnicity and nationality

Introduction

Racism and conflict between ethnic and national groups have long been a feature of human societies. We can illustrate this with a number of examples.

In 1601 Queen Elizabeth I issued a proclamation saying that 'Negroes and blackamoors' should be deported from England because they were 'infidels' and they were contributing to economic and social problems such as poverty and famine.

According to the historian Philip D. Curtin (1965), in the eighteenth century some 9.5 million Africans were transported across the Atlantic to become slaves in North and South America and the Caribbean. John Taylor, a writer and traveller, described the black slaves in Jamaica as 'these ignorant pore souls' who differed 'from bruite beast, only by their shape and speech'. In 1884, long after the abolition of slavery, the *Encyclopaedia Britannica* continued to express similar views. It claimed that the African Negro occupied the lowest position in the evolutionary scale and this was supposedly demonstrated by their abnormally long arms and lightweight brains.

Another group who were widely seen as inferior in nineteenth-century Britain were the Irish. Frederick Engels, Karl Marx's friend and collaborator, described the Irish in *The Condition of the Working Class in England*. Writing in 1844–5, he said:

> *The southern facile character of the Irishman, his crudity, which places him but little above the savage, his contempt for all human enjoyments, in which his very crudeness makes him incapable of sharing, his filth and poverty, all favour drunkenness.*

Engels, 1973, first published 1844

Over half a century later, in 1901, the London writer Joseph Bannister was no less critical of a different group of people in his book *England Under the Jews*. He described Jews as 'Yiddish money pigs' who were unwilling to take baths and so were particularly prone to skin and blood diseases. Bannister believed that Britain was becoming dominated by Jews, and in a private letter to a Jew he said 'It is a pity that

some kind of vermin exterminator could not be invented by which your vile breed could be eliminated.'

Anti-Semitic feeling (hostile feelings towards the Jewish people) went beyond mere words in Hitler's Nazi Germany. In *Mein Kampf* (completed in 1927) Hitler outlined his view that the true Germans were a racial group called the Aryans. The Aryan race had been corrupted by contact with inferior races such as the Slavs and Jews, but Hitler aimed to put this right by creating an Aryan 'master race'. In 1935 the Nuremberg Laws withdrew the civil rights of Jews and forbade mixed marriages between Jews and Aryans. The 'Final Solution' to the Jewish 'problem' involved gassing millions of Jews (along with gypsies, homosexuals, and others) in concentration camps such as Auschwitz, Belsen and Dachau.

In the 1990s, after the end of communist rule in Yugoslavia, civil war broke out between the Muslims, the Croatians and the Serbs. The conflicts largely concerned the boundaries and ethnic composition of new states as Yugoslavia broke up. In parts of Bosnia whole ethnic groups were driven out of an area so that it might be claimed by another group. This process became known as ethnic cleansing. Many thousands died as the Bosnian Serbs tried to seize territory from the Muslims and besieged towns and cities such as Gorazde, Srebrenica and Sarajevo. In the late 1990s Serbia engaged in ethnic cleansing on a massive scale in Kosovo, another region of the former Yugoslavia. Hundreds of thousands of ethnic Albanians were driven from their homes and became refugees in neighbouring states. In response, the military alliance of NATO (including the United States, the United Kingdom, France and Germany) went to war with Serbia.

As the situation in the former Yugoslavia shows, examples of conflict and inequality between racial, ethnic or national groups are by no means confined to history. In Northern Ireland there is conflict between Catholics and Protestants, in Sri Lanka between Tamils and the Sinhalese. In Spain some Basques seek an independent state, and in East Timor guerrilla leaders strive to regain independence from their Indonesian invaders. In Burundi and Rwanda, two ethnic groups – the Hutus and the Tutsis – have been in conflict for decades, resulting in the deaths of many thousands of people. In 1994–6 there was renewed violence, and large numbers of Tutsis were massacred by the Hutus. In Britain racially motivated attacks against British Asians and Afro-Caribbeans continue, and in Germany Turkish migrant workers are similarly victimized.

In Britain, France and other European countries, extreme right-wing parties such as the British National Party, the National Front and Le Pen's Front National, which oppose immigration and blame social problems on ethnic minorities, continue to attract support. In the USA, evidence suggests that many years after the enactment of civil rights legislation American blacks and Hispanics are still seriously disadvantaged in areas such as employment and education.

In this chapter we will examine some of the reasons why conflict and inequality between racial, ethnic and national groups continue to occur. We start by considering the view that there is a biological basis for distinguishing 'races' which explains the conflicts and inequalities that arise. (The word 'race' is placed in inverted commas because, as we shall see, there is debate over whether there is any scientific basis for distinguishing so-called 'races'.)

'Race'

Biological theories of 'race' attempt to establish a relationship between phenotype, or physical characteristics, such as hair and skin colour, and genotype, or the underlying genetic differences between groups of humans. As science has developed, the dominant thinking about this relationship has changed.

Michael Banton – theories of 'race'

Michael Banton has described the various attempts that have been made to divide human beings into different biological or racial groups (Banton, 1987). He distinguishes three main types of theory:

1 those which see 'race' as lineage
2 those which see it as type
3 those which see it as subspecies.

Race as lineage

According to Banton the word 'race' was not used in English until 1508 when it appeared in a poem by the Scotsman William Dunbar. At that time 'the Bible was accepted as the authority on human affairs' and ideas on racial difference were therefore based on biblical teaching. This meant that it was generally accepted that all humans were ultimately descended from Adam and Eve. The idea of 'race' as lineage adopted a monogenesist view: humans belonged to a single species and had a common origin.

However, it was believed that there were different groups of humans who had become differentiated at some point in the past. Biblical events such as the Flood and the fall of the Tower of Babel had contributed to humans becoming dispersed around the globe. This had resulted in distinctive lineages or lines of descent which corresponded to differences in physical appearance and geographical origin between human groups. People had become different as the result of migration to different environments, but ultimately because 'God had guided the course of events'.

In some respects the idea of 'race' as lineage implied that all humans were basically equal and, according to Banton, this influenced ideas on slavery. Slave owners had 'mistrust and ethnocentric contempt' for their slaves but this did not stem 'from assumptions about racial superiority'. There was agreement among supporters and opponents of slavery alike that 'the Negro was no more amenable to the regimentation of slavery than any other man'. Nevertheless, the idea of 'race' as lineage did produce views which suggested that 'races' were unequal in some ways.

Some claimed that God had made people different in order to make them suited to particular areas of the earth. For example, many thought that only Africans could work effectively in the extreme heat of the tropics. Banton argues that 'The message was that each people was adapted to its own environment and therefore should stay where they were.'

In the seventeenth and eighteenth centuries British and American writers rarely used the word 'race' when writing about human groups; however a few were beginning to do so and were starting to suggest that certain 'races' were superior to others. In 1748 the English philosopher David Hume said that 'Negroes' were the only 'race' that had never developed a major civilization and this indicated that they were 'naturally inferior to the Whites'.

Such views were to become much more common in the nineteenth century as a new approach to classifying groups of humans gained in popularity.

'Race' as type

The idea of 'race' as type is based upon a belief that all humans do not share a common origin and that humanity is divided into distinctive groups. It is therefore a polygenetic theory, that is a theory that humanity has several origins rather than one.

Some versions of this theory suggested that humans from different 'races' could not interbreed and produce fertile children. Banton says 'It assumed that racial differences had existed from some very early period of prehistory when different stocks had been created either by God or by some natural catastrophe.' The idea of 'race' as type gained in popularity as people of European origin came into closer contact with other groups. Banton argues:

> As the evidence about the diversity of human forms accumulated, more and more writers tended to refer to various kinds of type, and, indeed the construction of typologies of various kinds became a characteristic of nineteenth-century scholarship.
>
> Banton, 1987

This new approach to 'race' developed in different countries at around the same time but some of the most influential views originated in America.

The Philadelphian doctor Samuel James Morton based his arguments upon the measurement of skull sizes. In 1839 Morton distinguished five 'races':

1 Caucasian (from Europe, India and parts of North Africa and the Middle East)
2 Mongolian (Chinese and Eskimos)
3 Malay (from Malaysia and the Polynesian Islands)
4 American (native Americans from North and South America)
5 Ethiopian (from sub-Saharan Africa).

From his measurements Morton claimed that 'Caucasians' had the largest cranial capacity and 'Ethiopians' the smallest. Morton equated cranial capacity with the size of the brain, and the size of the brain with intellectual development. He believed therefore that Europeans were more advanced than sub-Saharan Africans.

Morton's ideas were developed further by J.C. Nott and G.R. Gliddon in their book *Types of Mankind*, published in Philadelphia in 1854. Nott and Gliddon believed that there were distinctive groups of humans of a relatively permanent kind. These separate types gave rise to differences in behaviour between groups of humans. Furthermore, different types of human were naturally antagonistic to one another. According to Nott and Gliddon, prior to any biblical writings the Ancient Egyptians had already classified humans into four types. They also claimed that 'certain Types have existed (the same as now) in and around the valley of the Nile, from ages anterior to 3500 years BC'. 'Types' – or 'races', as Nott and Gliddon also called them – were 'separated in physical organization', and those which were most different such as 'Blacks and Whites' did 'not amalgamate perfectly'.

Nott and Gliddon clearly believed in the superiority of white races. They claimed that Caucasians (who are supposed to originate from the Caucasus mountains) 'have in all ages been the rulers' and they had shown themselves to be the only humans capable of developing democracy. On the other hand, dark-skinned 'races' were 'only fit for military governments'.

Nott and Gliddon's work was typical of that of many other writers in asserting that there were distinct biologically different 'races'. These races behaved in different ways: some races had remained 'pure' and untainted by interbreeding; and some of them were superior to others.

Banton comments that Nott and Gliddon's notions of racial purity and of racial inferiority and superiority were close to the racial views of the Nazis.

An even bigger influence on Nazi thinking was the French writer Arthur de Gobineau. Writing in the 1850s he claimed that there was a distinctive Aryan race which had migrated from a homeland in the East and which was superior to all other races. According to Gobineau, the Aryans had then spread out and were responsible for establishing most of the world's major civilizations. These included the civilizations of Egypt, Rome, China, Greece, Assyria and even Mexico and Peru.

'Race' as subspecies

The idea of 'race' as subspecies combines elements of the idea of 'race' as lineage and that of 'race' as type. The origins of this conception of 'race' are to be found in the work of the British biologist Charles Darwin and his theory of evolution.

According to Banton, Darwin saw a species as 'a class which was distinctive because its members inherited common characters but inherited them in different combinations which were subject to continual modification'. Members of the same species can breed with one another and produce fertile offspring. However, because species are constantly changing and evolving it is possible for different branches, subgroups or subspecies to develop. Where groups within a species become geographically separated and breed only within that group, they can develop their own distinctive characteristics.

Darwin observed in the Galapagos Islands that certain types of bird and turtle varied slightly from island to island: they were developing distinctive subspecies by breeding only with animals from the same island. When subspecies evolved in different ways they could eventually become so distinctive that the offspring of animals from two different subspecies were infertile.

Darwin saw evolution as a slow process resulting from natural selection. Those members of a species that were best adapted to their environment were most likely to breed and therefore to pass on their genetic characteristics to future generations. There was also an element of sexual selection involved. Females would tend to select the most attractive males of their species with which to breed. Gradually the characteristics that made members of a species or subspecies more likely to breed and produce offspring became increasingly typical of the group as a whole.

Different human 'races' could develop in the same way as different subspecies of animal. Natural selection, sexual selection and chance variations in genes could result in distinct human groups with different physical appearances. Thus, although all humans had a common origin they could evolve to form different races.

Banton does not accept that the term 'race' is a useful one. He says that 'Race as a folk-concept differentiating present-day groups on the basis of their appearance has no theoretical value' (Banton, 1997). Some reasons why it may have no theoretical value will be explored below.

Herbert Spencer – human subspecies and social evolution

The idea of 'race' as subspecies became increasingly popular in the latter part of the nineteenth century. The English functionalist sociologist Herbert Spencer developed his ideas about social evolution at the same time as Darwin was developing his ideas about biological evolution (Spencer, in Andreski (ed.), 1971). In applying evolutionary ideas to the study of society Spencer developed influential ideas about the relationship between 'race' and human social development.

The mixture of races

Spencer believed that societies could sometimes benefit from the mixing of races. He said 'Sundry instances point to the conclusion that a society formed from nearly-allied peoples of which the conquering eventually mingles with the conquered, is relatively well fitted for progress.' The fusion of different characteristics can make the society adaptable and able to benefit from the best characteristics of the various races of which its population is made up. Spencer gives the example of the Hebrews who:

> not withstanding their boasted purity of blood, resulted from a mixing of many Semitic varieties in the country east of the Nile and who, both in their wanderings and after the conquest of Palestine, went on amalgamating kindred tribes.
>
> Spencer, 1971

The Romans, he claimed, gained strength from amalgamating with 'other Aryan tribes, Sabini, Sabelli and Samnites'. England too had benefited from the interbreeding of closely related groups including 'different divisions of the Aryan race' and 'varieties of Scandinavians'.

However, the outcome was rather different when societies were composed of mixed races that were less closely related. Following the principles of 'race' as subspecies, Spencer commented:

> If instead of different species, remote varieties are united, the intermediate organism is not infertile; but many facts suggest the conclusion that infertility results in subsequent generations: the incongruous workings of the united structures, though longer in showing itself, comes out ultimately.
>
> Spencer, 1971

According to Spencer, the dangers of mixing very different human subspecies were not just biological: the societies that resulted were likely to be highly unstable. Mexico and other South American republics were examples. Spain had an incongruous mixture of 'Basques, Celtic, Gothic, Moorish [and] Jewish' groups. Such societies required strong central government to keep the diverse 'racial groups from engaging in conflict with one another' and Spencer believed that too much government regulation hindered social evolution.

The evolutionary scale

According to Spencer then, societies could consist of one race, but often consisted of a mixture of several. The precise mixture helped determine whether or not a society became more evolved and civilized. Spencer developed a complex scheme for categorizing societies based on whether they had a complex or simple structure, and whether they were stable or unstable:

1 A simple society was 'a single working whole' which was not divided into different sections, groups or tribes.

2 A compound society was one where 'the simple groups have their respective chiefs under a supreme chief'.

3 Doubly compound societies were more complex still, with a number of compound societies united under a single government.

Table 4.1 shows Spencer's classification system (although it omits trebly compound societies which Spencer discussed separately).

Spencer left the reader in no doubt that simple societies were less developed and therefore inferior to more complex ones. He described them as 'uncivilized' and referred to some as 'savage tribes'. More complex societies had evolved further, were more civilized and better adapted to their environment.

The degree to which different societies had evolved was, in Spencer's eyes, influenced by race. Weaker tribes tended to be conquered by stronger ones in a struggle for survival. Among aboriginal tribes – the lowest groups on his evolutionary scale – the merged societies resulting from the conquest of one tribe by another were unstable and tended to break up. Among 'superior races' these complex societies were more stable. As a consequence they could evolve further. The most complex and therefore

Table 4.1   Herbert Spencer's Evolutionary Typology

SIMPLE SOCIETIES			
Headless	Occasional headship	Vague and unstable headship	Stable headship
Nomadic: (hunting) Fuegians, some Australians, Wood-Veddahs, Bushmen, Chépángs and Kusúndas of Nepal *Semi-settled*: most Esquimaux *Settled*: Arafuras, Land Dyaks of Upper Sarawak River	*Nomadic*: (hunting) some Australians, Tasmanians *Semi-settled*: some Caribs *Settled*: some Uaupés of the upper Rio Negro	*Nomadic*: (hunting) Andamanese, Abipones, Snakes, Chippewayans (pastoral), some Bedouins *Semi-settled*: some Esquimaux, Chinooks, Chippewas (at present), some Kamschadales, Village Veddahs, Bodo and Dhimáls *Settled*: Guiana tribes, Mandans, Corados, New Guinea people, Tannese, Vateans, Dyaks, Todas, Negas, Karens, Santals	*Nomadic*: *Semi-settled*: some Caribs, Patagonians, New Caledonians, Kaffirs *Settled*: Guaranis, Pueblos
COMPOUND SOCIETIES			
	Nomadic: (pastoral) some Bedouins *Semi-settled*: Tannese *Settled*:	*Nomadic*: (hunting) Dacotahs (hunting and pastoral), Comanches (pastoral), Kalmucks *Semi-settled*: Ostayaks, Beluchis, Kookies, Bhils, Congo-people (passing into doubly compound), Teutons before fifth century *Settled*: Chippewas (in past times), Creeks, Mundrucus, Tupis, Khonds, some New Guinea people, Sumatrans, Malagasy (until recently), Coast Negroes, Inland Negroes, some Abyssinians, Homeric Greeks, Kingdoms of the Heptarchy, Teutons in fifth century, Fiefs of tenth century	*Nomadic*: (pastoral) Kirghiz *Semi-settled*: Bechuanas, Zulus *Settled*: Uaupès, Fijians (when first visited), New Zealanders, Sandwich Islanders (in Cook's time), Javans, Hottentots, Dahomans, Ashantees, some Abyssinians, Ancient Yucatanese, New Granada people, Honduras people, Chibehas, some town Arabs
DOUBLY COMPOUND SOCIETIES			
	Nomadic: *Semi-settled*: *Settled*: Samoans	*Nomadic*: *Semi-settled*: Tahitians, Tongans, Javans (occasionally), Fijians (since firearms), Malagasy (in recent times), Athenian Confederacy, Spartan Confederacy, Teutonic Kingdoms Kingdoms from sixth to ninth centuries, Greater Fiefs in France of the thirteenth century *Settled*:	*Nomadic*: *Semi-settled*: *Settled*: Iroquois, Araucanians, Sandwich Islanders (since Cook's time), Ancient Vera Paz and Bogota peoples, Guatemalans, Ancient Peruvians, Wahhábees (Arab), Omán (Arab), Ancient Egyptian Kingdom, England after the tenth century

Source: S. Andreski (ed.) (1971) *Herbert Spencer*, Thomas Nelson, London, pp. 150–2

the most evolved societies of all were trebly compound. These were 'Ancient Mexico, the Assyrian Empire, the Egyptian Empire, the Roman Empire, Great Britain, France, Germany, Italy, Russia'.

To Spencer, social life and the evolutionary process involved the 'survival of the fittest'. Those individuals, groups and species that were not well adapted to their environment would die out. The historian Christopher Bolt notes that a number of nineteenth-century writers tried to justify the decline in numbers of the native populations of New Zealand and the Americas. They argued that the native populations were not well adapted and so could not survive. Bolt comments:

> *With a large degree of wishful thinking, some Victorians maintained that if the survival-of-the-fittest principle operated as it should, the Negro population of North America and the West Indies might soon follow these tribes towards extinction.*
>
> Bolt, 1971

The limitations of nineteenth-century ideas on 'race'

Although more sophisticated than theories of 'race' as type, the idea of 'race' as subspecies has also been used to suggest that certain 'races' are superior to others. All the approaches to 'race' examined so far have based their analysis on phenotypical differences in physical appearance between groups of humans. However, nineteenth-century scientists did not possess the scientific knowledge necessary to relate phenotypical differences to underlying genotype or genetic differences. Advances in genetics after the Second World War made this possible.

Steve Jones – genetics and evolution

Genetic differences

The geneticist Steve Jones (1991, 1994) has examined theories of 'race' in the light of increasing understanding of human genetics. There are 50,000 genes in each human being and these genes determine the differences between humans. Genetic research has found some differences between groups of humans. For example, changes in fewer than ten genes determine skin colour. According to Jones, climatic variations have led to the evolution of differences in these genes amongst people from different climatic areas. Ultraviolet light from the sun allows humans to produce vitamin D in the skin. Vitamin D is essential to avoid the disease rickets. Dark-skinned people do not manufacture vitamin D as easily as light-skinned people do. In less sunny climates those with dark skins are less likely to

survive into adulthood and are therefore unable to pass on their genes by having children.

There are genetic differences too between Europeans and the Japanese. Europeans are more tolerant of alcohol because their livers are more capable of breaking it down. In Japan a genetic variant of the liver enzyme is less effective at coping with alcohol. The Japanese drink less alcohol than the Europeans because when they do drink they tend to feel nauseous and their faces go red.

Genetic research also suggests that Africans:

> *are on a branch of the human family that split off from the others early on, and most of the rest of us are more closely related to each other than we are to the populations so far tested in Africa.*
>
> Jones, 1991

In the Pacific there seem to be two main genetic groups. One consists of the Australian aborigines and the people of New Guinea. Genetics suggests they have been settled in that area for a very long time. The peoples of other Pacific islands, on the other hand, are more closely related to East Asians and may have moved to the area more recently.

The absence of 'races'

Despite describing the existence of genetic differences between human groups, Jones does not believe that there is any genetic justification for distinguishing 'races'. He gives a number of reasons for this:

1 First, he suggests that to be able to show that there are different 'races' 'then the different peoples should be quite distinct from one another in a large sample of their genes, not just those for skin colour'. However, this is not the case. Geneticists have not found that the genes governing skin colour are related to other genetic patterns. Jones says 'The patterns of variation in each system are independent of each other. Our colour does not say much about what lies under the skin'.

2 Second, genetic diversity has relatively little to do with 'race'. About 85 per cent of the variations in human genes result from the differences between individuals from the same country. A further 5–10 per cent of genetic diversity comes from differences between countries in the same continent and populated by the same supposed 'race' (for instance, differences between the English and the Spanish, or between Nigerians and Kenyans). Jones concludes:

> *The overall genetic differences between 'races' – Africans and Europeans, say – is no greater than that between different countries within Europe or within Africa. Individuals – not nations and not races – are the main repository of human variation.*
>
> Jones, 1991

3 Third, overall, humans are much more homogeneous than other species. For example, one of Jones's areas of expertise is the genetic variations between snails. His research shows that variations between the snail populations in different Pyrenean valleys are greater than the variations between Australian aboriginals and English people. He says 'If you were a snail it would make good biological sense to be a racist: but you have to accept that humans are tediously uniform animals.'

Social definitions of 'race'

Steve Jones believes that many attitudes towards 'race' have no scientific basis. He argues:

> Humanity can be divided into groups in many ways: by culture, by language and by race – which usually means by skin colour. Each division depends to some extent on prejudice and, because they do not overlap, can lead to confusion.
>
> Jones, 1991

He gives the example of a secretary in Virginia in the USA. In 1987 she took her employers to court on the grounds that they had discriminated against her because she was black. The court ruled that she could not be black because she had red hair. She then got a job with a black employer and took him to court for discriminating against her because she was white. Again she lost the case. The court held that she could not be white because she had attended a black school.

Societies use different definitions of 'race'. Under apartheid in South Africa anyone who had just a single white ancestor was regarded as non-white or coloured, no matter what their actual skin colour was. In Haiti, on the other hand, the former ruler Papa Doc claimed that he lived in a white nation. Although most of the inhabitants had a dark skin colour nearly everyone could claim one or more white ancestors.

Some supposed 'races' are figments of the imagination. Genetic research suggests, for example, that there is no such thing as an 'Aryan race' and there is no evidence of a distinct Caucasian 'race' with its origins in the Caucasus mountains.

Attitudes to 'race'

Jones notes that thinking about 'race' has usually gone beyond classifying human groups. He says 'It is a tiny step from classifying people to judging them.' According to him the idea of 'distinct pure races which differed in quality had a disastrous impact'. Hitler's attempt to eradicate Jews was based upon 'scientific' claims that they were an inferior 'race'. In 1923 the US President Calvin Coolidge passed

immigration laws establishing quotas ensuring that most immigrants were from western and northern Europe. This policy was based on the claim that there would be racial deterioration if 'Nordic' people interbred with those from other 'races'. Jones concludes that 'Much of the story of the genetics of race – a field promoted by some eminent scientists – turns out to have been prejudice dressed up as science.'

To Jones issues such as racism are moral issues rather than scientific ones, as modern science has shown that there can be no biological argument for racism. There are variations in human genotypes which affect physical characteristics (phenotypes). However, they are not sufficiently significant to allow different 'races' to be identified and they are not related to the culture, behaviour or morality of different groups of humans.

John Richardson and John Lambert – sociology and 'race'

Like Steve Jones, John Richardson and John Lambert (1985) criticize biological approaches to 'race'. They describe the idea of pure 'races' as 'misleading in the extreme' and deny that clearcut, biologically different 'races' can be distinguished. However, they do not deny that 'race' should be studied by sociologists.

Whatever the scientific limitations of the concept, it is widely believed that 'races' exist and this belief influences the behaviour of many members of particular societies. Richardson and Lambert refer to W.I. Thomas's dictum that 'if people define a situation as real, it is real in its social consequences'. Since people define 'race' as real it has social consequences. The study of these consequences forms an important part of the sociology of 'race'.

The doctrine of racial superiority

As well as attacking some biological definitions of 'race', Richardson and Lambert also criticize the idea that some 'races' can be seen as superior to others. They outline three main problems with the doctrine of racial superiority:

1 There is no clear connection between biological differences and differences in behaviour and culture in groups of humans. Richardson and Lambert do not deny that biology has some bearing on social and cultural behaviour but claim that any links are 'remote and indirect'.

2 Social explanations of behavioural and cultural differences between human groups are far more convincing than biological ones. Biology is much less important in shaping human behaviour than animal

behaviour. Richardson and Lambert say 'Unlike animals, human beings are not so rigidly bound to inbuilt instincts or innate biological triggers; on the contrary, human survival and progress is enhanced if cultural flexibility prevails'. The same 'race' can produce very different cultures in different parts of the world. (An example might be Afrikaners in South Africa who developed a different culture under the apartheid system to the more liberal culture of The Netherlands, which is where their ancestors originated from.)

3 It is impossible to find any objective criteria to measure the 'superiority' or 'inferiority' of human groups. The Victorian Britons who argued for the superiority of white Europeans assumed that their urban, industrial societies were superior to other 'primitive' ones. However, as Richardson and Lambert comment:

claims of 'progress' appear less convincing when we consider the subsequent problems of industrial pollution, personal alienation, and the possibility of nuclear warfare. The African pygmy or Mongolian herdsman is arguably in a more 'harmonious' relationship with his physical environment than is the urban inhabitant of London or New York.

Richardson and Lambert, 1985

In any case, if cultural achievements and technological developments are a measure of superiority and inferiority, history shows that different 'races' have been the most advanced at particular points in time. There were highly developed African civilizations such as the Ashanti and Zimbabwe when Europe was still in the 'Dark Ages'. Richardson and Lambert quote Goldthorpe who claims that in 1600 China was perhaps the most developed nation, followed by India and Arabia. The evidence does not therefore support the belief that Europeans are innately superior to people from other parts of the world.

The social construction of 'race'

To Richardson and Lambert, and to most other sociologists, 'race' is a social construct: it has no biological basis. It has more to do with 'what people make of physical differences' and the 'everyday or commonsense notions which influence them'. How people define 'races' and their attitudes to different 'races' are influenced by the dominant belief systems of the society in which they live. For example, stereotypes about particular groups vary from place to place and time to time. Furthermore:

In some societies, at certain times, people are found to attach little weight to racial differences, while in other contexts we might find intense hostility and pronounced patterns of racial 'exclusion' and 'inclusion'.

Richardson and Lambert, 1985

In Richardson and Lambert's view, though, people do not just passively accept definitions of 'race' in a particular society. Through their actions and interactions with others they may reinforce or challenge existing beliefs about 'race', or they may help to create new beliefs. At the same time their beliefs and actions 'take place within particular historical and cultural contexts which tend to limit human choices and make certain types of cultural response and behaviour more likely than others'.

In later sections of this chapter we will analyse in more detail how 'race' is socially constructed. In particular in the sections on racism we will examine the way in which stereotypical beliefs about 'races' are created and sustained (see pp. 237–49).

Ethnicity is usually seen as defining groups in terms of their cultural characteristics rather than their supposed biological differences. In a later section we will discuss the concept of ethnicity which many see as a more valid way of classifying human groups than 'race' (see pp. 222–37).

Migration and 'race' relations

Human groups which regard themselves as biologically or culturally different often live in close proximity to one another. Some sociologists have seen the process of migration and the social relationships and social changes that result from it as the key to understanding race relations. Before discussing these theories, we will look briefly at patterns of migration.

Stephen Castles and Mark J. Miller – international migration

Patterns of migration 1600–1945

Castles and Miller (1993) have described world migration patterns both before and after the Second World War. They note that 'population movements in response to demographic growth, climatic change and the development of production and trade have always been part of human history'. Nations have sometimes sought to encourage immigration as part of 'nation building'. Migration has also been caused by warfare, and enforced migration has taken place as a result of deportation and enslavement.

From the sixteenth to the nineteenth century much migration was directly or indirectly related to colonialism. Colonial migrations are illustrated in Figure 4.1. Large numbers of people moved from the countries of the colonial powers in Europe to the colonies. For example Spanish and Portuguese settlers moved to South America.

The slave trade resulted in some 15 million Africans being taken as slaves across the Atlantic, resulting in the black population of North and South America and the Caribbean. The slaves were either abducted by sailors or exchanged with African traders or chiefs for manufactured goods. They were made to work in plantations and mines, and as servants. Products such as tobacco, coffee, cotton and sugar were produced in the colonies and most of what was produced was transported back to Europe.

In much of the Caribbean the native population of Caribs and Arawaks was completely wiped out. Slavery was abolished in 1834 in British colonies, in 1863 in Dutch colonies, and not until 1865 in some states of the USA.

Following the abolition of slavery more use was made of indentured servants who contracted to work for their employers for a number of years. In the Indian subcontinent more than 30 million were recruited as indentured workers by the British and they were taken to work in areas as diverse as East Africa, Trinidad, Guyana and Malaya. The Dutch also used indentured workers in the Dutch East Indies. As Castles and Miller point out, such movements of people during the colonial period have often left a legacy of ethnic division and conflict in former colonies. For example, Asians in Africa and Chinese in south-east Asia have experienced considerable hostility from the majority populations.

In North America the vast majority of the population are descended from immigrants; there are few surviving native Americans. Most black Americans are descended from the original slave population. In the nineteenth and early twentieth centuries there was also large-scale migration from Europe. Between 1800 and 1860 nearly two-thirds of migrants to the USA were from Britain, and over one-fifth were German. In the second half of the nineteenth century there were more migrants from Italy, Ireland, Spain and Eastern Europe.

Until 1880 anyone could migrate to the USA, but then restrictions were introduced. They were first placed on the entry of Chinese and Asians, and in

Figure 4.1 Colonial migrations from the seventeenth to the nineteenth century

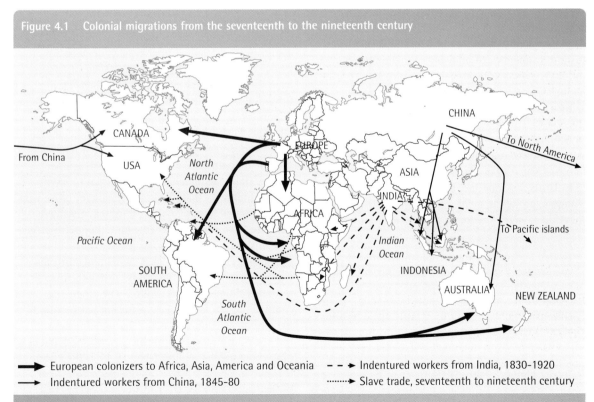

➤ European colonizers to Africa, Asia, America and Oceania
➤ Indentured workers from China, 1845–80
– – ➤ Indentured workers from India, 1830–1920
·······➤ Slave trade, seventeenth to nineteenth century

Source: S. Castles and M.J. Miller (1993) *The Age of Migration: International Population Movements in the Modern World*, Macmillan, Basingstoke, p. 47

1920 they were extended to Europeans and Latin Americans.

Canada and Australia are also largely populated by the descendants of migrants. Most of the early emigrants to Canada came from northern Europe but there was some migration to Canada by Japanese, Indians, Chinese and blacks from the USA. British colonization of Australia started in 1788. In the second half of the nineteenth century some Indians, Chinese and South Pacific Islanders settled in Australia, but in 1901 the parliament passed a 'White Australia Policy', with the aim of preventing non-whites from emigrating to Australia.

In the nineteenth and early twentieth centuries there was considerable migration within Europe. For example, large numbers of workers moved to Germany from Poland, and Italy and France imported workers from a variety of countries including Belgium, Italy, Portugal and Spain. Between the First and Second World Wars there was less migration in Europe but in France there was immigration from Italy, Poland and Czechoslovakia.

Castles and Miller sum up saying:

> *The period from about 1850 to 1914 was an era of mass migration. It was also a time of industrialisation and economic growth in Western Europe and the USA. Industrialisation was a cause of both emigration and immigration.*

Castles and Miller, 1993

In the interwar years 'xenophobia and economic stagnation' led to a decline in migration. There was hostility to the idea of allowing more immigration and little economic need for more workers.

Migration to highly developed countries since 1945

Castles and Miller argue that there have been two main phases of migration to highly developed countries since 1945. The first phase lasted until the early 1970s, a period in which there was strong economic growth in developed countries. In this phase there were three main types of migration:

1 Some people migrated from the southern and eastern fringes of Europe to the more affluent countries of the north and west. The richer countries were facing a labour shortage and wanted to recruit cheap labour. Those who migrated were often denied citizenship rights. Belgium and Switzerland recruited workers from Italy, and France recruited from Spain. In Germany the guestworker system was established. The main sources of guestworkers were Italy, Greece, Turkey, Morocco, Portugal, Tunisia and Yugoslavia. By 1973 there were 2.6 million guestworkers who were allowed into Germany only on condition that they stayed for restricted periods, and sometimes they were restricted to doing specific jobs. They had few civil rights, were not allowed to settle in Germany and could not bring their families with them.

2 The second type of migration involved emigration from colonies or former colonies to colonial powers. Again the motive was to recruit cheap labour to overcome a labour shortage in advanced industrial nations. France had large-scale immigration from Algeria, Morocco, Tunisia and West African colonies such as Mali and Senegal. The Netherlands had immigration from Indonesia and Surinam, and Britain from the Caribbean and the Indian subcontinent. (Britain is discussed separately on pp. 210–14.) This type of migration was usually permanent and the migrants were either already citizens, or they became citizens, of the countries to which they moved.

3 The third type involved migration to North America and Australia. A 1965 amendment to the Immigration and Nationality Act in the USA was intended to remove racist bias in the law. It led to an increase in migration to the USA by the Asian and Latin American kin of US citizens. There was also considerable migration to Canada from Britain, Germany, Italy and The Netherlands, and to Australia from Britain, Italy, Greece and Malta.

The globalization of migration since the 1970s

Castles and Miller claim that there has been a major shift in migratory patterns since the early 1970s. In 1973 oil-producing countries increased the price of oil, causing recessions in most rich capitalist countries. This resulted in a reduced demand for labour in Western Europe so recruitment of labour from former colonies slowed down. However, in Britain, France, The Netherlands and Germany ethnic minorities became more established as family members joined the original migrants and children were born in the countries to which their parents had migrated. Southern European countries such as Greece, Italy, Spain and Portugal started to have more immigrants than emigrants. Some of those who had emigrated in earlier years returned, and these countries also began to receive immigrants from Asia and Africa.

Outside Europe, the USA, Canada and Australia continued to receive immigrants, although Australia restricted numbers quite severely. Oil-producing countries in the Middle East attracted workers from rich and poor countries alike. Throughout the world there was also an enormous increase in the number of asylum-seekers and refugees. In 1980 there were 8.2 million refugees; by 1992 this had risen to an estimated 20 million. Over this period people fled from many countries including Afghanistan, Lebanon, Uganda, Zaïre, Namibia, Argentina and

Chile. The collapse of communism in the USSR and Eastern Europe also led to very large population movements. Over a quarter of a million people sought asylum in Germany in the first seven months of 1992, many from Romania and Yugoslavia.

According to Castles and Miller there has been a 'globalization of international migration'. By the 1980s and 1990s all regions of the world were experiencing substantial movements of people. Labour migration, especially in the Middle East and Asia, was often being accompanied by 'rigid control of foreign workers, the prohibition of settlement and family reunion, and the denial of basic rights'. However, the European experience suggested that pressures for longer stays to be allowed would grow and 'It therefore seems reasonable to predict that countries everywhere will become more ethnically diverse and cosmopolitan through migration.'

Migration to Britain

Immigration until 1945

Britain has long had an ethnically diverse population. John Richardson points out:

> The early Roman invaders encountered a mixed population of Britons, Picts and Celts, and when the Romans finally withdrew from these shores in 410 AD the succeeding centuries witnessed a series of forays and scattered settlements by varied groups of Angles, Saxons, Jutes, Danes and Vikings. This diversity was significantly enhanced by the arrival of the Normans.
>
> Richardson, 1990

Many other groups have migrated to Britain. Jews arrived in England with the Norman Conquest, though they were expelled by Edward I in 1290. In 1440 Richard II decided to tax the 'alien' population. It was found that they consisted mainly of Scots, Irish, French and 'Doche' – people from north Germany and the Low Countries (now Belgium and The Netherlands). In the sixteenth, seventeenth and eighteenth centuries England accepted large numbers of Protestant refugees fleeing from religious persecution in Europe. Many were French and Dutch Protestants. From 1680 there was an influx of Huguenots (French Protestants) to England.

The next waves of migration mainly involved the Jews and the Irish. By 1660 a small Jewish community had re-established itself in London. The main period of Jewish immigration to Britain took place between 1870 and 1914. In that period 120,000 Jews fled persecution in Eastern Europe to settle in Britain. In the eighteenth century the Irish also had a small community in London. Between 1820 and 1910 there was a massive emigration from Ireland. Nearly half the population left to escape starvation and poverty in their native country. Although many went to the USA, others settled in British cities such as Liverpool, London, Glasgow and Manchester.

In the nineteenth century there were few restrictions on immigration to Britain, but in 1905 the Aliens Act excluded immigrants 'without visible means of support'. However, the policy collapsed during the First World War when thousands of Europeans and members of the armed forces from British Commonwealth countries were allowed temporary residence.

In 1920 a new Aliens Act introduced strict regulations banning 'aliens' from being admitted to Britain without the permission of a customs officer and excluding those who were considered unfit or who could not support themselves and their families. People with sufficient money or who were sponsored by a British citizen were allowed entry. In the late 1930s these laws prevented most Jews who wanted to flee to Britain to escape Nazi persecution from entering the country.

During the Second World War it again proved impossible to control the entry of refugees. Along with British troops, large numbers of Polish, Belgians and French were evacuated to Britain from Dunkirk. Refugees also came to Britain from Czechoslovakia, Norway, Greece and Denmark. The Polish made up the largest group of all: by the end of 1945 there were nearly 250,000 Poles in Britain.

The biggest groups of immigrants to Britain since the Second World War have come from the Asian subcontinent and the Caribbean. We deal with this period of migration in a later section (see pp. 211–15).

Stephen Small – black people in Britain before 1945

Stephen Small (1994) points out that there have been black people (by which he means 'people of African-Caribbean and Asian origin') in Britain for many centuries. Some of the earliest blacks to come to Britain arrived with the armies of the Romans and some of them held senior positions. From the middle of the sixteenth century the numbers of blacks in Britain increased, until 1601 when Elizabeth I decided to expel all blacks on the grounds that they were causing economic problems.

Despite Elizabeth's policy, by 1715 there was a black community of some 15,000 in Britain. Many came to work as soldiers, servants and sailors. In the early nineteenth century there were usually over a thousand Lascars – Indian seamen employed by the British East India Company – in London. Some blacks arrived in Britain as slaves with their white masters, although they were more likely to be employed as servants than as slaves. Some of those who were slaves 'continually fled their masters, seeking refuge in small but cohesive communities across England's ports'.

In 1772 a ruling by Lord High Chief Justice Mansfield held that nobody, including slaves, could be removed from Britain by force, which meant that the rights of slave owners were restricted. In Britain the slave trade was abolished in 1807 and slavery in 1838. Slavery was abolished later in the USA (in 1865), so in the intervening years some black American slaves fled to Britain to seek their freedom.

By no means all blacks in Britain in the nineteenth century came from low-status backgrounds. Some 'were the children of African dignitaries who were sent to England to be educated: others were the children of white masters in the Caribbean'. There were also politically active Asians who set up the London Indian Society which campaigned for Indian independence. In 1892 Dadabhai Naoroji, a mathematics professor at London University, became the first Asian MP.

At the end of the First and Second World Wars some blacks from Commonwealth countries, and some American-Africans who had fought in the British army or as allies of the British, settled in Britain.

Small points out that some writers and historians have emphasized the hostility and discrimination experienced by blacks in Britain. Apart from Elizabeth I expelling blacks in 1601, there were attempts to 'repatriate' blacks to Sierra Leone in the 1780s, and in both 1823 and 1925 laws were passed prohibiting blacks from working on British ships. In 1919 there were anti-black riots in Liverpool and Cardiff, and again in Liverpool in 1948.

Other writers have claimed that despite such racism there has been considerable cooperation between working-class whites and blacks. Runaway slaves were often 'supported by the "London mob", and working-class whites helped them with food and shelter'. In the nineteenth century black British people were involved both in the Chartist movement (which campaigned for working-class political rights) and in the struggle to gain acceptance for trade unions.

Most black immigration to Britain has taken place since 1945 and we will examine this period in the next section. However, as Small says:

It is important to recognize the long-standing multi-racial and multi-cultural nature of Britain, and the contribution of black people to the development of British society and culture.

Small, 1994

New Commonwealth immigration to Britain 1945–61

The Nationality Acts of 1914 and 1948 imposed no restrictions on immigration to Britain from Commonwealth and Empire countries. Subjects of the British Empire had the right to enter Britain, vote, work and join the armed forces. Nevertheless there were relatively few people in Britain of Afro-Caribbean or Asian origin in the first few years after the Second World War. In 1953 the Civil Service estimated there to be 15,000 people of West African ethnic origin in Britain, 9,300 of Indian or Pakistani origin, and 8,600 of West Indian origin. Yet even in 1953 these ethnic minority groups were starting to increase quite rapidly.

In the aftermath of the Second World War, Britain was experiencing a serious labour shortage. The government set up a working party to explore the possibility of employing more people from the Commonwealth in Britain. It suggested that female workers could be recruited for the health service.

In 1948 the first ships carrying groups of immigrants from Commonwealth countries arrived in Britain. The very first was the *Empire Windrush* which carried 492 Jamaicans to Britain to seek work. London Transport recruited thousands of workers from Barbados, Trinidad and Jamaica. In some cases it paid the fares to enable its new workers to get to Britain. The British Hotels and Restaurants' Association also ran a recruitment campaign in the West Indies. Some private companies set out to recruit New Commonwealth workers as well. Textile companies in northern England advertised in the press in the Indian subcontinent. Woolf's rubber company in Southall recruited in the Punjab. Many, though by no means all, New Commonwealth immigrants were recruited to do relatively low-paid and unskilled jobs which employers could not fill with white British workers.

Table 4.2 shows estimated net immigration from New Commonwealth countries between 1953 and 1962. Although most of the earliest migrants in this period were from the West Indies, by 1962 they were outnumbered by immigrants from Pakistan and India. Most of the first immigrants from south-east Asia were men, with their families being more likely to follow later. Early migration from the West Indies included a higher proportion of women than that from India and Pakistan, and a second generation, born in Britain, developed more quickly. There were also long-established Afro-Caribbean communities in cities such as Cardiff, Liverpool and London.

Table 4.2		Estimated net immigration from the New Commonwealth, 1953–62			
	West Indies	India	Pakistan	Others	Total
1953	2,000				2,000
1954	11,000				11,000
1955	27,500	5,800	1,850	7,500	42,650
1956	29,800	5,600	2,050	9,350	46,800
1957	23,000	6,600	5,200	7,600	42,400
1958	15,000	6,200	4,700	3,950	29,850
1959	16,400	2,950	850	1,400	21,600
1960	49,650	5,900	2,500	–350	57,700
1961	66,300	23,750	25,100	21,250	136,400
1962[1]	31,800	19,050	25,080	18,970	94,900

[1] First six months up to introduction of controls

Source: Z. Layton-Henry (1992) *The Politics of Immigration*, Blackwell, Oxford, p. 13

Politics and immigration control

In some areas there was tension between the recently arrived ethnic minorities and the white population. In 1958 there were 'race riots' involving clashes between the Afro-Caribbean population of Notting Hill in London and local whites. E. Ellis Cashmore (1989) argues that in Notting Hill and elsewhere 'From 1957 ethnic-minority groups became targets for sporadic unprovoked attacks.' Cashmore says 'It would be difficult to maintain that the violence of 1958 actually signified the beginning of racial conflict.' Even before then there had been considerable debate about the 'colour bar', the banning of 'coloured' people from jobs or places. (For example, landlords sometimes used notices saying 'Europeans Only' or 'No Coloureds' to exclude Asians and Afro-Caribbeans from renting their property.)

Such issues served to highlight immigration and race relations as subjects of political controversy. Even in the 1940s some politicians had raised the possibility of introducing immigration controls. In 1954 and 1955 the issue was raised again by both Conservative and Labour politicians, and a working party was set up to consider the issue. However, no action was taken at that time.

In the aftermath of the Notting Hill 'race riots', though, the campaign to introduce controls gained momentum. An opinion poll in May 1961 found 73 per cent in favour of the introduction of controls. In 1962 the Commonwealth Immigrants Act was introduced. Commonwealth citizens were denied the right of entry unless they met certain criteria. If they did they were issued with vouchers of one of three types:

1 'A' vouchers were given to those who could show that they had a job in Britain before they arrived.

2 'B' vouchers went to those who were held to have qualifications or skills that were in short supply in Britain, for example medical qualifications.

3 'C' vouchers were issued on the grounds of individual merit. Some went to people who had served in the British armed forces.

The 1962 Act was justified by many commentators on the grounds that the large number of immigrants was adding to Britain's economic problems. However, Cashmore points out that the Act 'did not cover migrants from the Irish Republic, so it would seem that economic considerations were not really paramount'. It was directed at black immigration rather than all immigration.

Cashmore also argues that the Act:

marked the start of the 'numbers game', as it was called, since the abiding concern of politicians, the media and the majority of the white population was with the actual numbers of New Commonwealth immigrants entering the country and not with the quality of the relations between settlers and native whites.

Cashmore, 1989

The 1962 Act was introduced by a Conservative government, but the election of a Labour Government in 1964 made no difference to the overall direction of policy. In 1965 it tightened up on the issuing of work vouchers, thus further restricting immigration. In 1967 large numbers of East African Asians entered Britain, particularly from Kenya. The Kenyan government had introduced an 'Africanisation' policy and many Asians fled to Britain. East African Asians had not been covered by the 1962 Act so the government rushed through new legislation. The 1968 Commonwealth Immigrants Act restricted entry to Britain for East African Asians who held British passports. Under the Act all Commonwealth citizens with British passports became subject to immigration controls unless they had at least one parent or grandparent who had been born in the UK, or who was a citizen of the UK and its colonies. Andrew Pilkington comments:

The act proved to be racially discriminatory in nature. For its effects were to allow Kenyan whites to enter Britain but to prevent Kenyan Asians from doing so until they were lucky enough to be granted one of the limited number of vouchers issued each year.

Pilkington, 1984

In 1968 the Conservative shadow cabinet minister, Enoch Powell, made a famous speech in which he predicted that a multiracial Britain would prove to be disastrous. Powell claimed that Britain must be 'literally mad' to be allowing dependants of migrants to be entering Britain. He argued that it would eventually lead to racial conflict and serious violence. He said 'As I look ahead I am filled with foreboding. Like the Roman I seem to see "the River Tiber foaming with much blood"' (quoted in Layton-Henry, 1992). Powell was sacked from his job in the shadow cabinet, but the Conservative Party won the 1970 election and proceeded to restrict immigration even more.

The 1971 Immigration Act replaced employment vouchers with work permits for non-patrials (people without close family connections to the UK). Unlike the vouchers, the permits did not allow permanent residence or grant the right of settlement in Britain for dependants. Patrials, who had a parent or grandparent born in Britain, retained full citizenship rights. In practice, New Commonwealth citizens from the Indian subcontinent and the West Indies were far less likely to be patrials than the predominantly white population of Old Commonwealth countries such as Australia and New Zealand.

Despite the new Act the British government was forced to accept immigration by Ugandan Asians expelled from Uganda by its president, General Idi Amin, in 1972. Some 27,000 were accepted by Britain while others went to India and Canada.

Further changes were made to immigration laws under Margaret Thatcher's premiership in the 1980s. The 1981 British Nationality Act specified three categories of citizenship:

1   British
2   British Dependent Territories
3   British Overseas.

Once again those who were born in Britain, or who had parents or grandparents born in Britain, were granted British citizenship. Permanent settlers were also given British citizenship. British citizenship passed to children born overseas only if the parents were born in the UK. This excluded first-generation settlers from the Asian subcontinent and the West Indies. Someone who married a British citizen had to live in Britain for three years before they could apply for citizenship.

The Act was strongly criticized by the Labour Party. Roy Hattersley, its spokesperson on home affairs, condemned it as racist and sexist. Both the rules on children born outside the UK and on residence qualifications for prospective spouses were seen as discriminatory against Asians and Afro-Caribbeans.

In 1988 the Immigration Act made it more difficult for the families of immigrants to come to Britain. It repealed the automatic right of the families of men who had been settled in Britain before 1973 to join them in Britain. Dependants would only be allowed in if it could be shown that they could be provided with adequate housing and financial support and would not have to rely on state benefits. The Act came in for some heavy criticism. In the House of Lords, for example, Lord McNair described it as:

> *another mean-minded, screw-tightening, loophole-closing concoction imbued with the implicit assumption that almost anybody who seeks to enter this demi-paradise of ours has some ulterior, sinister, and very probably criminal motive and the sooner we get rid of him the better.*
>
> Quoted in Cohen, 1994, p. 64

In 1993 the Asylum and Immigration Appeals Act was introduced. This was designed to try to reduce the numbers of people seeking asylum. Asylum-seekers apply to enter a country in order to escape persecution in the country they are fleeing from. The British government which introduced the Act claimed that the system was being abused by 'economic migrants' – people who were not fleeing persecution but simply seeking a higher standard of living in Britain. The Act removed the right of appeal for visitors to Britain who were refused entry. Asylum-seekers retained the right of appeal, but they had to appeal within 48 hours of a decision by an immigration officer not to admit them. This might be difficult for asylum-seekers who were unlikely to have either access to legal advice or a detailed knowledge of the regulations. Asylum-seekers lost their rights to public housing while they were awaiting a decision. They were also required to be fingerprinted, and regulations specified that their applications would be refused if they failed to disclose all relevant information. In February 1996 new restrictions were introduced on the eligibility of asylum-seekers for social security payments.

Attempts to limit the number of asylum-seekers were also made through the extension of the need for visas for visitors to Britain from an increasing number of countries. Between 1985 and 1989 visa requirements were introduced for people from Sri Lanka, India, Bangladesh, Pakistan and Turkey. By the mid-1990s visas were required for people visiting Britain from over 100 countries. As Robin Cohen points out, it might be difficult for people who were being persecuted by a regime to apply for visas to leave the country. He says:

> *Now refugees were required to carry a passport from the very authorities who might be persecuting them. As to a visa, a visit to an accessible British embassy might well be interpreted as an act of dissent in itself.*
>
> Cohen, 1994, p. 83

Another rule which made it difficult to obtain asylum was introduced in 1987. Airlines and shipping companies were made responsible for ensuring that anyone they brought to UK entry points had valid documents. Failure to comply could result in large fines.

The introduction of new legislation led to some politically embarrassing incidents which revealed the inhumanity of the legislation and the way it was being applied. In 1993 the Home Office decided to deport Joy Gardner, who had arrived in Britain in 1987. Although she had married a British citizen, the marriage only lasted one month. Nevertheless she had a son who was born in Britain and her mother and several other relations were also in the country. Joy Gardner was seized, handcuffed and gagged in order to be deported. To the anger of many people, she died while the Metropolitan Police were attempting to carry out the deportation. In another case a British citizen, Koyobe Alese, was mistakenly deported after being stopped for a driving offence. In 1993 over half of the 323 passengers on a pre-Christmas flight from Jamaica to London were detained by the British immigration authorities on the grounds that they might be 'Yardies' – members of Jamaican organized crime groups.

Cohen believes that the British government has followed a deliberate policy of trying to prevent asylum-seekers even reaching Britain. Not only have those with legitimate reasons for being in Britain risked victimization, but many genuine refugees have had to face persecution in their own countries because of the unwillingness of Britain's authorities to allow entry into the country. For example, Cohen points out that in 1989 Britain forcibly deported from Hong Kong 51 Vietnamese people who had fled their country. Britain has also been more reluctant than many other countries to accept refugees from conflicts in places such as Bosnia and Kurdistan.

Britain's laws on refugees and migration have been affected by membership of the European Union. The EU (formerly the European Community) has always allowed the free movement of people between member states, and since 1993 citizens of each member state have become citizens of the EU as well. However, the EU has adopted what has become known as a 'fortress Europe' policy which has tried to largely exclude non-EU citizens from entry to the community.

In 1990 five of the original members of the EU signed the Schengen Agreement which tried to create common policies over issues relating to migration and asylum. Britain did not sign, preferring to retain its own restrictive rules. However, it did sign the Dublin Convention in 1990. This prevented asylum-seekers from applying for asylum in more than one

EU country. According to Cohen, it was an attempt to make sure that asylum-seekers could not try to take advantage of any weak link in Europe's borders by making multiple applications to different states. Thus, while membership of the EU has made movement within the community easier, it has done little for the plight of asylum-seekers from elsewhere.

British migration since 1961

As a consequence of some of the changes discussed above, immigration from the New Commonwealth (including Pakistan) declined from 136,000 in 1961 to 68,000 in 1972 and 22,800 in 1988. It rose slightly to 27,000 in 1992. The majority were allowed to come to Britain as the dependants of British citizens rather than as immigrants in their own right. In Table 4.3, the 1996 figures show that nearly half of those accepted for settlement in Britain were from Asia, but there were also significant numbers accepted from Africa, the Americas and Europe. The table shows that the vast majority were relatives of British citizens.

There is little doubt that many of the immigration rules have been specifically designed to limit the numbers of Asian and Afro-Caribbean migrants to Britain. This is despite the fact that there are many migrants from other parts of the world and that historically there is no substance to claims that migration might lead to 'overcrowding' in Britain.

Writing in 1992, Richard Skellington and Paulette Morris noted that:

> The word 'immigrant' is often wrongly used to refer only to black people. The majority of immigrants are white – from Eire or the Old Commonwealth (Australia, New Zealand and Canada) or from other European countries.
>
> Skellington and Morris, 1992

They point out that the 1981 census found that, of 3.4 million people in Britain who were born elsewhere, 1.9 million were white. Furthermore they note that strict limitations on immigration to Britain from the New Commonwealth could not be justified in terms of Britain becoming 'overcrowded'. Emigration has generally exceeded immigration. Government figures show that between 1978 and 1992 there was a net outflow of British citizens of over 120,000 (although, overall, including non-British citizens, there was a small net inflow of a mere 7,000). Figure 4.2 shows patterns of net migration for the United Kingdom from 1901 to 1994 with projections for later years. It shows that historically the UK has tended to be a net exporter of people.

The number and origin of asylum-seekers vary considerably from year to year. In 1996, for example,

Table 4.3   Acceptances for settlement in the UK: by region of origin and category of acceptance

	Thousands				
	1981	1986	1991	1995	1996
Asia	30.0	22.8	25.2	26.1	27.9
Africa	4.1	4.1	9.6	12.0	13.0
Americas	6.3	6.4	7.2	8.2	8.5
Europe[1]	6.6	5.2	5.6	4.2	7.5
Oceania	4.5	5.4	2.4	3.4	3.5
Other[2]	7.5	3.8	3.9	1.5	1.4
All regions	**59.1**	**47.8**	**53.9**	**55.5**	**61.7**
Of which:					
Wives	16.7	14.1	19.0	19.9	21.5
Husbands	6.7	6.8	11.6	12.7	12.4
Children	14.4	10.3	9.1	8.6	10.7
Four years' employment	6.7	3.3	3.4	4.1	3.9
Refugees	3.4	1.5	0.8	0.7	1.1
Other	11.2	11.8	10.1	9.5	12.0

1 Includes all EEA countries throughout the period covered. EEA nationals are not obliged to seek settlement and the figures relate only to those who chose to do so.
2 Mainly British overseas citizens and stateless persons and in 1981 to 1991 acceptances where the country was not separately identified; in 1995 and 1996 these are included in the relevant geographical areas.

Source: *Social Trends* (1998), London, HMSO, p. 37

Figure 4.2   Net migration to/from the United Kingdom

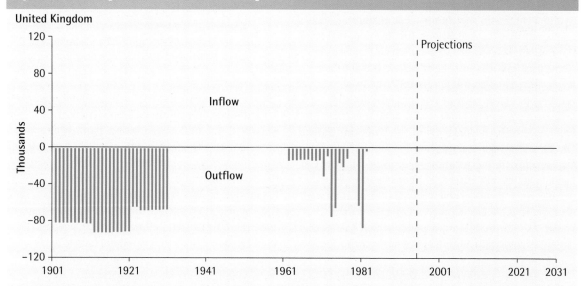

1 Includes net civilian migration and other adjustments. Ten-year averages are used before 1931 and between 1951 and 1971. A twenty-year average is used between 1931 and 1950. Data prior to 1971 are for calendar years; data after 1971 are mid-year estimates and projections.
2 1994-based projections.

Source: *Social Trends* (1997), HMSO, London, p. 35

there were some 30,000 applications, with over a third of applicants from Africa. Around 2,200 were accepted as refugees and granted asylum, and about 5,000 were granted exceptional leave to remain in Britain for a time. In 1995 there were 44,000 applicants, with just 1,300 accepted as refugees and 4,400 given leave to remain. Thirteen per cent of the applicants in 1995 were fleeing from Nigeria, 8 per cent from Somalia.

Robin Cohen (1994) argues that Britain's policies towards migration have not just been based on excluding black and Asian immigrants. At various times a range of groups, some of them white, have been seen as unsuitable for immigration to Britain. The reasons are tied up with nationalistic conceptions of British identity, which will be explored later in the chapter (see pp. 268–70).

Britain's ethnic minority population

It is only comparatively recently that the British government has started collecting data specifically on ethnic minority groups. The 1991 census included a question asking people to assign themselves to an ethnic group from a list of options as shown in Table 4.4. There were a number of problems with this:

1 The options were by no means exhaustive: for example, no 'Irish' category was included and a considerable number of respondents described themselves as belonging to the ethnic group category 'other'.

2 The figures are based upon self-assigned ethnic groups, and are therefore shaped by the subjective views of the respondents.

3 The question mixed up nationality (e.g. Bangladeshi), and skin colour (e.g. Black other).

4 The figures do not distinguish between people from distinctive cultural groups but with the same national origin (e.g. Indian Sikhs and Hindus).

Nevertheless, because the census is more comprehensive than any other survey, it provides perhaps the most reliable estimate of the size of the ethnic minority population in Britain.

Table 4.4 shows that in 1991 just over 2 million people described themselves as belonging to an ethnic minority group. Of these 890,000 described themselves as black, and 1.48 million as Indian, Pakistani or Bangladeshi.

Britain's ethnic minority population is not evenly distributed throughout the country. The 1991 census found that more than 50 per cent live in the

Table 4.4 Population: by ethnic group and age in Great Britain, 1991						
	Percentages and thousands					
	0–15	16–29	30–44	45–59	60 and over	All ages (= 100%) (thousands)
Ethnic group						
Ethnic minority group						
Black Caribbean	21.9	27.6	20.0	19.6	10.9	500
Black African	29.3	32.1	26.7	9.2	2.7	212
Black other	50.6	30.8	12.4	4.2	2.1	178
Indian	29.5	23.9	25.9	13.8	6.8	840
Pakistani	42.6	24.0	19.2	10.4	3.7	477
Bangladeshi	47.2	23.3	14.8	11.4	3.3	163
Chinese	23.3	29.7	29.4	12.0	5.7	157
Other Asian	24.4	25.2	33.0	13.3	4.1	198
Other	41.7	24.9	19.9	8.5	5.0	290
All ethnic minority groups	33.0	26.0	22.6	12.6	5.8	3,015
White	19.3	20.4	21.2	17.0	22.1	51,874
All ethnic groups	20.1	20.7	21.2	16.8	21.2	54,889

Source: *Social Trends* (1994), London, HMSO, p. 26

south-east of England. Some 60 per cent of the black population and just over 30 per cent of the Indian, Pakistani and Bangladeshi population live in London. Elsewhere the highest concentration of ethnic minorities is in the West Midlands (8 per cent). Lancashire, West Yorkshire and Greater Manchester also have sizeable ethnic minority populations.

In contrast, less than 1 per cent of the population claimed to belong to an ethnic minority in Scotland, Wales, south-west England and north England. In rural areas less than 1 per cent of the population was found to be from ethnic minority backgrounds compared to over one-third of the population in the London boroughs of Tower Hamlets, Hackney and Brent.

In 1994 the *Fourth National Survey of Ethnic Minorities* was carried out by the Policy Studies Institute (Modood *et al.*, 1997). It collected data from a representative sample of 5,196 people of Caribbean and Asian origin and a comparative group of 2,868 white people. As Table 4.5 shows, the survey revealed that, not surprisingly, a growing proportion of members of ethnic minorities had been born in Britain: in 1994, 62 per cent of the population of Caribbean origin had been born in Britain compared to 54 per cent in 1982. The figures were lower for other groups, reflecting the timing of migration. In 1994, 47 per cent of those of Indian origin were born in Britain. The equivalent figures were 41 per cent for African Asians, 52 per cent for Pakistanis and 44 per cent for Bangladeshis. In all groups the vast majority of children were born in Britain.

Although the major ethnic minorities in Britain are well established and many were born in Britain, some sociological approaches to 'race' and ethnicity have seen the process of migration as

important in understanding the position of ethnic minorities in societies. These approaches will now be examined.

Migration and assimilation

One influential approach to studying relationships between ethnic groups or race relations focuses on the process of migration by ethnic minority groups to a new society. It has sometimes been called the immigrant-host model because it tends to conceive of relationships between ethnic groups as between a dominant 'host' society and a smaller immigrant group.

The immigrant-host approach has usually adopted an optimistic view of race relations. Sociologists using this perspective have usually believed that eventually the immigrant group will adapt to the way of life of the host society and will be assimilated into it. Conflict based on 'race' and ethnicity will tend to decline or even disappear with the passage of time.

The immigrant-host model has sometimes been seen as similar to a functionalist view of society. Some sociologists who have used it see the host society as characterized by a basic consensus and a shared culture. The immigrant group is seen as temporarily disrupting the consensus and shared culture, before the society gradually adapts to the newcomers and the immigrants adapt to the society. The emphasis is usually on the second of these processes: the immigrants are expected to fit in with their new society more than their society is expected to adapt to them.

Thus, like functionalism, the immigrant-host model emphasizes stability, shared moral values and slow evolutionary change involving a process of adaptation. Furthermore, one of the pioneers of

Table 4.5 Proportion of ethnic minority population born in Britain, by age

	Caribbean	Indian	African Asian	Pakistani	Bangladeshi	Chinese
Children (0-15)	96	94	94	88	78	88
Working age (16-59)	53	34	14	28	13	14
Elderly (60 plus)	2	1	4	1	-	-
All ages (1994)	62	47	41	52	44	34
All ages (1982)	54	43	24	42	31	n.a.
Weighted count	*3,333*	*2,722*	*1,697*	*2,200*	*820*	*753*
Unweighted count	*2,429*	*2,835*	*1,708*	*3,599*	*1,923*	*459*

Analysis based on all individuals in survey households

Source: T. Modood *et al.* (1997) *Ethnic Minorities in Britain*, PSI, London, p. 21

this general approach, Robert E. Park, followed functionalists in using biological analogies in his work.

Robert E. Park – race relations and migration

The nature of race relations

Robert E. Park was a leading member of the Chicago School of Sociology, based at Chicago University, which developed influential theories of social life during the 1920s and 1930s. At the time Chicago was a rapidly growing city and large numbers of people from diverse groups were migrating to Chicago both from within the USA and from other countries. The Chicago sociologists engaged in detailed empirical research in their city, and it was in this context that Park developed his theory of race relations.

Park describes race relations as:

> the relations existing between peoples distinguished by marks of racial descent, particularly when these racial differences enter into the consciousness of the individuals and groups so distinguished, and by doing so determine in each case the individual's conception of himself as well as his status in the community.

Park, 1950

'Race relations' only existed where people had a sense of belonging to different groups and there was some conflict between them. Thus there were, according to Park, no race relations in Brazil. Although Europeans and Africans lived together in Brazil, there was almost no 'race consciousness' and therefore little potential for conflict.

Park believed that different 'races' originated with the dispersal of a once-concentrated population. The great dispersion was partly stimulated by the search for a more abundant food supply, and it was 'like the migration of plants and animals, centrifugal'. Each dispersed human group then 'developed, by natural selection and inbreeding, those special physical and cultural traits that characterize the different racial stocks'.

Eventually the centrifugal dispersion of humans was replaced by a centripetal force that brought people from the different 'racial stocks' together. European migration and conquest created race relations in many parts of the world and the mixing of different groups in cities had the same effect. Thus, Park says, 'It is obvious that race relations and all that they imply are generally, and on the whole, the products of migration and conquest.'

Interracial adjustments

Park claimed that a complex process of interracial adjustment followed migration or conquests that brought different 'races' into contact. This process involved 'racial competition, conflict, accommodation and assimilation'.

Competition was a universal, biological phenomenon: the 'struggle for existence'. Just as plants might struggle for sunlight, humans struggled for scarce and prized goods and, in particular, land. Park says:

> the invasion by one race or one people of the territories occupied and settled by another involves first of all a struggle for mere existence, that is to say a struggle to maintain a place on the land and in the habitat which has been invaded.

Park, 1950

Failure in this struggle could lead to extinction both in plant or animal species and in human 'races'. For example, the native population of Tasmania 'seem to have been hunted like wild animals by the European immigrants as were, at one time, the Indians in the USA'. Competition does not always take such an extreme form as this but it continues so long as there are different 'races' which have 'racial consciousness'.

Competition is a struggle by groups and individuals in the ecological order; conflict is a struggle between individuals in the social order. Park gives the example of conflict between 'negroes' and whites in the southern states of the USA over 'jobs and places of relative security in the occupational organization of the community in which they live'.

If competition and conflict divide 'races', then accommodation and assimilation bring them together. Conflict ceases, at least temporarily, when the status and power of different 'races' have become fixed and are generally accepted.

Accommodation allows people 'to live and work on friendly terms' but it does not ensure that relations will remain harmonious. The groups with less power and status may eventually decide that their position is unsatisfactory and they may seek to improve it through engaging in competition.

On the other hand assimilation provides a permanent solution to the problems created by race relations. Assimilation can involve two processes:

1 first, 'a process that goes on in society by which individuals spontaneously acquire one another's language, characteristic attitudes, habits and modes of behaviour';

2 second, 'a process by which individuals and groups of individuals are taken over and incorporated into larger groups'.

Park claimed that Italians, French and Germans had resulted from the assimilation of a variety of racial groups and that the USA had been able to assimilate a variety of groups with 'ease and rapidity'.

Park was unclear about whether assimilation was inevitable or not. In one article he said 'The race relations cycle which takes the form, to state it abstractly, of contacts, competition, accommodation and eventual assimilation, is apparently progressive and irreversible.'

However, he recognized that, at the time he was writing, Japanese and 'negro' Americans had not assimilated into American society. He suggested that this was because both groups had 'a distinctive racial hallmark' in the form of physical differences from white Americans. The Irish, for example, could become 'indistinguishable in the cosmopolitan mass', but for other groups the situation was different. Park argues:

> *Where races are distinguished by certain external marks these furnish a permanent physical substratum upon which and around which the irritations and animosities, incidental to all human intercourse, tend to accumulate and so to gain strength.*
>
> Park, 1950

An evaluation of Park

Although Park was generally optimistic about race relations in the long run, he seemed to believe that conflict would not necessarily disappear between all racial groups. Unlike some sociologists who have used the immigrant-host perspective, he did not believe that the migrants would necessarily adapt to the lifestyle of the hosts. For example, he was well aware that in some societies immigrants from Europe had become dominant, and in some cases had wiped out the indigenous population completely.

Nevertheless in several ways Park's work is open to criticisms that have been levelled at all immigrant-host theories. We will discuss these after the next section.

Sheila Patterson – Dark Strangers

The immigrant-host framework

In the 1950s Sheila Patterson conducted a study of first-generation immigrants from the West Indies in Brixton, London. She conducted interviews with 250 whites and 150 Afro-Caribbeans, and also did some observation and participant observation. She distinguished between a 'race situation' and an 'immigrant situation'. A 'race situation' involved clear divisions between racial groups, and was characteristic of South Africa where she had also carried out research. An 'immigrant situation' was less clearcut. In Britain she found:

> *The immigrant-host framework ... seemed to offer a far more satisfactory mode of interpreting the dynamics which were clearly taking place on both sides, the complex motivations of behaviour, the fluid, undefined, and uninstitutionalized relationships.*
>
> Patterson, 1965

In Britain the relationship between the hosts and the immigrants was not fixed but was evolving all the time.

Unlike 'conquest societies', Britain was 'a homogeneous and peaceable society' in which she found that 'social relations are harmonious and voluntarily ordered among the great majority of the society's members'. In such a situation both the hosts and the immigrants had common aims. These were accommodation, integration and assimilation. The whole process involved adaptation whereby the hosts and immigrants adapted to living together.

However, in Patterson's view, adaptation was rather different for the hosts and immigrants. She assumed that the immigrants would do more adapting than the hosts. For the immigrant group adaptation involved considerable changes in lifestyle through resocialization and acculturation. For the hosts it was 'a more passive process of acceptance' which was 'largely unconscious'.

Accommodation, integration and assimilation

Patterson saw accommodation as the first stage of adaptation involving only 'minimal adaptation and acceptance'. She suggested some ways in which the West Indian immigrants in Brixton could accommodate themselves to the lifestyle of the host society:

1 In employment:

> *One might hope to find West Indian workers settling into a job with one firm; generally conforming to British workers' customs and accepting their viewpoints; joining the union where this is customary.*
>
> Patterson, 1965

On the employers' side, organizations could be expected to judge their West Indian workers on merit and to begin to give promotions to the most able and senior.

2 In housing, West Indian landlords might start to enforce 'certain standards of domestic hygiene and behaviour among their tenants' while white landlords could start to accept West Indian tenants.

3 In social life, West Indians would need to adopt British habits such as 'queuing' and 'becoming regular and welcome clients in a local pub'.

4 Furthermore, 'One might expect to find West Indian men marrying sooner, and taking a more permanent interest in their children's security and education.'

5 West Indians would have to become less sensitive so that they would cease 'to regard ignorant but well-meaning remarks about their colour, country, or way of life as deliberate insults'.

Again the changes required of the host population were rather less demanding. Patterson says 'local people might be expected to be used to the presence of coloured people in public places, and not to stare at them or draw away from them in the streets, shops or pubs', and 'to offer new West Indian neighbours the customary welcome and cup of tea'. They should also begin to lose stereotypical views of West Indians and to judge individuals on their merits.

At the time of writing, in the 1960s, West Indians had not been in Britain long enough to move beyond the accommodation stage, but longer-established immigrant communities could reach a stage of pluralistic integration. In this stage:

the incoming group as a whole ... adapts itself to permanent membership of the receiving society in certain major spheres of association, notably in economic and civil life.

Patterson, 1965

The host society accepts the immigrants as a permanently settled group and tolerates the group retaining a distinctive culture such as a different religion or pattern of family life. Patterson cites French-Canadians and Anglo-Canadians as examples of ethnic groups living in pluralistic integration.

The final stage of adaptation is assimilation. In this stage there is complete adaptation by the immigrants or minority group to the society, and complete acceptance of them by the society. Assimilation may lead to physical amalgamation in which interbreeding leads to a complete disappearance of the distinctive features of the immigrant group and their hosts. Patterson gives the example of the Huguenots in Britain.

Accommodation in Brixton

Having set out the stages through which immigrant groups can pass on the road to assimilation, Patterson then examined how far West Indian migrants had progressed in Brixton in the 1950s.

In employment she found that the labour shortage had forced employers to accept West Indians as employees and that they had not laid them off in large numbers when there was a small recession in 1956–8. Furthermore she found that, 'a minority of exceptional individual migrants have begun to move up from the bottom of the industrial ladder'. However, there was still considerable opposition to the employment of West Indians by white workers. For example, one white worker commented 'Look at those darkies

at the exchange; they get sent out to jobs while local people are unemployed.'

There was also conflict resulting from the 'well-meant but rough humour' of some white workers. This was sometimes expressed in 'Nicknames such as "Sambo" and "Darkie", jocular references to "Jungle Jim", jokes about "pidgin English", and "doesn't it come off when you wash?"' Such observations did not prevent Patterson believing that 'the cockney's live-and-let-live attitude would eventually overcome the problems created by "nicknames" and "jocular references"'.

In housing, the rising number of West Indian landlords and increasing acceptance of West Indian tenants by white landlords had reduced the problems faced by newly arrived immigrants. However, there were still problems: for example, notices on tobacconists' boards advertising rooms, which said 'Sorry, no coloured' or 'English only'.

In social life Patterson found that 'Social relationships between migrants and the local population in Brixton are ... still mainly restricted to casual contacts in the streets, shops, buses, and public houses.' But there were real signs of progress. Local shops had accepted the West Indians as customers and in some cases had started stocking goods such as calypso records and West Indian food to supply their new customers. West Indians had adopted certain pubs as their locals and become 'welcome as regular customers'.

Some West Indians had adapted to what Patterson saw as the British way of life by establishing 'various forms of the elementary family unit', and the more prosperous were quite likely to be formally married. Patterson noted, though, that many family units had proved 'impermanent'. Few West Indians and whites had intermarried, so there was little short-term prospect of physical amalgamation. However, she did find that 'A minority of male migrants ... have been associating with white "misfits" and declassed women, usually drawn from the provinces or other parts of London.'

Conclusion

Overall Patterson found that West Indian migrants and the host community had not generally progressed beyond the accommodation stage. In some areas though, particularly employment, progress had been considerable and she felt optimistic about the future. It was possible that the white residents' feelings of 'strangeness and uncertainty' about the immigrants would result in 'a more rigid class-colour identification' but Patterson did not think it likely. According to her, the West Indian immigrant community was small and quite widely dispersed; individuals were starting to be upwardly mobile; and in some respects they had a similar culture to white British. She could therefore 'hazard the guess that over the next decades in Britain the West Indian migrants and their children will follow in the steps of the Irish' and achieve almost complete assimilation into British society.

John Richardson and John Lambert – a critique of the immigrant-host model

Strengths and weaknesses of the immigrant-host model

Richardson and Lambert (1985) are generally critical of the immigrant-host model, but do believe that it has some strengths. They believe that the process of migration can influence relationships between ethnic groups and that it is therefore well worth studying. They argue:

> The model effectively drew attention to the dislocation caused by migration, it bravely addressed the complexities of assimilation, and it demonstrated the dynamic processes of change, rather than settling for a misleadingly static view of black-white conflict.
>
> Richardson and Lambert, 1985

It raised important issues and, although it 'failed to supply satisfactory answers to all the issues, at least it stimulated further development of the debates'.

Richardson and Lambert identify four main flaws or limitations in the immigrant-host model:

1 First, they argue that it tends to be unclear about the status of the different stages that are usually outlined. Sometimes it is seen as inevitable that a society will move through these stages with a gradual movement towards assimilation; at other times the process seems less than inevitable. Both Patterson and Park recognized that there could be long delays before a society moved on to the next stage and that sometimes reversals were possible. However, at times Park also suggested that the 'race relations cycle' was an inevitable process. Thus some of the theories contradict themselves. Richardson and Lambert argue that concepts like accommodation and assimilation 'are not really spelled out, and in practice it remains difficult to identify the exact stage of "adjustment" which has been reached'.

2 Second, Richardson and Lambert question the assumption built into these theories that assimilation is desirable. The theories tend to assume that migrant groups will, or should want to, give up their distinctive cultures to become fully integrated into the host society. They tend to neglect the possibility that both the immigrants and the hosts might value the cultural diversity of a multicultural society. The model also places most of the emphasis on the

migrants changing and does not see the need for major changes in the host society. It can therefore be seen as ideologically biased in supporting the cultural domination of the majority ethnic group in a society.

3 Third, the immigrant-host model attaches little importance to the existence of racism as a cause of ethnic conflict and inequality. Many writers argue that, in Britain and elsewhere, ethnic conflict results from the deeply and widely held racist views of the host society. The hosts are far more than suspicious or cautious about the newcomers: they have been brought up to have stereotypical views and hostile attitudes. In Brixton, for example, it could be argued that the 'nicknames' and 'jocular remarks' described by Patterson were evidence of outright racism on the part of the white Londoners and were scarcely indicative of a 'live-and-let-live' attitude. (Racism is discussed in detail on pp. 237–49.)

4 Fourth, the immigrant-host model has been criticized by conflict theorists for assuming that there is a consensus in the host society. It hides divisions between males and females and different classes as well as between ethnic groups. It tends to ignore the cultural diversity and the wide variations in values that may already exist in the host society. For example, some groups may be very strongly opposed to immigration and hold entrenched racist views while other groups might welcome cultural diversity and be in favour of relaxing or removing immigration controls.

Conclusion

While processes of migration remain important, it can be argued that they are becoming less important in Britain. As discussed above (see p. 216), increasing proportions of the main ethnic minority groupings have been born in Britain and are not migrants. They can be seen as belonging to one of an increasingly diverse range of British cultures. It is no longer possible (if it ever was) to see Britain as possessing one dominant culture from which other cultures diverge. As will be discussed later, some sociologists see Britain as possessing a range of increasingly well-established new ethnicities (see pp. 272–6). These may be hybrids of different cultural traditions. They are too far removed from the process of migration to be seen in terms of an immigrant-host model.

Stephen Castles and Godula Kosack – a Marxist view of migration

In a 1973 study of migration to France, Germany, Britain and Switzerland, Castles and Kosack advanced a very different theory of migration from the immigrant-host model. Rather than seeing relations between immigrants and hosts in terms of cultural differences, they argued that migration had to be examined in the context of the international capitalist system.

They found that immigrants in the four countries studied had a number of similarities. These were a 'subordinate position on the labour market, concentration in run-down areas and poor housing, lack of educational opportunities, widespread prejudice, and discrimination from the subordinate populations and authorities'. Castles and Kosack argued that these similarities showed that the diverse immigrant groups 'had the same function and position in society, irrespective of their original backgrounds'.

Migration and the international economic system

Castles and Kosack regard migration as resulting from the development of the international economic system. According to them the richer European nations have exploited the poorer nations of the world causing their underdevelopment.

From colonial times onwards the Third World has been used as a source of cheap, easily exploited labour and cheap raw materials. The colonies were not allowed to develop, or in some cases even maintain, industries that competed with those of their European masters. Development has also been uneven in Europe, leaving potential migrants in some of the more impoverished rural areas of southern Europe. The poor in the Third World have then been used as a reserve army of labour by successful capitalist nations during periods of economic prosperity and high employment.

Migration tends to increase the inequalities between richer and poorer nations. Those who migrate are a valuable resource: they are usually young and vigorous. The society into which they were born has had to pay to maintain them during their childhood when they were not able to contribute to the wealth of their nation. Castles and Kosack therefore see 'migration as a form of development aid for the migration countries' which are able to take advantage of the labour which has cost them little or nothing to produce.

In the countries experiencing immigration the process of migration tends to benefit certain groups and to harm others. Although immigration to Western Europe has not been great enough to actually reduce wages, the extra supply of workers has helped to prevent wages rising as much as they might have done. The immigrants have increased competition for manual jobs. As a result:

> *workers are likely to lose from the tendency for immigration to restrain increases in the general wage rate. By the same token, capitalists gain, as profit rates are kept high.*
> Castles and Kosack, 1973

'Race prejudice' and the working class

As well as directly serving the interests of the ruling class by reducing its wage bills, immigration can also help to cement its power in capitalist societies. According to Castles and Kosack, prejudice against immigrants has three main functions:

1 First, it serves to 'conceal and legitimate the exploitation' of immigrant workers 'by alleging that they are congenitally inferior'. Injustice and discrimination that would otherwise be unacceptable are tolerated if they are directed at a supposedly inferior group.

2 Second, immigrant workers are often used as scapegoats for the problems created by the capitalist system. They are a convenient explanation for problems such as unemployment and housing shortages. In reality, though, such problems result from 'the deficiencies of capitalist society, which is unable to provide adequate living conditions and to guarantee security to the whole of the working population'.

3 Third, 'race prejudice' serves to divide the working class. Workers are persuaded to accept discriminatory measures against immigrant workers and this means that there is little prospect of the working class uniting to oppose capitalist power. Castles and Kosack argue:

> *The traditional class consciousness based on collective ideals and actions tends to be replaced by a sectional consciousness of the indigenous workers. Indeed, the change may go even further: the orientation towards collective action designed to improve the position of all workers may be replaced by aspirations for individual advancement, without any change in the non-egalitarian structure of society.*
> Castles and Kosack, 1973

Castles and Kosack conclude that immigration benefits the ruling class by reducing its labour costs and by preventing the working class from seeking to change the status quo which works to the advantage of the richest and most powerful members of society. (We discuss Marxist views on 'race' and ethnicity further on pp. 258–9.)

Stephen Castles and Mark J. Miller – *The Age of Migration*

The increase in migration

In a more recent study published in 1993, Castles, writing with Mark Miller, has described the internationalization of migration since 1973. He was more optimistic in the later study about the effects of migration than he was in 1973.

Castles and Miller argue that migration has increased as Third World countries have become more and more involved in the world capitalist system. In Third World countries that are developing, there is considerable migration from rural to urban areas, and as this happens more people acquire 'the financial and cultural resources necessary for international migration'.

Rich capitalist countries have tried to restrict migration, but are unable to do so completely. There are considerable numbers of illegal immigrants to some richer countries, for example to the USA from Mexico. In any case most countries now have established ethnic minority populations so that 'even if migration were to stop tomorrow' cultural pluralism would affect the countries 'for generations'.

There are enormous pressures encouraging migration and, as a result, 'Most highly developed countries and many less-developed ones have become far more culturally diverse than they were even a generation ago.'

The consequences of cultural pluralism

Castles and Miller argue that many countries now have no choice but to come to terms with the existence of a variety of ethnic groups within their national boundaries. 'Marginalisation and isolation' of ethnic minority groups have served only to strengthen their ethnic identity and, for some minorities, their culture has become 'a mechanism of resistance'. Consequently, 'Even if serious attempts were made to end all forms of discrimination and racism, cultural and linguistic differences will persist for generations.'

Although the discrimination and exclusion of ethnic minority groups are undesirable in themselves, the cultural pluralism they engender opens up new possibilities. A new global culture develops, encouraged by the mass media, international travel and migration. People become more familiar with the cultures of different societies and ethnic groups. Therefore 'difference need no longer be a marker for strangeness and separation, but rather an opportunity for informed choice among a myriad of possibilities'. International migration might even, Castles and Miller suggest, 'give hope of increased unity in dealing with the pressing problems which beset our small planet'.

To Castles and Miller then, it is no longer possible for most countries to adopt the 'monocultural and assimilationist models' that were advocated by supporters of the immigrant-host theories.

However some countries have been relatively isolated from international migration for many years. With the break-up of the USSR and the Soviet bloc in Eastern Europe, a number of countries have suddenly been exposed to enormous social changes. In such a situation 'narrow traditional cultures seem to offer a measure of defence' for those subject to these pressures. Hence exclusionary nationalism has led to civil war in areas such as the former Yugoslavia.

Ethnicity – the problem of classification

Like the immigrant-host model, sociological approaches based on the idea of ethnicity place great emphasis on culture. They distinguish human groups primarily according to the distinctiveness of their lifestyles. They tend to attach little importance to 'race' as a biological difference between humans, although they do recognize that it is important when groups of humans *believe* they belong to a particular 'race'.

However, unlike the immigrant-host model, approaches based around the idea of ethnicity do not assume that in the long term immigrant groups will assimilate by adopting the culture of the host society. The ethnicity approach implies that migrant groups will very often retain large elements of their original culture, although they may modify it in a new setting. In fact ethnicity studies are not just confined to migrant groups. Nation-states can contain distinctive ethnic groups without migration having taken place. These groups may or may not be thought of as 'races'.

In this section we will begin by discussing definitions of ethnicity and we will then examine a number of studies of ethnic groups in Britain. We will then evaluate the ethnicity approach.

Defining ethnicity

The origins of the term ethnicity

Thomas Hylland Eriksen (1993) points out that ethnicity derives from the Greek word *ethnos* which is itself derived from another Greek word *ethnikos*. This meant pagan or heathen. The term ethnic had this meaning in English until around the middle of the nineteenth century when it started being used as an alternative to 'race'. However, Eriksen argues that in modern anthropology and sociology an ethnic group is usually seen as being culturally rather than physically distinctive. This is certainly reflected in the views of the next writer we will look at, J. Milton Yinger.

J. Milton Yinger – a definition of ethnicity

J. Milton Yinger (1981) argues that there is a difference between physically defined and socially defined 'races'. He argues that physically distinct 'races' may exist in theory but in practice the boundaries between physical 'races' have become so blurred that groups of humans with a distinct phenotype are difficult to distinguish.

Yinger says that biological 'races' are 'of relatively little interest to the social scientist', though they may be of some interest to 'the biologist and physical anthropologist'. Socially defined 'races' consist of ethnic groups who are seen by themselves or others as having distinct biological characteristics, whether or not they really do form a distinct biological group.

To Yinger an ethnic group (or as he calls it, an ethnie) exists in the 'fullest sense' when:

> a segment of a larger society is seen by others to
> be different in some combination of the following
> characteristics – language, religion, race and
> ancestral homeland with its related culture; the
> members also perceive themselves in that way; and
> they participate in shared activities built around
> their (real or mythical) common origin or culture.
>
> Yinger, 1981

Yinger's definition is a fairly broad one and essentially any group which believes itself to be an ethnic group and which acts in terms of that belief *is* an ethnic group.

Yinger says that 'phenomena on many different levels of generality' can be called ethnic groups. These can be of three main types:

1 First, he claims that an immigrant population sharing 'a common former citizenship' can be the basis for an ethnie. In America, Koreans, Filipinos and Vietnamese are examples of this type of ethnie.

2 Second, an ethnic group can also consist of 'a subsocietal group that clearly shares a common descent and cultural background'. He gives as examples native American groups such as the Oneida Indians and the Iroquois, Turkomans in Iran, and Albanians in the former Yugoslavia.

3 Third, an ethnie can be composed of:

> pan-cultural groups of persons of widely different
> cultural and societal backgrounds who, however,
> can be identified as 'similar' on the basis of
> language, race or religion mixed with broadly
> similar statuses.
>
> Yinger, 1981

In America, Hispanics from different Latin American countries are sometimes seen as forming one ethnic group. In Britain, Asians are sometimes seen in the same way, despite linguistic and religious differences and despite originating from different countries.

John Richardson – ethnicity and other classification systems

Richardson (1990) identifies three main classification systems:

1 'race'
2 black/white
3 ethnicity.

He argues that there are some advantages in using ethnicity rather than 'race' and black/white. Like most sociologists he disputes the existence of clearcut biological groups in the population. He therefore rejects the use of the concept of 'race'. He also raises a number of problems with using the term black. It can be a confusing term since sometimes it is used to refer only to those of Afro-Caribbean origin, and sometimes in countries like Britain it is used more broadly to refer to disadvantaged minorities. However, when it is used in the latter sense, it is still not usually seen as appropriate to apply it to groups such as the Chinese, Cypriots and people from the Middle East, even though they are sometimes as disadvantaged in Western industrialized societies as groups who are commonly referred to as black.

Another problem is that many Asians do not regard themselves as 'black'.

In some ways then, Richardson sees ethnic groups as a more acceptable term than the available alternatives. He sees ethnicity as based upon cultural differences between groups and says:

> This classificatory approach is attractive in so
> far as it highlights socio-cultural criteria
> (unlike the conventional 'race' systems) and
> it accommodates a potentially wide range
> of groups (unlike the two-category
> black/white model).
>
> Richardson, 1990

Nevertheless, Richardson believes that there are serious problems with the idea of ethnicity as well. In particular it can be very difficult to distinguish clearly between ethnic groups. Many groups are themselves subdivided and they may overlap with other groups. Ethnic groups can be distinguished in different ways leading to different classifications. Thus, for example, territorial origin could lead to distinctions between Bangladeshis, Pakistanis and

Indians, whereas religious affiliation would lead to a distinction between Hindus, Sikhs and Muslims. Linguistic criteria could produce a third system of classification.

Conclusion

Whatever these problems, it can be argued that the idea of ethnic groups is the least unsatisfactory way of dealing with the problem of classification. It is more flexible and adaptable than other approaches, and can accommodate changes in people's perceptions about the groups to which they belong. Groups such as the Irish in England can be accommodated within the ethnicity framework whereas they cannot under the other alternatives.

This approach is not limited to describing immigrant groups and different facets of ethnicity (such as language, religion and territorial origin), and can be used as the basis of classification as appropriate to the sociological issue or issues under consideration. Above all it recognizes that social divisions between such groups are created, maintained, altered and challenged by humans and that they are not the inevitable product of supposed biological differences.

The idea of 'race', though, remains a useful term when ethnic groups are *thought* by themselves or by others to be distinguished by phenotype.

Studies of ethnicity

Studies of ethnicity often take the form of ethnographic studies, that is studies of the lifestyles of groups of people. Such studies do not always focus on migrants and their descendants, but in Britain the main focus has been on people of Caribbean and South Asian origin.

Migrants from the Caribbean and from South Asia were the subject of a number of early studies. These studies usually compared the lifestyles of Afro-Caribbeans or South Asians in Britain with their lifestyles in their native lands in order to evaluate the extent to which the British context had affected their cultures.

Later studies, which have taken place since a second generation (and then later generations) of British-born Afro-Caribbeans and South Asians has become established, have tended to examine the extent to which traditional cultures have changed across the generations.

The studies we will look at are only a small sample of the numerous studies that have been undertaken, but they are fairly typical of the genre.

Roger and Catherine Ballard – Sikhs in the Punjab and in Leeds

Phases of development of South Asian communities

Between 1971 and 1974 the Ballards conducted research into the lifestyles of Sikhs in Leeds and in the Jullundur Doab area of the Punjab (Ballard and Ballard, 1977). Although their research was confined to studying Sikhs, they claim to identify four phases of development which are common to most South Asian communities in Britain:

1 The pioneer phase took place before the Second World War and involved a small number of early migrants establishing the first South Asian communities in Britain.

2 The second phase involved mass migration mainly by males in the post-war era.

3 The third phase started around 1960. During this phase increasing numbers of wives came to Britain, the communities became more established and some South Asians began to move into better housing. The Ballards call this the phase of family reunions.

4 The fourth stage involved a further consolidation and improvement in housing for some and the development of a substantial British-born second generation. For Sikhs in Leeds this stage started around 1970, but in the early 1970s Pakistani and Bangladeshi groups in Leeds were only just entering the third phase.

Pioneers

Many of the very earliest Sikh migrants were pedlars and hawkers from the Bhatra caste who arrived in Britain in the early 1920s. By the 1930s there were small communities of Punjabis in most large British cities.

For example, Darshan Singh was an important early settler in Leeds. In 1938 he had accumulated enough money to buy a shop/warehouse. Like other successful pioneer settlers he then acted as a sponsor, encouraging relatives to come and settle and helping them once they arrived. Darshan Singh came from the Ramgarhia caste of craft workers and his influence resulted in most of Leeds's Sikhs belonging to the same caste.

Muslims and Gujaratis also became established in Leeds. Ex-sailors were the most important pioneers in these communities.

Mass migration

Mass migration started in the 1950s. The pioneers provided a foundation for new migrants, often offering them hospitality and accommodation while they looked for work. The Sikh migrants in this period did not think of themselves as permanent settlers. They tended to come from neither the poorest nor the most prosperous sections of Punjabi society. The poorest could not afford the fare to Britain, and the most prosperous had no reason to leave.

Living standards are relatively good in the Punjab but as families grow larger land is divided out and some people end up with holdings that are too small to sustain a family. Misfortune or a shortage of land could prompt one or more men to go abroad in search of earnings to help sustain their families back in the Punjab.

The first post-war migrants were almost exclusively male. According to the Ballards they 'regarded their villages of origin as the only meaningful arena of social interaction and tended to view Britain as a social vacuum, a cultural no-man's land'. The migrants wanted to live as cheaply as possible in order to maximize the amount of the money they could send home.

This led to the formation of all-male households, usually with 'a single landlord who assumed a kind of patriarchal authority over its members'. The landlords bought their houses as a temporary investment with no intention of staying in Britain. Large, cheap houses which accommodated a considerable number of tenants could generate a substantial income, and when they were sold they could provide the ex-landlord with a large lump sum to take back to the Punjab.

Family reunions

The Ballards identify a number of reasons why South Asian immigrants were reluctant to bring their families to Britain.

The migrants' original intention had not been to settle in Britain and many were worried about the influence British culture would have on their families if they joined them in Britain: British culture was seen as 'morally degenerate'. In any case new immigration laws could make family reunions problematic.

Furthermore, separation of husbands and wives was not as traumatic as it might be for Westerners. Sikh families, and South Asian families generally, do not place as much emphasis on the bond between wives and husbands as Western families do. The wives in Asia 'were still part of the joint household, under the care of the father or brother of the absent husband'. There has been a long tradition in the Punjab of men leaving their families for long periods, sometimes to work as soldiers.

However, 'male migrants were constantly homesick for their families and despite the quasi family ties of the all male household, life for the settler was ascetic'. Sikhs put less emphasis on purdah, or the seclusion of women, than Muslims, so Sikhs tended to be less worried about their wives coming to Britain. By 1971 the vast majority of Sikh men in Leeds were living with their wives whereas Muslim and Hindu all-male households were still quite common.

Many of the earliest male migrants had made little attempt to preserve traditional Sikh culture and values. Few took part in religious rituals and many did not bother wearing turbans or growing long hair and beards. Seeing their stay as temporary, and without having to worry about their family being corrupted by Western culture, they felt little need to try to protect themselves from Western influences. However, once they were joined by their families, Sikhs in Leeds became more concerned to ensure that their traditional family life and religion were preserved.

Far from encouraging assimilation, the establishment of a more permanent Sikh community led to a more distinctive ethnic identity. The Ballards comment:

> Throughout the 1960s, the Sikhs set about recreating as many of the institutions of Punjab society as possible. This was a strong contrast to the earlier period where they merely utilised those cultural values which eased their survival.
>
> Ballard and Ballard, 1977

For example, liaisons with white women by Sikh men began to be condemned more strongly, and regular attendance at Sikh temples became the norm.

As the Sikh community became more established and less money was sent home to the villages, it also became more prosperous. Standards of housing improved and many Sikhs set up their own businesses. The Punjabi population created an 'elaborate infra-structure of services and businesses' including goldsmiths, travel agents, cinemas and grocers' shops.

Although the Sikh community became increasingly entrenched and the likelihood of returning to Asia decreased, the belief in an eventual return (which has been called the myth of return) persisted. According to the Ballards, this provided a valuable justification for preserving Sikh culture. After all, the preservation of the culture would make the eventual return smoother. It also offered some psychological protection against racism since it was believed it would only have to be tolerated on a temporary basis pending the return to Asia. Thus the Ballards say that 'The importance of return as a real goal has gradually faded and instead it has become a central charter for the maintenance of Sikh ethnicity in Britain.'

The second generation

As a second generation born in Britain became a feature of more and more Sikh families, changes in lifestyle began to take place. Many moved out of the inner city and bought houses in suburban areas north of Leeds. Parents became increasingly concerned about their children's education and more eager for them to stay on at school and obtain higher qualifications. More wives, including those with children, started taking paid employment.

Although the Sikhs adopted some aspects of Western materialism and came to value individual educational achievement, this did not undermine traditional values within the family. Nor did it prevent strong family networks extending across different households.

The second generation of British-born and British-educated children 'have been exposed to socialisation in two very different cultures at home and at school'. The Ballards suggest that many people believe that this leads to very strong tensions between parents and children and long-lasting conflict between the generations. Their research, however, found that the conflict was often only temporary. Children would start wearing British-style clothes, following contemporary fashions, and some would start to argue about the need to visit relatives and worship at the temples. A few would contemplate running away from their family.

However, these behaviours often represented little more than a temporary period of teenage rebellion. The research found that even in the case of the runaways:

> almost all young Sikhs, as well as members of other South Asian groups, do eventually return to seek solutions within the context of their families. They have all been socialised into a deep-rooted loyalty to the family and they find the outside world alien and unsympathetic in comparison.
>
> Ballard and Ballard, 1977

Generally the second generation have modified their parents' values to make them more applicable to a British context, but they have not abandoned them. Many young Sikhs become skilled at multiple presentations of self, changing their behaviour between the family and the outside world of work or education. The experience of racism makes Sikhs believe that 'however much they try to conform, they can never really be British because of the colour of their skins'. This encourages a strong sense of ethnic identity and leads many young Sikhs to be

determined to bring up their own children with a strong 'sense of Punjabi identity'.

Conclusion

The Ballards claim that their account of Sikhs in Leeds is applicable to most groups of immigrants to Britain from rural areas of south-east Asia. They argue, though, that well-qualified professionals from urban areas adopted Western values and tried to assimilate into British society. However, they suggest that, faced with discrimination, these groups too have developed a greater ethnic consciousness. The Ballards say 'peasants and professionals are coming closer together'.

Nevertheless, the Ballards are critical of approaches to the sociology of ethnicity that place too much emphasis on racism and other external constraints in explaining the behaviour of ethnic minorities. Such approaches ignore 'the culturally determined preferences of the group concerned'. Both internal preferences and external constraints are important in shaping the lifestyle of ethnic minorities and neither should be ignored.

For example, Sikhs and other Asian groups have not maintained a distinctive ethnic identity just because they have been the victims of racism. The first generation had no intention of adopting Western lifestyles and this has had a strong bearing on the development of the communities.

While the first generation was more divided according to such factors as kinship, religion and caste, the second generation was somewhat different. Born in Britain and having experienced racism throughout their lives, they felt a greater sense of identity with other South Asians, whatever the differences between them. Thus, according to the Ballards, the second generation was, in the 1970s, 'moving towards the establishment of an over-arching South Asian ethnic group'. This ethnic identity may have been prompted by external hostility but was still actively being created through the choices being made by young Asians in Britain.

Roger Ballard – Sikhs and Mirpuri Muslims

Divisions in the Asian community

In an article published in 1990, Roger Ballard updated his earlier work and described changes in Asian communities in the late 1970s and 1980s. In the earlier study, he and Catherine Ballard had suggested that South Asians in Britain were being drawn closer together. In his later article, Ballard stresses that there are strong divisions between South Asian groups in Britain. He argues:

As it becomes increasingly obvious that settlers of different backgrounds are following varied, and often sharply contrasting social trajectories, so it is becoming steadily more difficult, and increasingly inappropriate, to make generalisations which are valid for all 'Asians' in Britain.

Ballard, 1990

He notes that there are divisions according to class, caste, region of origin, religion and different experiences of migration. In order to try to explain these divisions he compares the Sikhs who originated in Jullundur Doab in India (who are discussed above) with Muslims from the Mirpur District in Kashmir, Pakistan.

Differences between the Sikhs and Muslims

Both the Jullunduris and Mirpuris migrated to Britain from predominantly rural areas, and in both groups the main aim of the early migrants was to earn money to send back to Asia. However, after arrival in Britain they followed different paths.

The Sikhs were reunited with their families earlier than the Muslims and enjoyed more economic success. As described above, many Sikhs set up their own businesses, and others aspired to – and succeeded in gaining – middle-class jobs and statuses. By 1990 most had moved away from inner cities and their children were enjoying educational success comparable with that of middle-class white children.

Most of the Mirpuri Muslims became 'international commuters' during their early years as migrants. They would work for a time in Britain before returning home to spend some time with their families. They would then return to Britain to earn more money. A few set up their own businesses, although they were not as numerous nor as successful as those of the Sikhs. However, most relied upon unskilled or semi-skilled work in industries such as textiles and engineering. Their wages were comparatively low and from the 1970s onwards they were more likely to be hit by unemployment.

Even after being joined by their families most were unable to afford to buy homes away from the inner cities. Their children enjoyed less academic success than their Sikh counterparts.

Economic reasons for the differences

Having described the differences, Ballard then sets out to explain them. One important reason for the greater success of the Sikhs was the greater prosperity of their region of origin. Jullundur Doab is a relatively affluent agricultural area with fertile land and a good infrastructure. Mirpur also has fertile land

but it has a higher population density so landholdings tend to be small, it is difficult to irrigate and the infrastructure is poor.

As a consequence of these differences, migrants from Jullundur Doab tended to have more craft and business skills and higher educational qualifications than the Mirpuris. They also tended to be more literate.

Relying on unskilled and semi-skilled work in traditional manufacturing industries made the Mirpuris much more likely to lose their jobs once recession hit Britain. However, Ballard does not believe that such differences in economic situation can, on their own, account for the contrasting fortunes of the two groups. He argues that cultural differences may also be part of the explanation.

Cultural reasons for the differences

Ballard is very cautious about attributing too much importance to cultural factors. He expresses concern about the possibility of resorting to 'sweeping and inevitably stereotypical assertions about the allegedly "conservative" or "liberal" characteristics of the two religious traditions'. Nevertheless, he does believe that differences in religion and in community and family life could partly explain differences in the fortunes of South Asian groups. Ballard identifies three important cultural differences:

1 Muslims are allowed to marry close kin and often do so, whereas it is not permitted for Sikhs and Hindus. This means that kinship networks for Muslims tend to be more close-knit and geographically limited in scope.

2 The tradition of purdah is stronger in Islam than in Sikhism and it places greater restrictions on women in public places. As a result, Muslim women in Pakistan are less likely to travel long distances or to take up paid employment outside the home than Sikh women in India.

3 Sikhs and Hindus cremate their dead whereas Muslims bury them. Consequently Muslims tend to develop stronger ties to a particular village or region where their ancestors are buried.

Together these factors make Muslim families less geographically mobile and more close-knit and even inward looking. As a result, the male Mirpuri immigrants were rather more cautious about bringing their wives and children to Britain than the Sikh men. As international commuters, sometimes for up to 15 years, the Muslim men used up a lot of their money on travel. Furthermore, a higher proportion of their income was sent back to Asia to be spent or invested there. By the time the men decided that their families should settle in Britain the administrative obstacles had become greater, slowing down family reunions even more.

Muslim families have therefore had less time to become established in Britain and improve their living standards than some other groups of Asians. Once in Britain, Muslim wives were less likely to take paid employment, thus limiting the earning-power of the family. Thus, although the differences in the economic success of the two groups have been influenced by economic factors and the structural features of society, cultural factors such as religion and kinship patterns have had a part to play as well.

Conclusion

Ballard stresses at the end of his article that his account is rather over-simplified. He points out that 'Sikhs' and 'Mirpuris' are not homogeneous groups. For example, members of different Sikh castes such as the Jat (peasant-farmers) and the Ramgarhia (craft workers) have followed rather different paths. Furthermore, not all Jullunduris are Sikh and many British Pakistanis come from regions other than Mirpur.

Nevertheless, Ballard's work does show that it may only become possible to explain inequalities between ethnic groups if sociologists can develop a sophisticated understanding of cultural differences, as well as examining wider structural forces.

Ken Pryce – West Indians in Bristol

The study

Between 1969 and 1974 Ken Pryce conducted a study of West Indians in Bristol (Pryce, 1979). He relied mainly upon participant observation to collect his data but supplemented this with other methods including interviewing. His study was based mainly on St Paul's, a poor inner-city area of Bristol with a large West Indian community. Most of the population studied were, like Pryce himself, of Jamaican origin.

Like Ballard, Pryce compared the behaviour of the ethnic minority in Britain with the lifestyle in the country of origin. Although most of his study is descriptive, he does make use of some Marxist concepts in explaining the behaviour of West Indians in Britain. Like most ethnographers of South Asians in Britain, Pryce found the ethnic group he studied to be far from homogeneous. However, he found that West Indians were not divided according to such factors as nationality, religion, language or region of origin, but were differentiated according to the subcultures they had adopted in Britain.

All West Indians in Britain faced a series of problems in adapting to life there. They tried to solve these problems by forming a number of distinctive subcultures which helped them cope in different ways with their situation.

Jamaican origins

Most of the original immigrants to Britain who settled in Bristol were poor, working-class Jamaicans. Modern Jamaica was originally established as a plantation society, ruled by Britain, where African slaves were put to work in the service of British economic interests. According to Pryce, the culture of slaves was very much shaped by the experience of slavery and was influenced much more by Western culture than by African. He says:

Not only was the African culture of the slaves destroyed, but the plantation economies, being dependent parts of the larger metropolitan economy, had the effect of extending British capitalist modes and ways of thinking to the Caribbean.

Pryce, 1979

African slaves lost both their religion and their patterns of family life: most were converted to Christianity, and under slavery it was impossible to maintain stable families. The slaves adopted the British language of their masters and, in Pryce's view, they internalized European values. He believes that Jamaican culture came to value all things European, particularly those that were British, while African culture was rejected and even despised. He says 'In Jamaica, the closer symbols, mannerisms, appearances and institutions approximate and conform to British standards, the higher their value and prestige.'

In modern Jamaica, family life among the lower classes is characterized by instability and by the comparative rarity of formal marriage. Although the higher classes generally adopt the 'monogamous nuclear family and Christian marriage', the same is not true of the poor. When men and women become partners and decide to live together, they do not usually get married immediately. Indeed many never get married because they tend to split up, with the wife returning to her mother, taking any children with her. If the couple stay together long enough, they may get married eventually, but this may be years after they have had their children.

To Pryce, the instability of marriage in Jamaica stems 'directly from the institution of slavery'. Although Jamaica is very largely Protestant it has incorporated other elements into its religion. An important feature of Jamaican religion is 'its cultic diversity and the recrudescence of non-Christian features, typically confined to the masses'.

Thus Pentecostalism, which is popular in Jamaica, is based upon a literal interpretation of the Bible but it also emphasizes the importance of possession by the Holy Spirit.

Rastafarianism is based largely upon the Old Testament. Founded by Marcus Garvey in the early decades of the twentieth century, it preaches that black Africans living outside Africa will eventually return to their continent of origin and will be freed from the oppression and exploitation they have suffered at the hands of whites.

When in the 1950s a considerable number of Jamaicans emigrated and settled in Bristol, they brought with them religious beliefs and patterns of family life that were to have a strong influence on their lives in Britain.

Orientations and subcultures

From his study of Bristol, Pryce found two main orientations to society within the West Indian community. These were the expressive-disreputable orientation and the stable law-abiding orientation. The main difference between them was that those adhering to the former were unwilling to earn a living through regular work, whereas those adhering to the latter did seek regular employment.

All West Indians in Britain faced difficulty in finding well-paid, secure jobs and in affording comfortable accommodation. All faced problems of discrimination and rejection by white society, yet they responded in different ways:

1 Those who adopted the expressive-disreputable orientation rejected the society which rejected them.

2 Those who adopted the stable law-abiding orientation were more willing to accept or at least tolerate their situation and some adopted the values of white society wholeheartedly.

Within the expressive-disreputable orientation Pryce distinguished two subcultures:

1 the hustlers

2 the teenyboppers.

Within the stable law-abiding orientation there were four subcultures:

1 the in-betweeners

2 the mainliners

3 the proletarian respectables

4 the saints.

We will now look at each of these subcultures. Pryce's overall theory is illustrated in Figure 4.3.

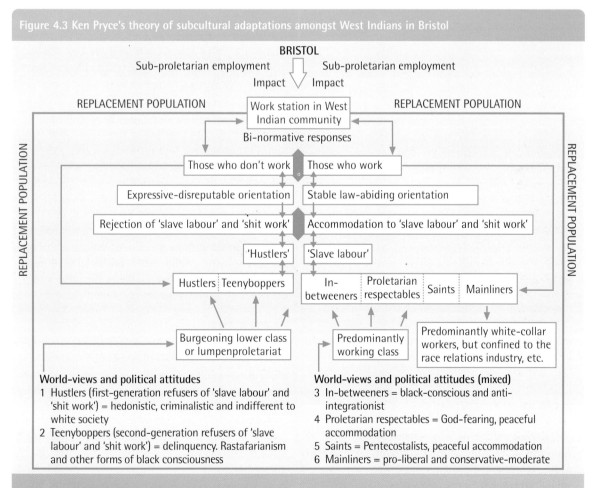

Figure 4.3 Ken Pryce's theory of subcultural adaptations amongst West Indians in Bristol

Source: K. Pryce (1979) *Endless Pressure*, Penguin, Harmondsworth, p. 271

Hustlers

Hustlers have conventional aspirations. They want to achieve material success. However, they have become disillusioned with trying to do so through conventional means. Many have experienced the 'humiliating effect of racial discrimination' and have become demoralized by the experience. Originally many of those who became hustlers wanted to work hard to earn enough to return home, but they found it impossible to get jobs doing anything other than 'white man's shit work'. They earned too little to save up money and they became increasingly resentful of their situation.

Pryce argues that slavery produced a strong antipathy amongst black Jamaicans to taking orders from white bosses. Being dominated by whites threatened the West Indian male's sense of masculinity. In Britain the response to discrimination has been to develop 'a dread of having to work as a menial' and 'abhorrence of having to take orders from a "cheeky white man" indifferent to him as an individual'.

Rejecting what they see as 'slave labour', they turn to hustles to earn a living. Most hustles are illegal. They involve selling drugs, acting as prostitutes' pimps, or 'conning others'. Some hustlers sell fake marijuana. Another earns a living by putting on dances, but he may sell tickets by claiming a famous reggae star is to appear when there is no chance of this happening. The odd hustler resorts to less subtle tactics by carrying out an armed robbery. Earning a living through hustles, rather than through more conventional means, 'restores the hustler's sense of pride and his feeling of mastery and autonomy'. He is reliant upon his own wits to make money and dependent on nobody.

Hustlers, and others of the expressive-disreputable orientation, believe it is very important to be strong and to be able to cope with pressure from difficult circumstances. Strength helps the hustler to avoid 'getting in a plight'. Pryce defines a plight as:

> *any form of misfortune or predicament involving loss of face – e.g. desertion by one's wife or husband, imprisonment, being crossed in a love affair, having the bailiff on one's front step, having to pawn one's clothes, going hungry, sexual impotence, losing a fight with one's friends watching.*
>
> Pryce, 1979

The pressure of avoiding these plights means that people have to let off steam. This often takes place at a 'blues dance' where hustlers gather with teenyboppers and others to listen to loud reggae and soul, drink, dance and smoke marijuana.

Teenyboppers

According to Pryce, a teenybopper is:

> *a West Indian youth in his teens or very early twenties, who is male, homeless, unemployed and who in the language of liberals and social workers, is 'at risk' in the community – that is, a young West Indian who is either already a delinquent or is in danger of becoming one.*
>
> Pryce, 1979

Teenyboppers are often a product of the unstable family life that is characteristic of lower classes in the West Indies, and which is also found in some families in Britain. During the early stages of migration to Britain, children were often left behind to be raised by relatives such as aunts or grandmothers, and this loosened attachments to parents. In Britain the frequent break-up of relationships, the absence of fathers in many homes, and the presence in some cases of the mother's new partner, combined with poverty, 'militate against family cohesion'.

Conflict between children and parents breaks out over issues such as how late children can stay out and who they choose as friends. The teenyboppers end up leaving home early in their lives. They find the outside world hostile, and experience racism when they try to find regular work. They suffer from drift and alienation and sooner or later come into conflict with the law.

Unlike hustlers, teenyboppers tend to be much more politically conscious. Some get involved with radical political organizations. The teenybopper has a 'schizoid orientation towards both his own Negro roots, which he despises, and the white bourgeois values which he had been indoctrinated to venerate as culturally and morally superior'. However, he is rejected by white society and he 'responds to rejection with rejection'. Some teenyboppers turn to Rastafarianism with its promise of salvation through a return to Africa, while others are influenced more by Marxism and 'a hodge-podge of the ideas and doctrines of all left-wing revolutionary positions'.

In-betweeners

As their name suggests, although Pryce sees members of this group as stable and law-abiding, he also sees them as having characteristics in common with the expressive-disreputable groups. In-betweeners are described as being aged 18–35 and ambitious for material success. They have steady jobs and are usually quite well educated and qualified. They have, or would like to have, a stable and conventional family life.

However, they want to achieve these things without abandoning their black roots. They believe in the importance of 'black culture' and 'black pride'. They are against close integration with whites and many hope to return to the Caribbean to use their skills to improve society there. They mix with hustlers during their leisure time and may smoke marijuana, but generally they are not very involved in illegal activities.

Mainliners

Like in-betweeners, mainliners have conventional jobs, they aspire to material success and stable and conventional family lives. However, they have very different values. Mainliners are very law-abiding, politically conservative and in favour of integration with whites. Many work in jobs such as race relations officers, youth workers, and health visitors. A few have their own businesses or work as supervisors. They are 'mostly, literate, middle-aged, well established West Indian residents'. They have no desire to return to the West Indies, and they adapt to life in Britain by adopting the lifestyle and culture of the British middle class.

Mainliners are seen as traitors to blacks by in-betweeners, and are regarded with thinly disguised contempt by Pryce. He criticizes them for claiming to represent the West Indian community and becoming self-appointed leaders. He claims that they are 'not necessarily accepted as social equals by their white colleagues, who are almost always of a higher social class and better educated than they'. Pryce is particularly scathing when he says 'There is no doubt that many mainliners are nothing more than pretentious pen-pushers who are less concerned with achieving results than with gaining recognition for themselves as individuals.'

Proletarian respectables and saints

The final two groups, proletarian respectables and saints, are both working-class, hard-working, law-abiding and politically passive. Like other West Indians they suffer from discrimination but despite this they 'tenaciously pursue regular and stable employment'. The men usually have unskilled or semi-skilled manual jobs; the women have routine low-paid service jobs in areas such as catering or the NHS. Many of the first generation came to Britain with families, and their experience of work in the West Indies had led to them becoming accustomed to long hours, poor conditions and low pay. In Britain they may be slightly better off than they had been, so they struggle on despite hardship.

The saints are Pentecostalists. Their religion preaches that 'Sin is rebellion against the law of God' and that 'Salvation consists in deliverance from all sin and unrighteousness through faith and repentance, water baptisms, baptism of the spirit and

continuance of a godly life.' These beliefs provide powerful sanctions against criminality and deviance, but the religion also offers comfort in a racist society. Saints devalue the significance of life in this world and look to salvation in life after death, making discrimination and hardship that much easier to bear.

Conclusion

Pryce concludes that all the subcultures are ways of dealing with the work situation that confronts West Indians in Britain. They are attempts to deal with or escape from 'pressures of poverty and race' which in turn have their origins in slavery and colonialism.

For centuries blacks have been exploited as a cheap 'reserve pool' of labour by British capitalism. In the West Indians, political consciousness resulted from the anti-colonial struggle for independence. Immigration to Britain resulted not only in the importation of the Westernized values adopted by the slaves, but also in the introduction of anti-colonial attitudes. This is reflected not only in the criminality of the hustlers, but also in the political consciousness of most teenyboppers and some in-betweeners.

Evaluation

Pryce's work demonstrates the value of ethnographic studies in revealing cultural differences within ethnic minority groups. However, like most studies, it is geographically limited. Although Pryce claims that his findings are probably applicable to most British towns and cities with a sizeable West Indian population, his study was confined to Bristol and wider generalizations may not be justified.

His study also concentrated very much on the men in the community. The cultures of West Indian women were discussed in much less detail and assumed much less significance in his overall theory.

Although Pryce tried to link his ethnographic study in Britain with a discussion of West Indian culture in the Caribbean, his attempt to do so has been criticized. Errol Lawrence (1982) argues that Pryce is quite wrong to claim that slavery destroyed African culture and that West Indians have almost completely adopted Western, European culture. Lawrence believes, for example, that African rituals and a belief in spirit possession have had a strong influence on West Indian culture, and that African languages have influenced the way West Indians speak English.

Furthermore, to Lawrence, slaves did not simply passively accept slavery and the attempt to destroy their culture. As well as maintaining African elements in their lifestyle some slaves rebelled or ran away from their owners.

All the studies examined in this section are somewhat dated. More recent studies of ethnicity in

Britain have tended to adopt a rather different approach. A number have argued that it is no longer possible to see sharp distinctions in the culture of ethnic minorities and the white majority in Britain. They stress that members of ethnic minorities are very diverse and that there is increasing overlap between different cultures. Many such studies are linked to new theoretical approaches in the study of 'race' and ethnicity, and some are linked to a new emphasis upon issues of identity. Most have drawn upon the insights provided by studies of racism. These newer approaches to British ethnicity will be examined later in the chapter, once some of the theoretical developments on which they are based have been considered.

James McKay – primordial and mobilizationist explanations of ethnicity

So far in this section we have examined how ethnicity can be defined and have considered some ethnographic studies of ethnicity. However, we have not yet dealt with explanations of how ethnic groups come to be formed in the first place. James McKay (1982) and others have identified two main types of explanation of how ethnic groups form: primordial and mobilizationist.

Primordial approaches

McKay notes that the primordial approach was first proposed by the American sociologist Shils in 1957. Shils claimed that people often had a primordial attachment to the territory in which they lived, or from which they originated, to their religion and to their kin. This attachment involved strong feelings of loyalty and, Shils said, 'a state of intense and comprehensive solidarity' (quoted in McKay, 1982).

Some writers see primordial attachments as a basic feature of social life and a natural and inevitable phenomenon in human groups. From this point of view humans always divide the world into groups of insiders and outsiders, 'us' and 'them', and have an emotional and intuitive bond with those who belong to their group. This comes either from socialization or from some basic psychocultural need for belonging.

Primordial ethnic attachments may persist for centuries or millennia, and can be the basis for intense conflict between ethnic groups over long periods.

McKay suggests that a strength of the primordial approach is that it can account for 'the emotional strength of ethnic bonds', but he is also critical of it. He claims that this approach tends to be 'determin- istic and static':

1 It assumes that members of ethnic groups have little choice about their sense of attachment, whereas in reality ethnic attachments do vary in strength from individual to individual.

2 It tends to assume that all individuals will have an ethnic identity and thus offers no explanation for the existence of 'rootless cosmopolitans'.

3 The approach cannot easily deal with changes in ethnic identity amongst groups.

4 The primordial approach attaches so much importance to basic human emotions that it tends to 'talk as if ethnic and group identities existed in a political and economic vacuum'.

Mobilizationist perspectives

The mobilizationist approach suggests that there is nothing inevitable or natural about ethnicity. Ethnic identities are actively created, maintained and reinforced by individuals and groups 'in order to obtain access to social, political and material resources'. People use the symbols of ethnic identity to further their own ends, and ethnic groups tend to be formed when people believe they can gain some advantage by forming them.

For example, South Asians or Afro-Caribbeans in Britain might develop an ethnic identity because they believe that membership of an ethnic group offers practical and emotional support in a hostile, racist society. By forming ethnic groups it might be possible to achieve changes in the law or other political changes which strengthen their position.

McKay is perhaps slightly more sympathetic to this approach than the primordial model, but he still believes that it has its limitations. It tends to underestimate the emotional power of ethnic bonds and assumes that ethnicity is always related to common interests being pursued by the group. McKay argues that this is not always the case. He says 'the fact that some ethnic groups pursue political and economic interests does not mean that all ethnic groups have identical goals'.

Furthermore this approach sometimes confuses class and ethnic stratification, seeing the two as being little different. Ethnicity, though, involves more than class interests and can cut across class boundaries. In places such as Northern Ireland, South Africa and the Lebanon, ethnic conflicts have been stronger than conflict between classes and people have tended to identify with their ethnic group regardless of their social class.

Combining the approaches

McKay believes that the affective, emotional ties emphasized in the primordialist model and the instru- mental ties stressed in the mobilizationist model tend to be interrelated and that both are 'manifestations' of ethnicity. Rather than being irreconcilable opposites, the two theories can be combined. Ethnicity may be based primarily on mobilizationist, or primordialist, interests in different sets of circumstances. By producing a matrix based on combining the two, McKay is able to distinguish five types of ethnicity. These are illustrated in Figure 4.4.

Ethnic traditionalists

Groups of ethnic traditionalists are held together primarily by emotional ties. They often have a long history and their children are socialized to internalize their culture. They are not particularly concerned with pursuing social and economic interests but are more interested in maintaining a culture. They identify strongly with the ethnic group to which they belong. Examples include 'the Hutterite colonies of North America, and beleaguered minorities in the Middle East such as Armenians, Assyrians, Copts, Kurds, Shiites and Lebanese Christians'. These groups may have material interests but they have not been mobilized to pursue them collectively.

Ethnic militants

Both primordial and political and economic interests are strong amongst ethnic militants. For example, the Basques in Spain have their own language and their own cultural symbols such as flags. However, they also have a political movement which tries to gain greater autonomy or even independence from Spain.

Symbolic ethnics

Symbolic ethnics have quite weak ethnic attachments in terms of both primordial and political and economic factors. They have only token involvement in, or identification with, their ethnic group. In the USA, those of Scottish descent who sometimes attend a clan festival and the Irish who occasionally join a St Patrick's Day parade are examples of symbolic ethnics.

Ethnic manipulators

This type of group tries to promote its own political or economic interests but ethnic manipulators do not possess the same group solidarity and strong emotional ties as ethnic traditionalists and ethnic militants. Thus Scottish Nationalists in the 1970s were organized in a political party (the SNP), but its appeal was largely economic. It was not based upon an appeal to a distinctive Scottish culture but upon the claim that Scotland would be better off if it were ruled from Scotland rather than from Westminster.

Pseudo-ethnics

Pseudo-ethnics have the potential to become strong ethnic groups but that potential has not been realized. Leaders struggle to mobilize a sense of ethnic identity. Members of the group are more loyal to the state than to their ethnic group or potential ethnic group. For example, South Island secessionists in New Zealand want their part of the country to become independent,

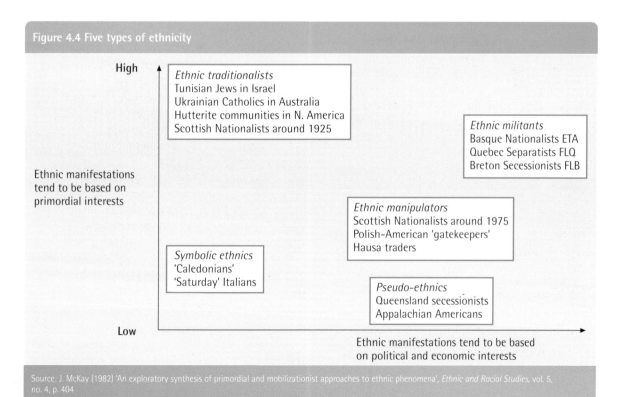

Figure 4.4 Five types of ethnicity

High

Ethnic traditionalists
Tunisian Jews in Israel
Ukrainian Catholics in Australia
Hutterite communities in N. America
Scottish Nationalists around 1925

Ethnic militants
Basque Nationalists ETA
Quebec Separatists FLQ
Breton Secessionists FLB

Ethnic manifestations tend to be based on primordial interests

Ethnic manipulators
Scottish Nationalists around 1975
Polish-American 'gatekeepers'
Hausa traders

Symbolic ethnics
'Caledonians'
'Saturday' Italians

Pseudo-ethnics
Queensland secessionists
Appalachian Americans

Low

Ethnic manifestations tend to be based on political and economic interests

Source: J. McKay (1982) 'An exploratory synthesis of primordial and mobilizationist approaches to ethnic phenomena', *Ethnic and Racial Studies*, vol. 5, no. 4, p. 404

but they have a difficult task because those who live there do not have a strong sense of primordial attachment to the island. McKay says:

> It could be said that ethnic militants and manipulators possess an ethnic trait which they utilize in order to obtain access to societal resources, whereas pseudo-ethnics try to make their pursuit of political and economic goals more legitimate by finding an ethnic foundation on which they can be based.
>
> McKay, 1982

Conclusion

McKay admits that his matrix model approach is not fully developed. It does not explain why ethnicity takes one form or another, but he believes that further research could help to develop causal theories based upon his matrix. He argues that the matrix can be used to examine how ethnic groups change over time and move from one part of the matrix to another. It can also be used to distinguish factions within ethnic groups. For example, McKay says 'Orthodox Jews, members of Jewish "defence" organizations, and militant Zionists have different types and degrees of ethnic organization and identification.'

Michael E. Brown – the causes of ethnic conflict

Ethnic conflict and the 'New World Order'

Although McKay's work has implications for understanding ethnic conflict, it does not directly address this issue. Michael E. Brown has drawn upon the work of a number of other writers in trying to explain the existence of ethnic conflict in the contemporary world (Brown, 1997, first published 1993). He starts by noting that in the early 1990s there was considerable optimism in many quarters about the prospects for ethnic relationships. With the collapse of communism in the Soviet Union and Eastern Europe, it was hoped that different states in the international community could work together to prevent or resolve conflict. For example, some people claimed that the international cooperation during the Gulf War – in which the USA and other countries (including Britain) repelled the Iraqi invasion of Kuwait – heralded the arrival of a 'New World Order'.

In the New World Order, states and ethnic groups would be reluctant to act in repressive or violent ways towards other states or ethnic groups because they would fear the consequences of the reaction from the international community. However, far from ushering in a new and more harmonious era, the end of the Cold War seems to have been followed by widespread and intense ethnic conflict. Brown points out that:

> The war in Bosnia-Herzegovina has received the most attention in the West because of the intense coverage it has received from the Western media, but equally if not more horrific conflicts are under way in Afghanistan, Angola, Armenia, Azerbaijan, Burma, Georgia, India, Indonesia, Liberia, Sri Lanka, Sudan and Tajikstan. Other trouble spots abound – Bangladesh, Belgium, Bhutan, Burundi, Estonia, Ethiopia, Guatemala, Iraq, Latvia, Lebanon, Mali, South Africa, Spain, and Turkey, for example – and the prospects for ethnic conflict in Russia and China cannot be dismissed.
>
> Brown, 1997, p. 80

Defining ethnicity

Brown tries to explain why such conflict has become prevalent, but first he tries to define ethnicity. He believes that six criteria must be met for a group of people to qualify as an ethnic group:

1 They must have a name that identifies them as a group.
2 They must 'believe in common ancestry'. It is not essential that this common ancestry is real or that genetic ties exist – it is the belief that matters.
3 They need to have shared beliefs about their collective past. These beliefs often take the form of myths.
4 They must have some degree of shared culture which is 'generally passed on through a combination of language, religion, laws, customs, institutions, dress, music, crafts, architecture, even food'.
5 The group has to have a sense of attachment to a specific territory.
6 Finally, members of the group must believe that they constitute an ethnic group.

Conflict between such groups can take a wide variety of forms. The conflict may take place through political processes with no violence involved. An example is the campaign of some French-Canadians to win autonomy for Quebec. On the other hand, the conflict may be very violent, as in the civil war in Bosnia. However, not all civil wars qualify as ethnic conflict. For example, the war between the Khmer Rouge and other groups in Cambodia is a war between political groups rather than ethnic ones. Nevertheless ethnic conflict is widespread.

The causes of ethnic conflict

Brown distinguishes between three main types of explanation for ethnic conflict, the systemic, the domestic and the perceptual.

Systemic explanations suggest that ethnic conflict results from 'the nature of the security systems in which ethnic groups operate'. An obvious systemic requirement before conflict is likely to occur is that the groups live close to one another. Brown suggests that fewer than 20 of the 180 or so states in the world are ethnically homogeneous. This creates the potential for an enormous amount of conflict, but, fortunately, not all ethnic neighbours end up in conflict. Using the ideas of the political scientist Posen, Brown suggests that conflict will not break out when national, regional or international authorities are strong enough to prevent it by controlling the potentially opposing groups. Without this control, conflict can occur when a particular group believes it is in their interests to resort to violence. This can happen if they believe they will be more secure by launching a pre-emptive strike rather than waiting to be attacked.

Conflict can also result when it is difficult to distinguish between the offensive and defensive forces of a potential adversary. When empires, such as the Soviet Union, break up, ethnic groups may have to provide for their own defence for the first time. Lacking sophisticated military equipment, they usually have to rely largely on infantry. Although infantry may be intended for defensive purposes, they can easily be seen as a potentially offensive force and encourage a pre-emptive strike. Furthermore, the break-up of empires often produces a situation in which ethnic groups are surrounded by other groups who are potentially hostile. Some groups develop state structures faster than others, and the faster-organizing group may seek to take advantage of the situation by seizing land. Many of these conditions existed in Bosnia, with Serbs trying to seize land from the Croats and from the Muslims, who were in the weakest position of all.

Where a newly independent ethnic state has nuclear weapons it is less vulnerable to external attack, and ethnic conflict between new nation-states is unlikely. Larger, newly independent, former Soviet states with nuclear weapons have tended to face less external threat than those without such weapons.

Domestic explanations of ethnic conflict relate to factors such as 'the effectiveness of states in addressing the concerns of their constituents, the impact of nationalism on inter-ethnic relations, and the impact of democratization on inter-ethnic relations'.

Using the ideas of Jack Snyder, Brown suggests that nationalistic sentiments are aroused in situations where people feel vulnerable because they feel they lack a strong state to protect them. In parts of Eastern Europe and the former USSR some groups have felt vulnerable because the state has been weak, or because they have found themselves in a state dominated by another, possibly hostile, ethnic group. Some ethnic minorities have been blamed for economic failures by the majority population and have responded by trying to establish their own states. Ethnic nationalism involves trying to establish

a nation-state based around a particular ethnic group. Such a state may not respect the rights of minorities and ethnic conflict is likely to result.

Drawing on a range of theories, Brown goes on to suggest that processes of democratization can produce problems in multi-ethnic societies. When an old regime has collapsed, and new arrangements are being discussed, there can be major problems if there are ethnic groups who feel they were mistreated under the previous regime. They may seek retribution for past wrongs or they may feel unable to work with members of other ethnic groups in a democratic system. Problems will be particularly acute where a powerful majority ethnic group rides roughshod over the wishes and interests of less powerful smaller groups. Politicians may seek to exploit ethnic differences to increase their support, and in doing so they will heighten people's consciousness of those differences and increase the significance they attach to them.

Perceptual explanations are concerned with the way in which ethnic groups perceive one another. Hostility can be increased through myths and false histories which distort and demonize members of another group. Brown uses the example of Serbs and Croats. He says:

> Serbs, for example, see themselves as heroic defenders of Europe and they see Croats as belligerent thugs; Croats see themselves as valiant victims of oppression and Serbs as congenital oppressors. Under such circumstances, the slightest provocation from either side simply confirms deeply held systems of belief and provides the justification for a retaliatory response.
>
> Brown, 1997, p. 88

Myths about other ethnic groups are particularly likely to develop where an authoritarian regime has suppressed the histories of ethnic minorities for a long time. Such regimes tend to suppress the critical examination of past history leaving little opportunity for myths to be challenged. It is not surprising therefore that Eastern Europe and the former USSR have seen high levels of conflict.

Conclusion

Brown concludes that ethnic conflict is most likely where ethnic groups are living in close proximity in an area where there is no strong central authority, particularly if the groups have hostile perceptions of one another based upon beliefs that they have been mistreated in the past. The end of the Cold War created such a situation in a number of regions, and no New World Order capable of limiting ethnic conflict has yet emerged.

However, Brown is not completely pessimistic. Conflict may lead to ethnic reconciliation. For example in Spain there has been a degree of reconciliation between the Spanish state and the Basques, Catalans and Galicians, who have all achieved some degree of autonomy. Peaceful separation sometimes takes place, an example being the separation of Czechoslovakia into Slovakia and the Czech Republic. However, there are also many situations in which different groups cannot agree on a constitutional settlement and ethnic war ensues. This may involve the slaughter of civilians and the creation of large numbers of refugees. Ethnic wars can also have chain-reaction effects. As new states are formed, a new problem can be created as another ethnic group finds itself in a minority in a new state. For example, when Georgia became independent from Russia the Ossetian minority began to seek their own state with other Ossetians in Russia.

Brown succeeds in identifying a number of reasons for the increase in ethnic conflict in areas of the world which have become politically unstable. His arguments are perhaps less convincing in explaining the revival of ethnic conflict and nationalism in some parts of the world (such as Western Europe) which have not experienced high levels of instability. Some commentators have linked such phenomena to a general process of globalization (see Chapter 9). Other explanations for ethnic conflict can be found in later sections on racism and nationalism (see pp. 254–62 and 263–8).

Ethnicity – an evaluation

The ethnicity approach certainly has some advantages over biological theories of 'race' and the immigrant-host model. Unlike the former it does not base its arguments upon physical distinctions, which modern genetics has found to be of little significance. Unlike the host-immigrant model, it does not assume that minority groups will assimilate by adopting the culture of the majority.

The ethnicity approach tends to be sympathetic to cultural diversity and to support multiculturalism – the belief that ethnic or cultural groups can peacefully co-exist in a society showing respect for one another's cultures. At least in theory, ethnographic studies allow the development of an insider's view of different cultures, and therefore facilitate a greater understanding of those cultures than is likely from other sociological approaches. Such studies also have the strength of recognizing the role that ethnic minorities have in shaping their own lives. They are not presented as the helpless captives of biology or the passive victims of racism. Ethnographic studies can reveal subtle variations and divisions within ethnic groups which are often lost in other approaches.

However, the ethnicity approach is far from perfect. Critics tend to argue that it places too much emphasis on the culture of ethnic minorities. While emphasizing how ethnic minorities shape their own lives, it sometimes neglects the wider forces which constrain members of ethnic minority groups. Racism and structural features of society – both of which may cause inequality – tend to be neglected. Writers like Pryce do mention colonialism and refer to social classes, but their arguments still centre on the culture of the groups being studied.

Marxists and other conflict theorists believe that the analysis of racism and inequalities stemming from the structure of society should be the starting point for an understanding of ethnic difference and inequality, and not a subsidiary theme. The ethnicity approach is sometimes criticized for offering unconvincing explanations of why people form ethnic groups in the first place. The racism approach and conflict theories claim to have superior explanations. We will examine racism and conflict approaches in the next sections.

The ethnicity approach has theoretical links to symbolic interactionism. Both tend to use participant observation as a research method and both emphasize the importance of seeing the social world from the actor's point of view. It is not surprising, then, that the ethnicity approach shares many of the limitations of symbolic interactionism. Not only does it tend to neglect social structure, but it also relies upon research methods that can be seen as subjective. The findings of participant observation studies depend very much upon the observer's interpretations and they are liable to be questioned.

For example, some sociologists question the view of researchers such as Pryce that West Indian family life is unstable and produces delinquency. Errol Lawrence (1982) attacks Pryce saying that he 'absolves the racist structures of the English education system by defining the Afro-Caribbean child's struggle against its racism as "maladjusted behaviour"'. Clearly Lawrence interprets the same behaviour very differently.

The ethnicity approach is often associated with multiculturalism. However, multiculturalism is not accepted as politically desirable by all sociologists. We will discuss the values underpinning multiculturalism in the final part of this chapter (see pp. 287–9).

Recently developing approaches have tended to question the belief that there are sharp dividing lines between ethnic groups. They see ethnic groups as in a constant state of flux with the boundaries between them shifting and the cultures intermingling. Theories of globalization suggest that the differences between cultures will become less marked as time progresses. Nevertheless, the widespread conflict between ethnic groups suggests that many people do believe they belong to an

ethnic group. For this reason it still seems to be worthwhile to study the cultural similarities and differences between groups of humans who feel they share a common ethnicity.

Racism

Introduction

Many of the ethnicity approaches discussed in the last section recognize the existence of racism and accept that racism influences the behaviour of ethnic minority groups. However, they place more emphasis on the choices made by members of ethnic minority groups than on the constraints that can result from the hostility and discrimination of the ethnic majority.

Sociological approaches that attach particular importance to racism emphasize the limitations imposed on ethnic minorities by such hostility and discrimination. The focus of attention is not the ethnic minority itself, but the wider society in which it is a minority group. There is more concern with the inequalities between ethnic groups than with cultural differences, and racism is therefore a particularly important concept in conflict approaches to 'race' and ethnicity.

In this section we will start by considering definitions of racism and related terms, before discussing the extent of racism. We will then examine explanations for the existence of racism.

Definitions

Prejudice and discrimination

The terms prejudice and discrimination are general ones that can be applied to many issues other than those to do with 'race' and ethnicity. For example, people may be prejudiced against people who are very short, or discriminate against other people because they are women.

In the *Dictionary of Race and Ethnic Relations* (1984) E.E. Cashmore defines prejudice as 'learned beliefs and values that lead an individual or group of individuals to be biased for or against members of particular groups'. Prejudice is therefore about what people think and is not necessarily translated into actions.

Discrimination, on the other hand, is about actions. Cashmore defines it as 'the unfavourable treatment of all persons socially assigned to a particular category'.

Both prejudice and discrimination are often based on stereotypes about particular groups of people. Stereotypes are over-simplified or untrue generalizations about social groups. For example, short people might be stereotyped as being unusually aggressive, and women as being weak and passive. When stereotypes imply negative or positive evaluations of social groups, they become a form of prejudice, and when they are acted on they become discrimination.

Early sociologists of 'race' and ethnicity often use the terms racial prejudice and racial discrimination to describe prejudice or discrimination directed at groups by virtue of their membership of a supposed racial or ethnic group. However, the use of these terms has become less common and racism has largely replaced them as the most widely used term.

Racism

Racism is a controversial term with no single, generally accepted definition. Robert Miles has discussed the origins of the term and identified a number of different ways in which it has been used (Miles, 1989, 1993).

According to Miles racism is a relatively new word. There was no entry for it in the *Oxford English Dictionary* of 1910. Its first use in English seems to date from the 1930s. At that time it was used as a description of the nineteenth-century theories which claimed that there were distinct, biologically differentiated 'races'. As scientists began to reject this view some termed their nineteenth-century counterparts who advocated it racists. Racism also came into use in the 1930s as a description of the beliefs of Hitler and the Nazi party in Germany.

This definition was an extremely narrow one. It meant that racism did not exist so long as it was not based upon a belief that there were biologically distinct races. The view that racism was a mistaken view about biological divisions between human groups was reflected in a definition used by UNESCO. During the 1950s and 1960s this organization arranged four conferences where experts from different countries came together to produce agreed statements about 'race' that could be issued by the UN. The fourth statement defined racism for the first time saying, 'Racism falsely claims that there is a scientific basis for arranging groups hierarchically in terms of psychological and cultural characteristics that are immutable and innate' (quoted in Miles, 1989). While broadening the definition to include beliefs about psychological and cultural differences, this still retained the idea that racism had to be based upon supposedly scientific theories.

This view was rejected by the British Weberian sociologist John Rex. Rex specifically stated that racist theories did not have to be based upon a scientific justification. He defined racism as 'deterministic belief systems about the differences between the various ethnic groups, segments or strata'. Racist theories attributed characteristics to human groups which were determined by factors beyond their control, and which could not be changed. Rex said:

> It doesn't really matter whether this is because of men's genes, because of the history to which their ancestors have been exposed, because of the nature of their culture or because of divine decree. Whichever is the case it might be argued that this man is an X and that, being an X, he is bound to have particular undesirable qualities.

> Rex, 1986

Rex's description of racism retains the idea that the word refers to theories about the differences between groups and the desirability or undesirability of these differences. Many contemporary definitions of racism do not limit the meaning of the term so that it refers only to theories and beliefs. Some also use racism to refer to behaviour which is based upon such theories and beliefs.

John Solomos, for example, defines it as 'those ideologies and social processes which discriminate against others on the basis of their putatively different racial membership' (Solomos, 1993). It need not be based upon any specific theory about biological or cultural superiority because, to Solomos, 'racism is not a static phenomenon'. People may hold stereotypical views about those from different supposed racial groups and may discriminate against them without necessarily believing the group to be inferior.

Some sociologists have described a new racism which does not involve clearly articulated beliefs about the superiority or inferiority of particular groups (see p. 260 for details).

A broad definition such as Solomos's perhaps comes closest to the meaning attached to racism in everyday language. People may be described as racist when they discriminate against members of other 'races' or express derogatory or stereotypical beliefs about them, regardless of what sort of theory, if any, underlies their actions or beliefs.

Precise definitions of racism continue to vary between contemporary sociologists. We will examine these differences as this section of the chapter develops.

Cultural racism

Richardson defines cultural racism as 'a whole cluster of cultural ideas, beliefs and arguments which transmit mistaken notions about the attributes and capabilities of "racial groups"' (Richardson, 1990). This definition is in line with many definitions of racism – for example it has much in common with Rex's definition. However, cultural racism always refers to the attributes of a society's culture rather than the beliefs held by individuals. An individual might hold racist beliefs, but it would only be an example of cultural racism if those beliefs were widely shared.

The idea of cultural racism is similar to some definitions of institutional racism which we will discuss later.

Racialism

To add to the confusion, some sociologists distinguish between racism and racialism. John Rex, for example, describes racialism as 'unequal treatment of various racial groups', as opposed to racism which involves beliefs about racial groups. In other words racialism involves actions, whereas racism does not; it is only concerned with what people think.

This distinction is not usually made in everyday language and has not been adopted by all sociologists.

Institutional racism

The term institutional racism is perhaps even more controversial than racism. Not only is it used in widely varying ways, but some have questioned whether institutional racism actually exists.

According to Miles, the idea of institutional racism originated in the work of American Black Power activists in the 1960s. In 1968 Carmichael and Hamilton defined racism as 'the predication of decisions and policies on considerations of race for the purpose of *subordinating* a racial group and maintaining control over that group'. Racism could be individual and overt, where people consciously and openly discriminated against blacks. However, it could also take the form of institutional racism. This was often covert or hidden. It did not require conscious discrimination since it took place as a result of 'the active and pervasive operation of anti-black attitudes' (quoted in Miles, 1989).

The idea of institutional racism was further developed by American sociologists such as Robert Blauner. Like Carmichael and Hamilton, Blauner argued that racism need not be conscious or based on individual prejudice. Blauner argued that racism was built into the way that major American institutions worked. Racism was 'located in the actual existence of domination and hierarchy', and it ensured the continued domination of particular races by others.

Like Carmichael and Hamilton, some sociologists have defined institutional racism in terms of the domination of blacks by whites and have not used it to apply to any racial groups.

Wellman argues that racism is concerned with protecting an advantaged position in society. Since, in American society at least, whites tend to be advantaged and blacks disadvantaged, only whites can be racist.

Another American sociologist, Katz, argues that all white Americans are inevitably racist regardless of their individual beliefs because racism is 'perpetuated by Whites through their conscious and/or unconscious support of a culture and institutions that are founded on racist policies and practices' (quoted in Miles, 1989).

In Britain, the term institutional racism has also been used in a variety of ways. David Mason (1982) identifies five of them:

1   The conspiracy version occurs when those in positions of power in public institutions deliberately set out to discriminate against racial groups. Mason cites the Scarman Report, which investigated the Brixton riots of 1981, in this context. Scarman denied that Britain was an institutionally racist society: 'If by that what is meant is that it is a society which knowingly, as a matter of public policy, discriminates against black people.'

2   The structural Marxist view of institutional racism does not depend upon the existence of conscious prejudice and discrimination. This argues that racism results from the consequences of state policy regardless of the intentions behind it. In other words if government policy results in inequality between racial groups, then this demonstrates that the state is racist whether or not individuals who hold positions in the state are racist as individuals.

The state acts to serve the interests of capitalists by trying to ensure profitability for their enterprises. In doing so it is bound to follow racist policies. For example, it might encourage the immigration of cheap easily exploited labour when it is needed, and then use that labour force as scapegoats for the failings of capitalism when unemployment rises and there is a shortage of adequate housing.

3   The unintended consequences approach to institutional racism has been particularly influential.

This argues that institutions in society can lead to racial disadvantage and inequality as a consequence of following policies that were not designed to be racist. For example, in a 1960s study of housing in Birmingham, Rex and Moore (1967) found that ethnic minority groups tended to end up in poor housing and had little success in obtaining council housing. This was partly because the council gave preference to those who had lived in the area longest. As fairly recent immigrants, most members of ethnic minorities were well down the list.

Similarly, Lord Scarman found that policing policies in Brixton in London, designed to reduce the number of 'street crimes' by stopping and searching suspects on the streets, resulted in discrimination against Afro-Caribbeans. Since they were most likely to be present on the streets when the police were looking for suspects, they were more likely to be stopped and arrested.

Neither of these policies may have been motivated by racial prejudice but both had the effect of discriminating against ethnic minorities. Sometimes it may be a question of what an organization does not do rather than the active policies it follows. For example, if job vacancies are not advertised in newspapers read by ethnic minority groups, then this can restrict their job opportunities even if the selection procedure adopted by an institution tries to provide equal opportunities.

A definition of institutional racism which incorporated at least an element of the unintended consequences approach was adopted by the Stephen Lawrence Inquiry (MacPherson, 1999). This was an inquiry into the racially motivated murder of Stephen Lawrence, a young black man, who was stabbed to death by a group of white youths in London on 22 April 1993. The inquiry also investigated the failure of the Metropolitan Police to convict anybody of the crime despite the availability of good evidence. The inquiry defined institutional racism as:

> The collective failure of an organisation to provide an appropriate and professional service to people because of their colour, culture, or ethnic origin. It can be seen or detected in processes, attitudes and behaviour which amount to discrimination through unwitting prejudice, ignorance, thoughtlessness and racist stereotyping which disadvantage minority ethnic people.

MacPherson, 1999, ch. 6, p. 11

4   The colonialism version of institutional racism suggests that the role in which racial or ethnic minority groups enter a society can result in institutional racism. Mason notes that John Rex argues that New Commonwealth immigrants to Britain were forced to take menial roles in keeping with their status as migrants from former colonies.

Robert Blauner has developed a similar argument about the consequences of black Americans with the status of former slaves taking positions in society. In both cases the initial disadvantages created long-term inequalities because the ethnic minority groups tended to be located at the bottom of their respective society's stratification systems and upward social mobility was very difficult.

5 The final type of institutional racism identified by Mason is political opportunism. This claims that institutional racism results not so much from prejudice but from the workings of the democratic process. Political groups will try to gain votes by taking advantage of 'race', like any other issue, to increase their popularity since the primary aim of all politicians is to win elections. Thus all major political parties in Britain have sought to win over voters by supporting immigration controls, and parties like the British National Party and National Front have sought electoral success by advocating openly racist views and policies.

Criticisms of the concept of institutional racism

In view of the wide variations in the way the term institutional racism has been used, it is not surprising that it has become a controversial concept. Even those who use it themselves tend to criticize sociologists who use the term in different ways.

Robert Miles (1989), for instance, sees institutional racism as 'exclusionary practices' which disadvantage racial groups but are no longer justified in terms of racist beliefs. Using this fairly narrow definition he criticizes wider definitions. He argues that broad definitions of institutional racism that see it as stemming from the structure of society are 'inseparable from a theory of stratification that is simplistic and erroneous'. They assume that all members of ethnic minorities are equally disadvantaged by the structural factors. Consequently these approaches to the concept are not able to account for the differences in success between ethnic minority groups.

Miles is particularly critical of approaches which suggest that institutional racism is simply 'what "white" people do'. These rely too much on attributing racism to individual behaviour and ignore the possibility that there are some structural constraints limiting opportunities for the victims of institutional racism. Furthermore, they limit the application of the concept to one historical situation – the institutional racism of 'whites' against 'blacks' – when racism can and has appeared in other contexts.

This last point is also raised by John Richardson. He suggests that some views on racism:

run the risk of transforming race relations in Britain into a simple morality play in which white 'villains' persecute black 'victims' (although in the wings there are black 'heroes' and 'heroines' waiting to rescue the victims).

Richardson, 1990

As Richardson points out, this denies the possibility of racism between ethnic minority groups or even that directed against whites.

Institutional racism – conclusion

Some sociologists take the existence of inequalities between ethnic groups as evidence of institutional racism. If, for example, Afro-Caribbeans do less well in the British education system than other groups, this could be seen as a clear indication that British education suffers from institutional racism.

However, this is not necessarily the case. Other factors such as social class or family background *could* account for the differences and it cannot be automatically assumed that the education system is responsible.

Structuralist accounts of institutional racism, though, tend to rely upon such evidence. If racism has nothing to do with the beliefs or actions of individuals and is simply the outcome of policies, whatever those policies were intended to achieve, then the only evidence that can be used to show that institutional racism exists is evidence of inequality.

The use of institutional racism in such a way tends to obscure the causes of inequalities between ethnic groups by attributing them to something that cannot be measured and is just assumed to be all-pervasive. For this reason, perhaps the term is most useful when it is used to refer to actual policies and practices in institutions which can be shown to have the effect of disadvantaging some groups.

This view is supported by John Richardson, who says that 'institutional racism implies that racism is found in the chief policies of our dominant institutions'. While some sociologists do not use the term unless it can be shown that there was a deliberate intention to discriminate, Richardson believes that this usage is too restrictive. He argues that:

regardless of the original intentions of the personnel involved, there is little doubt that their policies – or sometimes lack of policies – nevertheless have damaging social consequences for the less powerful ethnic and racial minorities.

Richardson, 1990

Racism and the law

In the 1960s and 1970s the British government passed laws making some forms of racial discrimination illegal. In this section we will outline that legislation and briefly consider how effective it has been.

The 1965 Race Relations Act

The 1965 Race Relations Act banned discrimination on the grounds of 'race, colour, or ethnic or national origin' in 'places of public resort' such as restaurants and on public transport. It also made it illegal to incite racial hatred in speech or writing.

The Act was widely criticized for being too limited. It did not cover discrimination in housing or employment – both of crucial importance to people's life chances. Furthermore the Race Relations Board which enforced the legislation had little power. Zig Layton-Henry (1992) says that 'It quickly found that most of the complaints it received were outside its jurisdiction, and even those it could deal with it had little power to enforce.'

The 1968 Race Relations Act

The 1968 Race Relations Act did extend the scope of the earlier Act to include employment, housing and the provision of commercial and other services. Discriminatory advertising and notices were banned. The Race Relations Board was given the power to investigate complaints of racial discrimination, institute conciliation procedures, and, if those did not work, take legal proceedings.

The 1968 Act certainly strengthened race relations legislation but it still had important limitations. The Race Relations Board had to wait for complaints to be made to it and could not investigate discrimination where the victims might not be aware that they had been unfairly treated. It still excluded some important areas of 'social' life, particularly the police: complaints against them on the grounds of racial discrimination continued to be investigated by the police themselves.

Zig Layton-Henry suggests that the small number of cases that were dealt with effectively by the Board indicate that it still lacked teeth. From April 1969 to April 1970, 982 complaints were investigated. In 734 cases it was decided that there was no discrimination, while 143 of the cases where it did find discrimination were related to advertising. Layton-Henry suggests that this was because the legislation was effective in dealing with discrimination in that area. However, the Board was less effective in dealing with discrimination in employment and housing. It is much harder to prove that discrimination has taken place in these areas, and consequently few cases were brought to court. In fact, of the 2,967 complaints investigated by the end of March 1972, only seven resulted in court cases. The penalties for those who were convicted usually involved the payment of very small sums in damages.

The 1976 Race Relations Act

The most recent legislation dealing with racial discrimination is the 1976 Race Relations Act. This introduced the idea of indirect discrimination: for example, using unjustifiable requirements or conditions which had the effect of discriminating against an ethnic minority group, even if the criteria of exclusion were not directly ethnic or racial ones. For example, if an employer stipulated that potential employees had to have been born in the UK or that they could not live in an inner-city area, then these policies could be seen as indirectly discriminatory since members of ethnic minorities are more likely to fall into these categories.

The Act also established the Commission for Racial Equality, which had the task of promoting racial harmony and could give legal assistance to those who believed they had been the victims of discrimination.

Layton-Henry says that the Commission for Racial Equality was 'a much more powerful body than its predecessors, with much greater scope and powers for strategic initiatives in enforcing the law'. In 1984 the Commission got Parliament to accept a new code of practice in employment, and it has conducted a wide range of revealing investigations into many different organizations including Hackney Council in London, St George's Hospital Medical School in London, and the National Bus Company. The Commission has exposed evidence of discrimination in the criminal justice system and has assisted local community relations councils.

However, like most other commentators, Layton-Henry believes that the Commission for Racial Equality has not achieved as much as might have been possible with stronger powers and more resources. It has continued to be difficult to bring prosecutions and, with limited resources, the Commission has often had to make difficult decisions about which cases and investigations to pursue and which to drop. Furthermore, Layton-Henry comments:

The return of the Conservatives in 1979 created a less favourable environment for the Commission's work as the new government was generally hostile to what it called the 'race relations industry' and reluctant to allocate resources to it.

Layton-Henry, 1992

Legislation against any sort of discrimination is likely to have a limited impact. It is often difficult to prove that actions were motivated by prejudice, and changes in a society's culture, although slower to produce change, may have a greater effect in the longer term. In the next section we will examine whether there is any evidence that legislation and/or cultural changes have led to a reduction in racism in Britain.

The extent of individual racism

The Institute of Race Relations 1969 Report

Some attempts have been made to discover how widespread racist beliefs are amongst individuals. In 1966–7, E.J. Rose and others (1969) carried out a study for the Institute of Race Relations which involved questionnaire research with a national sample of 2,500 people, and a more detailed study in five English urban areas which had large ethnic minority populations. The report was published in 1969.

The questionnaires included four key questions about racial prejudice. These were:

1 'If you had any choice would you particularly avoid having neighbours from any of these places – West Indies, India, Pakistan?'

2 'Do you think the majority of coloured people in Britain are superior, equal, or inferior to you?'

3 'Do you think the authorities should let or refuse to let a council house or flat to a family born in the West Indies, India or Pakistan?'

4 'Do you think a private landlord should let or refuse to let a house or flat to a family born in the West Indies, India or Pakistan?'

Respondents were then divided into categories:

1 those who gave no hostile answers to these four questions were defined as tolerant;

2 those who gave one hostile answer as tolerant-inclined;

3 those who gave two hostile answers as prejudiced-inclined;

4 those who gave three or four hostile answers as prejudiced.

Rose and his fellow researchers found that in the five boroughs studied 35 per cent of the sample were tolerant, 38 per cent tolerant-inclined, 17 per cent prejudiced-inclined and 10 per cent prejudiced. They found that:

1 women were slightly more tolerant than men;

2 the most prejudiced were in the 45–54 age group and the least prejudiced were under 35 and over 65;

3 skilled manual workers and their wives and the lower middle class were more prejudiced than other classes;

4 those with post-compulsory education were less prejudiced than others;

5 Conservative voters were more prejudiced than Labour voters who in turn were more prejudiced than Liberal voters;

6 tenants of private landlords were more prejudiced than owner-occupiers or council tenants.

Despite these differences, overall the study found that the most prejudiced in the population were not confined to specific social groups and could be found in all sections of society.

The biggest differences found between the 10 per cent of the population who were most prejudiced and the rest, were psychological. The most prejudiced people were 'much more prone than others to an authoritarian approach to life' and this approach to life involved 'an exaggerated need to submit to authority and acute hostility towards any outgroups'. These characteristics, the report suggested, stemmed from a hostility to ingroups and originally towards their parents. In trying to keep this hostility in check, individuals overcompensated and became hostile to outgroups. For this 10 per cent of the population, prejudice represented 'irrational "solutions" to personality inadequacies'.

The attitudes of those who were found to have less strong prejudice came from different causes. According to Rose *et al.*, it was the result either of misinformation about ethnic minority groups or of competition with ethnic minorities for scarce resources such as housing, hospital beds or school places.

Although little could be done about those with personality problems, the prejudice of others could be tackled by providing improved, more accurate information about ethnic minorities, and by providing more houses, hospital beds and school places, thus reducing competition for these resources.

The British Social Attitudes Surveys

More recent data, which gives some indication of changes in the amount of individual racism, has been produced by the *British Social Attitudes Surveys*. Since 1983 these annual surveys of a representative sample of the British population have included questions on racism. In general the results of the surveys offer some grounds for optimism.

Table 4.6 shows the percentage of respondents who described themselves as very prejudiced, a little prejudiced or not prejudiced at all. It shows that the

Table 4.6 How would you describe yourself?			
	1983 %	1987 %	1991 %
Very prejudiced	4	4	2
A little prejudiced	31	34	29
Not prejudiced at all	64	60	68

Source: R. Jowell *et al.* (1992) *British Social Attitudes Survey, 9th Report,* p. 183

percentage who described themselves as 'Not prejudiced at all' increased from 64 to 68 per cent between 1983 and 1991. Although this is a small increase, it does suggest some reduction in racism over that period.

Like the Institute for Race Relations study, the 1991 *British Social Attitudes Survey* found differences in prejudice according to party allegiance. Some 25 per cent of Labour supporters but 40 per cent of Conservative supporters admitted to being 'a little prejudiced' or 'very prejudiced'. Women were less likely than men to admit to being prejudiced.

The report found that older age groups were considerably more likely to express an objection than those from younger age groups, providing further ground for supposing that racial prejudice was decreasing.

The report found very little support for increased Asian or West Indian immigration but it found that large majorities supported the anti-discrimination laws. Furthermore, in 1991, 73 per cent of respondents thought that racial prejudice had either declined or remained as common as in the past. This compared to just 42 per cent in 1983. If these findings are to be believed, Britain is gradually becoming a less racist society, but the change has been slow and there is a very long way to go before individual racism will be eradicated.

More recent data has been provided by the Policy Studies Institute's (PSI) *Fourth National Survey of Ethnic Minorities* (Modood *et al.*, 1997). This included a sample of 2,867 white people who were interviewed in 1994. In this survey 26 per cent of white people said they were racially prejudiced against Asians, 20 per cent against those of Caribbean origin, 25 per cent against Muslims and 8 per cent against Chinese. Satnam Virdee (1997), who analysed the findings, speculates that the apparently greater prevalence of prejudice against Asians than Caribbeans might be due to 'the increasing adoption of a hybrid Caribbean/white identity by sections of the young white population' (see pp. 274–6 for details of a study supporting this view). The figures for racial prejudice are slightly lower than those for 1991 and again lend some credence to the belief that racial prejudice is declining. The survey found that men were more prejudiced than women against all ethnic minorities and that those aged 16–34 were less prejudiced than those aged over 34.

Much less optimistic findings were produced in an ICM poll of 1,042 British adults from all ethnic groups, conducted in July 1995. Two-thirds of the sample admitted they were racist and less than half the black and Asian respondents agreed that 'coloured people felt British' (quoted in Skellington and Morris, 1996).

The very different findings of this poll compared to the PSI survey may be due to differences in wording. Strangely, more people seem willing to admit to 'racism' than they are to 'prejudice'.

Conclusion – studies of individual racism

These studies give some indication of how willing people are to say they are racist or prejudiced and they give an indication of changes over time. They also provide interesting data about the distribution of racist beliefs in different social groups. However, they do not measure how many people act in a racist or racialist way.

Furthermore the studies have methodological limitations. They rely upon measuring the strength of the racist beliefs held by individuals, beliefs which respondents in questionnaire or interview research may be unwilling to admit. They are based upon the idea that racism is a characteristic of individuals, and perhaps a minority of individuals, rather than a feature of a society's culture or structure. They therefore add little to sociological understanding of cultural racism or institutional racism. At the very least they need to be supplemented by studies of these types of racism.

Racial harassment

One way of examining the actual incidence of racism is to study racial harassment. As part of the Policy Studies Institute's *Fourth National Survey of Ethnic Minorities*, questionnaire data was collected from interviews with 5,196 members of ethnic minorities on the incidence of racial harassment. Satnam Virdee noted that racial harassment had come to public attention partly because of some particularly vicious attacks. He gives the example of Rohit Duggal, a schoolboy in south-east London who was stabbed to death in a racially motivated attack. In all, according to Virdee, 15 people were killed in such attacks in Britain in the period 1992–4. However, Virdee argues that more everyday forms of harassment, such as racially motivated attacks on property and racist verbal abuse, can also have serious effects.

The findings of the PSI study are summarized in Table 4.7.

Virdee found that, although racially motivated physical attacks affected only about 1 per cent of the ethnic minority population, this would still involve about 20,000 attacks per year. He estimated that around 40,000 people had their property damaged for racially motivated reasons, and some 230,000 were racially abused or insulted. This compares with about 10,000 racially motivated incidents reported to the police in the same year. Most of the racial attacks –

Table 4.7 People who were subjected to some form of racial harassment in the last 12 months							
	Cell percentages						
	Caribbean	Indian	African Asian	Pakistani	Bangladeshi	Chinese	All ethnic minorities
Racially attacked	1	1	1	1	1	0	1
Racially motivated property damage	2	2	3	3	1	1	2
Racially insulted	14	9	12	11	8	16	12
Any form of racial harassment	15	10	14	13	9	16	13
Weighted count	1,567	1,292	799	862	285	391	5,196
Unweighted count	1,205	1,273	728	1,185	591	214	5,196

Source: T. Modood et al. (1997) Ethnic Minorities in Britain, PSI, London, p. 266

67 per cent – were committed by complete strangers, and 62 per cent of the racial insults came from strangers. However, most of the racial attacks on property were committed by neighbours (52 per cent) with 36 per cent committed by complete strangers. Some incidents took place at work – 8 per cent of racial attacks and 11 per cent of racial insults were committed by workmates.

Although racial insults may be less serious than racial attacks, they can still have important consequences. The researchers asked members of ethnic minorities about the effects of racial incidents. About one in seven said they had taken some measures in the previous two years to avoid racial harassment. Of this group, 58 per cent had 'Started to avoid going out at night', 54 per cent had 'Made home more secure', 35 per cent had 'Started to visit shops at certain times only', 23 per cent had 'Stopped children playing outside', 23 per cent had 'Stopped going out without partner', and 20 per cent had 'Started to avoid areas where only white people live'. Virdee concludes that for these people racial harass-ment 'has a significant impact on the quality of life they are able to lead'.

Racism and the press

Many sociologists argue that racism is not just a matter of individual prejudice but is also a feature of many societies' cultures and institutions. As we saw earlier, such sociologists tend to use the terms cultural racism and institutional racism. We will analyse a number of the theories of racism later in this section when we deal with different aspects of cultural racism (see, for example, pp. 259–60). In other chapters we will cover studies of the nature and extent of racism in the education system and criminal justice system (see Chapters 6 and 11). In the next section we will look at the mass media as an example of how racism may be found in important social institutions.

The mass media may play a significant role in shaping attitudes to 'race' in society as a whole and in creating or sustaining cultural racism.

Paul Hartmann and Charles Husband – racism and the press 1963–70

In a study of racism in the British press, Paul Hartmann and Charles Husband examined a sample of copies of *The Times*, *Guardian*, *Daily Express* and *Daily Mirror* published between 1963 and 1970 (Hartmann and Husbands, 1974). They analysed the content of their sample in order to discover how the issue of 'race' was portrayed in the press. The articles that made reference to 'race' in Britain were most likely to be about immigration, race relations, crime, legislation and discrimination.

From an analysis of the headlines of these stories they found that many contained words indicating violence or conflict. Some 10 per cent of the headlines contained violent words like 'murder', 'kill', 'shoot' or 'burn', and 12 per cent contained words suggesting conflict such as 'hate', 'crisis', 'row', 'clash' and 'threat'. Some 6 per cent contained what Hartmann and Husband called 'restrictive words' such as 'stop', 'curb', 'cut', 'ban' and 'bar'. In about 30 per cent of the headlines containing the word 'race', or a word derived from it (such as 'racial'), the headline also included a conflict or violent word.

Although many of the newspapers expressed opposition to racism in their editorials, the news coverage produced a negative image of ethnic minorities. Positive stories about 'race' relations were few and far between. Many stories associated ethnic minorities with conflict and violence or presented their presence in Britain as a problem. Hartmann and Husband comment:

> coloured people have not on the whole been portrayed as an intimate part of British society. Instead the press has continued to project an image of Britain as a white society in which the coloured population is seen as some kind of aberration, a problem, or just an oddity, rather than as 'belonging' to society.
>
> Hartmann and Husband, 1974

Teun A. van Dijk – racism and the press in the 1980s

Some years later Teun van Dijk carried out a similar study to that of Hartmann and Husband (van Dijk, 1991). He examined all copies of *The Times*, the *Guardian*, the *Daily Telegraph*, the *Daily Mail* and the *Sun* published between 1 August 1985 and 31 January 1986, and all copies of the same papers plus the *Independent* published in the first six months of 1989. In the earlier period there were 2,700 articles which made reference to ethnic minorities, but in the later period there were only 1,200.

In the 1985–6 period, no less than 974 of the stories concerned inner-city disturbances in which members of ethnic minorities were involved. The most frequently occurring words in these stories were 'police', 'riot', 'black' and 'race'. The dramatic and rather negative term 'riot' was preferred to more neutral terms such as 'unrest' or 'disturbance'. Van Dijk argues:

> the prominent presence of the concept of 'black' in the headlines suggests that the disturbances are defined primarily in terms of ethnic background or colour. They are not defined as 'urban' or 'social' forms of protest or unrest, or as actions of 'youths', but specifically attributed to black people, usually young males, despite the fact that about 30 per cent of the participants were white.
>
> van Dijk, 1991

Words such as 'murder', 'attack', 'death' and 'terror' appeared frequently in the headlines. Thus a fairly typical headline was 'West Indian Gang Invaded Pub in Revenge Riot' (*Daily Telegraph*, 23 August 1985). Like Hartmann and Husband, van Dijk found that ethnic minorities were frequently associated with violence or conflict in newspaper stories. Generally members of ethnic minorities were associated with negative actions and rarely portrayed as victims, as for example in racially motivated attacks. Whites, on the other hand, were quite often portrayed as victims and were less likely to be associated with negative actions.

Another story which received widespread coverage in 1985–6 was the Honeyford affair. Honeyford was a headmaster in a Bradford school who wrote a number of articles in which he claimed that white children were disadvantaged in schools where there was a majority of ethnic minority children. He attacked the idea of multicultural education, arguing that it could lead to the neglect of white culture. Honeyford was suspended but later reinstated. Van Dijk found that many headlines were sympathetic to Honeyford's position and critical of his opponents. For example, the *Daily Mail* on 17 October 1985 ran a story under the headline 'Rent-A-Rowdy Attack Forces Race Row Head out of College'. Van Dijk comments:

> These headlines first show that the tabloids tend to define as a 'mob' any group of people who engage in public actions which the tabloids do not like. In this case, this applies to a group of mostly Asian parents of the Bradford school, who picket the school, and demonstrate against Honeyford's return. For the tabloids, this legitimate protest is redefined as a violent battle, in which the opponents are implicitly qualified as irrational.
>
> van Dijk, 1991

In the 1989 coverage there was less frequent mention of violence. Van Dijk found that 'ethnic reporting in 1989 has become less negative and aggressive'. However, he admitted that this could just be due to the types of stories that featured in the news at that particular time.

Furthermore, there were still many stories which portrayed ethnic minorities as a threat. A *Sun* headline on 2 February 1989 stated 'Britain Invaded by an Army of Illegals'. Some of the stories emphasized a supposed cultural threat from ethnic minorities. Van Dijk comments that 'Whereas in 1985 the major villains were young rioting blacks, now the "threat" to British society comes from fundamentalist Muslims'. Islamic fundamentalism featured prominently in the news in that year because of the publication of Salman Rushdie's book *The Satanic Verses*. The Ayatollah Khomeini of Iran declared the book to be sacrilegious and he issued a *fatwa* or death sentence against Rushdie. Rushdie, a British citizen, was forced to go into hiding.

Although the findings for 1989 suggest there might have been some reduction in the amount of racism in the press, van Dijk's study indicates that the portrayal of ethnic minorities in at least some parts of the media continues to be predominantly negative.

John Solomos and Les Back – racism and popular culture

John Solomos and Les Back (1996) have examined images of 'race' in a wider range of media than just newspapers. They have studied the portrayal of 'race', ethnicity and nationality in a variety of eras and contexts. Their study covers British and German popular culture, and recent images that have been used worldwide.

John Bull, Britannia and the British Empire

The first part of their study examines British imperial propaganda. Solomos and Back define propaganda as, 'the transmission of ideas from dominant groups who control the means of communication, with the intention of influencing the receiver's attitudes and thus enhancing and maintaining their position and interests'. They claim that in the late nineteenth century popular representations relating to the British, the Empire and the colonies helped to form ideas both about what it meant to be British, and about how colonial people were different. Aspects of these ideas still persist today, albeit in a modified form, and influence contemporary racism.

In the late nineteenth and early twentieth century technological developments in the reproduction of images contributed to a big increase in advertising and the production of ephemera such as cigarette cards and postcards. The British Empire was celebrated in such media and even on items such as biscuit tins and matchboxes. Usually white men were portrayed as heroic explorers, enduring hardship to civilize the native 'other'. Explorers were associated with the marketing of particular products such as 'Stanley Boot Laces' (after the African explorer, Stanley). The icons of Britannia and John Bull were used particularly frequently.

Britannia originated in the mid-eighteenth century as a symbol of the British nation. It was closely associated with hatred of the French, with whom Britain was then at war. Britannia was associated with virtues such as patriotism, honesty and simplicity. The fact that Britannia was female encouraged negative stereotypes of the enemies of Britain who threatened to take advantage of Britannia's feminine vulnerability and undermine her virtue.

By 1915 Britannia was appearing on Vinolia toothpaste adverts, which implored the consumer to 'Buy British Goods'. She was presented against the backdrop of an idyllic scene from English rural village life. Part of the advert claimed that the toothpaste 'Cleans and Whitens Without Scratching'. Solomos and Back claim that such adverts 'embodied the nation in a racialised skin with phenotypic features and national attributes'. In other words they suggested that to be English was to be white. Furthermore the images associated with Britannia, such as the village scenes, were clearly English, and marginalized those in the Celtic fringes of Scotland, Ireland and Wales. It encouraged the sense that the

non-white and non-English could not claim to be true Brits.

The icon of John Bull was first used in the early eighteenth century. Like Britannia, by the end of the nineteenth century he had become an important emblem of national character. Products such as the John Bull Printing Outfit and John Bull Cycle Repair Outfit made him a familiar figure to adults and children alike. Solomos and Back say:

> John Bull was always presented as a proactive champion of Britain's interests abroad. This is manifested in images of his portly figure striding over a map of the world, carrying a packet of Coleman's Mustard or shouldering Cadbury's Cocoa Essence, bringing imperial goods to every table.
>
> Solomos and Back, 1996, p. 164

In an advert for England's Glory matches, he was portrayed as a boxer knocking out a French competitor. Like Britannia, John Bull was of course white, and by sporting a Union Jack his nationalism was always emphasized. Such products were saying, in effect, that by buying them you were purchasing a British identity.

Solomos and Back conclude that:

> imperial propaganda established some of the core symbols of British racism. It was also integrally connected with the fashioning of a national subject that possessed a distinct racial character, an imperial destiny and a standing in the world.
>
> Solomos and Back, 1996, p. 166

Representing the black presence in Britain

Imperial images and icons helped to establish a sense of what it meant to be British, but this was also established through the representation of those deemed to be outsiders. As the twentieth century progressed, black people assumed an increasingly important role of this type. In the early part of the century public commentators using the media encouraged the idea that the presence of blacks in Britain was a problem. According to Solomos and Back there was a lot of concern that 'race mixing', particularly sexual relationships between black and white people, might undermine British culture.

In 1935 the British Social Hygiene Council conducted a survey which received media attention. It raised concerns that black sailors were sexually demanding and promiscuous and that white women were becoming addicted to their sexuality. These themes were reiterated when many black GIs arrived in Britain with the US forces during the Second World War. Drawing on work by Clive Harris, Solomos and Back argue that 'racist discourse of this period is preoccupied with skin colour as the prime signifier of the subjectification of black people. The preservation of the English racial character was to be achieved by preserving its hue.' One symptom of this was that some people called for the 'half-caste' war babies of US servicemen to be sent to America.

During the 1950s much media coverage centred on the idea that black people were beginning to outnumber white people in some places in Britain. Particular areas of Birmingham, for example, became identified as predominantly black. The coverage was often critical of crude racism and criticized the 'colour bar' (black people being banned from certain places such as clubs, refused lodgings by landlords, etc.). However, it was still based upon the idea that skin colour was the primary marker of difference. Furthermore, it had the consequence that simply mentioning an area associated with a black popula-tion 'triggered a range of associated racial attributes (miscegenation/conflict) and cultural pathologies (drugs, vice, crime)'.

In the 1960s a lot of coverage saw black people as 'welfare scroungers'. They were portrayed as lazy spongers who had come to Britain to take advantage of its generous welfare system, while contributing nothing in return.

During the 1970s the focus of coverage shifted to emphasize the association of black people with crime. In particular the media gave a tremendous amount of coverage to 'muggings' supposedly committed by British Afro-Caribbeans (see Chapter 6 for details of a study of this issue). In the early 1980s there was a further shift as racist discourse stressed the link between black people and inner-city riots. This followed riots in areas such as Brixton in London, Toxteth in Liverpool and Moss Side in Manchester, and was despite the evidence that many whites were also involved. Black crime now came to be seen as crime against society itself.

Solomos and Back refer to the coverage of distur-bances in Lozells Road in Birmingham in 1985. The *Sun* carried a picture of a black man with a petrol bomb with the headline 'Hate of the Black Bomber'. The same photograph was carried by other newspapers and became 'the exemplary portrait of this "new folk devil"'.

As time passed, the dominant image of British blacks in the media changed. However, Solomos and Back believe that it retained two key elements. First, a black presence was seen as undermining British culture. Second, the cultural or racial charac-teristics of black people were seen as 'incompatible with the British way of life'. Media images were consistently racist even though the nature of the images changed.

Multiculturalism and media images

Solomos and Back believe that there have been significant changes in the way black people are portrayed by the media since the late 1980s. There has been an increase in the number of films made by black directors and producers. Television programmes such as the Cosby Show have provided more positive images of black people. However, this can sometimes give the misleading impression that inequalities between ethnic groups are a thing of the past.

A particularly important change is the increased use of multicultural images. As world markets have become more global, some advertisers have used multicultural images to associate their products with an anti-racist stance, as well as trying to make them appeal to a wide variety of people. For example, in 1995 British Airways had an advertising campaign in which a Danish bride in a white wedding dress, and an Indian bride wearing a red sari were shown side by side. The accompanying caption reads 'There are more things that bring us together than keep us apart.' Phillips have used pictures showing a blonde-haired white girl and a black boy pressing a switch on a TV together. Their caption says 'The Universal Language of Phillips'.

However, perhaps the best-known and most controversial advertising campaigns have been run by the Italian clothes manufacturer Benetton. One of their billboard posters shows a black, a white and an Oriental child sticking their tongues out (see Figure 4.5). Although such adverts appear to be entirely positive in promoting racial/ethnic harmony, Solomos and Back believe they can also be seen in a less positive light. In order to project this image of harmony, they need to present members of a variety of ethnic groups as being different. Benetton's

> *message of unity can only work if it has a constitutive representation of absolute racial contrast. The danger with such representations is that they rely upon a range of racial archetypes that are themselves the product of racism ... the concept of race is left unchallenged.*
>
> Solomos and Back, 1996, p. 187

A good example of how images of multicultural unity can have racist connotations is provided by another Benetton advert in which the hands of a black and of a white man are shown handcuffed together. In the USA people complained because it conjured up images of slavery, and in the USA and Britain some people associated the image with black criminality. In France a racist group threw a tear-gas cylinder into a Benetton shop after Benetton

Figure 4.5 United Colors? Benetton billboard poster, 1991

released a poster of a black woman breastfeeding a white baby. The group thought that it was advocating sex between white and black people. Others saw it as racist and sexist by presenting black women as the objects of white sexual desire. In some other countries Benetton's adverts have won prizes. The problem is that the portrayal of black or other ethnic minorities as different and exotic can evoke racist beliefs rather than ideas of harmony and unity.

Another example of how multicultural advertising can become associated with racist ideas is provided by Levi Strauss's advertising for 501 jeans. They make extensive use of black American music, especially blues, in their cinema and TV adverts. The adverts tend to be based around such characters as 'a youthful male rebel and his girl'. In such adverts being black is associated with stereotypes based around ideas of 'expressiveness, masculinity and sexuality'. Blackness becomes exotic and is linked with 'escape from the emotional and intellectual shackles of modernity'. It reaffirms black people

as different and associates them with 'exotic innocence'.

Solomos and Back believe that there can be a close relationship between racism and 'racial adulation'. For example, Mike Tyson's conviction for rape changed him from an admired boxer to a symbol of black sexuality and criminality. The British sprinter Linford Christie also gained respect and admiration for sporting prowess. However, this did not prevent the *Sun* newspaper from using him to evoke 'the long European history of viewing black men as hypersexual beings'. In 1992 the *Sun* carried a story about the size of Christie's 'Lunchbox' – or genitals. The story ran: 'His skin tight lycra shorts hide little as he pounds down the track and his Olympic-sized talents are a source of delight for women around the world.'

However, there are some media images that Solomos and Back believe can be unsettling and challenge racism and racial stereotypes. In a 1993 edition of Benetton's magazine *Colors* there was a series of articles questioning the nature of 'race'.

Figure 4.6 *Altered Image*: Toscani's portrait of a black Queen Elizabeth, spring 1993. This image was created for *Colors 4*, the first magazine dedicated entirely to racism. Courtesy of Colors.

There was a series of 'What If?' photographs showing a black Queen Elizabeth (see Figure 4.6), a black Arnold Schwarzenegger, an Oriental Pope John Paul II, and so on. To Solomos and Back these images forced people to think about why they found them implausible. In the case of the black Queen, for example, it exposed the way Englishness was associated with whiteness. In doing so it 'opens up a representational space which challenges the orthodoxies of race and nation'.

Conclusion

The work of Solomos and Back suggests that there are important continuities in the portrayal of 'race', ethnicity and nationality by the media, and that it is hard to avoid racism entirely even when you intend to do so. Racial stereotypes can be so strong and ingrained that they may sometimes be evoked by multicultural advertising. Nevertheless, Solomos and Back's analysis is not entirely pessimistic. More recent media portrayals of black people in Britain and elsewhere have become less crudely racist and more open to non-racist or anti-racist interpretations. Furthermore, the media and popular culture have made some successful attempts to challenge racist orthodoxy.

Inequalities between ethnic groups in Britain

In this section we examine the statistical evidence for the extent of inequality between ethnic groups in Britain, and the evidence for whether this inequality is increasing or decreasing. The inequalities may be caused by individual racism, cultural racism or institutional racism, but may also be the result of other factors such as cultural differences or class inequality. (Details of some inequalities between ethnic groups are discussed elsewhere in the book. See Chapter 11 for data on ethnic groups and educational achievement and Chapter 10 for information on ethnicity and unemployment.)

In 1994 Tariq Modood and others conducted research for the Policy Studies Institute (PSI) into inequality between ethnic groups in Britain (Modood *et al.*, 1997). They used data from questionnaires administered by interviewers to a sample of 5,196 people of Caribbean and Asian origin and 2,868 whites. The study also incorporated some figures from earlier surveys carried out by the PSI and its predecessor, Political and Economic Planning. These earlier studies were conducted in 1966–7, 1974–5 and 1982.

Employment and earnings

Table 4.8 shows the job levels of male employees in different ethnic groups in 1982 and 1994. It shows that, apart from Bangladeshis, all groups saw a rise in the proportions of men in professional, managerial or employer jobs. (No figures were produced for Chinese men in 1982 so comparisons cannot be made.) All ethnic groups saw a rise in the proportion of men who were in non-manual employment of some sort. The proportion of Caribbean and Indian men in professional/managerial employment or who were employers had risen particularly fast. However, significant disparities remained. There was a higher proportion of white men (30 per cent) in the highest category than for any other ethnic group apart from the Chinese (41 per cent). Pakistani (14 per cent), Caribbean (11 per cent) and Bangladeshi (7 per cent) men were particularly under-represented in top jobs. It is noticeable that there are big differences between ethnic groups, with the Chinese doing better than whites, and Pakistanis and Bangladeshis having fewest men in non-manual jobs.

Table 4.9 is produced from a combination of PSI studies and *Labour Force Surveys*. The figures may not all be strictly comparable due to differences in the methodologies used. Nevertheless it does give some indication of trends over time for male employees. It shows that the percentage of males in professional, managerial or employer jobs has risen for all groups since 1982. However, the percentage of white males in such jobs has risen consistently, while for ethnic minorities (excluding Pakistanis) the percentages have fallen since 1990.

As Table 4.10 shows, there are also big differences between women of different ethnic groups. White women enjoyed a rapid increase in the percentage holding professional, managerial or employer jobs, rising from 7 per cent in 1982 to 21 per cent in 1994. Only Chinese women (38 per cent in 1994) had a higher percentage in these jobs. Of the other ethnic groups, only African Asian women – with 14 per cent in professional, managerial or employer jobs – got into double figures. In all ethnic groups more than half of the women were employed in intermediate and junior non-manual work in 1994.

Modood believes that there has been some reduction in inequalities in job status between ethnic minorities and whites (Modood, 1997). He argues that ethnic minorities were initially downwardly mobile after emigrating to Britain, and only now are beginning to regain the occupational statuses they had prior to their arrival. Nevertheless, he believes that, overall, Indians and Caribbeans continue to suffer from relative occupational disadvantage compared to whites, while Pakistanis and Bangladeshis face 'severe disadvantage'. The disadvantages are particularly acute at the top of the occupational structure.

Other figures produced by Modood, and based upon the survey data, show that occupational inequalities between ethnic groups continue even when educational qualifications are taken into account. Table 4.11 shows that 40 per cent of white males with A levels or above gain work as professionals, managers or employers. African Asian men match this figure and Chinese men exceed it (61 per cent), but only 15 per cent of similarly well-qualified Caribbean men, 30 per cent of Indian men

Table 4.8 Job levels of male employees, 1982 and 1994 (percentages)

	White 1982	White 1994	Caribbean 1982	Caribbean 1994	Indian 1982	Indian 1994	African Asian 1982	African Asian 1994	Pakistani 1982	Pakistani 1994	Bangladeshi 1982	Bangladeshi 1994	Chinese 1994
Professional/managerial/employers	19	30	5	11	11	19	22	26	10	14	10	7	41
Other non-manual	23	21	10	20	13	28	21	31	8	18	7	22	26
Skilled manual and foremen	42	31	48	37	34	23	31	22	39	36	13	2	5
Semi-skilled manual	13	14	26	26	36	22	22	17	35	28	57	65	20
Unskilled manual	3	4	9	6	5	7	3	3	8	4	12	4	8
Non-manual	42	51	15	31	24	47	43	57	18	32	17	29	67
Manual	58	49	83	69	75	52	56	42	82	68	82	71	33

Note: For the sake of comparison with 1982, the self-employed are not included in the 1994 figures.
Source: T. Modood *et al.* (1997) *Ethnic Minorities in Britain*, PSI, London, p. 139

Table 4.9 Percentage of male employees in top SEG category (professional, manager or employer), 1982–94

Ethnic origin	1982 PSI Survey	1984–6 LFS	1988–90 LFS	1994 PSI Survey
White	19	24	27	30
Afro-Caribbean	5	5	12	11
African Asian	22	22	27	26
Indian	11	23	25	19
Pakistani	10	11	12	14
Bangladeshi	10	13	12	7

Source: T. Jones (1993) *Britain's Ethnic Minorities*, PSI, London, p. 82; and T. Modood *et al.* (1997) *Ethnic Minorities in Britain*, PSI, London, p. 135

and 34 per cent of Pakistani/Bangladeshi men were found to be in the highest occupational category. Amongst women, 24 per cent of white females with A levels or above were in the highest occupational category – twice the figure for Caribbean, Indian and African women.

Modood's research found, perhaps unsurprisingly, that white male full-time employees earned more than men in all ethnic minorities, with the exception of the Chinese. White men earned a mean of £331 pounds per week, Chinese men £336, African Asian men £335, Caribbean men £287, Pakistani men £227, and Bangladeshi men just £191.

More surprisingly, all groups of ethnic minority women, except Pakistani/Bangladeshi women, earned more than white women. The mean weekly earnings for white women were £244, compared to £181 for Pakistani/Bangladeshi women, £252 for Indian women, £254 for African Asian women, £267 for Caribbean women and £287 for Chinese women. Modood suggests that this undermines the argument that ethnic minority women are badly affected by double discrimination by virtue of being both female and black.

Writing in 1992, Heidi Safia Mirza argued that the achievements of young black women have been consistently underestimated. Many achieve high levels of educational attainment, and perhaps, despite racism, these achievements are beginning to be reflected in earnings.

Housing

Tenure patterns amongst ethnic minority groups have changed considerably since large-scale immigration from the New Commonwealth commenced in the 1950s. Early migrants found it difficult to obtain council housing because many councils had waiting lists based at least partly upon people's length of residence in an area. Newly arrived immigrants were likely to be towards the bottom of the lists. Some lacked the income or wealth necessary to become owner-occupiers and many relied upon finding accommodation in the private rented sector.

Immigrants from the West Indies tended to arrive in Britain before immigrants from South Asia, and as time passed they were in a stronger position than most Asians when it came to obtaining council housing. These early patterns of tenure are reflected in the changes in owner-occupation and renting from local authorities, shown in Tables 4.12 and 4.13.

Table 4.12 shows that there was a rise in owner-occupation for all groups except Pakistanis. Afro-Caribbeans and Bangladeshis increased their rate of owner-occupation during the 1980s but still had much lower rates than whites in 1994. In contrast, African Asians, Indians and Pakistanis had higher rates than whites.

Quite surprisingly a 1974 study found that South Asians and Afro-Caribbeans with manual jobs were more likely to be owner-occupiers than those with non-manual jobs. Trevor Jones (1993) suggests that this 'could partly be seen as a response to the closure of other housing opportunities, particularly at the early stages of settlement'. Facing the problem of residence qualifications in getting council housing and discrimination from white landlords in private rented accommodation, some relatively low-paid members of ethnic minorities turned to owner-occupation as the best option. For some there may also have been 'a positive drive towards home ownership associated with the drive towards self improvement and capital accumulation that is typical of immigrant communities'.

Table 4.10 Job levels of full-time female employees, 1982 and 1994 (percentages)

	White 1982	White 1994	Caribbean 1982	Caribbean 1994	Indian 1982	Indian 1994	African Asian 1982	African Asian 1994	Pakistani 1994	Chinese 1994
Professional/ managerial/employers	7	21	1	4	5	3	7	14	7	38
Intermediate and junior non-manual	55	58	52	76	35	61	52	66	60	55
Skilled manual and foremen	5	3	4	2	8	2	3	3	3	-
Semi-skilled manual	21	17	36	18	50	32	36	17	29	7
Unskilled manual	11	1	7	1	1	3	3	-	-	-
Non-manual	62	79	53	80	40	64	59	80	67	93
Manual	37	21	47	21	59	37	42	20	32	7

Source: Modood et al. (1997) Ethnic Minorities in Britain, PSI, London, p. 140

Table 4.11 Job levels of employees, by highest British qualification (base: employees excluding self-employed)

	White	Caribbean	Indian	African Asian	Pakistani/ Bangladeshi	Chinese
Male						
% in professional, managerial and employers category (prof. workers in parentheses)						
'A' level or higher	40 (12)	15 (18)	30 (16)	40 (26)	34 (22)	61 (36)
'O' level/CSE/other	21	15	21	17	11	–
No qualification	11	2	10	13	3	9
% in other non-manual category						
'A' level or higher	24	29	43	34	36	20
'O' level/CSE/other	26	25	37	37	26	62
No qualification	12	2	13	24	11	22
% in skilled manual category						
'A' level or higher	27	36	12	20	15	9
'O' level/CSE/other	28	37	18	11	9	–
No qualification	43	37	33	31	34	–
% in semi-skilled and unskilled manual category						
'A' level or higher	9	20	15	6	16	10
'O' level/CSE/other	25	23	24	35	54	38
No qualification	33	60	44	32	51	68
Weighted count	*612*	*314*	*241*	*205*	*167*	*83*
Unweighted count	*561*	*219*	*262*	*189*	*266*	*48*
Female						
% in professional, managerial and employers category (prof. workers in parentheses)						
'A' level or higher	24 (4)	11 (1)	12 (6)	19 (12)	11 (6)	32 (26)
'O' level/CSE/other	8	1	6	9	–	14
No qualification	10	–	4	1	–	17
% in other non-manual category						
'A' level or higher	60	75	77	77	81	63
'O' level/CSE/other	66	74	74	79	58	67
No qualification	44	36	27	39	19	45
% in skilled manual category						
'A' level or higher	–	1	4	5	3	–
'O' level/CSE/other	2	2	2	5	8	–
No qualification	6	6	3	5	3	–
% in semi-skilled and unskilled manual category						
'A' level or higher	17	12	7	–	5	5
'O' level/CSE/other	25	23	18	6	34	19
No qualification	39	59	65	54	78	38
Weighted count	*669*	*432*	*233*	*178*	*57*	*88*
Unweighted count	*633*	*322*	*226*	*149*	*66*	*48*

Source: Modood *et al.* (1997) *Ethnic Minorities in Britain*, PSI, London, pp. 102 and 106

Table 4.12 Percentage of households owner-occupied by ethnic group, 1982–94				
Ethnic group	1982 PSI Survey	1984–6 LFS	1988–90 LFS	1994 PSI Survey
White	59	60	65	67
Afro-Caribbean	41	38	46	50
African Asian	73	81	82	84
Indian	77	77	76	85
Pakistani	80	78	75	79
Bangladeshi	30	31	46	48

Source: J. Lakey, 'Neighbourhoods and Housing', in Modood et al. (1997) Ethnic Minorities in Britain, PSI, London, p. 215

Table 4.13 Percentage of households renting from local authority by ethnic group, 1982–94				
Ethnic group	1982 PSI Survey	1984–6 LFS	1988–90 LFS	1994 PSI Survey
White	30	28	25	20
Afro-Caribbean	46	47	41	33
African Asian	19	8	9	10
Indian	16	12	11	7
Pakistani	13	13	11	13
Bangladeshi	53	49	36	35

Source: J. Lakey, 'Neighbourhoods and Housing', in Modood et al. (1997) Ethnic Minorities in Britain, PSI, London, p. 199

Table 4.13 shows the small proportions of African Asians, Indians and Pakistanis living in council or social housing during the 1980s and 1990s. However, there was still a high proportion of Afro-Caribbeans and Bangladeshis living in such housing, despite big reductions in the availability of council houses. Amongst all groups reliance upon council housing fell during the 1980s, partly because the number of council houses declined as many were sold to their tenants.

Patterns of housing tenure seem to suggest that different ethnic minorities have rather different positions in the housing market. Other types of data on housing, though, seem to suggest that all ethnic minority groups are disadvantaged in terms of housing.

The 1994 PSI survey (Modood et al., 1997) found that 23 per cent of whites, 21 per cent of Indians, 9 per cent of Pakistanis/Bangladeshis, and 9 per cent of black Caribbeans lived in detached houses. All ethnic minority groups were more likely than whites to live in terraced houses.

There was also more overcrowding in ethnic minority households. In the 1994 PSI survey, some 2 per cent of white households were deemed to be overcrowded by virtue of having too few bedrooms, compared to 6 per cent of Caribbean, 13 per cent of Indian, 33 per cent of Pakistani, and 43 per cent of Bangladeshi households.

Jane Lakey, who compiled and discussed the PSI findings on housing, also examined data on the neighbourhoods in which ethnic minorities in Britain lived (Lakey, 1997). She found that in a number of ways ethnic minorities tended to live in more disadvantaged neighbourhoods. All ethnic minorities were more likely to live in areas of high unemployment than were whites. All non-Christian groups were more likely than Christians to feel they had inadequate access to places of worship. All

ethnic minorities were more likely than whites to complain of vermin infestation, and all minorities except Indians and African Asians were more likely than whites to express concern about graffiti or vandalism.

There were some issues that whites were more worried about than ethnic minorities (for example, street parking and the condition of paths and roads), but generally there was considerable evidence that ethnic minorities were less satisfied with their neighbourhoods. Lakey concluded that:

> ethnic minority households were not simply different from white ones in the neighbourhoods and housing, but … they were also disadvantaged. The extent of disadvantage was greater for some ethnic minority groups than for others, and the forms of disadvantage also varied between ethnic groups. Housing and neighbourhood disadvantage was compounded by a number of other problems faced by ethnic minority households, including low incomes and a history of settlement in poor areas.
>
> Lakey, 1997, p. 220

(For details of poverty statistics on ethnic groups see pp. 313–14.)

Inequalities between ethnic groups – conclusion

Data from this section and elsewhere in the book suggests that there has been some reduction in most types of inequality between whites and ethnic minority groups in Britain. Patterns of inequality vary by ethnic group, with African Asians and Indians generally faring better than Afro-Caribbeans and Bangladeshis. In all types of inequality there are important gender differences. For example, women from some ethnic minorities who are in employment have enjoyed considerable success in achieving high-status jobs, while their male counterparts have been less successful. It is therefore important not to generalize about ethnic minorities as a whole. Overall though, it is clear that ethnic minorities continue to

have poorer life chances than the white population in Britain (with the possible exception of the Irish).

Many sociologists attribute much of the inequality to racism, theories of which we will now examine.

Theories of racism

Psychological theories of racism

The Frankfurt School

Some influential theories of racism have assumed that racism is a characteristic of an abnormal minority of the population and that the abnormality which causes racism is psychological. One such psychological theory was developed by the Frankfurt Institute for Social Research, often known as the Frankfurt School. This was a group of social scientists who were originally based at Frankfurt, though some fled to the USA during the 1930s around the time of the Second World War.

The rise of fascism in Germany in the 1930s, with its strong anti-Semitism, prompted the School to investigate the origins of prejudice and discrimination. Perhaps the most influential research in this area was conducted by Theodor Adorno, who carried out a study to determine the causes of *The Authoritarian Personality* (1950).

The Frankfurt School often adopted an inter-disciplinary approach and much of its writing was influenced by the sociology of Marx and the psycho-analytic perspective of Sigmund Freud. Freud's work was particularly influential in developing theories of racism and prejudice.

Adorno's research was published in 1950 and it involved administering questionnaires to a sample of 2,000 Americans. Respondents were asked to agree or disagree with statements so that researchers could determine their attitudes towards religious and ethnic minorities, their views on politics and economics, and their moral values. About one-tenth of the total sample were interviewed in more depth. This sub-sample consisted of one group which had expressed the most prejudiced and authoritarian views and one group which had expressed the least prejudiced and authoritarian views. These groups were compared to determine what factors seemed to give rise to an authoritarian personality.

The Frankfurt School defined an authoritarian personality as one which involved 'stereotypic thinking, disguised sadism, the veneration of power' and 'the blind recognition accorded to anything that appeared forceful'. People with authoritarian person-alities submitted to those in authority and were

hostile to people who did not. They also tended to be hostile to any groups of people who were different from themselves, including members of ethnic minorities. They placed emphasis on 'traditional values ... externally correct behaviour, success, industry, competence, physical cleanliness, health, and uncritical conformist attitudes'. People with authoritarian personalities were seen as typical of those who were most likely to give uncritical support to Hitler in 1930s and 1940s Germany.

According to the research, such personalities had their origins in the way they had been brought up as children. The School argued:

> *Frequently the totalitarian characters are broken in their childhood, either by a strict father or by a general lack of love, and then repeat, for their part, that which had once been done to them, in order to be able to survive physically.*
>
> Adorno, 1950

Their loveless and rigid upbringings had forced these authoritarian personalities to be emotionally cool towards others, especially those who were different from themselves, and to value conformity. They found it difficult to sympathize with others and to tolerate difference. They were therefore intolerant of members of ethnic minorities.

John Dollard – frustration-aggression as the cause of prejudice

Like the Frankfurt School, Dollard was influenced by Freudian ideas and saw early upbringing as the key to explaining the development of racial prejudice (Dollard, 1939, 1957). Writing in 1957, in an attempt to explain racism in the Deep South of the USA, Dollard argued that those who are frustrated become aggressive and need an outlet for their aggression.

In socializing children, parents force them to suppress basic drives (which in Freudian theory come from the id) and frustration arises. The children, however, cannot take their frustration out on the parents because they rely upon them for physical survival. The frustration is stored up and later in life is directed against an alternative, more vulnerable target. In the Deep South black Americans fulfilled this function.

Criticisms of psychological theories

The theories of the Frankfurt School assume that racism and prejudice are confined to small numbers of abnormal individuals. However, many studies have found that some degree of racism is widespread in many societies and is not confined to an untypical minority. Many of the theories of racism which we will discuss next argue that racism is a product of a society's culture or its economic system, and is not therefore confined to a minority of individuals.

John Rex (1986) argues that Dollard's theory may be of some value in explaining why an individual 'should act competitively towards competitors'. He adds, though:

> It is not easy to see, however, why we should apply it more to a ruling group, like the Whites of the Deep South rather than to those whom they ruled and oppressed and frustrated.
>
> Rex, 1986

Since blacks in the Deep South suffered much more frustration than the whites, Dollard's theory would work better as an explanation of revolts by American blacks than as an explanation of discrimination by American whites.

E. Ellis Cashmore – *The Logic of Racism*

The study

In 1987, E. Ellis Cashmore published a study of racism in England in which he tried to understand *The Logic of Racism* from the viewpoint of English whites. It was based upon in-depth interviews with 800 people in the English Midlands. Although the main focus was on the views of ordinary working-class and middle-class whites, he also interviewed Afro-Caribbean and Asian British, and a number of local politicians and professionals, such as teachers, who had to deal with race relations issues in the course of their work.

Cashmore's main sample was based on four areas:

1 Newtown: an inner-city housing estate in Birmingham built during the 1960s. It had an overwhelmingly working-class population, nearly half of the population were under 30 and unemployment was high at 23.7 per cent. There was a large ethnic minority population of 13.4 per cent, most of whom were of Caribbean origin.

2 Chelmsley Wood: another working-class council estate but situated ten miles outside Birmingham and surrounded by suburban areas. Many people had

been rehoused there from Birmingham, and the biggest local employer was a nearby Rover factory. Like Newtown many of its residents were young with over 50 per cent being under 30. Its unemployment rate was lower than Newtown's at 16.3 per cent but was rising. Chelmsley Wood had a small ethnic minority population of 3.5 per cent.

3 Edgbaston: an area close to the centre of Birmingham but with an overwhelmingly middle-class population including many professionals and entrepreneurs. Unemployment was low at 4.2 per cent and there was a small but growing Asian population making up 6.1 per cent of all residents.

4 Solihull: a town ten miles west of Coventry with a very affluent population. Unemployment stood at just 4.2 per cent, less than 9 per cent of the houses were council houses and relatively few of the population were under 30 (38 per cent). Solihull had a very small ethnic minority population of around 1 per cent.

Cashmore examined the extent and nature of racism in different age groups in the white population in each of these four areas. The age groups were:

1 the middle-aged (21–50)

2 the young (under 21)

3 older people (over 50).

Racism and the middle-age groups

In Newtown most whites aged 21–50 expressed considerable suspicion of ethnic minorities and sometimes demonstrated outright hostility:

1 Many believed that ethnic minorities received preferential treatment over housing. A number of individuals felt that they personally had not been moved to a better council house or flat despite a long time on a waiting list because better residences had gone to ethnic minority groups.

2 A number of people also expressed resentment at the alleged nuisance caused by the noisiness of Afro-Caribbean neighbours who had parties or played music during the night.

3 Some residents feared street violence and held ethnic minorities responsible for its existence.

In Newtown the racism stemmed from competition over scarce resources, particularly housing, with some whites feeling they were missing out. Cashmore comments:

> Given that life in Newtown is a struggle at the best of times for many, some residents are inflamed at the idea of blacks and Asians being allocated housing and awarded grants.
>
> Cashmore, 1987

In Chelmsley Wood, 'race' was a less pressing issue because of the smaller ethnic minority population.

Whites saw them as less of an immediate threat because there were so few of them. Nevertheless, racism was still in evidence. In particular many whites criticized ethnic minorities for failing to assimilate by maintaining their own cultures and failing to mix with whites. Crude stereotypes of ethnic minority groups were common because the white residents of Chelmsley Wood had little direct contact with members of ethnic minorities. Cashmore describes the attitudes in the following way:

> ethnics are in society but not of it. Asians, for instance, are popularly seen as having an instrumental attitude to British society, which offers them opportunities for making money. Blacks, being less entrepreneurial, settle for less in the eyes of many white council residents. They are content to amble along in a parasitic way, sponging off the state and augmenting their unearned income with the spoils of robberies.
>
> Cashmore, 1987

The white middle class in Edgbaston and Solihull tended to see people in terms of their own individualistic and competitive values. As in Chelmsley Wood, Afro-Caribbeans were likely to be seen as spongers, but Asians were accorded more respect. Some at least were seen as hard-working and able to provide for themselves and their families.

Crude stereotypes were just as common in these areas as they were in Chelmsley Wood. There was 'an unquestioning acceptance of Asians as thrifty, hard working capitalists and West Indians as "lower-mentality" manual workers'. There was little direct competition for jobs or houses with ethnic minorities in the middle-class areas, and most of the residents had little direct experience of Asians or Afro-Caribbeans.

Conflict between ethnic groups seemed a remote problem for them and many believed that both conflict and racism were exaggerated. They accepted that there was some racism but believed that it was up to ethnic minorities to work hard and try to assimilate to overcome the racism. The white residents tended to disapprove of government legislation to ban discrimination, seeing it as unwarranted state interference in the operation of the free market. By-and-large they did not see themselves as racist.

However, a number of the employers interviewed by Cashmore did say that they had decided not to employ an Afro-Caribbean or Asian person in the past. This was not, they said, because they had any objection to employing them themselves, but rather because their customers or their existing workforce would not be happy with such an employee.

Although the racism of the white middle class seemed more restrained than that of some members of the working class, it is possible that it might affect the life chances of ethnic minorities more. Some of the middle-aged and middle-class residents of Edgbaston and Solihull were denying ethnic minorities opportunities and at the same time criticizing them for not making more attempt to succeed in British society.

Racism and the young

Perhaps the least racist white group of all were the young working class of Newtown. They had grown up alongside members of ethnic minorities and many felt that all youth in the area shared common grievances. Cashmore says that 'sheer familiarity and an apprehension of shared social conditions seems to foster a kind of mental assonance'. One of the Newtown youths, called 'John', saw 'no advantage in simply – and blindly – blaming his peers who have sat next to him at school and line up with him in dole queues'. The young had not experienced ethnic minorities as newcomers or immigrants so it was hard to see them as outsiders who were taking their jobs.

Nevertheless, there were social divisions along ethnic lines. Most of the youth of Newtown stuck to friends from their own ethnic group from the time they left school, and some of the young in Newtown did express racist views.

If racism and ethnic conflict were relatively muted in Newtown, the same was not found to be true of Chelmsley Wood. There, many white youths did blame ethnic minorities for unemployment and had highly stereotypical views of them. For example, one youth, 'Kevin', said 'They stink. Pakis really reek; you can tell one in a street a mile away. Blacks stink of sweat and a lot of them are pimps.'

Despite the small size of the ethnic minority population there was sometimes conflict between ethnic groups. In one reported incident a black woman was grabbed in a pub by a skinhead, and a black man in the pub hit him and knocked him out, prompting disputes between groups of whites, blacks and Asians in the street outside the pub.

Although there was little actual violence on this occasion, Cashmore describes conflicts of this kind as common. He argues that the lack of contact between whites and ethnic minorities leads to white youths relying largely upon the media for their beliefs about ethnic minorities. As a consequence they develop stereotypical views which rarely have a chance to be challenged through experience.

In the middle-class areas the youth often believed that the media exaggerated the amount of racism and discrimination. Most admitted that members of ethnic minorities suffered some problems but tended to argue that it was their own fault. The youth followed their parents in believing that individuals largely shaped their own lives and social conditions played little part in limiting people's opportunities. Thus, if ethnic minorities were less successful than whites, then it was mainly due to their lack of effort and their unwillingness to fit in with the culture of the host society.

However, not all the middle-class youths shared this view. In Solihull, for example, although living in an area remote from inner-city problems, a youth called 'Charles' suggested that the 'colour problem' was manufactured by the ruling class to divert attention from the problems of deprivation suffered by the poor. Another, called 'Kate', criticized older people for their unwillingness to tolerate different cultures.

However, although the views of middle-class youths were varied, most shared their parents' version of racism based upon a belief in the personal inadequacy of most individuals in ethnic minority groups.

Racism and older people

In Newtown, whites over 50 had experienced considerable changes during their lifetime. They had seen slum clearance programmes and the introduction of tower blocks. They had also seen considerable numbers of people from ethnic minorities settle in the area. Many believed that the standard of living in their area had declined and they were willing to blame this on ethnic minorities.

Their complaints were similar to those of whites from the middle-age group living in Newtown:

1 They believed that ethnic minorities caused excessive noise, and deprived white people of jobs and houses.

2 Ethnic minorities were also accused of organizing prostitution, running various rackets and contributing to a general decline.

Many residents, like 'Mrs Dobbs', did not put all the blame on ethnic minority groups for failing to assimilate. She also blamed the government and other authorities for allowing too much immigration and passing discrimination laws which, as she saw it, gave privileges to ethnic minorities which are not afforded to whites. People like Mrs Dobbs felt the area was being taken over by alien groups who were destroying the British way of life.

In Chelmsley Wood there was less fear of such a take-over. There were similar views to those in Newtown but they were expressed less strongly. Some residents thought that residential segregation was the answer to the problem: so long as ethnic minorities were kept at arm's length resentment could be minimized and problems limited. Here too the authorities were blamed for lax immigration control.

Whites over 50 in Edgbaston and Solihull followed those from the middle-age group in those areas in blaming ethnic minorities for any problems they faced. They believed that ethnic minority groups had made insufficient effort to integrate into white, English society and had been too keen on keeping their own distinctive cultures. Like the working class in the same age group, they did not approve of the Race Relations Acts. They did not believe that the government should intervene to regulate people's actions through such legislation, although they did support strong government action to restrict immigration. Cashmore comments:

> *The middle class elderly share few of the worries that infect the working class. Their views are not motivated by insecurity over their houses or their personal safety … They are, however, anxious about changes that threaten to upset the equilibrium they value so much. Too much cultural diversity can lead to the destruction of the homogeneous and standardized world in which they have prospered.*
>
> Cashmore, 1987

Conclusion

Cashmore found that racism was present in all classes and in all age groups. He therefore rejects psychological theories of racism which see it as a characteristic of pathological individuals with abnormal personalities. Instead he seems to see racism as the product of a type of natural conservatism. He says that 'most people are conservative for no reason more mysterious than that they want stability and order'.

Many people in Britain have experienced major social changes since the end of the Second World War. These changes include immigration from the New Commonwealth and with it the introduction of 'unfamiliar beliefs, languages and lifestyles'. Cashmore goes on to say:

> *If we accept that people are ordinarily conservative, then we can grasp a certain logic in their response to change … Racism in modern society typically arises in defence of the established order of things.*
>
> Cashmore, 1987

From Cashmore's point of view, racism takes different forms in different sections of society but everywhere it has the same roots.

John Richardson (1990) praises Cashmore's work for trying to understand racism rather than just condemning it or counting the number of people who are racist. Richardson also says that the study produced 'illuminating' empirical data. However, he also describes it as 'modest in conceptual and theoretical terms'. Certainly it made no attempt to find wider structural or historical roots of racism beyond a certain amount of innate conservatism.

Marxist theories of racism have usually taken a much broader, theoretical approach while paying less attention to the 'logic of racism' from the viewpoint of ordinary people.

Oliver C. Cox – a Marxist theory of racism

Ethnicity, 'race' and racism

Oliver C. Cox (1970 (1948)) developed an early theory of racism based on Marxist ideas. In 1948 he published his book *Class, Caste and Race* in which he rejected approaches that saw racism as something that had always existed and was a product of natural human sentiments.

To Cox the idea of 'race' was itself a human creation. Ethnic groups were any socially distinct groups which 'lived competitively in a relationship of superordination or subordination with respect to some other people or peoples within one state, country or economic area'. Ethnic groups could be divided into those that were distinguished by culture, and those that were distinguished by 'race'.

'Races' were identified according to physical characteristics but these characteristics did not have to reflect any real biological differences between groups. Cox said 'a race may be thought of as simply any group of people that is generally believed to be, and accepted as, a race in any given area of ethnic competition'. It was the belief in difference that was important, not any real differences that might exist.

To Cox racism was a comparatively recent phenomenon. It could not therefore have its origins in universal human sentiments which automatically made ethnic groups hostile to one another. He argued that 'one should miss the point entirely if one were to think of racial antagonism as having its genesis in some "social instinct" of antipathy between peoples'.

According to Cox there was no racism in ancient civilizations:

1 In Ancient Greece people were divided into Greeks and barbarians. The difference was not a racial one but was based on whether people were familiar with Greek language and culture. Those who were not familiar were barbarians.

2 In Ancient Rome citizenship was the key distinction. Freeborn people who possessed Roman citizenship could come from any part of the Empire and were not limited by ethnic or racial group.

3 The Roman Catholic Church distinguished between Christians and heathens and heretics on the basis of religious belief, and people from any racial group could convert to the religion and be accepted as equals. Even the early Portuguese explorers who were ruthless in their dealings with Africans did not see the latter as racially inferior; the Portuguese held

to the Christian belief that all people were equal in the eyes of God.

However, towards the end of the fifteenth century things changed and racism began to develop.

Capitalism and racism

In 1493, as a result of Spanish pressure, Pope Alexander VI issued a papal bull putting 'all the heathen peoples and their resources – that is to say, especially the coloured peoples of the world – at the disposal of Spain and Portugal'. At that point, according to Cox, racism was born.

To Cox racism is not 'an abstract, natural, immemorial feeling of mutual antipathy between groups, but rather a practical exploitative relationship with its socio-attitudinal facilitation'. In other words, racism is a set of beliefs used to justify and therefore to sustain the exploitation of one group by another. It had its origins in the development of capitalism with its need to systematically exploit labour power.

The 'capitalist exploiter, being opportunistic and practical, will utilize any convenience to keep his labour and other resources freely exploitable'. It was hard to justify the use of slave labour in terms of religious beliefs, which saw all humans as equal. It was therefore necessary to 'argue that the workers are innately degraded and degenerate, consequently they naturally merit their condition'.

Early capitalism went hand-in-hand with colonialism. As European nations conquered other areas of the world, they were able to exploit the workforce in the colonies and to justify their actions through racism. To Cox racism is always something developed by the exploiters against the exploited. He argues that 'race prejudice must be actually backed up by a show of racial excellence, secured finally by military might' and that 'the superior race controls the pattern of all dependent race prejudices'.

If racism is something developed to justify exploitation, it cannot be developed by those who are exploited. It is not only whites who are capable of racism, but by chance it was whites who developed capitalism, and therefore it was they who first developed it. According to Cox, if capitalism had not developed, then 'the world might never have experienced race prejudice'.

Criticisms of Cox

Many writers since Cox have agreed with him that racism is related to capitalism and colonialism. However, many have also denied that racism can only exist within capitalism and that colonialism and capitalism are the only causes of racism. Social psychologists tend to disagree with Cox that only white people can be racist, arguing that individuals from any ethnic group can be racist.

Cox's work has influenced some Marxists but most now reject his views as too simplistic. John Solomos says:

> the model of Marxism with which Cox was familiar was based on the conceptual baggage of 'base' and 'superstructure' and an instrumental view of the state as the agent of the capitalist class.
>
> Solomos et al., 1982

Cox saw racism as determined by the economic system. It existed because capitalism needed it to exist. The state acted in a racist way because the state was the instrument of the ruling class.

Many contemporary Marxists argue that such views are far too simplistic. The capitalist class is not all-powerful and the needs of the capitalist system do not in themselves determine everything that happens. An alternative approach has been developed at the Birmingham Centre for Contemporary Cultural Studies.

The Birmingham Centre for Contemporary Cultural Studies – a neo-Marxist theory of racism

A theoretical approach to racism

In a collection of articles called *The Empire Strikes Back*, published in 1982, a group of sociologists at the Birmingham Centre for Contemporary Cultural Studies developed a neo-Marxist approach to racism. In an introductory article, John Solomos, Bob Findlay, Simon Jones and Paul Gilroy outlined the main features of this approach.

They agreed with Cox that racism was influenced by colonialism but argued that racism predated colonialism and was shaped by many other factors. According to them the nature of racism in Britain was not fixed but changed as history progressed. They agreed with other Marxist writers that racism was connected to the exploitation of migrant labour in capitalist societies, but again argued that this was not the only important factor. To them, 'The construction of race as a "problem" has not come about by evolutionary means. It has emerged from a whole series of events: struggles, breaks, and discontinuities.' It was necessary to examine these complex events in order to understand racism.

Solomos et al. believed that it was necessary to examine the part played by ethnic minorities themselves in resisting and challenging racism and to consider how the working class came to accept racist beliefs. Racism was not something that was just imposed on exploited groups in society by an all-powerful ruling class. Although some exploited groups rejected racism, others accepted it and racist ideas were incorporated into their commonsense understanding of the world.

Like most Marxists, Solomos et al. accept that economic factors are important in shaping social life. In Britain in the 1970s and early 1980s, issues to do with 'race' developed against a backdrop of economic crisis and rising unemployment. However, Solomos et al. said that 'There is no one-to-one correspondence between the "crisis of race" and the economic crisis', pointing out that 'Economic decline preceded popular acknowledgement of crisis, and the expulsion of blacks as a solution to national problems has a long history in British political thought.'

A variety of historical and political factors shaped the situation, along with the development of the economy. The cultures of the working class and of ethnic minorities, and the policies followed by the British state all interacted to produce a particular form of racism in the 1970s and early 1980s.

According to Solomos et al. this period saw the emergence of a new racism which stressed the cultural differences between ethnic groups rather than biological superiority and inferiority of particular 'races'. It drew upon long-established beliefs about British nationalism which went back centuries, and which appealed to some sections of the white working class. In a later chapter in *The Empire Strikes Back*, Errol Lawrence tried to describe and explain the emergence of this new racism.

Errol Lawrence – the origins of racism in Britain

According to Lawrence, racist ideas have a very long history. Even before colonialism 'white' was associated with goodness and purity whereas 'black' was associated with evil. Hence, for example, the distinction between black and white magic. The Christian religion had always characterized non-Christians as pagans. In early contacts between Europeans and other peoples, non-Europeans were usually portrayed as uncivilized.

With the advent of colonialism racist ideas were developed further. Members of the British working class fought in the wars in which colonies were captured, and in the twentieth century they fought again in independence struggles in countries such as Kenya. Lawrence claims that by the time colonies were gaining independence colonial people had come to be seen as 'children needing protection or as the equally immature "brutal savage"'. Either way the newly independent states were seen as needing strong guidance from their former British 'masters'. Their success or failure was likely to be determined by the extent to which they adopted European culture and institutions.

According to Lawrence, in the 1970s in Britain the ruling class succeeded in 'reorganizing the common-sense racist ideologies of the white working class, around the themes of "the British nation", "the British people" and "British culture"'. The racist ideas that developed were not 'mere "relics" of a distant imperial past', but they did contain strong elements of ideologies developed during colonial times. These stressed the distinctive nature of British culture and the great traditions of British militarism which allowed Britain (and its working-class soldiers) to conquer large parts of the world.

Although the racist images 'are cross-cut by other contradictory images about the essential equality of all people ... they nevertheless tend to pull popular opinion towards racist opinions and interpretations'. This meant that 'Black cultures are still likely to be viewed as "primitive" in comparison to British "civilization"'.

The new racism

In the economic and political instability of the 1970s, 'immigrants' came to be seen as a cause of the problems. The emphasis was no longer on outright inferiority but more on difference. British strength came from its way of life, and the presence of 'aliens' with different cultures was sapping this strength and causing national decline. The British way of life was being undermined by 'foreigners' and it was unnatural for people with very different lifestyles to live together.

For example, the new racism attacked the family life of Afro-Caribbeans and Asians. Afro-Caribbeans were seen as incapable of maintaining stable families consisting of parents and children. Such families were viewed as the bedrock of British society. Asians, on the other hand, had unnaturally large extended families which led to overcrowding and the isolation of Asians from the beneficial effects of British culture.

From this point of view, individuals could not be truly British simply by having a British passport or even by being born in Britain. Rather they had to think of themselves as British and have a British lifestyle and values.

Neither Afro-Caribbeans nor Asians were seen as measuring up to these criteria. They had different 'identities', 'loyalties' and 'anti-British attitudes'. Their presence was therefore bound to cause conflict between the 'immigrants' and the real 'British'. According to the logic of the new racism, the only solution to the problem was for the 'immigrants' to leave Britain and return to the countries where their culture was more acceptable.

To Lawrence the new racism was a response to the crisis in British society. Unemployment, rising crime and the apparent breakdown of family life were all causes of concern, and ethnic minorities were convenient scapegoats for these problems. However, the new racism was not an automatic and inevitable consequence of economic change. It had to be created using elements of old racist ideas; it had to be accepted by, and make sense to, the white working class; and it had to overcome opposition from anti-racists.

Paul Gilroy – *There Ain't No Black in the Union Jack*

Paul Gilroy was one of the contributors to *The Empire Strikes Back* (see above). In 1987 his own book, *There Ain't No Black in the Union Jack*, was published. This extended the earlier analysis. Like Lawrence, Gilroy examined the new racism but he also discussed ethnic minority cultures. In doing so Gilroy was attempting to produce a more complete understanding of 'race' and ethnicity than studies that concentrated on racism or ethnicity alone. His study discusses a wide range of issues which overlap with the issues we consider in a number of sections in this chapter.

Race formation

Gilroy rejects both biological definitions of 'race' and studies of ethnicity which regard ethnic groups as having very strong and distinctive cultures which are slow to change. In his view, 'race' formation involves an ongoing process in which groups 'define themselves and organize around notions of "race"'. It is a 'continuous and contingent process' which varies from place to place and time to time. It is affected by racism but also by the conscious choices made by those who see themselves as belonging to racial groups.

Resistance to racism and political organization by 'races' play important roles in the process of 'race' formation. Gilroy says 'it is struggle that determines which definition of "race" will prevail and the conditions under which they will endure or wither away'. For example, in Britain the term 'black' had begun to be used to refer both to Afro-Caribbeans and Asians. This implies the possibility of Afro-Asian unity in a struggle against racism. More recently, however, 'black' has become more commonly used to refer to Afro-Caribbeans alone. To Gilroy 'This development has its origins in an understanding of "race" which stresses the obstacles to political accommodation erected between culture and ethnicity'. It has resulted from struggles over the meaning of 'race', and Gilroy believes it reflects the increasing influence of the new racism which puts great emphasis on cultural differences.

Although influenced by Marxism, Gilroy moves further from Marxist orthodoxy than the Birmingham Centre for Contemporary Cultural Studies had done in *The Empire Strikes Back*. He accepts that struggles over 'race' have been influenced by the development of capitalism – for example in its use of slave and migrant labour – but he denies that the exploitation of 'races' is a form of class exploitation.

Nor does Gilroy believe that conflict between 'races' is simply a form of class conflict. He says 'The processes of "race" and class formation are not identical. The former is not reducible to the latter even where they become mutually entangled.' Racial divisions are separate and distinct from class divisions and Gilroy talks of 'The evident autonomy of racism from production relations.' Indeed, to Gilroy class conflict is becoming less important in modern capitalist societies. Instead, conflict has become much more based around new social movements which are concerned with non-economic issues. Examples include the 'women's movements, youth movements, anti-nuclear and peace movements, ecological movements, and various urban and citizen movements'.

Racism

Gilroy agrees with Lawrence that there is a new form of racism in Britain and that it is based around cultural rather than biological distinctions. Gilroy sees this racism as intimately linked to 'discourses of patriotism, nationalism, xenophobia, Englishness, Britishness, militarism and gender difference'. The new racism involves specifying who may be regarded as a legitimate member of 'the Island Race' and who is considered an outsider. So-called 'immigrants', many of whom were actually born in Britain, are usually regarded as outsiders. They are portrayed as culturally different and therefore as threatening the British way of life. Their difference undermines a homogeneous British culture which is seen as having given Britain its strength.

This image of strength is stressed in celebrations of past military victories and was invoked during the 1982 war against Argentina over the Falklands. According to Gilroy, during that war the white residents of the Falklands were seen as coming from the same cultural community as white British people. They were portrayed as being genuinely British even though they lived 8,000 miles from Britain itself.

Similar attitudes prevailed in relation to Zola Budd. In 1984, Budd, a talented white South African distance runner, was given British citizenship because her grandfather had been British. Her application for citizenship was processed rapidly and accepted enthusiastically by the government. This contrasts with the much greater difficulties experienced by Asians and West Indians who try to secure British citizenship in order to emigrate to Britain. Indeed many Asians and Afro-Caribbeans who do have

British citizenship and may have been born in Britain are sometimes treated as more alien than whites from New Commonwealth countries like the Falklands and South Africa. When black protesters demonstrated against Zola Budd because she refused to denounce apartheid in South Africa, the *Sun* newspaper said that they should be 'returned to their original homelands' because 'There is no place for them in Britain.'

Gilroy believes that 'the link between crime and blackness has become absolutely integral' to the new racism. Through much of the 1950s and 1960s Afro-Caribbeans were not portrayed as being particularly prone to criminality. Their presence in Britain was portrayed as creating housing problems and they were certainly subject to much racial discrimination.

However, the turning point from which new racism developed was a speech by Enoch Powell. In 1968 he described the plight of an old white woman who had lived in a particular street all her life. Gradually, more and more blacks moved into her street. According to Powell, after she had refused a black neighbour's request to use her phone one night, she began to suffer verbal abuse from blacks in her area. Gilroy comments that in Powell's speech:

> *The anarchy represented by black settlement is counterposed to an image of England in which Britannia is portrayed as an old white woman, trapped and alone in the inner city.*
>
> Gilroy, 1987

She was surrounded by hostile aliens in her home – a corner of Britain had been taken over by outsiders. In Powell's view the aliens were liable to be criminals. In 1976 Powell argued that 'mugging' was a racial crime because it was predominantly carried out by blacks. This view of blacks as criminals was reinforced by media reporting of so-called 'muggings' and various inner-city disturbances in the 1970s and 1980s. (For details of a study of the 'panic' over mugging see Chapter 6.)

Ethnic absolutism

As we saw earlier in the chapter (see pp. 211–12), in his 1968 speech, Powell had said 'As I look ahead, I am filled with foreboding. Like the Roman, I seem to see "the River Tiber foaming with much blood".' The blood would be the inevitable consequence of immigration which led to people from different cultures living side-by-side.

Gilroy calls the view that there are completely different cultures ethnic absolutism. He criticizes people like Powell for believing that cultures are fixed and unchanging. For Gilroy there are many overlaps between black and white cultures in Britain, and indeed British culture, particularly youth culture, has become increasingly influenced by black culture. To him cultures are constantly changing and he attacks all those who analyse ethnic cultures as separate entities. This not only includes right-wing politicians who support the 'repatriation' of British blacks but also some left-wing thinkers and sociologists who study ethnicity. They too can be ethnic absolutists when they portray groups of Asians or Afro-Caribbeans as having quite distinct cultures from other British people.

Thus Gilroy is hostile to the sort of studies that we discussed in the 'Ethnicity' section of this chapter.

Black culture

In discussing black culture Gilroy concentrates on the music and youth culture of Afro-Caribbeans. He sees black culture as being formed partly as a response to racism and exploitation. For example, from slave songs to reggae, rap and hip-hop, black music and lyrics have expressed radical sentiments. However, black culture is much more than simply a reaction to racism: it is actively created in different contexts from diverse influences. Some of those influences are African and predate the large-scale exploitation of blacks by whites.

Black culture is an international culture which has been influenced by the diaspora, or dispersal, of African peoples throughout the world. In Britain there are strong Caribbean and Afro-American influences. Reggae music and the sound systems over which it is traditionally played have influenced black youth in Britain, as have North American traditions of soul and rap. Most styles of black music are based around African rhythms which were preserved in slave music and passed down to succeeding generations. Black music and culture not only have international origins, they are also influential throughout the world. Gilroy claims, for example, that 'Rastafari culture has been carried to locations as diverse as Poland and Polynesia, and hip-hop from Stockholm to Southall.'

Black culture has also influenced white youth. Gilroy attacks ethnic absolutists by pointing out how elements of black music have been adopted by whites. In the 1960s, mods and others started using black American slang words such as 'dig'. The Beatles' early records contained cover versions of rhythm and blues and rock and roll songs originally recorded by black American artists. Later, reggae rhythms started to be incorporated into mainstream pop music.

In Britain, Gilroy finds some evidence that racial divisions may be being weakened by music. In West London some Asians have become involved in hip-hop. White and black musicians worked together in the 1970s in groups like The Specials, who played ska music (a variation on reggae) and attacked racism in their lyrics. Gilroy quotes at length from David

Emmanuel's 1984 hit 'Cockney Translation'. In this song cockney and black slang are translated. For example, here are some of the lyrics:

> Cockney say scarper we scatter
> Cockney say rabbit we chatter
> We say bleach Cockney knackered
> Cockney say triffic we say wackard
> Cockney say blokes we say guys
> Cockney say alright we say Ites!
> We say pants Cockney say strides
> Sweet as a nut … just level vibes. Seen.

To Gilroy this suggested the increasing possibility of the black and white working classes working together to resist racism and class exploitation. Despite the differences between blacks and whites, their cultures were not completely separate and they influenced one another. Gilroy concludes on an optimistic note, suggesting that black and white cooperation offers an image of a better future. Eventually the different cultures may become so similar that people will no longer even think of each other as belonging to different 'races'.

Evaluation

Gilroy's work has been criticized by more conventional Marxists. They have criticized him for failing to define 'race' clearly and for continually referring to groups as 'races'. To Miles (1989) there is no biological basis for 'races'. 'Races' therefore do not exist and the term 'race' should not be used. He also criticizes Gilroy for arguing that class conflict has been replaced by 'race' conflict and other non-economic forms of conflict. To Miles and other Marxists class conflict is far from dead, and economic exploitation continues to be an important factor in the exploitation of ethnic minorities and the production of racism.

Whatever its limitations, Gilroy's work represents an important advance over most earlier approaches to 'race' and ethnicity. It combines the study of ethnic minority cultures with an examination of racism and in doing so avoids the narrow focus of many of the other studies we have examined in this chapter. Gilroy also discusses the relationship between 'race', racism, ethnicity and nationality in suggesting that in Britain racism has become increasingly closely connected with a form of British nationalism.

In some respects Gilroy's work anticipated a number of theoretical developments. These include the idea that new ethnicities are developing, that ethnic identities are not static but change continually, that identities are becoming fragmented, and that there is a complex relationship between 'race', ethnicity and nationality. These sorts of theoretical developments will be discussed below (see pp. 279–82). First, however, we will consider the issue of nationalism and identity.

Nationalism and identity

Nationalism

The importance of nationalism

Stuart Hall (1992) has pointed out that 'the great discourses of modernity', liberalism and Marxism, both led people 'to expect not the revival but the gradual disappearance of the nationalist passion'. In Marxist theory, classes, not nations, would become the great historical actors, while liberalism saw national differences being eroded by a global market in which trade linked all parts of the world.

A number of contemporary sociologists also claim that a process of globalization has been taking place. In this process national boundaries become less significant in social life: communication systems such as satellite TV transcend them. The world's financial markets are linked by technology so that movements in share prices in one country can instantaneously affect prices on the other side of the world. International organizations such as the UN and the EU also reduce the importance of nations, while travel gives individuals a less localized view of the world (see Chapter 9).

However, many people have argued that there has been a great resurgence of nationalism in recent decades. Individuals usually seem to identify more with their nation than with any other grouping. Nationalism could be seen as being present in the 'new racism' described by Gilroy in the preceding section, and in demands for independence by the Scottish and Welsh in Britain, the Basques in Spain and the Bretons in France. Nationalism was important in the collapse of the USSR, with demands for independence coming from Lithuania, Estonia, the Ukraine and elsewhere contributing to the break-up of the country. In the former Yugoslavia violent civil war raged as Croatians, Serbs and Muslims fought for territory in future independent states. Benedict Anderson claims that 'since World War II every successful revolution has defined itself in nationalist terms' and argues that:

> the 'end of the era of nationalism' so long
> prophesied is not remotely in sight. Indeed,
> nation-ness is the most universally legitimate
> value in the political life of our time.
>
> Anderson, 1983

Whether or not Anderson is right to attach so much importance to nationalism, it has certainly been neglected in much social theory and it is clearly an important feature of social life and one which shows little sign of becoming less important.

The definition of nationalism

Benedict Anderson argues that a nation is 'an imagined political community – and imagined as both inherently limited and sovereign':

1 It is imagined because most members of even a small nation never meet one another or hear one another yet they feel they all belong to one community. Whatever inequalities divide members of a nation it is 'always conceived as a deep, horizontal comradeship'.

2 It is limited in the sense that nations include some people who are regarded as belonging, while excluding others as outsiders. No nation claims to include the whole of humanity.

3 It is sovereign because nationalism seeks or celebrates independence and self-government for a group of people.

Anderson claims that racism and nationalism are quite different concepts:

1 Racism is based on 'dreams of eternal contamination'. It sees groups of people as having fixed, biological characteristics. For example, Jews, 'the seed of Abraham', are 'forever Jews no matter what passport they carry or what languages they speak and read'.

2 Nationalism, on the other hand, does not see individuals as inevitably belonging to a particular group of people. It is possible to become a member of a nation while it is not possible to become part of a 'race' to which the individual did not originally belong.

Anderson's view that racism and nationalism are quite different has not been accepted by most sociologists. Robert Miles (1989) argues that 'ideologies of racism and nationalism have a common historical origin'. Racism was originally used to justify the exploitation of non-Europeans in various parts of the world. With the end of colonialism, the kind of racism which saw distinct biological groupings in humanity was to some extent replaced by nationalism, in which individuals see their nation as superior to other nations. To Miles, racism and nationalism are similar because 'Both claim the existence of a natural division of the world's population into discrete groups which exist independently of class relations.' Both are used by people to justify beliefs that particular groups are superior to other groups.

However, Miles does acknowledge one important difference between nationalism and racism. He says 'the ideology of nationalism, unlike that of racism, specifies a particular political objective (national self-determination) and therefore a blueprint for political organisation on a world scale'. Thus, although Miles disagrees with Anderson about the relationship between nationalism and racism, he does agree that nationalism is based upon a belief that a group of people should have a sovereign state.

Thomas Hylland Eriksen (1993) examines the relationship between ethnicity and nationalism. To him 'Nationalism and ethnicity are kindred concepts.' Both are based upon the belief that a group of people is distinctive and has a shared culture. However, nationalism and ethnicity are different and the difference he identifies has a similar basis to the definitions of nationalism put forward by Anderson and Miles. Eriksen argues that a nationalist ideology 'is an ethnic ideology which demands a state on behalf of an ethnic group'.

Eriksen admits that this simple definition does pose certain problems when considering some examples of nationalism and ethnicity. Nationalism is sometimes used to try to unite diverse ethnic groups and it therefore 'stresses shared civil rights rather than shared cultural roots'. In Mauritius, for example, Mauritian nationalism is used to try to overcome the divisions between Hindus, Muslims, Chinese, French and Africans.

Another problem is that there are some marginal cases which could be seen as examples of nationalism *or* ethnicity. These may occur when some members of a group want full independence, while others want greater independence within an existing state. Scottish and Basque nationalism are both examples.

Although there is general agreement that nationalism is related to sovereignty, precise definitions vary and there is no agreement about the exact relationship between nationalism, 'race' and ethnicity.

Immanuel Wallerstein – the world system and peoplehood

Ambiguous identities

Wallerstein (1991) believes that in the modern world people have ambiguous identities. People from the same group will give varying answers when asked about their sense of identity. He gives some examples of this ambiguity by asking 'Are there Palestinians? Who is a Jew? Are Macedonians Bulgarians? Are Berbers Arabs? What is the correct label: Negro, Afro-American, Black (capitalized) black (uncapitalized)?' He points out that 'People shoot each other over the question of labels. And yet the very people who do so tend to deny that the issue is complex or puzzling or indeed anything but self-evident.' In an

attempt to understand the ways in which labels come to be used Wallerstein sets out to examine how different types of label relate to the development of 'the world system'.

'Race', nationality and ethnicity

To begin his analysis Wallerstein distinguishes between three ways of describing what he calls peoplehood. These are 'race', nation and ethnic group. He suggests:

> a 'race' is supposed to be a genetic category, which has a visible physical form. ... A 'nation' is supposed to be a sociopolitical category, linked somehow to the actual or potential boundaries of a state. An 'ethnic group' is supposed to be a cultural category, of which there are said to be certain continuing behaviours that are passed on from generation to generation and that are not normally linked in theory to state boundaries.
>
> Wallerstein, 1991

However, these terms are used very inconsistently and there are often arguments about whether a group of people is a racial, ethnic or national group. To Wallerstein all the terms are ideological: they are used to imply something about a group of people's past and to suggest how they should behave now. Thus a group which is persuaded that it is a national group may take action to secure its own state, whereas an ethnic group is more likely to defend its culture.

According to Wallerstein the use of different terms can be explained in terms of the world system – a concept which forms the basis of his whole theoretical approach.

The world system

Wallerstein argues that the development of capitalism led to the development of a world system. The capitalist economy gradually expanded so that every corner of the globe became part of an international economy. This international economy was and still is based upon the exploitation of some areas of the globe by other areas: the core areas, which have developed most, exploit the peripheral areas which are more distant from the centres of capitalist economic power. Core areas have traditionally been located in Europe, North America and Japan, while the peripheral areas have been located in what is often called the Third World. However, the system is not fixed and countries can experience a change in their position. They may become more prosperous and powerful and move inwards towards the core, or they may decline and move outwards towards the periphery.

Peoplehood and the capitalist world economy

Wallerstein claims that 'race', nation and ethnicity each correspond to a different feature of the capitalist world economy:

1 Wallerstein argues that '"race" is related to the axial division of labour' in the world economy. Before capitalism spread over the globe there was more genetic homogeneity in particular regions than there is today. For example, before the advent of colonialism and slavery, few Europeans lived in Africa and few Africans lived in Europe or the Americas. Racial categories began to be used to distinguish the workforces in the core and peripheral areas. Those from the more powerful core countries were held to be from more superior 'races' than those from the weaker peripheral countries. This helped to justify the exploitation of the supposedly inferior 'races' by the supposedly superior ones.

    Wallerstein cites South Africa as an example of how racial categories have continued to be constructed in line with distinctions between core and peripheral areas. When the country still had a system of apartheid, the Chinese population was designated as Asian and as non-white. However, visiting business people from the powerful core country of Japan were regarded as 'honorary whites', despite their apparent racial similarity to the Chinese South Africans.

2 Second, Wallerstein argues that 'nation' is related to the 'political superstructure' of the world system. Most modern states came into existence as a result of the world system. In 1450, for example, political entities such as the Holy Roman Empire, the Mogul Empire and the Burgundian Netherlands covered areas which are now divided into several distinct states. Turkey, Syria, Germany and Italy are among the many modern states that did not exist then. It was colonialism that led to the division of Africa into sovereign states.

    According to Wallerstein, nationalism only developed after sovereign states had been created as competitors in the world system. The states that compete often contain diverse groups of people and may be threatened by 'internal disintegration and external aggression'. Promoting nationalist sentiments helps the governments of states to prevent disintegration and to mobilize their populations to oppose external aggressors. Each state has a different position in the hierarchy of states which makes up the contemporary world system. Nationalist sentiments help to legitimate the position of the core nations in this hierarchy.

3 Third, ethnicity is related to 'the complex hierarchy within the labour segment'. Although all workers are exploited, some are exploited more than others. The most exploited often belong to ethnic minority groups. Different groups in the workforce have to behave differently to perform their tasks effectively in order to produce surplus value for their employers. Ethnicity involves cultural difference, which leads to different types of socialization in households belonging to different ethnic groups. These differences in socialization help to prepare workers from different ethnic groups for their different roles in capitalist economies.

Evaluation

Wallerstein's view that nationalism is a comparatively recent development is widely accepted. His views on racism have much in common with a number of Marxists. It is his views on ethnicity, however, which are perhaps the most implausible. He advances no evidence to show that members of different ethnic groups are socialized in their families to do different jobs in capitalist economies.

As we show elsewhere in this chapter, ethnic minorities in Britain are by no means confined to the lower reaches of the occupational structure (see pp. 286–7). While Wallerstein may be right to see the 'peoplehoods' of 'race' 'ethnicity' and 'nationality' as social constructions, some of his explanations as to how they develop are open to question.

David McCrone – *The Sociology of Nationalism*

In *The Sociology of Nationalism* (1998) David McCrone conducts a comprehensive review of sociological theories of nationalism. He finds that no one theory can account for the diverse forms that nationalism takes, but that a number of theories can contribute to the understanding of this phenomenon.

Civic and ethnic nationalism, state and nation

McCrone starts his analysis by distinguishing between civic nationalism and ethnic nationalism. In civic nationalism, nationalist sentiments are tied to belonging to a particular state. Thus in the USA many different ethnic groups share, to some degree, a sense of loyalty to the nation. It is their common citizenship that unites them rather than a common ethnic background. In other situations nationalism focuses more on ethnicity than on citizenship. For example, in the nationalism of the Serbs and Croats in the former Yugoslavia, it is a belief in a common ethnic origin which unites groups of people. However, McCrone admits that such a distinction can be criticized. Even in countries in which a civic concept of nationalism is dominant, ethnic groups sharing a common civic nationality may be hostile to one another. McCrone asks 'How is one to make sense of endemic racism against the "Other" in Western societies which profess overwhelmingly civic definitions of citizens'. An example would be racism directed against British Afro-Caribbeans and Asians by white British people. Ethnic pluralism can sometimes be at odds with civic nationalism.

McCrone also distinguishes between the nation and the state. Often they are seen as one and the same thing, as in the term nation-state, but this is not always the case. The state is essentially a political and administrative unit, but people may feel a sense of national identity which does not coincide with political boundaries. There are examples in Western societies of what McCrone calls 'stateless nations', where groups in particular regions seek greater autonomy or independent states. These include Scotland in the United Kingdom, Catalunya in Spain, and Quebec in Canada. Stateless nations need not necessarily have a strong ethnic identity. McCrone says that 'Scottishness is based upon living in a common territory', and not on a shared culture.

To McCrone the relationships between state and nation, territory and ethnicity are complex and consequently there can be no single theory of nation-alism. In order to make sense of this complexity McCrone broadly distinguishes four types of nation-alism. Each of these will now be discussed.

Nationalism and the development of the modern nation-state

This type of nationalism is related to the development of the nation-state in Western society. Examples of such states include the United Kingdom, France and the USA. This type of nation-state is generally seen as a product of modernity. The nation-state began to emerge with the decline of dominant religious thinking and a greater acceptance of secular authority. It is therefore often linked with the Enlightenment (see Chapter 15 for a description of the Enlightenment).

The emergence of the nation-state was also connected with the break-up of Empires, particularly the Austrian, Ottoman and Russian Empires. The territorial boundaries of nations came to demarcate the most important political units and, with these political divisions, nationalist sentiments became more important.

However different writers have provided a variety of explanations for the development of the Western nation-state. Some have seen its development as related to the growth of industrialism, others to the growth of capitalism. Some have argued that political leaders were important in promoting nationalist sentiment and creating the idea of a nation out of very little. On the other hand, some sociologists believe that existing ethnic divisions were important in providing a starting-point for the development of nation-states. McCrone argues that all these factors played some role in the development of the nation-

state. He accepts that economic changes played an important part, but is critical of those approaches that deny there were any ethnic or cultural factors involved. He believes that, where they existed, cultural and ethnic differences had to be highlighted by those who were trying to create nation-states. Ethnicity on its own was never enough to create a modern nation-state, but it could help. What was crucial was that ethnic nationalism, where it was important, was converted into a more civic form. McCrone says of nationalism:

> *the more implicit and embedded it is, the more powerful it can be. That is why what is called 'civic' nationalism is a much more powerful mobiliser in the long-term than its 'ethnic' variant.*
>
> McCrone, 1998, p. 171

Colonialism and nationalism

The second type of nationalism discussed by McCrone developed in colonies and post-colonial societies. Very often those opposed to colonial rule would appeal to a national identity in trying to mobilize opposition to colonial powers such as Britain and France. Anti-colonial movements often advocated and achieved secular states. However, with the economic failure of some of these states, nationalism in some post-colonial societies has become more associated with ethnicity and religion. People in many post-colonial societies have ambiguous identities, with nationality, religion and ethnicity all making claims on their loyalty. For example, in post-colonial Egypt people could think of themselves as Arab, Islamic or Egyptian. Different identities were in competition for people's allegiance. In countries like India and Algeria the nationalist movements which achieved independence made little appeal to religion or ethnicity. However, when they failed to deliver the 'economic, social and cultural liberation' that they promised, then secular liberation was 'outflanked by counter-risings which mobilised culture and religion'. A clear example is the overthrow of the secular Shah of Iran by the Islamic regime of Ayatollah Khomeini in 1979.

McCrone believes that a key component of post-colonial nationalism is what he calls 'the dialectic with the other'. Nationalists define their nation in terms of difference to somebody else, in this case the colonial power. The dialectical relationship between colonialism and post-colonialism can help explain the changing nature of nationalism. Although nationalism emerged in opposition to colonialism it often took the form of a kind of mirror image. While opposing colonialism and asserting the difference between the colony and the colonial power, it often took on the type of state structure and the ideology of the nation-state that had been introduced by the colonizer. Post-colonial states such as India adopted the 'Secularism, science and democracy' that were associated with colonialism. But other non-secular and non-scientific kinds of nationalism did not die out altogether. These have revived as the secular state – founded as a mirror image of colonialism – has failed to fulfil its promise.

Neo-nationalism

McCrone uses the term neo-nationalism to refer to nationalist independence movements in Western stateless societies such as the Basque country, Scotland and Quebec. He argues that this type of nationalism is hard to explain in terms of conventional theories. Most theories of Western nation-states assumed that the nineteenth century saw the successful establishment of distinct nations and that regional differences within nation-states would tend to disappear as time progressed.

Using the examples of Quebec, Catalunya and Scotland, McCrone argues that neo-nationalism develops when a set of circumstances coincide. It usually develops in areas with a strong civil society. (Civil society can be defined as the public life of a society as compared to the activities of the state and private life within households.) The key features of civil society are the economy and the family/domestic sphere. Neo-nationalism tends to develop in regions with strong economies rather than weak ones. It was noticeable that Scottish nationalism was given a boost by the discovery of North Sea oil. Neo-nationalism also tends to develop in areas where people have multiple national identities. Scots sometimes identify themselves as British, Catalans as Spanish and so on. McCrone comments that 'This plurality is a political resource which can be played in appropriate circumstances rather than a fixed characteristic.'

Neo-nationalism is normally based on relatively new political parties. There is usually no exact correspondence between support for such parties (for example, the Scottish National Party (SNP)) and independence. Some people who vote for such parties may not actually seek independence but may see the party as a way of gaining greater autonomy short of independence. This illustrates the ambiguity that is often present in such movements.

Finally, neo-nationalism tends to occur where the nation-states in which it develops are part of a larger supra-national organization such as the European Union or the North American Free Trade Association (NAFTA) (of which Canada is a member). Such organizations suggest that it is difficult to have a truly independent economy. If the British economy is closely integrated with the European economy, there seems less for Scotland to lose by becoming independent from the rest of Britain. An independent

Scotland within the EU appears to be a less risky proposition than a Scotland which simply goes it alone. Thus the closer links between societies involved in globalization actually create the space in which regional identities and independence movements can develop.

McCrone believes that neo-nationalism is largely civic rather than ethnic in nature. He denies that you can see neo-nationalism 'as a throwback to atavistic or ethnic forms of nationalism', or reduced 'to mere forms of pressure group politics'. Instead neo-nationalism must be seen as a 'multifaceted and adaptable ideology' which links issues of identity to issues of economic and cultural power.

Post-communist nationalism

The collapse of communism in the USSR and Eastern Europe led to major changes. Some states disappeared (for example, Yugoslavia and Czechoslovakia). Czechoslovakia was divided into the Czech Republic and Slovakia; East and West Germany were fused together; countries such as Poland, Latvia, Lithuania and Estonia regained their independence; and new states such as the Ukraine, Georgia and various central-Asian republics emerged out of what had been the Soviet Union. McCrone argues that there was a great deal of dissatisfaction with the communist regimes and nationalism became the focus of opposition to communism. A number of explanations have been suggested for why nationalism should be the focus.

One of the most common is what McCrone calls the deep freeze theory. This suggests that deep-seated, historic ethnic divisions were held in check by totalitarian communist regimes. When communism thawed out and opposition became possible, traditional rivalries between ethnic groups reappeared. An alternative theory suggests that politicians simply encouraged nationalist sentiment in order to secure popular support for their own leadership. For example, Slobodan Milosevic used the appeal of Serbian nationalism to increase his personal support. McCrone does not deny that both these theories have some merit but he believes that both are too simplistic. Instead he turns to the work of Roger Brubaker (1996) and argues that it provides the most satisfactory way of understanding post-communist nationalism.

Brubaker distinguishes three types of post-communist nationalism:

1 The nationalizing state is the form of nationalism in which a state, often a new one, tries to persuade its citizens to share a common identity. In Western Europe nationalizing states have been fairly successful in achieving a common identity based on citizenship, but not in Eastern Europe.

2 **National minorities** are groups who have a primary allegiance to another, often neighbouring, state. For example, there are significant groups of ethnic Hungarians in Romania and vice versa. National minorities are not so significant in Western Europe.

3 **National homelands** are the territories with which people who claim particular nationalistic ethnicities identify. Thus Romania is the national homeland for ethnic Romanians in Hungary.

Since there is rarely a perfect fit between nationalizing minorities, nationalizing states and national homelands in the former communist countries there is a lot of potential for nationalistic conflict and for politicians to emphasize or exploit national identities. This is particularly true of territories that used to be part of the Soviet Union. The Soviet Union officially classified people as belonging to different national minorities and so heightened a sense of national identity.

Having discussed Brubaker's analysis of nationalism, McCrone goes on to apply elements of it to a discussion of Yugoslavia. McCrone suggests that Yugoslavia failed to become established as a nationalizing state because too few people saw themselves as Yugoslavian. Members of the Communist Party, some of the young, and those from mixed parentage saw themselves as Yugoslavian, but most people did not. Furthermore, different areas of Yugoslavia corresponded reasonably closely with the national ethnic groups, Serbs and Croats. There was therefore a strong basis for establishing ethnic homelands with independent states.

The problem with Bosnia was that it had no dominant national ethnic group. The biggest group in the population (about 44 per cent) were Muslims, descendants of people who had converted to Islam when the area was part of the Ottoman Empire. Only a minority of ethnic Muslims actually practised Islam, but they had no ethnic allegiance to a Serbian or Croatian homeland. Bosnia-Hercegovina was a largely secular and pluralistic region with no ethnic basis for a nationalizing state. There was no strong sense of Bosnian citizenship. As McCrone says, this put the people of Bosnia-Hercegovina at a 'severe disadvantage when faced with enemies who aligned ethnicity, religion and citizenship in a much more potent and threatening way'. The consequence was a bloody civil war in which the people of Bosnia, especially the Muslims, were caught between the territorial ambitions of Serb and Croat nationalisms.

The future of nationalism

McCrone concludes that many early theorists of nationalism were quite wrong to believe that it would decline in importance. The ideology of nationalism, that people should have a nation-state to which they belong, has never been stronger. Other ideologies, such as socialism, have lost popularity while nationalism has become more popular. Nationalistic conflict remains possible in many parts of the world since only a minority of states are ethnically and culturally homogeneous. There are both stateless nations (where an ethnic group has no state of its own) and nationless states (where a territory is culturally heterogeneous). In some ways the power and importance of states have been undermined by globalization (see Chapter 9) and by supra-national bodies such as the European Union. However, nationalism has survived and prospered because it is a flexible, adaptable ideology. As societies undergo rapid change and there is more confusion and fluidity over identity (see below for a discussion of identity), nationalism can be an effective ideology for uniting groups of people. McCrone concludes:

> *Nationalist movements can, then, encapsulate cultural defence, the pursuit of political resources from the centre, as well as being vehicles for social identity in rapidly changing societies. It will not be possible to reduce any nationalism automatically to any one of these, but the rapidly increasing rate of social change makes it more rather than less likely as a potent vehicle of social protest.*
>
> McCrone, 1998, p. 182

Robin Cohen – British nationality and identity

Compared to countries in Eastern Europe and some other parts of the world Britain is a long-established state. Nevertheless Robin Cohen believes that what it means to be British is not clearcut (Cohen, 1994). He argues that there are a number of ways in which a British identity is ambiguous or unclear. His arguments illustrate how even in Western Europe the relationship between nationality and identity is far from straightforward.

Cohen discusses what he calls the fuzzy boundaries of being British. The idea of fuzzy boundaries originates from the idea of 'fuzzy logic' in mathematics. This is a method in which you proceed by trying to eliminate the uncertain edges of a problem to focus better on the problem itself. Similarly, Cohen believes, you can get to the core of what it means to be British by looking at the frontiers that divide Britons from others. These frontiers can be internal, such as the frontier between being British and being English, or external, such as the frontier between Britons and 'aliens'. Cohen identifies six frontiers:

1 The Celtic fringe. The Celtic fringe includes the Irish, Welsh and Scots. Despite the Act of Union between England and Scotland in 1707, Cohen believes that 'The Scots have always been regarded with an element of fear and not a little incomprehension by the English'. He believes that oil revenues have provided an important impetus towards independence in Scotland. The Welsh have a rather less strong sense of independent identity than the Scots. They would find it more difficult to prosper with economic independence and have less history as an independent nation. Nevertheless the Welsh language and events such as the Welsh National *Eisteddfod* provide some basis for a separate Welsh identity. Irish national consciousness is both much stronger and more problematic for England. Despite the strong Irish identity there are overlaps between being Irish and being English. Northern Ireland Unionists identify much more closely with England than Eire. Eire citizens can travel freely to the United Kingdom and vote in British elections. For the English the Celtic fringe is 'a familiar but inexplicit internal boundary'.

2 The dominions. A number of aspects of English and British identity are linked to the history of colonization. Large numbers of white British people settled in dominions such as Canada, New Zealand, Australia, South Africa and Rhodesia. All of these countries have achieved independence and, at least at some point in their history, have been ruled by the white settlers from Britain. Cohen believes that in all these countries a British identity became dominant. Many citizens of the countries managed to retain British passports, and their legal and education systems have usually retained close links with the corresponding British systems. White citizens of these countries are sometimes regarded as the 'kith and kin' of white British citizens. However, as Cohen points out, the association of British with white has become increasingly problematic. Although British immigration law and citizenship rules were influenced by a racist desire to maintain a white British identity (see pp. 211–13), they have not succeeded in maintaining what Cohen calls 'the myth of a racially exclusive British identity'. Even for racists, it is increasingly difficult to portray British identity in exclusively white terms. Despite independence, and the demise of an exclusively white British identity, some white communities in former colonies try to cling on to a British, and often a specifically English, identity.

3 Empire and Commonwealth. Cohen believes that the British Empire was about more than military conquest and political domination of other countries. It was also concerned with an attempt 'to establish a cultural and national superiority of worldwide proportions: an empire where, truly, the sun never set'. Despite independence, many former colonies have a legacy of colonization. Some of their institutions still follow the model established by the colonial power. The Indian civil service is one

example. Furthermore, the Commonwealth maintains institutional links between former colonies and the 'motherland'. Such connections have led to some former colonies, for example in the West Indies, retaining an element of British identity. Cohen argues, though, that British political leaders, particularly Margaret Thatcher, have attached little importance to the Commonwealth. On the other hand it continues to remain an important institution in relation to the monarchy.

4 The Atlantic connection. If Margaret Thatcher was unenthusiastic about the Commonwealth, she put much more emphasis on the so-called 'special relationship' between Britain and the USA. There are, of course, historical connections between Britain and the USA. Not only was America a British colony, but there are also large numbers of Americans descended from British emigrants. Although the USA is very culturally diverse, WASP (White Anglo-Saxon Protestant) culture remains the most influential of its cultures. Furthermore, English remains the dominant language in the USA. Cohen therefore concludes that 'a cousin-hood between the British and many Americans remains: a fuzzy frontier somewhere between a self-hood and an other-hood'.

5 Britain and Europe. Britain does not have the same linguistic links with Europe as it has with the USA. However, through the European Union, Britain's political ties with Europe are closer than those with the USA. While older British people tend to be resistant to the idea of closer European integration, this is not the case with the young. Cohen claims that:

the slow drip-feed of European integration is influencing the younger generation – who increasingly study, work, travel and holiday on the continent and who forget their kith and kin abroad, deride the British Empire and neglect the idealistic notion of a multiracial Commonwealth.

Cohen, 1994, p. 32

There is therefore something of a movement towards a more European identity for some young Britons.

6 Aliens. The frontier between the British and 'aliens' is less fuzzy than other frontiers. The maintenance of a British identity essentially rests upon defining some groups as 'others', people who do not belong, who have no claims to be British. Defining the alien involves 'a distinction between the self (the acceptable, the insider), and who the other (the stranger, the outsider, the alien) is'. As the fuzzy boundaries show, though, this distinction is not clearcut and can change over time.

Evaluation

Cohen's work illustrates the ambiguity, complexity and changing nature of one national identity – British identity. Colonialism and decolonization, migration, travel and political change have affected nearly all parts of the globe. It seems likely that the boundaries of national identity are fuzzy in many other countries apart from Britain. Nationalism is sometimes used as an ideology to try to remove some of the fuzziness. Issues of identity have become increasingly important in contemporary sociology and in the study of 'race', ethnicity and nationality in particular. Recent theories have suggested that identities have changed with the emergence of 'new ethnicities'. These theories will now be examined.

New ethnicities and identities

Cohen's work on the complexities of British and English identities has some similarities with recent work examining ethnic identities. Unlike traditional studies of ethnicities, this new approach emphasizes the changing nature of ethnic identities, and with these changes the creation of new ethnicities. The idea of new ethnicities has a good deal in common with some of Paul Gilroy's work (see pp. 260–2) but it tends to put less emphasis on racism and more on issues to do with identity. In this respect it is close to some postmodern theories which will be examined shortly (see pp. 279–82).

Stuart Hall – new ethnicities

Stuart Hall first used the term new ethnicities in an article originally published in 1989 (Hall, 1996). He relates the concept to developments in black cultural politics, particularly in Britain. In an earlier phase of black cultural politics, the term 'black' was used to refer to all people of Asian, Afro-Caribbean and African origin. It was used as a 'way of referencing the common experience of racism and marginalization in Britain and came to provide the organizing category of a new politics of resistance'. The experiences and interests shared by these black groups were seen as more significant than the cultural and other differences that divided them. The cultural politics resulting from this process involved challenging the negative representations of black people common in white British culture. Stereotypes of black people could be challenged in the printed media, TV, art, music and so on. To facilitate this challenge black people struggled to gain access to these media, which were dominated by whites.

The new cultural politics

By 1989 Hall believed that a new era in black cultural politics was emerging. Although the old struggles had been far from won and were continuing, new trends were developing alongside the old cultural politics. This change involved the 'end of the innocent notion of the essential black subject'. Hall explains that this involved 'the recognition of the extraordinary diversity of subjective positions, social experiences and cultural identities which compose the category "black"'. In other words, there was an increased awareness of differences between groups. These differences could be religious, class-based, ethnic, age-related, religious, to do with gender and sexuality, and so on. Hall puts particular emphasis on class, sexuality, gender and ethnicity. He argues that the representation of black people is increasingly focused on black people from a particular ethnic group, with a particular sexual preference, from a specific class background and for whom their masculinity or sexuality is significant. The new cultural politics tends to celebrate difference rather than ignoring it. He uses the example of the film *My Beautiful Laundrette* in which gender differences, class differences, ethnic differences and differences between gay and heterosexual people in an Asian community are featured strongly.

Films such as *My Beautiful Laundrette* challenge the idea that the major cultural division in society is between true Britons, who are white, and others. By showing the diversity of English people it challenges 'the exclusive and aggressive form of English identity [which] is one of the core characteristics of British racism today'. The new cultural politics of ethnicity shows that everybody speaks from a particular position in terms of their ethnicity and other characteristics. However, they are not confined to only speaking from that position. Asian film-makers, for example, need not just make Asian films for Asian audiences. Their films can explore issues other than those which are confined to ethnicity, and which are of interest to others beyond their own ethnic group.

The idea of new ethnicities therefore suggests that differences within ethnic groups provide the basis for a plurality of ethnic identities. In doing so they weaken the importance of the divisions between black/white, and show that all ethnic groups are internally differentiated. These differences (for example, differences in sexuality) cross-cut ethnicity and make people from different ethnic groups more aware of what they might have in common. At the same time they show the diversity of British people and challenge predominant conceptions of what it means to be British. Hall also briefly acknowledges that new ethnicities might involve novel forms of 'hybridization' and 'cut and mix'. Elements from different ethnic cultures might be combined to develop novel ethnic identities. This idea of hybridization is explored in greater detail in a later article which also tries to place the emergence of new ethnicities in a global context.

Stuart Hall – 'Our mongrel selves'

Capitalism and nationalism

In his article 'Our mongrel selves' (1992), Hall examines the relationship between capitalism, nationalism, ethnicity and identity. He argues that capitalism has had contradictory effects: it created the nation-state and with it nationalism, but in recent times capitalism has also promoted forces which have undermined national cultures. On the one hand, the global nature of the world has produced transnational imperatives. On the other hand, 'globalization seems to have led to a strengthening of "local" allegiances and identities'.

In Western Europe a number of countries have seen the development of movements calling for greater degrees of regional autonomy or complete independence; in Eastern Europe and the former USSR there has been 'a revival of ethnic nationalisms among peoples submerged for decades within the supra-nationalism of the Soviet sphere of influence'. Political changes such as the collapse of Soviet communism and the process of globalization have weakened nation-states and their attempts to impose a single all-embracing culture on diverse ethnic groups within their boundaries. The ethnic groups have taken advantage of the situation to reassert their distinctive identities.

To Hall, attempts to promote nationalism in the modern world can be very dangerous. Most modern nation-states 'are inextricably multicultural – mixed ethnically, religiously, culturally and linguistically'. When groups within the boundaries of a state assert their rights and celebrate their differences, it can lead to violent conflict. In the former Yugoslavia this has led to 'ethnic cleansing' – attempts to make whole areas 'ethnically pure' by killing or driving out members of other ethnic groups. In some states attempts to impose a single national culture on diverse groups lead to the development 'of an openly racist far right'. In France the Front National calls for the 'repatriation' of so-called 'immigrants', as do organizations such as the British National Party. In Germany, Turkish workers have been attacked and killed by right-wing nationalists.

However, Hall does not see nationalism as bad in itself. It has also been used by groups seeking independence from colonial powers which have oppressed them. Nationalism 'isn't necessarily either a reactionary or progressive force', it can be either.

Identity

According to Hall, the forces outlined above are causing people to have a confused sense of identity: a mixed-up view of who they are. The ethnic and cultural diversity of most countries, different nation-

alisms and the process of globalization, all contribute to the confusion. Many people have a number of identities simultaneously and may act and think in terms of belonging to a whole variety of groups. Hall says:

> *Modern people of all sorts and conditions, it seems to me, have had, as a condition of survival, to be members, simultaneously, of several overlapping 'imagined communities'; and the negotiations across and between these complex borderlines are characteristic of modernity itself.*

Hall, 1992

The novelist Salman Rushdie provides a good example of identity confusion. Born in Asia and brought up a Muslim, he is a British citizen who was condemned to death by the Ayatollah Khomeini of Iran for the allegedly anti-Islamic nature of his novel *The Satanic Verses*. Hall quotes Rushdie arguing that '*The Satanic Verses* celebrates hybridity, impurity, intermingling', and describing how mass migration has led to the creation of 'our mongrel selves'. Rushdie sees himself as representing a diverse mix of national, racial, religious, cultural and political identities.

Hall gives a graphic example of people's multiple identities, illustrating how issues of gender, politics and class can add to the confusion created by racial, ethnic and national differences. In 1991 the American president, George Bush, nominated a black conservative judge, Clarence Thomas, for the Supreme Court. A former colleague of Thomas, Anita Hill, then accused him of sexually harassing and propositioning her. People took different sides in the ensuing arguments according to their sense of identity. Hall says:

> *Some blacks supported Thomas on racial grounds; others opposed him on sexual grounds. Black women were divided, depending on whether their 'identities' as blacks or as women prevailed. Black men were also divided depending on whether their sexism overrode their liberalism. White men were divided, depending not only on their politics, but also on how they identified themselves with respect to racism and sexism. White conservative women supported Thomas, not only on political grounds, but also because of their opposition to feminism. White feminists, often liberal on race, opposed Thomas on sexual grounds. And because judge Thomas is a member of the judicial elite and Anita Hall, at the time of the alleged incident, was a junior employee, there were issues of social class position at work in these arguments too.*

Quoted in Pilkington, 1993, p. 63

Hall concludes that nationalism and ethnic absolutism are major threats to the modern world. With such pluralism in most parts of the world, tolerance of human diversity is essential if humans are to live together in anything approaching harmony. He says 'The capacity to live with difference is, in my view, the coming question of the 21st century.' In general terms new ethnicities facilitate living with difference by making ethnic absolutism and aggressive nationalism seem redundant. If there is no essential difference between different nationalities and ethnicities, if differences within ethnicities and nationalities are as important as differences between them, if many people have hybrid identities, then hatred and violence between groups become less likely.

Evaluation of Hall

Hall's influential work identifies important cultural changes in contemporary societies. However, aspects of it have been questioned. Solomos and Back argue that views such as those of Hall do not fully analyse 'the creation of new essentialisms on the basis of religion, ethnicity or race' (Solomos and Back, 1996). Hall fails to explain new ways in which people make absolute distinctions between different groups. These cannot all be attributed to a revival of nationalism brought about by global change. They might actually emerge out of the sorts of processes which create new ethnicities. Far from liberating people from their prejudices, they may encourage people to reassert them. Bhatt (1994, quoted in Solomos and Back, 1996) believes that intolerant and fundamentalist beliefs sometimes develop in minorities because they feel threatened by the sorts of processes outlined by Hall. They fear that their cultural distinctiveness will disappear as elements of other cultures become incorporated into their own. They may act to defend their own culture in ways that seem threatening and intolerant to people from other cultural traditions. A further criticism of Hall is that he tends to support his arguments with evidence from the work of particular black film-makers, artists, etc. Solomos and Back comment that Hall fails to show that 'new ethnicities' are important outside this context. The same, however, cannot be said of those who have conducted the sorts of empirical studies we will now examine.

Tariq Modood – new ethnicities and identities

Interview research

Tariq Modood and colleagues have conducted detailed empirical studies of ethnicity and identity in Britain (Modood, Beishon and Virdee, 1994 and Modood, 1997). In *Changing Ethnic Identities* Modood, Beishon and Virdee report on research involving semi-structured and group interviews with 74 British people of Caribbean or South Asian origin. The

interviews were conducted in 1993 and examined issues such as family life, religious belief and identity. Modood et al. argued that previous research in this area had tended to explain identity either in terms of a cultural affiliation to a particular ethnic group, or in terms of a political reaction to racism. Modood *et al.* believe that both ethnic origin and reactions to racism are important in forming identities but neither on its own is sufficient to explain the development of identities.

In their study Modood *et al.* found a wide variety of identities amongst the British. There were considerable differences between such aspects of identity as the importance attached to religion, to ethnic origin, and to being British. Amongst some, hybrid identities such as black-British and Asian-British were developing. Thus Modood *et al.* broadly accept the arguments of writers such as Stuart Hall that new ethnicities are beginning to emerge.

Amongst Caribbeans, most thought of themselves as Black. First generation British Caribbeans (that is, those born in the Caribbean) were most likely to describe themselves as West Indian, although a large minority used the term Black. A Black identity was most common amongst the second generation (who were born in Britain) but significant minorities preferred terms such as Black British. They tended to prefer describing themselves as Afro-Caribbean rather than as West Indian, and very few of the second generation thought the Caribbean island from which their parents had emigrated particularly significant. Many British Caribbeans felt there was considerable similarity between British and Caribbean culture. They tended to think Caribbean culture had less in common with South Asian culture than it had with British culture. Nevertheless, some second generation Caribbeans felt commonality with South Asians, based upon a common experience of racism. In this case they tended to see Black as a term covering both Caribbeans and South Asians. Some also thought that there were new fusions being created between Caribbean, Asian and/or white youth culture.

A number of Caribbeans pointed out that the way they thought of themselves varied from situation to situation. For example, for the first generation, island labels (for example, Jamaican or Antiguan) could be significant when mixing with others of Caribbean origin. One female respondent said she used to think of herself as Antiguan until she visited Antigua and people called her 'English girl'. Some of those interviewed commented that they felt British, but that this could be undermined by the experience of racism. One said 'We try to live British, but are not accepted as British'; another said 'If you are black they do not accept you as British even if we are here for another 100 years. White people don't see me as being British, I am always made conscious of that.' For one girl it was difficult to feel British because she felt excluded from many of the symbols and signs representing Britishness. She said 'Rule Britannia, Britannia rules the waves. Britons never, never, never will be slaves. Bull-shit, we were the slaves.' Nevertheless, many of those who were born in Britain did feel British even though they felt they were not fully accepted as such by some or all white people. Others rejected British identity in favour of an alternative.

Amongst South Asians 'the first generation, identified with their specific ethnic or religious identity rather than with a pan-Asian ethnicity of British nationality'. However, there were variations between groups. Most Punjabi Sikhs thought of themselves as Indian rather than as Sikh. Amongst other groups there was a wide range of identifications based on religion (Hindu or Muslim), region (for example, Gujarati or Punjabi), or nationality (Indian, Pakistani, or Bangladeshi). A few first-generation Pakistanis used hybrid terms such as Pakistani-British, but such terms were much more common in the second generation. Some of the second generation, though, simply saw themselves as 'Asian' and a small number as 'black'. This last group tended to have Caribbean friends with whom many shared a common interest in music. Some other young Asians thought there were wide cultural differences between themselves and Caribbeans.

Overall Modood *et al.* found a major difference between the first and second generations of South Asians. Most of the first generation 'had a strong sense of belonging to the society in which they were brought up and saw themselves as law-abiding, hard-working citizens at peace with British society but culturally distinct from it'. Only a few of the first generation took an active interest in developing a more British identity. In the second generation some:

> *saw themselves in terms of a bi-culturalism but the majority felt they were culturally more British than anything else. Few, however, felt they could call themselves British in an unproblematic way. By thinking of Britishness in terms of 'whiteness', backed up by violence, racial discrimination, harassment, abusive jokes and cultural intolerance, some white people made it very difficult for non-whites to identify with Britain in a positive way.*
>
> Modood *et al.*, 1994, p. 119

Despite this, those who had adopted a bi-cultural identity, such as British-Asian, managed to be positive about the British element of their identity while wishing to retain religious or ethnic elements of their identity as well.

Survey research

In later research, Modood (1997) analysed data from the 1994 PSI survey on ethnic minorities in Britain (see p. 216 for further details of this study). This provided statistical data on a large representative sample of ethnic minorities. Some of the main findings are summarized in Table 4.14. In the table the figures refer to rounded multiples of 10 per cent (thus 2 means approximately 20 per cent, 8 means approximately 80 per cent and so on).

The table shows that a large majority of all the groups thought of themselves as belonging to an ethnic minority. However, only a minority in all the groups, apart from the Chinese, did not think of themselves as British. Modood comments that ethnic identity, as revealed in this table, is more to do with 'whom one belongs with' than it is to do with people's actual behaviour. The highest scores tend to refer to membership (for example, membership of a religion) than to routine participation in activities like wearing ethnic clothes or speaking an ethnic minority language. Distinctive cultural practices were found to be more common amongst Caribbeans than South Asians. Amongst South Asians, Pakistanis and Bangladeshis were more likely to have distinctive, ethnically based cultural practices than Indians and African Asians. For example, they were more likely to see religion as very important, to wear Asian clothes, and to prefer schools of their own religion.

Modood *et al.* also examined changes between generations. Amongst South Asians generally, there was a progressive decline in cultural distinctiveness in the younger generation. Amongst Caribbeans it was more complex. For example, nearly 50 per cent of Caribbeans aged 35–49 did not think of themselves as British, yet a substantial minority (about one in six) of Caribbeans born in Britain did not even identify themselves as belonging to an Afro-Caribbean ethnic group. Amongst Asians diversity of identity was most evident between generations; amongst Caribbeans there was great diversity within generations as well as between them.

Conclusions

Modood and colleagues concluded that ethnic identity:

> *far from being some primordial stamp upon an individual, is a plastic and changing badge of membership. Ethnic identity is a product of a number of forces: social exclusion and stigma and political resistance to them, distinctive cultural and religious heritages as well as new forms of culture, communal and familial loyalties, marriage practices and coalitions of interests and so on.*
>
> Modood *et al.*, 1994, p. 119

Table 4.14 Ethnicity as 'difference': an overview

	Caribbean	Indian	African Asian	Pakistani	Bangladeshi	Chinese
Thinks of self as member of ethnic group	8	9	9	9	9	9
Has a religion other than one of the historic Christian churches	1	9	10	10	10	3
Women sometimes wear 'ethnic' clothes/ adornments (figures in parentheses refer to those who usually do)	3 (1)	9 (5)	9 (3)	10 (8)	10 (9)	-
Men sometimes wear 'ethnic' clothes/ adornments (figures in parentheses refer to those who usually do)	1 (-)	6 (1)	5 (-)	9 (1)	8 (1)	-
Uses a language other than English	2	9	9	10	10	8
Has visited country of origin of family in last 5 years	4	5	4	6	4	6
Parents chose one's spouse (16–34-year-olds only)	-	2	2	6	5	-
Would like quarter or more of pupils at child's school to be from own ethnic group	5	3	3	5	4	1
Would mind if a close relative were to marry a white person	1	4	3	5	4	1
Does not think of oneself as British	4	4	3	4	4	6

T. Modood (1997) 'Culture and Identity', in Modood *et al.* (1997) *Ethnic Minorities In Britain*, PSI, London.

They found an 'emerging and evolving plurality' of ethnicities, old and new. Modood (1997) does not believe that the changes are simply a watering-down of ethnic cultures and identities in a British context. While certain cultural practices (for example, religious practices or wearing ethnic clothes) might be less important for the second generation than the first, ethnic identities had become politicized rather than being taken for granted. Such identities are no longer based primarily around the private sphere of family life, but are more in the public sphere. The second generation is generally more willing than the first to campaign for political change and to assert its ethnic identity in public with pride. At the same time more of the younger generation than the old identify themselves as being at least partly British. New ethnicities have a little less to do with culture than traditional ethnicities and more to do with identity and politics. They are less distinctive and more likely to take on hybrid forms.

Les Back – new ethnicities and urban culture

Between 1985 and 1989 Les Back conducted ethnographic research into two council estates (which he calls 'Riverview' and 'Southgate') in south London

(Back, 1996). Riverview is a predominantly white area whereas Southgate is more ethnically mixed. Back worked as a youth worker in these areas, allowing him to do participant observation, but he also conducted semi-structured interviews with individuals and group interviews. His research examined both racism and the development of new ethnicities.

He found that in both Riverview and Southgate people thought about race and racism in relation to communities. Each area developed its own semantic system, or way of talking about race, which contained this community element.

In Riverview the main semantic system related to the idea of 'white flight'. This articulated the idea that long-established white residents were being forced to move out because the area was beginning to be 'swamped' by ethnic minority groups. As a consequence, the area was losing its sense of identity. The minorities in question were mainly black people and Vietnamese refugees. Alongside the white flight semantic system, there was a less widespread way of thinking about the area which saw it as 'a harmonious multi-ethnic district where belonging was determined by commitment to the area'.

In Southgate the dominant semantic system was what Back calls an 'our area system'. Both white and black people saw the area as harmonious. They recognized that racism existed, but saw it as absent from and irrelevant to their community. Alongside this a 'black community discourse' existed. This was a way of talking about the community which saw it as one in which black people had been able to organize and defend themselves from racism. This was accepted as legitimate by most white residents, but a few were more racist and did see the area in terms of 'white flight'.

Back therefore found that in both areas identities were related to communities as well as to ethnicity, age, etc. Amongst young people, a type of 'neighbourhood nationalism' was common. They felt solidarity towards, and shared a common identity with, other people from the area. Furthermore, in Southgate in particular a new type of hybrid black/white ethnicity was developing amongst young people. There were 'profound and vigorously syncretic cultural dialogues' in which white people stopped associating being white with being English. Some white youths even expressed a desire to be black. This did not refer to skin colour, but rather to black youth cultures to which the young white people were very attracted. This led to a remarkable situation in which black and white youths developed something of a shared identity based on mixed ethnicity. This can be illustrated with examples from Back's study.

Tony, who was a 17-year-old white male, had learnt to talk in the same way as local black people. Debbie, a white female, mainly had black friends. Like Tony, she had adopted black ways of talking and had her hair done in black styles. Mark, a white boy who was 15, admired a local reggae sound system called Saxon Studio. He too had adopted black ways of talking, especially Caribbean Creole dialects. All rejected racism. However, they did acknowledge that there were limits to them becoming black. They were aware that their skin colour was different from that of their black friends, and that they did not face the same racism as black people did. In a sense they were struggling to establish an identity which acknowledged their own whiteness, but which also acknowledged their connections to black culture and their opposition to white racism. Pauline, who was 16, said:

> I mean I don't see myself as white in the same way as the National Front people do, and I don't see myself as black – I mean white in the same way as my friends see themselves as black. I suppose I'm an English girl from London – well Southgate.
>
> Back, 1996, p. 142

Many of the black people in the study identified with their local area. They accepted that they were British, and felt they had much in common with local white youths. However, being British was seen largely as a statement of citizenship. They distanced themselves from an English identity, associating England with cultures that had little relevance to them.

Racism had not disappeared from either area. In Riverview, with its dominant white flight semantic system, racism was common amongst adult whites. Racist comments were sometimes used by white youths even against black friends, although they would claim that their comments were not to be taken seriously. However, racism was much stronger against the Vietnamese in the area. While white youths saw blacks as insiders who were part of the local community, the Vietnamese were seen as outsiders. They were seen as unwilling to mix with the locals and as possessing a culture that set them apart. Even amongst the young, then, the development of new ethnicities did not extend to the Vietnamese.

In Southgate there was very little racism amongst the young. Nevertheless, black youths did believe that white adults were fearful of them. They also believed that some white adults had stereotypical views of blacks, seeing them as 'over-emotional' or as 'highly sexed'.

Back concludes that new types of ethnicity are developing in some areas of Britain. They are not based simply on cultural traditions, nor are they simply a reaction to racism. He calls them liminal cultures. Liminality 'refers to a state of separation from the mundane aspects of life'. In social spaces away from mundane racism, boundaries of race and ethnicity become irrelevant and new 'racially and ethnically inclusive cultural forms' develop. However, these 'liminal and mixed cultures' tend to be unstable. They can only exist in certain conditions within certain communities and generally do not spread outside these limits and boundaries. Once people move outside the immediate locality it becomes more difficult to identify with and act according to a mixed black/white culture. Nevertheless, Back believes that such cultures can pose an important challenge to the idea that there is an absolute cultural divide between different ethnic groups. Liminal cultures show that cultural barriers are not insurmountable.

New ethnicities – conclusion

The main strength of studies of new ethnicities such as those of Modood and Back is that they try to combine insights from the study of identity, racism, ethnicity and community. They acknowledge that identities are shaped by the experience of racism, the cultural heritage of ethnic groups, and experience in local communities. The emphasis on diverse identity in much of the work on new ethnicities does run the risk of implying that people are free to choose whatever identity they wish. However, Modood and Back both acknowledge that such choices are limited and shaped by racism. Thus Back's optimism about the breakdown of racism in some multi-ethnic localities is tempered by his pessimism about the chances of such relationships extending into wider social spaces. Ethnic harmony is more difficult to achieve in society as a whole.

The study of new ethnicities succeeds in demonstrating some of the complexities of identity in contemporary societies. However, it does perhaps exaggerate the extent to which hybrid ethnic identities are new. For example, Jewish, Irish and other ethnic groups have long-established British communities which might be seen as involving hybrid ethnicities and identities. As they lack a historical perspective, the studies we have looked at cannot show that hybrid ethnicities are a genuinely novel phenomenon. However, some sociologists certainly believe that fundamental changes have taken place in the nature of ethnicity and identity. Many who support such beliefs have been strongly influenced by postmodernism.

Modernity, postmodernity, racism, ethnicity and identity

A number of sociologists have attacked modernity for causing racism. Far from seeing the Enlightenment belief in rationality as likely to undermine racist beliefs, they have argued that modernity has actually encouraged racism. Postmodern and post-structural theorists have also argued that racism arises out of a modern tendency to see the world in terms of binary oppositions, or pairs of opposites. Western modernity has contrasted itself with 'others' who are taken to be very different. Out of this process racism develops.

A number of advocates of post-structural and postmodern theories argue that traditional, modern sociology has tended to work with categories (such as 'race', ethnicity and nation) which are too rigid and inflexible to deal with a complicated contemporary world. They argue that postmodern analysis can break down these simplistic ways of thinking about issues and substitute new perspectives. It is claimed that these perspectives are more suited to understanding a world in which people have complicated, multiple and ambiguous identities. These approaches would agree that 'new ethnicities' are developing, but they go further than writers like Modood and Back, arguing that such changes should lead to whole new ways of thinking about racism and ethnicity.

Zygmunt Bauman – Modernity and the Holocaust

How modernity caused the Holocaust

In *Modernity and the Holocaust* (1989), Zygmunt Bauman argues that the Holocaust was a product of modernity. The mass extermination of Jews (and others) in Nazi Germany was not simply the result of anti-Semitism, an illogical racism directed against Jews. Rather the Holocaust was a product of the central features of modernity. Bauman says:

The truth is that every 'ingredient' of the Holocaust – all those many things that rendered it possible – was normal ... in the sense of being fully in keeping with everything we know about our civilization, its guiding spirit, its priorities ... of the proper ways to pursue human happiness together with a perfect society.

Bauman, 1989, p. 8

The links between modernity and the Holocaust take a number of forms:

1 The Holocaust was a product of modern, bureaucratic rationality (see Chapter 15 for a discussion of bureaucracy). The German bureaucracy (particularly the SS) was charged with the task of removing Jews from Germany. In keeping with the principles of modern bureaucracy, the people involved did not question the aims given to them by their political masters. They simply sought the most technically efficient means to achieve the objective. Moving Jews to Poland caused administrative problems for those Germans who had to govern the annexed territory. Another proposal was to send Jews to Madagascar, a colony of defeated France. However, this proved impractical as well. The distances involved and British naval capabilities meant that millions of Jews could not easily be sent there. Mass extermination was adopted simply because it was the most technically efficient means of getting rid of the Jewish presence in Germany. Bauman says 'The "Final Solution" did not clash at any stage with the rational pursuit of efficient, optimal goal-implementation. On the contrary, *it arose out of a genuinely rational concern, and it was generated by bureaucracy true to its form and purpose.*' Bureaucratic organization can be used to serve any end, and the modern ethos that bureaucrats should not question the purpose of their organization precludes them from taking steps to prevent events such as the Holocaust.

2 Evidence from Holocaust survivors suggests that most members of the SS responsible for carrying out the Holocaust did not appear to be psychologically disturbed sadists. They appeared to be relatively normal individuals. However, they were able to participate in such inhuman acts because they were authorized to do so by their superiors and because

the killing was routinized. They subjected themselves to the discipline of the organizations to which they belonged. Accepting organizational discipline is another feature of rational organization in modernity. The honour of civil servants depends upon their ability to follow the orders of their political masters, even if they disagree with those orders. Furthermore, modern, rational organization tends to make the consequences of individual actions less obvious. The part played by each member of a bureaucratic system may seem distant from the final consequences. Thus an official who designated people as 'non Aryan' in Nazi Germany would be unlikely to think of himself or herself as responsible for mass murder. Even the actual killing was sanitized by the use of gas chambers. Earlier methods had included machine-gunning victims. However, this was both inefficient and made the inhumanity of what was going on more obvious to the perpetrators. Gas chambers minimized such difficulties.

3 Modernity is based upon the existence of nation-states with clearcut boundaries. Jews were regarded as 'foreigners within' in European states. Bauman claims that 'in pre-modern Europe the peculiar flavour of Jewish *otherness* did not on the whole prevent their accommodation into the prevailing social order'. Premodern societies were divided by estates or castes, and Jews were just one more different group. Modern nation-states emphasize the homogeneity of the nation in order to foster nationalist sentiment. Their desire to maintain boundaries involves excluding alien others. This produces the conditions in which racism can thrive.

4 From the Enlightenment onwards, modern thinking has maintained that human societies can progress through the application of rational, scientific knowledge in planning society. The anti-Semitism that was expressed in an extreme form in the Holocaust was backed up by German scientists who could supposedly prove the inferiority of Jews. The mass extermination of Jews was justified on the grounds that it would improve German society. Such projects to transform society are typically modern and would not be considered in premodern societies which lacked such a sense of progress.

Conclusion

Bauman concludes that the possibility of the Holocaust was created by modernity. He does not deny that modernity has had its benefits, but he does believe that it created the conditions in which racism can thrive. This is particularly because modernity detaches morality from rationality and technical efficiency. In later work Bauman goes on to discuss postmodernity (Bauman, 1992). He argues that in postmodernity authority becomes dispersed amongst different groups of experts and is not centralized in the hands of the state. This returns more moral responsibility to the individual, who can now at least choose which authority to take notice of. Bauman therefore believes that postmodernity reduces the chances of events such as the Holocaust occurring. It opens up more opportunity for challenges to racism and more likelihood of the tolerance of diversity. Like postmodern theorists such as Lyotard (see Chapter 15), Bauman associates postmodernism with the acceptance of pluralism and the rejection of harmful attempts to direct the development of society.

Davis Goldberg – Racist Cultures

In his book Racist Cultures (1993), Davis Goldberg follows Bauman in relating racism to modernity. However, Goldberg does not focus on the Holocaust but looks more broadly at the development of racisms.

Premodern and modern societies

Goldberg argues that racism did not exist in premodern societies. For example, in classical Greece, slaves and barbarians were the victims of exclusion and discrimination. However, they were not differentiated from other people in terms of race but were simply seen as politically different. Similarly, he believes that people were not seen in racial terms in medieval Europe. To Goldberg the term 'race' only began to be used in the fifteenth century and only became important with the development of modernity.

Goldberg defines modernity as developing in the West from the sixteenth century onwards. He sees the 'modern project' as 'a broad sweep of socio-intellectual traditions', including:

> the commodification and capital accumulation of a market-based society, the legal formation of private property and systems of contract, the moral and political conception of rational self-interested subjects, and the increasing replacement of God and religious doctrine by reason and nature as the final arbiters of justificatory appeal.
>
> Goldberg, 1993, p. 3

These changes involved fundamental shifts in what Goldberg calls the conceptual order. The conceptual order was concerned with the way people thought about things, and in particular how they thought about their own identity in relation to others. Individuals no longer thought of themselves as the subjects of God, but, instead, as rational, independent individuals subject only to reason. Individuals developed a strong sense of themselves as possessing a cohesive identity. This sense of identity developed out of liberalism. This was because liberalism:

is committed to individualism for it takes as basic the moral, political and legal claims of the individual over and against those of the collective. It seeks foundations in universal principles applicable to all human beings or rational agents in virtue of their humanity or rationality.

Goldberg, 1993, p. 5

These principles would seem to be ill-suited to encouraging racism. If all people are united by reason, then there is little justification for treating them differently by virtue of their 'race'. Furthermore, liberalism is committed to the idea of progress through planned improvements in society, and it also 'takes itself to be committed to equality'. Goldberg adds that 'From the liberal point of view, particular differences between individuals have no bearing on their moral value, and by extension should make no difference concerning the legal or political status of individuals.'

Despite all this, Goldberg finds that many prominent liberal thinkers have been racist. The examples he cites include the philosophers David Hume and John Stuart Mill and the nineteenth-century British politician Benjamin Disraeli. Paradoxically, modernity and liberalism give rise to racism when, on the surface, it appears that they should do just the opposite. How does Goldberg explain this?

Liberals and racism

Goldberg argues that the emphasis on the rationality of humanity implied a comparison with the non-rational. The non-rational could be found both in premodern thought and in non-Western societies. Along with the development of colonialism, Western, rational liberals began to categorize other groups of humans as less rational or non-rational. Goldberg comments that the 'concept of race has served, and silently continues to serve, as a boundary constraint upon the applicability of moral principles'. Modern liberal beliefs in the morality of equality and liberty did not extend to those who were conquered, and in some cases enslaved, by the colonial powers such as Spain, France, Portugal and Britain. Goldberg says 'The rational, hence autonomous and equal subjects of the Enlightenment project turn out, perhaps unsurprisingly, to be exclusively white, European and bourgeois.'

Along with modernity's belief in rationality went scientific investigations based upon empiricism. Empiricism claims that it is possible to classify the world by carrying out detailed observations, and as such it has much in common with positivism (see Chapter 14 for a discussion of positivism). Empirical observations of humans formed the basis for classi-

fying them into different races. Specialized disciplines emerged which lent scientific respectability to racism. Biology and anthropology were combined to make claims that biological differences between groups of humans formed the basis for differences in culture. The supposedly primitive and non-rational cultures of some societies were taken as evidence of biological inferiority.

The dominant liberal ideas of modernity did see humans as having rights. For example, in the eighteenth century the French and American revolutions asserted the rights of American and French citizens. However, the belief in rights failed to protect non-whites from racism because those rights were seen as being limited to certain groups. Goldberg says:

The rights others as a matter of course enjoy are yet denied people of color because black, brown, red and yellow subjectivities continue to be disvalued; and the devaluation of these subjectivities delimits at least the applicability of rights or restricts their scope of application that people of color might otherwise properly claim.

Goldberg, 1993, p. 37

The West and its 'others'

Goldberg draws on the work of Edward Said (1985, first published 1978) in discussing how the devaluation of non-whites came about. In his book *Orientalism* Said explains how the West established a discourse (see Chapters 9 and 12 for a discussion of discourse) in which the Orient was portrayed in a stereotypical and largely negative way. The East was seen as mysterious and exotic, but also less rational than, and therefore inferior to, the West. The West defined the East as 'the other', that which it was not, and in doing so cemented its own sense of superiority. Following Said, Goldberg believes that, through the process of naming others as Orientals, the West was able to exercise power over them. By claiming to have knowledge about them, it denied those in Arab and other Eastern countries the opportunity to define who they were themselves. In doing so it effectively denied them the ability to act for themselves. Goldberg says:

Naming the racial Other, for all intents and purposes is the Other. There is, as Said makes clear in the case of the Oriental, no Other behind or beyond the invention of knowledge ... These practices of knowledge and naming construction deny all autonomy to those so named and imagined, extending power, control, authority and domination over them. To extend Said's analysis of the 'Oriental' to the case of race in general ... racialized social science knows ... what is best for the Other – existentially, politically, economically, culturally.

Goldberg, 1993, p. 150

Because Western social scientists and politicians claimed to understand the Orient better than Orientals themselves, they could claim to be in a better position to govern them – and make decisions that were in their interests – than they could themselves. Hence they could justify colonialism.

Racisms

Even though, in Goldberg's view, modernity caused racism, he does not believe that racism will simply disappear with the end of modernity. In fact he does not think that there is one racism, but rather many different racisms. He acknowledges that, as modern societies have developed, the nature of these racisms has changed. They have become less based upon biology, and more based upon cultural and other differences between racial groups. People justify excluding others in a variety of ways. Different tactics are needed to counter different racisms. Nevertheless, he does express some optimism that changes in society might be making it easier to challenge racisms. In general, he believes that there has been a trend towards postmodernism in Western societies. To Goldberg, postmodernism involved losing a single, unified sense of identity. People have more mixed, varied and insecure identities. This makes it more difficult to sustain the view that other people have unified identities based around their supposed 'race'. In these circumstances some people even start to contemplate taking on something of the identity of 'the Other' – that is, of those who are supposed to define who you are by being different. Goldberg concludes that:

> We must accordingly be prompted to think the once unthinkable: that whites ... be intellectually and culturally influenced by the thought of black people; that whites and blacks think through the conditions for being black, indeed, for whites to be black.
>
> Goldberg, 1993, p. 218

(The idea that whites might become black is examined by writers like Back, discussing new ethnicities, see pp. 274–6.)

Ali Rattansi – a 'postmodern' frame

In their discussions of 'race', racism, ethnicity and identity, Goldberg and Bauman are most concerned with criticizing modernity and its role in creating racisms. Ali Rattansi is more concerned with developing a postmodern approach to these issues. However, he is rather tentative in advocating postmodernism, and puts 'postmodern' in quotation marks to show that he has reservations about the term. Nevertheless he tries to outline a postmodern frame, or framework, for understanding Western 'racisms, ethnicities and identities'.

Decentering and de-essentialization

In Rattansi's view, a key element of any postmodern frame must involve a 'decentering and de-essentializing of the subject and the social' (Rattansi, 1994). To Rattansi, decentering the subject means rejecting the view that people have a strong and unambiguous sense of identity. People do not know who they are in an unproblematic way but tend to have confused, ambiguous and sometimes contradictory identities. The concept also involves rejecting the view that people can and do make sense of the world through the exercise of reason. Like other critics of Enlightenment thinking, Rattansi believes that subjective and emotional elements of humans are an integral part of the way humans understand and relate to the external world.

De-essentialization involves rejecting the belief that there are any fundamental or unchanging features of societies or humans. Thus Rattansi rejects the view that there is such a thing as human nature, and denies that there are features that are characteristic of all societies. Thus, for example, de-essentialization would reject the Marxist view that all societies can be understood in terms of their mode of production, and Parsons's view that all societies have the same functional prerequisites (see Chapter 15). Identities and societies are fluid; they change constantly and are therefore hard to pin down.

Nevertheless Rattansi does discuss factors that have helped to form Western identities. Like Goldberg he argues that Western identities have at least partly been formed by making comparisons with 'Others', particularly the non-white peoples who were colonized by Western imperial powers. In this context he argues that 'modernity cannot be understood without grasping racism as its other, "darker" side'.

Modern thinking not only produced racism out of a sense of superiority to its 'others', but it also insisted upon strong classification systems. The belief in the power and authority of rationality leads modernists to divide people into groups. However, Rattansi argues that a postmodern frame is bound to undermine classifications of people into races, ethnic groups or nations. By 'decentering and de-essentializing', it undermines the basis of racism or destructive nationalism. He says that 'there are no, unambiguous, water-tight definitions to be had of ethnicity, racism and the myriad terms in-between. Indeed, all these terms are permanently "in-between", caught in the impossibility of fixity and essentialization.'

Rattansi rejects the view that there are biological differences between 'races' and that there are clearcut cultural differences between ethnic groups or nationalities. He does not believe that such views are always destructive or harmful – sometimes they can be used to mobilize support for progressive changes. For example, he regards the use of the idea of an 'African race' by some black American activists as a useful resource in the struggle against white racism. Nevertheless, he argues that the idea of a distinctive African race could still be seen as racist.

Ethnicity and representation

Within a postmodern framework, the idea of ethnicity is not seen in absolute terms but as part of 'a cultural politics of representation'. Representation involves 'the construction and constant re-creation of ethnic identities through the production of images and narratives in visual texts of "popular" and "high" culture'. In other words, ethnic identities and ethnic groups are only created through people's active efforts to portray such groups as existing. They are more imagined than real. Nevertheless, they have real consequences. People use the representation of ethnic groups to try to gain advantages over other groups. People use the idea of ethnicity to claim superiority to, or authority over, other groups. They use the idea of ethnicity to mobilize support for their political projects. Although it is becoming less common, people sometimes try to represent group differences in terms of biological 'race' rather than cultural ethnicity. Rattansi calls this process racialization.

Because of the fluid nature of concepts such as ethnic groups and nations, a postmodern approach to these concepts should be based upon trying to deconstruct existing ideas on ethnicity and nationality. This involves taking the concepts apart and trying to show that they do not describe real groups at all. For example, conventional sociology might compare the examination performance and school exclusion rates of British Asians, Afro-Caribbeans and whites. It might conclude that teachers stereotype non-white pupils, place them in lower streams and so on (see Chapter 11 for examples of studies of this type). Rattansi attacks such studies for failing to deconstruct or take apart the categories involved. Not all teachers stereotype pupils. Not all pupils react in the same way when they are stereotyped. There are important differences and divisions within ethnic minority and white groups. To give just one example, female Afro-Caribbean pupils might react to schooling in a more compromising way than many

male Afro-Caribbean pupils who are more likely to rebel against racism.

A postmodern frame also criticizes the idea of institutional racism (see pp. 238–40 for a discussion of institutional racism). The idea of institutional racism, like concepts such as ethnicity, tends to over-generalize and ignore ambiguities and inconsistencies. Institutions such as the state, schools and hospitals tend to be 'fragmented and internally divided'. In some contexts they might operate in racist ways, in other contexts they do not. They are influenced by diverse professional ideologies (for example, those of psychiatry, medicine, education, and social work) which train their practitioners in different ways. Furthermore, in some places there is more effective resistance to racism than in others. Contradictions may arise in ideologies. For example, 'among teachers there is the popular liberal notion of treating individual students in supposedly "colour-blind" terms, which has the effect of ignoring the effects of racism and racialized economic disadvantage'. Ethnicity, 'race' and racism must be studied in specific local contexts since generalizations about these concepts are impossible.

Rattansi is generally supportive of ideas such as those of Stuart Hall that 'new ethnicities' are developing (see pp. 270–2). He agrees that ethnic identities are being combined in novel ways that undermine the old idea that there are clearcut distinctions between groups. Rattansi attributes this to the process of globalization. He also believes that there is a shift away from the use of the term 'black' to refer to all non-white people. The use of this term by disadvantaged minorities was part of a struggle to challenge racial or ethnic stereotypes, to substitute positive images and to try to gain access to the media for such views. Rattansi calls these processes 'a struggle over relations of representation'. This has largely been replaced by a new phase: 'a politics of representation'. This tries to move away from the idea of the 'essential black subject', that is the idea that all black people share a good deal in common. In the politics of representation, the '"positive" images are now regarded as suffocating the possibilities for exploring the huge variety of ethnic, sub-cultural and sexual identities pulsating in the minority communities'. Some of these developing cultures are themselves influenced by postmodern and post-structural thinking. An example is the 'postmodern rap' of the British South Asian rapper, Apache Indian.

Rattansi admits that this postmodern framing approach raises some questions that have yet to be answered. For example, he accepts that there may be question marks about the ability of this approach to challenge racism. Nevertheless, he does believe that the celebration of ethnic diversity and of new ethnicities is a positive and progressive development that allows the sociology of 'race' and ethnicity to move beyond the rather tired debates of the past

Kenan Malik – a critique of post-modern theories

Kenan Malik is highly critical of postmodern approaches to 'race' and denies that modernity can be seen as responsible for racism. He does not deny that racism has been a powerful and corrosive force in modern societies, but he does not see racism as a product of modernity itself. Furthermore, he does not believe that the celebration of difference, which he sees as a key feature of postmodern thinking, is the way to undermine racism. Instead, he argues that racism can best be tackled by reviving some of the principles on which modernity is based. In particular he believes that the application of universal principles is preferable to acknowledging and celebrating variety in human groups. Before examining Malik's own viewpoint though, we will discuss his comments on the sorts of postmodern theories we have looked at in this section.

Criticisms of other theories

First, Malik criticizes Bauman's claim that the Holocaust was a product of modernity. For Malik, the Holocaust arose in specific historical circumstances rather than being a product of modernity in general. If blame for the Holocaust can be attributed to anything, it should be to capitalism rather than reason. Modernity involves a belief in reason and the application of science, while capitalism involves economic relationships based upon the pursuit of profit. The two are not the same; indeed, capitalism may make it difficult to achieve the equality that was the objective of many modern thinkers. The inequalities produced by capitalism may encourage people to think of other 'races' as inferior, but this is not the same as saying that racism is produced by science and reason. As Malik says, 'By conflating the social relations of capitalism with the intellectual and technical progress of 'modernity', the product of the former can be laid at the door of the latter.'

Malik is also critical of the claim that the Holocaust can be blamed on modernity simply because modernity provides the technological means to accomplish mass extermination. Modern technology has also been used to alleviate problems such as famine and material poverty. The existence of advanced technology in itself cannot be held responsible for the political decision to use technology to exterminate people by gassing. Malik says:

I find it odious that scholars can in all seriousness equate mass extermination with the production of McDonald's hamburgers or of Ford Escorts, or make a comparison between technology aimed at improving the material abundance of society and political decisions which annihilate whole peoples and destroy entire societies.

Malik, 1996, p. 244

Second, Malik also criticizes the work of Goldberg. He agrees with Goldberg that racism was not present in premodern societies, but does not believe that it developed as an inevitable consequence of modern rationalism. There was no necessary connection between a scientific method and belief in rationality and the categorization of people by 'race'. Malik says:

Belief in reason, espousal of the scientific method and a universalistic conviction do not of themselves imply a racial viewpoint. That in the nineteenth century science, reason and universalism came to be harnessed to a discourse of race is a development that has to be explained through historical analysis; it is not logically given by the nature of scientific or rational thought.

Malik, 1996, p. 41

In reality, Malik claims, Enlightenment philosophy introduced the idea that humans could be equal and, in theory at least, its aims were 'to set all human beings free'. To Malik, what needs to be explained is why such philosophies changed to accept the idea of different races. Malik's explanation for this will be examined shortly.

Third, Malik criticizes the claims of writers such as Goldberg and Said that racism can be understood in terms of the concept of the 'Other'. Malik does not believe that modernity causes people automatically to compare themselves to other people, and that as a result racism develops. Malik suggests that such claims are so sweeping as be seriously misleading. In his view, it cannot be assumed that, over many centuries, Westerners have seen all non-Westerners as the 'Other' in the same way. Western views of other people have been related to specific contexts and circumstances. For example, different meanings have been given to the possession of a black skin at different times and at different places in modern history. At one time most Westerners thought that is was acceptable to enslave people with black skins. That is no longer the case. The meaning of 'otherness' is often disputed and contentious, and not all modern, post-Enlightenment thinkers have been persuaded of the truth of racist beliefs.

The origins of racism

Malik himself explains racism in terms of a clash between Enlightenment ideas and the social relations produced by capitalism. In the eighteenth century the universalistic Enlightenment idea that all humans were equal was widely held. For example, the French philosopher Rousseau, writing in 1770, distinguished between physical inequality (such as strength) and moral or political inequality. While the first type of inequality came from nature, the second type was created by humans and reflected both privilege and prejudice. In Rousseau's thinking – which was very much in line with the Enlightenment thinking from which modernity developed – there was no room for racism. There was prejudice against 'racial' groups in the eighteenth century, but liberals influenced by Enlightenment ideas were opposed, for example, to slavery.

Furthermore, a supposedly 'scientific' theory of racism only developed in the nineteenth century. Malik argues that this resulted from inequality within Western, capitalist society. While the Enlightenment had taught that people could be equal, people's experiences of society had shown them the develop-ment of a disadvantaged working class. These disadvantages seemed to be passed down from generation to generation, and this encouraged advantaged groups to believe that members of the working class were biologically inferior to themselves. This tendency was further encouraged by concern amongst the elite about the pace of social change, the apparent breakdown of traditional moral values and the danger of working-class unrest. In these circumstances it was the working class rather than non-Western others who were first seen as part of an inferior 'race'. Malik comments:

> For the Victorians race was a description of social distinctions, not of colour differences. Indeed, as I have already argued, the view of non-Europeans as an inferior race was but an extension of the already existing view of the working class at home.
>
> Malik, 1996, p. 91

A good example is the widespread view amongst the Victorian elite that the working-class Irish in the country were a biologically inferior group. It was the inability of capitalism to deliver the equality that modernity had promised that led to 'scientific' thinking becoming racist. It was only after the working class had begun to be thought of in racist terms that racial thinking began to be applied to non-European groups.

If Malik is right, then postmodernists have, at the very least, been too critical of modernity. There is no reason why rational modern thought cannot be turned against racism. It may be possible to combat racism in a more positive way than simply encour-aging an acceptance of human diversity. For Malik, postmodernists have abandoned the struggle to produce greater equality in favour of unequal diversity. Malik regards this as an undesirable and unnecessary admission of defeat (see pp. 287–9 for a discussion of values in theories of 'race', ethnicity and nationality).

Ethnic minorities in the labour market and stratification system

There is considerable evidence that ethnic minorities are disadvantaged in the British labour market. As we will see elsewhere in the book, ethnic minorities are more likely to suffer from unemployment (see Chapter 10). Furthermore, earlier in this chapter we saw that in general terms those from ethnic minori-ties tend to get paid lower wages and have lower-status jobs (see pp. 249–50). Although there are differences between ethnic groups, most groups continue to suffer from disadvantages even when factors such as fluency in English and educational qualifications are taken into account.

Discrimination in the labour market

The most straightforward explanation of disadvan-tage suffered by ethnic minorities in employment is that it results from the racism and prejudice of employers. In other words, employers discriminate against ethnic minority groups by either refusing to employ them, employing them only in low-status and low-paid jobs, or refusing to promote them.

Evidence to support this point of view is provided from a study by Colin Brown and Pat Gay (1985) carried out in 1984–5. They conducted research in London, Birmingham and Manchester, in which bogus applications were made for a variety of jobs by letter and by telephone. The supposed applicants were identified as being from ethnic minorities by the use of Hindu names for 'Asian' applicants and a Jamaican educational background for 'West Indian' applicants. In telephone applications ethnic accents were used to differentiate ethnic minority applicants from 'white' applicants.

Brown and Gay found that positive responses were significantly less common to applications from those who were identified as being from ethnic minorities. Some 90 per cent of white applicants, but only 63 per cent of Asian and 63 per cent of West Indian applicants, received positive responses.

Brown and Gay compared their results with those of similar studies carried out in 1973–4 and 1977–9. They found that the level of discrimination had remained about the same in all three studies. They concluded that 'there is no evidence here to suggest that racial discrimination in job recruitment has fallen over the period covered by these studies'. Similar studies have been repeated during the 1990s in local areas. Reporting on the findings of such studies, Modood comments that 'Objective tests suggest that the proportion of white people who are likely to carry out the most basic acts of discrimination has been stable at about a third for several decades' (Modood, 1997).

In the Policy Studies Institute's *Third National Survey* Brown tried to measure the experience of racial discrimination by ethnic minorities (Brown, 1984). Of those who were currently in the job market or who had worked in the last ten years, 26 per cent of West Indian men and 23 per cent of West Indian women claimed they had been refused a job for racial reasons. For Asians the corresponding figures were 10 per cent for men and 8 per cent for women. There was less evidence of racism affecting promotion. Only 11 per cent of West Indian men and 3 per cent of women claimed they had been refused a better job because of their 'race' or colour.

In the PSI's *Fourth National Survey of Ethnic Minorities* conducted in 1994, similar questions were repeated. The study found that 28 per cent of Caribbean people, 19 per cent of African Asians, 15 per cent of Indians, 7 per cent of Chinese, and 5 per cent of Pakistani/Bangladeshi people believed they had been refused a job for religious or racial reasons (Modood, 1997). Modood found a slight increase in reported discrimination of this type amongst Caribbeans, compared with the previous survey, but a slight decrease amongst South Asians.

These figures must be used with some caution. They rely upon the subjective beliefs of the respondents to the survey who might not be in a position to assess accurately whether they had been the victims of racial discrimination. Discrimination could be more common or less so than the figures indicate. However, the figures do suggest that at least some of the disadvantages experienced by ethnic minorities in the labour market could be the result of racism.

Ethnic minorities as an underclass

Some sociologists have tried to develop a more theoretical approach to explaining the position of ethnic minorities in the labour market and in society as a whole. Both British and American sociologists have suggested that ethnic minorities form an underclass. While some have defined an underclass in cultural terms, others have seen the underclass as a structural feature of society. The idea of an underclass is discussed in detail in other chapters (see pp. 91–6 for a discussion of the underclass in relation to stratification, and pp. 323–34 for a discussion of the underclass and poverty). In this section we will concentrate on the relationship between the concepts of underclass and ethnicity.

Charles Murray – *Losing Ground*

In his 1984 book, *Losing Ground*, Charles Murray argued that the USA had developed a black underclass. This underclass was distinguished by its behaviour. He claimed that increasing numbers of young blacks were withdrawing from the labour market: they were unwilling to work. At the same time there were increasing numbers of black single parents who had never been married.

Murray denied that such changes were the result of poverty and lack of opportunity. He argued that in the 1950s participation by blacks in the labour market was higher than in the 1960s, yet there was greater economic prosperity and lower unemployment in the 1960s than the 1950s.

To Murray the real reason for the changes in behaviour lay in welfare benefits. In his view Aid to Families with Dependent Children removed many of the incentives for men to work to support their families, and it enabled mothers to bring up their children on their own. The stigma of relying upon benefits had been reduced as more and more benefits were introduced for people with low incomes.

American critics of Murray have pointed out that the Aid to Families with Dependent Children was introduced some twenty years before the number of single-parent black families began to rise rapidly. Lydia Morris criticizes Murray for failing to explain the withdrawal of black youth from the labour market. The young unemployed have no automatic entitlement to benefit in the USA, so their behaviour cannot be explained in terms of the welfare system.

Some American sociologists have agreed with Murray that the USA has developed a black or ethnic minority underclass, but they have not agreed about the causes. They have attributed its development to structural forces rather than to the operation of the welfare system and the behaviour of welfare claimants. The most influential alternative view of the American underclass has been advanced by William Julius Wilson.

William Julius Wilson – *The Truly Disadvantaged*

In his 1987 book, *The Truly Disadvantaged* (1987), Wilson argues that blacks and Hispanics living in inner-city areas have come to form an underclass because of forces beyond their control. The disadvantages faced by urban blacks and Hispanics have historical roots and have created problems that continue to make it difficult to escape from the ghetto.

When poor blacks migrated from the rural south of the USA to the cities of the north, they faced the obstacle of racism when they tried to find work. The migrants had few skills and little prospect of career advancement. Their low levels of economic success encouraged whites to develop crude racial stereotypes which produced further problems for the ghetto poor. What work the blacks could find was largely unskilled and in manufacturing industry.

In the 1970s manufacturing industry began to decline, and the industry which survived the recession moved away from city centres. Service sector work increased but much of it required qualifications which ethnic minorities in the inner cities did not possess. Some blacks and Hispanics had enjoyed success, gained qualifications and secured well-paid jobs. However, these individuals moved out of the city centres to the suburbs, leaving behind the most disadvantaged. The poor had become trapped in areas where there were few opportunities to improve their lot. Wilson says:

> the underclass exists mainly because of large scale and harmful changes in the labor market and its resulting spatial concentration as well as the isolation of such areas from the most affluent parts of the black community.
>
> Wilson, 1987

In 1990, in an address to the American Sociological Association, Wilson abandoned the use of the term underclass (Wilson, 1991). Although he stuck by his analysis of the problems faced by ethnic minorities in the inner cities of the USA, he argued that the term underclass had become a liability. It had been adopted by right-wing commentators who had used it to indicate that the problems of the poor were of their own making. To Wilson the problems resulted more from impersonal economic forces, and the connotations the term had taken on were unfortunate. He therefore suggested that the groups he was describing should be called the ghetto poor rather than the underclass.

Some American critics have argued that Wilson underestimates the effects produced by racism. Their view is that the black middle class is small and that even those blacks with good jobs do less well than their white counterparts with similar qualifications. Problems for American blacks in the labour market are not confined to the poor.

The underclass in Britain

Some sociologists have argued that there is a British underclass composed mainly or exclusively of ethnic minorities. They have followed Wilson in arguing that the underclass has been created by structural forces, and have tended to be critical of sociologists such as Murray who see the underclass in cultural terms.

One of the most influential views of this type was advanced by Anthony Giddens (1973). Giddens argued that the underclass is composed of those with a disadvantaged position in the labour market. As well as lacking skills and qualifications, they may also have to face prejudice and discrimination. Women and ethnic minorities are most likely to suffer from these problems and are therefore most likely to be found in the underclass. As we saw in Chapter 2 (see p. 93), Giddens believes that migrants are very likely to end up in the underclass.

To Giddens, when ethnic minorities such as Asians and West Indians in Britain and Algerians in France are heavily concentrated in the lowest-paid jobs or are unemployed, then an underclass exists. When members of the underclass do have jobs they are mainly in the secondary labour market. (We discuss the concept of a secondary labour market in the next section.)

John Rex and Sally Tomlinson – the underclass in Birmingham

Giddens's ideas were further developed in a study of the Handsworth area of Birmingham conducted by John Rex and Sally Tomlinson and published in 1979. They argued that New Commonwealth immigrants to Britain largely went to Britain 'to fill the gaps in the less skilled and the less attractive jobs in manufacturing industry as well as in the less skilled jobs in the service industries'. During the 1950s and 1960s Britain experienced a shortage of labour, and immigration was encouraged to overcome the problem. The shortage was particularly acute in jobs requiring little skill, and immigrants were often employed in such jobs.

Rex and Tomlinson believe that there is not one but rather two distinctive labour markets in Britain. They support the dual labour market theory. This sees the primary labour market as consisting of jobs with high wages, good working conditions, job security and opportunities for on-the-job training and promotion. In contrast, the secondary labour market consists of jobs with low wages, poor working conditions, little job security and few opportunities for on-the-job training and promotion. Highly skilled jobs are usually located in the primary sector of the labour market, and less skilled jobs in the secondary. Skilled workers are usually more crucial to a company's success than workers with few skills, and so their loyalty to their employer is encouraged with high wages and opportunities for promotion.

Asian and West Indian immigrants were usually recruited to jobs in the secondary labour market. Because such jobs offer few promotion prospects or opportunities for training, they have tended to remain in a disadvantaged position in the labour market. For this reason ethnic minorities form an underclass in Britain.

Rex and Tomlinson acknowledge that not all members of ethnic minorities work in the secondary labour market but they offer evidence to show that they are disproportionately represented in such jobs. For example, using data from the 1971 census they found that in the West Midlands only 1 in 8 West Indian men, 1 in 6 Pakistanis, and 1 in 20 Indians were employed in vehicle manufacture, an industry which paid high wages. On the other hand, 33 per cent of West Indian men, more than 50 per cent of Indians, nearly 50 per cent of Pakistanis and 30 per cent of East African Asians worked in metal or metal goods manufacture; jobs in the metal industries tended to be poorly paid and offered few promotion prospects.

Rex and Tomlinson also found differences in the employment of women in the West Midlands in different ethnic groups. They say 'whereas the white woman typically becomes a secretary or a shopworker the immigrant woman works in a factory, or in a hospital and rather less frequently in service industries'.

In 1976 Rex and Tomlinson carried out a survey in Handsworth, Birmingham, in which structured interviews were conducted with a sample of 1,100 people. They found that 30 per cent of whites in Handsworth had white-collar jobs but only 9.5 per cent of West Indians and 5.1 per cent of Asians; 27.4 per cent of whites were in unskilled or semi-skilled manual work compared to 38.7 per cent of Asians and 44.1 per cent of West Indians. On the basis of their research, Rex and Tomlinson argued that ethnic minority groups:

> were systematically at a disadvantage compared with working-class whites and that, instead of identifying with working-class culture, community and politics, they formed their own organisations and became in effect a separate underprivileged class.

Rex and Tomlinson, 1979

In short, they formed an underclass which was perpetuated by the predominance of ethnic minorities in the secondary labour market.

Marxist approaches

Marxist sociologists agree with writers such as Giddens and Rex and Tomlinson (who use a broadly Weberian approach) that ethnic minorities are disadvantaged in capitalist societies. However, they do not agree that they form an underclass in Britain. They reject the importance attached to status in underclass theories and place more emphasis on the workings of the economy and the role of ethnic minorities in the economic system.

Stephen Castles and Godula Kosack – a reserve army of labour

In a study of immigrant workers in France, Germany, Switzerland and Britain, Stephen Castles and Godula Kosack found that the immigrants faced similar problems in the labour market to those identified in Handsworth by Rex and Tomlinson (Castles and Kosak, 1973). In these four European countries immigrants were found to be concentrated in low-paid jobs or in jobs with poor working conditions. Most were manual workers in unskilled or semi-skilled work and they suffered high rates of unemployment. Castles and Kosack claim that in Britain this situation is mainly due to discrimination. In France, Germany and Switzerland the migrant workers are foreigners in the country in which they are working and restrictive laws and regulations prevent them from gaining employment in the more desirable jobs.

Discrimination and restrictive regulations are, however, only the immediate causes of the plight of immigrants. The poor treatment of immigrants ultimately derives from the need in capitalist societies for a reserve army of labour: it is necessary to have a surplus of labour in order to keep wage costs down, since the greater the overall supply of labour, the weaker the bargaining position of workers. Furthermore, as Marxists, Castles and Kosack believe that capitalist economies are inherently unstable. They go through periods of boom and slump, and a reserve army of labour needs to be available to be hired and fired as the fluctuating fortunes of the economy dictate. After the Second World War capitalist societies exhausted their indigenous reserve army of labour; women, for example, were increasingly taking paid employment. Capitalist countries in Europe therefore turned to migrant labour and immigration to provide a reserve pool of cheap labour which could be profitably exploited.

Castles and Kosack do not believe that such workers form an underclass outside and below the main class structure. They regard them as being part of the working class. Like other workers they do not own the means of production and so share with them an interest in changing society. However, Castles and Kosack believe that immigrant and migrant workers are the most disadvantaged groups within the working class and as such they form a distinctive stratum. Thus Castles and Kosack believe that the working class is divided into two, with ethnic minorities constituting one working-class grouping and the indigenous white population the other.

This situation is beneficial to the ruling class in capitalist societies. Ethnic minorities are blamed for problems such as unemployment and housing shortages. Attention is diverted from the failings of the capitalist system. The working class is divided and cannot unite, develop class consciousness and challenge ruling-class dominance.

Annie Phizaklea and Robert Miles – class factions

Annie Phizaklea and Robert Miles (1980) have also advanced a Marxist analysis of the position of ethnic minorities in the labour market and class structure. On the basis of a study in South Brent, London, carried out in the mid-1970s, they agree with Castles and Kosack that migrant ethnic minority workers form a distinctive stratum within the working class. However, they deny that immigration and migrant labour have actually created divisions within the working class. They point out that the working class can also be seen as divided by gender and level of skill. Working-class women sell their labour for a wage in the same way as working-class men, but unlike working-class men they have unpaid domestic responsibilities. Skilled manual workers have always tried to defend their own interests and ensure that they enjoy higher wages than other manual workers.

To Phizaklea and Miles, the working class is not divided into two, but is split between a considerable number of class factions based upon gender, skill and ethnicity. Immigration did not divide a united working class; it added an extra dimension to existing divisions.

Andrew Pilkington – the underclass reconsidered

Despite the differences between the theories on ethnicity and employment examined so far, they share a good deal in common. Andrew Pilkington suggests:

> there is agreement that black workers are employed in predominantly nonskilled work, that they are locked into such work with few chances of escape and that this tends to segregate them from the indigenous workforce.

Pilkington, 1993

Pilkington believes that the underclass and Marxist theories are not supported by empirical evidence. He quotes figures from the *Labour Force Survey* for 1989–91. These showed that:

1 among West Indians and Guyanese, 32 per cent of men and 63 per cent of women were in non-manual occupations;

2 among Indians the figures were 59 per cent for men and 62 per cent for women;

3 among Pakistanis/Bangladeshis they were 40 per cent for men and 64 per cent for women.

Thus for women there was little difference in the proportions of ethnic minority groups in non-manual jobs. Amongst men, Indians were more likely than whites to have non-manual work and very substantial minorities of men in the other ethnic groups did not have working-class jobs. Pilkington therefore rejects the view that ethnic minorities are overwhelmingly trapped in jobs offering few prospects.

Pilkington also denies that ethnic minorities are segregated from the white workforce. He quotes a study of the labour market in Peterborough, conducted by Blackburn and Mann, in which it was found that 'the majority of immigrants are sharing jobs with the nativeborn', and that 'although immigrants receive less on average their conditions overlap very considerably with that of British workers' (quoted in Pilkington, 1984).

Pilkington fully accepts that ethnic minorities are disadvantaged in the labour market, but he does not agree that they are so disadvantaged that they constitute an underclass or subordinate stratum or faction of the working class. On the other hand, he believes that the situation is different for migrant workers in some other European countries. In France and Germany, for example, migrant workers can be seen to occupy a distinctive group at the bottom of the stratification system because 'they are predominantly located in nonskilled work with relatively few political rights'.

Conclusion

Recent figures confirm Pilkington's claim that ethnic minorities are not overwhelmingly concentrated in an underclass. (See, for example, the findings of the PSI's *Fourth National Survey* reported above, pp. 249–51.) Indeed, certain ethnic groups such as the Chinese and African Asians have been extremely successful in the labour market. Writers such as Heidi

Mirza warn of the dangers of labelling ethnic minorities in the labour market and elsewhere. Mirza points out that women of Caribbean origin have enjoyed considerable success in British society (see Chapter 11). That does not mean that the relatively successful groups are immune from discrimination – they might

have been even more successful if discrimination had been absent. However, any full explanation of inequalities in the labour market would need to take account of a range of factors other than discrimination. These would include gender, class, age and cultural differences.

Sociology, values and 'race' and ethnicity

Sociologists, like other members of society, are a product of their time and place. While sociologists may try to study society without being influenced by the commonsense beliefs of other members of society, they may find it difficult or even impossible to be completely objective. This was certainly true in the nineteenth century. Sociologists generally accepted the view of scientists and others that humanity was divided into distinct biological 'races', some of which were superior to others. Not surprisingly they tended to see themselves and their own 'race' as being at the top of the hierarchy.

Thus, to sociologists like Herbert Spencer (1971), white Europeans generally belonged to the most evolved 'races'. His beliefs did not stem from individual arrogance or ignorance. Colonialism undoubtedly contributed to persuading most Victorian English people that their 'race' was superior to the other 'races' that they and other European powers had conquered and ruled.

As large-scale migration between and within countries became more common, people from different 'races' increasingly lived close together. Sociologists supporting the immigrant-host model became less likely to claim that certain 'races' were superior to others. To them the problems of race relations were created by the difficulties encountered when immigrants or strangers settled in an established host society.

However, these views were still strongly influenced by the values of the sociologists who expressed them: it was always the 'immigrants' who were the problem, disrupting the harmony of the host society. The hosts were largely tolerant and some were even welcoming. Any fault lay with those who would not adapt to their new surroundings. From this point of view the hosts were generally willing to accept the strangers; they were not filled with racism or hatred.

The views associated with the immigrant-host model seem to remain common amongst British whites today. For example, as we saw earlier, Ellis Cashmore (1987) found that some people in Birmingham and the Midlands criticized 'immigrants'

for not fitting in with British ways. They resented it when 'immigrants' wanted to preserve their traditional cultures.

However, sociologists had begun to reject the idea that the culture of ethnic minorities was inferior to that of the white majority, and no longer assumed that 'immigrants' needed to change their cultures. Scientists had already discredited the idea that distinct 'races' existed. The mood of the times was moving in favour of greater tolerance of diverse cultures. In the USA the civil rights and Black Power movements encouraged ethnic minorities to take pride in their distinctiveness. In Britain legislation outlawed discrimination and made open racism less respectable and acceptable. Rather than just expecting 'immigrants' to integrate, new approaches to issues of 'race' and ethnicity seemed necessary.

One approach was to emphasize the desirability of ethnic pluralism. This suggested that the cultures of ethnic minorities should not necessarily change to allow integration, but rather they should remain distinctive and separate. Studies of ethnicity were carried out to develop a greater understanding of the diverse ways of life of different ethnic groups.

This approach produced policies of multiculturalism. From this viewpoint, schools, for example, should accommodate all ethnic groups: the diet, religious practices, clothing, beliefs and values of different ethnic groups should all be catered for in the education system.

Radical critics of this approach tended to dismiss it. James Donald and Ali Rattansi call it the 'saris, samosas and steel-bands syndrome'. It focused on the 'superficial manifestations of culture' and did not really address the underlying problems faced by ethnic minorities. Donald and Rattansi argue that multiculturalism ignores the 'continuing hierarchies of power and legitimacy'. If ethnic minorities are allowed or encouraged to wear saris, eat samosas and play in steel bands, that does not necessarily mean that their cultures have the same power and legitimacy as white culture. Donald and Rattansi argue that the 'limits to this approach were cruelly exposed by intellectual as well as political responses to *The*

Satanic Verses affair in the late 1980s'. Politicians and writers alike tended to side with Salman Rushdie against the British Muslim community who called for the book to be banned for blasphemy.

According to some sociologists, the emphasis on culture in multiculturalism has its own dangers. The new racism identified by Solomos *et al.* (1982) (see p. 259) and the ethnic absolutism described by Gilroy (1987) are based on the idea that ethnic groups are incompatible because their cultures are incompatible. Repatriation, which used to be justified on the grounds of biological difference, was supported by politicians like Enoch Powell on cultural grounds. Rivers of blood would flow simply because very different cultures could not mix.

Sociologists who stress the importance of racism suggest that the problems of 'race' and ethnicity cannot be solved by encouraging tolerance of different cultures. To some, racism is deeply ingrained in the minds, culture and institutions of whites. Whites possess most of the power in the USA, Britain and similar countries, and racism ensures they keep their power. From this point of view ethnic minorities have to fight to gain power rather than relying on the tolerance of well-meaning liberals. The policies associated with this approach are often called anti-racism. They involve seeking out, exposing and destroying the open or hidden racism present in society and its institutions.

Burnage High School in South Manchester became a notorious example of anti-racism in 1986 when Ahmed Iqbal Ullah was murdered by a white boy in the school playground, despite the school's vigorous anti-racist policy. Children in the school were taught about the evils of racism but that did not prevent the murder. The school banned white children from attending the funeral.

While nearly all sociologists today condemn racism, some disagree with some of the policies of anti-racism. Paul Gilroy argues that anti-racism has sometimes practised moralistic excesses. It has 'drifted towards a belief in the absolute nature of ethnic categories' and has therefore fallen into the trap of emphasizing 'race' to the exclusion of everything else. It sees the world in terms of black and white. Whites are the oppressors, blacks are the oppressed. All whites are racist, as are their institutions. Gilroy says:

The anti-racism I am criticizing trivializes the struggle against racism and isolates it from other political antagonisms – from the contradiction between capital and labour, from the battle between men and women. It suggests that racism can be eliminated on its own because it is readily extricable from everything else.

Gilroy, 1987

To Gilroy the views of some anti-racists are no longer plausible. Not only are issues of 'race' and ethnicity bound up with other issues, but racial and ethnic identities and cultures themselves cannot be separated into distinct and neat categories. Like Stuart Hall (1992) Gilroy believes that in the modern world there has been so much intermingling of different cultures that it is no longer appropriate to treat different 'races' as discrete groups. He says:

The outcomes of this cultural and political interaction reconstruct and rework tradition as they pursue their particular utopia. A vision of a world in which 'race' will no longer be a meaningful device for the categorization of human beings, where work will no longer be servitude and law will be disassociated from domination.

Gilroy, 1987

Postmodernists tend to share Gilroy's view that new types of ethnic identity are developing as the cultures of different ethnic groups are mixed. However, postmodernists tend to support a type of radical multiculturalism rather than hoping for the virtual disappearance of 'racial' differences. For example, Goldberg advocates a 'shift from the fundamental public commitment to ignore difference and particularity in the name of universality to a public celebration of diversity and an openly acknowledged and constantly recreated politics of difference' (Goldberg, 1993). Rather than treating everybody the same and pretending that there are no differences, we should acknowledge the differences. We should create space for different voices to be heard. For example, black lesbian females should have as much chance to express their views as white heterosexual males. Different religions, age groups, classes, ethnic groups, and people with different sexualities must all have a voice in contemporary society. They all need to record their own history, to express how they experience society and to celebrate their own identities. Their differences should not be suppressed under an Enlightenment philosophy that all people are fundamentally the same.

Kenan Malik (1996) strongly opposes this approach. He says 'The philosophy of difference is the politics of defeat, born out of defeat. It is the product of disillusionment with the possibilities of social change and the acceptance of the inevitability of an unequal, fragmented world'. He accuses postmodern thinkers of accepting and even encouraging the oppression of ethnic minority groups. From Malik's point of view, postmodernists sometimes seem to want such groups to remain oppressed. This is so that they can articulate their experiences and maintain their distinctive identities which are partly based on their oppression. Malik believes that a 'social revolution' is necessary. What is needed is a revolution in which people refuse to accept defeat and start to believe again that it is possible to intervene to make society better. Racism can be defeated by an active struggle against it.

Most postmodernists would not accept that their views are based upon accepting racism. They see the acceptance of diversity as liberating. Whatever the differences between postmodernists and writers such as Malik, their views are clearly very different from those of nineteenth-century sociologists. The same is true of multicultural and anti-racist views. All of these approaches would have been almost unthinkable in the nineteenth century, when the doctrine that some 'races' were superior to others dominated beliefs in sociology and society alike. That in itself suggests that sociology can contribute to the constructive development of social thought.

Poverty and social exclusion

Poverty and social exclusion

Introduction

The word poverty implies an undesirable state. It suggests that individuals or groups who are in poverty need to be helped so that their situation can be changed. Poverty, in other words, is a social problem. As we shall see later, however, for some groups in society, poverty can be useful. Generally speaking, though, poverty is considered to be an undesirable social problem for which a solution should be found.

1 The first step in finding the solution is to identify the problem. This requires a definition.

2 The second step is to assess the size of the problem. This involves the construction of ways to measure it.

3 Once the problem has been identified, defined and measured, the next step is to discover what causes it.

Therefore, only after we have found answers to the questions 'What is poverty?', 'What is the extent of poverty?', and 'What are the causes of poverty?', can the question 'What are the solutions to poverty?' be asked.

In this chapter we are going to examine some of the answers that social scientists have given to these four questions.

The definition and measurement of poverty

Since the nineteenth century, when rigorous studies of poverty first began, researchers have tried to establish a fixed standard against which to measure poverty. There have been three main areas of controversy over the basic principles on which such a standard can be based.

Absolute and relative poverty

First, researchers have disputed whether poverty should be measured in absolute or relative terms. Some writers have argued that there is a common minimum standard that can be applied to all societies below which individuals can be said to be 'in poverty'.

Measures of absolute poverty are usually based upon the idea of subsistence. In other words, people are in poverty if they do not have the resources to maintain human life.

Supporters of the concept of relative poverty, however, tend to dismiss this view. They argue that a definition must relate to the standards of a particular society at a particular time. According to this view, the point at which the dividing line that separates the poor from other members of society is drawn will vary according to how affluent that society is.

Material and multiple deprivation and social exclusion

The second area of controversy concerns whether poverty can be defined purely in material terms, or whether the definition should be wider. Some sociologists assume that poverty consists of a lack of material resources – in British society, for instance, a shortage of the money required to buy those commodities judged to be necessary to maintain an acceptable standard of living.

Other commentators, though, believe that poverty involves more than material deprivation. They see poverty as a form of multiple deprivation that can have many facets. For example, some have argued that inadequate educational opportunities, unpleasant working conditions, or powerlessness can all be regarded as aspects of poverty. None of these conditions is necessarily directly related to the income of the individual. Each implies that broader changes than simply increasing the income of the worst-off members of society are necessary if poverty is to be eliminated. Some commentators now favour the use of the term social exclusion to refer to a situation in which multiple deprivation prevents individuals from participating in important areas of society's activities. Thus the socially excluded might be unable to find work, take part in leisure activities or actively participate in a society's politics beyond voting at elections.

Inequality and poverty

The third area of controversy concerns the relationship between inequality and poverty. From one point of view, any society in which there is inequality is bound to have poverty. In other words, if all those individuals with below average incomes were defined as poor, then the only way that poverty could be eradicated would be to abolish all inequality in income. This is because if some people have higher than average incomes, inevitably others must fall below the average.

Most sociologists who adopt a relative definition of poverty accept that some reduction in inequality is necessary if poverty is to be reduced, but they do not believe it is necessary to abolish inequality altogether to solve this social problem. They argue that it is possible to establish a minimum standard, a poverty line, which might be below the average income. The poor within a society can then be defined as those whose income or resources fall so far short of the average that they do not have an acceptable standard of living. Thus it would be possible to have a society with some inequality where poverty no longer exists.

We will now look at these competing definitions and methods of measuring poverty, paying particular attention to the way that these definitions have been used, and the statistics they produce. The next section will therefore consider the questions, 'What is poverty?', and 'What is the extent of poverty?'

Absolute poverty

The concept of absolute poverty usually involves a judgement of basic human needs and is measured in terms of the resources required to maintain health and physical efficiency. Most measures of absolute poverty are concerned with establishing the quality and amount of food, clothing and shelter deemed necessary for a healthy life.

Absolute poverty is often known as subsistence poverty since it is based on assessments of minimum subsistence requirements. This means that those who use absolute measurements usually limit poverty to material deprivation.

Absolute poverty is generally measured by pricing the basic necessities of life, drawing a poverty line in terms of this price, and defining as poor those whose income falls below the line.

There have been many attempts to define and operationalize (put into a form which can be measured) the concept of absolute poverty. For example, in their 'Level of Living Index' Drewnowski and Scott (1966) define and operationalize basic physical needs in the following way:

1 nutrition, measured by factors such as intake of calories and protein;

2 shelter, measured by quality of dwelling and degree of overcrowding; and

3 health, measured by factors such as the rate of infant mortality and the quality of available medical facilities.

Some concepts of absolute poverty go beyond the notion of subsistence and material poverty by introducing the idea of basic cultural needs. This broadens the idea of basic human needs beyond the level of physical survival. Drewnowski and Scott include education, security, leisure and recreation in their category of basic cultural needs. The proportion of children enrolled at school is one indication of the level of educational provision; the number of violent deaths relative to the size of the population is one indication of security; and the amount of leisure relative to work time is one measure of the standard of leisure and recreation.

Criticisms of the concept of absolute poverty

The concept of absolute poverty has been widely criticized. It is based on the assumption that there are minimum basic needs for all people, in all societies. This is a difficult argument to defend, even in regard to subsistence poverty measured in terms of food, clothing and shelter. Such needs vary both between and within societies.

Thus Peter Townsend argues that 'it would be difficult to define nutritional needs without taking account of the kinds and demands of occupations and of leisure time pursuits in a society' (Townsend, 1970). For instance, the nutritional needs of the nomadic hunters and gatherers of the Kalahari Desert in Africa may well be very different from those of office workers in London. Within the same society, nutritional needs may vary widely, between, for example, the bank clerk sitting at a desk all day and the labourer working on a building site.

A similar criticism can be made of attempts to define absolute standards of shelter. Jack and Janet Roach give the following illustration:

City living, for example, requires that 'adequate' shelter not only protects one from the elements, but that it does not present a fire hazard to others and that attention be paid to water supplies, sewage, and garbage disposal. These problems are simply met in rural situations.

Roach and Roach, 1972

Thus, for instance, flush toilets, which may well be considered a necessary part of adequate shelter in the city, might not be considered essential fixtures in the dwellings of traditional hunting and gathering societies.

The concept of absolute poverty is even more difficult to defend when it is broadened to include the idea of basic cultural needs. Such 'needs' vary from time to time and from place to place, so that any attempt to establish absolute, fixed standards is bound to fail.

Drewnowski and Scott's basic cultural need for security is a case in point. In nineteenth-century England, younger relatives provided financial support for aged members of the working class, whereas today the same need is largely met by state old-age pensions and private insurance schemes. Increasing longevity, reductions in the size of families, and earlier retirement have altered the circumstances of the elderly. Definitions of adequate provision for old age have therefore changed since the last century. Thus, in terms of security, both the situation and expectations of the elderly in England have changed and are not strictly comparable over time.

A similar criticism can be made of attempts to apply absolute standards to two or more societies. For instance, recreational and leisure provision in the West may be measured in terms of the number of televisions, cinemas, parks and playing fields per head of the population. However, the concept of leisure on which this is based, and the items in terms of which it is measured, may be largely irrelevant for other societies: the Hopi and Zuñi Indians of the south-western USA, for example, have a rich ceremonial life and this forms the central theme of their leisure activities. Recreational needs are therefore largely determined by the culture of the particular society.

Any absolute standard of cultural needs is based in part on the values of the researchers which, in turn, reflect their particular cultures. Peter Townsend notes that when societies are compared in terms of recreational facilities, 'cinema attendance and ownership of radios take precedence over measures of direct participation in cultural events', such as religious rituals and other ceremonies (Townsend, 1970). This is a clear illustration of Western bias.

Budget standards and poverty

One common approach to measuring poverty is to use what has been called the budget standards approach. This involves calculating the cost of those purchases which are considered necessary to raise an individual or a family out of poverty. It has been used in some classic and contemporary studies of

poverty in Britain. The British government used it in calculating the level at which to set the means-tested benefit National Assistance (now called Income Support) when it was introduced in 1948. It has also been used by the US government in setting benefit levels.

Some of the earliest and most famous studies of poverty were conducted by Seebohm Rowntree in York (Rowntree, 1901, 1941, and Rowntree and Lavers, 1951). In his early work, the budget standards approach was originally based upon something very close to an absolute definition of poverty. (In Rowntree's later work, and in contemporary sociology, budget standards have been based upon more relative definitions of poverty.)

Seebohm Rowntree – trends in poverty

Rowntree's original method of defining or measuring poverty comes closest to the use of an absolute and material or subsistence definition in Britain.

Rowntree conducted a study of poor families in York in 1899 and drew a poverty line in terms of a minimum weekly sum of money 'necessary to enable families ... to secure the necessaries of a healthy life' (quoted in Coates and Silburn, 1970). The money needed for this subsistence level of existence covered fuel and light, rent, food, clothing, household and personal items, and was adjusted according to family size. According to this measure, 33 per cent of the survey population lived in poverty.

Rowntree conducted two further studies of poverty in York, in 1936 and 1950, based largely on a similar methodology. However, in the later studies he included allowances for some items which were not strictly necessary for survival. These included newspapers, books, radios, beer, tobacco, holidays

Table 5.1   Rowntree's studies of York

Causes of poverty	Percentage of those in poverty		
	1899	1936	1950
Unemployment	2.31	28.6	–
Inadequate wages	51.96	42.3	1.0
Old age	5.11	14.7	68.1
Sickness		4.1	21.3
Death of chief wage earner	15.63	7.8	6.4
Miscellaneous (incl. large family)	24.99	2.5	3.2
Totals	100	100	100
Percentage of survey population in poverty	33	18	1.5

Source: Adapted from K. Coates and R. Silburn (1970) *Poverty: The Forgotten Englishmen*, Penguin, Harmondsworth, London, p. 46

and presents. Despite the inclusion of the extra items, he found that the percentage of his sample population in poverty had dropped to 18 per cent in 1936 and 1.5 per cent in 1950. He also found that the causes of poverty had changed considerably over half a century. For example, inadequate wages, a major factor in 1899 and 1936, were relatively insignificant by 1950. Table 5.1 summarizes the results of Rowntree's surveys.

By the 1950s it appeared that poverty was a minor problem. 'Pockets' remained (for example, among the elderly), but it was believed that increased welfare benefits would soon eradicate this lingering poverty. The conquest of poverty was put down to an expanding economy (the 1950s were the years of the 'affluent society'), to government policies of full employment and to the success of the welfare state. It was widely believed that the operation of the welfare state had redistributed wealth from rich to poor and significantly raised working-class living standards.

Throughout the 1950s and 1960s researchers became increasingly dubious about the 'conquest of poverty'. Rowntree's concept of subsistence poverty, and the indicators he used to measure poverty, were strongly criticized. His measurement of adequate nutrition is a case in point. With the help of experts, Rowntree drew up a diet sheet that would provide the minimum adequate nutritional intake and, using this, he decided upon the minimum monies required for food. It was very unlikely, however, that this minimum budget would meet the needs of the poor. As Martin Rein argues, it was based on:

> an unrealistic assumption of a no-waste budget, and extensive knowledge in marketing and cooking. An economical budget must be based on knowledge and skill which is least likely to be present in the low-income groups we are concerned with.
>
> Rein, 1970

Rowntree's estimates further ignored the fact that most working-class people spent a smaller percentage of their income on food than his budget allowed. Nor did he allow for the fact that choice of food is based on the conventions of a person's social class and region, not upon a diet sheet drawn up by experts. Thus Peter Townsend argues that 'in relation to the budgets and customs of life of ordinary people, the make-up of the subsistence budget was unbalanced'.

Rowntree's selection of the 'necessaries of a healthy life' was based on his own opinions and those of the experts he consulted. In his original 1899 study, these necessities were very limited and genuinely included only the basic items necessary for living in an industrial society. However, as we saw earlier, in his later research he extended the range of

what he considered necessities quite considerably. In the 1936 survey, he expanded the idea of 'human needs' to include personal items such as a radio, a holiday, books and travelling. These items were estimated to cost 5 shillings (25 pence).

In his later work then, Rowntree used a measure of poverty significantly above subsistence level. Furthermore, the inclusion of such items as holidays anticipated the views of some of the supporters of relative poverty. Despite these alterations, Rowntree's studies revealed a dramatic decline in the amount of poverty. Rising living standards and improvements in the state benefits available to those on low incomes seemed to have reduced the poor to a very small fraction of the British population. In the 1960s, though, poverty was 'rediscovered' as researchers developed and applied the concept of relative poverty.

Jonathan Bradshaw, Deborah Mitchell and Jane Morgan – the usefulness of budget standards

Bradshaw *et al.* (1987) admit that the budget standards approach, which prices the necessities needed to avoid poverty, has its limitations. For example, they accept that it 'inevitably involves judgements – judgements about what items should be included, about the quantity of items that are required and about the price that should be fixed to the items'.

Nevertheless, they feel that the budget standards approach is useful because it focuses attention on the amount paid in benefits to the recipients of welfare. It offers sociologists the chance to assess whether benefit levels can provide adequately for people's needs.

Bradshaw *et al.* accept the criticism of Rowntree's work which points out that it is unrealistic to expect people to have a no-waste budget. To overcome this problem, they base their research on how people actually spend their money, rather than on how experts feel they ought to spend it. Bradshaw *et al.* used data from the *Family Finances Survey* to estimate how families spent their money. They then calculated what the families could afford to buy if they were receiving 110 per cent of basic Supplementary Benefit levels in 1986. (Supplementary Benefit was the main means-tested benefit in Britain in 1986.) The figure of 110 per cent of benefit levels, rather than 100 per cent, was used to allow for extra sources of income such as gifts, borrowing and part-time work. In 1986, 110 per cent of Supplementary Benefit for a family with two children under 11 gave the family a weekly income of £74.88.

At this level of income, the family was found to have a very low standard of living. They could not

Table 5.2   Items included and excluded from the Family Budget Unit (FBU) budgets

| Low-cost budget | | Modest but adequate budget | |
Examples of items included	Examples of items excluded	Examples of items included	Examples of items excluded
Basic furniture, textiles and hardware	Antiques, handmade or precious household durables	Basic designs, mass manufactured furniture, textiles and hardware	Antiques, handmade or precious household durables
First aid kit and basic medicine	Prescription, dental and sight care charges	Prescription charges, dental care, sight test	Spectacles, private health care
Fridge, washing machine, lawn mower and vacuum cleaner	Freezer, tumble-dryer, shower, electric blankets, microwave, food-mixer	Fridge-freezer, washing machine, microwave, food-mixer, sewing machine	Tumble-dryer, shower, electric blankets
Basic clothing (cheapest prices in C&A)	Secondhand, designer and high-fashion clothing	Basic clothing, sensible designs	Secondhand, designer and high-fashion clothing
TV, video hire, cassette player, basic camera	Hi-fi, children's TVs, compact discs, camcorders	TV, video hire, basic music system and camera	Children's TVs, compact discs, camcorders
Public transport, children's bikes	Car, adult bikes, caravan, camping equipment	Secondhand five-year-old car, secondhand adult bike, new children's bikes	A second car, caravan, camping equipment mountain bikes
Clocks, watches	Jewellery	Basic jewellery, watch	Precious jewellery
Haircuts	Cosmetics	Basic cosmetics, haircuts	Perfume, hair perm
	Alcohol/smoking	Alcohol – men 14 units, women 10 units (two-thirds HEA safe limit)	Smoking
Day-trip to Blackpool	Annual holiday	One-week annual holiday	Holiday abroad
Cinema twice a year, visiting museums or historic buildings about twice a year	Concerts, panto, ballet, or music lessons for children	Walking, swimming, cycling, football, cinema, panto every two years, youth club, scouts/guides	Fishing, water sports, horse-riding, creative or educational adult classes, children's ballet/ music lessons

Source: Household Budgets and Living Standards, Social Policy Research Findings, No. 31 (Nov. 1992).

afford a holiday and could only have a single one-day outing once a year. They could not afford to go to the cinema, nor to buy books, magazines or bicycles. Running a car was too expensive, and they could afford only one haircut per year.

The researchers examined the weekly menu of a family with two children. They went to Tesco's supermarket in Barrow and bought the shopping found to be typical of families on benefit. Despite buying the cheapest lines and assuming that no food would be wasted, they still found the diet to be 6,500 calories short of what a family needed for the week. The children's diets had too little iron and calcium, and all family members were eating too little fibre and too much fat.

Bradshaw *et al.* argue that studies such as theirs illustrate how deprived people living on benefits are compared to other members of society. They claim:

It is possible that the resurrection of budget standards methodology in the analysis of living standards in the UK could lead to a more considered review of the way we treat the seven million people in the UK dependent on Supplementary Benefit.

Bradshaw *et al.*, 1987

In the 1990s, Bradshaw established the Family Budget Unit (FBU) to continue and develop this approach. The unit distinguished between two levels of income: that which would produce a 'modest but adequate budget', and a 'low-cost budget'. Table 5.2 shows the items included and excluded from these standards. As can be seen from the table, the latter standard reflects contemporary expectations and consumption patterns in Britain. It includes, for example, some provision for leisure such as video hire, but makes no provision for an annual holiday.

The modest but adequate budget is rather more generous but excludes luxury items. Carey Oppenheim and Lisa Harker have compared these findings with levels of income support in Britain. They found that in 1995 income support would meet just 34 per cent of a modest but adequate budget for a single man, 26 per cent for a couple, 40 per cent for a lone mother with two young children and 66 per cent for a couple with two young children (Oppenheim and Harker, 1996).

Evaluation

Pete Alcock (1997) argues that the budget standards approach either relies upon accepting the opinion of experts about what constitutes an adequate budget, or it assumes that 'anyone seeing the evidence of the inadequacy of the weekly budget will recognise the existence of poverty'. Such an assumption is unlikely to be justified. Some will see the budget levels chosen as too generous, others as too mean. The definition is therefore either 'tautological ... or one based only on the judgement of experts'. Paul Spicker (1993) also argues that the approach of Bradshaw *et al.* has its limitations. He points out that people's quality of life is not entirely determined by how they spend money. For example, living standards can be improved by the unpaid labour of family members. Furthermore, no clear poverty line is identified in Bradshaw's work. However, Spicker does support the collection of data on what people actually spend rather than what experts say they should spend. He concludes that 'if there is a way to identify patterns of deprivation as a matter of fact with levels of income, this seems to be it'.

Relative poverty and deprivation

In view of the problems associated with absolute and subsistence standards of poverty, many researchers have abandoned them. Instead, they have defined and measured poverty in terms of the standards specific to a particular place at a particular time. In this section we will consider those definitions.

In a rapidly changing world, definitions of poverty based on relative standards will be constantly changing. Thus Samuel Mencher writes:

> *The argument for relative standards rests on the assumption that for practical purposes standards become so fluid that no definition of need, no matter how broad, satisfies the ever changing expectations of modern life.*
>
> Mencher, 1972

In Western society, products and services such as hot and cold running water, refrigerators and washing machines, medical and dental care, full-time education and motor cars are moving or have moved from being luxuries, to comforts, to necessaries. Thus, in Peter Townsend's words, any definition of poverty must be 'related to the needs and demands of a changing society'.

Moreover, some sociologists have argued that it is necessary to discuss poverty in terms of lifestyles. It is not sufficient to see poverty simply as lack of material possessions and the facilities necessary for material well-being. In contrast, these sociologists believe poverty also exists where members of society are excluded from the lifestyle of the community to which they belong.

Peter Townsend – poverty as relative deprivation

Peter Townsend has carried out a number of studies of poverty, including one of the most detailed ever undertaken in Britain (Townsend, 1979). During the 1960s and 1970s, he played a major part in highlighting the continuing existence of poverty, and in forcing the issue back on to the political agenda. He has also been the leading supporter of defining poverty in terms of relative deprivation: he stresses that poverty should be defined in relation to the standards of a particular society at a particular time. Furthermore, he believes that poverty extends beyond a simple lack of material resources. Townsend identifies three ways of defining poverty, which we will now examine.

The state's standard

The first is the state's standard of poverty, on which official statistics used to be based. Townsend calculates these figures on the basic rate of supplementary benefit (now income support), with the addition of housing costs for different types of household. All those who fall below this level are held to be in poverty, while those receiving income between 100 per cent and 139 per cent of benefit levels are held to be on the margins of poverty. Townsend, however, dismisses this standard as 'neither social nor scientific'. He sees it as being arbitrarily determined by the government of the day, and points out that from year to year it varies in relation to the average income of the population.

The relative income standard of poverty

Townsend calls the second definition of poverty the relative income standard of poverty. This is based upon identifying those households whose income falls well below the average for households with the same composition (the same numbers of adults and children). He defines those who receive 50 per cent or less of the average as poor, and those receiving 80 per cent or less as being in the margins of poverty.

(The British government has now adopted a relative income standard of poverty.) This definition has the benefit of being truly relative. As average income changes, then clearly the poverty line will change as well.

However, Townsend does not accept this definition either:

1 Again, he points out that the point at which such a poverty line is drawn is arbitrary: 60 per cent, 70 per cent or 90 per cent could be taken as the dividing line with no less and no more justification.

2 Nor does he believe that inequality and poverty are the same thing. For example, he argues that you cannot simply define, say, the poorest 20 per cent of the population as poor, because how badly off they are will depend on, among other factors, how developed the welfare system is. They might be considerably better off in a society like Sweden, which has a more highly developed welfare system than a country such as the USA.

3 Furthermore, Townsend wants to extend the concept of poverty beyond material disadvantage. Poverty, in his terms, involves the lifestyles associated with material shortage, and not the material shortage itself.

Relative deprivation

Townsend asserts that 'poverty can be defined objectively and applied consistently only in terms of the concept of relative deprivation'. He justifies this claim on the grounds that society determines people's needs: for example, it determines and conditions even the need for food. It affects the amount of energy that 'different sections of the population habitually expend not only at work but in community and family pursuits'. Their individual obligations as parents, wives or husbands, friends or neighbours, as well as the work they have to do, influence how many calories they have to consume each day. Society also determines what types of foodstuff are available and influences patterns of food consumption through its culture. For instance, tea is closely tied up with British culture and lifestyles: members of British society are expected to be able to offer visitors to their homes a cup of tea, and many workers would be outraged if management threatened to remove their right to a mid-morning tea break. Tea, Townsend reminds us, is 'nutritionally worthless' but 'psychologically and socially essential' in Britain.

Townsend argues that the concept of relative deprivation should be thought of in terms of the resources available to individuals and households, and the styles of living that govern how those resources are used. He believes that concentrating exclusively on income to assess a household's

material situation ignores other types of resources that might be available. It neglects capital assets (those who own their home may be better off than those who rent), and ignores occupational fringe benefits, gifts, and the value of public social services such as education and healthcare.

He also feels that it is necessary to move beyond consumption (the purchase of goods) to an examination of how resources affect participation in the lifestyle of the community. Townsend argues that poverty involves an inability to participate in approved social activities that are considered normal, such as visiting friends or relatives, having birthday parties for children, and going on holiday. The cost of such activities can vary greatly – a month on a Mediterranean cruise is considerably more expensive than a weekend's camping close to home – but, to Townsend, individuals suffer deprivation if they cannot afford even the cheapest form of such activities.

On the basis of these arguments Townsend defines poverty in the following way:

> *Individuals, families and groups in the population can be said to be in poverty when they lack the resources to obtain the types of diet, participate in the activities and have the living conditions and amenities which are customary, or at least widely encouraged or approved, in the societies to which they belong. Their resources are so seriously below those commanded by the average individual or family that they are, in effect, excluded from the ordinary living patterns, customs and activities.*

Townsend, 1979

Poverty in the United Kingdom

In *Poverty in the United Kingdom* (1979), Townsend used this definition to measure the extent of poverty in the UK. (He also collected figures on the basis of the other two definitions he had identified so that he could compare them with his own.) His research was based upon a social survey using questionnaires. In 1968–69, his researchers collected information on 2,052 households, containing 6,098 individuals, in 51 parliamentary constituencies in Britain.

The deprivation index

In order to put his definition of poverty into operation, Townsend devised a deprivation index This index covered a total of 60 specific types of deprivation relating to households, diets, fuel and lighting, clothing, household facilities, housing conditions and amenities, working conditions, health, education, the environment, family life, recreation and social activities. From this original list, he selected 12 items that he believed would be relevant to the whole of the population (and not just to certain sections of it), and calculated the percentage

Table 5.3	The deprivation index	
	Characteristics	% of population
1	Has not had a week's holiday away from home in last 12 months	53.6
2	Adults only. Has not had a relative or friend to the home for a meal or snack in the last four weeks	33.4
3	Adults only. Has not been out in the last four weeks to a relative or friend for a meal or snack	45.1
4	Children only (under 15). Has not had a friend to play or to tea in the last four weeks	36.3
5	Children only. Did not have party on last birthday	56.6
6	Has not had an afternoon or evening out for entertainment in the last two weeks	47.0
7	Does not have fresh meat (including meals out) as many as four days a week	19.3
8	Has gone through one or more days in the past fortnight without a cooked meal	7.0
9	Has not had a cooked breakfast most days of the week	67.3
10	Household does not have a refrigerator	45.1
11	Household does not usually have a Sunday joint (three in four times)	25.9
12	Household does not have sole use of four amenities indoors (flush WC; sink or washbasin and cold-water tap; fixed bath or shower; and gas/electric cooker)	21.4

Source: P. Townsend (1979) *Poverty in the United Kingdom*, Penguin, Harmondsworth, p. 250.

of the population deprived of them. The results of his findings are shown in Table 5.3.

Each household was given a score on a deprivation index. The more a household was found to suffer deprivation, the higher its score. Townsend then calculated the average score for households with different levels of income expressed as a percentage of basic supplementary benefit levels. He claimed to find a threshold for levels of income below which the amount of deprivation suddenly increased rapidly. This threshold was found to be at about 150 per cent of basic supplementary benefit levels. He therefore decided to classify all households that did not have this level of resources as 'suffering from poverty'.

Townsend adjusted the income deemed necessary for each family according to the numbers in it, whether adults were working, the age of any children, and whether any members were disabled. Because of the procedures he had followed, he felt able to claim that his figures and definition were 'scientific' and 'objective'.

On the basis of these calculations, Townsend found that 22.9 per cent of the population (or 12.46 million people) were living in poverty in 1968–9. This compared with 6.1 per cent in poverty according

to the state standard, or 9.2 per cent in poverty according to the relative income standard. Townsend found that poverty was much more widespread than other research had suggested.

Criticisms of Townsend's early research

Despite the enormous impact Townsend's early work has had on British poverty research, some writers have criticized it. David Piachaud (1981, 1987) argues that the index on which Townsend's statistics are based is inadequate. Piachaud writes, commenting on the items included in the index, that 'it is not clear what they have to do with poverty, nor how they were selected'. In particular, he questions the view that going without a Sunday joint and not eating fresh meat or cooked meals are necessarily associated with deprivation: it might reflect social and cultural differences. He claims that 'it is no indicator of deprivation if someone chooses to stay at home, eating salads and uncooked breakfasts'.

Dorothy Wedderburn (1974) also criticizes Townsend's index. She describes the decision to include certain items and exclude others as arbitrary. She would have preferred Townsend to carry out research into what was actually customary behaviour in society. As a result, she sees the index as reflecting Townsend's personal opinions: it is subjective and not an objective basis for measuring deprivation.

A problem that all researchers into poverty face is that of finding a point at which it is possible to draw a poverty line. Townsend claimed to have found such a point, below which deprivation starts to increase rapidly. Piachaud believes that the selection of this point (at 150 per cent of basic supplementary benefit levels) is as arbitrary as any other. He examined Townsend's data closely and disputed the view that deprivation starts to increase rapidly below this level of income. Other researchers, such as M. Desai (1986), have reanalysed Townsend's data, and have supported his claim that there is a poverty threshold.

Perhaps the most damaging criticism of Townsend advanced by Piachaud concerns the implications of his definition of poverty for measures designed to eradicate it. Using Townsend's deprivation index as a measure of poverty, all inequality of wealth and income could be removed from society, but poverty might still remain if people chose to become vegetarian or not to go on holiday. As Piachaud puts it, 'taken to its logical conclusion, only when everyone behaved identically would no one be defined as deprived'. To tackle what Townsend calls poverty would involve creating uniformity in people's behaviour, because Townsend did not attempt to discover whether it was choice or shortage of money which led to people in his survey scoring points on the deprivation index.

Amartya Sen (1981, 1985) argues that there is 'much to be said' for Townsend's concept of relative deprivation. However, Sen believes that relative deprivation, even including all its variants, cannot really be the only basis for the concept of poverty. He suggests that there is an:

> *irreducible core of absolute deprivation in our idea of poverty, which translates reports of starvation, malnutrition and visible hardship into a diagnosis of poverty without having to ascertain first the relative position.*
>
> Sen, 1985

Thus, if famine were very widespread in a society, it would make little sense to argue that there was no poverty on the grounds that there was little inequality since everybody was short of food.

Sen accepts that the resources needed to avoid absolute deprivation vary from society to society. The diet and shelter required in different circumstances will vary, but to him that does not prevent poverty researchers from determining when people have too little for their most basic needs. To Sen, then, 'the approach of relative deprivation supplements rather than supplants the analysis of poverty in terms of absolute dispossession'.

Townsend has defended himself against Sen. He has argued that Sen's concentration on absolute deprivation is politically dangerous. Potentially, at least, it gives governments in affluent societies an excuse to cut back their welfare states to an absolute bare minimum. Furthermore, Townsend claims that Sen offers no clear definition of absolute deprivation. Sen uses a variety of terms such as 'starvation', 'malnutrition' and 'hunger' to describe the situation where people's basic food needs are not being met. Yet 'starvation' and 'hunger' mean rather different things and Sen offers no clear criteria for determining when people's diets are inadequate and they are therefore in poverty.

More recently (Townsend, 1995), Townsend has continued to argue that an international poverty line can be based on a concept of relative deprivation. He claims that when absolute measures of poverty are used to compare nations, they tend to suggest that there is little poverty in richer countries. Since Townsend believes that poverty remains a substantial problem in countries such as the USA and Britain, he does not accept that absolute international poverty lines are adequate. Instead, he argues that international comparisons can be made by identifying a poverty threshold for each society, below which people start to suffer from relative deprivation. However, the problem remains that this still involves making comparisons on the basis of poverty lines that are unique to each country.

Despite Townsend's defence, Sen may have a point in arguing that different types of poverty should be distinguished. Most of Sen's research has been conducted in developing countries where absolute deprivation, however defined, remains a real problem. At least in terms of international comparisons, the idea of absolute deprivation as poverty may still be useful.

The London study

In his more recent research, Townsend has used slightly different research methods from those of his previous work (Townsend, Corrigan and Kowarzik, 1985). He has continued to define poverty in terms of relative deprivation, but he has amended the way the concept is operationalized.

In 1985–6, Townsend *et al.* used this new approach in a study of a sample of 2,703 Londoners. In this study, Townsend *et al.* (1987) distinguished between material deprivation and social deprivation.

Material deprivation covered dietary deprivation, clothing deprivation, housing deprivation, deprivation of home facilities, deprivation of environment, deprivation of location and deprivation at work.

Social deprivation covered lack of employment rights, deprivation of family activity, lack of integration into the community, lack of participation in social institutions, recreational deprivation and educational deprivation.

Initially, 77 items were included in the index to measure these different types of deprivation, but seven were excluded because the deprivation was found to affect more than 50 per cent of the population. In this way, Townsend *et al.* hoped to establish which activities in their index represented 'standard or majority norms, conventions and customs'.

Townsend *et al.* made greater allowances for variations in taste than was the case in Townsend's earlier study. For example, in measuring dietary deprivation different questions were used for meat-eaters and vegetarians. Scores from the material and social deprivation indexes were aggregated to produce an overall deprivation score for each household.

In the London research, Townsend *et al.* distinguished between objective and subjective deprivation. Objective deprivation was measured using the deprivation index. Subjective deprivation was measured by asking respondents the level of income their household required to escape poverty. Detailed information was also collected on the income received by each household.

The London findings

Townsend *et al.* followed Townsend's earlier study in trying to establish a threshold at which multiple deprivations began to increase. Table 5.4 shows the level of income needed to prevent multiple deprivation in comparison to the basic level of means-tested benefit, excluding housing costs. The level proved to be rather greater than in the earlier study, ranging from 203 per cent of benefit levels for a single person under 60, to 150 per cent for a couple with three children.

Self-assessments of how much money households needed to escape poverty proved to be very similar to the estimates made by the researchers. For example, the respondents estimated that £110 per week was needed by a couple with two children, while the researchers estimated £109 per week. For single parents, the equivalent figures were £80 and £81, and for a single person under 60, £60 and £64. However, there was a more substantial difference for a couple under 60. Respondents estimated their needs to be £104, while the researchers estimated £75.

Nevertheless, Townsend *et al.* concluded that their estimate of the poverty threshold was broadly similar to that of the population in their sample. Both methods of determining a poverty threshold showed that benefit levels were inadequate, with Londoners themselves suggesting that an average 61 per cent more than basic benefit levels was needed to escape poverty.

Joanna Mack and Stewart Lansley – *Poor Britain*

In between Townsend's earlier and later research, London Weekend Television financed a study of poverty built on Townsend's methods (Mack and Lansley, 1985). It was conducted by Joanna Mack and Stewart Lansley, and took account of many of the methodological criticisms of Townsend made by sociologists such as Piachaud. Although Townsend's later study in London did modify the methods to some extent, it still used a deprivation index consisting of items chosen by the researchers, and it still made no attempt to measure why people were not participating in some activities.

Mack and Lansley followed Townsend in defining poverty in relative terms, and in attempting to measure directly the extent of deprivation. Unlike Townsend, however, they tried to distinguish between styles of living which people could not afford, and those which they chose not to follow.

Furthermore, Mack and Lansley devised a new way of determining what were the 'necessities' of life in modern Britain. They accepted the point made by Piachaud that taste might influence whether some people went without items on a deprivation index. In order to overcome this problem, they decided to

Table 5.4	Weekly income required to surmount deprivation, as a percentage of basic means-tested assistance scales
Household type	Weekly income required, after deduction of housing costs, as a percentage of basic means-tested assistance scales
Single person under 60	203
Couple under 60	157
Couple with two children	151
Couple with three children	150
Single parent with one child	168

Note: Assumptions have had to be made about the ages of children so that basic rates could be estimated.

Source: P. Townsend (1993) *The International Analysis of Poverty*, Harvester Wheatsheaf, Hemel Hempstead, p. 61.

include in their research a question relating to each item that respondents said they lacked, asking them whether it was by choice, or through necessity, because of financial shortage. Those who said it was a matter of choice were not defined as being deprived of that item.

In addition, Mack and Lansley excluded some items from the index which groups with high income were as likely, or nearly as likely, to say they lacked by choice as groups on low incomes. They suggested that where these particular items were concerned, the cost of them depended to a significant extent on where people lived. (For example, the costs of a garden would be much greater for a resident in a fashionable and prosperous area of London than for a person living in an economically depressed northern town.) Lack of a television set was also ignored because the number who did not have this item was so small that no conclusions could be drawn from the data.

After the exclusion of such items, Mack and Lansley argued that their figures would accurately reflect the extent of involuntary deprivation.

Public perception of necessities

The second area in which this study tried to improve on Townsend's work was in the selection of items for inclusion in the index. Mack and Lansley wanted to avoid the accusation that their choice of items was purely arbitrary. They rejected Rowntree's use of experts to determine basic needs, and went beyond Townsend's subjective choices of what he thought was customary. They argued that it was possible to measure the standards of a society in order to provide a more objective basis for defining relative deprivation.

Table 5.5 The public's perception of necessities (% classing items as necessary)

	1990 %	1983 %	Change % +/−		1990 %	1983 %	Change % +/−
A damp-free home	98	96	+2	Hobby or leisure activity	67	64	+3
An inside toilet (not shared with another household)	97	96	+1	New, not secondhand, clothes	65	64	+1
Heating to warm living areas of the home if it's cold	97	97	0	A roast joint or its vegetarian equivalent once a week[3]	64	67	−3
Beds for everyone in the household	95	94	+1	Leisure equipment for children, e.g. sports equipment or bicycle[3]	61	57	+4
Bath, not shared with another household	95	94	+1	A television	58	51	+7
A decent state of decoration in the home[2]	92	–	–	Telephone	56	43	+13
Fridge	92	77	+15	An annual week's holiday away, not with relatives	54	63	−9
Warm waterproof coat	91	87	+4	A 'best outfit' for special occasions	54	48	+6
Three meals a day for children[1]	90	82	+8	An outing for children once a week[1]	53	40	+13
Two meals a day (for adults)[4]	90	64	+26	Children's friends round for tea/snack fortnightly[1]	52	37	+15
Insurance[2]	88	–	–	A dressing gown	42	38	+4
Fresh fruit[2]	88	–	–	A night out fortnightly	42	36	+6
Toys for children, e.g. dolls or models[1]	84	71	+13	Fares to visit friends in other parts of the country four times a year[2]	39	–	–
Separate bedrooms for every child over 10 of different sexes[1]	82	77	+5	Special lessons such as music, dance or sport[1,2]	39	–	–
Carpets in living rooms and bedrooms in the home	78	70	+8	Friends/family for a meal monthly	37	32	+5
Meat or fish or vegetarian equivalent every other day[3]	77	63	+14	A car	26	22	+4
Celebrations on special occasions, such as Christmas	74	69	+5	Pack of cigarettes every other day	18	14	+4
Two pairs of all-weather shoes	74	78	−4	Restaurant meal monthly[2]	17	–	–
Washing machine	73	67	+6	Holidays abroad annually[2]	17	–	–
Presents for friends or family once a year	69	63	+6	A video[2]	13	–	–
Out of school activities, e.g. sports, orchestra, scouts[1,2]	69	–	–	A home computer[2]	5	–	–
Regular savings of £10 a month for 'rainy days' or retirement[2]	68			A dishwasher[2]	4	–	–

Notes: The descriptions of items have been abbreviated
1 For families with children 2 Not included in the 1983 survey 3 Vegetarian option added in 1990 4 Two hot meals in the 1983 survey

Source: H. Frayman (1991) *Breadline Britain 1990s: The Findings of the Television Series*, London Weekend Television, London, p. 4.

Mack and Lansley asked respondents in their research what they considered to be necessities in contemporary Britain. Although the answers represented no more than the subjective opinions of members of society, they did at least give some indication of what the population considered to be customary, socially approved and of vital importance to social life. Furthermore, Mack and Lansley claimed to have discovered a large degree of consensus about what items were seen as necessities. Their findings, and those of a follow-up study (Mack and Lansley, 1992), are summarized in Table 5.5.

They decided to assume that an item became a necessity when it reached 50 per cent, because a majority of the population now classified it as one. The lack of a television, the lack of self-contained accommodation, the lack of a garden and the lack of money for public transport were excluded for reasons that have already been explained. This left them with a deprivation index of 22 items. Mack and Lansley went on to measure the extent of poverty, which they defined as 'an enforced lack of socially perceived necessities', on the basis of this index. Only those people who lacked three or more items were considered to be poor.

Mack and Lansley produced the following results, using a sample of 1,174 people who were questioned in February 1983. According to their calculations, there were 7.5 million people in poverty in Britain – 5 million adults and 2.5 million children – equivalent to 13.8 per cent of the population. Although this figure is substantially less than that reached by Townsend in 1968–9, it still shows that poverty remains a significant problem in contemporary Britain.

Because the figures were calculated on a different basis from those of Townsend, they were not strictly comparable, and did not therefore demonstrate that the amount of poverty had decreased. Indeed, Mack and Lansley thought that the amount of poverty had probably increased in the years preceding their study. They found that the share of national earnings from employment received by the poorest 40 per cent of the population had fallen from 15.6 per cent in 1965 to 10.2 per cent in 1976.

Mack and Lansley also pointed to a number of government decisions which had made the recipients of welfare payments worse off. In particular, they claimed that some policies of the Thatcher government would probably have increased the amount of poverty. Unemployment had risen, but the earnings-related supplement for the short-term unemployed had been abolished. Old-age pensions had risen more slowly than average wages, and there had been dramatic cuts in housing benefits after the autumn of 1983.

The follow-up study

Mack and Lansley carried out a follow-up study in 1990, using a sample of 1,800 people. Once again they conducted a survey to determine public perceptions of necessities. They found that these had changed. A weekly outing for children, children's friends round once a fortnight, a telephone and a best outfit for special occasions were all now seen as necessities by more than half the population. These were therefore added to the index. Televisions were also included.

Some new items were added which were also seen as necessities by the majority of respondents. These were:

1 a decent standard of decoration in the home
2 savings of at least £10 per week
3 home contents insurance
4 participation in out-of-school activities for children
5 fresh fruit and vegetables every day.

This produced an index of 32 items.

Changes between 1983 and 1990

The 1990 study found there had been a big increase in poverty. The numbers lacking three or more of the necessities, and therefore in poverty according to Mack and Lansley's definition, had risen from 7.5 million in 1983 to 11 million in 1990. The number in severe poverty, defined as lacking seven or more items, had gone up from 2.5 million in 1983 to 3.5 million in 1990.

Two-thirds of the poor in 1990 were found to be dependent on state benefits. Mack and Lansley argued that much of the increase in the numbers of poor resulted from specific changes in the benefits system:

1 Pensions were indexed to prices, rather than wages as in 1979, so that as wage earners became better off, pensioners became relatively poorer. Pensioners made up one-tenth of the poor in 1983, but one-fifth of the poor in 1990.
2 Invalidity benefit and income support (previously supplementary benefit) had also fallen well behind average earnings.
3 Two-thirds of single parents were found to be poor, compared to just under 50 per cent in 1983.
4 Many of the poor had been hit by the replacement of single payments with the social fund in 1988.

(We discuss these changes in benefits in more detail on pp. 343–4.)

Criticisms of Mack and Lansley

The inclusion of entirely new items in the 1990 index raises questions about the comparability of the data from the two studies. Obviously, the more items that are included as necessities, the greater the number of people who will be found to be lacking three or more necessities. Thus, at least part of the increase in poverty found in comparing the two studies may have resulted from the changes in the surveys rather than from changes in society.

Use of a public opinion poll to determine what are considered necessities is an advance over Townsend's approach which relies largely on the judgements of the researcher. However, even Mack and Lansley's method is heavily influenced by the choices made by the researchers. They have to choose what items to question the public about before they can determine what is considered deprivation. Many other items apart from those chosen could have been included.

The researchers also shaped the findings by defining poverty as lacking three or more items. If they had settled on two or four items as the dividing line they would have produced a different estimate of the total number in poverty. As David Piachaud (1987) points out, Mack and Lansley's approach 'still requires expert involvement in defining questions and determining answers'.

Piachaud also points out that there is a problem with individuals who spend their money on items that are not considered necessities. For example, some people could not afford to pay for an adequate diet or adequate housing because they spent large amounts of money on cigarettes or leisure pursuits. To Piachaud there needs to be 'some judgement about what margin, if any, needs to be allowed for non-necessities'. Again, this involves the use of the opinion of 'experts' and further undermines the claim that the results of such studies are based upon definitions of poverty supported by the general public.

Robert Walker (1987) attempts to overcome the problem of expert judgement by trying to 'democratize' the process of determining what necessities are. He argues that Mack and Lansley's approach fails to do justice to the complexity of the problem. The survey data they use gives respondents no chance to determine what quality of goods and services people need. For example, is a threadbare carpet adequate, or should it be in better condition? Moreover, Mack and Lansley gave the respondents no opportunity to include items they were not asked about, nor any chance to discuss the issues involved and reflect in depth on the necessities of contemporary living.

Walker therefore proposes that basic needs should be determined not by groups of experts, nor by survey methods, but by panels of ordinary people who are given the opportunity to have in-depth discussions. These members of the public could then produce costed descriptions of the minimum acceptable basket of goods and services needed by different family types.

In this way, a definition of poverty could be based upon a genuine consensus among a sample of the population, rather than being based upon the majority voting system used in Mack and Lansley's survey research. So-called experts would no longer define poverty in their own terms.

Pete Alcock is one writer who supports this approach. He argues that other approaches are flawed because:

absolute definitions of poverty necessarily involve relative judgements to apply them to any particular society; and relative definitions require some absolute core in order to distinguish them from broader inequalities. Both it seems have major disadvantages, and in pure terms neither is acceptable or workable as a definition of poverty.

Alcock, 1997, p. 72

Alcock prefers Bradshaw's approach because he sees it as combining the strengths of absolute and relative definitions of poverty, and because the definitions reached are based upon a consensus that implies that the political will exists to tackle the poverty uncovered.

An obvious problem with Walker's approach is the assumption that a consensus would be reached. It is quite likely that the members of the public on the panel would disagree about a minimum acceptable living standard. Furthermore, there would be no guarantee that the same living standard would be agreed by a different panel. Once again, an objective or 'democratic' definition of poverty would prove elusive.

Social exclusion

In recent years, some commentators have tried to broaden the issues involved in thinking about the most deprived groups in society by using the term social exclusion rather than poverty. In some ways, this represents an extension of Townsend's idea of relative deprivation, as it goes beyond confining the question of deprivation to commodities that can be directly purchased. Carol and Alan Walker define poverty as 'a lack of the material resources, especially income, necessary to participate in British society'. For them, social exclusion refers to the 'dynamic process of being shut out, fully or partially, from any of the social, economic, political and cultural systems which determine the social integration of a person in society' (Walker and Walker, 1997). Thus, for example, the socially excluded might include the unemployed who lack a role in the formal economic system; those who do not register to vote, who lack a role in the political system; and isolated elderly individuals who live alone and lack a role in the social system. Pete Alcock (1997) claims that the idea of social exclusion was first highlighted by the Child Poverty Action Group in Britain in the mid-1980s and has become an increasingly prominent issue in Europe. The EU's European Social Charter mentions the term 'social exclusion', and the EU also sponsored seminars on social exclusion during the 1990s. Alcock argues that:

> what the EU commentators were doing in their discussion of the problem of social exclusion was attempting to broaden the debate and research on poverty and deprivation beyond the confines and experiences of the poor to encompass the reaction to poverty by other social agencies and individuals throughout society. In this sense, they argue that, rather than being a state of affairs – as poverty has often been conceived – social exclusion is really a process involving us all.
>
> Alcock, 1997, p. 95

In other words, the idea of social exclusion forces us to consider the role of those who do the excluding (the comfortably-off majority), as well as those who are excluded. Brian Nolan and Christopher T. Whelan (1996) also stress that social exclusion is a dynamic concept. They say:

> talking of social exclusion rather than poverty highlights the gap between those who are active members of society and those who are forced to the fringe, the increasing risks of social disintegration, and the fact that, for the persons concerned and for society, this is a process of change and not a fixed or static situation.
>
> Nolan and Whelan, 1996

Adopting this focus has important consequences. For example, it implies policies that move beyond the '(re)distribution of resources to include the promotion of changes in social and economic structures' (Alcock, 1997). Better welfare payments on their own would not ensure that the excluded would receive the chance to participate in all areas of social, economic and political life. Roger Lawson (1995) describes social exclusion in Britain and America as becoming 'detached from the broader social and economic experiences of mainstream society'. He believes that social exclusion has been increasing because of the

'risks of family breakdown, reinforced gender inequalities ... more hostile and fearful relationships in local communities [and] the most disturbing of recent trends ... hardened racial cleavages and ... new forms of xenophobia and racism among the less privileged'. Tackling such problems would involve measures to deal with racism, to encourage a stronger sense of community, and to combat sex discrimination and other causes of gender inequality.

The term social exclusion was given further prominence in Britain when the Labour government launched a new Social Exclusion Unit in December 1997 to deal with social problems such as truancy and unemployment. In broad terms, its aims were to encourage social inclusion; in other words, to encourage people to participate in those areas of social life from which they were excluded. For example, it aimed to encourage truants to attend school, and unemployed people, particularly single parents and young people, to find employment.

Some problems with social exclusion

The concept of social exclusion plays a valuable role in broadening the debate about what constitutes a good quality of life to include more than purely material considerations. It also encourages policy-makers to coordinate a wide range of policies that try to improve the position of the disadvantaged. However, because of its breadth and because it is multi-dimensional, social exclusion is difficult to define precisely and measure reliably. As with relative poverty, there are even greater problems in using this concept to compare different societies which have different norms and patterns of social interaction. Tackling some aspects of social exclusion (for example, a decline in a sense of community) may be beyond the power of governments.

There is a risk that concern for the general notion of social exclusion might distract policy-makers from dealing with the specific material deprivation which is at the root of much social exclusion. Nolan and Whelan suggest that the EU may be keen on using the term social exclusion because it might be:

> more palatable, and perhaps more effective in terms of EU decision-making, to talk in terms of the need to accompany the integration of economies with measures to promote social integration and combat social exclusion rather than to highlight the possibility that economic integration could result in poverty for some vulnerable people and areas.
>
> Nolan and Whelan, 1996, p. 190

Social exclusion could thus be used to allow the EU to avoid doing anything directly about increased poverty that might be caused by a shift to Europe-wide free markets.

There is a related risk that the concept may be used to justify cutting welfare payments on the grounds that this will encourage the excluded to earn a living which will in turn lead to their greater involvement in society (see p. 346). It remains to be seen how successful such policies will be. Nolan and Whelan argue that social exclusion can be a useful concept because it 'may help to sensitize researchers and policy-makers to dynamics, processes, multiple disadvantages'. However, this does not mean that it can be used to replace the term poverty. Poverty still needs to be studied and highlighted because of its resonance in everyday language, because people feel they know what it means, and because, as an evaluative and emotive term, it encourages people to think something should be done about it. Thus they argue it would be undesirable to lose 'the spark that "poverty" ignites because of its everyday usage and evaluative content'.

Nevertheless, some sociologists have started making good use of the concept of social exclusion in explaining the causes of the predicament of the most disadvantaged in society. It also highlights important aspects of the problems faced by groups such as the disabled and ethnic minorities (see pp. 313–14).

Official statistics on poverty

Some countries use an official poverty line and produce regular statistics on poverty. The USA is an example. Other countries, such as Britain, do not have an official poverty line but do produce some statistics on low incomes.

Statistics on official poverty, or low incomes, are not necessarily based upon sophisticated sociological definitions of poverty. What is more, statistics from different countries are calculated in a variety of ways and therefore cannot always be compared.

Nevertheless, official statistics do provide valuable information about the extent of poverty, or at least low incomes. They also give some indication of how poverty is distributed between different social groups.

British statistics

Low Income Family statistics

Although Britain has never had an official poverty line it has published statistics on low incomes. Figures on Low Income Families were first produced by the then Department of Health and Social Security in the early 1970s. This set of figures was dropped by the Department of Social Security in 1988. However, the Institute for Fiscal Studies, an independent research institute, has continued to produce figures on Low Income Families since 1988 by extrapolating from official statistics.

Low Income Family statistics measure the numbers of families who are receiving different levels of income in relation to the main means-tested state benefit. They are calculated using figures from an annual government survey, the *Family Expenditure Survey*, and figures published by the Department of Social Security on benefits claimants. The basic state means-tested benefit was originally called national assistance, later supplementary benefit and is now called income support.

National assistance was first introduced in 1948 with the implementation of the Beveridge Report which laid the foundations of the welfare state. The level at which national assistance was first set was based upon the work of Seebohm Rowntree. Beveridge thought that Rowntree's 1899 poverty index was insufficiently generous and claimed to have based the initial benefit levels upon the 1936 index.

Frank Field (1982), however, argues that the benefits were set at a lower level than that which Rowntree's research indicated was necessary to raise people out of poverty. According to Field, for single men and women, benefits were set at 55 and 66 per cent of Rowntree's level respectively. Pensioners also received less than was necessary to raise them up to Rowntree's 1936 poverty line, but children were treated more generously.

National assistance and its later equivalents have been paid to those who can demonstrate that they have a low income. The benefit has been intended to provide a basic minimum income for those suffering material hardship. Figures have been produced by a number of different researchers on those receiving income at or below the level of these benefits and on those who receive 140 per cent or less of the basic benefit level.

As we saw earlier in this chapter, poverty researchers such as Townsend and Mack and Lansley argue that families need to be well above basic benefit levels to escape from poverty. The figures on both those receiving the same or less than basic benefit levels, and those receiving less than 140 per cent of basic levels, have been used by some commentators as a measure of poverty.

Advantages and disadvantages

When the Department of Social Security decided to discontinue publishing Low Income Family statistics it gave a number of reasons:

1 It argued that benefit levels were being used both to measure the extent of poverty and to alleviate poverty. This led to a paradox: if the government put benefit levels up, more people fell into the category Low Income Family, yet the poor were receiving more money. In other words, attempts to help the poor created more poverty.

2 It claimed that the use of the family as the unit of analysis overstated the extent of low income. Many households had more than one family living in them (for example, parents and married children), and the pooling of resources between family units could help to compensate for the low income of one unit.

3 140 per cent of benefit levels might be considered too generous as a measure of low income.

Christopher Giles and Steven Webb (1993) of the Institute for Fiscal Studies do not regard such criticisms as a justification for abandoning statistics on Low Income Families:

1 They point out that it is possible to adjust the figures to take account of the changes in the real value of benefit. They have produced such figures based on the 1979 benefit levels adjusted for inflation in later years (see below).

2 Giles and Webb see the second criticism as more serious, but any poverty figures are bound to run into the problem of the distribution of resources within households. Calculating the income of individuals, households or families as the basis for poverty statistics is problematic, whichever is used.

3 The third criticism is dismissed as unimportant. A 140 per cent of benefit levels does not have to be taken as the cut-off point between the poor and non-poor; 100, 110 or 120 per cent can be used as alternatives.

Some critics of the Conservative government have suggested that these figures were discontinued in 1988 for political reasons. If the Institute for Fiscal Studies had not carried on producing them, it would have been impossible to calculate changes in the numbers of 'poor', using official sources. Abandoning the figures could therefore be seen as a cynical attempt to hide an increase in poverty which had resulted from government policies.

Figures on Low Income Families do not correspond exactly to any sociological definition of poverty, but they do provide a rough guide to trends in poverty. Giles and Webb praise this measure for its simplicity and for the ease with which household size can be taken into account, since households with different compositions receive different levels of benefit. They also note that it is useful for determining the numbers of people who are slipping through the 'safety-net' of the welfare state, and receiving less than basic benefit levels.

Trends in Low Income Families

Figure 5.1 shows the numbers and percentages of the population with different levels of income in relation to benefit levels. There was a marked rise between 1979 and 1992 (the last available figure), with the percentage living at or below benefit levels rising from 14 to 24 per cent of the population. The percentage receiving less than 140 per cent of benefit levels rose from 24 to 33 per cent.

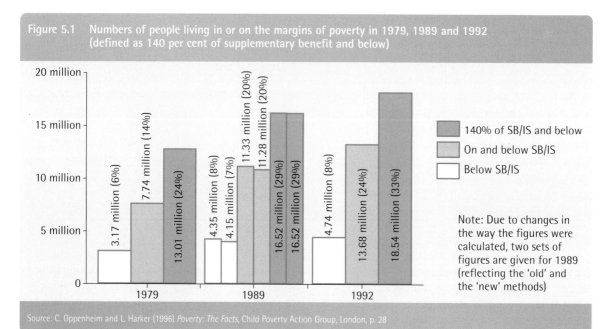

Figure 5.1 Numbers of people living in or on the margins of poverty in 1979, 1989 and 1992 (defined as 140 per cent of supplementary benefit and below)

Source: C. Oppenheim and L. Harker (1996) *Poverty: The Facts*, Child Poverty Action Group, London, p. 28

Carey Oppenheim and Lisa Harker (1996) attribute most of the increase in those living at or below income support levels to a rise in unemployment. Between 1979 and 1992, the numbers of pensioners on supplementary benefit/income support fell, but the numbers of lone parents, couples with children, the unemployed and the long-term sick on benefits all rose. The numbers of single people without children on very low incomes also rose.

As mentioned above, the Institute for Fiscal Studies has also calculated trends in Low Income Families using 1979 benefit levels as a base and allowing for inflation. On this measure, there was almost no increase in poverty between 1979 and 1992, largely because there was an increase in real terms in the value of income support/supplementary benefit over this period. However, Oppenheim and Harker argue that these figures are misleading. This is because those receiving income support/supplementary benefit have largely lost the right to single payments to help with the purchase of items such as cookers and beds. Now, claimants usually have to make do with loans instead. The Low Income Family statistics take no account of this change and therefore tend to underestimate any increase in poverty.

Homelessness

The figures discussed may be somewhat misleading because the *Family Expenditure Survey* on which they are based excludes people living in institutions such as nursing homes, residential homes, hospitals and prisons, and the homeless. Many of those excluded have low incomes and the homeless have some of the lowest incomes of all.

While there has probably been a reduction in the number of people resident in institutions, there has been a big increase in homelessness since the 1970s. Carol and Alan Walker (1997) report that there were 125,000 people registered as homeless by local authorities in 1995. However, there may be many more 'unofficial homeless'. N. Ginsburg estimates that, on the basis of the 1991 census, in addition to those living on the streets, there were 110,000 families who wanted a home of their own but were living with somebody else, 50,000 couples who wanted to live together but didn't, 140,000 sharing households when they didn't want to, and 22,000 living in bed and breakfast accommodation (quoted in Walker and Walker, 1997).

Not all these groups would be excluded from the statistics on Low Income Families, but, nevertheless, the rise in all types of homelessness would make a significant difference to the figures if the homeless were included. Indeed, it can be argued that some of the homeless are suffering from absolute poverty since they do not even have adequate shelter.

Households Below Average Income

The Conservative government discontinued its statistics on Low Income Families in 1988, and replaced them with figures on Households Below Average Income. So far figures for the period 1979–92/3 have been produced. These figures are based on household incomes both before and after housing costs, adjusted to take account of household size.

This method allows figures to be produced which show the number of households falling below different levels in relation to average income. For example, the number of households receiving 50 per cent or less of the average household income is sometimes taken as a measure of the numbers in poverty. It also allows trends in the income of richer and poorer sections of the population to be compared. The population is divided into ten groups of 10 per cent (or deciles) according to income, and the living standards of each decile can be tracked over time. Box 5.1 describes the levels of income required by different household types to be in each of these deciles.

Households Below Average Income statistics provide a useful measure of income inequality and can be used as one way of measuring relative poverty. Giles and Webb (1993) argue that the figures are useful because they are comprehensive and are not tied to benefit levels which are affected by political decisions. Figures such as the proportion of households receiving less than half the average income allow clear comparisons over time and between countries.

However, Giles and Webb note that the figures were never intended to be a measure of poverty and what they actually measure is simply income distribution. Peter Townsend has also attacked what he calls the 'relative income standard of poverty' (see pp. 296–7). Nevertheless, such statistics do provide useful information on inequality, and inequality is an important aspect of relative definitions of poverty.

Trends in income distribution

Figure 5.2 shows trends in the proportions of the population in Britain living in households which received less than 60 per cent, 50 per cent and 40 per cent of the average income between 1961 and 1993. It is based on data from the *Family Expenditure Survey*. It includes figures calculated before housing costs and after housing costs.

The statistics show a very large increase in the proportions falling below each level. For example, in 1961, 11 per cent of the population had an income of less than 50 per cent of the mean before housing costs, but this had nearly doubled to 20 per cent in

Box 5.1 Who would be where in income distribution deciles for different household types in Britain (1995 prices)

Bottom decile

Income support for a single person over 25 was £46.50 per week in 1995-6, for a childless couple £73 per week, and for a couple with two children £122.60. Anyone with just this income would be in the bottom decile. Pensioners with just the basic pension (£58.85 for a single pensioner, £94.10 for a couple) would also be here.

Decile 2

Benefit recipients with some Housing Benefit and pensioners with a small amount of private income would be in this decile.

Decile 3

A single pensioner with just £35 of occupational pension or Housing Benefit would make it into decile 3. They could be joined by a childless couple with one partner earning £10,000 gross per year or a couple with children and one partner earning £15,000.

Decile 4

Single people on very low earnings, pensioners with a little more private income, couples with slightly higher earnings than in decile 3, and some benefit recipients with earnings-related pensions or high levels of Housing Benefit would be in decile 4.

Decile 5

A single person earning just £8,500 would make it into decile 5. That is equivalent to about £4 per hour for a 40-hour week and weekly take-home pay of £130. A childless couple with one partner earning £15,000, or a couple with children and each partner earning £10,000, would also be here.

Decile 6

A single pensioner with an occupational pension of £5,000 gross would have enough to get into the top half of the income distribution. A couple of low earners on just £8,500 each would also make it. But for a couple with children, if only one was earning, gross pay of £23,000 would be required.

Decile 7

For a single person, £12,000 gross would be sufficient to place them in decile 7. The same earnings for a single-earner couple with children would put them in decile 2 or 3.

Decile 8

A single-earner couple with children would need more than £30,000 gross to make decile 8.

Decile 9

Both mother and father would need to earn around £20,000 per year for a couple with children to be in decile 9. A single person on average annual male earnings of around £19,000 per year would very comfortably make it into the upper half of this decile.

Top decile

This decile could include a single person earning £22,000 per year. But for a couple with children, if only one of them was earning, gross pay would have to be in excess of £50,000. A childless couple with each partner earning just £17,000 per year could join them in the richest decile.

Source: A. Goodman, P. Johnson, and S. Webb (1997) *Inequality in the UK*, Oxford University Press, Oxford, p. 61

Figure 5.2 Percentage of the population below 40 per cent, 50 per cent, and 60 per cent of national average income

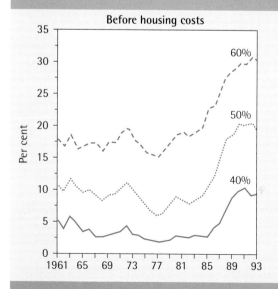

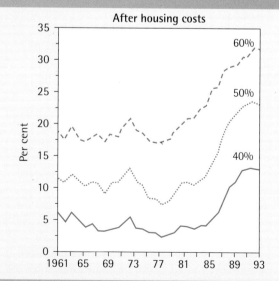

Source: A. Goodman, P. Johnson and S. Webb (1997) *Inequality in the UK*, Oxford University Press, Oxford p. 236

1992-3. In fact, whether you take those on 40, 50 or 60 per cent of income, before or after housing costs, there have been dramatic increases in the proportions on relatively low incomes, particularly since 1977.

This increase has been caused by significant shifts in income distribution. Figure 5.3 shows the changes in the real income and expenditure of decile groups between 1979 and 1992 after housing costs. It is based on research by Alissa Goodman and Steven Webb for the Institute for Fiscal Studies (Goodman and Webb, 1995). It shows that the poorest decile had a reduction in income of 18 per cent over the period and the next poorest decile a reduction of 1 per cent. In contrast, the richest decile had an increase in income of a massive 61 per cent, and the next richest an increase of 46 per cent. Thus, the richer the group the more they have benefited from changes, while the poorest 20 per cent have seen their position deteriorate. Strangely, the poorest decile has managed to increase expenditure substantially, despite a declining income. Oppenheim and Harker (1996) suggest that this may be due to them spending savings to meet a shortfall in income.

The composition of the bottom decile changed over the period covered. According to Goodman, Johnson and Webb (1997), the proportion of pensioners in the bottom decile fell from 40 to 20 per cent between 1961 and 1992-3, while the proportions of the single childless and couples with children rose. The proportion of the bottom decile who were

unemployed rose from 6 per cent to 31 per cent over the same period.

Another increasingly numerous group in the bottom decile were the self-employed, who rose from 8 to 15 per cent of the bottom decile. Goodman *et al.* suggest that this is because of 'an increasing number of low-skilled unemployed individuals trying to return to the labour market, being unable to find a job, and using self-employment as a way in'.

Official statistics and trends in British poverty – conclusion

Nearly all the official figures suggest there has been a rise in poverty over recent decades, particularly since 1979. There are more people living at or below the level of the basic means-tested benefit, more living below 140 per cent of that level, more earning less than 50 per cent of average income, and, after housing costs, the poorest 10 per cent of the population have become worse off in real terms. The proportion of the population living at or below the 1979 benefit level has changed very little in real terms, but the amount of homelessness has certainly increased, suggesting that absolute poverty has returned as a serious problem in Britain.

We examined some of the reasons for the changes in income distribution in Chapter 2 (see pp. 43–6), and we will explore more reasons for some of the other changes later in this chapter when theories of poverty are discussed (see particularly pp. 343–4).

International comparisons

Poverty in the European Union

Although the European Union prefers the term 'social exclusion' to poverty, it has not yet devised any way of comparing rates of social exclusion in different countries. Figures on poverty take two main forms. Some use the average income of the EU as a whole as a way of measuring poverty. In terms of the percentages of the population with income below 40 per cent of the EU average, Britain has relatively little poverty. In 1985, Britain had a lower poverty rate than Eire, Spain, Greece, Portugal, France and Germany, and a higher rate than Belgium, The Netherlands and Denmark.

However, a rather different picture emerges when poverty is calculated in terms of households with below average income and expenditure in each country. Figure 5.4 shows that in 1987–9, Britain had a higher proportion of households with an income less than 50 per cent of the national average than the nine other European countries included.

In addition, during the 1980s, European figures show a big increase in poverty in Britain whereas in most countries it was declining. Figure 5.5 shows that

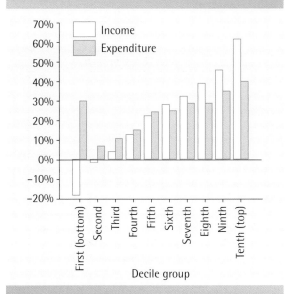

Figure 5.3 Changes in income and expenditure (after housing costs) across the income distribution (1979–92)

Source: C. Oppenheim and L. Harker (1996) *Poverty: The Facts*, 3rd edition, Child Poverty Action Group, London, derived from A. Goodman and S. Webb (1995) *The Distribution of UK Household Expenditure, 1979-92*, Institute for Fiscal Studies, London.

Britain experienced an increase of over 30 per cent in households in poverty during the 1980s, whereas in most countries poverty fell. One reason for this might be the declining proportion of government spending going on welfare in the 1980s and the low level of welfare spending in Britain compared to most countries in Europe.

The poverty index in the USA

The poverty index used by the Social Security Administration in the USA is based on the minimum cost of an adequate diet multiplied by three, since it is estimated that a typical poor family spends one-third of its income on food. The poverty line is drawn in terms of the minimum income required to buy 'a subsistence level of goods and services'.

Unlike Rowntree's definition, though, some account is taken of cultural variations in the consumption of food. Instead of estimating the cost of an ideal diet, the US government has carried out surveys into the actual dietary habits of the population and has based estimates of the cost of food on this information.

The US government first began keeping figures on poverty in 1959, when the poverty rate stood at 22.4 per cent. It dropped considerably during the 1960s, and levelled out at 11–12 per cent throughout much of the 1970s. Towards the end of the 1970s, the number officially estimated to be in poverty began to

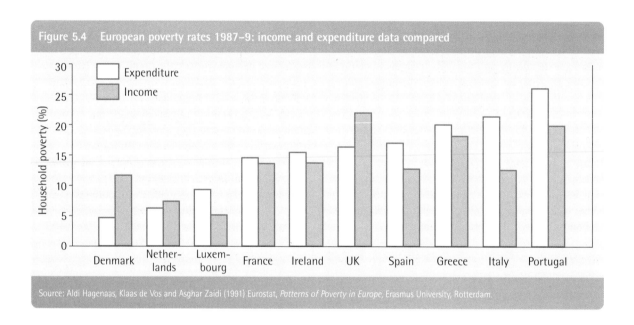

Figure 5.4   European poverty rates 1987–9: income and expenditure data compared

Source: Aldi Hagenaas, Klaas de Vos and Asghar Zaidi (1991) Eurostat, *Patterns of Poverty in Europe*, Erasmus University, Rotterdam.

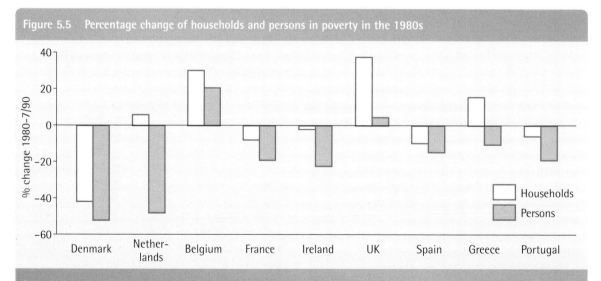

Figure 5.5   Percentage change of households and persons in poverty in the 1980s

Source: M. Cross, 'Generating the "new poverty": a European comparison' in R. Simpson and R. Walker (eds) (1993) *Europe: For Richer or Poorer?*, Child Poverty Action Group, London, p. 7.

rise, and it stood at 14 per cent in 1987. This represented some 36 million people. In 1991, there were slightly fewer in poverty, 33 million, again about 14 per cent of the population (Darby, 1996). In that year a family of four was seen as needing an income in excess of $14,463, and a single person $7,702.

The figures from the USA give little cause for optimism. They indicate that poverty has not fallen in the past twenty years or so. This is despite substantial rises in the living standards of most Americans. Douglas J. Besharov argues that in around 1973, 'the connection between economic growth and the reduction of poverty was broken' (Besharov, 1996). Like many official statistics though, they need to be used with caution. There have been numerous criticisms of the way that the American statistics are calculated.

The President's Commission on Income Maintenance Programs, a commission set up in 1968 to investigate poverty in the USA, makes several criticisms of the poverty index (President's Commission, 1989):

1 It does not reflect contemporary conventions of reasonable living standards. The minimum income assessed for a family to remain above the poverty line does not allow for many of the goods and services considered necessities by the population as a whole. According to the Commission, such 'necessities might include a car, an occasional dessert after meals, rugs, a bed for each family member, school supplies, or an occasional movie'.

2 No provision is made in the 'subsistence level goods and services' budget for medical care or insurance or for the purchase of household furnishings.

3 The Commission states that the monies deemed necessary for transportation 'would not cover even daily transportation for a worker'.

4 The Commission is particularly critical of the monies allocated for food, many of its criticisms echoing those made of Rowntree's food budget. It concludes that 'only about one-fourth of the families who spend that much for food actually have a nutritionally adequate diet'.

Figures suggest that, in relative terms, poverty in the USA has been increasing perhaps faster than official poverty. For example, between 1978 and 1987 the poorest 20 per cent of the population experienced an 8 per cent reduction in their share of the total national income, while the share of the richest 20 per cent went up by 13 per cent. As in Britain, the rich have been getting richer and the poor relatively poorer in recent years. Furthermore, according to Roger Lawson, the proportion of households receiving less than 50 per cent of median income has been increasing in the USA, from under 16 per cent in 1979 to around 18 per cent in 1986 (Lawson, 1995).

The social distribution of poverty

The chances of being in poverty in Britain (and indeed elsewhere) are not equally distributed. Some groups are much more prone to ending up in poverty than others, while the chances relating to particular groups change over time.

In this section we will briefly outline some of the variations in poverty rates.

Economic and family status

Figures 5.6 and 5.7 show the risk of poverty according to economic and family status in Britain in 1992–3. They are based on the numbers of individuals in households receiving below 50 per cent of average household income after housing costs. Figure 5.6 shows that participation in the labour market, at least on a full-time basis, greatly reduces the risk of poverty. Retirement and unemployment are both strongly associated with poverty.

Figure 5.7 shows that lone parenthood leads to a high risk of poverty: 58 per cent of lone parents are poor. Over a quarter of pensioner couples are poor, although the evidence suggests that the elderly are becoming less prone to poverty. As recently as 1988–9, 33 per cent of pensioner couples were poor by the definition used above. From 1988–9 to 1992–3, the proportion of couples with children living in poverty rose from 19 to 24 per cent, for lone parents there was a rise from 50 to 58 per cent, and for single people from 16 to 22 per cent.

Gender and poverty

Most figures on poverty are not broken down in terms of sex, but are based on households. However, it is possible to produce estimates of the numbers of men and women in poverty by using data on the proportions of men and women in households with particular economic and family statuses. There are more female than male pensioners, for example, and the vast majority of lone parents are female. On this basis, the Child Poverty Action Group estimates that there were about 5.2 million women, but only 4.2 million men, in poverty in 1992 (Oppenheim and Harker, 1996).

Within households, income may not be distributed equally. Women tend to have smaller independent incomes than men and there is no guarantee that women will share fully the income of their husbands or partners. Steven Webb has estimated that in 1991 women made up about two-thirds of the adults in the poorest households. Furthermore, in these households women's average independent income was just £99.90 per week, compared with £199.50 per week for men (quoted in Oppenheim and Harker, 1996). Research by P. Esam and R. Berthoud for the Policy

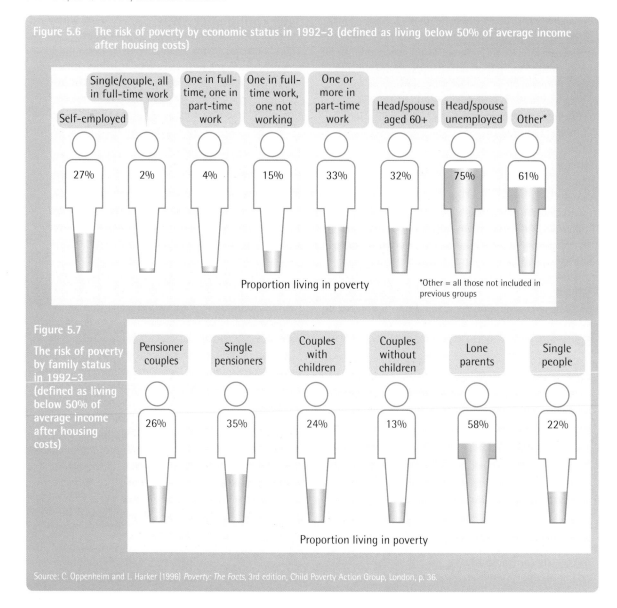

Figure 5.6   The risk of poverty by economic status in 1992–3 (defined as living below 50% of average income after housing costs)

Self-employed — 27%

Single/couple, all in full-time work — 2%

One in full-time, one in part-time work — 4%

One in full-time work, one not working — 15%

One or more in part-time work — 33%

Head/spouse aged 60+ — 32%

Head/spouse unemployed — 75%

Other* — 61%

Proportion living in poverty

*Other = all those not included in previous groups

Figure 5.7

The risk of poverty by family status in 1992–3 (defined as living below 50% of average income after housing costs)

Pensioner couples — 26%

Single pensioners — 35%

Couples with children — 24%

Couples without children — 13%

Lone parents — 58%

Single people — 22%

Proportion living in poverty

Source: C. Oppenheim and L. Harker (1996) *Poverty: The Facts*, 3rd edition, Child Poverty Action Group, London, p. 36.

Studies Institute estimated that in 1990–1 more than 4.6 million women had an independent income of less than £25 per week. This compared to just 0.4 million men (quoted in C. Oppenheim, 1993). Some of the reasons for the greater number of women living in poverty are listed here:

1   Women are less likely than men to have occupational pensions and income from investments.

2   Married women are less likely than married men to be working.

3   Women who are working are more likely than men to be low-paid. In 1994, women made up 64 per cent of of the employed who received less than £5.88 per hour, the Council of Europe's Decency Threshold (quoted in Oppenheim and Harker, 1996).

4   More women than men work part-time.

5   More women than men rely upon benefits as their main source of income.

6   Lone parents are vulnerable to poverty, and about nine out of ten lone parents are women.

7   The majority of pensioners are women.

Caroline Glendinning and Jane Millar (1994) give the following reasons for women having higher rates of poverty than men:

1   Women are disadvantaged in the labour market. They are seen as secondary workers because their primary role is seen as domestic (as housewives and mothers). They spend more time away from the labour market than men, and are more likely to have part-time jobs. The employment of married women is seen by some employers as less important than that of married men, so they are not expected to earn a family wage, that is, enough to support their spouse and children.

2   Women are 'disadvantaged in access to social security benefits'. Only 60 per cent of women are

entitled to maternity leave. Many women care for sick and elderly relatives, yet they receive very small state allowances for doing so. The intermittent and often part-time employment of women leaves many ineligible for unemployment benefit and redundancy pay.

3 Within the household men usually 'command more of the family resources (of money, of food, of space and so on) and this is legitimated by their status as breadwinners'.

Glendinning and Millar summarize their argument by saying:

The causes of poverty among women are thus a result of complex but mutually reinforcing threads, which have their origins in the limitations placed upon women by the current gendered division of labour and by the assumptions of female financial dependency upon men.

Glendinning and Millar, 1994

Ruth Lister (1995) argues that women are not just more likely to suffer poverty, they also have more responsibility for dealing with its effects. She says, 'it tends to be women who manage poverty and debt as part of their general responsibility for money management in low-income families'. This may lead to extra stress and ill health. Lister also suggests that women may suffer from 'time poverty' because of their continued responsibility for most domestic labour.

Ethnicity and poverty

Official statistics on ethnicity and poverty are not available. However, the Policy Studies Institute has produced figures on ethnicity and poverty using data from a survey of 5,196 people of Caribbean or Asian origin and 2,867 white people. The study, conducted by Richard Berthoud (1997), calculated figures on Households Below Average Income. The results are shown in Table 5.6.

The table shows that all ethnic minority groups were considerably more likely to experience poverty by this measure than white people, among whom 28 per cent of households were found to be in poverty. There were also big variations by ethnic group, with 34 per cent of households made up of those of Chinese ethnic origin in poverty compared with 82 per cent of Pakistani and 84 per cent of Bangladeshi households.

The conclusion is that poverty is common among most ethnic minority groups, despite the fact that there are relatively low proportions of pensioners among ethnic minorities. The poverty of these groups stems largely from labour market disadvantages, which lead to higher rates of unemployment and more people suffering from low pay.

Berthoud commented that he had been 'analysing household income for more than twenty years' and 'Pakistanis and Bangladeshis are by far the poorest group he has ever encountered'. He found that Pakistani and Bangladeshi households tended to be at high risk of being in poverty because of high rates of unemployment among the men and because relatively few of the women had paid employment. This was sometimes compounded by large family size.

This study provides the only British national data on poverty and ethnic minority groups, and the figures should be viewed with some caution. A single household member was asked to estimate total household income and, as Berthoud points out, both non-response and the fact that the person asked may not have known the income of every family member, may have distorted the findings. The study might have exaggerated the extent of poverty because its figures had higher estimates for families below average income than official figures. Nevertheless, the study does draw attention to the acuteness of the poverty suffered by some ethnic minority groups. Undoubtedly racism plays a part in creating high

Table 5.6 Households below average income							
	White	Caribbean	Indian	African Asian	Pakistani	Bangladeshi	Chinese
Below half average (%)	28	41	45	39	82	84	34
Between half and one and a half times average (%)	49	47	43	46	17	15	44
Above one and a half times average (%)	23	12	12	15	1	2	22
Weighted count, persons	5,954	2,910	1,322	1,520	1,469	674	660
Unweighted count, households	2,457	778	362	395	454	283	115

Source: T. Modood *et al.* (1997) *Ethnic Minorities in Britain: Diversity and Disadvantage*, Policy Studies Institute, London, p. 160

rates of poverty among ethnic minority groups (see pp. 254–62 for a discussion of racism).

The Policy Studies Institute study did not produce any figures on poverty among the Irish community in Britain, an ethnic minority group that is often neglected in research. There have, however, been local studies which include this group. Kaushika Amin and Carey Oppenheim (1992) quote a study carried out by Islington Council in 1987. The study measured material deprivation using indicators such as diet, working conditions, home facilities, clothing, housing and local facilities. It found that 37 per cent of the Afro-Caribbeans in Islington, 35 per cent of Asians and 47 per cent of Irish suffered material deprivation. This compared to 33 per cent of white people as a whole. (We examine inequality between ethnic groups in detail in Chapter 4.)

Pete Alcock argues that social exclusion is often as much a problem for ethnic minority groups as material deprivation (Alcock, 1997). It can involve lack of access to good quality housing, unequal access to healthcare and social services, and sub-standard education facilities. He says that 'deprivation in housing, health and education add significantly to the financial inequality of Black people in Britain, and they have remained important despite the introduction in the 1960s of race relations legislation'. Racial harassment may produce a sense of isolation and fear and thus exacerbate the social exclusion produced by other inequalities.

Poverty and disability

Another factor related to poverty which is often neglected is disability. Using data from a 1985–8 study of disabled people, it has been estimated that 47 per cent of disabled people were living in poverty (quoted in Oppenheim and Harker, 1996). Oppenheim and Harker suggest that such high rates of poverty are partly due to 'labour market exclusion and marginalization'. Most households containing a sick or disabled person receive no income from employment, and such households, not surprisingly, are much more likely than other households to depend on benefits. Oppenheim and Harker argue that they 'face the risks of poverty because of inadequate benefits'. Disabled people also tend to have higher spending costs on such items as special diets, transport, and heating than other people do.

Pete Alcock points out that disabled people may also suffer from social exclusion as well as material poverty. He notes that Townsend's pioneering research (see pp. 296–300) found that disabled people were likely to have poorer housing and fewer holidays. Alcock also argues that 'participation in social activities and leisure pursuits may be restricted by reduced mobility or sensory deprivation, leading to an overall

reduction in the quality of life of people with disabilities compared with most able-bodied people'. However, Alcock does not see the exclusion and poverty that are sometimes related to disability as being an inevitable consequence of the disability itself. Rather, they are caused by a society which discriminates against those with disability. This may be through active discrimination, or by failing to provide the resources and facilities which are necessary to minimize the impact of disability. He says:

> In the case of disability it is very much a case of non-reaction leading to problems for persons with disabilities. Modern industrial societies, and even modern welfare states, have largely been constructed on the basis that the people who inhabit them, who produce and reproduce them and benefit from them, are able-bodied. This is true of workplaces, public and private buildings, transport systems, information and telecommunication networks, retail outlets – indeed almost all venues for social interaction.
>
> Alcock, 1997, p. 193

The places where serious attempts have been taken to overcome these problems are few and far between and the welfare state generally fails to provide the extra resources which disabled people would need to overcome the social exclusion which can result. Furthermore, the carers of those with disabilities often find that they become excluded from areas of social life such as employment. They too are restricted in their movements and social interactions by the societal assumption that people are able-bodied.

The experience of poverty and social exclusion

Studies which try to measure the extent and social distribution of poverty and social exclusion are important because they help to establish the extent of the problem and to identify the groups who suffer most difficulty. However, they give little indication of what it is like to experience poverty and do not, therefore, really facilitate an understanding of the human costs involved. Furthermore, they do not allow the poor themselves any voice in academic research. In recent years, a number of researchers have conducted qualitative studies of poverty and social exclusion Many of those studies have been funded by the Joseph Rowntree Foundation.

Elaine Kempson – *Life on a Low Income*

The Joseph Rowntree Foundation, based in York, has long conducted studies of poverty in Britain. In 1995 it published an *Inquiry into Income and Wealth* which revealed growing wealth and income inequalities in Britain (Barclay, 1995, Hills, 1995). However, as one of the authors of the report, Sir Peter Barclay, pointed out, 'statistics barely lift the lid on the day-to-day reality of life for the millions of individuals and families at the bottom of the economic pile' (Barclay, in Kempson, 1996). As a consequence, the Foundation commissioned Elaine Kempson to review the findings of 31 qualitative studies funded by the Foundation. All the studies were completed in 1994 or 1995 and, in total, involved in-depth interviews with 2,100 people on low incomes and some 300 people whose work involved dealing with low-income groups. The studies focused on a range of issues, such as single homelessness, housing, nutrition and diet, disability, and debt and money management. The qualitative studies did not aim to pick out the worst cases of deprivation. Rather they sought to 'identify the general pattern that emerges and then use individual cases as illustrations' (Kempson, 1996). Kempson found that, despite the wide range of studies, the different reports gave a remarkably consistent picture of life on a low income. They tended to corroborate rather than contradict one another.

Making ends meet

Kempson comments that:

> *managing money on a low income takes skill; and the poorer people are, the more skill it takes. Not surprisingly some people fail to get it right first time, but far more remarkable is the way that millions of people succeed in managing budgets on incomes that are barely sufficient to cover even the necessities.*
>
> Kempson, 1996, p. 15

Some of the people who had most difficulty were those who had a sudden drop in income, but there were also problems for those who suffered long-term poverty. In some of these households, savings were used up and debt problems had mounted. Most of those on low incomes were not spendthrifts, indeed many planned expenditure with great care. In one study, which examined 74 low-income families, about two-thirds planned expenditure carefully. One example was Marion, a lone mother with four children who received income support. She said, 'I have to write everything out before I get paid. I write absolutely everything that I've got to buy, you know, for the week.' Planning usually meant cutting out luxuries, and some of the first things to go were 'treats' such as holidays, social activities and repairs and decorations to their homes. What 'luxuries' remained were seen as special treats. One girl, Nicola, who was 7, saw her two outings of the year – coach trips to Southport

and Skegness – in this light. This contrasted with a middle-class girl, Samantha, who had been to France twice in the year and Africa once. In addition, she had been on numerous trips and a number of weekends away.

Although poor parents tried to minimize the effect of low income on their children – often going without necessities themselves to do so – the children of the poor suffered a restricted social life. They were less likely to get involved in clubs, take part in extra-curricular activities at school or have their friends round.

Some groups did spend money on non-essentials. The single homeless, for example, drank a lot of alcohol, but this was untypical of other poor groups. Many people carried on smoking, but cut down. Kempson explained that they continued to smoke because they 'led stressful lives and smoking was the only way they reduced the stress, while people with more money went out for the evening or sat down with a drink at the end of the day'. Some people on low incomes bought lottery tickets or played the pools, but Kempson argues that for many this was the only chance they could see of significantly improving their situation, remote though that chance might be.

Apart from buying the odd non-essential item to make life bearable, the poor also had to cut down on essentials. This sometimes meant going without meals, buying the cheapest available food, having a poor (but cheap and filling) diet, switching the heating off and wearing extra clothes to keep warm in the house, and even, in the occasional case, sitting in the dark or using candles. Life for those on low incomes involves making difficult choices.

Borrowing money was an alternative to cutting down on essentials. Yet here, as one study found, there was a dual credit market. Those with reasonable and secure incomes could obtain credit from mainstream sources such as banks. Those on low incomes often had to turn to disreputable money lenders or pawn shops. In doing so, their borrowings became much more expensive, and they could soon find themselves with debts they had little chance of repaying. This produced another difficult choice: whether to put the needs of creditors or family first. One study of 74 low-income families with children found that only 12 had managed to 'keep their heads above water', while 20 families seemed 'to be drowning in a sea of financial problems'.

In some families the parents were simply unwilling to allow their children to go without necessities, even if this meant getting further and further into debt.

The effects of a low income

Kempson found that the research pointed to a wide range of negative consequences for those on low income. She summarized the findings, saying:

> the struggle to make ends meet not only affects family life, but can result in poor diet, lack of fuel and water, poor housing and homelessness, debt, poor physical health, and stress and mental health problems. The poorer people are, the more likely they are to face these problems.
>
> Kempson, 1996

The studies found that people often lost contact with friends because of the cost of socializing. In some families emotional support from spouses was essential, but in others the struggle to cope with little money led to arguments and sometimes even violence. The arguments sometimes drove children away, and could lead to them becoming homeless.

Many of the poor were aware that they had poor diets, and most were aware that their diets could be improved. For example, one respondent said:

> We try to eat 'proper' meals like meat and veg and that, but there isn't the money to do it all the time. So we eat properly once or twice a week, depending on the money, and the rest of the time we make do with things like sausages, pies, potatoes and things like beans. The meals aren't as good but they do the job, they'll fill them up and stop them from being hungry. It's the best I can do.
>
> Kempson, 1996

Health could also be affected by people cutting down on fuel and water. Many interviewers noted how cold people's houses were. Many of the poor feared their electricity being disconnected. For example, Ivy, who was 75 and a chronic asthmatic, turned the heating off in winter despite the effect on her medical condition. Some people used pre-payment meters, which helped them budget, but the costs were higher and there was the ever-present danger of running out of money to feed the meter. In the increasing proportion of homes with water meters people were starting to avoid using water even for essential purposes. Problems were exacerbated by a more commercial approach to debt collecting among some of the privatized utilities. They were less willing to compromise than in the past by finding ways short of disconnection to deal with their arrears.

Fear of losing their homes was a very real problem for some of the poor, particularly those who had become unemployed who had mortgages. The growth of home ownership in the 1980s, followed by a slump in house prices and increased unemployment, left some with mortgage debts greater than the market value of their house (negative equity) and without means to pay them off. Where people lost their homes and had to be rehoused, they were often sent to the most undesirable housing estates where crime and damp or unsuitable housing could affect physical and mental health.

Conclusions

Although Kempson's study paints a rather bleak picture of life on a low income, she does stress that individual circumstances vary a great deal. Some people can be relatively unscathed if they experience low income for a short period, have a supportive family and friendship networks, do not live in the poorest neighbourhoods, and so on. The very poorest suffered most, along with those who had a sustained period on low income. For many people, relatively modest increases in income would have made a tremendous difference to their lives.

Individualistic and cultural theories of poverty

In the previous sections we considered the questions 'What is poverty?' and 'What is the extent of poverty?' We are now going to look at some of the responses to the third question, 'What are the causes of poverty?'

Individualistic theories

The earliest theories of poverty were also perhaps the simplest. They placed the blame for poverty on the poor themselves. Those who suffered from very low incomes did so because they were unable or unwilling to provide adequately for their own well-being. From this point of view, neither society nor the social groups to which individuals belonged were accountable, and society should not therefore be responsible for providing for the needs of the poor. Such individualistic theories of poverty were particularly popular in the nineteenth century.

Herbert Spencer – 'dissolute living'

The nineteenth-century English sociologist, Herbert Spencer, was a severe critic of the poor. He dismissed the views of those who showed sympathy with the 'poor fellow' who was living in poverty. Why, he asked, did they not realize that he was usually a 'bad fellow', one of the 'good-for- nothings ... vagrants and sots, criminals ... men who share the gains of prostitutes; and less visible and less numerous there is a corresponding class of women' (Spencer, 1971).

According to Spencer, it was unnatural to help those engaged in 'dissolute living' to avoid the consequences of their actions. Those who were too lazy to work should not be allowed to eat. The key to explaining why particular individuals became poor lay in an examination of their moral character.

Spencer thought that the state should interfere as little as possible in the lives of individuals. If the Poor Law or welfare system gave the poor more than an absolutely minimum amount, laziness and moral decline would spread through the population. Individuals would be attracted to the easy life on offer to those not prepared to work for their own living. As a result, society would suffer. Its economy would not be successful.

Spencer believed strongly in the ideas of evolution that were so popular in late Victorian Britain. It was Spencer, not, as is often thought, the biologist Charles Darwin, who coined the phrase 'survival of the fittest'. If society were to evolve and become more successful, the most able and the hardest-working would have to be allowed to keep the rewards of their efforts. The weak, the incompetent and the lazy should be condemned to a life of poverty, because it was no more than they deserved. Poverty was a necessity for society, for without it the incentive to work would be missing.

'Scroungers'

Such explanations of poverty remain influential in modern Britain. According to Peter Golding and Sue Middleton (1978), most newspaper reporting of welfare claimants in the 1970s portrayed them as 'scroungers'. Their research unearthed numerous stories in the press about how those living on social security were enjoying comfortable, even extravagant lifestyles at the taxpayer's expense. This type of story continues to feature in the British press.

Individualistic explanations are accepted by a considerable proportion of the public in Britain, although their popularity has been declining. The European Commission conducted surveys of attitudes to poverty in Europe in 1976 and 1989. In the earlier survey, 43 per cent of respondents in Britain thought poverty was due to laziness. This figure had fallen to 18 per cent by the time of the later survey. In all EC countries, apart from Denmark, the proportion blaming poverty on laziness had declined, but Britain remained the country where people were most likely to explain poverty in this way.

Few sociologists today accept individualistic explanations of poverty. At the very least, sociologists see poverty as a characteristic of a social group such as a family or a community, and not as a characteristic of individuals. Some sociologists would go further and argue that it is not the generosity but the inadequacy of the welfare state, or the structure of society itself, which is responsible for the existence of poverty in the midst of affluence. For some, individualistic explanations of poverty are no more than an 'ideological smoke screen' to hide the injustices suffered by the poor. To the American writer William Ryan (1971), it is an example of 'blaming the victims' for what they suffer at the hands of others.

The New Right – *the culture of dependency*

The politics of the Conservative governments (1979–97) of Margaret Thatcher and John Major were associated with the ideas of the New Right. A central plank of their policies was the claim that the welfare state was leading to a culture of dependency.

Hartley Dean and Peter Taylor-Gooby, critics of the concept of a culture of dependency, have identified its key characteristics (Dean and Taylor-Gooby, 1992):

1 First, it assumes that people often act in ways that are motivated by rational calculations about the effort needed to secure rewards. If, for example, too much effort is required to secure a small rise in income, people will not bother to work.

2 Second, and to some extent contradicting the first point, people are strongly influenced by people around them, particularly those in the same neighbourhood. If few people go out to work in an area, then others living there may not bother to work themselves.

3 Third, the culture of dependency theory has a moral dimension. It extols the virtues of self-reliance and hard work, and denigrates dependence on others and laziness. For example, in 1987 John Moore, the then Secretary of State for Health and Social Security, said 'dependence in the long run decreases human happiness and reduces human freedom ... the well-being of individuals is best protected and promoted when they are helped to be independent'.

A few contemporary sociologists, such as David Marsland, have adopted the philosophy of the New Right and have used some of the thinking behind the concept of dependency culture to explain poverty.

David Marsland – poverty and the generosity of the welfare state

Marsland (1996) is rather dismissive of most of the approaches to poverty discussed in this chapter. He argues that a 'poverty lobby' has distorted the picture of deprivation in Britain and greatly exaggerated its extent. He claims that groups such as the Joseph Rowntree Foundation 'deliberately confuse poverty with inequality' and 'exaggerate the extent of poverty absurdly'. He accuses those who argue for the existence of widespread poverty as acting out of self-interest, and says that the 'legend of poverty is elaborated by mischief-makers and professional sentimentalists as an antidote to their own failed neurotic dreams'. He claims that these people completely fail to examine the evidence impartially, and 'the persistence of poverty guarantees a meaning for the lives of all those for whom the humdrum satisfactions of successful domesticity and useful practical work are either unavailable or never enough'.

Arguing for an absolute rather than relative definition of poverty, he suggests that steadily improving living standards resulting from capitalism have largely eradicated poverty. He sees inequality as a desirable feature of society because it rewards unequal effort and ability, and in doing so creates incentives for people to work harder. Furthermore, he believes the incomes of the least well-off groups in Britain have, in any case, been rising.

Marsland argues that, for most people, low income results from the generosity of the welfare state rather than from personal inadequacy as such (Marsland 1989). He is particularly critical of universal welfare provision: the provision of welfare for all members of society regardless of whether they are on low or high incomes. Examples of universal provision in Britain include education, healthcare and child benefits.

Marsland believes that such benefits have created a culture of dependency. He says 'the expectation that society, the state, the government, "they", will look after our problems tricks us into abdicating from self-reliance and social responsibility' (Marsland, 1989). He argues that welfare 'hand-outs' create incentives for staying unemployed; they ridicule competition and discourage self-improvement through education. Furthermore, by increasing public expenditure they take money away from investment in industry and thus hinder the production of wealth.

Marsland does not believe that all benefits should be withdrawn, but he does argue that they should be restricted to those in genuine need who are unable to help themselves. Benefits should be targeted at groups such as the sick and disabled, and should not be given to those who are capable of supporting

themselves. Such people make up only 5 to 8 per cent of the population, far fewer than the enormous proportion of the population who receive benefits. According to Marsland, reliance upon the huge, centralized bureaucracy of the welfare state 'weakens the vitality of the family, the local community, and voluntary associations, which are the natural arenas of genuine mutual help'. He concludes:

> *Critics of universal welfare provision are not blaming the poor, as welfarist ideologues allege. On the contrary, these are the foremost victims of erroneous ideas and destructive policies imposed on them by paternalists, socialists, and privileged members of the professional New Class.*
> Marsland, 1989

We will examine government policies that have been influenced by the New Right in a later section (see pp. 343–4).

Criticisms of Marsland

It is perhaps ironic that Marsland accuses the so-called 'poverty lobby' of failing to examine the evidence impartially. Marsland's own writing contains numerous personal attacks on those whose views he disagrees with. Some of these are based on unfounded claims about sociologists' motives which are backed up by no evidence whatsoever. For example, he fails to back up his claim that anti-poverty writers and campaigners act out of self-interest rather than a genuine concern for the plight of those on low incomes. Furthermore, where Marsland does use evidence, he is highly selective in the evidence he chooses to use. For example, he ignores the evidence that the real incomes of the poorest in Britain have been falling in recent years (see p. 344).

Bill Jordan (1989) argues that Marsland is wrong to attribute the culture of dependency to universal welfare provision. If such a culture exists, it is created by 'targeted', means-tested benefits received by only the very poor. He says that 'selective systems trap people in poverty and passivity, and exclude them from the opportunities and incentives enjoyed by their fellow-citizens'. If, for example, those in work have to pay for education and health-care, and the unemployed do not, then, 'many unskilled and partially disabled people will not be able to afford to work'.

Jordan claims that societies which rely upon means-tested benefits, such as the USA, tend to develop a large underclass which has little chance of escaping from poverty. If members of the underclass take low-paid jobs, they lose benefits and the right to free services, and they may end up worse off. In such societies the only way to persuade some people to work is to impose heavy penalties on them if they do not.

To Jordan, poverty does not result from an over-generous welfare system, but instead it is caused by a system which is too mean. He says that the only way to tackle poverty is to have 'universal provision, which brings everyone up to an acceptable level. Far from creating dependence it frees people from dependence.'

Hartley Dean and Peter Taylor-Gooby – *The Explosion of a Myth*

Dean and Taylor-Gooby (1992) have attempted to explode the 'myth' of dependency culture. They argue that it is 'based upon socially constituted definitions of failure', and does not really identify a difference between the independent and the dependent. Nobody is truly independent in contemporary Britain, or in similar societies. They say:

> When we speak of individual autonomy, or the sovereignty of the worker, the consumer or the citizen, we must remember that the human individual remains dependent upon other human individuals and social structures.
>
> Dean and Taylor-Gooby, 1992

For example, workers are dependent upon employers, consumers on those who supply the goods, and the citizen is dependent upon the state for 'physical security and the regulation of other human individuals and social structures'. The benefit claimant is not in a qualitatively different position to other members of society who are also dependent in various ways.

Dean and Taylor-Gooby's objections to dependency theory, though, are not simply philosophical. In 1990, they carried out 85 in-depth interviews with social security claimants of working age in south London and Kent. This research found that many benefit claimants had not lost interest in working. Only 14 of those interviewed showed little interest in working. Four of this group nevertheless hoped to come off benefits eventually, eight had health problems or caring responsibilities which prevented them from working, one had taken early retirement and only one had rejected the idea of working. He was a man in his fifties who described himself as an anarchist, who had rejected the work ethic after a career working as a technician in the oil industry.

Dean and Taylor-Gooby did find evidence that the benefits system discouraged some people from taking low-paid work. Over half of those interviewed made some reference to the problems associated with losing means-tested benefits if they went out to work. This seems to support Jordan's claim that it is means-tested benefits (like income support and family credit) rather than universal benefits which can create

disincentives to work. But there was no evidence that the disincentives had led to a dependency culture. For example, only 21 people said that their circle of friends and relatives contained many claimants. As Dean and Taylor-Gooby observe, 'clearly most respondents could not be said to be enmeshed in a claiming culture'.

According to this study, the ambitions, attitudes and social networks of most benefits claimants are little different from those of other members of society. They want to earn their own living and would prefer not to have to turn to the state for a basic income. For them, the state is a last resort, and one they would rather avoid. Dean and Taylor-Gooby conclude that 'the social security system does not foster a dependency culture, but it constructs, isolates and supervises a heterogeneous population of reluctant dependants'.

Dean and Taylor-Gooby's findings have been criticized for using a sample concentrated in the south of England where unemployment has generally been low. Critics argue that they might have obtained different results if they had studied the effects of social security in areas with higher rates of unemployment such as north-east England, Wales or Scotland.

The culture of poverty

Many researchers have noted that the lifestyle of the poor differs in certain respects from that of other members of society. They have also noted that poverty lifestyles in different societies share common characteristics. The circumstances of poverty are similar, in many respects, in different societies. Similar circumstances and problems tend to produce similar responses, and these responses can develop into a culture – that is the learned, shared and socially transmitted behaviour of a social group.

This line of reasoning has led to the concept of a culture of poverty (or, more correctly, a subculture of poverty), a relatively distinct subculture of the poor with its own norms and values. The idea of a culture of poverty was first introduced in the late 1950s by the American anthropologist, Oscar Lewis (1959, 1961, 1966). He developed the concept from his fieldwork among the urban poor in Mexico and Puerto Rico. Lewis argues that the culture of poverty is a design for living which is transmitted from one generation to the next.

A design for living

As a design for living which directs behaviour, the culture of poverty has the following elements:

1 On the individual level, in Lewis's words, the major characteristics are a strong feeling of marginality, of

helplessness, of dependence and inferiority, a strong present-time orientation with relatively little ability to defer gratification, a sense of resignation and fatalism.

2   On the family level, life is characterized by: free union or consensual marriages, a relatively high incidence of the abandonment of mothers and children, a trend towards mother-centred families and a much greater knowledge of maternal relatives. There are high rates of divorce and desertion by the male family head resulting in matrifocal families headed by women.

3   On the community level, 'the lack of effective participation and integration in the major institutions of the larger society is one of the crucial characteristics of the culture of poverty' (Lewis, 1961). The urban poor in Lewis's research do not usually belong to trade unions or other associations, they are not members of political parties, and 'generally do not participate in the national welfare agencies, and make very little use of banks, hospitals, department stores, museums or art galleries'. For most, the family is the only institution in which they directly participate.

Perpetuating poverty

The culture of poverty, then, is seen as a response by the poor to their place in society. According to Lewis, it is a 'reaction of the poor to their marginal position in a class-stratified and highly individualistic society' (Lewis, 1961).

The culture of poverty goes beyond a mere reaction to a situation. It takes on the force of culture because its characteristics are guides to action that are internalized by the poor and passed on from one generation to the next. As such, the culture of poverty tends to perpetuate poverty, since its charac- teristics can be seen as mechanisms that maintain poverty: attitudes of fatalism and resignation lead to acceptance of the situation, while the failure to join trade unions and other organizations weakens the potential power of the poor.

Lewis argues that, once established, the culture of poverty tends to perpetuate itself from generation to generation because of its effect on children. By the time slum children are aged 6 or 7, they have usually absorbed the basic values and attitudes of their subculture and are not psychologically geared to take full advantage of changing conditions or increased opportunities which may occur in their lifetime.

Lewis argues that the culture of poverty best describes and explains the situation of the poor in colonial societies or those societies in the early stages of capitalism, as in many developing countries. Although the culture of poverty is common in such societies, not everyone adopts it. In advanced capitalist societies and (the then) socialist societies, the

culture of poverty is non-existent, weakly developed or affects a fairly small minority. In the USA, for example, Lewis estimates that only 20 per cent of the poor adopt the lifestyle of the culture of poverty.

Other sociologists, however, have argued that the idea of a culture of poverty can be applied to most of the poor in advanced industrial societies. For example, in *The Other America*, Michael Harrington writes of the American poor:

> There is, in short, a language of the poor, a psychology of the poor, a world view of the poor. To be impoverished is to be an internal alien, to grow up in a culture that is radically different from the one that dominates the society.
>
> Harrington, 1963

Criticisms of the culture of poverty theory

Since its introduction, the culture of poverty theory has received sustained criticism. The actual existence of a culture of poverty has itself been questioned. Research in low-income areas in Latin American and African countries, which should have provided evidence of a thriving culture of poverty, has cast some doubt on Lewis's claims.

For example, William Mangin's (1968) research in the *barriadas* of Peru, shanty towns surrounding major cities, reveals a high level of community action and political involvement. Members of the *barriadas* often organize their own schools, clinics and bus cooperatives, have a high level of participation in community politics and show little of the family break-up described by Lewis.

Audrey J. Schwartz's (1975) research in the slum areas, or *barrios*, of Caracas in Venezuela revealed little evidence of apathy and resignation, present- time orientation or broken families, and she concluded that the subculture of the *barrios* did not perpetuate and maintain poverty.

Evidence from advanced industrial societies has cast further doubt on the culture of poverty thesis, and, in particular, its application to Western society. From their research in Blackston (a pseudonym for a low-income Black American community), Charles and Betty Lou Valentine state that 'it is proving difficult to find community patterns that correspond to many of the subcultural traits often associated with poverty in learned writings about the poor' (Valentine and Valentine, 1970). They found a great deal of participation in local government, constant use of welfare institutions and 'a veritable plethora of organizations' from block associations to an area- wide community council.

The research of the Valentines suggests that the lifestyle of the poor is more variable than had been previously thought. Similar conclusions about poverty in Britain are reached by Muriel Brown and Nicola Madge (1982). In their book, *Despite the Welfare State*, they review the findings of a major research project into deprivation conducted by the Social Science Research Council. Brown and Madge stated:

> All the evidence suggests that cultural values are not important for the development and transmission of deprivation. Generally speaking people do not necessarily bring up their children as they were brought up .... Further, there is nothing to indicate that the deprivations of the poor, racial minorities or delinquents, to cite but three examples, are due to constraints imposed by culture.
>
> Brown and Madge, 1982

More recent qualitative research in Britain, conducted for the Joseph Rowntree Foundation and summarized in a book by Elaine Kempson (1996), provides substantial support for the argument that no more than a small proportion of those on low income have a culture of poverty (for details of the research see above, pp. 314–16).

The research reported by Kempson found that there was:

> no lack of commitment to working, even among those who had been unemployed for some time. Getting a job was seen as the best chance people on low incomes had of improving their standard of living or repaying the money owed to creditors.
>
> Kempson, 1996

Indeed, some people went to extremes in their pursuit of work. One man, for example, visited the Job Centre four times a week, checked the local paper, visited local factories asking for work and had written over 100 letters. Some men visited factories in groups asking for work. However, such tactics were rarely successful, and many people on low income experienced considerable barriers to even looking for work. Age, lack of skills, poor health and disability and even having too little money to get on a bus to go and ask employers for work were all problems. This suggested that situational constraints were more important than culture in keeping people on low income. This view will now be examined.

Situational constraints – an alternative to a culture of poverty

The second and major criticism of the culture of poverty has centred around the notion of culture. Despite the research referred to above, there is evidence from both advanced and developing

industrial societies to support Lewis's characterization of the behaviour of the poor.

The use of the term 'culture' implies that the behaviour of the poor is internalized via the socialization process and once internalized is to some degree resistant to change. It also implies that aspects of the behaviour of the poor derive from values. Again, there is the suggestion of resistance to change.

Thus Lewis, with his notion of culture, suggests that, despite the fact that it was initially caused by circumstances such as unemployment, low income and lack of opportunity, once established, the subculture of low-income groups has a life of its own. This implies that if the circumstances which produced poverty were to disappear, the culture of poverty might well continue. This is made even more likely by Lewis's view that the culture of poverty is largely self-contained and insulated from the norms and values of the mainstream culture of society. The poor, to a large degree, therefore live in a world of their own.

Culture versus situational constraints

These arguments have been strongly contested. Rather than seeing the behaviour of the poor as a response to established and internalized cultural patterns, many researchers view it as a reaction to situational constraints. In other words, the poor are constrained by the facts of their situation – by low income, unemployment and the like – to act the way they do, rather than being directed by a culture of poverty.

The situational constraints argument suggests that the poor would readily change their behaviour in response to a new set of circumstances once the constraints of poverty were removed.

The situational constraints thesis also attacks the view that the poor are largely insulated from mainstream norms and values. It argues that the poor share the values of society as a whole, the only difference being that they are unable to translate many of those values into reality. Again, the situational constraints argument suggests that once the constraints of poverty are removed, the poor will have no difficulty adopting mainstream behaviour patterns and seizing available opportunities.

Mainstream values

In his classic study, *Tally's Corner*, Elliot Liebow strongly supported the situational constraints thesis (Liebow, 1967). The study is based on participant observation of black 'streetcorner men' in a low-income area of Washington DC, USA

The men are either unemployed, underemployed (working part-time), or employed in low-paid, unskilled, dead-end jobs as manual labourers, elevator operators, janitors, bus boys and

322 Chapter 5: Poverty and social exclusion

dishwashers. Their view of work is directed by mainstream values. The men want jobs with higher pay and status but they lack the necessary skills, qualifications and work experience. They regard their occupations from the same viewpoint as any other member of society. In Liebow's words, 'both employee and employer are contemptuous of the job'.

When streetcorner men blow a week's wages on a 'weekend drunk' or pack in a job on an apparent whim, the middle-class observer tends to interpret this behaviour as evidence of present-time orienta-tion and inability to defer gratification. Liebow, however, argues that it is not the time orientation that differentiates the streetcorner man from members of the middle class, but his future. Whereas middle-class individuals have a reasonable future to look forward to, the streetcorner man has none. His behaviour is directed by the fact that 'he is aware of the future and the hopelessness of it all'.

In the same way, Liebow argues that it is not inability to defer gratification that differentiates the streetcorner man from members of the middle class, but simply the fact that he has no resources to defer. Middle-class individuals are able to invest in the future, to save, to commit time and effort to their jobs and families, both because they have the resources to invest and because of the likelihood that their investment will pay off in the form of promotion at work and home ownership and home improvement. The streetcorner man lacks the resources or the promise of a pay-off if he invests what little he has. With a dead-end job or no job at all, and insufficient income to support his wife and family, he is 'obliged to expend all his resources on maintaining himself from moment to moment'.

Liebow argues that what appears to be a cultural pattern of immediate gratification, and present-time orientation is merely a situational response, a direct and indeed a rational reaction to situational constraints. Rather than being directed by a distinc-tive subculture, the behaviour of the streetcorner man is more readily understandable as a result of his inability to translate the values of mainstream culture – values which he shares – into reality.

Family life and situational constraints

Liebow applies similar reasoning to the streetcorner man's relationship with his wife and family. The men share the values of mainstream culture. They regard a conventional family life as the ideal and strive to play the mainstream roles of father and breadwinner. However, their income is insufficient to support a wife and family. Faced daily with a situation of failure, men often desert their families. Liebow writes, 'to stay married is to live with your failure, to be confronted with it day in and day out. It is to live in

a world whose standards of manliness are forever beyond one's reach.'

Increasingly, the men turn to the companionship of those in similar circumstances, to life on the streetcorner. Their conversation often revolves around the subject of marriage and its failure, which is explained in terms of what Liebow calls the theory of manly flaws. The failure of marriage is attributed to manliness, which is characterized by a need for sexual variety and adventure, gambling, drinking, swearing and aggressive behaviour. Men often boast about their 'manly flaws', illustrating their prowess with a variety of anecdotes, many of which have little relation to the truth. The theory of manly flaws cushions failure and, in a sense, translates it into success, for, at least on the streetcorner, manly flaws can bring prestige and respect. In Liebow's words, 'weaknesses are somehow turned upside down and almost magically transformed into strengths'.

On closer examination, however, Liebow found little support for the streetcorner man's rationale for marital failure. Marriages failed largely because the men had insufficient income to maintain them. The matrifocal families that resulted were not due to a culture of poverty, but simply to low income. The emphasis on manliness was not a valued aspect of lower-class culture, but simply a device to veil failure. Liebow concludes:

> The streetcorner man does not appear as a carrier of an independent cultural tradition. His behaviour appears not so much as a way of realizing the distinctive goals and values of his own subculture, or of conforming to its models, but rather as his way of trying to achieve many of the goals and values of the larger society, of failing to do this, and of concealing his failure from others and himself as best he can.
>
> Liebow, 1967

Liebow therefore rejects the idea of a culture of poverty or lower-class subculture, and sees the behaviour of the poor as a product of situational constraints, not of distinctive cultural patterns. The idea that situational constraints may shape the behaviour of the disadvantaged more than culture has been reiterated by some critics of the theory of the underclass (see the work of Blackman, discussed on pp. 332–3 and Craine, discussed on pp. 330–2).

Situational constraints and culture

A compromise between the extremes of Liebow on the one hand and Lewis on the other is provided by Ulf Hannerz (1969). He sees some virtue in both the situational constraints and cultural arguments.

Hannerz, a Swedish anthropologist, conducted research in a black low-income area of Washington

DC. In his book, *Soulside,* he argues that if a solution to a problem such as the theory of manly flaws becomes accepted by a social group, it is learned, shared and socially transmitted, and is therefore cultural. To some degree it is based on values, since the theory of manly flaws provides a male role model to which to aspire. This model is therefore not simply a cushion for failure, a thinly veiled excuse. To some degree, it provides an alternative to the mainstream male role model.

Like Liebow, Hannerz sees the theory of manly flaws as a response to situational constraints, but, unlike Liebow, he argues that if these constraints were removed, this 'model of masculinity could constitute a barrier to change'. However, Hannerz concludes that situational constraints are more powerful in directing the behaviour of the poor than cultural patterns. He argues that the cultural patterns that distinguish the poor exist alongside and are subsidiary to a widespread commitment to mainstream values. He does not see 'the ghetto variety of the culture of poverty as a lasting obstacle to change' (Liebow, 1967). Since the behaviour of the poor contains a cultural component, it may hinder change once the situational constraints are removed. There may be a cultural lag, a hangover from the previous situation, but Hannerz believes that this would only be temporary.

The underclass and poverty

In recent years, the concept of an underclass has become widely used and increasingly controversial. In Chapter 2 we discussed the underclass debate in terms of its relevance to theories of stratification. However, some theories based on the concept are also highly relevant to poverty. For example, similar ideas to those employed in individualistic and cultural theories of poverty have been used to explain the existence of an underclass.

Charles Murray – the underclass in Britain

As outlined in Chapter 2 (pp. 91–2), Charles Murray is an American sociologist who first developed ideas on the underclass in his home country. In 1989 he visited Britain and claimed that Britain too was developing an underclass. This section examines the debate surrounding his original article (Murray, 1989). The next section examines the debate relating to a subsequent article published in 1993.

Murray believes that members of the underclass are not simply the poorest members of society – they are those whose lifestyles involve a 'type of poverty'. According to Murray, this involves particular forms of behaviour. He says:

> When I use the term 'underclass' I am indeed focusing on a certain type of poor person defined not by his condition, e.g. long-term unemployed, but by his deplorable behaviour in response to that condition, e.g. unwilling to take the jobs that are available to him.
>
> Murray, 1989

Other types of 'deplorable behaviour' that are typical of the underclass are committing crimes and having illegitimate children. Murray does not claim that all poor people, nor all those who are unemployed or reliant upon benefit, engage in deplorable behaviour. It is only a minority who act in this way, but ultimately their behaviour will influence others. He claims:

> Britain has a growing population of working-aged, healthy people who live in a different world from other Britons, who are raising their children to live in it, and whose values are contaminating the life of entire neighbourhoods ... for neighbours who don't share those values cannot isolate themselves.
>
> Murray, 1989

Murray puts forward evidence in three areas to support his claims.

Illegitimacy

First, he looks at illegitimacy. He points out that in 1979, Britain had an illegitimacy rate of 10.6 per cent of births, which was low compared to most Western industrial societies. By 1988, though, it had risen to 25.6 per cent, higher than many comparable countries and not far behind the USA.

Murray cites figures to show that most illegitimate children are born to women from lower social classes and not to middle-class career women, and he suggests that in some areas the absence of a father has become the norm. For example, he relates a story about a girl in Birkenhead who was embarrassed when her father went to watch her in a school play because he was the only father there.

Murray notes that the majority of births are jointly registered to a mother and father (69 per cent in

1987), and of these 70 per cent give the same address, suggesting they live together. Even so, Murray does not believe that this undermines his argument. He questions whether relationships between cohabiting parents are as stable as those between married ones, although he admits that he has no evidence to show that the former are less stable. To Murray, the rising illegitimacy rate is important because illegitimate children will tend to 'run wild', and the lack of fathers results in 'a level of physical unruliness which makes life difficult'.

Crime

Second, Murray associates the development of an underclass with rising crime. Writing in 1989, he claimed that the rate of property crime in Britain at the time was at least as high and probably higher than that of the USA. In 1988, for example, England had a burglary rate of 1,623 per 100,000 of the population compared to a US rate of 1,309 per 100,000. Violent crime was lower in Britain, but Murray pointed out that it was rising rapidly, even though the proportion of young males in the population was falling.

Murray argues that crime is so damaging because communities become fragmented if rates of victimization are high. People become defensive and suspicious of one another and retreat into their homes. As crime becomes more common and more widely accepted, young boys start to imitate the older males and take up criminal activities themselves. As the crime rate rises further, the community becomes ever more fragmented and informal social controls which encourage conformity are weakened.

Unemployment

Murray does not see unemployment itself as a problem; instead, it is the unwillingness of young men to take jobs that creates difficulties. He says there is an 'unknown but probably considerable number of people who manage to qualify for benefit even if in reality very few job opportunities would tempt them to work'. Like illegitimacy and crime rates, unemployment is much higher in the lowest social class of unskilled manual workers, some of whom are becoming members of the underclass.

According to Murray, attitudes to work were changing in Britain at the end of the 1980s. Those in their thirties and forties who found themselves unemployed were generally much more committed to work than younger groups. The older generations of working-class males saw it as humiliating to rely on benefits, while the younger generations were happy to live off the state. Murray argues that 'talking to the boys in their late teens and early twenties about

jobs, I heard nothing about the importance of work as a source of self-respect and no talk of just wanting enough income to be free of the benefit system'.

In Murray's view, such attitudes are disastrous. He claims that 'when large numbers of young men don't work, the communities around them break down'. Young men without jobs are unable to support a family, so they are unlikely to get married when they father children and thus the illegitimacy rate rises. Supporting a family is one way for young men to prove their manhood. In the absence of family responsibilities they find other, more damaging ways to prove themselves, for example through violent crime.

Causes and solution

Murray sees the increase in illegitimacy as a consequence of changes in the benefits system. He calculates that, at 1987 prices, an unemployed single mother with a young child received just £22 in benefits in 1955. Furthermore, she had no special privileges on housing lists. The stigma of illegitimacy was also much greater. However, the value of benefits grew, the Homeless Person's Act of 1977 made pregnant women and mothers a priority in the allocation of housing, and the stigma of illegitimacy decreased. By the 1980s therefore, having an illegitimate child as a single mother and raising it alone had gone from 'extremely punishing' to 'not so bad'. There has always been a potential for rising illegitimacy because 'sex is fun and babies are endearing', but in earlier decades it had been held in check by the prohibitive financial and social costs of single motherhood. This was no longer true.

Crime, too, according to Murray, has become less severely punished. Official statistics show that, compared to earlier decades, criminals in the 1980s were less likely to be caught; if caught less likely to be convicted; and if convicted less likely to receive a severe penalty.

Murray offers no clear explanation as to why commitment to work should have declined among young men, but he does assert that providing more jobs will not solve the problem. He claims that some American cities in the second half of the 1980s had plenty of well-paid low-skilled jobs but members of the underclass were simply unwilling to take them.

Murray's solution to the problems he highlights is perhaps surprising given the causes he identifies. He does not, for example, suggest radical cuts in benefits or simply imposing stiffer sentences in the courts. He implies that such solutions are too drastic to be implemented or are impractical. For example, no political party in Britain supports the drastic cuts in benefits which would be needed to deal with illegitimacy, and the prison population might have to triple to deal effectively with crime.

What Murray suggests instead is that local communities should be given 'a massive dose of self-government'. They should take over responsibility for education, housing and criminal justice. With this power the local community would ensure that the problems were tackled. He says:

> *My premise is that it is unnatural for a neighbourhood to tolerate high levels of crime or illegitimacy or voluntary idleness among its youth: that, given the chance, poor communities as well as rich ones will run their affairs so that such things happen infrequently.*
>
> Murray, 1989

Charles Murray – *The Crisis Deepens*

Evidence of a deepening crisis

In 1993, the *Sunday Times* invited Murray to return to Britain to review how the situation had changed since his original visit. The result was the publication of a new article in which Murray argued that the crisis was deepening (Murray, 1994).

First, he noted that since the original article property crime had jumped by 42 per cent while the American rate had not changed. Consequently, by 1993, England and Wales had a much higher rate of property crime than the USA. Furthermore, violent crime had risen by 40 per cent, bringing it to the same level as the US rate in 1985.

Second, there had been a rise in the percentage of men in England and Wales who were economically active, from 9.6 to 13.3 per cent, although the unemployment rate remained almost unchanged.

Third, he found growing evidence of family instability. This took a number of forms. By 1992, the illegitimacy rate had risen to 31.2 per cent, and the divorce rate was almost as high as the marriage rate. On the other hand, the joint registration of illegitimate births by fathers as well as mothers had risen to 74 per cent in 1991 (compared to around 40 per cent in the late 1960s). In the early 1990s, about 70 per cent of jointly registered parents of illegitimate children lived at the same address. However, Murray did not think that this demonstrated evidence of strong relationships developing between most unmarried parents. He quotes a study based on the *General Household Survey* which found that the median duration of cohabitation was only about two years. This suggested that cohabitation rarely provided a stable relationship within which children could be raised.

Overall, in 1991, about 19 per cent of families with children in England and Wales were headed by lone parents, 6 per cent by a cohabiting couple and 75 per cent by a married couple. These figures covered all households with children. In households where a child was born in 1990, only 70 per cent were headed by a cohabiting couple. Murray also found that childbirth outside marriage was particularly common in local authority areas with a preponderance of unskilled manual workers. He concludes that 'the England in which the family has effectively collapsed does not consist just of blacks, or even the inner-city neighbourhoods of London, Manchester and Liverpool, but lower-working class communities everywhere'.

'New Victorians' and the 'New Rabble'

As well as discussing more recent evidence of a deepening crisis, Murray considers two possible scenarios for family life in Britain.

Under the first scenario, the breakdown of family life is seen as an inevitable feature of modernization. If this is the case, then there will be an inexorable rise in illegitimacy among all classes, including the upper middle class. Traditional family values will become increasingly rare throughout society and, he claims, it is therefore 'safe to predict that English society will be dysfunctional in ways that can now only be dimly imagined'.

However, Murray is hopeful that an alternative scenario will develop. Under the second scenario society will be increasingly split between a 'New Rabble' and 'New Victorians'. Illegitimacy will become the norm among the 'New Rabble', and:

> *inevitably, life in lower class communities will continue to degenerate – more crime, more widespread drug and alcohol addiction, fewer marriages, more dropout from work, more homelessness, more child neglect, fewer young people pulling themselves out of the slums, more young people tumbling in.*
>
> Murray, 1994

This bleak picture is counterbalanced by the 'New Victorians', particularly in the upper middle class, who will reassert traditional family patterns and values. They will rediscover the virtues and benefits of monogamous marriage, and along with this may go 'a revival of religion and of the intellectual; respectability of concepts such as fidelity, courage, loyalty, self-restraint, moderation, and other admirable human qualities that until recently have barely dared speak their names'. Murray actually found no statistical evidence to support the possibility that 'New Victorians' were growing in number in the upper middle class, but nevertheless he predicted that this was likely to happen.

Murray's solutions

Despite the positive aspects of the changes, British society will still be in deep trouble. It will be increasingly divided and the two groups will become increasingly segregated as the 'New Victorians' try to distance themselves from the 'New Rabble' by living in different areas. The values of the 'New Victorians' will only percolate down from the upper middle classes with changes in social policies.

As in his earlier article, Murray argues that the benefits system needs to be changed to get rid of disincentives to marriage and to discourage single parenthood. By living apart without being married, mothers and fathers can draw more benefit from the state. Single mothers can now afford to live on benefits, whereas in the past they could not. As a consequence, males who father children are often isolated from family life and the responsibilities of fatherhood, and are not socialized out of being barbarians. The benefits system, therefore, has to be changed so that it no longer penalizes marriage. Married couples in need must receive at least as much benefit as couples who live apart.

Furthermore, Murray suggests that you could improve the situation by 'eliminating benefits for unmarried women altogether' and restoring the benefits system that existed in 1960. Only in this way will women be forced to marry. People will have to avoid pregnancies outside marriage, or face drastic economic consequences.

Murray concludes that 'the welfare of society requires that women actively avoid getting pregnant if they have no husband, and that women once again demand marriage from a man who would have them bear a child .... It is all horribly sexist, I know. It also happens to be true.'

Critics of Murray

Murray's analysis of the underclass owes much to some of the theories of poverty we have already examined. Like New Right theories, it sees benefits as producing groups who are unable or unwilling to earn their own living. Like the culture of poverty theory, it sees the lifestyle of certain groups at the bottom of society as contributing to their own plight. On the other hand, it is unlike any single theory of poverty and it has become sufficiently influential to generate fierce criticism. The following criticisms were all made in response to Murray's original article.

Alan Walker – blaming the victims

Alan Walker (1990) argues that Murray puts forward totally inadequate evidence to support his case by relying upon 'innuendos, assertions and anecdotes'. Furthermore, Walker suggests that the best evidence

there is does not point to the existence of an underclass.

For example, research by Brown and Madge (1982), commissioned to investigate Sir Keith Joseph's claim that there was a 'cycle of disadvantage', found that at least 50 per cent of those born in a disadvantaged home did not end up disadvantaged themselves. This contradicts Murray's claims that supposed underclass attitudes and values would inevitably rub off on younger generations.

Walker also refers to official figures to attack Murray's views on illegitimacy. About 60 per cent of illegitimate births to women younger than 20 are registered by both parents. Lone parenthood is often short-lived. Research by John Ermisch (quoted in Walker, 1990) found that the median length of lone parenthood for a never-married woman in the early 1980s was less than three years. Most found a partner in a relatively short time. Most children born to such mothers do not spend the whole of their childhood with a single parent.

Walker argues that most of the so-called underclass have conventional attitudes. They want stable relationships and paid employment. It is not their values that prevent them from achieving their aims, but a lack of opportunities. In this context, Walker supports a type of situational constraints theory (see pp. 321–3 for a discussion of this type of theory). Walker criticizes government policy for the plight of the underclass. He says that Murray's theory 'diverts attention ... from the real problems: pauperization and social segregation as acts of government policy'.

In other words, Walker believes the poor are the victims of social policy rather than the cause of society's social problems.

Joan C. Brown – single motherhood

Joan C. Brown (1990) is critical of Murray's ideas on single motherhood. She quotes figures which show that, on average, divorced single mothers spend longer claiming benefits than never-married single mothers although Murray blames the latter group for the ills of the underclass.

She questions Murray's arguments about single motherhood becoming accepted as the norm in some neighbourhoods. Where there is a concentration of single mothers, it is usually due to council housing policy which allocates them to houses in particular areas, and nothing to do with neighbourhoods becoming tainted by values which undermine family life.

Furthermore, divorce has become very common in all strata of society and is not confined to lower classes. The *British Social Attitudes Survey* of 1983 found that 90 per cent of those aged 18–34 did not believe pre-marital sex to be wrong. Again, she concludes that it is not possible to argue that there are distinctive underclass attitudes which are confined to poor women.

Nicholas Deakin – Murray's tripod

Nicholas Deakin (1990) notes that Murray's argument rests upon a three-legged argument based on illegitimacy, crime and unemployment. Deakin believes that at least two of those legs are very shaky.

Murray describes illegitimacy as 'the purest form of being without parents', yet himself admits that many 'illegitimate children do indeed share a household with cohabiting but unmarried parents'. Like Walker and Brown, Deakin points out that single-parenthood 'is not a static condition, still less an immoral one' but simply 'a stage in the life which may lead in a variety of different directions'.

The second leg of the tripod rests upon the use of official statistics. However, these are well known for being highly unreliable so the data Murray uses are unconvincing. Deakin does not deny that there has been a big rise in unemployment but neither that nor a few anecdotes demonstrates that attitudes to work have changed amongst a supposed underclass.

Anthony Heath – underclass attitudes

The critics of Murray discussed so far raise serious doubts about Murray's evidence, but Anthony Heath has actually collected data to test the claim that the attitudes of the underclass are different (Heath, 1990). He used information from the *British Election Survey* of 1987 and the *British Social Attitudes Survey* of 1989. He confined his study to people of working age. He identified those in the surveys who did not have paid employment and who claimed income support and compared them to the rest of the sample.

Heath found that 86 per cent of the underclass said they would like to have a paid job compared to 57 per cent of those in families where at least one person was working. This suggests that Murray is wrong to argue that those reliant on benefits are less willing to work than others.

Heath also found that in most respects members of the underclass had similar attitudes towards marriage to other members of society. Some 22 per cent agreed that 'married people are generally happier than unmarried people' compared to 25 per cent of those from employed family units. Members of the underclass were more likely to agree that 'It is better to have a bad marriage than no marriage at all' (10 per cent compared to 2 per cent), and that 'Couples don't take marriage seriously enough when divorce is easily available' (61 per cent compared to 54 per cent). However they were less likely to agree that 'People who want children ought to get married' (47 per cent against 64 per cent).

Most of the evidence uncovered by Heath, then, suggests that the majority of the underclass (if they can be said to exist) have conventional aspirations. They want jobs and happy marriages, but they are slightly less likely than other members of society to believe that people should get married before having children.

Criticisms of *The Crisis Deepens*

Most of the commentaries on Murray's second article have been no less critical than those on the first.

Pete Alcock (1994) reiterates the sort of criticisms advanced by Alan Walker and Joan Brown. He notes that Murray's later writing concentrates on the issue of illegitimacy. He further notes that while Murray does advance some new evidence to support his case he still fails to substantiate his arguments. Alcock says:

> *Murray still does not address the points that most lone parents in Britain remain those separated or divorced (not the young mothers of illegitimate children), that most lone parents subsequently (re)marry, and that most illegitimate children are registered as living with both parents.*

Alcock, 1994

Alcock also points out that Murray makes many sweeping generalizations about the negative effects of lone parenthood which are unjustified. Two-parent families do sometimes produce poorly socialized children, just as lone parents can and do produce well-socialized children. In fact, Alcock argues, 'most of the unemployed, the perpetrators of crime and the cohabiting (or not) parents of illegitimate children have come from what must appear from all the evidence to be stable, married, family relationships'. Furthermore, Alcock is unconvinced by Murray's solution to the 'problem' of illegitimacy. Simply returning to the benefits system of the 1960s would not, as Murray seems to think, lead to a return to the society of the 1960s. Since society has changed in the meantime, people would be likely to respond differently to the old benefits system. In any case, people do not make decisions about their lives simply on economic grounds. As Alcock says, 'first-year sociology students soon learn that all the decisions we make, or think we make, are structured by a range of social, cultural and economic forces within which we move but without which we cannot step'.

Alcock believes that simply depriving unmarried mothers of their benefits would mean that 'many good parents and deserving children, by anyone's measure, will be cruelly deprived'. Murray could argue that the 'deserving' and 'undeserving' cases should be treated differently. However, Alcock points out that this might create perverse incentives. For example, if divorced single mothers received benefits and never-married single mothers did not, it would pay women with children to get married with the intention of getting divorced in order to claim benefits.

While some writers have rejected the idea of an underclass altogether, others have argued that there is an underclass, but have seen the group very differently.

Frank Field – *Losing Out*

The underclass and citizenship

Frank Field is a British Labour MP who has campaigned against poverty. Between 1997 and 1998 he was a minister in the Labour Government. In recent times he has advocated the radical reform of the benefit system in Britain. Like Charles Murray in 1989, he argues that Britain has a growing underclass among the poor (Field, 1989). In this early work, Field does not see the underclass as having a distinctive culture, nor does he see them as a pathological group undermining the well-being of society. Instead, he regards the underclass as the victims of social change and government policies.

Field links the growth of an underclass to the reduction of citizenship rights. In 1949, T.H. Marshall put forward the argument that whereas civil rights were largely established in the eighteenth century, and political rights (such as the right to vote) in the nineteenth century, social and economic citizenship rights were the main concern of the twentieth century. For example, the development of a welfare state provided citizens with the right to a basic living standard. Field regards this description of citizenship as an over-simplification but he accepted the general thrust of the argument.

He went on to claim, however, that since 1979 'the 300-year-old evolution of citizenship as an incorporating force in British society has been thrown into reverse'. This, in turn, has led to the growth of an underclass whose members are denied the economic and social citizenship rights enjoyed by others.

The composition of the underclass

According to Field, the underclass consists of three main groups:

1 The first group is the long-term unemployed. There is a continual flow of people into and out of unemployment, and those who are unemployed for a short time do not form part of the underclass. The two main groups among the long-term unemployed are school leavers who have never had a job and older workers who have been unemployed for long periods. With rising unemployment in the 1970s and 1980s, the unemployed swelled the ranks of the underclass considerably.

2 A second group that has been growing rapidly is single-parent families. Between 1979 and 1987, there was an increase of more than 200 per cent in the number of single mothers claiming welfare benefits. Some in this situation are only briefly dependent on benefits: it is those who are 'dependent on welfare for very long periods of time' who are part of the underclass.

3 The third group consists of elderly pensioners who depend on state benefits because they do not have an occupational pension. Field says that 'many of them live in the worst housing conditions, and their income does not adequately compensate for the extra expense arising from the disabilities that accompany extreme old age' (Field, 1989). Unlike the first two groups the elderly make up a declining proportion of the very poor.

What members of Field's underclass have in common is that they are all reliant upon state benefits which are too low to give them an acceptable living standard, and they have little chance of escaping from reliance upon benefits. Furthermore, their chances of escape have been declining as the forces that have created an underclass have also made the predicament of its members more difficult.

The causes of the underclass

Field attributes the development of the underclass to four main causes:

1 Rising levels of unemployment have made more people of working age reliant upon benefits and have led to a big increase in the numbers of long-term unemployed.

2 Social changes and government policy have widened the gap between higher and lower classes. Field specifically claims that Margaret Thatcher's government had a 'determination to widen class differences' in the 1980s.

3 Living standards in society as a whole have risen, but the poorest members of society have been excluded from the benefits enjoyed by the increasingly affluent.

4 There has been a change in public attitude towards those who have failed to be economically successful. The public has become less sympathetic and more inclined to blame the poor for their plight. According to Field, 'this has led to a psychological and political separation of the very poorest from the rest of the community.' A 'drawbridge' mentality has developed: successful members of the working class have cut themselves off from those who have had less success. The underclass is therefore becoming increasingly distinct from the working class.

Field devotes most of his attention to discussing the first three causes of the underclass and these will now be examined in more detail.

First, according to Field, the decline in manufacturing industry has led to an increase in unemployment among unskilled and semi-skilled workers. Their plight was worsened by changes in policy under the Conservatives. Unemployment benefit was restricted to the first six months of unemployment and was far from generous.

Second, inequality had increased under the Conservatives as a result of reductions in taxes for the better-off and reductions in benefits for the poor. In 1980, for example, Margaret Thatcher stopped increasing old-age pensions and invalidity benefit in line with wage rises (if they were greater than inflation). Instead, they were increased only in line with inflation. This meant that many groups reliant on benefits no longer shared in the general growth in prosperity in society. Field is also critical of changes in housing benefits and child benefits that reduced the amount which went to their recipients.

According to Field, there was a fundamental contradiction in the social security policies of the 1980s (policies which largely continued under John Major until 1997). The Conservative government wanted to discourage reliance upon benefits, but also wanted to target benefits on the most needy. The problem is that targeting, using means-tested benefits, increases dependency and creates a poverty trap from which it is difficult to escape. If the poor increase their earnings so that they no longer need to claim income support, they lose their entitlement to other benefits such as housing benefit. This means that overall they are not much better off. Single parents may have the additional problem of paying for childcare if they take up paid employment, which may leave them worse off than if they were drawing benefits. Field believes that such policies have created a large and growing underclass 'immobilized at the bottom of our society'.

Solutions

Field sees government policy as the main factor creating an underclass, and he sees changes in government policy as the main way of solving the problem. His proposals include a wide range of measures intended to reduce large-scale unemployment, to improve the living standards of those on benefits, to give claimants incentives to get off benefits and to reduce inequality.

In 1989, Field proposed moving civil service jobs to areas of high unemployment, targeting government purchases on such areas and improving training. The unemployed should be guaranteed employment training so that they can develop the skills necessary to work in a way that will allow their employers to compete internationally. Temporary work schemes should be set up for those who could not find work even after retraining.

Pensions and child benefit should both be increased. This would mean that many people would no longer need to claim means-tested benefits. Unemployment benefit should continue indefinitely for those willing to accept suitable jobs.

Income support should no longer take a spouse's earnings into account since this discourages many married people from finding work. Single parents should be allowed to earn more before their benefits are cut. Their benefit reductions should be based on a sliding scale, allowing them to keep more of their earnings and giving them a greater incentive to work. It should be possible to offset the costs of childcare against tax to ensure that paid employment is worthwhile for single parents.

Inequality should be reduced through a minimum wage of 55 per cent of the average earnings in a particular industry. Tax allowances for the better-off, such as tax relief on mortgages, should be cut or phased out. National Insurance should be changed so that there is no upper limit and high earners would therefore pay more.

Making welfare work

Field's more recent work (1996) has not used the term underclass, but has been concerned with the sort of issues raised by writers such as Charles Murray. In some respects, Field has moved towards accepting some of Murray's arguments while suggesting rather different solutions. He has agreed with Murray that welfare payments can encourage undesirable behaviour. In particular, he has developed his critique of means-tested benefits, describing them as 'the cancer within the welfare state, rotting decent values and overwhelming the honesty and dignity of recipients in almost equal proportions'. He argues that means tests tend to discourage both savings and work, because people lose benefits if their savings or earnings are too high. It also discourages honesty, because the low level of benefits creates big incentives to cheat the system.

Field's emphasis, however, has moved from increasing benefits to tackle poverty towards restructuring the benefits system to discourage qualities such as laziness and dishonesty. The only way this can be achieved is by developing a system which rewards good behaviour and punishes bad (rather than vice versa). Field says, 'welfare should aim to maximize self-improvement, without which all is lost. Work, effort, savings and honesty must all be rewarded rather than, as so often at present, being penalized by welfare's provisions.' The key to achieving this is, according to Field, the development of 'insurance benefits', in which people are rewarded for contributing to compulsory insurance schemes to meet their needs during unemployment, sickness, old age, and so on. The state can pay some contributions for those unable to earn a living, while some welfare provision may be withheld for those who refuse to work.

In 1989, Field's views on the underclass were very similar to many conflict theorists' views on poverty, which we will discuss shortly (see pp. 334–40). His more recent work owes something more to those right-wing thinkers who are critical of the behavioural effects of welfare. As a minister in the British Labour government elected in 1997, Field's ideas have had some impact on government policies, but his resignation in 1998 ensured that the impact was minimal. The policies of the Labour government will be examined at the end of this chapter (see pp. 345–6).

Other views on the underclass are examined elsewhere in the book. Some sociologists accept that there is a group of the poor at the bottom of the stratification system but do not accept that it is appropriate to call them an underclass. Others believe that there is an underclass but do not define it as consisting of long-term benefit claimants. These views were discussed in Chapter 2 (see pp. 93–5), while the relationship between the underclass and ethnicity is examined on pp. 282–5.

Qualitative studies of the underclass

Nearly all the views on the underclass examined here and elsewhere in the book rely largely on the use of statistical data. In some recent studies, however, researchers have tried to develop their understanding of those who are commonly regarded as members of the underclass

Steve Craine – the 'Black Magic Roundabout'
Steve Craine (1997) is highly sceptical about those sociologists who argue that there is an underclass among unemployed young people in Britain. He argues that most of the research on youth in Britain finds very little evidence of a large group of work-shy unemployed youths who turn to crime. He therefore conducted his own research in an inner-city area of Manchester he called 'Basildeane'.

The study involved research over ten years, between 1980 and 1990, of 39 unqualified school leavers. Nineteen were male, 20 were female. Steve Craine had been a youth worker in the area and he could therefore act as a participant observer as well as carrying out interviews. Most of the subjects of the study lived on a deprived estate known locally as 'the

jungle'. The area had very high unemployment as a result of a decline in local manufacturing, and decaying housing which had been neglected by the local authority.

The careers of the school leavers
Craine examined the way in which these young people's lives unfolded in terms of the concept of a 'career'. He looked at how they made choices about what to do next in the context of the situation in which they found themselves. Although some did turn to crime, this was not because that was the path they would ideally like to have taken. Rather, career choices were 'frequently desperate survival adaptations' taken in the context of structured inequality. Paraphrasing Marx, he says that 'participants were, indeed, active in the construction of their own history, but not as they pleased, nor under circumstances of their own choosing'.

Craine distinguishes between three types of transition for these school leavers (using concepts developed by Ken Roberts):

1 Three participants had a traditional post-school transition. That is, they went straight into employment. All three were married with children and were no longer living with parents by their mid-twenties. They came from homes where parents had stable jobs and their parents' workplace contacts had been useful in finding jobs.

2 The second group had a protracted transition. For four to seven years they moved between employment, unemployment and government schemes before finally finding more permanent employment. This group lost none of their commitment to the labour market and continued to struggle to find work despite frequent set-backs. They tended to come from families which were not regarded as the most 'rough' or the most 'respectable' in the area, but somewhere in the middle. In each of their families, at least one person was working.

3 The third and largest group experienced a cyclical transition. This 'entailed early careers in which participants became trapped on a (not so) merry-go-round of unemployment, government schemes and special programmes, youth jobs, work in the informal economy, more unemployment, more schemes, and so on'. Those trapped in this cycle called it the 'Black Magic Roundabout'.

Life on schemes
People who found themselves on the 'Black Magic Roundabout' were usually placed on schemes which offered no real training or prospect of employment. The schemes involved work such as clearing graveyards, cleaning up canals, decorating the homes of old people, and so on. Girls tended to be given

'feminized' work such as office, cleaning and care work, while boys were given the heavier manual tasks. Those on the schemes were derogatory about them and they believed that others saw them as having the lowest possible status. Craine says that 'trainees complained of inadequate facilities, lack of "proper" training, pointless "boring" and repetitive tasks and of being "treated like shit", like "some sort of moron", "like dirt"'.

All of those studied were derisive about the social and life skills training on the schemes, and many felt that their dignity was undermined by their movement into and out of dead-end schemes. One said 'it was like a bloody circus except we were the clowns'. Craine found that the schemes were ineffective in finding people work. In total, the 39 young people had been on nearly 90 schemes, for a total time of nearly 60 years. Only one person had gained access to a job through a scheme.

The hopelessness of the situation was expressed by people in various ways. One local graffiti artist had painted a 'piece' on a wall near the local careers office. Craine says, 'it displayed the familiar characters from the children's television series, *The Magic Roundabout*, but the faces of the various characters, Dylan, Dougal, Zebedee, etc., were grotesquely distorted with sinister, demonic eyes and embittered scowls, their faces drawn in pain or anguish'.

Craine discovered that this image was related to a local cult among the unemployed of watching daytime repeats of *The Magic Roundabout* on television. However, the idea of going round in a circle on the roundabout was also 'a pictorial metaphor for futility and alienation ... which concisely articulated the revolving door of cyclical post-school transitions'.

Underclass behaviour

In the context of the 'Black Magic Roundabout', some of the young people studied did engage in behaviour which some writers have associated with the underclass. Among the females, the choice was between domestic drudgery within male-dominated marriages, lone parenthood or alternative ways of earning an income. Nine of the girls had become lone parents by 1990, four were earning a living illegally (one through prostitution, one through fraud and drug dealing, and two through 'working on the side'), and the remainder were married or cohabiting with men. From their point of view, almost anything was better than the 'Black Magic Roundabout'. Becoming a mother or wife provided a more socially accepted role than being unemployed or on dead-end schemes, while illegal activities offered the only realistic prospect of earning a good living.

For the males, failure to find long-term work usually led to 'retreat into the norms, values and alternative status systems of their peer group subcultures. Participants built on a collective sense of identity constructed out of an exaggerated version of working-class machismo.' Most of them had fathered one or more children, but their macho emphasis on emotional detachment and their insecurity and lack of reliable income meant that only three of those undergoing cyclical transitions had established long-term relationships. Eight of the group had become involved in crime and the lives of some were made even more unstable by spending time in prison.

Among the long-term unemployed males, Craine found no lack of energy and imagination. That energy and imagination, however, was largely directed towards 'alternative careers'. These might start out as minor benefit fiddles, but later their illegal careers would progress further. Some were given work by two local 'hard' families, the Hattons and the Donoghues. This might involved acting as ticket touts, unlicensed street trading, or selling unofficial programmes at the GMex or other venues. For example, they sold poor-quality unofficial programmes at performances by the ice skaters Torvill and Dean. By wearing white coats, they appeared to be official programme vendors.

Craine argues that such alternative careers provided 'income, autonomy and status from living off their wits'. None of these was available from the opportunities provided by conventional work (because they could not obtain any), or on government schemes. The alternative careers often progressed beyond the initial stage. The next, 'intermediate stage' involved 'totting and hustling'. Totting was systematic benefit fraud; hustling activities included selling stolen goods, shoplifting and casual drugs dealing. The final stage involved more serious criminal activities: 'dealing' or systematic drug dealing; 'hoisting' or organized shoplifting; 'grafting' or organized burglary and other types of theft; and 'blagging' or robbery, armed or otherwise.

Conclusion

On the surface, Craine's study appears to provide ammunition for those who argue that there is an underclass problem caused by the cultural characteristics of its members. However, Craine argues that the culture he found is not passed down from generation to generation as Murray suggests. Rather it is a creative solution to an intolerable situation. Nor did Craine find that the welfare state encourages passivity. Rather, because benefits are too low for people to live on, it encourages people to earn their living in imaginative and entrepreneurial ways outside the law. Craine therefore found that 'benefit dependence, paradoxically, promotes a distorted "parody" of dominant values and encourages "the penny capitalism of the poor'". The development of alternative careers is not due to benefit dependence or pathological culture, but due to lack of legitimate opportunities. He explains it in terms of:

> *an inter-connected and cumulative ecology of disadvantage, which included: stigmatised residential location; (for some) absentee fathers; enduring poverty; transgenerational unemployment; negative policy interventions in housing benefits and training; plus the cynicism and alienation engendered by post-school labour market experiences.*
>
> Craine, 1997, p. 148

Not all of those on the 'Black Magic Roundabout' turned to crime or lone parenthood. Some were provided with 'forms of social support and policy intervention which helped to promote and sustain positive outcomes for disadvantaged young people'. In some cases, family members, housing professionals, or probation officers helped individuals gain access to legitimate opportunities. However, it is likely to be a minority of the disadvantaged young who go down such paths if:

> *we follow the New Right apologists of the underclass thesis and rest by our analyses and future policy agenda on empirically deficient notions of social pathology and individual moral defectiveness. In the meantime, socially excluded youth will continue to construct their own solutions and make their own history – no doubt fuelling further reactionary myths and stereotypes as they do.*
>
> Craine, 1997, pp. 151–2

Shane J. Blackman – the homeless and the underclass

Blackman's research

Steve Craine's work attacks New Right and other cultural explanations of the underclass by reiterating and developing the sorts of argument advanced by advocates of situational constraints theories. Like Craine, Shane Blackman is highly critical of New Right theories of the underclass. However, he goes one step further than Craine by rejecting the idea of an underclass altogether. Craine argues that the concept has been used 'as a means to heighten social fears and promote the idea of an "Other" with the aim of ensuring conformity among the working and middle classes' (Blackman, 1997). His claims are based upon a qualitative study of nearly 100 young people (79 per cent male and 21 per cent female) who visited an advice and information centre for young people in Brighton in 1992. His main focus was on

22 homeless people. He conducted ethnographic research and recorded his findings in a field diary.

The aspirations of the homeless

Blackman found that the young homeless had very similar aspirations to other members of society. A phrase used by many of them was, 'I am thinking of putting down roots'. They wanted permanent homes and some stability and security in their lives. Some of them gained employment during the study, for example in shops, labouring or doing voluntary work. Some undertook college courses. Between them, the 22 young homeless people had had a wide variety of previous jobs. Blackman found that 'it was certainly not the case, then, that these individuals avoided employment or lacked labour market experience', and that 'all the young people observed aspired to become part of the "normal" society'.

Nevertheless, they had become homeless and had not found themselves permanent housing or work. Furthermore, they sometimes engaged in behaviour, such as heavy drinking, which seemed to be making escape from homelessness more difficult. So how had they ended up in this situation and why were they unable to escape from it?

Reasons for their homelessness

Each individual had a different story to tell about their personal decline. These stories were 'often dramatic, depressing and sometimes horrific'. Many had become homeless because they 'had been abused, raped, exploited, violently shocked, or experienced bereavement, betrayal or rejection'. Unsurprisingly, none of them had actively sought out or desired homelessness. Once they had become homeless, though, they faced a number of obstacles to improving their lot:

1 They tended to suffer discrimination because they were homeless. It became more difficult to find work or housing if they had no address.

2 They faced problems if they took work in the formal economy. Most of the jobs they had a chance of getting were insecure or temporary, and so of little help in trying to obtain permanent accommodation. Also, they were reluctant to take such jobs because they would result in a loss of benefit. If they stopped claiming benefit it could be difficult to sign on again. There was no guarantee that the DSS would accept their claim and process it quickly.

3 The decline into homelessness had left many of these young people with a lack of self-confidence and a poor self-image. Blackman claims that many of them felt they were unintelligent because teachers, social workers and others had told them as much. Consequently, 'low esteem meets low expectation which brings about enduring self-labelling of personal underachievement'. This made it

difficult for them to have the self-belief to get out of their situation.

4 Their lack of self-belief was compounded by what Blackman calls the 'fear of fall'. Although to an outsider they seemed to have little to lose, they did have strong support and friendship networks among the other young homeless people in the area. One of the homeless said:

> If I could leave the world of the homeless, I'd do it today. Say if I leave, what happens if I don't make it again? I will end up having to move on. But if I stay homeless I have my friends, contacts, people I know. This is my world, why should I throw it away? It's all right for you, you've got other things. What I have may not seem much to you. It may not seem much to lose. But when you haven't got much – nothing really, then this seems a lot to lose.

Blackman, 1997

Some of them had made progress in the past by finding jobs or more secure accommodation, only to lose them and end up in an even worse situation. This was very dispiriting and discouraged them from taking a chance on the same happening again.

Surviving homelessness

The homeless in Brighton did engage in some types of behaviour which have been seen as being typical of the underclass. However, Blackman argues that such behaviour was a consequence of their homelessness, not a cause of it. It was a way of coping with their situation. For example, some of those studied did work illegally in the informal economy while claiming benefits. As we have seen above, though, this was hardly surprising given the lack of stable employment in the formal economy and the nature of the benefits system. In many cases, employers would only take them on if they did undeclared work. They were left with little choice other than to accept these jobs if they wanted to work at all.

Another example is that they would 'destruct a giro'. This involved going on a binge after receiving a giro cheque from the DSS. They would usually drink heavily, some took drugs, and they would spend all their money before they received their next payment.

Blackman found that some were ashamed of public drunkenness and other behaviour, but destructing a giro gave them a sense of autonomy and control that helped bolster their flagging self-esteem. For once they could consume products like other members of society. It was a particular source of pride if they could buy one of their friends a drink. Nevertheless, it could be self-defeating since it 'served to reinforce their feelings of social and economic dislocation, as they were cut free from the time discipline of the workplace or even their own more standard everyday routine'.

A few of the homeless did get involved in crime and prostitution, 'but such actions were not generally part of an organised activity and seemed more related to an individual's immediate economic circumstances'. When they were desperate their bodies were the last assets they had to exploit, so prostitution became their last resort. Few of them became involved in using hard drugs, and any drug dealing or property crime was haphazard rather than a systematic way of earning a living.

The homeless and the underclass

To outsiders the homeless in Brighton might have seemed dangerous, drunken and lazy. They appeared to be people who were making little effort to help themselves. Through his ethnographic research, Blackman was able to understand their behaviour from their point of view, and to see that it was largely a reaction to their situation rather than a way of life they chose. Blackman says, 'they were experiencing multiple problems in bleak cultural locations … They had become submerged in a localised subculture with specific strategies for coping with the difficulties in their everyday lives.'

In contradiction of Charles Murray's and similar theories of the underclass, they did not reject society's values. What made them different was that they had no stake in society and they shared the stigma of being homeless. What they needed was not a different culture, but jobs and homes. A few individuals in the study did find reasonably secure homes and Blackman found that this soon 'gave young people greater confidence to use the telephone to respond to jobs and housing advertisements' and their mental health improved. Blackman therefore rejected the underclass theory, arguing that it is an ideological device used to deny society's responsibility to the disadvantaged by claiming that some people are undeserving of government support. At the same time, it is used as a weapon to warn the respectable working class of their likely fate if they stop conforming and working hard. Like a number of other writers, Blackman sees members of the so-called 'underclass' as victims of society whose behaviour changes when they are given genuine opportunities to improve their lot.

Conflict theories of poverty

The sociology of poverty has increasingly come to be studied within a conflict perspective. Those working within this perspective argue that it is the failure of society to allocate its resources fairly that explains the continued existence of poverty. Poverty is not held to be the responsibility of those who suffer from it. Instead they are seen as the 'victims'.

To some extent conflict theorists disagree about the reasons why society has failed to eradicate poverty:

1 Some regard poverty as primarily the consequence of the failings of the welfare state.

2 Others place more emphasis on the lack of power and weak bargaining position of the poor which places them at a disadvantage in the labour market. The poor are either unable to sell their labour, or are prevented from receiving sufficient rewards from it to lift themselves out of poverty.

3 Many conflict theorists relate the existence of poverty to wider structural forces in society, in particular the existence of a stratification system.

4 Marxists tend to believe poverty is an inherent and inevitable consequence of capitalism. They cannot envisage the defeat of poverty without the total transformation of society.

Thus, although there are broad similarities between the sociologists we will look at in the following sections, there are also some areas of disagreement.

Poverty and the welfare state

Recent studies of poverty have found that those who rely upon state benefits for their income are among the largest groups of the poor. If poverty is defined in relative terms, and the definition that is advanced means that benefit levels do not raise the recipient above the poverty line, then a great deal of poverty can simply be attributed to inadequate benefits.

Nevertheless, it might be argued that the welfare state still makes a major contribution to reducing poverty, or at least to improving the relative position of those who are poor. It is widely assumed that one effect of the welfare state is to redistribute resources from the rich to the poor as, at first sight, it appears that both taxation and welfare payments do this.

Taxation

This view has been challenged by some conflict sociologists. Some taxes are certainly progressive, that is, they lead to the better-off paying a greater proportion of their income to the government than the lower income groups pay. Direct taxes, such as income tax, are levied at different levels according to income, and those on very low pay may not even reach the threshold at which tax must be paid.

However, indirect taxation (taxes levied on the purchase of goods) tends to be regressive. Taxes such as VAT (Value Added Tax) and duties on alcohol and tobacco tend to take up a greater proportion of the income of poorer sections of the community than richer ones.

Since 1978–9, the tax burden on the low-paid has increased, while the burden on the high-paid has been reduced. Direct taxation has become less progressive, indirect taxation has increased, and the relative position of those on low incomes has worsened. Official statistics showed that between 1979 and 1993–4, the real income of the poorest 10 per cent of the population fell by 13 per cent after housing costs, whereas for the richest 10 per cent it increased by 65 per cent. For the population as a whole, average real income growth, after housing costs, was 40 per cent (quoted in Oppenheim, 1997).

Christopher Giles and Paul Johnson (1994) have examined the effects of tax changes between 1985 and 1995 in a study for the Institute for Fiscal Studies. Table 5.7 shows the results. It divides the population into tenths or 'deciles', decile 1 being the poorest and decile 10 the richest. It shows that as a

Table 5.7	Impact of tax changes 1985–95, by decile group			
Decile	Percentage losing	Percentage gaining	Average gain/loss (£ per week)	Average gain/loss (% of net income)
1	66	7	-3.00	-2.9
2	44	13	-1.40	-1.4
3	47	23	-1.80	-1.5
4	43	40	-1.10	-0.8
5	37	50	0.70	0.4
6	33	57	1.60	0.7
7	29	64	3.10	1.2
8	25	69	4.40	1.5
9	23	72	6.30	1.8
10	20	76	31.30	5.8
All	37	47	4.10	1.7

Source: C. Giles and P. Johnson (1994) *Taxes Down, Taxes Up: The Effects of a Decade of Tax Changes*, The Institute for Fiscal Studies, London, p. 11.

result of tax changes the poorest decile has lost an average of £3 per week or 2.9 per cent of their income, while the richest decile has gained £31.30 or 5.5 per cent of their income.

The *Strategy of Equality*

Undoubtedly some welfare benefits primarily benefit those on the lowest incomes: income support, unemployment benefit and family credit are all directed at the poorest members of society. However, while they may prevent absolute poverty, some sociologists argue that welfare benefits do little to eradicate relative poverty.

Writing in 1982, Julian Le Grand suggested that the *Strategy of Equality* through the provision of social services had failed. From an examination of education, healthcare, housing and transport subsidies, he argued that the better-off members of British society had benefited considerably more than the poor. In education, the children of top income groups were more likely to stay on in education after the age of 16, and more likely to go to university. He calculated that the families in the top 20 per cent of income groups received nearly three times as much expenditure on their children's education as those in the bottom fifth.

In the field of healthcare, Le Grand claimed that those on higher incomes, again, benefit more from the services provided. The actual amounts spent on different income groups did not vary a great deal; however, lower socio-economic groups were more likely to suffer from illness, and therefore needed more medical care than the higher groups. It was this extra care that they did not receive. Le Grand found that 'the evidence suggests that the top socio-economic group receives 40 per cent more NHS expenditure per person reporting illness than the bottom one'.

The DHSS *Inequalities in Health Working Group Report*, better known as the *Black Report*, published in 1981, reached similar conclusions. It confirmed the inverse care law: those whose need is less get more resources, while those with a greater need tend to get less. For example, it found that doctors tend to spend more time with middle-class patients, and middle-class areas tend to have more doctors per head of the population than working-class areas.

Le Grand found a similar picture in relation to housing expenditure:

1   Poorer households received substantially greater benefits than richer ones from various forms of direct expenditure on housing. General subsidies on the supervision and maintenance of council housing and rent rebates and allowances (now replaced by housing benefits) favoured lower-income groups.

2   However, higher-income groups benefited considerably more from indirect expenditure. In particular, tax relief on mortgage interest payments provided a major saving for those homeowners who had mortgages.

3   Furthermore, capital gains tax was not charged on homes which were sold at a profit.

4   Improvement grants for houses were one form of direct expenditure which favoured the better-off.

Le Grand concluded that from housing policy, 'the richest group receives nearly twice as much as public subsidy per household as the poorest group'.

Writing in 1987, Le Grand argued that changes since the 1970s had done little to alter the overall picture:

1   Some changes resulted in improvements and services benefiting higher-income groups even more than they had done in the past: subsidies to council housing had been cut while mortgage tax relief had been expanded.

2   On the other hand, the replacement of rent rebates and allowances with housing benefits (which are means-tested) was likely to have benefited the poor.

3   The expansion of private education might also have cut state expenditure on the education of higher-income groups.

These changes more or less balanced each other out.

Le Grand reached a startling conclusion on the effects of expenditure on the social services, which is quite contrary to widely held assumptions. He said:

> It has failed to achieve full equality of whatever kind for most of the services reviewed. In those areas where data are available it has failed to achieve greater equality over time; and, in some cases, it is likely that there would be greater equality if there was no public expenditure on the services concerned.
>
> Le Grand, 1987

More recent changes in welfare

In recent years, some of the benefits enjoyed by the more wealthy have been removed or reduced. For example, privatization has limited the amount of subsidy paid by government and local authorities for public transport. Tax relief on mortgage interest payments was limited to the first £30,000 and the percentage relief was gradually reduced and eventually abolished. Taxation of company cars has been tightened up. In other areas, however, there is little evidence that changes have benefited the poor.

New ways have been introduced for the affluent to limit their tax bills. These took the form of TESSAs (Tax Exempt Special Savings Accounts) and PEPs (Personal Equity Plans), both of which are exempt from taxation. In 1999, the Labour government replaced these two schemes with a single scheme – the ISA (Individual Savings Account) – which restricts tax-free savings to an investment of £5,000 per year. This does make access to tax-free savings easier for the less affluent since money can be withdrawn without the loss of tax-free status. However, this is of little use to those who are too poor to have any money to save anyway.

Writing in 1997, George Smith, Teresa Smith and Gemma Wright noted some inequalities in education spending. The Additional Educational Needs formula used by the government tries to allow for the extra needs of children in poor areas. This affected about 17 per cent of the budget for schools in 1996, a fall from 24 per cent in 1990. However, the formula seems to work in inconsistent ways. For example, according to the formula, Harrow (a prosperous London suburb) had greater needs than Barnsley (a relatively poor Yorkshire town). Furthermore, due to a cut in 1994 in the allowance for areas with a large ethnic minority population, inner-city areas received reduced levels of funding. The poor have also lost out because of cuts in the provision of school meals and because local authorities no longer have the discretion to give free school meals to poor children whose families do not receive income support. According to Smith *et al.*, the children of the poor are more likely to be excluded from school than other children.

Norman Ginsburg (1997) notes that recent housing policy has been designed to encourage home ownership. The consequence has been that spending on new council housing has been severely restricted, and by 1996 some 1.7 million council or housing association homes had been sold to their tenants. The Conservative governments between 1979 and 1997 also pushed for increases in council rents towards market levels. Rents rose 36 per cent in real terms between 1988–9 and 1993–4. This was designed to encourage private landlords to rent out properties as well as to increase public revenues. However, the result has been increasing expenditure on housing benefit as the government has had to help the poorest meet these increased costs. This is despite cuts in the level and scope of housing benefit. Ginsburg notes that 'the government has capped housing benefit for private tenants, thereby pushing some households below the poverty line and even making some households homeless'.

Michaela Benzeval (1997) has found a growing health gap between the rich and poor in Britain. She says that 'throughout the 1980s and 1990s a considerable body of evidence accumulated that showed the poor health experience in terms of premature mortality and excess morbidity of people living in disadvantaged circumstances'. She quotes a variety of studies showing these inequalities. She argues that

Conservative government policies towards health focused on introducing 'market mechanisms' into the NHS and showed very little concern for health inequalities.

Overall, there is little reason to believe that government policies do any more now to redistribute resources to the poor than they did when Le Grand first discussed the failure of the *Strategy of Equality*. Indeed, Pete Alcock (1997) suggests that the Conservative governments of 1979–97 actively pursued a 'strategy of inequality'. They encouraged greater inequality between rich and poor. In doing so, they increased poverty and social exclusion. This was also reflected in changes in the labour market.

Poverty, the labour market and power

Not all of those who experience poverty in countries such as Britain and the USA rely on state benefits for their income. Nor can their poverty be primarily attributed to the failure of the social services to redistribute resources. A considerable proportion of the poor are employed, but receive wages that are so low that they are insufficient to meet their needs. In this section we examine the explanations that have been provided for some workers getting paid significantly less than even the average for manual work.

Market situation and poverty

In part the low wages of some groups can be explained in Weberian terms. Weber argued that a person's class position is dependent upon his or her market situation (Weber, 1947). It depends upon the ability of individuals and groups to influence the labour market in their own favour so as to maximize the rewards they receive.

The following explanations have been put forward to account for the market situation of the low-paid:

1 In advanced industrial societies, with increasing demand for specialized skills and training, the unemployed and underemployed tend to be unskilled with low educational qualifications. Liebow's 'streetcorner' men, with few skills or qualifications, can command little reward on the labour market.

2 With increasing mechanization and automation, the demand for unskilled labour is steadily contracting.

3 Competition from manufacturers in low-wage 'Third World' economies tends to force wages in Britain down.

4 Many, though by no means all, low-paid workers are employed either in declining and contracting industries or labour-intensive industries such as catering. It has been argued that the narrow profit margins of many such industries maintain low wage levels.

The dual labour market

Some sociologists and economists now argue that there are two labour markets. The dual labour market theory sees jobs in the primary labour market offering job security, promotion prospects, training opportunities and relatively high wages. By comparison, the secondary labour market offers little job security, few possibilities for promotion or training, and low wages.

The primary labour market tends to be found in large and prosperous corporations which to some extent can protect themselves against competition from smaller firms. The smaller companies may depend heavily on the corporations for business. They are in a weaker position and so cannot offer their employees the same advantages. Women and members of ethnic minority groups may be particularly concentrated in the secondary labour market and as a consequence are over-represented in low-paid jobs. (For further details and evaluation of the dual labour market theory see pp. 93–4 and 168–9.)

Changes in the labour market

Hartley Dean and Peter Taylor-Gooby (1992) argue that there were a number of changes in the labour market during the 1980s and early 1990s which made more people in Britain vulnerable to poverty:

1 Manufacturing industry declined. The proportion of GDP (gross domestic product – the total value of goods and services) produced by the manufacturing sector fell from 28 per cent in 1979 to 22 per cent in 1989. There was a corresponding increase in the service sector.

2 A considerable number of the new service sector jobs do not provide economic security. Many of the jobs are part-time and have low pay and little job security. Dean and Taylor-Gooby suggest that about one-third of the labour force was employed in 'peripheral' jobs in the mid-1980s. The idea of peripheral jobs is similar to the idea of jobs in the secondary labour market.

3 Economic change has affected particular parts of the country at different times, leading to regional unemployment and poverty. Unemployment rose in the North, Scotland, Wales, the Midlands and Northern Ireland in the early 1980s, but the South-East did not experience particular problems until the end of that decade and the start of the 1990s.

4 The decline of unionism has reduced the ability of workers to defend their rights and thereby ensure that their employment prevents them from falling into poverty. Union membership has declined, partly as a consequence of the increased employment of part-time workers who are less likely to be in unions. High unemployment and government legislation have also reduced union power. This is reflected in a fall in the number of days lost in strikes. (See Chapter 10 for a detailed discussion of unions·in Britain.)

Dean and Taylor-Gooby sum up by saying that these changes have 'created a pattern of employment that increases the vulnerability to dependency on last-resort social welfare of those unable to gain access to secure and well-paid jobs'.

Post-Fordism, globalization and poverty

Writing about poverty in all advanced industrial countries, Enzo Mingione (1996) argues that increases in poverty are linked to changes in the world economic system. He argues that there has been a shift from Fordist to post-Fordist production in the world economy. This involves a decline in heavy industry and mass production, and a shift to the service sector and those companies making smaller production runs of more specialized products. This results in a reduction in the number of full-time staff with secure employment and an increase in casual, insecure and temporary employment. (See Chapter 10 for a full account of post-Fordism.)

Globalization involves a reduction in the importance of national boundaries, a willingness of companies to shift investment overseas in search of cheap labour and freer trade, and consequently greater international competition. At the same time, there has been an increase in the number of women working or seeking employment. Together, such changes have made growing numbers of people vulnerable to poverty. Fewer people rely upon keeping their jobs over many years. With more women working, the idea of the family wage – a man earning enough to support a whole family – has decreased in importance. More families today rely upon having two earners. Unskilled female workers generally find it easier than men to secure jobs in the growing service sector. Mingione comments that 'the balance between the loss of stable manufacturing jobs and the growth in services is having a serious negative impact, particularly in de-industrializing cities'.

Secure jobs have also become harder to find as a result of the privatization of many welfare services. Subcontractors are less likely than local authority employers to provide workers with permanent jobs, partly because they have no guarantee of keeping contracts indefinitely. The problems of those who are poor are worsened by welfare systems that were designed when the advanced economies provided more permanent jobs. They tend to be ineffective at ensuring that people avoid poverty and social exclusion when their circumstances change quickly. Mingione also argues that the fragility of marriage in many countries, and the 'weakening of kinship networks', have reduced the 'community solidarity' which in earlier times helped people through such periods of hardship.

Poverty and power

The question of the power of the poor was examined by Ralph Miliband in an article entitled 'Politics and Poverty' (Miliband, 1974). In it, he argued that, in terms of power, the poor are the weakest group competing for the scarce and valued resources in society. Miliband stated that 'the poor are part of the working class but they are largely excluded from the organizations which have developed to defend the interests of the working class'. There are no organizations with the power of trade unions to represent the interests of the unemployed, the aged, the chronically sick or single-parent families. Because of their lack of income the poor do not have the resources to form powerful groups and sustain pressure.

Even if they were able to finance well-organized interest groups, the poor lack the economic sanctions to bring pressure to bear. Apart from low-paid workers, the main groups in poverty cannot take strike action and so threaten the interests of the powerful.

Their bargaining position is weakened still further by their inability to mobilize widespread working-class support, since non-poor members of the working class tend not to see their interests and those of the poor as similar. In fact, there is a tendency for members of the working class to see certain groups in poverty, such as the unemployed, as 'scroungers' and 'layabouts'. Efforts by the poor to promote their interests and secure public support are weakened by the 'shame of poverty', a stigma which remains alive and well.

Compared to other interests in society which are represented by pressure groups such as employers' federations, trade unions, ratepayers' associations and motoring organizations, the poor are largely unseen and unheard. More often than not they have to rely on others championing their cause, for example, organizations such as Shelter and the Child Poverty Action Group.

Ralph Miliband concludes that the key to the weak bargaining position of the poor is simply their poverty. He states that 'economic deprivation is a source of political deprivation; and political deprivation in turn helps to maintain and confirm economic deprivation'.

Poverty and stratification

Most conflict theorists move beyond explaining why particular individuals and groups are poor in an attempt to relate poverty to the organization of society as a whole. They claim that poverty is rooted in the very structure of society. The key concept used in this explanation is that of class, but some conflict theorists see class and poverty as less closely connected than others.

Peter Townsend – poverty, class and status

In the conclusion to *Poverty in the United Kingdom* (Townsend, 1979), Peter Townsend states 'the theoretical approach developed in this book is one rooted in class relations'. In particular, he sees class as a major factor determining 'the production, distribution and redistribution of resources', or, in other words, who gets what. However, according to his definition, poverty is also related to the cultural patterns of a society, the lifestyles which govern 'the expectations attaching to membership of society'. The relationship between different classes is not a sufficient explanation of poverty because it does not entirely explain how lifestyles develop and certain types of social behaviour become expected.

Townsend's use of the word 'class' is closer to that of Weber than of Marx. He argues that the distribution of resources is not always directly related to the interests of capital and capitalists. Some agencies of the state, he claims, act in their own interests, or act as checks on the operations of capitalists, and not simply as committees for handling the affairs of the bourgeoisie. For example, the civil service might be more concerned with preserving its own status and power than with maximizing profits for capitalists. Agencies such as the Health and Safety Executive, which is concerned with implementing the legislation governing health and safety at work and elsewhere, may limit the behaviour that is allowed in the pursuit of profit. The labour market, Townsend points out, is not just influenced by individuals and groups competing for higher pay, but also by institutions such as the Equal Opportunities Commission. They therefore also have an effect on the extent of poverty.

Townsend uses the Weberian concept of status to explain the poverty of those reliant on state benefits. The poor are a group who, in addition to lacking wealth, lack prestige. To Townsend, the low-status groups include retired elderly people, the disabled, the chronically sick, one-parent families and the long-term unemployed. As a consequence of their low status, their opportunities for access to paid employment are severely restricted. (These views are similar to Frank Field's arguments about the underclass, which we discussed on pp. 328–9.)

The internationalization of poverty

In his more recent writing (Townsend, 1993), Townsend has stressed the international dimension of poverty. International agencies such as the World Bank and the International Monetary Fund influence the distribution of resources in the world. The International Monetary Fund can impose conditions on governments which borrow money from it, which affect the poor. For example, they can ask governments to cut public expenditure by reducing the welfare programmes on which the poor rely.

Although these institutions mainly affect the poor in the 'Third World', others, such as the EC, have an important impact on the poor in the First World. For example, European employment legislation affects the rights of low-paid and part-time workers in member countries.

Furthermore, the internationalization of industry affects poverty in the First and Third Worlds alike. Cheap labour in Third World countries may be paid poverty wages. This can also create poverty in the First World as jobs are transferred from the high-wage economies of Europe, North America and Japan to low-wage economies, and, as a result, unemployment rises in the First World. Alternatively, First World workers may be forced to take pay cuts as a consequence of competition from low-wage economies in Africa, Asia and South America. These pay cuts may push them into poverty.

Townsend argues, therefore, that poverty can no longer be explained or understood by examining any one country in isolation.

Marxism, class and poverty

Marxist theories of poverty place less emphasis than most on differentiating the poor from other members of the working class. Rather than seeing them as a separate group, Ralph Miliband (1974) believes they are simply the most disadvantaged section of the working class. Westergaard and Resler go further, claiming that concentrating on the special disadvantages of the poor 'diverts attention from the larger structure of inequality in which poverty is embedded' (Westergaard and Resler, 1976). Marxists would see Townsend as failing to emphasize these wider structures sufficiently. Miliband concludes:

> *The basic fact is that the poor are an integral part of the working class – its poorest and most disadvantaged stratum. They need to be seen as such, as part of a continuum, the more so as many workers who are not 'deprived' in the official sense live in permanent danger of entering the ranks of the deprived; and that they share in any case many of the disadvantages which afflict the deprived. Poverty is a class thing, closely linked to a general situation of class inequality.*
>
> Miliband, 1974

Poverty and the capitalist system

To many Marxists, poverty can be explained in terms of how it benefits the ruling class. Poverty exists because it serves the interests of those who own the means of production. It allows them to maintain the capitalist system and to maximize their profits.

Poverty and the labour market

Members of the subject class own only their labour which they must sell in return for wages on the open market. Capitalism requires a highly motivated workforce. Since the motivation to work is based primarily on monetary return, those whose services are not required by the economy, such as the aged and the unemployed, must receive a lower income than wage earners. If this were not the case, there would be little incentive to work.

The motivation of the workforce is also maintained by unequal rewards for work. Workers compete with each other as individuals and groups for income in a highly competitive society. In this respect, the low-wage sector forms the base of a competitive wage structure. Low wages help to reduce the wage demands of the workforce as a whole, since workers tend to assess their incomes in terms of the baseline provided by the low-paid. J.C. Kincaid argues that 'standards of pay and conditions of work at the bottom of the heap influence the pattern of wages farther up the scale' (Kincaid, 1973). He maintains that low wages are essential to a capitalist economy since:

> *from the point of view of capitalism, the low-wage sector helps to underpin and stabilize the whole structure of wages and the conditions of employment of the working class. The employers can tolerate no serious threat to the disciplines of the labour market and the competitive values which support the very existence of capitalism.*
>
> Kincaid, 1973

If the low-wage sector were abolished by an increase in the real value of the wages of the low-paid, several of the possible consequences would be harmful to the capitalist class:

1   The delicate balance of pay differentials would be shattered. Other groups of workers might well demand, and possibly receive, real increases in their wages. This would reduce profit margins.

2   Wages within the working class might become increasingly similar. This might tend to unite a working class, previously fragmented and divided by groups of workers competing against each other for higher wages. A move towards unity within the working class might well pose a threat to the capitalist class.

3   If the real value of the wages of the low-paid were increased, the pool of cheap labour, on which many labour-intensive capitalist industries depend for profit, might disappear.

Containment and the working class

Since, from a Marxist perspective, the state in capitalist society reflects the interests of the ruling class, government measures can be expected to do little except reduce the harsher effects of poverty. Thus Kincaid argues that 'it is not to be expected that any government whose main concern is with the efficiency of a capitalist economy is going to take effective steps to abolish the low-wage sector'.

Despite claims to the contrary, there is little evidence that the welfare state has led to a major redistribution of wealth from the rich to the poor. Westergaard and Resler (1976) dismiss the theory that the welfare state, by using the power of the state to modify the workings of market forces, has created a more equal distribution of wealth. They argue that:

> The state's social services are financed largely from the wages of those for whose security they are primarily designed. They make for little redistribution from capital and top salaries ... they reshuffle resources far more within classes – between earners and dependants, healthy people and the sick, households of different composition, from one point in the individual's life cycle to another – than they do between classes
>
> Westergaard and Resler, 1976

The bulk of monies received by members of the working class have been paid or will be paid in the form of taxes by themselves or other members of that class.

Westergaard and Resler argue that the ruling class has responded to the demands of the labour movement by allowing the creation of the welfare state, but the system operates 'within a framework of institutions and assumptions that remain capitalist'. In their view, 'the keyword is "containment"'; the demands of the labour movement have been contained within the existing system. Westergaard and Resler argue that poverty exists because of the operation of a capitalist economic system which prevents the poor from obtaining the financial resources to become non-poor. In recent writing, John Westergaard argues that the welfare state continues to be subservient to the imperatives of a market economy. He argues that none of the changes that have been introduced to the welfare state in Britain 'have involved any breach of principle with the distributive logic of capitalism, and nor have they subverted the overall gearing of economic activity to property and labour market imperatives' (Westergaard, 1994). Indeed, from his point of view, the 1980s and early 1990s saw an intensification of the hold of market forces in Britain and a virtual abandonment of even the aim of redistributing wealth through the welfare state.

Kincaid summarizes the situation in the following way: 'It is not simply that there are rich and poor. It is rather that some are rich because some are poor.' Thus poverty can be understood only in terms of the operation of the class system as a whole since the question 'Why poverty?' is basically the same question as 'Why wealth?' Therefore, from a Marxist perspective, poverty, like wealth, is an inevitable consequence of a capitalist system.

Although the Marxist views of poverty discussed above were first advanced decades ago, they still provide one credible explanation for why poverty exists in capitalist societies. Indeed, with the increased emphasis on market forces in societies such as Britain, Westergaard may be right to assert that Marxist theories are more relevant than ever (Westergaard, 1994). However, they are less successful than other conflict approaches in explaining why particular groups and individuals become poor. They are not particularly sensitive to variations in income within the working class, and fail to differentiate clearly the poor from other members of the working class, or to provide an explanation for their poverty.

We have now outlined various responses to the first three questions posed at the beginning of this chapter. In the final section we will turn our attention to the fourth question: 'What are the solutions to poverty?'

Poverty and social exclusion – solutions and values

The culture of poverty and policies in the USA

Initially, we will consider government measures to deal with poverty and proposals to solve poverty, together with the ideologies that underlie them. First, the ideological aspects of the culture of poverty thesis will be examined. This theory provided the basis for US anti-poverty policies more than 30 years ago. However, the war on poverty that followed from it has some similarities with current 'New Labour' policies in Britain.

Like all members of society, sociologists see the world in terms of their own values and political beliefs, despite their attempts to be objective. This is particularly apparent in the area of poverty research.

Gans has suggested that 'perhaps the most significant fact about poverty research is that it is being carried out entirely by middle-class researchers who differ – in class, culture, and political power – from the people they are studying' (Gans, 1973).

Some observers argue that the picture of the poor presented by many social scientists is largely a reflection of middle-class value judgements. In particular, the idea of a culture of poverty has been strongly criticized as a product of middle-class prejudice. Charles A. Valentine in *Culture and Poverty*, a forceful attack on bias in poverty research, stated:

> Scarcely a description can be found that does not dwell on the noxiousness, pathology, distortion, disorganization, instability or incompleteness of poverty culture as compared to the life of the middle classes.
>
> Valentine, 1968

From this viewpoint, the poor themselves are a major obstacle to the removal of poverty. Therefore, it may be that at least a part of the solution to poverty is to change the poor, as, by implication, they are partly to blame for their situation. The direction in which the poor must be changed is also influenced by middle-class values: they must adopt middle-class norms and values. In short, as Valentine put it, 'the poor must become "middle class"'.

The war on poverty

Many observers argue that this line of reasoning formed the basis of the US government's policy towards poverty. In 1964, President Lyndon B. Johnson declared a war on poverty with the passing of the Economic Opportunity Act and the formation of the Office of Economic Opportunity to coordinate measures to fight poverty. The comments of the American anthropologist Thomas Gladwin represent the verdict of many social scientists on this campaign:

> The whole conception of the war on poverty rests upon a definition of poverty as a way of life. The intellectual climate in which it was nurtured was created by studies of the culture of poverty, notably those of Oscar Lewis ... [which] provide the basis for programs at the national level designed very explicitly to correct the social, occupational and psychological deficits of people born and raised to a life of poverty.
>
> Gladwin, 1967

The Office of Economic Opportunity created a series of programmes designed to re-socialize the poor and remove their presumed deficiencies:

1 The Job Corps set up residential camps in wilderness areas for unemployed, inner-city youth with the aim of 'building character' and fostering initiative and determination.

2 Many 'work experience' programmes were developed to instil 'work habits'.

3 The Neighbourhood Youth Corps created part-time and holiday jobs for young people.

4 A multitude of job training schemes were started to encourage the 'work incentive' and provide the skills required for employment.

The aim of many of these schemes was to undo the presumed effect of the culture of poverty by fostering ambition, motivation and initiative.

To counter the culture of poverty at an earlier age, government money was pumped into schools in low-income districts with the aim of raising educational standards. Operation Head Start, begun in January 1965, was intended to nip the culture of poverty in the bud. It was an extensive programme of pre-school education for the children of low-income families.

Much of the effort of the Office of Economic Opportunity was directed towards community action, the idea of local community self-help. The Office encouraged and financed self-help organizations run by the poor which covered a range of projects from job training and community business ventures to legal services and youth clubs. The idea was for the poor, with help, to pull themselves up by their own bootstraps, to throw aside the culture of poverty and become enterprising and full of initiative like their middle-class mentors.

In comparison with the above programmes, direct aid in the form of cash payments to the poor received a low priority. Edward James, in *America Against Poverty*, a study of the 1960s war on poverty, states that direct aid was the 'least popular anti-poverty strategy in America' (James, 1970).

Why the war on poverty was lost

The war on poverty was not designed to eradicate poverty by providing the poor with sufficient income to raise them above the poverty line. By changing the poor it was hoped to provide them with the opportunity to become upwardly mobile.

The war on poverty was a typically American solution reflecting the values of American culture with its emphasis on individual achievement in the land of opportunity. As Walter B. Miller neatly put it, 'nothing could be more impeccably American than the concept of opportunity' (Miller, 1962). The poor must make their own way: they must achieve the status of being non-poor, they must seize the opportunities that are available like every other respectable American.

By the late 1960s, many social scientists felt that the war on poverty had failed, as did the poor if the following comment by a welfare recipient is typical: 'It's great stuff this war on poverty! Where do I surrender?' (quoted in James, 1970). The poor remained stubbornly poor despite the energy and resolve of the Office of Economic Opportunity. Sociologists increasingly argued that solutions to poverty must be developed from stratification theory rather than the culture of poverty theory.

From this perspective, Miller and Roby argued that 'poverty programs should be recognized as efforts to engineer changes in the stratification profiles of the United States' (Miller and Roby, 1970). They and others argued that the very concept of poverty and the way in which it spotlights and isolates the poor disguised the true nature of inequality, and was counterproductive in providing solutions.

Once poverty is recognized as an aspect of inequality, and not merely a problem of the poor, solutions involve restructuring society as a whole. It can now be argued that the main obstacle to the eradication of poverty is not the behaviour of the poor but the self-interest of the rich.

Stratification and solutions to poverty

From the perspective of stratification theory, the solution to poverty involves a change in the stratification system. This war on poverty would be far harder to wage than the previous one since it would require considerable sacrifice by the rich and powerful.

The degree of change required is debatable and proposals reflect to some degree the values and political bias of the researchers. The suggestions put forward by Miller and Roby were rather vague. They advocated 'a re-allocation of American wealth to meet a reasonable set of priorities, a redistribution of goods and power to benefit the bottom half of the population'. However, they hastened to add 'we are not implicitly arguing the case for complete equality'.

Miller and Roby did not propose an alternative to the capitalist economic system. They assumed that the changes they proposed could take place within the context of American capitalism.

The war on poverty had its basis in traditional American liberalism.

1 It was American because of its insistence on individual initiative, its emphasis on opportunity and its distaste for direct provision of cash payments to the poor.
2 It was liberal because the reforms it attempted did not seek to alter the basic structure of society: American capitalism was taken for granted and any change in the situation of the poor must take place within its framework.

While the solutions to poverty proposed by American sociologists such as Miller and Roby were more radical and would involve modifications to the structure of society, they remain basically liberal. They would take place within the framework of capitalism and would not involve a fundamental change in the structure of society. Even so, they had little influence on the policies followed by Presidents Reagan, Bush and Clinton in the 1980s and 1990s.

The policies of Reagan, Bush and Clinton

According to Richard H. Ropers, the policies of Reagan and Bush involved drastic cuts in programmes for those on low incomes, increases in taxation for the low-paid and reductions for the wealthiest. James H. Johnson (1996) identifies four key aspects of these policies:

1 The government encouraged a laissez-faire business climate. This made it easier for businesses to shift production to different parts of the country or abroad. This led to the relocation of many jobs away from the inner cities leaving poor blacks and Hispanics in particular with few work opportunities.
2 There were very large cuts in federal aid to inner-city areas, particularly through cuts in resources allocated to community-based organizations. In Los Angeles, for example, aid was reduced from $370 million in 1977 to $60 million in 1990.
3 Criminal justice policy also disadvantaged the poor and socially excluded. Drastic sentences (such as a minimum five years in prison for using crack cocaine) and a crackdown on drug offences have led to more and more socially excluded people getting prison records. The records have only increased their exclusion as their chances of finding work have been further reduced.
4 A new emphasis on testing in the education system has led to increasing numbers of poor American children being put in special education classes. This has greatly increased the drop-out rate from education among those from poor backgrounds and so affected their long-term prospects. Again, black and Hispanic groups have been particularly badly affected.

Reagan and Bush's policies were based on New Right theories which were also influential in Britain. These are discussed in the next section. Reagan and Bush were both Republican Presidents, and Republicans are generally seen as more right wing and conservative than Democrats. In 1996, Bush was replaced by Bill Clinton of the Democratic Party, traditionally a party with greater sympathy for the poor. During his first presidential election campaign, Clinton pledged to 'end welfare as we know it' (quoted in Besharov, 1996) by giving the poor the training, education and childcare they needed to find work. However, during his 1996 campaign for re-election, he also promised 'an end to something for nothing' (quoted in Wattenburg, 1996) in the American welfare system.

By this he meant that families would receive government aid for two years only unless they went to work.

According to Lawrence M. Mead (1996), Clinton's approach embraces somewhat contradictory policies reflecting the values of American conservatives on the one hand and liberals on the other. He says 'conservatives would have the government *tell* the poor how to live, whereas liberals want to offer them the *chance* to get ahead'. Similar contradictions are also found in the policies of the 'New Labour' government of Tony Blair in Britain, which came to power in 1997.

Poverty and the expansion of welfare in Britain

In Britain, governments have not declared war on poverty. Between 1945 and 1979 successive governments were less averse than their American counterparts to providing cash payments to the poor, and to providing universal services (such as education and healthcare) to everyone regardless of ability to pay. Governments added to the provisions of the welfare state, partly with the aim of alleviating poverty. Critics argue that these developments were inadequate. According to Kincaid, benefits to the poor were 'pitifully low' and 'left millions in poverty' (Kincaid, 1973). The harsher edges of poverty may have been blunted by the welfare state, but poverty, at least in relative terms, remained. Welfare professionals may have cushioned some of the misery produced by poverty, but they had not solved the problem.

New Right solutions

After 1979, the Conservative governments of Margaret Thatcher and John Major followed a rather different course. Inspired by the ideas of the New Right, they decided to try to reduce welfare expenditure, move away from universal benefits and services, and target resources on the poor.

The intention was to free economic resources to create a more dynamic economy. As the economy grew, and living standards rose, economic success would 'trickle down' to those on low incomes so that their living standards would rise along with everyone else's. Reducing or replacing universal benefits would destroy the dependency culture which made people rely too heavily on state hand-outs. Means-tested benefits, such as income support, would go only to those who were not in a position to help themselves and who were in genuine need.

The welfare system was reformed in line with these policies in April 1987. Supplementary benefit was replaced by income support. Before 1987, the single-payments system allowed those on a low income to claim money for necessities such as household equipment, furniture, clothing and bedding, which they could not otherwise afford. This system was replaced by the social fund, under which loans rather than grants for such necessities became the norm. These loans had to be paid back out of benefits received. Only those who could afford to pay back the loans were offered them: some individuals were too poor to be given loans. The government argued that this system would make claimants more responsible and encourage them to plan ahead in managing household budgets. The government also cut the amount spent on housing benefit. Much of the money saved by the latter measure was spent on replacing family income supplement with family credit. Both were means-tested benefits designed to boost the incomes of those with low incomes, but family credit was more generous.

In September 1988, the Conservative government raised the age at which people became entitled to income support from 16 to 18. The intention was to prevent the young becoming victims of the dependency culture. In theory, all 16- and 17-year olds were guaranteed a place on a Youth Training Scheme that would provide them with an income.

Between 1992 and 1997 a whole range of further measures and changes were introduced. Marilyn Howard has outlined the main ones (Howard, 1997). In 1996, the Jobseeker's Allowance was introduced for the unemployed. Under this scheme, an unemployed person receives benefit only if they sign a Jobseeker's Agreement detailing how they intend to search for work. Those who do not comply can be instructed to undertake training schemes. The Jobseeker's Allowance lasts for only six months, whereas unemployment benefit could be claimed for a year. In 1995, Invalidity Benefit was replaced by Incapacity Benefit, designed to make it more difficult for people to claim that they are unfit for work and therefore eligible for the benefit. In 1990, full-time students lost their right to unemployment benefit and other means-tested benefits during their holidays. In 1994, a habitual residence test was introduced which has made it more difficult for people who have recently moved to Britain to receive benefit. Earnings-related elements, where benefits depend on previous earnings, have virtually disappeared from the benefits system. The Child Support Agency, introduced in 1993, has tried to shift the burden for supporting lone mothers from the state to absent fathers, who must now pay child maintenance. The government has also shifted much of the burden of responsibility for sickness benefits from themselves to employers. The Labour government has also increased its efforts to eradicate benefit fraud.

Criticisms of New Right policies

Critics argue that, far from reducing poverty, these measures increased it. Many of those reliant on welfare had their income cut. With the replacement of single payments by the social fund, some people were unable to buy necessities. The Child Poverty Action Group claimed that there were insufficient YTS places for all 16- and 17-year olds. Those who were not supported by their families and who could not find employment or a place on a training scheme could end up destitute and homeless.

The Conservative government claimed, however, that its policies benefited those on low incomes. According to government figures, the average income of the poorest 20 per cent of the population rose by 5.5 per cent in real terms between 1979 and 1985. This, the government claimed, supported its view that the benefits of economic growth would trickle down to those on low incomes.

However, the economist John Hills (1995) points out that the government's figures did not take account of changes in indirect taxes such as VAT and duties on petrol, alcohol and tobacco. Hills claims that when these are taken into account the real income of the poorest 20 per cent of households actually fell by 6 per cent between 1979 and 1986. Over the same period the richest 20 per cent of households saw their real income rise by 26 per cent. If his figures are correct, they seem to undermine the New Right's claim that prosperity will automatically solve the problem of poverty.

Most of the evidence contained in earlier sections of this chapter suggests that poverty increased from the late 1980s until 1997, again indicating that New Right policies may have added to the problem rather than solving it. Carey Oppenheim (1997) found no evidence of a 'trickle down' effect. In the introduction to the Child Poverty Action Group's 1997 book, *Britain Divided*, Alan Walker summarizes the effect of Conservative policies in the following way:

> *The fact is that many thousands of poor families can trace the start of their misfortune back to the recession of the early 1980s, a recession that was deepened and prolonged by government policies, and subsequent changes of administration have not improved their position but, rather, have been responsible for worsening it. As this book shows, poverty and social exclusion have increased remorselessly over the last 18 years and not one of the four Conservative Governments have had an explicit policy to combat them.*
>
> Walker and Walker, 1997, p. 1

The policies of the Labour government elected in 1997 will be examined on pp. 345–6

Welfare and redistribution as solutions to poverty

Some feel that the answer to poverty is to be found in improving welfare provisions. Mack and Lansley (1985) claimed that raising benefit levels can have a significant impact. To 'solve' the problem they estimated that supplementary benefit (now income support) would need to rise to 150 per cent of its then level, but the problem could be reduced by lower rises. On the basis of their opinion poll evidence they concluded 'People do accept that the problems of the poor should be tackled, and that the state has a responsibility to tackle them.'

Furthermore, the majority of the public declared themselves willing to make sacrifices to achieve this objective. Some 74 per cent said they would accept a 1 penny in the pound increase in income tax in order to help the poor. However, only 34 per cent were prepared to support a 5 pence in the pound increase for the same purpose, which would, according to Mack and Lansley, lift between one-third and one-half of the poor out of poverty. Mack and Lansley admit that poverty could not be eradicated in the lifetime of one parliament, but despite this they believe it is possible to make major inroads into the problem. There is enough public support for a policy to help the poor for a government to at least make a start without losing popularity.

Peter Townsend (1997) sees the solution to poverty resting on a wider range of measures. He argues that there is a need for a national plan to eradicate poverty. This would be in line with an agreement signed by the Conservative government at the United Nations Copenhagen Summit on Social Development in 1995. This agreement called for the signatories to eliminate absolute poverty, to greatly reduce relative poverty and to tackle the structural causes behind poverty.

Townsend believes that such a plan might ultimately require the development of a kind of international welfare state. With the progress of globalization it is increasingly difficult for individual countries to increase taxes and risk discouraging inward investment. Under such a framework national governments would then be able to:

1 Introduce limits on wealth and earnings and ensure that there were adequate benefits for the unemployed.

2 Ensure there was a link between benefit levels and average earnings to make sure that the relatively poor shared in increased prosperity.

3 Make sure that taxation was progressive, thus redistributing wealth from the rich to the poor.

4 Implement policies of job creation through the use of grants and by taking more government employees so that unemployment was greatly reduced.

Despite the radical nature of the changes he proposes, he stops short of suggesting revolutionary change. He says that 'it would be wrong to suggest that any of this is easy or even likely. The citadels of wealth and privilege are deeply entrenched and have shown a tenacious capacity to withstand assaults.'

Carol Walker and Alan Walker (1994) also argue for a wide range of measures to tackle poverty:

1 They criticize recent government emphasis in Britain on using means-tested benefit. They claim that such benefits as income support and housing benefit are difficult and costly to administer, tend to create disincentives to work and remain unclaimed by a sizeable minority of those who are entitled to them.

2 Walker and Walker would prefer a greater emphasis on universal benefits which, they claim, although expensive, are more effective at reducing poverty and encouraging people to escape from dependence on welfare.

3 To them, it is 'incomprehensible' that some people being paid benefits also have to pay tax. An integration of the tax and benefits systems could remove such anomalies and help ensure that everybody has the means to avoid poverty.

4 They would also like to see more policies aimed at preventing people from falling into poverty. In particular, they would like governments to have an 'active employment strategy' that would provide work for the unemployed and help to give disabled people and lone parents the opportunity to earn their own living.

Pete Alcock (1997) puts particular stress on the Walkers' final point in arguing that tackling poverty and social exclusion cannot be separated from governments' overall economic and social policies. He maintains that the purpose of the welfare state is not just to provide a safety net, or even to redistribute wealth. Rather, it is an integral part of maintaining the whole social and economic system. He says:

> the introduction of state welfare is the product of the process of economic adjustment within capitalist society in which state intervention in the reproduction and maintenance of major services, such as health and education, has become a necessary means of ensuring the continuation of existing economic forces, just as much as a means of redistributing resources to the poor.
>
> Alcock, 1997, p. 62

Capitalist societies such as Britain cannot do without welfare states, and the rich as well as the less fortunate benefit from the way the welfare state produces and reproduces workers. Those who see welfare simply as a way of redistributing wealth have missed the point that state policies can have a big impact by influencing the initial distribution of wealth. Thus policies on wealth, income, investment and employment can help to avoid the need for redistribution by preventing individuals from falling into poverty or suffering from social exclusion.

Marxist solutions

Given the sort of difficulties that Townsend mentions (see above), some Marxist sociologists do not accept that such changes are possible within a capitalist system. While capitalism remains, significant changes in the provisions of the welfare state are impossible. The 'walls of the citadels of wealth and privilege' will not be breached without a full-scale assault which seeks not merely to breach them, but to destroy them altogether. Because Marxists see poverty as simply one aspect of inequality, the solution to poverty does not involve reforms in the social security system, in the provision of additional payments or services to those defined as poor. Instead, it requires a radical change in the structure of society. Thus, Ralph Miliband argues that poverty will only be eradicated with the removal of inequality in general which 'requires the transformation of the economic structures in which it is embedded' (Miliband, 1974).

Westergaard and Resler (1976) take a similar view, maintaining that no substantial redistribution of wealth can occur until capitalism is replaced by a socialist society in which the forces of production are communally owned. As long as the free market system of capitalism determines the allocation of reward, they argue that inequality will remain largely unchanged.

Clearly Marxist views are ideologically based. Sociologists who adopt them are committed to the principles of socialism and equality. They regard capitalism as an exploitative system and condemn the inequality it generates. However, there seems little immediate prospect that the changes they propose will take place in Britain, the USA or other capitalist countries. A communist revolution does not seem imminent and neither former nor the few remaining communist countries have eradicated poverty altogether. Furthermore, the British Labour government elected in 1997 embarked on policies which are far removed from the radical proposals of Marxists.

'New Labour' – 'A hand up, not a hand-out'

The 'New Labour' government which took office in Britain in 1997 claimed that it had policies that would combat the problems of poverty and social exclusion. Tony Blair argued that what the poor needed was a 'hand up, not a hand-out'. In other words, they needed to be given the support they required to help themselves rather than simply depending on state benefits. Among the early policies introduced were the following:

1 The launch of a Social Exclusion Unit designed to help the socially excluded reintegrate into society. According to Patrick Wintour and Nick Cohen, the unit was to try to tackle truancy, discourage drug dependency by withdrawing benefits for those who refused drug rehabilitation courses, and allow tenants more control over big estates (Wintour and Cohen, 1997).

2 The money from a 'Windfall Tax' on the profits of privatized utilities, such as gas and electricity companies, was spent on providing more training and job opportunities for the young unemployed. This 'Welfare to Work' scheme gave people under the age of 25 who had been unemployed for more than six months one of four options. These were, first, subsidized employment with businesses (the companies getting £60 a week and £750 for training). Second, for those without qualifications, up to 12 months' full-time study. Third, six months' employment with a voluntary sector employer. Fourth, six months' work with the environmental taskforce. Those unwilling to take part risked losing their entitlement to benefit.

3 A scheme was introduced to give lone parents, who wanted it, advice and guidance on how to get back to work.

4 Another scheme was the introduction of after-school homework clubs designed for children who found it difficult to study at home.

Evaluation of New Labour policies

While all these changes offered new opportunities for poor and socially excluded people, some contained an element of compulsion because of the threat of lost benefits. Furthermore, the Blair government, in its early years in office at least, showed little willing-ness to increase benefits to raise the living standards of the poor. Its most controversial early measure was to reduce the benefits available to single parents in line with a policy the Conservative government had

intended to implement before it was voted out of office. 'New Labour' was elected promising that it would not exceed the previous government's spending plans and was therefore reluctant to commit itself to extra spending on the large welfare budget.

It was also elected promising there would be no increase in income tax rates. As a consequence it seems unlikely that the Labour government will initiate a significant redistribution of resources from rich to poor, or provide sufficient resources to lift those who remain dependent on welfare out of poverty. While some will benefit from improved opportunities, the success of policies such as those on unemployment may depend on whether the economy grows. In early 1998, Anthony Barnett and Patrick Wintour argued that, 'if the economy falters later this summer just as the New Deal starts, will the vacancies dry up? Only then will the entire experiment be truly put to the test' (Barnett and Wintour, 1998).

Whether or not the new policies will be successful remains to be seen. They do, however, seem to be based upon a mixture of ideological influences. On the one hand, Labour's policies appear to be based on the view that the poor and excluded need opportunities and that they will be willing to take advantage of these once they have the training, education, work experiences or childcare facilities they need. On the other hand, at least some claimants needed to be compelled to take advantage of the opportunities by the threat of lost benefit. While the former policies are associated with more left-wing sociologists, such as Peter Townsend, the latter are more typical of New Right theories and writers, such as Charles Murray.

If this novel mixture of contradictory ideologies produces policies that greatly reduce poverty and social exclusion, then it will have achieved more than the policies of the previous 30 years. However, if much of the research reviewed in this chapter is to be believed, it is difficult to see how these policies can be successful in achieving such aims without more resources being made available for those who, for one reason or another, are unable to work.

Crime and deviance

Crime and deviance

Introduction

In everyday language to deviate means to stray from an accepted path, and many sociological definitions of deviance simply elaborate upon this idea. In other words, we often find that deviance consists of those acts which do not follow the norms and expectations of a particular social group. Deviance may be positively sanctioned (rewarded), negatively sanctioned (punished), or simply accepted without reward or punishment.

In terms of the above definition of deviance, soldiers on the battlefield who risk their lives above and beyond the normal call of duty may be termed deviant, as may physicists who break the rules of their discipline and develop a new theory. Their deviance may be positively sanctioned: a soldier may be rewarded with a medal, and a physicist with a Nobel Prize. In one sense, though, neither is deviant since both conform to the values of society: the soldier to the value of courage, and the physicist to the value of academic progress.

By comparison, murderers not only deviate from society's norms and expectations, but also from its values, in particular the value placed on human life. Their deviance generally results in widespread disapproval and punishment.

A third form of deviance consists of acts that depart from the norms and expectations of a partic- ular society but are generally tolerated and accepted. The person with a house full of cats or someone with an obsession for collecting clocks would fall into this category. Usually their eccentricities are neither rewarded nor punished by others. Such people are simply defined as a 'bit odd' but harmless, and are therefore tolerated.

The sociological study of deviance

In practice, the field of study covered by the sociology of deviance is usually limited to deviance that results in negative sanctions. The American sociologist Marshall B. Clinard (1974) suggested that the term 'deviance' should be reserved for behaviour which is so much disapproved of that the community finds it impossible to tolerate. Although not all sociologists would accept this definition, it does describe the area usually covered by studies of deviance.

In terms of Clinard's definition, crime and delinquency are the most obvious forms of deviance. Crime refers to those activities that break the law of the land and are subject to official punishment; delinquency refers to acts that are criminal, or are considered antisocial, which are committed by young people. Social scientists who study crime are often referred to as criminologists.

However, many disapproved of, deviant acts are not defined as criminal. For example, alcoholism and attempted suicide are not illegal in Britain today. It is even the case that some criminal acts are not typically seen as deviant. Sometimes, outdated laws are left on the statute books even though people have long since stopped enforcing them. For example, under British law it is technically illegal to make or eat mince pies on Christmas Day, to shout 'taxi' to hail a cab, or for a salesperson to try to sell anything to a woman on a Sunday (Streeter, 1997).

The definition of deviance

Deviance is relative: there is no absolute way of defining a deviant act. Deviance can only be defined in relation to a particular standard and no standards are fixed or absolute. As such, what is regarded as deviant varies from time to time and place to place. In a particular society an act that is considered deviant today may be defined as normal in the future. An act defined as deviant in one society may be seen as perfectly normal in another. Put another way, deviance is culturally determined and cultures change over time and vary from society to society.

For instance, at certain times in Western society it has been considered deviant for women to smoke, use make-up and consume alcoholic drinks in public. Today this is no longer the case. In the same way, definitions of crime change over time. Homosexuality used to be a criminal offence in Britain. In 1969, however, homosexual acts conducted in private between consenting male adults over 21 were made legal, and in 1994 the age of consent was reduced to 18.

If we compare modern Western culture with the traditional cultures of the Teton Sioux Indians of the USA, we will see how deviance varies from society to society.

As part of their religious rituals during the annual Sun Dance ceremony, Sioux warriors mutilated their bodies: leather thongs were inserted through strips of flesh on their chests and attached to a central pole. Warriors had to break free by tearing their flesh, and in return were granted favours by the supernatural powers. Similar actions by members of Western society might well be viewed as masochism or madness.

Conversely, behaviour that is accepted as normal in Western society may be defined as deviant in Sioux society. In the West, the private ownership of property is an established norm: members of society strive to accumulate wealth, and substantial property holding brings power and prestige. Such behaviour would have incurred strong disapproval amongst the Sioux, and those who acted in terms of the above norms would be regarded as deviant. The Sioux's own norms prevented the accumulation of wealth. They had no conception of the individual ownership of land: the produce of the hunt was automatically shared by all members of the group. Generosity was a major value of Sioux culture, and the distribution rather than the accumulation of wealth was the route to power and prestige. Chiefs were expected to distribute gifts of horses, beadwork and weapons to their followers.

So far, the concept of deviance suggested is fairly simple: deviance refers to those activities that do not conform to the norms and expectations of members of a particular society. As studied by sociologists, it usually refers to those activities that bring general disapproval from members of society. Deviance is a relative concept: actions are only deviant with regard to the standards of a particular society at a particular time in its history.

However, as this chapter develops we will discover that this view of deviance will become more complex. First, however, we will consider some non-sociological explanations of deviance. These explanations pose straightforward questions such as 'Why do some individuals steal?' Often the answers are similarly straightforward, being based on the following lines of reasoning:

1 Deviant behaviour is different from normal behaviour. Therefore deviants are different from normal people.

2 Deviant behaviour is a social problem since it harms individuals and can have a disruptive effect on social life. Therefore deviants are a social problem.

3 Since they are abnormal, and their behaviour is undesirable, they must have some kind of pathology: they must be sick.

4 The answer to the question 'Why deviance?' therefore lies in diagnosing the illness from which the deviant is presumed to be suffering.

Much of this reasoning has strong moral overtones, since it is assumed that no normal person would have any desire to stray from the straight and narrow. The two main non-sociological diagnoses of the deviant are 'physiological' and 'psychological'. Both claim to have discovered scientifically the causes of deviance, just as doctors attempt to explain physical illness scientifically. Physiological theories claim that deviants have some organic defect or pathology: in other words they are born with some defect, or they develop one during their lives. (They might, for example, be affected by having a poor diet.) Psychological theories claim that it is the deviants' minds rather than their bodies that are ill: some emotional disturbance in their past has left them mentally unbalanced. This mental imbalance causes or influences their deviance.

In the next section we will look in more detail at these rival theories about what causes deviance.

Physiological and psychological theories of deviance

Physiological theories

Most physiological or biological explanations of deviance argue that particular individuals are more prone to deviance than others because of their genetic make-up. Genetically inherited characteristics either directly cause or predispose them towards deviance. Such theories are similar to the 'common-sense' notions that people whose eyes are close together, or whose eyebrows meet, cannot be trusted.

In the nineteenth century, 'scientific' explanations of human behaviour became increasingly popular. Cesare Lombroso, an Italian army doctor, was one of the first writers to link crime to human biology. In his book, *L'Uomo Delinquente*, published in 1876, Lombroso argued that criminals were throwbacks to an earlier and more primitive form of human being. He claimed to have identified a number of genetically determined characteristics which were often found in criminals. These included large jaws, high cheekbones, large ears, extra nipples, toes and fingers, and an insensitivity to pain. According to Lombroso, these were some of the outward signs of an inborn criminal nature. Later research found no support for Lombroso's picture of the criminal as a primitive biological freak.

Despite these crude beginnings, some criminologists have continued to support physiological theories. Sheldon and Eleanor Glueck, writing in the 1940s and 1950s, claimed to have found a causal relationship between physical build and delinquent activity. They argued that stocky, rounded individuals (a body type known as mesomorph) tend to be more active and aggressive than those with other builds, and that they are therefore more prone to committing crimes (described in Taylor, Walton and Young, 1973).

In the 1960s, British criminologists believed they had made an important breakthrough in the search for a scientific theory of crime. They claimed that they had found a precise genetic cause of criminality, chromosome abnormalities. Chromosomes transmit inherited characteristics from parents to children. Normally females have two X chromosomes, while males have one X and one Y. Occasionally, though, males have an extra Y chromosome. A number of researchers found that there was an unusually high proportion of men with this abnormality in high-security prisons for the mentally ill (described in Taylor, Walton and Young, 1973). They therefore concluded that chromosomal abnormalities predisposed people towards criminality.

More recently, biochemical theories of crime have been supported by some criminologists. Henry E. Kelly believes that chemical imbalances in the body can cause crime (Kelly, 1979). Hyperglycaemia, a condition in which there is too much sugar in the blood, may lead sufferers to commit crimes. Vitamin deficiencies may, according to Kelly, have the same effect. Chemical imbalances are partly the result of inherited characteristics, but they may also be caused by environmental factors such as a poor diet.

In *A Mind to Crime*, Anne Moir and David Jessel examine a wide range of biological theories that link biology to the mind, and the mind to criminality (Moir and Jessel, 1997). They argue that low intelligence (as measured in IQ tests) is largely inherited, and that it leads to impulsive behaviour. The impulsive person with a low IQ is unlikely to foresee the consequences of actions and is therefore more likely to commit crimes. Moir and Jessel maintain that crime and delinquency can be caused by low levels of serotonin – a chemical substance in the brain, which is involved in the operation of

neurotransmitters which allow communication between different parts of the brain. According to Moir and Jessel, serotonin has a role in toning down how people behave, inhibiting impulsive and anti-social behaviour. A lack of serotonin leads to Attention Deficit Disorder (ADD) in children, and their anti-social behaviour makes them prone to becoming delinquents.

Moir and Jessel argue that hormonal and other biological differences make males naturally more prone to criminality than women. They claim that 'the male mind – whether for reasons of evolution or something else – is wired and fuelled to be more criminal'. However, they also attribute some female crime to Premenstrual Syndrome (PMS) – this refers to behavioural changes which may be linked to hormonal changes before menstruation. They further claim that damage to parts of the frontal lobes of the brain can lead to 'aggressive, impulsive antisocial personality disorders', which make people very prone to criminal behaviour.

The modern supporters of biological theories of deviance are generally more cautious than their predecessors. They do not suggest that individuals are total prisoners of their genes. Instead they argue that biological factors predispose an individual to deviant behaviour. For example, Moir and Jessel argue that 'Genetic theory has advanced in sophistication, and we now know that environmental factors can interact with the genes, as it were switching the messages on or off.'

However, one study, conducted by the geneticist Hans Brunner in Holland, claimed to find a direct genetic link between genes and criminality (discussed in Jones, 1994). When Brunner studied the genes of individuals in a Dutch family who had been in trouble with the law, most of them had the same defect in one particular gene. The defect interfered with the transmission of electrical messages in the brain. Many members of the family had been convicted of impulsive, violent offences. The gene was passed down to men through the female line of the family; it was not present in the females of the family.

There is some evidence to suggest that there may be an element of inheritance in criminality. Studies of adoptions in Denmark have found that boys adopted at birth are more likely to become criminal if their biological father is also a criminal, than if he has no criminal convictions (discussed in Jones, 1998). In a study by Hutchings and Mednick it was found that half of the adopted boys who had become criminal had biological fathers who were also criminal, compared to a third of the non-criminal boys. Criminality amongst the boys was also associated with their adoptive parents being criminal, but the association was less strong than that with biological parents. This suggested that biology had more influence than environment.

Criticisms of physiological theories

Most sociologists tend to dismiss physiological or biological theories of deviance, arguing that any association between physical characteristics and deviant behaviour can be explained in other ways. For example, Taylor, Walton and Young provide an alternative explanation for the link between mesomorphism and delinquency. They suggest that:

> It may well be that lower working-class children, who are more likely to be found in the criminal statistics, are also by virtue of diet, continual manual labour, physical fitness and strength, more likely to be mesomorphic.
>
> Taylor, Walton and Young, 1973

Similarly they claim that males with chromosome abnormalities have a bizarre appearance and behave in ways that others find odd. These differences may exclude them from 'normal' social life, which in turn may lead them to crime.

A further problem for biological theories is that behaviour attributed to biological causes may not necessarily lead to criminal acts. The biochemistry of the body may indeed affect behaviour, but, as Kelly, Holborn and Makin point out, 'A diabetic at work without a recent insulin injection approaching the lunch break may become tense, erratic, short tempered, but that behaviour does not constitute a criminal act' (Kelly, Holborn and Makin, 1983). Impulsive or aggressive behaviour can be channelled in non-criminal directions. For example, aggression in a boxing ring, on a battlefield, or even in competitive business, may be socially acceptable, even desirable, behaviour. Behaviour only becomes criminal once a society has passed a law outlawing certain actions, and an individual has the law applied to their behaviour.

None of the biological theories can provide an entirely convincing explanation for crime. Brunner's study did find a specific genetic cause, but it was only linked to violent criminality in a single family. It may have little applicability in a wider context. Furthermore, in Brunner's study not all of those with the defect had been convicted of offences. The adoption studies provide some evidence of a genetic link to crime, but cannot explain how crime can be inherited.

It is undoubtedly true that the biochemistry of the brain and brain injuries can affect behaviour, but, on their own, biological factors cannot explain crime. The link between biology and criminality is indirect and mediated through social factors. For example, the geneticist Steve Jones argues that the link between male and female genetics and crime 'is such a distant one as almost to lack meaning; and most males, of course, are not criminal at all' (Jones, 1994).

Psychological theories

Psychological theories share certain similarities with biological theories:

1 They see the deviant as different from the population as a whole.
2 He or she is abnormal in a normal population.
3 The abnormality predisposes him or her to deviance.

However, psychological theories differ in that they see the deviant's sickness and abnormality as lying in mental processes rather than physical differences. The British psychologist Hans Eysenck includes a physiological element in his theory, but he places primary emphasis on the mind. He argues that there is a link between genetically-based personality characteristics and criminal behaviour. He maintains that individuals inherit different personality traits which predispose them towards crime. In particular, the extrovert is likely to break the law because 'he craves excitement, takes chances, often sticks his neck out, acts on the spur of the moment, and is generally an impulsive individual' (Eysenck, 1964). Furthermore, extroverts are harder to condition than introverts. It is more difficult for parents to socialize them to act in accordance with society's laws, norms and values.

John Bowlby (1946, 1953) took psychological theories in a different direction. He did not believe that deviance was inherited; rather he explained it in terms of a child's early socialization. In his book *Forty-four Juvenile Thieves* (1946), he maintained that children needed emotional security during the first seven years of their lives. This could be provided most effectively by a close, intimate and loving relationship with their natural mother. If the child was deprived of motherly love, particularly during the early years, a psychopathic personality could develop. Psychopaths tend to act impulsively, with little regard for the consequences of their actions. They rarely feel guilt, and show little response to punishment or treatment. Bowlby claimed that delinquents who were chronic recidivists (that is, they constantly broke the law, with little regard for the possible consequences) had suffered from maternal deprivation during their early years. Often they had been raised in orphanages, where they had been deprived of an intimate relationship with a mother figure. (You can read further details and criticisms of Bowlby's views in Chapter 3, pp. 132–3.)

Some psychologists have used the psychoanalytic theories of Sigmund Freud (1856–1939) to explain crime. In simple terms, Freud believed that the personality consisted of three parts: the id, the ego and the super-ego (Freud, 1973, first published 1916–17). The id contains basic biological urges (for example, the sex drive, desire for food and water, desire to keep warm). The ego is a conscious part of the mind which makes decisions. Sometimes it is able to restrain the desires of the id because it has learnt that the unrestrained pursuit of pleasure can lead to problems. For example, pursuing sexual pleasure without restraint might lead to danger or punishment. The super-ego consists of the conscience, which develops as a result of socialization. It is partly unconscious and it restricts the unrestrained pursuit of pleasure by producing feelings of guilt in people who want to do things that they have learnt to believe are wrong.

Freud believed that the development of a well-adjusted personality involved the resolution of the Oedipus complex in males, and the Electra complex in females. Most of his attention was focused on the Oedipus complex. Freud claimed that during the phallic stage of their development (around the age of $3\frac{1}{2}$ to 5 years) boys developed sexual desires for their mother. However, this is balanced by a fear of their father. Boys develop a fear of castration, believing that competition for their mother leaves them vulnerable to attack by their larger and more powerful father. The Oedipus complex is resolved by the boy developing an identification with his father, suppressing his sexual desire for his mother, and starting to imitate his father's behaviour.

According to some psychoanalysts, crime can result from an imbalance between the different parts of the mind, which is sometimes caused by a failure to resolve the Oedipus or Electra complex. Aichorn (1936) studied delinquent boys under his care in a home, and explained delinquency in terms of an underdeveloped super-ego. He attributed this to inadequate socialization caused by unloving or absent parents. In this respect, his ideas have some similarity with those of Bowlby. According to Aichorn, the failure of the super-ego to develop fully results in the delinquents lacking the same moral sense and feelings of guilt as those whose super-egos *have* developed fully.

Other writers have suggested that crime can result from an overdeveloped super-ego. Glover (1949) believed that children might identify with very strict parents, repress conflicts to the unconscious part of their mind, and consequently become neurotic and guilt-ridden. Occasionally this could lead to criminal behaviour, such as damaging the property of someone towards whom the offender felt angry.

Sometimes this condition was associated with the repression of childhood desires, which might be acted out in later life. An example could be an adult man stealing women's underwear from a clothesline.

Hewitt and Jenkins (1946) studied 500 juveniles and divided them into three types:

1 Those with an overdeveloped super-ego tended to be shy and inhibited. They were not likely to be involved in crime.

2 Those with an underdeveloped super-ego tended to be aggressive and unsociable. Not surprisingly, they were likely to get in trouble with the law.

3 The third group had a dual super-ego. They had not been effectively socialized into the morality of society as a whole, but they had been socialized into the morality of a delinquent gang. Thus they were likely to engage in criminal or delinquent behaviour because they believed it to be morally acceptable.

Criticisms of psychological theories

As with biological theories, many sociologists tend to dismiss psychological explanations of deviance:

1 They argue that such theories neglect social and cultural factors in the explanation of deviance. For example, Eysenck may have mistaken differences in values for personality types. His description of extrovert characteristics is very similar to the subterranean values, which, according to Matza, direct delinquent behaviour. Values are learned rather than being genetically determined. (We discuss Matza's views on pp. 361–3.)

2 Some sociologists argue that the methodology of many of the studies is suspect. There is little agreement amongst psychologists about what constitutes mental health and how to measure personality characteristics.

3 Many sociologists reject the priority given to childhood experience. They dismiss the view that the individual is the captive of his or her early experience, or conditioning, which is simply acted out in later life, since this approach ignores a vast number of social factors which influence behaviour during a person's life.

4 Marshall B. Clinard (1974) rather scornfully likens psychological theories of deviance to the older notion of 'possession by devils'. The devil has been replaced by the character defect; exorcism by the priest has been replaced by treatment by the psychiatrist.

5 Psychoanalytic theories have often been criticized as being unscientific. The parts of the mind described by Freud cannot be directly observed. They relate to inner processes in the mind which are not directly accessible to the researcher. Stephen Jones points out the difficulties associated with the research methods used by psychoanalysts. He says, 'Techniques such as hypnosis, dream analysis and

verbal association are ultimately subjective and psychoanalysts do not agree on how to use them' (Jones, 1998). It is also difficult to make predictions on the basis of psychoanalytic theories, so the theories are difficult to test.

Despite the problems associated with psychological theories of crime, psychological processes are obviously involved in criminality. Thus the question marks surrounding them are more to do with whether the particular theories have correctly identified the psychological factors involved in crime, rather than whether psychology is important at all. Although Freudian theory is unfashionable in academic circles, individuals have found psychotherapy to be effective, and most people do now accept that there are

unconscious parts of the mind. Nevertheless, psychological theories should be used very carefully. For example, theories such as Bowlby's can be used to justify the view that women with children should not go out to work. Psychoanalytic theories could be used to blame criminality on single-parent families. Biological and psychological theories risk portraying criminals as 'sick' and therefore in need of a cure. The suggested cures have ranged from psychoanalysis to castration – for sex offenders whose behaviour is blamed on hormones. Such 'treatments' tend to ignore the evidence that criminality is widespread in society, and not confined to small groups of people who have been convicted and who are deemed to be suffering from a sickness (see pp. 363–72 for a discussion of the extent of criminality).

Deviance – a functionalist perspective

The functions of deviance

Rather than starting with the individual, a functionalist analysis of deviance begins with society as a whole. It looks for the source of deviance in the nature of society rather than in the biological or psychological nature of the individual.

At first sight it seems strange that some functionalists should argue that deviance is a necessary part of all societies, and that it performs positive functions for social systems. After all, deviance breaks social norms and values. With the functionalist emphasis on the importance of shared norms and values as the basis of social order, it would appear that deviance is a threat to order and should therefore be seen as a threat to society. All functionalists agree that social control mechanisms, such as the police and the courts, are necessary to keep deviance in check and to protect social order. However, many argue that a certain amount of deviance has positive functions: that it even contributes to the maintenance and well-being of society.

Crime as inevitable

Emile Durkheim developed this argument with his discussion of crime in *The Rules of Sociological Method* (Durkheim, 1938, first published 1895). He argued that crime is an inevitable and normal aspect of social life. Crime is present in all types of society; indeed the crime rate is higher in the more advanced, industrialized countries. According to Durkheim, crime is 'an integral part of all healthy societies'. It is

inevitable because not every member of society can be equally committed to the collective sentiments (the shared values and moral beliefs) of society. Since individuals are exposed to different influences and circumstances, it is 'impossible for all to be alike'. Therefore not everyone is equally reluctant to break the law.

Durkheim imagined a 'society of saints' populated by perfect individuals. In such a society there might be no murder or robbery, but there would still be deviance. The general standards of behaviour would be so high that the slightest slip would be regarded as a serious offence. Thus the individual who simply showed bad taste, or was merely impolite, would attract strong disapproval from other members of that society.

Crime as functional

Crime is not only inevitable, it can also be functional. Durkheim argued that it only becomes dysfunctional (harmful to society) when its rate is unusually high or low. He argued that all social change begins with some form of deviance. In order for change to occur, yesterday's deviance must become today's normality. Since a certain amount of change is healthy for society (so that it can progress rather than stagnate), so is deviance. If the collective sentiments are too strong, there will be little deviance, but neither will there be any change, nor any progress. Therefore, the collective sentiments must have only 'moderate energy' so that they do not crush originality: both the originality of the criminal, and the originality of the genius. In Durkheim's words:

to make progress individual originality must be able to express itself. In order that the originality of the idealist whose dreams transcend this century may find expression it is necessary that the originality of the criminal, who is below the level of his time, shall also be possible. One does not occur without the other.

Durkheim, 1938, p. 71

Thus the collective sentiments must not be too powerful to block the expression of people like Jesus, William Wilberforce (who was instrumental in the abolition of slavery), Martin Luther King (the American civil rights campaigner), Mother Theresa (who worked with the poor in India), Nelson Mandela (who helped remove apartheid in South Africa) or Princess Diana (in her campaign against land mines).

Durkheim regarded some crime as 'an anticipation of the morality of the future'. In this way, terrorists or freedom fighters may represent a future established order – consider the examples of Robert Mugabe, a freedom fighter who later became prime minister of Zimbabwe, and Nelson Mandela, an African National Congress leader who became president of post-apartheid South Africa.

If crime is inevitable, what is the function of punishment? Durkheim argued that its function was not to remove crime in society but to maintain the collective sentiments at their necessary level of strength. In Durkheim's words, punishment 'serves to heal the wounds done to the collective sentiments'. Without punishment, the collective sentiments would lose their power to control behaviour, and the crime rate would reach the point where it became dysfunctional. Thus, in Durkheim's view, a healthy society requires both crime and punishment; both are inevitable, both are functional.

The positive functions of deviance

Durkheim's views have been developed by a number of sociologists. Albert K. Cohen (1966) analysed two possible functions of deviance:

1 Deviance can be a safety valve, providing a relatively harmless expression of discontent. In this way social order is protected. For example, Cohen suggests that 'prostitution performs such a safety valve function without threatening the institution of the family'. It can provide a release from the stress and pressure of family life without undermining family stability, since relationships between prostitutes and their clients usually avoid strong emotional attachments.
2 Cohen also suggests that certain deviant acts are a useful warning device to indicate that an aspect of society is malfunctioning. This may draw attention to the problem and lead to measures to solve it. Thus, truants from school, deserters from the army, or runaways from young-offender institutions, may

'reveal unsuspected causes of discontent, and lead to changes that enhance efficiency and morale'.

Durkheim and Cohen have moved away from the picture of the deviant as psychologically or biologically abnormal. Durkheim suggested that society itself generates deviance for its own well-being. Cohen argues that certain forms of deviance are a natural and normal response to particular circumstances. However, Durkheim did believe that excessively high rates of crime did suggest that something had gone wrong with society. This view was taken up and developed by Robert K. Merton's famous work in the 1930s.

Robert K. Merton – social structure and anomie

Merton (1968, first published 1938) argued that deviance results not from 'pathological personalities' but from the culture and structure of society itself. He begins from the standard functionalist position of value consensus – that is, all members of society share the same values. However, since members of society are placed in different positions in the social structure (for example, they differ in terms of class position), they do not have the same opportunity of realizing the shared values. This situation can generate deviance. In Merton's words, 'the social and cultural structure generates pressure for socially deviant behaviour upon people variously located in that structure'.

Cultural goals and institutionalized means

Using the USA as an example, Merton outlined his theory as follows. Members of American society share the major values of American culture. In particular they share the goal of success, for which they all strive and which is largely measured in terms of wealth and material possessions. The 'American Dream' states that all members of society have an equal opportunity of achieving success, of owning a Cadillac, a Beverley Hills mansion and a substantial bank balance. In all societies there are institutionalized means of reaching culturally defined goals. In America, the accepted ways of achieving success are through educational qualifications, talent, hard work, drive, determination and ambition.

In a balanced society an equal emphasis is placed upon both cultural goals and institutionalized means, and members are satisfied with both. But in America great importance is attached to success, and relatively little importance is given to the accepted ways of achieving success. As such, American society is unstable and unbalanced. There is a tendency to reject the 'rules of the game' and to strive for success by any available means. The situation becomes like a game of cards in which winning becomes so important that the rules are abandoned by some of the players. When rules cease to operate, a situation of normlessness or anomie results. In this situation of 'anything goes', norms no longer direct behaviour, and deviance is encouraged. However, individuals will respond to a situation of anomie in different ways. In particular, their reaction will be shaped by their position in the social structure.

Responses to cultural goals

Merton outlined five possible ways in which members of American society could respond to success goals:

1 The first and most common response is conformity. Members of society conform both to success goals and the normative means of reaching them. They strive for success by means of accepted channels.

2 A second response is innovation. This response rejects normative means of achieving success and turns to deviant means, in particular, crime. Merton argues that members of the lower social strata are most likely to select this route to success. They are least likely to succeed via conventional channels, and so there is greater pressure upon them to deviate. Their educational qualifications are usually low and their jobs provide little opportunity for advancement. In Merton's words, they have 'little access to conventional and legitimate means for becoming successful'. Since their way is blocked, they innovate, turning to crime which promises greater rewards than legitimate means.

Merton stressed that membership of the lower strata is not, in itself, sufficient to produce deviance. In some more traditional European societies those at the bottom of the social structure are more likely to accept their position since they have not internalized mainstream success goals. Instead they have developed distinctive subcultures which define success in terms that differ from those of the wider society. (In Chapter 2, pp. 75–6, and Chapter 5, pp. 319–21, we discuss traditional working-class subculture and the 'culture of poverty'.) Only in societies such as the USA, where all members share the same success goals, does the pressure to innovate operate forcefully on the lower classes.

Finally, Merton argues that those who innovate have been 'imperfectly socialized so that they abandon institutional means while retaining success-aspirations'.

3 Merton uses the term ritualism to describe the third possible response. Those who select this alternative are deviant because they have largely abandoned the commonly-held success goals. The pressure to adopt this alternative is greatest for members of the lower middle class. Their occupations provide less opportunity for success than those of other members

of the middle class. (We analyse the market situation of the lower middle class in Chapter 2, pp. 66–9.) However, compared with members of the working class, they have been strongly socialized to conform to social norms. This prevents them from turning to crime. Unable to innovate, and with jobs that offer little opportunity for advancement, their only solution is to scale down or abandon their success goals. Merton paints the following picture of typical lower-middle-class 'ritualists'. They are low-grade bureaucrats, ultra-respectable but stuck in a rut. They are sticklers for the rules, follow the book to the letter, cling to red tape, conform to all the outward standards of middle-class respectability, but have given up striving for success. Ritualists are deviant because they have rejected the success goals held by most members of society.

4 Merton terms the fourth, and least common, response, retreatism. It applies to 'psychotics, autists, pariahs, outcasts, vagrants, vagabonds, tramps, chronic drunkards and drug addicts'. They have strongly internalized both the cultural goals and the institutionalized means, yet are unable to achieve success. They resolve the conflict of their situation by abandoning both the goals and the means of reaching them. They are unable to cope, and 'drop out' of society, defeated and resigned to their failure. They are deviant in two ways: they have rejected both the cultural goals and the institutionalized means. Merton does not relate retreatism to social-class position.

5 Rebellion forms the fifth and final response. It is a rejection of both the success goals and the institutionalized means, and it replaces them with different goals and means. Those who adopt this alternative wish to create a new society. Merton argues that 'it is typically members of a rising class rather than the most depressed strata who organize the resentful and rebellious into a revolutionary group'.

To summarize, Merton claimed that his analysis showed how the culture and structure of society generate deviance. The overemphasis upon cultural goals in American society, at the expense of institutionalized means, creates a tendency towards anomie. This tendency exerts pressure for deviance, a pressure which varies depending on a person's position in the class structure.

Evaluation of Merton

Critics have attacked Merton's work for neglecting the power relationships in society as a whole, within which deviance and conformity occur. Laurie Taylor argued:

It is as though individuals in society are playing a gigantic fruit machine, but the machine is rigged and only some players are consistently rewarded. The deprived ones either resort to using foreign coins or magnets to increase their chances of winning (innovation), or play on mindlessly (ritualism), give up the game (retreatism), or propose a new game altogether (rebellion). But in the analysis nobody appeared to ask who put the game there in the first place and who takes the profits.

Taylor, 1971

Thus Taylor criticized Merton for not carrying his analysis far enough: for failing to consider who makes the laws and who benefits from the laws. To continue Taylor's analogy, the whole game may have been rigged by the powerful with rules that guarantee their success. These rules may be the laws of society.

Merton has also been criticized for assuming that there is a value consensus in American society and that people only deviate as a result of structural strain. His theory has been attacked as being too deterministic because it fails to explain why some people who experience the effects of anomie do not become criminals or deviants. Some critics believe that Merton's theory over-predicts and exaggerates working-class crime, and under-predicts and underestimates middle-class or white-collar crime. Taylor, Walton and Young (1973) believe that Merton's theory cannot account for politically motivated criminals (such as freedom fighters) who break the law because of commitment to their cause rather than the effects of anomie.

However, some sociologists have defended Merton's theory. Robert Reiner (1984) points out that Merton himself has acknowledged that not all Americans accept the success goals of the American Dream. Nevertheless, such goals are sufficiently widespread in the lower strata to account for their deviance. Reiner also notes that 'Merton was well aware both of the extensiveness of white-collar crime in the suites, and of the way that official statistics disproportionately record crimes in the streets'.

Merton explained white-collar crime by suggesting that American society placed no upper limit on success. However wealthy people were, they might still want more. Nevertheless, Reiner maintains that Merton's view that there was more working-class crime remains quite plausible, since those failing to become wealthy in legal ways will be under more pressure to find alternative routes to success. Reiner also believes that Merton's theory can be developed to accommodate most of the criticisms. Thus Taylor, Walton and Young's political criminals could be included in Merton's rebellion adaptation. Subculture theorists, whose work will be examined shortly, have also criticized Merton. However, as Reiner points out, their work represents an attempt to refine and develop Merton's theory rather than rejecting it altogether.

Despite the criticisms, Merton's theory remains one of the more plausible attempts to explain crime rates in whole societies. For example, it could be argued that the influence of Thatcherism and New Right thinking in Britain after 1979 encouraged a greater emphasis on individual success and therefore contributed to a rise in property crime. Similar arguments could be applied to former communist countries as they have changed to free market economies, stressing the importance of competition and individual success. Joachim J. Savelsberg (1995) argues that Merton's strain theory can help to explain the rapid rises in the crime rate in post-communist Poland, Czechoslovakia, East Germany and Russia. Poland is an example of how dramatic these rises sometimes were. Poland had its first free elections in 1989. Between 1989 and 1990 the official crime rate in Poland increased by no less than 69 per cent.

Merton's work, however, can hardly explain all crime. Since his original work, other sociologists have modified and built on his theory in order to try to develop more complete explanations for crime and delinquency.

Structural and subcultural theories of deviance

Structural theories of deviance are similar to Merton's theory. They explain the origins of deviance in terms of the position of individuals or groups in the social structure.

Subcultural theories explain deviance in terms of the subculture of a social group. They argue that certain groups develop norms and values which are to some extent different from those held by other members of society. For example, some groups of criminals or delinquents might develop norms that

encourage and reward criminal activity. Other members of society may regard such activities as immoral, and strongly disapprove of them. Subcultural theories claim that deviance is the result of individuals conforming to the values and norms of the social group to which they belong. Members of subcultures are not completely different from other members of society: they may speak the same language, wear similar clothes, and attach the same value to family life. However, their subculture is sufficiently different from the culture of society as a whole to lead to them committing acts that are generally regarded as deviant.

Often, structural and subcultural theories are combined, as in Albert Cohen's analysis of delinquency. The development of subcultures is explained in terms of the position of groups or individuals in the social structure.

Albert K. Cohen – the delinquent subculture

Cohen's work (1955) was a modification and development of Merton's position. From his studies of delinquency, he made two major criticisms of Merton's views on working-class deviance:

1 First, he argued that delinquency is a collective rather than an individual response. Whereas Merton sees individuals responding to their position in the class structure, Cohen saw individuals joining together in a collective response.

2 Second, Cohen argued that Merton failed to account for non-utilitarian crime – such as vandalism and joy-riding – which does not produce monetary reward. Cohen questioned whether such forms of delinquency were directly motivated by the success goals of the mainstream culture. He agreed, however, that Merton's theory was 'highly plausible as an explanation for adult professional crime and for the property delinquency of some older and semi-professional thieves'.

Cohen began his argument in a similar way to Merton. Lower-working-class boys hold the success goals of the mainstream culture, but, due largely to educational failure and the dead-end jobs that result from this, they have little opportunity to attain those goals. This failure can be explained by their position in the social structure. Cohen supported the view that cultural deprivation accounts for the lack of educational success of members of the lower working class. (We outline the theory of cultural deprivation in Chapter 11.)

Stuck at the bottom of the stratification system, with avenues to success blocked, many lower-working-class boys suffer from status frustration – that is, they are frustrated and dissatisfied with their low status in society. They resolve their frustration, not by turning to criminal paths to success, as Merton suggested, but by rejecting the success goals of the mainstream culture. They replace them with an alternative set of norms and values, in terms of which they can achieve success and gain prestige. The result is a delinquent subculture. It can be seen as a collective solution to the common problems of lower-working-class adolescents.

The delinquent subculture not only rejects the mainstream culture, it reverses it. In Cohen's words, 'the delinquent subculture takes its norms from the larger culture but turns them upside down'. Thus, a high value is placed on activities such as stealing, vandalism and truancy, which are condemned in the wider society. Cohen described the delinquent subculture in the following way: 'Throughout there is a kind of *malice* apparent, an enjoyment of the discomfiture of others, a delight in the defiance of taboos.' He illustrates this theme with the example of a boy defecating on the teacher's desk.

But the delinquent subculture is more than an act of defiance, a negative reaction to a society that has denied opportunity to some of its members. It also offers positive rewards. Those who perform successfully in terms of the values of the subculture gain recognition and prestige in the eyes of their peers. Thus stealing becomes, according to Cohen, not so much a means of achieving success in terms of mainstream goals, but 'a valued activity to which attaches glory, prowess and profound satisfaction'. Cohen argued that, in this way, lower-working-class boys solve the problem of status frustration. They reject mainstream values, which offer them little chance of success, and substitute deviant values, in terms of which they can be successful. Cohen thus provides an explanation for delinquent acts which do not appear to be motivated by monetary reward.

Like Merton, Cohen began from a structural perspective: because there is unequal access to opportunity, there is greater pressure on certain groups within the social structure to deviate. However, he parted company from Merton when he saw some delinquency as being a collective response directed by subcultural values. In this way he showed how pressure from the social structure to deviate was reinforced by pressure from the deviant subculture.

Evaluation of Cohen

Steven Box (1981) believed that Cohen's theory was only plausible for a small minority of delinquents. He questioned Cohen's view that most delinquent youths originally accepted the mainstream standards of success. Rather than experiencing shame and guilt at their own failure, Box argued, they feel resentment at being regarded as failures by teachers and middle-class youths whose values they do not share and cannot accept. They turn against those who look down on them; they will not tolerate the way they are insulted.

Cohen has also been criticized for his selective use of the idea of lower-class subculture. David Bordua (1962) argued that he used it to explain the educational failure of lower-working-class youngsters, with the notion of cultural deprivation, but he did not use it to explain delinquency. Thus, whereas cultural deprivation is passed on from one generation to the next, this does not seem to happen with the delinquent subculture. It appears to be created anew by each generation reacting to its position in the social structure.

Despite such criticisms, Cohen's ideas continue to offer insights into delinquency. Even Cohen's critics would generally accept that the search for status remains an important factor in the formation of delinquent subcultures.

Richard A. Cloward and Lloyd E. Ohlin – *Delinquency and Opportunity*

In *Delinquency and Opportunity* the American sociologists Cloward and Ohlin combined and developed many of the insights of Merton and Cohen (Cloward and Ohlin, 1961). While largely accepting Merton's view of working-class criminal deviance, they argued that he had failed to explain the different forms that deviance takes. For example, why do some delinquent gangs concentrate on theft while others appear preoccupied with vandalism and violence?

Cloward and Ohlin argued that Merton had only dealt with half the picture. He had explained deviance in terms of the legitimate opportunity structure but he failed to consider the illegitimate opportunity structure. In other words, just as the opportunity to be successful by legitimate means varies, so does the opportunity for success by illegitimate means. For example, in one area there may be a thriving adult criminal subculture which may provide access for adolescents; in another area this subculture may not exist. Thus, in the first area, the adolescent has more opportunity to become a successful criminal.

By examining access to, and opportunity for entry into, illegitimate opportunity structures, Cloward and Ohlin provided an explanation for different forms of deviance.

They began their explanation of working-class delinquency from the same point as Merton: that is, there is greater pressure on members of the working class to deviate because they have less opportunity to succeed by legitimate means. Cloward and Ohlin then distinguished three possible responses to this situation: the 'criminal subculture', the 'conflict subculture' and the 'retreatist subculture'. The development of one or other of these responses by young people depends upon their access to, and performance in terms of, the illegitimate opportunity structure.

Structure and subculture

1 Criminal subcultures tend to emerge in areas where there is an established pattern of organized adult crime. In such areas a 'learning environment' is

provided for the young: they are exposed to criminal skills and deviant values, and presented with criminal role models. Those who perform successfully in terms of these deviant values have the opportunity to rise in the professional criminal hierarchy. They have access to the illegitimate opportunity structure. Criminal subcultures are mainly concerned with utilitarian crime – crime which produces financial reward.

2 Conflict subcultures tend to develop in areas where adolescents have little opportunity for access to illegitimate opportunity structures. There is little organized adult crime to provide an 'apprenticeship' for the young criminals and opportunities for them to climb the illegitimate ladder to success. Such areas usually have a high turnover of population and lack unity and cohesiveness. This situation tends to prevent a stable criminal subculture from developing. Thus access to both legitimate and illegitimate opportunity structures is blocked. The response to this situation is often gang violence. This serves as a release for anger and frustration, and a means of obtaining prestige in terms of the values of the subculture.

3 Finally Cloward and Ohlin analysed Merton's retreatist response in terms of legitimate and illegitimate opportunity structures. They suggested that some lower-class adolescents form retreatist subcultures, organized mainly around illegal drug use, because they have failed to succeed in both the legitimate and illegitimate structures. In this sense they are double failures: they have failed to become successful by legitimate means and they have failed in terms of either criminal or conflict subcultures. As failed criminals or failed gang members, they retreat, tails between their legs, into retreatist subcultures.

Evaluation of Cloward and Ohlin

Cloward and Ohlin have produced the most sophisticated version of structural and subcultural theory. By combining the work of Merton and Cohen, and adding the notion of the illegitimate opportunity structure, they attempted to explain the variety of forms that deviance might take. Nevertheless, they may not have provided a convincing explanation for every type of deviant subculture.

Taylor, Walton and Young commented that 'It would be amusing, for instance, to conjecture what Cloward and Ohlin would have made of the Black Panthers or the hippies' (Taylor, Walton and Young, 1973). They argued that Merton, Cohen, and Cloward and Ohlin share one major fault in common: they all assume that everybody in America starts off by being committed to the success goal of achieving wealth. Taylor, Walton and Young believe that there is a much greater variety of goals which individuals pursue. A man or a woman, for example, may refuse to take a new job or accept a promotion which offers higher pay, because it would disrupt their family life, reduce the amount of leisure time they enjoyed, or result in greater stress. Furthermore, Taylor, Walton and Young claimed that some groups, such as hippies, made a conscious choice to reject the goal of financial success; they did not simply react to their own failure.

Nevertheless, it is clear that some people in the USA, Britain and elsewhere place considerable emphasis on material success. The marketization of capitalist societies (see pp. 402–6 for a discussion of crime and marketization) may have made these theories increasingly relevant. For example, Cloward and Ohlin's analysis of illegitimate opportunity structures could be applied to the organization of the supply of illegal drugs in towns and cities. Nigel South (1997) believes that the British drug trade is largely based around disorganized crime (which can be compared to Cloward and Ohlin's conflict subcultures), although some of the trade is based around professional criminal organization (more akin to criminal subcultures). Some drug users themselves could be seen as part of a retreatist subculture. Thus, once again, it is possible to use classic theories to understand contemporary patterns of criminality.

Walter B. Miller – lower-class subculture

The final two theories to be examined in this section explain crime in terms of class-based subcultures. The first of these theories, that of Walter Miller, sees crime as a product of lower-class culture. The second sees it as a product of underclass culture.

Miller (1962) did not believe that a deviant subculture arose from the inability of the members of lower social strata to achieve success. Instead he explained crime in terms of the existence of a distinctive lower-class subculture.

Miller believed that members of the American lower class had long had their own cultural traditions which differed significantly from those of members of the higher strata. He claimed that their values and way of life, which are passed on from generation to generation, actively encourage lower-class men to break the law.

Focal concerns

This distinctive cultural system, which may be termed 'lower-class', includes a number of focal concerns – that is, major areas of interest and involvement. Included in these focal concerns are 'toughness', 'smartness' and 'excitement':

1 Toughness involves a concern for masculinity, and finds expression in courage in the face of physical threat and a rejection of timidity and weakness. In practice, this can lead to assault and battery in order to maintain a reputation for toughness.

2 Smartness involves the 'capacity to outsmart, outfox, outwit, dupe, "take", "con" another'. It is expressed in the repertoire of the hustler, the conman, the cardsharp, the pimp, the pickpocket and the petty thief.

3 Excitement involves the search for thrills, for emotional stimulus. In practice, it is sought in gambling, sexual adventures and alcohol, all of which can be combined in a night out on the town.

This 'heady mixture' can result in damage to limb, life and property.

Two factors tend to emphasize and exaggerate the focal concerns of lower-class subculture in the lives of adolescents: first, their tendency to belong to a peer group which demands close conformity to group norms; and second, the concern of young people with status, which is largely achieved in terms of peer group norms. Thus the status of a lower-working-class youth can depend on his reputation for toughness and smartness in the eyes of his friends.

Delinquency and focal concerns

Miller concluded that delinquency is simply the acting out, albeit in a somewhat exaggerated manner, of the focal concerns of lower-class subculture. It resulted from socialization into a subculture with 'a distinctive tradition, many centuries old with an integrity of its own'.

Although this subculture has a life of its own, Miller did give reasons for its origin and maintenance. It stems from, and is partly sustained by, the necessity for a pool of low-skilled labour. Low-skilled workers need to be able to endure routine, repetitive and boring activity, and to tolerate recurrent unemployment. Lower-class subculture enables these workers to live with this situation. Its focal concerns provide satisfactions outside work which offset the dissatisfaction produced by work: the emphasis on excitement in the subculture compensates for the boredom of work.

Evaluation of Miller

Miller presented a picture of members of the lower class living in a world of their own, totally insulated from the rest of society. They appear to pursue their focal concerns with no reference to the mainstream culture. Many sociologists would disagree with this view. In his criticism of Miller, David Bordua stated:

Miller seems to be saying that the involvements in lower-class culture are so deep and exclusive that contacts with agents of middle-class dominated institutions, especially the schools, have no impact.

Bordua, 1962

(We analyse the concept of lower-class subculture in more detail in Chapter 5, pp. 319–23, and Chapter 11.)

Some studies have found working-class cultures in Britain with values significantly at odds with those of the middle class and the criminal justice system. For example, Owen Gill's study of *Luke Street*, a working-class area of Liverpool, found that the local residents did not believe it was wrong to commit some crimes (Gill, 1977). Stealing from houses that were not occupied was thought to be acceptable, and provoking the local police in various ways was widely accepted. Some sociologists, though, deny that there are significant differences in the values of different classes, which relate to crime. John Braithwaite argues that 'predatory crimes', which involve direct harm to the victims, are seen as wrong in all classes in Western societies (Braithwaite, 1989). He points to studies of delinquency, such as those conducted by West (1982), which show that even parents who are themselves criminals tend to disapprove of criminal activity by their children.

The underclass and crime

Charles Murray – welfare, culture and criminality

Many contemporary sociologists have pointed to a shrinking demand for unskilled labour in contemporary capitalist societies. This suggests that the proportion of the population making up a lower class might be declining, and that the relevance of Miller's theory might be decreasing. Communities such as that described by Owen Gill may no longer exist, at least not in the same form. However, some sociologists have suggested that, as the lower class have declined in number, some of the unemployed and unemployable have come to constitute an underclass. Some accounts of the underclass, such as that of Charles Murray (1989), do not accept that the underclass share the same values as other members of society. They see the underclass as responsible for a high proportion of crime, and explain their criminality in terms of their rejection of mainstream values and norms. Murray largely attributes the development of such values to the generosity of welfare states. The payments provided by welfare states have made it possible for young women to become single parents and for young men to reject the idea that it is important to hold down a job (see pp. 91–6 and 323–8 for further details on Murray).

Inequality, the underclass and crime

Although not a supporter of Murray's theory, Stephen Jones argues that there is 'a growing underclass who inhabit the run-down areas found in most American cities' (Jones, 1998). He believes that this gives rise to rather different criminal activities to those found in the lower class in America in the 1950s. He says, 'Gangs are now divided far more on racial grounds and their major activities centre on drugs. Disputes over territory are based on seemingly rational economic grounds rather than expressions of male machismo' (Jones, 1998).

Ian Taylor (1997) also believes that an underclass exists in American and British cities. However, he does not explain either the existence of the underclass or any involvement in criminality in the same way as Murray. He argues that the marketization of American and British society, the declining demand for unskilled labour, and rising inequality are all responsible for the development of an underclass. Young, unskilled, working-class males have been particularly affected by the long-term effects of increasing inequality and declining job opportunities. Taylor describes the situation in Britain in the following way:

> Many of the older industrial areas of England, Scotland, and Wales ... began to be plagued by quite unknown levels of theft and burglary, car stealing, interpersonal violence, and also by a crippling sense of fear and insecurity, which cuts thousands of their residents off from the pleasures of the broader consumer society and the compensations of friendship and neighbourhood.
>
> Taylor, 1997, p. 285

To Taylor, then, underclass criminality is a consequence of material deprivation rather than an unacceptable culture.

Evaluation of underclass theories of crime

Underclass theories have been extensively criticized. In both Britain and America, some people have questioned the view that there is a distinctive underclass culture, and some that there is an underclass at all. Some sociologists have seen the idea of an underclass as far more applicable in the USA than in Britain. Others have accepted that an underclass may exist, but deny that it has an ethnic component (see pp. 91–6, 283–7 and 323–8). Perhaps the strongest arguments against underclass theories of criminality have been against the sort of theory espoused by Charles Murray. For example, Henrik Tham (1998) has compared welfare policies and official crime rates in Britain and Sweden in the 1980s and 1990s. In Sweden, compared to Britain, there was less increase in inequality and less use of imprisonment; and Sweden's generous welfare payments were maintained at a much higher level than in Britain. However, crime rates increased more rapidly in Britain than they did in Sweden. Tham argues that this evidence undermines Charles

Murray's claim that the generosity of welfare payments can be held responsible for underclass crime. Rather, Tham argues, crime is more closely related to increases in inequality. Tham himself recognizes that the use of official crime rates is open to criticism, but his work does offer more support for theories such as those of Ian Taylor, than for cultural interpretations of the underclass.

Further criticisms of Murray are to be found in the work of Jane Mooney (1998). Mooney has reviewed research in Britain in order to evaluate Murray's claim that single parenthood is associated with criminality. She finds that 'there is not a single substantial scrap of evidence' that such a link exists. She quotes a leaked cabinet paper which found no direct association between single parenthood and criminality, and points out that 'The five million crimes reported to the police every year, with another ten million or more unreported, cannot conceivably be blamed on that fraction of single mothers who are on income support and have adolescent sons.' Mooney accepts that poverty may be linked to criminality, and that many single parents are poor, but denies that single parenthood as such is important. She believes that such views are blaming the victims of social inequality for society's ills. According to her own research into single parenthood in London, single mothers tend to be victims of crime, not perpetrators. Thus, about one in five single mothers in her research had been violently attacked in the previous year – twice the average rate for all women in her study.

In this section we have considered subcultural and structural theories which tend to see deviant behaviour as produced by forces beyond an individual's control. Pressurized by their position in the social structure, by their membership of a deviant subculture, a lower class or underclass, or by their presence in an area of social disorganization, individuals stray from the path of convention. In the following section we will look at a very different theory of delinquency, which includes some important criticisms of and modifications to subcultural theories.

David Matza – delinquency and drift

The American sociologist David Matza (1964) attacked some of the assumptions on which subcultural and structural theories are based, and produced his own distinctive explanation of delinquency. His work suggests that many sociological theories of delinquency are misleading in two ways:

1 They make deviants appear more distinctive than they really are.
2 They present an over-deterministic view of the origins of deviance. (Determinism is the doctrine that states that people have little or no freedom to direct their own actions since they are controlled by external forces.) 'Trapped by circumstances', the individual is automatically propelled down the path of deviance. Matza believes that this view ignores the choices and alternatives which are always available for human action.

In contrast to subculture theories, Matza argues that male delinquents are not in opposition to society's norms and values. In fact, to a considerable extent, they are committed to the same norms and values as other members of society. Society has a strong moral hold over them and prevents them from engaging in delinquent activities for most of the time. Matza backs up this claim by noting that delinquents often express regret and remorse when faced with what they have done. Furthermore, his own research suggests that most delinquents in training school express disapproval of crimes such as mugging, armed robbery, fighting with weapons, and car theft. Far from being committed to crime, delinquents are only occasional, part-time law-breakers; they are 'casually, intermittently, and transiently immersed in a pattern of illegal activity'.

Techniques of neutralization

If delinquents are generally committed to conventional norms and values, then how is it possible for them to contemplate illegal acts? Matza claims that in certain circumstances they are able to 'neutralize' the moral bind of society: they are able to convince themselves that the law does not apply to them on this particular occasion. Deviance becomes possible when they use techniques of neutralization which temporarily release them from the hold that society has over them.

Techniques of neutralization include:

1 Denial of responsibility for a deviant act – the delinquents may remove responsibility from themselves by blaming their parents or the area in which they live.
2 Denial of injury resulting from the act – the delinquents may argue that joy-riding does not harm anyone, it is just a bit of mischief, and that they were borrowing rather than stealing the car.

3   Denial that the act was basically wrong – an assault on a homosexual or a robbery from an extortionate store-owner can be presented as a form of 'rough justice'.

4   Condemnation of those who enforce the rules – the police may be seen as corrupt, or teachers as unjust and hypocritical.

5   Appeal to higher loyalties – the delinquents may argue that they broke the law not out of self-interest but to help their family or friends.

Matza argues that the use of techniques of neutralization throws serious doubts on the idea of deviant subcultures:

1   Techniques of neutralization are evidence of guilt and shame which indicates at least a partial acceptance of mainstream norms and values. If there really were a delinquent subculture, there would be no need to resort to techniques of neutralization, since there would be no guilt to neutralize.

2   Techniques of neutralization often employ one set of mainstream norms to justify breaking others. Thus, assaulting homosexuals is justified since it supports mainstream norms of sexual behaviour. Again, this shows some degree of commitment to mainstream culture.

Subterranean values

Once potential delinquents have freed themselves from the normal constraints society exercises over them, delinquency becomes a possibility. They are in a state of drift and may or may not break the law. Whilst the state of drift explains why people can break the law, it does not explain why they should wish to.

Matza explains the attraction to deviance in terms of subterranean values. This set of values encourages enjoying yourself, acting on the spur of the moment, self-expression, being aggressive and seeking excitement. These values, according to Matza, exist throughout society, alongside formal values which encourage hard work and planning for the future. The 'respectable' member of society will only act in accordance with subterranean values during leisure activities, such as drinking in a bar, visiting the bowling alley, or playing football. Delinquents do not hold different values to other members of society; they simply express subterranean values at the wrong place and time. For example, they may seek excitement at school, or they could be aggressive while at work. Again, Matza stresses that delinquents share more in common with other members of society than earlier theories would suggest.

The mood of fatalism and the mood of humanism

So far, Matza has explained why delinquency is possible, and why it is attractive to some adolescents. This is not sufficient, however, to explain why they embark on delinquency. Before this is likely, some 'preparation' may be necessary: they may have to learn some of the skills they will require (such as those needed to break into a car) from more experienced delinquents. They also need a strong push to step over the dividing line between deviance and conformity for the first time. As they drift, they may be pushed towards or away from deviance, according to the circumstances.

The final decision to step over the line comes when adolescents experience the mood of fatalism. They feel powerless: other people are pushing them around, telling them what to do. To overcome this feeling, they need to take some action that will make things happen, and 'restore their mood of humanism'. They wish to stop feeling like a victim of circumstances, and to prove to themselves that they too are human beings who can influence events around them. Committing a delinquent act assures them of at least some response, even if it is a negative one. At the very least, they can expect their action to be noticed, and to lead to a police investigation. Once they have taken this step, it becomes easier to contemplate other delinquent acts, but Matza emphasizes that delinquency never becomes more than an occasional activity.

The subculture of delinquency

Matza uses the term subculture of delinquency, rather than delinquent subculture. Although he has done no more than reverse the order of the words, the concept he uses is quite different from the traditional view of a subculture:

1   The norms and values of the subculture of delinquency allow delinquent acts, but do not demand them of members of the group.

2   The conventional values of society have a considerable influence on the behaviour of the delinquent.

3   The subculture of delinquency is a loose-knit group of adolescents. Individuals frequently drift into and out of the group; they are not committed, full-time members.

Evaluation of Matza

Matza's work is radically different from previous explanations of delinquency. He rejects the view that delinquents are pathological, that they are different from other members of society, that they are sick. He denies that deterministic theories can explain human behaviour. Instead he stresses the choices that are available to all human beings, including delinquents. His work is important in challenging the assumptions on which earlier theories were based. Nevertheless, Matza himself has been criticized.

Taylor, Walton, and Young (1973) raised doubts about the view that those who use the techniques of neutralization are never challenging the dominant values in society. They pointed out that denying your behaviour is wrong is quite different from explaining it away as the result of sickness or an accident. It may indeed represent a complete rejection of society's norms and values; 'A homosexual who says he cannot help being a homosexual because he is sick is very different from the homosexual who denies the fact of harm to the victim, who declares that "gay is 'good'".

Steven Box (1981) questioned the evidence that Matza used in support of his theory. Box suggested that it may not be possible to take the statements of delinquents at face value: when they express regret and remorse for their offences they may not be sincere; when they explain the reasons for their acts they may be attempting to justify themselves, rather than to provide an accurate account of their motives.

Stephen Jones (1998) believes that Matza's theory is quite good at explaining occasional delinquency that is not particularly serious. On the other hand, it is not particularly good at explaining violence. Jones says that Matza:

is nowadays considered to have had a somewhat romanticised view of crime. It is clear that, while everyone engaged in delinquency at some stages in their lives, there is a hard core who continue to commit serious offences on a regular basis, sometimes even lasting into adulthood.

Jones, 1998, p. 169

Despite these drawbacks, Matza's work has raised some important questions about deviance. In particular, it has questioned the view that deviants always hold quite untypical values, and it has tried to overcome the pitfalls of overly deterministic theories. Now we will consider the relationship between deviance and official statistics.

Deviance and official statistics

Many theories of deviance are based in part on official statistics provided by the police, the courts, and other government agencies involved in law enforcement. In countries such as Britain and the USA these statistics consistently show that some groups are more involved in crime than others. The working class, the young, males, and members of some ethnic minorities are all more likely to commit crimes than the middle class, the elderly, females, and whites – according to official data. Some sociologists have taken these figures at face value and have then proceeded to explain why such groups should be so criminal. Merton, Cohen, Cloward and Ohlin, and Miller (see pp. 354–60) all assume that working-class men are the main offenders, although they differ in their explanations as to why this should be so. If it could be shown that the reliability of the figures is open to question, it would raise serious doubts about their theories.

In Britain, official statistics on crime are published annually. They provide criminologists, the police, the courts, the media, and anyone else who is interested, with two main types of data:

1 They provide information on the total number of crimes 'known to the police'. This information is often taken as an accurate measure of the total amount of crime. The data allow comparisons to be made between crimes, and with previous years.

Often the figures receive widespread publicity through the media. The statistics often, though not always, show increases in crime over previous years, and they may lead to concern that the country is being engulfed in a crime wave.

Figure 6.1 shows long-term trends in crimes recorded by the police in Britain from 1876 to 1996. It shows that rates remained very low until the 1950s, but have increased rapidly in the period since then.

Figure 6.2 shows trends since 1971 in more detail. It shows that the crime rate appears to have increased rapidly for most of the period since 1971 in England, Wales and Northern Ireland. However, it does show some decline in the mid-1990s, particularly in England and Wales.

Table 6.1 provides a detailed breakdown of notifiable offences recorded by English and Welsh police forces (for April to March periods) from 1993 to 1998. It also shows percentage changes from the previous year. It shows that overall violent crime rose over this period, but other types of crime declined.

2 The official statistics provide information on the social characteristics of those who have been convicted of offences, such as their age and gender. It is on these figures that a number of theories of crime have been based.

Each of these sets of figures will now be examined in detail.

Figure 6.1 Crimes recorded by the police, 1876-1996

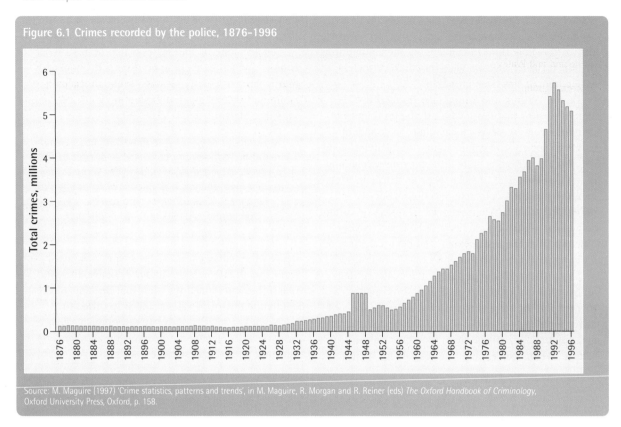

Source: M. Maguire (1997) 'Crime statistics, patterns and trends', in M. Maguire, R. Morgan and R. Reiner (eds) *The Oxford Handbook of Criminology*, Oxford University Press, Oxford, p. 158.

Figure 6.2 Notifiable offences* recorded by the police

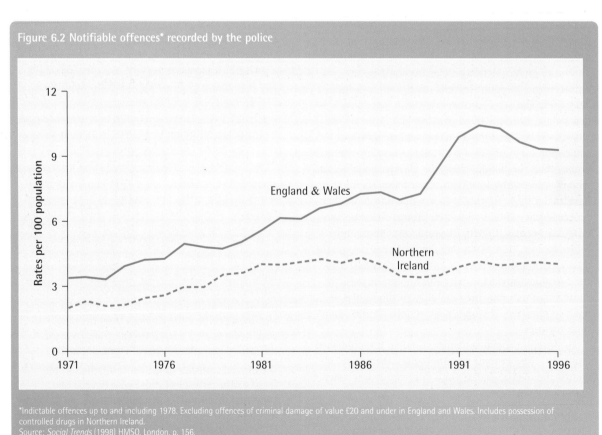

*Indictable offences up to and including 1978. Excluding offences of criminal damage of value £20 and under in England and Wales. Includes possession of controlled drugs in Northern Ireland.
Source: *Social Trends* (1998) HMSO, London, p. 156.

Table 6.1 Notifiable offences recorded by the police, by offence

England and Wales

Offence group	April 1993 to March 1994	April 1994 to March 1995	April 1995 to March 1996	April 1996 to March 1997	April 1997 to March 1998
	Number of offences				
Violence against the person	209,336	212,134	219,291	243,646	256,070
Sexual offences	32,390	31,177	29,887	32,120	34,151
Robbery	58,281	60,431	70,497	72,266	62,652
Total violent crime	*300,007*	*303,742*	*319,675*	*348,032*	*352,873*
Burglary					
Burglary in a dwelling	707,774	661,194	638,631	581,985	501,593
Burglary other than in a dwelling	622,689	575,791	595,843	545,042	486,839
Total burglary	*1,330,463*	*1,236,985*	*1,234,474*	*1,127,027*	*988,432*
Theft and handling of stolen goods					
Theft from the person	49,121	52,309	60,347	59,352	57,894
Theft of pedal cycle	184,344	172,324	168,482	147,160	140,031
Theft from shops	272,748	269,652	282,452	278,050	273,509
Theft from vehicle	902,030	827,196	817,229	778,269	695,498
Theft of motor vehicle	583,512	524,094	513,927	466,783	400,524
Vehicle crime	*1,485,542*	*1,351,290*	*1,331,156*	*1,245,052*	*1,096,022*
Other theft and handling stolen goods	702,525	662,386	623,867	594,085	577,517
Total theft and handling stolen goods	*2,694,280*	*2,507,961*	*2,466,304*	*2,323,699*	*2,144,973*
Fraud and forgery	158,628	140,180	134,394	135,975	136,232
Criminal damage	911,675	909,359	932,719	938,735	861,846
Other notifiable offences	42,974	48,156	51,741	57,210	60,981
Total all offences	*5,438,027*	*5,146,383*	*5,139,307*	*4,930,678*	*4,545,337*
	Percentage change from corresponding period in previous year				
Violence against the person	2.9	1.3	3.4	11.1	5.1
Sexual offences	11.4	-3.7	-4.1	7.5	6.3
Robbery	5.7	3.7	16.7	2.5	-13.3
Total violent crime	*4.3*	*1.2*	*5.2*	*8.9*	*1.4*
Burglary					
Burglary in a dwelling	-3.5	-6.6	-3.4	-8.9	-13.8
Burglary other than in a dwelling	-4.7	-7.5	3.5	-8.5	-10.7
Total burglary	*-4.2*	*-7.0*	*-0.2*	*-8.7*	*-12.3*
Theft and handling of stolen goods					
Theft from the person	20.4	6.5	15.4	-1.6	-2.5
Theft of pedal cycle	-15.8	-6.5	-2.2	-12.7	-4.8
Theft from shops	-3.4	-1.1	4.7	-1.6	-1.6
Theft from vehicle	-6.4	-9.0	-1.5	-4.8	-10.6
Theft of motor vehicle	-3.5	-8.3	-1.2	-9.2	-14.2
Vehicle crime	*-5.3*	*-10.2*	*-1.9*	*-6.5*	*-12.0*
Other theft and handling stolen goods	-5.8	-5.7	-5.8	-4.8	-2.8
Total theft and handling stolen goods	*-5.7*	*-6.9*	*-1.7*	*-5.8*	*-7.7*
Fraud and forgery	-5.7	-11.6	-4.1	1.2	0.2
Criminal damage	0.4	-0.3	2.6	0.6	-8.2
Other notifiable offences	11.6	12.1	7.4	10.6	6.6
Total all offences	*-3.7*	*-5.4*	*-0.1*	*-4.1*	*-7.8*

Source: *Home Office Statistical Bulletin*, Issue 22/98, Research, Development and Statistics Directorate, Home Office, UK, 13 October 1998, p. 11.

Unrecorded crime

It is quite obvious that not all crimes that take place are recorded by the police. There is much evidence of a substantial 'dark figure' of unrecorded crimes.

Before a crime is recorded, at least three things must happen:

1 It must come to someone's attention that a crime has taken place.

2 It must be reported to the relevant agency.

3 That agency must be willing to accept that the law has been broken.

Not all crimes, though, have a specific victim who is aware that they have been wronged. If you return home to find a broken window and valuable items missing from your house, it will not take you long to work out that you have been burgled. Crimes such as tax evasion, however, do not have a single victim to report the offence. In this case the victim is the community as a whole which has been deprived of tax revenue. The extent of this type of crime is difficult to measure, since it can only be uncovered by investigation. However, it is possible to estimate the amount of crime of which victims are aware, but which is not reported to the police, or not recorded as crime by them.

Victimization studies

In 1983, the Home Office Research and Planning Unit published the first *British Crime Surveys*. These studies contain data on crime in Britain. The first study was conducted in 1981, and by 1998 seven surveys had been completed and published. The most recent of these was conducted in 1997. The studies attempt to overcome some of the limitations of the annual criminal statistics. Instead of relying on police records, the Home Office carries out victimization studies. These involve asking individuals if they have been the victim of crime in the previous year. People are also asked whether they reported the crimes, and whether the police recorded them. The 1997 survey used a sample of 14,947 adults, aged 16 or over, in England and Wales. The studies confirm that the criminal statistics are highly unreliable.

Information was collected on a range of offences committed during 1997. The survey found that only 44 per cent of these crimes were reported to the police. Figure 6.3 shows that the rate of reporting varied considerably by type of crime – 97 per cent of vehicle thefts were reported, 57 per cent of robberies, but just 26 per cent of acts of vandalism.

Forty-four per cent of those who did not report the crime did not do so because they thought the offence was too trivial; 33 per cent said that the police would not have been able to do anything; 22 per cent said that the police would not be interested; and 11 per cent said that it was a private matter or that they had dealt with it themselves. About 3 per cent mentioned fear of reprisals, and just over 1 per cent fear or dislike of the police.

Once an offence had been reported, the police did not always accept that an offence had taken place. Indeed, overall it was estimated that 46 per cent of incidents reported to the police were not recorded by them as crimes in the categories of crime used in the

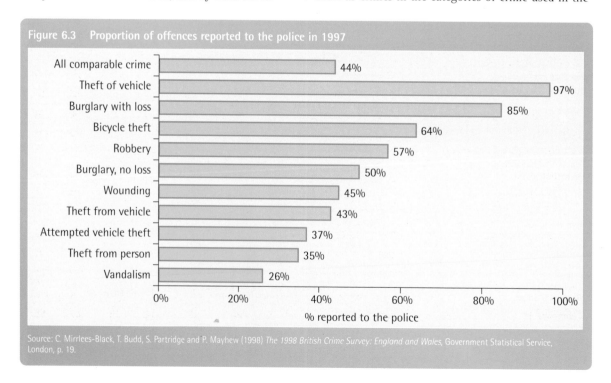

Figure 6.3   Proportion of offences reported to the police in 1997

All comparable crime	44%
Theft of vehicle	97%
Burglary with loss	85%
Bicycle theft	64%
Robbery	57%
Burglary, no loss	50%
Wounding	45%
Theft from vehicle	43%
Attempted vehicle theft	37%
Theft from person	35%
Vandalism	26%

% reported to the police

Source: C. Mirrlees-Black, T. Budd, S. Partridge and P. Mayhew (1998) *The 1998 British Crime Survey: England and Wales,* Government Statistical Service, London, p. 19.

British Crime Survey. While some were recorded as a different type of crime, which was not included in the survey, many were 'no-crimed'. That is, the police decided not to record it because it was too trivial, or they thought the incident had not taken place, or there was insufficient evidence to proceed, or because the victim did not want the matter to be taken further. The survey found that the official figures on the numbers of different types of crime taking place were very misleading. Since rates of reporting and recording varied so much between crimes, the official figures did not reflect the extent of different crimes uncovered by the survey. Clearly it would not be sensible to rely on the official figures, given these variations in non-reporting.

Table 6.2 compares crimes found by the *British Crime Survey* in 1997 and crimes recorded by the police, and makes comparisons with 1995. It shows, for example, that, of all crimes found in the survey,

84 per cent of vehicle thefts and 57 per cent of burglaries with loss were recorded by the police, but that only 10 per cent of thefts from the person and 14 per cent of attempted burglaries were recorded.

The Home Office research also provides a useful comparison with trends in crime revealed by official statistics. Figure 6.4 shows an increase of 67 per cent in crimes recorded by the police, compared to an increase of 56 per cent in crimes uncovered by the survey, between 1981 and 1997. This suggests that police figures have slightly exaggerated the rise in crime over this period. However, the broad trends revealed are similar, with both recorded and non-recorded crime falling between 1995 and 1997. Between these years, the police recorded a 12 per cent fall in the crimes covered by the survey; the survey found a fall of 15 per cent. The biggest falls, according to the *British Crime Survey*, were in attempted vehicle theft (down 27 per cent), theft of

Table 6.2 Comparison of *British Crime Survey* and crimes recorded by the police									
	1997 Police	1997 BCS	% BCS reported	% recorded of reported	% recorded of all BCS	% change 1995 to 1997 Police	BCS	% change 1981 to 1997 Police	BCS
Figures in 000s									
Vandalism	443	2,917	26	58	15	−4	−15	121	7
All comparable property theft (acquisitive crime)	1,751	6,261	50	56	28	−17	−15	51	99
Burglary:	519	1,639	64	49	32	−19	−7	48	119
Attempts and no loss	140	976	50	29	14	−17	−0.1	90	160
With loss	379	664	85	67	57	−20	−15	37	77
All vehicle thefts:	1,022	3,483	47	62	29	−15	−19	57	99
Theft from vehicle	552	2,164	43	59	25	−16	−14	63	68
Theft of vehicle	316	375	97	87	84	−21	−25	10	31
Attempted thefts	154	943	37	44	16	3	−27	447	425
Bicycle theft	151	549	64	43	27	−18	−17	19	154
Theft from the person	60	590	35	29	10	−4	−12	71	36
All comparable violence:	256	1,022	49	51	25	11	−13	150	53
Wounding	205	714	45	63	29	18	−17	143	41
Robbery	52	307	57	30	17	−11	−2	183	89
All comparable	2,450	10,199	44	54	24	−12	−15	67	56

Source: C. Mirrlees-Black, T. Budd, S. Partridge and P. Mayhew (1998) *The 1998 British Crime Survey: England and Wales,* Government Statistical Service, London, p. 26.

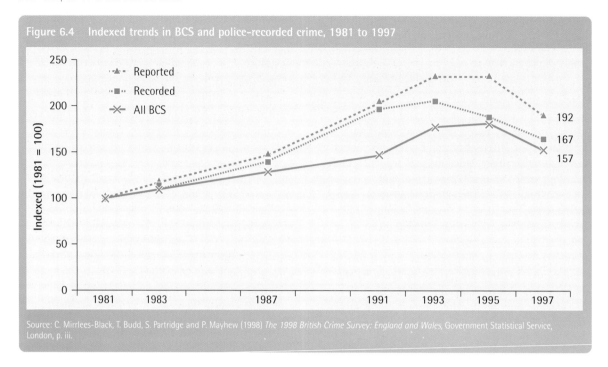

Figure 6.4   Indexed trends in BCS and police-recorded crime, 1981 to 1997

Source: C. Mirrlees-Black, T. Budd, S. Partridge and P. Mayhew (1998) *The 1998 British Crime Survey: England and Wales*, Government Statistical Service, London, p. iii.

vehicles (down 25 per cent), and wounding (down 17 per cent). According to police figures, though, woundings actually rose by 18 per cent between 1995 and 1997.

Despite recent falls, the *British Crime Surveys* suggest that, overall, there have been considerable increases in crime since 1981. Falls in some types of crime, particularly car-related crime, may be partly due to better security. The *British Crime Survey* suggests that the fall in woundings may have been due to more woundings being classified as common assaults.

Although victimization studies provide an indication of trends in crime and an estimate of how many crimes remain unrecorded, the data from them are not entirely reliable. Jock Young (1988) points out three main problems with victimization studies:

1 In most victimization studies a substantial minority, usually 20–25 per cent, refuse to cooperate with researchers. Those who do not take part are likely to be untypical of the population as a whole, and their absence from the data is likely to distort the figures. (In the 1998 *British Crime Survey* there was a non-response rate of 21.3 per cent.)

2 Victims may be more likely to conceal certain types of crime because of embarrassment or a misplaced sense of guilt. Crimes such as domestic violence and sexual crimes might be particularly prone to under-recording.

3 Changing public perceptions might affect the willingness of the public to regard acts as criminal. For example, people may have become less tolerant of crimes of violence or acts of vandalism, and they

would therefore be more likely to report less serious acts to researchers. On the other hand, the opposite might have taken place, so that the figures underestimate any increase in crime.

Given these problems, the trends revealed in victimization studies should be treated with caution, although they are probably more reliable than those shown in official statistics because they include so many crimes which are not reported.

The characteristics of offenders – self-report studies

It is clear, then, that there are many offences which are not known to the police, or are not recorded by them. An even smaller proportion of offenders are successfully prosecuted and find their way into the official statistics. In 1996, only 26 per cent of indictable offences in England and Wales were cleared up (*Social Trends*, 1998, p. 162). It is possible, at least in theory, that the people who are caught, tried and convicted are a representative cross-section of all those who commit offences. On the other hand, it could be that some sections of society are much more likely to be convicted than others, irrespective of whether they have committed more crimes.

A number of sociologists have devised an alternative to official statistics for discovering the characteristics of criminals. Self-report studies use questionnaires or interviews to collect information about individuals, and ask them to admit to the number of crimes they have committed. The data collected can then be compared with official conviction rates to discover which offenders are most likely to be convicted.

Steven Box (1981) has reviewed forty such studies on delinquency, conducted in a number of different countries. On the basis of this evidence, Box rejects the view presented in the official statistics that working-class youths are much more likely to engage in delinquency than middle-class youths. He says 'we should be very sceptical of those who continue to argue that delinquency is located at the bottom of the stratification system'.

In a more recent study, conducted by Graham and Bowling (1995), it was found that social class had no influence on whether young British males and females would admit to having committed offences. However, it was found that those from lower classes were more likely to admit to more serious offences.

Of course, it is possible that those replying to questionnaires or interviews might not be truthful about the amount of crime they commit. Various tests have been carried out to check on the results of these studies. These tests range from the use of lie detectors, to questioning adolescents' friends about crimes they claim to have taken part in. Generally it has been found that about 80 per cent of those who reply tell the truth. Self-report studies are not, therefore, entirely reliable. However, they do locate many more offenders than those who are convicted and appear in official statistics. As such they are probably considerably more reliable than the latter.

Bias in official statistics

Self-report studies suggest that there may be consistent police bias against working-class delinquents and in favour of middle-class delinquents. Some indication of why this might be so is provided by William Chambliss's classic study of two American delinquent gangs from the same city (Chambliss, 1973).

The 'roughnecks' were a group of working-class delinquents. They often got involved in fights, they siphoned petrol from parked cars, and frequently went shoplifting. Both the police and the community regarded them as a 'bad bunch of boys'. The police looked on them with suspicion, and all of them were arrested at least once.

The 'saints', in contrast, came from respectable, middle-class homes. None of them ever received so much as a ticket for a motoring offence from the police, though they were stopped and questioned on a number of occasions. Chambliss claimed that the 'saints' actually carried out more delinquent acts than the 'roughnecks', and some of their actions were of a very serious nature. They often drove when drunk, stealing was not uncommon, and they even placed barricades across roads just after sharp bends to catch out unsuspecting motorists.

On the basis of this study, Chambliss claims that the police frequently do not take middle-class delinquency seriously. The 'saints' did not conform to the police's image of typical delinquents. With the help of their middle-class parents when necessary, they were able to persuade the authorities that their activities were harmless pranks rather than serious delinquent acts.

White-collar crime

So far it has been suggested that official statistics do not give an accurate picture of the extent of delinquency among middle- and working-class adolescents. Unfortunately, few self-report studies have been conducted on adults so it is not possible to compare official statistics and the findings of self-report studies on adult crime. Even so, there is evidence that offences committed by adults of high social status are less likely to lead to arrests and convictions than those committed by adults of low social status.

Edwin Sutherland was the first sociologist to study what has come to be known as 'white-collar crime' (Sutherland, 1960). Sutherland defines white-collar crime as 'crimes committed by persons of high social status and respectability in the course of their occupations'. Such crimes include bribery and corruption in business and politics, misconduct by professionals such as doctors and lawyers, the breaking of trade regulations, food and drug laws, and safety regulations in industry, the misuse of patents and trademarks, and misrepresentation in advertising.

There is evidence to suggest that such offences are widespread. In business in the UK, for example, the Guinness affair in 1987 involved senior executives making illegal deals on the Stock Exchange, in order to inflate artificially the value of Guinness shares, which were to be exchanged for shares in Distillers in a takeover. Ernest Saunders, the chairman of Guinness at the time of the offences, received a prison sentence. Ian Taylor argues that in Britain there has been:

> an enormous explosion of fraud and corruption that has accompanied the construction of a free market economy since 1979, and which has escalated since the Big Bang of 27 October 1986, when the London Stock Exchange was significantly opened up to a largely unregulated system for the marketing of financial securities.
>
> Taylor, 1992

One common type of fraud is insider dealing, in which shares in a company are bought by individuals who know that the company is about to be the subject of a takeover bid. These individuals illegally use their knowledge to make a killing on the stock market. Some of the most significant crimes of this type took place in the USA in the 1980s. A number of employees of the investment bank Drexel Burnham Lambert were involved in the issuing of junk bonds. These are bonds issued with high yields in order to finance takeover bids, but often with little financial backing behind them to give security to investors. Using illegal insider trading, Drexel Burnham Lambert was able to make $800 million in 1986 alone (Punch, 1996). The leading participant, Michael Milken, served several years in prison and paid fines totalling $650 million. However, he is still believed to be extremely wealthy, having made no less than an estimated $1 billion over a five-year period.

In an even more spectacular example of the losses that can result from irresponsible financial deals, in 1998 it was found that an investment fund, or hedge fund, Long-Term Capital Management (LTCM), had made losses running into billions of US dollars. They had borrowed some $900 billion, more than 250 times their capital, to gamble on such things as future interest rates in Europe. Such was the scale of the collapse that it threatened the whole Western banking system. In November 1998, major Western governments decided to put together a $3.5 billion rescue package. Larry Elliot puts such sums of money in context by comparing the amounts spent on propping up LTCM with those pledged for disaster relief in November 1998 when disastrous floods hit Central America. Thousands were killed and the economies of countries such as Honduras were devastated, yet Western governments initially pledged help of just $100 million in emergency aid, less than a thirtieth of that being spent bailing out LTCM (Elliot, 1998).

A number of prominent businessmen have been accused of fraud when their businesses got into debt and collapsed. Peter Clowes was one such businessman who was convicted of fraud in 1992: some of the £113 million invested in his businesses by others was spent on personal luxuries such as a yacht. In 1993, Asil Nadir fled Britain and went to Cyprus to escape prosecution on fraud charges involving £25 million, arising from the collapse of his company Polly Peck.

Perhaps the best-known businessman accused of fraud was Robert Maxwell. He was the owner of Mirror Group newspapers and numerous other businesses before his mysterious drowning near the Canary Islands in 1991. Maxwell had used money from the pension fund of Mirror Group employees to stave off the collapse of his business empire. When it finally collapsed, it left debts of some £2 billion.

The inadequacy of the City regulation of business and banking was also illustrated with the bankruptcy of BCCI (the Bank of Credit and Commerce International) in 1991. The bank lost more than $10 billion in trading that was not recorded in its accounts, and by making fictitious loans.

Corruption on a massive scale took place during the 1970s when enormous amounts of money were lent, perfectly legally, by banks to governments in less developed countries such as the Philippines (where President Marcos invested vast sums in bank accounts abroad) and Mexico (where it has been estimated $40 billion went missing). The end result of such loans and the corruption that they encouraged was a worldwide debt crisis in which many poorer nations ended up heavily indebted to richer countries (George, 1988).

Offences committed by businesses do not just involve loss of money; some also result in injury, disability or loss of life. In 1984, an escape of poisonous gas from a chemical plant at Bhopal in India killed more than 3,000 people and caused permanent injury to a further 20,000. The escape of gas was caused by inadequate safety procedures at the plant, which was owned by a subsidiary of the US multinational corporation Union Carbide. No criminal charges were brought against the company when it agreed to pay $470 million in compensation to victims and their families.

Another tragic example of the consequences of negligence was the *Herald of Free Enterprise* disaster: 188 people died when the P&O car ferry sank after setting sail from Zeebrugge harbour with its bow doors open.

Inadequate safety precautions can lead to death tolls which dwarf that from street crimes. For example, in the year ending March 1998, 748 people were murdered in Britain, according to police statistics (*Home Office Research Bulletin*, 22/98, 13 October 1998). However, according to Michael Streeter (1997), in the late 1990s the effects of asbestos (which can cause the fatal lung disease mesothelioma) alone killed about 3,500 people per year in Britain. According to Streeter, the number of deaths resulting from exposure to asbestos were rising and were spreading beyond the traditional victims – building-site workers – to groups such as clerical workers and teachers, who had been exposed during construction work at their places of employment. The actions which resulted in these deaths may not have been illegal, but their consequences in terms of loss of life were very serious.

Serious injuries can also result from inadequate safety precautions, which may or may not contravene regulations. According to Barrie Clement (1997), figures from the British Health and Safety Executive show that in 1996 100 people were blinded at work, and 1,158 had an amputation as a result of an accident. However, the Health and Safety Executive only actually investigated six of the blindings. There were 302 fatal accidents at work in 1996.

John Braithwaite (1984) has studied corporate crimes committed by pharmaceutical companies and has discovered that they are alarmingly common.

The US Securities and Exchange Commission encouraged drug companies to reveal 'questionable payments' (or, in plainer language, bribery) in return for a promise that they would not be prosecuted. All the major companies had spent substantial amounts on such payments. American Hospital Supply had apparently spent $5.8 million on bribery. For example, it had bribed Mexican health inspectors not to enforce the Mexican Health Code at its plant in that country. Braithwaite found extensive negligence and fraud in the testing of drugs: test results were sometimes falsified, or results for tests that had never taken place were simply made up. There was a great deal of evidence of unsafe manufacturing practices being used, which could lead to faulty heart pacemakers or non-sterile medical products being distributed.

The most dramatic example of the possible effects of crimes like these is the 'thalidomide affair'. This drug was manufactured by Chemie Grunethal of Germany; it was used as a sleeping pill or tranquil-lizer. However, the use of the drug by pregnant women led to over 8,000 seriously deformed babies being born throughout the world. Despite numerous examples of adverse reactions from clinical tests, the drug was marketed with little delay, the advertising proclaiming that it was 'completely safe'. The company was slow to withdraw the product even when the drug's disastrous effects were known.

White-collar crimes involving politicians and state officials come to light from time to time. The 'Watergate' affair is one of the best-known examples. The US President Nixon was forced to leave office in 1974 as a result of his involvement in the break-in and attempted bugging of the offices of political opponents, and his involvement in using illegal sources of money to fund political campaigns. In another US political scandal, 'Irangate', government officials were found to have been involved in the exchange of arms for hostages with the government of Iran, which went against stated US policy.

In Britain, accusations have been made that members of the Thatcher government knowingly allowed companies to export products for military use, including parts for a 'supergun' to the govern-ment of Iraq. This contravened the British govern-ment's own ban on such exports during the Iran–Iraq war.

Another member of the Conservative government, Jonathan Aitken, was found to have accepted hospitality at the Paris Ritz from Mohammed Al Fayed in return for asking questions in Parliament.

Aitken was later imprisoned for conspiracy to pervert the course of justice, as a result of trying to cover up what had happened.

Michael Woodiwiss (1993) claims that the US government has a history of promoting drug trafficking. During the Vietnam war, 'opponents charged that the CIA was knowingly financing its operations from opium money'. This was confirmed in a book written by Orrin DeForest, a senior investiga-tions officer with the CIA. To raise more money, army officers allowed heroin to be smuggled back to America in the corpses of American soldiers. The bodies were cut open and had up to 25 kg of heroin concealed inside.

Gregg Barak (1994) accuses the US government of backing, at various times, repressive dictators in the Philippines, Brazil, South Korea, Cuba, Iran and Argentina; of helping to overthrow or undermine democratically elected governments in countries including Chile, Jamaica, Guatemala and Nicaragua; and of the use of illegal means to deal with domestic protest movements, such as the Black Panthers, the American Indian Movement, and anti-war movements during the 1960s.

More recently, in 1998, President Clinton ordered the bombing of a chemical factory in Sudan on the grounds that it was manufacturing chemical weapons. However, according to Ed Vulliamy and colleagues (1998), America's own tests could find no evidence that chemical weapons were being made there. The result was to destroy some of Sudan's capacity to produce desperately needed medicines.

British intelligence organizations have also been accused of engaging in illegal activities. For example, in his book *Spycatcher* (which the British government tried to suppress), Peter Wright claimed that during the period when Harold Wilson was prime minister the security services were involved in numerous unauthorized buggings and burglaries (Wright, 1987).

A number of factors combine to reduce the apparent extent and seriousness of white-collar crime:

1 It is difficult to detect: many white-collar crimes are 'crimes without victims'.

2 In cases of bribery and corruption, both parties involved may see themselves as gaining from the arrangement, both are liable to prosecution, and therefore neither is likely to report the offence.

3 In cases where the victim is the public at large (such as misrepresentation in advertising), few members of the public have the expertise to realize that they are being misled, or a knowledge of the legal procedure to redress the wrong. In such cases, detection and prosecution are often left to a government agency which rarely has the personnel or finances to bring more than a few cases to court in the hope of deterring the practice.

White-collar crimes, if detected, are rarely prosecuted. In the thalidomide affair no individual was ever found guilty of a criminal offence. Only one court case, in Canada, for compensation for one deformed baby, was ever completed. With their massive resources and skilled lawyers, the companies involved used delaying tactics to such an effect that every other case was settled out of court.

Often white-collar crimes are dealt with administratively by the various boards, and commissions and inspectorates are appointed to deal with them. 'Official warnings' rather than prosecutions are frequently the rule. In the case of professionals, their own associations usually deal with misconduct and, again, prosecution is rare. In extreme cases, doctors and lawyers may lose their licence to practise, but more often than not their professional associations simply hand down a reprimand.

The sociological study of white-collar crime provides some support for the view that there is one law for the rich and another for the poor. Edwin Sutherland (1960) argues that there is a consistent bias 'involved in the administration of criminal justice under laws which apply to business and the professions and which therefore involve only the upper socio-economic group'. The matter is neatly summarized by Willy Sutton, a professional bank robber, who stated:

> Others accused of defrauding the government of hundreds of thousands of dollars merely get a letter from a committee in Washington asking them to come in and talk it over. Maybe it's justice but it's puzzling to a guy like me.
>
> Quoted in Clinard, 1974, p. 266

Official statistics probably underestimate the extent of white-collar and corporate crime to a far greater degree than they underestimate the extent of crime in general. As a result, official statistics portray crime as predominantly working-class behaviour. Many sociological theories have seen social class as the key to explaining criminal deviance. This conclusion may not be justified in view of the nature of criminal statistics, which may give a misleading impression about the relationship between class and crime. Different classes may commit different types of crime, but it is not possible to be certain that lower classes are significantly more prone to crime than higher ones.

Statistics and theories of crime

All the theories of crime and deviance examined so far assume that criminals and deviants are a small minority of the population, and attempts have been made to explain crime in terms of the differences between the criminals and the remainder of the population. Thus criminals and deviants have particular biological characteristics, a defective upbringing, a particular place in the social structure, and so on.

However, studies of crimes that do not appear in the official statistics suggest that crime is very widespread in all social strata. In the USA, the President's Commission on Law Enforcement and the Administration of Justice found that 91 per cent of those questioned in a survey admitted to having committed crimes for which they could have been imprisoned (President's Commission, 1989).

Mike Maguire comments that:

> Depending upon the age, sex, and other social characteristics of those questioned, as well as the wording of the questions, self-report studies have generally found that between 40 and almost 100 per cent will admit to having committed at least one criminal offence during their lifetimes.
>
> Maguire, 1997, p. 175

Studies of a wide range of occupations and industries suggest that crime is a normal feature of working life, from managing directors to shop-floor workers.

If most members of society are deviant, at least occasionally, then new ways of looking at deviance, new questions about deviance, and perspectives which differ radically from those so far considered are needed. Accordingly we will now analyse an alternative perspective on crime and deviance.

Deviance – an interactionist perspective

The interactionist perspective differs from previous approaches in two ways:

1 First, it views deviance from a different theoretical perspective.

2 Second, it examines aspects of deviance which have been largely ignored by previous approaches. It directs attention away from deviants as such and the motivations, pressures and social forces which are supposed to direct their behaviour. Instead it focuses upon the interaction between deviants and those who define them as deviant. The interactionist perspective examines how and why particular individuals and groups are defined as deviant, and the effects of such a definition upon their future actions. For example, the interaction between the

deviant and various agents of social control, such as parents, teachers, doctors, police, judges and probation officers, may be analysed; and the effects upon the individual of being defined as a criminal or delinquent, or as mentally ill, or as an alcoholic, prostitute or homosexual may be examined.

The interactionist approach emphasizes the importance of the meanings the various actors bring to, and develop within, the interaction situation. Thus it may examine the picture of the 'typical delinquent' held by the police and note how this results in a tendency to define lower-class rather than middle-class law-breakers as delinquents.

Meanings are not, however, fixed and clearcut. They are modified and developed in the interaction process. Thus, from an interactionist perspective, the definition of deviance is negotiated in the interaction situation by the actors involved. For example, whether or not a person is defined as mentally ill will depend on a series of negotiations between him or her and a psychiatrist.

The approaches so far considered, with their emphasis on deviants simply reacting to external forces largely beyond their control, are close to a positivist position. Interactionists reject the positivist approach. They stress the importance of factors internal to the individual. Individuals do not react passively to external forces: they attach meanings to events before deciding how to respond.

Howard S. Becker – labelling theory

The definition of deviance

One of the most influential statements on deviance is contained in the following quotation from Howard S. Becker (1963), one of the early exponents of the interactionist approach. Becker argued:

> social groups create deviance by making the rules whose infraction constitutes deviance, and by applying those rules to particular people and labelling them as outsiders. From this point of view, deviance is not a quality of the act the person commits, but rather a consequence of the application by others of the rules and sanctions to an 'offender'. The deviant is one to whom the label has successfully been applied; deviant behavior is behavior that people so label.
>
> Becker, 1963, p. 9

Becker is suggesting that in one sense there is no such thing as a deviant act. An act only becomes deviant when others perceive and define it as such.

The act of nudity in Western society provides an illustration. Nudity in the bedroom, where the actors involved are husband and wife, is generally interpreted as normal behaviour. Should a stranger enter, however, nudity in his or her presence would usually be considered deviant. Yet, in particular contexts, such as nudist camps or certain holiday beaches, nudity in the presence of strangers would be seen as perfectly normal by the participants. A male spectator at a cricket match who 'streaked' across the pitch may be viewed as 'a bit of a lad' but, if he stood and exposed himself to the crowd, he might be regarded as 'some kind of a pervert'. Thus there is nothing intrinsically normal or deviant about the act of nudity. It only becomes deviant when others label it as such.

Whether or not the label is applied will depend on how the act is interpreted by the audience. This in turn will depend on who commits the act, when and where it is committed, who observes the act, and the negotiations between the various actors involved in the interaction situation.

Becker illustrated his views with the example of a brawl involving young people. In a low-income neighbourhood, it may be defined by the police as evidence of delinquency; in a wealthy neighbourhood as evidence of youthful high spirits. The acts are the same but the meanings given to them by the audience differ. In the same way, those who commit the act may view it in one way; those who observe it may define it in another. The brawl in the low-income area may involve a gang fighting to defend its 'turf' (territory). In Becker's words, they are only doing what they consider 'necessary and right, but teachers, social workers and police see it differently'.

If the agents of social control define the youngsters as delinquents and they are convicted for breaking the law, those youngsters then become deviant. They have been labelled as such by those who have the power to make the labels stick. Thus, Becker argued, 'Deviance is not a quality that lies in behavior itself, but in the interaction between the person who commits an act and those who respond to it.' From this point of view, deviance is produced by a process of interaction between the potential deviant and the agents of social control.

Possible effects of labelling

Becker then examined the possible effects upon an individual of being publicly labelled as deviant. A label defines an individual as a particular kind of person. A label is not neutral: it contains an evaluation of the person to whom it is applied. It is a master status in the sense that it colours all the other statuses possessed by an individual. If individuals are labelled as criminal, mentally ill or homosexual, such labels largely override their status as parent, worker, neighbour and friend. Others see them and respond to them in terms of the label, and tend to assume they have the negative characteristics normally associated with such labels.

Since individuals' self-concepts are largely derived from the responses of others, they will tend to see themselves in terms of the label. This may produce a self-fulfilling prophecy whereby 'the deviant identification becomes the controlling one'. (We examine the self-fulfilling prophecy theory in more detail in Chapter 11.)

Becker outlined a number of possible stages in this process:

1 Initially the individual is publicly labelled as deviant. This may lead to rejection from many social groups. Regarded as a 'junkie', a 'queer', a 'nutter', a 'wino' or a 'tearaway', he or she may be rejected by family and friends, lose his or her job and be forced out of the neighbourhood.

2 This may encourage further deviance. For example, drug addicts may turn to crime to support their habit since 'respectable employers' refuse to give them a job.

3 The official treatment of deviance may have similar effects. Ex-convicts may have difficulty finding employment and be forced to return to crime for their livelihood. Becker argued:

> the treatment of deviants denies them the ordinary means of carrying on the routines of everyday life open to most people. Because of this denial, the deviant must of necessity develop illegitimate routines.
>
> Becker, 1963

4 The deviant career is completed when individuals join an organized deviant group. In this context they confirm and accept their deviant identity. They are surrounded by others in a similar situation who provide them with support and understanding.

5 Within the group, a deviant subculture develops. The subculture often includes beliefs and values which rationalize, justify and support deviant identities and activities. For example, Becker states that organized male homosexual groups provide the individual with a rationale for his deviance:

> explaining to him why he is the way he is, that other people have also been that way, and why it is all right for him to be that way.
>
> Becker, 1963

The subculture also provides ways of avoiding getting into trouble with conventional society. The young thief, socialized into a criminal subculture, can learn various ways of avoiding arrest, from older and more experienced members of the group. Becker argued that, once individuals join an organized deviant group, they are more likely than before to see themselves as deviants and to act in terms of this self-concept. In this context the deviant identification tends to become 'the controlling one'.

Jock Young – labelling and marijuana users

The value of Becker's approach to the labelling of deviance can be seen from its application by Jock Young (1971) in his study of 'hippie' marijuana users in Notting Hill in London. Young examined the meanings which coloured the police view of the hippies, how their reaction to the hippies was directed by these meanings, and the effects upon the hippies of this reaction. The police tend to see hippies as dirty, scruffy, idle, scrounging, promiscuous, depraved, unstable, immature, good-for-nothing drug addicts. Young argued that police reaction to the hippies in terms of these meanings can 'fundamentally alter and transform the social world of the marijuana smoker'. In particular, drug-taking, which begins as 'essentially a peripheral activity of hippie groups', becomes a central concern.

Police action against marijuana users tends to unite the latter and make them feel different. As such, they rationalize and accept their difference. In self-defence, they retreat into a small, closed group. They exclude 'straights', not only for reasons of security (secrecy about marijuana use is important to avoid arrest), but also because they develop a deviant self-concept which makes it more difficult to include members of conventional society.

In this context, deviant norms and values develop. Having been defined and treated as outsiders, the hippies tend to express and accentuate this difference. Hair is grown longer, clothes become more and more unconventional. Drug use becomes transformed from a peripheral to a central activity, especially as police react more strongly against the deviance they have helped to create.

Young argued that, because of increased police activity, 'drug taking in itself becomes of greater value to the group as a symbol of their difference, and of their defiance of perceived social injustices'. In this situation a deviant subculture evolves and deviant self-concepts are reinforced, all of which makes it increasingly difficult for the hippies to re-enter conventional society.

Howard Becker – the origins of 'deviant' activity

Howard Becker's approach stressed the importance of the public identification of a deviant. It suggested that a deviant label can lead to further deviance, and can even change individuals' self-concepts so that they come to regard themselves as deviant for the first time.

However, Becker argued that this process is by no means inevitable. Ex-convicts do get jobs and go 'straight'; drug addicts do sometimes give up their habit and re-enter conventional society.

Furthermore, Becker tried to explain how individuals get involved in deviant activities in the first place. He conducted his own study of marijuana smoking in order to explain how the habit could start, and noted that various conditions had to be met if the first experimentation with the drug was to lead to regular use.

As an interactionist, Becker emphasized the importance of the subjective meanings given to experiences. Thus the physical experiences that result from taking drugs are interpreted by the individual as he or she interacts with others. With regard to marijuana, Becker says, 'The user feels dizzy, thirsty; his scalp tingles, he misjudges time and distance.' These effects will not necessarily be defined as pleasurable: other experienced smokers will need to reassure the new user that the effects are indeed desirable, and should be sought again.

Unlike the other theories of crime and deviance that we have looked at in this chapter, Becker examined becoming deviant as a process. Merton (1968) identified a single cause of deviance (anomie) to explain deviance throughout a person's life; Becker stressed that the reasons for deviance might change as time passes and circumstances alter. Thus the reason why someone tries marijuana for the first time could be quite different from the reasons for continuing after being caught and labelled. Becker used what he calls a 'sequential' approach to the explanation of deviance, and at any stage in the sequence it is possible that the deviant will return to conformity.

Edwin M. Lemert – societal reaction – the 'cause' of deviance

Like Becker, Edwin M. Lemert (1972) emphasized the importance of societal reaction – the reaction of others to the deviant – in the explanation of deviance. Lemert distinguished between 'primary' and 'secondary' deviation.

Primary deviation

Primary deviation consists of deviant acts before they are publicly labelled. There are probably any number of causes of primary deviation and it is largely a fruitless exercise to inquire into them for the following reasons:

1 Samples of deviants are based upon those who have been labelled and are therefore unrepresentative. For example, it makes little sense to delve into the backgrounds of convicted criminals to find the cause of their deviance, without examining criminals who have not been caught.

2 Many so-called deviant acts may be so widespread as to be normal in statistical terms. Thus, most males may at some time commit a homosexual act, engage in delinquent activities, and so on.

In fact, Lemert suggested that the only thing that 'known' deviants probably have in common is the fact that they have been publicly labelled as such.

Not only is the search for the causes of primary deviation largely fruitless, but primary deviation itself is relatively unimportant. Lemert argued that it 'has only marginal implications for the status and the psychic structure of the person concerned'. Thus Lemert suggested that the odd deviant act has little effect on individuals' self-concepts and status in the community, and does not prevent them from continuing a normal and conventional life.

Secondary deviation

The important factor in 'producing' deviance is societal reaction – the public identification of the deviant, and the consequences of this for the individual concerned. Secondary deviation is the response of the individual or the group to societal reaction.

Lemert argued that studies of deviance should focus on secondary deviation, which has major consequences for the individual's self-concept, status in the community and future actions. In comparison, primary deviation has little significance. Lemert argued that 'In effect the original "causes" of the deviation recede and give way to the central importance of the disapproving, degradational, and isolating reactions of society.'

Thus, Lemert claimed that societal reaction can be seen as the major 'cause' of deviance. This view, he argued, 'gives a proper place to social control as a dynamic factor or "cause" of deviance'. In this way, Lemert neatly reverses traditional views of deviance: the blame for deviance lies with the agents of social control rather than with the deviant.

Stuttering and societal reaction

Lemert was particularly convincing in his paper entitled 'Stuttering among the North Pacific coastal Indians', which examines the relationship between societal reaction and deviance. Previous research had indicated a virtual absence of stuttering among North American Indians: indeed most tribes did not even have a word for this speech irregularity. However, Lemert's investigation of deviance in various tribes living in the North Pacific coastal area of British Columbia revealed evidence of stuttering both before and after contact with whites. In addition, the languages of these tribes contained clearly defined concepts of stutterers and stuttering. It is particularly significant that their inland neighbours, the Bannock and Shoshone, had no words for stuttering, and research, using a large-scale sample of members of these tribes, found no evidence of actual stuttering.

The North Pacific coastal Indians had a rich ceremonial life, involving singing, dancing and speech-making. Their legends and stories were filled with references to famous orators and outstanding speeches. From an early age, children were initiated into ceremonial life, and parents stressed the importance of a faultless performance. There were rigorous and exacting standards to be met; rituals had to be performed exactly as they should be. If they did not meet these standards, children shamed their parents and suffered the ridicule of their peers. In particular, there was a highly developed sensitivity to any speech defect. Children and parents alike were anxious about any speech irregularity and responded to it with guilt and shame. Lemert concluded that stuttering was actually produced by societal reaction. The concern about, and the reaction to, speech irregularities actually created them. He argued that the culture, both past and present:

> seems favorable to the development of stuttering, that stutterers were and still are socially penalized, that parents tended to be specifically concerned or anxious about the speech development of their children, that children were anxious about ritual performances involving solo verbal behavior.
>
> Lemert, 1962

In other American Indian societies, where such concerns were largely absent, stuttering was unknown. Thus Lemert argued that societal reaction, prompted by a concern about particular forms of deviance, can actually produce those forms of deviance.

Erving Goffman – deviance and the institution

In general, interactionists view the various institutions for the treatment of deviance - the prisons, mental hospitals and reform schools - as a further set of links in a long chain of interactions which confirm the label of deviance, both for the individual so labelled and for society as a whole. In a series of trendsetting essays, Erving Goffman examined the treatment of mental patients in institutions (Goffman, 1968). He argued that, although the stated aim of such institutions is to cure and rehabilitate, a close examination of interaction patterns within the institutions reveals a very different picture.

Mortification

Goffman is particularly concerned with how, via a series of interactions, pressure is placed upon inmates to accept the institution's definition of themselves. Upon entry, 'he begins a series of abasements, degradations, humiliations, and profanities of self. His self is systematically, if often unintentionally, mortified.'

This mortification process strips inmates of the various supports which helped to maintain their former self-concepts. Often their clothes (an important symbol of identity) are removed. Their possessions (a further symbol of identity) may be taken away and stored for the duration of their stay. They may be washed, disinfected and their hair may be cut. They may then be issued with a new 'identity kit', such as regulation clothes and toilet articles. Such standardized items tend to remove individuality and define the inmate simply as a member of a uniform mass.

Once the entry phase is over, the inmate settles down to an endless round of mortifying experiences. Each day is strictly timetabled into a set of compulsory activities controlled by the staff. Inmates are allowed little freedom of movement, few opportunities to show initiative or take decisions. Throughout their stay, their actions are scrutinized and assessed by the staff in terms of the rules and standards which they have set. Many of these regulations can be degrading. For example, in some mental hospitals, a spoon is the only utensil provided for the patients to eat with.

Goffman summarized what mental hospitals, in particular, and treatment institutions, in general, 'say' to the inmates about themselves:

> In the mental hospital, the setting and the house rules press home to the patient that he is, after all, a mental case who has suffered from some kind of social collapse on the outside, having failed in some over-all way, and that here he is of little social weight, being hardly capable of acting like a fully-fledged person at all.
>
> Goffman, 1968

The effects

Not surprisingly, inmates in treatment institutions become anxious as their day of release approaches. At best, they have not been prepared for life on the outside; at worst, they have accepted the institution's definition of themselves as hopeless, hapless deviants. A small minority become institutionalized: they believe themselves unable to function in the outside world, cling to the security of the institution and go to great lengths to remain inside.

Despite this, Goffman argued that the effects of the institution upon the majority of inmates are not usually lasting. There is a period of temporary disculturation, which means that the former inmate must re-learn some of the basic 'recipes' for living in the outside world. However, the most lasting and important consequence is the label 'ex-mental patient' or 'ex-convict'. This, rather than the experience of being inside, makes re-entry into conventional society difficult.

Goffman reached the rather pessimistic conclusion that many treatment institutions 'seem to function merely as storage dumps for inmates'. Like societal reaction in general, treatment institutions serve to reinforce rather than reduce deviance. He did, however, stress that some ex-patients were able to successfully fight against the label. They did not see themselves as mentally ill, and could convince others that they had returned to normality. They survive despite the handicap of their stay in the institution.

Goffman's research took place several decades ago, and may not be so applicable today. However, his work helped to produce some of the improvements that have taken place since he was writing.

Deviance and the interactionist perspective – policies, criticisms and evaluation

Labelling theory and social policies

Stephen Jones (1998) has reviewed the policy implications of interactionist and labelling theories. He argues that they have two main implications. First, they suggest that as many types of behaviour as possible should be decriminalized. Second, they imply that, when the law has to intervene, it should try to avoid giving people a self-concept in which they view themselves as criminals. This might involve trying to keep people out of prison or warning people rather than prosecuting them.

Both of these approaches have had some influence. For example, in Britain, *The Independent* newspaper started a campaign in 1997 to legalize cannabis. In countries such as the Netherlands some 'soft' drugs have been effectively legalized.

However, in Britain, the main impact of such thinking has probably been on juvenile justice. Jones suggests that there have been rather inconsistent policies in this area, but there have been some attempts to avoid stigmatizing young offenders. These have included using cautions rather than prosecutions, introducing separate juvenile courts (with the Children and Young Person's Act, 1993) and having anonymity for young offenders.

For adults, the only measure of this nature was contained in the Rehabilitation of Offenders Act, 1974. This allowed offenders to withhold from employers information about most offences, once a period of time (which depended on the offence) had

elapsed. However, as Jones points out, such policies became less popular during the 1990s. In some quarters there has been a renewed emphasis on the public shaming of offenders in order to deter others. Examples of this include writing to men accused of kerb crawling, so that wives have a chance of learning of their offence, and the naming of paedophiles in local newspapers (starting with the *Bournemouth Evening Echo* in 1996). This suggests that, whatever the strengths and weaknesses of labelling theory, its influence declined in the 1990s.

Evaluation of the theory

In terms of sociological theory, in the 1960s the interactionist view of deviance enjoyed wide popularity. For many sociologists, the work of writers such as Becker, Lemert and Goffman became the accepted, orthodox perspective on deviance. Nevertheless, in the 1970s it began to provoke strong criticism. Interactionists rallied to the defence of their work and attempted to show that the criticisms were unjustified.

The definition of deviance

The first line of criticism attacked the interactionist definition of deviance. Becker and Lemert argued that deviance was created by the social groups who defined acts as deviant. Taylor, Walton and Young (1973), however, claimed that this view was mistaken. To them, most deviance can be defined in terms of the actions of those who break social rules, rather than in terms of the reaction of a social audience.

For example, it is true that in some circumstances deliberately killing another person may be regarded as justified: you may be acting in self-defence, or carrying out your duties as a soldier. But, whoever makes up the social audience, a 'premeditated killing for personal gain' will always be regarded as deviant in our society. As Taylor, Walton and Young put it, 'we do not live in a world of free social meanings': in many circumstances there will be little or no freedom of choice in determining whether an act is regarded as deviant or not.

The origins of deviance

A second, related criticism of interactionism is that it fails to explain why individuals commit deviant acts in the first place. Lemert claimed that it was not necessary to explain primary deviance, since it is very common and it has no impact on a person's self-concept. Many sociologists do not accept this claim.

Although most people do commit deviant acts from time to time, different individuals tend to turn to different types of deviance. One person might steal, another might break health and safety legislation, and a third might smoke marijuana. Clearly it is important to explain why individuals should choose to turn to one form of deviance rather than another.

Furthermore, it is clear that many deviants realize they are breaking the norms of society, whether or not they are caught and labelled. As Taylor, Walton and Young argue:

> while marijuana smokers might regard their smoking as acceptable, normal behaviour in the company they move in, they are fully aware that this behaviour is regarded as deviant in the wider society.
>
> Taylor, Walton and Young, 1973

Taylor, Walton and Young therefore suggest that it is necessary to explain why the marijuana smokers decide to take the drug despite their knowledge that it would be condemned by most other members of society.

It can also be argued that it is wrong to assume that primary deviance will have no effect on someone's self-concept. Even if people keep their deviance secret, they know that they are capable of breaking the law, and this could well affect both their opinion of themselves and their later actions.

Labelling as deterministic

The third major criticism of the interactionist perspective is that it is too deterministic. It assumes that, once a person has been labelled, their deviance will inevitably become worse. The labelled person has no option but to get more and more involved in deviant activities. Thus, Ronald Ackers stated:

> One sometimes gets the impression from reading the literature that people go about minding their own business, and then – 'wham' – bad society comes along and slaps them with a stigmatized label. Forced into the role of deviant the individual has little choice but to be deviant.
>
> Quoted in Gibbons and Jones, 1975, p. 131

Critics like Ackers are suggesting that individuals might simply choose to be deviant, regardless of whether they have been labelled. Thus, labelling does not cause most terrorists to turn to crime: they are motivated by their political beliefs to break the law.

As Alvin W. Gouldner notes in his critique of Becker (Gouldner, 1975), the interactionists tend to portray the deviant as someone who is passive and controlled by a 'man-on-his-back', rather than as an active 'man-fighting-back'. If individuals can choose to take part in deviance, they may also decide to ignore a label and to give up deviance 'despite' it.

The Swedish sociologist Johannes Knutssen (1977) argues that interactionists have not produced sufficient evidence to show that labelling will amplify deviance. Knutssen feels that labelling theorists have taken the effects of labels to be 'self-evident-truths', without producing the research findings necessary to support their case.

Labelling, laws and law enforcement

The final major criticism is that interactionists fail to explain why some people should be labelled rather than others, and why some activities are against the law and others are not. Why, to use Becker's example, should the police regard a brawl in a low-income neighbourhood as delinquency, and in a wealthy neighbourhood as no more than youthful high spirits? Why should laws against robbery be enforced strictly, when factory legislation is not? Why should it be illegal to smoke marijuana but not cigarettes? The critics of labelling theory claim that it does not provide satisfactory answers to these types of question.

A defence of interactionism

Interactionists have not taken this barrage of criticism lying down. In an article entitled 'Labelling theory reconsidered' (Becker, 1974), Becker attempted to defend himself against these attacks. In 1979, Ken Plummer advanced the claim that labelling theory had been 'misunderstood' and unfairly criticized.

Ken Plummer accepts the criticism that it is largely the nature of the act that defines deviance, while insisting that the reaction of a social audience to a deviant act is still important. He acknowledges that rule-breaking behaviour can be regarded as deviant whether or not it is discovered and labelled. He calls this form of deviance societal deviance. Plummer defines this as behaviour which breaks the laws of society, or which is commonly sensed by most of society's members to be deviant. For example, homosexuality is commonly regarded as deviant, and so by this definition a secret homosexual would be a deviant. Nevertheless, Plummer suggests that it is never certain whether a particular act or individual will be regarded as deviant by a social audience.

Situational deviance consists of those acts which others judge to be deviant, given the context in which they take place. A member of a rugby team who drinks heavily might be regarded as 'one of the lads', while in different situations others who actually drink less might be seen as alcoholics. Plummer therefore accepts that deviance depends partly on what you do, but, he reminds the critics, it also depends on the social reaction.

The second criticism – that interactionists ignore the initial causes of deviance – is dismissed by Plummer. He points out that, in practice, interactionists have devoted considerable attention to explaining primary deviance. For example, Becker tries to explain how it is possible to get involved in marijuana smoking. Some versions of labelling theory start their account of deviance at the point when labelling first occurs, but many interactionists deal with the earlier stages of becoming deviant. Becker himself claimed that he regretted calling his approach 'labelling theory'; he preferred it to be seen as an interactionist approach which did not concentrate exclusively on labels.

Plummer finds it even more difficult to accept that interactionist theories of deviance are deterministic. He points out that the whole interactionist perspective places great stress on the choices open to individuals as they interpret what happens around them and decide how to respond. It is quite different from a positivist approach which sees people's behaviour as directed by external forces beyond their control. As Plummer puts it:

> To take a theory that is sensitive to self, consciousness and intentionality and render it as a new determinism of societal reaction could only be possible if the theory were totally misunderstood in the first place.
>
> Plummer, 1979

He notes that Goffman's mental patients provide an excellent example of labelled deviants who fight against and often overcome the labels that are thrust on them against their will (see pp. 376–7 for further details). Becker saw the deviant as passing through a series of stages in his or her deviant career. At no stage does he say that it is inevitable that a person will continue to be a deviant – indeed Becker stresses that a deviant career could be abandoned at any stage.

The final major criticism of labelling theory is also rejected by Plummer. He believes that the labelling perspective opened up the whole question of who had the power to make society's rules and apply them to particular individuals. It raised for the first time the very issues that critics claimed it ignored. Nevertheless, it can be argued that interactionists do not satisfactorily answer these questions. Because of their emphasis on social action, they are not particularly concerned with the distribution of power in society as a whole.

Whatever the limitations of the interactionist perspective on deviance, it has made an important contribution to this area of sociology. It has shown that the definition of deviance is not a simple process. It challenges the view of the deviant as an abnormal, pathological individual. It questions positivistic and deterministic theories of crime. Finally, it raises the issue of who has the power to label acts and individuals as deviant. As such, it had a considerable influence even on some later, radical, sociologists who rejected the interactionist approach to deviance. Furthermore, it was a major source of inspiration for more recent theories, such as new left realism (see pp. 391–9) which includes the response to deviant and criminal behaviour as an important component of its theory.

Deviance – a phenomenological perspective

Aaron V. Cicourel – the negotiation of justice

The phenomenological approach to deviance has some similarities to the interactionist perspective. Both phenomenology and interactionism:

1 emphasize the importance of the way that the law is enforced;

2 are concerned with the process of labelling individuals as deviant;

3 concentrate on studying the subjective states of individuals rather than the structure of society as a whole.

However, interactionists and phenomenologists approach the study of deviance in different ways. Phenomenologists do not claim to produce causal explanations; they seek to understand what a phenomenon is. Thus, phenomenologists attempt to discover what deviance is by examining the way in which some acts and individuals come to be defined or labelled as deviant. Unlike interactionists, they stop short of claiming that labelling causes people to commit more deviant acts.

Ethnomethodology is an American sociological perspective which attempts to apply the principles of phenomenology to the study of society. The work of the American ethnomethodologist Aaron V. Cicourel on the treatment of delinquency in two Californian cities provides a good example of how this perspective has been applied to the study of deviance (Cicourel, 1976).

Defining delinquency

The process of defining a young person as a delinquent is not simple, clearcut and unproblematic. It is complex, involving a series of interactions based on sets of meanings held by the participants. These meanings can be modified during the interaction, so each stage in the process is negotiable.

The first stage is the decision by the police to stop and interrogate an individual. This decision is based on meanings held by the police of what is 'suspicious', 'strange', 'unusual' and 'wrong'. Such meanings are related to particular geographical areas. Inner-city, low-income areas are seen as 'bad areas' with a high crime rate; consequently behaviour in such areas is more likely to be viewed as suspicious. Interrogation need not lead to arrest. The process is negotiable but depends largely on the picture held by the police of the 'typical delinquent'. If the appearance, language and demeanour of the young person fit this picture, she or he is more likely to be arrested.

Once arrested, the young person is handed over to a juvenile officer (probation officer) who also has a picture of the 'typical delinquent'. If the suspect's background corresponds to this picture, she or he is more likely to be charged with an offence. Factors assumed to be associated with delinquency include 'coming from broken homes, exhibiting "bad attitudes" toward authority, poor school performance, ethnic group membership, low-income families and the like'.

It is not surprising, therefore, that Cicourel found a close relationship between social class and delinquency. Most young people convicted of offences had fathers who were manual workers. On a seven-class occupational scale, Cicourel found that one-third came from class 7.

Cicourel explained the preponderance of working-class delinquents by reference to the meanings held by the police and juvenile officers, and the interactions between them and the juveniles. When middle-class juveniles were arrested, there was less likelihood of them being charged with an offence: their background did not fit the standard picture of the delinquent. Their parents were better able to negotiate successfully on their behalf. Middle-class parents can present themselves as respectable and reasonable people from a nice neighbourhood, who look forward to a rosy future for their child. They promise cooperation with the juvenile officers, assuring them that their son or daughter is suitably remorseful.

As a result, the middle-class juvenile is often defined as ill rather than criminal, as accidentally straying from the path of righteousness rather than committed to wrongdoing, as cooperative rather than recalcitrant, as having a real chance of reforming rather than being a 'born loser'. He or she is typically 'counselled, warned and released'. Thus, in Cicourel's words, 'what ends up being called justice is negotiable'.

Cicourel based his research on two Californian cities, each with a population of around 100,000. The socio-economic characteristics of the two populations were similar. In terms of structural theories, the numbers of delinquents produced by the pressures of the social structure should be similar in each city. However, Cicourel found a significant difference in the numbers of delinquents arrested and charged. He argues that this difference can only be accounted for by the size, organization, policies and practices of the juvenile and police bureaus.

For example, the city with the highest rate of delinquency employed more juvenile officers and kept more detailed records on offenders. In the second city, the delinquency rate fluctuated sharply. Cicourel argues that in this city the response of the police to delinquency 'tends to be quite variable depending on publicity given to the case by the local paper, or the pressure generated by the mayor or chief or Captain of Detectives'. Thus, societal reaction can be seen to directly affect the rate of delinquency.

Cicourel argues that delinquents are produced by the agencies of social control. Certain individuals are selected, processed and labelled as deviant. Justice is the result of negotiation in the interaction process. The production of delinquents is also dependent on the ways in which police and juvenile bureaus are organized, their policies, and the pressures that are brought to bear on them from local media and politicians.

In view of these observations, Cicourel questions structural and subcultural theories of deviance which see deviance as a product of pressure from the social structure. He concludes:

> *The study challenges the conventional view which assumes 'delinquents' are 'natural' social types distributed in some ordered fashion and produced by a set of abstract 'pressures' from the 'social structures'.*
>
> Cicourel, 1976

Criticisms of Cicourel

Cicourel's study provides some useful insights into juvenile justice in the USA. He attempts to show how the meanings held by the various officials lead to some individuals being defined as delinquent.

However, critics such as Taylor, Walton and Young (1973) argue that he fails to explain how these meanings originate. He fails to show why, for instance, the police see the 'typical delinquent' as coming from a low-income family. In common with other phenomenologists and ethnomethodologists, he does not explain who has power in society, and how the possession of power might influence the definition of crime and deviance.

The same cannot be said of Marxists, whose theories on deviance we will now examine.

Who breaks the law? Who gets caught?

Corporate crime

Sociologists who have been strongly influenced by Marxism tend to argue that crime is widespread in all social strata. As we discovered in an earlier section (see pp. 369–72), there are many examples of illegal behaviour by white-collar criminals and corporations. Laureen Snider argues that 'Many of the most serious antisocial and predatory acts committed in modern industrial countries are corporate crimes' (Snider, 1993). Snider claims that corporate crime does more harm than the 'street crimes', such as burglary, robbery and murder, which are usually seen as the most serious types of crime. Writing in 1993, she pointed out that figures suggest that corporate crime costs more, in terms of both money and lives, than street crime.

For example, in a typical year in the USA about 20,000 people are murdered, and in Britain about 600. This compares in the USA with an annual death toll of 14,000 from industrial accidents (many resulting from breaking safety regulations), 30,000 from 'unsafe and usually illegal' consumer products, 100,000 from occupationally induced diseases, and 'hundreds of thousands of cancer deaths are caused by legal and illegal environmental pollution'. In Britain, workplace accidents account for 600 deaths and 12,000 injuries annually.

According to Snider, street crime involves losses of around $4 billion each year in the USA. However, losses from corporate crime are more than twenty times greater. In recent years, 312 US savings and loan companies have been unable to pay their debts, due to fraudulent activities such as insider dealing, failing to disclose accurate information in accounts, and racketeering. The General Accounting Agency has estimated the total cost of bailing out these companies as a minimum of $325 billion and, more probably, around $500 billion. This means it is likely to cost every household in the USA $5,000.

Despite the enormous costs of corporate crime, both the penalties and the chances of prosecution for those involved in it are usually small. Snider argues that enforcement agencies are expected to balance the costs of enforcing regulations (for example, in lost profits or jobs) with the benefits. Prosecutions are normally used as a last resort, and it is more likely to be small businesses which are taken to court rather than the big corporations which do most harm.

Quoting from a variety of studies, Snider notes that under US anti-trust legislation there were 1,551 prosecutions from 1890 to 1969, but only 4.9 per cent of offenders received a prison sentence. In fact, for the first 71 years of the laws no business leaders were imprisoned – the only people sent to jail were labour leaders. Some 80 per cent of the fines imposed were under $5,000.

Crime and the ruling class in Seattle

In an important study of crime in Seattle, Washington, William Chambliss (1978) argues that organized crime is not merely the servant of the ruling class but rather an integral part of it. His research covered nearly ten years, from 1962 to 1972, and was based on interviews with a variety of informants, including police officers, government officials, professional thieves, racketeers and prostitutes. Chambliss argues that crime occurs throughout all social strata. The major differences between strata are the types of crimes committed and the nature of law enforcement.

Chambliss claims that power, in the form of money and influence, is the key factor which determines who gets arrested and who does not. During the time of his study, over 70 per cent of the arrests in Seattle were for public drunkenness. Skid row rather than upper-class suburbia preoccupied the police. The courts and the jails were filled with the poor and the powerless.

Chambliss claims that the major crime syndicate in Seattle was made up of leading businessmen, political leaders and law enforcement officers. The syndicate organized illegal gambling, bookmaking, prostitution, pornography and the sale and distribution of drugs. Its tentacles spread throughout the ruling class. The vice president of a local bank helped the syndicate to conceal its large tax-free profits, and sat on the board of a syndicate-owned 'shark' loan company. Those who threatened to 'blow the whistle' on the syndicate's activities were murdered. Drowning was a favourite method since it could be conveniently glossed over as suicide by the coroner – a brother-in-law of a member of the syndicate.

Pay-offs and bribes to local politicians and government officials were standard practice, with the result that local government bureaucracy turned a blind eye to the syndicate's activities. Complaints from residents in low-income areas about the presence of brothels and gambling casinos in their neighbourhoods were ignored by the powers that be. From this type of evidence, Chambliss reaches the following conclusions:

1 Those who operate organized crime in American cities are not members of some 'criminal class' – they belong to the economic and political elite.

2 It is not only the small minority of active syndicate members within the ruling class who profit from crime. The class as a whole benefits, since monies

gained from illegal activities are used to finance legal business operations.

3 Corruption of local political and law enforcement agencies is essential for organized crime to flourish.

4 Criminal acts which favour ruling-class interests will not be penalized; those that do not will be subject to legal sanctions.

Why break the law? Why enforce the law?

Capitalism and crime

Many Marxists see crime as a natural 'outgrowth' of capitalist society. They argue that a capitalist economic system generates crime for the following reasons:

1 The economic infrastructure is the major influence upon social relationships, beliefs and values. The capitalist mode of production emphasizes the maximization of profits and the accumulation of wealth.

2 Economic self-interest rather than public duty motivates behaviour.

3 Capitalism is based on the private ownership of property. Personal gain rather than collective well-being is encouraged.

4 Capitalism is a competitive system. Mutual aid and cooperation for the betterment of all are discouraged in favour of individual achievement at the expense of others. Competition breeds aggression, hostility, and – particularly for the losers – frustration.

William Chambliss (1976) argues that the greed, self-interest and hostility generated by the capitalist system motivate many crimes at all levels within society. Members of each stratum use whatever means and opportunities their class position provides to commit crime. Thus, in low-income areas, the mugger, the petty thief, the pusher, the pimp and the prostitute use what they have got to get what they can. In higher-income brackets, business people, lawyers and politicians have more effective means at their disposal to grab a larger share of the cake.

Given the nature of capitalist society, and particularly American society, David Gordon (1976) argues that crime is rational, it makes sense. In a 'dog eat dog' society, where competition is the order of the day, individuals must fend for themselves in order to survive. This is particularly true for the American poor, since the USA has minimal welfare services compared to other advanced industrial societies. Gordon concludes that 'Most crimes in this country share a single important similarity – they represent rational responses to the competitiveness and inequality of life in capitalist societies.'

Selective law enforcement

From a Marxist viewpoint, the selective enforcement of the law has a number of important consequences. As noted above, the occasional prosecution of ruling-class crime perpetuates the fiction that the law operates for the benefit of society as a whole, that the state represents the public interest, and that the extent of ruling-class crime is small. Conversely, frequent prosecution of members of the subject class has equally important consequences.

David Gordon argues that the practice of law enforcement in the USA supports the capitalist system in three ways:

1 By selecting members of the subject class and punishing them as individuals, it protects the system which is primarily responsible for their criminal deviance. Individuals are defined as 'social failures' and as such they are responsible for their criminal activities. In this way, blame and condemnation are directed at the individual rather than the institutions of capitalism. Gordon argues that the practice of law enforcement serves to 'reinforce a prevalent ideology in this society that individuals, rather than institutions, are to blame for social problems'.

2 The imprisonment of selected members of the subject class 'legitimately' neutralizes opposition to the system. American blacks are heavily over-represented amongst those arrested for 'street crimes' such as robbery and aggravated assault. A New York chief of police neatly summarized the situation when he compared the role of the police in Harlem (the main black ghetto in New York City) to that of an army of occupation. Few have the insight of one black ex-convict who sums up Gordon's view of imprisonment when he states:

> It didn't take me any time to decide I wasn't going back to commit crimes. Because it's stupid, it's a trap, it only makes it easier for them to neutralize you.
>
> Quoted in Gordon, 1976, p. 208

3 Gordon argues that defining criminals as 'animals and misfits, as enemies of the state', provides a justification for incarcerating them in prisons. This keeps them hidden from view. In this way the most embarrassing extremes produced by the capitalist system are neatly swept under the carpet. If something were really done to help those who broke the law, if their problems were made public, the whole system might be questioned. But, Gordon concludes:

> By keeping its victims so thoroughly hidden and rendering them so apparently inhuman, our system of crime and punishment allows us to forget how sweeping a 'transformation' of our social ideology we would require in order to begin solving the problem of crime.
>
> Gordon, 1976

Gordon argues that the selective enforcement of the law serves to maintain ruling-class power and to reinforce ruling-class ideology. Further arguments in support of this view can be added to those he outlines:

1   The selective application of the law gives the impression that criminals are mainly located in the working class. This serves to divert attention from ruling-class crime.

2   It can also serve to divert the attention of members of the subject class from their exploitation and oppression.

3   It directs a part of the subject class's frustration and hostility (produced by this situation of exploitation) on to the criminals within their own class. The muggers, murderers and thieves can provide a scapegoat for the frustrations of the alienated masses.

4   This provides a safety valve, releasing aggression which might otherwise be directed against the ruling class.

5   It also serves to divide the subject class, particularly in low-income areas, where there is a tendency for people to see their enemies as the criminals within their own class.

Finally, what effect does selective law enforcement have upon crime itself? From his study of Seattle, William Chambliss reaches the following conclusion. Law enforcement agencies are:

> *not organized to reduce crime or to enforce public morality. They are organized rather to manage crime by cooperating with the most criminal groups and enforcing laws against those whose crimes are minimal. By cooperating with criminal groups law enforcement essentially produces more crime.*
>
> Chambliss, 1978

Criticisms of conventional Marxism

Marxist theories have come in for heavy criticism from a number of quarters:

1   Feminist sociologists have argued that Marxist theories put undue emphasis upon class inequality. From their point of view, Marxist theories ignore the role of patriarchy in influencing the way the criminal justice system operates. Marxists have also been accused of neglecting the importance of racism in the enforcement of laws.

2   Marxists have been criticized for assuming that a communist system could eradicate crime. Before the end of communism in the Soviet Union and Eastern European countries, crime had not been eradicated.

3   Stephen Jones (1998) points out that capitalism does not always produce high crime rates. For example, in Switzerland, which has long embraced a capitalist system, crime rates are very low.

4   Some Marxists have a rather simplistic view of the distribution of power in capitalist societies. While the group which Marxists define as a ruling class might have a disproportionate amount of power, it may be misleading to see them as monopolizing power. A range of non-Marxist theories suggest that the distribution of power is more complex than Marxists tend to believe (see Chapter 9). Stephen Jones points out that the activities of capitalists are sometimes criminalized. He gives the example of insider trading. If it were not illegal, capitalists would be free to make substantial profits out of their knowledge about proposed mergers and takeovers. The illegality of such activity suggests that capitalists cannot always get the laws they want.

5   'Left realists' tend to see Marxist theories as putting undue emphasis on corporate crime, at the expense of other types of crime. Left realists argue that crimes such as burglary, robbery and other violent crimes cause greater harm than Marxist theories seem to imply. The victims of such crimes are usually working-class, and the consequences can be devastating for them. To left realists, Marxism offers a rather one-sided view of crime and, in doing so, offers no way of dealing with the types of crimes which are of most concern to most members of the population. (We will discuss these views in more detail on pp. 391–9.)

6   Postmodern criminology rejects Marxist criminology as a 'metanarrative' which is neither believable nor defensible. These views will be examined later in the chapter (see pp. 423–7).

Conventional Marxist approaches have become rather unfashionable in sociology and criminology. Nevertheless, they have influenced a range of other approaches to the sociology of crime and deviance. Some of these will be examined in the next section.

There are a number of critical perspectives that have developed since the heyday of conventional Marxism. Some of these have drawn their inspiration in large measure from Marxism, despite using elements from other theories. These can be referred to as neo-Marxist approaches. Others owe rather less to Marxism and are perhaps better defined as radical theories of crime and deviance. Some feminist approaches (examined on p. 424) can also be seen as radical theories.

Neo-Marxism

Neo-Marxist sociologists of crime and deviance accept that society is characterized by competing groups with conflicting interests. Furthermore, they are all critical of existing capitalist societies, and they share a concern about the unequal distribution of power and wealth within such societies. However, none accept that there is a simple and straightforward relationship between the infrastructure of society and deviance. Although most of these sociologists (including Taylor, Walton and Young, Paul Gilroy, and Stuart Hall) have been strongly influenced by Marxism, their work differs in important respects from that of the Marxists we have examined so far. It can therefore be termed a neo-Marxist approach to deviance.

Ian Taylor, Paul Walton and Jock Young – *The New Criminology*

In 1973, Taylor, Walton and Young published *The New Criminology*. It was intended to provide a radical alternative to existing theories of crime and deviance. In some respects, Taylor, Walton and Young's views are similar to those of the Marxist writers who have just been examined:

1   They accept that the key to understanding crime lies in the 'material basis of society'. Like Marx, they see the economy as the most important part of any society.

2   They believe that capitalist societies are characterized by inequalities in wealth and power between individuals and that these inequalities lie at the root of crime.

3   They support a radical transformation of society: indeed, they suggest that sociological theories of crime are of little use unless they contribute in a practical way to the 'liberation of individuals from living under capitalism'.

However, in important respects they differ from more conventional Marxist approaches. As such, we can see *The New Criminology* as a neo-Marxist perspective on crime.

Crime, freedom and political action

Much of Taylor, Walton and Young's work is concerned with criticizing existing theories of crime. Marx himself is judged by them to have produced inadequate explanations of crime. He is criticized for coming close to providing an economically determin-

istic theory. Although they believe that economic determinism is untypical of Marx's work in general, they claim that, when he tried to explain crime, he saw the criminal as driven to crime by the poverty into which capitalism forced some sections of the population.

Taylor, Walton and Young insist that criminals choose to break the law. They reject all theories that see human behaviour as directed by external forces. They see the individual turning to crime 'as the meaningful attempt by the actor to construct and develop his own self-conception'.

The New Criminology denies that crime is caused by biology, by anomie, by being a member of a subculture, by living in areas of social disorganization, by labelling, or by poverty. It stresses that crimes are often deliberate and conscious acts with political motives. Thus the Women's Liberation Movement, the Black Power Movement and the Gay Liberation Front are all examples of 'people-fighting-back' against the injustices of capitalism.

Furthermore, many crimes against property involve the redistribution of wealth: if a poor resident of an inner-city area steals from a rich person, the former is helping to change society. Deviants are not just the passive victims of capitalism: they are actively struggling to alter capitalism.

Like conventional Marxists, Taylor, Walton and Young wish to see the overthrow of capitalism and its replacement with a different type of society. Unlike conventional Marxists, they refer to the type of society they wish to see as 'socialist' rather than 'communist'. They place greater emphasis than many Marxists on freedom in any future society. They wish to see a society in which groups which are now seen as deviant are tolerated. They believe that hippies, ethnic minorities, homosexuals, and perhaps even drug users, should simply be accepted in an ideal society, and not turned into criminals by persecution.

In capitalist society, people have severe restrictions placed upon their behaviour. Taylor, Walton and Young urge support and sympathy for groups who struggle to escape from the chains with which capitalism limits their freedom. Indeed, they conclude *The New Criminology* by saying that the purpose of criminology should be to create societies in which human diversity is tolerated without being seen as criminal.

A 'fully social theory of deviance'

In the final chapter of *The New Criminology*, Taylor, Walton and Young attempt to outline what they believe would be a fully social theory of deviance. From their critical examination of earlier theories they conclude that deviance needs to be explained from a number of angles simultaneously. They claim that other writers, including Marxists, have tended to give incomplete, or one-sided explanations of crime. To Taylor, Walton and Young, a complete theory needs to examine both the way society as a whole is organized, and the way that individuals decide to carry out criminal acts. They identify seven aspects of crime and deviance which they believe should be studied:

1 The criminologist first needs to understand the way in which wealth and power are distributed in society.

2 He or she must consider the particular circumstances surrounding the decision of an individual to commit an act of deviance.

3 It is necessary to consider the deviant act itself, in order to discover its meaning for the person concerned. Was the individual, for example, showing contempt for the material values of capitalism by taking drugs? Was he or she 'kicking back' at society through an act of vandalism?

4 Taylor, Walton and Young propose that the criminologist should consider in what ways, and for what reasons, other members of society react to the deviance. How do the police or members of the deviant's family respond to the discovery of the deviance?

5 The reaction then needs to be explained in terms of the social structure. This means that the researcher should attempt to discover who has the power in society to make the rules, and explain why some deviant acts are treated much more severely than others.

6 Taylor, Walton and Young then turn to labelling theory. They accept that it is necessary to study the effects of deviant labels. However, they emphasize that labelling may have a variety of effects. The amplification of deviance is only one possible outcome. Deviants may not even accept that the labels are justified: they might see their actions as morally correct and ignore the label as far as possible.

7 Finally, Taylor, Walton and Young say that the relationship between these different aspects of deviance should be studied, so that they fuse together into a complete theory.

Evaluation of The New Criminology

The New Criminology has attracted criticism from a number of quarters:

1 Feminist sociologists have criticized it for concentrating on male crimes and ignoring gender as a factor in criminality.

2 Some 'new left realist' criminologists have accused The New Criminology of neglecting the impact of crime on the victims, of romanticizing working-class criminals (who in reality largely prey on poor people rather than stealing from the rich), and of failing to take street crimes seriously (see pp. 391–9 for a discussion of left realism).

In 1998, 25 years after The New Criminology was published, Paul Walton and Jock Young edited and contributed to a new book evaluating the impact of their earlier work. In general, the original authors defended their earlier work, although they admitted that some criticisms were justified.

Paul Walton argues that the main achievement of The New Criminology was to 'deconstruct previous theories and reveal their self-seeking or selfless character in an attempt to construct the elements of a social theory of deviance' (Walton, 1998). According to Walton, the central aim of The New Criminology was an attempt to undermine 'correctionalism' – that is, the belief that the sociology of crime and deviance should be used to try to get rid of deviant or criminal behaviour. Walton believes that such a desire merely reflects ideological bias. People want to get rid of behaviour which their own ideology says is wrong.

To Walton, many traditional theories of crime 'acted as little more than an academic justification for existing discriminatory practices in the penal and criminal justice system'. The New Criminology advocated greater tolerance of a wider variety of behaviour. Although Walton believes that traditional forms of correctionalist criminology have survived, The New Criminology did succeed in opening up a new, radical approach to criminology. He accepts that some of the newer approaches in criminology – such as feminism, left realism and postmodernism – have been somewhat critical of The New Criminology (see pp. 391–9 and 423–7). Furthermore, he accepts some of their criticism, such as the feminist view that The New Criminology neglected gender. However, he argues that even these more recent approaches were all built on foundations laid by The New Criminology. Walton says that 'realist criminology, feminist criminology and postmodern criminology are all committed to creating a more just and equitable society'. In that respect they are a continuation of the traditions of The New Criminology.

Jock Young is now a leading proponent of left realist criminology, which has been critical of The New Criminology. However, like Walton, he defends its role in attacking conventional theories of crime and deviance. He stresses that The New Criminology emphasized the importance of explaining both the actions of offenders and the workings of the criminal justice system. It did not, as some critics seem to believe, put sole emphasis on the way in which the state defines some people's behaviour as criminal and ignores the crimes of others. In this respect he sees *The New Criminology* as a precursor to his later approach, new left realism (see pp. 391–9).

Young also believes that, in some respects, *The New Criminology* anticipated some of the arguments of postmodern sociology (see pp. 423–7). For example, it encouraged the acceptance of diversity, it acknowledged that crime and deviance took a variety of forms, which could not be explained by one overarching theory, and it recognized the creativity and originality of those who created different subcultures.

Like Walton, then, Young does not see *The New Criminology* as perfect, but he does see it as an advance on previous theories. Certainly it had some influence on the work of other sociologists. However, Taylor, Walton and Young had only sketched the main features of a theoretical approach to explaining crime and deviance. It was left to other sociologists to try to put their 'fully social theory of deviance' into practice.

Policing the Crisis – mugging, the state, and law and order

Stuart Hall, Chas Critcher, Tony Jefferson, John Clarke and Brian Roberts have attempted to provide a detailed explanation of the crime of 'mugging' in Britain (Hall et al., 1979). Like Taylor, Walton and Young, their work is influenced by a Marxist perspective, yet differs from traditional Marxist views. *Policing the Crisis* comes close to providing what Taylor, Walton and Young called a 'fully social theory of deviance'. The wide-ranging argument presented in the book deals with the origins and nature of mugging, the social reaction to the crime, and the distribution of power in society as a whole. The only aspect of crime that is dealt with in less detail is the effect of labelling on the deviants themselves.

Hall *et al.* differ from Taylor, Walton and Young in two important ways:

1 They do not share their belief that most crimes are political acts, especially since most of the victims of street crime are 'people whose class position is hardly distinguishable from that of the criminals'. 'Muggers' rarely choose the rich as victims – rather they tend to rob from individuals who share their own disadvantaged position in society.

2 They are perhaps more heavily influenced by the work of the Italian Marxist Antonio Gramsci than directly by the work of Marx himself. The influence of Gramsci will become increasingly apparent as this section develops.

'Mugging', the media and moral panic

In the 13 months between August 1972 and August 1973, 60 events were reported as 'muggings' in the national daily papers. Dramatic individual cases of such crimes were highlighted in the media. On 15 August 1972, Arthur Hills was stabbed to death near Waterloo Station in London. For the first time, a specific crime in Britain was labelled a 'mugging' in the press. On 5 November 1972, Robert Keenan was attacked by three youths in Birmingham. He was knocked to the ground, and had some keys, five cigarettes and 30p stolen. Two hours later, the youths returned to where he still lay, and they viciously kicked him and hit him with a brick.

It was stories such as these which highlighted an apparently new and frightening type of crime in Britain. Judges, politicians and the police lined up with the media in stressing the threat that this crime posed to society. Many commentators believed that the streets of Britain would soon become as dangerous as those of New York or Chicago. The Home Secretary in the House of Commons quoted an alarming figure of a 129 per cent increase in muggings in London in the previous four years.

Hall *et al.* argue that there was a 'moral panic' about crime. (A moral panic is an exaggerated outburst of public concern over the morality and behaviour of a group in society.) They try to explain why there should be such a strong reaction to, and widespread fear of, mugging. They reject the view that the panic was an inevitable and understandable reaction to a new and rapidly increasing form of violence. As far back as the nineteenth century, footpads and garrotters (who half-strangled their victims before robbing them) had committed violent street crimes similar to those of the modern mugger. Violent robberies were not, therefore, a new crime at all – indeed, as recently as 1968, an MP had been kicked and robbed in the street without the crime being labelled a 'mugging'.

Hall and his colleagues note that there is no legal crime called 'mugging'. Since legally there is no such crime, it was not possible for the Home Secretary to accurately measure its extent. They could find no basis in the criminal statistics for his figure of a 129 per cent rise over four years. From their own examination of the statistics there was no evidence that violent street crime was rising particularly fast in the period leading up to the panic. Using the nearest legal category to 'mugging' – robbery, or assault with intent to rob – the official statistics showed an annual rise of an average of 33.4 per cent between 1955 and 1965, but only a 14 per cent average annual increase from 1965 to 1972. This type of crime was growing more slowly at the time the panic took place than it had done in the previous decade.

For these reasons Hall *et al.* could not accept that the supposed novelty or rate of increase of the crime explained the moral panic over it. They argued that both 'mugging' and the moral panic could only be explained in the context of the problems that were faced by British capitalism at the start of the 1970s.

Capitalism, crisis and crime

Economic problems produced part of the 'crisis'. Many Marxists believe that capitalism faces deeper and deeper crises as time passes. Marx believed that only labour power produced wealth. In capitalist societies labour was exploited because the bourgeoisie kept a proportion of the wealth created by the workforce in the form of profit or surplus value. In order to compete with other manufacturers, capitalists needed to invest in new and more efficient machinery. However, as this mechanization took place, less and less labour power would be needed to manufacture the same quantity of goods. Since surplus value was only created through labour power, the dwindling workforce needed to be increasingly exploited if profits were to be maintained. Eventually this problem would lead to a declining rate of profit, rising unemployment and falling wages. According to Hall et al., such a crisis hit Britain at the time of the mugging panic.

The crisis of British society, however, went beyond economic problems. It was also a crisis of 'hegemony', a term first used by Antonio Gramsci. Hegemony is the political leadership and ideological domination of society. (We discuss Gramsci and hegemony in more detail in Chapter 9.) According to Gramsci, the state tends to be dominated by parts of the ruling class. They attempt to win support for their policies and ideas from other groups in society. They try to persuade the working class that the authority of the state is being exercised fairly and justly in the interests of all. A crisis in hegemony takes place when the authority of the state and the ruling class is challenged.

In 1970-2 the British state faced both an economic crisis and a crisis of hegemony. From 1945 until about 1968 there had been what Hall et al. call an inter-class truce: there was little conflict between the ruling and subject class. Full employment, rising living standards, and the expansion of the welfare state secured support for the state and acceptance of its authority by the working class. As unemployment rose and living standards ceased to rise rapidly, the basis of the inter-class truce was undermined. It became more difficult for the ruling class to govern by consent.

Hall et al. provide a number of examples of the challenge to the authority – to the hegemony – of the state:

1 Northern Ireland degenerated into open warfare.
2 There was a growth in student militancy and increased activity from the Black Power movement.

3 The unions posed perhaps the biggest single threat: in 1972 there were more workdays lost because of strikes than in any year since 1919. The miners were able to win a large pay-rise by using flying pickets, which prevented coal reaching key industries and power stations.

Since the government was no longer able to govern by consent, it turned to the use of force to control the crisis. It was in this context that street crime became an issue. Mugging was presented as a key element in a breakdown of law and order. Violence was portrayed as a threat to the stability of society, and it was the black mugger who was to symbolize the threat of violence.

In this way the public could be persuaded that society's problems were caused by 'immigrants' rather than the faults of the capitalist system. The working class was effectively divided on racial grounds, since the white working class was encouraged to direct its frustrations towards the black working class.

Crisis and the control of crime

The government was also able to resort to the use of the law and direct force to suppress the groups that were challenging them. Force could be justified because of the general threat of violence. Special sections of the police began to take action against the 'mugger'. The British Transport Police was particularly concerned with this crime. In February 1972, six months before the 'mugging' panic began, it set up a special squad to deal with violent crime on the London Underground. Hall et al. claim that the police in general, and this special squad in particular, created much of the 'mugging' that was later to appear in the official statistics. Following the argument of interactionists, they suggest that the police amplified, or made worse, the deviance they were supposed to be controlling.

They give examples of police pouncing unannounced on black youths of whom they were suspicious. Often this would provoke a violent reaction in self-defence by the youths, who would then be arrested and tried for crimes of violence. Many of the 'muggers' who were convicted following incidents like these had only police evidence used against them at trial. 'Victims' of their crimes were not produced because, Hall et al. imply, there were no victims in some cases. The societal reaction to the threat of violence led to the labelling of large numbers of young blacks as deviants. Labelling helped to produce the figures that appeared to show rising levels of black crime, which in turn justified stronger police measures.

Hall et al. do not claim that the reactions to crime, 'mugging', and other 'violence' were the result of a conspiracy by the ruling class. The police, the government, the courts and the media did not consciously plan to create a moral panic about street crime; the panic developed as they reacted to changing circumstances.

Neither were the media directly manipulated by the ruling class or the government: different newspapers included different stories, and reported 'mugging' in different ways. Nevertheless, there was a limited range of approaches to the issue in the press. Most stories were based on police statements or court cases, or were concerned with the general problem of the 'war' against crime. Statements by the police, judges and politicians were therefore important sources of material for the press. Consequently the newspapers tended to define the problem of 'mugging' in similar ways to their sources: criminal violence was seen as senseless and meaningless by most of the press. It was linked to other threats to society, such as strikes, and was seen as a crime which needed to be stamped out as quickly as possible.

A number of judges who stressed the need for deterrent sentences to turn back the tide of crime were quoted directly. Assistant Commissioner Woods of the Police Federation was widely quoted when he said that 'mugging' was a 'reflection of the present violent society', and declared that 'we are not going to let the thugs win'.

However, if the crisis in Britain produced the conditions in which a moral panic was likely, the media were largely responsible for 'orchestrating public opinion', and directing its attention and anger against the black mugger.

Black crime

Although *Policing the Crisis* concentrates on the moral panic about crime, Hall *et al.* also make some attempt to explain black criminality. Many immigrants to Britain from the Commonwealth arrived in the 1950s and early 1960s. They were actively encouraged to come to the country during a period of full employment and labour shortage. London Transport, for example, recruited large numbers of West Indians to fill low-paid jobs which might otherwise have remained vacant.

The recession in the early 1970s hit immigrant groups hard. They became a 'surplus labour force', many of whom were not required for employment. Thus, Hall *et al.* estimate that, at the time in question, black unemployment was twice the national average, and for school leavers it was four times higher than normal. Those who remained in employment often had to do menial and low-paid jobs, which some referred to as 'white man's shit work'. Some opted out of the employment market altogether. They turned to 'hustling' for money, using petty street crime, casual drugs dealing, and prostitution to earn a living. Hall

et al. do not find it surprising that some of this surplus labour force became criminals. They claim:

> *a fraction of the black labouring class is engaged in the traditional activity of the wageless and the workless: doing nothing, filling out time, trying to survive. Against this background is it not too much to say that the question 'Why do they turn to crime?' is a practical obscenity?*
> Hall *et al.*, 1979

From this point of view, street crime is seen as a survival strategy employed by an unwanted reserve army of labour.

Policing the Crisis – an evaluation

Policing the Crisis provides a sophisticated analysis of the crime of 'mugging' from a neo-Marxist perspective:

1 It suggests that the moral panic about mugging was not a rational response to a new and rapidly growing crime, but a response to the economic crisis and the crisis of hegemony for the British state.

2 The societal reaction to this crime can only be understood as part of the shift by the dominant class from ruling the country by consent, towards ruling it by force.

3 One result of the increasingly repressive policies and the greater use of the law, was the labelling of black 'muggers', and the amplification of the crime.

4 The media focused public concern about violence on to black 'immigrants', and in doing so disguised the real reasons for the crisis.

5 The rise in black criminality was largely the result of police labelling, but some West Indians were forced into crime in order to survive, as unemployment left them little alternative.

Given the range of issues that this study deals with, it is not surprising that other sociologists have raised criticisms. David Downes and Paul Rock (1988) have identified two major weaknesses:

1 They argue that the book contradicts itself. It appears to claim simultaneously that black street crime was not rising quickly, that it was being amplified by police labelling, and that it was bound to rise as a result of unemployment. According to this criticism, Hall *et al.* are trying to have their cake and eat it. They change their view on whether these crimes were rising or not, according to how it fits their argument.

2 Downes and Rock believe that *Policing the Crisis* fails to show that the moral panic over 'mugging' was caused by a crisis of British capitalism. They point out that there have been numerous moral panics – for example, about the violence of teddy boys, and mods and rockers, and in 1979-80 about widespread strikes in the 'winter of discontent'.

the average officer probably spends less than an hour a day on investigation and follow-up work.

3 Evidence from victimization studies and other sources shows that over 90 per cent of crimes known to the police are notified to them by the public. Most crimes that are cleared-up are also solved as a result of information received from the public. However, research suggests that public confidence in the police has declined, particularly in inner-city areas and amongst members of ethnic minorities. For example, the Policy Studies Institute found that in 1983 75 per cent of black British people in London, aged 15-24, thought that the police fabricated evidence; 82 per cent thought they used violence on suspects; and 66 per cent thought they made false records of interviews (quoted in Kinsey, Lea and Young, 1986). As trust breaks down between the police and some sections of the public, the flow of information from the victims of crime dries up.

4 Lacking the information that is necessary to solve crime, the police resort to new policing methods. They drift towards what Kinsey, Lea and Young call military policing. Without the support of the community, the police have to resort to tactics such as stopping and searching large numbers of people in an area or using surveillance technology to find suspects. This leads to the mobilization of bystanders. Even those who are not directly involved with the police come to see police officers as part of an alien force intent upon criminalizing local residents almost regardless of their guilt. As a result, a vicious circle is initiated: declining information leads to more military-style policing, and information provided by the public is reduced further. This process is illustrated in Figure 6.5.

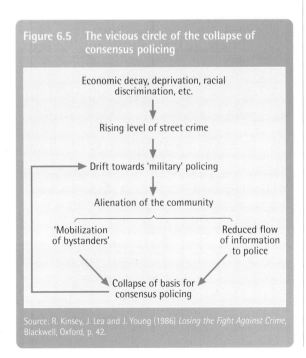

Figure 6.5 The vicious circle of the collapse of consensus policing

Economic decay, deprivation, racial discrimination, etc.
↓
Rising level of street crime
↓
Drift towards 'military' policing
↓
Alienation of the community
↓
'Mobilization of bystanders'   Reduced flow of information to police
↓
Collapse of basis for consensus policing

Source: R. Kinsey, J. Lea and J. Young (1986) *Losing the Fight Against Crime*, Blackwell, Oxford, p. 42.

A good example of this process occurred in 1981. The Brixton riots were sparked by a police operation, Swamp 81, in which the streets of Brixton were flooded by police stopping and searching people suspected of offences.

Improving policing

How then can the police improve their performance and begin to clear up more crime? Kinsey, Lea and Young argue that the key to police success lies in improving relationships with the community so that the flow of information on which the police rely increases. To achieve this, they propose that minimal policing should be used. This is:

a style of policing under a system of democratic accountability in which information is freely given by the public and where the police are sufficiently trusted to do the job they are paid for – the full and proper investigation of crime.

Kinsey, Lea and Young, 1986

This approach involves maximizing the role of the public in shaping police policy. Kinsey, Lea and Young believe that the public should have much more power to shape policing through democratically elected police authorities. These should be able to issue guidelines and direct the police towards dealing with the crimes that are of most public concern. The public should play a major role in determining which incidents the police become involved in. Unless directed to take action by police authorities, the police should only respond to public requests for help.

Kinsey, Lea and Young see little role for stopping and searching suspects and little point in having police on the beat. Such police practices either antagonize the public on whom the police rely, or are ineffective. It is only very rarely that police on the beat actually discover crimes.

The police should spend as much of their time as possible actually investigating crime. Kinsey, Lea and Young believe that, if the police act in these ways, they can regain the trust of the public and become more effective in clearing up the crimes that are of most public concern.

Over-policing and under-policing

Although he has argued that the public should establish priorities for the police, Jock Young (1992) has also identified areas which he believes are over-policed and under-policed. In other words, he thinks that the police and the state devote too much of their time and energy to dealing with certain types of crime, and not enough to others. In the former category are minor drug offences and juvenile 'status' crimes, such as under-age drinking; in the latter there are a wide range of offences where he believes tighter control by the state is necessary. These include racially motivated attacks, corporate crime, pollution, and domestic crimes of physical and sexual abuse.

Tackling the social causes of crime

Jock Young (1992, 1997) does not believe that crime can be dealt with simply by improving the efficiency of the police. As we saw in earlier sections, he and other left realists see the problem of crime as rooted in social inequalities. Only if those inequalities are significantly reduced will the problem of crime be reduced.

Young and Matthews (1992) argue that 'objectives within the criminal justice system are linked to wider social and political objectives of greater equality, opportunity and freedom of choice'. Young (1992) suggests that improving leisure facilities for the young, reducing income inequalities, raising the living standards of poorer families, reducing unemployment and creating jobs with prospects, improving housing estates, and providing 'community facilities which enhance a sense of cohesion and belonging' all help to cut crime.

Young does not believe that the criminal justice system is the main source of crime control. He says, 'It is not the "thin Blue Line", but the social bricks and mortar of civil society which are the major bulwark against crime' (Young, 1997). Young insists that 'social causation is given the highest priority'. Order will only arise in a just society, and all solutions must therefore address the question of whether they enhance social justice. Long-term problems, therefore, need to be addressed, but more immediate measures can be taken, so long as they enhance the overall aim of increasing social justice.

The multi-agency approach

Left realists have not tended to say a great deal about how the wider social causes of crime, such as excessive income inequality, can be tackled. They have concentrated on suggesting shorter-term and more readily achievable ways of reforming institutions. However, such proposals are not limited to the police.

Young (1992) advocates a 'multi-agency' approach. For example, councils can improve leisure facilities and housing estates, while the family, the mass media and religion have a role in improving the 'moral context' which permits so much crime. Social services, victim support schemes and improved security can help alleviate the problems of actual or potential victims. In Young's view, the public also have a vital role to play in dealing with crime.

The square of crime

As we have seen in the above discussion, left realists have examined many facets of crime. These include the causes of crime, the nature of crime statistics, policing, public attitudes towards crime and the police, the chances of being a victim of crime, and so on. In recent years these elements have been brought together into one theoretical approach to the understanding of crime. This has been called the square of crime.

As Figure 6.6 shows, the square of crime involves four elements:

1 the state and its agencies
2 the offender and their actions
3 informal methods of social control (sometimes called 'society' or 'the public')
4 the victim

Left realists believe that crime can only be understood in terms of the inter-relationships between these four elements. Roger Matthews states:

> *crime is, in an important sense, a socially-constructed phenomena. Its meaning is profoundly influenced by considerations of time and space. Its construction is based upon the interaction of four key elements – victims, offenders, the state and the public.*
> Matthews, 1993

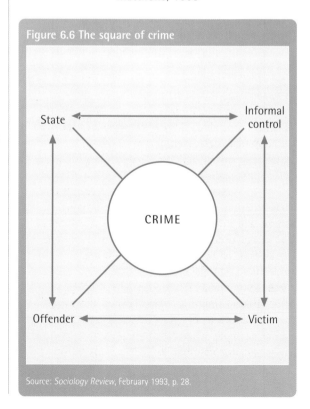

Figure 6.6 The square of crime

State — Informal control

CRIME

Offender — Victim

Source: *Sociology Review*, February 1993, p. 28.

The idea that crime is socially constructed, that social factors determine who and what are considered criminal, is nothing new. Labelling theorists, phenomenologists and Marxists all agree that this is the case. The idea that crime needs to be examined from different angles is not new either. For example, *The New Criminology* (Taylor, Walton and Young, 1973) proposed just such an approach, and Young acknowledges that in this respect it served as a precursor to left realism (Young, 1997).

However, left realism claims to go beyond these approaches in a number of ways. Left realists pay far more attention to victims and public opinion than the approaches mentioned above. *The New Criminology* pays little or no attention to victims, in examining crime. Matthews and Young (1992) claim that many other theories concentrate on just one part of the square of crime: labelling theory on the state, control theory on the public, positivism on the offender, and victimology on the victim. Left realists do not accept that one element of the square of crime is always of prime importance. The importance of different elements varies from crime to crime. Matthews says:

> *Each particular form of crime will have a different set of determinants within this framework and will involve a different combination of the key elements within the square. Thus corporate crime and street crime involve different types of victim–offender relation and are regulated by a different combination of formal and informal controls.*
>
> Matthews and Young, 1992

Multiple aetiology

Whatever the type of crime, though, left realists believe that each of these four elements is crucial, and together they determine what crime is, as well as what causes it and how it might be dealt with. Jock Young calls this the principle of multiple aetiology – that is, it is caused by several different factors. Crime by its very nature is a product of formal and informal rules, of actions by offenders, and of reactions by victims and the state and its agencies. It is therefore important to try to understand why people offend, what makes the victims vulnerable, the factors that affect public attitudes and responses to crime, and the social forces that influence the police.

For example, when examining changes in violent behaviour in a country, both alterations in the amount of violence and in public and police attitudes about what constitutes serious violence have to be examined. Young says:

> *Deviance and control cannot be studied independently of each other. You cannot study changes in policing without changes in patterns of crime ... Systems of social control profoundly affect deviance and changes in deviance patterns of control.*
>
> Young, 1992

The idea of the square of crime can be illustrated by considering the different elements that go to make up crime. For crime to exist there must be laws prohibiting behaviour. The existence or otherwise of those laws is influenced by the public. For an infraction to take place there must be an offender (or someone perceived as an offender) and, usually, a victim.

A variety of social factors influence the behaviour of the victim. For many offences it is the victim who decides whether the offence is reported. Victims will be influenced by prevailing social values in deciding whether they think an offence is immoral, illegal and worth reporting. The relationship between victim and offender might affect both the victim's willingness to report the crime and the impact that the crime has on him or her. For example, wives might be unwilling to report the domestic violence of their husbands, or they might see the behaviour as 'normal'. The crimes of a spouse will have a different impact to those of a stranger.

The response of the police or other authorities then determines whether the offender is defined as criminal or not. Public opinion can have an impact on the behaviour of authorities. As labelling theorists point out, the decisions and actions of the criminal justice system can influence the future behaviour of those convicted of crime. Changes in any of these areas can affect the crime rate and the problems which criminality poses for society.

Evaluations of left realism

Since left realism is highly critical of many existing theories of crime and deviance, it is not surprising that it has itself been the subject of criticism.

Failure to explain the causes of crime

Gordon Hughes (1991) attacks left realism on a number of counts, but argues that its major failing is in its attempts to explain the causes of street crime. On one level, left realists have simply failed to carry out the necessary research. Hughes says, 'The empirical investigation of offenders' motives remains the yawning gap in the NLR research on crime.' The concentration on victimization studies has prevented left realists from gathering their own data on the motives of offenders. The data they have collected are largely quantitative and statistical and cannot reveal the subjective states of offenders. Thus, according to Hughes, 'NLR offers no empirical account of the subjective worlds of the street criminal but, instead, appears to rely for the most part on speculation.'

The reliance upon subculture theory

Hughes also criticizes left realism for its reliance upon subculture theory. He says, 'NLR uses subcultural analysis without any fundamental or radical revision.' By doing so, it falls into the trap of repeating some of the errors of the original subculture theories. For example, it assumes that there are shared values throughout society and that it is only when these break down that crime becomes likely. It is equally possible to argue that crime stems from the existence of many different sets of values, some of which tolerate certain types of crime. To Hughes, left realism tends to concentrate on the criminal subculture in terms of Cloward and Ohlin's categories (see pp. 358–9), or the adaptation of innovation in terms of Merton's approach (see pp. 354–6). In doing so, it neglects other responses to relative deprivation such as retreatism or ritualism. Hughes also claims that concentrating upon the criminal subculture in relation to ethnic minorities might lead to 'a further fanning of the stereotype, "black = criminal".'

Hughes concludes that the work of left realists tends to over-simplify the causes of crime; it 'reduces law-breaking to the effects of deprivation and selfishness', while giving less sophisticated explanations of the various responses to deprivation than those offered by Albert Cohen, Merton or Cloward and Ohlin.

Relative deprivation

Stephen Jones (1998) argues that left realism fails to explain why some people who experience relative deprivation turn to crime, while others do not. According to Jones, the theory of relative deprivation tends to over-predict the amount of crime. There is less crime, particularly property crime, than might be expected if the theory was correct. In fact, Jones also believes that the theory serves better as a theory of property crime than of violent crime. It is easy to understand why the sufferers from relative deprivation might turn to theft or burglary to solve their material problems; it is less easy to see what they might gain from violence. Furthermore, Jones does not believe that the left realist solution to crime, of reducing inequality, would get rid of relative deprivation. Many people might still feel deprived even if the gap between them and the better-off had narrowed.

The focus on victims

While left realists are certainly right to point out that other approaches have tended to neglect victims, some commentators think that there are flaws in their emphasis on victims. Stephen Jones (1998) argues that left realists only listen to victims on certain issues. Thus, while they take victims' accounts of their fear of crime at face value, they do not ask victims about the causes of crime. Instead they impose their own explanations, which might have little credibility to victims. Jones says, 'victims are only empowered at the level of providing information'.

Furthermore, to Jones, left realists only really take account of the views of certain types of victims. Their studies have been concentrated on urban areas where crime rates are high. This might give a misleading impression of how harmful crime is, since it neglects suburban and rural areas where crime has much less impact on people's lives.

Corporate and organized crime

Left realists are certainly aware of corporate crime and see it as a major problem. However, Vincenzo Ruggiero (1992) argues that they have neglected its investigation, and that this type of crime cannot be readily understood within the framework of their theory. He says that they do not consider how crime can be integrated into work carried out for corporations. Nor do they examine the ways in which offenders can themselves be the victims of criminal organizations (for example the drug-taker being exploited by the pusher, or the prostitute by the pimp). Victims tend to be seen as the victims of aberrant individuals within the square of crime, not as the victims of corporations or 'central and local authorities'. Lip service is paid to issues such as corporate crime but they are not integrated into the theory.

Stephen Jones (1998) expresses a similar point in a different way. Jones believes that the emphasis on street crime means that left realists are accepting legal, police and popular definitions of what constitutes real crime, and which crimes are important. Labelling theory and Marxism encouraged a consideration of how certain types of harmful behaviour, often carried out by people with power, were not criminalized. Left realists have concentrated on conventionally defined crime, ignoring the issue of what is defined as crime, and therefore risk losing 'many of the supposed advances in criminological theory over the last 40 years'.

The strengths of left realism

Most of the critics acknowledge that left realist criminology has made some contribution to the development of sociological theories of crime and deviance. Gordon Hughes sees it as having the following strengths:

1 It has revived some useful sociological concepts such as relative deprivation.
2 It has promoted debate and theoretical development within the subject.
3 It has highlighted the problems that street crime can cause for weak members of society.
4 It has explored the position of victims much more than most previous theories, and it 'avoids the worst excesses of both "the right" and "the left" in neither glorifying nor pathologizing the police and other state agencies' (Hughes, 1991). Overall, though, Hughes concludes:

> In its efforts to expunge itself of its own past sins of romanticism, NLR has jettisoned many of the valuable gains made by radical theory over the past two decades.
>
> Hughes, 1991

Left realism and social policy

Whatever its merits (or lack of them) new left realism has probably had more influence on policies concerning crime than most sociological theories. A number of its proposals have been adopted. For example, the police in Britain increasingly employ civilians to do routine tasks, thus giving them more time to investigate crime. The police have also begun to put more emphasis on crimes such as domestic violence.

More generally, there are similarities between the policies of the 'New' Labour Party in Britain and the theories of left realism. Labour's slogan 'Tough on Crime, Tough on the Causes of Crime' echoes the ideas of left realists. However, British Labour Party policies have also been influenced by other theories, and they have been less obviously designed to reduce inequality, which left realists see as a key factor underlying crime rates.

Some aspects of left realist policy proposals, such as increasing police accountability, have not been seriously attempted. Indeed, Stephen Jones argues that 'the removal of discretion from policing is impossible' (Jones, 1998), so increases in accountability could only go so far. Thus, the effectiveness of the policies of Tony Blair's Labour government will not be a true test of the effectiveness of left realist policies. Nevertheless, in some areas these policies may provide some evidence as to whether left realism can do anything to alleviate problems associated with crime, where other approaches seem to have had little success.

Right realist criminology

Attempts to find 'realistic' solutions to the problems of crime have not been confined to left-wing sociologists. Right-wing sociologists have also tried to develop new theoretical approaches to explain and suggest solutions to crime. Right realist theories are particularly associated with American sociologists such as James Q. Wilson and Richard Hernstein. James Q. Wilson was an advisor to President Reagan. Although not popular amongst British social scientists, right realist views have had some influence on British governments and certainly have similarities to some populist views about what should be done about crime in Britain. Right realist views are very different to left realist views and, as we will see, have been strongly attacked.

James Q. Wilson – *Thinking About Crime*

Poverty, rationality, community and crime

In *Thinking About Crime* (1975), James Q. Wilson attacked many of what he took to be conventional views about crime amongst social scientists. He denies that trying to get rid of poverty will lead to major reductions in crime. He argues that, in the 1960s in the USA, major anti-poverty programmes were accompanied by enormous increases in the amount of crime. He therefore believes that crime can neither be explained nor tackled by welfare programmes or policies designed to redistribute wealth and income. He points out that many poor people (for example, those who are elderly or sick) do not commit crimes, and so poverty itself cannot be considered a cause of crime.

Wilson concentrates particularly on what he calls 'predatory street crime', such as burglary, robbery, theft and murder. He argues that the general public are far more concerned about such crimes than they are about victimless crime or white-collar crime. Furthermore, street crimes are particularly important because they undermine communities, and successful communities are the best protection against rising crime.

Wilson sees crime as being the result of rational calculations. People will commit crime if the likely benefits exceed the likely costs. This might suggest that harsher sentences and more police are the answer to crime. From this viewpoint you might think that, if punishments were greater and there was more chance of being caught, then people would commit fewer crimes. However, Wilson believes that such an approach can have only a limited impact. In reality, the chances of getting caught for a particular crime are quite small. If offenders do not believe that they are going to get caught, or if punishments only take place long after offences, then even severe penalties will not deter people. Certain and swift penalties are likely to be effective, but, until they can be assured by the criminal justice system, other types of measure are also needed.

There are other ways of changing the balance between the gains and losses of committing crimes. One example is the prescription of methadone to heroin addicts. This offers addicts an alternative and less destructive substitute drug, which helps to limit the side-effects of giving up heroin. Combined with a clampdown on the supply of heroin, leading to an increase in price, the heroin problem can be contained. The costs of taking the drug are increased, while the costs of giving up are reduced. At the same time, former addicts have more chance to enjoy the benefits of a conventional lifestyle.

Another effective way of dealing with crime is to try to prevent the disintegration of communities. This is more effective than trying to rely upon deterrent sentencing. Where strong communities exist, they can deter crime, because people who are disgraced by being found to be involved in crime will lose their standing in the community. Where a community is strong, this loss will be important to people and they will try to avoid it. The problem is that crime itself undermines communities. Wilson says:

> *Predatory street crime does not merely victimize individuals, it impedes and, in the extreme case, even prevents the formation and maintenance of community. By disrupting the delicate nexus of ties, formal and informal, by which we are all linked with our neighbours, crime atomizes society and makes its members mere individual calculators estimating their own advantage.*
>
> Wilson, 1975, p. 21

This tends to lead to even higher crime rates. In the absence of a community, people no longer gain by conforming to the community's values.

Broken windows

In a later article written with George Kelling, Wilson spells out how to avoid the collapse of community as a consequence of criminality (Wilson and Kelling, 1982). They believe that it is crucial to try to maintain the character of neighbourhoods and prevent them from deteriorating. If a single window, broken by vandals, goes unmended; if incivilities such as rudeness and rowdiness on the streets go unchallenged; then problems will quickly grow. More windows will be vandalized, unruly youths will start hanging around on the streets, and law-abiding citizens will become afraid to go out. Freed from close observation by respectable members of the community, those inclined to criminality will commit more and more street crimes.

On the other hand, if residents believe that attempts are being made to maintain law and order, they will be more likely to report crime and discourage incivilities and anti-social behaviour in public places. Informal social controls will be maintained, and street crime will not get out of hand. The crucial role of the police, then, is to stop an area from deteriorating by clamping down on the first signs of undesirable behaviour. They should try to keep drunks, prostitutes, drug addicts and vandals off the streets. They should try to make law-abiding citizens feel safe. Their role is to maintain public law and order in areas where it has yet to break down. Controversially, Wilson and Kelling believe that it is a waste of valuable resources to put much effort into the worst inner-city areas. Once law and order have broken down, the police are unlikely to be able to restore it by arresting people. Their time is better spent concentrating on those areas where there is still hope.

Wilson and Hernstein – *Crime and Human Nature*

In a more recent book written with Richard Hernstein (Wilson and Hernstein, 1985), Wilson's work has taken a slightly different tack. Wilson and Hernstein claim that there is a substantial biological element in causing crime. They argue that some people are born with a predisposition towards crime. Their potential for criminality is more likely to be realized if they are not properly socialized. If parents fail to teach them right from wrong, and particularly if they fail to punish them immediately for misbehaving, those who are prone to crime become much more likely to commit criminal acts in later life. In close-knit nuclear families, children can be conditioned to have a conscience, which will keep them out of trouble with the law. Where such families are absent (for example, in single-parent families), effective socialization is unlikely. Furthermore, they believe that the quality of socialization has declined with the development of a more permissive society in which anything goes.

Despite the role they see for biology and socialization, Wilson and Hernstein still believe that people possess free will. Ultimately they choose whether to commit crimes, by weighing up the costs and benefits. Unfortunately, an over-generous welfare system discourages people from putting in the hard work necessary to hold down a job. It is too easy to live off benefits. At the same time, in an increasingly affluent society the potential gains from crime are constantly increasing. For many people the benefits of crime come to outweigh the costs, and the crime rate rises.

In dealing with such problems the authorities should be pragmatic. Just as they should concentrate on neighbourhoods which have a chance of being saved, so they should concentrate on individuals who can be turned away from crime. Habitual and professional criminals may be beyond redemption, and for them lengthy sentences may be the only answer. For others, early intervention can be effective in deterring them from taking up crime on a more permanent basis.

Evaluation of right realism

Some aspects of right realist thinking have been influential. In parts of both the USA and Britain 'Zero Tolerance' policing has been influenced by the idea that it is effective to clamp down at the first sign that an area is deteriorating. The idea of Zero Tolerance is that, by proceeding against minor offences, the police will discourage the people in a locality from moving on to more serious crime. However, in a review of research on the ideas of Wilson and Kelling, Roger Matthews found little evidence that tolerating broken windows and public incivilities led to an increase in crime (Matthews, 1992). Matthews argued that the level of incivility was determined by the level of crime, and not the other way round.

Stephen Jones (1998) argues that factors such as lack of investment are far more important in determining whether a neighbourhood declines. Jones also argues that the approach advocated by Wilson and Kelling would lead to an unfair criminal justice system. The police would concentrate their attention on minor offenders, and sometimes on people who have not broken the law at all but are merely rude or unruly. More serious offenders would be given less police attention and would therefore be more likely to get away with their offences. Furthermore, even if particular neighbourhoods could be made more orderly, there is a danger that the uncivil, disorderly and criminal members would simply move their activities to a neighbouring area with a less strong sense of community.

Jones is just as critical of the work of Wilson and Hernstein. He dismisses the biological elements of their theory as based upon outdated and already discredited theories. He argues that they ignore issues of class, ethnicity and gender, fail to consider the role of inequality and unemployment in causing crime, and neglect white-collar and corporate crimes (many of which can be very harmful). He points out that, in the USA, elements of a right realist approach have been adopted, For example, repeat offenders have become subject to the 'three strikes and you're out rule' in some states. This stipulates that after three serious offences an offender should automatically get a life sentence. However, despite such measures and a rapid increase in levels of imprisonment, the crime rate has risen inexorably in the USA. This comes as no surprise to the next group of theorists we will consider, for they concentrate on the very issues that Jones accuses right realists of neglecting.

Marketization, globalization, inequality and crime

Some left realists, such as Jock Young, have touched upon how changes in Western societies in the 1980s and 1990s might have encouraged rises in the crime rates. These issues have been developed further by sociologists considering the impact of marketization, globalization and rising inequality on society. These themes have generally been developed by left-of-centre sociologists sympathetic to the view that the New Right policies of political leaders such as Margaret Thatcher and Ronald Reagan have done immense harm. Politically, their views tend to stand

somewhere between those of Marxists and left realists: they tend to want more radical changes than those prescribed by left realists, but they stop well short of advocating a total transformation of society. They tend to refer to themselves as social democratic or socialist criminologists, or sociologists of crime and deviance They are particularly critical of the increasing importance of market forces in Western capitalist societies, and have analysed the impact this has had on society in general and crime in particular.

Ian Taylor – *The Political Economy of Crime*

Ian Taylor argues that:

> In Britain, as in the United States, an understanding of the pattern of crime is inextricably connected to an understanding of the political economy, not just of unemployment, but more broadly of the new inequality characteristic of free market societies.
>
> Taylor, 1997, p. 285

Furthermore, he does not believe that such changes are confined to Britain and the USA. They are also typical of Europe. He says:

> As we approach the end of the century, the advance of 'economic liberalism' – or of a free market, untrammelled (and, indeed, encouraged) by Governments – is observable right across Europe – from Ireland to Russia, from Spain to 'social-democratic' Scandinavia.
>
> Taylor, 1998a, p. 19

Taylor is interested in how changes in the global economy and the ways in which politicians have responded to these changes have affected crime.

Social changes

Taylor identifies a number of important changes in the world economy, in the responses of governments, and in culture:

1 Multinational corporations have shifted their activities from country to country in the search for profitability. Taylor generally agrees with the theory of post-Fordism (see Chapter 10) which suggests that mass production of standardized products is no longer a viable way to ensure long-term profit. These changes have reduced the job security of full-time workers and increased the amount of part-time, temporary and insecure employment.

2 The deregulation of stock exchanges and opening-up of world markets to increased competition have made it more difficult for governments to exercise control over the economies of the countries they govern. Increased economic instability has resulted.

3 The state has reduced its role in social and economic planning, and its involvement in 'the provision of public goods in areas like health and welfare, transport, housing and urban planning' (Taylor, 1997). Some of these areas have been increasingly opened up to market forces and competition, and there have been cut-backs in the provision of welfare.

4 The European Community has increasingly become an exclusively economic community, which puts primary emphasis upon economic growth and, in particular, on trying to gain an increasing share of world markets. Ruggiero, South and Taylor comment

that, in Europe, 'the emphasis on the market is leaving little space for the development of public and state institutions, and for their consequent production of social cohesion and social justice' (Ruggiero, South and Taylor, 1998). Instead it has become 'dominated by corporations, monopolies and oligarchies'.

5 These changes have resulted in a change in society's cultures towards marketization. Increasingly, ordinary members of society are encouraged to see social life in market terms – to calculate the economic costs and benefits of making particular decisions. This includes criminals. People are also encouraged to see themselves as consumers who are entitled to be able to buy what they want. In the media, in particular, there is:

> a discourse which identifies the viewer or the listener as a consumer of 'goods', and which glorifies the idea of choice across a range of different market places (unlimited tourist experiences, multiple channel television; a range of private health and personal insurance schemes, etc.).
>
> Taylor, 1998a, p. 20

Taylor does not believe that marketization and the idea of the consumer completely pervade European societies, but he does believe that they are increasingly influential.

These changes have had a profound impact on crime.

The impact on crime

Marketization and opportunities for criminality

The development of capitalism has produced new opportunities for criminal activity. The deregulation of financial markets has provided increased opportunities for crimes such as insider trading, where financiers use privileged knowledge of proposed takeovers to make a financial killing. Taylor (1997) lists numerous examples, including the case of the Wall Street stockbrokers, Drexel, Burnham and Lambert. They were accused of manipulating the US stock market and committing various frauds and, in 1990, agreed to pay $650 million to the Securities and Exchange Commission as punishment for their activities. In Britain, the collapse of Barings Bank in 1996, after their futures trader, Nick Leeson, had lost some £860 million, is perhaps the best-known example of financial crime. Deregulation has also encouraged the development of 'tax havens', such as the Cayman Islands, which are not just used for avoiding tax, but also for laundering and hiding money gained through criminal activities.

According to Taylor, marketization has also increased opportunities for various types of crime based directly upon the growth of market, consumer societies. Examples include insurance fraud by claimants and salespeople, and 'VAT, customs and pension scheme fraud' (Taylor, 1997). The development of the European Community has provided enormous scope for defrauding the European Commission of money by making false claims for various subsidies and other payments. Taylor quotes an estimate that the European Commission loses some $7 billion per year due to fraud.

Changes in employment and unemployment

Other crimes are related to the changing nature of employment and unemployment. Taylor (1998b) believes that there has been a fundamental shift in employment patterns in capitalist societies. Both mass manufacturing and the public sector have experienced substantial job losses, even in the most successful capitalist countries such as Germany. Furthermore, there is little prospect of anything like a return to full employment. Taylor notes that the latest economic thinking suggests that Britain could enjoy economic growth of 3 per cent a year, without any increase in employment opportunities. 'Jobless growth' can take place because high technology businesses can meet rising demand through the use of new technology, without taking on more workers. Many of the jobs that are created are flexible, temporary or part-time. Taylor agrees that there has been a shift towards post-Fordist employment patterns.

These changes have two main effects:

1 In the areas most affected by unemployment, Taylor describes 'the massively destructive effects that this joblessness clearly has had on the self respect of individuals and communities'. This effect has been so strong because unemployment has become a more or less permanent feature of some areas. There is little hope of a major improvement, and the longer high levels of unemployment last, the greater the cumulative effects. Lack of opportunity and hope leads some to turn to crime. Taylor points out that officially-recorded burglary increased by 122 per cent between 1979 and 1991, theft/handling stolen goods by 95 per cent, and robberies by 262 per cent.

2 Changing patterns of work have created more opportunities and incentives for criminal activity based on work. Ruggiero, South and Taylor (1998) believe that subcontracting encourages the employment of people who are working illegally, such as illegal immigrants, those who are fraudulently claiming benefit, or those who are employed in conditions or at wage levels which fail to conform to national laws. Such practices are particularly common in the clothing, food and building industries. Subcontractors often feel that

they have to break the rules so as to cut costs, in order to get and retain contracts in very competitive industries.

Materialism and inequality

While the precise nature of employment opportunities is related to particular types of crime, the overall increase in criminality is underpinned by growing materialism and widening inequality. On the one hand, success is increasingly portrayed in terms of achieving a lifestyle associated with the consumption of expensive consumer goods. Taylor says:

> *Television programmes and magazines (for example* Hello! *magazine, the quintessential product of our times) seem obsessed by the lifestyles of individuals who have been successful in business or the media; great interest is shown in the material goods that have been acquired by the successful (from items of clothing to cars) and in the various pleasures of personal consumption in which they indulge.*
>
> Taylor, 1998b

On the other hand, inequalities have widened rapidly. For example, Taylor quotes British government figures showing that, in 1988-9, the most affluent 20 per cent of the population received 41 per cent of national income, compared to 35 per cent ten years earlier. Meanwhile, the share of the bottom 10 per cent fell from around 10 per cent to 6.9 per cent over the same decade. Taylor sees the prevalence of crimes such as car theft as related to these changes. Stealing a car allows someone to possess one of the most highly prized of consumer goods, even if only on a temporary basis.

Drugs and globalization

Perhaps the area of crime where globalization and marketization have had the biggest impact is the drugs trade. Drawing on Mike Davis's book *City of Quartz* (1988), Taylor (1997) argues that cities such as Los Angeles have been badly affected by deindustrialization and lack of opportunities for young working-class men. At the same time, the culture of entrepreneurship encouraged many young blacks, who confronted the additional problem of racism, to pursue illegitimate opportunities in the drugs business. In the 1980s, new opportunities opened up in Los Angeles because of a shift in the 'cocaine trail' from Florida to California. As crack cocaine became increasingly popular, there were opportunities to set up 'crack houses' in which crack was distilled and cut. Towards the end of the 1980s it was estimated that there were more than 10,000 members of drugs gangs in Los Angeles, and about one gang-related killing per day.

But it was not just poverty and inequality in inner cities and the culture of entrepreneurship which encouraged the drugs trade – there were also factors connected to globalization. In a globalized economy, countries such as Peru, Colombia, Sri Lanka and Burma have been left behind. Some Third World countries such as Brazil, Mexico, South Korea and Taiwan have developed substantial industries, but other countries have not. The less successful countries have turned to the production of drugs, because crops from which drugs are derived require little technology or investment, and can command high prices when used to produce drugs. Meanwhile, the massive profits of the global drugs trade can be hidden in the growing offshore tax havens such as the Cayman Islands.

Dealing with crime

Taylor accepts that left realists have provided some useful suggestions as to how to deal with the crime problem. These include greater police accountability and a multi-agency approach to dealing with problems (see pp. 396–7). However, he thinks that more emphasis needs to be placed on:

> 'the big issues' – the realities of market society with all its social and cultural effects (joblessness; the homelessness, poverty and deprivation) at the heart of civil society; the massive subversion of institutions, especially local authorities but also the whole apparatus of welfare state provision with respect to health, income support, and so on that until the late 1970s were working, however imperfectly, in the public interest.

> Taylor, 1998b, p. 253

But Taylor does not believe there can simply be a return to the past. Too much has changed to make that possible. Nevertheless, he does believe that there is a need to try to 'reinvent the lost sense of community, public civility and/or sense of shared citizenship that characterised English life before the free market experiment'. One way to move towards achieving this would be to try to restructure the labour market in the hope that more people would find employment and thus gain a role in community life. He advocates the adoption of a Europe-wide four-day week, creating a need for millions more employees.

Taylor is critical of right-wing policies which simply advocate locking up more criminals. Instead he supports greater public investment in crime prevention. He gives the example of a 1980s programme on the Paris Metro, in which redecoration, the frequent removal of litter, and patrolling by security officers greatly improved the environment and helped to cut crime. Taylor believes that, in

Britain, free-market ideas have become so entrenched that it is difficult to get any sort of public expenditure on the type of scheme adopted on the Paris Metro. He believes that effective measures to deal with crime are unlikely, unless that culture is changed.

Evaluation of Taylor

Taylor's work has the great merit of trying to explain crime in the context of important changes in capitalist societies. Unlike many previous theorists, he does not try to develop a general theory of crime, which could be applicable to any place or time, but he discusses it in the context of recent trends towards globalization and marketization. Furthermore, many of his arguments seem very plausible. However, he does tend to produce rather generalized arguments which lack a detailed examination of criminal motivation. It is therefore difficult to evaluate how directly any increase in criminality can be linked to the changes he discusses.

Furthermore, some of his suggested solutions to crime seem open to criticism. The adoption of a four-day week in Europe might harm the competitiveness of European countries, since employers might have to turn to less well qualified and more inexperienced workers to make up for the shortfall in labour. In areas where there is a shortage of skilled workers there might be problems in meeting the demand for certain skills. While it might be seen as desirable to reinvent a sense of common citizenship, it is difficult to see how it can be achieved if marketization has advanced as far as Taylor believes.

Elliot Currie – lessons from the United States

The crime problem in the USA

The American sociologist Elliot Currie has tried to provide 'Lessons from the United States' in explaining crime in Europe (Currie, 1998). Currie argues that 'we in the United States constitute a sort of natural laboratory – an ongoing experiment in the social and economic consequences of market-driven social policy'. Like Ian Taylor, Currie argues that marketization has had a major impact and has been largely responsible for rising crime. He points out that, according to official figures, American 15–24-year-olds are 73 times more likely to be murdered than their counterparts in Austria, 44 times more likely than in Japan, and 20 times more likely than in Britain. The prison population of the USA is more than three times greater per head of population than in Britain (which itself has the highest rate of imprisonment in Europe). The US prison population exceeded one million people in 1993 and has continued to rise. Despite this, crime, particularly violent crime, has carried on increasing, and Currie describes the USA as 'a country reeling, saddened and sickened by this plague of violence'.

Market society

Currie attributes these trends directly to economic and social policies that were introduced by Presidents Reagan and Bush in the 1980s and early 1990s. These policies led to the establishment of what Currie calls a market society. A market society is more than a society in which market mechanisms, such as the use of supply and demand, are used to run economic affairs. In a market society, 'the pursuit of private gain increasingly becomes the organising principle for all areas of social life … all other principles of social or institutional organisation become eroded or subordinated to the overarching one of private gain' (Currie, 1998). People come to depend on the market to meet their psychic and cultural needs as well as their economic ones. Thus they increasingly gain a sense of identity and personal satisfaction from the consumption of consumer goods. Currie does not believe that any society conforms perfectly to his description of a market society, but he sees the USA as coming closest, and believes it has moved ever closer to that description over recent years.

The links between market society and increasing crime

Currie believes that there are five main interlinked reasons why market society leads to high crime rates:

1 Currie argues that 'Market society promotes crime by increasing inequality and concentrated economic development.' According to Currie, there was an unprecedented increase in economic inequality in the USA during the 1980s and 1990s. For example, he quotes figures showing that the top 1 per cent of income earners in the USA enjoyed an 85 per cent rise in their pre-tax income in the 1980s, while the poorest 20 per cent had a decline in real incomes of 12 per cent. The tax burden of the rich was cut, that of the poor increased. He attributes this to changes in the labour market as well as government policy. The number of very well-paid jobs has increased, but so has the number of very poorly-paid and insecure jobs. Legislation has lowered the real value of the legal minimum wage; some jobs have been moved to low-wage economies in Asia and the Caribbean; and unions have become too weak to bargain effectively for their members. Faced with restricted opportunities to escape from poverty by legitimate means, the poor increasingly turn to crime.

2 Currie says that 'Market society promotes crime by eroding the capacity of local communities to provide "informal" support, mutual provision and effective socialisation and supervision of the young.' He argues that, in the USA, rising housing costs, combined with the loss of full-time employment opportunities, have made some neighbourhoods socially unstable. There are high rates of geographical mobility out of many low-income areas, which makes it hard for a sense of community to develop. Poor people become concentrated in the cheapest areas of cities and their poverty acts as a drain on their ability to look after their children adequately. They are constantly struggling to make ends meet, and most of their neighbours are in the same position. People cannot afford to help each other out. Economic strain and social disorganization (the lack of a stable community) combine to produce high crime rates.

3 Currie's third claim is that 'Market society promotes crime by stressing and fragmenting the family.' Currie notes that conservative writers on crime have often blamed inadequate families for high crime rates, but, to Currie, it is the stresses of market society which prevent families from coping and surviving. The lack of employment for less-skilled men reduces the pool of marriageable men in low-income areas. For low-income families it is often necessary for both partners to work, and sometimes for each to have to try to hold down more than one job at a time. A single salary is unlikely to meet their needs. Single parents have a particular struggle trying to earn enough to support their children. This leads to a lack of leisure time, and parents being absent from home and their communities for much of the week. The resulting strains can lead to family break-up or the inadequate socialization of children. Parents are 'burdened by overwork' and become unable to contribute to or benefit from informal support networks with other parents.

4 Fourth, Currie says, 'Market society promotes crime by withdrawing public provision of basic services from those it has already stripped of livelihoods, economic security and "informal" communal support.' Benefits in the USA and in Britain have been cut. According to Currie, they are now at a level where they are insufficient to raise families dependent on them out of poverty. Furthermore, cuts in public services lead to the withdrawal of preventative health and mental health care and drug rehabilitation programmes. Social services are also less able to intervene to prevent child abuse. The lack of resources for social services stores up problems which in the end produce a higher crime rate.

5 The final link between market society and crime is: 'Market society promotes crime by magnifying a culture of Darwinian competition for status and resources and by urging a level of consumption that

it cannot provide for everyone through legitimate channels.' This claim has some similarities to Robert Merton's anomie theory (see pp. 354-6), but writers like Currie and Ian Taylor believe that the competitive culture has developed much further than it had when Merton was writing in the 1930s. According to Currie, by the 1990s the dominant values involved 'the consumerist values of immediate gratification in the pursuit of material satisfaction – some American delinquents will cheerfully acknowledge that they blew someone away for their running shoes'. The emphasis on consumerism leads to a chronic neglect of other values which might encourage 'social order and personal security'. The values of material success and consumption particularly affect the young and, for the more disadvantaged youth, the increased emphasis on consumption has coincided with a reduction in opportunities for material success. Currie describes this as 'a recipe for disaster', a disaster which has already happened in the USA and which is increasingly affecting Europe.

Evaluation of Currie

Currie puts forward a powerful and plausible argument about the links between market society and criminality. However, he fails to back up his arguments with much evidence. For example, he details no research which shows the increased influence of consumer values amongst the young, or which shows that community life and parenting have been undermined by social and economic changes. Currie tends to assume that stronger communities and better parents existed before the 1980s – an assumption which should have been backed up by some research.

However, some researchers have been carrying out empirical research into the links between market economies and crime. John Hagan (1994) has reviewed American research and has found ample evidence for the sorts of links proposed by Currie. Hagan believes that concentrated areas of poverty, increasing race-linked inequality, and increased residential segregation of the deprived have all been caused by the adoption of free-market policies. To Hagan, these processes have led to certain areas being deprived of the social capital (such as job opportunities, networks of contacts with potential employers, and stable families) which makes young people more likely to seek non-criminal careers. Hagan quotes a number of ethnographic and qualitative studies, all of which seem to support the contention that growing inequality is linked to growing crime.

Some support for the idea that crime can be linked to marketization can also be found in British studies. One such study will now be examined.

Dick Hobbs and Colin Dunningham – entrepreneurship and glocal organized crime

Entrepreneurial criminals and crime networks

In an ethnographic study of organized crime in Britain, conducted during the 1990s, Dick Hobbs and Colin Dunningham examine how criminal careers are related to wider economic changes (Hobbs and Dunningham, 1998). They argue that organized crime increasingly involves individuals together in loose-knit networks, who treat their criminal career rather like they would a business career. They are constantly on the look-out for new business opportunities, and often mix legitimate and illegitimate enterprise. Just as Fordist mass production has given way to post-Fordist flexible production in the formal economy (see Chapter 10 for a discussion of Fordism and post-Fordism), similar changes have taken place in organized crime. The large criminal organizations of the 1960s (such as those of the Krays and the Richardson brothers in London) have largely disappeared.

As part of their study, Hobbs and Dunningham carried out research in a depressed post-industrial town, which they called 'Downtown'. They found no evidence that there was any large criminal organization in the area. Instead, individuals with extensive criminal contacts acted as 'hubs', connecting the diverse activities of different loose groupings of criminals. Nevertheless, Hobbs and Dunningham see criminal activities as being firmly rooted in local contexts. Criminal entrepreneurs develop their careers, at least initially, in local areas. They rely very much on networks of contacts to find opportunities to make money. Eventually some become involved in wider networks – for example, those involving drug smuggling. They may even emigrate, but generally they retain strong local links. Thus, Hobbs and Dunningham do not believe that organized crime is increasingly dominated by large multinational or even global criminal organizations (such as the Mafia). Instead it works as a glocal system. That is, there are some global connections involved but it remains locally based. They particularly studied criminals with contacts in Downtown, the run-down area in which their study was based. Hobbs and Dunningham illustrate their claims with a number of case studies.

Case studies

Bill and Ben started their careers separately as burglars. They ended up in prison together, and on their release started working together stealing from building sites. They quickly progressed to stealing plant machinery from sites and developed a close relationship with building workers and contractors in the local area, to whom they sold most of the stuff they had stolen. This proved profitable and, after about five years, Ben diversified into property development, arranging fraudulent mortgage deals, and the importation of cannabis. However, disputes with business partners led to the collapse of the cannabis business and, faced with financial problems, Ben had to go back to being a small-time crook.

Bill was more successful. He bought a share in a pub which proved very profitable. He made a lot of money stealing from lorry compounds. He would drive a lorry equipped with false numberplates into a secure compound and pay for the night's stay. He would then leave, but a number of associates would hide in the lorry. When the security guards had gone, they would proceed to break into other lorries and move goods from them into their own lorry. Bill would return at opening time and drive away with the now lucratively laden vehicle. Bill built up contacts with local businesses and criminals through his pub and started supplying imported amphetamines. He also got involved in selling stolen designer clothes and CDs.

Dave Peters was one of the most successful criminals they studied. He started his career by collaborating with various criminal organizations which imported cannabis. He soon progressed to running a team of burglars and became involved in managing a chain of pubs. He made so much money that he moved to the Costa del Sol from where he ran a shipping business. Amongst other activities, the shipping business supplied Dave Peters's growing chain of clubs which he bought throughout Europe. Despite these international connections, he also kept a warehouse near Downtown, which acted as a centre for the disposal of stolen goods.

Ned was another successful criminal. To those who did not know him better, he was a successful local businessman who drove a Mercedes, lived in an expensive house, and spent much of his time at a local leisure club. However, Ned had made much of his money by fixing greyhound races, dealing in cannabis through a local network, and disposing of stolen goods. He was given a nine-month prison sentence when the police found him in possession of stolen whisky. After that, he changed to a career as a plumber and was able to secure large contracts by using bribes. He became involved with a gang who carried out armed robberies, but he feared another gaol term and took to acting as a police informer as insurance against further convictions. His legitimate business interests flourished, but he continued occasional involvement in activities such as drug importation, disposing of stolen goods, and selling counterfeit currency.

Conclusion

Hobbs and Dunningham believe that their study shows how legal and illegal businesses become intermeshed in local entrepreneurial networks. While they tie into broader networks, local contacts and knowledge remain crucial to these criminals. The criminals described in the case studies are in many ways exemplary entrepreneurs. They are very flexible and are constantly looking for profitable openings in various markets. They are products of a 1980s and 1990s enterprise culture which has opened up illegitimate opportunities in some of the places where legal paths to success have become severely restricted.

Evaluation

All of the studies examined in this section have drawn upon older theories of crime and deviance. The Marxist critique of capitalism, Merton's discussion of anomie, and Cloward and Ohlin's discussion of illegitimate opportunities have all influenced the writers discussed above. However, Taylor, Currie, Hagan, and Hobbs and Dunningham all try to place their theories and studies in the context of changes in contemporary economies, and they all believe that social changes have strengthened the link between crime and capitalism. While the theories are not particularly original, they do seem to highlight important changes in the nature of crime. They would be more convincing if they used detailed comparisons with the 1970s and earlier to show that the criminality they try to explain is quantitatively or qualitatively different from what has gone before. If they could do this, they would be able to demonstrate more convincingly that marketization is responsible for much of the contemporary crime 'problem'.

Gender and crime

Gender and patterns of crime

Writing in 1977, Carol Smart stated:

Our knowledge is still in its infancy. In comparison with the massive documentation on all aspects of male delinquency and criminality, the amount of work carried out on the area of women and crime is extremely limited.

Smart, 1977

She put forward a number of reasons for this neglect:

1 Women tend to commit fewer crimes than men, so female offenders are seen as less of a problem for society.

2 Most crimes committed by women seem to be of a comparatively trivial nature and may therefore be considered unworthy of research.

3 Sociology and criminology have both tended to be dominated by males. In the main they have been studied by men and the studies have been about men.

4 Traditional criminology is motivated by a desire to control behaviour that is regarded as problematic. Since women's criminality has been seen as much less problematic than men's, it has received correspondingly less attention.

Although the years since Smart's study have seen much more interest in the study of female crime and deviance, some general theories in this area of sociology continue to neglect gender as a factor influencing criminality. This is despite the fact that official figures suggest that gender is perhaps the most significant single factor in whether an individual is convicted of crime. Sociological theories which fail to explain this relationship could therefore be seen as inadequate.

According to official statistics, in 1996, 261,100 men were found guilty of indictable offences and 142,600 were cautioned. In the same year, 38,000 women were found guilty and 48,200 were cautioned (Annual Abstract of Statistics, HMSO, London, 1998, pp. 88-9). Based on these figures, in 1996 just 17.6 per cent of known offenders were female. Figure 6.7 shows that, in all age groups, males are far more likely to be found guilty of, or cautioned for, indictable offences.

Table 6.3 shows the percentages of males and females, in different age groups, found guilty of, or cautioned for, indictable offences. It also gives the numbers of crimes committed by males and females in all age groups. The table shows that, in 1996, males were 64 times more likely than women to be found guilty of, or cautioned for, sexual offences; 22 times as likely for burglary; 12 times as likely for robbery; more than 9 times as likely for criminal damage; and more than 5 times as likely for violence against the person.

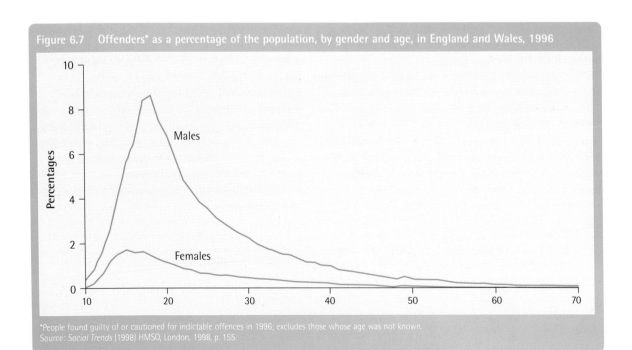

Figure 6.7   Offenders* as a percentage of the population, by gender and age, in England and Wales, 1996

*People found guilty of or cautioned for indictable offences in 1996; excludes those whose age was not known.
Source: *Social Trends* (1998) HMSO, London, 1998, p. 155.

| Table 6.3 | Offenders found guilty of, or cautioned for, indictable offences in England and Wales: by gender, type of offence and age, 1996 | | | | | |

	Percentages					
	10-13	14-17	18-20	21-34	35 and over	All aged 10 and over (= 100%) (thousands)
Males						
Theft and handling stolen goods	7	24	16	38	16	153.7
Drug offences	-	12	23	54	11	72.8
Violence against the person	4	22	15	42	17	43.9
Burglary	8	31	20	36	5	40.5
Criminal damage	8	24	16	39	13	11.7
Sexual offences	4	14	7	30	45	6.4
Robbery	6	38	22	30	5	6.0
Other indictable offences	1	8	16	56	19	70.1
All indictable offences	4	20	17	44	15	405.1
Females						
Theft and handling stolen goods	10	26	12	34	18	54.5
Drug offences	-	9	18	57	16	8.7
Violence against the person	8	34	10	34	14	7.9
Burglary	15	39	14	25	6	1.8
Criminal damage	7	29	10	37	17	1.2
Sexual offences	10	18	11	32	29	0.1
Robbery	8	51	17	20	4	0.5
Other indictable offences	1	11	15	54	20	11.5
All indictable offences	8	23	13	39	17	86.3

Source: *Social Trends* (1998) HMSO, London, p.161.

Such figures are neither unusual nor surprising. In Britain, there has been a long-standing tendency for men to commit many more crimes than women, and a similar pattern is repeated in many other countries. Frances Heidensohn (1997) quotes American research which shows that, in 1993, females accounted for only 24 per cent of arrests of those aged under 18, and 19 per cent of those in older age groups. Her own research, conducted in the mid-1980s, found that females made up 20 per cent or less of offenders in a variety of European countries. Heidensohn also quotes a number of historical studies of offenders in Britain, which show women accounting for small proportions of the total number of law-breakers. Thus, one study of the Home Counties in 1782-7 found that women made up just 12 per cent of those convicted; another found that women accounted for a steady 17 per cent of convictions from 1860 to 1890. However, one study, which examined cases at the Old Bailey from 1687-1912, did find that 45 per cent of defendants

were women (Feeley and Little, 1991, quoted in Heidensohn, 1997). This study may be unrepresentative because it concentrated on one court.

Official figures such as these have raised three main questions about gender and crime:

1 Do women really commit fewer crimes than men, or are the figures misleading? Some sociologists have suggested that women's offences are consistently under-recorded by the authorities.

2 Although women continue to commit comparatively few crimes, some people have suggested that the proportion of crimes committed by women has been increasing. According to a number of commentators, this alleged increase has resulted from 'women's liberation'. Is this so?

3 Why do those women who do break the law commit crimes?

In the following sections we examine the answers that sociologists have given to these questions.

Official statistics, criminality and gender

Pollak – the 'masked' female offender

Writing in 1950, Otto Pollak argued that official statistics on gender and crime were highly misleading. He claimed that the statistics seriously underestimated the extent of female criminality. From an examination of official figures in a number of different countries, he claimed to have identified certain crimes that are usually committed by women but which are particularly likely to go unreported.

1   He assumed that nearly all offences of shoplifting and all criminal abortions were carried out by women, and then asserted that such crimes were unlikely to come to the attention of the authorities.

2   He also argued that many unreported crimes were committed by female domestic servants.

3   Pollak accepted official definitions of crime when he pointed out all the offences of prostitution that were not reported. Male clients of prostitutes were assumed to have engaged in no illegal activities.

4   He even went so far as to suggest that women's domestic roles gave them the opportunity to hide crimes such as poisoning relatives and sexually abusing their children.

Pollak then went on to give reasons as to why there should be an under-recording of female crime:

1   He argued that the police, magistrates and other law enforcement officials tend to be men. Brought up to be chivalrous, they are usually lenient with female offenders, so fewer women appear in the statistics. However, he regarded this as only a minor factor.

2   Second, and to Pollak more important, women are particularly adept at hiding their crimes. He attributed this to female biology. Women have become accustomed to deceiving men because traditional taboos prevent women from revealing pain and discomfort resulting from menstruation. Furthermore, women also learn to mislead men during sex. Men cannot disguise sexual arousal when they get an erection, whereas women can take part in sexual intercourse whilst faking interest and pleasure.

Criticisms of Pollak

Not surprisingly, Pollak's totally inadequate analysis has been subject to fierce criticism. Frances Heidensohn (1985) points out just a few of the numerous flaws in his argument:

1   She notes that later research indicates that much shoplifting is committed by men.

2   Changes in the law have reduced the number of illegal abortions.

3   Even at the time that Pollak was writing there had been a very large reduction in the number of female domestic servants.

4   Heidensohn draws attention to the number of crimes committed against prostitutes by male customers, and the frequency of male crimes in domestic life. All the evidence indicates that men are considerably more likely than women to commit violent and sexual offences in the privacy of their home.

5   Pollak's statistical analysis is based upon little evidence and many unsupported assumptions. The same can be said of his attempt to explain the supposed 'masking' of female crime. For example, Heidensohn comments that the 'concealment of menstruation is by no means universal and changed sexual mores have long since made nonsense of his view of passive, receptive females brooding vengeance'.

Heidensohn regards Pollak's work as being based upon an unsubstantiated stereotypical image of women, and notes his unwillingness to attribute male crime to a biological predisposition to aggression and violence.

However, although the claim that women are naturally more likely to conceal crimes can be readily dismissed, the possibility that women are treated more leniently by the legal authorities warrants closer examination.

Criminality, sex and the law

In theory at least, the vast majority of laws are sex-blind: the possibility of being charged, or the type of offence for which you are charged, does not depend upon your sex. However, there are a few laws that only apply to members of one sex. For example, in Britain, only men can be convicted of rape or offences of homosexuality. On the other hand, only women can be convicted of infanticide or soliciting as prostitutes. In reality, only a very small proportion of crimes come into one of these categories and legal definitions therefore make little difference to the overall statistics for male and female crime.

Leniency towards female offenders

Since Pollak's work, there have been numerous self-report studies in which individuals are asked about what crimes they have committed. (For further comments on this type of study see pp. 368–9.) Although such studies have their methodological limitations, they do give some indication of the extent of unreported crime and the chances that different groups have of escaping the discovery and prosecution of their offences.

Some self-report studies have supported Pollak's claim that female offenders are more likely to escape conviction than males. Writing in 1981, Anne

Campbell pointed out that female suspects were more likely than male suspects to be cautioned rather than prosecuted. Official statistics show that this remains true. In 1996, of males recorded as offending, 35 per cent were cautioned and 65 per cent convicted. In the case of women, 56 per cent were cautioned and 44 per cent were convicted.

A study by Hilary Allen (1989), based upon an examination of 1987 criminal statistics, showed apparent leniency towards female offenders. For example, 73 per cent of women, but only 54 per cent of men, found guilty of indictable motoring offences, were given fines. This difference very largely resulted from more men being given prison sentences. Allen has also found evidence that women sometimes escape prison in very serious cases (including manslaughter), where a male defendant might have been expected to receive a gaol term (Allen, 1987). In 1976, Campbell compared a self-report study on her own sample of 66 urban schoolgirls, aged 16, with similar data on a sample of 397 16-year-old males, collected by West and Farrington. These sources of data showed that 1.33 offences were committed by males for every 1.0 committed by females. This contrasted with 1976 official figures on convictions, which showed 8.95 male convictions for every female conviction (Campbell, 1981).

On the surface these data provide support for the 'chivalry' thesis, which claims that police and courts are lenient towards female offenders.

Evidence against the 'chivalry' thesis

In contrast, most other researchers have not found support for the chivalry thesis. Steven Box (1981) has reviewed the data from self-report studies in Britain and the USA. Although a few of these studies indicate some leniency towards females, the majority do not. He is able to conclude that:

> the weight of evidence on women committing serious offences does not give clear support to the view that they receive differential and more favourable treatment from members of the public, police or judges.
>
> Box, 1981

He goes on to say 'it would not be unreasonable to conclude that the relative contribution females make to serious crime is fairly accurately reflected in official statistics'.

All self-report studies rely upon the respondent's ability and willingness to tell the truth. Some researchers have tried to measure crime more directly, using observation. Abigail Buckle and David P. Farrington carried out a small-scale observational study of shoplifting in a British department store in south-east England in 1981 (Buckle and Farrington, 1984). Shoplifting is one crime where numbers of female offenders nearly match numbers of male offenders in the official statistics. This study found that 2.8 per cent of the 142 males observed shoplifted, but only 1.4 per cent of the 361 females did so. Obviously this study uses far too small a sample to draw firm conclusions, but, as one of the few attempts to measure crime directly, it does provide some evidence against the chivalry thesis.

Sentencing policy

Another approach to evaluating the 'chivalry' thesis is to examine sentencing policy. In 1983, David P. Farrington and Alison Morris conducted a study of sentencing in Magistrates Courts. They started out by noting that some official figures did imply more leniency towards women. For example, in 1979, 6.6 per cent of men but only 2 per cent of women found guilty of indictable crimes were imprisoned. Farrington and Morris examined data on sentencing for 408 offences of theft in Cambridge in the same year. Some 110 of these offences were committed by women.

Although men received more severe sentences than women, the research found that the differences disappeared when the severity of offences was taken into account. Farrington and Morris concluded 'There was no independent effect of sex on sentence severity' (Farrington and Morris, 1983).

However, these findings were not replicated in a study carried out by Roger Hood in the West Midlands in 1989, which used a sample of 2,884 male and 433 female defendants in Crown Courts (Hood, 1992). Hood compared the sentencing of men and women, controlling for variables which he had found affected the sentencing of men. He found that white women were given custodial sentences 34 per cent less often than men in similar cases, and black women 37 per cent less often.

As we will discover in later sections, though, this does not necessarily mean that women are always treated sympathetically by the legal system.

Criminal justice as biased against women

A rather different point of view is put forward by those who argue that women are treated more harshly by the criminal justice system than men.

This view can be supported by evidence which suggests that male offenders are sometimes treated more sympathetically than their female victims. This is particularly the case with rape trials. Carol Smart argues that such trials 'celebrate notions of male sexual need and female sexual capriciousness' (Smart, 1989). She quotes the following statements by trial judges in rape cases in support of this claim:

*It is well known that women in particular and
small boys are likely to be untruthful and
invent stories.*

Judge Sutcliffe, 1976

*Women who say no do not always mean no. It is
not just a question of how she says it, how she
shows and makes it clear. If she doesn't want it
she only has to keep her legs shut.*

Judge Wild, 1982

*It is the height of imprudence for any girl to hitch-
hike at night. That is plain, it isn't really worth
stating. She is in the true sense asking for it.*

Judge Bertrand Richards, 1982

Quoted in Smart, 1989

Sandra Walklate (1995) believes that, in effect, it is
the female victim rather than the male suspect who
ends up on trial. Women have to establish their
respectability if their evidence is to be believed.
Walklate quotes a study by Adler (1987) which found
that women who were single mothers, had a criminal
record, were punks, had children in care, lived in a
commune or supported the Greenham Common peace
camp (an all-female protest camp against nuclear
weapons) were all regarded by courts as lacking in
respectability and therefore credibility. Walklate
agrees with Carol Smart that rape trials continue to
see things from the male point of view, which accepts
that men become unable to restrain their sexual
desires once women give them any indication they
might be available for sex.

Many researchers have claimed that men are
treated leniently in cases of domestic violence. In a
pioneering study of domestic violence by Dobash and
Dobash it was found that police officers were 'very
unlikely to make an arrest when the offender has
used violence against his wife' (Dobash and Dobash,
1979). Sandra Walklate points out that, since this
study, the police, encouraged by feminist
campaigners, have made attempts to take domestic
violence more seriously. The Metropolitan Police have
set up Domestic Violence Units to monitor the way
the police deal with such cases, and in British police
forces generally there is an increased emphasis upon
prosecuting offenders. Nevertheless, Walklate believes
that there 'is clearly a long way to go before we can
say that such policies really represent empowerment
for women'.

Double standards in criminal justice

A number of empirical studies and commentaries on
gender and crime have reached the conclusion that
males and females are treated differently and
inequitably by the justice system, but not always to
the detriment of women. Basing her arguments on a
review of available evidence, Heidensohn (1985)
suggests that women are treated more harshly when
they deviate from societal norms of female sexuality.
Sexually promiscuous girls are more likely to be
taken into care than similar boys. On the other hand,
courts may be reluctant to imprison mothers with
young children.

To Heidensohn, the justice system is influenced by
attitudes to gender in society as a whole. These are
based upon 'dual' and 'confused' assumptions about
women, which see women as 'virgin and whore,
witch and wife, Madonna and Magdalene'.

As we noted earlier, Hilary Allen's study of
sentencing (Allen, 1987, 1989) found that women
were treated quite leniently in the case of motoring
offences. She found that women were more likely to
escape with low-tariff punishments across a range of
offences and were certainly less likely to get sent to
prison. However, she also found that women were
more likely than men to be put on probation for
some offences.

Like Heidensohn, Allen argues that the policies are
tied up with conventional definitions of femininity
and masculinity. Men's offences are often put down
to aggression or greed. Men are more likely to be
fined and imprisoned partly because they are seen as
being less central to family life than women. The loss
of money from a fine or the loss of a parent through
imprisonment is regarded as less problematic for a
family if the offender is a man than if it is a woman.

Women are seen as being less inherently deviant
than men, and courts find it harder to understand
their criminal activity. Consequently courts are more
likely to order reports on female offenders in the
search for 'underlying psychological meanings'.
Probation may be used instead of a fine, with the
intention of helping the female offender. In this case,
though, what could be seen as 'chivalry' by the
courts could also be seen as disadvantaging women
and reinforcing sexist ideologies about masculinity
and femininity.

Similar conclusions are reached by Pat Carlen
(1997). She argues that:

> *the majority of British born women who go to
> prison in England, Wales and Scotland are less
> likely to be sentenced for the seriousness of their
> crimes and more according to the court's
> assessment of them as wives, mothers and
> daughters. If they are young and their parents or
> state guardians believe them to be beyond control,
> if they are single, divorced or separated from their
> husbands, or if their children are in residential
> care, they are more likely to go to prison than
> those who, though their crimes may be more
> serious, are living more conventional lives.*

Heidensohn, 1997, p. 158

Carlen quotes from her own earlier research into Scottish sheriffs (judges). In interviews, the sheriffs stated that they were unlikely to send women who were good mothers to prison, but were much more inclined to punish childless women, or women whose children were in care, with a custodial sentence.

Although women who conform to the ideals of femininity held by male judges sometimes get off relatively lightly, others are less lucky. Some alternatives to prison, such as community service, are unsuitable for women who cannot get childcare, so they tend to get prison sentences as the only practicable option. Carlen claims that some pregnant women who are very poor or homeless are sent to prison so that their children are born in what the courts see as more desirable surroundings.

If writers such as Heidensohn, Allen and Carlen are correct, then the British criminal justice system is highly gendered. That is, its decisions (whether they benefit men or women) are at least partly based on the sex and gender characteristics (as well as the class and ethnicity) of those it deals with. As such, the idea of equality before the law is an illusion.

The causes of female crime and deviance

Physiological causes

Not surprisingly, some of the earliest attempts to explain female criminality were based upon physiological or biological theories. Indeed, one of the pioneers of biological theories of male crime, Caesare Lombroso, also attempted to explain female crime. (We provide more details of Lombroso's theories on pp. 349–50.) Writing with William Ferrero in *The Female Offender*, Lombroso devoted considerable attention to comparing anatomical features of female criminals and non-criminals (Lombroso and Ferrero, 1958, first published in English 1895). For example, he reported data comparing brains and skulls, the width of cheekbones, size of jaws and even the size of the thighs of prostitutes and 'normal women'! Nevertheless, his overall argument is that, rather than being the cause of female criminality, biology tends to prevent women from becoming criminal.

Writing about male crime, Lombroso had suggested that criminals could be identified through the presence of 'stigmata' or physical abnormalities, such as having an extra toe or nipple. Lombroso and Ferrero found few examples of such abnormalities amongst female criminals. To them this suggested that most female offenders were not true, biological, criminals. They broke the law only occasionally and their crimes were not serious. They claimed that women had a deficient moral sense, and were

inclined to be vengeful and jealous, but 'In ordinary cases these defects were neutralized by piety, maternity, want of passion, sexual coldness, by weakness and an underdeveloped intelligence.'

Nevertheless, they did believe that a few women were born criminals. These women were so exceptional and started life with such 'enormous' 'wickedness' that each was 'consequently a monster'. They tended to be more masculine than other women.

Lombroso's work has long been discredited. For example, Heidensohn comments:

> *his work was fanciful rather than scientific. His detailed measurements were not subject to any tests of significance and his 'analysis' of photographs of 'fallen women' is as objective as an adjudication in a beauty contest.*
>
> Heidensohn, 1985

Such criticisms have not prevented some later sociologists from seeking biological explanations both for women's conformity, and, when it occurs, their deviance. For example, Anne Moir and David Jessel (1997) explain some violent female crime as resulting from hormonal changes associated with Premenstrual Syndrome (PMS). Most sociologists, however, have rightly focused on possible social causes of female crime.

Female crime and women's liberation

Freda Adler – the 'new female criminal'

In 1975, the American writer Freda Adler claimed that women's liberation had led to a new type of female criminal and an increase in women's contribution to crime.

Adler starts by rejecting biological theories. For example, she denies a direct link between hormones, aggression and criminality. She points out that there are 'many passive men with normal androgen levels who are less aggressive than women' (Adler, 1975). (We discuss sex and gender differences and hormones on pp. 128–9.) She argues that differences in the behaviour of males and females are socially determined, and that changes in society have led to changes in that behaviour.

Adler quotes numerous statistics which appear to show increasing female involvement in crime, particularly in some crimes which have traditionally been committed mainly by men. She says that, in the USA between 1960 and 1972, robberies by women went up 277 per cent, men's by only 169 per cent. Embezzlement by women rose by 280 per cent in the same period, whereas for men the figure rose by a mere 50 per cent. Overall arrest rates for females were rising three times as fast as those for males, and particularly quickly among female delinquents.

To Adler this suggested that future generations of adult criminals would show a narrowing gap in the crime rates of males and females. She also claimed that similar trends of rising female crime could be discerned in Western Europe, New Zealand and India.

Why, then, were women becoming so much more involved in crime? Adler believed that the main reason was that women were taking on male social roles in both legitimate and illegitimate areas of activity. She stressed the pace and extent of change saying:

> There is a tide in the affairs of women as well as men, and in the last decade it has been sweeping over the barriers which have protected male prerogatives and eroding the traditional differences which once nicely defined the gender roles.
>
> Adler, 1975

As women entered the labour force in increasing numbers, they wanted increased representation in jobs previously reserved for men. The same applied in criminal careers: 'The female criminal knows too much to pretend, or return to her former role as a second-rate criminal confined to "feminine" crimes such as shoplifting and prostitution.' Instead, women were getting involved in robbing banks, mugging, loan sharking and even murder.

Adler's views proved to be very controversial, particularly as they could be used to imply that women's liberation was a bad thing. They stimulated considerable research into the question of whether women's crime was increasing.

Carol Smart – a critique of Adler

Carol Smart is amongst those who have responded to Adler's argument (Smart, 1979). She advances the following criticisms:

1 Adler incorrectly assumes that rates of delinquency are an accurate guide to future patterns of adult crime. This is a mistake since 'It is well known that juvenile delinquency and adult crime are quite different phenomena, involving largely different personnel, different motivations and different purposes.'

2 Extending the argument to include changes in female crime rates in countries as diverse as New Zealand and India ignores 'cultural variations, different criminal codes and legal systems, different methods of collating statistics and different degrees of "emancipation" for women'.

3 Smart points out that Adler's views are largely based upon official statistics, which are notoriously unreliable.

However, Smart then goes on to claim that official figures for England and Wales do not in any case support Adler's theory about crime and emancipation. Although women's crime did increase in proportion to men's from 1965 to 1975, it had increased more rapidly from 1935 to 1946 and from 1955 to 1965, before the women's liberation movement had made significant progress.

Criticisms of Smart

Smart's own views have themselves been the subject of criticism by Roy Austin (1981). He looked more closely at the official figures used by Smart. He agreed with her observations about indictable crime in general, but found that they did not apply to Class 1 offences (violence against the person and sexual offences), nor to Class 2 offences (burglary and robbery). In both these categories, 1965-75 had shown the most rapid increase in women's crime compared to men's. Since these were just the sort of crimes that Adler had claimed would increase with female liberation, the figures undermined Smart's case.

Steven Box and Chris Hale – liberation versus marginalization

Box and Hale (1983) are rather dismissive of Smart's and Austin's attempts to determine whether female liberation leads to rising crime. They say 'the Smart–Austin disagreement is based on analyses too weak to sustain either position'. Both of them made a number of mistakes:

1 They included sexual crimes in their figures. Some of these are sex-specific or include consensual sexual acts between adults (such as homosexuality) and are not therefore relevant to the debate.

2 Neither Austin nor Smart controlled for the changing proportions of males and females in the population.

3 Neither made any attempt actually to measure female liberation.

Methods

Box and Hale set out to avoid such mistakes in their own research. They allowed for changing proportions of males and females in the population, excluded sexual crimes, and used four measures of female liberation. They took declines in the birth rate and increases in the numbers of single women as indicators of liberation, since these suggested freedom from the patriarchal family. Increasing rates of participation in the labour force and rises in the number of female graduates and undergraduates were also taken as indicators of liberation.

Box and Hale were concerned that changes in police procedures might have affected the way in which female crime was dealt with, so that women's offences had become more likely to be recorded. They therefore examined changes in the number of women police officers as a possible indicator of changing police routine.

They also noted the argument that most female offenders who committed serious crimes tended to come from lower-class backgrounds. Such women were the least likely to be touched by emancipation. It was possible, therefore, that recession and increased economic marginalization could account for any increase in female crime. Rates of female unemployment were used as a way of indicating the amount of economic marginalization amongst women.

Findings

Official figures showed a large absolute increase in female indictable crime in 1951-79 in England and Wales. However, male crimes were increasing at the same time, and the proportion of violent crimes against the person committed by women had scarcely increased. On the other hand, property crime by women had increased from 13 per cent to 22 per cent of the total.

When Box and Hale came to examine the relationship between various measures of liberation and female crime, they found little evidence that liberation was causing crime. None of the variables measuring liberation was found to be statistically significant.

However, they did detect a statistical relationship between male crime rates and those of women. This suggested that social forces which had nothing to do with female liberation were acting to push up crime rates for both sexes.

Box and Hale also found a relationship between the increasing employment of women police officers and the recording of violent crime by women. They suggested that perhaps the theory that female liberation had increased women's crime had 'sensitized' the authorities to the 'problem' and resulted in female crimes of violence becoming more likely to be recorded.

Changes in the way acts were labelled could perhaps explain such changes as there had been in the figures. Box and Hale also found a relationship between unemployment rates and crime rates amongst women. This was particularly strong for property crimes.

Reviewing the debate about female crime and women's liberation, Box concluded:

> The major factor accounting for most of the increase in property offences seems to be economic marginalization. In other words, as women become economically worse off, largely through unemployment and inadequate compensatory levels of welfare benefits, so they are less able and willing to resist the temptations to engage in property offences as a way of helping to solve their financial difficulties.

Box and Hale, 1983

Evaluation

Like all the other studies discussed in this section, Box and Hale's work relies upon official statistics and, as such, the findings can only be tentative. Nevertheless, it is more sophisticated than other studies and Box is fairly convincing when he says 'Female liberation does not appear to have been the demonic phenomenon described by criminologists and accepted by the media, police and criminal justice officials.'

Official figures do not suggest that this statement has become any less true. In 1980, women made up 17.18 per cent of those convicted or cautioned for indictable offences. The figure had increased only very marginally to 17.6 per cent by 1996.

In a study of female offenders in the USA, Meda Chesney-Lind reaches a similar conclusion (Chesney-Lind, 1997). She found no evidence of any link between women's liberation and female criminality in the 1970s, arguing that poor, marginalized women were more involved in crime than liberated women. She does find some evidence of female involvement in drug-related crime, including violent crime, in the 1990s. However, she again argues that this has nothing to do with liberation. Rather, such criminal activities by women are usually connected to prostitution; women's involvement in criminality continues to be shaped by conventional gender roles.

Pat Carlen – women, crime and poverty

Sample and methods

In 1985, Pat Carlen conducted a study of 39 women aged 15-46 who had been convicted of one or more crimes (Carlen, 1988). She carried out lengthy and in-depth unstructured taped interviews with each of the women. Most were from the London area and 20 were in a prison or youth custody centre at the time of interviewing. Most of the women were working-class (as are most women with criminal convictions) and they had committed a range of offences. Twenty-six had convictions for theft or handling stolen goods, 16 for fraud or similar offences, 15 for burglary, 14 for violence, 8 for arson, 6 for drugs offences, and 4 for prostitution-related crime.

Like Box, Carlen does not believe that liberation has resulted in an increase in crimes by women. Most of her sample had been touched little by any gains that women had experienced in, for example, access to a wider range of jobs. Instead, most had experienced their opportunities becoming increasingly restricted. Carlen argues that the working-class background of most of her sample is fairly typical of female offenders convicted of more serious crimes, although she is aware that 'white-collar' female criminals might be escaping conviction for their offences. She says 'when women do break the law those from lower socio-economic groups are more liable to criminalization than are their middle-class sisters'.

By reconstructing the lives of such women from in-depth interviewing, Carlen hoped to identify the sets of circumstances that led to their involvement in crime.

Control theory

Carlen adopts control theory as her theoretical approach. Control theory has influenced a considerable number of criminologists and was first explicitly outlined by an American sociologist, T. Hirschi, in 1969. It starts with the assumption that humans are neither naturally wicked and prone to crime, nor are they naturally virtuous and prone to conformity. Instead, humans are essentially rational and they will turn to crime when the advantages seem to outweigh the disadvantages and are more appealing than the likely rewards of conformity.

According to Carlen, working-class women have been controlled through the promise of rewards stemming from the workplace and the family. Such women are encouraged to make what she calls the 'class deal' and the 'gender deal'. The class deal offers material rewards such as consumer goods for those respectable working-class women who work dutifully for a wage. The gender deal offers 'psychological and material rewards ... emanating from either the labours or the "love" of a male breadwinner'. When these rewards are not available, or women have not been persuaded that these rewards are real or worth sacrifices, the deals break down and criminality becomes a possibility.

Factors encouraging deviance

Carlen found that the women attributed their criminality to four main factors. These were drug addiction (including alcohol), the quest for excitement, being brought up in care, and poverty. She places particular emphasis on the last two factors: very often the abuse of drugs and the desire for excitement were the consequence of being brought up in care or of being poor.

In all, 32 of the women had always been poor, 4 of the remaining 7 were unemployed at the time of

being interviewed, and only 2 had good jobs. A majority of the women (22) had spent at least part of their lives in care.

Rejection of the class deal

Poverty and being brought up in care led to the women rejecting the class and gender deals. Few of the women had experience of the possible benefits of the class deal. They had never had access to the consumer goods and leisure facilities which society portrays as representing the 'good life'.

Attempts to find a legitimate way of earning a decent living had been frustrated. For example, six of the women had been through the Youth Training Scheme, but they had returned to being unemployed at the end of their training. A number had gained qualifications in prison but had found them to be of no use in finding a job. Many had experience of day-to-day 'humiliations, delays and frustrations' in trying to claim benefits. They had 'a strong sense of injustice, oppression and powerlessness'. Crime was a way of resisting the injustices and trying to solve the problems of poverty. The women had little to lose by turning to crime, and potentially a good deal to gain.

Rejection of the gender deal

According to Carlen, women generally are deterred from committing crime because they are brought up to see themselves as the 'guardians of domestic morality'. They also have less opportunity to commit crimes because they are more closely supervised than males, first by parents and later by husbands. Patriarchal ideology promises women happiness and fulfilment from family life. For most of the women in the study, though, the gender deal had not been made, or had been rejected. They had been freed from family life, or so closely supervised that they felt oppressed by the family. Carlen says:

> when young girls have been brought up in situations where absolutely no rewards (and many severe disabilities) have been seen to emanate from familiness, when, too the technologies of gender discipline have been unusually harsh or oppressive, women's adult consciousness has been constituted within an immediate experience of the fundamental oppression inherent in the gender deal ... they have resisted it.
>
> Carlen, 1988

Some of the women had been sexually or physically abused by their fathers. Eight of them had been physically attacked by male partners. For the 22 women who had been in care there had been little opportunity to 'acquire the psychological commitment to male-related domesticity'. Spending time in care broke attachments to friends and family and reduced some of the potential social costs of isolation which could result from crime. Running away from care, usually with no money, or leaving care, sometimes homeless and unemployed, could easily lead on to crime. Carlen describes the situation of women leaving care in the following way:

Ill-equipped (both materially and by their previous experiences) for living on their own, many of the women had soon begun to think that crime was the only route to a decent standard of living. They had nothing to lose and everything to gain.

Carlen, 1988

Convictions and prison sentences merely served to restrict the women's legal opportunities even further and make the attractions of crime greater.

Conclusion

Carlen's study was based upon a small sample of mainly working-class women involved in fairly serious crimes. It is therefore dangerous to generalize from her findings. Nevertheless, her study does provide strong support for the view that criminal behaviour becomes more likely when society's mechanisms of social control break down. Other sociologists have examined social control mechanisms to explain why women seem so much more likely to conform than men.

Female conformity

Frances Heidensohn – women and social control

As earlier sections have indicated, however inaccurate official statistics may be, it seems clear that women do commit fewer serious crimes than men. Frances Heidensohn (1985) has tried to explain why this should be so. Like Pat Carlen, she uses control theory as the basis of her explanation. Building on the work of other sociologists, she argues that male-dominated patriarchal societies control women more effectively than they do men, making it more difficult for women to break the law. Control operates at home, in public and at work.

Control of women at home

Being a housewife directly restricts women by limiting their opportunities for criminality. Heidensohn describes domesticity as 'a form of detention'. The endless hours spent on housework and the constant monitoring of young children leave little time for illegal activities. A 'very pervasive value system' persuades women that they must carry out their domestic responsibilities dutifully or they will have failed as mothers and wives. Women who challenge the traditional roles of women within the

family run the risk of having them reimposed by force. Heidensohn says 'many observers confirm that wife-battering is in fact an assertion of patriarchal authority'.

If they are the main or only wage earner, men may also use their financial power to control women's behaviour. Daughters as well as wives are more closely controlled by the family. They are usually given less freedom than boys to come and go as they please or stay out late at night and are expected to spend more time doing housework.

Control of women in public

In public, women are controlled by the male use of force and violence, by the idea of holding on to a 'good' reputation, and by the 'ideology of separate spheres'.

Women often choose not to go out into public places because of the fear of being attacked or raped. Heidensohn quotes the 1986 *Islington Crime Survey*, which found that 54 per cent of women, but only 14 per cent of men, often or always avoided going out after dark because of fear of crime. She quotes Susan Brownmiller's claim that rape and fear of rape 'is nothing more or less than a conscious process of intimidation by which all men keep all women in a state of fear' (quoted in Heidensohn, 1985). Heidensohn stops short of endorsing this view but does argue that the sensational reporting of rapes and the unsympathetic attitude of some police and judges to rape victims act as forces controlling women.

Women also tend to limit their behaviour in public places because of the risk of being labelled unrespectable, of being seen as a 'slag, slut or bitch'. The wrong sort of 'dress, demeanour, make-up and even speech' can damage a girl's reputation in the eyes of men (Heidensohn, 1985).

The ideology of separate spheres, which sees a woman's place as being in the home, 'has become part of the system that subtly and sometimes brutally confines women'. Women are not expected to raise their concerns in public and place them on the political agenda. If they try, they may be ridiculed and told to return to where they belong – in the home. Such a fate befell the Greenham Common women who, during the 1980s, protested about the siting of American nuclear weapons in Britain.

Control of women at work

At work, women are usually controlled by male superiors in the hierarchy, and workers' own organizations – trade unions – are also dominated by men.Women may also be intimidated by various forms of sexual harassment that discourage female employees from asserting themselves or from feeling at home at work. Sexual harassment 'ranges from whistles and catcalls and the fixing of pinups and soft porn pictures, to physical approaches and attacks which could be defined as possibly indecent and criminal'. Heidensohn quotes surveys which find that up to 60 per cent of women have suffered some form of sexual harassment at work.

Conclusion – conformity and deviance

Heidensohn's argument about the causes of conformity by women fits in well with Carlen's views on the causes of deviance. Both are based on control theory and both agree that crime and deviance by women take place when controls break down and women lose the real or imagined incentives to conform. Heidensohn suggests that some female criminals may be those who have 'perceived the bias of the system and decided to push against it'.

For other women it is the restrictions themselves that force them into reliance upon crime. She says 'women are particularly vulnerable because they are so economically exploited'. If they lose the 'protection' of a man they may turn to crimes such as prostitution as the only way to earn a reasonable living.

Evaluation

Many of Heidensohn's arguments are based upon generalizations, some of which do not apply to all women. She does not always support her claims with strong empirical evidence. Furthermore, she admits that many of the empirical tests of control theory have been carried out on juvenile offenders rather than adults, and that control theory does sometimes portray women as being passive victims (Heidensohn, 1997). However, she does present a plausible explanation of why such a gap remains between men's and women's crime rates. In doing so she highlights some of the inequalities between men and women that remain.

(A discussion of feminist postmodernism is included below on pp. 423–7.)

Masculinities and crime

Early feminist approaches in criminology highlighted the neglect of women in criminological theory. At the same time they paved the way for a consideration of how masculinity could help in explaining crime. While traditional criminological studies have been written by men, about men and (arguably) for men, few have explicitly examined the links between masculinity and crime. They have tended to concentrate on crimes committed by males and to ignore crimes committed by females, but have not considered what it might be about masculinity which leads to an apparently higher crime rate.

The few studies that have made links between masculinity and crime have tended to use very simple models. Thus Tim Newburn and Elizabeth A. Stanko argue that 'the dominant theoretical models have rarely gone beyond the simple association of masculinity with, say, machismo' (Newburn and Stanko, 1994). Theorists such as Walter Miller did relate crime to a working-class, male-dominated culture of toughness, but his analysis remained unsophisticated (Miller, 1962) (see pp. 359–60 for a discussion of his work). Others, such as Lombroso and Ferrero, who first published their work in the nineteenth century, have related gender differences in crime to biological differences (Lombroso and Ferrero, 1958). However, quite apart from their other faults (see p. 413 for a discussion), such theories completely ignore how social factors shape what it means to be thought of as a 'real man' or a 'real woman'.

Of the increasing number of attempts to discuss the relationship between criminality and masculinities, James W. Messerschmidt's is perhaps the most influential.

James W. Messerschmidt – *Masculinities and Crime*

Biology, sex roles and radical feminism
Messerschmidt starts his analysis by criticizing what he sees as the failure of previous criminology to deal with the relationship between masculinity and crime (Messerschmidt, 1993). Previous attempts to address this issue have been based either on biology or on what he calls sex-role theory. Messerschmidt rejects biological accounts on the grounds that cross-cultural comparisons do not reveal any universal masculine characteristics. For example, he believes that studies of aggression in men show that men are not naturally aggressive. There are societies in which men are not particularly aggressive; there are aggressive people with low levels of male hormones; and there are many individual males who are far from aggressive. Following writers such as Kessler and McKenna

(see pp. 134–5), Messerschmidt even rejects the view that there is a clearcut distinction between two genders. Some societies, for example, have a third gender, the berdache (see p. 135 for a description of the third gender).

Sex-role theories do not rely upon biological arguments, but to Messerschmidt they are still flawed. Such theories argue that differences in male and female behaviour result simply from men and women being socialized differently. Thus if, for example, men are socialized to be more aggressive, they are more likely to commit violent crimes. Messerschmidt argues that such theories portray men and women as being far too passive. He says that 'men and women are active agents in their social relations'. They do not simply act out the roles they have been taught, but make active decisions about how to behave as circumstances change.

Sex-role theories also ignore the influence of social structures, institutions and power relations on social life. To Messerschmidt, any adequate theory must pay attention to the way factors such as these shape social life. He is also critical of some feminist theories. He believes that radical feminists often succeed in introducing power and social structure into their analysis, but they analyse gender issues in too simplistic a way. Their arguments tend to be too generalized and are often applied to all men and all women. He says that their:

> focus on alleged differences between men and women acted to obscure differences amongst men. For example, the social experiences of African-American men differ from those of white men due to racist and classist structures that systematically disadvantage African-American men.
>
> Messerschmidt, 1993, p. 45

They also tend to neglect variations in power relations between men and women at different places at different times. Thus Messerschmidt believes that a theory explaining why men commit crimes should take account of different masculinities – the different ways that people have perceived being masculine. Different conceptions of masculinity tend to lead to different social actions, in general, and different types of criminality, in particular.

Messerschmidt's approach

Messerschmidt adopts a version of Anthony Giddens's structuration theory (see Chapter 15) as a theoretical approach for understanding gender and crime. Like Giddens, he believes that social structures exist, but they only exist through structured social action. In other words, people's actions are needed to reproduce social structures. If they change the way they behave, the structures change. For example,

patriarchal structures will change if men and women start behaving differently in families and sharing housework equally. On the other hand, pre-existing structures do shape social action. For example, the relatively low wages available to most women in a gendered labour market encourage those women who are involved in partnerships with men to concentrate on domestic tasks, because their partner can earn more through paid employment. To Messerschmidt, structures both constrain and enable. Patriarchal structures often enable men to act in ways which restrict the options open to women, although such structures do change and they do not make it impossible for women to act in ways that are considered unfeminine.

Messerschmidt sees class, race and gender structures as the most important social structures. Thus he emphasizes that women and men from different classes and ethnic groups are in different positions in social structures.

Gender structures

In terms of gender relations, Messerschmidt identifies three key social structures which are instrumental in channelling the behaviour of males and females:

1 The gender division of labour has changed over time and affects social groups differently. Since industrialization the gender division of labour has created roles such as mother/housewife and male breadwinner. The 'good provider' has become one of the dominant types of masculinity. For middle-class men this type of masculinity becomes centred on 'technical knowledge, rationality and calculation', as these are the characteristics needed to hold down a well-paid job. In the USA, though, African-American men were largely excluded from such roles as a result of racism. As a consequence, African-American women have been more likely to be in paid employment than white middle-class women.

   He goes on to say that 'White working class masculinities were organized around holding a steady job, bringing pay home reliably, skill and endurance in paid labour'. Since the Second World War the gender division of labour has changed. Increased material expectations have led many families to have dual wage earners. They feel they need to have two wage earners to achieve an acceptable standard of living. Having a wife who is working is no longer seen as showing that the husband is an inadequate man because he cannot provide for his family on his own. Nevertheless, unequal structures remain, with men largely retaining the better-paid jobs and having less domestic responsibility.

2 Gender relations of power 'are embedded in, and reinforced by, the gender division of labor'. It gives men more control over material resources. However, men also have more power than women because

they 'control the economic, religious, political, and military institutions of authority and coercion in society'.

3   There are also structures relating to sexuality. These tend to devalue homosexuality and, in contemporary societies, 'dominant ideology marks heterosexual performance as a hallmark of one's identity as a man'. As we will see, this has important consequences for male criminality.

Accomplishing masculinity

Despite the existence of different gender structures, gendered social action does not follow automatically from them. Rather, gender is something people do, something they accomplish. In everyday life they try to present themselves in their interactions as adequate or successful men or women. They constantly monitor and adjust their social actions in the light of the circumstances. Messerschmidt says:

> masculinity is accomplished, it is not something done to men or settled beforehand. And masculinity is never static, never a finished product. Rather, men construct masculinities in specific social situations (although not in circumstances of their own choosing); in doing so men reproduce (and sometimes change) social structures.
>
> Messerschmidt, 1993, p. 80

From this viewpoint, a man chatting with his mates at a bar, a man having sex with his female partner, a man discussing a business deal, or a man playing a sport, are all trying to accomplish masculinity. However, men do not all construct the same type of masculinity. An individual's situation may or may not provide easy access to dominant forms of masculinity. Some men are not in a position to accomplish certain highly-valued types of masculinity and must try to find alternative ways to be real men. Messerschmidt says, 'Although masculinity is always individual and personal, specific forms of masculinity are available, encouraged, permitted depending on one's class, race, and sexual preference.'

Hegemonic and subordinated masculinities

Following the work of Connell (see pp. 191–6), Messerschmidt divides masculinity into two main types: hegemonic and subordinated masculinities. Hegemonic masculinities are the dominant and most highly-valued types of masculinities. Subordinated masculinities are less powerful and carry lower status – examples include homosexual masculinity and the masculinity of African-Americans.

The nature of hegemonic masculinity varies from place to place and time to time, but it is generally

based upon the subordination of women. Hegemonic men benefit from their power over women. Men with less dominant forms of masculinity may also try to get benefits from power over women, but it is less easy for them to do so. Nevertheless, they too may engage in practices which try to maintain dominance over women (and perhaps succeed).

The importance of this for crime is that criminal behaviour can be used as a resource for asserting masculinity. Indeed, Messerschmidt goes as far as arguing that:

> crime by men is a form of social practice invoked as a resource, when other resources are unavailable, for accomplishing masculinity. By analysing masculinities, then, we can begin to understand the socially constructed differences among men and thus explain why men engage in different forms of crime.
>
> Messerschmidt, 1993, p. 85

Thus, to Messerschmidt, the idea of masculinity is absolutely central to explaining crime – indeed he seems to see the main motivation behind male crime as involving a desire by men to show that they are masculine.

Using a wide variety of research findings largely from other sociologists' studies, Messerschmidt then proceeds to analyse why different groups of males turn to different types of crime in attempts to be masculine in different ways.

Masculinities and crime in youth groups

White middle-class boys tend to enjoy educational success and frequently also display some sporting prowess. In these ways they are able to demonstrate the possession of some characteristics of hegemonic masculinity. However, this is achieved at a price. Characteristics such as independence, dominance and control largely have to be given up in school. In order to achieve success, white middle-class boys are, to an extent, emasculated, their masculinity is undermined. They have to act in relatively subservient ways to schoolteachers. However, outside school they try to demonstrate some of the characteristics that are repressed within school. This involves engaging in pranks, acts of vandalism, excessive drinking and minor thefts.

Because of their background, white middle-class boys are usually able to evade becoming labelled as criminals by the authorities. Messerschmidt quotes Chambliss's classic study, which compares the 'saints' and the 'roughnecks', as an example (see p. 369 for details). Such young men adopt an accommodating masculinity within school. This is a 'controlled, cooperative, rational gender strategy of action for institutional success'. Outside, they adopt more of an oppositional masculinity, which goes against certain middle-class norms but asserts some aspects of hegemonic masculinity they are denied in school. They are able to express their masculinity in ways that are socially approved by teachers and parents in school, and by peer groups out of school.

White working-class boys also experience school as emasculating. However, they have less chance of academic success and so cannot easily access the type of masculinity based on academic success, which is accessible to middle-class youth. They therefore tend to construct masculinity around the importance of physical aggression. It is important to be tough or hard and to oppose the imposition of authority by teachers and others. Their masculinity can also be expressed through violence against gay men, non-whites, or others who fail to match their conception of what it means to be masculine. Theirs is an oppositional masculinity both inside and outside school. Messerschmidt quotes the 'lads' in Paul Willis's study of anti-school peer groups as an example (see Chapter 11 for details of this study).

The third group, lower working-class, ethnic minority boys, have great problems finding reasonably-paid, secure employment. They do not expect to be able to express their masculinity as breadwinners by holding down a steady job and supporting a family. Their parents may be too poor to buy them consumer goods with designer labels which confer status. With little chance of asserting their masculinity through success within school or work, the focus of these young men's lives is the street. They are unable to access the advantages of hegemonic masculinity through legitimate means and instead turn to violence and crime. They use violence inside and outside school to express their masculinity. They become more involved in serious property crime than white working-class youths. This at least offers some possibility of the material success associated with hegemonic masculinity.

Messerschmidt quotes a number of American studies showing how robbery is used to make the offenders feel more masculine than their victims, how gang and turf warfare is part of an attempt to assert masculine control, and how rape is sometimes used to express control over women.

Messerschmidt describes the particularly horrific case of the 'Central Park Jogger Rape', which took place in New York in 1989. Four adolescent African-Americans beat and repeatedly raped a young, white, female jogger, before dragging her unconscious to a ravine and leaving her for dead. Messerschmidt says, 'Such group rape helps to maintain and reinforce an alliance among the boys by humiliating and devaluing women, thereby strengthening the fiction of masculine power.'

Of course, men in such groups do not necessarily resort to rape. They may be able to establish their masculinity through consenting sexual conquests instead. Like their white middle-class and working-class counterparts, lower working-class, ethnic minority males do masculinity within the limits of the social structures that constrain them. Their recourse to a more violent and aggressive form of masculinity reflects the 'social conditions of poverty, racism, negated future' which limit their options.

Types of 'real men'

Messerschmidt also discusses how different types of masculinity can be expressed by different adult males in a variety of contexts.

On the street, pimping is one way to express masculinity. Pimps usually exercise strong control over the prostitutes they 'run'. By getting the women to turn most of their earnings over to them, they can also enjoy a degree of material success. They have more chance of expressing their masculinity in this way than by struggling to find and keep low-paid work. Furthermore, they can assert their masculinity by adopting 'the cool pose of the badass', which involves 'use of "poses" and "postures" that connote control, toughness and detachment'. They are loud and flamboyant and make sure that they display their success through using luxury consumer goods. For black pimps this is a way 'to transcend class and race domination', because they can assert their ability to earn money through work, and their power to exercise authority and control. However, their lifestyle and flashy displays are despised by more successful, white middle-class men, and, in effect, they only end up confirming their status as inferior men.

In the workplace, working-class men assert their masculinity through resisting the authority of managers. They find ways of working together to slow down production or to allow petty pilfering of goods from work. They also tend to use various forms of sexual harassment to demonstrate their superiority to women. This might involve 'acts such as sexual slurs, pinches or grabs, and public displays of derogatory images of women'. This helps to cement a shop-floor masculinity based around heterosexuality.

The expression of masculinity is less crude amongst senior managers, but it is present none the less:

> [The] old boys network, whereby some men are helped by other men to achieve career success ensures women are largely excluded from the higher echelons of business. The men who are rewarded with career success must demonstrate hegemonic masculine characteristics based upon being 'ambitious, shrewd and nearly amoral'.
>
> Messerschmidt, 1993, p. 134

They must place their success above other values, and to achieve success they must do whatever is necessary to make their company profitable. In this sort of masculine culture it is not surprising that corporate and white-collar crimes are accepted, even encouraged, when they are the only way to guarantee profits. Messerschmidt quotes an engineer at Ford explaining why nobody questioned the continued production of the Pinto model in the USA. This car was prone to bursting into flames if it was in a rear-end collision, and many people died as a result, but it continued in production. The engineer explained that safety 'didn't sell', and that anyone questioning the production of the Pinto would, quite simply, have been sacked.

The corporate executive has to keep his job if he is to maintain his sense of himself as a successful breadwinner. He resorts to corporate crime when his position is under threat and his masculinity risks being compromised.

Like shop-floor workers, corporate executives also try to express their masculinity through exercising control over women. However, because of their power, they do not need to resort to cruder forms of sexual harassment. They can hire sexually attractive secretaries and other female staff. They may use offers of promotion, or threats of dismissal, to obtain sexual favours from them. However, Messerschmidt does admit that 'sexual harassment is by no means automatic. Women often enter into genuine and humane relationships with men in the work-place, not withstanding the fact that these men may be in supervisory positions vis-à-vis the woman.'

The family is another area where men express different types of masculinity and dominance over women. Messerschmidt argues that relatively powerless men use wife-beating, violent rape, and even murder to reassert masculine control when their masculinity is threatened by women. Thus, much violence occurs when the man perceives that his wife has not carried out her duties, obeyed his orders, or shown him adequate respect.

Such assertions of masculine control occur in all types of family, from all ethnic groups and classes. However, what Messerschmidt calls 'force-only rapers' are particularly common in middle-class households. In such cases the man uses only the amount of force necessary to get his wife or partner to engage in sex against her will. Such rapes, he claims, are essentially about sexuality rather than

masculine power. The men feel that their masculinity has been undermined by the unwillingness of their wife to have sex with them. They can restore their sense of their own masculinity by enforcing sex on 'their' woman.

Evaluation of Messerschmidt

Messerschmidt's work provides some valuable insights into the relationship between masculinity and crime. It uses a sophisticated theoretical approach which allows for the existence of different types of masculinity and for the way that these masculinities can change. It makes plausible attempts to link different types of crime to different types of masculinity and it appears to provide a basis for explaining why men are more criminal than women. Tony Jefferson describes Messerschmidt's work as 'a brave attempt' (Jefferson, 1997).

However, Jefferson criticizes Messerschmidt's work on a number of grounds. He argues that Messerschmidt fails to explain why particular individuals commit crimes rather than others. For example, only a small minority of African-American men carry out rapes. Jefferson therefore believes that, despite efforts to the contrary, Messerschmidt's work ends up with a rather over-determined view of men. It tends to assume that all men in particular circumstances will be socialized to express their masculinity in particular ways. He says 'This emphasis on constraints rather than action explains the ultimately deterministic feel to the analyses.'

Other criticisms apart from those expressed by Jefferson can also be added. Messerschmidt seems to advance rather stereotypical and negative views of men in general, and of working-class and non-white men in particular. There is no room in his book for men who might commit politically motivated crimes in a fight against an oppressive government, and little for men who reject the idea that being a real man involves asserting control over women.

Other writers, such as Bob Connell (1995) (see pp. 191–6), do not always portray men in such a negative light. Furthermore, perhaps Messerschmidt exaggerates the importance of masculinity in the explanation of crime. If Messerschmidt is to be believed, then nearly all crimes committed by men are an expression of their masculinity. While Messerschmidt may be right that it is difficult to understand male crime without reference to masculinities, he may be wrong to assume that it can be explained by this alone.

Postmodernism and criminology

As in other areas of sociology, postmodern perspectives have started to influence the study of crime and deviance. It is perhaps less obvious what such approaches can contribute to an understanding of crime and deviance than with some other topics, but nevertheless attempts have been made to see how useful postmodernism might be. One of the most influential postmodern approaches to criminology attempted to combine postmodernism with feminism to produce a new way of thinking about crime.

Carol Smart – postmodern feminism and female criminality

Traditional criminology

In an article entitled 'Feminist approaches to criminology, or postmodern woman meets atavistic man' (Smart, 1995, first published 1990), Carol Smart examines the relationship between postmodernism, feminism and criminology. She starts by attacking both traditional approaches in criminology (such as biological, psychological and subcultural theories) and newer approaches, such as left realism (see pp. 391–9). To Smart they all share certain central characteristics and they all adopt a version of positivism. First, they all try to find the causes of criminality. Second, the aim of all of them is to try to eradicate crime. Third, they all assume that scientific methods are the best way of finding the truth about crime. Finally, they all believe that it is possible to develop a metanarrative – a master theory – which will explain crime.

Smart does not reject some of the aims of approaches such as left realism. She thinks that left realists have their hearts in the right places when they want to 'reduce the misery to which crime is often wedded' and they seek 'policies which are less punitive and oppressive'. The trouble is:

> that science is held to have the answer if only it is scientific enough. Here is revealed the faith in the totalizing theory, the master narrative which will eventually – when the scales have fallen from our eyes or sufficient connections have been made – allow us to see things for what they really are.
>
> Smart, 1995, p. 35

Conventional criminology is based on a modernist paradigm. Such a paradigm assumes there will be progress, that sciences such as criminology can deliver knowledge that is superior to all other knowledge. It arrogantly believes that 'it is only a matter of time before science can explain all from the broad sweep of societal change to the motivations of the child molester'.

Deconstructing positivism and modernism

Smart rejects the modernist paradigm and more specifically traditional, positivist approaches. She argues that the modernist approach is 'male or phallagocentric', with a typical masculine obsession with control and domination over others (in this case criminals). It is politically suspect because it denies a voice to anyone other than the scientific criminologist. The voices of 'lesbians and gays, black women and men, Asian women and men, feminists and so on' are drowned out by the strident assertions of the scientists, who are usually white, Western men.

Traditional criminology panders to the requirements of often oppressive states who will not provide money for research which does not correspond to their often oppressive agenda. To Smart, no general theory of crime is ever possible, no matter how much research is done and how sophisticated scientific methods become. Modernism is an 'exhausted mode' of thinking. It has failed to deliver the goods, and failed to reduce crime rates for governments.

A central reason for this is that it has been quite wrong to see crime as a single type of phenomenon. Different crimes involve very different types of behaviour. Often, some of the most important characteristics of behaviours which are lumped together in the category 'crime' have nothing to do with them being against the law. Postmodern approaches are better able to deconstruct such behaviours, to show that they are not what they seem. Thus, Smart says:

> The thing that criminology cannot do is deconstruct 'crime'. It cannot locate rape and child sexual abuse in the domain of sexuality, nor theft in the domain of economic activity nor drug use in the domain of health. To do so would be to abandon criminology to sociology, but more importantly it would involve abandoning the idea of a unified problem which requires a unified response – at least at the theoretical level.
>
> Smart, 1995, p. 39

If criminology admitted that there was no single type of activity that constituted crime, there would be no need for criminology, and criminologists would be out of jobs. Smart does not therefore regard it as surprising that criminologists try to stick to the myth that a theory of crime is possible. However, she believes that feminist theory offers potentially

424 Chapter 6: Crime and deviance

superior approaches to studying the various types of behaviour that are categorized as crimes.

Feminist approaches to criminology

Smart draws on the work of Sandra Harding (1986, 1987) in distinguishing three types of feminism: feminist empiricism, standpoint feminism, and feminist postmodernism:

1 Feminist empiricism argues that previous work has been largely written about men by men. It argues that the balance of research is sexist, with women largely being left out. It therefore believes that more empirical research needs to be carried out about women. Smart notes that there has been a big increase in criminological studies of women (some of them have been discussed in this chapter). However, Smart believes that such an approach makes little difference to criminology as a whole. Conventional criminology can carry on using the methods and theories and simply acknowledge that it is writing about men and not humanity as a whole. Feminist criminologists can fill in the gaps in knowledge about women, but without allowing the discipline to progress in any other way.

2 Standpoint feminism offers a more radical challenge. This approach believes that true knowledge can be created by listening to the oppressed and disadvantaged. Women who are actively engaged in the struggle against patriarchal society can understand how the society works. Standpoint feminist criminologists have listened to, for example, female victims of rape, sexual harassment and domestic violence. The accounts of female victims are intended to replace the dominant accounts of such crimes, which have previously come largely from male police officers and male criminologists.

   While Smart welcomes the attempt to see the world from the viewpoint of the subjugated, she does not believe that it goes far enough. For example, it is unable to explain the involvement of men in crime and it cannot understand masculinity. This is because it cannot examine the viewpoint of dominant groups in society.

3 Smart is convinced that the best feminist approach is feminist postmodernism. Feminist postmodernism rejects the view that there is one scientific, criminological theory that can explain crime. It rejects the view that all men, or all women, are essentially the same. There is no essence of humanity, masculinity or femininity which can explain crime. Indeed, crime itself has no core of essential characteristics through which it can be understood. People have fractured identities. Individuals have many different aspects to their identity, involving their ethnicity, class, gender, age, experiences, etc. Everyone is different. Similarly, crimes are very different acts committed by very different people for very different reasons.

Criminology needs to be de-essentialized, it must stop looking for essential characteristics which do not exist. Smart says, 'The core element of feminist postmodernism is the rejection of the one reality which arises from "the falsely universalizing perspective of the master" (Harding, 1987).'

Standpoint feminism seeks to substitute the truth of the oppressed for the truth of the oppressors. Feminist postmodernism:

> does not seek to impose a different unitary reality. Rather it refers to subjugated knowledge, which tell different stories and have different specificities. So the aim of feminism ceases to be the establishment of the feminist truth and becomes the aim of deconstructing Truth and analysing the power effects that claims to truth entail.
>
> Smart, 1995, p. 45

What Smart argues, then, is that postmodern feminist criminologists should take apart the claims made by other theorists and practitioners about crime. They should show how male criminologists, police, judges, and so on, make false claims about crime and how it should be dealt with. Their claims are designed to, and often do, give them power over others. Smart follows Foucault's ideas on power (see Chapter 9) in arguing that power exists in all social relationships and derives from discourses, and from claims to the possession of knowledge. Power is not concentrated in any one place, it is not monopolized by any one group. Power, including the power of men, can only be challenged by resistance in each place, each time it is used. Knowledge which claims to be the truth has to be challenged.

Smart uses the example of rape to illustrate her ideas. She says that postmodern feminists can challenge the way rape is portrayed in court cases. They can attack the way that the vagina is portrayed as a passive and vulnerable receptacle, and the penis as a weapon. They can attack the view of judges that women dressed in short skirts are 'asking for it', and undermine the idea that men cannot control their sexual urges once they have gone so far. They can examine the way in which male and female sexualities are portrayed in courts, the media and elsewhere. They can reveal the inconsistencies and contradictions involved in these portrayals, and by doing so challenge and undermine the prevailing discourses through which power is exercised over women.

Conclusion

Smart concludes by arguing that criminology has little to offer feminism. Its modes of analysis are outdated and of little use. Criminology has been revived by feminism, particularly postmodern feminism, and not the other way round. Therefore she believes that 'It might be that criminology needs feminism more than the reverse' and 'it is very difficult to see what criminology has to offer to feminism'.

Pat Carlen – a critique of postmodern feminist criminology

Carlen (1992) is sympathetic to some of the arguments advanced by Carol Smart. She accepts that it is unlikely that one theory could explain all crime, and agrees that there is no fundamental essence which distinguishes criminal behaviour from all other behaviour. She agrees with Smart that standpoint feminism is wrong to assume that the truth can be discovered simply by letting oppressed women speak for themselves. However, she does not believe that all attempts to explain or even to control crime can be seen as part of a failed, male, modernist project.

Attempts to produce theories of crime can illuminate the causes of specific crimes committed by particular groups of women. Furthermore, they can be used in support of progressive policies which can tackle injustice. Nor does Carlen believe, as some postmodernists do, that you should simply respect and celebrate the lifestyles of different groups of oppressed women. For example, her own research (see pp. 415–17 for details of some of her work) revealed connections between female criminality, homelessness and drug addiction. Using this knowledge to try to reduce homelessness and drug addiction, and therefore crime, is seen by Carlen as progressive rather than regressive. It is not the imposition of the phallocentric, modernist view of the world on reluctant women, but a genuine attempt to understand people's problems and help them to overcome them. Carlen comments:

> Women with drink or drug addictions often choke to death on their own vomit. Others have Aids as a result of either sharing needles or engaging in prostitution to fund their habits. Sleeping rough, nursing bleeding sores and suffering withdrawal symptoms are not particularly life-enhancing processes either. Not one woman of the many I have known with addictions has celebrated her addictive state; many have themselves referred to 'destructive lifestyles', 'abusing my body' and 'killing myself'.
>
> Carlen, 1992, p. 63

Just because such views might be shared by the criminal justice system and conventional criminologists does not mean that they are wrong. Deconstructing such views will not do anything to alleviate the deprivations faced by such women.

To Carlen, trying to explain crime does not mean that you inevitably fall into an essentialist trap. You do not inevitably end up with the same biases as the more sexist male criminologists or the more oppressive parts of the criminal justice system. You can recognize that crime and criminals are very different, that no one theory will do, without abandoning the attempt to explain crime. Carlen has no objection to the sort of critical deconstruction of bias in the criminal justice system advocated by Carol Smart. However, she does not believe that criminology should confine itself to only conducting that sort of study. To do so would risk losing sight of what she sees as the fundamental aim of feminist criminology, which is:

> To ensure that the penal regulation of female lawbreakers does not increase their oppression as unconventional women, as black people and as poverty-stricken defendants still further; and to ensure that the penal regulation of lawbreaking men is not such that it brutalizes them and makes them behave even more violently or oppressively towards women in the future.
>
> Carlen, 1992, p. 66

Evaluation

Both Smart and Carlen claim that feminist criminology can be used to promote social justice. However, they believe that different theoretical and methodological approaches can best achieve this. While Smart advocates a methodology based on deconstruction and a theory based on postmodernism, Carlen supports more conventional methodologies and more traditional theories which claim to be able to explain crime. Perhaps both approaches can help illuminate the relationship between gender and crime. For example, they could be used to understand both why some men commit rapes, and how the actions of rapists and victims are dealt with by the courts. Of the two theorists, Carlen seems the more willing to accept the use of a variety of approaches in studying crime and criminal justice.

John Lea – *Criminology and Postmodernity*

Although not himself a postmodernist, John Lea has reviewed the ways in which postmodernism has been, or could be, applied to criminology (Lea, 1998). Lea believes that criminology is an obvious target of attack for postmodernists. This is because:

> Criminology and penology were central pillars of the postwar 'grand narratives' of social engineering and welfare reformism, the blueprints for the good society that are now so discredited. The crisis of modernity is a part of the crisis of criminology.
>
> Lea, 1998, p. 163

Scientific theories held the promise of solving the problem of crime. Instead, the crime rate rose almost inexorably. If the scientific study of crime did nothing to help control it, postmodernists may argue that the time has come to abandon the objective of the scientific explanation and control of crime. To Lea, postmodernism has the potential to contribute to understanding three aspects of crime: the nature of crime, explaining the causes of crime and controlling crime.

The nature of crime

Lea suggests that deconstruction is the main method that postmodernists advocate for understanding the nature of crime. Postmodernists such as Carol Smart (discussed above) see traditional criminology as obscuring the nature of crime by seeing all crime as the same sort of phenomenon. Lea says, 'taking the example of rape, deconstruction exposes how the definition of an activity such as rape involves its repression of its other characteristics – as a form of sexuality'. However, such an approach raises its own problems. The idea that rape is essentially a form of sexuality could itself be deconstructed to show that this definition repressed other aspects of rape (for example, that it was to do with power, or to do with crime after all). This raises the problem of infinite regress. Every deconstruction could itself be deconstructed in a process that would be never-ending and would lead nowhere. In practice, what has to happen is that deconstruction stops at some point. Smart stops at the point of saying that rape is to do with sex, but such a decision seems arbitrary and simply reflects Smart's own preconceptions about rape.

An alternative approach to deconstruction is similar to that of standpoint feminism (see p. 424), where a particular social group is held to be the key to understanding a phenomenon. Thus, lesbians, gays, members of ethnic minorities, working-class women, disabled men, or whoever, might be seen as having a privileged viewpoint from which to deconstruct particular crimes. However, this seems to be reverting to a form of foundationalism (the belief that there is a firm foundation for some absolute truth), which postmodernists reject. Furthermore, the views of oppressed groups might have been distorted or contaminated by the ideologies of more powerful groups. Thus, for example, gays and lesbians might have been persuaded by heterosexuals that heterosexuality is more normal than homosexuality.

A third type of deconstruction suggests that the search for truth is abandoned in favour of knowledge that works – that is effective in achieving some objective. Thus, if a particular theory of crime can be applied to reduce crime, it should be accepted, whether or not the theory stands up to close examination. However, as Lea points out, what works is very much influenced by the distribution of power in society. So, for example, a theory that much sex between married men and women was in fact rape by the man would be resisted and rejected by men, who have more power than women. Thus, you would end up accepting only those theories that reflected the desires and interests of the powerful. Lea says, 'what began as a radical critique of dominant discourses of power ends up prostrating itself before them. What "works" in any situation is precisely a product of the dominant relationship of power!'

Lea believes that criminology has long included a type of deconstruction in the form of labelling theory. Criminologists have already critically examined the nature of crime, and postmodern advocates of deconstruction have not produced a coherent and superior alternative. Furthermore, criminology already has its own ways of analysing the influence of power on the definition of crime. Deconstruction can show that power is always involved in defining crime, but this has long been acknowledged by Marxist, feminist and various other critical types of criminology. Such approaches can relate the definition of crime to the distribution of power in particular societies at particular times. Postmodern deconstruction is less satisfactory because all it can do is show how some sort of power relationship is always involved in definitions of crime.

The causes of crime

Lea, quoting the ideas of Lyotard (see Chapter 15), argues that postmodern approaches to the causes of crime reject the idea that some grand theory or grand narrative can explain crime. Carol Smart, for example (see pp. 423–5), rejects what she calls 'positivist' approaches in criminology. Instead, postmodern theories can only look for 'local truths', explanations of particular, individual examples of crime.

Postmodernists tend to reject the idea that different crimes can be linked together and common factors which cause them can be found. Each criminal act is, in effect, to be regarded as a unique event. Postmodernists also tend to see crime, like everything else, as part of a process of 'the experimental creation of lifestyles' and a 'process of free self-creation'. Individuals may choose an identity as a bank robber or a heroin addict. From this postmodern viewpoint, crime is simply a product of 'the general condition of freedom itself'.

Lea finds such an approach to explaining criminality unsatisfactory. While it avoids being deterministic, it goes to the opposite extreme and abandons any claim to be able to explain crime in general. It is unable to explain, for example, why certain groups are likely to resort to certain types of crime rather than others. While crime might be widespread, certain types of crime are more associated with particular groups: corporate crime with corporate executives, street crimes with the marginal and oppressed. Postmodern criminology cannot explore such links.

The control of crime

In this area, Lea sees postmodernism as making a more useful contribution. According to Lea, postmodernism argues that there has been a move away from formal methods of social control based on a centrally planned criminal justice system. Under modernity, the control of crime was based on the idea that all citizens share certain rights, and that these should be administered impartially by the police, courts, welfare agencies and so on. However, it was also recognized that informal social control, which worked through social pressure, was also important. The state intervened to buttress informal social control outside the criminal justice system through 'a variety of social rights to welfare and education, parental and children's rights and so on'. Various types of treatment and 'care' were used where informal social control was not working, in addition to punishment through the criminal justice system.

Lea believes that things have changed with the move towards a postmodern society. He says:

> *If postmodernisation has any meaning then it lies in the hypothesis that decentralised informal mechanisms come to dominate and partially replace formal centralised institutions and their accompanying discourses or grand narratives, and at the same time that formal criminal justice institutions operate in an increasingly informal way.*
>
> Lea, 1998, p. 181

Increasingly, for example, private security firms, such as those responsible for watching over shopping malls, replace the police in providing private security. Control is achieved less through punishing offenders than by denying some people access to places where they might offend. In some American estates and in blocks of flats in Britain, for example, security firms exclude undesirables from entering. There has been a decline in the idea of public space in which anyone can move freely without being watched, monitored or vetted. Closed-circuit television (CCTV) is not just confined to private spaces, but is increasingly used to monitor the streets of towns and cities as well.

In some ways, such changes can be seen in a postmodern light as celebrating diversity. Different groups are confined to certain areas of towns or cities. Lea says 'the blacks in the ghetto and the whites in the protected central city and the segregated and secured suburbs are all, equally, manifestations of difference'.

In each area people are treated differently. There is a move away from seeing people as citizens with rights, and a move towards seeing them as consumers or customers. Policing policies tend to become more localized in focus. Ghettos and suburbs are seen as having different policing needs and are treated differently. Thus the criminal justice system starts to take account of people's diverse lifestyles and needs.

Lea sees some of these changes as welcome. In postmodern societies there seems more likelihood that policing can become sensitive to the needs of minorities. However, such a change also carries dangers. There is a danger that the ghettos will either be left alone to fend for themselves, or that they will be repressed through military-style policing. If people are treated as consumers, then those with no spending power are less likely to get their needs met. No one can afford private security in the areas where people are most likely to be the victims of crime.

In the end the acceptance and celebration of difference are unlikely to solve the problems of the most disadvantaged. They are left at the mercy of the forces of global capitalism. Although there are some advantages in abandoning the idea of citizenship rights in favour of valuing difference, it is ultimately self-defeating. Rather than liberating people, it condemns the weak to be neglected. Although different social groups, such as ethnic minorities, gays, women, inner-city dwellers and so on, demand slightly different things from the criminal justice system, they are all seeking some form of justice. Thus, to Lea, controlling crime must rely upon retaining some notion of justice, and some idea of the basic rights of citizens. Without this it is likely to be the voices of the powerful which drown out the demands of others.

Evaluation

Lea accepts that postmodernism can offer something to criminology in describing changes in society. It has identified some novel developments in the way crime is controlled. However, he does not believe that it offers a viable method for studying crime, or an acceptable approach to dealing with it. He agrees with Pat Carlen (1992) that postmodern criminology has failed to demonstrate that it should supersede other approaches.

Sociology, values and deviance

It is clear from this chapter that the sympathies of many sociologists tend to lie with the deviant. This will inevitably influence their research. In a paper entitled 'Who's side are we on', Howard Becker argues that it is impossible to conduct research 'uncontaminated by personal and political sympathies' (Becker, 1970). Like many sociologists, he believes that a value-free sociology is not possible. Becker claims that his sympathies are with the 'underdog', the deviant who is labelled by the agencies of social control. These sympathies tend to colour the views of the entire interactionist school. The villains of the piece are the agents of social control: the police, the judges, the probation and prison officers, the doctors and the psychiatrists – those who process the deviants and slap on the labels. In terms of their critical view of control agencies, Becker claims that, politically, 'interactionist theories look (and are) rather Left'.

Alvin Gouldner takes a rather different view. He accuses the interactionists of adopting a 'bland liberal position' which advocates cosmetic reform rather than radical change (Gouldner, 1971). In criticizing the agencies of social control they fail to attack the real causes of deviance which lie in society itself. Gouldner argues that this failure is due to the interactionists' ideological stance. Their liberal views lead them to regard the basic foundations of society as sound. More radical commitments would demand fundamental changes in the structure of society rather than the less repressive measures of social control which the interactionists advocate.

Gouldner claims that many members of the interactionist school have a romantic identification with the more colourful and exotic deviants. He suggests that they 'get their kicks' from a 'titillated attraction to the underdog's exotic difference'. He claims that 'theirs is a school of thought that finds itself at home in the world of hip, drug addicts, jazz musicians, cab drivers, prostitutes, night people, drifters, grifters and skidders: "the cool world"'. Gouldner argues that this identification by largely middle-class sociologists with the 'cool underworld' colours their choice of research subjects, their perspectives and conclusions. It leads at best to rather bland sympathies with the underdog, and a relatively mild reproach to the agencies of social control to lay off and leave the deviants alone. Gouldner regards this as a poor substitute for a radical critique of society as a whole.

Functionalists such as Merton (1968) have also been accused of 'bland liberalism' by their more radical critics. Merton's view of society is critical, but the changes indicated by his conclusions suggest reform rather than radical change. He sees inequality of opportunity as the major cause of crime and delinquency, and implies that measures to increase equal opportunity will solve many of society's problems. With a basic commitment to US society in the first place, and a belief that its foundations are fundamentally sound, Merton is directed towards criticism and reform rather than condemnation and radical change. This may well have prevented him from questioning the system itself, and, as Laurie Taylor (1971) suggested, asking basic questions such as 'Who made the rules in the first place?'

If the interactionists and functionalists can be accused of liberal bias, the same can hardly be said of some of the Marxists. Commitment to radical change reverberates through their writings. Starting from the value judgement that private property is theft, Marxist sociologists reject the basic structure of class society. Their political views result in a condemnation of ruling-class crime and a sympathetic treatment of the crimes of the subject class. When Marxists such as Frank Pearce (1976) refer to the 'naked barbarity' of capitalism, it is clear that commitments other than scientific objectivity direct and influence their choice of subject matter, their methods of analysis and their conclusions.

The 'New Criminology' of Taylor, Walton and Young is, if anything, even more idealistic than conventional Marxist theories. These writers wish to 'create a society in which the facts of human diversity, whether personal, organic or social, are not subject to the power to criminalize' (Taylor, Walton and Young, 1973). However, they do not make it clear which laws could be abolished and which, if any, need to be retained.

New left realists (including Jock Young, one of the authors of *The New Criminology*) label such approaches as left idealism and attack them as hopelessly romantic. Left realists advocate a more sober analysis and are less sympathetic to the criminal. Their research suggests that criminals should be seen, not as Robin Hood figures redistributing wealth and thereby helping the working class, but as further damaging the already difficult lives of inner-city residents. Kevin Stevenson and Nigel Brearly summarize Young's change of heart well when they discuss his changing views on drug use: 'Young's view of illegal drug use has shifted from a libertarian concern with the rights to self-determination of young drug users to the concerns of an anxious parental generation' (Stevenson and Brearly, 1991). Left realists still describe themselves as socialist, and still seek a more egalitarian society, but they opt for limited reform rather than radical or even revolutionary changes.

Feminist criminologists start by attacking previous criminology as having an in-built male bias. They see it as having been written by men, about men and for men. Since the 1970s, research by women has begun to redress the imbalance. However, in doing so some feminist sociologists have in turn been influenced by their values and have made questionable generalizations about the attitudes and behaviour of men. For example, when Brownmiller claimed that rape was 'nothing more or less than a conscious process of intimidation by which all men keep all women in a state of fear' (Brownmiller, 1975), she certainly allowed the strength of her feelings to influence her analysis.

Some feminists, such as Carol Smart (1995), have moved towards embracing postmodern theories. As such, they have not just rejected the male-dominated content of criminology, they have rejected the whole idea of explaining crime. Smart believes that criminology can offer little to the postmodern feminist interested in crime.

Postmodernists have something in common with earlier approaches to criminology. Like interactionist sociologists, they tend to be interested in exotic and marginal groups in society. Like Taylor, Walton and Young (1973), they celebrate diversity and difference. They believe that all social groups should have a chance to create their own identities. However, unlike interactionists and the New Criminologists, they do not believe that it is possible to try to engineer reforms or revolutions to improve society. They believe that any attempt to do so will create more problems than it will solve. Any attempts to do something about crime must be local and individual. Postmodernists reject any grand narrative which claims to explain or provide solutions for crime in general. Their critics argue that, in trying to avoid imposing any one set of values on society, postmodernists lose sight of the idea that criminology can be used to promote social justice. Writers such as John Lea (1998) believe that, far from being progressive, postmodernism tends to be inherently regressive, because it denies the possibility of trying to do anything to change societies, which he believes are ridden with inequality and injustice.

Since the issues of crime, deviance and conformity are essentially about what humans consider to be right and wrong, it is hardly surprising that values impinge on this area of study to a very great extent. Many of the theories examined in this chapter reflect how their authors think society ought to be arranged, as much as how they think it actually is.

Chapter 7

Religion

Religion

Introduction – definitions of religion

1 'In the beginning was the Word, and the Word was with God, and the Word was God.' The God of Christianity is a supreme being, his word is the ultimate truth, his power is omnipotent. His followers worship him and praise him and live by his commandments.

2 The Dugum Dani live in the Highlands of New Guinea. They have no god, but their world is inhabited by a host of supernatural beings known as mogat. The mogat are the ghosts of the dead. They cause illness and death and control the wind and the rain. The Dugum Dani are not pious – they do not pray. Their rituals are not to honour or worship the mogat but to placate and appease them.

3 The Teton Sioux lived on the northern prairies of the USA. The worlds of nature, on which they were dependent, were controlled by the Wakan powers. The powers were stronger and more mysterious than those of people. They caused the seasons to change, the rains to fall, the plants to grow and the animals to multiply. In this way they cared for the Sioux. The Sioux did not worship the Wakan powers but invoked their aid: they appealed to the powers for assistance or protection.

Religious beliefs of one sort or another are present in every known society but their variety seems to be endless. Any definition of religion must encompass this variety. However, it is difficult to produce a definition broad enough to encompass this variety without incorporating phenomena that are not normally thought of as religions. Two main approaches have been adopted in tackling this issue: those that rely upon functional and those that use substantive definitions.

1 One way of defining religion is to see it in terms of the functions it performs for society or individuals. An example of this approach is provided by Yinger who defined religion as 'a system of beliefs and practices by means of which a group of people struggles with the ultimate problems of human life' (quoted in Hamilton, 1995). However, Hamilton notes two main problems with such a definition. First, it allows the inclusion of a wide variety of belief systems in the category 'religion'. For example, by this definition communism could be regarded as a religion even though it explicitly rejects religious beliefs. Second, it is based upon assumptions about the roles and purposes of religion. However, these roles and purposes might vary between societies and it should be the job of sociology to uncover them by empirical investigation, not to assume what they are from the outset. Third, phrases such as 'the ultimate problems of human life' are open to varied interpretations. Hamilton points out that for some people the ultimate problems of life might be 'simply how to enjoy it as much as possible, how to avoid pain and ensure pleasure' (Hamilton, 1995). It is clear that many other aspects of social life, apart from religion, address such issues – for example, medicine and leisure.

2 Other approaches are based upon substantive definitions, that is they are concerned with the content of religion rather than its function or purpose. Substantive definitions can take a number of forms.

Durkheim (1961) defined religion in terms of a distinction between the sacred and the profane. Sacred objects produce a sense of awe, veneration and respect, whereas profane objects do not. However, as critics have pointed out, in some cases explicitly religious objects are not treated with respect.

A common approach to a substantive definition of religion is to define it in terms of supernatural beliefs. Thus Roland Robertson states that religion 'refers to the existence of supernatural beings that have a governing effect on life' (Robertson, 1970). A supernatural element is combined with institutional aspects of religion in Melford Spiro's definition of religion as 'an institution consisting of culturally patterned interaction with culturally postulated superhuman beings' (Spiro, 1965). However, as Hamilton points out, such definitions run into problems because certain belief systems which are commonly regarded as religions, such as Buddhism, do not contain a belief in supernatural beings.

All definitions emphasize certain aspects of religion and exclude others. Functional definitions tend to be too inclusive – it is too easy to qualify as a religion; while substantive ones tend to be too exclusive – it is too difficult to qualify as a religion. We will look at a variety of definitions throughout the chapter and it should be borne in mind that the definitions tend to reflect the theoretical assumptions and the specific arguments being advanced by individual sociologists. This is particularly evident in the debate on secularization (the question of whether religion has declined). Varying definitions allow the advocates and critics of the theory to include evidence that supports their case and exclude evidence that contradicts it.

The problems of definition should not, however, be exaggerated. The disputes tend to occur over phenomena that can be considered to be on the fringes of religion (such as New Age movements) and there is general agreement that such belief systems as Hinduism, Islam, Buddhism, Christianity, Buddhism and Judaism are religions.

Religion – a functionalist perspective

The functionalist perspective examines religion in terms of society's needs. Functionalist analysis is primarily concerned with the contribution religion makes to meeting these needs. From this perspective, society requires a certain degree of social solidarity, value consensus, and harmony and integration between its parts. The function of religion is the contribution it makes to meeting such functional prerequisites – for example, its contribution to social solidarity.

Emile Durkheim

The sacred and the profane

In *The Elementary Forms of the Religious Life*, first published in 1912, Emile Durkheim presented what is probably the most influential interpretation of religion from a functionalist perspective (Durkheim, 1961). Durkheim argued that all societies divide the world into two categories: the sacred and the profane (the non-sacred). Religion is based upon this division. It is 'a unified system of beliefs and practices related to sacred things, that is to say things set apart and forbidden'.

It is important to realize that:

> *By sacred things one must not understand simply those personal things which are called gods or spirits; a rock, a tree, a spring, a pebble, a piece of wood, a house, in a word anything can be sacred.*
>
> Durkheim, 1961

There is nothing about the particular qualities of a pebble or a tree that makes them sacred. Therefore sacred things must be symbols, they must represent something. To understand the role of religion in society, the relationship between sacred symbols and what they represent must be established.

Totemism

Durkheim used the religion of various groups of Australian aboriginals to develop his argument. He saw their religion, which he called totemism, as the simplest and most basic form of religion.

Aboriginal society is divided into several clans. A clan is like a large extended family with its members sharing certain duties and obligations. For example, clans have a rule of exogamy – that is, members are not allowed to marry within the clan. Clan members have a duty to aid and assist each other: they join together to mourn the death of one of their number and to revenge a member who has been wronged by someone from another clan.

Each clan has a totem, usually an animal or a plant. This totem is then represented by drawings made on wood or stone. These drawings are called churingas. Usually churingas are at least as sacred as the species which they represent and sometimes more so. The totem is a symbol. It is the emblem of the clan, 'It is its flag; it is the sign by which each clan distinguishes itself from all others.' However, the totem is more than the churinga which represents it – it is the most sacred object in aborigine ritual. The totem is 'The outward and visible form of the totemic principle or god.'

Durkheim argued that if the totem 'Is at once the symbol of god and of the society, is that not because the god and the society are only one?' Thus he suggested that in worshipping god, people are in fact worshipping society. Society is the real object of religious veneration.

How does humanity come to worship society? Sacred things are 'considered superior in dignity and power to profane things and particularly to man'. In relation to the sacred, humans are inferior and dependent. This relationship between humanity and sacred things is exactly the relationship between humanity and society. Society is more important and powerful than the individual. Durkheim argued that 'Primitive man comes to view society as something sacred because he is utterly dependent on it.'

But why does humanity not simply worship society itself? Why does it invent a sacred symbol like a totem? Because, Durkheim argued, it is easier for a person to 'visualize and direct his feelings of awe toward a symbol than towards so complex a thing as a clan'.

Religion and the 'collective conscience'

Durkheim believed that social life is impossible without the shared values and moral beliefs that form the collective conscience. In their absence, there would be no social order, social control, social solidarity or cooperation. In short, there would be no society. Religion reinforces the collective conscience. The worship of society strengthens the values and moral beliefs that form the basis of social life. By defining them as sacred, religion provides them with greater power to direct human action.

This attitude of respect towards the sacred is the same attitude applied to social duties and obligations. In worshipping society, people are, in effect, recognizing the importance of the social group and their dependence upon it. In this way religion strengthens the unity of the group: it promotes social solidarity.

Durkheim emphasized the importance of collective worship. The social group comes together in religious rituals full of drama and reverence. Together, its members express their faith in common values and beliefs. In this highly charged atmosphere of collective worship, the integration of society is strengthened. Members of society express, communicate and understand the moral bonds which unite them.

According to Durkheim, the belief in gods or spirits, which usually provide the focus for religious ceremonies, originated from belief in the ancestral spirits of dead relatives. The worship of gods is really the worship of ancestors' souls. Since Durkheim also believed that souls represent the presence of social values, the collective conscience is present in individuals. It is through individual souls that the collective conscience is realized. Since religious worship involves the worship of souls, Durkheim again concludes that religious worship is really the worship of the social group or society.

Criticisms of Durkheim

Durkheim's ideas are still influential today, although they have been criticized:

1 Critics have argued that Durkheim studied only a small number of Aboriginal groups which were somewhat untypical of other Aboriginal tribes. Is may therefore be misleading to generalize about

Aboriginal beliefs from this sample, never mind generalizing about religion as a whole.

2 Most sociologists believe that Durkheim has overstated his case. While agreeing that religion is important for promoting social solidarity and reinforcing social values, they would not support his view that religion is the worship of society. Durkheim's views on religion are more relevant to small, non-literate societies, where there is a close integration of culture and social institutions, where work, leisure, education and family life tend to merge, and where members share a common belief and value system. His views are less relevant to modern societies, which have many subcultures, social and ethnic groups, specialized organizations, and a range of religious beliefs, practices and institutions. As Malcolm Hamilton puts it, 'The emergence of religious pluralism and diversity within a society is, of course, something that Durkheim's theory has great difficulty dealing with' (Hamilton, 1995).

3 Durkheim may also overstate the degree to which the collective conscience permeates and shapes the behaviour of individuals. Indeed, sometimes religious beliefs can be at odds with and override societal values. Malcolm Hamilton makes this point strongly:

> The fact that our moral sense might make us go against the majority, the society, or authority, shows that we are not quite so dependent upon or creatures of society as Durkheim claims. Society, powerful as it is, does not have the primacy that Durkheim believes it has. Ironically, it often seems to be the case that religious beliefs can have a much greater influence upon and hold over the individual than society does since it is often out of religious convictions that individuals will fly in the face of society or attempt to withdraw from it, as in the case of many sectarian movements.
>
> Hamilton, 1995, p. 105

Bronislaw Malinowski

Like Durkheim, Malinowski uses data from small-scale non-literate societies to develop his thesis on religion (Malinowski, 1954). Many of his examples are drawn from his fieldwork in the Trobriand Islands off the coast of New Guinea. Like Durkheim, Malinowski sees religion as reinforcing social norms and values and promoting social solidarity. Unlike Durkheim, however, he does not see religion as reflecting society as a whole, nor does he see religious ritual as the worship of society itself. Malinowski identifies specific areas of social life with which religion is concerned, and to which it is addressed. These are situations of emotional stress that threaten social solidarity.

Religion and life crises

Anxiety and tension tend to disrupt social life. Situations that produce these emotions include crises of life such as birth, puberty, marriage and death. Malinowski notes that in all societies these life crises are surrounded with religious ritual. He sees death as the most disruptive of these events and argues that:

> *The existence of strong personal attachments and the fact of death, which of all human events is the most upsetting and disorganizing to man's calculations, are perhaps the main sources of religious beliefs.*
>
> Malinowski, 1954

Religion deals with the problem of death in the following manner. A funeral ceremony expresses the belief in immortality, which denies the fact of death, and so comforts the bereaved. Other mourners support the bereaved by their presence at the ceremony. This comfort and support check the emotions which death produces, and control the stress and anxiety that might disrupt society. Death is socially destructive since it removes a member from society. At a funeral ceremony the social group unites to support the bereaved. This expression of social solidarity reintegrates society.

Religion, prediction and control

A second category of events – undertakings that cannot be fully controlled or predicted by practical means – also produces tension and anxiety. From his observations in the Trobriand Islands, Malinowski noted that such events were surrounded by ritual.

Fishing is an important subsistence practice in the Trobriands. Malinowski observed that in the calm waters of the lagoon 'fishing is done in an easy and absolutely reliable manner by the method of poisoning, yielding abundant results without danger and uncertainty'. However, beyond the barrier reef in the open sea there is danger and uncertainty: a storm may result in loss of life and the catch is dependent on the presence of a shoal of fish, which cannot be predicted. In the lagoon, 'where man can rely completely on his knowledge and skill', there are no rituals associated with fishing, whereas fishing in the open sea is preceded by rituals to ensure a good catch and protect the fishermen. Although Malinowski refers to these rituals as magic, others argue that it is reasonable to regard them as religious practices.

Again we see ritual used for specific situations that produce anxiety. Rituals reduce anxiety by providing confidence and a feeling of control. As with funeral ceremonies, fishing rituals are social events. The group unites to deal with situations of stress, and so the unity of the group is strengthened.

Therefore we can summarize by saying that Malinowski's distinctive contribution to the sociology of religion is his argument that religion promotes social solidarity by dealing with situations of emotional stress that threaten the stability of society.

Criticisms of Malinowski

Malinowski has been criticized for exaggerating the importance of religious rituals in helping people to cope with situations of stress and uncertainty. Tambiah (1990, discussed in Hamilton, 1995) points out, for example, that magic and elaborate rituals are associated with the cultivation of taro and yams on the Trobriand Islands. This is related to the fact that taro and yams are important because men must use them to make payments to their sisters' husbands. Men who fail to do so show that they are unable to fulfil significant social obligations. These rituals are therefore simply related to the maintenance of prestige in that society and have little to do with cementing solidarity or dealing with uncertainty and danger. A particular function or effect that religion sometimes has, has been mistaken for a feature of religion in general.

Talcott Parsons

Religion and value consensus

Talcott Parsons (1937, 1964, 1965a) argued that human action is directed and controlled by norms provided by the social system. The cultural system provides more general guidelines for action in the form of beliefs, values and systems of meaning. The norms which direct action are not merely isolated standards for behaviour: they are integrated and patterned by the values and beliefs provided by the cultural system. For example, many norms in Western society are expressions of the value of materialism. Religion is part of the cultural system. As such, religious beliefs provide guidelines for human action and standards against which people's conduct can be evaluated.

In a Christian society the Ten Commandments operate in this way. They demonstrate how many of the norms of the social system can be integrated by religious beliefs. For example, the commandment 'Thou shalt not kill' integrates such diverse norms as the ways to drive a car, to settle an argument and to deal with the suffering of the aged. The norms that direct these areas of behaviour prohibit manslaughter, murder and euthanasia but they are all based on the same religious commandment.

In this way, religion provides general guidelines for conduct which are expressed in a variety of norms. By establishing general principles and moral beliefs, religion helps to provide the consensus which Parsons believes is necessary for order and stability in society.

Religion and social order

Parsons, like Malinowski, sees religion as being addressed to particular problems that occur in all societies. He argues that in everyday life, people 'go about their business without particular strain'. If life were always like this, 'religion would certainly not have the significance that it does'. However, life does not always follow this smooth pattern. The problems that disrupt it fall into two categories:

1 The first 'consists in the fact that individuals are "hit" by events which they cannot foresee and prepare for, or control, or both'. One such event is death, particularly premature death. Like Malinowski, and for similar reasons, Parsons sees religion as a mechanism for adjustment to such events and as a means of restoring the normal pattern of life.

2 The second problem area is that of 'uncertainty'. This refers to endeavours in which a great deal of effort and skill have been invested, but where unknown or uncontrollable factors can threaten a successful outcome. One example is humanity's inability to predict or control the effect of weather upon agriculture. Again, following Malinowski, Parsons argues that religion provides a means of adjusting and coming to terms with such situations through rituals which act as 'a tonic to self-confidence'.

In this way, religion maintains social stability by relieving the tension and frustration that could disrupt social order.

Religion and meaning

As a part of the cultural system, religious beliefs give meaning to life; they answer, in Parsons's rather sexist words, 'man's questions about himself and the world he lives in'. This function of religion is particularly important in relation to the frustrations we discussed in the last section, which threaten to shatter beliefs about the meaning of life and so make human existence meaningless. Why should a premature death occur? It is not something people expect to happen or feel ought to happen. Social life is full of contradictions that threaten the meanings people place on life. Parsons argues that one of the major functions of religion is to 'make sense' of all experiences, no matter how meaningless or contradictory they appear.

A good example of this is the question of suffering: 'Why must men endure deprivation and pain and so unequally and haphazardly, if indeed at all?' Religion provides a range of answers: suffering is imposed by God to test a person's faith; it is a punishment for sins; and suffering with fortitude will bring its reward in Heaven. Suffering thus becomes meaningful.

Similarly, the problem of evil is common to all societies. It is particularly disconcerting when people profit through evil actions. Religion solves this contradiction by stating that evil will receive its just deserts in the afterlife.

Parsons (1965a) therefore sees a major function of religion as the provision of meaning to events that people do not expect, or feel ought not, to happen – events that are frustrating and contradictory. Religion 'makes sense' of these events in terms of an integrated and consistent pattern of meaning. This allows intellectual and emotional adjustment. On a more general level, this adjustment promotes order and stability in society.

Criticisms of the functionalist approach

The functionalist perspective emphasizes the positive contributions of religion to society and tends to ignore its dysfunctional aspects. With its preoccupation with harmony, integration and solidarity, functionalism neglects the many instances where religion can be seen as a divisive and disruptive force. It bypasses the frequent examples of internal divisions within a community over questions of religious dogma and worship – divisions that can lead to open conflict. It gives little consideration to hostility between different religious groups within the same society, such as Catholics and Protestants in Northern Ireland or Hindus and Muslims in India. In such cases religion can be seen as a direct threat to social order. As Charles Glock and Rodney Stark state in their criticism of functionalist views on religion:

> We find it difficult to reconcile the general theory with considerable evidence of religious conflict. On every side it would seem that religion threatens social integration as readily as it contributes to it. The history of Christianity, with its many schisms, manifests the great power of religion not merely to bind but to divide.
>
> Glock and Stark, 1965

The Marxist perspective on religion, which we are going to consider next, provides an interesting contrast to functionalist views.

Religion – a Marxist perspective

In Marx's vision of the ideal society, exploitation and alienation are things of the past. The means of production are communally owned, which results in the disappearance of social classes. Members of society are fulfilled as human beings: they control their own destinies and work together for the common good. Religion does not exist in this communist utopia because the social conditions that produce it have disappeared.

To Marx, religion is an illusion which eases the pain produced by exploitation and oppression. It is a series of myths that justify and legitimate the subordination of the subject class and the domination and privilege of the ruling class. It is a distortion of reality which provides many of the deceptions that form the basis of ruling-class ideology and false class consciousness.

Religion as 'the opium of the people'

In Marx's words, 'Religion is the sigh of the oppressed creature, the sentiment of a heartless world and the soul of soulless conditions. It is the opium of the people' (Marx, in Bottomore and Rubel, 1963). Religion acts as an opiate to dull the pain produced by oppression. It is both 'an expression of real suffering and a protest against suffering', but it does little to solve the problem because it helps to make life more bearable and therefore dilutes demands for change. As such, religion merely stupefies its adherents rather than bringing them true happiness and fulfilment.

Similarly, Lenin argued 'Religion is a kind of spiritual gin in which the slaves of capital drown their human shape and their claims to any decent life' (cited in Lane, 1970).

From a Marxist perspective, religion can dull the pain of oppression in the following ways:

1 It promises a paradise of eternal bliss in life after death. Engels argued that the appeal of Christianity to oppressed classes lies in its promise of 'salvation from bondage and misery' in the afterlife. The Christian vision of heaven can make life on earth more bearable by giving people something to look forward to.

2 Some religions make a virtue of the suffering produced by oppression. In particular, those who bear the deprivations of poverty with dignity and humility will be rewarded for their virtue. This view is contained in the well-known biblical quotation, 'It is easier for a camel to pass through the eye of a needle, than for a rich man to enter the Kingdom of Heaven.' Religion thus makes poverty more tolerable by offering a reward for suffering and promising compensation for injustice in the afterlife.

3 Religion can offer the hope of supernatural intervention to solve the problems on earth. Members of religious groups such as the Jehovah's Witnesses live in anticipation of the day when the supernatural powers will descend from on high and create heaven on earth. Anticipation of this future can make the present more acceptable.

4 Religion often justifies the social order and a person's position within it. God can be seen as creating and ordaining the social structure, as in the following verse from the Victorian hymn 'All things bright and beautiful':

> The rich man in his castle,
> The poor man at his gate,
> God made them high and lowly,
> And ordered their estate.

In this way, social arrangements appear inevitable. This can help those at the bottom of the stratification system to accept and come to terms with their situation. In the same way, poverty and misfortune in general have often been seen as divinely ordained as a punishment for sin. Again, the situation is defined as immutable and unchangeable. This can make life more bearable by encouraging people to accept their situation philosophically.

Religion and social control

From a Marxist viewpoint, religion does not simply cushion the effects of oppression, it is also an instrument of that oppression. It acts as a mechanism of social control, maintaining the existing system of exploitation and reinforcing class relationships. Put simply, it keeps people in their place. By making unsatisfactory lives bearable, religion tends to discourage people from attempting to change their situation. By offering an illusion of hope in a hopeless situation, it prevents thoughts of overthrowing the system. By providing explanations and justifications for social situations, religion distorts reality. It helps to produce a false class consciousness that blinds members of the subject class to their true situation and their real interests. In this way it diverts people's attention from the real source of their oppression and so helps to maintain ruling-class power.

Religion is not, however, solely the province of oppressed groups. From a Marxist perspective, ruling classes adopt religious beliefs to justify their position both to themselves and to others. The lines 'God made them high and lowly/And ordered their estate' show clearly how religion can be used to justify social inequality, not simply to the poor, but also to the rich. Religion is often directly supported by the ruling classes to further their interests. In the words of Marx and Engels, 'the parson has ever gone hand in hand with the landlord'. In feudal England the lord of the manor's power was frequently legitimated by pronouncements from the pulpit. In return for this support, landlords would often richly endow the established church.

Evidence to support Marxism

There is considerable evidence to support the Marxist view of the role of religion in society.

The caste system of traditional India was justified by Hindu religious beliefs. In medieval Europe, kings and queens ruled by divine right. The Egyptian Pharaohs went one step further by combining both god and king in the same person. Slave-owners in the southern states of America often approved of the conversion of slaves to Christianity, believing it to be a controlling and gentling influence. It has been argued that in the early days of the Industrial Revolution in England, employers used religion as a means of controlling the masses and encouraging them to remain sober and to work hard.

A more recent example which can be used to support Marxism has been discussed by Steve Bruce (1988). He has pointed out that, in the USA, conservative Protestants – the 'New Christian Right' – consistently support right-wing political candidates in the Republican Party, and attack more liberal candidates in the Democratic Party. In 1980 they 'targeted' 27 liberal candidates for attack; 23 of them lost. The New Christian Right supported Ronald Reagan in his successful campaign for the presidency in 1984. In the 1988 presidential campaign, however, Reagan was unsuccessfully challenged for the Republican nomination for president by a member of the New Christian Right, Pat Robertson. Robertson is one of a number of television evangelists who have tried to gain new converts to their brand of Christianity and who spread their political and moral messages through preaching on television.

According to Bruce, the New Christian Right have supported 'a more aggressive anti-communist foreign policy, more military spending, less central government interference, less welfare spending, and fewer restraints on free enterprise'. Although Bruce emphasizes that they have had a limited influence on American politics, it is clear that they have tended to defend the interests of the rich and powerful at the expense of other groups in the population.

The limitations of Marxism

Conflicting evidence suggests that religion does not always legitimate power; it is not simply a justifica-

tion of alienation or a justification of privilege, and it can sometimes provide an impetus for change. Although this is not reflected in Marx's own writing, nor in much of Engels's earlier work, it is reflected in Engels's later work and in the perspectives on religion advanced by more recent neo-Marxists. We will examine these views after the next section, which considers the relationship between religion and communism.

Furthermore, the fact that religion sometimes acts as an ideological force in the way suggested by Marx, does not explain the existence of religion. As Malcolm Hamilton points out:

> To say, however, that religion can be turned into an instrument of manipulation is no more to explain it than saying that because art or drama can be utilised for ideological purposes this explains art or drama.
>
> Hamilton, 1995, p. 84

In contrast, approaches such as those used by Stark and Bainbridge (1985) do try to find an explanation for the almost universal presence of religion in society in basic human needs. Their views will be examined shortly (see pp. 445–6).

Religion and communism

Marx stated that 'Religion is only the illusory sun which revolves round man as long as he does not revolve round himself' (Marx and Engels, 1957). In a truly socialist society individuals revolve around themselves, and religion – along with all other illusions and distortions of reality – disappears.

Whatever the merits of this prophecy, it certainly does not reflect the situation in the socialist Israeli kibbutzim. Many kibbutzim are fervently religious and their members appear to experience no contradiction between religion and socialism.

In the USSR under communism the strength of religion was harder to gauge. After the revolution of 1917 the communist state placed limits on religious activity and at times persecuted religious people. Soviet law restricted religious worship to designated churches and other places of prayer. Religious instruction of children was banned. Geoffrey Hosking estimated that there were more than 50,000 Russian Orthodox churches before the 1917 revolution, but by 1939 only about 4,000 remained (Hosking, 1988). Writing in 1970, David Lane claimed that there were about 20,000 Russian Orthodox churches in 1960, but nearly half of these had been closed by 1965 due to the policies of Khrushchev.

On the surface such figures suggest that religion had declined, but this may have been due to the activities of the ruling elite rather than to a loss of faith by the population. Lane claimed that religion probably had little hold over the population, but it had, nevertheless, shown a certain resilience to communism. This resilience was reflected in one estimate which placed the number of baptized Orthodox Christians in the period 1947–57 at 90 million, which is roughly the same as in 1914. In 1988, Geoffrey Hoskins argued that 'The Soviet Union is already a much more "religious" country than Britain or most of Western Europe.'

When President Gorbachov instituted a policy of *glasnost*, or openness, restrictions on religion were relaxed. In 1989 and 1990, unrest in a number of Soviet republics suggested the continued strength of religious belief. The Roman Catholic Church in Lithuania was one source of demands for independence. In 1990, conflict between Soviet Muslims in Azerbaijan and Soviet Christians in Armenia led to troops being deployed to restore order.

When the USSR began to divide and Communist Party rule was abandoned, religious convictions became even more evident. In 1991, David Martin described how church bells were used to summon millions of people to link arms around the Baltic states of Latvia, Lithuania and Estonia. In other former communist countries there were 'enormous gatherings in Poland to celebrate the feast of the Assumption and the passionate pilgrimages of the Serbs to monastic shrines at Kosova' (Martin, 1991b).

Opinion poll figures suggest that religion remained important to large proportions of the population during the communist eras in the USSR and Eastern Europe, and that religion has become stronger since the demise of communism. Quoting data from the International Social Survey Program, Andrew Greeley notes that, in 1991, 47 per cent of the Russian population claimed to believe in God (Greeley, 1994). The strength of the religious revival is revealed by the fact that 22 per cent of the population were former non-believers who had converted to a belief in God. Similarly, Mikl[ó]s Tomka found that, in 1978, 44.3 per cent of the population of Hungary claimed to be religious, and that this had risen to 76.8 per cent by August 1993 (Tomka, 1995).

One society which has retained communism throughout the 1990s is Fidel Castro's Cuba. However, even such a staunch communist as Castro was forced to acknowledge the continuing appeal of religion when he invited Pope John Paul to Cuba in January 1998. The Pope addressed large and enthusiastic crowds, suggesting that Roman Catholicism remained strong despite some 40 years in which the communist state had discouraged religious participation and belief.

These examples suggest that there is more to religion than a set of beliefs and practices which develop in societies based on the private ownership of the means of production. (See Chapter 15 for an analysis of religion within the general framework of Marxist theory.)

Engels and neo-Marxists – religion as a radical force

Engels – Christianity and social change

Roger O'Toole, commenting on the Marxist sociology of religion, argues that 'Beginning with the work of Engels, Marxists have undoubtedly recognized the active role that may be played by religion in effecting revolutionary social change' (O'Toole, 1984). Thus, in *On the History of Early Christianity*, Engels compared some of the early Christian sects that opposed Roman rule to communist and socialist political movements (Marx and Engels, 1957). He said, 'Christianity got hold of the masses exactly as modern socialism does, under the shape of a variety of sects.' While Christianity originated as a way of coping with exploitation among oppressed groups, it could become a source of resistance to the oppressors and thus a force for change.

Otto Maduro – the relative autonomy of religion

Maduro is a contemporary neo-Marxist. While accepting many aspects of Marx's analysis of religion, he places greater emphasis on the idea that religion has some independence, or 'relative autonomy', from the economic system of the bourgeoisie (Maduro, 1982). He denies that religion is always a conservative force and, indeed, claims that it can be revolutionary. He says, 'Religion is not necessarily a functional, reproductive or conservative factor in society; it often is one of the main (and sometimes the only) available channel to bring about a social revolution.'

Maduro claims that, up until recently, Catholicism in Latin America tended to support the bourgeoisie and right-wing military dictatorships which have represented its interests. The Catholic Church has tended to deny the existence of social conflicts between oppressive and oppressed classes. It has recognized some injustices, such as poverty and illiteracy, but has suggested that the solution lies with those who already have power. The Catholic Church has also supported members of the clergy who have assisted private enterprise and government projects; it has celebrated military victories but failed to support unions, strikes, and opposition political parties.

On the other hand, more recently, Catholic priests have increasingly demonstrated their autonomy from the bourgeoisie by criticizing them and acting against their interests. Maduro believes that members of the clergy can develop revolutionary potential where oppressed members of the population have no outlet for their grievances. They pressurize priests to take up their cause, and theological disagreements within a church can provide interpretations of a religion that are critical of the rich and powerful.

All of these conditions have been met in Latin America and have led to the development of liberation theology (for further details of liberation theology see p. 451).

Bryan S. Turner – a materialist theory of religion

Bryan Turner (1983) follows Marx in arguing that religion rises from a material base: that is, he agrees that religion relates to the physical and economic aspects of social life. Unlike Marx, however, Turner does not believe that religion has a universal role in society, nor does he believe that religion is always an important part of ruling-class ideological control. He questions the belief that religion has always been a powerful force persuading subject classes to accept the status quo.

Religion and feudalism

Marxists have tended to assume that, in the feudal period, religion (in particular, Roman Catholicism in Europe) was a belief system that played a fundamental part in integrating society. Turner rejects the view that religion was as important for serfs and peasants as it was for feudal lords. On the basis of historical evidence he claims that the peasantry were largely indifferent to religion: their main concern was simply survival.

By comparison, religion played an important part in the lives of the ruling class, the feudal lords. In feudalism, wealth consisted of, and power derived from, the ownership of land by private individuals. For the ruling class to maintain its dominance it had to pass on property to an heir. Usually a system of primogeniture was used: the eldest son of a landowner inherited all his father's land. This prevented the splitting-up of estates, which would have reduced the concentration of power in the hands of particular individuals. It was therefore vital to the workings of feudalism and the maintenance of a dominant class that there was a legitimate male heir for each landowner. Premarital promiscuity and adultery both jeopardized the production of such an heir. Marriage and the legitimacy of children were

propped up and defended by the church. Thus, in Turner's words, 'religion has the function of controlling the sexuality of the body in order to secure regular transmission of property via the family'. Without religion it would have been difficult to ensure there were recognized legitimate heirs who could retain concentrated landholdings in their family's possession.

A secondary function of religion under feudalism also stemmed from primogeniture. There was a surplus of younger sons who did not inherit land. In military feudalism, sons might meet an early death, so it was necessary to have a number of heirs in case one or more were killed. But those who did not receive an inheritance had to have some means of support. Monasteries provided one solution to the problem of the surplus males.

Religion and capitalism

Turner believes that, in modern capitalism, religion has lost the one vital function that it had for the ruling class. Today, he claims, individual and family property is much less important for the maintenance of ruling-class power. Property has become depersonalized – most wealth is concentrated in the hands of organizations (such as banks, pension funds and multinational corporations) rather than in the hands of individuals. In these circumstances, religion is no more than an optional extra for modern capitalist societies. Since the transmission of property via the family is no longer vital to the system, society can tolerate, and the church can accept, divorce and illegitimacy.

Turner's views on religion are similar to the more general views on the dominant ideology thesis advanced by Abercrombie, Hill and Turner (1980). They believe that modern capitalist societies do not possess a widely-accepted ruling-class ideology, and that such an ideology is not necessary for the continuance of capitalist domination: the ruling class use coercion and naked economic power to maintain their position. Abercrombie et al. therefore question Marx's beliefs about the importance of religion in producing false class consciousness in capitalist societies. (For more details on the dominant ideology thesis see Chapter 9.)

Having discussed Marxist and materialist views on religion, we will now turn to a consideration of the relationship between gender and religion. Some feminist theories of religion have similarities with Marxist theories.

Gender, feminism and religion

Introduction

Feminist theories of religion follow Marxist theories in arguing that religion can be an instrument of domination and oppression. However, unlike Marxism, they tend to see religion as a product of patriarchy (see pp. 150–6 for a discussion of patriarchy) rather than as a product of capitalism. They see religion as serving the interests of men rather than those of a capitalist class. Indeed, such a view of religion is not confined to female and feminist sociologists. For example, Anthony Giddens argues that:

> The Christian religion is a resolutely male affair in its symbolism as well as its hierarchy. While Mary, the mother of Jesus, may sometimes be treated as if she had divine qualities, God is the father, a male figure, and Jesus took the human shape of a man. Woman is portrayed as created from a rib taken from a man.
>
> Giddens, 1997, p. 449

The secondary and often subordinate role of women in Christian doctrine is also typical of most other religions. Karen Armstrong argues that 'None of the major religions has been particularly good to women. They have usually become male affairs and women have been relegated to a marginal position' (Armstrong, 1993). Although women may have made significant advances in many areas of life, their gains in most religions have been very limited.

Women continue to be excluded from key roles in many religions (although the Church of England finally allowed the ordination of women priests in 1992). This is despite the fact that women often participate more in organized religion (when they are allowed to) than men. Steve Bruce points out that, according to the 1991 *British Social Attitudes Survey*, 65 per cent of regular church attenders in Britain and Northern Ireland were women, compared to 35 per cent who were men.

Feminist writers are therefore interested in how women came to be subservient within most religions and how religion has been used to cement patriarchal power. More recently, some sociologists have examined how women have begun to try to reduce the imbalance between males and females within religion.

Gender inequality in religion

The origins of gender inequality

A number of writers have noted that, historically, women have not always been subordinate within most religions. Karen Armstrong, for example, argues that in early history 'women were considered central to the spiritual quest' (Armstrong, 1993). In the Middle East, Asia and Europe, archaeologists have uncovered numerous symbols of the Great Mother Goddess. She was pictured as a naked pregnant woman and seems to represent the mysteries of fertility and life. As Armstrong puts it:

> The Earth produced plants and nourished them in rather the same way as a woman gave birth to a child and fed it from her own body. The magical power of the earth seemed vitally interconnected with the mysterious creativity of the female sex.
>
> Armstrong, 1993, p. 8

There were very few early effigies of gods as men. As societies developed religious beliefs in which there were held to be many different gods and goddesses, the Mother Goddess still played a crucial role. Armstrong says she was:

> absorbed into the pantheons of deities and remained a powerful figure. She was called Inanna in Sumner, in ancient Mesopotamia, Ishtar in Babylon, Anat or Asherah in Canaan, Isis in Egypt and Aphrodite in Greece. In all these cultures people told remarkably similar stories about her to express her role in their spiritual lives. She was still revered as the source of fertility.
>
> Armstrong, 1993, p. 9

Not surprisingly, since they had goddesses, these societies also had female priests.

However, the position of women in religion began to decline as a result of invasions. Armstrong says:

> In Mesopotamia, Egypt and India, Semitic and Aryan invaders from the north brought with them a male-orientated mythology which replaced the Goddess with more powerful masculine deities. These invasions had begun as early as the fourth millennium but became more and more devastating.
>
> Armstrong, 1993, p. 21

Armstrong argues that an Amorite myth dating from about 1750 BC marked the start of the eventual decline of the goddess. In it the goddess Tiamat, the goddess of the sea, is replaced by the male god of Babylon, Marduk. Male gods such as the Hebrew Yahweh became increasingly important and they introduced a 'more martial and aggressive spirituality'.

The final death knell of goddesses came with the acceptance of monotheism – belief in a single god rather than many. This originated with Yahweh, the god of Abraham. Furthermore, this 'God of Israel would later become the God of the Christians and the Muslims, who all regard themselves as the spiritual offspring of Abraham, the father of all believers'.

Jean Holm – inequality in major religions

Jean Holm has reviewed some of the ways in which women are subordinate or exploited in contemporary religions and devalued by different religious beliefs (Holm, 1994). She argues that, while the classical teachings of many religions have stressed equality between men and women, in practice women have usually been far from equal. She says, 'Women do, of course, have a part to play in many religions, but it is almost always subordinate to the role of men, and it is likely to be in the private rather than the public sphere.' She gives a number of examples.

In Japanese folk religions women are responsible for organizing public rituals, but only men can take part in the public performances. In Chinese popular religion women are associated with Yin and men with Yang. However, Yang spirits are more important and powerful. In Buddhism, both men and women can have a religious role as monks and nuns respectively. However, all monks are seen as senior to all nuns. Orthodox Judaism only allows males to take a full part in ceremonies. In Islam, in some regions, women are not allowed to enter mosques for worship, and men have made all the legal rulings. Christianity has also been male-dominated. Holm says:

> Many of the most influential ideas were worked out by (celibate) men in the first five centuries of the church's history, and the significant developments of the medieval Church and the Reformation were also shaped by men.
>
> Holm, 1994, p.xiii

In Hinduism only men can become Brahmanic priests. Sikhism is perhaps the most egalitarian of the major religions since all offices are equally open to men and women. However, even in Sikhism, only a small minority of women have significant positions within the religion.

Women's second-class status is often related to female sexuality. Holm comments that 'Menstruation and childbirth are almost universally regarded as polluting. In many traditions women are forbidden to enter sacred places or touch sacred objects during the menstrual period.' For example, Hindu women are prohibited from approaching family shrines when pregnant or menstruating. Muslim women are not allowed to touch the Koran, go into a mosque or pray during menstruation.

Despite documenting these inequalities, Holm is not entirely pessimistic. As we will see later, she does detect evidence of changes in which the inequality between men and women in religion is being slowly reduced (see below, p. 443).

Feminist perspectives on religion

Simone de Beauvoir – religion and *The Second Sex*

Jean Holm describes some of the inequalities between males and females within different religions. However, she goes into little detail about why such inequalities exist. The French feminist Simone de Beauvoir provides such an explanation in her pioneering feminist book *The Second Sex* (1953, first published 1949). To Beauvoir, religion acts for women in very similar ways to those in which Marx suggested religion could act for oppressed classes. De Beauvoir says, 'There must be a religion for women as there must be one for the common people, and for exactly the same reasons.' Religion can be used by the oppressors (men) to control the oppressed group (women) and it also serves as a way of compensating women for their second-class status.

De Beauvoir notes that men have generally exercised control over religious beliefs. She says, 'Man enjoys the great advantage of having a God endorse the code he writes.' That code uses divine authority to support male dominance. As de Beauvoir says, 'For the Jews, Mohammedans, and Christians, among others, man is master by divine right; the fear of God will therefore repress any impulse towards revolt in the downtrodden female.'

However, in modern societies, 'religion seems much less an instrument of constraint than an instrument of deception'. Women are deceived by religion into thinking of themselves as equal to men despite their evident inequality. In some ways women are portrayed by religion as being closer to God than men, even if they are unlikely to hold positions of power within religions. As mothers, women have a key religious role: 'a mother not only engenders the flesh, she produces a soul for God.' Women are taught to be relatively passive, but in some ways this makes them appear more godly than the men whose 'agitation for this and that is more than absurd, it is blameworthy: why remodel this world which God himself created.'

Like Marx's proletariat, religion gives women the false belief that they will be compensated for their sufferings on earth by equality in heaven. In these ways the subjugation of women through religion helps to maintain a status quo in which women are unequal. Women are also vital to religion because it is they who do much of the work for religious organizations and introduce children to religious beliefs. Thus, de Beauvoir concludes:

Religion sanctions woman's self-love; it gives her the guide, father, lover, divine guardian she longs for nostalgically; it feeds her day-dreams; it fills her empty hours. But, above all, it confirms the social order, it justifies her resignation, by giving hope of a better future in a sexless heaven. This is why women today are still a powerful trump in the hand of the Church; it is why the Church is notably hostile to all measures likely to help in women's emancipation. There must be religion for women; and there must be women, 'true women' to perpetuate religion.

de Beauvoir, 1953, p. 591

Nawal El Saadawi – *The Hidden Face of Eve*

Patriarchy, Islam and the limited role of religion

Simone de Beauvoir writes from the perspective of a Western, Christian woman. Nawal El Saadawi is an Egyptian feminist writer and a leading advocate of women's rights in the Arab world. She was sacked from her post as Egypt's Director of Public Health by the then ruler Sadat, and has been imprisoned for her political activities. In *The Hidden Face of Eve* (1980), she discusses female oppression in the Arab world and elsewhere and considers the importance of religion in creating and perpetuating oppression.

El Saadawi recounts some of her personal experience of oppression. For example, she describes in chilling terms her terror as a young girl when her parents forced her, without warning or explanation, to undergo 'female circumcision', where part of her clitoris was amputated. She argues that Arab girls are often victims of sexual aggression by men (often their fathers, brothers or other relations). She also discusses prostitution, slavery and abortion and argues that all of these areas provide evidence of patriarchal dominance of Arab men over Arab women.

She notes that oppressive practices such as female circumcision have often been attributed to the influence of Islam. However, El Saadawi denies that the oppression of women is directly caused by religion in general, or Islam in particular. Female circumcision has been practised in a considerable number of countries, not all of them Islamic. Authentic religious beliefs tend to be opposed to any such practices because, 'if religion comes from God, how can it order man to cut off an organ created by Him as long as that organ is not diseased or deformed?' Authentic religion aims at 'truth, equality, justice, love and a healthy wholesome life for all people, whether men or women'.

Furthermore, other religions are often more oppressive than Islam. She says, 'If we study

Christianity it is easy to see that this religion is much more rigid and orthodox where women are concerned than Islam.' To El Saadawi, the oppression of women is caused by 'the patriarchal system which came into being when society had reached a certain stage of development'. Nevertheless, she does see religion as playing a role in women's oppression. Men do distort religion to serve their own interests, to help justify or legitimate the oppression of women.

The origins of oppressive religion

El Saadawi argues that religion started to become patriarchal through the misinterpretation of religious beliefs by men. She cites the Greek mythological story of Isis and Osiris. The male Osiris is overpowered by the evil Touphoun. His body is cut into small pieces and dispersed in the sea, and his sexual organ is eaten by fish. Despite this, Isis (who is female) is able to reassemble Osiris's body. To El Saadawi, this story clearly implies female superiority, but it has been interpreted quite differently by men. They have emphasized the superiority of Osiris because he was created from the head of the god Zeus, who was greater than Osiris, according to Homer and other writers, because he was more knowledgeable. In reality, El Saadawi says, all the male gods were created by, or given the ability to move by, the greatest deity of them all, the goddess Isis.

Similar distortions have entered the story of Adam and Eve, which is accepted by both Christians and Muslims as part of the story of creation. Eve is usually portrayed by males as a temptress who created sin in the world, but was created from Adam's spare rib. However:

if we read the original story as described in the Old Testament, it is easy for us to see clearly that Eve was gifted with knowledge, intelligence and superior mental capacities, whereas Adam was only one of her instruments, utilized by her to increase her knowledge and give shape to her creativity.

El Saadawi, 1980, pp. 105–6

Like other writers, El Saadawi argues that forms of religion that were oppressive to women developed as monotheistic religions (believing in a single god) became predominant. Such religions 'drew inspiration and guidance from the values of the patriarchal and class societies prevalent at the time' (El Saadawi, 1980). For example, the Jewish religion drew upon the patriarchal power of Abraham to produce a situation in which 'A Hebrew household was embodied in the patriarchal family, under the uncontested and undivided authority of the father.'

Islamic society also developed in a patriarchal way through the dominance of a male minority who owned herds of horses, camels and sheep. As a consequence, 'Authority in Islam belonged to the man as head of the family, to the supreme ruler, or the Khalifa (political ruler), or Imran (religious leader).' Although the Koran stipulated that both men and women could be stoned to death for adultery, this fate was very unlikely to befall men. This was because men were permitted several wives (but women were not permitted several husbands) and because men could divorce their wives instantaneously. There was therefore little need for men to commit adultery. Even today in countries such as Egypt women are still subject to extremely restrictive marriage laws.

El Saadawi describes Christ as a revolutionary leader who opposed oppression. Early Christianity had stricter moral codes than other religions, and codes which treated the sexes fairly equally. Nevertheless, at a later stage:

> the religious hierarchies that grew and fattened on the teachings of Christ allowed the system of concubinage to creep in once more. Despite the limitations placed by Christianity on man's sexual freedom, woman was maintained in her inferior underprivileged status as compared with him. The patriarchal system still reigned supreme and grew even more ferocious with the gradual shift to a feudal system.
>
> El Saadawi, 1980, p. 119

In the fourteenth century, for example, the Catholic Church declared that women who treated illnesses, without special training, could be executed as witches.

Conclusion

El Saadawi concludes that female oppression is not essentially due to religion but due to the patriarchal system that has long been dominant. Religion, though, has played its part. She says:

> The great religions of the world uphold similar principles in so far as the submission of women to men is concerned. They also agree in the attribution of masculine characteristics to their God. Islam and Christianity have both constituted important stages in the evolution of humanity. Nevertheless, where the cause of women was concerned, they added a new load to their already heavy chains.
>
> El Saadawi, 1980, p. 211

The only way for women to improve their lot is to struggle for their own liberation. Arab women have been doing this for longer than their Western counterparts. As early as fourteen centuries ago Arab women successfully campaigned against the universal use of the male gender when referring to people in general in the Koran. El Saadawi believes that any recent gains in the position of Arab women have been due to a combination of social, economic and political changes and their own struggles. She argues that women have benefited from socialist revolutions wherever they have taken place. Revolutions will further the cause of women even more if the positive aspects of the Koran can be emphasized and the patriarchal misinterpretations abandoned. Thus El Saadawi is not hostile to religion itself, but only to the domination of religion by patriarchal ideology.

Women and resistance to religious oppression

Signs of hope

Apart from El Saadawi, the theorists examined above have tended to portray women as the passive victims of religious oppression, and religions themselves as being universally oppressive. Increasingly, however, sociologists have come to acknowledge that women can no longer be seen as being so passive. Jean Holm (1994), acting as editor of a book dealing with women and different religious traditions, sees 'signs of hope' in the religious situation of women. Rita Gross (1994) detects that there are signs that a 'post-patriarchal' Buddhism might be developing in Western countries.

Leila Badawi (1994) notes aspects of Islam that are positive for women. Unlike Christian women, Islamic women keep their own family name when they get married. Muslims also have considerable choice over which interpretation of Islam, or school of law, they give their allegiance to. Some schools of law have much more positive attitudes to women than others.

Alexandra Wright notes that Reform Judaism has allowed women to become rabbis since 1972 (Wright, 1994). Holm notes that even in 1994 there were already three female Anglican bishops. Some Christian religions, particularly Quakerism, have never been oppressive to women. Kanwaljit Kaur-Singh points out that 'Sikh Gurus pleaded the cause of the emancipation of Indian womanhood and did their best to ameliorate the sordid condition of women' (Kaur-Singh, 1994).

Thus it should not be assumed that all religions are, and always have been, equally oppressive to women. Furthermore, even apparently oppressive practices may be open to varied interpretations. One example is the veiling of Islamic women.

Helen Watson – the meaning of veiling

Perspectives on veiling

Helen Watson argues that 'For non-Muslim writers, the veil is variously depicted as a tangible symbol of women's oppression, a constraining and restricting form of dress, and a form of social control, religiously sanctioning women's invisibility and subordinate socio-political status' (Watson, 1994). However, this is not the viewpoint of many Muslim women and writers. To them, hijab, or religious modesty, actually has advantages for women, which can reduce, or allow them to cope with, male oppression.

The veil has the potential both to constrain and to liberate. Watson accepts that Islamic interpretations of the Koran's advocacy of modesty have been interpreted differently for men and women. Primary emphasis has been placed upon the need for women to be modest because their seductiveness might lead men astray. Furthermore, some Islamic feminists argue that the Koran makes no clear statement of the need for women to wear a veil in the presence of men who are not relatives. Rather, the practice is based upon a misinterpretation of the Koran by those who wanted to maintain patriarchal relationships that predated Islam. To some the practice is 'at odds with the reforming and egalitarian inspiration and ethos of Islam'.

Nevertheless, by examining three personal responses to veiling by different women, Watson maintains that wearing veils can be used in a positive way by Islamic women in a globalized world. As Western culture tries to influence Islamic countries, and more Muslims live in the Western world, the veil can take on new meanings for women.

The experience of veiling

The first example studied by Watson was Nadia, a second-generation British-Asian woman studying medicine at university. Nadia chose herself to start wearing a veil when she was 16. She was proud of her religion and wanted others to know that she was Muslim. She felt that 'It is liberating to have the freedom of movement to be able to communicate with people without being on show. It's what you say that's important, not what you look like.' She found that, far from making her invisible, wearing a veil made her stand out, yet it also helped her to avoid 'lecherous stares or worse' from men.

The second woman, Maryam, was a middle-aged, lower-class Algerian living in France, who had migrated there ten years earlier with her husband. When she was growing up in Algiers her relatives wore Western-style clothes. Maryam thought that

times had changed and it was now appropriate for her to wear a veil. She thought, 'It is difficult enough to live in a big foreign city without having the extra burden of being molested in the street because you are a woman.' Her husband was happy with her decision because it made him worry about her less when she was going to work. Maryam was also keen to wear a veil because she wanted to follow the example of women in Iran. She described the 1979 Islamic revolution there as 'the people's struggle to throw out their corrupt ruler, rid the country of the ill effects of Western influences and make a better society'. She continued, 'These things all had the result of making me more aware of the importance of Islam and my conduct and duty as a mother and a wife for the future of the next generation.'

The third woman interviewed by Watson, Fatima, was a vegetable seller in Cairo. She was in her late seventies. She took a less positive view of the trend towards wearing veils amongst Egyptian women. She thought it was 'just a trend'. When Fatima was a young woman, women still took the idea of modesty seriously without feeling the need to dress so traditionally. Fatima did not think that 'this new veiling is a religious duty. A woman's modest conduct is more important than what she wears.' She was in favour of an increased emphasis on morality amongst Islamic women, though, and was happy for people to turn against some of the less desirable Western values. However, she thought that the issue of whether to wear a veil should always be a matter of choice rather than of law.

Conclusion and evaluation

Watson concludes that veiling is often a reaction against an increasingly pervasive Western culture. Some Muslim men too have begun to reject Western-style clothes – for example, by refusing to wear ties. All this can be seen as '"a sign of the times" which entails the assertion of independence, separate identity and a rejection of western cultural imperialism'. Rather than seeing the veil as a sign of male oppression, it has become 'a reaction against the secular feminism of the West, and as part of the search for an indigenous Islamic form of protest against male power and dominance in public society'.

Watson's work serves as a caution to sociologists who interpret in simplistic terms the practices of religions which are not their own. It shows that the meaning of religion needs to be carefully interpreted. In studies of religion, account needs to be taken of the meaning of religion to its believers; it is not just based upon reading holy texts and observing religious practices. Watson's work suggests that practices that may appear oppressive can take on a variety of meanings. Nevertheless, her conclusions should be treated with some caution. Her observations are based upon studying only three women. She appears to have made no attempt to find Muslim women who felt they were forced into wearing the veil against their will by men or patriarchal society.

Attempts by women to subvert patriarchy by changing the meaning of traditional practices may not always succeed in liberating women from domination through religion. There is always a danger that they might have the opposite effect.

Rodney Stark and William Sims Bainbridge – religion and compensators

Unlike functionalist sociologists such as Durkheim, the American sociologists Stark and Bainbridge see religion as meeting the needs of individuals rather than those of society as a whole (Stark and Bainbridge, 1985). Unlike Marx, they see religion as meeting universal human needs rather than those that stem from class inequality and exploitation. Unlike feminists, they do not see religion as primarily serving the interests of men rather than women. Furthermore, they reject the view, shared by the classic sociologists of religion, that the development of industrial capitalist societies would, one way or another, ultimately undermine religion (see p. 486). Stark and Bainbridge claim that religion helps to meet universal human needs. As such, changes in society cannot diminish its appeal.

Human desires

They start with the basic premise that 'Humans seek what they perceive to be rewards and try to avoid what they perceive to be costs.' In short, people do what they believe will be good for them. This provides quite a straightforward basis for human decision making but individuals may still face problems:

1 Many of the things that people desire, for example wealth and status, are scarce and cannot be attained by everyone.

2 Some things that people strongly desire may not be available at all. One such desire, and one that is crucial for their theory, is a desire for life after death. Even without convincing evidence that eternal life is possible, people continue to want it, and it is here that the roots of religion lie.

Compensators

Stark and Bainbridge recognize that religion might not actually provide people with eternal life, but what it does offer is a 'compensator'. A compensator is 'the belief that a reward will be obtained in the distant future or in some other context which cannot be verified'. They are a type of IOU – if individuals act in a particular way they will eventually be rewarded. In the absence of immediate rewards people are liable to turn to compensators.

Some political activists would like society to be transformed. If there is little evidence that the transformation is likely, they may develop the belief in a future revolution as a compensator. Similarly, a compensator is exchanged for a reward when a parent persuades a child that working hard now will eventually lead to fame and riches. Some compensators are quite specific – for example, the promise of a cured wart; others are more general. The promise of eternal life is an example of a general compensator.

Compensators and the supernatural

Sometimes individuals want rewards that are so great and so remote from everyday experience that the possibility of gaining them can only be contemplated alongside a belief in the supernatural. Stark and Bainbridge say:

> Since time immemorial humans have desired to know the meaning of existence. Why are we here? What is the purpose of life? Where will it all end? Moreover, people have not just wanted answers to these questions; they have desired particular kinds of answers – that life has meaning. But for life to have a great design, for there to be intention behind history, one must posit the existence of a designer or intender of such power, duration, and scale as to be outside the natural world of our senses.
>
> Stark and Bainbridge, 1985

Only belief in a god allows us to have answers to our most fundamental questions. According to this viewpoint, religion consists of organizations which offer 'general compensators based on supernatural assumptions'.

Religious pluralism and secularization

Since religion answers universal questions, and it offers compensators that meet universal human needs, religion can neither disappear nor seriously decline. If churches compromise their beliefs in the supernatural they become less appealing as a source of compensators. Thus 'for religious organizations to move markedly in the direction of non-supernaturalism is to pursue the path to ruin'. If this happens, people turn to different religious organizations, and particularly to new sects and cults that have a greater emphasis on the supernatural. (We will discuss sects and cults later, see pp. 460–2.)

According to Stark and Bainbridge, American society has become characterized by religious pluralism as people have sought new sources of compensators. They quote J. George Melton's 1978 *Encyclopedia of American Religions* which listed no fewer than 1,200 different religious groups. Stark and Bainbridge deny that there are many people who lack beliefs and they do not believe that secularization has taken place or will take place in the future. (In general terms secularization means the decline of religion. For a detailed definition of secularization see pp. 469–70.) They claim that 'the majority of people who say they have no religious affiliation express considerable belief in the mystical and supernatural'. In other words, they have not lost their need for supernatural compensators. Furthermore, Stark and Bainbridge quote survey evidence which suggests that 60 per cent of those whose parents had no religious affiliation claim a religious affiliation for themselves. Where agnosticism or atheism existed, they were not passed on to succeeding generations.

Stark and Bainbridge – an evaluation

Stark and Bainbridge have provided an original and comprehensive attempt to develop a sociological perspective on religion. Their work has provided a number of insights into religious organizations and religious change. However, it has not been without critics.

Roy Wallis and Steve Bruce argue that the available evidence contradicts their theory (Wallis and Bruce, 1986). New religious movements have not gained sufficient recruits to replace those lost from more established religions. (The evidence for and against the theory of secularization is examined in detail on pp. 470–93.)

Wallis and Bruce also criticize Stark and Bainbridge for ignoring social and cultural influences on the questions that individuals ask and the rewards they seek. It is by no means inevitable that people seek the kinds of reward for which religion offers compensators. Society, culture and socialization might create the need for religion rather than universal human desires. Wallis and Bruce say:

> *since most people are born into a social world in which religious beliefs already exist, belief in another world with supernatural characteristics opens up the possibility of wanting things there as well as rather than instead of here.*
>
> Wallis and Bruce, 1986

By reducing their explanation of religion to supposedly universal needs, Stark and Bainbridge neglect the social factors that help to create and sustain religion. For example, they neglect the possibility that religion might be related to sustaining the power and dominance of men. This possibility was examined in the previous section on gender.

Religion and social change

There are a number of possible relationships between religion and social change. Religion may be a factor that impedes social change, or it may help to produce it. Another possibility is that religion itself has no influence on changes in society, but that there is nevertheless a causal relationship between the two. From this point of view, it is social change in society as a whole that leads to changes in religion.

Religion as a conservative force

Functionalists and Marxists have generally dismissed the possibility that religion can cause changes in society. They believe that religion acts as a conservative force and that it is changes in society that shape religion, not vice versa.

Religion can be seen as a 'conservative force' in two senses, depending on the meaning attached to the word 'conservative'. The phrase conservative force is usually used to refer to religion as preventing change and maintaining the status quo. Functionalists have claimed that it acts in this way because it promotes integration and social solidarity. As we discovered in previous sections, from a functionalist perspective, religion provides shared beliefs, norms and values, and helps individuals to cope with stresses that might disrupt social life. In these ways it facilitates the continued existence of society in its present form. Marx had similar views, although he saw religion as maintaining the status quo in the interests of the ruling class rather than those of society as a whole.

'Conservative' may, however, be used in another way: it can refer to traditional beliefs and customs. Usually if religion helps to maintain the status quo it will also maintain traditional customs and beliefs. For example, the stance of successive popes against the use of contraception has restricted the growth of artificial methods of birth control in Roman Catholic countries. But in some circumstances religion can support social change while at the same time promoting traditional values. This often occurs when there is a revival in fundamentalist religious beliefs.

Conservatism, fundamentalism and social change

Recent years have seen the rise of fundamentalist religious beliefs in different parts of the world. Donald Taylor (1987) defines fundamentalism as involving the following:

1   A group of people perceive a challenge to an ultimate authority, usually a god, in which they believe.
2   These people decide that the challenge cannot be tolerated.
3   They reaffirm their belief in the authority that is being challenged.
4   They oppose those who have challenged the established beliefs, and often they use political means to further their cause.

According to this view, fundamentalism involves the reassertion of traditional moral and religious values against changes that have taken place and those who support the changes. If fundamentalists are successful, they succeed in defending traditional values, but at the same time they change society by reversing innovations that have taken place.

However, it should be borne in mind that religions are usually open to many different interpretations. Those claiming to be returning to the original teachings of a religion may well disagree with one another. Thus Fred Halliday, commenting on Islamic fundamentalism, says that 'no such essential Islam exists: as one Iranian thinker puts it, Islam is a sea in which it is possible to catch almost any fish one wants' (Halliday, 1994). In other words, each partic-ular fundamentalist interpretation of a religion is only one amongst many.

In a book of articles edited by Lionel Caplan (1987), fundamentalism was identified among a wide variety of religious groups throughout the world. These included Sikh fundamentalists in the Punjab, Hindu fundamentalism amongst Sri Lankans in Britain, and Islamic fundamentalism in Turkey. Steve Bruce has analysed fundamentalism amongst Protestant groups in Northern Ireland, Scotland and the USA (Bruce 1985, 1986, 1988).

However, perhaps the most dramatic example of fundamentalism causing social change through the imposition of a return to traditional values has been in Iran. Under the last Shah, Iranian society underwent a process of change. One aspect of this change was the liberalization of traditional Islamic attitudes to women. In 1979 the Iranian revolution, which was partly inspired by Islamic fundamentalism, took place and these changes were reversed. In this case, it can be argued, religious beliefs contributed to producing revolutionary change. Religion did not therefore act as a conservative force in one sense of the word. Nevertheless, in terms of supporting traditional values, it did act as a conservative force. The two meanings of the word conservative should therefore be distinguished.

Changes in society and religion

Most sociologists agree that changes in society lead to changes in religion:

1   Talcott Parsons (1937, 1964, 1965a), for example, believed that, as society developed, religion lost some of its functions (for further details, see pp. 434–5).
2   Marx believed that a change in the infrastructure of society would lead to changes in the superstructure, including religion. Thus Marx anticipated that, when a classless society was established, religion would disappear (Marx and Engels, 1957).
3   Bryan Turner (1983) claims that religion lost its function of facilitating the smooth transfer of property from generation to generation when feudalism gave way to capitalism.
4   As later sections of this chapter will show, supporters of the secularization theory think that industrialization has led to profound changes that have progressively reduced the importance of religion in society (see pp. 469–93).
5   A number of sociologists have claimed that changes involved in the advent of postmodernism and globalization have produced changes in religion (see pp. 493–500).

So far, then, it appears to be generally agreed that, first, religion helps to maintain the status quo, and that, second, changes in religion result from changes in the wider society. Some sociologists, however, have argued that religion can cause social change.

Max Weber – *The Protestant Ethic and the Spirit of Capitalism*

Both functionalists and Marxists emphasize the role of religion in promoting social integration and impeding social change. In contrast, Weber (1958, first published in English 1930) argued that in some circumstances religion can lead to social change: although shared religious beliefs might integrate a social group, those same beliefs may have repercussions which in the long term can produce changes in society.

Marx is generally regarded as a materialist. He believed that the material world (and particularly people's involvement with nature as they worked to secure their own survival) shaped their beliefs. Thus, to Marx, the economic system largely determined the beliefs that were held by individuals. In Marxist terms, the mode of production determined the type of religion that would be dominant in any society.

Unlike Marx, Weber rejected the view that religion is always shaped by economic factors. He did not deny that, at certain times and in certain places, religion may be largely shaped by economic forces, but he denied that this is always the case. Under certain conditions the reverse can occur, that is, religious beliefs can be a major influence on economic behaviour.

Weber's social action theory argues that human action is directed by meanings and motives. (See Chapter 15 for a discussion of Weber's general theory.) From this perspective, action can only be understood by appreciating the world view – the image or picture of the world held by members of society. From their world view, individuals obtain meanings, purposes and motives that direct their actions. Religion is often an important component of a world view. In certain places and times, religious meaning and purposes can direct action in a wide range of contexts. In particular, religious beliefs can direct economic action.

Capitalism and ascetic Protestantism

In his most famous book, *The Protestant Ethic and the Spirit of Capitalism* (1958), Weber examines the relationship between the rise of certain forms of Protestantism and the development of Western industrial capitalism. In the first part of his argument Weber tries to demonstrate that a particular form of Protestantism, ascetic Calvinist Protestantism, preceded the development of capitalism. He also tries to show that capitalism developed initially in areas where this religion was influential. Other areas of the world possessed many of the necessary prerequisites yet they were not amongst the first areas to develop capitalism. For example, India and China had techno-logical knowledge, labour to be hired, and individuals engaged in making money. What they lacked, according to Weber, was a religion that encouraged and facilitated the development of capitalism. The first capitalist nations emerged among the countries of Western Europe and North America that had Calvinist religious groups. Furthermore, most of the earliest capitalist entrepreneurs in these areas came from the ranks of Calvinists.

Having established a relationship – a correlation between Calvinism and capitalism – by comparing religion and economic development in different parts of the world, Weber goes on to explain how and why this type of religion was linked to capitalism.

Calvinist Protestantism originated in the beliefs of John Calvin in the seventeenth century. Calvin thought that there was a distinct group of the elect – those chosen to go to heaven – and that they had been chosen by God even before they were born. Those who were not among the elect could never gain a place in heaven however well they behaved on earth.

Other versions of Christianity derived from the beliefs of Martin Luther. Luther believed that individual Christians could affect their chances of reaching heaven by the way that they behaved on earth. It was very important for Christians to develop faith in God, and to act out God's will on earth. In order to do this they had to be dedicated to their calling in life. Whatever position in society God had given them, they must conscientiously carry out the appropriate duties.

At first sight, Lutheranism seems the doctrine more likely to produce capitalism. However, it encouraged people to produce or earn no more than was necessary for their material needs. It attached more importance to piety and faith than to the accumulation of great wealth.

The doctrine of predestination advocated by Calvin seems less likely to produce capitalism. If certain individuals were destined for heaven regard-less of their earthly behaviour – and the rest were equally unable to overcome their damnation – there would be little point in hard work on earth.

Weber points out, though, that Calvinists had a psychological problem: they did not know whether they were amongst the elect. They suffered from a kind of inner loneliness or uncertainty about their status, and their behaviour was not an attempt to earn a place in heaven, but rather to convince themselves that they had been chosen to go there. They reasoned that only the chosen people of God would be able to live a good life on earth. If their behaviour was exemplary they could feel confident that they would go to heaven after death.

Therefore, the interpretation that the Calvinists put on the doctrine of predestination contributed to them becoming the first capitalists.

The Protestant ethic

The Protestant ethic which Weber describes (and which enabled Calvinists to convince themselves that they were amongst the elect) developed first in seventeenth-century Western Europe. The ethic was ascetic, encouraging abstinence from life's pleasures, an austere lifestyle and rigorous self-discipline. It produced individuals who worked hard in their careers or callings, in a single-minded manner. Making money was a concrete indication of success in one's calling, and success in one's calling meant that the individual had not lost grace in God's sight.

John Wesley, a leader of the great Methodist revival that preceded the expansion of English industry at the close of the eighteenth century, wrote:

> *For religion must necessarily produce industry and frugality, and these cannot but produce riches. We must exhort all Christians to gain what they can and to save all they can; that is, in effect to grow rich.*
>
> Quoted in Weber, 1958, p. 175

These riches could not be spent on luxuries, fine clothes, lavish houses and frivolous entertainment, but in the glory of God. In effect, this meant being even more successful in terms of one's calling, which in practice meant reinvesting profits in the business.

The Protestants attacked time-wasting, laziness, idle gossip and more sleep than was necessary – six to eight hours a day at the most. They frowned on sexual pleasures; sexual intercourse should remain within marriage and then only for the procreation of children (a vegetable diet and cold baths were sometimes recommended to remove temptation). Sport and recreation were accepted only for improving fitness and health, and condemned if pursued for entertainment. The impulsive fun and enjoyment of the pub, dance hall, theatre and gaming house were prohibited to ascetic Protestants. In fact anything that might divert or distract people from their calling was condemned. Living life in terms of these guidelines was an indication that the individual had not lost grace and favour in the sight of God.

The spirit of capitalism

Weber claimed that the origins of the spirit of capitalism were to be found in the ethic of ascetic Protestantism. Throughout history there had been no shortage of those who sought money and profit: pirates, prostitutes and money lenders in every corner of the world had always pursued wealth. However, according to Weber, both the manner and purpose of their pursuit of money were at odds with the spirit of capitalism.

Traditionally, money seekers engaged in speculative projects: they gambled in order to gain rewards. If successful they tended to spend money frivolously on personal consumption. Furthermore, they were not dedicated to making money for its own sake. Weber argued that labourers who had earned enough for their family to live comfortably, and merchants who had secured the luxuries they desired, would feel no need to push themselves harder to make more money. Instead, they sought free time for leisure.

The ascetic Protestant had a quite different attitude to wealth, and Weber believed that this attitude was characteristic of capitalism. He argued that the essence of capitalism is 'the pursuit of profit and forever renewed profit'.

Capitalist enterprises are organized on rational bureaucratic lines. Business transactions are conducted in a systematic and rational manner with costs and projected profits being carefully assessed. (We examine Weber's views on rational action in detail in Chapter 15, and in this chapter, pp. 450–1.)

Underlying the practice of capitalism is the spirit of capitalism – a set of ideas, ethics and values. Weber illustrates the spirit of capitalism with quotes from two books by Benjamin Franklin, *Necessary Hints to Those that Would be Rich* (1736) and *Advice to a Young Tradesman* (1748). Franklin writes 'Remember that time is money.' Time-wasting, idleness and diversion lose money. 'Remember that credit is money.' A reputation for 'prudence and honesty' will bring credit, as will paying debts on time. Business people should behave with 'industry and frugality', and 'punctuality and justice' in all their dealings.

Weber argued that this spirit of capitalism is not simply a way of making money, but a way of life which has ethics, duties and obligations. He claimed that ascetic Protestantism was a vital influence in the creation and development of the spirit and practice of capitalism: a methodical and single-minded pursuit of a calling encourages rational capitalism. Weber wrote that 'restless, continuous, systematic work in a worldly calling must have been the most powerful conceivable lever for the expansion of the spirit of capitalism'. Making money became both a religious and a business ethic. The Protestant 'interpretation of profit-making justified the activities of the businessman'.

Weber claimed that two major features of capitalist industry – the standardization of production and the specialized division of labour – were encouraged by Protestantism. The Protestant 'uniformity of life immensely aids the capitalist in the standardization of production'. The emphasis on the 'importance of a fixed calling provided an ethical justification for this modern specialized division of labour'.

Finally, Weber noted the importance of the creation of wealth and the restrictions on spending it, which encouraged saving and reinvestment:

> *When the limitation of consumption is combined with this release of acquisitive activity, the inevitable result is obvious: accumulation of capital through an ascetic compulsion to save. The restraints that were imposed on the consumption of wealth naturally served to increase it, by making possible the productive investment of capital.*
>
> Weber, 1958

The ascetic Protestant way of life led to the accumulation of capital, investment and reinvestment. It produced the early businesses that expanded to create capitalist society.

Materialism and Weber's theory

Weber, then, believed that he had discovered and demonstrated that religious beliefs could cause economic change. He claimed that he had found a weakness in Marx's materialism which implied that the economic system always shaped ideas.

However, it should be stressed that Weber did not discount the importance of the economy and material factors. He said, 'It is, of course, not my aim to substitute for a one-sided materialistic an equally one-sided spiritualistic causal interpretation of culture and of history'. Capitalism was made possible not just by Calvinist Protestantism, but also by the technology and economic system of the countries in which it developed. Material factors were as important as ideas in its development; neither could be ignored in any explanation.

Religion, modernity and rationality

As well as proposing an explanation for the origins of capitalism, Weber also had a good deal to say about the likely consequences of the changes produced by the development of Protestantism. His theories have had a tremendous influence on general ideas about changes in Western societies, and in particular on the concepts of modernity and secularization. Modernity refers to both a historical period and a type of society which is often seen as developing along with industrialization, science and capitalism (see p. 8). Secularization refers to the decline of religion (see below, pp. 469–70). Robert Holton and Bryan Turner (1989), for example, argue that the central themes of all of Weber's sociology were 'the problems of modernization and modernity, and that we should regard rationalization as the process which produced modernism'.

As we have seen above, in *The Protestant Ethic and the Spirit of Capitalism* Weber argued that ascetic Protestantism helped to produce modern capitalism. With that went an emphasis on rational calculation since pursuing the maximum possible profit required an appraisal of the profits that would be produced by following different lines of action. The capitalist would then follow whatever path would produce the greatest profit. Weber distinguished between formal rationality and substantive rationality (Weber, 1964). Formal rationality involved calculating the best means to achieve a given end, and the calculations had to be in a numerical form. Substantive rationality involved action designed to meet some ultimate goal, such as justice, equality or

human happiness. Capitalist behaviour put primary emphasis upon the formal rationality of accounting in the pursuit of profit maximization. Substantive rationality, including the morality provided by religious beliefs, tended to fade into the background in capitalist societies.

To Weber, rationality would not be confined to capitalist enterprise in the modern world. As Holton and Turner point out, it would also involve 'a rational legal system, the separation of the home and the work-place, rational financial management, and the emergence of a rational system of administration'. Weber's ideas on bureaucracy are a good example of his belief that modern societies would be increasingly characterized by rationality (see Chapter 15). However, to Weber, and to many later sociologists, rationality can be at odds with the faith that is required by religion.

Religions do not expect their followers to try to test their beliefs scientifically, nor do they expect religious beliefs to be based upon weighing up the costs and benefits of joining a religious group. Followers should simply believe in the truth of their religion. In the rationalized modern world, though, Weber thought that it would be increasingly difficult for followers of religion to maintain their faith. Discussing Protestant sects in the USA, Weber said, 'closer scrutiny revealed the steady progress of the characteristic process of "secularization" to which all phenomena that originated in religious conceptions succumb' (Weber in Gerth and Mills (eds), 1948). In short, ascetic Protestantism would contribute to the development of capitalism, which required a rational approach to social life, which would in turn undermine religion. Protestant religions therefore contained the seeds of their own destruction. As Malcolm Hamilton puts it:

> *Once on its way, the modern economic system was able to support itself without the need of the religious ethic of ascetic Protestantism which in many ways could not help but sow the seeds of secularization in modern society by its own promotion of worldly activity and consequent expansion of wealth and material well-being. Calvinistic Protestantism was its own gravedigger.*
>
> Hamilton, 1995, p. 152

Weber – an evaluation

The ideas of Weber and other sociologists on modernity, rationality and secularization will be discussed later in the chapter. The following discussion therefore concentrates on his specific ideas relating to *The Protestant Ethic and the Spirit of Capitalism*.

Since its publication Weber's book has received both criticism and support from researchers:

1   Sombart (1907), an early critic, argued that Weber was mistaken about the beliefs held by Calvinists. According to Sombart, Calvinism was against greed and the pursuit of money for its own sake.

Weber himself countered this argument. He pointed out that it was not the beliefs of Calvinists that were important in themselves. The doctrine of predestination was not intended to produce the rational pursuit of profit, but nevertheless that was one of its unintentional consequences and the evidence was in the way that ascetic Protestants actually behaved.

2   A second criticism points to parts of the world where Calvinism was strong, but capitalism did not develop until much later. For example, Switzerland, Scotland, Hungary and parts of the Netherlands all contained large Calvinist populations but were not among the first capitalist countries.

Gordon Marshall (1982) dismisses this criticism. He argues that the critics demonstrate a lack of understanding of Weber's theory. Weber did not claim that Calvinism was the only factor necessary for the development of capitalism. His theory cannot therefore be disproved simply by finding Calvinist countries that failed to become capitalist comparatively early. In his own study of Scotland, Marshall found that the Scottish had a capitalist mentality but were held back by a lack of skilled labour and capital for investment, and by government policies that did not stimulate the development of industry.

3   A potentially more damaging criticism of Weber's theory originates from Marxist critics such as Kautsky (1953). Kautsky argues that early capitalism preceded and largely determined Protestantism. He sees Calvinism as developing in cities where commerce and early forms of industrialization were already established. In his view Protestantism became the ideology capitalists used to legitimate their position.

This is a chicken and egg question – which came first: Calvinism or capitalism? The answer depends upon how capitalism is defined. To Weber, pre-capitalist money-making ventures were not organized rationally to ensure continued profit.

Marshall (1982) disputes this. He suggests that the medieval merchant classes behaved quite rationally considering the conditions of the time. It was not their psychological attitude that encouraged them to make what Weber saw as risky investments, but the situation they faced. In England the risks involved in trading were balanced by investments in land. Buying landed estates was not an example of conspicuous consumption, but of the prudent spreading of investments. In the Netherlands too, the business classes spread their risks but more money went into merchant trading because of the price of land. Even so, defenders of Weber insist that a distinctive rational capitalist entrepreneur did not emerge until after Calvinism.

4   A fourth criticism of Weber does not deny that Calvinism was an important factor which helped lead to capitalism, but questions the view that it was the religious beliefs of Calvinists that led to them becoming business people. According to this view, non-conformist Calvinists devoted themselves to business because they were excluded from holding public office and joining certain professions by law. Like the Jews in Eastern and central Europe, they tried to become economically successful in order to overcome their political persecution.

In reply to this criticism, supporters of the Protestant ethic thesis argue that only Calvinist minorities developed the distinctive patterns of capitalist behaviour which involved rational planning for slow but sure capital growth; only they could develop capitalist businesses before capitalism was established.

Despite the considerable effort devoted to discussing Weber's theory by historians and sociologists alike, no agreement has been reached about its accuracy. Nevertheless, whatever the merits of this particular study, Weber does successfully highlight the theoretical point that ideas – in this case religious ideas – can conceivably lead to economic change.

Religion and social change – conclusion

Many sociologists do now accept that religion can be a force for change. Despite the examples that can be used to support the functionalist and Marxist view that religion promotes stability, other examples contradict their claims.

G.K. Nelson (1986) points to a number of cases where religion has undermined stability or promoted change:

1   In Northern Ireland, Roman Catholicism has long been associated with Irish Republicanism.

2   In the USA in the 1960s the Reverend Martin Luther King and the Southern Christian Leadership Council played a leading role in establishing civil rights and securing legislation intended to reduce racial discrimination.

3   Also in the 1960s, a number of radical and revolutionary groups emerged within the Roman Catholic Church in Latin America. They preached liberation theology, arguing that it was the duty of church members to fight against unjust and oppressive right-wing dictatorships. Thus, in 1979, Catholic revolutionaries supported the Sandinistas when they seized control in Nicaragua.

4   In Iran, Islamic fundamentalism played a part in the 1979 revolution, led by the Ayatollah Khomeini.

5   Poland provides another example of religion stimulating change. The Roman Catholic Church

opposed the communist state in Poland, and it supported the attempts of the free trade union Solidarity to achieve changes in Polish society. In 1989 the communist monopoly on power was broken when Solidarity was allowed to contest and win many seats in the Polish parliament.

6 In South Africa, Archbishop Tutu was a prominent opponent of apartheid.

Examples such as these lead Nelson to conclude that 'far from encouraging people to accept their place, religion can spearhead resistance and revolution'. In many cases when religion has been a force for change in society, the society that results may be strongly influenced by that religion.

Engels (Marx and Engels, 1957), unlike Marx, did realize that in some circumstances religion could be a force for change. He argued that groups which turned to religion as a way of coping with oppression could develop into political movements which sought change on earth rather than salvation in heaven. Some contemporary neo-Marxists have followed Engels and developed this view (see pp. 438–9 for further details).

Religion and revolutionary movements

Leland W. Robinson (1987) argues that in some circumstances revolutionary movements deliberately try to use religion in their attempts to change society. He claims that three things are necessary if this is to happen:

1 The classes with the potential to become revolutionary need to have a predominantly religious world view. In the Third World this is often the case, particularly in Latin America, the Near East and South Asia. Europe is less religious and revolutionary movements have not usually tried to use religion. There are, however, exceptions, such as the role of the Roman Catholic Church in undermining the communist state in Poland.

2 The main religion needs to have a theology that can be interpreted in such a way that it can be used against those in power. Buddhism tends to stress the separation of religion and society into different spheres. Christianity and Hinduism have more revolutionary potential. For example, Gandhi used the Hindu concept of Sarvodaya (the welfare of all) to attack British colonial rule and to inspire rural peasants and the urban poor to turn against the British.

3 It is also necessary for the clergy and the revolutionary classes to have close contacts. Robinson argues that in countries such as Paraguay the clergy usually come from and remain in close contact with local communities. Here they have opposed the repressive regime of Stroessner. In Cuba the Catholic Church was so remote from ordinary

people that it did not support Castro's communist revolution of 1956–9. A 1957 survey of 4,000 agricultural workers in Cuba found that only 7.8 per cent said that they had had any dealings with the Catholic clergy.

Where the above three factors are present, revolutionaries are able to make use of religion. This becomes even more likely in situations where the revolutionary classes all share the same religion, where this is different to the religion of those in power, and where there are no alternative organizations available through which to express dissent. In many countries in South America, such as Guatemala, Chile and El Salvador, where the police and military have been used to crush other organizations such as trade unions, religion is the only remaining outlet for dissent.

Conservative or radical religion?

Merideth B. McGuire (1981) also examines the factors which influence the type of role that religion plays in society, commenting 'The question is no longer "Does religion promote social change?" but rather, "In what way and under what conditions does it promote rather than inhibit change?"' Unlike Leland, McGuire does not concentrate exclusively on the revolutionary potential of religion. She identifies four main factors that determine the potential of religion to change society:

1 The first factor is the beliefs of the particular religion. Religions that emphasize adherence to strong moral codes are more likely to produce members who are critical of society and who seek to change it. If a religion stresses concern with this world, it is more likely to result in actions by its members which produce change than a religion which confines itself to a concern with sacred and spiritual matters. Thus Protestantism can have more impact on social change than Buddhism.

2 The second factor is the culture of the society in which a religion exists. In societies where religious beliefs are central to the culture (such as in Latin America), anyone wishing to produce change tends to use a religious legitimation for their actions. In Britain, however, religion plays a less central role in societal culture, so it tends to play a less important role in justifying changes in society.

3 What McGuire describes as the social location of religion is the third important factor. This concerns the part that religion plays in the social structure. Again, the greater the importance of religion, the greater its potential to play a part in producing change. Where an established church or other religious organization plays a major role in political and economic life, there is considerable scope for religion having an impact on processes of change.

4 The final factor is the internal organization of religious institutions. According to McGuire, religions with a strong, centralized source of authority have more chance of affecting events. On the other hand, the central authority might try to restrain the actions of parts of the organization. For example, in 1978 at the Puebla Conference in Mexico, the Pope clashed with Latin American Roman Catholic bishops who were advocating liberation theology.

McGuire provides only a sketchy outline of the factors determining whether religion acts as a conser-vative force maintaining the status quo or as a force for change. Nevertheless she does provide a starting point for analysing the relationship between religion and social change.

In the next section we will examine different types of religious organization and the wide variety of ideologies that have been supported by different organizations. We will also discover that conservative and radical ideologies tend to be associated with different types of religious organization.

Religious organizations

Individuals may have their own religious beliefs without belonging to any particular organization: they may form their own personal and unique relationship with a god or some source of spiritual power. However, many members of society express their religious beliefs through organizations, and the organizations tend to shape those beliefs. Social factors influence the types of organization that are created, who joins them and how they develop. At the same time, religious organizations may themselves influence society.

Before we examine these issues, it is necessary for us to distinguish between the different types of religious organization. There have been a number of attempts to categorize them, but no system fits perfectly the infinite variety of such organizations that have existed throughout the world. Nevertheless, it is possible broadly to distinguish some main types of religious organization.

The church

Ernst Troeltsch in 1931 was one of the first writers to try to distinguish different types of religious organi-zation. Troeltsch used the term church to refer to a large religious organization. Individuals do not have to demonstrate their faith to become members of a church – indeed, often they are born into it. In some churches the practice of baptism ensures that all the children of members are automatically recruited before they are old enough to understand the faith.

In principle a church might try to be universal – to embrace all members of society – but in practice there might be substantial minorities who do not belong. Because of its size, members of a church are drawn from all classes in society, but the upper classes are particularly likely to join. This is because, in Troeltsch's words, a church usually 'stabilizes and determines the political order' (Troeltsch, 1981).

Churches are sometimes closely related to the state. For example, the Roman Catholic Church in the Middle Ages had important political, educational and social functions. Even in contemporary Britain the Queen is both head of the Church of England and head of state. Churches are likely to be ideologically conservative and support the status quo: an opinion poll in 1988 found that 63 per cent of active lay members of the Church of England supported the Conservative Party, which received only 43 per cent of the total votes in the 1987 election (quoted in Davie, 1989).

This type of organization accepts and affirms life in this world: members can play a full part in social life and are not expected to withdraw from society. In many circumstances a church will jealously guard its monopoly on religious truth, and will not tolerate challenges to its religious authority. For example, the Roman Catholic Church at one time used the Inquisition to stamp out heresy. Churches are formal organizations with a hierarchy of professional, paid officials.

Steve Bruce argues that the concept of a church is primarily useful in describing pre-modern Christian societies. He says, 'The notion of the church derives its force from the growth of Christianity and the historic forms of Catholic, Orthodox, and Coptic churches. These bodies sought to be co-extensive with their societies' (Bruce, 1996). However, in 1517 Martin Luther, a German priest, began to question some of the teachings and practices of the medieval church. This led to the Reformation in which competing religious views developed, including the Protestant Church of England established by Henry VIII. A plurality of sects with competing doctrines also developed. To Bruce, the development of religious pluralism in societies undermines the maintenance of the church type of religious organi-zation. He says, 'when a population becomes divided between a number of organizations, that fragmentation undermines the conditions for the church form' (Bruce, 1995). This is because it becomes more difficult for the state to lend exclusive support to one religion, and because a single set of religious beliefs is no longer taken for granted and reinforced by all groups in society. Thus, for Bruce, churches, in the sense meant by Troeltsch, are essentially historical phenomena which cannot continue to exist in modern societies. Indeed, Bruce sees the Church of England as a denomination rather than a church.

A number of examples can illustrate Bruce's point. A variety of organizations, which call themselves churches or which could be seen as churches, do not conform to the characteristics outlined by Troeltsch:

1 The percentage of the population who are members of a church can vary widely. For example, according to the *UK Christian Handbook*, in Britain in 1995 just 1,785,273 people were members of Anglican churches. Some 82 per cent of these were in the Church of England.

2 Many churches today do not claim a monopoly of the religious truth – other religions are tolerated. In Britain there is a growing diversity of religious groupings that are tolerated by the Church of England.

3 Furthermore, the ecumenical movement, which seeks unity between varying Christian religious groups, demonstrates the extent to which churches are now willing to compromise their beliefs.

4 Churches are not always ideologically conservative and they do not always support the dominant groups in a society: the General Synod of the Church of England clashed with the British Conservative government in the l980s and l990s over issues such as poverty and conditions in Britain's inner cities. Davie claims that there is a growing gap within the Church of England between lay members, who tend to be conservative, and senior officials such as bishops, who tend to be more radical (Davie, 1989).

5 In some circumstances the churches are not connected to the state, and may even act as a focus of opposition to it. Before the overthrow of communism in Poland the Roman Catholic Church opposed the communist government, and in many parts of Latin America liberation theology has also led to conflict between the Catholic Church and the state.

Roland Robertson argues that throughout the world there has been an increase in church–state tensions (Robertson, 1987). Far from identifying closely with the state, churches are increasingly distancing themselves from it. Robertson notes tensions between the state and Shiite fundamentalists in the Middle East, Coptic Christians in Egypt, Maronite Christians in Lebanon, Sikhs in India and Islamic fundamentalists in Pakistan, Indonesia and the Philippines. He points out that many churches are transnational organizations, their activities are not confined to a single country. He argues that, in the modern 'world system', nation-states interact with each other by pursuing non-religious, secular national interests. In international trade and diplomacy there is little room for the consideration of theological issues. Consequently national governments tend to come into conflict with the moral concerns of domestic churches and transnational religious organizations.

There are some ways in which contemporary churches retain some of their traditional characteristics, at least in some societies. Churches in industrial societies tend to be larger and more conservative than other religious groups. Some industrialized societies have retained fairly strong churches that continue to conform to most of the characteristics outlined by Troeltsch. Roy Wallis and Steve Bruce claim, of the Roman Catholic Church, 'In those places where it is dominant, e.g. Spain, Portugal and the Republic of Ireland, it acts as a universal church, claiming authority over the society as a whole' (Wallis and Bruce, 1986). In the Republic of Ireland the bishops continue to receive state support for the moral teachings of Catholicism, and as recently as 1983 they were able to denounce a well-established Pentecostal Protestant religious group as a dangerous cult which should not be tolerated.

In other countries, though, the Catholic Church is not in a position to act in such ways and has to co-exist peacefully with a plurality of other religions, making no special claims on the state. Similarly, in Iran there is close identification between Islam and the state, but in countries such as Turkey the Muslim religion has much less influence on the state and politics.

Denominations

Troeltsch's original categorization of religious organizations included only churches and sects. It did not include 'denominations'. As Troeltsch based his work on an analysis of religion in sixteenth-century Europe, his classification was not capable of describing the variety of religions in the USA, or for that matter in modern Britain. According to Stark and Bainbridge (1985), the term denomination is usually used to refer to an organization that shares several but not all of the supposed features of a church. It is often seen as a kind of watered-down church which has some similarities to a sect (we will discuss sects in the next section).

In a study of religion in the USA, H.R. Niebuhr (1929) was the first sociologist to differentiate clearly the denomination from the church. A denomination has been seen as having the following features:

1 Unlike a church, a denomination does not have a universal appeal in society. For example, in Britain in 1995 Methodists could claim 401,087 members, and there were 195,200 Baptists.

2 Like churches, denominations draw members from all strata in society, but, unlike churches, they are not usually so closely identified with the upper classes. Often a considerable number of denominations exist within a particular society. In the USA there is no established church, but a large range of denominations.

3 Unlike a church, a denomination does not identify with the state and approves the separation of church and state.

4 Denominations do not claim a monopoly of the religious truth. They are prepared to tolerate and cooperate with other religious organizations.

5 Denominations are usually conservative: members generally accept the norms and values of society, although they may have marginally different values from those of the wider society. Some denominations place minor restrictions on their members. For instance, Methodists are discouraged from drinking and gambling, but drinking in moderation is tolerated, and drinkers are not excluded from the denomination.

6 In other respects, denominations have the same characteristics as churches: new members are freely admitted and they have a hierarchy of paid officials.

Steve Bruce (1995) sees the lack of a claim to a monopoly of the religious truth as the defining feature of denominations. Furthermore, he sees them as increasingly important. He says:

> The last two hundred years has seen gradual evolution of churches and sects into denominations. The church form has been made untenable by the gradual increase in cultural pluralism and by the unwillingness of the state to continue to force reluctant people into the state church.
>
> Bruce, 1995, p. 9

The blurring of boundaries between religious organizations as they change has made the concept of the denomination no less problematic than the concept of the church. It covers a wide range of organizations from Jehovah's Witnesses to Methodists, from Pentecostalists to Baptists. Some organizations are classified as sects by some sociologists but as denominations by others.

Stark and Bainbridge (1985) are highly critical of the concept of a denomination. They argue that the addition of denominations to the distinction between church and sect only 'renders fluid and uncertain an intellectual scheme that was supposed to be a solid basis for analysis'. Indeed, they claim that the division of religious organizations into discrete types obscures rather than clarifies the differences between them (see pp. 460–2 for further details of their argument).

Sects

According to Troeltsch, sects have characteristics that are almost diametrically opposed to those of churches:

1 They are both smaller and more strongly integrated than other religious organizations.

2 Rather than drawing members from all sections of society and being closely connected to the state, Troeltsch claimed that sects are 'connected with the lower classes, or at least with those elements in Society which are opposed to the State and Society'.

3 Far from being conservative and accepting the norms and values of society, sects are 'in opposition to the world'. They reject the values of the world that surrounds them, and their detachment may be 'expressed in the refusal to use the law, to swear in a court of justice, to own property, to exercise dominion over others, or to take part in war'.

4 Sect members may be expected to withdraw from life outside the sect, but at the same time they may wish ultimately to see changes take place in the wider society.

5 Members of a sect are expected to be deeply committed to its beliefs. They may be excluded from the sect if they fail to demonstrate such a commitment.

6 Young children cannot usually enter the sect by being baptized if they are not old enough to understand the significance of the ceremony. They must join voluntarily as adults, and willingly adopt the lifestyle and beliefs of the sect. In particular they must sacrifice 'worldly pleasures' in order to devote themselves to their religious life. In this sense, sects exercise a stronger control over individuals' lives than, for example, the modern Church of England. Sects share this characteristic with religions such as Islam in countries where religious beliefs still have a strong hold over social life.

7 Like churches such as the Roman Catholic Church in Europe in the Middle Ages, sects tend to believe that they possess a monopoly of the religious truth.

8 Unlike churches, though, they are not organized through a hierarchy of paid officials. If central authority exists within a sect, it usually rests with a single charismatic leader, whose personality and perceived special qualities persuade the followers to adhere to his or her teachings.

Sects were originally groups which broke away from the dominant religion in a society because of a disagreement over the interpretation of the religion. Steve Bruce describes the process of sect formation in the following way:

> *From time to time the church would face dissent or revolt. People would protest against ecclesiastical pomp and wealth or would seek to live out a more radical form of the faith. Those who could not be contained within the church – for example, as a religious order – broke away to form 'sects'. As they often challenged the state as much as the church, they were met with repression. For this, if for no other reason, sects were normally small.*

Bruce, 1995, p. 3

To Bruce, the original sects were a product of the 'upheavals of the reformation' (Bruce 1996) but, as noted above, some of them developed to become denominations which were tolerated as religious diversity became more accepted. However, Bruce also acknowledges that sects can prosper in modern societies where people have more opportunity to form their own subcultures. Even with the greater toleration of contemporary societies, though, some sects may come into serious conflict with the wider society and its values.

One example was the People's Temple, an American sect of the 1970s. When this sect came to an end it had just 900 members. It was founded in California by the Reverend Jim Jones and, although it recruited a considerable number of relatively affluent whites, it had a particular appeal to black ghetto dwellers of northern California.

The sect had a radical ideology: it claimed to be based upon a Marxist philosophy and it strongly opposed prejudice and discrimination. Many members withdrew from participation in the outside world in the early stages of the sect's development, giving over their homes and property to Reverend Jones. Some continued to work outside, but eventually the sect became completely isolated as its members moved to set up a commune at 'Jonestown' in the rainforests of Guyana.

The degree of integration within the group was tragically illustrated when in 1978 the entire membership died after taking cyanide. Some committed suicide on the orders of their leader; others were murdered by being tricked into taking the poison.

In common with many other sects, members were expected to demonstrate their faith – in this case by such acts as signing confessions to crimes they had not committed, suffering public humiliations if Jones believed they had done something wrong, and drinking unidentified liquids of an unpleasant colour. Jones exercised strict control over his followers. His charismatic leadership was strengthened by fraudulent attempts to demonstrate his religious powers. 'Miracle

healings' would take place where followers would pretend to have been instantly cured of cancer by spitting out pieces of chicken liver they had concealed in their mouth. Careful scrutiny of members' dustbins allowed Jones to claim divine fortune-telling powers.

In the 1990s there were a number of religious movements in which there were deaths of some of the followers in violent circumstances. Perhaps the best-known example of this was the Branch Davidians. Founded by their charismatic leader, David Koresh, they established a commune at Waco in Texas. Koresh demanded absolute loyalty from members. In February 1993 the Bureau of Alcohol, Tobacco and Firearms attempted to search their premises only to be met by gunfire. Four AFT agents were killed and 16 were wounded. After a lengthy siege the FBI attempted to arrest those inside using armoured vehicles. A fire started, resulting in the deaths of more than 80 Branch Davidians including 22 children. A subsequent investigation found that sect members had started the fire themselves, although survivors insist that this was not the case.

Although the People's Temple and the Branch Davidians are extreme examples of sects, many other religious organizations display similar characteristics. But there are also numerous exceptions. It is possible to find sects of vastly different sizes, with a wide variety of ideologies, contrasting attitudes to the outside world, varying degrees of control over their membership, and with or without a professional clergy and a charismatic leader.

Bryan Wilson (1982) accepts that Troeltsch's description of sects may have been accurate in relation to European countries, until quite recently. However, it does not account for or adequately describe the proliferation of sectarian groups in Europe and the USA in recent decades. Some of the new religious movements, which come close to Troeltsch's description of sects, will be examined shortly.

Cults

According to Steve Bruce (1995), Troeltsch mentioned 'mysticism' as another tradition within Christianity in addition to the church and sect. Bruce describes it in this way, 'Unlike the other forms, this was a highly individualistic expression, varying with personal experiences and interpretations.' To Bruce, this corresponds to the idea of a cult, which he sees as a 'loosely knit group organised around some common themes and interests but lacking any sharply defined and exclusive belief system'. A cult tends to be more individualistic than other organized forms of religion because it lacks a fixed doctrine. Cults tolerate other beliefs and indeed their own beliefs are often so vague that they have no conception of heresy. Cults often have customers rather than members and these customers may have relatively little involvement with any organization once they have learnt the rudiments of the beliefs around which the cult is based.

This rather general description corresponds fairly closely to one type of new religious movement identified by Wallis (1984) – the World-Affirming Movement (see pp. 459–60). It is rather different from the definition of cult advanced by Stark and Bainbridge (1985) (see pp. 460–2). Many aspects of the New Age movement are based around cults (see below, pp. 466–9). The different ways in which the word cult is used will be explored in greater depth in the next sections.

New religious movements, sects and cults

There have been numerous attempts to refine the basic distinctions between church, denomination, sect and cult in the light of the wide variety of small religious, spiritual or mystical groups that have sprung up since the 1960s. Eileen Barker (1985) suggests that they could be classified according to the religious tradition from which they originate. For example, Hari Krishna and the disciples of Bhagwan Rajneesh take their inspiration from the Hindu religion, Zen groups from Buddhism, and the Children of God from Christianity. The Unification Church (better known as the Moonies) combines elements from Taoism, Confucianism, Spiritualism and Buddhism, although it is based primarily around the Bible. Other groups have an occult, pagan or

witchcraft source. Some groups have little connection with previous religions but are part of what Barker calls the Human Potential Movement, which attempts to liberate human potential through some technique – Primal Therapy, for example, uses screaming.

However, Barker also points out that some groups 'are so idiosyncratic that they would appear to defy any classification'. She cites a Japanese group who regarded Thomas Edison (the American inventor) as a minor god, and the Kennedy Worshippers who numbered around 2,000 and saw the assassinated president of the USA, John F. Kennedy, as a god.

Barker suggests that another way of classifying new religious movements is according to the degree of commitment shown by their members. The People's Temple (see p. 456) is at one extreme, while some other movements, such as Transcendental Meditation (see p. 459), require little more of their members than to attend a short course. Eileen Barker puts forward these classification schemes as no more than tentative suggestions. Other sociologists, such as Roy Wallis, have developed much more detailed systems of classification.

Roy Wallis – *The Elementary Forms of the New Religious Life*

The development of a range of new religions and the revival of some old ones, in the 1970s, led Roy Wallis to categorize these new religious movements (Wallis, 1984). His views are illustrated in Figure 7.1. He divides new religious movements into three main groups. Like Troeltsch, the principal criterion he uses to categorize religious organizations is their relation-

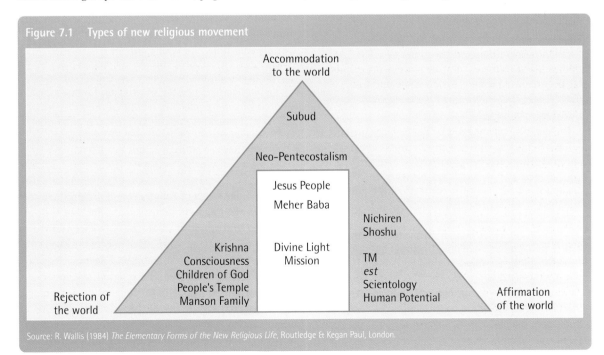

Figure 7.1 Types of new religious movement

Accommodation to the world

Subud

Neo-Pentecostalism

Jesus People
Meher Baba

Krishna Consciousness
Children of God
People's Temple
Manson Family

Divine Light Mission

Nichiren Shoshu

TM
est
Scientology
Human Potential

Rejection of the world

Affirmation of the world

Source: R. Wallis (1984) *The Elementary Forms of the New Religious Life*, Routledge & Kegan Paul, London.

ship to the outside world. He therefore distinguishes between them according to whether the movement and its members reject, accommodate or affirm the world. He represents his typology with a triangle, and notes the existence of some groups (those in the central box) which do not fit neatly into any single category.

World-rejecting new religious movements

The world-rejecting new religious movements have most of the characteristics of a sect described by Troeltsch:

1 They are usually a clearly religious organization with a definite conception of God. For example, the Unification Church, better known as the 'Moonies' – after their leader Reverend Sun Myung Moon – pray in a conventional way to a 'Heavenly Father'.

2 In other respects, though, such groups are far from conventional. Their ideology is invariably highly critical of the outside world, and the movement expects or actively seeks change.

3 Some groups are millenarian: they expect God's intervention to change the world. The Nation of Islam in the USA are a case in point. They prophesy that in the year 2000 Allah will destroy the whites and their religion.

4 In order to achieve salvation, members are expected to have a sharp break from their conventional life when they join the movement. Organizations of this type act as total institutions, controlling every aspect of their members' lives. (For more details on total institutions see pp. 475–6.) As a result, they often develop a reputation for 'brainwashing' their members, since families and friends find it hard to understand the change that has taken place in a member.

5 Limited contact with the outside world might be allowed, to facilitate fund-raising. Moonies in San Francisco help to support the group by selling flowers, and members of other movements distribute literature or sell records for the same purpose. Sometimes they simply beg for money, claiming to be collecting for charity.

6 The leadership of the groups may be quite prepared to have contacts with the outside world in an attempt to try to change society without waiting for divine intervention. Jim Jones, leader of the ill-fated People's Temple, had close contacts with Californian politicians. Louis Farrakhan, leader of the Nation of Islam, became heavily involved in US politics. In particular, Farrakhan supported the black Democratic Party presidential candidate, the Reverend Jesse Jackson, in his attempts to promote policies designed to benefit disadvantaged minorities. Farrakhan himself, though, was strongly criticized for making apparently anti-Semitic comments.

7 Although they are usually radical, there can be conservative elements in the beliefs and actions of such organizations. The Unification Church is strongly anti-communist, and has supported South Korean military dictatorships. Many of the movements are morally puritanical, forbidding sex outside marriage, for example. The 'Moonies' are particularly strict about restricting sex to monogamous marriage.

8 World-rejecting new religious movements vary enormously in size: the 'Moonies' have an international following while other groups are small and locally based.

9 Most of them tend to be based around some form of communal lifestyle, and as such develop unconventional ways of living. The commune of the ill-fated Branch Davidians in Waco, Texas is a case in point.

Thus, despite the variations within these groups, none of them are content with the world as it is.

Wallis sees most world-rejecting new religious movements as sects. He defines sects as groups that claim to be uniquely legitimate and which advocate religious doctrines that are widely regarded as deviant. They have 'an authoritative locus for the attribution of heresy' and are hostile to the state and non-members.

World-accommodating new religious movements

The world-accommodating new religious movements are usually offshoots of an existing major church or denomination. For example, neo-Pentecostalist groups are variants of Protestant or Roman Catholic religions, while Subud is a world-accommodating Muslim group.

Typically these groups neither accept nor reject the world as it is, they simply live within it. They are primarily concerned with religious rather than worldly questions. As Wallis puts it:

The world-accommodating new religion draws a distinction between the spiritual and the worldly in a way quite uncharacteristic of the other two types. Religion is not constructed as a primarily social matter; rather it provides solace or stimulation to personal interior life.

Wallis, 1984, p. 35

The religious beliefs of followers might help them to cope with their non-religious social roles, but the aim of the religion is not to create a new society nor to improve the believers' chances of success in their lives. Instead, world-accommodating sects seek to restore the spiritual purity to a religion, which it believes has been lost in more conventional churches and denominations. Many of the members of these organizations were, before joining, members of churches or denominations with which they had become disillusioned. Pentecostalists hold that the belief in the Holy Spirit has been lost in other Christian religions. The Holy Spirit speaks through Pentecostalists, giving them the gift of 'speaking in tongues'.

It is the spiritual and religious aspects of world-accommodating groups that differentiate them from other religious organizations, but they can still be seen as denominations. According to Wallis, denominations have a 'respectable' set of religious beliefs and are tolerant of the existence of other religions. Most of the members of world-accommodating groups live conventional and conforming lives outside their religious activities.

This is demonstrated by Ken Pryce's study of West Indians in the St Paul's district of Bristol. He found that Pentecostalists lived respectable lives. They usually had, or wished to have, normal jobs. Unlike some members of the local community, they did not earn their living from prostitution or by selling drugs, and they did not belong to radical political movements.

World-affirming new religious movements

The world-affirming new religious movements are very different from all other religious groups, and may indeed lack some of the features normally thought to be central to a religion. Wallis says that such a group 'may have no "church", no collective ritual of worship, it may lack any developed theology or ethics' (Wallis, 1984). However, these groups do claim to be able to provide access to spiritual or supernatural powers, and in that sense can be regarded as religions.

Rather than rejecting existing society or existing religions, world-affirming groups accept the world as it is and they are not particularly critical of other religions. What they offer the follower is the potential to be successful in terms of the dominant values of society by unlocking spiritual powers present in the individual. Salvation is seen as a personal achievement and as a solution to personal problems such as unhappiness, suffering or disability. Individuals usually overcome such problems by adopting some technique that heightens their awareness or abilities.

World-affirming movements are not exclusive groups: they seek as wide a membership as possible. Rather than trying to convert people as such, they try to sell them a service commercially. Followers carry on their normal lives except when undergoing training; often courses are held at weekends or at other convenient times so as not to cause disruption. There is little social control over the members, or customers, and they are not normally excluded from the group if they fail to act in accordance with its beliefs.

An example of a world-affirming new religious movement is provided by Transcendental Meditation or TM. TM is based upon the Hindu religion, but during at least some periods of its development the religious elements have been played down. First introduced to the West in the late 1950s, it achieved prominence in 1968 when the Beatles met its leading proponent, the Maharishi Mahesh Yogi.

TM involves a meditational technique whereby a follower is given a personal mantra on which to concentrate for 20 minutes in the morning and evening. It is claimed that this technique can provide 'unbounded awareness' which can have beneficial effects for individuals and for society. Some followers of TM claim that in areas where as little as 1 per cent of the population have been initiated, crime, accidents and sickness are all reduced. Initiation is a simple matter and can take place in just a couple of hours with further follow-up sessions lasting just a few hours more. An advanced course in the powers of TM, the Siddi programme, claims to provide occult powers such as the ability to levitate. In the USA, the course costs several thousand dollars.

As with some other new religious movements, there have been attempts to make deliberate use of TM's teachings to solve social problems. Teachers have been dispatched to areas of civil unrest in the hope of converting local leaders who, it was hoped, would in turn use their new powers to overcome the area's problems. In the 1992 and 1997 British general elections, hundreds of followers of TM stood for parliament as representatives of the Natural Law Party, offering the voters harmonious rule in line with the natural laws of the universe as discovered by the Maharishi.

Within some world-affirming groups there is an inner-core of followers who attach great significance to the teachings of the movement and start to live more as members of a world-rejecting movement. TM, for instance, has developed an exclusive inner-group of members trained in advanced techniques who have characteristics a little closer to those of world-rejecting sects.

In addition, other world-affirming groups may think that their beliefs have a potential beyond helping individuals achieve success. They may believe that their training, if sufficiently widespread, could contribute to solving problems such as racial conflict, or even world hunger. Such political aims are not, however, the main concern of world-affirming new religious movements – they are merely a possible by-product of their teachings.

According to Steve Bruce, who has developed Wallis's views, there are two main types of world-affirming new religious movement. There are 'those which add a spiritual dimension to what had been a western secular psychotherapy and those which tailor an initially oriental product for Western sensibilities' (Bruce, 1995). TM is a good example of the latter type. Bruce uses Insight as an example of the former type. Insight involves taking training courses which allow individuals to discover a 'centre' within themselves that contains the answer to all our questions and the solution to our problems. It enables individuals to free themselves from guilt and anxiety, to think positively about themselves and to live fulfilling lives.

To Wallis, most world-affirming new religious movements are cults. Cults are like sects in that they have religious beliefs that are widely regarded as deviant, but, unlike sects, cults tolerate the existence of other religions. Cults are 'loosely structured, tolerant, and non-exclusive'. They have a rapid turnover in membership and are relatively undemanding on their followers.

The 'middle ground'

Wallis realizes that no religious group will conform exactly to the categories he outlines. He says 'all actual new religious movements are likely to combine elements of each type to some extent' (Wallis, 1984). Indeed, he points to a number of groups that occupy an intermediate position, such as the Healthy Happy Holy Organization (3HO), and the Divine Light Mission. Comparing them to the three main groups, he says 'They combine in various degrees all three types, and more particularly elements of the conventional society and the counter-culture.'

3HO, for example, is similar to world-accommo-dating new religious movements in that it is an offshoot of an established religion, in this case Sikhism. As in world-affirming movements, it employs techniques that it is claimed will bring personal benefits such as happiness and good health. In common with TM, 3HO hopes that its teachings will have spin-offs for the outside world: in fact, nothing less than world unity. 3HO is not exclusive. Classes are provided for those who are not full members so that they can receive benefits from the teachings. Even fully committed members are expected to have conventional marriages and to hold down conventional jobs.

On the other hand, 3HO does have some characteristics in common with world-rejecting movements. The organization has a clear concept of God. Members dress unconventionally in white clothing and turbans. They live in communes or ashrams, but the ashrams do not involve total sharing: individuals pay for their own room and board. Some restrictions are placed on behaviour: members of 3HO are vegetarians and abstain from alcohol, tobacco and mind-altering drugs.

Occupying as it does the middle ground, 3HO allows its followers to combine elements of an alternative lifestyle with conventional marriage and employment.

Roy Wallis – an evaluation

James A. Beckford (1985) commends Wallis's scheme for recognizing that new religious movements do not always fit neatly into one category or another, and for outlining the differences in the types of individuals recruited by different types of movement (we outline Wallis's views on recruitment on pp. 462–3). However, Beckford also offers some criticisms of Wallis:

1 He argues that Wallis's categories are difficult to apply. It is not made clear whether the teachings of the movement or the beliefs and outlooks of the individual members distinguish the different orientations to the world.

2 Beckford feels that Wallis pays insufficient attention to the diversity of views that often exists within a sect or cult.

3 Beckford also questions the worth of defining some groups as 'world-rejecting'. In his view, no group can afford to reject the world altogether since they rely upon contacts with the wider economic system for their very survival.

Nevertheless Beckford does not deny that a typology, or list of types, of new religious movements is useful. In contrast, Stark and Bainbridge, whose views we examine next, reject the idea of using a typology to distinguish new religions.

Rodney Stark and William Sims Bainbridge – un–ideal types

The problems of typologies

According to Stark and Bainbridge (1985), none of the typologies of new religious movements, sects, churches and denominations developed by other sociologists is a sound basis for categorization. All of them consist of lists of characteristics that each type is likely to have. However, these characteristics are not found in every religious organization placed in each category. Not all churches try to convert all members of society and not all sects are exclusive.

Such characteristics used to distinguish organizations are correlates – sets of characteristics that tend to be found together in the same organizations. They are not however attributes – characteristics that an organization must have if it is to be defined as a church, denomination, sect or cult. Defining types of organization in terms of correlates tends to lead to confusion since most organizations are in some ways exceptions to the rule.

Stark and Bainbridge therefore argue that typologies of religious organization should be abandoned altogether. Instead, they adopt the ideas of Benton Johnson, an earlier sociologist of religion. Johnson argued that religious organizations could be compared in terms of a single attribute and could be placed at any point on a continuum in terms of this attribute. Johnson said:

> A church is a religious group that accepts the social environment in which it exists. A sect is a religious organisation that rejects the social environment in which it exists.
>
> Quoted in Stark and Bainbridge, 1985, p. 23

Thus they claim that religious groups can be compared in terms of the degree of conflict that exists between them and the wider society. The use of such a definition allows clear comparisons. For example, the Catholic Church in the USA is nearer to the sect end of the continuum than the Catholic Church in the Republic of Ireland. It also allows changes over time to be clearly described: organizations might change and become more, or less, in tension with the social environment.

Sects and cults

Stark and Bainbridge then go on to argue that there are different kinds (they are careful to avoid using the word types) of religious movement in a high degree of tension with their social environment:

1 Sects are groups that are formed as an offshoot of an existing religion as a result of division or schism within that religion.

2 Cults, on the other hand, are new religions, or at least they are new in a particular society. Some result from cultural importation, where a religion from other societies is introduced into a society in which it had not previously been practised. Thus, Eastern religions introduced into the USA are examples of imported cults. Some cults, though, are entirely new. These result from cultural innovation; they are unconnected to existing religions.

Stark and Bainbridge go on to suggest that cults exhibit different degrees of organization and can be divided into three types:

1 Audience cults are the least organized and involve little face-to-face interaction. Contacts are often maintained through the mass media and the occasional conference. Many of the members of the audience for such cults may not know each other. Astrology is an example of an audience cult, as is the belief in UFOs.

2 Client cults are more organized and usually offer services to their followers. In the past they tended to offer 'medical miracles, forecasts of the future, or contact with the dead', though more recently they have 'specialised in personal adjustment'. Scientology, for example, offers its clients the opportunity to clear 'engrams' (repressed memories of painful experiences) from the brain, while the Reich Foundation offers the promise of the 'monumental orgasm'.

3 Cult movements involve followers much more. They try to satisfy all the religious needs of their members and, unlike client and audience cults, membership of other faiths is not permitted. They do, however, vary considerably in their power. Some require little more than occasional attendance at meetings and acceptance of the cult's beliefs, but others shape the whole of a person's life. The Reverend Sun Myung Moon's Unification Church is an example of a cult movement. Many client cults become cult movements for their most dedicated followers – for example, practitioners of TM who take the Siddi programme (see p. 459 for a short description of TM).

A well-publicized example that would probably fit Stark and Bainbridge's definition of a cult movement was the Heaven's Gate cult. They were a doomsday cult with an interest in computer technology and science fiction. They started in the mid-1970s and required members to refrain from sex, drugs and alcohol. The leader, Marshall Applewhite, who liked to be addressed as 'Do' or 'The Representative' even had himself castrated so that he did not become distracted by physical pleasures. The group believed that the earth was about to be recycled to become a garden for some future generation. The leader told his followers that they needed to leave their earthly bodies so as to get closer to heaven. When the comet Hale-Bopp passed close to earth in 1997, the cult members committed suicide, believing that their spirits would ascend to a spacecraft which was following close behind the comet.

Cults and compensators

Stark and Bainbridge argue that different types of cult offer different types of rewards and compensators for their followers. In line with their general theory of religion (discussed on pp. 445–6), they believe that religious organizations exist to meet the needs of individuals.

Audience cults offer very weak compensators which may provide 'no more than a mild vicarious thrill or social entertainment'. Watching Uri Geller allegedly bend a spoon through psychic power does not promise the audience any great improvement in their lives.

Client cults, on the other hand, offer more valuable specific compensators. Stark and Bainbridge say 'If astrologers really could improve our life chances by telling us the right day to make investments, get married, or stay away from the office, those would indeed be valuable rewards.'

However, these cults do not offer general compensators such as an explanation of the meaning of life or the promise of life after death. General compensators are provided by cult movements.

Conclusion

Stark and Bainbridge offer a different, and they would claim superior, method of distinguishing religious organizations to that of Wallis. They make some useful distinctions between different types of cult; however, in doing so, they contradict themselves. They develop their own typology and fail to notice that some groups will not conform to all the characteristics they attribute to audience cults, client cults or cult movements

Reasons for the growth of sects, cults and new religious movements

Religious sects and cults are not a new phenomenon: they have existed for centuries. Steve Bruce traces the emergence of the first sects to the Reformation of the church in the sixteenth century and the upheavals that accompanied it (Bruce, 1995). Despite this, most existing sects and cults originated in the twentieth century, and the 1960s in particular saw the appearance of many new organizations. Table 7.1 shows the date of origin of the 417 native-born sects and 501 cults uncovered in the early 1980s in the USA by Stark and Bainbridge.

Although it is widely believed that these types of religious movement are more common in the USA than in Europe, Stark and Bainbridge uncovered

Table 7.1	When American sects and cults formed: percentage formed in the indicated period	
Historical period	Sects (405)*	Cults (484)*
1899 and before	19	7
1900–1929	22	8
1930–1949	23	10
1950–1959	16	14
1960–1969	14	38
1970–1977	3	23
	100	100

*No date of founding known for 12 sects and for 17 cults.

Source: R. Stark and W.S. Bainbridge (1985) *The Future of Religion*, University of California Press, Berkeley, p. 131.

evidence that there were proportionately more in some European countries. For example, they claimed that in the late 1970s in the USA there were 2.3 cult movements per million inhabitants, compared to 3.2 per million in England and Wales. In England and Wales they found no fewer than 153 different cult movements.

The growth of sects and cults can be explained either in terms of why particular individuals choose to join, or in terms of wider social changes. In reality these reasons are closely linked, since social changes affect the number of people available as potential recruits.

Marginality

Max Weber provided one of the earliest explanations for the growth of sects (Weber, 1963). He argued that they were likely to arise within groups that were marginal in society: members of groups outside the mainstream of social life often feel that they are not receiving the prestige and/or the economic rewards they deserve. One solution to this problem is a sect based on what Weber called 'a theodicy of disprivilege' (a theodicy is a religious explanation and justification). Such sects contain an explanation for the disprivilege of their members and promise them a 'sense of honour' either in the afterlife or in a future 'new world' on earth.

Bryan Wilson (1970) has pointed out that a variety of situations could lead to the marginalization of groups in society, which in turn could provide fertile ground for the development of sects. These situations include defeat in war, natural disaster or economic collapse. Radical and undesirable changes such as these are not the only circumstances that can encourage sect development.

In part, the growth of sects in the USA in the 1960s was accomplished through the recruitment of marginal and disadvantaged groups. The Black Muslims, for example, aimed to recruit 'the negro in the mud', and the sect seemed to offer hope for some of the most desperate blacks.

However, for the most part, in the 1960s and 1970s the membership of the world-rejecting new religious movements was drawn from amongst the ranks of young, white, middle-class Americans and Europeans. Wallis (1984) does not believe that this contradicts the theory that marginal members of society join world-rejecting sects. He argues that many of the recruits had already become marginal to society. Despite their middle-class backgrounds, they were usually 'hippies, drop-outs, surfers, LSD and marijuana users'. Their marginality may have been further increased by arrests for drug use or activities involved with radical politics. They were attracted to the communal lifestyle which the sect offered.

Relative deprivation

However, this does not explain why quite affluent middle-class youth should become marginal members of society in the first place. The concept of 'relative deprivation' can be used to explain their actions. Relative deprivation refers to subjectively perceived deprivation: that which people actually feel. In objective terms the poor are more deprived than the middle class, but in subjective terms certain members of the middle class may feel more deprived than the poor. They do not lack material wealth, but feel spiritually deprived in a world they see as too materialistic, lonely and impersonal. According to Wallis (1984), they therefore seek salvation in the sense of community offered by the sect.

Stark and Bainbridge (1985) also employ the concept of relative deprivation in explaining the origin of sects. They define sects as organizations which break away from an established church, and they believe that it is the relatively deprived who are likely to break away. Splits take place when churches begin to compromise their beliefs. When the more successful members of a religion try to reduce the amount of tension between that religion and the outside world, the less successful resent it and break away.

Social change

A number of sociologists, such as Bryan Wilson (1970), argue that sects arise during periods of rapid social change when traditional norms are disrupted, social relationships come to lack consistent and coherent meaning, and the traditional universe of meaning is undermined.

Wilson uses the example of the early Methodist movement, which had the characteristics of a sect. He sees the rise of Methodism as the response of the urban working class to the 'chaos and uncertainty of life in the newly settled industrial areas'. He claims that they had to evolve 'new patterns of religious belief to accommodate themselves to their new situation'. In a situation of change and uncertainty, the sect offers the support of a close-knit community organization, well-defined and strongly sanctioned norms and values, and a promise of salvation. It provides a new and stable universe of meaning which is legitimized by its religious beliefs.

More generally, Steve Bruce (1995, 1996) attributes the development of a range of religious institutions including sects and cults to a general process of modernization and secularization. He believes that the weakness of more conventional institutionalized religions has encouraged some people to consider less traditional alternatives. In the Middle Ages the church form of organization was dominant. With the Reformation, splits within the church led to the creation of the new sects.

As modern societies developed and faith in traditional sources of authority (such as churches) declined, religious pluralism and diversity were increasingly tolerated. The denomination became the characteristic form of religion – a watered-down version of the intolerant beliefs of churches and sects which believed that only they knew the truth. More recently, in what Bruce believes is a more secular world in which people are less likely to hold strong commitments, cults have become more popular. These require fewer sacrifices and less commitment than churches and sects and are therefore more tolerable to a modern clientele. However, a small number of people are willing to join the stricter sects. Bruce's views on specific types of new religious movement will be examined below.

The growth of new religious movements

Wallis (1984) has pointed to a number of social changes which he believes accounted for the growth of new religious movements in the 1960s. Some of these had important effects on youth in particular:

1 The growth of higher education and the gradual lengthening of time spent in education created an extended period of transition between childhood and adulthood. Youth culture developed because there was an increasing number of young people who had considerable freedom but little in the way of family or work responsibilities.

2 At the same time there was a belief that developing technology would herald the end of poverty and economic scarcity.

3 Radical political movements were also growing in the 1960s, providing an alternative to dominant social norms and values.

Wallis claims that in these circumstances world-rejecting new religious movements were attractive because of the potential they seemed to offer for 'A more idealistic, spiritual and caring way of life, in the context of more personal and loving social relationships.' It has also been suggested that the growth of such movements was related to secularization. In general terms secularization means a decline in the importance of religion in society. (For details of the relationship between sects and secularization see pp. 485–6.)

Steve Bruce (1995) sees world-rejecting movements as having a particular appeal to the young. Many had become disillusioned by the failure of the counter-culture in the 1960s to radically change the world. The hippie culture and the commune movement had disintegrated largely because of drugs and exploitation of the movement. The disillusioned young people sought another path to salvation through religion rather than peace and love.

Wallis (1984) provides only a very sketchy explanation of recruitment to world-accommodating religious movements. He claims that those with a substantial stake in society, but who nevertheless have reasons for being dissatisfied with existing religions, tend to join them.

World-affirming new religions, as we saw earlier, are very different from the other types. They do not involve a radical break with a conventional lifestyle, they do not strongly restrict the behaviour of members, and they offer material and practical advantages to their followers. For all of these reasons they might be expected to appeal to different groups in society, and to develop in different circumstances.

World-affirming new religious movements usually develop after world-rejecting ones, and more of them have survived longer. Research suggests that members of groups such as Erhard's Seminar Training have members with above-average incomes and education who are somewhat older than members of world-rejecting groups. To Wallis, what they offer is a 'means of coping with a sense of inadequacy among social groups which are, by the more obvious indicators, among the world's more successful and highly rewarded individuals'. It is primarily the emphasis placed upon individual success in terms of status, income and social mobility that stimulates these 'religions' to develop.

Actually achieving success may in another sense motivate individuals to join these groups. Individuals may feel that in the successful performance of their social roles (such as their jobs) they lose sight of their real selves. A world-affirming religious movement might allow the rediscovery of this real 'self'.

Bryan Wilson (1976) has argued that these religions offer immediate gratification for those who take part. Wallis suggests that those who are social-ized into being dedicated to their work, and who have internalized the Protestant work ethic, find it hard to enjoy their leisure activities while feeling free from guilt. In an increasingly leisure- and consumer-orientated society, Wallis believes that world-affirming organizations offer a path to guilt-free spontaneously-enjoyed leisure.

Steve Bruce (1995, 1996) believes that world-affirming new religious movements are predomi-nantly a response to the rationalization of the modern world. Because of rationalization, 'Modern life is so fragmented that many people find it increasingly difficult to draw on their public roles for a satisfying and fulfilling sense of identity' (Bruce, 1995). Jobs, for example, are simply a means to an end, to earn a living, and offer little sense of satisfac-tion or fulfilment. People no longer have a sense of calling to their work and may not identify strongly with their workmates. People have, however, been encouraged to value achievement, yet many lack the opportunities to be as successful as they would like. World-affirming movements can offer a solution. They provide a technique which claims to be able to bring people both success and a spiritual element to their lives.

The explanations provided above offer some general reasons why world-affirming movements should be popular in advanced industrial societies, but do not explain why particular individuals should join, nor why they are popular at particular periods of time. More specific theories have been devised to account for what Wallis calls movements of the middle ground.

Several sociologists studying these movements have claimed that they help to reintegrate people into society, while allowing them to retain some elements of an alternative lifestyle. These movements appeal to those members of the counter-culture or world-rejecting religious movements who have become disillusioned, or feel they need to earn a living in a conventional way. They offer a stepping-stone back towards respectability. Thus Mauss and Peterson describe the members of one such group, the Jesus Freaks, as 'penitent young prodigals' (quoted in Wallis, 1984, p. 75).

These middle-ground groups were particularly successful from the mid-1970s onwards, when economic recession and the decline in the numbers of people willing to adopt alternative lifestyles provided a large pool from which recruitment might take place.

The development of sects

Sects as short-lived organizations

In 1929, H.R. Niebuhr made a number of observa-tions about the way in which religious sects changed over time. He argued that sects could not survive as sects beyond a single generation. Either they would change their characteristics, compromise and become denominations, or they would disappear altogether. He advanced the following arguments to support this view:

1 Sect membership was based upon voluntary adult commitment: members chose to dedicate themselves to the organization and its religion. Once the first generation started to have children, though, the latter would be admitted as new members when they were too young to understand the teachings of the religion. These new members would not be able to sustain the fervour of the first generation. Consequently the sect might become a denomination.

2 Sects that relied upon a charismatic leader would tend to disappear if the leader died. Alternatively, the nature of the leadership would change: no

longer would the charisma of an individual hold the sect together. This would allow the bureaucratic structure of a denomination with its hierarchy of paid officials to emerge.

3 Niebuhr argued that the ideology of many sects contained the seeds of their own destruction. Sects with an ascetic creed would encourage their members to work hard and save their money. As a result the membership would be upwardly socially mobile, and would no longer wish to belong to a religious group which catered for marginal members of society. Once again the sect would have to change or die: either becoming a denomination or losing its membership.

According to Niebuhr, then, there was no possibility of a sect surviving for long periods of time without losing its extreme teachings and rejection of society. One example that illustrates this well is that of the Methodists before they became a denomination: as the Methodist membership rose in status in the nineteenth century, the strict disciplines of the sect and its rejection of society were dropped, and it gradually came to be recognized as a denomination. A number of sects have also disappeared because of the mass suicide (or murder) of their members. The examples of the People's Temple and the Branch Davidians have been discussed above (see p. 456).

The life cycle of sects

However, Bryan Wilson (1966) rejects Niebuhr's view that sects are inevitably short-lived. He points out that some sects do survive for a long time without becoming denominations. To Wilson, the crucial factor is the way the sect answers the question 'What shall we do to be saved?' Sects can be classified in terms of how they answer this question. Only one type, the conversionist sect, is likely to develop into a denomination. Examples include the evangelical sects, typical of the USA, which aim to convert as many people as possible by means of revivalist preaching. Becoming a denomination does not necessarily compromise its position. It can still save souls.

The other types of sect cannot maintain their basic position in a denominational form. Adventist sects, such as the Seventh Day Adventists and Jehovah's Witnesses, provide an example of the reason why. Adventist sects await the Second Coming of Christ, who will judge humanity and establish a new world order. Only sect membership will guarantee a place in the new order. The rich and powerful and those who follow conventional religions will be excluded from Christ's kingdom on earth. Adventists sects are founded on the principle of separation from the world in the expectation of the Second Coming. To become a denomination they would have to change

this basic premiss. Separation from the world and denominationalism are not compatible.

Thus Wilson concludes that a sect's prescription for salvation is a major factor in determining whether or not it becomes a denomination.

Internal ideology and the wider society

Roy Wallis (1984) takes a more complex view of the paths followed by sects: he feels the chances of sects surviving, changing or disappearing are affected both by the internal ideology of the sect and by external social circumstances.

Since Wallis distinguishes a variety of different types of sect, he argues that they are likely to follow different paths. According to him, the development of sects may involve them changing from one type of sect to another, rather than becoming denominations. Wallis does not believe that there is any single or inevitable path that any type of sect will follow, and he suggests that the changes that do take place may be specific to a particular historical period.

World-rejecting sects do often change their stance as time passes. Like Niebuhr, Wallis sees the possibility that such groups may soften their opposition to society and become more world-accommodating. This seems to have been particularly common in the 1970s when economic recession discouraged some members from dropping-out and rejecting society altogether. The Children of God, for example, weakened their opposition to other religions and no longer thought of non-members as servants of Satan.

Wallis accepts that charismatic leaders have difficulty in retaining personal control over a religious movement indefinitely, and that this may also result in changes. If the organization grows, a process which Weber described as the routinization of charisma can take place. A more bureaucratic organization develops so that some of the leader's personal authority becomes vested in his (or untypically her) officials or representatives. Nevertheless the changes may stop well short of denominationalization.

Wallis also recognizes that sects can disappear. World-rejecting sects may actually be destroyed by the charismatic leader, as in the case of Jim Jones's People's Temple. Social changes may lead to the members becoming less marginal in society, so threatening the base on which the sect was founded. However, as new groups in society become marginal, new sects will arise.

According to Wallis, then, world-rejecting sects do tend to be unstable, but new ones emerge, and those that do survive may become more world-accommodating while continuing to exist as sects.

World-affirming movements are less likely than world-rejecting ones to be based on a charismatic leader or to have members who are marginal or deprived. They also require less sacrifice and commitment from members, and for this reason are not so likely to disappear. Instead, since their services are often sold as a commodity, they are vulnerable to a loss of support from their consumers. To the extent that they sell themselves in the market-place, they are subject to the same problems as a retailer. If the public no longer needs, or gains benefits from, their services, they will lose customers. To Wallis, though, world-affirming movements are more likely to change to attract a new clientele than to cease to exist.

Transcendental Meditation (TM), for example, initially emphasized its spiritual elements, and in the second half of the 1960s it succeeded by identifying closely with the counter-culture. In the 1970s the counter-culture declined and TM tried to broaden its appeal by emphasizing the practical benefits – the worldly success – that the meditation claimed to offer.

Wallis points out that consumers might tire of a product that fails to deliver its promises. One response is to try to gain an inner-core of committed followers. TM did just this through the Siddi programme and perhaps in this way helped to guarantee a permanent following.

Wallis believes that world-affirming movements are flexible and they can change relatively easily as they seek to survive and prosper. In some circumstances they can also become more religious and spiritual (like world-rejecting movements) for at least an inner-core of followers.

The position of the movements of the middle ground is by its very nature more precarious. Since they are in an intermediate position they are likely to shift between being world-rejecting and world-affirming, depending upon circumstances and the needs and wishes of the membership. This can lead to splits within the movements or the establishment of rival organizations. One British movement of this type, the Process, was founded in 1963 and split into two separate groups in 1973. If these splits do not take place it is likely that such movements fluctuate between the two extremes, continuing in one form or another, but not establishing a clear and permanent ideology and identity.

Wallis says little about how world-accommodating movements develop, but these seem the most stable of the new religious movements. Indeed, some are not particularly new: Pentecostalism has survived little-changed since the early years of the twentieth century. As Wallis points out, this type of 'new' religious movement has most in common with denominations.

Thus, although Wallis does not agree with Niebuhr that sects inevitably disappear or become denominations, his work does suggest that there may be tendencies in these directions. Those religious movements that are most similar to denominations are the likeliest to remain stable. World-rejecting movements, which have most in common with the type of sects Niebuhr described, are the least likely to survive for long periods in their original form.

The New Age

Examples of the New Age

The New Age is a term that has been applied to a range of ideas which started to become prominent in the 1980s. Although some of these beliefs were organized as new religious movements (particularly as world-affirming new religious movements) and as cults of various types (particularly client cults and audience cults), in many cases they were not closely attached to particular organizations (Heelas, 1996, Bruce 1995). Rather, New Age ideas were spread through aspects of the culture of particular societies in films, shops, seminars, meetings, music, television programmes, public lectures and so on.

Examples of New Age beliefs include interest in clairvoyance, contacting aliens, belief in 'spirit guides' and 'spirit masters', various types of meditation and psychotherapy, beliefs in paganism, magic, tarot cards, ouija, astrology and witchcraft, an interest in self-healing and natural or traditional remedies for ill health (for example, yoga, aromatherapy, reflexology), spiritually inclined ecology such as a belief in Gaia (the Greek goddess who has been used to represent the sacred and interconnected nature of all life), and so on. Manifestations of the New Age can be found in places such as the annual Mind, Body and Spirit Convention, which has been held in London since 1977; in publications on topics such as Feng Shui, mysticism and Shamanism; in the music of groups such as Kula Shaker; in shops that sell tapes of sounds from nature which can be used for relaxation or meditation; in communes such as the Findhorn community in Scotland (which grew vegetables with the help of plant spirits rather than fertilizers); and in more conventionally organized groups such as the Scientologists and some Buddhist groups.

The themes of the New Age

What have such a diverse range of activities and beliefs got in common? Paul Heelas (1996) believes that the central feature of the New Age is a belief in self-spirituality. People with such beliefs have turned away from traditional religious organizations in the search for the spiritual and instead have begun to look inside themselves. The New Age 'explains why life – as conventionally experienced – is not what it should be; it provides an account of what it is to find perfection; and it provides the means for obtaining salvation'. However, that salvation does not come from being accepted by an external god, it comes from discovering and perfecting yourself. Often this means going beyond your conscious self to discover hidden spiritual depths. Heelas says:

> Perfection can be found only by moving beyond the socialized self – widely known as the 'ego' but also as the 'lower self', 'intellect' or the 'mind' – thereby encountering a new realm of being. It is what we are by nature.
>
> Heelas, 1996, p.19

In this process we find our spiritual core. New Agers tell people that 'You are Gods and Goddesses in exile' who only need to cast off the cloaks that hide this to uncover their true potential. There are many different ways to (in the word of a Doors song) 'break on through to the other side'. These include 'psychother-apies, physical labour, dance, shamanic practices, magic, or for that matter, fire-walking, sex, tennis, taking drugs or using virtual-reality equipment'.

According to Heelas, the New Age values personal experience above 'truths' provided by scientists or conventional religious leaders. In this respect detraditionalization is a key feature of the New Age: it rejects the authority that comes from traditional sources and sees individuals and their sense of who they are as the only genuine source of truth or understanding. A good example of this attitude was a notice above the door of Bhagwan Shree Rajneesh's Ashram (commune) at Puna, which said 'Leave your minds and shoes here.'

The New Age stresses that you can become responsible for your own actions, you do not need to be governed by preconceived ideas. It also emphasizes freedom to discover your own truth and discover your own way to the truth. Although many aspects of the New Age draw on traditional mystical and religious teachings, these are seen as ways of getting in touch with your own spirituality rather than as doctrines that must be rigidly followed. They allow the discovery of truth as an abstract concept, as an inner and spiritual phenomenon, rather than revealing a particular and specific version of the truth. According to Heelas, the movement believes that 'the same wisdom can be found at the heart of all religious traditions'.

Variations within the New Age

Although Heelas detects many common themes in the New Age, as outlined above, he also discerns some variations in New Age beliefs. Following Roy Wallis's typology of new religious movements (see pp. 457–60), Heelas distinguishes between aspects of the New Age which tend towards the world-affirming

and those which are more world-rejecting. The former type stress how the New Age can help you experience the best of the outer world. For example, New Age teachings might help you to be successful in business. Harper Collins (the publishers of this book) in the 1990s ran company-wide courses following the New Age 'Values and Vision' training of Tishi. Transcendental Meditation now has its own University of Management in Holland. There are numerous other examples and all claim to be able to help companies to become more profitable and individuals more successful.

World-rejecting aspects of New Age stress how to experience the best of the inner world, how to achieve inner spirituality and turn away from any concern with worldly success.

Most New Age beliefs, though, offer the best of both worlds, claiming that you can become both successful and spiritually fulfilled. Not surprisingly, then, the radicalism of different New Age beliefs differs considerably. While some almost celebrate capitalism, others are strongly opposed to aspects of it. This is particularly true of ecologically inclined parts of the movement. Nevertheless, Steve Bruce believes that even these types are less radical than some of the new religious movements of earlier decades. Bruce says of environmentalism:

> it is critical of aspects of the modern world, especially those such as pollution that can be seen as side-effects of greed and over-consumption, and in that sense the New Age is 'alternative', but there is little of the blanket condemnation of the present world found in out-and-out world-rejecting new religions.
>
> Bruce, 1995, p. 109

Heelas also detects differences between those aspects of the New Age which stress that you make your own truth through experience and those which believe that there is some external cosmic order which can be discovered, or that you need the help of 'gurus, masters, facilitators or trainers'.

The appeal of the New Age

Both Steve Bruce and Paul Heelas agree that the New Age can best be explained as a development of modernity. In other words they agree that the key characteristics of the New Age are derived from, or at least closely related to, what they see as the most recent stages of the development of Western societies (see Chapter 15 for a discussion of modernity).

Steve Bruce claims that the New Age appeals most to affluent members of society, particularly the 'university-educated middle classes working in the "expressive professions": social workers, counsellors, actors, writers, artists, and others whose education and work causes them to have an articulate interest in human potential'. They may have experienced personal development themselves and therefore find it plausible to believe that there is the potential for further development for themselves or others. These are also the sorts of people who have been most exposed to a belief in individualism, which is characteristic of modern societies. Modern societies are relatively egalitarian and democratic so the views and beliefs of individuals are given more credence than was once the case, whereas the views of experts and traditional authorities are regarded with more scepticism. Bruce says:

> This is the importance of the New Age. It illustrates the zenith of individualism. Individualism used to mean the right to act as one wished provided it did not harm others and the right to hold views radically at odds with the consensus. It has now shifted up in abstraction from a behavioural and ethical principle to an epistemological claim [a claim about how you know what is true and what is not]. It is now asserted as the right to decide what is and what is not true.

> Bruce, 1995, p. 122

The New Age is a symptom of the extreme relativism of knowledge; that is, what you believe comes to depend simply on your subjective point of view and is not based upon general acceptance of definite claims by scientists and experts. It is also, in Bruce's eyes, a symptom of the decline of traditional religion. If people have little faith in the claims of scientists, they have even less in those of traditional religious leaders.

Paul Heelas (1996) reaches broadly similar conclusions. He sees the main appeal of the New Age as stemming from aspects of mainstream culture. However, it provides a more critical, radicalized and more religious, sacrilized version of mainstream culture. On the surface it appears to reject mainstream culture but in fact it is based on an extreme emphasis on the individualism that is typical of modernity. This individualism leads to people becoming 'disembedded, desituated or detraditionalized selves'. People have no roots in the locality where they were born or brought up. They no longer have unquestioning faith in political, moral or religious codes, or in the leaders who espouse them. People are thrown back on their own resources to make sense of the world and to create their own identity.

The individualism of modernity takes two forms:

1 Utilitarian individualism encourages people to seek to maximize their own happiness and material success. This is linked both to the desire for consumer goods and to those aspects of the New Age which aim to provide people with techniques to make them more successful in business or in their careers.

2 Expressive individualism emphasizes the importance of being yourself, discovering your authentic or true self. This links to those aspects of the New Age which are more inner-directed.

Heelas examines four more specific ways in which modernity might link to the appeal of the New Age:

1 Modernity gives people a 'multiplicity-of-roles'. For example, they have work roles, family roles, roles as consumers, as members of various organizations, as friends and so on. In the modern world there may be little overlap between these roles; people are unlikely to live close to, and socialize primarily with, their workmates, or to live in the same community all their lives, or to work with members of their family. Because of this, people may end up with a fragmented identity – they have no central, core concept of who they are. The New Age offers ways of finding an identity.

2 Consumer culture encourages people to try to become the perfect person by, for example, wearing the right clothes, using the best make-up, having the healthiest diet, etc. This creates a 'climate of discontent' as people fail to achieve the perfection portrayed by the advertisers. This encourages people to try new ways of gaining perfection, including those offered by the New Age.

3 Following Bryan Wilson (see p. 463), Heelas suggests that periods of rapid social change, in which traditional norms and values are disrupted, might lead people to seek certainty and security in religious or spiritual beliefs.

4 The decline of conventional religion, particularly Christianity, leaves people without strong spiritual alternatives to the New Age when they are seeking solutions to the problems created by modernity.

Heelas sees the last of these explanations as the least important. However, he believes that all may have some role to play in explaining the appeal of the New Age. All are linked to modernity, but people experience modernity in very different ways. Some people experience modernity as (in a phrase used by Weber) an 'iron cage'. They feel trapped by the power of bureaucracies, the routines of work and the demands of success in capitalist societies. Yet, for all its demands, modernity does not offer most people a satisfying sense of identity – of who they are and why they exist. The New Age offers a solution.

Others experience modernity as a 'crumbling cage' where they have too much freedom, too few guidelines about how to behave. Again, the New Age offers possible solutions for people prepared to look within themselves for the answers.

Of course there are other ways of dealing with the dilemmas of modernity. As Heelas acknowledges, some people – for example, Christian fundamentalists in the USA – turn to traditional religion. Others might throw themselves into their work or become entranced by consumer culture. Nevertheless, the popularity of the New Age is only made possible by the nature of modernity. Heelas concludes:

Basically, the appeal of the New Age has to do with the culturally stimulated interest in the self, its values, capacities and problems. Whereas traditionalized religiosity, with its hierarchical organization, is well-suited for the community, detraditionalized spirituality is well-suited for the individual. The New Age is 'of' the self in that it facilitates celebration of what it is to be and to become; and 'for' the self in that by differing from much of the mainstream, it is positioned to handle identity problems generated by conventional forms of life.

Heelas, 1996, pp. 173–4

The New Age – conclusion

On the surface the New Age seems to contradict the views of sociologists such as Weber that the modern world would become increasingly rational. There

seems to be little rationality in the claim by the New Ager Shirley Maclaine that she is responsible for the birth of her parents (quoted in Heelas, 1996), or that spirit guides, astrology or messages from 'an energy personality essence no longer focused in physical reality' (quoted in Bruce, 1995) can help us to live our lives better. But if Bruce and Heelas are correct, then the rationality of modernity also brought with it an individualism in which apparently non-rational beliefs could flourish.

Some writers disagree with Bruce and Heelas, seeing the existence of such beliefs as evidence that we have moved beyond modernity into an era of postmodernity (see pp. 495–500 on postmodernity and religion). There is no agreement either on whether the New Age is evidence of the resurgence of spiritual belief or a manifestation of secularization (see pp. 499–500). But Bruce and Heelas seem to be on strong ground in arguing that the New Age is related to a decline in traditional beliefs and that it is closely linked with other social and cultural developments in modern societies.

Secularization

Support for the secularization thesis

Although sociologists have disputed whether religion encourages or inhibits social change, most agree that changes in society will lead to changes in religion. Furthermore, many have claimed that social change would lead to the weakening or even disappearance of religion.

In the nineteenth century it was widely believed that industrialization and the growth of scientific knowledge would lead to secularization, which very broadly can be defined as the process of religious decline. August Comte (1986), the French functionalist sociologist, believed that human history passed through three stages. Each stage was characterized by a different set of intellectual beliefs:

1 In the first, theological stage, religious and superstitious beliefs would be dominant.

2 These would be weakened as society passed into the second, metaphysical stage, during which philosophy would become more important.

3 Religious belief would disappear altogether in the final, positive stage, in which science alone would dominate human thinking and direct human behaviour.

Durkheim did not agree that religion was doomed to total obsolescence. He once commented that there was 'something eternal in religion' (Durkheim, 1961). Nevertheless, he did anticipate that religion would be

of declining social significance. In an industrial society in which there was a highly specialized division of labour, religion would lose some of its importance as a force for integrating society. Social solidarity would increasingly be provided by the education system rather than the sort of religious rituals associated with the more simple societies.

Weber too anticipated a progressive reduction in the importance of religion. He thought that in general people would act less in terms of emotions and in line with tradition, and more in terms of the rational pursuit of goals. Rationalization would gradually erode religious influence (Weber, 1958, 1963, Gerth and Mills, 1954) (for further details see Chapter 15).

Marx did not believe that industrial capitalism as such would herald the decline of religion, but he did believe that it would set in motion a chain of events that would eventually lead to its disappearance (Marx, 1950). Religion, according to Marx, was needed to legitimate inequality in class societies, but capitalism would eventually be replaced by classless communism, and religion would cease to have any social purpose.

Many contemporary sociologists have followed in the footsteps of the founders of the subject. They have argued that science and rationality, the decline of traditional values, and the increasingly specialized division of labour, would tend to undermine religion in particular and faith and non-rational beliefs in general. These views are largely based upon an analysis of the nature of modernity.

Modern societies are seen to be incompatible with the retention of a central role for religion. That is not to say that supporters of the secularization thesis necessarily believe that religion will disappear completely. Instead they argue that in some sense religion will decline in significance. For example, Bryan Wilson – for over thirty years a leading advocate of secularization – defines secularization as 'the process whereby religious thinking, practice and institutions lose social significance' (Wilson, 1966).

Problems with the secularization thesis

Despite widespread support for the theory of secularization, a number of doubts have been raised:

1 Some sociologists have questioned the belief that religion was as important in the past as has been widely assumed. If pre-industrial societies were not truly religious, then religion may have declined little, if at all.

2 The role of religion in different modern societies varies considerably. It is possible that secularization is a feature of the development of some modern societies, but not of others. For example, religion appears to be much more influential in the USA than it is in the UK. There are also disagreements about how far you might expect the process of secularization to have spread. For example, would you expect Asian, African, and Latin American countries to have experienced secularization, or would you expect it to be limited to North America and Western Europe? The crucial question here is which countries are perceived to be 'modern'.

3 The concepts of religiosity and secularization are not given the same meanings by different sociologists. Problems arise in evaluating the theory of secularization because of the absence of a generally agreed definition. Glock and Stark argue that 'Perhaps the most important attribute of those who perceive secularization to be going on is their commitment to a particular view of what religion means' (Glock and Stark, 1969). Thus one researcher might see the essential characteristic of religion as worship in a religious institution. As a result she or he may see a decline in church attendance as evidence of secularization. Another might emphasize religious belief, which is seen as having nothing necessarily to do with attending a religious institution. A third might see the issue in terms of the role religion plays in shaping public life, for example politics and education; while a fourth might see it in terms of the extent to which religious teaching has influenced the moral values of a society.

4 Even if modernity does lead to secularization, you cannot necessarily conclude that contemporary societies will become increasingly secular. Some advocates of the theory of postmodernism argue that, in moving beyond modernity, societies will also move beyond the secular. Faith and religion will be rediscovered in a world in which the achievements of science and rationality have less appeal than they once had (see Chapter 15 for a discussion of modernity and postmodernity).

The question of secularization will now be discussed in terms of some of the varying definitions of the concept that have been used, before returning to a more general discussion of the issues raised by this concept.

Institutional religion – participation

Statistical evidence

Some researchers have seen religious institutions and the activity associated with them as the key element in religious behaviour. From this viewpoint they have measured the importance of religion in society in terms of factors such as church attendance, church membership and participation in ceremonies such as marriages which are performed in church.

In these respects, a good deal of the statistical evidence does seem to point towards secularization. However, the evidence needs to be examined carefully: some of it does not appear to support the secularization thesis; the evidence varies between countries; and the reliability and validity of many of the statistics are open to question. (For an explanation of the terms validity and reliability see Chapter 14.)

We will now examine the statistics relating to different types of participation in institutional religion.

Church attendance in Britain

Some of the strongest evidence for the secularization thesis as applied to Britain seems to come from church attendance statistics. Figure 7.2 shows long-term trends in church attendance in England and Wales and Scotland according to a variety of surveys and studies, some of which are discussed below.

The earliest available survey statistics on church attendance originate from the 1851 'Census of Religion'. This found just under 40 per cent of the adult population attending church. In England and Wales the figures dropped to 35 per cent by the turn of the century and 20 per cent in 1950.

In 1979 and 1989 two new Church Censuses were carried out. In both of these, clergy were asked to make comparisons with five years earlier and estimate changes in the size of their congregations. The 1979 census was based on average attendance during the month of November. The 1989 census was based upon an attempt to collect information from every Christian church in England on Sunday 15 October of that year. A church was defined as 'a body of people meeting on a Sunday in the same premises primarily for the purposes of public worship at regular intervals'. 'Church' was used in a very wide sense – the study included figures on Anglicans, Roman Catholics, Orthodox religions, Christian denominations and the House Church movement (in which small groups get together to pray in each others' homes or in other buildings that are not normally used for religious purposes). Altogether 390,000 'churches' were discovered, 70 per cent of

which returned the questionnaires on which the statistics were based (Brierley, 1991). Using these surveys and estimates provided by individual religious organizations, estimates have been produced in the *UK Christian Handbook: Religious Trends 1998/99* (Brierley, ed., 1997) for adult church attendance between 1980 and 1995 in England. The results are given in Table 7.2 and include estimates for the year 2000 based on previous trends.

The overall attendance figures are repeated along with membership figures in graph form in Figure 7.3. These figures show a continuing drop in church

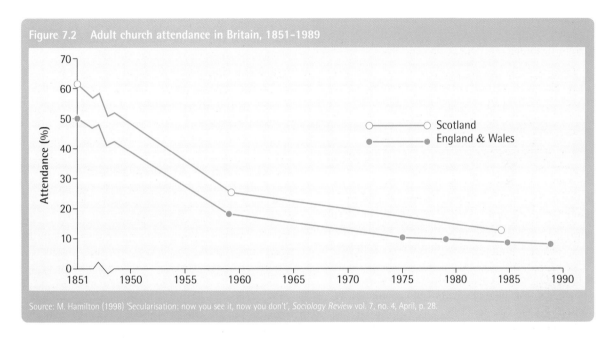

Figure 7.2   Adult church attendance in Britain, 1851–1989

Source: M. Hamilton (1998) 'Secularisation: now you see it, now you don't', *Sociology Review* vol. 7, no. 4, April, p. 28.

Table 7.2   Adult church attendance in England, 1980–2000

England	1980	1985	1990	1995	2000
Anglican	968,000	920,900	917,600	854,000	831,800
Baptist	201,300	196,200	197,700	195,200	192,000
Catholic	1,601,400	1,424,200	1,346,400	1,100,800	972,700
Independent	164,200	176,500	179,700	184,900	190,000
Methodist	437,900	420,800	395,200	350,500	321,800
New churches	50,300	81,000	114,200	156,100	198,000
Orthodox	7,200	8,400	9,600	10,800	12,000
Pentecostal	147,200	152,400	164,700	171,900	179,000
United Reformed	139,000	121,400	104,100	97,900	91,500
Other churches	97,700	81,400	83,000	75,700	73,000
TOTAL	3,814,200	3,583,200	3,512,200	3,197,800	3,061,800
% of adult population	*10.2%*	*9.3%*	*9.0%*	*8.1%*	*7.7%*

Source: P. Brierley (ed.) (1998) *UK Christian Handbook: Religious Trends 1998/99*, Christian Research, p. 2.12.

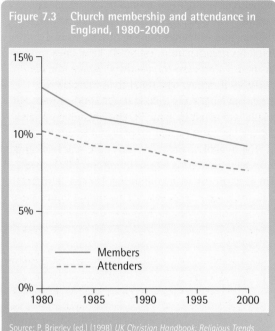

Figure 7.3   Church membership and attendance in England, 1980–2000

Members
Attenders

Source: P. Brierley (ed.) (1998) *UK Christian Handbook: Religious Trends 1998/99*, Christian Research, p. 2.13.

Church membership in Britain

Tables 7.4 to 7.8 show the number of church members, the number of separate congregations or churches, and the number of ministers in the UK and its constituent countries from 1980 to 1990. Figures 7.4 to 7.7 show some of these statistics in graph form. Both the tables and graphs include projections to the year 2000. The data reveals substantial falls in the membership of Anglican, Roman Catholic and Presbyterian churches, although membership of Orthodox churches has risen. Overall membership of these churches fell by nearly 1.2 million between 1980 and 1995, or by around 19 per cent.

According to the *UK Christian Handbook*, by 1995 only 10.8 per cent of the UK adult population were members of Anglican, Catholic, Orthodox or Presbyterian churches. In England the figure was just 7.5 per cent, compared to 8.8 per cent in Wales, 25.3 per cent in Scotland and 72.9 per cent in Northern Ireland.

attendance overall, particularly among Anglican, Baptist, Catholic and United Reformed churches. This appears to indicate a sustained process of secularization. Table 7.3 shows total adult attendance in Great Britain from 1980 to 2000. Again, the figure for 2000 is based on projections. This shows a drop in attendance from 10.9 per cent of the population in 1980 to 8.7 per cent in 1995.

Attendance at special Christian ceremonies such as baptisms and marriages has also declined. In 1900, 65 per cent of children born alive in England were baptized. By 1970 it was down to 47 per cent and in 1993 had fallen as low as 27 per cent (Bruce, 1996). There has also been a noticeable drop in the number of marriages conducted in church. According to Bruce, nearly 70 per cent of English couples were married in the Church of England at the start of the twentieth century. By 1990 it had fallen to 53 per cent. According to the *UK Christian Handbook*, 47 per cent of marriages in England and Wales in 1995 took place in a religious building.

Table 7.3   Total adult church attendance in Great Britain, 1980–2000

Great Britain	1980	1985	1990	1995	2000
TOTAL (millions)	4.77	4.51	4.38	3.98	3.79
	10.9%	10.1%	9.6%	8.7%	8.2%

Source: P. Brierley (ed.) (1998) *UK Christian Handbook: Religious Trends 1998/99*, Christian Research, p. 2.12.

Table 7.4   Total institutional churches

Membership					
	England	Wales	Scotland	N Ireland	**Total UK**
1980	3,749,987	289,038	1,358,679	879,747	**6,277,451**
1985	3,309,455	262,056	1,259,759	891,801	**5,725,071**
1990	3,101,081	239,515	1,175,601	892,624	**5,408,821**
1995	2,934,360	206,593	1,053,542	894,342	**5,088,837**
2000[1]	2,632,510	184,521	960,885	897,340	**4,675,256**

Churches					
	England	Wales	Scotland	N Ireland	**Total UK**
1980	21,885	3,241	3,021	1,504	**29,651**
1985	21,638	3,118	2,923	1,482	**29,161**
1990	21,478	2,996	2,863	1,537	**28,874**
1995	21,392	2,840	2,757	1,517	**28,426**
2000[1]	21,212	2,729	2,650	1,533	**28,124**

Ministers					
	England	Wales	Scotland	N Ireland	**Total UK**
1980	19,246	1,406	3,108	1,523	**25,283**
1985	18,637	1,290	2,847	1,501	**24,275**
1990	18,378	1,197	2,748	1,452	**23,775**
1995	17,015	1,150	2,573	1,434	**22,172**
2000[1]	16,183	1,103	2,370	1,457	**21,113**

[1] Estimate

Source: P. Brierley (ed.) (1998) *UK Christian Handbook: Religious Trends 1998/99*, Christian Research, p. 2.8.

The above figures do not include Free churches such as Baptist, Methodist and Pentecostal churches. Here the pattern of changes in membership is more variable. There have been rises in membership of new churches and Pentecostal churches but falls in the membership of Baptist, Independent, Methodist and other 'other' Free churches. The figures are given in Tables 7.9–7.15. Overall, Free Church membership declined slightly between 1980 and 1995, falling by around 3,400 or by just under 0.3 per cent.

Membership of some non-Christian churches and other religious organizations has been increasing. Table 7.16 shows members and congregations of non-Trinitarian religions. This shows a significant increase in membership from over 350,000 in 1980 to over 520,000 in 1995 – an increase of around 47 per cent. Much of this increase is accounted for by the rises in the numbers of Jehovah's Witnesses, Mormons and Scientologists. (Scientologists are sometimes classified as a cult.) Some other groups, including Theosophists, Unitarian churches and Spiritualists, have declined.

Table 7.17 provides statistics on major religions other than Christianity in the UK. This shows substantial increases in membership of some non-Christian religions. The number of Muslims has increased by 274,000, Sikhs by 200,000, Hindus by 35,000 and Buddhists by 28,000. There have been declines in some groups – for example, Jews – but overall membership of these religions has increased by some 545,000, or over 70 per cent. While much of this increase may be explained by births to parents following these religions, and by immigration, some has been due to conversions. For example, some people from a Christian background have converted to Buddhism.

New religious movements, which take the form of sects or cults, involve much smaller numbers than the major non-Christian religions. The *UK Christian Handbook* lists 18 such movements and has estimated

Table 7.5	Anglican[1] membership, churches and ministers				
Membership					
	England	Wales	Scotland	N Ireland	**Total UK**
1980	1,817,290	131,553	67,655	162,960	**2,179,458**
1985	1,553,446	116,976	62,756	162,765	**1,895,943**
1990	1,398,863	108,365	58,619	162,130	**1,727,977**
1995	1,472,627	95,985	55,136	161,525	**1,785,273**
2000[2]	1,286,310	87,150	49,800	160,830	**1,584,090**
Churches					
	England	Wales	Scotland	N Ireland	**Total UK**
1980	16,927	1,698	312	462	**19,399**
1985	16,629	1,639	317	440	**19,025**
1990	16,440	1,595	313	476	**18,824**
1995	16,362	1,540	320	452	**18,674**
2000[2]	16,227	1,503	316	459	**18,505**
Ministers					
	England	Wales	Scotland	N Ireland	**Total UK**
1980	11,101	802	237	332	**12,472**
1985	10,796	752	244	366	**12,158**
1990	11,130	700	240	304	**12,374**
1995	10,577	710	244	250	**11,781**
2000[2]	10,191	691	242	283	**11,407**

[1] These figures are more than just the Church of England, although in 1995 the Church of England membership was 82 per cent of the total
[2] Estimate

Source: P. Brierley (ed.) (1998) *UK Christian Handbook: Religious Trends 1998/99*, Christian Research, p. 2.8.

Table 7.6	Roman Catholic mass attendance, churches and priests				
Mass attendance					
	England	Wales	Scotland	N Ireland	**Total UK**
1980	1,601,365	56,956	296,329	502,403	**2,457,053**
1985	1,424,235	58,169	285,031	513,905	**2,281,340**
1990	1,346,416	54,819	283,899	515,710	**2,200,844**
1995	1,100,845	47,387	249,180	518,005	**1,915,417**
2000[1]	972,705	46,356	243,260	521,510	**1,783,831**
Churches					
	England	Wales	Scotland	N Ireland	**Total UK**
1980	3,016	209	476	459	**4,160**
1985	3,109	217	478	464	**4,268**
1990	3,174	213	485	467	**4,339**
1995	3,147	205	464	470	**4,286**
2000[1]	3,140	206	464	472	**4,282**
Priests					
	England	Wales	Scotland	N Ireland	**Total UK**
1980	6,788	340	1,175	707	**9,010**
1985	6,427	332	1,111	647	**8,517**
1990	6,083	311	1,050	643	**8,087**
1995	5,490	279	936	720	**7,425**
2000[1]	5,133	265	876	700	**6,974**

[1] Estimate

Source: P. Brierley (ed.) (1998) *UK Christian Handbook: Religious Trends 1998/99*, Christian Research, p. 2.8.

Table 7.7 Orthodox membership, congregations and priests

Membership

	England	Wales	Scotland	N Ireland	Total UK
1980	187,227	9,409	6,366	163	**203,165**
1985	203,280	8,686	11,585	190	**223,741**
1990	240,281	8,512	16,950	225	**265,968**
1995	258,466	6,093	23,732	269	**288,560**
2000[1]	285,450	5,615	29,055	300	**320,420**

Congregations

	England	Wales	Scotland	N Ireland	Total UK
1980	160	4	5	2	**171**
1985	185	5	8	2	**200**
1990	203	6	10	2	**221**
1995	243	7	15	3	**268**
2000[1]	268	7	18	3	**296**

Priests

	England	Wales	Scotland	N Ireland	Total UK
1980	162	4	2	0	**168**
1985	180	3	4	0	**187**
1990	182	3	7	0	**192**
1995	201	2	11	0	**214**
2000[1]	217	2	13	0	**232**

[1] Estimate

Source: P. Brierley (ed.) (1998) *UK Christian Handbook: Religious Trends 1998/99*, Christian Research, p. 2.8.

Table 7.8 Presbyterian membership, churches and ministers

Membership

	England	Wales	Scotland	N Ireland	Total UK
1980	144,105	91,120	988,329	214,221	**1,437,775**
1985	128,494	78,225	900,387	214,941	**1,322,047**
1990	115,521	67,819	816,133	214,559	**1,214,032**
1995	102,422	57,128	725,494	214,543	**1,099,587**
2000[1]	88,045	45,400	638,770	214,700	**986,915**

Churches

	England	Wales	Scotland	N Ireland	Total UK
1980	1,782	1,330	2,228	581	**5,921**
1985	1,715	1,257	2,120	576	**5,668**
1990	1,661	1,182	2,055	592	**5,490**
1995	1,640	1,088	1,958	592	**5,278**
2000[1]	1,577	1,013	1,852	599	**5,041**

Ministers

	England	Wales	Scotland	N Ireland	Total UK
1980	1,195	260	1,694	484	**3,633**
1985	1,234	203	1,488	488	**3,413**
1990	983	183	1,451	505	**3,122**
1995	747	159	1,382	464	**2,752**
2000[1]	642	145	1,239	474	**2,500**

[1] Estimate

Source: P. Brierley (ed.) (1998) *UK Christian Handbook: Religious Trends 1998/99*, Christian Research, p. 2.8.

Figure 7.4 Percentage changes since 1980 in the Anglican Church

Members, Churches, Ministers

Source: P. Brierley (ed.) (1998) *UK Christian Handbook: Religious Trends 1998/1999*, Christian Research, p. 2.9.

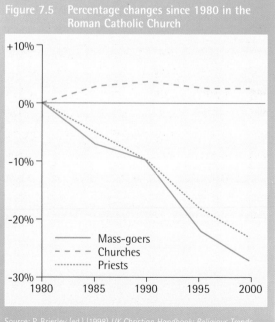

Figure 7.5 Percentage changes since 1980 in the Roman Catholic Church

Mass-goers, Churches, Priests

Source: P. Brierley (ed.) (1998) *UK Christian Handbook: Religious Trends 1998/1999*, Christian Research, p. 2.9.

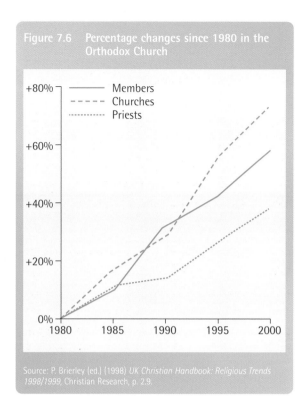

Figure 7.6 Percentage changes since 1980 in the Orthodox Church

Source: P. Brierley (ed.) (1998) *UK Christian Handbook: Religious Trends 1998/1999*, Christian Research, p. 2.9.

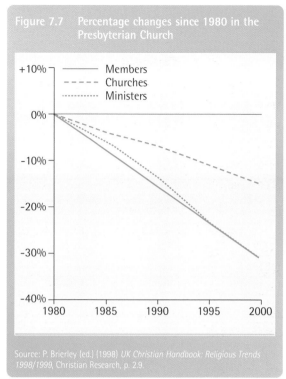

Figure 7.7 Percentage changes since 1980 in the Presbyterian Church

Source: P. Brierley (ed.) (1998) *UK Christian Handbook: Religious Trends 1998/1999*, Christian Research, p. 2.9.

Table 7.9 Total Free Church membership

Membership					
	England	Wales	Scotland	N Ireland	Total UK
1980	972,893	166,394	78,892	57,716	**1,275,895**
1985	973,781	148,450	77,015	57,147	**1,256,393**
1990	1,007,302	136,895	79,667	59,755	**1,283,619**
1995	1,015,466	124,698	71,550	60,767	**1,272,481**
2000[1]	1,022,817	112,332	71,128	61,662	**1,267,939**

Churches					
	England	Wales	Scotland	N Ireland	Total UK
1980	15,912	2,569	1,087	697	**20,365**
1985	15,994	2,436	1,111	698	**20,339**
1990	16,479	2,304	1,128	704	**20,715**
1995	16,487	2,206	1,109	724	**20,626**
2000[1]	16,497	2,073	1,119	735	**20,524**

[1] Estimate

Source: P. Brierley (ed.) (1998) *UK Christian Handbook: Religious Trends 1998/99*, Christian Research, p. 2.10.

Table 7.10 Baptist membership and churches

Membership					
	England	Wales	Scotland	N Ireland	Total UK
1980	162,892	51,814	17,564	7,545	**239,815**
1985	172,573	43,963	18,214	8,349	**243,099**
1990	166,353	37,820	18,103	8,645	**230,921**
1995	162,975	34,194	18,083	8,155	**223,407**
2000[1]	164,295	29,847	17,955	8,220	**220,317**

Churches					
	England	Wales	Scotland	N Ireland	Total UK
1980	2,221	827	181	88	**3,317**
1985	2,279	785	191	93	**3,348**
1990	2,547	743	195	103	**3,588**
1995	2,413	715	208	112	**3,448**
2000[1]	2,413	678	215	121	**3,427**

[1] Estimate

Source: P. Brierley (ed.) (1998) *UK Christian Handbook: Religious Trends 1998/99*, Christian Research, p. 2.10.

Table 7.11 Independent[1] membership and churches

Membership

	England	Wales	Scotland	N Ireland	Total UK
1980	109,619	74,644	38,395	14,223	**236,881**
1985	113,205	66,785	35,457	14,122	**229,569**
1990	114,453	61,112	36,280	13,680	**225,525**
1995	112,468	53,599	27,572	12,605	**206,244**
2000[2]	114,113	46,808	26,846	12,595	**200,362**

Churches

	England	Wales	Scotland	N Ireland	Total UK
1980	2,596	908	528	263	**4,295**
1985	2,538	859	521	259	**4,177**
1990	2,483	817	519	266	**4,085**
1995	2,402	780	470	258	**3,910**
2000[2]	2,346	736	466	261	**3,809**

[1] Total of Brethren, congregational and other independent churches
[2] Estimate

Source: P. Brierley (ed.) (1998) *UK Christian Handbook: Religious Trends 1998/99*, Christian Research, p. 2.10.

Table 7.12 Methodist membership and churches

Membership

	England	Wales	Scotland	N Ireland	Total UK
1980	463,086	25,963	8,240	23,268	**520,557**
1985	422,969	23,026	7,200	21,095	**474,290**
1990	404,381	20,627	7,133	19,591	**451,732**
1995	358,610	18,293	6,312	17,872	**401,087**
2000[1]	329,355	15,650	5,750	16,065	**366,820**

Churches

	England	Wales	Scotland	N Ireland	Total UK
1980	7,639	553	79	210	**8,481**
1985	7,173	501	78	203	**7,955**
1990	6,855	451	77	179	**7,562**
1995	6,422	418	76	176	**7,092**
2000[1]	6,033	367	75	161	**6,636**

[1] Estimate

Source: P. Brierley (ed.) (1998) *UK Christian Handbook: Religious Trends 1998/99*, Christian Research, p. 2.10.

Table 7.13 New churches membership and congregations

Membership

	England	Wales	Scotland	N Ireland	Total UK
1980	9,337	300	400	100	**10,137**
1985	32,351	1,000	1,500	500	**35,351**
1990	71,039	1,740	2,775	1,900	**77,454**
1995	100,766	2,400	3,460	2,975	**109,601**
2000[1]	124,100	3,100	4,200	3,800	**135,200**

Churches

	England	Wales	Scotland	N Ireland	Total UK
1980	219	4	4	1	**228**
1985	649	15	15	5	**684**
1990	1,120	27	28	16	**1,191**
1995	1,479	36	40	25	**1,580**
2000[1]	1,803	44	46	35	**1,928**

[1] Estimate

Source: P. Brierley (ed.) (1998) *UK Christian Handbook: Religious Trends 1998/99*, Christian Research, p. 2.10.

Table 7.14 Pentecostal[1] membership and churches

Membership

	England	Wales	Scotland	N Ireland	Total UK
1980	105,888	8,154	4,310	8,716	**127,068**
1985	113,893	8,881	4,557	9,338	**136,669**
1990	133,669	10,902	5,717	12,211	**162,499**
1995	163,045	11,651	6,681	15,154	**196,531**
2000[2]	174,861	12,660	7,140	16,815	**211,476**

Churches

	England	Wales	Scotland	N Ireland	Total UK
1980	1,568	172	93	71	**1,904**
1985	1,684	171	98	71	**2,024**
1990	1,801	171	98	77	**2,147**
1995	2,036	163	112	88	**2,399**
2000[2]	2,154	156	117	93	**2,520**

[1] Total of main-line Afro-Caribbean and Oneness Apostolic churches
[2] Estimate

Source: P. Brierley (ed.) (1998) *UK Christian Handbook: Religious Trends 1998/99*, Christian Research, p. 2.10.

Table 7.15   Other churches[1] membership and churches

Membership

	England	Wales	Scotland	N Ireland	Total UK
1980	122,071	5,519	9,983	3,864	**141,437**
1985	118,790	4,795	10,087	3,743	**137,415**
1990	117,407	4,694	9,659	3,728	**135,488**
1995	117,602	4,561	9,442	4,006	**135,611**
2000[2]	116,093	4,267	9,237	4,167	**133,764**

Churches

	England	Wales	Scotland	N Ireland	Total UK
1980	1,669	105	202	64	**2,040**
1985	1,671	105	208	67	**2,051**
1990	1,673	95	211	63	**2,042**
1995	1,735	94	203	65	**2,097**
2000[2]	1,748	92	200	64	**2,104**

[1] Total of Central, Holiness, Lutheran and overseas nationals churches and denominations
[2] Estimate

Source: P. Brierley (ed.) (1998) *UK Christian Handbook: Religious Trends 1998/99*, Christian Research, p. 2.10.

Table 7.16   Non-Trinitarian church membership, UK, 1980-95

	1980	1990	1995
Christadelphians	22,000	20,000	19,500*
Christian Community	1,060	800*	600
Church of Christ, Scientist	15,000*	11,000	9,500
Church of God International	5	35	75
The Family	200	200	200*
Global Church of God	–	–	50
Jehovah's Witnesses	85,321	116,612	131,000
Liberal Catholic Church	1,830	1,550	1,400
London Church of Christ	–	1,000	1,500
Church of Jesus Christ of Latter-Day Saints (Mormons)	114,458	159,789	171,000
New Church	2,161	1,712	1,450
Philadelphia Church of God	–	–	50
Reorganized Church of Jesus Christ of Latter Day Saints	2,000*	1,824	1,446
Church of Scientology	30,000	75,000	121,800
Spiritualists	52,404	45,000	40,000*
Theosophists	5,122	4,700	4,500
Unification Church (Moonies)	597	385	390*
Unitarian and Free Christian Churches	11,000	8,500	6,700
The Way	300	600*	750
Other non-Trinitarian	10,000	10,000	10,000
Total	**353,558**	**458,657**	**521,867**

* Estimate
Source: Compiled from P. Brierley (ed.) (1998) *UK Christian Handbook: Religious Trends 1998/99*, Christian Research, pp. 10.2–10.5.

Table 7.17   Major religions other than Christianity, UK, 1980-95

	1980	1990	1995
Ahmadiyya Movement	7,250	7,700	7,900
Bahá'ís	3,000	5,000*	6,000
Buddhists	17,000	31,500	45,000
Hindus	120,000	140,000	155,000
International Society for Krishna Consciousness	300	425	600
Jains	6,000*	10,000	10,000
Jews	110,915	101,239	93,684
Muslims	306,000	495,000	580,000
Satanists	100	280	420
School of Meditation	4,820	7,000*	9,000
Sikhs	150,000	250,000	350,000
Zoroastrians	1,350*	2,000	2,500
Other religions	9,000	15,000	20,000
Total	**735,735**	**1,066,149**	**1,281,014**

* Estimate
Source: Compiled from P. Brierley (ed.) (1998) *UK Christian Handbook: Religious Trends 1998/99*, Christian Research, pp. 10.12–10.15.

the membership of these organizations along with that of other new religious movements. As Table 7.18 shows, membership of such movements rose by nearly 5,000 between 1980 and 1995, an increase of approximately 130 per cent.

All of the above figures should be viewed with some caution. Many of the figures are estimates, and, as we will see below, interpreting religious statistics is difficult and controversial.

Nevertheless they do give some indication of membership trends. Overall there does seem to have been a decline in membership of religious organizations in the UK. Institutional, Christian religions have declined most, while many non-Christian and smaller religions have gained members. Using statistics from *Religious Trends 1998/99* (Brierley, 1998), and taking institutional churches, Free churches, non-Trinitarian churches, major religions other than Christianity, and new religious movements together, membership fell from 8,646,464 to 8,172, 993 between 1980 and 1995 in the UK. This was a fall of 473,471 or approximately

Table 7.18	Membership of new religious movements, UK, 1980-95		
	1980	1990	1995
The Aetherius Society	100	100	120
Brahma Kumanis	700	900	1,000
Chrisemma	–	–	20
Creme	250	375	450
Da Free John	35	50	55
Eckankar	250	350	400
Elan Vital	1,250	1,800	2,100
Fellowship of Isis	150	250	300
The Barry Long Foundation	–	400	400
Life Training	–	200	300
Mahikari	–	220	250
Outlook Seminar Training	–	75	90
Pagan Federation	500	900	1,100
The Raelin Movement	100	100	100
Sahaja Yoga	220	280	330
Shinnyeon UK	10	30	50
Solara	–	140	160
3HO	60	60	60
Others	250	1,000	1,500
Total	**3,825**	**7,285**	**8,785**

Source: Compiled from P. Brierley (ed.) (1998) *UK Christian Handbook: Religious Trends 1998/99*, Christian Research, pp. 10.6-10.8.

5.5 per cent. This seems to offer some support for the theory of secularization but, as we shall see, critics of the theory see such figures as far from conclusive.

Religious participation in the USA

A very different impression is given by statistics on religious participation in the USA. There, rates of religious participation are much higher than those in Britain and on the surface do not provide support for theories of secularization. Writing in 1993, C. Kirk Hadaway, Penny Marler, P.L. Church and Mark Chaves noted that rates of self-reported church attendance in the USA were around 40 per cent. By this measure, Protestants had about the same attendance rates in the early 1990s as they had in the 1940s. Rates of attendance for Catholics in the USA did decline in the 1960s and early 1970s, but had not fallen any further. For example, in 1991 a poll conducted by Princeton Religious Research Centre found that 42 per cent of Americans claimed to have attended a church or synagogue in the previous week; 45 per cent of Protestants and 51 per cent of Catholics claimed to have done so.

Interpreting the evidence on participation and membership

Most of the long-term evidence on membership and attendance in Britain seems to support the secularization theory. Although recent years have seen a growth in smaller religious organizations, compared to the nineteenth century and early decades of the twentieth century there is little doubt that fewer people attend a place of worship or belong to a religious organization. In the USA, though, the evidence seems to support the views of those who question the secularization thesis. However, the evidence from both countries is far from conclusive and needs to be used with care. As Grace Davie says, 'Religious statistics are notoriously hard to handle' (Davie, 1989).

Both the reliability and the validity of the statistics are open to question. Nineteenth-century church attendance figures for Britain pose special problems because the methods of data collection used do not meet today's standards of reliability. More recent British figures may be hard to trust as well. Some commentators argue that attendance and membership figures may be distorted by the ulterior motives of those who produce them. Some churches – for example, the Roman Catholic Church – may underestimate the numbers in their congregation in order to reduce the capitation fees they have to pay to central church authorities. Others, particularly Anglican churches, may overestimate the figures to produce impressive totals, particularly where there may be a risk of a church with a small congregation being closed down.

Membership figures can be calculated in different ways, and various churches, denominations and other religious groups use different criteria:

1 Members of the Roman Catholic Church in Britain and the Church of England are normally taken to be those who have been both baptized and confirmed. The numbers may therefore include people who, although officially members, have taken no part in church life since their confirmation.

2 The Church of Wales, on the other hand, bases its figures on those attending Easter Communion.

3 Figures giving the numbers who are held to be members of the Jewish religion simply document the number of Jewish heads of household, regardless of how often or whether they attend a synagogue.

Because of these variations, statistics on church membership are highly unreliable, and the trends indicated by the figures may be misleading.

In the USA the attendance statistics are based on survey evidence. Hadaway, Marler and Chaves (1993) have questioned the reliability of the evidence. They conducted a detailed study of church attendance in a part of Ohio. In most of the churches they were able to get attendance counts from the clergy, in others they estimated attendance by counting cars in church car parks. They compared these results with findings from their own telephone poll. Their conclusion was that, overall, actual church attendance was about half that claimed in polls. Twice as many people claimed to attend church or a synagogue as actually did so. People exaggerated their church attendance, probably because church attendance was seen as socially desirable behaviour, and people were unwilling to admit their lack of attendance.

The decline in church attendance in Britain can be interpreted in a number of ways:

1   David Martin claims that the relatively high attendances in Victorian Britain may have been influenced by non-religious factors. He believes that in the nineteenth century church-going was a sign of middle-class respectability to a greater extent than it is today. Many Victorians may have attended church to be seen, rather than to express deep religious convictions (Martin, 1969).

2   Some sociologists argue that a decline in institutional religion cannot be taken as indicating a decline in religious belief and commitment. Religion today may be expressed in different ways. Religion may have become increasingly privatized; people develop their own beliefs and relationship with God and see religious institutions as being less important.

3   It is also possible that many individuals who hold religious beliefs, and whose behaviour is also partly directed by such beliefs, are not formally registered as church members.

Table 7.19	Belief in God in Great Britain and Northern Ireland, 1991		
	Position	Britain (%)	Northern Ireland (%)
'I don't believe in God'	1	10	1
'I don't know whether there is a God and I don't believe there is any way to find out'	2	14	4
'I don't believe in a personal God but I do believe in a higher power of some kind'	3	13	4
'I find myself believing in God some of the time but not at other times'	4	13	7
'While I have doubts, I feel that I do believe in God'	5	26	20
'I know God really exists and I have no doubts about it'	6	23	57
'I don't know' and 'No answer'	7	2	7

Source: British *Social Attitudes Survey* (1992).

Statistics on participation in religious institutions provide only one type of indicator of the religious commitment of individuals and may be only tenuously linked to the strength of religious beliefs. Those, like Bryan Wilson (1966), who see such figures as a measure of secularization are influenced by the traditional view that a religious person is one who goes to church. As Peter Glasner argues, 'These studies have in common the identification of religion with "church-orientated" religion' (Glasner, 1977).

We will now examine some evidence relating to religious belief and activity outside the context of religious organizations.

Belief, church-going and atheism

Opinion poll evidence is perhaps the simplest type of data relating to religious beliefs. However, there are a variety of questions that can and have been asked about religious beliefs, and the questions asked determine the impression given by the data.

Opinion poll data generally finds that many more people retain religious beliefs than are members of religious organizations or regular attenders at places of worship. In 1991 the *British Social Attitudes Survey* found that 62 per cent of people believed in 'God' at least some of the time, while a further 13 per cent believed in a 'higher power of some kind', and 14 per cent were uncertain about whether God existed. Only 10 per cent in Britain and a mere 1 per cent in Northern Ireland denied the existence of God outright.

As with all opinion poll data, there are question marks over the strength of the relationship between what people say and what they do. As Malcolm Hamilton says, saying you believe in God:

> does not mean that it has any consequences for behaviour, is held with any conviction, or has any real meaning. What the surveys show is not that people are religious but that they have a propensity to say yes to this sort of survey question.
>
> Hamilton, 1998, p. 29

Furthermore, opinion poll data can also be used to support the secularization theory. Steve Bruce points out that the *British Social Attitudes Survey* found in 1991 that 12 per cent of people in Britain said that they had given up believing in God, whereas only 6 per cent said they had started believing in God, having previously been non-believers (Bruce, 1995). Furthermore, by looking at the results of a number of surveys conducted between 1957 and 1991, Bruce was able to show a decline in the belief in sin, the soul, hell, heaven, life after death and the devil (see Table 7.20).

Less strong support for secularization is provided by Peter Brierley (1991), who has used data from the 1989 English Church Census and elsewhere to estimate the percentages of the population who are Christian and non-Christian. He has also divided Christians up into church-goers, nominal Christians (church members who do not attend regularly), and notional Christians (those who say they are Christian but who are neither church members nor attenders). Non-Christians are divided into the secular and those who hold non-Christian religious beliefs. Figure 7.8 shows Brierley's estimates with the figures for 1980 shown in brackets.

As Brierley says, 'The diagram shows that change in the British religious scene is relatively slow – a

percentage point or two over a decade.' There is some evidence that the population is moving away from participation in institutional Christian religion but retaining religious beliefs. There is also evidence of an increase in atheism and agnosticism, but the change is slight. (We will examine the data relating to religion in the USA later, see pp. 487–8.)

Religious belief and participation may be the most obvious areas in which to look for evidence in favour of or against secularization. However, some theorists deny that these are crucial to the secularization thesis. For example, José Casanova (1994) argues that these aspects of religion are essentially irrelevant to secularization. For him, it is the role of religion that is important, in particular the process of differentiation (see p. 482). We will now examine aspects of theories of secularization which focus more on the role of religion in society.

Institutional religion – disengagement, differentiation and societalization

Disengagement

Some researchers, as we have just noted, have seen the truly religious society in terms of full churches. They have therefore seen empty churches as evidence of secularization. Others have seen the truly religious society as one in which the church as an institution is directly involved in every important area of social life. In terms of this emphasis, a disengagement or

Table 7.20	Belief in sin, the soul, heaven, life after death, the devil and hell, in Britain, 1957–1991			
	1957	1981	1987	1991
Sin	–	69	51	–
Soul	–	59	50	–
Heaven	–	57	48	46
Life after death	54	45	43	27
Devil	34	30	31	24
Hell	–	27	29	24

Source: S. Bruce (1995) 'Religion and the sociology of religion' in M. Haralambos (ed.) *Developments in Sociology*, vol. 11, p. 5.

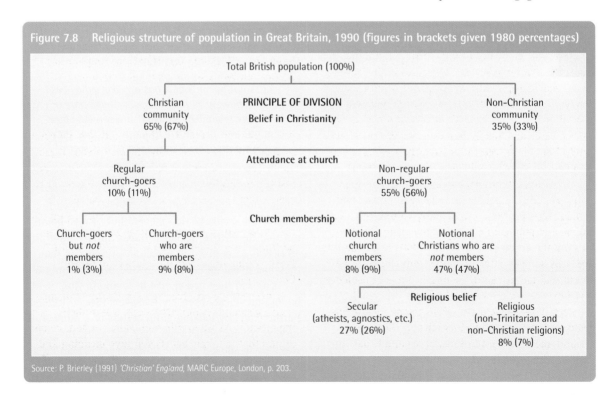

Figure 7.8 Religious structure of population in Great Britain, 1990 (figures in brackets given 1980 percentages)

Source: P. Brierley (1991) *'Christian' England*, MARC Europe, London, p. 203.

withdrawing of the church from the wider society is seen as secularization. David Martin sees this view as concerned with decline in the power, wealth, influence and prestige of the church (Martin, 1969). Compared to its role in medieval Europe, the church in contemporary Western society has undergone a process of disengagement. In the Middle Ages, there was a union of church and state. Today, apart from the right of bishops to sit in the British House of Lords, the church is hardly represented in government.

Steve Bruce argues that the state churches have lost their power as they have become more distant from the British state (Bruce, 1995). This distancing has given them the freedom to be more critical of governments. For example, during the period of Conservative government from 1979 to 1997, the Church of England criticized nuclear weapons policy, and lack of help for the poor in the inner cities. However, the government took little or no notice of the views expressed by church leaders.

Nevertheless, the power of the church in the Middle Ages need not necessarily be seen as a golden age of religion. As David Martin suggests, 'the height of ecclesiastical power can be seen either as the triumph of the religious or its more blasphemous secularization'. Thus, today, the church's specialization in specifically religious matters may indicate a purer form of religion, untainted by involvement with secular concerns such as politics. Martin also suggests that there has been a shift in the focus of religion away from 'the institutions of the state and the economy' towards 'the needs and sentiments of people' (Martin, 1969).

The concept of disengagement is, however, questioned by José Casanova. Casanova is actually a supporter of the theory of secularization, but only in the sense that he believes differentiation has taken place (see below, p. 482). He does not believe that religion has withdrawn from public and political life. Indeed, in his book *Public Religions in the Modern World*, he claims that 'Religion in the 1980s "went public" in a dual sense. It entered the "public sphere" and gained, thereby, publicity' (Casanova, 1994).

Increasing attention was paid to religion by politicians, social scientists and the general public, and religious leaders were increasingly willing to enter public and political debate. Casanova says that 'During the entire decade of the 1980s it was hard to find any serious political conflict anywhere in the world that did not show behind it the not-so-hidden hand of religion.' Examples included the conflict between Jews and Muslim Arabs in the Middle East, between Protestants and Catholics in Northern Ireland and between Muslims, Serbs and Croats in Bosnia. Religion played an important part in the revolts that led to the collapse of communism in

Eastern Europe and the former USSR. The 'Moral Majority' of fundamentalist Christians became influential in the USA. The Salman Rushdie affair (when the Iranian leader Ayatollah Khomeini declared Rushdie's book *The Satanic Verses* blasphemous to Islam and issued a fatwa, or religious death sentence) highlighted a clash between religious and secular values in Britain.

Furthermore, Casanova says:

> *religious activists and churches were becoming deeply involved in struggles for liberation, justice, and democracy throughout the world. Liberation theologies were spreading beyond Latin America, acquiring new forms and names, Asian and African, Protestant and Jewish, black and feminist.*
>
> Casanova, 1994, p. 3

Casanova therefore believes that there has been a deprivatization of religion. Before the 1980s, religion was becoming confined to the private sphere. It was becoming a matter of personal conscience, and religious organizations were withdrawing from trying to influence public policies. From the 1980s, this was reversed, with religions again trying to exert an influence on public life.

Casanova does not believe that this undermines all aspects of the theory of secularization. Nevertheless, he does dismiss that element of the theory which sees secularization as involving the confinement of religious influence to the private sphere. Public religions have returned to playing an important role in politics. The privatization of religion is a 'historical option', which has been followed in some societies at some times, but it is not an inevitable or irreversible aspect of modernity. Since the 1980s the privatization of religion has become an increasingly unpopular option.

Structural and social differentiation

An alternative to the view that disengagement equals secularization is provided by Talcott Parsons (1951, 1960, 1965a). Parsons agrees that the church as an institution has lost many of its former functions. He argues that the evolution of society involves a process of structural differentiation: various parts of the social system become more specialized and so perform fewer functions. (This idea forms part of Parsons's theory of social evolution, outlined in Chapter 15.)

However, the differentiation of the units of the social system does not necessarily lessen their importance. As we saw in a previous section, Parsons argues that religious beliefs still give meaning and significance to life. Churches are still the fount of religious ethics and values.

As religious institutions become increasingly specialized, Parsons maintains that their ethics and values become increasingly generalized. In American society, for instance, they have become the basis for more general social values.

Steve Bruce (1995) discusses essentially the same process as Parsons, although in Bruce's case he terms it social differentiation. Unlike Parsons, he sees it as a feature of secularization that stems from the rationalization of the modern world. In the fourteenth century the medieval church tried to assert control over activities like money lending, defining them as sinful. Social differentiation means that the church now has much less opportunity to involve itself in non-religious spheres. Indeed, to Bruce, social life becomes dominated by the logic of capitalist production with its emphasis on calculability, efficiency and profit. Religious faith and morality become less and less significant in the culture and institutions of modern societies. He says:

> Modernization sees the freeing of economic activity from religiously sanctioned controls and the development of the world of work as an autonomous sphere driven only by its own values. Gradually other aspects of life go the same way. Education, social welfare, health care, and social control have mostly passed out of church control, and where churches still run such activities they do so in ways that differ little from secular provision.
>
> Bruce, 1995, p. 128

Unlike Parsons, Bruce sees differentiation as affecting individuals as well as institutions. Modern societies have become increasingly egalitarian. People no longer have fixed roles which are ascribed at birth. There are no longer rigid hierarchies in which everybody knows their place. There is much greater occupational and geographical mobility. People frequently mix with strangers without knowing their status. As a result, it is increasingly difficult for people to see themselves as subject to the power of an omnipotent God. Bruce says, 'The idea of a single moral universe in which all manner and conditions of people have a place in some single grand design became less and less plausible.' Institutional religion therefore exercises a less significant hold over individuals.

José Casanova (1994) sees differentiation as a key feature of modernity and as the core of any theory of secularization. Differentiation initially involved the separation of religion from the state and from economic activity. This came about as a result of four factors:

1 The Protestant Reformation which, in those societies it affected, led to religion making less strong claims for control over the state and civil society.

2 The establishment of modern nation-states which claimed sovereignty over a given territory and which were unwilling to concede part of their sovereignty to external religious centres of power (such as the Papacy).

3 The growth of modern capitalism – the church found it impossible to establish control over the economic sphere.

4 The scientific revolution which undermined church claims to a monopoly of knowledge.

Indeed the strength of churches suffered most in societies where the church held out against developments in science (such as Newton's contribution to physics). Religion lost credibility where it stuck to biblical orthodoxies which became increasingly untenable in the light of new knowledge.

In caesaropapist societies (where an absolute ruler also claimed exclusive religious legitimacy) there was a rapid decline in the popularity of religion once the absolute ruler finally lost authority.

In societies with an established church which has tried to retain its authority over society (such as Spain, where the Catholic Church tried to retain its predominance for much of the period of rule by the fascist leader General Franco (1939–75)), the decline of church-based religion has been quite marked. In other societies where a plurality of religions has been tolerated and the church–state link has been broken early, religion has remained more popular.

Once differentiation between the sacred and the secular had taken place this opened the way for differentiation of other parts of society from one another. Casanova therefore argues that 'The differentiation and emancipation of the secular spheres from religious institutions and norms remains a general modern structural trend. Indeed this differentiation serves precisely as one of the primary distinguishing characteristics of modern structures' (Casanova, 1994). However, Casanova does not believe that the differentiation of religion from other spheres (which is his definition of secularization) necessarily implies that religion will decline in other ways.

Societalization

Bruce (1995) uses the term societalization (a term first used by Bryan Wilson) to refer to a process in which social life becomes fragmented and ceases to be locally based. Like social differentiation, he sees this as a consequence of a general process of modernization. Modern societies do not have close-knit communities. People's lives are increasingly dominated by large impersonal bureaucracies, and in suburbs people rarely know and mix with their immediate neighbours. People interact with one another at the level of society as a whole rather than within local communities.

According to Bruce, the decline of community undermines religion in three ways. First, without a strong sense of community, churches can no longer serve as the focal point for communities. For example, large proportions of the community will not turn out for a local wedding or funeral at the parish church because most people will not know the betrothed or the deceased.

Second, people's greater involvement with the broader society in which they live leads them to look far more widely for services. They are less likely to turn to the local priest or vicar for practical or emotional support.

Third, the cultural diversity of the society in which people live leads them to hold beliefs with less certainty. Bruce says 'Beliefs are strongest when they are unexamined and naïvely accepted as the way things are.' In a society where we no longer get constant reinforcement of a particular religious view:

> *Religious belief is now obviously a matter of choice. We may still choose to believe, but we cannot easily hide from ourselves the knowledge that we choose God rather than God choosing us. God may still be respected and loved but that he no longer need be feared means that one major source of motivation for getting religion right has been removed.*
>
> Bruce, 1995, p. 131

According to Bruce, then, fundamental changes in social life in modern societies lead to institutional religion losing its social base, many of its social roles and its main source of legitimation. However, Bruce may exaggerate the extent of change and the consequences for religion. For example, there has been a long-standing debate about whether, and to what extent, there has been a decline of community, with many commentators questioning the view that there has been a straightforward movement from strong to weak communities (see, for example, Slattery, 1985). Bruce asserts the decline of community without examining the evidence in detail. Similarly, some writers have questioned the dominance of religious world views in the past (see below, p. 490). However, Bruce is certainly correct to point out that there has been a growth of religious diversity in many modern societies. The significance of this will now be considered.

Institutional religion – religious pluralism

Some researchers imply that the truly religious society has one faith and one church. This picture is influenced by the situation in some small-scale, non-literate societies, such as the Australian aboriginals, where the community is a religious community. Members share a common faith and at certain times of the year the entire community gathers to express this faith in religious rituals.

In terms of Durkheim's view of religion, the community is the church (Durkheim, 1961). Medieval European societies provided a similar picture: there the established church ministered to the whole society.

A number of sociologists essentially follow this line of thinking. Steve Bruce (1992) argues that religious pluralism results from a variety of sources, all of which have 'undermined the communal base to religious orthodoxy'. England expanded to incorporate Scotland and Ireland, which had different religious traditions, while migration has led to a plurality of religious groups in both North America and Europe. Industrialization reduced the contact between social classes and helped to create new, predominantly working-class versions of Christianity such as Methodism.

Modernization and industrialization bring with them the social fragmentation of society into a plurality of cultural and religious groups. As we have seen above, Bruce believes that the consequence is that the state can no longer support a single religion without causing conflict. The plurality of religions reminds individuals that their beliefs are a personal preference, a matter of choice, and no longer part and parcel of their membership of society.

Wade Roof and William McKinney (1987) have reached broadly similar conclusions about the development of religion in the USA. They quote figures, shown in Table 7.21, which show Protestantism declining and an increase in the percentage of the population with no religious preference or who believe in religions other than Protestantism, Catholicism or Judaism. Roof and McKinney quote a 1976 Gallup survey which showed that 4 per cent of the American population said they had been involved in TM, 3 per cent in yoga, 2 per

Table 7.21	Trends in religious preference in the USA, 1952–85		
	1985	1952	Percentage change
Protestant	57	67	– 15
Catholic	28	25	+ 12
Jewish	2	4	– 50
Other	4	1	+ 300
None	9	2	+ 350

Source: Princeton Religion Research Center (February 1986) *Emerging Trends*, vol. 8, no. 2, quoted in W.C. Roof and W. McKinney (1987) *American Mainline Religion*, Rutgers University Press, New Brunswick, p. 16.

cent in mysticism, and 1 per cent claimed involvement in Eastern religions. They argue that religious pluralism has meant that religion 'has lost force as an integrative influence'. Like Bruce, they believe that religious pluralism has created a 'new voluntarism', where religious beliefs become a matter of choice for the individual. They also refer to a 1978 Gallup poll in the USA in which 81 per cent of those questioned agreed with the statement, 'An individual should arrive at his or her own religious beliefs independent of any churches or synagogues.'

On the other hand, it could be argued that a truly religious society is simply one in which religious beliefs and institutions thrive. It is not necessary for everyone to share the same religious beliefs for religion to be important. Northern Ireland is a case in point. There the divisions between Catholics and Protestants are associated with higher rates of church membership and attendance than in other parts of the UK. In some modern societies (such as the USA) it could be that having such religious pluralism exercises a strong influence on society in general, encouraging a toleration of diversity in which a plurality of beliefs can thrive. However pluralism is perceived in modern societies it largely stems from two sources: from the existence of different ethnic groups with their own religious traditions, and from the growth of new sects and cults. These will now be examined.

Ethnicity and religious diversity

Steve Bruce (1996) acknowledges that certain ethnic groups often retain strong religious beliefs. However, he does not see this as an argument against the secularization thesis. This is because Bruce believes that religion remains strong because of its social importance rather than because the members of the group have deep religious convictions as individuals.

Bruce claims that religion tends to serve one of two main purposes for ethnic groups: cultural defence or cultural transition:

1 Religions take on the role of cultural defence where:

> there are two (or more) communities in conflict and they are of different religions (for example, Protestants and Catholics in Ulster, or Serbs (Orthodox), Croats (Roman Catholic) and Bosnian Muslims in what used to be Yugoslavia), then the religious identity of each can call forth a new loyalty as religious identity becomes a way of asserting ethnic pride.
>
> Bruce, 1996, p. 96

From Bruce's point of view, it is their ethnic identity that is important rather than religiosity. In Northern Ireland he cites the example of Ian Paisley's Democratic Unionist Party. It represents Northern Ireland Protestants who strongly support the union of Northern Ireland within the UK. (They opposed the peace proposals in 1998–9.) Most of the activists in this party are members of the evangelical Protestant Free Presbyterian Church. Only a tiny percentage of the Northern Irish population, about 1 per cent, are Free Presbyterians, but Ian Paisley's party gets much more support than that. This is because, according to Bruce, ethnic Protestants identify themselves with the party's opposition to a united Ireland, not because they are attracted to the religious convictions of the party's activists.

2 Cultural transition:

> involves religion acquiring an enhanced importance because of the assistance it can give in helping people cope with the shift from one world to another. It might be that the people in question have migrated; it might be that they remain in the same place while that place changes under their feet.
>
> Bruce, 1996, p. 96

Religion is used as a resource for dealing with situations where people have to change their identity to some extent. For example, Asian and Afro-Caribbean migrants to Britain and their descendants can use mosques, temples and churches as centres for their communities, and their religion as a way of coping with the ambiguities of being Asian or black and British.

However, Bruce believes that religion loses this role where a group becomes increasingly integrated into the host community. For example, Irish Catholics who migrated to England and Scotland were originally subject to considerable hostility and discrimination from the host population. Catholicism was very important to this group for several generations. However, as Irish Catholics have increasingly married outside their own ethnic group and have enjoyed increasing success, prosperity and acceptance by other members of the population, the importance of their religion as a focus for community identity has declined considerably.

Bruce concludes that 'Cultural defence and cultural transition may keep religion relevant but they will not create a religious society out of a secular one.'

However, this interpretation is not shared by everybody. The historian Callum G. Brown (1992) questions Bruce's claim that it can be seen as evidence of secularization when religion has a role in cultural defence or cultural transformation for particular ethnic groups. He sees 'ethnic defence' as a key function of religion in the modern world. Brown denies that there was ever a 'golden age' in which religion provided a single, unifying world view for all members of a society. There has always been some diversity in religious outlooks and there have always been some who were sceptical or hostile towards religion. The role of religion has changed, but that is not the same thing as decline. Brown says that 'Religion adapts to different social and economic contexts. It is not static, unchanging and unyielding to different situations. Such changes that churches undergo do not necessarily mean secularisation.' In particular, he argues that contemporary religion might draw its strength from individual communities (including ethnic communities) rather than from society as a whole. A religiously plural society can also be a non-secular society and both the USA and Britain are examples.

Certainly, there is plenty of evidence that religion can and often does remain strong amongst ethnic groups even though it has to adapt to a changed situation if migration or social changes have taken place. George Chryssides (1994) argues that in Britain the religions of immigrant groups and their descendants have had three main paths open to them. The first option is apostasy, where a particular set of religious beliefs is abandoned in a hostile environment. The second is accommodation, where religious practices are adapted to take account of the changed situation. The third option is renewed vigour, where the religion is reasserted more strongly as a response to the actual or perceived hostility to it. Examples of all three responses can be found.

Chryssides cites the case of Morris Cerello – a Sikh who converted to Christianity – as an example of apostasy. An example of accommodation might be a Sikh who removed his turban because he believed it would improve his chances at a job interview. Those who insist on strong religious orthodoxy from their children could be practising their religion with renewed vigour.

Chryssides acknowledges that ethnic minority religions have faced difficulties in Britain. They have had to establish places of prayer and deal with situations where religious observation might be difficult. However, the general pattern has been characterized by accommodation and renewed vigour rather than apostasy. Buildings have been bought and converted into mosques and temples and religious beliefs and practices have been retained or adapted rather than abandoned. For example, many Islamic women have found ways to dress modestly while incorporating Western elements into their clothing. Religious marriage ceremonies have been adapted to meet the requirements for a legal marriage under British law.

The vigour of ethnic minority religions in Britain is demonstrated by the existence of some first-generation converts to them. Chryssides notes that Buddhism has been particularly successful in attracting new followers who have been brought up within the Christian tradition.

Some writers argue that there has been a revival of religion, which directly contradicts the claims of the advocates of the secularization thesis. For example, Gilles Kepel, in a book called *The Revenge of God* (1994), argues that there has been a resurgence of Judaism, Christianity and Islam in the modern world. According to Kepel, this has affected these religions whether they are the religion of a minority or a majority in a particular society. Thus, for example, British Muslims have retained or strengthened their faith, not as a way of coping with a cultural transition, but because they have been influenced by a worldwide Islamic revival.

Furthermore, Kepel sees all the religious revivals as reactions against modernity. He says, 'they complain about the fragmentation of society, its "anomy", the absence of an overarching ideal worthy of their allegiance ... [They] consider that in the final analysis the modernism produced by reason without God has not succeeded in creating values.' If Kepel is correct, far from reducing religion to a source of identity for some ethnic groups, modernity encourages people to rediscover religion as a way of coping with the social changes produced by modernity.

Sects, cults and secularization

The continuing proliferation of sects has been interpreted by some researchers in much the same way as the spread of denominations and religious pluralism in general. It has been seen as a further fragmentation of institutional religion and therefore as evidence of the weakening hold of religion over society.

Accurate measurements of the numbers of sects and the size of their memberships are not available, but estimates have been made. Although Roy Wallis (1984) believed that there was a decline in new religious movements in the late 1970s and early 1980s, more recent figures suggest that they have been growing. Amongst established sects, Jehovah's Witnesses' membership rose from 62,000 in 1970 to 116,000 in 1990 and 131,000 in 1995. Furthermore, estimates made by *Religious Trends 1998/99* (Brierley, 1998) suggest that membership of what they define as new religious movements more than doubled between 1980 and 1995 (see Table 7.18, p. 478). There are certainly more sects today than there were before the Second World War.

Stark and Bainbridge (1985) have shown that the 1960s had the highest rate of cult formation in the USA. Some 23 per cent of the cults they uncovered were formed between 1970 and 1977, 38 per cent in the 1960s, 14 per cent in the 1950s, and the remaining 25 per cent before 1950.

Despite contradictions in the evidence, the apparent vitality of sects seems to provide evidence against the secularization theory. World-rejecting sects are perhaps the most religious type of organization, since they demand greater commitment to the religion than other organizations. If they are stronger than in the past, it suggests that religion retains a considerable appeal for the populations of advanced industrial societies. Andrew Greeley (1972) believes that the growth of new religious movements represents a process of resacrilization: interest in, and belief in, the sacred is being revived. Societies such as Britain and the USA are, if anything, becoming less secular.

Rodney Stark and William S. Bainbridge (1985) also deny that secularization has taken place. They believe that some established churches may have lost part of their emphasis on the supernatural, but secularization never advances far because new religious groups with more emphasis on the supernatural constantly emerge. Stark and Bainbridge put forward statistical evidence to support this claim. According to their figures on religious activity in different states of the USA, cults thrive where conventional religions are weak. For example, in California relatively few people are church-goers but many believe in supernatural phenomena. (For further details of Stark and Bainbridge's theory of religion see pp. 445–6 and pp. 460–2.)

Nevertheless other sociologists see the growth of sects as evidence of secularization. Peter Berger (1970) argues that belief in the supernatural can only survive in a sectarian form in a secular society. In order to maintain a strong religious belief and commitment, individuals must cut themselves off from the secularizing influences of the wider society, and seek out the support of others of like mind. The sect, with its close-knit community organization, provides a context in which this is possible. From this viewpoint, the sect is the last refuge of the supernatural in a secular society. Sects are therefore evidence of secularization.

Bryan Wilson (1982) takes a similar view, maintaining that sects are 'a feature of societies experiencing secularization, and they may be seen as a response to a situation in which religious values have lost social pre-eminence'. In other words, sects are the last outpost of religion in societies where religious beliefs and values have little consequence.

Bryan Wilson is particularly scathing in his dismissal of the religious movements of the young in the West, such as Krishna Consciousness which emerged during the 1960s in the USA. He regards them as 'almost irrelevant' to society as a whole, claiming that 'They add nothing to any prospective reintegration of society, and contribute nothing towards the culture by which a society might live.'

By comparison, Methodism, in its early days as a sect, provided standards and values for the new urban working class, which helped to integrate its members within the wider society. In addition, its beliefs 'steadily diffused through a much wider body of the population'.

In contrast, Wilson feels that the new religious movements show no such promise. Their members live in their own enclosed, encapsulated little worlds. There they emphasize 'hedonism, the validity of present pleasure, the abandonment of restraint and the ethic of "do your own thing"'. Wilson is scornful of their 'exotic novelty' which he believes offers little more than self-indulgence, titillation and short-lived thrills. He believes that movements which seek the truth in Asian religions and emphasize the exploration of the inner self – such as Krishna Consciousness – can give little to Western society. They simply 'offer another way of life for the self-selected few rather than an alternative culture for mankind'. Rather than contributing to a new moral reintegration of society, they just provide a religious setting for 'dropouts'. They do not halt the continuing process of secularization and are 'likely to be no more than transient and volatile gestures of defiance' in the face of a secular society.

Similar conclusions are reached by Roy Wallis (1984) and Steve Bruce (1995, 1996). According to Wallis, 'new religious movements involve only a very small proportion of the population ... and even then often for only very brief periods during the transition to adulthood'. For those who join world-affirming movements the motives for joining are largely secular anyway: they wish to get on in the world rather than pursue other-worldly concerns. Wallis claims that for most of the population new religious movements are 'a matter of profound indifference'.

Steve Bruce argues that new religious movements only recruit very small numbers compared to the massive decline in mainstream Christian religions. World-rejecting new religions have affected the smallest numbers of people, while world-accommo-dating ones have influenced a greater number of people. Yet it is these religious movements that have the least impact on people's lives. To Bruce, 'people who chant in Soka Gakki or meditate in TM or attend est seminars or Insight weekends' carry on their lives very much as normal and there 'are no consequences for the operation of the social system' (Bruce, 1996).

Secularization and the New Age

Steve Bruce has also commented on the significance, or in his view the lack of significance, of the New Age. Like new religious movements, he sees the New Age as posing little or no threat to the validity of the theory of secularization. Although it affects more people than sects, 'it cannot aspire to promote radical and specific change because it does not have the cohesion and discipline of the sect' (Bruce, 1996). In fact, he believes that the New Age is simply an extreme form of the individualism that is characteristic of modern societies. As such it has a role as 'symptom and as a cause in the erosion of faith in orthodoxies and the authority of professional knowledge'.

However, Bruce does accept that toned-down aspects of New Age beliefs may become accepted as parts of the 'cultural mainstream'. For example, New Age has had some impact on people's concern for the environment and willingness to give credence to alternative medicines.

It could be argued that Bruce underestimates the significance of the effects he identifies. If substantial numbers of people are willing to question scientific orthodoxy and place some trust in beliefs which require a degree of faith, this in itself could be taken as evidence against the secularization theory. Paul Heelas (1996) certainly regards the New Age as rather more significant than does Bruce. He quotes a 1993 Gallup opinion poll which found that in Britain 26 per cent of people believed in reincarnation, 40 per cent in some sort of spirit, 17 per cent in flying saucers and 21 per cent in horoscopes; while a 1989 Gallup poll found that no less than 72 per cent had 'an awareness of a sacred presence in nature'.

Using a broad definition of the New Age, then, there appears to be at least a minimal level of belief in some of its claims amongst a high proportion of the population. Some New Age magazines are quite successful (*Body, Mind and Spirit* sells about 60,000 per month in Britain), and in the USA there were some 4,000 New Age bookshops by 1989. Heelas argues that aspects of New Age beliefs are deeply embedded in contemporary Western culture. They are a 'radicalized' version of 'humanistic expressivism'. The New Age might not be much like a traditional religion, but to Heelas it provides a strong argument against the view that modern societies have become secular and rational. It is just that individuals have turned within themselves in the search for spirituality rather than looking to the external authority of church religions.

Institutional religion – the secularization of religious institutions in the USA

Will Herberg – denominations and internal secularization

According to Will Herberg (1960), the main evidence for secularization in the USA is not to be found in a decline in participation in religion, but in a decline in the religiosity of churches and denominations

themselves. The major denominations have increasingly emphasized this world as opposed to the other world; they have moved away from traditional doctrine and concern with the supernatural; they have compromised their religious beliefs to fit in with the wider society. Because of this, they have become more like the secular society in which they are set.

Herberg claims that the major denominations in America have undergone a process of secularization. They increasingly reflect the American 'way of life' rather than the word of God. For the typical church-goer, religion is 'something that reassures him about the essential rightness of everything American, his nature, his culture and himself'. But, from Herberg's viewpoint, this has little to do with the real meaning of religion.

Herberg's views on religion in the USA have been challenged on a number of grounds. Roof and McKinney accept that Herberg's analysis had much merit when it was written in the 1950s but they argue that 'it failed to ring true in the America of the 1980s' (Roof and McKinney, 1987). In particular, not all religious groupings seem to have turned their back on what Herberg would see as authentic religion. Like other commentators, Roof and McKinney note the growth of conservative Protestant religions (sometimes called the New Christian Right) which seem to combine a serious commitment to religious teachings, a strong element of theological doctrine and a refusal to compromise religious beliefs. As such, they seem to directly contradict Herberg's claims about secularization within religious institutions.

Institutional religion – the New Christian Right

Roof and McKinney categorize the following religious groups in America as conservative Christians: Southern Baptists, Churches of Christ, Evangelicals/Fundamentalists, Nazarenes, Pentecostalists/Holiness, Assemblies of God, Churches of God and Adventists. Using survey data they estimated that conservative Protestants made up 15.8 per cent of the American population in 1984. Their evidence suggests that these groups have been growing since the 1920s. In 1967 the Southern Baptist Convention overtook Methodists as the largest Protestant denomination. Roof and McKinney quote a 1976 Gallup poll which found that 34 per cent of the population said they had been 'born again'.

Roof and McKinney's data also shows that conservative Protestants are more likely than any other religious group in the USA to attend church and believe in God. They have rejected any move towards liberal values and instead have strongly supported traditional morality. Conservative Protestants have been strong opponents of abortion, extra-marital or pre-marital sex, homosexuality and the relaxation of divorce laws. They have supported literal interpretations of the Bible, campaigning against the teaching of evolutionary biology on the grounds that it contradicted the biblical account of God's creation of the earth.

A number of sociologists have noted the many ways in which conservative Protestants have succeeded in publicizing and promoting their views in the USA. According to James Davison Hunter (1987), by the early 1980s they had set up 450 colleges and 18,000 schools, established 275 periodicals, 70 evangelical publishing houses and 3,300 Christian bookshops. They had also started 65 television stations and intervened in numerous political campaigns.

Hunter does not claim that the growth of conservative Protestantism disproves the secularization thesis, but he does believe that it challenges it. He says:

> Secularization may yet prove to be the ultimate design for contemporary society, but that is unlikely. Minimally, one can say that it is not a straight-line occurrence, as is often assumed; cycles of secularity and religious upsurge are evident.
>
> Hunter, 1987

The limited impact of conservative Protestantism

A different view is taken by Steve Bruce (1988, 1996) who argues that the New Christian Right has had very little impact. Very few of its members who have stood for national office have won their elections. No more than five senators have supported the New Christian Right and they have failed to get any new Federal legislation passed. Opinion polls have showed no shift towards their views on moral issues. In Bruce's view they have achieved no more than to 'remind cosmopolitan Americans that fundamentalists were not extinct and still had some rights' (Bruce, 1996).

Furthermore, Bruce believes that the strength of religious beliefs among evangelical Christians in the USA has gradually been watered down. He quotes a study by James Hunter which found that 77 per cent of young evangelical Americans thought that playing cards was morally wrong in 1951; by 1982 none thought so. Similarly, over the same period and amongst the same group, moral objections to social dancing declined from 91 per cent to 0 per cent, to drinking alcohol from 98 per cent to 17 per cent, and

to smoking marijuana from 98 per cent to 17 per cent (quoted in Bruce, 1996).

If Bruce is to be believed, the New Christian Right may have slowed down the process of secularization within its own religious institutions, but it has failed to do any more than that. Indeed he believes that the only reason the New Christian Right gets so much attention is that its members are unusual for holding strong religious convictions in a largely secular world.

Internal secularization in Britain

Less attention has been devoted to the possibility that British churches and denominations have undergone secularization. However, Steve Bruce (1988) does believe that British mainstream churches have abandoned, or at least watered down, a number of their religious convictions. These include beliefs in the virgin birth, Christ's bodily resurrection (the former Bishop of Durham, David Jenkins, called it a 'conjuring trick with a bag of bones'), heaven and hell, and the expectation that Christ would return to earth. Bruce also points out that most British Christian churches have ceased to claim a monopoly of the religious truth.

In the previous sections we have examined approaches to secularization largely in terms of institutional religion. Our focus now changes to a more general view of the role of religion in Western society and is concerned with the influence of religious beliefs and values on social norms and values, social action and consciousness. As in previous sections, assessments of the importance of religion depend largely on the observer's interpretation of what constitutes a 'religious society' and religiously motivated action.

Religion and society – desacrilization

A number of sociologists have argued that the sacred has little or no place in contemporary Western society, that society has undergone a process of desacrilization. This means that supernatural forces are no longer seen as controlling the world, action is no longer directed by religious belief, and human consciousness has become secularized.

Disenchantment

Weber's interpretation of modern society provides one of the earliest statements of the desacrilization thesis. He claimed that modern society is 'characterized by rationalization and intellectualization and, above all, by the "disenchantment of the world"' (Weber, in Gerth and Mills (eds), 1948). The world is no longer charged with mystery and magic; the supernatural has been banished from society. The meanings and motives that direct action are now rational.

Weber's concept of rational action and his view that modern society is undergoing a process of rationalization are examined in detail in Chapter 15. Briefly, rational action involves a deliberate and precise calculation of the importance of alternative goals and the effectiveness of the various means of attaining chosen goals.

For example, if an individual's goal is to make money, he or she will coldly and carefully calculate the necessary initial investment and the costs involved in producing and marketing a commodity in the most economical way possible. His or her measurements will be objective: they will be based on factors that can be quantified and accurately measured. He or she will reject the means to reach that goal which cannot be proven to be effective.

Rational action rejects the guidelines provided by emotion, by tradition or by religion. It is based on the cold, deliberate reason of the intellect, which demands that the rationale for action can only be based on the proven results.

Science and reason

A number of sociologists have accepted Weber's interpretation of the basis for action in industrial society. In *Religion in a Secular Society* (1966), Bryan Wilson stated that 'Religious *thinking* is perhaps the area which evidences most conspicuous change. Men act less and less in response to religious motivation: they assess the world in empirical and rational terms.'

Wilson argued that the following factors encouraged the development of rational thinking and a rational world view:

1 Ascetic Protestantism, which 'created an ethic which was pragmatic, rational, controlled and anti-emotional'.

2 The rational organization of society, which results in people's 'sustained involvement in rational organizations – firms, public service, educational institutions, government, the state – which impose rational behaviour upon them'.

3 A greater knowledge of the social and physical world, which results from the development of the physical, biological and social sciences. Wilson maintained that this knowledge was based on reason rather than faith. He claimed that:

> Science not only explained many facets of life and the material environment in a way more satisfactory [than religion], but it also provided confirmation of its explanation in practical results.
>
> Wilson, 1966

4 The development of rational ideologies and organizations to solve social problems. Ideologies such as communism and organizations such as trade unions offer practical solutions to problems. By comparison, religious solutions, such as the promise of justice and reward in the afterlife, do not produce practical and observable results.

Wilson argues that a rational world view is the enemy of religion. It is based on the testing of arguments and beliefs by rational procedures, on assessing truth by means of factors that can be quantified and objectively measured. Religion is based on faith and as such is non-rational. Its claim to truth cannot be tested by rational procedures.

Peter Berger (1970) develops some of Weber's and Wilson's ideas within the framework of the sociology of knowledge. He maintains that people in Western society increasingly 'look upon the world and their own lives without the benefit of religious interpretations'. As a result there is a secularization of consciousness. Berger argues that the 'decisive variable for secularization' is 'the process of rationalization that is the prerequisite for any industrial society of the modern type'. A rational world view rejects faith which is the basis of religion. It removes the 'mystery, magic and authority' of religion.

Steve Bruce (1988) stresses the specific role of scientific beliefs themselves in undermining religion. He argues that technological advances reduce the number of things that need to be explained in religious terms. It has given individuals a greater sense of control over the natural world and less need to resort to supernatural explanations or remedies. He says:

> We may still go to church to celebrate the successful conclusion of the harvest but we use chemical fertilisers and weed-killers rather than prayer to ensure a good crop. When all the conventional medical solutions have been exhausted, we may pray for the health of a loved one but only a very few small sects reject conventional medicine and trust instead to the Lord.
>
> Bruce, 1988

However, he also discusses the importance of rationalization in general. He says:

> a world of rationality is less conducive to religion than a traditional society. Everything is seen as potentially improvable. Everything can be made more efficient. We find it very easy to talk about means and procedures but very difficult to discuss transcendental means.
>
> Bruce, 1996, p. 48

Bruce acknowledges that such events as the death of a loved one or an injustice suffered may lead people to turn to God. There are some things even in the modern world that science and rationality cannot deal with. However, when people do turn to God, they do so as individuals. Furthermore, they tend to do so as a last resort after the rational, scientific alternatives have all been fully exhausted. Thus:

When we have tried every cure for cancer, we pray. When we have revised for our examinations, we pray. We do not pray instead of studying, and even committed believers suppose that a research programme is more likely than a mass prayer meeting to produce a cure for AIDs.

Bruce, 1996

Although the argument that scientific rationalism has triumphed over religion and superstition appears strong, not everybody finds it convincing. For example, the development of New Age beliefs seems to suggest that the non-rational has a place in contemporary societies (see pp. 466–9 and 499–500). Furthermore, there is plenty of evidence which appears to point to a religious revival on a global scale (see p. 492).

Also, the theory of postmodernism suggests that societies have begun to move beyond the scientific rationality of modernity, partly because they have started to mistrust science. People are increasingly aware of the failures of science (including the failure to find a cure for AIDs) and, more importantly, the negative side-effects that can be produced by science and technology. Examples might include global warming, air pollution, increasing cancer rates, the depletion of the ozone layer, and so on. In these circumstances people may turn to religion, of one sort or another, as an alternative to science, which some see as creating as many problems as it solves. The relationship between religion and postmodern society will be examined shortly (see pp. 495–500).

In this section we have considered the desacrilization thesis, that is the view that religion and the sacred have largely been removed from the meanings that guide action and interpret the world, and from the consciousness of humanity. This view is difficult to evaluate since it is largely based on the impressions of particular researchers rather than 'hard' data. In addition, it compares industrial society with often unspecified pre-industrial societies in which, presumably, religion provided a guide to action and a basis for meaning. We will deal with the problems involved in this approach in the next section.

Religion in pre-industrial societies

As we saw in the previous sections, the term 'secularization' has been used in many different ways.

Whichever way it has been used, though, the supporters of the theory of secularization have tended to take it for granted that pre-industrial societies were highly religious. Some researchers have challenged this view.

Larry Shiner (1971) notes that those who argue that the social significance of religion has declined have 'the problem of determining when and where we are to find the supposedly "religious" age from which decline has commenced'.

The anthropologist Mary Douglas (1973) argues that the use of supposedly 'religious', small-scale non-literate societies as a basis for comparison with modern 'secular' societies is unjustified. She states that:

The contrast of secular with religious has nothing whatever to do with the contrast of modern with traditional or primitive … The truth is that all varieties of scepticism, materialism and spiritual fervour are to be found in the range of tribal societies.

Douglas, 1973

It is simply an illusion concocted by Westerners that 'all primitives are pious, credulous and subject to the teaching of priests or magicians'.

In the same way, the search for the golden age of religion in the European past may provide an equally shaky standard for comparison. From his study of religion in sixteenth- and seventeenth-century England, K.V. Thomas states:

We do not know enough about the religious beliefs and practices of our remote ancestors to be certain of the extent to which religious faith and practice have actually declined.

Quoted in Glasner, 1977, p. 71

Secularization – international comparisons

David Martin – *A General Theory of Secularization*

Most sociologists studying secularization have concentrated on making observations about, and researching into, particular modern industrial societies. They have, nevertheless, often assumed that secularization is a universal and perhaps inevitable process. Bryan Wilson (1966) claims, for example, 'Secularization, then, is a long term process occurring in human society.' However, even Wilson, a leading advocate of theories of secularization, admits that 'The actual patterns in which it is manifested are culturally and historically specific to each context.' The nature and extent of the changes in the role of religion in society may vary so much in different parts of the world that it is misleading to see secularization as a single process.

By concentrating on Britain and the USA, sociologists have had a rather narrow view of social change and religion. For instance, they have not accounted for the revival over recent years of Islamic fundamentalism in Iran and other countries. David Martin has taken a wider view than most sociologists by looking at the changing role of religion in a range of societies (Martin, 1978). Martin's research shows very different patterns of religious practice in various advanced industrial countries. In some cases it shows marked differences within single societies. Martin argues that the role and strength of religion in modern societies are determined by a number of factors:

1 The first important factors are the degree of religious pluralism and the dominant religion. Societies where the Roman Catholic Church claims a monopoly of the religious truth are usually very different to those where Protestantism and Catholicism both have a major foothold, or where there is a greater variety of denominations and churches.

2 The political system of a society and the relationship between church and state both have a significant impact on the importance of religion within that society.

3 The third major factor is the extent to which religion helps to provide a sense of national, regional or ethnic identity.

We will now study a number of examples which illustrate Martin's general theory of secularization.

Variations in religious participation

The level of participation in religion varies widely in Protestant societies. In the USA, 40 per cent or more of the adult population attend church each Sunday; in England the figure is just over 10 per cent; while in Sweden it falls as low as 5 per cent. Martin explains these variations in the following way:

1 In the USA there is a high degree of religious pluralism and no official connection between church and state. There is also a plurality of immigrant groups of different ethnic origin. Religious participation is therefore not confined to higher-status groups who can support a religion closely identified with the state. A plurality of religions flourish as ethnic minorities try to maintain their separate identities. While participation in religion is very high, religion does not play a vital role in the functioning of society. Social solidarity is cemented more by patriotism and by a belief in the American way of life than by shared religious beliefs.

2 In Britain there is an association between the Church of England and the state. However, there is also considerable religious pluralism. Protestant-dissenting denominations draw membership and support from lower social classes who may not be attracted to the established church. Attendance is quite low because of the association of church and state, but not as low as in Sweden where the church is virtually a department of state. In some parts of Britain, such as Wales and Scotland, attendances are higher than the average because of an association between religion and nationalism.

3 Sweden has the lowest attendance figures because of the dominance of a single church and its association with the state. As a result of this close association, and the lack of alternative religious organizations, church attendance is largely confined to higher social classes.

In all of these societies, then, religion retains some influence. Where a church retains important functions, religious participation tends to be low, but participation is much higher in societies where religion appears to have lost many of its functions.

In Roman Catholic countries such as France, Spain, Italy and Portugal, the church still has an important role in society. It influences government policy in areas such as education and laws relating to marriage, divorce, contraception and abortion. Attendances at church are high and, according to Martin, Catholic societies are generally less secular than Protestant ones. There is little religious pluralism and what divisions there are tend to be within the Roman Catholic Church rather than between different religious organizations.

However, such societies frequently have deep social divisions: often there is a strong, and predominantly lower-class, atheist opposition to Catholicism. These divisions are reflected in such conflicts as the Spanish Civil War and the 1968 student protests in Paris, while France and Italy also have sizeable communist parties.

Other countries like the Netherlands, West Germany and Switzerland are split between a Protestant majority and a large Catholic minority, in a ratio of approximately 60:40. In these countries the Roman Catholic minority tends to be among the less affluent, so the ruling elite and Catholicism are not closely connected. Participation in religion is high because it provides a sense of identity for the two main subcultures. Religion plays an important role in such areas of social life as education, where separate Protestant and Catholic schools may be retained.

Religion in the Third World

Martin has also drawn attention to the contrasting fates of religions in different Third World countries (Martin, 1991a, 1991b). In some Latin American countries the Roman Catholic Church remains a key institution in society, and Protestantism has made few converts. In countries such as Mexico and Argentina,

Protestants make up only about 2 per cent of the population. In Brazil, on the other hand, about 20 per cent of the population have become Protestant, and by 1985 there were more Protestant than Catholic ministers. Most ministers represent strongly religious versions of Protestantism such as Pentecostalism and Seventh Day Adventism. Martin argues that Pentecostalism attracts the small shopkeepers and craft workers who have moved to the cities and whose means of earning a living fit in well with a religion that emphasizes self-discipline and thrift.

In Islamic societies religious change also varies from country to country. In Tunisia and Egypt the state has become more secular: Islamic beliefs do not have a great influence on political decisions. In Iran the Islamic revolution of 1979 took the country in the opposite direction with religious leaders gaining most of the political power. In other countries there is a continuing conflict between the religious and the secular. In the Sudan, for example, there are strong advocates of religious pluralism and tolerance, but there are others who wish to see an Islamic state established. In Turkey attitudes towards religion are ambivalent. Some see religion as a cause of 'backwardness'. Others see it as the vital foundation on which the moral values of the society rest.

Prospects for religion

Far from predicting the demise of religion, Martin argues that it is likely to increase in importance. If anything, the future is likely to see the forces of secularization in retreat. Impetus towards secularization originated in north-western Europe, and here the factors which undermined religion have disappeared:

1 First, religion is no longer so closely associated with rich and powerful elites in society. It has therefore become more acceptable to people from lower classes.

2 Second, rationalism has lost some of its appeal. There is increasing interest in the mystical, the supernatural and the religious.

Outside Europe many countries retain strong religious influences on society. From Martin's viewpoint, 'There is no inevitable tilt to history down which every society is sociologically fated to fall.' Secularization is not an automatic and universal process.

Contemporary religious revivals

Martin's views are reflected in some more recent contributions to the debate over secularization which have argued that there is little evidence of a general trend towards secularization in the world as a whole. Gilles Kepel claims that any trend towards secularization was reversed in around 1975 (Kepel, 1994). Furthermore, the various religious revivals were very ambitious – they were aimed at 'recovering a sacred foundation for the organization of society – by changing society if necessary'. He uses the examples of Christians in the USA and Europe, Jews in Israel, and Muslims throughout the world to support his case.

Since 1978, when Pope John-Paul II became Pope, Catholicism has been less willing to concede ground to the secular forces. In Italy, young people have been attracted to the Catholic group, Communion and Liberation, which demands strong personal commitment from Catholics. In France, Catholic 'charismatic renewal' groups have tried to initiate a re-Christianization of society. In former communist countries such as Czechoslovakia and Poland the Roman Catholic Church has enjoyed great popularity.

In the USA the evangelical 'New Christian Right' have succeeded in attracting increasing numbers of Americans to their campaigns to reassert Christian values (see above, pp. 487–8, for a discussion of their significance).

In Israel, groups such as the Lubavitch have campaigned against the watering-down of traditional Jewish beliefs. Political parties based upon the Jewish religion have come to exercise an important influence on Israeli politics by holding the balance of power in parliament between the major political parties. In doing so they have forced the Jewish state to take religious beliefs seriously.

Islamization movements have had success in many parts of the world. For example, the Islamic Salvation Front won elections in Algeria in 1992. Amongst the Palestinians, radical Islamic groups such as Hamas have been prominent in opposing Israeli occupation of the West Bank. Kepel also points to the Salman Rushdie affair. The campaign by British Muslims against Rushdie's book *The Satanic Verses* indicates how Islamic values continue to be important even in Western Europe.

To Kepel, all of the above are examples of attempts to counter secularism. They are a reaction to the apparent failure of attempts to base the policies of nation-states upon secular principles. He says, 'They regard the vainglorious emancipation of reason from faith as the prime cause of the ills of the twentieth century, the beginnings of a process leading straight to Nazi and Stalinist totalitarianism.' As such, they are very much a reaction against modernity. However, Kepel does not regard them as being equally successful. He says, 'It is far more difficult to expel secularism from Western society than from today's Jewish or Muslim world.'

Nevertheless, Kepel's work suggests that it might be appropriate to see the modern world as characterized by a continuing conflict between the secular and the sacred, rather than being characterized by the inevitable triumph of the former over the latter.

Secularization – conclusion

As the views of sociologists such as Martin and Kepel illustrate, the secularization thesis has not been definitively proved or disproved. This is partly because sociologists from Weber to Wilson and from Comte to Casanova have used the term 'secularization' in many different ways. This has led to considerable confusion since writers discussing the process of secularization are often arguing about different things.

Martin (1969) states that the concept of secularization includes 'a large number of discrete, separate elements loosely put together in an intellectual hold-all'. He maintains that there is no necessary connection between the various processes lumped together under the same heading. Because the range of meaning attached to the term 'secularization' has become so wide, Martin advocates its removal from the sociological vocabulary. Instead, he supports a careful and detailed study of the ways in which the role of religion in society has changed at different times and in different places.

Glock and Stark (1969) argue that researchers have been unable to measure the significance of religion because they have not given adequate attention to defining religion and religiosity. Until they have clearly thought out and stated exactly what they mean by these terms, the secularization thesis cannot be adequately tested.

There is some evidence that contemporary theorists of secularization do pay more attention to differentiating between different issues that have been considered under the heading 'secularization'. For example, Steve Bruce (1995, 1996), a strong advocate of the theory of secularization, accepts that religion can remain an important part of individual beliefs, but he believes that religion has lost its social and political significance.

José Casanova distinguishes between three aspects of secularization:

1 Secularization as differentiation. In these terms secularization takes place when non-religious spheres of life (such as the state and the economy) become separate from and independent of religion.

2 Secularization as a decline of religious beliefs and practices. In this case secularization takes place when fewer individuals take part in religious activities or hold religious beliefs.

3 Secularization as privatization. With this type of secularization, religion stops playing any part in public life and does not even try to influence how politicians make decisions or individuals in society in general choose to live their lives.

Casanova believes that recent history shows that religious beliefs and practices are certainly not dying out, and that 'public religions' have increasingly re-entered the public sphere. Thus, to him, it is only in the first sense that secularization has taken place. Religion no longer has a central position in the structure of modern societies, but neither does it fade away.

Most theorists who either support or attack the theory of secularization are now willing to admit that the theory cannot be unproblematically applied to all groups in all modern societies. It can therefore be argued that the national, regional, ethnic and social class differences in the role of religion discussed by Martin and others make it necessary to relate theories to specific countries and social groups.

Religion and globalization

While the debate around secularization shows the need to examine the differences between religions in different societies, the theory of globalization suggests that religion in different societies needs to be understood in the context of changes in the world as a whole. There are a number of different theories of globalization (see Chapter 9), but all suggest that the boundaries between societies are becoming less important, that social life within individual societies is increasingly influenced by events elsewhere in the world, and that some social changes are evident throughout the world rather than being confined to particular places. A number of writers have attempted to understand how such changes have influenced religion.

Peter Beyer – globalization, religion, particularism and universalism

Peter Beyer sees globalization as involving a situation in which 'peoples, cultures, societies, and civilizations previously more or less isolated from one another are now in regular and almost unavoidable contact' (Beyer, 1994). This has two contrasting effects. On the one hand, there is an increased danger of clashes between different cultures – now found within the same society – which might misunderstand or be hostile to one another. On the other hand, the increased contact between cultures and religion might reduce the differences between them and therefore reduce the likelihood of conflict.

Global society is characterized by a clash between particularism and universalism. Particularism involves an emphasis on the distinctive characteristics of particular groups. These differences might be national, regional, cultural or religious. Universalism involves an emphasis on similarities between people or societies or values, which result from their common humanity. In this situation religions can take one of three directions:

1 Religion might take a relatively marginal role in global society. Unable to provide an overarching set of values and beliefs that can be shared by all members of society, it might retreat into a limited and privatized role. According to Beyer, globalization leads to the world being dominated by specialized sub-systems. He says, 'Thus, for instance, the world capitalist economy operates in terms of money, the global political system in terms of bureaucratically organized power, the scientific system in terms of verifiable truth.' All of the systems are instrumental in aiming for increased efficiency and the rational achievement of ends.

There is no obvious role for religion as a sub-system of global society. While religious ritual used to be seen as essential for the success of harvests, for good health or military success, this is no longer the case. Without a global role, religion tends to be left merely to deal with personal questions such as the meaning of life. When religion follows this path, it loses its public role and 'Privatized religion continues to develop in a myriad of pluralistic directions across the full range of religious possibilities.' Individuals choose the sect, cult, denomination or major world religion they wish to follow.

However, religion is not inevitably confined to the private sphere.

2 The main sub-systems of modernity and globalization create some problems. The global economy, global science and the global political system offer little in the way of an identity for individuals and social groups. Identities tend to be relativized: people lack a single overriding sense of who they are. They may have a number of separate roles (such as a job and family roles) but no single source of identity. Furthermore, in a pluralistic world, in which different cultures and religions live close together and have increasing contact with one another, it becomes difficult to assert that one culture is better than others.

Religion can adopt an important role in dealing with these problems. Individuals and social groups can use religion to give them a central source of identity. They can use it to reassert their superiority over other social groups. They can use religious affiliations to mobilize groups to seek power and influence in a globalized society in which they feel marginalized or threatened. Very often religions which assert particularistic differences are closely associated with nationalism. Thus, according to

Beyer, Israel, Iran, India and Japan are all examples of countries where conservative or fundamentalist religions have been associated with nationalism.

3 The third option is for religion to attempt a more universalistic approach. Beyer calls this the liberal option. In this case religion attempts to be more ecumenical – it tries to bring together different faiths and beliefs. Instead of emphasizing difference, it emphasizes common values or beliefs which are, or it believes should be, shared globally. Examples of such beliefs might be a belief in universal human rights or in some conception of social justice. Beyer sees liberation theology as a good example of this type of development. Although based upon Catholicism, its interests are as much political as religious, with its concern for the poverty of disadvantaged groups in Latin America. Indeed, many of the problems of the poor can be attributed to the operation of the global capitalist system. Another example of the universalistic approach is religious environmentalism where different religious groups can be united in trying to save what may be seen as a divinely created earth.

Beyer concludes that globalization will not lead to the demise of religion. However, it does limit its influence. It is no longer integral to powerful sub-systems such as the global economy, the political system and science. While it remains important to systems of communication, it can only really try to influence events in the world rather than directly shaping them. For example, Beyer says that:

> with peace and justice issues, many religious people and organizations will become deeply involved in the problems; but the proffered solutions are going to be political, educational, scientific, economic, and medical – assuming, of course, that the global system does not collapse along with its biological environment.
>
> Beyer, 1994, p. 222

Samuel P. Huntington – *The Clash of Civilizations*

Samuel Huntington sees religion as developing a rather greater role in the modern world than Beyer. Although he does not use the term 'globalization' he discusses the same processes as those identified by globalization theorists. For example, he says, 'the world is becoming a smaller place. The interactions between peoples of different civilizations are increasing; these increasing interactions intensify civilization consciousness' (Huntington, 1993). Like some other theorists of globalization, he believes that the increasing contacts between different groups can sometimes have the effect of intensifying the emphasis upon differences rather than bringing groups closer together. In Huntington's theory, the groups are civilizations rather than nation-states or religions as such. However, there are often close relationships between religions and civilizations.

Civilizations

To Huntington, a 'civilization is a cultural entity'. He says, 'Civilizations are differentiated from each other by history, language, culture tradition, and, most important, religion.' The civilizations he distinguishes are 'Western, Confucian, Japanese, Islamic, Hindu, Slavic-Orthodox, Latin American and possibly African civilization'.

In the contemporary world, sources of identity that are not religious or based on civilization have declined in significance. The end of the Cold War and the collapse of communism have meant that people are less divided by political differences. Economic change, improved communications, travel and migration have weakened the nation-state. On the other hand, regional economic cooperation (for example in the EU and the North American Free Trade Area) strengthens civilization consciousness. Huntington says, 'In much of the world religion has moved in to fill this gap, often in the form of movements that are labelled "fundamentalist". Such movements are found in Western Christianity, Judaism, Buddhism and Hinduism, as well as Islam.' Because of this, Huntington believes that, far from the world becoming secularized, there is evidence of unsecularization.

Clashes between civilizations

Huntington believes that there will increasingly be clashes between civilizations. He argues that 'As people define their identity in ethnic and religious terms, they are likely to see an "us" versus "them" relation existing between themselves and people of different ethnicity or religion.'

Geographical closeness increases the likelihood of clashes. Thus there tend to be high rates of conflict along the borders (or fault lines) between civilizations. Hence there were clashes in the former Yugoslavia where Orthodox, Christian and Muslim civilizations met. In the Middle East there are clashes between Islam, Judaism and Western Christianity. Huntington sees the Gulf War of 1990 as partly a clash between Arabs and the West (although there were Arab nations on both sides). In Asia there is the clash between Muslims and Hindus in the Indian subcontinent. China has repressed Buddhists in Tibet and Muslim minorities in China itself.

Increasingly, political leaders use an appeal to civilization consciousness to try to mobilize support. Thus, Saddam Hussein argues that Islamic countries should unite against American imperialism, and the Orthodox Serbs appealed for support from Orthodox Russia in the Bosnian conflict.

According to Huntington, then, most of the conflict in the world can now be related to religious divisions rather than political ones. For example, 'In the 1930s the Spanish Civil War provoked intervention from countries that politically were fascist, communist and democratic. In the 1990s the Yugoslav conflict is provoking intervention from countries that are Muslim, Orthodox and Western Christian.'

Implications for the future

Huntington does not argue that sources of conflict and identity other than civilizations and their religions will disappear or become insignificant. However, he does believe that civilizations will become more important than ideology and other sources of conflict. The implication is that religion will become more rather than less important in global terms. Although at the moment Western Christian civilization is dominant, in the future it will increasingly be challenged. China, for example, has developed nuclear weapons, and Islamic countries such as Pakistan, India, Iran and Iraq have been trying to develop them (India carried out underground nuclear tests in 1998). There is the possibility of an arms race between Eastern civilizations based on Islamic and Confucian religions.

However, as there is no likelihood of a world or global civilization developing, the different civilizations will have to learn to live with one another. Unfortunately, Huntington's theory gives little reason for optimism that they will do so.

High modernity, postmodernity and religion

Advocates of secularization, such as Steve Bruce, argue that the development of modernity led to secularization. According to the arguments advanced by such writers, the role of religion becomes marginalized in modernity because science and rationality supplant faith in religious beliefs, and because the differentiation of institutions largely relegates religion to a private sphere. This would suggest that theories which argue that modernity has changed, or that it has been replaced by postmodernity, might imply that there is the potential for a religious revival. Thus theories of high modernity or postmodernity might be able to partly explain the apparent revival of religion discussed in the sections above. David Lyon, for example, notes that 'Religion, then, is reappearing in sociological accounts of post- or late-modern societies' (Lyon, 1996). Two theories in which religion has reappeared will now be examined, followed by a discussion of whether the New Age can be seen as a postmodern phenomenon.

Anthony Giddens – high modernity and religious revival

The main features of high modernity

In *The Consequences of Modernity* (1990) and *Modernity and Self-Identity* (1991) Anthony Giddens argues that modern societies have moved into a new phase of high modernity. He sees this as a development of modernity and a radicalization of certain features of modernity. However, although high-modern societies develop out of modern ones, they are significantly different.

Like Steve Bruce, Giddens sees modernity as involving rationalization and differentiation. However, high modernity takes these a step further.

First, there is increased reflexivity. This involves the constant monitoring of social life in order to improve it. People become increasingly willing to change their beliefs, practices and institutions in the light of new knowledge and experience. The Enlightenment (see Chapter 15) seemed to offer the promise of certainty through scientific knowledge. However, high modernity leads to an unsettling uncertainty because of this constant willingness to change. It also produces a tendency to undermine the traditional. Giddens says, 'Modern institutions differ from all preceding forms of social order in respect of their dynamism, the degree to which they undercut traditional habits and customs' (Giddens, 1991). Sociology itself is part of the reflexivity. It involves critically analysing social arrangements rather than taking them as given and retaining them simply because they are traditional.

Second, there are fundamental changes in the organization of space and time. The separation of time and space involves a process whereby 'The advent of modernity increasingly tears space away from place by fostering relations between "absent" others, locationally distant from any given situation of face-to-face interaction' (Giddens, 1990). In other words, new communications technology (such as the internet and satellite communications) and the globalization of social life (see Chapter 9 for a discussion of globalization) mean that social relation-

ships increasingly take place between people who live and work in different parts of the globe.

Third, and closely related to the separation of time and space, disembedding occurs. By this Giddens means 'the "lifting out" of social relations from local contexts of interaction and their restructuring across indefinite spans of time-space' (Giddens, 1990). What happens in a particular locality may be shaped by events far away. For example, hill sheep farmers may be affected by the fall-out from a nuclear accident thousands of miles away (as in the case of Chernobyl), or a factory may have to close because of economic changes in other continents.

People can no longer place their trust in people whom they know from their immediate locality. Instead they must trust that expert systems will prove reliable and effective in meeting their needs. For example, people trust that the systems are in place to ensure that an aeroplane they fly on has been properly serviced and the pilot properly trained. They do not need to know the mechanics and the pilot personally to have sufficient confidence to place their lives in their hands.

Religion and high modernity

At first sight, Giddens's description of high modernity does not appear to be a place where religion will flourish. Traditional beliefs (such as religions) are questioned. Technical systems and science are highly developed and very important. As local communities become less significant, religious beliefs are less likely to be reinforced by the communities in which people live. Indeed, in The *Consequences of Modernity* Giddens does suggest that religion faces an uphill task. He admits that secularization does not involve the disappearance of religion. However, he says:

> *Yet most of the situations of modern social life are manifestly incompatible with religion as a pervasive influence upon day-to-day life. Religious cosmology is supplanted by reflexively organised knowledge, governed by empirical observation and logical thought, and focused upon material technology and socially applied codes. Religion and tradition were always closely linked, and the latter is even more thoroughly undermined than the former by the reflexivity of modern social life, which stands in direct opposition to it.*
>
> Giddens, 1990, p. 109

In essence, Giddens does little more than restate conventional versions of the secularization thesis using his own terminology. However, in his 1991 book, *Modernity and Self-Identity*, he adopts a rather different position. Here he argues that high modernity provides the conditions for a resurgence of religion. He says, 'Religious symbols and practices are not only residues from the past; a revival of religious or, more broadly, spiritual concerns seems fairly widespread in modern societies.' But why should this be? The answer largely lies in the consequences of modernity for the individual sense of self. As tradition loses its grip on social life, individual selves become increasingly reflexive. That is, people make more conscious choices about who they are and what they wish to become. They do not simply accept their position in society and their sense of self that comes from socialization. However, individuals face problems in developing their sense of self.

First, rational knowledge has replaced the certainty that comes from tradition with the certainties of science. Nevertheless, in every field, there are competing experts making divergent claims about what is true and what is not. Individuals have to choose between the claims of these experts in many areas of their life. Examples might include conflicting advice on the most fashionable clothes, the most healthy diet or the best moral values. High modernity is therefore characterized by increasing doubt in people's minds about all sorts of aspects of their lives. As Giddens puts it, 'Modernity institutionalises the principle of radical doubt and insists that all knowledge takes the form of hypotheses: claims which may very well be true, but which are in principle always open to revision' (Giddens, 1991).

Second, what Giddens calls 'existential questions' – questions about why people exist – tend to be separated from everyday life in high modernity. People whose condition or behaviour makes you think about the purpose of existence tend to be kept apart from others in institutions or some physically separate place. Giddens says, 'The mad, the criminal and the seriously ill are physically sequestered from the normal population, while "eroticism" is replaced by "sexuality" – which then moves behind the scenes to become hidden away.' As a result, 'The sequestration of experience means that, for many people, direct contact with events and situations which link the individual lifespan to broad issues of morality and finitude are rare and fleeting.' People are isolated from thinking about death, what happens to you after you die, why you should act in a 'sane' way, why you should conform, and from sex itself, and they are therefore in somewhat of a moral vacuum.

As people try to make sense of their lives and themselves in a reflexive way but within a moral vacuum, 'Personal meaninglessness – the feeling that life has nothing worthwhile to offer – becomes a fundamental psychic problem in circumstances of late modernity.' Religion and spirituality can step in to fill the vacuum that has been left, although it can also be filled by various forms of '"Life politics" –

concerned with human self-actualisation'. Thus people might feel a sense of personal fulfilment through joining an ecological movement and trying to live in harmony with the earth, rather than through joining a religious movement.

Religious movements are another way of overcoming this sense of meaninglessness. Unlike the past, though, and typical of other aspects of high modernity, there is now a great choice of religious beliefs and movements to consider. Reflexive individuals have to decide for themselves which cult, sect, denomination or church, or which New Age beliefs to follow (if any). Religions offer 'a return of the repressed', since they directly address issues of the moral meaning of existence which modern institutions so thoroughly tend to dissolve'.

Fundamentalism

There is one type of religious revival which Giddens sees as particularly worrying – fundamentalism. He sees religious fundamentalism of various types as a response to the way in which high modernity undermines certainty and detraditionalizes society. It is a relatively new phenomenon – the term 'fundamentalism' has only come to be widely used in the past 30 years or so – and it represents a rejection of key aspects of high modernity. He describes it as 'tradition defended in the traditional way – but where that mode of defence has become widely called into question' (Giddens, 1994).

Fundamentalists – for example, some Protestant fundamentalists in the USA – simply assert that they are right through an appeal to traditional beliefs. They react against a globalized world in which differences and disputes are usually resolved by discussion and dialogue by refusing to compromise or even consider that they might be wrong. They assert their religious beliefs and will allow no contradictions. To Giddens, such an approach to religion is dangerous in the contemporary world because of the diaspora or dispersal of different people across the globe and the rapid communications and increased levels of migration and travel. In a globalized world the different ethnic and religious groups who live in close proximity have to be more tolerant of one another if serious conflict is to be avoided.

Evaluation of Giddens

James A. Beckford identifies both strengths and weaknesses in Giddens's views on religion and high modernity (Beckford, 1996). To Beckford it is a strong theory because it appears to account for both the traditional types of religion (for example, traditional fundamentalism) and novel types (such as cults). It also appears convincing because 'Giddens regards the survival of religion as a central consequence of high modernity rather than as an awkward or incidental freak show on the side.'

Nevertheless, it does seem contradictory that religion should revive in a society characterized by the use of rational thought to monitor every aspect of life. To Beckford, Giddens can only explain this by reverting to untestable claims about the needs of individuals. Basically, religion comes down to the need for some moral certainty and some sort of answer to existential questions such as why we are here. Beckford says, 'he seems to posit the existence of a "real" self, which is resistant to the pressures of high modernity'. This argument has a 'distinctly functionalist ring about it' since it is based on the idea that people have basic needs which must be met. Beckford goes on to say that:

> the repressed morality asserts itself. This 'volcanic' or emergent vision of moral agency is inadequate insofar as it runs the risk of implying that the real moral agent is pre- or even non-social. It is difficult to avoid the suspicion that the 'return of the repressed' is a rabbit pulled out of a theoretical hat when all other tricks have failed to make sense of the persistence of religion at a time when, according to the theory of high modernity, religion's chances of survival are extremely slim.
>
> Beckford, 1996, pp. 36–7

Certainly, this interpretation would seem to fit with the apparent change in Giddens's views on the fate of religion, noted earlier in this section.

Zygmunt Bauman – religion and postmodernity

Although Bauman (1992) is a theorist of postmodernity, his analysis of religion has some similarity to that of Giddens. Like Giddens, Bauman sees contemporary societies as developing out of key features of modernity. He also agrees with Giddens that there is increased reflexivity in the contemporary world and that this poses problems for individuals. Furthermore, he follows Giddens in arguing for a religious revival that results from the problems faced by individuals. Nevertheless, Bauman's characterization of changes in society and his explanations for any religious revival are rather different to those of Giddens.

To Bauman, modernity was characterized by a search for universal truths. Postmodernity tears down or deconstructs any claims to universal truth. He sees postmodernity as a 'state of mind' in which there is a 'universal dismantling of power-supported structures'. People no longer accept that others have authority over them and that they must live their lives according to rules imposed by any form of external authority. To Bauman, postmodernity:

> means licence to do whatever one may fancy and advice not to take anything you or the others do too seriously. … It means a shopping mall overflowing with goods whose major use is the joy of purchasing them; and existence that feels like a life-long confinement to the shopping mall. It means the exhilarating freedom to pursue anything and the mind-boggling uncertainty as to what is worth pursuing and in the name of what one should pursue it.
>
> Bauman, 1992, p. vii

This uncertainty raises problems with morality and ethics. Modernity tried to put ethical problems on one side. They were reduced to or replaced by rules or laws. People were encouraged to behave in particular ways because the rules (for example, of bureaucracies) or laws of society said they should. The rules and laws were justified on rational grounds as providing the best means for achieving given ends. Thus Bauman says, 'Modernity was, among other things, a gigantic exercise in abolishing individual responsibility other than that measured by the criteria of instrumental rationality and practical achievement.'

However, once postmodernity has torn away the belief that there can be a rational basis for perfecting society, it leaves individuals with no external rules to govern their lives. This leads to a renewed emphasis on the ethical and the moral, but now it is personal ethics and morality that are important. Bauman says:

> The ethical paradox of the postmodern condition is that it restores to agents the fullness of moral choice and responsibility whilst simultaneously depriving them of the comfort of universal guidance that modern self-confidence once promised. … In a cacophony of moral voices, none of which is likely to silence the others, the individuals are thrown back on their own subjectivity as the only ultimate ethical authority.
>
> Bauman, 1992, p. xxii

Morality becomes privatized, a matter of personal choice. Yet morality cannot be abandoned altogether. Individuals still seek to evaluate themselves and their own worth. They still want to make their lives meaningful. In modernity individuals tended to have what Bauman calls 'life-projects', things they wished to achieve, ambitions they wanted to fulfil. In postmodernity people seek a process of 'self-constitution'. Rather than achieving things, they want to be somebody. They want to be 'visible' to others. They want to get noticed and to be admired or respected. Uncertain about their own worth, people want the reassurance of people noticing and admiring them. They need to think of the lifestyle they adopt, the things they consume and the moral beliefs they adopt as superior to those of other people.

In the absence of any one set of rules about how you should behave, what is good taste or which moral beliefs are true, people have only two possible sources of reassurance. First, they can seek justification for their choices from 'experts' in a particular field. There may be many competing experts but to have some outside support is better than to have none. Second, they can rely upon a 'mass following' supporting their choices. You can try to be a trendsetter, or at least to follow the crowd so that you are not too out of step with others, too unfashionable.

With all these choices available, and with individuals responsible for their own morality, people turn to experts in morality, religious leaders, for some guidance. Bauman concludes that there is a 'typically postmodern heightened interest in ethical debate and increased attractiveness of the agencies claiming expertise in moral values (e.g., the revival of religious and quasi religious movements)'.

Evaluation of Bauman

James A. Beckford (1996) is even more critical of Bauman than he is of Giddens. He sees his analysis as rather contradictory. Some types of religion or quasi-religion might seem to fit aspects of his theory. Thus the 'playfulness of some New Age beliefs' seems to fit in with the supposed lack of seriousness in postmodern consumer culture. However, to Beckford, it is simply contradictory for Bauman to say that postmodernity undermines faith in external authorities and that it makes people seek the authority of religious experts for their beliefs. Beckford says, 'This sounds suspiciously like an argument about the appeal of authority and moral principles at a time – postmodernity – when such things were not supposed to be important.'

According to Beckford, Giddens, Bauman and other theorists who believe that there has been a fundamental change in contemporary societies in recent times are faced with a problem. They need to explain the 'continuous importance of religion throughout history' in the context of claims about major changes in social life. Beckford does not believe that there has been a massive religious revival, because he does not believe that there was any preceding massive decline in religion. If he is right, then perhaps the theorists of postmodernity and high modernity have exaggerated the extent of change in social life. It is a view that would probably attract some sympathy from Paul Heelas who has examined the significance of the New Age for theories of postmodernity.

Paul Heelas – postmodernity and the New Age

Why the New Age appears postmodern

Paul Heelas (1996) argues that in a number of ways the New Age does appear to have characteristics that are associated with postmodernism:

1 First, it seems to involve de-differentiation and detraditionalization. Scott Lash (1990) has argued that postmodernism involves de-differentiation – that is, a breakdown in traditional categories such as those between high culture and popular culture. The New Age appears to involve a breakdown in the distinction between traditional religious beliefs and popular culture. Furthermore, Heelas says, 'dedifferentiation is a major theme of the movement. In most versions of New Age thought, inner spirituality does not acknowledge difference. All people are held to share the same inner spirituality, together with the spirituality of the natural order as a whole.' The New Age is detraditionalized simply because it rejects the established traditions of conventional religions such as Christianity.

2 Like postmodernism, the New Age appears to accept relativism. It does not accept one set of ideas as revealing the whole truth, and it is prepared to accept that there is merit in the viewpoints of different groups. The same characteristics are thought to be typical of postmodernism, which rejects metanarratives that claim to provide definitive guides to the truth and how social life should be organized.

3 The New Age seems to have strong links with the consumer culture that writers like Bauman see as central to postmodernism. New Agers can 'consume' different practices from week to week. For example, people might 'participate in "shamanic" weekends, followed by some "Zen", or "yoga", and then a visit to some "Christian"-inspired centre'.

4 Like postmodernism, the New Age emphasizes the importance of experience over the achievement of particular ends. Heelas suggests that both consumers – for example, when they are shopping – and New Agers might experience 'euphoric intensities' which lead to the 'disintegration of the subject'. They become so involved in their activities that they forget who they are and simply enjoy the experience.

5 Heelas points out that some writers have made the simple link that both the New Age and the idea of postmodernity are all about the advent of a new era.

Why the New Age is not postmodern

Despite the apparent similarities and connections between postmodernism and the New Age, Heelas rejects the idea that the New Age is postmodern. He argues that the New Age has a very strong, central metanarrative at its heart. Although it rejects what he calls cultural metanarratives (for example, about how society should be developed), it replaces them with an 'experiential metanarrative'. This metanarrative does claim to be able to reveal absolute truths and to provide people with the basis for planning their lives.

Although there might be different paths towards the type of inner wisdom that New Agers seek, a core set of beliefs exists which allows people to make judgements about themselves and others. Heelas says that the New Age 'shows a considerable degree of unity in its basic discourse of self-spirituality'. Furthermore, committed New Agers do not think of these beliefs as trivial, playful or no more important than the consumer goods they choose to buy. They treat their beliefs as serious ones just as others might treat more conventional religions. They do differentiate between their spirituality and less important parts of their lives.

Heelas also points out that many aspects of New Age beliefs are not particularly new. There is a long tradition of similar thinking going back to the theosophy movement (founded in India towards the end of the nineteenth century) which was an early form of self-religion. In any case, many New Age beliefs derive from ancient sources.

Heelas concludes that the New Age can be seen as emphasizing an individualism which 'involves the ascription of value and truth to the self'. Individualism is a key feature of Western culture and of modern societies. Because of this there is no justification in regarding the New Age as postmodern. Heelas says that 'the New Age is quite clearly an aspect of modernity'. Indeed, he argues that there is no clearcut division between a modern and a postmodern era. You can find examples from social life in the past which seem postmodern, and examples from the present which do not appear to be postmodern at all. Heelas says it is 'much more profitable to think in terms of a dynamic interplay between de-traditionalisation and re-traditionalisation, tradition-maintenance and tradition-construction than it is to think in terms of nineteenth-century-like periodisations'.

History, including the history of religion, is more complicated than the idea that we have moved from modernity to postmodernity would suggest.

Sociology, values and religion

Throughout this chapter it is evident that the ideological commitments of particular researchers have influenced their definition of religion and their view of its role in society. In terms of their value judgements, they have considered some aspects of religion as worthy of study and dismissed others as irrelevant.

The influence of ideology in the study of religion is clearly evident in Marxist perspectives. Marx believed that people's salvation lay in their own hands. People would find salvation when they fulfilled their true nature. Fulfilment could only be found in a truly socialist society, a society created by people. Marx's utopian vision left no room for religion. Since religion had no place in the ideal socialist society, it must be a response to the flaws of non-socialist societies. From this set of beliefs and values, the Marxist analysis of religion follows a predictable course: religion represents either a salve to the pain of exploitation or a justification for oppression. In either case, it is a distortion of reality which people can well do without.

The conservative tendencies of functionalism, with its preoccupation with social order, provide a similarly predictable analysis. The concern of the functionalist approach with discovering the basis of stability and order in society leads to an emphasis on particular aspects of religion. From this perspective,

religion is seen as reinforcing social norms and values and promoting social solidarity, all of which are required for a stable and smooth-running social system. By its very nature, functionalist theory tends to discount the divisive and disruptive effects of religion, and it ignores the role of religion as an agency of social change.

The intrusion of value judgements into research is particularly clear in the secularization debate. Many of the arguments are based on particular researchers' judgements of the 'truly religious society', in terms of which they evaluate what they see in contemporary society. Thus Will Herberg sees the religion of American denominations as a poor substitute for true religion. Max Weber observes industrial society in the early twentieth century and pictures a rather pathetic and disenchanted populace without the support of the deep spirituality which religion provides. By contrast, Talcott Parsons rather smugly observes American society in the middle years of the twentieth century, notes its high moral standards and assumes they must be based ultimately on Christian values.

Such divergent interpretations may say as much about the observers as the reality of their subject matter.

As well as being influenced by their personal values, sociologists are also influenced by fashions in academic argument. The increasing importance of the concepts of postmodernism and globalization has led many sociologists to feel the need to reconsider how the sociology of religion should be approached. In a way, this has revitalized this area of sociology. So long as the theory of secularization went relatively unchallenged, sociologists of religion seemed to be studying a peripheral area of society that was declining in significance.

Theories of postmodernity and globalization leave more room for religion to be seen as an important feature of contemporary society. On the surface they seem to be buttressed by the evidence of religious revival on a global scale. However, this evidence needs to be approached with caution. Sociologists,

like other people, tend to interpret the evidence to fit their preconceptions, and some theorists of postmodernity and globalization may have exaggerated the importance of religion. Similarly, however, advocates of secularization may have underestimated the continuing significance of religion. As James A. Beckford says, 'from time to time sociology is swept by enthusiasm for novel concepts or theories' (Beckford, 1996).

It is important that the most recent fashions are regarded with as much scepticism as the older ones. Without this scepticism sociology would become stuck with the favoured concepts of a particular generation of sociologists, whether they remained appropriate to changing societies or not.

Chapter 8

Families and households

Families and households

Introduction

The family has often been regarded as the corner-stone of society. In pre-modern and modern societies alike it has been seen as the most basic unit of social organization and one which carries out vital tasks such as socializing children. Until the 1960s few sociologists questioned the importance or the benefits of family life. Most sociologists assumed that family life was evolving as modernity progressed, and the changes involved made the family better-suited to meeting the needs of society and of family members.

A particular type of family, the nuclear family (based around a two-generation household of parents and their children), was seen as well-adapted to the demands of modern societies. From the 1960s, an increasing number of critical thinkers began to question the assumption that the family was necessarily a beneficial institution. Feminists, Marxists and critical psychologists began to highlight what they saw as some of the negative effects and the 'dark side' of family life.

In the following decades the family was not just under attack from academic writers – social changes also seemed to be undermining traditional families. Rising divorce rates, cohabitation before marriage, increasing numbers of single-parent families and single-person households, and other trends have all suggested that individuals may be basing their lives less and less around conventional families.

Some have seen these changes as a symptom of greater individualism within modern societies. They have welcomed what appears to be an increasing choice for individuals. People no longer have to base their lives around what may be outmoded and, for many, unsuitable, conventional family structures. Others, however, have lamented the changes and worried about their effect on society. Such changes were seen as both a symptom and a cause of instability and insecurity in people's lives and in society as a whole. This view was advocated by traditionalists who wanted a return to the ideal of the nuclear family. For them, many of society's problems were a result of the increased family instability.

Some postmodernists have begun to argue that there has been a fundamental break between the modern family and the postmodern family. They deny that any one type of family can be held up as the norm to which other family types can be compared. While modern societies might have had one central, dominant family type, this is no longer the case. As a result, it is no longer possible to produce a theory of 'the family'. Different explanations are needed for different types of family.

Alongside these developments in society and sociology, family life has become a topic of political debate. What was once largely seen as a private sphere, in which politicians should not interfere, is now seen as a legitimate area for public debate and political action. As concern has grown in some quarters about an alleged decline of the family, politicians have become somewhat more willing to comment on families. Sometimes they have devised policies to try to deal with perceived problems surrounding the family.

In short, the family has come to be seen as more problematic than it was in the past. The controversies that have come to surround families and households are the subject of this chapter.

We begin by examining the assumption of the 'universality' of the family.

Is the family universal?

George Peter Murdock: the family – a universal social institution

In a study entitled *Social Structure* (1949), George Peter Murdock examined the institution of the family in a wide range of societies. Murdock took a sample of 250 societies, ranging from small hunting and gathering bands to large-scale industrial societies. He claimed that some form of family existed in every society and concluded, on the evidence of his sample, that the family is universal.

Murdock defined the family as follows:

The family is a social group characterized by common residence, economic co-operation and reproduction. It includes adults of both sexes, at least two of whom maintain a socially approved sexual relationship, and one or more children, own or adopted, of the sexually cohabiting adults.

Murdock, 1949

Thus the family lives together, pools its resources and works together, and produces offspring. At least two of the adult members conduct a sexual relationship according to the norms of their particular society.

Such norms vary from society to society. For example, among the Banaro of New Guinea, the husband does not have sexual relations with his wife until she has borne a child by a friend of his father. The parent–child relationship, therefore, is not necessarily a biological one. Its importance is primarily social, children being recognized as members of a particular family whether or not the adult spouses have biologically produced them.

Variations in family structure

The structure of the family varies from society to society. The smallest family unit is known as the nuclear family and consists of a husband and wife and their immature offspring. Units larger than the nuclear family are usually known as extended families. Such families can be seen as extensions of the basic nuclear unit, either vertical extensions – for example, the addition of members of a third generation such as the spouses' parents – and/or horizontal extensions – for example, the addition of members of the same generation as the spouses, such as the husband's brother or an additional wife. Thus the functionalist sociologists Bell and Vogel define the extended family as 'any grouping broader than the nuclear family which is related by descent, marriage or adoption'.

Either on its own or as the basic unit within an extended family, Murdock found that the nuclear family was present in every society in his sample. This led him to conclude that:

The nuclear family is a universal human social grouping. Either as the sole prevailing form of the family or as the basic unit from which more complex forms are compounded, it exists as a distinct and strongly functional group in every known society.

Murdock, 1949

However, as we will discover in the following sections, Murdock's conclusions might not be well-founded.

Kathleen Gough – the Nayar

Some societies have sets of relationships between kin which are quite different from those which are common in Britain. One such society was that of the Nayar of Kerala in Southern India, prior to British rule being established in 1792. Sociologists disagree about whether this society had a family system or not, and thus whether or not it disproves Murdock's claim that the family is universal.

Kathleen Gough (1959) provided a detailed description of Nayar society. Before puberty all Nayar girls were ritually married to a suitable Nayar man in the *tali*-rite. After the ritual marriage had taken place, however, the *tali* husband did not live with his wife, and was under no obligation to have any contact with her whatsoever. The wife owed only one duty to her *tali* husband: she had to attend his funeral to mourn his death.

Once a Nayar girl reached or neared puberty she began to take a number of visiting husbands, or 'sandbanham' husbands. The Nayar men were usually professional warriors who spent long periods of time away from their villages acting as mercenaries. During their time in the villages they were allowed to visit any number of Nayar women who had undergone the *tali*-rite and who were members of the same caste as themselves, or a lower caste. With the agreement of the woman involved, the *sandbanham* husband arrived at the home of one of his wives after supper, had sexual intercourse with her, and left before breakfast the next morning. During his stay he placed his weapons outside the building to show the other *sandbanham* husbands that he was there. If they arrived too late, then they were free to sleep on the veranda, but could not stay the night with their wife. Men could have unlimited numbers of *sandbanham* wives, although women seem to have been limited to no more than 12 visiting husbands.

An exception to the family?

Sandbanham relationships were unlike marriages in most societies in a number of ways:

1 They were not a lifelong union: either party could terminate the relationship at any time.

2 *Sandbanham* husbands had no duty towards the offspring of their wives. When a woman became pregnant, it was essential according to Nayar custom that a man of appropriate caste declared himself to be the father of the child by paying a fee of cloth and vegetables to the midwife who attended the birth. However, it mattered little whether he was the biological parent or not, so long as someone claimed to be the father, because he did not help to maintain or socialize the child.

3 Husbands and wives did not form an economic unit. Although husbands might give wives token gifts, they were not expected to maintain them – indeed it was frowned upon if they attempted to. Instead, the economic unit consisted of a number of brothers and sisters, sisters' children, and their daughters' children. The eldest male was the leader of each group of kin.

Nayar society, then, was a matrilineal society. Kinship groupings were based on female biological relatives and marriage played no significant part in the formation of households, in the socializing of children, or in the way that the economic needs of the members of society were met.

In terms of Murdock's definition, no family existed in Nayar society, since those who maintained 'a sexually approved adult relationship' did not live together and cooperate economically. Only the women lived with the children. Therefore, either Murdock's definition of the family is too narrow, or the family is not universal.

Gough claimed that marriage, and by implication the family, existed in Nayar society. In order to make this claim, though, she had to broaden her definition of marriage beyond that implied in Murdock's definition of the family. She defined marriage as a relationship between a woman and one or more persons in which a child born to the woman 'is given full birth-status rights' common to normal members of the society.

Matrifocal families – an exception to the rule?

Murdock's definition of the family includes at least one adult of each sex. However, both today and in the past, some children have been raised in households that do not contain adults of both sexes. Usually these households have been headed by women.

A significant proportion of black families in the islands of the West Indies, parts of Central America such as Guyana, and the USA do not include adult males. The 'family unit' often consists of a woman and her dependent children, sometimes with the addition of her mother. This may indicate that the family is not universal as Murdock suggests, or that it is necessary to redefine the family and state that the minimal family unit consists of a woman and her dependent children, own or adopted, and that all other family types are additions to this unit.

Female-headed families are sometimes known as matriarchal families and sometimes as matrifocal families, although both of these terms have been used in a number of senses. We will use the term matrifocal family here to refer to female-headed families.

The causes of matrifocal families

Matrifocal families are common in low-income black communities in the New World. In the USA in 1985, 51 per cent of all black children lived with their mothers but not with their fathers. The percentage is also high in other New World societies. For example, Nancie González (1970), in her study of Livingston, Honduras in 1956, found that 45 per cent of black Carib families had female heads. (See pp. 545–6 for comments on lone parenthood and ethnicity in Britain.)

The high level of matrifocal families has been seen as a result of one or more of the following factors:

1 Melville J. Herskovits (1958) argued that the West African origin of New World blacks influenced their family structure. In traditional West Africa, a system of polygyny (a form of extended family with one husband and two or more wives) and considerable female economic independence meant that the husband played a relatively marginal role in family life. Herskovits maintained that this pattern continues to influence black family life.

2 A second argument sees the system of plantation slavery as a major factor accounting for matrifocal families. M.G. Smith (1962) noted that, under slavery, the mother and children formed the basic family unit. Families were often split with the sale of one or more of their members, but mothers and dependent children were usually kept together. The authority of the male as head of the family was eroded because he was subject to the authority of the plantation owner who, with his white employees, had the right of sexual access to all female slaves. Formed under slavery, the model of the matrifocal family is seen to have persisted.

3 A third argument sees the economic position of blacks in the New World as the basic cause of the matrifocal family. Elliot Liebow (1967), whose views are outlined in Chapter 5 (pp. 321–3), saw female-

headed families as resulting from desertion by the husband because he has insufficient funds to play the role of father and breadwinner.

4 A final argument accepts that poverty is the basic cause of matrifocal families but states also that matrifocality has become a part of the subculture of the poor. This view is contained in Oscar Lewis's concept of the culture of poverty (Lewis, 1961). From his research in a low-income black area of Washington DC, Ulf Hannerz (1969) argued that female-headed families are so common that to some degree they have become an expected and accepted alternative to the standard nuclear family. According to this argument, matrifocal families are not simply a product of poverty but also of culture. (See Chapter 5, pp. 319–23, for a general discussion of the relationship between poverty, culture and family structure.)

Can we then see the matrifocal family as an exception to Murdock's claim that the family is universal, or, if it is accepted as a family, as an exception to his claim that the nuclear family is a universal social group? In order to decide this, we will first consider the arguments that support Murdock, and then the arguments against him.

Support for Murdock

1 Statistically, the female-headed family is not the norm either within black communities or in the societies in which they are set.

2 The matrifocal family is often a nuclear family that has been broken. Particularly in the USA, it is usually a product of separation or divorce. It did not begin life as a matrifocal family.

3 Some sociologists believe that the mainstream model of the nuclear family is valued by blacks and regarded as the ideal.

4 Many sociologists view the female-headed family as a family 'gone wrong', as a product of social disorganization and not, therefore, as a viable alternative to the nuclear family. It has been accused of producing maladjusted children, juvenile delinquents and high-school dropouts. Since it does not appear to perform the functions of a 'proper family', it is regarded as a broken family and not as a viable unit in its own right.

Arguments against Murdock

The following arguments support the view that the matrifocal family should be recognized as an alternative to the nuclear family:

1 Simply because in statistical terms the matrifocal family is not the norm, does not mean it cannot be recognized as an alternative family structure. In many societies that practise polygyny, polygynous marriages are in the minority, yet sociologists accept them as a form of extended family.

2 As Hannerz (1969) argued, in low-income black communities matrifocal families are to some extent expected and accepted.

3 Members of matrifocal families regard the unit as a family.

4 The matrifocal family should not be seen simply as a broken nuclear family. From her West Indian data, González (1970) argues that the female-headed family is a well-organized social group which represents a positive adaptation to the circumstances of poverty. By not tying herself to a husband, the mother is able to maintain casual relationships with a number of men who can provide her with financial support. She retains strong links with her relatives who give her both economic and emotional support. González states that 'By dispersing her loyalties and by clinging especially to the unbreakable sibling ties with her brothers, a woman increases her chances of maintaining her children and household'. In a situation of poverty, 'the chances that any one man may fail are high'.

5 The supposed harmful effects on the children of the matrifocal family are far from proven (see pp. 541–4 for a discussion of lone parenthood).

The above arguments suggest that the matrifocal family can be regarded as a form of family structure in its own right. If these arguments are accepted, it is possible to see the matrifocal family as the basic, minimum family unit and all other family structures as additions to this unit.

The female-carer core

This view is supported by Yanina Sheeran. She argues that the 'female-carer core' is the most basic family unit. She says:

> The female-carer unit is the foundation of the single mother family, the two parent family, and the extended family in its many forms. Thus it is certainly the basis of family household life in Britain today, and is a ubiquitous phenomenon, since even in South Pacific longhouses, pre-industrial farmsteads, communes and Kibbutzim, we know that female carers predominate.

Sheeran, 1993, p. 30

In Britain, for example, Sheeran maintains that children usually have one woman who is primarily responsible for their care. These primary carers are often but not always the biological mother; they may 'occasionally be a grandmother, elder sister, aunt, adoptive mother or other female'. The primary carer may get help from female relatives, childminders, nannies, or from their husbands or male partners. Sheeran does not therefore deny that men play some part in childcare, but she does deny that their role is as important as that of women. She is sceptical of claims by some sociologists that men's involvement in childcare in Britain has greatly increased (see the discussion of the symmetrical family, pp. 529–31, for an example of such a view).

Sheeran seems to be on strong ground in arguing that a female-carer core is a more basic family unit than that identified by Murdock, since in some societies families without an adult male are quite common. However, she herself admits that in Britain a small minority of lone-parent households are headed by a man. According to figures quoted by her from the *General Household Survey* of 1989–90, about 13 per cent of British households consisted of a lone mother with dependent children, and about 2 per cent of lone fathers with dependent children. Mukti Jain Campion, writing in 1995, notes that figures indicated that at that time there were in the region of 100,000 lone fathers in Britain and about 1.5 million in the USA. Thus it is possible to argue that the female-carer core is not the basis of *every* individual family, even if it is the basis of *most* families in all societies.

Matrifocal families, and one-parent families in general, are becoming more common in Britain. We will consider the significance of this development later in this chapter (see pp. 541–4).

Gay families

Another type of household that may contradict Murdock's claims about the universality of the family, as defined by him, is gay and lesbian households. By definition, such households will not contain 'adults of both sexes, at least two of whom maintain a socially approved sexual relationship' (Murdock, 1949). Such households may, however, include children who are cared for by two adult females or two adult males. The children may have been adopted, be the result of a previous heterosexual relationship, or they may have been produced using new reproductive technologies involving sperm donation or surrogate motherhood. A lesbian may have sex with a man in order to conceive a child to be raised by her and her female partner.

Most children of gay couples result from a previous heterosexual relationship. Lesbian mothers are rather more common than gay fathers, due to the difficulties gay men are likely to have in being granted custody or given adopted children. However, Mukti Jain Campion quotes a study which claimed that over 1,000 children were born to gay or lesbian couples in San Francisco between 1985 and 1990,

and that there were many more people living with gay partners who had conceived children in hetero-sexual relationships. Thus, while households consisting of gay partners and one or more children may not be very common, they do exist. This raises the question of whether such households should be regarded as families.

Rather like lone-parent families, households with gay parents are seen by some as not being 'proper' families. In most Western societies the gay couple will not be able to marry and any children will have a genetic connection with only one of the partners. However, Sidney Callahan (1997) argues that such households should still be seen as families. He argues that, if marriage were available, many gay and lesbian couples would marry. Furthermore, he believes that the relationships involved are no different in any fundamental way from those in heterosexual households. Callahan therefore claims that gay and lesbian households with children should be regarded as a type of family, at least where the gay or lesbian relationship is intended to be permanent. He concludes, 'I would argue that gay or lesbian households that consist of intimate communi-ties of mutual support and that display permanent shared commitments to intergenerational nurturing share the kinship bonding we observe and name as family' (Callahan, 1997).

The universality of the family – conclusion

Whether the family is regarded as universal ultimately depends on how the family is defined. Clearly, though, a wide variety of domestic arrange-ments have been devised by human beings which are quite distinctive from the 'conventional' families of modern industrial societies. As Diana Gittins puts it, 'Relationships are universal, so is some form of co-residence, of intimacy, sexuality and emotional bonds. But the *forms* these can take are infinitely variable and can be changed and challenged as well as embraced' (Gittins, 1993).

It may be a somewhat pointless exercise to try to find a single definition that embraces all the types of household and relationship which can reasonably be called families.

Having examined whether the family is universal, we will now examine various perspectives on the role of families in society.

The family – a functionalist perspective

The analysis of the family from a functionalist perspective involves three main questions:

1 First, 'What are the functions of the family?' Answers to this question deal with the contributions made by the family to the maintenance of the social system. It is assumed that society has certain functional prerequisites or basic needs that must be met if it is to survive and operate efficiently. The family is examined in terms of the degree to which it meets these functional prerequisites.

2 A second and related question asks 'What are the functional relationships between the family and other parts of the social system?'

3 It is assumed that there must be a certain degree of fit, integration and harmony between the parts of the social system if society is going to function efficiently. For example, the family must be integrated to some extent with the economic system. We will examine this question in detail in a later section when the relationships between the family and industrialization are considered.

The third question deals with the functions performed by an institution or a part of society for the individual. In the case of the family, this question considers the functions of the family for its individual members.

George Peter Murdock – the universal functions of the family

Functions for society

From his analysis of 250 societies, Murdock (1949) argued that the family performs four basic functions in all societies, which he termed the sexual, reproductive, economic and educational. They are essential for social life since without the sexual and reproductive functions there would be no members of society, without the economic function (for example, the provision and preparation of food) life would cease, and without education (a term Murdock uses for socialization) there would be no culture. Human society without culture could not function.

Clearly, the family does not perform these functions exclusively. However, it makes important contributions to them all and no other institution has yet been devised to match its efficiency in this respect. Once this is realized, Murdock claimed, 'The immense utility of the nuclear family and the basic reason for its universality thus begin to emerge in strong relief.'

Functions for individuals and society

The family's functions for society are inseparable from its functions for its individual members. It serves both at one and the same time and in much the same way. The sexual function provides a good example of this. Husband and wife have the right of sexual access to each other, and in most societies there are rules forbidding or limiting sexual activity outside marriage. This provides sexual gratification for the spouses. It also strengthens the family since the powerful and often binding emotions which accompany sexual activities unite husband and wife. The sexual function also helps to stabilize society. The rules which largely contain sexual activity within the family prevent the probable disruptive effects on the social order that would result if the sex drive were allowed 'free play'. The family thus provides both 'control and expression' of sexual drives, and in doing so performs important functions, not only for its individual members, but also for the family as an institution and for society as a whole.

Murdock applied a similar logic to the economic function. He argued that, like sex, it is 'most readily and satisfactorily achieved by persons living together'. He referred in glowing terms to the division of labour within the family whereby the husband specializes in certain activities, the wife in others. For example, in hunting societies men kill game animals which provide meat for their wives to cook and skins for them to make into clothing. This economic cooperation within the family not only goes a long way to fulfilling the economic function for society as a whole, but also provides 'rewarding experiences' for the spouses working together, which 'cement their union'.

Murdock argued that his analysis provides a 'conception of the family's many-sided utility and thus of its inevitability'. He concluded that 'No society has succeeded in finding an adequate substitute for the nuclear family, to which it might transfer these functions. It is highly doubtful whether any society will ever succeed in such an attempt.'

Criticisms of Murdock

Murdock's picture of the family is rather like the multi-faceted, indispensable boy-scout knife. The family is seen as a multi-functional institution which is indispensable to society. Its 'many-sided utility' accounts for its universality and its inevitability.

In his enthusiasm for the family, however, Murdock did not seriously consider whether its functions could be performed by other social institutions and he does not examine alternatives to the family. As D.H.J. Morgan notes in his criticism, Murdock does not answer 'to what extent these basic functions are inevitably linked with the institution of the nuclear family' (Morgan, 1975).

In addition, Murdock's description of the family is almost too good to be true. As Morgan states, 'Murdock's nuclear family is a remarkably harmonious institution. Husband and wife have an integrated division of labour and have a good time in bed.' As we will see in later sections, some other researchers do not share Murdock's emphasis on harmony and integration.

Talcott Parsons – the 'basic and irreducible' functions of the family

Parsons (1959, 1965b) concentrated his analysis on the family in modern American society. Despite this, his ideas have a more general application since he argued that the American family retains two 'basic and irreducible functions' which are common to the family in all societies. These are the 'primary socialization of children' and the 'stabilization of the adult personalities of the population of the society'.

Primary socialization

Primary socialization refers to socialization during the early years of childhood which takes place mainly within the family. Secondary socialization occurs during the later years when the family is less involved and other agencies (such as the peer group and the school) exert increasing influence.

There are two basic processes involved in primary socialization: the internalization of society's culture and the structuring of the personality.

Unless culture is internalized – that is, absorbed and accepted – society would cease to exist, since without shared norms and values social life would not be possible. However, culture is not simply learned, it is 'internalized as part of the personality structure'. The child's personality is moulded in terms of the central values of the culture to the point where they become a part of him or her. In the case of American society, personality is shaped in terms of independence and achievement motivation, which are two of the central values of American culture.

Parsons argued that families 'are "factories" which produce human personalities'. He believed that they are essential for this purpose since primary socialization requires a context which provides warmth, security and mutual support. He could conceive of no institution other than the family that could provide this context.

Stabilization of adult personalities

Once produced, the personality must be kept stable. This is the second basic function of the family: the stabilization of adult personalities. The emphasis here is on the marriage relationship and the emotional security the couple provide for each other. This acts as a counterweight to the stresses and strains of everyday life which tend to make the personality unstable.

This function is particularly important in Western industrial society, since the nuclear family is largely isolated from kin. It does not have the security once provided by the close-knit extended family. Thus the married couple increasingly look to each other for emotional support.

Adult personalities are also stabilized by the parents' role in the socialization process. This allows them to act out 'childish' elements of their own personalities which they have retained from childhood but which cannot be indulged in adult society. For example, father is 'kept on the rails' by playing with his son's train set.

According to Parsons, therefore, the family provides a context in which husband and wife can express their childish whims, give and receive emotional support, recharge their batteries, and so stabilize their personalities.

Criticisms of Parsons

This brief summary of Parsons's views on the family is far from complete. Other aspects will be discussed later in this chapter (pp. 524–5) (see also Chapter 3, p. 132), but here we will consider some of the arguments which criticize his perspective:

1 As with Murdock, Parsons has been accused of idealizing the family with his picture of well-adjusted children and sympathetic spouses caring for each other's every need. It is a typically optimistic, modernist theory which may have little relationship to reality.

2 His picture is based largely on the American middle-class family which he treats as representative of American families in general. As D.H.J. Morgan (1975) states, 'there are no classes, no regions, no religious, ethnic or status groups, no communities' in Parsons's analysis of the family. For example, Parsons fails to explore possible differences between middle- and working-class families, or different family structures in ethnic minority communities.

3 Like Murdock, Parsons largely fails to explore functional alternatives to the family. He does recognize that some functions are not necessarily tied to the family. For instance, he notes that the family's economic function has largely been taken over by other agencies in modern industrial society. However, his belief that its remaining functions are

'basic and irreducible' prevents him from examining alternatives to the family.

4 Parsons's view of the socialization process can be criticized. He sees it as a one-way process, with the children being pumped full of culture and their personalities being moulded by powerful parents. He tends to ignore the two-way interaction process between parents and children. There is no place in his scheme for the children who twist their parents around their little finger.

5 Parsons sees the family as a distinct institution which is clearly separated from other aspects of social life. Some contemporary perspectives on the family deny that such clearcut boundaries can be established (see pp. 581–2). The family as such cannot therefore be seen as performing any particular functions on its own in isolation from other institutions.

Critical views of the family

The view that the family benefits both its members and society as a whole has come under strong attack. Some observers have suggested that, on balance, the family may well be dysfunctional both for society and its individual members. This criticism has mainly been directed at the family in Western industrial society.

Edmund Leach – *A Runaway World?*

In a lecture entitled *A Runaway World?* (1967) Edmund Leach presented a pessimistic view of the family in industrial society. Leach, an anthropologist, had spent many years studying small-scale pre-industrial societies. In such societies the family often forms a part of a wider kinship unit. An extensive network of social relationships between a large number of kin provides practical and psychological support for the individual. This support is reinforced by the closely-knit texture of relationships in the small-scale community as a whole.

By comparison, in modern industrial society, the nuclear family is largely isolated from kin and the wider community. Leach summarizes this situation and its consequences as follows:

> In the past kinsfolk and neighbours gave the individual continuous moral support throughout his life. Today the domestic household is isolated. The family looks inward upon itself; there is an intensification of emotional stress between husband and wife and parents and children. The strain is greater than most of us can bear.
>
> Leach, 1967

Thrown back almost entirely upon its own resources, the nuclear family becomes like an overloaded electrical circuit. The demands made upon it are too great and fuses blow. In their isolation, family members expect and demand too much from each other. The result is conflict. In Leach's words, 'The parents and children huddled together in their loneli-

ness take too much out of each other. The parents fight; the children rebel.'

The family and society

Problems are not confined to the family. The tension and hostility produced within the family find expression throughout society. Leach argued that the 'isolation and the close-knit nature of contemporary family life incubates hate which finds expression in conflict in the wider community'. The families in which people huddle together create barriers between them and the wider society. The privatized family breeds suspicion and fear of the outside world. Leach argued that 'Privacy is the source of fear and violence. The violence in the world comes about because we human beings are forever creating barriers between men who are like us and men who are not like us.'

Only when individuals can break out of the prison of the nuclear family, rejoin their fellows and give and receive support will the ills of society begin to diminish. Leach's conclusion is diametrically opposed to the functionalist view of the family. He stated that 'Far from being the basis of the good society, the family, with its narrow privacy and tawdry secrets, is the source of all our discontents.'

R.D. Laing – *The Politics of the Family*

In *The Politics of the Family* (1976) and a number of other publications (for example, Laing and Esterson, 1970, Laing, 1971), R.D. Laing presented a radical alternative to the functionalist picture of the 'happy family'. Laing was a phenomenological psychiatrist: he was concerned with interaction within the family and the meanings that develop in that context. His work was largely based on the study of families in which one member has been defined as schizophrenic.

Laing argues that the behaviour of so-called schizophrenics can only be understood in terms of relationships within the family. Far from viewing schizophrenia as madness, he argues that it makes sense in terms of the meanings and interactions that develop within the family. As such it can be seen as reasonable behaviour.

Laing maintains that the difference between so-called 'normal' and 'abnormal' families is small. It therefore follows that a lot can be learned about families in general by studying those labelled as abnormal.

Exploitation in the family

Laing views the family in terms of sets of interactions. Individuals form alliances, adopt various strategies and play one or more individuals off against others in a complex tactical game. Laing is preoccupied with those interaction situations that he regards as harmful and destructive. Throughout his work he concentrates on the exploitative aspects of family relationships. The following example illustrates his approach (Laing, 1971).

Jane is defined as schizophrenic. She is in a perpetual reverie, her own little dream world, which consists of a game of tennis. It is a mixed doubles match; she is the ball. Jane sits motionless and silent and eats only when fed. The adults in the family are in a state of conflict, her father and his mother being ranged against her mother and her mother's father. The two halves of the family communicate only through Jane; she is the go-between. The strain eventually becomes too much for her and she escapes into her dream world. However, as her 'dream' shows, even in this world she cannot escape from the clutches of the family. The game of tennis symbolizes the interaction patterns in the family.

With examples such as this, Laing shows how the family can be a destructive and exploitative institution.

Laing refers to the family group as a nexus. He argues that 'the highest concern of the nexus is reciprocal concern. Each partner is concerned about what the other thinks, feels, does' (Laing, 1962). Within the nexus there is a constant, unremitting demand for mutual concern and attention. As a result there is considerable potential for harm: family members are in an extremely vulnerable position.

Thus, if a father is ashamed of his son, given the nature of the nexus, his son is deeply affected. As he is emotionally locked into the nexus, he is concerned about his father's opinion and cannot brush it off lightly. In self-defence he may run to his mother who offers protection. In this way, Laing argues that 'A family can act as gangsters, offering each other mutual protection against each other's violence.'

Reciprocal interiorization

From interaction within the nexus, reciprocal interiorization develops: family members become a part of each other and the family as a whole. They interiorize or internalize the family. Laing argues that 'To be in the same family is to feel the same "family" inside' (Laing, 1971). The example of Jane illustrates this process – her little world is an interiorization of family interaction patterns.

Laing regards the process of interiorization as psychologically damaging since it restricts the development of the self. Individuals carry the blueprint of their family with them for the rest of their life. This prevents any real autonomy or freedom of self; it prevents the development of the individual in his or her own right. Self-awareness is smothered under the blanket of the family. As a result of family interiorization, Laing states, 'I consider most adults (including myself) are or have been more or less in a hypnotic trance induced in early infancy' (Laing, 1971).

The family 'ghetto'

Like Leach, Laing argues that problems in the family create problems in society. Due to the nature of the nexus and the process of interiorization, a boundary or even a defensive barrier is drawn between the family and the world outside. This can reach the point where 'Some families live in perpetual anxiety of what, to them, is an external persecuting world. The members of the family live in a family ghetto as it were' (Laing, 1962). Laing argues that this is one reason for so-called maternal over-protection. However, 'It is not "over" protection from the mother's point of view, nor, indeed, often from the point of view of other members of the family.'

This perception of the external threat of a menacing society tends to unite and strengthen the nexus. The barrier erected between the family and the world outside may have important consequences. According to Laing, it leads family members, particularly children, to see the world in terms of 'us and them'. From this basic division stem the harmful and dangerous distinctions between Gentile and Jew, black and white, and the separation of others into 'people like us' and 'people like them'.

Within the family children learn to obey their parents. Laing regards this as the primary link in a dangerous chain. Patterns of obedience laid down in early childhood form the basis for obedience to authority in later life. They lead to soldiers and officials blindly and unquestioningly following orders. Laing implies that without family obedience training, people would question orders, follow their own judgement and make their own decisions. If this were so, American soldiers might not have marched off to fight what Laing regards as a senseless war in Vietnam in the 1960s, and we might no longer live in a society which Laing believes is largely insane.

Despite Laing's preoccupation with the dark side of family life, he stated in an interview with David Cohen in 1977:

> I enjoy living in a family. I think the family is still the best thing that still exists biologically as a natural thing. My attack on the family is aimed at the way I felt many children are subjected to gross forms of violence and violation of their rights, to humiliation at the hands of adults who don't know what they're doing.
>
> Quoted in Cohen, 1977, pp. 216–17

Criticisms of Leach and Laing

Leach and Laing in their different ways have presented a radical alternative to the functionalist perspective on the family, but their work is open to a number of criticisms:

1   Neither has conducted detailed fieldwork on the family in contemporary industrial society and in fact Laing's research is limited to investigations of families in which one member has been defined as schizophrenic.

2   Both talk about 'the family' with little reference to its position in the social structure. For example, there is no reference to social class in Laing's work and therefore no indication of the relationship between class and family life.

3   Leach examined the family over time, but the work of Laing lacks any historical perspective.

4   Both authors examine the Western family from their particular specialized knowledge: Leach from his work on family and kinship in small-scale non-Western societies, and Laing from his study of schizophrenia and family life. This inevitably colours their views. In itself, this is not a criticism, but it is important to be aware of the source of their perspectives.

5   To some degree, Leach and Laing both begin with a picture of a society out of control or even gone mad. Leach, in *A Runaway World?* (1967), implies that society has got out of hand; Laing goes even further by suggesting that many aspects of contemporary society are insane. Such views of society will produce what many consider to be an extreme and unbalanced picture of the family. However, it is possible to accuse the functionalists of the opposite bias. For example, Parsons gave the impression of an immensely reasonable society ticking over like clockwork. In this context a well-adjusted, contented family is to be expected.

Leach and Laing have provided a balance to the functionalist view which has dominated sociological thinking on the family for many years. Laing, in particular, has given important insights into interaction patterns within the family. In doing so he may, as D.H.J. Morgan suggests, have come 'closer to family life as it is actually experienced than do many of the more orthodox presentations' (Morgan, 1975).

In the next section we will consider the Marxist view of the family.

Marxist perspectives on the family

Friedrich Engels – the origin of the family

The earliest view of the family developed from a Marxist perspective is contained in Friedrich Engels's *The Origin of the Family, Private Property and the State* (Engels, 1972, first published 1884).

Like many nineteenth-century scholars, Engels took an evolutionary view of the family, attempting to trace its origin and evolution through time. He combined an evolutionary approach with Marxist theory, arguing that, as the mode of production changed, so did the family.

During the early stages of human evolution, Engels believed that the means of production were communally owned and the family as such did not exist. This era of primitive communism was characterized by promiscuity. There were no rules limiting sexual relationships and society was, in effect, the family.

Although Engels has been criticized for this type of speculation, the anthropologist Kathleen Gough argues that his picture may not be that far from the truth. She notes that the nearest relatives to human beings, the chimpanzees, live in 'promiscuous hordes', and this may have been the pattern for early humans.

The evolution of the family

Engels argued that, throughout human history, more and more restrictions were placed on sexual relationships and the production of children. He speculated that, from the promiscuous horde, marriage and the family evolved through a series of stages, which included polygyny, to its present stage, the monogamous nuclear family. Each successive stage placed greater restrictions on the number of mates available to the individual.

The monogamous nuclear family developed with the emergence of private property, in particular the private ownership of the means of production, and the advent of the state. The state instituted laws to protect the system of private property and to enforce the rules of monogamous marriage. This form of marriage and the family developed to solve the problem of the inheritance of private property. Property was owned by males and, in order for them to pass it on to their heirs, they had to be certain of the legitimacy of those heirs. They therefore needed greater control over women so that there would be no doubt about the paternity of the offspring. The monogamous family provided the most efficient device for this purpose. In Engels's words:

> It is based on the supremacy of the man, the express purpose being to produce children of undisputed paternity; such paternity is demanded because these children are later to come into their father's property as his natural heirs.
>
> Engels, 1972

Evidence for Engels's views

Engels's scheme of the evolution of the family is much more elaborate than the brief outline described above. It was largely based on *Ancient Society*, an erroneous interpretation of the evolution of the family by the nineteenth-century American anthropologist, Lewis Henry Morgan. Modern research has suggested that many of its details are incorrect. For example, monogamous marriage and the nuclear family are often found in hunting and gathering bands. Since humanity has lived in hunting and gathering bands for the vast majority of its existence, the various forms of group marriage postulated by Engels (such as the promiscuous horde) may well be figments of his imagination.

However, Gough argues that 'the general trend of Engels's argument still appears sound' (Gough, 1972). Although nuclear families and monogamous marriage exist in small-scale societies, they form a part of a larger kinship group. When individuals marry they take on a series of duties and obligations to their spouse's kin. Communities are united by kinship ties and the result is like a large extended family. Gough argues that:

> It is true that although it is not a group marriage in Engels's sense, marriage has a group character in many hunting bands and in most of the more complex tribal societies that have developed with the domestication of plants and animals. With the

> development of privately owned, heritable property, and especially with the rise of the state, this group character gradually disappears.
>
> Gough, 1972

(Further aspects of Engels's views on the family are examined in Chapter 3, p. 142.)

Eli Zaretsky – personal life and capitalism

Eli Zaretsky (1976) has analysed more recent developments in the family from a Marxist perspective. He argues that the family in modern capitalist society creates the illusion that the 'private life' of the family is quite separate from the economy. Before the early nineteenth century the family was the basic unit of production. For example, in the early capitalist textile industry, production of cloth took place in the home and involved all family members. Only with the development of factory-based production were work and family life separated.

In a society in which work was alienating, Zaretsky claims that the family was put on a pedestal because it apparently 'stood in opposition to the terrible anonymous world of commerce and industry'. The private life of the family provided opportunities for satisfactions that were unavailable outside the walls of the home.

Zaretsky welcomes the increased possibilities for a personal life for the proletariat offered by the reduction in working hours since the nineteenth century. However, he believes that the family is unable to provide for the psychological and personal needs of individuals. He says 'it simply cannot meet the pressures of being the only refuge in a brutal society'. The family artificially separates and isolates personal life from other aspects of life. It might cushion the effects of capitalism but it perpetuates the system and cannot compensate for the general alienation produced by such a society.

Furthermore, Zaretsky sees the family as a major prop to the capitalist economy. The capitalist system is based upon the domestic labour of housewives who reproduce future generations of workers. He also believes that the family has become a vital unit of consumption. The family consumes the products of capitalism and this allows the bourgeoisie to continue producing surplus value. To Zaretsky, only socialism will end the artificial separation of family private life and public life, and produce the possibility of personal fulfilment.

Next we will examine the family from a feminist viewpoint.

Feminist perspectives on the family

The influence of feminism

In recent decades feminism has probably had more influence on the study of the family than any other approach to understanding society. Like Laing, Leach and Marxists, feminists have been highly critical of the family. However, unlike other critics, they have tended to emphasize the harmful effects of family life upon women. In doing so they have developed new perspectives and highlighted new issues.

Feminists have, for example, introduced the study of areas of family life such as housework and domestic violence into sociology. They have challenged some widely-held views about the inevitability of male dominance in families and have questioned the view that family life is becoming more egalitarian. Feminists have also highlighted the economic contribution to society made by women's domestic labour within the family. Above all, feminist theory has encouraged sociologists to see the family as an institution involving power relationships. It has challenged the image of family life as being based upon cooperation, shared interests and love, and has tried to show that some family members, in particular men, obtain greater benefits from families than others.

Recently, some feminists have questioned the tendency of other feminists to make blanket condemnations of family life and have emphasized the different experiences of women in families. Some have rejected the idea that there is such a thing as 'the family' rather than simply different domestic arrangements. They have, however, continued to identify ways in which domestic life can disadvantage women.

In later sections of this chapter we will consider the impact of feminism on the study of conjugal roles, domestic labour, social policy and marriage. In the next section, however, we will examine some of the feminist theoretical approaches to understanding the family.

Marxist feminist perspectives on the family

Marxists such as Engels and Zaretsky have acknowledged that women are exploited in marriage and family life but they have emphasized the relationship between capitalism and the family, rather than the family's effects on women. Marxist feminists use Marxist concepts but see the exploitation of women as a key feature of family life. The next few sections will examine how these theories have been applied to the family. (More details of the Marxist feminist approach can be found in Chapter 3, pp. 148–50.)

The production of labour power

Margaret Benston stated that:

> *The amount of unpaid labor performed by women is very large and very profitable to those who own the means of production. To pay women for their work, even at minimum wage scales, would involve a massive redistribution of wealth. At present, the support of the family is a hidden tax on the wage earner – his wage buys the labor power of two people.*
>
> Benston, 1972

The fact that the husband must pay for the production and upkeep of future labour acts as a strong discipline on his behaviour at work. He cannot easily withdraw his labour with a wife and children to support. These responsibilities weaken his bargaining power and commit him to wage labour. Benston argues that:

> *As an economic unit, the nuclear family is a valuable stabilizing force in capitalist society. Since the production which is done in the home is paid for by the husband–father's earnings, his ability to withhold labour from the market is much reduced.*
>
> Benston, 1972

Not only does the family produce and rear cheap labour, it also maintains it at no cost to the employer. In her role as housewife, the woman attends to her husband's needs, thus keeping him in good running order to perform his role as a wage labourer.

Fran Ansley (1972) translates Parsons's view, that the family functions to stabilize adult personalities, into a Marxist framework. She sees the emotional support provided by the wife as a safety valve for the frustration produced in the husband by working in a capitalist system. Rather than being turned against the system which produced it, this frustration is absorbed by the comforting wife. In this way the system is not threatened. In Ansley's words:

When wives play their traditional role as takers of shit, they often absorb their husbands' legitimate anger and frustration at their own powerlessness and oppression. With every worker provided with a sponge to soak up his possibly revolutionary ire, the bosses rest more secure.

Quoted in Bernard, 1976, p. 233

Kathy McAfee and Myrna Wood make a similar point in their discussion of male dominance in the family. They claim that 'The petty dictatorship which most men exercise over their wives and families enables them to vent their anger and frustration in a way which poses no challenge to the system' (quoted in Rowbotham, 1973).

Ideological conditioning

The social reproduction of labour power does not simply involve producing children and maintaining them in good health. It also involves the reproduction of the attitudes essential for an efficient workforce under capitalism. Thus, David Cooper argues that the family is 'an ideological conditioning device in an exploitive society' (Cooper 1972). Within the family, children learn to conform and to submit to authority. The foundation is therefore laid for the obedient and submissive workforce required by capitalism.

A similar point is made by Diane Feeley (1972), who argues that the structure of family relationships socializes the young to accept their place in a class-stratified society. She sees the family as an authoritarian unit dominated by the husband in particular and adults in general. Feeley claims that the family with its 'authoritarian ideology is designed to teach passivity, not rebellion'. Thus children learn to submit to parental authority and emerge from the family preconditioned to accept their place in the hierarchy of power and control in capitalist society.

(Marxist views on the role of the family in capitalist society mirror Marxist analysis of the role of education – see Chapter 11.)

Criticisms

Some of the criticisms of previous views of the family also apply to Marxist approaches. There is a tendency to talk about 'the family' in capitalist society without regard to possible variations in family life between social classes, ethnic groups, heterosexual and gay and lesbian families, lone-parent families, and over time. As D.H.J. Morgan notes in his criticism of both functionalist and Marxist approaches, both 'presuppose a traditional model of the nuclear family where there is a married couple with children, where the husband is the breadwinner and where the wife stays at home to deal with the housework' (Morgan, 1975). This pattern is becoming less common and the critique of this type of family may therefore be becoming less important.

Marxist feminists may therefore exaggerate the harm caused to women by families and may neglect the effects of non-family relationships (apart from class) on exploitation within marriage. Thus, for example, they say little about how the experience of racism might influence families. They also tend to portray female family members as the passive victims of capitalist and patriarchal exploitation. They ignore the possibility that women may have fought back against such exploitation and had some success in changing the nature of family relationships. Furthermore, they are not usually prepared to concede that there may be positive elements to family life. As we shall see, difference feminists are more prepared to accept that there may be some positive advantages for some women, in some families.

Radical feminist perspectives on the family

There are many varieties of radical feminism. As Valerie Bryson says, 'the radical feminist label has been applied in recent years to a confusingly diverse range of theories' (Bryson, 1992). She says 'it is the site for far ranging disagreements at all levels of theory and practice'. However, Bryson does identify some key characteristics which distinguish radical feminists from other feminists:

1 'It is essentially a theory of, by and for women' and therefore 'sees no need to compromise with existing perspectives and agendas'. Radical feminist ideas

tend to be novel rather than adaptations of other theories such as Marxism.

2 'It sees the oppression of women as the most fundamental and universal form of domination'. Society is seen as patriarchal, or male-dominated, rather than capitalist, and women are held to have different interests to those of men.

Radical feminists do not agree on the source of male domination, but most do see the family as important in maintaining male power. We will now analyse one major radical feminist theory of the family.

Christine Delphy and Diana Leonard
– Familiar Exploitation

Types of feminism

Delphy and Leonard (1992) are unlike most radical feminists in that they attach considerable importance to material factors in causing women's oppression. In this respect they have some similarity with Marxist feminist theories. In particular, Delphy and Leonard attach special importance to work and say that their approach 'uses Marxist methodology'. Nevertheless, they see themselves as radical feminists since they believe that it is men, rather than capitalists or capitalism, who are the primary beneficiaries of the exploitation of women's labour. To them, the family has a central role in maintaining patriarchy. They say:

> We see the familial basis of domestic groups as an important element in continuing the patriarchal nature of our society: that is, in the continuance of men's dominance over women and children.
>
> Delphy and Leonard, 1992

The family as an economic system

Delphy and Leonard see the family as an economic system. It involves a particular set of 'labour relations in which men benefit from, and exploit, the work of women – and sometimes that of their children and other male relatives'. The key to this exploitation is that family members work not for themselves but for the head of the household. Women in particular are oppressed, not because they are socialized into being passive, nor because they are ideologically conditioned into subservience, but because their work is appropriated within the family. Delphy and Leonard argue that 'It is primarily the *work* women do, the uses to which our bodies can be put, which constitutes the reason for our oppression.'

Delphy and Leonard identify the following features as the main characteristics of the family as an economic system:

1 Every family-based household has a social structure that involves two types of role. These are head of household and their dependents or helpers. Family households have members who are connected by kinship or marriage. Female heads of household are uncommon. Figures indicate that only about one in ten adult women in Britain aged 16 to 60 heads a household. Most of these women are single or widows and there are no other adults present. Only one in 25 women aged 16 to 60 heads a household which contains other adults. Where a male adult relative is present it is usually he who takes over as head of household. In the case of married women, even if she has the main income and owns the house, 'she is at least semi-subordinate, owing her husband respect and obedience and having responsibility for domestic (and sexual and emotional) labour'.

2 The male head of household is different from other members because he 'decides what needs doing in a given situation' and assigns tasks to other members or delegates to them. Other family members may change his mind about decisions, but it is his mind to change. He makes the final decision.

3 The head of household provides maintenance for other family members, and they receive a share of family property on his death. However, they have to work for him unpaid.

4 The type and amount of work family members have to do are related to sex and marital status. Female relatives have to do unpaid domestic work; wives in addition have to carry out 'sexual and reproductive work'. Although the precise allocation of tasks varies from household to household, domestic work remains a female responsibility.

5 Money and resources for maintenance, and money inherited by dependents, are not related to the amount of work done. A man must provide for his dependents' basic needs, and may be very generous, but, unlike an employer, he does not purchase labour power by the hour, week or amount produced. The amounts inherited by family members are more related to position – with, for example, sons inheriting more than daughters – than to work.

6 The relations of production within the family often, therefore, involve payment in kind (such as a new coat or a holiday) rather than payment in money.

7 The economic relationships rarely involve formal contracts or bargaining. This means that family members must use informal methods of negotiation. For example, 'Wives and children have to study their husbands and fathers closely and handle them carefully so as to keep them sweet'. The male heads have to find informal ways of motivating their workers and, if possible, 'foster their subordinates' feelings of affection for them'.

8 'The head of the family may have a near monopoly over, and he always has greater access to and control of, the family's property and external relations.'

9 When dependents, particularly wives, have paid employment outside the home they still have to carry out household tasks, or pay others out of their wages to do housework or care for children for them.

Domestic labour

Having outlined how the family works as an economic system, Delphy and Leonard go on to examine in more detail who contributes to and who benefits from family life. They admit that most men do some housework but that such tasks are usually done by women. They claim that 'time-budget studies show ... that the amount of time women spend on domestic work has not declined this century and they still do twice as much each day as men in all western and eastern bloc countries even when they have paid employment'. Furthermore, there is 'a clear order of responsibility to care for children, the sick and elderly'. This responsibility always falls on female relatives, where they are available, except in special circumstances (for example, if the wife is disabled).

On the other hand, when men marry, they end up doing only half the housework they did as bachelors. However much they may decide to 'help' their wives, husbands do not assume responsibility for housework.

Supporting husbands

As well as carrying out housework and caring for children, the sick and older people, women also contribute a great deal to their husbands' work and leisure by providing 'for their emotional and sexual well-being'. Drawing on the work of a British sociologist, Janet Finch, Delphy and Leonard describe some of the types of help provided by wives. Sometimes they provide direct help – for example, doing office work for a self-employed husband, proofreading books if their husband is an author, or doing constituency work if he is an MP. They may stay at home to answer the phone or arrange dinner parties for colleagues of their husband.

Wives also give moral support, 'observing and moderating his emotions, arranging entertainment and relaxation, and supplying personal needs'. Wives are there to listen when their husbands unburden themselves of their work problems. They provide 'trouble-free sex', which is important since 'men frequently unwind best post-coitally'. Wives also make the house into a home so that it is 'comfortable, warm and undemanding'. Women even control their own emotions so that they can provide emotional care for husbands. They 'flatter, excuse, boost, sympathize and pay attention to men', all to give them a sense of well-being.

In contrast, men make little contribution to their wives' work. They find it 'psychologically, socially or legally impossible' to work under their wives' direction. They might give some assistance to working wives, but the husband's career remains the central one.

Consumption

Delphy and Leonard believe, then, that wives contribute much more work to family life than their husbands. Despite this, they get fewer of the material benefits of family life than men. Men retain ultimate responsibility for family finances, and women consume less than male family members. The (usually) male head of household has the 'decision-making

power' to determine what goods are produced or bought for the family and who uses them. For instance, 'the food bought is the sort *he* likes, and he gets more of it and the best bits'. Husbands get more leisure time, more access to the family car, or to the best car if there is more than one; and sons get more spent on their education than daughters. In every area of family consumption it is the status of different family members which shapes who gets what.

Empirical evidence

Delphy and Leonard use four main sources to try to back up their claims. Three of these are studies of British factory workers and their families. They use Goldthorpe and Lockwood's 1962 study of affluent workers in Luton (see pp. 79–81 for further details), a 1970s study of 500 workers and their wives in a Bristol company which made cardboard packing cases, and a 1980s study of redundant steel workers in Port Talbot, Wales. They also use data from Christine Delphy's own studies of French farming families.

Although the studies did not always contain the data needed to test their theories, they found support for their arguments in a number of areas. The following are a few examples:

1 In Bristol, the researchers found that husbands did not want their wives to take paid employment and often discouraged them from doing so. Wives had little influence on their husbands' patterns of work.

2 In Port Talbot, most men strongly resisted doing housework, even though they were unemployed. They saw redundancy as a threat to their masculinity and did not want it further undermined by doing 'women's' jobs in the house. Only 25 per cent of the sample gave more than occasional help with housework and in no case did the husband take the main burden of housework. The Port Talbot study also found that the husband usually retained control of the family finances.

3 Delphy's research revealed that wives' labour was vital to the success of French farms. Farms owned by bachelors enjoyed considerably less success than those owned by married men. Nevertheless, wives had little autonomy and were given the 'arduous, least-valued tasks'. Wives had very little say in how the farm was run and farms were usually handed down to sons.

Conclusion and summary

Delphy and Leonard believe that the family is a patriarchal and hierarchical institution through which men dominate and exploit women. Men are usually the head of household, and it is the head who benefits from the work that gets done. Women provide '57 varieties of unpaid service' for men, including providing them with a 'pliant sexual partner and children if he wants them'. Wives do sometimes resist their husband's dominance – they are not always passive victims – but 'economic and social constraints' make it difficult for women to escape from the patriarchal family.

Delphy and Leonard do not think that there are simple solutions to the problems created by the family. Individual men may love their wives, but that does not stop them from exploiting them. Single mothers cannot escape from patriarchy 'because they are often poor and their situation is always difficult'. Lesbians 'may be downright ostracized and physically attacked'. In the end, they admit that they do not know what strategy feminists should use to change the family, but they believe that women should continue to struggle to improve their lives, both inside and outside family life.

Evaluation

Delphy and Leonard provide a comprehensive analysis of the family from a radical feminist perspective. They highlight many ways in which the family can produce or reinforce inequalities between women and men. However, their work can be criticized both theoretically and empirically:

1 Theoretically, Delphy and Leonard do not succeed in demonstrating that inequality is built into the structure of the family. Their argument is based upon the assumption that *all* families have a head, usually a man, and it is the head who ultimately benefits from family life. However, they do not show theoretically or empirically that all families have a head who has more power than other family members. They fail to acknowledge that there may be some families in which power is shared. It may well be possible to find inequalities in every household, but that does not necessarily mean that one person is dominant. Ironically, they make similar, false assumptions to those found in the work of the functionalist George Peter Murdock (see pp. 504–6).

2 Empirically, their work is based upon unrepresentative data. The three British studies used are all of manual workers, and two of them are rather dated. Most researchers have found less gender inequality in middle-class families than in working-class families, so these studies may have an in-built bias towards supporting their theory. Furthermore, they were not specifically directed at testing Delphy and Leonard's theory. The relevant data are often therefore absent from the research.

3 Delphy's study of French farming families was specifically directed at testing their theories, but farming families are hardly typical of other families. Family members tend to work in the family business – the farm – and few wives have an independent source of income which could reduce marital inequality.

Delphy and Leonard tend to make rather sweeping statements about inequality which may not apply equally to all families. In doing so they perhaps overstate their case by denying the possibility of exceptions.

Laura M. Purdy – 'Babystrike!'

Feminism and motherhood

Like Delphy and Leonard, Laura M. Purdy (1997) believes that women are disadvantaged and exploited in family relationships. Unlike Delphy and Leonard, she believes that these disadvantages largely result from childcare responsibilities rather than from material inequalities. Purdy argues that in recent years feminists have placed less emphasis on criticisms of families and marriage, while issues such as pornography and sexual harassment have come to be seen as more important. She says, 'critiques of marriage and family seem almost forgotten as feminists, like society at large, now seem generally to assume that all women – including lesbians – will pair up and have children'. Some recent accounts of the family in the popular media suggest that it is possible for women to 'have it all'. They can combine a successful career with a rewarding family life and successful and satisfying child-rearing. Purdy questions whether it is really possible to 'have it all' and whether family life in general, and child-rearing in particular, are really the paths to female self-fulfilment.

Purdy suggests that it is generally assumed that women should want to form couples (whether hetero-sexual or lesbian) and have children. Couples who choose not to have children are thought of as eccentric and selfish. Young women never 'hear that some people shouldn't have children, either because they don't really want them, because they are not able to care for them well, or because they have other projects that are incompatible with good child-rearing'. Purdy believes that feminism should try to counter the assumption that having children is necessarily desirable.

The disadvantages of motherhood

According to Purdy, there are a number of disadvantages for women in having children. Having children is extremely expensive and can increase the burden of poverty on women who are already poor. Having children represents a commitment for women for the rest of their lives, and a particularly onerous commitment during the first 18 years. According to an American study quoted by Purdy, men still do only 20 per cent of domestic work, despite big increases in female employment. This makes it very difficult for women to compete on equal terms in the labour market or to try to fight for greater equality. She asks, 'How can women energetically fight the entrenched sexism in society and pursue positions of power and prestige if their time and energy is mostly taken up with children's needs, needs that cannot and ought not be ignored?'

Purdy believes that society in general takes it for granted that women will have children and therefore perform the vital function of reproducing the species. The only way to bring home to men the sacrifices of child-rearing is for women to stop having children. In other words, Purdy advocates a babystrike. Only then would men take women's demands for equality within families seriously. Only then would social arrangements change so that women were able to combine having children with successful careers.

Evaluation

The idea of a babystrike is a novel suggestion for focusing male attention on the disadvantages suffered by women. Purdy makes an important point in drawing attention to the particular problems posed for women by the responsibilities of childcare. However, she places perhaps too much emphasis on one factor – that of child-rearing – in creating and perpetuating women's disadvantages in families. Other feminists, perhaps with some justification, would not accept that children are the only, or even the main, reason for women being unequal within families. They certainly would not accept that women only start to suffer inequality once they have children. Like a number of other theorists of the family, Purdy may exaggerate the effects of one particular source of inequality while neglecting others.

Difference feminism

Neither Marxist nor radical feminism is particularly sensitive to variations between families. Both approaches tend to assume that families in general disadvantage women and benefit men (and, in the case of Marxist approaches, benefit capitalism). Both can be criticized for failing to acknowledge the variety of domestic arrangements produced by different groups, and the range of effects that family life can have.

Increasingly, however, feminists have begun to highlight the differences between groups of women in different family situations. Thus, they have argued that women in single-parent families are in a different situation to women in two-parent families; women in lesbian families are in a different position to women in heterosexual families; black women are often in a different family position to white women; poor women are in a different position to middle-class women, and so on. Feminists who analyse the family in these terms have sometimes been referred to as 'difference feminists'. Difference feminists have been influenced by a range of feminist theories including liberal feminism (see pp. 136–9), Marxist feminism and radical feminism. Their work often has affinities with postmodern theories of the family (see pp. 582–4) and with ideas relating to family diversity (see pp. 537–49). However, they share a sufficiently distinctive approach to be considered a separate feminist perspective on the family.

Michèlle Barrett and Mary McIntosh – *The Anti-social Family*

One of the earliest examples of a theory of the family put forward by difference feminists is provided by the work of Michèlle Barrett and Mary McIntosh (1982). Their work was influenced by Marxist feminism but moves beyond the kinds of Marxist feminist views discussed earlier (see pp. 514–15). Barrett and McIntosh believe that the idea of 'the family' is misleading, given the wide variations that exist in life within families and the varieties of household types in which people live. (Family and household diversity is discussed on pp. 537–49.) If there is no one normal or typical family type, then it may be impossible to claim that the family always performs particular functions either for men or for capitalism.

The 'anti-social' family

Barrett and McIntosh do believe that there is a very strong ideology supporting family life. To them 'the family' is 'anti-social' not just because it exploits women, and benefits capitalists, but also because the ideology of the family destroys life outside the family. They say 'the family ideal makes everything else seem pale and unsatisfactory'. People outside families suffer as a consequence. Family members are so wrapped up in family life that they neglect social contact with others. 'Couples mix with other couples, finding it difficult to fit single people in.'

Life in other institutions (such as children's homes, old people's homes and students' residences) comes to be seen as shallow and lacking in meaning. Barrett and McIntosh argue that homes for the handicapped could be far more stimulating for, say, Down's syndrome sufferers, if it were not for life in institutions being devalued by the ideology of the family.

Like other feminists, they point out that the image of the family as involving love and mutual care tends to ignore the amount of violent and sexual crime that takes place within a family context. They note that 25 per cent of reported violent crimes consist of assaults by husbands on their wives, and many rapes take place within marriage.

They do not deny that there can be caring relationships within families, but equally they do not think that families are the only places in which such relationships can develop. In their view, the ideology that idealizes family life:

> *has made the outside world cold and friendless, and made it harder to maintain relationships of security and trust except with kin. Caring, sharing and loving would all be more widespread if the family did not claim them for its own.*
>
> Barrett and McIntosh, 1982

Linda Nicholson – 'The myth of the traditional family'

Like Barrett and McIntosh, Linda Nicholson (1997) believes that there is a powerful ideology which gives support to a positive image of family life. She argues that this ideology only supports certain types of family while devaluing other types. Nicholson contrasts what she calls the 'traditional' family with 'alternative' families. She is an American feminist and her comments largely refer to the USA, but they may be applicable more generally to Western societies.

The 'traditional' family

Nicholson defines the traditional family as 'the unit of parents with children who live together'. The bond between husband and wife is seen as particularly important, and the family feels itself to be separate from other kin. This family group is often referred to as the nuclear family (see pp. 524–5). When conservative social commentators express concern about the decline of the family, it is this sort of family they are concerned about. They tend to be less worried about any decline of wider kinship links involving grandparents, aunts, uncles and so on.

According to Nicholson, the nuclear family is a comparatively recent phenomenon. It first developed among upper classes in the eighteenth century. For middle-class groups this type of family only became popular in the nineteenth century. Working-class people often aspired to form nuclear families in the nineteenth century, but their low income usually prevented them from doing so. They frequently had to share accommodation with others from outside the nuclear family. Indeed, it was not really until the 1950s and the post-Second World War boom that nuclear family households became the norm for working-class families. Thus Nicholson argues that the conventional family is actually a very recent phenomenon for most people.

However, even in the 1950s, some groups lacked the resources to form nuclear families. This was the case for people with few or outdated skills and for many African Americans who were the victims of racism in the labour market.

Alternative families

Alternative family forms were already developing even before the traditional family reached its zenith. Nicholson says that:

> *even as a certain ideal of family was coming to define 'the American way of life', such trends as a rising divorce rate, increased participation of married women in the labor force, and the growth of female-headed households were making this way of life increasingly atypical. In all cases such trends preceded the 1950s.*
>
> Nicholson, 1997, p. 35

Some of these changes actually altered what was perceived as a 'traditional' family. For example, it came to be seen as 'normal' for married women to work, even if they and their partners had small children. Other changes, though, were seen as producing alternative families. Alternatives to traditional families included, 'Not only gays and lesbians but heterosexuals living alone; married couples with husbands at home caring for children', as well as stepfamilies, single parents, heterosexual couples living together outside marriage, and gay or lesbian couples with or without children.

The merits of different family types

Alternative families, or alternatives to traditional families, tend to be devalued. They are seen as less worthy than traditional families. However, Nicholson rejects this view. Alternative families are often better than traditional ones for the women who live in them. For example, poor black women in the USA derive some benefits when they live in mother-centred families, often without men. They develop strong support networks with other friends and kin, who act as a kind of social insurance system. They help out the families who are most in need at a particular time if they are in a position to do so.

Such families do have disadvantages. If they have some good fortune and come into money, each family is expected to share resources. This makes it difficult for individual families to escape poverty. Furthermore, the lack of stable heterosexual partnerships means that 'children frequently do not have the type of long-term relationships with father figures which is normative within middle-class households'.

Traditional families also have advantages and disadvantages. Because both partners now tend to work, they have tremendous time pressures, making it difficult to carry out satisfactory and rewarding childcare. Children who are the victims of abuse by parents have relatively little opportunity to turn to other relatives for help. Traditional families place a heavy burden of expectation on the partners, and, with work and childcare commitments, it may be difficult for them to provide the love and companionship each partner expects. The traditional family also precludes and excludes gay and lesbian relationships.

However, traditional families do have some advantages. Their small size tends to encourage intimacy between family members, and, when the relationships work, they can be rewarding and long-lasting.

Traditional families can be economically successful because they are not under strong requirements to share their resources with others.

Conclusion

The fact that they have some advantages does not mean that traditional families are better than alternative types. From Nicholson's point of view, different types of family suit different women in different circumstances. She believes that the distinction between traditional and alternative families should be abandoned. The distinction implies that traditional families are better, when this is often not true. In any case, the idea of the traditional family misleadingly implies that such families have long been the norm, when in fact they have only become popular in recent times, and have never been totally dominant.

By the late 1990s so many people lived in alternatives to traditional families that the idea of the traditional family had become totally outdated. Nicholson therefore concludes that all types of family and household should be acknowledged and accepted because they could suit women in different circumstances. She advocates the celebration of greater choice for people in deciding on their own living arrangements.

Cheshire Calhoun – lesbians as family outlaws

Like Linda Nicholson, Cheshire Calhoun develops a type of difference feminism influenced by postmodernism (Calhoun, 1997). Unlike Nicholson, she focuses on lesbian families rather than looking at the merits of a variety of family forms for women. Calhoun is a postmodern, difference feminist from the United States.

Calhoun argues that feminist theories have generally neglected sexual orientation as a source of oppression distinct from gender oppression. However, Nicholson believes that sexual orientation can be an important source of oppression and that family ideology contributes to that oppression.

Conventional feminist views

Calhoun starts by noting conventional feminist views on the family. Such views see the family as an important source of female oppression for a variety of reasons. These include the ways in which families make women financially dependent upon men, the way family ideology encourages women to put the family before their own interests, inequalities in the amount of domestic work done by men and women, and the way in which family ideology 'often masks gender injustice within the family including battery, rape and child abuse'.

Calhoun accepts that this sort of feminist analysis is accurate but says that 'This picture ... is not, in fact, a picture of *women's* relation to the family, but is more narrowly a picture of *heterosexual* women's relation to the family, marriage and mothering.' Lesbians who live outside heterosexual families can hardly be directly exploited by relationships within such families. Indeed lesbians are uniquely placed to avoid dependence on men within families. However, Calhoun does believe that they are disadvantaged by the ideology of the heterosexual family.

Some lesbian feminists have argued that lesbians should avoid forming families. They have argued that, because women are exploited in heterosexual marriages, marriage and family life are inevitably patriarchal. Similarly they have argued that, because mothering disadvantages heterosexual women – by, for example, limiting their opportunities in the labour market – lesbian women should also avoid becoming mothers. Calhoun disagrees. She believes that it is not family life itself that leads to the exploitation of women, rather it is family life within patriarchal, heterosexual marriages that is the problem. Lesbian marriage and mothering can avoid the exploitative relationships typical of heterosexual marriage. Indeed, lesbian partners may be able to develop forms of marriage and family life which can point the way to creating more egalitarian domestic relationships.

This view is in stark contrast to a more conventional view that lesbians and gays cannot develop proper marriages or construct genuine families. According to Calhoun, gays and lesbians have historically been portrayed as 'family outlaws'. Their sexuality has been seen as threatening to the family. They have been portrayed as 'outsiders to the family and as displaying the most virulent forms of family-disrupting behaviour'. However, Calhoun believes that the anxiety among heterosexuals about gays and lesbians has in fact been caused by anxiety about the state of the heterosexual nuclear family. Rather than recognizing and acknowledging the problems with such families, heterosexuals have tried to attribute the problems to corrupting outsiders or outlaws: that is, gays and lesbians.

Crises of heterosexual families

Calhoun believes that there have been three historical periods when heterosexual families have been seen as in crisis and consequently gays and lesbians have become a focus of critical attention:

1 In the period from the 1880s to the 1920s, conventional heterosexual family life was challenged by early feminists who campaigned for greater legal rights for women, such as the right to institute divorce proceedings and the right for married women to own property. Some medical theorists attributed these campaigns to women who were too masculine. They developed 'a new gender category variously labelled the sexual invert, the intermediate sex, the third sex ... the man-woman'. This group of women was distinguished by masculine traits such as short hair, smoking and drinking, being aggressive and so on. Calhoun describes this category as 'the precursor to the contemporary categories "lesbian" and "homosexual"'. Most men were unable to accept that the challenge to male supremacy within the family could be mounted by normal women seeking greater equality, and so blamed it on women who deviated from conventional gender norms.

2 From the 1930s to the 1950s, the economic depression and the Second World War were the main sources of a crisis in heterosexual families. During the depression many men lost their jobs and, with it, their breadwinner role. There was also a drop in marriage rates. During the war there were long separations for many married couples, and divorce and desertion became much more common. To Calhoun, all of this represented a 'cultural crisis in masculinity'. With increasing numbers of men unable to sustain their masculinity through being the breadwinning heads of families, there was a 'shift in the cultural construction of masculinity from being gender-based to being sexuality-based'. The key aspect of masculinity now became being

heterosexual, not being head of a family. The distinction between (desirable) heterosexuality and (undesirable) homosexuality was reinforced in panics about homosexual child molesters in the periods from 1937 to 1940 and from 1949 to 1955. Once again, a crisis in the heterosexual family was blamed on the corrupting influence of homosexual outsiders on conventional family life.

3 In the 1980s and 1990s a whole range of factors undermined heterosexual family life. These included rising divorce rates and single-parent families becoming so common that 'Father's Day cards now include ones addressed to mothers, and others announcing their recipients as "like a dad"'.

Extended kinship networks have become increasingly important for the urban poor, and the idea of the family headed by a heterosexual couple with their offspring has been undermined by new reproductive technology. Calhoun says:

Increasingly sophisticated birth control methods and technologically assisted reproduction using in-vitro fertilization, artificial insemination, contract pregnancy, fertility therapies, and the like undermine cultural understandings of the marital couple as a naturally reproductive unit, introduce nonrelated others into the reproductive process, and make it possible for women and men to have children without a heterosexual partner.

Calhoun, 1997, pp. 142–3

According to Calhoun, modern family life is essentially characterized by choice. Lesbians and gays introduced the idea of chosen families. You can choose who to include in your family without the restrictions of blood ties or the expectation of settling down with and marrying an opposite-sex partner. Now, however, heterosexuals also construct 'chosen families' as they divorce, remarry, separate, choose new partners, adopt children, gain stepchildren and so on.

Rather than seeing the above changes in a positive light, many commentators have seen them as a threat to families and the institution of marriage. This time there have been two main types of family outlaw who have been scapegoated and blamed for the changes. These are 'the unwed welfare mother and ... the lesbian or gay whose mere public visibility threatens to undermine family values and destroy the family'. In Britain, for example, the Local Government Act of the late 1980s made illegal 'the teaching in any maintained school of the acceptability of homosexuality as a pretended family relationship' (quoted in Calhoun, 1997). Similarly, in 1990, the US Congress passed a law prohibiting the federal government from using funds to promote homosexuality.

Conclusion

Calhoun concludes that such scapegoating of lesbians and gays is used to disguise the increasingly frequent departures from the norms of family life by heterosexuals. She says:

> claiming that gay and lesbian families are (or should be) distinctively queer and distinctively deviant helps conceal the deviancy in heterosexual families, and thereby helps to sustain the illusion that heterosexuals are specially entitled to access to a protected private sphere because they, unlike their gay and lesbian counterparts, are supporters of the family.
>
> Calhoun, 1997, p. 146

Thus the ideology of the heterosexual family has played an important part in encouraging discrimination and prejudice against gays and lesbians.

To Calhoun, gay and lesbian relationships, with or without children, are just as much family relationships as those of heterosexual couples. She does not believe that arguing for them to be accepted as such in any way legitimates the heterosexual, patriarchal family that has been so criticized by radical and Marxist feminists. In the contemporary world, heterosexual families engage in 'multiple deviations from norms governing the family'. A wide variety of behaviours and family forms have become common and widely accepted. Accepting gays and lesbians as forming families involves the acceptance of just one more variation from traditional conventional families. It has the potential benefit of reducing the anti-gay and anti-lesbian prejudice that has been promoted in the name of preserving the family.

Difference feminism – conclusion

The feminists discussed in this section all avoid the mistake of making sweeping generalizations about the effects of family life on women. They tend to be sensitive to the different experiences of family life experienced by women of different sexual orientations, ethnic groups, classes and so on (although each writer does not necessarily discuss all the sources of difference that affect how families influence women's lives). In these respects they can be seen as representing theoretical advances upon some of the Marxist and radical theories discussed earlier.

However, *some* difference feminists do sometimes lose sight of the inequalities between men and women in families by stressing the range of choices open to people when they are forming families. By stressing the different experiences of women they tend to neglect the common experiences shared by most women in families. Nevertheless, this general approach may be right to suggest that it is possible (if not common) for both men and women to develop rewarding and fulfilling family relationships.

This section has examined the family from a variety of perspectives. The focus now changes to various themes that are significant to our understanding of the family as a unit of social organization. The first theme is the effect of industrialization and modernization on the family.

The family, industrialization and modernization

The pre-industrial family

A major theme in sociological studies of the family is the relationship between the structure of the family and the related processes of industrialization and modernization. Industrialization refers to the mass production of goods in a factory system which involves some degree of mechanized production technology. Modernization refers to the development of social, cultural, economic and political practices and institutions which are thought to be typical of modern societies. Such developments include the replacement of religious belief systems with scientific and rational ones, the growth of bureaucratic institutions, and the replacement of monarchies with representative democracies (see p. 8 for an introduction to the concept of modernity).

Some sociologists regard industrialization as the central process involved in changes in Western societies since the eighteenth century; others attach more importance to broader processes of modernization. However, there are a number of problems that arise from relating the family to industrialization or modernization:

1 The processes of industrialization and modernization do not follow the same course in every society.

2 Industrialization and modernization are not fixed states but developing processes. Thus the industrial system in nineteenth-century Britain was different in important respects from that of today. Similarly, British culture, society and politics are very different at the turn of the millennium from how they were two hundred years earlier.

3 Some writers dispute that we still live in modern industrial societies and believe that we have moved

into a phase of postmodernity. The issue of the family and postmodernity will be examined later in the chapter (see pp. 582–4).

Further difficulties arise from the fact that there is not one form of pre-industrial, or pre-modern, family, but many.

Much of the research on the family, industrialization and modernization has led to considerable confusion because it is not always clear what the family in modern industrial society is being compared to. In addition, within modern industrial society there are variations in family structure. As a starting point, therefore, it is necessary for us to examine the family in pre-modern, pre-industrial societies in order to establish a standard for comparison.

The family in non-literate societies

In many small-scale, non-literate societies, the family and kinship relationships in general are the basic organizing principles of social life. Societies are often divided into a number of kinship groups, such as lineages, which are groups descended from a common ancestor. The family is embedded in a web of kinship relationships. Kinship groups are responsible for the production of important goods and services. For example, a lineage may own agricultural land which is worked, and its produce shared, by members of the lineage.

Members of kinship groups are united by a network of mutual rights and obligations. In some cases, if individuals are insulted or injured by someone from outside the group, they have the right to call on the support of members of the group in seeking reparation or revenge. Many areas of an individual's behaviour are shaped by his or her status as kin. An uncle, for example, may have binding obligations to be involved with aspects of his nephew's socialization and may be responsible for the welfare of his nieces and nephews should their father die.

Something of the importance of family and kinship relationships in many small-scale societies is illustrated by the following statement by a Pomo Indian of northern California:

> *What is a man? A man is nothing. Without his family he is of less importance than that bug crossing the trail. In the white ways of doing things the family is not so important. The police and soldiers take care of protecting you, the courts give you justice, the post office carries messages for you, the school teaches you. Everything is taken care of, even your children, if you die; but with us the family must do all of that.*
>
> Quoted in Aginsky, 1968

In this brief description of the family in small-scale, pre-industrial society we have glossed over the wide variations in family and kinship patterns which are found in such societies. Even so, it does serve to highlight some of the more important differences between the family in kinship-based society and the family in industrial society.

The 'classic' extended family

A second form of pre-industrial, pre-modern family, sometimes known as the classic extended family, is found in some traditional peasant societies. This family type has been made famous by C.M. Arensberg and S.T. Kimball's study of Irish farmers, entitled *Family and Community in Ireland* (Arensberg and Kimball, 1968).

As in kinship-based societies, kinship ties dominate life, but in this case the basic unit is the extended family rather than the wider kinship grouping. The traditional Irish farming family is a patriarchal extended family, so-called because of the considerable authority of the male head. It is also patrilineal because property is passed down through the male line. Within the family, social and economic roles are welded together, status being ascribed by family membership.

On the farm, the father–son relationship is also that of owner–employee. The father–owner makes all important decisions (such as whether to sell cattle) and directs the activities of all the other members of the extended family. He is head of the family and 'director of the firm'.

Typically, the classic extended family consists of the male head, his wife and children, his ageing parents who have passed on the farm to him, and any unmarried brothers and sisters. Together they work as a 'production unit', producing the goods necessary for the family's survival.

Some people have argued that, as industrialization and modernization proceed, kinship-based society and the classic extended family tend to break up, and the nuclear family – or some form of modified extended family – emerges as the predominant family form.

Talcott Parsons – the 'isolated nuclear family'

Structural isolation

Talcott Parsons argued that the isolated nuclear family is the typical family form in modern industrial society (Parsons, 1959, 1965b, Parsons and Bale, 1955). It is 'structurally isolated' because it does not form an integral part of a wider system of kinship relationships. Obviously there are social relationships between members of nuclear families and their kin but these relationships are more a matter of choice than binding obligations.

Parsons saw the emergence of the isolated nuclear family in terms of his theory of social evolution. (This theory is outlined in Chapter 15.) The evolution of society involves a process of structural differentiation. This simply means that institutions evolve which specialize in fewer functions. As a result, the family and kinship groups no longer perform a wide range of functions. Instead, specialist institutions such as business firms, schools, hospitals, police forces and churches take over many of their functions.

This process of differentiation and specialization involves the 'transfer of a variety of functions from the nuclear family to other structures of the society'. Thus, in modern industrial society, with the transfer of the production of goods to factories, specialized economic institutions became differentiated from the family. The family ceased to be an economic unit of production.

The family and the economy

Functionalist analysis emphasizes the importance of integration and harmony between the various parts of society. An efficient social system requires the parts to fit smoothly rather than abrade. The parts of society are functionally related when they contribute to the integration and harmony of the social system.

Parsons argued that there is a functional relationship between the isolated nuclear family and the economic system in industrial society. In particular, the isolated nuclear family is shaped to meet the requirements of the economic system. A modern industrial system with a specialized division of labour demands considerable geographical mobility from its labour force. Individuals with specialized skills are required to move to places where those skills are in demand. The isolated nuclear family is suited to this need for geographical mobility. It is not tied down by binding obligations to a wide range of kin and, compared to the pre-industrial families described above, it is a small, streamlined unit.

Status in the family

Status in industrial society is achieved rather than ascribed. Individuals' occupational status is not automatically fixed by their ascribed status in the family or kinship group. Parsons argued that the isolated nuclear family is the best form of family structure for a society based on achieved status.

In industrial society, individuals are judged in terms of the status they achieve. Such judgements are based on what Parsons termed universalistic values that is values that are universally applied to all members of society. However, within the family,

status is ascribed and, as such, based on particularistic values, that is values that are applied only to particular individuals. Thus a son's relationship with his father is conducted primarily in terms of their ascribed statuses of father and son. The father's achieved status as a bricklayer, schoolteacher or lawyer has relatively little influence on their relationship since his son does not judge him primarily in terms of universalistic values.

Parsons argued that, in a society based on achieved status, conflict would tend to arise in a family unit larger than the isolated nuclear family. In a three-generation extended family, in which the children remained as part of the family unit, the following situation could produce conflict. If the son became a doctor and the father was a labourer, the particularistic values of family life would give the father a higher status than his son. Yet the universalistic values of society as a whole would award his son higher social status. Conflict could result from this situation, which might undermine the authority of the father and threaten the solidarity of the family.

The same conflict of values could occur if the nuclear family were extended horizontally. Relationships between a woman and her sister might be problematic if they held jobs of widely differing prestige.

The isolated nuclear family largely prevents these problems from arising. There is one main breadwinner, the husband–father. His wife is mainly responsible for raising the children and the latter have yet to achieve their status in the world of work. No member of the family is in a position to threaten the ascribed authority structure by achieving a status outside the family which is higher than the achieved status of the family head.

These problems do not occur in pre-modern, pre-industrial societies. There, occupational status is largely ascribed, since an individual's position in the family and kinship group usually determines his or her job. Parsons concluded that, given the universalistic, achievement-orientated values of industrial society, the isolated nuclear family is the most suitable family structure. Any extension of this basic unit may well create conflict which would threaten the solidarity of the family.

As a consequence of the structural isolation of the nuclear family, the conjugal bond – the relationship between husband and wife – is strengthened. Without the support of kin beyond the nuclear family, spouses are increasingly dependent on each other, particularly for emotional support. As we outlined previously, Parsons argued that the stabilization of adult personalities is a major function of the family in modern industrial society. This is largely accomplished in terms of the husband–wife relationship.

William J. Goode

In *World Revolution and Family Patterns* (1963), William J. Goode surveyed the relationship between family structure and industrialization in various parts of the world. Like Parsons, he argued that industrialization tends to undermine the extended family and larger kinship groupings. Goode offered the following explanations for this process:

1 The high rate of geographical mobility in industrial society decreases 'the frequency and intimacy of contact among members of the kin network'.

2 The relatively high level of social mobility also tends to weaken kinship ties. If members of a working-class family become upwardly mobile, for example, they may adopt the lifestyle, attitudes and values of their new social class. This would tend to cut them off from their working-class kin.

3 Many of the functions once performed by the family have been taken over by outside agencies such as schools, business and welfare organizations. This reduces the dependency of individuals on their family and kin.

4 The importance of achieved status in industrial society means that the family and kinship group have less to offer their members. The family cannot guarantee its members a job or directly provide the necessary education and training to obtain one. The highly specialized division of labour in industrial society makes it even more difficult for an individual to obtain a job for a relative. As Goode states, 'He may not be in a suitable sector of the occupational sphere, or at a level where his influence is useful' (Goode, 1963).

Ideology and the nuclear family

However, Goode did not regard the pressures of industrialization as the only reason for the breakdown of extended family ties. He argued that the move to nuclear families had been 'far more rapid than could be supposed or predicted from the degree of industrialization alone'.

Goode believed that the ideology of the nuclear family had encouraged its growth, particularly in non-Western societies. This is due partly to the prestige of Western ideas and lifestyles. Since the nuclear family is found 'in many areas where the rate of industrialization is slight', Goode recognized 'the independent power of *ideological* variables'. He also argued that the spread of the nuclear family is due in part to the freedom it affords its members. In this type of family people owe fewer obligations to their kin.

The extended family and role bargaining

Goode applied the concept of role bargaining to his study of the family. This means that individuals attempt to obtain the best possible 'bargain' in their relationships with others. They will attempt to maximize their gains. In terms of family relationships, this means they will maintain relationships with kin and submit to their control if they feel they are getting a good return on their investment of time, energy and emotion.

With respect to the extended family and industrialization, Goode argued that 'It is not so much that the new system is incompatible, as it offers an alternative pattern of payments.' In other words, extended family patterns can operate in industrial society. Although it costs time and money, the rapid transport system in modern society means that 'the individual can maintain an extended kin network if he wishes to do so'. However, the 'alternative pattern of payments' offered by industrial society provides a better bargain for many people. They gain more by rejecting close and frequent contacts with kin beyond the nuclear family, than by retaining them.

Goode used the concept of role bargaining to explain social class differences in family structure. From his world survey, Goode found that extended family patterns are most likely to occur in the upper classes. Since members of ruling classes and elites have an important influence on appointments to top jobs, the retention of family ties makes economic sense. In Goode's terms, it is an effective role bargain. By comparison, members of the lower strata 'have little to offer the younger generation to counteract their normal tendency to independence'.

Goode concluded that extended kinship ties are retained if individuals feel they have more to gain than to lose by maintaining them.

Criticism of Parsons and Goode

So far, the arguments examined in this section suggest that modernization and industrialization led to a shift from predominantly extended to predominantly nuclear family types. The nuclear family is portrayed by writers such as Parsons and Goode as being well-adapted to the requirements of modern industrial societies. Furthermore, the nuclear family is generally portrayed in a positive light. David Cheal sees this view as being closely related to the modernist view of progress (Cheal, 1991).

Cheal describes modernism as 'a self-conscious commitment to, and advocacy of the world-changing potential of modernity'. Writers such as Parsons and Goode put forward a modernist interpretation of the family. Cheal attacks Parsons in particular.

Parsons saw the change towards a nuclear family as part of the increased specialization of institutions. The family was seen as an increasingly well-adapted specialist institution which interacted with other specialist institutions such as those of the welfare state. Cheal is very sceptical of the modernist view of the family advocated by Parsons. He claims that the faith in progress expressed by writers like Parsons and Goode ignored contradictions within modernity. Changes in different parts of society did not always go hand-in-hand. For example, increased employment of women in paid employment did not lead to men sharing domestic tasks equally. From Cheal's point of view, there is nothing inevitable about modern institutions developing in such a way that they functioned well together. Furthermore, Cheal argues that:

Parsons's generalizations about family life were often seriously parochial, reflecting narrow experiences of gender, class, race and nationality. Inevitably, that resulted in Parsons drawing some conclusions that have not stood up well to empirical investigation, or to the passage of time.

Cheal, 1991, p. 34

Peter Laslett – the family in pre-industrial societies

The family in kinship-based society and the classic extended family represent only two possible forms of family structure in pre-industrial society. Historical research in Britain and America suggests that neither was typical of those countries in the pre-industrial era.

Peter Laslett, a Cambridge historian, has studied family size and composition in pre-industrial England (Laslett, 1972a, 1972b, 1977). For the period between 1564 and 1821 he found that only about 10 per cent of households contained kin beyond the nuclear family. This percentage is the same as for England in 1966. Evidence from America presents a similar picture.

This surprisingly low figure may be due in part to the fact that people in pre-industrial England and America married relatively late in life and life expectancy was short. On average, there were only a few years between the marriage of a couple and the death of their parents. However, Laslett found no evidence to support the formerly accepted view that the classic extended family was widespread in pre-industrial England. He states that 'There is no sign of the large, extended co-residential family group of the traditional peasant world giving way to the small, nuclear conjugal household of modern industrial society.'

The 'Western family'

Following on from his research in England, Laslett began to draw together the results of research into pre-industrial family size in other countries (Laslett,

1983, 1984). He reached the conclusion that the nuclear family was not just typical of Britain. He uncovered evidence that there was a distinctive 'Western family' found also in northern France, the Netherlands, Belgium, Scandinavia and parts of Italy and Germany. This type of family was typically nuclear in structure: children were born relatively late, there was little age gap between spouses, and a large number of families contained servants. This family type contrasted with Eastern Europe and other parts of the world (such as Russia and Japan) where the extended family was more common.

According to Laslett, it was at least possible that the predominance of the nuclear family was a factor that helped Western Europe to be the first area of the world to industrialize. He reversed the more common argument that industrialization led to the nuclear family, claiming that the nuclear family had social, political and economic consequences which in part led to industrialization.

Family diversity in pre-industrial societies

Although Laslett has successfully exploded the myth that the extended family was typical of pre-industrial Britain, his conclusions should be viewed with some caution.

Michael Anderson (1980) points out some contradictory evidence in Laslett's own research. Laslett's research might have shown average household size to be under five people, but it also revealed that a majority of the population in pre-industrial Britain (53 per cent) lived in households consisting of six or more people. Anderson also referred to other research that suggests a much greater variety of household types than Laslett's theory of the Western family implies. For instance, research has shown that in Sweden extended families were very common. Furthermore, there is evidence of considerable variation within Britain: the gentry and yeoman farmers, for example, tended to have much larger households than the average.

For these reasons, Anderson is critical of the idea of the 'Western family'. He believes pre-industrial Europe was characterized by family diversity without any one type of family being predominant.

Michael Anderson – household structure and the Industrial Revolution

Michael Anderson's own research into the effects of industrialization on families does not, however, support the view that during industrialization extended families began to disappear (Anderson, 1971, 1977).

Using data from the 1851 census of Preston, Michael Anderson found that some 23 per cent of households contained kin other than the nuclear family – a large increase over Laslett's figures and those of today. The bulk of this 'co-residence' occurred among the poor. Anderson argues that co-residence occurs when the parties involved receive net gains from the arrangement. He states:

> If we are to understand variations and changes in patterns of kinship relationships, the only worthwhile approach is consciously and explicitly to investigate the manifold advantages and disadvantages that any actor can obtain from maintaining one relational pattern rather than another.
>
> Anderson, 1971, p. 77

Extended families and mutual aid

Preston in 1851 was largely dependent on the cotton industry. Life for many working-class families was characterized by severe hardship, resulting from low wages, periods of high unemployment, large families, a high death rate and overcrowded housing. In these circumstances, the maintenance of a large kinship network could be advantageous to all concerned:

1 In the absence of a welfare state, individuals were largely dependent on kin in times of hardship and need. Ageing parents often lived with their married children, a situation that benefited both parties. It provided support for the aged and allowed both the parents to work in the factory, since the grandparents could care for the dependent children.

2 The high death rate led to a large number of orphans, many of whom found a home with relatives. Again the situation benefited both parties. It provided support for the children who would soon, in an age of child labour, make an important contribution to household income.

3 A high rate of sickness and unemployment encouraged a wide network of kin as a means of mutual support: with no sickness and unemployment benefits, individuals were forced to rely on their kin in times of hardship.

4 Co-residence also provided direct economic advantages to those concerned. Additional members of the household would lower the share of the rent paid by each individual.

5 Finally, the practice of recruiting for jobs through kin encouraged the establishment of a wide kinship network. Anderson notes that the system of '"Asking for" a job for kin was normal in the factory towns and the employers used the kinship system to recruit labour from the country.'

Anderson's study of Preston indicates that, in the mid-nineteenth century, the working-class family

functioned as a mutual aid organization. It provided an insurance policy against hardship and crisis. This function encouraged the extension of kinship bonds beyond the nuclear family. Such links would be retained as long as they provided net gains to those involved. Anderson concludes that the early stages of industrialization increased rather than decreased the extension of the working-class family.

Elizabeth Roberts – family life and duty

Like Anderson, Elizabeth Roberts has studied family life in Lancashire (Roberts, 1984). She conducted a study of working-class women in three Lancashire towns: Preston, Barrow and Lancaster. The study used oral history techniques, interviewing people about their past lives, in order to examine family life between 1890 and 1940.

Like Anderson, Roberts found that extended kinship links remained very strong in working-class families, with family members helping each other out in many different ways. However, her findings differ from Anderson's in two important respects:

1 Roberts found evidence of a great deal of support being given by working-class women to family members in other households as well as to the family members with whom they lived.

2 She denies Anderson's claim that family relationships are largely based upon self-interest. Roberts found that women often gave practical, emotional and even financial support to other family members without getting or expecting much in return. Indeed, providing this help often cost the giver a good deal in time, effort and sometimes money. Roberts therefore argues that family relationships were based rather more on emotions and values than calculating self-interest. People helped their relatives because they felt affection or a sense of duty towards them, and not just because they had something to gain.

Evaluation

Janet Finch (1989) suggests a number of possible explanations for the differences in the findings of Roberts and Anderson:

1 Their studies refer to different time periods. Finch advances the possibility that family life had become less harsh and had stabilized by the end of the nineteenth century, giving people more opportunity to give unselfish support to their kin.

2 The differences could relate to gender. Roberts's study was based upon studies of women and it could be that women are more likely than men to have a strong sense of duty towards relatives.

3 The differences could be a result of using different research methods. Anderson largely used

quantitative data from census returns; Roberts used qualitative data from in-depth interviews. Interviews would be more likely to reveal a sense of duty towards relatives than statistical data.

Finch concludes that the two studies do not necessarily have to be seen as contradictory. It may be that they highlight different aspects of family life in which:

> *Feelings of affection and concepts of duty are taken into calculations about mutual advantage based on material considerations. The result is patterns of support whose basis is probably far more complex than it appears to an outsider and which also perhaps includes the expectation that love and affection themselves will be reciprocated.*
>
> Finch, 1989

Whatever the basis of support between kin, Roberts and Anderson are in agreement that nineteenth-century industrialization did not destroy extended family relationships. This conclusion is also supported by the next research that we will consider, that of Young and Willmott.

Michael Young and Peter Willmott – four stages of family life

Michael Young and Peter Willmott conducted studies of family life in London from the 1950s to the 1970s. In their book, *The Symmetrical Family*, they attempt to trace the development of the family from pre-industrial England to the 1970s (Young and Willmott, 1973). Using a combination of historical research and social surveys, they suggest that the family has gone through four main stages. In this section we will concentrate on their analysis of the working-class family.

Stage 1 – the pre-industrial family

Stage 1 is represented by the pre-industrial family. The family is a unit of production: the husband, wife and unmarried children work as a team, typically in agriculture or textiles. This type of family was gradually supplanted as a result of the Industrial Revolution. However, it continued well into the nineteenth century and is still represented in a small minority of families today, the best examples being some farming families.

Stage 2 – the early industrial family

The Stage 2 family began with the Industrial Revolution, developed throughout the nineteenth century and reached its peak in the early years of the twentieth century. The family ceased to be a unit of production since individual members were employed as wage earners. Throughout the nineteenth century, working-class poverty was widespread, wages were low and unemployment high. Like Anderson, Young and Willmott argue that the family responded to this situation by extending its network to include relatives beyond the nuclear family. This provided an insurance policy against the insecurity and hardship of poverty.

The extension of the nuclear family was largely conducted by women who 'eventually built up an organization in their own defence and in defence of their children'. The basic tie was between a mother and her married daughter, and, in comparison, the conjugal bond (the husband–wife relationship) was weak. Women created an 'informal trade union' which largely excluded men. Young and Willmott claim that 'Husbands were often squeezed out of the warmth of the female circle and took to the pub as their defence.'

Compared to later stages, the Stage 2 family was more often headed by a female. However, this resulted more from the high male death rate than from desertion by the husband.

The Stage 2 family began to decline in the early years of the twentieth century but it is still found in many low-income, long-established working-class areas. Its survival is documented in Young and Willmott's famous study entitled *Family and Kinship in East London*. The study was conducted in the mid-1950s in Bethnal Green, a low-income borough in London's East End. Bethnal Green is a long-settled, traditional working-class area. Children usually remain in the same locality after marriage. At the time of the research, two out of three married people had parents living within two or three miles of their residence.

There was a close tie between female relatives. Over 50 per cent of the married women in the sample had seen their mothers during the previous day, over 80 per cent within the previous week. There was a constant exchange of services such as washing, shopping and babysitting, between female relatives. Young and Willmott argued that in many families the households of mother and married daughter were 'to some extent merged'. As such they can be termed extended families, which Young and Willmott define as 'a combination of families who to some degree form one domestic unit'.

Although many aspects of the Stage 2 family were present in Bethnal Green, there were also indications of a transition to Stage 3. For example, fathers were increasingly involved in the rearing of their children.

Stage 3 – the symmetrical family

In the early 1970s, Young and Willmott conducted a large-scale social survey in which 1,928 people were interviewed in Greater London and the outer metropolitan area. The results formed the basis of their book, *The Symmetrical Family*.

Young and Willmott argue that the Stage 2 family has largely disappeared. For all social classes, but particularly the working class, the Stage 3 family predominates. This family is characterized by 'the separation of the immediate, or nuclear family from the extended family'. The trade union of women is disbanded and the husband returns to the family circle.

Life for the Stage 3 nuclear family is largely home-centred, particularly when the children are young. Free time is spent doing chores and odd jobs around the house, and leisure is mainly 'home-based', for example, watching television. The conjugal bond is strong and relationships between husband and wife are increasingly 'companionate'. In the home, 'They shared their work; they shared their time.' The nuclear family has become a largely self-contained, self-reliant unit.

Young and Willmott use the term symmetrical family to describe the nuclear family of Stage 3. 'Symmetry' refers to an arrangement in which the opposite parts are similar in shape and size. With respect to the symmetrical family, conjugal roles, although not the same – wives still have the main responsibility for raising the children, although husbands help – are similar in terms of the contribution made by each spouse to the running of the household. They share many of the chores, they share decisions, they work together, yet there is still men's work and women's work. Conjugal roles are not interchangeable but they are symmetrical in important respects.

Reasons for the rise of the symmetrical family

Young and Willmott give the following reasons for the transition from Stage 2 to Stage 3 families:

1 A number of factors have reduced the need for kinship-based mutual aid groups. They include an increase in the real wages of the male breadwinner, a decrease in unemployment and the male mortality rate, and increased employment opportunities for women. Various provisions of the welfare state such as family allowances, sickness and unemployment benefits, and old-age pensions have also reduced the need for dependence on the kinship network.

2 Increasing geographical mobility has tended to sever kinship ties. In their study of Bethnal Green, Young and Willmott showed how the extended kinship network largely ceased to operate when young couples with children moved some 20 miles away to a new council housing estate.

3 The reduction in the number of children, from an average of five or six per family in the nineteenth

century to just over two in 1970, provided greater opportunities for wives to work. This in turn led to greater symmetry within the family since both spouses are more likely to be wage earners and to share financial responsibility for the household.

4 As living standards rose, the husband was drawn more closely into the family circle since the home was a more attractive place. It became more comfortable with better amenities and a greater range of home entertainments.

Class and family life

Young and Willmott found that the home-centred symmetrical family was more typical of the working class than the middle class. They argue that members of the working class are 'more fully home-centred because they are less fully work-centred'. Partly as compensation for boring and uninvolving work, and partly because relatively little interest and energy are expended at work, manual workers tend to focus their attention on family life. Young and Willmott therefore see the nature of work as a major influence on family life.

The 'Principle of Stratified Diffusion'

In *The Symmetrical Family* Young and Willmott devise a general theory which they term the Principle of Stratified Diffusion. They claim that this theory explains much of the change in family life in industrial society. Put simply, the theory states that what the top of the stratification system does today, the bottom will do tomorrow. Lifestyles, patterns of consumption, attitudes and expectations will diffuse from the top of the stratification system downwards.

Young and Willmott argue that industrialization is the 'source of momentum', it provides the opportunities for higher living standards and so on. However, industrialization alone cannot account for the changes in family life: it cannot fully explain, for example, why the mass of the population has chosen to adopt the lifestyle of Stage 3 families. To complete the explanation, Young and Willmott maintain that the Principle of Stratified Diffusion is required.

Industrialization provides the opportunity for a certain degree of choice for the mass of the population. This choice will be largely determined by the behaviour of those at the top of the stratification system. Values, attitudes and expectations permeate down the class system; those at the bottom copy those at the top.

A Stage 4 family?

Applying the Principle of Stratified Diffusion to the future (writing in 1973), Young and Willmott postulated the possible development of a stage 4 family. They examine in detail the family life of managing directors, which, in terms of their theory, should diffuse downwards in years to come. Managing directors are work-centred rather than home-centred – 'my business is my life' being a typical quote from those in the sample. Their leisure activities are less home-centred and less likely to involve their wives than those of Stage 3 families. Sport was an important area of recreation, particularly swimming and golf. The wife's role was to look after the children and the home. As such the managing director's family was more asymmetrical than the Stage 3 family.

Young and Willmott suggest that changes in production technology may provide the opportunity for the Stage 4 family to diffuse throughout the stratification system. As technology reduces routine work, a larger number of people may have more interesting and involving jobs and become increasingly work-centred. Young and Willmott admit that 'We cannot claim that our 190 managing directors were representative of managing directors generally.' However, given the evidence available, they predict that the asymmetrical Stage 4 family represents the next major development.

Evaluation

A number of features of Willmott and Young's work are open to criticism. Many feminists have attacked the concept of the 'symmetrical family', arguing that there has been little progress towards equality between husband and wife (see pp. 552–63 for details). There is also little evidence that the 'Principle of Stratified Diffusion' has led to the 'Stage 4 family' becoming typical of all strata. Married women have continued to take paid employment and few working-class families can afford to adopt the lifestyle and family arrangements of managing directors. Later research by Peter Willmott has not used or supported the concept of the 'Stage 4 family', as we will see on p. 532.

The middle-class family

Contacts with kin

Many of the arguments examined in preceding sections suggest that the middle-class family should be less attached to kin beyond the nuclear unit than its working-class counterpart. The middle-class job market is more geographically mobile and more financially secure. There is therefore less opportunity and less need to maintain a wide kinship network. However, a number of studies have shown that middle-class families maintain close contacts with kin beyond the family.

Research conducted in the late 1950s by Willmott and Young in Woodford, a largely middle-class

London suburb, showed that, despite the fact that kin were more geographically dispersed, compared to Bethnal Green, fairly regular contacts were maintained (Willmott and Young, 1960). In Bethnal Green, 43 per cent of husbands and wives had seen their mothers in the previous 24 hours, compared to 30 per cent in Woodford. Although in Woodford there was less frequent contact with parents while the latter were employed, the frequency of contact was much the same as in Bethnal Green when parents retired. On retirement, middle-class parents often moved to Woodford to live near their married children.

In their study of Swansea, South Wales, conducted in the early 1960s, Rosser and Harris found that levels of contact between parents and married children were similar to those in Bethnal Green (Rosser and Harris, 1965). This applied to both middle- and working-class families. Despite the wider dispersal of kin in Swansea, improved transportation facilities (particularly the family car) made frequent contact possible. Rosser and Harris state that 'The picture that emerges, then, is of a vigorous kinship grouping wider than the elementary (nuclear) family, similar to that described in the Bethnal Green studies.' As in Bethnal Green, the Swansea families exchanged services with kin beyond the nuclear family and provided each other with support in times of need.

Quantity and quality of contacts

A major problem in studies of the family is the difficulty of measuring the importance of kin beyond the nuclear family. In a study of middle-class family life also carried out in Swansea, Colin Bell questions whether the frequency of actual face-to-face contacts between kin provides an accurate assessment (Bell, 1968). Bell points to the importance of contact by telephone and mail. He also distinguishes between the quantity and quality of contacts. For example, bumping into mum on a street corner in Bethnal Green may have far less significance than a formal visit to mother by her middle-class daughter.

In his study, Bell found a lower level of direct face-to-face contact with kin beyond the nuclear family than in either the Woodford sample or Rosser and Harris's middle-class sample. Despite this relatively low level of contact, he argues that, compared to the working class, 'Middle-class kin networks may have fewer day-to-day demands but I think that there is little evidence to suggest that they necessarily show any different affective quality.' Thus direct contact may be less frequent but the emotional bonds are the same.

Bell makes a similar point about the provision of services for kin beyond the nuclear family. They may not be as numerous as those provided in the working class, but they may be just as significant. He found that aid from parents, especially the son's father, was particularly important during the early years of marriage. It often took the form of loans or gifts to help with the deposit on a house or the expenses of the first baby. Bell concludes that kin beyond the nuclear family still play an important part in the lives of many middle-class families.

Similar conclusions were reached by Graham Allan in research conducted in a commuter village in East Anglia in the early 1970s (Allan, 1985). Although he found some evidence that the relationship between working-class wives and their mothers was particularly close, in general there was little difference between the middle- and working-class kinship networks. In both cases relationships were characterized by a 'positive concern' for the welfare of the kin regardless of the frequency of face-to-face contacts.

Contemporary family networks

Peter Willmott – networks in London

In research conducted during the 1980s in a north London suburb, Peter Willmott found that contacts with kin remained important in both the middle and working class (Willmott, 1988). In the area he studied, about a third of the couples had moved to the district in the previous five years. Only a third of all the couples had parents or parents-in-law living within ten minutes' travelling distance. However, despite the distance between their homes, two-thirds of the couples saw relatives at least weekly. Working-class couples saw relatives more frequently than middle-class couples, but the differences were not great.

Maintaining contact was relatively easy for most families because so many had access to cars. Most also had homes that were sufficiently spacious for relatives to come and stay. Some 90 per cent had telephones which enabled them to keep in touch with relatives even if they did not meet face-to-face.

Willmott also found that 'relatives continue to be the main source of informal support and care, and that again the class differences are not marked'. For example, nearly 75 per cent had relatives who sometimes helped with babysitting and 80 per cent looked to relatives to help them when they needed to borrow money.

Margaret O'Brien and Deborah Jones – families and kinship in East London

Margaret O'Brien and Deborah Jones conducted research in Barking and Dagenham, East London, in the early 1990s (O'Brien and Jones, 1996). They collected survey data on 600 young people and their parents in this predominantly working-class area. They compared their findings with a 1950s study of the same area conducted by Peter Willmott (1963).

They found that, compared with the 1950s, this area had developed a greater variety of types of family and household. Of the young people surveyed, 14 per cent lived with a step-parent, and 14 per cent lived in lone-parent families. According to census statistics, over one-third of births in the area took place outside marriage. There were many dual-earner families, with 62 per cent of women in their sample working in paid employment, and 79 per cent of men. In Willmott's 1950s study, family life was much more homogeneous. Then, 78 per cent of people were married, and just 1 per cent were divorced. Most single people were young and lived with their parents.

Despite the move towards a greater plurality of family and household types, O'Brien and Jones did not find that there had been any major erosion in the importance attached to kinship. In both Willmott's and O'Brien and Jones's research, over 40 per cent of the sample had grandparents living locally. In the 1990s, 72 per cent of those studied had been visited by a relative in the previous week, and over half the sample saw their maternal grandparent at least weekly. Twenty per cent had a large network of local kin numbering over ten relatives.

O'Brien and Jones conclude that there has been a pluralization of lifestyles, an increase in marital breakdowns and a big rise in dual-earner households. However, they also found that 'kin contact and association do not appear to have changed significantly since Willmott's study of the borough in the 1950s'. This suggests a greater continuity in kin relationships, at least among the working class in London, than that implied by some other studies.

Families and kinship in the 1980s and 1990s

All of the above studies have been based upon specific geographical areas at a particular point in time. The *British Social Attitudes Surveys* of 1986 and 1995 contained a number of questions on families and kinship (reported in Jowell *et al.* (eds) (1989) and McGlone *et al.*, 1996). The surveys used large representative samples of the British population. The results of these two surveys have been analysed by Francis McGlone, Alison Park and Kate Smith (1998).

Changes affecting families

McGlone *et al.* start by noting that a number of important changes that might affect family life took place between 1986 and 1995. Some of these were:

1 An increase in the proportion of elderly people in the British population, as people live longer and the birth-rate declines; and an increased emphasis by the government on families looking after their elderly rather than the welfare state.

2 Greater emphasis by the government and others upon trying to eradicate what some have seen as 'poor parenting', by getting kin beyond children's parents involved in looking after them.

3 Increases in the levels of divorce, cohabitation, lone parenthood, and births outside marriage.

4 An increase in the proportion of families living in poverty and reliant upon benefits, partly as a consequence of more family members experiencing unemployment.

5 A larger proportion of married women taking paid employment outside the home.

6 Young people have started entering the labour force later, and older men are more likely than before to experience unemployment.

7 The labour market has changed so that there are relatively few unskilled jobs for manual workers (especially men) but there is more demand for the highest-qualified workers. More people work part-time or in non-permanent employment.

8 As a consequence of some of these changes, the young often stay reliant upon their families for longer than they did in the past.

Given the scope of these changes, you might expect there to be very major differences in family relationships and the strength of kinship networks. However, McGlone *et al.* actually found considerable continuity between 1986 and 1995.

Contacts with relatives in 1995

The *British Social Attitudes Surveys* revealed that even in 1995 contacts with relatives remained quite frequent. For example, in 1995, 47 per cent of people without dependent children and 50 per cent of those with dependent children saw their mothers at least once a week (see Table 8.1). And 35 per cent of those without children and 45 per cent of those with children saw their fathers at least once a week. (All

figures refer to the proportions of those with living relatives of the type specified.)

The proportions were even higher for those who lived within one hour's drive of their relatives. Amongst this group, for example, 75 per cent of those without children under 16 saw their mother, and 63 per cent saw their father, at least once a week. Amongst those with children, 70 per cent saw their mother and 69 per cent saw their father at least once a week. Telephone contact was also common. Amongst women with a dependent child, 78 per cent talked to their mother at least once a week, 54 per cent to their father, 45 per cent to an adult sibling, and 39 per cent to another relative.

In line with other studies, it was found that there were significant social class differences. Tables 8.2 and 8.3 show that contacts were more frequent for manual workers than for non-manual workers, particularly among those with dependent children. The difference between manual and non-manual workers was partly explained by a tendency for manual workers to live closer to relatives but, even when this was taken into account, some differences remained.

Changes in contact over time

Although contacts with relatives remained frequent in 1995, a comparison with 1986 did find that they had declined somewhat. In 1986, 59 per cent of those with dependent children saw their mother at least once a week, declining to 50 per cent in 1995. Contacts with all other relatives had fallen as well. However, the falls were partly accounted for by people living further apart. As Table 8.4 shows, the fall in contact with mothers was less for those who lived within an hour's driving distance than for the group as a whole. Contacts with fathers remained unchanged and those with adult siblings had increased.

What fall there had been was largely accounted for by non-manual workers. This was particularly true of

Table 8.1	Proportion who see specified relative at least once a week, by whether there is a dependent child (1995)							
	No child under 16		All with child under 16		Age of child in household			
					Under 5		5 to 15	
	%	Base	%	Base	%	Base	%	Base
Mother	47	535	50	478	51	226	48	252
Father	35	385	45	395	47	206	44	189
Adult sibling	25	1,097	36	543	41	245	33	298
Other relative	31	1,250	45	552	49	242	42	310

Note: The base for each percentage comprises all those with the specified relative (non-resident)
Source: F. McGlone, A. Park and K. Smith (1998) *Families and Kinship*, Family Policy Studies Centre, London, p. 12.

Table 8.2	Proportion with a dependent child who see specified relative at least once a week, by social class (1995)			
	Manual workers		Non-manual workers	
	%	Base	%	Base
Mother	65	193	39	271
Father	59	160	36	223
Adult sibling	46	235	28	291
Other relative	57	224	37	314

Note: The base for each percentage comprises all those with the specified relative (non-resident) and dependent children.

Source: F. McGlone, A. Park and K. Smith (1998) *Families and Kinship*, Family Policy Studies Centre, London, p. 14.

Table 8.3	Proportion without a dependent child who see specified relative at least once a week, by social class (1995)			
	Manual workers		Non-manual workers	
	%	Base	%	Base
Mother	48	230	47	279
Father	37	173	33	189
Adult sibling	28	540	21	509
Other relative	38	571	24	629

Note: The base for each percentage comprises all those with the specified relative (non-resident) and with no dependent children.

Source: F. McGlone, A. Park and K. Smith (1998) *Families and Kinship*, Family Policy Studies Centre, London, p. 14.

Table 8.4	Proportion with a dependent child who see specified relative living within one hour's journey time at least once a week (1986 and 1995)			
	1986		1995	
	%	Base	%	Base
Mother	76	269	70	328
Father	69	196	69	253
Adult sibling	55	300	56	336
Other relative	70	313	64	383

Note: The base for each percentage comprises all those with the specified relative who lives within one hour's journey time (non-resident) and dependent children.

Source: F. McGlone, A. Park and K. Smith (1998) *Families and Kinship*, Family Policy Studies Centre, London, p. 17.

middle-class families where the woman was in full-time paid employment. It appeared that in many dual-earner families there was too little time to maintain regular weekly contact with parents and other relatives. There was no significant change in maternal and paternal contacts among manual workers.

Families and help

As earlier studies suggested, even where there was a lack of contact between family members, that did not necessarily mean that kinship networks had become unimportant. The *British Social Attitudes Surveys* of 1986 and 1995 asked people who they would go to for help with things such as doing household and garden jobs, support during illness, and borrowing money. For household jobs and help while ill, most said they would turn first of all to a spouse or partner, while turning to other relatives was the second most popular choice. For borrowing money, the most popular options were borrowing from other relatives or from a bank. Amongst those who had received help in the previous five years, a high proportion had got that help from relatives. For example, 59 per cent of those without a child under 16 and 71 per cent of those with a child, who had received a loan or gift of money, had got it from a parent or in-law, and over a third of those who had received help when ill had got it from one of these sources.

McGlone *et al.* conclude that family members remain the most important source of practical help. While people tend to turn first to a spouse or partner, after that they turn to other relatives, with friends or neighbours being less important.

Attitudes to families

Here, McGlone *et al.* found that 'the majority of the adult population are very family-centred'. Table 8.5 summarizes the results of the study in this area. It shows that less than 10 per cent thought that friends were more important to them than family members. The vast majority thought that parents should continue to help children after they had left home, and around 70 per cent thought that people should keep in touch with close family members. A majority thought that you should try to keep in touch with relatives like aunts, uncles and cousins, even if you did not have much in common with them.

Conclusions

McGlone *et al.* found that families remain very important to people in contemporary Britain. They argue that their study confirms the results of earlier research showing that families remain an important source of help and support, and that family contacts are still maintained even though family members tend to live further apart. Their research suggests that

Table 8.5 Attitudes towards the family, by whether there is a dependent child								
	No child under 16		All with child under 16		Age of child			
					Under 5		5 to 15	
% agreeing	%	Base	%	Base	%	Base	%	Base
People should keep in touch with close family members even if they don't have much in common	74	1,407	68	595	66	265	69	330
People should keep in touch with relatives like aunts, uncles and cousins even if they don't have much in common	59	1,414	49	594	42	264	54	330
People should always turn to their family before asking the state for help	54	1,394	42	594	36	264	46	329
I try to stay in touch with all my relatives, not just my close family	50	1,381	43	583	42	259	43	324
I'd rather spend time with my friends than with my family	15	1,370	11	584	9	263	13	321
Once children have left home, they should no longer expect help from their parents	15	1,413	6	596	8	264	4	332
On the whole, my friends are more important to me than members of my family	8	1,393	7	588	8	264	6	324

Source: F. McGlone, A. Park and K. Smith (1998) *Families and Kinship*, Family Policy Studies Centre, London.

the 'core' of the family does not just include parents and children – in most households grandparents are part of the core as well. They also found that differences between social classes remained significant, with the working class still more likely to have frequent contacts than the middle class. Despite all the social changes affecting families between 1986 and 1995, kinship networks beyond the nuclear family remain important to people.

Janet Finch – family obligations and social change

Janet Finch has studied changes in family life using a slightly different viewpoint from that of the studies discussed above (Finch, 1989). In a review of research conducted by many different sociologists she has discussed the changing nature of family obligations. Her work is particularly concerned with the extent to which members of a family feel obliged to offer assistance to their kin and feel a sense of duty towards them. This also involves considering what help is given, as well as the reasons behind the decision to give help.

Finch examines the extent to which relatives feel an obligation to provide accommodation by sharing households, and to give economic, emotional or moral support, practical help, financial assistance and personal care (for example, by nursing a sick relative). She considers the possibility that there was a 'Golden Age' before the Industrial Revolution in

which family obligations were much stronger and family members helped each other far more.

The myth of a 'Golden Age'

Overall, Finch argues that the idea of a 'Golden Age' of the family which was undermined by the Industrial Revolution is a myth. For example, she says that there is no evidence that people automatically assumed responsibility for elderly relatives in pre-industrial times, and 'most elderly people who are married have always lived only with their spouse'. Also, when primogeniture (inheritance by the first-born son) was the main principle governing inheritance, parents made little or no financial provision for children other than the eldest son in their wills.

Some changes have certainly taken place: far fewer children are permanently looked after by relatives other than their own parents; and in the last 50 years a smaller proportion of the single elderly have been living with relatives. However, such changes are largely a result of demographic trends. Because life expectancy has risen, there are fewer orphans and more elderly people in the population. Because average family size has gone down since the nineteenth century, there are fewer children with whom the rising numbers of elderly might live.

In any case, according to Finch, much of the assistance given in the past was based upon mutual self-interest rather than a selfless sense of obligation to family members. People who took relatives' children into their households often employed them as servants. When kin outside the immediate nuclear family have lived with each other in the past this has often been for the purpose of sharing housing costs. Before, during and since the Industrial Revolution most kin relationships have not been characterized by unconditional giving by some relatives to others, but have been based upon 'reciprocal exchange on the basis of mutual advantage'.

One exception to this general rule has been the relationship between parents and children. It has been and remains common for parents to help their children without expecting equivalent support in exchange.

Factors influencing family obligations

Finch stresses that the extent and nature of family obligations felt by people vary enormously from one family to another and are shaped partly by interpersonal relationships between the individuals involved. Nevertheless, family obligations are influenced by social factors such as region, gender, ethnicity, generation and the economic situation of the family and its members. Kin relationships remain special to people, and people generally feel more of a sense of duty to members of their family than to anybody else. However, having independence is also important to members of families and reliance upon kin is usually seen as a last resort rather than the first. The family can offer a safety net in times of need and it can offer mutual benefits, but people try to avoid relying upon it too much.

These characteristics of family relationships are not new, according to Finch. Although the circumstances in which family relationships are made have changed enormously since pre-industrial times, there is no evidence that in general there is less sense of obligation to kin than there was in the past.

The isolated nuclear family?

The evidence we have presented so far under the heading of 'The family, industrialization and modernization' provides a somewhat confusing picture. On the one hand there is Talcott Parsons's isolated nuclear family, and on the other a large body of evidence suggesting that kin beyond the nuclear family play an important part in family life and that the importance of that role may not have been greatly diminishing.

In America, a number of researchers have rejected Parsons's concept of the isolated nuclear family. Sussman and Burchinal, for example, argue that the weight of evidence from a large body of research indicates that the modern American family is far from isolated. They maintain that the family can only be properly understood 'by rejection of the

isolated nuclear family concept' (Sussman and Burchinal, 1971).

Parsons replied to his critics in an article entitled 'The normal American family' (Parsons, 1965a). He argued that close relationships with kin outside the nuclear family are in no way inconsistent with the concept of the isolated nuclear family. Parsons stated that 'the very psychological importance for the individual of the nuclear family in which he was born and brought up would make any such conception impossible'.

However, he maintained that the nuclear family is structurally isolated. It is isolated from other parts of the social structure such as the economic system. For example, it does not form an integral part of the economic system as in the case of the peasant farming family in traditional Ireland.

In addition, the so-called 'extended families' of modern industrial society 'do not form firmly structured units of the social system'. Relationships with kin beyond the nuclear family are not obligatory – they are a matter of individual choice. In this sense, 'extended kin constitute a resource which may be selectively taken advantage of within considerable limits'. Thus, extended families do not form 'firmly structured units' as in the case of the classic extended family or the family in kinship-based societies.

Evidence from Rosser and Harris's Swansea research supports Parsons's arguments. Rosser and Harris maintained that the nuclear family is 'a basic structural unit of the society' and, although kinship relationships beyond the nuclear family are important to individuals, in terms of the social structure as a whole they are 'not of major and critical importance' (Rosser and Harris, 1965).

The Swansea study revealed a 'vast variation' in kinship relationships. Members of some families were in daily contact with kin beyond the nuclear family; members of other families rarely saw their relatives. Janet Finch's review of family research also found a great variety of relationships within families (Finch, 1989). This is the expected finding in view of Parsons's emphasis upon individual choice. However, as we will see later in the chapter, it may be that nuclear families no longer (if they ever did) make up a vital structural unit in contemporary societies either. There is evidence that the decision to form a nuclear family is increasingly also a matter of choice (see pp. 563–5).

The 'modified extended family'

In order to clear up the confusion surrounding the term 'isolated nuclear family', Eugene Litwak argues that a new term, the modified extended family, should be introduced to describe the typical family in modern industrial society. Litwak defines the modified extended family as:

> *a coalition of nuclear families in a state of partial dependence. Such partial dependence means that nuclear family members exchange significant services with each other, thus differing from the isolated nuclear family, as well as retain considerable autonomy (that is not bound economically or geographically) therefore differing from the classical extended family.*

Quoted in Morgan, 1975, p. 65

The 'modified elementary family'

Graham Allan accepts Litwak's view that kin outside the nuclear family continue to be important in industrial society (Allan, 1985). On the basis of his own research in a commuter village in East Anglia, he argues that in normal circumstances non-nuclear kin do not rely on each other. In many families there may be little exchange of significant services most of the time. However, in most families the members do feel an obligation to keep in touch. For example, very few married children break off relationships with their parents altogether, and brothers and sisters usually maintain contact. Although significant services are not usually exchanged as a matter of course, kin frequently recognize an obligation to help each other in times of difficulty or crisis.

Unlike Litwak, Allan believes that these kinds of relationships are confined to an inner or 'elementary' family, consisting of wives and husbands, their parents, children, brothers and sisters. The obligations do not extend to uncles, aunts, nephews, nieces, cousins or more distant kin. Allan therefore prefers the term modified elementary family to 'modified extended family', since to him it more accurately describes the range of kin who are important to an individual.

The 'dispersed extended family'

On the basis of research carried out in London in the 1980s, Peter Willmott reached broadly similar conclusions to Litwak and Allan. He claims that the dispersed extended family is becoming dominant in Britain (Willmott, 1988). It consists of two or more related families who cooperate with each other even though they live some distance apart. Contacts are fairly frequent, taking place on average perhaps once a week, but less frequent than they were amongst extended families who lived close together. Cars, public transport and telephones make it possible for dispersed extended families to keep in touch. Members of dispersed extended families do not rely on each other on a day-to-day basis.

Like Litwak, Willmott sees each nuclear family unit as only partially dependent upon extended kin. Much of the time the nuclear family is fairly self-sufficient but in times of emergency the existence of extended kin might prove invaluable. Thus Willmott argues that, in modern Britain, 'although kinship is largely chosen, it not only survives but most of the time flourishes'.

The research discussed by McGlone *et al.* (1998) reaches broadly similar conclusions. Kinship networks outside the nuclear family are still important. Indeed they argue that the core of families with dependent children includes not just the nuclear family but also grandparents. Despite all the social changes that could have weakened kinship, people still value kinship ties and for the most part try to retain them even when they live some distance from their relatives.

In this section we have focused on the changes in household composition and kinship networks that have accompanied industrialization in Britain. We will now examine the extent to which the idea of a 'typical family' is accurate.

Family diversity

Although some historians such as Michael Anderson (1980) have pointed to a variety of household types in pre-industrial times and during industrialization, it has generally been assumed that a single type of family is dominant in any particular era. Whether the modern family is regarded as nuclear, modified extended, modified elementary or dispersed extended, the assumption has been that this type of family is central to people's experiences in modern industrial societies. However, recent research has suggested that such societies are characterized by a plurality of household and family types, and that the idea of a typical family is misleading.

The 'cereal packet image' of the family

Ann Oakley (1982) has described the image of the typical or 'conventional' family. She says, 'conventional families are nuclear families composed of legally married couples, voluntarily choosing the parenthood of one or more (but not too many) children'.

Leach (1967) called this the 'cereal packet image of the family'. The image of the happily married couple with two children is prominent in advertising, and the 'family-sized' packets of cereals and other types of product are aimed at just this type of grouping. It tends also to be taken for granted that this type of family has its material needs met by the male breadwinner, while the wife has a predominantly domestic role.

The monolithic image of the family

The American feminist Barrie Thorne has attacked the image of the 'monolithic family'. She argues that 'Feminists have challenged the ideology of "the monolithic family", which has elevated the nuclear family with a breadwinner husband and a full-time wife and mother as the only legitimate family form' (Thorne, 1992). She argues that the focus on the family unit neglects structures of society that lead to variations in families. She says, 'Structures of gender, generation, race and class result in widely varying experiences of family life, which are obscured by the glorification of the nuclear family, motherhood, and the family as a loving refuge.' The idea of 'The Family' involves 'falsifying the actual variety of household forms'. In fact, according to Thorne, 'Households have always varied in composition, even in the 1950s and early 1960s when the ideology of The Family was at its peak.' By the 1990s, such an ideology was more obviously inappropriate since changes in society had resulted in ever more diverse family forms.

Households in Britain

The view that such images equate with reality has been attacked by Robert and Rhona Rapoport (1982). They drew attention to the fact that in 1978, for example, just 20 per cent of families consisted of married couples with children in which there was a single breadwinner.

As Table 8.6 shows, since the Rapoports first advanced the idea of family diversity, there has been a steady decline in the proportion of households in Great Britain consisting of married couples with dependent children, from 38 per cent in 1961 to just 23 per cent in 1998. There has been a corresponding increase in single-person households in the same period, with the proportion of households of this type rising from 11 per cent in 1961 to 28 per cent in 1998. Furthermore, the proportion of households that were single-parent households with dependent children more than tripled, from 2 per cent in 1961 to 7 per cent in 1998. The total number of lone-parent households rose from 6 per cent to 10 per cent over the same period. Single-parent families are discussed in more detail on pp. 541–4.

Types of diversity

The fact that the 'conventional family' no longer makes up a majority of households or families is only one aspect of diversity identified by the Rapoports. They identify five distinct elements of family diversity in Britain:

Table 8.6 Households: by type of household and family

	1961	1971	1981	1991	1998[1]
One person	%	%	%	%	%
Under pensionable age	4	6	8	11	14
Over pensionable age	7	12	14	16	14
Two or more unrelated adults	5	4	5	3	3
Single family households Couple[2]					
No children	26	27	26	28	28
1–2 dependent children[3]	30	26	25	20	19
3 or more dependent children[3]	8	9	6	5	4
Non-dependent children only	10	8	8	8	7
Lone parent[2]					
Dependent children[3]	2	3	5	6	7
Non-dependent children only	4	4	4	4	3
Multi-family households	3	1	1	1	1
All households[4] (=100%) (millions)	16.3	18.6	20.2	22.4	23.6

1 At spring 1998.
2 Other individuals who were not family members may also be included.
3 May also include non-dependent children.
4 Includes couples of the same gender in 1998.

Source: *Social Trends* (1999) HMSO, London, p. 42.

1 First, there is what they term organizational diversity. By this they mean there are variations in family structure, household type, patterns of kinship network, and differences in the division of labour within the home. For example, there are the differences between conventional families, one-parent families, and dual-worker families, in which husband and wife both work.

There are also increasing numbers of reconstituted families. The reconstituted family is the second 'emerging form' identified by the Rapoports. These families are formed after divorce and remarriage. This situation can lead to a variety of family forms. The children from the previous marriages of the new spouses may live together in the newly reconstituted family, or they may live with the original spouses of the new couple. Although it might be seen to reflect a failure to create a happy family life, some adults in a reconstituted family may find positive aspects of reconstitution.

On the basis of a study conducted in Sheffield, Jacqueline Burgoyne and David Clark (1982) claim that some individuals in this situation see themselves as 'pioneers of an alternative lifestyle'. They may choose to remain unmarried to their new partner, and may find advantages in having more than two parental figures in their children's lives. Sometimes they believe that step-siblings gain from living together. Some couples in the Sheffield study felt a considerable sense of achievement from the successful reconstitution of a family. (For further details on divorce, see pp. 566–72.)

2 The second type of diversity is cultural diversity. There are differences in the lifestyles of families of different ethnic origins and different religious beliefs. There are differences between families of Asian, West Indian and Cypriot origin, not to mention other ethnic minority groups. (We discuss ethnic family diversity in more detail on pp. 544–8.) Differences in lifestyle between Catholic and Protestant families may also be an important element of diversity.

3 There are differences between middle- and working-class families in terms of relationships between adults and the way in which children are socialized.

4 There are differences that result from the stage in the life cycle of the family. Newly married couples without children may have a different family life from those with dependent children and from those whose children have achieved adult status.

5 The fifth factor identified by the Rapoports as producing family diversity is cohort. This refers to the periods at which the family has passed through different stages of the family life cycle. Cohort affects the life experiences of the family. For example, those families whose children were due to enter the labour market in the 1980s may be different from other families: the high rates of unemployment during that period may have increased the length of time that those children were dependent on their parents.

Regional diversity

In addition to these five aspects of diversity identified by the Rapoports, David Eversley and Lucy Bonnerjea (1982) point to regional diversity. They argue that there tend to be distinctive patterns of family life in different areas of Great Britain:

1 In what they term 'the sun belt' (the affluent southern parts of England) two-parent upwardly mobile families are typical. Eversley and Bonnerjea claim that this area attracts family builders.

2 They describe a number of coastal regions as the 'geriatric wards'. Much of the south coast (from Cornwall to Sussex, for example) has a disproportionate number of retired couples without dependent children, and widows and widowers.

3 Older industrial areas suffering from long-term decline tend to have fairly conventional and traditional family structures.

4 Inner-city areas tend to have greater concentrations of both one-parent and ethnic minority families.

5 What they describe as 'newly declining industrial areas' (particularly likely to be found in the Midlands) have more diverse family patterns.

6 The final type of region identified by Eversley and Bonnerjea is the truly rural area. Here, the family-based farm tends to produce strong kinship networks.

Gay and lesbian families

Since the Rapoports' pioneering volume on family diversity in Britain, other forms of diversity have developed or become more prominent. Gay and lesbian households may have become more common-place – certainly there are more openly gay and lesbian households than there were several decades ago. As Jeffrey Weeks, Catherine Donovan and Brian Heaphey argue, 'During the past generation the possibilities of living an openly lesbian and gay life have been transformed' (Weeks, Donovan and Heaphey, 1999). As discussed earlier (see p. 507), many sociologists believe that such households, where they incorporate long-term gay or lesbian relationships, should be seen as constituting families.

According to Weeks et al., homosexuals and lesbians often look upon their households, and even their friendship networks, as being chosen families. Some see their relationships as involving a greater degree of choice than those in more conventional heterosexual families. They choose who to include in their family and negotiate what are often fairly egalitarian relationships. Some see their families as an alternative type of family which they are consciously developing. Weeks et al. argue that this may be part of wider social changes in which 'we culturally prioritize individual choice and the acceptance of diversity. Commitment becomes increasingly a matter of negotiation rather than ascription.' (Their views are similar to those of Anthony Giddens – see pp. 578–9 for details.)

New reproductive technologies

Unlike gay and lesbian relationships, new reproductive technologies add an entirely new dimension to family diversity. It was not until 1978 that the first 'test-tube baby', Louise Brown, was born. The process is called *in vitro* fertilization and involves fertilizing an egg with a sperm in a test-tube, before implanting in a woman's womb. The woman may or may not be the woman who produced the egg.

Surrogate motherhood involves one woman carrying a foetus produced by the egg of another woman. This raises questions about who the parents of a child are, and questions about what constitutes a family. As noted earlier (see pp. 521–3), Calhoun sees this as undermining the centrality of the reproductive couple as the core of the family, and it introduces a greater range of choices into families than was previously available. John Macionis and Ken Plummer (1997) show how new reproductive technologies can create previously impossible sets of family relationships. They quote the case of Arlette Schweitzer, who in 1991 gave birth in South Dakota in the USA to her own grandchild. Her daughter was unable to carry a baby and Arlette Schweitzer acted as a surrogate mother. She gave birth to twins, a boy and a girl. Macionis and Plummer ask, 'is Arlette Schweitzer the mother of the twins she bore? Grandmother? Both?' Such examples, they say, 'force us to consider the adequacy of conventional kinship terms'. They note that such technologies have largely been made available to heterosexual couples of normal child-rearing age, but they have also been used by lesbians, homosexuals, and single and older women. The implication of new reproductive technologies is that biology will no longer restrict the possibilities for forming or enlarging families by having children. They therefore add considerably to the range of potential family types and thus contribute to growing diversity.

A global trend

According to Rhona Rapoport (1989), the decline of conventional family forms and the increasing diversity are part of a global trend. She quotes figures showing a movement towards diverse family structures in very different European countries. In Finland, the percentage of households consisting of a nuclear family declined from 63.8 per cent in 1950 to 60 per cent in 1980. In Sweden, the decline was from 52.4 per cent in 1960 to 42.6 per cent in 1980, and in East Germany from 56.7 per cent in 1957 to 48.7

per cent in 1977. She also points to an enormous increase throughout Europe in the proportion of married women who have paid employment, which suggests that men's and women's roles within marriage are changing and consequently new family forms are developing. These conclusions are broadly shared by a study of diversity in Europe.

Diversity and European family life

At the end of the 1980s the European Co-ordination Centre for Research and Documentation in Social Sciences organized a cross-cultural study of family life in 14 European nations (Boh, 1989). These were Belgium, Finland, France, the German Democratic Republic and Federal Republic of Germany (the study was carried out before re-unification), Great Britain, Hungary, Italy, the Netherlands, Norway, Poland, Sweden, and the then Soviet Union and Yugoslavia.

The findings of individual national studies were analysed and compared by Katja Boh. She tried to 'trace the tendencies in changes of family patterns' in order to:

> answer the crucial question whether these tendencies converge, which would mean that family patterns in European family life are becoming more similar, or the recent political and economic developments have produced differences contributing to a greater diversity in family life patterns.
>
> Boh, 1989

Evidence of diversity

In most aspects of family life Boh found a wide range of patterns in different countries:

1 The likelihood of married women working varied greatly, with well over 80 per cent in work in the Soviet Union, but less than one-third in Belgium and the Netherlands.

2 Marriage rates appeared to be diverging. In 1932, Poland had the highest rate at 8.3 marriages per thousand of the population; Norway had the lowest at 6.2. By 1984 the gap between the highest rate (10.3 in the USSR) and the lowest (4 in Sweden) was much greater.

3 Boh noted that cohabitation as an alternative to marriage was becoming common in Sweden and Finland but remained comparatively rare in Belgium and Italy.

4 She also discovered that the number of children born per woman was greatest in the Soviet Union and Poland and lowest in the Federal Republic of Germany and the Netherlands.

5 As discussed previously, single parents are much more common in some European countries than in others. Boh found that the highest rates in 1981 were in Finland, while the lowest were in the Soviet Union.

Common trends

Although most of the evidence showed that family life was very different in different European countries, some evidence did point to certain trends being widespread. All European countries had experienced rising divorce rates and many had made it easier to get divorced. Cohabitation appeared to have become more common in most countries, and the birth rate had declined everywhere.

Convergence in diversity

The existence of diverse patterns of family life in Europe, but with some common trends, seems at first sight to be contradictory. However, Katja Boh argues that, together, they produce a consistent pattern of convergence in diversity. While family life retains considerable variations from country to country, throughout Europe a greater range of family types is being accepted as legitimate and normal. This has been caused by:

> Increasing gender symmetry in work patterns, more freedom in conjugal choice and a more hedonistic view of marriage and love, premarital and experimental sexuality, higher marriage instability and alternative forms of 'living together', decreasing fertility and change in forms of parenting.
>
> Boh, 1989

Boh concludes:

> Whatever the existing patterns are, they are characterized by the acceptance of diversity that has given men and women the possibility to choose inside the boundaries of available options the life pattern that is best adapted to their own needs and aspirations.
>
> Boh, 1989

Before evaluating whether there has really been a move towards diversity, and discussing the significance of the changes that have taken place, we will examine two particularly important sources of diversity – lone parenthood and ethnicity – in greater detail.

The increase in single parenthood

As mentioned earlier, single-parent families have become increasingly common in Britain. According to government statistics, in 1961, 2 per cent of the population lived in households consisting of a lone parent with dependent children, but by 1998 this had more than tripled to 7 per cent (*Social Trends*, 1999). Between 1972 and 1996-7 the percentage of children living in single-parent families increased from 7 per cent to 19 per cent (*Social Trends*, 1998).

According to Hantrais and Letablier (1996), Britain has the second highest rate of lone parenthood in Europe. It is exceeded only by Denmark, and rates in countries such as Greece, Portugal and France are much lower than those in Britain. Nevertheless, throughout Europe and in advanced industrial countries such as Japan and the USA, the proportions have generally been increasing since at least the 1980s.

Although useful, figures on the proportions living in single-parent families need to be interpreted with caution. They provide only a snapshot picture of the situation at one point in time and do not represent the changing family life of many individuals. Many more children than the above figures seem to suggest spend part of their childhood in a single-parent family, but many fewer spend all of their childhood in one. Children may start their life living in a single-parent family. However, the single parent may well find a new partner and marry them or cohabit with them. The child will then end up living with two parents.

Greg Duncan and Willard Rodgers estimated – from survey data on children born between 1967 and 1969 in the USA – that less than a third of children born into a single-parent family stayed in one throughout their childhood (Duncan and Rodgers, 1990). The *British Household Panel Survey* revealed that about 15 per cent of lone mothers stopped being lone parents each year. This was usually because they had established a new relationship (quoted in *Social Trends*, 1998).

It should also be noted that many children who live in a single-parent household do see and spend time with their other parent. Furthermore, even in two-parent families, one parent (usually the mother) might be responsible for the vast majority of the childcare. In terms of children's experience, then, the distinction between single-parent and two-parent households is not clearcut.

The causes of single parenthood

Lone parenthood can come about through a number of different routes. People who are married can become lone parents through:

1 divorce
2 separation
3 death of a spouse.

Lone parents who have never been married:

1 may have been living with the parent of the child when the child was born, but they subsequently stopped living together.
2 may not have been living with the parent of the child when the child was born.

Official statistics give some indication of the frequency of the different paths to lone-parenthood, but do not provide a complete picture.

Official figures for Britain show that the largest proportion of female lone parents in 1995-7 were single, with about a third being divorced and just under a quarter separated. The figures for those who were single do not differentiate between those who were cohabiting when the child was conceived and those who were not. These proportions have changed over time. Between 1971 and 1995-7, according to official statistics, the proportion of lone mothers who were single rose from 21 per cent to 33 per cent, the proportion who were divorced rose from 16 per cent to 38 per cent, while the proportion who were widowed fell from 21 per cent to just 6 per cent. The proportions among lone fathers were somewhat different in 1995-7, with more becoming lone parents through being widowed. It should be noted, though, that lone fathers make up only a small minority of lone parents. Only 1 per cent of the family households in the 1996 *General Household Survey* were headed by lone fathers, compared to 18 per cent that were headed by lone mothers (Thomas, Walker, Willmott and Bennett, 1998).

Clearly, then, the rise in lone motherhood is closely related both to increases in the divorce rate and to an increase in births outside marriage. The causes of the rise in divorces are discussed later in this chapter (see pp. 568–72). The increase in single lone mothers may partly result from a reduction in the number of 'shotgun weddings' – that is, getting married to legitimate a pregnancy. Mark Brown (1995) suggests that in previous eras it was more common for parents to get married, rather than simply cohabiting, if they discovered that the woman was pregnant. Marriages that resulted from pregnancy were often unstable and could end up producing lone motherhood through an eventual divorce or separation. Now, the partners may choose to cohabit rather than marry and, if their relationship breaks up, they end up appearing in the statistics as a single, never-married, parent.

According to figures quoted by Brown, there has been a marked increase in jointly registered births outside marriage. In 1971 just 45 per cent of births were jointly registered in England and Wales but this had increased to 76 per cent by 1992. Of these, nearly three-quarters were registered by couples living at the same address. Brown also points out that some lone mothers may intend to cohabit with the father of their child but may be prevented from doing so if they cannot find or afford accommodation together.

The absence of cohabitation does not necessarily imply that the parents do not have a close relation-

ship. Some writers see the rise of single parenthood as a symptom of increased tolerance of diverse family forms. For example, the Rapoports (1982) claim that the single-parent family is an important 'emerging form' of the family which is becoming accepted as a legitimate alternative to other family structures.

However, there is little evidence that a large number of single parents see their situation as ideal and actively choose it as an alternative to dual parenthood. Burghes and Brown conducted research into 31 lone mothers and found that only a minority of the pregnancies were planned. None of the mothers had actively set out to become lone mothers and all of them attributed the break-up of their relationship to 'violence in the relationship or the father's unwillingness to settle down' (Burghes and Brown, 1995). In this small sample, all aspired to forming a two-parent household, but they had failed to achieve it despite their preference.

A number of Conservative politicians have argued that the increase in single parenthood is a consequence of the welfare state. John Selwyn Gummer claimed that there are 'perverse incentives' for young women to become pregnant so that it increases their chance of being allocated council housing. In July 1993, two other Conservative ministers, Peter Lilley and John Redwood, expressed concern about the cost of welfare payments to single-parent families and the possibility that the availability of such payments encouraged single parenthood. In 1993, the then Home Secretary, Michael Howard, expressed approval for a policy in New Jersey in the USA, in which welfare benefits were withdrawn from lone mothers (discussed in McIntosh, 1996).

The view that welfare payments create lone motherhood has been closely associated with Charles Murray's view of the underclass (discussed on pp. 91–2 and 323–8). According to Mary McIntosh, the US President Bill Clinton has suggested that Murray's explanation for the development of the underclass is basically correct. New Labour politicians in Britain have been less willing to openly suggest that lone motherhood is caused by welfare payments. However, they have developed a 'New Deal' for lone parents which encourages them to find employment rather than relying upon benefits (discussed in the Green Paper, *Supporting Families*, 1998). (See pp. 576–7 for a discussion of New Labour policies on families.)

However, there are a number of reasons for supposing that the welfare state is not responsible for the increases:

1 Some commentators do not believe that lone parenthood gives advantages to those seeking local authority housing. In 1993, John Perry, policy director of the Institute of Housing, said:

I've not been able to find a single housing authority which discriminates in favour of single parents over couples with children. The homeless get priority, but there is no suggestion that a homeless single parent gets priority over a homeless couple.

Quoted in *The Independent on Sunday*, 11 July 1993

2 As the next section indicates, single parents who are reliant upon benefits tend to live in poor housing conditions and to have low standards of living. There is little material incentive to become a single parent.

3 There is evidence that a large majority of single parents do not wish to be reliant on state benefits. They would prefer to work for a living but find it impractical to do so. A 1991 DSS survey found that 90 per cent of single parents would like to work at some point in the future and 55 per cent would start work immediately if they could obtain suitable help with childcare (quoted in the *Observer*, 11 July 1993). The 1998 British government Green Paper, *Supporting Families*, quoted figures showing that 44 per cent of lone mothers had paid employment and 85 per cent of the remainder would like to be employed.

David Morgan suggests that the rise in lone parenthood could partly be due to changing relationships between men and women. He says important factors causing the rise could include 'the expectations that women and men have of marriage and the growing opportunities for women to develop a life for themselves outside marriage or long-term cohabitations' (Morgan, 1994).

A longer-term trend that helps to account for the increase could be a decline in the stigma attached to single parenthood. This is reflected in the decreasing use of terms such as 'illegitimate children' and 'unmarried mothers', which seem to imply some deviation from the norms of family life, and their replacement by concepts such as 'single-parent families' and 'lone-parent families', which do not carry such negative connotations. The reduction in the stigma of single parenthood could relate to 'the weakening of religious or community controls over women' (Morgan, 1994).

The consequences of single parenthood

Single parenthood has increasingly become a contentious issue, with some arguing that it has become a serious problem for society. For example, in a letter to *The Times* in 1985, Lady Scott said:

A vast majority of the population would still agree, I think, that the normal family is an influence for good in society and that one-parent families are bad news. Since not many single parents can both earn a living and give children the love and care they need, society has to support them; the children suffer through lacking one parent.

Quoted in Fletcher, 1988, p. 151

Similar sentiments have been expressed by British Conservative politicians and, when they were in government, such views began to influence social policies (see pp. 574–6). New Labour politicians have been less inclined to condemn single parenthood outright, but the Labour government's 1998 Green Paper, *Supporting Families*, did say that 'marriage is still the surest foundation for raising children'.

Sociologists such as Charles Murray have even gone so far as to claim that single parenthood has contributed to creating a whole new stratum of society, the underclass – a claim we consider in detail on pp. 91–6. Mary McIntosh says that 'Over recent years, the media in the United Kingdom have been reflecting a concern about lone mothers that amounts to a moral panic' (McIntosh, 1996). She claims that, as a group, lone mothers have been stigmatized and blamed for problems such as youth crime, high taxation to pay for welfare benefits, encouraging a culture of dependency on the state, and producing children who grow up to be unemployable. She says, 'Perhaps the most serious charge is that they are ineffective in bringing up their children.'

However, while most commentators agree that single parenthood can create problems for individual parents, many sociologists do not see it as a social problem, and some believe that it is a sign of social progress. As Sarah McLanahan and Karen Booth have said:

Some view the mother-only family as an indicator of social disorganization, signalling the 'demise of the family'. Others regard it as an alternative family form consistent with the emerging economic independence of women.

McLanahan and Booth, 1991

Single parenthood and living standards

However single parenthood is viewed, there is little doubt that it tends to be associated with low living standards. The *General Household Survey* of 1996 found that single-parent families were disadvantaged in comparison to other British families. In 1996, 60 per cent of lone-mother families had a gross weekly income of below £150 per week, compared to 7 per cent of married couples (Thomas *et al.*, 1998).

Many of these differences stem from the likelihood of lone-parent families relying upon benefit. British government figures show that, in 1961, one in six lone parents received government benefits; by 1993, over three-quarters did so. According to DSS figures from 1993, the average single parent with one child received just £67.55 per week in income support, although they might in addition receive extra child allowance and housing benefit to cover rent or mortgage payments.

Other effects

More controversial than the low average living standards of lone parents is the question of the psychological and social effects on children raised in such families. McLanahan and Booth have listed the findings of a number of American studies which seem to indicate that children are harmed by single parenthood. These studies have claimed that such children have lower earnings and experience more poverty as adults; children of mother-only families are more likely to become lone parents themselves; and they are more likely to become delinquent and engage in drug abuse (McLanahan and Booth, 1991).

The findings of such studies must be treated with caution. As McLanahan and Booth themselves point out, the differences outlined above stem partly from the low income of lone-parent families and not directly from the absence of the second parent from the household.

In a review of research on lone parenthood, Louie Burghes notes that some research into the relationship between educational attainment and divorce suggests that children in families where the parents divorce start to do more poorly in education before the divorce takes place. Burghes argues that this implies that 'it is the quality of the family relationships, of which the divorce is only a part, that are influential' (Burghes, 1996).

The more sophisticated research into the effects of lone parenthood tries to take account of factors such as social class and low income. These studies find that 'the gap in outcomes between children who have and have not experienced family change narrows. In some cases they disappear; in others, statistically significant differences may remain. Some of these differences are small' (Burghes, 1996).

E.E. Cashmore has questioned the assumption that children brought up by one parent are worse off than those brought up by two. Cashmore argues that it is often preferable for a child to live with one caring parent than with one caring and one uncaring parent, particularly if the parents are constantly quarrelling and the marriage has all but broken down.

Cashmore also suggests that single parenthood can have attractions for the parent, particularly for mothers, since conventional family life may benefit men more than women. He says:

> Given the 'darker side of family life' and the unseen ways in which the nuclear unit serves 'male power' rather than the interests of women, the idea of parents breaking free of marriage and raising children single-handed has its appeals.

Cashmore, 1985

It can give women greater independence than they have in other family situations. However, Cashmore does acknowledge that many lone mothers who are freed from dependence on a male partner end up becoming dependent on the state and facing financial hardship. He concludes that 'Lone parents do not need a partner so much as a partner's income.'

David Morgan does believe that the evidence suggests that the children of single parents fare less well than those from two-parent households (Morgan, 1994). He qualifies this by saying that 'we still do not know enough about what causes these differences'. As with the effects of financial hardships, the children could be affected by the stigma attached to coming from a single-parent family. Morgan argues that 'It is possible, for example, that school teachers may be more likely to label a child as difficult if they have the knowledge that a particular child comes from a single-parent household.'

For Morgan, it is very difficult to disentangle the direct and indirect effects on children of being brought up in a single-parent household, and therefore dangerous to make generalizations about such effects.

Ethnicity and family diversity

Ethnicity can be seen as one of the most important sources of family diversity in Britain. Ethnic groups with different cultural backgrounds may introduce family forms that differ significantly from those of the ethnic majority.

British sociologists have paid increasing attention to the family patterns of ethnic minority groups. They have been particularly concerned to establish the extent to which the family relationships typical of the societies of origin of the ethnic minorities have been modified within the British context. Thus, sociologists have compared ethnic minority families in Britain both with families in the country of their origin and with other British families.

Although some changes in the traditional family life of these groups might be expected, the degree to which they change could provide important evidence in relation to the theory of increasing family diversity. If it is true that cultural diversity is becoming increasingly accepted in Britain, then these families could be expected to change little. If, however, the families of ethnic minorities are becoming more similar to other British families, then family diversity resulting from ethnic differences might be only temporary.

Statistical evidence

Statistical evidence does suggest that there are some differences in the prevalence of different household types in different ethnic groups.

The Policy Studies Institute's *Fourth National Survey of Ethnic Minorities*, which was conducted in England and Wales in 1994, also found significant differences between the families and households of different ethnic groups (Modood *et al.* 1997, see p. 216 for further details of the survey). Table 8.7 shows the marital status of different ethnic groups among adults under 60. It shows that whites and Caribbeans had higher rates of divorce and cohabitation than other groups, and that Indians, African Asians, Bangladeshis and Pakistanis were the ethnic groups who were most likely to be married.

The survey also found marked differences in the parental status of families with children. These are shown in Figure 8.1. The survey found that 90 per cent of South Asian families with children had married parents. Amongst whites, 75 per cent of families had married parents; amongst Caribbean families, less than 50 per cent had married parents, and a third had single, never-married mothers.

Using data from previous surveys, Tariq Modood *et al.* were able to calculate the proportions of families with children in different ethnic groups which were headed by lone parents at different points in time. Table 8.8 shows that there had been a substantial increase in lone parenthood in all three ethnic groups, but that the increase had been most noticeable in ethnic minorities. The rate amongst South Asian families had risen most quickly, but from a very low base, so that by 1994 they were still by far the least likely group to have formed lone-parent families.

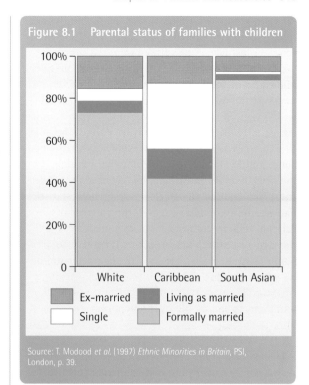

Figure 8.1 Parental status of families with children

Legend:
- Ex-married
- Single
- Living as married
- Formally married

Source: T. Modood *et al.* (1997) *Ethnic Minorities in Britain*, PSI, London, p. 39.

Table 8.8 Proportion of families with children which were lone-parent families, 1974–94

	White	Caribbean	South Asian
1974 (household definition)	n.a.	13	1
1982 (household definition)	10	31	5
1994 (household definition)	16	36	5

Source: T. Modood *et al.* (1997) *Ethnic Minorities in Britain*, PSI, London , p. 40.

Table 8.7 Marital status, adults under 60

	White	Caribbean	Indian	Percentages African Asian	Pakistani	Bangladeshi	Chinese
Single	23	41	21	21	19	22	34
Married	60	39	72	72	74	73	62
Living as married	9	10	3	2	3	1	1
Separated/divorced	7	9	3	3	3	1	3
Widowed	1	2	2	1	2	3	–
Weighted count	*4,194*	*1,834*	*1,539*	*960*	*1,053*	*344*	*467*
Unweighted count	*4,187*	*1,298*	*1,560*	*951*	*1,709*	*815*	*271*

Note: Analysis based on all individuals in survey households, who were neither dependent children, nor 60 or more.

Source: T. Modood *et al.* (1997) *Ethnic Minorities in Britain*, PSI, London , p. 24.

Rates amongst Caribbean families had also risen rapidly and were probably the highest rates at the time of all three surveys (there were no figures for whites in the 1974 survey). It is significant that very high rates of single parenthood were not present amongst families of Caribbean origin in 1974. This would suggest that diversity of family types amongst ethnic minorities has developed over time. The family types of ethnic minorities have not remained static and Modood *et al.* conclude that ethnic minority families in Britain changed rapidly between the 1970s and the 1990s. However, as both statistics and qualitative studies suggest, the patterns of different ethnic groups do remain somewhat different. There has not been a convergence to a single, typical, British family type, characteristic of all ethnic groups.

We will now examine the significance of variations in family life by ethnic group.

South Asian families

Roger Ballard (1982, 1990) has examined South Asian families in Britain and compared them to families in South Asia itself. Migration from this area began in the 1950s and was mainly from the Punjab, Gujerat and Bengal. Although there are important differences in family life within these groups, which stem from area of origin, religion and caste, Ballard identifies some features generally held in common.

Families in South Asia are based traditionally around a man, his sons and grandsons, and their respective wives and unmarried daughters. These family groups ideally live and work together in large multi-generational households, sharing both domestic and production tasks. In practice, in the past many households were not as large as might be expected. A high death rate limited the number of generations living together, and sons might establish different households after their father's death when the family land was divided up.

Changes in South Asian families

Ballard found that some changes had taken place in Asian families in Britain. Women were increasingly working outside the home, and production was less frequently family-based because wage labour provided the most common source of income. Ballard claims that married couples in Britain expect more independence from their kin. In some families extended kinship networks are less important than they traditionally are because some of the kin remain in South Asia or live in distant parts of Britain. Families were also split into smaller domestic units, partly because British housing was rarely suited to the needs of large groupings.

The strengthening of South Asian families

Despite these changes, Ballard says:

> It should not be assumed that such upheavals have either undermined or stood in contradiction to family unity. On the contrary migration has taken place within the context of familial obligations and has if anything strengthened rather than weakened them.
>
> Ballard 1982

Many migrants found that British culture seemed to attach little value to family honour and placed relatively little emphasis on maintaining kinship ties. As a result, many first-generation immigrants became conservative and cautious in their attitudes to family life. They were vigilant in ensuring that standards of behaviour in the family did not slip and kept a close check on their children.

Ballard found that many children had the experience of two cultures. They behaved in ways that conformed to the culture of the wider society for part of the time, but at home conformed to their ethnic subculture. Although children increasingly expected to have some say in their marriage partners, they generally did not reject the principle of arranged marriages.

The majority of families relied on wage labour, but some of the more successful began to establish family businesses (such as buying a shop) which provided a new focus for the family's economic activities.

Ballard found that, despite the distances involved, most families retained links with their village of origin in Asia. Extended kinship links could stretch over thousands of miles. He found that money was sometimes sent to help support family members who remained in Asia.

In Britain, despite the housing problems, close family ties remained. By living close together, or buying adjoining houses and knocking through a connecting door, people were able to retain strong family links.

Ballard concluded that South Asians had suffered comparatively little disruption to family life as a result of settling in Great Britain.

Asian families in the PSI *National Survey*

Data on families collected in the Policy Studies Institute's *Fourth National Survey of Ethnic Minorities* was analysed by Richard Berthoud and Sharon Beishon (1997). They found that British South Asians 'were more likely to marry and marry earlier than their white equivalents. Few of them lived as married and separation and divorce were relatively rare.' Nearly all South Asian mothers were married and 'a relatively high proportion of South Asian couples, including many with children, lived in the same house as the young man's father'. Nevertheless, there was some evidence that family patterns were changing.

There were some divorces and some single parents in Asian communities, and another sign of change was a fall in the number of children born to each married couple. The study also found some evidence of changing attitudes to family life, with, for example, young people expecting more say in the choice of marriage partner than their parents had expected.

Cypriot families in Britain

Robin Oakley (1982) conducted a study of Cypriot families in Britain. This group numbers around 140,000, and in some areas, particularly London, the Cypriot community has been established since just after the First World War. Most of the immigration took place in the 20 years following the Second World War.

According to Oakley, Cypriots traditionally have very strong extended family ties, and parents retain strong connections with married children. There are taboos against seeking outside help to solve family problems, and families are not child-centred – children are expected to pull their weight like other family members. Oakley found little evidence that these patterns had changed significantly among British Cypriot families despite the length of time some of them had been in Britain. There were relatively few elderly Cypriots in Britain and for this reason extended kinship links were somewhat weaker than in Cyprus itself.

Families in the West Indies

Research into the family life of West Indians in Britain and in the Caribbean has found greater diversity in their cultural patterns. Jocelyn Barrow (1982) argues that there are three main West Indian family types in the Caribbean:

1 The conventional nuclear family, or 'Christian marriage', which is often little different from nuclear families in Britain. Families of this type tend to be typical of the more religious or economically successful groups in the population.

2 The second main type found in the West Indies, the common-law family, is more frequently found among the less economically successful. An unmarried couple live together and look after children who may or may not be their biological offspring.

3 The third type Barrow calls the mother household, in which the mother or grandmother of the children is head of the household and, for most of the time at least, the household contains no adult males. This type of household often relies a good deal on the help and support of female kin living nearby to enable the head of the household to fulfil her family responsibilities.

West Indian families in Britain

To a large extent, research has shown that a similar mixture of family types exists in Britain amongst West Indian groups. Geoffrey Driver (1982), however, has found that in some cases what appears to be a nuclear family is rather different beneath the surface. He uses the example of a family called the Campbells. In this family the wife took on primary responsibility both for running the household and for being the breadwinner after her husband lost his job. In reality, then, this was a mother-centred family, even though it contained an adult male.

Barrow (1982) found that mother-centred families in Britain, whether or not they contained an adult male, could rely less on the support of female kin than they could in the West Indies. They were much less likely to live close to the relevant kin, and in some cases appropriate kin were still in the West Indies, and could not therefore be called upon to provide assistance.

However, Barrow discovered that equivalent networks tended to build up in areas with high concentrations of West Indians. Informal help with childcare and other domestic tasks is common among neighbours, and self-help projects such as pre-school playgroups are frequent features of West Indian communities.

Mary Chamberlain (1999) studied the importance of brothers, sisters, uncles and aunts to Caribbean families in the United Kingdom and the Caribbean. She found that siblings often played a significant part in the upbringing of their younger brothers and sisters or of their nephews and nieces. Like Barrow, she found that distance from kin made it difficult or even impossible for relatives to play such a signifi-cant role in childcare as they played in many families in the Caribbean. Nevertheless, some British Afro-Caribbeans were able to choose to live close to their relatives, and brothers, sisters, aunts and uncles played a greater role in the upbringing of children than is typical of white British families.

Berthoud and Beishon, who analysed the data from the PSI survey, found some distinctive features of black family life in Britain, but also a great deal of variety between families. They say that 'the most striking characteristic is a low emphasis on long-term partnerships, and especially on formal marriage' (Berthoud and Beishon, 1997). British Afro-Caribbean families had high rates of divorce and separation and were more likely than other groups to have children outside of marriage. Among this group there were also high proportions of lone mothers, but Afro-Caribbean lone mothers were much more likely than those from other groups to have paid employment. Nevertheless, over half of Caribbean families with children were married or cohabiting in long-term relationships.

Ethnicity and family diversity – conclusion

The general picture provided by these studies, then, suggests that immigrants and their descendants have adapted their family life to fit British circumstances, but have not fundamentally altered the relationships on which their traditional family life was based. This would suggest that the existence of a variety of ethnic groups has indeed contributed to the diversity of family types to be found in Britain. These ethnic minorities have succeeded in retaining many of the culturally distinctive features of their family life.

Nevertheless, there is also evidence of changes taking place in the families of ethnic minorities, and British culture may have more effect on future generations. Each ethnic group contains a variety of different family types, which are influenced by factors such as class and stage in the life cycle, which relate to diversity in white families. David Morgan warns that:

> while seeking to recognize ethnic diversity in a multicultural society, ethnic boundaries may be too readily or too easily constructed by, say, white Western analysts. There may be oversimplified references to 'The Chinese family', 'The Muslim family' and so on just as, in the past, there have been oversimplified references to 'the Jewish family'.
>
> Morgan, 1996, p. 62

Ethnic minority families have not just contributed to family diversity through each group having its own distinctive family pattern, they have also contributed to it through developing diverse family patterns within each ethnic group. The Cypriot example, though, demonstrates the considerable resilience of the culture of an ethnic group, some of whom have been settled in Britain for well over half a century.

Robert Chester – the British neo-conventional family

In a strong attack upon the idea that fundamental changes are taking place in British family life, Robert Chester (1985) argued that the changes had been only minor. He claimed that the evidence advanced by writers such as the Rapoports was misleading, and that the basic features of family life had remained largely unchanged for the vast majority of the British population since the Second World War. He argued:

> Most adults still marry and have children. Most children are reared by their natural parents. Most people live in a household headed by a married couple. Most marriages continue until parted by death. No great change seems currently in prospect.
>
> Chester, 1985

Percentage of people versus percentage of households

Chester believed that a snapshot of household types at a particular time does not provide a valid picture of the British family.

The first point that Chester made is that a very different picture is produced if the percentage of people in various types of household is calculated, instead of the percentage of households of various types. Households containing parents and children contain a greater percentage of the population than the percentage of households they make up. This is because family households tend to have more members than other types of household.

Chester's arguments were based upon figures from 1981. As Table 8.9 shows, the way the figures are calculated does make a difference. In 1981, 40 per cent of households were made up of two parents and children, but over 59 per cent of people lived in such households. In 1998, 30 per cent of households consisted of two parents plus children, but 49 per cent of people lived in such households. Despite the decline, very nearly half were still living in nuclear, two-generation households, with a further 24 per cent living in couple households.

The nuclear family and the life cycle

The second point made by Chester was that life cycles make it inevitable that at any one time some people will not be a member of a nuclear family household. Many of those who lived in other types of household would either have experienced living in a nuclear family in the past, or would do so in the future. He said, 'The 8 per cent living alone are mostly the elderly widowed, or else younger people who are likely to marry.' He described the parents–children household as 'one which is normal and is still experienced by the vast majority'.

The 'neo-conventional family'

According to Chester, there was little evidence that people were choosing to live on a long-term basis in alternatives to the nuclear family. However, he did accept that some changes were taking place in family life. In particular, many families were no longer 'conventional' in the sense that the husband is the sole breadwinner. He accepted that women were increasingly making a contribution to household finances by taking paid employment outside the home.

However, he argued that, although 58 per cent of wives, according to his figures, worked, often they only did so for part of their married lives, and frequently on a part-time basis. Many gave up work for the period when their children were young; a minority of married mothers (49 per cent) were employed, and only 14 per cent of working married mothers had full-time jobs. Because of such figures he argued that 'The pattern is of married women withdrawing from the labour force to become mothers, and some of them taking (mostly part-time) work as their children mature.'

Although he recognized that this was an important change in family life compared to the past, he did not see it as a fundamental alteration in the family. He called this new family form – in which wives have some involvement in the labour market – the neo-conventional family. It was little different from the conventional family apart from the increasing numbers of wives working for at least part of their married lives.

Family diversity – conclusion

While Chester makes an important point in stressing that nuclear families remained very common and feature in most people's lives, he perhaps overstated his case. As Table 8.9 shows, there has been a continuing reduction in the proportion of people living in parents-and-children households, from 59 per cent in 1981 to 49 per cent in 1998. The percentages of people living alone or in lone-parent households have increased. Thus, since Chester was writing, there has been a slow but steady drift away from living in nuclear families in Britain.

In 1990, the position was summed up by Kathleen Kiernan and Malcolm Wicks who said that 'Although still the most prominent form, the nuclear family is for increasing numbers of individuals only one of several possible family types that they experience during their lives.' Similarly, in 1999, Elizabeth Silva

and Carol Smart argue that fairly traditional family forms remain important. They note that:

in 1996 73 per cent of households were composed of heterosexual couples (with just under 90 per cent of these being married), 50 per cent of these households had children, and 40 per cent had dependent children ... only 9 per cent of households with dependent children were headed by lone parents.

Silva and Smart, 1999, p. 3

Nevertheless, they argue that 'personal choices appear as increasingly autonomous and fluid'. The idea that family diversity indicates a new era of choice was first advanced by the Rapoports in 1982. They argued that it was increasingly acceptable to form alternative households and families to conventional nuclear ones. They said:

Families in Britain today are in a transition from coping in a society in which there was a single overriding norm of what family life should be like to a society in which a plurality of norms are recognized as legitimate, indeed, desirable.

Rapoport and Rapoport, 1982

The passage of time does not seem to have made their argument less valid. Indeed, a growing number of sociologists have tried to link ideas of choice and diversity with their particular views on modernity and postmodernity. (These views will be examined on pp. 577–84.)

Having surveyed the ways in which the structure of the family may have changed over the years, we will now investigate whether the functions of the family have also changed.

Table 8.9	Households and people in households in Great Britain, 1981 and 1998			
Type of household	% of households 1981	% of people 1981	% of households 1998	% of people 1998
One person	22	8	28	12
Married couple	26	20	28	24
Married couple with dependent children	32	49	23	40
Married couple with independent children	8	10	7	9
Lone parent with dependent children	4	5	7	8
Other	9	8	7	8

Source: *Social Trends* (1982 and 1999) HMSO, London.

The changing functions of the family

The loss of functions

Many sociologists argue that the family has lost a number of its functions in modern industrial society. Institutions such as businesses, political parties, schools, and welfare organizations now specialize in functions formerly performed by the family. Talcott Parsons argued that the family has become:

on the 'macroscopic' levels, almost completely functionless. It does not itself, except here and there, engage in much economic production; it is not a significant unit in the political power system; it is not a major direct agency of integration of the larger society. Its individual members participate in all these functions, but they do so as individuals, not in their roles as family members.

Parsons, 1955, p. 16

However, this does not mean that the family is declining in importance – it has simply become more specialized. Parsons maintained that its role is still vital. By structuring the personalities of the young and stabilizing the personalities of adults, the family provides its members with the psychological training and support necessary to meet the requirements of the social system. Parsons concluded that 'the family is more specialized than before, but not in any general sense less important, because society is dependent more exclusively on it for the performance of certain of its vital functions'. Thus the loss of certain functions by the family has made its remaining functions more important.

This view is supported by N. Dennis (1975) who argues that impersonal bureaucratic agencies have taken over many of the family's functions. As a result, the warmth and close supportive relationships that existed when the family performed a large range of functions have largely disappeared.

Dennis argues that, in the impersonal setting of modern industrial society, the family provides the only opportunity 'to participate in a relationship where people are perceived and valued as whole persons'. Outside the family, individuals must often interact with strangers in terms of a number of roles. Adopting roles such as employee, customer, teacher and student, they are unable to express many aspects of themselves or develop deep and supportive relationships. Dennis argues that:

marriage has become the only institution in which the individual can expect esteem and love. Adults have no one on whom they have the right to lean for this sort of support at all comparable with their right to lean on their spouse.

Dennis, 1975

Young and Willmott make a similar point, arguing that the emotional support provided by family relationships grows in importance as the family loses many of its functions. They claim that the family:

can provide some sense of wholeness and permanence to set against the more restricted and transitory roles imposed by the specialized institutions which have flourished outside the home. The upshot is that, as the disadvantages of the new industrial and impersonal society have become more pronounced, so the family has become more prized for its power to counteract them.

Young and Willmott, 1973, p. 269

The maintenance and improvement of functions

Not all sociologists would agree, however, that the family has lost many of its functions in modern industrial society. Ronald Fletcher, a British sociologist and a staunch supporter of the family, maintained that just the opposite has happened. In *The Family and Marriage in Britain* (1966), Fletcher argued that not only has the family retained its functions but those functions have 'increased in detail and importance'. Specialized institutions such as schools and hospitals have added to and improved the family's functions, rather than superseded them.

1 Fletcher maintained that the family's responsibility for socializing the young is as important as it ever was. State education has added to, rather than removed, this responsibility since 'Parents are expected to do their best to guide, encourage and support their children in their educational and occupational choices and careers'.

2 In the same way, the state has not removed the family's responsibility for the physical welfare of its members. Fletcher argued that 'The family is still centrally concerned with maintaining the health of its members, but it is now aided by wider provisions which have been added to the family's situation since pre-industrial times'.

Rather than removing this function from the family, the state provision of health services has served to expand and improve it. Compared to the past, parents are preoccupied with their children's health. State health and welfare provision has provided additional support for the family and made its members more aware of the importance of health and hygiene in the home.

3 Even though Fletcher admitted that the family has largely lost its function as a unit of production, he argued that it still maintains a vital economic function as a unit of consumption. Particularly in

the case of the modern home-centred family, money is spent on, and in the name of, the family rather than the individual. Thus the modern family demands fitted carpets, three-piece suites, washing machines, television sets and 'family' cars.

Young and Willmott (1973) make a similar point with respect to their symmetrical Stage 3 family (see pp. 529–30). They argue that 'In its capacity as a consumer the family has also made a crucial alliance with technology.' Industry needs both a market for its goods and a motivated workforce. The symmetrical family provides both. Workers are motivated to work by their desire for consumer durables. This desire stems from the high value they place on the family and a privatized lifestyle in the family home. This provides a ready market for the products of industry.

In this way the family performs an important economic function and is functionally related to the economic system. In Young and Willmott's words, 'The family and technology have achieved a mutual adaptation.'

Neo-Marxist views

This economic function looks rather different from a neo-Marxist perspective. Writers such as Marcuse (1972) and Gorz (1965) argue that alienation at work leads to a search for fulfilment outside work. However, the capitalist-controlled mass media, with its advertisements that proclaim the virtues of family life and associate the products of industry with those virtues, simply creates 'false needs'. With pictures of the 'Persil mum' and the happy family in the midst of its consumer durables, the myth that material possessions bring happiness and fulfilment is promoted. This myth produces the obedient, motivated worker and the receptive consumer that capitalism requires. The family man or woman is therefore ideal material for exploitation. (We analyse Marcuse's views in more detail in Chapter 10.)

Feminism and economic functions

Feminist writers have tended to disagree with the view shared by many sociologists of the family that the family has lost its economic role as a unit of production and has become simply a unit of consumption. They tend to argue that much of the work that takes place in the family is productive but it is not recognized as such because it is unpaid and it is usually done by women. The contribution to economic life made by women is frequently underestimated.

The radical feminists Christine Delphy and Diana Leonard (1992) accept that industrialization created new units of production such as factories, but deny that it removed the productive function from the

family. Some productive functions have been lost, but others are performed to a much higher standard than in the past. They cite as examples 'warm and tidy rooms with attention to décor, and more complex meals with a variety of forms of cooking'. The family has taken on some new productive functions, such as giving pre-school reading tuition to children, and functions such as washing clothes and freezing food have been reintroduced to the household with the advent of new consumer products.

They also point out that there are still a fair number of families which continue to act as an economic unit producing goods for the market. French farming families, which have been studied by Christine Delphy, are a case in point. (We discussed Delphy and Leonard's work in more detail earlier, see pp. 516–18. Housework is discussed in more detail on pp. 552–63.)

Summary and conclusions

In summary, most sociologists who adopt a functionalist perspective argue that the family has lost several of its functions in modern industrial society but they maintain that the importance of the family has not declined. Rather, the family has adapted and is adapting to a developing industrial society. It remains a vital and basic institution in society.

Others dispute the claim that some of these functions have been lost, or argue that new functions have replaced the old ones. From all these viewpoints the family remains a key institution.

All the writers examined here have a tendency to think in terms of 'the family' without differentiating between different types of family. They may not, therefore, appreciate the range of effects family life can have or the range of functions it may perform. Postmodernists and difference feminists certainly reject the view that there is any single type of family which always performs certain functions (see pp. 582–4 for a discussion of postmodernism and pp. 519–23 for a discussion of difference feminism).

The writers discussed also tend to assume that families reproduce the existing social structure, whether this is seen as a functioning mechanism, an exploitative capitalist system, or as a patriarchal society. Yet families are not necessarily supportive of or instrumental in reproducing existing societies. With increasing family diversity, some individual families and even some types of family may be radical forces in society. For example, gay and lesbian families sometimes see themselves as challenging the inegalitarian relationships in heterosexual families (see pp. 562–3 for a discussion of lesbian families).

In this section we have discussed the various functional roles that the family performs; in the next section we focus on the various roles within the family.

Conjugal roles

A major characteristic of the symmetrical family – which Young and Willmott (1973) claimed was developing when they were writing in the 1970s – was the degree to which spouses shared domestic, work and leisure activities. Relationships of this type are known as joint conjugal roles, as opposed to segregated conjugal roles.

In Young and Willmott's Stage 2 family, conjugal roles – the marital roles of husband and wife – were largely segregated. There was a clearcut division of labour between the spouses in the household, and the husband was relatively uninvolved with domestic chores and raising the children. This segregation of conjugal roles extended to leisure. The wife associated mainly with her female kin and neighbours; the husband with his male workmates, kin and neighbours. This pattern was typical of the traditional working-class community of Bethnal Green.

In the Stage 3 symmetrical family, conjugal roles become more joint. Although the wife still has primary responsibility for housework and child-rearing, husbands become more involved, often washing clothes, ironing and sharing other domestic duties. (In fact, from their research Young and Willmott found that 72 per cent of husbands did housework other than washing up during the course of a week.) Husband and wife increasingly share responsibility for decisions that affect the family. They discuss matters such as household finances and their children's education to a greater degree than the Stage 2 family.

Young and Willmott argue that the change from segregated to joint conjugal roles results mainly from the withdrawal of the wife from her relationships with female kin, and the drawing of the husband into the family circle. We looked at the reasons they gave for this in a previous section (see pp. 529–30). The extent to which conjugal roles have been changing and what this indicates about inequalities between men and women have been the subject of some controversy. These controversies will now be discussed.

Inequality within marriage

Although much of the recent research on conjugal roles has been concerned with determining the degree of inequality between husband and wife within marriage, there has been no generally accepted way of determining the extent of inequality. Different researchers have measured different aspects of inequality. Some have concentrated on the division of labour in the home: they have examined the allocation of responsibility for domestic work between husband and wife and the amount of time spent by spouses on particular tasks. Others have tried to measure the distribution of power within marriage.

Young and Willmott are amongst those who have argued that conjugal roles are increasingly becoming joint. However, most sociologists who have carried out research in this area have found little evidence that inequality within marriage has been significantly reduced.

Conjugal roles, housework and childcare

The symmetrical family

Young and Willmott's views on the symmetrical family (see above) have been heavily criticized. Ann Oakley (1974) argues that their claim of increasing symmetry within marriage is based on inadequate methodology. Although the figure of 72 per cent (for men doing housework) sounds impressive, she points out that it is based on only one question in Young and Willmott's interview schedule: 'Do you/does your husband help at least once a week with any household jobs like washing up, making beds (helping with the children), ironing, cooking or cleaning?' Oakley notes that men who make only a very small contribution to housework would be included in the 72 per cent. She says, 'A man who helps with the children once a week would be included in this percentage, so would (presumably) a man who ironed his own trousers on a Saturday afternoon.'

Ann Oakley – housework and childcare

A rather different picture of conjugal roles emerged in Oakley's own research (1974). She collected information on 40 married women who had one child or more under the age of 5, who were British or Irish born, and aged between 20 and 30. Half of her sample were working-class, half were middle-class and all lived in the London area.

She found greater equality in terms of the allocation of domestic tasks between spouses in the middle class than in the working class (see Table 8.10). However, in both classes few men had a high level of participation in housework and childcare: few marriages could be defined as egalitarian. In only 15 per cent of marriages did men have a high level of participation in housework, and in childcare in only 25 per cent.

Table 8.10 Husband's participation in domestic tasks

	High	Medium	Low
Husband's participation in housework			
Working class	10%	5%	85%
Middle class	20%	45%	35%
Husband's participation in childcare			
Working class	10%	40%	50%
Middle class	40%	20%	40%

Source: Adapted from Ann Oakley (1985) *The Sociology of Housework*, 2nd edition, Basil Blackwell, Oxford, p. 137.

Middle-class couples

Stephen Edgell (1980) tested Young and Willmott's theory of the symmetrical family by examining conjugal roles in a sample of 38 middle-class couples.

The symmetrical family was thought by Young and Willmott to be particularly typical of the middle class, but Edgell found little evidence to support this view. None of the couples in his sample was classified as having joint conjugal roles in relation to housework, although 44.6 per cent did have joint conjugal roles in relation to childcare. In these cases

most childcare tasks were shared, although women might still spend more time on them.

Survey data

The studies of both Oakley and Edgell are based on small samples which are not representative of the population as a whole. However, studies with much larger samples have been undertaken as part of the *British Social Attitudes Survey*. Using a sample of over 1,000 married respondents, it asked who usually carried out household tasks. Table 8.11 shows the results from the 1984 and 1991 surveys. Like Edgell's study, it found more sharing of child-rearing than household tasks. It also showed some movement towards a more egalitarian household division of labour over time. In terms of the household tasks there was more sharing of responsibilities and there were more households in which men did most of the washing and ironing, cooking, cleaning, shopping and washing up.

However, the number of households in which men were mainly responsible for these tasks remained as small minorities in 1991. Repairing household equipment was the only type of task that was more likely to be carried out by men.

The most recent *British Social Attitudes Survey* also included comparative data from Europe, but only included data on a restricted range of household

Table 8.11 Household division of labour by marital status in Great Britain, 1984 and 1991

	Married people Actual allocation of tasks					
	Mainly man 1984	1991	Mainly woman 1984	1991	Shared equally 1984	1991
Household tasks						
(percentage allocation)						
Washing and ironing	1	3	88	84	9	12
Preparation of evening meal	5	9	77	70	16	20
Household cleaning	3	4	72	68	23	27
Household shopping	6	8	54	45	39	47
Evening dishes	18	28	37	33	41	37
Organization of household money and bills	32	31	38	40	28	28
Repairs of household equipment	83	82	6	6	8	10
Child-rearing						
(percentage allocation)						
Looks after the children when they are sick	1	1	63	60	35	39
Teaches the children discipline	10	9	12	17	77	73

Source: *Social Trends* (1986) p. 36, and *British Social Attitudes Survey* (1992) pp. 7, 102, 103.

tasks (Jowell *et al.*, 1998) (see Table 8.12). This showed a small reduction in the gendered nature of washing and ironing in Britain (it was a mainly female task in 84 per cent of households in 1991, while the equivalent figure for 1997 was 79 per cent). There was also a small reduction in the tendency for men to be responsible for making repairs around the house (although the precise wording of the relevant question changed between surveys). Washing and ironing were less female-dominated in Britain than in other countries, but in Sweden looking after sick family members was considerably less likely than it was in Britain to be a mainly female activity.

Divisions of labour in north-west England

The Lancaster Regionalism Group also used survey data collected in 1988 to investigate the household division of labour (Warde *et al.*, 1990). The study, carried out by a group based at Lancaster University, was confined to north-west England, and the sample of 323 households was predominantly middle-class and contained disproportionate numbers of couples aged 36–59. This was because the questionnaires were administered by A-level Sociology students to their parents. The sample cannot therefore be considered representative, but in some other respects the methods used were an improvement on previous studies.

The Lancaster Group decided to include questions on who last carried out household tasks as well as who usually did them. They argued that when people stated that tasks were usually shared, this might disguise the fact that in many cases the task would still be carried out by women more often than men. In fact, the main effect of using this type of question was to reveal that children made a greater contribution to housework than is usually found.

The questionnaire covered a wide range of tasks, 45 in all, and yielded predictable results. The researchers found that 'Husbands tend to do a very much larger proportion of tasks concerned with home

maintenance, home improvement and car maintenance.' On the other hand, 'Women do the vast proportion of routine housework, domestic production and childcare.' Women cooked the last meal in 79 per cent of households, last washed the clothes in 87 per cent, tidied up in 72 per cent and bathed the children in 71 per cent.

The Lancaster researchers also decided to examine the popularity of different household tasks. Clearly some tasks are less pleasant and less interesting than others, and they wanted to see whether the male or female partner was likely to get the unpopular jobs. From a list of 20 tasks, ironing, washing clothes and washing dishes were most frequently chosen as things that were never enjoyed. Although men had last washed the dishes in 23 per cent of households, in only 5 per cent had they last done the ironing, and in only 3 per cent had they last washed the clothes. Respondents were not asked whether they enjoyed cleaning the toilet but, as Alan Warde, one of the researchers, puts it, 'cleaning lavatories is the bottom line – the least pleasant and least prestigious of all tasks'. It was also overwhelmingly women's work: women had last done this in 81 per cent of households.

As well as finding out who did what, and how popular tasks were, these researchers also decided to ask whether people thought that their household's division of labour was fair. They found a considerable proportion of men, 42 per cent, who thought that they were doing less than their fair share. Thus there was some evidence that attitudes had changed but 'the actual pattern of behaviour remains much as it was in an earlier generation'.

Mary Boulton – women and childcare

All of the above studies have focused simply upon the allocation of tasks in the home. Mary Boulton (1983) argues that they exaggerate the extent of men's involvement in childcare, and she denies that

Table 8.12 Household division of labour, 1997					
% saying always or usually the woman:	Western Germany	Britain	Irish Republic	Netherlands	Sweden*
Washing and ironing	88	79	85	87	80
Looking after sick family member	50	48	50	47	38
% saying always or usually the man:					
Makes small repairs around the house	80	75	69	78	82
Base (households with partners only)	*1,604*	*601*	*607*	*1,255*	*883*
For Sweden the base varies for the different tasks and this is the smallest unweighted base.					
Source: R. Jowell *et al.* (1998) *British and European Social Attitudes, Fifteenth Report*, Ashgate, Aldershot, p. 32.					

questions about who does what give a true picture of conjugal roles. To her, childcare:

> *is essentially about exercising responsibility for another person who is not fully responsible for herself and it entails seeing to all aspects of the child's security and well-being, her growth and development at any and all times.*
>
> Boulton, 1983

Boulton claims that, although men might help with particular tasks, it is their wives who retain primary responsibility for children. It is the wives who relegate non-domestic aspects of their lives to a low priority. From her own study of 50 young married mothers in London who did not have full-time jobs, only 18 per cent of husbands gave extensive help with childcare, while 36 per cent gave moderate help and 46 per cent minimal help. Husbands therefore had a major share of the responsibility for childcare in less than 20 per cent of the families she studied.

Elsa Ferri and Kate Smith – *Parenting in the 1990s*

Some empirical support for Boulton is provided by a study conducted by Elsa Ferri and Kate Smith (1996). They have produced data based upon the *National Child Development Survey*. This survey followed, as far as possible, the lives of everybody born in Great Britain in a specific week in 1958. The data comes from the 1991 survey when those involved were 33 years old. By that time, the sample included 2,800 fathers and 3,192 mothers.

The survey found that it was still very rare for fathers to take primary responsibility for childcare. In both the sample of mothers and the sample of fathers it was very rare in dual-earner families, no-earner families, or families where only the mother worked, for the man to be normally responsible for the children or to look after them when they were ill. In almost every category the man was the main carer in 4 per cent or less of families (see Tables 8.13 and 8.14). Even when the woman had paid employment outside the home and the man did not, it was still more common for the woman than the man to take main responsibility for routine childcare or childcare in the event of illness. This suggests that the increasing employment of married women outside the home had made comparatively little impact on the contributions of their male partners to childcare. Contrary to some other studies, the study found that men with working-class jobs or backgrounds made more contribution to childcare than those with middle-class jobs or backgrounds.

The study also found little evidence of the development of egalitarian gender roles in relation to other types of housework. Ferri and Smith say, 'Thus,

Table 8.13 'Who is normally responsible for generally being with and looking after children': by parents' employment situation

Cohort fathers:	Dual earner: wife ft	wife pt	Single earner: wife home	wife works	No earner
	%	%	%	%	%
Mostly father	2	1	<1	16	3
Mostly wife	24	42	68	21	45
Shared equally	72	57	32	61	53
Someone else	2	–	<1	2	–
Total	100	100	100	100	100
(n)	(397)	(993)	(1,008)	(44)	(78)
Cohort mothers:	Dual earner: mother ft	mother pt	Single earner: mother home	mother works	No earner
	%	%	%	%	%
Mostly mother	32	52	72	26	45
Mostly husband	1	<1	–	9	1
Shared equally	66	48	28	64	54
Someone else	1	–	–	1	–
Total	100	100	100	100	100
(n)	(532)	(1,261)	(953)	(66)	(83)

Source: E. Ferri and K. Smith (1996) *Parenting in the 1990s*, Family Policy Studies Centre, London, p. 15.

Table 8.14 'Who is normally responsible for looking after children when ill': by parents' employment situation

| Cohort fathers: | Dual earner: | | Single earner: | | No earner |
	wife ft	wife pt	wife home	wife works	
	%	%	%	%	%
Mostly father	2	1	<1	11	4
Mostly wife	45	65	76	36	45
Shared equally	52	34	23	50	51
Someone else	1	–	–	2	–
Total	100	100	100	100	100
(n)	(396)	(992)	(1,010)	(44)	(78)
Cohort mothers:	**Dual earner:**		**Single earner:**		**No earner**
	mother ft	mother pt	mother home	mother works	
	%	%	%	%	%
Mostly mother	54	69	80	48	66
Mostly husband	1	1	–	2	–
Shared equally	44	30	20	50	34
Someone else	1	–	–	–	–
Total	100	100	100	100	100
(n)	(531)	(1,260)	(953)	(64)	(83)

Source: E. Ferri and K. Smith (1996) *Parenting in the 1990s*, Family Policy Studies Centre, London, p. 16.

for example, two-thirds of full-time working mothers said they were responsible for cooking and cleaning, and four out of five for laundry.'

Conjugal roles and hours worked

Examining who does what within the home has been the most common method employed by sociologists studying conjugal roles. However, it can be argued that this may give a misleading picture, for it does not indicate how time-consuming different tasks are. It may be that the tasks carried out by women take up less time than those carried out by men.

Young and Willmott

In *The Symmetrical Family*, Young and Willmott collected information on how husbands and wives spent their time. They asked members of their sample to keep a record of time spent on different tasks, including paid employment and domestic work. The results, shown in Table 8.15, draw a rather different picture to that of other studies of the way tasks are allocated.

In this study, it seemed to be 'women not in paid work' (that is, housewives without a job) who did least work, although women with part- and full-time jobs did rather more work than men. Overall, the

Table 8.15 Average hours of paid and unpaid work (diary sample: married men and women aged 30 to 49)

	Men	Women working full-time	Women working part-time	Women not in paid work
Total for week				
Paid work, travel to work and household tasks	59.4	63.3	61.1	45.5

Source: M. Young and P. Willmott (1973) *The Symmetrical Family*, Penguin, Harmondsworth, p. 111.

differences between men's and women's work time were not that great.

Criticisms of Young and Willmott

Graham Allan (1985) has suggested that Young and Willmott's study might underestimate the hours spent on work by women. He points out that the study involved married couples aged between 30 and 49. It therefore excluded younger married women who would be more likely to have young children, and who might therefore spend more time on domestic tasks.

Allan's criticism of Young and Willmott's work seems to be supported by Ann Oakley's estimates of the amount of time spent on housework by the women in her study (Oakley, 1974). Oakley's sample were all aged between 20 and 30 and had young children. None of the sample spent less than 48 hours each week on housework. The woman who spent least time on these tasks was the only one in the sample who had a full-time job. The average number of hours spent on housework each week was 77, and this figure included five women who had part-time paid jobs.

Hours worked and social change

None of the above studies made any attempt to measure directly changes in hours worked by husbands and wives over time. Jonathan Gershuny (1992) has examined how social changes have affected the burden of work for British husbands and wives. Perhaps the most important change affecting this area of social life has been the rise in the proportion of wives taking paid employment outside the home. Sociologists such as Oakley have argued that women have increasingly been taking on a dual burden: they have retained primary responsibility for household tasks while also being expected to have paid employment. As Gershuny points out, this could lead to increased inequality between husbands and wives as a rising proportion of women suffer from this dual burden.

Gershuny examined 1974 and 1975 data from the BBC Audience Research Department, and 1987 data from an Economic and Social Research Council project, to discover how the share of work had changed. As Figure 8.2 shows, in 1987 the husbands of working women continued to do less than half the total paid and unpaid work done by their spouses. However, in other household types husbands did more than half the total work, and in all categories the husbands' share of work had risen.

Gershuny looked particularly closely at the possibility that the dual burden of working women was increasing the inequality in hours worked. Although the dual burden remained, men did seem

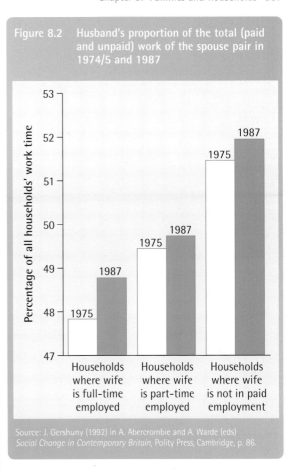

Figure 8.2 Husband's proportion of the total (paid and unpaid) work of the spouse pair in 1974/5 and 1987

Source: J. Gershuny (1992) in A. Abercrombie and A. Warde (eds) *Social Change in Contemporary Britain*, Polity Press, Cambridge, p. 86.

to be making more effort to do housework when their wives were in paid work. Husbands of wives with full-time employment increased the average time spent daily on cooking and cleaning from around 20 minutes in the mid-1970s to more than 40 minutes in 1987.

Types of work

Although Gershuny found that total working hours for husbands and wives were 'about the same', he noted that 'there is still differential specialization'. Simple figures on the amount of work done by husbands and wives do not give an accurate picture of the nature of their respective responsibilities. Graham Allan (1985) suggests that the work that women carry out in the home may be tedious and less satisfying than the more creative tasks that are frequently done by men. He says 'much female domestic work is monotonous and mundane, providing few intrinsic satisfactions'.

However, it can, of course, be argued that much paid work outside the home carried out by men is also alienating, although it is not usually as socially isolating as looking after young children. Gershuny's evidence shows that men were starting to take on more of the mundane household tasks, but such tasks continued to be primarily a female responsibility.

Leisure time

Another way of measuring inequality in time allocation between males and females is to examine who
has most leisure. This is the approach used by Oriel
Sullivan in a study of 380 British heterosexual
couples who kept time-budget diaries in 1986
(Sullivan, 1996). Sullivan distinguished between
patterns of time-use at the weekend and during
weekdays. Not surprisingly she found that men spent
more time on paid work while women spent more
time on housework and childcare (see Figure 8.3).
Although men did spend a little more time on socializing, sleeping, relaxing and eating than women, the
difference was not great. Sullivan comments on:

> *how similar the overall proportion of time spent
> on leisure activities is for the two sexes. The extra
> time that women spend on domestic tasks is
> almost exactly equivalent at the overall level to
> the extra time that men spend doing paid work,
> leaving the same proportion of leisure time (more
> or less) free for both.*

Sullivan, 1996, p. 84

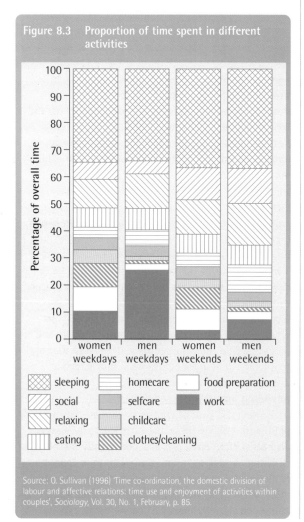

Figure 8.3 Proportion of time spent in different activities

Percentage of overall time (y-axis, 0–100)

Categories: sleeping, social, relaxing, eating, homecare, selfcare, childcare, clothes/cleaning, food preparation, work

Bars: women weekdays, men weekdays, women weekends, men weekends

Source: O. Sullivan (1996) 'Time co-ordination, the domestic division of labour and affective relations: time use and enjoyment of activities within couples', *Sociology*, Vol. 30, No. 1, February, p. 85.

Conjugal roles and power

Decision making

Another approach to studying conjugal roles is to
examine power within marriage. This has usually
been attempted through an examination of who
makes the decisions. In terms of a common sexist
phrase, it is a question of who 'wears the trousers' in
the family. Edgell, in his study *Middle-Class Couples*
(1980), interviewed both husbands and wives about
who made the decisions, and also asked them which
decisions they thought were the most important.
Wives dominated in those areas of decision making
concerning interior decorations, domestic spending
and children's clothes. All of these areas, though,
were considered unimportant. Men dominated three
areas of decision making – those relating to moving
house, finance and the car – all of which were
regarded as important. These findings are shown in
Table 8.16.

Decisions relating to money closely reflected the
overall pattern that Edgell discovered. He found that,
typically, the husband decided the overall allocation
of financial resources and had most say in the case
of decisions involving large sums of money, whereas
the wife, in every family in the sample, tended to
make the minor decisions.

Agenda setting and ideological power

As we discover in Chapter 9, power is a complex
concept and may be measured in a number of ways.
Power can be exercised through agenda setting, that
is deciding what questions and issues are discussed
(what Steven Lukes (1974) calls the 'second face of
power'), as well as through actually making
decisions. Nothing in Edgell's research (see above)
indicated that wives enjoyed more of this type of
power to compensate for their lack of influence over
important decisions. Husbands usually set the agenda
for marital debate. The possibility of moving house to
another area, for example, was only raised when it
became desirable in order to improve the husband's
career prospects.

Nor did wives seem to possess more ideological
power – that is, the ability to persuade people to do
things that are against their interests (Lukes's third
face of power). Many, though not all, wives in the
study accepted that traditional gender roles should be
maintained, and that the husband should be the
dominant 'partner'. When asked about her attitude to
sexual equality, an industrial scientist's wife replied
that 'women generally like to be dominated by men,
this is instinctive', while a dentist's wife said 'most
women would become too hard and lose sight of the
fact that they were female'. Edgell found that about
half of the husbands, but surprisingly even more of

Table 8.16   The importance, frequency and pattern of decision making in different areas of family life

Decision area	Perceived importance	Frequency	Decision maker (majority pattern)
Moving	Very important	Infrequent	Husband
Finance	Very important	Infrequent	Husband
Car	Important	Infrequent	Husband
House	Very important	Infrequent	Husband and wife
Children's education	Very important	Infrequent	Husband and wife
Holidays	Important	Infrequent	Husband and wife
Weekends	Not important	Frequent	Husband and wife
Other leisure activities	Not important	Frequent	Husband and wife
Furniture	Not important	Infrequent	Husband and wife
Interior decorations	Not important	Infrequent	Wife
Food and other domestic spending	Not important	Frequent	Wife
Children's clothes	Not important	Frequent	Wife

Source: S. Edgell (1980) *Middle-class Couples*, Allen & Unwin, London, p. 58.

the wives – about two-thirds – regarded sexual equality as a bad thing.

Graham Allan (1985) neatly summarizes the way in which ideological factors limit women's power in many marriages when he describes 'the taken-for-granted assumptions which emphasize the predominance of the male over the female in almost every sphere of domestic life'. In any struggle for power within the family, he claims, 'the female is chronically disadvantaged from the start by the socially constructed framework of values and norms which constrain her options'.

Dual-career families

A more recent study by Irene Hardill, Anne Green, Anna Dudlestone and David Owen (1997) attempted to discover whether there had been any shift towards more egalitarian power relationships in marriages since the work of Edgell. The researchers carried out semi-structured interviews in dual-career households around the Nottingham area. Their sample originated through approaches to five employers of managerial and professional staff in Nottingham – a university, a bank, the health service and two major private-sector companies. In all of the households, both partners had professional or managerial jobs. The sample therefore consisted of households where you might expect the careers of both partners to be important.

The households were classified into those where the husband's career took precedence in making major household decisions (such as what part of the country to live in), those where the wife's career took

precedence, and those where neither career clearly took precedence over the other. In this latter group, for example, the couple might have moved more than once, sometimes to accommodate the husband's career, sometimes to accommodate the wife's. In 19 households the man's career came first, in 5 households the woman's career took precedence, and in 6 neither career was clearly prioritized. It was most likely to be the man who decided where the couple were to live, and men tended to make decisions about cars. However, husband and wife usually made a joint decision about buying or renting a house.

Overall, the study found 'evidence of career-related decisions and decisions relating to infrequent, lifestyle decisions being made either by female partners or jointly by both partners in about a third of case study households'. Although men still dominated in most households, this was not the case in a significant minority of households. There was therefore some evidence of a small move towards more egalitarian relationships.

Conjugal roles – money management

Jan Pahl – systems of money management

Jan Pahl (1989, 1993) was the first British sociologist to conduct detailed studies of how couples manage their money. Her study was based upon interviews with 102 couples with at least one child under 16. The couples were interviewed individually and together to discover any disparities between the accounts of the partners. In all of the cases both partners had at least some form of income from employment or benefits. The sample, although small, was fairly representative of the population as a whole in terms of employment, class, housing and ownership of consumer goods. However, the very rich were under-represented.

The couples were divided into two groups: those who had joint bank accounts and those who did not. These groups were further divided into two categories: those where the husband made most of the important financial decisions, paid the bills and examined the bank statements; and those where the wife carried out these roles. Table 8.17 shows the main results in a statistical form. It also shows how happy or unhappy the men and women were with their marriage (the husbands' answers are in brackets).

Table 8.17	Marital happiness by control of finances: wives' answers (husbands' answers in brackets)			
	Wife control	Wife-controlled pooling	Husband-controlled pooling	Husband control
Marriage described as:				
Happy/ very happy	13 (13)	23 (25)	37 (35)	13 (16)
Average/ unhappy	1 (1)	4 (2)	2 (4)	9 (6)
Total number of couples	14	27	39	22

Source: J. Pahl (1993) 'Money, marriage and ideology: holding the purse strings?' *Sociology Review*, September, p. 8.

Husband-controlled pooling was the most common pattern (39 couples). In this system, money was shared but the husband had the dominant role in deciding how it was spent. This system was often found in high-income households, especially if the wife did not work. It was also common if the woman worked part-time or if she had a lower-status job than her husband.

Wife-controlled pooling was the second most common category, involving 27 couples. In this system, money was shared but the wife had the dominant role in deciding how it was spent. This group tended to be middle-income couples, especially where the wife was working and had a better-paid job than her husband or was better-educated.

Husband control was found in 22 couples. Amongst these couples the husband was usually the one with the main or only wage, and often he gave

his wife housekeeping money. Some of these families were too poor to have a bank account, in others only the husband had one. Sometimes the women worked, but their earnings largely went on housekeeping. In some systems of husband control, the husband gave his wife a housekeeping allowance out of which she had to pay for all or most of the routine costs of running the household.

Wife control was the least frequent pattern, found in just 14 couples. This was most common in working-class and low-income households. In a number of these households neither partner worked and both received their income from benefits. In most of these households neither partner had a bank account and they used cash to pay any bills.

Inequality and money management

According to Pahl, the most egalitarian type of control is wife-controlled pooling. In households with this system the male and female partners tend to have similar amounts of power in terms of decision making, and they are equally likely (or unlikely) to experience financial deprivation. They also tend to have similar amounts of money to spend on themselves.

Wife-controlled systems sound like they give women an advantage over men. However, they tend to be found in households where money is tight and there is little, if anything, left over after paying for necessities. Often women will go short themselves (for example, by eating less, delaying buying new clothes and spending little on their leisure) rather than see their husbands or children go short.

Husband-controlled systems tend to give husbands more power than their wives. In these households men usually spend more on personal consumption than wives.

Where husband-controlled pooling occurs, men tend to have more power than women, but the inequality is not as great as in systems of husband control. In the highest-income households there is usually sufficient money to meet the personal expenditure of both partners.

Overall, then, Pahl found that just over a quarter of the couples had a system (wife-controlled pooling) associated with a fair degree of equality between the partners. This would suggest that in domestic relationships, as in a number of other areas, women have not yet come close to reaching a position of equality.

Carolyn Vogler – changes in money management systems

Other research has largely confirmed Pahl's overall finding. Carolyn Vogler used data from the Economic and Social Research Council's *Social Change and Economic Life Initiative* (see Chapter 10 for details) to examine the extent to which money management systems had changed over time (Vogler, 1994).

She used interview data from a large sample of 1,211 couples and compared their financial arrangements with those of their parents. She found that the housekeeping allowance system had declined considerably (from 36 per cent to 12 per cent of couples) whereas some form of pooling had increased from 19 per cent to 50 per cent. However, the housekeeping allowance system had often been replaced with a female-managed system, but usually only in low-income households in which women were struggling to make ends meet. Furthermore, only 20 per cent of respondents used a form of joint pooling that gave a reasonable level of equality between the sexes. Most of the rest were male-dominated.

Vogler therefore estimated that there had been an increase in the proportion of relationships with egalitarian financial arrangements, from about 6 per cent to around 20 per cent, leaving a big majority where a significant degree of inequality remained. Vogler concluded that increased female participation in paid employment had not eradicated inequality in patterns of money management. She argues that further progress towards equality requires 'effective challenges towards the husband's traditional status as the main breadwinner in the family'.

Conjugal roles – invisible and emotional work

Marjorie L. DeVault – *Feeding the Family*

In an interesting qualitative study of domestic labour, the American sociologist Marjorie L. DeVault carried out an in-depth study of one area of domestic work, *Feeding the Family* (DeVault, 1991). She conducted in-depth interviews with 30 women and 3 men who lived in 30 households. The household members were from a variety of ethnic and class backgrounds.

DeVault found that feeding the family involves much more than tasks like shopping, cooking and washing up – the sort of tasks traditionally included in questionnaires about the domestic division of labour. It also involves planning and staging the meal as an event. There is therefore a great deal of 'invisible work' involved, as well as that which is visible and obvious.

Although some women said that they enjoyed planning meals, others found it a considerable burden. For example, a woman called Jean said, 'My biggest peeve about cooking, preparing three meals a day, is trying to figure out what to put on the table.' For the interviewees, planning meals involved thinking of food that would satisfy other family members. Very often they had to take account of the

tastes and preferences of husbands and children, which were sometimes different. DeVault says:

> Responding to these individual preferences is not a personal favor, but a requirement of the work. Family members may not eat if they don't like what is served, so women usually restrict their planning to items that have been successful in the past.
>
> DeVault, 1991, p. 40

Women may be particularly concerned that children eat appropriate and healthy foods even if they generally prefer less healthy food. This often involves being creative so that healthy food is served in a guise that is palatable to the children. In trying to balance the requirements of different family members, the food preferences of the woman preparing the food can get lost. Women responsible for cooking learn what food goes down well and what does not. Their work 'requires constant monitoring and adjustment'. Indeed, it is difficult for them to relax; once a particular meal has been completed it is soon time to start planning the next one.

It is also difficult to relax during meals. Meals are family events and have to be made to work by the participants. The woman who has prepared the meal tends to take a leading role in trying to ensure that the meal goes smoothly to the satisfaction of all family members. An important part of organizing the meal as a social occasion involves organizing talk. In different households this might involve initiating appropriate conversations or remaining quiet, if that is what the husband prefers. In some working-class households, DeVault found that conflict arose between men who did not want conversation around the dinner table and women who did want it. Organizing talk can be a demanding task, which again makes it difficult for the person responsible to relax and enjoy their food.

DeVault acknowledges that it is not always women who do all the work of feeding the family, but it is most common for them to be mainly responsible. It is a demanding and time-consuming task, which involves much more than the physical labour involved. She concludes, '"Doing a meal," then, requires more than just cooking; it takes thoughtful foresight, simultaneous attention to several different aspects of the project, and a continuing openness to ongoing events and interaction.'

Jean Duncombe and Dennis Marsden – emotion work

Drawing on the work of other sociologists, Jean Duncombe and Dennis Marsden (1995) identify another invisible element of women's domestic work, emotion work. The term 'emotion work' was first used by Arlie Hochschild (1983) to describe the sort of work that workers such as airline hostesses do in trying to keep passengers happy. Duncombe and Marsden also try to develop the work of N. James (1989), who discussed how 'from a very early age girls and then women become subconsciously trained to be more emotionally skilled in recognising and empathising with the moods of others'.

Hochschild and James were mainly interested in emotion work in paid employment. Duncombe and Marsden examine the implications of their ideas for relationships between heterosexual partners.

Their research was based on interviews with 40 white couples who had been married for 15 years. They asked the couples, separately and together, how their marriage had survived for so long in an age of high divorce rates. They found that many women expressed dissatisfaction with their partner's emotional input into the relationship and the family. Many of the women felt emotionally lonely. A number of the men concentrated on their paid employment, were unwilling to express feelings of love for their partner, and were reluctant to discuss their feelings. Most of the men did not believe there was a problem. They did not acknowledge that emotion work needed to be done to make the relationship work.

Duncombe and Marsden found that many of the women in the study were holding the relationship together by doing the crucial emotion work. In the early stages of the relationship, the partners, but particularly the women, deep act away any doubts about their emotional closeness or suitability as partners. At this stage any doubts are suppressed because they feel in love and are convinced of the worth of the relationship. Later, however, 'with growing suspicions, they "shallow act"' to maintain the 'picture for their partner and the outside world'. Shallow acting involves pretending to their partners and others that the relationship is satisfactory and they are happy with it. They 'live the family myth' or 'play the couple game' to maintain the illusion of a happy family. This places a considerable emotional strain on the woman but it is the price to pay for keeping the family together. However, eventually some women begin to 'leak' their unhappiness to outsiders. In the end this may result in the break-up of the relationship and separation or divorce.

In the meantime, women's greater participation in emotion work can be 'a major dimension of gender inequality in couple relationships'. With married women increasingly having paid employment, they can end up performing a triple shift. Having completed their paid employment they not only have to come home and do most of the housework, they also have to do most of the emotion work as well. As

women have gained paid employment this type of inequality has not reduced. Progress in this area would require even more fundamental changes. Duncombe and Marsden say:

> In fact if we consider what would be a desirable future, the most important change would be for boys and men to become meaningfully involved in the emotional aspects of family life and childcare from an early age. And this would require not only a massive reorganization of work and childcare but also a deep transformation in the nature of heterosexual masculinity.

Duncombe and Marsden, 1995, p. 33

Evaluation

Both DeVault and Duncombe and Marsden identify important and neglected aspects of gender roles. Their work is important in opening up discussions of gender relationships to include a consideration of the emotions – an area that has often been neglected by sociologists. However, it cannot be assumed on the basis of such small samples that women do most of the emotion work in all families. There are likely to be some atypical families in which men are more emotionally involved.

Gillian Dunne – the division of labour in lesbian households

In an interesting departure from studies of conjugal roles in heterosexual households, Gillian Dunne (1999) conducted a study of the division of labour in lesbian households. She examined 37 cohabiting lesbian couples who took part in in-depth, semi-structured interviews. Dunne found that 'A high level of flexibility and even-handedness characterized the allocation of employment responsibilities in partnerships.' A number of the couples were responsible for the care of one or more children, making it difficult for both to work full-time. However, unlike most heterosexual couples, one of the partners did not usually take primary responsibility for childcare. The birth-mother of the child was not necessarily the main carer, and the partners often took turns to reduce their paid employment to spend more time with the children.

The women were also asked to keep time-budget diaries. These revealed that in most households there was a fairly equitable division of time on household tasks. In 81 per cent of households neither partner did more than 60 per cent of the housework. Where the division of tasks was more skewed towards one partner than the other, it was usually the case that the one who did less housework spent much longer in paid employment.

Many of the women felt that their sameness as women and the lack of different gender roles made it easier to share tasks equitably. One of the women said, 'I suppose because our relationship doesn't fit into a social norm, there are no pre-set indications about how our relationship should work. We have to work it out for ourselves.'

Dunne concludes that the boundaries between masculinity and femininity and the hierarchical nature of gender relationships, with men being dominant, help to produce conventional domestic divisions of labour in heterosexual households. The best way to change this is to give greater value to 'feminine' tasks such as childcare and housework.

Many middle-class women have avoided the consequences of men's lack of involvement in housework by employing other women to help with domestic tasks. Their career opportunities have been gained at the expense of low-paid, exploited, working-class cleaners, nannies, childminders, etc. To Dunne, this is not an acceptable solution since it helps to perpetuate the exploitation of women in what she sees as a patriarchal society. Dunne says:

we have a common interest in dissolving gender as a category of both content and consequence. This involves acting upon our recognition that gender has a social origin, is possessed by men as

well as women and can thus be transcended by both. In practical terms, this means recognizing and celebrating the value of women's traditional areas of work rather than accepting a masculine and capitalist hierarchy of value which can lead to women passing on their responsibilities to less powerful women.

Dunne, 1999, p. 80

Inequality within marriage – conclusion

Dunne's study of lesbian households suggests that equitable domestic divisions of labour can be achieved. However, it is not easy to achieve them in the context of a culture that still differentiates quite clearly between masculinity and femininity.

Most of the evidence suggests that women are still a long way from achieving equality within marriage in contemporary Britain. They are still primarily responsible for domestic tasks and they have less power than their husbands within marriage. In terms of the amount of hours spent 'working', though, the general picture of inequality seems to be less clearcut. Husbands of wives with full-time jobs do seem to be taking over some of the burden of housework, although the change is slow and some inequality remains.

Marriage and marital breakdown

Many social and political commentators in Western societies have expressed concern about what they see as the decline of marriage. Many see this as a threat to the family, which in turn they see as the bedrock of a stable and civilized society. A number of threats to marriage have been identified. They fall into two main categories: threats resulting from alternatives to marriage, and threats resulting from the breakdown of marriages.

On the surface, the evidence for a crisis in the institution of marriage seems compelling. However, as we will see, the evidence needs to be interpreted carefully and it may not indicate as big a crisis in family life as some commentators believe.

'Threats' from alternatives to marriage

First, it is argued that marriage is becoming less popular – decreasing numbers of people are getting married. More people are developing alternatives to conventional married life. These alternatives can take a number of forms.

Marriage rates

Writing in the 1980s, Robert Chester was amongst those who noted that marriage rates among young adults had declined in many Western countries (Chester, 1985). First Sweden and Denmark began to have falling marriage rates among the under thirties. The trend continued in Britain, the USA and West Germany in the early 1970s, and later spread to France. Between 1981 and 1990 the marriage rate in Britain for all age groups fell from 7.1 per year per thousand of the eligible population, to 6.8. In 1995 it had fallen to under 6 (*Social Trends*, 1998). As Figure 8.4 shows, marriage rates, overall, fell in European Union countries between 1960 and 1975, and in all except Denmark they fell further between 1975 and 1994.

However, Chester did not see these sorts of figures as conclusive evidence of a decline in the popularity of marriage. He said, 'Mainly we seem to be witnessing a delay in the timing of marriage, rather than a fall-off in getting married at all.' He thought that future generations might marry less frequently, but he believed that there would be only a small (if any) reduction in marriage rates.

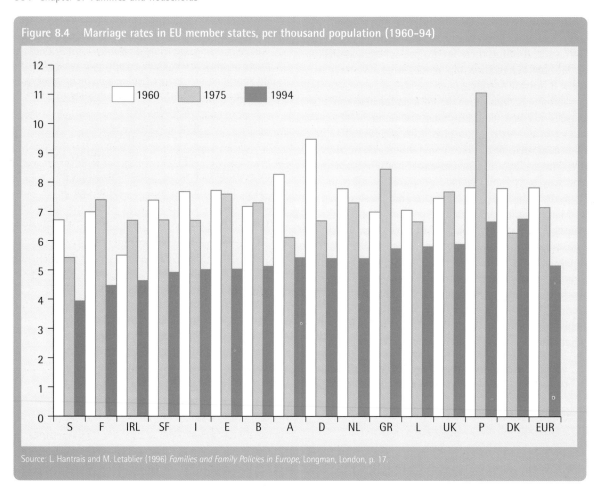

Figure 8.4   Marriage rates in EU member states, per thousand population (1960-94)

Source: L. Hantrais and M. Letablier (1996) *Families and Family Policies in Europe*, Longman, London, p. 17.

Although the marriage rate has declined, much of the decline does seem to be due to people delaying marriages rather than never getting married. According to British government statistics, in 1961 the average age at first marriage in the UK was 25.4 years for men, and 25.2 years for women. In 1996 the average age at first marriage was considerably older: 28.5 years for men and 26.3 years for women (*Social Trends*, 1999). Some commentators are keen to point out that most people do get married at some stage of their lives. According to Jon Bernardes:

> It is important to realize that around 90 per cent of all women marry in the UK today compared to 70 per cent in the Victorian era. Britain has one of the highest rates of marriage in the European Union. By the age of 40 years, 95 per cent of women and 91 per cent of men have married.

Bernardes, 1997, p. 137

Cohabitation

One alternative to marriage is cohabitation by couples who are not legally married. The percentage of non-married women aged 18 to 49 who were cohabiting doubled between 1981 and 1996-7, from 12.5 per cent to 25 per cent. Furthermore, the average length of cohabitation also increased, rising from 18 months in 1979 to 28 months in 1993-4 (*Social Trends*, 1998).

However, Chester (1985) argued that in most cases cohabitation is only a temporary phase: most of those who cohabit get married eventually. In some cases one or both of the partners is separated but not divorced from a previous spouse, and so is not free to get married. Others see the period of cohabitation simply as a trial marriage, and intend to get married if it proves satisfactory. Most cohabiting couples intend to and do get married if they have children. Chester concluded that 'In practice, only about 2 per cent of single women aged between 18 and 49 are living and bearing children in "consensual unions" which may be permanent.'

Evidence that can be used to support Chester's view can be found in a 1981 study of a representative sample of the people of Sheffield and Aberdeen. Jacqueline Burgoyne and David Clark (1984) asked their sample whether they thought that cohabitation outside marriage was a good idea. Some 38 per cent thought it was if cohabitation was a prelude to marriage, but this figure was reduced to only 15 per cent if it was a permanent alternative to marriage.

A rather different view is taken by Joan Chandler (1993). She sees the increase in cohabitation as rather more significant and says, 'The time couples spend cohabiting is lengthening and increasingly they appear to be choosing cohabitation as a long-term alternative to marriage.' Chandler suggests that this is reflected in the increasing proportions of children born out of marriage – partners no longer feel as much pressure to marry to legitimize a pregnancy. She argues:

> Many of today's parents have detached childbearing and rearing from traditional marriage and 28 per cent of children are now born to unmarried mothers. However, many fewer are born to residentially lone parents, as 70 per cent of these children are jointly registered by parents who usually share the same address.
>
> Chandler, 1993

Although Chandler sees cohabitation as increasingly popular, she does point out that it is nothing new. Unofficial self-marriage (where people simply declare themselves to be married – sometimes called 'living over the brush') was very common in past centuries. She quotes research which estimates that as many as a quarter to a third of couples lived in consensual unions in Britain in the eighteenth century.

Recent survey evidence suggests that cohabitation is increasingly accepted as a long-term alternative to marriage. In the 1998/9 *British and European Social Attitudes Survey* (conducted in 1987) 64 per cent of the sample agreed that 'It is all right for a couple to live together without intending to get married' (Jowell *et al.*, 1998).

Single-person households

Another alternative to marriage is to live on your own. Many single-person households may be formed as a result of divorce, separation, the break-up of a partnership involving cohabitation, or the death of a partner. However, others may result from a deliberate choice to live alone. There is statistical evidence that single-person households are becoming more common. According to government statistics, in 1961 4 per cent of households in Great Britain consisted of a single person under pensionable age; by 1996-7 this had tripled to 12 per cent (*Social Trends*, 1998). Over the same period the proportion of households consisting of a single person over pensionable age increased from 7 per cent to 15 per cent, although this was largely due to an ageing population and women being widowed, rather than a matter of choice.

Jon Bernardes (1997) believes that there are strong social pressures discouraging people from remaining single because society portrays marriage as the ideal state. He says, 'Predominant ideologies emphasize the "normality" of forming intimate partnerships and the "abnormality" of remaining single for too long'. However, despite Bernardes's claims, the increasing frequency of single-person households among those below retirement age does suggest that there is greater acceptance of a single status as an alternative to marriage or cohabitation.

John Macionis and Ken Plummer (1997) claim that among women aged 20 to 24 in the USA the proportion who were single (although not necessarily living alone) increased from 28 per cent in 1960 to 67 per cent in 1994. They comment that 'Underlying this trend is women's greater participation in the labour force: women who are economically secure view a husband as a matter of choice rather than a financial necessity.' On the other hand, in Britain at least, the very high proportion of people who marry at least once suggests that few people rule out altogether the option of getting married.

Communes

Another alternative to the marriage-based household in Western societies is the commune. Andrew McCulloch defines communes as 'experimental household groups which practise an ideology of sharing' (McCulloch, 1982). In the USA communes are relatively commonplace – McCulloch quotes a 1975 study by J. Jerome that put the number at 25,000 – but they are much less numerous in Britain.

McCulloch's own research over a five-year period uncovered 67 communes, but only six of them survived over the full five years, and he believed that by the end of the research there were only 50 left.

The values of members of communes pose a significant challenge to marriage and the family. As McCulloch puts it, those who form or join communes are often looking for somewhere where they can 'be themselves' and live collectively rather than in small, isolated, nuclear family units. However, in numerical terms, communes represent very little threat to traditional familial and marital values.

One reason why communes tend to be short-lived is the problem of new generations and how they fit into the communal group. Many communes encourage the free development of sexual relationships between their members, and this raises the question, 'at what age does the child become a sexual participant in the group and what are the consequences of this?'

One solution to this type of problem is the formation of collective rather than communal households. Collective households consist of a number of nuclear family units and, although there may be a considerable amount of sharing between the units, there are limits on what is shared. McCulloch claims that this type of household is becoming increasingly popular, and is often a successful solution to the problems of urban living. Ideologically, however, it seems less of a radical departure from traditional marriage than the communal household.

Marital breakdown

The second type of threat to contemporary marriage is the apparent rise in marital breakdowns. The usual way of estimating the number of such breakdowns is through an examination of the divorce statistics, but these statistics do not, on their own, provide a valid measure of marital breakdown.

Marital breakdown can be divided into three main categories:

1 Divorce, which refers to the legal termination of a marriage.
2 Separation, which refers to the physical separation of the spouses: they no longer share the same dwelling.
3 So-called empty-shell marriages, where the spouses live together, remain legally married, but their marriage exists in name only.

These three forms must be considered in any assessment of the rate of marital breakdown.

Divorce statistics

Despite minor fluctuations, there was a steady rise in divorce rates in modern industrial societies throughout the twentieth century.

In 1911, 859 petitions for divorce were filed in England and Wales, of which some three-quarters were granted a decree absolute. Table 8.18 presents statistics on divorce for England and Wales from 1961 to 1997.

The dramatic increase in petitions in 1971 was due in part to new divorce legislation. This increase did not simply represent a backlog of couples waiting to legally end an unsatisfactory marriage, since the number of petitions continued to rise during the following years. The figures show a rising divorce rate over the whole period, although in the 1990s the divorce rate seems to have stabilized (at a historically very high level) at around 13 per thousand married people. This figure may not appear very high until it is compared with the marriage rate. Figure 8.5 shows the United Kingdom rates for first marriages, remarriages and divorces between 1961 and 1996. It shows that by 1996 there were nearly as many divorces as first marriages, and nearly as many remarriages as divorces.

In 1996 there were 351,514 marriages but 157,588 divorces, meaning that there were more than half as many divorces as marriages (*Annual Abstract of Statistics*, 1999). According to Joan Chandler, 'If trends continue, approximately 40 per cent of marriages presently being formed will end in divorce' (Chandler, 1993). The proportion of marriages that are remarriages has also been rising. For example, 15 per cent of all marriages in the UK in 1961 were remarriages for one or both partners; by 1996 this figure had risen to approximately 41 per cent (*Annual Abstract of Statistics*, 1999).

Table 8.18 Divorce in England and Wales	1961	1971	1976	1981	1986	1987	1988	1989	1990	1991	1992	1993	1994	1995	1996	1997
Petitions filed (thousands)																
England and Wales	32	111	145	170	180	183	183	185	192	179	190	184	176	174	178	164
Decrees nisi granted (thousands)																
England and Wales	27	89	132	148	153	150	155	152	158	153	149	161	154	156	158	148
Decrees absolute granted (thousands)																
England and Wales	25	74	127	146	154	151	153	151	153	156	157	163	155	153	155	146
Persons divorcing (per thousand married people)																
England and Wales	2.1	6.0	10.1	11.9	12.9	12.7	12.8	12.7	12.9	13.5	13.7	13.9	13.4	13.1	13.8	-

Source: *Social Trends* 23 (1993) and *Annual Abstract of Statistics* (1999) pp. 42–3.

Figure 8.5   Marriages and divorces in the UK

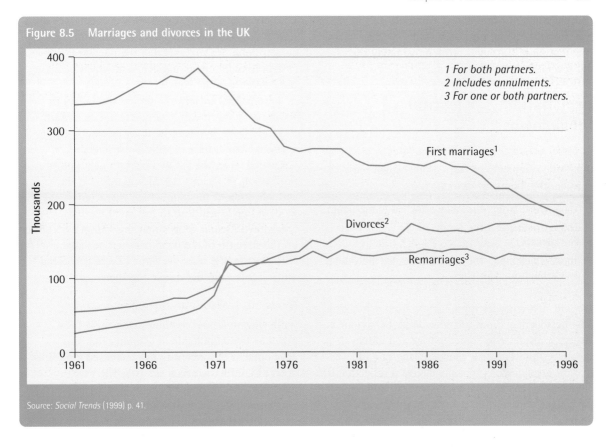

1 For both partners.
2 Includes annulments.
3 For one or both partners.

First marriages[1]

Divorces[2]

Remarriages[3]

Source: *Social Trends* (1999) p. 41.

Whichever way the figures are presented, the increase in divorce is dramatic.

Britain's divorce rate is also very high in comparison with most other industrial societies: in the European Community only Denmark had a higher rate in 1990. Elsewhere, the USA also has a higher rate than Britain. However, an increase in the divorce rate has been experienced in nearly all industrial societies over the past few decades and is by no means unique to Britain.

Separation statistics

Reliable figures for separation are unobtainable. In Britain, some indication is provided by applications to a magistrates' court for a legal separation order, but many spouses separate without going to court, and for these there are no figures available.

Chester estimates that the number of recorded separations increased during the 1960s by about 65 per cent. This does not necessarily mean an increase in separations since the number of unrecorded separations is unknown. Although the numbers are small compared with divorce, there was a marked increase in judicial separations in the 1970s and early 1980s. In 1972, 133 were granted; in 1984, 4,445. However, from this high point, numbers fell and there were only 1,199 judicial separations in 1996 and a mere 589 in 1997.

Empty-shell marriages

Estimates of the extent of empty-shell marriages can only be based on guesswork. Even where data exist, the concept is difficult to operationalize (that is, put into a measurable form). For example, if a couple express a high level of dissatisfaction with their relationship, should this be termed an empty-shell marriage?

Historical evidence gives the impression that empty-shell marriages are more likely to end in separation and divorce today than in the past. William J. Goode argues that in nineteenth-century America:

> *People took for granted that spouses who no longer loved one another and who found life together distasteful should at least live together in public amity for the sake of their children and of their standing in the community.*
>
> Goode, 1971

Even though an increasing number of empty-shell marriages may end in separation and divorce today, this does not necessarily mean that the proportion of such marriages, in relation to the total number of marriages, is decreasing.

In view of the problems involved in measuring marital breakdown it is impossible to be completely confident about overall rates of breakdown. However, levels of divorce are now so high that it is probably true that more marriages break down today than they did several decades ago.

Explanations for marital breakdowns

In *When Marriage Ends* (1976), Nicky Hart argues that any explanation of marital breakdown must consider the following factors:

1 those which affect the value attached to marriage;
2 those which affect the degree of conflict between the spouses;
3 those which affect the opportunities for individuals to escape from marriage.

We will first consider these factors from a functionalist perspective. From this viewpoint, behaviour is largely a response to shared norms and values. It therefore follows that a change in the rate of marital breakdown is to some degree a reflection of changing norms and values in general, and, in particular, those associated with marriage and divorce.

The value of marriage

Functionalists such as Talcott Parsons and Ronald Fletcher argue that the rise in marital breakdown stems largely from the fact that marriage is increasingly valued. People expect and demand more from marriage and consequently are more likely to end a relationship which may have been acceptable in the past. Thus Ronald Fletcher argues that 'a relatively high divorce rate may be indicative not of lower but of higher standards of marriage in society' (Fletcher, 1966).

The high rate of remarriage apparently lends support to Parsons's and Fletcher's arguments. Thus, paradoxically, the higher value placed on marriage may result in increased marital breakdown.

Conflict between spouses

Hart (1976) argues that the second set of factors that must be considered in an explanation of marital breakdown are those which affect the degree of conflict between the spouses. From a functionalist perspective it can be argued that the adaptation of the family to the requirements of the economic system has placed a strain on the marital relationship. It has led to the relative isolation of the nuclear family from the wider kinship network. William J. Goode argues that, as a result, the family 'carries a heavier emotional burden when it exists independently than when it is a small unit within a larger

kin fabric. As a consequence, this unit is relatively fragile' (Goode, 1971). Edmund Leach (1967) makes a similar point. He suggests that the nuclear family suffers from an emotional overload which increases the level of conflict between its members.

In industrial society, the family specializes in fewer functions. It can be argued that, as a result, there are fewer bonds to unite its members. The economic bond, for example, is considerably weakened when the family ceases to be a unit of production. N. Dennis (1975) suggests that the specialization of function which characterizes the modern family will lead to increased marital breakdown. Dennis argues that this can place a strain on the strength of the bond between husband and wife. Put simply, when love goes, there is nothing much left to hold the couple together.

Modernity, freedom and choice

Colin Gibson (1994) combines elements of the previous two arguments in claiming that the development of modernity has increased the likelihood of conflict between spouses. The way modernity has developed has put increasing emphasis upon the desirability of individual achievement. Gibson argues that people now live in an 'enterprise and free-market culture of individualism in which the licence of choice dominates'. He adds that 'A higher divorce rate may be indicative of modern couples generally anticipating a superior standard of personal marital satisfaction than was expected by their grandparents.'

People increasingly expect to get most of their personal satisfaction from their home life and 'television programmes reinforce the feeling that togetherness is the consummate life style'. However, the emphasis on togetherness is somewhat undermined by 'the Thatcherite manifesto of unfettered self-seeking interest', so that conflict between spouses becomes more likely if self-fulfilment is not delivered by the marriage.

Individualistic modernity and the ideology of the market emphasize consumer choice, and, if fulfilment is not forthcoming through your first choice of marriage partner, then you are more likely to leave and try an alternative in the hope of greater satisfaction. In the past it was difficult for women in particular to escape from unsatisfactory marriages, but with greater independence – resulting from paid employment and other sources – this is no longer the case. Gibson says, 'Greater freedom to judge, choose and change their mind has encouraged women to become more confident and assertive about what they expect from a marriage.' They increasingly exercise that freedom by leaving marriages that fail to live up to what they expect.

The ease of divorce

So far we have considered the factors which affect the value attached to marriage and those which affect the degree of conflict between spouses. The third set of factors that Hart considers essential to an explanation of marital breakdown are those which affect the opportunities for individuals to escape from marriage. This view is backed up by the *British and European Social Attitudes Survey* carried out in 1997 (Jowell *et al.*, 1998). It found that 82 per cent of their sample disagreed with the view that 'Even if there are no children a married couple should stay together even if they don't get along.'

If, as the functionalists argue, behaviour is directed by norms and values, a change in the norms and values associated with divorce would be expected. It is generally agreed that the stigma attached to divorce has been considerably reduced. This, in itself, will make divorce easier.

Goode (1971) argues that the change in attitudes towards divorce is part of the more general process of secularization in Western societies. (Secularization refers to the declining influence of the church and of religious belief in general – we discuss secularization in more detail in Chapter 7, pp. 469–93.) During the nineteenth century, the church strongly denounced divorce, insisting that the phrase 'till death do us part' be taken literally. During the twentieth century, despite a strong rearguard action, the church had to accommodate the rising divorce rate by taking a less rigid view.

However, the official church position is probably less important than the declining influence of religious beliefs and values in general in industrial society. Many sociologists argue that secular (that is non-religious) beliefs and values increasingly direct behaviour. In terms of divorce, Goode argues that this means that 'Instead of asking, "Is this moral?" the individual is more likely to ask, "Is this a more useful or better procedure for my needs?"'

A similar view is taken by Colin Gibson (1994), who also believes that secularization has weakened the degree to which religious beliefs can bind a couple together and make divorce less likely. He says, 'Secularization has also witnessed the fading of the evangelical bond of rigid morality which intertwined the cultural fabric of conformist social mores and habits and the declared public conscience.' Along with a decline in religious beliefs, there has also been a decline in any set of shared values that might operate to stabilize marriage. He describes the change in the following way:

> Within our pluralistic society it has become increasingly difficult to sustain an identifiable common culture containing generally held values, aspirations and symbols. George Formby and his ukulele had a cultural identity embracing men and women, rich and poor, young and old; the vocal form of Madonna does not offer the same symbolic universality.
>
> Gibson, 1994, p. 216

In the absence of any central, shared beliefs in society, anything goes, and there is little or no stigma attached to divorce.

Divorce legislation

The changing attitudes towards divorce have been institutionalized by various changes in the law which have made it much easier to obtain a divorce. In Britain, before 1857, a private act of parliament was required to obtain a divorce. This was an expensive procedure beyond the means of all but the most wealthy.

Since 1857, the costs of obtaining a divorce have been reduced and the grounds for divorce have been widened. Divorce legislation was influenced by the idea of matrimonial offence, the notion that one or both spouses had wronged the other. This was the idea behind the Matrimonial Causes Act of 1857 which largely limited grounds for divorce to adultery. Although divorce legislation in 1950 widened the grounds to include cruelty and desertion, it was still based on the same principle.

The Divorce Reform Act, which came into force in 1971, no longer emphasized the idea of matrimonial offence and so avoided the need for 'guilty parties'. It defined the grounds for divorce as 'the irretrievable breakdown of the marriage'. This made divorce considerably easier and accounts in part for the dramatic rise in the number of divorces in 1971 (see Table 8.18).

New legislation relating to divorce was introduced at the end of 1984. This reduced the period a couple needed to be married before they could petition for divorce, from three years to one year. It also altered the basis on which financial settlements were determined by the courts. From 1984 the conduct of the partners became something the courts could take into account. If the misbehaviour of one partner was responsible for the divorce, they could be awarded less than would otherwise have been expected. The intention behind this seemed to be to counteract what some saw as the anti-male bias in maintenance payments from men to their ex-wives.

The Family Law Bill of 1996 ended the reliance upon showing that one or both partners were at fault in order to prove that the marriage had broken down. Instead, the partners simply had to assert that the marriage had broken down and undergo a 'period of reflection' to consider whether a reconciliation was possible. Normally this period was one year, but for those with children under 16, or where one spouse asked for more time, the period was eighteen months. The bill also encouraged greater use of mediation, rather than relying on solicitors, to resolve issues such as the division of money and arrangements for children.

Despite a reduction in costs, divorce was still an expensive process during the first half of the twentieth century. It was beyond the means of many of the less wealthy. This was partly changed by the Legal Aid and Advice Act of 1949 which provided free legal advice and paid solicitors' fees for those who could not afford them. The economics of divorce were further eased by the extension of welfare provisions, particularly for single parents with dependent children. Although many consider these provisions far from generous, they do provide single-parent families with the means to exist without the support of the second partner.

Women, paid employment and marital conflict

Along with other perspectives she examines, Nicky Hart (1976) presents a Marxist alternative, although it does not form the theoretical basis of her work. She argues that the increasing divorce rate can be seen as a 'product of conflict between the changing economic system and its social and ideological superstructure (notably the family)'.

In advanced capitalist industrial societies, there is an increasing demand for cheap female wage labour. Wives are encouraged to take up paid employment not only because of the demand for their services, but also because the capitalist-controlled media has raised material aspirations – the demand for goods that families desire. These material aspirations can only be satisfied by both spouses working as wage earners. However, conflict results from the contradiction between female wage labour and the normative expectations that surround married life. 'Working wives' are still expected to be primarily responsible for housework and raising children. In addition, they are still expected, to some degree, to play a subservient role to the male head of the household. These normative expectations contradict the wife's role as a wage earner since she is now sharing the economic burden with her husband. Conflict between the spouses can result from this contradiction, and this conflict can lead to marital breakdown.

Official statistics seem to support the view that it is largely wives' dissatisfaction with marriage that accounts for the rising divorce rate. In 1989, 73 per cent of divorce petitions were filed by wives, and just 27 per cent by husbands. This was a dramatic change in comparison with 1946 when wives accounted for 37 per cent of petitions and husbands for 63 per cent.

The social distribution of marital breakdown

Income, class and unemployment

This section concludes with an examination of the variation in divorce rates between different social groups within society.

Marital breakdown is not spread evenly across the population: the changes that have influenced the rate of marital breakdown do not affect all members of society in the same way, but are mediated by the social structure. For example, changes in society are filtered through the class system and, to some degree, affect members of different classes in different ways. As a result there are class variations in rates of marital breakdown.

In the USA, there is an inverse relationship between income and marital breakdown: the lower the family income, the higher the rate of separation and divorce. Low income can place a strain on the marital relationship. It has been argued that, in poverty areas, expectations of marital success are lower, as is the stigma attached to marital breakdown. It has been suggested that marital breakdown has become self-perpetuating in many low-income groups.

In Britain, the situation is similar. Table 8.19 shows the results of a study by Haskey (1984) of the social class of a sample of 2,164 divorcing couples in England and Wales in 1979. It shows that, in general, non-manual workers have considerably lower divorce rates than manual workers, although skilled manual workers do have a lower rate than skilled non-manual workers. The divorce rate is particularly high

Table 8.19	Divorce and social class in England and Wales
Social class of husband	**Standardized divorce rate**
I Professional	47
II Intermediate	83
IIIN Skilled, non-manual	108
IIIM Skilled, manual	97
IV Partly skilled	111
V Unskilled	220
Armed forces	270
Unemployed	225
All social classes	100

Source: Quoted in J. Burgoyne, R. Ormrod and M. Richards (1987) *Divorce Matters*, Penguin, Harmondsworth, p. 34.

amongst the unskilled and the unemployed, suggesting that material hardship may be an important factor shaping British divorce rates. However, Haskey notes that the divorce rate is also very high amongst families where the husband is in the armed forces and therefore in secure and reasonably well-paid employment. This suggests that specific occupations might encourage divorce.

In a review of research on divorce, Colin Gibson quotes British research from 1990, which involved interviewing 5,000 people. This found that, in the year after becoming unemployed, people had a 130 per cent greater chance of separating from their spouses than other people (quoted in Gibson, 1994). The psychological trauma and financial hardship associated with unemployment might both play a part in explaining this association since both could place a marriage under strain.

Age

Apart from social class, a number of other factors are associated with the variations in divorce rates. There is an inverse relationship between age at marriage and divorce: the lower the age at marriage, the higher the rate of divorce. Colin Gibson refers to research which suggests that half of those who are under 20 when they marry will be divorced within 25 years (quoted in Gibson, 1994).

A number of reasons have been given for this. There may be greater economic pressure on the teenage marriage since the spouses are only just beginning their working lives and their wages are likely to be low. Compared to all marriages, a higher proportion of teenage marriages are undertaken to legitimize a pregnancy. In addition, teenagers are more likely to change their outlook and so 'grow apart'. They are less likely to have the experience to select a compatible partner and less likely to be aware of the responsibilities that marriage entails.

Another part of the reason may again be related to social class. Working-class couples are more likely than the middle class to marry as teenagers, and their class rather than age at marriage may be the main factor influencing their divorce rate.

The marital status of parents

There is an association between individuals' likelihood of getting divorced and the marital status of their parents. If one or both spouses have parents who are or have been divorced, there is a greater possibility that their own marriage will end in divorce.

The usual explanation is that marital conflict produces psychological instability in the children, who express this instability in their own marriage. However, Hart argues that the experience of having divorced parents may reduce the individual's aversion to divorce. In addition, divorced parents may be more likely, if not to encourage the divorce, at least not to oppose it as strongly as non-divorced parents.

Background and role expectations

Statistics indicate that the chances of marital breakdown are increased if the spouses have different social backgrounds – for example, if they come from different classes or ethnic groups. Conflict may result from partners having different marital role expectations which stem from the subculture of their particular social group. When spouses share similar backgrounds, there is a greater likelihood that their friends will be similar and this will tend to reinforce the marriage. In Goode's words, it is probable 'that those who are alike in many respects will share a similar and approving circle' (Goode, 1971).

In advanced industrial society, the increasing rate of social and geographical mobility results in greater opportunities for marriage between individuals of differing social backgrounds and therefore in a greater potential for marital conflict.

Occupations

Finally, various studies have indicated a relationship between particular occupations and high rates of divorce. Nicky Hart (1976) finds that long-distance lorry drivers, sales representatives and some engineers and technicians, whose jobs require frequent separation from their spouses, have higher-than-average divorce rates. In a later review of research, Colin Gibson (1994) also argues that long separations between spouses are associated with high divorce rates. Apart from the possibility of lessening the dependence of the spouses upon each other, such jobs provide the husband in particular with a greater opportunity to meet members of the opposite sex away from the company of his spouse.

T. Noble (1970) finds a similar relationship between particular occupations and high rates of divorce. Actors, authors, artists, company directors and hotel-keepers have high divorce rates, which, Noble argues, result from their high degree of involvement in their work and low involvement in their marriage.

We have examined only some of the many factors associated with the variation in divorce rates. The researcher is faced with a multitude of factors and it is difficult to establish which are more important than others. With reference to the particularly rapid rise in the overall rate of marital breakdown in recent years, Hart (1976) assigns priority to the changing role of women in society. We consider this in detail in Chapter 3.

Conclusion

A decline in the rate of marriage, increasing cohabitation outside marriage, the existence of communes, the rising number of single-parent families and single-person homes, and the apparent increase in marital breakdown, all seem to suggest the decline of marriage as an institution in modern Britain. Yet all of these changes are open to different interpretations, and none – at least on its own – seems likely to make marriage obsolete in the near future.

It is easy to exaggerate the extent to which there has been a retreat from marriage. Robert Chester says, 'On the evidence, most people will continue not only to spend most of their lives in a family environment, but also to place a high value on it' (Chester, 1985).

The socialist feminist sociologists Pamela Abbott and Claire Wallace (1992) are also rather sceptical of the belief that the family and marriage are in danger of falling apart. They suggest that this view has been encouraged by the 'New Right' (right-wing politicians and thinkers whose views and policies are discussed on pp. 574–6). To Abbott and Wallace, such people have succeeded in setting the agenda of public debate about the family by trying to portray it as under serious threat from moral decay in society as a whole, and they have carefully interpreted the evidence to support their case. Abbot and Wallace say:

> We are told how many marriages end in divorce, how many children live in single-parent families and so on. Yet we can also look at these statistics another way – to show the stability of the family. Six out of ten couples who get married in the 1990s, according to present trends, will stay together until one of them dies. Seven out of eight children are born to parents living together, three-quarters of whom are legally married. Only one in five children will experience parental divorce by the time he or she is 16; that is, four out of five children born to a married couple will be brought up by them in an intact family. In 1985, 78 per cent of British children under 16 were living with both natural parents who were legally married.
>
> Abbott and Wallace, 1992

Abbott and Wallace recognize the increasing diversity of family forms but see the alleged decline of the family and marriage as having been exaggerated for political ends.

C.C. Harris (1983) draws a cautious conclusion based upon the ambiguous evidence. He says 'the case that marriage and the family in Britain are at present in a process of "deinstitutionalization" is simply not proven'. Instead he recognizes that there has been an increase in the number of people living outside of households based on married couples. He believes that it is possible to detect, particularly from the delaying of marriage, 'the emergence of a period of extra-familial independence among young adults' and argues that the recognition of 'dysfunctional' aspects of married life has led a small minority of the population to begin to explore alternatives, at least for a temporary phase of their lives.

The family, politics and social policy

International comparisons

Until recently, sociologists have paid little attention to the relationship between social policy and the family. As Graham Allan (1985) points out, Britain does not have a government ministry responsible for family affairs, and traditionally it has not had a specific package of government policies aimed at the family. Most European countries have both of these.

Adrian Wilson (1985) has given examples from a variety of societies and historical periods of how the state has tried to directly shape family life:

1 In the USSR the post-revolutionary communist government of the 1920s took measures intended to weaken and ultimately destroy the family. Divorce and abortion were made much easier to obtain.

2 In Romania, under the communist regime of Ceausescu, family life was encouraged. Those who remained unmarried after the age of 25 had to pay extra income tax – a measure intended to increase the birth rate.

3 In China, on the other hand, couples had to apply for permission to have more than one child, and there were penalties for those who did not make their contribution to solving the problem of over-population.

4 In Britain, though, the family has usually been regarded as an area where it is inappropriate for the state to interfere too much, since, as Allan puts it, 'the state is concerned with regulation, control and coercion; the family is thought of as an area for love, intimacy and personal fulfilment'. In short, the family belongs to the private sphere, and should therefore, for the most part, be left alone. However, since the 1980s, British politicians of the major parties have increasingly seen fit to make tentative forays into commenting on and sometimes intervening in family life.

Bias towards conventional families

Despite the traditional British belief that politicians should not interfere in the family, state policies have always had an impact on family life. Taxation, welfare, housing and education policies all influence the way in which people organize their domestic life. The policies adopted can encourage people to live in certain types of household and discourage them from living in other types. Furthermore, in recent decades the family has come to be seen as a legitimate and important subject of public debate.

Feminists and other radical critics of government policies have sometimes seen them as biased. They have argued that they tend to favour the traditional nuclear family in which there are two parents – a male breadwinner and a wife who stays at home when there are young children. Allan argues that 'Much state provision ... is based upon an implicit ideology of the "normal" family which through its incorporation into standard practice discourages alternative forms of domestic organization from developing' (Allan, 1985). To Allan, these policies encourage 'the standard form of gender and generational relations within families'. In other words, they assume that one family member will put primary emphasis during their life on childcare rather than work; that families will usually take care of their elderly and sick; and that wives are economically dependent on their husbands.

Daphne Johnson (1982) argues that schools are organized in such a way that it is difficult for single-parent families and dual-worker families to combine work with domestic responsibilities. School hours and holidays mean that families with children find it difficult for the adult members to combine the requirements of employers with their domestic responsibilities.

Roy Parker (1982) claims that state assistance (of a practical rather than financial nature) tends not to be given to the elderly and sick if they live with relatives. It is assumed that the family will care for them. In both the care of the elderly and infirm and the care of children, this generally means that wives will be expected to take up these domestic responsibilities, or at least to work only part-time. It can be argued that, in recent years, Parker's argument has become increasingly valid, at least in terms of its application to elderly people. The state has encouraged families to take responsibility for their elderly members, either in practical or financial terms. Furthermore, the elderly are increasingly required to use their savings to pay for their care in old age rather than receiving free care from the state.

The situation in relation to childcare is less clearcut. A voucher system has been introduced which helps subsidize the costs of childcare for children attending nurseries as they approach school age. However, it is not possible to offset the costs of childcare against earnings to reduce the size of tax bills. This reduces the incentive for mothers (or the primary carer) to seek paid employment, since any childcare costs have to be paid out of income from employment which is liable to taxation. On the other hand, the Working Families Tax Credit (introduced in 1999) does allow help with childcare, but only in low-income families where both partners are in paid employment. This discourages women in these families from staying at home to look after their children.

In public housing policy the formal emphasis is usually upon making children's needs a priority. However, Lorraine Fox Harding believes that in practice married couples with children tend to be favoured over single parents with children. Single parents are usually provided with the least desirable housing. Furthermore, Fox Harding says, 'Most dwellings are constructed for the nuclear family and are planned and designed by men. Units are privatised and self-contained. The centrality of family housing reinforces dominant notions of family and non-family households' (Fox Harding, 1996). Few council or other public houses have been built to accommodate groups larger than conventional nuclear families.

The traditional conjugal roles of wives in the 'conventional' family are further reinforced by other parts of the taxation and benefits systems. For example, married women can only receive invalidity pensions if they can show that their physical condition prevents them from doing housework – a rule that does not apply to men and single women. Until 1986 married women also could not claim the Invalid Care Allowance; it was taken for granted that they could and should carry out 'caring' family roles, and they were not therefore given financial compensation for doing so. The taxation system continues to give an extra tax allowance to married couples over and above the allowances due to cohabiting couples or individuals. However, the value of this allowance has been gradually reduced.

Fox Harding believes that regulations relating to maternity leave and pay reinforce traditional gender roles. In Britain, unlike some European countries, fathers have no right to paid or unpaid leave from work on the birth of a child, whereas women do have such rights. (At the time of writing the government was considering giving men the right to three months' unpaid leave.) Furthermore, 'Benefits for pregnancy and the period after childbirth are inadequate, reflecting the assumption that women have the support of a male partner' (Fox Harding, 1996).

In 1993 the Child Support Agency was established. It oversees the payment of maintenance by 'absent' parents to the parents responsible for looking after the children. Its work therefore covers divorced, separated and never-married couples who live apart. The agency was set up to make sure that fathers in particular would find it more difficult to escape financial responsibility for their children. In this respect it can be seen as supporting the traditional family by imposing financial costs on those who do not live in one.

The Child Support Agency has been highly controversial and highly criticized. For example, many argue that its main aim is not to help children but rather to save the Treasury money, since maintenance payments usually reduce the benefits paid to single mothers. Indeed, in its first year the agency was set a target of saving £530 million of taxpayers' money. However, it was clear that Conservative ministers supported the agency, not just to save money, but also because they saw it as helping to uphold moral values relating to parental responsibility. As we will see, the Labour government elected in 1997 in some ways continued to support such policies on similar grounds.

As Fox Harding notes, cut-backs in welfare provision in the 1980s and 1990s had the effect of extending family responsibilities beyond the immediate, nuclear family. This was in contrast to earlier decades of the twentieth century when there was a tendency for the state to take over responsibilities that had previously been left to families. Fox Harding gives the example of care of the elderly and care of children aged 18-25. In both cases cuts in benefits have put the onus on families to help, even though they have not been made legally responsible for doing so. Fox Harding also sees the increased emphasis on absent parents supporting their offspring as an example of the state's attempt to extend familial responsibilities.

Policies which do not support conventional families

Not all government policies can be seen as supporting conventional families or traditional gender roles within them. For example, there have been some measures which might be seen as undermining traditional male dominance within families. Fox Harding points out that in 1991 the House of Lords ruled that men were no longer exempt from being charged with raping their wives. Traditional patriarchal authority relations within families have been further undermined by increasing intolerance of men using violence to discipline their wives or children.

The gradual liberalization of divorce laws by the state shows a willingness to accept that marriage does not guarantee the long-term stability of a family. Some legal concessions have been made to recognize the rights of cohabitees who are not married. Lorraine Fox Harding says, 'there are some rights which have been extended to cohabitees, such as succession to tenancies and inheritance in certain circumstances, and the right to have orders made to restrain violence'. However, in other respects, cohabitees are given no specific rights other than those stemming from more general laws, and cohabiting gay or lesbian couples have no legal rights relating specifically to such relationships.

Pamela Abbott and Claire Wallace – the family and the New Right

Pamela Abbott and Claire Wallace (1992) have examined the view of the family and social policy that was put forward by the New Right in Britain and the USA in the 1980s. Instead of arguing that government policy was biased in favour of the conventional family, the New Right argued that government policy was undermining it and policies had to be changed.

In Britain, New Right thinking was promoted by individual journalists and academics – for example, Paul Johnson and Roger Scruton – and by 'think tanks' such as the Centre for Policy Studies and the Adam Smith Institute. In the USA a variety of pressure groups have campaigned to reassert traditional morality and family relationships. Abbott and Wallace describe them as a 'Pro-Family' movement and say that it 'developed out of an alliance of political, religious, anti-feminist and pro-life anti-abortion groups'. In Britain, the 'Pro-Family' movement has not been as strong, but an anti-abortion movement, individuals like Victoria Gillick (who campaigned to stop doctors prescribing contraceptives to girls under 16 without parental consent), and organizations like Families Need Fathers (which is opposed to divorce) have supported similar causes to their American counterparts.

Abbott and Wallace argue that the New Right advocates 'liberal economic policies with support for conservative social moral values'. Members of the New Right see the family as being under threat from permissiveness, social changes and government policies, and this in turn threatens the stability of society. To them the family operates properly when it remains stable and the wife is responsible for socializing children so that they conform to society's norms and values. The husband, as principal breadwinner, is disciplined by the need to provide for his family. The New Right sees many signs of the family becoming unable to carry out its proper role. These include 'working mothers (who by taking paid work fail to put the needs of their children first), increased divorce rates, higher numbers of single-parent families and open homosexuality'. It argues that such changes have played a major role in causing social problems such as crime, delinquency and drug abuse.

The New Right and politics

In trying to influence political debate and the actions of governments, the New Right has tried to change what it sees as harmful social policies. Abbot and Wallace argue that in both Britain and the USA the New Right has attacked the welfare systems for encouraging deviant lifestyles and family forms. For example, welfare payments have allowed mothers to bring up their children in single-parent families, taxation policies have discriminated against married couples, divorce laws have made it easier to end marriage, and abortion laws and the relaxation of laws against homosexuality have undermined traditional morality.

Indeed, from this point of view, government policy has further undermined the family by taking from conventional families and giving to deviant households. Welfare payments to single mothers have driven up taxation to the point where wives with young children are forced to take paid employment to make ends meet. As a result, even those who wish to live in conventional nuclear families, with the mother at home, are unable to do so, and more children are socialized in unsatisfactory ways.

The New Right has been in a position to influence social policy because of the election of political leaders sympathetic to its views. These include Ronald Reagan, president of the USA from 1980 to 1988, and Margaret Thatcher, who was prime minister of Britain throughout the 1980s. Abbott and Wallace say of Reagan:

> *He put himself firmly on the side of the 'pro-family' movement in supporting both the patriarchal nuclear family as necessary and inevitable and in seeing welfare reforms as at least partly responsible for the decline of the American family.*
>
> Abbott and Wallace, 1992

In Britain, Margaret Thatcher also supported many aspects of New Right thinking on the family. She agreed that the family was a vital institution for maintaining social stability. In a speech in May 1988, Thatcher said:

> *The family is the building block of society. It's a nursery, a school, a hospital, a leisure place, a place of refuge and a place of rest. It encompasses the whole of society. It fashions beliefs. It's the preparation for the rest of our life and women run it.*
>
> Quoted in Abbott and Wallace, 1992

Soon after coming to office, Thatcher set up a Family Policy Group consisting of Ferdinand Mount, a prominent New Right academic, and senior cabinet ministers. Abbott and Wallace describe the group's recommendations in the following way:

> *They thought that mothers with young children should be encouraged to stay at home, that financial disincentives against motherhood should be removed to facilitate this, that the tax/benefits system should be orientated more towards the family ... they also suggested that the family, in the widest sense, should be encouraged to take on responsibility for the disabled, the elderly and unemployed 16-year-olds.*
>
> Abbott and Wallace, 1992

The New Right and policies

On the surface, it would appear that the New Right had a major impact on government policy on both sides of the Atlantic. Abbott and Wallace do identify some policies that were influenced by its ideas. In America, for example, in 1984 new legislation required states to ensure that biological fathers contributed to supporting their offspring when they did not live with the mother.

In Britain, from April 1988, benefits were withdrawn from 16–18-year-olds who did not take up a place on a training scheme. This was partly to try to force families to take responsibility for maintaining unemployed teenagers. Conservative governments also followed policies supporting 'community care' for the elderly and disabled rather than care in state institutions. In practice this meant care by family members, and usually women. The 1988 budget changed taxation so that cohabiting couples could no longer claim more in tax allowances than a married couple. It also prevented cohabiting couples from claiming two lots of income tax relief on a shared mortgage when a married couple could only claim one.

However, in many other ways the New Right failed to achieve the changes it wanted. Abbott and Wallace say that, in the USA, 'few of the policies of the pro-family movement were implemented. Nor did the traditional two-parent patriarchal family consistently benefit from economic policies.'

In Britain the New Right also had limited success. In terms of moral policies, divorce was actually made easier in 1984 and legislation was enacted which gave 'illegitimate' children the same rights as those born within marriage. In terms of economic policies, some changes seem to have given a relative advantage to single parents. From 1987 to 1988 the extra benefit payable to single parents was increased, while the Child Benefit payable to all mothers was frozen. Family Credit, introduced to replace Family Income

Supplement in 1988, allowed single parents claiming it to earn more before benefit starts to be reduced.

Conservative governments did not introduce any tax or benefits policies to encourage mothers to stay at home with young children and, to Abbot and Wallace, many Thatcherite policies actually undermined family life. Such policies include the freezing of Child Benefit, economic policies which forced up unemployment, the emphasis on home ownership and opposition to the provision of council housing, and cuts in education spending and the real levels of student grants. All of these policies have hit the finances of many families, with the result that, far from encouraging self-reliance, 'Many families and individuals have had their ability to care for themselves reduced, not increased.'

To Abbott and Wallace, the main purpose of government policies under Thatcher was to reduce public spending; maintaining the traditional family was very much a secondary consideration. For example, the 1988 Immigration Act abolished the rights of British and long-settled Commonwealth citizens to be joined by their wives and children unless it could be shown that they could be maintained without relying upon welfare payments. In practice, Abbott and Wallace claim, the policies ended up making more families dependent on welfare and 'the main outcome was the polarisation between the poor and the better off'. They conclude:

> the welfare and economic policies advocated by the New Right – insofar as they have been implemented by the Thatcher and Reagan administrations – have been more concerned with reasserting the rights of middle-class men and maintaining capitalism than they have been with a genuine concern for men, women and children and the quality of their lives.
>
> Abbott and Wallace, 1992

The family under John Major's government

Margaret Thatcher left office in 1990 and was replaced as prime minister by John Major. Major remained in office until the Labour Party displaced the Conservatives in government in the election of 1997.

Ruth Lister (1996) has reviewed the approach to the family adopted by John Major. Lister notes that Major did take an interest in the family as an issue. He gave specific responsibility for family matters to a cabinet member (Virginia Bottomley), although he did not establish a cabinet sub-committee to examine policies in this area. He also ended the erosion in the value of Child Benefit in an apparent attempt to give extra support to families with children. The Child

Support Agency, which tried to get absent fathers to pay maintenance costs for their children, was also launched during Major's period in office.

Furthermore, a White Paper concerned with adoption came down strongly in favour of giving priority to married couples, and against allowing adoption for gay and lesbian couples. Many of Major's cabinet ministers made strong attacks upon single parents, particularly at the 1993 Conservative Party conference. Ruth Lister describes this as an 'orgy of lone-parent bashing'. John Major himself launched a 'Back to Basics' campaign at the same conference, which included an emphasis on the virtues of conventional family life.

However, the Back to Basics campaign floundered when there were a number of embarrassing revelations about the personal lives of several Conservative MPs and ministers. According to Lister, from 1994 John Major encouraged his cabinet colleagues to tone down their rhetoric criticizing single parents. In the end the Major government actually introduced few policies which had much impact on shaping families and family life. Major's period in office saw a considerable concern about families, but little change in government policies. Ruth Lister therefore concludes that the Major government:

> is more likely to be remembered for the 'moral panic' about the breakdown of the 'family' and for the backlash against lone parent families that it helped to unleash, together with the legacy it inherited in the form of the Child Support Act, than for any distinctive policies of its own directed towards families and women. It is thus family politics rather than family policies that have thrived in the first half of the 1990s.
>
> Lister, 1996, p. 29

The family and 'New Labour'

Family values

Although support for 'family values' has traditionally been associated with more right-wing thinkers and political parties, it has begun to exercise some influence over the British Labour Party. Elizabeth Silva and Carol Smart claim that the 'political mantra on the family is not peculiar to Conservative governments but has also become a theme of New Labour in Britain' (Silva and Smart, 1999). They quote Tony Blair's 1997 conference speech in which he said, 'We cannot say we want a strong and secure society when we ignore its very foundations: family life. This is not about preaching to individuals about their private lives. It is addressing a huge social problem.' He went on to cite teenage pregnancies, families unable to care for their elderly members, poor parental role models, truancy, educational under-achievement and even unhappiness as amongst the social problems which could stem from the failure to achieve successful family life. Blair went on to pledge that the government would examine every area of government policy to see how it could strengthen family life.

Silva and Smart suggest that Blair was really talking about a specific type of family life. They say, 'Strong families are, of course, seen as conjugal, heterosexual parents with an employed male breadwinner. Lone mothers and gay couples do not, by definition, constitute strong families in this rhetoric.' However, they do believe that Blair and the Labour government recognized that social change had occurred and that it was not possible to follow policies that pretended that most people continued to live in conventional families.

Supporting Families

This concern with families led to the Labour government setting up a committee, chaired by the home secretary Jack Straw, to produce a consultation paper or Green Paper. This was published in 1998 under the title *Supporting Families*. The Green Paper suggested a whole range of measures to provide 'better services and support for parents', such as a National Family and Parenting Institute to coordinate and publicize services available to families. It suggested a greater role for health visitors in helping out families. It also made proposals which would help people to balance the requirements of work and their home life. These included longer maternity leave, a right to three months' unpaid leave for both parents, and a right to time off (from employment) for family reasons.

The paper included measures designed to strengthen marriage and to reduce the number of marriage breakdowns. These included giving registrars a greater role in advising married couples, and improvements to the information couples received before marriage. It also suggested making pre-nuptial agreements (for example, about who gets what in the event of divorce) legally binding.

The paper suggested that it was necessary to take measures to cut teenage pregnancies because these

were associated with wider social problems. With regard to single parents, the Green Paper heralded the introduction of a New Deal. This involved ensuring that single parents received personal help and advice to assist them in returning to paid employment if they wished to do so. For low-income families a Working Families Tax Credit was to be introduced which allowed them to claim some tax relief against a proportion of the childcare costs they incurred by going to work.

Conclusion

In general the measures proposed and introduced by the Blair government in its early years were based around strengthening conventional families. However, they certainly moved away from the idea that families should have a single earner and that women should stay at home to look after children. As described above, a number of measures were taken to help parents combine paid work with domestic responsibilities. The Green Paper said:

> We also need to acknowledge just how much families have changed. Family structures have become more complicated, with many more children living with step-parents or in single parent households. They may face extra difficulties and we have designed practical support with these parents in mind.
>
> *Supporting Families*, 1998, p. 4

It accepted that single parents and unmarried couples could sometimes raise children successfully, but none the less said that 'marriage is still the surest foundation for raising children and remains the choice of the people in Britain'. No mention was made of providing support for single people.

Despite a toning down of the rhetoric criticizing unconventional families and non-family groups, the policies of 'New Labour' continue to idealize stable, long-lasting marriage and nuclear families. Furthermore, the stress on trying to maintain such domestic arrangements in the face of trends that seem to undermine them, largely reflects the family agenda originally pushed to the forefront of politics in Britain by the New Right.

Families, modernity and postmodernity

Much of this chapter has suggested that significant changes have taken place in family life in Europe and North America (as well as elsewhere) over the last few decades. Although some sociologists have stressed that it is important not to exaggerate the

extent of the changes, all acknowledge that at least some changes have taken place. A number of sociologists have related the changes to the concepts of modernity or postmodernity. They have seen them as part and parcel of changes in society as a whole.

Although the sociologists examined in this section disagree about whether social changes should be seen as part of the development of modernity or as part of a postmodern stage in the development of society, there are some similarities in the sorts of changes they relate to the development of the family.

Anthony Giddens – *The Transformation of Intimacy*

In an influential book, the British sociologist Anthony Giddens argues that major changes have taken place in intimate relationships between people (particularly relationships between sexual partners). He relates these changes to the development of what he calls high modernity (his concept of high modernity is discussed in Chapter 15).

Romantic love

Giddens argues that pre-modern relationships in Europe were largely based around 'economic circumstance' (Giddens, 1992). People got married to particular people largely to provide an economic context in which to produce a family. For the peasantry, life was so hard that it 'was unlikely to be conducive to sexual passion'. Married couples, according to research quoted by Giddens, rarely kissed or caressed. The aristocracy also married for reasons to do with reproduction and forming economic connections between families.

However, in the eighteenth century the idea of romantic love began to develop, first among the aristocracy. Romantic love involved idealizing the object of the love and, for women in particular, telling stories to themselves about how their lives could become fulfilled through the relationship. The idea of romantic love was closely connected to the emergence of the novel as a literary form. Romantic novels played an important part in spreading the idea of romantic love. It was also related to the limitation of family size. This allowed sex, for women, to gradually become separated from an endless round of (at the time very dangerous) pregnancy and childbirth. Romantic love contains the idea that people will be attracted to one another and this attraction will lead to the partners being bound together.

In theory, romantic love should be egalitarian. The bond is based upon mutual attraction. In practice, however, it has tended to lead to the dominance of men. Giddens says, 'For women dreams of romantic love have all too often led to grim domestic subjection.' Sex is important in romantic love, but a successful sexual relationship is seen as stemming from the romantic attraction, and not the other way round. In the ideal of romantic love, a woman saves herself, preserves her virginity, until the perfect man comes along.

Plastic sexuality

Giddens argues that in the most recent phase of modernity the nature of intimate relationships has undergone profound changes. Virginity for women is no longer prized, and few women are virgins on their marriage day. Plastic sexuality has developed. With plastic sexuality, sex can be freed from its association with childbirth altogether. People have much greater choice over when, how often and with whom they engage in sex. The development of plastic sexuality was obviously connected to the development of improved methods of contraception. To Giddens, however, it began to emerge before these technological developments and has more social than technical origins. In particular, as we will see, it was tied up with the development of a sense of the self that could be actively chosen.

Confluent love and the pure relationship

The emergence of plastic sexuality changes the nature of love. Romantic love is increasingly replaced by confluent love. Confluent love is 'active contingent love' which 'jars with the "for-ever", "one-and-only" qualities of the romantic love complex'.

In earlier eras, divorce was difficult or impossible to obtain and it was difficult to engage openly in pre-marital relationships. Once people had married through romantic love they were usually stuck with one another however their relationship developed. Now people have much more choice. They are not compelled to stay together if the relationship is not working. The ideal which people increasingly base relationships on is the pure relationship, rather than a marriage based upon a romantic passion. Pure relationships continue because people choose to stay in them. Giddens says, 'What holds the pure relationship together is the acceptance on the part of each partner, "until further notice", that each gains sufficient benefit from the relationship to make its continuance worthwhile.' Love is based upon emotional intimacy and only develops 'to the degree to which each partner is prepared to reveal concerns and needs to the other and to be vulnerable to that other'. These concerns are constantly monitored by people to see if they are deriving sufficient satisfaction from the relationship to continue it. Marriage is increasingly an expression of such relationships once they are already established, rather than a way of achieving them.

However, pure relationships are not confined to marriage or indeed to heterosexual couples. In some cases and in some ways gay and lesbian relationships may come closer to pure relationships than heterosexual ones. Furthermore, pure relationships do not have to be based upon exclusivity if both partners agree that they will not limit their sexual relationships to one another.

In general, Giddens sees pure relationships as having the potential for creating more equal relationships between men and women. They have an openness and a mutual concern and respect which makes it difficult for one partner to be dominant. However, that does not mean that Giddens has an entirely positive view of contemporary marriage and other intimate relationships – far from it. He documents a whole range of emotional, psychological and physical abuses that can occur within contemporary relationships. The pure relationship is more of an ideal than a relationship that has actually been achieved by most intimate couples. But Giddens does think there is a trend towards such relationships, because their development is intimately bound up with the development of modernity.

Modernity and self-identity

Giddens sees institutional reflexivity as a key, perhaps the key, characteristic of modernity. In pre-modern times institutions were largely governed by tradition. They carried on in certain ways because they had operated that way in the past. Modernity involves the increasing application of reason. Reason is used to work out how institutions could work better. Reflexivity describes the way in which people reflect upon the institutions that are part of the social world and try to change them for the better.

Increasingly, such reflexivity reaches into all areas of social life, including very personal areas. For example, publications such as the *Kinsey Report* (a survey of sexual behaviour among Americans) opened up sex to critical reflection. An increasing number of manuals, magazine columns and so on are written to help people reflect upon and try to improve their sex lives. Giddens says, 'the rise of such researches signals, and contributes to, an accelerating reflexivity on the level of the ordinary, everyday sexual practices'.

Reflexivity extends into the creation of self-identity. People can increasingly choose who they want to be. They are no longer stuck with the roles into which they are born and confined by the dictates of tradition. Within the limits of the opportunities available to them, people can increasingly shape who they are and who they think themselves to be. Giddens argues that there is a 'reflexive project of the self' which 'is oriented only to control. It has no morality other than authenticity, a modern day version of the old maxim "to thine own self be true"'. People want to discover who they really are, and trying different relationships can be an important part of this process. Seeking a pure relationship may, for example, allow an individual to try to decide whether they are truly homosexual, heterosexual or bisexual.

People have far more choice of lifestyle than in the past, and trying different ones may be part of creating a self-identity. Giddens says, 'Today, however, given the lapse of tradition, the question "Who shall I be?" is inextricably bound up with "How shall I live?"'

Conclusion

If Giddens's analysis is correct, then it certainly seems to explain the increasing rates of divorce and other relationship breakdowns and the greater pluralism of family forms. The continuing popularity of marriage could be seen as part of the quest for the pure relationship. Certainly Giddens seems to be on strong ground in arguing that there is more sense of choice in personal relationships than in the past.

However, Giddens may underestimate the degree to which factors such as class and ethnicity continue to influence the form that relationships take. Furthermore, other sociologists, while agreeing that there is now more choice, see this as resulting from somewhat different processes to those discussed by Giddens. Furthermore, some see the changes in a much more negative light than Giddens does.

Ulrich Beck and Elisabeth Beck-Gernsheim – *The Normal Chaos of Love*

Another influential interpretation of changes in relationships and family life has been put forward by the German sociologists Ulrich Beck and Elisabeth Beck-Gernsheim (1995, first published in German in 1990). Beck and Beck-Gernsheim follow a similar line of argument to Giddens in claiming that changes in family life and relationships are being shaped by the development of modernity. They also follow Giddens in arguing that modernity is characterized by increasing individual choice, in contrast to an emphasis upon following tradition in pre-modern societies. However, they characterize this process as involving individualization rather than reflexivity, and see it as having rather different consequences from those outlined by Giddens.

Individualization

Individualization involves an extension of the areas of life in which individuals are expected to make their own decisions. Beck and Beck-Gernsheim say, 'The proportion of possibilities in life that do not involve decision-making is diminishing and the proportion of biography open to decision-making and individual initiative is increasing.' Like Giddens, they contrast this increasing choice with a pre-modern era in which choice was much more limited and tradition much more important in shaping social life. They trace the origins of the process of individualization back to a range of factors including the influence of the Protestant ethic (see pp. 447–51), urbanization and secularization.

Most important of all, though, was an increase in personal mobility, both social and geographical. As modern societies opened up, moving place and moving jobs became easier, and this presented individuals with more choices about how to run their lives. In the second half of the twentieth century this process went on to a new stage in which there was a rapid increase in available choices. The reasons for this included the opening up of educational opportunities, the improvement in the living standards of the lower classes, which freed them from the daily grind of trying to survive in poverty, and improved labour market opportunities for women. The latter change has led to new uncertainties in gender roles and has particularly affected intimate relationships.

Choice in families and relationships

If pre-modern societies gave people little choice about their roles in families and marriages, they did at least provide some stability and certainty. Beck and Beck-Gernsheim say that for individuals the 'severing of traditional ties means being freed of previous constraints and obligations. At the same time, however, the support and security offered by traditional society begin to disappear.' In the absence of such supports and security, individuals have to try to create personal relationships that will provide for their needs. Beck and Beck-Gernsheim say that the nuclear family seems to offer 'a sort of refuge in the chilly environment of our affluent, impersonal, uncertain society, stripped of its traditions and scarred by all kinds of risk. Love will become more important than ever and equally impossible.' It is important because people believe that they can express and fulfil their individuality through a loving relationship. Love offers the promise of an 'emotional base' and a 'security system' which are absent in the world outside. However, contemporary societies prevent the formation of such relationships.

Love in the context of successful family relationships has come to depend on individuals finding a successful formula. It can no longer be based upon norms and traditions since these no longer exist in a form that is generally or even widely accepted. People try out a range of arrangements, such as cohabitation, marriage and divorce, in their search for love. In each relationship they have to work out solutions for how to order their relationships anew. Beck and Beck-Gernsheim describe the situation in the following way:

it is no longer possible to pronounce in some binding way what family, marriage, parenthood, sexuality or love mean, what they should or could be; rather these vary in substance, norms and morality from individual to individual and from relationship to relationship. The answers to the questions above must be worked out, negotiated, arranged and justified in all the details of how, what, why or why not, even if this might unleash the conflicts and devils that lie slumbering among the details and were assumed to be tamed. ... Love is becoming a blank that lovers must fill in themselves.

Beck and Beck-Gernsheim, 1995, p. 5

The causes of conflict

The amount of choice in itself causes the potential for conflict, but there are other factors that make it even more likely. Earlier periods of industrial, modern societies were based upon relatively clearcut gender roles involving a male breadwinner and a female carer and homemaker. Industrial work by men was founded upon the assumption of a wife who was carrying out housework and childcare tasks. With increased opportunities for women in education and employment, this has changed. Now, both men and women might seek fulfilling careers.

Furthermore, the demands of the capitalist workplace contrast markedly with those of domestic life. Beck and Beck-Gernsheim comment that 'Individual competitiveness and mobility, encouraged by the job market, run up against the opposite expectations at home where one is expected to sacrifice one's own interests for others and invest in a collective project called family.' The family is the arena in which these contradictions and conflicts are played out. Men and women argue over who should do the housework, who should look after the kids and whose job should take priority. The results of the arguments are unlikely to satisfy both parties. In the end one person's career or personal development has to take a back seat. In a world where individualization has proceeded so far this is bound to cause resentment.

Conclusion

Beck and Beck-Gernsheim believe that these contradictions lead to '*The Normal Chaos of Love*'. Love is increasingly craved to provide security in an insecure world, but it is increasingly difficult to find and sustain. The quest for individual fulfilment by both partners in a relationship makes it difficult for them to find common ground. Beck and Beck-Gernsheim conclude pessimistically that 'perhaps the two parallel lines will eventually meet, in the far distant future. Perhaps not. We shall never know.'

Giddens's conclusions seem a little over-optimistic, those of Beck and Beck-Gernsheim seem rather too pessimistic. Some couples do manage to work out their differences and produce mutually satisfactory relationships. However, Beck and Beck-Gernsheim may be right to suggest that the apparent greater choice over relationships can create problems in making them work.

David H.J. Morgan – past-modern sociology and family practices

Past-modern sociology

David Morgan has attempted to develop an approach to studying the family which takes account of recent changes in family life without fully embracing postmodernism (Morgan, 1996, 1999). He borrows the term past-modern from R. Stones (1996) to characterize his approach. He claims that this approach draws upon a wide variety of influences including feminism, postmodernism and interactionism. It tries to avoid the sort of modern approach to studying 'the family' which assumes that families have a fixed structure and clear boundaries between themselves and the outside world. He would reject, therefore, the kinds of approaches used by Parsons (see pp. 509–10 and 524–5) and by Young and Willmott (pp. 529–31), which tend to see a single dominant type of family evolving alongside the development of modern societies.

On the other hand, Morgan is also opposed to an extreme version of postmodernism 'that would threaten to empty sociological enquiry (of any kind) of any content' (Morgan, 1999). Morgan believes that you should acknowledge the changes taking place in family lives, but that you should not reject the use of all empirical evidence. He says, 'the assemblage of carefully collected "facts" about family living is not to be despised but neither is it to be seen as the culmination of family analysis'.

Changes in family living

Morgan believes that modern approaches to studying family living have become outdated because of changes in families and societies. Both are increasingly characterized by 'flux, fluidity and change'. 'The family' is not a static entity which can be frozen at a moment in time so that its form can be clearly analysed. Rather, it is constituted by ongoing processes of change, and overlaps considerably (and in changing ways) with the society that surrounds it. In the conventional sociological way of thinking about families:

> family living is not about hospital waiting lists, size of classrooms or the availability of public transport. Yet such matters, in the experiences of individual members, may be at least as much to do with routine family living as the matters subsumed under the statistical tables [such as those about household size, divorce rates and so on].
>
> Morgan, 1999, p. 15

Morgan's alternative approach attempts to take account of the blurred boundaries between families and the outside world, and the constantly changing nature of family life.

Family practices

Morgan believes that the study of the family should focus on family practices rather than, for example, family structure. Family practices are concerned with what family members actually do, and with the accounts they give of what they do. Unlike some postmodernists, Morgan does not believe that what families do should be reduced to the descriptions of what they do. He believes there is a social reality that really exists and can be described and analysed by sociologists. That reality is independent of sociologists' descriptions of it. However, that should not stop sociologists from also discussing the way in which people talk about and describe their own family lives.

Morgan goes on to outline the central themes brought out by the idea of family practices:

1 The first is 'A sense of interplay between the perspectives of the social actor, the individual whose actions are being described and accounted for, and the perspectives of the observer'. For example, researchers should examine how far individuals see themselves as members of families, and they should consider where people draw the boundary between their family and non-family members.

2 The second is 'A sense of the active rather than the passive'. People do not just occupy particular roles, they actively construct their lives. Gender, class and family relationships are all worked out by people in the course of their actions, they are not predetermined. Even something as apparently passive as sleeping involves actively working out what are seen as appropriate sleeping arrangements for different family members.

3 The next thing that the idea of family practices is supposed to convey is 'A focus on the everyday'. Routine family practices, such as how breakfast is organized and consumed, can tell you as much, if not more, about family life as examining less mundane events, such as weddings.

4 Morgan also believes that examining family practices should place 'A stress on regularities'. Although family life may change frequently, there are often regular patterns that reoccur, particularly in the daily routines. Sociologists should not lose sight of these regularities, which may well be part of the taken-for-granted life of families.

5 Despite the importance of regularities, Morgan also believes that there should be 'A sense of fluidity'. Family practices will flow into practices from other spheres of social life. He says:

> Thus a family outing might consist of a variety of different family practices while also blending with gendered practices, leisure

*practices and so on. Further, the family outing
may well be linked in the perceptions of the
participants to other such outings, to
anticipated future outings and the planning
involved in each case.*

Morgan, 1999, p. 18

6   Finally, the idea of family practices involves 'An
    interplay between history and biography'. The focus
    should not be entirely upon the experience of family
    life on an everyday basis, it should also be linked to
    a consideration of the historical development of
    society as a whole. Family outings, for example, are
    linked to 'a wider historical framework to do with
    the development of leisure, transportation and
    shifting constructions of parenthood and childhood'.

Although a little vague, Morgan's past-modern
approach does offer the possibility of analysing family
life in a way which is sensitive to contemporary
changes but which also rests upon detailed evidence.
It suggests that some of the older debates about
family structure and the 'typical' or 'conventional'
family may be becoming less useful for understanding
family life today. It also offers the possibility of
examining areas of family life (such as outings and
use of health services) which have not usually been
the focus of study for sociologists of 'the family'.

Judith Stacey – the postmodern family

The shift to the postmodern family

Unlike Giddens, Beck and Beck-Gernsheim, and
David Morgan, the American sociologist Judith
Stacey believes that contemporary societies such as
the USA have developed the postmodern family
(Stacey, 1996). Like the other writers examined in this
section, she associates changes in the family with a
movement away from a single dominant family type
and with greater variety in family relationships. She
says, 'I use the term postmodern family ... to signal
the contested, ambivalent, and undecided character of
our contemporary family cultures.' She goes on, 'Like
postmodern culture, contemporary Western family
arrangements are diverse, fluid, and unresolved. Like
postmodern cultural forms, our families today admix
unlikely elements in an improvisational pastiche of
old and new.' She does not see the emergence of the
postmodern family as another stage in the development of family life; instead it has destroyed the idea
that the family does progress through a series of
logical stages. It no longer makes sense to discuss
what type of family is dominant in contemporary
societies because family forms have become so
diverse. Furthermore, there can be no assumption

that any particular form will become accepted as the
main, best, or normal type of family.

Stacey believes that this situation is here to stay. It
will be impossible for societies to go back to having
a single standard (such as the heterosexual nuclear
family) against which all families are compared and
judged. Societies will have to come to terms with
such changes and adapt to cope with the greater
variety and uncertainty in family life. Although some
commentators deplore the decline of the conventional, heterosexual nuclear family, diversity is here
to stay. Social attitudes and social policies will have
to adjust to this diversity if postmodern families are
to have a good chance of facilitating fulfilling lives
for their members.

Postmodern families in Silicon Valley

Stacey's claim that the postmodern family is characteristic of the USA is based upon her own research
into family life in Silicon Valley conducted during
the mid-1980s. Silicon Valley in California is the
'global headquarters of the electronics industry and
the world's vanguard postindustrial region' (Stacey,
1996). Usually trends in family life in the USA take
on an exaggerated form in Silicon Valley. For
example, divorce rates in this area have risen faster
than in other areas of the country. Trends there are
generally indicative of future trends elsewhere.

Most sociologists have tended to argue that
higher-class and middle-class families lead the way
in new family trends and that working-class families
then follow later (see, for example, Willmott and
Young's idea of the symmetrical family, pp. 529–32).
Stacey's research suggests that the reverse might be
true with the rise of the postmodern family. Her
research focused on two working-class extended-kin
networks in Silicon Valley, and uncovered the way in
which these families had become adaptable and
innovative in response to social changes.

According to Stacey, the modern family was
largely based around the idea of the male as the
primary breadwinner, earning a 'family wage'. In
other words, the man earned enough to keep the
whole of the family. However, this sort of family life
only became available to working-class families
relatively late in the twentieth century. It was not
until the 1960s that some working-class men started
earning enough to keep a whole family. Furthermore,
the situation was to be short-lived. By the late 1970s,
economic changes began to threaten the viability of
families dependent on a working-class male wage
earner. The two central people in each of the kinship
networks studied by Stacey's research were Pam and
Dotty: working-class women who had to adapt their
family life to changing personal circumstances and
the changing society that surrounded them.

Pam and Dotty

Both Pam and Dotty got married to manual workers around the end of the 1950s and the start of the 1960s. Both their husbands were of working-class origin but both worked hard and worked their way up in the electronics industry until they had middle-class jobs. Despite this, neither husband was earning enough to maintain their family in the sort of middle-class lifestyle they desired. Pam took on some cleaning and childcare work, but she kept it a secret from her husband to avoid injuring his male pride in being the sole breadwinner. Dotty took on a range of temporary and low-paid jobs.

In the early 1970s, Pam and Dotty both started courses at their local college – courses designed to give them a chance of getting better work. At the college they were exposed to feminist ideas for the first time and this encouraged them to take steps to change their marriages and family life. Both were unhappy with aspects of their marriage. Both husbands took little part in family life and were unwilling to help with housework. Dotty's husband, Lou, physically abused her. For these reasons both women left their husbands.

Pam got divorced, studied for a degree, and pursued a career working for social services. Some time later Pam became a born-again Christian and remarried. Her second marriage was a more egalitarian one and her family network was far from conventional. In particular, she formed a close relationship with her first husband's live-in lover and they helped each other out in a range of practical ways.

Dotty eventually took her husband back, but only after he had had a serious heart attack which left him unable to physically abuse her. Furthermore, the reconciliation was largely on Dotty's terms and her husband had to carry out most of the housework. Dotty meanwhile got involved in political campaigns in the community, particularly those concerned with helping battered wives. Later she withdrew from political campaigning and took part-time work in an insurance office. However, her husband and two of her adult children died. One of her deceased daughters left four children behind and Dotty successfully obtained custody of the children, against the wishes of her son-in-law, who had abused members of his family. Dotty then formed a household with one of her surviving daughters, who was a single mother.

These complex changes in the families of Pam and Dotty showed how two working-class women developed their family life to take account of changes in their circumstances in a rapidly changing environment. Stacey comments that by the end of the study, 'Dotty and Pamela both had moved

partway back from feminist fervour, at the same time both had moved further away from the (no longer) modern family.' Furthermore, none of Pam's or Dotty's daughters lived in a conventional, modern nuclear family.

The working class and the postmodern family

Stacey found that the image of working-class families clinging on to conventional family arrangements longer than the middle class was quite erroneous. She says, 'I found postmodern family arrangements among blue collar workers at least as diverse and innovative as those found within the middle-class.'

The women she studied had drawn upon the traditions of working-class and African American women being supported by their female kin (such as mothers, daughters, sisters and aunts) to find new ways of dealing with the changes to their family circumstances. In post-industrial conditions, when jobs were less secure and workers were expected to work 'flexibly', women drew on such traditions to find ways of coping with uncertainty and change. Stacey says that the working-class women she studied were:

> Struggling creatively, often heroically, to sustain oppressed families and, to escape the most oppressive ones, they drew on "traditional" premodern kinship resources and crafted untraditional ones. In the process they created postmodern family strategies.

> Rising divorce and cohabitation rates, working mothers, two-earner households, single and unwed parenthood, along with inter-generational female-linked extended kin support networks appeared earlier and more extensively among poor and working-class people.

Stacey, 1996, p. 29

Gay and lesbian families

As well as the working-class women Stacey studied in Silicon Valley, her ideas also draw upon an analysis of gay and lesbian families. She argues that gay and lesbian families have also played a pioneering role in developing the postmodern family. In the early 1970s, gay and lesbian organizations were often strongly anti-family, but by the late 1980s this attitude had been reversed. There was a major 'gay-by boom' – that is a boom in babies and children being looked after by gay and lesbian couples.

Stacey quotes research which suggests that by the late 1980s between 6 and 14 million children were being brought up in gay and lesbian families. Gay and lesbian families are themselves extremely diverse, but because of the prejudice they sometimes face they form a 'new embattled, visible and necessarily self-conscious, genre of postmodern kinship' (Stacey, 1996).

Furthermore, 'self-consciously "queer" couples and families, by necessity, have had to reflect much more seriously on the meaning and purpose of their intimate relationships'. This forced reflection makes them more creative and imaginative in developing family forms to suit their circumstances, and it makes them more likely to include people from outside conventional nuclear family relationships in their family circle. Stacey believes that:

> gays and lesbians improvisationally assemble a patchwork of blood and intentional relations – gay, straight, and other – into creative, extended kin bonds. Gay communities more adeptly integrate single individuals into their social worlds than does the mainstream heterosexual society, a social skill quite valuable in a world in which divorce, widowhood and singlehood are increasingly normative.
>
> Stacey, 1996, p. 143

Within this creativity and flexibility, gay and lesbian couples have increasingly asserted a right to claim, if they wish, aspects of more conventional family relationships for themselves. This has involved, for example, claiming custody of children, lesbian women intentionally becoming pregnant so that they can raise a child with their partner, and trying to have same-sex marriages legally recognized. Slowly they have made gains on all these fronts, although at the time Stacey was writing same-sex marriage had not become legal in the USA. (A court case over the legality of same-sex marriage was pending in Hawaii.)

Stacey argues that research indicates that gay and lesbian relationships are at least as suitable for raising children as heterosexual marriages. Generally, research finds that there is virtually no difference in the psychological well-being and social development of children with gay or lesbian carers and those with heterosexual carers. Stacey says, 'The rare small differences reported tend to favor gay parents, portraying them as somewhat more nurturant and tolerant, and their children in turn, more tolerant and empathetic, and less aggressive than those raised by non-gay parents.'

Stacey believes that children raised in gay and lesbian families are less likely to be hostile to homosexual relationships and more likely to try them for themselves. However, she regards this as an advantage rather than as a problem. This is because it discourages intolerance of families who are different, and, in a world of increasing family diversity, this is essential. It also allows people more freedom to explore and develop their sexuality, free from what Adrienne Rich has called 'compulsory heterosexuality' (quoted in Stacey, 1996).

Conclusion

Stacey does not believe that the development of the postmodern family has no disadvantages. She acknowledges that it does create a certain degree of unsettling instability. Nevertheless, she generally welcomes it as an opportunity to develop more egalitarian and more democratic family relationships. As we will see in the next section, such views are controversial and many commentators mourn the decline of stable, conventional families.

As we have seen earlier in the chapter (see pp. 548–9, for example), it is questionable whether diversity and what Stacey calls the postmodern family have really become that common. It is possible that Stacey exaggerates the extent of change. Neither gay and lesbian families nor families in Silicon Valley are likely to be typical American families or typical of families in contemporary societies.

Research conducted by O'Brien and Jones (1996) into working-class families and kinship in East London suggests rather more continuity in the family patterns of the working class than that found by Stacey (see p. 532). Nevertheless, Stacey does identify some important trends and raises interesting possibilities about the strategies that families will adopt in the future to cope with a rapidly changing social world.

Sociology, values and the family

Like those they write about, sociologists are members of society and members of families. They too have been exposed to family ideologies which suggest that a particular type of family (usually the heterosexual nuclear family) is the ideal. Increasingly this view has been challenged and any consensus about the best way to organize family life has been undermined.

Nevertheless, the ideology of the conventional nuclear family remains powerful and influential.

Sociologists' views of the family are unlikely to be free from their beliefs about what the family ought to be. In fact, Talcott Parsons's picture of the isolated nuclear family is essentially no different from an idealized image of a perfect, modern, heterosexual nuclear family. It can be argued that the concept of the isolated nuclear family owes more than a little to his values.

When functionalists such as Parsons were devising their theories of the family, the dominance of the nuclear family was largely unquestioned. Here, as in all areas of sociology, functionalist perspectives have been accused of having a conservative bias. With their emphasis on the universality and inevitability of the family, they justify its existence. With their preoccupation with the positive aspects of the family, they provide it with legitimation. As Barrington Moore argues, these views may say more about the hopes and ideals of sociologists than the reality of their subject matter. He states:

> Among social scientists today it is almost axiomatic that the family is a universally necessary social institution and will remain such through any foreseeable future … I have the uncomfortable feeling that the authors, despite all their elaborate theories and technical research devices, are doing little more than projecting certain middle-class hopes and ideals onto a refractory reality.
>
> Quoted in Morgan, 1975, p. 3.

In other words, the view that the family is here to stay through time immemorial may be primarily a reflection of middle-class values.

D.H.J. Morgan argues that functionalist perspectives on the family 'give emphasis to the limits of human activity rather than the potentialities' (Morgan, 1975). In doing so they adopt a conservative stance. By emphasizing the universal necessity for the family and the vital functions it performs for the social system, they imply that individuals must accept the inevitable. Members of society must form families and act accordingly within the limits set by the requirements of the social system.

Although functionalist views on the family are no longer particularly influential in sociology, similar views are still influential in society. New Right perspectives on the family have a remarkable similarity to those of functionalists. Both approaches see the nuclear family as the ideal, neither believes that there are viable alternatives to living in families, neither examines the ways in which families can harm individuals, and both see families as vital to producing social stability.

However, they do differ in the extent to which they see the family as under threat. For example, Fletcher (1988) saw the rising divorce rate as an indication that people value family life, and happy families split up only to be reformed as even happier families. Members of the New Right, on the other hand, see divorce as just one symptom of a serious

moral decline. As the family breaks down and single parenthood becomes more common, they see a danger of the young being inadequately socialized and becoming an ever greater problem for society.

Functionalists and the New Right can both be accused of having a very idealized picture of life in nuclear families. For the most part, they have made little attempt to actually investigate family life, simply assuming that all is sweetness and light. This cosy image has been shattered by sociologists and psychiatrists who have studied some of the less savoury aspects of life in families. In R.D. Laing's studies of schizophrenia (Laing, 1976, Laing and Esterson, 1970), feminist studies of domestic violence, and Marxist and feminist research on labour and power within households, an alternative image of the family has been presented. From this point of view the family is, or at least can be, exploitative, violent and psychologically damaging.

Unlike functionalists, feminists, Marxists and other radical critics cannot be accused of seeing the family through rose-tinted spectacles. However, they can be accused of letting their value judgements direct their theories and research. Marxists start with the assumption that capitalism is evil; feminists with the assumption that society is patriarchal and that women are exploited by men. From these starting points their sociology follows a predictable path. Evidence is gathered to confirm their theories and they usually display little self-doubt in their dedication to their particular perspective.

A rather different and arguably less judgemental view is advocated by some sociologists who have written about family diversity. They neither want to preserve the traditional family, nor to dismiss it as a harmful institution. Instead they believe that all domestic living arrangements should be accepted and respected whether they are nuclear families, communes, extended families, gay and lesbian couples, single-person or single-parent households. Rhona Rapoport describes this as the secular pluralist orientation (Rapoport, 1989). She sees it as 'characterised by tolerance towards the diversity of family forms' and argues that it will 'be followed by people advocating human rights'.

Such views are largely echoed by theorists of the postmodern family. Judith Stacey generally welcomes the increased diversity, choice and creativity which she believes are involved in contemporary family life. She says, 'In theory, the postmodern family condition of pluralism and flexibility should present a democratic opportunity in which individuals' shared capacities, desires, and convictions could govern the character of their gender, sexual and family relationships' (Stacey, 1996). However, she warns that problems such as discrimination and poverty may make it difficult for all but the most affluent to take full advantage of the new freedom.

Stacey also recognizes that the ideology of the conventional, heterosexual nuclear family and the social policies that often accompany the ideology may continue to make life difficult for those who want to construct alternative family lives. Certainly even political parties such as the British Labour Party, with some sympathy for the view that family diversity should be accepted, find it difficult to abandon the rhetoric supporting conventional families (see pp. 576–7).

The views of writers such as Rapoport and Stacey sound as if they are less value-laden, less ideological than those of most other sociologists. However, even their views are influenced by a particular set of values, in this case libertarian values. Furthermore, as Rapoport admits:

> *Problems may arise as regards limits. The norm of free choice may be applicable to adults, but where children are involved the main issue is to serve their best interests in some form of domestic arrangement.*
>
> Rapoport, 1989

What is in the best interests of children, or for that matter adults, will always to some extent be a value judgement.

Power, politics and the state

Power, politics and the state

Introduction

In this chapter we are mainly concerned with the nature and distribution of power in modern industrial societies.

Many sociologists argue that political sociology is the study of power in its broadest sense. Thus Dowse and Hughes state that 'politics is about "power", politics occurs when there are differentials in power' (Dowse and Hughes, 1972). In terms of this definition, any social relationship that involves power differentials is political. Political relationships would extend from parents assigning domestic chores to their children to teachers enforcing discipline in the classroom; from a manager organizing a workforce to a general ordering troops into battle.

However, the traditional study of politics has concentrated on the state and the various institutions of government such as Parliament and the judiciary. Sociologists have been particularly concerned with the state, but they have examined it in relation to society as a whole, rather than in isolation.

Sociologists often distinguish between two forms of power, authority and coercion:

1 Authority is that form of power which is accepted as legitimate – that is, right and just – and therefore obeyed on that basis. Thus, if members of British society accept that Parliament has the right to make certain decisions and they regard those decisions as lawful, parliamentary power may be defined as legitimate authority.

2 Coercion is that form of power which is not regarded as legitimate by those subject to it. Thus, from the point of view of some Basque nationalists, the activities of the Spanish police and army in the Basque province may be regarded as coercion.

However, the distinction between authority and coercion is not as clearcut as the above definitions suggest. It has often been argued that both forms of power are based ultimately on physical force, and that those who enforce the law are able to resort to physical force whether their power is regarded as legitimate or not.

We will begin by looking at Max Weber's influential views on power and types of authority.

Max Weber – power and types of authority

Max Weber defined power as:

> *the chance of a man or a number of men to realize their own will in a communal action even against the resistance of others who are participating in the action.*
>
> Weber, in Gerth and Mills, 1948, p. 180

In other words, power consists of the ability to get your own way even when others are opposed to your wishes.

Weber was particularly concerned to distinguish different types of authority. He suggested that there were three sources: charismatic, traditional, and rational–legal.

Charismatic authority

Charismatic authority derives from the devotion felt by subordinates for a leader who is believed to have exceptional qualities. These qualities are seen as supernatural, super-human, or at least exceptional compared to lesser mortals.

Charismatic leaders are able to sway and control their followers by direct emotional appeals which excite devotion and strong loyalties. Historical examples which come close to charismatic authority might include Alexander the Great, Napoleon and Fidel Castro. More ordinary people, such as teachers or managers, may also use charisma to exercise power.

Traditional authority

Weber called the second type of authority traditional authority. In this case authority rests upon a belief in the 'rightness' of established customs and traditions. Those in authority command obedience on the basis of their traditional status which is usually inherited. Their subordinates are controlled by feelings of loyalty and obligation to long-established positions of power.

The feudal system of medieval Europe is an example of traditional authority: monarchs and nobles owed their positions to inherited status and the personal loyalty of their subjects.

Rational–legal authority

The final type of authority distinguished by Weber was rational–legal authority. In this case, unlike charismatic and traditional authority, legitimacy and control stem neither from the perceived personal qualities of the leader and the devotion they excite, nor from a commitment to traditional wisdom. Rational–legal authority is based on the acceptance of a set of impersonal rules.

Those who possess authority are able to issue commands and have them obeyed because others accept the legal framework that supports their authority. Thus a judge, a tax inspector or a military commander are obeyed because others accept the legal framework that gives them their power. The rules on which their authority is based are rational in the sense that they are consciously constructed for

the attainment of a particular goal and they specify the means by which that goal is to be attained. For example, laws governing the legal system are designed to achieve the goal of 'justice'.

Ideal types

Weber stressed that, in reality, authority would never conform perfectly to any of his three types. His three categories are ideal types, each of which defines a 'pure' form of authority. In any particular example, authority may stem from two or more sources. It is therefore possible to find examples of authority which approximate to one of these types, but it is unlikely that a perfect example of any could be found.

Weber's attempts to define power and authority have been highly influential. The pluralist view of power and the state has adopted Weber's definition as a basis for measuring who has power in modern industrial societies.

Pluralists concentrate on the will (or desires) of individuals or groups to achieve particular ends. The wishes that people have are then compared to actual decisions taken by a government. The group whose wishes appear to be carried out are held to possess greater power than those who oppose them. Therefore, power is measured by comparing the stated wishes of individuals or groups who seek to influence government policy, with the actions taken by their government. (Pluralist views on power and the state are discussed fully below, see pp. 593–601.)

Steven Lukes – a radical view of power

Despite the acceptance of Weber's definition of power by many sociologists, some writers believe that it is too narrow. Steven Lukes (1974) has put forward a radical view of power as an alternative. He argues that power has three dimensions or faces, rather than just one.

Decision making

Like pluralists, Lukes sees the first face of power in terms of decision making, where different individuals or groups express different policy preferences and influence the making of decisions over various issues. Lukes would accept that if a government followed the policies advocated by the trade unions, this would represent evidence that the unions had power. However, he believes that it is misleading to concentrate entirely on decisions taken, for power can be exercised in less obvious ways.

Non-decision making

The second face of power does not concern decision making, but rather focuses on non-decision making Power may be used to prevent certain issues from being discussed, or decisions about them from being taken.

From this point of view, individuals or groups exercising power do so by preventing those who take a decision from considering all the possible alternative sources of action, or by limiting the range of decisions they are allowed to take.

For example, a teacher might offer students the opportunity to decide whether to do a piece of homework that week or the following week. The class appears to have power, for they have been given the opportunity to reach a decision. In reality, however, most power still rests with the teacher who has limited the options open to the students. The students are not free to decide whether or not they do this particular piece of work, nor can they choose to reject doing homework altogether.

Shaping desires

The third face of power strays even further from an emphasis on decision making, and the preferences expressed by members of society. Lukes claims that power can be exercised by shaping desires, manipulating the wishes and desires of social groups. A social group may be persuaded to accept, or even to desire, a situation that is harmful to them.

Some feminists would argue that men exercise power over women in contemporary Britain by persuading them that being a mother and housewife are the most desirable roles for women. In reality, feminists claim, women who occupy these roles are exploited by, and for the benefit of, men.

Lukes's definition of power

Having examined the nature of power, Lukes is able to conclude that power can be defined by saying that 'A exercises power over B when A affects B in a manner contrary to B's interests.' In other words, Lukes argues that power is exercised over those who are harmed by its use, whether they are aware they are being harmed or not.

Lukes has been responsible for refining the concept of power, and showing that it has more than one dimension. As he himself admits, though, what is in a person's interests, or what is good for them, is ultimately a matter of opinion. A mother and housewife might deny that her role in society is any less desirable than that of her husband. She might also deny that she is being exploited.

Despite this problem, the radical definition of power has become increasingly influential. Marxist sociologists in particular have used this definition to attack the evidence used by sociologists advocating other perspectives.

We will develop this issue of defining and measuring power as the various theories are examined in detail. Next, however, we will analyse the role of the state in relation to power.

The state

Definitions of the state

The definition of the state is probably less controversial than the definition of power. Weber provided a definition with which most sociologists are in broad agreement. He defined the state as 'a human community that (successfully) claims the monopoly of the legitimate use of physical force within a given territory' (Weber, in Gerth and Mills, 1948).

In modern Britain, the state rules over a clearly-defined geographical area, which includes England, Northern Ireland, Wales and Scotland (although there is now some devolution of power to Scotland, Wales and Northern Ireland).

Only the central authority is believed by most members of society to have the right to use force to achieve its ends. Other groups and individuals may resort to violence, but the actions of terrorists, football 'hooligans' and murderers are not seen as legitimate. The state alone can wage war or use the legal system to imprison people against their will.

On the basis of Weber's definition, the state can be said to consist of the government or legislature which passes laws, the bureaucracy or civil service which implements governmental decisions, the police who are responsible for law enforcement, and the armed forces whose job it is to protect the state from external threats.

Many sociologists see the state as consisting of a wider set of institutions and, in Britain, would include welfare services, and the education and health services. Some go even further and see nationalized industries (such as the Post Office) as part of the state. However, in developing their theories of the state most sociologists have concentrated upon the more central institutions such as the government and the civil service.

The twentieth-century world came to be dominated by nation-states which laid claim to territory in every corner of the world (see pp. 263–70 for a discussion of nationalism). However, although states which conform to Weber's definition have existed for thousands of years, and include ancient Greece, Rome and Egypt, and the Aztecs of Central America, the state is a comparatively new feature of many societies. Anthropologists have discovered a number of stateless 'simple' societies. These are sometimes called acephalous or headless societies.

Stateless societies

In the 1930s, E.E. Evans-Pritchard (1951) carried out a study of the Nuer society in Africa. The society consisted of some 40 separate tribes, none of which had a head or chief.

Only a few decisions had to be taken which affected the tribe as a whole, such as whether to mount a raid on a neighbouring tribe, or whether to initiate young men into adult status. Such decisions appear to have been reached informally through discussions between members of the tribe.

Each tribal grouping was based on a particular geographical area, but they did not claim exclusive rights to using that land. More than half the Nuer lived in tribal areas in which they had not been born.

There was no legal system as such, and there were no particular individuals charged with special responsibility for policing the community. Instead, men who believed they had been wronged were expected to challenge the offender to a duel to the death.

In this society there was no government or other institution which claimed a monopoly of the legitimate use of force, and the society was not based upon a clearly defined territory. As such, Nuer society can be seen as stateless.

The feudal state

A number of commentators believe that the modern centralized state is also a relatively new feature of many parts of Europe. They suggest that it did not develop until after the feudal period.

Under feudalism the legitimate use of force was not concentrated in the hands of a centralized authority. While, in theory, the monarch ruled at the centre, in practice, military power and the control of particular territories were in the hands of feudal lords in each region. Gianfranco Poggi has described how, for example, in the Maconnâis in feudal France, the King was a 'dimly perceived, politically ineffective figure' (Poggi, 1978). The Count of the Maconnâis had originally been granted land by the King in return for providing warriors, but by the twelfth century lesser feudal lords, to whom the Count had granted territory, effectively ruled their own territo-

ries and monopolized military power. Thus the state was not centralized in any one place, but located in many separate centres throughout the nation.

Only in the seventeenth century did the French monarchy successfully establish its authority over the aristocracy in the regions. Furthermore, it was only in the nineteenth century that transport and communications had developed sufficiently for it to become possible for the centralized state to exercise close control over the far-flung corners of its territory.

The modern state

The centralized state developed comparatively recently in many areas of the world. However, its importance in modern, industrialized societies increased dramatically in the nineteenth and twentieth centuries.

In Britain, for instance, in this period the state greatly extended its involvement in, and control over, economic affairs, and the provision of welfare, healthcare and education. These developments are reflected in the rising proportion of Gross National Product (the total amount of economic activity in a society that can be measured in monetary terms) spent by the government. The economists C.V. Brown and P.M. Jackson (1982) have calculated that government spending as a proportion of Gross National Product (GNP) has risen in Britain, from 8 per cent in 1890, to 29 per cent in 1932, to 40.2 per cent in 1966, and to 51.4 per cent in 1976. By 1997-8 it had gone back down to 38.3 per cent (*Independent Budget Review*, 10 March 1999).

The increasing importance of the state in industrial societies has prompted sociologists to devote considerable attention to this institution. In particular they have debated which groups in society control the state and in whose interests the state is run. We will now examine the competing sociological perspectives on power and the state, beginning with a functionalist perspective.

Power – a functionalist perspective

Most sociological theories of power follow Weber's definition in two important respects:

1 Weber's definition implies that those who hold power do so at the expense of others. It suggests that there is a fixed amount of power, and, therefore, if some hold power, others do not. This view is sometimes known as a constant-sum concept of power. Since the amount of power is constant, power is held by an individual or group to the extent that it is not held by others.

2 The second important implication of Weber's definition is that power-holders will tend to use power to further their own interests. Power is used to further the sectional interests of particular groups in society. This view is sometimes known as a variable-sum concept of power, since power in society is not seen as fixed or constant. Instead it is variable in the sense that it can increase or decrease.

Talcott Parsons – the variable-sum concept of power

Power and collective goals

Talcott Parsons's view of power was developed from his general theory of the nature of society. He began from the assumption that value consensus is essential for the survival of social systems. From shared values derive collective goals, that is, goals shared by members of society. For example, if materialism is a major value of Western industrial society, collective goals such as economic expansion and higher living standards can be seen to stem from this value. The more Western societies are able to realize these goals, the greater the power that resides in the social system. Steadily rising living standards and economic growth are therefore indications of an increase of power in society.

Parsons's view of power differentials within society also derived from his general theory. Since goals are shared by all members of society, power will generally be used in the furtherance of collective goals. As a result, both sides of the power relationship will benefit and everybody will gain by the arrangement. For instance, politicians in Western societies will promote policies for economic expansion which, if successful, will raise the living standards of the population as a whole.

Thus, from this viewpoint, the exercise of power usually means that everybody wins. This forms a basis for the cooperation and reciprocity that Parsons considered essential for the maintenance and well-being of society.

Authority and collective goals

As we saw in Chapter 7, Parsons regarded power differentials as necessary for the effective pursuit of collective goals. If members of society pool their efforts and resources, they are more likely to realize their shared goals than if they operate as individuals. Cooperation on a large scale requires organization and direction, which necessitate positions of command. Some are therefore granted the power to direct others.

This power takes the form of authority. It is generally regarded as legitimate since it is seen to further collective goals. This means that some are granted authority for the benefit of all.

Parsons's views may be illustrated by the following example.

One of the major goals of traditional Sioux Indian society was success in hunting. This activity involved cooperation and power relationships. During the summer months the buffalo – the main food supply of the tribe – were gathered in large herds on the northern plains of North America. The buffalo hunt was a large-scale enterprise under the authority and control of marshals who were appointed by the warrior societies. An effective hunt required considerable organization and direction and was strictly policed. In particular, the marshals were concerned to prevent excitable young warriors from jumping the gun and stampeding the herd, which might endanger the food supply of the entire tribe. Marshals had the authority to beat those who disobeyed the rules and destroy their clothes and the harness of their horses. Thus, by granting power to the marshals, by accepting it as legitimate, and obeying it on that basis, the whole tribe benefited from the exercise of their authority.

Power in Western democracies

Parsons's analysis of the basis of political power in Western democracies provides a typical illustration of his views on the nature of power. He argued that:

> *Political support should be conceived of as a generalized grant of power which, if it leads to electional success, puts elected leadership in a position analogous to a banker. The 'deposits' of power made by constituents are revocable, if not at will, at the next election.*
>
> Parsons, 1967, p. 339

Just as money is deposited in a bank, members of society deposit power in political leaders. Just as depositors can withdraw their money from the bank, so the electorate can withdraw its grant of power from political leaders at the next election. In this sense, power resides ultimately with members of society as a whole. Finally, just as money generates interest for the depositor, so grants of power generate benefits for the electorate since they are used primarily to further collective goals. In this way, power in society can increase.

Many sociologists have argued that Parsons's views of the nature and application of power in society are naïve. They suggest that he has done little more than translate into sociological jargon the rationalizations promoted by the power-holders to justify their use of power. In particular, they argue that Parsons has failed to appreciate that power is frequently used to further sectional interests rather than to benefit society as a whole. We will analyse these criticisms in detail in the following sections.

Power and the state – a pluralist perspective

Pluralism is a theory which claims to explain the nature and distribution of power in Western democratic societies. Classical pluralism was the original form that this perspective took, but it has been heavily criticized. Some supporters of this perspective have modified their position and have adopted an elite pluralist view which takes account of some of these criticisms.

We will first describe and evaluate classical pluralism, before considering elite pluralism at the end of this section.

Classical pluralism

This version of pluralism has important similarities with the Parsonian functionalist theory. Pluralists agree with Parsons that power ultimately derives from the population as a whole:

1 They accept that the government and state in a Western democracy act in the interests of that society and according to the wishes of its members.

2 They see the political systems of countries such as the USA, Britain and France as the most advanced systems of government yet devised, and regard them as the most effective way for a population to exercise power and govern a country.

3 They regard the exercise of power through the state to be legitimate rather than coercive, since it is held to be based upon the acceptance and cooperation of the population.

Pluralists, however, part company from Parsons in three important respects.

The nature of power

First, pluralists follow Weber in accepting a constant-sum concept of power. There is seen to be a fixed amount of power which is distributed among the population of a society. They do not accept Parsons's variable-sum concept of power, which sees it as a resource held by society as a whole.

Sectional interests

Second, they deny that democratic societies have an all-embracing value consensus. They would agree with Parsons that members of such societies share some interests and wishes in common. For example, most citizens of the USA share a commitment to the constitution of the country and the political institutions such as the presidency, the Congress and the electoral system.

However, pluralists do not accept that members of society share common interests or values in relation to every issue. They believe that industrial society is increasingly differentiated into a variety of social groups and sectional interests, and, with the increasingly specialized division of labour, the number and diversity of occupational groups steadily grow. Groups such as doctors, teachers, business people and unskilled manual workers may have different interests. Each group may be represented by its own union or professional association, and these groups may put forward conflicting requests to the government.

Pluralists do not deny the existence of class, or division based on age, gender, religion or ethnicity. However, they do deny that any single division dominates any individual's wishes or actions. According to their view, each individual has a large number of different interests. A male manual worker might not just be a member of the working class, he might also be a car owner, a mortgage payer, an avid reader of library books and a father of two children in higher education. Therefore, while he has certain interests as a manual worker, other interests stem from other aspects of his position in society. As a car owner he has an interest in road tax and petrol prices being kept low, as a mortgage payer in interest rates being reduced, as a library user in more government expenditure on this service, and as a father in higher student grants. Another range of interests could be outlined for a female professional.

To the founder of the pluralist perspective, the nineteenth-century French writer de Tocqueville (1945, first published 1835), a democratic political system requires that individuals have a large number of specific interests. He believed that democracy would become unworkable if one division in society came to dominate all others. Such a situation could lead to a tyranny of the majority: one group in society would be in a permanent majority and the interests and wishes of the minority could be totally disregarded.

Northern Ireland could be seen as a contemporary example of this situation, where the population is split between a majority of Protestants and a minority of Catholics. Most individuals identify so strongly with their religious groupings that other interests are seen to be of secondary importance. The existence of a permanent majority of Protestants prevents a democratic system similar to that in the rest of the UK – that is, operating in such a way that each member of the Catholic minority has as much influence on government policy as each member of the Protestant majority.

The state

The third difference to the functionalist view follows from the pluralists' denial that a complete value consensus exists. Since individuals have different interests, political leaders and the state cannot reflect the interests of all members of society in taking any single decision.

To pluralists the state is seen as an honest broker which takes account of all the conflicting demands made on it by different sections of society. The state mediates between different groups, ensuring that all of them have some influence on government policy, but that none gets its own way all the time. On one particular occasion the government might take a decision which favours car owners, such as deciding to build a new motorway. On another it might decide against such a project in order to take account of the protests of environmentalists. On a third, the government might reach a compromise, concluding that the road is necessary but changing the route in order to protect an area of particular environmental importance. Pluralists argue that every group over a period of time has its interests reflected in governmental decisions, but because of the divisions within society it is not possible for the state to satisfy everyone all of the time. In Raymond Aron's words, 'government becomes a business of compromise'.

Classical pluralism – political parties and interest groups

Political parties

From a pluralist perspective, competition between two or more political parties is an essential feature of representative government. Political parties are organizations which attempt to get representatives elected to positions in parliaments or their local equivalents. Pluralists claim that competition for office between political parties provides the electorate with an opportunity to select its leaders and a means of influencing government policy.

This view forms the basis of Seymour M. Lipset's definition of democracy. According to Lipset:

Democracy in a complete society may be defined as a political system which supplies regular constitutional opportunities for changing the governing officials, and a social mechanism which permits the largest possible part of the population to influence major decisions by choosing among contenders for political office.

Lipset, 1981, first pub. 1959, p. 27

For efficient government, Lipset argued that competition between contenders for office must result in the granting of 'effective authority to one group' and the presence of an 'effective opposition' in the legislature as a check on the power of the governing party.

Pluralists claim that political parties in democratic societies are representative for the following reasons:

1 The public directly influences party policy, since, in order to be elected to govern, parties must reflect the wishes and interests of the electorate in their programmes.

2 If existing parties do not sufficiently represent sections of society, a new party will usually emerge, such as the Labour Party at the turn of the century in Britain, or the Referendum Party (which campaigned at the 1997 election against Britain accepting a single European currency).

3 Parties are accountable to the electorate since they will not regain power if they disregard the opinions and interests of the public.

4 Parties cannot simply represent a sectional interest since, to be elected to power, they require the support of various interests in society.

However, as Robert McKenzie stated, political parties must not be seen 'as the sole "transmission belts" on which political ideas and programmes are conveyed from the citizens to the legislature and the executive' (McKenzie, 1969). During their time in office and in opposition, parties 'mould and adapt their principles under innumerable pressures brought to bear by organized groups of citizens which operate for the most part outside the political system'. Such groups are known as interest or pressure groups.

Interest groups

Unlike political parties, interest groups do not aim to take power in the sense of forming a government. Rather they seek to influence political parties and the various departments of state. Nor do interest groups usually claim to represent a wide range of interests. Instead their specified objective is to represent a particular interest in society.

Interest groups are often classified in terms of their aims as either protective or promotional groups:

1 Protective groups defend the interests of a particular section of society. Trade unions such as the National Union of Mineworkers (NUM), professional associations such as the British Medical Association, and employers' organizations such as the Confederation of British Industry are classified as protective groups.

2 Promotional groups support a particular cause rather than guard the interests of a particular social group. Organizations such as the RSPCA, Friends of the Earth and the Lord's Day Observance Society are classified as promotional groups.

3 Membership of promotional groups is potentially larger and usually more varied than that of protective groups since they require only a commitment to their cause as a qualification for joining.

4 By comparison, membership of protective groups is usually limited to individuals of a particular status: for example, miners for membership of the NUM.

In practice, the distinction between protective and promotional groups is not clearcut, since the defence of an interest also involves its promotion.

Interest groups can bring pressure to bear in a number of ways:

1 By contributions to the funds of political parties, such as trade union contributions to the Labour Party.

2 By illegal payments to elected representatives and state officials – in other words, bribery. In 1994 it was revealed that at least one MP in Britain had received payments from Mohammed Al-Fayed in return for asking questions on his behalf in the House of Commons. Although not illegal, this example does suggest that money has sometimes been used to buy access to MPs and government ministers.

3 By appealing to public opinion. An effective campaign by an interest group can mobilize extensive public support, especially if it attracts widespread coverage by the mass media, and its arguments are seen to be valid. Certain conservation groups have successfully adopted this strategy. In the mid-1990s, protesters campaigning for rights for the disabled chained themselves to buses at the entrance to Downing Street. Another example is the campaign launched by rock musicians at the 1999 Brit Awards for the cancellation of a large part of the Third World's debt.

4 By various forms of civil disobedience or direct action. This approach has been used by a wide variety of interest groups. Examples include the gay rights group OutRage! interrupting a sermon by the Archbishop of Canterbury, hunt saboteurs trying to prevent fox hunting, and anti-roads protesters building tree-houses and tunnels to prevent work taking place.

5 By the provision of expertise. It has often been argued that, in modern industrial society, governments cannot operate without the specialized knowledge of interest groups. By providing this expertise, interest groups have an opportunity to directly influence government policy. In Britain, representatives of interest groups now have permanent places on hundreds of government advisory committees.

Interest groups and democracy

Pluralists see interest groups as necessary elements in a democratic system for a number of reasons.

Voting in elections involves only minimal participation in politics for members of a democracy. Classical pluralists believe that as many people as

possible should participate as actively as possible in politics. They do not believe that in Britain, for instance, voting once every five years is an adequate level of participation. Interest groups provide the opportunity for many individuals – who are not members of political parties – to participate in politics. For example, many members of the Friends of the Earth limit their active interest in politics to participation in the activities of this organization.

Interest groups are also necessary because even those who have voted for a government may not agree with all its policies. In a party-political system it is necessary to choose between the overall packages offered by the opposing parties. Interest groups make it possible to alter some parts of a governing party's policies while retaining those with which a majority of the population agree.

Clearly it is also vital that those who voted for a losing party have some opportunity to allow their voice to be heard. To the classical pluralist, the large number and diversity of pressure groups allow all sections of society to have a say in politics.

Before an election, a party seeking office outlines its proposed policies in a manifesto. The electorate can choose who to vote for on the basis of the alternative manifestos put forward. However, manifestos cannot be completely comprehensive: new issues not covered by them may arise. In the 1979 election in Britain no reference was made to the Falkland Islands in the manifestos of the major parties, since the Argentinian occupation of the islands had not been anticipated.

Interest groups provide the means through which the public can make their views known to a governing party as circumstances change and new issues arise. Furthermore, interest groups can mobilize public concern over issues that have been neglected or overlooked by the government. The British interest group Shelter draws the attention of the public and government alike to the plight of the homeless, while the Animal Liberation Front campaigns for the rights of voteless and voiceless animals.

According to classical pluralists, then, all sections of society and all shades of political opinion are represented and reflected in a wide variety of groups in Western democracies. Anyone who feels that they are being neglected by the government can form a new pressure group in order to rectify the temporary flaw in the operation of the democratic system.

Measuring power

Pluralists have provided empirical evidence to support their claim that Western societies are governed in accordance with democratic principles. The evidence they advance is based upon an attempt to show that a government's policies reflect a compromise between the wishes of the various sectional interests in society. They therefore concentrate upon the first face of power: decision making.

Pluralists compare the decisions taken by a government with the wishes of its general public, and the wishes expressed by different groups in the population. By examining evidence from opinion polls and the stated policy preferences of interest groups, pluralists reach the conclusion that countries such as Britain and the USA are genuinely democratic.

Robert A. Dahl – *Who Governs?*

One of the most famous studies supporting the pluralist view is *Who Governs?* by Robert A. Dahl (1961). Dahl investigated local politics in New Haven, Connecticut. He examined a series of decisions in three major issue areas:

1 urban renewal, which involved the redevelopment of the city centre;

2 political nominations, with particular emphasis on the post of mayor;

3 education, which concerned issues such as the siting of schools, and teachers' salaries.

By selecting a range of different issues, Dahl claimed that it should be possible to discover whether a single group monopolized decision making in community affairs.

Dahl found no evidence of one group dominating decision making, but concluded that power was dispersed among various interest groups. He discovered that interest groups only became directly involved in local politics when the issues were seen as directly relevant to their particular concerns. Dahl claimed that the evidence showed that local politics was a business of bargaining and compromise, with no one group dominating decision making.

For example, business interests, trade unions and the local university were involved in the issue of urban renewal. The mayor and his assistants made the major decisions in consultation with the various interest groups and produced a programme that was acceptable to all parties concerned.

Dahl rejected the view that economic interests dominated decision making. He concluded:

Economic notables, far from being a ruling group, are simply one of many groups out of which individuals sporadically emerge to influence the policies and acts of city officials. Almost anything one might say about the influence of economic notables could be said with equal justice about half a dozen other groups in New Haven.

Dahl, 1961, p. 72

Power in Britain

Similar studies on national politics have been conducted by pluralist researchers in Britain. In an important study using the decision-making approach, Christopher J. Hewitt (1974) examined 24 policy issues which arose in the British Parliament between 1944 and 1964. The issues covered four main policy areas:

1 foreign policy (e.g. the Suez crisis of 1956);

2 economic policy (e.g. the nationalization of road haulage);

3 welfare policy (e.g. the Rent Act of 1957);

4 social policy (e.g. the introduction of commercial television).

Hewitt compared the decisions reached by Parliament with the views of the interest groups involved and contemporary public opinion. In some cases the decisions favoured certain interest groups to the exclusion of others. In other cases government decisions favoured some groups but 'substantial concessions were made to the opposing interests'. However, Hewitt found that no one interest group consistently got its own way. He stated that 'Neither the business group nor any other appears to be especially favoured by the government.'

Poll data on public opinion were available on 11 of the 24 issues included in the study. In only one case – the abolition of capital punishment in 1957 – did the decision of Parliament oppose public opinion.

Hewitt's study suggested that both a variety of specialized interests and public opinion in general are represented in the British Parliament. He concluded that:

[the] picture of national power that is revealed suggests a 'pluralist' interpretation since a diversity of conflicting interests are involved in many issues, without any one issue being consistently successful in realizing its goals.

Hewitt, 1974

The CBI

A study of the relationship between government and the Confederation of British Industry (CBI) by Wyn Grant and David Marsh (1977) reached similar conclusions.

The CBI was created in 1965 from an amalgamation of three employers' federations. Membership of the CBI includes most of the top 200 manufacturing companies in Britain. It has direct channels of communication with government ministers and powerful civil servants, and is concerned with furthering the interests of private industry, particularly the manufacturing sector. In order to assess its influence on government, Grant and Marsh examined four pieces of legislation from 1967 to 1972:

1 The CBI fiercely opposed the Iron and Steel Act of 1967 which renationalized the iron and steel industry. Its views were rejected by the Labour government and, according to Grant and Marsh, the CBI 'fought an almost entirely unsuccessful defensive action'.

2 The Clean Air Act of 1968 aimed to reduce air pollution. The two main interest groups involved were the CBI and the National Society for Clean Air. The CBI was successful in obtaining various modifications to the bill, and the resulting act was a compromise between the views of the two interest groups.

3 The Deposit of Poisonous Wastes Act of 1972 was concerned with the disposal of solid and semi-solid toxic wastes. The Conservative government was under strong pressure from conservation groups and, in particular, the Warwickshire Conservation Society, which mobilized strong public support. Although the CBI obtained some important concessions, it by no means got all its own way. Grant and Marsh observed: 'It would seem, then, that a new interest group (the Warwickshire Conservation Society) with hardly any permanent staff can exert as much influence over a specific issue as the CBI.'

4 The Industry Act of 1972 was directed at regional development. The CBI was particularly concerned to prevent the government from having the right to buy shares in private industry. Its members were suspicious of any measures that might give the government more control over private industry. The TUC, on the other hand, favoured direct government investment, particularly in labour-intensive service industries, to ease the problem of unemployment. In practice, neither interest group appears to have had much influence, although the TUC were happier than the CBI with the final act. The government pursued a relatively independent policy, which was a response to 'the immediate demands of economic and political situations' rather than to the pressures of either interest group.

Grant and Marsh conclude that 'the CBI has little consistent direct influence over the policies pursued by government'. Despite its powerful membership and its access to the highest levels of government, 'the CBI's ability to influence events is limited by the government's need to retain the support of the electorate and by the activities of other interest groups'.

Pluralism and contemporary British politics

Although there have been no detailed studies of recent policies from a pluralist perspective, it is possible to argue that there is plenty of evidence of governments taking note of a variety of interest groups. It also appears that the government often follows policies supported by public opinion.

Although balancing a range of interests may not have been particularly typical of Margaret Thatcher's period as prime minister (1979-91), it has been more characteristic of John Major's period in office (1991-7), and that of Tony Blair (1997-). For example, John Major tried to balance the views of pro- and anti-Europeans by his policy of 'wait and see' over whether Britain should enter a single European currency. The 'New Labour' Party under Tony Blair has openly tried to respond to the views of a wide range of pressure groups and to take account of a range of sectional interests. His government has, for example, taken account of the views of trade unions by introducing minimum wage legislation and by giving unions a right to recognition by the employer where certain conditions are met.

On the other hand, the Blair government has not reinstated all the trade union laws repealed under the Conservatives – measures which would have been strongly opposed by the CBI and other groups. Furthermore, the Labour government has actively tried to include business leaders in the government and to take account of business interests and wishes.

In his 1999 budget speech, the chancellor of the exchequer tried to emphasize the even-handedness of the government's approach. He said:

> With this last budget of the twentieth century, we ... leave behind the century-long sterile conflicts between governments of the left that have too often undervalued enterprise and wealth creation, and governments of the right, too often indifferent to public services and fairness.
>
> Gordon Brown, quoted in *The Independent Budget Review*, 10 March 1999, p.12

In the budget there were cuts in Corporation Tax (which reflected the wishes of businesses); increases for pensioners (which reflected the wishes of many unions and groups such as Help the Aged); and increases in petrol prices (which pleased many environmental organizations, although hauliers demonstrated against the rises). Although not all pressure groups were pleased by the budget, it does appear to give an example of how a wide range of groups may have their views taken into account by contemporary governments.

Pluralism – a critique

A large body of evidence from studies such as those of Dahl in the US, and Hewitt and Grant and Marsh in Britain, appears to support the classical pluralist position. However, there are a number of serious criticisms of pluralism. These criticisms are concerned both with the methods pluralists use to measure power, and empirical evidence which seems to contradict their claim that power is dispersed in Western democracies.

Non-decisions and safe decisions

Marxists and other conflict theorists have suggested that pluralists ignore some aspects of power. In particular it is argued that they concentrate exclusively on the first face of power, decision making.

John Urry (in Urry and Wakeford, 1973), for example, believes that pluralists ignore the possibility that some have the power to prevent certain issues from reaching the point of decision. As a result of this non-decision making, only safe decisions may be taken – decisions which do not fundamentally alter the basic structures of capitalist societies.

From this point of view, it is in the interests of the powerful to allow a variety of interest groups to influence safe decisions. This fosters the illusion of real participation and helps to create the myth that a society is democratic. It disguises the real basis of power and so protects the powerful.

Pluralists can also be criticized for ignoring what Steven Lukes (1974) has identified as the third face of power. They do not take account of the possibility that the preferences expressed in opinion polls or by pressure groups might themselves have been manipulated by those with real power. In Marxist terms, the decisions might reflect the false class consciousness of members of society who do not realize where their own true interests lie. Real power might therefore rest with those who control institutions such as the media and the education system, which can play a part in shaping individuals' attitudes and opinions.

The consequences of decisions

Other writers have identified further ways in which power can be measured. Westergaard and Resler argue that 'Power is visible only through its consequences' (Westergaard and Resler, 1976). Government legislation may fail to have its intended effect. Despite an abundance of legislation aimed at improving the lot of the poor, Westergaard and Resler believe that there has 'been little redistribution of wealth':

1 Studies of actual decisions might give the impression that the interests of the poor are represented in government decisions.
2 Studies of the results of those decisions might provide a very different picture.

In any case, many sociologists deny that governments in Western democracies monopolize power. A government might, for example, seek to reduce the level of unemployment in order to secure victory at the next election. However, it is not within the government's power to control all the actions of large corporations, who can decide whether to close existing factories, making some of their workforce redundant, or to invest their profits overseas. This may be increasingly true if some theorists of globalization are to be believed (see pp. 624–33).

Contradictory evidence

The above points pose fundamental questions about the pluralists' method of measuring power, but pluralism can also be criticized on its own terms. Some of the evidence suggests that some interest groups have more influence over government decisions than others. Decision making by governments does not always appear to support the view that power is equally distributed among all groups in society, or that the state acts impartially as an 'honest broker'.

In Britain, a study by David Marsh and David Locksley (1983) contradicts the evidence supporting pluralism, for it suggests that the interest groups representing industry have more influence than other groups with respect to some issues. For example, in 1978 the CBI was successful in discouraging the then Labour government from introducing legislation that would have resulted in workers sitting on the boards of companies. In a similar fashion in 1975, pressure from the CBI and the City of London played a major part in persuading the Labour government to drop proposals to nationalize the 25 largest industrial companies in Britain.

Marsh and Locksley also claim that trade unions have had a considerable amount of influence over legislation relating to prices and wages policies, and industrial relations, although they have had much less impact on other areas of government policy. In recent years, though, the influence of unions has certainly declined. It can be argued that the wishes of trade unions were consistently ignored by the governments of Margaret Thatcher and John Major from 1979 to 1997. For some 18 years these pressure groups representing many millions of workers had very little influence on government decisions affecting them.

If anything, promotional groups seem to possess much less influence than protective groups. In a study of nuclear power policy, Hugh Ward (1983) found that 'the anti-nuclear movement in Britain has been very unsuccessful'. Interest groups such as Friends of the Earth failed to persuade successive governments not to build more nuclear power stations. Ward claims that the Central Electricity Generating Board, the UK Atomic Energy Authority, and GEC (General Electric Company) carried much more influence with those governments than the promotional pressure groups opposing expansion.

Although the British government has now stopped ordering new nuclear power stations, this may have as much to do with the high costs of producing power using nuclear energy compared with more conventional sources. Other anti-nuclear campaigns have not enjoyed success in achieving their objectives. Despite the considerable support that the Campaign for Nuclear Disarmament (CND) was able to gain in the 1980s, British governments went ahead with ordering Trident nuclear submarines as a replacement for Polaris. Thus it seems that, while governments may take account of the views of pressure groups, they may choose not to do so.

Unrepresented interests

Classical pluralists assume not only that interest groups have equal power, but also that all major interests in society are represented by one group or another. This latter assumption is also questionable.

The fairly recent emergence in Britain of consumer associations and citizens' advice bureaus can be seen as representing the interests of consumers against big business, and of citizens against government bureaucracies. It cannot be assumed that such interests were absent, unthreatened or adequately represented before the existence of such organizations. For instance, the unemployed are a group who, unlike employers and employees, still lack a protective pressure group to represent them.

Reappraisals of classical pluralism

It is not surprising that, given the strength and number of criticisms advanced against classical pluralism, some of its supporters have modified their positions. David Marsh originally provided evidence to support classical pluralism, but later rejected the pluralist approach in favour of what he describes as the fragmented elite model (Grant and Marsh, 1977, Marsh, 1983, Budge, McKay and Marsh, 1983).

Robert A. Dahl (1984) still supports the ideal of a pluralist democracy, but now accepts that it has certain dilemmas. He does not believe that the USA conforms perfectly to that ideal. The central dilemma is the unequal distribution of wealth and income. Dahl now argues that this provides an unequal distribution of power. Wealthy individuals find it easier to take an active and effective part in political life. He also notes that the owners and controllers of large corporations exercise considerable power in making decisions. Dahl therefore calls for increasing democratic control over business, and a reduction in inequalities in wealth and income.

Elite pluralism

Some pluralists, however, have responded to criticisms by adapting the theory to take account of some of the weaknesses of classical pluralism.

David Marsh has described a number of attempts to explain the distribution of power and the operation of the state as elite pluralist theories (Marsh, 1983). These theories share important similarities with classical pluralism:

1 They see Western societies as basically democratic.
2 They regard government as a process of compromise.
3 They agree that power is widely dispersed.

On the other hand:

1 They do not accept that all members of society have exactly the same amount of power.
2 They do not concentrate exclusively on the first face of power.
3 They see elites, the leaders of groups, as the main participants in decision making.

Representative elites – J.J. Richardson and A.G. Jordan

J.J. Richardson and A.G. Jordan (1979) have analysed the British government from an elite pluralist perspective. They argue that consultation among various groups has become the most important feature of British politics. Interest groups are not the only groups involved: government departments, and nationalized and private companies can also play an important part in the negotiations which determine policy. As far as possible the government tries to minimize the conflict between the representatives of organized groups, and to secure the agreement of the different sides concerned with a particular issue.

In these circumstances the participation of the mass of the population is not required to make a country democratic. Members, and indeed non-members of organizations, have their sectional interests represented by the elites, such as trade union leaders and the senior officials of promotional groups.

Unequal influence

However, Richardson and Jordan do not claim that all groups have equal power, or that all sections of society have groups to represent them. An important factor governing the degree of influence an interest group has is whether it is an insider or an outsider group:

1 Insider groups are accepted by the government as the legitimate representatives of a particular interest in society, and are regularly consulted on issues deemed relevant to them.
2 Outsider groups lack this recognition and are not automatically consulted.

According to Richardson and Jordan, the wishes of insider groups, such as the National Farmers' Union and the CBI, carry more weight with the government than those of outside groups, such as CND.

Richardson and Jordan also point out that some groups in society are in a better position to take action to force policy changes on the government than others. In the 1970s the NUM exercised considerable power through the use and threatened use of strikes which posed serious problems for the government by endangering energy supplies.

In contrast, Richardson and Jordan are also prepared to admit that some interests are not effectively represented at all. While teachers have well-organized unions to represent their views to the government over educational issues, parents have no equivalent organizations.

Despite these apparent drawbacks to democracy in Britain, Richardson and Jordan believe that other factors ensure that the government does not ignore the interests of significant sections of the population. This is because groups who are neglected by the government tend to organize more to force the government to take their views into account.

For example, until comparatively recently, governments of most industrial societies showed little interest in environmental issues. When the problems of pollution and the destruction of the environment became more acute, new interest groups such as Greenpeace and Friends of the Earth sprang up to force these issues on to the political agenda. Situations where an interest in society is not represented will, therefore, be only temporary.

Measuring power

The elite pluralist position is also more sophisticated than classical pluralism in dealing with the problem of measuring power. Like classical pluralists, Richardson and Jordan stress the importance of examining decisions to determine whose wishes are being carried out. But they also examine the second face of power: they discuss who has influence over what issues reach the point of decision. They are prepared to accept that it is possible for well-organized groups to keep issues off the political agenda for a time.

To illustrate their point they quote an American study by M. Crenson. This study compared two Indiana cities, East Chicago and Gary, which had similar levels of air pollution resulting from industrial activity. In East Chicago, action was taken against this problem as early as 1949; whereas, in Gary, industrialists successfully prevented the problem from emerging as an issue until the middle of the 1950s. Gary relied heavily on one industry – steel – and the importance of this industry to the city persuaded officials not to take action.

Once again, though, Richardson and Jordan do not believe that non-decision making seriously undermines democracy. They claim that 'there is evidence that it is increasingly difficult to exercise this power'. They believe that in modern democracies it is possible for interest groups to force issues on to the political agenda even against the wishes of the government and other organized interests. Among the British examples they cite are those of the Smoke Abatement Society persuading the government to pass the Clean Air Act in 1956, and the Child Poverty Action Group reviving poverty as an issue in the early 1970s.

One reason why new issues can rapidly become important in the political arena is the existence of backbench MPs, who do not hold government office. They are keen to further their careers by showing their talents through advocating a new cause.

Wyn Grant – pressure groups and elite pluralism

In recent work, Wyn Grant (1999) has supported what is essentially an elite pluralist position. Focusing on the role of pressure groups he notes a number of important changes in British politics:

1 The power of the pressure groups – which were most influential in the 1970s – has declined. Thus the TUC and the CBI have lost their central role in discussions with the government, although they still retain some influence.

2 The number of pressure groups has greatly expanded so that very few interests can now claim to be unrepresented.

3 Pressure groups no longer focus so exclusively on Westminster and on changing government policy. There are now 'multiple arenas' in which they try to exert influence. These include the European Union and the courts, and in the future will include the devolved parliaments in Wales, Scotland and Northern Ireland. Some pressure groups try to influence people's activities directly rather than trying to get the government to act. For example, the oil company Shell was persuaded not to dump its disused oil rig Brent Spar in the North Sea partly by boycotts of products encouraged by environmental pressure groups.

4 Linked to the above point is an increased use of various forms of direct action. Examples include the firebombing of milk tankers in Cheshire by radical, vegan, animal rights campaigners, the release of mink from mink farms by the Animal Liberation Front, the attempts by anti-roads campaigners to prevent road building, and the attempts of farmers to blockade ports to prevent the importation of Irish beef. Such methods have mixed results, but some, at least, are effective. Direct action not only gains publicity; it can

sometimes increase the costs of activities like building roads or farming mink so that economic disincentives are created.

5 Despite the increase in direct action, there has also been an increase in the number of pressure groups consulted by governments. Some groups previously regarded as outsider groups (such as Greenpeace) have become accepted by governments as suitable groups to consult over matters that concern them. Nevertheless, Grant still believes that a distinction between insider and outsider groups remains valid. Like other elite pluralists, he believes that insider groups tend to have more influence than outsider groups, although the latter group can sometimes achieve their objectives through direct action.

Grant concludes that, 'For all the talk of a "new" Britain and a "new" politics, there is much that looks like "business as usual" in the world of pressure group politics' (Grant, 1999). Pressure groups still help to ensure that Britain is essentially democratic, but it remains true that some groups have more influence than others.

Elite pluralism – a critique

Clearly, elite pluralism does answer some of the criticisms advanced against classical pluralism. It allows for the possibility that, at least temporarily, some interests may not be represented and some groups may have more power than others. It acknowledges that all individuals may not play an active part in politics, and it does not rely exclusively on measuring the first face of power, decision making. However, the analysis of elite pluralists may not be satisfactory in at least three ways:

1 In showing that democracies do not work perfectly, their own evidence raises doubts about the basic pluralist view that power is widely dispersed in Western industrial societies.

2 While they note the existence of elite leaders, they fail to discuss the possibility that these elites monopolize power and use it in their own interests.

3 Elite pluralists take account of two faces of power, but ignore the third. They do not discuss the power of some members of society to influence the wishes of others.

Elite theory

Elite theory differs from both pluralism and functionalism in that it sees power in society as being monopolized by a small minority. Elite theory sees society as divided into two main groups: a ruling minority who exercise power through the state, and the ruled.

There are, however, a number of ways in which elite theorists differ. They do not agree as to whether elite rule is desirable or beneficial for society; they differ in their conclusions about the inevitability of elite rule; and they do not agree about exactly who constitutes the elite or elites.

Classical elite theory

Elite theory was first developed by two Italian sociologists: Vilfredo Pareto (1848–1923) and Gaetano Mosca (1858–1911). Both saw elite rule as inevitable and dismissed the possibility of a proletarian revolution leading to the establishment of a communist society. As such they were arguing against Marx's view of power and the state.

Because of the inevitability of elite rule neither saw it as desirable that any attempt should be made to end it. Pareto and Mosca agreed that the basis of elite rule was the superior personal qualities of those who made up the elites. Pareto believed that elites possessed more cunning or intelligence, while Mosca

saw them as having more organizational ability. Since people were unequal, some would always have more ability than others, and would therefore occupy the elite positions in society.

According to both theorists, apart from the personal qualities of its members, an elite owes its power to its internal organization. It forms a united and cohesive minority in the face of an unorganized and fragmented mass. In Mosca's words, 'The power of the minority is irresistible as against each single individual in the majority.' Major decisions that affect society are taken by the elite. Even in so-called democratic societies, these decisions will usually reflect the concerns of the elite rather than the wishes of the people. Elite theorists picture the majority as apathetic and unconcerned with the major issues of the day. The mass of the population is largely controlled and manipulated by the elite, passively accepting the propaganda which justifies elite rule.

Although there are broad similarities between the work of these classical elite theorists, there are also some differences.

Vilfredo Pareto

Pareto (1963, first published 1915-19) placed particular emphasis on psychological characteristics as the basis of elite rule. He argued that there are two main types of governing elite, which (following his intellectual ancestor and countryman, Machiavelli) he called lions and foxes:

1 Lions achieve power because of their ability to take direct and incisive action, and, as their name suggests, they tend to rule by force. Military dictatorships provide an example of this type of governing elite.

2 By comparison, foxes rule by cunning and guile, by diplomatic manipulation and wheeling and dealing. Pareto believed that European democracies provided an example of this type of elite.

Members of a governing elite owe their positions primarily to their personal qualities – either to their lion-like or fox-like characteristics.

Major change in society occurs when one elite replaces another – a process Pareto called the circulation of elites. All elites tend to become decadent. They 'decay in quality' and lose their 'vigour'. They may become soft and ineffective with the pleasures of easy living and the privileges of power, or too set in their ways and too inflexible to respond to changing circumstances.

In addition, each type of elite lacks the qualities of its counterpart – qualities which in the long run are essential to maintain power. An elite of lions lacks the imagination and cunning necessary to maintain its rule and will have to admit foxes from the masses to make up for this deficiency. Gradually foxes infiltrate the entire elite and so transform its character. Foxes, however, lack the ability to take forceful and decisive action, which at various times is essential to retain power. An organized minority of lions committed to the restoration of strong government develops and eventually overthrows the elite of foxes.

Whereas, to Marx, history ultimately leads to and ends with the communist utopia, to Pareto, history is a never-ending circulation of elites. Nothing ever really changes and history is, and always will be, 'a graveyard of aristocracies'.

A critique of Pareto

Pareto's view of history is both simple and simplistic. He dismisses the differences between political systems such as Western democracies, communist single-party states, fascist dictatorships and feudal monarchies as merely variations on a basic theme. All are essentially examples of elite rule and, in comparison with this fact, the differences between them are minor.

Pareto fails to provide a method of measuring and distinguishing between the supposedly superior qualities of elites. He simply assumes that the qualities of the elite are superior to those of the mass. His criterion for distinguishing between lions and foxes is merely his own interpretation of the style of elite rule.

Nor does Pareto provide a way of measuring the process of elite decadence. He does suggest, however, that if an elite is closed to recruitment from below it is likely to rapidly lose its vigour and vitality and have a short life. Yet, as T.B. Bottomore (1993) notes, the Brahmins – the elite stratum in the Indian caste system – were a closed group which survived for many hundreds of years.

Gaetano Mosca

Like Pareto, Gaetano Mosca (1939) believed that rule by a minority was an inevitable feature of social life. He based this belief on the evidence of history, claiming that in all societies:

> two classes of people appear – a class that rules and a class that is ruled. The first class, always the less numerous, performs all political functions, monopolizes power and enjoys the advantages that power brings, whereas the second, the more numerous class, is directed and controlled by the first.
>
> Mosca, 1939

Like Pareto, Mosca believed that the ruling minority were superior to the mass of the population. He claimed that they were 'distinguished from the mass of the governed by qualities that give them a certain material, intellectual or even moral superiority', and he provided a sociological explanation for this superiority, seeing it as a product of the social background of the elite.

Unlike Pareto, who believed that the qualities required for elite rule were the same for all time, Mosca argued that they varied from society to society. For example, in some societies courage and bravery in battle provide access to the elite; in others the skills and capacities needed to acquire wealth.

Elite theory and democracy

Pareto saw modern democracies as merely another form of elite domination. He scornfully dismissed those who saw them as a more progressive and representative system of government. Mosca, however, particularly in his later writings, argued that there were important differences between democracies and other forms of elite rule. By comparison with closed systems such as caste and feudal societies, the ruling elite in democratic societies is open. There is therefore a greater possibility of an elite drawn from a wide range of social backgrounds. As a result, the interests of various social groups may be represented in the decisions taken by the elite. The majority may therefore have some control over the government of society.

As he became more favourably disposed towards democracy, Mosca argued that 'the modern representative state has made it possible for almost all political forces, almost all social values, to participate in the management of society'. But he stopped short of a literal acceptance of Abraham Lincoln's famous definition of democracy as 'government of the people, by the people, for the people' (quoted in Bottomore, 1993). To Mosca, democracy was government of the people; it might even be government for the people, but it could never be government by the people. Elite rule remained inevitable. Democracy could be no more than representative government, with an elite representing the interests of the people.

Despite his leanings towards democracy, Mosca retained his dim view of the masses. They lacked the capacity for self-government and required the leadership and guidance of an elite. Indeed Mosca regretted the extension of the franchise to all members of society, believing that it should be limited to the middle class. He thus remained 'elitist' to the last.

Elite theory and the USA – C. Wright Mills

Whereas Pareto and Mosca attempted to provide a general theory to explain the nature and distribution of power in all societies, the American sociologist C. Wright Mills (1956) presented a less ambitious and less wide-ranging version of elite theory. He limited his analysis to American society in the 1950s.

Unlike the early elite theorists, Mills did not believe that elite rule was inevitable; in fact he saw it as a fairly recent development in the USA. Unlike Pareto, who rather cynically accepted the domination of the masses by elites, Mills soundly condemned it. Since he saw elite rule as based upon the exploitation of the masses, he adopted a conflict version of elite theory. Because the elites and the masses had different interests, this created the potential for conflict between the two groups.

The power elite

Writing in the 1950s, Mills explained elite rule in institutional rather than psychological terms. He rejected the view that members of the elite had superior qualities or psychological characteristics which distinguished them from the rest of the population. Instead he argued that the structure of institutions was such that those at the top of the institutional hierarchy largely monopolized power. Certain institutions occupied key pivotal positions in society and the elite comprised those who held 'command posts' in those institutions.

Mills identified three key institutions:

1 the major corporations
2 the military
3 the federal government

Those who occupied the command posts in these institutions formed three elites. In practice, however, the interests and activities of the elites were sufficiently similar and interconnected to form a single ruling majority, which Mills termed the power elite. Thus the power elite involved the 'coincidence of economic, military and political power'. For example, Mills claimed that 'American capitalism is now in considerable part military capitalism.' As tanks, guns and missiles poured from the factories, the interests of both the economic and military elites were served. In the same way, Mills argued that business and government 'cannot now be seen as two distinct worlds'. He referred to political leaders as 'lieutenants' of the economic elite, and claimed that their decisions systematically favoured the interests of the giant corporations.

The net result of the coincidence of economic, military and political power was a power elite which dominated American society and took all decisions of major national and international importance.

Elite unity

However, things had not always been so. The power elite owed its dominance to a change in the 'institutional landscape'.

In the nineteenth century economic power was fragmented among a multitude of small businesses. By the 1950s, it was concentrated in the hands of a few hundred giant corporations 'which together hold the keys to economic decision'.

Political power was similarly fragmented and localized and, in particular, state legislatures had considerable independence in the face of a weak central government. The federal government eroded the autonomy of the states, and political power became increasingly centralized.

The growing threat of international conflict led to a vast increase in the size and power of the military. The local, state-controlled militia were replaced by a centrally-directed military organization.

These developments led to a centralization of decision-making power. As a result, power was increasingly concentrated in the hands of those in the command posts of the key institutions.

According to Mills, the cohesiveness and unity of the power elite were strengthened by the similarity of the social backgrounds of its members and the interchange and overlapping of personnel between the three elites. Members were drawn largely from the upper stratum of society; they were mainly Protestant, native-born Americans, from urban areas in the eastern USA. They shared similar educational backgrounds and mixed socially in the same high-prestige clubs. As a result, they tended to share similar values and sympathies, which provided a basis for mutual trust and cooperation.

Within the power elite there was frequent interchange of personnel between the three elites: a corporation director might become a politician and vice versa. At any one time, individuals might have footholds in more than one elite.

Elite dominance

Mills argued that American society was dominated by a power elite of 'unprecedented power and unaccountability'. He claimed that momentous decisions such as the American entry into the Second World War and the dropping of the atomic bomb on Hiroshima were made by the power elite with little or no reference to the people.

Despite the fact that such decisions affected all members of society, the power elite was not account-able for its actions, either directly to the public or to any body which represented the public interest. Mills saw no real differences between the two major political parties – the Democrats and the Republicans – and therefore the public was not provided with a choice of alternative policies.

In Mills's analysis, the bulk of the population was pictured as a passive and quiescent mass controlled by the power elite which subjected it to 'instruments of psychic management and manipulation'. Excluded from the command posts of power, the 'man in the mass' was told what to think, what to feel, what to do and what to hope for by a mass media directed by the elite. Unconcerned with the major issues of the day, 'he' was preoccupied with 'his' personal world of work, leisure, family and neighbourhood. Free from popular control, the power elite pursued its own concerns – power and self-aggrandizement.

Elite self-recruitment in Britain

C. Wright Mills's view of the elites in the USA can also be applied to Britain. A number of researchers have found that the majority of those who occupy elite positions in Britain are recruited from the minority of the population with highly privileged backgrounds. This appears to apply to a wide range of British elites, including politicians, judges, higher civil servants, senior military officers, and the directors of large companies and major banks. There are high levels of elite self-recruitment: the children of elite members are particularly likely to be themselves recruited to elite positions.

There is also evidence that there may be some degree of cohesion within and between the various elites. Individuals may occupy positions within more than one elite: cabinet ministers and other MPs may hold directorships in large companies. Individuals

may move between the elites: the former businessman Geoffrey Robinson became a minister in Tony Blair's first cabinet in 1997. Directors may also sit on the boards of a number of different companies.

Elites are also likely to have a common educational background: many members of elites attended public schools and went to Oxford or Cambridge University. John Rex argues that this type of education serves to socialize future top decision makers into a belief in the legitimacy of the status quo. It creates the possibility that the elites will be able to act together to protect their own interests. Rex suggests:

> *the whole system of 'Establishment' education has been used to ensure a common mind on the legitimacy of the existing order of things among those who have to occupy positions of power and decision.*
>
> Rex, 1974

The following studies provide evidence for the existence of such elites in Britain.

'Top decision makers'

In a study conducted in the 1970s, Tom Lupton and Shirley Wilson traced the kinship and marital connections of six categories of 'top decision makers'. These categories were ministers, senior civil servants, and directors of the Bank of England, the big five banks, city firms and insurance companies (Lupton and Wilson, 1973).

Lupton and Wilson constructed 24 kinship diagrams, usually covering three generations and indicating relationships by birth and marriage. Seventy-three of the top decision makers appeared on these diagrams, accounting for 18 per cent of the total number of people included in the 24 extended-family groupings. Clearly there were close kinship and marital ties between the elites examined, and certain families were disproportionately represented in the ranks of top decision makers.

Members of Parliament

Table 9.1 shows the result of research by George Borthwick *et al.* into the educational background of Conservative MPs. It compares the new MPs elected in the 1979, 1983 and 1987 elections with those first elected to Parliament before 1979, but who remained MPs after the 1979 election. It therefore highlights changes in background. It shows some decline in the number of public school-educated MPs, but neverthe-less over half of the 1987 entry had been to public schools and 44 per cent had been to Oxford or Cambridge University.

John Scott (1991) points out that cabinets, particu-larly Conservative ones, are even more educationally unrepresentative than the House of Commons as a whole. For example, four-fifths of Mrs Thatcher's 1983 cabinet were educated at public schools (no less than one-third of whom had been to Eton and Winchester).

The 1997 general election did lead to a substantial change in the make-up of the House of Commons.

Research by David Butler and Dennis Kavanagh (1997) reveals that there was a much higher proportion of public-school-educated MPs in the Conservative Party than in the Labour Party which formed the government. As Table 9.2 shows, 67 of

Table 9.1 Educational background of Conservative MPs

	Number	Public school %	Eton %	Oxford %	Cambridge %	Other universities %
Pre-1979	261	75	17	30	25	17
1979 entry	78	59	14	21	14	32
1983 entry	104	55	6	19	19	38
1987 entry	57	53	7	30	14	32

Source: G. Borthwick, D. Ellingworth, C. Bell, and D. MacKenzie, (1991) 'The social background of British MPs', *Sociology*, November, p. 71.

Table 9.2 Educational background of candidates, 1997 election

	Labour Elected	Labour Defeated	Conservative Elected	Conservative Defeated	Liberal Democrat Elected	Liberal Democrat Defeated
Type of education						
Elementary	–	–	–	–	–	–
Elementary +	2	–	–	–	–	–
Secondary	48	19	5	48	5	66
Secondary+ Poly/College	86	54	9	74	6	162
Secondary + University	215	120	42	154	16	253
Public school	2	–	9	17	1	8
Public school + Poly/College	5	4	9	28	2	10
Public school + University	60	24	91	154	16	94
TOTAL	418	221	165	475	46	593
Oxford	41	11	46	59	11	38
Cambridge	20	16	38	45	4	25
Other universities	214	117	49	204	17	284
All universities	275 (66%)	144 (65%)	133 (81%)	308 (65%)	32 (70%)	347 (59%)
Eton	2	–	15	20	1	–
Harrow	–	–	–	5	–	–
Winchester	1	–	1	3	–	–
Other public schools	64	28	93	169	18	102
All public schools	67 (16%)	28 (13%)	109 (66%)	197 (42%)	19 (41%)	102 (17%)

Source: D. Butler and D. Kavanagh (1997) *The British General Election of 1997*, Macmillan, Basingstoke, p. 203.

the 418 Labour MPs elected had been to public schools (just two of these had been to Eton), and 109 of the 165 successful Conservative candidates were public-school-educated. Thus 16 per cent of Labour MPs were educated at public schools compared to 66 per cent of Conservative MPs. Nevertheless, even in the Labour Party those with public school backgrounds were over-represented compared to in the population as a whole. There were also high proportions of MPs who had attended Britain's elite universities, Oxford and Cambridge: 61 Labour and 84 Conservative MPs were Oxbridge graduates.

The occupational backgrounds of MPs elected in 1997 were by no means exclusively from elite groups. A wide range of professions was represented. Nevertheless, the Labour cabinet did include wealthy members of the business elite such as Geoffrey Robinson and Lord Sainsbury. As Table 9.3 shows, there were very few MPs with manual occupations. Even in the Labour Party – traditionally the party of the working class – only 13 per cent of their MPs had manual jobs; and the Conservative Party and the Liberal Democrats each had only a single MP with a manual occupation.

Overall there is no doubt that the election of over 400 Labour candidates reduced the domination of the House of Commons by members of elites, but that did not mean there were not still significant numbers of people from elite backgrounds in Parliament and in government.

Elite theory in the USA and Britain – an evaluation

The evidence provided by C. Wright Mills and by numerous researchers in Britain has shown that those occupying elite positions have tended to come from privileged backgrounds, and that there have been important connections between different elites. However, the significance of these findings is open to dispute.

Some Marxists claim that they provide evidence for a ruling class based upon economic power, rather than a ruling elite based upon the occupation of 'command posts'.

Furthermore, it has been argued that these versions of elite theory fail to measure power adequately: they do not show that these elites actually have power, nor that they exercise power in their own interests against the interests of the majority of the population.

Robert A. Dahl (1973) has criticized Mills from a pluralist perspective. He claimed that Mills had simply shown that the power elite had the 'potential for control'. By occupying the command posts of major

institutions it would certainly appear that its members have this potential. But, as Dahl argued, the potential for control was not 'equivalent to actual control'. Dahl maintained that actual control can only be shown to exist 'by examination of a series of concrete cases where key decisions are made: decisions on taxation and expenditures, subsidies, welfare programs, military policy and so on'. If it can then be shown that a minority has the power to decide such issues and to overrule opposition to its policies, then the existence of a power elite will have been established. Dahl claimed that, by omitting to investigate a range of key decisions, Mills failed to establish where 'actual control' lies. As a result, Dahl argued that the case for a power elite remains unproven.

Dahl's criticism of C. Wright Mills applies with equal force to British studies of elite self-recruitment. Furthermore, the British studies make no attempt to measure the second and third faces of power (they make no reference to non-decision making nor do they discuss how the wishes of the population may be manipulated by elites). As such, studies of elite self-recruitment may reveal something about patterns of social mobility but they provide little direct evidence about who actually has power.

Both C. Wright Mills's work and most British studies of elite self-recruitment are very dated. Studies conducted in the 1980s and 1990s are thin on the ground. Some of the more recent research on political elites, which we discussed earlier, and work by John Scott on the 'upper class' (see pp. 51–5) suggest that elite self-recruitment is still common in Britain, but the evidence only covers a limited range of elites.

Fragmented elites – government in Britain

A distinctive elite theory of power and the state is provided by Ian Budge, David McKay and David Marsh (1983). Along with C. Wright Mills they accept that elite rule takes place in modern democracies, but they deny that the elite is a united group. Rather they believe that there are a large number of different fragmented elites which compete for power. They state that 'The evidence points to a variety of groups, interests and organizations all exercising considerable influence over policies but divided internally and externally.'

Budge et al. deny that power is concentrated only in the hands of a state elite centred on the prime minister and the cabinet. They point out that political parties may be divided between different factions or groups. Traditionally there have always been divisions between the 'left wing' and 'right wing' of

Table 9.3   Occupational background of candidates, 1997 election

	Labour Elected	Labour Defeated	Conservative Elected	Conservative Defeated	Liberal Democrat Elected	Liberal Democrat Defeated
Professions						
Barrister	12	7	20	47	4	6
Solicitor	17	11	9	41	2	27
Doctor/dentist/optician	3	2	2	4	4	11
Architect/surveyor	–	–	2	9	–	7
Civil/chartered engineer	3	2	–	4	1	10
Accountant	2	2	3	24	1	26
Civil service/local government	30	19	5	7	2	28
Armed services	–	–	9	10	1	11
Teachers:						
University	22	4	1	3	2	19
Polytechnic/college	35	17	–	2	1	19
School	54	37	7	19	4	85
Other consultancies	3	4	2	1	1	10
Scientific/research	7	2	1	2	–	7
TOTAL	188 (45%)	107 (48%)	61 (37%)	173 (36%)	23 (50%)	266 (45%)
Business						
Company director	7	3	17	51	2	25
Company executive	9	13	36	90	7	66
Commerce/insurance	2	9	7	33	1	39
Management/clerical	15	8	1	15	1	30
General business	4	7	4	22	–	41
TOTAL	37 (9%)	40 (18%)	65 (39%)	211 (44%)	11 (24%)	201 (34%)
Miscellaneous						
Miscellaneous white collar	69	29	2	16	1	57
Politician/political organizer	40	9	15	20	5	13
Publisher/journalist	29	10	14	27	4	18
Farmer	1	2	5	13	1	7
Housewife	–	–	2	4	–	9
Student	–	4	–	2	–	8
TOTAL	139 (33%)	54 (24%)	38 (23%)	82 (17%)	11 (24%)	112 (19%)
Manual workers						
Miner	12	–	1	–	–	–
Skilled worker	40	20	–	9	1	14
Semi/unskilled	2	–	–	–	–	–
TOTAL	(13%)	(9%)	(1%)	(2%)	(2%)	(2%)
GRAND TOTAL	418	221	165	475	46	593

Source: D. Butler and D. Kavanagh (1997) *The British General Election of 1997*, Macmillan, Basingstoke, p. 205.

the Labour Party over issues such as how many industries should be nationalized. Budge *et al.* claim that there were similar divisions in Conservative cabinets in the early 1980s, between supporters of Thatcherite policies and the 'wets', urging a more cautious approach.

Furthermore, governments cannot always rely on the support of backbench MPs: in the 1974-9 Labour government only 19 per cent of Labour MPs did not vote against government policy at some time. To complicate matters even further, the House of Lords has the power to delay, and sometimes effectively kill, legislation.

For these reasons, Budge *et al.* claim that elites within Parliament are too divided to be able to be the dominant force in British politics.

These divisions are further increased by the civil service. Ministers tend to rely on their civil servants for information and advice, to be guided by civil servants, and to develop departmental loyalties. Those representing spending ministries such as education and defence may, as a result, compete with each other to gain a larger share of the total government budget. Civil servants also have more direct methods of exercising power. Even when decisions have been reached, they have considerable room for manoeuvre in interpreting and implementing them.

Budge *et al.* use a very broad definition of the state. To them it includes not only central government, but also local government and a range of semi-independent institutions and organizations. Local government, they argue, has both the ability and the will to challenge central authority. For example, Britain continues to have a considerable number of local education authorities which retain at least some grammar schools, despite the attempts of successive Labour governments to abolish them.

Further constraints on central government stem from the independence of the judiciary and the police. Judges have considerable discretion in interpreting the law, to the extent that they can have a major impact upon the effects of government legislation. To give just one example, judicial decisions have limited the scope of the Race Relations Act of 1971 so that it does not outlaw racial discrimination in private clubs. The police have almost as much independence. Budge *et al.* point out that chief constables 'are wholly responsible for all decisions' in their force. If senior police officers do not effectively enforce a particular law, government decisions will have little impact.

Yet another important limitation on the government is the existence of a large number of Quangos (Quasi-Autonomous Non-Governmental Organizations). These range from organizations such as the Jockey Club, to the Trustees of National Museums, the BBC and nationalized industries. Although most of these organizations rely to some extent on government funding, they still have freedom to take an independent line. For example, at times the BBC has broadcast programmes against the wishes of, or critical of, the government.

According to this view, then, there are a wide variety of elites within what can be broadly defined as the state, who limit the degree of power held by the government. But Budge *et al.* do not see power as confined to the state. In common with elite pluralists they point out that some pressure groups have considerable power. In particular, the unions have sometimes been able to thwart the government through strikes, while the CBI and financiers have been able to veto some governmental decisions by using their financial power.

The government also has to contend with the elites of international organizations such as NATO and the EC (now the EU), and it is bound by the decisions of the Court of Justice of the EC. In 1976, for example, the British government was forced by that court to introduce tachographs (which can read whether the drivers have broken EC regulations) into commercial vehicles.

Summary and critique

The fragmented elite theory sees power resting with a very wide variety of elites, government ministers, backbench MPs, senior civil servants, officials in local government, the chairpersons of nationalized industries, the leaders of other quangos, senior judges and police officers, top union officials, powerful business people, and those occupying the senior positions in international organizations to which Britain belongs. Since the elite are fragmented and divided rather than cohesive and united, Budge *et al.* do not believe that any single group in society monopolizes power. They would agree with pluralists that a wide variety of groups and interests are represented in society, but they would disagree that this adds up to a truly democratic government. As they put it, 'fragmentation does not guarantee effective popular control'.

Budge *et al.* may exaggerate the extent to which some elites act independently of political leaders. Since their study was published in 1983 the number of quangos in Britain has rapidly increased. For example, new funding councils for various parts of the welfare state have been introduced, along with NHS trusts, and some schools and all colleges have become formally independent of local authorities and the national government. Yet most such quangos still rely very heavily on government funding and in many the government has a role in appointing officials.

The Further Education Funding Council (FEFC) is a case in point. This organization determines the funding of further education and sixth-form colleges, and as such appears to have considerable power. However, its members are not elected: they are directly appointed by the government. In 1994, two of its members were former Conservative politicians and four were businessmen, including Anthony Close from Forte – a business which contributed £80,500 to the Conservative Party in 1992.

The government not only determines the personnel involved, it also sets the overall budget and has directly intervened in the affairs of the FEFC by, for example, withholding funds from colleges unless they persuaded their staff to accept new contracts. Thus, while quangos might seem to produce independent elites, which can come into conflict with the political elite, their autonomy can sometimes be illusory, with the governmental elite remaining the dominant force.

The fragmented elite theory is also open to the same criticisms as the work of C. Wright Mills. It tends to assume that those in elite positions actually exercise power. Budge *et al.* back their analysis up with numerous examples but do not provide systematic evidence on the basis of distinguishing the three faces of power.

Marxists and some other conflict theorists would claim that all elite theory fails to identify the underlying basis for power. In particular, Marxists argue that power derives from wealth in the form of owning the means of production, rather than from the occupation of senior positions in society. We will examine Marxist views on power and the state in the next section.

Power and the state – Marxist perspectives

Marxist perspectives, like elite theory, see power as concentrated in the hands of a minority in society. Marxist theorists also agree with those elite theorists who see power being used to further the interests of the powerful.

Marxist theories stress that the powerful and the powerless have different interests and that these differences may lead to conflict in society. Unlike elite theory, though, Marxist approaches do not assume that power rests with those who occupy key positions in the state. They see the source of power as lying elsewhere in society. In particular, Marxists put primary emphasis upon economic resources as a source of power.

A wide variety of Marxist theories of power have been developed. We start this section by examining the work of Marx himself, and his friend and collaborator Engels, before going on to consider the views of those who have developed less orthodox Marxist views.

Marx and Engels on power and the state

According to Marx, power is concentrated in the hands of those who have economic control within a society (Marx 1974, 1978; Marx and Engels, 1950b). From this perspective, the source of power lies in the economic infrastructure:

1 In all class-divided societies the means of production are owned and controlled by the ruling class. This relationship to the means of production provides the basis of its dominance. It therefore follows that the only way to return power to the people involves communal ownership of the means of production.

2 In a communist society, power would be more equally distributed amongst the whole of the population, since the means of production would be communally owned rather than owned by individuals.

As we have seen in previous chapters, in capitalist society ruling-class power is used to exploit and oppress the subject class, and much of the wealth produced by the proletariat's labour power is appropriated in the form of profit or surplus value by the bourgeoisie. From a Marxist perspective, the use of power to exploit others is defined as coercion. It is seen as an illegitimate use of power since it forces the subject class to submit to a situation which is against its interests. If ruling-class power is accepted as legitimate by the subject class, this is an indication of false class consciousness.

Ruling-class power extends beyond specifically economic relationships. In terms of Marxist theory, the relationships of domination and subordination in the infrastructure will largely be reproduced in the superstructure (see p. 11 for a definition of these terms). The state (as part of the superstructure) reflects the distribution of power in society. The decisions and activities of the state will favour the interests of the ruling class rather than those of the population as a whole.

Despite the general thrust of the arguments of Marx and Engels, there are, as we will see, some inconsistencies in their statements about the state.

The origins and evolution of the state

Engels claimed that in primitive communist societies the state did not exist. Kinship (or family relationships) formed the basis of social groupings (Engels 1884, in Marx and Engels, 1950b). These societies were essentially agricultural, and no surplus was produced beyond what was necessary for subsistence. It was therefore impossible for large amounts of wealth to be accumulated and concentrated in the hands of a few. There was little division of labour, and the means of production were communally owned.

Only when societies began to produce a surplus did it become possible for a ruling class to emerge. Once one group in society became economically dominant, a state developed.

Engels believed that the state was necessary to 'hold class antagonisms in check'. In primitive communist societies all individuals shared the same interests; in class societies, a minority benefited from the existing social system at the expense of the majority. According to Engels, the exploited majority had to be held down to prevent them from asserting their interests and threatening the position of the ruling class. Thus in ancient Athens the 90,000 Athenian citizens used the state as a method of repressing the 365,000 slaves.

The simplest way the state could control the subject class was through the use of force or coercion. Engels pointed to the police, the prisons and the army as state-run institutions used to repress the exploited members of society.

Engels believed that coercion was the main type of power used to control the population in early states. In ancient Athens and Rome, and the feudal states of the Middle Ages, ruling-class control of the state was clearly apparent. For example, the feudal state consisted exclusively of landowners; serfs possessed neither private property nor political rights.

However, Engels believed that more advanced forms of the state were less obviously a coercive tool of the ruling class. Indeed, Engels described democracies as the 'highest form of state', for with such a state all members of society appear to have equal political power. Each individual in societies with universal suffrage can vote, and in theory therefore has as much influence over government policy as every other individual. According to Engels, this would tend to mean that the existing social order would be perceived as fair, just and legitimate, since the state would be seen to reflect the wishes of the population. As such, the state would not need to rely so heavily on the use of force: in most cases the authority of the state would be accepted by the population.

In reality, however, Engels believed that democracy was an illusion. Real power continued to rest with the owners of the means of production, and not with the population as a whole.

One way in which the ruling class could ensure that the state continued to act in its interest was through corruption. Troublesome officials who threatened to follow policies harmful to the bourgeoisie could be bribed. A second way to determine government policies was through the use of the financial power of capitalists. The state often relied upon borrowing money from the bourgeoisie in order to meet its debts. Loans could be withheld if the state refused to follow policies beneficial to the bourgeoisie.

The end of the state

Marx and Engels did not believe that the state would be a permanent feature of society. Since they believed its purpose was to protect the position of the ruling class and to control the subject class, they argued that it would become redundant once classes disappeared. In the immediate aftermath of the proletarian revolution, the proletariat would seize control of the state. They would use it to consolidate their position, establish communal ownership of the means of production, and destroy the power of the bourgeoisie. Once these objectives had been achieved, class division would no longer exist, and the state would 'wither away'.

The views of Marx and Engels on the state are neatly summed up in the *Communist Manifesto*, where they say 'The executive of the modern state is but a committee for managing the common affairs of the whole bourgeoisie' (Marx and Engels, 1950a, first published 1848).

However, Engels did accept that in certain circumstances the state could play an independent role in society, where its actions would not be completely controlled by a single class. Engels argued that, at particular points in history, two classes could have roughly equal power. He claimed that in some monarchies of seventeenth- and eighteenth-century Europe the landowning aristocracy and the rising bourgeoisie were in opposition to each other and both were equally powerful. In this situation the state could take an independent line since the warring classes effectively cancelled each other out.

Furthermore, in his more empirical studies Marx recognized that there might be divisions within states in capitalist countries. For example, in *The Class Struggles in France 1848-1850* (Marx, in Marx and Engels, 1950a), Marx acknowledged a difference in interests between finance capitalists on the one hand and the industrial bourgeoisie on the other. Finance capitalists (many of whom were large landowners) had an interest in the government of France retaining the huge debt it had at the time, since financiers could benefit from lending money to the French state. On the other hand, the industrial bourgeoisie were being harmed by the taxes needed to service the debt.

Marx and Engels inspired many later Marxists to devote a great deal of attention to the study of power and the state, but their original work is sometimes vague, and is sometimes inconsistent. It has been interpreted in different ways. Furthermore, the work of the founders of Marxism has not been entirely free from criticism from more contemporary sociologists adopting this perspective. Consequently a number of contrasting Marxist theories of the state have been developed. These differ over the precise way in which they see the bourgeoisie controlling the state, the extent to which they believe the state enjoys independence from ruling-class control, and the importance they attach to this institution for maintaining the predominance of the bourgeoisie in capitalist societies.

Ralph Miliband – the capitalist state

The British sociologist Ralph Miliband (1969) followed Marx and Engels in seeing power as being derived from wealth. He rejected the pluralist view that in 'democracies' equal political rights give each member of the population equal power. He referred to political equality as 'one of the great myths of the epoch' and claimed that genuine political equality was 'impossible in the conditions of advanced capitalism' because of the power of those who own and control the means of production.

Miliband followed conventional definitions of the state, seeing it as consisting of the institutions of the police, the judiciary, the military, local government, central government, the administration or bureaucracy, and parliamentary assemblies. He believed that it was through these institutions that 'power is wielded', and that this power was exercised in the interests of the ruling class.

Miliband believed that the state could sometimes act as the direct tool or instrument of those who possess economic power. They used it to preserve their economic dominance, maintain their political power and stabilize capitalist society by preventing threats to their position. However, Miliband did accept that in some circumstances direct intervention by the wealthy was not necessary in order for the state to act in their interests.

Elites and the ruling class

To Miliband the state was run by a number of elites who ran the central institutions. These elites included cabinet ministers, MPs, senior police and military officers, and top judges. Together he saw them as

largely acting to defend the ruling class or bourgeoisie: he believed that all the elites shared a basic interest in the preservation of capitalism and the defence of private property. In some ways Miliband's views are similar to those of the elite theorist C. Wright Mills, but Miliband sees elites as acting in the interests of capitalists and not just in their own interests.

Miliband attempted to justify his claims by presenting a wide range of empirical evidence:

1 First, he tried to show that many of those who occupy elite positions are themselves members of the bourgeoisie. For example, he pointed out that in America, from 1899 until 1949, 60 per cent of cabinet members were businessmen, and this occupational group also made up about 33 per cent of British cabinets between 1886 and 1950.

2 Obviously the above figures do leave a considerable proportion of the state elite who are not from business backgrounds. To take account of this point, Miliband advanced his second type of evidence, which attempts to show that the non-business person in the state elite will, in any case, act in the interests of the bourgeoisie. He argued that groups such as politicians, senior civil servants and judges are 'united by ties of kinship, friendship, common outlook, and mutual interest'. The vast majority come from upper- or middle-class families. Most share similar educational backgrounds since they have attended public schools and Oxford or Cambridge University. As such they have been socialized into identifying with the interests of the ruling class. Furthermore, even those few recruits to elite positions who come from working-class backgrounds will only have gained promotion by adopting the values of the ruling class. They will have undergone a process of bourgeoisification, and will have come to think and act as if they were members of the bourgeoisie.

3 Third, Miliband claimed to be able to show that the actions of the state elites have, in practice, tended to benefit the ruling class. He pointed out that judges saw one of their primary duties as the protection of private property. He suggested that Labour governments have done little to challenge the dominance of the ruling class. Although the 1945 Labour government nationalized a number of industries, it stopped far short of what many of its supporters would have wished. The existing owners were generously compensated, and the appointment of business people to run the industries meant that they were operated in a capitalistic way which, if anything, assisted private industry.

Legitimation

Miliband also advanced an explanation as to why the majority of the population should accept a state which acts against their interests. He examined various ways in which the subject class was persuaded to accept the status quo. In effect, he considered the third face of power, claiming that the economic power of the ruling class enabled them to partly shape the beliefs and wishes of the remainder of the population. He believed that this took place through the process of legitimation, which he regarded as a system of 'massive indoctrination'. Miliband argued that the capitalist class sought to:

> persuade society not only to accept the policies it advocates but also the ethos, the values and the goals which are its own, the economic system of which it is the central part, the 'way of life' which is the core of its being.
>
> Miliband, 1969, p. 211

Miliband illustrated his argument with an analysis of advertising, by means of which capitalist enterprises promote both their products and the 'acceptable face' of capitalism. He argued that all advertising is political since it serves to further the power and privilege of the dominant class. Through advertisements, giant, privately-owned corporations, such as ICI, BICC, Unilever, ITT and the major banks and oil companies, promote the view that their major concern is public service and the welfare of the community. Profits are a secondary consideration and portrayed mainly as a means of providing an improved service.

The image of the corporation and its products is made even rosier by association in advertisements with 'socially approved values and norms'. Miliband argued that capitalism and its commodities are subtly linked via advertisements to 'integrity, reliability, security, parental love, child-like innocence, neighbourliness, sociability'. With these kinds of associations, the exploitative and oppressive nature of capitalism is effectively disguised.

Finally, advertising promotes the view that the way to happiness and fulfilment involves the accumulation of material possessions – in particular, the acquisition of the products of capitalism. The individual is encouraged to 'be content to enjoy the blessings which are showered upon him' by the 'benevolent, public-spirited and socially responsible' capitalist enterprise.

Miliband argued that advertising provides one example of the ways in which capitalism is legitimated. He regarded the process of legitimation as essential for the maintenance of capitalist power. If successful, it prevents serious challenge to the basis of that power: the private ownership of the means of production. In the following chapters, we will examine further aspects of the process of legitimation in detail.

To sum up, Miliband argued that there is direct interference by members of ruling elites in the state.

Their dominance is further cemented through the socialization of state personnel from non-elite backgrounds into the values of the elite, and the manipulation of the beliefs of the mass of the population so that they will lend support to pro-capitalist policies.

Nicos Poulantzas – a structuralist view of the state

Nicos Poulantzas (1969, 1976) has criticized Miliband's view of the state and has provided an alternative Marxist interpretation which places less stress on the actions of individuals and more on the role of social structure. A structuralist approach emphasizes the importance of social structure, and minimizes the importance of the actions of individuals in society. As such, Poulantzas saw much of the evidence advanced by Miliband as irrelevant to a Marxist view of the state.

The state and the capitalist system

Poulantzas described the state as 'the factor of cohesion of a social formation': in other words, the state was vital for maintaining the stability of the capitalist system. As part of the superstructure, it would automatically tend to serve the interests of the ruling class. It was not necessary for members of the ruling class to occupy elite positions within the state: the existence of a capitalist system was itself sufficient to ensure that the state functioned to benefit the ruling class. Similarly, the background of members of the state elite was of little importance: it was not their class origin but their class position which determined their behaviour. Since they occupied positions in a state, which inevitably functions to benefit the bourgeoisie, their job would ensure they acted in the interests of the bourgeoisie regardless of their background. They would not take actions harmful to capitalist interests.

Relative autonomy

Poulantzas took this argument a stage further. He claimed that:

> the capitalist state best serves the interests of the capitalist class only when members of this class do not participate directly in the state apparatus, that is to say when the ruling class is not the politically governing class.
>
> Poulantzas, 1969, p. 73

Poulantzas argued that the ruling class did not directly govern, but rather its interests were served through the medium of the state. As such, the state was relatively autonomous. To some degree it was free from the ruling class's direct influence, independent from its direct control. However, since the state was shaped by the infrastructure, it was forced to represent the interests of capital.

Poulantzas argued that the relative autonomy of the state was essential if it was to effectively represent capital. The state required a certain amount of freedom and independence in order to serve ruling-class interests. If it were staffed by members of the bourgeoisie, it might lose this freedom of action. The following reasons have been given for the relative autonomy of the capitalist state:

1   As a group the bourgeoisie is not free from internal divisions and conflicts of interest. To represent its common interests the state must have the freedom to act on behalf of the class as a whole.

2   If the bourgeoisie ruled directly, its power might be weakened by internal wrangling and disagreement, and it might fail to present a united front in conflicts with the proletariat. The relative autonomy of the state allows it to rise above sectional interests within the bourgeoisie and to represent that class as a whole. In particular, it provides the state with sufficient flexibility to deal with any threats from the subject class to ruling-class dominance.

3   To this end the state must have the freedom to make concessions to the subject class, which might be opposed by the bourgeoisie. Such concessions serve to defuse radical working-class protest and to contain the demands within the framework of a capitalist economy.

4   Finally, the relative autonomy of the state enables it to promote the myth that it represents society as a whole. The state presents itself as a representative of 'the people', of 'public interest' and 'national unity'. Thus, in its ideological role, the state disguises the fact that essentially it represents ruling-class interests.

Repressive and ideological state apparatus

Poulantzas did not disagree with Miliband about the importance of legitimation. However, he went much further in seeing this process as being directly related to the state. He used a broader definition of the state than Miliband. He divided it into the repressive apparatus – the army, government, police, tribunals and administration – which exercises coercive power, and the ideological apparatus – the church, political parties, the unions, schools, the mass media and the family – which is concerned with the manipulation of values and beliefs, rather than the use of force.

Most writers do not see institutions such as the family as constituting part of the state. Poulantzas argued that they should be categorized in this way for the following reasons:

1   Like the repressive institutions of the state, they are necessary for the survival of capitalism. Without them the proletariat might develop class consciousness and challenge the capitalist system.

2   The ideological apparatus depends ultimately on the repressive apparatus to defend and maintain it. He gave the example of the defence of education through the French police and army intervening against the student revolts in Paris in 1968.

3   Poulantzas argued that changes in the repressive apparatus of the state lead to changes in the ideological apparatus. In fascist Germany, for instance, the state took direct control of much of the ideological apparatus.

4   He claimed that the ultimate communist aim – the 'withering away' of the state – would only be achieved with the abolition of institutions such as the family.

Criticisms of Poulantzas

Miliband (1972) tried to defend himself against the criticisms made by Poulantzas, and he put forward his own criticisms of the latter's work. In particular he accused Poulantzas of structural super-determinism. In other words, Miliband did not believe that ultimately all aspects of the behaviour of the state were determined by the infrastructure. Such a theory, he claimed, could not account for the differences between fascist and 'democratic' states within capitalist systems.

Furthermore, Miliband argued that Poulantzas's theory was not backed up by empirical evidence. It was not sufficient to simply assert that the state must act in the interests of capitalism.

Miliband also questioned the definition of the state proposed by Poulantzas. He expressed great scepticism about the claim that institutions such as the family could be seen as part of the state. He accepted that they might have an ideological role, but denied that they are in any sense directly controlled by the state. Although he agreed that they are part of the political system, he argued that they possess so much independence or autonomy that it is ridiculous to see them as part of the state.

It can also be argued that the theory of relative autonomy is impossible to prove or disprove. If the theory is accepted, any action the state takes can be interpreted one way or another as benefiting the bourgeoisie. If it does not appear to directly benefit them, it can be dismissed as a mere concession to the proletariat. Some neo-Marxists argue that concessions can be more than token gestures. To writers such as Gramsci, the working class do have some power and can influence the actions of the state. (We will analyse neo-Marxist views later in this chapter.)

Evidence to support Marxism

Marxist writers have adopted more sophisticated methods of measuring power than either pluralists or elite theorists. They have examined all three faces of power identified by Steven Lukes (1974), and have also extended the concept to include the effects of decisions.

The effects of decisions

As we saw earlier, the decision-making approach to measuring power used by pluralists has been heavily criticized. Marxists such as Westergaard and Resler (1976) argued that power can only be measured by its results: if scarce and valued resources are concentrated in the hands of a minority, that group largely monopolizes power in society. Westergaard and Resler maintained that 'power is visible only through its consequences; they are the first and final proof of the existence of power'. Put simply, the proof of the pudding is in the eating: whoever reaps the largest rewards at the end of the day holds the largest share of power.

Westergaard and Resler claimed that the marked inequalities that characterize British society 'reflect, while they also demonstrate, the continuing power of capital'. The concentration of wealth and privilege in the hands of the capitalist class therefore provides visible proof of its power. Legislation on taxation, which could lead to the redistribution of wealth, is not usually enforced effectively. Furthermore, loopholes in the law often allow the wealthy to avoid paying much of their tax.

Westergaard and Resler believed that the welfare state does little to redistribute income, for it is largely financed out of the taxes paid by the working class. More recent research conducted by Westergaard (1995) suggests that, if anything, the 1980s and early 1990s saw increased inequality in Britain (see pp. 122–3).

Apart from information on the distribution of wealth and income, Westergaard and Resler used detailed examples to show that the activities of the state represent the interests of the ruling class.

Concessions to the working class

In Britain, as in other advanced capitalist societies, the state has implemented a wide range of reforms which appear to directly benefit either the subject class in particular or society as a whole. These include legislation to improve health and safety in the workplace, social security benefits such as old-age pensions and unemployment and sickness benefit, a national health service, and free education for all.

However, these reforms have left the basic structure of inequality unchanged. They have been largely financed from the wages of those they were intended to benefit and have resulted in little redistri-

bution of wealth. They can be seen as concessions, which serve to defuse working-class protest and prevent it from developing in more radical directions which might threaten the basis of ruling-class dominance. In Westergaard and Resler's words, 'Their effects are to help contain working-class unrest by smoothing off the rougher edges of insecurity.'

Non-decision making

Marxists have also been concerned to examine the second face of power: non-decision making. John Urry, in criticizing Dahl, argued that he:

> ignores the process by which certain issues come to be defined as decisions and others do not. The study of decisions is the failure to study who has the power to determine what are decisions.

> Urry, in Urry and Wakeford, 1973

Many Marxists believe that the range of issues and alternatives considered by governments in capitalist societies is strictly limited. Only safe decisions are allowed – those which do not in any fundamental way challenge the dominant position of the bourgeoisie. The sanctity of private property is never questioned; the right of workers to keep the profits produced by their labour is never seriously proposed; and communism is never contemplated as a realistic alternative to capitalism.

Ideology

According to Marxists, the ability of the ruling class to suppress such questions is related to the third face of power. Numerous studies claim that the bourgeoisie are able to produce false class consciousness amongst the working class. Westergaard and Resler (1976) argued that ruling-class ideology promotes the view that private property, profit, the mechanisms of a market economy and the inequalities which result are reasonable, legitimate, normal and natural. If this view is accepted, then the dominance of capital is ensured since 'no control could be firmer and more extensive than one which embraced the minds and wills of its subjects so successfully that opposition never reared its head'.

Westergaard and Resler claimed that, because of the pervasiveness of ruling-class ideology, the capitalist class rarely has to consciously and actively exercise its power. Capitalism and the inequalities it produces are largely taken for granted. A capitalist economy guarantees a disproportionate share of wealth to a minority and generates an ideology which prevents serious questioning of the established order. As a result, issues that might threaten the dominance of capital are usually prevented from reaching the point of actual decision. The capitalist class is therefore able to enjoy the advantage and privilege 'merely because of "the way things work", and because those ways are not open to serious challenge'.

If anything, the plausibility of such arguments increased in later decades of the twentieth century. Countries such as Britain and the United States embraced capitalist free markets more wholeheartedly. The regimes of leaders such as Ronald Reagan and Margaret Thatcher tried to reduce government spending on welfare and state intervention. Margaret Thatcher's Conservative government in Britain (1979-91) privatized numerous state-owned industries and tried to introduce competitive, capitalist-like relationships into parts of the welfare state such as the National Health Service (NHS).

However, this does not mean that Marxist views are immune from criticism.

Criticisms of Marxism

Marxists provide a considerable amount of evidence to support their views. However, the Marxist theory of the state cannot explain why the state became stronger rather than 'withering away' in communist countries. Furthermore, Marxists fail to take account of the possibility that there are sources of power other than wealth. Some conflict theorists deny that wealth is the only source of power, despite seeing economic power as important. If they are correct, then Marxists certainly exaggerate the degree to which those with economic power dominate state decisions and determine the effects of those decisions.

We will now consider the state from a neo-Marxist viewpoint.

Neo-Marxist approaches to power and the state

A number of writers have put forward theories of the state and the distribution of power in society which are heavily influenced by Marxism, but which differ in some significant way from the original writings of Marx and Engels. This section examines the work of two such writers: the early twentieth-century sociologist Antonio Gramsci, and the contemporary British sociologist David Coates.

Antonio Gramsci – hegemony and the state

Antonio Gramsci (1891-1937) is among the most influential twentieth-century theorists who have themselves been influenced by Marx. Gramsci was an Italian sociologist and political activist. A leader of the Italian Communist Party, he is partly remembered for the part he played in the Turin Factory Council Movement, in which industrial workers in that city unsuccessfully attempted to seize control of their workplaces. From 1926 until his death, Gramsci was imprisoned by Mussolini's fascist government, and his main contributions to sociological theory are contained in his *Prison Notebooks* written during that time (Gramsci, 1971).

Gramsci parted company with conventional Marxists in arguing against economic determinism: he did not believe that the economic infrastructure determined to any great degree what occurred in the superstructure of society. He talked of a 'reciprocity between structure and superstructure': although the infrastructure could affect what took place in the superstructure, the reverse was also possible.

Gramsci did not deny that the economic infrastructure of society was important: it provided the general background against which events took place. An economic crisis might increase political awareness amongst the proletariat, for instance. However, he felt that the actions of groups trying to maintain or change society were at least as important.

Political and civil society

Unlike traditional Marxists, Gramsci divided the superstructure of society into two parts: political society and civil society. Political society consisted of what is normally thought of as the state. This was primarily concerned with the use of force by the army, police and legal system to repress troublesome elements within the population. Civil society consisted of those institutions normally thought of as private, particularly the church, trade unions, the mass media and political parties.

In a novel way Gramsci claimed that 'the state = political society + civil society'. He used a very broad definition of the state, for he did not think of it in terms of particular institutions but rather in terms of the activities of a dominant class in society.

Hegemony

At one point in his work Gramsci described the state as:

> the entire complex of practical and theoretical activities with which the ruling class not only justifies and maintains its dominance, but manages to maintain the active consent of those over whom it rules.

Gramsci, 1971, p. 244

If the ruling class managed to maintain its control by gaining the approval and consent of members of society, then it had achieved what Gramsci called hegemony. Hegemony was largely achieved, not through the use of force, but by persuading the population to accept the political and moral values of the ruling class. Here Gramsci stressed the importance of ideas in society: effective ruling-class control was only maintained to the extent that the ruling class could retain command of the beliefs of the population through civil society.

Gramsci's view on how hegemony could be maintained comes close to Marx's view of false class consciousness. However, unlike the views Marx sometimes expressed, Gramsci did not see the ruling class as ever being able to impose entirely false beliefs and values on the population, nor did he see the state as ever being able to act as a simple instrument or tool of ruling-class dominance. The state could only remain hegemonic if it was prepared to compromise and take account of the demands of exploited classes, and, for the following three important reasons, ruling-class hegemony could never be complete.

Historic blocs

In the first place, Gramsci saw both the ruling and subject classes as being divided. The ruling class was divided into groups such as financiers, small and large industrialists and landowners, while industrial workers and agricultural peasants represented a major division within the subject class. No one group on its own could maintain dominance of society. Hegemony was only possible if there was some sort of alliance between two or more groups.

Gramsci called a successful alliance – which achieved a high level of hegemony – a historic bloc; but because of the different elements it contained it would always be something of a compromise between the groups involved.

Concessions

The second reason why the hegemony of one group would never be complete was that the state always had to make some concessions to the subject class. Gramsci said, 'hegemony undoubtedly presupposes that the interests and tendencies of the groups over which hegemony is to be exercised are taken into account'. From this point of view, the ruling class had to make concessions in order to be able to rule by consent instead of relying on the use of force. It had to adopt some policies that benefited the subject class.

Dual consciousness

If the ruling class were able to indoctrinate the population completely, then clearly it would not be necessary for them to make concessions. However, Gramsci maintained that this was never possible. He believed that individuals possessed dual consciousness. Some of their ideas derived from the ruling class's control over civil society and its ability to use institutions such as the church and schools to persuade people to accept that capitalism was natural and desirable. However, in part, individuals' beliefs were also the product of their activities and experiences. To a limited extent they would be able to see through the capitalist system, and realize that their interests lay in changing it. For example, their day-to-day experience of poor working conditions and low wages would encourage them to believe that, at the very least, some reforms of the system were necessary.

The overthrow of capitalism

According to Gramsci, then, power derived only in part from economic control; it could also originate from control over people's ideas and beliefs. Since the ruling class was unable to completely control the ideas of the population, it could never completely monopolize power. Similarly the subject class would always have some influence over the activities of the state. The activities of political society would benefit them to the extent that they were able to realize where their interests lay and wrest concessions from the ruling class.

Like Marx, Gramsci looked forward with anticipation to a proletarian revolution, but he saw such a revolution arising in a rather different way. He did not accept that the contradictions of the capitalist economic system made a revolution a foregone conclusion.

The revolutionary seizure of power in Tsarist Russia by the Bolsheviks was only possible because of a complete absence of ruling-class hegemony in that country. The rulers lacked the consent of the subject classes and so those classes were able to overthrow them with a direct frontal attack. Gramsci termed such a violent revolutionary seizure of power a 'war of manoeuvre', in which direct action was taken to secure victory.

In most advanced capitalist countries, though, he saw the ruling class as having much more hegemony than they had possessed in Russia. Consequently countries such as Italy and Britain needed a good deal more preparation before they would have the potential for a proletarian revolution. Gramsci called such preparation a 'war of position' – a kind of political trench warfare in which revolutionary elements in society attempted to win over the hearts and minds of the subject classes. It was only when individuals had been made to realize the extent to which they were being exploited, and had seen through the ideas and beliefs of the ruling class, that a revolution was possible. For this to happen, 'intellectuals' had to emerge within the subject classes to mould their ideas and form a new historic bloc of the exploited, capable of overcoming ruling-class hegemony.

David Coates – *The Context of British Politics*

Gramsci's views on the state are reflected in a number of later studies, including David Coates's book on British politics (Coates, 1984). Coates does place more emphasis on economic factors than Gramsci, but nevertheless eventually draws conclusions which are similar to Gramsci's. We will discuss his examination of the economic influences on the British state first, before considering those aspects of his work which can be seen as 'Gramscian'.

The state and multinationals

Coates starts his work by attempting to show the limitations on the state which are produced by the international capitalist system. He tries to demonstrate that each capitalist country cannot be analysed separately, since capitalism is not limited by national boundaries.

Multinational corporations with branches in a number of different countries form an increasingly important part of the modern capitalist system. The British government's freedom of action is limited by these companies. The multinationals' decisions about where to invest money and where to open and close factories can have a tremendous impact on the British economy. The largest multinationals, such as General Motors, wield massive economic power: General Motors has a greater turnover than the total wealth produced by the Danish economy.

Attempts to control multinationals are unlikely to be successful. If, for example, a government introduces exchange controls to prevent the companies moving profits abroad, then such controls can be bypassed through transfer pricing. This involves one part of a company selling commodities to a part of the same company in another country at unrealistically high or low prices. Through this technique, multinationals effectively move resources from country to country whatever laws a particular government passes.

In any case, if the government is not to risk jeopardizing the high proportion of investment in Britain which comes from abroad, it cannot afford to pursue policies which would seriously threaten the interests of foreign capitalist companies operating in Britain.

The actions of the British government are further restricted by the major international financial institutions and the World Bank. These organizations are intended to oversee the world's banking, financial and monetary systems. In the 1970s a British Labour government was forced to seek a loan from the IMF (International Monetary Fund), but in order to secure it the government had to comply with the IMF's instructions on how the British economy should be managed. (Global influences on states are discussed again later in the chapter, see pp. 624–33.)

The state and finance capital

Like the elite pluralists Richardson and Jordan (1979), Coates stresses the international influences on the British government. Unlike them, and in common with traditional Marxists, he emphasizes the economic limitations on governments. These constraints come not only from abroad but also from within British society.

Coates claims that finance capital (the banks, insurance companies and financial trusts in the City of London) has a particularly strong influence on the British government. He calculates that in 1981 such institutions controlled assets worth some £562 billion, which represents about £10,000 for every member of the population. He suggests that all governments rely to a considerable extent upon the support of these institutions. If, for example, the latter choose to sell sterling it can rapidly cause a currency crisis as the value of the pound falls.

If the government takes measures which harm the City of London's position as a major financial centre in the world, it risks enormous damage to the British economy as a whole. This is because Britain imports more manufactured goods than it exports, and much of the difference in the balance of payments is made up by invisible earnings, such as the income from the sale of insurance policies worldwide provided by Lloyds of London, and other financial services.

In comparison to financiers, Coates claims, industrial capital (in this case British-owned industry) has less influence over government policy. The CBI, for example, failed to persuade the government to reduce the value of the pound and reduce interest rates in the late 1980s. Both of these measures would have benefited industry. The first would have made British goods cheaper and easier to sell abroad; the second would have cut companies' costs by reducing the price of borrowing money. Both, however, would have made Britain less attractive as a financial centre for foreign investors.

Using such evidence, Coates claims that finance capital has had more influence over the British government than industrial capital, and the consequences have been the decline of British manufacturing industry and rising unemployment.

Divisions in the ruling class

These aspects of Coates's work have much in common with traditional Marxism, although they do place more emphasis on international constraints on the state. In other respects his work is much closer to that of Gramsci. He explicitly rejects the instrumentalist view of the state put forward by Miliband, and the structuralist relative-autonomy approach advocated by Poulantzas.

In the first case, Coates argues that the state cannot be a simple instrument of the ruling class, since the ruling class itself is divided in such a way that different 'fractions' of capital have different interests. Small and large industrialists, multinational and domestic concerns, finance and industrial capital, all place conflicting demands on the state. Often the state cannot serve one section of the ruling class without damaging another.

Coates rejects the structuralist view because he does not accept that the existence of a capitalist system ensures that ultimately the state will have to act in the interests of the ruling class as a whole. As he puts it, 'what capitalism generates around the state is not a set of unavoidable imperatives so much as a set of conflicting demands'. These conflicting demands stem not just from divisions within the ruling class, but also from divisions between classes.

Dual consciousness

Coates points out that capitalism produces not just an economic system but also a civil society. He follows Gramsci in seeing civil society as consisting of private institutions, such as the family, as well as the social relationships between a whole variety of groups. All of these groups make demands on the government, and they include workers and their unions, ethnic minorities and women, as well as capitalists.

Like Gramsci, Coates sees the exploited and oppressed groups as possessing dual consciousness. To some extent they are taken in by attempts to legitimate the capitalist system, but to some extent they also see through that system. According to Coates, individuals in Britain in exploited classes hold contradictory beliefs. They may accept the basic arrangements of capitalism, such as wage labour, but nevertheless believe that the rich have too much power. They may be racist and sexist, but remain committed to human dignity and equal rights and opportunities for all. Many are loyal to parliamentary democracy, but strongly believe that ordinary people have little influence over government.

In this situation the state has to try to maintain its hegemony despite the existence of some degree of class consciousness among the population.

Hegemony

Coates follows Gramsci in seeing the state as the institution which attempts to cement an alliance or historic bloc of different sections of the population, which is capable of maintaining hegemony. Again, he

agrees with Gramsci that this may involve making real concessions to exploited and oppressed groups. Coates argues that the ruling class do not monopolize power entirely. Trade unions, for example, can sometimes exercise a genuine influence on government policy. He sees the nationalizations and improvements made in the welfare state under the 1945 Labour government as representing real working-class gains, and not just token concessions.

According to Coates, most British governments have been able to maintain a high degree of hegemony. They have achieved this by succeeding in getting the population to accept a 'national project'. Most people have been willing to go along with state policies which appear to offer some benefit to all sections of the population. Until the 1980s this was fairly easy in a rapidly expanding world capitalist economy: in the 1950s and 1960s full employment, rising wages and the provision of welfare services such as health and education produced a fairly stable society.

However, Coates is not convinced that ruling-class hegemony will remain easy to maintain in the future. He saw Mrs Thatcher's Conservative Party policies as an attempt to produce a new national project based upon an appeal to improve Britain's economic competitiveness by reducing public spending. Coates believed that the economic weakness of the British economy in the world capitalist system (which was in recession in the late 1980s) produced a crisis for the British state. Its legitimacy was increasingly questioned, and he doubted that Thatcherism would be successful in re-establishing ruling-class hegemony.

Evaluation

Coates's work provides a good example of how neo-Marxist theories of power and the state have become increasingly sophisticated. He identifies a wide range of groups, institutions and processes through which power is exercised and the activities of the state are influenced. The groups involved include members of the working class and trade unions as well as different fractions of capital at home and abroad. He denies that one group monopolizes power, or that all power stems from wealth, but agrees with other Marxist and neo-Marxist theorists that power is very unequally distributed.

Although his work may now be somewhat dated, it can be applied to more contemporary British politics. For example, the power of finance capitalists was never more evident than in 1992 when Britain was forced to leave the Exchange Rate Mechanism (ERM). The ERM was intended to limit the fluctuations in exchange rates for a number of European currencies to those specified by the member states.

Despite the financial muscle of the members (which included Germany, France and Italy, as well as the UK), currency speculators forced Britain to withdraw when speculation by them in sterling meant that the currency could no longer be sustained within the agreed bands.

Although a Labour government was elected in 1997, it went out of its way, both in opposition and in power, to reassure the financial markets that it would do nothing to undermine their interests. For example, Labour leaders promised to stick to the spending plans outlined by the previous government for three years after taking office, and it also promised not to increase income tax. This would suggest that there is limited scope for left-wing governments to adopt radical policies in contemporary capitalist societies. This issue has been debated by theorists of globalization and others who have discussed the extent to which the nation-state retains the autonomy to act as it chooses (see pp. 624–33).

Abercrombie, Hill and Turner – *The Dominant Ideology Thesis*

Writers such as Gramsci and Coates emphasize the role played by ideas and beliefs as sources of power, in addition to economic factors. However, some Marxists following a more traditional line reject this view. Abercrombie, Hill and Turner (1980) deny that there is a coherent dominant ideology in capitalist societies, and question the view that any such ideology is the main factor holding advanced capitalist societies together. In a rather similar way to Gramsci, they suggest that members of the subject and ruling classes often hold contradictory views. For example, members of the subject class may support the welfare state, but believe in the importance of economic freedom and competition between individuals and companies; similarly they are often strongly nationalistic, but this does not square with the existence of multinational corporations.

Furthermore, Abercrombie *et al.* claim to have evidence that members of the subject class actually reject those elements of a dominant ideology that can be identified. They quote a number of studies to support their point. Paul Willis's study of education, *Learning to Labour* (1977), shows that working-class boys reject much of what schools teach them and attach greater value to manual labour than to more highly-rewarded non-manual jobs. Hugh Beynon's study, *Working for Ford* (1973), revealed that many factory-floor workers are alienated from work and feel exploited.

Such evidence might be taken as support for Gramsci's theory of dual consciousness, but Abercrombie *et al.* see it in a very different light. They

argue that it shows the importance of economic power, for if so many people reject ruling-class ideology, then it must be the ruling class's wealth rather than their ideological control that allows them to retain their dominance in society. Abercrombie *et al.* argue that it is factors such as the threat of unemployment, the risk of poverty and the possibility of being imprisoned that make the exploited conform in capitalist societies.

Tom Bottomore – elites and classes

Tom Bottomore (1993) provides an example of a contemporary neo-Marxist approach to power and the state. Bottomore agrees with more conventional Marxists that power is largely concentrated in the hands of an economically dominant upper class. However, he believes that in some circumstances non-economic elites may have considerable power. Furthermore, although he rejects pluralist accounts of power, he does believe that a more equitable distribution of power might be achieved through reformed democratic systems.

Power and the global economy

Bottomore claims that:

> The world economy is dominated by 500 of the largest multinational corporations, by the nation states in which they have their headquarters, and by those institutions of world capitalism such as the World Bank and the International Monetary Fund which determine and regulate economic development on a world scale.
>
> Bottomore, 1993, p. 119

According to Bottomore, the earth's wealth has become more concentrated than ever before and, as a consequence, upper classes and elites have become increasingly dominant. He attributes this increased concentration of power to the following factors:

1 Multinational companies have grown both in size and power. These companies allow small numbers of people – that is, their senior executives – to wield enormous amounts of power.

2 New Right governments and thinking, which became dominant in the 1980s and 1990s, 'lauded the role of a business elite, asserted an extreme individualism, and accepted or even welcomed a gross commercialization of social life and the growth of inequality'. This gave ideological support to the dominance of capitalism and capitalists, and created improved opportunities for the accumulation of profit.

3 Communist regimes in Eastern Europe and the USSR collapsed leaving yet more markets for capitalists to exploit. Furthermore, the collapse of the regimes seemed to suggest that there was no alternative to free-market capitalism.

Elite rule and class rule

All of these factors appeared to point to an increasingly powerful ruling class. However, Bottomore argues that power does not always stem from economic control. He is prepared to accept that power has sometimes stemmed partly from the possession of military force (as in the case of military dictatorships), or through the occupation of key party positions (as in the case of communism in the USSR or Nazism in Germany). Nevertheless, both military and political elites in totalitarian regimes base their power to a considerable extent on the control of the economy.

Furthermore, by the 1990s, such sources of power had become relatively unimportant. Bottomore says, 'it is evident that in the present-day world, dominated by the leading capitalist countries, classes and class relations have the most potent influence on the character of political rule'.

Bottomore believes that small groups of people, who dominate the crucial decisions in the contemporary world, act like elites, but should be seen 'more accurately as "upper classes"'. They act like elites because they try to ensure that the political system operates in such a way as to minimize the effectiveness of those who oppose the policies they support.

They do this in a number of ways:

1 Party politics plays down the importance of issues and transforms politics into 'media circuses' in which the personality of party leaders is given undue importance.
2 Summit meetings are held to give the largely illusory impression that the leaders of the largest capitalist countries are serious about dealing with major problems facing the world. In fact, summits are largely media events, and little usually changes as a result of them.
3 Political parties in many countries have increasingly concentrated power in their own hands to the exclusion of the mass of the population.
4 In countries like Britain, the political elites generally oppose electoral reform which would allow the views of minorities to be better represented in Parliament.
5 Political leaders are usually hostile to, and take little notice of, social movements which act outside of mainstream politics.
6 Transnational institutions such as the European Union are remote from the mass of the population and do not have directly-elected officials in the most powerful positions.

Participatory democracy

Although Bottomore sees power as largely stemming from wealth, and he believes that capitalists and the political elites are becoming increasingly powerful, he does not follow some other Marxists in claiming that the only way to improve the situation is a communist revolution. Instead, Bottomore believes that progress can be made by developing a participatory democracy.

Such progress may be possible because capitalism already faces a number of problems:

1 Economic crises and instability are becoming more acute and difficult to control in a global capitalist economy.
2 The world capitalist economy faces serious environmental problems (such as global warming) which will make it more difficult to achieve a continued growth in profitability.
3 Opposition to the logic of global capitalist development is growing, particularly in new social movements such as those engaged in ecological and environmental campaigns (see pp. 643–7).

In this situation Bottomore believes that there is scope for significant improvements which would involve a considerable dispersal of power. He argues for a 'radical devolution of power within nation states themselves, to regional and local authorities whose policies can be more closely observed and influenced by the public'.

Active, participatory democracy can also be enhanced through the activities of social movements. These may operate outside conventional parliamentary and pressure-group politics and can involve more and more people in shaping their own societies. People are increasingly well-educated and have the leisure time to devote to the 'self-regulation of their forms of life'. If participatory democracy is successful, then 'social movements of many different kinds are likely to have a growing influence, encouraging the necessary dissolution of the mystique of political elites and at the same time undermining the real dominance of upper classes'.

Evaluation

Bottomore's work provides an updated neo-Marxist approach to power, which takes account of changes such as the development of social movements and the apparent globalization of the economy. It offers an alternative to communist revolution (which seems increasingly unlikely to happen) as a path towards a society in which power is more equally distributed. However, his work uses a mixture of Marxist class theory and elite theory, and, as a result, it appears confused at times. For example, he does not make the links between political elites and upper-class power (which stems from wealth) particularly clear. His claim that the upper classes are getting ever more powerful seems to contradict his view that power could be decentralized and that new social movements could have a growing role in politics. Furthermore, like the other theories examined so far, Bottomore says little about how the state itself may exercise power. This issue is examined in the next section.

State-centred theories of power

The approaches we have considered so far have been society-centred: they see the state and its actions as shaped by external forces in society as a whole. We will now look at an alternative perspective which has a completely different viewpoint.

Eric A. Nordlinger – the autonomy of democratic states

Society-centred and state-centred approaches

According to Eric A. Nordlinger (1981), theories of power and the state are either society-centred or state-centred. To Nordlinger, all the perspectives on the state and power examined so far are society-centred, and society-centred approaches have 'a pervasive grip upon citizens, journalists and scholars alike'. Pluralism sees the state's actions as determined by the democratic will of the people; elite theory sees its actions as shaped by the wishes of a small group of powerful people; Marxism sees the state as shaped by the interests of a ruling class. Although some Marxist and neo-Marxist theories concede that the state may have some autonomy, they do not go far enough, because, in the final analysis, the state is portrayed as being unable to go against ruling-class interests.

Nordlinger criticizes all these approaches saying:

> the possibility that the state's preferences have at least as much impact on public policy as do society's is ignored; the state's having certain distinctive interests and divergent preferences is not considered; the state's many autonomous actions are not calculated; the state's numerous autonomy-enhancing capacities and opportunities are not examined.
>
> Nordlinger, 1981

Nordlinger argues that society-centred approaches have been so dominant that a very distorted and one-sided view of the state and power has been produced. Although society can and does influence the state, the reverse sometimes happens. This is what Nordlinger describes as the state-centred approach to the theory of power. The state acts independently or autonomously to change society.

This is true of democracies, as well as other types of state, even though they are supposed to be under the control of the electorate.

The autonomy of the democratic state takes three forms.

Type 1 state autonomy

Type 1 state autonomy occurs when the state has different wishes to those of major groups in society, and implements its preferred policies despite pressure for it not to do so. For example, state policy in Sweden is often formulated by Royal Commissions. About 80 per cent of those who serve on the Commissions are civil servants, and the recommendations are usually followed even when they are unpopular with the electorate or are opposed by elites outside the state. In Norway, public–private committees which formulate public policy are often chaired by civil servants and, again, their recommendations are normally accepted whatever the opposition to them.

To Nordlinger there are many ways in which the state can enhance its autonomy from society. These include:

1 using secretive systems of decision making;
2 using honours, appointments or government contracts to persuade opponents to accept proposals;
3 using the state's resources to counter resources used by opponents (for example, using the funds in the state bank to prop up a currency that is being undermined by speculators);
4 threatening to change a range of policies in such a way as to harm the interests of opponents of the state's policies;
5 taking actions or issuing statements which cause mistrust among different groups of opponents.

Because the state has considerable power of its own, it is sometimes able to utilize it to prevent effective opposition.

Type 2 state autonomy

Type 2 state autonomy occurs when the state is able to persuade opponents of its policies to change their mind and support the government. Nordlinger argues that this is quite common and examples of it can be found in classical pluralist studies such as Dahl's *Who Governs?* (see p. 596). Although Dahl claimed that the authorities in New Haven were responsive to public opinion and the policies they adopted were shaped by interest groups, Nordlinger believes that the authorities played an active role in manipulating public opinion. For example, Dahl himself pointed out that there had been little or no interest in a programme of urban renewal until the mayor put the issue on the agenda and persuaded various interest groups to support him. None of the interest groups agreed with his proposals when they were first put forward. From this viewpoint, then, Dahl's own evidence showed that the state could act autonomously in shaping public opinion, rather than having its policies shaped by public opinion.

Type 3 state autonomy

Type 3 state autonomy occurs when the state follows policies which are supported, or at least not opposed, by the public or powerful interest groups in society. Very often, significant groups in society may be unsure of what policies to support and leave it up to the state to decide. For example, between 1948 and 1971 the USA's grain farmers, industrial workers and exporters made little attempt to influence America's international monetary policy. Although the policy affected them a great deal, they were unable to predict the effects of the state's policies and so were content to accept whatever policies the state adopted.

On many issues concerned with the state itself there is considerable apathy on the part of the public, and the state has considerable freedom of manoeuvre, even though the issues may be of great importance. Nordlinger suggests that such issues tend to include 'possible changes in the state units' formal powers relative to one another, policy implementation responsibilities, budgetary allotments, staffing, organization, and standard operating procedures'.

Nordlinger's views suggest that the state has considerable autonomy over many issues, whether there is opposition from society or not. While he recognizes that the autonomy is only partial, he perhaps goes further in attributing independence to the state than other state-centred approaches. His theory is backed up by a limited number of empirical examples.

Other sociologists have conducted more detailed research in their attempts to show that the state acts as an independent source of power.

Theda Skocpol – *Bringing the State Back In*

The autonomy of states from society

Theda Skocpol (1985) is perhaps the most influential of the state-centred theorists. She has written extensively about the state as a source of power and is a strong supporter of what she calls *Bringing the State Back In*. She argues that pluralists, functionalists, Marxists and neo-Marxists have all tended to see the state as shaped by external pressures and have neglected the possibility that the state can shape society. Like Nordlinger, she is critical of such approaches. For example, she says:

virtually all neo-Marxist writers on the state have retained deeply embedded society-centred assumptions, not allowing themselves to doubt that, at base, states are inherently shaped by classes or class struggles and function to preserve and expand models of production. Many possible forms of autonomous state action are thus ruled out by definitional fiat.

Skocpol, 1985, p. 5

To Skocpol, states can have considerable autonomy and, as actors, have the potential capacity to achieve their policy goals. These goals 'are not simply reflective of the demands or interests of social groups, classes or society', for states can have their own goals and pursue their own interests.

Skocpol believes that one of the main aims of states and parts of states is to increase their own power. She suggests that 'We can hypothesize that one (hidden or overt) feature of all autonomous state actions will be the reinforcement of the prerogatives of collectivities of state officials.' 'Policies different from those demanded by societal actors will be produced' as states 'attempt to reinforce the authority, political longevity, and social control of the state organizations.'

Skocpol gives a number of examples of states acting in pursuit of their own interests.

In 1968 in Peru there was a coup organized by career military officers who used state power to plan economic growth, weaken opposition groups in society, and try to impose order. In Britain and Sweden, according to Skocpol, the civil services often oppose the policies of elected politicians and have some success in ensuring that their policies are not implemented in such a way as to undermine the power of the state. In the USA, both the White House and the State Department are fairly insulated from public opinion and democratic control, and they often act autonomously. Skocpol's own research had found that in the USA after the First World War, the Department of Agriculture was a powerful part of the state which acted independently in the pursuit of its own interests.

State capacities

Although all states have the potential to achieve their own goals, their capacity to do so will be affected by a number of factors:

1 Skocpol says that 'sheer sovereign integrity and the stable administrative control of a given territory are preconditions for any state's ability to implement policies'. Unless a state can largely command the territory for which it is responsible, it will have no power base from which to achieve its aims.

2 States that have a reliable and substantial source of income are more powerful than those that do not. For example, if a state relies heavily upon the export of a single commodity or product (as some Third

World states do), then it is vulnerable to a decline in demand for the product or a reduction in its value. On the other hand, economies that export a wide variety of products have a more reliable income.

3 States that govern rich societies obviously have more potential for raising domestic taxes than those that govern poor societies. This can strengthen their power base.

4 States that are forced to borrow large amounts of money can end up in a weaker position than those that have sufficient revenue to finance their activities.

5 States also tend to increase their power if they can recruit many of the most able and highly-educated members of society into their ranks. Not only does this tend to improve the organization of the state, it also deprives non-state organizations and groups of the personnel who would be most likely to challenge and undermine the state's power.

Skocpol believes that whether a state becomes powerful or not partly depends upon how well organized groups in society are. She criticizes Marxists for claiming that states always reflect the interests of a dominant class, saying:

> the political expression of class interests and conflicts is never automatic or economically determined. It depends on the capacities classes have for achieving consciousness, organization, and representation. Directly or indirectly, the structures and activities of states profoundly condition such class capacities.

Skocpol, 1985, p. 25

To Skocpol, Marxist political sociology 'must be turned, if not on its head, then certainly on its side'. The state shapes the activity of classes as much as classes shape the activity of the state.

States' capacities are profoundly affected by their relationships with other states. Large and powerful armed forces increase the capacity of a state to defend its own territory or seize the territory of other states. Control over territory is the basis of the state's ability to raise revenue and finance its activities. States can be weakened by wars, especially if they incur crippling costs or they suffer military defeats. External threats can result in internal weakness and sometimes contribute to the state losing its autonomy from society.

States and social revolutions

In her most substantial empirical study, Skocpol (1979) compared revolutions in France (1788), China (1911) and Russia (1917). She argues that in all these cases the activities of the states and the weak position that the states found themselves in played a vital role in causing revolutions. The Chinese, Russian and French states acted in ways which undermined their own

power and produced a situation where the state was overthrown by particular classes. Although class conflict was important in all of the revolutions, none of them could be understood without considering the role of the state as an autonomous actor. All three were 'imperial states – that is, differentiated, centrally coordinated administrative and military hierarchies functioning under the aegis of the absolute monarchies'. Although there were differences in the circumstances that led to the revolutions, Skocpol argues that, in all of them, 'The revolutionary crises developed when old-regime states became unable to meet the challenges of evolving international situations.'

In the following section we will analyse the French revolution in more detail to illustrate Skocpol's argument.

France

France fought two wars in the middle years of the eighteenth century: the War of the Austrian Succession (1740–8) and the Seven Years War (1756–63). Both were expensive and France had little military success – in fact in the Seven Years War it lost a number of colonies to Britain.

In eighteenth-century France around 85 per cent of the population were peasants, but agriculture was not highly developed. France had a lower per capita income than Britain and other European competitors, restricting the wealth available for the state to tax. Furthermore, the tax system was inefficient, with numerous exemptions and deductions for the elites who collected the taxes. Consequently the French state got into financial trouble. This was further exacerbated by French involvement in the American War of Independence, when France sided with the American colonists against their British rulers.

In 1797 an Assembly of Notables was called and the finance minister proposed a new land tax to deal with the problem. The Notables rejected the proposal but advocated the establishment of a new body representing landowners, a body which would have to approve any new taxes. When the king refused there were demonstrations and protests in different parts of the country. The king then summoned the Estates General, which consisted of various elites, but this body was unable to reach any agreement about what to do. While most members of the Estates General wanted to restrict the power of the king, they could not agree on how to do it. Consequently the French state was effectively paralysed and its weakness allowed popular protests to take place. Skocpol says:

> By the summer of 1789, the result was the 'Municipal Revolution', a nation-wide wave of political revolutions in cities and towns throughout France, including of course the celebrated 'fall of the Bastille in Paris'. In the

context of simultaneous political crises of 1788-9, crowds of artisans, shopkeepers, journeymen, and labourers roamed the cities searching for arms and grain and demanding both bread and liberty.

Skocpol, 1979, pp. 66-7

The French monarch was overthrown and replaced by revolutionary government.

Conclusion

According to Skocpol, in France, Russia and China, it was the weakness of the state which ultimately caused the revolutions. She comments that 'In all three cases ... the ultimate effect of impediments to state-sponsored reforms was the downfall of monarchical autocracy and the disintegration of the centralized administrative and military organizations of the state.' In each case the state could have acted differently by introducing more effective reforms earlier to prevent the development of a revolutionary situation. Each regime was brought down by a combination of external pressures from other states and the way 'agrarian relations of production and landed dominant classes impinged upon state organizations'. While class relationships were important, none of the revolutions could be understood without reference to the actions taken by the states involved.

In all three countries the revolutions led to the collapse of the old regimes, but they were replaced sooner or later by regimes with even more centralized power and more autonomy than the old states: the Napoleonic regime in France, and communist regimes in China and Russia. According to Skocpol, these were all clear examples of states which could exercise power and which could sometimes act to pursue their own interests rather than the interests of groups within society.

Evaluation of state-centred theories

One of the problems with state-centred theories may be that they are often unclear about their precise theoretical position. Thus Bob Jessop argues:

In their eagerness to criticize society-centred analysis, they have failed to distinguish three different sorts of claim about the state. It is not clear whether they are: (a) rejecting the so-called society-centred approach in its entirety and arguing that the state should be the independent variable; (b) bending the stick in the other direction for polemical purposes, one-sidedly emphasizing the importance of the state as a crucial causal factor; or (c) suggesting that a combination of society and state-centred perspectives will somehow provide a complete account of state–society relations.

Jessop, 1990, p. 287

Most critics are prepared to accept that the actions of the state should be taken into account in studies of power. However, many believe that Skocpol and similar writers exaggerate the importance of the state in an attempt to support their approach. Furthermore, Jessop argues that it is artificial and misleading to see the 'state' and 'society' as being quite separate institutions. He sees state and society as so intimately connected that it is not possible to completely separate them in accounts of power.

Both Jessop and McLennan argue that state-centred approaches offer misleading analyses of the so-called society-centred approaches which they are attacking. Jessop claims that they rest on a '"straw-man" account of the society-centred bias in other studies'. In reality, Jessop suggests, other theories do take account of the power of the state. McLennan (1989) argues in similar fashion that many Marxists, such as Poulantzas, recognize that the state has 'relative autonomy' and that its actions are not entirely determined by society. McLennan concludes that 'Pragmatically it is always degrees of autonomy we are dealing with.'

This is true both of Skocpol's work and of many Marxist theories of power, and the theoretical difference between these approaches has been greatly exaggerated by many of the advocates of a state-centred approach.

Globalization and the power of the nation–state

A number of sociologists and others have begun to argue that the analysis of power cannot be confined to examining the distribution of power within particular nation-states. This is reflected in some of the theories we discussed earlier in this chapter. In his Gramscian discussion of British politics, David Coates (1984) recognizes that the actions of the British state are limited by the operation of the international capitalist system (see pp. 617–19), as does Tom

Bottomore in his discussion of elites and upper classes (Bottomore, 1993, pp. 619–20). Similarly, the state-centred theories – such as that of Skocpol, discussed above – acknowledge that state power is affected by the actions of other states.

State-centred theories do, however, tend to emphasize the autonomy of individual states and the significance of their actions. Approaches which claim that globalization has taken place tend to see the power that exists outside nation-states as restricting their activities and limiting their power. From this point of view, power relationships increasingly cut across national boundaries, and states lose some of their capacity to act independently and shape social life within their boundaries.

There are many advocates and some critics of the theory of globalization. We will start by examining the ideas of one of the strongest supporters of the theory, Kenichi Ohmae, before considering the ideas of those who take a less extreme position.

Kenichi Ohmae – *The Borderless World*

As a management consultant and 'business guru', Kenichi Ohmae (1994) is primarily concerned with the significance of globalization, which he alleges is taking place, for large corporations. However, his analysis also encompasses changes in the distribution of power and the role of nation-states. He is one of the most uncompromising and wholeheartedly enthusiastic advocates of globalization and so his views form a convenient starting point.

The inter-linked economy

According to Ohmae, political borders have become increasingly insignificant in a globalized world, particularly in the most developed economic regions. In particular, Ohmae sees the United States, Japan and Europe as forming one, giant, inter-linked economy (ILE), which is being joined by rapidly developing countries such as Taiwan, Singapore and Hong Kong. He claims that the ILE 'is becoming so powerful that it has swallowed most consumers and corporations, made traditional national borders almost disappear, and pushed bureaucrats, politicians, and the military towards the status of declining industries'.

Ohmae sees such developments as stemming from an opening up of the world economy so that trade between people in different nation-states becomes very easy. This in turn is a consequence of rapid improvements in communications. Through such developments as cable and satellite TV, cheaper, easier and more frequent international travel, and (since Ohmae was writing) the rapid development of the internet, individuals are increasingly able to see what people consume in other countries. It has also become much easier for individuals to buy what they want from other countries. Ohmae says:

> *Today, of course, people everywhere are more and more able to get the information they want directly from all corners of the world. They can see for themselves what the tastes and preferences are in other countries, the styles of clothing now in fashion, the sports, the lifestyles.*
>
> Ohmae, 1992, p. 19

In the past, governments could exercise considerable control over the flow of information to their citizens. Now this is no longer possible. If people see that what they are getting is substandard they will look abroad for something better or insist upon improvements. For example, in Japan the population grew dissatisfied with the standard of their housing. According to Ohmae, 10 million Japanese travel abroad each year. Seeing how others live led them to insist that the government take steps to improve the standard of the housing available to them.

The lack of control governments now have over information is paralleled by the lack of control they can have over the economy. It is becoming increasingly difficult for governments to protect their domestic industries from foreign competition. It is difficult to enforce attempts to impose tariff barriers designed to prevent imports, and, in any case, it is counterproductive. Tariffs are only effective in some low-income economies. India, for example, protects its domestic car industry from external competition. The end result is over-priced and outdated cars which consumers do not like. In higher-income countries, people demand access to the best goods produced anywhere in the world. According to Ohmae, this is not only good for the consumer, it is good for the country's economy as well.

According to Ohmae, most wealth is no longer produced by manufacturing, and most jobs are created when economies are open to investment from any companies, be they domestic, foreign or multinational. He says, 'such functions as distribution, warehousing, financing, retail marketing, systems integration and services are all legitimate parts of the business system and can create as many, and often more, jobs than simply manufacturing operations'.

Global citizens and regional links

Individuals have become global citizens. They, 'want to buy the best and the cheapest products, no matter where in the world they are produced'. Regional economic links have become more important than national economies, and distant parts of the world are connected through business and other ties. Californian businesses often have stronger links with Asian businesses than with businesses in other areas of the USA. Hong Kong has strong links with parts of Canada, since many business people from Hong Kong moved to Canada because they feared the consequences of Hong Kong reverting to Chinese control. There are clusters of investment by Japanese companies in Alsace-Lorraine and South Wales.

If national governments try to limit or stifle these links, they undermine economic growth and incur the displeasure of their citizens. Nor can governments use economic policies to control their economies in the way they used to. Financiers can move money around the globe in vast quantities almost instantaneously. Governments cannot set tax rates or interest rates, or try to fix the value of their currency without taking account of these facts.

National policies can soon be rendered ineffective if financiers and corporations move their currency or their businesses elsewhere. Indeed, Ohmae argues that corporations should no longer see themselves as being based in a particular society. To be successful they have to produce the best products in the world. The development costs of being the best are often enormous and only global success will repay the initial investment. To achieve such success they need to have footholds throughout the inter-linked economy and adapt their businesses and products to meet local conditions. This cannot be achieved unless businesses lose their sense of being based primarily in a single country.

Governments and consumers

According to Ohmae, then, governments have largely lost their power to regulate and control both their national economies and information within their boundaries. Another important governmental function, providing military security, is also becoming redundant. In the inter-linked economy it makes little sense for nations to fight over territory. Invading your neighbour would involve destroying property owned by your own citizens, and disrupting economic activity which contributes to your own country's wealth. States such as Singapore have little in the way of armed forces, yet they do not live in fear of external military threats.

In Ohmae's view of the world, power has shifted decisively from governments to individual consumers. Both governments and companies alike have to accommodate the demands of consumers if they are to get re-elected, or win and keep customers. It is a world in which there is a plurality of cultures, in which 'People vary in how they want to live.' Regimes that try to maintain or impose a single, national culture (such as communist regimes) are doomed to failure.

If states have lost much of their economic role and power, and their role in controlling information, and if they are losing their military role, and no longer have a national culture to protect, are they still necessary? Do they still have any power? Ohmae thinks they are necessary and that they retain some limited powers. They are necessary, essentially, to produce the conditions in which consumers, workers and corporations can thrive in the global economy. They are still necessary to provide the infrastructure (such as roads and a legal system) which makes it possible for businesses to operate. Above all, though,

they need to try to ensure the best possible education for their citizens. Ultimately, Ohmae believes that economic success results from having a highly-educated, entrepreneurial and well-informed population. To achieve these limited objectives, governments still need to raise taxes. However, if their taxes are too high, the effect will be counterproductive, since businesses will simply relocate elsewhere.

Evaluation

Ohmae's view of a world in which political borders are largely irrelevant and power is transferred to consumers is open to many criticisms. Ohmae ignores the continuing role of nation-states in controlling access to their territories as markets for businesses. Although there has been movement towards freer trade in the world economy, completely free trade has not yet come close to fruition. The three biggest capitalist blocs of Japan, North America and the European Union continue to restrict the trade allowed with each other and with nations outside these blocks.

Ohmae surely exaggerates the decline in the importance of the military capability of states. Neither consumers nor corporations have the ability to use military force to impose their will on others. As Nigel Harris says, 'States have a monopoly within their territory of the use of physical power while companies rarely have more than security guards' (Harris, 1992). Individual consumers have even less ability to impose their will on others through the use of force.

Even if Ohmae is correct in believing that the power of the nation-state has declined, it is surprising that he attributes so much power to consumers. Many other theorists of globalization argue that power has shifted to corporations rather than to consumers (see below). Some theorists, such as Hirst and Thompson, raise serious questions about whether globalization has taken place, while others, such as Giddens, accept that globalization has happened, but make far less extreme claims about the decline of state power. Some of these alternative views will now be considered.

Globalization and transnational corporations

As long ago as 1971, Raymond Vernon published a book claiming that the power of nation-states was being eclipsed by the power of multinational (now often called transnational) corporations. Vernon said, 'Suddenly, it seems, the sovereign states are feeling naked. Concepts such as national sovereignty and national economic strength appear curiously drained of meaning' (Vernon, 1971).

Vernon believed that the power of nation-states was declining, but he saw it as shifting to corporations rather than consumers. Multinational and transnational corporations are defined in different ways by different writers, but, as a minimum definition, they are business organizations which operate in more than one country. Most of the larger transnational corporations operate in numerous countries and their activities involve vast sums of money. For example, the 1995 United Nations Conference on Trade and Development found that global sales by the foreign affiliates of transnational corporations amounted to $5.2 trillion, which was more than the total value of all goods and services traded in the world (which amounted to $4.8 trillion) (*World Investment Report*, 1995).

In view of the increased popularity of theories of globalization, it is not surprising that some sociologists have argued that power has shifted to such corporations in a globalized world. One such sociologist is Leslie Sklair.

Leslie Sklair – *Sociology of the Global System*

Leslie Sklair (1993, 1995) believes that states retain some power but that any understanding of the global system must focus primarily upon transnational corporations (TNCs).

Transnational practices

Sklair points out that 'The largest TNCs have assets and annual sales far in excess of the Gross National Products of most of the countries in the world' (Sklair, 1993). In 1992 there were 135 TNCs with annual sales of more than $10 billion. He claims that:

> *such well-known companies as Ford, General Motors, Shell, Toyota, Volkswagen, Nestle, Sony, Pepsico, Coca Cola, Kodak, Xerox (and many others most of us have never heard of) have more economic power at their disposal than the majority of the countries of the world.*
>
> Sklair, 1993, p. 7

Sklair's model is based upon the idea of transnational practices. He defines these as 'practices that originate with non-state actors and cross state borders'. These are distinguished from international relations which involve the relations between nation-states. According to Sklair, transnational practices are increasingly important, compared to international relations.

Transnational practices take place in three main spheres:

1 the economic
2 the political
3 the cultural-ideological

These correspond to the practices of:

1 the transnational corporation
2 the transnational capitalist class
3 the culture-ideology of consumerism

Sklair sees the transnational corporation as the vehicle of the global system. He points to the enormous wealth of such corporations and the crucial role they have in most national economies.

The transnational capitalist class is the driver of the global system. This class consists of executives of TNCs, 'globalizing state bureaucrats', 'capitalist-inspired politicians and professionals' and 'consumerist elites (merchants, media)' (Sklair, 1995). It is seen as making system-wide decisions which affect the whole of the global system, and it attempts to make decisions which further its own interests within the system. Although it includes some politicians based in particular nation-states, the class opposes protectionism, which puts national interests above those of the class as a whole.

The culture-ideology of consumerism involves the worldwide spread of the ideology, which stresses the benefits of consumerism. It has become so important because of the near-universal spread of the mass media. Sklair says that cheap televisions, cassettes and radios 'now totally penetrate the First World, almost totally penetrate the urban Second and Third Worlds, and are beginning to penetrate deeply into the countryside in every country' (Sklair, 1995).

TNC power

Like Ohmae, then, Sklair largely sees the decline of the power of the state as a consequence of the development of capitalism. Unlike Ohmae, he believes that power largely rests with TNCs rather than consumers. Sklair claims that:

> *Effective TNC control of global capital and resources is almost complete. There are few important national resources that are entirely exempt from economic transnational practices. Transnational capitalist classes rule directly, through national capitalist political parties or social democratic political parties that cannot fundamentally threaten the global capitalist system, or they exert authority indirectly to a greater or lesser extent as the price levied on the non-capitalist states as a sort of entrance fee into the global capitalist system.*
>
> Sklair, 1995, p. 95

To Sklair, consumers are effectively indoctrinated by the ideology of the corporations. Far from ensuring that a globalized world acts in their interests, they, for the most part, tamely consume the products that capitalist ideology pushes. He

628 Chapter 9: Power, politics and the state

says that 'The control of ideas in the interests of consumerism is almost total.'

Despite his more extreme claims, Sklair does recognize both that there is some opposition to the capitalist global system and that nation-states retain some power. There are some anti-global social movements which challenge the ideology of consumerism, including environmental movements. However, Sklair does not believe that they have the power to mount a serious challenge to global capitalism.

States are less powerless. Sklair admits, for example, that the United States of America remains enormously powerful, certainly compared to some Third World states and even the larger TNCs. He says:

> All the Fortune 500 corporations [the biggest corporations in the world] do not have the same economic impact on the United States, for example, as a few copper TNCs have had on Chile, or fruit companies on Central America, or mining corporations on Southern Africa.
>
> Sklair, 1995, p. 99

In a few parts of the world, such as China, TNCs have had little success in gaining power at the expense of the state.

Evaluation

Sklair's analysis is more subtle and better supported by evidence than that of Ohmae. It also recognizes that the global system may have serious disadvantages. It seems more plausible to argue that power has shifted to TNCs than to say, as Ohmae does, that consumers are virtually all-powerful. Nevertheless, Sklair may well exaggerate the power of TNCs. His emphasis is on companies involved in production and he says little about the significance of global financiers, bankers and speculators. Yet finance capitalism involves bigger and more rapid flows of resources than does investment abroad by TNCs.

Other theorists such as Jeffrey Frieden (1991) attribute much more importance to finance capitalism. Furthermore, Sklair concentrates almost exclusively on economic aspects of globalization. A slightly broader view is taken by Kevin Bonnett.

Kevin Bonnett – globalization, power and politics

Globalization

Kevin Bonnett (1994) argues that 'Power in Britain (or in any other advanced country) can no longer be understood as first and foremost existing *within* the society.' Nation-states are a comparatively recent historical creation: Italy and Germany did not become unified states until the late nineteenth

century and many colonies did not become autonomous states until they achieved independence a few decades ago.

In some parts of the contemporary world – for example, in the former Yugoslavia – nation-states have broken up and, increasingly throughout the world, power is exercised *across* nation-states rather than *within* them. Bonnett says, 'Many of the economic, political, military and ideological powers that shape our lives work across nations – and increasingly they operate on a global scale.' Multinational corporations, international financial markets, transnational communications systems (such as satellite TV) and transnational organizations (such as the EU) all operate outside of the control of individual nation-states, yet have a profound influence on what goes on within them.

Bonnett acknowledges that international forces – such as colonial empires and international trade – have been significant for centuries, but he believes that, recently, global forces have become more important. He claims that 'What is new is the scale and intensity of ... links and the fact that space and time are "shrunk" by the speed and relative cheapness of travel and electronic communications.'

Globalization and nationalism

While global forces seem to weaken the power of the nation-state from outside, they can also do so from within. Transnational and global relationships may also strengthen 'localism or small scale nationalism'. Ethnic and national groups seeking independence from large states can look to transnational organizations or systems of security to assist them in asserting their independence and claiming nationhood. Thus, 'The Baltic states and other parts of the former USSR have found it possible to proclaim independence – by virtue of links to wider economic and military networks', such as the EU and NATO. In Western Europe, Scottish nationalists have stressed the practicality of becoming independent from England while remaining within the EU. Bonnett says:

> It has come to seem that almost any people with a shared culture or language now comes to define itself as a nation. And once they define themselves as a nation, the logical step in the contemporary world is to become a nation-state – claiming sovereign independence and national self-determination.
>
> Bonnett, 1994

From this point of view, the power of nation-states is under threat from two directions.

Internationalism threatens to reduce the power of states to exercise power independently, while small-scale nationalism and localism threaten to undermine the unity of existing states.

Evaluation

By including a discussion of nationalism and localism, Bonnett adds a useful extra dimension to our examination of globalization. However, in one sense, nationalism involves reasserting the importance of nation-states and their governments, albeit in smaller nation-states than exist at present. The revival of nationalism cannot therefore be seen as unambiguously undermining the power of states, since, while attacking the power of existing states, it claims power for new ones (see pp. 263–70 for a discussion of nationalism).

Unlike Sklair, Bonnett makes little attempt to qualify his claims about the globalization of the world and he certainly fails to consider evidence that globalization might not be taking place. The same cannot be said of the next theorists to be considered, who are amongst those who have started to question whether globalization is happening at all.

Paul Hirst and Grahame Thompson – questioning globalization

'Inter-national' economies and globalized economies

Paul Hirst and Grahame Thompson's *Globalization in Question* (1996) makes an attempt to test the theory of globalization empirically. Like Sklair, they put the role of transnational corporations (TNCs) or multina-tional corporations (MNCs) at the forefront of their argument. They start their analysis by distinguishing between a globalized economy and an inter-national economy

They argue that a globalized economy consists of a system in which 'distinct national economies are subsumed and rearticulated into the system by international processes and transactions. The inter-national economic system becomes autonomized and socially disembedded, as markets and production become truly global.' In other words, nation-states become almost irrelevant to patterns of economic activity, and the existence of national boundaries makes little or no difference to patterns of trade.

In an inter-national economy, though, 'processes that are determined at the level of the national economy still dominate and international phenomena are outcomes that emerge from the distinct and differ-ential performance of the national economies'. The world is made up of interacting national economies.

TNCs and MNCs

Hirst and Thompson regard corporations as a key test of whether the world economy is global or inter-national. They distinguish between MNCs (multina-tional corporations) and TNCs (transnational corporations). In MNCs the national base is important

and they are effectively regulated by their home government. In contrast, TNCs are globally based and 'footloose'. They have an international management team and are potentially willing to base their operations, including if necessary their headquarters, anywhere in the world.

Hirst and Thompson then use their own data (based on an analysis of the sales, assets and profits of 500 corporations in 1987, and the sales and assets of more than 5,000 corporations in 1992-3) to test whether corporations are still MNCs or have become TNCs. According to their analysis, both sets of data show that home-based activities dominate in terms of such measures as the number of subsidiaries and affiliates, the location of assets, and the place where profits are produced. For example, in 1992-3, 75 per cent of both German and Japanese manufacturing corporations' sales were in the home region/country. The corresponding figure for the UK was 65 per cent, and for the USA 67 per cent. They conclude that MNCs are dominant in a largely inter-national economy.

Nation-states and power

Hirst and Thompson adopt a more balanced position when discussing economic governance and nation-states. They accept that 'the combined effects of changing economic conditions and past public policies of dismantling exchange controls have made ambitious and internationally divergent strategies of national economic governance far more difficult'. States have to adopt increasingly similar policies if they are to succeed in the contemporary world.

Furthermore, Hirst and Thompson admit that states have a reduced capacity 'to act autonomously on their societies'. They give the example of the socialist government of France in the 1980s. It tried to combat unemployment and recession by pumping money into the economy, but the negative reaction of foreign investors and financiers forced it to abandon the policy.

Along with the loss of economic power, Hirst and Thompson believe that there has also been a loss of military power. This is because it has become inconceivable for most developed nations to pursue policies through military force in a post-cold war but nuclear era. It is simply too risky to embark on military campaigns with the possibility of a nuclear response.

States may even have lost some ideological power. With increasingly heterogeneous populations, states are less able to call on nationalist loyalty. The diversity of populations makes it difficult to produce loyalty to any one set of values.

Although Hirst and Thompson believe that the state's capacities have been reduced and in some ways changed, they do not believe that they have been eliminated altogether. The state retains a role as a 'facilitator and orchestrator of private economic actors':

> it still retains one central role that ensures a large measure of territorial control – the regulation of populations. People are less mobile than money, goods or ideas: in a sense they remain 'nationalized', dependent on passports, visas, and residence and labour qualifications.
>
> Hirst and Thompson, 1996, p. 171

It is this quality which gives the state democratic legitimacy. It can claim to speak for a body of people and thus can play a crucial role in negotiating international agreements. Hirst and Thompson see such agreements as crucial in the contemporary international economy. They conclude that 'Politics is becoming more polycentric, with states as merely one level in a complex system of overlapping and often competing agencies of government.'

Evaluation

Hirst and Thompson can be criticized on a number of grounds. First, their analysis of TNCs and MNCs leaves room for alternative interpretations. They themselves point out that 'The fact that only 30 per cent or so of company activity is conducted abroad does not tell us anything about the strategic importance of that 30 per cent to the overall business activity of firms.' Furthermore, the definition of the 'home region' on which the above figures are based is extremely broad. Thus the German 'home region' is taken to include the rest of Europe and the Middle East and Africa, the US home region includes Canada, and the Japanese home region covers the whole of south-east Asia.

Hirst and Thompson perhaps use an over-restrictive definition of TNCs in order to allow them to arrive at the conclusion that there are few genuine TNCs. Furthermore, as Anthony Woodiwiss (1996) points out, Hirst and Thompson are arguing against a rather extreme view of the 'borderless world' (derived from the writings of Ohmae), which is not representative of the more qualified accounts of globalization.

Second, aspects of their argument seem to point in the opposite direction to the conclusions they reach. Their emphasis on inter-national regulation just adds plausibility to the theory of globalization since increased inter-national regulation is only necessary because of globalization.

Third, Woodiwiss argues that they are so keen to find evidence to support their ideas that they tend to ignore potentially contradictory evidence. In particular, they neglect the transnational influences on economies other than those involving corporations (for example, tourism and changes in exchange rates).

Despite these problems, Hirst and Thompson do succeed in raising serious doubts about the more extreme versions of globalization. They show that

home markets remain important to corporations and that most do retain strong attachments to their country of origin. They also show that the continued control over territory and ability to represent populations mean that states continue to have sources of power which are not available to other institutions.

Anthony Giddens – globalization and high modernity

Unlike Hirst and Thompson, Anthony Giddens generally supports the theory of globalization. Indeed, as we will see, he explicitly criticizes Hirst and Thompson. However, Giddens is also critical of the extreme version of the theory advanced by Ohmae, as he steers a path between those who deny globalization has taken place and those who think it has completely transformed the world.

Globalization and time–space distanciation

Anthony Giddens defines globalization as 'the intensification of worldwide social relationships which link distant localities in such a way that local happenings are shaped by events occurring many miles away and vice versa' (Giddens, 1990). This often includes events which take place in other nation-states and which may be outside the control of any state. He sees this process as involving 'time–space distanciation', in which interaction is stretched across space so that people no longer have to be physically present to interact with one another. Technological innovations such as the internet and satellite communications make this possible and reduce the time it takes to communicate with people in other parts of the world. National boundaries become less significant and states less able to control what happens in the world.

Competition and the global economy

Part of this process involves increasing competition between businesses in different societies. Businesses have to compete globally if they are to be successful. They cannot rely upon monopolizing their own domestic market. This is because the opening up of world trade prevents national governments from protecting businesses from foreign competition.

Giddens puts forward some evidence to support his claim that globalization is taking place. He attacks Hirst and Thompson's views by arguing that world trade is more important and more open than ever before. According to Giddens (1999), only 7 per cent of the Gross Domestic Products of the richest nations consisted of exports in 1950. By 1970 it was 12 per cent, and by 1997 it had risen further to 17 per cent. Furthermore, Giddens also points out that a much-expanded role has developed for world financial markets. According to Giddens, 'Over a trillion dollars a day is turned over in currency exchange transactions.' Furthermore, institutional investors who can shift money around the world extremely rapidly have become incredibly powerful. According to his figures, in the USA in 1996 they held assets of $11.1 trillion. Even if Hirst and Thompson are right to point out that much trade is regional, Giddens is convinced that 'there is a "fully global economy" on the level of financial markets'.

Nation-states and power

Where do these economic changes leave the governments of nation-states? Giddens believes that the changes do restrict their power. Nation-states have to compete to attract inward investment from major transnational corporations and they have to keep institutional investors happy. They cannot therefore afford to levy very high taxes in order to pay for expensive welfare programmes. If they tried to tax too highly, businesses would go elsewhere and deprive the government of the business revenue they need to fund their welfare programmes. Giddens says:

> The new period of globalization attacks not only the economic basis of the welfare state but the commitment of its citizenry to the equation of wealth with national wealth. The state is less able to provide effective central control of economic life.
>
> Giddens, 1994, p. 140

However, this does not lead Giddens to agree with writers such as Ohmae that the nation-state has lost its power and become insignificant. Giddens asks, 'Is the nation-state becoming a fiction as Ohmae suggests, and government obsolete? They are not, but their shape is being altered' (Giddens, 1999). It is true that governments lose some economic power, but other powers are retained, even enhanced.

Giddens believes that governments can sometimes use nationalist sentiments to increase the support they gain from their populations. Furthermore, he believes that 'Nations retain, and will for the foreseeable future, considerable governmental, economic and cultural power, over their citizens and in the external arena.' However, he believes that to exercise such powers they increasingly need to collaborate with other states, with transnational actors, and with regions and localities within their own states. Each of these has become more important, and national governments, without being stripped of power, do increasingly share it with other groups and organizations.

Evaluation

Giddens provides perhaps the most balanced analysis of globalization. Although parts of his argument are not particularly well backed up with evidence, he does show an awareness of the continuing power of states and of some of the limitations that have been put on that power.

David Held – democracy and the cosmopolitan order

David Held (1993) is a British sociologist who has given detailed consideration to the implications of globalization for the state. His work adds an extra dimension to the views already considered, because it includes a discussion of how democratic systems can try to come to terms with the limitations on them stemming from globalization. He talks of the 'progressive enmeshment today of states and societies in regional and global networks', and considers how democracy can be developed in a world in which the nation-state does not have all the power.

Examples of globalization

Generally Held makes stronger claims than Giddens does about the impact of globalization.

He argues that, in terms of economics, governments find it hard to control their own economy. For instance, countries cannot determine their own interest rates without reference to those in other countries. If a government wants to cut interest rates to stimulate its economy, it may be unable to do so if other countries keep their rates high, thus attracting investment to them. World financial markets can undermine the value of a country's currency, forcing its government to change policy to take account of the new circumstances. Furthermore, multinational companies are using marketing and production systems that are global in scale. The same products are sold throughout the world and production can be moved from one country to another regardless of the wishes of national governments.

Ecological issues cut across national boundaries as well. The destruction of rain forests, air pollution and nuclear disasters can all lead to environmental damage in other parts of the world. With more people travelling, health issues such as AIDS become difficult to address in one country without taking account of the situation in others.

Like other writers on globalization, Held also points to the increased power of international and transnational organizations. He notes that the 'European Community, the North Atlantic Treaty Organization or the International Monetary Fund diminish the range of decisions open to given national "majorities".' Military issues also take on a global dimension, with the existence of spy satellites for gathering intelligence, and intercontinental missiles. With the ending of the cold war, as a result of the collapse of communism in Russia and Eastern Europe, there are closer contacts and more complex interconnections between groups of nations which were formerly hostile to one another.

Held points out that some countries are in a particularly weak position when trying to maintain their independence and autonomy. Many Third World countries are heavily in debt to the First World and they rely upon them for aid and military protection. They are left 'vulnerable and dependent on economic forces and relations over which they have little, if any, control'.

Overall, then, nations have become less and less isolated and at the same time less able to control their own affairs. This has serious implications for democracy.

Globalization and cosmopolitan democracy

Democracy is based upon the assumption that a group of people can exercise control over their own affairs. As it becomes more difficult to confine issues within national boundaries, it becomes harder to operate democracy along these lines. As well as bringing people together, globalism can create 'fragmentation' and 'disintegrative trends'. Closer global ties bring diverse cultures together and can increase the chances of conflict and war between people of different cultures and national identities. As the old power blocs of the cold war become less dominant, people assert their local and regional, ethnic or nationalist identities, threatening democracy. Globalization can 'weaken old political and economic structures without necessarily leading to the establishment of new systems of regulation'.

Held argues that these problems can only be tackled by producing a new democratic system which enables people in different nations and localities to decide together how they are going to tackle issues which cut across national boundaries.

In fact, since the Second World War it has been recognized that some form of international law and global institutions might be necessary to create order in the world and deal with international issues. In the post-war period the World Bank and the International Monetary Fund were introduced to try to regulate aspects of the world's monetary and economic systems, and the United Nations was established. Although the UN has tried to intervene in issues throughout the world, Held argues:

> The image of international regulation projected by the charter (and related documents) was one of 'states still jealously "sovereign"', but linked together in a 'myriad of relations'; under pressure to resolve disagreements by peaceful means and according to legal criteria.
>
> Held, 1993, pp. 33-4

Because of the emphasis on sovereignty of states, though, the UN has not been able to act effectively in most of the situations it has tried to deal with. Members of the Security Council have been able to veto any policy they disapproved of and, with China, the USA, Russia, the UK and France all as permanent members, there has rarely been agreement. Nevertheless, the UN has, according to Held, been useful. It has:

> provided a vision, in spite of its limitations, of a new world order based upon the meeting of governments and, under appropriate circumstances, of a supranational presence in world affairs championing human rights.
>
> Held, 1993, p. 36

Despite its having had some success, Held does not believe that the UN, or a similar body, can produce democracy in the new, globalized world. Instead, he proposes a cosmopolitan model of democracy in which people can participate in decisions taken at different levels. Some decisions would be taken by new regional parliaments representing areas such as Africa and Latin America. The existing European Parliament could be strengthened. Some transnational issues could be resolved by referendums held in those areas of the world affected by particular issues.

Individuals would be protected in the cosmopolitan model of democracy by the 'entrenchment of a cluster of rights, including civil, political, economic and social rights, in order to provide shape and limits to democratic decision-making'. These rights would be incorporated into the constitutions of nation-states and international bodies. Such rights would be upheld by international courts which would have strong powers to punish governments which refused to conform to them. Ultimately the world would need 'an authoritative assembly of all democratic states and societies – a re-formed UN, or a complement to it – would be an objective'.

Conclusion and evaluation

Held admits that his proposals have many possible pitfalls. People might wish to ask questions about a new democratic international assembly – questions such as 'Would it have any teeth to implement decisions? How would democratic international law be enforced?' and 'Would there be a centralized police and military force?' However, Held believes that most concerns could be 'met and countered' and that the establishment of the sort of international body he proposes is not beyond the bounds of possibility.

Held's views are perhaps somewhat idealistic. While many states are affected by global issues, that does not necessarily mean that they have the same interests in relation to those issues. For example, poor Third World countries have an interest in changing some aspects of the global economy which benefit the rich First World, and which the latter therefore wants to retain. The disagreements among member states of the EU and the inability of the UN to take effective action in places such as Bosnia, Kosova and Chechnya suggest that Held's vision of

international democracy and cooperation will not easily become reality. Nevertheless, he may be right to point out that democracy must tackle the problem of globalization if power is not to become more distant from the citizens of nation-states. Identifying the problem is easier than finding the solution, but it could at least be seen as a step in the right direction.

Michael Mann – the sources of social power

In recent work, Michael Mann (1986, 1993) has started an ambitious project which aims to develop new theories of power and of sociological theory in general. However, far from simply entering current debates about power and sociological theory in an abstract way, he has tied his theory of social life to an account of the development of societies from 10,000 BC to the present day. In doing so, he has returned to the all-embracing questions about societal development which so concerned the 'classical' sociologists, Marx, Weber and Durkheim. Furthermore, Mann has a considerable advantage over these eminent sociologists, since he has access to up-to-date historical and archaeological evidence which was unavailable to them.

Mann's work incorporates elements from the theories of power discussed in the two preceding sections of this chapter:

1 He agrees with writers such as Skocpol that the state can be an independent source of power, arguing that 'political power' is as important as ideological, military and economic power.

2 He follows theories of globalization in claiming that theories of power cannot be confined to examining how power is distributed within national boundaries. Like Held and others, Mann believes that networks of power can stretch across countries and across the globe. He does not, however, see this as a particularly new phenomenon, claiming that networks of power have long extended across sizeable geographical areas.

In some ways Mann's work represents a more fundamental challenge to theories of power than state-centred approaches and the theory of globaliza-tion, for Mann starts his analysis by attacking perhaps the most basic concept of sociology, that of 'society'.

The non-existence of 'society'

Mann says 'if I could, I would abolish the concept of "society" altogether'. Although he continues to use the word 'society' for the sake of convenience, he is anxious to point out that 'societies are not unitary. They are not social systems (closed or open); they are not totalities.' Mann claims that it logically follows

from this standpoint that non-existent societies cannot be divided into parts or sub-systems, as they are by Parsons, nor can they be analysed in terms of 'levels', as in the Marxist division between the infrastructure and the superstructure. Furthermore, he rejects the idea of societal evolution because of his belief that societies are not unitary.

How, then, is Mann able to justify his rejection of so many central concepts in sociological theory? His main argument is very simple: human behaviour is not, and has never been, exclusively related to, or caused by, a particular territory in which an individual lives. In the modern world, for example, the development of the mass media has led to many aspects of culture extending across national boundaries. Nor is the spread of cultural influences particularly new: for centuries, major religions such as Islam and Christianity have had an influence which transcends national boundaries.

Like theorists of globalization, Mann claims that a society such as Britain is not a political unit which can be analysed independently. Britain is a member of the military alliance NATO, and of the economic grouping of nations, the EU. Many companies in Britain are owned by multinational corporations which are based abroad. Through trade, the British economy is affected by other countries, and cultural products from all parts of the world are imported. In order to understand the culture, politics, military activity and economics of Britain, then, it is necessary to consider what happens in other parts of the world. Throughout history, according to Mann, trade, war and conquest have ensured that there has never been an isolated society.

Power networks and types of power

On the basis of such observations, Mann reaches the view that 'societies are constituted of multiple overlapping and intersecting sociospatial networks of power'. In order to understand social life, sociologists need to study the way that humans enter into social relationships which involve the exercise of power.

Since power is so central to his theory, Mann spends some time explaining what he means by the word and distinguishing different forms of power. He sees power as the ability to pursue and attain goals through mastery of the environment. Power, in this sense, can take two separate forms:

1 Distributional power is power over others. It is the ability of individuals to get others to help them pursue their own goals. Distributional power is held by individuals.

2 In contrast, collective power is exercised by social groups. Collective power may be exercised by one social group over another: for example, when one nation is colonized by another. It may also be exercised through mastery over things: for example, the ability to control part of nature through an irrigation scheme.

Having distinguished between different types of power, Mann goes on to explain the two main ways in which it can be exercised:

1 Extensive power is 'the ability to organise large numbers of people over far-flung territories in order to engage in minimally stable cooperation'. An example of extensive power would therefore be the influence over believers exercised by a major religion.

2 Intensive power, on the other hand, is the ability 'to organise tightly and command a high level of mobilization or commitment from the participants'. Thus a religious sect might be seen as having intensive power in comparison to the more extensive power of a church.

In the final part of Mann's analysis of different types of power, he identifies a difference between authoritative and diffused power:

1 Authoritative power is exercised when conscious, deliberate commands are issued, and those to whom they are issued make a conscious decision to follow them. A football player following a referee's instructions to leave the field would be an example of authoritative power.

2 Diffused power spreads in a more spontaneous way. It involves power relationships, but ones which operate without commands being issued. Mann uses the example of market mechanisms: a company can go out of business not because someone commands that it does, but because it is unable to compete with other companies producing the same types of product. Often this type of power produces behaviour that appears as 'natural' or 'moral', or as resulting from 'self-evident common interests'.

By combining the distinctions between intensive and extensive, and authoritative and diffused power, Mann is able to distinguish four principal types of power. Examples of the four types of power are given in Table 9.4.

Table 9.4	Michael Mann – examples of social power	
	Authoritative	Diffused
Intensive	Army command structure	A general strike
Extensive	Militaristic empire	Market exchange

Source: M. Mann (1986) *The Sources of Social Power*, vol. 1, Cambridge University Press, Cambridge, p. 9.

The sources of power

So far, this account of Mann's theory has explained the types of power that he believes exist, but not where that power comes from. Central to his approach is the simple idea that power can have four sources: these can be economic, ideological, political and military.

Mann follows Marx in thinking that economic power is important, but he does not attribute the primary role to it that Marx does, because of the importance of the three other sources. Ideological power involves power over ideas and beliefs; political power concerns the activities of states; and military power the use of physical coercion. In Marxist theory these sources of power are often seen as being united. From a Marxist point of view, the group that has economic power – those who own the means of production – will also have ideological power through their ability to promote false class consciousness. Furthermore, the economically ruling class will exercise control over the state and will therefore have political power; and, through the state, it will also monopolize military power.

However, Mann disagrees with the Marxist view, claiming that each source of power can be independent of the others. Ideological power can be wielded by churches or other religious organizations, which may have little or no economic power. The political power of a state does not ensure that it will have ideological power. In communist Poland, for example, much of the population appeared to attach more importance to the ideas of the Roman Catholic Church and the free trade union Solidarity than to those of the communist state. Even political and military power are not necessarily tied together. In feudal Europe, military power rested mainly in the hands of individual lords and not with the state. In modern societies, in a *coup d'état* the army actually takes power from the political rulers. Thus, in Chile, General Pinochet led a military coup in which power was seized from President Allende's elected government.

Of course, Mann accepts that in a particular society at a particular time, two or more of the four sources of power might be monopolized by a social group, but all power never rests in one set of hands. Since no society is completely independent, networks of power will stretch across national boundaries, thus preventing a single group within a society from having all the power.

An example of Mann's approach

In his explanation of social changes Mann explains how these various sources of power are related to each other. For example, he demonstrates how, shortly after AD 1300, an innovation in military strategy led to a number of important social changes in Europe, and in particular a weakening in the influence of feudalism.

At the battle of Courtrai, Flemish infantrymen were faced by an attack from French mounted knights. At the time, semi-independent groups of armoured mounted knights were militarily dominant and the normal tactic for infantry who were attacked by them was to flee. On this occasion, though, the Flemings were penned against a river and had no alternative but to fight. By adopting a close-knit formation, the pike phalanx of the Flemings was able to unseat many of the knights and secure victory.

As a result, feudal mounted armies lost their dominance, and societies such as the Duchy of Burgundy, which did not adapt to the changed circumstances, declined. Furthermore, the change led to a centralization of state power and a reduction in the autonomy of feudal lords. It became recognized that mixed armies of cavalry, infantry and artillery were the answer to the pike phalanx, and states could more easily provide the resources to maintain this type of army than could individual lords. Thus changes in the nature of military power led to an extension of the political power of the state.

On the surface, it might appear that this significant episode in history is an example of military technology determining the course of social change, but Mann believes that ideological and military factors were also important. He suggests that pike phalanxes could not have succeeded unless the individuals in them were convinced that those on either side of them would stand firm. In societies such as Flanders and Switzerland, such trust was likely to develop because of the way of life of the burghers and free peasants there. Furthermore, the different types of army produced by the Flemings and the Swiss on one side, and feudal societies on the other, were related to their respective abilities to produce an economic surplus to finance their armies. Thus the four sources of social power were all linked: an extension of military power was related to the nature and distribution of ideological and economic power and led to an increase in the political power of the state. In this example, military power was particularly important, but, according to Mann, in other episodes in history, any of the other three sources of power can assume a more central role.

Conclusion

Other theories of power and the state tend to emphasize a particular source of power. Marxism stresses the importance of economic power, pluralism stresses ideological power in democracies, and elite and state-centred theories emphasize political power. Mann's approach argues that any complete theory must embrace all of these, as well as including military power.

Michel Foucault – power/knowledge

The nature of power

The work of Michel Foucault (1926-1984) provides an influential and novel view of power. Like Mann, he saw power as something that is not concentrated in one place or in the hands of particular individuals. However, he goes much further from conventional views of power than Mann does. Foucault's complex (and sometimes obscure and contradictory) writings suggest that power is found in all social relationships and is not just exercised by the state. Nevertheless, much of his work is concerned with the way in which the state develops its ability to classify and exercise power over populations.

To Foucault, power is intimately linked with knowledge: power/knowledge produce one another. The extension of the power of the state therefore involves the development of new types of knowledge which enable it to collect more information about and exercise more control over their populations. This involves the development of discourses: ways of talking about things which have consequences for power. However, Foucault does not just think of power in coercive terms: as well as restricting people, power can enable them to do things. Furthermore, and paradoxically, he only sees power as operating when people have some freedom. Power never allows total control and, indeed, constantly produces resistances and evasions as people try and often succeed in slipping from its grasp.

Foucault's ideas will now be examined in more detail.

Madness and Civilisation

Much of Foucault's early work was taken up with an account of how the state increasingly tried to regulate and control populations. Before the eighteenth century, governments made little attempt to control, regulate or even monitor the behaviour of the mass of the population. Few statistics were produced, and few records kept.

In *Madness and Civilisation* (1967) Foucault describes how such phenomena as unemployment, poverty and madness started to be seen as social problems by states in the eighteenth century. Before that, the mad were largely free from state interference. Although they were sometimes cast out of towns, they were permitted to wander as they wished in rural areas. Alternatively they were put to sea together in 'ships of fools'. However, this system of dealing with the mad was replaced by places of confinement (such as madhouses) in which the mad, the poor and the sick were separated and isolated from the rest of the population.

Foucault argues that this was due to a new concern in European culture with a sense of responsibility for such social problems and a new work ethic. It was felt that something should be done with the mad; and others were punished for the new sin of laziness.

By the start of the nineteenth century, however, the policy of confining these diverse groups together came to be seen as a mistake. For example, although the unemployed were forced to work in the madhouses, this just led to them doing some of the work needed in the local area, thus increasing unemployment and making the problem worse. Consequently, new methods were used to separate the different groups of undesirables.

New scientific disciplines, such as psychiatry, were developed to categorize people (as sane or mad, and as suffering from different illnesses). In this process the discourses of the social sciences came to be involved in power relationships. According to Madan Sarup, by discourse Foucault meant 'practices that systematically form the objects of which they speak' (Sarup, 1988).

From this viewpoint, the practices of psychiatry (and, connected to them, the knowledge contained in theories) created the mentally ill. Psychiatry was a discourse and a tactic used to control particular groups in the population. The technique of classifying people as mentally ill was an important part of the state's gradual development of systems of administration. Administration allowed the monitoring of people and hence offered the potential for controlling their behaviour.

However, classifying and monitoring people did not just involve a straightforward coercive use of power by the state. Rather it created the possibility of localized power/knowledge relationships that took place at an individual level. For example, power/knowledge related to the discourse of psychiatry created the possibility of power being exercised in individual interactions between psychiatrists and their patients. In Foucault's view, though, the power is part of the discourse of psychiatry, and not something which is held by individual psychiatrists.

Discipline and Punish

Many of the themes first explored in *Madness and Civilisation* were explored further in a later book, *Discipline and Punish* (1991, first published 1975). In this book, Foucault traces the changes in the nature and purposes of punishment in the eighteenth century. His book starts with a graphic account of the execution of the French murderer Damiens in Paris in 1757. Damiens was first placed on a scaffold where pieces of flesh were torn from him using red-hot pincers. Lead, oil, resin wax and sulphur were melted together and then poured on to the flesh wound. Each of his four limbs was then attached to a separate horse so that they could pull him apart. However, initially this failed, and a knife had to be used on Damiens to make it easier for the horses to pull his body apart. Still alive, his head and the trunk of his body were tied to a stake and set on fire.

By the late eighteenth century such public punishments were starting to die out. Punishment was increasingly hidden. People were executed behind closed doors using swifter methods (such as the guillotine or hanging), and many people were locked away in prisons. Here they were subjected to a regime involving a strict timetable of work, sleep, education and so on.

Changes in punishment

Foucault argues that these changes involved a fundamental shift in the nature of punishment. In the early eighteenth century, punishment focused on the body, it involved the direct infliction of pain as a way of making the offender suffer for his crimes, and as a way of discouraging others. By the late eighteenth and early nineteenth century, this had changed. It was no longer the body that was the main focus of punishment, but the soul. The punishment consisted of a loss of rights – particularly the right to liberty – rather than the suffering of pain. The certainty of being caught was intended to deter people, rather than the public humiliation of execution or being placed in the stocks.

Furthermore, the intention was to reform the offender rather than simply to make him suffer.

Foucault admits that there was not a clearcut break between these two systems of punishment (executions continued to be used, for example), but he argues that, nevertheless, there was a definite shift from one approach to another.

What was being judged also subtly changed. In the earlier period people were judged for what they had done. By the later period they were judged for what sort of a person they were. The motivation behind the crime began to be taken into account because of what it revealed about the offender. The punishment used varied according to the motivation. Foucault says:

> The question is no longer simply: 'Has the act been established and is it punishable?' But also: 'What is this act, what is this act of violence or this murder? To what level or to what field of reality does it belong? Is it a phantasy, a psychotic reaction, a delusional episode, a perverse action?' It is no longer simply: 'Who committed it?' But: 'How can we assign the causal process that produced it? Where did it originate in the author himself? Instinct, unconscious, environment heredity?'
>
> Foucault, 1991, p. 19

A whole range of experts were involved in answering these questions: experts such as psychologists and psychiatrists, educationalists, and members of the prison service. Control over punishment became fragmented and wrapped up in their specialist knowledge. Foucault says, 'A corpus of knowledge, techniques, "scientific" discourses is formed and becomes entangled with the practice of the power to punish.'

In such extracts, Foucault, then, tries to show that, even as the state developed techniques for controlling populations, it also ceded power to the experts who had the knowledge deemed necessary to exercise power in ways suitable for reforming people.

The exercise of power/knowledge

However, Foucault does not argue that such knowledge/power relationships are entirely '"negative" mechanisms that make it possible to repress, to exclude, to prevent, to eliminate'. Instead, he believes that there are also 'positive' aspects to them. They can be positive in the sense that they make it possible for certain things to be achieved. Foucault gives the example of how punishments can be used to motivate workers to step up their efforts and provide more of the labour power that society might need.

Foucault is also insistent that power is not something simply possessed by individuals. He says, 'power is exercised rather than possessed'. An individual does not simply hold power; they can use

power if they can muster the right 'dispositions, manoeuvres, tactics, techniques' to achieve what they want. Furthermore, power is only exercised by getting people to do something, when they have a choice not to. It is not simply physical coercion, where there are no options open to those over whom power is exercised. In fact (in a later work) Foucault makes it clear that he thinks there are very few circumstances in which people have no choice. In most circumstances somebody would have a choice of resisting by the possibility 'of committing suicide, of jumping out through the window, of killing the other' (Foucault, 1988, quoted in Hindess, 1996).

From Foucault's point of view, then, it is always possible to resist the exercise of power, to refuse to go along with what others are trying to get you to do. When attempts are made to exercise power, the result always has an element of uncertainty. Indeed, he believes that power can sometimes be reversed. At one point in his work he argues that the fact 'that I am older and that at first you were intimidated can, in the course of the conversation, turn about and it is I who can become intimidated before someone, precisely because he is younger' (Foucault, 1988, quoted in Hindess, 1996).

In *Discipline and Punish* Foucault reiterates his belief that power/knowledge are virtually inseparable. He says:

> we should admit that power produces knowledge ... that power and knowledge directly imply one another; that there is no power relation without the correlative constitution of a field of knowledge, nor any knowledge that does not presuppose and constitute at the same time power relations.
>
> Foucault, 1991, p. 27

Partly because power is so wrapped up with knowledge, there is almost always some chance to resist the exercise of power by challenging the knowledge on which it is based. For example, a psychiatric patient could question the accuracy of a psychiatrist's diagnosis.

Because power/knowledge imply one another, power relationships are present in all aspects of society. They 'go right down into the depths of society ... they are not localised in the relations between the state and its citizens or on the frontier between classes' (Foucault, 1991).

Thus Foucault would see most of the views of power discussed in this chapter as inadequate because they are too limited in scope. Marxism is too limited because it only focuses on class relationships of power. Pluralism and elite theory are inadequate because they concentrate on power exercised by the state. None of them look at power in the everyday activities of people and the commonly-used discourses involved in interaction.

Government and discipline

Although Foucault does not believe that power/knowledge is only exercised through the state, that does not mean that he thinks that power/knowledge is absent from the state. Attempts are made by states and other authorities to govern, manipulate and control behaviour. Although never entirely successful, sophisticated techniques can be devised to do this.

In *Discipline and Punish*, for example, Foucault goes into considerable detail about the way in which activities overseen by the state involve power/knowledge. For example, he discusses the panopticon, a prison design proposed by the English philosopher Jeremy Bentham. Although never fully implemented, aspects of it were incorporated into the design of some prisons, as illustrated in Figure 9.1. The key feature of the

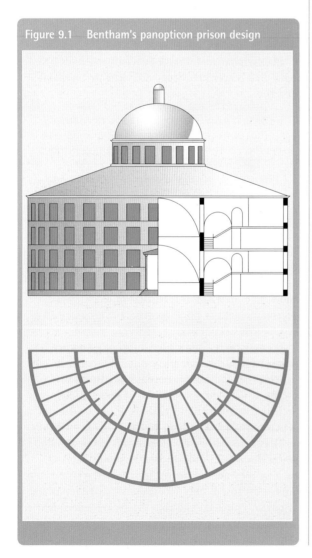

Figure 9.1   Bentham's panopticon prison design

panopticon was a central tower which allowed prison warders to see into every cell and therefore to observe the activities of all the inmates. The use of backlighting would mean that the warders would be able to see into cells without the inmates knowing whether they were being observed at any particular time. Inmates would therefore have to restrain their activities and act in a disciplined manner all the time, just in case they were being watched.

Foucault sees discipline as an important feature of modern societies. Techniques of surveillance are used to check on people's behaviour in places such as schools, hospitals and elsewhere. However, the possibility of being watched also encourages self-discipline: people become accustomed to regulating and controlling their own actions, whether or not somebody is checking up on them.

Discipline gives people the ability to regulate and control their own behaviour. According to Foucault, it is based upon the idea that humans have a soul that can be manipulated. This is far more effective than trying to punish individual bodies by inflicting extreme pain, in the way described earlier in the execution of Damiens. Instead of punishing bodies, you try to produce docile bodies – bodies which pose no threat to order because they are self-disciplined.

Discipline is an important part of governing, but it is not confined to the activities of the government. It is also present in the activities of organizations (from nineteenth-century factories to contemporary corporations). Furthermore, it is never entirely successful. As Barry Hindess describes it, 'The suggestion is, then, that we live in a world of disciplinary projects, and all of which suffer from more or less successful attempts at resistance and evasion. The result is a disciplinary, but hardly disciplined society' (Hindess, 1996).

In Foucault's view, government extends far beyond the activities of the state and, particularly, the passing and enforcement of laws. Attempts at government through discipline are almost ubiquitous features of modern societies, but such attempts are never completed and never entirely successful. The unruly pupil, the worker who sabotages machinery, and the psychiatric patient who denies their diagnosis are as much a feature of modern society as the disciplined citizen with a docile body.

Evaluation

Foucault's work provides a number of important insights into the nature of power. For example, he succeeded in showing that knowledge is closely connected to power, he demonstrates that power can be found in many social relationships other than those involving the state, and he makes the important observation that power is unlikely to be absolute. He is aware that people often resist or evade attempts to exercise power.

In many ways, then, his work is subtler than that of other writers, such as some Marxists (who tend to see power as concentrated in the hands of an economic ruling class), elite theorists (who see it as concentrated in the hands of those in key positions), and pluralists (who focus on the decisions of the state to the exclusion of other ways of exercising power).

However, it can be argued that Foucault underestimates the importance of the sources of power discussed in some of these theories. For example, he neglects the power than can be exercised through the control of economic resources, such as the power to shut down a plant by shifting production elsewhere. He neglects the power that can be exercised through the use of military force. On a smaller scale, he might exaggerate the power of a mental patient to resist or evade their diagnosis; and, of course, the power of prisoners is usually strictly limited and does not include the power to change their sentence. Foucault tends to focus too much on the power associated with knowledge rather than other types and sources of power.

Foucault's work on power is in some ways contradictory. On the one hand, it documents the increased ability of governments and others to watch, record, manipulate or even control the activities of populations. On the other hand, it insists that power is only exercised when people have some freedom, and it claims that resistance is always possible. Thus his work seems to point in opposite directions. It also involves a strange definition of power which directly contradicts more conventional definitions. In most views of power (such as Weber's, discussed on pp. 588–9), power is exercised precisely when people do not have freedom to act as they choose rather than when they do.

Despite these problems, Foucault certainly succeeded in developing ideas that have proved to be provocative and have stimulated both research and theorizing. He has also provided an interesting analysis of how modern societies develop techniques of social control.

Postmodernism, politics and new social movements

There are a variety of postmodern approaches to politics. Most, like Foucault, see politics as involving a wider range of activities than those confined to the state and political parties. They all tend to identify a difference between modern politics and postmodern politics. They vary in the sort of changes they associate with postmodern politics and the significance they attach to those changes.

We will start by examining some of the more extravagant claims made by postmodernists, and then discuss postmodern theories that make more modest claims about changes in the nature of power and politics. The most extreme view of all is perhaps that of Jean Baudrillard. He goes way beyond Foucault's claim that power is dispersed, arguing that power has disappeared and politics is no longer real.

Jean Baudrillard – the end of politics

Perhaps the most extreme postmodern view of power and politics is advanced by Jean Baudrillard (1983). Baudrillard's basic position is that signs (such as words and visual images) no longer reflect or represent reality. Instead, signs have become totally detached from reality and indeed disguise the fact that reality no longer exists. In this process, politics becomes simply about the manipulation and exchange of signs to produce the appearance of a non-existent reality. We have entered an era of simulacra: signs which mask the fact that reality no longer exists.

Examples of the end of politics

Baudrillard gives a number of examples of this process:

1 Party politics in Western democracies gives the impression of offering a real choice between different parties with differing policies. In reality this is an illusion. The differences between parties (such as the Republicans and Democrats in the USA) are minuscule, and the same homogeneous political elite occupy state positions whoever wins the election. Having elections maintains the impression that political conflict continues to exist.

2 To Baudrillard, wars have also lost their reality: they have become simulacra. That is not to say that they do not have real effects. Baudrillard concedes that 'the flesh suffers just the same, and the dead ex-combatants count as much there as in other wars'. However, wars do not exist in the sense that they involve 'the adversity of adversaries, the reality of antagonistic causes, the ideological seriousness of war – also the reality of defeat or victory'.

Baudrillard gives the example of the bombing of Hanoi by the USA during the Vietnam war. He thinks that this bombing had no military purpose, since America had already decided to withdraw its forces, but it did allow the Vietnamese to pretend to be reaching a compromise and the Americans to feel less bad about leaving. The bombing was a simulacrum because it hid the reality that nothing was at stake – the bombing could make no difference to the outcome.

3 Baudrillard seems to believe that contemporary politicians have no real power. He describes Presidents Johnson, Nixon, Ford and Reagan as puppet presidents who lacked the power to change the world. Their main purpose was to maintain the illusion that politics continued as normal. To Baudrillard they were simply the 'mannequins of power'.

4 Baudrillard believes that even the most potentially devastating political conflict, the cold war, hid the absence of power. In the cold war the possession of vast arsenals of nuclear weapons by the main (supposed) protagonists (the USA and the USSR) was irrelevant. The destructiveness of the weapons cancelled each other out and made any actual war impossible. The situation therefore 'excludes the real atomic clash – excludes it beforehand like the eventuality of the real in the system of signs'.

Baudrillard therefore believes that real power and actual politics have disappeared into a system of signs which is based around simulacra – signs which have no relationship to an actual reality. He talks of 'the impossibility of a determinant position of power', and describes 'power itself eventually breaking apart … and becoming a simulation of power'.

Evaluation

Baudrillard's claims are so extravagant that they are hard to justify. He provides no definition of power, so it is difficult to evaluate his claim that it has disappeared. Nevertheless, Baudrillard admits that people are killed in real wars, and he does not justify his claim that there are no real victors and vanquished in wars. For example, the USA did lose the Vietnam war, and a regime to which it was hostile did take control of the government. By any reasonable definition of power and politics, this was a political defeat for the USA and a victory for their Vietnamese enemies, since the Vietnamese regime did gain power against the wishes of the US government.

There are many similar examples which seem to contradict Baudrillard's arguments.

Baudrillard may have more of a point in arguing that it often makes little difference which political party wins elections in countries such as the USA. However, he still fails to show that there are no significant differences between the policies of different parties. Baudrillard tends to make sweeping generalizations backed up by examples whose significance is debatable. He does not systematically examine the evidence which might support or refute his case. For this reason, his claims, while interesting, are open to serious doubt. Even other postmodernists do not go as far as arguing that power has disappeared and that politics is just an illusion. They do, however, claim to have identified some important changes in power and politics in a postmodern era. (For further evaluation of Baudrillard, see Chapter 15.)

Jean-François Lyotard – the decline of metanarratives

Politics and language-games

As discussed elsewhere (see Chapter 15 for a detailed account), Jean-François Lyotard associates postmodernism with a decline of metanarratives. By this he means that people no longer place their faith in big, all-embracing stories about how the world works or about society. In politics they lose their belief in political ideologies such as Marxism and fascism. However, it is not just particular sets of political beliefs that lose people's support; rather, people become sceptical that any set of beliefs can provide an effective understanding and resolution of the problems of humanity. People no longer think that a perfect society is attainable.

The implication of this view is that politics will become less about arguments over major ideologies and will become more localized and limited in scope. Lyotard sees knowledge in general as the main source of power in postmodern societies. As people lose their faith that any one metanarrative can provide comprehensive knowledge, knowledge breaks down into a series of different, specialist language-games. Politics therefore becomes increasingly linked to specialist language-games and less concentrated in the hands of states.

Furthermore, knowledge itself becomes evaluated more according to whether it is useful, rather than whether it is true. That is, if knowledge can be used to achieve certain specific aims, then it is accepted, whether or not it can be shown to be true in terms of scientific theories. Lyotard says that knowledge 'will continue to be, a major, perhaps the major – stake in the competition for power' (Lyotard, 1984).

Useful knowledge is not confined to states, and is increasingly possessed by multinational corporations and by other organizations and individuals that are part of civil society. Lyotard is aware that power can be exercised through coercion (which could be exercised, for example, by state-controlled military forces), but he sees such power as becoming much less important than that exercised by those who possess the most useful knowledge.

Evaluation

Lyotard's work opens up a number of ideas on power and politics, which have been developed and reiterated by later postmodernists. These include the equation of power with knowledge; the possibility that the state loses much of its power; the idea that politics becomes fragmented; and the idea that people become concerned with single issues rather than grand ideologies.

While there may be some truth in all of these ideas, they are also open to criticism. For example, this sort of approach tends to ignore military power; it may underestimate the power of nation-states (see pp. 621–4); and it ignores the continuing importance of some 'metanarratives'. For example, nationalist metanarratives remain a powerful force in areas such as Serbia; and religious metanarratives remain powerful in Islamic Iran.

Some critics have argued that most Western societies are dominated by the idea of free-market capitalism, which is no less of a metanarrative than the ideology of communism. Such examples suggest that centralized state power and big issues remain important in contemporary politics. (For further evaluation of Lyotard, see Chapter 15.)

Nancy Fraser – postmodern politics and the public sphere

The public sphere

Nancy Fraser argues that there has been a shift from predominantly modern to predominantly postmodern politics in contemporary societies. She argues that such a shift involves a change in the public sphere. She defines the public sphere as those aspects of social life other than the economy and the activities of the state. She describes it as 'the space in which citizens deliberate about their common affairs' and as 'a site where social meanings are generated, circulated, contested and reconstructed' (Fraser, 1995). Fraser believes that the public sphere has undergone important changes which involve a transition in the nature of politics.

The public sphere in modern societies

According to Fraser, in modern societies three main assumptions were made about the public sphere:

1 It was assumed that democratic debate was possible between people even if they had different statuses. Thus a poor person with a low-status job had as much chance to participate in debate in the public sphere as someone who was rich, successful and in a high-status job.

2 It was thought preferable to try to integrate everyone into one arena in which the concerns, the

preferences and the beliefs of the public were discussed. It was thought undesirable for groups to discuss issues separately from one another. It was believed that 'a single, comprehensive public sphere is always preferable to a nexus of multiple publics'.

3 In the modern conception of the public sphere it was believed that people should discuss what was in the public interest, what was good for everyone, rather than arguing for their own private interests and what was good for them.

Fraser questions all of these modern assumptions about the public sphere:

1 In practice, inequalities between members of the public restricted the chances disadvantaged groups had to make their voices heard and their opinions count. What Fraser calls 'protocols of style and decorum'- ways of talking and acting – served to mark out higher-status individuals from lower-status ones. Lacking the appropriate protocols, women and those from ethnic minorities and lower classes found it difficult to get their views listened to and respected.

2 In a situation where substantial inequalities exist, Fraser denies that it is desirable to have public debate confined to a single, overarching public sphere. She believes it is far better to have multiple public spheres in which members of different social groups or those with specialist interests discuss issues with one another. In these groups people can develop alternative competing views to those of the political mainstream, and then compete to get their views on to the political agenda. Fraser says:

members of subordinated social groups – women, workers, people of color, and gays and lesbians – have repeatedly found it advantageous to constitute alternative publics. I have called these "subaltern counterpublics" in order to signal that they are parallel discursive arenas where members of subordinated groups invent and circulate counter discourses.

Fraser, 1995, p. 291

Eventually groups such as feminists may succeed in getting their ideas taken seriously and effecting some changes in society.

3 Fraser also rejects the idea that people should not push their private interests in the public sphere. She argues that what starts out as being a private interest can come to be accepted as an issue of public concern. For example, when feminists started raising the issue of sexual harassment their ideas were not taken seriously. Most people considered the behaviour they complained of to be no more than 'innocent flirting'; others saw it as a purely personal matter.

Fraser argues that the personal and the private can be political, and you cannot presume in advance that certain things should be off limits for public debate. Furthermore, labelling issues like sexual harassment as private simply serves to perpetuate and reinforce the power of privileged groups – in this case, men. The divide between the public and the private is an artificial division of modern societies and it should not be allowed to shape public, political debate. People themselves should be the only arbitrators of what should be discussed in the public sphere and it should not be limited by any conception of what is in the public interest.

Postmodernism and the public sphere

Fraser therefore believes that modern assumptions about the public sphere need to be replaced by postmodern ones. These should involve:

1 The elimination of the inequalities between social groups which prevent people from having equal power in public, political debate.

2 The acceptance and encouragement of different groups having their own debates.

3 The rejection of the idea that supposedly 'private' issues should be off limits for public debate.

Fraser therefore advocates a pluralistic politics in which the widest possible participation takes place. She sees politics as operating outside the formal mechanisms of party politics and parliamentary government, and sees it as involving a wide variety of groups talking, discussing and arguing. She sees issues such as gender, ethnicity and sexuality as very important in postmodern politics. Class also remains important, but it is no longer the dominant issue it once was. To Fraser, inequalities stemming from class, race, gender and sexuality cut across each other and influence debates in the public sphere. The interplay of different types of inequality is character-istic of postmodern politics. She illustrates these points with reference to the discussion of the issue of Clarence Thomas in US politics (this case is also referred to in Chapter 4, see p. 271).

Clarence Thomas and postmodern politics

Clarence Thomas is a US judge who was nominated in 1991 to be appointed to the Supreme Court of the USA. Clarence Thomas is black and has generally conservative views. His nomination was generally supported by right-wing politicians. However, after being nominated, a black woman, Anita Hill, accused him of sexually harassing her some years earlier when she was working with him in a junior position.

The argument over whether Thomas should be confirmed in his appointment was played out in the public sphere, even though it involved behaviour – sexual harassment – which some saw as a private issue. It involved issues of race, gender and class

differences. The struggle over the appointment involved trying to present the case as a particular sort of issue (a class, gender or race issue). It showed the importance of language in postmodern politics because the argument rested upon the words used to define the issue.

The Senate Judiciary Committee, which reviewed the proposed appointment, initially decided not to publicize the accusations made by Hill. However, pressure from feminist groups, who accused the committee of sexism, brought the issues into the open for public debate. The feminists succeeded, therefore, in getting the question of sexual harassment accepted as being of legitimate public concern. However, the White House, who proposed Thomas in the first place, managed to argue that other aspects of Judge Thomas's private life (including a claim that he had admitted watching pornographic movies when he was a law student) were not relevant to public debate.

Anita Hill was not so successful in ruling her private life out of bounds for public scrutiny. Fraser says, 'Soon the country was awash in speculation concerning the character, motives, and psychology of Anita Hill.' She was accused by different people of being 'a lesbian, a heterosexual erotomaniac, a delusional schizophrenic, a fantasist, a vengeful spurned woman, a perjurer, and a malleable tool of liberal interest groups'.

Anita Hill had some success in presenting herself as a woman who was the victim of discrimination and inappropriate behaviour by a man. Although they were both black, Judge Thomas had more success in using the issue of race to defend himself. Fraser describes how he claimed that the hearings were 'a "high-tech lynching" designed to stop "an uppity Black who deigned to think for himself". He spoke about his vulnerability to charges that played into racial stereotypes of black men as having large penises and unusual sexual prowess.' In doing so, he tried (largely successfully) to make Anita Hill appear to be behaving like a white racist. Fraser says, 'the result was it became difficult to see Anita Hill as a black woman'. The position of black *women* became marginalized. Thomas succeeded in claiming some of the protections of privacy that had historically been given to white men. Hill was not able to get the same protections. This was not, perhaps, too surprising given that, historically, 'black women have been highly vulnerable to sexual harassment at the hands of masters, overseers, bosses and supervisors'.

Class issues were also involved in the case. As Hill's superior when he was alleged to have harassed her, it could be argued that Thomas was trying to exploit his superior class position to obtain sexual favours. However, supporters of Thomas in the media portrayed the issue quite differently. They depicted Anita Hill as a professional, intellectual yuppie, while Judge Thomas was depicted as an ordinary bloke with down-to-earth and commonsense views. This depiction ignored the fact that Hill was born into rural poverty.

In the end, Thomas was confirmed as a Supreme Court judge.

Conclusion

Fraser claims that this whole episode neatly illustrates the nature of postmodern politics. It shows how arguments over how issues are defined are crucial. It shows how arguments over what should be allowed into the public sphere and what should be kept private are of key importance. It demonstrates how inequalities between a range of social groups continue to shape postmodern politics in debates in the public sphere. It shows how debates in the public sphere influence the activities of the state. Finally it shows how, in the public sphere, a wide variety of different voices can be heard.

The Thomas/Hill case led to:

> the fracturing of the myth of homogenous 'communities'. The 'black community', for example, is now fractured into black feminists versus black conservatives versus black liberals versus various other strands of opinion that are less easy to fix with ideological labels. The same thing holds true for the 'women's community'. This struggle showed

> *that women don't necessarily side with women just because they are women.*
> Fraser, 1995, p. 307

Postmodern politics is more complicated than modern politics ever was.

Evaluation

Fraser makes some useful observations about contemporary politics. Certainly she seems on strong ground in arguing that issues relating to what should be private and what can be public are important, and in claiming that gender, ethnicity and sexuality are important political issues as well as class. However, she may exaggerate the difference between modern and postmodern politics.

Although they might have been less prominent in the past, issues such as gender and ethnicity have not been absent from politics in previous eras. (Examples include arguments over the introduction of voting rights for women and campaigns to abolish slavery.) Furthermore, there has always been a plurality of groups (such as pressure groups) trying to get their particular issues to the top of the political agenda. If there has been a move towards the sort of postmodern politics described by Fraser, then it may be a matter of degree rather than a clearcut break with a very different system of modern politics.

New social movements and the new politics

Postmodern theories of power and politics, such as that of Fraser, stress the fragmentation and widening of political debate, and relate it to a decline in the importance of conventional party politics. These themes can all be linked to the emergence and development of what have come to be known as new social movements, which are seen by some sociologists as a key aspect of changes in the nature of politics in contemporary capitalist societies. The main characteristics of new social movements will be outlined first, before discussing a range of views on the significance of these movements.

Simon Hallsworth – 'Understanding new social movements'

Simon Hallsworth provides a useful introduction to the main characteristics of new social movements.

Defining new social movements

According to Hallsworth, the term 'new social movements' is generally applied to 'movements such

as feminism, environmentalism, the anti-racist, anti-nuclear and civil rights movements which emerged in liberal democratic societies in the 1960s and 1970s' (Hallsworth, 1994). They are movements which are 'held to pose new challenges to the established, cultural, economic and political orders of advanced ... capitalist societies'. The term is not usually applied to movements supporting traditional values (such as the anti-abortion movement), to long-established social movements (such as trade unions), or to conventional political parties. It is sometimes used broadly to incorporate religious movements like the Moonies, the Human Potential Movement and some ostensibly non-political groups such as New Age travellers.

New social movements and issues

New social movements tend to have an issue basis. They are focused on particular social issues. These broadly divide into two types of issues:

1 The first type are concerned with issues to do with 'the defence of a natural and social environment perceived to be under threat'. In this category are

animal rights groups (such as the Animal Liberation Front), anti-nuclear groups (such as the Campaign for Nuclear Disarmament) and environmental groups (such as Greenpeace, and Friends of the Earth). They tend to be opposed to 'a perceived tendency inherent in the logic of the modern industrial order to plunder and annihilate the natural world'. The more radical ones believe that their campaigns can show the way towards a quite different sort of society, in which people live in more harmonious ways with animals, the natural environment and each other. Others have more modest aims, such as encouraging recycling to limit damage to the environment.

2   The second type have a 'commitment to furthering the provision of rights to historically marginalised constituencies in societies such as women, ethnic minority groups and gay people'. Feminist, anti-racist and gay rights groups (such as OutRage!) come into this category, as do groups campaigning for the rights of the disabled.

The novel features of new social movements

New social movements represent a departure from conventional party and pressure-group politics in a number of ways:

1   Such groups have tried to extend the definition of what is considered political to include areas such as individual prejudice, housework and domestic violence.

2   They have generally rejected the development of bureaucratic organizations in favour of more informal structures. Hallsworth says, 'they are usually characterised by low levels of bureaucracy, decision-making premised upon the idea of full participation, the appointment of few (if any) full-time officials, and a blurring of the social distance between officials and other members'. They are not content to delegate to, or be represented by, elites. Instead they seek a participatory democracy.

3   New social movements tend to be diverse and fragmented, with many organizations and informal groups concerned with the same issues. There is no central leadership to coordinate the activities of the different groups. Feminism provides a good example of this (see pp. 136–9 for a discussion of different types of feminism).

4   Unlike political parties, they do not seek power for themselves. Unlike traditional pressure groups (like unions and employers' organizations), they do not use threats to withdraw resources (such as labour power or capital) to achieve their objectives. Instead they use a wide range of tactics, from illegal direct action (sometimes including bombs) to civil disobedience. They also use a variety of means, such as publishing books and appearing on television, to win people over to their causes.

5   New social movements tend to pursue very different values to conventional politicians. Generally, economic issues related to improving people's material living standards are not given much prominence. They are mainly concerned with what Hallsworth and others call 'post materialist values'. These are more to do with the quality of life than with material comfort. They are the product of societies in which it is assumed that people's basic material needs (such as food and shelter) can be easily met.

6   According to Hallsworth, members of new social movements tend to have certain social characteristics which distinguish them from members of more conventional political organizations. Most members tend to be young (particularly between 16 and 30). They also tend to be from neither traditional working-class nor upper-class backgrounds. Instead they are mainly from a new middle class, 'who tend either to work principally in the public/service sector of the economy (such as teachers, social workers, nurses etc.) or who are born to parents who work in the public sector'. Those who are outside conventional employment, particularly students and the unemployed, are also over-represented in these movements.

Conclusion

Hallsworth concludes that new social movements:

> may be conceived as the heralds of distinctly new forms of politics in western liberal democratic societies. Considered in this way their uniqueness is apparent in the novelty of the issues they have sought to contest; in the post-material values they have sought to advocate; in their distinctive organisational form and structure; in the form of political activity with which they are associated; as well as by the distinctive profile of their membership.
>
> Hallsworth, 1994, p. 10

However, different sociologists have disputed both how significant these movements are and what their significance is. Some of these disagreements will now be examined.

Stephen Crook, John Pakulski and Malcolm Waters – social movements and postmodernization

Crook, Pakulski and Waters associate the development of social movements with a process they define as postmodernization. This involves a clear shift from the politics of modern societies to a new politics of postmodernizing societies. Although postmodernization is an ongoing process and may not yet be complete, they do believe that 'New politics marks both a substantive and permanent change in the political complexion of advanced societies' (Crook, Pakulski and Waters, 1992).

Old politics in modern societies

According to these writers, politics in modern societies had a number of key features:

1 It was dominated by political parties drawing their support from particular classes.

2 Politics was largely concerned with the sectional interests of these classes.

3 Politics was dominated by the activities of elites who were supposed to represent the interests of particular socio-economic groups.

4 The state was the key focus of political activity and the exercise of power. In Europe the bureaucratic-corporatist state was developed. Corporatism involved allowing the representatives of the two sides of industry (capital and labour, or employers and workers) access to state decision-making through their organizations. In Britain, for example, these were principally the CBI (Confederation of British Industry) and the TUC (Trades Union Congress). Negotiations between these groups were used to reach compromise solutions and blunt the impact of class conflict.

5 In the old politics, political activity was seen as belonging to a separate, specialized sphere of social life, which was not the concern of ordinary people in their everyday activities.

New politics in postmodernizing societies

However, according to Crook et al., old politics of this sort has largely given way to a new politics which is very different.

New politics has the following characteristics:

1 The class basis of support for political parties declines. Left-wing parties can no longer rely upon working-class support, and right-wing parties can no longer rely on members of the middle and upper classes voting for them. The electorate becomes more volatile and identifies less with a particular class.

2 Politics becomes less concerned with sectional interests and more concerned with moral issues that affect everyone. For example, a concern with animal rights, world peace or ecology is not confined to particular classes but is based upon a universal appeal to moral principles. Furthermore, people's political views become associated with their choice of lifestyle rather than with class membership. Thus ecological movements will be supported by those who choose to live green lifestyles (for example, by recycling their products or cycling rather than using cars) rather than by people from any particular class.

3 The new politics moves away from people relying upon elites to represent them. In the new politics, social movements encourage everyone to become involved in campaigns over certain issues. The members of new social movements are often suspicious of leaders and want to retain democratic control over their own organizations.

4 The new politics is not focused on the activities of the state, nor is it based upon the incorporation of sectional interest groups into state decision making. Unions and employers' organizations lose some of their influence on government, and the focus of politics moves from the state to civil society.

5 This change is so great that the new politics 'spills over and fuses with the socio-cultural arena ... protests combine with leisure activities and merge into a total counter-cultural *Gestalt*'. Political views do not just reflect your lifestyle; choosing to live in a particular way is a political statement and a form of political activity.

Postmodernization and the shift to new politics

What then has caused the shift to the new politics?

Perhaps the most important factor is what Crook et al. call class decomposition. Members of social classes become less similar to one another. There is progressive social differentiation: that is, even people from the same backgrounds become increasingly dissimilar to one another. Members of the bourgeoisie become divided between owners and managers, the working class becomes divided according to the region they live in, their level of skill, and 'a growing diversity of lifestyles and consumption patterns'. The middle class also becomes increasingly heterogeneous, with divisions between professional, administrative and technical workers and between state employees and those working in private industry.

New social movements do tend to attract particular groups in the population, such as the young, the geographically mobile, the well-educated and those in creative and welfare professions. However, according to Crook et al., this represents 'socio-cultural rather than socio-economic' divisions. It is related to lifestyle and consumption patterns rather than class divisions. (For more details of Pakulski's views on class, see pp. 119–22.)

Another important cause of the shift to the new politics is the increasing importance of the mass media in postmodernizing societies. As the media come to penetrate all areas of social life, politics becomes increasingly about the manipulation of words and symbols in the mass media. In this situation, political issues are:

> *always contextualized, and linked with the global issues and general values, often in the form of such doom scenarios as nuclear holocaust and greenhouse disaster. This dramatizes them, adds a sense of urgency, and generates mass anxiety which proves to be an exceptionally potent propellant for action.*
>
> Crook, Pakulski and Waters, 1992, p. 156

The media therefore contribute to people taking a more global outlook, which makes it less likely that they will confine their political concerns to narrow sectional interests.

Conclusion

Crook *et al.* conclude that postmodernization has led to a permanent shift in politics, resulting in 'the increased diversity of political processes – more open organizational structures, more diverse elites, more fluid and fragmented alliances and loyalties, and more complex networks of communication'. They go on to argue that 'Even if the inevitable normalization strips the new politics of some of its formal idiosyncrasies, the diversity that constitutes a major departure from the class-structured partisan politics of the past will persist.'

Evaluation

Crook *et al.* identify some significant trends in contemporary politics, but they may exaggerate them. Some writers argue that there has been little if any decomposition of classes (see pp. 122–3). Others have questioned the view that the class basis of voting has significantly declined (see pp. 659–62). Trade unions and employers may still have an important role in contemporary politics and, from a Marxist point of view, writers such as Crook *et al.* ignore the continuing powerful influence of the capitalist economy on politics (see pp. 609–19). Perhaps a more balanced view of new social movements and new politics is taken by the next writer to be considered, Anthony Giddens.

Anthony Giddens – social movements and high modernity

Like Crook *et al.*, Anthony Giddens (1990) believes that important changes have been taking place in politics in contemporary societies. Unlike Crook *et al.*, Giddens believes that these changes are part of developments in modernity rather than part of a transition to postmodernity. As modernity has developed, and moved into a phase which he calls high modernity or radicalized modernity, changes have taken place; these have been changes in emphasis rather than complete transformations.

Giddens characterizes modernity as having four institutional dimensions, illustrated in Figure 9.2:

1 Capitalism is 'a system of commodity production centred upon the relation between private ownership of capital and propertyless wage labour'. The analysis of capitalism has been the focus of much of the sociology developed by Marxists.

2 Industrialism is 'the use of inanimate sources of material power in the production of material goods, coupled to the central role of machinery in the production process'.

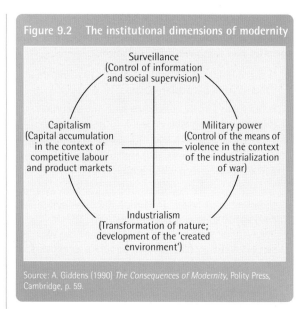

Figure 9.2   The institutional dimensions of modernity

Surveillance
(Control of information
and social supervision)

Capitalism
(Capital accumulation
in the context of
competitive labour
and product markets

Military power
(Control of the means of
violence in the context
of the industrialization
of war)

Industrialism
(Transformation of nature;
development of the 'created
environment')

Source: A. Giddens (1990) *The Consequences of Modernity*, Polity Press, Cambridge, p. 59.

3 Surveillance 'refers to the supervision of the activities of subject populations in the political sphere'. Following Foucault (see pp. 635–9), this may take place in workplaces, prisons, schools and similar institutions. It is largely the concern of nation-states and, with the advent of modern societies, the ability of states to monitor their populations greatly increases.

4 Military power concerns 'control of the means of violence'. This again is largely the prerogative of the nation-state, and the development of military technology leads to the industrialization of war and increases the ability of the nation-state to use violence.

According to Giddens, social movements develop which correspond to these four institutional dimensions. These are illustrated in Figure 9.3.

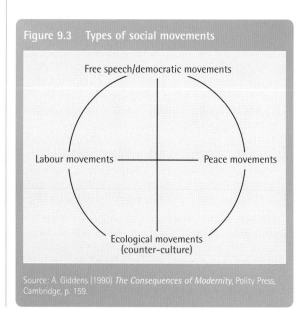

Figure 9.3   Types of social movements

Free speech/democratic movements

Labour movements

Peace movements

Ecological movements
(counter-culture)

Source: A. Giddens (1990) *The Consequences of Modernity*, Polity Press, Cambridge, p. 159.

Social movements concerned with each of the four dimensions have existed throughout the modern period. However, in high, or radicalized, modernity the emphasis in political activity shifts away from labour movements, which were most prominent in the early period of modernity:

1 Labour movements correspond to the institution of capitalism. They are specifically concerned with 'attempts to achieve defensive control of the workplace through unionism and to influence or seize state power through socialist political organisation'.

2 Free speech/democratic movements correspond to the institutional dimension of surveillance. Like labour movements, they have a long history within modernity. In earlier periods they were often closely linked to labour movements. At the same time as trying to gain economic improvements for their members, they often also tried to win them greater rights to democratic participation. In recent times, free speech/democratic movements have tended to become separated from labour movements and have campaigned in their own right. A British example is Charter 88, which campaigns for, amongst other things, the introduction of a Bill of Rights for British citizens.

The other two types of movement – ecological and peace movements – Giddens describes as 'newer in the sense that they have come to increasing prominence in relatively recent years'. However, he does not believe that they are completely new; both have a history dating back to much earlier in the modern period.

3 Peace movements are concerned with the means of violence. Pacifist movements go back to earlier wars, such as the First World War, when the industrialization of war meant that war was becoming increasingly destructive. However, peace movements have become more prominent because of the 'growth in high-consequence risks associated with the outbreak of war, with nuclear weaponry forming the core component in contemporary times'.

4 Ecological movements correspond to the institutional realm of industrialism. The 'created environment' is therefore their area of concern. Like peace movements, they are not completely new. In the nineteenth century, ecological movements were linked with romanticism and were mainly intended to 'counter the impact of modern industry on traditional modes of production and upon the landscape'. In the late twentieth century they assumed greater prominence, partly because of the increased risks associated with possible global ecological catastrophes (such as global warming, and the depletion of the ozone layer).

Conclusion

Giddens therefore sees globalization (see pp. 630–1) and increases in risk as major factors leading to the increasing prominence of social movements concerned with peace and ecology. However, he stresses that such movements are not entirely new, and nor have they replaced other actors as a source of power or the location of political activity.

To Giddens, party politics, the nation-state, and the economic power of business remain crucially important in high-modern societies. Discussing how power can be exercised to improve modern societies, he says:

> *Peace movements, for example, might be important in consciousness raising and in achieving tactical goals in respect of military threats. Other influences, however, including the force of public opinion, the policies of business corporations and national governments, and the activities of international organisations, are fundamental to the achieving of basic reforms.*
>
> Giddens, 1990, p. 162

Social movements might be increasingly important, but they have not eclipsed or replaced other political arenas.

Evaluation

Giddens's views are based upon a rather abstract model of modernity and its institutional dimensions, which is not really supported by detailed empirical evidence. Because his discussion is pitched at a high level of generality, he goes into little detail about such issues as the background and objectives of those who join social movements, and the way they are organized.

Nevertheless, his work is useful because it shows an awareness of continuities in the development of politics and social movements, which are neglected by some other writers – writers who may exaggerate the degree to which such movements are genuinely novel.

Voting behaviour

If Giddens's analysis is correct, then the state remains an important source of power, and party politics remains at least as important as the campaigns of social movements. In parliamentary democracies governments are formed through competition between political parties in elections. This process is the subject of this section, which focuses on patterns of voting in Britain.

Butler and Stokes – partisan alignment

Until the 1970s, patterns of voting in post-war Britain were predictable. Most psephologists (those who study voting behaviour) agreed on the basic characteristics of British voting and on the explanation of these characteristics. David Butler and Donald Stokes (1974) were perhaps the most influential psephologists during the 1960s and early 1970s and their views became widely accepted.

There were two main features of the British political system at this time: partisan alignment and a two-party system. These were closely related to each other and, together, seemed to make it relatively easy to explain British voting.

Class and partisan alignment

The theory of partisan alignment (strong adherence to a particular party) explained voting in the following way:

1 It suggested that class, as measured by a person's occupation, was the most important influence on voting.

2 It claimed that most voters had a strongly partisan self-image: they thought of themselves as 'Labour' or 'Conservative'.

3 This sense of identity led to voters consistently casting their votes for the party with which they identified. Few people changed their votes from election to election, there was little electoral volatility, and there were few floating voters who were prepared to consider changing their allegiance.

Using the evidence from Butler and Stokes's research into the 1964 election, Ivor Crewe found that 62 per cent of non-manual workers voted Conservative, and 64 per cent of manual workers voted Labour (Sarlvick and Crewe, 1983).

Butler and Stokes themselves produced a range of figures which appeared to confirm that most voters had a strongly partisan self-image, and that this self-image was closely related to voting. In 1964, for example, only 5 per cent of those they questioned did not claim to identify with a party. Of those who did identify with a party only 12 per cent said they identified 'not very strongly', while 41 per cent identified 'fairly strongly' and 47 per cent 'very strongly'. In the local elections in May 1963, 85 per cent of those with a Conservative partisan self-image voted Conservative, and 95 per cent of those who identified with the Labour Party voted Labour.

The strength of these political ties was reflected in the low swings (percentage changes in votes) between Conservative and Labour in successive elections. In the general elections of the 1950s the average swing was just 1.6 per cent. Few people changed the party they voted for because of the strength of their attachment to one or other of the major parties. As late as 1974 Butler and Stokes felt justified in saying 'class has supplied the dominant basis of party allegiance in the recent past'.

The two-party system

The second main feature of British voting patterns, the two-party system, was perhaps even more striking: together the Labour and Conservative parties dominated the political scene. In no election between 1945 and 1966 did their combined vote fall below 87.5 per cent of those cast, and the third most popular party, the Liberals, gained in excess of 10 per cent of the vote only once (in 1964).

The results did not surprise psephologists. If class determined voting, and there were two classes, then inevitably there would be two dominant parties to represent those classes. The Conservatives gained so many votes because middle-class non-manual voters identified with that party, while the Labour Party enjoyed similar levels of support among working-class manual voters. There was little room left for a third party. The Liberals were not believed to represent any particular class, and therefore could not rely on strongly partisan support from any particular section of the electorate. This was reflected in the very low vote they received in some elections: in 1951 the Liberals gained only 2.5 per cent of the votes cast.

Political socialization

So far we have examined the evidence for partisan alignment and the existence of a two-party system. However, this does not explain why there should be such a strong relationship between class and voting.

The explanation provided by Butler and Stokes was essentially very simple. To them, political socialization held the key to explaining voting. As children learned the culture of their society, they also learned the political views of parents and others with whom they came into contact. Butler and Stokes stated quite emphatically that 'A child is very likely indeed to share the parents' party preference.'

They saw the family as the most important agent of socialization, but, by the time an individual was old enough to vote, other socializing institutions would have had an effect as well. Butler and Stokes argued that schooling, residential area, occupation and whether they belonged to a union would all influence the way people voted. The Conservative Party could expect to get most support from those who:

1 attended grammar or public schools;

2 lived in middle-class areas where many people were homeowners;

3 were not members of unions.

Labour support would be most likely to come from those who:

1 attended secondary modern schools;
2 lived in working-class areas (and particularly on council estates);
3 were union members.

The most important factor, though, was whether voters had a manual or non-manual occupation.

All of these factors were important because they influenced the extent to which voters came into contact with members of different classes and therefore whether they mixed with partisan Labour or Conservative supporters. Generally speaking, all of these factors reinforced the effects of the voter's class background. For instance, children with parents who voted Labour were more likely to go to secondary modern schools and become trade union members.

In emphasizing the effects of socialization, Butler and Stokes were denying that the policy preferences of an individual were important. Voters were not thought to pay much attention to the detailed policies outlined in party manifestos. They did not choose who to vote for on the basis of a rational assessment of which package of policies on offer would benefit them most. They voted emotionally, as an expression of their commitment to a particular party. To the extent that they had preferences for policies, these were largely shaped by the parties themselves: voters would trust their party to implement the best policies.

The 'problem' of deviant voters

The partisan alignment theory of voting was so widely accepted that in 1967 Peter Pulzer claimed that 'Class is the basis of British party politics; all else is embellishment and detail' (Pulzer, 1967). However, the partisan alignment theory could not explain the existence of deviant voters: those who did not conform to the general pattern.

Throughout the post-war period a significant number of the British electorate have been deviant voters. Deviant voters are normally defined as manual workers who do not vote Labour, and non-manual workers who do not vote Conservative. In other words, deviant voters are those who do not vote for the party which is generally seen as representing their class.

The precise number of deviant voters fluctuated between elections, but generally there have been considerably more manual workers who did not vote Labour than non-manual workers who did not vote Conservative. According to Ivor Crewe, in the 1959 election 34 per cent of manual workers voted Conservative and 22 per cent of non-manual workers voted Labour (Sarlvick and Crewe, 1983).

The existence of deviant voters was important to psephologists both because of their political significance and the challenge they posed for the dominant partisan alignment theory:

1 They were politically important because they were central to determining the results of elections. (For most of the period since the war, manual workers have formed a majority of the population; if there had been no deviant voters, the Labour Party would have won every election.)
2 They were important for theories of voting because their existence seemed to directly contradict the claim that class was the basis of politics.
3 Consequently, considerable attention was devoted to studying these voters and explaining their behaviour.

Deferential voters

One of the earliest explanations of working-class Conservative voting was given in the late nineteenth century by Walter Bagehot. He argued that the British are typically deferential to authority and prone to defer decision making to those 'born to rule' whom they believe 'know better'. Hence the attraction of the Conservative Party which, particularly in the nineteenth century, was largely staffed from the ranks of the landed gentry, the wealthy and the privileged. The Conservatives represented traditional authority, and Bagehot argued that party image, rather than specific policies, was the major factor affecting voting behaviour. This led to the existence of the deferential voter.

In the early 1960s, Robert McKenzie and Alan Silver (1972) investigated the relationship between deferential attitudes and working-class support for the Conservative Party. They claimed that deference accounted for the voting behaviour of about half the working-class Tories in their sample.

Secular voters

Those working-class Tories whose support for the Conservative Party could not be accounted for by deferential attitudes were termed secular voters by McKenzie and Silver. Secular voters' attachment to the Conservative Party was based on pragmatic, practical considerations. They evaluated party policy and based their support on the tangible benefits, such as higher living standards, that they hoped to gain. They voted Conservative because of a belief in that party's superior executive and administrative ability.

McKenzie and Silver suggested that working-class support for the Conservatives had an increasingly secular rather than a deferential basis. They argued that this change helped to explain the increasing volatility of British voting patterns. Secular voters were unlikely to vote simply on the basis of party loyalty. Almost all the deferentials but only half the seculars stated that they would definitely vote Conservative in the next election. The seculars were waiting to judge specific policies rather than basing their vote on traditional party loyalties.

The theory of the secular voter proved to be highly influential and is very similar to many later theories of voting. McKenzie and Silver believed that secular voters made up quite a small, though increasing, section of the electorate. However, despite their small numbers, they represented a fundamental challenge to the partisan alignment theory since their motives for voting for a particular party were quite different from those of a partisan party supporter.

Contradictory socializing influences

Butler and Rose (1960) offered some explanations of deviant voting which were quite consistent with the theory of partisan alignment. They suggested that contradictory socializing influences on individuals would reduce their sense of loyalty to the party of their class. If, for example, one parent voted Labour and the other Conservative, there would be a considerable chance of their children becoming deviant voters in later life. Social mobility could also lead to deviant voting if individuals ended up in a different class to that of their parents. For example, individuals from a working-class background who experienced upward social mobility and gained middle-class jobs might vote according to their background rather than according to their current class position.

Embourgeoisement

Another explanation of deviant voting, which was broadly consistent with the theory of partisan alignment, suggested that a change was taking place within the working class. After the Labour Party was defeated in a third consecutive election in 1959, some psephologists began to consider the possibility that defeat had become inevitable for Labour in general elections.

Butler and Rose suggested that one section of the manual workforce was increasingly adopting middle-class attitudes and lifestyles. Affluent workers were enjoying living standards equal or even superior to those of the middle class, and consequently were more likely to identify themselves as middle-class and support the Conservative Party. (This argument is a version of the embourgeoisement theory which we discussed in Chapter 2.) In effect, Butler and Rose were suggesting, not that partisan alignment was less strong, but that the boundary between the middle and working classes had shifted so that some manual workers could now be considered middle-class.

A study by Eric Nordlinger (1966) found no support for this explanation. The Labour voters in Nordlinger's sample earned on average slightly more than the working-class Tories, although the factor which appeared to differentiate the two groups was not income as such, but the *degree of satisfaction* with income. Working-class Tories were found to be much more satisfied with their levels of income than their Labour counterparts. Satisfaction would lead to a desire to maintain the status quo, and hence support for the Conservative Party with its more traditional image. Dissatisfaction would lead to a desire for change, and hence support for Labour, with its image as the party of change.

The argument that working-class affluence leads to Conservative voting was further discredited by Goldthorpe et al.'s study of affluent workers in Luton (Goldthorpe et al., 1968a). Goldthorpe et al. found that affluence does not lead to middle-class identification nor to support for the Conservative Party. Of the affluent workers in Luton who voted in the 1955 and 1959 elections, nearly 80 per cent voted Labour, which is a significantly greater percentage than for the working class as a whole.

Goldthorpe et al. found that the most common reason given for Labour support was 'a general "working-class" identification with Labour' and a feeling that the Labour Party more closely represented the interests of the 'working man'. However, there appeared to be little of the deep-seated party loyalty which is supposed to be characteristic of the traditional working class. Like their attitude to work, the Luton workers' support for Labour was largely instrumental. They were primarily concerned with the pay-off for themselves in terms of higher living standards.

Cross-class attachments

Goldthorpe et al. argue that affluence as such reveals little about working-class political attitudes. They maintain:

> the understanding of contemporary working-class politics is found, first and foremost, in the structure of the worker's group attachments, and not, as many have suggested, in the extent of his income and possessions.
>
> Goldthorpe et al., 1968a

The importance of 'group attachments' is borne out by their research. Those affluent workers who voted Conservative usually had white-collar connections. Either their parents, siblings or wives had white-collar jobs or they themselves had previously been employed in a white-collar occupation. These 'bridges' to the middle class appeared to be the most important factor in accounting for working-class

Conservatism in the Luton sample. Attachments with and exposure to members of another class seemed to have a strong influence on cross-class voting.

This idea was developed by Frank Parkin (1968). He argues that, through greater exposure to members of the middle class than their Labour counterparts, working-class Tories internalized the dominant value system which the Conservative Party represents.

Bob Jessop (1974) found support for this view from a survey conducted in the early 1970s. He argued that members of the working class vote Conservative 'because they are relatively isolated from the structural conditions favourable to radicalism and Labour voting' – that is, from the conditions which serve to insulate manual workers from the middle class and the dominant value system. Such structural conditions are found in their most extreme form in the mining, shipbuilding and dock industries. Traditionally, workers in these industries formed occupational communities in single-industry towns. Insulation from members of the middle class both at work and in the community led to the development of a working-class subculture which provided an alternative to the dominant value system. In this setting, strong loyalties to the Labour Party developed.

These views did nothing to alter the widespread acceptance of the partisan alignment theory of voting. In line with that theory, writers such as Parkin tried to explain deviant voting in terms of political socialization. They added to the sophistication of the theory by examining situations in which individuals might experience contradictory socializing influences, but they did not change the basic framework within which voting was explained.

Middle-class radicals

Frank Parkin (1968) was one of the few writers who also analysed the reasons for deviant voting by middle-class Labour supporters. His explanation was quite different from that for working-class Conservatism. He found that these middle-class radicals were likely to have occupations 'in which there is a primary emphasis upon either the notion of service to the community, human betterment or welfare and the like or upon self-expression and creativity'. Such occupations include teaching and social work. Since Labour is seen as the party mainly concerned with social welfare, voting Labour is a means of furthering the ideals which led people to select these occupations.

Middle-class Labour voters tend to be outside the mainstream of capitalism. Parkin states that their 'life chances rest primarily upon intellectual attainment and personal qualifications, not upon ownership of property or inherited wealth'. As such they have no vested interest in private industry, which the Conservative Party is seen to represent.

In this case, individuals were seen to be voting for the party that was most likely to serve their interests and beliefs. They were not voting according to political socialization: they themselves were actively evaluating what the competing parties had to offer.

Parkin's explanation for this group of deviant voters comes closer to the theories of voting that were to become popular in the 1970s and 1980s than to the theory of Butler and Stokes. In the next section we will look at various attempts to analyse the patterns of voting in Britain since 1974.

Patterns of voting since 1974

During the 1970s, and particularly from 1974 onwards, important changes started to take place in the pattern of British voting. In the following sections we will outline briefly the changes that took place and then examine possible explanations for these changes:

1   The first major change appeared to be the declining influence of class on voting behaviour. The distinction between manual and non-manual workers no longer appeared to account for the way most of the electorate voted. There seemed to be much more volatility than in early elections, with a substantial proportion of the electorate changing the party it voted for from election to election.

2   The second and closely related change was the rapid increase in the numbers of deviant voters. Studies suggest that in the 1983 and 1987 elections a

minority of manual workers voted Labour, while the Conservative share of the non-manual vote has been less than 60 per cent in every election since 1974.

3   The third change may help to explain the second: Britain might have changed from a two-party to a three-party system. In 1981 four leading members of the Labour Party broke away to form the new Social Democratic Party. They then joined with the Liberal Party to fight the 1983 election together. The resulting Alliance succeeded in gaining 26.1 per cent of the votes cast, only just over 2 per cent behind Labour's 28.3 per cent share. For the first time since the war the combined Labour and Conservative stranglehold over voting was seriously threatened. A third party (or in this case an alliance of two 'third' parties) seemed to have a real chance of forming a government at some future date.

The Alliance did less well in 1987 but still polled 22.6 per cent of the votes cast. After 1987 the Liberals and the SDP merged to form the Liberal Democrats. In 1992 their vote declined further to 18.3 per cent, but this was still much higher than their share of the vote in any election between 1945 and 1970. In 1997 their vote increased marginally to 18.6 per cent, but the number of seats they won jumped up to 46, twice as many as in their previous best post-war performance (23 seats in 1983).

4 The final change that appeared to be taking place was the decline of the Labour Party. Labour had done badly in 1979, gaining only 36.9 per cent of the votes cast, but the 1983 result was even more disastrous. At that election Labour received a lower share of the popular vote than at any time since 1918. It even seemed as if Labour could hardly be considered a national party any longer: it won only three non-London seats in the entire south-east of England. Labour's strength was increasingly confined to the traditional heartlands of its support in the depressed industrial regions of Wales, Scotland and the north of England.

A number of commentators speculated that Labour's decline might be permanent. If conventional explanations of voting behaviour were correct, then a number of social changes were threatening the basis of the Labour vote. By 1983 non-manual workers outnumbered manual workers. Employment in industry, and particularly 'heavy' industries such as mining and shipbuilding, was declining. This was precisely where Labour had traditionally enjoyed its most loyal support. As early as 1981 Peter Kellner claimed that 'the sense of class solidarity which propelled Labour to victory in 1945 has all but evaporated' (Kellner, 1981).

As we will see, the view that Labour was in permanent decline was hardly borne out by the result of the 1997 election.

We will now consider a number of attempts to explain these changes. As psephologists took account of the alterations in voting behaviour, the emphasis placed upon political socialization by Butler and Stokes was increasingly rejected. It was replaced by an emphasis on the policy preferences of individual voters.

Bo Sarlvik and Ivor Crewe – partisan dealignment

Ivor Crewe was amongst the first commentators to criticize the approach of Butler and Stokes and to identify changing trends in British voting. In this section we will discuss his work with Bo Sarlvik, published in 1983. In later sections we will review Crewe's work on the 1987 and 1992 elections.

Sarlvik and Crewe argued that Butler and Stokes could not explain the reduction of class-based voting since 1974. Evidence suggested that embourgeoisement could not account for the decline in partisanship. Nor could Sarlvik and Crewe find any evidence that there had been a sudden and dramatic increase in voters whose parents had different party loyalties. They accepted that there had been more social mobility, but it was nothing like enough to account for the rise in deviant voting.

The decline in partisan voting

Tables 9.5 and 9.6 summarize some of the main findings of the *British Election Studies*, which have been conducted by a number of different researchers using survey techniques to collect standardized information about a large sample of voters. (The 1997 figures are based on a BBC/NOP exit poll.) The findings appear to confirm Crewe's theory that partisan dealignment has taken place in Britain.

Sarlvik and Crewe originally defined partisan dealignment as a situation where:

> none of the major occupational groups now provides the same degree of solid and consistent support for one of the two major parties as was the case in the earlier post-war period.
>
> Sarlvick and Crewe, 1983

In later writings, however, Crewe distinguished between partisan dealignment and class dealignment. Partisan dealignment referred to a decline in the percentage of the electorate who had a strong sense of loyalty to a particular party; class dealignment referred to a decline in the relationship between the working class and Labour voting and the middle class and Conservative voting.

Table 9.6 shows different measures of the strength of the relationship between class and voting, including a measure of the amount of absolute class voting. This is the percentage of voters who were middle-class and voted Conservative or who were working-class and voted Labour. In other words, it measures the percentage of non-deviant voters. In 1983 non-manual Labour voters were in a minority of voters at 47 per cent.

The Alford Index is another measure of the degree to which class influences voting, on a scale of 1 to 100. For Labour, if the score were 100, then all manual workers who voted would vote Labour. If the score were 0, Labour would gain the same proportion of votes in the middle class as in the working class. For the Conservatives, if the score were 100, then all non-manual workers who voted would vote Conservative. If the score were 0, the Conservatives would gain the same proportion of votes in the working class as in the middle class. By this measure, the decline in partisan voting in the working class

Table 9.5 Occupational class and party choice, 1964–97 (per cent)

	1964 Non-manual	Manual	1966 Non-manual	Manual	1970 Non-manual	Manual
Conservative	62	28	60	25	64	33
Labour	22	64	26	69	25	58
Liberal	16	8	14	6	11	9

	February 1974 Non-manual	Manual	October 1974 Non-manual	Manual	1979 Non-manual	Manual
Conservative	53	24	51	24	60	35
Labour	22	57	25	57	23	50
Liberal	25	19	24	20	17	15

	1983 Non-manual	Manual	1987 Non-manual	Manual	1992 Non-manual	Manual	1997 Non-manual	Manual
Conservative	55	35	54	35	56	36	37	24
Labour	17	42	20	45	24	51	37	58
Liberal, etc.	28	22	27	21	21	14	20	13

Source: D. Denver (1994) *Elections and Voting Behaviour in Britain*, 2nd edition, Harvester Wheatsheaf, London, p. 61, and D. Denver (1997) 'The results: how Britain voted', in A. Geddes and J. Tonge (eds) *Labour's Landslide*, Manchester University Press, Manchester.

Note: 'Liberal, etc.' in the last row refers to the Liberal-SDP Alliance in 1983 and 1987 and to the Liberal Democrats in 1992 and 1997.

Table 9.6 Measures of class voting, 1964–92

	Alford index (Labour)	Alford index (Conservative)	Absolute class voting
1964	42	34	63
1966	43	35	66
1970	33	31	60
Feb 1974	35	29	55
Oct 1974	32	27	54
1979	27	25	55
1983	25	20	47
1987	25	19	49
1992	27	20	54

Source: D. Denver (1994) *Elections and Voting Behaviour in Britain*, 2nd edition, Harvester Wheatsheaf, London, p. 62.

has been dramatic. It fell substantially between 1964 and 1983, dropping from 42 to 25.

From such evidence, Sarlvik and Crewe concluded that most voters were no longer strongly loyal to a party on the basis of their class, and that there was much greater volatility in the electorate. In the four elections of the 1970s, for example, less than half of the electorate (47 per cent) voted Labour or voted Conservative four times in a row.

The causes of partisan dealignment

First, Sarlvik and Crewe argued, factors other than class seemed to be increasingly related to voting. Such factors included whether voters rented or owned their housing, and whether they were members of trade unions. In 1979 the Conservatives were 51 per cent ahead of Labour among non-manual workers who were not in trade unions, but only 7 per cent ahead of those who were members. Labour was 33 per cent ahead of the Conservatives among manual trade union members, but actually 1 per cent behind among non-union manual workers.

Sarlvik and Crewe believed that class boundaries were being blurred by factors such as these. There were fewer 'pure' members of the working class who had manual jobs, lived in council houses and belonged to trade unions; and fewer 'pure' members of the middle class who had non-manual jobs and were non-unionized. The increasing numbers of unionists in the middle class and the increasing numbers of homeowners in the working class had reduced the level of partisan alignment among individuals with the traditional party of their class, and had resulted in class dealignment as well.

The second explanation of partisan dealignment put forward by Sarlvik and Crewe provided a more fundamental challenge to the theories of Butler and Stokes. They argued that it was misleading simply to see the voters as captives of their socialization, unable to make rational choices about which party to vote for. Instead, Sarlvik and Crewe claimed that voters' active decisions about which party's policies best suited them had to be included in any explanation of voting. From their analysis of the 1979 general election, Sarlvik and Crewe argued that 'voters' opinions on policies and on the parties' performances in office "explain" almost twice as much as all the social and economic characteristics taken together'.

According to Sarlvik and Crewe, the main reason why the Conservatives won in 1979 was simply that the electorate was unimpressed with the performance of the previous Labour government and supported most Conservative policies. Some issues were particularly important. Sarlvik and Crewe found that Conservative proposals designed to limit the power of trade unions and plans to privatize some state-funded industries were the most important policies which persuaded Labour voters to switch to the Conservatives.

Despite the significance Sarlvik and Crewe attached to the policy preferences and active choices of the electorate, they did not claim that class was of no importance. They stated that 'The relationships between individuals' social status and their choice of party have by no means vanished. But as determinants of voting they carry less weight than before.' Traditional theories could not be completely rejected: Sarlvik and Crewe still saw class as the most important aspect of a person's social status, but parties which wished to win elections could not just rely on the loyalty of their supporters – their policies had to appeal to voters as well.

Himmelweit, Humphreys and Jaeger – a consumer model of voting

Some psephologists went much further than Sarlvik and Crewe in rejecting the partisan alignment theory of voting. Himmelweit, Humphreys and Jaeger (1985) based their findings upon their own longitudinal study of voting, which followed a group of men who were 21 in 1959, through to the October election of 1974.

In their book *How Voters Decide* Himmelweit *et al.* argued that an understanding of voting should be based on analysing members of the electorate's deliberate selection of a party to vote for, and not on political socialization. They emphasized the rational choices made by voters. They believed that people

decided how to vote by deciding what they wanted, and how far each party met their requirements.

To explain this theory, Himmelweit *et al.* compared an elector's choice of party with a consumer making a purchase. For example, someone choosing a new car will take a number of factors into account, such as price, comfort, performance, size, running costs and reliability. Some factors will be more important to a particular individual than others: one potential purchaser might put most emphasis on price and running costs, while another is primarily concerned with performance and size. Consumer choice is not always easy: you might want both cheapness and high quality. If you cannot have both, you will have to compromise.

Himmelweit *et al.* argue that choosing a party involves the same sort of process. Certain policies will be more important to you than others. One party will come closer to your views in their stated policy than another. No single party is likely to advocate all the single policies that you support. Consequently you will have to weigh up which party offers the most attractive package, taking into account the importance you attach to each issue.

Of course, a voter may not have 'perfect knowledge' of all the policies on offer, but there is more to buying products than examining the labels and listening to the claims of advertisers. Potential purchasers may have had some previous experience of the product and if it has proved satisfactory in the past they are more likely to buy it again, even if it is not exactly suited to their needs. In a similar way, voters have experience of previous governments and they can judge the parties on the basis of past performance. One reason for the rise in 'deviant' voting, according to Himmelweit *et al.*, was the increasingly negative judgements made by voters on the parties they had previously chosen: they decided to opt for new brands because their old choices proved so unsatisfactory.

The image Himmelweit *et al.* provided of the voters, then, is of very calculating individuals trying to achieve their objectives as best they can. However, they did not altogether dismiss more emotional factors in voting. These factors can be compared to brand loyalty, and advice from friends and relatives about products. You may identify with a particular product which you have used before and which you trust; you may also be influenced by what people you know tell you about products, and their recommendations. Similarly, when voting, you may have some loyalty to a party, and you may be influenced by the political preferences of others.

However, these factors (which are similar to Butler and Stokes's concepts of party alignment and political socialization) were considered of little importance by Himmelweit *et al.* They argued that such factors were only important if your policy preferences cancelled each other out. In other words, only if two or more parties offered you equally attractive sets of policies would you be influenced by party loyalty or the opinion of others. By 1974, Himmelweit *et al.* thought that party loyalty had a minimal impact on the electorate, although they accepted that it may have been more important before then.

Himmelweit *et al.* provided statistical support for their consumer model of voting. They claimed that 80 per cent of voting in the October 1974 election could be predicted on the basis of their model.

If Himmelweit *et al.*'s theory is correct, it has important implications for the political parties. It suggests that all the parties have a chance of winning elections if they can tailor their policies to fit those preferred by a majority of the electorate. Regardless of how badly Labour did in 1983, such a consumer model does not suggest that its decline is necessarily permanent or irreversible. According to this theory of voting, the parties are competing for the votes of the whole of the electorate, and not just for those of a small number of floating voters.

Criticisms

This radical new explanation of voting has been heavily criticized. Paul Whiteley (1983) describes the study as unreliable, since it was based on a small and unrepresentative section of the population. By 1974, Himmelweit *et al.*'s sample consisted of just 178 respondents, all of whom were male, aged about 37, and some 75 per cent of whom were non-manual workers. It cannot be assumed that the factors influencing the voting of this group will be typical of the factors influencing the voting of the rest of the population.

A more fundamental objection to explaining voting in terms of policy preference is raised by David Marsh (1983). He points out that this type of explanation cannot fully account for voting unless it explains why people prefer certain policies in the first place. These types of theory deny the importance of class, but fail to suggest alternative influences on the choice of policy.

Heath, Jowell and Curtice – the continuing importance of class

Heath *et al.*'s conclusions contradict those of many other psephologists because they use different and more sophisticated research methods (Heath, Jowell and Curtice, 1985).

Redefining class

The first, and perhaps most important, methodological change involves the definition and measurement of class. Heath *et al.* argue that defining the middle class as non-manual workers and the working class as manual workers is theoretically inadequate. They claim that classes can be more adequately defined in terms of economic interests, that is, according to their situation in the labour market. They therefore use a version of John Goldthorpe's neo-Weberian class scheme to distinguish five classes. (See pp. 114–17 for further details of Goldthorpe's class scheme.)

The five classes are:

1 The salariat, which consists of managers, administrators, professionals and semi-professionals who have either considerable authority within the workplace or considerable autonomy within work.

2 Routine non-manual workers, who lack authority in the workplace and often have low wages.

3 The petty bourgeoisie, which consists of farmers, the owners of small businesses, and self-employed manual workers. Their situation depends upon the market forces that relate to the goods and services they supply. They are not wage labourers and they are not affected in the same way as other workers by employment and promotion prospects. This group cuts across the usual division between manual and non-manual workers.

4 'Foremen' and technicians, who either supervise other workers or who have more autonomy within work than the fifth class.

5 Manual workers – Heath *et al.* do not separate manual workers in terms of the degree of skill their job requires since they do not believe that skill levels have a significant impact on voting.

Apart from using new class categories, another important feature of Heath *et al.*'s work is the way they deal with the voting of women. Nearly all of the previous studies classified women voters according to the occupation of their husband if they were married. Heath *et al.* argue that women's own experience of the workplace will have a greater impact on their voting than that of their husband.

Table 9.7 summarizes Heath *et al.*'s findings on class voting in the 1983 election.

The continuing importance of class

The results suggest a stronger relationship between class and voting (in 1983) than the results of studies using conventional definitions of class:

1 The working class remained a stronghold of Labour support.

2 'Foremen' and technicians (who would normally be categorized as part of the skilled working class) were strongly Conservative.

Table 9.7	Class voting in the 1983 election			
Class	Conservative	Labour	Alliance	Others
Petty bourgeoisie	71%	12%	17%	0%
Salariat	54%	14%	31%	1%
Foremen/ Technicians	48%	26%	25%	1%
Routine non-manual	46%	25%	27%	2%
Working class	30%	49%	30%	1%

Source: A. Heath, R. Jowell and J. Curtice (1985) *How Britain Votes*, Pergamon, Oxford, p. 20.

3   The petty bourgeoisie (some of whom would normally be defined as manual workers) were the strongest Conservative supporters.

4   The salariat and routine non-manual workers gave most of their support to the Conservatives, but it was also in these classes (as well as in the working class) that the Alliance gained its greatest share of the votes.

Examining the results of one election does not reveal whether or not class-based voting has declined. Heath *et al.* therefore attempt to measure the strength of the relationship between class and voting since 1964. It is more difficult to measure this relationship using a fivefold division of the population into classes, so they decided to measure the strength of the relationship between class and voting by measuring the likelihood of the salariat voting Conservative and the working class voting Labour.

From their figures they calculated an odds ratio which determines the relative likelihood of a class voting for the party it could be expected to. The figures in Table 9.8 show how many times more likely it is for the working class to vote Labour and the salariat to vote Conservative than vice versa.

Table 9.8 produced some unexpected findings. There appear to have been wide variations in the relationship between class and voting, but no long-

Table 9.8	Odds ratio for working class voting Labour and salariat voting Conservative in general elections, 1964–83						
Election	1964	1966	1970	1974 (Feb)	1974 (Oct)	1979	1983
Odds ratio	9.3	7.3	3.9	6.1	5.5	4.9	6.3

Source: Adapted from A. Heath, R. Jowell and J. Curtice (1985) *How Britain Votes*, Pergamon, Oxford, p. 20.

term dealignment. According to this measurement, 1983 was an average election and not a year in which the influence of class was at its lowest since the Second World War.

Changes in the class structure

Heath *et al.* claim that much of the change in levels of support for the different parties is the result of changes in the distribution of the population between classes. For example, the working class has shrunk as a proportion of the electorate while the salariat and routine non-manual groups have grown. However, changes in the class structure alone cannot explain all the changes in levels of support for the parties in elections. Heath *et al.* calculated what percentage of the votes each party would have gained in 1983 if they had kept the same levels of support in each class as they had in 1964. The results are summarized in Table 9.9.

Table 9.9	Changes in party support 1964–83 and predicted share of the vote in 1983 if parties had retained the same level of support in each class from 1964		
	Labour	Conservative	Liberal Alliance
% vote 1964	44	43	11
% vote 1983	28	42	25
Predicted % vote in 1983 given changes in the class structure	37	48.5	12.5

Source: Adapted from A. Heath, R. Jowell and J. Curtice (1985) *How Britain Votes*, Pergamon, Oxford, p. 20.

On these figures, the Labour Party did even worse than expected, the Conservative Party failed to take advantage of changes in the social structure, while the increase in Liberal/Alliance support was far greater than would be anticipated. Consequently Heath *et al.* conclude that factors other than changes in the social structure must have affected patterns of voting.

Rejection of consumer theory

Heath *et al.* reject the view that detailed policy preferences account for these changes. They measured people's views on various policies and asked them where they thought the major parties stood on these issues. They also asked voters which issues they thought were most important:

1   Unemployment and inflation came top of the list, and on both Labour had the most popular policies.

2   The Alliance proved most popular on the third most important issue (whether there should be more

spending on welfare or tax cuts), while Labour and the Conservatives tied a little way behind.

3 Conservative and Alliance policies proved most popular on the fourth most important issue, defence.

On the basis of this evidence, Labour should have won a handsome victory. If the six most important issues were taken into account, Labour and the Conservatives would have received the same share of the vote. Heath *et al.* therefore reject the consumer theory of voting; their evidence suggests that it cannot explain the Conservative victory in 1983.

Party images

Despite rejecting the consumer theory, Heath *et al.* do not deny that the actions taken by a political party affect the vote it obtains, but they believe that it is not the party's detailed policies that matter, but its overall political stance in the eyes of the electorate. They say, 'It is not the small print of the manifesto but the overall perception of the party's character that counts.' If voters believe that a party has the same basic ideology as they have, they will be likely to vote for it. From this point of view, Labour lost so badly in 1983 because many voters believed it had moved too far to the left, despite the extent to which they agreed with its policies.

Class, ideology and voting behaviour

Heath *et al.* use a more complex model of ideology than the simple left/right distinction that is usually employed. They argue that there are two main dimensions to ideological differences on issues:

1 Class issues are mainly economic: they concern such questions as whether industries should be nationalized or privatized, and whether income and wealth should be redistributed. The ideology which supports nationalization and redistribution can be called left-wing, and the opposite right-wing.

2 Liberal issues concern non-economic questions such as whether there should be a death penalty, whether Britain should retain or abandon nuclear weapons, and whether there should be a strong law-and-order policy or not. For the sake of convenience, the ideology which supports the death penalty, the retention of nuclear weapons and strong law-and-order policies will be called 'tough', while its opposite will be called 'tender'.

In terms of these differences, the Labour Party supports left-wing and tender policies, the Conservative Party supports right-wing and tough policies, and (according to Heath *et al.*) the Alliance was perhaps slightly to the right of centre on class issues and more tender than tough on liberal issues. Liberal supporters have a distinctive ideological

position and, according to Heath *et al.*, it is one that is becoming increasingly popular with the electorate.

From their analysis of changes in voters' ideology, Heath *et al.* find that there have been distinct shifts. On average, voters increasingly support right-wing economic policies, but more tender social policies. These changes seem to have benefited the Alliance more than the other major parties, both of whom have experienced a significant move away from their ideology on one of the two dimensions. The study finds that the main reason for the high level of Alliance support in 1983 was the increasing proportion of voters whose ideological position roughly coincided with that party's.

Summary

The complex and highly sophisticated theory of voting devised by Heath *et al.* differs from both the partisan alignment and consumer theories. Class remains very important but it does not directly determine the party voted for. It is not specific policies that matter, but the class of the voters and how they perceive the ideological position of the parties. From this point of view, the prospects for the parties in the future will be partly determined by changes in the class structure, but they can also affect their chances of success by the way they present themselves to the electorate.

Criticisms of Heath, Jowell and Curtice

Ivor Crewe (1986) has attacked the work of Heath *et al.* In particular he criticizes their use of an odds ratio table based upon the chances of the working class voting Labour and the salariat voting Conservative. Crewe says, 'their odds ratio is a two-party measure applied to a three-party system'. It fails to take account of the growth of support for centre parties – the Liberals and the Alliance – in the elections of 1979 and 1983. Furthermore, Crewe points out that in 1983 the working class and the salariat combined made up a minority of the electorate (45 per cent).

The response to criticisms

Heath *et al.* (1987) have answered these criticisms. They argue that odds ratios are more appropriate for measuring the relationship between class and voting than the class index of voting used by Crewe. In Crewe's index all voters who do not vote Conservative or Labour are seen as a kind of deviant voter and are used as evidence that classes have lost their 'social cohesion or political potential'.

Heath *et al.* point out that the centre parties can increase their share of the vote without any change in social classes. For example, if the Labour or Conservative Party change their policies, and thereby appeal less to potential centre-party voters, they can lose support without the electorate changing their views. Heath et al.'s odds ratio avoids this problem because the level of support for centre parties does not directly affect the ratio. It measures the strength of class-based voting in the class-based parties. It does not fall into the trap of assuming that a vote cast for somebody other than a Labour or Conservative Party candidate indicates a decline in the relationship between class and voting.

Heath et al. are happy to acknowledge that the odds ratio used in their original study measured the relationship between class and voting in a minority of the electorate. To counter this problem they calculated odds ratios for a number of other classes. They found the same 'trendless fluctuations' in the relationship between class and voting revealed in their original study. Once again they discovered no evidence that class was exerting less influence on voting behaviour than it had in the past.

Ivor Crewe – the 1987 election and social divisions

According to Crewe's figures, in 1987 the percentage of people voting for the party representing their class increased marginally (Crewe, 1987a, 1987b). Compared to 1983 the combined percentage of non-manual Labour voters rose from 47 per cent to 48 per cent. Nevertheless, deviant voters still made up a majority of the electorate (52 per cent). Crewe argues that the election largely confirms his analysis of trends in voting behaviour. He claims it shows that divisions continue to grow within both the middle and working classes.

Divisions in the middle class

Using data from a Gallup survey commissioned by the BBC, Crewe found that the Conservatives lost support in the middle class. In both the 'core' middle class of professionals, administrators and managers, and the 'lower' middle class of office and clerical workers, the Conservative vote fell 3 per cent compared to 1983. These data would seem to suggest that the Conservative Party was losing support from all sections of the middle class. However, Crewe claimed to have discovered a major split in the class between university-educated and public-sector non-manual workers on the one hand, and non-university-educated and private-sector non-manual workers on the other. As Table 9.10 shows, the Conservatives lost 9 per cent of their vote amongst the university-educated middle class and 4 per cent amongst those working in the public sector.

Thus Crewe believes that 'new divisions' are opening up in the middle class. Education and the sector in which individuals work are both starting to

Table 9.10	The new divisions in the middle class: voting in 1987					
	University-educated		Public sector		Private sector	
	1987	1983–7	1987	1983–7	1987	1983–7
Conservative	34%	−9%	44%	−4%	65%	+1%
Labour	29%	+3%	24%	–	13%	–
Liberal/SDP	27%	+4%	32%	+4%	22%	−1%

Source: I. Crewe (1987) 'A new class of politics', Guardian, 15 June.

exercise a strong influence on voting patterns, resulting in an increasingly divided middle class.

Divisions in the working class

As we discovered in an earlier section (see pp. 652–4), Crewe has believed for some time that the working class is divided. Labour has been losing support in the 'new working class' who live in the south of the country, own their own homes, are non-union members and work in the private sector. Crewe found that these divisions continued to be very important in 1987. For example, the Conservatives led Labour by 46 per cent to 26 per cent amongst the working class in the south of England, and by 44 per cent to 32 per cent amongst working-class homeowners. Crewe claims that the Labour Party:

> had come to represent a declining segment of the working class – the traditional working class of the council estates, the public sector, industrial Scotland and the North ... It was a party neither of one class nor one nation, it was a regional class party.
>
> Crewe, 1987a

Policy preference and voting

Crewe also examined the influence of policies on voting in 1987. On the surface he found little support for his belief that policy preference was becoming more important in shaping voters' behaviour. When asked to name the two issues that concerned them most, respondents were most likely to mention unemployment, followed by defence, the NHS and education. On all of these issues, except defence, Labour policies enjoyed more support than Conservative policies. Crewe says, 'Had electors voted solely on the main issues Labour would have won.'

Crewe therefore revised his earlier position that policy preference was crucially important in shaping voting. Instead, Crewe argued that voters attach more importance to their own prosperity than they do to issues that they identify as problems for society as a whole. He said, 'when answering a survey on the important issues respondents think of public problems; when entering the polling booths they think of family fortunes'.

The Gallup survey found that 55 per cent believed that the Conservatives were more likely to produce prosperity than other parties; only 27 per cent thought they were less likely to do so. Furthermore, respondents were more likely to say that opportunities to get ahead, the general economic situation and their household's financial situation had improved, than they were to say the reverse. Thus Crewe believed that the main reason that the Conservatives won in 1987 was that people felt more prosperous and they trusted the Conservatives to deliver rising living standards.

Anthony Heath, John Curtice, Geoff Evans, Roger Jowell, Julia Field and Sharon Witherspoon – *Understanding Political Change 1964-87*

Heath *et al.* conducted the *British Election Study* into the 1987 election. Their findings were published in the book *Understanding Political Change* (Heath *et al.*, 1991). In it they examined how voting and voters had changed between 1964 and 1987. They discussed a number of influential ideas on voting and political change by using data from successive election studies. In doing so they challenged many of the ideas put forward by other psephologists. In particular they raised doubts about whether the social psychology had changed much at all. Society and politics might have changed, but Heath *et al.*'s findings suggested that the reasons why people voted in particular ways had not altered much over more than two decades.

Volatility and party identification

First, Heath *et al.* examined the proposition that voters had become more volatile and less willing to identify with a party and remain loyal to it. In 1964, 88 per cent of those questioned said they identified very or fairly strongly with a political party. By 1987 this had declined to 71 per cent. On the other hand, there was no clear trend in the percentage of respondents who thought of voting for another party during the campaign and who could not therefore be considered party loyalists. In 1964, 25 per cent of those asked thought of voting for another party; in 1983 the figure was the same, 25 per cent; and in 1987 it had increased only marginally to 28 per cent. Thus, while some figures suggested a small but significant decline in partisan alignment, other figures were more ambiguous.

The research reached more clearcut conclusions on electoral volatility. Between the 1959 and 1964 elections 18 per cent of those who voted in both elections changed who they voted for; between the 1983 and 1987 elections 19 per cent of those who voted in both changed their choice of party. Heath *et al.* used three different measures of volatility but obtained similar results for all of them. They said:

All three measures show much the same changes over time, the differences being rather modest and showing no clear trend towards increasing volatility. Volatility was at its highest on all three measures between 1970 and 1974, but since then it has fluctuated.

Heath, *et al.*, 1991

Policy preference, parents and voting

In examining the extent to which party preference influences voting, Heath *et al.* note that the strength of the relationship will be influenced by the degree to which the policies of parties differ. If, for example, Labour and Conservative have very different manifestos at an election, more people are likely to vote for a centre party such as the Liberals (now the Liberal Democrats), leaving Labour and Conservative supporters polarized in their views. If Labour and Conservatives put forward less distinct sets of proposals at an election, they are likely to pick up votes from centre parties, and the voters for the two main parties are likely to have less distinctive views.

Heath *et al.* compared the 1964 and 1979 elections to examine changes in the relationship between policy preference and voting, since the Liberals polled about the same proportion of the votes in those two elections and the perceived differences between Labour and the Conservatives were at a similar level in the two elections. They found that policies seemed to have had a considerable amount of influence on voting in the 1979 election. This appeared to be in line with the theory that voters were becoming more rational and were increasingly influenced by their policy preferences. However, Heath *et al.* also found that 'issues were rather important in 1964'. The different policies of Labour and the Conservatives on nuclear weapons and on privatization versus nationalization both exercised a considerable influence on voting in that year. Heath *et al.* conclude that 'voters were rational and sophisticated in the 1960s just as they are today'. Thus Heath *et al.* accept the importance of policy preference for voting but deny that this is anything new.

They also examined the influence of parents on voting, and again found that there seemed to be relatively little change from the 1960s. While there had been a small decline in the likelihood of children voting the same way as their parents, this could be explained by an increase in social mobility which meant that children ended up in a different class from that of their parents. Where children remained in the same class there was no evidence that political socialization in childhood had become less important.

The findings of Heath *et al.* on party identification, volatility, policy preference and the influence of parents on voting represent a challenge to the view of Crewe and others that a major change in the factors influencing voting took place in the 1970s. Heath *et al.* found that a similar mix of factors influenced voting in the 1970s and 1980s as in the 1960s. The idea that a fundamental change had taken place was not supported by the evidence.

Class-based voting

As in their earlier study, Heath *et al.* discussed the view that class was becoming less closely related to voting. They distinguished between absolute and relative class voting. Absolute class voting measures the proportion of people voting for the class their party is commonly held to represent: in other words, the percentage of voters who are not 'deviant voters'. Table 9.11 is based on the five-class model used by Heath *et al.* in their earlier study, but with the working class and 'foremen' and technicians combined to form the working class, and the other three classes (petty bourgeoisie, routine non-manual workers and the salariat) combined to form the middle class.

Table 9.11 shows, and Heath *et al.* acknowledge, that absolute class voting has declined. However, it has declined rather less than it first appears if

Liberals and other centre parties are regarded as class-based parties representing the middle class. Heath *et al.* argue that it is legitimate to see them in this way since they draw a comfortable majority of their votes from middle-class voters. Thus, to Heath *et al.*, absolute class voting has declined, but not to the extent that psephologists such as Crewe have claimed.

On the other hand, Heath *et al.* are unwilling to concede that relative class voting has declined, at least since 1970. Using an odds ratio which compares the chances of the salariat voting Conservative with the chances of the working class voting Labour (this statistical measure is explained further on p. 656), they found that there was little change between the 1983 and 1987 elections. They therefore confirmed their earlier claim that there had been 'trendless fluctuations' in relative class voting, although this time they did say that these fluctuations had been typical only since 1970. They say, 'Looking ... at the Conservative:Labour log odds ratio, we see that this declined rapidly between 1964 and 1970. There is however no further decline after 1970.'

Heath *et al.* therefore modify their position from that expressed in the earlier work, *How Britain Votes*. They say that there has been a 'modest' decline in the relationship between class and voting, but much less than that claimed by many other commentators. However, one reason for this has simply been an increase in the number of candidates standing for centre parties. In 1964, 1966 and 1970 the Liberals contested only just over half the seats in the general elections. In later elections they, or other centre parties, have stood in nearly all constituencies. Simply by having a greater number of candidates they have attracted more votes away from the more clearly class-based parties, and thus they have weakened the apparent relationship between class and voting. Any change in the relationship has more to do with political changes than any alteration in the psychology of the electorate.

Divisions within classes

Heath *et al.* examine Crewe's claims that there is a 'new working class' and that new divisions have opened up in the middle class. They concede that housing tenure has a relationship with voting, but deny that this is anything new. According to their figures, living in a council house influenced people to vote Labour as much in 1964 as it did in 1987. Similarly, being an owner-occupier was just as likely to influence somebody to be a Conservative voter in 1964 as it was in 1987.

Union membership, or non-membership had some influence on voting, as did ethnicity (people from an ethnic minority were more likely to vote Labour), but

Table 9.11	Absolute class voting, 1964–87	
	Middle-class Conservative plus working-class Labour as percentage of all voters	Middle-class Conservative or Liberal plus working-class Labour as percentage of all voters
1964	64.0	70.7
1966	64.4	69.9
1970	60.2	64.4
February 1974	55.5	66.5
October 1974	57.4	68.6
1979	56.7	64.3
1983	51.7	66.9
1987	51.6	66.3

Source: A. Heath *et al.* (1991) *Understanding Political Change*, Pergamon Press, Oxford, p. 65.

there was no evidence that the strength of either of these relationships had increased. Indeed, membership or non-membership of a trade union seemed to be becoming less of an influence on voting.

However, region had become more important. In 1964, region had little effect on working-class voting patterns, but in 1987 the working class living in the south were becoming proportionately more likely to vote Conservative, while those in the north, and in Wales and Scotland were becoming proportionately more inclined to vote Labour.

Heath *et al.* conclude that 'the working class is certainly fragmented' but, with the exception of regional differences, this fragmentation is nothing new.

Heath *et al.* found more evidence that there were new divisions in the middle class. In particular, they found that 'welfare and creative professionals' were increasingly inclined to vote Labour, while other members of the middle class were likely to remain loyal to the Conservatives. They also found that having had higher education was increasingly associated with non-Conservative voting in the middle class. Longer-established divisions in the middle class were based on religion (with members of the Church of England being more likely than others to vote Conservative) and social background (with middle-class people from working-class backgrounds more likely than others to vote Labour).

Overall, Heath *et al.* found that neither the middle class nor the working class were 'internally homogeneous', but this was nothing new and most of the divisions within the classes dated back at least as far as the 1960s.

'Pocket-book voting'

As we discussed earlier, another theory proposed by Crewe was that people voted according to their own economic interests: they voted for the party they thought would be best for their standard of living. Heath *et al.* examined this theory, calling it pocket-book voting.

They did find that people who had voted Conservative in 1983 were less likely to vote Conservative again in 1987 if they felt that their own standard of living, or the standard of living in the country as a whole, had fallen. However, Heath *et al.* questioned the theory that voting was directly related to living standards. People were much more likely to mention the government's general competence or incompetence as a reason for changing their vote than they were to mention standards of living. Furthermore, those who did mention their own standard of living were also very likely to mention the interests of the social class to which they belonged. This suggested that they tended to see their own self-interest as tied to the interests of their class as a whole. Heath *et al.* claim that 'pocket-book voting and class voting may not be rivals but rather may be different aspects of the same phenomenon'.

Conclusion

Heath *et al.* conclude that, between 1964 and 1987, voting was affected by social changes (such as the contraction of the working class) but there had been little change in the factors shaping voting. Class, non-class social factors, policy preferences and party images all had an influence and no one factor could explain voting in either 1964 or 1987. Many of the apparent changes were due either to social change or to political change, and not to changes in the motivation of voters. Many social factors had been working against the Labour Party, reducing the percentage of the population likely to vote for them. Other changes had benefited the Liberal Party and other centre parties. Politically, the success of the Liberals (and the SDP) had increased volatility and led to the apparent reduction in the importance of class. Part of this success, though, was simply due to the increased number of candidates these parties had put up at elections.

As in their study of the 1983 election. Heath *et al.* calculated the effects of changes on Labour's electoral prospects. Comparing 1964 and 1987, the effects of social changes plus the increased number of Liberal candidates and the extension of the franchise to those aged over 18 could be expected to have disadvantaged the Labour Party by 8.4 per cent, advantaged the Liberal/Alliance by 8.9 per cent, and made no overall difference to the Conservative vote. Obviously these changes made it difficult for Labour to win elections. Nevertheless, Labour did better in 1987 than it had done in 1983.

Criticisms of *Understanding Political Change*

In a review of *Understanding Political Change*, Ivor Crewe was rather less critical than he had been of Heath's earlier work in *How Britain Votes*. He even praised aspects of the book saying:

> *The technical accuracy and theoretical interest of what Heath* et al. *have to say about volatility, tactical voting and other supposed consequences of partisan alignment are for the most part unchallengeable. Analysis and interpretation are authoritative, sophisticated and almost painfully cautious.*

Crewe, 1992

This more positive tone was hardly surprising since, as Crewe acknowledged, the conclusions of *Understanding Political Change* were rather closer to his own views than those of the earlier study. Crewe said of the change in emphasis, 'Earlier confidence has given way to caution: the missionary's impatience with the old primitives has mellowed into the old cleric's self-doubt and scepticism.'

Crewe notes that Heath and his collaborators gave less weight to the political values of parties and voters than they had done earlier and put more emphasis on social and political changes. Nevertheless, Crewe recognized that there were still considerable differences between himself and Heath *et al.*, and he identifies a number of weak spots in their analysis:

1 He argues that Heath *et al.* only take a very limited number of political changes into account. For example, while they analyse the extension of the vote to 18-20-year-olds and the expansion in the number of Liberal candidates, they take no account of things such as changes in party leaders, or the impact of the press and other media. They give no good reason for excluding some possible influences on voting while paying close attention to others.

2 They fail to consider the possibility that voting behaviour had shaped some of the factors they had analysed rather than the other way round. For example, the rise in the number of Liberal candidates

could be seen as resulting from the great success enjoyed by Liberal candidates in by-elections between 1970 and 1974. Heath *et al.* may have got cause and effect the wrong way round. In other words, the rise in the number of candidates was caused by increased popularity and not vice versa.

3 Crewe continues to insist that the relationship between class and voting had become much less strong. He admits that measures of relative class voting give some indication of how ideologically distinctive classes are. Nevertheless, absolute measures are also important. For example, if Labour support fell to 25 per cent in the working class, but to 0 per cent in the middle class, this would show up as a strengthening of the class basis of voting in odds ratio tables. What this would fail to make clear was the fact that Labour could no longer be seen as the party of the working class since it was attracting just a quarter of their votes. To Crewe, then, absolute measures of class voting are vital for measuring the 'political cohesion of a single class'. According to Heath *et al.*'s own figures, Labour's share of the working-class vote fell from 68 per cent in 1964 to 48 per cent in 1984, and Crewe believes that such figures cannot but be taken to show that the working class lost some of its political solidarity.

The 1992 election

The results of the 1992 election are given in Table 9.12. They show that, although the Conservatives won the election, their vote dropped by 0.4 per cent, compared to the 1987 election. Labour's vote rose by 3.6 per cent and the Liberal Democrats lost 2.0 per cent of the vote, compared to the Alliance's share in 1987. The Conservatives were returned to office with an overall majority for the fourth successive time, having already held office for 13 years. Nevertheless, their overall majority was cut from 101 to 21, and Crewe calculates that, 'had a mere 1,702 people voted Labour rather than Conservative in the eleven most marginal Conservative seats, the government would have lost its overall majority' (Crewe, 1992).

On the surface, then, the decline of the Liberal Democrat vote seemed to firmly establish Labour as the only serious alternative to the Conservatives, and the small size of the Conservatives' overall majority seemed to give Labour grounds for optimism. However, many commentators interpreted the result quite differently. What the result meant for Labour, and for the future of British politics generally, was keenly debated.

Richard Rose – Labour's 'shattering' defeat

Labour's advantages

Richard Rose (1992) argues that the result of the 1992 election 'was shattering for Labour not only because it thought it was going to win but because, by all the old rules, it *should* have won'. From this point of view, Labour fought the election under very favourable conditions, yet it still ended up about 8 per cent behind the Conservatives. Rose identifies a number of factors which were working to increase the Labour vote in 1992:

1 Labour had been a relatively united party between 1987 and 1992, and the left wing, which had lost Labour votes in previous elections, no longer had much influence in the party.

2 The centre parties had been damaged by the arguments which surrounded the merger of the largest sections of the Liberal and Social Democratic Parties to form the Liberal Democrats. Labour therefore had a good opportunity to win votes from former Liberal and SDP voters.

Table 9.12 The 1992 general election

	Total number of votes	MPs elected	Share of UK vote (%)	Share of GB vote (%)
Conservative[a]	14,049,508	336	41.8	42.8
Change from 1987	+313,171	−39	−0.4	−0.4
Labour	11,557,134	271	34.4	35.2
Change from 1987	+1,527,190	+42	+3.6	+3.7
Liberal Democrat[b]	5,998,446	20	17.8	18.3
Change from 1987	−1,342,706	−2	−4.8	−4.8
Welsh/Scottish Nationalists[c]	786,348	7	2.3	2.4
Change from 1987	+245,886	+1	+0.6	+0.7
Others[d]	433,870	0	1.3	1.3
Change from 1987	+282,353	0	+0.8	+0.8
Northern Ireland parties[e]	785,093	17	2.3	–
Change from 1987	+54,941	0	+0.1	–
Total	33,610,399	651	United Kingdom turnout	77.7
Change from 1987	+1,080,835	+1	Change from 1987	+2.3

Notes

a The figures for the Conservative Party exclude 11 candidates in Northern Ireland who polled a total of 44,608 votes.
b The Liberal Democrats exclude 73 candidates standing for the 'Liberal Party' who polled 64,744 votes: they are compared with the Liberal/SDP Alliance in 1987.
c The figures for the Nationalists include 3 joint Plaid Cymru/Green candidates.
d The figures for 'others' exclude all candidates and votes in Northern Ireland: they include 253 Green candidates (170,047 votes), 73 Liberal Party candidates (64,744 votes), 300 candidates for the Natural Law Party (60,617 votes), and 220 'other' candidates who polled a total of 138,462 votes.
e The figures for Northern Ireland include all candidates and votes including Conservative (11 candidates), Natural Law (9), Workers (8) and 'others' (8), as well as the Ulster Unionists, the Democratic Unionists, the Popular Unionists, the SDLP, Sinn Fein and the Alliance.

Source: I. Crewe (1992) 'Why did Labour lose (yet again)?' Politics Review, September, p. 2.

3 The 1992 election was held because the government had come to the end of its five-year term and was unable to put it off any longer. The conditions under which the Conservatives were forced to seek re-election were very far from ideal for them. In particular, 'The economy was in prolonged recession and unemployment had risen sharply in the South of England', which was the heartland of Tory support. If a sense of economic well-being helped governments to win elections, then the poor economic situation seemed likely to be a serious handicap to the Conservatives.

4 The Conservative election campaign was widely seen as lacking in inspiration. It seemed 'at times even defeatist', suggesting that the Conservatives themselves were far from confident of success. This was hardly surprising since the opinion polls consistently indicated that Labour would win.

5 The Conservative Party had 'experienced two leadership contests, first to remove Margaret Thatcher and then to choose the relatively unknown John Major as her successor'. The elections had exposed divisions within the Conservative Party and had resulted in their leader being much less

experienced than the leader of the main opposition party, Neil Kinnock.

Taken together, these factors meant that Labour expected to win. The question, therefore, was why they failed to do so.

A structural realignment in electoral competition

Rose observes that 'Election outcomes can be influenced both by short-term actions of party leaders and long-term structural change.' In 1992 the short-term factors were in Labour's favour. However, according to Rose, the long-term structural factors had so undermined Labour's vote that they outweighed any advantages that Labour enjoyed.

Figure 9.4 shows trends in votes for the three main parties since the war. To Rose, this figure demonstrates that there has been a significant change since 1974. Before that date, Conservative and Labour shares of the vote had been fairly similar. From 1974 onwards, though, the Labour average declined, while the Conservative vote stayed at about

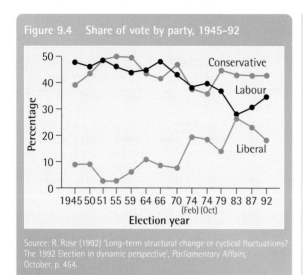

Figure 9.4   Share of vote by party, 1945-92

Source: R. Rose (1992) 'Long-term structural change or cyclical fluctuations? The 1992 Election in dynamic perspective', *Parliamentary Affairs*, October, p. 454.

the same level. In the six general elections between February 1974 and 1992, the Conservative vote ranged between a low of 35.8 per cent in October 1974 and a high of 43.9 per cent in 1979. The Labour range was between a low of 27.6 per cent in 1983 and a high of 39.2 per cent in October 1974. Rose calculates that 'the mid point of the Conservative range is 6.4 per cent above that of Labour', and he notes that since 1979 the Conservative vote has usually been near the top of its range whilst the Labour vote has been near the bottom of its range. From these figures he concludes that there has been a structural realignment in electoral competition. Labour's 'normal vote', ignoring short-term influences, has fallen to 33-4 per cent, while the Conservative 'normal vote' has stayed as high as 40-1 per cent.

Structural changes

Rose identifies the following changes which, in his view, had led to Labour's long-term electoral decline:

1 Cities, which used to be Labour strongholds, have declined as population centres, leaving Labour with fewer urban constituencies where it can rely on winning.

2 In 1951, 28 per cent of people were homeowners. By 1992 this figure had risen to almost 75 per cent. Since homeowners are more likely to vote Conservative than council tenants, this has reduced the normal level of Labour support.

3 Standards of living have risen sharply since 1951. Gross Domestic Product per capita has gone up 139 per cent even after allowing for inflation. Many more people own a range of consumer goods which were the prerogative of a rich minority in 1951. The number of poor, who are traditionally Labour supporters, has fallen substantially.

4 Educational standards have also risen fast. Between 1950 and 1992 the proportion of young people

staying on to receive tertiary education nearly tripled. There are fewer voters with a very poor education – another group which has traditionally been prone to voting Labour.

5 Perhaps more controversially, Rose also claims that:

> Structural changes in British society since 1951 have replaced an old system of class relations with new divisions of life style and taste. In 1951 the distinction between cloth caps and bowler hats, the civilian equivalent of officers and other ranks, was marked in many ways from manners and accents to voting.
>
> Rose, 1992

Without the old class system, Labour cannot rely on solid support from the working class. The working class is in any case shrinking, from over two-thirds of the electorate in the 1950s to under a half by the 1990s.

6 Trade union membership has declined. It fell by a quarter in the 1980s alone, and union members have always been more inclined to vote Labour than non-union members.

Together these changes have been steadily undermining Labour support, making it increasingly difficult for Labour to win elections.

Political problems for Labour

Writing in 1992, Rose believed that Labour's long-term problems could well be compounded by shorter-term political problems by the time of the next election:

1 The economy might well be in a better state than in 1992.

2 There was no guarantee that Labour would maintain party unity for a further five years, and any splits could have serious consequences in lost votes.

3 Labour could try for an electoral pact with the Liberal Democrats but, to Rose, political problems made such a pact 'impossible to conceive', at least until after the second general election of the 1990s. In any case, research suggested that voters who defected from the Liberals or Liberal Democrats were just as likely to change to voting Conservative as voting Labour.

4 In Scotland, Labour was very successful in 1992, but at a future election a number of its seats could come under threat if there was any further revival of support for the Scottish Nationalist Party.

Rose also points out that, despite Labour increasing its share of the vote in 1987 and again in 1992, it still had a mountain to climb. Even if Labour gained a further 3.4 per cent of the vote in the next election (its average increase in the previous two), it would still poll fewer votes than the Conservatives.

Rose does say that it was not inevitable that the Conservatives would win the next election, but he also says, 'the hope for a Labour majority in Parliament in 1996 can be described as "Micawberism run mad", a passive hope that someday something will turn up'. He implies that if Labour could not win in 1992, when nearly all the short-term factors favoured the party, then its future prospects were dismal.

Conclusion

Rose's analysis is not particularly sophisticated and not backed up by his own detailed empirical research. Nevertheless, his case appeared quite convincing and he was not alone in suggesting that Labour was in trouble. Most other psephologists, though, did not go quite as far as him in writing off Labour's future chances.

Ivor Crewe – the 1992 election

A devastating setback for Labour

Ivor Crewe (1992) reaches broadly similar conclusions to Rose about the performance of the parties in the 1992 election. According to Crewe, the election was not a total success for the Conservatives even though they won their fourth consecutive election. It was the lowest share of the vote with which the Conservatives had won an election since 1922 and, with a 2 per cent swing in its favour, 'Labour came very close to toppling the Conservative government.' Nevertheless, the election was a 'devastating setback for the Labour party'. It was its third worst percentage vote since the Second World War (with only the 1983 and 1987 elections being worse) and, despite its gains, it still ended up 7.4 per cent behind the Conservatives.

Like Rose, Crewe argues that factors were working very much in Labour's favour. He identifies the following reasons why Labour might have been expected to win:

1 Unlike the previous two elections, the 1992 election was fought during a recession, which harmed the electoral chances of the government. Labour did not have the problem of being blamed for widespread strikes (as it had as a result of the 'Winter of Discontent' in 1978-9); it did not have the problem of 'left wing extremism and weak leadership' (as it did in 1983); and it did not have an unpopular unilateral nuclear disarmament policy (as it did in 1987). The government had to contend with adverse publicity about 'unemployment, bankruptcies and house repossessions', all of which 'soared throughout 1992'.

2 In the early 1980s most Tory policies had been fairly popular, but by 1992 the Conservatives had implemented a number of very unpopular measures.

The 'poll tax' became 'the worst policy disaster of any post-war government' and the government was eventually forced into replacing it. The government's economic policy 'was almost as great a shambles' and 'educational and health reforms were too long delayed for their claimed benefits to make an impact by election day'.

3 The Labour Party had transformed itself into a 'united disciplined, moderate and modern' party, while its main competitor for anti-Conservative votes, the Liberal/SDP Alliance, had lost support because of difficulties over merging to become the Liberal Democrats.

4 The Labour Party managed to get 'caring' issues such as health, education and unemployment to the top of the agenda during the election campaign, and it was on these issues that it enjoyed the most favourable image with the electorate.

Like Rose, Crewe concludes that Labour should have won, and he identifies the key question about the election as 'Why did Labour lose yet again?'

Class and voting

One possible reason for Labour losing could have been continuing class dealignment, resulting in a further erosion of working-class support.

Table 9.13 shows the patterns of class voting in 1992 and the changes from the preceding two elections, according to opinion poll evidence. The figures show that Labour enjoyed the biggest swing in 1992, compared to 1987, amongst professional and managerial workers. But it also regained a considerable number of working-class votes, with a 4.5 per cent swing, compared to an overall swing of about 2 per cent. Crewe admits, therefore, that 'by conventional definitions class voting slightly increased'. The proportions voting for their traditional classes went up: 47 per cent of those voting being working-class Labour voters or middle-class Conservative voters, compared to 44 per cent in 1987.

Furthermore, the split between the 'traditional' and 'new' working class became less apparent. As Table 9.14 shows, the Conservative lead over Labour amongst the working class in the south was cut from 18 to 2 per cent; a 12 per cent Conservative lead amongst working-class owner-occupiers became a 1 per cent Labour lead; and amongst working-class non-union members Labour also regained the lead from the Conservatives.

Although Crewe argues that 'the rise in class voting should not be exaggerated' – since under half of those voting still cast their vote along class lines – the election provided little support for theories of class dealignment. Labour voting did increase in the middle class, weakening the relationship between class and voting in that class; but, in the working

Table 9.13 Class voting in 1992

	Con	Lab	Lib Dem	Con lead over Lab	Swing to Lab
Professional/ managerial (ABs)					
Vote in 1992	55	23	22	+32	+5.5
Change from 1987	-1	+10	-9	-11	
Change from 1979	-9	+2	+6	-11	+5.5
Office/clerical (C1s)					
Vote in 1992	50	29	21	+21	+1.0
Change from 1987	+2	+4	-6	-2	
Change from 1979	-4	-1	+5	-3	+1.5
Skilled manual (C2s)					
Vote in 1992	41	40	19	+1	+3.0
Change from 1987	-2	+4	-2	-6	
Change from 1979	0	-4	+4	+2	-2.0
Semi-skilled/unskilled manual (DEs)					
Vote in 1992	31	55	14	-24	+4.5
Change from 1987	-1	+8	-7	-9	
Change from 1979	-3	+2	+1	-5	+2.5
Unemployed					
Vote in 1992	27	56	17	-29	+0.5
Change from 1987	+1	+2	-4	-1	
Change from 1979	-13	+7	+6	-20	+10.0

Source: I. Crewe (1992) 'Why did Labour lose (yet again)?' *Politics Review*, September, p. 5.

class, traditional patterns of voting returned to some extent. Labour's defeat could not therefore be put down to a loss of support in the working class.

Issues and voting

Crewe's figures also suggest that issues may not have influenced the election result to the extent that would be expected by policy preference theories of voting. As in his analysis of the 1987 election, Crewe found that Labour policies tended to be more popular on the issues which people said were most important to them. When asked to select two issues, health, unemployment and education were the most frequently mentioned by opinion poll respondents. On all of them Labour enjoyed a healthy lead over the Conservatives.

Defence – which had been mentioned as one of the two most important issues by 35 per cent in 1987 – was mentioned by only 3 per cent in 1992. Conservative policies on defence were much more popular than Labour's, and the decline in the importance of defence to the electorate must have benefited Labour.

The economy and economic well-being

The economy did not appear to be a particularly important issue for most voters. Only 11 per cent mentioned prices as one of the two most important issues and 10 per cent mentioned taxation. However, as Crewe had observed about the 1987 election, what people say is important to them when asked by opinion pollsters may not be the same as what actually influences them when they come to vote. A feeling of economic well-being may be crucial to governments seeking re-election.

Table 9.14 Working-class voting in 1992

	The new working class				The traditional working class			
	Lives in South	Owner occupier	Non-union member	Works in private sector	Lives in Scotland or North	Council tenant	Union member	Works in public sector
Conservative	40	40	37	32	26	22	29	36
Labour	38	41	46	50	59	64	55	48
Liberal Democrat	23	19	17	18	15	13	16	16
Con or Lab majority	Con	Lab	Lab	Lab	Lab	Lab	Lab	Lab
in 1992	+2	+1	+9	+18	+33	+42	+26	+12
Con or Lab majority	Con	Con	Con	Lab	Lab	Lab	Lab	Lab
in 1987	+18	+12	+2	+1	+28	+32	+18	+17
Swing to Labour 1987–92	+ 8.0	+ 6.5	+ 5.5	+ 8.5	+ 2.5	+ 5.0	+ 4.0	- 2.5 (to Con)

Source: Gallup/BBC survey (10–11 June 1987); Gallup post-election survey (10–11 April 1992).

However, at first sight even this explanation does not seem to account for Labour's surprising failure: 30 per cent of respondents believed that their living standards had fallen during the preceding year, and only 25 per cent thought they had improved.

Nevertheless, Crewe believes that voters' perceptions about the comparative abilities of Labour and the Conservatives to deliver economic prosperity played a crucial part in determining the result. If people did not feel that the Conservatives were making them better off (as they did in 1987), they did feel that they would be worse off under Labour. In general they blamed economic problems on world recession or on Mrs Thatcher, rather than John Major who had replaced her as Conservative leader. Many feared the economic effects of electing a Labour government even though they thought Labour had better policies on most non-economic issues. In an exit poll (conducted on voters leaving the polling station), 53 per cent thought the Conservatives were the party most likely to take the right decisions on the economy, whereas only 35 per cent saw Labour as the best party in this respect.

With one exception, the opinion polls leading up to the election predicted that Labour would get a bigger share of the vote than the Conservatives. Even the exit polls considerably underestimated the margin of Conservative victory. In part, these inaccuracies may have been due to the limitations of the opinion polls themselves, but there was also evidence of a late swing from Labour to the Conservatives. Amongst those who changed their mind at the last minute, income tax, the economy, prices and interest rates were much more likely to be seen as important than they were by other voters. During the campaign the Conservatives attacked Labour, claiming that if a Labour government were elected it would result in a 'double whammy' of more taxes and higher prices. The evidence suggests that this part of the Conservative campaign had some success in spreading fear of the financial consequences of a Labour government, causing a last-minute switch which contributed to Labour's defeat.

Other factors

As well as concern about Labour's competence to run the economy, Crewe identifies a number of other factors that may have contributed to the result:

1   Public perceptions of the leadership qualities of the Conservatives' John Major and Labour's Neil Kinnock may have been important. One poll found that 52 per cent thought Major would make the better leader, compared to 23 per cent who named Kinnock. To Crewe, 'Kinnock was a serious electoral liability'.

2   Despite the widespread view that Labour managed its campaign better, it was the Conservatives who gained support during the run-up to the election. Across a whole range of issues Conservative policies

gained in popularity as the campaign progressed. Crewe suggests that the electorate either developed a view that the Conservatives had more 'general governing competence than Labour' or it feared that Labour might be incompetent.

3   A third factor which was cited by many as influencing the outcome was the coverage of the election by the press. Most papers supported the Conservatives and some were particularly strong in doing so. On election day the *Sun* published a front-page picture of Neil Kinnock's head superimposed on a light-bulb with the headline, 'If Kinnock wins today will the last person to leave Britain please turn out the lights.' Some people argued (including the *Sun* itself) that this was crucial in persuading a number of *Sun* readers in marginal constituencies to change their minds at the last minute and vote Conservative, and therefore allow the Conservatives to retain a slender overall majority.

Crewe finds some support for this view. Amongst *Sun* readers there was a big swing of 7.5 per cent to the Conservatives at the last minute. However, this was unlikely to have saved any more than six seats. Its effects should not be exaggerated because there was also a big swing amongst readers of the non-aligned *Independent* (7 per cent) and a rather small swing (2.5 per cent) amongst readers of the strongly pro-Tory *Daily Express*. Although the press did make a difference, it was not a decisive one.

Conclusion

Although Crewe saw the election as a 'devastating setback' for Labour, since it had lost despite fighting the election 'in as ideal conditions as an opposition could hope to find', his findings were not quite as pessimistic about Labour's prospects as Rose's. Crewe believed that the Conservatives might well have lost their overall majority if the opinion polls had not misleadingly shown Labour to be ahead. Fear of a Labour government (rather than great enthusiasm for a Tory government) 'galvanised Conservative support'. There was a high turn-out amongst Conservative supporters, and waverers who were considering voting for the Liberal Democrats returned to the Conservative fold to avoid a Labour victory.

Nevertheless, Labour did not deprive the Conservatives of an overall majority, despite the conditions under which the election was fought, a result which scarcely suggested that Labour could be confident of its future electoral prospects.

Heath, Jowell and Curtice – 'Can Labour win?'

Heath, Jowell and Curtice (1994) were involved in conducting the *British Election Study* for the 1992 election, as they had been in 1983 and 1987. They carried out two surveys on the 1992 election. One was a cross-section survey in which a sample of voters were interviewed in the week following the election. The second was a panel survey in which respondents interviewed in 1987 were re-interviewed in 1992. The second survey excluded voters who were too young to vote in 1987, but panel surveys provide a better indication than other types of survey as to why people change their votes from election to election. (Panel surveys are a type of longitudinal study – this kind of research is discussed in Chapter 14.)

The size of Labour's task

Like Richard Rose and Ivor Crewe, Heath *et al.* start their analysis by noting that Labour lost despite factors operating in its favour, such as the recession, the unpopularity of the poll tax, the weakness of the Liberal Democrats, the merits of the Labour campaign and the greater popularity of its policies compared to 1987. They say, '1992 seemed to be Labour's best chance of victory since 1974. But the party still lost with nearly eight points less of the popular vote than the Conservatives.'

Nevertheless, Heath *et al.* believed that the 1992 election did offer some hope to Labour supporters. They argued that, in order to deprive the Conservatives of an outright victory in the next election, Labour would need a swing of just 0.5 per cent in its favour. On the other hand, it would need a 4.1 per cent swing to win an overall majority. This would be a higher swing than Labour had achieved in any election since 1945.

In Labour's favour was the need to win a smaller share of the vote than the Conservatives in order to win an overall majority. Labour tends to be stronger in seats with a smaller electorate so it could win more seats than the Conservatives for the same number of votes. To win outright on the current constituencies, Labour would need to be just over 0.5 per cent ahead of the Conservatives, whereas the Conservatives would need to be more than 6.5 per cent ahead of Labour to gain an overall majority.

Heath *et al.* point out that one problem for Labour was that boundary changes were due to take place before the next election. If votes were cast as they had been in 1992, these would be likely to give the Conservatives around 12 extra seats while depriving Labour of 5 seats. On the other hand, Labour stood to gain more than the Conservatives from any revival in Liberal Democrat fortunes, since the latter were challenging the Conservatives in far more constituencies than they were challenging Labour.

Heath *et al.* therefore argued that there was 'a mountain Labour has to climb' to win an overall majority, but the 'lower slopes are rather gentler'. Depriving the Conservatives of an overall majority would be relatively easy for Labour if it could continue to progress from its 1992 position. However, as Heath *et al.* noted earlier, Labour did fight the 1992 election under very favourable conditions, making it seem unlikely that it could do even better in the future.

In order to explore future prospects in more depth, Heath et al. went on to consider different theories of voting and their relevance for the different parties.

Volatility

Heath *et al.* comment that the likelihood of a big swing to Labour would be greater if the electorate were becoming more volatile. However, they found little evidence that this was happening. According to their findings, 22 per cent of people changed how they voted between 1987 and 1992, a slight increase on the 19 per cent who changed between 1983 and 1987. Nevertheless, this was still lower than the 24 per cent who changed the way they voted between the 1970 and February 1974 elections.

Social change and Labour's chances

Heath *et al.* agree with commentators like Rose that Labour is handicapped by social changes which undermine Labour's electoral base. According to their figures, the declining size of the working class could have been expected to cost Labour a 6 per cent share of the vote between 1964 and 1992.

As with volatility, though, the theory of class dealignment could be seen as giving Labour some hope. If voters are becoming less and less influenced by class when deciding which party to support, then a decline in the size of the working class need not be a major disadvantage for Labour. As in their earlier work, though, Heath *et al.* are generally critical of theories of class dealignment. Their figures suggest that there was no change in the amount of relative class voting, comparing the working class and salariat between the 1987 and 1992 elections. (For a definition of relative class voting, see p. 660.) They therefore 'conclude that class remains important, and that the declining size of the working class is indeed an important long-term problem for Labour'.

There are some social changes which have benefited Labour, including the increasing size of the ethnic-minority electorate and an increase in those receiving higher education (both groups are more likely to vote Labour), and a decline in the number of regular church-goers (who tend to vote Conservative). Overall, though, Labour's prospects have certainly been harmed by social changes.

Social attitudes

Table 9.15 details the proportions of people agreeing with a number of statements about government policy. According to Heath *et al.*, it shows that:

> on the face of it, the electorate was more left-of-centre on a number of key issues (though not all) at the time of the 1992 general election than they had been at the time of Labour's last election victory in 1974.
>
> Heath, Jowell and Curtice, 1994

For example, more people favoured spending money to get rid of poverty, putting money into the NHS, and giving workers more say at their places of work. Nearly as many people favoured the redistribution of wealth to working people in 1992 (48 per cent) as had done in 1974 (54 per cent). Heath *et al.* thought that some of the apparent shift to the left might be illusory and result from 'people's perceptions that the status quo had shifted to the right'.

Nevertheless, to the extent that voting is influenced by attitudes to issues, Labour could draw some comfort. There was little evidence that Labour's ideological position was becoming more unpopular or unacceptable to the electorate.

Party identification and political factors

If policies were not a major problem for Labour, trends in party identification were. Table 9.16 shows that identification with the Conservatives and Liberals was at a similar level in 1964 and 1992. On the other hand, Labour appeared to lose the loyalty of many of its supporters in the late 1970s and early 1980s, and it had failed to win them back. To Heath *et al.*, the sudden change in Labour Party identification was so swift that it could not have resulted from long-term social trends. Rather it was a consequence of short-term political failure by the Labour Party. The 'Winter of Discontent', the formation of the SDP and disagreements over nuclear weapons within the party 'not only cost the party votes in the short-term but also broke the long-term bond that formerly linked them to the party'.

Labour's prospects

Although not denying the enormous task Labour faced in trying to gain an overall majority in a future election, Heath *et al.* saw Labour as having more chance of success than either Richard Rose or Ivor Crewe did. From their analysis it appeared to be crucial that Labour should persuade more people to identify with the party.

Writing in 1994, Heath *et al.* found evidence that this might be happening:

1 John Major's standing in the opinion polls had declined to make him the 'most unpopular Prime Minister for the longest period in opinion poll records', and Labour's then leader, John Smith, was much more popular than his predecessor Neil Kinnock had been.

Table 9.15 Long-term trends in attitudes

	October 1974	1979	1987	1992
Percentage agreeing that the government should ...				
Redistribute income and wealth to ordinary working people	54	52	50	48
Spend more money to get rid of poverty	84	80	86	93
Nationalize more companies	30	16	16	24
Privatize more companies	20	38	31	23
Not introduce stricter laws to regulate trade unions	–	16	33	40
Give workers more say in running places where they work	58	55	76	79
Put more money into the NHS	84	87	90	93
Percentage agreeing that ...				
Welfare benefits have not gone too far	22	17	34	46

Source: A. Heath, R. Jowell and J. Curtice (1994) 'Labour's last chance?' in Heath *et al.* (eds) *Labour's Last Chance? The 1992 Election and Beyond*, Dartmouth Publishing, Aldershot, p. 285.

Table 9.16 Trends in party identification

	Conservative %	Labour %	Liberal %	None %
1964	41	42	12	5
1966	39	45	10	5
1970	42	42	8	7
February 1974	38	39	14	6
October 1974	36	39	15	7
1979	39	38	12	9
1983	37	31	19	11
1987	39	32	17	11
1992	42	34	13	8

Notes

Liberal represents Liberal 1964–79; Liberal, SDP or Alliance 1983–87; Liberal Democrat 1992.

The figures are adjusted to take account of the sampling variation in the survey estimates. They do not sum to 100% because of 'other' parties.

Non-voters excluded.

Source: A. Heath, R. Jowell and J. Curtice (1994) 'Labour's last chance?' in Heath *et al.* (eds) *Labour's Last Chance? The 1992 Election and Beyond*, Dartmouth Publishing, Aldershot, p. 287.

2 The Conservatives had damaged their image as a result of splits within the party over Britain's relationship with the EC.

3 In September 1992 the actions of currency speculators had forced Britain to withdraw from the Exchange Rate Mechanism (which was supposed to protect the exchange rate of the pound).

4 A number of ministers were forced to resign or were dismissed between 1992 and 1994 as a consequence of 'either sexual scandals or failures in office'.

5 Perhaps most damaging of all, the Conservatives undermined their image as a low tax party by raising a number of taxes and by imposing VAT on domestic fuel.

Opinion poll evidence suggested that the Conservatives were losing support. One poll in 1993 found that only 33 per cent of people believed that the government was competent; and a succession of polls put Labour over 10 per cent ahead of the Conservatives. Furthermore, over four polls in 1993, Gallup found that on average only 30 per cent of the electorate identified with the Conservatives while 36 per cent identified with Labour.

Heath *et al.* remind readers that Labour enjoyed a big lead in most of the opinion polls before the 1992 election, but it still lost. They also say that 'we would expect mid-term disaffection from a governing party to dissipate somewhat and be replaced by a "homing tendency" at the following general election'. The Conservatives could expect to regain much of their support by the time voters actually got the chance to choose a new government. However, Heath *et al.* also raise the possibility that a major change could be taking place in British politics. They say:

It is at least plausible that the period since 1992 may have inflicted long term damage to the public's image of and affection for the Conservative Party of the kind inflicted on Labour some ten to fifteen years earlier.

Heath, Jowell and Curtice, 1994

If that were the case, the Conservative and Labour parties might return to being fairly evenly matched in their quest for election victories.

The 1997 general election

The election result

The result of the 1997 general election certainly gave psephologists food for thought. It appeared to offer strong confirmation of some theories, while making others seem completely implausible. In particular, it appeared to make a nonsense of the claims of some psephologists (such as David Rose)

that, after the 1992 result, Labour had an almost impossible task to win an overall majority. David Butler and Dennis Kavanagh comment that 'The result was all the more striking, considering the many analyses in the immediate aftermath of the 1992 election that Labour faced too high a mountain to climb' (Butler and Kavanagh, 1997). The implications for some theories, though, were not so clearcut.

The results of the election are given in Table 9.17.

Table 9.17	The results of the 1997 general election			
Party	Share of vote	Change	Number of seats	Change
Conservative	31.4	−11.4	165	−178
Labour	44.4	+9.2	419	+145
Lib Dem	17.2	−1.1	46	+28
Others	7.0	+3.3	11	+5

Note: Change in the number of seats won is based on the 'notional' number of seats that each party would have won in 1992 had the new constituency boundaries been in operation. The Speaker is counted as a Labour candidate although she was not opposed by the other major parties.

Source: D. Denver (1997) 'The results: how Britain voted', in A. Geddes and J. Tonge (eds) *Labour's Landslide*, Manchester University Press, Manchester, p. 9.

The results marked a considerable change from previous elections. As David Denver says, 'By any standards the result was dramatic' (Denver, 1997a). Some of its most dramatic characteristics have been pointed out by Denver and others:

1 Labour won its first general election victory for some 23 years, with its highest share of the vote since 1966. It won an overall majority in the Commons of 179 – their biggest ever overall majority. (The previous best was 146 in 1945.) It was the biggest majority for any government since 1935. Labour won 'many seats that would normally have been considered as certain Conservative wins' (Denver, 1997a). As Table 9.17 shows, there was a massive swing to the Labour Party (9.2 per cent) and an even larger swing away from the Conservatives (-11.4 per cent). According to Denver, the swing from Conservative to Labour was 10.3 per cent – the biggest swing between the two since the Second World War.

2 The Conservative Party suffered a very bad defeat. Andrew Geddes and Jonathon Tonge (1997) point out that the Conservatives got their lowest share of the vote since 1832. David Denver (1997a) notes that seven cabinet ministers lost their seats, the Conservatives lost over half their seats overall, and they won no seats in Wales or Scotland. Although they got a higher share of the vote than the Labour Party had managed in their worst post-war

performance (28 per cent in 1983), the scale of the change in fortunes from one election to another was certainly the biggest in post-war history.

3 There was no dramatic change in the fortunes of the third party (the Liberal Democrats) in terms of the share of the vote. However, there was a big increase in the number of seats they won. They increased their number of MPs from 18 to 46, with an increase in their share of the vote of less than 1 per cent. This was almost certainly due to a big increase in tactical voting. Considerable numbers appeared to vote for someone other than their first-choice candidate in order to defeat a Conservative candidate (see below). It was also a successful election for minor parties and independent candidates. The share of the vote gained by 'others' increased by 3.3 per cent to 7 per cent. The independent 'anti-sleaze' candidate Martin Bell defeated the Conservative Neil Hamilton in what was considered a very safe Conservative seat. David Denver notes that Martin Bell became the first candidate without links to a political party to be elected an MP in a general election since 1945. A new party, the Referendum Party (which was opposed to Britain joining a single European currency and was led by the businessman James Goldsmith), won 2.7 per cent of the vote.

The limits to the landslide

However, it is possible to exaggerate the novel features of the 1997 election. In particular, the scale of Labour's victory in terms of their overall majority was disproportionate to the scale of their success in terms of votes cast. Andrew Geddes and Jonathan Tonge (1997) note that the number of seats won by Labour was partly a product of the first-past-the-post voting system. In this system the candidate with the most votes in each constituency wins the seat, and the votes cast for losing candidates effectively count for nothing. The system tends to favour the most successful parties and makes it very difficult for minor parties to win seats unless their support is concentrated in specific areas of the country (as is the case with the Scottish Nationalist Party, for example).

Labour won 63 per cent of the seats with 44 per cent of the votes cast. Geddes and Tonge calculate that 'Under a strictly proportional system, Labour would have been denied an overall majority, possessed 128 fewer MPs and been confronted by thirty-nine extra Conservative and sixty-six Liberal Democrat MPs.'

John Curtice and Michael Steed observe that Labour's share of the vote was lower than any it achieved between 1945 and 1966, including three elections it lost during that period. Furthermore, the turnout was, at 71.2 per cent, the lowest since the war. Less than a third of the electorate (30.9 per cent) actually voted for the Labour Party.

Overall, then, it was the swing from the Conservatives to Labour that was the most notable feature of the election rather than the proportion of votes that the Labour Party gained.

The *British Election Study* of 1997

The significance of the 1997 general election was the focus of the book *Critical Elections* which was based on the *British Election Study* (Evans and Norris (eds), 1999). The 1997 *British Election Study* was the eleventh in a series of studies dating back to 1964. The 1997 study used a sample of 2,733 in England and Wales and 882 in Scotland. A number of psephologists used data from the 11 studies to evaluate whether 1997 represented a radical break from previous elections. All based their articles upon a framework for analysing elections outlined by Pippa Norris and Geoffrey Evans (1999a).

Pippa Norris and Geoffrey Evans – 'Understanding electoral change'

Pippa Norris and Geoffrey Evans argue that it is possible to distinguish between three main types of elections: maintaining elections, dealigning elections and realigning elections. Dealigning elections can be subdivided into two types, deviating and secular; whilst realigning elections can also be divided into two types, secular and critical (see Figure 9.5).

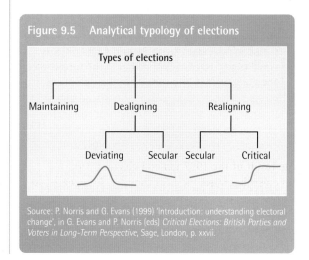

Figure 9.5 Analytical typology of elections

Types of elections

Maintaining   Dealigning   Realigning

Deviating   Secular   Secular   Critical

Source: P. Norris and G. Evans (1999) 'Introduction: understanding electoral change', in G. Evans and P. Norris (eds) *Critical Elections: British Parties and Voters in Long-Term Perspective*, Sage, London, p. xxvii.

1   Maintaining elections are elections in which no major changes take place in the nature of voting, in the nature of the competing parties or in the issues which are of key importance in politics. There may be small shifts in the share of votes gained by each party but these are due to short-term political factors rather than long-term trends or fundamental changes. Thus, while the governing party might change, the fundamental character of politics does not.

Norris and Evans comment that the big swing from Conservative to Labour in 1997 makes it implausible that 1997 could be seen as a maintaining election.

2   Dealigning elections take place when 'the social psychological bonds linking parties and voters loosen' (Norris and Evans, 1999a). These are of two types:

Deviating elections result when 'particular personalities, issues or events produce a temporary sharp reversal in the "normal" share of the vote for major parties'. They often contain strong protest votes against a party in power and can involve a sudden surge in support for minor parties. One example was the 1989 European elections, when the Green Party achieved a much higher share of the vote in Britain than it has received before or since. Deviating elections do not signal a long-term change except in as much as they show that the electorate has become more volatile. Short-term political factors have most influence on the outcome.

Norris and Evans say that:

> The 1997 election can be most plausibly regarded as a deviating election if it is interpreted primarily as an expression of negative protest against the 18 years of Conservative rule, prompted by the pervasive problems of sexual and financial sleaze, internal leadership splits and the sense of economic mismanagement which afflicted the Major administration after the 'Black Wednesday' ERM debacle.

Norris and Evans, 1999a, p. xxix

(For details about 'Black Wednesday', see pp. 618–19.) If this analysis was correct, then the Labour Party could expect electoral difficulties in the future once the Conservatives had sorted out their problems.

Secular dealignment describes elections which involve a 'long term, incremental and cumulative progressive weakening in party-voter bonds'. Such elections may involve a long-term process of class dealignment, where voters cease to automatically support a party which they believe represents their class interests. Bo Sarlvick and Ivor Crewe argued in 1983 that there had been a 'decade of dealignment' in British politics (see pp. 652–4), and they therefore saw elections in the 1970s and 1980s as involving secular dealignment.

If the 1997 election could be seen in these terms, then Labour's victory would be a product of continuing trends. They were able to win because of the gradual erosion of loyal support for both parties. However, like a victory based upon a deviating election, one victory, however big, would not guarantee future success. A volatile and fickle electorate with few loyalties could as easily turn against the Labour Party as it had against the Conservatives in 1997.

3   Realigning elections involve evolutionary or revolutionary change in the social and psychological bonds between voters and parties. In such elections a significant part of the electorate begin to identify with particular parties, when they did not do so before.

Secular realignment is characterized by 'an evolutionary and cumulative strengthening in party support over a series of elections'. From this viewpoint, Labour's 1997 victory was a case of 'one more heave'. They had picked up support in the 1987 and 1992 elections and this process continued in 1997 as they had further improved their appeal to the electorate. Norris and Evans say that 'Such an interpretation would rest on broadened Labour support for non-traditional constituencies for the parties, such as among women or younger voters, due to the process of value change in the British electorate.'

Critical elections involve the biggest changes of all. They are 'those exceptional contests which produce abrupt, significant and durable realignments in the electorate with major consequences for the long-term party order'. They affect the agendas of several governments and not just the one elected in the critical election. Critical elections have three related features:

i.   There is some realignment in the 'ideological basis of party competition'. Issues which were not important in previous elections might become central to the political agenda. Alternatively, one or more parties might shift their ideological position so much that they 'leapfrog' over other parties. Thus, for example, a traditionally left-wing party might move so far that they become more right-wing than a party of the ideological centre. Another alternative is that a new party with significant support might become established for the first time.

ii. There will be 'some realignments in the social basis of party support'. For example, particular classes, ethnic groups or regions will change from predominantly supporting one party to supporting another.

iii. Finally, there will be 'realignments in the partisan loyalties of voters'. Large numbers of people become loyal to a party for the first time or shift their loyalty from one party to another.

There are a number of ways in which the 1997 election could be interpreted as a critical election which changed the face of British politics. It could be argued that the election saw a major shift to the right by the Labour Party, with the consequence of widening its social appeal to members of the middle class and gaining many new partisan supporters. Britain's role in the European Union emerged as an important issue while other issues declined in importance. For example, defence policies became less controversial with the end of the cold war between Russia (and previously the Soviet Union) and the West.

In their introductory chapter, Norris and Evans reserved judgement about whether 1997 was a critical election or not. We will now review the findings of the other social scientists who examined data from the *British Election Study* of 1997, before returning to the conclusions reached by Norris and Evans.

Ian Budge – changes in party policy and ideology

The first issue examined by one of the researchers was the question of how far the Labour Party had changed its policies and ideology. Ian Budge (1999) examined the major policy positions of the Labour Party, the Conservative Party and the Liberal Democrats (previously the Liberals and the Liberal/Social Democrat Alliance) in every election since 1945. Each sentence in the manifestos was analysed in terms of whether it adopted a left-wing or a right-wing stance. Budge then calculated whether, overall, the manifesto had a preponderance of left-wing or right-wing policies. Table 9.18 gives some indication of the sorts of policies that were judged to be left-wing or right-wing. Figure 9.6 charts the findings of the study.

Table 9.18 shows some significant movements in party ideology. Between 1992 and 1997 the Labour Party manifesto moved sharply to the right, so that for the first time in post-war history there were more right-wing than left-wing policies. Furthermore, Labour had leapfrogged over the Liberal Democrats, so that Labour's manifesto was the more right-wing.

However, Budge did not conclude that these changes were necessarily indicative of a critical election. The Liberal Democrats held their position on the centre-left, and the 'Conservatives kept, broadly speaking, their Thatcherite right-wing posture'. The Labour Party certainly changed its stance, but it deviated 'only from their leftward shift of position in 1992'. Having temporarily shifted to more left-wing policies in the previous election, Labour continued its general move to the right which had begun in 1983.

Table 9.18	Budge's left–right coding scale	
Codings of manifesto sentences		
Right emphases (sum of %s for)	Minus	Left emphases (sum of %s for)
Pro-military		Decolonization
Freedom, human rights		Anti-military
Constitutionalism		Peace
Effective authority		Internationalism
Free enterprise		Democracy
Economic incentives		Regulate capitalism
Anti-protectionism		Economic planning
Economic orthodoxy		Pro-protectionism
Social services limitation		Controlled economy
National way of life		Nationalization
Traditional morality		Social services expansion
Law and order		Education expansion
Social harmony		Pro-labour

Source: I. Budge, 'Party policy and ideology: reversing the 1950s?' in G. Evans and P. Norris (eds) (1999) *Critical Elections: British Parties and Voters in Long-Term Perspective*, Sage, London, p. 5.

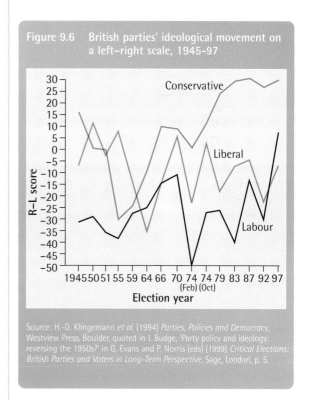

Figure 9.6 British parties' ideological movement on a left–right scale, 1945-97

Source: H.-D. Klingemann *et al.* (1994) *Parties, Policies and Democracy*, Westview Press, Boulder, quoted in I. Budge, 'Party policy and ideology: reversing the 1950s?' in G. Evans and P. Norris (eds) (1999) *Critical Elections: British Parties and Voters in Long-Term Perspective*, Sage, London, p. 5.

Budge does not believe that this change will necessarily be permanent. Having established a stronger electoral position, the Labour Party might well move back towards more left-wing policies, perhaps with a renewed emphasis on welfare spending. Budge therefore believes that 1997 can best be interpreted as a deviating election rather than a critical one, at least in terms of party ideology.

Pippa Norris – the ideology of MPs

Research by Pippa Norris (1999a) examines whether the shift to the right in Labour's manifestos is reflected in the ideology of Labour politicians. She uses survey data about more than 1,000 candidates and MPs from the major parties who stood in the 1992 and 1997 elections. The surveys included a range of questions that were used to measure the ideological stances of different candidates. For example, they were asked how far they agreed or disagreed with statements such as 'Ordinary working people get their fair share of the nation's wealth' and 'There is one law for the rich and one law for the poor' and 'Private enterprise is the best way to solve Britain's economic problems.'

Norris found strong evidence that there had been a shift to the right amongst Labour politicians. Compared to MPs and candidates in 1992, those in 1997 were more likely to agree that private enterprise could solve economic problems, and to disagree that major public services should be in public ownership, and that the government should be responsible for providing jobs. In all these respects there was evidence of a drift to the right.

Furthermore, Norris also detected a trend away from a liberal stance and towards what she calls a 'populist stance' on moral and social values. For example, Labour politicians became increasingly likely to endorse 'censorship to uphold moral standards' while fewer expressed tolerance of political rights for anti-democratic parties. Many more Labour MPs agreed that "young people today don't have enough respect for traditional values".

One exception was the issue of homosexuality where there was a move towards greater tolerance. By comparing the views of Labour MPs first elected in 1997 with those who had already been in Parliament, she found that these shifts were more marked among the new MPs. She also found them to be more evident amongst younger Labour MPs than older ones. Indeed, amongst all parties, MPs under 35 tended to be more right-wing than their older counterparts.

Overall, Norris found a convergence in the values of politicians from the three major parties, with some shift towards the centre from the Conservatives, the Liberal Democrats maintaining their centre-left position, and Labour being close to them. Comparing these results with the values of the British electorate as revealed in the election studies, she found that Labour politicians were 'closer to the median British voter than the average Conservative politician'. Labour seemed to have had some success in capturing the middle ground. Indeed, Conservative politicians expressed views which were so far to the right on economic issues that, in 1997, the views of Conservative voters were actually closer to those of Labour and Liberal Democrat politicians than they were to Conservative politicians.

Norris concludes that, in terms of the values of MPs, 'the new House does represent a decisive break with the past pattern of party competition'. With Labour and Liberal Democrat politicians having an ideological position close to the bulk of the British electorate, 'the Conservatives occupy a lonely but distinctive position on the right'. Nevertheless, the attitudes of the younger politicians suggest that the House of Commons might drift further right as younger politicians take the places of older ones.

Paul Webb and David Farrell – the ideology of party members

Webb and Farrell (1999) examine whether the changes in party manifestos and in the ideology of MPs and candidates were reflected in the ideology of party members. Labour saw an increase in party membership from 279,530 in 1992 to 405,000 in 1997, while the Conservative membership fell from 500,000 to 400,000 over the same period. Liberal Democrat membership held steady at around 100,000.

Webb and Farrell found some movement in the values of Conservative members. Generally they had moved a little to the right in the 1980s and then back to the left in the 1990s. However, changes amongst Labour members had been greater. Webb and Farrell say, 'After moving fairly sharply left between 1987 and 1992, they then lurched even more dramatically to the right between 1992 and 1997.' Like Labour MPs and candidates, Labour members also became more inclined to support authoritarian social and moral views. Webb and Farrell argue that the influx of new members joining the party after Tony Blair became leader accounts for much of this change.

Amongst members of all parties Webb and Farrell found that extreme views had become less common. They say, 'In general terms, the gap between party members and voters diminished considerably in the 1990s.' In the past, Conservative members tended to have more right-wing views than Conservative voters, while Labour members tended to have significantly more left-wing views than Labour voters. By 1997 the differences between members and voters were the smallest they had been for decades.

Webb and Farrell therefore argue that the 1997 election may have represented a 'critical realignment in the predominant pattern of party competition in

Britain'. However, they suggest that there is no guarantee that this state of affairs will persist. It is always possible that changing circumstances will produce new ideological splits between political leaders, party members and voters in each party.

Ivor Crewe and Katrina Thompson – dealignment or realignment?

Ivor Crewe and Katrina Thompson (1999) use *British Election Study* data to examine whether the dealignment Crewe had claimed to detect in earlier elections (see pp. 652–4 and 658–9) had continued in 1997. Realignment might have taken place if significant numbers of voters had started to identify with particular parties, when they had not done so in the past. There would be evidence of realignment if the big increase in the Labour vote represented a corresponding increase in its number of loyal supporters. If this had taken place, then it might indicate that 1997 was a critical election because it had changed the level of support the parties could expect at future elections.

On the other hand, 1997 might be no more than a deviating election if the Conservatives had been 'defeated by a temporary protest of dissatisfied voters' (Crewe and Thompson, 1999).

On the surface, the 1997 election did provide evidence of a dramatic realignment. According to Crewe and Farrell, it saw the biggest change in party identification since 1964. Conservative identifiers went down from 45 per cent to 39 per cent between 1992 and 1997, while Labour identifiers rose from 33 per cent to 46 per cent. The percentage of Conservative identifiers was the lowest it had been since 1964. All of this seemed to indicate that Labour had replaced the Conservatives as the natural majority party, only able to be defeated in exceptional circumstances. If that was the case, then 1997 would certainly have been a critical realigning election.

However, Crewe and Farrell interpret the data differently. They argue that questions about party identification measure little more than current voting preferences. Party identification changes in line with voting and says little about long-term commitments. According to Crewe and Farrell, a better indication of partisanship is found in those who *strongly* identify with a particular party.

Figure 9.7 shows a long-term trend towards declining partisanship, or what Crewe calls partisan dealignment. In 1964, 44 per cent of voters very strongly identified with a political party; by 1997 it was just 16 per cent. Furthermore, in 1997 it was the youngest voters – those in the 18-24 age group – whose partisanship was the weakest. While Labour benefited from a large swing in votes, it could not

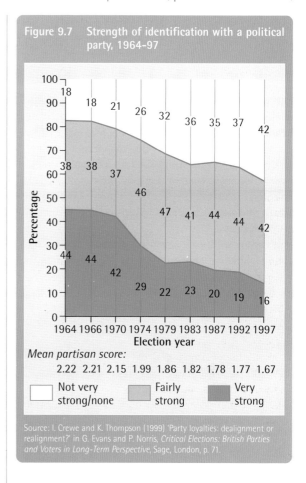

Figure 9.7   Strength of identification with a political party, 1964-97

Mean partisan score:

2.22 2.21 2.15 1.99 1.86 1.82 1.78 1.77 1.67

☐ Not very strong/none   ▨ Fairly strong   ▧ Very strong

Source: I. Crewe and K. Thompson (1999) 'Party loyalties: dealignment or realignment?' in G. Evans and P. Norris, *Critical Elections: British Parties and Voters in Long-Term Perspective*, Sage, London, p. 71.

claim to have gained a large block of loyal and partisan followers.

Crewe and Farrell note that the Labour Party continued to enjoy very high levels of popularity in the period after the election. With so many new supporters, the aftermath of the election provided the potential for substantial realignment towards the Labour Party. Crewe and Farrell describe an 'opportunity to harden the overwhelming but soft partisanship of young voters into a New Labour generation; but these same voters are open to conversion to another party if the government is perceived to fail.'

Labour's success was caused by 'ideological convergence' with other parties, as it shifted towards the ideological middle ground. It was not based on attracting loyal support from particular social groups, or based on specific policy issues. The electoral success and post-election popularity of Labour were largely based upon short-term political factors, such as a divided Conservative Party and a 'buoyant economy', rather than more long-term or fundamental factors. For Crewe and Farrell, then, 1997 was a potentially realigning election, but not one that in itself involved a critical realignment.

Geoffrey Evans, Anthony Heath and Clive Payne – class and voting in 1997

Part of Crewe and Sarlvick's original argument that dealignment was taking place suggested that class dealignment was occurring (see pp. 652–4). This view was questioned by Heath, Jowell and Curtice in their study of the 1983 election (see pp. 655–8), and in some subsequent work by these writers. This issue was discussed by Geoffrey Evans, Anthony Heath and Geoff Payne (1999) in relation to the 1997 election.

Evans et al. used a seven-class model devised by John Goldthorpe and Anthony Heath, rather than the simple division between manual and non-manual workers. They found that in 1997 unprecedented proportions of the service classes and other non-manual classes voted Labour.

Table 9.19 shows that, in 1997, over a third of the higher service class and over 40 per cent of the lower service class voted Labour, as did nearly half (49 per cent) of routine non-manual workers. Labour did even better amongst working-class voters but, compared to elections in the 1960s, the gap between the support Labour got from middle- and working-class voters was much narrower. Evans et al. note that Labour did no better amongst the working class in 1997 than they had in the 1960s, but between 1964 and 1997 their middle-class support more than doubled.

Table 9.19   Class by party vote for elections, 1964–97 (per cent)

Election	Base	Party	Higher service	Lower service	Routine non-manual	Petty bourgeoisie	Foremen & technicians	Skilled working class	Unskilled working class
1964	1,359	Con	65	61	59	74	37	25	26
		Lab	18	20	26	15	48	70	66
		Lib	17	19	15	11	15	5	8
1966	1,413	Con	66	56	49	67	35	22	25
		Lab	19	29	41	20	61	73	70
		Lib	15	15	10	13	4	5	5
1970	1,303	Con	66	60	51	69	39	33	32
		Lab	22	32	40	20	56	63	61
		Lib	12	8	9	11	5	4	7
1974 Feb	1,858	Con	59	51	45	68	39	23	24
		Lab	17	26	29	18	39	59	61
		Lib	24	23	26	14	22	18	15
1974 Oct	1,746	Con	57	47	44	70	35	20	22
		Lab	17	30	32	13	52	62	65
		Lib	26	23	24	17	13	18	13
1979	1,410	Con	61	61	52	77	44	28	34
		Lab	24	19	32	13	45	58	53
		Lib	15	20	16	10	11	14	13
1983	2,877	Con	60	53	53	71	44	33	29
		Lab	8	16	20	12	28	47	49
		Lib/SDP	32	31	27	17	28	20	22
1987	2,860	Con	63	50	51	64	39	31	31
		Lab	11	19	26	16	37	48	48
		Lib/SDP	26	31	23	20	24	21	21
1992	2,131	Con	66	50	54	66	41	37	28
		Lab	16	21	30	17	45	50	60
		Lib Dem	18	29	16	17	14	13	12
1997	1,822	Con	44	37	33	43	21	14	18
		Lab	34	42	49	40	62	67	69
		Lib Dem	22	21	18	17	17	19	13
Change 1992–97		Con	-22	-13	-21	-23	-20	-23	-10
		Lab	+18	+21	+19	+23	+17	+17	+9
		Lib Dem	+4	-8	-2	0	+3	+6	+1

Source: G. Evans et al. (1999) 'Class, Labour as a catch-all party?' in G. Evans and P. Norris, Critical Elections: British Parties and Voters in Long-Term Perspective, Sage, London, p. 90.

Evans *et al.* measured the overall relationship between class and voting, using a composite measure of 'changes in the odds ratios between classes and parties across elections' (see p. 656 for a description of odds ratios). The results are given in Figure 9.8.

In Figure 9.8 the 1964 election is taken as a base and other figures show how strong the class and voting relationship was in comparison to 1964. The figure shows what Evans *et al.* describe as 'a generally declining trend from the highest point in 1964 to the lowest in 1997 with some fluctuations in-between'. In 1997, for example, the class–voting relationship was only about 60 per cent as strong as it had been in 1964.

Unlike some of the earlier studies involving Anthony Heath, Evans *et al.* were prepared to admit that class was exercising a decreasing influence on voting patterns by the end of the millennium. However, they argued that this change was largely the result of changes in the Labour Party and its relationship with working-class voters. Statistically, much of the variation in the relationship between class and voting was caused by changes in the relationship between class and Labour voting. Evans *et al.* suggested, therefore, that it might be the changing character of the Labour Party that was largely responsible for the weakening relationship between class and voting. In particular, it might be caused by changes in the ideology and policies of Labour so that it became a party appealing to all classes (a 'catch-all party') rather than one which aimed its appeal specifically at the working class.

Evans *et al.* noted that the study by Ian Budge (see pp. 673–4) had found that the Labour Party had moved well away from a left-wing ideology by 1997 in an attempt to appeal to middle-class voters. Evans *et al.* looked at data from the *British Election Studies* which measured whether voters thought there was a 'good deal', 'some', or 'not much' difference between the parties. In 1997 only 33 per cent of voters thought there was a good deal of difference between the parties. This compares to 46 per cent giving this reply in 1964 and as many as 82 per cent in 1983 and 84 per cent in 1987.

In general, then, it appeared that the voters accurately perceived that the ideological gap between the parties had narrowed by 1997. Evans *et al.* attribute the decline in class-based voting to this reduction in the perceived ideological gap between the parties. In particular, the Labour Party attracted so many middle-class votes in 1997 because it had largely abandoned left-wing policies which would appeal to working classes but alienate middle classes.

The big fluctuations in the class and voting relationship between elections did not suggest that the changes were part of an inevitable and long-term trend in society. Rather they were a product of short-term political changes within parties. If this was the case, then the relationship between class and voting might strengthen in the future if a more clearcut ideological division between the Conservative and Labour parties returned.

Evans *et al.* therefore conclude that the dip in class voting in 1997 does not show that it was a critical election since it did not necessarily signal a

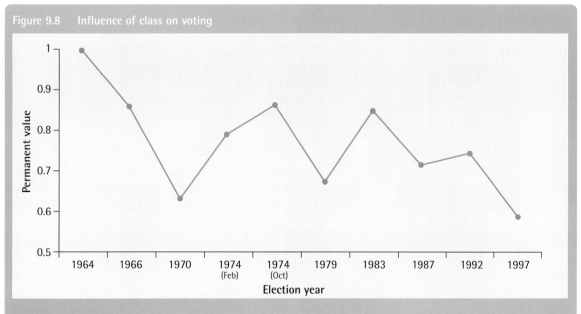

Figure 9.8   Influence of class on voting

Source: G. Evans et al. (1999) 'Class, Labour as a catch-all party?' in G. Evans and P. Norris, Critical Elections: British Parties and Voters in Long-Term Perspective, Sage, London, p. 93.

permanent change. They say, 'The future strength of class voting therefore depends more upon party strategy and electoral appeals than upon secular trends in society.'

Non-class cleavages and voting

If there was no critical change in class voting in 1997, did a critical change take place in the relationship between other social factors and voting? Researchers examined the *British Election Studies* for any major shift in voting according to ethnicity, gender and region. In the process, they were able to examine at least parts of Crewe's earlier arguments that sectoral cleavages might be replacing class divisions as a major influence on voting (see p. 653). Crewe saw region as one important sectoral cleavage but did not see ethnicity and gender as particularly significant.

Ethnicity

Shamit Saggar and Anthony Heath (1999) looked at the relationship between ethnicity and voting. Using data that went back to 1974, they found no evidence of a major shift in the voting of ethnic minorities. Labour attracted between 72 per cent and 83 per cent of ethnic-minority votes in the six elections between October 1974 and 1997; the Conservatives between 7 per cent and 18 per cent. In 1997 an overwhelming 84.8 per cent of blacks and Asians voted Labour, 11.3 per cent voted Conservative and 3.2 per cent voted for the Liberal Democrats. Saggar and Heath

conclude that the 1997 election reinforced existing patterns of ethnic-minority voting and that there was no evidence of a critical realignment.

Gender

Pippa Norris (1999b) found more evidence of changes in the relationship between gender and voting. In the 1960s and 1970s, women in Britain were proportionally more likely to vote Conservative and less likely to vote Labour than men.

In most countries, women have traditionally given more support to right-wing parties than men. Recent studies in a number of countries have suggested that the gender gap in voting is reducing. In some countries, such as the USA, the traditional gender pattern has been reversed. Women have gone from being more right-wing than men to being more left-wing.

Figure 9.9 shows the gender gap in post-war British elections. It calculates 'the difference in the Conservative-Labour lead among women minus the Conservative-Labour lead among men' (Norris, 1999b). For example, if the Conservatives had an 8 per cent lead over Labour among women but a 3 per cent lead among men, the gender gap would be 5 per cent. The figure shows that the gender gap has fluctuated considerably, from about 17 per cent in 1951 and 1955, to just around 2 per cent in 1987 and about 4 per cent in 1997. However, the figure does indicate a gradual reduction in the gender gap. Women are no longer much more inclined to vote Conservative than men.

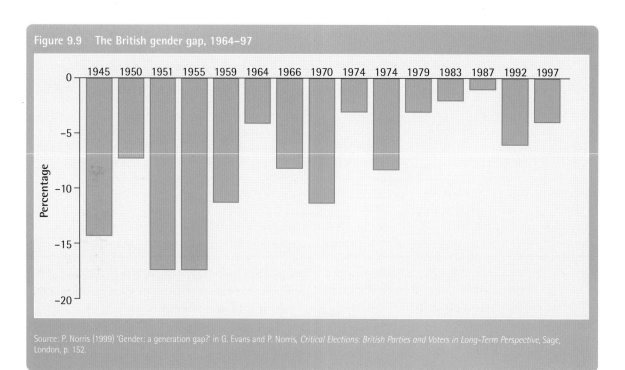

Figure 9.9   The British gender gap, 1964–97

Source: P. Norris (1999) 'Gender: a generation gap?' in G. Evans and P. Norris, *Critical Elections: British Parties and Voters in Long-Term Perspective*, Sage, London, p. 152.

Norris finds that the relationship between gender and voting is influenced by age. Older women are more likely to vote Conservative than older men, whereas younger women are more likely to vote Labour than younger men. Norris argues that:

The most plausible reason for this we can suggest is that the younger generation of women spent their formative years during the height of the second wave women's movement, the social revolution in sex roles which occurred in the 1960s, and the change in cultural values associated with feminism.

Norris, 1999b, p. 162

As older generations of women die and younger generations reach voting age we might therefore expect the gender-gap in voting to be reversed so that women become more inclined to vote Labour than men. Norris concludes that 1997 was not a critical election in terms of gender and voting. Women were still more likely to vote Conservative overall than men were. However, she does anticipate a gradual 'secular realignment' in patterns of gender and voting in line with the leftward drift she has detected among women.

Region and voting

John Curtice and Alison Park (1999) detected two main features of the geography of voting in the 1997 election:

1 The swing from Conservative to Labour was bigger in the southern parts of England than in the northern parts.

2 There was a good deal of tactical voting. In particular, in constituencies where either a Liberal Democrat or a Labour candidate seemed well-placed to unseat a Conservative MP, anti-Conservative voters seemed to switch to the party which had the best chance of defeating the Conservatives.

One consequence of these shifts was that the Conservatives lost more seats than they would have done if the fall in their vote had been evenly spread. Curtice and Park believe that the trends in the 1997 election represented dealignment rather than realignment. Between the mid-1950s and the mid-1980s regional factors exercised an increasing influence on voting. Even when factors such as class were taken into account, Labour gained more support in the north while the Conservatives increased their support in the south. The 1997 election reversed these trends and therefore reduced the influence of region in shaping people's voting preferences. Curtice and Park calculate that, between 1987 and 1997, a quarter of the regional gap in voting preferences disappeared, although southerners were still more likely to vote Conservative than northerners.

Curtice and Park examine a number of possible explanations for the narrowing of regional differences in voting.

First, they consider the idea that it was due to economic differences. While earlier recessions had generally had the most adverse effects on industrial jobs in northern constituencies, by the mid-1990s there were increasing numbers of job losses in services and in the south. So perhaps a sense of economic gloom had spread to the south and turned voters against the Conservative government. However, Curtice and Park found that at the time of the election those in the south of England were more likely than those in the north to believe that the economy was improving. They therefore dismissed this as a way of explaining the narrowing regional gap in voting.

Second, they considered the possibility that the change resulted from the Labour Party deliberately targeting southern voters. As part of their modernization strategy, the Labour Party set out to shed policies that were unpopular with southern voters. In particular, Labour abandoned its commitment to nationalization (which had been Clause 4 of its constitution), distanced itself from trade unions, and promised not to increase income tax.

Curtice and Park found some evidence to support this second theory. Data from the *British Election Study* of 1997 found that, throughout the country, Labour was perceived as being more right-wing than it had been in previous elections. People had noticed the changes in policy and this had affected people's image of the party.

Furthermore, by 1997, those in the south saw the Labour Party as more right-wing than those in the north. This could explain why Labour gained more ground in the south of the country, where much of the electorate was hostile to the more left-wing positions Labour had adopted in previous elections. Curtice and Park comment that 'overall, Labour's modernization project was particularly successful in overcoming negative perceptions and associations that the southern voter had of the party in the 1980s'.

In terms of tactical voting, Curtice and Park estimate that in 1997 nearly 5 per cent of voters switched to their second-preference party (either Labour or Liberal Democrats) in order to defeat a Conservative candidate. In contrast, in 1992 only about 3.5 per cent of voters did this, and in the previous two elections only about 3 per cent. So there was a significant increase in tactical voting. If this were to continue into future elections, then 1997 could be seen as a critical election.

However, this could not be seen as evidence of a critical realignment. The willingness to vote tactically is most common amongst those who do not have strong partisan loyalty to one party. The increase in tactical voting was therefore indicative of dealignment, particularly among those with left-of-centre views. Curtice and Park argue that:

> never before had Labour and the Liberal Democrats
> been felt to have so much in common. And as a
> result, more voters were relatively indifferent in
> their feelings towards the two parties while at the
> same time disliking the Conservatives.
>
> Curtice and Park, 1999, p. 144

Curtice and Park conclude that most of the evidence points to 1997 as a dealigning election. The north–south divide became less significant, and the closing of the ideological and policy gap between Labour and the Liberal Democrats weakened some people's attachment to either of these parties. The main reason for these changes was that people's perceptions of the parties had changed. The electorate's reasons for choosing to vote for a particular party had not altered radically, but people thought that the Labour Party had changed, making it more attractive to southern voters in particular. This would suggest that the ideological image of parties is an important factor shaping voting behaviour.

Geoffrey Evans – the issue of Europe

Geoffrey Evans (1999) used *British Election Study* data to examine the importance of policies on European integration in the 1997 election. Europe was certainly a significant issue to the political parties. The Conservatives were split over attitudes to Europe. The Euro-sceptic wing of the party opposed further integration in general, and the entry of sterling into a common European currency (the Euro) in particular. Some other senior Conservatives were Euro-enthusiasts and were strongly in favour of more integration. The Labour Party, which had adopted a stance opposed to European integration in the 1980s, was more pro-Europe than the Conservatives by the time of the 1997 election. Although the Labour manifesto did not commit a Labour government to accepting a common currency, it was not hostile to the possibility.

Evans found that, in 1997, Labour voters were more pro-Europe than Conservative voters. In 1992 there had been little difference in the attitudes to Europe among Conservative and Labour voters, and in previous elections it was Labour voters who were more anti-Europe and Conservative voters more pro-Europe. Thus the views of voters supporting these parties had shifted in line with the changing policies of the parties.

Although Evans found that views on Europe seemed to have only a small influence on voting, the issue did cut across traditional class allegiances. Working-class voters who were hostile to Europe were a little more likely to vote Conservative in 1997, compared to pro-Europe working-class voters. Conversely, Labour had more success among pro-Europe middle-class voters than among those who were anti-Europe. Because working-class voters tend to be more hostile to Europe than middle-class ones, the reversal in party policies towards Europe served to weaken the relationship between class and voting. Evans concludes that 'Europe now cross-cuts the left–right basis of voting and because of party realignment on the issue now serves to reduce the effects of class on vote.'

Pippa Norris and Geoffrey Evans – was 1997 a critical election?

Pippa Norris and Geoffrey Evans (1999b) reviewed the findings of all the researchers who analysed the 1997 *British Election Study* in order to decide whether 1997 was a critical election or not.

In terms of the result, they argue that factors such as the large swing from Conservative to Labour, the high level of volatility, and the big increases in the seats won by Labour and the Liberal Democrats do suggest that 1997 was a critical election. However, they point out that 'Labour's landslide was largely the product of the exaggerative qualities of the electoral system rather than landslide of votes.' Despite the size of their majority, Labour got significantly fewer than half of the votes cast.

In terms of changes in party politics, they see the ideological shift in Labour's position as the most significant feature of the election. For only the second time in post-war politics (the other occasion being 1964) Labour manifesto policies were more right-wing than those of the Liberal Democrats (previously the Liberals). Labour also had more right-wing than left-wing policies overall. Labour had broken with many of its socialist policies and adopted 'social liberalism … emphasizing market incentives, opportunities and civic responsibilities within a devolved state'.

Furthermore, this shift in policies was in line with changes in the views of party members and MPs. Younger MPs were particularly supportive of 'New Labour' policies. The closeness of the Labour and Liberal Democrat policies, compared to the distinctively right-wing policies of the Conservatives, was also a new feature of party competition in 1997.

However, Norris and Evans argue that there is little evidence of any major realignment of the electorate. The evidence points instead to increased dealignment. Fewer voters were strongly identifying with parties in 1997 than in previous elections. Class had declined in significance, but largely because Labour had adopted less left-wing policies. Labour's reversal of policy to become more sympathetic to

European integration lost them some working-class support, thus contributing to class dealignment. Regional and gender factors were exercising a less strong influence on voting, while ethnic minorities continued to offer strong support for Labour.

Overall, Norris and Evans believe that the most significant change in 1997 was the ideological dealignment involved in Labour's move to the centre. However, it was not clear in the aftermath of the election whether this would be a permanent change, or whether Labour would drift back towards more left-wing policies once they were more confident of success in future elections.

In terms of social changes and the relationship between parties and the electorate, Norris and Evans conclude that 'The most consistent evidence suggests a pattern of continuing secular dealignment in the British electorate due to political changes in party competition.' The 1997 election could not, therefore, be regarded as a critical election. It represented a deepening of previous trends towards dealignment and not a radical break with the past.

However, Norris and Evans did think that there was some possibility that 1997 could turn out to have been an important turning point. If Labour could achieve a sense of partisan loyalty amongst the large number of young voters who supported them in 1997, then they might have set in motion processes leading to an eventual realignment of party support in their favour.

Evaluation

Norris and Evans and the other writers who analysed the results of the 1997 *British Election Study* put primary emphasis upon the ideological shift in the Labour Party in explaining the result of the 1997 election. In doing so they rather downplay the role of other possible factors, particularly those relating to the unpopularity of the Conservative Party.

Anthony King (1998) argues that the main factor explaining the 1997 result was the unpopularity of the Conservative Party. He sees the exit of Britain from the Exchange Rate Mechanism (ERM) as the event which triggered the Conservatives' 'loss of reputation'. In previous elections some people had been unwilling to vote against the Conservatives

because they believed that the Conservatives were the only party who could be trusted to run the economy competently.

On 16 September 1992 – so-called 'Black Wednesday' – Britain was forced to leave the ERM as the result of speculators such as George Soros selling sterling and buying other currencies. This was despite the assertions of the Conservative chancellor, Norman Lamont, that Britain would not be forced to leave. Although the economy was actually quite successful in the period leading up to the 1997 election, the Conservatives were not seen as responsible. Economic success had followed when the Conservatives had been forced, against their will, to abandon the main plank of their economic policy. After Black Wednesday, Conservative ratings in opinion polls plummeted and never recovered.

Other problems added to the Conservatives' difficulties by the time of the 1997 election. King says that the Conservatives had:

> forfeited their reputation for economic competence – and their reputations for almost everything else besides – and they also managed to give the impression that they did not desperately care about, or were actively opposed to the great public services on which the great majority of the British people depend. (They also managed, in passing, to appear weak, hopelessly disunited, sleazy and disreputable.)
>
> King, 1998, p. 205

Labour won the election in the sense that they provided an apparently united, moderate and competent alternative to the Conservatives, but they only attracted so much support because the Conservatives had such a poor image.

If King's analysis is correct, then short-term political factors were more important than the changing ideology of the Labour Party, or deep-seated changes in the electorate. However, the loss of the Conservatives' reputation for economic competence could have longer-term repercussions, making it more difficult for them to win successive general elections in the future than it had been in the period from 1979 until 1997.

Sociology, power, politics, the state and values

As in all areas of sociology, those who adopt a particular perspective on power and politics often claim objectivity and accuse their opponents of ideological bias. As Geraint Parry noted, the early elite theorists such as Pareto and Mosca believed they

had established 'a neutral, "objective" political science, free from any ethical consideration' (Parry, 1969). From this standpoint, they dismissed Marxism as little more than ideology. Marxists have replied in a similar vein accusing elite theorists of merely translating ruling-class ideology into sociological jargon. However, it is doubtful whether any perspective has a monopoly on objective truth. It is possible to argue that all views on power, politics and the state owe something to the ideology and values of those who support them.

The ideological basis of Marxism is clearly visible. Marx was not only a sociologist but a political radical committed to the cause of the proletarian revolution. His writings reveal a vehement hatred of what he saw as the oppressive rule of the bourgeoisie. Marxists are committed to the idea of political equality, believing that it can only be realized in an egalitarian society based on communist principles.

From this standpoint, Marxists condemn the representative democracies of Western capitalist societies. Any reform in the political system which leaves the economic base of capitalism unchanged is seen as merely a concession to the proletariat which serves to maintain the status quo. Given their commitment to communism, it is noticeable that many Marxist writers were far more restrained in their criticisms of political inequality in the former USSR than they were in their criticisms of the West.

From the point of view of elite theory, Marxism is merely wishful thinking. Given the inevitability of elite rule, the egalitarian society is an illusion. However, the early elite theorists are just as vulnerable to the charge of ideological bias. Parry suggests that Pareto and Mosca began with a formula that was little more than a statement of conviction. They then scoured the history books selecting information that fitted their preconceived ideas. These ideas owed much to Pareto and Mosca's evaluation of the masses. They regarded the majority of people as generally incompetent and lacking the quality required for self-government.

Elite theory has often been seen as an expression of conservative ideology. With its assertion of the inevitability of elite rule, it can serve to justify the position of ruling minorities. Attempts to radically change the status quo, particularly those aimed at political equality, are dismissed as a waste of time. The removal of one elite will simply lead to its replacement by another.

Thus, as Parry observed, early elite theory 'offered a defence, in rationalistic or scientific terminology, of the political interests and status of the middle class' (Parry, 1969). In fact, Mosca went as far as to suggest that members of the working class were unfit to vote.

Despite their claims to objectivity and neutrality, the early elite theorists were strongly opposed to socialism. T.B. Bottomore argued that 'Their original and main antagonist was, in fact, socialism, and especially Marxist socialism' (Bottomore, 1966). Thus the debate between Marxists and elite theorists can

be seen, at least in part, as a battle between rival ideologies.

Pluralism can be seen as an expression of either conservative or liberal ideology, depending on the point of view of the observer. By implying that Western democracies are the best form of representative government that can be hoped for in complex industrial societies, elite pluralists can be seen to advocate the maintenance of the status quo. The inference from their argument is leave well alone. As Bottomore stated, the elite pluralist conception of democracy as representative government is limited and restricted compared to the idea of direct participation.

A commitment to this idea might well result in a very different analysis of Western political systems. This is evident from Bottomore's own work. He regarded the pluralist view of democracy as a poor substitute for the real thing. His belief that direct participation in politics by all members of society is a realistic alternative to representative government may well be influenced by a commitment to this ideal.

Frank Parkin suggested that 'pluralism is quite plausibly regarded as a philosophy which tends to reflect the perceptions and interests of a privileged class' (Parkin, 1972). Pluralism claims that all major interests in society are represented. However, in an unequal society, the interests of the rich and powerful are likely to be better served than those of the underprivileged. With its emphasis on the representation of all interests, pluralism tends to disguise this situation. It is likely to divert attention from the inequalities that result from the operation of the political process. By doing so it may help to maintain the status quo and provide support for the privileged.

While it has often been seen as a reflection of conservative ideology, pluralism has also been interpreted as a liberal viewpoint. Liberalism is a philosophy which accepts the basic structure of Western society while advocating progressive reforms within that structure. These reforms are directed by a concern for individual liberty and a desire to improve the machinery of democratic government.

Many pluralists admit that Western democracies have their faults, and are concerned to correct them. Thus Arnold Rose admits that the USA is not 'completely democratic' (Rose 1967) and looks forward to a number of reforms to make the existing system more representative. But he accepts that the basic framework of American society is sound and therefore does not advocate radical change.

Pluralism has found particularly strong support in the USA, and many of the important pluralist writers, such as Dahl and Rose, are American. To some degree their writings can be seen as a reflection of American culture. Since the Declaration of Independence, American society has emphasized the liberty of the individual rather than social equality. In this respect, it is significant that the USA has no major socialist party, unlike most of its West European counterparts.

This emphasis on liberty rather than equality is reflected in pluralist theory. From a pluralist perspective, democracy is a system of government which provides freedom for members of society to organize in the defence and promotion of their interests. Westergaard and Resler claim that pluralists 'value liberty more than equality' (Westergaard and Resler, 1976) and see the free-enterprise capitalist system as 'a bulwark of liberty'. The values of liberty and freedom of the individual are enshrined in the 'American Dream'. As a result, the writings of American pluralists may owe more than a little to the ethos of their society.

While Marxists, elite theorists and pluralists have argued over the values implicit in each other's theories, some postmodernists have argued that strongly-held political ideologies are being abandoned. Furthermore, they welcome this development, arguing that political ideologies create more problems than they solve.

Lyotard (1984), for example, rejects all metanarratives (or big stories) about how society is and how it should be run. He believes that a commitment to an ideology is always dangerous. People who are committed to certain political beliefs will commit inhuman acts in support of their ideology. Political leaders such as Stalin (the second leader of communist USSR) have been responsible for the murder of millions in the name of political ideology. Lyotard welcomes a change to a world in which people no longer believe in political metanarratives. Lacking such strong values, people are less likely to be able to justify the murder of others. To Lyotard, in a postmodern world people turn away from claiming to know absolute truths about society and they become more pragmatic. They believe only in those things that work and have a practical value.

Foucault's work also provides a radical departure from more conventional theories of power. By arguing that power/knowledge are inseparable and that power is all around, Foucault implies that the world cannot be changed by the political ideologies of states and governments. Power is highly dispersed, it is everywhere, and the only way to make any changes is in a piecemeal, localized way. This view can be seen

as implying fairly conservative values in which radical and widespread change cannot be achieved.

However, some sociologists claim that writers such as Lyotard and Foucault have failed to escape from the grip of value-laden ideologies. By denying the desirability or possibility of pursuing large-scale or radical changes in society, they become conservatives by default. If nothing can, or should, be changed, then the implication is that the status quo must be accepted. Madan Sarup, for example, says:

> *Politically, it is clear that thinkers like Lyotard and Foucault are neo-conservatives. They take away the dynamic on which liberal social thought has traditionally relied. They offer us no theoretical reason to move in one social direction rather than another.*
>
> Sarup, 1988, p. 140

The label of neo-conservatism is not, however, appropriate for all those calling themselves postmodernists. Others, such as Nancy Fraser (1995), remain committed to ideological struggles, and in many ways offer highly radical views supporting extensive changes in society.

However, Fraser rejects the idea that there is one ideology or issue which should subsume all others. She sees class, race and gender issues as all being important. She supports those whom she sees as struggling against class inequality, racism and sexism. Unlike Marxists, however, she does not see the struggle as an economic one, but rather as one to do with discourse – the way people talk and think about these issues.

In their own way, sociologists like Fraser are as committed to values as Marxists. Like Marxists, they believe in radical change and strive for liberation. Unlike Marxists, they are more likely to support a variety of causes (such as anti-racism, feminism, gay liberation and ecology) rather than one (proletarian revolution). As such, they reflect the plurality of new social movements discussed earlier in the chapter (see pp. 643–7).

Despite the recent developments in theories of power and in politics itself, it is still possible to discern a basic division between those influenced by conservative and those influenced by more radical values. Some of the issues and the terminology have changed, but the basic stances have not.

Chapter 10

Work, unemployment and leisure

Work, unemployment and leisure

The nature of work

Defining work and non-work

The concept of work appears easy to define, but in reality it is not. Keith Grint claims that 'no unambiguous or objective definition of work is possible' (Grint, 1991). He examines a number of definitions to illustrate his point:

1 First, he considers whether work can be seen as 'that which ensures individual and societal survival by engaging with nature'. One problem with this definition is that many activities commonly regarded as work – for example, writing sociology books! – may not be seen as essential or necessary for a society's survival.

2 Grint argues that work cannot be defined simply as employment. Many activities in which people are employed are also done by people who are not employed. Examples include washing up, ironing, childminding, car maintenance, decorating and even breastfeeding.

3 Grint denies that work can be defined as 'something we have to do' whether we like it or not. Eating and drinking come into this category but are not usually seen as work.

4 Work cannot be seen as non-leisure activities. Activities which are leisure for some may be work for others, such as playing football. In any case, work and leisure can take place simultaneously and be hard to separate. A round of golf for a manager with an important customer may combine work and leisure. In some societies work and leisure run together in nearly all activities. Grint refers to the anthropologist Malinowski's study of the Trobriand Islands where it was found that there 'is no separation between the work of gardening and the associated rituals – they are one and the same process'.

Grint concludes that work is socially defined: any definition has to be specific to a particular society at a particular time. He says 'Work, then, in its physical features and its linguistic descriptions is socially constructed ... there are aspects of social activities which we construe as work and this embodies social organization.'

In modern Western societies Grint sees employment as a type of work, but not the only type. Whether other activities are seen as work depends upon 'whose interpretation of the activity carries the most weight'. Grint himself, for example, clearly defines housework as work, but he recognizes that some people do not and he says:

> *the subordinate and gendered status of domestic labour and its popular classification as non-work is a valuable reminder of the significance of patriarchal ideology in the evaluation of work.*
>
> Grint, 1991, p. 40

In other words it is men's definitions of work which have usually carried the most weight, with the result that much of the effort expended by women has not been seen as work.

Attitudes to work in pre-industrial societies

Attitudes towards work have varied historically and from society to society. Furthermore, they vary within society and may be the focus for considerable conflict. These varying attitudes reflect the values and sometimes the interests of those who hold them.

According to Keith Grint, the ancient Greeks regarded work as part of 'the sphere of necessity' as opposed to 'the sphere of freedom'. It was looked down upon, and a good deal of the work was performed by slaves. He says:

> *anyone who had to work at an occupation all the time was ignoble, and ... the essence of ennoblement lay in the realm of politics, a realm based on but untarnished by, the labour of other, lesser mortals.*
>
> Grint, 1991, p. 15

In hunter–gatherer societies the situation is somewhat different. Grint claims that productive activity is kept to the minimum necessary. There is no work ethic and, as soon as there is enough food, hunting and gathering stop. In fact such societies often have no concept of work as such, and 'Work and non-work are not so much merged as irrelevant terms to describe the activity.'

In pre-industrial Britain, before the advent of factories, most work took place in or close to the home. Agriculture and domestic textile production were the two most common types of work for lower classes. A number of historians and sociologists have argued that pre-industrial workers did only as much work as they felt they had to. Shoshana Zuboff says:

> Work patterns were irregular, alternating between intense effort and idleness. Most work activities emanated from the home, and the distractions of the family, the taverns, and the social web of the community limited any undivided attention to work.
>
> Zuboff, 1988, p. 31

Domestic textile workers retained considerable control over their work and they frequently resisted efforts to get them to work harder. There was a widespread practice of 'St Monday'. People would work extra hard for part of the week in order to have Monday off. This custom often followed on from weekend drinking sessions, and early industrial entrepreneurs such as James Watt found that their workers would be drunk if they tried to force them to work on Monday.

Higher classes, too, had little enthusiasm for physical labour. Zuboff argues that three influences produced a contempt for labour which went back as far as the Middle Ages:

1 The Greek and Roman tradition, which saw labour as associated with slavery.

2 'The barbarian heritage that disdained those who worked the land and extolled the warrior who gained his livelihood in bloody booty.'

3 A Jewish and Christian tradition which 'admired contemplation over action'. It is notable that the Bible sees work as punishment for sin. Since Adam and Eve were expelled from the Garden of Eden, humans have had to earn their living by the sweat of their brow.

Until a few centuries ago, then, work was generally an irrelevant concept, or was seen as something to be avoided altogether or at least minimized. Until relatively recently, working hours for individuals were not regular. Yet many contemporary studies of the unemployed have shown that many of them miss work a great deal, and not just because their income

drops (see pp. 750–5). Modern Western attitudes towards work are therefore very different from those in ancient, hunter–gatherer or pre-industrial societies. This raises the question of where these contemporary attitudes have come from.

The origin of contemporary attitudes to work

Following the ideas of Weber (1958), some sociologists have argued that Protestantism had an important role in producing a contemporary work ethic. Weber argued that certain forms of Protestantism, particularly those based on Calvinism, encouraged a distinctive attitude to work. Calvinists saw their work as a calling from God and they worked with dedication and commitment to convince themselves that God had chosen them to go to heaven. (Weber's ideas are examined in detail in Chapter 7, pp. 447–51.)

The Protestant work ethic, as it is sometimes known, encouraged a much more positive attitude towards work than had been the case before. The elevation of work to a moral duty was encouraged by Victorian Englishmen such as Samuel Smiles. Keith Grint (1991) quotes Smiles's doctrine that 'Heaven helps those who help themselves.' The belief of such Victorians in saving money and not wasting it, working hard and living a sober life, closely resembles the beliefs of early Calvinists.

The Industrial Revolution itself was the second major source of modern attitudes to work. The historian E.P. Thompson (1967) argues that large-scale, machine-powered industry necessitated the introduction of new working patterns and with them new attitudes. According to Thompson, pre-industrial work was regulated by task orientation: the necessities of the job determined when and how hard people worked. For example, the changing seasons regulated agricultural work, while domestic textile workers determined how hard they worked and when they completed their tasks. Work and leisure were intermingled so there was 'no great sense of conflict between labour and passing the time of day'.

With industrialization, the expensive machinery had to be kept in use to repay the capital costs, and employers therefore sought to impose, and eventually succeeded in imposing, regular work patterns on employees.

These patterns of work were based around time rather than tasks. Thompson says 'Time is now currency: it is not passed but spent.' Workers who were used to a considerable amount of control over their work patterns experienced the new working day in the factory, with its emphasis on punctuality, as oppressive. They resented having to work to the clock. The early factory owners had considerable problems trying to persuade people to take jobs in the factories. When they had recruited workers they often regarded their reluctant employees as work-shy and lazy. They therefore sought to change their attitudes and get them to accept new working patterns. According to David Lee and Howard Newby:

> *workers brought up under the assumptions of 'task orientation', were subject to massive indoctrination on the folly of 'wasting' time by their employers, a moral critique of idleness which stemmed from the Puritan work ethic.*
>
> Lee and Newby, 1983, p. 29

Many contemporary attitudes to work can be traced back to such Victorian ideas. These include the unemployed demanding the right to work, students and young adults working hard to progress in their career, and employers penalizing workers who are persistently late. However, both during the Industrial Revolution and since, some individuals and groups have questioned the virtue of devoting themselves to work, or the wisdom of feeling guilty if they are 'wasting time'. For example, Keith Grint quotes the Russian anarchist Kropotkin who attacked the Victorian work ethic, saying:

> *let us begin by satisfying our needs of life, joy and freedom. And once all will have experienced this well-being we will set to work to demolish the last vestiges of the bourgeois regime, its morality derived from the account book.*
>
> Quoted in Grint, 1998, p. 20

Clearly, Kropotkin's views are emotive and value-laden, but the same can be said of those who have glorified hard work.

Different sociological views on work, leisure and unemployment have also been strongly influenced by the values of their authors. Indeed, sociologists who are strongly committed to an ideal of work and leisure often produce the most interesting and influential views on the subject. Karl Marx (whose ideas on work are similar to those of Kropotkin) is a case in point, and we will examine his views in the next section.

Work and leisure – conflict perspectives

Karl Marx – alienated labour

To Marx (1818–83), work – the production of goods and services – held the key to human happiness and fulfilment. Work is the most important, the primary human activity. As such it can provide the means either to fulfil people's potential or to distort and pervert their nature and their relationships with others.

In his early writings (particularly the *Economic and Philosophical Manuscripts*, first published in 1844) Marx developed the idea of alienated labour. At its simplest, alienation means that people are unable to find satisfaction and fulfilment in performing their labour or in the products of their labour. Unable to express their true nature in their work, they are estranged from themselves: they are strangers to their real selves. Since work is a social activity, alienation from work also involves alienation from others. Individuals are cut off from their fellow workers.

Marx believed that work provided the most important and vital means for people to fulfil their basic needs, their individuality and their humanity. By expressing their personality in the creation of a product, workers can experience a deep satisfaction. In seeing their product used and appreciated by others, they satisfy their needs and thereby express their care and humanity for others. In a community in which everyone works to satisfy both their individual needs and the needs of others, work is a completely fulfilling activity. In Marx's words, 'each of us would in his production have doubly affirmed himself and his fellow men'.

Apart from possibly the dawn of human history, Marx argued that this ideal has yet to be realized. Throughout history, humanity's relationship to its work has been destructive both to the human spirit and to human relationships.

The origins of alienation

Marx speculated that the origin of alienation is to be found in an economic system involving the exchange of goods by a method of barter. Within such a system the products of labour become commodities, articles of trade. With the introduction of money as a medium of exchange, they become commodities for buying and selling, articles of commerce. The products of labour are mere 'objects' in the market, no longer a means of fulfilling the needs of the individual and the community. From an end in themselves, they become a means to an end: a means for acquiring the goods and services necessary for survival. Goods are no longer a part of the individual who produces them. In this way 'the worker is related to the *product of his labour* as to an *alien* object'.

Alienation springs initially from the exchange of goods in some form of market system. From this develops the idea and practice of private property, the individual ownership of the means of production. Marx argues that 'although private property appears to be the basis and the cause of alienated labour, it is rather a consequence of the latter'. Once the products of labour are regarded as commodity objects, it is only a short step to the idea of private ownership. A system of private property then feeds back into the forces that produced it and heightens the level of alienation. This can be illustrated by capitalist economies in which the ownership of the means of production is concentrated in the hands of a small minority. Alienation is increased by the fact that workers do not own the goods they produce.

From the idea that workers are alienated from the product of their labour stem a number of consequences. Workers become alienated from the act of production, their actual work. Since work is the primary human activity, they become alienated from themselves. As a result, the worker:

> does not fulfil himself in his work but denies himself, has a feeling of misery rather than well-being, does not develop freely his mental and physical energies but is physically exhausted and mentally debased. The worker therefore feels himself at home only during his leisure time, whereas at work he feels homeless.

Marx, in Bottomore and Rubel, 1963, p. 169

Work ceases to become an end in itself, a satisfaction and fulfilment of human needs. It simply becomes a means for survival. As a means to an end, work cannot produce real fulfilment.

Alienated from the product of their work, the performance of their labour and from themselves, workers are also alienated from their fellows. They work to maintain the existence of themselves and their families, not for the benefit of the community. Self-interest becomes more important than concern for the social group.

Marx regarded the economic system, the infrastructure, as the foundation of society, which ultimately shaped all other aspects of social life. He divided the infrastructure into two parts: the 'means of production' and the 'relations of production'.

The means of production are the more important since, according to Marx, 'The social relations within which individuals produce, *the social relations of production, are altered, transformed, with the change and development of the material means of production*'. The means of production are the means used for producing goods. Thus, under feudalism – an

agrarian economy – land is the most important part of the means of production. Under capitalism, the raw materials and machinery used to manufacture the products of industry are major aspects of the means of production.

The relations of production are the social relationships associated with the means of production. In a capitalist economy, the relationship of the two main groups in society to the means of production is that of ownership and non-ownership. The capitalists own the means of production; the workers simply own their labour which, as wage earners, they offer for hire to the capitalists.

Alienation and capitalism

Marx argued that the nature of work in society can only be understood by examining it in terms of the infrastructure. He believed that a capitalist infrastructure inevitably produced a high level of alienation.

In a capitalist economy, a small minority own the means of production. Workers neither own nor have any control over the goods they produce. Like their products, workers are reduced to the level of a commodity. A monetary value is placed on their work and the costs of labour are assessed in the same way as the costs of machinery and raw materials. Like the commodities they manufacture, workers are at the mercy of market forces, of the law of supply and demand. During an economic recession many workers will find themselves jobless with few means of support. However, the unemployed are not alienated in the conventional Marxist sense of the word. Alienation is a consequence of wage labour.

Wage labour is a system of slavery involving the exploitation of workers. Only labour produces wealth, yet workers receive, in the form of wages, only a part of the wealth they create. The remainder is appropriated (taken) in the form of profits by the capitalists. Thus, the majority of society's members, the proletariat, usually work for and are exploited by a minority, the bourgeoisie.

Capitalism is based on self-interest, avarice and greed. It is a system of cut-throat competition concerned with the maximization of profit rather than the satisfaction of real human need. Trapped within this system, both capitalists and workers are alienated from their true selves. Members of both groups are preoccupied with self-interest in a system that sets individual against individual in a struggle for survival and personal gain.

Marx saw two important characteristics of industrial society – the mechanization of production and a further specialization of the division of labour – as contributing to the alienation of the workforce. However, he stressed that the capitalist economic system, rather than industrialization as such, is the primary source of alienation.

Marx argued that the mechanization of production reduces the physical effort involved in work but 'The lightening of the labour even becomes a sort of torture, since the machine does not free the labourer from work, but deprives it of all interest.' Mechanization and associated mass production reduce the need for skill and intelligence and remove from work 'all individual character and consequently all charm for the workman. He becomes an appendage of the machine, and it is only the most simple, most monotonous, and most easily acquired knack, that is required of him.'

Industrial society also involves a further specialization of the division of labour. People are trapped in their occupational roles since they must specialize in a particular activity in order to earn their living. In Marx's words, 'each man has a particular exclusive sphere of activity, which is forced upon him from which he cannot escape'. Freedom and fulfilment are not possible when people are imprisoned in a specialized occupation, since only a limited part of themselves can be expressed in one job. As we will see, this is very different from Durkheim's assessment (see pp. 691–3).

Communism and the end of alienation

Marx's solution to the problem of alienated labour is a communist or socialist society in which the means of production are communally owned and the specialized division of labour is abolished. He believed that capitalism contained the seeds of its own destruction: the concentration of alienated workers in large-scale industrial enterprises would encourage an awareness of exploitation, of common interest, and facilitate worker organization to overthrow the ruling capitalist class. In a communist society workers would at one and the same time produce goods for themselves and the community, and so satisfy both individual and collective needs.

Evaluation

Marx's theory of alienation has been criticized in a number of ways. His views on alienation under communism have been regarded as simplistic and naive by many critics. In his analysis of East European communism, Milovan Djilas (1957) argued that, although the means of production were communally owned, they were controlled by and for the benefit of a ruling elite. He claimed that 'Labour cannot be free in a society where all material goods are monopolized by one group.'

Marx also gives little indication of how the specialized division of labour can be abolished in socialist society. He simply states that:

in a communist society, where nobody has one exclusive sphere of activity but each can become accomplished in any branch he wishes, society regulates the general production and thus makes it possible for me to do one thing today and another thing tomorrow, to hunt in the morning, fish in the afternoon, rear cattle in the evening, criticize after dinner, just as I have a mind, without ever becoming hunter, fisherman, shepherd or critic.

Marx, in Bottomore and Rubel, 1963, p. 97

Marx thus pictures a society in which members are able to train for those jobs that interest them and move from one task to another, as the mood takes them.

Many critics have questioned the practical possibility of such a system. Furthermore, the collapse of communism in the former USSR and Eastern Europe during the late 1980s and early 1990s suggests that the abolition of the specialized division of labour is unlikely to take place.

Marx has also been attacked for his work on alienation by some Marxists. Some have argued that this early part of his work is too abstract and philosophical. As defined by Marx, alienation is impossible to measure. Workers cannot be asked if they are alienated since their alienation would prevent them from realizing that they were. It is therefore also impossible to support or disprove his theory. Marxists such as Louis Althusser (1969) have therefore dismissed this part of Marx's writings as unscientific. They argue that only Marx's later writings, focusing on economics and exploitation, provide a proper basis for a scientific Marxist understanding of society.

We will deal with further criticisms of Marx's views as the chapter progresses, but for an examination of the concept of alienation within the general framework of Marxist theory, see Chapter 15.

Herbert Marcuse – alienation from work and leisure

Herbert Marcuse (1972) was a neo-Marxist who tried to develop Marx's original theory of alienation. Although he accepted much of Marx's work, Marcuse placed less emphasis than Marx himself on the centrality of work to people's lives. He put more stress on the consumption of products.

When Marx first outlined his views on alienated labour – in 1844 – workers in industry worked between 12 and 16 hours a day. Alienated in the factory, workers had few opportunities for fulfilment in leisure. They had time for little else save what Marx described as 'animal functions' – eating, sleeping and procreating. Existing on subsistence wages, often in appalling living conditions, workers had few means for self-fulfilment in leisure even if they did have the time. Marx regarded non-work time as simply a means for the workforce, the fodder of capitalism, to recover and recuperate from its labour – and reproduce itself.

Advanced industrial society has seen a significant reduction in working hours – in Western Europe and America industrial employees work on average between 40 and 46 hours a week – and a steady rise in the living standards of the population as a whole. It would appear that the opportunity for self-fulfilment in leisure has greatly increased, but many neo-Marxists argue that this opportunity has not been realized.

Leisure and 'false needs'

In *One Dimensional Man*, Marcuse discusses both capitalist societies and the former communist societies of Eastern Europe. He argues that all advanced industrial societies crush the potential for personal development. Work is 'exhausting, stupefying, inhuman slavery'. Leisure simply involves 'modes of relaxation which soothe and prolong this stupefaction'. It is based on and directed by false needs, which are largely imposed by a mass media controlled by the establishment. Needs are false if they do not result in true self-fulfilment and real satisfaction. If the individual feels gratified by the satisfaction of false needs, the result is merely 'euphoria in unhappiness' – a feeling of elation on a foundation of misery. Marcuse claims that:

> *Most of the prevailing needs to relax, to have fun, to behave and consume in accordance with the advertisements, to love and hate what others love and hate belong to this category of false needs.*
>
> Marcuse, 1964, p. 5

Members of society no longer seek fulfilment in themselves and in their relationships with others. Instead, 'The people recognise themselves in their commodities; they find their soul in their automobile, hi-fi set, split-level home, kitchen equipment.' The circle is now complete: industrial man or woman is alienated from every sphere of his or her life.

Marcuse presents a very pessimistic view of the nature of leisure in industrial society. He pictures a mindless 'happy robot' compulsively chasing false needs. He suggests that the term happy consciousness, which describes the false belief that 'the system delivers the goods', is more appropriate today than Marx's phrase false class consciousness. Relative affluence and the extension of leisure have

simply changed chains of iron into chains of gold. Ruling classes and ruling elites have strengthened their hold over the workforce by making its exploitation more bearable.

False needs serve to divert attention from the real source of alienation. Their satisfaction simply coats the bitter pill with sugar. At one and the same time false needs provide a highly motivated labour force which works for the money to consume, and a ready market for the products of industry.

C. Wright Mills – white-collar alienation

C. Wright Mills rejected some aspects of the Marxist perspective on society. He believed that US society was dominated by a ruling elite rather than a ruling class which owned the means of production. Nevertheless he accepted that there was a conflict of interest between the main groups in society: the ruling elite and the mass of the population. Furthermore, in a study of the American middle classes entitled *White Collar* (1951), Mills applied Marx's concept of alienation to non-manual workers.

Mills stated that the expansion of the tertiary sector (the service sector) of the economy in advanced capitalist societies had led to a 'shift from skills with things to skills with persons'. Just as manual workers became like commodities by selling their 'skills with things', a similar process occurred when non-manual workers sold their 'skills with persons' on the open market.

Mills referred to this sector of the economy as the personality market. A market value was attached to personality characteristics and, as a result, people sold pieces of their personality. Therefore, managers and executives were employed not simply because of their academic qualifications and experience, but for their ability to get on with people. The salesperson was given a job for his or her apparent warmth, friendliness and sincerity.

However, because aspects of personality were bought and sold like any other commodity, individuals were alienated from their true selves. Their expression of personality at work was false and insincere. Mills gave the example of a girl working in a department store, smiling, concerned and attentive to the whims of the customer. He stated 'In the course of her work, because her personality becomes the instrument of an alien purpose, the salesgirl becomes self-alienated.' At work she is not herself.

In the salesroom, in the boardroom, in the staffroom, in the conference room, men and women were prostituting their personalities in pursuit of personal gain. Mills regarded American society as a 'great salesroom' filled with hypocrisy, deceit and insincerity. Rather than expressing their true person-alities and feelings, people assumed masks of friend-liness, concern and interest in order to manipulate others to earn a living.

Mills's pessimistic view of the sale of personality in American capitalist society is summarized in the following quotation:

> *The personality market, the most decisive effect and symptom of the great salesroom, underlies the all-pervasive distrust and self-alienation so characteristic of metropolitan people ... People are required by the salesman ethic and convention to pretend interest in others in order to manipulate them ... Men are estranged from one another as each secretly tries to make an instrument of the other, and in time a full circle is made – one makes an instrument of himself and is estranged from It also.*
>
> Mills, 1951

In this way people were alienated from themselves and from each other.

Although several decades old, there is little reason to suppose that Mills's analysis is any less applicable today than it was then.

Criticisms of conflict perspectives

Conflict perspectives on the nature of work and leisure are open to a number of criticisms:

1 They are based partly on a rather vague picture of what people could and ought to be. It can be argued that this view says more about the values of particular sociologists than it does about people's essential being. Many of the arguments are grounded in assumptions about human nature which are impossible to prove.

2 They tend to ignore the meanings held by members of society. If people claim fulfilment in work and/or leisure, there is a tendency to dismiss their views as a product of false class consciousness. This applies particularly to Marxist views.

3 Conflict perspectives are very general. As Alasdair Clayre (1974) notes, they tend to lump together diverse occupations and leisure activities and create a simple model of people in industrial societies.

Possible correctives to these shortcomings will be dealt with in later sections, but we will now look at work from a functionalist perspective.

Emile Durkheim – *The Division of Labour in Society* – a functionalist view

Where Marx was pessimistic about the division of labour in society, Emile Durkheim (1858–1917) was cautiously optimistic. Marx saw the specialized division of labour as trapping workers in their occupational role and dividing society into antago-nistic social classes. Durkheim saw a number of problems arising from specialization in industrial society, but believed that the promise of the division of labour outweighed the problems. He outlined his views in *The Division of Labour in Society*, first published in 1893 (Durkheim, 1947).

Pre-industrial society – mechanical solidarity

Durkheim saw a fundamental difference between pre-industrial and industrial societies. In the former there is relatively little social differentiation: the division of labour is comparatively unspecialized. Most people are involved in hunting and gathering. Social solidarity in pre-industrial societies is based on similarities between individual members. They share the same beliefs and values and, to a large degree, the same roles. This uniformity binds members of society together in a close-knit communal life.

Durkheim refers to unity based on resemblance as mechanical solidarity. He describes the extreme of mechanical solidarity in the following way:

> *Solidarity which comes from likeness is at its maximum when the collective conscience completely envelops our whole conscience and coincides with all points in it. But at that moment our individuality is nil. It can be borne only if the community takes a small toll of us.*
>
> Durkheim, 1947

In a society based on mechanical solidarity, members are, as it were, produced from the same mould.

Industrial society – organic solidarity

Solidarity in industrial society is based not on unifor-mity but on difference. Durkheim referred to this form of unity as organic solidarity. Just as in a physical organism the various parts are different yet work together to maintain the organism (for example, the heart, liver and brain in the human body), so, in industrial society, occupational roles are specialized yet function together to maintain the social unit.

Where Marx saw the division of labour as divisive, Durkheim believed it could increase the interdependence of members of society and so reinforce social solidarity. In order to produce goods and services more efficiently, members of industrial society specialize in particular roles. Specialization requires cooperation. For example, a large range of specialists are required to design, manufacture and market a particular product. Members of society are dependent on each other's specialized skills and this interdependence forms the basis of organic solidarity.

However, the interdependence of skills and the exchange of goods and services are, in themselves, insufficient as a basis for social solidarity. The specialized division of labour requires rules and regulations – a set of moral codes which restrain the individual and provide a framework for cooperation. The exchange of goods and services cannot be based solely on self-interest, 'for where interest is the only ruling force each individual finds himself at war with every other'.

Durkheim saw the development of contract as a beginning of the moral regulation of exchange. Two parties enter into a legal agreement based on a contract for the exchange of goods and services. Contracts are governed by a general legal framework and grounded in shared beliefs about what is just, reasonable, fair and legitimate; but Durkheim saw the growth of contract as only a beginning. It was insufficient as a moral foundation for industrial society.

Anomie

Durkheim believed that the specialized division of labour and the rapid expansion of industrial society contained threats to social solidarity. They tended to produce a situation of anomie which, literally translated, means normlessness.

Anomie is present when social controls are weak, when the moral obligations that constrain individuals and regulate their behaviour are not strong enough to function effectively. Durkheim saw a number of indications of anomie in late nineteenth-century industrial society: in particular, high rates of suicide, marital break-up and industrial conflict. Such behaviour indicates a breakdown of normative control.

Industrial society tends to produce anomie for the following reasons. It is characterized by rapid social change which disrupts the norms governing behaviour. In Durkheim's elegant phrasing, 'The scale is upset; but a new scale cannot be immediately improvised. Time is required for the public conscience to reclassify men and things.'

In particular, Durkheim argued that the customary limits to what people want and expect from life are disrupted in times of rapid change. Only when desires and expectations are limited by general agreement can people be happy, since unlimited desires can never be satisfied.

In industrial society people become restless and dissatisfied, since the traditional ceiling on their desires has largely disintegrated. Increasing prosperity resulting from economic expansion makes the situation more acute. Durkheim states:

> *With increased prosperity desires increase. At the very moment when traditional rules have lost their authority, the richer prize offered these appetites stimulates them and makes them more exigent and impatient of control.*
>
> Durkheim, 1947

A new moral consensus about what people can reasonably expect from life is required. This will involve the regulation of competition in the exchange of goods and services. Exchange must be governed by norms regulating prices and wages, which involve a general agreement on issues such as a fair and reasonable return for services. This agreement will set limits on people's desires and expectations.

Not only rapid social change but the specialized division of labour itself tends to produce anomie. It encourages individualism and self-interest since it is based on individual differences rather than similarities. There is a tendency for the individual to direct his or her own behaviour rather than be guided and disciplined by shared norms.

Although Durkheim welcomed this emphasis on individual freedom, he saw it as a threat to social unity, since it tends to erode a sense of duty and responsibility towards others – factors which Durkheim saw as essential for social solidarity. He maintains, 'If we follow no rule except that of a clear self-interest in the occupations that take up nearly the whole of our time, how should we acquire a taste for any disinterestedness, or selflessness or sacrifice?'

Occupational associations and anomie

Whereas Marx's solution to the problem of alienation was radical – the abolition of capitalism and its replacement by socialism – Durkheim believed that the solution to anomie could be provided within the existing framework of industrial society. The self-interest which dominates business and commerce should be replaced by a code of ethics which emphasizes the needs of society as a whole. In Durkheim's words, 'economic activity should be permeated by ideas and needs other than individual ideas and needs'.

Durkheim sees occupational associations as the means to subject economic activity to moral regulation. Various industries should be governed by freely elected administrative bodies on which all occupations in the industry are represented. These bodies would have the power 'to regulate whatever concerns the business: relations of employers and employed – conditions of labour – wages and salaries – relations of competitors one to the other and so on'.

Such associations would solve the problem of anomie in two ways:

1 They would counter individualism by reintegrating individuals into a social group which would re-establish social controls.

2 By establishing a consensus about the rewards various members of society could reasonably and justifiably expect, normative limits would be placed on individual desire. This consensus would form the basis for rules to regulate economic activity.

In particular, Durkheim believed that inheritance as a mechanism for distributing property would gradually die out because of its 'fundamental injustice'. Property would be owned by occupational associations and exchanged by means of contracts. Economic rewards would be based on the contribution of the services of various occupations to the well-being of the community. Then, 'the sole economic inequalities dividing men are those resulting from the inequality of their services'.

Durkheim envisaged a delicate balance between the state and occupational associations. In the absence of occupational associations, the state might assume despotic powers and, conversely, without some form of state regulation, each association might assume despotic control over its members. In addition, the state would coordinate and regulate economic activity on a national level and enforce a common morality – a moral consensus – which is essential for social solidarity.

This vision of an efficiently functioning organic solidarity was influenced by Durkheim's view of professional associations – the voluntary associations which administer the practice of professionals such as doctors and lawyers. In professional associations he saw many of the features that were lacking in industry and commerce. These included a clearly established code of conduct, which is binding on all members, and a sense of duty, responsibility and obligation to the community as a whole. Durkheim saw such professional ethics as the key to a future moral order in industrial society.

The professions – a prototype for a future moral order?

As outlined in Chapter 2 (pp. 60–1), the functionalist view of the professions largely mirrors Durkheim's optimism. The professional association integrates individual members into an occupational group.

Through its control of training and education, the association establishes both professional competence and professional ethics. Control of occupational behaviour in terms of these ethics is established by the power of the association to bar particular members from practising if they break the established code of conduct. For example, doctors can be struck off the register and barred from practice for professional misconduct.

Professional ethics emphasize altruism: a regard for others rather than a narrow self-interest. Professionals are supposed to be concerned with serving the community in general, and their clients in particular, rather than supporting sectional interests or furthering their own interests. Thus lawyers are the guardians of the law in the interests of society as a whole; doctors, directed by their Hippocratic oath, are concerned first and foremost with the health of the community. The relatively high rewards (in terms of income and prestige) received by professionals reflect their important contribution to the well-being of society. This functionalist view of professionals thus provides a model for Durkheim's future moral order.

However, this optimistic view has been attacked by other sociologists. Those adopting or influenced by a Weberian approach see professions as groups organized to defend their own interests rather than as groups serving society as a whole (see pp. 61–2). Macdonald, for example, sees professionalism as a project adopted by certain groups of workers in order to improve their status and strengthen their market situation (see pp. 61–2). From this point of view, professionalism is not a characteristic inherent in certain types of job, but a status actively achieved through the efforts of groups of workers.

From the viewpoint of radical conflict theorists and Marxists, professions serve the interests of powerful groups in society (see pp. 62–3). Far from acting as a prototype for a future moral order, they act to preserve the existing moral order and maintain the position of the powerful.

The critical views of the professions we have just outlined suggest that Durkheim's moral reintegration of a society based on organic solidarity will require more fundamental changes than occupational associations. Durkheim sees differences in reward based on a consensus on the occupation's value to the community. However, he underestimates the possibility that, once some are more equal than others, they have the power to define their services as more worthy and valuable than others, and in doing so further their own interests.

Technology and work experience

In this section we return to issues raised by Marxist approaches to work. We will look at the meaning and experience of work, but examine these factors largely in terms of specific occupations, rather than in terms of society as a whole. In particular, we will consider the influence of production technology on the organization of work, and on the behaviour and attitudes of workers.

Robert Blauner – alienation and technology

In a famous study published in the 1960s entitled *Alienation and Freedom*, the American sociologist Robert Blauner examined the behaviour and attitudes of manual workers in the printing, textile, automobile and chemical industries (Blauner, 1964). He saw production technology as the major factor influencing the degree of alienation that workers experienced.

Blauner defined alienation as 'a general syndrome made up of different objective conditions and subjective feelings and states which emerge from certain relationships between workers and socio-technical settings of employment'.

Objective conditions refer mainly to the technology employed in particular industries. Subjective feelings and states refer to the attitudes and feelings that workers have towards their work. This information is obtained from questionnaires.

Blauner claimed to account for attitudes towards work in terms of production technology. Thus, different forms of technology produced different attitudes towards work and, therefore, varying degrees of alienation. Blauner divided the concept of alienation into four dimensions:

1 the degree of control workers have over their work;
2 the degree of meaning and sense of purpose they find in their work;
3 the degree to which they are socially integrated into their work;
4 the degree to which they are involved in their work.

In terms of these four dimensions, the alienated worker has a sense of powerlessness, meaninglessness, isolation and self-estrangement

Craft technology

Blauner first examined the printing industry, arguing that it typifies pre-industrial craft technology. (His study was conducted at a time when neither mechanical nor computerized typesetting was widespread.

Most typesetting was done by hand and required considerable skill.) Questionnaire data from workers in the four industries studied showed that printers had the highest level of job satisfaction. For example, only 4 per cent of printing workers found their work dull and monotonous, compared to 18 per cent in textiles, 34 per cent in the automobile industry and 11 per cent in the chemical industry.

Blauner argued that, in terms of his four dimensions of alienation, printers were non-alienated workers: they had control over their work and therefore did not experience a sense of powerlessness. Work was done by hand rather than by machine.

The nature of print technology meant that the worker was largely free from external supervision. Self-discipline, rather than control from supervisors or managers, largely determined the quality of the product, the speed of work and the quantity of output.

Compared to many industries, printing did not involve a highly specialized division of labour or a standardized product. These factors contributed to the relatively high degree of meaning and purpose printers found in their jobs. By working on a large segment of the product, they could see and appreciate their contribution to the finished article – the newspaper, book or magazine.

Largely because of the nature of print technology, the printer identified with the craft and other craft workers. Print technology encouraged printers to develop their skills and take a pride in their work. They were not tied to a machine and this allowed them to move around the shop floor and talk to others. In terms of the third dimension of alienation – the degree of social integration – printers were not socially isolated.

Due to their control over their work, the meaning they found in work and their integration into an occupational community, printers did not experience self-estrangement from work.

Mechanization – machine minding

If the printing industry represented pre-industrial production, the textile industry was typical of the early stages of industrialization. Most textile workers were machine minders.

In terms of the first dimension of alienation – degree of control – textile workers experienced a sense of powerlessness. They were tied to their machines with little freedom of movement. Their tasks were routine and repetitive, requiring little judgement or initiative and offering few opportunities to take decisions.

Production technology in textiles provided little opportunity for meaning and purpose in work. The product was standardized and the worker performed only a few routine operations. The work involved little skill and variety and the individual worker's contribution to the finished product was small. These factors largely prevented workers from taking a pride in and deriving a sense of purpose from their work.

Blauner argued that the objectively alienating factors of textile technology should result in textile workers feeling isolated and self-estranged. However, this was not the case. Blauner explained this in terms of the community setting of the industry. The workers in his survey lived in small, close-knit communities, united by ties of kinship and religion. The majority of the adults worked in the textile mills. They felt a part of the industry because they were a part of the community.

Mechanization – assembly-line production

Blauner argued that alienation was found in its most extreme form in assembly-line production in the automobile industry. His data indicated that 34 per cent of manual workers in the industry found their jobs dull and monotonous, but this figure rose to 61 per cent for those working directly on the assembly line.

Workers on the line had little control over their work. The line determined the speed of work and afforded little freedom of movement. The particular job, tools and techniques used were 'predetermined by engineers, time-study technicians and supervisors'. Decisions were taken out of the worker's hands and there was little call for skill, judgement or initiative. As a result they experienced a sense of powerlessness.

Mass production on assembly lines afforded little opportunity for experiencing meaning and purpose in work. The product was standardized, the work was routine and repetitive, and tasks were highly fragmented – broken down into their simplest components, with each worker specializing in a small number of operations.

Workers on assembly lines were socially isolated. They did not feel a part of the company for which they worked nor did they integrate into an occupational community of workmates. They were tied to the line, working as individuals rather than in groups. They had little opportunity to socialize with their fellow workers. Unable to identify with the product or with a particular skill, they did not form occupational communities like the craft printers.

Assembly-line technology produced a high level of self-estrangement. In fact many workers felt hostility towards their work. The only aspects of the job that were liked by those in the survey were levels of pay and security of employment. The high degree of alienation produced an instrumental attitude to work – work was simply a means to an end. Hostility

and an instrumental approach to work accounted in part for the relatively high level of strikes and unrest in the automobile industry.

Automation

Finally, Blauner examined work in the chemical industry, which involved the most recent developments in production technology. The oil and chemical industries employed automated continuous-process technology whereby the raw materials entered the production process, the various stages of manufacture were automatically controlled and conducted by machinery, and the finished product emerged 'untouched by human hand'.

Blauner believed that automation reversed the 'historic trend' towards increasing alienation in manufacturing industry. It restored control, meaning, integration and involvement to the worker. Although the product was manufactured automatically, the worker had considerable control over and responsibility for production. Work in chemical plants involved monitoring and checking control dials which measured factors such as temperature and pressure. Readings indicated whether or not adjustments had to be made to the process. Blauner stated that these decisions required 'considerable discretion and initiative'.

Work also involved the maintenance and repair of expensive and complicated machinery. Skilled technicians ranged freely over the factory floor; there was considerable variety in their work compared to routine machine minding and assembly-line production. In direct contrast to assembly-line workers, none of the process workers felt that they were controlled or dominated by their technology. (Today, many assembly lines are automated and have similarities with the automated production systems of the chemical factories described by Blauner.)

Compared to craft work, Blauner argued that, in continuous-process technology, 'the dominant job requirement is no longer manual skill but responsibility'. This emphasis on responsibility restored meaning and purpose to work; it was an 'important source of satisfaction and accomplishment'.

Process technology halted the increasingly specialized division of labour. It integrated the entire production process and, since workers were responsible for the overall process, they could see and appreciate their contribution to the finished product. Their sense of purpose was increased by the fact that process workers operated in teams with collective responsibility for the smooth running of the machinery. Again, this encouraged the individual worker to feel a part of the overall production process.

Unlike the assembly-line worker, the process worker did not experience social isolation. The integration of maintenance and repair workers into a team and its movement around the factory floor furthered the integration of the workforce. Since physical effort was no longer involved in actual production, management no longer needed to police the workforce to drive it to greater effort. The line between management and workers tended to become blurred, since their relationship was based on consultation rather than coercion.

Both management and workforce were concerned with the trouble-free operation of production machinery. To further this shared goal, the consultation of workers 'with supervisors, engineers, chemists and other technical specialists becomes a regular, natural part of the job duties'.

Blauner argued that the technology of automated production integrates the workforce as a whole. This has important consequences for industrial relations. Blauner claimed that the process worker would be 'generally lukewarm to unions and loyal to his employer'. Unlike craft workers, process workers did not identify with a craft as such and form strong unions on the basis of this identification; unlike assembly line workers, they did not simply work for money and consequently strongly support unions as a means to increase their wage packets.

Because the process workers were non-alienated in terms of the first three dimensions of alienation, they were involved in their work. Blauner claimed that process work provided 'an opportunity for growth and development'. He concluded that 'Since work in continuous process industries involves control, meaning and social integration, it tends to be self-actualizing instead of self-estranging'.

Automation and class consciousness

Blauner saw automation as reversing a trend towards instability and division within the working class. Unlike assembly-line production, automation produced the non-alienated worker; it replaced dissent (disagreement) between workers and management with consensus (agreement). Repressive and coercive control was succeeded by consultation and cooperation. Militant trade union activity was transformed into loyalty to the firm.

These factors combined to transform the worker. His or her social personality was increasingly like that of 'the new middle class, the white-collar employee in bureaucratic industry'. Blauner concluded that automation had led to a 'decline in the worker's class consciousness and militancy, a development that reflected the growing consensus between employers and employees and the increase in the worker's feeling that he had a stake in industry'.

In this way, automation was increasingly integrating the working class into the structure of capitalist society.

The importance of technology

Blauner admitted that technology did not completely shape the nature of work. He stated that 'Whereas technology sets limits on the organization of work, it does not fully determine it, since a number of different organizations of the work process may be possible in the same technological system'.

However, he did see technology as the major factor influencing the behaviour and attitudes of workers. It therefore followed that a reduction in levels of alienation, as Blauner defined it, would largely involve changes in production technology.

He suggested that variation of work organization within a given technology would go some way to solving the problem. For example, job rotation, 'a policy that permitted the worker to move from one subdivided job to another', would have the effect of 'adding variety to his work and expanding his knowledge of the technical process'.

Similarly, job enlargement, which reversed the trend towards task fragmentation and increased the worker's area of responsibility, would have some beneficial results. For instance, Blauner pointed to a job enlargement scheme at IBM where machine operators were given the added responsibility of setting up and inspecting their machines. He claimed that this 'not only introduced interest, variety and responsibility and increased the importance of the product to the worker, it also improved the quality of the product and reduced costs'.

Blauner argued, though, that such variations on existing technology were insufficient to solve the problem of alienation. What was needed was a new technology, designed not only to produce goods at minimum economic cost, but also at minimum personal cost to the worker.

Criticisms of Blauner

Blauner's study can be criticized on a number of points:

1 From a Marxist perspective, Blauner ignored the basic cause of alienation – the objective position of the worker in the relations of production in a capitalist economic system. From this perspective, the printer and the process worker are just as alienated as the assembly-line worker. All are exploited wage labourers. Blauner's solutions to alienation will therefore leave the basic cause untouched. At best they will produce a 'happy robot', who may feel satisfied at work, but will still be alienated from it.

2 The second major criticism of Blauner's study involves his use of questionnaire data. He relied heavily on this information for measuring the degree of alienation experienced by workers. It is extremely difficult to interpret the results of questionnaires. For example, if workers state that they like a job,

this may mean that they are satisfied with one or more of the following factors: wages, occupational status, social relationships at work, the amount of interest and involvement the job provides, the present job in comparison with past jobs, and so on. It may be possible to design a sophisticated questionnaire, which separates out the various factors involved, but problems still remain.

As Blauner admitted, the way a question is worded 'may favor one response rather than another' and 'the meaning of the question may not always be the same to the worker as it is to the interviewer'. In addition, there is a tendency for all workers to express satisfaction with their jobs. Since a person's self-image is partly determined by occupation, an admission of dissatisfaction with work might well undermine his or her self-respect.

3   A third criticism is advanced by Keith Grint (1998), who suggests that Blauner greatly exaggerates the influence of a particular type of work within each industry. For example, Blauner emphasized that alienation was common among all workers in car plants. However, he himself pointed out that only 18 per cent actually work on the assembly lines which are deemed responsible for causing the alienation.

4   Grint also suggests that Blauner's own arguments undermine his claims about the impact of technology at work. In discussing women's work and alienation, Blauner said that 'women have, on the average, less physical stamina than men' but he also argued that, since 'working women often double as housewives and mothers, it is to be expected that they would be fatigued by their work'. Grint says, 'His assumption is conventionally patriarchal and simultaneously self-contradictory'. Not only does he make a totally unsupported claim about women's stamina, but he also proceeds to argue against his own view that the fatigue of women workers is down to their sex. In the process he shows that factors other than technology, such as outside domestic responsibilities, have a strong influence on attitudes to work.

Theo Nichols and Huw Beynon – the chemical industry

Theo Nichols and Huw Beynon (1977) agree that Blauner exaggerated the extent to which technology shaped work. They do so by directly contradicting Blauner's claims about the chemical industry. In a study of seven chemical plants in Britain they found little evidence that alienation had decreased and that the amount of skilled and rewarding work had increased. In six of the seven plants, control-room operatives were a minority of the workforce.

Nichols and Beynon claimed that about 50 per cent of the work in the chemical industry in Britain involved virtually no skill. A manager at one of the plants they studied, a fertilizer factory, distinguished between 'scientific work' and 'donkey work'. Of the

180 workers at that factory only 40 did scientific work. The rest were largely unskilled labourers who spent their working day loading, packing, sealing and then humping around the factory heavy bags of fertilizer. The company had introduced job rotation for these workers but Nichols and Beynon found little evidence that this had reduced alienation. One worker commented:

> *You move from one boring, dirty, monotonous job. And then to another boring, dirty, monotonous job. And somehow you're supposed to come out of it all 'enriched'. But I never feel 'enriched' – I just feel knackered.*
>
> Nichols and Beynon, 1977

Nichols and Beynon also denied that monitoring and checking control dials was fulfilling work. In many plants, control-room operatives worked alone and felt isolated. Many expressed boredom with their work: much of the time they had nothing to do but stare at the dials. Most found it difficult to concentrate and sometimes this led to stress. The operatives were responsible for very expensive machinery – and there was the constant danger of a major accident. During an incident at an ammonia plant the control-room operatives had been given just a few seconds' warning before a major explosion. Ten men were injured, one was permanently disabled and another suffered from nervous tension because of the accident. Nichols and Beynon concluded that work in control rooms 'is noisy and it can be stressful and lonely', although they concede that it 'is not as arduous as packing bags'.

Nichols and Beynon provided a very different picture of the chemical industry from that provided by Blauner. Consequently they did not accept that automated continuous-process technology increased the skills required of workers, produced more job satisfaction and reduced alienation. They believed that, if anything, the reverse was true.

Serge Mallet – automation and class conflict

Another sociologist who has strongly disagreed with some of Blauner's conclusions is the French Marxist Serge Mallet (1975). Where Blauner saw automation reducing the possibility of class conflict, Mallet saw just the opposite.

Although he largely agreed with Blauner that automation led to a greater integration of workers in the factory, Mallet argued that this would not lead to a more general integration of workers into capitalist society. He maintained that automation would highlight the major contradiction of capitalism: the collective nature of production and the private ownership of the means of production. Since workers in automated industry had greater control over and responsibility for production, they would tend to see themselves as the real controllers of industry. The consultation and cooperation between process workers, technicians and operating managers would tend to unite them and encourage a recognition of common interests. The conflict between their interests and those of the higher-level managers and owners of the company would therefore be brought sharply into focus.

Workers would increasingly question the basis of ownership and control and demand worker control of the enterprise. This would revitalize the trade union movement which would no longer be represented by centralized, bureaucratic organizations distanced from the shop floor. Instead, union power would be decentralized and based on syndicalist principles, that is worker control at the level of the company.

Mallet saw workers in automated production forming the vanguard of the class struggle. He believed that they would provide an example which the working class as a whole would tend to follow. Mallet's work was published in 1975. Developments in work and trade unionism since then do not seem to have supported his claims.

Duncan Gallie – automation reconsidered

Automation and workers' attitudes in Britain and France

In a study entitled *In Search of the New Working Class* (1978), Duncan Gallie attempted to test the theories of Blauner and Mallet. If either Blauner or Mallet were correct, automated technology should have had important consequences, whatever its national or regional setting. Gallie selected four oil refineries for investigation: two in France and two in Britain. By designing his research in this way, he hoped to assess the impact of technology, independent of the influence of national or regional variations. In Britain, for example, he selected refineries in very different areas: one was in Kent, a prosperous area in south-east England, the other in Grangemouth in Scotland, an area with a history of high unemployment.

Gallie's findings provided little support for either Blauner or Mallet. He discovered significant differences between the British and French workers, differences that could only be accounted for by the distinctive histories of the two societies and by the nature of British and French working-class subculture and national culture. Gallie stated that 'The emergence of new forms of technology occurs,

not in some form of social vacuum, but in societies with well-established institutional arrangements, and with distinctive patterns of social conflict.'

Wage rates and differentials

Gallie's findings may be summarized as follows. Both British and French workers were paid high wages compared with other manual workers. Blauner and Mallet had argued that pay was no longer a central concern for workers in automated industry, but, while over 90 per cent of the British workers were satisfied with their pay and living standards, over 66 per cent of the French workers were dissatisfied. The latter expressed their feelings in the form of strikes. From 1963 to 1972, 24 strikes brought production to a halt in the two French refineries, pay being the major issue in most of the stoppages. Only one strike closed down production in the British refineries over the same time period.

The difference in levels of satisfaction over pay can partly be explained by the methods of establishing wage rates. In France part of the workers' wages was made up of a 'merit bonus' which was based on length of service and 'good behaviour'. This system produced mistrust and ill-feeling since workers saw it as a means of management coercion and control.

Attitudes to work

Gallie found little support for Blauner's picture of non-alienated workers who were involved in their work. In both Britain and France, 'The commonest attitude towards work in all our refineries was one of indifference.'

Though many of the hardships of mechanized mass production had been removed, others had taken their place. Continuous-process industry involves round-the-clock production, which requires shift work. Workers believed that this disrupted their family and social life, and produced ill-health.

A second problem in all refineries involved staffing levels, since it is difficult to determine adequate levels for automated technology. Such problems threaten the stability and harmony which Blauner saw as typical of automated industry. In general, these problems were settled peacefully in British refineries whereas in France they were a source of conflict between workers and management.

Management and workers

Where Blauner saw increasing cooperation and consensus between management and workers, Mallet saw increasing conflict between workers and junior-level management on one side and higher-level management on the other. Blauner's picture was closest to the situation in British refineries. There, workers largely identified with management objectives such as increasing the efficiency of the firm. They felt that management was concerned with their interests and welfare and not simply with profits for the benefit of shareholders. By comparison, the French workers believed that management was largely concerned with shareholders' interests and cared little for the welfare of workers. Their attitude towards management tended to be antagonistic, based on a view of 'us and them'.

Gallie found little evidence to support Mallet's claims about the demand for worker control. Only a very small minority of French workers and an even smaller minority of British actually wanted worker control. However, the French workers did want more participation in decision making than their British counterparts. For example, they were more likely to want a say in high-level financial decisions, whereas the British defined such issues as management's job.

Explanations of differences between British and French workers

Gallie argued that a number of factors explained the variation in attitudes between British and French workers:

1 Working-class subcultures in the two countries differed. In particular, 'French workers were more committed to egalitarian values than their British equivalents.'

2 Management 'styles' and philosophy differed. French management retained a tighter, more autocratic control over decision making and tended to be paternalistic. (Paternalism refers to a style of authority whereby those in control act like a father, distributing rewards and punishments at their discretion, based on the belief that they know what is best for those subject to their authority.) French management had considerable discretion in deciding the size of each worker's 'merit bonus', which formed an important part of his or her income. By comparison, British management operated on a 'semi-constitutional' basis. Wages were formally negotiated and there were no discretionary payments by management.

3 There were important differences in the negotiating machinery and union representation in the two countries. In France, wages were negotiated at national level; in Britain, the important negotiations were at plant level. As a result, British workers were more directly involved in the decision-making process. Gallie argues that in general:

The less participative the decision-making system, the less will workers regard it as legitimate. A lower degree of legitimacy will in turn be associated with a higher degree of generalized distrust of management's motives.

Gallie, 1978, p. 207

4 The major unions in Britain and France had very different conceptions of their role. Gallie describes the French unions as unions of ideological mobilization: they were committed to the overthrow of capitalism and saw their main role as raising the consciousness of workers. In Britain, unions saw their major role as directly representing the wishes of their members, and as such they were mainly concerned with negotiating for better pay and conditions.

Gallie argues that, as a result of the above factors, 'The British workers had an image of the firm that was essentially "co-operative" while the French workers had an image that was essentially "exploitive".'

Automation and class – conclusions

A number of important conclusions stem from Gallie's study. The British refineries were closer to Blauner's picture; the French closer to that drawn by Mallet. This led to a rejection of the theories of both authors. Automated production, in and of itself, does not necessarily lead to a closer integration of the workforce into capitalist society, as Blauner suggested, nor does it necessarily herald the emergence of class consciousness and class conflict, as Mallet predicted. In fact, automated technology itself appears to have had little effect on wider social issues. Management style, the nature of decision making, trade union philosophy and organization and working-class subculture appear to be far more important.

Gallie concluded that if the changes predicted by either Blauner or Mallet do occur, it will not be for the reasons that either suggests. He stated:

Rather, it will depend on changing cultural expectations within the working class, on changes in management attitudes, and on changes in trade union objectives. Similarly, it will follow from our argument that if these developments do occur, the automated sector will not be particularly distinctive. Rather, it will be participating in a very much broader movement occurring within industry in the particular society.

Gallie, 1978

The last phrase in this quotation is particularly important. Although both France and Britain share a capitalist mode of production, the response of workers to that fact will be modified by the factors which Gallie describes, factors which differ considerably between the two countries.

This finding has important implications for the study of work. It suggests that studies which concentrate simply on an analysis of work in capitalist systems are inadequate. They require, in addition, an analysis of the peculiarities of the particular society in which capitalist economies are set.

Computers, technology and changes in work

Technological determinism

Many recent studies of work and technology have paid particular attention to the impact of computers on patterns of work. However, they have not confined themselves to looking at this specific type of technology, but have also examined the nature of the relationship between work and technology in general. In doing so they have considered questions raised in the work of sociologists such as Blauner and Gallie.

The key issue in these debates is the question of technological determinism. Keith Grint says that 'technological determinism considers technology to be an exogenous and autonomous development which coerces and determines social and economic organisations and relationships' (Grint, 1991). In other words, a particular technology forces work to be organized in a particular way. It therefore has a direct impact on such things as the extent to which workers are alienated, and class relationships in society as a whole.

Blauner's theories are often taken as a good example of technological determinism. Although Blauner describes technology as simply 'the most important single factor' shaping an industry, much of his work does give technology a determining role.

Social determinism

At the opposite extreme is social determinism. Grint describes this as assuming that 'technological changes are themselves socially engineered and/or that work relationships are, in any case, derived from, and ultimately determined by, cultural and/or social aspects'. In other words, outside social factors determine how technology is developed and used, and what it means for relationships at work. Duncan Gallie's work is a good example of social determinism. For him, technology in itself had 'very little importance for the social integration of the workforce' (Gallie, 1978).

Contemporary commentators on computer technology and changes at work tend not to adopt such extreme positions. Most argue for something in between technological and social determinism. In the discussion that follows, we will start with those theories that are closer to a position of technological determinism and move towards those that come closer to social determinism.

Shoshana Zuboff – *In the Age of the Smart Machine*

The power of technology

Shoshana Zuboff is an American sociologist who has studied the impact of computers on patterns of work in the USA (Zuboff, 1988). She attaches very great importance to information technology and argues that it has enormous potential to transform work. Indeed she believes that technology has always shaped social life to a considerable degree. She sees medieval castles, telephones and light bulbs as examples of technologies that have altered social life in fundamental ways. For example, the telephone allows intimate conversation without physical presence, and the electric light 'rescues the night from darkness'. In her view, the widespread adoption of computers in the workplace will have no less of an impact.

However, Zuboff is not simply a technological determinist. She does not believe that computers in themselves will determine the nature of work. The choices made by humans have had and will continue to have an important role. We will discuss the precise relationship she sees between technology and human choice later in this section. First, however, we will review the research on which her conclusions are based.

Zuboff's research

Zuboff decided to conduct research in places of work that were introducing new information technology. She was interested in examining the impact of computer technology as workers were experiencing its introduction. Between 1981 and 1986 she studied eight organizations which were either introducing information technology or extending its role. These were: two pulp mills and one pulp and paper mill (Piney Wood, Tiger Creek and Cedar Bluff); part of a telecommunications company (Metro Tel); the dental claims operation of Consolidated Underwriting Insurance; the Brazilian office of Global Bank; the pharmaceuticals company DrugCorp; and an office dealing with stock and bond transfer at Universal Technology. This range of institutions allowed Zuboff to study the impact of new technology amongst blue-collar workers, clerical workers and managers. She used a mixture of small-group discussions, interviews and participant observation.

Computers and manual work

For manual workers, information technology was affecting the whole experience of working. Physical effort was becoming less important and manual skills were declining in significance. According to Zuboff, skilled manual workers had traditionally used skills based on the physical experience of manipulating things and they developed 'experience-based knowledge'. They used their bodies in '*acting-on* equipment and materials'. At paper mills such as Tiger Creek, computers completely changed the skills required. Workers now controlled the production process through manipulating abstract symbols on computer screens. One said:

> *With computerization I am further away from my job than I have ever been before. I used to listen to the sounds the boiler makes and know just how it was running. I could look at the fire in the furnace and tell by its color how it was burning ... I feel uncomfortable being away from these sights and smells. Now I only have numbers to go by.*
>
> Zuboff, 1988, p. 63

Information technology was challenging the assumptions of manual workers about the nature of their work. Intellective skills were replacing manual ones so that, although some old skills became redundant, new ones were replacing them. According to Zuboff, one of the main effects of computer technology is to 'informate' the workplace. That is, it greatly increases the quantity of information available to workers and managers. How managers choose to use that information determines whether the increase in new skills outweighs the loss of old skills.

White-collar work

While blue-collar workers act on materials, white-collar workers 'act with' other people. They are important for coordinating the activities of a company. Although their work is much less physical than that of blue-collar workers, it has not always been entirely abstract. For example, taking a file out of a filing cabinet does contain a physical element to it.

In Consolidated Underwriting and the stock and bond transfer department of Universal Technology, computerization had similar effects for clerical workers. Paper files were replaced by computer screens. The workers lost personal contacts with customers and other workers, and increasingly worked on their own at a screen, processing data. In both offices the possibility of using initiative was taken away from the workers and many felt that they were over-qualified for the work they were now doing. A number of the clerks complained of 'eye strain, nervous exhaustion, physical strain, irritability, enervation, sedentariness, back pain,

short tempers and intolerance'. Zuboff explains this in the following way:

> *Automation meant that jobs which had once allowed them to use their bodily presence in the service of interpersonal exchange and collaboration now required their bodily presence in the service of routine interaction with a machine. Jobs that had once required their voices now insisted that they be mute.*
>
> Zuboff, 1988

Some of the clerical workers were asked to draw pictures illustrating the experience of work before and after computerization. Two of these pairs of drawing are reproduced below. They graphically illustrate how the workers felt they were affected by the technological changes.

Figure 10.1   A transfer assistant, before and after computerization

Before

After

'Before I was able to get up and hand things to people without having someone say, what are you doing? Now, I feel like I am with my head down, doing my work.'

Source: S. Zuboff (1988) *In the Age of the Smart Machine*, Basic Books, New York, p. 146.

Figure 10.2 A benefits analyst, before and after computerization

Before

After

'My supervisor is frowning because we shouldn't be talking. I have on the stripes of a convict. It's all true. It feels like a prison in here.'

Source: S. Zuboff (1988) *In the Age of the Smart Machine,* Basic Books, New York, p. 147.

The effects of information technology were rather different at Global Bank Brazil. At the insurance company and the stock and bond office it was used to increase the volume of work through automation. At the bank the computers were used to informate. They made more information available to workers and this was used to improve the quality of the service they provided. Bankers had easier access to details of customers' accounts on a database and this allowed them to take a more active role in helping customers to manage their finances. Interpersonal contacts with customers remained important, but they were now supported by more objective data about their financial affairs. Much of the routine work was carried out by the computers, meaning there was less need for routine clerical workers.

Authority and the 'information panopticon'

Just as information technology was sometimes used to automate and sometimes to informate, it could also be used to make work more or less hierarchical.

Some of the companies studied by Zuboff used computers to introduce what she calls the information panopticon. The panopticon was an architectural design devised by the British philosopher Jeremy Bentham. It consisted of a central tower from which activities in all wings of the building could be centrally monitored. The design was used in some prisons and factories because it facilitated control over the workers or inmates. (These views are influenced by the work of Foucault, see pp. 635–9.) Information technology can be used for a corresponding purpose.

Zuboff argues that the principles of centralized monitoring have now become a feature of the way some companies have used information technology. Indeed, according to her analysis, information technology makes the behaviour of workers much more transparent than it has ever been before. At Metro Tel, the telecommunications company, computers were used to allocate tasks to workers, calculate the time they should take and monitor workers' efficiency. At Cedar Bluff, the 'Overview System' allowed management to monitor all the decisions made by workers operating the plant's equipment, and to determine who was at fault when something went wrong.

When they were used to create an information panopticon, computers were reinforcing the authority of managers and strengthening hierarchies. For example, at Metro Tel, craft workers were closely monitored by supervisors, supervisors by lower-level management, lower-level management by the next level of managers up, and so on.

Computers undermining hierarchy

In some of the companies studied by Zuboff, computers were having a very different effect. Information technology was breaking down traditional hierarchies.

At DrugCorp, a computer-conferencing system called DIALOG was introduced in 1978. Workers throughout the company used computer communications to contribute ideas and raise issues about particular areas of the company's work. Workers from different levels in the hierarchy could subscribe to each of the conferences. Having subscribed, they could contribute ideas to the conference or take ideas from it at will.

The system was mainly designed to help research and development and to encourage innovation in the development of new products. According to Zuboff, DIALOG 'helped create a new culture of information sharing and discussion'. It helped to break down barriers between different levels in the hierarchy. Lower and higher levels began to share knowledge and information rather than simply giving and receiving instructions. As at Global Bank Brazil, knowledge became a collective resource, being used to its maximum potential to help the company.

In fact, towards the end of her research, senior managers at DrugCorp replaced DIALOG with a less flexible system of computer-based communications, which mainly involved sending routine electronic mail. It was, Zuboff believed, a retrograde step, a case of how 'the old world tries to suffocate the new'.

Technology and choice

Zuboff concludes from her study that managers can choose to use the new technology to go in either of two opposite directions. They can use it to informate – spread information more widely, undermine traditional hierarchies and make an organization more creative; or they can use it to automate – monitor employees more closely, reinforce traditional hierarchies and make the organization more rigid.

Zuboff argues that there is an 'interplay between essence and choice in the computerized workplace'. The technology has an essence, it has particular capabilities, but how it is put to use is chosen by managers. She compares this to a kaleidoscope. A change in an organization's technology 'wields the power of the hand at the turning rim'. It 'lays open new choices' and challenges the old orthodoxies. However, whereas the fragments in the kaleidoscope fall into place at random, in an organization the final shape of things is determined by managerial decisions.

In this context Zuboff does not sound particularly like a technological determinist. However, at other points in her book she clearly indicates what sorts of choices she thinks will have to be made in the future. At Piney Woods, one of the managers had asked 'Are we all going to be working for a smart machine, or will we have smart people around the machine?' Zuboff believes that more smart people will be needed. According to her, the traditional, rigid and hierarchical organization is unlikely to prosper and may be forced to adapt. She says:

> *it is unlikely that a traditional organization will achieve the efficiencies, standards of quality, or levels of innovation that have become mandatory in an environment marked by the competitive challenges of global markets and deregulation.*
>
> Zuboff, 1988

Firms will be forced to use the information that computers can provide constructively. While they can choose not to in the short term, in the long term they will need to use smart people rather than trying to replace them with the machine.

Jon Clark, Ian McLoughlin, Howard Rose and Robin King – *The Process of Technological Change*

Determinism and choice

Jon Clark, Ian McLoughlin, Howard Rose and Robin King (1988) have examined the impact of new technology through a study of telephone exchanges in Britain. Like Zuboff, they are opposed to simple technological determinism, insisting that human choices are a crucial part of technological innovation. However, they also argue that the technology itself has a strong influence on work.

Unlike Zuboff, they see the choices that humans have as being limited once the technology has been introduced and established. During the process of introducing it, though, they do believe that there is considerable scope for influencing the way the technology will ultimately affect work. While Zuboff tends to assume that managers determine how technology is used, Clark *et al.* note that non-managerial workers can also exert considerable influence.

Engineering systems

The theory developed by these sociologists is based upon the concept of an engineering system. An engineering system does not just consist of the technology (the hardware and the software) but also of the way it is set up or 'functionally arranged (configured) in certain specific ways' within an organization. The systems and working practices that surround the technology exert a strong influence on how it is used. Thus Clark *et al.* say:

> *while agreeing that outcomes cannot be explained in terms of the capabilities of 'the technology', we suggested that it was equally erroneous to reject the notion that it can have an independent influence.*
>
> Clark *et al.*, 1988

The technology does influence work, but it is not the only influence.

Technology in telephone exchanges

Clark *et al.*'s study examined the replacement of electro-mechanical Strowger telephone exchange systems with the semi-electronic TXE4 system. The researchers used self-report diaries, semi-structured interviews and observation in eight British Telecom exchanges that were making the change.

The old Strowger systems connected callers in a step-by-step mechanical process. The machinery required a considerable amount of routine mainte-nance. Some of the maintenance required was predictable and could be organized in advance by supervisors. Apart from the routine work, the engineers also corrected faults that cropped up. The process of connecting calls could be seen and heard by engineers looking for faults. Physical familiarity with the machinery was vital in correcting the faults, so experience was essential for repairing the equipment. Maintenance engineers could expect to progress to a senior grade as they became more experienced. Supervisors usually rose from the shop floor so, like senior engineers, they had considerable experience of the technology.

TXE4 systems are rather different. They are quiet when operating and it is not possible to physically observe switches being made to connect calls. Calls are connected through a matrix and a fault tends to affect a greater number of calls than a fault in a Strowger exchange.

Technology and skills

Clark *et al.* argue that the technical features of these two systems had a strong influence on the skills required to accomplish work tasks. (They call these skills skill in the task.) For example, TXE4 exchanges required 'mental diagnostic skills' as opposed to the 'refined manual skills' necessitated by the Strowger exchanges. The new exchanges produced a more 'abstract working relationship with the equipment'. The new skills were more easily developed through formal training programmes than through experience. TXE4 exchanges were more suited to teamwork since faults could not be isolated from the rest of the system while one person worked to correct them.

However, the technology had a much less direct impact on skills in the person – the way skills are distributed to individuals with particular occupational positions. Managers, unions and the work groups of supervisors and maintenance workers had a good deal of influence over how skills came to be distributed. Conflict and negotiation determined how the overall 'engineering system' incorporated the new technology.

For example, in two of the British Telecom areas studied, the maintenance workers' union, the POEU, was influential in determining which staff were retrained to carry out the sophisticated maintenance work on the new equipment. In the event it was the senior technicians who received the training. This left the junior technicians with little chance of promotion. Experience alone was no longer sufficient to develop the skills required at senior levels. The position of supervisors was also weakened. Many were unfamiliar with the technical details of TXE4 exchanges, so they found it hard to monitor and exercise detailed control over the work of the senior technicians.

In the third British Telecom area, the POEU branch was much less powerful and not so well-organized. Here, senior technicians had less success in defending their position.

Conclusion

Once the technology had been set up and was in routine operation, it became very hard for the different groups of workers to change their relationship to the technology. Clark *et al.* conclude, therefore, that there are critical junctures at which groups can intervene to try to influence the way technology is used. Although the nature of the work tasks is largely determined by the nature of the technology, who does the tasks is not, and can be altered at these critical junctures. After this point, 'social chances become frozen within a given technology'.

Keith Grint is amongst those who have attacked this view of the relationship between work and technology. He denies that the nature of work ever becomes 'frozen'. Grint says 'inasmuch as technology embodies social aspects it is not a stable and determinate object ... but an unstable and indeterminate artefact whose precise significance is negotiated but never settled' (Grint, 1998).

We will discuss Grint's own views at the end of this section. First, however, we will examine the theory of Rob Kling. Like Grint, he does not believe that theories such as that of Clark *et al.* have distanced themselves sufficiently from technological determinism.

Rob Kling – the consumption of technology

The varied effects of computers

The American sociologist Rob Kling (1991, 1992) is critical of the types of theory we have examined so far in this section. He disagrees with Zuboff that computer technology is necessarily going to transform society in a particular direction, or indeed at all. He also accuses Zuboff, amongst others, of using evidence which is 'carefully selected to fit ... her logic of social change'.

Nor does he agree with Clark *et al.* that technological innovation has predictable effects once it has been set up and is operating routinely. Instead, Kling argues that technology can have very many different effects and these depend partly upon how it is used or 'consumed'. In other words, even after being designed, purchased and operated routinely, computers can be used in different ways. Sometimes computers transform social relationships at work and in the wider society, but they can also reinforce existing relationships or have a negligible impact. Sometimes computers deskill work; at other times they make work more skilled. He is therefore opposed to deterministic theories of the relationship between computers and social change.

Studies of computerization

Kling cites a number of studies to illustrate the diverse effects of computerization. In a study of the introduction of an 'Urban Management Information System' to local government in an American city there was little evidence that it achieved any of its stated aims. These aims were: improving efficiency by providing easier access to data; improving management; and reducing paperwork. Instead, Kling found 'UMIS's primary value was in *enhancing the welfare agency's image* when it dealt with federal funders and auditors.'

In another study, Rob Kling and Tom Jewett examined computerization in a mortgage bank (Western Mortgage) and in the sales department of a big pharmaceuticals company (Coast Pharmaceuticals). In both companies the introduction of new computer systems during 1987 led to an expansion of the range of jobs done by clerical workers. At Coast Pharmaceuticals the workers changed from 'order entry clerks' to 'customer service representatives'. In their new role they had more responsibility and greater contact with customers. At Western Mortgage, clerical workers' jobs changed from manually entering information on ledgers to entering it directly on computers. Although they learned some new computer skills, the change restricted their movement around the office and gave them less opportunity for casual social contacts. Unlike the workers at Coast Pharmaceuticals, they remained fairly routine clerical workers and the new technology had relatively little impact.

With Suzanne Iacano, Rob Kling studied a high technology manufacturing firm (PRINTCO) in the early 1980s. Many of the staff they talked to claimed that their new computerized inventory control system saved money and increased efficiency. However, nobody had actually estimated any savings involved, nor could they give any evidence that these savings were real. Kling and Iacano claimed that this system was really used so that material-control managers could 'gain control over the purchasing staff and ... help production line managers battle with projections made by marketing staff. Workplace discipline was tightened and material-control managers increased their influence in the firm.

Conclusion

Rob Kling believes that computers can have very diverse effects on work. They can have a larger or smaller impact, and they can increase or decrease skills in particular jobs. He denies that there has been

a 'computer revolution' changing work in very fundamental ways. The effects vary from job to job. There have been 'some major structural transformations in banking' and major changes in the work of copy typists, but most white-collar work has been altered in 'interesting procedural ways without radically restructuring the organization of work'. In other areas such as schooling there have been 'negligible changes'. Many of the benefits claimed for new computer systems are exaggerated and some may not be real at all.

The effects of computerization are strongly influenced by what Kling calls the 'social organization of access to information systems', or how, in effect, the technology is used or consumed. He gives the example of university students using computers. If the 'chemistry lab' model is used, and students have to use computers at fixed times, it will tend to regiment their lives. Technology will have a very different effect if a 'library model' is used, and students can complete their computer work at their own convenience. The technology might be identical, but the effects are different.

On the other hand, Kling does at times claim that the precise nature of the technology can have a significant impact. In particular, different software packages can require different types of worker to use them. For example:

> some database management systems require that each new capability be programmed by a skilled programmer (e.g. Revelation). Others, which have powerful commands on menu systems (such as Paradox), allow the moderately skilled to navigate through databases in complex ways.
>
> Kling, 1992

Thus systems such as Revelation will employ a small number of very skilled programmers and deskilled operatives, while Paradox requires routine white-collar workers to increase their skills. So, although Kling argues that the same technology can be consumed in different ways leading to different results, he also believes that the technology itself has an independent effect on the outcome.

(We will examine the question of whether work has been deskilled in detail in later sections. See pp. 707–13.)

Keith Grint and Steve Woolgar – discourse and computers

Technology and discourse

Grint and Woolgar (1992, 1997) have perhaps gone further than other sociologists in attacking techno-logical determinist accounts of the effects of computers. In a debate with Kling they have argued that he attributes too little importance to the interpretation of the meaning of technology by human actors. They point out that, although Kling says that particular technology can be consumed in different ways, he nevertheless identifies a technical core which has at least an influence on the uses to which new technology can be put. For example, they quote Kling's argument about one type of database encouraging deskilling when another does not.

To Grint and Woolgar, a technology cannot be separated from the interpretation put on it by actors. They argue that the discourse surrounding a technology – the way people talk about it and determine what it is – is what in the end decides the effects it has. They say, 'Discourse is foundational to social action not, as Kling would have it, some impoverished effort to look at mere talk.'

By looking at the way people talk about technology, sociologists can study who has the power to get their version of what the technology means accepted. Those who succeed in getting their version accepted exercise power and are likely to be able to use the technology to favour their own interests. According to this view, the 'nature and capacity' of a technology never become completely fixed but are 'essentially indeterminate, both during conception, design, and development and beyond the point of sale and use'.

The capacity of technology

Keith Grint (1992) gives the following example to illustrate these views. If a new technology is introduced, capitalists may argue that the essential capacity of the technology is that it can increase productivity while reducing costs. On the other hand, an anti-capitalist may claim that it inherently has the capacity to reduce the effort required of workers. To both sides their analysis is objective and, used in any other way, the technology is being misused and its inherent capacity distorted.

From Grint's point of view the technology has no inherent capacity: it simply has different meanings which depend on the audience looking at it. The disagreement between the two sides in the example above is not just about how the technology is deployed, it is also about what it can do – what its capacity is. Grint says:

We do not have contrary interpretations of the same machine; what the machine is and what it will do are social constructions such that we actually construct different machines.

Grint, 1992, p. 62

Grint goes on to acknowledge that which interpretation is accepted is not a matter of chance. The power

to define what technology is, is not equally distributed. He argues:

What tends to happen is that so called 'experts' are endowed with sufficient status to persuade the majority of lay people that they are right and the rest of us are wrong. After all, if an expert tells us ... that you cannot get leukaemia by working in a nuclear power station (despite the rumours), or that there is no link between ill health and unemployment (despite the rumours) ... who are we to believe?

Grint, 1992, p. 63

Evaluation

Grint and Woolgar raise important questions about how technology is used and show that there are always choices involved in deploying it. Some people have argued that they go too far in appearing to suggest that technological capacity is entirely a matter of interpretation.

In a defence of his own work, Rob Kling (1992) pointed out that guns have certain capacities which, for example, flowers do not. It is harder to kill people with flowers than guns. Grint and Woolgar replied to this criticism that even in the case of a gunshot wound there are social processes involved in interpreting what has happened. They say, 'John F. Kennedy's assassination is a classic example of the difficulty of providing an irrefutable, "objective" account of the damage caused by "the bullet".' They conclude, 'we do not argue that the bullet (technology) is irrelevant but that the process by which it achieves relevance is irredeemably social'.

Their discourse analysis of technology has some similarity with the perspective of ethnomethodology. Like ethnomethodology, their analysis is not always clear about how certain groups get their definitions of social reality, or the capacity of a technology, accepted and why. Thus, although Grint says that 'experts' tend to have more chance of getting their own way in this respect, he also seems to argue that all social groups have a good chance of getting their definitions accepted. He claims:

power can be regarded as a consequence of action rather than a cause. Thus, control over work organisations and their technologies is grounded in the actions of subordinates not the commands of superordinates: if subordinates refuse to act, or refuse to accept superordinate definitions of technological capacity, then superordinate power rapidly dissolves.

Grint, 1992, p. 63

It is doubtful whether the experience of most workers would match this view. Certainly Harry Braverman, whose views we will examine next, would be likely to dismiss it as fantasy.

The labour process and the degradation of work

Between the mid-1970s and the mid-1980s much of the research in the sociology of work was devoted to an analysis of the labour process. Paul Thompson defines the labour process as 'the means by which raw materials are transformed by human labour, acting on the objects with tools and machinery' (Thompson, 1993). The preceding discussions of technology, work orientation, automation and computerization clearly touch upon the labour process, but they do not directly address the issues raised by the most influential figure in labour process theory, Harry Braverman. Braverman published his book *Labor and Monopoly Capitalism: The Degradation of Work in the Twentieth Century* in 1974, and since then a vast amount of literature has been produced which discusses his views.

Within this literature the emphasis has been, in Paul Thompson's words, on 'Who owns, controls and designs work' and the 'consequences of these social relations on forms of technology and the divisions of labour'. We will examine Braverman's theory first, before considering the critical responses to it.

Harry Braverman – a Marxist view of the labour process

Braverman (1974) followed Marx in arguing that work within capitalist society was alienating. However, Braverman did not believe that work had been equally degraded during all periods of capitalism: he claimed that the twentieth century had seen a particularly rapid degradation of work.

Braverman discussed automation and class, but he did not see changes in the labour process as being a direct consequence of automation; instead he saw automation as a consequence of attempts to change the labour process. In particular, Braverman believed that the level of skill required in work had been progressively reduced under capitalism, mainly because employers have used deskilling as a method of controlling the workforce.

Braverman based his argument upon the observation that usually under capitalism, 'what the worker sells, and what the capitalist buys, is not an agreed amount of labor, but the power to labor over an agreed period of time'. In other words, an employee is not normally paid to expend a certain amount of effort, or to produce a certain number of goods, but rather to give up a certain number of hours to work for the employer. In early periods of capitalism, capitalists made workers labour for very long hours

in order to get them to produce more and increase profits or surplus value, but this was not the most effective way to increase productivity.

Braverman claimed that human labour power is 'infinite in potential': the amount that people can produce is almost unlimited. However, in simply buying the workers' time the employer is not guaranteeing that that potential is realized. What is actually produced is:

limited by the subjective states of the workers, by their previous history, by the general social conditions under which they work as well as the particular conditions of the enterprise, and by the technical setting of their labor.

Braverman, 1974

Braverman argued that the development of the labour process under capitalism had been shaped by employers' attempts to overcome these limitations.

Deskilling and the reduction of labour costs

Braverman accepted that all societies have had social divisions of labour in which some individuals carry out separate and specialized roles. However, he claimed that only modern capitalism has produced the manufacturing divisions of labour or the 'breakdown of the processes involved in the making of the product into manifold operations performed by different workers'. By breaking the work involved in production down into its constituent parts, the capitalists can reduce labour costs. They no longer need to employ skilled craft workers at high rates of pay to make a whole product: unskilled workers can carry out the simplest parts of production. The more the work is divided up and broken down, the smaller the proportion of work requiring skilled labour. Thus, for example, in modern factories, complex consumer products can largely be produced by unskilled workers because each worker need understand only part of the production process. As a consequence, work is deskilled.

Braverman saw deskilling as the product of management decisions rather than technology. In particular he believed that the scientific management of Frederick W. Taylor had had a profound impact upon the organization of work in capitalism.

Scientific management and control over production

Taylor first published his views in the early part of the twentieth century in the USA, and Braverman analysed the consequences of the principles upon which scientific management was based:

1 Taylor's first principle was that management should gather together all the traditional knowledge of working people in a particular industry and reduce this knowledge to 'rules, laws, and formulae'. To Braverman, this greatly diminished the power of workers and their control over production because managers took from them the knowledge necessary to make production possible.

2 Taylor's second principle was that 'brain work' should be taken away from the factory floor and carried out in a planning department. Braverman called this the 'separation of conception from execution', and he argued that it made the detailed control of the labour process by management easier.

3 The third principle was that management should plan out and give written instructions to every worker, specifying exactly what they should do.

To Braverman, when all three steps were followed, the management achieved control over the workforce. Although the workers as human beings retained their critical faculties, they had lost their skills and overall knowledge of the production process, so there was little they could do to resist the employers. Braverman believes that under modern capitalism:

> *labor power has become a commodity. Its uses are no longer organized according to the needs and desires of those who sell it, but rather according to the needs of its purchasers, who are, primarily, employers seeking to expand the values of their capital.*
>
> Braverman, 1974

Management 'concessions'

Management does make some attempt to respond to the problems created for employees by deskilled and degrading work. It does so not out of charity, but out of self-interest. It needs to prevent resistance from workers.

One way of doing this is to use industrial psychology and the human relations school of management to habituate workers to oppressive working conditions. Braverman does not therefore regard human relations management as an alternative to scientific management but as a way of making the tight control of scientific management slightly more tolerable.

Braverman accepted that another way of making workers accept new management techniques is the concession of higher wages to some employees. However, as these higher wages are paid to a shrinking proportion of the workforce, and to workers who are increasingly productive, they do not threaten the profitability of the capitalist enterprise.

Braverman was extremely pessimistic about the position of workers. He saw them as increasingly

trapped, without the possibility of challenging management control. He said:

> *the working class is progressively subjected to the capitalist mode of production, and to the successive forms which it takes,* only as the capitalist mode of production conquers and destroys all other forms of organization of labor, and with them the alternatives for the working population.
>
> Braverman, 1974

Evidence for deskilling

As well as discussing the general processes through which skill is destroyed, Braverman also provided some more specific evidence to support his case. Official census statistics in the USA appeared to show an increase in the number of semi-skilled or skilled manual workers, but Braverman questioned the validity of these statistics. He pointed out that in the 1930s the basis on which the statistics were calculated was changed so that any operatives who tended or minded machines became classified as semi-skilled, despite the fact that the training needed to carry out their job might be minimal. Many such workers learned to do their job in two to twelve weeks, which hardly compares with the apprenticeship of traditional craft workers which would last several years. As the number of such craft workers has declined rapidly, so the overall level of skill within the working class has been dramatically reduced.

Braverman also believed that the falling number of rural labourers had led to a deskilling of the workforce. In 1900, 17.7 per cent of the working population of the USA were in the category 'farm laborers and foremen'. By 1970 this had declined to 1.7 per cent. Farm labourers have always been classified as unskilled so, as their numbers fell as a proportion of the working population, the skills of American workers might appear to be rising. In reality, Braverman claimed, farm labourers were far more skilled than the operatives in industry who were classified as semi-skilled. He said, of the farm labourer, 'he was the product of years of farm life and had a mastery of a great many skills involving a knowledge of land, fertilizer, animals, tools, farm machinery, construction skills, etc.'

Braverman was aware that official figures in the USA, and indeed in other capitalist countries, showed that an increasing proportion of the workforce was employed in non-manual occupations. Again, on the surface, this might seem to contradict the deskilling thesis. However, he believed that many non-manual jobs have themselves been deskilled. For example, he claimed that professional workers such as draughts-people, technicians, engineers, nurses and teachers have lost some of their skills (see p. 63 for further details of this argument). He went further in arguing that routine white-collar workers such as clerks, secretaries and retail sales workers have been so deskilled that they have now become members of the proletariat. (For a full discussion of the proletarianization thesis, see pp. 66–9.) Overall, Braverman estimated that some 70 per cent of the labour force in the USA were members of the proletariat whose work had undergone a process of degradation involving the removal of skill, responsibility and control.

Between the proletariat and the bourgeoisie is an intermediate group of lower-level managers, marketing and finance specialists, engineers and technicians, who exercise authority and control over the workforce. They are themselves, though, subject to the overall control of top management and the bourgeoisie. Braverman believed that control and skill have become polarized. There has been an increase in control and skill for some of the intermediate group, but, as Braverman put it, 'the mass of workers gain nothing'.

Responses to Braverman

Reactions to Braverman's provocative theory have been both numerous and varied. Some sociologists have been highly supportive of Braverman and have presented evidence that seems to bear out his claims. Others have argued that Braverman paints an over-simplified picture of change, although they accept that there have been some areas of work which have been deskilled. Some sociologists have been much more critical and have suggested that in recent years work has been reskilled not deskilled.

We will examine the evidence to support Braverman before considering the main areas of critical debate arising from his work.

Labour and Monopoly Capital has prompted some Marxist sociologists to carry out case studies of changes in the labour process to provide support for Braverman. For example, in the book *Case Studies on the Labor Process*, edited by Andrew Zimbalist (1979), a number of American writers tried to show how work had been degraded in occupations as diverse as carpentry, coalmining, car assembly, jewellery making and clerical work in insurance.

Deskilling in the printing and typesetting industries

Andrew Zimbalist (1979) himself carried out a case study on the printing industry. He described how in the nineteenth century printing remained the preserve of craft workers. Before the 1880s typesetting was carried out entirely by hand and was a highly-skilled job which required both manual and mental skill. However, employers progressively introduced new technology, such as semi-automatic typesetting machines, which cut out some of the manual skills required by typeset-

ters. In the 1950s photo-typesetting machines were introduced, and gradually these machines were developed and the skills necessary to operate them were reduced. The third generation of these machines introduced word-processing and, according to Zimbalist, this destroyed the traditional craft of typesetting. At the *Washington Post* and the *New York Times* the new technology was used to break the power of print workers' unions: it removed most of the skill from their work and reduced their independence so that they could be controlled more closely by management.

Similar processes have taken place in Britain. In the 1980s, Rupert Murdoch successfully challenged the power of the printing unions by moving the production of his newspapers (*The Times*, *Sunday Times*, *Sun* and *News of the World*) to a new printing works at Wapping which used advanced computer-based printing technology. This allowed journalists and advertising copy-writers to type material directly into computers without print union members being involved. It enabled Murdoch to dismiss print union workers and replace them with members of the Electricians Union, the EETPU, who agreed to a no-strike deal.

As we indicated in an earlier section of this chapter (see pp. 694–7), Blauner used printing and typesetting as an example of a traditional craft occupation. Zimbalist's work and the Wapping example show how even one of the last strongholds of craft work has been deskilled and the power of the workers and their control over the labour process have been drastically reduced.

However, this example could also be used to challenge some of Braverman's assumptions. The deskilling of printing and typesetting took place long after the development of scientific management, suggesting that he may have exaggerated its influence. Furthermore, in neither Britain nor the USA did print workers accept their deskilling passively. Although they were eventually unable to protect the craft skills of their jobs, they did fight and delay new working practices. These and other criticisms of Braverman will now be examined.

The craft worker and deskilling

Some critics of Braverman argue that his theory simply does not fit the facts. Braverman may have greatly exaggerated the importance of craft work in the nineteenth century. As Paul Thompson points out:

A large proportion of the industrial population was, and is, in non-factory manual occupations like transport and mining. Although they had a specific type of skill and control of their own, it could not be compared with factory work concerned with discrete operations on separate machines.

Thompson, 1983

Craig Littler (1983) notes that industries such as food processing and tobacco were set up using semi-skilled and unskilled labour from the start and never used craft workers. Braverman has also been accused of having a romantic image of a 'golden age' of work and of making invalid claims about the amount of skill and autonomy that were necessary for workers in the past. Thompson suggests that craft workers' skills 'could frequently be exaggerated compared to non-craft workers'.

Evidence of deskilling

Braverman can also be criticized on the ground that a good deal of evidence suggests that deskilling has not been taking place, at least not in recent years.

An important study of the relationship between skill and occupational change was conducted as part of the Social Change and Economic Life Initiative, which was funded by the Economic and Social Research Council (Penn, Rose and Rubery (eds), 1994). This study examined the local labour markets in six localities in Britain: Aberdeen, Kirkcaldy, Rochdale, Coventry, Swindon and Northampton.

Questionnaire data was collected from nearly 4,000 employees in a total sample of over 6,000. The study examined data relevant to both Braverman's theory of deskilling and theories of post-Fordism (see pp. 713–17 for a discussion of post-Fordism).

Duncan Gallie (1994) was one of the researchers who analysed the results of the study. He used five measures to examine changes in skill:

1 The qualifications that employees claimed were necessary to get their job.
2 The length of training received after completing full-time education.
3 How long it took employees to learn to do their job well.
4 Whether people had supervisory responsibilities.
5 How skilled people thought their own work to be.

The distribution of skills by social class are summarized in Table 10.1. The table shows that the service class had substantially higher levels of skill than other classes, with non-skilled manual workers having very much lower levels of skill than the three intermediary classes. Amongst the three intermediary classes, different types of skill were prominent. For example, lower non-manual workers were the most likely of the three to require qualifications equivalent to O level and above; supervisory and technical workers were most likely to be responsible for the work of others; and skilled manual workers were the most likely to consider their job skilled, to have received training and to need more than a month to learn to do their job.

Gallie notes that the service class has been expanding while the non-skilled manual class has been contracting, indicating a general movement towards more skilled occupations. However, this does not measure patterns of skill change within each class. Here again there was evidence of some upskilling.

Overall, 52 per cent of employees claimed that the skill required in their job had increased over the last five years, compared to just 9 per cent who said it had decreased; 60 per cent said that the responsibility required in their job had increased, while only 7 per cent said it had decreased. The class which appeared to have done worst on these measures was the non-skilled manual class. Even in this group, though, a higher proportion said that their work had become more skilled rather than less in the previous five years (33 per cent as opposed to 15 per cent). Amongst the service class as many as 67 per cent reported a skills increase whereas just 4 per cent reported a decrease.

Another possible source of skill reduction was the move away from employment in manufacturing and towards employment in services. However, Gallie found little difference in the experience of upskilling in manufacturing (53 per cent said they had been upskilled in the last five years) and services (50 per cent said they had been upskilled). Furthermore,

Table 10.1 Skill characteristics by class (%)					
	Service	Lower non-manual	Supervisory/ technical	Skilled manual	Non-skilled manual
O level equivalent currently required	85	61	50	51	12
No training	34	52	49	43	76
Learnt to do the job in less than a month	10	21	24	17	52
Responsible for work of others	65	22	64	27	13
Consider job skilled	91	68	70	86	40

Source: D. Gallie (1994) 'Patterns of skill change: upskilling, deskilling or polarization?' in R. Penn, M. Rose and J. Rubery, *Skill and Occupational Change*, Oxford University Press, Oxford, p. 48.

service-sector workers tended to be slightly more skilled than workers in manufacturing. Gallie therefore concludes that 'the transition from a manufacturing to a service-based economy does not of itself have major implications for patterns of skill'.

Gallie therefore found little evidence to support Braverman's deskilling theory – upskilling was much more common. Overall, though, Gallie found that the best description of the situation was one of skill polarization. He says, 'Those that already had relatively high levels of skill witnessed an increase in their skill levels, whilst those with low levels of skill saw their skills stagnate.' Part-time female workers were amongst those least likely to experience skill increases, while people who worked with advanced technology were amongst those most likely to benefit from skill increases.

Scientific management and managerial control

Another area of criticism concerns the importance of Taylorism and scientific management as methods used to control the workforce. All Braverman's examples were taken from the USA and on this basis he assumed that scientific management was the main method of control used in all capitalist countries.

Craig Littler (1983) has pointed out that Taylorism had much less influence in Britain than it had in the USA. Although scientific management was influential in Britain, it was only in the 1930s that it began to be used by a considerable number of employers. Littler also believes that Braverman attributed too much importance to Taylorism in some industries where there was a move away from craft skills. He says that 'Even within a traditional metal working firm ... with all the signs of craft deskilling, the transition to non-craft working had largely occurred before Taylor's disciples set foot on the factory floor.'

Conflict and methods of control

Many sociologists who are sympathetic to Marxism do not disagree with Braverman that capitalists try to control the labour process, but they do deny that scientific management is the predominant method of control, and that control is necessarily complete.

For example, Richard Edwards (1979) described the workplace as a contested terrain in which both the degree of control achieved by the management, and the type of control used, will vary. Edwards pointed out that unions and informal methods of control are also used by employers as they seek to get their own definitions of 'a fair day's work' accepted. Although Edwards portrayed management as ultimately being quite successful in controlling the labour process, the type of control used has had to be adapted to take account of worker resistance and changed circumstances.

According to Edwards, nineteenth-century capitalism was characterized by small firms with relatively few resources. They relied upon simple control exercised by the entrepreneurial owners of the businesses, and perhaps a small number of supervisors and managers. Edwards argued that 'These bosses exercised power, personally intervening in the labor process often to exhort workers, bully and threaten them, reward good performance, hire and fire on the spot.'

As production became concentrated in the hands of a smaller number of larger firms, towards the end of the nineteenth century, simple control became less effective. Furthermore, in the early decades of the twentieth century the American labour movement became better-organized and more able to resist simple control. Employers turned to more sophisticated structural control methods.

The first type of structural control to be used was technical control. Under this method, machinery directed the labour process. For example, on production lines the pace of work and nature of the tasks performed are largely determined by the machinery of the production line itself.

Edwards believed that, since the Second World War, the second type of structural control, bureaucratic control, has gradually replaced technical control. It developed first as a way of controlling the increasing number of non-manual workers who could not readily be controlled by technical means. This type of control 'rests on the principle of embedding control in the social structure or social relations of the workplace'. Workers are controlled through the creation of complex hierarchies in which there are clear lines of authority, and the behaviour of different workers within the hierarchy is constrained by written rules. Competition for promotion is used to divide the labour force. Within the hierarchy, workers are encouraged to be in conflict with each other rather than uniting to challenge management control.

Unlike Braverman, Edwards saw the use of technology and bureaucratic hierarchies as more important than scientific management as control strategies. He also saw techniques of control as passing through different stages rather than a single method being dominant throughout the history of capitalism. Edwards did accept, though, that simple and technical control continued to exist in some capitalist enterprises.

Andy Friedman – control and worker resistance

A rather more critical view of Braverman was taken by Andy Friedman (1977). Although he saw control over the labour process as a vital influence upon managerial strategies, he accepted that other factors were also important. Furthermore, he argued that worker resistance to management could do more than change the type of control used over them; it could also reduce the amount of control that managers had over some sections of the workforce.

Friedman's work was based upon a distinction between 'direct control' and 'responsible autonomy'. Under direct control every aspect of a worker's labour is tightly controlled and directed by management (as was the aim of scientific management). However, there is no guarantee that management will be able, as Braverman assumed, to maintain direct control. It may be forced to concede some degree of responsible autonomy.

Friedman defined responsible autonomy as 'the maintenance of managerial authority by getting workers to identify with the competitive aims of the enterprise so that they will act "responsibly" with a minimum of supervision'. In other words, some workers can be left to monitor their own work and use their initiative so long as they are willing to accept the need to work for the profitability of the company.

Workers may be able to force management to accept responsible autonomy if they are well-organized, and particularly if they are central workers. The skills and capacities of central workers are essential to the long-term profitability of the company. Skilled workers are the most likely to be central workers, while unskilled workers are more likely to be peripheral. (This is because the latter are less essential to the company's profits since they can easily be replaced.)

Although workers' resistance is the most important factor determining the amount of autonomy that workers have, other factors such as market forces can have an impact. For example, where companies operate in an uncertain market – where what is produced needs to be changed frequently to meet consumer demand – a flexible workforce with responsible autonomy may be needed.

Friedman believed that responsible autonomy and direct control have existed side by side during all stages of capitalism, and indeed both may be present within a single enterprise at a particular time. However, he believed that, overall, capitalism had moved towards granting more workers responsible autonomy, and he did not agree with Braverman that deskilling was an inevitable consequence of the development of capitalism. For instance, in a study of Coventry car workers, Friedman found considerable autonomy under the gang system. Employees worked in groups with their own elected gang leader, who was free to negotiate directly with management on behalf of the gang.

Friedman's work raises the question of whether changes in work in recent years contradict Braverman's claim that capitalism would progressively degrade work. We will deal with this issue in a later section (see p. 717). However, Friedman did share with Braverman the assumption that at least some degree of control is maintained over the workforce and, like Braverman, he saw the attempt to control the workforce as central to the way work is organized.

Braverman, Edwards and Friedman may all have exaggerated the importance of control over the workforce for management. New technology might be introduced for the straightforward reason that products can be produced more cheaply because fewer workers are required. It may have little to do with how easy it will be to control the workforce using the new technology. Furthermore, it cannot be assumed that attempts to control the workforce will be successful. As we will discover in the next section, some workers may be able to defend the definition of their work as skilled even when it goes against the interests of their company.

Skill, worker resistance and power

Braverman's theories prompted a sociological interest in the concept of skill. Although Braverman questioned the definitions of skill used in the US census, he did not produce a clear definition of skill himself. He appeared to assume that it could be objectively measured, but later writers have suggested that the definition of skill is, at least in part, a social construction. Groups of workers, and indeed management, may try to impose definitions of skill in their own interests. Some workers may be able to retain the definition of their work as skilled even when the skills required for it are reduced; others may never gain recognition for the skills required in their jobs.

A number of feminist critics of Braverman have argued that he failed to recognize the amount of skill required in some work done predominantly by women. Veronica Beechey (1983) points out that 'There are, for instance, forms of labour which involve complex competencies and control over the labour process, such as cooking, which are not conventionally defined as "skilled"'. Beechey suggests that in some areas where women have been brought into the labour force they might be doing highly-skilled work which is not recognized as such by employers. This raises questions about the extent to which deskilling has taken place.

Furthermore, Braverman assumes that deskilling, when it does occur, is a consequence of managerial strategies. Some feminist writers argue that male-dominated trade unions can have as much impact. Sylvia Walby (1986) has described how men have been far more successful than women in protecting their skills, and the definition of their jobs as skilled, in engineering, textiles and clerical work.

In a study of the engineering and textile industries in Rochdale, Roger Penn (1983, 1984) describes how some groups of skilled manual workers were able to protect the skills of their work, not just from female workers but also from management. Penn argues that these workers successfully used techniques of social exclusion even when management had the technical means to deskill their jobs. Social exclusion involves the prevention of management from controlling the labour process. It also involves the prevention of other workers (particularly less skilled workers) from taking over parts of the skilled workers' jobs.

Penn believes that workers in occupations in which factory production preceded automation were able to develop techniques of social exclusion within the factory and were able to defend their skills. Engineers and mule spinners came into this category and they successfully resisted deskilling for many decades. In particular areas of the country, such as Rochdale, local conditions (particularly a

shortage of skilled labour) allowed the engineers to protect their skills until as late as the 1960s. In other parts of the country, engineering was deskilled decades earlier. For other occupations which were originally skilled, automation and factory production occurred simultaneously. Groups such as weavers and cardroom workers were not well enough organized to resist deskilling.

Penn's work shows that management is not always free to impose the labour process it desires upon workers. Workers can do more than force management to change its control strategy: they can successfully resist deskilling for many decades. Penn accuses Braverman of a type of determinism in seeing deskilling as the inevitable result of the capitalists' need to control the labour force. Like some feminist critics, he claims that Braverman pays too little attention to the power of male trade unions.

Flexibility and post-Fordism

A number of writers have argued that, since the 1970s, there have been important changes in industry and work in general. They put forward a quite different perspective on work from that supported by Braverman: they believe that changes in work in recent years have *increased* the amount of skill required by many workers. What is more, they see a number of factors other than the need to control the workforce as shaping the organization of work by employers. From this point of view, there has been a trend away from the techniques of production associated with 'Fordism'.

Fordism

Fordism is named after Henry Ford, the American car manufacturer who pioneered mass production. It involves the use of a moving assembly line which controls the pace of work. Under this system, workers perform repetitive assembly tasks which require little training or skill. The parts used are designed so that they can be assembled easily. Machines are used to produce standardized parts for products which are mass-produced. Products made using this system tend to be relatively cheap. Labour costs are held down because there is little need to employ skilled labour. Because of the large number of products produced, overheads and capital costs, such as the cost of machinery, are relatively low.

From Braverman's point of view, such production methods, when combined with scientific management, do indeed deskill work and make it easier for

management to control the labour process. However, Braverman's views are called into question if, as some now believe, Fordism is outdated and is being replaced.

Post-Fordism and flexible specialization

Michael J. Piore (1986) is amongst those who believe that capitalist countries have entered a post-Fordist era. He claims that much work is now organized according to the principles of flexible specialization. Many of these principles originated in Japan but have been adopted by employers in other capitalist countries, partly as a response to the success of Japanese business.

According to Piore, manufacturers have used new technology, particularly computers, to make manufacturing more flexible. For example, computer numerical-controlled machine tools can be reprogrammed to perform different tasks. This enables manufacturers to make goods in small batches economically: it no longer costs vast amounts to shift from the production of one product to the production of another.

According to Piore, new technology helps industry to meet changing demands. Consumers are increasingly demanding more specialized products, and the demand for mass-produced articles is decreasing.

Piore believes that these developments have resulted in changes in patterns of work and management. As companies become more flexible, they require more flexible and skilled workers. He says:

*These developments seem to be producing an
employment structure in which low-skilled
repetitive tasks are reduced (eliminating semi-
skilled jobs), but the highly skilled work involved in
designing products or in shifting from one product
to another remains, albeit often in a new form
more closely linked to the computer.*

Piore, 1986, p. 158

More flexible working requires a more flexible
organizational structure. Firms are organized less
hierarchically with more communication between
departments. Managerial practices also change. Many
companies have adopted the Japanese *kan-ban* or
just-in-time system whereby large stocks of parts
are no longer held in reserve. Instead they are
delivered just before they are needed, to the
appropriate workers. Apart from cutting costs, this
also allows the product to be changed very quickly.

Workers in companies that are changing along
these lines need to be more broadly trained, as their
work becomes increasingly varied. Because of their
long training and the importance of their skills to
their companies, they enjoy more job security, and
management makes greater attempts to enlist their
cooperation.

Some firms have adopted another Japanese
technique, quality circles. In quality circles, groups
of workers and managers meet together periodically
to discuss how the production or performance of the
company can be improved.

Other initiatives may include workers' representatives sitting on company boards, and profit-sharing
schemes which enable workers to benefit from any
success the company enjoys.

Flexible specialization, then, increases the skills
needed by the workforce, and, unlike industries where
scientific management techniques are used, workers
may cooperate with management in organizing the
labour process. By implication, job satisfaction
increases and industrial conflict decreases.

The theory of flexible specialization also implies a
move away from the concentration of capital in giant
corporations, and an increase in the number and
importance of small businesses. Another supporter of
the flexible specialization theory, C. Sabel (1982),
points to the Third Italy region as an example of how
industry is likely to develop in the future. This region
in the north of Italy enjoyed considerable economic
success in the 1970s. It is based upon networks of
small- and medium-sized firms which cooperate
together, making use of each other's specialist skills.
The Italian clothing firm Benetton is used by Sabel as
an example of flexible specialization. It changes its
products frequently and uses a wide range of
suppliers in order to respond to the rapidly changing
demands of the fashion market.

The flexible firm – core and peripheral workers

Similar views have been developed by the British
economist John Atkinson (1985) in his theory of the
flexible firm. Atkinson believes that a variety of
factors have encouraged managers to make their
firms more flexible. Economic recession in the 1970s
and 1980s, and the consequent reduction in trade
union power, technological changes, and a reduction
in the working week have all made flexibility more
desirable and easier to achieve.

According to Atkinson, flexibility takes two main
forms:

1 Functional flexibility refers to the ability of
   managers to redeploy workers between different
   tasks. It requires the employment of multi-skilled
   employees who are capable of working in different
   areas within a firm. Such flexible workers form the
   core of a company's workforce. They are employed
   full-time and have considerable job security. The
   core is usually made up of 'managers, designers,
   technical sales staff, quality control staff,
   technicians and craftsmen'. These are shown as 'A' in
   Figure 10.3.

2 Numerical flexibility is provided by peripheral
   groups. It refers to the ability of firms to reduce or
   increase the size of their labour force. The first
   peripheral group have full-time jobs but enjoy less
   job security than core workers. These workers might
   be 'clerical, supervisory, component assembly and
   testing', and they are easier to recruit than core
   workers because their skills are common to
   employment in many different firms. These are
   shown as 'B' in Figure 10.3. The second peripheral
   group of workers are even more flexible. They are
   not full-time permanent employees. They may work
   part-time, on short-term contracts, under temporary
   contracts or under a government training scheme.
   (These are shown as 'C' in Figure 10.3.) Atkinson
   believes that flexible firms are making increasing use
   of external sources of labour. More work is
   subcontracted ('D'), and the self-employed ('E') and
   agency temporaries ('F') are also used.

Figure 10.3 shows how Atkinson sees the flexible
firm, and the wide range of labour sources that are
available to increase functional and numerical
flexibility.

Atkinson does not go as far as Piore in believing
that the trend towards flexibility increases the skills
and autonomy of the workforce. He certainly believes
that core workers benefit from the changes. They
learn a greater variety of skills and increase their
functional flexibility. Management also allows participation by core workers in the decision-making
processes of the firm.

On the other hand, the further away workers are
from the core group, the less likely they are to enjoy
such benefits. Peripheral workers may not be required

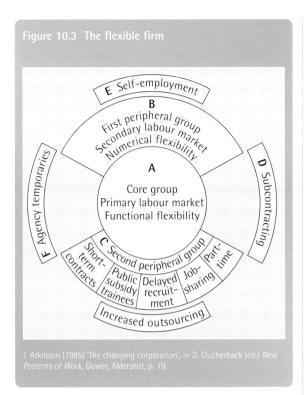

Figure 10.3 The flexible firm

E Self-employment

B
First peripheral group
Secondary labour market
Numerical flexibility

D Subcontracting

F Agency temporaries

A
Core group
Primary labour market
Functional flexibility

C Second peripheral group

Short-term contracts

Public subsidy trainees

Delayed recruitment

Job-sharing

Part-time

Increased outsourcing

J. Atkinson (1985) 'The changing corporation', in D. Clutherback (ed.) *New Patterns of Work*, Gower, Aldershot, p. 19.

to broaden their skills, and employers may give them little opportunity to participate in decision making.

Like Piore, Atkinson offers no support for the view of Braverman that work has been deskilled. Unlike Piore, Atkinson does not imply that most workers have their skills increased or broadened in flexible companies. Peripheral workers usually require less skill, and have their work more closely controlled than core workers.

(For a description of David Harvey's theory of 'flexible accumulation' (Harvey, 1990), which partly draws upon theories of post-Fordism, see Chapter 15.)

Criticism and evaluation of theories of flexibility

Theories about the increasing flexibility of work have been controversial because they contradict the widely-held belief among sociologists that work is becoming less satisfying and less skilled. Anna Pollert (1988) is one of the strongest critics – indeed, she has tried to 'dismantle' the theory of flexibility. Pollert argues that the theory of flexibility 'conflates and obscures contradictory processes within the organisation of work'. She believes that the theory is certainly over-simplified and at times inaccurate.

Production methods

In the first place, Pollert does not believe that Fordist production methods have ever been as dominant as

flexibility and post-Fordist theories imply. Small-batch production was important throughout the twentieth century, and companies with the flexibility to produce specialized products are nothing new. Pollert does not believe either that there has been any marked reduction in the importance of mass production. She says:

> one can look at a whole range of industries which are based upon mass and large batch production and continue to sell well to large markets: food, drinks, flat-pack furniture, DIY goods, toiletries, records, toys – the list covers most consumer goods.
>
> Pollert, 1988

She also points out that the success of Japanese business is largely the result of producing cheap, well-designed and reliable products rather than specialist products in small numbers. The spread of flexibility in industry is in any case limited by the cost of new technology. Computer-controlled machinery is very expensive and often only big firms can afford it. For example, in the clothing industry only the large manufacturers have the resources to adopt computer-aided design and computer-controlled cutting systems.

Flexibility and skill levels

Second, Pollert questions the view that flexibility, where it has been introduced, has led to the workforce requiring more skills. Basing her argument upon a number of empirical studies, she claims that flexibility can have a wide variety of effects upon work. She says that more flexible production may lead to 'continuing dependence on traditional skills, deskilling, skill increases and skill polarisation'. Management and workers may well come into conflict as a result of the introduction of new technology or management proposals for new working practices. Pollert points out that either side 'can wrest gains and suffer costs in the negotiation of change'. Once again, Pollert finds the theory of flexibility over-simplified.

The peripheral workforce

Third, Pollert attacks Atkinson's claim that companies are making increasing use of a peripheral workforce. On the basis of a number of statistical studies, Pollert argues that the amount of temporary work has fluctuated, but has not increased dramatically: part-time workers declined as a proportion of the manufacturing workforce between 1979 and 1986, and there is little evidence that subcontracting increased in the first half of the 1980s. Peripheral workers of these types have always been an important part of the labour force, and clearcut increases in these types of employment would be expected if Atkinson was correct about the move towards numerical flexibility.

Skill levels and new technology

Stephen Wood (1989) also criticizes Piore and Atkinson. Like Anna Pollert, he questions the view that the changes associated with flexibility have led to workers needing greater skills. His own study of two British steel-rolling mills found that new technology did help to increase the range of products produced, but it did not increase significantly the skills needed by workers. He suggests that many of the workers who do highly-skilled jobs with the new technology were skilled workers to start with and have not had their skills increased. In other cases, flexibility for workers means little more than having to move between semi-skilled jobs that require very little training.

Wood accuses supporters of theories of flexibility of greatly exaggerating their case. He questions the degree to which there has been a move towards specialized production by asking 'What proportion of the cars of even the British royal family or president of the USA are custom-built?' He attacks Piore and Sabel for ignoring the negative consequences of changes in work for the British workforce in the 1980s. These include 'job losses, unemployment, tightening of performance standards, labour intensification, changing employment contracts and reduction of the power of trade unions and workers' representatives'.

The extent of flexibility

Shirley Dex and Andrew McCulloch (1997) have examined evidence of the extent of flexible working in Britain. They include a wide range of job types in their definition of flexible working. These are: self-employment, part-time work, temporary work, fixed-term contracts, zero-hours contract employment, seasonal work, shift work, homeworking, Sunday working, teleworking, working only in term-time and job-sharing. They use data from the *Labour Force Survey*, the *British Household Panel Survey* (1991–3) and from surveys of employers.

Overall they found that there had been some increase in flexible working, but it was not as great as some people have suggested. Although in 1994 about half of all women and a quarter of all men were in flexible employment, according to their estimates, this did not represent a massive increase in flexibility compared to earlier periods. Overall, flexible working increased from about 30 per cent of the workforce in 1981 to about 38 per cent in 1994. Most of the increase took place in the early 1980s, and by the 1990s there was little evidence of flexible working continuing to grow. Indeed, there

seemed to have been something of a trend back towards full-time jobs.

Dex and McCulloch therefore believe that there has been a polarization between core and peripheral jobs, as postulated in some theories of flexibility and post-Fordism. However, they do not believe that flexible working will become much more common than it already is.

Multi-tasking and the intensification of labour

Like Dex and McCulloch, Paul Thompson (1993) is less critical of theories of flexibility than sociologists such as Pollert and Wood . He accepts that 'The modern worker does frequently have to be more flexible.' He suggests that teamworking could be here to stay, and he detects a move away from Taylorism and scientific management. Nevertheless, he thinks that the 'extent and novelty of flexibility has been grossly exaggerated'.

Thompson argues that many jobs have not been reskilled but have simply been expanded to include a greater range of tasks, each of which requires little skill. He found evidence of this multi-skilling or multi-tasking in his own research at the Leyland Volvo bus plant. He also claims that it is typical of fast-food outlets such as McDonald's. Workers are expected to be able to perform a variety of tasks involved in preparing and selling the food, but there is little skill involved and virtually no opportunity for workers to use their initiative. They have to follow very detailed sets of rules telling them how to do their jobs.

Thompson acknowledges that some of the old methods of controlling and monitoring workers have been relaxed, but new methods of control have been put in their place. Some companies use new technology to monitor the performance of workers; others award daily or weekly scores to encourage staff to work harder. Nissan UK uses a 'Neighbour Watch' system which involves workers monitoring each other.

Companies also use more intensive recruitment processes, such as detailed psychological tests, and workers are expected to conform more closely to 'corporate culture and norms'.

Japanese companies and those using similar management methods have also succeeded in making workers work harder. As Thompson points out, policies such as just-in-time are intended to get rid of the slack in the production process. Production targets are regularly increased as the pace of the work gets faster and faster.

Overall, Thompson believes that important changes are taking place in work, but they are not as the supporters of flexibility describe them. The changes are more limited than they first appear; they do not always lead to reskilling; and they frequently result in an intensification of work. To Thompson, ideas such as post-Fordism are unwarranted generalizations. The claims about changes in work are far too sweeping. In different countries, companies and sectors of the economy, the extent and nature of changes can be very different.

Flexibility and control

Braverman claimed that, in the twentieth century, management tightened its control over the labour process, but theories of flexibility imply that management increasingly shares control with core workers. Maryellen R. Kelley (1989) has tried to evaluate these competing claims in a study of management and new technology. She studied industries in the USA which used programmable automation involving computer-controlled machinery. Her study was based upon responses to questionnaires from production managers in 1,015 plants, of which 43 per cent had adopted programmable automation. The data were collected in 1986–7.

Kelley distinguished between three types of control:

1 In factories using 'strict Taylorist' control, machines were programmed by engineers or management. If Braverman was correct, this would be the predominant type of control.

2 Worker-centred control existed where blue-collar or manual workers programmed the machines. If theories of increasing flexibility were correct, this type of control would be predominant.

3 In factories where manual and non-manual workers both played a part in programming, shared control existed.

As Table 10.2 shows, no one pattern of control was dominant, and Kelley concluded that neither Braverman nor flexibility theories were supported by her research. Worker-centred control was found to be more common in relatively small plants, and 70 per cent of the plants with worker-centred control did concentrate on producing small batches. This might seem to support theories of flexibility; however, over 50 per cent of factories using strict Taylorist control also specialized in small batches. Furthermore, because worker-centred control was more common in small plants, only 11.8 per cent of the workforce benefited from this type of control.

Class and post-Fordism

Some writers who are not wholly unsympathetic to the theory of post-Fordism nevertheless criticize it for over-simplifying changes and for ignoring the role of class conflict in society as a whole. Many accounts of flexibility and post-Fordism seem to portray it as a universal feature of contemporary societies, which is an inevitable result of developments in capitalist economies. Ash Amin notes that critics think the theories are 'based on arbitrarily derived guiding principles and universal claims based on partial truths, thus denying the key aspects of history as complex and heterogeneous' (Amin, 1994). Thus, while post-Fordism or flexible firms might be present in some specific places, there is no simple, overall trend in the nature of work that can be identified.

John Tomaney argues along similar lines that the nature of different workplaces varies considerably. Furthermore, he argues that 'A determining characteristic of the nature of workplace change is the balance of forces existing between management and labour' (Tomaney, 1994). The ways in which work and workplaces are organized will therefore be different, depending on whether management or workers have the upper hand. Tomaney does not believe that there has been a general move from mass production to flexible specialization or post-Fordism. However, there has been some reduction in the bargaining power of some groups of workers compared to the 1950s and 1960s; but even this varies from time to time and place to place.

The future of work

Braverman's theory of the degradation of work, and Piore and Atkinson's theory of flexible specialization reach very different conclusions about the direction that work is moving in. Braverman adopted a Marxist approach and was very pessimistic. Piore and Atkinson used more conventional economic theories and reached predominantly optimistic conclusions. Nevertheless, criticisms of the theories suggest that they share a common fault: all three writers claim that work is developing in one particular direction. They ignore evidence which shows that work may develop in different ways in different industries and types of employment: while much work is becoming less skilled and more tightly controlled, other work is retaining or increasing its skill content and becoming more flexible.

Table 10.2 Types of control in US manufacturing plants		
	Plants %	Total employment %
Strict Taylorist	24.0	47.1
Shared control	44.8	41.1
Worker centred	31.2	11.8

Source: M.R. Kelley (1989) 'Alternative forms of work automation under programmable automation', in S. Wood (ed.) *The Transformation of Work?* Unwin Hyman, London, p. 239.

Conflict and cooperation at work

Having looked at various theories concerning the changing nature of work in society, we will now consider a different aspect of this subject: conflict and cooperation.

Forms of conflict

Conflict at work can take many different forms:

1   Conflict may occur between managers and non-managerial workers or between different groups of non-managerial workers. The former type of conflict has usually been the focus of sociological study, because it has often been assumed that those in positions of authority at work have different interests from those of their subordinates; but conflict is also common between groups of workers. For example, semi-skilled and skilled workers may clash over such issues as wage differentials and job demarcation.

2   Conflictual behaviour by workers can take a variety of forms. These include sit-ins, working to rule, refusal to work overtime, absenteeism, leaving the job, working with less than normal effort, and striking.

3   As Richard Hyman points out, many of the actions taken by workers may be a response to management behaviour. Employers and managers may initiate conflict. Hyman says, 'conflict with the employee can take the form of plant closure, sacking, victimization, blacklisting, speed-up, safety hazards, arbitrary discipline and so on' (Hyman, 1984).

In one form or another, conflict is a common feature of work. It is not, though, by any means universal. In many places of work employees routinely obey instructions and carry out their work tasks without perceiving a conflict of interests between themselves and their employers, and without engaging in conflictual behaviour. In some places of work managers enlist the assistance of other workers in increasing the efficiency and success of the company, and consult workers' representatives on proposed changes.

Some sociologists emphasize the extent to which there is cooperation based upon common interests at work; others emphasize the extent of conflict based upon different interests. These different perspectives will now be examined with particular reference to the role of trade unions in society.

Consensus and cooperation in work

From a functionalist perspective, society is character-ized by shared interests. As we saw in Chapter 2, functionalists such as Talcott Parsons and Kingsley Davis and Wilbert E. Moore do not believe that there

should be any conflict of interests between employers, managers and other workers (see pp. 27–8 for details).

Talcott Parsons claimed that work is dominated by the fundamental goal of 'success'. He believed that there is a value consensus in industrial societies based upon individual achievement and economic efficiency. Workers at all levels in a company will recognize that it is necessary for individuals to carry out specialized tasks according to their ability, and that it is necessary for the activities of a company to be coordinated by workers who hold positions of authority. If a company is successful, everyone benefits: shareholders receive larger dividends as the company becomes more profitable; workers can enjoy higher wages and job security.

From this point of view, conflict damages everyone's interests since it prevents the success of the company. If there is conflict, it is due to minor malfunctions in the system, and the removal of conflict can be achieved with reform of industrial relations rather than a radical change in the structure of industrial society. From this point of view, it might eventually be possible to eliminate strikes completely.

Pluralism, trade unions and the institutionalization of industrial conflict

From the pluralist perspective, differences of interest do exist in industrial societies. For example, employees have an interest in increasing their wages, while employers have an interest in keeping wages low so that profits can remain high. However, employees also want to keep their jobs and it is therefore against their interests to press for wages that will make their industry bankrupt. Moreover, as consumers, workers may realize that excessive wage demands will lead to inflation, which in turn will devalue their wage packets. In this situation it is possible for different interest groups such as employees and employers to resolve their differences through negotiation.

Pluralists believe that power in industrial societies is dispersed between many different interest groups, all of which have some power. Trade unions form the major groups representing the interests of employees. A number of sociologists who support the pluralist position have argued that it is largely through trade unionism that the working class has been integrated into capitalist society. Conflict between employers and employees exists, but it has been institutionalized in terms of an agreed set of rules and procedures. The net result is increasing stability in industrialized society. No longer is the working class seen as a threat to social order; there is less and less chance of the type of conflict that Marx predicted. (See pp. 593–7 for an outline of pluralist views.)

Ralf Dahrendorf – industrial democracy

The German-born sociologist Ralf Dahrendorf (1959) argued that pluralism 'provides an opportunity for success for every interest that is voiced'. He believed that the voice of the working class was growing louder through its formal associations. He saw a trend towards a more equal balance of power between employers and employees, and the development of what he termed industrial democracy. Dahrendorf made the following case.

Democracy in industry begins with the formation of workers' interest groups. In particular, interest groups are necessary to represent workers, since employers cannot negotiate with a disorganized collection of employees.

For workers' interest groups to be effective, they must be recognized as legitimate by employers and the state. This has been an uphill struggle in capitalist societies. In nineteenth-century Britain, employers strongly resisted the formation of trade unions, often insisting that their workers sign a document declaring that they were not union members. In America, particularly during the 1930s, organized crime syndicates were sometimes employed by companies to prevent their workforce from forming trade unions. However, by the latter half of the twentieth century, unions were generally accepted as legitimate by employers and the state. Dahrendorf regarded this as the major step towards industrial democracy and the institutionalization of industrial conflict.

With the formation of workers' interest groups, a number of processes occurred which furthered the integration of the working class into the structure of capitalist society:

1 Negotiating bodies were set up for formal negotiation between representatives of employers and workers. Such negotiations took place within a framework of agreed-upon rules and procedures. Conflict was largely contained and resolved within this framework.

2 Should negotiations break down, a machinery of arbitration was institutionalized, in terms of which, outside bodies mediate between the parties in dispute.

3 Within each company, workers were formally represented, for example by shop stewards, who represented their interests on a day-to-day basis.

4 There was a tendency 'towards an institutionalization of workers' participation in

industrial management'. Dahrendorf gave the example of workers appointed to the board of directors in certain European countries.

In the above ways, the voice of labour was heard in capitalist enterprises, and there was a trend towards joint regulation of industry by workers and employers.

Trade unions and the integration of the working class

Some sociologists have argued that trade unions help to integrate the working class into capitalist societies, making them less likely to become a radical or revolutionary force.

These views may be illustrated by the role of unions in British society in the 1970s. Not only were unions involved in decision-making processes at the shop-floor level, but they were regularly consulted by central government. Union officials frequently sat on government advisory committees, and cabinets had regular meetings with members of the TUC to discuss important national and international issues. Although there were sometimes confrontations between the government and unions, there was also a good deal of cooperation.

Some sociologists have referred to this as an era of corporatism. Although there is no one agreed definition of corporatism, it involves the government consulting and cooperating with employers and trade unions in the formulation of economic policy. From 1962, one of the main forums in which these groups worked together was the National Economic Development Council. In 1975, the National Enterprise Board was established, through which employers, unions and government developed policies jointly for firms receiving state aid.

The Labour government of 1974–9 cooperated with the TUC during most of its term in office through the 'Social Contract'. Under the Social Contract the TUC agreed to moderate wage demands and to try to avoid strike action, in return for being able to influence government economic policies.

The picture which emerges is of fully-fledged interest groups – trade unions – effectively representing workers' interests. Industrial conflict has been institutionalized and the working class has been integrated into both the capitalist enterprise and society as a whole. However, as we will show in a later section (see pp. 593–7), this picture does not square easily with the large number of strikes that took place in the 1970s. Furthermore, the Labour government's attempts to control wage rises led to the 'Winter of Discontent' of 1978–9, in which employees such as lorry drivers, health service workers and local authority workers took strike action.

This was followed by the electoral success in 1979 of the Conservatives under Margaret Thatcher. Successive Conservative governments made little attempt to incorporate unions in decision-making processes. This suggests that the era of corporatism was no more than a temporary phase: industrial capitalist societies may not be able to institutionalize conflict between employers and employees permanently. Although the Labour government elected in 1997 was less hostile to unions than the Conservative regimes that preceded it, there was no attempt to return to the corporatist days of the 1970s. Indeed, 'New Labour' tried to distance itself from its union links in order to avoid alienating the middle class and voters who were not union members (see p. 730 for a fuller account).

Conflict and consent at work – Marxist perspectives

Marxist sociologists agree that employers and the working class have fundamentally different interests. They believe that workers are exploited by the bourgeoisie because they are not paid the full value of their labour. The bourgeoisie exploits workers by extracting surplus value (the difference between the value of the work done and the wages paid).

Thus, to Marx, capitalism entailed the need for companies to be profitable. If they were not, capital would not be invested in them and they would not survive. To be profitable they had to be based upon the extraction of surplus value and the exploitation of workers.

This conflict of interests provides the basis upon which conflict can develop within work.

Profit, conflict and control

This point of view has been developed by Craig R. Littler and Graeme Salaman (1984). In order to achieve the maximum amount of profit, employers need to control their labour force to make them as productive as possible. They therefore tend to make labour 'as unskilled as is feasible, cheapen it and regulate it so that workers are constrained to act according to the specifications of the employer'. By doing these things, though, employers create the conditions which can lead to conflict. Littler and Salaman say, 'Such tendencies create an increasingly serious disadvantage: the loss of employee good will, the emergence of worker resistance, and high levels of labour turnover and absenteeism.'

Many Marxists who have studied the labour process argue that employers cannot afford to allow worker resistance and conflict to reach excessive levels. They require at least some degree of consent and cooperation from the workforce. Littler and Salaman say, 'the enterprise, quite obviously, reveals at one and the same time relations of co-operation and integration, and relations of conflict and exploitation'. Cooperation is needed so that workers expend enough effort to be productive and so that management can coordinate those efforts.

The manufacture of consent

In a study based on participant observation in a machine shop in the USA, which was published in 1979, Michael Burawoy argued that employers have been able to manufacture consent by abandoning very strict control over the labour process. In this way they have disguised exploitation at work, persuaded workers that they enjoy rights and benefits at work, and they have given workers the chance to adapt to the control exercised over them:

1 Workers are unable to see that they are being exploited at work because employers can blame low wages or job losses on the market and not on themselves. For example, they can claim that the workers cannot expect excessive wage rises or the preservation of all jobs if the company is to compete successfully with others.

2 Burawoy suggested that the state's legal regulation of industry limits the actions that management can take and protects it from trying to control work too closely. In doing so, the state protects management from itself and prevents excessive conflict. Although writing about the USA, Burawoy's point can be applied to Britain. Such laws as the Employment Protection Act and the Sex Discrimination Act encourage workers to believe that their rights are being protected. They can see themselves as what Burawoy calls 'industrial citizens', protected from exploitation by the law.

3 According to Burawoy, management increasingly allows workers to engage in 'making out'. It does not control the workforce too closely and gives them the chance to relieve boredom and avoid fatigue while still meeting or exceeding management production targets. Rules are not enforced too severely and work is not monitored too closely, so that workers do not feel oppressed. The workers themselves – through 'making out' activities – create the conditions under which they are willing to cooperate with management and cope with their jobs. As such they contribute to the creation of their own acceptance of exploitation.

Coercion and control

Other Marxist sociologists, though, do not agree that workers are so willingly persuaded to consent to their own exploitation. From this point of view, cooperation within work is not chosen by workers but is forced upon them by coercion.

For example, Richard Hyman (1984) points out that strikes were much more common in Britain in the 1970s than they were in the 1980s. He attributes this to the coercive pacification of the workforce under Mrs Thatcher's Conservative governments. Changes in trade union law and increasing unemployment weakened the bargaining power of workers so that they had little choice but to cooperate with management: workers have no hope of forcing management to accept their demands if they can be replaced easily and have little chance of finding a new job if sacked. (For further details of Hyman's views in relation to strikes, see pp. 725–6.)

Variations in conflict and consent

A more complex view of conflict and consent at work is advanced by P.K. Edwards and Hugh Scullion in a study published in 1982. In a comparison of seven factories in Britain they try to show that the amount of conflict and consent varies depending upon a range of factors.

In two clothing factories there was little conflict. Management rigidly controlled the workforce yet, for the most part, this control was accepted by the workers. In a large metals factory, management control was less severe, yet conflict between management and workers was much more evident.

According to Edwards and Scullion, the degree to which workers consent to management direction or come into conflict with it depends upon the precise techniques of managerial control used, and the circumstances of particular groups of workers. For example, in the clothing factories workers tended to accept the tight controls as natural and inevitable. Many of them had come straight from school, and had no experience of other work. Dissatisfied workers tended to leave the companies. The workforces had not organized themselves to challenge management, and individual workers were too isolated to try to change the status quo.

In the large metals factory the management was in a much weaker position. The company that owned the factory was not very profitable and the wages they paid were comparatively low. Management could not try to control the skilled workers, upon whom it relied, too closely because they were difficult to replace. The skilled workers were well-organized. They saw the management as incompetent and often came into conflict with it. They resented the low wages and on a number of occasions successfully challenged management attempts to increase control over the labour process.

To Edwards and Scullion, then, neither conflict nor consent are typical of the workplace. Both are possible, depending on particular circumstances. Where management does achieve a high degree of control, it can be the result of coercion or achieving consent, or a combination of both tactics. Like the other Marxists examined in this section, Edwards and Scullion believe that differences of interest between management and workers mean that the potential for conflict is always present at work. Unlike writers such as Burawoy, they do not believe that managers have been successful in manufacturing consent and controlling the workforce at all places of work.

Trade unions and the power of labour

Marxist perspectives

In terms of his hopes for the future of the working class, Marx saw both danger and promise in the formation of trade unions. He feared that they might be 'too exclusively bent upon the local and immediate struggles with capitalism'. In other words, trade unions could become preoccupied with furthering the interests of their particular members. In doing so they could lose sight of the overall struggle between capital and labour.

In spite of this, Marx believed that unions contained the potential to become 'organized agencies for superseding the very system of wage labour and capital rule'. By uniting workers in a struggle against employers, unions could provide help to create class consciousness. Cooperation between unions against employers on a local level could lead to class solidarity on a national level. In this way unionism could eventually lead to the formation of revolutionary political parties which would seize power.

Trade union consciousness

Marx's optimism was shared by few of his successors. For example, Lenin (who was the first leader of the USSR after the 1917 revolution) argued that unions were limited to developing trade union consciousness, that is a recognition of shared interests by members of a particular union, rather than an awareness of the common interests of the working class as a whole. This would tend to limit union demands to improvements in wages, hours and working conditions within specific industries. Lenin feared that unions were becoming increasingly self-interested, furthering the interests of their particular members at the expense of other workers.

However, he did believe that 'the trade unions were a tremendous step forward for the working class' (Lenin, 1969). He saw them as an important part of the class struggle, but argued that trade union consciousness could only be widened by linking unions to a political party representing the interests of the working class as a whole.

Modern Marxists and other commentators who would like to see unions have more power are often pessimistic about the role of unions in the class struggle. For example, Richard Hyman argues that 'Management still commands; workers are still obliged to obey. Trade unionism permits debate around the terms of workers' obedience; it does not challenge the fact of their subordination' (Hyman, 1984).

Having considered the various perspectives' views on the role of trade unions in society, we will now look at what might occur when cooperation between employers and employees breaks down.

Types of industrial conflict

As we noted earlier, there are a number of different types of industrial conflict. In the following sections we will concentrate on two specific types of conflict: strikes and industrial sabotage.

Strikes

Strikes are an obvious expression of industrial conflict. Richard Hyman (1984) isolates five elements in the definition of a strike:

1 It is an actual stoppage of work, which distinguishes the strike from activities such as overtime bans and go-slows.

2 It is a temporary stoppage of work – employees expect to return to work for the same employer after the strike is over.

3 It is a collective act involving a group of employees and as such it requires a certain amount of worker solidarity and organization.

4 It is the action of employees, and this distinguishes the strike from so-called 'rent strikes' and refusals by students to attend lectures.

5 It is nearly always a calculative act – an act that is specifically designed to express grievances, to seek a solution to problems, to apply pressure to enforce demands.

Strikes may be official or unofficial. Official strikes have the recognition and backing of the union; unofficial strikes, sometimes known as wildcat strikes, do not.

Strikes sometimes bring results. In a study of strikes, Richard Hyman concludes that they 'regularly prove highly effective in speeding negotiations towards an acceptable conclusion'. Paul Edwards (1995) quotes evidence, based on Confederation of British Industry figures, which shows that in Britain in the 1980s negotiations involving strikes led to higher pay settlements than those that did not. However, whether pay rises more than compensated for earnings lost during strikes is debatable.

Strike statistics

Strikes make news. From the 1950s to the mid-1980s, the impression often given by the mass media in Britain was that of a strike-prone workforce ready to stop work at the drop of a hat. However, this may have been a misleading impression. The Donovan Commission – a government-sponsored investigation into the UK's industrial relations record – found that even in the 1960s Britain's strike rate was only about average among comparable countries (quoted in Hyman, 1984).

More recent figures are given in Table 10.3. They show that Britain had a relatively high strike rate from 1988 to 1992 (98 working days lost per 1,000 employees) but a much lower rate for the 1993–7 period (just 26 days lost per 1,000 employees). Only Austria, Portugal, Switzerland and Japan had a lower rate between 1993 and 1997 (of the countries listed in the table). Between 1988 and 1992, 12 listed countries had a lower rate than Britain and, in terms of working days lost, Britain's rate was about average amongst advanced capitalist economies.

Statistics on strike activity require careful interpretation:

1 Hyman (1984) points out that British statistics are based on reports provided by employers. Some employers may be more conscientious in recording stoppages than others. Some may leave certain disputes unrecorded to give the impression of good industrial relations. Others may include every single stoppage in the hope of providing evidence for legal restrictions on strikes.

2 Different countries use different definitions when compiling strike statistics. In the UK a strike is only included in the statistics if at least 10 workers have been involved and the strike has lasted at least one day, or 100 or more working days have been lost. Political strikes are not included. By contrast, in Austria, the Netherlands and Japan there are no restrictions on the size of strike for it to be included in the statistics. Germany uses a similar definition to Britain's but includes political strikes and excludes strikes by civil servants. In the USA only strikes

Table 10.3 Labour disputes: working days not worked per thousand employees[a] in all industries and services, 1988-97

	1988	1989	1990	1991	1992	1993	1994	1995	1996	1997	Average[b] 1988-92	Average[b] 1993-97	Average[b] 1988-97
United Kingdom	166	182	83	34	24	30	13	19	57R	10	98	26	62
Austria	3	1	3	19	8	4	0	0	0	6	7	2	4
Belgium	66	44	34	22	65	18	24	33	49	–	46	–	–
Denmark	41	23	42	30	27	50	33	85	32	41	33	48	40
Finland	88	98	446	230	41	10	309	495	11	56	184	175	180
France	107	177	65	46	36	48	39	299R	57R	–	85	–	–
Germany[c]	2	4	15	5	47	18	7	8	3	–	16	–	–
Greece	442R	614R	1,505R	378R	183R	101R	41R	27R	46R	23	627	47	327
Ireland	177	62	266	100	218	68	27	132R	110R	69	165	82	120
Italy	226	300	342	195	180	235	236	64R	135R	83	248	151	201
Luxembourg	0	0	0	0	0	0	0	60	2	–	0	–	–
Netherlands	2	4	37	17	15	8	8	115	1	2	15	27	21
Portugal	67	127	44	37	58	25	30	20	16R	25	66	23	44
Spain	1,399	417	283	486	701	248	728	163	171	190	644	295	469
Sweden	199	101	191	5	7	54	15	177	17	7	102	54	80
EU average	206R	157R	142R	88R	105R	69R	97R	95R	53R	–	138	–	–
Iceland	929	747	2	31	3	1	867	1,889R	0	291	341	609	479
Norway	45	9	79	1	207	19	54	27	278	4	68	77	73
Switzerland	0	0	1	0	0	0	4	0	2	0	0	1	1
Turkey	264	415	480	536	151	74	31	601	31	20	366	147	249
Australia	266	184	210	250	148	100	76	79	131	75	211	92	150
Canada	423	312	427	216	183	130	136	131	276	290	313	194	253
Japan	4	5	3	2	5	2	2	1	1	2	4	2	3
New Zealand	313	163	279	85R	99	20	31	42	52R	18	189	33	108
United States	42	153	55	43	37	36	45	51	42	38	66	42	54
OECD average	124R	142R	108R	75R	70R	49R	61R	77R	51R	–	103	–	–

a Employees; some figures have been estimated.
b Annual averages for those years within each period for which data are available, weighted for employment.
c From 1993 data cover the entire Federal Republic of Germany; earlier data represented West Germany only.
R revised
– not available

Source: J. Davies (1999) 'International comparisons of labour market disputes in 1997', *Labour Market Trends*, National Office For Statistics, London, April, p.176.

involving more than 1,000 workers for at least a day or a complete shift feature in the statistics. Clearly, international comparisons should take account of these differences.

3 Whether a strike qualifies for inclusion is often a matter of interpretation. Keith Grint (1998) notes that a 1974 strike by dockers in favour of May Day being a public holiday was defined as an industrial dispute, while an engineering strike against the sequestration of union funds was not. The annual figures are determined by such interpretations.

4 Finally, there are a number of ways of measuring the significance of strikes. These include the actual number of stoppages, the number of workers involved in strikes, and the number of working days 'lost' through strike action. Table 10.4 gives statistics for these three measures for Britain from 1900 to 1998.

Table 10.4	British strike statistics (annual averages), 1895-1998		
Year	No. of Stoppages	Workers involved	Working days lost
1895–9	777	–	7,470,000
1900–4	484	–	2,888,000
1905–9	445	–	4,204,000
1910–14	932	993,250	16,120,000
1915–19	890	1,060,600	10,378,000
1920–4	857	1,061,000	30,277,000
1925–9	393	472,000	13,207,000
1930–4	412	289,000	3,980,000
1935–9	863	359,000	1,938,000
1940–4	1491	499,000	1,813,000
1945–9	1881	507,000	2,235,000
1950–4	1701	584,000	1,903,000
1955–9	2530	742,000	4,602,000
1960–4	2512	1,499,000	3,180,000
1965–9	2380	1,213,000	3,920,000
1970–4	2884	1,567,000	14,039,000
1975–9	2310	1,658,000	11,663,000
1980–4	1363	1,297,000	10,487,000
1985–9	890	783,000	3,939,000
1990–4	334	223,000	824,000
1995–6	240	269,000	859,000
1997	216	129,000	235,000
1998	166	91,000	282,000

Source: K. Grint (1998) *The Sociology of Work*, 2nd edition, Polity Press, Cambridge, p. 162; and *Labour Market Trends*, National Office for Statistics.

The figures show that there can be wide fluctuations from year to year. A single major strike can affect the figures a great deal. For example, in 1984 the miners' strike accounted for 22.4 million working days lost, 83 per cent of the total for the year.

However, despite the fluctuations, some trends can be detected. Figure 10.4 shows strike trends between 1895 and 1995–6, by averaging figures over five-year periods. The 1980s saw a substantial reduction in strikes, however measured. Furthermore, as Table 10.4 shows, the figures have fallen further since 1995–6. The year 1997 saw the smallest number of days lost through strikes in the UK since records began in 1891. Although the number of working days lost due to strikes increased slightly in 1998, strikes were still at a historically very low level.

Changes in patterns of striking

Some sociologists have tried to make sense of strike statistics by dividing recent British industrial relations history into periods. J. Durcan, W.E.J. McCarthy and G.P. Redman (1983) have identified four distinct phases of strike activity between 1945 and 1973:

1 They describe 1945–52 as the period of post-war peace. Unions tried to cooperate with the Labour government in the attempt to reconstruct British industry. There were relatively few strikes.

2 Durcan et al. call the second phase – 1953–9 – the return of the strike. The Labour government lost office and unions were less willing to cooperate with the Conservatives. There was a feeling among workers that the era of post-war austerity was over and they began to demand regular wage rises. Wage demands were also fuelled by rising prices.

3 The period 1960–8 is termed the shop-floor revolt. There were few large-scale strikes but a rising

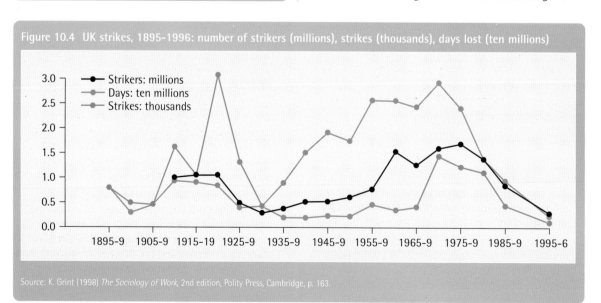

Figure 10.4 UK strikes, 1895-1996: number of strikers (millions), strikes (thousands), days lost (ten millions)

Source: K. Grint (1998) *The Sociology of Work*, 2nd edition, Polity Press, Cambridge, p. 163.

number of small-scale strikes in nearly every industry. There was increasing confidence among shop stewards who organized strikes in individual plants.

4 The fourth phase, 1969–73, is described as the formal challenge. Large-scale official disputes became more common and the number of striker-days lost reached record levels.

Hyman argues that Durcan *et al.* identify some of the main trends, but tend to over-simplify the developments. He says, 'Rather than distinct phases, it may be more accurate to speak of overlapping and at times contradictory tendencies, each dominant to a greater or lesser degree at particular points of time' (Hyman, 1984).

Nevertheless, Hyman himself claims to be able to identify three phases since 1973:

1 The years 1974–6 were those of the Social Contract. In the summer of 1975 the TUC agreed to cooperate with the Labour government in trying to curb pay claims. In return the government formulated economic policy in consultation with the TUC.

2 During 1977–9 there was a revival of struggle. Inflation caused a decline in the real value of wages and public-sector employees in particular went on strike to protect their wages.

3 Hyman describes the third of his phases as the era of coercive pacification in which the actions of Mrs Thatcher's Conservative governments pushed unions onto the defensive. Force was used to pacify the unions and reduce their willingness and ability to strike.

The replacement of Margaret Thatcher with another Conservative prime minister, John Major, made little difference to the relationship between government and unions. In 1997, a Labour government was elected. Historically, the Labour Party has had close links with the trade union movement. However, as we will see, Tony Blair's Labour government has distanced itself from unions to a greater extent than previous Labour governments.

The Thatcher and post-Thatcher eras will now be examined in more detail.

Richard Hyman – Thatcherism and the attack on unions in the 1980s

Hyman claims:

> All post-war British Governments regardless of party (with the partial exception of Heath's first two years) had shared a commitment to the consensual management of a 'mixed economy'. Thatcherite conservatism broke with the commitments of previous Governments.
>
> Hyman, 1984

According to Hyman, the Conservatives blamed union extremists for Britain's economic problems and tried to reduce the power of the unions. They believed that policies designed to create full employment left unions with too much bargaining power. The Conservatives were determined that the government should intervene less in the economy. Instead, market forces should be allowed to control economic developments. Hyman says:

> The succession of anti-union laws, the attacks on public welfare, the 'privatization' of state industries and services, the deliberate creation of mass unemployment, are all logical reflections of a passionate faith in the virtues of competitive capitalism.
>
> Hyman, 1984

The government developed what Hyman calls a multi-pronged offensive. The first part of this involved changes in trade union laws:

1 The 1980 Employment Act outlawed secondary picketing by strikers: it became illegal for them to picket anywhere other than their own place of work. Secondary action, taken in sympathy with another group who were in dispute, became liable for claims for damages, except in special circumstances. Secondary action was only immune from claims for damages where it involved employees of a customer or supplier of the company where industrial action was being taken.

2 The 1982 Employment Act narrowed the definition of a trade dispute to one which was 'wholly or mainly' about terms and conditions of employment. Disputes that were not covered by immunities became liable to claims for damages. Furthermore, it became possible for courts to grant injunctions telling unions not to engage in unlawful strikes or other types of industrial dispute. If they failed to comply, unions were subject to large fines and their funds could be sequestrated (temporarily confiscated). The act also enabled companies to selectively fire striking workers without it being regarded as unfair dismissal.

3 The Trade Union Act of 1984 made it necessary for secret ballots to be held before industrial action could take place, if the action was to be legal. Social security laws were also amended so that the benefits strikers' families received were calculated on the assumption that strikers were receiving strike pay, whether or not they were.

4 More recent legislation has further tightened restrictions on unions. The 1990 Employment Act specified that actions involving more than one employer had to be preceded by a separate ballot for each employer involved. Under this Act unions were made responsible for unofficial strike action taken by their members and therefore became liable for claims for damages in such disputes. The pre-entry

closed shop was also made illegal: it was no longer possible to make membership (or non-membership) of a union a precondition of a job offer.

5 The Trade Union Reform and Employment Rights Act of 1993 gave union members the right not to have union subscriptions taken from their pay without their written consent. It required strike ballots to be conducted postally and independently scrutinized. It also established a new Citizen's Right to take legal action to restrain illegal industrial action.

These changes made it much more difficult for unions and their members to take strike action and sustain it. They placed severe limits upon the legality of strikes and meant that unions and strikers could face prohibitive costs. Not surprisingly they led to a more cautious approach to industrial action by some unions, and so contributed to a fall in the number of strikes, although the legislation itself caused some industrial unrest.

According to Hyman, the government's second line of attack involved the removal of legal protections for employees. For example, fair wages clauses in government contracts were removed. The power of Wages Councils to set minimum wages in some industries was first of all reduced and then, in 1993, the Wages Councils were abolished altogether.

The third part of the offensive was to reduce the amount of consultation between government and unions. Hyman believed that the disdain shown by the government for trade unions forced the TUC to withdraw from the National Economic Development Council in 1982. The removal of union membership rights at GCHQ in Cheltenham in 1984 led to unions cutting more links with the government.

Fourth, according to Hyman, the Conservative government attacked public-sector employees. Budgetary controls on local authorities and nationalized industries forced them to offer low wage increases and stricter conditions of employment. Hyman points to examples such as British Leyland, where he considers there was 'a systematic attack on shop steward organisation'; British Steel, where the number employed was halved; and British Rail, where 'a succession of disputes has been provoked over pay and working conditions'.

Hyman recognizes that some of these policies led in the short term to serious disputes, such as the steel strike in 1980, and the miners' strike in 1984–5. Nevertheless, he believes that in the long term they weakened unions and reduced the number of strikes. In both the disputes mentioned above, unions failed to get significant concessions from the government.

Finally, Hyman argues that the rapid rises in unemployment in the early 1980s led to a weakening of union power and a reduction in the effectiveness

of strikes. Union members became more concerned about keeping their jobs, and less willing to risk losing them by striking.

Summing up his argument, Hyman says:

each defeat discourages others from the risk of a strike. This negative demonstration effect is part of a process which may be termed 'coercive pacification'; sustained mass unemployment and a governmental offensive have systematically undermined most workers' collective strength and confidence.

Hyman, 1984

Evaluation of Hyman

Keith Grint (1991) questions the view that Conservatism under Thatcher and Major has been the principal cause of a reduction in union power. He points out that the fall in official strike figures started before 1979 when the Conservatives returned to power.

Furthermore, declines in strike activity have not been confined to Britain but have occurred in all large Western societies, with the exception of Denmark, Finland and New Zealand. These international trends clearly cannot be attributed to British politics. Grint also argues that strikes do not necessarily show that unions are strong, and a lack of strikes that they are weak. He describes some strikes as 'last-ditch defences' by workers faced with the prospect of unemployment, while, in the period from 1979 to 1991, British workers' wages kept substantially ahead of inflation and productivity. This hardly seems to indicate union weakness.

Grint does not claim that government policies have had no impact on the union movement, but he sees other factors as having a stronger influence. In particular, he believes that the overall economic situation has the biggest effect on strikes and union power.

Paul Edwards – reasons for the decline of strikes

Like Grint, Paul Edwards (1995) takes a broader view than Hyman in trying to explain the possible causes of the reduction in the number of strikes in Britain. He identifies the following factors as being significant:

1 Changing economic conditions. Edwards believes that high inflation contributed to the high strike rates in the 1970s. Workers felt the need to go on strike so that their wages did not decline in value in real terms. The fall in inflation to low levels in the 1990s might help to account for the lower strike rate.

2 Occupational change. Strikes may have been reduced because the numbers of workers in strike-prone industries (such as mining) have been greatly reduced. He calculates that, had employment in

coalmining stayed at 1971 levels, then you could have expected about 405 more strikes in the 1986-90 period than there actually were.

3 The law. This may have played some part in reducing strike activity, but Edwards thinks that its effects can be exaggerated. Research has been conducted into whether the law has reduced strikes, once economic and labour market changes have been taken into account. This research has produced contradictory results. Some studies have found that the law has had an independent effect on top of other factors; other research has found no independent effect from the law. Edwards argues that if the law has had much effect it is because it has 'indirectly shaped assumptions about the desirability and efficacy of action'. Of the legal changes, compulsory strike ballots may have had most effect. Edwards believes that ballots themselves can sometimes be used as an effective bargaining counter, prompting an improved offer from employers which can form the basis of an agreement before a strike takes place.

4 Better industrial relations. Edwards sees this as the most difficult factor to measure. Improved industrial relations might involve increasing trust and better communications between management and workers. Alternatively, it might simply involve workers being too afraid to strike or just being pragmatic and realistic about what pay rises and other concessions they are likely to achieve. Edwards sees little evidence of more trust and better communications but he does find some evidence that fear might have reduced strikes. Research suggests, for example, that management is increasingly willing to use dismissal to discipline workers.

It seems likely, then, that a combination of factors has led to the fall in the strike rate, with only some of them directly related to conscious attempts by Conservative governments to reduce union power.

Paul Smith and Gary Morton – union exclusion in the 1980s and 1990s

Like Hyman and Edwards, Smith and Morton (1993) have examined the effects of government policies on union power and have noted how employment legislation has been used to weaken unions. However, they have also considered in detail how employers have used the legislation and how changes in work have affected unions. They use John Goldthorpe's concepts of union inclusion and exclusion.

Inclusion involves allowing unions to participate in decision making; exclusion involves isolating and marginalizing unions. For much of the 1970s British governments tried inclusion: for example, negotiating the 'Social Contract' with union leaders. According to Smith and Morton, the 1980s and 1990s saw a move towards the exclusion of unions. This was not just a direct effect of government

legislation but also resulted from employers using the increased freedom of manoeuvre offered to them by changed circumstances.

Smith and Morton note that union membership fell from 13.2 million in 1979 to 10.04 million in 1990. At the same time the number of strikes was falling and union power was apparently on the wane. Some employers have excluded unions by derecognition: refusing to recognize unions as the legitimate representatives of workers and refusing to negotiate with them. This is particularly common in shipping and provincial and national newspapers. Half the larger ships owned by UK companies are sailed under flags of convenience and are not therefore subject to union agreements. Companies such as Cunard and Sealink have withdrawn from national collective agreements with shipping unions. Similarly, News International and Associated Newspapers are amongst the major newspaper groups which no longer negotiate with the National Union of Journalists.

Other employers have not gone so far but have employed partial exclusion policies. They have recognized the right of unions to exist but have tried to minimize their influence. This has been achieved in a number of ways:

1 Some companies have introduced performance-related pay. Under this system, workers are paid according to their individual work performance. Collective agreements negotiated with unions become less important or completely redundant. A similar method of reducing union influence is to issue individual contracts to employees. Since their conditions are different it becomes very difficult for unions to negotiate on behalf of large groups of workers. Many privatized companies have used these techniques. British Telecom, for example, has introduced both performance-related pay and individual contracts for managerial staff and is extending the latter to sales staff.

2 A second way in which union influence has been reduced is through the use of subcontracting. When work is subcontracted, non-unionized labour taking over the work may replace unionized labour. The theories of post-Fordism and the flexible firm (discussed on pp. 713–17) both suggest that firms are making more use of subcontracting.

Increased subcontracting has also resulted from government policy. A number of areas of government and local authority employment have become subject to compulsory competitive tendering: private companies are given the opportunity to bid to take over the work. Smith and Morton comment that in local authorities this has led to 'widespread wage cuts and worsened conditions accomplished with relatively little union resistance'.

3 The unions' collective bargaining power has been further undermined as large organizations have been

split into smaller units. Many large companies have handed over bargaining power to subsidiaries. Examples include Cadbury, Courtaulds, Pilkington, Prudential and United Biscuits. These changes make it easier for employers to pick off more troublesome groups of workers without risking a dispute throughout the whole company or organization. For example, in the public sector, London Transport was divided into 13 subsidiaries in 1989. When one of them, London Forest Travel, succeeded in opposing wage cuts and worsened conditions, much of its operation was closed down.

4　Another technique that has been used is the replacement of full-time permanent employees with workers on fixed-term contracts. British Coal and the BBC are among the organizations to have done this. In British Telecom, catering, transport, cleaning and security are all now provided by contract and often non-unionized labour.

Smith and Morton argue, then, that such union exclusion policies are an important part of the current restructuring of work, 'the object of which is to consolidate the *de facto* redistribution of power to employers'. By implication, it therefore makes it more difficult for unions to take industrial action, including going on strike. However, Smith and Morton do qualify their claims, saying that 'To date, employers' exclusion policies have been tentative and exploratory.' They also say that 'The result of union exclusion policies cannot be predetermined' and unions' own responses to them will partly determine the extent to which they will undermine union power.

Peter Ackers, Chris Smith and Paul Smith – unions in the new workplace

Some of the themes developed by Smith and Morton are developed further by Peter Ackers, Chris Smith and Paul Smith (1996). They look at factors affecting unions and the response of the unions to them.

Ackers *et al.* identify a range of factors which have undermined unions and reduced membership. Unionization tends to be most successful where you find 'large-scale and highly bureaucratic employment situations; limited scope for occupational mobility; the need to defend skill structures; and specific sectoral conditions such as close-knit occupational and/or geographical communities'. All of these conditions have been undermined.

Manufacturing industry has contracted, making workplaces smaller. Bureaucratic public industries have been privatized. Occupational mobility has increased, and sectors with close-knit communities or workers have declined rapidly. Self-employment and part-time work (which are unlikely to be unionized) have both increased, and there has been a general move towards services.

In the UK, unions have been affected by the proliferation of new factories owned by foreign transnational corporations. Japanese firms such as Nissan and Sony have invested in Britain, as have a range of US firms like IBM, Hewlett Packard and Motorola. Many of the US firms are non-union companies, and Japanese companies often insist on having a single-union deal so that they only have to negotiate with one union. According to Ackers *et al.*, about half of the new multinational-owned factories have no unions at all; many of the others have single-union deals or try to develop cooperative relationships with unions.

The relationship between workers and management has also been affected by new management theories which followed from the free-market policies of Margaret Thatcher. New management techniques have tried to undermine or bypass unions by developing the relationship between individual employees and management. Individualized contracts (where each individual has their own conditions of service) and staff evaluation schemes reduce the role of unions.

Information technology has also had an impact. It has been used by management to communicate directly with employees (for example, by using e-mail), thus reducing their reliance on information from their union. It also allows them to try to encourage loyalty to the company by promoting a corporate culture. Information technology can be used to monitor the behaviour of employees, making it more difficult for them to act in ways which the company disapproves of, and workers can be dispersed and fragmented by working alone (and sometimes at home) at computer terminals.

Ackers *et al.* believe that there has been some move towards 'flexibility', which weakens unions. An extreme case is the supermarket chain Asda, which no longer has full- and part-time employees. Instead it has 'key-timers' who are called up by the company, with only two hours' notice, when it wants them to work. It is difficult for such workers to get together and form unions.

Contracting out of public services has made it impossible for some workers to bargain directly with those who are ultimately paying for their work. Even among those who have a permanent, full-time job in a large company, teamworking has made it more difficult for unions to retain their importance in bargaining. Teamworking involves 'a move away from strict control hierarchies' and it is 'supposed to delegate responsibility for task allocation and scheduling to groups of workers'. This reduces solidarity and consciousness amongst groups of workers. Working in teams, employees have been 'empowered' to sort out problems themselves. By throwing responsibility on to workers it makes it more difficult to blame management and to justify strike or other industrial action.

Some unions have responded to these changes by adopting a 'new realism'. The most right-wing unions, such as the electricians' union, the EETPU, have accepted no-strike deals and single-union agreements in an attempt to win members from other unions. Other unions have gone less far, but have also tried to be more conciliatory to management. At the same time they have tried to arrest the decline in union membership. Ackers *et al.* comment that:

> the TUC and the two great general unions, the TGWU and the GMB, emphasised more modest overtures to management, in the form of reform proposals for 'single-table-bargaining', and by stressing 'link' campaigns to win the growing peripheral workforce of part-time women and ethnic minorities – with limited success.

> Ackers, Smith and Smith, 1996, pp. 26–7

Generally, unions struggled to be successful in the 1980s and 1990s and had to adopt pragmatic policies. Thus, 'by the late 1980s a common practical agenda emerged of opportunist mergers, overtures to employers, recruitment campaigns, and improved public images and individual services for workers'. Unable to rely upon a traditional sense of solidarity, unions have had to show that they can offer benefits for individual workers as well as bargaining for their collective interests.

The Social Change and Economic Life Initiative – trade unionism in recession

Although they qualify their remarks, writers such as Smith and Morton clearly see trade unionism as losing influence in the 1980s and 1990s. A somewhat different picture is provided by research carried out as part of the Economic and Social Research Council's Social Change and Economic Life Initiative (Gallie, Penn and Rose (eds), 1996). The research included a survey of managers' attitudes at 935 workplaces in six locations, and case study research on particular organizations (see p. 710 for more details of the overall research programme involved).

Gallie *et al.* acknowledge that, on the surface, there was ample evidence of union decline. For example, union membership declined from 13.2 million in 1979 to 10.04 million in 1990. New legislation had hit the unions hard and the number of strikes had also declined. However, the research found that, despite the national decline, there was no marked loss of union influence at workplace level.

Duncan Gallie and Michael Rose examined the data from the employers' survey (Gallie and Rose,

1996). They found that few employers were hostile to unions. In only 5 per cent of all the organizations (and 2 per cent of those that actually had unions) did managers disapprove of union membership. In 28 per cent of organizations employers actively encouraged people to join unions. Gallie and Rose comment that they found a 'general impression that managers in unionised plants were generally sympathetic, rather than hostile, to the unions'. In more in-depth follow-up interviews, 64 per cent of managers found contacts with shop stewards helpful, compared to just 5 per cent who found them conflictual. The most common reason for managers being positive about unions was that they helped to improve communications with the staff. Other reasons given were that unions helped to build up trust and that they made negotiations more rational.

There was little evidence, then, that unions were marginal in most places of work by the 1990s. Furthermore, the evidence did not suggest that there had been a major decline in union influence. There were big variations between individual workplaces, but most managers thought that union influence had increased rather than decreased. For example, in 51 per cent of establishments the managers thought that union influence over pay had not changed, 13 per cent thought their influence had decreased, but 36 per cent thought it had increased. In terms of influence over work organization, 33 per cent thought union influence had grown and 12 per cent believed it had declined.

In the interviews it emerged that, where managers believed that union influence had increased, they thought that this had particularly affected pay bargaining, disciplinary procedures and redundancy agreements. Where their influence had decreased, this was thought to apply particularly to recruitment, controlling the pace of work and the allocation of workers to different tasks. Gallie and Rose conclude that 'Despite their loss of power at national level, our evidence suggests that the unions retained their influence relatively well in those workplaces where they had a presence.'

Broadly similar conclusions were reached by Michael Rose (1996) in an examination of case studies of industrial relations in 'sunrise' industries around Swindon. The Swindon area is relatively affluent and contains a number of new, high-technology industries. The four case studies included a subsidiary of an American multinational corporation, an electronics firm (which was non-union), the headquarters of a British multinational corporation and a public-sector research centre. These were just the sorts of companies which theories of post-Fordism and flexibility would suggest had been deeply affected by the reorganization of work. They were also the sorts of companies which had tended to introduce new management techniques, particularly those associated with human resource management (HRM). HRM involves trying to communicate directly with employees, and motivating and relating to people as individuals rather than through union representatives.

The non-union firm had succeeded in avoiding union representation, but only by providing very good conditions of service and rewards for employees. In the public-sector research establishment, support for unions seemed to be growing; and in the other organizations there was little hostility to unions. In some of the companies employees were concerned about the intensification of their work, and there was little evidence that employers had succeed in gaining the trust of their workers.

This research suggests that, where unions exist, they will continue to enjoy a reasonable level of support from employees, and that flexibility, post-Fordism and new management techniques will not usually lead to workers trusting employers more than unions.

The unions under the Labour government

If the decline of unionism seems to be more of a national than a local phenomenon, did the election of a Labour government in 1997 herald a new era of national influence for trade unions?

The Labour Party and the trade union movement in Britain have always had close links. Originally the Labour Party grew out of the trade union movement, and the party still receives a substantial proportion of its funds from the unions, and the unions retain a constitutional role within the party – although one of declining significance. Nevertheless, the Labour Party in the late 1980s and 1990s began to distance itself from trade unions. For example, the right of union leaders to use block votes (where they got one vote for every union member) at party conferences was withdrawn. The prime minister Tony Blair in particular tried to distance the party from its union associations to avoid alienating potential middle-class supporters.

Consequently, Labour's manifesto for the 1997 election did not propose reversing most of the legislation introduced by the Conservatives. The only policy that directly benefited unions concerned union recognition. A bill was introduced in 1999 which obliged employers to recognize unions, and therefore to negotiate with them, where more than half the workforce were union members.

The Labour government also recognized unions at GCHQ in Cheltenham, part of the British intelligence services. Union recognition had been withdrawn by the Conservatives on the grounds that it threatened national security.

Another policy which unions supported was the acceptance of the Social Chapter – this was European Union legislation which the Conservatives had opted out of. This provided for, amongst other measures, a maximum working week for most employees. The Labour government also introduced a minimum wage – a policy supported by the unions, although, at just £3.60 an hour, it was lower than the unions would have liked.

Despite these changes, Tony Blair was careful to point out that he did not want a return to the type of unionism that had been typical of the 1970s. He gave a speech to a TUC session on industrial relations in May 1999 in which he expressed his support for 'new unionism' (reported in *The Independent*, 25 May 1999). New unionism should be based upon 'partnership' between management and unions in achieving a common goal of a successful business. He called for an end to 'us and them' conflict between unions and management, and announced a £5 million government contribution to a partnership fund to train managers and union officials to work closely together.

Certainly the early years of Blair's government did not see a return to the high levels of strikes seen in earlier decades. Whether this was due to improved industrial relations or simply the relatively weak position of unions is more uncertain. The next section will examine the causes of strikes and the reason for the decline in their numbers in recent years.

The causes of strikes

In the previous section we examined changes in the numbers of strikes in Britain as a whole. In this section we will analyse both the reasons for some groups of employees being more strike-prone than others, and the factors that contribute to individual strikes.

Strikes are not spread evenly throughout the labour force. In Britain, from 1966 to 1970, the number of days lost through strikes, relative to the size of the workforce in particular industries, was greatest in the dock industry, followed by the car industry, shipbuilding and coalmining. Table 10.5 gives the figures for 1996 and 1997. It shows that the patterns of striking had changed to some extent.

In 1996, 'transport, storage and communication' had by far the highest strike rate, followed by the manufacture of coke and petroleum products, followed by the manufacturing of transport equipment, other manufacturing and public administration.

In 1997, the manufacturing of coke and petroleum products had the highest rate, followed by the manufacturing of transport equipment, and the manufacturing of 'other non-metallic mineral products'. Mining experienced relatively few strikes in these years. Although some areas of manufacturing

Table 10.5 Working days lost in the UK, per thousand employees, 1996 and 1997

Industry group	Working days lost per 1,000 employees[a] 1996	1997
All industries and services	58	10
Mining, energy and water	8	9
Manufacturing	24	21
Services	70	8
Agriculture, hunting, forestry and fishing	–	–
Mining and quarrying	25	26
Manufacturing of:		
Food products, beverages and tobacco	6	16
Textiles and textile products	8	2
Leather and leather products	–	–
Wood and wood products	–	–
Pulp, paper and paper products; printing and publishing	10	–
Coke, refined petroleum products and nuclear fuels	257	249
Chemicals, chemical products and man-made fibres	2	–
Rubber and plastic products	4	1
Other non-metallic mineral products	–	49
Basic metals and fabricated metal products	6	5
Machinery and equipment not elsewhere classified	20	9
Electrical and optical equipment	3	6
Transport equipment	114	130
Manufacturing not elsewhere classified	114	2
Electricity, gas and water supply	–	–
Construction	10	19
Wholesale and retail trade; repair of motor verhicles, motorcycles and personal and household goods	–	–
Hotels and restaurants	4	1
Transport, storage and communication	679	27
Financial intermediation	10	22
Real estate, renting and business activities	–	–
Public administration and defence; compulsory social security	113	22
Education	69	15
Health and social work	3	3
Other community, social and personal service activities, private households with employed persons, extra-territorial organizations and bodies	3	5

– Nil or negligible.
a Based on the latest mid-year (June) estimates of employee jobs.

Source: J. Davies (1998) 'Labour disputes in 1997', *Labour Market Trends*, National Office for Statistics, June, p. 303.

remained prone to strikes, in 1996 there were considerably higher rates of striking in services than in most areas of manufacturing or mining, energy and water.

A number of explanations have been put forward to account for why there has been a historical tendency for certain industries to be more strike-prone than others. In an early study of strikes in 11 countries, Clark Kerr and Abraham Siegel (1954) found that miners, dockers and seamen had the highest strike records. They argued that community integration was the key to explaining strike activity in these occupations.

Miners, dockers and seamen tended to live in occupational communities which were relatively isolated from the wider society. In such communities, a consciousness of kind developed which involved a strong awareness of shared grievances, a close emotional commitment to trade unionism, and a high level of working-class solidarity. Shared grievances and worker solidarity, set in the context of a close-knit community, tended to make strike action (a collective act requiring some degree of solidarity) more likely.

Some doubt is thrown on Kerr and Siegel's theory by Stephen Hill's study of London dockers (Hill, 1976). Hill found little evidence of the community integration that is supposed to be typical of dockland life. The London dockers were remarkably like the affluent workers studied by Goldthorpe and Lockwood (see pp. 79–81). Their lifestyle was largely privatized and their orientation to work and trade unions primarily instrumental. Whatever the merits of Kerr and Siegel's explanation, it is not supported by Hill's particular case study. (For further details of Hill's research see Chapter 2, p. 81.)

High strike rates cannot be assumed to follow automatically from certain types of employment. British coalmining no longer has a high strike rate. Since the 1970s and early 1980s coalmining in Britain has been drastically reduced. Most pits have been closed and the remaining ones have been privatized. The miners lost a bitter national dispute in 1984–5, since when the National Union of Mineworkers (NUM) has become much weaker than it was. Paul Edwards describes this strike as 'a major turning point. New work practices were introduced; though these provoked resentment, workers lacked the willingness and ability to strike over them' (Edwards, 1995).

Coal is a much less important source of fuel in power stations and other places than it was, and Britain's remaining deep mines struggle to compete with cheap, imported coal. For these reasons, miners have a very weak bargaining position compared to that enjoyed in earlier decades, and striking may be seen as more likely to result in job losses than pay rises. The circumstances of particular industries can therefore affect the propensity of the workers to strike, although, according to Edwards, in the early 1990s mining was still more strike-prone than other industries.

Dock work is another area where striking has declined. Edwards notes that, in the 1970s, on average half of all dockers were involved in strikes every year. In 1980 there were 90 dockers strikes; by 1988 there were just 15. As in mining, the number of jobs has declined rapidly. Employment in dock work fell from around 80,000 in the 1950s to around 10,000 in 1989. A national dockers strike in 1989 attempted to defend dock workers' conditions (based on the National Dock Labour Scheme which the government decided to abolish). The strike failed and dockers were forced to accept new contracts. Their position was undermined by technical developments such as the increased use of containers, which reduced the need for their labour and changed the nature of their job. Like miners, their position was greatly weakened by changes that they could not prevent or control.

In the car industry, strikes have continued, but at a lower level than in the 1970s. They started declining in the 1980s. Edwards (1995) attributes this to three changes:

1 The contraction of the industry. Many plants were closed, undermining the occupational communities which had served as the basis for strikers' solidarity.

2 Aggressive management imposed new working practices and directly attacked unions, for example by dismissing union officials.

3 The introduction of new technology weakened the bargaining position of some groups of skilled workers such as sheet metal workers and tool makers.

Edwards concludes that 'technical and organizational change' plays a major role in affecting the level of strikes, and that the type of employment in itself is not crucial. He also sees the bargaining position of workers as a crucial factor, with those in weak positions unlikely to risk their jobs by striking.

Strikes and technology

The role of technology has been seen as important in explaining strike rates by writers other than Edwards. This explanation has been used to explain the high frequency of strikes in the car industry. It is based on the type of arguments developed by Robert Blauner (see pp. 694–7): assembly-line technology produces a high level of alienation which leads to hostile relationships between workers and management. Strikes, as an expression of industrial conflict, will therefore be more likely in industries employing this kind of production technology.

This explanation is unable, however, to account for variations in strike activity within the same industries in different countries. As Richard Hyman notes, 'Why does the strike record for the British motor industry contrast so markedly with the comparative harmony in Germany or Japan, when the technology of car assembly is internationally uniform?' (Hyman, 1984). The weakness of the technological argument has already been seen in Duncan Gallie's account of British and French oil refineries (see pp. 698–9). Despite working with similar technologies, the French workers had a far higher strike record than their British counterparts.

Strikes and negotiating procedures

A third explanation for variations in strike activity deals with the effectiveness of the negotiating machinery available for settling disputes. This view suggests that the better-developed the negotiating machinery the lower the strike rate will be. However, in a 1980 study of British workplaces (for details, see below), Daniel and Millward (1983) examined a number of aspects of negotiating procedures. Contrary to the arguments advanced above, they found that establishments with an agreed negotiating procedure were more likely to experience industrial action than those with no agreed procedures.

Factors associated with high strike rates

Neil Millward, Mark Stevens, David Smart and W.R. Hawes (1992) conducted a study of industrial relations in Britain in 1990, based upon structured interviews with management and workers at 2,061 places of employment. Similar studies were carried out earlier in 1980 and 1984 (Stevens and Millward, 1983, and Millward and Stevens, 1986). In the first of these studies, Stevens and Millward (1983) found that strikes were more common in establishments with a large number of manual workers; small establishments had fewer strikes. They also found that the greater the percentage of the workforce who were members of unions, the more likely they were to go on strike. The sex of the workforce made little difference in establishments with few union members, but, in highly unionized places of work, those with a predominantly male workforce were most likely to go on strike. Share ownership schemes for employees appeared to make strikes among manual workers less likely.

In the most recent of the studies, Millward *et al.* (1992) again found that relatively high levels of industrial action were found in larger establishments and in those with a high proportion of the workers in unions. They also found that industrial action was more likely where there were several unions in a particular workplace. In 1990 they found that industrial action was much more common in the public sector than in the private sector. Comparing the 1990 study with the earlier ones, they found a big decline in the incidence of industrial action. They suggested that this was partly due to the decline in the proportion of workplaces that were unionized, and in the proportion of workers who were in unions in those places that were unionized. They also suggested that economic changes and changes in the law might have had an impact.

Although the findings of these surveys are interesting, they were largely based upon quantitative data and provided no direct evidence of the motivation of strikers.

Strikers' definition of the situation

The explanations for variations in strike levels between different industries that we have just outlined have been criticized by Richard Hyman. He argues that they largely ignore the strikers' definition of the situation. For example, workers in one industry may define strikes as a last resort, while those in another may see strikes as a routine and even natural part of industrial life.

Hyman argues that workers do not simply react to production technology or negotiating procedures and predictably strike or not strike as the case might be. They define their work situation and the act of striking in a particular way. Hyman does not deny that factors such as production technology can influence behaviour, but he maintains that they are translated into action via the meanings given to them. Thus an explanation of the strike-prone British car industry and the relatively strike-free situation in the same industry in Japan and Germany requires a knowledge of the meanings and definitions that workers give to industrial life.

Disputes over wages and redundancies

So far, the discussion of strikes has concentrated on the question of why some industries are more strike-prone than others. In the remainder of this section we consider the reasons for strikes in general.

The biggest single cause of strikes has traditionally been disputes over wages. The statistics in Figure 10.5, produced by the National Office for Statistics, show that disputes over pay remain a very important cause of strikes. However, disputes over redundancies have become increasingly important and in 1993 involved many more workers than disputes over pay. Clearly this was related to the recession. Workers may have become more defensive, trying to protect their jobs rather than trying to improve their living standards by increasing their wages. High unemployment may have made workers reluctant to strike over pay. Low inflation may have made industrial action over pay seem less necessary.

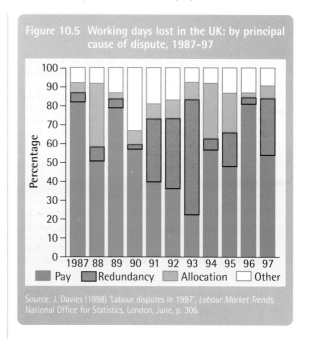

Figure 10.5 Working days lost in the UK: by principal cause of dispute, 1987–97

Source: J. Davies (1998) 'Labour disputes in 1997', *Labour Market Trends*, National Office for Statistics, London, June, p. 306.

Given the importance of pay as a cause of disputes in earlier years, sociologists devoted considerable attention to explaining why pay seemed to have preoccupied workers. From one point of view, the emphasis on pay was not surprising, because of the widespread instrumental orientation of the labour force. From their analysis of a strike at the Pilkington glass factory in St Helens in 1970, Tony Lane and Kenneth Roberts (1971) argued that the promise of a quick financial reward was a major factor accounting for the rapid spread of the strike around the factory.

However, even when a strike is mainly concerned with money, it inevitably involves questions of power. A strike itself is a power struggle and it may well reflect discontent with the nature of authority and control in the day-to-day running of industry. As Lane and Roberts argued, workers sell more than their labour. 'He' also 'undertakes to abide by a set of rules, he submits to a system of authority'. This involves a sacrifice of certain areas of freedom, a sacrifice which will not be lost on the worker even if he or she does define work in primarily instrumental terms. Lane and Roberts state that 'If he treats his *labour* as a commodity it does not follow that he expects himself, as a person, to be treated as a commodity.'

Disputes over authority and control

It can be argued that, to some degree, discontent about the nature of authority and control in industry underlies all strikes. In some disputes, it is clearly a central issue. From his analysis of the Ford strike of 1969, Huw Beynon states 'It was, as the Halewood stewards never tired of saying, not a money strike but a strike of principle' (Beynon, 1973). The principle concerned control.

Ford had offered the workers a package which, in financial terms, was very acceptable. It involved a wage rise, holiday benefits and lay-off payments. In Beynon's words, 'This would have suited the lads. A pay increase, a holiday bonus and a bit of security. That sounded great.'

However, the package also placed important restrictions on the power of the workforce. It included a 'good behaviour clause', which stated that many of the benefits would be cancelled for a six-month period for any 'unconstitutional action' by a group of workers. This covered activities such as unofficial strikes, overtime bans and restriction of output in general. In addition, workers were required to give 21 days' notice of an official strike. As one shop steward told Beynon, 'If they get away with this one it will be all up. We'll be back to Victorian times. The ball and chain won't be in it.' In the case of the Ford strike, economic considerations took second place to the principle of control.

A somewhat different approach to the explanation of strikes involves an analysis of events immediately preceding a strike. This approach was used by Alvin Gouldner in his study entitled *Wildcat Strike* (Gouldner, 1957). The strike he observed was preceded by a growing sense of grievance and by mounting tension which finally exploded into an outright stoppage of work. New machinery and new management had been introduced into the company and this altered the relationship between management and workers. New rules were enforced and supervision was tightened up. What had been seen as an easy-going relationship with management was now seen by the workers as rigid and coercive.

Dissatisfaction with the new regime mounted until it was finally expressed in strike action. Interestingly, the strikers' demands were for higher wages. They did not regard it as legitimate to challenge management's authority to manage. They expressed their discontent in terms of a wage demand, which they felt was legitimate according to the rules of the game. In the end, the workers accepted a wage rise as compensation for the new authority structure.

Strikes as normal

The view that the outbreak of a strike is an emotional outburst in response to accumulated grievances and growing tension in the workplace does not explain the origins of all strikes. Lane and Roberts's analysis of the Pilkington strike indicates that it was not preceded by a build-up of discontent. Morale was not particularly low, labour turnover was not particularly high, there was no change in the number of disputes in the factory, things were 'normal'. Lane and Roberts state:

> This means of course that workers can be drawn into a strike without being conscious of an exceptionally wide range of grievances, and without being subject to unusual stress on the shop floor. A strike, in other words, can gather momentum under 'normal' working conditions.

Lane and Roberts, 1971

This leads Lane and Roberts to regard strikes as a normal feature of industrial life. The Pilkington workers were dissatisfied with wage levels and relationships with management but these were facts of working life. And it is the facts of working life that Lane and Roberts see as the basis for strikes. They conclude that 'The nature of work, the terms of the employer–employee relationship, the integration of the trade unions into the power structure, all make strikes inevitable.' However, this argument cannot explain why strikes became so much less frequent in Britain in the 1990s than they had been in earlier decades. Additional factors are necessary to transform potential conflict into actual conflict.

Industrial sabotage

Laurie Taylor and Paul Walton define industrial sabotage as:

> that rule-breaking which takes the form of conscious action or inaction directed towards the mutilation or destruction of the work environment (this includes the machinery of production and the commodity itself).

Taylor and Walton, 1971

Drawing on a wide range of data from the writings of journalists, historians and sociologists, Taylor and Walton classify acts of industrial sabotage in terms of the meanings and motives that direct them. They identify three main motives: 'attempts to reduce tension and frustration'; 'attempts at easing the work process'; and 'attempts to assert control'.

They argue that each type of sabotage indicates the prevalence of distinctive strains or problems within the workplace.

Attempts to reduce tension and frustration

Taylor and Walton provide the following example to illustrate the first type of sabotage. Two seamen were cleaning out sludge from the tanks of a ship. They had been working for a week and only had two buckets for the purpose. With more buckets the job could have been considerably shortened but the foreman told them he lacked the authority to issue any from the ship's stores. Tired and frustrated, the seamen picked up their buckets and smashed them to smithereens against the bulkhead. This action provided a release for tension and frustration.

Saboteurs in similar situations explain their actions in the following way. They have reached the end of their tether, and often an incident occurs which they feel is the last straw. Sabotage makes them feel better: it gets things off their chest. Such actions are usually spontaneous and unplanned. In the above example, the seamen didn't say a word, they just looked at each other and, with a single thought, smashed their buckets.

Taylor and Walton argue that such forms of sabotage 'are the signs of a powerless individual or group'. They tend to occur in industries where unions are absent or ineffective, and where there is little or no history of collective industrial action. In this situation there are few opportunities to remove the source of grievances. Sabotage provides a means of temporarily releasing frustration when workers lack the power to remove its source.

Attempts at easing the work process

The motive directing the second type of sabotage is simply to make work easier. Taylor and Walton give the example of workers in an aircraft factory whose job was to bolt the wing to the fuselage of the plane. When the bolt did not align with the socket some workers used a 'tap' to recut the thread of the socket. This provided the extra thousandth or so of an inch to enable the bolt to be screwed into the socket. The plane was seriously weakened by this procedure and, with sufficient vibration, the bolt could fall out. Despite the fact that taps were officially banned and regular inspections were held to stamp out their use, workers continued to use them.

Taylor and Walton argue that this type of sabotage is typical of industries in which workers have to 'take on the machine', where they work against the clock, and wages are dependent on output. By cutting corners, workers can increase output and, from their point of view, cut through red tape and get on with the job.

Attempts to assert control

The third type of sabotage directly challenges authority and is used by workers in an attempt to gain greater control. Usually it is planned and coordinated. Taylor and Walton give the example of car workers in Turin. A series of strikes had failed to bring production to a halt, so the strikers turned to vandalism and violence to secure their objectives. They smashed production lines and intimidated strike breakers.

Taylor and Walton suggest that this form of sabotage was most common during the early stages of industrialization before trade unions were fully established. For example, machine smashing by groups such as the Luddites in England during the 1820s and 1830s was used as a strategy for raising wages. Taylor and Walton argue that 'In functional terms we could describe trade-union negotiation as taking over from sabotage and other forms of direct action and institutionalizing conflict through collective bargaining.' However, judging from investigations into a number of industries, sabotage (as an attempt to assert control) still regularly occurs.

In *Working for Ford*, a study of Ford's Halewood plant on Merseyside, Huw Beynon (1973) notes a number of examples of sabotage directed by a desire for greater control. During Beynon's research, management refused to accept joint consultation with the unions about the organization of work on the shop floor. Management decided issues such as the speed of particular jobs and manning levels. In their demand for greater control, workers would sometimes pull out the safety wire to stop the assembly line. Action such as this forced management to allow workers some control over the speed of the line.

A similar strategy was used by workers in the paint shop, who sanded down the cars after an early coat of paint. If they believed that they were having to work too quickly or that there were insufficient people to do the job, they would sand paint off the style lines – the angles on the body that give the car its distinctive shape. Usually they won the point and got what they wanted.

Taylor and Walton (1971) argue that sabotage directed by a desire to assert control tends to occur in the following situations:

1 Where there is a history of militancy.
2 Where there is a general recognition of who is to blame for grievances.
3 Where there are few opportunities for effective protest through official channels.

Motives for sabotage can and often do overlap. The examples from Halewood may be seen as attempts both to reduce frustration and assert control. Taylor and Walton expected sabotage motivated by a desire for control to increase in Britain. Writing in 1971, they stated:

> There appears to be a systematic government and official trade-union campaign not only to reduce strike activity but at the same time to implement productivity agreements which tend to reduce the workers' area of autonomy within the factory.
>
> Taylor and Walton, 1971

If the weapons in the workers' armoury are blunted in this way, the desire for control may be increasingly channelled into industrial sabotage.

P.K. Edwards and Hugh Scullion – the social organization of industrial conflict

Most studies of industrial conflict concentrate on one particular type of conflict – for instance, strikes or industrial sabotage. Edwards and Scullion (1982) argue that each type of industrial conflict cannot be examined in isolation: companies that have low levels of one type of conflict may have high levels of another. They believe that both the level and the type of industrial conflict experienced in different companies are closely related to the strategies used by management to control the labour process.

Edwards and Scullion examined industrial conflict in seven British factories, using unstructured interviews, observation and content analysis of company records. They studied many types of behaviour which could be seen as involving conflict between management and workers: labour turnover, absenteeism, breaches of factory discipline, industrial sabotage, the withdrawal of cooperation and effort by workers, and strikes. All of the factories had some conflict but the type of conflict varied.

Labour turnover and absenteeism

In two clothing factories industrial conflict mainly took the form of labour turnover and absenteeism. Both were small firms and the workforce was strictly controlled. At an underwear factory, workers resented the use of disciplinary measures by management. At a hosiery factory, the tedium of the work caused discontent among workers, yet management was able to control most aspects of workforce behaviour.

There was little collective organization in the workforces. Both factories paid workers according to piecework, so there was little point in industrial sabotage or withdrawing effort. Many of the workers were young women and the easiest way to escape from the frustrations of their work was simply to leave. A high rate of labour turnover was tolerated by the management because it was quite easy to replace workers who left. Absenteeism was not a major problem because workers could easily be moved from one part of the factory to another, and payment by piecework meant that wage costs were not affected.

Control of the shop floor

The situation was very different in a large metals factory. Labour turnover was lower than in the clothing factories and absenteeism was rare. In most other respects, though, there was a good deal of industrial conflict.

The company that owned the factory was doing badly and the wages of the skilled craft workers were declining compared to those paid by other employers. The company, though, relied upon their skilled workers to maintain continuous production. They could not afford a high rate of labour turnover amongst workers who were difficult to replace at the wage levels they were able to pay. The workers on the shop floor were well-organized and, with this combination of circumstances, managers had difficulty in maintaining control over some aspects of the labour process.

Absenteeism in the large metals factory was rare. Work was carried out under a gang system whereby a group of workers agreed to fulfil a quota for production. Shop stewards were responsible for organizing each gang of workers in order to meet this quota; and, with the considerable bargaining power of the workers, they were able to ensure that the quotas were not very demanding. Therefore, it was often possible for a gang to finish work early and leave the factory, or even to organize rotas so that workers took unofficial days off. In these circumstances absenteeism was unnecessary.

Similarly, there was little point in industrial sabotage when workers already enjoyed so much control. Conflict tended to arise when management tried to reassert control over the labour process by, for example, trying to prevent early leaving or trying to reduce manning levels. Workers responded to these measures by withdrawing cooperation or staging short strikes, steps which usually succeeded in getting management to back down.

Sophisticated control

In a factory that Edwards and Scullion refer to as the 'process factory' there was relatively little industrial conflict. Managers operated a system of sophisticated control. Workers had to work shifts and the shift system was potentially a source of conflict. However, employees were selected carefully and the requirements of the shift system were explained to them before they were taken on. Managers regularly consulted workers; they did not require workers to clock in or out and they allowed work groups some independence. Employees also received a guaranteed annual salary. Nevertheless, the behaviour of workers was closely monitored and quiet warnings would be issued if they stepped too far out of line. In general this system of sophisticated control succeeded in producing a loyal workforce who were reluctant to take action against management.

One cause of conflict that did remain was the rigidity of the shift system. Management was unwilling to grant time off for personal reasons and this led to some absenteeism. Even this form of conflict was kept within strict limits since absences were carefully recorded and action was taken if an individual's absence record came to be regarded as unsatisfactory. There were shop stewards in the process factory but they usually worked harmoniously with management. They rarely became a focus for organized resistance to management control.

Management strategies and other influences on conflict

Edwards and Scullion's study shows that the presence or absence of industrial conflict is closely related to the strategies used by management to control the workforce. Particular strategies produce particular types of conflict. For example, strong control tends to produce absenteeism and rapid labour turnover. Where workers enjoy considerable control over the labour process, withdrawal of cooperation and the occasional strike are more likely to result. Sophisticated control techniques, if used carefully, can minimize the amount of conflict.

Edwards and Scullion do not claim, though, that management control strategies are the only factor determining the level and type of industrial conflict. The profitability of a company, the local labour market, the strength of workers' organizations and the characteristics of the workforce all play a part in patterns of industrial conflict. Workers may compromise more if their company faces bankruptcy or if alternative employment is hard to find. They may take action more frequently if they are represented by powerful unions or shop stewards. Young and unskilled workers may be less assertive than older and skilled workers. Thus, to Edwards and Scullion, patterns of industrial conflict cannot be fully understood without reference to the complex set of circumstances at each place of work.

In the first part of this chapter we have looked at the issue of work; in the second part we will consider the issue of 'no work' – that is, unemployment.

Unemployment

Unemployment statistics

Since the 1970s unemployment has become an important political issue. Government statistics show that in the 1980s and 1990s unemployment reached higher levels than at any time since the Second World War. Between 1948 and 1966 the official unemployment rate in the UK averaged less than 2 per cent of the workforce. It increased slightly in the 1960s, and in the 1975–8 period rose to above 6 per cent. After a drop it rose again to 4.8 per cent in 1980, and then nearly doubled in two years to 9.5 per cent in 1982.

Unemployment reached a peak in 1985 and 1986: in both years 11.8 per cent of the workforce were out of work. Unemployment figures then began to fall steadily, reaching 5.8 per cent in 1990. They reached another peak of 10.8 per cent in January 1992 before falling slowly to just 4.5 per cent in April 1999.

In the period 1948–66 the number of people out of work averaged about 350,000. By 1979 the figure was 1,200,000, and it then rose rapidly to reach an average of 3,289,000 in 1986. By March 1989 unemployment figures had fallen below 2 million, but they rose again to exceed 3 million in 1993. There were 1,290,700 unemployed in April 1999 (source: Office for National Statistics enquiry line).

Figure 10.6 shows trends in unemployment between 1979 and 1997. The figures on which it is based are seasonally adjusted, that is they take account of variations in the labour market in particular months to reveal the underlying trend.

Official statistics as an overestimation

Although most commentators would accept that official unemployment figures provide a general indication of trends in unemployment, they need to be treated with great caution. Some critics of the statistics have argued that they exaggerate the amount of unemployment. For example, in October 1985, Sir Michael Edwardes, the former chair of British Leyland, Lord Young, the then Employment Secretary, and Jeffrey Archer, the novelist and former vice-chair of the Conservative Party, all claimed publicly that up to one million people were included in the unemployment statistics who should not be. This was because they were working and claiming benefit illegally or were not genuinely looking for work.

However, such claims might themselves be exaggerated. In a survey of 1,000 unemployed people in 1982, the Economics Intelligence Unit found that only 8 per cent said that they had done any paid work (quoted in Watts, 1983). In a study of the Isle of Sheppey, R.E. Pahl (1984) found that the unemployed were no more likely to engage in officially unrecorded 'informal work' than those with paid employment.

It is difficult to measure the number of people claiming to be unemployed who are not seriously looking for work. However, in a review of the evidence, Kevin Hawkins claims that 'there is no evidence to suggest that any more than a small minority of the unemployed are unconcerned about getting another job' (Hawkins, 1984).

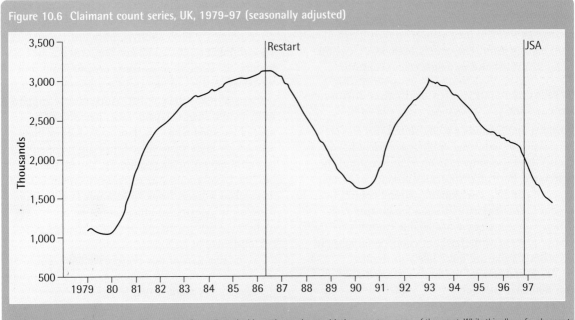

Figure 10.6 Claimant count series, UK, 1979-97 (seasonally adjusted)

Note: The series has been adjusted, taking account of past discontinuities, to be consistent with the current coverage of the count. While this allows for changes to the benefit rules, it has not been adjusted for the impact of changes in the way the rules are applied. It does not yet take account of the direct benefit rule changes arising from JSA which removed an estimated 15–20,000 claimants from the count, cumulatively, over the period October 1996 to March 1997.

Source: K. Sweeney and D. McMahon (1998) 'The effect of Jobseekers' Allowance on the claimant count', *Labour Market Trends*, National Office for Statistics, London, April, p. 202.

Official statistics as an underestimation

Sociologists usually argue that official unemployment statistics underestimate the amount of unemployment rather than exaggerate it. Certainly government figures can be misleading because the basis on which they are calculated has been changed.

Between 1979 and 1987, Margaret Thatcher's Conservative governments changed the method of calculating unemployment statistics 19 times, and nearly all of these changes removed substantial numbers from the unemployment register. For example:

1 After November 1982, those who were not eligible for benefits were excluded from unemployment figures.

2 In March 1983, men over 60 who were claiming long-term supplementary benefit (now called income support) were no longer required to sign on and so were no longer recorded as unemployed.

3 In September 1988, benefit regulations were changed so that most people under 18 became ineligible for income support, resulting in some 90,000 being taken off the unemployment register.

As a consequence of these and other changes, the underestimation of unemployment through the exclusion of those who cannot claim benefits may be considerable.

Another important change took place in October 1996 when unemployment benefit was replaced by the Jobseeker's Allowance. This reduced the entitlement to contributions-based benefits (paid at more than the basic level of benefit) from 12 months to 6 months. It provided extra measures to encourage people to look for work and introduced more stringent checks on eligibility for benefit. Kate Sweeney and Denis McMahon (1998) estimated that these changes removed 15–20,000 claimants from the count for each month between November 1996 and March 1997.

Furthermore, there is strong evidence that many people who are unemployed and would like to obtain a job do not bother to register because they are not entitled to claim any benefits. This applies particularly to many married women.

Unemployment figures have been further reduced by various training schemes which remove young people in particular from the unemployment register. For example, according to the *Employment Gazette* there were 270,000 people on youth training schemes in May 1994 and a further 138,000 receiving Training for Work. There were 137,600 people involved in the New Deal in March 1999.

In view of the changes outlined above, it is clear that officially recorded trends in unemployment cannot be taken at face value. They may have consistently underestimated the extent of unemployment in recent decades. To give one example: while the Department of Employment claimed that 3,276,861 people were unemployed in

October 1985, a TUC estimate put the figure at around 4,500,000.

The Department of Employment's own *Labour Force Survey* uses a social survey to collect information on unemployment, using the International Labour Office's (ILO) definition of unemployment. This defines the unemployed as those who were without work in a particular week, who were available to start work in the next fortnight, and who were waiting to start a job or had looked for work in the previous month. Although this excludes some people without a job who would like one but who have not recently been seeking work (including people on training schemes), it is a broader definition than that based on benefit claimants used for the standard government statistics. The British government has now accepted that this is the best measure of unemployment trends and ILO-based figures are now generally used by the government instead of claimant-based statistics.

According to figures based on the ILO definition, there were 1,822,000 unemployed in the UK in January to March 1999, compared to just 1,290,700 according to the claimant-count statistics. Figure 10.7 shows unemployment, according to ILO-based figures, between 1987 and 1998.

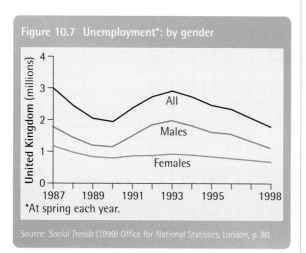

Figure 10.7 Unemployment*: by gender

*At spring each year.

Source: *Social Trends* (1999) Office for National Statistics, London, p. 80.

The social distribution of unemployment

Unemployment is not equally distributed among groups in the population. Despite the limitations of official figures, it is possible to discern overall patterns.

Class

Table 10.6 (based on the *Labour Force Survey* and the ILO definition of unemployment) shows that lower social classes are generally more likely to experience unemployment. For example, in the winter of 1998–9,

non-manual workers had just half the average rate of unemployment (3.1 per cent as opposed to 6.2 per cent). Professionals had the lowest rate at 1.7 per cent, followed by managers and administrators at 2.4 per cent. The highest rates were 9.4 per cent for 'Others' (which included most unskilled manual workers and those who did not state their previous occupation), and 8.2 per cent for plant and machine operatives (which was nearly five times the rate for professionals). In the recession of the early 1990s there was concern that the problem of unemployment was spreading beyond the working class and industry into middle-class and service-sector jobs. However, throughout the period, upper middle-class workers continued to have much lower rates than working-class ones.

Gender

The official figures show higher rates of unemployment for men than for women. In April 1999 there were 986,200 men registered as unemployed (an unemployment rate of 6.2 per cent) compared to 304,000 women (a rate of just 2.3 per cent). According to these figures the unemployment rate for men was more than two and a half times that of women. However, these statistics for women are likely to be an underestimate, given that married women are sometimes ineligible for the benefits that would lead to them being registered.

The ILO statistics give a significantly different picture. In the January–March 1999 period, ILO-based figures put male unemployment at 1,126,000 (6.9 per cent) and female unemployment at 696,000 (5.4 per cent). The female rate by this measure was much closer to the male rate than it was according to the claimant count. Even ILO figures probably underestimate the number of unemployed women, since considerable numbers of married women may wish to work but do not actively seek employment.

Although unemployment may still be higher for men, it should be noted that women are more likely than men to do part-time jobs, and full-time employment may be elusive for women.

Age

Table 10.7 gives unemployment rates as a percentage of the economically active males and females in each age group. It is based on the ILO definition of unemployment. The figures show high rates of unemployment for the young, particularly for men under 25, and low rates for women over 40. Although the rates for men in older age groups were generally lower than the average, men between 55 and 64 have generally experienced fairly high unemployment rates and their rates have sometimes exceeded the male average.

Table 10.6 ILO unemployment rates: by previous occupation

UNITED KINGDOM	All in employment	Manual	Non-manual	Managers and administrators 1	Professional 2	Associate professional and technical 3	Clerical and secretarial 4	Craft and related 5	Personal and protective services 6	Selling 7	Plant and machine operatives 8	Other 9
All												
Spring 1992	9.7	12.6	5.1	4.6	2.6	5.0	6.6	13.1	7.9	7.9	13.2	14.0
Spring 1993	10.3	13.2	5.6	4.9	3.5	5.0	7.3	14.3	8.1	9.1	13.3	14.4
Spring 1994	9.6	12.2	5.1	4.8	2.8	4.5	6.1	12.8	7.9	8.8	12.9	13.3
Spring 1995	8.6	10.5	4.7	3.9	2.7	4.0	5.8	10.2	7.4	8.4	10.7	12.9
Spring 1996	8.2	10.0	4.3	3.8	2.4	4.1	5.4	9.3	6.7	7.3	10.0	12.9
Spring 1997	7.1	8.3	3.6	3.2	1.9	3.0	4.7	7.2	5.9	6.2	8.4	11.0
Winter 1997/8	6.3	7.4	3.0	2.6	1.7	2.3	4.0	5.9	5.8	5.6	7.9	9.9
Spring 1998	6.1	7.2	3.1	2.4	1.6	2.5	4.1	5.9	5.2	6.0	8.4	9.1
Summer 1998	6.6	7.0	3.1	2.4	1.7	2.4	4.5	5.7	5.4	5.6	7.6	9.0
Autumn 1998	6.2	6.9	3.1	2.3	1.9	3.0	4.2	5.4	5.1	5.4	7.6	9.2
Winter 1998/9	6.2	7.1	3.1	2.4	1.7	2.9	3.7	5.7	5.2	6.2	8.2	9.4
Changes Win 97–Win 98	-0.1	-0.2	0.0	-0.2	0.0	0.6	-0.3	-0.2	-0.6	0.6	0.3	-0.5
Male												
Spring 1992	11.5	14.5	5.5	5.1	3.0	6.8	10.1	13.3	10.4	9.1	13.0	20.4
Spring 1993	12.4	15.4	6.2	5.2	4.0	6.4	12.1	14.7	11.4	11.3	13.2	20.5
Spring 1994	11.4	14.1	5.6	5.1	3.2	5.8	9.0	13.2	10.9	10.8	12.6	19.0
Spring 1995	10.1	12.1	5.0	4.1	3.1	5.0	9.2	10.4	10.2	9.9	10.7	18.3
Spring 1996	9.7	11.5	4.8	4.1	2.9	5.3	8.9	9.5	8.7	9.1	10.1	18.6
Spring 1997	8.1	9.3	3.7	3.2	2.1	4.1	7.4	7.3	7.7	6.9	8.6	15.2

Winter 1997/8	13.5	7.4	6.5	7.2	6.0	6.2	2.8	1.6	2.9	3.2	8.0	7.0
Spring 1998	12.6	8.2	6.9	6.3	5.9	6.0	2.8	1.4	2.4	3.0	7.9	6.8
Summer 1998	11.6	7.3	6.5	6.7	5.6	6.8	3.1	1.6	2.4	3.1	7.5	7.2
Autumn 1998	12.1	7.4	6.1	6.9	5.2	6.7	3.7	1.7	2.3	3.1	7.5	6.8
Winter 1998/9	12.7	8.0	6.9	7.3	5.6	6.0	3.7	1.8	2.3	3.2	7.9	7.0
Changes Win 97–Win 98	-0.8	0.6	0.4	0.2	-0.4	-0.2	0.9	0.2	-0.6	0.0	-0.1	0.0
Female												
Spring 1992	7.0	14.0	7.2	6.6	11.0	5.5	3.0	2.1	3.7	4.7	8.5	7.3
Spring 1993	7.8	13.9	7.9	6.2	10.4	5.6	3.5	2.7	4.2	5.0	8.6	7.6
Spring 1994	7.4	13.8	7.6	6.3	9.0	5.1	3.1	2.2	4.3	4.7	8.2	7.3
Spring 1995	7.0	10.8	7.5	5.9	8.2	4.6	2.9	1.9	3.4	4.3	7.2	6.8
Spring 1996	6.7	9.6	6.3	5.6	8.3	4.2	2.9	1.6	3.2	3.8	6.9	6.3
Spring1997	6.2	7.9	5.8	5.0	6.6	3.8	2.0	1.6	3.0	3.4	6.0	5.8
Winter 1997/8	5.7	9.9	5.2	5.1	4.6	3.2	1.8	1.7	2.0	2.9	6.0	5.4
Spring 1998	5.1	9.2	5.6	4.7	5.9	3.4	2.1	1.8	2.2	3.1	5.7	5.3
Summer 1998	5.8	8.7	5.1	4.7	6.6	3.6	1.8	1.9	2.4	3.1	5.9	5.8
Autumn 1998	5.6	8.7	4.9	4.2	7.9	3.3	2.2	2.2	2.2	3.1	5.6	5.4
Winter 1998/9	5.3	9.1	5.8	4.1	6.4	2.9	2.1	1.5	2.4	3.0	5.4	5.2
Changes Win 97–Win 98	-0.4	-0.8	0.6	-0.9	1.8	-0.3	0.3	-0.1	0.5	0.0	-0.6	-0.2

Denominators are all persons in employment in relevant occupation plus ILO unemployed who last worked in relevant occupation. Includes those who did not state their current or previous occupation.

Source: *Labour Market Trends* (1999) Office for National Statistics, London, May, p. s45.

Table 10.7   ILO unemployment rates*: by gender and age, 1991–8

United Kingdom	Percentages							
	1991	1992	1993	1994	1995	1996	1997	1998
Males								
16–17	15.4	17.7	18.5	18.8	18.9	21.2	19.3	18.0
18–24	15.7	19.0	21.1	19.2	17.7	17.1	14.8	13.0
25–44	8.0	10.5	10.9	10.2	9.0	8.7	7.0	5.8
45–54	6.3	8.4	9.4	8.6	7.4	6.4	6.1	4.8
55–59	8.4	11.2	12.3	11.6	10.2	9.9	8.0	6.7
60–64	9.9	10.2	14.2	11.6	9.9	8.9	7.6	7.0
65 and over	5.9	4.9	4.6	3.7	–	4.1	4.0	–
All aged 16 and over	9.2	11.5	12.4	11.4	10.1	9.7	8.1	6.8
Females								
16–17	14.3	14.0	15.1	17.1	15.6	15.1	16.0	15.2
18–24	10.5	11.0	12.9	11.8	11.5	10.2	9.7	9.3
25–44	7.1	7.3	7.3	7.0	6.7	6.3	5.4	5.2
45–54	4.6	5.0	5.0	5.0	4.5	4.1	3.8	3.1
55–59	5.5	4.5	6.0	6.5	4.7	4.2	4.8	3.5
60 and over	4.4	3.1	3.9	2.9	–	–	2.0	2.0
All aged 16 and over	7.2	7.3	7.6	7.3	6.8	6.3	5.8	5.3

* At spring each year.

Source: *Social Trends* (1999) Office for National Statistics, London, p. 81.

Unemployment should not, therefore, just be seen as a problem for the young.

It has been generally accepted that youth unemployment was one of the most serious unemployment problems of the 1980s and 1990s. However, there is evidence to suggest that unemployment is more likely to be a long-term problem for older members of the workforce.

Ethnicity

The evidence concerning ethnicity and unemployment is more straightforward. Table 10.8 is based on data from the Labour Force Survey for spring 1997 to winter 1997–8. It shows that ethnic minorities suffer from higher rates of unemployment. The survey found that just 6 per cent of whites were unemployed, compared to over 21 per cent of Pakistanis/Bangladeshis and 19 per cent of blacks. The unemployment rate for Indians and other ethnic minorities also exceeds the national average, although the rate for Indians was the closest to the white rate. Unemployment is particularly common among younger members of ethnic minorities, with

Table 10.8   ILO unemployment rates[1]: by ethnic group and age, 1997–8[2]

Great Britain	Percentages				All aged
	16–24	25–34	35–44	45–59/64[3]	16–59/64[3]
White	13	6	5	5	6
Black	39	18	12	16	19
Indian	18	7	6	7	8
Pakistani/ Bangladeshi	29	16	13	26	21
Other groups[4]	22	13	10	8	13
All ethnic groups[5]	14	7	5	5	7

1 Unemployment based on the ILO definition as a percentage of all economically active.
2 Combined quarters: spring 1997 to winter 1997–98
3 Men up to the age of 64, women up to the age of 59.
4 Includes those of mixed origin.
5 Includes those who did not state their ethnic group.

Source: *Social Trends* (1999) Office for National Statistics, London, p. 82.

no less than 39 per cent of black people aged 16–24 unemployed at that time.

Region

There are considerable variations in the regional distribution of unemployment. Unemployment tends to be highest in regions that have traditionally relied upon the heavy industries; these were badly hit in the recessions of the late 1970s and early 1980s.

The recession at the start of the 1990s hit the usually more prosperous areas in the south of England and service-sector jobs harder, but it was still the north of England, Northern Ireland and Wales which bore the brunt of unemployment. This is reflected in the official figures for March 1999, which showed that Merseyside had the highest rate of unemployment at 8.8 per cent, followed by Northern Ireland at 7.3 per cent, Scotland, and Yorkshire and Humberside (at 5.6 per cent) and Wales at 5.5 per cent. The lowest rates were the south-east of England at 2.6 per cent, the east of England at 3.2 per cent, and the south-west of England at 3.3 per cent. Nevertheless, the gap between unemployment rates in different regions of the UK narrowed in the 1990s, and there were some pockets of relatively high unemployment in the south of England. London had a rate of 5.2 per cent, exceeding the UK average of 4.6 per cent.

Disability and unemployment

The *Labour Force Survey* defines a work-limiting disabled person as somebody who has 'a health problem which they expect to last for more than a year and which limits the kind or amount of work they might do' (*Social Trends*, 1999). Table 10.9 shows the economic activity status of those fitting

Table 10.9	Economic activity status of disabled[1] people: by gender, spring 1998		
United Kingdom		**Percentages**	
	Males	**Females**	**All**
In employment			
Working full-time	33	16	25
Working part-time	5	18	11
All in employment	38	34	37
Unemployed[2]	7	4	6
Economically inactive	54	61	58
All disabled (=100%) (millions)	2.8	2.4	5.3

1 Work-limiting disabled. Males aged 16 to 64, females aged 16 to 59.
2 Based on the ILO definition.

Source: *Labour Force Survey*, Office for National Statistics, London.

this definition in spring 1998. It shows that nearly 60 per cent of this group were economically inactive and a further 6 per cent were unemployed.

Statistically, then, you are most likely to suffer from unemployment if you are a young, unskilled male worker living in Northern Ireland, Wales or northern England, particularly if you are disabled. White, middle-aged, professional workers living in the south-east of England are much less likely to be unemployed.

The causes of unemployment, and government policy

Economists distinguish between a number of types of unemployment.

Frictional unemployment

Frictional unemployment occurs when workers change jobs but do not move immediately to their new job. They are unemployed for a short time as they search for work or wait to take up a new position. Economists regard frictional unemployment as inevitable in a changing economy and it is not usually seen as a serious problem.

Structural unemployment

Structural unemployment occurs when jobs are available and there are workers seeking employment, but the workers do not match the jobs. There are two main types of structural unemployment: regional and sectoral.

1 Regional unemployment exists where unemployed workers do not live in the areas where suitable vacancies are available. In the second half of the 1980s, as unemployment fell, it became difficult to fill some vacancies in south-east England because of labour shortages in that region, despite high unemployment in other parts of Britain.

2 Sectoral unemployment exists when the unemployed lack the appropriate skills or qualifications to fill vacancies. As old industries decline and new ones develop, some workers are left with obsolete skills. In Britain, workers in such industries as textiles, coalmining, shipbuilding and iron and steel, who have been made redundant, have found it difficult to find work which matches their skills.

Cyclical unemployment

Both frictional and structural unemployment occur when vacancies are available for the unemployed. Although these types of unemployment accounted for some of the unemployment during recent decades in Britain, clearly they could not account for it all. The number of unemployed far exceeded the number of vacancies: the supply of labour exceeded the demand for workers by employers. Such a situation is sometimes called cyclical unemployment.

All Western economies experience fluctuations, with periods of depression and boom following one another. These economic cycles may be short-term, with minor fluctuations over four- to six-year periods, or they may be long-term. For example, the British economy experienced a major depression in the 1930s, which was followed by a post-war economic boom in the 1950s and 1960s, which in turn was followed by recession in the 1970s and 1980s. The early 1990s saw a recession, while economic growth returned in the late 1990s.

This raises the question of why Britain experienced such severe depressions in the 1970s and 1980s, which led to such rapid rises in unemployment in those decades. We will consider different explanations for these depressions later in this section. We will also examine why unemployment fell in the mid- to late 1990s.

Although unemployment had fallen by the late 1990s, it had not reached the very low levels of the 1950s and 1960s. Some writers claim that capitalist, industrial economies have changed in such a way that full employment will never occur again. In particular, it has been suggested that new technology has permanently reduced the demand for labour.

Technological change and deindustrialization

Recent decades have seen a continuing decline in the importance of manufacturing industry. In June 1975 there were 7.35 million workers in manufacturing industry; by December 1998 there were just over 4 million. In December 1998 there were just 4.3 million employed in all production industries (which include mining, quarrying, electricity, water and gas supply) – less than a quarter of the total workforce which numbered over 18 million. Employment in services has increased greatly. For example, in December 1998, over 2.5 million people were employed in health and social work services alone. Some have seen these changes as representing a deindustrialization of Britain, with serious implications for future levels of unemployment.

In 1979, Clive Jenkins and Barrie Sherman predicted the collapse of work. They estimated that over 25 years there would be a job reduction of 5 million, or some 23 per cent of the labour force. They acknowledged that service-sector jobs would increase, but predicted that new technology would lead to a large reduction in manufacturing employment.

Jenkins and Sherman attached particular importance to microprocessors. Products incorporating microchips would require fewer parts. Machines using the new technology would be easier

to maintain and test. Computers would result in more efficient stock control, thereby decreasing the amount of stock held in warehouses. Fewer clerical staff would be required because microcomputers and computer-controlled machines would drastically reduce the numbers involved in the direct production of goods. As a result of such changes, a typical company could cut its workforce by 50 per cent.

Jenkins and Sherman give the example of television production. When Thorn Electrical Industries decided to copy Japanese television manufacturers by changing to new technology, this resulted in the workforce at assembly plants being cut by half, while maintaining the same level of output.

Colin Gill (1985) has suggested that new technology threatens to reduce the workforce in numerous occupations. Amongst the groups threatened are printers, welders, draughtspeople, laboratory technicians, engineers, sales staff, warehouse workers, postal staff, supervisors and mineworkers.

Not only did Gill anticipate a decline in manufacturing industry, but he also said that 'the prospects for continued employment growth in the existing service industries look bleak'. He suggested that the concentration of retailing in large supermarkets and other shops would tend to reduce employment. He believed that employment in banking, insurance and professional services would be hit by new information technology, which would allow routine aspects of these jobs to be automated. In other areas there was no guarantee of increased employment. The level of government employment largely depends upon government policies, and in the 1980s the British government was reluctant to expand the workforce in areas such as education and health.

The recession of the early 1990s seemed in line with some of Gill's pessimism. Redundancies in areas such as financial services, hotels and distribution increased considerably, and white-collar workers added significantly to the ranks of the unemployed. However, economic revival in the later 1990s seemed to suggest that a move towards a more service-based economy did not inevitably mean high levels of unemployment, although it may be that the reduction in unemployment will not last.

Despite the strong arguments advanced to support the view that technological change has led to rising unemployment, other commentators attach more importance to weaknesses in the British economy. For example, Kevin Hawkins (1984) points out that many industrial jobs have moved to other countries rather than disappearing altogether. Britain has lost manufacturing jobs at the same time as consumers have bought increasing amounts of imported goods. British industry has found it difficult to compete successfully with overseas competition. Jobs have been created in Japan, other European Community countries, and newly industrialized countries of the Third World, such as Taiwan and Hong Kong, but not in Britain.

From this point of view, high unemployment levels are not inevitable. They could be reduced if Britain's economy and industry could become more efficient and competitive.

Theories of unemployment – market liberal theory

During much of the period since 1945 it was accepted by Labour and Conservative governments alike that the government could and should maintain low levels of unemployment. Much of this thinking stemmed from the work of the British economist J.M. Keynes (1936).

Keynes argued that unemployment in the 1930s was caused by a lack of demand in the economy. If too few goods were purchased, then production would be cut back and jobs would be lost. If the demand for goods were increased, then the process would be reversed and unemployment would fall. It was therefore the duty of the government to manage demand in the economy; an increase in government spending could cut unemployment.

Successive governments were committed to a mixed economy. Government control over key industries would allow the government to manipulate the economy so that mass unemployment could be avoided.

In the 1970s the consensus about broad economic policy was eroded. Governments faced the problem of rising inflation as well as rising unemployment. Measures designed to reduce unemployment could lead to increased inflation. The Conservative Party under Margaret Thatcher turned to market liberal economic theories, which challenged Keynes's view that the government could solve economic problems by increasing demand in the economy.

Monetarism

The most influential economist advocating market liberal policies was the American Milton Friedman. He advocated monetarist policies to control inflation. He believed that inflation was caused by too much money chasing too few goods. The government could reduce or even eliminate the problem by reducing the money supply, that is, allowing less money to circulate in the economy. This necessitated cutting back on government spending and not expanding it, as Keynes advocated.

To Friedman, there was a natural rate of unemployment in any economy. The government could not reduce unemployment below the natural rate without causing excessive inflation unless there were other fundamental economic changes. The natural rate of unemployment was affected by such factors as the level of unemployment benefit and the flexibility of wage rates.

Classical free market economists such as Adam Smith had argued that unemployment could not exist in the long term. The unemployed would be prepared to work for lower wages in order to get a job, and at lower wage rates it would be profitable for employers to take workers on. The demand for and supply of labour would come into balance and unemployment would disappear.

Friedman pointed out that there was not, in reality, a totally free market in labour. Unions could use their power to drive up wages so that they were artificially high, and unemployment benefits would discourage people from working for low wages. Other important factors would be the mobility of the labour force, and the availability and cost of information about job vacancies.

Government economic policy

These views were reflected in the policies of the Conservative governments of Margaret Thatcher and John Major from 1979. They tried to cut public expenditure, reduce the power of unions by changes in the law, and make benefits for the unemployed less generous. The overall policy was intended to reduce the role of the state in economic affairs and leave market forces to determine the way the economy developed.

It was hoped that these policies would make British industry more competitive, allowing efficient industry to prosper. The burden of taxation on successful industries would be reduced if the government ceased to subsidize inefficient industries. Nationalized industries were to be privatized and public subsidies to inefficient 'lame duck' industries would be withdrawn. The costs of employing people would fall as unions lost power and the bargaining position of workers became weaker. Employers would therefore employ more people. As benefits were cut, the incentives to take low-paid work would increase.

Criticisms of Conservative policies

Critics of these policies have argued that, far from reducing unemployment, they actually caused it to increase. John MacInnes (1987) points out that the short-term effects hardly supported the claim that the measures would produce lower unemployment levels: 'employment in manufacturing fell by 21 per cent shedding 1.5 million jobs between December 1979 and December 1982. Total employment fell by 2 million (9 per cent) in the same period.'

MacInnes accepts that a world recession would have led to rising unemployment whatever policies the government followed, but he claims that the slump in Britain was deeper than in other advanced industrial countries, and he attributes this to government policies. He argues that the government simply lowered demand in the economy, and this 'dampened economic activity sufficiently to reduce inflationary pressures, but at the cost of a large drop in output, slower growth and much higher unemployment'.

MacInnes acknowledges that after 1983 unemployment figures fell, but he questions the claim that this demonstrates the long-term success of Margaret Thatcher's free-market policies. He puts forward the following arguments:

1 Compared to other countries, Britain's employment record was poor. Between 1980 and 1986 total UK employment fell by 3 per cent, but by rather less (2 per cent) in the European Community as a whole. In the USA employment rose by 10 per cent over the same period.

2 Some of the decline in unemployment was due to changes in the definition of unemployment, and increased numbers on government programmes such as the Youth Training Scheme.

3 All of the increased employment between March 1983 and September 1986 was due to a rise of some 388,000 in the number of part-time jobs. MacInnes calculates that over this period the number of full-time jobs actually fell by over 50,000.

He therefore concludes that the recovery after 1983 'did little to reverse the rise in unemployment', which he believes the government's policies had encouraged.

After MacInnes made the above comments, unemployment rose again, suggesting that he was right to question the claim that free-market policies would solve the problem. The number of full-time employees fell by more than a million between March 1991 and March 1993, during the recession of the early 1990s. Furthermore, a number of commentators, such as Frank Field, have argued that the government had abandoned any attempt at pursuing full employment. Indeed, Norman Lamont, the first chancellor in John Major's government, described unemployment as 'a price well worth paying' to achieve other economic goals such as reducing inflation. However, it is possible that some Conservative policies contributed to the fall in unemployment in the late 1990s (see below).

Marxist theories of unemployment

Unlike Keynes and supporters of market liberal theories, Marx saw unemployment as resulting from the capitalist system itself. He did not believe that, in the long term, capitalist economies could be managed to eliminate unemployment, nor did he think that market forces would reduce unemployment of their own accord (Marx, 1950a, 1950b, 1974, 1978). Marx saw unemployment as an endemic problem of capitalism, and one which would get progressively worse.

However, he did not believe that capitalist economies always had and would have high levels of unemployment. He believed that such economies went through cycles. Periods of expansion in which there was full employment were followed by periods of crisis during which unemployment rose. Recoveries from crises were only temporary. Each successive crisis would be worse than the previous one until eventually the capitalist system was destroyed.

Marx believed that capitalist economies worked in the following way. The bourgeoisie are primarily interested in maximizing the amount of surplus value produced. (Surplus value is the difference between the costs of producing commodities and the price the bourgeoisie are able to sell them for.) In order to be successful, members of the bourgeoisie must compete with each other. To succeed they must invest some of their profits in new machinery which can produce goods more efficiently. In this process they accumulate capital in the form of the machinery used in production.

During booms, the over-accumulation of capital takes place. The bourgeoisie install new machinery, but as their businesses expand they find that there are not enough workers to operate it. Because workers are scarce, competition between firms for workers forces them to raise wages. Increased wage levels inevitably mean that the rate of profit falls, since the higher the wages the smaller the proportion of the total costs of production that becomes surplus value. As the rate of profit falls, the confidence of the bourgeoisie is reduced, and they are less willing to invest in new technology. Furthermore, at the new and higher rates of pay, much of the old machinery that is being used is no longer profitable and has to be scrapped.

The boom is followed by a slump. With the lack of new investment, and old machinery being taken out of production, unemployment inevitably rises. Eventually unemployment forces down wage rates, which means that profitability, business confidence and investment increase, and the economy starts to expand again.

Capitalists require workers who can be hired during booms, and fired during slumps. Marx refers to the part of the workforce who are used in this way as the reserve army of labour. The unemployed are the victims of the cyclical way in which the capitalist economy works.

The processes described above explain why Marx thought that capitalism went through periods of crisis in which unemployment rose. However, they do not explain why he thought that these crises would get progressively worse.

According to Marx's labour theory of value, it is only labour power, or work, which actually creates wealth or surplus value. As production becomes increasingly mechanized, the bourgeoisie invest a greater proportion of their capital in machinery. Labour costs decline as a proportion of the bourgeoisie's expenditure on production. Rises in productivity can increase the surplus value produced by each worker, but, as the price of investment in new machinery rises, it becomes increasingly difficult for profits to remain high. To maintain profits each worker has to be exploited at a higher rate.

To Marx, this situation cannot continue indefinitely. Workers will eventually realize they are being exploited, develop class consciousness, and overthrow the capitalist system.

Clearly, Marx's predictions that capitalism would collapse have not come true. Indeed, the economic systems of some former communist countries, such as the Soviet Union, came closer to collapse under communism than have the economies of most advanced capitalist countries. Nevertheless, capitalist economies have not proved as manageable as economists like Keynes believed.

Governments have not been able to manipulate economies in such a way that mass unemployment has become a thing of the past. Furthermore, economic crises continue to hit the capitalist system periodically. For example, in the late 1990s, Japan and the economies of south-east Asia experienced major problems.

Britain's economic decline

Marx's general theory of capitalism claims to explain why mass unemployment occurs periodically in capitalist economies, but it does not explain why Britain should have suffered particularly severe economic problems.

The British Marxist historian E.J. Hobsbawm (1970) argues that Britain's economic decline can be traced back to the nineteenth century. He claims that Britain suffered from being the first country to industrialize. British industry invested heavily in machinery in the earliest stages of industrialization and failed to modernize in response to competition. The costs of scrapping obsolete equipment discouraged new investment. This lack of investment prevented Britain from competing effectively with developing competitors such as West Germany and the USA.

The British bourgeoisie were able to prevent the rate of profit falling too low in the nineteenth and early twentieth centuries because the British Empire provided a market for British goods, even if they were not produced competitively. Furthermore, the British economy tended to move increasingly into trade and finance where profits were more predictable than in manufacturing. Much British capital went abroad and was used to improve the efficiency of overseas competitors. Hobsbawm concludes, 'Britain, we may say, was becoming a parasitic rather than a competitive economy, living off the remains of world monopoly, the underdeveloped world, and her past accumulations of wealth.'

In *The British Economic Disaster*, Andrew Glyn and John Harrison (1980) note that some of the economic trends noted by Hobsbawm continued in Britain after 1945. Investment in new machinery was low, investment abroad was high. Although the sun set on the British Empire after the war, Britain continued to trade with ex-colonies with whom it had preferential tariffs. This continued to protect British industry from overseas competition, but discouraged capitalists from investing in Britain. Adequate profits could be made without taking too many risks.

Glyn and Harrison, though, attach more importance to the labour market and trade unions than Hobsbawm. They argue that Britain suffered from greater labour shortages than competitors. Japan and the rest of Europe had reserves of underemployed agricultural labour on which it could draw, whereas Britain did not. When combined with strong union organization, this led to real wages rising faster than in competitor countries. Wages rose faster than productivity, which squeezed profits, discouraged investment in Britain, encouraged investment abroad and ultimately led to 'Britain's economic disaster' and mass unemployment in the 1970s and 1980s.

The decline of unemployment in the late 1990s

As detailed above (see pp. 737–9), unemployment in Britain fell in the late 1990s. Robin Marris (1999) noted that in March 1999 claimant unemployment was at its lowest for 19 years. Unlike for much of the previous two decades, Britain's unemployment rate was lower than that of most other European Union countries. Britain's rate was 5.4 per cent, above that for the USA (which was about 3 per cent), but considerably below the rates for countries such as France, Germany and Italy. Richard Jackman (1998) noted that, between 1988 and 1998, unemployment in Britain fell by about 3 per cent, whereas it rose by about 2 per cent in Italy, France and Germany.

Jackman examines a number of possible explanations for this change:

1 It could be due to the way the figures are calculated. The change could be an artefact of changing definitions of unemployment. However, Jackman rejects this view. Britain's unemployment has also fallen relative to other countries when the ILO definition is used rather than the claimant count. The ILO definition provides a standardized measure which allows different countries to be compared.

2 The improvement could simply be the result of economic cycles. Britain might be experiencing an upturn in its economy at a slightly different time from other countries, with the likelihood that unemployment would start rising again before too long. Jackman argued that there was 'no way of telling whether the present reduction of unemployment is a consequence of a structural improvement in the labour market or whether it is simply the result of a cyclical upturn in the economy'. However, he did detect some indication that changes in the labour market might partly explain the reduction in unemployment. In the late 1990s inflation remained relatively low, suggesting that falling unemployment was not the result of a short-term boom.

3 The third possibility is that the change could be the result of a genuine improvement in the supply side of the economy, that is the supply of labour. The reduction in trade union power and the removal of some protections for workers (such as Wages Councils which set minimum wages for some industries) could have made labour cheaper and more flexible.

Reductions in benefits may also have had an effect. By 1998, UK unemployment benefit levels were just 30 per cent of the wages of the average unskilled manual worker, and about half the average level in the European Union. These factors could have increased both the demand from employers and the willingness of claimants to take up paid employment. The latter trend could have been further promoted by changes in benefits rules as well as levels. In particular, the introduction of the Jobseeker's Allowance in 1996 obliged claimants to attend interviews every two weeks, at which they had to provide evidence that they had been looking for work.

Although Jackman suggests that such policies may have helped to reduce unemployment, he is still critical of the policies. He argued that, by 1998, there was little scope for cutting unemployment further by making labour markets more flexible or by making it more difficult to claim benefits. Furthermore, he claimed that the reduction of unemployment had been bought at considerable cost. He says, 'These achievements have been bought at the cost of greatly increased income inequality (resulting largely from increased wage inequality) and a greater incidence of poverty (due in part to reduced unemployment benefits).' Thus the greater availability of work had not solved the problems of the poorest in society.

Furthermore, research by Duncan Gallie and Caroline Vogler (1994) found little evidence that unemployment could be explained in terms of supply-side problems. In general, they did not find that the unemployed were reluctant to take work or were fussy about the sort of work they took. They used data from 1986 and 1987 surveys which were part of the Social Change and Economic Life Initiative (see p. 710 for details of this study).

They found that the unemployed were more likely than the employed to say they would want to work even if they had no financial need to do so. The unemployed were also found to be flexible about the sort of work they would accept. Only 12 per cent of the unemployed wanted a higher-than-average wage for their type of work before they would accept a job. Substantial minorities were willing to be flexible about where they lived or about retraining: 40 per cent said they would be willing to move outside the area to find work; and 45 per cent had seriously considered retraining.

Thus, according to this research, a high proportion of the unemployed provided a relatively cheap and flexible pool of labour available to employers when demand for employment picked up. This raises questions about how far policy changes affecting the supply side of the economy could explain the reduction in unemployment in the late 1990s, a decade or so later.

A 1997 report by the Council of Churches for Britain and Ireland (CCBI) expressed scepticism that the fall in unemployment would be permanent. The report argues that falling unemployment without high inflation has been experienced during previous economic cycles and has not led to permanently low unemployment. Furthermore, if the fall is due to more flexible labour markets in which it is easier to hire people, the corollary is that it is also becoming easier to fire people. If this is the case, then any future economic downturn could see a rapid increase in the number of unemployed.

The Labour government and unemployment policies

Whatever the merits or otherwise of Conservative policies relating to unemployment, the election of a Labour government in 1997 represented a development of those policies rather than a radical break with them. Despite the Labour Party's traditional commitment to full employment, Tony Blair's Labour government committed themselves to reducing unemployment rather than eradicating it. For example, in January 1999, the education secretary David Blunkett made a speech arguing that it was unrealistic for governments to aim for full employment any more (reported in *The Times*, 1 February 1999).

The Labour government introduced a number of new policies designed to help or encourage the unemployed back into work and to encourage employers to take them on:

1 The main plank of Labour's policy was the New Deal. This scheme, which cost some £3.5 billion, was funded by a windfall tax – a one-off tax on the profits of privatized utilities such as gas and electricity companies. The programme started in 12 pilot areas in January 1998 and was later extended nationally.

   This scheme initially required unemployed young people to receive a four-month 'Gateway' of specialist advice. After that they were offered four options: a subsidized job in the private sector, full-time education, employment in the voluntary sector (for example, with a charity), or work with an environmental task force. If somebody refused all these options, then they would lose the right to benefit.

   Employers were given a subsidy by the government to take on people under 25 who had been unemployed for six months or more. In 1998 the New Deal was extended to people over 25 who had been out of work for more than two years, to single parents and to people with disabilities. According to government figures (Employment Service, *New Deal Statistics First Release*, May 1999), by March 1999, 266,300 people had started the New Deal, and 128,700 had left or finished the scheme, of whom 44 per cent had entered unsubsidized employment.

2 In February 1999 the government announced the creation of 12 employment zones in high unemployment areas (Birmingham, Brent, Brighton and Hove, Doncaster, Haringey, Liverpool and Sefton, Middlesborough, Newham, Nottingham, Plymouth, Southwark and Tower Hamlets). In these zones each person who had been long-term unemployed (at least a year) was to be given a personal adviser who was able to provide money to help individuals seek work

3 In January 1999 the government announced that it planned to withdraw benefits from any claimant who refused to attend interviews. The scheme was to be initially introduced in 12 pilot areas and would apply to all claimants there, including the disabled and lone parents. Each claimant would have their own personal adviser who would help them determine what benefits they were entitled to. The scheme was intended both to reduce fraud and to help claimants back to work.

4 Some steps were taken to make employment more attractive to the low-paid. A minimum wage was introduced in 1999, guaranteeing £3.60 an hour to employees over the age of 21 and £3.00 pounds an hour to those aged 18–21. Furthermore, in the budget of 1999, the threshold at which you started paying tax was raised and a new starting rate of tax of 10 per cent was announced. These measures were intended to make it more worthwhile to take low-paid work – by reducing the number of low-paid workers who had to pay tax at all, and reducing the tax bill for the rest.

Labour policies were designed to provide carrots and sticks for the unemployed. The carrot was the promise of guaranteed work (voluntary, private-sector or with the environmental task force) or full-time education, along with the promise of more take-home pay from low-paid work. The stick was the possible withdrawal of benefits. In addition, employers were offered financial incentives to take on workers.

On the surface, by 1999 these measures were enjoying some degree of success. By the start of 1999, more than 35,000 employers had signed up for the New Deal (quoted in *The Times*, 1 February 1999), and there was some fall in ILO unemployment among 18–24-year-olds, from an average of 13.1 per cent in 1997 to 12.2 per cent in the winter of 1998–9 (*Employment Gazette*, May 1999). Nevertheless, youth unemployment remained much higher than unemployment in older age groups.

Whether Labour policies will succeed in creating long-term jobs and a sustained drop in unemployment remains to be seen. Certainly in the early years of the administration they were helped by a buoyant economy. A truer test of the policies will occur if and when the overall economic picture becomes less rosy.

The effects of unemployment

The effects on society

Numerous claims have been made about the effects of mass unemployment on society. Usually the effects have been seen as detrimental to society. Adrian Sinfield (1981) argues that unemployment 'devalues or debases the standard or quality of life in society'.

He believes it does so in the following ways:

1 Those remaining in work feel less secure and may have their standard of living threatened. This is partly because of short-time working and reductions in the amount of overtime, and partly due to the reduced bargaining power of workers which leads to downward pressure on wages.

2 The workforce becomes less willing to leave an unsatisfactory or unsatisfying job because of the fear that they will be unable to find new employment. It becomes less mobile and the number of frustrated and alienated workers increases.

3 Divisions within society are likely to grow. The unemployed and those in unsatisfying work may blame weak groups in society for their problems. Male workers accustomed to full-time work, for example, may attribute their unemployment to married women entering the labour market. Immigrants and ethnic minorities may be used as scapegoats, with the result that racial tensions increase.

4 Sinfield believes that high unemployment reduces the chance of equality of opportunity being achieved. With a surplus of labour, employers need no longer make an effort to recruit women, ethnic minorities, the young, the old, the disabled and handicapped, or former inmates of prisons or mental hospitals. For example, writing in 1981, Sinfield claimed that the proportion of firms which had more than 3 per cent registered disabled in their workforce had fallen from two-thirds to one-third with the rise of mass unemployment.

John Lea and Jock Young (1984) argue that unemployment among the young leads to the marginalization of some members of society. Those who have never worked feel that they have no stake in society. Since they are not members of unions they lack the institutional means to express their discontent. According to Lea and Young, this helped to create a subculture of despair in some inner-city areas of Britain and contributed to the urban riots of the 1980s. (See pp. 393–4 for further details of Lea and Young's views.)

Many social problems have been linked to unemployment. Sheila Allen and Alan Watson say:

> Links between unemployment and a wide range of social problems have been made by academics, politicians and journalists. Ill-health, premature death, attempted and actual suicide, marriage breakdown, child battering, racial conflicts and football hooliganism are a few of the examples that have been cited.
>
> Allen and Watson, 1986

Many of these can be seen as the effects of unemployment on the individual rather than on society, and some of these will be examined in the next section. However, clearly they also have implications for society. If unemployment does cause or contribute to these problems, then it may threaten the stability of society by undermining the family, and causing racial tension and crime.

Solving these problems also has economic costs. For instance, greater expenditure may be required on the NHS to finance the treatment of those who become ill due to unemployment. Unemployment has direct economic costs as well. John MacInnes (1987) points out that government expenditure on benefits rises with increased unemployment. The government also loses the taxation revenue it would have received if the unemployed had been in work.

Despite the strength of many of these claims about the negative effects of unemployment, they should be treated with some caution. Allen and Watson suggest that each problem linked with unemployment may be caused by 'a complex of interacting factors which belie any simple cause effect relationship promulgated in popular debate' (Allen and Watson, 1986). As we will see in the next section, it can be difficult to isolate the effects of unemployment from other variables.

The personal effects of unemployment

Financial effects

Perhaps the most obvious effects of unemployment are financial. Melanie White (1990) quotes a study by the Office of Population, Censuses and Surveys which found that over two-thirds of families with parents under 35 were in debt after three months' unemployment.

The severity of the financial impact of unemployment has been due to two main factors:

1 There has been an increase in the number of long-term unemployed – those who have been out of work for a year or more. At the start of the 1990s, claimants lost their right to claim unemployment benefit after 12 months. They then had to rely upon means-tested income support, which is paid at a lower rate. Then in 1996 unemployment benefit was changed to a 'Jobseeker's Allowance'. This allowance ceased after just six months, after which time the unemployed became reliant upon other benefits if they were eligible for them. The longer a person is out of work, the greater their financial hardship is likely to be, as savings are eaten up and financial problems mount.

2 Relative to wages, unemployment benefits have been declining. Even if the actual living standards of the unemployed are higher than they were in the 1930s, the amount of relative poverty caused by unemployment in the 1980s has been considerable. (See pp. 296–303 for a discussion of relative poverty.)

Duncan Gallie and Caroline Vogler's research (1994) for the Social Change and Economic Life Initiative found that many of the unemployed experienced considerable financial difficulties (see p. 710 for details of this research project). In this research, respondents were asked how difficult they found it to make ends meet: 61 per cent of the unemployed said that they found this quite difficult or very difficult, compared to just 15 per cent of those in secure higher-paid jobs and 32 per cent of those in insecure, low-paid work. Only 32 per cent of the unemployed had had a holiday in the previous 12 months, compared to 76 per cent of those in secure and well-paid employment; 73 per cent of the unemployed had cut back on clothing to save money, and 38 per cent had even had to cut back on food. The unemployed were found to be significantly worse off even than those in low-paid, insecure work, and, not surprisingly, very much poorer than those with more secure and better-paid jobs.

Social effects of unemployment

Many of the effects of unemployment are less easily measured than the financial ones. Leonard Fagin and Martin Little (1984) argue that the unemployed lose more than money when they lose their job:

1 They claim that work gives people a sense of identity – of who they are and what their role in society is. It is a source of relationships outside the family. Unemployment tends to reduce social contacts.

2 Work also provides obligatory activity. In a study of unemployed men in London, Fagin and Little claimed that 'most of the men we saw found immense difficulties in creating a framework which would impose on them a regular, purposeful activity'. They found it hard to occupy themselves.

3 A closely related aspect of work which is lost with unemployment is its ability to structure psychological time. Work divides the day and week into time periods, and Fagin and Little found that the unemployed had difficulty organizing their time without this framework. The men they studied spent more of their time in bed, but their sleep was restless and they felt more tired than they did when they were working.

4 Fagin and Little also point out that work provides opportunities to develop skills and creativity, and it provides a sense of purpose. This sense of purpose tended to be lost with unemployment and was reflected in men making statements such as 'I'm surplus to requirement', 'I'm marginal, a nobody, and nobody gives a bugger', and 'I'm on the scrap heap at fifty-five'.

5 Finally, Fagin and Little suggest that income from work provides freedom and control outside work. In particular, it creates the possibility of engaging in leisure activities that cost money.

Such effects can place strain on the personal relationships of the unemployed. Richard Lampard (1994) used data from the Social Change and Economic Life Initiative (see p. 710) to estimate the effects of unemployment on the likelihood of marriages breaking up. He found that the marriage of someone who was unemployed was 70 per cent more likely to break up during a 12-month period than the marriage of somebody who had never been unemployed.

Leisure and unemployment

One possible gain from being unemployed is the increase in leisure time. However, P. Kelvin, C. Dewberry and N. Morley Burber found that only certain types of leisure activities increased with unemployment (quoted in Kay, 1989). The unemployed spend more time watching television, doing housework, reading, and engaging in practical activities and hobbies. Kelvin et al. found no change in playing games, religious activities, creative activities and general outdoor leisure. Social life and 'going out' both decreased, as did active participation in sport and spectating at sports events. Predictably, the unemployed spent more time watching sport on television.

Overall, Kelvin et al. found that leisure was not an adequate substitute for work, because most of the leisure was solitary and passive and failed to compensate for the loss of social contacts at work. They concluded that 'the "leisure" activities of the unemployed are at best palliatives for boredom, and mostly, for most of the unemployed, they are inadequate as that'.

Duncan Gallie, Johnathan Gershuny and Carolyn Vogler (1994) researched the leisure activities of the unemployed as part of the Social Change and Economic Life Initiative. Like Kelvin et al., they found that the unemployed spent more time on some leisure activities and less on others. Unlike Kelvin et al., they found that men were slightly more likely to watch and play sport once they became unemployed, although women were less likely to take part in these activities.

Expensive pastimes such as visiting the theatre, concerts, cinemas and pubs all declined, while watching television and reading books increased. Overall, unemployed men spent something like two hours a day, and women an hour and a half a day, more than the employed on passive leisure activities like watching TV, listening to the radio, reading papers and 'sitting around'. These researchers also found that unemployed people had fewer social contacts with people outside the home. Many of the friends of the unemployed were also unemployed, whereas the social networks of the employed consisted mainly of other people who had jobs.

Psychological reactions to unemployment

Many commentators from the 1930s onwards have claimed that the unemployed react to the loss of work in a series of stages. The psychological reactions are often quite different amongst the newly unemployed compared to those who have been out of work for some time. Fagin and Little (1984) claim to have identified four main stages:

1   The first, which they call the phase of shock, was experienced by only a small number of their sample. It consisted of a sense of disbelief and disorientation.

2   The second stage, that of denial and optimism, was more common. In this stage, the unemployed are positive and optimistic. They see unemployment as a temporary situation and resolve to take advantage of it. They tend to seek work enthusiastically during this stage, but there is also a sense of being on holiday. If financial problems are not immediate, the unemployed tend to use some of their free time constructively in leisure pursuits. This stage is particularly common amongst workers who felt little attachment to their jobs, and they may even feel relieved to have escaped from them.

3   Fagin and Little found that nearly all of those who remained unemployed went through the third stage, anxiety and distress. The unemployed become more concerned about finding work and anxious about their futures.

4   The final stage was resignation and adjustment. The long-term unemployed eventually come to terms with their situation. They accept that their prospects of finding work are slim, lower their expectations for the future, and become apathetic.

Although many researchers have identified similar sequences of psychological reaction amongst the unemployed, Peter Kelvin and Joana Jarrett (1985) warn that such descriptions may over-simplify the effects of unemployment. They stress that reactions to unemployment vary with individual circumstances. Furthermore, some of the reactions may be caused by poverty rather than unemployment as such. They refer to research carried out in the 1930s which showed that not all the long-term unemployed became apathetic. Those whose incomes remained high often remained 'unbroken' (quoted in Kelvin and Jarrett, 1985).

Similarly, Adrian Sinfield (1981) argues that unemployment affects different groups in different ways, depending upon their previous experiences, expectations, and the social groups they belong to. For example, a young person with no experience of full-time work might experience unemployment differently from an older worker made redundant after decades of working life.

Some support for the view that the experience of unemployment will vary is provided by research carried out by Johnathan Gershuny (1994) as part of the Social Change and Economic Life Initiative. The research was based upon questions from the General

Health Questionnaire which focused on mild depression. The questions asked about such issues as whether people had suffered a loss of confidence or whether they felt unable to enjoy themselves.

The research also looked at a range of experiences which it has been claimed are linked to psychological well-being. Respondents were asked whether they felt they had time on their hands, whether they met a range of people, whether they felt they did something useful, whether they felt respected and so on. The research found that the unemployed were less likely to feel positive about these aspects of their life and less likely to have varied social contacts than the employed.

The research also found that the unemployed had poorer psychological health than the employed. However, the psychological well-being of the unemployed who had wide social contacts and felt positive about how they spent their time was better than amongst the unemployed who did not have these advantages. Nevertheless, even amongst the unemployed group with the most fulfilling lives there was worse psychological health than the average for employed people. Thus, while unemployment affects people to varying degrees, it does seem to do psychological harm to a big majority.

Physical health and unemployment

Perhaps the most dramatic claims about the effects of unemployment relate to health. In a review of research on this subject Jeremy Laurance (1986) refers to studies which have reached the following conclusions:

1   Unemployed school leavers in Leeds were found to experience poorer mental health than those who got jobs.

2   A study based upon the 1971 census in Britain found a 20 per cent higher mortality rate amongst unemployed men compared to the employed, even when social class and age were controlled.

3   Researchers in Edinburgh in 1982 found that the suicide and attempted suicide rate was 11 times higher for unemployed men than for employed men.

4   National studies of child development in Britain have found that the children of the unemployed are on average shorter than other children of the same age.

Laurance refers in some detail to a study by a GP in Calne, a small country town in Wiltshire. Employment in the town was dominated by a large sausage factory. After it closed, and unemployment rose, consultation rates increased by 20 per cent, and outpatient referrals to hospital went up by 60 per cent.

Laurance is aware that none of the studies actually proves that unemployment causes health problems. Many variables can affect health, and not all of them can be controlled in research. Furthermore, the studies do not explain how and why unemployment might lead to ill-health. Nevertheless, he concludes that there is at least strong circumstantial evidence that the effects of unemployment can go beyond the financial and psychological.

More recent research shows that unemployed men continue to suffer higher mortality rates than those with jobs. For example, the 1997 Council of Churches for Britain and Ireland report, *Unemployment and the Future of Work*, reports research, based upon longitudinal data produced by the Office of Population, Censuses and Surveys, which showed that between 1971 and 1989 there was 'significantly raised mortality amongst unemployed men in all social classes'.

Youth and the effects of unemployment

Many of the resources that the British government has allocated to dealing with unemployment have been directed at young people. Most, though not all, training schemes have been set up for school leavers. This implies that unemployment is a particularly serious problem for the young.

This view is supported by Paul Willis (1984). On the basis of a study conducted in Wolverhampton in 1984, he argues that a 'new social condition' has been created for youth in areas of high unemployment. Unemployment disrupts the normal transition to adulthood. The young unemployed are denied the opportunity to become independent from parents and often experience long periods of poverty. They are denied the opportunity to take on family responsibilities, and planning for marriage is postponed.

Willis believes that financial hardship prevents the young unemployed from enjoying a normal social life. Without work, leisure activities have less meaning and increasing amounts of time are spent at home. Young people are left in limbo, in a state of 'suspended animation', unable either to look forward to or make the transition to adult status. They become bored, frustrated and demoralized. This often leads to stress and conflict within the family.

Not all researchers agree with Willis that unemployment hits the young hardest. Ken Roberts (1986) accepts that young people do not enjoy unemployment, but he believes that they are better-equipped to deal with it than older unemployed workers. He says 'as newcomers to the workforce young people have no established occupational identities to shatter'. Since they have not experienced work, they do not lose the sense of identity that work provides for older unemployed people. Very often,

many of the peers of the young unemployed will also be out of work, so the sense of deprivation they experience will be muted. Indeed, financially they may be better off on training schemes or claiming benefits than they were at school. Many can also rely upon generous support from their families. Roberts claims that research evidence suggests that young people suffer less psychological and physical harm from unemployment than older people.

In research involving interviews with 551 16–20-year-olds in Liverpool, Manchester, Wolverhampton and London in 1979–81, Kenneth Roberts, Maria Noble and Jill Duggan (1984) found that many of the young were not committed to finding full-time permanent work. Over half of the periods of unemployment experienced by those they studied were caused by youths leaving work voluntarily. Some of them preferred intermittent employment and were less than keen to stay forever in what were often unskilled, low-paid and tedious jobs.

Despite these findings, Roberts *et al.* do not claim that youth unemployment does not cause problems. None of their sample actually enjoyed being out of work. Even if unemployment did not cause much psychological damage, it did lead to boredom. The young unemployed had the 'daily dilemma of what to do and where to go'.

There is evidence to suggest that, even with these qualifications, Roberts *et al.* underestimate the impact of unemployment on the young. For example, in a study of 1,150 unemployed 17-year-olds carried out in 1982, Peter Warr, Michael Banks and Philip Ullah (1985) produced strong evidence that unemployment was affecting their health. They found the unemployed youths to be suffering from significantly higher levels of psychological distress than their employed counterparts examined in other studies. Some 82 per cent of the symptoms described by the unemployed youths were said to have started at or after the time when they became unemployed.

Gender and the effects of unemployment

Most of the research on the effects of unemployment has been carried out into male unemployment. Official figures tend to disguise the extent of female unemployment and it tends to be assumed that unemployment is a particular problem for men.

Sinfield (1981) suggests that female employment rather than unemployment is often seen as the problem. Women are expected to be primarily committed to being housewives and mothers rather than workers. The increasing employment of married women outside the home has sometimes been held responsible for rises in male unemployment. Work is often seen as a central source of identity for men, but as less important for women.

Women might be expected to suffer less from unemployment because domestic life offers them a sense of identity and purpose.

In the 1980s, research started to challenge such assumptions. Using data from questionnaires and interviews carried out in Brighton in 1983, Felicity Henwood and Ian Miles (1987) compared the situations of unemployed men and women. They collected data on access to certain types of experience. These were:

1 Meeting a broad range of people.
2 Keeping busy most of the day.
3 Feeling they were contributing to society.
4 Believing they received respect from society.
5 Having things to do at regular times during the day.

Henwood and Miles found that unemployed men and women had less access to these experiences than the employed. Amongst the unemployed in their sample they detected no significant sex differences; women were as deprived of these experiences by unemployment as men.

A lack of these experiences also affected housewives who were not seeking work outside the home. Although their lives were more structured and they had more sense of purpose than unemployed women, they were as deprived of social contacts and things to keep them busy during the day. This research suggests that unemployment is at least potentially as damaging for women as it is for men, and that housewives suffer some of the problems associated with unemployment.

It is sometimes assumed that working women suffer few financial hardships from unemployment. In a study of women made redundant from a clothing factory in Castleford and another in Harrogate, Angela Coyle (1984) challenged this assumption. She found that, even in families where the husband had the highest wage, the wife's wage was usually 'a crucial component of family household income'. Furthermore, Coyle points out that many women are divorced, widowed, separated or unmarried, and they rely upon their own wage.

In terms of psychological effects, she did find that some women turned their attention to domestic work after being made redundant. For a short time this helped them, but after a while they began to feel isolated. They missed the social contacts and sense of purpose provided by employment outside the home.

Married women often resented returning to a state of financial dependence on men. She also noted that many women took work in the first place to escape from the restrictive limitations of their domestic roles. She says 'the family may soften the blow of job loss, but in the end the family appears to be the trap'.

There is also evidence that young women find unemployment just as traumatic as men. In Warr, Banks and Ullah's study (described above) of 1,150 unemployed 17-year-olds, the 'Females consistently reported more distress, depression and anxiety, and among the white subsample were considerably more concerned than males about the stigma of being unemployed.' The females were also found to be more committed to finding work than the males.

The effects on communities

The social and personal effects of unemployment can perhaps best be illustrated by examining how they interact when unemployment impinges upon a whole community. This is likely to happen when a community relies heavily upon a single source of employment which is abruptly closed down. With the closure of many pits in the UK in recent years, a number of mining communities have been hit in this way.

Studying mining communities

In the early 1990s, Chas Critcher, Bella Dicks and Dave Waddington (1992) studied two pit villages in Yorkshire. In one village the pit had been shut for six months; in the other for two years. In these villages they conducted unstructured interviews. In spring 1992 they conducted a survey in these and two other pit villages, one of which was 'safe' from closure and another where closure was threatened. They used a 21-item questionnaire to measure the level of stress in the four communities. The questionnaire contained questions on psychological symptoms such as anxiety, physical symptoms such as high blood pressure, and behavioural symptoms such as sleeplessness.

Stress and personal problems

The results of their survey of stress levels are presented in Table 10.10. They suggest that job security in the 'safe' village helped to keep stress down, while pit closure and even threatened pit closure raised stress considerably. The stress resulting from the loss or threatened loss of a job was made worse because others in the community were also suffering from stress and so would find it more difficult to give support. Critcher *et al.* say:

> *A woman who worked in the pit canteen described to us how miners had sustained her through her husband's serious illness and the death of her father. She feared the loss of such moral support as much as her loss of earnings.*

Critcher, Dicks and Waddington, 1992

Table 10.10 Levels of personal stress in four mining communities (based on a 10 per cent sample)			
	Medium stress	High stress	Medium/High combined
Closed six months	28	13	41
Closed two years	21	13	34
'Threatened'	15	13	28
'Safe'	16	5	21

Source: C. Critcher, B. Dicks and D. Waddington (1992) 'Portrait of despair', *New Statesman and Society*, 23 October, p. 17.

However, that is not to say that loss of earnings did not have a major impact. In the pit village where the closure had taken place six months earlier, 46.2 per cent of the ex-miners remained unemployed. In the village where closure had taken place two years earlier the picture was scarcely better: 45.7 per cent were still unemployed. Many of those who had found work had been forced to accept 'low pay and job insecurity in the building trade or driving'.

The search for work contributed to high stress levels. One man described how he became anxious after numerous unsuccessful job applications. Although he eventually found work cleaning public buildings, it was not before he had started suffering from palpitations and had been put on beta blockers by his doctor. As financial pressures built up, 'Cars were sold, and holidays abroad became a distant memory.' With no local employment there was little demand for the houses. They became impossible to sell, preventing people from moving in search of job opportunities elsewhere.

Although most of those made redundant in the pits were men, women in the community suffered just as much. The wives of the miners had 'to bear the brunt of family poverty and male despair'. They were faced by 'the hourly presence of an often demoralised partner'. When the women found work to help the family budget, their male partner sometimes resented their own loss of status as a breadwinner. Women were also particularly anxious about the prospects for their children. The end result was that:

many of these women were isolated in a spiral of anxiety and financial hardship, unable to salvage much hope at all for the future, other than a natural optimism and a belief that somehow they would come through.

Critcher, Dicks and Waddington, 1992

Social and economic problems

Not surprisingly, the widespread personal problems in the two villages caused social and economic problems for the communities as a whole. The local economy suffered. Some local shops, pubs and services closed down or shed staff as the spending power of local consumers fell. The appearance of the villages began to deteriorate and community facilities started to decay. Informal mechanisms of social control began to break down. A crime prevention officer in one of the villages reported a 27 per cent increase in crime in one year, and thought that the following year's increase would be more than 35 per cent. Burglary, car theft, joy-riding and petty theft were increasing in both the villages, and there was evidence that drug-taking was also rising. Marriages and family life were coming under increasing stress.

The overall picture presented by Critcher *et al.* of the village six months after closure was of 'a community struggling to come to terms with a total disorientation of its established patterns of work, family and communal life'. In both villages the impact of pit closure was enormous. They conclude:

When we talk of the devastation of mining communities, there is only slight exaggeration. Some do manage to adjust to radically changed circumstances. Others just get by. Some are driven to despair.

Critcher, Dicks and Waddington, 1992

Leisure

The sociology of leisure is a comparatively new area of sociology. Although early sociologists had made passing references to leisure, it was only in the 1970s that it started to be studied as a distinct topic. Early contributions to this debate tended to concentrate on the relationship between leisure and other areas of social life, particularly work and the family. We will look at these first.

Stanley Parker – the influence of work on leisure

Stanley Parker (1976) defined leisure as a residual category of time: it is the time left over after other obligations have been attended to. He distinguished five aspects of people's lives:

1 Work is the time spent in paid employment.

2 Work obligations refer to time that is taken up as a consequence of employment, but is not actually spent working. Travel to and from work is an example of a work obligation.

3 Non-work obligations involve such activities as housework and childcare.

4 Time is also occupied by physiological needs. People have to spend time engaged in activities such as eating, sleeping, washing and defecating.

5 The time left over is defined as leisure.

Although work only takes up part of people's lives, Parker argued that leisure activities are 'conditioned by various factors associated with the way people work'. In particular, he suggested that the amount of autonomy people have at work (the amount of freedom to take decisions and organize their work), the degree of involvement they have in work, and their level of intrinsic job satisfaction, are directly related to their leisure activities.

Parker based his findings on a series of interviews he conducted with bank clerks, childcare officers and youth employment officers, plus published material on a range of occupations studied by sociologists. He saw the relationship between work and leisure as falling into three main patterns: the extension pattern, the neutrality pattern and the opposition pattern.

The extension pattern

In the extension pattern work extends into leisure: there is no clear dividing line between the two. Activities in both spheres are similar, and work is a central life interest rather than family and leisure. Time for activities which can be defined exclusively as leisure is short and is used mainly for the 'development of personality' – for example, reading 'good' literature or going to the theatre.

This pattern is associated with occupations providing a high level of autonomy, intrinsic job satisfaction and involvement in work. Jobs that typify this pattern include business, medicine, teaching, social work and some skilled manual trades. For example, outside statutory office hours, business-people often entertain clients and colleagues at the dinner table or on the golf course – contexts in which business and pleasure are combined. Parker found that the social workers in his survey spent much of their free time in activities connected with their work. Some helped to run youth clubs; others met to discuss clients' problems.

The neutrality pattern

In the neutrality pattern a fairly clear distinction is made between work and leisure. Activities in the two

spheres differ, and family life and leisure, rather than work, form the central life interest.

This pattern is associated with occupations providing a medium to low degree of autonomy, which require the use of only some of the individual's abilities, and where satisfaction is with pay and conditions rather than work itself. Hours of leisure are long, compared to the extension pattern, and are used mainly for relaxation. Leisure is often family-centred, involving activities such as family outings.

Occupations typically associated with the neutrality pattern include clerical workers and semi-skilled manual workers.

The opposition pattern

In the opposition pattern work is sharply distinguished from leisure. Activities in the two areas are very different and leisure forms the central life interest.

This pattern is associated with jobs providing a low degree of autonomy, which require the use of only a limited range of abilities and which often produce a feeling of hostility towards work. Hours of leisure are long and are used mainly to recuperate from and compensate for work. The opposition pattern is typical of unskilled manual work, mining and distant water fishing.

The data for Parker's opposition pattern was drawn mainly from two studies: *Coal is Our Life* by N. Dennis, F. Henriques and C. Slaughter (1956), a study of coalminers in Featherstone, Yorkshire; and *The Fishermen* by Jeremy Tunstall (1962), a study of distant water fishermen in Hull. Both occupations have a high death and injury rate, and involve work in extreme and demanding conditions, all of which produce high levels of stress.

The leisure activities of the miners and fishermen revolved around drinking in pubs and working men's clubs in the company of their workmates. The authors of both studies saw this form of leisure as a means of relief and escape from the demands and dangers of work. Tunstall stated 'Fishermen say "Of course fishermen get drunk. Anybody who does what we do has to get drunk to stay sane."' Dennis *et al.* described the miners' leisure as 'vigorous' and 'predominantly frivolous' in the sense of 'giving no thought to the morrow'. They argued that the insecurity produced by the high rate of death and injury encourages an attitude of living for the moment, which is expressed in having a good time down at the working men's club.

Parker's theory of work and leisure was first published in 1972, and since then he has moderated his position to accept that other factors exert an influence on leisure patterns. Nevertheless, he has remained convinced that work is the most important factor shaping leisure. This assumption and other features of his work can be challenged on a number of grounds.

Criticisms of Parker

First, Parker tends to ignore factors other than work which shape leisure patterns. For example, Rhona and Robert Rapoport (1975) believe that family lifestyle is the most important influence on leisure. For example, adolescents tend to have rather different leisure pursuits to middle-aged parents or retired people. Parker also ignores the influence of class on leisure patterns. His opposition pattern may represent a traditional working-class lifestyle, expressed in an extreme form by miners and distant water fishermen, rather than a response to particular occupations. In any case, the lifestyles of miners and fishermen may have changed considerably since the research on which Parker's views are based. With rising living standards and the decline of traditional industries, close-knit occupational communities of groups such as miners and fishermen may be rapidly disappearing.

National culture is another factor that can affect leisure patterns. Research on the leisure of managers illustrates this point. American managers fit squarely into the extension pattern: the manager's life is portrayed as all work and no play, with a working week of over 60 hours. Even when leisure was used purely for relaxation, nearly three-quarters of the managers in one survey stated that they saw 'leisure time as a refresher to enable you to do better work'.

This subordination of leisure to work is not reflected in Britain. A survey by John Child and Brenda Macmillan (1973) of 964 British managers revealed that only 2.3 per cent mentioned that leisure time was used 'to improve their careers and performance in their jobs'. Nearly a quarter specifically stated that leisure was a means to escape from and forget about work.

British managers come closest to Parker's neutrality pattern. Child and Macmillan found that they worked some 20 hours a week less than their American counterparts. They used their relatively long hours of leisure for relaxation and enjoyment. Playing and watching sport, home improvements and hobbies such as photography were major leisure-time activities. Child and Macmillan concluded that 'British managers preferred to compartmentalize their lives so that the job is forgotten during their leisure time.'

Child and Macmillan argue that a large part of the differences can be explained in terms of the cultures of the two societies. American culture places a greater emphasis on the work ethic, on the importance of individual achievement and self-improvement, and upon work as a means to these ends.

A second line of criticism suggests that Parker's analysis is rather deterministic: it does not allow for individual choice in leisure activities and the wide variety of leisure pursuits engaged in by people who have the same jobs. John Clarke and Chas Critcher say of Parker's theory, 'it fails to allow adequately for human agency and tends to reduce social behaviour to the level of a cultural reflex, in this case to the influence of work' (Clarke and Critcher, 1985).

Clarke and Critcher also advance a third criticism of Parker, that his work does not deal successfully with the leisure patterns of women. They believe that housework should be seen as a form of work, and not as a non-work obligation. Parker does not explain the influence of housework on leisure and he does not take account of the open-ended nature of domestic obligations for many women. Clarke and Critcher suggest that in some cases women may not feel able to lay claim to any leisure 'once they have accepted the overwhelming responsibilities of motherhood'. Gender differences as well as work influence patterns of leisure.

Ken Roberts – a pluralist perspective on leisure

Ken Roberts (1978, 1986) takes a rather broader view of leisure than Stanley Parker. He does not deny that work and the life cycle influence leisure, but he sees other factors as important as well. He stresses the variety of leisure patterns that are available to individuals, and he sees leisure as involving freedom to choose. Indeed, Roberts defines leisure in terms of choice. He says, 'Leisure is not the whole of non-work but, within this area, includes only those activities (and inactivities) that are relatively self-determined.' In other words, individuals are only engaging in leisure when they feel they are choosing what to do themselves.

Things which people have to do, or feel they have to do, cannot be leisure. Some activities, such as paid employment and physical necessities like eating or sleeping, clearly do not count as leisure according to this definition. To Roberts, activities such as tending the garden and paying a visit to ageing relatives only count as leisure if they are done freely and not out of a sense of obligation.

Roberts accepts the claim of pluralists that Britain and other advanced industrial societies are essentially democratic. (For a full discussion of pluralism see pp. 593–601.) There are many different groups in society and an enormous variety of leisure interests. The latter are affected by class, age, sex, marital status, education and many other factors. All groups in society have the opportunity to pursue their interests within the limits laid down by the law. The public simply take part in the leisure activities they enjoy.

758 Chapter 10: Work, unemployment and leisure

Leisure and choice

Roberts argues against theories which claim that the public have their leisure interests manipulated by others. He denies that the state and commercial enterprises impose patterns of leisure on people. He says 'The providers have no captive audience.' The state provides some facilities but this does not guarantee that it can shape patterns of leisure. Roberts points out:

> members of the public can pick and choose. They do not have to use country parks, Forestry Commission nature trails, art centres or sports halls. People only use the facilities that they find useful, and if the public sector does not satisfy their tastes, individuals can turn to commercial provision or self-help.
>
> Roberts, 1978, p. 83

Individuals can also join pressure groups to encourage the government to subsidize the types of leisure pursuits that they most enjoy.

According to Roberts, commercial providers of leisure have to respond as much as the government does to public tastes. However much they try to manipulate the public through advertising or other means, people are free to choose the goods and services they buy. The declining public demand for bowling-alleys has forced many to close down, while the commercial sector has had to respond to new leisure interests. For example, travel firms have responded to the increasing demand for cheap package holidays abroad.

If neither the state nor private companies provide the leisure opportunities the public wants, then individuals can provide their own: there are 'participant-run dart and domino leagues, golf clubs and photography societies, while kids play street football and arrange their own informal games'.

Social factors and leisure

Although he stresses the freedom of choice in leisure activities, Roberts does not deny that social factors influence patterns of leisure. People choose to engage in leisure pursuits that fit in with their personal circumstances, lifestyle and the social groups to which they belong.

Roberts uses data from a survey he conducted in 1972 to examine the factors influencing leisure. The sample used consisted of 474 economically active males in Liverpool. On the basis of his evidence, Roberts claims that work has relatively little influence on people's leisure pursuits. He also points out that, even excluding the unemployed, about half the population do not have paid work. The young, retired and full-time housewives do not have their leisure influenced by work, simply because they are not 'working'.

Roberts also disagrees with Stanley Parker that work is the central factor shaping leisure amongst those who do have a job. In all occupational groups television takes up the largest single block of leisure time, and alcohol, tobacco, gambling and sex are popular throughout the occupational structure.

Roberts accepts that class affects leisure, but rejects the view that it is the dominant influence. Activities such as going to the theatre are predominantly middle-class, but they take up only a minute amount of leisure time. Low income limits the leisure activities of some groups, but he claims that nearly everyone has enough money to participate in a sport and have a holiday of some sort.

Family life cycle and leisure

Roberts attributes far more importance to the family life cycle than he does to work. For example, he found that unmarried people under 30 spent less time watching television and more time socializing than their married counterparts.

However, Roberts does not argue that life cycle is the only important factor influencing patterns of leisure:

1 He recognizes gender as being important and suggests that women have less leisure time than men.

2 He found that education also had a strong influence. Those who had stayed on longer in education watched less television and spent more time outside their homes with friends.

3 Finally, he argues that styles of marriage are important. Married couples who have joint conjugal roles tend to engage in home-centred leisure, while those with segregated conjugal roles tend to go out more. (For a definition of joint and segregated conjugal roles see p. 552.)

Roberts's views differ from Parker's in the emphasis he places on the variety of factors influencing leisure. To Roberts, leisure is defined as a matter of choice and is characterized by diversity. There are social influences on leisure, but compared to work it is an area of life in which individuals enjoy great freedom. In some ways his work anticipated some themes in postmodern perspectives on leisure (particularly the emphasis on choice), which will be examined shortly.

John Clarke and Chas Critcher – leisure in capitalist Britain

John Clarke and Chas Critcher (1985) have developed a neo-Marxist approach to the sociology of leisure. Their work has been influenced by the Italian Antonio

Gramsci, who himself developed Marx's theories. (For a discussion of Gramsci's work see pp. 615–17.)

Clarke and Critcher argue that writers such as Roberts greatly exaggerate the degree of freedom and choice involved in leisure. They accept that individuals do have some freedom in their leisure activities, but they believe that they are limited and constrained by capitalism. Leisure is an arena of struggle between different social groups (in particular classes) but it is not an equal struggle. The bourgeoisie are in a stronger position to shape leisure than subordinate classes.

Capitalism and leisure

Clarke and Critcher claim that the very existence of capitalism shapes the nature of work and leisure. Before the Industrial Revolution there was no clear dividing line between these two spheres of life. Those working in agriculture and domestic textile production could to a large extent determine when and how hard they worked. For example, there was the widespread practice of taking Monday off, which was known as 'St Monday'. Leisure and work could sometimes be combined: people often drank alcohol whilst working.

The Industrial Revolution and the development of capitalism initially had two main effects: they removed many of the opportunities for leisure, and led to a clear demarcation between work and leisure.

Investment in industrial machinery required people to work increasingly long hours and any flexibility was lost. The machinery had to be used to the full to get the maximum return from the investment, and the workforce had to be present at the same time. With the excessive working hours, working-class leisure became largely confined to the tavern.

By the 1880s leisure began to grow: working hours were reduced and living standards rose. However, the freedom and flexibility of leisure in pre-industrial times did not return.

According to Clarke and Critcher, the two most important influences on leisure became the state and capitalist enterprise. Both began to play a crucial role in defining leisure and determining the leisure opportunities available.

The state plays an important role in licensing certain leisure activities, such as pubs, wine bars, casinos and betting shops, and 'undesirables' are excluded from holding licences. Films and videos are censored or cleared for release. Health and safety legislation regulates the conditions under which leisure goods and services can be consumed. Through these measures the state is empowered to ensure that leisure is safe and orderly, but at the same time limits are placed upon the ways that leisure time can be spent.

Another important area of state involvement in leisure is its regulation of public space. There is inequality of access to private space, particularly housing, for leisure purposes, and the disadvantaged tend to use public spaces such as the street and parks for leisure. In these circumstances the young, ethnic minorities and the working class in general have part of their recreation controlled by the police, who might deem some of their activities on the street as inappropriate. Clarke and Critcher suggest that conflict over the use of public space was one factor contributing to the urban riots of the early 1980s in Britain.

They also claim that the state is concerned to prevent disorderly leisure which might be a threat to social stability. Working-class leisure patterns are discouraged. Middle-class tastes and culture are promoted and subsidized by the state. Leisure centres have had some success in increasing working-class involvement in sport, but in general there is a middle-class and male bias in the sports that are promoted. The Sports Council's most funded sports are squash, swimming, athletics, sailing, rowing, tennis and golf.

Summing up, Clarke and Critcher say, 'in relation to both body and mind, the state has pushed policies aimed at drawing subordinate social groups into "rational recreation" in order to curb the potential dangers of free time'.

If people are engaged in officially sanctioned leisure pursuits they cannot be engaged in violence, riots or political agitation.

The commercialization of leisure

Perhaps the most important aspect of leisure under capitalism, according to Clarke and Critcher, is its commercialization. Leisure has become big business and an important source of profit for the bourgeoisie.

The commercial provision of leisure is dominated by large companies which have a wide variety of leisure interests. For example, the Rank Organization is involved in the film industry, and in the manufacture of hi-fi equipment and videos, through subsidiaries like Bush and Wharfedale; it has interests in dancing, bowling and bingo; and it owns hotels, marinas and Butlins.

Clarke and Critcher claim that such large corporations have the power to influence consumers' needs. The leisure industry creates new products and services and then tries to persuade consumers that they should purchase them.

In some areas of leisure provision, a few large companies dominate the market and restrict consumer choice. In the brewing industry, the 'big six' – Watney Mann, Bass Charrington, Allied, Scottish and Newcastle, Whitbread and Courage – have taken over many smaller breweries and closed them down. They have reduced the number of beers available, closed pubs, and tightened their control over the remaining pubs by replacing tenants with salaried managers. At the same time they have tried to change the character of pubs, altering the layouts and replacing traditional pub games with more profitable juke boxes and fruit machines.

Although Clarke and Critcher believe that the state and private enterprise have restricted choice and manipulated tastes, they do not believe that they have completely dominated leisure. They claim that leisure, like other areas of social life, has been affected by class struggle. The state and private enterprise have tried to establish their hegemony or domination of leisure, but they have not been entirely successful. In some areas they have met with effective resistance.

For instance, the Campaign for Real Ale resisted the large brewers' attempts to replace natural with keg beers and to some extent reversed the trend towards reducing the range of beers available. Similarly, the state has not always been successful in persuading the working class and other subordinate groups to accept participation in the leisure pursuits that it has promoted.

Criticisms of 'class domination' theories

Despite Clarke and Critcher's qualifications to their argument, they clearly see leisure as being a far more restricted area of social life than pluralists such as Roberts. However, Roberts himself dismisses what he calls class domination theories of leisure.

To Roberts (1978) leisure choices in Britain are as free as can be expected in any society. Companies try to make a profit out of leisure, but they can only succeed if they provide what consumers want. The state may intervene in leisure, but in doing so it tends to increase choice rather than restrict it. Roberts argues:

> if recreational opportunities are to be made available to economically disadvantaged groups, public provision is a logical if not the only method. If the state did not subsidize sport and other forms of recreation that involve the use of land, the majority of children would be unable to participate.
>
> Roberts, 1978

The pluralist and neo-Marxist perspectives on leisure offer quite different interpretations of this area of social life. Perhaps both tend to generalize and pay too little attention to evidence that contradicts their respective theories.

Gender and leisure

All of the theories of leisure examined so far have been accused of neglecting or dealing inadequately with the question of gender. As Sheila Scraton puts

it, 'Until the 1980s women were largely absent as focuses of leisure analyses except as appendages to men or unproblematically defined as part of the nuclear family' (Scraton, 1992).

Since the start of the 1980s, feminist sociologists have begun to examine women's leisure in its own right and have devoted increasing attention to the question of the relationship between gender and leisure patterns.

A number of feminists have criticized earlier work that made reference to this issue but failed to explore it in great depth. Eileen Green, Sandra Hebron and Diana Woodward (1990) say that Parker's early work was based almost entirely around the leisure of male workers. They note that Ken Roberts suggests that gender is important and accepts that women have less leisure than men, but his work contains only short discussions of the issue. Clarke and Critcher's work has been rather better received by feminist writers, but Green et al. nevertheless say that it shows a 'surprising lack of engagement with well-known feminist work in the area'.

Gender and patterns of leisure

All feminist writers on gender and leisure agree that there are important differences between men's and women's leisure. They argue that not only do men and women tend to take part in different types of leisure, but women also have less access to leisure opportunities than men.

Tables 10.11 and 10.12 present the findings of structured interview research from the General Household Surveys of 1987, 1990, 1993 and 1996. Table 10.11 shows that in 1996 the only sports, games and physical activities that women took more part in than men were swimming, keep fit/yoga and horse riding. Some 54 per cent of men but only 38 per cent of women had participated in one activity other than walking in the previous four weeks.

Table 10.12 shows less variation in home-based leisure patterns between women and men. Both had very high rates of participation in watching television, visiting or entertaining friends or relatives, and listening to the radio, records and tapes. However, there was a marked difference between participation in DIY, predominantly done by men, and dressmaking, needlework or knitting, overwhelmingly done by women. This seems to reflect traditional conjugal roles. Women were more likely to read books, while men were slightly more likely to do gardening.

Furthermore, these tables do not reveal differences in the amount of time available to men and women for leisure nor differences in the circumstances in which women and men can engage in leisure.

Table 10.11 Trends in participation in sports, games and physical activities in the four weeks before interview: by sex, 1987–96

Persons aged 16 and over, Great Britain

Active sports, games and physical activities*	Men				Women			
	1987	1990	1993	1996	1987	1990	1993	1996
	Percentage participating in the 4 weeks before interview							
Walking	41	44	45	49	35	38	37	41
Any swimming	–	14	15	13	–	15	16	17
Swimming: indoor	10	11	12	11	11	13	14	15
Swimming: outdoor	4	4	4	3	3	4	3	3
Keep fit/yoga	5	6	6	7	12	16	17	17
Snooker/pool/billiards	27	24	21	20	5	5	5	4
Cycling	10	12	14	15	7	7	7	8
Weight training Weight lifting	7	8	9	9 2	2	2	3	3 1
Any soccer	10	10	9	10	0	0	0	0
Golf	7	9	9	8	1	2	2	2
Running (jogging, etc.)	8	8	7	7	3	2	2	2
Ten-pin bowls/skittles	2	5	5	4	1	3	3	3
Badminton	4	4	3	3	3	3	2	2
Tennis	2	2	3	2	1	2	2	2
Any bowls	2	3	3	2	1	1	2	1
Fishing	4	4	4	3	0	0	0	0
Table tennis	4	3	2	2	1	1	1	1
Squash	4	4	3	2	1	1	1	0
Horse riding	0	1	0	0	1	1	1	1
At least one activity (excluding walking)†	57	58	57	54	34	39	39	38
At least one activity†	70	73	72	71	52	57	57	58
Base = 100%	9,086	8,119	8,062	7,186	10,443	9,455	9,490	8,510

* Includes only activities in which more than 1.0% of all adults participated in 4 weeks before interview in 1996.
† Total includes those activities not separately listed.

Source: *General Household Survey* (1996) Office for National Statistics, London, p. 219.

Feminist research, which is discussed below, suggests that in both these respects women are severely disadvantaged.

Liberal and radical feminist perspectives on leisure

While all feminist perspectives see women as disadvantaged in relation to leisure, different feminist approaches disagree about the extent of the problem,

the causes of it, and solutions to it. Sheila Scraton, though not herself a liberal feminist, has described how liberal feminists see the problem (Scraton, 1992). (The liberal feminist perspective on society is discussed on pp. 137–8.)

Scraton claims that liberal feminists focus on unequal opportunities to participate in leisure, and particularly unequal access to leisure facilities. They believe that these inequalities result from the process

Table 10.12 Selected leisure activities: participation rates in the four weeks before interview: by sex and age

Persons aged 16 and over, Great Britain: 1996

Leisure activities	16–19	20–24	25–29	30–44	45–59	60–69	70 and over	Total
				Age				
	Percentage participating in the 4 weeks before interview							
Men								
Watching TV	99	99	100	99	99	99	98	99
Visiting/entertaining friends or relations	97	98	97	97	95	94	91	95
Listening to the radio	93	93	94	93	91	85	78	90
Listening to records/tapes	97	96	94	88	75	67	51	79
Reading books	51	59	57	61	58	60	57	58
Gardening	20	21	36	53	60	68	59	52
DIY	33	40	64	67	64	57	42	58
Dressmaking/needlework/knitting	4	4	2	4	3	3	3	3
Base = 100%	418	472	651	1,980	1,729	947	989	7,186
Women								
Watching TV	99	98	99	98	99	99	99	99
Visiting/entertaining friends or relations	98	99	99	98	97	96	94	97
Listening to the radio	97	95	94	90	86	81	75	87
Listening to records/tapes	99	96	92	90	76	62	42	77
Reading books	74	71	70	71	72	72	66	71
Gardening	10	21	34	50	58	54	40	45
DIY	15	24	23	39	34	21	11	30
Dressmaking/needlework/knitting	16	29	39	37	46	47	36	37
Base = 100%	412	567	790	2,392	1,957	1,077	1,316	8,511
Total								
Watching TV	99	98	99	99	99	99	98	99
Visiting/entertaining friends or relations	98	98	98	97	96	95	93	96
Listening to the radio	95	94	94	92	88	83	76	88
Listening to records/tapes	98	96	93	89	75	65	46	78
Reading books	63	66	64	66	65	66	62	65
Gardening	15	21	35	52	59	61	48	48
DIY	25	34	50	52	48	38	24	42
Dressmaking/needlework/knitting	9	15	14	22	26	27	22	22
Base = 100%	830	1,039	1,441	4,372	3,686	2,024	2,305	15,697

Source: *General Household Survey* (1996) Office for National Statistics, London, p. 219.

of socialization through which women and men learn distinctive gender roles. Thus 'discriminatory practices based on stereotypical assumptions about gender' prevent women from enjoying the same opportunities as men.

Liberal feminists seek to change this situation by highlighting these discriminatory practices and getting them changed. Scraton cites initiatives by the Sports Council as an example. The Sports Council has identified women as one 'target group' who are not taking advantage of the opportunities available, and has initiated campaigns to encourage more women to participate in sports.

Liberal feminism is a reformist perspective: it claims that gender inequalities can be successfully tackled through gradual piecemeal reform, without requiring fundamental changes in society. Amongst the reforms advocated, and sometimes achieved, by liberal feminists are the provision of childcare facilities, special transport arrangements and women-only sessions at leisure centres.

More radical feminists tend to welcome these sorts of initiatives but argue that they cannot lead to fundamental changes. As Scraton puts it, 'Critical feminist theory argues, however, that women's access to existing structures and institutions will not challenge the deep rooted gender inequalities that have become institutionalised and fundamental to social practices.'

Radical feminists believe that the structure of society prevents equality between men and women, and that only changes in the social structure can end this inequality. One such approach will now be examined.

Eileen Green, Sandra Hebron and Diana Woodward – a socialist feminist perspective

Green *et al.* describe themselves as socialist feminists, but their work is perhaps based more on feminist ideas than socialist ones (Green, Hebron and Woodward, 1990). They say that 'the concept of patriarchy is central to our theoretical analysis' and much of their work is concerned with showing how men restrict the leisure opportunities of women. Their work is based partly on a review of other studies and partly on their own research. They studied a total of 707 women in Sheffield, using questionnaires, interviews and discussion groups. The interviews and discussion groups were also conducted with the male partners of the women being studied.

The definition of leisure

Green *et al.* start by arguing that the definitions of work and leisure used by male sociologists are inappropriate. Such definitions tend to be based on men with full-time jobs and fail to take account of the situation of women. To many of the women interviewed, leisure was a 'vague and amorphous concept'. They found it hard to separate leisure from other aspects of their lives, but often saw it as a state of mind. Many women regarded it as doing things that they enjoyed or as the chance to please themselves. They did not see leisure in terms of particular periods of time or as specific activities.

Green *et al.* claim that it is much harder for women to forget about work and put aside specific time periods for their leisure. Women tend to have open-ended domestic responsibilities, particularly when they have young children. Whether they have paid employment or not, they are invariably 'on call' to tend to the needs of other family members. According to Green *et al.*, some women with part-time jobs actually saw those jobs as a form of leisure. For example, working in a bar on a Saturday night could be seen as an opportunity to socialize and escape from domestic chores.

Thus Green *et al.* claim that studies of women show that leisure can only be defined subjectively: there is no objective way of separating work and leisure independently of the opinions of those being studied.

Patterns of work and leisure

From their own research, Green *et al.* reached a number of conclusions about patterns of work and leisure for men and women:

1 Overall, men have more time for leisure than women. Women found it harder to plan their leisure because their domestic responsibilities were open-ended.

2 Women had less money than men, and many wives were still financially dependent on their husbands. This restricted the types of leisure they could engage in.

3 The attitudes of men further restricted the options open to women. Green *et al.* say, 'many groups of women are expected to choose their leisure time activities mainly from within the limited range of home and family-oriented activities which are socially defined as acceptable, womanly pursuits'.

Thus the emphasis in Green *et al.*'s theory is on the constraints imposed on women's leisure.

Leisure and social control

According to Green *et al.*, the constraints which limit women's leisure stem from structural features of patriarchal capitalist societies. Systems of social control prevent women from having the same freedom with regard to leisure as men. Green *et al.* argue:

> social control operates at a number of levels across what may be seen as a continuum ranging from non-coercive forms to actual physical violence. In addition such forms of control are closely related to ideologies of gender and gender-appropriate behaviour.
> Green, Hebron and Woodward, 1990

Physical violence and sexual attacks outside the home make women afraid to venture out, particularly if they are on their own and it is dark. This makes it difficult for women to engage regularly in leisure outside their home, especially in winter. Husbands or partners may use anything from physical violence to mild disapproval to persuade women to limit their leisure to what they see as respectable activities. In the Sheffield study, men seemed much more willing to allow their wives, partners or daughters to go to activities such as yoga, keep-fit and night-school classes, than to pubs and clubs.

Many venues for leisure activities outside the home are dominated by males, and women may feel uncomfortable in them. Green *et al*. claim that men use joking, ridicule and sexual innuendo to put women down in leisure venues where they are unwelcome. In their study, 80 per cent of the women said that they felt uncomfortable in a pub on their own; 90 per cent in wine bars.

Along with financial constraints and hostility from men, ideology also controls women's behaviour and limits their activities. Women themselves often accept patriarchal ideology and monitor their own and each other's behaviour to make sure it does not exceed the boundaries of feminine respectability. For example, mothers feel guilty about leaving their children and so tend to give up previous leisure pursuits once their first child is born. One woman in Sheffield remarked, 'As soon as I had my baby I felt different, I didn't feel as though I could go to a nightclub.'

Relationships between mothers and their married daughters enable women to support one another but can encourage the maintenance of traditional gender roles across generations.

If married women's leisure is not constrained by any of the above systems of social control, then it is likely to be restricted simply by lack of time. Some 97 per cent of the married women interviewed in Sheffield did the majority of the housework. Women with paid employment tended to do a 'double shift' of housework and paid work.

Other influences on leisure

Green *et al*. do not claim that gender is the only influence on leisure, nor do they think that all women are in the same position. Their study of Sheffield found that class and income level, age, ethnic group, and 'work and domestic situation' all had an effect.

Women from higher classes and higher-income levels tend to have more opportunity to engage in expensive leisure pursuits. Higher-class women participate more in sport, yoga and keep-fit than women from lower classes.

Single, young employed women have perhaps the most freedom. Although their employment limits the time they have for leisure, they have more financial independence than married women and usually less

responsibility for housework and childcare. Single women have weaker ideological restrictions on their leisure outside the home, and they have no husbands to frown on their behaviour.

The Sheffield research suggested that getting married depressed participation rates in sport even more than having children. Having children does have a big impact though. Women's recreation often becomes family recreation and not something for them to enjoy purely on their own account. For example, mothers tend to go swimming with their children rather than on their own.

Gender, ethnicity and leisure

Ethnic-minority women have their leisure limited not just by virtue of their gender but also as a result of their ethnicity. As well as sexual harassment, they are 'subjected to racial oppression in the form of institutionalised discrimination as well as random interpersonal acts of harassment and racial attack'. As a consequence they may be even more unwilling than other women to go out to leisure activities. Green *et al*. quote a study conducted for the Greater London Council (GLC) which found that 54 per cent of all London women, but only one-third of Afro-Caribbean women, travelled for pleasure each week.

Although women from Asian and Afro-Caribbean ethnic minorities share common problems which result from racism, they have different cultural traditions which affect their leisure. In traditional Asian rural kinship systems, 'Personal preferences and autonomy are rigorously subordinated to the interests of the household unit, which is hierarchically ordered under the authority of the eldest male.' Although the situation of Asian women in Britain is very varied, 'there are clear cultural and religious barriers to their attainment of autonomy and sexual equality, above and beyond those faced by most white and Afro-Caribbean women'.

For example, Green *et al*. claim that Asian men are reluctant to encourage women to be mobile, and this is reflected in figures from the GLC's study which showed that two-thirds of Asian women felt unsafe walking in public places and 95 per cent would not go out alone after dark.

Afro-Caribbean women are rather less restricted in their leisure. Green *et al*. say that they have more power in their families than Asian women and this encourages independence. They say that black women 'are able to draw on the historical tradition of the powerful matriarch, mainstay of the family, as a source of confidence and inspiration'. Leisure is less home-based than for Asian women but is still limited. As well as fear of racially motivated attacks, financial hardship, inadequate state facilities for childcare (especially for single mothers), and the demands of factory employment all create problems for many Afro-Caribbean women. In addition, 'Isolation from an extended network of female kin removes a source both of childcare and of leisure companions.'

Conclusion

The work of Green *et al.* suggests that a number of factors work alongside gender to shape women's opportunities, or lack of opportunities, to enjoy leisure. Although the emphasis is very much on the constraints on women, Green *et al.* are not entirely pessimistic. They found that women do have some success in making opportunities for leisure. This partly stems from 'women's informal sociability', that is, their ability to 'develop and maintain friendships at school, in the workplace, outside the school gates, at the shops and bus stop, and in any number of other unpromising leisure venues where women meet regularly'.

Women are also slightly more active than men in voluntary organizations and are more likely to attend night classes. Although these are relatively 'safe' and acceptable forms of leisure activity, which do not challenge gender stereotypes, they do offer women some opportunities to increase their independence from men. Furthermore, some women are being more ambitious and are trying to challenge male domination of leisure. Green *et al.* say:

> we did talk to women who are making real inroads into the male bastions of leisure, and to many others who are managing to claim some time and pleasure for themselves in the face of very limited resources.
>
> Green, Hebron and Woodward, 1990

Modernity, postmodernity and leisure

A number of sociologists in recent years have begun to relate leisure to the concepts of modernity and postmodernity. Some have argued that we are entering an era of postmodernity, and as a result the nature of leisure is changing. In this section we will concentrate on the work of three writers. Chris Rojek (1995) has some reservations about using the concept of postmodernity, but nevertheless uses it as the basis for his views on changes in the nature of leisure. John Urry (1990) uses the idea of postmodernity to understand changes in tourism. Sheila Scraton and Sheila Bramham (1995) examine how the ideas of modernity and postmodernity have been applied to understanding leisure, but they are quite critical of the claim that there has been a shift to postmodernity.

Chris Rojek – *Decentring Leisure*

In his book, *Decentring Leisure* (1995), Rojek explores the changing nature of leisure in advanced capitalist societies. He argues that in order to understand leisure better it needs to be decentred. By this he means that leisure should not be seen as a clearly demarcated aspect of social life which can be studied in its own right. The experience of leisure cannot be separated out from other experiences. There are a number of reasons for this.

First, leisure can best be understood by examining it within the context of the sort of society in which it exists. What counts as leisure and the purpose of leisure have changed over time, and the idea of leisure only has meaning within the society within which it is located.

Second, in postmodernity the meaning of leisure becomes less clear. Modern societies had a relatively clear idea about what leisure was. Leisure was associated with the idea of freedom and tended to be seen as involving escape from more constrained and limited areas of social life such as work or education.

With the advent of postmodernity, the distinction between leisure and other areas of social life, such as work, becomes much more confused. The purpose of leisure becomes much less clear. Leisure overlaps with other areas of social life and its meanings become far more diverse than 'escape' and 'freedom'.

Rojek bases his argument upon the idea of a general shift from modern societies towards postmodern societies. However, he is careful to avoid saying that there has been any definite break between modernity and postmodernity. To Rojek, postmodernity retains a good deal in common with modernity and there were postmodern elements in modern societies.

Furthermore, there are no clearcut divisions between leisure in different sorts of societies. Capitalism, modernity and postmodernity tend to push leisure in different directions, but they do not inevitably produce different types of leisure. Concepts such as capitalism, modernity and postmodernity draw attention to particular aspects of leisure while neglecting others. Each therefore 'encompasses some aspects of leisure and culture while at the same time leaving other aspects in the semi-darkness'. Nevertheless, despite these reservations, Rojek does identify some general differences between modern and postmodern leisure.

Modern and postmodern leisure

Rojek identifies five main differences between modern and postmodern leisure:

1 The modernist view of leisure is that it 'is segmented from the rest of life as a charmed realm of self-fulfilment and life satisfaction'. It is work that is the foundation of modern societies. Work and leisure are contrasted as two separate realms, but with postmodernity they come together. For example, more and more people work in leisure industries, people can experience fun and enjoyment at work, they can even see going to work as a leisure pursuit. Conversely, people can experience 'routine and confinement' when they are engaged in activities that are supposed to be leisure pursuits.

2 Modern societies tend to contrast authentic with inauthentic experience. They celebrate the authentic as being superior to the inauthentic. For example, going to see an authentic historical building, say the Tower of London, is superior to visiting a model of it or looking at a picture. In modern culture there is also an emphasis on the planning of leisure. Leisure is organized and given a sense of purpose for the participants.

However, in postmodern leisure, people are less likely to seek the authentic experience. Virtual reality machines, models and representations of things, 'simulation and hyperreality', are fully accepted as valid in leisure activities. Furthermore, leisure is less planned and purposeful. People are less likely to pursue leisure activities for particular purposes, but take part in them just for the sake of it. Leisure becomes an end in itself rather than an escape from work or part of planned activities designed to achieve goals such as self-improvement.

3 Postmodernism 'outflanks the notion of the integrated self which underpins modernist thought'. For example, in modernist thought people pass through different stages in the life cycle. At each stage people have a strong sense of who they are and engage in leisure pursuits appropriate to their age-group identity. Young people will go out socializing, middle-aged people will have more home-centred leisure, older people will spend more times on hobbies, and so on. To Rojek, such assumptions do not apply with postmodernism. For example, older people might continue to go to night clubs, discos and rock concerts, and young people might well engage in more sedate pursuits associated in modern thinking with older age groups.

4 Postmodernism breaks down a whole series of barriers between areas of social life. Rojek says:

The barriers between home and abroad, public and private life, work and leisure, childhood and old age, male roles and female roles, white and ethnic cultures cease to be treated as given 'facts' of life. Instead there is more emphasis on ambivalence, variability, flexibility and individualism.

Rojek, 1995, p. 172

Societies become more pluralistic in the lifestyles and identities of their members, and less rigid in terms of who can adopt the particular identities. Identity politics becomes more important for people. They can pick and choose who to be and are not even limited by their biological make-up. For example, white people can choose to listen to and identify with the music of black people, men can dress as women and vice versa. Leisure plays a central role in identity politics. In leisure activities people can construct their own identities, they can choose who to be. In modern societies leisure reflects who you are. The sort of leisure you engage in is shaped by factors such as your job, your sex and your ethnic group. With postmodernism your leisure increasingly creates your identity – you become who you are through your leisure.

5 In modernity there tends to be a sharp distinction between providers and consumers of leisure. There is assumed to be a hierarchical relationship between the two. The providers of leisure are the experts and they organize leisure for the consumers. With postmodernism this distinction and the hierarchical relationship breaks down. People are no longer content to let others organize their leisure for them. People increasingly cooperate to organize their own leisure. In the past, higher-class males were largely responsible for organizing leisure and imposing their preconceptions about leisure on others. Increasingly, women, ethnic minorities, and other groups who were assumed to be passive consumers, actively shape and organize their own leisure.

On the whole, Rojek welcomes the tendency towards more postmodern patterns of leisure. Modernist leisure held out great promises for people. It seemed to offer them a 'realizable utopia' involving a 'longed-for state of freedom, choice and life satisfaction'. However, the utopia was never achievable. Modern leisure was too planned and constraining, too limited and restricted by the statuses of the participants. In pursuing it we simply discovered that 'our images of freedom, choice and life-satisfaction are barred by undreamt-of contingencies and hazards. Leisure becomes one more problem in an existence already surrounded with problems. We feel deceived and short-changed.'

A postmodern approach to leisure helps to avoid some of these problems. We no longer necessarily expect leisure to supply a sense of escape, choice and freedom. However, we actually experience greater choice and freedom than in modern leisure. Our expectations are lowered but our experiences improve, making people more satisfied than before.

Evaluation of Rojek

Rojek's work tends to be rather abstract and make very general statements about the nature of leisure. As such it exaggerates and simplifies the changes in leisure that he claims have taken place. Although Rojek denies that there is a clearcut distinction between modern and postmodern leisure, he nevertheless ends up characterizing them as being very different. Furthermore, he provides little in the way of systematic evidence that a shift in leisure has taken place. In some ways a rather more convincing account of postmodern leisure is provided by Sheila Scraton and Peter Bramham, even though they are more critical of postmodern ideas.

Sheila Scraton and Peter Bramham – leisure and postmodernity

Modernity

According to Sheila Scraton and Peter Bramham, 'Leisure has been seen as a product of modernity, and of industrial capitalism which demarcated time, as defined by the clock, into segments to be bought and sold like any other commodity, at market rates' (Scraton and Bramham, 1995). Drawing on the work of the historian E.P. Thompson (1967), they argue that, before industrialization and the advent of modernity, there was no clear distinction between work and leisure. Time was governed by the cycles of the seasons and those of night and day. Work activities and leisure activities were intermingled.

However, with the advent of the factory system and the new system of paying workers for their time rather than for what they produced, a strong distinction between work time and non-work time began to be established.

According to Scraton and Bramham, 'Modernity, or industrial society was essentially a class based or mass society.' Fordist production techniques, which used assembly lines for the mass production of standardized products, became dominant. Systematic, rational planning is also a feature of modernity and these aspects of modernity influenced the development of leisure.

Modernity and leisure

Scraton and Bramham argue that 'Organised leisure was part and parcel of the modern project. It was the time left over from work and paid employment which could be filled with acceptable free-time activities or relaxations supporting existing economic and political arrangements.' The state and the voluntary sector became involved in organizing leisure which was supposed to benefit individuals and/or society.

One focus of the policies was youth, particularly working-class males, who were seen as an actual or potential problem. Such institutions as youth clubs and the Scouts were designed to keep young people occupied and out of trouble. Leisure quangos, which

were connected to the state but not directly run by it, began to develop. These included organizations such as the Countryside Commission, the Arts Council and the Sports Council. They promoted what were deemed to be healthy, useful and culturally acceptable leisure. Leisure was designed to be 'rational or recuperative'. It could lead to self-improvement or help people recover from the exertions of paid employment. Leisure professionals paid particular attention to helping disadvantaged groups to benefit from leisure. Such groups were seen to include the elderly and the disabled as well as the working class.

However, the idea of rational, planned, organized leisure for the masses began to lose some of its influence after the Second World War. Scraton and Bramham suggest that:

> The influence of American culture through rock and roll, teenage subcultures, the women's movement and the presence of distinctive minority ethnic groups and diverse cultural patterns, all raised questions about the homogeneous and unidirectional nature of rational leisure and highlighted the growing fragmentation and diversity of free time tastes and activities.
>
> Scraton and Bramham, 1995, p. 20

These developments heralded changes which some researchers came to characterize as the development of postmodern leisure.

Postmodern leisure

Scraton and Bramham identify a number of features of post-war leisure which have come to be seen as postmodern:

1 If modern leisure is based on organizations planning leisure, postmodern leisure is based on individuals buying products and services. Modern leisure was disciplined whereas postmodern leisure is more concerned with self-indulgence. You do what you want to do rather than what others tell you is good for you. Postmodern leisure has been compared to the shopping mall where you are spoilt for choice and are encouraged to indulge yourself as much as possible.

2 Drawing on the work of the postmodernists Baudrillard and Lyotard (see Chapter 15), Scraton and Bramham argue that the idea of postmodern leisure is associated with fragmentation and the breakdown of the distinction between high culture and popular culture (see Chapter 12 for a discussion of these terms). Political, social and cultural elites can no longer dictate to the masses what is good for them. Furthermore, people do not participate in leisure *en masse*. There is an enormous variety of subcultural groups pursuing their own leisure pursuits, from trainspotters to bungee jumpers and from scuba divers to stamp collectors.

3   Scraton and Bramham also draw on the work of
    Giddens. Although Giddens prefers the concept of
    high modernity to postmodernity (see Chapter 15),
    Scraton and Bramham believe that Giddens's
    theories are similar to those of postmodernists. To
    Giddens (1991), lifestyle becomes increasingly
    important in modern societies. Giddens defines
    lifestyles as involving the creation of a sense of
    identity rather than meeting utilitarian needs, such
    as needs for food, housing, a regular income and so
    on. Leisure becomes an expression of the pursuit of
    a particular lifestyle. Leisure becomes playful, a
    means to express who you are, rather than the
    pursuit of self-improvement or relaxation. Scraton
    and Bramham say, 'The importance of rational
    recreation, games and team spirit, fair play and
    traditional sporting values are undermined by
    individualism, privatisation and commercialism.'
    People's identities become more wrapped up in the
    sort of consumer goods they consume and their
    choice of pastimes, rather than in their jobs, their
    families or their community.

4   If modernity led to an increasingly clear distinction
    between work and leisure, postmodernity has the
    opposite effect. Work increasingly intrudes into
    home life through such technology as the laptop
    computer, mobile phones and fax machines. At the
    same time, work sometimes becomes an extension of
    leisure activities. In addition to the points made by
    Scraton and Bramham, it can also be argued that
    people increasingly use their leisure interests to set
    up businesses or to choose careers.

    More and more of the economy becomes devoted to
    the provision of leisure services. Jobs such as being a
    holiday rep, working in a bar or working in the
    music or entertainments industries can allow
    individuals to have fun at work and to treat work as
    an extension of their leisure.

    Scraton and Bramham illustrate these sorts of
    changes with the example of swimming pools.
    Swimming in Victorian public baths was a serious
    activity designed to provide physical education for
    the masses. Now:

    *swimming has been transformed into water-based
    fun in leisure pools, with water chutes, slides,
    wave machines, inflatables, fountains, popular
    music, aqua-rhythm classes [aerobics in the pool]
    with laser lights, stylish swimming costumes,
    casually overviewed by spectators in tropicana
    restaurants, grazing on fast-foods, whilst drinking
    diet-cokes.*

    Scraton and Bramham, 1995, p. 22

5   Postmodern leisure also involves an increased
    concern with the body. While the rational leisure of
    modernity was concerned with bodily health and
    fitness, postmodern leisure associates this with the
    individual's pursuit of particular lifestyles and
    identities. Scraton and Bramham argue that 'working
    out' on multi-gyms, exercise bikes and similar

devices is 'all part of the postmodern quest to
develop a distinctive lifestyle, desired body shape
and social identity. Appearance and image are all.'

Drawing on the work of Featherstone (1991), Scraton
and Bramham note the role of homeopaths, doctors,
aerobics instructors and the like in advising people
on how to achieve their desired body image and
lifestyle.

6   Another aspect of postmodern leisure is the way in
    which it draws upon the sort of simulations or
    simulacra discussed by the postmodern writer
    Baudrillard (1983). To Baudrillard, simulacra are
    representations of things that do not exist (see
    Chapter 15). Simulacra include theme parks such as
    Disneyworld which represent invented, media
    characters and places. In postmodern leisure, people
    increasingly seek simulated experiences, for example
    in video or virtual reality machines.

    Nostalgia for the past also becomes an increasingly
    important part of people's leisure because people
    have lost the faith in the future that was
    characteristic of modernity. The heritage industry
    becomes increasingly important and more people visit
    places that purport to recreate the past. An example
    is the Jorvik centre in York, which claims to reproduce
    the sights, sounds and even smells of the Vikings.

John Urry – *The Tourist Gaze*

The nature of tourism

Scraton and Bramham's discussion of theme parks
and the heritage industry draws, in part, on the
work of John Urry (1990) on tourism. Urry does not
see postmodernism as involving a shift to a
completely new type of society, nor does he see it as
something that affects all aspects of society to the
same extent. For example, he relates changes in the
economy more to the idea of post-Fordism than to
postmodernism.

Urry sees postmodernism as a trend confined to
some aspects of society's culture. There is no sharp
break between modernism and postmodernism, with
elements of postmodernism present in previous eras.
Nevertheless, he does claim that there are distinctive
emerging trends in the culture of tourism which can
legitimately be identified as postmodern.

Both in modern and postmodern culture, tourism
has always had some distinctive features. In particular, it involves people travelling to look at or gaze
at a place away from their normal places of residence
and work. Tourism involves a temporary stay away
from one's places of work and residence, with the
intention of returning home after a short period.

In modern culture there is a fairly sharp distinction between work and tourism, just as such societies
distinguish sharply between work and leisure in
general. Tourism is a type of economic activity, but it
contains elements that are different from the normal

purchase of goods and services. Tourists do purchase goods (such as meals), and pay for a variety of services, but these are not the central reasons for being a tourist.

The essence of being a tourist is to gaze upon something 'because there is an anticipation, especially through daydreaming and fantasy, of intense pleasures, either on a different scale or involving different senses to those customarily encountered' (Urry, 1990). Tourists are particularly keen to gaze on things that are out of the ordinary, and they often try to capture the gaze on film, video or a postcard.

Tourism is largely, then, about the consumption of signs, or images that represent something else. These images are socially constructed and are shaped to a considerable extent by mass media and their portrayal of different sights. Thus literature, films, TV and so on represent places in particular ways which give them a meaning for tourists. Urry gives the following examples:

> When tourists see two people kissing in Paris what they capture in the gaze is 'timeless romantic Paris'. When a small village in England is seen, what they gaze upon is the 'real olde England'.

Urry, 1990, p. 3

The consumption of signs and images is particularly characteristic of postmodern culture. Indeed, Scott Lash and John Urry (1994) have written of a general movement towards the increased importance of signs in the economy. In this sense, tourism has in a way anticipated the emergence of postmodern culture long before it developed in most other areas of social life.

While all tourists are seeking 'the gaze' that does not mean that all tourists are alike. First, they can be seeking different types of gaze. Second, the nature of tourism has changed somewhat, with a move from predominantly modern types of tourism towards postmodern or 'post-tourism'.

Types of gaze and tourist experience

Urry distinguishes between the collective gaze and the romantic gaze:

1   In the collective gaze the presence of large numbers of people is part of the tourist experience. If other people were not there, the experience would be deemed less satisfactory and less enjoyable. In the collective gaze, 'Other people give atmosphere or a sense of carnival to a place' (Urry, 1990). Examples include British seaside resorts and cosmopolitan cities, where the other people are part of the attraction.

2   The romantic gaze, on the other hand, requires an absence of other people, particularly other tourists. Urry says, 'the emphasis is upon solitude, privacy and

a personal, semi-spiritual relationship with the object of the gaze'. Tourists looking for an authentic wilderness or wishing to experience the beauty of a mountain scene have no wish to have their gaze disrupted by the presence of hordes of other tourists.

Changes in tourism

Having discussed the nature of different types of tourism, Urry identifies a number of changes that are characteristic of a shift away from modern types of tourism towards postmodern types. He sometimes refers to those who prefer postmodern tourism as post-tourists.

1   First, there is a shift away from the collective gaze of modern tourism towards the romantic gaze of postmodern tourism. Modern tourism developed as a mass-market product. In the British seaside resorts that developed after the Industrial Revolution, the urban working classes were taken en masse to places such as Blackpool, Morecambe, Brighton and Southend. Later, with the development of cheap air travel and the package holiday, the collective gaze was typical of the experience of tourists going to the Spanish costas and many other southern European resorts.

Increasingly, however, tourists wish to escape from the collective tourist gaze. This is particularly true of the service class: that growing class of professionals and managers who work in services rather than manufacturing industry. This group seeks to differentiate itself from the mass of people by avoiding consuming mass-market products. They prefer products that are seen as 'natural'. Such products include:

> health foods, real ale, real bread, vegetarianism, nouvelle cuisine, traditional, non-western science and medicine, natural childbirth, wool, lace and cotton rather than man-made fibres, antiques rather than 'man-made' reproductions, restored houses/warehouses, jogging, swimming, cycling, mountaineering, and fell-walking rather than organised, contrived leisure.

Urry, 1990, pp. 94–5

Part of this reaction against the modern involves a search for the authentic. In terms of holidays it involves trying to get away from the tourist masses to experience a place as it really is. If there are too many tourists the place being visited will simply become another tourist destination; it will change its character because of the presence of the tourists.

Thus the postmodern tourist will seek out the 'real Spain' of rural villages visited by few tourists rather than the mass-market resorts on the coast. The postmodern tourist wants to engage in the romantic gaze in obscure destinations like Syria or Bolivia. Specialist holiday companies and companies which arrange independent travel become increasingly important with the advent of postmodern tourism. Even the bigger companies that run package tours have set up subsidiaries to provide holidays that cater for more individual tastes.

2 Postmodern tourism involves a particular attraction to the countryside. The countryside is seen as attractive because it is perceived as getting away from the artificial, planned nature of towns and cities. Urry says it is 'thought to embody some or all of the following features: a lack of planning and regimentation, a vernacular quaint architecture, winding lanes and a generally labyrinthine road system, and the virtues of tradition and the lack of social intervention.'

To Urry, many of the supposed characteristics of the countryside are myths. In Britain, for example, much of the countryside has been very much shaped by human intervention in the form of agriculture. It is very difficult to actually gaze upon the 'unspoilt' countryside, with the prevalence of motorways, concrete farm buildings, farm machinery and so on. Nevertheless, this is not what tourists see when they gaze upon the countryside – their gaze is selective. Such tourists are particularly keen to visit ordinary parts of the countryside and try to avoid country attractions developed to cater for tourists.

3 Postmodern tourists do not just try to retreat from modernity by going to the countryside, they also look back to the past. According to Urry, there has been an enormous expansion of the heritage industry. Urry calculated that in 1990 there were already 464 museums that included industrial material, and 817 museums relating to rural history in the UK.

Postmodern heritage tourists are not just interested in great monuments and historic houses but also in sites relating to the everyday life of the past. Again, there is a search for the authentic, real life of people in the past. There is an interest in the mundane and everyday. Nearly anything can be seen as suitable for the tourist gaze. Places with little apparent tourist appeal, such as Wigan and Bradford, have developed their own heritage attractions and tourist industries.

Urry sees these developments as relating to a nostalgic interest in the past, particularly in people's past working lives, which have changed or disappeared as a result of the rapid deindustrialization of Britain in the 1970s and 1980s. Suddenly, much of manufacturing industry became history.

However, Urry also sees the changes as being part of postmodernism's tendency to break down boundaries 'particularly between the frontstage and backstage of people's lives'. People become interested not only in the public life of kings, queens, politicians and so on, but also in the family and working lives of ordinary people.

4 Urry argues that in a postmodern culture tourism becomes less differentiated from other aspects of life. Following the claims of Scott Lash (1990), Urry believes that modernity is characterized by differentiation whereas postmodernity is characterized by dedifferentiation.

In modern societies and modern culture, spheres of life such as work and leisure, tourist and non-tourist activities are sharply differentiated. In pre-modern and pre-industrial societies, work, leisure and family life were intermingled. In modern industrial societies, where people increasingly worked outside the home for set hours, these different spheres became more easily distinguishable.

In postmodernism, though, the situation changes. In terms of leisure and tourism there is a dedifferentiation of the distinction between 'the cultural object and the audience so that there is an active encouragement of audience participation. Examples include the "living theatre" and the development of game shows on TV where "anybody can be a star for five minutes"' (Urry, 1990).

There is also a weakening in the distinction between high and low culture, so that even advertising images come to be seen as art. In terms of tourism, 'Almost everywhere has become a centre of "spectacle and display"'. It therefore becomes difficult to escape from tourist sites, and people constantly encounter tourist attractions whilst going about their everyday domestic and work lives.

Furthermore, more distant objects of the tourist gaze – for example, for Europeans, the Taj Mahal – become familiar through the media. With a multitude of TV channels and media available, it becomes easy to access representations of objects that are subject to the tourist gaze.

5 Although an important part of postmodern tourism is the search for the authentic, there is also an important element of playfulness about much of it. Sometimes there is an awareness that the search for true authenticity has become problematic. On occasions, postmodern tourists even enjoy the lack of authenticity of an object. For example, Urry says 'When the miniature replica of the Eiffel Tower is purchased, it can be simultaneously enjoyed as a piece of kitsch, an exercise in geometric formalism and as a socially revealing artefact.'

The postmodern tourist is aware that many supposedly authentic experiences (for example, folk dances) are simply staged for tourists and may bear little resemblance to dances that take place when tourists are absent. Sometimes postmodern tourists enjoy tourist sites and tourist events precisely because they are the sorts of things that tourists are not supposed to enjoy. Urry gives examples such as tours of Sydney which are designed to be 'boring', and the Leprosy Museum in Bergen. Urry asks, 'It is an interesting question whether it is in fact possible to construct a postmodern tourist site around absolutely any object.'

Urry does not conclude that the modern tourist and the collective gaze have disappeared. Many people still enjoy package holidays to mass-market destinations. But he does believe that there has been a trend away from these types of tourism towards more postmodern types.

Sheila Scraton and Peter Bramham – an evaluation of postmodern theories of leisure and tourism

Scraton and Bramham are happy to acknowledge that many of the changes described by postmodern theories of tourism and leisure have taken place. However, they argue that these changes affect some groups more than others. In particular, postmodern leisure and tourist practices are largely the preserve of more affluent members of society.

Many people do not enjoy the choices which postmodern theories suggest are available to everybody. Many do not have the time or the money to engage in playful, postmodern pursuits. For example, Scraton and Bramham deny that shopping can always be seen as providing the opportunity to construct a personal identity through making elaborate lifestyle choices. They say:

For many women shopping remains functionally about trying to feed and clothe a family on a restricted income. It takes place in local shops, markets and Oxfam and the transport costs alone constrain any choice there may be to enter the bright lights of the shopping mall.

Scraton and Bramham, 1995, p. 29

The types of leisure activities people engage in are not just restricted by lack of resources. Leisure remains gendered. They point out that video games and virtual reality technology are mostly enjoyed by men, and most games involve aggression and violence. Sex tourism to countries like Thailand is almost exclusively male-orientated, although it is young women who are exploited through it.

Racism is another important feature of society that restricts leisure choices. Scraton and Bramham quote research which suggests that racism is endemic in many sports, making it difficult for ethnic-minority men and women to fulfil their potential. Scraton and Bramham therefore conclude that:

By focusing on pleasures, fantasies and pastiche, postmodernism neglects many people's lives which remain influenced by their experiences of poverty, gender and racism. This is political and social reality and if we are to study and understand leisure in times of change we must explore postmodern leisure but without losing sight of persistent social inequalities.

Scraton and Bramham, 1995, p. 34

Sociology, values and work and leisure

As with every topic in sociology, it is not possible to be objective and neutral about subjects such as work, unemployment and leisure. Throughout this chapter it is apparent that the range of views presented owes much to the values and ideology of particular sociologists. At times this is obvious – for example, with Marx's passionate condemnation of work in capitalist society; at others it is less apparent – for example, with Blauner's relatively restrained analysis of work in the USA.

As with Marxist perspectives in general, Marxist views of work and leisure are based on a radical utopian ideology:

1 It is radical because it looks forward to a fundamental change in the structure of society.

2 It is utopian because it looks forward to an ideal society.

3 It is ideological because, in the last analysis, it is based on a set of values about what people ought to

be, about the nature of human fulfilment and how best it can be realized.

In evaluating and analysing work and leisure in industrial society, Marxists use their picture of the communist utopia as a point of reference, as a standard of comparison. Since work and leisure in industrial society fall far short of this ideal, Marxist views are openly critical.

However, their ideological content should not lead to the outright dismissal of such views. Marx's concept of alienation has been one of the most stimulating and productive ideas in sociology. Ideology can produce important insights. Richard Hyman's interpretation of industrial conflict in capitalist society is strongly influenced by a commitment to an egalitarian society organized on lines similar to those outlined by Marx (Hyman, 1984). It provides an important balance to the more orthodox functionalist view.

It can be argued that sometimes ideology intrudes too far into analysis.

In *Alienation and Freedom*, Robert Blauner (1964) stated that he studied work 'from the viewpoint of the intellectual observer with his own values and conceptions of freedom and self-realization'. His viewpoint can be seen as an expression of American liberalism. He was largely uncritical of the structure of capitalist society and, by implication, accepted it as just and fundamentally sound. His proposals for change are based on liberal ideology in that they involve reform rather than radical change.

The changes in production technology which he advocated to improve the quality of work can take place within the existing framework of industrial society. Blauner's liberal views tended to focus his attention on the workplace rather than the wider society.

Whether their views are radical or liberal, many sociologists regard work in industrial society as largely unfulfilling. In particular, they have tended to contrast the independent, creative, presumably fulfilled craft workers of pre-industrial days with the factory worker in industrial society. The 'alienated' factory worker suffers by comparison.

Robert Blauner argued that this comparison is based on a romanticized picture of craft work and an idealization of pre-industrial society in general. He noted that less than 10 per cent of the medieval labour force was made up of craft workers, whereas the vast majority of workers were peasants engaged in monotonous drudgery. Blauner argued that an idealized view of the past is partly responsible for the concept of the alienated worker in modern industrial society.

If pre-industrial work was idealized in some of the early sociology of work, leisure is more likely to be idealized today. Some postmodernists portray leisure as an area in which people can exercise freedom, choice and self-expression. According to such accounts, it is through leisure that people can construct almost any identity they choose. In contemporary societies people choose from a multitude of leisure activities and even shopping is portrayed as a means of self-fulfilment by some sociologists.

It can be argued that such views are more than a little influenced by the values of a consumer society which encourages everyone to purchase as many consumer goods as they can. Some postmodern views of leisure could therefore be seen as reflecting the interests and values of capitalist corporations, which benefit from such a consumer culture. Scraton and Bramham (1995) therefore add some balance to the discussion of leisure by reminding postmodern sociologists that some people's opportunities to consume are restricted by poverty, racism and gender differences.

Like any areas of social life, work, unemployment and leisure can look very different when approached from different theoretical perspectives which focus on different facets of society.

Education

Education

Introduction

In its broadest sense, education is simply one aspect of socialization: it involves the acquisition of knowledge and the learning of skills. Whether intentionally or unintentionally, education often also helps to shape beliefs and moral values.

In small-scale non-literate societies, such as hunting and gathering bands, education was hard to distinguish from other aspects of life. Young people learned their 'lessons' largely by joining in the social group. Knowledge and skills were usually learned informally by imitating examples provided by adults. Although adults sometimes instructed their young, they did so as part of their daily routine. Thus boys accompanied their fathers on hunting trips, while girls assisted their mothers with cooking and gathering vegetables.

In more complex pre-industrial societies, such as those of medieval Europe, specialized educational institutions slowly developed, along with the specialized role of the teacher. However, such developments provided formal education for only a small minority of the population, such as future members of the clergy and the sons of the wealthy. Formal education for the masses was not provided until industrialization was well under way.

The expansion of British education

In Britain, free compulsory education conducted in formal institutions staffed by full-time professionals began in 1870. Although the state had contributed to the provision of education as early as 1833, only with Forster's Education Act of 1870 did it assume full responsibility. In 1880 school attendance was made compulsory up to the age of 10. With the Fisher Education Act of 1918 the state became responsible for secondary education, and attendance was made compulsory up to the age of 14. The school-leaving age was raised to 15 in 1947, and to 16 in 1972.

The raising of the school-leaving age was obviously accompanied by an expansion of schooling. For most of the twentieth century, though,

education also expanded as a result of people continuing in education after the compulsory period of attendance, or returning to education later in life. In 1900 only 1.2 per cent of 18-year-olds entered full-time further or higher education; by 1938 the figure had reached 5.8 per cent.

However, the first explosion of post-compulsory education came in the 1950s, 1960s and early 1970s. The *Robbins Report* of 1963 established the principle that all those capable of benefiting from higher education should be entitled to it. New universities were built, polytechnics were established, and the Open University gave adults fresh educational opportunities. Children of school-leaving age were encouraged to stay on in school sixth forms, or to attend college. By 1990, 36 per cent of 16–18-year-olds were in full-time education in Britain.

The growth in higher education slowed down in the late 1970s and early 1980s, but rapid growth resumed in the late 1980s and early 1990s. Most existing universities expanded, as did the polytechnics which were given university status in 1993.

Table 11.1 indicates that in 1997 expenditure on education amounted to the vast sum of £36 billion – more than 10 per cent of all government expenditure.

Educational policy in Britain

In the post-war period there have been a number of key concerns in British educational policy:

1　There has been a concern with widening access to and participation in education. In terms of secondary education this was a particular concern in the immediate post-war period, and, as we have seen, this was reflected in the gradual raising of the school-leaving age. From the 1960s the main focus of attention on widening participation switched to higher education, while in the late 1990s more attention was focused on further education.

2　A second area of concern has been promoting equality of opportunity. The Labour governments of the 1960s and 1970s adopted some policies that were designed to reduce class differences in educational attainment. In particular they introduced comprehensive education. Comprehensive schools replaced the tripartite system, under which children

Table 11.1 Expenditure of government in real terms, by function, 1987–97

United Kingdom	£ billion at 1997 prices[1]				
	1987	1991	1995	1996	1997
Social protection	96	109	133	132	131
Health	33	37	43	44	44
Education	31	33	36	36	36
Defence	30	30	24	24	23
Public order and safety	12	15	17	16	16
General public services	9	13	16	16	15
Housing and community amenities	11	11	9	7	6
Recreation, culture and religion	4	5	5	4	4
Other economic affairs and environmental protection[2]	24	26	28	28	24
Gross debt interest	30	22	28	29	30
All expenditure	280	301	338	335	331

1 Adjusted to 1997 prices using the GDP market prices deflator.
2 Includes expenditure on transport and communication, agriculture, forestry and fishing, mining, manufacture, construction, fuel and energy and services.

Source: *Social Trends* (1999) Office for National Statistics, London, p. 116.

were sent to different types of school according to their supposed aptitude at the age of 11. Many children sat an intelligence test, the eleven-plus, which was supposed to distinguish the academically able (who went to grammar schools) from those with a more practical orientation (who went to secondary moderns). A small minority went to technical schools designed to cater for those with technical abilities.

Where comprehensives were introduced, the three-tier system was replaced by single schools which catered for all the state-educated children in a particular area. The intention was to ensure that all children received the same opportunities because they were attending the same type of school. The old divisions between predominantly middle-class grammar schools and working-class secondary moderns would disappear.

Comprehensive schools were only introduced gradually and never became universal. By the 1980s some critics argued that comprehensives were failing to eradicate class differences in educational achievement. Others argued that the introduction of comprehensives had failed to tackle non-class sources of unequal educational opportunities. In particular, it had failed, on its own, to do anything to reduce gender and ethnic differences in educational opportunities. In the last two decades of the twentieth century more attention was focused on these sources of educational inequality than on class. However, these issues were tackled on a more piecemeal basis than class inequalities had been.

The election of a Conservative government in 1979 represented something of a turning point in British educational policy. Even before the election some Labour politicians were beginning to move away from an emphasis on equality of opportunity. However, the New Right ideas of Margaret Thatcher and some of her colleagues shifted the focus of educational policy firmly towards the issues of standards, vocational training and choice.

The government argued that too much attention had been paid to promoting equality of opportunity, and not enough to improving educational standards. From this point of view, the education system would be successful if it raised overall levels of achievement, rather than reduced inequalities in achievement. This would be accomplished by introducing greater competition into the education system, which in turn would be achieved by giving parents and students greater choice. By exercising their choices the consumers of educational services would ensure that successful institutions thrived, while those that were failing their customers would be forced to improve or risk going out of business.

Competition would also cut costs by making schools, colleges and universities more efficient. At the same time, the Conservative government wanted to ensure that education met the needs of employers. They reasoned that Britain's economic success depended upon having a workforce with the sort of education and skills that were necessary to compete effectively with other capitalist nations. To this end, a renewed emphasis was placed upon basic skills (such as maths and English) in the school system, and upon job-related or vocational education. These sorts of policies came to be known as the new vocationalism.

The election of a Labour government in 1997 did not lead to a reversal of the policy aims introduced by Conservative administrations. The emphasis on standards and vocational training remained, although the new government did show less faith in competition in the education system than its Conservative predecessors. There was also renewed concern for issues relating to equality of opportunity. There was therefore a mixture of continuity with the policies introduced under Margaret Thatcher and John Major, and a return to some of the policy objectives of previous Labour administrations.

The British educational system

The numerous changes in educational policy have left a complicated and diverse education system, which varies from locality to locality. Both Northern Ireland and Scotland have their own education systems which are significantly different to those in England and Wales. In Northern Ireland the eleven-plus and grammar schools have been retained in most areas.

Scotland has its own exams, with Scottish Highers being used instead of A levels. In England and Wales there is a bewildering range of educational institutions. Local education authorities have been able to exercise considerable discretion in organizing the local educational system, and in the 1980s and 1990s schools and other institutions gained some rights to choose alternative paths.

Research by Caroline Benn and Clive Chitty (1997) has examined the overall structure of British secondary education. The research is partly based upon government statistics and partly upon their own survey of 1,560 educational institutions. The survey was conducted in 1994 and the research was largely based on questionnaires. Benn and Chitty discussed a number of ways in which the British education system varied from locality to locality:

1 There were variations in terms of the extent to which the system was comprehensive. They estimated that in 1994 over 99 per cent of Scottish and Welsh state secondary schools were comprehensive, compared to 82.9 per cent in England, and none in Northern Ireland.

2 In England in particular there is a wide variety of school types. The percentages of children in these types, in 1994, are shown in Table 11.2. Benn and Chitty found that 9.6 per cent of children were being educated in private schools. These included fee-paying boarding schools (including the most prestigious ones, like Eton), fee-paying day schools, and City Technology Colleges (CTCs) which, though state-funded, are technically private institutions. Some 2.8 per cent were still being educated in secondary modern schools, and 3.6 per cent in selective grammar schools. Selective grant maintained schools (schools which had opted out of local authority control following the 1988 Education Act) accounted for 3.9 per cent of the school population. About 79 per cent of secondary children were being educated in comprehensive schools. A small number of children were attending technical and other schools specializing in particular aspects of the curriculum.

3 Another source of variation results from the existence of voluntary and denominational schools. These schools were originally funded partly from foundation donations or bequests, and in some cases were connected to particular religious denominations. Although such schools are now usually entirely funded by the state, they tend to retain a degree of autonomy – particularly over such matters as finances and criteria for selecting pupils – which most other state-funded schools do not have. Some denominational schools will only allow pupils from their denomination (usually Church of England or Roman Catholic) to attend, while others have more open selection criteria. Some of these schools have become grant maintained (having opted out of local authority control), while others have not. In

1994 about 10 per cent of pupils were being educated in voluntary or denominational schools.

4 Another variation from area to area involves the age ranges educated at particular institutions. In some areas pupils stay in the same secondary school from the age of 11 to the end of the sixth form. An increasing number of schools, however, have no sixth form and 16–19-year-old students are educated in sixth-form, further education or tertiary colleges.

Sixth-form colleges tend to specialize in academic education for 16–19-year-olds; tertiary colleges in a wider range of courses for 16–19-year-olds; while general further education colleges often offer a wide range of academic and vocational courses for adults and 16–19-year-olds alike. In some areas, 16–19-year-olds have a choice of attending a college or a school with a sixth form; in other areas all school sixth forms have been replaced by colleges.

Benn and Chitty found that, in 1994, about 15 per cent of schools were in tiered schemes where children attended primary, middle and upper schools. Middle schools usually cover the ages of 9–13 or 8–12, thus spanning the age range usually attending primary and secondary schools.

5 A final source of diversity concerns gender. Some schools are single-sex, others are mixed. A few schools have a mixed sixth form but are single-sex for those under 16.

Table 11.2 Numbers of children in different types of secondary school in England, 1994		
Type of school	Overall number	Overall percentage
Comprehensive		79.0
Comprehensive secondary	2,399,445	73.9
Middle deemed secondary	161,056	5.0
Selective, non-comprehensive and private		21.0
Grammar	116,193	3.6
Grant maintained selective*	128,214	3.9
Technical	2,198	0.1
Other	35,820	1.0
Modern	90,672	2.8
Private	312,502	9.6
Total	3,246,100	100.0

* GM school numbers are approximate and are based on research estimates that one-third of GM schools are using selective entry methods. All other GM comprehensive schools are included in the comprehensive total.

Source: C. Benn and C. Chitty (1997) *Thirty Years On: Is Comprehensive Education Alive and Well or Struggling to Survive?* Penguin, Harmondsworth, p. 88.

The mix of different school types and proportions being educated in different systems is constantly changing and is affected by government policies. For example, after coming to power in 1997, the Labour government decided to do away with grant maintained status for schools, and to encourage, though not compel, the remaining grammar schools to abandon selection on the grounds of academic ability (see pp. 816–18).

Because the vast majority of pupils attend a school close to their home (boarding pupils are an exception), and because of the diversity of systems from area to area, Britain can be seen as having many local education systems rather than one national system. Thus Ron Glatter, Phillip Woods and Carl Bagley (1997) believe that competition between schools needs to be studied in terms of the 'local competitive arena', rather than in a national context.

Higher education is largely based around independent universities, each of which grants its own degrees and has considerable autonomy, despite being largely reliant upon government funds. However, there are also a range of higher education colleges, some of which specialize in particular areas such as agriculture, teacher training, the arts or technology. Some higher education courses are now taught in further education colleges; and institutions such as the Open University give people the chance to study for higher-level qualifications at home.

However, because so many full-time students move to a new area to take higher education courses, higher education involves competition for students at a national rather than a local level. Indeed there is some international competition, with most British universities making efforts to attract foreign students.

This brief introduction to British educational policy and the British educational system provides some important background to the next few sections which examine different perspectives on education. These perspectives have both influenced and been influenced by the development of educational policies and the education systems in Britain and elsewhere. Educational policies and educational systems will be discussed and evaluated in much greater detail as the chapter develops.

Education – a functionalist perspective

Two related questions have guided functionalist research into education:

1 The first asks 'What are the functions of education for society as a whole?' Given the functionalist view of the needs of the social system, this question leads, for example, to an assessment of the contribution made by education to the maintenance of value consensus and social solidarity.

2 The second question asks 'What are the functional relationships between education and other parts of the social system?' This leads to an examination of the relationship between education and the economic system, and a consideration of how this relationship helps to integrate society as a whole.

As with functionalist analysis in general, the functionalist view of education tends to focus on the positive contributions education makes to the maintenance of the social system.

Emile Durkheim – education and social solidarity

Writing at the turn of the last century, the French sociologist Emile Durkheim saw the major function of education as the transmission of society's norms and values. He maintained:

Society can survive only if there exists among its members a sufficient degree of homogeneity; education perpetuates and reinforces this homogeneity by fixing in the child from the beginning the essential similarities which collective life demands.

Durkheim, 1961, pp. 87–8

Without these 'essential similarities', cooperation, social solidarity, and therefore social life itself would be impossible. A vital task for all societies is the welding of a mass of individuals into a united whole – in other words, the creation of social solidarity. This involves a commitment to society, a sense of belonging, and a feeling that the social unit is more important than the individual. Durkheim argued that 'To become attached to society, the child must feel in it something that is real, alive and powerful, which dominates the person and to which he also owes the best part of himself.'

Education, and in particular the teaching of history, provides this link between the individual and society. If the history of their society is brought alive to children, they will come to see that they are part of something larger than themselves: they will develop a sense of commitment to the social group.

Durkheim's views can be illustrated by educational practices in the USA. There, a common educational curriculum has helped to instil shared norms and values into a population with diverse backgrounds. It has provided a shared language and a common history for immigrants from every country in Europe. The American student learns about the Founding Fathers, about the Constitution, and about Abraham Lincoln, who personifies the American values of equality of opportunity and achievement in his journey from the humble origins of a log cabin to the White House. By beginning their school day with an oath of allegiance to the Stars and Stripes, the symbol of American society, the students are socialized into a commitment to society as a whole.

Education and social rules

Durkheim argued that, in complex industrial societies, the school serves a function which cannot be provided either by the family or the peer group. Membership of the family is based on kinship relationships; membership of the peer group on personal choice. Membership of society as a whole is based on neither of these principles.

Individuals must learn to cooperate with those who are neither their kin nor their friends. The school provides a context where these skills can be learned. As such, it is society in miniature, a model of the social system. In school, the child must interact with other members of the school community in terms of a fixed set of rules. This experience prepares him or her for interacting with members of society as a whole in terms of society's rules.

Durkheim believed that school rules should be strictly enforced. Punishments should reflect the seriousness of the damage done to the social group by the offence, and it should be made clear to transgressors why they were being punished. In this way, pupils would come to learn that it was wrong to act against the interests of the social group as a whole. They would learn to exercise self-discipline, not just because they wanted to avoid punishment, but also because they would come to see that misbehaviour damaged society as a whole. Science, and particularly social sciences like sociology, would help the child to understand the rational basis on which society was organized. Durkheim stated:

> It is by respecting the school rules that the child learns to respect rules in general, that he develops the habit of self-control and restraint simply because he should control and restrain himself. It is a first initiation into the austerity of duty. Serious life has now begun.
>
> Durkheim, 1961, p. 149

Education and the division of labour

Finally, Durkheim argued that education teaches individuals specific skills necessary for their future occupations. This function is particularly important in industrial society with its increasingly complex and specialized division of labour.

The relatively unspecialized division of labour in pre-industrial society meant that occupational skills could usually be passed on from parents to children without the need for formal education. In industrial society, social solidarity is based largely on the interdependence of specialized skills – for example, the manufacture of a single product requires the combination of a variety of specialists. This necessity for combination produces cooperation and social solidarity.

Thus schools transmit both general values, which provide the 'necessary homogeneity for social survival', and specific skills, which provide the 'necessary diversity for social cooperation'. Industrial society is thus united by value consensus and a specialized division of labour whereby specialists combine to produce goods and services.

David Hargreaves – Durkheim and the modern school

Durkheim's views have influenced some modern sociologists and educationalists. David Hargreaves (1982) has criticized the modern comprehensive school from a Durkheimian point of view. He claims that contemporary schools place far too much stress on developing the individual, and not enough on the duties and responsibilities that the individual should have towards group life in the school.

Furthermore, Hargreaves argues that many schools fail to produce a sense of dignity for working-class pupils. If pupils do not achieve individual success in competitive exams, they will tend to rebel and fail to develop a sense of belonging within the school. If the school fails them in not providing a sense of dignity and belonging, pupils may form subcultures which reject the values of the school, and therefore of the wider society. (See p. 848 for a discussion of Hargreaves's work on subcultures.)

According to Hargreaves, these problems can be solved if greater stress is placed upon the social role of the individual pupil within the school. Hargreaves says, 'To acquire dignity a person must achieve a sense of competence, of making a contribution to, and of being valued by, the group to which he or she belongs.' Hargreaves proposes a number of changes to the curriculum in order to create a sense of competence and belonging:

1 He argues that pupils should have some freedom to pursue fields of study in which they have a special

interest or talent. In this way all pupils will develop a sense of their own worth.

2 In addition there should be compulsory parts of the curriculum: community studies would help pupils to have a clear view of their role in society.

3 Expressive arts, crafts and sports should also play a vital role. In putting on plays and taking part in team games like hockey and football, pupils would experience satisfaction by contributing to collective enterprises. They would develop a sense of loyalty to the school, and learn to respect one another for the contribution each could make to the school.

Criticisms of Durkheim

Durkheim's views on education are open to a number of criticisms. As Hargreaves's work suggests, it is far from clear that education in modern Britain succeeds in transmitting shared values, promoting self-discipline, or cementing social solidarity. Durkheim also assumes that the norms and values transmitted by the education system are those of society as a whole, rather than those of a ruling elite or ruling class.

Hargreaves shows more awareness of the existence of a variety of cultures and values in society, and points to some of the limitations of contemporary education. However, Hargreaves's proposals for changes in the curriculum are controversial. Many contemporary changes in education seem designed to encourage individual competition and to train pupils for particular vocations. It could be argued that sport and community studies are not the best subjects to study as a preparation for future working life.

Although Durkheim and Hargreaves both criticize education based upon individual competition in an exam system, other functionalists see competition as a vital aspect of modern education (a view also supported by New Right perspectives, see pp. 794–801). We will now examine their views.

Talcott Parsons – education and universalistic values

The American sociologist Talcott Parsons (1961) outlined what has become the accepted functionalist view of education. Writing in the late 1950s, Parsons argued that, after primary socialization within the family, the school takes over as the focal socializing agency: school acts as a bridge between the family and society as a whole, preparing children for their adult role.

Within the family, the child is judged and treated largely in terms of particularistic standards. Parents treat the child as their particular child rather than judging her or him in terms of standards or yardsticks that can be applied to every individual.

However, in the wider society the individual is treated and judged in terms of universalistic standards, which are applied to all members, regardless of their kinship ties.

Within the family, the child's status is ascribed: it is fixed by birth. However, in advanced industrial society, status in adult life is largely achieved: for example, individuals achieve their occupational status. Thus the child must move from the particularistic standards and ascribed status of the family to the universalistic standards and achieved status of adult society.

The school prepares young people for this transition. It establishes universalistic standards, in terms of which all pupils achieve their status. Their conduct is assessed against the yardstick of the school rules; their achievement is measured by performance in examinations. The same standards are applied to all students regardless of ascribed characteristics such as sex, race, family background or class of origin. Schools operate on meritocratic principles: status is achieved on the basis of merit (or worth).

Like Durkheim, Parsons argued that the school represents society in miniature. Modern industrial society is increasingly based on achievement rather than ascription, on universalistic rather than particularistic standards, on meritocratic principles which apply to all its members. By reflecting the operation of society as a whole, the school prepares young people for their adult roles.

Education and value consensus

As part of this process, schools socialize young people into the basic values of society. Parsons, like many functionalists, maintained that value consensus is essential for society to operate effectively. In American society, schools instil two major values:

1 the value of achievement
2 the value of equality of opportunity

By encouraging students to strive for high levels of academic attainment, and by rewarding those who succeed, schools foster the value of achievement itself. By placing individuals in the same situation in the classroom and so allowing them to compete on equal terms in examinations, schools foster the value of equality of opportunity.

These values have important functions in society as a whole. Advanced industrial society requires a highly motivated, achievement-oriented workforce. This necessitates differential reward for differential achievement, a principle which has been established in schools. Both the winners (the high achievers) and the losers (the low achievers) will see the system as just and fair, since status is achieved in a situation where all have an equal chance. Again, the principles that operate in the wider society are mirrored by those of the school.

Education and selection

Finally, Parsons saw the educational system as an important mechanism for the selection of individuals for their future role in society. In his words, it 'functions to allocate these human resources within the role-structure of adult society'. Thus schools, by testing and evaluating students, match their talents, skills and capacities to the jobs for which they are best suited. The school is therefore seen as the major mechanism for role allocation.

Criticisms of Parsons

Like Durkheim, Parsons fails to give adequate consideration to the possibility that the values transmitted by the educational system may be those of a ruling minority rather than of society as a whole. His view that schools operate on meritocratic principles is open to question – a point which we will examine in detail in later sections.

Kingsley Davis and Wilbert E. Moore – education and role allocation

Like Parsons, Davis and Moore (1967, first published 1945) saw education as a means of role allocation, but they linked the educational system more directly with the system of social stratification. As outlined in Chapter 2, Davis and Moore see social stratification as a mechanism for ensuring that the most talented and able members of society are allocated to those positions that are functionally most important for

society. High rewards, which act as incentives, are attached to those positions. This means, in theory, that all will compete for them and the most talented will win through.

The education system is an important part of this process. In Davis's words, it is the 'proving ground for ability and hence the selective agency for placing people in different statuses according to their capacities'. Thus the education system sifts, sorts and grades individuals in terms of their talents and abilities. It rewards the most talented with high qualifications, which in turn provide entry to those occupations that are functionally most important to society.

Criticisms of Davis and Moore

General criticisms of Davis and Moore's theory have been examined in Chapter 2 (see pp. 28–9). With respect to the relationship between education and social stratification, there are a number of more specific criticisms:

1 The relationship between academic credentials and occupational reward is not particularly close. In particular, income is only weakly linked to educational attainment.

2 There is considerable doubt about the proposition that the educational system grades people in terms of ability. In particular, it has been argued that intelligence has little effect upon educational attainment.

3 There is considerable evidence to suggest that the influence of social stratification largely prevents the educational system from efficiently grading individuals in terms of ability.

We will consider these points in detail later.

Education – a liberal perspective

The liberal view of education is not a sociological perspective as such. Rather it is a view adopted by many educationalists. Unlike functionalism, it focuses on education in relation to the individual rather than society. From this viewpoint, the main purpose of education is held to be the promotion of the well-being of the individual, and only indirectly the improvement of society.

John Dewey – education and human potential

One of the most influential proponents of the liberal view of education was the American educationalist and philosopher, John Dewey (1953).

Dewey argued that it was the job of education to encourage individuals to develop their full potential as human beings. He particularly stressed the development of intellectual potential. Schooling for all would help to foster the physical, emotional and spiritual talents of everyone, as well as their intellectual abilities.

Dewey was critical of the rote learning of facts in schools, and argued for progressive teaching methods. People should learn by experience: by doing things rather than being told. In this way they would not just gain knowledge but would also develop the skills, habits and attitudes necessary for them to solve a wide variety of problems.

Furthermore, individuals would develop the ability and motivation to think critically about the world around them.

For Dewey, and similar educationalists, a progressive education system is a vital part of a successful democracy. Since in a democracy power rests with the people, it is necessary for the people to be able to think for themselves when exercising their power. Liberal education would be incompatible with a dictatorship, where free and critical thought could threaten the authority of the state. Dewey hoped that the education system he proposed would promote flexibility and tolerance, and individuals would be able to cooperate together as equals.

The liberal perspective and educational policies

Some liberals hope that education will help to reduce inequality. By developing the potential that exists within all human beings, the stratification system would become more open. Although liberals acknowledge that there is a need for reform, they believe that, with relatively minor modifications, education can come to play a full and successful role in industrial societies.

Liberal views have influenced a number of educational policies in both the USA and Britain.

In the 1960s in the USA, Lyndon B. Johnson stated, 'The answer to all our national problems comes down to a single word: education' (quoted in Bowles and Gintis, 1976). As a result, specially designed programmes of education for the underprivileged became the keynote of Johnson's war on poverty. However, as Chapter 5 on poverty indicates, there is a wide gap between liberal ideals and what actually happens.

In the 1960s and 1970s Britain saw a movement towards progressive, child-centred education which was based largely upon liberal principles. Each child was held to be unique, and education was designed to foster equally the talents of each unique individual. In 1975, however, William Tyndale, a junior school in Islington, London, hit the headlines when teachers went on strike after the report of a government inspection of the school. Government inquiries and press reports criticized the school for its progressive style of education, arguing that lack of discipline had produced a situation in which children were failing to develop even basic skills in reading, writing and arithmetic.

This episode set the tone for the new vocationalism which developed in the 1980s and remained influential in the 1990s, and which can partly be seen as a reaction against liberal and progressive

education. (For details of the new vocationalism, see pp. 803–5.)

Liberal education has come under attack from Marxist sociologists as well as right-wing politicians. Marxists argue that the liberal view of education tends to ignore the inequalities in society which make liberal ideals impossible to achieve without major social changes.

Ivan Illich – *Deschooling Society*

Illich differs from the conventional liberal approach in that he advocates far more radical changes to the education system. In *Deschooling Society* (1973, first published 1971) he takes liberal views to their logical conclusion by arguing that formal schooling is unnecessary, and indeed harmful to society.

Although Illich was not a sociologist by training or profession – he studied theology and philosophy and spent several years as a Roman Catholic priest in New York – *Deschooling Society* is an important contribution to the sociology of education.

The educational ideal

Illich begins with his views on what education should be. First, there is the learning of specific skills such as typing, woodwork and speaking a foreign language. Next there is education as such, which is not concerned with the acquisition of particular skills. Education should be a liberating experience in which individuals explore, create, use their initiative and judgement and freely develop their faculties and talents to the full.

Illich claims that schools are not particularly effective in teaching skills and, in practice, diametrically opposed to the educational ideals in which he believes. He argues that the teaching of skills is best left to those who use those skills in daily life. He gives the example of Spanish-speaking teenagers in New York, many of whom were high-school dropouts, who were employed to teach Spanish to schoolteachers, social workers and ministers. Within a week they had been trained to use a teaching manual designed for use by linguists with university qualifications; and within six months they had effectively accomplished their task. However, the employment of such 'skill teachers' is largely prevented by a system which demands professionals – that is, officially trained, specialized and certificated teachers.

The educational reality

Illich's main attack is on the failure of schools to match his educational ideals. He regards schools as repressive institutions which indoctrinate pupils, smother creativity and imagination, induce conformity and stultify students into accepting the interests of the powerful. He sees this hidden curriculum operating in the following way:

1 Pupils have little or no control over what they learn or how they learn it. They are simply instructed by an authoritarian teaching regime and, to be successful, must conform to its rules. Real learning, however, is not the result of instruction, but of direct and free involvement by the individual in every part of the learning process. In sum, 'most learning requires no teacher'.

2 The power of the school to enforce conformity to its rules and to coerce its inmates into acceptance of instruction stems from its authority to grant credentials which are believed to bring rewards in the labour market. Those who conform to the rules are selected to go on to higher levels in the educational system. Illich states, 'Schools select for each successive level those who have, at earlier stages of the game, proved themselves good risks for the established order'. Conformity and obedience therefore bring their own rewards.

3 Finally, students emerge from the educational system with a variety of qualifications which they and others believe have provided them with the training, skills and competence for particular occupations. Illich rejects this belief. He argues that 'The pupil is "schooled" to confuse teaching with learning, grade advancement with education, a diploma with competence'.

Education and social problems

Illich sees the educational system as the root of the problems of modern industrial society. Schools are the first, most vital and important stage in the creation of the mindless, conforming and easily manipulated citizen. In schools, individuals learn to defer to authority, to accept alienation, to consume and value the services of the institution, and to forget how to think for themselves. They are taught to see education as a valuable commodity to be consumed in ever-increasing quantities.

These lessons prepare pupils for their role as mindless consumers, to whom the passive consumption of the goods and services of industrial society becomes an end in itself. Responding to advertisements and the directives of the powerful, they invest time, money and energy in obtaining the products of industry. Deferring to the authority of professionals, individuals consume the services of doctors, social workers and lawyers. Trained to accept that those in authority know what is best for them, individuals become dependent on the directives of governments, bureaucratic organizations and professional bodies.

Illich maintains that modern industrial society cannot provide the framework for human happiness and fulfilment. Despite the fact that goods are pouring from the factories in ever-increasing quantities, and despite the fact that armies of professionals provide ever more comprehensive programmes to solve social ills, misery, dissatisfaction and social problems are multiplying. The establishment offers a solution which is at once simple and self-defeating: the consumption of even more goods and services. Illich concludes:

> As long as we are not aware of the ritual through which the school shapes the progressive consumer – the economy's major resource – we cannot break the spell of this economy and shape a new one.
>
> Illich, 1973

Deschooling

Illich proposes a simple yet radical solution. As the title of his book – *Deschooling Society* – suggests, the answer lies in the abolition of the present system of education. Since schools provide the foundation for all that is to follow, deschooling lies 'at the root of any movement for human liberation'.

In place of schools, Illich offers two main alternatives:

1 First, skill exchanges, in which instructors teach to others the skills they use in daily life. Illich argues that skills can best be learned by drills involving systematic instruction.

2 Second, and most important, Illich proposes learning webs, which consist of individuals with similar interests who 'meet around a problem chosen and defined by their own initiative' and who proceed on a basis of 'creative and exploratory learning'.

Illich concludes that deschooling will destroy 'the reproductive organ of a consumer society' and lead to the creation of a society in which people can be truly liberated and fulfilled.

Although in sympathy with much of what Illich says, Marxists such as Bowles and Gintis (1976) argue that Illich has made a fundamental error. Rather than seeing schools as the basis of the problem and their removal as the solution, Bowles and Gintis argue that 'The social problems to which these reforms are addressed have their roots not primarily in the school system itself, but rather in the normal functioning of the economic system.' From their viewpoint, deschooling would only produce 'occupational misfits' and 'job blues', which are hardly sufficient to transform society as a whole. From a Marxist perspective, liberation involves a revolutionary change in the economic infrastructure of society.

Social democratic perspectives on education

The social democratic view on education is not
simply a sociological theory. According to the Centre
for Contemporary Cultural Studies at Birmingham
University (CCCS, 1981), this perspective has been
developed by a number of individual groups. In the
Centre's opinion, social democratic thinking has been
reflected in the work of sociologists such as A.H.
Halsey, economists such as John Vaizey, Labour Party
politicians, and the teaching profession. For most of
the post-war period, British educational policies have
been dominated by this approach.

Equality of opportunity

Social democrats accept the basic institutions of
parliamentary democracies such as Britain, but argue
that state intervention is necessary to reduce inequalities produced by the free-market economy. They
disagree with functionalists that education provides
genuine equality of opportunity.

Halsey believes that education fails to offer the
same opportunities to lower social classes as it does
to higher classes. Halsey's work, which we will
examine in detail later in the chapter (see pp. 842–3),
indicates that the children of parents with the least
material resources tend to be found disproportionately among the 'failures' of the education system.

A.H. Halsey, Jean Floud and C. Anderson (1961)
were highly critical of the tripartite system of
education introduced in 1944. As mentioned earlier
in the chapter, under this system children attended
three types of school: grammar schools (for the
academically able), technical schools (for those seen
as having specifically technical abilities) and
secondary moderns (for the less academically able).
Selection procedures were partly based on an intelligence test, the eleven-plus. The majority of children
went to secondary modern schools. Halsey et al.
claimed that in these schools children failed to
develop their potential, and this meant that Britain
increasingly lacked the highly educated and trained
workforce that a modern industrial society requires.

From this point of view, the education system was
not just failing to provide equality of opportunity, it
was failing to develop the potential of individuals.
Social democratic perspectives suggest that the liberal
ideal of individual development is compatible with
the aim of social justice, but in the post-war period
neither was being achieved.

Some social democratic theorists argued that
education could actually create greater equality, as
well as promoting equality of opportunity, if the
system were run properly. In his book *The Future of*

Socialism, the Labour Party politician Anthony
Crosland (1981) argued that a fairer education
system would also 'equalise the distribution of
rewards and privileges so as to diminish the degree
of class stratification'. If educational success or
failure no longer depended upon class background,
then the amount of social mobility would increase to
the extent that class distinctions would become
progressively blurred.

Economic growth

Social democratic perspectives also seemed to offer
another advantage to parliamentary democracies. By
making societies more meritocratic, and ensuring that
everyone could develop their potential, each
individual would be able to make the maximum
possible contribution to society. In doing so they
would encourage economic growth which would
bring prosperity to all.

This point of view was most clearly stated by the
American economist Theodore W. Shultz (1961). He
argued that skills and knowledge were forms of
capital. Capital investment in humans could have the
same effects as capital investments in machinery. If
more were spent on education, the productivity and
efficiency of the workforce would increase, and the
extra money spent would soon be repaid by the extra
contribution made to the economy. Shultz claimed
that his theory could be illustrated by American
agriculture, where farms with a less educated
workforce were not as productive as those with a
more educated workforce.

Many of the policies of British governments since
the Second World War appear to have followed the
path outlined by social democratic theory. As we
indicated in the introduction to this chapter, in the
decades leading up to the 1980s expenditure on
education rose substantially. The raising of the
school-leaving age and the expansion of higher
education were designed both to expand opportunities and to ensure a more skilled workforce.

The tripartite system of 1944 was originally
intended to provide more opportunities for all social
classes. However, social democratic critics argued that
this system was wasting talent in secondary modern
schools, and this was one of the reasons why Labour
governments progressively introduced comprehensive
schools. Other measures, such as compensatory
education and Educational Priority Areas, were
intended to assist working-class pupils who might be
disadvantaged by their home background. (For
further details, see p. 835.)

More recently, under Tony Blair's Labour government, a range of new policies have been introduced, which seem very much in line with social democratic thinking, although they can also be seen as related to a 'post-Fordist' perspective on education (see pp. 813–16). New measures have been introduced to make it easier to get rid of selective education and grammar schools. By October 1998, 161 grammar schools remained (quoted in *The Independent*, 22 October 1998). In 1998 the government introduced measures allowing a parental ballot over the replacement of selective education with comprehensive education where 20 per cent of parents in an area signed a petition calling for a ballot.

Other measures included extra money for inner-city schools to set up computer learning centres (announced in the 1999 Budget), and Education Action Zones which would provide extra resources for education in certain deprived areas. (These and other 'New Labour' policies are examined on pp. 816–18.)

Functionalist theories of education had suggested that education was already fulfilling the functions required of it. Social democratic theories acknowledged the limitations of education, but held up the vision of a much improved society that could result if the deficiencies of education were recognized and put right. It was claimed that education could help individuals achieve their potential, provide equality of opportunity, and produce a more egalitarian and prosperous society.

However, in the 1970s and 1980s, the hostility of some pupils to school, the continuing differences in educational achievement between classes, and economic recession, all raised serious doubts about the validity of the social democratic perspective. Numerous criticisms were advanced.

Criticisms and evaluation of social democratic theory

Equality of opportunity

First, even social democratic theorists themselves began to realize the limited inroads that had been made into reducing inequality of opportunity. In their book *Origins and Destinations*, A.H. Halsey, A. Heath and J.M. Ridge (1980) found little evidence of increasing equality of opportunity (at least amongst males, to whom their study was confined), despite the changes that had been made to the education system (see pp. 822–3). Recent studies confirm that great inequalities in educational achievement remain between social classes. As Marxist theories became more prominent in the sociology of education, it was argued that education could not possibly compensate for the inequalities in society as a whole.

Economic growth

A second type of criticism raised questions about the effectiveness of education in promoting economic growth.

In 1976, in a speech at Ruskin College, the Labour prime minister James Callaghan initiated what became known as the 'Great Debate' on education. He claimed that education was failing to meet the needs of industry.

With the election in 1979 of Margaret Thatcher's Conservative government, the political criticisms became stronger. New Right thinkers who influenced Conservative policies argued that the emphasis on equality of opportunity and on liberal ideals of developing individuals' potential were reducing educational standards. Comprehensives were believed to be holding back the most talented and contributing to the reduction in standards.

Furthermore, the New Right believed that the curriculum was not directed towards the skills required by employers. Far from promoting industrial growth, excessive expenditure on education was thought to be putting industry at a disadvantage. Profits from industry were not being reinvested in industry, but instead were wasted on an inefficient education system.

These views were reflected in a number of changes in education which we will examine later in the chapter (see pp. 801–6).

Workforce skills

A further area of criticism raises questions about the educational requirements of the workforce in advanced industrial societies. As Chapter 10 shows, sociologists over recent years have debated whether work has been reskilled or deskilled in advanced industrial societies (see pp. 707–11). If it has become deskilled (if the workforce requires less training), it is difficult to attribute the growth of education to the needs of the economy. Furthermore, there is doubt about the extent to which formal education is necessary for training the workforce.

From an examination of studies analysing the relationship between education and the economy, Randall Collins (1972) concluded that only a minor part of the expansion of education in advanced industrial societies can be seen as directly serving the demands of industry for skills, training and knowledge. Writing about American society, Collins claimed that only 15 per cent of the increase in education of the US labour force during the twentieth century could be attributed to shifts in the occupational structure – a decrease in the proportion of jobs with low-skill requirements and an increase in the proportion of jobs with high-skill requirements.

However, it could be argued that the *same* jobs have greater skill and knowledge requirements as industrial society develops. For example, plumbers, clerks, doctors and managers today may require greater expertise and technical skills than they did at the turn of the last century. Again Collins doubts that the rapid expansion of education is primarily a response to these requirements. He argues, 'It appears that the educational level of the US labour force has changed in excess of that which is necessary to keep up with the skills requirements of jobs.' Collins concludes that the contribution of education to the economic system in advanced industrial societies has been exaggerated.

Collins reaches the following conclusions about the relationship between education and the economy:

1 Studies from various countries suggest that, once mass literacy has been achieved, education does not significantly affect economic development.

2 Most occupational skills are learned 'on the job', and, where specific training is required, firms provide their own apprenticeship and training schemes.

3 Higher education for particular professions such as medicine, engineering and law may be considered 'vocationally relevant and possibly essential'. However, much higher education – for example, schools of business administration – represents an attempt to achieve 'professionalization'. As such, education serves to raise the status of the occupation, rather than to transmit the knowledge and skills necessary for its performance.

Collins's conclusions are controversial, and some sociologists believe that education is becoming increasingly important in advanced industrial economies. Writing in 1990, M. White (1990) claimed that learning specific vocational skills was becoming less important for economic growth, but high levels of general education were becoming more important. In a rapidly changing economy, 'versatile and adaptable people capable of continuing to learn' were essential. Only with a good education would individuals be 'sufficiently flexible to respond to the opportunities, and cope with the hazards' of the future.

Post-Fordism and education

White's views are similar to those of some sociologists who argue that fundamental changes in the nature of the world's economy have resulted in education becoming increasingly important for producing economic success. Phillip Brown, A.H. Halsey, Hugh Lauder and Amy Wells (1997) have described a 'new consensus' among educationalists and sociologists that there is an increasingly global economy in which the general educational standards of a nation's population are vital to

economic success. According to this view (which Brown *et al.* describe rather than advocate), since the 1970s economic globalization has taken place (see Chapter 9 for a discussion of globalization). Nation-states cannot control or limit economic competition by restricting imports to protect domestic businesses. If businesses are to succeed, they need to compete effectively with foreign companies by producing goods and services which are better than those of competitors.

The biggest contribution that governments can make to economic success is to ensure that the workforce have high levels of educational qualifications. Specific vocational qualifications are less important than developing intellectual ability, because of the rapidly changing nature of the global economy. Workers need to be flexible enough to change the work they do in response to global competition and changes in the demand for particular goods or services. Businesses and their workers have to adapt to new opportunities as they arise and cannot rely upon doing the same sort of work throughout their working lives. Brown *et al.* say that 'there is now widespread agreement that a high-quality general education is more appropriate to conditions of rapid technological change than a narrowly specialized vocational education'.

Brown *et al.* admit, though, that there are a variety of views on whether specific vocational education is important as well as raising the general level of education in the population. There are also differences between the advocates of what Phillip Brown and Hugh Lauder call 'neo-Fordist' and 'post-Fordist' approaches to education in a global economy (see pp. 797–8 and 813–16). In particular, some 'neo-Fordists' are opposed to the social democratic view that increased spending on education will lead to economic prosperity. Nevertheless, most sociologists do accept that education has some bearing on the economic success or failure of nations in a world which many see as increasingly globalized.

Globalization, the economy and education

Some advocates of the theory of globalization agree with social democratic theories that education is crucial to economic growth. However, from their point of view, it may be difficult to combine policies designed to achieve economic growth with those designed to promote equality of opportunity. This is because workers are not just competing with other workers in their own country for high-status and highly-paid jobs; they are also competing with workers in other countries.

An example of this sort of view is provided by Robert B. Reich (1997, first published 1991). He claims that 'national borders no longer define our economic fates'. Individuals therefore compete with other individuals throughout the world for the best jobs. Those who are successful can reap immense rewards, while those who lack the skills that are in demand can find that their work has little value in the global labour market. This leads to a polarization of income between the rich and the poor. Many routine jobs in manufacturing have been lost in the richer capitalist countries and have shifted to developing nations. This is because wages are so much lower in the latter than the former. In countries such as the Philippines and the Dominican Republic workers can be paid a fraction of what they would be paid in the USA.

However, one group, which Reich calls 'symbolic analysts', have been particularly successful in the global economy. Symbolic analysts include researchers, management consultants, public relations experts, political consultants, film producers, scriptwriters and so on. What they have in common is that they 'manipulate oral and visual symbols' – an increasingly important role in a world in which communications and transport have developed so rapidly. From this point of view, educating people to do the work of symbolic analysts is crucial to economic success.

If Reich is correct, then it may have become impossible for national governments to shape the nature of educational competition and therefore to try to ensure that an education system promotes social justice and equal opportunities. However, some sociologists are sceptical about aspects of the theory of globalization, and it may be that the theory has exaggerated any reduction in the power of national governments (for a critique of the theory of globalization, see Chapter 9). (For further discussion of the relationship between education and the economy, see pp. 787–91, 797–9 and 813–16.)

Marxist criticisms

Birmingham University's Centre for Contemporary Cultural Studies (CCCS, 1981) has developed a comprehensive critique of social democratic policies from a Marxist point of view. According to its analysis, social democracy has contradictory aims: it is not possible to pursue equality of opportunity and equality at the same time. This is because equality of opportunity inevitably means that some will be more successful than others.

In the Centre's view, even the Labour Party has done no more than pay lip-service to the idea of equality. Changes such as the introduction of comprehensive schools gave the impression of giving greater opportunities to the working class without really doing so. Labour governments were attempting to promote social cohesion rather than trying to transform society.

The writers from the Centre claim that many of the changes in education in recent decades have been designed to benefit the capitalist economy at the expense of the working class. They would have much preferred the working class to have greater control over its own education. They argue that in the nineteenth and early twentieth centuries there was a close relationship between working-class education and radical political movements. Chartists and early feminists such as the suffragettes used education to promote awareness among the working class and women of injustice in society. They encouraged political agitation and attempts to improve society. State education, on the other hand, has done as little to promote class or gender consciousness as it has done to promote equality.

Given the number and strength of criticisms levelled at social democratic perspectives, it was not surprising that new perspectives on education were developed. In terms of British politics, the main challenge to social democracy came from the Conservative Party. In terms of sociology, conflict theorists (and particularly Marxists) argued that education played a very different role in society from that suggested by functionalists, liberals and social democrats.

Education – conflict perspectives

All the perspectives on education that we have examined so far have assumed that education either does – or could – function for the benefit of society as a whole. Liberal and social democratic views accept that there are limitations to the existing education system, but they specify the ways in which it could be altered and improved.

Conflict perspectives on education, in contrast, are based upon the view that groups within existing societies have fundamentally different interests. Thus, however education is organized in contemporary societies, some people will benefit from it more than others. This does not mean that conflict sociologists deny that education could be improved, but it does mean that many of them believe that significant improvements can only be achieved if they are accompanied by wider social changes.

Samuel Bowles and Herbert Gintis – schooling in capitalist America

The American economists and sociologists Bowles and Gintis (1976) argue that the major role of education in capitalist societies is the reproduction of labour power. In particular, they maintain that there is 'close "correspondence" between the social relationships which govern personal interaction in the work place and the social relationships of the education system'. According to Bowles and Gintis, this correspondence principle provides the key to understanding the workings of the education system. Work casts a 'long shadow' over the education system: education is subservient to the needs of those who control the workforce – the owners of the means of production.

The hidden curriculum

The first major way in which education functions is to provide capitalists with a workforce which has the personality, attitudes and values that are most useful to them. Like Marx, Bowles and Gintis regard work in capitalist societies as both exploitative and alienating; yet, if capitalism is to succeed, it requires a hard-working, docile, obedient, and highly-motivated workforce, which is too divided and fragmented to challenge the authority of management.

The education system helps to achieve these objectives largely through the hidden curriculum. It is not the content of lessons and the examinations that pupils take which are important, but the form that teaching and learning take and the way that schools are organized. The hidden curriculum consists of those things that pupils learn through the experience of attending school, rather than the stated educational objectives of such institutions. According to Bowles and Gintis, the hidden curriculum shapes the future workforce in the following ways:

1 It helps to produce a subservient workforce of uncritical, passive and docile workers. In a study based upon 237 members of the senior year in a New York high school, Bowles and Gintis found that the grades awarded related more to personality traits than academic abilities. They found that low grades were related to creativity, aggressiveness and independence, while higher grades were related to perseverance, consistency, dependability and punctuality.

Far from living up to the liberal ideal of encouraging self-development, the American education system was creating an unimaginative and unquestioning workforce which could be easily manipulated by employers.

2 Bowles and Gintis claim that the hidden curriculum encourages an acceptance of hierarchy. Schools are organized on a hierarchical principle of authority and control. Teachers give orders, pupils obey. Students have little control over the subjects they study or how they study them. This prepares them for relationships within the workplace where, if workers are to stay out of trouble, they will need to defer to the authority of supervisors and managers.

3 At school, pupils learn to be motivated by external rewards, just as the workforce in a capitalist society is motivated by external rewards. Because students have so little control over, and little feeling of involvement in, their school work, they get little satisfaction from studying. Learning is based upon the 'jug and mug' principle. The teachers possess knowledge which they pour into the 'empty mugs', the pupils. It is not therefore surprising that many pupils do not enjoy the process of schooling. Instead they are encouraged to take satisfaction from the external reward of a qualification at the end of their studies. The qualification offers the promise of employment, or better-paid employment than would otherwise have been the case.

The subsequent creation of a workforce motivated by external rewards is necessary, according to Bowles and Gintis, because work in capitalist societies is intrinsically unsatisfying. It is not organized according to the human need for fulfilling work, but according to the capitalist's desire to make the maximum possible profit. As a result, the workers must be motivated by the external reward of the wage packet, just as the pupil is motivated by the external reward of the qualification.

4 Bowles and Gintis claim that another important aspect of the hidden curriculum is the fragmentation of school subjects. The student, during the course of the school day, moves from one subject to another: from mathematics to history, to French, to English. Little connection is made between the lessons: knowledge is fragmented and compartmentalized into academic subjects.

This aspect of education corresponds to the fragmentation of the workforce. Bowles and Gintis believe that most jobs in factories and offices have been broken down into very specific tasks carried out by separate individuals. In this way, workers are denied knowledge of the overall productive process, which makes it impossible for them to set up in competition with their employers. Furthermore, a fragmented and divided workforce is easier to control, and this control can be maintained because of the principle of 'divide and conquer'. It becomes difficult for the workforce to unite in opposition to those in authority over them.

The benefits of the education system for capitalism

Bowles and Gintis believe, then, that the hidden curriculum produces a passive and obedient workforce, which accepts authority without question, which is motivated by external rewards, and which is fragmented. They also argue that the formal parts of the curriculum correspond to the needs of capitalist employers.

Bowles and Gintis claim that capitalism requires a surplus of skilled labour. This maintains a high rate of unemployment and ensures that workers of all levels of skill have to compete with each other for jobs. Employers can pay low wages through being able to threaten dismissal and replacement by the reserve army of skilled workers. Since the mental requirements of most jobs are quite low, and most skills can be learned on the job, education tends to over-educate the workforce.

Apart from the direct benefits provided by the education system, just outlined, Bowles and Gintis argue that education also has indirect benefits for capitalism through the legitimation of inequality. By making society appear fair and just, class consciousness does not develop and the stability of society is not threatened.

The illusion of equality of opportunity

From the functionalist perspective of Parsons and Davis and Moore, industrial societies are open and meritocratic: they provide genuine equality of opportunity. Social democratic theorists do not accept that this situation exists, but they do believe that changes to education could bring meritocracy closer to being a reality.

Bowles and Gintis reject the view that capitalist societies are meritocratic and deny that they can become so within a capitalist framework. They believe that class background is the most important factor influencing levels of attainment.

The idea that we all compete on equal terms is an illusion. Although education is free, and open to all, and despite the fact that individuals can apply for jobs at will, Bowles and Gintis claim that some have much greater opportunities than others. The children of the wealthy and powerful tend to obtain high qualifications and highly-rewarded jobs, irrespective of their abilities. The education system disguises this, with its myth of meritocracy. Those who are denied success blame themselves, and not the system which has condemned them to failure.

Intelligence, educational attainment and occupational reward

Bowles and Gintis base their argument on an analysis of the relationships between intelligence (measured in terms of an individual's intelligence quotient or IQ), educational attainment, and occupational reward. They argue that IQ accounts for only a small part of educational attainment.

At first sight this claim appears incorrect. A large body of statistical evidence indicates a fairly close

relationship between IQ and educational attainment. But is IQ the causal factor? Does a high IQ directly cause educational success? If it did, then people with the same IQ should have roughly the same level of educational attainment. Bowles and Gintis examined a sample of individuals with average IQs. Within this sample they found a wide range of variation in educational attainment, which led them to conclude that there is hardly any relationship between IQ and academic qualifications.

What then accounts for differences in attainment between people with similar IQs? Bowles and Gintis found a direct relationship between educational attainment and family background. The causal factor is not IQ, but the class position of the individual's parents. In general, the higher a person's class of origin, the longer he or she remains in the educational system and the higher his or her qualifications.

But why do students with high qualifications tend to have higher-than-average intelligence? Bowles and Gintis argue that this relationship is largely 'a spin-off, a by-product' of continued education. The longer an individual stays in the educational system, the more his/her IQ develops. Thus IQ is a *consequence* of length of stay, not the cause of it.

The above evidence led Bowles and Gintis to conclude that, at least in terms of IQ, the educational system does not function as a meritocracy.

They apply a similar argument to the statistical relationship between IQ and occupational reward. In general, individuals in highly-paid occupations have above-average IQs. However, Bowles and Gintis reject the view that IQ is directly related to occupational success. Within their sample of people with average IQs, they found a wide range of income variation. If IQ were directly related to occupational reward, the incomes of those with the same IQ should be similar.

Again Bowles and Gintis found that family background was the major factor accounting for differences in income. They conclude that IQ itself has little direct effect on income variation. Thus, at least in terms of IQ, they reject the view that the placement of individuals in the occupational structure is based on meritocratic principles.

Finally, Bowles and Gintis examined the relationship between educational credentials and occupational reward. Again there is a large body of statistical evidence which indicates a close connection between the levels of qualification and occupational reward. Bowles and Gintis reject the view that this connection is a causal one. They argue, for example, that high qualifications, in and of themselves, do not lead directly to highly-paid jobs.

They found that the main factors accounting for occupational reward were the individual's class of origin, race and sex. There is considerable evidence to show that educational qualifications are far more valuable on the job market to the white male than to the white female, to the white male than to the black male, to the middle-class male than to the working-class male.

The apparent connection between occupational reward and educational qualifications is simply due to the fact that, in general, white middle-class males obtain higher educational qualifications than other social groups, and also obtain higher occupational rewards. Their IQ has little effect upon either their educational attainment or their occupational reward; their academic qualifications have little effect upon their future income. Thus Bowles and Gintis conclude:

> the intellectual abilities developed or certified in school make little causal contribution to getting ahead economically. Only a minor portion of the substantial statistical association between schooling and economic success can be accounted for by the school's role in producing or screening cognitive skills.
>
> Bowles and Gintis, 1976

The myths of education

If Bowles and Gintis's analysis is correct, then the educational system can be seen as a gigantic myth-making machine which serves to legitimate inequality. It creates and propagates the following myths:

1 Educational attainment is based on merit.
2 Occupational reward is based on merit.
3 Education is the route to success in the world of work.

The illusion of meritocracy established in schools leads to the belief that the system of role allocation is fair, just and above-board. In particular, the 'emphasis on IQ as the basis for economic success serves to legitimate an authoritarian, hierarchical, stratified and unequal economic system'.

Education creates the myth that those at the top deserve their power and privilege, that they have achieved their status on merit, and that those at the bottom have only themselves to blame. In this way the educational system reduces the discontent that a hierarchy of wealth, power and prestige tends to produce.

Thus Bowles and Gintis conclude that 'Education reproduces inequality by justifying privilege and attributing poverty to personal failure.' It efficiently disguises the fact that economic success runs in the family, that privilege breeds privilege. Bowles and Gintis therefore reject the functionalist view of the relationship between education and stratification put forward by Talcott Parsons and Davis and Moore.

Class conflict and education

Bowles and Gintis devote less attention to explaining how education and work correspond than they do to describing the similarities between them. Nevertheless, Bowles and Gintis do make some attempt to explain how such a close fit has come about. They admit that there has been conflict over the American educational system, and that in the past it has not always fitted neatly with the economy. They also admit that members of the working class have at certain times tried to shape the education system themselves.

However, Bowles and Gintis deny that the conflict has produced any notable working-class victories. They claim that representatives of the ruling class have intervened at crucial times to ensure that their interests continue to be served. Any compromises that have taken place have come down heavily in favour of the ruling class, not the working class.

Bowles and Gintis also claim that working-class demands for changes in education have been of limited scope. They suggest that the working class is likely to be fairly content with the type of education system Bowles and Gintis have described because it fosters the attitudes and abilities that are appropriate for work in a capitalist society and, as such, it meets day-to-day needs. Furthermore, the role of the education system in legitimating inequality prevents members of the working class from seeing beyond their own life experiences. Exploited groups are not encouraged to see how the education system and the society it is part of could be transformed to serve working-class interests.

Education in communist societies

Bowles and Gintis provide a comprehensive Marxist view of education in a capitalist society, but their discussion of education in the former communist societies is more sketchy. However, they do express some criticisms of how education worked in the USSR and Eastern Europe under communist regimes.

They argue that there were similarities between the communist education systems and that of the USA. In particular, education in communist countries was also hierarchical and it encouraged some of the same personality traits as the American system. This was due to the failure of these societies to attain true communism. Bowles and Gintis state that 'These countries have abolished the private ownership of the means of production while replicating the relation-ships of economic control, dominance and subordina-tion characteristic of capitalism.'

The communist countries reduced inequalities, but a minority of state officials still controlled the means of production. Bowles and Gintis believe, therefore, that only when there was genuine economic democracy, in which workers took control of the means of production, would a truly socialist education system develop.

Criticisms and evaluation of Bowles and Gintis

The work of Bowles and Gintis has been highly controversial. It has been criticized by Marxists and non-Marxists alike. The critics tend to agree that Bowles and Gintis have exaggerated the correspondence between work and education, and have failed to provide adequate evidence to support their case:

1 M.S.H. Hickox (1982) questions the view that there is a close correspondence between education and economic developments. He points out that in Britain compulsory education was introduced long after the onset of industrialization. Despite the fact that for a long time capitalists did not employ a workforce which had had its attitudes and values shaped by education, the development of capitalism did not appear to be affected.

2 Phillip Brown, A.H. Halsey, Hugh Lauder and Amy Wells (1997) argue that, even if education used to produce the sorts of behaviour and personality required by capitalist employers, this may no longer be the case. They suggest that changes in the nature of work organizations have reduced the importance of bureaucratic control and increased the importance of teamworking. However, the exam system in which people are judged and compete with one another as individuals discourages the development of teamworking skills.

3 Bowles and Gintis can be criticized for their claims about the way that schools shape personality. They did not carry out detailed research into life within schools. They tended to assume that the hidden curriculum was actually influencing pupils. There are, however, numerous studies which show that many pupils have scant regard for the rules of the school, and little respect for the authority of the teacher. Paul Willis (1977) (see pp. 791–4) showed that working-class 'lads' learned to behave at school in ways quite at odds with capitalism's supposed need for a docile workforce.

4 Bowles and Gintis have been criticized for ignoring the influence of the formal curriculum. David Reynolds (1984) claims that much of the curriculum in British schools does not promote the development of an ideal employee under capitalism. The curriculum does not seem designed to teach either the skills needed by employers, or uncritical passive behaviour which makes workers easy to exploit. He says:

The survival in schools of a liberal, humanities-based curriculum, the emphasis upon the acquisition of knowledge for the purposes of intellectual self-betterment rather than ... material gain, the limited swing to science

within higher education, the continuing high status of 'pure disciplines' as against work-related applied knowledge, the decline in commercially important foreign languages at sixth form level ... all suggests a lack of correspondence.

Reynolds, 1984, p. 293

It might be added that the popularity of sociology as an A level subject in Britain could hardly be seen as promoting unthinking workers! Even if the hidden curriculum could be shown to encourage docility, the presence of Bowles and Gintis themselves within the formal curriculum would undermine their claims about education.

5 A further area of criticism concerns the extent to which education legitimates inequality by creating the appearance that success and failure are based upon merit. M.S.H. Hickox (1982) refers to a study by Richard Scase in which only 2.5 per cent of a sample of English workers expressed the view that educational qualifications were an important factor in determining social class. Most of those interviewed placed a far greater emphasis on family background and economic factors. This would suggest that education has not succeeded in legitimating inequality in Britain.

6 Bowles and Gintis have been attacked for failing to adequately explain how the economy shapes the education system. David Reynolds (1984) suggests that it is simply not possible for British capitalists, or the 'capitalist state' to exercise detailed control over British schools. Local authorities have a considerable amount of freedom in the way they organize schools, and, once they 'shut the classroom door', teachers are not subject to close supervision. Reynolds claims that 'a large number of radicals have been attracted into teaching', and because of their independence they have not moulded education to suit the needs of capitalism.

Bowles and Gintis developed their theory of education in the 1970s, and their views have become less influential in later decades. However, it can be argued that, since critics first responded to their theory, the British education system has developed in such a way that their analysis may have become more relevant. For example, local authorities have lost some of their power over education because they no longer run colleges, and some schools have opted out of local authority control. The freedom of teachers has been restricted by the introduction of a national curriculum, and education has become more explicitly designed to meet the needs of employers. These changes will be discussed later in the chapter (see pp. 803–5).

Whatever the merits of Bowles and Gintis's work, many sociologists sympathetic to Marxism have, however, felt the need to modify their approach. Some have denied that parts of the superstructure, such as education, are exclusively shaped by the infrastructure; others have stressed that pupils and students are not simply the passive recipients of education.

Marxism, struggle, and the relative autonomy of education

In response to the criticisms of Bowles and Gintis, Marxists such as Henry Giroux (1984) have advocated a modified approach to the analysis of education within a broadly Marxist framework. Giroux makes the following general points:

1 He argues that working-class pupils are actively involved in shaping their own education. They do not accept everything they are taught, nor is their behaviour entirely determined by capitalism. Pupils draw upon their own cultures in finding ways to respond to schooling, and often these responses involve resistance to the school.

2 Giroux claims that schools can be seen as 'sites' of ideological struggle in which there can be clashes between cultures. Different classes, ethnic and religious groups all try to influence both the content and process of schooling. From this point of view the nature of education is not simply determined by the needs of capitalism, but is influenced by a continuing struggle between the groups involved.

3 The education system possesses relative autonomy from the economic infrastructure. Unlike Bowles and Gintis, Giroux argues that education has partial independence from the needs or requirements of capitalist industry. For example, he points out that in the USA in the early 1980s the education system produced more graduates than were required. Many became unemployed or had to take low-paid jobs that required little training. In this way the myth that education provided equal opportunity and the chance for upward mobility was undermined. Giroux stresses, however, that the independence of education is only partial: in the final analysis, education cannot go against the fundamental interests of capitalism.

Criticisms of relative autonomy

Although in some respects Giroux's work is more subtle than that of Bowles and Gintis, Andy Hargreaves (1982) believes that it fails to solve the problems associated with Marxist theories of education. To Hargreaves there is a massive contradiction built into the theory of resistance and relative autonomy: it claims that education is free to develop in its own way and is influenced by numerous social groups, yet it is still determined by the economy.

Hargreaves criticizes Giroux for failing to spell out in what circumstances education can develop independently, and how and when economic factors

become paramount. He describes Giroux's theory as one in which 'anything goes'. Pupils might be indoctrinated with bourgeois ideology at school, or fight against the authority of the teachers. Both fit the theory of relative autonomy. It therefore becomes impossible to prove the theory wrong: any facts can be made to fit it. As Hargreaves says of such theories, 'they appear to want to have it both ways, to assert both the dependence and independence of schooling; to have their cake and eat it'.

Paul Willis – *Learning to Labour*

In an important and much discussed study, Paul Willis (1977) developed a distinctive, neo-Marxist approach to education. Like Giroux, Willis recognizes the existence of conflict within the education system, and he rejects the view that there is any simple, direct relationship between the economy and the way the education system operates. Like Bowles and Gintis, Willis focuses on the way that education prepares the workforce, but he denies that education is a particularly successful agency of socialization. Indeed, Willis argues that education can have unintended consequences for pupils – consequences which may not be completely beneficial to capitalism.

Despite some similarities with the work of Giroux, Willis's study is more sophisticated and it contains an extra dimension. As well as drawing upon Marxist sociology, Willis adopted some of the research techniques associated with symbolic interactionism. He used a wide variety of research methods in his study of a Midlands school in England in the 1970s. He used 'observation and participant observation in class, around the school and during leisure activities, regular recorded group discussions, informal interviews and diaries'.

In the course of his research Willis did not just rely upon abstract analysis of the relationship between education and the economy, but tried to understand the experience of schooling from the perspective of the pupils. He soon found that schools were not as successful as Bowles and Gintis supposed in producing docile and conformist future workers.

The counter-school culture

The school Willis studied was situated on a working-class housing estate in a predominantly industrial small town. The main focus of his study was a group of 12 working-class boys whom he followed over their last 18 months at school, and their first few months at work. The 12 pupils formed a friendship grouping with a distinctive attitude to school. The 'lads', as Willis refers to them, had their own counter-school culture, which was opposed to the values espoused by the school.

This counter-school culture had the following features. The lads felt superior both to teachers, and to conformist pupils, whom they referred to as 'ear 'oles'. The lads attached little or no value to the academic work of the school, and had no interest in gaining qualifications. During their time at school, their main objective was to avoid going to lessons, or, when attendance was unavoidable, to do as little work as possible. They would boast about the weeks and months they could go without putting pen to paper. They resented the school trying to take control over their time – they constantly tried to win 'symbolic and physical space from the institution and its rules'.

While avoiding working, the lads kept themselves entertained with 'irreverent marauding misbehaviour'. 'Having a laff' was a particularly high priority. Willis described some of the behaviour that resulted:

> During films in the hall they tie the projector leads into impossible knots, make animal figures or obscene shapes on the screen with their fingers, and gratuitously dig and jab the backs of the 'ear 'oles' in front of them.
>
> Willis, 1977, p. 31

In class:

> there is a continuous scraping of chairs, a bad tempered 'tut-tutting' at the simplest request, and a continuous fidgeting which explores every permutation of sitting or lying on a chair.
>
> Willis, 1977, p. 13

Throughout school, the lads had an 'aimless air of insubordination ready with spurious justification and impossible to nail down'.

To the lads, the school equalled boredom, while the outside world, particularly the adult world, offered more possibilities for excitement. Smoking cigarettes, consuming alcohol and avoiding wearing school uniform were all ways in which they tried to identify with the adult world. In the diaries they kept, school warranted no more than a footnote in the description of the day. Going out at night was seen as far more important. Many of them also had part-time jobs, which were more than just ways of earning cash: they were a means of gaining a sense of involvement in the male, adult world.

The lads' counter-culture was strongly sexist, emphasizing and valuing masculinity, and downgrading femininity. It is significant that the lads regarded the ear 'oles as cissies, lacking true masculine attributes. In addition, the counter-culture was racist, seeing members of ethnic minorities as inferior.

According to Willis, the lads were anxious to leave school at the earliest possible moment, and they looked forward eagerly to their first full-time jobs.

While the ear 'oles took notice of career lessons and were concerned about the types of job they would eventually get, the lads were content to go on to any work, so long as it was a male manual job. To them, all such jobs were pretty much the same and it made little difference whether they became tyre fitters, bricklayers' mates or factory workers. All of these jobs were considered 'real work', in contrast to the 'pen pushers'' jobs which the ear 'oles were destined for.

Manual labour was seen by the lads as more worthy than mental labour. The sacrifices of working hard at school were simply not worth the effort. They saw little merit in years of extra study in which their freedom and independence were lost, and during which they would have little cash in their pockets.

Having described the counter-school culture, Willis observes that the education system seems to be failing to manipulate the personalities of pupils to produce ideal workers. They neither defer to authority nor are they obedient and docile. Education does not produce pupils who believe in individual achievement: instead they reject the belief that hard work and striving for individual success can bring worthwhile rewards. They have very little in common with the types of student that the work of Bowles and Gintis suggests the American education system produces.

Yet Willis believes, paradoxically, that the lads were well prepared for the work that they would do. It was their very rejection of school which made them suitable for male, unskilled, or semi-skilled, manual work.

Shop-floor culture and counter-school culture

When Willis followed the lads into their first jobs, he found important similarities between shop-floor culture and the counter-school culture. There was the same racism and sexism, the same lack of respect for authority, and the same emphasis on the worth of manual labour. Having a 'laff' was equally important in both cultures, and on the shop-floor, as in the school, the maximum possible freedom was sought. The lads and their new workmates tried to control the pace at which they worked, and to win some time and space in which they were free from the tedium of work.

According to Willis, both the counter-school culture and the shop-floor culture are ways of coping with tedium and oppression. Life is made more tolerable by having a 'laff' and winning a little space from the supervisor, the manager or the teacher. In both settings, though, the challenges to authority never go too far. The lads and workers hope to gain a little freedom, but they do not challenge the institution head-on. They know that they must do a certain amount of work in the factory or risk dismissal, and they realize that the state can enforce school attendance if it is determined to do so.

Having described and compared the counter-school culture and the shop-floor culture, Willis analyses the significance of his findings for an understanding of the role of education in society.

Willis does not see the education system as simply being a successful agency of socialization which produces false class consciousness. He does believe that education reproduces the sort of labour force required by capitalism, but not directly or intentionally. He says that state schools, and the oppositional culture within them, are 'especially significant in showing a circle of unintended consequences which act finally to reproduce not only a regional culture but the class structure and also the structure of society itself'.

The lads are not persuaded to act as they do by the school, nor are they forced to seek manual labour; rather they actively create their own subculture, and voluntarily choose to look for manual jobs. They learn about the culture of the shop-floor from fathers, elder brothers and others in the local community. They are attracted to this masculine, adult world, and respond to schooling in their own way because of its lack of relevance to their chosen future work.

Capitalism and the counter-school culture

In the final part of his book, Willis discusses the significance of the counter-school culture for capitalist society. Once again he does not simply argue that the lads' culture is entirely beneficial to capitalism, nor does he think it is entirely harmful. Willis claims that in some ways the lads see through the capitalist system, but in other ways they contribute to their own exploitation and subordination.

Willis identifies a number of insights into the workings of capitalism that the lads have, which he calls penetrations. The lads see through at least part of the ideological smokescreen that tends to obscure the true nature of capitalism:

1 He says that they recognize that capitalist society is not meritocratic. They understand that they are unlikely to be upwardly socially mobile to any great extent.

2 The lads show an appreciation of the limitations of a strategy of pursuing individual achievement for improving their own lives. Willis claims that only collective action can dramatically change the position of the working class, and in their loyalty to their mates at school or on the shop floor the lads recognize this. Willis states that 'no conceivable number of certificates among the working class will make for a classless society, or convince industrialists

and employers – even if they were able – that they should create more jobs'.

3 The lads can see through careers advice. They know that most of the jobs likely to be available in their area require little skill, and that their studies at school will not prepare them for their work. Even if they worked hard at school, the qualifications they would get would be quite limited. They might be able to move into clerical work, or gain an apprenticeship, but the sacrifices would hardly be worth the small amount of extra pay.

4 They have come to understand the unique importance of manual labour power. In a sense they have followed in the footsteps of Karl Marx and found for themselves that it is labour power that creates wealth.

On the other hand, Willis does not believe that the lads have seen through all of the ideological justifications for capitalism. Given their antipathy to non-manual labour (the work of 'pen pushers'), their critical understanding of capitalism is limited to what they can learn through their own experience. They have no overall picture of how capitalism works to exploit them.

Willis is particularly critical of their sexism and racism. Their attitudes to women and ethnic minorities merely serve to divide the working class, making it easier for it to be controlled. Furthermore, the lads' willing entry into the world of manual work ultimately traps them in an exploitative situation. At school they prepare themselves to cope with manual labour, but in doing so they condemn themselves to 'a precise insertion into a system of exploitation and oppression for working-class people'.

In his wide-ranging research, then, Willis tries to show that it is the rejection of school which prepares one section of the workforce (semi-skilled and unskilled manual labourers) for its future role. This is done through the actively created and chosen counter-school culture of some working-class pupils. The reproduction of labour power through education works in an indirect and unintentional way. The lads are not simply suffering from false class consciousness – in part they understand their own alienation and exploitation – yet in the end their own choices help to trap them in some of the most exploitative jobs that capitalism has to offer. As Willis says, 'Social agents are not passive bearers of ideology, but active appropriators who reproduce existing structures only through struggle, contestation and a partial penetration of those structures.'

Paul Willis – criticism and evaluation

Undoubtedly Willis's study has been influential. Liz Gordon, for example, claims that it 'has provided the model on which most subsequent cultural studies investigation within education has been based'(Gordon, 1984). Furthermore, she believes that it has encouraged Marxists to pay more attention to the details of what actually happens within education, and it has helped to overcome a tendency to provide over-simplified accounts of the role of education in society. Nevertheless Willis has his critics.

David Blackledge and Barry Hunt (1985) advance three main criticisms:

1 They suggest that Willis's sample is inadequate as a basis for generalizing about working-class education. Willis chose to concentrate on a mere 12 pupils, all of them male, who were by no means typical of the pupils at the school he studied, never mind of schoolchildren in the population as a whole.

2 In a related criticism they accuse Willis of largely ignoring the existence of a whole variety of subcultures within the school. Blackledge and Hunt point out that many pupils came somewhere in between the extremes of being totally conformist and being totally committed to the counter-school culture. They say:

> Willis … seems to accept at face value the lads' view that the conformists in the school cannot, at the same time as being involved in their school work, also take an interest in some of the things that are at the centre of the world of the lads – music, clothes, the opposite sex, drink, etc.
>
> Blackledge and Hunt, 1985, p. 216

As we will see in a later section, some interactionist studies have uncovered a wide variety of pupil subcultures and ways of reacting to school (see pp. 848–9).

3 Blackledge and Hunt suggest that Willis misinterpreted some evidence. For example, by examining Willis's own evidence they argue that there is little basis for claiming that the lads develop the same attitudes to work as previous generations

of workers. They point to some differences between one of the lads, Joey, and his father. They say:

> Joey's father obviously takes a pride in his work and derives considerable self-respect from it … He clearly enjoys the recognition by management that he is doing a demanding job well and has a good, friendly relationship with them … Joey … unlike his father … is not on good terms with other social groups and classes … (management for the father; conformists, teachers and ethnic minorities for the son); rather he displays a contempt for anyone who is not part of his own small world.
>
> Blackledge and Hunt, 1985, pp. 209–10

With such strong differences between the working father and the son at school, Blackledge and Hunt find it hard to understand how Willis believes that schooling becomes a preparation for the world of adult, male, manual work.

Willis might also be criticized for adopting some Marxist concepts uncritically. For example, Willis assumes that the workers he studies are exploited, and, in claiming that the lads have 'penetrated' aspects of capitalism, he assumes that his highly critical stance towards modern British society is almost self-evidently true.

Furthermore, it is questionable how far Willis's findings would apply in contemporary Britain. With a big decline in the availability of unskilled male manual work since the 1970s, it is likely that male working-class attitudes to education may have changed. The belief that education is largely irrelevant to finding work may have become less widespread as the labour market has changed. Nevertheless, in trying to combine an ethnographic study of the school with an analysis of the role of education, Willis demonstrated how it is possible to move beyond the limited focus of most studies of education.

New Right perspectives on education

Equal opportunities in the 1980s and 1990s

Both the social democratic and the more radical Marxist perspectives on education were influential in the late 1960s and early 1970s. In Britain, however, from the middle of the 1970s, governmental concern with equality and equality of opportunity was gradually replaced by a growing emphasis on other issues.

Successive governments showed little interest in adopting policies that attempted to compensate for class inequalities. Interest in gender and ethnic inequalities remained strong, and in many areas new policies were adopted to try to reduce these inequalities. However, these initiatives tended to be locally based. While many individual schools, colleges, higher education institutions and local education authorities adopted equal opportunities policies, which were particularly aimed at eliminating racism and sexism, governments paid less attention to developing policies concerned with these issues. Instead, the main focus of national policy-making shifted elsewhere and concentrated on the needs of industry and the economy. This change in emphasis also developed in several other capitalist countries – for example, in New Zealand and the USA.

New Right thinking is largely based on theories derived from economics, particularly from those that advocate market systems as a way of distributing resources. Market systems are driven by individuals making decisions about what to buy or consume. Because consumers have a choice, the providers or producers of the goods or services have to respond to the preferences of consumers. If they fail to do so, consumers will go elsewhere and the producers will go out of business.

Publicly-funded education, however, has not normally been provided by commercial enterprises, but instead has been run by bureaucracies which are accountable to elected politicians. In Britain, for example, education has largely been run by local education authorities accountable to local authorities and ultimately accountable to national government.

Some theorists, known as public choice theorists – such as J. Buchanan and G. Tullock (1962) – have tried to analyse bureaucratic and democratic systems of control to see what effects such systems are likely to have on the efficiency and effectiveness of publicly-run services. They have argued that bureaucracy and democracy are likely to produce inefficient and ineffective services. For example, public choice theorists claim that, under these systems, *producers* rather than *consumers* tend to dominate decision making.

Public services often act as a monopoly: consumers cannot freely choose an alternative provider of free education, health services or refuse collection. Furthermore, because they are publicly funded, the providers cannot go out of business. They therefore have little incentive to respond to the needs of consumers. Instead it is the producers who tend to dominate decision making: producer capture takes place. For example, education comes to reflect the interests of teachers and the bureaucrats who run the system, rather than the consumers – the pupils and parents – whom the system is intended to benefit.

According to public choice theory, groups such as teachers and other employees in educational bureaucracies have an interest in increasing expenditure on education, to make their jobs more secure and improve their promotion prospects. Through pressure groups, such as trade unions, they can persuade governments to follow the policies they favour through the promise of political support. For example, governments might agree to increase expenditure on education in the belief that this will win them votes from teachers and local authority workers.

According to public choice theory, everyone acts according to their own interests. Politicians want votes, teachers and bureaucrats want secure jobs, and it is their interests which become dominant in conventional state education systems. As a result, state expenditure on education increases, which results in rising taxes. This in turn damages the economy. Businesses end up being over-taxed and unable to compete with businesses in other countries. At the same time pupils and parents have little control over education. They have to accept the state education that is on offer and they have little chance to change or shape it. However, New Right thinkers believe that if competition and market systems are introduced into education all of these problems can be remedied.

Perhaps the most influential advocates of the introduction of market forces into education are the US political scientists Chubb and Moe, whose work will now be discussed.

John E. Chubb and Terry M. Moe – 'Politics, markets and the organization of schools'

In their article 'Politics, markets and the organization of schools' (1997, first published 1988), John E. Chubb and Terry M. Moe put forward their case for the introduction of market forces into education.

The need for reform

Chubb and Moe start by noting that there has been a 'long-simmering discontent about declining test scores, loose academic standards and lax discipline' in the US education system. Similar concerns have also been expressed in Britain (see, for example, p. 801 on the Great Debate). In the USA a variety of solutions have been proposed to remedy the situation. These solutions include 'clear school goals, rigorous academic requirements, an orderly climate, strong instructional leadership by the principal teacher', and so on. However, Chubb and Moe believe that all of these solutions are inadequate. All of them are aimed at improving the internal organization of schools, whereas the real solutions involve changing the overall institutional framework within which schools work.

Attempts to impose particular values and ways of operating on schools are doomed to failure. Some schools might have some success in reforming, but they will lack incentives to continually improve and there can be no guarantee that all or even most schools will take steps to improve. However, according to Chubb and Moe, improvements will almost inevitably follow if there is a move towards a market system within education.

Public and private schools

In order to support their arguments, Chubb and Moe compare how public schools (in the USA, state-run schools are called public schools) and private schools are run.

Public schools 'are controlled by democratic authority and administration'. Although individual schools have their own elected school boards, state and federal government play a crucial role in the overall direction of schooling. In any public school, therefore, a wide range of people can be seen as the 'constituents' – that is, the people who have a legitimate say in how the school should be run. These include local and national politicians and administrators, students, parents, and citizens in general, who vote in elections or pay taxes.

Public education is not supposed to be responsive simply to the needs of those who use the services of the school; it is intended to serve wider public purposes as determined by politicians. Usually, the only way of influencing school policy is through expressing your opinion and hoping that your views are taken into account by those in authority. In theory it is possible for the parents of public-sector children to take their children out of the school. However, there are usually only two ways of doing this. One is to pay for private schooling, but many parents are not willing to do this or cannot afford it. The other is to move house to an area with a school the parents prefer. Moving house, though, involves considerable cost, and many factors other than the quality of the local school influence where people choose to live.

Schools themselves tend to have little freedom and autonomy under a public system of this type because they are accountable to a large group of constituents. These constituents all have their own self-interests and sometimes these will conflict with the interests and wishes of parents and pupils. Politicians need to attract support in order to win elections. To do this they must try to take actions which take account of the wishes of a variety of interest groups. The better-organized the interest groups, the more likely they are to influence the government. Chubb and Moe argue that these interest groups:

include teachers' unions and associations of administrators, but also a vast array of groups representing more specialized interests – those of minorities, the handicapped, bilingual education, drivers' education, schools of education, book publishers, and accrediting and testing organizations among them.

Chubb and Moe, 1997, p. 366

Generally these groups have a vested interest in maintaining existing educational systems, since change costs them money and might undermine their position in the education system. They all want as big a share as possible of the public money that funds education.

The government bureaucrats who run the education system also have 'incentives to expand their budgets, programs, and administrative controls'. These vested interests tend to undermine the autonomy of schools, restricting their ability to respond to the needs and wishes of parents. At the same time they encourage ever-increasing expenditure on a school system which is unlikely to be providing what parents want.

Private schools have a great deal more room for manoeuvre than public ones. Instead of being shaped by a diverse group of constituents, they are responsible to a smaller and more clearly defined group of consumers: the parents who are paying the fees for children to attend the school. These consumers have two ways of influencing school policies. The most direct way is to remove their children from the school or to choose a different school for their children to attend in the first place. Because schools rely upon the fees paid by parents, this creates a strong incentive for the schools to change if they are failing to attract sufficient pupils. It also encourages schools to allow parents a second way of influencing their policies – that is, through listening to their views.

Because they need to please their clientele in order to survive, private schools have good reason to consult parents and listen to what they have to say. They become responsive to what parents want. Because they need the fees, they are much more likely to create a match between what they provide and what the parents are looking for. Furthermore, private schools are not constrained by governmental and bureaucratic interference. They have much more freedom to change and adapt to what their customers want than public schools do. Also, they have incentives to keep costs down. The cheaper the fees, the more customers they will attract, so long as they can keep providing the sort of high-quality education that parents want. The fact that parents are willing to pay for private education when they could get public education free demonstrates that private schools must be successful in meeting parents' needs.

Evidence

Chubb and Moe support their claims with research evidence. They collected data from 60,000 students in more than 1,000 schools, and in about 500 of these schools they also collected data from 30 teachers, the principal and some other staff members. They found that private schools were less likely than public ones to be responsible to outside administrators; more likely to be closely controlled by school boards; and they had more freedom to hire and fire staff. They also found that parents tended to be more supportive of the private schools and their aims than parents of children in public schools; that staff were more satisfied with the leadership of the principal in the private sector; and that private schools had clearer goals.

Conclusion

Chubb and Moe conclude that:

> *Public schools are products of our democratic institutions. They are subordinates in a hierarchic system of control in which diverse constituency groups and public officials impose policies on local schools. It is no accident that public schools are lacking in autonomy, that principals have difficulty leading and that school goals are heterogeneous, unclear and undemanding.*
>
> Chubb and Moe, 1997, p. 378

The only way to overcome these problems is to change the way the schooling system is organized. This can only be done effectively if public schools become subject to the same sorts of incentives for improvement and responsiveness as are characteristic of the private sector. Power needs to be decentralized 'to the producers and immediate consumers of educational services', so that schools can get on with providing the sort of education their customers want. Chubb and Moe suggest that this could be achieved through a voucher system. All parents could be given a voucher entitling them to purchase for their children education of a value determined by the government. This would encourage public and private sector schools to compete in an open market for children to attend their schools. Successful schools could grow, while the unsuccessful would need to improve to survive. All schools would become more flexible and responsive, although Chubb and Moe concede that 'broad democratic guidance' would be needed to oversee the system.

Phillip Brown and Hugh Lauder – neo-Fordism and the New Right

Chubb and Moe concentrate on the organization of schools in supporting their New Right policies, whereas Phillip Brown and Hugh Lauder (1997) examine the broader relationship between New Right thinking and the development of the economy. Brown and Lauder are not themselves supporters of the New Right – indeed they are critical of New Right ideas. However, their work does help to explain the broader context in which New Right thinking emerged.

Changes in the economy

Brown and Lauder believe that economic globalization has taken place since the 1970s (see Chapter 9 for a discussion of globalization). It has become increasingly difficult for countries to regulate their own economies. Capital investment has become more footloose: companies are willing to invest wherever they can get the best deal. Multinational corporations (MNCs) have no loyalty to the country in which their businesses originated. Instead, mass production has come to be 'located in countries, regions, or communities which offer low wage costs, light labour-markets legislation, weak trade unions, and "sweeteners" including "tax holidays" and cheap rents'. In this situation there is a tendency for countries to undercut one another in trying to attract businesses.

However, at the same time the importance of mass production in the global economy has declined. Brown and Lauder are generally sympathetic to the ideas put forward by advocates of the theory of post-Fordism. According to this view, companies increasingly seek profits through the flexible production of expensive, high-quality goods and services. Consumers are no longer willing to consume standardized and mass-produced products in large numbers. Instead, consumers have rapidly-changing tastes and they are increasingly willing to pay for high-quality products that reflect these changing tastes. From this point of view, economic success requires a highly-skilled, highly-educated and flexible labour force. Only such a labour force can meet the challenges presented by the new global economy.

Although governments agree that there is a need for improved education in order to compete in the global economy, there are distinctive views about how these improvements can be achieved. According to Brown and Lauder, New Right governments in countries such as Britain, the USA and New Zealand adopted a neo-Fordist approach to improving the education system.

Neo-Fordism and education

The neo-Fordist, New Right response to globalization blames excessive welfare spending and social democratic policies towards education for economic decline. From this point of view the economies of countries such as Britain have been damaged by spending too much on the education system and by placing too much emphasis on equality of opportunity. High levels of government expenditure have forced up tax rates, discouraging foreign companies from investing in these countries.

Too much emphasis on equality of opportunity has also led to a decline in educational standards. Rather than concentrating on policies that would ensure that educational standards were improved for all groups, these countries have concentrated on reducing inequality in the educational standards achieved by different groups. According to the New Right, this has tended to drag down the standards of the most able while still failing to ensure that the least able gained at least basic skills and some educational qualifications.

To the New Right, the path to economic success is through cutting the costs of education while creating incentives to improve standards. This will provide two benefits. First, it will lower taxes, making a country more attractive for inward investors. Second, it will provide investors with the skilled, educated and trained workforce they need. To the New Right, the best way of achieving this is through the introduction of greater choice and market forces, or marketization, into education. As argued by Chubb and Moe, consumers will benefit by being given greater choice in the education system, and by schools having incentives to respond to consumer choices. In a marketized education system public money follows the choices made by parents and students, giving successful schools the money to expand, and failing schools the incentive to improve. At the same time, competition will drive down the costs of educating children.

According to Brown and Lauder, this neo-Fordist approach is intended to create an enterprise culture in which people learn to compete from the earliest stages in their life, and they are encouraged to use their initiative in the pursuit of economic success. Flexibility is achieved by making it easier to hire and fire workers. There is more emphasis on trying to continue mass production by using cheap labour than on competing by having the best-educated workforce.

For example, in the 1990s, John Major's Conservative government decided to opt out of the Social Chapter of the Maastricht Treaty of the European Union. The Social Chapter guaranteed certain rights for workers (such as a maximum working week). John Major and others argued that it would price British workers out of their jobs. They would become more expensive than employees in countries where such rights did not exist.

Brown and Lauder do not believe that the New Right's drive to cut educational costs will disadvantage the children of middle-class and upper-class parents. On the contrary, they believe that such parents will be best-placed to take advantage of the competitive school system. They will be more likely to get their children into the successful schools, while working-class parents and parents from disadvantaged minorities will be more likely to end up with their children being educated in less successful schools.

From the point of view of the New Right, though, the success of some schools will encourage excellence throughout the system. All schools will be forced to aspire to the standards of the most successful if they are to attract sufficient students. Even if marketization does not benefit all parents and pupils equally, in the long term it is the only way to achieve cheap, efficient and effective education. (Brown and Lauder have also analysed more left-wing contemporary perspectives on education, which they describe as post-Fordist – see pp. 813–16.)

Criticisms of New Right perspectives on education

Some of the general criticisms of the New Right perspective on education will be introduced here. More detailed criticisms will be developed in evaluating the ways in which such theories have been applied in educational policies in Great Britain.

Hugh Lauder – criticisms of New Right policies

Hugh Lauder criticizes New Right policies which advocate the marketization of education on a number of grounds:

1 Even with a voucher system it would be misleading to believe that parents would be genuinely equal in the education market. Some parents have more knowledge and understanding of the education system and more money. They are in a better position than other parents to manipulate education markets to get the most out of them. Lauder says:

> different groups enter the market on vastly different terms in both material and cultural capital. Which groups will operate successfully in the market will be determined, not so much by participation per se, but by the cultural capital, the knowledge of the rules of the game, that 'consumers' bring to the market.
>
> Lauder, 1997, p. 388

For example, middle-class parents will be more likely to get their children into the schools with the best reputations, or to pay extra for them to attend more prestigious schools. To Lauder, this will increase inequality in the education system and will also negatively affect standards (see pp. 806–10 for examples from Britain which support his views).

2 Lauder believes that state-run comprehensive systems – where a mix of children attend the same sort of school – raise standards rather than depress them. For example, he quotes research by McPherson and Williams which found that the mix of people from different class backgrounds in Scottish comprehensive schools raised the academic

standards of the least able, whereas the most able did just as well as they might be expected to do in other systems. On the other hand, in a market system, children from lower-class backgrounds will tend to end up in the schools that are failing to compete effectively. Such schools will be caught in a spiral of decline. With falling numbers they will lack the money to improve, and this will result in declining achievement for significant sections of the school population.

3 The existence of some schools which fail to compete effectively is particularly important given that choosing a school for children to attend is not the same as buying other products. Education takes place over many years and during that time the performance of the school might improve or get worse. The choice of the 'best' school at a particular point in time may not ensure that your child gets the best education throughout their primary or secondary schooling. Those who fail to make the right choice or fail to get their first preference might end up trapped in an unsatisfactory school.

4 Lauder also argues that the operation of educational markets might actually reduce choice. The decision of a relatively small number of parents not to send their children to a particular school might render it economically unviable. If the school closes down as a result, choice in the area will be restricted.

5 A number of sociologists have pointed out that choice of school is limited by geographical location. For practical reasons most parents have to send their children to a local school, and in rural areas the choice may be restricted to a single school. Because of the limited choices involved there may be very little competition.

6 Another problem with the marketization of education is that schools are limited in their ability to expand by taking on more pupils. They are constrained by the size of their buildings and the land they have. They may not have access to the capital required to expand if they are successful. Building may take a considerable time, and there is no guarantee that the school will remain popular in the long term.

Stewart Ranson – criticisms of marketization

More possible problems with marketization are identified by Stewart Ranson (1996, first published 1993).

Ranson believes that marketization can be damaging in terms of the sorts of values that it produces. According to Ranson, it encourages an 'atrophied psychology of possessive individualism'. Markets are based upon the assumption that each individual will pursue an 'instrumental rationality' in which their sole concern will be to maximize their own self-interest. Ranson believes that when individuals do act in this way it is because the market encourages them to do so. It undermines values that stress the importance of selflessness and cooperation

with others. The marketization of education is therefore based on, and encourages, 'a degraded and distorted psychology of human nature'.

Ranson does not just object to the introduction of markets into education on the grounds that it encourages anti-social values; he also believes that the nature of education makes it unsuitable for the imposition of market values. He argues that, unlike buying, say, a cassette, decisions relating to education can change the nature of the product being purchased. Educational institutions have 'chameleon-like qualities'. For example, if many people choose to send their children to a particular school because it is small and can treat its pupils as individuals, then the school is likely to grow, thus changing the characteristics that attracted people to it in the first place.

Because education markets are shaped by individual decisions, they are unpredictable, and rational decisions may result in unintended consequences. For example, a parent may wish to send their child to a school because of its mixed intake of children from different social classes and ethnic groups. However, like-minded parents from similar backgrounds may make the same decision, making the social mix of the school more homogeneous.

Ranson believes that consumer choice can end up empowering the producers (that is, the schools) to control the market. For example, the most successful and over-subscribed schools may start choosing the pupils they wish to accept.

Consumer choice may also reduce as a result of markets. Markets may force many or all institutions to compete for the same sort of students, making institutions increasingly homogeneous. For example, all schools might end up stressing academic qualities and exam results in an attempt to attract the academically able middle-class pupils who are likely to enhance the school's performance in educational league tables. Parents who want a more vocationally orientated school might lose that option as a result of the operation of educational markets.

Like many other commentators, Ranson sees markets in education as socially divisive. Hierarchies of schools are likely to develop and only individuals with the appropriate cultural capital (the knowledge and techniques necessary to manipulate the market) are likely to benefit. Those lacking the necessary knowledge, skills and social contact will have little prospect of getting their children into the best schools.

Unlike Chubb and Moe, Ranson believes that it is far better to plan the education system through strongly democratic local politics. In this way people can get the sort of education they want, rather than being restricted by free markets.

Together, all the individual decisions taken in educational markets can produce consequences that were neither intended nor desired. These consequences might include the restriction of choice, the creation of strong hierarchies, a reduction of educational opportunities for the disadvantaged, and so on. To Ranson, they can only be avoided through non-market methods of controlling education.

Will Bartlett and Julian Le Grand – the nature of quasi-markets

While Lauder's and Ranson's criticisms relate specifically to education, others have analysed marketization more generally. Will Bartlett and Julian Le Grand (1993) have examined the theory of quasi-markets.

Quasi-markets are the types of structures set up by governments who try to introduce market forces – for example, competition – into state-provided services. They are not real markets because they are not actually paid for by the consumers spending their own money. They are publicly funded, but individual consumers can influence where the public money goes through their choices. They cannot, however, directly determine exactly how much money goes to particular providers – for example, schools – because levels of funding are set by government bureaucracies.

Bartlett and Le Grand have identified a number of potential problems with this system:

1 In quasi-markets there is usually a single ultimate purchaser of services, that is the government. This restricts the bargaining position of the providers (schools and colleges). This can lead to a situation where 'A purchaser that exploits its monopoly power to drive a hard bargain may sour relationships with providers, lower their morale and motivation.' In effect, the situation is imbalanced because providers are subject to market pressure while purchasers are not.

2 Because of the above, the prices paid for educational or other services in quasi-markets are not the result of market forces. They are determined by negotiation or fixed by the rules of bureaucracies. Quasi-markets cannot therefore reflect the prices that consumers are prepared to pay for products, and they are therefore less responsive to consumer demands than real markets are likely to be.

3 Quasi-markets can be adversely affected by opportunistic behaviour by suppliers. Markets rely upon information for consumers to make their choices. If people have no information about what goods or services are best, they have no way of making rational decisions.

In education, attempts have been made to provide information through, for example, league tables of exam results. However, it is expensive to provide information, and it creates incentives for providers to manipulate the information on which consumers base their decisions. For example, schools and colleges may have incentives to manipulate league tables by excluding pupils who are unlikely to do well and entering people for easy exams which they are unlikely to fail.

4 Suppliers also have an incentive to engage in moral hazard. This involves reducing the quality of what they provide, in order to cut costs, while still meeting the criteria needed to receive funding. In educational quasi-markets there are strong incentives to persuade pupils or students to choose an institution, and strong incentives to maintain standards that are acceptable to those providing the funding, but incentives to maintain the highest possible standards for students or pupils once they have chosen the institution are weaker. This is particularly the case where institutions are struggling financially and need to find savings.

5 There are further potential problems which result from the possibility of cream-skimming. Cream-skimming is 'discrimination by either purchasers or providers against the more expensive users', such as 'the disruptive child from a deprived background'. Such children will not only use up more of a school's resources because they will require more individual attention, but they will also depress the school's performance by lowering league table results.

The government can try to make allowances for this by providing educational institutions with different amounts of money for different types of pupils and students – for example, students with special needs. However, the prices are artificially set by the government, and administering such schemes can be expensive; and they create incentives to classify more students in groups that attract extra money. Such schemes may also encourage cream-skimming of those who fall into the better-funded categories but whose extra needs are not that great. Furthermore, such schemes can also lead to a polarization between those schools which successfully cream-skim and those which do not, leading to pupils in the latter schools being at a marked disadvantage.

In general, the fact that quasi-markets are only partially subject to market forces makes it difficult to ensure that they deliver efficient, effective and high-quality services in line with consumers' requirements. Whatever rules are imposed on the market, the institutions that provide the services have incentives to maximize income and perfor-mance, as measured by league tables and other indicators, while putting less effort into anything that is not measured or does not produce revenue. Critics argue that this can lead to institutions making decisions that are harmful to the education of their pupils and students. Furthermore, many critics argue that the marketization of education tends to lead to greater inequality of opportunity. While some benefit from attending the successful schools, others are harmed by attending the unsuccessful ones.

The general arguments put forward by critics of New Right perspectives will be illustrated in a later section which evaluates the impact of New Right reforms in Britain. First, however, those reforms will be described.

The New Right and educational policies in Britain

New Right perspectives certainly influenced the types of policies introduced by a number of governments in different parts of the world in the 1980s and 1990s. However, policies were rarely based purely on New Right perspectives alone. As we will see, a range of other factors influenced the actual policies that were implemented. New Right perspectives and the policies that partially resulted from them will be examined and evaluated together in this part of the chapter.

The 'Great Debate'

Although, in Britain, Conservative governments of the 1980s and 1990s introduced modifications to the education system which reflected the new priorities, the change in thinking began under the last Labour government of the 1970s. In 1976 the Labour prime minister James Callaghan made a speech at Ruskin College calling for a 'Great Debate' on education. It was followed by a Green Paper (a government discussion document) on education. The paper argued:

> It is vital to Britain's economic recovery and standard of living that the performance of the manufacturing industry is improved and that the whole range of government policies, including education, contribute as much as possible to improving industrial performance and thereby increasing the national wealth.
>
> Quoted in Finn, 1987, p. 106

In a period of rising unemployment and the apparent decline of Britain's economy, the concern was that education was failing to produce appropriately skilled and motivated young workers. The social democratic view of education – that it should promote equality of opportunity – was deemed to be less important than the needs of industry. This emphasis, and the policies that followed from it, have become known as the new vocationalism.

The New Right and British education

Education and economic growth

Despite the fact that the 'Great Debate' was initiated by a Labour prime minister, it was in tune with some of the thinking of the New Right and the Conservative governments after 1979. Although the

latter rejected the social engineering implied in the idea that education could be used to make society more egalitarian, they did think that education could promote the social changes that they wanted to see. In particular, the New Right argued that education should be largely concerned with promoting economic growth through concentrating on improving the skills of the workforce.

Some employers believed that education was failing to meet their needs, and the New Right believed that unemployment was rising partly because many school leavers were unemployable. However, the objectives were not to be achieved by 'throwing money at the problem', for, as Dan Finn puts it, the New Right saw a 'bloated public sector which was strangling the wealth-creating element of the economy' (Finn, 1987). Extra resources for education could only come from the profits of British industry and so reduce Britain's competitiveness.

In the first year of the Thatcher government, education expenditure was cut by 3.5 per cent, and changes designed to overcome the supposed deficiencies of social democratic policies began to be made.

Competition, choice and standards

If the overall aim of New Right policies was to use education to promote economic growth, the mechanisms through which this was to be achieved were encouraging competition, increasing choice (particularly parental choice), and an emphasis on raising standards. At the same time the education system would be made more efficient, eliminating waste and saving the taxpayer money. These aims were made quite explicit in the handbook *Britain 1993*, published by HMSO. This described the aims of the government's education reforms as:

- *to raise standards at all levels of ability;*
- *to increase parental choice of schools and improve the partnership of parents and schools;*
- *to make further and higher education more widely accessible and more responsive to the needs of the economy;*
- *to achieve the best possible return from the resources invested in the education service.*

Quoted in Burgess, 1994, p. 71

An important part of the New Right's philosophy – and one which has exercised a strong influence on educational reforms – has been its hostility to state bureaucracies. New Right thinking generally holds that state-run institutions are inherently inefficient. They waste money because they do not have to make a profit and they therefore have no interest in restricting their expenditure. The introduction of market forces through competition between institutions forces them to become more efficient.

For example, educational institutions have to compete to attract students or pupils. The ones that fail to attract the students lose funding. As a consequence, they either have to raise their standards or face the possibility of having to close. The greater the choice offered to parents as to which school their children attend, the greater the competition between schools. The greater the competition, the greater the incentive for schools to improve.

Stephen J. Ball quotes a New Right educationalist, Stuart Sexton, outlining these principles. Sexton was an adviser to the Conservative education ministers Mark Carlisle and Keith Joseph. Writing in his 1987 pamphlet *Our Schools – A Radical Policy*, Sexton said:

> To produce the quality and choice that we expect in education, to improve our schools, we need to change the way that we fund and manage them. Making the education service fully responsive to parental choice and student needs, with a direct financial relationship between provider and consumer, is the way to better standards, and a far better way than administrative tinkering and political exhortation.
>
> Quoted in Ball, 1990, p. 44

Testing and examining

One of the important mechanisms through which the New Right hoped to increase competition was through the increased use of testing and examining, and the publication of results. This was designed to provide information for parents to help them make informed choices about the school they chose for their children.

However, Conservative governments of the 1980s and 1990s only supported the use of certain types of test. They generally opposed coursework and allowing pupils' teachers to assess their work. Instead they favoured national, standardized tests and examinations. Conservative governments supported the use of traditional unseen examination and test papers, designed so that direct comparisons could be made between schools.

To encourage greater competition, Conservative governments also introduced league tables detailing how successful a school had been according to certain measures. League tables were first introduced

in 1992 and included information on performance in public examinations (GCSE and A levels), attendance rates and national performance tests – for example, those measuring numeracy and literacy in primary schools. This enabled the consumers of education (pupils, students and their parents) to take exam success rates and other factors into account when choosing schools or colleges.

Stephen Ball (1990) argues that in some respects the advocacy of standardized tests and examinations goes against New Right thinking. The New Right are generally 'against imposing uniformity on schools' and they 'value diversity'. However, in this case, most New Right educationalists thought that the advantages of being able to make direct comparisons between educational institutions outweighed the disadvantages of imposing a centralized state-run system of testing and examination.

Curriculum content – the New Right and traditionalism

Although the New Right and the Conservative governments of the 1980s and 1990s supported radical changes in the way education was organized, and sought to introduce a more business-orientated curriculum, in other areas they supported the teaching of very traditional subjects. According to Stephen Ball (1990), they proposed the teaching of subjects such as Latin and Greek and opposed social science subjects, peace studies, and personal, social and health education. They were also hostile to multicultural education, which encourages pupils to develop a knowledge of the culture of ethnic minorities. Similarly they were against the widespread teaching of ethnic minority languages (such as certain Asian languages), and instead emphasized the importance of European languages such as French, Italian, Spanish and German.

Again, in this area there is some contradiction between New Right philosophy and the policies pursued. New Right thinking would suggest that there should be a free market in the choice of curriculum content by the consumers of education. This choice, while absent in public schools, was available in private schools, which were never compelled to conform to the National Curriculum (see below for a discussion of the National Curriculum).

However, educational policies have also been influenced by philosophies other than those of the New Right, and by individuals who do not identify wholeheartedly with New Right thinking. In particular, there has been an emphasis on retaining the traditional values, organizations, and curriculum content of the British education system. The New Right was not the only force shaping educational policy under the Conservative governments.

The New Right and the control of education

In a study of the introduction of one of the most important recent changes in the education system, the 1988 Education Reform Act, Richard Johnson argues that the legislation 'did not derive straightforwardly, from New Right theories' (Johnson, 1991). Rather, 'A multitude of practicalities intervened: political divisions, administrative dilemmas, strong opposition.' Opposition came, for example, from LEAs and from teachers and their unions. There were also divisions within Conservative ranks. For example, Mrs Thatcher's first education secretary, Keith Joseph, and more radical New Right thinkers favoured a voucher system. Under this system, parents would be given a voucher by the state with a fixed value. It could be used to pay for education in either a privately-owned or a publicly-run school. However, this measure was never adopted because opposition to it was too strong.

In the next section we will briefly describe the main educational changes introduced in Britain between 1979 and 1994. As we have seen in this section, these changes were largely, but not completely, shaped by the New Right. After we have examined the nature of the changes made, we will evaluate some of the most important ones in detail.

Changes in education 1979–97

Schooling

Some steps were taken to prevent the ending of selective schooling. The Education Act of 1976, which compelled LEAs to draw up plans for comprehensive reorganization, was repealed. An Assisted Places Scheme was introduced, which paid for state pupils to be educated at independent schools, in the hope that this would encourage the most able to develop their talents.

The most far-reaching package of changes was introduced in the 1988 Education Reform Act. The following measures were all introduced through this legislation:

1 Testing and attainment targets were introduced for children of 7, 11, 14 and 16, in the hope that standards would rise as schools competed with each other to succeed in reaching the targets.

2 For the first time the government laid down a National Curriculum, which required pupils to study mathematics, English, science, history, geography, technology, music, art and physical education, plus a foreign language for 11-16-year-olds. This was intended to ensure that pupils concentrated on what the government saw as key subject areas. Since its introduction, a number of changes have been made to the National Curriculum. We discuss these changes later.

3 The Act emphasized the idea of parental choice – in theory, at least, parents were given the right to send their children to the school of their choice, to further encourage schools to compete and concentrate on improving their results. A policy of open enrolment compelled every school to recruit pupils up to the maximum that could be accommodated in its buildings.

4 The Act allowed the establishment of City Technology Colleges (CTCs). These would be inner-city educational institutions specializing in technology. They would be sponsored by private industry, so that the state did not pay the full costs of building the colleges, and they would be independent of LEAs. CTCs would cater for the 11-18 age groups and compete with existing state schools. Only 15 CTCs were ever established – largely because of the lack of financial support from companies who it had been hoped would make substantial contributions to help set up CTCs.

5 Existing schools were allowed to opt out of local authority control and instead be funded directly from central government. Opting out created a new category of grant maintained schools which were self-governing. Opting out had to be supported by parents in a ballot. By April 1996, 643 secondary schools had opted out and become grant maintained. They were responsible for just under 20 per cent of secondary children (quoted in Woods, Bagley and Glatter, 1998). In September 1999 grant maintained schools returned to local authority control (see pp. 816–17).

6 The 1988 Act also gave greater autonomy to schools in the way they spent their money. Local management of schools gave the responsibility for managing at least 85 per cent of school budgets to headteachers and governors, thus reducing the power of LEAs. Schools also became responsible for hiring, firing and disciplining staff.

7 Under the new system of formula funding, the financing of schools was largely based upon the number of enrolments. This was intended to reward successful schools which attracted large numbers of pupils, while giving less successful schools the incentive to improve. At least 80 per cent of local education authority budgets had to be allocated on the basis of pupil numbers. For the remaining 20 per cent of the budget, some allowance could be made for factors that affected the costs of running the school, such as their size and the state of the school's buildings.

There were a number of other important changes in schooling which were not introduced in the 1988 Education Reform Act:

1 The Technical and Vocational Education Initiative (TVEI) was started as a pilot scheme in 1983 in 14 LEAs. It was a scheme for 14-18-year-olds which ran alongside the conventional curriculum and included work experience. The TVEI became available to all secondary schools in 1986 and was later extended to include sixth-form, further education and tertiary colleges. Roger Dale (1986) suggests that it was associated with the aim of producing pupils who had a better understanding of work and the economy – pupils who could get jobs and carry them out successfully.

2 The Certificate for Pre-Vocational Education (CPVE) was similar to TVEI in stressing preparation for work. CPVE, first taught in 1985-6, was for those over 16 who were uncertain of what work they wished to do. It offered work experience and was taught in schools and colleges. CPVE taught practical skills, but could be combined with taking exams in traditional subjects, although in practice it tended to be taken by pupils who were unsuccessful in the compulsory period of education. The CPVE was not a great success and was later replaced by other vocationally-orientated qualifications such as GNVQs and NVQs.

3 In 1986 the National Council for Vocational Qualifications was set up, with the aim of introducing standardized vocational qualifications related to working in particular occupations. By 1990, about 170 NVQs (National Vocational Qualifications) had been established, with more being added to the list as time progressed. NVQs are intended to reward practical achievement, with qualifications being gained by demonstrating 'competencies'. NVQs have four levels, ranging from Level 1 (the equivalent of GCSE) to Level 4 (the equivalent of postgraduate-level study). After an initial two-year pilot scheme, GNVQs (General National Vocational Qualifications) were introduced nationally in 1993. These were intended to provide a vocationally-orientated alternative to traditional academic exams such as GCSEs and A levels.

4 One change that went against the general trends was the introduction of a new qualification for 16-year-olds in 1988. The General Certificates of Secondary Education (GCSEs) replaced the two-tier system of O levels for more academic pupils, and CSEs (Certificates of Secondary Education) for students judged to be less able. These qualifications generally contrasted with government policy in that they led to all students being entered for the same examination: GCSEs did not differentiate between academic and non-academic pupils. However, there were exceptions in some subjects (such as mathematics) where students could take different versions of GCSE exams with varying levels of difficulty. As time progressed, more subjects followed this path and had different exams for students of different abilities.

GCSEs also went against the general thrust of government policy by incorporating a considerable amount of coursework in the assessment methods. They therefore tended to encourage more student-centred teaching methods, rather than the traditional 'chalk and talk' teaching which tends to be favoured by the New Right. Although the government later placed restrictions on the proportion of GCSE and A level marks that could be awarded through coursework (restricting it to 20 per cent), a coursework component remained in the assessment of most subjects.

The 1993 Education Act made further changes. Many were quite minor but some of the most significant changes are listed below:

1 There were changes to the process of becoming an opted-out or grant maintained school, making it easier to change status.

2 Parents of children with special needs were given more power in choosing a school for their children.

3 Secondary schools were given the right to specialize in particular parts of the curriculum (such as music or science) if they wished.

4 A new School Curriculum and Assessment Authority was formed (through the merger of existing bodies), with responsibility for overseeing all matters relating to exams and assessment in schools.

5 LEAs were given new powers to deal with truancy, and truancy league tables were introduced.

6 The secretary of state was given powers to appoint Education Associations to take over the running of 'ailing' schools.

Together, these measures were intended to develop further the policies already introduced. They would increase the variety of schools available, enhance parental choice and try to ensure the improvement of educational standards.

Further and higher education

As well as initiatives in schools, there were important changes in further and higher education during the same period:

1 The 1993 Education Act compelled further education colleges to become independent, self-governing bodies, funded by the Further Education Funding Council rather than by LEAs. As in schools, funding was to be based largely on the recruitment of students, thus encouraging competition between further education colleges and other institutions, such as schools with a sixth form.

2 The 1993 Education Act also allowed polytechnics to become universities.

3 The government allowed higher education to expand rapidly in the late 1980s and early 1990s, but this

expansion was financed partly through cutting back on grants to students. The value of student grants was gradually reduced from 1990 onwards. Instead of relying entirely on grants, students were given the opportunity to take out low-cost loans which had to be repaid once they had graduated and gained reasonably well-paid employment.

4   As in other areas of education, measures were introduced to make higher education more influenced by industry. The 1988 Education Reform Act established a Polytechnic and Colleges Funding Council and a University Funding Council, both of which had strong representation from commerce and industry.

Training

A whole range of changes were introduced into training programmes. Some of these initiatives started even before the Conservatives took office in 1979. Many of them shifted power away from schools and colleges and towards the Department for Employment and new organizations which had closer links with employers than with educators.

1   Many of the early changes were associated with the extension of the activities of the Manpower Services Commission (MSC) (which later became the Training Commission). This organization was created in 1973 by the Employment and Training Act. It was made answerable to the secretary of state for employment, not the education minister, and given responsibility for the selection and training of people for employment, and for ensuring that employers had a suitable supply of labour.

2   Its earliest measures were the Job Creation Programme of 1975, which provided temporary jobs for some of the unemployed; and the 1976 Work Experience Programme, which placed some of the young unemployed on six-month work placements. As unemployment rose, the MSC both expanded its activities and became involved in educational areas that would previously have been the responsibility of the Department of Education and Science.

3   The Youth Opportunities Programme (YOP) of 1978 included both work experience and short training courses. Mrs Thatcher's Conservative government was initially hostile to the MSC, but with unemployment rising rapidly it decided to extend YOP. Trainees on this scheme were entitled to one day a week off-the-job training, although not all received it. One area of training which the MSC started to develop was social and life skills, which aimed to develop positive attitudes to work, discipline, getting to work on time, and getting on with other trainees and employees at places of work.

4   In 1983 the Youth Training Scheme (YTS) replaced YOP. YTS was a one-year training scheme, again combining work experience with education for school leavers.

5   In 1986 YTS was extended to a two-year scheme. This scheme was designed to achieve the development of four 'outcomes'. Peter Raggatt and Lorna Unwin describe these as 'competence in job skills; competence in a range of transferable core skills; ability to transfer skills and knowledge to new situations; personal effectiveness' (Raggatt and Unwin, 1991). Raggatt and Unwin argue that the two-year YTS scheme met with hostility from employers who complained that 'its emphasis and the development, assessment and recording of the four outcomes was too time consuming and bureaucratic'.

6   Partly as a result of objections by employers, YTS was replaced in 1990 with Youth Training. The only requirement in this scheme was for employers to ensure that trainees followed some sort of training programme which led towards a Level 2 NVQ.

7   At the end of 1988 a White Paper entitled *Employment for the 1990s* announced the government's intention to set up a new type of organization to develop training. These were to be Training and Enterprise Councils or TECs. The first of these came into operation in 1990 and a network covering the whole of Britain was soon established. TECs are a national network of independent companies run by chief executives recruited from private industry. They are expected to deliver training and enterprise in their locality. TECs took over the running of Training Commission programmes such as Youth Training and Employment Training (a scheme for unemployed adults), but they were also given the job of evaluating the economic needs of their area and trying to stimulate economic development. Two-thirds of the board of each TEC has to consist of senior managers from major companies.

8   In 1991, pilot schemes for training credits were introduced. Initially piloted in 11 areas, these training credits were given to all 16-17-year-olds who left full-time education. They entitled school leavers to spend a specified sum of money on training provided by employers, colleges or other bodies. The aims were to increase the amount of training that early school leavers received, and to make training providers more responsive to the needs of school leavers by giving young people the financial power to shape the sort of training they received.

These lists of educational and training initiatives since 1979 are by no means exhaustive. Nevertheless, they do summarize most of the main changes that took place under Conservative governments up to 1997. We will now look at some of these measures in more detail by examining sociological studies which have attempted to evaluate the effects of these changes, and in some cases to reveal the hidden agenda that may have encouraged their introduction.

Critical evaluations of the educational reforms

Stephen J. Ball, Richard Bowe and Sharon Gewirtz – competitive advantage and parental choice

The study

Between 1991 and 1994 Stephen Ball, Richard Bowe and Sharon Gewirtz conducted a study of 15 schools in three neighbouring LEAs (Ball *et al.*, 1994, Gewirtz *et al.*, 1995). The study included a mixture of LEA-controlled schools, grant maintained schools, two church schools and a CTC. The institutions served a variety of areas, some with mainly middle-class populations and some with a higher concentration of working-class residents. Some areas had substantial ethnic minority populations and others did not.

Ball *et al.* visited the schools, attended meetings, examined documents and interviewed a sample of teachers. They interviewed about 150 parents who had children in primary schools, who were at the point of making the choice about the secondary schools their children should attend. They also interviewed some primary headteachers, and examined LEA documents about changing patterns of choice. Ball *et al.*'s study attempted to discover the effects that parental choice and the encouragement of competition between schools were having on the education system, and particularly on opportunities for different social groups.

The effects on schools

The study found that the changes were having significant effects on secondary schools. This was particularly true of those schools that were under-subscribed: they had to try to do something to arrest their decline. More successful schools could afford to be fairly complacent but they too were starting to change some of their practices.

Most schools were 'paying a lot more attention to what parents want for their children's education. Or more precisely what schools *think* that parents want.' However, it was not the case that schools were equally keen to attract all students. The publication of league tables meant that schools were much more keen to attract academically able pupils who would boost the school's league table performance and thus improve its reputation. Thus according to Ball *et al.*, 'In a sense there is a shift of emphasis from student needs to student performance: from what the school can do for the students to what the student can do for the school.'

This emphasis has encouraged some schools to reintroduce streaming and setting and to direct more

resources to children who are likely to be successful in examinations and tests. In some cases it has led to pupils being seen as commodities by the school, and this being communicated to the pupils. In one school, students had been known to point out to teachers that the school received £2,200 for each of them attending that school (Gewirtz *et al.*, 1995).

As schools have concentrated on the more able pupils, they have paid less attention to those with Special Educational Needs (SENs). Indeed, Ball *et al.* argue that 'some of the money and energy previously devoted to educational endeavours like SEN work are now focused on marketing activities'. In an effort to attract pupils, some schools have taken to publishing glossy brochures and some have brought in public relations firms. Staff are expected to devote more time and energy to marketing activities such as open evenings.

Ball *et al.* believe that these changes have led to 'a significant shift in the value framework of education'. Gewirtz *et al.* see this as involving an overall shift from comprehensive to market values, although individual schools have been affected to different degrees. This shift involves a number of characteristics which are summarized in Figure 11.1.

Neighbouring schools have ceased to cooperate with each other and instead there is 'suspicion and hostility' between them as they compete for pupils.

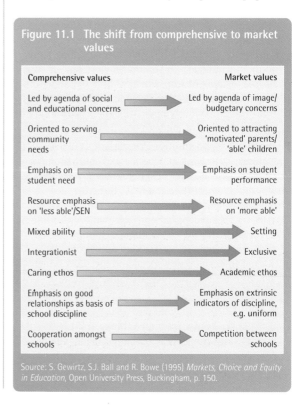

Figure 11.1 The shift from comprehensive to market values

Comprehensive values	Market values
Led by agenda of social and educational concerns	Led by agenda of image/ budgetary concerns
Oriented to serving community needs	Oriented to attracting 'motivated' parents/ 'able' children
Emphasis on student need	Emphasis on student performance
Resource emphasis on 'less able'/SEN	Resource emphasis on 'more able'
Mixed ability	Setting
Integrationist	Exclusive
Caring ethos	Academic ethos
Emphasis on good relationships as basis of school discipline	Emphasis on extrinsic indicators of discipline, e.g. uniform
Cooperation amongst schools	Competition between schools

Source: S. Gewirtz, S.J. Ball and R. Bowe (1995) *Markets, Choice and Equity in Education*, Open University Press, Buckingham, p. 150.

As competitive, market systems are introduced, 'commercial rather than educational principles are increasingly dominant in making curriculum and organisation and resource allocation decisions'. In line with market values, 'shrewdness rather than principles is rewarded' (Ball *et al.*, 1994). Budgetary concerns, such as cutting costs, are seen as more important than educational and social issues (Gewirtz *et al.*, 1995). More attention is devoted to the image of the school, particularly to making it seem to have a traditional and academic focus. Maintaining good relations between staff and pupils has become less of a priority in some schools than maintaining a favourable image – for example, by strictly enforcing rules about school uniform.

The education market and degrees of choice

Gewirtz *et al.* found that parents were not equally able to take advantage of the supposed opportunities for choice in making decisions about their children's education. Significant choices before the age of 16 were really confined to expressing a preference for a particular secondary school. The amount of real choice involved in this decision was limited both by the availability of schools and by the ability of parents to discriminate between them.

Gewirtz *et al.* argue that three broad groups can be distinguished in terms of their ability to discriminate between schools:

1 Privileged/skilled choosers are strongly motivated to choose a school for their children and they have the necessary skills to do so. They have the ability to understand the nature of different schools and to evaluate the claims made by schools in their publicity. They are likely to devote considerable time and energy to finding out about different schools and their admission criteria. They can maximize the chances of getting their children into their preferred schools. For example, they are more likely to find out if certain schools will only accept their child if they put that school as their first choice. Sometimes they plan well ahead and make sure that their children start their schooling at a primary school which is a feeder school for a particularly successful secondary school.

Privileged/skilled choosers often have the money to make a range of choices that will assist their children's education. These choices may include moving house or paying for private education.

Privileged/skilled choosers are usually middle-class and some – for example, teachers – benefit from inside knowledge of the education system. This group tends to seek out the most successful 'cosmopolitan schools', which are often over-subscribed and draw their intake from a wide area.

2 Semi-skilled choosers 'have strong inclination but limited capacity to engage with the market' (Gewirtz *et al.* 1995). They are just as concerned to get the best possible education for their children but they do not have the same level of skill as their privileged/skilled counterparts. They tend to lack the 'experiences or inside knowledge of the school system and the social contacts and cultural skills to pursue their inclination to choice "effectively". They are less "at ease" in the medium of school choice than the privileged/skilled choosers.'

For example, they are less likely to appeal if they do not get their children into their first-choice school. They are more likely to accept rumours about schools and their local reputation at face value than to probe deeper, and they can have difficulties interpreting league table results. This group are less likely to be middle-class than privileged/skilled choosers, and are more likely to choose a local school than a successful cosmopolitan one.

3 The disconnected choosers are not inclined to get very involved with the education market. They are concerned about their children's welfare and education but 'they do not see their children's enjoyment of school or their educational success as being facilitated in any way by a consumerist approach to school choice'.

They tend to consider a small number of options, and frequently just the two closest schools to where they live. They may not own a car or have easy access to affordable public transport, making the local schools seem the only realistic options. They tend to believe that there is little difference between schools, and to put more emphasis on the happiness of their child than on the academic reputation of the school. Gewirtz *et al.* comment that 'happiness is generally a matter of social adjustment, friendship and engagement with "the local", rather than the achievement of long-term goals or the realization of specific talents'.

Other types of chooser also take account of such factors, but do not concentrate on them to the same extent as disconnected choosers. The result is that disconnected choosers are more likely to send their children to the local school where their friends are going, rather than travel further afield to a supposedly better school. Disconnected choosers are likely to be working-class and are more likely than other choosers to send their children to an under-subscribed school.

These differences result in certain groups being more likely to benefit from the education market than others. Generally, the higher a person's social class, the more likely they are to benefit from the best state schooling (or to be able to choose private schooling). The market leads to a hierarchy of schools and, even without selection by academic ability, can lead to a growing division between predominantly middle-class and working-class schools. Indeed, Gewirtz *et al.* believe that genuinely open choice does not exist.

Different groups of parents restrict their choice to particular types of school. These different groups choose from different circuits of schooling.

Circuits of schooling

According to Gewirtz *et al.* there are four distinctive circuits of schooling. These are:

1 'Local, community, comprehensive schools', which are mainly attended by local pupils and which support a comprehensive school ethos.

2 'Cosmopolitan, high profile, elite, maintained schools' – some are openly selective, some may be grant maintained schools, and they succeed in attracting students from outside their immediate locality.

3 Private day schools which cater for fee-paying pupils who live within commuting distance.

4 Catholic schools designed to cater specifically for children of that faith.

Parents tend to make their choice from within one of these circuits of schooling. Disconnected choosers tend to consider the first circuit of schooling, whereas the privileged/skilled choosers are more likely to make their choice from the second and/or the third circuit. Because there are different types of chooser and different circuits of schooling, 'choice is very directly and powerfully related to social class differences ... choice emerges as a major new division in maintaining and reinforcing social-class divisions and inequalities'. According to Gewirtz *et al.*, the impression of choice is largely illusory. Not only is it restricted by the schools available in any particular area, it is also limited by the class-based nature of the way the system of choosing operates.

Conclusion

Ball *et al.* (1994) conclude that the encouragement of parental choice, the publication of exam results in league tables, open enrolment, formula funding and other policies designed to make education more market-orientated have all served to make education less egalitarian. Those whose children are already advantaged in the system seem to be gaining even more benefits, while those who are already disadvantaged are losing further ground.

At the same time the ideology of educational institutions is changing in such a way that schools are becoming more concerned with attracting the gifted and the advantaged than with helping the disadvantaged. According to Ball *et al.*'s research:

> *we are likely to end up with a more socially differentiated and divisive system of education. In any market there are winners and losers. In this market we may all end up losing out!*

Ball *et al.*, 1994

(For more discussion of this research, see pp. 838–40.)

Ron Glatter, Phillip Woods and Carl Bagley – 'Diversity, differentiation and hierarchy'

The study

Another study of the marketization of schooling, and particularly the effects of introducing greater choice of school, has been conducted by Ron Glatter, Phillip Woods and Carl Bagley (1997). They conducted research in three areas, each of which formed what they call a local competitive arena. Each of these areas was relatively discrete, with most pupils going to a school within the area, although some did attend schools in neighbouring areas.

Glatter *et al.* believe that educational markets are essentially local, with real competition only taking place between schools within travelling distance of one another. For this reason the amount of choice and the nature of the choice open to parents depend upon the choices available locally. Their study therefore aimed to discover whether the changes in the education system had increased, reduced or made no difference to the amount of choice in particular localities. They also examined whether schools had become more hierarchical – that is, whether clearer differences in the status of different schools had emerged. They looked at how schools had responded to the changes and they collected questionnaire data on parental attitudes about diversity.

Competition in different areas

The first area, which they call Marshampton, was a town with a population of about 120,000, with a relatively high proportion of middle-class and professional people. The area contained one long-established private school and, before the changes, six LEA state schools, one of which was a selective grammar school. In response to the educational changes, all the LEA schools had opted for grant maintained status, having opted out of local authority control. Thus the marketization of education had produced a change in the types of school available, but no greater diversity since all the schools had decided to change status.

Furthermore, Glatter *et al.* detected a move towards uniformity. The schools without sixth forms were all hoping to open their own sixth forms to give their schools greater status and academic credibility. Market pressures were pushing all the schools in a similar direction. A clear hierarchy of schools had emerged in the area, with less successful schools under-subscribed. However, Glatter *et al.* found that it was extremely difficult for the less successful schools to improve their position in the hierarchy, because of problems such as a poor reputation and cuts in their budgets. Thus competition was not doing much to improve standards, particularly for those attending the less popular schools.

The second area was Northern Heights, a predominantly working-class area with a substantial Bangladeshi population. It was located in a larger LEA area, Northborough. Northborough had a wide range of secondary schools consisting of two boys' and one girls' grant maintained schools, one boys' and one girls' LEA school, three Roman Catholic schools, three special schools and one independent school.

There were three co-educational comprehensive schools run by the LEA in Northern Heights itself. One of these was an over-subscribed, academically-orientated school, while the other two concentrated more on pastoral matters and were under-subscribed. All three of these schools were seeking to offer more of a vocational curriculum to their pupils. About two-thirds of parents in Northern Heights sent their children to one of these schools, while about a third of the residents chose to send their child to a school outside the immediate area.

This area, then, did offer plenty of diversity and choice, and this had been increased since some schools had chosen to opt out of LEA control. However, some parents could not get their first choice, and the element of choice was by no means new. Northborough had adopted a policy of open enrolment, allowing children to choose their school, as early as 1977.

East Greenvale was a semi-rural area with numerous villages and three small towns. Each of these towns had an LEA-controlled 13-18 co-educational comprehensive school. The vast majority of children chose to go to the nearest school. Because of the geographical distance between the schools, each operated as almost a local monopoly. Each school was fairly content with the number of pupils they could attract and informally agreed not to 'poach' students from other areas. There was little differentiation between the schools and little opportunity for exercising choice.

Conclusions

The research of Glatter *et al.* demonstrates the extent to which local factors largely determine how the educational market operates. The geography of different areas, the number and nature of existing schools, and the tactics adopted by schools combine to determine how much and what sort of competition there is in particular areas. The introduction of markets into education has unpredictable and varied effects, but in two of the areas of the study it made

no marked difference to the real choices available to parents.

Glatter *et al.* conclude that the 'secondary school system is not dramatically moving in the direction of greater diversity or reduced hierarchy'. Furthermore, in their study of parents' attitudes, Glatter *et al.* found no real evidence that parents sought diversity. All parents sought 'a caring, child-centred focus', although some parents did want their child's school to stress a more academic focus.

Tony Edwards and Geoff Whitty – traditional and modern versions of academic excellence

Tony Edwards and Geoff Whitty (1997) have considered the impact of educational changes in terms of the effects they have had on ideas of educational excellence. In particular they have looked at the role of private schooling in shaping perceptions of what good schooling is, and the effects of a more competitive environment on private schools.

Private schools

Edwards and Whitty note that fees in private schools have risen faster than inflation. In 1993-4 day pupils paid between £3,300 and £8,400 per year, while boarders' fees ranged from £6,900 to £11,400. Edwards and Whitty argue that in the past the main reason why parents were willing to pay fees was because of the image of elite boarding schools. This image included the 'attractions of social exclusiveness, and the consequent opportunities to acquire polish and useful acquaintances'. The emphasis in these schools has traditionally been on acquiring these kinds of cultural advantages rather than on academic excellence.

The emphasis on classics helped a disproportionate number of pupils from private boarding schools to get into Oxford or Cambridge University (Oxbridge), where Latin used to be important as part of the entrance test. Such schools also often had specific scholarships for their pupils to go to Oxbridge. However, by the 1970s such factors were becoming less important in gaining admission to Oxbridge, and the boarding schools began to concentrate more on academic excellence. In the 1980s and 1990s a number of changes introduced by Conservative administrations pushed all private schools further in this direction.

The Assisted Places Scheme was justified on the grounds that it provided opportunities for those who could not afford fees to fulfil their potential in private education. At the same time it allowed the private schools to raise their academic standards by recruiting some of the most able pupils who did not have privileged parents.

The National Curriculum is largely based upon the type of academic education provided at fee-paying schools. It therefore ensures that there is considerable similarity between what is studied at private and state schools. Testing and league tables provide direct comparisons between levels of achievement in schools. Private schools are likely to seek to achieve good results to justify their fees – something they had less need to do when information on exam results was less widely available. Private schools have therefore been forced to compete with the more successful state schools.

The emphasis on exams

The result of these changes has been to push all schools towards an emphasis on success in public exams, particularly GCSEs and A levels. This has reinforced the idea that an academic education is the only worthwhile type of education. Edwards and Whitty therefore argue that 'The effects of "free" parental choice in English conditions are still being powerfully shaped by the continuing prestige of the kind of education associated with elite private schooling.' The convergence between state and private education has reduced choice rather than increased it.

Edwards and Whitty note that there have been attempts to value a more vocationally orientated curriculum. These have included the TVEI initiative (see p. 804), the establishment of City Technology Colleges and the introduction of GNVQs. However, none of these have come close to gaining parity of esteem for vocational students. The marketization of education has simply reinforced the separating of 'academic "sheep" from vocational "goats"', so that vocational courses are very largely 'chosen' by those who cannot achieve success on academic ones. Like some of the other sociologists examined in this section, then, Edwards and Whitty believe that markets have done little to encourage diversity or provide people with real choices.

The National Curriculum

The introduction and development of the National Curriculum

As we outlined earlier, the National Curriculum was introduced in 1988. It required 11-16-year-old pupils to study mathematics, English, science, history, geography, technology, music, art, physical education and a foreign language. Of these, English, mathematics and science were defined as core subjects. Schools were expected to spend about 10 per cent of teaching time on English, 10 per cent on

mathematics and 10–20 per cent on science. The remaining subjects were defined as foundation subjects and each would take up around 10 per cent of school time, with the exception of physical education, which would take up 5 per cent. All schools were expected to spend a minimum of 70 per cent of teaching time on the National Curriculum, with any remaining time being used for religious education and other subjects.

The National Curriculum also included attainment targets, which would outline what children were expected to understand, know and do at four key stages, at the ages of 7, 11, 14 and 16. These abilities would be regularly tested and there would be standardized tests for all pupils at each of these stages. The results of these tests would be published so that parents could compare the success of schools.

In fact, these proposals were never implemented in full. Teachers' unions (particularly the National Union of Teachers) opposed some of the testing procedures and boycotted them. Partly as a consequence of such opposition, the government ordered Sir Ron Dearing to examine the workings of the National Curriculum and propose reforms. In 1994 the findings of the *Dearing Report* were accepted. These greatly simplified the testing procedures and drastically slimmed down the National Curriculum itself. From 1994 it was decided that the National Curriculum should be confined to the three core subjects of English, mathematics and science.

Common criticisms of the National Curriculum

Denis Lawton (1989) identified a number of the most frequent criticisms made of the original National Curriculum. These were:

1 It was too bureaucratic. Many of the documents relating to the National Curriculum seemed more concerned with controlling the activities of teachers than improving the standard of what pupils learned.

2 It greatly centralized power in the hands of the secretary of state for education. It therefore undermined local democratic control of education and limited the choices open to parents. With one exception, they could no longer significantly affect the content of their children's education by choosing which school they attended, since all schools had to teach a very similar curriculum.

3 The exception was private schools which were not subject to the National Curriculum. Thus the government could be accused of only providing choice for those rich enough to afford private schooling.

4 The content of the National Curriculum was accused of being very traditional and unimaginative. Different groups objected to the exclusion of particular subjects. Lawton points out that it

'neglected important areas of learning such as political understanding, economic awareness, moral development, and many other cross-curricular themes'.

5 Many objected to the publication of test results. Schools that did badly risked losing pupils (and, with them, funding) and therefore entering a spiral of decline. This resulted in an unfair disadvantage to those left in the unsuccessful schools.

6 Some critics were worried that testing at 7 and 11 would lead to the labelling of some children as failures at an early age, damaging their future educational prospects.

The National Curriculum and power

The first two criticisms outlined above suggest that the National Curriculum was in conflict with the objectives of the New Right: it did not seem to be increasing choice and making education subject to market forces by freeing it from state bureaucracy. Geoff Whitty notes that some people have explained this apparent inconsistency by suggesting that the changes were:

> as much about increasing central government control at the expense of the teaching profession and local government, as they are about increasing the power of local communities, which are linked with parents in the government's rhetoric.
>
> Whitty, 1989

Whitty himself suggests that the government's policies were not entirely inconsistent with the New Right's beliefs in the merits of the free market. From the New Right's point of view, it was sometimes necessary to use state power to get rid of state intervention in particular areas. In the short term the state could be used to attack and weaken those who opposed New Right thinking. This included left-wing LEAs and teachers' unions. The government could therefore ensure that:

> the pervasive collectivist and universalistic welfare ideology of the post-war era is restrained. In this way, support for the market, self-help, enterprise and the concept of the 'responsible' family and a common 'national identity' can be constructed.
>
> Whitty, 1990

In the long-term, then, the National Curriculum could free parents 'from dependency on professional experts' and persuade them to exercise choices in ways consistent with the government's free-market ideology.

From Whitty's point of view, the National Curriculum is therefore designed to shift power in the short term away from opponents of the government and towards the state. However, in the long term it can be used to reduce the need for state intervention, since it ensures that parents will make the right curriculum choices when greater power is given to them.

The National Curriculum, class and cultural diversity

Long before the government decided to introduce a National Curriculum, sociologists were debating the merits of having different types of curriculum in schools. Some supported the use of a single curriculum for all pupils. For example, in 1975 Denis Lawton proposed a common culture curriculum. He accepted that there were important subcultural differences between social classes, but maintained that there were sufficient similarities to form a school curriculum based on a common culture. He claimed that 'A heritage of knowledge and belief which includes mathematics, science, history, literature and, more recently, film and television is shared by all classes.'

However, it can be argued that no common curriculum can afford realistic solutions to the problem of inequality of educational opportunity in a stratified society. The very existence of stratification tends to prevent a common culture, since class subcultures largely arise from the position of social groups in the stratification system. Whatever the content of the curriculum, it is bound to be more familiar to and therefore easier to understand for particular social groups.

Some critics have claimed that the National Curriculum favours higher social classes and disadvantages ethnic minorities in its choice of subject content and in the way it is organized. We will now examine the National Curriculum in terms of how it affects ethnic minority groups.

The National Curriculum and ethnicity

Conrad MacNeil discusses the National Curriculum from a 'black perspective'. Writing in 1988, he argued:

> The culture reflected in it is no more than prevailing white Anglo-Saxon and totally excludes the significant input from the Caribbean, the African and Indian continents and elsewhere. Furthermore, it reflects an imperialist and Eurocentric concept of a static Anglo-Saxon culture which no longer exists.
>
> MacNeil, 1990

He gave a number of examples to support his claims:

1 In history the emphasis was on British history and carried the risk of having 'the same old diet of colonial domination' in which it is claimed that British colonialism benefited rather than harmed the peoples who were colonized. Asian, Afro-Caribbean and African history was neglected.

2 In terms of languages, MacNeil noted that there were 12 languages in the UK spoken by over 100,000 people, but less than half of them were European. However, the language component in the National Curriculum placed the emphasis on the teaching of European languages, discouraging, for example, Asian pupils from studying Asian languages without studying a European language other than English as well.

3 Similarly, in literature, the culture of ethnic minorities would be neglected, with the works of distinguished black writers largely forgotten, and the emphasis on traditional English writers such as Shakespeare, Milton, Hardy and Dickens.

Barry Troyna and Bruce Carrington (1990) identify another area in which the National Curriculum might disadvantage ethnic minorities. The 1988 Act specifically said that any new religious education syllabus had to reflect the dominance of Christian religious traditions and could not treat all major religions in the same way.

The National Curriculum and differentiation

As well as defining certain types of knowledge as worth acquiring while excluding other types, the National Curriculum provided standards against which the performance of pupils could be measured. Richard Johnson (1991) argues that this is the main way in which the introduction of a National Curriculum will affect class differences in education. He says that the introduction of standardized testing at an early age 'means that individual children will be ranked and ordered as never before'. He describes the National Curriculum as 'a mechanism for differentiating children against fixed norms'.

Once differentiated, other reforms in education mean that children are likely to end up studying different courses, often in different institutions. Thus grammar schools, CTCs, private schools and grant maintained schools are likely to recruit successful, mainly middle-class children, while working-class children are more likely to end up in schools that have remained in local authority control. After the age of 16, pupils can be directed in different ways: academic, middle-class pupils towards traditional A levels; and less academically successful, working-class pupils towards new vocational courses and training programmes.

To Johnson, the National Curriculum did not encourage equality of opportunity, despite the fact that it forced all children in the state sector to study the same subjects. Instead, the renewed emphasis on testing and increased differentiation between types of school undermined the principles of comprehensive schooling and represented a move back to the era of grammar schools and secondary moderns. He says, 'As so often in the history of English education,

institutional separations will become social segregations, especially on lines of class and race.'

Youth training schemes

Dan Finn – the hidden agenda of YTS

The new vocationalism involved in the various youth training schemes has been strongly attacked by some critics. Dan Finn (1987) refuses to accept that it is really designed to achieve its stated objectives. Finn claims that in 1983 confidential government papers leaked to the London magazine *Time Out* showed that the real purpose of the Youth Training Scheme (YTS) was to restrict the number of workers joining trade unions, so reducing the bargaining power of the workforce. YTS would also directly reduce the wage levels of young workers.

The government paid employers for 'training' people on YTS, but in fact the trainees could be used as a source of cheap labour. Furthermore, the small allowances paid to people on YTS would depress wage levels generally for young workers. The scheme would also reduce embarrassing unemployment statistics, since those participating were not classified as unemployed. In addition, the government hoped that it would help to reduce crime and social unrest (for example, riots) by taking up the free time of young people.

Finn denies that there was any truth in the claim that school leavers were unemployable. He believes that their unemployment was simply the result of a lack of jobs. He points out that many school pupils have experience of the world of work and prove themselves capable of holding down part-time jobs even before they leave school. In a survey of fifth-form pupils in Rugby and Coventry, he found that 75 per cent had had some experience of working: they could hardly be totally ignorant of the world of work.

Finn regards the various youth training schemes as a way of coping with the surplus of labour in the 1970s and 1980s. Rather than being left to their own devices, swelling the unemployment statistics, school leavers would be taught the values and attitudes that would make them an easily exploited workforce. The schemes would help to lower the employment expectations of the working class so that they would 'know their place'.

John Clarke and Paul Willis – the transition from school to work

John Clarke and Paul Willis (1984) have reached similar conclusions. They argue that the new vocationalism is a way of producing people who want to work, but are kept in 'suspended animation' before work becomes available. They see the schemes as resulting from a 'crisis of profitability' in British industry. Trainees can be used as a substitute for full-time employees who would have to be paid more and would be eligible for redundancy payments.

Phillip Cohen – social and life skills

Phillip Cohen (1984) has produced an interesting analysis of the content of education received on training schemes, looking particularly at social and life skills training. Rather than 'reskilling' the population – training them in specific skills like bricklaying – Cohen sees these courses as deskilling the workforce. The schemes claim to teach 'transferable skills', but Cohen regards these as no more than a type of 'behavioural etiquette'. Trainees are taught that their chances of securing a job are determined by how well they can manage the impression of themselves given to others. The true nature of the labour market, and the fact that unemployment is a structural feature of society, are disguised. Individuals are persuaded that the 'personal' problem of unemployment results from their failure to 'market' themselves to employers.

Cohen uses an example from social and life skills literature to illustrate his point. In the example – a cartoon story – a white boy and a black girl ring up to enquire about a job. The girl does everything right. She is polite, she explains exactly what information she requires, she takes a pen and paper with her to write down details, and she has prepared a clear explanation of why she wants the job. She thanks the potential employer, even though he shows no interest in employing her. The boy does everything wrong, forgetting who he wants to speak to and running out of money for the phone box. He also admits that it is not really the sort of job he is looking for. Despite the contrasts, both are equally unsuccessful: neither gets the job.

Cohen argues that the message of this story is that you should hide your feelings and if necessary be untruthful to secure work. Individuals must be in control of their own emotions and should not be 'uncool' by 'being yourself'. Encouraging this type of behaviour fosters an inner detachment, so that there is no personal disappointment from failure. It allows the individual to cope with powerlessness without challenging the powerful. In short, it is intended to produce a workforce who will work anywhere, or who will accept unemployment, but in doing so must submerge their own personality.

'New Labour' and post-Fordist perspectives on education

Introduction

New Right thinking has undoubtedly had an enormous influence on the development of educational policies in Britain and elsewhere. However, the election in 1997 of a Labour government in Britain raised the possibility that educational policy would take a new direction. As we will see, there were significant changes, but aspects of New Right policies and the new vocationalism were retained. In particular, the emphasis on driving up standards and on allowing 'choice' in the education system was retained, as was a desire to limit government expenditure and keep taxes relatively low.

However, the new approach did accept that an increase in government spending on education could be justified; it placed less faith in market competition to achieve improvements; and it showed a greater concern with issues of inequality and social justice. It did not place as much emphasis on equality and justice, though, as Marxist and even social democratic perspectives have done in the past (see pp. 787–94 and 783–6).

The perspective behind these policies was less clear than the idea of marketization which was perhaps the main principle shaping New Right policy. However, Phillip Brown and Hugh Lauder claim to have discerned a post-Fordist perspective behind the thinking of the Labour Party in Britain and other left-of-centre parties elsewhere.

Phillip Brown and Hugh Lauder – globalization and the post-Fordist perspective on education

Neo-Fordism and post-Fordism

As discussed earlier, Phillip Brown and Hugh Lauder (1997) believe that globalization has affected approaches to educational policy (see pp. 797–8). According to Brown and Lauder, globalization has led to an increased awareness of the need to have education policies that enable a country to compete globally. They believe that the New Right response has been to develop policies based upon a neo-Fordist approach.

In neo-Fordism the emphasis is upon cutting costs for potential investors: by cutting public expenditure so as to reduce taxation; by weakening the bargaining position of workers and encouraging them to be more 'flexible'; by creating an 'enterprise culture'; and by tailoring training to meet the specific needs of employers. While neo-Fordism is one coherent response to the forces of globalization, it is not the only possible one. Brown and Lauder say, 'There is no hidden-hand or post-industrial logic which will lead nations to respond to the global economy in the same way, despite the fact that their fates are inextricably connected' (Brown and Lauder, 1997).

Countries such as Germany, Japan and Singapore have adopted rather different, post-Fordist policies, rather than the neo-Fordist policies of countries such as the USA, New Zealand and Britain under right-wing governments. Brown and Lauder identify the policies of left modernizers, including the American president Bill Clinton and the British Labour Party in the 1990s, as having a post-Fordist perspective on education.

A summary of Brown and Lauder's views on the differences between neo-Fordism and post-Fordism are provided in Table 11.3.

Left modernizers

Left modernizers set their ideas in the context of a belief in the existence of a post-Fordist world economy. (See Chapter 10 for a detailed discussion of post-Fordism.) In this type of economy, markets change rapidly, and companies and their workers need to be flexible to meet frequent changes in consumer demand for different products. Companies are successful where they can produce high-quality products to meet these changing demands and are flexible enough to respond quickly to changes.

Left modernizers believe that in a post-Fordist economy there is a need for 'commitment to invest-ment in human capital and strategic investment in the economy as a way of moving towards a high-skilled, high-waged, "magnet economy"' (Brown and Lauder, 1997). Left modernizers believe that economic success cannot come from simply undercutting other countries in the price of goods. Such an approach is unlikely to succeed because the poorest countries of the world can always supply labour at lower wages than the richer countries. Successful countries will be able to protect the working conditions of employees – for example, through minimum wage legislation – if they succeed in establishing a high-skill, high-wage economy.

Success can only be achieved by producing higher-quality goods and services than are available elsewhere. Because they have to compete on a global level, companies usually have to be the best in the world to sell in large numbers. This can only be

Table 11.3   Post-Fordist possibilities: alternative models of national development

Fordism	Neo-Fordism	Post-Fordism
Protected national markets.	Global competition through: productivity gains, cost-cutting (overheads, wages).	Global competition through: innovation, quality, value-added goods and services.
	Inward investment attracted by 'market flexibility' (reduce the social cost of labour, trade union power).	Inward investment attracted by highly skilled labour force engaged in 'value-added' production/services.
	Adversarial market orientation: remove impediments to market competition. Create 'enterprise culture'. Privatization of the welfare state.	Consensus-based objectives: corporatist 'industrial policy'. Cooperation between government, employers and trade unions.
Mass production of standardized products/low-skill, high-wage.	Mass production of standardized products/low-skill, low-wage 'flexible' production.	Flexible production systems/small batch/niche markets; shift to high-wage, high-skilled jobs.
Bureaucratic hierarchical organizations.	Leaner organizations with emphasis on 'numerical' flexibility.	Leaner organizations with emphasis on 'functional' flexibility.
Fragmented and standardized work tasks.	Reduce trade union job demarcation.	Flexible specialization/multi-skilled workers.
Mass standardized (male) employment.	Fragmentation/polarization of labour force. Professional 'core' and 'flexible' workforce; (i.e. part-time, temps, contract, portfolio careers).	Maintain good conditions for all employees. No 'core' workers receive training, fringe benefits, comparable wages, proper representation.
Divisions between managers and workers/low-trust relations/collective bargaining.	Emphasis on 'managers' right to manage'. Industrial relations based on low-trust relations.	Industrial relations based on high trust, high discretion, collective participation.
Little 'on the job' training for most workers.	Training 'demand' led/little use of industrial training policies.	Training as a national investment/state acts as strategic trainer.

Source: P. Brown and H. Lauder (1997) 'Education, globalization and economic development', in A.H. Halsey, H. Lauder, P. Brown and A. Wells, *Education: Culture Economy Society*, Oxford University Press, Oxford, p. 175.

achieved with a workforce that has received the best possible education and training. From this point of view, to achieve success it is well worth investing in education and training – sometimes using government money to help crucial, high-technology sectors of the economy.

However, left modernizers accept that there are not unlimited resources available for education and investment in business. It is therefore important to concentrate on improving the quality of education without necessarily simply spending more money on it. Standards can be raised in other ways as well. The state must assume responsibility for ensuring that educational standards are as high as possible and must be intolerant of educational institutions that fail to achieve these objectives.

Left modernizers see a number of advantages to this approach:

1 It will produce a 'magnet economy', that is the skills and productivity of workers will attract considerable investment from abroad.

2 Economic success will largely solve the problem of unemployment. Although there will always be some who lack the skills to hold down jobs, programmes of retraining and education for adults can ensure that everybody has the chance to learn the necessary skills to have a good chance of finding work. In a rapidly changing globalized world, they will need to be flexible and accept the need for retraining if their skills become outdated and there is no longer a demand for them in the global economy.

3 Such policies will also lead to a reduction in inequality. Left modernizers believe that inequality largely stems from differences in the value of the skills possessed by different groups. By giving everybody the right to a high-quality education and access to retraining where necessary, there will be greater opportunities for everyone, skill inequalities will be reduced, and therefore inequality generally will decline.

Evaluation of left modernizers

Brown and Lauder do not question the general belief that a high-skill, high-wage economy is necessary. Furthermore, they support the general principle that investment in education can have beneficial effects. However, they also believe that there are flaws in the approach:

1 Brown and Lauder argue that training large numbers of skilled and educated workers will not in itself ensure economic success. Companies take a range of other factors apart from the skills of the labour force into account when making investment decisions, and, with growing competition from rapidly-developing Asian countries (such as Taiwan and South Korea), there is no guarantee that Britain can achieve anything approaching full employment.

Indeed, there is the risk that the workforce might become over-educated, and that there might not be enough jobs for all the expensively-educated graduates and highly-trained workers.

2 Brown and Lauder question the claim that increasing the skills of the workforce and improving educational standards will necessarily lead to a reduction in inequality. They argue that wage levels are shaped more by 'differences in labour-market power' than by levels of skill. Powerful groups are able to get their work defined as more skilled than less powerful groups, whatever the actual skills involved (see pp. 61–2 for similar views).

3 Brown and Lauder believe that the influence of a global labour market makes it increasingly important that governments intervene directly to reduce inequality. In a global economy the winners are likely to be extremely successful and highly paid, while the losers will be very unsuccessful and poor. Inequalities are likely to widen. Trying to raise everybody's educational standards will certainly not eliminate these inequalities and will be unlikely to reduce them very much. Brown and Lauder point out that a wealth of research shows that class inequalities have a major impact on people's performance in the education system. Those from deprived backgrounds are likely to take less advantage of improved opportunities for education and training than those from privileged backgrounds.

Brown and Lauder therefore conclude that improved educational and training opportunities are not enough. While they are necessary, they need to be supplemented by policies which will ensure that nobody is too deprived to have a good chance of succeeding in the education system. To achieve this, it is important that there is a 'social wage which delivers families from poverty'. Only with a guaranteed minimum income, and the security from deprivation that that brings, can all members of society have a fair chance to develop their potential.

Evaluation

Brown and Lauder raise some important questions about the adequacy of an increasingly important perspective on education. In some ways their ideas are reminiscent of the views of Marxist and social democratic sociologists, who have long argued that educational inequality cannot be effectively dealt with without dealing with inequality in the wider society.

However, Brown and Lauder's proposals are modest compared with some suggestions for redistributing wealth that have been put forward by radical sociologists. While what they propose might reduce poverty, research suggests that it is not just the poor who are disadvantaged in the education system. Even those in secure working-class jobs with wages comfortably above poverty levels may tend to do less well than most of their middle-class counterparts (see pp. 822–7 on class inequalities in education). In this case, any significant move towards equality of educational opportunity would require much greater redistribution than anything envisaged by Brown and Lauder, or likely to be introduced by 'left modernizers'.

'New Labour' and educational policies in Britain

Introduction

The election of Tony Blair's 'New Labour' Party in Britain in 1997 certainly led to some changes in the direction of educational policy towards the sort of post-Fordist approach outlined by Brown and Lauder. There was clearly a change in emphasis from the policies pursued by the preceding Conservative governments which had been in power since 1979. However, just as the Conservative governments did not always pursue policies in line with New Right thinking, Labour policies have also sometimes diverged from the post-Fordist perspective. This section will describe the policies adopted by the Labour government in its early years in office, before briefly evaluating them.

Labour's educational philosophy

Labour politicians in Britain in the 1990s certainly stressed the importance of education. Before the 1997 election, the leader of the party, Tony Blair, said that his priorities were 'Education, Education and Education'. In a speech on 16 June 1999, David Blunkett, the secretary of state for education and employment, outlined why education was so important. He said:

> Competitive pressures are intensifying. Ours is an increasingly complex and technologically driven world. As a country we need the effort and skill of all our people to compete and succeed. The sheer pace of change is adding to pressures. In today's job market, people have to constantly adapt – train and retrain – to stay ahead. Those who lack the skills to do so – those who, through lack of a basic education, are not even on the first rung of the training ladder – will become increasingly vulnerable.
>
> Blunkett, 1999, p. 1

In this quote, David Blunkett neatly encapsulates the main features of a post-Fordist perspective on education. These are: the belief in the importance of education in a global economy; the belief that education and training are vital to economic success; the claim that workers need to be flexible and to seek frequent retraining, if necessary; and the need for the unqualified to receive education to provide them with opportunities in society. Later in the speech Blunkett emphasized the link between education and opportunities in employment. He said, 'We know that failure at school is strongly linked to failure at work and in life more generally.' He also stressed the importance of an adequate educational foundation for children, and the need for continuing education throughout people's lives.

However, Blunkett did not believe that educational improvements could simply be imposed by governments. He argued that 'empowered and self-reliant individuals, strong families, self-sustaining communities' were necessary. Echoing elements of New Right thinking, he implied that over-reliance upon the state was a bad thing. It was better if the state encouraged people to help themselves and each other.

Educational policies

These concerns were reflected in a range of policies introduced by Labour. A number were designed to try to ensure that standards of education were improved:

1 In its election manifesto the government pledged to reduce class sizes to 30 in all primary schools, and, once elected, it spent extra money in an attempt to achieve this.

2 All schools were required to draw up Home–School Contracts, to involve parents in trying to ensure that children did their best at school, and to ensure that schools met their obligations to parents and their children.

3 A literacy and numeracy hour was introduced in primary schools to try to ensure that all children got a solid grounding in basic skills.

4 Ambitious targets were set for pupil achievement. For example, there was a target that, by 2002, 80 per cent of 11-year-olds would achieve government-set standards in English, and 75 per cent would reach the expected level in maths.

5 A National College for School Leadership was announced in 1999. Its objective was to ensure that all headteachers and other senior managers in schools were of a high standard.

6 The government took a tough line on inspection, retaining Chris Woodhead (appointed under the Conservatives) as Chief Inspector of Schools (head of the Office for Standards in Education) and extending his remit to include pre-school education and colleges.

Woodhead was a controversial figure, unpopular with teaching unions, partly because he expressed the view that there were large numbers of inadequate teachers. For a short time the government adopted a policy of 'naming and shaming': identifying the worst performing schools to try to shame them into improving.

7 The government supported *direct intervention by government agencies*, allowing them to take over schools or even local education authorities that were held to be failing pupils and students. Measures were introduced to allow the private sector to take over these functions on a temporary basis.

8 The government announced in 1998 a plan to set up *homework clubs*, and aimed to have them established in half of all secondary schools and a quarter of primary schools by 2003. The aim was to raise standards by encouraging all pupils to continue their learning outside school hours.

9 In 1999 the government announced its intention to set up a *Learning and Skills Council* to oversee most aspects of post-16 education and training, with the aim of improving standards. It was to take over many of the responsibilities of the Further Education Funding Council and of TECs. It was to operate through local Learning and Skills Councils throughout the country.

A number of other policies were designed to reduce inequality of opportunity as well as trying to improve school standards:

10 Extra spending went into *Education Action Zones*. These were established in areas of high deprivation and low levels of educational achievement in an attempt to boost the educational achievements of the deprived. The first 12 zones came into existence in September 1998, extended to 25 the following year. In the zones, money from the government and from private-sector sponsors could be spent on attracting teachers to the areas through higher pay, setting up homework clubs, and providing extra help to pupils. Education Action Zones can also deviate from the National Curriculum. In April 1999 it was announced that some of the worst-performing inner-city schools could become individual Education Action Zones, sometimes in conjunction with their feeder primary schools.

11 Another measure focused on the most deprived was the establishment of *social exclusion units*. These aimed to tackle a variety of causes of social exclusion, one of which was truancy from school.

12 Steps were implemented to make it easier to get rid of grammar schools and to end selection in other schools. The Conservatives had allowed up to 50 per cent of the children at comprehensives to be selected by academic ability. In 1998 the Labour government announced that a petition signed by 20 per cent of parents would trigger a ballot over whether grammar school status or selection should be retained. The

Labour government declared itself against selection, which has often been seen as socially divisive and harmful to the education of working-class children, but it did not insist that selection was ended.

13 Labour also *abolished grant maintained status* for schools, insisting that such schools either returned to local authority control or took on voluntary-aided status. The policy was partly designed to reduce educational inequality by removing the possibility that grant maintained schools could be seen as elite institutions cream-skimming the brightest students.

The central plank of the government's unemployment policy was the New Deal. The aim of this was to get the unemployed – particularly the young, single parents and the long-term unemployed – back to work. To this end, substantial amounts of money were made available for training or to subsidise employers taking on workers. Like some of the other policies, it was designed to tackle social exclusion (see p. 749 for more details of the New Deal).

Evaluation of Labour policies

Despite the large number of innovations, the Labour government retained many Conservative measures and continued to express approval for some aspects of Conservative policy and New Right thinking. For example, they continued to stress the importance of parental choice and of competition to improve standards. They retained league tables and City Technology Colleges and most aspects of the marketization of further education.

Expenditure on education was increased, but only to the extent that allowed the government to stick to quite strict spending limits. There were no increases in taxation to allow for increased educational expenditure. One controversial, money-saving policy was to introduce tuition fees for higher education students, initially of £1,000 per year. The government also decided to phase out student grants altogether, replacing them with tuition fees. Although the poorest students were exempt from paying fees, critics of these policies argued that they would discourage those from working-class backgrounds from staying on in education. Such students would be more likely to be daunted by the prospect of running up debts of many thousands of pounds while at university, and would be unlikely to receive voluntary financial help from their parents.

Although it is too early to evaluate the effectiveness of these policies, it is possible to suggest how they might be criticized by those supporting alternative perspectives on the education system:

1 From the *New Right* point of view, the Labour policies limit consumer choice by getting rid of

some of the diversity in schooling (for example, by getting rid of grant maintained schools). They threaten to undermine academic excellence by trying to phase out selection. They risk tax rises through excessive spending on education, and they could produce excessive bureaucratic interference in the education system with some power returning to LEAs.

2 From a *Liberal* point of view, Labour policy involves far too much emphasis on the economic role of education and too little on the importance of developing individual potential. From this point of view the education system under current and previous governments is too centralized and gives too little opportunity for the system to be tailored to individual and local needs. Furthermore, there is too much emphasis on exams and testing and not enough on other aspects of education.

3 From a *Marxist* point of view, Labour policies will fail to achieve their objectives. Inequality of opportunity will not be eradicated simply by tinkering with the education system itself and providing a few more resources in the most deprived areas. Instead, much greater efforts would be necessary to redistribute

wealth and power. Without such changes, children from working-class backgrounds will continue to bring such disadvantages with them that they are never likely to achieve anything like as much as their middle-class counterparts.

4 The *social democratic* view is perhaps the most similar to that of the British Labour Party – indeed much of their thinking stems from a social democratic tradition. However, even from this viewpoint there are faults in Labour policies. The party has failed to eradicate selection in the education system, even though it has discouraged it, and it has done nothing to eradicate streaming and setting. Tuition fees for higher education could be seen as likely to increase inequality of educational achievement between classes. From this perspective it would be better to have more democratic planning of education rather than retaining reliance upon market forces.

As the policies have time to take effect, research will help to reveal how far they have achieved their objectives. It is also likely that a number of critics will begin to attack aspects of the left-modernizing perspective which underlies the changes.

Postmodern perspectives on education

Robin Usher and Richard Edwards – *Postmodernism and Education*

Education and modernity

In their book, *Postmodernism and Education* (1994), Robin Usher and Richard Edwards discuss the implications of postmodernism for education. They start by arguing that 'Education is very much the dutiful child of the Enlightenment and, as such, tends to uncritically accept a set of assumptions deriving from the Enlightenment.'

They refer to the work of Lyotard, the leading proponent of postmodernism (see Chapter 15), who believed that, from the modern perspective, education promised to liberate the whole of humanity from ignorance and backwardness. According to the promises of modernity, education would help to spread the rational and scientific beliefs that would free people from the grip of tradition and superstition. Individuals had always had the potential to think for themselves and to make rational decisions, but they were prevented from doing this in pre-modern societies by the influence of superstition and tradition.

According to Usher and Edwards, the task of education under modernity was 'one of "bringing out", of helping to realise this potential, so that subjects

became fully autonomous and capable of exercising their individual and intentional agency'. Within modernity, education is the key to developing individuals and, in doing so, making social progress possible.

Usher and Edwards follow writers such as Lyotard in arguing that modernity is characterized by a belief in metanarratives of human progress (see Chapter 15 for a discussion of metanarratives). It is education which expresses and disseminates the big stories about progress and helps to give people their belief in progress itself and their faith in science and reason as the ways of achieving it.

Postmodernism/postmodernity and education

If Edwards and Usher are fairly clear about the close relationship between education and modernity, they are less clear about its relationship with postmodernity. Indeed they are rather unclear about what postmodernity is. They say:

> *To talk about postmodernity, postmodernism or the postmodern is not therefore to designate some fixed and systematic 'thing'. Rather, it is to use a loose umbrella term under whose broad cover can be encompassed at one and the same time a condition, a set of practices, a cultural discourse, an attitude and a mode of analysis.*

Usher and Edwards, 1994, p. 7

If it is unclear what postmodernism, postmodernity and the postmodern are, it is clearer what they are against. They are opposed to any belief that there is a firm foundation to knowledge; they are critical of any attempt to impose one version of the truth on people; and they are against believing that science and rationality can solve all human problems. Thus, Usher and Edwards say, 'postmodernism teaches us to be sceptical of foundationalism in all its forms, of totalising and definitive explanations and theories and thus of the dominant taken-for-granted paradigms in education, whether these be liberal, conservative or progressive'.

Postmodernism would therefore be suspicious of the liberal claim that human potential can be achieved through education, of the conservative claim of functionalists that education can produce shared values and social solidarity, and of the radical claims of social democrats that education can produce equality of opportunity and a just society. To Usher and Edwards, postmodernism also denies that there is any single best curriculum that should be followed in schools. If there is no one set of truths that can be accepted, then there is no basis for saying that one thing should be taught in all schools whereas other things should be excluded. Instead they argue that education should teach many different things and should accept that there can be different truths. Rather than providing any definitive blueprint for education, postmodernism simply suggests that there should be no attempt to impose one set of ideas on all education.

The future of education

How then might the education system develop? Usher and Edwards outline four possibilities:

1 Modern education systems could continue. The liberal view that education can help individuals fulfil their potential could be retained and the current education system could continue largely unchanged.

2 An alternative is that a conservative perspective could be imposed on the education system. The education system could be reshaped so that it tried to stress traditional values and to impose one set of values on everybody. This could occur as a reaction to the uncertainty and differences between people, which are part of postmodernity.

3 Education could be shaped to reflect the capitalist system. The content of education could be modified so that the primary emphasis is upon knowledge that is useful and helps to make a profit, rather than the main emphasis being on seeking truth. This has some affinity with postmodernism in that it defines knowledge in terms of usefulness rather than truth (see Lyotard's views on the changing nature of knowledge, in Chapter 15), but it still imposes one version of how education should be

developed, rather than accepting that education can encompass variety.

4 The final possibility is that education could reflect aspects of postmodernism by taking account of cultural pluralism – the needs of different groups. It could acknowledge the importance to individuals of shaping their own education to meet their personal needs and wishes. Usher and Edwards say, 'Examples here might be the emphasis on lifelong learning, the recognition and exploration of cultural difference, of educational provision for and by marginalised and oppressed groups.'

This would not entirely remove modern elements from the education system. For example, teaching people to be tolerant and accepting of people from different cultures could be seen as part of the modern, humanist, liberal tradition which tries to use education to turn individuals into better people.

Nevertheless, it would go some way towards undermining what Usher and Edwards see as the elitism of modern education. According to them, modern education was largely run by and for dominant groups such as white, wealthy males. If pluralism were accepted and minority interests catered for, this would no longer be the case.

The fourth possibility generally finds favour with Usher and Edwards, but they are careful not to put it forward as a definitive statement of how postmodern education should develop. They are conscious of trying to avoid the 'danger of simply replacing one totalising, oppressive discourse with another ... Therefore any reconfiguration is provisional and open to question.'

Nevertheless, they do concede that different educations are necessary for different people, including groups who are relatively powerless and currently have little influence on the education system.

Robin Usher, Ian Bryant and Rennie Johnston – postmodernism and adult education

In *Adult Education and the Postmodern Challenge* (1997), Robin Usher, writing on this occasion with Ian Bryant and Rennie Johnston, focuses particularly upon postmodernism and adult education. This book reiterates many of the points made in the earlier work by Usher and Edwards. It contrasts the nature of modernity and postmodernity, discusses how postmodernity undermines claims to a single truth, and suggests that this will lead to greater diversity within education. However, it goes further in suggesting how elements of postmodernism have already become evident in adult education, and it extends the analysis to discuss how adult education is linked to postmodern consumption.

According to Usher *et al.*, adult education has been particularly responsive to the postmodern trend towards greater choice and diversity. Compared to schooling, there is much more use of flexible and distance learning. This allows greater tailoring of the content and pace of education to meet individual needs.

Postmodernity is characterized by the decentring of knowledge: a move away from seeing any particular knowledge as central to all knowledge and superior to other forms of knowledge. This is reflected in the vast range of courses provided for adults by educational institutions. It is also reflected in increased uncertainty about what adult education is for. Liberal adult education, designed to develop people's potential as human beings or to encourage certain humanistic values, competes with a more vocational model which sees adult education as preparation for work. However, both models are beginning to be challenged by education becoming simply another form of consumption.

Education, consumption and identity

According to Usher *et al.*, postmodernism involves a decentring of the self. People no longer have a single, overarching sense of identity, of who they are. People's class, religion, place of birth, nationality and so on no longer define, on their own, who people are and how they see themselves. People are increasingly free to create their own identities and to change them almost at will. They do this partly by consuming different products, from the vast array of consumer products available, and by choosing particular lifestyles.

Increasingly, adult education has become simply another consumer product involved in lifestyle choices. Thus, for example, a woman may choose to study Italian to give herself a more cosmopolitan and sophisticated identity; or study alternative therapies such as acupuncture because she want to identify herself with New Age lifestyles. (See pp. 466–9 for a discussion of postmodern identities, and Chapter 12 for a discussion of the New Age.) In these circumstances, adult education becomes more of a playful, leisure activity, rather than the purposive, goal-orientated activity it was under modernity. Usher *et al.* say:

> *As education in the postmodern becomes detached from legitimising grand narratives, it becomes increasingly implicated with specific cultural contexts, on localised and particularistic knowledges, on the needs of consumption and the cultivation of desire and on the valuing of a multiplicity of experience as an integral part of defining a lifestyle. ... in postmodernity knowledge is valued for its 'interest' and its role in supporting the play of difference.*
>
> Usher, Bryant and Johnston, 1997, p. 15

However, Usher *et al.* do also acknowledge that another trend within postmodernism is for knowledge to become a commodity that can be bought and sold. Knowledge is also valued if it is useful and can therefore be exchanged for money in the labour market. Knowledge is no longer valued because it provides 'the truth', though, or because it helps to make people more rational. Essentially, enjoying yourself and making money become most important to people.

Modern educators and intellectuals might scoff at these concerns as being unimportant, trivial and lacking in seriousness. Usher *et al.* do not agree. Indeed they believe that postmodern education can play an important role in helping oppressed groups. Because of its openness, it gives a chance for education to feature the concerns of the oppressed. Furthermore, being able to consume is important to many groups trying to escape from disadvantage and oppression. Usher *et al.* say, 'There are many examples of oppressed groups who see empowerment in terms of the increased consumption of desired goods and images; as adult educators we ought to recognise this and at the very least not deny it.'

According to Usher *et al.*, adult education is no longer a well-defined field with clear goals. It increasingly overlaps with other areas of life, including leisure and work, and has a multiplicity of meanings and purposes for those involved.

Michael W. Apple – postmodernism, education, power and economics

The problems with postmodernism

Michael W. Apple (1997, first published 1993) welcomes some aspects of the postmodern perspective. He agrees, for example, that it may be misleading to believe that a single grand theory or metanarrative can explain everything about education, and he agrees that issues such as consumption and identity are increasingly important in contemporary societies. However, he also believes that postmodernists concentrate too much on local struggles over education and in doing so lose sight of the bigger picture. He claims that, while postmodernists focus on 'clever rhetorical and cultural battles ... over what counts as "appropriate" knowledge and what counts as "appropriate" forms of teaching and knowing', the education system as a whole is being shaped by wider political and economic forces. Postmodernists tend to ignore these forces and therefore neglect the sorts of insights into education offered by Marxists and neo-Marxists.

While Apple himself would not like to see Marxist perspectives emphasized to the exclusion of postmodern ones, he does not believe that the postmodern approach can afford to ignore what he calls the 'political economy' of education. Whilst postmodernists and cultural theorists are busy arguing amongst themselves, the education system is being shaped by powerful political and economic forces.

At times Apple is somewhat scathing about aspects of postmodernism and the cultural theory that it uses, saying, 'It moves from theory to theory rapidly, often seemingly assuming that the harder something is to understand or the more it rests on European cultural theory (preferably French) the better it is.' In the process, it 'has often lost any but the most rhetorical connections with the multiple struggles against domination and subordination'.

Power relationships

Apple gives an example of the sort of power relationships ignored by postmodernists. He claims that those types of knowledge that are valued by postmodernists, particularly cultural theory, are not particularly highly valued or important in the exercise of power. Instead he believes that 'technical/administrative knowledge' has been given the highest value, and the possession of such knowledge is used by people to gain positions of power and influence.

This type of knowledge is the type deployed in running large corporations in a competitive global economy. Apple says:

> An advanced corporate economy requires the production of high levels of technical/administrative knowledge because of national and international economic competition, and to become more sophisticated in the maximization of opportunities for economic expansion, for communicative and cultural control and nationalization, and so forth.

Apple, 1997, p. 600

Students learn this sort of knowledge when being educated in rapidly developing subjects such as market research and human relations. In the USA there have been cuts in humanities and arts subjects while business-related subjects have been expanding.

However, perhaps the most significant US example of this sort of trend is the TV programme *Channel One*. *Channel One* provides 'news' and commercials. It supplies free videos and TVs to each classroom and a satellite dish for schools which agree that over a three- to five-year period at least 90 per cent of pupils will watch at least 90 per cent of the broadcasts. The schools are monitored to ensure that they comply with the agreement. The offer is hard for cash-strapped schools to refuse and *Channel One* has been very successful. However, *Channel One* broadcasts essentially pro-capitalist, pro-business propaganda and in doing so is shaping the way schoolchildren see the world.

Apple concludes that social scientists should not allow postmodernism to make them forget the extent to which capitalism and economic power shape the world. He argues that the way contemporary societies are run 'is still capitalism and that makes a difference to our daily lives', and he says, 'The world may be a text, but some groups seem to be able to write their lines on our lives more easily than others.'

Postmodernism and education – evaluation and conclusion

Because postmodernists are anxious to attack all grand theories (or metanarratives), they try to avoid claiming that their approach is a coherent theory at all. It is largely based upon criticizing other approaches. Nevertheless, postmodernists are unable to avoid putting forward some of their own views, but it is often unclear what exactly they are trying to say.

For example, there is often ambiguity over whether they are describing changes in the education system or advocating change in a particular direction, or both.

It can be argued that, whichever is being claimed, there are serious problems with their analysis. For example, if their ideas are seen as descriptions of actual changes in education, then they may be inaccurate. Developments in the British education system have in some respects (such as the National Curriculum) involved the centralization of power in the hands of the government rather than increased diversity and choice (see pp. 810–12). Some social scientists question whether policies purportedly designed to achieve greater consumer choice have actually had such an effect (see pp. 806–10).

Postmodernists advance little empirical evidence to support the claim that adult education has become about choice of lifestyle rather than gaining qualifications for work. For sociologists such as Apple, commercialization and commodification of education are more important trends than consumer choice.

If their theories are more about how they would like to see the education system change, then they ignore powerful economic and political forces which may work to prevent the sort of changes they would like to see. If education is increasingly dominated by business, then it is unlikely that the curriculum will be increasingly influenced by the interests of local, oppressed groups. Feminists, gay rights activists, anti-racists, campaigners for disabled rights and so on may influence some university courses, but they are unlikely to be able to shape mainstream schooling. Furthermore, as Apple implies, qualifications relating to these sorts of subjects are unlikely to produce knowledge that has the same status and power as qualifications related to business.

Differential educational achievement

Class and achievement

Research reveals that the higher the social class, the higher the levels of educational achievement are likely to be. The children of parents in higher social classes are more likely to stay on in post-compulsory education, more likely to achieve examination passes when at school, and more likely to gain university entrance. These sorts of differences were a feature of British education throughout the twentieth century, and the evidence suggests that they remain very significant at the turn of the century. Whether there has been any reduction in the inequalities is more debatable, but some research suggests that the inequalities remain almost as great as ever, despite improvements in overall levels of achievement.

A.H. Halsey, A.F. Heath and J.M. Ridge – *Origins and Destinations*

One of the most thorough studies of class inequalities in education used a sample of 8,529 males born between 1913 and 1952 and educated in England and Wales. A.H. Halsey, A.F. Heath and J.M. Ridge (1980) found clear class differences. They divided their sample into three groups according to the father's occupation:

1 the service class who worked as professionals, administrators and managers;

2 the intermediate class who were clerical or sales workers, the self-employed and lower-grade technicians and foremen;

3 the working class including manual workers in industry and agriculture.

Halsey *et al.* found that a boy from the service class, compared to a boy from the working class, had four times as great a chance of being at school at 16, eight times the chance at 17, and ten times the chance at 18. Furthermore, his chance of going to university was eleven times greater.

Staying on until 16

By examining different cohorts (that is, groups born in different time periods), they found that there had been some reduction in staying-on rates until 16 or over, but little evidence of a reduction in class inequalities in other respects.

Halsey *et al.* looked at length of stay in education and access to university places. All of those in their sample passed through the education system before

the raising of the school-leaving age to 16, so they examined how many stayed on until that age. Here they did find some reduction in class inequalities, as Table 11.4 shows.

The rate of attendance for the working and intermediate classes more than trebled, while for the service class it increased by 50 per cent. However, Halsey *et al.* found no reduction in inequalities when examining who stayed on to 18 or over. As Table 11.5 shows, the rates more than doubled for all social classes, but it was the service and intermediate classes who gained most, and the working class least.

Table 11.4	Percentage staying in education until the age of 16 or over			
	Date of birth			
Class	1913–22	1923–32	1933–42	1943–52
Service class	52.4	61.0	77.3	78.6
Intermediate class	16.1	23.9	34.6	48.5
Working class	9.2	9.6	19.8	31.6

Source: A.H. Halsey, A.F. Heath and J.M. Ridge (1980) *Origins and Destinations*, Clarendon Press, Oxford, p. 136.

Table 11.5	Percentage staying in education until the age of 18 or over			
	Date of birth			
Class	1913–22	1923–32	1933–42	1943–52
Service class	15.7	20.0	32.2	38.2
Intermediate class	6.1	6.2	5.9	14.4
Working class	3.1	2.3	3.8	6.4

Source: A.H. Halsey, A.F. Heath and J.M. Ridge (1980) *Origins and Destinations*, Clarendon Press, Oxford, p. 140..

Halsey *et al.* suggest that credentialization has taken place, whereby the basic levels of education required to improve the chances of getting a well-paid job have gradually increased. In terms of attendance rates at 16, the working class caught up to some extent, but few stayed on long enough to gain sufficient qualifications to be upwardly socially mobile.

University entrance

The final area that Halsey *et al.* examined was class and university entrance. Once again they found evidence of increased opportunities for all classes because of the expansion of university places. Yet, as Table 11.6 shows, there was again little difference in the rates at which different classes were able to take advantage of these opportunities. Furthermore, as Halsey *et al.* point out, in absolute terms the service class gained much more than the working class. For both groups, attendance at university more than trebled, but for the service class this represented an absolute increase of 19.2 per cent; for the working class a mere 2.2 per cent.

Overall, then, Halsey *et al.* found only one area (rates of attendance at 16 or over) in which the relative chances of the highest and lowest classes were becoming more meritocratic, and even that might have been rendered insignificant by credentialization. In other respects, there was no evidence of an increasingly meritocratic society.

Halsey *et al.*'s figures should, however, be viewed with some caution. They are based entirely on a male sample, and the inclusion of female pupils might have made a significant difference to the findings. Furthermore, they are somewhat dated and do not show the effects of more recent changes.

Recent figures on class and achievement

Government figures

More recent figures from an official government survey, the *Labour Force Survey*, show that participation rates vary considerably by class. As Table 11.7 shows, in 1997/8, 80 per cent of those from professional backgrounds entered higher education at 18 or 19, compared to just 14 per cent of those from unskilled backgrounds. Thus those from the highest class had more than five times the chance of those from the lowest class of going on to degree-level courses. Such figures do suggest some narrowing of the gap in participation rates in higher education, but they show that children from professional backgrounds remain much more likely than any other group to benefit from the expansion of higher education.

Table 11.8 shows very big differences in the educational qualifications achieved by those in different socio-economic groups (the rough equivalent of social classes). It is based on another government survey, the General Household Survey, and figures are taken from 1995 and 1996. It shows that 66 per cent of professionals had degree-level qualifications or their equivalent, compared to less than 1 per cent of those in unskilled manual work.

Table 11.6	Attendance at university			
	Date of birth			
Class	1913–22	1923–32	1933–42	1943–52
Service class	7.2	15.9	23.7	26.4
Intermediate class	1.9	4.0	4.1	8.0
Working class	0.9	1.2	2.3	3.1

Source: A.H. Halsey, A.F. Heath and J.M. Ridge (1980) *Origins and Destinations*, Clarendon Press, Oxford, p. 188.

Table 11.7	Participation rates* in higher education, by social class, 1991/2–1997/8						
Great Britain				Percentages			
	1991/2	1992/3	1993/4	1994/5	1995/6	1996/7	1997/8
Professional	55	71	73	78	79	82	80
Intermediate	36	39	42	45	45	47	49
Skilled non-manual	22	27	29	31	31	31	32
Skilled manual	11	15	17	18	18	18	19
Partly skilled	12	14	16	17	17	17	18
Unskilled	6	9	11	11	12	13	14
All social classes	23	28	30	32	32	33	34

* The number of home domiciled initial entrants aged under 21 to full-time and sandwich undergraduate courses of higher education in further education and higher education institutions expressed as a proportion of the averaged 18- to 19-year-old population. The 1991 census provided the population distribution by social class for all years.

Source: *Social Trends* (1999) Office for National Statistics, London, p. 61.

824 Chapter 11: Education

Table 11.8 Highest qualification level attained, by sex and socio-economic group

Economically active persons aged 25–69 not in full-time education, in Great Britain: 1995 and 1996 combined

Highest qualification level attained[1]	Socio-economic group[2]							
	Professional	Employers and managers	Intermediate non-manual	Junior non-manual	Skilled manual and own account non-professional	Semi-skilled manual and personal service	Unskilled manual	Total
	%	%	%	%	%	%	%	%
Degree or equivalent								
Men	65	24	30	12	2	1	1	16
Women	68	22	24	4	4	1	0	11
Total	66	24	26	5	2	1	0	14
Further education below degree level								
Men	17	19	20	13	10	7	2	14
Women	11	19	28	5	4	4	1	11
Total	16	19	25	6	9	5	1	12
GCE A level or equivalent[3]								
Men	7	17	16	24	15	10	7	15
Women	7	13	9	12	10	8	4	10
Total	7	16	12	14	14	9	5	12
GCSE grades A–C or equivalent[3]								
Men	5	19	20	29	24	22	20	21
Women	4	23	21	39	28	23	14	27
Total	5	20	20	37	25	23	16	24
GCSE grades D–G or equivalent/commercial qualifications/apprenticeship								
Men	0	5	4	7	14	12	12	9
Women	3	8	7	18	14	12	10	12
Total	1	6	6	16	14	12	11	10

Foreign or other qualifications								
Men	3	3	3	2	3	2	4	3
Women	7	2	2	2	3	4	2	2
Total	4	2	3	2	3	2	2	2
No qualifications								
Men	2	12	7	14	33	45	55	23
Women	0	13	9	21	38	47	69	26
Total	2	12	8	20	34	46	64	25
Bases = 100%								
Men	693	2,089	994	570	2,939	1,117	255	8,657
Women	210	999	1,686	2,465	647	1,427	507	7,941
Total	903	3,088	2,680	3,035	3,586	2,544	762	16,598

1 Those who never went to school are excluded.
2 Excludes no answers, members of the Armed Forces, full-time students and those who had never worked.
3 Including FE qualifications.

Source: M. Thomas et al. (1998) *Living in Britain: Results from the 1996 General Household Survey*, Office for National Statistics, London, p. 95.

It is not entirely surprising that professionals are so likely to have degrees, since qualifications of this level are often a requirement of their job. But it is striking that those in manual jobs have so few qualifications. According to these figures, nearly two-thirds of unskilled manual workers have no qualifications at all, while nearly half of semi-skilled manual workers and over one-third of skilled manual and own-account non-professionals are unqualified.

Participation in higher education has been increasing for all social classes. As Table 11.7 (see p. 823) shows, between 1991/2 and 1997/8 participation amongst 18- and 19-year-olds rose from 23 per cent to 34 per cent. The proportion of lower classes participating rose faster than that for higher classes, but from a very low base. Although the participation rate for the children of unskilled manual workers more than doubled over this period, it was still the case that only 14 per cent were participating in 1997/8. Children from professional backgrounds still had a participation rate that was more than five times that of those from unskilled manual backgrounds: 80 per cent of the former were receiving a higher education, compared to 14 per cent of the latter. Those from partly-skilled and skilled manual backgrounds also had low participation rates of less than 20 per cent.

Teresa Smith and Michael Noble – educational inequality from the 1980s to the 1990s

The 1980s and the 1990s saw an increase in the proportions staying on at school or college after 16, and in the number being successful in GCSEs, in England. Teresa Smith and Michael Noble (1995) have examined data to see whether these changes resulted in a reduction in class inequalities. By looking at data from different LEAs, and classifying LEAs as advantaged, disadvantaged, or in-between, they were able to see how these changes had affected more and less deprived areas. Figures 11.2 and 11.3 show the results.

The figures show that in both cases the advantaged areas benefited slightly more than the disadvantaged areas from these changes. For example, in terms of those gaining five or more GCSEs at grade C or above, there was an increase of approximately 50 per cent in all three area types: the advantaged, medium and deprived. However, Smith and Noble point out that 'this means that the *actual rate* diverges with the more advantaged areas ending up further ahead'. This is because 50 per cent of an already high figure is more than 50 per cent of a lower figure. Although the figures are based upon aggregate figures for whole LEAs, and not on individuals, they do show that inequalities between areas were not decreasing. Other studies suggest that the same is true of individuals.

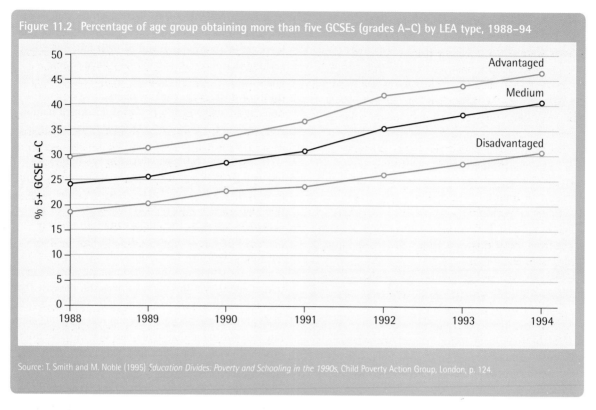

Figure 11.2 Percentage of age group obtaining more than five GCSEs (grades A–C) by LEA type, 1988–94

Source: T. Smith and M. Noble (1995) *Education Divides: Poverty and Schooling in the 1990s*, Child Poverty Action Group, London, p. 124.

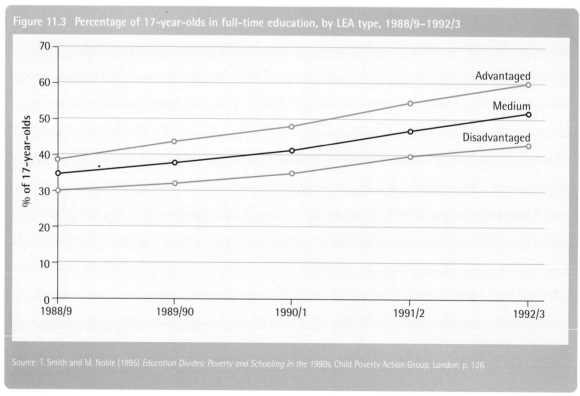

Figure 11.3 Percentage of 17-year-olds in full-time education, by LEA type, 1988/9–1992/3

Source: T. Smith and M. Noble (1995) *Education Divides: Poverty and Schooling in the 1990s*, Child Poverty Action Group, London, p. 126.

John Bynner and Heather Joshi – class differences, 1950s-1990s

In a study carried out by John Bynner and Heather Joshi (discussed in Norton, 1999) at the City University in London it was found that class differ-ences in educational achievement had persisted between the 1950s and 1990s.

The study compared 11,000 people in Britain born in March 1958 with 9,000 born in April 1970. Although more people were achieving high educational qualifications in the second cohort, the inequalities between the highest and the lowest classes were as great as they had been in the earlier cohort. For example, amongst those born in 1970 they found that daughters from an unskilled manual background, whose father had left school before he was 16, ended up on average with qualifications three levels lower than those achieved by daughters from a professional background. (For example, GCSE qualifications are three levels lower than degree qualifications.)

Children from lower classes who were born in 1950 generally did find work on leaving school, albeit often unskilled or semi-skilled work. Amongst those from lower classes born in 1970, many more ended up unemployed.

The existence of big inequalities in educational achievement in Britain is well established. Such inequalities are also found in other countries. It is also well established that there has been little, if any, decline in these inequalities over recent decades. We will now examine a number of possible causes of the existence and persistence of class inequalities in education.

Intelligence, class and educational achievement

The most obvious explanation for differences in educational achievement is the intelligence of the individual. In Britain, the 1944 Education Act established the tripartite system of education. Children were allocated to one of three types of school – grammar, technical, or secondary modern – largely on the basis of their performance in an intelligence test, the eleven-plus.

Educational psychologists (such as Sir Cyril Burt) were influential in the establishment of this system. Burt's research appeared to show that intelligence was largely inherited and could be measured by the use of a test. It therefore made sense to send children to the type of school best suited to their abilities. Grammar schools provided an academic education for those with a high measured intelligence, while secondary schools catered for those with a lower measured intelligence.

In the eleven-plus exam there was a strong correlation between results and social class, with middle-class children getting higher average scores. Consequently more middle-class children gained places at grammar schools.

Burt's research into intelligence was later discredited – many of his results had simply been invented – and the tripartite system was gradually replaced by comprehensives which all children attended regardless of ability. In most areas the eleven-plus was phased out. Nevertheless, many studies continue to show that there is a correlation between measured intelligence and achievement in education. Working-class children continue to score less well in intelligence tests than middle-class children. This might lead to the conclusion that lower intelligence continues to explain class differences in achievement.

However, there are many reasons for not jumping to such a simplistic conclusion. As Bowles and Gintis (1976) have argued, simply because above-average intelligence is associated with high academic qualifications, it does not necessarily mean that one causes the other. Before reaching any conclusions, it is necessary to examine questions such as 'What is intelligence?', 'How is it measured?', 'Where does it come from?'

What is intelligence?

The American psychologist Arthur Jensen (1973) defines intelligence as 'abstract reasoning ability', and argues that it is 'a selection of just one portion of the total spectrum of human mental abilities'. It is the ability to discover the rules, patterns, and logical principles underlying objects and events, and the ability to apply these discoveries to solve problems.

Intelligence is measured by intelligence tests which give an individual's intelligence quotient or IQ. Such tests are designed to measure abstract reasoning ability, and so exclude questions such as 'Which is the highest mountain in the world?' which test knowledge and memory rather than the ability to reason. Thus a simple IQ test may ask for the next number in the following sequence: 2, 4, 6, 8. This question requires individuals to discover the pattern underlying the sequence of numbers and to apply their discovery to solve the problem.

Despite their widespread use, there is a large body of evidence to suggest that IQ tests are not a valid measure of intelligence, particularly when they are used to compare the intelligence of members of different social groups.

Culture and intelligence

Many researchers argue that IQ tests are biased in favour of the middle class, since they are largely constructed by and standardized upon members of this group. If it is accepted that social classes and other social groups have distinctive subcultures and that this affects their performance in IQ tests, then comparisons between such groups in terms of measured intelligence are invalid.

This argument is best illustrated by the testing of non-Western populations with Western IQ tests. The Canadian psychologist Otto Klineberg (1971) gave a test to Yakima Indian children living in Washington State, USA. The test consisted of placing variously shaped wooden blocks into the appropriate holes in a wooden frame 'as quickly as possible'. The children had no problem with the test but produced low scores because they failed to finish within the required time. Klineberg argues that this does not indicate low intelligence but simply reflects the children's cultural background. Unlike Western culture, the Yakima do not place a high priority on speed.

Such examples suggest that Western IQ tests are inappropriate for non-Western people. The same argument has been applied to the use of IQ tests within Western societies which contain different subcultural groups, including social class subcultures. Thus, the British psychologist Philip Vernon states that 'There is no such thing as a culture-fair test, and never can be' (Vernon, 1969). This suggests that conclusions based on comparisons of the average measured IQ of different social groups must be regarded at best with reservation.

Genes and intelligence

There is general agreement that intelligence is due to both genetic and environmental factors: it stems partly from the genes individuals inherit from their parents, and partly from the environment in which they grow up and live. Environmental influences include everything from diet to social class, from quality of housing to family size. Some social scientists, such as Arthur Jensen (1973) and Richard Hernstein and Charles Murray (1994) in America, and Hans Eysenck (1971) in Britain, argue that IQ is largely inherited. They variously estimate that between 60 and 80 per cent of intelligence is genetically based.

Studies of identical twins raised in different environments show that they have different IQ scores. Since the twins are genetically identical, it can be argued that differences in their IQs are caused by environmental factors. But this does not allow an accurate measurement of how much of the IQ score of each twin is due to environmental factors, and prevents a reliable estimate of the genetic and environmental component of intelligence.

Despite objections to their views, Eysenck, Jensen, and Hernstein and Murray maintain that genetically-based intelligence accounts for a large part of the difference in educational attainment between social groups. Eysenck claims that 'What children take out of schools is proportional to what they bring into the schools in terms of IQ' (Eysenck, 1971). Jensen is more cautious when he suggests that 'genetic factors may play a part in this picture' (Jensen 1973). However, he does argue that there is better evidence for the influence of genes on educational attainment than there is for the influence of environmental factors.

Hernstein and Murray (1994) are concerned with inequality in general and not just inequality of educational attainment, although they see educational qualifications as one of the factors that create more general inequality. According to Hernstein and Murray, American society is increasingly meritocratic. People's class positions are increasingly determined by their intelligence. The education system itself is increasingly meritocratic. For example, the top US universities are now much less likely to admit people simply because they come from a wealthy family, than they were in the past. Much more attention is now paid to standardized tests in determining who will get the prized places at universities such as Harvard.

Environment and intelligence

Those who argue that differences in IQ between social groups are due largely to environmental factors make the following points. It is not possible to estimate the degree to which IQ is determined by genetic and environmental factors. Research has indicated that a wide range of environmental factors can affect performance in IQ tests. Otto Klineberg summarizes some of these factors:

> *The successful solution of the problems presented by the tests depends on many factors – the previous experience and education of the person tested, his degree of familiarity with the subject matter of the test, his motivation or desire to obtain a good score, his emotional state, his rapport with the experimenter, his knowledge of the language in which the test is administered and also his physical health and well-being, as well as on the native capacity of the person tested.*
>
> Klineberg, 1971

In the following sections we will examine evidence which indicates that the relatively low test scores of certain social groups are due, at least in part, to the factors outlined by Klineberg.

Given all the criticisms that were made of Eysenck and Jensen in the 1970s, it is perhaps surprising that the same sorts of argument were revived by Hernstein and Murray in the 1990s. Their ideas have promoted just as much criticism as those of their predecessors, and the evidence and arguments used to support their claims are as unconvincing as those of Eysenck and Jensen.

Many researchers now conclude that, given the present state of knowledge, it is impossible to estimate the proportions of intelligence due to heredity and environment. Measurement of possible genetically-based differences in IQ between social groups would involve the exposure of large numbers of individuals born into those groups to identical environments. Since this is neither morally acceptable nor practically possible, the debate will probably never be resolved.

In one sense the whole IQ debate can be seen as a storm in a teacup. It has been regarded as important because of the assumption that IQ directly affects educational attainment and level of income. If Bowles and Gintis (1976) are correct, this is not the case. They find that IQ is 'nearly irrelevant' to educational and economic success. Thus differences in IQ between social classes and ethnic groups, whether due mainly to environmental or genetic factors, may well have little real significance.

Class subcultures and educational attainment

Various studies have shown that, even when IQ is held constant, there are significant differences in educational attainment between members of different social groups. Thus working-class students with the same measured IQ as their middle-class counterparts are less successful in the educational system. It has therefore been suggested that class stratification is directly related to educational attainment. In particular, it has been argued that the subcultures and the distinctive norms and values of social classes influence performance in the educational system.

Values, class and educational attainment

This position was first spelt out in detail by the American sociologist Herbert H. Hyman (1967) in an article entitled 'The value systems of different classes', written in the 1960s. He argued that the value system of the lower classes creates 'a self-imposed barrier to an improved position'.

Using a wide range of data from opinion polls and surveys conducted by sociologists, Hyman outlined the following differences between working- and middle-class value systems:

1 Members of the working class place a lower value on education. They place less emphasis on formal education as a means to personal achievement, and they see less value in continuing school beyond the minimum leaving age.

2 Members of the working class place a lower value on achieving higher occupational status. In evaluating jobs, they emphasize 'stability, security and immediate economic benefits' and tend to reject the risks and investments involved in aiming for high-status occupations. Job horizons tend, therefore, to be limited to a 'good trade'.

3 Compared to their middle-class counterparts, members of the working class believe that there is less opportunity for personal advancement. This belief is probably the basis for the lower value

placed on education and high occupational status. Hyman argues that, although it is based on a realistic assessment of the situation – since the working class does indeed have less opportunity – the belief itself reduces this opportunity still further.

The values Hyman outlined did not characterize all members of the working class – a sizeable minority did not share them. This minority included many manual workers with white-collar parents – a fact which influenced their choice of reference group. Such workers identified more with the middle class and as a result tended to have higher aspirations.

In general, however, Hyman concluded that 'the lower-class individual doesn't want as much success, knows he couldn't get it even if he wanted to, and doesn't want what might help him get success'. Thus, the motivation to achieve, whether in school or outside it, will generally be lower for members of the working class.

Jobs, attitudes and educational attainment

In 1970, the British sociologist Barry Sugarman related certain aspects of middle- and working-class subcultures more directly to differential educational attainment. He provided an explanation for differences in attitude and outlook between the two classes, arguing that the nature of manual and non-manual occupations largely accounted for these differences.

Sugarman claimed that many middle-class occupations provided an opportunity for continuous advancement in income and status. This encouraged planning for the future: for example, the investment of time, energy and money in training to meet the requirements of higher-status jobs.

By comparison, working-class jobs reached full earning capacity relatively quickly, but provided fewer promotion prospects and less income for investment. In addition they were less secure. Manual workers were more likely to be laid off or made redundant than white-collar workers. The absence of a career structure in many working-class jobs meant that individual effort had less chance of producing improvements in income, status and working conditions. Collective action in the form of trade union pressure provided a more effective strategy.

Sugarman argued that differences in the nature of jobs tended to produce differences in attitude and outlook. Since they had less control over the future, less opportunity to improve their position, and less income to invest, manual workers tended to be fatalistic, concerned with immediate gratification, and present-time oriented. Since they were more dependent on joint action to improve wages and working conditions, they tended to emphasize collectivism rather than individualism.

Sugarman argued that these attitudes and orientations were an established part of working-class subculture. Pupils from working-class origins would therefore be socialized in terms of them. This may have accounted, at least in part, for their low level of educational attainment.

1 Fatalism involves an acceptance of the situation rather than efforts to improve it; as such it will not encourage high achievement in the classroom.

2 Immediate gratification emphasizes the enjoyment of pleasures of the moment rather than sacrifice for future reward, and will tend to discourage sustained effort with its promise of examination success. It will also tend to encourage early school-leaving, for the more immediate rewards of a wage packet, adult status and freedom from the disciplines of school.

3 Present-time orientation may further reduce the motivation for academic achievement, whereas an emphasis on long-term goals and future planning can encourage pupils to remain longer in full-time education by providing a purpose for their stay.

4 Finally collectivism involves loyalty to the group rather than the emphasis on individual achievement which the school system demands.

Sugarman therefore concluded that the subculture of pupils from working-class backgrounds places them at a disadvantage in the educational system.

Class subcultures – problems of methodology

Before continuing the theme of this section, it is important to make a number of criticisms of the concept of social class subculture and the methodology used to establish its existence:

1 The content of working-class subculture is sometimes derived from observation. In contrast to the behaviour of many members of the middle class, aspects of working-class behaviour appear to be directed by the attitudes, norms and values outlined above. However, this behaviour may simply be a response in terms of mainstream culture to the circumstances of working-class life. Thus, members of the working class may be realistic rather than fatalistic, they might defer gratification if they had the resources to defer, and they might be future-oriented if the opportunities for successful future planning were available.

From this point of view, members of the working class share the same norms and values as any other members of society. Their behaviour is not directed by a distinctive subculture. It is simply their situation which prevents them from expressing society's norms and values in the same way as members of the middle class. (This view is examined in detail on pp. 321–3.)

2 The content of working-class subculture is sometimes derived from interviews and questionnaires. Hyman's data were largely obtained from these sources. Barry Sugarman gave a questionnaire to 540 fourth-year boys in four London secondary schools, and his conclusions are largely based on data from this source.

However, what people say in response to interviews or questionnaires may not provide an accurate indication of how they behave in other situations. As Robert Colquhoun (1976) notes in his criticism of Sugarman, it cannot simply be assumed that 'a response elicited in a questionnaire situation holds in the context of everyday life situations'. Thus, social class differences in response to interviews and questionnaires may not indicate subcultural differences which direct behaviour in a wide range of contexts.

3 Finally, in a criticism of American studies, R.H. Turner (discussed in Colquhoun, 1976) notes that social class differences reported from interviews and questionnaire data are often slight. Sociologists tend to ignore similarities between classes and emphasize the differences.

J.W.B. Douglas – *The Home and the School*

The warnings contained in the above criticisms are applicable to an important early longitudinal study (that is, a study of the same group over time) by J.W.B. Douglas and his associates, *The Home and the School* (1964). The study was based partly on questionnaire data and utilized the concept of social class subculture. In *The Home and the School*, Douglas examined the educational careers of 5,362 British children born in the first week of March 1946, through primary school to the age of 11. In a second publication, *All Our Future*, he followed the progress of 4,720 members of his original sample through secondary school up to the age of 16 in 1962.

Douglas divided the students into groups in terms of their ability, which was measured by a battery of tests including IQ tests. He also divided the students into four social-class groupings, and found significant variations in educational attainment between students of similar ability but from different social classes. Comparing the attainment of 'high ability' students, Douglas found that 77 per cent of upper middle-class, 60 per cent of lower middle-class, 53 per cent of upper working-class and 37 per cent of lower working-class students gained good certificates at GCE O level. Comparing students of lower ability, he found even larger attainment differences related to social class.

Douglas also found that length of stay in the educational system was related to social class. Within the 'high ability' group, 50 per cent of the students from the lower working class left secondary school in their fifth year, compared with 33 per cent from the upper working class, 22 per cent from the lower middle and 10 per cent from the upper middle class. Again, social class differences were greater for lower-ability students.

Parental interest in education

Douglas related educational attainment to a variety of factors, including the student's health, the size of the family, and the quality of the school. The single most important factor appeared to be the degree of parents' interest in their children's education. In general, middle-class parents expressed a greater interest, as indicated by more frequent visits to the school to discuss their children's progress. They were more likely to want their children to stay at school beyond the minimum leaving age and to encourage them to do so. Douglas found that parental interest and encouragement became increasingly important as a spur to high attainment as the children grew older.

Douglas also attached importance to the child's early years since, in many cases, performance during the first years of schooling is reflected throughout the secondary school. He suggested that, during primary socialization, middle-class children receive greater attention and stimulus from their parents. This forms a basis for high achievement in the educational system. Douglas concluded, 'We attribute many of the major differences in performance to environmental influences acting in the pre-school years.'

Pre-school socialization

Apart from this general observation, Douglas did not examine pre-school socialization in detail. A large amount of research, mainly conducted by psychologists, has explored the relationships between child-rearing practices, social class and educational attainment. Although the results of this research are far from conclusive, there is some measure of agreement on the following points:

1 Behaviour patterns laid down in childhood have important and lasting effects. In particular, the child's personality is largely shaped during the years of primary socialization.

2 There are social class variations in child-rearing practices.

3 These variations have a significant effect upon attainment levels in the educational system.

Compared to working-class child-rearing practices, those of the middle class have been characterized as follows:

1 There is an emphasis on high achievement.

2 Parents expect and demand more from their children.

3 They encourage their children to constantly improve their performance in a wide range of areas, from childhood games to talking and table manners.

4 By rewarding success, parents instil a pattern of high achievement motivation into their children.

By giving their children greater individual attention and setting higher standards for them to attain, parents provide a stimulating environment which fosters intellectual development. In this way, middle-class child-rearing practices lay the foundation for high attainment in the educational system.

Criticisms

The above views have been strongly criticized. A number of arguments have been advanced to suggest that working-class parents are not necessarily less interested in their children's education just because they go to their children's schools less frequently than their middle-class counterparts. Tessa Blackstone and Jo Mortimore (1994) make the following points:

1 Working-class parents may have less time to attend school because of the demands of their jobs. Blackstone and Mortimore say:

> *frequency of visits to their child's school may indicate more about the relatively flexible working hours of fathers in non-manual occupations than about their levels of interest in their child's education.*
> Blackstone and Mortimore, 1994

2 Working-class parents may be very interested in their children's education but they are put off going to school because of the way teachers interact with them. Blackstone and Mortimore argue that it is possible that:

> *working-class parents feel ill at ease or the subject of criticism when they visit school. Teachers represent authority and parents who have had unhappy experiences at school or with authority figures may be reluctant to meet them.*
> Blackstone and Mortimore, 1994

3 Blackstone and Mortimore also quote evidence from the *National Child Development Study* which found that 89 per cent of middle-class but only 75 per cent of working-class children attended a school with a well-established system of parent–school contacts. Thus it was easier for the middle-class parents to keep in touch with the educational progress of their children.

Even if Douglas were right that big variations in child-rearing practices between social classes exist (which is far from established), the view that behaviour patterns laid down in childhood have a lasting effect has been challenged. In an important article entitled 'Personal change in adult life', Howard

S. Becker (1971) shows that behaviour can change radically depending on the situation. He argues that changes in behaviour patterns in adult life show clearly that human action is not simply an expression of fixed patterns established during childhood. If Becker's view is correct, educational attainment is a reflection of what happens in the classroom rather than what happens in the cradle.

Basil Bernstein – speech patterns

In this section we have examined possible subcultural differences between social classes which may account for differential educational attainment. We conclude the section with a consideration of class differences in speech patterns and their relationship to educational attainment.

Since speech is an important medium of communication and learning, attainment levels in schools may be related to differences in speech patterns. Much of the early work in this area was conducted by the English sociologist Basil Bernstein (1961, 1970, 1972). He distinguished two forms of speech pattern which he termed the elaborated code and the restricted code. In general, members of the working class are limited to the use of restricted codes, whereas members of the middle class use both codes.

Restricted codes are a kind of shorthand speech. Those conversing in terms of the code have so much in common that there is no need to make meanings explicit in speech. Married couples often use restricted codes since their shared experience and understandings make it unnecessary to spell out their meanings and intentions in detail.

Bernstein stated that restricted codes are characterized by 'short, grammatically simple, often unfinished sentences'. There is limited use of adjectives and adjectival clauses, of adverbs and adverbial clauses. Meaning and intention are conveyed more by gesture, voice intonations and the context in which the communication takes place.

Restricted codes tend to operate in terms of particularistic meanings, and as such they are tied to specific contexts. Since so much is taken for granted and relatively little is made explicit, restricted codes are largely limited to dealing with objects, events and relationships that are familiar to those communicating. Thus the meanings conveyed by the code are limited to a particular social group: they are bound to a particular social context and are not readily available to outsiders.

In contrast, an elaborated code explicitly verbalizes many of the meanings that are taken for granted in a restricted code. It fills in the detail, spells out the relationships and provides the explanations omitted by restricted codes. As such, its meanings tend to be universalistic: they are not tied to a particular

context. In Bernstein's words, the meanings 'are in principle available to all because the principles and operations have been made explicit and so public'. The listener need not be plugged in to the experience and understanding of the speaker since the meanings are spelled out verbally.

To illustrate his points, Bernstein gave the example of stories told by two 5-year-olds, one with a working-class, the other with a middle-class background. The children were given four pictures on which to base their story. In the first, several boys are playing football. In the second, the ball breaks a window. The third shows a woman looking out of the window and a man making a threatening gesture in the boys' direction. The fourth picture shows the boys retreating from the scene.

Using an elaborated code to spell out the detail in the pictures, the middle-class child describes and analyses the relationships between the objects, events and participants, and his or her story can be understood by the listener without the aid of the pictures.

The working-class child, using a restricted code, leaves many of his or her meanings unspoken, and the listener would require the pictures to make sense of the story. This story is therefore tied to a particular context, whereas the first story is free from context and can be understood with no knowledge of the situation in which it was created.

Bernstein explained the origins of social-class speech codes in terms of family relationships and socialization practices, and the nature of manual and non-manual occupations. He argued that working-class family life fosters the development of restricted codes. In the working-class family, the positions of its members are clearcut and distinct: status is clearly defined in terms of age, sex and family relationship. This clarity of status therefore requires little discussion or elaboration in verbal communication. Father can simply say 'Shut up' to his children, because his position of authority is unambiguous.

By comparison, members of middle-class families tend to relate more as individuals rather than in terms of their ascribed status as father, son, mother and daughter. Relationships tend to be less rigid and clearcut and based more on negotiation and discussion. As a result, meaning has to be made more explicit, intentions spelled out, rules discussed, decisions negotiated. Middle-class family relationships therefore tend to encourage the use of an elaborated code.

Bernstein also saw a relationship between the nature of middle- and working-class occupations and speech codes. He argued that working-class jobs provide little variety, offer few opportunities to participate in decision making, and require manual rather than verbal skills. In a routine occupation in the company of others in a similar situation, the manual worker is discouraged from developing an elaborated code. By comparison, white-collar occupations offer greater variety, involve more discussion and negotiation in reaching decisions and therefore require more elaborated speech patterns.

Speech patterns and educational attainment

Bernstein used class differences in speech codes to account in part for differences in educational attainment:

1 Formal education is conducted in terms of an elaborated code. Bernstein stated that 'the school is necessarily concerned with the transmission and development of universalistic orders of meaning'. This places working-class children at a disadvantage because they are limited to the restricted code.

2 The restricted code, by its very nature, reduces the chances of working-class pupils successfully acquiring some of the skills demanded by the educational system.

Bernstein did not dismiss working-class speech patterns as inadequate or substandard: he described them as having 'warmth and vitality', 'simplicity and directness'. However, particularly in his earlier writings, he did imply that, in certain respects, they are inferior to an elaborated code. He suggested that an elaborated code is superior for explicitly differentiating and distinguishing objects and events, for analysing relationships between them, for logically and rationally developing an argument, for making generalizations and handling higher-level concepts. Since such skills and operations form an important part of formal education, the limitation of working-class pupils to a restricted code may provide a partial explanation for their relatively low attainment.

Class and classification systems

In later work, Bernstein (1996) develops these ideas and tries to make links between classification systems and social class. He attempts to show that working-class children are more likely to classify things in terms of personal meanings and experiences, whereas middle-class children are more likely to classify things in terms of abstract principles.

He reports a study of 29 middle-class and 29 working-class children who were shown pictures of different types of food. He found that the working-class children were likely to classify foods on grounds such as 'I cook this for my mum' or 'I have this for breakfast'. On the other hand, the middle-class children were likely to use criteria such as whether the foods were vegetables, fruits or meats. When asked to re-classify the foods in a different

way, the working-class children continued to use criteria related to personal experience, while the middle-class children changed to using personal criteria as well.

Bernstein concludes that middle-class children can easily adopt two different ways of classifying things, whereas working-class children tend to concentrate upon one classification system. This gives middle-class children something of an advantage in the education system, since they feel more comfortable with abstract systems of classification which are frequently used in education.

To back up these claims, Bernstein quotes a study conducted by Whitty, Rowe and Aggleton (1994, quoted in Bernstein, 1996). In this study, students in four schools in England were given questionnaires in which they were asked to describe the meaning of new cross-curricular themes which had been introduced into English schooling. These themes included such things as economic and industrial understanding, health education and environmental education. Once again, working-class children tended to describe them in terms of personal meanings, whereas middle-class children described them in more abstract terms.

Educational psychology and speech patterns

Some educational psychologists have attached even more importance than Bernstein to speech patterns in explaining differences in educational achievement between classes. In particular, American psychologists such as Martin Deutsch, Carl Bereiter and Siegfried Engelmann (discussed in Labov, 1973) argue that the speech patterns of members of low-income groups are central to any explanation of their educational attainment. Where Bernstein is cautious, they state categorically that the speech patterns of low-income blacks and whites in America are inferior in practically every respect to those of members of higher-income groups.

Thus Bereiter states that the speech of many low-income children 'is not merely an underdeveloped version of standard English, but is a basically non-logical mode of expressive behaviour'. He argues that it is hopelessly inadequate to meet the requirements of the educational system, particularly with its failure to deal with higher-level concepts. Bereiter concludes that the speech patterns of the lower class retard intellectual development, impede progress in school, and directly contribute to educational failure.

Criticisms

Both Bernstein's ideas and the more extreme claims of psychologists such as Bereiter have provoked strong criticism. In a detailed critique of Bernstein's views, Harold Rosen (1974) attacks his arguments step by step. He states that Bernstein's view of social class is vague: at times he talks about the working class in general as having a restricted code; at others he specifies the lower working class. Bernstein lumps together all non-manual workers into a middle class whose members from top to bottom appear equally proficient in handling an elaborated code. He thus ignores possible variety within these classes.

Rosen also criticizes Bernstein's characterizations of working- and middle-class family life and work situations, demanding evidence for his assertions. Rosen notes a further lack of hard evidence for elaborated and restricted codes: Bernstein provides few examples to actually prove their existence.

Finally, Rosen accuses Bernstein of creating the myth that the supposed middle-class elaborated code is superior in important respects to working-class speech patterns. Rosen concludes that 'It cannot be repeated too often that, for all Bernstein's work, we know little about working-class language.'

Chris Gaine and Rosalyn George (1999) also criticize Bernstein for a lack of evidence and for using simplified distinctions between the working class and middle class. They suggest that, even if there was a homogeneous working class in the 1960s, when Bernstein's work began, this is not the case now. They say, 'Given the changes in the British class structure ... it would be unwise to describe it as anything other than multi-layered and blurred.' They therefore believe that it is far too simplistic to assume that the working class have one, dominant speech pattern.

In this section we have examined possible subcultural differences between social classes which may account, in part, for the different attainment levels of members of these groups in the educational system. We will examine the implications and policies that stem from this view in the next section.

Cultural deprivation and compensatory education

The picture of working-class subculture is not an attractive one. It is portrayed as a substandard version of mainstream middle-class culture. Its standard deteriorates towards the lower levels of the working class, and at rock bottom it becomes the culture of poverty, which we outlined in Chapter 5.

From this portrayal, the theory of cultural deprivation was developed. This states that the subculture of low-income groups is deprived or deficient in certain important respects and this accounts for the low educational attainment of members of these groups. This theory places the blame for educational failure on the children and their family, their neighbourhood and the subculture of their social group.

The so-called culturally deprived child is deficient or lacking in important skills, attitudes and values which are essential to high educational attainment. His or her environment is not only poverty-stricken in economic terms but also in cultural terms. The following quotation from Charlotte K. Brooks is typical of the picture of the culturally deprived child which emerged in Britain and the USA in the early 1960s:

> he is essentially the child who has been isolated from those rich experiences that should be his. This isolation may be brought about by poverty, by meagreness of intellectual resources in his home and surroundings, by the incapacity, illiteracy, or indifference of his elders or of the entire community. He may have come to school without ever having had his mother sing him the traditional lullabies, and with no knowledge of nursery rhymes, fairy stories, or the folklore of his country. He may have taken few trips – perhaps the only one the cramped, uncomfortable trip from the lonely shack on the tenant farm to the teeming, filthy slum dwelling – and he probably knows nothing of poetry, music, painting, or even indoor plumbing.
>
> Quoted in Friedman, 1976, p. 121

The catalogue of deficiencies of the culturally deprived child includes linguistic deprivation, experiential, cognitive and personality deficiencies, and a wide range of 'substandard' attitudes, norms and values.

Cultural deprivation and equality of education

The theory of cultural deprivation poses problems for the ideal of equality of opportunity in education. It had been argued that the provision of similar educational opportunities for all would give every student an equal opportunity to fulfil his or her talents. In the USA the high school provided a uniform system of secondary education. In Britain, supporters of the comprehensive school argued that the replacement of the tripartite system of secondary education – the grammar, technical and secondary modern schools – with the comprehensive system would go a long way towards providing equality of educational opportunity. A single system of secondary schools should provide the same opportunities for all.

However, it became increasingly apparent that a uniform state educational system would not provide everyone with an equal chance, since many would enter and travel through the system with the millstone of cultural deprivation hanging round their necks.

This realization slowly changed the notion of equality of educational opportunity. Formerly it had been argued that equality of opportunity existed when access to all areas of education was freely available to all. Now it was argued that equality of opportunity only existed when the attainment levels of all social groups were similar. The emphasis had changed from equality of access to equality of *results*.

Compensatory education and positive discrimination

From the viewpoint of cultural deprivation theory, equality of opportunity could only become a reality by compensating for the deprivations and deficiencies of low-income groups. Only then would low-income pupils have an equal chance to seize the opportunities freely provided for all members of society.

From this kind of reasoning developed the idea of positive discrimination in favour of culturally deprived children: they must be given a helping hand to compete on equal terms with other children. This took the form of compensatory education – additional educational provision for the culturally deprived. Since, according to many educational psychologists, most of the damage was done during primary socialization, when a substandard culture was internalized in an environment largely devoid of 'richness' and stimulation, compensatory education should concentrate on the pre-school years.

This thinking lay behind many of the programmes instituted by the Office of Economic Opportunity during President Johnson's war on poverty (from the 1960s to the early 1970s). Billions of dollars were poured into Operation Head Start, a massive programme of pre-school education, beginning in Harlem and extended to low-income areas across America. This and similar programmes aimed to provide planned enrichment – a stimulating educational environment to instil achievement motivation and lay the foundation for effective learning in the school system.

The results were very disappointing. In a large-scale evaluation of Operation Head Start, the Westinghouse Corporation concluded that it produced no long-term beneficial results.

During the late 1960s and early 1970s the Office of Economic Opportunity tried a system of performance contracting. Experts were contracted to raise the educational standards of low-income pupils on a payment-by-results basis. Highly-structured intensive-learning programmes were often used, similar to those developed by Bereiter and Engelmann at the University of Illinois. (Bereiter and Engelmann devised a programme of pre-school language education which drilled young children in the use of standard English.)

Again the results were disappointing. Performance contracting sometimes produced short-term improvements but its effects were rarely lasting.

From its evaluation of performance contracting, the Office of Economic Opportunity concluded that

'the evidence does not indicate that performance contracting will bring about any great improvement in the educational status of disadvantaged children' (quoted in Jensen, 1973).

Despite such gloomy conclusions, there is still support for compensatory education. Some argue that it has failed either because the programmes developed have been inappropriate or because the scale of the operation has been insufficient.

Educational Priority Areas

In Britain, compensatory education began in the late 1960s with the government allocating extra resources for school building in low-income areas and supplements to the salaries of teachers working in those areas.

Four areas – parts of Liverpool and Birmingham, Conisbrough and Denaby in the then West Riding of Yorkshire, and Deptford in south-east London – were designated Educational Priority Areas (EPAs). Programmes of compensatory education were introduced in the EPAs. These were based mainly on pre-school education and additional measures in primary schools to raise literacy standards. Although it is difficult to evaluate the results, reports from the EPAs were generally disappointing.

A.H. Halsey, who directed the EPA projects, argues that positive discrimination in England has yet to be given a fair trial. It has operated on a shoestring compared to American programmes – for example, in 1973 only one-fifth of 1 per cent of the total education budget was spent on compensatory education. Writing in 1977, Halsey stated, 'Positive discrimination is about resources. The principle stands and is most urgently in need of application.'

Compensatory education in the 1980s and 1990s

In Britain, in the 1980s and 1990s extra resources were made available for areas deemed to be suffering from deprivation. Local education authorities were allocated extra money according to an index called Additional Educational Needs (AEN). For example, from 1990 to 1994 this index was based upon the percentage of children who were from lone-parent families, the percentage who were dependent on income support, and the percentage whose parents were born outside the UK. According to Teresa Smith and Michael Noble (1995), AEN made up about 10.5 per cent of the education grant to LEAs before 1990, but changes introduced in 1990 raised this figure to 25 per cent.

Smith and Noble are supportive of the principle that extra resources should be made available to deprived areas, but are somewhat critical of the way the scheme worked. According to them, the scheme was particularly beneficial to certain London boroughs which had high proportions of lone mothers and ethnic minorities, even though these boroughs were not particularly deprived. On the other hand, some northern areas which were quite deprived did not score highly on the index. Under the AEN system, in 1992 the affluent London borough of Harrow received more extra funding per head than much poorer areas such as Barnsley or Liverpool.

In 1994 the proportion of the total education budget given for AEN was cut to 17 per cent, and the way of calculating the figures was altered to take less account of the proportion of ethnic minority children in the area.

There is little evidence that AEN has made a significant difference to educational performance. As discussed earlier (see p. 825), Smith and Noble found no evidence of a narrowing of the gap in educational achievement between affluent and deprived areas, even though the deprived areas would have received more funds under AEN than other areas. To Smith and Noble, this was not entirely surprising, since in the period in question there was a marked increase in inequality in British society as a whole (see pp. 43–9 for a discussion of rising inequalities). In these circumstances it would be hard for extra resources in the education system to overcome the effects of rising inequality in society generally.

The most recent attempt to provide extra assistance for the education of those in deprived areas in Britain is the introduction of Education Action Zones by the Labour government (see p. 817). These have certain similarities with the Educational Priority Areas of the 1970s. Like the earlier scheme, they provide extra resources to try to improve education in inner-city areas, and attempt to raise standards by compensating the beneficiaries for their deprivation. Whether these schemes will prove any more successful than their predecessors in raising educational achievement amongst the deprived remains to be seen.

Criticisms of compensatory education

Despite continuing support for compensatory education, criticism of the idea and its theoretical basis has been strong. .

Despite the AEN scheme, compensatory education was not generally favoured by Conservative governments in Britain between 1979 and 1997. Rather than trying to equalize outcomes in the education system, the Conservatives encouraged increased competition, with the stated aim of raising standards throughout the education system. Some critics of these policies argued that Conservative reforms from 1979 increased class inequality (see, for example, pp. 806–10).

The theory of cultural deprivation has also been strongly attacked by those who are in favour of reducing class inequalities in education. It has been seen as a smokescreen which disguises the real factors that prevent equality of educational opportunity. By placing the blame for failure on the child and his or her background, it diverts attention from the deficiencies of the educational system. William Labov argued that Operation Head Start is 'designed to repair the child rather than the school; to the extent it is based upon this inverted logic, it is bound to fail' (Labov, 1973).

Some of the more recent schemes have focused more upon improving schools, but they have still tended to assume that there is something wrong with the pupils and that this is an important factor behind their educational failure.

Even schemes which take account of possible inadequacies in schools can be criticized for diverting attention from the inequalities in society. D.C. Morton and D.R. Watson (1973) argued that patching-up operations such as programmes of compensatory education cannot remove inequality of educational opportunity which is rooted in social inequality in society as a whole. They claimed that compensatory education serves as 'a diversion from the pursuit of a genuine egalitarian policy'. In their view, equality of educational opportunity can only be possible in a society without social inequality. Compensatory education merely tinkers with a small part of the existing system; what is required is a radical change in the system as a whole.

Morton and Watson's comments may be just as applicable today as they were when they were first written, especially as evidence suggests that inequality has increased in Britain and the USA, compared to the 1970s.

Pierre Bourdieu – cultural capital and differential achievement

The cultural deprivation theory has been criticized for assuming or implying that higher-class cultures are superior to working-class culture. By implication, members of the working class are themselves to blame for the failure of their children in education.

In France, Pierre Bourdieu and his colleagues at the Centre for European Sociology in Paris have developed their own distinctive cultural explanation for achievement, and of the role of education in society (Bourdieu, 1971, 1973, 1974, 1984, 1994, Bourdieu and de Saint-Martin, 1974, Bourdieu and Passeron, 1977). Unlike cultural deprivation theory, this approach, cultural capital theory, is strongly influenced by Marxism. As such, it does not assume that the culture of higher social classes is in any sense superior to that of the working class.

Bourdieu argues that working-class failure is the fault of the education system and not working-class culture. The education system is systematically biased towards the culture of dominant social classes; it devalues the knowledge and skills of the working class.

Cultural reproduction

According to Bourdieu (1971, 1974), the major role of the education system is cultural reproduction. This does not involve the transmission of the culture of society as a whole, as Durkheim argued, but, instead, the reproduction of the culture of the 'dominant classes'. These groups have the power to 'impose meanings and to impose them as legitimate'. They are able to define their own culture as 'worthy of being sought and possessed', and to establish it as the basis for knowledge in the educational system.

However, this evaluation of dominant culture is 'arbitrary'. There is no objective way of showing that it is any better or worse than other subcultures in society. The high value placed on dominant culture in society as a whole simply stems from the ability of the powerful to impose their definition of reality on others.

Bourdieu refers to the dominant culture as cultural capital because, via the educational system, it can be translated into wealth and power. Cultural capital is not evenly distributed throughout the class structure, and this largely accounts for class differences in educational attainment. Students with upper-class backgrounds have a built-in advantage because they have been socialized into the dominant culture.

Bourdieu claims that 'The success of all school education depends fundamentally on the education previously accomplished in the earliest years of life'. Education in school merely builds on this basis: it does not start from scratch but assumes prior skills and prior knowledge. Children from the dominant classes have internalized these skills and knowledge during their pre-school years. They therefore possess the key to unlock the messages transmitted in the classroom; in Bourdieu's words, they 'possess the code of the message'.

The educational attainment of social groups is therefore directly related to the amount of cultural capital they possess. Thus middle-class students have higher success rates than working-class students because middle-class subculture is closer to the dominant culture.

Bourdieu is somewhat vague when he attempts to pinpoint the skills and knowledge required for educational success. He places particular emphasis on style, on form rather than content, and he suggests that the way in which pupils present their work and themselves counts for more than the actual scholastic content of their work. He argues that, in awarding grades, teachers are strongly influenced by 'the intangible nuances of manners and style'. The closer the student's style to that of the dominant classes, the more likely the student is to succeed. The emphasis on style discriminates against working-class pupils in two ways:

1 Because their style departs from that of the dominant culture, their work is penalized.

2 They are unable to grasp the range of meanings that are embedded in the 'grammar, accent, tone, delivery' of the teachers. Since teachers use 'bourgeois parlance' as opposed to 'common parlance', working-class pupils have an in-built barrier to learning in schools.

The habitus

In later work Bourdieu (1984, 1994, first published 1990) develops his ideas in terms of the concept of habitus.

Habitus refers to the lifestyle, the values, the dispositions and the expectations of particular social groups. A particular habitus is developed through experience. Individuals learn what to expect out of life, how likely they are to succeed in different projects, how others will respond to them if they behave in particular ways, and so on. Because different social groups have different experiences and chances in life, the habitus of each group will be different.

Individuals internalize the values, the behaviour and expectations of the habitus, and it shapes their future actions. They are not total captives of a habitus, they are free to act as they choose, but it does lead them towards making certain choices, regarding certain types of behaviour as normal, and so on. Individuals have to react to particular events, many of which are novel, but they tend to do so in terms of behaviours that they have come to see as '"reasonable", "common-sense", behaviours' (Bourdieu, 1994). Bourdieu therefore argues that 'the habitus is an infinite capacity for generating products – thoughts, perceptions, expressions and actions – whose limits are set by the historically and socially situated conditions of its production'.

According to Bourdieu, the habitus is closely linked to the development of taste, which in turn is closely related to education.

Taste, class and education

In *Distinction: A Social Critique of the Judgement of Taste* (1984), Bourdieu discusses the development of and importance of taste.

Using survey data as evidence, Bourdieu claims that people's tastes – for example, tastes in art, films, music and food – are related both to upbringing and to education. He claims to show that there is 'a very close relationship linking cultural practices (or the corresponding opinions) to educational capita (measured by qualifications); and secondarily, to social origin (measured by father's occupation)'. Different tastes are associated with different classes, and class factions have different levels of prestige:

1 Legitimate taste has the greatest prestige and includes serious classical music and fine art.
2 Middlebrow taste consists of 'the minor works of the minor arts'- for example, Gershwin's *Rhapsody in Blue.*
3 Popular taste includes 'light music or music devalued by popularization' (Bourdieu, 1984). Bourdieu gives the examples of *The Blue Danube* and Petula Clark (who was a popular singer in the 1960s).

Through upbringing and education, people learn to be able to express good taste. Those with legitimate taste can mix in the most culturally advantaged circles.

According to Bourdieu, the education system attaches the highest value to legitimate taste. Those who are brought up with legitimate taste find it easier to succeed in the education system and they are likely to stay on longer. Furthermore, the longer they stay on, the more legitimate taste they are likely to acquire. Once you have acquired a certain amount of legitimate taste through upbringing and education, then you can cultivate it further on your own. You end up with 'a "disinterested" propensity to accumulate experience and knowledge which may not be directly profitable in the academic market' (Bourdieu, 1984).

Good taste on its own does not guarantee educational success or a well-paid job, but it certainly helps. For example, it helps you get into the most prestigious schools. It also shapes teachers' perceptions of their pupils. Unconsciously teachers recognize different tastes and the types of behaviour typical of different classes. They value and reward legitimate taste more than middlebrow taste, and, in turn, middlebrow taste is valued more than popular taste. Such tastes may not even be part of the formal curriculum but they play an important role in giving those from higher-class backgrounds more chance of success.

The social function of elimination

Bourdieu claims that a major role of the educational system is the social function of elimination (Bourdieu, 1973, 1974, Bourdieu and Passeron 1977). This involves the elimination of members of the

working class from higher levels of education. It is accomplished in two ways:

1 by examination failure
2 by self-elimination

Due to their relative lack of dominant culture, working-class pupils are more likely to fail examinations, which prevents them from entering higher education. However, their decision to vacate the system of their own free will accounts for a higher proportion of elimination. Bourdieu regards this decision as 'reasonable' and 'realistic'. Working-class students know what is in store for them. They know that the dice are loaded against them. Their attitudes towards education are shaped by 'objective conditions', and these attitudes will continue 'as long as real chances of success are slim'.

These arguments lead Bourdieu to conclude that the major role of education in society is the contribution it makes to social reproduction – the reproduction of the relationships of power and privilege between social classes. Social inequality is reproduced in the educational system and as a result it is legitimated. The privileged position of the dominant classes is justified by educational success; the under-privileged position of the lower classes is legitimated by educational failure.

The educational system is particularly effective in maintaining the power of the dominant classes since it presents itself as a neutral body based on meritocratic principles providing equal opportunity for all. However, Bourdieu concludes that, in practice, education is essentially concerned with 'the reproduction of the established order'. This it does by ensuring working-class failure and the success of the higher class.

Stephen J. Ball, Richard Bowe and Sharon Gewirtz – cultural capital and educational choice

Bourdieu' s work on the importance of cultural capital in education has been very influential and has been used in a number of empirical studies. One such study is Sharon Gewirtz, Stephen J. Ball and Richard Bowe's study of 15 schools in neighbouring LEAs in England (see pp. 806–8 for full details of the study) (Ball, Bowe and Gewirtz 1994, Gewirtz, Ball and Bowe 1995). The study examines the impact of educational reforms, such as the introduction of open enrolment into the English education system. It discusses whether the increased emphasis on parental choice and market forces has led to greater equality of opportunity.

The education market and middle-class parents

According to Ball *et al.*, the educational reforms in England have altered the position of parents and pupils. With LEAs having less control over the allocation of pupils to schools, there is more opportunity for parents to manipulate the market. In particular, middle-class parents 'are exploiting the market in education and bringing their social and cultural advantages to bear'. They are in a better position than working-class parents to ensure that their children go to the school of their choice. There are a number of reasons for this.

First, middle-class parents possess more cultural capital than most working-class parents. They are more likely to have the knowledge and contacts to 'play the system'. Ball *et al.* found from their interviews that strategies used by the middle class included: attempting to make an impression with the headteacher at the open day; making a private appointment to visit the headteacher; knowing how to mount a successful appeal; and, most commonly, putting in multiple applications.

Second, gaining knowledge of the education system and manipulating it to your own advantage requires 'a great deal of stamina – to research, visit schools, make multiple applications and appeal'. Middle-class parents have their stamina 'sustained by knowledge, contacts, time and money'. Those with inside contacts in the education system, such as teachers and their relatives, are in a particularly good position.

As discussed earlier (see pp. 806–8), Gewirtz *et al.* distinguish between predominantly middle-class 'privileged/skilled choosers, semi-skilled choosers (who tend to come from intermediate classes), and disconnected choosers (who tend to be working-class). Generally, the more skilled the chooser, the more cultural capital they have. They are more able to decipher the subtler cultural messages provided by the school about its ethos. They have an advantage in identifying the best schools as well as in trying to find places for their children in them.

Third, middle-class parents' advantages are not entirely cultural. They also have material advantages over their working-class counterparts. These advantages are:

1 Middle-class parents can afford to pay for the public transport necessary to send their children to more distant schools. They may also be able to pay for taxis and they are more likely to have cars to take their children to school.

2 They are more likely to be able to move house so that they live in the immediate catchment area of a successful school with a good reputation.

3 They are more able to afford extra help or coaching to get children into grammar schools. Of course, they are also much more likely to be able to pay to have their children educated privately.

4 Middle-class parents are more likely to be able to afford to pay for childcare for younger children. This gives them more time to take their older children to more distant schools, and to visit schools so that they can make an informed choice about which school they want their children to attend.

Working-class and ethnic minority parents

Ball *et al.* did not find that working-class parents were any less interested in their children's education than their middle-class counterparts. However, they tended to lack the cultural capital and material advantages which enabled many middle-class parents to influence which secondary school their children attended.

Many working-class parents preferred to send their children to the nearest school because of 'a complex pattern of family demands and structural limitations'. Not only was it more difficult for them to secure a place for their children in a distant but successful school, but they actually placed considerable value on the advantages of obtaining a schooling close to home. Ball *et al.* say:

They want their children to go to a school which is easily accessible and does not involve long and dangerous journeys; a school where friends', neighbours', and relatives' children also go; a school which is part of their social community, their locality.

Ball, Bowe and Gewirtz, 1994

In Bourdieu's terms, they want to attend a school which is in tune with the habitus of their background.

Some – though by no means all – ethnic minority parents also suffer disadvantages in trying to manipulate the system to get their children into the best possible schools. If they were born abroad they may have limited experience of British education. Furthermore, there are disadvantages for those who do not feel confident enough about their English language skills to be able to negotiate the system, or who do not have the necessary contacts to assist them in working it. As Ball *et al.* put it, 'Their cultural capital is in the wrong currency and they are less able to accumulate the right sort.'

Conclusion

Ball, Gewirtz and Bowe's study illustrates how the sorts of cultural factors identified by Bourdieu can have an impact on class differences in education. However, it also suggests that they interact with material factors which can directly affect the educational prospects of different groups. Bourdieu himself is aware that material factors are also important. For example, he discusses how differences in income, as well as in culture, help to shape the tastes of different class groups (Bourdieu, 1984). Some theories place primary emphasis on the effects of material inequality on educational success. One such theory is that of Raymond Boudon.

Raymond Boudon – class position and educational attainment

In *Education, Opportunity and Social Inequality* (1974) the French sociologist Raymond Boudon argues that inequality of educational opportunity is produced by a two-component process.

The primary and secondary effects of stratification

We dealt with the first component, which he refers to as the primary effects of stratification, earlier (see pp. 829–34). It involves subcultural differences between social classes, which are produced by the stratification system.

However, although Boudon agrees that differences in values and attitudes between social classes produce inequality of educational opportunity, he argues that the secondary effects of stratification are probably more important.

The secondary effects stem simply from a person's actual position in the class structure – hence Boudon uses the term positional theory to describe his explanation. He maintains that, even if there were no subcultural differences between classes, the very fact that people start at different positions in the class system will produce inequality of educational opportunity.

For example, the costs involved and the benefits to be gained for a working-class boy and an upper middle-class boy in choosing the same educational course are very different, simply because their starting positions in the class system are different. If the upper middle-class boy chose a vocational course such as catering or building, his choice would probably lead to social demotion: the job he would obtain as a result of the course would be of a lower status than that of his father. However, the situation would be very different for the working-class boy who selected a similar course. The course might well lead to social promotion, compared to the occupational status of his father. Thus there are greater pressures on the upper middle-class boy to select a higher-level educational course, if only to maintain his present social position.

These pressures are compounded by the boys' parents. Boudon suggests that parents apply the same cost–benefit analysis as their children to the selection of courses. As a result, there will probably be greater pressure from upper middle-class parents for their son to take a course leading to professional status, whereas working-class parents would be more likely to settle for a lower-level course for their son.

The costs and benefits of education

Boudon also relates the costs and benefits of course selection to family and peer group solidarity.

If a working-class boy chose to become a barrister and followed the required courses, this would tend to weaken his attachment to his family and peer group. He would move in different circles, live a different lifestyle, and still be continuing his education when most or all of his friends had started work. His choice would therefore result in certain costs to family and peer group solidarity.

However, the same choice of career would result in benefits for the upper middle-class boy. His friends would probably be following similar courses and aiming for jobs at a similar level. His future occupation would be of a similar status to that of his father. Thus, if the upper middle-class boy chose to become a barrister and selected the appropriate educational course, his choice would reinforce family and peer group solidarity. Again, position in the class system directly affects the individual's educational career.

Boudon's positional theory argues that people behave rationally: they assess the costs and benefits involved when choosing how long to stay in the educational system and what courses to take. For people in different positions in the stratification system, the costs and benefits involved in choosing the same course are different. As a result, Boudon argues 'even with other factors being equal, people will make different choices according to their position in the stratification system'.

In a complex and sophisticated analysis, Boudon attempts to assess the relative importance of the primary and secondary effects of stratification on educational attainment. He finds that, when the influences of primary effects (subcultural differences) are removed, although class differences in educational attainment are 'noticeably reduced', they still remain 'very high'.

If Boudon's analysis is correct, the secondary effects of stratification are more important in accounting for differential educational attainment. Thus, even if all subcultural differences were removed, there would still be considerable differences in educational attainment between social classes and a high level of inequality of educational opportunity.

Boudon's work has important implications for practical solutions to the problem of inequality of educational opportunity. Even if positive discrimination worked, and schools were able to compensate for the primary effects of stratification, considerable inequality of educational opportunity would remain.

Boudon argues that there are two ways of removing the secondary effects of stratification.

A common curriculum and equality of opportunity

The first involves the educational system. If it provided a single compulsory curriculum for all students, the element of choice in the selection of course and duration of stay in the system would be removed. Individuals would no longer be influenced by their class position since all students would take exactly the same courses and remain in full-time education for the same period of time.

Boudon argues that the more branching points there are in the educational system – points at which students can leave or choose between alternative courses – the more likely working-class students are to leave or choose lower-level courses. Thus, if there were not a branching point at the age of 16 in British secondary education, inequality of educational opportunity would be reduced, since a greater proportion of working-class students leave at 16 compared to middle-class students of similar ability.

Boudon supports this point with evidence from Europe and the USA. There are fewer branching points in the American educational system, compared to European systems, and statistics suggest that inequality of educational opportunity is lower in the USA.

Boudon argues that the gradual raising of the school-leaving age in all advanced industrial societies has reduced inequality of educational opportunity, but present trends indicate that this reduction will, at best, proceed at a much slower rate.

An egalitarian society and equality of opportunity

Boudon's second solution to the problem of inequality of educational opportunity is the abolition of social stratification. He sees moves in the direction of economic equality as the most effective way of reducing inequality of educational opportunity. As a result, he argues that 'the key to equality of opportunity lies outside rather than inside the schools'; but, since there is little evidence that economic inequality in Western industrial societies is decreasing, Boudon sees no real evidence to suggest that class differences in educational attainment will decrease significantly in the foreseeable future.

Boudon concludes that 'For inequality of educational opportunity to be eliminated, either a society must be unstratified or its school system must be completely undifferentiated.' Since there is little

hope of either occurring in Western society, Boudon is pessimistic about prospects for eliminating inequality of educational opportunity.

Teresa Smith and Michael Noble – material factors and British education

Polarization in education

Despite the differences between them, the theories discussed above – Boudon's theory, the theory of cultural deprivation, and cultural capital theory – all attach importance to cultural factors. However, it is possible that material factors, such as family income, play a part independently of culture in determining levels of attainment.

Lower social classes may lack the money to provide their children with the same educational opportunities as middle- and upper-class parents. The changes to education in Britain introduced in the 1980s and 1990s may have made material inequalities even more relevant to educational opportunities.

As we saw earlier (see pp. 806–10), some critics of the marketization of education argue that it increases the importance of money in determining educational success. Smith and Noble (1995) suggest that marketization is likely to produce an increased polarization between successful, well-resourced schools in affluent areas, and under-subscribed, poorly-resourced schools in poor areas. They suggest that, if this is the case, then new policies will 'reduce rather than increase opportunities for children from poor families, by concentrating socially disadvantaged children in a limited number of increasingly unpopular schools'. Being able to afford to live in the areas with the best schools becomes more important.

The costs of education

Greater resources may give many other advantages to parents. Having money allows them to provide children with more educational toys, a greater range of books, a superior diet, more space in the home to do homework, greater opportunities for travel, private tuition, and access to private fee-paying schools. Thus, affluent parents can provide their children with advantages both before they attend school and during their school career.

'Free' state education has costs for parents. Smith and Noble point out that parents may struggle to pay for the hidden costs, and there have been cut-backs in the provision of help to those who are poor. Amongst the hidden costs are school clothing, meals, transport to and from school, and sometimes equipment, materials and school trips. There has been some provision to supply these free to the children of the poorest in Britain, but in recent years there have been cuts in these areas. Poor children may be entitled to clothing grants, but it is not compulsory for LEAs to provide them.

Smith and Noble found that in the 1990s a number of LEAs were cutting back on the number of grants and the actual amount they provided. Help with transport costs is automatically provided for children under the age of 8 who live more than two miles from school, and to older children who live more than three miles from school. For those who live nearer, help with bus fares is at the discretion of LEAs, and this may lead to some poor children walking nearly three miles to school.

Smith and Noble have found that schools struggling to make ends meet are increasingly imposing charges for trips, materials and equipment. By law, children should not be charged for anything essential to their school curriculum, but there is evidence of increasing pressure being put on parents to make 'voluntary' contributions. Children who have to make do with second-rate equipment and materials, and who are unable to go on trips enjoyed by most of their classmates, will have a less rich educational experience than other children.

Poor children remain entitled to free school meals. However, according to Smith and Noble there have been cut-backs in this service to save money. Cash cafeterias, where children pay cash for the items they choose, have become increasingly common. The value of the free school meal entitlement is sometimes insufficient to cover the cost of a full meal in such cafeterias. Smith and Noble also point out that there is considerable stigma attached to receiving free school meals in some schools, and in these circumstances the educational progress of recipients might be hindered.

Staying on in education

As Boudon suggests, decisions on whether to stay on in education are crucial to determining people's educational prospects. For poor children, it may be essential that grants are provided to help their families to support them in post-compulsory education.

Writing in 1995, Smith and Noble noted that Educational Maintenance Allowances and Further Education Awards were available in some LEAs. Both were means-tested, that is, they only went to the poorest students. However, both types of award were optional. Most LEAs did provide them, but there were big variations in the likelihood of getting an award in different areas. In 1993, for example, 74 in every 1,000 16- and 17-year-olds in Wales received an Educational Maintenance Award, compared to just 11 in 1,000 in the south-east outside London. In 1991 the average award was about £440 per year, and it is debatable whether this would be adequate to meet the costs of continuing in education.

Cultural or material factors?

Halsey, Heath and Ridge (1980) attempted to measure the importance of cultural and material factors. (For further details of the study, see pp. 822–3.) They distinguished between family climate, which involved cultural factors, and material circumstances. Family climate was measured in terms of levels of parental education, and attitudes to education; material circumstances were measured in terms of family income.

Halsey et al. found that both cultural and material factors had some effect on the educational attainment of children:

1 Family climate was important in determining what type of secondary school a child attended. Once a child was at school, however, family climate had little effect on the child's progress.

2 Material circumstances played a key role in determining how long children stayed at school. Halsey et al. stated, 'on this analysis, class inequalities in school leaving had virtually nothing to do with family climate. Material disadvantage is far more important.'

As Table 11.9 shows, the decision as to whether to stay on in post-compulsory education is a key factor in children's educational careers. Once children chose

Father's social class	Percentage staying at school until 16 or older	Percentage of those staying on to 16 or later passing one or more O levels	Percentage staying on to 18 or later	A level success rate: percentage of those who stayed to 18 or later and passed one or more A levels
Service class	70	83.1	28.2	93
Intermediate	32.6	74	7.7	90
Working class	26.8	71	3	93

Table 11.9 Social class, post-compulsory education and exam success

Source: A.H. Halsey, A.F. Heath and J.M. Ridge (1980) *Origins and Destinations*, Clarendon Press, Oxford.

to stay on after 16, most had some exam success: those from working-class backgrounds had almost as high a success rate as those from service-class backgrounds.

Halsey *et al.* suggest that a successful way of raising the educational achievement of the working class would be to offer grants to sixth-form students to encourage those from relatively poor backgrounds to stay on. The findings of this study tend to support the view that material circumstances affect the length of stay in education, which in turn has a crucial effect on the levels of achievement attained. It seems likely, however, that cultural and material factors work together to shape educational opportunities, a view accepted by most sociologists.

Education – an interactionist perspective

The explanations of differential achievement that we have examined so far all suggest that pupils' progress in education is strongly influenced by factors over which individuals have little control. Intelligence and home background are presented as largely determining the performance of pupils within the education system.

Yet the most obvious place to look for an explanation of differential educational achievement is within the education system itself. None of the previous approaches is based upon an examination of schooling, but it is widely assumed that schools play an important part in determining educational success and failure. Many parents (at least those who can afford it) spend considerable sums of money so that their children can attend fee-paying schools. It is highly unlikely that they would do so if they did not believe that such schools would offer their children some advantage.

Before the establishment of comprehensives many parents were also anxious that their children gained a place at a grammar school, assuming that this would prove advantageous for their children. Supporters of the comprehensive system hoped that, when all children in state education attended the same type of school, class inequalities in educational achievement would be greatly reduced. This did not happen. Despite comprehensives, class inequalities remain, and this has led to an emphasis on examining the differences in treatment that pupils receive, even when they are attending the same school.

Interactionists have illuminated the processes within the education system which result in different levels of achievement. Interactionists – far more than any other types of sociologists – have researched into the details of day-to-day life in schools.

As we saw in previous sections, psychologists and sociologists have explained performance in the education system in terms of intelligence, cultural and material deprivation, and social stratification. All of these approaches are, from the interactionist point of view, deterministic: that is, they see human behaviour as directed and determined by forces beyond the control of the individual. Individuals are held to react in a predictable way to external stimuli such as the directives of subcultures or the pressures of stratification systems.

Self-concept and meanings

To interactionists, the explanation of human behaviour needs to take account of the subjective states of individuals, and the meanings that individuals attach to external stimuli. For example, a pupil who achieves a poor test result might interpret the result in different ways and attach different meanings to it:

1 They might attribute the result to their own lack of ability and resign themselves to continued failure in the education system.

2 They might believe that the result has been caused by them failing to work sufficiently hard, and they might resolve to work with renewed effort.

3 On the other hand, they might attach little or no importance to the result, or they could deny the validity of the test and continue to believe that they have considerable ability despite the result.

Within education, as in society as a whole, other people are perhaps the most important source of external stimuli: their words and actions will constantly be interpreted and given meanings. To interactionists, your view of yourself, or self-concept, is produced in interaction with others. The self-concept of the pupil is influenced by the other pupils and the teachers with whom she or he interacts. The self-concept of a pupil may be modified if others constantly contradict it. For example, pupils who consider themselves to be a 'joker' may be forced to reconsider if nobody laughs at their jokes.

Interaction may be particularly important as the pupil develops the aspects of his or her self-concept concerned with academic ability.

Social roles

Another important interactionist concept is that of social roles. Within schools there are the obvious roles of pupils and teachers, but to interactionists these roles are not fixed and unchangeable.

Teachers may disagree with each other about the sort of person who makes the ideal teacher, and about the types of behaviour that are consistent with the pupil role.

Similarly, pupils may have different ideas about what makes the ideal teacher, or, for that matter, the ideal pupil. They may be unable to live up to the model of the ideal pupil held by their teachers. As a result, pupils may start to develop new patterns of behaviour. They may form subcultures in which the pupil role becomes modified, and types of behaviour which are punished by their teachers are rewarded by their peers.

Cultural deprivation theories also use the idea of subculture, but in a very different way. To interactionists, subcultures emerge from interaction within school as pupils develop ways of coping with school life. Subcultures are actively produced by those who are members of them. In cultural deprivation theory, however, the subcultures that influence educational attainment exist prior to the child going to school, and those who fail in the education system are the passive victims of the limitations of their own upbringing.

These general concepts provide the framework for interactionist studies of education. We will now examine the findings of these studies.

Typing, labelling and the self-fulfilling prophecy

One of the most important aspects of the interactionist theory of education concerns the ways in which teachers make sense of and respond to the behaviour of their pupils.

In their book, *Deviance in Classrooms* (1975), David H. Hargreaves, Stephen K. Hester and Frank J. Mellor analyse the ways in which pupils come to be typed or classified. Their study is based upon interviews with teachers, and classroom observation in two secondary schools. They examined the way in which teachers 'got to know' new pupils entering their first year at the school.

Initially, teachers have limited knowledge about their new pupils as individuals. They may know about the types of catchment area from which pupils originate, and have a general image of first-year pupils, but apart from this they can only start to build up a picture as the school year progresses. Hargreaves *et al.* distinguish three stages of typing or classification.

The first stage consists of speculation. The teachers make guesses about the types of pupils they are dealing with. The researchers noted seven main criteria on which initial typing was based. Teachers distinguished pupils according to:

1 their appearance
2 how far they conformed to discipline
3 their ability and enthusiasm for work
4 how likeable they were
5 their relationships with other children
6 their personality
7 whether they were deviant

Hargreaves *et al.* stress that in the speculation phase teachers are only tentative in their evaluations, and they are willing to amend their views if initial impressions prove to be misleading. Nevertheless, they do form a working hypothesis – a theory about what sort of child each pupil is.

Each hypothesis is then tested in the second phase, which Hargreaves *et al.* call elaboration. Gradually the hypotheses are either confirmed or contradicted, but either way the teachers become more confident in their judgements as their typing is refined.

When the third stage is reached, stabilization takes place. By this time the teacher feels that 'He "knows" the pupil; he understands him; he finds little difficulty in making sense of his acts and is not puzzled or surprised by what he does or says.' By this time, all the pupil's actions will be evaluated in terms of the type of pupil they are thought to be. Some pupils will be regarded as deviants, and for them it will be difficult for their behaviour to be seen in a positive light.

Typing and social class

Although Hargreaves *et al.* do emphasize that typing is a gradual process, other sociologists have suggested that it can be much more abrupt.

In a study of an American kindergarten, R.C. Rist (1970) found that as early as the eighth day of school the children were permanently seated at three separate tables. Furthermore, table 1 was reserved for 'fast learners', tables 2 and 3 for the less able. According to Rist, though, it was not, in reality, ability which determined where each child sat, but the degree to which they conformed to the teacher's own middle-class standards. For example, the teacher seemed to take account of whether the children had neat and clean appearances, and whether they were known to come from an educated family in employment. In other words, the kindergarten teacher was evaluating and labelling pupils on the basis of their social class, not on the abilities they demonstrated in class.

Similar claims were made by Howard Becker (1971). He interviewed 60 teachers from Chicago high schools and found that they tended to classify and evaluate students in terms of a standard of the 'ideal pupil'. This standard included the teachers' views of what constituted ideal work, conduct and appearance. Teachers perceived students from non-manual backgrounds as closest to this ideal; those from lower working-class origins as furthest from it. They interpreted the behaviour of lower-class students as indicating a lack of interest and motivation, and saw them as unrestrained and difficult to control.

Becker argues that, simply by perceiving certain students in this way, teachers experience problems in working with them. He concludes that the meanings in terms of which students are assessed and evaluated can have significant effects on interaction in the classroom and attainment levels in general.

The effects of typing

In itself the typing or labelling of pupils might not be that important, but many sociologists claim that it has important effects upon the progress of pupils. Teachers are in a position to affect their pupils' progress in a number of direct and indirect ways.

For example, Aaron V. Cicourel and John I. Kitsuse (1971) conducted a study of the decisions of counsellors in an American high school. The counsellors play an important part in students' educational careers since they largely decide which students should be placed on courses designed for preparation for college entry. Although the counsellors claimed to use grades and the results of IQ tests as the basis for classifying students in terms of achievement, Cicourel and Kitsuse found significant discrepancies between these measures and the ways in which students were classified.

Like Becker, Cicourel and Kitsuse found that the student's social class was an important influence on the way he or she was evaluated. Thus, even when students from different social backgrounds had similar academic records, counsellors were more likely to perceive those from middle- and upper middle-class origins as natural 'college prospects', and place them on higher-level courses.

Cicourel and Kitsuse argue that counsellors' classifications of students' ability and potential are influenced by a whole range of non-academic factors, such as the students' appearance, manner and demeanour, assessments of their parents, and reports from teachers on their conduct and adjustment. Cicourel and Kitsuse suggest that a counsellor's evaluation of an individual as a 'serious, personable, well-rounded student with leadership potential' may

often have more effect than his or her grades upon his or her educational career. Cicourel and Kitsuse conclude that such procedures do not uphold the 'ideal of equal access to educational opportunities for those of equal ability'.

In an article based on the same research, Cicourel and Kitsuse examine the meanings employed by counsellors in the definition of students as 'conduct problems'. Again they found a range of factors which subtly combine to create the counsellors' picture of a conduct problem. These include 'the adolescent's posture, walk, cut of hair, clothes, use of slang, manner of speech'. Again social class is an important basis for classification, since the characteristics used to type a conduct problem tend to be found in students from low-income backgrounds.

In British schools, teachers often differentiate between pupils by making decisions about what exams to enter them for and what streams or bands to place them in. These decisions can influence the options open to pupils and the extent of their progress in similar ways to those discovered by Cicourel and Kitsuse. We will consider this particular question of banding and streaming in the next section.

Teachers can also affect pupil progress in other ways apart from determining what classes they are placed in and what courses they take. Two closely related theories – the self-fulfilling prophecy theory and the labelling theory – both suggest that pupil behaviour can be changed by the way that teachers react to them.

The labelling theory suggests that typing leads to labels being attached to pupils.

The self-fulfilling prophecy theory argues that predictions made by teachers about the future success or failure of pupils will tend to come true because the prediction has been made. The teacher defines the pupil in a particular way, such as 'bright' or 'dull'. Based on this definition, the teacher makes predictions or prophecies about the behaviour of the pupil: for example, that she or he will get high or low grades.

The teachers' interaction with pupils will be influenced by their definition of the pupils. They may, for example, expect higher-quality work from, and give greater encouragement to, the 'bright' pupils. The pupils' self-concepts will tend to be shaped by the teachers' definition. Pupils will tend to see themselves as 'bright' or 'dull', and act accordingly. Their actions will, in part, be a reflection of what the teacher expects from them. In this way the prophecy is fulfilled: the predictions made by the teacher have come to pass. Thus the pupil's attainment level is to some degree a result of interaction between himself or herself and the teacher.

There have been a number of attempts to test the validity of the self-fulfilling prophecy theory. The most famous one was conducted by Robert Rosenthal and Leonora Jacobson (1968) in an elementary school in California. They selected a random sample of 20 per cent of the student population and informed the teachers that these children could be expected to show rapid intellectual growth. They tested all pupils for IQ at the beginning of the experiment. After one year the children were re-tested and, in general, the sample population showed greater gains in IQ. In addition, report cards indicated that teachers believed that this group had made greater advances in reading skills.

Although Rosenthal and Jacobson did not observe interaction in the classroom, they claimed that 'teachers' expectations can significantly affect their pupils' performance'. They suggested that teachers had communicated their belief that the chosen 20 per cent had greater potential to the children, who responded by improving their performance. Rosenthal and Jacobson speculated that the teachers' manner, facial expressions, posture, degree of friendliness and encouragement conveyed this impression, which produced a self-fulfilling prophecy.

Despite the plausibility of the self-fulfilling prophecy theory, it has been criticized. One area of criticism concerns the evidence. Rosenthal and Jacobson have been strongly attacked for the methodology they used in their study. In particular, it has been suggested that the IQ tests they used were of dubious quality and were improperly administered. In a review of research in this area, C. Rogers summarizes the findings. He says:

> Some show effects only with younger children, some only with older ones. Some show effects with urban children, but not suburban. Some show quantitative but not qualitative effects on pupil–teacher interactions, while others show the exact opposite.
>
> Rogers, 1982

Notwithstanding these contradictions, Rogers claims that the overall evidence, on balance, suggests that the self-fulfilling prophecy is a real phenomenon. However, it can be argued that it is not the inevitable phenomenon that Rosenthal and Jacobson make it appear.

Some interactionists have come to realize that not all pupils will live up to their labels. In a study of a group of black girls in a London comprehensive school, Margaret Fuller (1984) found that the girls resented the negative stereotypes associated with being both female and black. They felt that many people expected them to fail, but, far from living up to their expectations, they tried to prove them wrong. The girls devoted themselves to school work in order to try to ensure their success.

This particular interactionist, then, recognizes that negative labels can have a variety of effects. However, this observation weakens the forcefulness of the labelling theory. It seems that labels will usually have an effect, but the type of effect they have is not predictable. Fuller's work avoids some of the pitfalls of the cruder versions of labelling theory, which are rather deterministic in suggesting the inevitability of failure for those with negative labels attached to them. Her views are more in keeping with the non-deterministic interpretations of behaviour, which are, for the most part, typical of interactionist research.

Banding and streaming

Labelling and self-fulfilling prophecy theories suggest ways in which teachers' reactions to individual pupils can affect their educational careers. It is also possible, though, that whole groups of pupils, not just individuals, can be treated in different ways. Despite the fact that, under the comprehensive system, all state-educated pupils attend the same type of school, this may not mean that they receive the same type of education. In many comprehensive schools, pupils are placed, for at least part of the time, in different classes according to their supposed abilities.

Stephen J. Ball – banding at *Beachside Comprehensive*

In his book *Beachside Comprehensive* (1981), Stephen J. Ball examines the internal organization of a comprehensive school. At Beachside a system of banding was introduced for first-year pupils. Pupils were placed in one of three bands on the basis of information supplied by their primary schools. The first band was supposed to contain the most able pupils, and the third band the least able. However, Ball found that factors other than academic criteria were influential in determining the bands in which the children were placed. In particular, for pupils of similar measured ability, those whose fathers were non-manual workers had the greatest chance of being placed in the top band.

Ball observed that most pupils were conformist and eager when they first entered the school, but gradually the behaviour of the children began to diverge. He attributed this process to teachers having stereotypical views of the different bands. Band one was seen as likely to be hard-working, dedicated and well-behaved. Band three was not expected to be particularly troublesome, but the pupils were expected to have considerable learning problems. Band two was expected to be the most difficult to teach and the least cooperative.

According to Ball, the effect of these views was a progressive deterioration in the behaviour of most band two pupils, which was reflected in higher levels of absence, more non-conformist behaviour and a lack of effort being put into homework.

As a result of teacher expectations, different bands tended to be taught in different ways and encouraged to follow different educational routes. Band one pupils were 'warmed-up': they were encouraged to have high aspirations and to follow O level courses in subjects with a high academic status. In contrast, band two children were 'cooled-out' and directed towards more practical subjects and towards CSE exams. The end result was that band two pupils were much less likely than their band one counterparts to take O levels, to stay on at school after the age of 16, or to take A levels.

Ball admits that not all band two children failed. Some were able to overcome the difficulties that placement in this band produced. Nevertheless, there was a strong relationship between banding and performance. Given that there was also a strong relationship between social class and banding, Ball claims that 'working-class pupils tend to percolate downwards in the processes of academic and behavioural differentiation'.

Nell Keddie – streaming and classroom knowledge

While Ball examined the workings of a banding system, a study by Nell Keddie (1973) looked at the operation of streaming in a single subject in a large London comprehensive school. As well as looking at the classification and evaluation of students, Keddie also studied the ways in which knowledge was evaluated and classified. She tried to work out the criteria used by teachers to categorize and evaluate classroom knowledge.

Keddie discovered that knowledge defined by teachers as appropriate to the particular course was considered worthwhile; knowledge from the student's experience which did not fit this definition was considered of little consequence. Knowledge presented in an abstract and general form was considered superior to particular pieces of concrete information. The knowledge made available to students depended on the teacher's assessment of their ability to handle it. Thus those students who were defined as bright were given greater access to highly evaluated knowledge.

Like other interactionists, Keddie found a relationship between perceived ability and social class. Pupils were streamed into three groups in terms of ability. There was a tendency for pupils from higher-status white-collar backgrounds to be placed in the 'A' stream, and for those from semi-skilled and unskilled manual backgrounds to be relegated to the 'C' stream.

Keddie observed the introduction of a new humanities course designed for all ability levels. Despite the fact that all streams were supposed to be taught the same material in the same way, Keddie found that teachers modified their methods and the information they transmitted, depending on which stream they were teaching. There was a tendency to withhold 'higher grade' knowledge from 'C' stream pupils. Some teachers allowed the 'C' stream pupils to make more noise and do less work than those in the 'A' stream.

Keddie argued that teachers classified students in terms of a standard of the 'ideal pupil', similar to that described by Becker (see p. 845). The middle-class pupils in the 'A' stream were closest to this ideal and were therefore given greater access to highly evaluated knowledge. This resulted in 'the differentiation of an undifferentiated curriculum'.

Keddie then examined the students' definition of the situation, and she accounted for the 'success' of 'A' stream students in the following way. 'A' stream students were more willing to accept on trust the validity of the teacher's knowledge and to work within the framework imposed by the teacher. By comparison, 'C' stream pupils would not suspend their disbelief if the teacher made statements that did not match their own experience. For example, one pupil objected to a teacher's portrayal of the 'British family' because it did not fit his own experience.

From the teachers' viewpoint, such objections slowed down the transmission of the 'body of knowledge' they were concerned with getting across. Many of the questions asked by 'C' stream pupils were defined by teachers as irrelevant and inappropriate, as were their attempts to relate their personal experience to the course. In general, 'C' stream pupils were less willing to work within the guidelines set by teachers. Keddie ironically commented, 'It would seem to be the failure of high-ability pupils to question what they are taught in schools that contributes in large measure to their educational achievement.'

Keddie concluded that classifications and evaluations of both pupils and knowledge are socially constructed in interaction situations. Appropriate knowledge is matched to appropriate pupils. This results in knowledge defined as high-grade being made available to students perceived as having high ability. It results in pupils perceived as having low ability (in practice, mainly working-class pupils) actually being denied knowledge which is essential for educational success.

Pupil subcultures and adaptations

From an interactionist point of view, pupils experience school in different ways. They are treated differently by their teachers, given different labels, and often placed in different bands or streams. The pupils attach different meanings to their education and find a variety of ways to relate to their experiences. Schools usually lay down a set of standards and indicate to their pupils how they are expected to behave.

However, not all pupils are able and willing to conform to the image of the ideal pupil held by teachers. If they fail to do so, pupils may well form their own subcultures which reject some of the values of the school.

David Hargreaves – streaming and pupil subcultures

In an early study of a secondary modern school, David Hargreaves (1967) related the emergence of subcultures to labelling and streaming. Pupils labelled as 'troublemakers' were placed in lower streams; those whose behaviour was more acceptable in higher streams. Those with negative labels attached to them had been defined as failures: first, by being placed in a secondary modern which was seen as a second-rate institution; and second, through the streaming system. Many teachers regarded them as no more than 'worthless louts'.

Faced with the problem of being unable to achieve high status within the school, such pupils attempted to protect their sense of worth and retain a positive self-concept. Students labelled as troublemakers tended to seek out each other's company, and within their group awarded high status to those who broke the school rules. Thus, disrupting lessons, giving cheek to teachers, failing to hand in homework, cheating and playing truant all brought prestige. According to Hargreaves, then, two distinctive subcultures emerged within the school: the conformists and the non-conformist delinquents.

Peter Woods – pupil adaptations

Peter Woods (1979, 1983) argues, however, that schools are more complex than Hargreaves's work would suggest. Woods based his ideas upon a study of 'Lowfield', a secondary modern in a rural area of the Midlands.

Following Merton's typology of adaptations (see pp. 354–6), Woods suggests that pupils' ways of dealing with school life depend upon whether they accept or reject the aim of academic success and the institutional means which specify the appropriate forms of behaviour within the school. Going beyond Merton, Woods points out that pupils may accept goals and means with a greater or lesser degree of enthusiasm, and for different reasons. In all, Woods identifies no fewer than eight different modes of adaptation to the school:

1 Ingratiation is the most positive adaptation. Pupils who try to ingratiate themselves identify completely with teachers, and try to earn their favour. Such pupils care little about other pupils' attitudes to them and they may be regarded by other pupils as 'creeps' or 'teacher's pets'.

2 Compliance is a less strong positive adaptation to the school. Woods regards this adaptation as typical of new pupils in secondary schools. It is also common among older pupils who are studying for external exams, who comply for instrumental reasons, that is in order to achieve success in their exams.

3 Opportunism is an adaptation which often develops in the second year at school and may be a temporary phase before the pupil develops a stable attitude to the school. Opportunist pupils fluctuate between trying to gain the approval of their teachers and their peer group.

4 Ritualists are deviant to the extent that they reject the goals of education, but they are not difficult to control. They will 'go through the motions' of attending school, and will not break school rules, but they are not concerned either to achieve academic success, or to gain the approval of teachers.

5 Other pupils develop more deviant adaptations. Retreatists reject both the goals and the means laid down by the school, but without outright rebellion. They try to pass the time by daydreaming in lessons, 'mucking about' or 'having a laugh', but they are not consciously trying to oppose the values of the school.

6 According to Woods, a very common adaptation in later years at the school is colonization. This is characterized by 'indifference to goals with ambivalence about means'. Colonizers attach no great importance to academic success, but will try to get away with just enough to 'keep their noses clean'. They want to avoid trouble, but will copy or cheat if they think there is little chance of discovery.

7 Intransigence represents one of the most difficult adaptations for schools to cope with. Intransigent pupils are indifferent to academic success, and reject the accepted standards of behaviour. They are much less afraid than the colonizers to hide their deviance.

8 The final adaptation, rebellion, involves the rejection of both goals and means and their replacement with alternatives. In this case, school life is directed towards quite different objectives from those sanctioned by the school. For example, some girls might devote their school life to showing concern for their personal appearance, or discussing boys. Some boys might only be interested in escaping school to enter the world of unskilled manual work (see, for example, the description of Paul Willis's study, pp. 791–3).

Like many other interactionists, Woods relates his views in a very general way to social class, arguing that the more conformist adaptations tend to be typical of middle-class pupils, the less conformist of the working class. Middle-class pupils will, according to Woods, tend to find both the goals and means encouraged by the school to be more in keeping with the cultural values of their families than will working-class pupils.

Criticisms of Peter Woods

Complicated though Woods's adaptational model is, some interactionists nevertheless feel that it fails to do justice to the complexities of interaction within schools. V.J. Furlong (1984) suggests that pupils do not consistently act in accordance with a subculture or a particular type of adaptation. He stresses that individual pupils will behave differently in different contexts. For example, teachers tend to be seen as 'strict' or 'soft', and even normally conformist pupils might resort to deviant activities when faced with a 'soft' teacher and encouraged to be disruptive by fellow pupils.

A further limitation of the adaptational and subcultural approaches is suggested by M. Hammersley and G. Turner (1984). They point out that there may well be no single set of aims or values accepted by those in authority within a school. Not all teachers share a middle-class view of the world and middle-class values. Some may be in sympathy with at least some of the activities of 'deviant' pupils, and be less than enthusiastic about the most conformist among those they teach.

The interactionist perspective – an evaluation

The interactionist approach to the sociological study of education undoubtedly has advantages over some approaches. It is based upon far more detailed empirical evidence than, for example, functionalist and Marxist theories of the role of education in society. It has provided many insights into the day-to-day life of schools and other educational institutions. Furthermore, it is more sophisticated than some of the more deterministic theories of educational achievement. It shows that children's educational careers are not necessarily determined by such factors as IQ and home background.

Peter Woods (1983) claims that the interactionist perspective also has practical applications. He believes that it provides information which could lead to better teaching and a reduction in conflict and deviance within schools.

However, as in other areas of sociology, interactionist work has limitations. Some studies tend to be rather descriptive and do not always explain the phenomena they describe. For example, the description of different pupil adaptations advanced by Peter Woods does not fully explain why individuals adopt one particular adaptation rather than another.

Similarly it is difficult to support the interactionist contention that meanings and definitions of situations are simply constructed in classroom interaction. It is difficult to account for the apparent uniformity of meanings which result from a multitude of interactions. If meanings are negotiated in interaction situations, more variety would be expected. For example, is it simply coincidence that the 60 high school teachers interviewed by Becker all appear to hold the same concept of the 'ideal pupil'?

The relative uniformity of meanings that lie behind what counts as knowledge and ability, suggests that such meanings are not simply constructed in the classroom but rather they have a wider and more fundamental basis. In addition, many interactionists refer to the existence of class differences in education, but they fail to explain how those class differences originate. In these respects, symbolic interactionism can be accused of having too narrow a focus, of failing to take account of factors external to the school which might constrain or limit what happens within education.

Some attempts have been made to combine ethnographic studies of schools with sociological perspectives that do take into account wider factors related to the overall structure of society. One such attempt was made by Willis (see pp. 791–3).

Another study, by R. Sharp and A. Green (1975), highlights some of the limitations of interactionism. From their study of a number of classes in an infant school they found that a variety of constraints affected teachers' behaviour.

The school favoured a progressive pupil-centred education which treated each individual as unique and discouraged the differentiation of pupils according to ability. However, even in the classrooms of teachers who were in full support of this philosophy, the teachers did start to stratify individuals and to treat groups of pupils differently. This was because of the constraints under which the teachers worked, particularly the high pupil–teacher ratio (that is, the large size of the classes).

Sharp and Green conclude that the meanings held by the individuals concerned do not, on their own, determine what happens within education, and that interactionism needs to broaden its concerns to take account of such factors as the educational policies of the state which determine the conditions in which teachers and pupils work.

Gender and educational attainment

Developing views on gender and educational attainment

Although much of the earliest research on inequality of educational attainment focused on class, by the late 1970s gender inequality was becoming increasingly researched. By the late 1980s under-achievement by females was probably attracting more concern than under-achievement by the working class. However, in the mid-1990s there was a quite sudden reversal of the concern with *female* under-achievement. Instead concern became more directed at *male* under-achievement. In part, this change of focus was prompted by changes in the statistics of educational achievement, most of which suggested that, on average, females were doing better than males in most aspects of education.

However, there is disagreement over whether this change of emphasis is really justified, with some feminists arguing that female under-achievement should not be neglected.

Gaby Weiner, Madeleine Arnot and Miriam David (1997) have tried to summarize the changing discourses surrounding educational debates in Britain, and to relate these to changing discourses concerned specifically with gender and education. Their ideas are summarized in Table 11.10.

In the most recent phase, they see the new emphasis on male disadvantage as part of a wider discourse concerned with improving school standards. Some of their ideas will be discussed in more detail later in this section (see pp. 862–3).

Statistics on gender and differential achievement

Girls have long been more successful than boys in the early years of education. However, in the past, boys tended to out-perform girls in most areas after the age of 16. This is no longer the case.

Table 11.11 shows the results of National Curriculum tests at key stages 1, 2 and 3 (for 7-, 11- and 14-year-olds) in 1997. At all stages girls do better (or are assessed as better by teachers) in English, and they do better than boys in maths at key stage 1, and slightly better than boys at science in key stage 2. The difference in maths and science scores is small, but girls' advantage in English is quite marked.

In terms of GCSEs, greater female success in education has become more apparent. Table 11.12 shows that in 1996/7 a higher percentage of girls got a grade C or above in every subject apart from biological sciences and economics (where boys did marginally better), and mathematics, where boys and girls did equally well. Overall, girls got a grade C or above in 58 per cent of the GCSEs they entered, compared to 49 per cent for boys.

Girls have long passed more exams at 16 than boys.

Figure 11.4 shows the proportions of males and females gaining A level passes. It shows that in the late 1980s the percentage of girls achieving 2 or more A levels or 3 or more Scottish Highers exceeded the percentage of boys achieving the same qualifications.

Table 11.10	Parallel educational discourses	
Historical period	**Prevalent discourses of education**	**Prevalent discourses of gender and education**
1940s, 1950s	equality of opportunity: IQ testing (focus on access)	weak (emphasis on equality according to 'intelligence')
1960s, 1970s	equality of opportunity: progressivism/mixed ability (focus on process)	weak (emphasis on working-class male disadvantage)
1970s to early 1980s	equality of opportunity: gender, race, disability, sexuality, etc. (focus on outcome)	equal opportunities/anti-sexism (emphasis on female disadvantage)
Late 1980s, early 1990s	choice, vocationalism and marketization (focus on competition)	identity politics and feminisms (emphasis on femininities and masculinities)
Mid-1990s	school effectiveness and improvement (focus on standards)	performance and achievement (emphasis on male disadvantage)

G. Weiner, M. Arnot and M. David (1997) 'Is the future female? Female success, male disadvantage, and changing gender patterns in education', in A.H. Halsey et al. (eds) *Education: Culture Economy and Society*, Oxford University Press, Oxford, p. 622.

Table 11.11 Pupils reaching or exceeding expected standards, by key stage and gender, 1987

England	Percentages			
	Teacher assessment		Tests	
	Males	Females	Males	Females
Key stage 1[1]				
English	75	85	–	–
Mathematics	82	86	82	85
Science	84	86	–	–
Key stage 2[2]				
English	57	70	57	70
Mathematics	63	65	63	61
Science	68	70	68	69
Key stage 3[3]				
English	52	70	48	67
Mathematics	62	65	60	60
Science	60	63	61	60

1 Percentage of pupils achieving level 2 or above.
2 Percentage of pupils achieving level 4 or above.
3 Percentage of pupils achieving level 5 or above.

Source: *Social Trends* (1999) Office for National Statistics, London, p. 63

Table 11.12 Percentage of pupils achieving GCSE grade A–C, by subject and gender, 1996/7

Great Britain	Percentage achieving grade A*–C		
Subject group	All	Males	Females
Biological science	82	84	81
Chemistry	87	87	88
Physics	88	88	88
Science single award[1]	20	18	22
Science double award[2]	49	48	49
Other science[2]	47	46	51
Mathematics	47	47	47
Computer studies	58	56	62
Information systems[2]	54	52	57
Design and technology[2]	46	39	54
Craft, design and technology[3]	43	41	55
Technology[2]	54	51	58
Combined syllabuses[2,4]	47	44	53
Business studies	52	48	56
Home economics	42	26	45
Art and design	61	52	70
Geography	54	51	58
History	57	53	61
Area studies[2]	29	24	35
Economics	62	62	61
Humanities[2]	41	32	49
Religious studies	54	46	60
Social studies	51	42	55
English	56	48	64
Welsh[5]	58	48	67
English literature[2]	61	53	68
Welsh literature	62	53	70
Drama	67	57	74
Communication studies[2]	53	42	61
Modern languages			
French	50	42	57
German	55	47	62
Spanish	54	44	60
Other languages[6]	69	63	74
Classical studies	85	83	88
Creative arts[2]	48	37	59
Physical education	50	50	50
Vocational studies	50	41	55
General studies[2]	63	61	65
Modern studies[7]	58	52	63
Music	69	63	74
All entries	53	49	58
English and Mathematics[8,9]	41	38	44
English, Maths and a science[8,9]	38	36	41
English, Maths, Science and Modern languages[10]	36	31	40
Mathematics and Science[10]	42	41	42
Any subject	74	70	78

1 Standard grade in General science in Scotland.
2 England and Wales only.
3 Craft and design, Graphic communications and Technological studies in Scotland.
4 Includes Design and technology, or Technology or Information systems with other subjects for England.
5 Welsh as a first language.
6 Includes Welsh as a second language.
7 Scotland only.
8 English or Welsh as a first language in Wales.
9 Totals for Wales, and subsequently Great Britain are slight undercounts.
10 England and Scotland only.

Source: *Education and Training Statistics for the UK, (1998)* DfEE, London, p.70.)

Figure 11.4 Proportions of males and females gaining A level passes, 1975/6–1996/7

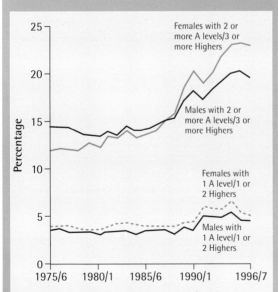

Females with 2 or more A levels/3 or more Highers

Males with 2 or more A levels/3 or more Highers

Females with 1 A level/1 or 2 Highers

Males with 1 A level/1 or 2 Highers

Note: Based on population aged 17 at the start of the academic year. Data up to 1990/1 relate to school leavers. From 1991/2 data relate to pupils of any age for Great Britain and school leavers for Northern Ireland and exclude sixth-form colleges in England and Wales which were reclassified as FE colleges from 1 April 1993.

Source: *Social Trends* (1999) Office for National Statistics, London, p. 55.

Since then, females have widened the achievement gap still further.

Another change is an increased tendency for females to stay on in education or training. In 1986, 41 per cent of males but just 33 per cent of females stayed on in education or training until they were 18. In 1997 there was little difference between the sexes, with 62 per cent of males and 60 per cent of females still in education or training at 18 (source: *Social Trends*, 1999).

In higher education the change has been even more dramatic. Table 11.13 shows that in 1970/1 males outnumbered females in higher education by more than 2:1. By 1996/7 females outnumbered males. However, there were still more males studying for postgraduate qualifications, and there is evidence that males continue to dominate in some of the more prestigious subject areas (see pp. 857–62).

Figures for those currently studying for or recently achieving qualifications suggest, then, that inequality between males and females is much less marked than it has been in the past. However, this does not mean that in the population as a whole men and women have similar levels of qualifications. The improvements in female achievement in the current generation will take many years to produce a population in which males and females have similar levels of achievement.

Table 11.14 shows the overall distribution of qualifications, and it shows that, overall, men remain much better qualified than women. For example, amongst whites in 1997-8, 54 per cent of men had A levels or higher qualifications, compared to 36 per cent of women. Amongst Indians, Pakistanis and Bangladeshis, 39 per cent of men and 25 per cent of women had qualifications at those levels. Amongst blacks, the gap was narrower: 42 per cent of men and 35 per cent of women had A levels or higher qualifications.

The evidence suggests, then, that women have substantially lower levels of educational qualifications than men; but, for those currently passing through the education system, the gap between the achievement of men and women is not great. In many areas females are marginally out-performing males, while at some of the highest levels (such as postgraduate qualifications) men retain an advantage. Furthermore, considerable differences remain in the types of subject studied by males and females. In some cases males may be more likely than females to be doing the prestigious subjects and those that offer the best career prospects (see pp. 857–62).

Table 11.13 Students[1] in further and higher education, by type of course and gender, 1970/1–1996/7[2]

United Kingdom	Thousands							
	Males				Females			
	1970/1	1980/1	1990/1	1996/7[2]	1970/1	1980/1	1990/1	1996/7[2]
Further education[3]								
Full-time	116	154	219	414	95	196	261	445
Part-time	891	697	768	638	630	624	986	938
All further education	1,007	851	987	1,052	725	820	1,247	1,383
Higher education[4]								
Undergraduate								
Full-time	241	277	345	491	173	196	319	528
Part-time	127	176	193	168	19	71	148	224
Postgraduate								
Full-time	33	41	50	75	10	21	34	63
Part-time	15	32	50	113	3	13	36	102
All higher education[5]	416	526	638	912	205	301	537	980

1 Home and overseas students.
2 1996/7 figures are not directly comparable with other years since those refer to enrolments rather than headcounts. Includes 1994/5 further education data for Wales.
3 Excludes adult education centres.
4 Includes Open University.
5 Data for 1996/7 include students whose level of study is unknown.

Source: *Social Trends* (1999) Office for National Statistics, London, p. 60.

Explanations for under-achievement by females

A variety of explanations have been advanced for female under-achievement in education, and we will consider the most significant ones in the following sections. Most of these explanations are based upon the assumption that it is girls who are less successful, and so are most relevant to explaining under-achievement in earlier decades. However, some of the processes discussed may still be preventing female pupils from achieving their full potential.

Innate ability

One possible explanation for female under-achievement is that there are differences in innate ability between males and females. However, while researchers have looked for evidence that girls have lower levels of ability than boys, many test results suggest that, if anything, girls have more innate ability than boys. Harvey Goldstein (1987) points out that, on average, girls performed better in the eleven-plus. Some LEAs, in fact, adjusted girls' scores downwards in order to ensure that grammar schools were not predominantly occupied by girls.

When separate tests are carried out for different types of ability, girls also tend to perform better than boys overall. Goldstein summarizes the results for girls and boys aged 11 as follows:

broadly speaking, for achievement in mathematics and reading the average differences are small, while for both verbal and non-verbal reasoning tests the girls have higher average scores than boys.

Goldstein, 1987

Some researchers suggest that this is because girls mature earlier intellectually than boys. At the time Goldstein was writing, by the age of 16 boys had overtaken girls in their average scores for mathematics and reading, although girls continued to do better in reasoning tests.

As Goldstein points out, though, the idea that such tests can measure innate ability is largely discredited (for a critique of IQ tests, see pp. 827–9). Furthermore, there are many processes which might have accounted for the comparative deterioration of girls in terms of mathematics and reading. Girls' experience of schooling may well explain the decline of their comparative performance in these areas.

From a review of the available evidence, Paul Trowler (1995) also raises strong doubts about the usefulness of biological explanations of female under-achievement. He does not think that there is much difference in male and female abilities amongst primary schoolchildren, but he acknowledges that most studies show that, at the age of 11, girls do slightly better than boys in tests of verbal skills, whilst boys perform slightly better in tests of visuo-spatial skills. However, Trowler points out that there

Table 11.14 Highest qualification held,[1] by gender and ethnic group, 1997–8[2]

Great Britain	Percentages						
	Degree or equivalent	Higher education qualification[3]	GCE A level or equivalent	GCSE grades A to C or equivalent	Other qualification	No qualification	All
Males							
Indian/Pakistani/Bangladeshi	18	5	16	14	25	22	100
Black	14	6	22	18	24	16	100
White	14	8	32	18	14	15	100
Other groups[4]	20	5	17	15	27	15	100
Females							
Indian/Pakistani/Bangladeshi	9	5	11	18	25	33	100
Black	9	12	14	27	22	16	100
White	11	9	16	29	15	20	100
Other groups[4]	12	8	15	17	33	15	100

1 Men aged 16 to 64, women aged 16 to 59.
2 Combined quarters: spring 1997 to winter 1997/8.
3 Below degree level.
4 Includes those who did not state their ethnic group.

Source: *Social Trends* (1999) Office for National Statistics, London, p. 65.

is very little difference in overall IQ scores for males and females. Differences in specific abilities might well be a product of social rather than biological processes. He concludes that:

> Obviously there are differences between males and females – physical, hormonal, genetic and so on. Even the less obvious ones can be established in a scientific way. The problem comes when trying to establish a link between social behaviour (e.g. women being better at languages) and these scientifically validated physical characteristics. It is very difficult, if not impossible, to say for sure that they are causally linked.

Trowler, 1995, p. 181

In the absence of convincing evidence for gender differences in attainment being the result of innate differences, we turn next to more plausible, alternative explanations.

Early socialization

Early socialization may well account for any eventual relative failure of girls. Fiona Norman and her colleagues (Norman et al. 1988) point out that, before children start school, conditioning and sex stereotyping have already begun. From the types of play that girls and boys are encouraged to engage in and the types of toys they are given, different sets of aptitudes and attitudes can be developed.

Girls may have their educational aspirations affected through playing with dolls and other toys which reinforce the stereotype of women as 'carers'. Boys tend to be encouraged to be more active than girls, and this may be reflected in their attitudes in classrooms. Furthermore, boys are more likely to be given constructional toys which can help develop scientific and mathematical concepts. Stereotypes of men and women can be further reinforced by the media, through comics, books, television and various types of advertising.

One possible consequence of early gender stereotyping is that girls may come to attach less value to education than boys. Research conducted by Sue Sharpe (1976) into a group of mainly working-class girls in London in the early 1970s found that the girls had a set of priorities which were unlikely to encourage them to attach great importance to education. She found that their concerns were 'love, marriage, husbands, children, jobs, and careers, more or less in that order'. Sharpe argued that, if girls tended to see their future largely in terms of marriage rather than work, then they might have little incentive to try to achieve high educational standards.

In the 1990s Sharpe repeated her research and found that girls' priorities had changed (Sharpe, 1994). The changes may help to explain why the educational attainment of girls at school is now greater than that of boys (see pp. 862–4 for more details).

Material factors

There is little doubt that the cultural factors involved in socialization play some part in explaining gender differences in educational attainment. It is less clear what part material factors might play, since obviously both boys and girls come from families at every level of the stratification system.

However, J.W.B. Douglas (1964) and colleagues suggested that in some families more resources are devoted to the education of sons than daughters. If parents believe that their son's future depends more upon his work than their daughter's, they may be less willing to finance post-compulsory education for daughters than for sons. This is a comparatively under-researched area and whether such differences continue today is unclear.

Socialization in school

Most research into gender and education has focused on factors internal to schools. Many sociologists have claimed to detect bias against girls in the educational system.

Glenys Lobban (1974) claims that the early years of some educational reading schemes reinforce the gender stereotyping found in wider society. From a study of 179 stories in six reading schemes, Lobban found that only 35 stories had heroines, compared to 71 which had heroes. Girls and women were almost exclusively portrayed in traditional domestic roles and it was nearly always men and boys who took the lead in non-domestic tasks. In at least three of the schemes females took the lead in only three activities in which both sexes were involved: hopping, shopping with parents, and skipping. Males took the lead in seven joint activities: exploring, climbing trees, building things, looking after pets, sailing boats, flying kites and washing cars. Summarizing the findings and the likely effects of the reading schemes, Lobban says:

> The girls who read them have already been schooled to believe, as our society does, that males are superior to females and better at everything other than domestic work, and the stories in the schemes cannot but reinforce the damage that our society does to girls' self-esteem.

Lobban, 1974

Lobban's research was conducted in the 1970s, but more recent research has also found evidence of gender stereotyping. In 1992, Lesley Best and her students examined a sample of 132 books for pre-school-age children in an attempt to discover whether gender bias in children's books had decreased.

They found that in these 132 books, 792 male and 356 female characters were portrayed. There were 94 male heroes but just 44 heroines. Some 75 per cent of the female characters featured in the book were portrayed in family situations, compared to just 15 per cent of the male characters; and men were shown in 69 different occupations, but women in only 18. Some characters were shown in non-traditional roles – there were two female sailors, a female jockey, and a male babysitter, for example – but they were the exception rather than the rule.

Lesley Best concluded that, despite the existence of a few non-sexist books, little had changed since Lobban's research. She says:

> it would seem that there is little attempt made in pre-school books to widen the horizons for either sex by presenting more women in a broad range of jobs or more men taking on a caring role.
>
> Best, 1993

Although considerable efforts have been made to eliminate gender stereotyping – for example, by some LEAs, teachers and publishers – there is evidence that the efforts have not been successful.

John Abraham conducted research in a comprehensive school in 1986. He found that gender stereotyping remained. After analysing the three main maths textbooks used he found them to be:

> extremely male-dominated. Moreover, male and female agency was extremely stereotyped. There were many more males represented in active roles. Women tended to be shopping for food or buying washing machines, whilst men tended to be running businesses or investing.
>
> Abraham, 1995, p. 113

In French textbooks there was also some gender stereotyping. However, unlike the maths books, women were sometimes shown using the subject in paid employment. In the maths books, the roles for women did not suggest any positive attractions of being a female mathematician. Maths was largely used in domestic roles. In the French books, female-dominated jobs such as being an air hostess, a secretary or a model suggested that French could be useful to women in paid employment.

Research which only examines the content of reading schemes or textbooks is rather limited in scope. It does not reveal what effects such books have on children. Recent research has tended to emphasize that children are not simply the passive recipients of socialization processes. Instead, they are actively involved in shaping their own conceptions of what it means to be masculine or feminine. Abraham's study is itself an example of this, and further aspects of his study will be discussed later (see pp. 865–6).

Behaviour in the classroom – self-confidence and criticism

The active and dominant males in the reading schemes may be reflected in the behaviour of boys and girls in the classroom. From their own classroom observations and from the analysis of other studies, Barbara G. Licht and Carol S. Dweck (1987) reached some interesting conclusions about sex differences in the self-confidence of young children in education.

Licht and Dweck found that girls lack confidence in their ability to carry out intellectual tasks successfully. Despite the superior performance of young girls compared to boys in primary schools, it was the girls who generally expected to encounter most difficulty when learning new things. According to Licht and Dweck, boys are able to shrug off failures by attributing them to a lack of effort on their part, or unfair assessment by teachers. Girls, on the other hand, constantly underestimate their ability, fail to attach significance to their successes, and lose confidence when they fail.

This is because girls blame failure on their own intellectual inadequacies, while explaining success in terms of luck. In doing this, girls fail to convince themselves that they are capable of succeeding, and they come to avoid challenging new situations in which they fear they will fail.

Licht and Dweck do not think that this situation is the result of conscious discrimination by teachers. Indeed, they found that, in line with their own experiences of how girls performed, most primary school teachers expected greater success from their girl pupils. However, by examining fourth- and fifth-grade American classes, Licht and Dweck found differences in the ways that boys and girls were evaluated.

There was very little difference between the sexes in the amount of praise and criticism that girls and boys received for their academic achievements and failures. Boys, however, were criticized much more frequently for lacking neatness in their work, for failing to make sufficient effort and for misbehaviour in the classroom. Licht and Dweck concluded that girls begin to lose confidence because they get less criticism from teachers. The boys in their study were given ways of explaining away their failures in terms of behaviour that could be modified; the girls had no such excuses to make for themselves.

Michelle Stanworth – gender differences in further education

Michelle Stanworth (1983) examined the later stages of the education system in a study of A level classes in a further education college. She interviewed teachers and pupils from seven different classes in the humanities department. Her findings suggested that in the sixth form a number of the attitudes displayed by teachers would impede the educational progress of girls. These attitudes were not confined to male teachers – they were also typical of their female colleagues.

Teachers found it much more difficult to remember the girls in their classes. Without exception, all the pupils whom teachers said it was difficult to name and recall were girls. Quiet boys were remembered, but quiet girls seemed to blend into the background and make little impression on their teachers.

Stanworth found that teachers held stereotypical views of what their female pupils would be doing in the future. Only one girl was seen as having the potential to enter a professional occupation. Interestingly, she was the most assertive of the girls in the classroom but her academic performance was not particularly good. The most academically successful girl was described by one teacher as being likely to become a 'personal assistant for someone rather important'. Even for this girl, marriage was suggested as one of the most significant aspects of her future life; and male teachers mentioned nothing other than marriage as the future for two-thirds of the female pupils.

When asked which students were given the most attention by teachers, the pupils themselves named boys two and a half times as often as girls, although girls outnumbered boys by nearly two to one in the classes studied. The pupils reported that boys were four times more likely to join in classroom discussions, twice as likely to seek help from the teacher, and twice as likely to be asked questions.

Furthermore, girls were consistently likely to underestimate their ability, while boys overestimated theirs. Pupils were asked to rank themselves in terms of ability in each class. In 19 of the 24 cases in which teachers and pupils disagreed about the ranking, all of the girls placed themselves lower than the teachers' estimates, and all but one boy placed themselves higher.

Stanworth found, then, that interaction in the classroom seemed to disadvantage girls considerably. They were encouraged to take less part in classes, and got less attention from teachers, and as a consequence lacked faith in their own ability. Teachers had an important role in these processes, but pupils themselves contributed to the interaction which, according to Stanworth, 'Played an active part in the regeneration of a sexual hierarchy, in which boys are the indisputably dominant partners.'

Dale Spender – *Invisible Women*

Perhaps an even stronger attack on the education system is made by Dale Spender in her book *Invisible Women* (1983). Spender claims that education is largely controlled by men who use their power to

define men's knowledge and experiences as important, and women's knowledge and experiences as insignificant. Thus, in economics, for example, the contribution of women's often unpaid work to the world's economy is usually ignored. Women who have made a notable contribution to human progress (such as Ada Lovelace who helped to develop computer software) are also ignored. Indeed, Spender sees the whole curriculum as being riddled with sexism, which is bound to undermine girls' self-confidence and hinder their progress.

Quoting from a variety of studies, Spender goes on to argue that girls get less attention than boys in the classroom. She taped some of her own classes in which she consciously tried to divide her time equally between the sexes, yet she still found that only 38 per cent of her time was spent interacting with girls.

Spender argues that girls have to wait longer than boys for what attention they do receive in the classroom, and that female contributions to discussion and debate are usually treated dismissively by the males present. Boys are often abusive and insulting to girls, yet teachers fail to rebuke them. Male pupils play an important part in damaging girls' education. Spender claims that 'boys do not like girls ... they find them inferior and unworthy, and even despicable'. Boys communicate their low regard for the girls in the classroom, forcing them to retreat into keeping a low profile.

Although she concentrates on what happens in the education system, Spender does not hold the system entirely responsible for the educational failure of girls. She points out that 'girls were just as familiar with the roles they were supposed to play, before they were allowed to attend schools', and today children learn to behave in masculine and feminine ways before they are old enough to start their formal education. Spender sees male dominance in society as a whole as the basic cause of girls' difficulties in education, but schools help to reinforce that dominance and ensure that it continues. Spender concludes:

> mixed-sex education is preparation for 'real life' ... for in real life it is men who dominate and control; but this is not equality of educational opportunity; it is indoctrination and practice in the art of dominance and subordination.
>
> Spender, 1983

Criticisms of Stanworth and Spender

These strong condemnations of the education system are not entirely accepted by some sociologists. Gay J. Randall (1987) points out that Stanworth's work was based upon interviews and not direct classroom observation. It therefore gives some indication of what pupils perceive to be happening in classrooms, but does not actually establish, for example, that teachers give more attention to girls. Randall also quotes Sara Delamont who accuses Spender of using inadequate data and failing to specify most of her research methods so that the findings could be checked in later research.

Randall's own research failed to find such clearcut bias as that of Stanworth and Spender. She observed classes which involved practical work in workshops and laboratories in an 11-18 comprehensive school. In a class of ten girls and nine boys she did find that the boys occupied the central position in the class more often than girls when teachers were giving an initial demonstration of the work they were to do. However, in the lessons she observed, she found that girls had more contact with teachers than the boys did. In one lesson, girls averaged 49 seconds contact with the teacher, compared to boys' 43 seconds; in another, girls averaged 3 minutes 45 seconds, and boys just 56 seconds of individual attention.

Although the above study was only small-scale, it does suggest that some caution should be exercised in considering claims that girls are always disadvantaged in classroom interaction. Randall suggests that, perhaps in the laboratory, where pupils can talk to teachers on an individual level, girls are more forthcoming than they are when it would involve speaking in front of the whole class.

Some research has supported the claim that, overall, males dominate in classrooms, but has argued that it is not all boys who dominate. Jane and Peter French (1993, first published 1984) give an example from a class of 10-11-year-olds they studied. They found that three particular boys received most of the attention while the rest of the boys received no more attention than the girls. These boys seemed to have adopted a successful tactic of making comments that were likely to bring further questions to them from the teacher. For example, when discussing what time they got up in the morning, one boy attracted considerable attention to himself by saying that he got up at 'four thirty' – as it transpired, to feed his large number of pet animals. French and French's study suggests that pupils' tactics are as important as teacher prejudices in determining who gets attention in the classroom, and that it may be a small number of vociferous boys who benefit rather than boys in general.

More recent studies of gender in education have tended to move away from an exclusive focus on achievement. However, they do suggest that any processes that might disadvantage girls in the education system are likely to be more subtle than those identified by Spender and Stanworth. These will be discussed later in this section.

Gender and subject choice

Statistics on subject choice

Although inequalities of educational achievement between males and females may have declined, differences in the subjects studied by them remain considerable. To some extent the National Curriculum limits these differences. Since its introduction, school pupils have had fewer options, because much of the curriculum has to be followed by all pupils. When choices are available to pupils, though, some subjects remain predominantly a male preserve, while others are mainly done by women.

Table 11.15 shows entries for A levels in England and Wales, and for Scottish Highers, in 1996/7.

Males outnumbered females in all science and technical subjects apart from biology and 'other science'. Men also predominated in geography, economics and physical education. Female entries outnumbered male entries in all other subjects. English, modern languages and social studies were subjects with particularly high proportions of female entries.

It could be argued that men's predominance in subjects such as economics, maths, computer studies and most physical sciences meant that they were more likely than females to be doing the most prestigious subjects and those most likely to lead to well-paid and powerful jobs.

Similar patterns are found in higher education, as shown in Table 11.16.

In 1996/7 males were more likely to gain first degrees in physical and mathematical sciences, engineering and technology, and architecture, building and planning. In all other areas – apart from veterinary science and agriculture, where there were the same number of men and women gaining degrees – women predominated.

It is noticeable that women have made significant inroads into some traditionally male areas – indeed, have overtaken them. They have, for example, overtaken men in gaining degrees in medicine and dentistry, and in business and financial studies. Male dominance in scientific and technical subjects, however, remains.

Socialization and subject choice

Many of the factors that influence levels of attainment in education also influence the choice of subjects studied. Cultural factors, particularly early socialization, may encourage boys to develop more interest in and aptitude for technical and scientific subjects. When choosing which subjects to study, females and males may well be influenced by what they have learned about femininity and masculinity.

Table 11.15 Entries for A levels[1] in England and Wales, and for Scottish Highers, by subject and gender, 1996/7

Great Britain Subject group	Number of entries (000s) All	Males	Females
Biological sciences	66.0	25.8	40.2
Chemistry	52.3	28.5	23.8
Physics	43.2	32.8	10.4
Other science	10.8	4.8	6.0
Mathematics	87.5	54.3	33.2
Computer studies	14.8	12.1	2.7
Craft, design and technology[2]	18.8	14.4	4.4
Business studies[3]	42.3	19.7	22.6
Home economics	2.7	0.1	2.5
Art and design	41.7	15.7	26.0
Geography	49.8	27.4	22.4
History	47.9	21.2	26.7
Economics	23.2	14.9	8.2
Religious studies	9.0	2.3	6.7
Social studies[4]	76.5	24.7	51.9
English	68.1	25.3	42.8
Welsh[5]	0.6	0.1	0.4
English literature[4]	59.0	17.7	41.3
Welsh literature	0.4	0.1	0.3
Drama	1.9	0.5	1.4
Communication studies[4]	27.7	10.1	17.5
Modern languages	52.0	15.9	36.0
French	28.8	8.4	20.5
German	12.1	3.7	8.3
Spanish	5.9	1.7	4.2
Other languages	5.2	2.1	3.0
Classical studies[6]	7.7	3.2	4.5
Creative arts[7]	6.7	2.7	3.9
Physical education	16.5	10.6	5.9
Vocational studies[4]	5.5	2.7	2.8
General studies[4]	73.5	35.9	37.6
Modern studies[8]	8.2	3.2	5.0
All entries	914.1	426.7	487.4

1 Includes AS equivalent for England.
2 Craft and design, Graphic communication and Technological studies in Scotland.
3 Includes Accounting, management and information studies and Secretarial studies in Scotland.
4 England and Wales only.
5 Welsh as a second language.
6 Includes Classical Greek, Gaedhlig i.e. Gaelic (Learners) and Latin.
7 Includes music.
8 Scotland only.

Source: Education and Training Statistics for the UK (1998) DfEE, London, p.71.

Table 11.16 Students[1] obtaining higher education qualifications,[2] by type of course, gender and subject group, 1996/7[3]

Thousands

United Kingdom	Sub-degree[5]	First degree[4]	PHDs & equivalent	Postgraduate[4] Masters and others	Total	Total higher education
All						
Medicine & Dentistry	–	5.8	0.9	1.8	2.7	8.5
Subjects allied to Medicine	13.1	14.5	0.5	3.6	4.1	31.7
Biological sciences	1.5	15.4	1.6	1.9	3.5	20.3
Vet. science, Agriculture & related	1.5	2.8	0.3	0.9	1.2	5.6
Physical sciences	1.2	14.1	1.8	2.3	4.1	19.4
Mathematical sciences	5.5	13.0	0.6	3.6	4.2	22.7
Engineering & Technology	6.2	23.0	1.8	5.8	7.5	36.8
Architecture, Building & Planning	2.2	7.5	0.1	3.0	3.1	12.8
Social sciences	7.9	31.3	0.8	12.9	13.7	52.9
Business & Financial studies	18.9	29.6	0.3	19.0	19.3	67.8
Librarianship & Info science	0.8	3.3	–	1.9	2.0	6.1
Languages	1.4	16.5	0.5	2.6	3.1	21.0
Humanities	0.6	10.3	0.5	2.3	2.8	13.7
Creative arts and Design	4.6	18.0	0.1	2.9	3.0	25.6
Education	1.1	2.0	0.3	2.9	3.2	6.2
IT and INSET	2.7	12.1	–	25.6	25.7	40.5
Combined general	7.4	36.3	0.1	6.4	6.5	50.2
Unknown[6,7]	10.5	2.8	–	1.2	1.2	14.5

Males

Medicine & Dentistry	–	2.8	0.5	0.8	1.3	4.1
Subjects allied to Medicine	1.3	3.1	0.3	0.9	1.2	5.6
Biological sciences	0.6	5.9	0.8	0.8	1.6	8.1
Vet. science, Agriculture & related	0.9	1.4	0.2	0.5	0.7	3.0
Physical sciences	0.7	8.8	1.4	1.5	2.9	12.4
Mathematical studies	4.0	9.5	0.5	2.7	3.2	16.7
Engineering & Technology	5.5	19.7	1.5	4.8	6.3	31.5
Architecture, Building & Planning	1.8	5.9	0.1	1.9	2.0	9.7
Social sciences	2.1	13.8	0.5	5.9	6.4	22.3
Business & Financial studies	7.4	14.3	0.2	11.2	11.4	33.2
Librarianship & Info science	0.4	1.3	–	0.7	0.7	2.4
Languages	0.4	4.7	0.2	0.9	1.2	6.3
Humanities	0.3	4.8	0.3	1.2	1.5	6.5
Creative arts & Design	2.0	7.5	0.1	1.2	1.3	10.8
Education	0.3	0.9	0.1	1.0	1.2	2.4
ITT and INSET	0.8	2.5	–	8.0	8.0	11.3
Combined general	3.0	15.9	0.1	4.1	4.2	23.2
Unknown[6,7]	5.2	1.1	–	0.6	0.6	6.9
All subjects	36.8	123.8	6.8	48.9	55.7	216.3

Females

Medicine & Dentistry	–	3.0	0.4	0.9	1.3	4.4
Subjects allied to Medicine	11.8	11.4	0.3	2.7	2.9	26.1
Biological sciences	0.9	9.5	0.8	1.1	1.9	12.2
Vet. science, Agriculture & related	0.7	1.4	0.1	0.4	0.5	2.6
Physical sciences	0.5	5.2	0.5	0.8	1.3	7.0
Mathematical sciences	1.5	3.5	0.1	0.9	1.0	6.0
Engineering & Technology	0.7	3.4	0.2	1.0	1.2	5.3
Architecture, Building & Planning	0.5	1.5	–	1.1	1.1	3.1
Social sciences	5.7	17.6	0.3	7.0	7.3	30.6
Business & Financial studies	11.5	15.3	0.1	7.8	7.9	34.6
Librarianship & Info science	0.4	2.0	–	1.2	1.2	3.7
Languages	1.0	11.8	0.2	1.7	1.9	14.7
Humanities	0.3	5.5	0.2	1.1	1.3	7.1
Creative arts & Design	2.6	10.5	–	1.6	1.7	14.8
Education	0.7	1.1	0.1	1.9	2.0	3.8
ITT and INSET	1.9	9.6	–	17.6	17.6	29.2
Combined general	4.4	20.4	–	2.2	2.3	27.0
Unknown[6,7]	5.3	1.7	–	0.7	0.7	7.7
All subjects	50.4	134.4	3.4	51.7	55.1	239.9

1 Includes students on Open University courses.
2 Excludes qualifications from the private sector.
3 Includes 1995/6 data for higher education institutions in England and further education colleges in Scotland.
4 Excludes some 3.9 thousand first degree and 0.9 thousand postgraduate qualification awards in higher education institutions not broken down further.
5 Excludes students who successfully completed courses for which formal qualifications are not awarded.
6 Includes further education institutions in England for which a subject breakdown is not available.
7 Includes further education institutions in Wales for which the standard subject breakdown above is not available.

Source: *Education and Training Statistics for the UK* (1998) DfEE, London, p. 75.

In her 1970s study, Sue Sharpe (1976) found that the girls she questioned were most inclined to choose office work as their preferred future employment, followed by a group of occupations which included teachers, nurses, bank clerks and shop assistants – all traditionally areas with high levels of female employment.

The girls interviewed rejected many jobs (such as mechanics, electricians, driving instructors and engineers), either because they defined them as 'men's' work, or because they felt that employers and society at large defined them as such. In these circumstances it was hardly surprising that most girls saw little point in studying subjects that are traditionally the province of men.

Schools and subject choice

Sue Sharpe also recognized, though, that the education system itself plays a part in directing girls towards 'feminine' subjects. Although she admitted that schools were improving in this respect, she believed that girls tended to be steered towards arts subjects, and particularly to subjects such as cookery, needlework and typing.

Teresa Grafton and her colleagues (Grafton *et al.*, 1987) carried out a study of a co-educational comprehensive school in south-west England. They found that in the first and second years nearly all girls chose cookery and needlework from the craft options available, while nearly all boys chose metalwork and woodwork. It was not compulsory for them to make these choices, but the school made it clear that there were only limited places available for members of either sex who wanted to study non-traditional subjects. In this way it was made clear what were regarded as the 'normal' choices.

In the fourth year subject choices could once more be made. The way the timetable was organized meant that the combinations pupils could opt for were limited. For example, in one set of choices, traditional girls' subjects (needlework and commercial skills) competed with traditional boys' subjects (woodwork and metalwork). Guidelines were issued to third-year tutors which stressed that all subjects were open to both sexes but 'prior discussion' was necessary for boys who wanted to take the 'family and child option', while girls had to show a 'sincere desire' to take metalwork and woodwork.

Grafton *et al.* recognized that factors outside the school were important in influencing subject choice: pupils were guided by parents, siblings and friends. The researchers also describe the choices as being 'clearly closely related to sexual divisions in the home and in the labour market'. Nevertheless, the organization of the school timetable and the sorts of advice that pupils received from teachers played a major part in directing the girls towards traditional and predictable subject areas.

Science and gender

Alison Kelly (1987) has attempted to explain why science tends to be seen as masculine, and she identifies two main reasons.

First, Kelly argues that the way science subjects are packaged makes them appear boys' subjects. She claims that most science textbooks have very few women portrayed in them. From her observations of classes she found that teachers tended to use examples that were likely to be more in keeping with boys' experiences. For instance, cars were used as an example to illustrate acceleration when bicycles might have been more familiar to both sexes. In another lesson, a demonstration of eclipses was accomplished with the aid of a football. This was preceded by a conversation between the male teacher and the male pupils about the previous Saturday's football results. In such circumstances girls may feel less at home in science classrooms than boys.

However, Kelly argues that the second factor, the behaviour of pupils rather than teachers, makes the greatest contribution to turning sciences into boys' subjects. Boys tend to dominate science classrooms, grabbing apparatus before girls have a chance to use it, and shouting out answers to the questions directed at girls. In these respects, science classrooms represent a small-scale version of society as a whole. Kelly argues:

> Boys act as if they have automatic priority over the resources of the laboratory, whether they be the apparatus, the teacher's attention, or just the physical space. One of the general principles of a patriarchal society – that males are more important than females – is acted out in the science classroom in a way which limits girls' opportunities to learn.
>
> Kelly, 1987

Anne Colley – the persistence of gender inequalities in subject choice

Anne Colley (1998) has reviewed the reasons why differences in subject choice persisted in secondary schools in the late 1990s. She notes that the National Curriculum led to some reduction in gender differences because it restricted choices up to the age of 16, but, even so, substantial differences remained at GCSE level and even greater ones at A level. Colley identifies perceptions of gender roles, subject preferences and choice and the learning environment as the most significant factors.

Perceptions of gender roles

Colley argues that research has shown that certain attributes are seen as desirable for men and a quite different set are seen as desirable for women. Masculinity is positively associated with 'self-reliance, individualism, ambition, dominance, the ability to lead, which have been summarised as instrumental'. On the other hand, femininity has been positively associated with 'kindness, being affectionate, being eager to soothe hurt feelings, reflecting a dimension of expressiveness'. Despite all the changes in society in recent decades, these remain the dominant definitions of masculinity and femininity. Colley accepts that biological differences could lie behind these gender roles. However, any biological differences are indirect and operate through social roles which have a more immediate and direct influence upon gendered behaviour.

Colley acknowledges that individuals accept conventional masculinity and femininity to different degrees. Some evidence suggests that parents' attitudes and the way they socialize their children have a significant influence on the extent to which children differentiate between masculine and feminine roles. Certainly children vary in the degree to which they see masculinity and femininity as distinctive and different. Colley's own research has shown that this influences choice of school subjects. Girls who adhered to traditional ideas of female roles were more likely to be attracted to humanities and music as subject choices, whereas they tended to dislike physical education. On the other hand, boys who had conventional ideas of masculinity were attracted to physical education but they tended to dislike English.

Colley sees socialization and attitude to gender roles as more important than ability. For example, although girls do better than boys in most GCSE subjects, this is not the case for biology, where boys do better. However, girls are more likely than boys to go on to do biology as an A level. This may be because biology is the one science subject about living things (which is seen as a feminine concern), whereas as other sciences are concerned with inanimate things (seen as a more masculine concern).

Subject preferences and choice

According to Colley, ideas about gender interact with the way subjects are perceived and taught in shaping subject choices. The images of the different subjects and the aspects of them that are stressed influence whether they can be seen as masculine or feminine. Colley uses the example of computer studies.

In 1992 only 14 per cent of those starting university computer courses were female. Computing involves working with machines rather than working with people, so this gives it something of a masculine image to start with. However, this is exacerbated by boys tending to dominate in computer studies classes, so girls get less chance to use the computers. Furthermore, the sorts of tasks set by teachers and the rather formal way in which computers are first introduced tend to put girls off. Pupils are rarely given the chance to work together in computer classes and tasks tend to be rather abstract. For both these reasons girls find it difficult to like computer classes and to gain confidence in the subject. While there is no evidence that girls are any less competent, the way in which the subject is taught and boys' dominance in the classroom make girls feel less confident.

Even if subjects tend to be seen as masculine or feminine, this can change depending upon the content of the curriculum. For example, music – traditionally seen as a feminine subject – has become more popular with boys in recent years. The main reason seems to be the increased use of computers and electronic instruments, which have led to music being seen as a more technological and therefore masculine subject.

The learning environment

As well as the image of subjects, the overall learning environment also influences subject choices. One factor which might be important is whether a school is single-sex or mixed. Colley reports research by Lawrie and Brown (1992) which found that girls in a mixed school tended to see maths as more difficult than girls in a single-sex school did. Furthermore, girls in the all-girl school were more than twice as likely as those in the mixed school to go on to study A level maths. However, this research only compared two schools, so it is dangerous to generalize from the findings.

Other research has reached contradictory conclusions about whether all-girl schools help to make it easier for girls to be attracted to scientific and technical subjects. There is some evidence, though, that girls are more confident in such subjects when they are taught in single-sex classes within mixed schools. For example, there have been some successful experiments with girl-only computing sessions in schools, where girls were encouraged to work alongside their friends. Colley comments that 'participation was encouraged by undertaking computing activities on their own terms in a manner which fits their preferred style of working'.

Conclusion

Colley concludes that subject choice continues to reflect:

> *adult male and female social roles and the abilities and attributes assigned to males and females on the basis of these roles in the gender stereotypes of academic subject areas. The information contained in these stereotypes is acquired during socialisation and reinforced by prevailing beliefs, observations of the status quo, and educational practices which themselves are influenced by the same stereotypes.*
>
> Colley, 1998, pp. 32-3

These stereotypes need to be challenged in the education system itself if differences in the subject choices of males and females are to be reduced. Ways need to be found to make subjects seen as masculine attractive to girls, and subjects seen as feminine attractive to boys.

Reasons for the under-achievement of males

Female improvement, moral panic or male under-achievement?

As discussed earlier (see p. 852), by the mid-1990s there was increasing concern that males were under-achieving in the education system. In fact, the educational achievements of both males and females have been increasing over recent decades, with more people gaining higher-grade GCSEs, passing A levels, and getting degrees. However, the performance of females has improved faster than the performance of males, which, as we have seen, has led to females gaining more qualifications than males in some areas.

These changes can be interpreted in a number of ways.

The improved achievement of women

First, they could be seen primarily in terms of the improvements in female achievement. A number of general factors might account for the improved performance of females in education:

1 Changes in the labour market – with the decline of heavy industry, the increase in service-sector work, the increasing employment of 'flexible' part-time workers and workers on fixed-term contracts have all increased employment opportunities for women. The rapid rise in the employment of married women, especially since the Second World War, has increased the incentives for women to gain educational qualifications.

2 These changes may be reflected in changing attitudes amongst females. When Sue Sharpe repeated her 1970s research on teenage girls in the 1990s (see p. 854) she found that their priorities had changed. They no longer attached primary importance to marriage and having children, and instead 'almost unanimously endorsed the importance of having a job or career and, in this respect, emphasised being able to support themselves'. They therefore attached much more importance to education than their counterparts had in the 1970s.

3 The women's movement and female sociologists have drawn attention to gender inequalities in education. In doing so they have encouraged teachers to become more aware of the issue and have persuaded some to change their practices so that they are less likely to disadvantage female pupils and students. Some schools and local education authorities have taken initiatives designed to improve educational opportunities for girls.

The moral panic about men

Second, these changes could be seen as no more than a moral panic or a backlash against feminist views on education.

Gaby Weiner, Madeleine Arnot and Miriam David (1997) are somewhat sceptical about the sudden discovery of male under-achievement. They argue that the media have created a misleading moral panic which exaggerates and distorts the extent and nature of any problem. They say:

> *Rather than celebrating girls' achievements and aspirations, we now have a discourse of male disadvantage in which boys are viewed as falling behind in academic performance. The discourse also has powerful class and racial dimensions, with the impact of black and/or male working-class under-achievement interpreted as a threat to law and order.*
>
> Weiner, Arnot and David, 1997, p. 620

Although the media are also concerned about the under-achievement of white, middle-class boys, they see black and working-class under-achievement as a particular problem because it is likely to lead to unqualified, unemployable black and working-class men turning to crime. In short, the discourse links male under-achievement to ideas about the existence of an underclass (see pp. 323–33 for a discussion of the underclass).

Weiner *et al.* accept that some changes have taken place. For example, the introduction of GCSEs has led to more females taking and succeeding in exams at 16; and the National Curriculum has reduced gender differences in subject choice up to 16. However, the differences in subject choice emerge at A level, and boys continue to get higher grades than girls in A levels. Thus Weiner *et al.* believe that female rather than male under-achievement is still characteristic of the education system at higher levels. They say:

what we have is a rather more complex picture than hitherto indicated: it seems neither so bleak (for boys) nor as rosy (for girls) as has been depicted in the media and elsewhere. Girls have clearly made improvements since the 1970s in examination performance up to 16, but patterns are not nearly so clear-cut post 16.

Weiner, Arnot and David, 1997, p. 628

What is occurring is simply a 'backlash' against female success (see p. 185 for a discussion of the idea of an anti-female backlash). Men feel threatened by even the possibility that women might become equal and have used the question, '*What about the boys!* effectively achieving a swift reassertion of male educational interests.'

Weiner *et al.* put forward a strong case in arguing that concern about male under-achievement might be exaggerated. Certainly there is little evidence that females are becoming much more successful than males in the higher reaches of the education system. Nevertheless, some males have always found it difficult to achieve success in the education system. The new concern with male performance in education might be useful for highlighting some problems that they face. It can also be argued that it is just as valid to explore ways of raising the achievement of boys as it is for raising that of girls.

The under-achievement of men

The third way of looking at these changes is to see them in terms of the under-achievement of males. From this point of view, males are achieving less than they could and should do in the education system. Although this is usually portrayed as a new problem, many of the possible reasons for any under-achievement may not be new at all. Indeed, some of them may be class-related, and may in the past have been seen as primarily class issues rather than as problems of masculinity (for example, see Paul Willis's work, pp. 791–4).

Whether the changes outlined above are interpreted as improvements in female achievement, as grossly exaggerated by a moral panic, or as indicating male under-achievement, it is clear that some changes have taken place. Most attempts to explain them have used the approach which sees them as indicative of male under-achievement. One such attempt will now be examined.

Eirene Mitsos and Ken Browne – boys' under-achievement

The achievement of boys and girls

Eirene Mitsos and Ken Browne (1998) do believe that boys are under-achieving in education, although they also believe that girls are disadvantaged. The

evidence of boys' under-achievement, according to Mitsos and Browne, is that:

Girls do better than boys in every stage of National Curriculum SAT [Standard Assessment Tests] results in English, maths and science, and they are now more successful than boys at every level in GCSE, outperforming boys in every major subject ... except physics.

Mitsos and Browne, 1998, p. 27

They point out that girls are now more likely to stay on in education after reaching 16, and to go on to higher education. However, they note that girls are still under-represented in science and engineering subjects; they do less well in A levels than boys with the same GCSE grades; in society as a whole women are less well qualified than men; and women still do less well in paid employment than men with similar qualifications. Thus Mitsos and Browne adopt a balanced position. There are problems for women in education, which prevent them from fulfilling their potential, but there are also problems for men. At least some of the problems faced by each sex are rather different.

Reasons for improvements in girls' achievement

First, Mitsos and Browne discuss why girls' achievement has improved so much in recent years. They identify five main reasons:

1 The '*women's movement* and *feminism* have achieved considerable success in improving the rights and raising the expectations and self-esteem of women'. Women are more likely to aspire to careers that require high levels of qualifications, and are therefore motivated to succeed in education.

2 Sociologists have highlighted some of the disadvantages faced by girls, and, as a result, equal opportunity programmes have been developed, which have improved opportunities for girls.

3 The increase in service-sector jobs considered suitable for women, and the decline in predominantly male, unskilled work, have opened up job opportunities for women, providing added incentives for them to gain qualifications.

4 Evidence suggests that girls are more motivated and hard-working than boys in doing school work. Mitsos and Browne claim that 'Research shows that the typical 14-year-old girl can concentrate for 3–4 times as long as her fellow male student', and that girls tend to be better organized than boys. Girls' greater motivation and organizational skills may give them an advantage in coursework which now counts for more in assessments than it did in the past.

5 Mitsos and Browne say that 'by the age of 16 girls are estimated to be more mature than boys by up to two years'. They therefore take exams more seriously than boys do.

Reasons for boys' under-achievement

Mitsos and Browne then go on to suggest a range of reasons why boys do less well than they could:

1 Teachers may tend to be less strict with boys, giving them more leeway with deadlines and expecting a lower standard of work than they get from girls. This can allow boys to under-achieve by failing to push them to achieve their potential.

2 Boys are more likely to disrupt classes. They are considerably more likely to be sent out of the classroom than girls, resulting in them losing learning time in class. Furthermore, boys are much more likely to be expelled: some 80 per cent of those permanently excluded from schools are boys.

3 The culture of masculinity encourages boys to want to appear macho and tough. They are therefore more likely to develop an *anti-education*, anti-learning subculture, where school work is seen as "unmacho". This is the sort of subculture adopted by the 'lads' in Paul Willis's classic study (see pp. 791–4). Because of this tendency, boys may lack the dedication and perseverance necessary to succeed in coursework.

4 The decline in male manual work may result in many working-class boys lacking motivation. They see little point in trying hard at school if it is unlikely to result in the sort of job they would be seeking. The lack of opportunities for some groups of men may lower the self-esteem and confidence of boys from the same groups.

5 Paradoxically, though, research suggests that most boys overestimate their ability. Mitsos and Browne quote research which shows that at GCSE level boys tend to overestimate the grades they will achieve, while girls tend to underestimate them. These over-confident boys may not work hard enough to achieve the sort of results they expect to get.

6 Some evidence suggests that girls are more likely than boys to spend their leisure time in ways which complement their education and contribute to educational achievements. Mitsos and Browne say, 'To simplify and generalise: while boys run around kicking footballs, playing sports or computer games and engaging in other aspects of "laddish" behaviour, girls are more likely to read or stand around talking'. Girls therefore tend to develop their linguistic skills more than boys and, since 'School is essentially a linguistic experience', this puts boys at a disadvantage.

Mitsos and Browne put particular emphasis on reading. Women are more likely to read books than men, and mothers are more likely than fathers to read to their children. Girls are therefore more likely than boys to have same-sex role models to encourage them to read. Furthermore, when they are young, girls are more likely than boys to read fiction. It is mostly fiction that is read in the early years at primary school. This may give girls an early advantage in reading.

Conclusion

Mitsos and Browne conclude that, underlying the factors that contribute to male under-achievement, is 'an identity crisis for men'. With an increase in female employment and a decline in some traditional areas of men's work, it has become more difficult for boys to see their future in terms of being a family's breadwinner. For some males at least, 'The future looks bleak and without clear purpose to them.'

However, Mitsos and Browne are careful to balance such comments with a recognition of continuing disadvantages for girls in education and women in society as a whole. They say that 'girls still have marked disadvantages such as underrating themselves and lacking confidence in their ability, getting less of teachers' time and having to tolerate the dominance of boys in the classroom'. Once they leave school, they find that men still hold most of the highest-status and powerful positions in society.

Evaluation

Mitsos and Browne offer some interesting ideas about the reasons why boys may not do as well as they could in education. Many of them seem quite plausible. However, they do not discuss or evaluate the research on which their claims are based. Sometimes they fail to give references to the relevant research, making it very difficult to evaluate how well-based the claims are. Furthermore, they tend to list individual points rather than developing an overall theoretical framework. Their work can be seen as a number of preliminary suggestions to explain boys' under-achievement. As they themselves admit, much more research needs to be done in this area before any firm conclusions can be reached.

New directions in the study of gender and schooling

Many recent studies of gender and education have moved away from simply looking at reasons for differential achievement between males and females. Instead they have looked more generally at how gender shapes and is shaped by educational institutions. These studies have implications for explaining differential achievement, but this is not their primary focus. Such studies are characterized by some or all of the following:

- A tendency to look at a wide range of processes related to gender within schools.
- An increased emphasis on the active role played by pupils and students in the creation of gender relationships, rather than simply looking at alleged gender discrimination by teachers.
- Greater consideration of the way children form identities, rather than a narrow focus simply on academic achievement.
- The inclusion of some consideration of class and/or ethnicity as variables which interact with gender in shaping school relationships.

The following studies all exemplify at least some of these characteristics.

John Abraham – *Divide and School*

The study

In *Divide and School*, John Abraham (1995) describes the results of an ethnographic study of the process of schooling in a mixed-sex comprehensive school, which had fairly equal proportions of middle- and working-class pupils. The study was conducted in 1986. Abraham considered factors relating to both class and gender, but not ethnicity since the school pupils were almost all white. The school was an academically successful one. The study focused on fourth-year pupils, and used questionnaires, interviewing, participant observation and secondary sources.

'Typical boys', 'typical girls'

Eight teachers in the school were asked to identify and describe pupils who were typical boys and typical girls. One was unwilling to do so, but the other seven all made similar comments. Abraham divides the comments into five categories:

1 Least typical boys were thought to be 'effeminate, softly spoken, like a girl, immature'.

2 Most typical boys were identified as those from a group known to some of the teachers as 'the cowboy faction'. This group were not academically able or dedicated; they were mischievous, frequently got into trouble and flirted with girls a lot.

3 The most typical girls were seen as 'lacking in confidence, neat, fussy, conscientious, more ready to accept the teacher's wishes, very quiet and very pleasant but doesn't say much and very studious'.

4 The least typical girls were 'scruffy and not at all feminine, bolshy, hang around with boys, don't have girls as friends'.

5 The final group was seen as the most typical of girls in some respects but the least typical in other

respects. They were the most deviant of the girls; they were quite aggressive and unwilling to follow school rules. They were more concerned with their appearance and boyfriends than doing school work.

Teachers, boys and girls

Overall, though, teachers expected more bad behaviour from boys than from girls. Boys received considerably more bad behaviour notes and reports that they had missed assignments than girls did.

However, Abraham's own research suggested that there was little difference between boys and girls in their willingness to spend time on homework. Girls and boys were about equally conscientious in doing maths homework, and girls only slightly more conscientious over English. It appeared that the pupils were judged as much on teachers' gender expectations as they were on actual behaviour. Girls were expected to be more conscientious, so they were perceived as being so. Boys tended to be disciplined more, but this was not entirely a product of teacher stereotyping. The most anti-school boys tended to challenge authority in direct ways and to plan disruption so as to maximize discomfort to the teacher. The most anti-school girls were more likely to push rules to the limit, but to take care not to overstep the boundaries that would get them into serious trouble.

There was some evidence that boys got more attention in class, but this was not always the case. In maths classes and some English classes, teachers asked boys considerably more questions than girls, but this was not the case in French, where questions were fairly equally distributed. However, girls were more likely to take the initiative and ask questions than boys were. Nevertheless, overall it was boys who received the lion's share of attention. Quite often, though, some of this attention was more about classroom management than about academic progress. Teachers felt they needed to constantly involve and check up on the more disruptive boys, while most of the girls could be trusted to be getting on with their work.

Abraham concludes that:

> The result was a polarization of involvement between the sexes. It was expected that boys would dominate and be attention seekers, but that girls would be quiet and conscientious. The teachers tended to work with these as 'givens' rather than challenge them because that seemed the most viable management strategy in coping with the immediacy of many classroom situations.
>
> Abraham, 1995, p. 69

Dealing with the unruly boys could have had the effect of holding back the academic progress of the more conscientious girls. Furthermore, in other areas of the school, boys tended to dominate, restricting opportunities for girls. Many of the fourth-year boys played football at lunchtime, taking up most of the available space for children to use. Girls were largely confined to using the space on the outside to walk around chatting to each other.

Pupils and gender relations

Abraham does not see the gender relations in the school as simply a product of teacher stereotypes. The pupils actively created their own subcultures and they were influenced by class as well as gender. Most of the particularly disruptive girls and boys were from working-class backgrounds. Amongst the girls, dress codes developed as an important signifier of their membership of a deviant group. Amongst the boys (known as 'the lads' or the cowboys), a culture of masculine toughness was important.

In many ways these groups used quite conventional definitions of masculinity and femininity as resources with which to construct their own subcultures. It was rather different for another subculture within the school, 'the gothic punks'. This was a mainly male, but mixed, group, who liked to dress in black (in contravention of the school uniform rules), grow their hair long and sometimes dye it black, and listen to music. The boys in the group rejected the idea that science and technology were boys' subjects and did not enjoy sports like football and rugby. They were more interested in art and music as school subjects. The gothic punks were not particularly academic, although many came from middle-class backgrounds. Nor were the boys amongst them seen as particularly masculine. Many teachers and pupils saw them as somewhat effeminate and they were not particularly popular.

Despite being disruptive, 'the lads' were quite popular with some of their male teachers who shared, for example, an interest in football. They also earned a certain amount of respect from many of their male peers.

There was pressure on girls from teachers and other pupils to conform to conventional definitions of femininity. For example, girls who spent a lot of time with boys tended to be seen as 'untypical girls' by teachers and labelled as 'slags' or 'whores' by other girls.

Abraham concludes that 'as an institution the school tended to reinforce, rather than challenge traditional gender norms', although the gothic punks showed that pupils themselves did not always live up to teachers' expectations of masculinity and femininity.

Paul Connolly – *Racism, Gender Identities and Young Children*

The study

Another study which emphasizes the diverse influences on gender in schools is Paul Connolly's study of three classes of 5- and 6-year-olds in a multi-ethnic inner-city primary school (Connolly, 1998). The study was carried out in 1992–3, using observation, interviews with parents, staff and governors, and group interviews with the children. Connolly also used secondary sources such as files produced by the school.

Connolly emphasizes that schooling could not be understood simply in terms of gender relationships. In particular, he examined how ethnicity also shaped social relationships in the school. Although his research was based in the school, Connolly paid particular attention to the wider context in which the schooling took place. He did not see the social relationships within the school as just a product of the education system. Young though the children were, they brought with them to school ways of thinking about masculinity, femininity and ethnicity which played an important role in developing the internal school relationships. Of course, teachers' attitudes and behaviour played a role as well. There was evidence of some sexism from teachers, but Connolly stresses the complexities of the factors shaping what went on in the school.

Black boys

Because he had a particular interest in the relationship between ethnicity and gender, Connolly focuses primarily on ethnic minority boys and girls.

The teachers in the school were well aware that it was located in a deprived area. They were concerned about the maintenance of discipline and they brought with them to their work assumptions about different groups. For example, Connolly found that teachers were more likely to criticize the behaviour of black boys than that of other groups. Connolly says:

> *There were many examples gained from observations throughout the school year, where Black boys would be sent to stand outside the classroom, told to stand up or move in assemblies, and be singled out and instructed to stand by the wall or outside the staffroom during playtime. While Black boys were not the only ones to be disciplined in this way, they were significantly over-represented in these processes.*
>
> Connolly, 1998, p. 79

According to Connolly, teachers were influenced in their perceptions of black boys 'by the broader discourses on "race", crime and the inner city'. Some teachers thought that some of the black male children they were teaching were in danger of growing up to be violent criminals and they saw them as a threat to school discipline. By picking on them they were trying to nip their behaviour in the bud. However, they also took more positive steps to encourage them to participate enthusiastically and actively in school activities. There was a particular pride taken in the school football teams, in which some of the black boys who were perceived to be badly behaved were players. The emphasis on football, though, created a 'specifically masculine ethos within the school'.

However, it was not just a question of the boys being labelled by teachers and them living up to their labels. The black boys also brought with them to school their own values and attitudes – for example, those relating to masculinity. This contributed to the black boys' sense of identity as much as the behaviour of teachers.

One particular group of black boys, whom Connolly dubs the 'Bad Boys', drew upon common perceptions of black male children to base their behaviour upon ideas of 'hyper-masculinity'. They were successful in establishing themselves as some of the toughest in the school, as among the best footballers, and as some of the most attractive to girls in games of 'kiss-and-chase'. This earned them considerable respect from their male peers in the school. It therefore encouraged them to concentrate on non-academic ways of earning status and so limited their educational progress.

Black girls

Some negative stereotypes were not just confined to boys. Like black boys, black girls were perceived by teachers as potentially disruptive but likely to be good at sports. They were more likely to be singled out for punishment than other girls. However, teachers did tend to believe that black girls were good at some subjects, such as music and dancing. One girl, for example, was often chosen to come to the front of the class to sing her favourite songs.

Despite the predominant perception within the school that girls were more passive than boys, some of the black girls were willing to challenge this. Although boys used various techniques of intimidation to try to maintain their dominance within the school, some of the black girls got together from time to time to turn the tables on the boys. For example, on one occasion eight of the black girls 'captured' a white boy whom they found particularly troublesome. They paraded him around the playground.

The teachers at this school tended to 'underplay the Black girls' educational achievements and focus on their social behaviour'. Like their black male counterparts, they were quite likely to be disciplined

and punished even though their behaviour did not always seem to justify it. However, this was not the case with all the girls. One of the black girls, Whitney, came from a higher-class background than the others and she was seen as approaching the ideal of a model pupil. Consequently, her work was valued, she received more encouragement than other black girls and she was less likely to be disciplined for bad behaviour.

South Asian boys

South Asian boys developed rather different identities to black boys. On the local estates, white residents tended to see Asians as an 'alien wedge' who were more distinctive and different than black people. Asians were seen as having different family lifestyles, which were more close-knit than those of the rest of the community. They were also seen as different by virtue of being able to speak languages other than English, and because of religion. Aspects of these views were reproduced amongst the teachers in the school.

Some teachers contrasted what they saw as the close and supportive Asian families with the high rates of single parenthood amongst other groups in the area. However, some teachers also believed that Asian parents might lack the parenting skills necessary to help their children develop social skills. South Asian boys tended to be seen as immature rather than as seriously deviant. Misbehaviour was often seen as 'silly' rather than as a threat to order. Much of their bad behaviour went unnoticed by teachers and was not punished to the same extent as that of black boys.

Partly because of their inability to be seen as challenging the school, the identity of South Asian boys was 'feminized'. They were seen as relatively passive and conformist. Some were even described as 'little' by teachers, and some teachers thought that particular South Asian boys needed 'looking after' because they were vulnerable. Because of this there was a tendency for other boys who wanted to assert their masculinity to pick on South Asian boys and attack them. This reaffirmed their feminized identity and made it very difficult for them to assert their masculinity. They were largely excluded from football – one of the key arenas for asserting masculine identity. Those who did join in football games were sometimes subject to racial abuse.

The South Asian boys had difficulty in gaining status as males. This made it difficult for them to enjoy school and feel confident. However, teachers did have high expectations of their academic work. They expected them to be reliable and keen. They were often praised, and encouraged to try hard and take their work seriously.

South Asian girls

South Asian girls were seen as likely to be even more obedient and hard-working than South Asian boys, and, furthermore, than black and white girls. Teachers more or less took it for granted that South Asian girls would produce a reasonable standard of work and that they would be conscientious. (However, Connolly's own observations showed that 'the behaviour of South Asian girls pointed towards a similar mix of work and avoidance of work and obedience and disruption, making their behaviour largely indistinguishable from that of their female peers'.)

All of this suggested that South Asian girls would have advantages over other girls. Teachers' expectations were high and this would encourage the girls to live up to them. On the other hand, though, teachers felt there was little need to give these girls special help. They expected them to cope without it. Teachers got no extra status from helping South Asian girls to achieve academic success. It was expected of them. Some teachers spent more time trying to get pupils from other groups to do well. This was because the teachers would get more of a sense of achievement if these pupils' work improved against the odds.

Like South Asian boys, South Asian girls had high status in terms of their perceived academic ability, but they had a relatively low status among their peers. In some ways they were viewed as extremely feminine because they were regarded as 'quiet, passive, obedient and helpful'. However, they were also regarded as 'the Sexual Other in relation to discourses on boyfriends and the related discursive themes of intimacy, love and marriage'. They were not expected to get involved in games of 'kiss-and-chase' nor were they seen as potential girlfriends by black boys and white boys. Their culture was seen as too alien and inferior by other pupils for them to be seen as possible girlfriends.

Conclusion

Connolly's study shows how gender and ethnicity interact in creating identities amongst young children, and it highlights some of the ways in which this might influence educational achievement. It shows that children themselves are instrumental in creating the gender identities found within schools. Important though teachers' gender and ethnic stereotypes are in shaping the school, these stereotypes are themselves partly shaped by wider discourses in the community and can be challenged or modified by pupils themselves. It shows the danger of trying to explain the difference in educational achievement between boys in general and girls in general in terms of general theories which fail to take account of other social divisions such as class and ethnicity. The next section will examine ethnic differences in achievement in detail.

Ethnicity and educational attainment

Ethnicity and levels of attainment

The educational performance of ethnic minorities has become a widely debated issue, although it is only comparatively recently that reliable data on ethnicity and educational achievement have become available. Most of the numerous studies that have now been carried out have found that, overall, ethnic minorities tend to do less well than other members of the population. However, this hides important variations between and within ethnic groups, with some ethnic minorities being particularly successful.

The *Swann Report*

In the 1980s the government-sponsored *Swann Report* (1985) found important differences between ethnic minority groups. As Table 11.17 shows, from a survey of five LEAs it was found that Asians did almost as well as the whites or 'others'. Asians were slightly less likely than 'others' to get five or more graded results in O level or CSE examinations, but in other respects were just as successful. The *Swann*

Report noted, though, that one Asian group (those of Bangladeshi origin) did particularly badly.

The average performance of West Indians was considerably worse than that of whites. Only 5 per cent of the West Indians in the *Swann Report* study passed an A level, and only 1 per cent went to university.

The Policy Studies Institute (PSI) survey

The Policy Studies Institute's *Fourth National Survey of Ethnic Minorities* (Modood *et al.*, 1997), conducted in 1994, found that the educational qualifications of ethnic minorities had improved considerably compared to the 1980s.

The survey used a sample of 5,196 people of Caribbean and Asian origin and of 2,867 white people. Tables 11.18 and 11.19 show the results of the survey. Amongst men it was found that Chinese, African Asians and Indians were better qualified than whites, while Caribbeans, Pakistanis and Bangladeshis were the least well qualified. However a substantial number of Caribbean men had vocational qualifications such as a trade apprentice-ship, an ONC or an HNC.

The same broad pattern was found amongst women, although women overall were less well qualified than men. The exception was Caribbean

women who were more likely to have A level/below degree-level qualifications than white women, although only a small proportion had degrees. This points to the importance of distinguishing between the educational performance of men and women within each ethnic group, as well as considering differences between ethnic groups. As with men, women of Indian, African Asian and Chinese origin all had high proportions of advanced qualifications, particularly degrees. Indian women were the most likely to have degrees, but relatively few had A level standard qualifications. Bangladeshi women were the least well qualified, followed by Pakistani women.

The PSI study also compared the qualifications of those born in Britain, or who were 15 or less at the time of migration, with the qualifications of migrants who came to Britain aged 16 or older. Here, there were signs that considerable progress had been made in the educational achievements of some Caribbeans.

As Table 11.20 shows, the qualifications of Caribbeans who had been born in Britain or were 15 or less when they migrated were almost as good as those of whites. Second-generation British Caribbean men were gaining more higher-level qualifications than their female counterparts. Overall, the qualifications of the second generation were much better than those of the migrants' generation, suggesting that overall figures might exaggerate any under-achievement by ethnic minorities in British education. However, Bangladeshis and Pakistanis had made least progress, and still achieved well below other ethnic groups.

Table 11.17 School leavers in five LEAs, 1981–2 (percentages)

	Asians	West Indians	All others (5 LEAs)	All maintained school leavers in England
CSE and O levels				
No graded results	19	19	19	11
At least 1 graded result (but fewer than 5)	64	75	62	66
5 or more graded results	17	6	19	23
A levels				
No A level pass	87	95	87	86
At least 1 A level	13	5	13	14
Intended destination				
University	4	1	4	4
Other full-time further education	30	27	14	21
Employment	39	51	64	64
Not known	28	22	18	11

Source: *Swann Report* (1985).

Table 11.18 Highest qualification of men aged 16–64

	Percentages							
	White	Caribbean	Indian	African Asian	Pakistani	Bangladeshi	Chinese	All ethnic minorities
None or below O level	31	44	35	32	48	60	31	40
O level or equivalent	14	15	16	20	21	20	20	18
A level to below degree (vocational in parentheses)	44(33)	35(29)	25(12)	29(10)	20(11)	10(3)	22(15)	26(16)
Degree	11	6	24	20	11	10	26	15
Degree (1991 census)[1]	10	4	15[2]	15[2]	8	7	22	1,
Weighted count	1,049	648	554	423	418	151	179	2,374
Unweighted count	943	453	543	364	573	294	99	2,326

1 The census figures are for 18–64-year-olds and overseas qualifications have been interpreted in the light of British standards.
2 The census figure for Indians and African Asians is a combined one for these two groups.

Source: T. Modood (1997) 'Qualifications and English language', in T. Modood *et al.* (eds) *Ethnic Minorities in Britain: Diversity and Disadvantage*, Policy Studies Institute, London, p. 65.

Modood sums up the findings, saying:

Comparing the two generations, then, it is quite clear that there has been remarkable progress in the acquisition of qualifications, and that nearly every group of both men and women have participated in this. This progress, however, confirms the division observed in the migrant generation. There the Pakistanis and Bangladeshis were amongst the less well qualified, and this is still true of the second generation.

Modood, 1997, p. 71

Ethnic minorities were found to be more likely than whites to stay on in post-compulsory education. Table 11.21 shows that, for all ethnic minority

Table 11.19 Highest qualification of women aged 16–59

	Percentages							
	White	Caribbean	Indian	African Asian	Pakistani	Bangladeshi	Chinese	All ethnic minorities
None or below O level	38	34	40	32	60	73	25	41
O level or equivalent	25	29	21	25	22	17	29	24
A level to below degree (vocational in parentheses)	29(15)	34(25)	19(8)	27(6)	11(4)	7(2)	30(12)	24(12)
Degree	8	3	19	15	7	3	17	11
Degree (1991 census)1	5	3	7[2]	7[2]	3	2	25	6
Weighted count	1,181	773	605	337	396	125	188	2,424
Unweighted count	1,126	585	573	311	525	273	102	2,369

1 The census figures are for 18–59-year-olds and overseas qualifications have been interpreted in the light of British standards.
2 The census figure for Indians and African Asians is a combined one for these two groups.

Source: T. Modood (1997) 'Qualifications and English language', in T. Modood *et al.* (eds) *Ethnic Minorities in Britain: Diversity and Disadvantage*, Policy Studies Institute, London, p. 66.

Table 11.20 Highest qualification of those born in the UK or 15 years old or less at time of migration (base: 25–44-year-olds)

	Percentages							
	White	Caribbean	Indian	African Asian	Pakistani	Bangladeshi	Chinese	All ethnic minorities
Highest qualification of those born in UK or 15 years old or less on migration								
None or below O level	30	26	31	24	54	74	[11]	30
O level or equivalent	22	30	24	17	18	14	[34]	25
A level or equivalent or higher (degrees in parentheses)	49(12)	45(7)	45(15)	59(23)	26(11)	12(4)	[55(27)]	44(12)
Proportion with higher British qualifications (degrees in parentheses)								
Men	62(16)	57(8)	54(18)	64(32)	30(12)	11(5)	[64(42)]	35(17)
Women	39(9)	37(8)	35(11)	52(12)	20(10)	12(-)	[42(7)]	29(8)
Weighted count	1,048	663	292	244	192	33	77	1,501
Unweighted count	1,051	552	303	219	281	90	39	1,484

Note: Figures in square brackets denote degrees and small sample size.

Source: T. Modood (1997) 'Qualifications and English language', in T. Modood *et al.* (eds) *Ethnic Minorities in Britain: Diversity and Disadvantage*, Policy Studies Institute, London, p. 70.

Table 11.21 Participation in full-time education, 16–24-year-olds				
	Percentages			
	White	Caribbean	Indian/ African Asian	Pakistani/ Bangladeshi
16–19-year-olds in full-time education				
Men	43	46	81	71
Women	56	57	66	54
20–24-year-olds in full-time education				
Men	7	18	38	31
Women	12	18	25	19
Weighted count	403	318	456	360
Unweighted count	313	162	311	447

Source: T. Modood (1997) 'Qualifications and English language', in T. Modood et al. (eds) *Ethnic Minorities in Britain: Diversity and Disadvantage*, Policy Studies Institute, London, p. 76.

Table 11.22 Admissions to higher education by ethnic group and type of institution, 1992		
Level of representation among admissions compared to the proportion of the 15–24 age group in Britain (Census, 1991)		
Chinese	*Over*-represented in admissions to university	(+109%)
	Over-represented in admissions to polytechnic	(+86%)
Indian	*Over*-represented in admissions to university	(+19%)
	Over-represented in admissions to polytechnic	(+91%)
Black African	*Over*-represented in admissions to university	(+14%)
	Over-represented in admissions to polytechnic	(+243%)
Black Caribbean	*Under*-represented in admissions to university	(−63%)
	Over-represented in admissions to polytechnic	(+43%)
Pakistani	*Under*-represented in admissions to university	(−19%)
	Over-represented in admissions to polytechnic	(+48%)
Bangladeshi	*Under*-represented in admissions to university	(−45%)
	Under-represented in admissions to polytechnic	(−8%)
White	*Under*-represented in admissions to university	(−1%)
	Under-represented in admissions to polytechnic	(−7.5%)

Source: A. Pilkington (1997) 'Ethnicity and education', in M. Haralambos (ed.) *Developments in Sociology Volume 13*, Causeway Press, Ormskirk, p. 105; derived from T. Modood and M. Shiner (1994) *Ethnic Minorities and Higher Education*, Policy Studies Institute, London.

groups (except Pakistani and Bangladeshi women), both males and females were more likely to be in full-time education amongst 16-24-year-olds than whites were. Modood suggests that this might partly be due to whites in this age group having found full-time employment. It might also be partly because members of ethnic minorities tend to get qualifications slightly later in life than whites. Nevertheless, Modood believes that the research indicates that all ethnic minorities have a strong drive towards achieving qualifications.

Research on university admissions also suggests that inequalities between the achievements of ethnic groups remain substantial, although they have probably been declining in recent years. Research by Modood and Shiner (1994, discussed in Pilkington, 1997) found that Chinese, Indians and black Africans all had above-average rates of admission to higher education institutions in 1992. However, as Table 11.22 shows, Bangladeshis did much worse than the average, and whites slightly worse. For both Pakistanis and black Caribbeans the picture was more complicated. They were less likely than the average to be admitted to universities but more likely to be admitted to the somewhat less prestigious polytechnics (most have now become universities but are still less likely to be among the most prestigious institutions).

Overall, then, there is evidence of declining inequality of achievement; but there is clear evidence of continuing under-achievement amongst Bangladeshis and Pakistanis, and some (though not clearcut) evidence of under-achievement amongst black Caribbeans.

We will now examine attempts to explain differences in educational attainment between ethnic groups.

Innate ability and attainment

As in the case of class and gender, some commentators have attributed differences in levels of achievement to IQ. Arthur Jensen (1973) and Hans Eysenck (1971) have both argued that blacks have genetically inherited levels of intelligence which are lower than those of whites.

Hernstein and Murray (1994) are a little more circumspect, describing themselves as 'agnostic' over whether differences between black and white

Americans in IQ scores are caused by genetic or environmental factors. However, they do argue that there is a good case that the differences might be genetic in origin. In a review of research, Hernstein and Murray found that, on average, blacks scored 16 points lower in IQ tests than whites. They argue that, far from being the victims of discrimination, black Americans actually do better in the educational system than you would expect given their IQ.

A strong case can be made for environmental factors accounting for this difference (for example, in America blacks are more likely to live in poverty than whites). However, Jensen, Eysenck and Hernstein and Murray all point to evidence which suggests that differences in IQ remain when environments are equalized. When blacks and whites of similar income levels and occupational statuses are compared, blacks on average still have slightly lower test scores.

Jensen, Eysenck and Hernstein and Murray are mistaken in believing that this provides strong evidence of blacks having inferior innate intelligence to whites. It is impossible to control all the possible environmental factors that could affect IQ scores. Bodmer (1972) suggests that over 200 years of prejudice and discrimination against blacks prevents an equalization of environment with whites.

Andrew Pilkington argues against the idea of a genetic basis for IQ differences between ethnic groups. He suggests that it is 'questionable whether race is a biologically meaningful concept' (Pilkington, 1997) (see pp. 204–6 for details of similar arguments). If it is not, then it is hard to see how supposedly 'racial' differences can be related to genetics. It is also questionable whether IQ tests really measure intelligence.

In Britain, IQ differences between blacks and whites are smaller than in the USA, and what differences there are can largely be explained by differences in socio-economic status. Like Bodmer, Pilkington argues that racism may well be responsible for any remaining differences. Pilkington also points out that evidence suggests that IQ is not fixed by genetics. In many parts of the world IQ scores have been rising, and the gap between IQ scores of different ethnic groups has been narrowing.

Members of the Swann Committee examined the evidence in Britain (Swann, 1985). When they took into account environmental factors they found that differences in IQ scores between ethnic groups were sharply reduced. Indeed they argued that the differences were so insignificant that they could question the 'good sense or good will' of anyone who claimed that the differences mattered.

Cultural and material factors and attainment

A much more plausible explanation of ethnic differences in educational attainment is that they are due to various cultural factors.

Language

One such factor is language. In some Asian households English is not the main language used. In some West Indian households 'Creole' or 'patois' (variations upon conventional English) are spoken.

However, recent research evidence does not support the view that language is an important factor. A study by Geoffrey Driver and Roger Ballard (1981) found that, by the age of 16, Asian children whose main home language was not English were at least as competent in English as their classmates. The *Swann Report* found that linguistic factors might hold back the progress of a few West Indian children, but for the vast majority they were of no significance (Swann, 1985).

The Policy Studies Institute's *Fourth National Survey of Ethnic Minorities* (Modood et al., 1997), conducted in 1994, did find evidence that lack of fluency in English was a significant problem for some groups. The degree of fluency was judged by the interviewers who conducted the research. The results are shown in Table 11.23 which reveals that there were high proportions of older age groups who were not 'fairly good' or fluent English speakers. Only 4 per cent of Bangladeshi women aged 45–64 were judged to be able to speak English well or fluently. However, older age groups are likely to have finished gaining educational qualifications, and the figures for the youngest age group (16-24-year-olds) are more significant.

Amongst men, nearly everyone spoke English well or fluently. Amongst women, 16 per cent of Pakistanis and 20 per cent of Bangladeshis were not fluent English speakers. Modood did not try to link linguistic fluency with educational attainment, but it is possible that lack of fluency in English amongst some Bangladeshi and Pakistani females could reduce their chances of gaining high-level qualifications.

Family life

A number of writers suggest that the nature of family life affects levels of attainment among ethnic minorities. From this point of view, West Indians are held to have a family life which fails to encourage children to do well in education, and in which there is an inadequate provision of toys, books and stimulation from parents. It has also been suggested that the West Indian population in Britain has a high proportion of one-parent families and a high proportion of working

Table 11.23 Fluency in English, by age

	Percentages									
	Men					Women				
	Indian	African Asian	Pakistani	Bangladeshi	Chinese	Indian	African Asian	Pakistani	Bangladeshi	Chinese
English spoken fluently or fairly well										
16–24-year-olds	99	99	96	97	100	96	98	84	80	98
25–44-year-olds	88	94	81	75	82	73	92	47	27	82
45–64-year-olds	68	87	56	54	50	53	71	28	4	47
Weighted count	544	420	388	149	179	583	332	358	123	186
Unweighted count	534	360	527	291	98	557	304	472	269	101
Those who came to live in Britain over age 25	60	81	42	59	(48)	42	54	20	5	(34)
Weighted count	172	98	70	38	38	144	70	68	37	51
Unweighted count	185	103	120	78	24	162	82	99	87	29

Source: T. Modood (1997) 'Qualifications and English language', in T. Modood *et al.* (eds) *Ethnic Minorities in Britain: Diversity and Disadvantage*, Policy Studies Institute, London, p. 61.

women who leave their children without close parental supervision in the early years of their life.

In a study of West Indians in Bristol, Ken Pryce (1979) described family life as 'turbulent', and he argued that 'West Indians lack a group identity and a tight, communal form of group life based on a sense of collective interdependence, and mutual obligation amongst kinsmen.'

In contrast to West Indian families, Asian families are widely believed to be more close-knit and supportive of their children's education. In a summary of his report, though with 'some caution', Lord Swann suggested that 'the Asian family structure, more tightly knit than either the white or the West Indian, may be responsible for their higher levels of achievement' (Swann, 1985).

Geoffrey Driver and Roger Ballard (1981) claim that the majority of the original South Asian immigrants to Britain came from rural areas and had little formal education. However, their research suggests that parents soon developed high aspirations for their children's education, and that parental attitudes may have contributed to their children's educational success. They say of Asian parents' attitudes to their children, 'Not only have they encouraged them to work hard at school, but they have generally been prepared to give considerable support to their children's efforts to gain further qualifications.' Driver and Ballard conclude that membership of the Asian ethnic minority is a 'positive resource' which helps rather than hinders their education.

Despite the plausibility of the above arguments, some commentators are cautious about them. The *Swann Report* was unable to comment in detail upon the effects of West Indian family life because, it argued, there was insufficient evidence to reach firm conclusions.

Furthermore, most researchers agree that the majority of West Indians are very concerned about their children's education. Ken Pryce found in Bristol that 'The majority of West Indian parents have great academic aspirations for their children.' In a study based upon a sample in the Handsworth area of Birmingham, John Rex and Sally Tomlinson (1979) did not find clear evidence that Asians were more interested in the education of their children than West Indians. From a sample of 400 white adults, 395 West Indians and 305 Asians, 89.1 per cent of the white parents, 79 per cent of the West Indians and 69.4 per cent of the Asians had made a recent visit to their children's school.

Andrew Pilkington (1997) argues that cultural explanations for differences in educational achievement should be treated with caution, but cannot be dismissed out of hand. He says, 'There are clearly a series of problems in pointing to cultural differences. The boundaries between ethnic groups are fuzzy; there is a great deal of difference within ethnic groups; and there is the danger of overstating differences.' There is also a danger of 'ethnocentrism', with white commentators being critical of ethnic minority cultures simply because they are different from their own cultures. Furthermore, cultural explanations distract attention away from possible failings in the education system itself.

However, Pilkington argues that there are real cultural differences. For example, it is well established that Afro-Caribbeans have much higher rates of single parenthood and divorce than Asians. Pilkington believes that, despite these differences, 'Both Afro-Caribbean and Asian culture are more effective than that of the white working class in encouraging children to stay on after post compulsory schooling.' He believes that there is strong evidence that the cohesiveness of Asian families may assist in the high educational achievement of some Asian groups, and that Afro-Caribbeans may have family cultures that are not as conducive to educational success. He is careful to put these comments in context, arguing that deprivation and racism are important factors that contribute to shaping cultures, and that it is important to tackle these factors rather than blaming parents for children who do not do well in education.

Apart from the uncertainties over the precise nature of ethnic minority family life and its effects, the cultural arguments may also be criticized for ignoring other factors affecting educational attainment, particularly material factors and the workings of the education system itself.

Social class and attainment

As we saw in earlier sections, class appears to be related to educational achievement, with members of lower social classes gaining fewer qualifications and leaving the education system earlier than higher classes. Poor educational performance by ethnic minorities could, at least in part, be a result of their social class rather than their ethnicity.

The Swann Committee investigated this question and found that low average levels of achievement by West Indian children were influenced considerably by 'socio-economic factors' (Swann, 1985). The Committee claimed that, when these factors were taken into account, the degree of under-achievement by West Indian children was reduced by 'around 50 per cent and very possibly more'.

Some support for these conclusions is provided by Trevor Jones's analysis of the *Labour Force Survey* (Jones, 1993). He found that class makes a significant difference to the likelihood of staying on in education after 16. For example, 47 per cent of ethnic minority children, aged 16-19, from unskilled or semi-skilled manual backgrounds, were in full-time education in 1988-90, compared to 69 per cent of those from professional, managerial or employer backgrounds. The high concentrations of ethnic minorities in low social classes could therefore affect their staying-on rates.

Research by Drew (1995) used data from the *Youth Cohort Study* to examine ethnic and class differences in educational achievement. The *Youth Cohort Study* was a study of 28,000 people who reached school-leaving age in 1985 or 1986. Table 11.24 shows the results of an analysis of the grades achieved in O levels and CSEs (now replaced by GCSEs).

Drew conducted a statistical analysis of the relative importance of class, gender and ethnicity in shaping educational attainment, and found that class was easily the most important factor. However, it is clear from the table that some differences remain even when class is taken into account, with Afro-Caribbeans doing slightly less well than other groups, and Asians from intermediate and manual backgrounds getting rather better qualifications than whites and Afro-Caribbeans from the same classes.

Although class certainly accounts for some, and perhaps much, of the inequality in education between ethnic groups, it may not account for it all. The *Swann Report* and many other commentaries have suggested that racism may also be an important cause of the inequality.

Racism and the education system

The final area in which explanations for the differential levels of educational achievement between ethnic groups have been sought is the education system itself.

The *Swann Report*

The *Swann Report* (Swann, 1985) certainly attached some importance to the role of the education system in explaining under-achievement. It accepted that only a small minority of teachers were consciously racist, but thought that there was a good deal of 'unintentional' racism. Teachers, and the books and other materials they used, sometimes supported a negative image of ethnic minorities.

Bernard Coard – racism and under-achievement

Perhaps the strongest attack on the British education system's treatment of ethnic minorities has been advanced by Bernard Coard (1971). He claims that the British education system actually makes black children become educationally subnormal by making them feel 'inferior in every way'. He says of the black child:

> *In addition to being told he is dirty and ugly and 'sexually unreliable' he is told by a variety of means that he is intellectually inferior. When he prepares to leave school, and even before, he is made to realize that he and 'his kind' are only fit for manual, menial jobs.*
>
> Coard, 1971

Table 11.24 Average exam score, by ethnic origin, sex and socio-economic group

	Average exam score			Standard deviation of exam scores	
	Male	Female	No. of cases	Male	Female
Afro-Caribbean:					
Professional	27.1	24.9	12	7.5	8.2
Intermediate	21.1	18.1	68	13.5	11.9
Manual	14.3	15.6	115	11.6	12.5
Other*	12.1	16.1	49	11.5	11.1
All	(16.4)	(16.8)	(244)	(12.7)	(12.1)
Asian:					
Professional	30.7	27.8	17	23.2	16.0
Intermediate	27.2	25.9	95	14.2	16.3
Manual	23.3	22.5	189	16.6	13.9
Other	12.9	14.1	133	11.0	11.4
All	(21.2)	(20.9)	(435)	(16.0)	(14.7)
White:					
Professional	30.4	32.3	2,118	16.7	15.7
Intermediate	23.7	25.6	3,903	16.2	15.3
Manual	17.6	20.6	5,218	14.2	14.5
Other	13.0	13.4	1,430	14.0	13.4
All	(20.9)	(23.4)	(12,669)	(16.1)	(15.8)
Professional:					
Afro-Caribbean	27.1	24.9	12		
Asian	30.7	27.8	17		
White	30.4	32.3	2,118		
Intermediate:					
Afro-Caribbean	21.1	18.1	68		
Asian	27.2	25.9	95		
White	23.7	25.0	3,903		
Manual:					
Afro-Caribbean	14.3	15.6	115		
Asian	23.3	22.5	189		
White	17.6	20.0	5,218		
Other:					
Afro-Caribbean	12.1	16.1	49		
Asian	12.9	14.1	133		
White	13.0	13.4	1,430		

* This group includes all those who did not report sufficient information for their socio-economic grouping to be established.

Source: D. Drew (1995) 'Race', Education and Work: The Statistics of Inequality, Avebury, Aldershot, p. 79.

Coard goes on to explain some of the ways in which this takes place:

1 West Indian children are told that their way of speaking is second-rate and unacceptable, the implication being that they themselves are second-rate as human beings.

2 The word 'white' is associated with good; the word 'black' with evil. Coard gives an example of a children's book in which the 'white unicorn' and the 'white boys' are able to repel an attack by the violent and evil 'black pirates'.

3 The content of the education children receive tends to ignore black people. Reading books often contain only white people, and when blacks do feature they are normally shown in subservient social roles such as servants. Coard claims that the people whose lives are studied and acclaimed (the heroes and figures from history and the present day) are white. Black culture, music and art are all conspicuous by their absence from the curriculum.

4 The attitudes to race conveyed in the classroom are reinforced by the pupils outside it. In playground arguments, white children may describe West Indian children as 'black bastards'.

Coard believes that these experiences have important consequences for the child. He believes that black children develop an 'inferiority complex', a 'low self-image', and 'low expectations in life'. Teachers expect black children to fail, and this produces a self-fulfilling prophecy in which they live 'up' to the expectations once they have been labelled. Not only are black children placed in lower streams and bands, and in schools for the educationally subnormal, but they themselves expect to fail and, as a result, they do so. (For a full description of labelling and interactionist approaches to education, see pp. 843–9.)

Coard's views on the British education system have caused considerable controversy. They have been both supported and criticized by other writers. Coard's analysis was based upon impressionistic evidence and personal experience, but his argument that teachers hold stereotypical views of ethnic minorities has been supported by the research of Elaine Brittain (1976). Based upon a postal questionnaire, using a sample of 510 teachers in primary and secondary schools in Britain, Brittan's research found that two-thirds of teachers perceived West Indian children as having low ability and being a disciplinary problem.

More direct evidence that teachers may consciously or unconsciously discriminate against ethnic minorities is provided by a detailed study of primary schools which we will now examine.

Cecile Wright – racism in multi-racial primary schools

In 1988–9 Cecile Wright (1992) conducted an ethnographic study of four multi-racial inner-city primary schools. The study involved: classroom observation of a total of 970 pupils and 57 staff; observation outside the classroom; informal interviews with all the observed teachers, some support staff and the four headteachers; interviews with the parent or parents of 38 children; and an examination of test results in three of the schools.

Wright found that 'the vast majority of the staff … seemed genuinely committed to ideals of equality of educational opportunity'. However, despite these ideals, there was considerable discrimination in the classroom.

Asians in primary schools

In nursery units Asian children were largely excluded from group discussions because teachers assumed that they would have a poor command of English. When they did involve the Asian pupils, the teachers tended to speak to them in simplistic, childish language.

In general, in all classes 'Asian girls seemed invisible to the teachers.' They received less attention than other pupils, and teachers sometimes expressed 'open disapproval of their customs and traditions'. For example, they disapproved when Asian girls tried to maintain some privacy when they had to get changed in the classroom for PE. Another example of insensitivity was when one teacher was handing out letters for pupils to take to their parents so that they could give permission for their children to go on a school trip. The teacher said to the Asian girls, 'I suppose we'll have problems with you girls. Is it worth me giving you a letter, because your parents don't allow you to be away from home overnight?'

Wright concluded that such comments from teachers made Asian pupils increasingly isolated from other pupils, who picked up on teachers' comments and became hostile to the Asians. It led to the Asian pupils themselves being ambivalent towards the school. For example, when Asian culture and celebrations were introduced into the school curriculum, Asian pupils 'expressed some pride' in having their culture acknowledged but they were also 'concerned that this often exacerbated the teasing, ridicule and harassment which they felt they received daily, particularly from the white children'.

Afro-Caribbeans in primary schools

Despite the hostility of teachers towards Asian cultural traditions, and their assumptions that Asians would have poor language skills, teachers did expect them to have some academic success. The same was not true of Afro-Caribbean children. For these children there were 'expectations of bad behaviour, along with disapproval, punishment and teacher insensitivity to the experience of racism'. In one class, for example, an Afro-Caribbean pupil called Marcus was frequently criticized for shouting out answers to questions, whereas white pupils engaging in the same behaviour were not.

Generally, 'Afro-Caribbean boys received a dispro-portionate amount of teachers' negative attentions.' Compared to white boys whose behaviour was the same, they were more likely to be sent out of class, to be sent to see the headteacher or to have privileges withdrawn. Afro-Caribbean Rastafarian children 'were seen by some teachers as a particular threat to classroom management' and were treated even more harshly.

Conclusion

All the schools made attempts to take account of the multicultural nature of their intake in what they taught. However, they often failed to achieve their objectives in doing so. Teachers would mispronounce words or names relating to ethnic minorities, causing white children to laugh and black children to be embarrassed. Wright comments that 'This situation unintentionally served to make topics or areas of knowledge associated with ethnic minority values and culture appear exotic, novel, unimportant, esoteric or difficult.'

The problems of the ethnic minority children in the primary schools were further exacerbated by racism from other children. White children often refused to play with Asian children 'and frequently subjected them to threatening behaviour, name calling and hitting'. Both Asian and Afro-Caribbean children sometimes had to suffer 'intimidation, rejection and the occasional physical assault'.

Wright concludes that 'some black children are relatively disadvantaged' in primary schools. She argues that the earliest years of education provide 'the foundations of emotional, intellectual and social development', and that these early disadvantages might well hold back the children in later stages of their education.

Racism reconsidered

The emphasis upon the faults of the education system reflected in the above pieces of research should be treated with some caution:

1 Teachers do not necessarily behave in the classroom in ways which reflect the negative stereotypes of ethnic minorities that they might hold. In a study of an inner-city secondary modern school, Martin Hammersley (unpublished) found that racist

comments in the staffroom did not lead to racism in the classroom. In the classes he observed he found no evidence of explicit discrimination, nor of 'covert' discrimination, although he accepted that covert discrimination was more difficult to identify.

2 It certainly cannot be assumed that all teachers are racist. In a review of research into this area, Monica J. Taylor (1981) admits that some teachers have negative views of West Indians, but she says, 'it would also appear that many teachers are sensitively and actively concerned to evolve a consistent and fair policy towards the treatment of their black pupils'.

3 It has been questioned whether black pupils have a low self-image which could contribute to their educational failure. Maureen Stone (1981) conducted a survey of a sample of 264 West Indian children aged 10-15 in Greater London. Using observation and interviews she found no evidence that West Indian children had a low self-concept or lacked self-esteem. Many of the pupils in her study were hostile to teachers and believed that teachers discriminated against them. However, since this did not appear to prevent the West Indian children from maintaining a positive image of themselves, it could not have produced a self-fulfilling prophecy that resulted in low levels of achievement. The *Swann Report* also examined the evidence in this area and concluded that low self-esteem among ethnic minorities was not widespread (Swann, 1985).

As we saw in an earlier section (see pp. 844–6), some sociologists believe that labelling theories of educational success or failure are too deterministic. Labelling theory seems to give those labelled little choice as to how they respond to labels: if they are defined as failures, they will fail. Stone's research and the findings of Lord Swann both indicate that labels might not be accepted by those who are labelled. Some sociologists therefore emphasize the positive and active part that pupils themselves play in determining how they react to the educational system.

The studies we will examine next place emphasis on the variety of ways in which ethnic minorities respond to racism in the education system.

Heidi Safia Mirza – *Young, Female and Black*

The study

In *Young, Female and Black*, Heidi Mirza (1992) describes the results of a study of 198 young women and men, including 62 black women aged 15-19 who were the main focus of the study. They all attended two comprehensive schools in south London. Mirza conducted observation in the school, used questionnaires to obtain basic data on the sample, and conducted informal interviews both with members of the sample and with parents. She used secondary sources such as school records and exam results. She carried out detailed case studies of three black women.

The myth of under-achievement

Mirza argues that there is a 'myth of underachievement' for black women. The girls in her sample did better in exams than black boys and white pupils in the school, and Mirza believes that in general the educational achievements of black women are underestimated.

Mirza also challenges the labelling theory of educational under-achievement. Although there was evidence of racism from some teachers, she denies that this had the effect of undermining the self-esteem of the black girls. When asked whom they most admired, 48 per cent of the black girls named themselves and over half named somebody who was black. Some of the girls felt that some teachers put them down and did not give them a chance to prove themselves. However, 'Although the girls were resentful of these attitudes, there was little evidence that they were psychologically undermined by this different treatment.'

Types of teacher

A few teachers Mirza describes as 'overt racists'. One, for example, used the term 'wog' to one of the girls. The girls tried to avoid these teachers if possible and were certainly not prepared to accept their negative definitions of black people.

Another group, whom Mirza describes as 'the Christians', tried to be 'colour blind', recognizing no differences between ethnic groups. Although the behaviour of this group was less damaging than that of the overt racists, it did have its problems. For example, a number of the teachers who fell into this category opposed the setting up of a Multi-Racial Working Party because they believed there was no problem of racism to address. Teachers in this group sometimes failed to push black pupils hard enough for them to achieve success. Sometimes they gave black girls reports that were more glowing than their achievements justified, preventing them from identifying and putting right their own weaknesses before exams came around.

A few of the teachers were active anti-racists, described by Mirza as 'the crusaders'. However, Mirza describes their campaigns as 'often misguided and over-zealous'. They put more effort into promoting these campaigns in the staffroom than they did into preparing for the classroom. Attempts to make classes relevant to black pupils sometimes resulted in no

more than bemusement. For example, one teacher introduced a role play into a class, which involved a girl who had been playing truant meeting her social worker. Although designed to reflect the experiences of black people, none of the black girls in the class had played truant or ever had a social worker.

Another group were described as 'the liberal chauvinists'. Like the crusaders they were well-intentioned. They wanted to help black pupils, but their 'help' was patronizing and often counterproductive. They felt they understood their problems and knew what was best for them. For example, one teacher stopped a girl entering for all her exams because it was felt she could not cope with the workload. The teacher believed that the girl's mother overworked her at home, helping out with household chores. In reality the pupil was desperate to enter all her exams because she needed them to get on to a social work course. This ambition was thwarted by the teacher's insistence that she did fewer subjects.

Summarizing the actions of the Liberal chauvinists, Mirza says:

> there were numerous examples of teachers' negative assessments, most of which were based on what they believe to be 'informed judgements. These negative assessments often led to the curtailment of opportunities that should have been available to the black girls in the study in view of their ability and attainment.'
>
> Mirza, 1992, p. 78

The final group identified by Mirza was a group of four black teachers. Mirza found that this group were effective teachers who were liked and respected by their pupils from all ethnic groups. Although they showed no favouritism to black pupils, they could be 'of immense value when it came to advising and understanding the girls' needs'.

Conclusion

Overall, Mirza found that the black girls in her study had positive self-esteem, were concerned with academic success and prepared to work hard. They did sometimes encounter open racism, but most of the teachers were genuinely trying to meet the girls' needs. However, most were failing to do so, and in the process were making it difficult for the girls to fulfil their potential. The girls had:

> to look for alternative strategies with which to 'get by'. These strategies, such as not taking up a particular subject or not asking for help, were employed by the girls as their only means of challenging their teachers' expectations of them, and as such were ultimately detrimental to the education of the pupils concerned.
>
> Mirza, 1992, p. 83

Mirza therefore believes that it was not the effects of labelling as such that held the girls back, nor was it the culture of the girls. Instead they were simply held back by the well-meaning but misguided behaviour of most of the teachers, and in particular by the power that teachers could exercise over pupils. In the end, however much they rejected the beliefs of their teachers, the girls 'were in no position in the "power hierarchy" to challenge any negative outcomes' that came from the way the teachers interpreted the girls' behaviour.

Mairtin Mac an Ghaill – ethnic minorities in the sixth form

Mairtin Mac an Ghaill (1992) conducted an ethnographic study of 25 Afro-Caribbean and Asian students studying A levels in a sixth-form college in a Midlands city from 1986 to 1988. He used observation and carried out interviews with the students, their parents, their teachers, and representatives of the black community in the area.

To different degrees, all the students 'spoke of the pervasiveness of white racism in relation to, *inter alia*, British immigration laws, the housing and labour markets, welfare institutions, policing and media presentation'. However, they disagreed over the extent of racism within education, with some arguing that 'they experienced little personal racial antagonism', and others believing that 'their schools, as part of the wider society, were seen as significant institutions in reproducing racial exclusiveness'.

Their beliefs about the extent of racism, though, did not directly determine their attitudes to education and their levels of academic success. Those who believed they were labelled as likely failures, and who felt that they were the victims of most racism, were not necessarily those who had the most negative attitudes to education and nor were they those who put least effort into their academic work. The way that students 'perceived and responded to schooling' varied considerably and was influenced by the ethnic group to which they belonged, their gender, and the class composition of their former secondary schools.

Schooling and class

Some of the students had been to predominantly working-class inner-city schools, some to more suburban schools, and one to a private school. Eight females and four males went to single-sex schools. These varying experiences of schooling had affected the attitudes of individual students to the education system. The girl who went to a private school hated it and saw the other girls there as racist snobs. However, she reacted against this situation. She said,

'The place could have made me fail but I was determined to prove them wrong about black people.'

Many of those who went to the inner-city schools identified an anti-academic culture at the schools and linked this with high rates of unemployment in the area. One Asian male, for example, said that teachers treated them as a problem, but without realizing that 'they are one of the main causes of our problems'. Teachers did not expect them to do well, but this student believed that 'It's just as bad for the white kids in many ways.'

Some of the girls thought they benefited from going to single-sex suburban schools. Although there was some racism, the environment was more academic and girls had greater chances of success in science subjects since there were no boys to dominate lessons.

Most pupils saw their parents as a major reason for their success in education. Mac an Ghaill says, 'The students explicitly identified with their parents, seeing them as their main support and source of inspiration.' This contradicts the claims of some sociologists that parental culture holds some members of ethnic minorities back in the education system. However, a few of the girls did believe that their gender was a handicap at home. They were expected to do much more domestic work than their brothers, leaving them less time for their studies.

Gender and ethnicity

Gender also affected their experiences at school. Some of the students felt that Afro-Caribbean boys were treated particularly badly. Teachers saw them as a threat and disciplined them more than other groups. One Afro-Caribbean boy said:

> *The teachers treated black boys much worse than Asians and whites. Like, if we were standing together, they would break us up, saying gangs were bad. But they didn't seem to feel threatened in the same way with Asian and white boys.*
>
> Ghaill, 1992

Some students felt that teachers saw Asian girls as having more academic potential than Afro-Caribbean girls. An Afro-Caribbean student called 'Deborah' claimed, 'There's no way that a black girl would be encouraged to do the good subjects. It was music and sport for us.'

Survival strategies

All of the ethnic minority students experienced problems in the education system, but they experienced them differently depending on their gender and their ethnic group. Nevertheless, all of these students had enjoyed some success. They had done so through adopting a variety of survival strategies.

Some of the girls had banded together in their schools and used 'resistance within accommodation'. They would help each other out with academic work and would try to do work that would get them good marks. However, they were less willing to conform to school rules relating to dress, appearance and behaviour in class.

Some of the other ethnic minority pupils were less hostile to their schools and tried to become friendly with specific teachers. They tried to avoid other teachers who were racist, to prevent conflict. As one Asian student said, 'You keep your head down. What choice have you? My mates knew who the racist teachers were and kept out of their way.'

Although only a small-scale study, Mac an Ghaill's research shows the importance of seeing how class, gender and ethnicity interact within the school system. He argues that 'we need to move beyond mono-causal explanations and direct our research to the multifaceted dimensions of a class-based school system that is racially and gender structured'.

This research also shows that negative labelling does not necessarily lead to academic failure amongst ethnic minority students. Although such labelling creates extra barriers, some students are able to overcome these barriers and 'In so doing, they are rejecting the model of white society presented by teachers and are resisting incorporation into white cultural identities.'

Conclusion

The various explanations examined above are not necessarily mutually exclusive. It is probable that a number of factors work together in producing the lower levels of achievement found in some ethnic minority groups. The *Swann Report* concluded that racial discrimination inside and outside school, along with social deprivation, were probably the main factors. Although the *Swann Report* attached little importance to cultural factors, it seems possible that they play some part in explaining differences in levels of achievement between ethnic minorities, as well as between ethnic minorities and the rest of the population.

Similar conclusions are reached by Andrew Pilkington. He says:

> *IQ is not a major factor but there is evidence to suggest that a range of social factors are significant: economic deprivation which itself stems at least in part from racial discrimination; culture which needs to be located in an economic context; ineffective schools; and racism in schools.*
>
> Pilkington, 1997, p. 121

Given the highly controversial nature of this issue it is not surprising that such varied explanations exist, and that a definitive answer to the question of why some ethnic minorities do poorly in education has not been reached.

Sociology, values and education

As members of society, sociologists, like everyone else, are committed to, or at least influenced by, political ideologies and values. To some degree, this will affect their choice of theoretical perspective, their methodology, and interpretation of data. Much of the criticism within the sociology of education has been levelled at the ideological assumptions and value judgements which are presumed to underlie the various viewpoints. We will now briefly examine this criticism.

Functionalist perspectives are often criticized for having a conservative bias: a prejudice in favour of maintaining things the way they are. The functions of education outlined by Durkheim, Parsons, and Davis and Moore are often similar to the 'official version' presented by government departments. As such they are accused of uncritically accepting the establishment view, and, in doing so, supporting it. Their conservative viewpoint may prevent them from considering many of the possible dysfunctional aspects of education. A more radical political standpoint and less

apparent commitment to the dominant values of their society might well produce a very different picture of the role of education in society.

During the 1950s and 1960s, sociologists were preoccupied with the question of inequality of educational opportunity, particularly in relationship to class. They felt it was morally wrong, and their views also fitted with government policy which was concerned with getting the best return on investment in education. The 'wastage of talent' involved in unequal educational opportunity reduced the efficiency of the educational system in meeting the demands of the economy. It has been argued that a commitment to liberal and social democratic theories, with their emphasis on reform rather than radical change, influenced this type of research, directing the questions asked and the answers provided.

Both social democratic theory and liberalism are concerned with reform within the framework of existing social institutions. They do not advocate radical change. Thus theories such as cultural deprivation and solutions such as compensatory education suggest a reform of existing institutions rather than a revolutionary change in the structure of society. Many sociologists appeared to operate from the viewpoint that education was a good thing and that reforms in the educational system would lead to progressive social change in a society which, while far from perfect, was heading in the right direction.

Particularly during the late 1960s and 1970s, sociologists such as Michael Flude argued that reforms such as compensatory education can 'be seen as a part of a persuasive liberal ideology that diverts attention from the exploitive and alienating practices of dominant classes and the need for fundamental social change' (Flude, 1974).

The ideological basis of some reforms has also been attacked by interactionists. Supporters of compensatory education have been accused of basing their views on a commitment to middle-class values. Thus lower working-class subculture is judged to be deficient because it is evaluated in terms of middle-class standards. Nell Keddie (1973) suggests that the uncritical acceptance by many sociologists of teachers' definitions of knowledge and ability is based on the fact that both teachers and sociologists share the same middle-class prejudices. She maintains that the middle-class values of many sociologists limit their vision and therefore prevent them from asking important questions.

However, the interactionists themselves have been criticized for their value judgements, for their commitment to cultural relativism, and for what Bill Williamson calls their 'romantic libertarian anarchism' (Williamson, 1974). By this he means that the views of some interactionists seem to be coloured by an unrealistic commitment to a vision of society without government, in which everybody is free to express themselves in their own way, in which all knowledge and all views are equally valid. Williamson suggests that this view is a romantic dream with little or no chance of translation into practice. As such it diverts attention from a realistic consideration of the nature of power in society.

By comparison with the above viewpoints, the ideological bases of Marxist perspectives are clearcut. They begin from the value judgement that capitalist societies are exploitative, repressive and anti-democratic. This should not, however, detract from their usefulness. They lead to interpretations of the role of education in society which might not be possible if society as a whole were not examined from a critical stance. As Bowles and Gintis state, 'As long as one does not question the structure of the economy itself, the current structure of schools seems eminently reasonable' (Bowles and Gintis, 1976). Many of the questions that Marxists such as Bowles

and Gintis ask derive directly from their commitment to socialism. At worst, their answers provide a fresh and stimulating view of the role of education in capitalist society.

From 1979 until 1997 government policies in Britain were quite different from those of the 1960s. The government changed from being concerned with promoting equal opportunities, to being concerned with standards and the needs of industry. The ideology behind New Right thinking was highly individualistic and was opposed to the idea that the state could try to rectify individual failure. As Phillip Brown *et al.* put it, 'The New Right take the view that individuals are the authors of their own poverty, and that state action to ameliorate their own situation would be counterproductive' (Brown *et al.*, 1997).

However, few sociologists have adopted the values of the New Right and supported the thrust of Conservative government policy. Most have criticized the philosophy behind educational reforms without necessarily dismissing all the changes that have taken place.

The majority of sociologists remain committed to the promotion of equality of opportunity within education. The rise of feminism has pushed the issue of gender and education towards the top of the sociological agenda. Similarly, concern in society as a whole about racial conflict and the under-achievement of some ethnic minorities, has led to a growing interest in the educational attainment of ethnic minority groups. Feminist and anti-racist values have increasingly come to influence the sociology of education, and, most recently, the under-achievement of boys has reached the political agenda. The abolition of class inequalities is no longer seen as sufficient to eradicate inequality of opportunity within education.

With the election of a Labour government in 1997, there was something of a return to the concern with equal opportunities, characteristic of earlier periods. However, by the late 1990s the language had changed, with concern being expressed for 'social exclusion' and improving standards rather than for poverty and class inequality. Furthermore, the new government continued to emphasize the importance of parental choice and to encourage some aspects of competition in the education system. The ideology behind their thinking and policies involved a mixture of individualism and collectivism. Both the state and the individual had to work hard to improve education.

Postmodern theories of education claim to be getting away from ideologically-based theories. They generally deny that any of the 'metanarratives' about education put forward by other perspectives can be seen as valid. They are merely viewpoints and no viewpoint is better than any other. Phillip Brown *et al.* describe the postmodern view, saying, 'there is little or no justification for claiming that one specific theory or view of knowledge is a better representation of knowledge than any other' (Brown *et al.*, 1997). For postmodernists, truth and power are inseparable and any move to choose to teach one truth rather than another involves an attempt by one group to exercise power over others. It is for that reason that they believe in encouraging different groups to develop their own education so that diversity is the order of the day.

While denying that their own approach is ideological, or based on a 'metanarrative', they claim that it will help to lead to the liberation of oppressed groups. For the first time, the oppressed will be able to develop their own knowledge, and children will be able to see the world from the viewpoint of the oppressed. However, postmodern theories have been accused of being as ideological as all other perspectives, as well as being self-contradictory. They are contradictory because they deny the possibility of any grand theory, while putting forward their own view of liberation. Phillip Brown *et al.* say, it 'has been difficult to reconcile the relativism and nihilism of a set of theories denying the possibility of human progress with a politics of difference advancing the liberation of women and people of colour' (Brown *et al.*, 1997). The postmodern perspective is ideological precisely because it includes claims about certain groups being oppressed and about the need for their liberation.

The recognition that values enter into all theories of education does not, though, mean that the perspectives are not of any value. The point of having an education system is to try to achieve objectives which have been defined by someone as desirable. Opening up the debate about why and whether education is valuable can contribute to making it better-suited to the needs of individuals and society.

Culture and identity

Culture and identity

Introduction

The definition of culture

In the introductory chapter (see pp. 3–4) culture was defined as being the whole way of life found in a particular society. It was suggested that culture was learned and shared by members of a society. However, the concept of culture is a complicated one. In his book *Keywords*, Raymond Williams, a leading theorist of culture, claims that 'Culture is one of the two or three most complicated words in the English language' (Williams, 1976).

The word 'culture' has in fact been used in a number of different ways both by sociologists and in everyday conversation. All the ways in which it has been used implicitly or explicitly contrast culture with nature. The things that humans produce or do are cultural, whereas the things that exist or occur without human intervention are part of the natural world. Christopher Jencks describes culture in this sense as 'all which is symbolic: the learned ... aspects of human society' (Jencks, 1993). However, the various definitions differ over what aspects of human life and its products should be seen as part of culture.

Jencks distinguishes four main senses in which the word culture is now used:

1   Culture is sometimes seen as a state of mind. Someone becomes cultured if they move towards 'the idea of perfection, a goal or an aspiration of individual human achievement or emancipation'. From this perspective, culture is seen as a quality possessed by individuals who are able to gain the learning and achieve the qualities that are seen as desirable in a cultured human being. This definition is reflected in the views of writers such as Matthew Arnold (see p. 899).

2   The first definition is rather an elitist one in that it sees some aspects of what is human as superior to other aspects. The second definition is also elitist, but rather than seeing some *individuals* as superior to others it sees certain *societies* as superior to others. In this sense, culture is closely related to the idea of civilization. Some societies are more cultured or more civilized than others. This view of culture is closely linked to evolutionary ideas, such as those of

Herbert Spencer (see pp. 202–4) who saw Western societies as more evolved than other societies.

3   The third definition sees culture as 'the collective body of arts and intellectual work within any one society'. As Jencks points out, this is a fairly commonsense definition and is widely used. From this point of view, culture is to be found in theatres, concert halls, art galleries and libraries, rather than in all aspects of human social life. Culture in this sense is sometimes called high culture.

4   The final definition sees culture as 'the whole way of life of a people'. This definition of culture is adopted by Ralph Linton who says, 'The culture of a society is the way of life of its members; the collection of ideas and habits which they learn, share and transmit from generation to generation' (Linton, 1945).

The fourth definition is the one most usually adopted by contemporary sociologists. Culture in this sense virtually incorporates the whole of the subject matter of sociology. Thus it is hard to see the sociology of culture as being very distinct from other areas of sociology. When the third definition is adopted it is easier to identify a distinctive area of sociology which is the sociology of culture. It includes, for example, the sociology of art, the sociology of music and the sociology of literature.

Types of culture

These definitions of culture (particularly the third and fourth) can be developed further through a brief examination of the different types of culture that have been identified by sociologists.

High culture

High culture, as mentioned above, is usually used to refer to cultural creations that have a particularly high status. They are regarded by arbiters of cultural taste as the epitome of the highest levels of human creativity. The products of long-established art forms are usually seen as examples of high culture. They include such things as opera, the work of highly regarded classical composers such as Beethoven and

Mozart, the painting of artists such as Leonardo da Vinci, and critically acclaimed literature such as the work of Shakespeare and John Milton. For many who use the term, high culture is seen as aesthetically superior to lesser forms of culture such as the next three we will consider.

Folk culture

Folk culture refers to the culture of ordinary people, particularly those living in pre-industrial societies. Dominic Strinati says that folk culture is often taken to arise 'from the grass roots, is self-created and autonomous and directly reflects the lives and experiences of the people' (Strinati, 1995). Examples of folk culture include traditional folk songs and traditional stories that have been handed down from generation to generation. Folk culture has been seen by some theorists as being less worthwhile than high culture but nevertheless as worthy of some respect. Strinati describes this view in the following way: 'folk culture can never aspire to be art, but its distinctiveness is accepted and respected'. It is at least an authentic culture and not one that is artificially created.

Mass culture

For its critics mass culture is seen as less worthy than folk culture. If folk culture is seen as characteristic of pre-modern, pre-industrial societies, mass culture is a product of industrial societies. Mass culture is essentially a product of the mass media, and examples include popular feature films, television soap operas and recorded pop music. As we shall see, some critics of mass culture see it as debasing for the individual and destructive of the fabric of society. If folk culture was created by ordinary people, mass culture is only consumed by them. From this viewpoint, the audience become passive members of a mass society, unable to think for themselves.

Popular culture

The term popular culture is often used in a similar way to the term mass culture. Popular culture includes any cultural products appreciated by large numbers of ordinary people with no great pretensions to cultural expertise: for example, TV programmes, pop music, mass-market films such as *Titanic* and the *Star Wars* series, and popular fiction such as detective stories. However, while mass culture is usually used as a pejorative term – a term of abuse – this is by no means always the case with the term popular culture. While some do see popular culture as shallow or even harmful, others, including some postmodern theorists, argue that it is just as valid and just as worthwhile as high culture.

Subculture

Finally, subculture is a term widely used in sociology to refer to 'groups of people that have something in common with each other (i.e. they share a problem, an interest, a practice) which distinguishes them in a significant way from other social groups' (Thornton, 1997). The term has been applied to a wide range of groups, including communities who live close together and have a shared lifestyle, youth groups who share common musical tastes and enjoy the same leisure activities (for example, ravers), ethnic groups, people who share the same religious beliefs, members of the same gang, and so on. Some theorists, particularly functionalists, have tended to emphasize the degree to which culture, in the sense of lifestyle, is shared by members of a society. Many other theorists emphasize one or more aspects of cultural pluralism or subcultural variety in society.

Identity

The definition of identity

The concept of identity has been defined as 'A sense of self that develops as the child differentiates from parents and family and takes a place in society' (Jary and Jary, 1991). It refers to the sense that someone has of who they are, of what is most important about them. Important sources of identity are likely to include nationality, ethnicity, sexuality (homosexual, heterosexual, bisexual), gender and class. Although it is individuals who have identities, identity is related to the social groups to which the individual belongs and with which they identify. However, there is not always a perfect match between how a person thinks of themselves and how others see them. Personal identity may be different from social identity. For example, a person perceived by others to be male may see themselves as a woman trapped in a man's body

The importance of identity

The concept of identity has become increasingly important in sociology. Early sociologists rarely used the concept, although their work often implied a theory of identity. For example, most early studies of social class in Britain tended to see class identity as central to people's sense of who they were. Studies of class consciousness (see, for example, pp. 75–89) often assumed that class identity was normally strong. They downplayed the importance of other identities such as gender, sexuality and ethnicity. Some sociologists believe that studies such as these operated with a modern conception of identity. People's identities were seen as fairly stable, as widely shared within social groups, and as based upon one or two key variables, such as class and nationality.

More recently, post-structuralist and postmodern theories of identity have adopted very different theories (see pp. 922–32). They tend to suggest that people's identities have many different facets, that they frequently change and can contain considerable contradictions. For example, people may act in more 'masculine' ways in some situations and more 'feminine' ways in other situations. Furthermore, the meaning of 'feminine' and 'masculine' identities has become less clearcut. There may now be many different ways to be manly or womanly, rather than just one (see, for example, pp. 191–6).

According to these sorts of perspectives, people actively create their own identities. Identities are no longer reducible simply to the social groups to which people belong. People have a great deal of choice about what social groups to join and, through shopping and other forms of consumption, people can shape and sometimes change their identities. To some writers, most individuals in contemporary societies no longer have a stable sense of identity at all – their identities are fragmented (see pp. 925–6).

Identity and culture

The concept of identity is closely related to the idea of culture. Identities can be formed through the cultures and subcultures to which people belong or in which people participate. However, different theories of identity see the relationship between culture and identity in rather different ways. Those influenced by modern theories of culture and identity are more likely to see identity as originating in a fairly straightforward way from involvement in particular cultures and subcultures. For example, people living in Britain would be expected to have a strong sense of British identity. Theories influenced more by postmodernism tend to stress the complexity of being British and the diversity of ways in which, for example, British people from different ethnic or national origins interpret British identity.

Stephen Frosh describes the view that identity draws from culture but is not simply formed by it in the following way:

> Recent sociological and psychological theory has stressed that a person's 'identity' is in fact something multiple and potentially fluid, constructed through experience and linguistically coded. In developing their identities people draw upon culturally available resources in their immediate social networks and in society as a whole. The process of identity construction is therefore one upon which the contradictions and dispositions of the surrounding socio-cultural environment have a profound impact.
>
> Frosh, 1999, p. 413

The issue of identity will be explored in much greater depth towards the end of the chapter. First, however, we will examine a number of perspectives on culture.

Culture – functionalist perspectives

Functionalist sociologists have generally had little to say about culture in the sense of the arts, but have been interested in culture in the sense of norms, values and lifestyles. Functionalists have generally approached the issue of societal culture from an evolutionary perspective. Their emphasis has been on the changing nature of culture as society evolved. However, the first view to be considered – that of Durkheim and Mauss – tries to go back to the origins of human culture.

Emile Durkheim and Marcel Mauss – *Primitive Classification*

The need for classification

In *Primitive Classification* (1963, first published 1903) Emile Durkheim and Marcel Mauss considered some of the most basic questions about how human culture arises. To Durkheim and Mauss, culture only becomes possible once humans are able to distinguish between things and classify them. At birth, humans cannot classify things and experience simply 'a continuous flow of representations'. This makes it difficult to separate one thing from another. In order to develop a culture humans have to develop a system for classifying things. Without one, they cannot make sense of the world around them.

The origin of classification systems

But where does the model on which classification is based come from? Durkheim and Mauss claimed that the model comes from the structure of society. Because social structures are based upon divisions between social groups, people begin to classify the rest of the world in terms of such divisions.

Durkheim and Mauss believed that Australian aboriginals had the simplest and most primitive societies. They considered that such societies provided important evidence about how human systems of classification might have developed. By examining the work of other anthropologists, Durkheim and Mauss found that the Port Mackay aboriginals had perhaps the simplest classification system of all. The Port Mackay aboriginals were divided into two social groups or moieties. These were called the *Youngaroo* and the *Wootaroo*. Because their society was divided into two groups, they divided everything else into two groups corresponding to their moieties. For example, alligators and the sun were classified as *Youngaroo*, whereas kangaroos and the moon were *Wootaroo*.

Other aboriginal groups had more complicated systems. For example, the *Wakelbura* of Queensland classified everything into four groupings. This was because their society was divided into four groups: two moieties – the *Mallera* and *Wutaru* – each of which was subdivided into two marriage clans – the *Kurgila* and *Banbey* in the *Mallera* moiety, and the *Wongu* and *Obu* in the *Wutaru* moiety. The *Wakelbura* classification system reflects these divisions, with two primary classes of things, each of which was further subdivided into two. Furthermore, this affected even what people were allowed to eat. The *Banbey*, for example, were only allowed to eat food that was classified as Banbey (including kangaroos, dogs, small bees and honey).

Complex classification systems

As the complexity of societies increases, so does the complexity of classification. For example, the Zuni Sioux of North America have an eight-fold classification system based upon eight points of the compass. For example, 'the pelican, crane, grouse, sagecock, the evergreen oak, etc. are things of the north; the bear, coyote, and spring grass are things of the west'.

Although such classification systems might appear primitive, they are the basis for all classification and indeed all culture. Like much more advanced and even scientific classification systems, they describe hierarchies, establish relationships between groups of things, and organize the world to make it comprehensible. Thus all understanding is based upon social relationships. Durkheim and Mauss say:

> *Far from being the case ... that the social relations of men are based upon logical relations between things, in reality it is the former which have provided the prototype for the latter. ... The first logical categories were social categories; the first classes of things were classes of men.*
>
> Durkheim and Mauss, 1963, p. 82

Religion and classification

In other work, Durkheim is equally insistent on arguing that culture has a social origin. In *The Elementary Forms of the Religious Life* (1961, first published 1912) he extended the arguments of

Primitive Classification to incorporate religion. He argued that religion is based upon a basic division of the world into the sacred and the profane. He again used the example of Australian aboriginals and advanced the argument that the totem system is concerned with the worship of society (see pp. 432–3 for a full discussion).

In simple societies, Durkheim believed that religion was the basis for the collective conscience – the shared moral beliefs and values of a society. Although Durkheim does not use the term 'culture' to refer to the collective conscience, what he describes is very similar to the way the term culture is used by some other writers. Durkheim says, 'The totality of beliefs and sentiments common to average citizens of the same society forms a determinate system which has its own life; one may call it the *collective* or *common* conscience' (Durkheim, 1947). As discussed in Chapter 10, Durkheim believed that the collective conscience exerts a very strong influence on people in pre-industrial societies. These societies are characterized by mechanical solidarity. People feel a sense of solidarity because they are similar to one another. There is little division of labour. (See Chapter 10 for further details.)

As society evolves, the division of labour becomes more specialized. People are no longer so similar to one another. However, they do depend upon one another. For example, teachers need farmers to grow food, and farmers need teachers to educate their children. Durkheim describes this situation of interdependence as organic solidarity. In a society of organic solidarity a collective conscience – a shared culture – is still necessary. However, the collective conscience tends to be less strong than it was under mechanical solidarity. Individuals have to be different to carry out their specialized roles. (For example, a boxer needs to be more aggressive than a nurse.)

A specialized division of labour can encourage excessive individualism (which Durkheim calls egoism) or even a situation of normlessness (which he calls anomie). Anomie can result from changes in society which disrupt existing relationships and bring existing values into question. This can lead to social problems such as a high suicide rate (see Chapter 14). Nevertheless, it is still possible for society to maintain a collective conscience. Durkheim suggests that the education system and professional associations can help to cement social solidarity amongst people in industrial societies (see Chapter 11 on education and Chapter 10 for more on professional associations).

Conclusion

To Durkheim, then, a shared culture, or collective conscience, is necessary if a society is to run smoothly. This shared culture exists over and above the wishes and choices of individuals, and it constrains their behaviour. It is passed down from generation to generation. Durkheim says that the collective conscience 'does not change from generation to generation, but, on the contrary, it connects successive generations with one another. It is thus entirely different from particular consciences, although it can be realised only through them.' People must conform to the culture of their society if they are to avoid the risk of punishment. Although society needs a shared culture, the specialized division of labour and rapid pace of industrial societies can place it under threat and positive steps may have to be taken to support it.

Criticisms and evaluation of Durkheim

Durkheim's work has been extensively criticized. Rodney Needham questions Durkheim and Mauss's work on primitive classification on the grounds that 'there is a simple lack of correspondence between form of society and form of classification' (Needham, 1963). For example, Port Mackay moieties are actually divided into marriage clans. You would therefore expect them to adopt a four-fold classification system rather than a binary one. Durkheim and Mauss ignore this evidence because it fails to support their case.

There have also been criticisms of Durkheim's work on religion (see p. 433) and on suicide (see Chapter 14). In general, Durkheim's work has been criticized for exaggerating the extent to which human culture is determined by social structure. His work leaves little room for human creativity and does little to address subcultural differences between groups. However, Durkheim did pave the way for developing a social theory of culture, and he encouraged many later writers to examine the ways in which social factors might shape culture.

Talcott Parsons – culture and social structure

Talcott Parsons's theory of culture is integral to his theories of society as a whole. His views will therefore be discussed only briefly here, but more details can be found in other chapters (see pp. 26–7, 434–5, and Chapter 15).

Culture and the social system

In *The Social System* (1951) Parsons defined cultural objects as 'symbolic elements of the cultural tradition, expressive symbols or value patterns'. Culture therefore includes such things as the language of a society, symbols such as flags, and beliefs about right and wrong, as well as things such as the art and literature of a society. Parsons thus adopted a broad definition of culture. He distin-

guished culture from the physical environment and from the individual personality. However, it is culture that links these different elements of a social system together. Individuals can only interact socially once a culture which allows communications between them has developed. Furthermore, people interpret the physical world through the symbols, such as words, that are part of their culture. Parsons said:

> a social system consists in a plurality of individual actors interacting with each other in a situation which has at least a physical or environmental aspect, actors ... whose relation to their situations including each other is defined and mediated in terms of a system of culturally structured and shared symbols.
>
> Parsons, 1951, pp. 5-6

To Parsons, human society is not possible without a shared culture. It allows people to communicate, to understand each other and to work towards shared goals. The existence of a shared culture is a functional prerequisite – a basic need – of any society that is to survive. He said, 'the high elaboration of human action systems is not possible without relatively stable symbolic systems'.

Culture and socialization

Parsons and Bales (1955) argued that culture is passed on to children through socialization, particularly through primary socialization in the family (see pp. 509–10). Parsons (1951) argued that socialization allows people to learn about different statuses and roles. Statuses in society indicate to others what sort of behaviour to expect from someone. For example, pupils would expect somebody with the status of a teacher to treat them in an impartial way when marking their work. Roles, such as the roles of mother or father, carry certain expectations with them and guide people as to how they should behave in accordance with society's culture. (For a discussion of culture, status and roles, largely based upon Parsons's ideas, see pp. 3–6.)

However, Parsons and Bales did accept that culture is not simply passed down to children and never modified. Culture constrains and limits behaviour, but it can change in interaction. If it is not repeated and reinforced in actual behaviour, culture can change. Parsons and Bales said:

> The common culture then acts as a control on behavior, and vice versa ... But the common culture also requires maintenance, reconstruction, and so on – it requires overt interaction in real space and time, with all the physical constrictions so imposed, in order to be built, and in order to survive and grow.
>
> Parsons and Bales, 1955, p. 301

Culture and social change

Despite such statements, Parsons generally saw culture as slow to change. He recognized that not everyone will share exactly the same culture, but he believed that most members of society must share most aspects of any particular culture if the society is to function smoothly and survive. Like Durkheim, though, Parsons did believe that major changes in culture do take place as societies gradually evolve. In particular, Parsons argued that, as societies change from being simple to being more complex, there is a change in the values underlying the social system.

In simple societies pattern variables A are dominant. These are largely based upon ascription – people are evaluated and rewarded according to who they are. For example, individuals will help other people or give them a job because they are members of the same family or clan.

In more complex societies the values associated with pattern variables B become dominant. These are based upon achievement – people are rewarded according to what they have achieved and what they can do. Thus a person might be given a job because they have passed the necessary exams and gained relevant experience, rather than because they happen to belong to the same family as the person making the appointment (see Chapter 15 for further details). To Parsons, societies with a culture based upon achievement are fairer and more efficient than those based upon ascription.

Criticisms and evaluation of Parsons

Parsons has often been accused of exaggerating both the extent to which contemporary societies possess a common culture and the extent to which people conform to the culture into which they are socialized. While such criticisms may be largely justified, Parsons did make it clear that he did not believe that everybody shares an identical culture. However, contemporary societies may possess such cultural diversity that they raise questions about how much culture needs to be shared. In Britain, for example, there is a great deal of ethnic, regional and religious diversity, yet British society continues to function without any signs of imminent disintegration. It may be that Parsons's views are more applicable to fairly homogeneous societies than to heterogeneous ones. If that is the case then his views cannot be applied to all social systems as he claims.

Marxist theories of culture and identity

Karl Marx on culture

Like Durkheim, Marx made little explicit use of the concept of culture. However, contained within his extensive writings there are a number of ideas that could be seen as forming a theory of culture (in the sense of the lifestyle of a society). Furthermore, Marx also developed some ideas on art and literature.

The origins of culture

Like functionalists, Marx argued that human culture has a social origin and cannot be seen as deriving directly from nature or from innate instincts in human beings. Culture comes from humanity's creation of the first societies. Unlike Durkheim, though, Marx did not see culture developing in terms of primitive classification systems that derive from social structure. Instead he believed that culture had a material origin in human labour.

As a materialist Marx believed that material circumstances and economic activity shaped human consciousness. In the *Economical and Philosophical Manuscripts* (first published 1844) Marx argued that 'the animal is immediately identical with its life-activity. It is its *life-activity*. Man makes his life-activity itself the object of his will and of his consciousness. He has conscious life-activity' (quoted in Baxandall and Morawski (eds), 1974). In this passage, Marx is arguing that animals do not possess a consciousness separate from activities such as hunting or building nests. While animals produce things, they do so only to meet their immediate needs. However, humans do more than this.

Once humans get together and form social groups they engage in productive activity even when they have no need to. Marx said, 'man produces even when he is free from physical need and only truly produces in freedom therefrom. ... Man, therefore, also forms things in accordance with the laws of beauty.' Because humans, once they form social groups, produce more than they need to do for simple physical survival, they begin to produce things for their aesthetic appeal. They produce things because they give pleasure rather than because they meet needs such as hunger or thirst.

To Marx, culture originates in human productive activity. As humans extend the work they do beyond their survival needs, they start to develop self-consciousness. This allows them to actively create their own culture. In *Capital* (first published

1867), Marx elaborated further on this theme. He suggested that the imagination and creativity of the human worker are qualitatively different from the mechanical behaviour of bees or other animals. He said:

> the poorest architect is categorically distinguished from the best of bees by the fact that before he builds a cell in wax, he builds it in his head. The result achieved at the end of a labor process was already present at its commencement, in the imagination of the worker in its ideal form. More than merely working an alteration in the form of nature, he also knowingly works his own purposes into nature.
>
> Quoted in Baxandall and Morawski (eds), 1974, p. 54

Alienation and culture

According to Marx, when humans live in freedom, they fulfil themselves through the creative activity of producing things using their imagination. However, problems arise when human freedom is restricted by the existence of private property. Some humans start to accumulate large amounts of private property at the expense of others, and the propertyless begin to lose their freedom. They lack the means of production such as the tools or the land necessary to produce enough for their own physical survival. Instead they have to work for others who do own the means of production. They lose freedom to organize their productive activity or work. They are compelled to work for the owners of the means of production in order to survive. In short, they become alienated.

As discussed elsewhere (see Chapter 10), alienation involves a sense of estrangement from the work that people do (the act of production), from other workers, from what they are producing (the end product) – because they no longer own it – and even from their own essential humanity. Alienated workers are unable to freely express their own humanity by using their creativity in their work.

Culture as ruling-class ideology

Marx developed these ideas further by claiming that in class-stratified societies culture can be seen as little more than ruling-class ideology. From this point of view culture is simply an expression of the distorted view of the world advanced by the dominant class. It is part of the superstructure of society. The superstructure is shaped by the economic base or infrastructure. The ruling class – the owners of the means of production – use their economic power to shape society's culture. In a famous passage in *The German Ideology* (first published 1846) Marx and Engels argued that:

> *The ideas of the ruling class are, in every age, the ruling ideas: i.e. the class which is the dominant material force in society is at the same time its dominant intellectual force. The class which has the means of material production at its disposal, has control at the same time over the means of mental production, so that in consequence the ideas of those that lack the means of mental production are, in general, subject to it. The dominant ideas are nothing more than the ideal expression of the dominant material relationships grasped as ideas.*
>
> Quoted in Bottomore and Rubel (eds), 1963, p. 93

Contemporary Marxists have used such statements as the basis for developing Marxist theories of institutions such as the mass media (see Chapter 13).

However, the writings of Marx and Engels are open to a range of interpretations and they do not always state that the cultural superstructure of society is entirely shaped by the infrastructure. At other times Marx, or Marx and Engels, argued that the infrastructure influences, or perhaps sets limits on, what happens in the cultural superstructure, but does not totally determine it. Elements within the infrastructure can influence one another as well (see Chapter 15 for an elaboration of these views).

One interpretation of Marx, then, sees all culture in capitalist societies as a product of ruling-class ideology. The working class are seen as suffering from false class consciousness and their beliefs and culture will therefore be shaped by the ruling class. This theory has been called 'the dominant ideology thesis' (Abercrombie *et al.*, 1980). Other interpretations see the working class and other cultures as possessing some independence or relative autonomy from ruling-class domination and from the economic base.

Culture as the reflection of class differences

A further interpretation of Marx emphasizes class differences between cultures. From this point of view, different classes will always tend to have different cultures because their conditions of material existence are different. The different experiences of living as members of the ruling class or the working class will produce a different view of the world and hence a different culture. Stefan Morawski describes this interpretation of Marx and Engels's views in the following way: 'Ideology will here be considered as the statement or symptomatic expression of a pattern of social class attitudes, interests, or habits of thought' (Morawski, 1974). Thus working-class literature will be different from literature produced by the ruling class.

However, Engels accepted the possibility that aspects of culture such as literature could, in the work of some writers, rise above the class origins of the writer and demonstrate revealing insights into society. An example is Engels's discussion of the German writer Goethe.

According to Engels, at times Goethe's work is restricted by his class background. His comfortable and respectable background as the 'Frankfurt alderman's cautious child, the privy councilor of Weimar' sometimes leads Goethe to celebrate German life. However, at other times, Goethe is 'the poet of genius, who is disgusted by the wretchedness of his surroundings' (quoted in Baxandall and Morawski (eds), 1974).

Here, Engels raises the possibility that people can see through false class consciousness and produce cultural works that show an appreciation of the oppression and exploitation found in class societies. Thus, literature and other forms of art and aspects of culture tend to reflect the experiences of different class groups, but they can sometimes rise above this to uncover something approaching the truth about society.

Marx and Engels believed that eventually the culture of society as a whole would change. Class consciousness would develop in the working class and they would begin to see through the distorted ideology of the ruling class. Capitalism would be replaced by communism and, in the absence of exploitation and ruling-class domination, humans would be able to return to creating things that expressed their true humanity.

(The strengths and weaknesses of the work of Marx and Engels will become clear as we discuss the way their ideas have been used by later Marxists. Criticism and evaluation of Marx and Engels relevant to their theories of culture can also be found on p. 437, pp. 609–20, and Chapter 15.)

Marxist and neo-Marxist theories of the general cultures of societies are examined elsewhere in the book (see, for example, pp. 33–6, 436–9 and Chapter 15). This section will therefore concentrate on Marxist theories of the arts, and particularly literature.

Marxist theories of the arts

John Berger – oil paintings and private property

Ruling-class art

One of the most straightforward Marxist theories of art is advanced by John Berger (1972). In *Ways of Seeing* he argues that oil painting – the dominant medium for painters between 1500 and 1900 – came to reflect the world view of the ruling classes. Berger says that 'The art of any period tends to serve the ideological interests of the ruling class.' He claims that in the period 1500-1900, 'a way of seeing the world, which was ultimately determined by new attitudes to property and exchange, found its visual expression in the oil painting'.

Oil paintings had special characteristics that made them particularly suitable for portraying ruling-class ideology. According to Berger, oil painting has a 'special ability to render the tangibility, the texture, the lustre, the solidity of what it depicts. It defines the real as that which you can put your hands on.' This was important because oil painting came to be primarily concerned with the depiction of wealth or property.

Because of the sense of tangibility that oil painting can produce, it gave substance to the sense of ownership that the ruling class wanted to portray in their paintings. Although paintings had always

portrayed things of value, in earlier periods they were usually related directly to the glory of God. As capitalist society developed, painting focused more directly on the wealth and power of the ruling class, elevating money above religious considerations. Berger says:

> *Works of art in earlier traditions celebrated wealth. But wealth was then a symbol of a fixed social or divine order. Oil painting celebrated a new kind of wealth – which was dynamic and which found its only sanction in the supreme buying power of money.*
>
> Berger, 1972, p. 90

The ruling class were able to impose their own view of the world, simply because it was very largely they who commissioned paintings. Large numbers of paintings were commissioned by the wealthy – most of mediocre quality. It was more important to the buyers of the paintings that they portrayed them and their wealth in the way they wanted, than that the painting was of a high quality. Berger says, 'Hack work is not the result of either clumsiness or provincialism; it is the result of the market making more insistent demands than the art.'

Examples of ruling-class art

Berger gives a number of examples to illustrate his claims.

In earlier periods, paintings of Mary Magdalene tended to emphasize the importance of her story. This was that 'she so loved Christ that she repented of her past and came to accept the mortality of the flesh and the immortality of the soul'. However, by the time of the dominance of oil paintings, the typical portrait of her had changed. She was now portrayed as a woman to be owned by men – simply another possession. Berger says, 'She is painted as being, before she is anything else, a takeable and desirable woman.'

Still-life paintings were more obviously about possessions. These tended to portray such things as tables laden with luxurious foods as testament to the high living of those who had commissioned them.

Paintings of animals were also popular. However, they were not usually animals in the wild but 'livestock whose pedigree is emphasized as proof of their value'.

Landscapes were used to celebrate the property of the rich. Berger uses the example of *Mr and Mrs Andrews*, painted by Gainsborough (see Figure 12.1). The Andrews insisted on being included in the landscape which featured land owned by them. According to Berger, 'They are landowners and their proprietary attitude towards what surrounds them is visible in their stance and their expressions.'

Low-life paintings

Of course, not all oil paintings portrayed the property of the rich. However, even some that portray the poor reflect ruling-class ideology. Pictures of 'low life', such as pictures of debauched groups in taverns, were popular with the growing bourgeoisie in the sixteenth to nineteenth centuries. The point of such pictures, though, was to tell a moral tale about how the rich deserved their success while the poor had only themselves to blame for their misfortune. Berger says that such paintings 'lent plausibility to a sentimental lie: namely that it was the honest and hard-working who prospered, and that the good-for-nothings deservedly had nothing'.

Rembrandt

Despite the emphasis that Berger puts upon ruling-class ideology in shaping oil painting, he does accept that some paintings were able to transcend the narrow concerns of the bourgeoisie. However, such works are exceptional and can only be painted by those who undergo a struggle to free themselves from dominant ways of thinking about the world. According to Berger, one painter who succeeded in this respect was Rembrandt.

In his early work Rembrandt succumbed to the dominant artistic style propagated by the bourgeoisie.

In an early self-portrait (see Figure 12.2) Rembrandt portrays himself with his first wife. He is essentially showing off his wife and, to Berger, 'The painting as a whole remains an advertisement for the sitter's good fortune, prestige and wealth.'

In a self-portrait painted thirty years later, when he was an old man (see Figure 12.3), Rembrandt portrays himself in a more sombre and reflective mood and includes none of the trappings of material success. Berger says, 'All has gone except a sense of the question of existence, of existence as a question.' Rembrandt has succeeded in shaking off ruling-class ideology and painting something of more universal and lasting significance.

Evaluation of Berger

Janet Wolff (1981) argues that Berger provides a rather crude and over-simplified explanation of oil paintings. She considers that his study lacked 'an adequate and systematic analysis'. However, Wolff does acknowledge that 'the intervention into the discipline of art history has proved to be extremely critical and influential, and it has stimulated a good deal of more detailed analysis'. Many other Marxist theories of art and literature have adopted a broadly similar approach, but have tried to refine the sorts of arguments put forward by Berger. One example is the work of Lucien Goldmann.

Lucien Goldmann – class and literature

The expression of class world views

In his best-known work, *The Hidden God* (1964), Goldmann develops a sociological account of the French writers Pascal and Racine. Unlike Berger, Goldmann does not believe that artistic products tend to reflect ruling-class ideology in a simple way. Instead, he argues that works of art (in this case great works of literature) reflect the world view of particular social classes. He says, 'the most important group to which any individual may belong, from the point of view of intellectual and artistic activity and creation, is that of the social class, or classes of which he is a member'. He justifies this claim by saying that humans in subject classes have to devote most of their effort to physical survival, while those in more dominant classes have to devote their time to maintaining their dominance. Class therefore tends to be prominent in people's thinking about the world.

To Goldmann, most people have only an incoherent and partial class consciousness. However, a few individuals are more perceptive than this. They are:

Figure 12.1 *Mr and Mrs Andrews*, by Gainsborough, c.1748-9, National Gallery, London

Figure 12.2 *Self-portrait with Saskia*, by Rembrandt, 1635–9, Gemaldegalerie, Dresden
Figure 12.3 (inset) *Self-portrait as an Old Man*, by Rembrandt, Gallerie Degli Uffizi, Florence

exceptional individuals who either actually achieve or who come very near to achieving a completely integrated and coherent view of the social class to which they belong. The men who express this vision on an imaginative or conceptual plane are writers and philosophers.

Goldmann, 1964, p. 17

Pascal and Racine

Goldmann sees Pascal and Racine as examples of just such exceptional individuals. He argues that they shared a particular tragic vision of the world, which reflected the position of a specific class grouping in French society in the seventeenth century. Goldmann refers to this class as the *noblesse de robe.*

The *noblesse de robe* consisted of members of legal and administrative professions who were not directly employed by the monarchy but were tied to the state, which was partially under the control of the monarchy. The world view of the *noblesse de robe* was therefore likely to partially reflect the world view of the monarchy.

However, the sort of functions they performed in, for example, the legal profession, inclined them towards a rather different world view, which was more rationalistic and less inclined to accept the traditional authority of the monarchy. Their world view therefore contained contradictory elements characteristic of both the monarchy and the rising bourgeoisie, who had a more rationalistic outlook. According to Goldmann, it was this contradictory ideology that was reflected in the tragedies written by Pascal and Racine.

The central feature of the tragedies was 'that everything which God demands is impossible in the eyes of the world, and that everything that is possible when we follow the rules of this world ceases to exist when the eye of God lights upon it'. In short, it was impossible to succeed in the world *and* to please God. This reflected the impossibility of acting as members of the bourgeoisie and pleasing the king. Thus the literature of Pascal and Racine directly reflected and expressed the contradictions of the class position of the *noblesse de robe.*

Evaluation of Goldmann

Janet Wolff argues that Goldmann provides a relatively sophisticated and subtle Marxist interpretation of literature. She says:

He relates literature and ideology to class structure without using a simple reductionist equation, but instead insists that social life is a totality. The relationship between literary production is not defined as causal or crudely deterministic, but is presented as mediated through social groups and their consciousness.

Wolff, 1981, p. 58

Wolff notes that Goldmann uses the idea of the exceptional individual, who can articulate a class consciousness which others can only partially grasp. To Wolff, this is a considerable advance on the much more deterministic approach of Berger.

However, Goldmann's work is not above criticism and, from a number of viewpoints, may be seen as inadequate.

First, it rather assumes without strong justification the primacy of class in shaping experience. To feminists, for example, gender is more important than class in influencing art. Other social groupings, such as ethnic groups and age groups, may also exert an influence on the production of literature and other art forms.

Second, Goldmann's work assumes that a class can possess an ideology, that individuals can develop a coherent and consistent view of the world, and that the meaning of a text can be clear to those who interpret it. All of these claims are challenged by a variety of post-structuralists and postmodernists who are deeply critical of such neat assumptions.

Third, despite the autonomy that Goldmann attributes to individual authors, he still advances a rather monocausal account of literature. It is doubtful whether one single factor, such as the expression of the world view of a particular class, can explain the content of art forms like literature. As this chapter develops, a range of other influences upon culture will be discussed.

Neo-Marxist theories of culture

A number of writers have developed what can be described as new or neo-Marxist theories of culture. All of these approaches have been significantly influenced by Marxism, but all tend to argue that culture possesses considerable autonomy or independence from economic influences, and that there is no straightforward correspondence between class and culture.

Raymond Williams – *Culture and Society*

One of the most influential figures in the development of cultural studies in Britain has been Raymond Williams. In a series of important books, Williams (1961, 1965, 1978) examined the relationships between society, culture and art, using some

aspects of Marxist theories in the development of
his ideas.

Class consciousness and culture

In *Culture and Society* (1961) Williams questions two
main aspects of Marxist theories of culture.

First, he argues that the use of the ideas of
infrastructure and superstructure is misleading. He
says, 'Structure and superstructure, as terms of an
analogy, express at once an absolute and fixed
relationship. But the reality which Marx and Engels
recognize is both less absolute and less clear.'

Williams does not deny that economic factors
influence culture, but he does deny that they
determine culture in a straightforward way. He says:

> *A Marxist theory of culture will recognize diversity
> and complexity, will take account of continuity
> within change, will allow for chance and certain
> limited autonomies, but, with these reservations,
> will take the facts of the economic structure and
> the consequent social relations as the guiding
> string on which a culture is woven.*
>
> Williams, 1961, p. 261

In Williams's work there is much more room for
historical detail and individual and group creativity
than in some Marxist theories.

Second, Williams argues that Marxist theories of
culture have been too concerned with art and literature. As such they have had too narrow a focus. For
Williams, Marxist theory emphasizes the interdependence of all aspects of social reality, and such a
narrow field as art and literature should not be taken
as synonymous with culture. He therefore argues that
'Marxists should logically use "culture" in the sense
of a whole way of life, a general social process.'

Working-class culture and bourgeois culture

Williams's own studies include an analysis of
working-class culture. During the Industrial
Revolution and the nineteenth century there was
relatively little art and literature produced by the
working class, but they did develop their own distinctive lifestyles and institutions. To Williams, the basis
of working-class culture was the commitment to
acting collectively. Individual members of the working
class were too weak to defend themselves individually
and too restricted in their life chances to achieve
success through individual effort. Therefore, working-
class culture has taken shape through 'the collective
democratic institution, whether in the trade unions,
the cooperative movement, or a political party'.

While Williams draws this general contrast
between collective working-class and individualistic
bourgeois culture, he does not believe that there is
an absolute and clearcut distinction between them.

There is some overlap between bourgeois and
working-class culture. He says, 'there is both a
constant interaction between these ways of life and
an area which can properly be described as
belonging to or underlying both'. Furthermore,
cultures are not the automatically determined
products of class structures. Rather they are actively
created by people who are responding to their
economic circumstances.

Residual and emergent, alternative and oppositional culture

In a later work Williams (1978) tries to develop his
ideas on the relationship between class and culture
further. As in his earlier work, he denies that there is
ever a monolithic, totally dominant ruling-class
ideology in society. While there may be a dominant
ideology, it is always likely to be challenged by
alternative ideologies. There may be residual ideologies (the ideology of a class which is declining but
still important) or emergent ideologies (the ideologies of new groups that are outside the ruling class).
Residual and emergent ideologies may be either
oppositional (opposed to the dominant ideology) or
alternative (they co-exist with the dominant
ideology without challenging it). Thus, to Williams,
there is nothing inevitable about groups outside the
ruling class either accepting or rejecting the
dominant ideology. Both responses are possible, and
of course people may accept some aspects of the
dominant ideology while rejecting others.

Evaluation of Williams

Williams's ideas encouraged other writers to take
working-class cultures seriously and therefore to
study them. Such writers tried to move away from
deterministic versions of Marxism and to take
account of specific historical circumstances and
human creativity. Nevertheless, they did not really
resolve the question of the precise relationship
between the economy and culture.

Furthermore, many contemporary theorists (for
example, most postmodernists) argue that it is
difficult to distinguish such a thing as working-class
culture, and they would certainly deny that the
working class retains a collective culture such as
that described by Williams (see, for example,
pp. 119–21). For such theorists, even if working-class
culture was important in modern societies, it is no
longer so in postmodern societies. Although this
might not invalidate Williams's historical studies of
working-class culture, it does raise questions about
whether his theories are useful for understanding
contemporary society. Other research suggests that
working-class lifestyles remain culturally distinctive
(see pp. 74–89).

The Birmingham Centre for Contemporary Cultural Studies

In Britain, perhaps the most influential source of neo-Marxist ideas on culture in the 1970s and 1980s was the Birmingham Centre for Contemporary Cultural Studies (CCCS) (see pp. 259–60 and Chapter 11 for examples of their work). The CCCS extended the study of culture to an examination of youth cultures, incorporating elements of Marxism within the analysis.

Resistance through Rituals

In *Resistance through Rituals* (Hall and Jefferson (eds), 1976) John Clarke, Stuart Hall, Tony Jefferson and Brian Roberts (1976) outline a theoretical approach to the study of youth cultures. They do so within a broadly Marxist framework, arguing that material circumstances impose limits on the sorts of cultures that people can develop. However, they allow considerable room for human creativity in producing culture.

Cultures and material life

According to Clarke *et al.*:

> the 'culture' of a group or class is the distinctive 'way of life' of the group or class, the meanings, values and ideas embodied in institutions, in social relations, in systems of beliefs, in mores and customs, in the uses of objects and material life.
>
> Clarke *et al.*, 1976, p. 10

Individuals are born into particular cultures and these tend to shape the way in which they see the world – their maps of meaning, as Clarke *et al.* term it. However, these maps of meaning and their associated cultures change as history unfolds and as members of social groups actively create cultures and innovate. But groups cannot just create new cultures at will. Cultures always relate to experiences and sets of material circumstances and are always partly shaped by pre-existing cultures. Furthermore, cultures exist in hierarchical relationship to one another. The culture of dominant groups is always likely to be more powerful than the cultures of less powerful groups. But Clarke *et al.* deny that a whole society's culture will ever be dominated by one ruling-class ideology.

Hegemony

Clarke *et al.* draw extensively on the theories of the Italian Marxist Gramsci (see pp. 615–17). Gramsci argued that in order to achieve political and ideological domination (which he called hegemony) powerful classes always had to struggle against competing ideologies and make compromises with other less powerful classes. Dominant ideology can always be opposed and hegemony is never complete. Clarke *et al.* adopt a similar position. They say:

> Other cultural configurations will not only be subordinate to this dominant order: they will enter into struggle with it, seek to modify, negotiate, resist or even overthrow its reign – *its* hegemony. The struggle between classes over material and social life thus always assumes a continuous struggle over the distribution of 'cultural power'.
>
> Clarke *et al.*, 1976, p. 12

It might be an unequal struggle, but it is a struggle none the less. Subordinate cultures will generally try to win space, to make room for their own distinctive lifestyles, values and institutions away from the influence of more powerful cultures. An example is the traditional working-class neighbourhood, dating from the 1880s, with its distinctive physical layout – 'the networks of streets, houses, corner shops, pubs and parks' – and social relationships – 'the networks of kin, friendship, work and neighbourly relations'. The working class exercised considerable informal control over these areas.

Youth subcultures

To Clarke *et al.* youth subcultures often represent creative attempts to try to maintain or win autonomy or space from dominant cultures. They win 'cultural space in the neighbourhood and institutions, real time for leisure and recreation, actual room on the street-corner'. They are partly shaped by the parent culture of the class from which they originate (for example, working class or middle class), but they are distinct from it.

Youth cultures create their own distinctive style: for example, by choosing a style of dress and listening to a particular type of music. The styles adopted by individual cultures represent an attempt to '"solve", but in an imaginary way, problems which at the concrete material level remain unresolved'.

The example of Teddy boys can illustrate these arguments.

Tony Jefferson – Teddy boys

Tony Jefferson (1976) argues that the youth culture of Teddy boys (or Teds) represented an attempt to recreate the sense of working-class community which came under threat in the post-war period from urban redevelopment and growing affluence in some sections of the working class.

Unskilled working-class youth felt that their social status was being undermined and that their 'territory' was under threat from the urban planners and from a growing ethnic minority presence in their neighbourhood. They responded by forming groups in which members had a strong sense of loyalty to one another and were willing to fight over their territory. Their style of dress incorporated Edwardian-style jackets, bootlace ties and suede shoes. Jefferson sees aspects of this style as part of an attempt to buy status. For example, Edwardian-style jackets were originally worn by 'upper-class dandies' in Edwardian times, and by wearing them Teds hoped that some of the status of this group would rub off on them.

Bootlace ties appeared to come from American Western films, in which they were worn by the 'slick city gambler whose social status was, grudgingly, high because of his ability *to live by his wits* and outside the traditional working class mores of society'. Like their counterparts in the Westerns, the Teddy boys felt themselves to be outsiders who needed to live by their wits. They were seeking something of the status of the city gambler and so adopted part of their dress.

To Clarke *et al.* youth cultures do not solve the fundamental problems of working-class youth, but they do offer 'imaginary solutions'. Working-class youth can at least feel that they are doing something to protect their territory, gain status and recreate community. They also challenge and resist dominant ideologies without really threatening them. Youth cultures are part of the continuing struggle for cultural hegemony, born out of class cultures, but distinct from them. They are actively created by their members who develop their own styles as a way of expressing their situation and its contradictions, or their aspirations.

Evaluation of the CCCS

The work of the CCCS was important, not just in trying to develop a neo-Marxist approach to culture, but also in encouraging sociologists to take popular culture seriously. In analysing such things as the dress sense of Teddy boys it attempted to integrate elements of semiology (sometimes called semiotics) (see pp. 906–8) into neo-Marxist studies of culture. However, the neo-Marxist elements of their approach have rather fallen out of fashion. They have been seen as exaggerating the importance of class at the expense of other social divisions.

Postmodernists tend to follow the CCCS in taking popular culture seriously, but they do not follow them in seeing class as important. They see popular culture more in terms of straightforward consumption and lifestyle choices. Different subcultures are not unsuccessful attempts to win space from dominant cultures, because there is no dominant culture. Subcultures are simply an expression of the freedom of consumers to create their own cultures.

Neo-Marxist theories such as those developed by the CCCS tend to fall between two stools. To conventional Marxists they fail to fully acknowledge the importance of the economic base in shaping culture. To postmodernists they fail to fully accept the freedom that people have to invent cultures. Nevertheless, their work certainly helped to inspire the further development of cultural studies.

Culture and civilization

The culture and civilization tradition

Sociological perspectives are not the only ones that have been influential in the development of ideas about culture. Another influential source of ideas has been a tradition of thinking which has been influenced by disciplines such as literary criticism. This has been called the culture and civilization tradition.

This tradition is based upon an attempt to evaluate the worth of different cultures, just as a literary critic might evaluate the worth of different books. It has generally been critical of popular culture while extolling the virtues of high culture, and even, to a lesser extent, folk culture. The civilization tradition in general supports an elitist approach to culture in which the culture of the masses is seen as inferior to the culture of elite groups. It also tends to see high culture as in decline or under threat. However, different writers blame different causes for the deterioration of culture.

The culture and civilization tradition emerged out of concern about the effects of industrialization, urbanization and modernization in the nineteenth century. The massive changes introduced by the Industrial Revolution led to acute anxiety that the finer aspects of civilization were being undermined. John Storey (1993) argues that it was the emergence of a distinctive culture of subordinate classes that was the main source of anxiety.

The industrial working class in the growing towns and cities was able to develop:

an independent culture at some remove from the direct intervention of the dominant classes. Industrialization and urbanization had redrawn the cultural boundaries. No longer was there a shared common culture, with an additional culture of the powerful. Now for the first time in history, there was a separate culture of the subordinate classes of the urban and industrial centres.

Storey, 1993, pp. 20-1

Matthew Arnold – *Culture and Anarchy*

Matthew Arnold (1822–88) was the first significant writer in the culture and civilization tradition. Arnold was a poet and literary critic who also taught at Rugby School and was a school inspector. However, he was best known for his book *Culture and Anarchy* (1960, first published 1869).

Culture – the 'study of perfection'

To Arnold, culture was 'the study of perfection' which led to 'a *harmonious* perfection, developing all sides of our humanity' and a '*general* perfection, developing all parts of our society'. People became cultured through the pursuit of perfection.

From Arnold's perspective, the pursuit of perfection was becoming uncommon in nineteenth-century England. People were becoming too materialistic and too concerned with machinery and its products. Arnold described the 'worship of machinery and of external doing', and complained of the dangers of equating civilization with material wealth. A truly civilized culture could only be attained through 'getting to know, on all the matters which most concern us, the best which has been thought and said in the world; and through this knowledge, turning a stream of free and fresh thought upon our stock notions and habits'. Through studying the finest poetry and literature people could develop their humanity, come closer to perfection, and in doing so help to improve society.

Reading was the key to this. Arnold comments that 'a man's life of each day depends for its solidity and value on whether he reads during that day, and far more still, on what he reads during it'.

Arnold clearly saw some reading as more worthy than other reading. Only the best was good enough, and the popular tastes of the mass of the population were certainly not uplifting and cultured. Indeed Arnold saw the urban working class as a dangerous and largely uncultured group. They had lost deference for their social superiors and insisted upon being able to do as they liked. This had resulted in dangerous political protests and threatened a descent into anarchy which could destroy civilization and culture. Arnold warned of how there was:

> a body of men, all over the country ... beginning to assert and put in practice an Englishman's right to do what he likes; his right to march where he likes, meet where he likes, enter where he likes, hoot as he likes, threaten as he likes, smash as he likes.
>
> Arnold, 1960, p. 76

The solution to the problem of the working class was to educate them. Without education they would be unable to gain culture and therefore unable to play a constructive rather than destructive role in society.

Evaluation of Arnold

John Storey is fairly scathing about Arnold's work. He argues that its basic concern is not culture, but to advocate 'social order, social authority, won through cultural subordination and deference' (Storey, 1993). It is an argument for putting the working class back in their place by denying their developing culture any validity. However, Arnold was unwilling to actually take any part in politics to advance his cause – that is, the propagation of culture to maintain social order. Storey suggests that this gave him little chance of achieving his objectives and made his writings fairly pointless. Storey says:

> Arnold's small circle would appear to be nothing more than a self-perpetuating intellectual elite. If they are never to engage in practical politics, and never to have any real influence on the mass of humankind, what is the purpose of all the grand humanistic claims to be found scattered throughout Arnold's work?
>
> Storey, 1993, p. 26

All this elite could do was to congratulate each other on their own good taste, their own culture.

Elitist views of culture have increasingly been challenged in recent years (see pp. 900–1), and working-class culture during the Industrial Revolution has been viewed with more respect by some historians. For example, in *The Making of the English Working Class* (1963), E.P. Thompson portrays working-class culture during the Industrial Revolution as resourceful, creative and certainly no less worthy than the culture of higher classes.

F.R. Leavis – culture and civilization in the 1930s

F.R. Leavis wrote extensively about the decline of culture in the 1930s. He drew heavily upon the work of Matthew Arnold and in many ways his work can be seen as applying Arnold's views in a twentieth-century context. By the time he was writing, parts of the mass media had developed, and they became the focus of some of his strongest attacks.

In *Culture and Environment* (1977, first published in the 1930s) F.R. Leavis and Denys Thompson look back approvingly to culture in pre-industrial times. They argue that there was a rich culture amongst ordinary people which developed naturally out of people's ordinary lives. However, this had been lost as a result of industrialization and modernization. Leavis and Thompson say:

What we have lost is the organic community with the living culture it embodied. Folk-songs, folk-dances, Cotswold cottages and handicraft products are signs and expressions of something more: an art of life, a way of living, ordered and patterned involving social arts, codes of intercourse and a responsive adjustment, growing out of immemorial experience, to the natural environment and the rhythm of the year.

Quoted in Storey, 1993, p. 32

The decline of culture

In 'Mass civilisation and minority culture' (first published 1930), Leavis explores the impact of the loss of folk culture on the appreciation of art and literature. Leavis claims that, in the past, even what is thought of as 'high-brow' culture was accessible to the masses. Thus, it was not just a cultural elite who went to watch Shakespeare's plays when they first appeared, but also a mass of ordinary people. It was true, perhaps, that they did not appreciate all the subtleties of Shakespeare, but they could enjoy his plays on a simpler level than the more cultured members of the audience.

According to Leavis, the situation was very different by the 1930s. Leavis believed that in all eras it was 'often a very small minority' on which 'the discerning appreciation of art and literature depends ... [it is] only a few who are capable of unprompted, first-hand judgement' (Leavis, 1930, in J. Storey (ed.), 1994). Only this small minority was capable of distinguishing great art from the mundane and the valueless, simply by virtue of their innate aesthetic judgement. They alone could determine who were the contemporary successors to writers such as Shakespeare, Dante and Baudelaire – the writers whose work would stand the test of time. A slightly larger group could learn to distinguish between good and bad literature and art and develop some ability to appreciate the greatness of the best works. However, they could never take a lead in the formation of aesthetic judgements about new works of art.

The culture of the elite and the culture of the masses

According to Leavis, the preservation of culture depended upon the retention of the elite minority with the most discriminating taste. Yet in the 1930s both the taste of this group and the culture of the masses had come under serious threat.

Elite culture was threatened by the mass of cultural products being created. There was too much for anyone to take in. Their aesthetic sensibilities would be swamped. Leavis writes:

A reader who grew up with Wordsworth moved among a limited set of signals (so to speak): the variety was not overwhelming. So he was able to acquire discrimination as he went along. But the modern reader is exposed to a concourse of signals so bewildering in their variety and number that, unless he is especially gifted and especially favoured, he can hardly begin to discriminate.

Quoted in Storey (ed.), 1994, p.16

Serious though this problem was, to Leavis it was made much worse by the impact of social and cultural changes on the rest of the population. Leavis argued that cultural damage was being done by the consequences of modernization, such as the development of the motor car, the spread of American culture, the break-up of families, and 'the effects of better salesmanship, and more mass-production and standardisation'.

Leavis was highly critical of the dominant media of the day – radio broadcasting and films. He criticized both as 'passive diversion' which discouraged people from thinking for themselves and using their minds constructively. Films came in for the strongest criticism. They were described as involving 'surrender, under conditions of hypnotic receptivity, to the cheapest emotional appeals' judgement'.

Criticism and evaluation of Leavis

Leavis's work is open to a number of criticisms:

1 He may have exaggerated the attractiveness and harmony of pre-industrial folk culture. Raymond Williams (1963) argued that Leavis ignored the illiteracy, poverty and short life-expectancy of ordinary people in pre-industrial England. Without money, education or many years of life they were hardly in a position to develop their appreciation of art and literature very much.

2 Leavis fails to consider the possibility that cultural products such as films and rock music might be worthwhile art forms in their own right. In later decades some critics began to take the cinema seriously and to argue that it was no less worthy than fine art and literature.

An example of rock music being taken seriously is the work of Michael Gray (1973) on the lyrics and, to a lesser extent, the music of Bob Dylan. Gray argued that Bob Dylan's work was perhaps the most artistically accomplished work since that of D.H. Lawrence. He describes Dylan as 'A great artist', and argues that:

It is time it was more generally recognized that to use rock music, as Dylan has done, is not to be, ipso facto, *lacking in such high seriousness; and the corollary is to analyse, not shudder at, what Dylan has achieved.*

Gray, 1973, p. 19

Since the time Gray was writing, a number of rock musicians and other artists working in popular culture have had their work taken sufficiently seriously for it to become the subject of academic analysis.

3 Dominic Strinati (1995) develops this line of argument further, suggesting that elitist theories such as that of Leavis fail to justify their claims that high culture has superior characteristics. From this point of view, it is not just a question of *some* popular culture being taken seriously; instead *any* products of popular culture may be seen as great art by those who particularly like them.

Strinati describes the elitist view as based on 'a set of unexamined values which shape the perception of popular culture held by their adherents'. He goes on to say that 'Elitist judgements fail to take seriously both alternative interpretations of popular culture, those which can be developed from alternative vantage points outside the elite, and the value these alternatives possess'. Thus, for example, if a punk believes that the music of the Sex Pistols is greater art than that of Beethoven, or a dance music fan believes that Massive Attack's CD *Protection* is greater than Mozart's concertos, there is ultimately no way of determining who is right. It is simply a matter of taste, as there are no agreed criteria for fans of classical music and popular music on how the merits of music should be judged.

4 As the above point implies, the elitist view of culture does not therefore consider the possibility that taste might simply be a social construct. According to Bourdieu (1984), what is regarded as good taste is related to the habitus of particular social groups. (Habitus refers to the habits, lifestyles and behaviour typical of and familiar to particular social groups such as classes. See Chapter 11 for a discussion of Bourdieu.)

The lifestyles of higher classes encourage them to value particular cultural products, styles of speaking, and so on, above others. There is nothing inherently superior in these forms, but because they are associated with privileged classes they gain a higher status. The lower classes lack the cultural capital of the higher classes – that is, they do not possess the values and taste necessary to gain acceptance by privileged groups. They find it difficult to be successful in education (which is largely based on the culture of higher classes) and to be upwardly mobile in society.

5 Finally, Leavis may exaggerate claims that societies were developing a type of mass culture. The arguments about mass culture spread outside the rather elitist sphere of literary criticism and began to influence some sociological thinking as well. However, as we shall see, this line of thinking has been extensively criticized.

Mass culture

In 1950s America there was considerable concern about the impact of what was called mass culture. In many ways the writing that emerged out of this concern was similar to the work of writers such as Leavis. However, the concerns of mass culture went wider than art, which was the main focus of the work emerging from literary criticism. The critics of the 1950s were also somewhat less elitist than Arnold and Leavis. They were more likely to be radicals, supporting change in society, rather than conservatives seeking a return to a lost 'golden age' when high culture still had a dominant influence. Two writers, Bernard Rosenberg and Dwight Macdonald, can be used to exemplify this approach.

Bernard Rosenberg – mass culture in America

The debasement of culture

Bernard Rosenberg (1957) mounted one of the strongest attacks on mass culture in America. Rosenberg argued that, although American society had raised most people's living standards to unprece-

dented levels, it had done so at the expense of debasing culture. New technology had removed most of the repetitive and dehumanizing manual drudgery that used to take up so much of people's time. It had given them more leisure, and yet people felt less fulfilled than before. Rosenberg described the situation in the following, rather dramatic way:

Before man can transcend himself he is being dehumanized. Before he can elevate his mind, it is being deadened. Freedom is placed before him and snatched away. The rich and varied life he might lead is standardized. ... The mass grows. We are more alike than ever; and feel a deeper sense of entrapment and loneliness.

Rosenberg, 1957, p. 5

Technology and mass culture

What, then, was responsible for this lamentable state of affairs? According to Rosenberg, technology was the ultimate culprit. In communist countries (such as the USSR) and capitalist countries (such as the USA) alike, new media technology had allowed the development of mass culture. With individuals left with considerable free time, the mass media (such as films, radio and cheap popular fiction) had stepped in to fill people's spare time. Soap operas, detective stories and popular magazines provided standardized and undemanding entertainment. Even in universities those who could simplify their subject and make it easy to understand were becoming popular.

Rosenberg was particularly scathing about popular self-help books which promised to teach people the skills necessary for success with little effort on their part. A series of 'How to' books promised to teach you how to do things such as 'using your imagination to originate a new selling idea' or 'How to draw upon an "inner power" to make sales.' Rosenberg comments that 'Success is still the bitch goddess of American society. The purveyors of mass culture allege that it too can be achieved through passive absorption.'

According to Rosenberg, then, people were no longer being challenged to think for themselves and risked becoming an uncritical, easily-manipulated mass. Rosenberg warned that 'At its worst, mass culture threatens not merely to cretinize our taste, but to brutalize our senses while paving the way to totalitarianism.'

Like others of his generation, Rosenberg thought that the rise of Fascism in Germany in the 1930s had only been possible because Germany had become a mass society in which Hitler was able to exploit the passivity of the population and manipulate them through the mass media.

Dwight Macdonald – 'A theory of mass culture'

Dwight Macdonald adopted a similar line of argument to Rosenberg, but developed his ideas in more detail.

Types of culture

Macdonald distinguished between folk art, high culture and mass culture.

He saw folk art as the 'culture of the common people' in pre-industrial societies. It 'grew from below. It was a spontaneous, autochthonous expression of the people, shaped by themselves, pretty much without the benefit of high culture, to suit their own needs' (Macdonald, 1957). Folk culture did not produce great art, but in its own limited way it had some merit, and it was at least authentic. It emerged out of genuine communities in which people interacted with one another.

High culture was not so explicitly defined. Macdonald took its meaning as almost self-evident. However, Macdonald did not just see the classic works of great artists, musicians and writers (for example, Leonardo da Vinci, Beethoven and Shakespeare) as being examples of high culture. He also included the

work of twentieth-century avant-gardists in the category of high culture (the term avant-garde refers to artists who develop challenging and original work in a given field). Rosenberg includes in the avant-garde the painter Picasso, the poet Rimbaud, the composer Stravinski, and the writer James Joyce. High culture is seen as the product of great individuals who are able to produce work that appeals to a minority who can appreciate work of this calibre.

Mass culture is very different from either folk culture or high culture. It has little, if any, merit. It is designed to appeal to the lowest common denominator. It is unchallenging and has nothing of significance to say. It does not express a genuine culture in the way that folk art does, nor achieve the intrinsic artistic value of high culture. It is simply standardized, commercial kitsch imposed by businesses on the masses to make a profit. (Kitsch is a German word for popular culture. It tends to be used as a term of abuse, implying that what it refers to is mindless and worthless.) Macdonald said:

> Mass culture is imposed from above. It is fabricated by technicians, hired by businessmen; its audiences are passive consumers, their participation limited to the choice between buying and not buying. The Lords of kitsch, in short, exploit the cultural needs of the masses to make a profit and/or to maintain their class rule.
>
> Macdonald, 1957, p. 60

Like elite theorists such as Leavis, Macdonald saw mass culture as a threat to high culture. Like Rosenberg, he saw mass culture as creating a risk of totalitarianism. Macdonald thought that mass society and mass culture had made communist rule in the Soviet Union possible, and had facilitated Hitler's rise to power. It was not just culture that was at stake, but political control as well. Indeed, Macdonald follows something similar to a Marxist line of argument in seeing mass culture as a possible tool of the ruling classes.

The problem of mass culture

Why was mass culture such a problem? Macdonald made a number of claims:

1 He believed that bad culture would drive out good People found mass culture easier to understand. It took less mental effort. It therefore tended to undermine high culture. Macdonald said:

> It threatens high culture by its sheer pervasiveness, its brutal, overwhelming, quantity. The upper classes, who begin by using it to make money from the crude tastes of the masses and to dominate them politically, end by finding their own culture attacked and even threatened with destruction by the instrument they have thoughtlessly employed.
>
> Macdonald, 1957, pp. 61-2

2 As a result, mass culture would end up creating a single, homogenized, culture. High culture would be vulgarized and incorporated in a simplified form into mass culture. For example, the high culture of the theatre was undermined by the mass culture of the cinema. Macdonald observed that plays were increasingly put on simply to try to sell movie rights. If the plays were too sophisticated to have the potential to be made into films, they would not be staged. Mass cultural forms, like detective stories, were adopting a bogus intellectual style to make them seem more artistically important than they really were. Macdonald cites the work of Dorothy M. Sayers as an example.

To Macdonald the distinction between high culture and mass culture was breaking down so that it was getting harder to distinguish between the two.

3 Macdonald believed that the triumph of mass culture would lead to increased alienation amongst those who created cultural products. There was a greater division of labour in media such as the cinema, when compared with the theatre, so that individuals were reduced to carrying out rather mechanical tasks relating to one small aspect of the film.

4 Macdonald claimed that mass culture was leading to 'adultized children and infantile adults'. He quoted research which suggested that American adults were increasingly reading comics and comic strips in newspapers. Adults were also watching children's television programmes, like *The Lone Ranger*, in large numbers, while children were gaining easy access to adult-orientated films and television. The result, according to Macdonald, was the creation of infantile adults – unable to cope with adult life without turning to escapist mass culture for leisure – and over-stimulated children, who grew up too fast.

5 Even more seriously, Macdonald believed that mass culture was undermining the fabric of society. It was creating a mass society, in which individuals were atomized. They were losing their involvement in small social groups and losing opportunities to interact with one another in a meaningful way. Instead, people were becoming isolated individuals relating only to centralized systems and organizations such as the mass media, political parties and companies. Macdonald said, 'The mass man is a solitary atom, uniform with and undifferentiated from thousands and millions of other atoms who go to make up "the lonely crowd" as David Riesman well calls American society'.

Conclusion

Macdonald's conclusions are those of a gloomy pessimist. He sees little sign that high culture can survive, arguing that even the efforts of the avant-garde are under threat from mass culture. Most

people had become trapped in a self-perpetuating mass society and mass culture, their sensibilities and will to resist dulled by several generations' output of mindless mass culture. Only 'heroes' could resist such pressure, and they were few and far between. Nevertheless, Macdonald did not see the situation as completely hopeless. It was still possible that, despite their dwindling number and influence, a small cultural elite could keep the flame of high culture alight.

Evaluation of mass culture theory

The idea that mass culture is harming society remains influential today. However, it has come under increasing attack and has generally fallen out of favour amongst sociologists of culture. In the 1970s Edward Shils (1978) argued that advocates of mass culture theory were wrong to say that there had been a decline in working-class and lower middle-class culture. He did not deny that most mass culture was not particularly enlightening, but he thought it less damaging for lower classes than the 'dismal and harsh existence of earlier centuries' (quoted in Storey, 1997).

Increasingly, though, sociologists have not just argued that mass culture is not as bad as its critics make out; they have begun to attack the idea that it is appropriate to evaluate cultures as superior or inferior to one another. Furthermore they have criticized the idea that it is possible to distinguish between just two cultures, high culture and mass culture. Herbert J. Gans is a case in point (see below).

Herbert J. Gans – the plurality of taste cultures

Herbert J. Gans attacked the idea that cultural experts had any right to try to impose their judgements about culture on others. He said, 'all people have a right to the culture they prefer' (Gans, 1974). Gans was an early advocate of the view that America had a large number of different taste cultures, all of which were equally worthwhile. Rather than simply distinguishing between worthwhile high culture and worthless mass or popular culture, he identified a range of different cultures, each of which had their own intrinsic worth. Gans identifies five main taste cultures.

High culture

High culture consisted of art, music and 'serious' literature (in fiction, for example, the seriousness was demonstrated by an emphasis 'on character development over plot, and the exploration of basic philosophical, psychological and social issues'). To Gans, high culture was intended for small audiences and he emphasized the importance of the creativity of the creators of the culture (writers, artists, film directors and so on). Gans admitted that high culture did pay more attention to 'abstract social, political, and philosophical questions and fundamental societal assumptions more often, more systematically, and more intensively than do other cultures'. However, more popular cultures also addressed moral issues and paid attention to areas such as the problems of earning a living, which were neglected by high culture.

Upper-middle culture

Upper-middle culture was the culture of upper-middle-class, well-educated professionals and managers who had no special knowledge of or involvement in high-culture arts and literature. These people were less concerned with innovative music, literature and art than those involved in high culture. They wanted more plot in the fiction they read. They wanted the heroes in their books to achieve their goals in competition with other people. They enjoyed some of the writing of authors such as Norman Mailer and Arthur Miller, and read publications like *Harper, New Yorker* and *Vogue*. Broadway theatre and foreign films were also favoured by those with upper-middle-class culture.

Many women involved in this culture were interested in women's liberation and the cultural products of its advocates. According to Gans, on the one hand upper-middle-class culture rejected anything that was too experimental or too abstract, and on the other hand it rejected anything considered too 'vulgar' or populist. Gans believed that this was the fastest-growing culture in America (at the time he was writing) because of the expansion of college education.

Lower-middle culture

Lower-middle culture was the 'dominant taste culture' in the USA. It attracted those in lower professions, such as teaching, and those in administrative jobs. This taste culture was less interested in art, serious film, literature and so on than the other taste cultures examined so far. However, its followers were prepared to watch television series derived from upper-middle culture films (for example, *M.A.S.H.*), and to read magazines like *Cosmopolitan*, or the novels of Harold Robbins.

This taste culture wanted substance that was easy to understand and enjoyable. People who were part

of this culture would accept elements of high culture if they met these criteria. Thus, for example, they might own reproductions of the more popular paintings of artists such as Van Gogh and Degas (famous for his paintings of ballet dancers).

Gans argued that lower-middle culture was increasingly breaking up into different groups. There were traditional and progressive factions. Traditionalists objected to open discussion of sexuality in lower-middle-class culture, whereas progressives were in favour of it.

Low culture

Low culture was 'the culture of the older lower-middle class, but mainly of the skilled and semi-skilled factory and service workers, and of the semi-skilled white collar workers'. They rejected anything with the pretensions of high culture and stressed substance above all else. They liked stories with morals about individual and family problems, and films with plenty of action. The male hero in low culture films:

> is sure of his own masculinity, is shy with 'good' women and sexually aggressive with 'bad' ones. He works either alone or with 'buddies' of the same sex, depends partly on luck and fate for success, and is distrustful of government and all institutionalized authority.
>
> Gans, 1974, p. 91

Gans cites Clark Gable and John Wayne as examples. The mass media are important for transmitting low culture. Members of this taste culture enjoy television programmes such as the *Beverly Hillbillies*, rock and country music, and tabloid newspapers with sensational headlines.

Quasi-folk, low culture

Quasi-folk, low culture is described as 'a blend of folk culture and of the commercial low culture of the pre-World War II era'. It represents the tastes of many blue-collar workers and the rural poor. It is described as 'a simpler version of low culture, with the same ... emphasis on melodrama, action comedies and morality plays'. Comics, old Westerns and soap operas are amongst the cultural forms that are popular.

Age and ethnicity

As well as these five main, well-established and class-based cultures, Gans also discusses cultures based on age groups or ethnic groups.

According to Gans, youth cultures had existed for some time, but in the 1960s they became more diverse and influential. Some youth cultures were total cultures, while others were partial cultures. By total cultures Gans meant a whole lifestyle outside of mainstream society, whereas partial cultures involved tastes of groups who remained within mainstream society.

Total cultures

There were five main types of total culture: a drug and music culture; a communal culture, which involved living in communes; a political culture, which was divided into many groups but which had in common the desire to overthrow American capitalism; a religious culture, based on religious sects or cults such as the Jesus freaks; and a neo-dadaist culture, concerned with experimenting with a mixture of new artistic, social and political ideas. Although these total youth cultures did not have many followers, they were highly visible and attracted a lot of concern from those in mainstream culture.

Partial cultures

Gans saw the partial cultures as part-time versions of the total cultures. They were more likely to have become commercially exploited, and were closer to mainstream tastes. However, they shared with total cultures a critical perspective on conventional lifestyles and a preference for radical music and other art forms.

According to Gans, black culture rose to greater prominence in the 1960s, although black Americans had, of course, always had their own culture. In the 1960s the civil rights movement prompted black Americans to be more proud of their culture and to produce more of their own music, television programmes, films and so on.

Finally, Gans discussed ethnic cultures. Each group of immigrants brought their own cultures with them but they tended to be less important to children born in America than they were to the original immigrants. However, Gans detected a revival of ethnic cultures amongst such groups as Italians and Poles.

The hierarchy of tastes

Gans was aware that there was no straightforward distinction between these cultures. Individuals might choose to consume cultural products from different taste cultures, and certain types of cultural product might be popular in different taste cultures. Nevertheless, he did believe that an overall taste structure existed.

There was a hierarchy of tastes, with high culture at the top and other cultures ranged below it. But Gans did not see this hierarchy as based on merit. It was largely the product of differences in the class, status and power of those who belonged to the different taste cultures. Thus, high culture and upper-middle culture were seen as better because they were

the cultures of the highest class and most powerful groups in American society. These groups were more able to fund and protect their cultures than other groups. For example, Gans notes that sexually explicit material is produced in both high culture (for example, James Joyce's book *Ulysses*) and in low culture (for example, hard-core pornography films and magazines).

In 1973 the US Supreme Court ruled that pornographic material could be acceptable if it had 'some redeeming social value'. This allowed sexually explicit high culture to continue untroubled by agencies of law enforcement, while low-culture pornography was criminalized.

Conclusion

Gans concluded by attacking critics of mass culture for trying to impose their own values on others. He argues that all of the different cultures examined by him fulfil the needs of their audiences for information and entertainment. In a pluralistic and democratic society they are all worthy of respect.

However, Gans did not entirely avoid his own value judgements. He did suggest that there were ways in which high culture could be seen as superior to other cultures. For example, high culture could deal with more aspects of life because its public was better educated than the public for other cultures. Thus high culture could consider philosophical issues whereas low culture could not. High culture might also be better able to provide adequate information to help people solve both personal and social problems.

Evaluation

Gans not only provides a strong critique of mass culture theory, he also develops his own conflict theory of culture and taste. His work represents a major advance on theories of mass culture because it recognizes that different cultures can be useful for different audiences, and because it recognizes that there is a plurality of cultures rather than just two.

Gans acknowledges the importance of class, ethnicity and gender in contributing to cultural diversity. His work is in some ways a precursor to postmodern theories of culture which emphasize plurality and diversity (see pp. 916–21). However, for some, his work retains an element of elitism. By arguing that high culture does have some advantages over other cultures, Gans fails to rid himself entirely of judgements about which cultures are more valid.

At an empirical level Gans's work provides an interesting description of American cultures in the 1970s. Clearly this description may not be applicable to different societies at different times, and his work may perhaps lack detailed arguments about why different groups have different tastes.

Dominic Strinati – a critique of mass culture theory

While Gans criticized mass culture theory by developing his own alternative approach to culture, Dominic Strinati (1995) is simply concerned with evaluating the theory of mass culture. Strinati is even more critical than Gans and attacks mass culture theory on a number of different grounds:

1 Strinati believes that mass culture theory is just as elitist as the approaches adopted by writers like F.R. Leavis and Matthew Arnold. He says that it 'fails to recognize that mass culture can be understood, interpreted and appreciated by other groups in distinct and "non-elitist" social and aesthetic positions within society'. It makes the false assumption that the masses are 'cultural dopes' willing to consume any old rubbish put before them by the mass media.

    However, the consumers of mass culture are often critical and reject many products (such as films and television programmes) which they find insufficiently interesting or entertaining. Consumers of mass culture are not a passive and undifferentiated mass. They are discriminating in what they choose to consume, and active in deciding how they are going to react (see Chapter 13 for research which supports such claims).

2 According to Strinati, mass culture theory sees all popular culture as homogeneous – it is all the same. Strinati argues that this is far from being the case, and in reality there is a very wide variety of styles and genres. To take just one example, popular music can hardly be seen as homogeneous when it includes 'rap, soul, jazz, sampling, novelty songs and "serious ballads"'.

3 Strinati does not agree with mass culture theorists like Macdonald that it is possible to distinguish an authentic and superior 'folk culture' from an inauthentic and inferior mass culture. For example, folk blues and country music are not part of 'pure' cultures untainted by outside influences. All have

been affected by a range of musical traditions. Furthermore, authenticity does not determine how much an audience enjoys its music. Pop music may be just as enjoyable and seen by its audience as just as good as any of the types of supposedly 'authentic' popular music.

4 The theory of mass culture rests upon the assumption that there is a reasonably clearcut boundary between high culture and mass culture, but this is not the case. Strinati says:

> the boundaries drawn between popular culture and art, or between mass, high and folk culture, are constantly being blurred, challenged and redrawn. These boundaries are not given, nor are they consistently objective and historically constant. Rather, they are contested, discontinuous and historically variable.
>
> Strinati, 1995, pp. 45-6

What was once considered mass culture might increase in status and come to be taken seriously as art. Strinati gives the examples of jazz music, the films of Alfred Hitchcock, and rock-and-roll records which have attained the status of classics.

Cultural politics

To Strinati, the theory of mass culture is a product of cultural politics rather than an objective assessment of the merits of different cultures. It represents a backlash by intellectuals who feel threatened by the growth of popular culture.

Mass culture threatens the hierarchy of taste by giving everybody the chance to choose what they think are the best books, films, music, paintings or images and so on. This undermines 'the symbolic power of intellectuals over the standards of taste which are applied to the consumption of cultural goods'. It is hardly surprising that they choose to fight a rearguard action to defend their cultural power. To Strinati, though, their arguments are unconvincing and unlikely to preserve the authority of their elitist judgements.

Structuralism

Structuralism is an influential approach to the study of culture, which originated in theories of linguistics. Structuralist approaches to culture see language as the key to understanding the social world. They see the social world as a linguistic phenomenon. Most social life is conducted through language, and, from a structuralist point of view, shaped by it. Structuralist thought began with the work of the French linguist, Ferdinand de Saussure.

Ferdinand de Saussure – semiology

Signs

Ferdinand de Saussure (1857–1913) is usually seen as the founder of semiology (sometimes called semiotics), or the science of signs. Saussure defines semiology as '*A science that studies the life of signs within society*' (Saussure, 1966, first published in English in 1959). Saussure defines a sign as 'the combination of a concept and a sound image'. Signs, then, consist of two parts. For example, the sign 'tree' consists of:

1 The concept of tree – the sort of object that is referred to as a tree.

2 The sound-image of tree. This is not the physical sound made when somebody says the word 'tree' but the 'psychological imprint of the sound'. You can recite the word 'tree' to yourself in your imagination without actually saying it, and the ability to do this means that the sound-image is a psychological phenomenon rather than the physical sound when the word is spoken.

Saussure then goes on to use the word signified to denote a concept, and the word signifier to denote the sound-image. Signified and signifier together form a sign.

The relationship between signifier and signified

Saussure argued that there is an arbitrary relationship between signifier and signified. There is no necessary reason why particular signifiers should be used to denote particular concepts. This is demonstrated by the fact that different languages use different words to signify the concept of tree. He says, 'nothing would prevent the association of any idea with any sequence of sounds'.

Although the signifier has no necessary connection with the signified, people cannot choose what words to use to signify particular concepts. Thus an individual cannot decide to start calling trees dogs and continue to be understood by others. Signs are handed down from one generation to the next. Saussure comments that 'No society, in fact, knows or has ever known language other than as a product inherited from preceding generations.' He therefore sees language as a social phenomenon shared by members of a social group and passed down to children. Therefore, it is largely immutable – it tends to be fixed and unchanging. Saussure accepts that some changes in language are possible over long periods of time. However, even then, there tend to be only small shifts in the meaning of particular signifiers.

Langue and parole

Saussure does not see language as simply a collection of unrelated signifiers. Signifiers are defined in terms of other signifiers. For example, the signifier 'animal' helps to define the signifier 'dog'. Furthermore, language can only be used if there are some rules governing how different signifiers are strung together to communicate ideas. Each language therefore has a structure consisting of the grammatical rules, words, the meanings that link words together, and so on. Saussure calls this overall structure the langue. He distinguishes it from parole, which refers to the actual use of language.

The sentences in this book, the words spoken by sociology students in classrooms, the discussions people have in pubs and in their homes are all examples of parole. All require the existence of a langue to make the parole possible. Saussure compares this to the game of chess. In chess the langue consists of the rules governing initial placement of pieces, the movement of pieces, taking opponents' pieces, winning the game, and so on. The parole consists of the actual moves chosen by particular players.

Linguistics

To Saussure, linguistics involves examining parole – examples of the use of language – to understand the underlying structure or langue. A language should be studied as an integrated system with its own logic and structure. It should not be seen in terms of its links with an external reality. Thus the sign 'dog' should be seen in terms of its relationship with other signs, such as 'animal' and 'bark', rather than in terms of its relationship with the actual creature it describes.

Saussure therefore emphasizes that people experience the world in terms of signs which have particular meanings, rather than experiencing it in a direct material way. John Storey has described the implications of this aspect of Saussure's work. He says:

> The function of language is to organize and construct our access to reality. It therefore also follows from this that different languages in effect produce a different mapping of the real. When a European gazes at a snowscape, he or she sees snow. An Eskimo looking at the same snowscape would see so much more, the reason being that Eskimos have over fifty words to describe snow. Therefore an Eskimo and a European standing together surveying the snowscape would in fact be seeing two quite different conceptual schemes.
>
> Storey, 1997, pp. 70-1

Evaluation

Saussure effectively founded the disciplines of semiology and linguistics. However, his work has attracted some criticism. Norman Fairclough (1989, discussed in Strinati, 1995) argues that Saussure exaggerates the extent to which language is shared by members of a society. Fairclough also argues that Saussure neglects the importance of power. More powerful members of society may try to define their own language as superior to other forms, creating the possibility of conflict over what forms of language are afforded the highest status.

However, there is no doubt that Saussure influenced the work of other writers. His ideas laid the foundations for the whole discipline of semiology which now extends to the analysis of signs other than words (for example, clothing and food). In this sort of study there is an attempt to uncover the meaning system of a set of signs in a way that is similar to the way in which Saussure examined the langue of a language.

Saussure's ideas also influenced the work of structuralists such as Lévi-Strauss, by suggesting to them that human thinking and social relationships could be shaped by underlying structures similar to those that are integral to a langue. The work of Lévi-Strauss will be examined shortly, but first we will consider an example of how semiotics has been used to understand culture.

Dick Hebdige – *Subculture: The Meaning of Style*

Subculture and style

Dick Hebdige (1979) used semiotics in order to try to understand the meaning of a number of post-war British youth subcultures. To Hebdige, it was possible to understand the meaning of the quiff of the Teddy boy, the safety pins of punks or the music of the mods.

Each youth subculture developed its own style and each took everyday objects and transformed their meaning. Hebdige says, '"humble" objects can be magically appropriated; "stolen" by subordinate groups and made to carry "secret" meanings: meanings which express, in code, a form of resistance to the order which guarantees their continued subordination'.

Teddy boys transformed the meaning of Edwardian suits and pointed boots. Punks transformed the meaning of safety pins and ripped jeans. They became gestures of defiance against society. They came to signify membership of particular subcultures and the whole complex set of meanings that each subculture expressed. Each subculture defines itself in opposition to mainstream culture. Each subculture is spectacular: it creates a spectacle and is intended to get noticed.

Skinheads and mods

Like Saussure, Hebdige believes that meanings derive from internal systems of differences. Just as a dictionary defines words in terms of their differences and similarities to other words, so the meaning of clothing is defined in terms of differences and similarities to other types of clothing. For example, skinheads wore 'cropped hair, braces, short, wide levi jeans or functional sta-prest trousers, plain or striped

button-down Ben Sherman shirts and highly polished Doctor Martin boots'. Their appearance was a kind of exaggerated version of the working-class manual labourer and expressed the image of the 'hard' working-class man.

On the other hand, mods adopted a more respectable appearance, which reflected aspirations to be upwardly mobile and join the middle class. However, their dress and style were certainly different to those of most middle-class people. Despite their 'apparently conservative suits in respectable colours', their style expressed an 'emotional affinity with black people' and a love of the world of 'cellar clubs, discotheques, boutiques and record shops', which was outside the 'straight world' of the respectable middle class.

The mods' dress allowed them to move fairly easily between work and leisure, but at the same time they disrupted the conventional meanings of some of the clothes they wore. Hebdige says:

> Quietly disrupting the orderly sequence which leads from signifier to signified, the mods undermined the conventional meaning of 'collar, suit and tie', pushing neatness to the point of absurdity ... they were a little too smart, somewhat too alert, thanks to amphetamines.
>
> Hebdige, 1979, p. 52

Black subcultures

Black British people also developed distinctive subcultures based upon differences and similarities to other styles of dress. In the first post-war phases of immigration from the West Indies, the first-generation migrants adopted smart and conventional dress which reflected their aspirations to succeed in Britain. They wore, 'rainbow mohair suits and picture ties ... neatly printed frocks and patent leather shoes'. However:

> all hopes of ever really fitting in were inadvertently belied by every garish jacket sleeve – too loud and jazzy for contemporary British tastes. Both the dreams and the disappointments of an entire generation were thus inscribed in the very cut (ambitious and improbable) of the clothes in which it chose to make its entrance.
>
> Hebdige, 1979

By the 1970s, the disappointments that stemmed from racism and high levels of unemployment began to be expressed in the clothes and subcultural style of Rastafarians. British Rastafarians expressed their alienation from British culture by adopting simple clothes with an African feel to them. Army surplus stores provided garments able to express 'sinister guerrilla chic'. The key themes of Rastafarian style were resistance to the dominance of white culture and the expression of black identity.

Punk

Reggae, Rastafarianism and their associated styles influenced white youth culture, but their association with blackness precluded their wholesale adoption by white youths. In the 1970s, white youth developed their own subculture – punk – which Hebdige analyses in detail.

To Hebdige, punk almost rewrote the rules of semiology, in certain respects changing the way signs were used to convey meaning. Punk drew some meaning from reggae and Rastafarianism. Some punk groups, such as The Clash, incorporated reggae rhythms into their music, and some punks wore the red, gold and green of Rastafarians.

Punk also adopted an element of the Rastafarian opposition to being seen as British (rather than African). Punks explicitly attacked conventional notions of being British – for example, in the Sex Pistols songs *Anarchy in the UK* and *God Save the Queen*.

But punk also defined itself in opposition to certain types of music. It disliked the empty commercialism of the Glam Rock of people such as Alvin Stardust and Gary Glitter, but it was also critical of artists who were seen as pretentious (such as David Bowie and Roxy Music). Punk attacked the existing music industry and tried to break down the barrier between performer and audience. It celebrated the amateurish nature of many punk bands and encouraged anybody who could play a couple of chords on a guitar to form their own band.

Behind punk was a claim to 'speak for the neglected constituency of white lumpen youth', and a desire to 'act out alienation'. It was undoubtedly British, but it 'was predicated upon a denial of place. It issued out of nameless housing estates, anonymous dole queues, slums-in-the-abstract. It was blank, expressionless, rootless.' Unlike Rastafarianism, it gave no hope for the future. There was no equivalent to the return to Africa which held the promise of redemption for British rastas. Instead, there was simply, in the Sex Pistols' words, no future.

Punk and chaos

Hebdige comments that 'The punk subculture, then, signified chaos at every level.' Part of this chaos involved radical departures in the way signifiers were used. It was not just that punks took such ordinary objects as safety pins, bin liners and toilet chains and transformed them into fashion accessories. They were also able to detach symbols from their conventional meanings. For example, some punks and punk groups took the swastika as a signifier, but it 'was wilfully detached from the concept (Nazism) it conventionally signified'. Used by punks, the swastika was no longer a symbol of racism – most punks were strongly anti-

racist. Instead it was used simply to signify a lack of meaning. Hebdige says, 'the central value "held and reflected" in the swastika was the communicated absence of any such identifiable values'.

Signifying practices

Hebdige argues that conventional semiotics is unable to deal with the meaning of punk, where signifiers were separated from what they signified. He therefore uses the idea of signifying practice to understand the nature of signs in punk subculture.

According to the idea of signifying practice, the traditional relationship between langue (the structure of language) and parole (individual uses of language) is reversed. Langue is no longer seen as more important than parole. Rather than meaning deriving from the overall structure of language, it derives more from the position of the person using it. Thus the meaning of the swastika no longer comes from its relationship to other signifiers (such as 'racism' or 'Nazism') but from the fact that it was punks who were using the concept. The idea of signifying practices sees language as something that is fluid and capable of changing its meaning. Language is always in the process of being used; its meaning changes, and it is never fixed as it appears to be in dictionaries. Punk is an example of the 'triumph ... of the signifier over the signified'.

Punk and the ruling class

Although Hebdige draws primarily on semiology to develop his ideas on youth subcultures, he also makes use of Marxist ideas. He sees all subcultures 'as a form of resistance ... in which the experienced contradictions and objections to ... ruling ideology are obliquely represented in style'. Although they might pose no major threat to the ruling class, they do produce what Hebdige calls 'noise' – an alternative source of ideas which interferes with ruling-class attempts to create the impression of societal harmony.

Evaluation

Hebdige provides a stimulating attempt to understand the meaning of different subcultures and to develop semiology as a sociological tool. However, his work is only as good as his interpretations, and subcultures could be interpreted in different ways. There is no evidence in his work that the Teddy boys, mods or punks actually saw their own subcultures in the same way as Hebdige saw them. He did not, for example, conduct in-depth interviews with members of subcultures to check that their views corresponded with his own. To more conventional sociologists this could be seen as a limitation of his work. To postmodernists and post-structuralists Hebdige is wrong to assume that it is possible to attribute any one meaning to punk. Rather, punk is open to a range of interpretations each of which is equally valid.

Claude Lévi-Strauss – structuralism, myths and kinship

Structures

Saussure's attempts to uncover the basic structure of signs and language influenced the development of structuralism. Structuralism analyses the basic structures underlying human thinking and human social groups. The anthropologist Claude Lévi-Strauss (1963, 1986, first published 1963) was the first to develop structuralism, using it to understand such things as kinship systems and myths.

Lévi-Strauss believes that there are certain structures which underlie all human thinking and social arrangements. While these structures cannot be directly observed, they can be revealed in human culture, which is shaped by these structures. Since the structures are common to all humans, evidence of them can be found universally. Thus the myths of the Ancient Greeks and North American Indians (or native Americans) reflect the same structures. Similarly, all kinship systems are based upon the same basic structures. The details of different myths or kinship systems may be very different, but the fundamental structure is the same.

Kinship

Lévi-Strauss argues that 'kinship phenomena are *of the same type* as linguistic phenomena' (Lévi-Strauss, 1963). By this he means that kinship systems are based upon certain laws which apply to all cultures. Just as Saussure believed that all languages had the same relationship between signifiers and the signified, Lévi-Strauss believed that all kinship systems had the same basic relationships.

According to Lévi-Strauss, all kinship systems have sets of relationships, and, like a language, each part of the system only has meaning when related to other elements. Thus, for example, the position of wife can only exist if related to the position of husband, and the position of mother can only exist in relation to the position of son or daughter. Furthermore, the same basic parts of kinship systems are found everywhere. Lévi-Strauss says:

> *the recurrence of kinship patterns, marriage rules, similar prescribed attitudes between certain types of relatives, and so forth, in scattered regions of the globe and in fundamentally different societies, leads us to believe that, in the case of kinship ... the observable phenomena result from the action of laws which are general but implicit.*
>
> Lévi-Strauss, 1963, p. 34

So what then is the basic structure of kinship? Lévi-Strauss believes that it involves three types of family relationship: 'a relationship between siblings, between spouses, and a relation between parent and child'. In addition there is an avuncular relationship between uncle or aunt and nephew or niece. This derives automatically from the existence of relationships between parents and children and between siblings.

This basic structure is 'a direct result of the universal presence of an incest taboo'. The incest taboo prohibits sexual relationships between close relatives such as siblings and parents and children. The existence of this taboo means that 'a man must obtain a woman from another man who gives him a daughter or a sister'. The basic kinship structure needs to exist to establish which members of society are not the kin of an individual – and with whom that individual can therefore have a legitimate sexual relationship.

Within different kinship structures the strength of one relationship will tend to determine the strength of others. In the Trobriand Islands, for example, sibling relationships are fairly weak, so children have closer relationships with their fathers than they do with uncles. In Tonga, on the other hand, sibling relationships are seen as more important than spouse relationships. Consequently boys have close relationships with uncles – sometimes closer than the relationship with their own father.

Binary oppositions

To Lévi-Strauss, kinship systems are not the only aspects of culture which are universal. He also claimed to find certain binary oppositions, or pairs of opposites, which structure all human thinking.

These binary oppositions stem from the way that humans tend to divide up the world into 'segments so that we are predisposed to think of the environment as consisting of a vast number of separate things belonging to named classes' (Leach, 1970). Examples of such binary oppositions are nature/culture, man/woman, good/bad. The categories in each binary opposition are mutually exclusive; something cannot be part of nature and culture at the same time. However, the existence of binary oppositions sometimes causes contradictions. Myths are used to try to resolve these contradictions.

Myths

Many myths incorporate elements related to food. Eating food is an essential part of human culture and, according to Lévi-Strauss (1986, first published 1963), humans consume food in ways related to the opposition between nature/culture. Raw food is seen as part of nature. Animals, which are part of nature, eat food in raw form. Cooking, on the other hand, transforms food into a part of culture because it is something that humans do to food. Left to their own devices, meat or vegetables will rot as part of a natural process. Like raw food, rotted food is seen as part of nature.

Lévi-Strauss argues that food in different states is found in many myths. The discovery of fire and the cooking of food features prominently in some of them. It is used to make sense of the transition of humans from being animals – which eat raw food, and are therefore part of nature – to being humans who are cultured and have the means to cook food.

Another fundamental problem dealt with in myths is the origin of human beings. In many, if not all, cultures it is believed that humanity had an autochthonous origin, that is that the first humans were created autonomously without being born to a mother and father. In some cultures humans are seen as coming from the earth, in others as being created by God. This belief contradicts human experience which shows that humans come into being as the result of a union between a man and a women.

This problem is dealt with in the Oedipus myth 'which relates the original problem – born from one or born from two? – to the derivative problem; born from different or born from same?' (Lévi-Strauss, 1963). In the Greek Oedipus myth, Oedipus marries his mother Jocasta, kills his father Laios, and slays the Sphinx, a monster who does not want men to live.

Lévi-Strauss notes that the meaning of Oedipus is 'swollen-foot' and that in mythology people who are born from the earth are either unable to walk or are clumsy walkers. He therefore believes that Oedipus represents autochthonous birth even though he was born with a mother and a father. The myth is unable to resolve the contradiction between autochthonous and bisexual reproduction, but it does express the contradiction in mythical form. Furthermore, although the contradiction is not resolved, humanity does survive, as the creatures which threaten it (such as the Sphinx) are killed.

As with other myths, Lévi-Strauss does not see the Oedipus myth as the product of a particular culture. He argues that the basic structures of this myth are to be found in very different and widely separated societies. The details of the story may vary, but the structure remains the same. It is therefore a product of the basic structures of human thought, particularly the existence of certain binary oppositions.

Lévi-Strauss concludes that myths serve as an 'intermediary entity' between parole (particular stories or myths) and langue (the basic structures of thought and the human brain). Myths express the structure in the form of particular stories and make it possible to deal with, and sometimes resolve, the contradictions in binary oppositions.

Evaluation

Dominic Strinati (1995) argues that Lévi-Strauss tends to use highly selective evidence in support of his theories. While he uses plenty of examples to back up what he says, he tends to ignore any evidence that contradicts him. For example, Strinati says, 'his analysis of Oedipal myths is only successful because he selects those features of the stories which suit his case, and ignores others which contradict the notion that they are expressions of a universal mental structure'. If they truly expressed a universal mental structure, then all examples would support his theories and there would be no need to be selective.

Because Lévi-Strauss is seeking evidence of universal mental structures his arguments are reductionist: that is, they try to reduce all culture to being the product of fixed mental structures. Lévi-Strauss therefore neglects the importance of history in shaping cultures and makes little attempt to explain the variety of human cultures that exist. Strinati says:

> Downplaying the importance of history means that the problems posed for any analysis of popular culture by historical variations in cultures and societies are simply not addressed. Indeed, it could be argued that it is impossible to understand the formal structures of language or myth outside of their social and historical contexts.
>
> Strinati, 1995, p. 121

Strinati also accuses Lévi-Strauss's structuralism of being deterministic. It allows no room for human creativity and simply assumes that all culture is automatically shaped by unconscious mental structures whatever the wishes of individuals. Furthermore, the meaning of culture is always open to interpretation, and this very fact 'suggests that the importance of the human subject cannot be so easily dismissed'.

Finally, Strinati attacks Lévi-Strauss's claim that humans always think in terms of binary oppositions – for example, that between nature and culture. Strinati admits that all societies have to respond to the existence of nature, but they do not necessarily see it as the opposite of culture. Different societies understand nature in different ways; it does not have the same meaning for everybody and it is not always seen in terms of a binary opposition with culture. This point could be extended to all of Lévi-Strauss's examples of binary oppositions. There are plenty of occasions when humans think in more subtle terms than distinguishing between pairs of opposites.

Some of the criticisms of Lévi-Strauss are addressed in the work of the next writer to be examined, Will Wright.

Will Wright – the structure of the American Western

Wright and structuralism

In his book *Sixguns and Society* (1975), Will Wright takes his inspiration from Lévi-Strauss's structuralism in analysing Western films. Although influenced by the work of Lévi-Strauss, Wright's approach does differ.

First, he does not see the structure of the Western as a reflection of the basic structures of the mind. To Wright, Westerns reflect the structure of society at particular times rather than unchanging mental structures. The structure of Westerns therefore changes as society changes. According to Wright, the characters in myths represent certain social principles and they 'act out a drama of social order' (Wright, 1994, first published 1975). A fight between two people, for example, is not just a fight between individuals, but might represent 'a conflict of principles – good versus evil, rich versus poor, black versus white'.

Second, Wright does not follow Lévi-Strauss in believing that all human thought is shaped by the existence of binary oppositions. Much literature is complex. It may be based upon similarities and differences between three or more characters rather than stark contrasts between pairs of opposites. However, Wright does believe that binary oppositions are central to the nature of myths, and he sees Westerns as a type of myth.

The use of binary oppositions simplifies myths and ensures that the message they carry gets across. Wright comments, 'when two characters are opposed in a binary structure their symbolic meaning is virtually forced to be both general and easily accessible because of the simplicity of the differences between them'.

Wright then proceeds to analyses the structure of Westerns and finds that there are three main types: the classical plot, the transitional plot and the professional plot. Of these most attention is paid to the classical plot – the original plot from which alternative types diverged later in the development of the genre.

Classical Westerns – *Shane*

Classical plots dominated Westerns from 1930 to 1955. A good example of this type of plot is the film *Shane*. In this film, the hero, Shane, stops for water at a small farm. The couple who run the farm (the Starretts) are initially suspicious of Shane, and he leaves. Shortly afterwards, the Rikers, who are big cattle ranchers in the area, arrive and tell the Starretts that they must leave the land so that they can extend their cattle ranch. At this point Shane

returns and tells the Rikers to leave. Shane becomes more friendly with the Starretts who are grateful for his intervention.

In the local town the next day Shane refuses to fight with one of the Rikers' cowboys. In the evening several farmers gather at the Starretts' farm to discuss how to resist the aggression of the Rikers. Shane is introduced but is accused of cowardice by one of the farmers who witnessed the incident with the Rikers' cowboy earlier in the day.

However, the following day, Shane is confronted by the Rikers' men in the saloon. He refuses to back down when challenged by them and, with the aid of some of the farmers who are there, defeats Riker's men in a fight. Riker hires a gunfighter and takes revenge by burning one of the farms.

Most of the farmers are ready to give up the fight but Joey Starrett persuades them to stay and he resolves to kill Riker. Shane tries to persuade Starrett that it is too dangerous for him to fight Riker, but Starrett is insistent. Shane knocks Starrett unconscious to prevent him challenging Riker. Shane goes into town, kills the hired gunfighter and two of the Riker brothers and effectively defeats the Rikers. Shane then leaves the area despite Joey Starrett shouting to him to come back.

The classical plot

Wright argues that the basic plot of this Western is common to all Westerns with a classical plot. Wright sees this as consisting of 13 elements which are always present:

1 *'The hero enters a social group.'*

2 *'The hero is revealed to have an exceptional ability.'*

3 *'The society recognizes a difference between themselves and the hero; the hero is given a special status.'*

4 *'The society does not completely accept the hero.'*

5 *'There is a conflict of interests between the villains and society.'*

6 *'The villains are stronger than society; the society is weak.'*

7 *'There is a strong friendship or respect between the hero and a villain.'*

8 *'The villains threaten society.'*

9 *'The hero fights the villains.'*

10 *'The hero defeats the villains.'*

11 *'The society is safe.'*

12 *'The society accepts the hero.'*

13 *'The hero loses or gives up his special status.'*

Wright, 1994, first published 1975, pp. 123–5

Wright identifies four main binary oppositions in this plot:

1 An opposition between people inside and people outside society. The farmers in Shane are inside society, and Shane outside, with the ranchers (the Rikers) being seen as largely outside society.

2 An opposition between good and bad. The villains – the Rikers – are bad; the farmers and Shane are good.

3 An opposition between the strong and the weak. The hero and the villains are strong; the society (represented by the farmers) is weak.

4 An opposition between wilderness and civilization. This is similar to the opposition between societal insiders and outsiders except that the villains are seen as part of civilization along with the farmers. Shane represents the wilderness.

Why then did the classical Western have these sorts of plots involving these oppositions? Wright interprets them as a reflection of American capitalism. In America at the time of these Westerns, big business was unpopular. Big businesses were seen as responsible for the Wall Street Crash (a plunge in share values) in 1929, and for the subsequent recession.

In classical Westerns big business is represented by ranchers. Big business was seen as harming individuals with small businesses (represented by the farmers), who were trying to earn a living to keep their families. The solution was to be found in the actions of heroic individuals who could save America from the corruption within society coming from big business. Shane, of course, represents the heroic individual.

The transitional plot

As American society changed, the Western changed too. The transitional plot was an intermediate stage. In this sort of Western the hero starts as a societal insider, but discovers society to be corrupt. The hero therefore moves away from society and civilization and aligns himself (the hero is always male) with the wilderness. However, society is always too strong and ultimately prevents escape. According to Wright, the 1954 film *Johnny Guitar* was the last Western with a transitional plot.

The professional plot

After 1954 the transitional plot was replaced by the professional plot. This is similar to the transitional plot except that the hero is initially dedicated to some form of professional activity.

According to Wright, this sort of plot reflected the increased importance of technocratic professionals in American corporations, who felt their lives to be too restricted by the demands of those organizations. Instead of doing what they wished, they had to follow the aims laid down by corporations. The heroes of the professional plot are unwilling to have their individualism crushed by society, though in the end they cannot avoid it.

Evaluation

Wright's work is not open to the charges of reductionism and determinism which have been effectively levelled at Lévi-Strauss. He shows more awareness of how particular historical circumstances might shape the nature of the Western film. However, he may still be too dogmatic in arguing that certain narrative structures are associated with particular eras. For example, John Storey argues that the 1990 film *Dances with Wolves* (in which a cavalry officer rejects the army and goes to live among the Sioux) is a good example of a transitional plot.

It can also be argued that Wright underestimated the sheer diversity of Westerns. In the 1960s and 1970s, Westerns with diverse plots expressing quite different ideologies were made. For example, *The Cowboys* (a John Wayne film) was made to support American involvement in the Vietnam War, whereas *The Culpepper Cattle Co.* was an anti-war Western. Some films had the main aim of providing a more realistic view of the West (for example, *Will Penny, Doc*, and *Little Big Man*), while others harked back to the classical plot (for example, *Red River, She Wore a Yellow Ribbon*, and *Valdez is Coming*).

The criticisms of Wright, though, are rather less damaging than those of Lévi-Strauss. Wright did at least try to relate the structure of films to their changing historical context; he just over-simplified the relationship. Lévi-Strauss made much more sweeping claims than Wright – claims which are all the more difficult to support.

Post-structuralism

Derrida, Lacan and Foucault

Post-structuralism is a rather general term used to refer to the work of writers such as Jacques Derrida (see pp. 159–60), Jacques Lacan (see pp. 158–9) and Michel Foucault (see pp. 635–9).

At first sight these writers have little in common since they wrote about somewhat different issues using a variety of theoretical approaches. Jacques Lacan is influenced by psychoanalysis and is concerned with gender differences in early human development. Jacques Derrida's work is based more upon linguistics and focuses on the meaning of language. Michel Foucault's work was wide-ranging and considered issues as diverse as the development of prisons, sexuality, madness and, more generally, the relationship between power and knowledge.

However, they are grouped together as post-structuralists because their work includes some broad philosophical similarities. They are seen as post-structuralists because their work has developed out of a rejection of the idea of structures. Nevertheless, it owes a lot to the emphasis on language found in the work of semiologists and structuralists such as Saussure and Lévi-Strauss.

Post-structuralism and Lévi-Strauss

Post-structuralists reject Lévi-Strauss's belief that it is possible to find certain fixed structures in society which reflect the human mind. They also reject the Marxist view that society has certain structures (such as a class structure) which shape social relationships. Foucault, for example, saw power/knowledge as the key to understanding how society is shaped (see p. 637). Power/knowledge has no fixed form but constantly changes in the course of interaction. Power is not to be found in social structures, but is intimately linked to the way people talk about things and create particular discourses (see p. 635 for a discussion of discourse).

Language, meaning and subjectivity

Chris Weedon argues that post-structuralists 'share certain fundamental assumptions about language, meaning and subjectivity' (Weedon, 1994, first published 1987). The emphasis on language is to be found in Lacan's idea of the symbolic order (see pp. 158–9), Derrida's discussion of *différence* (see pp. 159–60) and Foucault's discussion of discourse. All agree that the way people understand society and the way society works are shaped by language. As Weedon puts it, 'Language is the place where actual and possible forms of social organization and their likely social and political consequences are defined and contested.'

However, post-structuralists insist that language does reflect or describe some underlying reality or structure. They argue that it is language that creates reality rather than reflecting it.

Madan Sarup says that 'In post-structuralism, broadly speaking, the signified is demoted and the signifier made dominant' (Sarup, 1988). Sarup points out that Derrida 'believes in a system of floating signifiers pure and simple, with no determinable relation to any extra-linguistic referents at all'. While, for example, Lévi-Strauss looked for the meaning behind myths, post-

structuralists deny that any fixed meaning is present.

Derrida argues that the meaning of a text (anything that contains meaningful signs) depends upon how a particular reader interprets it. Thus, if two people interpret a film or book as having different meanings, each interpretation is equally valid. As Madan Sarup says, 'While structuralism sees the truth as "behind" or "within" a text, post-structuralism stresses the interaction of reader and text' (Sarup, 1988).

Meaning is always related to the particular context in which it is being discussed. Outside that context the meaning might be quite different.

Post-structuralist feminism

Although post-structuralists do not believe that it is possible to see behind signs and language to find the truth, many believe that the particular meanings that gain acceptance are of crucial importance. Chris Weedon, a post-structuralist feminist, gives some examples.

Weedon (1994) argues that the outcome of rape trials in the United Kingdom is largely determined by the meaning given to the idea of 'natural justice' and the meaning attributed to the word 'rape'. The dominance of masculine definitions of natural justice leads to a situation where men are unlikely to be convicted of rape. This is because it is seen as 'natural' for a man to continue with sex even when a woman says no. From this point of view, it is unjust for courts to find men guilty where women may have appeared to encourage sex. Weedon says, 'courts often endorse the view of rape as an active endorsement of male sexuality in the face of female "provocation". In the view of some judges, this may take the form of going out alone at night, wearing a mini-skirt or being a prostitute.' From Weedon's point of view it is important to challenge this view of natural justice so that courts are more likely to find rapists guilty and punish them.

As a post-structuralist Weedon sees arguments over language as having a key social and political role. Changing the accepted interpretation of a word or sign in particular contexts can have a crucial role in promoting greater social justice. This process can make use of Derrida's idea of deconstruction (see pp. 159–60), in which the meaning of signs is taken apart and found to be contradictory.

Post-structuralism and identity

As well as attacking the idea that signs have any fixed meaning, post-structuralists also reject the idea that individuals have a fixed sense of who they are – that is, of identity. Post-structuralists use the idea of the subject.

According to Chris Weedon, in conventional views of the subject, '"Subjectivity" is used to refer to the conscious and unconscious thoughts and emotions of the individual which are unique, fixed and coherent and make her what she is.'

Weedon and other post-structuralists reject this view. They argue that individuals do not have a unique, fixed or coherent idea of who they are or sense of identity. Instead their identity is shaped through involvement in particular discourses. From this point of view, experience shapes your subjectivity, but experience itself is only understood in terms of the discourses that surround it. For example, a person does not simply experience 'family life' in a direct way. Instead they make sense of it through the discourses – the ways of thinking and talking about the family – that they come into contact with.

Somebody influenced by feminist discourse will experience being a 'mother' or a 'wife' very differently from somebody influenced by more traditional discourses of the family. Since there are a wide range of discourses available, and each of these may be challenged and changed over time, individuals do not have a settled sense of who they are. Chris Weedon suggests that even the identity of being a woman has no fixed meaning. What people understand by womanhood, and how women see themselves as women, changes as they come into contact with continually changing and contested discourses of femininity (see pp. 921–32 for a fuller discussion of identity).

Post-structuralism attacks the foundations on which most types of social science have been based, and instead focuses on the fluid and indeterminate meaning of language. By undermining conventional approaches in social science post-structuralism paved the way for postmodern theories of society and culture. These will be examined shortly.

Lawrence Grossberg –
The Deconstruction of Youth

An example of post-structural analysis is provided by Lawrence Grossberg's discussion of the changing meaning of 'youth' (Grossberg, 1994, first published 1986). To Grossberg, the meaning of youth does not simply reflect a changing reality. Instead the meaning helps to create the reality it describes. If people come to think of 'youth' in a particular way, then people who think of themselves as young will tend to act in ways that are consistent with this view. The signifier 'youth' has subtly changed its meaning and has started to reshape how youth actually behaves.

Youth practices and discourses

Grossberg outlines three main phases in the development of youth discourses and practices:

1 Following the Industrial Revolution, discourses about young people were more concerned with the ideas of childhood and adulthood than with the idea of youth. Childhood was seen as a time of innocence. Children needed to be provided with protection against the premature loss of innocence. Schools, medical institutions and the family became the three types of institution responsible for protecting children and preparing them for the adult world. Children were kept away from work until they were deemed old enough to become adults and leave school. However, once they reached the necessary age, they were expected to adopt an adult outlook swiftly and to take on adult responsibilities.

2 After the Second World War there was a baby boom. It became important to delay the entry of the baby boomers into the labour market so that unemployment did not rise. The idea of youth or adolescence as an extended transitional period between childhood and adulthood became increasingly important. A growing number of young people carried on in the educational system for increasing periods of time.

   However, the discourses surrounding youth were rather ambiguous. Youth was seen as 'on the one hand, a time of fun, a time in which one could take risks and, on the other hand, a potential threat'.

   In this period, youth managed to carve out its own space and its own cultures, particularly those related to rock-and-roll. Grossberg notes that rock-and-roll managed to find space to exist outside institutions run by adults. He says, 'the physical spaces which it appropriated and created as its own: the street, the jukebox, the party and the "hop/dance" ... all attempt to exist outside of the family and of the school'. Young people took the new discourse of youth and used it to create their own culture.

3 From the late 1970s, though, things were beginning to change. This was characterized by the 'sliding of the signifier of "youth" from rock and roll to video-computers'. Young people lost some of their overt rebellion and belief that they could change the world, and replaced it with cynicism. Youth became more knowledgeable about the adult world, and more obsessed with becoming part of it. Young people lost the desire to celebrate youth in its own right, which was typical of the earlier post-war period. They 'returned to a conception of youth as training for adulthood with its own leisure activities, its own fun, but without any special significance'.

   The leisure activities themselves have changed. Political activities have been superseded by hanging around in shopping malls, and experimentation with mind-altering drugs has become less significant than getting drunk. Idealism and rebellion are out of fashion, copying adults is in.

Grossberg largely attributes this change in the meaning of youth to the way in which adults have helped to shift the discourse of youth. As the baby boomers reached middle age and were unwilling to give up their idea of themselves as youthful, they redefined youth as an attitude of mind rather than simply in terms of age. Some tried to hang on to their youth by working out at the gym.

Many aspects of youth culture became incorporated into adult-controlled institutions. For example, rock music has been incorporated into adverts and has become an integral part of commercial television (for example, MTV). The boundaries between youth and adulthood have become somewhat blurred in these new discourses, making it more difficult for youth to retain a distinctive identity. According to Grossberg, as youth move away from identities based on music towards those based on video-computer technology, they are denying their youthfulness. They are trying to be more adult than the adults by knowing more than them about grown-up technology.

Evaluation of post-structuralism

Post-structuralism focused attention on the importance of language, which was certainly neglected by many other sociologists (including functionalists and Marxists). But the focus on language is the greatest weakness of post-structuralism as well as its greatest strength.

Their emphasis on language leads post-structuralists to neglect material reality. For example, Marxists would argue that material wealth has just as much influence on society as discourse or ways of talking about things. In the end capitalists have the power to determine which television programmes or films are made and promoted. To socialist and Marxist feminists it is the wealth of men rather than the way language is used that keeps women oppressed.

Like other sociological approaches which deny the existence of absolute truth (such as postmodernism and ethnomethodology (see Chapter 15)), post-structuralism advocates relativism. It argues that the 'truth' depends simply on who you listen to, which discourse is accepted. Because signifiers are defined in terms of other signifiers, they cannot represent reality.

This creates a problem shared with other relativist approaches: there is no reason to accept post-structuralism above other sociological perspectives. From a post-structuralist viewpoint each perspective is simply a different discourse and there is no way of testing which are true and which are false.

Post-structuralists clearly believe that their own discourse is superior to other discourses. Some see certain perspectives (for example, feminism) as being more valid than others (for example, functionalism). However, the philosophy underlying their own perspective prevents them from being able to show why their views should be accepted above the views of others. (For an evaluation of Foucault, see pp. 635–9; for an evaluation of post-structuralist and postmodern feminism, see pp. 157–63.)

Modernity, postmodernity and culture

Stephen Crook, Jan Pakulski and Malcolm Waters – postmodernization

Stephen Crook, Jan Pakulski and Malcolm Waters (1992) argue that contemporary societies are undergoing a process of postmodernization. They are in the process of changing from modern to postmodern societies. Crook et al. trace the changes involved in this process by comparing modern and postmodern culture.

Modern culture

According to Crook et al. there are three main characteristics of modern culture: differentiation, rationalization and commodification.

1 Differentiation involves the separating out of different parts of society. Economic, political, social and cultural spheres become increasingly distinct from one another. Drawing on the ideas of Max Weber, Crook et al. argue that different aspects of society come to be judged in terms of different criteria. Science is judged in terms of truth; morality and law in terms of goodness and justice; and art in terms of beauty. Each sphere develops its own specialist institutions and occupations.

Initially, the patronage of the rich enabled people to become professional musicians, composers, sculptors and artists. Later, specialist institutions such as art schools developed to train future generations of cultural specialists. Other institutions, such as theatres, art galleries, and concert halls, were established to make cultural products more widely available.

Culture was therefore separated or differentiated from other aspects of life. It was produced by specialists, trained in particular institutions, and it was consumed in specific places. This formed the basis for distinguishing between folk culture (which could be found among ordinary people) and high culture, which was the product of these specialist individuals and institutions.

However, as modernity progressed, new types of popular culture developed, such as the music hall, the charabanc (coach) trip or the seaside holiday resort. In these, too, culture was differentiated from other areas of life, but it had no pretensions to being high culture.

There have been some attempts to break down the division between high culture and everyday life. Avant-garde artists have tried to shock people out of their cultural complacency by portraying everyday objects as art. For example, in 1917 Marcel Duchamp displayed a urinal as a work of art with the title 'Fountain'. He attributed the work to the sanitary engineer who designed the urinal. However, such protests against the splitting of art and life had little impact in modern societies.

2 According to Crook *et al.*, rationalization also shaped modern culture, but not as completely as differentiation. Music has been increasingly influenced by harmonic rationalization, in which mathematics has been used to help compose harmonic music. There has also been a considerable rationalization of the reproduction of music and other art forms.

   Technology has been used to make it possible to recreate or copy culture. For example, the piano allowed the reproduction of a version of complex music on a single instrument. Radios and record players allowed broadcasts and copies of original music to be consumed more widely. Printing technology allowed the reproduction of works of art to become rationalized – you no longer relied upon the efforts of individual artists to see a copy of a picture.

   While some have seen these developments as undermining the distinction between high culture and everyday life, Crook *et al.* disagree. People may be able to sit in their living room listening to Beethoven on their hi-fi while gazing at a print of the *Mona Lisa*, but this simply serves to reinforce the status of high culture. It gives legitimacy to the idea that certain individuals were the greatest artists or composers.

   Nevertheless, in modernity the rationalization of culture can only proceed so far, since the individual creativity of the great artist is still valued.

3 The commodification of culture involves turning cultural products into commodities that can be readily bought and sold. From the viewpoint of mass

culture theories (see pp. 901–3) this undermines aesthetic values and threatens the purity of high art. It brings to the masses an inferior and debased culture which then threatens the unique qualities of high art.

Crook *et al.* do not agree with this view. To them the development of taste is a key feature of modern culture. Taste only develops when people have enough resources to make some choices about what they consume. In early modernity only the highest classes could do this, but as modernity progresses the possibility of choosing what to consume spreads to all classes. This does not undermine hierarchies of taste. The taste of higher social classes is still valued above that of lower classes. In modernity classical music is still seen as superior to the latest pop music.

Postmodernization

In modern societies, culture is differentiated from other areas of social life and high culture is differentiated from popular culture. However, postmodernization reverses these trends. According to Crook *et al.*, an intensification of some of the processes at work in modernity leads to postmodernization. Differentiation, rationalization and commodification are superseded by hyperdifferentiation, hypercommodification and hyper-rationalization. Although each of these develops from, and intensifies the processes of, modernity, they have the effect of reversing some of the trends evident in modernity. This leads to a new type of culture. Crook *et al.* call this new culture postculture.

Hypercommodification

Hypercommodification involves all areas of social life becoming commodified. In modern societies certain areas of social life such as family life, your class background and community ties were not commercialized and were major sources of identity. They influenced what you consumed because they influenced taste. Thus, for example, different families from different classes and different localities would tend to eat different types of food, wear different types of clothes and buy different types of furniture. Hypercommodification undermines these differences.

First, all areas of social life are invaded by commodities. Family activities like eating are invaded by the marketing of products. Consumption increasingly takes place within the home and members of the same family become more inclined to consume different things. Often children have their own television sets, and they might sit in different rooms to their parents, watching different programmes and adverts, and even eating different foods.

Instead of a uniform family culture, each family member chooses their own lifestyle. Similarly, members of the same class no longer tend to share the same tastes. They can increasingly choose from a range of lifestyle options. Different lifestyles themselves become freed from their association with specific groups. For example, people from many different backgrounds choose to live 'green' lifestyles which express their concern for the environment, or choose to follow particular sports or even particular teams.

According to Crook et al., style, unlike taste, is not constrained or shaped by external social factors like class. Styles are systems of signs: the style you choose says something to others about what sort of a person you are. Styles are shaped only by personal preference – essentially everybody can become whoever they choose.

Hyper-rationalization

Hyper-rationalization involves the use of rationalized technology to spread cultural consumption more widely and to privatize it. Technology such as the Walkman and satellite TV allows greater individual choice about what you listen to or watch. Video and cassette recorders extend choice over when and where the cultural products you like are consumed. Again this allows individuals to choose their own lifestyle. Public cultural events such as theatres and music halls, where people gather to consume cultural products simultaneously, become less important.

Following the ideas of Baudrillard (see Chapter 15) Crook et al. argue that this erodes the distinction between authentic and inauthentic culture. Media images come to dominate society. Media copies and reproductions begin to replace the authentic, real thing they represent. Eventually images and signs lose their connection with reality and become what Baudrillard calls simulacra (see Chapter 15 for a definition of simulacra).

Hyperdifferentiation

Crook et al. argue that 'In postmodernization a thousand flowers bloom.' A fantastic variety of cultural forms develop, with no particular type being dominant. For example, popular music has fragmented into a wide variety of styles, each with its own audience choosing its own preferred style, to go with its chosen lifestyle. As variety becomes the order of the day, it becomes difficult for any particular style to claim to be superior to all others.

Furthermore, hypercommodification leads to the incorporation of high culture into cultural forms that have not traditionally enjoyed much prestige. For example, classical music is used as background music in advertising, films and television programmes.

The increased fragmentation of culture – hyperdifferentiation – leads ultimately to dedifferentiation, in which distinctions between different types

of culture break down. In particular, the distinction between high culture and popular culture is undermined in postmodernizing societies. Not only does high culture get incorporated into popular culture, but popular culture increasingly claims to be serious art. Each cultural style has its own devotees who see their own preferred styles and art forms as better than others. High culture no longer has an exclusive claim to legitimacy.

Conclusion

Crook et al. claim that postculture is characterized above all by fragmentation. Variety and choice are the main features of postculture where lifestyle preferences replace a hierarchy of tastes based on class and other social differences.

Crook et al. did not believe that postculture had become completely dominant at the time they were writing (1992). They saw postmodernization as an ongoing process, but did not deny that elements of modern culture remained important. Nevertheless, they clearly believed that postmodernization was gaining momentum, and envisaged a time when it would have largely undermined modern culture.

Dominic Strinati – postmodernism and popular culture

Crook et al. are enthusiastic advocates of the claim that contemporary societies are moving towards postmodernity. Dominic Strinati (1995) is much more sceptical. However, he does provide a commendably clear explanation and discussion of how theories of postmodernism analyse popular culture. He argues that there are five main features of postmodern analysis of popular culture, and he illustrates these arguments with reference to a variety of cultural products. He also examines factors that might have produced postmodern popular culture.

The main features of postmodernism

Strinati identifies the main features of postmodernism as the following:

1 The first is 'The breakdown of the distinction between culture and society'. This involves the development of a 'media-saturated society'. In such a society the mass media are extremely powerful. Rather than reflecting reality the media become so all-consuming that they create our sense of reality. Computer technology helps to create virtual realities which 'potentially replace their real life counterparts'. Increasingly, economic activity is concerned with buying and selling media images rather than physical products.

2 The second main feature of postmodernism is 'An emphasis on style at the expense of substance'. Thus,

particular products become popular because they have designer labels which evoke an attractive lifestyle, rather than because they are useful. Society develops a 'designer ideology'. Surface qualities assume more importance than anything deeper. For example, Strinati says that in popular culture:

surface and style, what things look like, playfulness and jokes, are said to predominate at the expense of content, substance and meaning. As a result, qualities like artistic merit, integrity, seriousness, authenticity, realism, intellectual depth and strong narratives tend to be undermined.

Strinati, 1995, p. 225

For example, a film will tend to be successful if it is visually appealing, whether the plot is any good or not.

3 There is a 'breakdown of the distinction between art and popular culture'. In postmodern culture 'anything can be turned into a joke, reference or quotation'. Thus, elements of what used to be thought of as 'high culture' become incorporated into popular culture. The pop artist Andy Warhol, for example, produced a famous print consisting of thirty representations of Leonardo da Vinci's *Mona Lisa*. The work is called 'Thirty are better than One', and it undermines the special aura and uniqueness of the original by emphasizing how easy it is to produce endless copies of the print.

Strinati says that 'postmodern popular culture refuses to respect the pretensions and distinctiveness of art'. Art has become incorporated into everyday life in societies dominated by signs. Consequently, there is no longer anything special about art.

The critics of mass culture in the earlier decades of the century were deeply worried about just such a development (see pp. 901–3). If postmodernists are right, the worst fears of these critics have come true. However, postmodernists see no reason to be unhappy about this; they welcome the fun, spontaneity and variety of the new postmodern culture in which art is part of life.

4 A fourth feature of postmodern culture is the development of 'Confusions over time and space'. Following the ideas of David Harvey (see Chapter 15), Strinati believes that rapid travel, almost instantaneous communications, and the speed with which capital, information and cultures flow from society to society all lead to confusions over time and space. The media make it possible to witness events on the other side of the globe almost as if you were there. As a result people's sense of space becomes confused.

Postmodern culture also confuses people's sense of time. For example, architecture is often nostalgic and incorporates styles from previous eras. Theme parks recreate the past and try to create the future. Postmodern films often avoid following a story from start to beginning (linear time), but jump around

between past, present and future in a confusing way. The title and content of the film *Back to the Future* show how conventional ideas of linear time can be undermined in postmodern culture.

5 Finally, postmodern culture involves 'The decline of metanarratives'. Drawing on the ideas of Lyotard (see Chapter 15), Strinati sees postmodernism as involving a decline in people's faith in any big stories, or big ideas about the world. Postmodernism is 'sceptical of any absolute, universal and all-embracing claim to knowledge', such as 'religion, science, art modernism and Marxism'. It denies that there is any sense of progress in history. In popular culture this manifests itself in the use of collage, where elements from very different sources are brought together in particular cultural artefacts. Postmodern films often mix different genres, and postmodern buildings mix different styles. The implicit message is that no style or genre is better than any other. Everything is equally valid and the search for a single truth is both pointless and dangerous.

Reasons for the emergence of postmodernism

Strinati identifies three main reasons for the emergence of postmodernism:

1 Capitalist societies have placed an increasing emphasis on consumerism. In the earlier stages of capitalism there was more emphasis on production, on developing the productive capacity of machinery, and on meeting people's basic needs. Advanced capitalist societies have, on average, much higher living standards and there is much more emphasis on getting people to consume products that can be produced in very high numbers. A more affluent population with more leisure time needs to be entertained and persuaded to spend money if companies are to continue to make profits. The media are central to these processes, and consequently media images increasingly dominate society.

2 'New middle-class occupations' have developed which have an interest in promoting postmodern culture. These occupations include design, marketing, advertising and creative jobs in the various media. These jobs involve persuading people about the importance of taste. Once people are persuaded of this, then they will need the expertise of those who claim to be experts in their fields, and they will usually access this expertise through the media.

Strinati also sees groups such as teachers, social workers, lecturers and therapists as important because of their involvement with 'notions of psychological and personal fulfilment and growth'. Such ideas also encourage people to take lifestyle seriously. They therefore encourage them to consume the goods and services required for the lifestyle that they decide is best for them.

Strinati concludes that, for the new occupations in the middle class, 'Their quest for cultural power leads them towards postmodernism and away from the cultures of other classes, such as the high culture of the traditional middle-class intelligentsia.'

3 According to Strinati, postmodernism also comes about because of the 'erosion of collective and personal identities'. There has been a gradual disappearance of identities based upon such things as class, local communities, religion and the nation-state. Yet they have not been replaced by alternative sources of identity. People's identities become more personal and individual, and 'popular culture and the mass media come to serve as the only frames of reference available for the construction of collective and personal identities'. (See pp. 921–32 for a detailed discussion of identity.)

An evaluation of postmodern theories of culture

As well as describing postmodern theories of culture, Dominic Strinati also evaluates them. In doing so he raises a considerable number of problems with postmodern theories of popular culture in particular and culture in general:

1 Strinati argues that postmodernists greatly exaggerate their case in suggesting that the mass media 'take over "reality"'. He says, 'The mass media are important, but not that important.' He sees exaggerated claims about the importance of the media as a product of the ideology of those who make a living from the media. They are based on little empirical evidence; there is no reason to suppose that most people cannot distinguish between image and reality. For example, few people believe that the characters in soap operas are real. Postmodernism also fails to explain exactly why the media are so important, and it ignores other areas of social life, such as work and families, which are also important.

2 Postmodern theory also exaggerates the importance of the media in shaping what people consume. People do not just buy products because of their image or the designer label attached to them; they also buy them because they are useful. Furthermore, less affluent members of society simply cannot afford to buy expensive products for the kudos attached to a brand name. What is more, not all sections of society have a culture which attaches importance to the image of products.

3 Strinati questions the logic of postmodernism's claim that metanarratives are in decline. This is because he argues that postmodernism is itself a metanarrative. Strinati says that postmodernism:

> *presents a definite view of knowledge and its acquisition, together with a general account of the significant changes it sees occurring in modern societies. It presumes to tell us something true about the world, and knows why it is able to do this.*
>
> Strinati, 1995, p. 241

These are just the characteristics that postmodernists use to describe other metanarratives, of which they are so critical. The popularity of postmodernism therefore undermines the postmodernists' claim that metanarratives are in decline.

4 Strinati has more time for the postmodernists' claim that concepts of time and space have been affected by such things as faster travel and communications. However, he argues that some people have less opportunity to experience these changes than others. The poorer people of the world do not have access to computer technology, satellite communications or jet travel. In any case, some changes date back to the early decades of the century (for example, aeroplanes and the cinema), considerably before postmodernity is supposed to have developed.

As in other areas, postmodernists do not provide detailed evidence that people's consciousness has changed. There are no studies which actually show that people have confused ideas about space and time.

5 Strinati does believe that 'Postmodernist claims about the breakdown of the distinction between art and popular culture do have a certain plausibility.' However, he argues that these claims can only be applied to the culture of the new middle-class occupations which he sees as largely responsible for the emergence of postmodernism.

Generally people still find it possible to distinguish between what they consider art and what they see as popular culture. Furthermore, postmodernists themselves distinguish between 'modern' and 'postmodern' cultural products. If they can do this, then 'the potential for cultural discrimination must remain under postmodernism'.

If postmodernists prefer postmodern films, buildings, television programmes and so on to modern ones, it remains open for other groups of people to retain their own preferences, which may be quite different to those of postmodernists.

Strinati believes that 'Rather than dismantling the hierarchy of aesthetic and cultural taste, postmodernism erects a new one, placing itself at the top.' Postmodern cultural products often contain 'clever' references to a variety of styles and genres from previous eras. Only clever, well-informed people (particularly postmodernists), who are familiar with all these different styles and genres, can fully appreciate the subtleties of postmodern art and popular culture.

6 Finally, Strinati evaluates postmodern claims about actual changes in popular culture. He argues that postmodern elements are most common in advertising and architecture, but that in other areas they have had a more limited impact. He looks particularly at the cinema.

Strinati notes that many films, which can be seen as postmodern in some respects, can be seen as modern in other respects. For example, the *Back to the Future* films may have confusions over space and time, but they also have strong narratives (story lines) – a feature supposed to be characteristic of modern films. Even *Blade Runner*, the archetypal postmodern film, is partly based upon themes that predate the emergence of postmodernism by many decades.

Blade Runner follows the theme of Mary Shelley's novel *Frankenstein*, which explored the tragic consequences of trying to replicate human life (the characters in *Blade Runner* are 'replicants' – near-perfect reproductions of human beings).

Strinati believes that many of the supposedly postmodern aspects of the contemporary cinema are nothing new. For example, even early silent films parodied other genres, taking some ideas from music hall. Films which involve nostalgia for the past have also long been made. Westerns and gangster films are two examples.

Dominic Strinati concludes that there are many examples of a postmodern influence on aspects of

popular culture, but they are only examples. They are not important or numerous enough to justify the rather grand and generalized claims made by many postmodernists. Strinati says, 'While it cannot be dismissed completely, postmodernism seems subject to severe theoretical and empirical limitations. It is certainly inadequate as a basis for developing a sociology of popular culture.'

This is partly because Strinati believes that any adequate theory must take account of two main factors: the tastes of audiences, and the need for the culture industry to make a profit. He says that 'it is doubtful whether power and control over production by themselves are sufficient to determine patterns of cultural consumption.' However, they do have an important role in determining what is produced: a role that is wholly neglected by postmodernists. (For an example of a theory of postmodernity which does not neglect power and control over production, see the work of David Harvey, discussed in Chapter 15.)

Identity

Introduction – the nature of social identity

Richard Jenkins argues that social identity is 'our understanding of who we are and of who other people are, and, reciprocally, other people's understanding of themselves and of others' (Jenkins, 1996). Identity is something that is negotiable and is created in the process of human interaction. It involves making comparisons between people and therefore establishing similarities and differences between them. Those who are believed by themselves and others to be similar, share an identity, which is distinguishable from the identity of people who are believed to be different and who do not, therefore, share the same identity.

To Jenkins, 'social identity is about meanings', and these meanings are socially constructed rather than being about essential differences between people. For example, Jenkins discusses the transition to being an old-age pensioner or senior citizen. The change in identity and the social role that accompanies it are based upon an arbitrary distinction between those who are 64 and those who are 65, but it has a tremendous impact on a person's identity. Jenkins says:

> Imagine, for example, the morning of your sixty-fifth birthday. With it, as well as birthday cards, will come retirement, a pension, a concessionary public transport pass, special rates every Tuesday at the hairdresser. ... Although it will be the same face you will see in the bathroom mirror, you will

> no longer be quite the person that you were yesterday. Nor can you ever be again.
> Jenkins, 1996

According to Jenkins, identity is an integral part of social life. It is only by distinguishing the identities of different groups that people are able to relate to other people. An awareness of different identities provides some indication of what sort of person you might be dealing with, and therefore how you can relate to them.

The understanding you have of different identities might be limited, or wrong altogether, but it is a vital part of social life and it makes interaction possible. Jenkins comments that:

> More often than not, men and women going about their everyday lives are concerned with specific *social identities*. We talk, for example, about whether people are born gay or become gay as a result of the way they have been brought up. About what it means to be 'grown up'. About what the difference is between Canadians and Americans. We observe the family who have just moved in around the corner and shake our heads: what can you expect, they come from the wrong part of town. We watch the television news and jump to all sorts of conclusions about current events on the basis of identifications such as 'Muslim', 'fundamentalist Christian', or whatever.
> Jenkins, 1996, p. 5

Jenkins concludes that 'Without social identity, there is, in fact, no society.'

Although most sociologists would agree with Jenkins that identity is an integral and crucial part of society, there is disagreement amongst them about the factors that shape identity in contemporary societies and the ways in which the nature of social identity has developed over time. An influential way of thinking about identity has been suggested by Stuart Hall, and it provides a convenient starting point for a discussion of the controversies surrounding the nature of identity.

Stuart Hall – three concepts of identity

In 'The question of cultural identity' (1992), Stuart Hall argues that ideas on identity have passed through three main stages in which particular conceptions of identity were dominant in thinking about society. These are:

1 The Enlightenment subject
2 The sociological subject
3 The post-modern subject

Pre-modern identities

Hall argues that the early stages of modernity 'gave rise to a new and decisive form of individualism, at the centre of which stood a new conception of the individual subject and its identity' (Hall, 1992). In pre-modern societies identities were largely based around traditional structures, particularly related to religion. Your position in society and your identity came from the position you were born into, which was seen as reflecting the will of God. People were not regarded as being unique individuals with their own identity, but simply part of the 'great chain of being'. This concept saw every living thing as having a place in the scheme of things. There was a hierarchy stretching from God at the pinnacle, through kings and less significant human beings, to animals, plants and inanimate objects at the bottom. Your identity came from your place in the scheme of things rather than from any individual or personal attributes.

The Enlightenment subject

However, with the advent of modernity, this changed. Between the sixteenth and eighteenth centuries a new conception of identity became dominant. This new conception of identity had two key features:

1 The individual subject was seen as 'indivisible'. Each person had an identity in their own right, and this identity was unified and could not be broken down into smaller, constituent parts.

2 The identity of each individual was unique.

The individual was not part of something bigger – the great chain of being – but was seen as having a distinct identity of their own.

According to Hall, this conception of identity stemmed from the ideas of the French philosopher, Descartes (1596–1650).

Descartes believed that there was a basic distinction between the mind and matter. He had a dualistic conception of humans: they were divided into two separate parts, the mind and the body. Each individual's mind was separate from every other individual's mind; consequently each individual was unique. The distinctiveness of the individual mind was expressed in Descartes' famous saying, 'Cogito, ergo, sum' – 'I think, therefore I am.'

The individual, in this conception of identity, was a unified, whole person with the ability to think for themselves. The individual saw themselves as distinct and separate from other people, complete in their own right. The individual was rational, able to work out things for themselves on the basis of logic, and not limited by their position in society or traditional beliefs. Hall describes it thus:

> *The Enlightenment subject was based on a conception of the human person as a fully centred, unified individual, endowed with the capacities of reason, consciousness and action, whose 'centre' consisted of an inner core which first emerged when the subject was born, and unfolded with it, while remaining essentially the same – continuous or 'identical' with itself – throughout the individual's existence. The essential centre of the self was a person's identity.*
>
> Hall, 1992, p. 275

The sociological subject

By the nineteenth century a more sociological conception of the subject and individual identity began to develop. Hall sees this as resulting from changes in society.

As industrialization and urbanization began to take hold, society became more complicated. It became increasingly based upon organizations and structures which shaped the lives of individuals. By the early twentieth century, for example, companies run by individual entrepreneurs were giving way to corporations owned by shareholders and run by complex administrations. Furthermore, 'The individual citizen became enmeshed in the bureaucratic and administrative machineries of the modern state.'

Each individual was no longer seen as being so unique and separate from other individuals. Rather, the relationship between the individual and society was mediated through 'group processes and ... collective norms'. For example, an individual's identity was seen as being tied up with their membership of a particular social class, a specific occupational grouping, their origins in a particular region, their nationality, and so on.

Symbolic interactionism and identity

Hall sees the theory of symbolic interactionism as a good example of this conception of individual identity. From the viewpoint of symbolic interactionism, individual identity is only formed in interaction with others. A person's view of themselves, or self-concept, is partly a product of how others see that person.

The symbolic interactionist George Herbert Mead called the self-concept the 'I' (see Chapter 15). Another interactionist, Charles Horton Cooley (discussed in Hall, 1992), saw humans as having a 'looking-glass self'; their sense of who they were reflected the reactions of other people to them.

From the interactionist viewpoint, people still possessed their own individuality, but it was not an individuality wholly distinct from society. Identity acts as a bridge between the social and the purely individual. By possessing a particular identity, individuals internalize certain norms and values that accompany that identity. It allows their behaviour to be predictable to others and in turn makes behaviour in society more patterned and regular.

This sort of view can be illustrated with the example of social class. A particular class identity would encourage people to behave in particular ways. Traditional working-class and middle-class identities differed, and they were associated with different subcultures (see pp. 75–6). The existence of these subcultures gave substance to and reinforced the class structure of society. Hall comments that 'Identity thus stitches (or, to use a current medical metaphor, "sutures") the subject into the structure. It stabilizes both subjects and the cultural worlds they inhabit, making both reciprocally more unified and predictable.'

This general approach to identity was not confined to interactionists. For example, functionalists such as Parsons saw identity in terms of the existence of social roles which fitted individual personalities into the social system (see Chapter 15).

Change in late modernity – the postmodern subject

According to Hall, the symbolic interactionist theory of identity and the idea of the sociological subject might have been appropriate analyses in modernity, but they have become increasingly inappropriate in late modernity or the postmodern era (Hall is somewhat unclear as to whether the contemporary era is late-modern or postmodern).

According to Hall, contemporary societies are increasingly characterized by the existence of fragmented identities. People no longer possess a single, unified conception of who they are, but instead possess 'several, sometimes contradictory or unresolved, identities'. This fragmentation of identity has a number of sources.

Modernity and change

Modern societies have always been characterized by rapid change. In late-modern societies the pace of change increases, which makes it difficult for people to retain a single, unified sense of who they are.

New social movements

In the past, social class provided something of a 'master identity', which overarched other identities and formed the basis for political conflict. However, in the 1960s and 1970s people began to organize around issues other than class. New social movements developed (see pp. 643–7) concerned with a variety of issues and identities. Hall lists 'feminism, black struggles, national liberation, anti-nuclear and ecological movements' as examples. Instead of people feeling part of a single class, their identity became fragmented in terms of their gender, ethnicity, religion, age, nationality, views on ecology, and so on.

Identity politics

With the rise of new social movements, identity itself became a political issue. Identity politics, as it became known, is concerned with the differences between groups of people, and with allowing individuals to express those differences. It emphasizes the importance of hearing different voices, particularly those of oppressed groups such as gays and lesbians, black women, the disabled, and so on.

Feminism

Feminism had a particularly important role. It paved the way in opening up what were previously thought of as private issues (like housework and domestic violence) to public debate. Feminism therefore 'exposed, as a political and social question, the issue of how we are formed and produced as gendered subjects. That is to say, it politicized subjectivity, identity and the process of identification (as men/women, mothers/fathers, sons/daughters).'

In its early phases feminism replaced the idea of all humans having the same identity, 'mankind', with the idea that men and women were different. It encouraged women to unite as 'sisters' and tried to substitute gender as the 'master identity' instead of class. However, more recently, difference feminism has emphasized the differences between women (for example, women from different ethnic origins). This has led to a further fragmentation of identity (see pp. 519–23 for a discussion of difference feminism).

Disciplinary power and surveillance

Another important factor in fragmenting identities is highlighted in the work of Foucault (see pp. 635–9). According to Foucault, societies were becoming increasingly characterized by 'disciplinary power' and 'surveillance'. The behaviour of individuals was increasingly watched, monitored and, where necessary, punished. Such techniques originated in prisons and hospitals, but have since spread to encompass many aspects of society. Since people are monitored and treated as individuals rather than as members of social groups, they become increasingly isolated. This makes it more difficult for them to form coherent identities based upon social interaction.

Globalization

A final, very important, factor in creating fragmented identities is the process of globalization. Hall suggests a number of ways in which globaliza- tion might affect identity.

The ease and frequency with which people move around the world, and improvements in communica- tions and the 'global marketing of styles, places and images' can lead to a 'cultural supermarket effect'. People are no longer confined to developing identi- ties based upon the place in which they live, but can choose from a very wide range of different identities. They can adopt the clothes, ways of speaking, values and lifestyles of any group they choose.

On the other hand, global consumerism can also lead to increasing homogeneity, or similarity, between people. Products are marketed worldwide, and the most successful (for example, Coca-Cola) can be found more or less anywhere.

There are therefore contradictory trends within globalization, but both can undermine previously existing identities. The homogenization of the global consumer undermines identities rooted in membership of particular social groups. The ability to make greater choices about identity means that people living in close proximity and even belonging to the same social groups can have quite different identities. Globalization thus opens up a number of possibilities.

Globalization and different sources of identity

Hall then goes on to review the actual effects of globalization on identity. He argues that in modern societies nationality was an important source of identity. Most nation-states emphasized the importance of the nation and tried to use national identity to create solidarity among citizens of different classes, ethnic origins and so on. With globalization, this has not proved so easy or effective. There have been three main responses to globalization in relation to nationality:

1 In some places people have tried to reaffirm national identity as a defensive mechanism. They have perceived a threat to their national identity, from, for example, immigration. Thus, in Britain, such a reaction has created 'a revamped Englishness, an aggressive little Englandism, and a retreat to ethnic absolutism in an attempt to shore up the nation'.

2 The first reaction to globalization is found among ethnic majorities, but ethnic minorities sometimes react in defensive ways as well. In response to racism and exclusion, ethnic minorities have sometimes placed a renewed emphasis upon their ethnic identities and culture. In Britain this has involved 're-identification with cultures of origin (in the Caribbean, India, Bangladesh, Pakistan); the construction of strong counter-ethnicities – as in the symbolic identification of second generation youth, through the symbols and motifs of Rastafarianism, with their African origin'.

3 A third reaction to globalization is the construction of new identities. A British example is the construction of a 'black' identity, embracing British Afro-Caribbeans and Asians. The black British identity represents an alternative to the re- identification with cultural origins, as a response to racism and exclusion. In this case identity becomes hybrid, mixing more than one existing identity into a new identity (see pp. 272–6).

The first two responses to globalization have had the effect of reviving ethnicity as a source of identity, often in opposition to existing nationalism. In several parts of the world ethnic groups have demanded their own nation-states, as bigger nation-states (such as the USSR and Yugoslavia) have broken up. (This has led to considerable violence and even civil war in places such as Bosnia and Kosovo.)

Hall sees this strident nationalism, based upon real or imagined ethnic differences, as a worrying trend. He argues that the idea of ethnic purity is largely a myth. Nearly all populations come from a variety of ethnic backgrounds. This has become increasingly true in the twentieth century with the large-scale migration of great numbers of people. Most cultures are hybrid ones and attempts to create 'pure' ethnic identities are very dangerous in such circumstances. (See pp. 271–2 for more discussion of Hall's ideas on ethnicity and nationality, and pp. 222–82 for a general discussion of ethnicity, nationality and identity.)

Conclusion

Hall concludes that, in line with postmodern theory, identity has become decentred. Individuals can no longer find a core or centre to their identity, based on class or existing nation-states. Globalization in particular has had 'a pluralizing impact on identities, producing a variety of possibilities and new positions of identification, and making identities more positional, more political, more plural and diverse; less fixed, unified or trans-historical'. It is this uncertainty and diversity that have led some groups to make a more stable or unified identity by trying to create a renewed emphasis upon their ethnicity.

Zygmunt Bauman – 'From pilgrim to tourist – or a short history of identity'

Zygmunt Bauman (1996) goes much further than Hall in advocating a postmodern view of identity. According to Bauman, identity has not just become fragmented, it has ceased to have any stable base whatsoever. Identity has become simply a matter of choices, and not even choices that are necessarily consistent or regular. Individuals can change their identity as and when they choose.

Modern identity as pilgrimage

According to Bauman, under modernity identity could be seen as similar to a pilgrimage. In a pilgrimage a person maps out their future life. They have a goal – to reach the place of pilgrimage. All of their actions are geared towards achieving that goal. They must not be distracted along the way by enjoying hospitality or engaging in leisure activities. They need a singleness of purpose. They must treat the world around them as if it were a desert, free from distractions. Furthermore, in the desert sand they can see their footprints stretching back into the distance, reassuring them about how far they have come.

To Bauman, the formation of identity in modern societies was very much like a pilgrimage. People's life strategies were based upon having a clear sense of who they wanted to become. Their lives were geared towards achieving their desired identity. This identity was usually related to their occupation. They worked in this job and tried to have a successful career. They mapped out their future, looking ahead to achieving their career goals, and looking backwards to see how far they had come since embarking on their career.

Postmodernity – 'the world inhospitable to pilgrims'

Pilgrims require a degree of certainty in the world. They have to know that the place of pilgrimage will be there when they arrive, otherwise the pilgrimage will be pointless. Postmodernity undermines pilgrimage as a life strategy by creating uncertainty.

In postmodern societies change is so rapid that there can be no certainty that particular positions, or even particular professions, will still exist in 10, 20 or 30 years' time. Bauman says:

not only have jobs-for-life disappeared, but trades and professions which have acquired the confusing habit of appearing from nowhere and vanishing without notice can hardly be lived as Weberian 'vocations' – and to rub salt into the wound, the demand for the skills needed to practice such professions seldom lasts as long as the time needed to acquire them.

Bauman, 1996, p. 24

In this situation there is no point in embarking on a pilgrimage. The destination – the job that a successful career will lead to – will have disappeared long before getting there. Because jobs change so rapidly, a person's career achievements so far may well be irrelevant to future jobs and will quickly be forgotten. Similarly, for the pilgrim in a desert, a storm may well come along and blow the sand around to cover up the tracks. The pilgrim can no longer see how far they have progressed.

Postmodern life strategies

In this situation new life strategies are required. These strategies abandon the idea of creating any single, central or permanent identity. Instead, people change their identity at will, putting little commit-ment into achieving an identity which may at any time become obsolete. Bauman identifies four postmodern life strategies:

1 The stroller (or *flaneur*) is somebody who strolls around cities observing and being entertained by the spectacle of city life. He or she has no particular objective in mind but strolls simply as a leisure pursuit. The stroller is a postmodern 'playful consumer' who has replaced the 'heroic producer' (or worker) of modernity.

   Shopping malls have been created as the haunt of the postmodern stroller. Shopping malls are there so that you can 'stroll while you shop and ... shop while you stroll'. You can sample an endless range of products and consume whatever you wish, construct whatever identity you choose, and change it the following day if you want. With developments such as multi-channel television and the Internet the stroller does not even have to leave the comfort of their armchair to enjoy their pastime.

2 The second life strategy is that of the vagabond. In past times, the vagabond wandered from place to place refusing to be tied down to any one place. The authorities disliked the vagabonds because they were unpredictable. They had no particular goals in their wandering so you could never predict where they would turn up. This was quite different from the utterly predictable movements of the pilgrim.

   The vagabond is always a stranger wherever they wander, and has no settled place in the world. In a postmodern world it makes sense to wander from identity to identity without settling on any one. Indeed postmodern society makes it more or less impossible to settle. Bauman says:

> Now there are few 'settled' places left. The 'forever settled' residents woke up to find the places (places in the land, places in society and places in life), to which they 'belong', no longer existing or no longer accommodating, neat streets turn mean, factories vanish together with jobs, skills no longer find buyers, knowledge turns into ignorance, professional experience becomes liability, secure networks of relations fall apart and foul the place with putrid waste.
>
> Bauman, 1996, p. 29

It is little wonder that becoming a wandering vagabond, changing identity at will, becomes an attractive option.

3 The tourist represents the third strategy. Like the vagabond, the tourist moves from place to place. However, their movements are a little more purposeful. They know where they want to go. But they are not like the pilgrim. They do not travel to meet some ultimate goal. They simply go to places to gain new experiences, to see somewhere different or do something they have not done before.

In postmodern societies people do not devote themselves to working on creating and cementing a particular identity. Like the tourist seeking new experiences, the equivalent postmodern life strategy involves trying out new identities and always looking for something new to sample.

4 The final strategy is that of the player. This involves treating life as a game. Games are played to win, but the result has no lasting consequences. Win or lose, you forget the last game and move on to another one. Similarly, in postmodern societies people can play the game of having particular identities for a time. (For example, they might be a left-wing radical student in their youth but change their politics in middle age.)

While a person will try to play each identity game well, that will not stop them from changing the game and playing at a new identity once they decide a particular game is over.

Conclusion

Bauman concludes that:

> All four intertwining and interpenetrating postmodern life strategies have in common that they tend to render human relations fragmentary ... and discontinuous; they are all up in arms against 'strings-attached' and long-lasting consequences, and militate against the construction of lasting networks of mutual duties and obligations.
>
> Bauman, 1996, p. 33

There are no solid, lasting identities. The only duty of the postmodern citizen is to 'lead an enjoyable life' by changing identity at will.

Evaluation of Hall and Bauman

Despite the differences between them, Stuart Hall and Zygmunt Bauman both argue that there has been a general movement away from relatively stable identities, based upon social factors such as class, towards more fragmented identities. Bauman in particular stresses the extent to which people can choose identities, while Hall places more emphasis on the increasing importance of ethnicity in shaping identity. These views have been criticized on a number of grounds:

1 Some sociologists deny that class has lost its importance as a source of identity. For example, Marshall, Newby, Rose and Vogler (1988) argue that in Britain people still see themselves as members of classes and that class continues to influence people's beliefs as well as their life chances (see pp. 88–9).

Similarly, in a discussion of class, politics and identity, Frank McDonough argues that 'pronouncing the death of class in British society does seem premature' (McDonough, 1997). McDonough accepts that there have been some changes in, for example, working-class life, including a growth in consumerism. However:

> this cultural revolution has not completely led to the working class no longer feeling working class. When account is taken of what the working class say about class, we find they still do not feel middle class. They still believe that class has a detrimental impact on their life. They still consider class to be an important part of British life.
>
> McDonough, 1997, p. 223

McDonough also believes that class divisions remain important in British politics.

2 Some feminists argue that gender remains the dominant source of identity. Although difference feminists stress the variety of identities that women have (see pp. 519–23), radical feminists continue to see gender as the principal source of identity, as well as the main source of exploitation in patriarchal societies (see pp. 136–7 and 145–7 for discussions of radical feminism). They therefore contradict Bauman's view that identities are freely chosen rather than related to social factors, and they suggest that gender is a more important source of identity than Hall's work seems to imply.

3 Richard Jenkins (1996) argues against Hall's view that reflexivity – reflecting upon your identity – is distinctively modern. According to Jenkins, long before modernity people were self-conscious about their identity and would seek to change it. Jenkins says:

Saint Augustine's Confessions, *written more than 1,500 years ago, is a testament to the possibilities for reforging the self, offered as an example for others. Going back nearly another thousand years, one can understand Buddhism as a project for the reformation of selfhood.*

Jenkins, 1996, p. 10

To Jenkins there is nothing new about being self-conscious about your identity – it is a universal feature of being human.

4 Jenkins also believes that writers such as Bauman greatly exaggerate the degree to which identities are fragmented, short-lived and freely chosen in contemporary societies. He is as sceptical about the claim that there is a distinctive postmodern type of identity as he is about the claim that modernity ushered in a radical change in identity.

Jenkins accepts that there have been some changes in identity – for example, feminism has increased the importance of gender as a source of identity – but he denies that the changes are fundamental. He says that 'Most commentators on postmodernism are on a historicist mission by any other name, substituting a meta-narrative of fragmentation for the old story of progress. In the pursuit of such grand themes, the mundane is likely to be overlooked.' Jenkins is accusing postmodernists of doing exactly what they object to other theorists doing – producing grand theories or metanarratives which are not soundly based.

Unlike postmodernists, Jenkins believes that identity remains rooted in social experience and the membership of social groups, and that it is not something that can just be changed at will. His ideas will now be examined.

Richard Jenkins – identity as a social product

Individual and collective identity

Richard Jenkins argues that identities contain elements of the 'individually unique' and the 'collectively shared' (Jenkins, 1996). While each individual has an identity which is personal to them, those identities are shaped through membership of social groups. The individual elements of identity emphasize difference, the collective elements similarities, but the two are closely related.

Using the ideas of symbolic interactionists such as George Herbert Mead (see Chapter 15), Jenkins argues that identity is formed in the process of socialization. Through this process people learn to distinguish the socially significant similarities and differences between themselves and others.

In childhood, certain identities take on primary importance and are relatively stable throughout

people's lives. Jenkins says that 'selfhood, humanness, gender, and, under some circumstances, kinship and ethnicity, are primary identities, more robust and resilient to change in later life than other identities'.

Although all social identities can change, they are much less easy to change than postmodernists such as Bauman suggest. Furthermore, 'social identity is never unilateral' – people's identities are always formed in relationship to other people.

Drawing on the ideas of the interactionist Erving Goffman, Jenkins argues that in everyday life people are concerned to manage impressions of themselves – to give the impression of themselves they want others to see. Identities are formed as people try to get others to see them as they want to be seen. They may or may not be successful. If unsuccessful they may find it difficult to sustain the identity they prefer. (These ideas are based partly on labelling theory – see pp. 372–6.)

Identities are not just concerned with our own impressions of ourselves, but also with our impressions of others, and others' impressions of us. Identity is both internal – what we think our own identity is – and external – how others see us. Identities are formed and stabilized in a dialectical relationship between these internal and external factors – they interact to produce an identity.

External factors – how others see us and react to us – may contradict and undermine, or support and strengthen our view of ourselves. Either way, identity emerges out of this relationship between ourselves and others. Jenkins says:

Your external definition of me is an inexorable part of my internal definition of myself – even if only in the process of rejection or resistance – and vice versa. Both processes are among the routine everyday practices of actors. Nor is one more significant than the other.

Jenkins, 1996, p. 27

Power and identity

To Jenkins, identity formation is not simply related to individual interactions. It is also related to larger social groups. Interaction leads to the construction of boundaries, or dividing lines, between different social groups which carry different identities. For example, the distinction between men and women, and between working class, middle class and underclass, has implications for people's identities.

The ability to claim identities for yourself and to attribute particular identities to others is essentially a question of power. Some groups have more power than other groups to claim identities for themselves and to attribute identities to others. For example, the poor and the unemployed, living in inner-city areas, may have little power to resist being seen as part of an 'underclass'.

Furthermore, identities are closely related to social positions, particularly in organizations. Organizations classify people by job title and rank and people are not simply free to choose their own position within organizations. A cleaner at the BBC cannot simply choose to become Director General in order to change his or her identity.

The existence of identities associated with particular social groups and positions in organizations means that identity is never completely fluid and simply a matter of choice. Jenkins says, 'Social identities exist and are acquired and allocated within power relations. Identity is something *over* which struggles take place and *with* which stratagems are advanced.'

The Black Power movement in the USA, and feminist and gay liberation movements are examples of groups organizing to change the widely-held perceptions of particular social identities. They were not simply the struggles of individuals to gain a more positive social identity. They were (and are) the struggles of social groups which sought a more positive social identity for the group as a whole.

Conclusion and evaluation

While Jenkins's views have some differences to those of Hall (for example, over whether reflexivity first developed with modernity), they are particularly antagonistic towards the claims of postmodernists such as Bauman.

Jenkins's work seems to be on strong ground in arguing that humans are not simply free to choose their own identity, that some identities (such as gender) are not easy to change, and that identities are social as well as individual. He puts forward a strong case in arguing that any change in the nature of identity associated with a supposed shift to postmodernity, has been exaggerated. However, some sociologists argue for a position between that of Bauman and that of Jenkins. The work of one such sociologist will now be considered.

Harriet Bradley – *Fractured Identities*

In a review of studies of identity and inequality, Harriet Bradley argues that neither modern nor postmodern conceptions of identity are adequate on their own. She says, 'A key objective is to pull together classical or modernist approaches to understanding inequalities with the newer perspectives inspired by postmodernism and post-structuralism' (Bradley, 1997).

As a starting point, Bradley identifies a number of differences between these two approaches.

Modernist and postmodern approaches to identity

1   Modernist approaches emphasize the importance of structures (such as class structures or patriarchy) in explaining identity. Postmodern approaches emphasize choice.

2   Modernist approaches tend to suggest that society is polarizing (for example, between rich and poor). Postmodern approaches see societies, and the identities of its members, fragmenting into many different groups.

3   Modernist approaches tend to see class or gender as key sources of identity. Postmodern approaches often argue that class is disappearing. They deny that women are in any sense a unified group with a single identity. They argue that there are numerous different sources of identity. More stress is placed in postmodern thinking on 'race', ethnicity, nationality, culture and religion, as diverse, but interconnected, sources of identity.

4   Modernist approaches see societies as relatively predictable, with a degree of social order. Postmodern approaches emphasize 'chaos and confusion, the limitless welter of apparently unique events'.

5   Modernist approaches stress material sources of power, particularly control over resources such as money. Postmodern approaches emphasize the importance of the cultural and symbolic. From the postmodern point of view, power stems from the control over discourse – over how people talk and think about issues or social groups. Meanings are seen as central.

The problems of modernist and postmodern approaches

Bradley believes that neither modernist nor postmodern positions on any of these issues are entirely satisfactory. For example, she says, 'Societies are chaotic, but also orderly; behaviour is infinitely variable, but also regular and predictable; social relations change, but are also stable and persistent.'

Similarly, she argues that structured social inequalities remain important; they have not disappeared. However, such inequalities no longer shape identities in as straightforward a way as they used to; there is more fluidity and choice involved in identity. But choice is not absolute: it is constrained by the existence of certain dynamic relationships. Bradley prefers the term 'dynamic' to the term 'structure', because she believes that the idea of structure exaggerates the degree to which social relationships are solid and fixed. There are, for example, class dynamics which affect people's life chances and identities, but these do not stand still. Class dynamics are in constant process of change.

Furthermore, power does not just come from meanings and discourse, important though these are.

Bradley says, 'It would be nice if the social world were no more than a contestation of meanings, so that, merely by renaming the world, we could change it.' But this is not the case. A number of feminists have contributed to 'rewriting history from female points of view; yet it must be acknowledged to have had as yet rather little effect on the massive exploitation of women by entrepreneurs around the world'. She goes on: 'men are able to dominate women not only by dominating them in discourse, but also by controlling the distribution of social wealth' – for example, by giving them lower-paid jobs.

Nevertheless, exploitation cannot begin to be challenged until oppressed groups are able to attack the discourses that portray the oppression as inevitable or desirable. Women had to challenge the discourse of female inferiority before liberation of women became a possibility; black people had to challenge the discourse of slavery, and so on. Bradley argues that 'both materiality and meaning are aspects of constraining power relations', and it makes no sense to emphasize one to the exclusion of the other.

Four aspects of inequality

In her study, Bradley examines four aspects of inequality: class, gender, 'race' and ethnicity and age. Although she sees these as the most important types of inequality and sources of identity, she accepts that there are other important social divisions: examples include sexuality and disability.

Although these inequalities and sources of identity can be analysed separately, in practice they interact with each other in a dynamic way. She says:

> It has become almost a commonplace to say that classes are gendered and that gender relations are class-specific. Similarly the other dimensions of 'race'/ethnicity and age impinge on individual class and gender experience and in any particular concrete example it is hard to separate out the different elements.
>
> Bradley, 1997, p. 19

Bradley does not see any one source of inequality as being of primary importance. She sees all as significant. This contrasts with Marxists who see class as central, feminists who see gender as central, and some anti-racists who believe that 'race'/ethnicity is most important.

Inequalities and identities

How do these inequalities relate to identity? Bradley does not believe that there is a straightforward relationship between inequality and identity. The importance of inequalities for identity varies over time and with individual circumstances.

Bradley accepts that postmodernists have a point in arguing that there is a good deal of choice over identity and that identities are to some extent fragmented. However, Bradley still sees identities as rooted in membership of social groups. It will be difficult for a young Afro-Caribbean woman to see herself as white, upper-class, elderly or male.

Furthermore, social factors tend to bring certain identities to prominence while reducing the significance of others. Although precise predictions about the identities that people will adopt are impossible, it *is* possible to discern more general trends. Bradley says:

> For example, it is suggested that changes in work and the break-up of old urban communities are currently acting to weaken class identities. Or again, for Afro-Caribbeans in Britain 'race' is arguably a more potent source of identity than class because it is so visible.
>
> Bradley, 1997

Three levels of identity

Identities tend to be grounded in inequalities, social divisions and differences. However, the importance of particular inequalities, divisions and differences for identity varies from place to place, from time to time, and from individual to individual. Bradley therefore believes that it is useful to conceive of identity as working at three different levels:

1 Passive identities are 'potential identities'. The potential exists for them to become important, in the way that individuals see themselves and others see them, but the identity is lying largely dormant. Bradley sees class identity in this way. Most British people accept that class inequalities exist, but most of the time they do not see themselves as members of a class. However, events or circumstances can raise consciousness of class and its importance as a source of identity.

2 Active identities 'are those which individuals are conscious of and which provide a base for their actions. They are positive elements for an individual's self identification although we do not necessarily think of ourselves continually in terms of any single identity.' For example, a woman who is experiencing sexual harassment from a man is likely to respond to the experience in terms of her gender identity, but at other times another identity might be to the fore.

3 Politicized identities exist where they provide 'a more constant base for action and where individuals constantly think of themselves in terms of an identity'. Such identities are formed through political action, through campaigners highlighting the importance of the identity and using it as a basis for organizing collective action. For example, feminists succeeded in transforming gender into a politicized identity for many women in the 1970s and 1980s; and at times gay rights campaigners have achieved the same kind of politicized identity for many gays and lesbians.

Having outlined her general theory of identity, Bradley then goes on to examine the significance of class, gender, 'race'/ethnicity and age in producing identities in contemporary Britain.

Class and identity

As discussed above, Bradley does not see class as the strongest source of identity in contemporary Britain. She sees it as being mainly a source of passive identity. This is partly because class is less visible and obvious in the everyday world than age, 'race'/ethnicity and gender. However, Bradley does not agree with the argument of postmodernists that class is dying out or disappearing. Rather, there is evidence of class both polarizing and fragmenting.

Bradley quotes a number of studies which show that, far from being reduced, inequalities in countries such as Britain are increasing. Put simply, the rich are getting much richer, while the poor are becoming slightly worse off (see pp. 46–9 and 334–6 for summaries of studies that reach similar findings). This creates the potential for class to be an increasingly important source of identity.

However, Bradley also detects evidence that class is fragmenting. She argues that Weber's ideas on class status and party (see pp. 36–9) can be used as a basis for understanding a situation in which there is a plurality of classes which are cross-cut by different status groups (such as ethnic groups), and in which many political organizations and pressure groups are no longer based on class.

The class structure has fragmented, with the development of an 'underclass' (which Bradley sees as a marginal group outside the class structure), and a big increase in self-employment. Furthermore, 'Classes are split by region, public or private sector membership, gender or ethnic origins, amongst other things.'

Bradley therefore concludes that 'neither class, as a set of lived economic relationships, nor class analysis, as a set of social categories, is dead. But there must be recognition of how class relations are shaped by other forms of inequality.'

Gender and identity

In discussing theories of gender, Bradley notes a move away from theories which saw women as a single group, united by their common experience of oppression, towards theories which see women (and indeed men) as being fragmented into different groups. The former type of theory included radical, Marxist and liberal feminisms (see pp. 136–8), while the latter sort includes Black, postmodern and difference feminism (see pp. 138–9, 157–63 and 519–23).

Bradley believes that both types of theory are important and that both provide insight into the formation of identity. She notes that some commen-

tators in the popular media believe that inequality between women and men is a thing of the past. Bradley denies that this is so, and believes that the common experience of disadvantage and sexism provides a basis for a common identity for women.

However, not all women experience disadvantage to the same extent or in the same ways. For example, Black feminists have suggested that the family is experienced differently by white and black women. White feminists see the family as a source of patriarchal oppression. Black feminists experience the black family (which is quite likely to be headed by a woman) as a source of solidarity and as a bulwark against oppression.

To Bradley, gender – both as a general category, and in terms of differences between groups of women and groups of men – is a very important source of identity in contemporary Britain. Furthermore, gender is an active politicized identity for women as a result of the influence of feminism.

More recently, gender has started to become politicized for men. Men used to take the experience of being male for granted – it was seen as the norm and being female was seen as a deviation from the norm. However, masculinity has started to be politicized, with the development of men's movements, and demands for male rights (for example, rights over access to children after divorce), and in a 'backlash' against feminism (see p. 185).

That does not mean that all men and all women experience gender as their main source of identity in all circumstances. Like other sources of identity, it interacts with a variety of other sources. There is a plurality of ways to be a woman or to be a man – as well as class and 'race'/ethnicity, age and sexuality are also important. For example, Bradley argues that:

> *For a post-pubescent exploring the pleasures (and problems) of her newly sexualized body in relation to young men, the experience of womanhood is quite different from that of an ageing post-menopausal woman, struggling to adjust to bodily changes in a culture that puts a high value on youth and fertility.*
>
> Bradley, 1997

Similarly, gay men and lesbians will have different experiences of masculinity or femininity, and have rather different identities from their heterosexual counterparts. Thus, while gender is a crucial source of identity, its interactions with other sources of identity are very important.

'Race'/ethnicity and identity

Like gender, 'race'/ethnicity has become a more important source of identity in contemporary societies than class, and it is more likely to produce active and politicized identities. Sometimes this is partly due to the visibility of skin colour differences between supposed 'races', but this is not always the case. For example, the violence and 'ethnic cleansing' in the former Yugoslavia have occurred between different white ethnic groups.

To a considerable extent the importance of 'race'/ethnicity as a source of identity depends upon how it is used politically to mobilize groups and provide them with a sense of belonging and history. For example, the Black Power movement of the 1960s led to many British and American people from diverse non-white ethnic groups identifying with an oppressed, non-white minority. However, by the 1970s a stronger sense of African identity had developed among black British and American people. By the 1980s:

> the move towards ethnic particularism might lead people to identify more narrowly, say with a specific Caribbean island or region in the Indian sub-continent. In the 1990s political thinking ... may encourage people to adopt 'hyphenated' identities: Mexican-American, British-Indian and so forth.
>
> Bradley, 1997, p. 137

This can lead to people having somewhat confused ethnic identities, particularly if they move from a former colony in which they were born to a Western society. Once again, though, political mobilization is important. For example, the identity of a British Muslim has assumed more importance than other identities (such as being Pakistani) among some people of Asian origin in Britain as a result of the revival of Islam as a world religion (see p. 492 for a discussion of Islamic revival).

For dominant ethnic groups, such as white people in Britain or the USA, ethnic identity is a rather less politicized identity. It tends to be taken as the norm and only becomes an active part of identity in certain circumstances. In Britain, Scottish and Welsh ethnic identities are more active and politicized than an English identity, but an English identity can become important in some contexts (such as sporting events or foreign travel).

Age and identity

Bradley describes age as 'the neglected dimension of inequality'. As a source of identity, age is important for individuals. Young people have legal constraints on what they are allowed to do; older people face ageism; and there are, of course, physiological differences between age groups which affect identity.

However, Bradley sees age as 'more problematic' as 'a basis of collective social identity'. Political parties are not usually organized to represent age

groups, and only a few pressure groups are concerned with age. Furthermore, 'Age as an issue is very low on the political agenda.' Thus, to Bradley, age is primarily part of individual identity and only rarely becomes part of an active or politicized identity. She identifies two main reasons for this:

1 Individuals move through different age groups and are aware that they will not stay young, middle-aged or old for ever. The temporary nature of their membership of an age group mitigates against the development of a stable, long-lasting identity.

2 Unlike other types of stratification, the most powerful group is in the middle. The most disadvantaged age groups, the young and the old, are likely to have little in common to form a basis for making common cause with one another.

However, there are some examples of age becoming a more active identity. Some aspects of youth culture express a sense of conflict with adults. Bradley quotes the classic song by the Who, 'My Generation':

> People try to put us down
> Just because we get around.
> The things they do look awful cold
> Hope I die before I get old.

Nevertheless, the more political aspects of youth culture are more likely to be related to other aspects of stratification than to age, particularly 'race'/ethnicity. (See, for example, the work of Paul Gilroy, pp. 260–2.) Political parties may have specific sections for the young (for example, Young Conservatives), but they are not wholly or mainly concerned with age-related issues.

Despite the limited importance of age as an active or politicized source of identity amongst the young, Bradley does note two examples of youth-related issues coming to the fore:

1 In 1960s America, Britain and other European countries, the radical student movement was partly based around age-related issues. This included demands for educational reform, sexual liberation and an end to what was seen as the bureaucratic and materialistic culture of the middle-aged.

2 In Britain in the 1990s something of a 'coalition of various youth interests (New Age travellers, ravers, environmental groups and "tribes")' got together to campaign against the Criminal Justice Bill. However, Bradley suggests that the unifying theme of this coalition – the 'right to party' – may not be sufficiently political to form the basis for a more lasting movement.

Amongst older people there have been some examples of political mobilization. In America a radical group called the Grey Panthers have campaigned for the rights of the elderly. However, only a very small minority of older people get involved in political activities related to age. Their circumstances vary widely. They may be affluent or very poor, relatively young and vigorous or extremely elderly and very frail. In these circumstances it is hard for them to identify strongly with each other, let alone with the young (the other disadvantaged age group). Bradley does suggest that the old may become more political in the future, as the generation who were involved in the feminist and student movements of earlier decades reach retirement age.

Conclusion

Bradley concludes that in contemporary societies stratification systems and identities are becoming both polarized and fragmented. There is increasing polarization between the rich and the poor and between the young and the (increasingly long-lived) old. There is also some polarization between ethnic groups – with the re-emergence of nationalist and fascist groups determined to advocate racist policies – and between the affluent and poor elderly.

Inequality has not gone away. Sexism and racism continue to exist alongside ageism, class inequality and other sources of disadvantage. Gender and 'race'/ethnicity are somewhat in the ascendancy over class as sources of active and politicized identities. Age remains more important in terms of individual identities than collective ones. However, all are still important as sources of identity and there is fragmentation and division in each of them.

As a result, people in contemporary societies tend to have fractured identities. They lack a single identity that overarches all others. Nevertheless, people's identities are still essentially social. While there is an element of choice over identity this is not as great as postmodernists believe. Bradley says, 'Few of us can, as yet, choose to be English, male and middle class if we were born Indian, female and working class.'

To Bradley, the fracturing of identities is not new. There have always been divisions between and within different sources of identity, which have made it possible for individuals to have fractured identities. However, recent changes in society have led to increased fragmentation, and people have become more aware of the multiple sources of identity open to them.

Bradley concludes that both modernist and postmodern theories are necessary to understand identity and social change. She says:

A reworked version of modernist analysis, benefiting from the critical insights of postmodern and post-structuralist thought, offers the best hope for an adequate understanding of the double and contradictory nature of contemporary society, both fragmenting and polarizing. Such an approach must grasp the persisting nature of social hierarchies as well as exploring the interplay of relationships which gives rise to the fractured identities characteristic of post-capitalist societies.

Bradley, 1997, p. 214

Culture, identity and values

It is not surprising that in studying culture sociologists have found it difficult to detach themselves from their own cultural values. Like all members of society, sociologists tend to be socialized into seeing certain cultures, particularly their own, as superior to others. A cultural critic such as Matthew Arnold was certainly influenced by his elite upbringing, his work in a public school and the tradition of literary criticism in which certain types of culture were seen as civilized while others were not. The prejudice in favour of elite culture continued in the twentieth century with the work of mass culture critics such as Macdonald.

Sociologists are not just influenced by their upbringing, though. As writers such as Bradley stress, your identity can develop throughout your life and is not fixed from childhood onwards. The identity you have shapes the way you see the world

and, in the case of sociologists, can influence the theories they develop.

Part of the process of developing an adult identity may involve becoming committed to a particular political ideology, which may in turn shape your prejudices about culture. Thus the Marxist sociologist Lucien Goldmann was impressed with the work of Pascal and Racine because their work was such a good expression of the world view of a particular class. The socialist ideas of Raymond Williams led him to take the everyday culture of the working class seriously, and therefore to believe that 'culture' was not just to be found in paintings, literature, music and the like.

Values are not just influenced by your upbringing and the political ideology you follow. They are also influenced by the era in which you live. For some earlier generations of sociologists class was seen as the most important feature of society, and culture could only be explained and evaluated if class assumed a central role in the analysis.

More recently, however, class has rather fallen out of fashion as an explanation for sociological phenomena, or as a central source of identity for sociologists. Indeed, consumption may have become more important to some sociologists' sense of identity. The enormous choice of goods open to affluent middle-class professionals (such as university sociology lecturers) may have made more of an impression on them than any experience of oppression or class conflict.

It is not entirely surprising, then, that some sociologists have embraced postmodern ideas so wholeheartedly. For the advocates of postmodernism all culture is equally valid. There is no distinction between high culture and mass culture. It is just as worthy to visit a shopping mall as it is to visit an opera house; just as valid to watch an episode of a soap opera as it is to watch a play by Shakespeare. All leisure activities and all cultures are worthwhile. The only criterion for evaluating them is whether they are enjoyable.

While such a viewpoint may be preferable to highly elitist views of writers such as Arnold, it is important that sociologists remember that not everybody has the same chance to shape their identity and sample cultures at will as they do. Inequalities continue to shape people's life chances, the cultures they develop, the art forms they prefer and the identities they establish. While no one identity may be better than any other, as Harriet Bradley points out, identities are not simply a matter of choice.

Chapter 13

Communication and the media by Paul Trowler

Communication and the media by Paul Trowler

Introduction: defining the 'mass media'

At one time a good definition of the mass media would have been this:

> The methods and organizations used by specialist social groups to convey messages to large, socially mixed and widely dispersed audiences.

This definition is still useful in some ways. It distinguishes the mass media (communication from a single point to many other points) from interpersonal media (communication from a single point to another single point) and also from network media, which are flexible enough to allow permutations of communication between single, small or large numbers of points in any direction. It also serves to describe the different channels or modes of communication and the ways in which such communication is received: radio, television, film, print and so on.

In the last two decades of the twentieth century, however, this definition became rather less useful. This is because modern communications media have become less 'mass' in character. New technologies – many of which are relatively cheap to produce and purchase – have greatly increased the potential for small-scale communication to specialist audiences. This contrasts with the 'mass' communications media of the past such as large-circulation national magazines and television channels which broadcast programmes to an audience of millions, with little competition from others.

In the last ten years or so there has been an enormous change in the nature of the media and the ways people interact with them. For example, cable, terrestrial and satellite television channels plus widespread cheap access to the Internet and digital technology have spread rapidly from the USA to many other parts of the world. In addition, communication no longer has to be one-way: audiences are now able to interact with the media to some extent, so they are able to exercise some control over the form and sometimes the content of the messages they receive.

In his book *Understanding Media* (1964) the Canadian sociologist Marshall McLuhan suggested that developments in communication were the main force for change in human society. For example, when printing was invented and when electronic media were developed, important social changes began to take place. For McLuhan, therefore, the real importance of the media lies not in their content, but in the way they themselves alter our social world. Today, we see a dynamic and complex relationship between communications media and social change.

Another problem with definitions of 'mass' media like the one at the beginning of this chapter is their assumptions about the nature of the audience. The word 'mass' has its roots in theories of 'mass society' (see Chapter 12). Oliver Boyd-Barrett and Chris Newbold (1995) point out that the concept of 'mass' implies 'great size, homogeneity, lack of distinctiveness or individuality and ... mindless, even irresponsible response'.

Early sociology of the media tended to concentrate on newspapers and television and paid particular attention to news content. More recent sociology has also studied other media and a broader range of content of those media. It has shown that audience responses to media content can be highly individual. Such responses can include pleasure or anger, changes in behaviour, increased understanding, or some other experience.

Many sociologists now believe that each of us makes our own interpretations of media messages. However, they also believe that these interpretations are influenced by our particular social contexts: such things as our ethnicity, our gender and our occupation. Many postmodernist sociologists regard media messages (or 'texts', as such sociologists call them) as polysemic: in other words, each media message or text is capable of being interpreted in a variety of ways. Many sociologists also stress the influence of the immediate context of viewing on our interpretation of media messages: for example, whether a message is viewed at home or elsewhere, alone or with others, while doing nothing else or engaged in other activities.

For these and many other reasons it is extremely difficult to devise a satisfactory definition of communication media. It is important, therefore, to bear this in mind when we study sociological theories about the content, influence and effects of media communications.

Role and influence of the media: structure and content

Pluralist theories

'Pluralism' is a label generally applied to theories of the media that were popular in the first 70 years of the twentieth century. (See Chapter 9 for a more detailed description of pluralism.)

Pluralists argue that society is made up of many interacting but competing sections. These sections of society have more or less equal access to resources and influence, and they are policed by a benign and neutral state operating in the public interest. According to pluralists, different parts of the media cater to these various sections of society. The media reflect society: just as there is diversity within society, so there is diversity in media content. Because the media *reflect* society in this way, they are unlikely to have much effect in changing society.

Pluralism appears in the work of many media commentators, particularly in the ideas of media workers themselves. Indeed, many of the early studies of media content and effects that came to be labelled 'pluralist' were funded by the media industry. A more recent example of this is Martin Harrison's (1985) study of the work of the Glasgow Media Group (see p. 937).

An example of a pluralist author who is also a media professional is Nicholas Jones, who is a correspondent on BBC radio news. Jones (1986) argues that radio news is neutral, fair and balanced: in other words, his claim is that, taken as a whole, radio news reporting does not take sides, it reports all relevant views about an event and it gives such views equal emphasis. Jones examined the media's reporting of industrial disputes and claimed that any *apparent* bias in reporting depends on how successful workers or management are in obtaining suitable media coverage of their argument. Jones believes that industrial disputes are increasingly about publicity: each side tries to gain media approval in the hope that this will help it win its case.

An illustration: Katz and Lazarsfeld

Personal Influence by Elihu Katz and Paul Lazarsfeld is a classic pluralist text. It was published in 1955 and based on data collected in 1945. The basic question underlying this study is how far the media influence opinions and attitudes, particularly political opinions and voting behaviour. Katz and Lazarsfeld note that:

> *fundamentally all communications research aims at the study of effect [but] there are a variety of possible effects that the mass media may have upon society, and several different dimensions along which effects may be classified.*
>
> Katz and Lazarsfeld, 1955, p. 124

They argue that in general the media have a rather limited influence. This is because the mass communication process can be affected in unpredictable ways by five 'variables':

1 Variable exposure, access or attention to media messages. Personal, political, practical or technological factors can shape the nature and extent of an individual's or group's exposure to any particular message or medium.

2 The type of medium used to convey the message has an important impact on the power of the message. For example, television footage of starving children may have a more powerful effect than a newspaper report about the same event.

3 The nature of the content, and the form, presentation and language of the message will have important consequences for its effect. This is illustrated by the national response to the killing of black teenager Stephen Lawrence after its reporting in the press and media, and the subsequent changes to recruitment and training practices in the police service.

4 Beliefs and attitudes among members of the audience can modify or completely distort the meaning of a given message:

> *For example, a prejudiced person whose attitude towards an out-group is strongly entrenched may actively resist a message of tolerance in such a way that the message may be perceived as a defence of prejudice or as irrelevant to the subject of prejudice entirely.*
>
> Katz and Lazarsfeld, 1955, p. 127

5 Leaders and opinion-makers within communities can mediate messages received from the mass media. For example, people tend to vote in the way their spouses, parents, fellow club members or fellow

employees vote, not in the way the dominant media messages tell them to vote. Thus, pluralists argue that power and status are of little relevance in this context: 'Some individuals of high social status apparently wield little independent influence and some of low status have considerable personal influence' (Katz and Lazarsfeld, 1955).

Criticisms of pluralism

The next section examines the main criticisms of this kind of pluralist thinking, particularly those made by Marxist and neo-Marxist writers. However, here are two important criticisms that are often made.

First, it is claimed that pluralist theorists are frequently part of, or funded by, the media industries themselves. Early pluralists, called 'administrative researchers', were funded in this way, which raised questions about their impartiality (Boyd-Barrett, 1985). More recently, Greg Philo (1986), Director of the Glasgow Media Group, has accused the major pluralist critic of their work, Martin Harrison, of more or less being a spokesperson for Independent Television News (ITN), which provided Harrison with selective access to transcripts of its news coverage and used him in its own interests.

Second, the pluralist claim that the media are generally diverse and neutral is criticized in terms of what Jay Blumler and Michael Gurevitch (1995) call the 'emergent shared culture' of politicians and press and television journalists.

Blumler and Gurevitch claim that journalists and politicians depend on one another and adapt to one another's requirements. Politicians need journalists to help them persuade people to adopt a certain view (of themselves, their party or what they are trying to achieve). Journalists need politicians for the interviews, news, action and comment that they require. Rules and understandings emerge on both sides and a certain degree of trust is built up. Patterns of behaviour develop and become simply 'what is expected'. Interaction between journalists and politicians becomes predictable and taken for granted.

The result, though, is that journalistic diversity narrows, journalistic 'objectivity' is compromised, and media content becomes prey to professional 'spin doctors'. It was for these reasons that Guardian newspaper journalists refused for a time to participate in the parliamentary 'lobby' system. This system formed a major part of the shared culture by giving newspapers access to privileged (and heavily 'spun') information as long as the sources of such information were not disclosed.

However, as we shall see, the main difficulty with the pluralist model is that it *assumes* rather than *demonstrates* that media content as a whole is highly diverse. The two theories examined below challenge this assumption and so reach quite different conclusions about the nature of media effects.

Marxist theories

Marxist theories sharply contradict pluralism (see Chapter 15). In *The German Ideology* Karl Marx states that 'in every epoch, the ruling ideas are the ideas of the ruling class' (Marx and Engels, 1970, first published 1846). Contemporary Marxists believe that the media are the means by which the ideas of the ruling class maintain their dominance as the 'ruling ideas'.

Marxists argue, for example, that ruling ideas are very apparent in advertising: adverts help promote manufactured goods by stimulating aspirations about lifestyles and ways of behaving generally. They attach connotative codes to material objects: in other words, advertised products are associated with a range of positive attitudes, feelings and desires within an audience, which help the products to sell.

Politically the 'ruling ideas' set the agenda, excluding some possibilities and normalizing others so that they become 'just common sense'.

Ruling ideas control the information we have about the world and even shape our leisure activities. Marxists claim that this is largely because the capitalist class has access to the resources which enable its members to present their ideas as 'normal'. Consequently, there is a striking lack of diversity within media messages. Although media sources and messages *appear* diverse, in reality there is centralized ownership: a few media corporations own and operate most media.

These media corporations are huge and they dominate the industry. The many businesses within these corporations support and promote each other's operations (this is called synergy). Thus, for example, the *Sun* newspaper will promote the interests of BskyB television because Rupert Murdoch's News Corporation has controlling interests in both (Belfield, Hird and Kelly, 1994). In this way, films like *Star Wars* are able to obtain saturation coverage on a global basis.

Ben Bagdikian (1997) has pointed out that if each of the USA's daily newspapers, magazines, radio and television stations and book publishers were owned by separate individuals there would be 25,000 owners. In fact, only ten corporations dominate ownership of daily newspapers, magazines, broadcast and cable television, books and films. Figure 13.1 illustrates the diversity of the holdings of one of these corporations, Time Warner.

There is much evidence to suggest that the process of monopolization described by Marx has taken place in the media industry. According to Bagdikian, in the 1980s there were 50 dominant media corporations in

Figure 13.1 Time Warner Select US Holdings, 1998

Film
Castle Rock Entertainment
Fine Line Features
HBO Pictures
New Line Cinema
Turner Original Productions
Warner Bros. Studios (including a
    library of 6,000 films, Looney
    Tunes cartoons, and 29,000
    television programme episodes)

Home Video
HBO Home Video
New Line Home Video
Warner Home Video (world's leading home
    video distributor)
Warner/Reprise Home Video

Cable Television
Cable News Network (CNN)
CNN Airport Network
CNNfn
CNN Headline News
CNN/SI
Cartoon Network
Cinemax
Comedy Central
Court TV
Home Box Office
TBS Superstation
TNT
Turner Classic Movies (TCM)
Time Warner Home Theater (pay-per-view)
Time Warner Cable (in 12 million homes,
    including 1.1 million subscribers in New
    York city) 24-hour cable news channels
    in New York, Rochester, Tampa, and
    Orlando

Television
Castle Rock (producer of *Seinfeld*)
Hanna-Barbera Cartoons
Kids WB!
New Line Television
Telepictures Productions (producer of
    Jenny Jones & *The Rosie O'Donnell
    Show*)
WB Television Network
Warner Bros. Domestic Television
    Distribution
Warner Bros. Television (biggest
    producer of network prime time
    programming, including *ER*, *Friends*,
    and *Murphy Brown*)
Warner Bros. Television Animation

Publishing
Backbay Books
Book-of-the-Month Club
Bullfinch Press
Children's Book of the Month Club
History Book Club
Leisure Arts
Little Brown
Oxmoor House
Paperback Book Club
Sunset Books
Time Life Books
Time Warner Audio Books
Time Warner Electronic Publishing
Warner Books

Magazines
More than 30 magazines, including:
Baby Talk
Coastal Living
Cooking Light
DC Comics
Entertainment Weekly
Food & Wine
Fortune
Health
Hippocrates
Inside Stuff
In Style
Life
MAD
Money
Parenting
People
People en Espanol
Progressive Farmer
Southern Living
Southern Accents
Sports Illustrated
Sports Illustrated for Kids
Sunset, the Magazine of Western Living
Teen People
This Old House
Time
Time for Kids
Weight Watchers
Who Weekly
Your Company

Other Entertainment Holdings
CNN Radio
HBO Store
Time Warner Telecom
Warner Bros. Consumer Products
Warner Bros. Studio Stores (185 stores)

Music
American Recordings
Asylum Records
Atlantic Classics
Atlantic Nashville
Atlantic Records
Beggars Banquet
Big Beat
Celtic Heartbeat
Columbia House Music Club
Curb Records
East/West Records
Elektra Records
Giant Records
Interscope
Lava
Matador Records
Maverick Records
Mesa/Bluemoon
Qwest Records
Reprise Records
Rhino Records
Sire Records
Slash Records
Tag Records
Tommy Boy
Warner Bros. Music
Warner Music Group
Warner Nashville
Turner Music Publishing
Warner/Chappell Music (owner of more
    than 1 million songs)
WEA Corp. (home entertainment
    distribution)
WEA Manufacturing (CD, cassette
    production)

Multimedia
CNN Interactive (http://www.cnn.com)
Pathfinder (more than 50 Websites;
    http://www.pathfinder.com)
Road Runner (high-speed Internet service
    provider affiliated with
    Time Warner Cable)
Time Warner Interactive
    (http://www.timewarner.com)

Sports
Atlanta Braves (Major League Baseball)
Atlanta Hawks (National Football League)
Atlanta Thrashers (National Hockey
    League)
Goodwill Games
Turner Sports
World Championship Wrestling

Source: D. Croteau and W. Hoynes (2000) *Media Society: Industry, Images and Audiences*, Pine Forge, London, pp. 43-4.

the USA, and at that time they tended to concentrate on one medium only. By 1990 the number had fallen to 23; by 1997 it was 10. Mergers and acquisitions continue, so that by the early years of the twenty-first century we can expect even fewer to dominate. Bagdikian writes:

> In the last five years a small number of the country's largest industrial corporations have acquired more public communications power – including ownership of the news – than any private business has ever before possessed in world history. ... [Together they] have created what is, in effect, a new communications cartel within the United States.
>
> Bagdikian, 1997, pp. xii, ix

In January 2000, Time Warner (whose diverse interests are summarized above) merged with America Online, the world's biggest Internet service provider. This is the largest take-over ever (a friendly one in this case). The new company, AOL Time Warner, will be headed by Steve Case who said, 'By joining forces ... we will fundamentally change the way people get information, communicate with others, buy products and are entertained' (quoted in the *Guardian*, 11 January 2000).

Similarly, Oliver Boyd-Barrett and Terhi Rantanen (1998) note that the influence of news organizations is increasingly global in scale. In addition, the same individuals tend to appear on the boards of different corporations, both within the media and in other crucial sectors of the economy. This is partly because large corporations themselves are no longer just media corporations but are involved in many sectors of the capitalist economy: Sony owns Columbia, Westinghouse owns CBS, General Electric owns NBC, and so forth.

For most Marxists, it is the logic of capitalism that dictates the content and effects of the mass media. The poor and the powerless are not a profitable market for large capitalist corporations and so they are largely ignored. In the USA the *Saturday Evening Post* was driven out of business because it failed to attract advertisers: its readership was simply not attractive to them. The same thing happened in the UK to the *News on Sunday*, which described itself in its Editorial Charter as a:

> socialist publication [which] will remain independent of all political parties and institutions. [It] recognizes that Britain is a society based on the unequal ownership of wealth, prosperity and power, and will seek to inform the readers of such inequalities, their causes and effects.

Launched in 1987, the *News on Sunday* closed after only seven months.

Bagdikian also shows that capitalism's corporate logic means that the interests of the affluent extend into news coverage too. For example, the news media pay close attention to any drop in the stock market which may harm the interests of the minority of the population with significant shareholdings, but they pay almost no attention to a decline in the buying power of the minimum wage, which dropped by 35 per cent between 1987 and 1994 in the USA.

This 'logic of capitalism' argument even appeals to researchers who are not Marxists. In *Television and Beyond* (1990) Ellen Wartella and others show that there is extremely little diversity in children's programming as a result of the same capitalist logic. They conducted a survey of all audio-video programming available to children in the Champaign–Urbana area of Illinois in the USA. The survey results showed extremely limited variety (different programmes across different types of media) and extremely limited diversity (different types of programming within one medium). Diversity was only available to those families who could afford cable television:

> The most striking characteristic of these data is their clear indication that there is no diversity of children's programming on commercial television. All the weekday commercial children's programmes are cartoons; two thirds of these are toy related. ... Weekend commercial television provides minimal diversity: only 3 of the 28 commercial children's programmes over the weekend are not cartoons.

Wartella *et al.*, 1990, pp. 51–4

Those who could afford to subscribe to cable, however, had access to a far wider variety of programmes, including live action, comedy, drama, quiz shows, instructional programmes, and so on. The study thus confirms the predictions made by earlier authors such as Garnham (1986), who foresaw the polarization of society into one section rich in media and information, and another section poor in media and information:

> A two-tier market divided between the information rich, provided with high-cost specialized information and cultural services, and the information poor, provided with increasingly homogenized entertainment series on a mass scale.

Garnham, 1986, p. 38

For another strand of Marxist thinking, however, the processes involved are less subtle than those just described. The direct manipulation of media content by corporation chiefs is well documented. For example, newspaper editors working for Rupert Murdoch tell stories about his telephone calls directing the content of the front page. They admit that this influences their decisions and leads to self-censorship (Evans, 1994).

Ken Auletta (1991) tells how in the USA the purchase of NBC News by General Electric led to conflicts about the content and role of the television news - conflicts which the new owners won. Stories abound of the 'dumbing down' of news output after their being taken over by conglomerates.

Criticisms of Marxism

Marxist perspectives tend to underestimate the state's regulation of the media, which can set limits to media ownership, and hence control of content. For example, Rupert Murdoch was excluded from bids for the fifth national terrestrial television channel in the UK (Channel 5) because of his extensive media ownership.

In Europe, European Union competition law was applied to a proposed joint pay-television venture between the Kirch Group, Deutsche Telekom and Bertelsmann. The proposal was ruled incompatible with European competition rules because it would have inhibited the entry of others into the German market: Kirch already had a cable monopoly and the other two firms dominated programming and pay-television. Jeanette Steemers concludes:

> Broadcasting is far from dead, but its future health with regard to market dominance, and the safeguarding of plurality and diversity, depends on the outcome of regulatory efforts at both a national and EU level.

Steemers, 1999, p. 245

A related point is that Marxist perspectives usually focus on media ownership. If, however, we consider audiences, it soon becomes clear that terrestrial television is the 'most consumed' medium. In general, people spend seven times longer watching television than reading newspapers.

The IPA *Trends in Television Report* for the fourth quarter of 1998 showed a gradual increase in the amount of television being watched, with viewing up to an average of 3.61 hours per day. This took the average above 3.59 for the first time since 1994.

For pluralists, the dominance of television is reassuring because it is precisely the medium over which national government and regulative bodies like the Independent Television Commission and Broadcasting Standards Commission have the most control.

Table 13.1 Media concentration (TV, newspapers and radio) by time use, 1993/4	
Media group	**% share of audience**
BBC	19.7
News International	10.6
ITV Network	9.4
Daily Mail Trust	7.8
Mirror Group Newspapers	7.6
United Newspapers	5.7
Carlton Communications	3.1
Channel 4	2.9

Source: T. Congdon *et al.* (1995) *The Cross Media Revolution,* John Libbey, London.

According to pluralist theories, the content of the media is largely dictated by market demand rather than by ruling ideas and the interests of the affluent. Thus, *control* rather than *ownership* is the important factor in determining the output of the media.

Market share and profitability are of main interest to managers, not social or political influence. For example, although Rupert Murdoch's News Corporation bought Fox Television in the mid-1980s, it became successful by broadcasting anti-establishment programmes like *Married ... with Children* and *The Simpsons*. These series challenged 'traditional' family values, in sharp contrast to bland programmes on other channels such as *The Cosby Show*. Profits rose and Fox did well, beating the powerful and well-established CBS on viewing figures for 18–49-year-olds in 1993.

Ignoring or manipulating the demands of the market can prove expensive, as News Corporation also discovered when it took over *TV Guide*

magazine and moved its editorial content downmarket. It lost sales of half a million copies in the first year of ownership. There had been a place in the market for serious journalism in this listings magazine. By removing it the magazine lost its distinctiveness and its market share.

We shall look at postmodernist theories in detail below (see pp. 949–50). Postmodernists argue that power is not concentrated in a few hands; rather, power *circulates* in a fluid way. For example, public opinion triumphed over corporate interest, with the *assistance* of the media, when Shell decided to dismantle and recycle the Brent Spar oil platform in 1998.

The Brent Spar was a massive structure used by Shell in its oil-drilling operations. It had ceased to be useful and was simply going to be dumped on the ocean floor, despite its enormous bulk and hazardous polluting chemicals. Shell's change of mind was the result of a public outcry over the threat of environmental damage. Temporary alliances were formed between different interest groups and included individuals not usually involved in pressure politics.

This example shows that, as such issues arise, some groups become active and mobilize their forces to do battle. The outcomes of these battles are not predetermined and the role of the media varies from one to another.

Neo-Marxist theories: cultural hegemony

Neo-Marxist arguments place less emphasis than Marxist ones on the logic of capitalism to explain the content and effects of the mass media. Rather, they stress the idea that the culture of the dominant class is reproduced in taken-for-granted ways through the mass media. This is part of what is known as cultural hegemony: the domination of one set of ideas over others.

This hegemonic model is a more sophisticated version of Marxism. It is associated with the work of the Italian Marxist Antonio Gramsci. Such thinkers view ideology (see below) as more important than the simple pursuit of economic interest. Most people (journalists and others) genuinely act according to their beliefs, which are not necessarily determined by (although they are linked to) their class position. Dominance is instead accomplished at the *unconscious* level.

Neo-Marxists argue that the media *make* meanings and organize them into systems or codes which help to make the world comprehensible to viewers and readers: they provide order and help us link together what would otherwise appear to be separate events. However, only a relatively small number of codes –

organized into an ideology – are used to interpret reality: these become taken-for-granted sets of ideas. They are so taken for granted that they are 'invisible' to those who use them to interpret the world.

This hegemonic view does not suggest that there is no space available for competing viewpoints: the media-propagated ideology is dominant, but it is not monopolistic. The social world does involve struggle between competing ideologies and there are challenges to current social organization.

Stuart Hall and cultural hegemony

Stuart Hall argues that each culture in society has a different way of classifying the world. All of the ways in which a culture communicates, including the communications of the mass media, contain systems of signs which represent aspects of its world view. Different kinds of meaning can be given to the same set of events. As a result:

> In order for one meaning to be regularly produced, it had to win a kind of ... taken-for-grantedness for itself. That involved marginalizing, downgrading or de-legitimating alternative constructions. Indeed, there were certain kinds of explanation which, given the power of and credibility acquired by the preferred range of meanings, were literally unthinkable or unsayable.
>
> Hall, 1995, p. 355

According to Hall, the media encode the meanings of the powerful. They are able to do this because they – or at least the majority of them – operate within a framework of consensus (agreement). This consensus is *constructed*: it is an educated, learnt consent, to which the media are central. This is rarely the result of conscious or deliberate manipulation by the state or by powerful interests: if this were the case (and were seen to be the case by the population at large) the legitimacy of media messages would be undermined. Rather, it is unconscious, taken for granted. For instance:

> When phrasing a question ... a broadcasting interviewer simply takes it for granted that rising wage demands are the sole cause of inflation, he is both 'freely formulating a question' on behalf of the public and establishing a logic which is compatible with the dominant interests in society. ... The ideology has 'worked' in such a case because the discourse has spoken itself through him/her.
>
> Hall, 1995, p. 363

Cultural hegemony and the social construction of meaning

Hall's approach fits very closely with the direction sociology took during the 1980s. This new direction became known as the 'linguistic turn': the examina-tion of the ways in which patterns of communication in society shape our view of reality.

Jonathan Potter and Margaret Wetherell (1987) use a newspaper article as an example of this approach:

> *Islamic Terrorists Blow Up Plane*
> In Beirut last night the hijackers of the British Airways 727 finally released the passengers and crew. As the gunmen left they detonated a large quantity of explosive and the plane was quickly gutted by fire. This followed a period of intense negotiation in which the authorities made it clear that they were not going to meet the hijackers' main demands.

Potter and Wetherell make a number of points about this article. First, a newspaper reader would be very familiar with this type of story. It fits into a stereo-typical pattern which we categorize as 'hijackings'. Second, some of the terms in the story are loaded with evaluations: 'the gunmen', 'hijackers' and 'terrorists' all have negative associations. Third, the combined effect is to place this story firmly into ways of thinking and understanding the world, in much the way that Stuart Hall suggests.

Discourse analysis

Norman Fairclough (1995) shows how discourse analysis can uncover the role of the media in the production of cultural hegemony. (For a discussion of discourse analysis, see p. 635.)

In his study of a 1993 edition of the television programme *Crimewatch UK*, Fairclough describes how a crime is re-enacted for the cameras, how the presenter comments on it and appeals for help, and how at the end a police officer provides further information. Friends, family and sometimes victims themselves are included in the presentation, as are members of the rescue services. Thus, there are three 'voices': police, journalists and 'ordinary people'. The commentary to the re-enactment provides immediacy by using the historic present tense ('It's six o'clock and Claire is ...'), and by appealing directly to the viewer ('Were you in the vicinity?'). The personal lives of victims are described in detail and witnesses speak in everyday language ('It suddenly dawned on me ...'), so that the presentation is made more like a soap opera. Another kind of programme, the biography, is also appealed to ('She was in the Duke of Edinburgh Scheme'), as are police programmes like *Inspector Morse*.

In discourse analysis this is referred to as intertex-tuality: the styles, methods and content of different sorts of texts (in this case, television programmes) are drawn upon and are made to do interpretive work in other contexts. Fairclough demonstrates the complex nature of *Crimewatch*'s discourse in this regard, with its mix of reconstruction, drama, narrative, public appeal, police work and biography.

According to Fairclough, *Crimewatch* and programmes like it represent 'an intervention into the fraught relationship in contemporary society between the state and the people'. Politicians and state institutions have lost much of their public credibility, and there is a crisis of legitimacy for the police, who are often portrayed as corrupt and inept, in contrast to a nostalgic vision of 'the bobby on his beat' in the past. *Crimewatch* is fighting a rearguard action in this context, reconstructing a relationship of trust and cooperation. The programme presents the work of policing as a joint effort between police, journalists and ordinary people: 'We have, then, a crossing of boundaries and a merging of voices and practices which powerfully domesticates and so legitimizes police work.'

The key point of this approach is that discourse does not just represent reality, it *creates* it. A problem with discourse analysis, however, is that it represents only the analyst's reading: in this case Fairclough's. Messages are polysemic and audience reception studies (discussed below) show how complex it is to decode media messages. Fairclough acknowledges this at the end of his account of how *Crimewatch* legitimizes police work and redefines the relationship between the public and the state: 'Or at least appears to do so: it would be fascinating to know what audiences make of this programme.'

The Glasgow Media Group and cultural hegemony

The Glasgow Media Group has made many studies of television news. It has concluded that the world view of journalists serves to predetermine and structure what is to be taken as important or significant and what interpretation is to be placed upon it. This fundamentally affects the character and content of 'the news'. The Group's studies examine the evidence to test and illustrate the cultural hegemony argument.

In *Bad News* (1976), *More Bad News* (1980), *Really Bad News* (1982) and *War and Peace News* (1985) content analysis of television output, and the quantification of types of stories and the way they are presented, are used to demonstrate the partial nature of television news reporting (see Chapter 14 for a discussion of content analysis). They conclude that:

- The discourse of broadcast news is 'ideologically loaded'. Phrases which evoke attitudes and emotions ('connotative codes') - such as 'trouble', 'radical', 'pointless strike', etc. - all structure listeners' perspectives on stories.
- Visuals are similarly loaded with connotative codes.

The camera recording from behind police lines encourages the viewer to identify with the police. The contrast between calm studio shots of managers being interviewed and groups of strikers shouting over each other at the factory gates reinforces dominant messages of dangerous strikers.

- Stories are reported in a way that reproduces the viewpoint of powerful interests because these interests have greater access to the media. Their viewpoints appear 'normal' to journalists.
- Media professionals set the agenda about the most important issues of the day. For example, the effects of strikes are more likely to be reported than their causes. Picket-line violence is emphasized rather than police violence and intimidation. Such dominant themes are likely to recur in the news and serve to reinforce each other.
- Content analysis by the Group suggests that news coverage of party politics is sympathetic towards the political centre ground. What media professionals see as 'extremism' will be treated unsympathetically or remain unreported.

In these ways and others, television news very largely echoes the interests and attitudes of the dominant class in society. The effects of this world view are two-fold. First, it defines what counts as 'news', whose opinions are important enough to be sought, who should be interviewed and so on. Second, it provides journalists with a way of interpreting events and 'explaining' them.

In *War and Peace News* (1985) and *Getting the Message* (1993) the Glasgow Media Group added some elements from traditional Marxist theory to their analysis of media bias. For example, they stress the pressures on broadcasting journalists to present the establishment viewpoint, even if it does not accord with their own view. Sometimes, however, journalists can 'escape' these pressures and present a critical point of view or even one that is anti-establishment. Jonathan Dimbleby is named specifically as a television journalist whose views are out of the ordinary for a journalist, and who has been able to use the media to express them.

In their 1990 publication *Seeing and Believing*, the Glasgow Media Group moved from studies of media content to audience studies, usually using group discussions and various group exercises. Here they note, in agreement with Stuart Hall, that audiences do not always accept or believe what they are told. Their cultural background, their experience (of actually being on a picket line, for example) and other characteristics can enable them to 'read' media messages in a variety of ways.

The Glasgow Media Group has moved from a position which simply 'read off' or assumed media effect from an examination of media content. It now theorizes what it calls a circuit of communication. This circuit is a system of communication in which production, content and reception of messages are constantly affecting each other, although in unequal ways.

Criticisms of cultural hegemony

Theories of cultural hegemony are criticized by pluralists, who point out that not all journalists share a dominant ideology. Many journalists attempt to expose the unacceptable sides of capitalism. The Watergate scandal, which toppled from power the US president Richard Nixon, is just one example of the sort of work of such reporters. Similarly, in the late 1990s, press reporting of Tory 'sleaze' was instrumental in triggering the downfall of three Conservative politicians: Neil Hamilton, Jonathan Aitken and Jeffrey Archer.

The model of cultural hegemony assumes a single unified culture among media professionals, but this is highly questionable. Postmodern perspectives argue that organizations have multiple cultures, many of which can be in conflict. An example of such cultural complexity in a media organization is provided by journalist Mike Royko, who describes the purchase of the *Chicago Sun-Times*, a successful quality newspaper, by Rupert Murdoch's News Corporation:

> *We knew that there had been publications that he basically left alone, like the* Village Voice, *and we thought that he might do that here, since this was a very successful quality newspaper. But as soon as his people started coming in, it was clear that this wasn't their intention. They came in like a bunch of pirates. It's unusual for a Chicago newspaper guy to view somebody coming in as a bunch of thugs – I mean, we're generally thought of as pretty hard-nosed newspaper people.*
>
> Quoted in Belfield and Hird, 1994, p. 79

Pluralists argue that the media cannot reflect the views of the dominant class in Britain because sections of that class are highly critical of much of the political and other reporting of the broadcast media. Like media professionals, the dominant class is itself extremely varied in character. Those on the political right frequently argue that there is a liberal 'bias' in the BBC and some of the other media.

In 1986 the Conservative Party Chairman Norman Tebbitt complained bitterly about the BBC's reporting of an American bombing raid on Libya. Other examples include a *Panorama* programme during the Falklands dispute (April 1982) which was criticized by some as anti-British; and another about right-wing infiltration of the Conservative Party (called *Maggie's Militant Tendency*), broadcast in January 1984. The latter caused extreme anger in the government. It resulted in a court case brought by two Conservative MPs. The case was settled out of court and an apology was made by the BBC.

Organizational factors: media occupations and professionals

The internal characteristics of media organizations provide useful information which helps to explain media content and effects. For instance, Johnathan Bignell (1997) points out that 'news' is not a fixed category: how it is interpreted depends on the type of media involved. Quality newspapers have more foreign news, tabloids more personality-based news. It is the professional workers within media organizations who make selections based on the values within their organization. Galtung and Ruge (1965) describe the conscious and unconscious criteria used by journalists in this process. The more criteria a potential story fulfils, the more likely it is that the story will be printed. Here are some of the criteria that Galtung and Ruge list:

- Frequency: short-lived events are preferred to long processes.
- Threshold: the more intense the event, the more preferred it is (for example, a very large annual increase in road deaths as opposed to a small one).
- Unambiguity: the more easily interpreted an event is, the better, particularly if it fits into a known category of news stories, such as 'royal stories'.
- Meaningfulness: relevance to the assumed reader.
- Consonance: the story's closeness to the assumed reader's expectations or desires (for example, the demand for news about a royal marriage).
- Unexpectedness: unexpected events are preferred to expected ones.
- Reference to elite nations: stories about powerful (rather than powerless) nations are preferred.
- Reference to elite persons: stories about powerful or famous people are preferred to stories about powerless or obscure people.
- Reference to persons: stories which can be simplified by personifying the issues into one or more people are desirable, especially if there is conflict between these people.
- Reference to something negative: bad news is more 'newsworthy' than good news.

Media organizations: structure and agency

The above approaches have their limitations. Oliver Boyd-Barrett (1995) points out that media professionals are also influenced by social structures over which they have limited control. He claims that studies such as that of Galtung and Ruge (1965) fail to explore the origin of the sets of values they identify. They stress what is known as active gatekeeping: the systematic inclusion or exclusion of certain types of content. They attribute too much to human agency and remain unaware of the structural constraints placed upon it. As Boyd-Barrett puts it, 'news values have to be explained as well as identified'. Cultural hegemony theories are able to do this in terms of the dominant world view which shapes the perceptions and choices of media professionals.

There are other sets of structural factors which condition media content. First, there are recurrent practices within organizations, which have grown up over a long period of time. They are not necessarily obvious to media professionals or to audiences because they are so taken for granted. Lawrence Grossberg *et al.* provide an example from American television:

> In the television industry ... the evening news programme ... will open with a teaser of the top few stories and a brief tape clip [and] will feature a half-dozen hard news stories, all or almost all with tape; none ... longer than 90 seconds. There will be a male and female anchor (the male ... older than the female), a weather person, and a sports anchor. One or two will be members of a minority group. ... The news team will send us off with a 'feel good feature'. The form is set and so familiar we rarely notice it, much less stop to ask why. A large part of the answer ... is that there are industrywide constraints – unwritten 'rules' that characterize what TV is. ... They maintain themselves because they are familiar, taken for granted ... by both those in the industry and the audience.
>
> Grossberg *et al.*, 1998, p. 62

CBS president Rob Wood said that his freshest ideas came in his early years at the top. After a time 'you learn the rules too well and don't think in new directions' (Turow, 1982).

Second, there are the constraints of production processes, which frequently affect what is possible. The origins of much news coverage, for example, often lie in official sources such as press conferences, parliamentary reports and camera coverage, interviews with government ministers and so on. Regular 'diary' events provide a staple diet for news organizations, reappearing each year. The demand for a constant, predictable supply of news to the newsroom demands that this is so. Technical conditions often influence what is *not* in the news: the absence of cameras or the costs associated with news-gathering in distant places will mean that some stories never reach the newsroom.

Role and influence of the media: audiences and their responses

This section explores the relationship between media messages and the audience. Sociological thinking about this relationship has developed from simple models of cause and effect to increasingly complex models about the nature of media texts, the audience and 'effects'.

The hypodermic model

This early model makes an analogy between media messages and a drug injected by a hypodermic syringe. The medium itself (television, newspapers, film, etc.) is the syringe; the medium's message or content is what is injected. The audience is the patient. This medical model of media influence is found in the titles of books, even recent ones. The concept of narcotization also draws on this model: narcotization refers to the political, physical and mental apathy supposedly induced by the 'mass' media. The Frankfurt School's Herbert Marcuse writes in *One Dimensional Man* (1964) that 'the hypnotic power of the mass media deprives us of the capacity for critical thought which is essential if we are to change the world'.

Shannon and Weaver's (1949) early model of media effect, shown in Figure 13.2, is essentially a hypodermic model, although they recognize that external factors ('noise') may introduce differences between the message transmitted and that received.

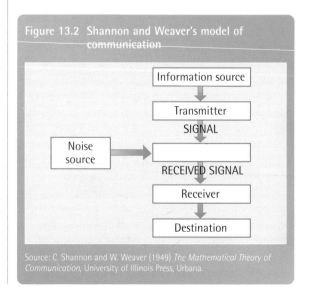

Figure 13.2 Shannon and Weaver's model of communication

Source: C. Shannon and W. Weaver (1949) *The Mathematical Theory of Communication*, University of Illinois Press, Urbana.

The hypodermic model is now out of favour, but in early studies of the media it was usually at least implicit. Laboratory studies conducted by psychologists like Bandura, Ross and Ross (1963) looked for simple cause-and-effect relationships between a media message and audience response. They concluded that film images are as effective in teaching aggression as real-life models, particularly in boys, who tended to imitate the postures, actions and words of film aggressors they had seen.

For Bandura and his colleagues, their experiments confirmed the 'imitative' model of media effects. This is a development of the social learning approach, which suggests that people learn new behaviours through their observation of the behaviour of others (Miller and Dollard, 1941). This is a very simple hypodermic model, to which Bandura added the idea that learning is more effective if the observed behaviour is reinforced in the daily life of the observer, including via media messages. Attractive film characters behaving in particular ways and being rewarded for their behaviour are ways in which imitative behaviour can be reinforced. This is referred to as the disinhibitory effect.

The problems with this kind of approach are, first, that it is unable to define what it means by 'violence' or other behaviours that are supposedly imitated:

There appears to be considerable confusion as to what is filmed aggression. For some it is an adult hitting a ... doll, for others a prize fight, and for [others] ... it is Westerns or war shows. Few investigators, if any, seem to be concerned that different types of filmed aggression will have different effects on different types of children.

Noble, 1975, p. 141

Second, as we have already discussed, audiences are highly diverse and have different responses.

Third, the imitative or social learning model tends to concentrate on short-term effects only, and ignores the cumulative effects of exposure to many messages in the normal course of daily life.

Fourth, the model largely fails to take into account the different 'uses' audience members make of media content and the different ways there are of interacting with the medium (for example, whether a television programme is watched closely or used as background).

Fifth, the model ignores other media effects. Eysenck and Nias (1978) point out that media messages may enable individuals to express and discharge powerful emotions safely and thus prevent behaviours that might otherwise have happened. Media messages may desensitize individuals to the effects of violence (for example, by not showing them), but they may also *sensitize* individuals to

violence when its effects are shown, thus perhaps preventing violence in real life.

However, despite all these problems, this model of media effects is still very popular. The mass media themselves tend to reproduce it when they report crimes that were supposedly 'caused' by the media. Politicians and campaigners against sex and violence in the media also assume this model when they argue for greater censorship or complain about particular programmes.

The normative model and the two-step flow

'Normative' refers to ways of behaving that come to be considered as 'normal' and that regulate social interaction. The normative model is a more sophisticated *social* theory of media influence than the hypodermic model.

Studies in the 1940s and 1950s like Robert Merton's *Mass Persuasion* (1946) and Katz and Lazarsfeld's *Personal Influence* (1955) (see pp. 936–7) discovered that a two-step flow process of media influence was operating. The first step is when a media message actually reaches a member of the audience. The second step is its interpretation and influence, which are affected by social interaction. Such social interaction means that other people, but especially those whose views are respected ('opinion leaders'), shape how an individual responds to the media and any effects that the media have.

An extension of the two-step flow idea is the multi-step flow model, which recognizes that there are successive stages in the social interpretation of media messages. Such messages are discussed and used in everyday life and become integrated into the cultural world. An example of this process is provided by Dorothy Hobson (1990). Hobson describes her research on 'Jacqui', a telephone sales manager for an internationally known pharmaceutical company. Jacqui described how women in her office spent some of their working day:

Somebody would say something like 'Who saw Coronation Street *last night?' and Anita would say 'Oh, I saw it!', and you'd sort of have Mary sitting there going 'Oh, my God!', and making comments about* Coronation Street *and doing some stupid impression beneath the desk and you'd say 'Shut up Mary, shut up!', and everybody would go 'Ssh, ssh, Anita, tell us what happened.' ... Anita ... would go into great detail about what had happened and ... everybody would sit and listen and if you'd seen it the night before and she missed bits out you'd say 'Er, wait a minute, he wasn't very happy about that', or whatever.*

Hobson, 1990, p. 78

The conversation quickly turned to their own lives and interests and to discussions of what they would do if they were in the same circumstances as the characters. Women in the office were enticed to watch these programmes just so that they could join in the discussions.

Hobson's kind of approach is useful because it focuses clearly on media audiences and what they do with messages. However, it pictures people as strongly conditioned by their environment, particularly by opinion leaders and by social norms. In practice people can create and change norms, break them and redefine them. The theory is also unclear about whether the norms are based on consensus or whether they are imposed on people by powerful groups within society.

The uses and gratifications model

This model stresses that different people use the media in different ways in order to obtain different sorts of pleasure or fulfil different sorts of needs. Individuals are viewed as active interpreters and choice-makers, rather than as passive receivers of media messages. For example, two people watching a party political broadcast might be satisfying very different needs, or obtaining very different gratifications.

Dennis McQuail (1972) suggested that there were the following types of uses and gratifications available from the media:

- Diversion: an escape from routine.
- Personal relationships: (a) surrogate membership of a community like that in *Brookside* or *Coronation Street*, or (b) by enabling us to operate better in a real community, like Jacqui's workmates.
- Personal identity: helping us to explore and confirm our identity - for example, the person who sees using the Internet as confirming their self-image as up-to-date and efficient. Media use may also challenge and weaken one's sense of identity.
- Surveillance: the feeling of knowing what's going on - for example, information from the news about the chancellor's annual budget.

In his early work, James Lull (1990) also adopted the uses and gratifications model. He made a list of the social uses of television, shown in Table 13.2.

It is clear that men and women use the media in different ways and obtain different types of gratifications from it. Some types of media and media messages may not be gratifying at all for some women. Likewise, older retired people and younger people are likely to derive different gratifications from media content. (These points are discussed in more detail below.)

Table 13.2   The social uses of television
Structural
Environmental: background noise; entertainment
Regulative: punctuation of time and activity; talk patterns
Relational
Communication facilitation: experience common ground; conversational entrance; anxiety reduction; agenda for talk; value clarification
Affiliation/avoidance: physical, verbal contact/neglect; family solidarity; family relaxant; conflict reduction; relationship maintenance
Social learning: decision making; behaviour modelling; problem solving; value transmission; legitimization; information dissemination; schooling
Competence/dominance: role enactment; role reinforcement; substitute role portrayal; intellectual validation; authority exercise; gatekeeping; argument facilitation
Source: J. Lull (1990) *Inside Family Viewing: Ethnographic Research on Television's Audiences*, Routledge, London.

However, the uses and gratifications approach fails to raise important questions about *why* people have particular needs or *why* they choose particular forms of gratifications. In particular it suggests that 'needs' are pre-existent; in fact the media can also *create* needs (for example, advertising can be very effective in creating a need for a particular product). Like the hypodermic model it treats people as asocial and does not recognize that needs are partly socially created (in this it is different from the normative approach). It focuses on individual differences, personality and psychology, and ignores the cultural context and social background which structures audience responses. The uses and gratifications approach is functionalist (see p. 10) in character, suggesting that the media perform a function but ignoring the dysfunctional nature of the media.

The interpretative model

In the interpretative model, audiences are believed to 'filter' media messages. Not only do people use the media in different ways; they also attend to and receive media messages in a selective way, ignoring, reacting to, forgetting or reinterpreting messages according to their own viewpoint. In other words they actively interpret the media message. James Halloran (1970) points out that this approach helped researchers to 'get away from the habit of thinking in terms of *what media do to people*, and to substitute for it the idea of *what people do with the media*'.

One important way in which people engage with media messages is intertextually; that is, they may read one text in relation to others (Fiske, 1988), or they may use one message system (for example, newspaper accounts of the lives of stars) to engage with another (for example, a television programme which includes one of those stars as an actor). Fiske (1988) notes that in watching a soap opera a viewer will move between different levels:

- Engagement: 'I felt I was really there with the characters.'
- Detachment: 'He will die on this journey because I've heard the actor wants to leave the series.'
- Referential: 'That man is very much like my own boss.'

According to Fiske, any one text is necessarily read in relationship to others: an audience brings a range of textual knowledge to bear.

David Buckingham: reading audiences

The ways in which people interpret the media partly depend on their level of media literacy. David Buckingham (1993) suggests that someone with only a low level of television literacy might be able to do the following:

- Distinguish between voices on a soundtrack or between figures and backgrounds.
- Understand the principle of editing and follow a narrative.
- Relate sound and image tracks together.
- Grasp elements of 'television grammar' such as camera angles and movements.

This sort of understanding of television might be typical of a child. However, Buckingham suggests that someone with a higher level of television literacy might be able to:

- Understand the codes or 'rhetoric' of television language.
- Categorize programmes into types and understand their different conventions.
- Describe different models of narrative structure and be aware of the way narrative time is manipulated through editing.
- Infer character traits and construct psychologically coherent characters from a few clues.
- Be aware of how viewers are invited to identify with characters.
- Understand the production process and the circulation and distribution of programmes.
- Infer the motivations and intentions of producers.

Clearly, these different levels of media literacy will influence the interpretation process. In some ways they are similar to Bernstein's elaborated and

restricted codes of language (see Chapter 11). The elaborated code (high media literacy) allows for greater possibilities of understanding and expression than the restricted code (low media literacy).

Although the interpretative model was a useful step forward in understanding media effects, it has a number of problems. Media messages are much stronger than this model often suggests: they carry a dominant and powerful influence. Also, media messages are not isolated. They are repeated frequently and are reinforced in different ways in different media: they have a cumulative impact.

Similarly, the model sees individuals as interpreting messages in a very isolated way. In fact people belong to cultures and subcultures which provide them with particular ways of looking at the media. A person's subculture strongly influences whether they accept, alter or reject the dominant meaning of a media message.

The structured interpretation model

This model builds on the interpretative model discussed above. It agrees that the audience can interpret media messages in different ways, but suggests that there is a preferred reading or dominant message. This preferred reading is structured by the cultural context of the audience.

So, for example, a news item about the Queen Mother's birthday may be capable of being interpreted in different ways, but one of these is 'easier' than the others because of the way in which the story is presented and because of the general culture in which the item is produced and consumed ('encoded' and 'decoded', to use the jargon). In the UK, the preferred reading might be admiration for a very old woman who still selflessly performs public duties in the national interest.

However, complications exist because there are numerous subcultures involved when a single mass media message (or 'text') is received. To understand a text, researchers cannot just 'read' it themselves but must understand how it is read by different audiences within different subcultures. These subcultures could be associated with age, gender, race, class, religion, geography, etc. Some of these audiences are sophisticated and have the ability to read a text in more than one way.

Ien Ang (1991) notes that audiences have traditionally been seen as an undifferentiated mass, in the same way as we think of 'the population' or 'the nation'. Ang says that we must avoid this sort of model and instead take account of the everyday practices and experiences of audiences themselves. The structured interpretation model attempts to do this.

David Morley and the *Nationwide* audience

David Morley's (1980) study was important because it related 'meaning' to social location. The study focused on audience reception of the daily television magazine programme *Nationwide*, and explored the reactions and readings of a panel of respondents.

Morley played a recording of a single programme to 18 groups. The different groups had very different educational, social and economic backgrounds. A second programme was shown to a further 11 groups, which this time included some from trade union and management training centres.

Morley concluded that different socio-economic classes interpret the meaning of a television programme in different ways, although there is no one-to-one relationship between class location and reading.

The media messages in the study were encoded in such a way as to make perfect sense to the bank managers among the respondents. However, the trade unionists among them saw the *Nationwide* coverage as biased towards management. Younger management trainees saw the coverage as favouring the unions. Meanwhile, middle-class students criticized the programme for its superficiality, and the group of mainly black working-class students saw it as too detailed and boring. Thus, one group approached the programme for information, the other for entertainment. Morley concludes:

> *These examples of the totally contradictory readings of the same programme item ... do provide us with the clearest examples of the way in which the 'meaning' of a programme or a 'message' depends upon the interpretive code which the audience brings to the decoding situation.*
>
> Morley, 1992, p. 112

According to Morley, the production of a meaningful message by media professionals in television discourse is always the result of 'work'. It always contains more than one potential 'reading': that is, it is polysemic.

Finally, the activity of 'getting meaning' from the message is also complex, however transparent and 'natural' it seems. Morley shows that social location is important in providing a set of cultural 'tools' which we use, usually unconsciously, to decode media messages. These include the language, concepts and assumptions associated with a subculture, other social location or ideological position. Developing Morley's work, Croteau and Hoynes (2000) refer to these as *discursive resources* and point out that different groups of people in society have access to different sets of discursive resources for decoding media messages.

This raises a question about whether the structured interpretation model adopts an over-determined view of individuals, whose attitudes and views are largely conditioned by the social groups to which they belong. Instead of seeing the audience as an undifferentiated mass, as earlier models have done, or even seeing them as divided by class, age, etc. as this one does, postmodernists argue that we need to see them as people interacting with the media in specific social situations. In this way the same person will perceive and react to the same media message in different ways in different contexts. It is therefore difficult or impossible to make generalizations about 'the audience' as such.

Understanding audience reception: the third phase

Pertti Alasuutari (1999) suggests that we can categorize the audience reception approaches examined above under two headings, and that a third approach to understanding the reception of media messages is about to mature.

The 'first generation' of reception research, at its peak during the 1970s, is associated with Hall's notion of encoding and decoding. The 'new' aspect of this compared to many previous studies was its recognition that media texts undergo a process of 'translation', both when they are assembled by specialist groups in the media and when they are read by the audience. Hall noted that before a message can be put to a use or satisfy a need it must be meaningfully decoded. The emphasis on this process, rather than on simplistic 'effects', marked the start of increasingly sophisticated audience reception studies.

Morley's *Nationwide* research also fits this model and confirms Hall's suggestion that media messages can be decoded differently:

- The hegemonic code is the 'preferred reading' encoded by the media professionals.
- The professional code interprets messages according to the culture of the professional group to which the viewer belongs.
- The negotiated code modifies but does not totally reject the preferred reading.
- The oppositional code is one in which the viewer comprehends the message but rejects it.

Crucial to all this is the concept of the interpretative community: the culturally coherent group that tends to decode messages in a consistent way.

The second generation of reception studies, from the 1980s, usually relied on ethnographic approaches (see Chapter 14) to studying the audience. Such studies often focused on the politics of gender as it related to media messages. So, for example, Lull (1990), Morley (1986) and Silverstone (1991) concentrated on the social uses and the gendered nature of television, particularly within the family. The emphasis of such studies is on the everyday life of a small group of people – not the characteristics of a larger interpretative community – and its implications for the reception of media messages. Some of these studies are discussed below.

Now a 'third generation' of audience reception studies is developing. Influenced by postmodernist thinking and the 'linguistic turn' in sociology and cultural studies (see p. 941), it adopts what Alasuutari calls 'a constructionist view'. This has begun to question the very notion of 'the audience' itself.

Similarly, the media themselves are now seen as an important part of the culture, rather than as a series of separate message generators. As a result, emphasis is placed on the discourses within which 'the public', 'the audience' and 'the world' are understood by audiences and programme makers, and how audiences and programme makers understand themselves. These more recent studies are rooted in a postmodernist approach to understanding the world and the changing nature of the world itself.

Postmodernity, postmodernism and the media

While 'postmodernism' is a philosophical approach to understanding the world, 'postmodernity' is a description of what the world is like, at least as depicted by postmodernists. (For a more detailed discussion of postmodernity, see Chapter 15.)

Postmodernity is a condition which is media-saturated: the media are not just one aspect among many of that condition but are its intimate, defining aspect. In postmodernity the norm is complexity: there are many meanings and not one deep, profound meaning. Access to the multitude of messages transmitted via the media provides access to these meanings.

For Jean Baudrillard (1988) the communication/media revolution has meant that people are engulfed by information to such an extent that the distinction between reality and the word/image which portrays it breaks down into a condition he calls hyperreality. In this condition – another key characteristic of postmodernity – words, images and the information they convey become open to multiple interpretations, mirroring the breakdown of 'objectivity'.

Media messages are not simply interpreted in one way by a passive audience, but are read in many ways by different portions of the audience or even by the same people at different times. Lash notes that 'everyday life becomes pervaded with a reality – in TV, adverts, video, communication, the Walkman, cassette decks in automobiles, and now, increasingly, CDs, CDV, and DAT – which increasingly comprises representations' (Lash, 1990).

Sherry Turkle (1996) echoes Jean Baudrillard when she talks about television as part of the postmodern 'culture of simulation', where we learn to identify with the simulated world of television more readily than we do with the 'real' world around us. For instance, the bar featured in the television series *Cheers* figured so prominently in the imagination because most people do not have a neighbourhood place where 'everybody knows your name'. Instead, they identified with the place on the screen. Recently it was given life off the screen as well. Bars designed to look like the one on *Cheers* have sprung up all over the USA, most poignantly in airports, the most anonymous of places. Here, no one will know your name, but you can always buy a drink or a souvenir sweatshirt.

According to Turkle, such simulation has laid the groundwork for the next development in the relationship between reality and simulation. Computers and the virtual worlds they now provide are already adding another dimension to the mediated experience of reality.

The global and the local

Postmodernity removes the distinction between the global and the local by linking them with technologies associated with travel and communication, particularly media technologies. Television news in particular plays an increasingly important global role. The globalization of television news has led to its domination by a mainstream Anglo-American point of view, largely as a result of the limited number of news agencies around the world. Although Oliver Boyd-Barrett (1998) argues that there is an increasing diversity of such news agencies, he concludes that a few major agencies such as Agence France-Presse, Associated Press, World Television News and Reuters - located primarily in the USA, the UK and France - have dominance in the provision of news.

Baudrillard claims that one effect of all this is to blur the distinction between image and reality, as we saw in the example of the *Cheers* bar. Another is to undermine traditional concepts and old certainties like 'duty', 'authority', 'hierarchy' and so on. This is because values are seen as relative, not absolute.

According to theories of postmodernity we create our own set of values and understandings from the global information around us. In particular the search for a 'true' or authentic self gives way to a 'playfulness' in which personal identity is experimental, expressed and invented through choices of lifestyle. Lifestyles are chosen primarily by selecting those on offer through the media.

Criticisms of postmodernism

Postmodernism has been criticized and attacked from a variety of different points of view (see Chapter 15). For example, Frank Webster (1999) claims that there has been no profound change in society as a result of the 'information explosion'. To think in this way is to see technological change as causing social change. This ignores the fact that technologies, like media messages, are interpreted and used in particular ways in particular social contexts, and that technology and society interact with each other.

Webster also argues that postmodernist accounts of the information-rich society fail to ask – much less answer – some important questions: 'What sort of information has increased? Who has generated what kind of information, and for what purposes and with what consequences has it been generated?'

According to Lerner (1994) the failure of postmodernism to answer such questions has had the effect of obscuring poverty, oppression and various forms of inequality around the world, thus foiling attempts to make the world better and more egalitarian.

Role and influence of the media: images and social groups

Popular discussions of the media often focus on their impact on particular social groups. The discussions usually concern whether the media have a negative impact on the social position of women, for example, or minority ethnic groups, social classes, young or old people and people with disabilities.

A useful way of looking at this issue is to consider the different phases that media messages pass through: this is known as the 'message trajectory'. Four such phases can be readily identified:

1 The media institutions and the message formulation stage.
2 The media message content: the nature of the 'text'.
3 The audience: behaviour and reception.
4 The effects or impact of the message.

The following sections discuss these four phases in relation to the various social groups listed above. However, in reality of course each of these groups intersects with others: any individual will simultaneously be a member of several social groups - for example, young and disabled. It is important to remember this; otherwise instances of multiple discrimination can remain hidden.

For example, it is known that people with disabilities are under-represented in television output, and this may be particularly true if they are from ethnic minorities. A large content analysis of more than six weeks of UK-produced television output showed that there were no disabled characters from minority ethnic groups (Cumberbatch and Negrine, 1992).

Media institutions and the message formulation stage

Gender

Creedon (1989) points out that there has been a 'gender switch' in media industries, so that the media are dominated by 'pink collar' workers (that is, women).

However, Croteau and Hoynes (2000) show that in the USA in the mid-1990s women occupied only 6 per cent of top newspaper management positions, wrote only 19 per cent of front-page stories, occupied only 20 per cent of news director posts in television stations, and presented only 20 per cent of television news reports.

Comparable figures apply in other media and the percentages are similar or more pronounced in other nations. Women remain nearer the bottom of the pyramid of power and influence in the media.

Radical feminists (see pp. 136–7) argue that this male domination means that the media continue to produce those images of women which men desire. Media content reflects the nature of media organizations and patriarchal (male-dominated) society in general. Media messages are the powerful talking to the less powerful, men talking to women.

Those issues which are of particular concern to women - such as discrimination at work and in education, sexual harassment, the problems of child care, social isolation, police attitudes in rape cases, and so on - are therefore frequently ignored or trivialized. According to some researchers this is due to conscious manipulation by males; according to others it is the result of patriarchal cultural hegemony.

Ethnicity

What about ethnicity in media organizations? Although there is a high proportion of black and Asian television presenters (BSC, 1999), there are very few representatives of ethnic minorities in more senior management positions. Samir Shah, head of the BBC's current affairs television output from 1987, says:

> *The BBC is a very white institution. At practically all the meetings I attend, I'm the only non-white face present ... we tend to get most of the non-white faces down in the canteen, and that's not good enough. Changes have to be made everywhere, right up to Board level.*
>
> Quoted in Pines, 1992, p. 162

In North America the situation is rather different. Colle (1973) describes the causes and effects of the increasing integration of minority ethnic groups into the media. These include new legislation to provide equality of opportunity in employment practices, a changing social climate, the work of groups campaigning for minority rights, and the positive actions and non-discriminatory policies of key organizations. These factors have combined to open the American media, at least in part, to previously excluded minorities.

Class, age and disability

Those people in senior positions in media organizations are mostly middle-class and usually older than most other media workers. People with disabilities are rather poorly represented within media institutions. Anne Karpf notes in *Doctoring the Media*:

> *Employment is the nub of the problem. As long as media images of disability continue to be shaped by able-bodied people, and intended for an able-bodied audience, the stereotypes will flow. The employment of people with disabilities in broadcasting and their media image are inextricably linked. When in 1986 Fairplay organized a survey of British TV companies, it found that, although most had equal opportunities policies, very few had a programme to implement them. What's more, they often cast able-bodied actors as disabled characters, producing unconvincing portrayals which the disability movement likens to those of blacked-up actors of the past.*
>
> Karpf, 1988, p. 120

Media message content: the nature of the 'text'

Media representations of social groups vary considerably. The treatment of minority ethnic groups is very different, for example, in popular newspapers to the treatment in television comedy and film. Changes in social attitudes and awareness over the years have led in some cases to marked differences in the representation of particular social groups in the same media. This provides the source for much of the humour in the *Austin Powers* films.

The explosion in demand for media 'software' – programming content – means that no matter how old or challenging to contemporary views, many programmes are continuously recycled by cable and satellite companies. This diversity makes generalizing about media representations of social groups both difficult and hazardous.

Gender

The relative numbers of women and men portrayed in the media depend very much on the particular medium and type of programme. On terrestrial and satellite television, for example, males outnumber females in all programme types (BSC, 1999), but a higher percentage of those females are likely to be portrayed in major roles.

Soap operas have a relatively high proportion of women, though they are still outnumbered by men: there are as many as seven men to three women in some soap operas. Cartoons have a particularly low number of women (often stylized as cats, etc.). In advertisements there are three all-male ads for every one all-female ad. Some types of comedy programme have almost no women, while others have very few men.

However, numbers alone are not the most important criterion. The nature of the representation is important. Bretl and Cantor (1988) note that males are still more likely than females to be shown in higher-status occupations, depicted away from the home, associated with different types of products, and assigned more credibility as authorities rather than consumers.

The most striking difference Bretl and Cantor describe is in the narration of voice-overs: 90 per

Table 13.3 Level of appearance, by gender (terrestrial television)						
	Male		Female		Total	
Level of appearance	N	%	N	%	N	%
Major role	1,482	16	1,080	23	2,562	18
Minor role	1,475	16	693	15	2,168	16
Incidental/interviewee	6,217	68	2,922	62	9,139	66
Totals	9,174	100	4,695	100	13,869	100

Source: BSC (1999) *Monitoring Report 7*, Broadcasting Standards Commission, London, p. 100.

cent of narrators were male, reinforcing the 'male = authoritative' association. Where female narrators were used this was typically in the promotion of products associated with care of the body.

Diana Meehan (1983) suggests that there are essentially only ten female character types presented in the American drama serials she studied:

1 *The Imp*, a rebellious tomboy character.

2 *The Goodwife*, the homemaker

3 *The Harpy*, an assertive, even aggressive single woman.

4 *The Bitch*, who is manipulative, dangerous and deceitful.

5 *The Victim*, in need of rescue.

6 *The Decoy*, who appears to be a victim but can overcome her difficulties.

7 *The Siren*, who lures her male victim to disaster.

8 *The Courtesan*, who is at least close to being a prostitute.

9 *The Witch*, who is powerful and dangerous.

10 *The Matriarch*, an older woman with power, prestige and authority.

Meehan also argues that women are portrayed as extremes more than men: as either good or evil, with the 'good' ones portrayed as lacking a strong sexual appetite, submissive and domesticated. Male characters, by contrast, are portrayed in more subtle ways.

Similar stereotypical representations are present in some kinds of music. Karen Saucier's (1986) careful content analysis of the lyrics of the top 40 country songs of 1981 describes the words of these songs as a 'three minute soap opera'.

Saucier was concerned to analyse the gender representations within these songs. She found that 95 per cent presented a male–female relationship theme (getting together or breaking up); 8 per cent concentrated on male sexual prowess; and 8 per cent gave advice about love relationships. A woman was usually portrayed in terms of 'her man', with no status in terms of property or economic role in the community or workplace. The only acceptable role for a woman was housewife, mother or lover.

Men were commonly depicted as using alcohol to deaden the pain of loss or failure, while women were often depicted as using their sexuality as a resource in situations where men have the power. She concludes:

> *The symbolic world offered by country music lyrics represents a rather bleak, limited world for both men and women in regard to status, role and power. The only aspect of their lives that is somewhat under their control is the relationship between themselves and their lover.*

Saucier, 1986, p. 163

According to Eugene Provenzo (1991), video games too provide strictly limited representations of roles for both males and females. He notes that games designed for Nintendo and others have extremely stereotyped representations of males and females, probably more so than in other media. Women are usually anonymous and are generally portrayed as passive. The games are generally 'macho' in orientation, with both males and females usually depicted as young and physically 'ideal'.

Non-fictional television programmes also tend to present a limited range of images of women. While newsreaders are increasingly likely to be women, Pat Holland (1987) argues that this trend can be linked to the growing 'intimization' of television news. This new stress on intimacy and emotion – traditionally regarded as female attributes – has provided an employment opportunity for women, whereas the earlier 'rationalistic' approach to the news was more clearly linked to male values.

However, while news and weather presenters are much more likely to be female than in the past, they are usually young and attractive. Such trends are not difficult to associate with the domination of news provision by global corporations discussed above (see pp. 937–40).

Marjorie Ferguson (1983) conducted a detailed content analysis and interview study of three of the largest-selling women's magazines.

According to Ferguson, women's magazines convey a 'cult of femininity'. They instruct women in values and attitudes about being a woman. They tell women what to do and how to think about themselves, about their men, colleagues, children, neighbours and bosses. The novice is instructed in how to achieve her chosen ends: what to wear, how to act, and what to buy to be a *femme fatale*, super-cook or office boss.

While Ferguson claims that it is only women who are instructed in this way, a similar approach is now being applied to men. However, this does not suggest that there is increasing equality in representations of gender roles; rather, the growth in magazines aimed at men simply increases gender stereotyping.

Ethnicity

It is very difficult to generalize about representations of ethnicity in the media. This is because some subsections of broadcast, print and film media are oriented to and sensitive towards questions of ethnicity (for example, programmes or even whole satellite channels dedicated to Asian issues, magazines for those with Caribbean roots, etc.) and represent minority ethnic groups in appropriate ways. Even parts of the 'white establishment' media can be sympathetic and campaign for better treatment of minorities in the media (Wilcox, 1992).

However, there is much research evidence to suggest that newspapers in particular tend to stereotype the cultural values and norms of behaviour of some minority groups. Stories are often cast in terms of the threat posed by minority ethnic groups: by their increasing numbers, criminality or in some other way, as Table 13.4 indicates.

Television, meanwhile, portrays a particularly restricted range of social roles for minority ethnic groups.

The Broadcasting Standards Commission (1999) found that in terrestrial and satellite television members of minority ethnic groups appeared in 42 per cent of programmes, accounting for 7 per cent of all

people with a speaking role. They were best represented in children's programmes. The occupation portrayal of members of minority ethnic groups in television programming is strongly skewed, as Table 13.5 reveals.

Class

Glennon and Butsch (1982) studied television representations of social class lifestyles in family contexts between 1941 and 1978. They collected information about 218 family series. All of these were American prime-time programmes, mostly (86 per cent) situation comedies, but there were also family dramas, adventure serials and cartoons. Their uniting

Table 13.4 Frequencies of headline depictions of minority and majority groups, August 1985–January 1986

	The Times	Sun	Telegraph	Mail	Guardian
MEC: neutral	22	11	20	15	26
MEC: negative	19	25	32	16	14
MEC: positive	4	1	4	4	5
Majority: neutral	23	0	9	6	20
Majority: negative	9	1	14	6	7
Majority: positive	3	0	10	2	7
State/parties: neutral	26	4	11	10	21
State/parties: negative	2	0	4	2	2
State/parties: positive	4	1	3	1	3
Police/judiciary: neutral	31	2	13	12	34
Police/judiciary: negative	21	4	6	8	25
Police/judiciary: positive	4	1	13	4	2
Neutral: MEC	10	3	7	10	11
Negative: MEC	11	7	14	8	16
Positive: MEC	10	3	13	3	7
Neutral: majority	3	1	3	4	7
Negative: majority	5	7	6	5	2
Positive: majority	1	0	2	0	2
Neutral: state/parties	3	0	2	0	2
Negative: state/parties	1	1	3	0	0
Positive: state/parties	0	0	1	0	0
Neutral: police/judiciary	12	1	5	7	6
Negative: police/judiciary	6	11	23	21	13
Positive: police/judiciary	2	2	2	3	3

MEC = Individuals from a minority ethnic community
Emboldened section = Individual or group was the active agent
Non-emboldened section = Individual or group had actions done to them
Majority = Individuals from the majority community

Source: T. van Dijk (1991) *Racism and the Press*, Routledge, London.

Table 13.5 Occupational status of people from minority ethnic groups (terrestrial television)

Occupation	Black N	Black %	Asian N	Asian %	Other N	Other %	Total N	Total %
Arts, media and entertainment	116	22	76	31	11	8	203	22
White-collar office	13	2	15	6	3	2	31	3
Educationalist, academic	4	1	3	1	5	4	12	1
Travel and leisure	10	2	3	1	9	6	22	2
Health and caring	35	7	19	8	15	11	69	8
Legal	3	1	3	1	–	–	6	1
Police including private detectives	37	7	1	*	7	5	45	5
Other uniformed services	14	3	–	–	6	4	20	2
Domestic staff	4	1	–	–	–	–	4	*
Blue-collar worker	7	1	1	*	1	1	9	1
Sportsperson	32	6	2	1	2	1	36	4
Clergy, religious leader	4	1	2	1	2	1	8	1
Politician/spokesperson	10	2	2	1	4	3	16	2
Shop and stall owner/assistant	6	1	8	3	3	2	17	2
Pensioner/retired	3	1	–	–	–	–	3	*
Student	9	2	14	6	2	1	25	3
Under 16 years	29	6	12	5	7	5	48	5
Housewife	2	*	2	1	–	–	4	*
Unemployed	6	1	–	–	1	1	7	1
Criminal	11	2	–	–	4	3	15	2
Others	14	3	7	3	7	5	28	3
Cannot code	154	29	74	30	48	34	276	30
Not applicable	3	1	–	–	3	2	6	1
Total	526	102	244	99	140	99	910	99

Source: BSC (1999) *Monitoring Report 7*, Broadcasting Standards Commission, London, p. 119.

feature was that the main characters were members of a family and most of the interactions portrayed were within the family.

The study found that:

- Working-class families were under-represented and middle-class families over-represented.
- Almost half had professional heads of household (two-thirds were either managers or proprietors: in reality a quarter of the American workforce in 1970).
- Blue-collar workers were portrayed as heads of household in 4 per cent of the series (36 per cent in reality).
- Glamorous and successful families were portrayed most: many of the families were portrayed as extremely wealthy.
- In the few working-class families represented, some were portrayed as upwardly mobile; others were portrayed with an unintelligent father (Glennon and

Butsch argue that these two themes undermine the dignity of working-class family life).

- The effort of moving from a working-class to a middle-class family lifestyle was underestimated.

Glennon and Butsch made some attempt to analyse the way these classes were portrayed. For example, they note that:

- In the middle-class families, parents were usually portrayed as coping effectively with problems.
- Many working-class fathers were portrayed in a comic way, laughed at by the rest of the world.

However, it is not appropriate for large content-analysis studies like that of Glennon and Butsch to make these kinds of judgements. That is because they often hide assumptions about what messages mean in the first place (for example, 'portrayed as unintelligent' is itself a judgement made by the researcher). Neither do they tell us anything about how these messages are received by the audience.

Studies of representations of social class in non-fiction television have been conducted by the Glasgow Media Group (particularly 1976, 1980 and 1982). Their findings are summarized in detail on pp. 942–3. It is interesting to note that for the Glasgow Media Group the working class are generally portrayed as 'trouble' on television news, in very much the same way as working-class youth (see below). From a neo-Marxist perspective this is no surprise: the media are simply acting against counter-hegemonic groups in an effort to sustain ideological dominance.

Age

In late Victorian and Edwardian times adolescents came to be seen as potentially dangerous, ready to go on the rampage unless they were kept employed. Geoff Pearson's (1983) analysis of newspaper reporting shows how the music hall and the cinema were seen as offering opportunities to go astray. These forms of mass media were very important in the past and received the same sort of criticisms as videos have done in recent times.

Pearson argues that contemporary images usually categorize youth as a problem. This is often contrasted in the media with a Golden Age (usually 20 years ago) when young people knew their place, there was little crime and people respected the police. Pearson's account of his search through press archives reveals that, no matter what the date, this same story is told: the Golden Age is *always* 20 years previously. The media are in a permanent panic about whatever manifestation of 'youth as a problem' is current: the Hooligans of Victorian times, the Teds of the 1950s or the Travellers of today.

In the 1950s, for example, Teds were portrayed in the media as outcasts, frequently in trouble and wandering the streets. Paul Rock and Stan Cohen have argued that the image of the Ted in the press can be understood as the personification of evil: 'He seems to stalk like some ... monster through much of the otherwise prosaic newspaper reporting of the fifties' (Rock and Cohen, 1970).

What about media images of older people? Susan Sontag (1978) points out that there is a 'double standard of ageing': women are required to match up to a youthful ideal all their lives but men are not. There are very positive images of ageing for men. This gender distinction needs to be taken into account in any discussion of media representation of the elderly.

Lambert *et al.*'s (1984) content analysis of British television over a two-week period showed that 50 per

cent of programmes included people over the age of 60. Most images of the elderly were those of 'world leaders': politicians, business people, experts, administrators and judges. These were almost exclusively men. Similarly, news anchor men and quiz masters tended to be older and to be portrayed as having authority.

Biggs (1993) summarizes recent research on age stereotyping in British television, in entertainment and other non-current affairs broadcasting. He finds that soap operas are dominated by middle-aged or older people. Sit-coms (situation comedies) tend to present older people as enfeebled, vague and forgetful, or as cantankerous battleaxes. There are, however, examples of 'reverse stereotyping' in which older people are portrayed as exceptions to the rule.

Despite all this, Biggs concludes that recently the media have promoted an active image of ageing. However, there is still a lack of concern about the problems of age and ageing. As we saw above, there is limited news value in long-term issues such as ageing.

Signorelli's (1989) content analysis of over 14,000 American television characters between 1969 and 1981 found that the very old and the very young were under-represented in prime-time dramatic fiction. Older characters were less likely to be presented as 'good', but less likely to be involved in violence than younger characters. Some 70 per cent of older men and 80 per cent of older women were treated discourteously and as low-status persons. However, representation is patchy. For example, Dail (1988) found that older women in soap operas were likely to be portrayed in a positive way.

This patchiness is also found in other media. On Radio 4, for example, there are more older men than older women. In sports broadcasting there is a tradition of the positively-portrayed older man 'moving on' into semi-retirement (with a bit of commentating on the side). Examples are Ian Botham, Viv Richards and Ted Dexter. One or two examples of women in the same position do exist (for example, Sue Barker, Virginia Wade) but their numbers are far smaller.

As in other aspects of media representations, there is evidence of considerable change over time. In industrialized countries around the world, people aged over 50 have become a larger part of the population, as birth rates decline and life expectancy increases. These same people are increasingly likely to be affluent in retirement as a result of economic and social changes.

Featherstone and Hepworth (1995) show how the magazine *Retirement Choice* presents positive images of ageing, in recognition of the new large market. However, they are still critical of representations of age within its pages. Ageing is represented as 'an extended plateau of active middle age ... a period of youthfulness and active consumer lifestyles'. The message *Retirement Choice* propagates is that the ageing process is a matter of making the right lifestyle (and hence consumer) decisions. Difficult issues such as decline and dependency are avoided.

Disability

The Broadcasting Standards Commission (1999) showed that people with disabilities appeared in 7 per cent of their sample of television programmes and accounted for 0.7 per cent of all those who spoke. They were most represented in broadcast films, drama and soap opera. Disabled males in television output outnumbered females by about 3 to 1, and only 1 in 10 were from minority ethnic groups. As with women, when they did appear they were more likely to be in a major role than those 'without' disabilities. American productions were twice as likely to portray people with disabilities as British ones.

Longmore (1987) listed the following forms of representation of disabled people on television:

- disability or physical handicap as an emblem of evil;
- the disabled as monsters;
- disability as a loss of one's humanity;
- disability as total dependency and lack of self-determination;
- the image of the disabled as a maladjusted person;
- disability with compensation or substitute gift (for example, the blind having compensatory powers);
- disability leading to courageousness or achievement;

Table 13.6 Attitudes shown towards characters in dramatic fiction		
Attitude	Able-bodied characters %	Disabled characters %
Sympathy	7	34
Pity	2	12
Patronizing	14	30
Sadness	3	16
Fear	7	16
Avoidance	3	9
Attraction	43	33
Respect	51	39
Mocking	8	10
Abuse	13	15

Multiple coding means that totals are more than 100%

Source: Adapted from G. Cumberbatch and R. Negrine (1992) *Images of Disability on Television*, Routledge, London.

- disability and sexuality: as a sexual menace, deviancy, danger stemming from loss of control.

Cumberbatch and Negrine (1992) add the following to Longmore's list:

- disability as an object of fun or pity;
- the disabled as the object of charity.

These authors suggest that what is missing among these stereotyped representations:

is the portrayal of people with disabilities as an integral part of life. ... When people with disabilities do appear on the screen, their presence and their actions are determined by the nature of the disabilities ... he/she is much less likely to appear as a person, an individual, who happens also to have a disability.

Cumberbatch and Negrine, 1992, p. 90

The audience: behaviour and reception

Our discussion of media images of social groups has highlighted the importance of reception analysis: of understanding how the audience interpret and use media content, in what circumstances and why. This section examines these things in relation to the five groups examined above.

Gender

Recent radical feminists have tended to adopt a fairly optimistic approach to understanding women's relationship to the media. They regard women as empowered readers of media messages, and stress the processes women use to decode media messages and their ability to resist and even gain pleasure from such messages. For example, Ang's (1985) study of the female audience of *Dallas* identified the pleasures that women obtained from the programme.

Recent studies have also stressed the importance of the television viewing context. For example, Hargrave (1999) shows that adults viewing television with children are more likely to react negatively to sex scenes than when viewing alone or with other adults.

Context also relates to the relationship between a particular audience and a specific medium. For many authors the technologies of the mass media are themselves highly gendered: in other words, they are clearly associated with a gender identity. Gender identity in this context refers to the beliefs, values and feelings people have about themselves and about media technology and content.

Skirrow (1986) uses the related concept of gender valence, which is a measure of the degree to which media technology or content involves male or female gender identities. For example, according to Skirrow, video games 'are particularly unattractive [to women] since they are part of a technology which … is identified with male power, and they are about mastering a specifically male anxiety in a specifically male way'.

Similarly, Turkle (1988) argues that women 'use their rejection of computers … to assert something about themselves as women. … It is a way to say that it is not appropriate to have a close relationship with a machine.' The computer is a cultural symbol of what a woman is not. In rejecting computers women are rejecting something they see as gender-coded.

Gray (1987) notes that people say that women generally avoid computers and video games because they are too complex. However, women routinely use other complex equipment (which men often claim not to be able to operate) like sewing machines, microwave ovens and washing machines. For Gray an important factor in all this is men's domination of domestic leisure, which alienates women from the technology associated with it.

By contrast, the telephone is the key technology that many women would hate to lose because it is a way of 'saving the sanity' of those who have a sense of isolation in their homes. Similarly, Hobson (1980) suggests that radio has a female gender valence and is particularly important for working-class women with young children, as it helps structure their day and links them with the outside world.

Gender identities and gender valence can change over time. Lisa Lewis's (1990) discussion of videos provides an interesting example. She notes that the streets are usually no-go areas for young women, and girls are usually pushed into 'bedroom culture'. Yet here, too, they find male dominance. For example, most videos on MTV are designed around male adolescence: 'Ideologies of rebelliousness, independence … sexual promiscuity … street culture … and female conquest'. As a result, music videos have had a male gender identity.

Arguably the popularity of girl bands and solo female singers has changed this. Their challenging, subversive style can be interpreted by their female audiences as a strategy of opposition. Girls often imitate the image, demeanour and argot (vocabulary and delivery style) of these stars. They develop female friendships and solidarity by these means: a 'gendered support system for girls'. Of course, such imitation is also promoted by the fashion industry and others who target this group.

Recent sociological studies of women's magazines have tended to shift away from criticism of their sexist images, sexist ideology and negative effects on women's socialization (see p. 952). Hermes (1995), for example, shows that women derive a lot of pleasure from reading these magazines and find them useful. Readers find them relaxing and educative, and they also believe that the magazines connect them to the wider world. Readers tend to change in the way they use these magazines and the magazines tend to change over time with their readers. Hermes's study is a postmodernist one which sees readers as intelligent, diverse and active in their approach to the text.

Ethnicity

The interpretative model of media messages highlights the polysemic nature of media texts (see p. 948). This is particularly evident with issues of ethnicity. Let us take as an example *The Cosby Show*, the most popular American television comedy in history.

A successful upper-middle-class black family (the Huxtables) are presented extremely favourably in a variety of comedy situations. The lead actor, Bill Cosby, is himself popular, rich and successful and in the show the boundaries between the real Cosby and the fictional Dr Huxtable are blurred (as the title of the show illustrates).

The programme could be interpreted in terms of the Huxtable family (and Bill Cosby) as positive representations of what American black people can become, as positive role models. Alternatively, the programme could be read as depicting an extremely unrepresentative group of black people who are isolated from, and ignore, the problems of racism, deprivation and under-achievement that disproportionately affect black people in the USA.

Jhally and Lewis (1992) demonstrate the importance of understanding social differentiation within the audience and the need to distinguish between types of response to media messages. One interesting finding of their study was the degree to which respondents viewed *The Cosby Show* as real. Both black and white respondents had no difficulty in making statements about black people based on their experience of the Huxtables. The authors note that:

> The line between the TV world and the world beyond the screen has, for most people, become exceedingly hazy. We watch at one moment with credulity, at another with disbelief. We mix scepticism with an extraordinary faith in television's capacity to tell the truth. We know that the Huxtables are not real yet we continually think about them as if they were.

Jhally and Lewis, 1992, p. 133

The overall response to *The Cosby Show* was heavily conditioned by the ethnicity of the person watching it. Black interviewees tended to discuss the show in terms of racial stereotyping. Generally, they contrasted the portrayal of the Huxtables very favourably with other programmes containing representations of minorities. *The Cosby Show*, however, confronts black viewers with a difficulty. Do they go along with the show's fiction that 'there are black millionaires all over the place', thus ignoring the deep racial divisions in the USA? Or do they consult their own experience for a more realistic view of American blacks, but then leave themselves open to charges of stereotyping and fatalism?

For white viewers there is no such problem. They come to believe that there is room for minorities to succeed purely by their own efforts. This, for Jhally and Lewis, is simply a more sophisticated form of racism: other blacks have failed to succeed where the Huxtables have not, and their lack of success must, therefore, be their own fault.

Jhally and Lewis conclude that the overall effect of *The Cosby Show* is negative, for it masks persistent divisions of race and class in the USA.

Ethnicity, identity construction and the media

Marie Gillespie (1995) shows how television and video are used to recreate the culture of South Asians in London and how these media are also leading to cultural change. Her study is an account of young Punjabis (14–18-year-olds) living in Southall, West London, where Punjabis comprise the largest single Asian community outside the Indian subcontinent. Her work took place from 1988 to 1991, during which time the *fatwa* (death sentence) was pronounced against Salman Rushdie, the Gulf War was fought and communism in Eastern Europe collapsed.

Gillespie found that the young people use television and video to redefine their ethnicity. A range of choices are available to young Punjabis, from *Neighbours* to Indian sacred soaps like the *Mahabharata*. This encourages the young people to compare, contrast and criticize cultures, including those of their parents. They dream of an essentially American lifestyle represented in advertisements for Coca-Cola and Levi jeans. However, they are not duped, neither do they live in a fantasy world. They are able to reflect on cultural differences even when they are drawn into a programme and identify with its characters, as tends to happen with *Neighbours*. For example, one young girl uses *Neighbours* as a kind of mirror to reflect on gender roles:

> *You can see that families in* Neighbours *are more flexible, they do things together as a family, they don't expect that girls should stay at home and do housework and cooking, boys and girls are allowed to mix much more freely. ... Indian families do go out together to eat ... but most of us can only go out with the family, they can't go out with their mates like the boys do. ... Boys live on the outside and girls on the inside.*

Gillespie, 1995, p. 169

News reports of the Gulf War had the same kind of function, but in relation to religion and national and international loyalties. The young people were torn between identifying with the Iraqi Muslims or with the USA and its allies; between whether or not to adopt their parents' view of the conflict (itself based on their experience of colonialism); and whether or not to adopt a critical stance towards the reporting of the war. This highlighted their sense of hybrid national and cultural identity, but at the same time gave them the freedom to make choices; a sense of uncertainty, but also of global interconnectedness.

Television and video thus enable the young people to 'stand outside' their parents' culture and to judge it against a large number of alternatives. They could also go on to change it, to construct new and original versions of ethnicity, and to define what it is to be a young British Asian. These young people are informed and active 'readers' of media texts, not passive receivers. The effect of the media is, on the whole, to empower them.

Social class and audience reception

Ann Gray (1992) shows how class and gender interact in the use of the media. Gender identities influence media use, of course, but so do the social contexts of use and the gendered relationships of power in the household. Gray shows the importance of class, gender and viewing context for the use of television and video. Her in-depth research into the video use of 30 women of different social classes shows clear differences between social classes I (professional) and II (intermediate) compared to IIIn (skilled non-manual) and IIIm (skilled manual), though Gray was not able to come to firm conclusions about social classes IV (partly skilled) and V (unskilled).

Social classes IIIn and IIIm had a far greater reported use of television and video than social classes I and II. The differences between the viewing habits of men and women were much clearer in IIIn and IIIm than in I and II. The higher the social class, the more concern there was about children using the television and video 'too much' and the more effort was made to control their use. The lower the social class, the more television and video were an accepted (and dominant) part of life and conversation. The higher the social class, the more preference there was for 'classics' and British productions (a perceived sign of quality).

In all classes, however, the context was important and affected how women used video. The context of viewing could be all the family together, children only, male and female together, male only, or female only. In all classes women tended to give control of viewing to men, citing their employment as justification.

Men enjoyed documentaries, current affairs and (especially in classes IIIn and IIIm) sport. Politics, space, science, science fiction, and action adventure were also 'men's domains' in the all-male context. Men tended to archive tapes and to organize their viewing more than women. Soap operas, weepies, romance and costume drama were enjoyed by the women watching alone in all classes.

However, women with higher education were more likely to have similar tastes to their partners. For classes I and II, men and women agreed that the following was a correct representation of taste:

Positive	Negative
classics	popular
quality	trash
important	trivial
British	American

In contrast, classes IIIn to V agreed that the following was important:

'Male' genres	'Female' genres
hard	soft
tough	soppy
real	fantasy
serious	silly
factual	fictional

However, all the women enjoyed programmes that stressed personal relationships, believable characters and a strong story. So, across the classes there is this polarity:

Male	Female
heroic	romantic
public	domestic
societal	familial
physical	emotional

Age and the reception of messages

Barry Gunter and Jill McAleer (1997) investigated children's use and reception of television in the home. They note that for 4–24-year-olds the number of hours spent watching television remained relatively constant between 1982 and 1994 at around 2.8 hours per day – less than all other age groups. This contrasts with the viewing practices of older, retired people as reported by Gauntlett and Hill (1999), who found that older people tended to 'allow' themselves to watch more television as their social contacts and mobility diminished.

Gunter and McAleer found no strong evidence that television displaces other activities. Instead, they found that the more the children have access to different media in the home, the more they do. Sometimes children performed two activities at the same time, such as reading and watching television.

Similarly, older people derived particular benefits from television:

It was both comfort and company in times of illness and grief, although its reminder of happier times made it a double-edged, bittersweet pleasure. Older viewers felt that television kept them in touch with the world, and mentally active. Television gave these viewers a 'virtual mobility'; its ability to show them other parts of the world was frequently acknowledged.

Gauntlett and Hill, 1999, p. 207

David Buckingham: children and television

We have seen how the level of 'media literacy' affects the sophistication with which people are able to 'read' media messages. One hypothesis is that children are likely to be less media literate than adults and so are more vulnerable to a 'hypodermic' effect of media messages. However, David Buckingham's (1993) work on children and advertising tends to contradict this view.

Children are clearly aware of the functions of advertising and sceptical about it. For example, 8-year-old Ben said, 'They're trying to persuade people to buy things or do things'; and Nancy, also 8, said, 'That's why they advertise it, because they can't get anyone to buy it, so they just try and ... make it look really good.' While children also gave some more imaginative reasons for advertising (for example, 'to allow the actors to change their clothes' and 'to allow people to go to the toilet'), all the children except one who gave this sort of reason *also* gave answers like Ben's and Nancy's.

Buckingham came to a number of conclusions. While children said that they pestered their parents to buy things they had seen, this was done with the realization that they probably would not get them (they were 'trying it on'). They did not seriously ask for things they knew they would not get. They substituted these with requests they knew were more realistic. At Christmas time children consciously used advertisements to help them because they knew they would be asked what they wanted for Christmas and so they needed to generate a list. This finding confirms the 'uses and gratifications' model rather than the 'hypodermic model' of media effects (see pp. 944–6).

According to Buckingham, children saw 'other people' as being influenced by advertisements, but they hardly ever saw themselves as influenced in this way. These 'other people' were usually children younger than themselves. Children were critical, even cynical, about free gifts and the quality of merchandise being advertised generally. They applied their own interpretations to the content of advertisements. People appearing in adverts were described as 'ugly', 'stupid', 'prattish', 'wallies' and 'boring old has-beens'. (Ten-year-old Anne complained that adverts showing women doing the washing and ironing were sexist, and Donna, also 10, was unhappy about the fact that boys' sports got most prominence.)

Children applied their well-developed television literacy (see p. 947) to advertisements. They were able to read the intentions of the advertisers (seeing who the advert was aimed at) and discuss technical aspects of its production. They were 'wise consumers'. Some reported that before buying a toy they had seen on television they tested those their friends had bought. Others reported comparing prices of similar goods in different shops. Children often remembered an advert very well, but could not associate it with any particular product.

Although these results suggest that children are very active in interpreting, modifying and even rejecting advertising messages, Buckingham qualifies this conclusion. First, although these sorts of responses to advertisements give children mental defences against the hypodermic injection of the message, there is no guarantee about when, or if, such defences will be used while watching television or buying goods. Children may have defences, but they may not use them.

Second, the methods used in this study made it more likely that these defences would be shown. Buckingham said that the children interviewed seemed to be competing with each other to see who could be the most cynical and clever about adverts.

Third, while children were generally sceptical about advertising, they displayed a great enthusiasm for watching adverts. Buckingham suggests that children derive a great deal of pleasure from adverts. They enjoy using catchphrases, parodying adverts and singing the songs in adverts – although they often invent new words! Buckingham partly agrees with the conclusion reached by Nava and Nava (1990) that 'young people consume commercials independently of the product which is being marketed'.

Disability and the reception of media messages

Cumberbatch and Negrine (1992) held discussion groups with people who themselves had disabilities, with carers, with families of those with disabilities and with able-bodied people, about their responses to images of disability on television and in films. They also conducted a survey about attitudes towards people with disabilities. Their findings confirm those of audience reception studies in other areas, such as Hartmann and Husband's (1974) study of responses to media representations of black people. Real-life contact with a minority group represented in media messages, or being a member of such a group, gives a particular perspective on the message and enables members of the audience to 'read' it in alternative ways.

Effects or impact of the message

Gender

How theorists interpret the effects of media messages largely depends on the model of media content and influence they subscribe to. The impact of media content on gender roles, for example, is quite clear to those who adopt fairly simple hypodermic and social learning models of media influence. For instance, Provenzo argues that sexist representations in video games have important influences on males:

> [Males] come to assume from the images provided by the games (as well as other sources from the media and the general culture) that women are indeed the 'weaker sex' and constantly in need of aid or assistance. Thus the games not only socialize women to be dependent, but also condition men to assume dominant gender roles.
>
> Provenzo, 1991, p. 100

Similarly, Frueh and McGhee (discussed in Tuchman, 1978) also adopted a simple model of 'effect'. They interviewed American kindergarten children about the amount of time they spent watching television, testing the extent and direction of their sex-typing. Traditional sex-role stereotyping was positively correlated by Frueh and McGhee with heavy viewing. According to this research, women are persuaded to accept and 'go along' with their role: they undergo a process of 'modelling', that is, imitating a role model seen on television. Beuf's (1974) study argues that some girls aged between 3 and 6 have abandoned their ambitions even by that early age.

The implication of this kind of work is that, because of the small number of high-status females in the media available for girls to imitate, the ambitions of real women are limited. The power of the media in this respect is strong, according to Beuf, because the average American girl will have spent more time in front of the television by the time she is 15 than she will have spent in the classroom.

Beuf also argues that women suffer anxiety and stress because advertising and soap operas create concerns in women about their body image, the need to purchase products to keep them attractive and the competition with other women to get and keep a man.

According to socialist feminists (see p. 137), media content sustains and perpetuates the capitalist system and the support-role of women. Big business effectively controls the editorial content of women's magazines, in particular. That women are portrayed in traditional ways is in the interests of the capitalist class: it justifies using women as a reserve labour force. Kath Davies argues thus:

Since those who control the media are almost all (rich) men, there is every incentive for them to present the capitalist, patriarchal scheme of things as the most attractive system available – and to convince the less privileged that the oppression and limitations of their lives are inevitable.

Davies, 1987, p. 3

However, such straightforward capitalist manipulation of the media is not considered particularly important by many other socialist feminists. Most adopt either a cultural hegemony model of influence or the more sophisticated 'logic of capitalism' version of Marxism in explaining the influence of the media on women (see pp. 937–43).

Angela McRobbie (1991) is in the latter category. She notes how women's magazines have to attract advertising - their articles on makeup surrounded by adverts for eyeliner, hair-mousse and lipstick. Fashion and celebrity, prominent in such magazines, are also tied into the system of consumption. It is part of the 'inner logic' of these magazines that consumption is a natural feature of readers' experience, so that it is seen as extremely unusual not to be interested in 'hairstyles, "cleansing" and all the other intimate rituals that are an intrinsic part of being a woman in contemporary consumer culture' (McRobbie, 1991).

Liberal feminists' interest in sex roles usually leads them to adopt content analyses of the media, though they tend to take for granted the *effects* of the stereotyped content they usually find. Gaye Tuchman argues that the media in general, and television advertisements in particular, perform the symbolic annihilation of women:

The analyses of television commercials support the ... hypothesis ... [that] commercials neglect or rigidly stereotype women.

Tuchman *et al.* (eds), 1978

However, media content can be changed by a conscious process of rooting out those elements in society which perpetuate such stereotypes. Tuchman believes that this is increasingly the case:

The mass media deal in symbols and their symbolic representations may not be up to date. A time lag may be operating. ... As values change, we would expect the images of society presented in the media to change.

Tuchman *et al.* (eds), 1978

Ethnicity

In terms of ethnicity, too, the model of media effects adopted by a researcher will have important consequences for the way they gather and interpret

their data. Van Dijk (1991) provides an example. He reports the initial results of a study of the effects of press reports on 'race' on people's perceptions of race issues. Based on interviews designed to reveal how people recall and re-tell press stories, the conclusions are as follows:

- People recall stories even from years ago: time is not a major factor.
- Where an event is massively reported, individuals can integrate the story into their understanding of reality and their more general knowledge about, for example, a particular group of immigrants.
- Where the reader has a good understanding of the issues already, stories are more likely to be recalled and integrated into their ideas.

According to Van Dijk, virtually no reader challenges the interpretation of immigration issues put forward in the press (and which come from elite groups in society). The possibility that different audiences will interpret the text in different ways (as reception analysis would suggest) is discounted by Van Dijk.

The hypodermic model can give rise to fears that the attitudes which are 'injected' into the audience will quickly result in action; that media-inspired racial prejudice, for example, will turn into racial discrimination; or worse, that race hatred will turn into race killings.

However, most studies suggest that direct experience affects the impact of media messages. Hartmann and Husband's (1974) study on children's attitudes towards race is a case in point. Part of the sample they selected for study lived in the West Midlands and Yorkshire (where there is a high density of Asian groups), and another part lived in Teesside and Glasgow (where there is not). Hartmann and Husband found that children in Teesside and Glasgow were more likely to view race relations in terms of 'conflict', 'threat' and 'numbers' because virtually all their information on the issue came from the media rather than actual experience.

Recent studies have emphasized the importance of class and other differences in audiences in conditioning the nature of media effects. If it is the case (as the Glasgow Media Group and others suggest) that the media encode a culturally skewed view of the world, then this will be interpreted differently by different sections of the audience. In terms of social class and gender, for example, Andrea Press concludes:

Because the vast majority of television characters are middle class or upper class, my study indicates that television seems to support what I call a 'hegemony of middle-class realism' for working-class women, and as such may operate in part to blind working-class women to the realities of their own situation in society. When their experience is addressed directly ... working-class women are moved to articulate their difference from, and reality apart from, these images. ... For middle-class women, however, already living the middle-class material life depicted in the vast majority of television products, television's hegemonic importance rests more in the form of the family, and of women's role within it.

Press, 1995, p. 428

Age and media effects

We have already seen how Gillespie (1995) describes the importance of the mass media for young Punjabi Londoners. Dick Hebdige (1988), however, argues that any attempt to understand youth subcultures must take into account how the mass media structure the way society is perceived by the young people within them. Their subcultures are based both on the realities of their social situation and perceptions of it mediated by the mass media – see Figure 13.3.

From a neo-Marxist point of view, Hebdige argues that the media's role is to 'absorb' youth subcultures into mainstream society. Instead of allowing young people to resist capitalist society, the capitalist world attempts to neutralize them through incorporation. The mass media are an extremely important part of this process. The media portray members of youth subcultures as 'just normal kids underneath', the sons and daughters of Mr and Mrs Average, just going through a phase.

Another way of neutralizing youth resistance is what Hebdige calls the commodity form of incorpora-tion. Here, youth cultural signs (dress or music, for example) are converted into mass-produced objects and sold on the high street. In this process they lose their threatening and oppositional meanings. The capitalist market effectively takes artefacts away from

young people, alienating them from their own subculture. Furthermore, the market 'normalizes' the symbols of resistance by turning them into a 'leisure-time only' style.

Hebdige's is a neo-Marxist perspective. For some postmodernist writers like Gillespie (1995), however, the young are more empowered than Hebdige suggests, and the media are empowering rather than oppressive.

Disability and media effects

Cumberbatch and Negrine (1992) argue that the character of an audience conditions the effects of the stereotyped representations of people with disabilities on television and film. In particular, those with personal experience of living with disability are able to reject or reinterpret dominant readings. For those without this experience television's treatment of disability tends to mean that it is seen as an 'issue' and as 'a problem'.

People with disabilities wish to be seen on television because they are part of life and not alien to it. They do not want to use the box as a soap box but as a 'window on the world' in which they exist. ... [But the] achievement of integration is one that more 'positive' imagery alone is unlikely to win single-handedly. Other major social changes would have to take place to accompany the desire to achieve that aim; and such changes would need to include the provision of access to all facets of life, something that will happen only, in the view of many discussants, when people with disabilities are asked about their attitudes, feelings and needs and are not just given what others think they need.

Cumberbatch and Negrine, 1992, p. 134

Cumberbatch and Negrine highlight an issue at the forefront of much recent thinking about media

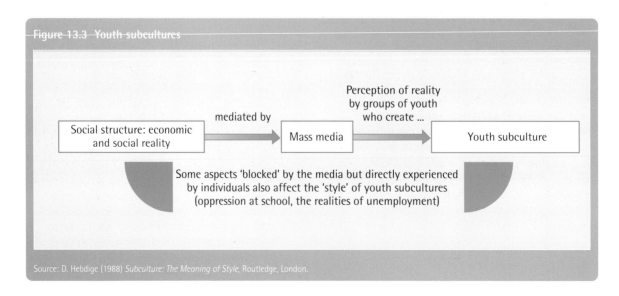

Figure 13.3 Youth subcultures

Social structure: economic and social reality → *mediated by* → Mass media → *Perception of reality by groups of youth who create ...* → Youth subculture

Some aspects 'blocked' by the media but directly experienced by individuals also affect the 'style' of youth subcultures (oppression at school, the realities of unemployment)

Source: D. Hebdige (1988) *Subculture: The Meaning of Style*, Routledge, London.

'effects': the idea that media messages should not be viewed as isolated from the social context in which they are propagated, but should be considered holistically, that is in combination with all surrounding circumstances. As Jenny Kitzinger says, 'Media power does not exist in a vacuum, and audience reception is not an isolated encounter between an individual and a message' (Kitzinger, 1999). Alasuutari (1999) too reminds us that media messages are simply part of social life. Studying them out of context is likely to result in misapprehensions about their role and power.

Sociology, values and communication media

Sociological studies of the media often reveal at least as much about the authors' attitudes to society, morality, parenting and education, etc., as they do about the media themselves.

One example of this concerns worries about media effects on children's aggressiveness and displays of violence. For those who subscribe to a hypodermic or social learning model of media effects, such as Michael Medved (1992) and Elizabeth Newson (1994), the issues about media effects are urgent and serious. Here the audience is regarded as largely passive and easily subject to manipulation by the specialist social groups who create media content.

These writers are quick to point to alleged links between the portrayal of violence in the media and subsequent real-life violence. Many feature films have been the focus of concerns of this sort. Every now and then there is a new moral panic about a film, though it is worth noting that these panics are propagated and sustained through other parts of the media, usually popular newspapers. These panics usually give rise to calls for action, often involving tighter media regulation by the state and more parental control. Underneath these calls are models of an ideal society based on shared (often religious) values and regulations imposed by the state.

In contrast, for authors such as Geoffrey Pearson (1983) and Martin Barker (1989; Barker et al., 1994) the focus of interest is on these worries themselves, not the alleged media effects. Both Pearson and Barker point out that with every new medium the claim is made that 'this time it is different, this time there are special dangers'. Pearson shows that the media have always portrayed a Golden Age (see p. 954) where such dangers did not exist. Barker and Pearson dismiss such concerns because they are based on simplistic models of cause and effect. They view the suggested 'solutions' as stemming from the authoritarian attitudes of those proposing them.

Barker, for example, talks about 'flexipanic', by which he means the flexible – but contradictory – use of argument by researchers and others who are motivated by worries about the media. An example of flexipanic concerns video and film. On the one hand, concern is expressed about video's ability to fast forward, provide slow motion and freeze frame, all of which enables viewers to go straight to the gory bits and linger over them. On the other hand, there is a simultaneous moral panic about feature films, whose realistic, gradual development of tension makes horror scenes even more shocking.

For some Marxists and neo-Marxists such as Stuart Hall (Hall et al. 1978, 1982) and the Glasgow Media Group (1982) these moral panics about the media are themselves part of an agenda about increasing state regulation at a time of crisis in capitalism. To them, such panics are 'really' about gaining public support for the extension and strengthening of state power. The reinforcement of the capitalist state in this way enables it to sustain itself during critical periods.

Beneath these different kinds of theory there are completely different sets of values and different models of the ideal society. Sets of values, often strongly felt, and theories about individuals and society which are rarely made explicit, clearly underpin the questions sociologists ask about the media, the methods they use and the sorts of answers they get. Theorists like Medved and Newson may claim that 'a wealth of scientific studies in recent years have removed most of the remaining doubts about the link between make-believe brutality and real-world aggression'. However, the fact is that the jury is still out on the media's role in this issue. One of the reasons why these things are so difficult to decide is precisely because our own values affect this area of sociological enquiry.

Chapter 14

Methodology

Methodology

Introduction

Any academic subject requires a methodology to reach its conclusions: it must have ways of producing and analysing data so that theories can be tested, accepted or rejected. Without a systematic way of producing knowledge the findings of a subject can be dismissed as guesswork, or even as common sense made to sound complicated. Methodology is concerned with both the detailed research methods through which data are collected, and the more general philosophies upon which the collection and analysis of data are based.

As we have seen in this book, most areas of sociology are riven with controversy. Methodology is no exception to this general rule. One of the main areas of disagreement concerns – in the most general terms – whether sociology should adopt the same methods as (or similar methods to) those employed in science.

Sociology first developed in Europe in the nineteenth century when industrialization resulted in massive social changes. Accompanying these social changes were intellectual changes during which science started to enjoy a higher reputation than ever before. Science appeared to be capable of producing objective knowledge that could be used to solve human problems and increase human productive capacity in an unprecedented way. It was not surprising, therefore, that many early sociologists chose to turn to science for a methodology on which to base their subject.

However, not all sociologists have agreed that it is appropriate to adopt the methodology of the natural sciences. For these sociologists, studying human behaviour is fundamentally different from studying the natural world. Unlike the subject matter of, for example, chemistry or physics, people possess consciousness, which means (from the point of view of some sociologists) that sociology requires a different type of methodology from science.

In the above terms, it was possible to identify two broad traditions within sociology:

1 Those who advocated the use of scientific and usually quantitative methods (numerical statistical methods).

2 Those who supported the use of more humanistic and qualitative methods.

However, it was never the case that all sociologists fitted neatly into these categories. Furthermore, as will become clear, there are divisions *within* these two broad camps as well as *between* them.

In recent years, some sociologists have questioned the need for such a rigid division between quantitative and qualitative methodology, and have advocated combining the two approaches. Other sociologists have advocated methods associated with critical social science or with postmodernism.

Critical social science tends to favour more qualitative methods but it is not exclusively associated with such methods. The central feature of critical social science is that it links research with trying to transform society. It therefore rejects the view of many sociologists – including many of the advocates of the two approaches discussed above – that researchers should be impartial. Instead, it sides with those it sees as the disadvantaged and oppressed groups in society. It seeks to develop any methods that will help to liberate these groups from their oppression.

Feminists are amongst the most influential of critical social scientists, and some feminists have argued that distinctive feminist methodologies should be adopted.

Postmodernists have developed their approaches to methodology relatively recently. They tend to reject the belief that researchers can ever discover some objective truth about the social world. Instead they believe that all that can be done is to examine the social world from the viewpoint of the different actors within it, and to deconstruct or take apart existing explanations of society. They reject the claims of traditional quantitative, qualitative and critical researchers that it is possible to determine the truth about society. Whatever method is used, researchers will be left with many different accounts of the social world, and no particular account can be singled out as being better than the others.

Critical social science and postmodernism will be examined in detail later in the chapter, but first the contrast between quantitative and qualitative approaches will be discussed in greater depth.

'Scientific' quantitative methodology

As the introduction suggested, some sociologists have tried to adopt the methods of the natural sciences. In doing so they have tended to advocate the use of quantitative methods. The earliest attempt to use such methods in sociology is known as positivism.

Positivism, Durkheim and sociology

The French writer Auguste Comte (1798–1857) was the first person to use the word 'sociology', and he also coined the term 'positive philosophy' (Comte, 1986, first published in the 1840s). Comte believed that there was a hierarchy of scientific subjects, with sociology at the pinnacle of that hierarchy. Comte was confident that scientific knowledge about society could be accumulated and used to improve human existence so that society could be run rationally without religion or superstition getting in the way of progress.

Emile Durkheim (1858–1917) advocated a similar methodology to that of Comte. He has been widely regarded as a positivist. Durkheim's classic study *Suicide* (1970, first published 1897) is often seen as a model of positivist research and it does indeed follow many of the methodological procedures of positivism. Certain aspects of Durkheim's work will be used to illustrate the positivist approach. However, strictly speaking Durkheim was not a positivist. As the discussion below will show, he did not follow the positivist rule which states that sociological study should be confined to observable or directly measurable phenomena.

1 Social facts

First, as a positivist, Comte believed that the scientific study of society should be confined to collecting information about phenomena that can be objectively observed and classified. Comte argued that sociologists should not be concerned with the internal meanings, motives, feelings and emotions of individuals. Since these mental states exist only in the person's consciousness, they cannot be observed and so they cannot be measured in any objective way.

Durkheim agreed that sociologists should confine themselves to studying social facts. He argued that 'The first and most fundamental rule is: *Consider social facts as things*' (Durkheim, 1938, first published 1895). This means that the belief systems, customs and institutions of society – the facts of the social world – should be considered as things in the same way as the objects and events of the natural world.

However, Durkheim did not believe that social facts consisted only of those things that could be directly observed or measured. To Durkheim, social facts included such phenomena as the belief systems, customs and institutions of society. Belief systems are not directly measurable or observable since they exist in the consciousness of humans. Nevertheless, Durkheim saw them as existing over and above individual consciousness. They were not chosen by individuals and they could not be changed at will. Social facts, such as the customs of a particular profession, were external to each individual and constrained their behaviour. That is, each person had their options limited by the existence of customs and practices.

In Durkheim's view, society is not simply a collection of individuals, each acting independently in terms of his or her particular psychology or mental state. Instead, members of society are directed by collective beliefs, values and laws – by social facts which have an existence of their own. Social facts therefore make individuals behave in particular ways. Durkheim's definition and use of the term 'social facts' distinguish him from positivists such as Comte. In many other respects, though, he followed the logic and methods of positivism. (The differences between Durkheim's approach and positivism are further discussed on p. 976.)

2 Statistical data

The second aspect of positivism concerns its use of statistical data. Positivists believed it was possible to classify the social world in an objective way. Using these classifications it was then possible to count sets of observable social facts and so produce statistics. For example, Durkheim (1970) collected data on social facts such as the suicide rate and membership of different religions.

3 Correlation

The third stage of positivist methodology entails looking for correlations between different social facts. A correlation is a tendency for two or more things to be found together, and it may refer to the strength of the relationship between them. In his study of suicide Durkheim found an apparent correlation between a particular religion, Protestantism, and a high suicide rate.

4 Causation

The fourth stage of positivist methodology involves a search for causal connections. If there is a strong correlation between two or more types of social phenomena, then a positivist sociologist might suspect that one of these phenomena was causing the other to take place. However, this is not necessarily the case, and it is important to analyse the data carefully before any such conclusion can be reached.

The example of class and criminality can be used to illustrate this point. Many sociologists have noted a correlation between being working-class and a relatively high chance of being convicted of a crime. This has led some (for instance, Robert Merton (1968)) to speculate that being working-class was one factor which might cause people to commit criminal acts. This can be illustrated simply as:

BEING WORKING-CLASS

causes

CRIME

However, there are other possibilities that might explain the correlation. It could be that a similar proportion of criminals come from all social classes but that conviction for crime causes criminals of middle-class origin to be downwardly socially mobile, and to become working-class, since their criminal records might prevent them from obtaining non-manual work. In other words it is being criminal that causes a person to become working-class, and not the other way round. This is illustrated as:

CRIME

causes

A PERSON TO BECOME WORKING-CLASS

Furthermore, there is the even more serious possibility that an apparent connection between two social phenomena might be a spurious or indirect correlation. This occurs when two or more phenomena are found together but have no direct connection to each other: one does not therefore cause the other. It may be that some third factor has a causal relationship to both the phenomena or factors being examined. For example, it may be that gender is related both to social class and to the likelihood of committing a crime, and that class and crime are not directly connected at all. Men may be more likely to commit crimes than women and may also be more likely to have manual jobs. Thus the original correlation discovered could be a product of the

concentration of men in the working class, as the diagram below illustrates:

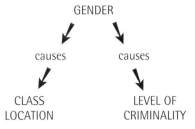

A further possibility is that the police discriminate against the working class and arrest more members of that class than of the middle class, even though the middle class are just as prone to crime.

Multivariate analysis

In order to overcome the problem of spurious correlation, Durkheim devised a technique known as multivariate analysis. This involves trying to isolate the effect of a particular independent variable upon the dependent variables. The dependent variable is the thing that is caused (in the example used above, crime); the independent variable(s) is/are the factor or factors that cause the dependent variable. In the diagram above, gender is an example of an independent variable.

To assess the influence of a particular independent variable – that is, to see if it is more or less important than another independent variable – it may be possible to produce comparisons where one variable is held constant, and the other is changed. For instance, the effect of gender on criminality could be isolated from the effect of class by comparing working-class men and women to see whether their crime rates were similar or different.

With the aid of computers and sophisticated statistical techniques, quantitative researchers can analyse the relative importance of many different variables. Durkheim had to make do with less sophisticated research procedures, but he used the same logic in his study of suicide. For example, he checked whether or not Protestantism was associated with a high suicide rate regardless of nationality by examining suicide rates in a range of countries.

Laws of human behaviour

Positivists believe that multivariate analysis can establish causal connections between two or more variables. If these findings are checked in a variety of contexts (for example, in different societies at different times), then the researchers can be confident that they have attained the ultimate goal of positivism: a law of human behaviour.

A scientific law consists of a statement about the relationship between two or more phenomena which is true in all circumstances. Thus Newton's three Laws of Motion were supposed to describe the ways in which matter would always move. Similarly, Comte and Durkheim believed that real laws of human behaviour could be discovered.

Durkheim claimed to have discovered laws of human behaviour that governed the suicide rate. According to Durkheim the suicide rate always rose during a time of economic boom or slump.

Comte believed he had discovered a law that all human societies passed through three stages: the theological, the metaphysical, and the positive. In the first stage humans believed that events were caused by the actions of gods; in the second, events were held to be caused by abstract forces; but, in the third, scientific rationality triumphed so that scientific laws formed the basis of explanation.

Positivists and Durkheim, then, believe that laws of human behaviour can be discovered by the collection of objective facts about the social world in a statistical form, by the careful analysis of these facts, and by repeated checking of the findings in a series of contexts. From this point of view humans have little or no choice about how they behave. What takes place in their consciousness is held to be irrelevant since external forces govern human behaviour: people react to stimuli in the environment in a predictable and consistent way. They may also have little or no awareness of the factors shaping their actions. These can be uncovered through studying statistical patterns. The implication is that humans react directly to a stimulus without attaching a meaning to it first. (A simple example would be that if a motorist saw the stimulus of a red light, he or she would automatically react to it by stopping.) It is this implication of the positivist approach that has attracted the strongest criticism, as will become clear as the chapter develops.

Positivism is based upon an understanding of science that sees science as using a mainly inductive methodology. An inductive methodology starts by collecting the data. The data are then analysed, and out of this analysis theories are developed. Once the theory has been developed it can then be tested against other sets of data to see if it is confirmed or not. If it is repeatedly confirmed, then Durkheim and positivists such as Comte assume they have discovered a law of human behaviour.

Karl Popper – falsification and deduction

Despite the undoubted influence of positivist methodology within sociology, the inductive method on which it is usually based has not, by any means, been accepted by all scientists. Indeed, many scientists now advocate and use an alternative, deductive approach. Although the logic of the deductive approach is similar in many ways to positivism, the differences have important implications.

This alternative methodology in both natural science and sociology is supported by Karl Popper in his book *The Logic of Scientific Discovery* (1959). The deductive approach reverses the process of induction. It starts with a theory and tests it against the evidence, rather than developing a theory as a result of examining the data.

Popper argues that scientists should start with a 'hypothesis' or a statement that is to be tested. This statement should be very precise, and should state exactly what will happen in particular circumstances. On the basis of the hypothesis it should be possible to deduce predictions about the future. Thus, for example, Newton's Law of Gravity enables hypotheses to be made about the movement of bodies of a given mass, and these hypotheses can then be used to make predictions which can be tested against future events.

According to Popper it matters little how a scientific theory originates. It does not, as positivists suggest, have to come from prior observation and analysis of data. Scientists can develop theories however they wish – their theories might come to them in dreams or in moments of inspiration. What is important, and what makes them scientific, is their ability to be tested by making precise predictions on the basis of the theory.

Popper differs from positivists in that he denies that it is ever possible to produce laws that will necessarily be found to be true for all time. He argues that, logically, however many times a theory is apparently proved correct because predictions made on the basis of that theory come true, there is always the possibility that at some future date the theory will be proved wrong, or 'falsified'. For example, to Popper, the hypothesis 'all swans are white' is a scientific statement because it makes a precise prediction about the colour of any swan that can be found. But, however many times the statement is confirmed – if five, five hundred or five thousand swans are examined and found to be white – the very next swan examined may prove to be black and the hypothesis will be falsified. Laws, whether of natural science or of human behaviour, do not, from this point of view, necessarily have the permanence attributed to them by positivists.

Popper suggests that scientists have a duty to be objective, and to test their theories as rigorously as possible. Therefore, once they have formulated hypotheses, and made predictions, it is necessary to try constantly to find evidence that disproves or falsifies their theories. In the natural sciences one method that has been developed in order to falsify theories is the laboratory experiment. This method, and its relevance to sociology, will now be examined. Popper's view of science will be evaluated later in the chapter (see pp. 1023–7).

The laboratory experiment and sociology

The word 'science' conjures up an image of researchers in white coats carrying out experiments in laboratories. This image is not usually associated, however, with sociology. Indeed sociologists very rarely carry out laboratory experiments even if they support the use of 'scientific' methods in their research. The reasons for this will be examined later, but first, why does the laboratory experiment enjoy such popularity in natural science?

The main reason why scientists use the laboratory experiment is because it enables them to test precise predictions in exactly the way that Popper advocates. Laboratories are controlled environments in which the researcher can manipulate the various independent variables however they wish. They can calculate the effects of a single independent variable while removing the possibility that any other factors are affecting the dependent variable they are studying. This is achieved through the use of a control with which to compare the experiment.

For example, if an experimenter wished to determine the importance of the independent variable, light, on the growth of plants, they could set up a laboratory experiment to isolate the effects of light from other independent variables. Thus the experimenter would set up an experiment and a control in which every variable other than the amount of light was held constant. Two sets of identical plants of the same species, age, condition and size would be kept at the same temperature, in an environment of the same humidity, planted in the same type and amount of soil, and given the same amount of water at the same time. The control group of plants would be exposed to a given intensity of light for a given period of time. The experiment group could be exposed to either more or less light than the control group. The results would be observed, measured and quantified. A single variable – light – would have been isolated to find the effects it had, independently of all the other variables.

The laboratory experiment allows researchers to be far more confident that they have isolated a particular variable than they would have been had they observed plants in the wild, where it would not be possible to regulate the various independent variables so tightly. Furthermore, the laboratory experiment facilitates replication: so long as the precise nature of

the experiment is recorded, other scientists can reproduce identical conditions to see if the same results are obtained.

From Popper's point of view the experimental method is extremely useful because it allows the sort of precision in the making and repeated testing of predictions that he advocates. Laboratory experiments are quite frequently used in some 'social sciences', particularly psychology, but sociologists almost never make use of them. There are two main reasons for this:

1 Laboratories are unnatural situations. Members of society do not, in the normal course of events, spend their time under observation in laboratories. The knowledge that they are being studied, and the artificiality of the situation, might well affect the behaviour of those involved and distort the results so as to make them of little use.

2 It is impractical to carry out experiments in laboratories on many of the subjects of interest to sociologists. It is not possible to fit a community – let alone a whole society – into a laboratory. Nor is it possible to carry out a laboratory experiment over a sufficiently long time span to study social change.

Field experiments

As a consequence of the above difficulties, when sociologists do carry out experiments they are normally outside a laboratory. Such experiments are known as field experiments. They involve intervening in the social world in such a way that hypotheses can be tested by isolating particular variables.

For example, Rosenthal and Jacobson (1968) tested the hypothesis that self-fulfilling prophecies could affect educational attainment by manipulating the independent variables of the pupils' IQ (intelligence quotient) scores known to teachers (see p. 846).

In an experiment into gender role socialization carried out at Sussex University, girl babies were dressed up in blue clothes, boy babies in pink, and the reactions of adults to their behaviour were recorded. Not only did the adults assume that the boys were girls, and vice versa, but they interpreted their behaviour differently depending upon the sex they presumed them to be. Thus restless 'boys' (in reality the girls dressed in blue) were regarded as wanting to be active and to play, while restless 'girls' were regarded as being emotionally upset and in need of comfort (reported in Nicholson, 1993).

In another experiment, Sissons observed the reactions of members of the public when they were asked for directions by an actor. The location of the experiment was held constant (it took place outside Paddington station), but the appearance of the actor varied. Halfway through the experiment the actor changed from being dressed as a businessman to being dressed as a labourer. Sissons found that the public were more helpful when the actor was dressed as a businessman rather than as a labourer (discussed in McNeill, 1985).

Brown and Gay (1985) conducted field experiments in which they made bogus applications for jobs by letter and telephone, identifying themselves as being from different ethnic groups (white, Asian and Afro-Caribbean). They found that the applications from supposedly non-white candidates were less likely to lead to a job interview than those from supposedly white candidates (see pp. 282–3).

Although field experiments overcome the problem of experiments taking place in an unnatural setting, these experiments do have other problems associated with them. First, it is not possible to control variables as closely as it is in the laboratory. Thus in Sissons's experiment, for example, it was not possible to carry out the two experiments at the same time and the same place, and, since they took place at different times, factors such as the weather and the time of day might have affected the results.

Second, in some field experiments the fact that an experiment is taking place can affect the results. This is often known as the Hawthorne Effect, after a famous experiment conducted at the Hawthorne works of the Western Electricity Company in Chicago and analysed by Elton Mayo (1933). The experiment was intended to test various hypotheses about worker productivity. Variables such as room temperature, the strength of the lighting and the length of breaks were varied, but, irrespective of whether working conditions were improved or made worse, productivity usually increased. It appeared that the workers were responding to the knowledge that an experiment was taking place rather than to the variables being manipulated.

To avoid the Hawthorne Effect (which can render the results of experiments worthless), it is necessary that the subjects of experimental research are unaware that the experiment is taking place. This, however, raises a further problem: the morality of conducting experiments on people without their consent. Some sociologists strongly object to doing this. Some experiments, such as Sissons's, may not have great moral implications, but others do. In Rosenthal and Jacobson's experiment (described above) the researchers may have held back the educational careers of some children by lying to their teachers.

Although field experiments open up greater possibilities than laboratory experiments, they are still likely to be confined to small-scale studies over short periods of time. Experimentation on society as a whole, or on large groups in society, is only likely to be possible with the consent of governments. Few

governments are willing to surrender their authority to social researchers who are keen to test the theories and hypotheses they have developed! In any case it would cost a fortune and funds for research are limited. In these circumstances sociologists normally rely upon studying society as it is, rather than trying to manipulate it so that their theories can be tested directly.

The comparative method

The comparative method, as its name suggests, involves the use of comparisons. These may be comparisons of different societies, of groups within one or more societies, and comparisons at the same or different points in time. Unlike the experiment, the comparative method is based upon an analysis of what has happened, or is happening in society, rather than upon the situations artificially created by a researcher. The data used in the comparative method may come from any of the primary or secondary sources discussed in detail later in this chapter.

The comparative method overcomes some of the problems involved with experimentation in 'social sciences'. Moral problems are not as acute as in experimentation, since the researcher is not intervening directly in shaping the social world. Furthermore, the researcher is less likely to affect artificially the behaviour of those being studied, since the data, at least in theory, come from 'natural' situations.

The comparative method uses a similar 'scientific' logic to that employed by positivists, or to that used in the deductive approach supported by Popper. Systematic comparisons can be used either to establish correlations and ultimately causal connections and supposed 'laws', or to rigorously test hypotheses.

This method can be used to isolate variables to try to uncover the cause or causes of the social phenomenon being studied. It can be a far less convenient approach than laboratory or field experimentation. There is no guarantee that the available data will make it possible to isolate variables precisely when comparing, for example, the development of two different societies. There may be many ways in which they differ, and determining which independent variables caused the differences in the societies may not be straightforward.

The comparative method is superior to the experiment, though, in that it allows the sociologist to study the causes of large-scale social change over long periods of time. The historical development of societies can be studied; this is not feasible using experiments.

The comparative method has been widely used in sociology, particularly but by no means exclusively by those advocating a 'scientific' quantitative approach to the subject. The major founders of the discipline – Marx, Durkheim and Weber – all employed the comparative method.

Marx (1974) compared a wide variety of societies in order to develop his theory of social change and to support his claim that societies passed through different stages (see Chapter 15 for further details).

Durkheim, too, used the comparative method in his study of the division of labour and the change from mechanical to organic solidarity (Durkheim, 1947, first published 1893) (see pp. 691–3 for further details). Durkheim's study of suicide (which is considered later in this chapter) is a classic example of how detailed statistical analysis – involving the comparison of different societies, different groups within society, and different time periods – can be used to try to isolate the variables that cause a social phenomenon (see pp. 974–6).

In *The Protestant Ethic and the Spirit of Capitalism* (1958, first published 1930) Weber systematically compared early capitalist countries in Western Europe and North America with countries such as China and India to try to show a correlation between early capitalism and Calvinism (see pp. 446–51).

Modern sociologists have followed in the footsteps of Marx, Durkheim and Weber. There are numerous examples of the use of this method throughout this book, including David Martin's comparison of secularization in different countries (see pp. 490–2), Cicourel's comparison of juvenile justice in two Californian cities (see pp. 379–80), Michael Mann's comparison of networks of power in different territories (see pp. 633–5), and Fiona Devine's comparison of affluent workers in Luton in the 1990s and similar workers in the 1960s (see pp. 81–3).

Interpretive and qualitative methodology

Despite the considerable influence of the 'scientific' approaches to sociological methodology described above, an alternative series of interpretive or qualitative approaches has long existed within sociology. These approaches claim either that 'scientific' approaches are inadequate on their own for collecting, analysing and explaining data, or that they are totally inappropriate in a subject that deals with human behaviour. Thus some sociologists who advocate the use of interpretive and qualitative approaches suggest that they should be used to supplement 'scientific' quantitative methodology; others that they should replace 'scientific' approaches.

Qualitative data

Quantitative data are data in a numerical form: for example, official statistics on crime, suicide and divorce rates. By comparison, qualitative data are usually presented in words. These may be a description of a group of people living in poverty, providing a full and in-depth account of their way of life, or a transcript of an interview in which people describe and explain their attitude towards and experience of religion.

Compared to quantitative data, qualitative data are usually seen as richer, more vital, as having greater depth and as more likely to present a true picture of a way of life, of people's experiences, attitudes and beliefs.

The interpretive approach

Sociologists who take an interpretive approach are usually the strongest advocates of qualitative data. They argue that the whole basis of sociology is the interpretation of social action. Social action can only be understood by interpreting the meanings and motives on which it is based. Many interpretive sociologists argue that there is little chance of discovering these meanings and motives from quantitative data. Only from qualitative data – with its greater richness and depth – can the sociologist hope to interpret the meanings that lie behind social action.

Some interpretive sociologists reject the use of natural science methodology for the study of social action. They see the subject matter of the social and natural sciences as fundamentally different. The natural sciences deal with matter. Since matter has no consciousness, its behaviour can be explained simply as a reaction to external stimuli. It is compelled to react in this way because its behaviour is essentially meaningless. Unlike matter, people have consciousness. They see, interpret and experience the world in terms of meanings; they actively construct their own social reality. Meanings do not have an independent existence, a reality of their own which is somehow separate from social actors. They are not imposed by an external society that constrains members to act in certain ways. Instead they are constructed and reconstructed by actors in the course of social interaction.

People do not react automatically to external stimuli as positivists claim. Instead, they interpret the meaning of a stimulus before responding to it. Motorists who see a red light will not automatically stop in response to this stimulus. They will attach a meaning to the stimulus before acting. Motorists might conclude that the light is a decoration on a Christmas tree, and not a traffic signal, or alternatively that it indicates that a nearby building is a brothel. Having established the meaning of the stimulus to their own satisfaction, the motorists will then decide how they wish to respond. Motorists being pursued by the police might jump a red light rather than stop. If the stimulus is regarded as a decoration, motorists might stop to admire it, or continue on their way without giving the light a second thought. Clearly, the motorist who concludes that the red light is advertising a brothel might respond in a variety of ways!

Whatever action is taken by an individual, advocates of interpretive sociology would argue that the causal explanation of human behaviour is impossible without some understanding of the subjective states of the individuals concerned. Thus a positivist might be content to discover what external factors led to a certain type of human behaviour, while an advocate of a more qualitative approach would be interested in the meaning attached to the behaviour by those engaging in it.

It is at this point that opponents of positivist and 'scientific' methods begin to diverge. While some, like Weber, regard the understanding of meaning as necessary to making causal explanations possible, others, such as phenomenologists, regard understanding as the end product of sociological research and they reject the possibility of producing causal explanations at all.

The implications of three qualitative interpretive sociological approaches for methodology will now be briefly examined. They are dealt with in more detail in the next chapter.

1 Max Weber

Weber defined sociology as the study of social action (Weber, in Gerth and Mills (eds), 1948). Action is social when it takes account of other members of society. Weber believed that an explanation of social action necessitated an understanding of the meanings and motives that underlie human behaviour. The sociologist must interpret the meanings given to actions by the actors themselves. For instance, in order to explain why an individual was chopping wood, the sociologist must discover the person's motives for doing so – whether they were doing it to earn money, to make a fire, to work

off anger or for some other motive. According to Weber, understanding motives could be achieved through *verstehen* – imagining yourself to be in the position of the person whose behaviour you were seeking to explain.

Weber's emphasis on meanings and motives is obvious throughout his work. For example, in *The Protestant Ethic and the Spirit of Capitalism* (1958), one of his main concerns was to interpret the beliefs and motives of the early Calvinists (see pp. 446–51). However, he was not simply concerned with understanding meanings and motives for their own sake. Weber wanted to explain social action and social change. He was interested in causality.

This can be seen clearly from The Protestant Ethic and the Spirit of Capitalism. Using the comparative method, Weber systematically compared the characteristics of early capitalist countries and technologically advanced oriental societies. By doing so he claimed to have isolated 'ascetic' Protestantism as a variable that contributed to the rise of capitalism. He saw the moral and religious beliefs and motives of the early Calvinists as one of the main factors accounting for the emergence of capitalism in the West. (For a fuller account of Weber's methodology, see Chapter 7.)

2 Symbolic interactionism

Symbolic interactionists do not reject the attempt to establish causal relationships within sociology; indeed they see this as an important part of the sociologist's work. However, they tend to believe that statistical data does not provide any great insight into human behaviour. Interactionists see human behaviour as largely governed by the internal processes by which people interpret the world around them and give meaning to their own lives.

In particular, interactionists believe that individuals possess a 'self-concept', or image of themselves, that is built up, reinforced or modified in the process of interaction with other members of society. Thus human beings have an image of what sort of person they are, and they will tend to act in accordance with that image. They might see themselves as caring or tough, honest or dishonest, weak or strong, and their behaviour reflects this sense of their own character.

The responses of others to an individual may make it impossible for him or her to sustain a particular self-concept; the self-concept will change, and in turn the behaviour of the individual will alter accordingly. Thus interactionists have tried to show how the labelling of people as deviant, or as educational successes or failures, can produce self-fulfilling prophecies in which their behaviour comes to live up (or down) to the expectations of others.

(For details of these labelling theories, see pp. 372–9 and 843–9.)

The implications of these views for sociological methodology have been developed by the American interactionist Herbert Blumer (1962). Blumer rejects what he regards as the simplistic attempts to establish causal relationships which characterize positivist methodology.

As an example, Blumer refers to the proposition that industrialization causes the replacement of extended families with nuclear families. He objects to the procedure of isolating variables and assuming that one causes the other with little or no reference to the actor's view of the situation. He argues that data on the meanings and interpretations which actors give to the various facets of industrialization and family life are essential before a relationship can be established between the two factors.

Blumer claims that many sociologists conduct their research with only a superficial familiarity with the area of life under investigation. This is often combined with a preoccupation with aping the research procedures of the natural sciences. The net result is the imposition of definitions on the social world with little regard for their relevance to that world. Rather than viewing social reality from the actor's perspective, many sociologists have attempted to force it into predefined categories and concepts. This provides little chance of capturing social reality, but a very good chance of distorting it.

In place of such procedures Blumer argues that sociologists must immerse themselves in the area of life that they seek to investigate. Rather than attempting to fit data into predefined categories, they must attempt to grasp the actor's view of social reality. This involves 'feeling one's way inside the experience of the actor'. Since action is directed by actors' meanings, the sociologist must 'catch the process of interpretation through which they construct their action'. This means that the researcher 'must take the role of the acting unit whose behaviour he is studying'.

Blumer offers no simple solutions as to how this type of research may be conducted. However, the flavour of the research procedures he advocates is captured in the following quotation:

> It is a tough job requiring a high order of careful and honest probing, creative yet disciplined imagination, resourcefulness and flexibility in study, pondering over what one is finding, and a constant readiness to test and recast one's views and images of the area.
>
> Blumer, 1962

(For a detailed discussion of symbolic interactionism see Chapter 15.)

3 Phenomenology

The nature of social reality

Phenomenology represents the most radical departure from the 'scientific' quantitative methodology examined at the start of the chapter. Phenomenologists go further than interactionists in that they reject the possibility of producing causal explanations of human behaviour. They do not believe that it is possible objectively to measure and classify the world. To phenomenologists, human beings make sense of the world by imposing meanings and classifications upon it. These meanings and classifications make up social reality. There is no objective reality beyond these subjective meanings.

Thus, for example, in Cicourel's study of juvenile justice (Cicourel, 1976) (examined on pp. 379–80), police and juvenile officers had the problem of classifying the behaviour of juveniles into the categories: delinquent and non-delinquent. Cicourel did not find this process to be objective: it largely depended on the stereotypes of the 'typical delinquent' held by the officials. As such, the data on convictions for various delinquent acts were a social product based upon the commonsense assumptions of the authorities who created the statistics.

At first sight, Cicourel's study might simply suggest that the statistics were invalid and that further research might well reveal the true rate of delinquency. However, phenomenologists reject this view. All statistics are social products which reflect the meanings of those who created them. The meanings are the reality which sociologists must examine. Crime statistics have no existence outside the meanings and interpretive procedures that produced them. To assume that there is a true crime rate that has an objective reality is to misunderstand the nature of the social world. From a phenomenological perspective, the job of the sociologist is simply to understand the meanings from which social reality is constructed.

Phenomenologists believe that the problem of classification is universal, and not unique to particular types of data. All people, all of the time, make decisions about how to classify things, and these decisions are the product of social processes. For example, on a simple level, what one person might classify as a 'chair' might be classified by another person as a 'wooden object', and by a third person who was involved in a pub brawl as 'a missile'. From this point of view all data are the product of the classification systems used by those who produce them. If the classification system were different, the data would be different.

Furthermore, to phenomenologists there is no way of choosing between different systems of classification and seeing one as superior to another. It is therefore pointless to use data which rest upon the interpretations of individuals in order to try to establish correlations and causal relationships. Thus, using official statistics to reach the conclusion that being working-class causes a person to commit crimes would not be justified. The figures would only show how crime was defined and classified, rather than what criminal actions had been carried out by particular groups within the population.

Phenomenologists believe that sociologists should limit themselves to understanding the meanings and classifications which people use to give order to and make sense of the world. With their exclusive emphasis upon meanings and the social construction of reality, phenomenologists concentrate almost entirely on the subjective aspects of social life which are internal to the individual's consciousness. They therefore tend to use rather different research methods from the more 'scientific' approaches.

The implications of the different approaches considered so far will now be discussed with reference to a particular area of social life: suicide.

The sociology of suicide

Arguably, the topic of suicide has received a disproportionate amount of attention from sociologists. A large number of books and articles have been written on the subject, whereas other areas of social life that could be seen as equally important – for instance, murder – have not been the subject of so much interest. The main reason for this is the fact that Durkheim used this topic to illustrate his own methodological approach.

Durkheim – *Suicide: A Study in Sociology*

In 1897 Durkheim published his book *Suicide: A Study in Sociology* (1970), and many studies of suicide have been, at least in part, a reaction to Durkheim's work. Some sociologists have tried to show how Durkheim's approach was successful in explaining suicide; others have tried to develop and improve his theory; others have rejected his whole approach. Suicide has become an area in which different methodological approaches have been tested and disputed.

Durkheim chose to study suicide for a number of reasons. In late nineteenth-century France, sociology was gradually becoming established as an academic discipline and Durkheim wanted to reinforce this process and show how his particular approach to the subject was superior to others. He wished to use his study to show how there was a sociological level of analysis which was distinct from other disciplines and which made an important contribution to the explanation of social phenomena.

Suicide was, and still is, widely regarded as a highly individual act. For example, it is often explained in terms of an individual's depression. It therefore appeared an unlikely candidate for sociological analysis with its emphasis on the social rather than the individual. There were established psychological theories of suicide. Durkheim attempted to show that suicide could not be fully explained by psychologists. Sociology could explain aspects of suicide which psychology could not.

Durkheim did not deny that particular circumstances would lead to a particular person taking his or her own life, but personal reasons could not account for the *suicide rate*. For example, he tried to show that there was no relationship between the incidence of insanity (which many psychologists associated with suicide) and the suicide rate. He found that Jews had higher rates of insanity than other religious groups, but they had lower rates of suicide.

Durkheim also chose to study suicide because of the availability of suicide statistics from a number of European countries. He regarded these statistics as social facts and so believed that they could be used to find the sociological causes of suicide rates. He could try to establish correlations, and, using the comparative method, could uncover the patterns that would reveal the causal relationships at work in the production of suicide rates. In this way he aimed to demonstrate that sociology was as rigorous a discipline as the natural sciences.

In order to achieve these objectives Durkheim first tried to show that suicide rates were relatively stable in a particular society over a period of time. As Table 14.1 shows, over the periods covered there was a remarkable consistency in the comparative suicide rates of the European societies in question. Durkheim felt able to claim that 'The suicide-rate is therefore a factual order, unified and definite, as is shown by both its permanence and its variability.' Furthermore, as will be discussed shortly, Durkheim found consistent variations in the suicide rate between different groups within the same society. He believed it was impossible to explain these patterns if suicide was seen solely as a personal and individual act.

Table 14.1	Rate of suicides per million inhabitants in different European countries					
		Period		Numerical position in:		
	1866–70	1871–5	1874–8	period 1	period 2	period 3
Italy	30	35	38	1	1	1
Belgium	66	69	78	2	3	4
England	67	66	69	3	2	2
Norway	76	73	71	4	4	3
Austria	78	94	130	5	7	7
Sweden	85	81	91	6	5	5
Bavaria	90	91	100	7	6	6
France	135	150	160	8	9	9
Prussia	142	134	152	9	8	8
Denmark	277	258	255	10	10	10
Saxony	293	267	334	11	11	11

Source: E. Durkheim (1970) *Suicide: A Study in Sociology*, Routledge & Kegan Paul, London, p. 50.

Durkheim then went on to establish correlations between suicides and other sets of social facts. He found that suicide rates were higher in predominantly Protestant countries than in Catholic ones. Jews had a low suicide rate, lower even than Roman Catholics. Generally, married people were more prone to suicide than those who were single, although married women who remained childless for a number of years ended up with a high suicide rate. Durkheim also found that a low suicide rate was associated with political upheaval. The suicide rate in France fell after the *coup d'état* of Louis Bonaparte, for example. War also reduced the suicide rate. After war broke out in 1866 between Austria and Italy, the suicide rate fell by 14 per cent in both countries.

Having established these correlations, Durkheim used multivariate analysis to isolate the most important variables and to determine whether there was a genuine causal relationship between these factors and suicide. For example, Durkheim recognized the possibility that it might be the national culture rather than the main religion of particular countries that accounted for their suicide rate. In order to test whether this was the case he checked on differences within the population of particular countries to see whether these differences supported his views on the importance of religion. The evidence supported Durkheim. For example, Bavaria, the area of Germany with the highest number of Roman Catholics, also had the lowest suicide rate. He also checked the relative importance of different factors: he found that high suicide rates

were correlated with high levels of education. However, he established that religion was more important than level of education. Jews had a low suicide rate despite having a high level of education.

Types of suicide

From his analysis of the relationship between suicide rates and a range of social factors, Durkheim began to distinguish types of suicide. He believed that the suicide rate was determined by the relationships between individuals and society. In particular, suicide rates were dependent upon the degree to which individuals were integrated into social groups and the degree to which society regulated individual behaviour. On this basis he distinguished four types of suicide: egoistic, altruistic, anomic and fatalistic, as illustrated in Figure 14.1.

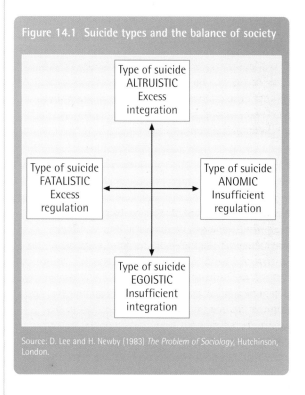

Figure 14.1 Suicide types and the balance of society

Source: D. Lee and H. Newby (1983) *The Problem of Sociology*, Hutchinson, London.

Egoistic suicide resulted from the individual being insufficiently integrated into the social groups and society to which he or she belonged. This, according to Durkheim, accounted for the discrepancy between the suicide rates of Protestants and Roman Catholics. He argued that the Catholic religion integrated its members more strongly into a religious community. The long-established beliefs and traditional rituals of the Catholic Church provided a uniform system of religious belief and practice into which the lives of its members were closely intertwined. The Catholic faith was rarely questioned and the church had strong controls over the conscience and behaviour of its members. The result was a homogeneous religious community, unified and integrated by uniform belief and standardized ritual.

By comparison, the Protestant Church encouraged its members to develop their own interpretation of religion. Protestantism advocated 'free inquiry' rather than the imposition of traditional religious dogma. In Durkheim's view, 'The Protestant is far more the author of his faith.' As a result, Protestants were less likely to belong to a community that was unified by a commitment to common religious beliefs and practices. Durkheim concluded that the higher rate of suicide associated with Protestantism 'results from its being a less strongly integrated church than the Catholic church'.

Durkheim also related egoistic suicide to 'domestic society' or family relationships. The unmarried and childless were less integrated into a family than the married and those with children. The former group had less responsibility for others and as a consequence were more prone to egoism and a high suicide rate.

Durkheim thought that anomic suicide was the other main type of suicide in industrial societies. Anomic suicides took place when society did not regulate the individual sufficiently. This occurred when traditional norms and values were disrupted by rapid social change which produced uncertainty in the minds of individuals as society's guidelines for behaviour became increasingly unclear. Not surprisingly, Durkheim found that suicide rates rose during periods of economic depression, such as the period following the crash of the Paris Bourse (stock exchange) in 1882. What was more surprising – and at first sight difficult to explain – was the rise in the suicide rate during a period of economic prosperity. The conquest of Rome by Victor-Emmanuel in 1870 formed the basis of Italian unity and led to an economic boom with rapidly rising salaries and living standards, but it also led to a rising suicide rate. Durkheim reasoned that both booms and slumps brought the uncertainty of anomie, and so more suicides.

Durkheim thought that egoism and anomie were problems that affected all industrial societies to a greater or lesser extent. Because of the highly special- ized division of labour in such societies they were less integrated than simple or 'primitive' societies.

Pre-industrial societies could suffer from the opposite types of suicide to egoistic and anomic: altruistic and fatalistic.

Altruistic suicide took place when the individual was so well integrated into society that they sacrificed their own life out of a sense of duty to others. In the past, Hindu widows would kill themselves at their husband's funeral (suttee); and in traditional Ashanti society some of the king's

followers were expected to commit suicide after the death of the monarch. Individuals were so strongly integrated into their society that they would make the ultimate sacrifice for the benefit of others.

The fourth and final type of suicide, distinguished by Durkheim as fatalistic suicide, occurred when society restricted the individual too much. It was the suicide 'of persons with futures pitilessly blocked and passions violently choked by oppressive discipline'. Durkheim thought that this type of suicide was of little importance in modern societies, but it was of some historical interest, being the cause of high suicide rates among slaves.

Durkheim, suicide and methodology

Durkheim's study of suicide illustrates his views both on society and on methodology. He believed it was essential to achieve the right amount of integration and regulation in society: 'primitive' societies tended to have too much of both; industrial societies too little of either. He used quantitative, 'scientific' methods, employing the comparative method in a highly systematic way. However, he did not simply follow the approach advocated by positivists. He used the supposedly objective statistics available on suicide to support the claim that unobservable forces shaped human behaviour. The total number of suicides was determined by such unobservable 'collective tendencies', which 'have an existence of their own' and are as 'real as cosmic forces'.

According to some of today's sociologists, such as Steve Taylor, Durkheim adopted a realist rather than a positivist view of science (realism is discussed on pp. 1026–7). However it is defined, it is nevertheless Durkheim's methodology in studying suicide that has attracted most attention from supporters and critics alike.

Positivist responses to Durkheim

Sociologists studying suicide who adopt positivist methods have generally praised most aspects of Durkheim's work. As early as 1930 Maurice Halbwachs carried out a review of his work. Halbwachs attempted to refine Durkheim's work and did not challenge the use of a 'scientific' approach in the study of suicide. Indeed he claimed that Durkheim had been able to provide 'a fully compre- hensive treatment of the phenomenon of suicide, which could be modified and added to, but which in principle seems unassailable' (Halbwachs, 1930).

Halbwachs could add to and modify Durkheim's work by making use of both the more recent suicide statistics that had become available and new methods of statistical analysis such as the use of correlation coefficients. On the whole he confirmed what Durkheim had found. However, he did argue that

Durkheim had overestimated the importance of religion in determining the suicide rate. Halbwachs claimed to have found that differences between living in urban and rural areas had more impact than differences between Catholics and Protestants.

Jack P. Gibbs and Walter T. Martin (1964) agreed with Durkheim and Halbwachs that suicide should be studied using scientific methods and statistical data. However, they believed that Durkheim himself had failed to use sufficiently rigorous methods. As noted earlier, Durkheim sometimes used concepts that could not be directly observed or measured and thus he did not entirely follow positivist methods. Gibbs and Martin picked up on this and attempted to rectify what they saw as a flaw in Durkheim's otherwise exemplary method. In particular they suggested that Durkheim failed to define the concept of 'integration' in a sufficiently precise and measurable way. They point out that 'one does not see individuals tied to society in any physical sense'. Consequently it was impossible to test the theory that lack of integration led to a high suicide rate.

Gibbs and Martin did not believe that integration itself could be measured directly. The type of data necessary to measure the durability and stability of social relationships was not available. They therefore proposed that 'status integration' could be used as an indicator of social integration. Status integration concerns the extent to which individuals occupy sets of social roles that are commonly found together. People with a high degree of status integration have job, family and other statuses that are commonly grouped together. Those with a high degree of status incompatibility have unusual sets of statuses. Thus, in their theory, an occupation in which 75 per cent of its members are married is compatible with marriage, but if only 35 per cent are married it is not compatible. Individuals with compatible statuses are deemed to be highly integrated since it is assumed that they will have more and stronger social relationships than those with incompatible statuses. To Gibbs and Martin, the greater the degree of status integration in a population, the lower the suicide rate will be.

Gibbs and Martin's theory shows that some commentators criticized Durkheim for being insufficiently positivist and for making too little use of statistical data. The theory itself, though, does not bear close examination. Gibbs and Martin do not provide any evidence to show that status integration can be used to measure the strength of people's social relationships. Nor do they justify the use of statistics alone to identify compatible statuses. Hagedorn and Labowitz point out that male ballet dancers and male lion tamers are both uncommon but the former could be expected to have more incompatible statuses (quoted in S. Taylor, 1982).

Interpretive theories of suicide

Interpretive sociologists tend to make much stronger attacks on Durkheim's study of suicide than positivists. They tend to reject many of the basic principles of Durkheim's approach rather than quibbling about particular details. On the whole, however, they do acknowledge the possibility of explaining the causes of suicide.

J.D. Douglas – *The Social Meanings of Suicide*

One of the best-known interpretive critics of Durkheim is J.D. Douglas (1967). Douglas particularly criticizes the use of official statistics in the study of suicide, questioning their validity. He points out that the decision as to whether a sudden death is suicide is made by a coroner and is influenced by other people, such as the family and friends of the deceased. Douglas suggests that systematic bias may enter the process of reaching a decision, and that this bias could explain Durkheim's findings. For example, when a person is well integrated into a social group, his or her family and friends might be more likely to deny the possibility of suicide, both to themselves and to the coroner. They may feel a sense of personal responsibility which leads them to try to cover up the suicide. With less well-integrated members of society this is less likely to happen. So, while it might appear that the number of suicides is related to integration, in reality the degree of integration simply affects the chances of sudden death being recorded as suicide.

Douglas sees suicide statistics as the result of negotiations between the different parties involved. However, he does suggest that the distortions in the statistics are systematic. By implication, it might be possible to reduce or allow for these distortions to produce more reliable statistics that could be used to explain suicide.

Douglas's second main criticism of Durkheim is that it was ridiculous for Durkheim to treat all suicides as the same type of act without investigating the meaning attached to the act by those who took their own life. Douglas points out that in different cultures suicide can have very different meanings. For example, if a businessman in a modern industrial society kills himself because his business has collapsed, it is a quite different act from the suicide of an elderly Innuit (Eskimo) who kills himself for the benefit of his society at a time of food shortage. Each act has a different motive behind it and a social meaning that is related to the society and context in which it took place.

In order to categorize suicides according to their social meanings Douglas suggests that it is necessary to carry out case studies to discover the meanings of particular suicides. These case studies could be based upon interviews with those who knew the person well, and upon the analysis of the suicide notes and diaries of the deceased. Although he did not carry out such research, Douglas nevertheless claims that the most common social meanings of suicide in Western industrial society are: transformation of the soul (for example, suicide as a way of getting to heaven); transformation of the self (suicide as a means of getting others to think of you differently); suicide as a means of achieving fellow-feeling (or sympathy); and suicide as a means of getting revenge by making others feel guilty.

In other societies other meanings might be more common.

Jean Baechler – suicide as problem solving

Douglas's approach has been developed further by the French sociologist Jean Baechler (1979). Baechler makes extensive use of case studies of suicide in existing literature, and he classifies suicides according to their meanings. He sees suicidal behaviour as a way of responding to and trying to solve a problem. Suicide is adopted when there seems to be no alternative solution. From this perspective it then becomes possible to classify suicides according to the type of solution they offer and the type of situation they are a response to: in other words, according to the end pursued by the suicidal individual. On this basis, Baechler divides suicides into four main types:

1 Escapist suicides take three forms. Some people take their own lives as a means of flight from an intolerable situation. For others, suicide is a response to grief about the loss of something in particular, perhaps a loved one or even a limb. Suicide may also be a means of self-punishment used by a person when they feel they have done wrong.

2 Aggressive suicides are a way of harming another person or people. There are four types of aggressive suicide. Vengeance suicides are intended to make another person feel guilty or to bring condemnation on them from society. For example, a wife might commit suicide to draw attention to her husband's cruelty. Crime suicides involve killing another person during the suicidal behaviour: for example, when someone shoots a spouse and then turns the gun on themselves. Blackmail suicides are used to persuade someone else to change their behaviour and treat the suicide victim better. Appeal suicides are used to show others that the person concerned is in need of help. Blackmail and appeal are often the ends pursued by those who make suicide attempts that either fail or are not entirely serious.

3 Oblative suicides are ways of achieving something that is particularly valued by the suicide victim.

Sacrifice involves giving up your own life to save another person. Transfiguration suicides are used by a person so that they can obtain a more desirable state: for example, to join a loved one in the afterlife.

4 Ludic suicides involve taking deliberate risks that might lead to death. There are two types: the ordeal and the game. Ordeals are ways by which an individual tries to prove themselves to others by showing their bravery. Games involve taking risks 'for the hell of it': for example, playing Russian roulette with nobody else present.

Baechler is more explicit than Douglas in suggesting that causes of suicide can be found. However, unlike Durkheim, he does not believe that suicide can be explained wholly or even mainly in terms of external factors. As Baechler puts it, 'Whatever the external factor considered, it always happens that the number of those who do not commit suicide is infinitely greater than the number of those who do.' Not everyone whose business fails, or whose spouse dies, or who is a Protestant in an urban area, kills themselves. Thus, to Baechler, suicide must always be at least partially explained through 'personal factors' that are particular to an individual.

Baechler's work differs from the studies of suicide examined so far in that he includes attempted suicides under his general definition of 'suicidal behaviour'. Other sociologists have paid even more attention to the implications of attempted suicide (see pp. 980–1).

Criticisms of interpretive theories

Interpretive sociologists have been criticized in a number of ways. Steve Taylor (1989) criticizes both Douglas and Baechler for failing to recognize the value of Durkheim's work. He also questions the worth of schemes that are designed to categorize suicides according to their social meanings. Commenting on Baechler, he points out that individual cases often fit a number of categories, depending on the interpretation the researcher makes of the victim's motives. There is no reason to believe that these interpretations are any more reliable than suicide statistics. Taylor also criticizes Douglas for contradicting himself. At some points Douglas implies that suicide statistics can never be reliable since it is always a matter of judgement whether a death is a suicide. At other times he suggests that causes of suicide can be found. It is difficult to see how this can be if it is impossible to be certain whether an act is a suicide. Phenomenological sociologists have taken this type of criticism to its logical conclusion by denying there can be any objective data on which to base an explanation of suicide.

J. Maxwell Atkinson – *Discovering Suicide*

Scientific and quantitative methods are completely rejected by some phenomenologists. This can be seen clearly from J. Maxwell Atkinson's study of suicide (Atkinson, 1978). Atkinson does not accept that a 'real' rate of suicide exists as an objective reality waiting to be discovered. Sociologists who proceed with this assumption will end up producing 'facts' on suicide that have nothing to do with the social reality they seek to understand. By constructing a set of criteria to categorize and measure suicide – in scientific language, by 'operationalizing' the concept of suicide – they will merely be imposing their reality on the social world. This will inevitably distort that world.

As Michael Phillipson observes, the positivist methodology employed by Durkheim and other researchers 'rides roughshod over the very social reality they are trying to comprehend' (Phillipson, 1972). Suicide is a construct of social actors, an aspect of social reality. Official statistics on suicide, therefore, are not 'wrong', 'mistaken', 'inaccurate' or 'in error'. They are part of the social world. They are the interpretations, made by officials, of what is seen to be unnatural death. Since the object of sociology is to comprehend the social world, that world can only be understood in terms of the categories, perceptions and interpretations of its members. Thus, with reference to suicide, the appropriate question for sociologists to ask is, in Atkinson's words, 'How do deaths get categorized as suicide?' (Atkinson, 1978).

Categorizing death

Atkinson's research focuses on the methods employed by coroners and their officers to categorize death. His data are drawn from discussions with coroners, attendance at inquests in three different towns, observation of a coroner's officer at work, and a part of the records of one particular coroner.

Atkinson argues that coroners have a 'commonsense theory' of suicide. If information about the deceased fits the theory, they are likely to categorize his or her death as suicide. In terms of this theory, coroners consider the following four types of evidence relevant for reaching a verdict:

1 They take into account whether or not suicide notes were left or threats of suicide preceded death.
2 Particular modes of dying are judged to be more or less likely to indicate suicide. Road deaths are rarely interpreted as an indicator for suicide, whereas drowning, hanging, gassing and drug overdose are more likely to be seen as such.
3 The location and circumstances of death are judged to be relevant. For example, death by gunshot is more likely to be defined as suicide if it occurred in

a deserted lay-by than if it took place in the countryside during an organized shoot. In cases of gassing, a suicide verdict is more likely if windows, doors and ventilators have been blocked to prevent the escape of gas.
4 Coroners consider the biography of the deceased, with particular reference to his or her mental state and social situation. A history of mental illness, a disturbed childhood and evidence of acute depression are often seen as reason for suicide. A recent divorce, the death of a loved one or relative, a lack of friends, problems at work or serious financial difficulties are regarded as possible causes of suicide. This, as Atkinson points out, is remarkably similar to Durkheim's notion of social integration.

Referring to the case of an individual found gassed in his car, a coroner told Atkinson, 'There's a classic pattern for you – broken home, escape to the services, nervous breakdown, unsettled at work, no family ties – what could be clearer.' Thus coroners' views about why people commit suicide appear to influence their categorization of death.

Coroners' commonsense theories of suicide contain explanations of the causes of suicide. If information about the deceased's background fits these explanations, then a verdict of suicide is likely. Atkinson provides the following summary of the procedures used to categorize unnatural death. Coroners 'are engaged in analysing features of the deaths and of the biographies of the deceased according to a variety of taken-for-granted assumptions about what constitutes a "typical suicide", a "typical suicide biography"', and so on. Suicide can therefore be seen as an interpretation placed on an event – an interpretation which stems from a set of taken-for-granted assumptions.

This view has serious implications for research that treats official statistics on suicide as 'facts' and seeks to explain their cause. Researchers who look for explanations of suicide in the social background or mental state of the deceased may simply be uncovering and making explicit the taken-for-granted assumptions of coroners. Atkinson found that coroners' theories of suicide were remarkably similar to those of sociologists and psychologists. Since coroners use their theories of the cause of suicide as a means for categorizing suicide, this similarity might be expected. Thus social scientists who look for the causes of suicide in the social situation or mental condition of those officially classified as suicides may simply be revealing the commonsense theories of coroners.

Criticisms of phenomenology

Phenomenological views have themselves been subject to criticism. Barry Hindess (1973) points out that the criticisms of suicide statistics advanced by phenomenologists can be turned against the sociological theories of phenomenologists themselves. If suicide statistics can be criticized as being no more than the interpretations of coroners, then studies such as that done by Atkinson can be criticized as being no more than the interpretation of a particular sociologist. Just as there is no way of checking on the validity of the verdicts reached by coroners, there is no way of checking on the validity of the accounts of how coroners reach their decisions advanced by phenomenological sociologists. Hindess therefore dismisses the work of such sociologists as being 'theoretically worthless', and he says of their work, 'A manuscript produced by a monkey at a typewriter would be no less valuable.' If phenomenological views were taken to their logical conclusion no sociology would be possible, and the attempt to understand and explain suicide would have to be abandoned.

Steve Taylor – beyond positivism and phenomenology

'Persons under trains'

Steve Taylor (1982, 1989, 1990) has tried to move beyond all the approaches that have been examined so far. However, his own study starts by confirming the view of many critics of Durkheim that suicide statistics are unreliable (Taylor, 1982).

Taylor conducted a study of 'persons under trains' – people who met their death when they were hit by tube trains on the London Underground. Over a 12-month period he found 32 cases where there were no strong clues as to the reason for the death. No suicide notes were left and no witnesses were able to state that the victim jumped deliberately. In effect, it was impossible to say with any certainty whether a suicide had taken place or not. Nevertheless, 17 cases resulted in suicide verdicts, 5 were classified as accidental deaths, and the remaining 10 produced open verdicts.

Taylor found that a number of factors made suicide verdicts more likely. People with a history of mental illness and those who had suffered some form of social failure or social disgrace were more likely to have their death recorded as suicide. When a person who had died had no good reason to be at the tube station, suicide verdicts were more likely. Taylor also found that the verdict was strongly influenced by the witnesses who testified to the dead person's state of mind. Where the witness was a close friend or family member they tended to deny that the person had reason to kill themselves and stress reasons why they might want to carry on living. Where the witnesses were less close to the person – for example, in one case their landlady – they were less likely to deny suicidal motives.

Taylor's methodology

Taylor, then, found strong evidence to support the view that suicide statistics cannot be taken at face value. Specific factors seemed to have influenced the verdicts reached and distorted suicide figures in particular ways. However, Taylor does not follow phenomenologists in arguing that such problems make it impossible to explain suicide. Taylor's own theory is not based upon statistical evidence but upon attempts to discover 'underlying, unobservable structures and causal processes'. This type of approach is based upon a realist conception of science, which is discussed later in this chapter. He develops his theory as an attempt to explain the key features of different types of suicide revealed in case studies.

Types of suicide

Taylor's theory is illustrated in Figure 14.2. He argues that suicides and suicide attempts are either 'ectopic' – they result from what a person thinks about themselves – or 'symphysic' – they result from a person's relationship with others. Suicides and suicide attempts are also related either to certainty or to uncertainty – people are sure or unsure about themselves or about others. Thus, like Durkheim, Taylor distinguishes four types of suicide connected to diametrically opposed situations. In Taylor's theory, however, they are situations faced by partic-

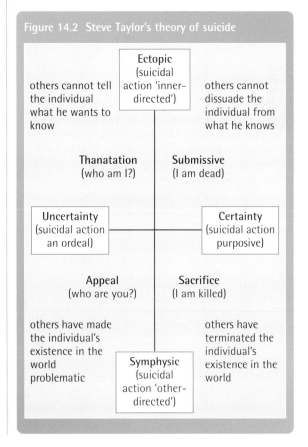

Figure 14.2 Steve Taylor's theory of suicide

ular individuals and are not related so closely to the wider functioning of society. We will now look at the four types of suicide that Taylor identified.

The first two types are ectopic or inner-directed suicides:

1 Submissive suicide occurs when a person is certain about themselves and their life; they believe that their life is effectively over and see themselves as already dead. Taylor says, 'The world of the submissive is one of constricting horizons; of closing doors, blind alleys and cul-de-sacs.' The terminally ill may commit submissive suicide. In other cases a person may have decided that their life is valueless without a loved one who has died. In this type of suicide the suicide attempt is usually deadly serious – the person is sure they wish to die.

2 Thanatation is a type of suicide, or suicide attempt, which occurs when a person is uncertain about themselves. The suicide attempt is a gamble which may or may not be survived, according to fate or chance. If the attempt does not result in death, the person learns that they are capable of facing death. In some cases the person may be exhilarated by the thrill of the risk taking and they may make several suicide attempts. Taylor gives as examples the novelist Graham Greene, who periodically played Russian roulette with a revolver, and the poet Sylvia Plath, who deliberately risked death by driving her car off the road.

The other two types are symphysic or other-directed suicides:

1 Sacrifice suicides occur when a person is certain that others have made their life unbearable. The person who takes their own life often attributes the blame for their death to others so that they will feel guilty or will suffer criticism from other members of society. For example, Taylor refers to a case in which a 22-year-old man killed himself because his wife was in love with his elder brother and she wanted a divorce. The man left letters making it clear that he felt that his wife and brother were responsible for his death.

2 Appeal suicides and suicide attempts result from the suicidal person feeling uncertainty over the attitudes of others towards them. The suicide attempts are a form of communication in which the victim tries to

show how desperate they are, in order to find out how others will respond. Suicide attempts may involve trying to persuade others to change their behaviour, or they may offer them chances to save the victim. Those who make the attempts 'combine the wish to die and the wish for change in others and improvement in the situation; they are acts both of despair and of hope'.

For example, a woman slashed herself with a bread knife in front of her husband after he had discovered her having sex with a neighbour. Her husband took her to hospital and she survived. She later said that she was unsure whether or not she would bleed to death but wanted to show her husband how much she loved him and to appeal for forgiveness through her actions.

In another case a man took an overdose of barbiturates in a car parked in front of his estranged wife's house. He left a note for his wife saying what he had done. However, a dense fog obscured the car so his wife did not see him when she returned to the house and therefore could not save him.

Taylor also refers to Marilyn Monroe's death. She had rung her doctor before taking her fatal overdose, and on previous occasions when she had rung him in an agitated state he had come round to calm her down. His failure to do so on this occasion removed any chance of discovery and rescue.

Evaluation of Taylor

Taylor's theory has some advantages over the other sociological theories examined so far. For example, it helps to explain why some suicide victims leave notes and others do not, why some suicide attempts seem more serious than others, and why some take place in isolation and others in more public places. However, his theory is hard to test. It rests upon the meanings given to suicidal actions by those who take part in them and these meanings can be interpreted in different ways.

For those whose suicide attempts result in death the meanings can only be inferred from circumstantial evidence, since they are no longer able to explain their motives. Individual suicides may result from a combination of motives, with the result that they do not fit neatly into any one category.

Quantitative and qualitative methodology

The preceding sections of this chapter have outlined and illustrated the differences between these two broad approaches to methodology. Ray Pawson has described the impression that such descriptions tend to give to many students. He says that many

students 'have their minds firmly fixed upon an image of a methodological brawl in which the beleaguered minority (the phenomenologists) have been for years trying to survive the onslaught of the wicked majority (the positivists)' (Pawson,

1989). He claims that such a view is highly misleading.

Pawson is correct to point out that the distinction between positivism and phenomenology has sometimes been exaggerated, and some of his points will be examined shortly. However, the disputes are real. When Hindess says that 'A manuscript produced by a monkey at a typewriter would be no less valuable' than the work of phenomenologists, he illustrates the strength of some of the methodological battles that have taken place. Nevertheless, a number of points should be made to put these disputes into perspective:

1 Even those who have strongly advocated and are closely associated with either a quantitative or qualitative approach have not necessarily stuck rigidly to their own supposed methodological principles. Douglas (1967) points out how Durkheim in his study of suicide strayed away from basing his analysis entirely on 'social facts', and dealt with the subjective states of individuals. For example, he gave mental sketches of what it felt like to be a Roman Catholic or a Protestant, in order to explain why their suicide rates should be so different.

At the other extreme, even one of the most ardent critics of quantitative methods, Cicourel (1976), has made extensive use of statistical data. In his study of juvenile justice in two Californian cities he collected statistics on law enforcement in the two cities, and he used a systematic comparison of the cities in order to explain their differing crime rates.

2 It can be argued that the 'methodological brawl'

mentioned above has come to an end. Pawson says that the idea that 'positivists and phenomenologists are always at logger heads is a sixties' hangover; nowadays it is much more accurate to describe the relationship between those who do qualitative and those who do quantitative research as one of truce' (Pawson, 1989). Many sociologists get on with actually doing research without worrying too much about the philosophical basis of that research. As the later sections on primary sources will show, practical difficulties have at least as much influence on the choice of research methods as theoretical considerations. Furthermore, many sociologists now advocate methodological pluralism (see pp. 1022–3), where a mixture of quantitative and qualitative methods is used.

3 Finally, new philosophies of science and new approaches to methodology have now made the disagreements of positivists and phenomenologists look somewhat outdated. The realist conception of science, which will be discussed in a later section (see pp. 1026–7), does not imply that science should be concerned only with that which can be observed directly. In this respect it does not exclude the use of qualitative methods in a 'social science' such as sociology. Critical social science, particularly feminism, and postmodern sociology offer distinctive perspectives on methodology which do not fit neatly into either camp in the disputes between positivist and interpretive sociologists.

We will now examine critical social science and postmodern approaches to methodology before looking at specific research methods.

Critical social science methodology

Lee Harvey – critical social research

The nature of critical social research

Critical social science embraces all those approaches in sociology which aim to be critical of society in order to facilitate social change. Criticism of some sort is present in most social science but, according to its advocates, critical social science goes beyond simply criticizing. According to Lee Harvey, the key characteristic of critical social science is that 'critique is an integral part of the process ... A critical research process involves more than appending critique to an accumulation of "fact" or "theory" gathered via some mechanical process, rather it denies the (literally) objective status of knowledge' (Harvey, 1990).

This approach does not believe that you can simply discover the truth by using the appropriate

quantitative or qualitative methods. Instead it believes that 'knowledge is a process' in which you move towards understanding the social world. Knowledge is never completed, it is never finished, because the social world is constantly changing. Furthermore, knowledge can never be separated from values. As members of the social world, researchers are bound to be influenced by their values and those of society. However, their aim should be to try to get beyond the dominant values of society, to try to see what is going on underneath the surface.

Thus, critical social scientists tend to believe that the way society appears to its members can be misleading. Things that are taken for granted need to be seen in a different light so that the true values underlying them can be revealed. Once this has been done, it may be possible to use the new knowledge to transform society.

Examples of critical social research

Harvey uses the example of feminist studies on housework to illustrate the approach. According to him, feminists have been able to show that housework should be seen as real work, just like paid work. Like paid work it creates things of value and it has a crucial role in the economy. Male-dominated commonsense views of housework have devalued it and seen it as unimportant. By revealing the true nature of housework, feminists have been able to encourage social changes in which women have demanded that the value of their unpaid work is recognized (see pp. 552–63 for a discussion of housework).

Critical research is particularly concerned with revealing oppressive structures so that such structures might be changed. Harvey says that 'It is important that the account be located in a wider context which links the specific activities with a broader social structural and historical analysis.' Thus, an analysis of housework can be linked to changes in the role of women in society with the rise of industrial capitalism (see pp. 144–5) and the development of patriarchy (see pp. 151–6).

There are numerous examples of critical social science. Harvey sees the work of Karl Marx (see, for example, pp. 33–6), C. Wright Mills's work on power elites (see pp. 603–4), and Paul Willis's study of working-class lads in the education system (see pp. 791–4) as examples. He divides critical social science studies into three main types, which concentrate on class, on gender and on ethnicity and racism. Of course, some of the best critical research examines all three simultaneously. However, these categories are by no means exhaustive, and critical social scientists also examine issues such as sexuality and disability – indeed any area where some social groups can be seen as systematically disadvantaged or oppressed.

The main features of critical research

Harvey sees critical research as having the following main features:

1 Abstract concepts and ideology
   It uses abstract concepts such as housework but goes beyond simply carrying out empirical studies based on such concepts. Thus, instead of just measuring who does housework tasks, critical research tries to examine how such concepts relate to wider social relationships. Housework is seen as a work relationship rather than as simply a set of tasks to be performed. In this way it tries to get beneath the surface of social reality. This involves trying to overcome the dominant ideology or ideologies. Distorted ideological beliefs may be related to dominant classes or to patriarchal or racist beliefs. They mask the material reality that lies behind these beliefs. In Marxist theory, for example, the ideology of wage labour as a free and fair exchange between employer and employee disguises the material advantages enjoyed by the employer as the owner of the means of production.

2 Totality, structure and history
   Each abstract concept and particular belief cannot be examined in isolation. According to Harvey it is necessary to relate each bit of a society to a totality. Harvey says, 'Totality refers to the view that social phenomena are interrelated and form a total whole.' For example, in *The New Criminology* (1973), Taylor, Walton and Young advocate trying to understand the actions of criminals in the context of society as a whole (see pp. 386–8).

   Critical social scientists see societies as possessing structures. Structures constrain or limit what people can do, but also make social actions possible. For example, the structures of capitalist societies make it difficult for members of the working class to set up their own businesses to compete with big capitalist companies. On the other hand, they make it possible for some capitalists to make substantial profits.

   Structures, though, are not static; they change. Studies of society therefore need to be related to particular historical contexts. You need to examine how particular societies have changed over time in order to understand them at any particular point in time. Thus studies of the working class need to take account of how the economy and the labour market have changed since the advent of capitalism (see pp. 75–88 for examples).

3 Deconstruction, essence and reconstruction
   Critical social researchers proceed through a process of deconstruction and reconstruction. In the process of deconstruction the different elements of particular areas of social life are taken apart in order to try to discover an essence. The essence is the 'fundamental concept that can be used as the key to unlocking the deconstructive process'. Thus, for example, the essence of capitalism, according to Marx, is 'the commodity form', while the essence of housework, according to Christine Delphy, is a set of work relationships in the context of family life.

   Reconceptualization – thinking of familiar aspects of social life in unfamiliar ways – is the key to discovering essences through deconstruction. This process is never finished. Harvey says that critical research:

involves a constant questioning of the perspective and analysis the researcher is building up. It is a process of gradually, and critically, coming to know through constant reconceptualization. This means that the selection of a core concept for analysis is not a once-and-for-all affair.

Harvey, 1990, p. 30

The process of deconstruction does not follow a pre-set path, as laid down by, for example, positivists. The development and testing of hypotheses and the collection of empirical data can all proceed 'in parallel'. The process involves 'a constant shuttling back and forwards between abstract concept and concrete data; between social totalities and particular phenomena; between current structures and historical development; between surface appearance and essence; between reflection and practice'. Some of the process does involve '"armchair" speculation', but empirical studies can also be carried out by whatever methods are most suitable.

Deconstruction leads to reconstruction. The researcher aims in the end to 'lay bare the essential relationships that are embedded in the structure'. They develop theoretical insights which allow the phenomena under investigation to be seen in a new way. A good example is Paul Willis's study of the transition from school to work among working-class 'lads'. Willis reveals how the 'lads'' rebellion at school serves as a preparation for the alienating shop-floor jobs they end up doing. According to Willis the 'lads' thereby actively contribute to maintaining their own oppression (see pp. 791–4 for details).

4 Praxis

Critical social research is not just a theoretical activity, it is also a form of praxis. Harvey defines praxis as 'practical reflective activity. Praxis does not include "instinctive" or "mindless" activity like sleeping, breathing, walking, and so on, or undertaking repetitive work tasks. Praxis is what changes the world'. The point of research is to improve the world. Researchers are interested in whether there is any potential for the oppressed groups being studied to come together to change their situation. If these groups come to understand their situation better, they are more likely to resist or challenge the structures that oppress them. To Harvey, far from being a neutral, uninvolved observer of society, the researcher should be an involved and committed participant in the social world. The involvement should be directed towards developing a radical praxis within oppressed social groups.

Research methods

Critical social science is not tied to any single research method. Critical social scientists have used a full range of methods including questionnaires, interviews, case studies, ethnography and semiology (see pp. 999–1003, 1003–8, 1008–14, 996–7 and Chapter 13 for discussions of these methods). However, this approach does tend to be sympathetic towards methods which allow the social world to be seen from the viewpoint of those who are oppressed.

Some feminists have advocated the use of interviews (see pp. 988–9); Goldthorpe and Lockwood (whom Harvey describes as critical social researchers) used questionnaires (see pp. 79–81); while critical ethnography is perhaps the most popular of all the methods used by such researchers (see pp. 1013–14). Unlike positivist and interpretive approaches to methodology, the emphasis is not so much upon the preferred technique, but upon the purpose of the research. Any method is permissible so long as it allows you to get beneath the surface of social life and has the potential for helping to change society. Harvey concludes that 'Although not susceptible to simple methodic prescriptions critical social research lies at the very heart of emancipatory sociological enquiry.'

Criticisms of critical social research

Martin Hammersley has identified a number of problems with critical social research:

1 First, he believes that there are problems in identifying sources of oppression in order to orientate research. Although critical social researchers identify a range of sources of oppression (principally class, gender and ethnicity) there may be others which they have not identified. Furthermore, it is not clear how they can clearly distinguish oppressor from non-oppressor. Hammersley says, 'many people may be simultaneously oppressor and oppressed' (Hammersley, 1992). If critical research is focused on understanding the viewpoint of the oppressed, it becomes difficult to carry out if oppressors might in some ways be oppressed themselves. It becomes hard to know who to interview or who to observe.

2 Hammersley believes that there are problems with the whole concept of oppression and differing ideas of needs and interests. There might be very different viewpoints on what a group needs and what their interests are. There may also be many different views on, and dimensions of, oppression. Hammersley believes that, in the end, needs, interests and what constitutes oppression are subjective judgements. As it is unlikely that all human needs and preferences can be met in society, some judgement has to be made about which needs and interests are legitimate and which are not.

3 Hammersley believes that critical researchers tend to argue that 'there is a single set of values that everyone would agree on if it were not for the effects of ideology on our thinking'. If this were the case, it might get around the problem of deciding who was oppressed. However, Hammersley argues that this could never be achieved. Individuals, never mind social groups, can be in two (or more) minds about what is just, fair or in their interests. Furthermore, the interests of different oppressed

groups might clash. For example, a religious minority might be oppressed in a society because of their beliefs. However, the religion might be highly patriarchal and oppress women within the religion. In such a case it becomes unclear whether the critical researcher should focus upon revealing the oppression of the religious minority, or of the women within that minority. If they try to do both they risk the contradictory position of arguing both that the religion should be tolerated and that its oppression of women should not be tolerated.

4 According to Hammersley, critical researchers try to establish the truth of their arguments either by getting oppressed groups to agree with their findings, or by showing that the findings have been successful in combating oppression. There are problems with both of these methods.

First, oppressed groups may not be able to evaluate the truth of social science theories because they may be suffering from some sort of false consciousness. How do you know that they have cast off false consciousness and can now see the truth?

Second, you cannot assume that even a correct theory will automatically produce social changes which overcome oppression. Many other factors apart from the production of theories will determine whether oppressed people are emancipated. As Hammersley says:

Theories are not simply applied but used in association with practical knowledge. And, if this is the case, the achievement of emancipation depends on much more than the truth of the theory, and so failure to achieve emancipation does not tell us that the theory is false.

Hammersley, 1992, p. 115

Because of the above points Hammersley denies that critical researchers have succeeded in producing an acceptable alternative to conventional methodology for establishing the truth. If this is the case, then critical research 'becomes simply research directed towards serving the interests of some particular group, whose interests may conflict with others, including those of other oppressed groups'.

Phil Carspecken – a defence of critical research

Despite the sorts of criticism advanced by writers such as Hammersley, some researchers argue that it is possible to produce an acceptable critical social science methodology. Writing in 1996, Phil Carspecken argues that critical researchers had failed to develop a detailed methodology. He attempts to put this right.

Carspecken believes that critical research need not be biased because the researchers engaging in it have value commitments. Critical researchers should not just look for the facts which fit their theories. Like researchers from other traditions they should be open to finding evidence which contradicts their theories and challenges their values. They should always be open to changing their standpoints in the light of what they find during the course of research. Furthermore, research needs to be systematic and careful. It should go through a number of stages to reach conclusions which can be widely accepted as being close to the truth. Carspecken suggests the following stages.

The process of research

1 Compiling the primary record. In the first stage the researcher immerses themselves in the social life of the group or site being studied. They take notes and may use video- or audio-tape. The researcher tries to develop a preliminary understanding of the social world from the viewpoint of those being studied.

2 Preliminary reconstructive analysis. In this stage the researcher starts to analyse what they found in the first stage. They look particularly for 'interaction patterns, their meanings, power relationships, roles, interactive sequences' and so on.

3 Dialogical data generation. At this stage the researcher starts talking to those being studied and discusses his or her preliminary findings with them. The subjects of research have an opportunity to influence the way the researcher is thinking and help him or her decide how convincing the initial ideas are. Carspecken says that this 'democratizes the research process'. Interviews and discussion groups will be used at this stage.

4 Discovering system relations. Once stage 3 is well under way the researcher now begins to broaden the study to try to link his or her specific findings to other parts of social life. For example, the relationships found in a school might be linked to the content of the mass media, the local labour market or changing conceptions of masculinity and femininity.

5 Using system relations to explain findings. Only in the final stage does the researcher being to produce causal explanations of what they have found. Links are made to social structures and particular attention may be made to 'class, race, gender and political structures of society'.

Establishing truth claims

Why, though, should people believe the results of such research? Will it not simply reflect the biases and values that the researcher started with?

Carspecken believes not. First, the features of social life uncovered by researchers are the basis on which the theories are developed. They are not simply based on the researcher's abstract ideas. Second, the subjects of the research have a chance to confirm or contradict the initial understandings developed by the researcher. Third, Carspecken develops a sophisticated analysis of how conclusions may be reached about whether the findings of research are true or not.

Like Popper (see pp. 968–9), Carspecken does not believe that social scientists can produce statements that will necessarily be regarded as true for all time. Even if everyone agreed that something was true, this view might be rejected in some future society. However, in essence, whether something is regarded as true or not ultimately depends upon whether people can agree that it is true. A truth claim – a claim that something is true – is always an act of communication. It is an attempt by one person or group to assert to other people that something is true. Establishing the truth is therefore a communicative process.

The way to check whether a truth claim stands up to scrutiny is to see whether other people agree with it. The only way to do that is to allow others a chance to accept or refute the truth claim. Traditional science considers truth claims by limiting those who are allowed to express an opinion on them to the scientists. Only experts have their views taken seriously. In critical research, those who are being studied have a say as well as other social scientists. In studying social life, the participants – the children in a classroom, the workers in an office, the members of families or whatever – are the experts. Checking whether they can be convinced by the social researchers' theory is a key part of testing whether it is true.

However, there are some problems involved in checking the findings of research by seeing whether people will agree with them or not. People often agree with things not because they believe them, but because of power relationships. Following the work of Habermas (1984), Carspecken believes that communications can be distorted where some of those communicating have power over others involved. To use a simple example, if someone holds a gun to your head and threatens to kill you, you are likely to agree with whatever they say regardless of whether you believe it.

Critical researchers should therefore be aware of these sources of distortion. They should try to ensure that they eliminate, as far as possible, power relationships between themselves and those being studied. Thus Carspecken believes that researchers should:

Establish supportive, nonauthoritarian relationships with the participants in your study. Actively encourage them to question your own perceptions. Be sure that participants are protected from any harm that your study could produce, and be sure that they know they are protected.

Carspecken, 1996, p. 90

However, researchers should also challenge beliefs that may result from power relationships. Thus, for example, women who believe that their husbands or male partners should be able to tell them what to do, could have their beliefs challenged by a researcher. The researcher would have to find out whether the women in question could be persuaded that the relationship was patriarchal.

The subjects of the research are not the only ones who need to be persuaded of the researcher's truth claims. Other social scientists and readers of the research need to be persuaded too. Of course, the research will be evaluated by people whose views are influenced by the power relationships in which the researcher is involved. He or she will therefore be unlikely to persuade everybody of the truthfulness of their work. Nevertheless, their aim should be to make the findings as convincing as possible.

While checks on the validity of truth claims do in the end come down to a matter of opinion, Carspecken does not believe that what people believe is just random. To him, what people will accept is affected by what is real. He argues that 'a single, real, world exists independently from any cultural categories used to describe it and act in relation to it'. This real world 'resists' human actions. People find that it allows them to behave in certain ways, and that in other ways it limits their behaviour. For example, if people believed that broken glass was not sharp, and acted towards it accordingly, they would soon find themselves cut and bleeding. It would be hard to sustain the belief that broken glass was not sharp, and cultural beliefs would be likely to change.

Beliefs tend to fall into line with reality because of people's experiences. Of course this does not always happen. People can believe things in spite of experiences which suggest that the beliefs are mistaken. Furthermore, many beliefs are far more complicated than the above example, and cannot easily be tested against experience. Nevertheless, the idea that a real world exists and that it can resist human actions allows Carspecken to claim that ultimately there can be a sound foundation for people trying to agree on what is true and what is not.

Feminist methodology

Approaches to feminist methodology

Perhaps feminist approaches to critical research are the most developed ones. There have been numerous attempts to develop feminist ways of doing or approaching research, but three approaches have been particularly influential:

1 The attack on 'malestream' research. This involves a criticism of previous, male-dominated, mainstream research. Often referred to by feminists as 'malestream' research, it is criticized for being based upon sexist or patriarchal principles.

2 The claim that there can be distinctive feminist research methods. This approach argues that the more conventional 'scientific' methods used by men are not particularly good at helping the researcher to understand social reality – particularly, though not exclusively, the reality of women.

3 The claim that feminism can reveal a distinctive epistemology, or theory of knowledge, which is superior to other epistemologies.

The attack on 'malestream' research

This is perhaps the least controversial of feminist approaches to methodology. Rather than trying to construct a completely new feminist approach, it tries to rectify the mistakes of previous, dominant and male-orientated research methodologies. From this point of view, research has generally been carried out about men, by men and for men. Pamela Abbott and Claire Wallace provide a comprehensive list of feminist criticisms of 'malestream' sociology. They say:

> Feminists have made a number of criticisms of sociology.
> 1 that sociology has mainly been concerned with research on men and by implication with theories for men;
> 2 that research findings based on all-male samples are generalised to the whole population;
> 3 that areas and issues of concern to women are frequently overlooked or seen as unimportant;
> 4 that when they are included in research they are included in a distorted and sexist way;
> 5 that sex and gender are seldom important explanatory variables;
> 6 that when sex and gender are included as variables they are just added on, ignoring the fact that the explanatory theories used are ones which have justified the subordination and exploitation of women.

Abbot and Wallace, 1997, p. 6

A number of examples included in this book can illustrate these points:

- According to Carol Smart (1977), the sociology of crime and deviance was, until the late 1970s, almost exclusively the sociology of male crime and delinquency (see p. 408).

- Studies such as those by Merton, Cohen, Miller and Cloward and Ohlin (see pp. 354–60) almost completely ignored women, yet assumed that they applied to criminals in general and not just male criminals.

- As Ann Oakley (1974) points out, housework was seen as too unimportant to be studied by social scientists until her own pioneering work.

- Michelle Stanworth (1984) criticizes John Goldthorpe's class scheme for, generally, allocating wives to classes based upon their husband's occupation (see p. 111).

- Male social scientists such as Talcott Parsons, sociobiologists and Lombroso and Ferrero have been accused as having sexist, biologically-based explanations of female behaviour (see pp. 132–3, 129–31 and 413).

- Class classification schemes have been accused by Arber, Dale and Gilbert (1986) of being based on male jobs and of being unable to usefully differentiate different types of female employment (see p. 116).

There have also been frequent criticisms of the use of sexist language in social research. For example, Margaret Eichler (1991) points out that terms such as 'men' and 'mankind' have often been used to refer to people in general.

Evaluation

These sorts of criticism of 'malestream' sociology have been very influential and widely accepted. The numbers of sociological studies of women, studies of issues important to women, and studies which examine female perspectives on social life, have proliferated. It has become much less common for sociologists to try to generalize about people of both sexes on the basis of male samples. The sociological study of women, by women and for women has become much more commonplace.

Sexist language in sociology has also become much less common. For example, the British Sociological Association's 'Ethical Guidelines' state that sexist language is unacceptable, and it is banned from the organization's journal *Sociology* (see the 'Notes for contributors' in any edition of this journal).

Although the problems of 'malestream' sociology have certainly not been eliminated, they have been greatly reduced and the arguments advanced for non-sexist sociology have become relatively uncontentious. Other feminist approaches to research methods, though, are much more contentious.

Feminist research methods

Ann Oakley – the masculine model of interviewing

Perhaps the best-known and most influential argument that there should be distinctive feminist research methods is advanced by Ann Oakley (1981). In particular she argues that there is a feminist way of conducting interviews which is superior to a more dominant, masculine model of such research.

By studying the instructions of various methodology books which describe the techniques of interviewing, Oakley is able to discover the main features of the masculine approach to interviewing. She says, 'the paradigm of the "proper" interview appeals to such values as objectivity, detachment, hierarchy and "science" as an important cultural activity which takes precedence over people's more individualised concerns'.

Although they can be friendly in order to establish some minimum rapport, interviewers must maintain their distance to avoid becoming too involved with respondents. Certainly any emotional involvement between interviewer and respondent must be avoided at all costs. The interviewees must be manipulated as 'objects of study/sources of data'. They must always have a passive role, and must never become active in shaping the interview. If the interviewee asks the interviewer questions, the interviewer should not answer and should make it clear that he or she is there to ask questions and not to answer them.

Interviewing of this type emphasizes the importance of producing reliable data that can be repeated and checked. Interviewers have to avoid expressing any opinion of their own. To do so will influence the answers of the respondents and lead to bias in the research.

The feminist approach to interviewing

Having outlined the masculine approach to interviewing, Oakley proceeds to suggest a feminist alternative. She draws upon her own experience of interviewing women about becoming mothers. She conducted 178 interviews, with most women being interviewed twice before the birth of their child and twice afterwards. In some cases Oakley was actually present at the birth. On average each of the women was interviewed for more than nine hours.

Oakley found that the women often wanted to ask her questions. Instead of avoiding answering them, Oakley decided to answer their questions as openly and honestly as she could. Some of the questions were about her and her research, others were requests for information about childbirth or childcare. In some cases the women were anxious about some aspect of childcare or childbirth, and often they had failed to get satisfactory answers from medical staff. In these circumstances Oakley found it impossible to refuse to answer their questions. She was asking a great deal of the interviewees at a difficult time in their lives, and it was only reasonable that she should give something back in return.

Oakley decided to make the research more collaborative. Instead of looking at the women as passive respondents, she wanted them to become her collaborators and friends. Indeed, it was often the interviewees who took the initiative in developing the relationship further. Many expressed an interest in the research and wanted to become more involved. Some rang her up with key pieces of information. Oakley claims that 'the women were reacting to my own evident wish for a relatively intimate and non-hierarchical relationship'.

She tried to make sure that she did not exploit the interviewees. She asked permission to record interviews and use the information. While she was at the mothers' houses she gave them help with childcare or housework if they needed it. She discussed her own experiences of childbirth with the women who were interested, and tried to offer advice on where they could get help with particular problems.

Oakley's objectives in adopting such an approach were not just to give some help to the women and to avoid exploiting them, in return for their participation. She also believed that it improved the quality of the research. It allowed her to get closer to the subjective viewpoints of the women being studied. It also played some role in trying to change and improve the experience of becoming a mother for the women involved. Oakley says:

> *Nearly three-quarters of the women said that being interviewed had affected them and the three most common forms this influence took were in leading them to reflect on their experiences more than they would otherwise have done; in reducing the level of their anxiety and/or in reassuring them of their normality; and in giving a valuable outlet for the verbalization of feelings.*
>
> Oakley, 1981, p. 50

Oakley concludes that interviewing that breaks down the barriers between researchers and their subjects is preferable to masculine, 'scientific' interviewing. She says that a feminist methodology:

requires, further, that the mythology of 'hygienic' research with its accompanying mystification of the researcher and the researched as objective instruments of data production be replaced by the recognition that personal involvement is more than dangerous bias – it is the condition under which people come to know each other and to admit others into their lives.

Oakley, 1981, p. 58

Evaluation of Oakley

Oakley's approach to interviewing has been quite influential amongst feminists and her ideas are widely quoted in books about methodology. Although generally sympathetic to her approach, some critics have argued that it is not original or distinctively feminist.

Ray Pawson argues that Oakley simply elaborated on conventional ways of conducting unstructured interviews. He says:

This vision of interviewing-as-fieldwork is precisely that urged from the traditional doctrines of interpretative, phenomenological or humanistic sociology. There is a time-honoured tradition of positivism-bashing in general and structured-interviewing bashing in particular, and this feminist approach is essentially a repetition of this literature.

Pawson, 1992, p. 119

The differences between structured and unstructured interviewing will be discussed later in the chapter (see pp. 1003–4). However, it can be argued that there are some features of Oakley's approach which go beyond conventional approaches to unstructured interviewing. For example, even unstructured interviewing is not normally supposed to involve advising and helping the interviewees, since it is thought that such interventions might affect the findings. Oakley's approach to feminist interviewing incorporates elements of critical research which are not typical of other types of interpretative research.

Feminist standpoint epistemology

Perhaps the most influential of feminist epistemologies is what has been called standpoint epistemology. From this point of view, the way in which women experience social life gives them unique insights into how society works. Sandra Harding says, 'The feminist standpoint epistemologies ground a distinctive feminist science in a theory of gendered activity and social experience' (Harding, 1986). That is, they believe that feminist knowledge can only come from examining the unique experiences of women in societies in which men and women experience social life in different ways.

Standpoint epistemology generally does not deny that it is possible to discover the truth about society. However, instead of believing that the truth can be established through the observation of facts and the discovery of statistical relationships, it seeks to find the truth through understanding women's experiences. Furthermore, it tends to believe that no one version of the truth can explain everything. Although women have certain experiences in common, there are also big differences between groups of women, and their different experiences need to be explored before a full picture of the social world can be produced.

Liz Stanley and Sue Wise are amongst the advocates of standpoint epistemology. They argue in favour of 'theory derived from experience' which is 'constantly subject to revision in the light of that experience' (Stanley and Wise, 1990). They say that feminist research should be 'not only located in, but proceeding from, the grounded analysis of women's experiences'. By examining their experiences the feminist researcher can understand the world.

According to Stanley and Wise, 'all knowledge, necessarily, results from the conditions of its production, is contextually located, and irrevocably bears the marks of its origins'. Generally speaking, sociology has usually expressed 'the practices and knowledge of highly particular white, middle-class, heterosexual men'. Feminist standpoint epistemology replaces this with the view of the world developed through the experiences of oppressed women. Oppressed women are in a special position, able through their experiences to see through the ideology of their male oppressors.

However, Stanley and Wise do not believe that all women experience the world in the same way. For example, black, lesbian and working-class women have different experiences to those of their white, heterosexual and middle-class counterparts. Stanley and Wise therefore support the view that feminist epistemology needs to look at different standpoints and should not try to pretend that one set of knowledge can deal with the experiences of very different groups of women. They are in favour of a plurality of feminist theories deriving from the study of different oppressed groups. No one theory should be allowed to be dominant.

Although Stanley and Wise accept the need for a plurality of theories, they do not go as far as some postmodernists who deny that any methodology can deliver a true picture of social life (see pp. 990–1). To Stanley and Wise the viewpoints of different women need to be examined simply because women do have real, different experiences. Feminist methodology needs to uncover these different and often previously neglected experiences in order to develop a fuller understanding of the social world.

Criticisms of feminist standpoint epistemology

Ray Pawson (1992) argues that such epistemologies run into major problems when those being studied continue to see the world in terms that the researcher finds unconvincing. Thus, for example, feminist researchers are unlikely to give much credence to women's views that it is 'natural' for women to do the housework and for men to be dominant. Sometimes, however much they try to persuade the women being studied to see things differently, the women may stick to beliefs which feminists see as reflecting patriarchal ideology. In such cases researchers may find themselves going against what their respondents believe, or, alternatively, having to accept views which they believe to be untrue.

According to Pawson a further problem with standpoint epistemology is that it puts all the emphasis upon studying the experiences of the oppressed. This effectively rules out studying the oppressors (in this case men), even though studying oppressors might reveal at least as much about the nature of oppression as studying the oppressed.

Pawson is also unpersuaded by the view that you can simply describe a plurality of different viewpoints. Sometimes the viewpoints of groups of women, grounded in different experiences, may contradict one another. Unless the researcher decides to say that one viewpoint is better than another, they end up having to accept contradictory beliefs. This leads them down the path of relativism. They are no longer trying to explain society as it really is; they are reduced to accepting all viewpoints as equally valid. Different feminist views of the world are only true for particular groups of women; none can claim to describe society as it really is for everybody. In these circumstances sociology loses any claim to be able to produce knowledge which is superior to the common-sense knowledge of ordinary members of society.

Pawson's criticisms tend to generalize about feminist methodologies and epistemologies and are not particularly sensitive to variations between them. Not all feminist standpoint epistemologies are relativistic; some do not see the viewpoints of all groups of women as equally valid. Indeed the accusation of relativism could be more justly directed against postmodern methodology (see pp. 990–1) than feminist methodology. Furthermore, as we have seen above, critical social scientists such as Phil Carspecken have tried to deal with some of the apparent problems with methodologies that take the viewpoint of the oppressed seriously (see pp. 985–6).

Critical and feminist approaches to methodology will be discussed further as the chapter develops.

Postmodern methodology

Varieties of postmodern methodology

There is no single type of methodology accepted by all postmodernists. However, it is possible to distinguish three broad positions adopted by the variety of writers who discuss postmodernism:

1 Some postmodernists, such as David Harvey (1990), see postmodernity largely in terms of changes in society. They do not believe that the nature of knowledge has changed or that radical new methodologies are needed to replace old ones. They therefore tend to use conventional methods and conventional sources of data. Thus Harvey analyses statistical economic data and tries to interpret cultural trends from a number of secondary sources. From the viewpoint of such writers, existing methodologies, whether quantitative or qualitative, are quite adequate for the analysis of society.

2 On the other hand, some writers make a sharp distinction between modern and postmodern epistemology. Modern epistemology (or theory of knowledge) tends to claim that the truth can be discovered by the use of the correct techniques. Those who advocate both deductive and inductive methods (see p. 968), and even critical social scientists (see pp. 982–6), believe that procedures can be used to evaluate what is true and what is not. While Popper and critical sociologists may not believe that the final truth can be established, they do at least believe that it is possible to rule out some knowledge as being untrue.

Epistemological postmodernists argue that there is no basis even for ruling out some knowledge as being untrue. Nevertheless, Lyotard (1984), for example, dismisses all knowledge based upon modern epistemologies as deriving from 'metanarratives' (see Chapter 15). Metanarratives are big stories about the world and are essentially opinions rather than objective knowledge.

Lyotard rejects the claims of all 'scientific' subjects and believes that all knowledge is essentially a form of story-telling. He sees all stories as equally valid and offers no way of distinguishing between true and untrue stories. The implication of this view is that postmodern methodology should simply consist of allowing different people to tell their stories. No attempt should be made to try to establish that any particular stories are better than any others.

Some postmodernists have tried to develop postmodern ethnography as a way of allowing the voices of diverse social groups to be heard (see pp. 1014–15 for a discussion of postmodern ethnography).

3 Postmodern ethnography allows epistemological postmodernists to collect some of their own data. However, much postmodern sociology is not so concerned with creating new knowledge as with attacking existing knowledge. Many such approaches have drawn on the work of Jacques Derrida as a basis for criticizing other sociologists' work (see Kamuf, 1991, for extracts from Derrida).

Derrida believes that language can never truly represent an external, objective reality. Language is simply a self-contained system in which words are defined in terms of other words. Because of this, scientists, sociologists and indeed anyone else should not be believed if they claim to have established the absolute truth. Therefore the work of such writers should be deconstructed.

Deconstruction involves examining texts (anything containing written language) and taking them apart. In this process Derrida believes that the inherent contradictions built into existing knowledge can be revealed (see pp. 159–60 for further details). The technique of deconstruction is often used by postmodernists to attack and try to undermine texts such as existing sociological theories. This strand of postmodern methodology is therefore based around the critique of secondary sources (see pp. 1016–22) rather than the creation of new knowledge.

Postmodern methodology – evaluation

Postmodern methodology has been widely accused of adopting a position of complete relativism. That is, it argues that knowledge simply depends upon your point of view, and that one person's view is as good as any other person's view. Modernist sociologists of various types continue to reject this view. For example, critical social scientists such as Phil Carspecken believe that there are ways of evaluating different truth claims (see above, pp. 985–6). Carspecken does believe that postmodern method-ology offers some insights but rejects its claim that there is no basis for producing objective knowledge. He believes that there are ways of convincing others of the validity of knowledge. Carspecken says, 'Few would want to say that their descriptions of society are nothing but interpretations, capable of persuading others only through the exertion of power (persua-sion) rather than argument' (Carspecken, 1996).

Ultimately argument is grounded in an external reality and the way that this reality prevents people from doing whatever they choose. Like realist theorists of science (see pp. 1026–7), critical social scientists like Carspecken continue to reject the extreme relativism of some postmodernists.

A number of writers have turned postmodern arguments on postmodernists. They have pointed out that, if there is no way of distinguishing fact from fiction, then there is absolutely no way of showing that postmodernists' stories about the social world are any better (or worse) than other stories (see Chapter 15). Similarly there is no way of showing that postmodern methodologies are any better (or worse) than more conventional methodologies.

Postmodern methodology will be discussed further as the chapter develops.

The research process

This part of the chapter will deal with the major issues involved in actually carrying out research. It begins with a consideration of how researchers go about selecting topics for research, and goes on to examine the practical and theoretical issues involved in collecting and analysing data.

Choosing a topic for research

Before embarking upon research, sociologists have to decide what they are going to study. This choice may be affected by a number of factors.

The values and beliefs of the researcher will obviously play some part. Sociologists are unlikely to

devote considerable time and energy to issues that they think are unimportant or trivial. For example, Peter Townsend's values have led him to regard poverty as an important problem in contemporary industrial societies (see pp. 296–300), while Paul Heelas believed that the New Age movement was worthy of attention (see pp. 466–9).

What a researcher believes is important may be influenced by developments within the discipline of sociology, or developments in the wider society. Sociology is a profession as well as a discipline, and many sociologists wish to advance their careers by criticizing or developing the work of fellow sociologists, or by trying to resolve some key sociological issue. This might explain why so many sociologists have followed Durkheim in studying suicide, while other areas of social life have been comparatively neglected.

Similarly, routine clerical workers have been studied more than some other sections of the stratification system. This group is often seen as a crucial test of Marxist and Weberian theories of stratification. Groups of less theoretical interest to sociologists, such as agricultural labourers, have been studied less often.

In the sociology of religion, apparent examples of religious revival, such as the revival of Islam and the New Christian Right in the USA, have been studied partly in order to evaluate the theory of secularization.

When there are major changes in society, sociologists are likely to study them. Sociology was born in the nineteenth century, largely out of a concern about the changes wrought by the Industrial Revolution. More recently, sociologists have studied apparent social changes in terms of theories and concepts such as postmodernism (see Chapter 15), post-Fordism and high modernity (see pp. 713–17).

Sociologists have also devoted more time in recent decades to studying unemployment than they did in the 1950s and 1960s when rates of unemployment were very much lower. In the sociology of work the impact of information technology has been a focus of attention (see pp. 700–6).

Specific government policies can also stimulate research. Hence, for example, the concern with the 'new vocationalism' in the contemporary sociology of education (see pp. 801–13), and the concern with 'social exclusion' in studies of social policy since the British Labour government established a Social Exclusion Unit (see p. 346).

A very important factor affecting the choice of research topic is the availability or otherwise of grants to finance it. Research funds may come from charitable foundations – such as the Nuffield and Rowntree foundations – from industry, or from government – in Britain usually via the Economic and Social Research Council (or ESRC). The European Union sometimes provides funds for sociological research.

Some small-scale research requires little funding, but major research projects can be very expensive, and the sort of research that gets done can be very strongly influenced by those who hold the purse strings. Payne et al. have suggested that the SSRC (the predecessor of the ESRC) 'had no pretensions to being anything other than a government organisation' (Payne et al., 1977). As an important source of funding for British sociology it tended to restrict the amount of sociological research that was critical of the government of the day.

Industrial providers of research grants tend to want some practical benefits from the money they spend, so research into organizations and industrial sociology is most likely to receive funding from this source.

Other practical difficulties apart from money can affect the topics chosen by sociologists for their research. The availability of existing data on a topic or the practicality of collecting data will both have an influence. Durkheim chose to study suicide partly because statistics were available from many European countries (see pp. 974–7). Some important groups in the population – for example, senior politicians and the directors of top companies – rarely form the basis of detailed studies. This is partly due to their unwillingness to reveal their activities to sociological scrutiny. Other relatively powerless groups, such as delinquent gangs, have been subject to detailed and frequent study.

Primary sources

Primary sources of information consist of data collected by researchers themselves during the course of their work. Secondary sources consist of data that already exist. Primary sources would include data collected by researchers using questionnaires, conducting interviews or carrying out participant observation. Secondary sources include official statistics, mass media products, diaries, letters, government reports, other sociologists' work and historical and contemporary records. Secondary sources will be discussed later.

Choosing a primary research method

Some of the factors that influence the choice of research topic can also influence the choice of research method used to study that topic. For example, the source of funding for a proposed project might well specify the type of method to be employed. Many funding bodies support the use of more quantitative methods. Janet Finch, for example, describes the 'dominance achieved by quantitative methods, and the (at best) secondary place which qualitative methods were accorded' (Finch, 1986) in the development of British social policy research. However, the most important factors influencing the choice of research method are the topic to be studied and the theoretical and practical considerations.

Some topics lend themselves more readily to the use of quantitative techniques such as questionnaires: for example, research into voting in Great Britain tends to involve large-scale studies using quantitative statistical techniques because of the sheer numbers necessarily involved in the research if the data are to be of any use. Other topics, such as behaviour in classrooms, lend themselves more readily to qualitative methods.

As the earlier sections of this chapter have shown, those who support a particular theoretical approach tend to use either quantitative or qualitative methods. This commitment may well be the major influence on their choice of research method.

Reliability

Many of the debates about the merits of particular research methods focus on questions of reliability and validity. In the natural sciences, data are seen to be 'reliable' if other researchers using the same methods of investigation on the same material produce the same results. By replicating an experiment it is possible to check for errors in observation and measurement. Once reliable data have been obtained, generalizations can then be made about the behaviour observed. No sociologist would claim that the social sciences can attain the standards of reliability employed in the natural sciences. Many would argue, however, that sociological data can attain a certain standard of reliability.

Generally speaking, quantitative methods are seen to provide greater reliability. They usually produce standardized data in a statistical form: the research can be repeated and the results checked. Questionnaires can be used to test precise hypotheses which the researcher has devised.

Qualitative methods are often criticized for failing to meet the same standards of reliability. Such methods may be seen as unreliable because the procedures used to collect data can be unsystematic, the results are rarely quantified, and there is no way of replicating a qualitative study and checking the reliability of its findings.

Validity

Data are 'valid' if they provide a true picture of what is being studied. A valid statement gives a true measurement or description of what it claims to measure or describe. It is an accurate reflection of social reality. Data can be reliable without being

valid. Studies can be replicated and produce the same results but those results may not be a valid measure of what the researcher intends to measure. For instance, statistics on church attendance may be reliable but they do not necessarily give a true picture of religious commitment.

Supporters of qualitative methods often argue that quantitative methods lack validity. Statistical research methods may be easy to replicate but they may not provide a true picture of social reality. They are seen to lack the depth to describe accurately the meanings and motives that form the basis of social action. They use categories imposed on the social world by sociologists – categories that may have little meaning or relevance to other members of society. To many interpretive sociologists, only qualitative methods can overcome these problems and provide a valid picture of social reality.

Practicality

Researchers are sometimes attracted to quantitative methods because of their practicality. Quantitative methods are generally less time-consuming and require less personal commitment. It is usually possible to study larger and more representative samples which can provide an overall picture of society. Qualitative research often has to be confined to the study of small numbers because of practical limitations. It is more suited to providing an in-depth insight into a smaller sample of people.

These points will be developed in the following sections.

Choosing a sample

Once a sociologist has chosen a topic for research and a method to carry out that research, she or he needs to decide upon a 'sample': that is, the actual individuals to be studied. All research involves some sort of sampling, some selection of who or what to study. Those researchers who advocate 'scientific' quantitative methods tend to support the use of sophisticated sampling techniques and often claim to be able to generalize on the basis of their findings. Those who support interpretive qualitative methods tend to study smaller numbers of people, so their studies are less likely to require complex sampling techniques.

A sample is a part of a larger population. It is usually selected to be representative of that population: those included in the sample are chosen as a cross-section of the larger group. The use of samples saves the researcher time and money since it reduces the number of individuals to be studied. If the sample is chosen carefully, it is possible to generalize from it: that is, to make statements about the whole relevant population on the basis of the sample.

The first stage in sampling involves identifying the relevant population. A population in this sense includes all the relevant sampling units. The sampling unit is the individual person or social group in that population. In a study of voting in Britain the relevant population would be all those entitled to vote, and the sampling unit would be the individual voter.

Having determined the sampling unit and the population, the researcher might then try to obtain or to produce a sampling frame. In a study of voting there is a ready-made sampling frame – the electoral register – since a sampling frame is simply a list of all the relevant sampling units in the population. It is important that the sampling frame is as comprehensive as possible: if it is not, the sample might be seriously distorted. Researchers have sometimes used telephone directories as a sampling frame for the population of a particular area, but the directory would not include those who have ex-directory numbers and those without a telephone. Since the latter would probably be people on low incomes, the results of a study on (for example) voting intentions based upon this sampling frame might be seriously misleading.

Often, even apparently comprehensive sampling frames contain omissions. For example, the electoral register does not include all adults living in Britain. Foreign nationals (except for some citizens of Eire), those who have failed to register as voters, and members of the House of Lords are among those who would be excluded. The introduction of the Poll Tax in the early 1990s led to large numbers of people avoiding enrolment on the electoral register in an attempt to get out of paying the tax.

Studies use imperfect sampling frames. The early *British Crime Surveys* used the electoral register (see pp. 366–8 for details of these surveys). Pat Mayhew (quoted in McNeill, 1988), the Principal Research Officer responsible for the Surveys, admits that the most comprehensive sampling frame now available is not the electoral register, but the Postcode Address File. Mayhew notes that the electoral register does not include many people in institutions (such as mental hospitals and prisons) who may be particularly prone to being the victims of crime.

Later *British Crime Surveys* did start using the Postcode Address File. However, even that is not perfect. A sample using this as a sampling frame would be likely to under-represent the homeless. Furthermore, researchers usually rely upon the 'Small User File' of the Postcode Address File and this excludes addresses which normally receive 25 or more items of mail per day. As Sara Arber (1993) points out, a few households which receive unusually large volumes of mail will not be included on samples using this sampling frame.

One government study, the census, avoids the problems of sampling by studying all, or very nearly all, members of a large population. By law every household in Britain has to complete a census form, although some individuals (including many of the homeless) may slip through the net.

Sociologists lack the resources to carry out such comprehensive studies as the census, and so they usually try to select a sample that contains the same proportions of people with relevant characteristics as are present in the population under consideration. If that population contains 60 per cent women and 40 per cent men, then the sample should contain 60 per cent women and 40 per cent men. Other important characteristics such as age, occupation, ethnic origin and religion are often taken into account by researchers as they select their sample.

Other, more specialized factors may be taken into account, depending upon the nature of the research. Opinion polls on voting intentions usually use a sample from a variety of constituencies chosen according to the share of the vote won by the major parties in those constituencies at the previous election. Thus a number of 'safe' Labour, 'safe' Conservative and more marginal seats would be included. Clearly the results would be distorted if the sample was chosen entirely from safe Labour seats.

In a study of education the researcher might wish to select the sample so as to ensure that the types of schools attended by those in the sample reflect the proportions in the population as a whole.

If sampling has been carried out satisfactorily, researchers should be able to generalize on the basis of the results. This means that they should be able to make statements about the whole population without having conducted research into every member of that population. For example, opinion pollsters often claim to be able to predict the results of an election in Britain to within a couple of percentage points on the basis of a sample of perhaps one or two thousand people.

Different methods of producing a sample will now be examined.

Types of sampling

Random and systematic sampling

This is the simplest way to select a large sample. Using random sampling the researcher ensures that each sample unit has an equal chance of being chosen to take part in the research. This is often achieved by assigning numbers to each sample unit and selecting members of the sample by using a random number table. The nearest everyday equivalent to this is picking numbers out of a hat.

A less time-consuming, though slightly less random, method is to select, say, every tenth or twentieth number on a list. Since this method is not truly random it is known as systematic sampling.

Random sampling is not ideal. It relies on statistical probability to ensure the representativeness of the sample. In simple terms, it is based upon the so-called 'law of averages', and a relatively large sample is needed for the researcher to be confident that the sample will be genuinely representative. Researchers therefore generally prefer to use the method we will discuss next: stratified random sampling.

Stratified random sampling

Stratified random sampling involves the division of the sampling frame into groups in order to ensure that the sample is representative. The researcher identifies the important variables that need to be controlled and allocates the sampling units to different groups according to these variables.

For example, the researcher might identify gender and class as important variables. In this case the population would be divided into working-class males, working-class females, middle-class males, middle-class females, upper-class males and upper-class females. The sample would then be selected at random from each of these groups ensuring that the proportions of the sample in each category were the same as the proportions in the population as a whole. If 20 per cent of the population were found to be working-class females, 20 per cent of the sample would be working-class females.

This is an effective method of choosing a representative sample because it allows the researcher to control the variables that are seen as important. It requires a smaller sample size to ensure representativeness than random sampling. However, stratified random sampling is often not practicable. Even if a sampling frame is available, it often does not contain the information necessary to divide the population into groups. Opinion pollsters can use the electoral register as a sampling frame but it does not provide information such as the occupations of the electorate. For this reason it cannot be used to produce a stratified random sample.

Quota sampling

Quota sampling allows researchers to control variables without having a sampling frame. When quota sampling is used, the interviewers are told how many respondents with particular characteristics to question, so that the overall sample reflects the characteristics of the population as a whole. For example, an interviewer might be required to administer a questionnaire to ten married females and ten married males aged between 20 and 35, five unmarried men and women of the same age group and so on. Once the quota for a particular category has been filled, responses will not be collected from those in that category.

This is a particularly useful method of sampling when the overall proportions of different groups within a population are known. Government population statistics could be used to set the quota for a representative sample of different age groups in the British population. As Sara Arber (1993) points out, it is also generally quicker and cheaper than using probability sampling. There is no need to revisit those chosen in your sample if they are not available on the first visit. If someone refuses to cooperate, you can simply find someone else with the same characteristics. When speed is of the essence – for example, if you want to conduct an opinion poll on voting on the day of an election – then quota sampling may be the only practical option.

Despite the simplicity of quota sampling, it does have both theoretical and practical drawbacks in some circumstances. Quota sampling is not truly random because each person within the population does not have an equal chance of being chosen. For example, a researcher stopping people on a particular street at a particular time can only question people who happen to be in that place at that time. The lack of genuine randomness may distort the results. For example, a researcher for a political opinion poll who questions people at 11 o'clock on Tuesday morning in a city centre would be unlikely to gain much response from those who work in the surrounding rural area.

Stopping people in the street may lead to a low response rate. Many people could refuse to cooperate, and those who do cooperate might be untypical of the population as a whole in a way that was not anticipated when the original quotas were set up.

Quota sampling usually requires the researcher to ask a number of personal questions to determine whether the respondent has the characteristics of a quota group on which information is required. Asking such questions at the start of an interview might put some interviewees off, and put others on their guard so that their responses are not as open and honest as they might otherwise have been.

Furthermore, practical problems can arise in filling quotas. In some circumstances people who have full-time jobs might prove more difficult to interview than people without jobs.

Despite these limitations quota sampling continues to be used because there are circumstances when random or stratified random sampling is not possible.

Multi-stage sampling

Multi-stage sampling can save the researcher time and money, although it reduces the extent to which the sample is genuinely random. It simply involves selecting a sample from another sample. It is often used in opinion polls on voting intentions. In the first stage a few constituencies, which, on the basis of previous research, appear to represent a cross-section of all constituencies, are selected. Some rural and some urban constituencies would be included and previous election results used to check that the constituencies selected are a reasonable mixture in terms of party support. In the second stage individual respondents are chosen from within these constituencies.

If multi-stage sampling was not used in this sort of research, opinion poll organizations would incur the prohibitive expense of sending researchers to every constituency in the country, to interview a mere three or four people in each to get an overall sample of 2,000. However, in multi-stage sampling the loss of randomness may be accompanied by an increase in sampling error.

Snowballing

Snowballing is a very specialized type of sampling and is usually only used when other methods are not practical. It involves using personal contacts to build up a sample of the group to be studied. For example, it was used by Laurie Taylor (1984) when he persuaded John McVicar, a former criminal, to obtain introductions to members of the London underworld of professional crime. Taylor then used these contacts to obtain introductions to more criminals. Clearly, such samples cannot be representative since, to have any chance of being included, those studied must be part of a network of personal contacts. But for groups such as professional criminals it is not easy to use other ways of obtaining a sample.

Non-representative sampling

Sociologists do not always try to obtain representative cross-sections of the population they wish to study. In terms of Popper's views of science (see pp. 968–9), researchers should try to disprove or falsify their theories. This means looking for untypical examples of a phenomenon which does not fit a particular theory. For example, in examining the view that differences in the behaviour of men and women are primarily shaped by biological rather than cultural differences, sociologists such as Ann Oakley have tried to find untypical examples of human behaviour (see p. 133). Feminist sociologists claim to have falsified the biological arguments about the behaviour of men and women by finding examples of societies in which women behave in ways more usually associated with men and vice versa. (For examples, see p. 133.)

Goldthorpe *et al.*'s rejection of the embourgeoisement hypothesis (see pp. 79–81) provides an interesting example of the use of a non-representa-

tive sample (Goldthorpe *et al.*, 1968a, 1968b, 1969). The embourgeoisement hypothesis stated that large numbers of affluent workers were becoming middle-class as a result of their rising living standards. On the basis of available evidence, Goldthorpe *et al.* doubted this claim. To test the embourgeoisement hypothesis they selected a sample from the most affluent manual workers. If any manual workers were becoming middle-class, it would be members of this 'untypical' group. The research results showed little or no evidence of embourgeoisement. Having chosen the group most likely to confirm the hypothesis, Goldthorpe *et al.* felt confident in rejecting the theory of embourgeoisement.

Fiona Devine (1992, 1994) used a sample of similar workers in a later study of Luton workers which examined how far the working class had changed in the intervening period (see pp. 81–3).

Some sociologists have argued that it is important to study the best-informed members of social groups rather than a cross-section of a group. Thus, the interactionist Herbert Blumer thought that you should seek and question the most acute observers of a group or aspect of social life since 'A small number of such individuals, brought together as a discussion group, is more valuable many times over than any representative sample' (Blumer, 1969).

Case studies and life histories

Case studies

In general, case studies make no claims to be representative. A case study involves the detailed examination of a single example of something. Thus a case study could involve the study of a single institution, community or social group, an individual person, a particular historical event, or a single social action.

Howard Becker has described one aim of case studies as the attempt 'to arrive at a comprehensive understanding of the group under study' (Becker, 1970). Ken Pryce's participant observation study of a single West Indian community in the St Paul's area of Bristol attempted, at one level, simply to understand that particular community (Pryce, 1979). Shane Blackman (1997) conducted a detailed ethnographic study of the homeless in Brighton in order to understand how that group experienced and saw the social world (see pp. 332–3).

However, case studies can be used, as Becker claims, 'to develop more general theoretical statements about regularities in social structure and process'. As mentioned above, a case study of a particular society can be used to falsify a general theory about social life. Thus Gough's study of Nayar society showed that family structures based upon a marital bond are not universal (Gough, 1959) (see pp. 504–5). Steve Craine's study of school leavers in Manchester was able to falsify the belief of some theorists that an underclass culture was passed down from generation to generation (Craine, 1997) (see pp. 330–2).

Case studies can also be used to produce typologies, or a set of categories defining types of a social phenomenon. Douglas (1967) suggests that case studies can be used to discover the different types of suicide by uncovering the different social meanings of suicide.

Case studies may be useful for generating new hypotheses which can then be tested against other data or in later studies. Paul Willis's study of a single school has produced a number of hypotheses about the relationship between education and capitalist societies, which have proved to be a useful focus for research and the development of theories by other sociologists of education (Willis, 1977) (see pp. 791–4). Dick Hobbs and Colin Dunninghan (1998) used their case studies of individuals involved in organized crime to develop hypotheses about the changes in the nature of local and global relationships in criminal networks (see pp. 406–7).

A major drawback of case study research is that it is not possible to generalize on the basis of its findings. It is impossible to determine how far the findings of a study into one example of a social phenomenon can be applied to other examples. Alan Bryman (1988) suggests that one way to overcome this problem is to carry out or use a number of case studies of the same type of phenomenon. An example is the work of P.K. Edwards and Hugh Scullion (1982) who conducted case studies of seven British factories in order to develop a more general theory about factors affecting industrial conflict (see pp. 736–7). Similarly Shoshana Zuboff (1988) carried out case study research in eight organizations in order to try to make generalizations about the impact of information technology (see pp. 700–3).

However, as Bryman points out, it may be difficult to make direct comparisons of the results of studies carried out either by different people, or by the same person at different times. The data are likely to be more systematic if a single researcher, or group, collects data on a number of social groups at the same time. However, if this is done, the research ceases to be a case study as such.

Life histories

Life histories are a particular type of case study – the whole study concerns one individual's life. They can be carried out using a variety of methods but most frequently use extended, unstructured interviews. Some life histories make considerable use of personal documents. The following are some examples: a study of the life of a Polish peasant conducted by Thomas and Znaniecki; Gordon Allport's 'Letters from Jenny', a study of an ageing woman; and Robert Bogdan's study of Jane Fry, a transsexual. (All of these examples are discussed in Plummer, 1982.)

Like case studies, life histories, by their very nature, use an untypical sample. However, Ken Plummer argues that they have a number of uses and can be of considerable value in developing sociological theory.

Plummer suggests that life histories can be used as a 'sensitizing tool'. They can help the researcher develop an understanding of the meaning of concepts used by those she or he is studying. The 'rich detail' of life-history data can help cut through the 'dense jargon' that makes so much theoretical sociology difficult to comprehend. The life history allows the researcher to see the world from the social actor's point of view. This viewpoint is one that may challenge the assumptions and preconceptions of outsiders. For example, Plummer claims that Bogdan's study shows how transsexualism can seem a rational and reasonable choice from the actor's point of view, rather than a sickness, as it appears to be to some psychiatrists.

Like case studies in general, life histories can be used to falsify existing theories or to inspire new ones. A number of life histories can be used together to develop a theory, test it and refine it, and then test it again. Plummer refers to this theoretical approach as 'analytic induction'. The first life history allows the researcher to make preliminary hypotheses. These can be tested in subsequent life-history research. Where the hypotheses are found wanting, they can be modified to fit the extra cases. As research proceeds, the sociologist develops increasingly useful theories and generalizations. (This approach is similar to the 'grounded theory' advocated by Glaser and Strauss (1967) (see p. 1012 for further details).

Some feminist researchers argue that life-history research is useful for helping women to understand their situation, and, once they have understood, helping them to change it. Thus Maria Mies found that discussing life histories with female victims of violence helped the women to understand 'that their own experience of violence was not just their individual bad luck, or even their fault, but there is an objective social basis for this private violence by men against women and children' (Mies, 1993).

For critical researchers generally, life-history research can help to raise people's consciousness and awareness of their own exploitation by encouraging them to reflect upon the factors that have shaped their life experiences.

Pilot studies

Having selected a research method and chosen a
method of selecting a sample, some sociologists carry
out a pilot study before embarking upon the main
research project. A pilot study is a small-scale
preliminary study conducted before the main research
in order to check the feasibility or to improve the
design of the research. Pilot studies are not usually
appropriate for case studies, but they are frequently
carried out before large-scale quantitative research in
an attempt to avoid time and money being wasted on
an inadequately designed project. A pilot study is
usually carried out on members of the relevant
population, but not on those who will form part of
the final sample. This is because it might influence
the later behaviour of research subjects if they had
already been involved in the research.

Pilot studies can be useful for a number of
reasons:

1 If interviews or questionnaires are to be used, the
   questions may be tested to make sure that they
   make sense to respondents – that is, they produce
   the sort of information required and are
   unambiguous. Michael Young and Peter Willmott
   (1961) used a pilot study involving over a hundred
   interviews before carrying out their research into
   family life in Bethnal Green. They found the pilot
   interviews useful for developing questions that
   returned to particular themes so that they could try
   to check the consistency of answers to reveal if any
   respondents were being untruthful.

   Pilot studies were carried out in the Economic and
   Social Research Council's *Social Change and
   Economic Life Initiative* study (which studied social
   change in six British local labour markets). They were
   used for 'testing questionnaire items, the placing of
   the work history schedule, interview length, and the
   contact procedure' (Gallie, 1994). The researchers
   believed that this helped them to improve the
   reliability and response rate of their research.

2 Pilot studies may help researchers develop ways of
   getting the full cooperation of those they are
   studying. In a pilot study for her research into
   housebound mothers, Hannah Gavron (1966) found
   that it was necessary to establish a rapport with the
   respondent if she was to get full, open and honest
   answers. She therefore spent some time chatting to
   the respondent informally before starting the
   interview.

3 Pilot studies may be used to develop the research
   skills of those taking part. When Rex and Moore
   (1979) studied immigrants in Birmingham they used
   their pilot study to train the amateur interviewers
   they were using.

4 The pilot study may determine whether or not the
   research goes ahead. The researchers might discover
   insurmountable practical problems which lead to

them dropping the project. In some cases a pilot
study might be used to convince a funding
organization of the usefulness of a particular
project. If the pilot study is unsuccessful, the full
study may be abandoned.

Social surveys

Social surveys can be defined as research projects
which collect standardized data about large numbers
of people. The data are usually in a statistical form,
and the most practical way of collecting such data is
through the use of questionnaires. Other types of
research method, such as unstructured interviewing
or observation, would be less suitable for collecting
standardized information about large groups because
they would be both time-consuming and difficult to
translate into a statistical form.

Stephen Ackroyd and John A. Hughes (1981) have
distinguished three main types of survey:

1 The first type, the factual survey, is used to collect
   descriptive information. The government census can
   be seen as a type of factual survey. The pioneering
   research done by Rowntree in his studies of poverty
   in York (see pp. 293–4) is a more sociological
   example. Rowntree's research was designed
   primarily to document the extent of poverty rather
   than to explain it, and this also applies to the more
   recent research on poverty by Mack and Lansley
   (1985, 1992) (see pp. 300–3 for further details of
   this study).

2 The second type, the attitude survey, is often carried
   out by opinion poll organizations. Instead of
   producing descriptive information about the social
   world, this type of survey attempts to discover the
   subjective states of individuals. Many polling
   organizations collect information about attitudes to
   political policies and personalities. Information on
   attitudes is often collected by sociologists interested
   in voting, for example Heath, Jowell and Curtice
   (1985, 1994) (see pp. 658–61). Sociologists who
   study stratification, such as Marshall, Newby, Rose
   and Vogler (1988), sometimes collect data on
   attitudes in order to examine the issue of class
   consciousness (see pp. 88–9 for further details).

3 The third type of survey, the explanatory survey, is
   more ambitious than the other types, since it goes
   beyond description and tries to test theories and
   hypotheses or to produce new theories. Most
   sociological surveys contain some explanatory
   element. Marshall *et al.* (1988), for example, tested
   the theory that routine white-collar workers had
   become proletarianized (see p. 69).

   Surveys such as that carried out by Townsend into
   poverty are designed to be both descriptive and
   explanatory. Townsend used survey data both to
   measure the extent of poverty and to develop
   theories to explain it (Townsend, 1979, 1993;
   Townsend, Corrigan and Kowarzik, 1985).

Researchers usually want to be able to generalize from social surveys, and so surveys are usually based on carefully selected samples. The success of any survey depends ultimately on the quality of the data it produces. Most social surveys use questionnaires as a means of data collection. The advantages and disadvantages of this method and the reliability and validity of the data it produces will now be examined.

Questionnaires

A questionnaire consists simply of a list of pre-set questions. In questionnaire research the same questions are usually given to respondents in the same order so that the same information can be collected from every member of the sample.

Administering questionnaires

Questionnaires may be administered in a number of ways. Often they are given to individuals by interviewers, in which case they take the form of structured interviews. This method was used by Goldthorpe et al. (1968a, 1968b, 1969) in their affluent worker study, and by Young and Willmott in their survey of family life in London, conducted in 1970 (Young and Willmott, 1973). (See Chapter 8, pp. 529–31.) It was also used by Gordon Marshall and colleagues in their study of class (Marshall et al., 1988), and in the ESRC *Social Change and Economic Life Initiative* (Scott, 1994) (see p. 729).

Structured interviews have the advantage of having a trained interviewer on hand to make sure that the questionnaire is completed according to the instructions and to clarify any ambiguous questions. But questionnaires administered by interviewers involve the problem of interviewer bias. This means that the responses given are influenced by the presence of the researcher. (See pp. 1006–7 for a discussion of interviewer bias.) In addition, this method is expensive compared to the following alternatives.

The postal questionnaire, as its name suggests, is mailed to respondents with a stamped addressed envelope for return to the researcher. It provides an inexpensive way of gathering data, especially if respondents are dispersed over a wide geographical area. The return rate, though, does not often exceed 50 per cent of the sample population and is sometimes below 25 per cent. This may seriously bias the results since there may be systematic differences between those who return questionnaires and those who do not. For example, the main response to a postal questionnaire on marital relationships might come from those experiencing marital problems and wishing to air their grievances. If most non-respondents were happily married, the researcher would be

unjustified in making generalizations about married life on the basis of the returns.

A second way, and one that obtains a far higher return rate, is when questionnaires are administered to a group, such as a class of students or workers at a union meeting. This method is less expensive than dealing with individual respondents while maintaining the advantages of the presence of an interviewer. However, the interviewer must ensure that respondents do not discuss questions within the group since this might affect their answers.

A third way of administering a questionnaire is to ask the questions over the telephone. This is often done by market research firms or marketing departments of companies, but it is not usually regarded as satisfactory by sociologists. Unless the researcher specifically wants a sample of people who have a telephone, the sample is unlikely to be representative of the population being studied.

Producing questionnaires and analysing the data

Questionnaires tend to be used to produce quantitative data. Sometimes researchers may not have very clear hypotheses and will ask a wide range of questions on a topic. However, they must have some idea of what factors are important or interesting before they can start to construct a questionnaire.

In the process of choosing questions, researchers have to operationalize concepts. In other words abstract concepts have to be translated into concrete questions which make it possible to take measurements relating to those concepts. Sociologists classify the social world in terms of a variety of concepts. For instance, social class, power, family, religion, alienation and anomie are concepts used to identify and categorize social relationships, beliefs, attitudes and experiences which are seen to have certain characteristics in common. In order to transpose these rather vague concepts into measuring instruments, a number of steps are taken.

First, an operational definition is established. This involves breaking the concept down into various components or dimensions in order to specify exactly what is to be measured. Thus, when Robert Blauner (1964) attempted to operationalize the concept of alienation, he divided it into four components – powerlessness, meaninglessness, isolation and self-estrangement (see pp. 694–7). Similarly, when Gordon Marshall and colleagues (1988) operationalized the concept of class, they adopted the definitions of class categories used by E.O. Wright and John Goldthorpe (see pp. 111–17).

Once the concept has been operationally defined in terms of a number of components, the second step involves the selection of indicators for each component. Thus an indicator of Blauner's component of powerlessness might be an absence of opportunities for workers to make decisions about the organization of work tasks. Marshall *et al.* selected indicators of class consciousness such as attitudes towards social inequality and towards industrial conflict.

Third, indicators of each dimension are put into the form of a series of questions that will provide quantifiable data for measuring each dimension. Thus indicators of class consciousness became questions such as 'Do you think the distribution of income and wealth is a fair one?' and 'Do you think there are any important issues which cause conflicts between those who run industry and those who work for them' (Marshall *et al.*, 1988).

Researchers have a number of choices to make during the process of operationalizing concepts in questionnaires. First they have to decide what form of question to ask.

Questions may be open-ended, such as: 'Under what circumstances do you think a person could move from one class to another?' Open-ended questions allow the respondents to compose their own answers rather than choosing between a number of given answers. This may be more likely to provide valid data since respondents can say what they mean in their own words. However, this kind of response might be difficult to classify and quantify. Answers must be interpreted carefully before the researcher is able to say, for example, that a certain percentage of respondents attribute good industrial relations to effective management, an efficient union, high pay or whatever.

A second type of question, sometimes known as a closed or fixed-choice question, requires a choice between a number of given answers. For example, the following question was asked to white people in Britain:

> *If a close relative were to marry an ethnic minority person would most white people –*
> *Would not mind*
> *Would mind a little*
> *Would mind very much*
> *Can't say*

Modood *et al.*, 1997, p. 316

Sometimes the respondent is asked to choose between two stated alternatives. For example:

> *In the past there was a dominant class which largely controlled the economic and political system, and a lower class which had no control over economic or political affairs. Some people say that things are still like this, others say it has now changed. What do you think? Has it changed, or stayed the same?*

Marshall *et al.*, 1988, pp. 294–5

A similar type of question requires the respondent to agree or disa1gree with a particular statement. For example:

> *A number of ideas have been put forward in order to overcome Britain's economic problems. (For each one indicate whether you agree or disagree.)*
> a. *Leaving it to market forces to revive the economy.*
> b. *Income policies which increase the wages of the low paid rather than the high paid.*
> c. *Increasing income tax in order to increase welfare benefits.*
> d. *Import controls to protect Britain from competition from abroad.*
> e. *Increased taxes on the profits of successful companies in order to maintain jobs in declining industries.*
> f. *Increased government spending to revive the economy.*

Marshall *et al.*,, 1988, p. 293

Compared to the open-ended type, fixed-choice questions provide responses that can be more easily classified and quantified. It requires relatively little time, effort and ingenuity to arrive at statements describing the percentages of respondents who gave different answers. However, fixed-choice questions do not allow the respondent to qualify and develop their answers. It is therefore difficult for researchers to know exactly what they are measuring. For example, when respondents agree that there are issues which divide management and workers, it is not clear what the respondents think those issues are. They might be quite different to the sorts of issues the researchers think might be divisive. Other questions can be added to clarify what respondents mean, but some sociologists would argue that in-depth, unstructured interviews would be better than structured ones for determining the extent and strength of class consciousness.

If open-ended questions are used, and the researcher wants the data to be in a statistical form, it becomes necessary to code the answers. Coding involves identifying a number of categories into which answers can be placed. The researcher usually examines the answers given and establishes the principal types of answer that have been provided. Thus, in the *British Crime Survey* of 1998, the answers to an open-ended question on the reasons why people had not reported crimes were put into classifications such as: 'Too trivial', 'Police couldn't do anything', 'Dealt with ourselves', Dislike/fear of police', 'Inconvenient to report', 'Police would not be interested', 'Fear of reprisal', 'Reported to other authorities' and 'Other answers' (Mirrlees-Black *et al.*, 1998).

Once the data have been collected and classified, it is necessary to analyse them. In an explanatory survey this often involves using multivariate analysis to determine the relationships between the variables. For example, in their study of educational achievement, A.H. Halsey and colleagues tried to measure the relative importance of cultural and material factors in producing educational success or failure (Halsey *et al.*, 1980) (see pp. 842–3 for further details).

Questionnaires are often designed to test a particular hypothesis. Goldthorpe *et al.* (1968a, 1968b, 1969) used questionnaires to test the embourgeoisement thesis; while Marshall *et al.* (1988) used them to test various theories of stratification. In such cases the data are analysed in relation to the hypotheses that are being tested. The analysis of data from descriptive or attitude surveys is often more straightforward. Sometimes it involves little more than statements about the percentages of respondents who gave particular replies.

The advantages of questionnaires

Questionnaire research is certainly a practical way to collect data. Although designing the questionnaire and carrying out pilot studies may take some time, once in use questionnaires can be used to collect large quantities of data from considerable numbers of people over a relatively short period of time. Thus Mack and Lansley (1985) in their initial study of poverty used a sample of 1,174 people (see pp. 300–3 for further details), while the *British Crime Survey* of 1998 (discussed on pp. 366–8) used a sample of 14,947 households (Mirrlees-Black *et al.*, 1998). Such large samples cannot be studied using more in-depth research methods without incurring prohibitive costs.

Even when questionnaires are administered by interviewers this involves relatively little personal involvement, or danger or sacrifice on the part of the researcher, when compared with some participant observation studies. The results of questionnaire research can be relatively easily quantified, and with the assistance of computers the data can be analysed quickly and efficiently. Using computers, the relationships between many different variables can be examined. Many sociological and other social science researchers use the *Statistical Package for Social Sciences* computer programme, which can rapidly produce complex statistical analyses.

To some quantitative researchers, however, the theoretical advantages are more important than the practical ones. Although relatively few sociologists today claim to be positivists, a considerable number support the use of quantitative data on the grounds that it can be analysed more 'scientifically' and objectively than qualitative data. Quantitative data can be considered more reliable than qualitative data. Since each individual respondent answers precisely the same questions in the same order, they

are all responding to the same stimuli. Any differences in response should, in theory, reflect real differences between respondents. Furthermore the figures produced can be checked by other researchers, and their reliability should therefore be high.

Only when the data are quantified by means of reliable measuring instruments can the results of different studies be directly compared. Thus studies of British elections over several decades have produced data that can be used to determine changing patterns of voting and changing social attitudes within the British electorate. Heath, Jowell and Curtice (1985, 1994) in their two studies of British elections were able to use data from their own and other election studies to reveal ideological shifts in the electorate, and to check the claim that class was becoming less important in determining voting behaviour (see pp. 655–7 and 667–70 for details).

From a positivist point of view, statistical data from questionnaires can be analysed so that new theories can be produced. More typically, however, such data are used to test existing hypotheses, since the researcher must have a reasonably clear idea of the sort of information that is important before they set the questions. Whether questionnaires are used inductively (as in the former case) or deductively (as in the latter), they can be used to try to establish causal relationships through multivariate analysis. Ivor Crewe (1987a) used statistical data to check his theory that housing tenure, among other factors, had an influence on voting behaviour independent of social class (see p. 658). Many sociologists regard questionnaires as a suitable method for testing precise hypotheses in a rigorous manner: for example, Marshall *et al.* (1988) used questionnaire data to back up their claim that they had falsified the proletarianization thesis (see p. 69).

As has already been mentioned, questionnaire research can generally use larger samples than qualitative methods. For this reason, sociologists who have carried out a social survey tend to feel more justified in generalizing about a wider population than those who have carried out an in-depth study of a smaller number of people. This is particularly likely where a questionnaire is used in conjunction with sophisticated sampling techniques so that the researcher can be confident that the sample is representative. Researchers into such areas of social life as poverty, voting, crime and stratification, who have carried out social surveys using questionnaires, have not hesitated to make claims about the British population as a whole, not just those questioned during the research.

Despite the importance of the theoretical points discussed above, questionnaires are not just used by positivists or those who strongly believe in the advantages of quantitative data. In many circumstances they are used when resources are limited and data are needed on large numbers of people. They are particularly useful when straightforward descriptive data are required. However, the validity of the statistical data, particularly when produced for explanatory surveys, has been questioned by some sociologists who advocate a more interpretive, qualitative approach. These criticisms will now be examined.

The disadvantages of questionnaires

Interpretive sociologists vary in their views on survey research and the data it produces. Weber's methodological position implies that such data can be one – but only one – of the types of data required in sociological research. Interactionists often see statistical data as inadequate for producing sociological explanations of human behaviour. Phenomenologists go further, for they see the data produced as an artificial creation of the researcher. Above all, critics argue that, despite the reliability of questionnaire data, it lacks validity. To phenomenologists in particular, the methodological assumptions on which questionnaires are based are entirely false. They put forward six main objections:

1 It cannot be assumed that different answers to the same question reflect real differences between respondents. However much care is taken with the wording of questions, respondents may interpret them differently. People who choose the same response may not mean the same thing. People who choose different responses may not mean different things. This may result from the wording of questions. For example, the word 'uptight' in low-income black American areas usually refers to a close relationship between friends, but when it entered the vocabulary of mainstream America it changed its meaning to anxious and tense. Even common words and phrases carry different associations for different groups. As Irwin Deutscher observes, 'Within a society, as well as between societies, the sociologist seeks information from and about people who operate verbally with different vocabularies, different grammars and different kinds of sounds' (Deutscher, 1977). Thus a questionnaire, which provides little opportunity to qualify meaning, might not provide comparable data when administered to members of different social groups.

2 In designing the questionnaire researchers assume that they know what is important. Respondents cannot provide information that is not requested, they cannot answer questions that are not asked. For this reason, it is difficult to develop hypotheses during the course of the research and researchers are limited to testing those theories that they have already thought of.

3 Questionnaire research involves the operationalization of concepts, and some interpretive sociologists argue that such procedures produce a distorted picture of

the social world. The process of breaking down a concept so that it can be quantified imposes sociological constructs, categories and logic on the social world. Thus, when Blauner sought to measure alienation (see pp. 694–7) he employed a concept which might have had no reality in the social world he sought to understand. Indeed Blauner admits that 'It is difficult to interpret a finding that 70 per cent of factory workers report satisfaction with their jobs because we do not know how valid or reliable our measuring instrument is' (Blauner, 1964). The workers were not allowed to reveal their attitudes to their work in their own way. As the phenomenologist Michael Phillipson observes, 'the instruments of the observer create the very order they are supposedly designed to reveal' (Phillipson, 1972).

4 The validity of the data may be reduced by the unwillingness or inability of respondents to give full and accurate replies to questions. Quite simply, respondents may lie. Attempts to check the accuracy of self-report studies on crime (see pp. 368–9) have found that some 20 per cent of respondents do not tell the truth. Even if respondents want to tell the truth they may be unable to do so because of faulty memory or because they lack the relevant information. Thus the British Crime Surveys may have underestimated the amount of unreported crime because victims may have been unaware or may have forgotten that they had been the victims of crime.

Furthermore, even when respondents are honest, and not hampered by ignorance or forgetfulness, there are some types of questions where the validity of the answers can still be queried. This is particularly true of questions about attitudes. It cannot be assumed that stated attitudes will be translated into actual behaviour.

For instance, in the 1930s La Pierre (1934) travelled to 251 establishments – such as restaurants, hotels and campsites – in the USA with two Chinese people. They were refused service or accommodation at only one of these places, yet when the same establishments were sent a questionnaire a few months later, only one said that they would accept Chinese customers.

When observation or participant observation is used, the researcher relies less on respondents' accounts and may therefore have more chance of producing valid data.

5 A fifth reason for doubting the validity of questionnaire data is the distance maintained between the researcher and the subject of the research, particularly in the case of postal questionnaires. As Alan Bryman puts it:

The quantitative researcher adopts the posture of an outsider looking in on the social world. He or she applies a preordained framework on the subjects being investigated and is involved as little as possible in that world. This posture is the analogue of a detached scientific observer.

Bryman, 1988

To a positivist this approach encourages objectivity, but to an interpretive sociologist it precludes the possibility of understanding the meanings and motives of the subjects of the research. Unlike participant observation, the researcher does not undergo similar experiences to the subjects of the research, and so cannot draw so easily on experience to understand the behaviour of those being studied. Using questionnaires it is not possible to see how people act and react towards each other, nor is it possible to examine the way in which self-concepts change during the course of interaction. Interactionists in particular do not believe that the researcher can gain genuine insights into the subjective states underlying the behaviour of those being studied unless the researcher gets close to those they are studying.

Some feminists and critical social scientists also object to questionnaire research on similar grounds. They believe that it is important to involve the subjects of research in the research process. This has a number of advantages. It allows the subjects to contribute to evaluating the research; it allows the researcher to avoid exploiting them; and it enables the consciousness of exploitation to develop.

For example, Victor Jupp and Clive Norris comment that critical researchers in criminology have a 'theoretical and political aversion to the highly formal quantitative and positivist approaches of conventional criminology' (Jupp and Norris, 1993). They associate such methods with using data to control criminals and deviants, whereas their aims are more directed at liberating people from the controls which restrict them. They see this as better achieved through methods which are 'qualitative, naturalistic and non-positivist and include life-history and other informal interviews, observational methods, especially participant observation, case studies and social history research'.

6 Finally, when open-ended questions are used, and the researcher requires quantitative data, the coding of answers will take place. As in the operationalization of concepts this involves researchers imposing their own order on the data. The differences in the precise answers given to questions are glossed over as answers which are not identical are placed together in a single category. This process obscures the differences that do exist between the answers.

Questionnaire research – conclusions

Despite the strength of these criticisms it is increasingly accepted by most sociologists that there is a place for survey research in sociology. After all, there would be little point in carrying out participant observation or in-depth interviewing to discover the percentages of males and females who watched television every evening.

Furthermore, even some feminists believe that quantitative questionnaire research has its uses. For example, Toby Epstein Jayaratne (1993) points out

that quantitative research, such as that which uses questionnaires, has been useful in documenting the extent of sexism in certain institutions. The critical social scientist Lee Harvey (1990) sees some questionnaire research (such as that undertaken by Goldthorpe et al.) as falling within the tradition of critical research.

It is usually when statistical data from questionnaires is used to try to establish causal relationships that opponents of quantitative research become most concerned about the validity of the data being used. However, such research does often provide useful data on social structures which may shape behaviour without individuals being aware of it. Thus studies of social class and social mobility produce findings about people's life chances which could not be produced using other methods (see pp. 97–105 for examples). When used alongside qualitative methods, questionnaire research can certainly make a crucial contribution towards developing as full a picture as possible of social life.

Interviews

Types of interview

Interviews take a number of forms depending upon how structured they are. A completely structured interview is simply a questionnaire administered by an interviewer who is not allowed to deviate in any way from the questions provided. The interviewer simply reads out the questions to the respondent. At the other extreme, a totally unstructured interview takes the form of a conversation where the interviewer has no predetermined questions. Most interviews fall somewhere between these two extremes.

Interviews of a more structured variety may allow the interviewer to probe the respondents' answers so that they can, if necessary, be clarified. The interviewer may also be allowed to prompt the interviewee, that is, give them extra guidance to help them answer the question. For example, Goldthorpe et al.'s team of researchers were able to prompt interviewees who could not decide how to answer a question about whether they had actively done anything to find a different job, by suggesting that they might have read job adverts in local newspapers (Goldthorpe et al., 1968a).

In more unstructured interviews the conversation develops naturally, unless the respondent fails to cover an area in which the researcher is interested. Eventually the interviewer will direct the conversation back to the areas he or she wishes to cover. Marjorie DeVault, for example, in her study *Feeding the Family*, had some questions which she made sure every interviewee answered, but she also allowed them to talk freely around one general question. She told them that she wanted to talk about 'all the housework that has to do with food: cooking, planning, shopping, cleaning up' (DeVault, 1991).

Some interviewers have a schedule of topics they wish to cover and they make sure that at some point the conversation comes back to these topics.

Some feminist researchers, such as Ann Oakley, are advocates of very unstructured interviews in which the researcher and person being interviewed become collaborators in the research and sometimes friends (see pp. 988–9). Critical social researchers also usually prefer unstructured interviewing.

As highly-structured interviews are very similar to questionnaires, the rest of our discussion of interviews will concentrate on interviews of a less structured variety.

Interviewing styles

Having a conversation with somebody is extremely common in human interaction, and it might be thought that interviewing requires no special preparation. However, the sociological researcher needs to overcome the problems of making contact with – and gaining the cooperation of – respondents. Having made contact, and persuaded a person to take part in the interview, the researcher then needs to try to ensure that the respondent gives full, honest and open answers.

Interviewers have used a variety of methods to make contact with respondents. They have telephoned in advance, written letters and turned up at interviewees' houses. At the initial point of contact it is important that the interviewers establish why they wish to carry out the interview and what the information is to be used for. They may also need to explain how the interviewee was selected and why they are suitable for research. Gavron (1966) used letters of introduction from the interviewee's doctor in order to establish contact. When she met them she explained the nature and purpose of her research.

The most common way of conducting interviews is to be non-directive: to refrain from offering opinions, to avoid expressions of approval and disapproval. Often an interviewer will spend some time trying to establish rapport or understanding between themselves and the interviewee. They may do this simply by talking informally before the interview proper starts. Once the interviewee feels that he or she is not going to be criticized or judged, that they can talk freely and can rely upon a sympathetic audience, it is hoped that they will talk with honesty and openness. Since the respondent does not have to answer the questions (and since they may be asked about private or personal aspects of their lives which they would not usually discuss

with a stranger), it is often argued that non-directive interviewing is the most effective type of interviewing.

In contrast, Howard Becker suggests that interviewers may be inhibited by adopting this relatively passive approach and a 'bland, polite style of conversation' (Becker, 1970). He suggests that on certain occasions a more active and aggressive approach can provide much fuller data. This involves the interviewer taking 'positions on some issues' and using 'more aggressive conversational tactics'.

Becker adopted these tactics in his interviews with Chicago schoolteachers (discussed on p. 845). He claims that American schoolteachers believe they have a lot to hide from what they regard as a 'prying, misunderstanding, and potentially dangerous public'. They are therefore unlikely to volunteer certain information. By adopting an aggressive stance, being sceptical, and at times even pretending to be stupid, Becker managed to prise out much of this information. In particular, he claimed to have uncovered the ways that teachers categorized and evaluated students in terms of their class and ethnic backgrounds – information they would have preferred to have kept hidden for fear of being accused of prejudice and discrimination. Becker states: 'I coerced many interviewees into being considerably more frank than they had originally intended.'

Becker suggests that this approach is particularly useful for one-off interviews. Similar information can be picked up more subtly over a series of interviews without running the risk of antagonizing respondents. The apparent success of Becker's rather unorthodox tactics suggests that there is no one best way of interviewing.

Some sociologists who, like Becker, reject non-directive interviewing believe that interviewers should be empathetic towards interviewees rather than aggressive. Thus the feminist researcher Ann Oakley (1981), in her study of childbirth and childcare, became closely involved with the women she was studying. She advised them and sometimes even gave them help, and she encouraged them to become actively involved in the research process (see pp. 988–9 for details).

Individual and group interviews

It is normal for a single interviewer to interview a single respondent. This has a number of advantages. It may be easier to establish rapport, confidentiality can be ensured, and the respondent is not distracted or influenced by the presence of other interviewees. In some circumstances, though, sociologists have carried out group interviews.

For example, Paul Willis (1977), in his study of education, interviewed several of the 'lads' together (see pp. 791–4 for further details). It can be argued that this might be more likely to produce valid data than a one-to-one interview. The lads' activities usually took place in a group context, and a group interview would reflect this. In group interviews Willis was able to observe interaction between the 'lads', and they felt more at ease than when talking alone to an older and middle-class interviewer.

James Holstein and Jaber Gubrium argue that group interviews are valuable because they 'allow diverse categorizations and sentiments to emerge, showing how participants flesh out, alter, or reconstruct viewpoints in response to challenges' (Holstein and Gubrium, 1995). They believe that having many voices present (which they call multivocality) broadens interviews and can make the participants more reflexive. They think more deeply about their answers and reflect critically upon them in their responses to others.

This view of interviewing is rather different to the view that sees interviews as simply uncovering the facts – as untainted by the interview process as possible. Instead it sees the interview as an active process in which knowledge is created through interaction. This type of group interview tends, therefore, to be favoured by interactionist, interpretive and critical sociologists.

A similar style of interview – the focus group – is also used by political parties who want more in-depth data on public opinion than that provided by opinion polls.

Interviews are not natural social situations. Some sociologists have sought ways to minimize the extent to which respondents may see them as artificial or unnatural, in the belief that this is essential for valid data to be obtained. Others believe that more valid data can be obtained by emphasizing and using the process of interaction that takes place within the interview.

The advantages of interviews

Interviews are seen as a useful research method by many different types of sociologist. Although they represent something of a compromise between more structured research methods like questionnaires and the more in-depth methods such as participant observation, they can be adapted to suit both the practical needs and theoretical preferences of different sociologists.

Those who support the use of more quantitative methods tend to prefer interviews to participant observation. Compared to participant observation, interviews can utilize larger samples, so generalizations are more justified. With some coding of responses it is possible to produce statistical data from interviews, and it is easier to replicate the

research and check results. Because there is usually some degree of structure in an interview it is easier to make direct comparisons than it is by using data from participant observation.

To sociologists who prefer more qualitative methods, interviews have clear advantages over questionnaires. The concepts and words used by interviewer and interviewee alike can be clarified; the researchers' concepts are less likely to be imposed on the social world; issues can be explored in greater depth; and the researcher does not limit the responses to fixed choices. For these reasons interviews can be useful for generating new hypotheses and theories which the researcher would not otherwise have thought of.

For example, when Elizabeth Bott (1971) started her interviews with 20 families in her investigation into conjugal roles, she had not considered the possibility that friendship networks might affect the type of conjugal relationship that developed. Had she been using questionnaires she would not have included the questions that would have been necessary to discover the information which she needed to formulate her theory.

The above arguments, though, do not explain why sociologists should sometimes choose to use interviews in preference to all other research methods. They are not as reliable as questionnaires and they are not as likely to produce valid data as participant observation. A major reason for the widespread use of interviews is their sheer practicality. There is no other method which allows access to so many different groups of people and different types of information. As Ackroyd and Hughes put it:

> Using as data what the respondent says about himself or herself potentially offers the social researcher access to vast storehouses of information. The social researcher is not limited to what he or she can immediately perceive or experience, but is able to cover as many dimensions and as many people as resources permit.
>
> Ackroyd and Hughes, 1981

In short, interviews are more flexible than any other research method. They can be used to extract simple factual information from people. They can be used to ask people about their attitudes, their past, present or future behaviour, their motives, feelings and other emotions that cannot be observed directly. Interviewers can explore each question or issue in as much depth or superficiality as they wish. The range of information available from interviews can be demonstrated from the following examples.

In their study of schizophrenia R.D. Laing and A. Esterson (1970) used in-depth interviews to study the past behaviour and emotional states of people with schizophrenia and their families (see pp. 510–12). The family is such a small and closed social grouping that participant observation is almost impossible without changing the family's behaviour.

Howard Becker (1963) used interviews to study 50 marijuana smokers. Via interviews he was able to try to explore the whole of the 'deviant career' of the drug users, from the time they first tried the drug to when they became regular users involved with a subculture of marijuana smokers. Interviewing allowed Becker to discuss the motives and circumstances that led to them trying the drug and continuing to use it.

Interviews are often used to carry out research into groups who might not otherwise consent to being the subject of research. Laurie Taylor (1984) could only produce data about professional crime in Britain because he was able to gain the trust of the criminals he interviewed. Clearly, participant observation would have been out of the question, and he would have been unlikely to have obtained a satisfactory response rate using postal questionnaires. Furthermore, because of Taylor's lack of familiarity with professional criminals he might have had difficulty deciding what questions to ask them. Once again, the flexibility and practicality of interviews are evident. Similar comments are applicable to the studies of criminal networks by Dick Hobbs and Colin Dunninghan (1998) (see pp. 406–7), which used life-history interviews with professional criminals connected with one particular locality.

Apart from their practicality, there are some theoretical advantages to interviews compared with other methods. From the viewpoint of some feminist and critical researchers, interviews allow close collaboration between interviewer and interviewee so that they can become partners in the research. Interviews allow the opportunity for critical reflection by all those involved, so that they can examine and sometimes change the perspectives through which they see the world. This is important for critical researchers, whose objective is to change the social world. Such opportunities may not always be possible in participant observation studies where the flow of social life limits time for reflection. Some sociologists have gone as far as arguing that the interviewing process itself creates new knowledge rather than just revealing data that was previously present in the interviewees' heads (Holstein and Gubrium, 1995).

The disadvantages of interviews

Stephen Ackroyd and John A. Hughes have observed that:

> *The foundations of interviewing are to be found in the mundane observation that people can report on what they feel, tell others about aspects of their lives, disclose what their hopes and fears are, offer their opinions, state their beliefs, answer questions about who they see regularly, what they did last week, how much they spend on food, and so on, to put it simply they can impart masses of information about themselves.*
>
> Ackroyd and Hughes, 1981

The problem is that these masses of information may be neither valid nor reliable. Interviews have many of the same drawbacks as questionnaires: the responses given may not be accurate and may not reflect real behaviour. Respondents may lie, may forget, or may lack the information required.

To give a simple example, some of the criminals interviewed by Laurie Taylor (1984) later claimed that they had made up fanciful stories about their escapades in order to see how gullible Taylor was.

However, even if respondents are not handicapped by forgetfulness or ignorance, and have no wish to deceive, they may still not give valid answers. As critics of questionnaire data have pointed out, interviewees may not act in accordance with their stated beliefs. When reflecting on past events they may alter their interpretation in the light of subsequent experience. Because interviews are artificial, Cicourel has asked whether they 'capture the daily life, conditions, opinions, values, attitudes, and knowledge base of those we study as expressed in their natural habitat' (quoted in Bryman, 1988).

David Matza's work on delinquents in the USA can illustrate the sort of problem that arises with interview data (Matza, 1964) (see pp. 361–3 for further details). Matza interviewed 100 delinquents in training school and found that a surprisingly large number of them disapproved of most crimes. Matza concluded that delinquents did not, on the whole, strongly reject society's values. Critics, however, have pointed out that, apart from the question of how truthful the delinquents were, Matza failed to take account of the possibility that they had modified their views as a result of their punishment. At the time of their offences they may have regarded the laws they were breaking contemptuously and only later did they change their minds.

Interviewees may also be influenced by the presence of the researcher. The answers given may be influenced by the way the interviewees define the situation. William Labov (1973), for instance, found that young black American children responded differently when interviewed in different contexts.

Interviewed by a white interviewer in a formal setting, the children said little when asked to describe a toy jet plane. This type of evidence had led some psychologists to conclude that these children were linguistically deprived and that this deprivation contributed to their failure in education. However, Labov produced evidence to show that the apparent linguistic deprivation was the result of interviewing techniques and not a genuine reflection of the children's linguistic ability. When the children were interviewed by a black interviewer in a formal setting they were more forthcoming. When the children sat on the floor with the interviewer, and they were able to bring their best friend with them, they opened up and became fluent and articulate.

Labov argued that when children defined the situation as hostile they were unable to demonstrate their real abilities. When they defined the situation as friendly they were able to give a much better account of themselves. Clearly such factors as the age, skin colour, sex, clothing and accent of the interviewer may affect the interviewees' definition of the interview, and so affect their behaviour.

A further problem with unstructured interviews is that there is more opportunity for the interviewer (usually without realizing it) to direct the interviewee towards giving certain types of response. Consciously or unconsciously, respondents might give the sort of answers that they believe the interviewer wants to hear, rather than saying what they truly believe. This problem is known as interviewer bias. It can never be totally eliminated from interview research simply because interviews are interaction situations.

Interviewer bias is demonstrated in a study conducted by Stuart A. Rice in 1914 (discussed in Deming, 1971). Two thousand destitute men were asked, among other things, to explain their situation. There was a strong tendency for those interviewed by a supporter of Prohibition to blame their decline on alcohol; but those interviewed by a committed socialist were much more likely to explain their plight in terms of the industrial situation. The interviewers apparently had their own views on the reasons for destitution, which they communicated to the respondents.

In order to conduct an interview successfully and interpret the responses correctly the interviewer must also be aware of the social conventions of those being interviewed. For example, certain activities may be regarded as more 'socially desirable' by members of one group than by members of another. As a result there may be differences between social groups in terms of their members' willingness to admit to particular activities.

The importance of this can be seen from a study conducted by Bruce Dohrenwend in New York to investigate the relationship between mental health and ethnicity (discussed in Phillips, 1971). Respondents were asked whether or not they had experienced a list of symptoms associated with mental illness. Compared with Jews, Irish and blacks, Puerto Ricans reported experiencing more of the symptoms and therefore appeared to have a higher rate of mental illness. Yet Dohrenwend found that the symptoms were regarded as less undesirable by Puerto Ricans than by members of the other ethnic groups. As a result they were more ready to admit to them. Such findings cast serious doubt on the validity of interview data and therefore on the use to which those data are put.

Interviews – conclusion

In all research methods the procedures used by the researcher influence the sort of data produced. Interviews are no exception. Nigel Fielding (1993b) argues that there are three main perspectives on the merits of interview data:

1   Positivists believe that interviews can produce valid and fairly reliable data so long as standardized interviews are used and care is taken to avoid interviewers letting their own views become known to interviewees. The greater the detachment and impartiality of the researcher, the more valid and reliable the data will be.

2   Symbolic interactionists, on the other hand, recognize 'No clear-cut distinction between research interviews and other forms of social action ... For interactionists, the data are valid when a deep mutual understanding has been achieved between interviewer and respondent.' From this viewpoint, the interactive nature of interviews helps the production of valid knowledge, rather than gets in the way.

3   From the viewpoint of ethnomethodologists, interviews 'do not report on an external reality displayed in respondents' utterances but on the internal reality constructed as both parties contrive to produce the appearance of a recognisable interview'. Interviews then become the objects of study rather than sources of data. Ethnomethodologists can study them to reveal the informal tacit understandings which shape the way interviews are conducted.

A fourth perspective – that of critical researchers and feminists – is not mentioned by Fielding. It can be argued that this perspective comes close to that of interactionists. However, in addition, critical and feminist researchers also see interviews as an opportunity for interviewers and interviewees to see through the ideologies of social life, to reflect together on the social world being studied, and, ultimately, to begin to change that reality so that it becomes less exploitative.

Despite the problems associated with interviews, they are unlikely to be abandoned as sources of data by sociological researchers. As the above perspectives suggest, they can be adapted to fit the theoretical preferences of different sociologists. Furthermore, as David Silverman points out, conversations are an integral part of social life, and as one of the main ways in which people communicate they are invaluable as a way of trying to understand society. Silverman says:

> They offer a rich source of data which provides access to how people account for their troubles and good fortunes. Human beings can never fully see the world through the eyes of another person, but talking to other people can certainly provide insights into their perspectives on social life. Perhaps only through participant observation can researchers develop greater insights.
>
> Silverman, 1985

Observation and participant observation

Observation

All sociological research involves observation of some sort. The use of observation is not confined to researchers advocating any particular methodological approach. Thus positivists believe that the social world can be objectively observed, classified and measured. Observation has also been frequently used by qualitative social researchers: numerous interactionist sociologists have observed interaction in the classroom when studying education. Similarly, in studying suicide, the ethnomethodologist J. Maxwell Atkinson (1978) observed the process of decision making in coroners' courts. However, there are limits to the situations in which social life can be observed in 'natural' settings without affecting the validity of the data produced.

There are a considerable number of social situations in which the presence of an observer is prohibited, or is unlikely to be allowed. Sociologists who study politics are not allowed to observe the deliberations of the British Cabinet, nor can they observe private conversations between members of the government and their senior officials. Sociologists interested in family life are unlikely to be allowed to observe interaction between married couples in the bedroom, nor is it likely that sociologists who study work will be able to observe the board meetings of large companies.

Even when observation is allowed, the researcher's presence might alter the behaviour of those being observed to such an extent that the data is of little use. In small, closely-knit social units such as families the observed can hardly be expected to act naturally with an observer present.

Despite this, in certain situations sociologists might judge that some useful and valid data can still be produced. For example, in his study of secondary schooling, David Hargreaves (1967) found that some teachers he observed altered their behaviour considerably. Some refused to talk to the class as a whole when he was present. But others appeared to carry on as normal, and Hargreaves believed that some of his data were therefore valid (see p. 848 for further details of Hargreaves's study). In such situations the longer the researcher observes, the more likely those being studied are to forget about his or her presence, and the more likely they are to act naturally.

Given the danger that the researcher will influence those being studied, valid data can most reasonably be expected to result when the presence of passive outsiders is quite normal. Thus, in courtrooms, in the Visitors' Gallery of the House of Commons, or on the terraces at a football match, a sociological researcher is able to blend into the background without any great difficulty. In other circumstances it may be necessary for the observer to get involved in the activities of those being studied. To be accepted, she or he will have to become a participant observer.

Ethnography and participant observation

Ethnography is the study of a way of life. It was first introduced into the social sciences by anthropologists who studied small-scale, pre-industrial societies. Bronislaw Malinowski's study of the Trobriand Islands (Malinowski, 1954) (pp. 433–4) is an example of an ethnographic study. Anthropologists increasingly recognized the need to get as close as possible to the societies they were investigating. More recently, the same approach has been applied to the study of groups within industrial society.

Ethnography can take various forms and is used by sociologists of different types. It is widely used by symbolic interactionists, and critical ethnography is a common type of study amongst critical social scientists (see pp. 1013–14). Ethnography can use different qualitative research methods, but the most common are in-depth interviews, participant observation, and the use of qualitative documents. It may also involve collecting some quantitative data. However, participant observation is often the most important single method used in ethnographic studies.

As a means for gathering data, participant observation has a long history in sociology. It has been used by researchers with widely differing theoretical perspectives. As such it is a research technique that has been adapted to meet the requirements of sociologists with various views on the nature of social reality. However, it has been particularly associated with the work of symbolic interactionists such as Herbert Blumer, Howard Becker and Erving Goffman. This method became widely employed in the USA in the 1960s and since then has been regarded by many sociologists as the most appropriate way of obtaining qualitative data.

Joining the group, collecting and recording the data

One of the most important decisions that participant observers have to make is how to approach the social group they wish to join. Researchers may decide to be an overt participant observer, where they declare their true identity and purpose, or a covert participant observer, where the fact that they are a researcher is not revealed. Sometimes researchers choose to be partially open but do not provide those being studied with the full story.

Some researchers strongly advocate being open from the start, arguing that it is both morally and practically the best way to carry out participant observation. The American sociologist Ned Polsky, in his study of *Hustlers, Beats and Others* (1967), suggests that it is morally correct to be truthful, and that the research can easily be ruined if the covert participant observer is uncovered. Another advantage is that the open researcher may be able to avoid participation in distasteful, immoral, or illegal behaviour. (For example, Howard Parker (1974), when studying Liverpool delinquents, could refuse to take part in the theft of car radios without damaging his relationship with the people he was studying.)

Furthermore, the researcher is free to ask questions without arousing suspicion. In a study of female sexuality and its relationship to masculinity among a group of students at a further education college, Beverley Skeggs was open about her research and argued that her 'age, clothing, attitude and marginal status as a part-time teacher enabled the students not to see me as part of the establishment' (Skeggs, 1991).

Sometimes researchers are less open without actually lying to those they are studying. William Foote Whyte (1955), in a classic study of an Italian American slum, simply described himself as a writer without elaborating further. Ken Pryce (1979), in his study of the West Indian community in Bristol, found that he could be quite open with some of the groups, but with others (such as those engaged in illegal activities) he had to be more guarded.

The main disadvantage of being open is that it may affect the behaviour of those being studied. 'Doc', one of the key members of the street-corner gang studied by Whyte, said to him, 'You've slowed me up plenty since you've been down here. Now, when I do

something, I would have to think that Bill Whyte would want to know about it and how to explain it. Before I used to do things by instinct' (Whyte, 1955). The knowledge that they are being observed can influence people's behaviour as they become more self-conscious and think about their actions.

An obvious advantage of covert participant observation is that the members of the group being studied are not likely to change their behaviour as a result of being studied, since they are kept in ignorance of the fact that they are being observed for research purposes. Some studies may not be possible without participant observation being covert, either because the group would change its behaviour too much, or because the researcher would not be allowed to join in the first place.

For example, Jason Ditton (1977) wanted to study thefts by bread van salesmen during the course of their work. Clearly the salesmen might have become much more cautious if they knew that they were being observed; indeed they might have stopped stealing altogether. Nigel Fielding (1993a) argues that he would not have been able to conduct his study of the National Front (a very right-wing and racist political party in Britain) without conducting covert research, because of the members' hostility to sociology. Another researcher, who called himself 'James Patrick', had to keep even his name secret as he feared for his personal safety when studying violent Glasgow gangs (Patrick, 1973). Similarly, William Chambliss (1978) needed to maintain secrecy when conducting a study of organized crime in Seattle (see pp. 383–4). Researchers have also had to keep their work secret when studying such groups as the Masons and certain religious sects.

If secrecy is maintained, then the researcher has little choice but to become a full participant in the group. However, if the researcher is open, there is an element of choice in the degree of involvement. Some researchers remain fairly detached. Others become much more involved. Ken Pryce found himself going to clubs and blues dances, drinking with and talking to local residents well past midnight during his study of West Indian life in Bristol (Pryce, 1979).

Becoming too much of a participant can cause difficulties. In particular the researcher may have the problem of 'going native'. They may become so much a part of the group that they are unable to stand back and analyse the situation objectively. Nigel Fielding argues that, in collecting data, 'One must maintain a certain detachment in order to take that data and interpret it.' On the other hand, those who experience this problem have at least achieved complete acceptance by the group and they may well have a true insider's view. Perhaps the most complete insider's view can be provided by those who become sociological researchers, and use their own experiences as a source of data. Simon Holdaway (1983) was a police officer for a number of years before becoming a sociologist, and could genuinely claim to provide a view from *Inside the British Police.*

The more detached participant observer can perhaps be more objective, but may not understand the behaviour of those being studied quite as well. Fielding comments that there can be a problem in some overt research of '"not getting close enough", of adopting an approach which is too superficial and which merely provides a veneer of plausibility for an analysis to which the researcher is already committed'. In other words the researcher avoids risking challenging their own preconceived ideas by not digging too deeply into the social world of those being studied. However, very often the researcher cannot predict how involved they will become. It depends to some extent upon how much rapport they build up with the subjects of their research.

To be successful, the participant observer must gain the trust of those observed. In his study of black 'street-corner' men in Washington DC (see pp. 321–2), Elliot Liebow (1967) had to win over Tally, the leader of the group. Only when Liebow had gained Tally's trust did Tally admit that he had lied to him at the start of their acquaintance.

The close and relatively long-lasting relationships established through participant observation provide greater opportunities for developing trust than are provided by other research techniques. Interviews and questionnaire surveys usually involve one-off, short-lived encounters. Particularly with groups such as low-income blacks and teenage gangs, a relationship of trust is necessary to secure cooperation. As Lewis Yablonsky notes from his research on teenage gangs, 'Their characteristic response to questionnaires investigating the gang's organization or personal activities is one of suspicion and distrust. To the gang boy every researcher could be a "cop"' (Yablonsky, 1973). In this type of situation participant observation is more likely to provide valid data than other research techniques.

Once the researcher has entered the group and gained its trust, he or she must then go about collecting the data and recording it. Much of this involves watching and waiting, and taking part where necessary, but some participant observers have supplemented the data gained in this way with some interviewing. This has the advantage of allowing the researcher to request the precise information required, without waiting for it to crop up in normal conversation. It is obviously only possible where the research is overt. Whyte (1955) used interviews with a 'key informant', 'Doc', to gain most of the background information required. Pryce (1979) made extensive use of formal and informal interviews.

Recording the data from interviews can be relatively straightforward: Pryce used a tape recorder. Recording data from participant observation is more difficult. Tape recorders would probably inhibit the natural behaviour of those being studied. Taking notes could have a similar effect, and may in any case be impracticable. Most researchers have to opt for the best means available: committing what has taken place to memory, and writing it down as soon as possible. Ditton (1977) used to retire to the lavatory to take notes in private. Pryce had to wait until he got home. He said:

> I had to rely heavily on memory, my method was to write down these observations as soon as possible after hearing or observing them. The rule of thumb I constantly exercised was to record them while they were still fresh in my mind, generally the same day ... I believe most of the information I recorded in this way was fairly accurate, if not accurate word for word, accurate in tone, flavour and in the emotions expressed.
>
> Pryce, 1979

Not all sociologists, though, would accept Pryce's claim.

The advantages of participant observation

Supporters of participant observation have argued that, compared to other research techniques, it is least likely to lead to sociologists imposing their reality on the social world they seek to understand. It therefore provides the best means of obtaining a valid picture of social reality.

With a structured interview (a predetermined set of questions which the interviewee is requested to answer) or a questionnaire (a set of printed questions to which the respondent is asked to provide written answers) sociologists have already decided what is important. With preset questions they impose their framework and priorities on those they wish to study. By assuming that the questions are relevant to the respondents they have already made many assumptions about their social world.

Although participant observers begin the work with some preconceived ideas (for example, they will usually have studied the existing literature on the topic to be investigated), at least they have the opportunity to directly observe the social world.

The value of this opportunity is clear from Whyte's observations: 'As I sat and listened, I learned the answers to questions I would not have had the sense to ask if I had been getting my information solely on an interviewing basis' (Whyte, 1955). Intensive observation over a period of years provided Whyte with a picture of what was important in the lives of the Italian Americans he studied. Without this exposure to their daily routine he would have remained ignorant of many of their priorities. Had he relied solely on interviews, this ignorance would have prevented him from asking important and relevant questions.

Liebow was particularly concerned about the danger of distorting the reality he wished to observe. He states that, from the outset of his research, 'there were by design, no firm presumptions of what was or was not relevant' (Liebow, 1967). He did his best simply to look and listen and to avoid any preconceptions of what was or was not important. Liebow chose participant observation because he believed that the method would provide a 'clear, firsthand picture' of the 'life of ordinary people, on their grounds and on their terms'. By observing what was said and done, where, when and by whom, he hoped to discover how a group of black street-corner men saw and organized their lives. Liebow claims that 'Taking this inside view makes it easier to avoid structuring the material in ways that might be alien to the material itself.'

In participant observation, it is also more difficult for the people being studied to lie or mislead the researcher than it is in other research methods. The researcher is on the spot and witnesses actual behaviour rather than relying upon people's accounts of their lives.

Where the researcher gains data from talking to those being studied, the validity of the data may be greater than in informal interviews. For example, the feminist researcher Beverley Skeggs argues that she was able to obtain valid data on the sexuality of young women because of the closeness of the relationship she developed with them. She says:

> *Their comments on their own sexual responses came from small soirées in my flat or their bedrooms. The discussions often became so intimate and animated that I think the idea that they were speaking for research purposes became lost in the desire to discuss contentious issues in a safe situation.*
>
> Skeggs, 1991, p. 128

Participant observation is a particularly appropriate method for symbolic interactionists because it allows an understanding of the world from the subjective point of view of the subjects of the research. Because researchers experience many of the same events as the observed, they are better able to put themselves in their position and to understand why they interact with others in particular ways.

Pryce felt that participant observation allowed him to understand and explain the subjective views of some West Indians in Bristol. He said, 'There is a tendency to either ignore or disregard the subjective feelings of members of the West Indian minority.' One of those subjective feelings was the belief of some that there was no point in trying to earn a living through ordinary employment, which was dismissed as 'slave labour' and 'shit work' (Pryce, 1979).

Howard Parker (1974) also believed that he could see the world through the eyes of those he studied – he felt justified in calling his book *View from the Boys*.

Interactionists believe that behaviour is largely governed by the self-concept held by an individual. Self-concepts are not fixed and static, but change during the course of interaction. Similarly, the meanings people attach to their own behaviour change as the context in which that behaviour takes place alters. Participant observation studies are often carried out over an extended period of time and it is therefore possible to study the process through which such changes happen.

This can be illustrated by Jock Young's study of marijuana smokers in Notting Hill (Young, 1971). He found that the behaviour, the meaning attached to that behaviour, and the self-concepts of those involved altered in response to police attempts to discourage marijuana smoking. The drug users in the area became more secretive, attached more importance to taking the drug, and in response to what they saw as persecution they saw themselves as being in opposition to some of society's values. (For further details, see p. 374.) Such changes and the way they came about would have been difficult to identify and explain on the basis of interview or questionnaire data.

Many interactionists see observation or participant observation as the best means of studying interaction. Much interaction takes place almost instinctively, and those involved cannot be expected to recall precise details if asked in an interview. Furthermore, it is difficult for complete participants to be detached and objective when discussing their relationships with others. It is easier, for example, for an outsider to comment on group relationships. Parker (1974) was able to describe in detail the relationships between members of delinquent gangs he studied. In St Paul's, Pryce (1979) was able to distinguish a number of different subcultures which a resident of the area might not have been fully aware of.

Critics of participant observation argue (as will be discussed later) that the findings of such studies lack objectivity, that they are unreliable and depend too much upon the interpretations of the observer. Defenders of this research method generally believe that these objections can be overcome, and that participant observation can be made sufficiently systematic to be regarded as being a reliable as well as valid research method.

Finally, participant observation provides in-depth studies that can serve a number of useful purposes. In particular, participant observation is useful for generating new hypotheses. Rather like unstructured interviews, participant observation can go in unexpected directions and so can provide sociologists with novel insights and ideas. Although less useful for testing hypotheses, because the type of data produced is not entirely under the control of the researcher, it may be useful for falsifying theories. Thus Parker's study of British delinquents (Parker, 1974) could be used to test how far Albert Cohen's explanation of American delinquency (see pp. 357–8) is applicable to Britain.

The limitations and disadvantages of participant observation

Participant observation has many practical disadvantages. It is often very time-consuming. Cicourel (1976) spent four years studying juvenile justice in California. Beverley Skeggs (1997) spent a total of 12 years conducting ethnographic research following the lives of women who had been on a 'caring' course at a further education college in England.

The researcher can usually only study a very small group of people and has to be physically present for the research to proceed. In personal terms such research may be highly inconvenient and demanding. The researcher may be required to move house, to live in an area they would not otherwise choose, and to mix with people they would rather avoid. They may find it necessary to engage in activities they dislike in order to fit in with the group, and they may even face personal danger. 'James Patrick' left Glasgow in a hurry when the gang violence began to sicken him and he felt concerned for his own safety (Patrick, 1973).

There are also limits on who can be studied using this method. Higher-class and more powerful groups in society, in particular, may exclude participant observers. Individual researchers may lack the skills, knowledge or personality to be accepted by a particular group.

More serious, though, are the theoretical objections that have been raised.

First, to quantitative researchers, the samples used in participant observation are too small and untypical for generalizations to be made on the basis of the findings. Any conclusions can only apply to the specific group studied. Thus Pryce (1979) would not have been justified in making generalizations about all West Indians in Britain on the basis of a study of Bristol.

Second, such studies cannot be replicated, so the results cannot be checked. It is therefore difficult to compare the results with the findings of other studies.

The data from participant observation rely upon the particular interpretations of a single individual, and are specific to a particular place and time.

Cicourel (1976) admits that his participant observation study relied heavily upon his own observational and interpretive skills. If the reader has little faith in Cicourel's skills, then he or she will have little reason to accept his findings. It is quite possible that a different researcher would have reached quite different conclusions. As Whyte admits, 'To some extent my approach must be unique to myself, to the particular situation, and to the state of knowledge existing when I began research' (Whyte, 1955).

Moreover the account of social life produced by participant observation is the result of a highly selective method of data collection. The participant observer usually records only a small fraction of all possible data that he or she could have used. The observer selects what to record and what to omit and imposes a framework upon the data in the process of interpreting it. Martyn Hammersley points out that an ethnographer could have produced many different descriptions of the same setting. He says, 'there are multiple, non-contradictory, true descriptions of any phenomenon' (Hammersley, 1992). In this situation it may be difficult to accept a particular researcher's description as reflecting anything more than a personal perspective.

A third theoretical objection is that the validity of the data is bound to be affected by the presence of the researcher, since the group being studied will not act naturally. This point is rejected by many participant observers. Whyte, for example, felt that eventually he was able to blend into the background so that social life carried on as normal around him.

To critics – particularly those who support the use of positivist methods – participant observation is simply 'unscientific'. It is not systematic or rigorous, its findings cannot be checked, the research cannot be replicated, it is a subjective rather than objective research method. However, some interactionist sociologists have suggested that this sort of qualitative research need not lack rigour.

Glaser and Strauss (1967) claim that qualitative research can be used to generate and refine what they called grounded theory. The whole process of collecting and analysing qualitative data can be systematic. Theories can be produced which are grounded in the data and in the real social world. In the early stages the researcher starts to develop categories and then further data are collected to see if they fit with these categories. Hypotheses begin to emerge as the initial hunches of the researcher are backed up or refuted by the data that is being produced. Causal explanations can be produced, and may be tested in follow-up studies.

Becker (1970) showed how this sort of approach can be used when he was studying the behaviour of medical students. From observing the behaviour and listening to the comments of medical students he began to distinguish between 'cynical' and 'idealistic' attitudes to medicine. In the former case, patients tended to be regarded as little more than animated visual teaching aids; in the latter, as human beings whose pain and suffering the students felt a duty to relieve. Having found that these categories seemed to work, Becker went on to observe how often and in what circumstances the students were cynical or idealistic. Noting that students tended to be idealistic when talking to other students, Becker advanced the hypothesis that 'Students have "idealist" sentiments' but 'group norms may not sanction their expression'. Becker says that it is perfectly possible to check the hypotheses produced by participant observation, and that this research method need not be unsystematic. He says of participant observation that 'the technique consists of something more than merely immersing oneself in data and having "insights"'.

In a book edited by Anslem Strauss and Juliet Corbin (1997) a range of individual studies apply grounded theory to research on topics as diverse as understanding chronic pain, cancer research, the activities of headhunting companies, abusive relationships and contemporary Japanese society.

However, writers such as Hammersley still question the ability of ethnographic research to develop theoretical understanding. Hammersley says, 'Grounded theorising seeks both to represent concrete situations in their complexity and to produce abstract theory. It thus operates under conflicting require-ments' (Hammersley, 1992).

Descriptive accounts can concentrate on the unique features of a particular social situation, but developing theory does require making some general-ization beyond the setting being studied. According to Hammersley this is only possible if a number of cases are studied to see whether they conform to a theory. Yet very few ethnographers have even attempted to compare a range of case studies using ethnographic methods, and those who have done so generally rely upon interviews rather than participant observation.

Furthermore, Hammersley believes that the claim of some ethnographers that they are developing theories 'presupposes that there are scientific laws of human social life … Yet few ethnographers today believe there are such laws.' To Hammersley, then, there is little basis for arguing that ethnography can be used to develop theory. However, this position is totally rejected by advocates of critical ethnography.

Critical ethnography

Critical ethnography is the sort of ethnography advocated by supporters of critical social science (see pp. 982–6). Unlike Hammersley, critical ethnogra-phers believe that ethnography can be used both to develop and to test theories, including theories that examine the structure of society as a whole.

Paul Willis's study of the transition from school to work among a group of working class 'lads' is sometimes seen as the first example of a critical ethnography (Willis, 1977) (see pp. 791–4). Willis relied largely upon data from interviews, but often other critical ethnographers have made use of partici-pant observation and other methodologies.

Since Willis's study there have been numerous examples of critical ethnographies. These include Sallie Westwood's study of female factory workers (Westwood, 1984), Beverley Skeggs's study of working-class women who had been to a further education college (Skeggs, 1997), and Mairtan Mac an Ghaill's study of the development of masculinity in an English state secondary school (Mac an Ghaill, 1994).

As discussed earlier in the chapter, critical social scientists believe that research should involve close collaboration between researchers and their subjects; that studying oppressed groups can help to reveal the hidden and oppressive structures of unequal societies; and that research can be instrumental in changing society. Steven Jordan and David Yeomans (1995) see critical ethnography as providing a way for researchers to understand the way oppression is experienced by the oppressed by sharing some of the same experiences. Carspecken argues that critical ethnographers are 'concerned about social inequali-ties, and we direct our work towards positive social change'. He goes on: 'We use our research, in fact, to refine social theory rather than merely to describe social life' (Carspecken, 1996).

Mairtan Mac an Ghaill's study *The Making of Men* (1994) illustrates the main features of critical ethnog-raphy. Mac an Ghaill tries to develop theories of masculinity (particularly those of R.W. Connell, discussed on pp. 191–6) by studying 11 heterosexual young men in a British state secondary school in the Midlands, and a second group of homosexual young men from a range of educational institutions in the same area. He tries to use elements of feminist methodology and argues for an approach to research based on 'collaboration, reciprocity and reflexivity'.

Mac an Ghaill tries to use the research process to challenge the assumption that heterosexuality is preferable to homosexuality, and he also encourages the young men to question dominant ideas on what makes you a true man. For example, he discusses with the homosexual students the way in which conventional ideas of masculinity largely prevent emotional closeness between men. In the course of his research he seems to have some success in encouraging the gay students to positively value their conceptions of masculinity, rather than being defensive in the face of hostility from heterosexuals. The study tries to relate changes in conceptions of masculinity to changes in the British education system and in the wider society.

An evaluation of critical ethnography

As with grounded theory and critical social research in general, Martyn Hammersley (1992) is hostile to critical ethnography. As discussed above, he sees problems in basing research around the concept of oppression and he questions the belief that the validity of theories can be checked by the subjects of research. However, some critical ethnographers have tried to develop rigorous approaches that overcome the sorts of objections commonly directed at this research method. One such approach has been developed by Patti Lather (1986).

Lather accepts that critical ethnography can sometimes be criticized for using circular arguments. The ethnographic description is used both for developing theory and for testing it. Experience comes to be interpreted in terms of the theory, yet the experience is also used to confirm the theory. To break out of the circle Lather recommends four procedures:

1 Triangulation involves the use of different research methods to cross-check the validity of the data. Thus, for example, participant observation can be used to check the validity of data gained from interviews (see pp. 1022–3 for a discussion of triangulation).

2 Construct validity involves a 'ceaseless confrontation with and respect for the experiences of people in their daily lives to avoid theoretical imposition' (Lather, 1986). From Lather's point of view this is only possible in ethnographic research; questionnaire-type research tends to be guilty of imposing theoretical constructs on the explanation of behaviour without examining whether they have real relevance in understanding people's lives (see criticisms of questionnaire research, pp. 1002–3).

3 Face validity is achieved through recycling your findings through at least some of those being studied, while being aware that they may be suffering from false consciousness. Although Hammersley is critical of doing this, Lather believes that it is useful as *one* check on the validity of findings. It helps ensure that the researcher has not fundamentally misunderstood the viewpoint of those being studied and therefore completely failed to grasp the framework within which they choose how to act.

4 Catalytic validity refers to 'the degree to which the research process reorients, focuses, and energizes participants towards knowing reality in order to transform it'. Again, this objective is rejected by critics of this type of research, but it does perhaps provide one indication of whether the research has gone beyond the commonsense understandings of the people being studied.

Critical ethnography certainly retains problems despite attempts by some sociologists to develop it and overcome objections. As Irlam Siraj-Blatchford (1995) points out, critical ethnography does tend to assume that you should study the oppressed. It therefore neglects the study of oppressors, who might be able to offer even more insight than the oppressed into the way oppression works.

Furthermore, critical ethnography has by no means overcome all the problems in testing the validity and reliability of data. However, the same is true of other research methods. Critical ethnographers such as Patti Lather and Phil Carspecken use the subjects of research as an additional check on data rather than as an alternative to conventional checks on the data.

Postmodern ethnography

While critical ethnography hopes to penetrate beyond common sense to reveal hidden structures of oppression, postmodern ethnography has no such aims. Some postmodernists do see themselves as opposing oppression, but they do so by undermining all claims to discover the truth, rather than by trying to replace commonsense truths with an analysis of oppressive structures.

Postmodern ethnography rejects any claim to trying to produce objective descriptions of social life, never mind explanations. However, it does follow critical ethnography in emphasizing cooperation with those being studied. Stephen A. Tyler describes postmodern ethnography as:

> a cooperatively evolved text consisting of fragments of discourse intended to evoke in the minds of both reader and writer an emergent fantasy of a possible work of common-sense reality, and thus to provoke an aesthetic integration that will have a therapeutic effect.
>
> Tyler, 1997, first published 1986, p. 254

Tyler seems to be arguing that postmodern ethnography should act very much like a work of literature. It is designed to stimulate the imagination, to make people think about the lives of other people, not to describe reality in any objective way. Indeed he argues that it is 'in a word, poetry – not in its textual form but in its return to the original context and function of poetry ... [which] evoked memories of the ethos of community'.

To Tyler this type of ethnography should acknowledge that there can be many different viewpoints within a social group. It is not the ethnographer's job to decide between these different viewpoints and produce a single account, but to record the variety of perspectives. A postmodern ethnography may take a form in which different versions are published together (as in the different gospels in the Bible), but the precise form it will take cannot be decided in advance. Instead, the researcher and those who are being studied must work together and find a format that will preserve the diversity of views in the social group.

The author is much less important than in traditional sociological studies. The author is not seen as being in a privileged, superior position to those being studied. She or he is not seen as having any special ability to make an analysis of social reality which can rise above the subjective views of those being studied. Tyler says, 'The whole ideology of representational significance is an ideology of power. To break its spell we would have to attack writing, totalistic representational signification, and authorial authority'. Like Jean-François Lyotard (see Chapter 15), Tyler seems concerned that any claims to have discovered the truth will be used to produce metanarratives – big stories about truth and fiction, right and wrong. These in turn may be used to dominate and oppress groups of humans.

Tyler admits that postmodern ethnography will not produce a coherent account of social life. It will be 'fragmentary' and will not be 'organized around familiar ethnological categories such as kinship, economy and religion'. However, he does not see this as a particular problem. For Tyler, the fragmentary nature of postmodern ethnography is desirable because 'We confirm in our consciousness the fragmentary nature of the post-modern, for nothing so defines our world as the absence of a synthesizing allegory'. In other words, people experience the social world as fragmented and cannot find any single way of understanding it. An individual's social life is experienced as many different stories which are not closely linked to one another. Tyler concludes that 'Post-modern ethnography captures the mood of the post-modern world, for it, too, does not move toward abstraction, away from life, but back to experience. It aims not to foster the growth of knowledge but to restructure experience'.

Postmodern ethnography – an evaluation

For an approach which advocates a move away from abstraction and back to experience, Tyler's description of postmodern ethnography is highly abstract.

He provides no concrete example of postmodern ethnography and no detailed suggestions as to how to conduct it. Furthermore his approach seems somewhat contradictory. He argues that postmodern ethnography should be more than 'an edited collection of authored papers' written by participants in social life, yet he wishes to give no special privilege to the ethnographer. Indeed it is unclear why an ethnographer is needed at all, since the opinions of the author are seen to be no better than those of the people being studied.

Furthermore, if ethnography should act like a poem, stimulating the imagination, it is again unclear why it is needed. Fiction can perform the task of stimulating the imagination at least as well as writing that claims to have some basis in real experience. Tyler's arguments could, therefore, be seen as self-defeating. By arguing that ethnography is really no different to fiction he makes a case for abandoning ethnography altogether.

Postmodern ethnography suffers from the same problem of extreme relativism (in which no view is better than any other) which afflicts a number of other versions of postmodernism (see Chapter 15).

Longitudinal research

In most sociological studies, researchers study a group of people for a relatively short period of time. They analyse their data, produce a report on their research and move on to new endeavours. However, some researchers study a group over an extended period, collecting data on them at intervals. Such studies are known as longitudinal or panel studies.

Longitudinal studies were first used by researchers in the USA in the 1940s to measure changes in public attitudes. It was seen as more reliable to follow a particular sample over a period of time when measuring changing attitudes, than to select a new sample from time to time. By using a 'panel' the researcher could be sure that changes in the attitudes measured would not result from changes in the composition of the sample.

Longitudinal studies originated as extended attitude surveys. Since then, they have usually been used to collect quantitative data in social surveys, though not necessarily about attitudes. Sometimes a particular age group or cohort is followed over a number of years. The *Child Health and Education Survey* has tried to follow the development of every child born in Britain between the 3rd and 9th of March 1958. Another longitudinal study was carried out by J.W.B. Douglas. In *The Home and the School* (1964) he followed the educational progress of a sample of children through their school careers (see pp. 830–1).

Another example is provided by D.J. West and D.P. Farrington's *Who Becomes Delinquent?* (1973). This study was concerned with 411 London schoolboys. It followed their development from age 8 to 18 in order to determine what factors were associated with delinquency.

Longitudinal studies are usually large-scale quantitative studies, but some qualitative studies also extend over considerable periods of time. Alan Bryman commented, 'There is an implicit longitudinal element built into much qualitative research, which is both a symptom and a cause of an undertaking to view social life in processual, rather than static terms' (Bryman, 1988). In other words, methods such as participant observation are based upon the assumption that social life should be explained in terms of an unfolding story. Parker's study of Liverpool delinquents provides a good example of this (Parker, 1974). Parker showed how the type of delinquency engaged in by 'the boys' changed as the research developed and the boys grew older.

A major advantage of any longitudinal study is its ability to pick up such changes; a study extending over a shorter time span cannot, and so the results can be misleading. Beverley Skeggs's study of a group of young women during and after studying at a further education college followed the women for a total of 12 years (Skeggs, 1991, 1997).

Supporters of longitudinal studies also see them as more likely to provide valid data than other types of research. As W.D. Wall and H.L. Williams (1970) point out, retrospective studies which ask people to report on past events in their lives rely upon fallible human memories. Wall and Williams also say, 'Human beings naturally seek for causes and may unconsciously fabricate or exaggerate something to

account for the present state of affairs.' Longitudinal studies help to overcome this problem because recent events are less likely to have been reinterpreted in the light of subsequent consequences.

Quantitative longitudinal studies often examine a large number of variables because the researchers are unsure what data may prove to be important or required later in the research. For example, West and Farrington (1973) collected information relating to no less than 151 variables in their study of delinquency. Although the researcher still has to decide what variables to study, examination of so many limits the extent to which they impose their own theories upon the research.

Longitudinal studies do, of course, have disadvantages. It may be necessary to select people who are accessible and willing to cooperate over an extended period. Furthermore, the size of the sample is liable to fall as some individuals become unwilling to continue to take part, or prove impossible to trace. Douglas's original sample of 5,362 children in 1957 was reduced to 4,720 by 1962 (Douglas, 1964). Since those who were lost may not have been representative of the sample as a whole, the results may have been distorted.

More serious criticisms question the overall validity of the data. Quantitative longitudinal studies collect data using such research methods as questionnaires and interviews. As earlier sections have shown, some sociologists question the validity of data collected in this way. A particular problem with longitudinal studies is that the subjects of the research are conscious of the fact that their behaviour is being studied. This may influence them and change their behaviour because they think more carefully about their actions.

Secondary sources

Secondary sources consist of data that have already been produced, often by people other than sociologists. Secondary data produced by the government are often used by sociologists. Organizations such as trade unions, companies and charities are a useful source of data, as are documents such as letters, diaries and autobiographies produced by individuals. The secondary sources used by sociologists may be contemporary or historical, and the data available from them may be primarily qualitative or quantitative. When sociologists refer to existing sociological studies by other writers in their own research, these become secondary sources.

Sociologists often use secondary sources for practical reasons. They can save time and money and they may provide access to historical data that cannot be produced using primary research because the events concerned took place before current members of society were born.

Secondary sources are invaluable to sociologists but have to be used with great caution. Their reliability and validity are open to question, and often they do not provide the exact information required by a sociologist.

Specific types of secondary sources will now be examined. At the end of the section there will be a general discussion on how to evaluate all types of secondary sources.

Official statistics

A vast range of statistics are produced by the government. In recent years the Government Statistical Service (which was set up in 1941) has coordinated the production of government statistics, but the production of large-scale statistical data goes back at least to 1801, when the first census was conducted.

Sociologists interested in demography have used statistical data from the census and elsewhere to examine a wide range of topics, which include birth and death rates, marriage and fertility patterns, and divorce. Sociologists who study deviance have used official crime and suicide statistics. The many official economic statistics are of interest to sociologists concerned with work. Figures on inflation, unemployment and employment, strikes and productivity have also been used. Indeed, almost every area of sociological research has found some use for official statistics.

Some statistics, such as unemployment figures, are published monthly; others, such as crime statistics, annually. Information from the census is produced once every decade. Other statistical surveys are carried out on an irregular basis: for example, the *British Crime Surveys*. One of the reference books that is most frequently consulted by sociologists in Britain is *Social Trends*, which has been produced annually since 1970 and summarizes statistical data on society.

Much of the statistical information made available by the government would not exist if it were left to sociologists. They lack the resources and power to carry out the work that goes into producing these data. For example, each household is compelled by law to return a census form, and has a legal duty to provide accurate information; it would be impossible for sociologists to obtain this information independently.

Official statistics are easily accessible and cost sociologists nothing to produce. Sociologists generally acknowledge that such statistics are useful, but they do not necessarily agree about what use can be made of them. Some sociologists do not accept the reliability and validity of official statistical data, while others are prepared to place more trust in them.

In the past, some positivists tended to accept official statistics uncritically. Durkheim (1970) believed that suicide statistics were sufficiently reliable and valid to measure the extent and social distribution of suicide (see pp. 974–7). Using official statistics, he tried to establish correlations between suicide and other 'social facts', and ultimately to discover causal relationships and laws of human behaviour.

Similarly, many of the early structural and subcultural theories of crime were based upon the assumption that the official crime statistics accurately identified the working class as the group most prone to criminal activity (see pp. 354–61).

Today sociologists are more cautious about the use of official statistics in areas of social life such as suicide and crime, but most would accept the reliability and validity of statistics from the census. (Earlier parts of this book have shown how inaccurate some official statistics can be – for instance, many crimes remain unreported and as such cannot be recorded in official data (see pp. 363–72).)

Victimization and self-report studies

Despite this, many researchers believe that problems like these can be overcome. For example, victimization or self-report studies use questionnaires administered to members of the population in order to determine the extent of reported and unreported crime. The British Crime Surveys provide examples of victimization studies (for example, Mirrlees-Black *et al.*, 1998) (see pp. 366–8 for further details). D.J. West and D.P. Farrington's longitudinal study of delinquency in London (West and Farrington, 1973) included a self-report study in which members of the sample were asked 38 questions about delinquent acts they might have carried out.

It is sometimes argued that on the basis of such studies it is possible to estimate the real amount of crime in society as a whole, and to calculate the extent of criminality in social groups. The figures can be used to determine the accuracy of official figures, and appropriate adjustments can then be made to them. Even so, as Peter Eglin points out, 'The question remains, however, whether an error estimate calculated for some set of, say, national statistics in some given year will be generalizable to other times or other places' (Eglin, 1987).

An even more serious problem concerns the question of the validity of the answers given by respondents in surveys. Stephen Box (1981) has noted that in self-report studies respondents may exaggerate their criminality, or alternatively they might be unwilling to admit to their crimes. In effect, self-report studies measure how many crimes people say they have committed, rather than the actual number.

Furthermore, in measuring the criminality or delinquency of an individual, the researcher has to decide what offences or actions to include in the list of questions. Among West and Farrington's 38 questions, for instance, respondents were asked about stealing school property worth more than 5p, and about annoying, insulting or fighting other people (strangers) in the street. The precise wording and number of questions included in the questionnaire ultimately determine the amount of crime or delinquency uncovered – and in any case respondents may interpret the questions in different ways.

Whether or not an offence is included in the statistics depends upon the choices made by the researcher. In the *British Crime Surveys* the researchers discounted certain events because they did not believe that they constituted crimes. The statistics produced by such studies are therefore of dubious validity.

However, several sociologists believe that self-report and victimization studies provide some indication of the real extent of crime, and that they help to correct the misleading impression (provided by the official figures) that crime is an overwhelmingly working-class phenomenon.

A phenomenological view

Ethnomethodologists and phenomenologists reject the use of statistics for measuring or determining the causes of the social facts to which they claim to refer. As earlier parts of this book show, sociologists such as Cicourel (1976) and Atkinson (1978) believe that statistics are the product of the meanings and taken-for-granted assumptions of those who construct them. Thus Cicourel claims that the stereotypes held by the police and juvenile officers lead to youths from lower social classes being more likely to be seen as delinquent. Justice is negotiable and statistics produced by official agencies are socially created (see pp. 379–80). Similarly, Atkinson has described how the commonsense theories held by coroners influence the way they categorize sudden deaths (see pp. 979–80). Both Cicourel and Atkinson regard official statistics as social creations.

This does not mean that official statistics are of no sociological interest. Indeed phenomenological sociologists believe they are important: they can be studied in order to discover how they are produced. This helps the sociologist to understand the commonsense theories, taken-for-granted assumptions, stereotypes and categorization procedures of officials involved in the production of the statistics. To writers such as Cicourel, this is the only use that can be made of official statistics, including those such as census statistics, which appear to be based upon far more objective categories. To Cicourel, all statistics involve classifying things as 'this' or 'that', and such decisions are subjective.

Cicourel's views may become less convincing, though, when applied to such data as the age and sex distribution of a population. There may be considerable room for interpretation when considering whether an act is criminal or a sudden death is a suicide. There is less room for interpretation when deciding whether somebody is male or female.

A conflict view

In response to both positivist and phenomenological views, a number of conflict sociologists have developed alternative perspectives on official statistics. They argue that official statistics are neither hard facts, nor subjective meanings. Instead they consist of information which is systematically distorted by power structures in society. Ian Miles and John Irvine argue that official statistics are 'developed in support of the system of power and domination that is modern capitalism – a system in which the state plays a particularly important role' (Miles and Irvine, 1979).

Miles and Irvine do not believe that statistics produced by the government are complete fabrications, because, as they point out, such a viewpoint would be unable to explain why the state frequently publishes figures that are embarrassing to the government. For instance, figures on inflation, crime and unemployment often seem to suggest that government policies are not working. The statistics are not complete distortions, but they are manipulated through the definitions and collection procedures used so that they tend to favour the interests of the powerful. Miles and Irvine say that official statistics are produced according to the needs of the various state agencies for information to coordinate their activities and justify their programmes. They are related to a single ideological framework underpinning the concepts and categories employed.

This view appeared to be supported when the Thatcher government appointed Derek Rayner in 1980 to review the British government's statistical services. Rayner proposed considerable cut-backs in the statistics produced and wanted them confined strictly to information directly needed by the government. Most of his recommendations were implemented. In the wake of the changes introduced following the report, 'The government was repeatedly accused of delaying, suppressing, abolishing and manipulating data for its own ends' (Levitas, 1996). Ruth Levitas mentions a number of examples.

The basis for calculating unemployment figures was frequently changed, almost always with the effect of reducing recorded levels of unemployment (see pp. 737–9 for a discussion of unemployment statistics). Figures on public expenditure were also manipulated. Income from the sale of public assets was artificially used to reduce recorded levels of expenditure, rather than being treated as income. Waiting lists for NHS patients were reduced by removing from the lists those who were unable to keep appointments for operations. Certain figures which might be damning to the government were not produced or published. For example, census statistics no longer included deaths by social class, which might have revealed a growing gap between the life expectancies of different classes. The government changed the data it produced on poverty, making it difficult to compare poverty rates with previous years (see pp. 305–9).

Levitas comments that 'By the end of the 1980s, public confidence in official statistics was at an all-time low.' Although some attempts have been made in the 1990s to make British official statistics less politically biased, critics continue to believe that they still reflect the ideology of the government. In the 1995 edition of the Central Statistical Office's annual publication *Social Trends*, an editorial by Muriel Nissel (the first editor of the publication), which was critical of government manipulation of statistical services, was withdrawn by the Office's director, Bill McLennan.

Conflict sociologists often question the categories used in official statistics. Thus, Theo Nichols (1996) argues from a Marxist point of view that the categories used in the census and other official statistics disguise the true nature of class in capitalism. Most have been based on the Registrar General's scale, which uses status as an indicator of social class. To Nichols (as a Marxist) class is based upon the relationship to the means of production. Thus the official statistics give the impression of a status hierarchy and disguise the existence of classes that are in opposition to each other as exploiters and exploited. (New classifications will be used for the census of 2001. These will be based on a largely Weberian view of class and, like the previous scheme, will include no separate category for a ruling class.)

Like phenomenologists, conflict sociologists tend to believe that official statistics are invalid for measuring the things they refer to, but that they do reveal something about those who produce them. However, rather than seeing them as based merely upon subjective meanings, conflict sociologists see them as reflecting the ideological frameworks that are produced by dominant social groups. Official statistics can therefore be analysed to uncover those frameworks and the power structures that produce them.

Historical sources

Historical documents are of vital importance to sociologists who wish to study social change which takes place over an extended period of time. There are limits to the period over which a sociological study using primary sources can extend, and past events may be important in understanding how contemporary patterns of social life came about.

One area in which historical statistical sources have been of considerable importance is the study of family life. Chapter 8 showed how the development of family life since before the Industrial Revolution has been a major topic of sociological inquiry. Peter Laslett (1972, 1977) made extensive use of parish records in order to discover how common nuclear and extended families were in pre-industrial England. Such data have been most useful in correcting the

assumption that extended family households were the norm in pre-industrial Britain (see p. 527). However, findings based upon such secondary sources need to be used with caution. Many parish records have not survived, and the documents that Laslett used relate only to particular villages which happened to have complete records. It may therefore be dangerous to accept generalizations based upon such findings.

Michael Anderson's research on the family (see pp. 527–8) is based upon early census statistics which are more readily available (Anderson, 1971). Nevertheless, Anderson chose to concentrate on one town, Preston, so the patterns of family life described are again not necessarily representative. Anderson also points out that census statistics do not provide an in-depth picture of family relationships. He lists the sort of descriptive, qualitative data that can be used to supplement statistical data in the historical study of the family as:

> *tracts, reports of missionary and charitable societies, descriptions of crimes, newspaper investigations into the condition of the people, parliamentary investigations and the evidence of some witnesses to them, speeches in parliamentary debates and some aspects of novels.*
>
> Anderson, 1980

Like qualitative data from primary research, qualitative secondary sources may be unreliable and are open to a number of interpretations. Many of the secondary sources mentioned above are highly subjective and are likely to reflect the ideologies of those who produced them. Nevertheless, they do reveal something of the perspectives of their producers.

Whatever the problems of historical research, without using historical documents sociologists would be confined to producing a rather static view of social life. Without such documents, Max Weber (1958) would have been unable to consider the influence of religion on the development of capitalism (see pp. 447–51), and Michael Mann (1986) would not have had the opportunity to discuss the relationship between different sources of social power throughout history (see pp. 633–5).

Life documents

Life documents are created by individuals and record details of that person's experiences and social actions. They are predominantly qualitative and may offer insights into people's subjective states. They can be historical or contemporary and can take a wide variety of forms. Ken Plummer illustrates this diversity when he says:

People keep diaries, send letters, take photos, write memos, tell biographies, scrawl graffiti, publish memoirs, write letters to the papers, leave suicide notes, inscribe memorials on tombstones, shoot films, paint pictures, make music and try to record their personal dreams.

Plummer, 1982

All of these sources, along with many others, have the potential to be useful to sociologists.

The use of life documents has a long history in sociology. Their use was popularized by W.I. Thomas and F. Znaniecki in their study *The Polish Peasant in Europe and America* (1919). Thomas and Znaniecki made use of 764 letters, a lengthy statement by one Polish peasant about his life, reports from social work agencies, court reports and articles from Polish newspapers. From such sources they tried to understand and explain the experience of migration for the hundreds of thousands of Polish people who moved to America in the early years of the twentieth century.

The study was widely regarded as a classic at the time but, according to Plummer (1982), it is now rarely mentioned and infrequently read. This is partly because life documents themselves have fallen out of favour as a source for sociologists. Those who favour more quantitative methods tend to regard life documents as an inadequate source of data. They are difficult to obtain and the ones that exist are likely to cover an unrepresentative sample of the population.

Like all data, personal documents are open to interpretation. They may say more about the subjective states of individuals than the events they are describing. It is unlikely that the husband, wife, or political opponent of a diary writer would describe events in quite the same way. Personal documents that are meant to be read by others (such as letters and autobiographies) may be written with an audience in mind. As Ponsonby once commented, 'letters may be said to have two parents, the writer and the recipient' (quoted in Plummer, 1982). Such documents may be designed more to justify actions than to make a real attempt to explain the writer's feelings or motives.

Diaries, when they are available, may have greater validity if they are not intended for public consumption. One way of overcoming the scarcity of diaries and the unrepresentative nature of examples that exist, is for the researcher to prompt those being studied to keep diaries. Young and Willmott (1973) asked the subjects of their research into family life in London to keep diaries, recording how much time they spent on different activities and how they felt about them. Oscar Lewis (1961), studying poverty in Mexico, persuaded a number of families to keep detailed diaries recording the events

of a single day. Such diaries may be more systematic than those obtained by chance; however, they may be less valid. The awareness that they will be used for research might influence the details included by their writers.

Despite these limitations, Plummer believes that personal documents should play a crucial role in sociology. Using them as a source avoids a preoccupation with abstract theories 'which can kill off any concern for the joy and suffering of active human beings'. Compared to other secondary sources, personal documents allow much greater insight into the subjective states of individuals, which in turn shape their behaviour.

Plummer supports symbolic interactionist approaches to studying social life. From this point of view some sort of participant observation may be the ideal method for studying social life. Where this type of research is not possible, life documents are the best alternative since they offer insights into the 'ordinary ambiguous personal meanings' that shape people's actions in their everyday lives. (More details of Plummer's theoretical standpoint are included in the section on case studies and life histories – see pp. 996–7.)

The mass media and content analysis

Many parts of the mass media are notoriously inaccurate. Sociologists would, for example, be unlikely to turn solely to a national newspaper for an objective account of social life in Britain. Although some parts of the mass media may provide sociologists with useful data, their main importance is as objects of study. Rather like the official statistics, mass media reports can be used to analyse the ideologies of those who produce them. Some sociologists have been highly critical of parts of the mass media for producing distorted images of society which might mislead the public or adversely affect the socialization of children.

There are a number of different approaches to carrying out content analysis, in which researchers analyse the content of documents. These may be largely quantitative, largely qualitative, or combine both approaches. Ray Pawson (1995) identifies four main approaches to carrying out content analysis:

1 Formal content analysis. Here the emphasis is upon objectivity and reliability. A systematic sample of texts is collected for study, a classification system is devised to identify different features of these texts, and these features are then counted. For example, G. Lobban (1974) conducted a study of the portrayal of gender roles in children's reading schemes. She listed and counted the toys and pets that children had, the

activities they engaged in, the skills they learned, and the roles that adults were shown in. The technique is reliable because other researchers can repeat the same techniques to check the findings. The same methods can also be replicated to carry out comparative studies. For example, Lesley Best (1993) repeated Lobban's research in the 1990s (see pp. 854–5).

The simplicity and reliability of quantitative content analysis makes it appealing. However, it is not without its problems. Simply counting the number of items tells you nothing about their significance, and the meanings of the texts or images being studied can only be implied. As Ray Pawson points out, there is an assumption that the audience are simply passive consumers of the message, and no attempt is made to examine how they actually interpret the messages in the text.

2   Thematic analysis. The second approach identified by Pawson is thematic analysis. Pawson says:

> *The idea is to understand the encoding process, especially the intentions that lie behind the production of mass media documents. The usual strategy is to pick on a specific area of reportage and subject it to a very detailed analysis in the hope of unearthing the underlying purposes and intentions of the authors of the communication.*
>
> Pawson, 1995

Thematic analysis is sometimes aimed at discovering the ideological biases of journalists and others involved in the production of mass media documents. Pawson cites the example of Keith Soothill and Sylvia Walby's study of newspaper reporting of sex crimes such as rape (Soothill and Walby, 1991). Soothill and Walby found that the reporting tended to emphasize the danger of being raped in public places and the pathological nature of individual rapists. It tended to ignore the prevalence of rape by partners and friends of victims, and the wider context of patriarchal power within which sex crimes take place. According to Pawson the main method involved in such studies is simply the repetition of examples.

Critics of such studies argue that they rarely use scientific samples, and they therefore tend to use examples selectively to fit the preferred interpretation of the researchers. Like formal content analysis there is no attempt to check whether consumers of the media interpret the messages in the same way as the researchers.

3   Textual analysis. Pawson describes this approach as involving examining the 'linguistic devices within the documents in order to show how texts can be influential in encouraging a particular interpretation'. This approach, for example, looks at how different words are linked together so that readers will interpret stories in a particular way. An example is the Glasgow Media Group's study of television reporting of strikes (Glasgow Media Group, 1976). It found that strikers tended to be described using verbs such as 'claim' or 'demand', while management tended to have verbs such as 'offer' or 'propose' applied to them. This meant that readers tended to view strikers as actively causing the strikes and being unreasonable, while managers were portrayed as being more reasonable and as the passive victims of the strikers. The linking of visual images and words can also be studied in this way.

As with thematic analysis, the main methodological problem with textual analysis is that it relies heavily upon the researcher's interpretation. This may not correspond to the interpretation of members of the audience or of other researchers. The method therefore lacks reliability.

4   Audience analysis. This approach overcomes some of the problems of earlier approaches by focusing on the responses of the audience as well as the content of the mass media. This then provides some check on the researcher's interpretation of the message and it recognizes that audiences actively interpret messages rather than just being passive. Sometimes audiences reject the messages apparently being advanced by the media.

Pawson discusses an early example of this approach, provided by a study of *Nationwide* (a British news programme) conducted by Morley (1980). He found, for example that groups such as shop stewards tended to be more critical and sceptical about *Nationwide*'s coverage of the news than groups such as bank managers.

Critics argued that Morley's study, which involved viewing and talking about *Nationwide* in groups, created a rather artificial research setting. Furthermore there is no guarantee that people are fully open and honest in discussing their reactions to the mass media with researchers. The messages of the media may have a long-term influence on people's interpretations of the social world around them, and such effects are difficult to pick up in audience research.

More thorough studies may try to combine a range of methods. The work of the Glasgow Media Group (1976) illustrates some of the benefits of combining methods. In their first study they combined formal, thematic, and textual analysis. They used quantitative counts to analyse the words used in newscasts and also looked in great detail at particular sentences. Their findings were used to develop a thematic understanding of the coverage of industrial relations. They did not carry out audience research, but there is no reason why such research could not be complemented by studies of the audience as well.

John Scott – assessing secondary sources

John Scott (1990a, 1990b) has provided some useful guidelines for evaluating secondary sources (or, as he calls them, documents). The criteria can be applied to all secondary sources, including existing sociological research. They offer systematic ways of trying to ensure that researchers use secondary sources with as much care as they employ in producing primary data.

Scott identifies four criteria:

1   Authenticity – this refers to the question of how genuine a document is. There are two aspects of authenticity: soundness and authorship. Scott says, 'A sound document is one which is complete and reliable. It should have no missing pages or misprints and, if it is a copy of an original it should be a reliable copy without errors of transcription' (Scott, 1990a). When the document is not sound, the researcher needs to consider carefully how far the omissions detract from its reliability and validity.

The question of authorship concerns who it was written by. Many documents are not actually produced by those to whom they are attributed. For example, many letters signed by the prime minister may have been written by civil servants and might reveal little about the prime minister's own views. The most extreme problem of authenticity occurs when documents are faked, as in the case of the so-called 'Hitler Diaries' which were originally authenticated as the work of the former German leader but which later proved not to be genuine.

2   Credibility – this issue relates to the amount of distortion in a document. Any distortion may be related to sincerity or accuracy. In a sincere document the author genuinely believes what they write. This is not always the case. The author may hope to gain advantage from deceiving readers. For example, politicians may distort accounts of their actions or motives in their diaries or memoirs to justify what they have done. Inaccuracy might result from unintended distortions, such as when an account is written some time after the events described and faulty memory makes absolute accuracy impossible.

3   Representativeness – Scott points out that 'Sampling of documents must be handled as carefully and as systematically as the sampling of respondents in a survey'. A researcher must be aware of how typical or untypical the documents being used are, 'in order to be able to assign limits to any conclusions drawn'.

Two factors which may limit the possibility of using representative documents are: survival and availability. Many documents do not survive because they are not stored, and others deteriorate with age and become unusable. This is obviously a particular problem when doing historical research in sociology. Other documents are deliberately withheld from researchers and the public gaze, and thus do not become available. For example, many official documents are not made available for 30 years; others which are classified as secret may never be made public. Individuals and private organizations may also be unwilling to make many of their documents available to researchers.

4   Meaning – this concerns the ability of a researcher to understand the document. At one level the researcher may have difficulty with literal understanding. It may be in a foreign language, in old-fashioned handwriting, or it could use archaic vocabulary which is difficult to comprehend.

Interpretative understanding is even more difficult to achieve: it involves 'understanding of what the document actually signifies'. For example, there has been a long-standing debate about whether suicide statistics signify more about suicides or about the officials who define certain acts as suicides (see pp. 974–81).

Some of the problems involved in deciphering meaning are discussed in the section on the mass media (see pp. 1020–1). Whether quantitative content analysis or qualitative semiotic analysis is chosen, interpretative understanding is always open to debate.

Scott shows that all secondary sources need to be evaluated and used with great care. Research using them needs to be as systematic and rigorous as research which produces primary data. The same care should be employed when reading and using existing sociology books and studies. In particular, as Scott points out, 'readers must always be aware of the interests and commitments of authors', since these may influence the way that secondary and other sources are interpreted and used.

Triangulation

As an earlier section indicated (pp. 981–2), it is difficult to see quantitative and qualitative methods as mutually exclusive. Increasingly sociologists are combining both approaches in single studies. As Bryman puts it:

The rather partisan, either/or tenor of debate about quantitative and qualitative research may appear somewhat bizarre to an outsider, for whom the obvious way forward is likely to be a fusion of the two approaches so that their respective strengths might be reaped.

Bryman, 1988

In reality, the degree to which quantitative and qualitative approaches are different has been exaggerated. Bryman points out that 'Most researchers rely primarily on a method associated with one of the two research traditions, but buttress their findings with a method associated with the other tradition.' The practice of combining quantitative and qualitative research has a long history, and is evident in the approach advocated by Weber (see p. 972).

Bryman has suggested a number of ways in which using a plurality of methods – a practice known as triangulation – can be useful:

1 Qualitative and quantitative data can be used to check on the accuracy of the conclusions reached on the basis of each.

2 Qualitative research can be used to produce hypotheses which can then be checked using quantitative methods.

3 The two approaches can be used together so that a more complete picture of the social group being studied is produced.

4 Qualitative research may be used to illuminate why certain variables are statistically correlated.

The following examples illustrate the advantages of combining research methods.

In her study of the Unification Church, or Moonies, Eileen Barker used participant observation, questionnaires and in-depth interviewing. She claimed that this combination of methods allowed her to 'see how the movement as a whole was organized and how it influenced the day-to-day actions and interactions of its members' (Barker, 1984). She tried to test hypotheses formulated from qualitative data using questionnaires.

Quantitative techniques have been used to systematically analyse data from observation or participant observation. For example, Delamont (1976) used the Flanders Interaction Analysis Categories in her studies of classroom interaction. These allowed her to categorize the different types of interaction and to time them in order to determine differences in the educational experience of boys and girls. She used qualitative data to explain the reasons for the quantitative relationships she found.

Amanda Coffey and Paul Atkinson (1996) note that qualitative data can be analysed in many different ways. Amongst them is the systematic coding of different types of data so that related pieces of data can be easily found and linked together. Furthermore, computer programmes such as *Ethnograph, QUALPRO and ATLAS/ti* are now sometimes used to make the analysis of qualitative data easier and more systematic.

The combination of methods is not just confined to the use of primary data. In a study of secondary schooling, Paul Corrigan (1981) used interviews, observation and historical and contemporary documents. These enabled him to place his analysis of school life within the context of the historical development of the education system in Britain.

Bryman (1988) believes that both qualitative and quantitative research have their own advantages. Neither can produce totally valid and completely reliable data, but both can provide useful insights into social life. He argues that each has its own place, and they can be most usefully combined. Generally, quantitative data tends to produce rather static pictures, but it can allow researchers to examine and discover overall patterns and structures in society as a whole. Qualitative data is less useful for discovering overall patterns and structures, but it does allow a richer and deeper understanding of the process of change in social life. Bryman says, 'A division of labour is suggested here in that quantitative research may be conceived of as a means of establishing the structural element in social life, qualitative research the processual.'

As the next section will show, the view that sociology should use both qualitative and quantitative methods does not necessarily preclude the possibility that it can be scientific.

Sociology and science

Scientific methodology

The early parts of this chapter described how sociologists have adopted varying views on the relationship between sociology and science. Positivists claim that science uses established methods and procedures, and that these methods and procedures can be applied to the social sciences. They believe that social facts can be observed objectively, measured and quantified.

Analysis of statistics can reveal correlations, causes and ultimately laws of human behaviour. From this point of view, sociological studies using such methods can be considered to be scientific. Positivists see the use of scientific methods as highly desirable, and they tend to be critical of those sociologists who study subjective and unobservable mental states.

Popper (1959) also sees it as highly desirable that sociology should be scientific, but argues that science is a deductive rather than inductive methodology. Scientists should make precise predictions on the basis of their theories so that they can strive conscientiously to falsify or disprove them. Popper rejects many sociological theories as being unscientific because they are not sufficiently precise to generate hypotheses that can be falsified. He is particularly critical of Marxism for failing to make precise predictions: for example, for failing to specify exactly when and under what circumstances a proletarian revolution would take place in capitalist societies. Marxism cannot be falsified since the day of the proletarian revolution and the dawning of the truly communist society is pushed further into the future. Marxism is an article of faith rather than a scientific theory.

Like positivists, then, Popper believes that it is possible for 'social sciences' in general, and sociology in particular, to become scientific by following a particular set of methodological procedures. He parts company with positivists in denying that science can deliver the final, incontrovertible truth, since the possibility of falsification always exists. Instead he believes that the longer a theory has stood the test of time, the more often researchers have failed to falsify it, the closer it is likely to be to the truth.

Phenomenologists reject the view that natural science methodology is appropriate to sociology. To phenomenologists, objective observation and measurement of the social world are not possible. The social world is classified by members of society in terms of their own stereotypes and taken-for-granted assumptions. In these circumstances the social world cannot be measured objectively; statistics are simply the product of the categorization procedures used. The best that sociologists can hope to do is to study the way that members of society categorize the world around them. They cannot collect meaningful statistical data and establish correlations, causal connections and laws. Indeed, phenomenologists reject the whole possibility of finding laws of human behaviour.

The social context of science

All of the views discussed so far are based upon the assumption that there are established methods and procedures that characterize science. However, as Kaplan (1964) has pointed out, it is necessary to distinguish between 'reconstructed logics' and 'logics in use'. Reconstructed logics consist of the methods and procedures scientists claim to use. Both positivism and Popper's methodological approach represent reconstructed logics. However, there is no guarantee that scientists actually do follow such guidelines. Logics in use refer to what scientists actually do during their research, and this may depart considerably from their reconstructed logics.

Michael Lynch (1983) has conducted research in a psycho-biological laboratory, which illustrates how scientists may be less objective than they claim. The scientists studied brain functioning by examining thin slices of rats' brains under microscopes. Photographs and slides of the brain slices were examined to see how useful they were in developing theories of brain functioning. Sometimes unexplained features were found in the photographs. Very often these were put down to some error in the production of the photograph or slide: they were seen as artefacts, rather than being a real feature of the rat's brain. (An artefact is something produced by the research process which does not exist in the phenomenon being studied.) Some of these features were held to be an error in staining, others were believed to be the result of scratching of the specimen when it was being sliced.

There was much discussion in the laboratory about whether these features were artefacts or not. In reaching their conclusions, the scientists were influenced by their existing theories, the types of features they were looking for and expected to find. If the visible marks on the slide or photograph did not fit their theories of how rats' brains functioned, they were much more likely to dismiss the marks as errors. Their interpretations of the data were guided by their theories. Far from following Popper's methodology and striving to falsify their theories, the researchers tried to use the evidence to confirm them. Many scientists may be reluctant to dismiss perhaps years of intellectual effort and research because a single piece of evidence does not support the theory that they have developed.

The social context of Darwin's theory of evolution

It may also be the case that the sorts of theories that are developed in the first place – and which scientists try to confirm rather than falsify – are influenced by social factors rather than the detached pursuit of objective knowledge. Roger Gomm (1982) has used Darwin's theory of evolution as an example to illustrate this.

Darwin claimed that species developed and evolved by a process of natural selection. Most followers of Darwin believed that this process took place gradually. Natural selection occurred through adaptation to the environment. Genetic differences between members of a species make some better-suited to survival in a particular environment. Those that have a better chance of survival are more likely to produce offspring and so shift the species towards their genetic characteristics. For example, giraffes with longer necks may have been more likely to survive and produce offspring than those with shorter necks because they were able to feed off leaves which other species and certain members of their own species could not reach.

Gomm points out that the ideas of natural selection and gradual evolution are not supported by all of the evidence. According to Gomm, Darwin himself did not believe that evolution was a gradual process, but that it was initiated by sudden genetic changes or mutations. Fossil records do not support the gradualist theory of evolutionary change; instead there appear to be rapid periods of genetic change and eras of mass extinction. Gomm claims that the popularity of 'gradualism' was not the result of careful interpretation of the evidence but 'because it lined up with a preference for gradual social and political change among the dominant social groups of the time'. Darwin's theories were often misused – for example, by the English functionalist sociologist Herbert Spencer – to indicate how societies should be run. Those in power did not want it to appear that revolutionary change was the answer to society's problems, because it could undermine their dominance.

The idea of natural selection suggests, as Herbert Spencer put it, 'survival of the fittest'. The weak – those unsuited to survival in a particular environment – must perish to ensure the healthy genetic development of a species. In this theory, competition is the key to genetic and evolutionary progress.

However, as Gomm points out, 'the idea of natural selection as a red in tooth and claw struggle for survival is only a half truth at best. It leaves out of account the extent to which individuals within a species cooperate with each other.'

In his book *Mutual Aid* (published in 1902) the Russian anarchist Prince Peter Kropotkin amassed a wealth of evidence to show that cooperation rather than conflict allowed animals to survive in flocks, herds or other groups. Many animals are best able to resist predators, or at least ensure that casualties are minimized, in such groupings.

Why then was Darwin's competitive vision of the natural world preferred to Kropotkin's equally carefully-argued cooperative vision? Gomm argues that it was because Darwin's views fitted more closely with the ideologies of dominant social groups in Victorian Britain:

1 It justified the free-market capitalist system and did not support socialist ideas which argued for state intervention in the economy.

2 It legitimated harsh social policies which saw the poor as 'unfit' and therefore as not worthy of much assistance. (See pp. 316–17 for details of Herbert Spencer's Darwinist views on poverty.)

3 Since evolution allowed species to be seen as superior or inferior, it allowed groups within the species to be placed on an evolutionary scale. Gomm argues that

the idea of evolution as progress 'allowed the Victorians to lay out the peoples of the world on an evolutionary ladder, with Australian Aboriginals at the bottom (least evolved) and Victorian intellectual males at the top'. It therefore justified the colonization of non-Western people on the grounds that the British Empire would civilize them.

A similar use of a scientific theory to legitimate the domination of one group by another (that is women by men) is provided by sociobiology (see pp. 129–31).

Thomas Kuhn – paradigms and scientific revolutions

The preceding section argues that the interpretation of evidence is governed by the theories that scientists hold, and that these theories themselves may be influenced by social and ideological factors. This suggests that in practice scientists operate in very different ways from those advocated by Popper or positivists.

Thomas Kuhn (1962) has developed an analysis of science which also sees it as being far from the objective pursuit of knowledge. In *The Structure of Scientific Revolutions*, Kuhn argues that science is characterized by a commitment to a scientific paradigm. A paradigm consists of a set of beliefs shared by a group of scientists about what the natural world is composed of, what counts as true and valid knowledge, and what sort of questions should be asked and what sort of procedures should be followed to answer those questions. A paradigm is a complete theory and framework within which scientists operate. It guides what evidence is collected, how that evidence is collected, and how it should be analysed and explained. When scientists work within a paradigm, they tend to look for data that supports and refines that paradigm. The way that scientists perceive the world around them is also governed by the paradigm – they see the world in ways that are consistent with the paradigm.

Kuhn does not believe that the same methods and procedures are found throughout scientific history; rather they are specific to particular sciences at particular times. Nor does Kuhn believe that scientists are entirely objective – paradigms are not accepted or rejected on the basis of evidence alone. Each paradigm has a social base, in that it is grounded in a community of scientists committed to a particular view of the world or some part of it. Established scientists trained to think within the framework provided by an established paradigm find it difficult to see the world in any other way. Furthermore, they have a vested interest in maintaining it, for their academic reputations and careers rest upon the work they have done within that paradigm. Consequently, scientists may ignore evidence that does not fit 'their' paradigm.

Scientific revolutions

Scientific beliefs do change, but, according to Kuhn, rather than changing gradually they are changed by scientific revolutions. In a scientific revolution one scientific paradigm is replaced by another: for instance, when Newton's paradigm in physics was replaced by Einstein's. Change in science is not a gradual process of accumulating new knowledge, but a sudden move from one paradigm to another. This occurs when an accepted paradigm is confronted by so many 'anomalies', or things it cannot explain, that a new paradigm is developed, which does not suffer from the same anomalies. A community of scientists may resist the change, but, once a new generation of scientists who have been trained within the new paradigm start practising, the new paradigm is accepted. A science then returns to its 'normal' state in which the paradigm is elaborated and developed, but the framework that it lays down is largely unquestioned.

Kuhn's work raises serious questions about other views of science. To Kuhn a scientific subject is one in which there is, at least most of the time, an agreed paradigm. There is no guarantee, however, that the accepted paradigm is correct: it may well be replaced by a new paradigm in the future. Scientific training has more to do with learning to see the physical world in a particular way than it has to do with a commitment to discovering the truth through objective research.

If Kuhn's view of science is accepted, then it is doubtful if sociology can be seen as a science. The sociological community has not accepted one paradigm, or, in sociological vocabulary, one 'perspective'. Marxists, functionalists, feminists, interactionists, ethnomethodologists and postmodernists all see the social world in different ways: they ask different questions and get different answers. Even within a perspective there is a lack of consensus. There are many variations within Marxism and feminism, while within functionalism Durkheim and Parsons reached different conclusions on many issues, and they did not analyse societies in the same ways.

In this situation, sociology can be regarded as 'pre-paradigmatic' – a single paradigm has not yet been accepted – and, as such, sociology is pre-scientific. It could, of course, become scientific if sociologists were to agree upon a perspective that all practitioners of the subject could accept. Given the present state of the subject, such an outcome seems highly unlikely.

Whether it is desirable for sociology to become a science is questionable. Sociology seems to exist

almost in a permanent state of revolution, but the constant conflict may help to push the subject forward at a rapid pace.

Criticisms of Kuhn

Although influential, Kuhn's work has been criticized. It has been seen as having little relevance to social science and as being based upon inadequate evidence. Anderson, Hughes and Sharrock argue that Kuhn is doing no more than describing natural science, and his views have little relevance to sociology. Furthermore, they believe that he has underestimated the degree to which there is conflict and disagreement in natural science. Most of the time alternative paradigms are debated. Anderson et al. claim that a careful examination of the history of science shows that 'The periods of revolution grow in size while those of settled "normality" contract' (Anderson et al., 1986).

The realist view of science

From the discussion so far, it would appear that it is either impossible or undesirable for sociology to be a science. Despite the claims of positivists and Popper, it seems inappropriate for a subject that deals with human behaviour to confine itself to studying the observable, to ignore the subjective, to try to falsify theories or to make precise predictions. However, partly in response to such problems, the realist theory of science – which stresses the similarities between social and natural science – has been developed. Realists such as Roy Bhaskar (1979), Russell Keat and John Urry (1982), and Andrew Sayer (1984) argue that none of the above points disqualifies sociology from being a science. They believe that positivists, Popper, and indeed Kuhn, are mistaken about the nature of science.

'Closed' and 'open' systems

Sayer (1984) argues that there is a difference between closed and open systems as objects of scientific study. Within closed systems all the relevant variables can be controlled and measured. In scientific laboratory experiments closed systems may be produced; and certain branches of science such as physics and chemistry have much more scope for the study of closed systems than others.

There are many areas of science in which all the relevant variables cannot be controlled or measured. As a result it is not possible to make the precise predictions advocated by Popper. For example, doctors cannot predict with certainty who will become ill; seismologists cannot predict exactly when an earthquake will occur; and meteorologists cannot predict the weather with anything like absolute precision. In all of these cases the reasons for the lack of precision are similar – some of the variables cannot be measured, or the processes involved are too complex for accurate predictions to be made.

Sociology has similar problems. Within society as a whole, or within a social group, innumerable variables may influence what happens. Thus sociologists cannot be expected to predict exactly what the divorce rate will be in five years' time, or whether a revolution will occur within a given period of time.

Human consciousness

However, even if it is accepted that a science does not need to make predictions, this still leaves the problem of human consciousness to be dealt with. As outlined earlier, positivists believe that a science should confine itself to the study of the observable, whereas interpretive sociologists believe that reference must be made to internal and unobservable meanings and motives in explaining human behaviour. Realists point out, though, that science itself does not confine itself to studying observable phenomena. As Keat and Urry say, scientists may 'postulate the existence of entities which have not been observed, and may not be open to any available method of detection' (Keat and Urry, 1982).

Viruses, sub-atomic particles and magnetic fields all form part of scientific theories, despite the impossibility (at present) of directly observing them. Scientists cannot easily observe continental drift, because it takes place too slowly, nor can they see the mechanisms that produce it, because they are below the earth's surface. Darwin could not observe evolution, because it took place too slowly.

Causality

To realists, then, both Popper and positivists have failed to define science accurately, and so the objections raised by interpretive sociologists to seeing sociology as a science become irrelevant. Realists see science as the attempt to explain the causes of events in the natural or social world in terms of underlying and often unobservable structures, mechanisms and processes. Realists produce causal explanations and explain them in terms of such structures, mechanisms and processes. An example of a mechanism or process in science would be Darwin's idea of natural selection. In sociology, examples include ideas on the concentration of capital and the pauperization of the proletariat.

To realists, explaining the mechanisms through which events take place is a vital part of causal explanation. This requires the researcher to specify which factors or variables determine whether these mechanisms operate. For example, in different conditions the concentration of capital might be slowed down, speeded up or halted. Similarly, in Darwin's theory of evolution the actual consequences

of the operation of natural selection depend upon the precise and changing environmental conditions in which species evolve.

According to realists, events take place and mechanisms operate within the context of structures. Keat and Urry argue that a structure is a 'system of relationships which underlie and account for the sets of observable social relationships and those of social consciousness' (Keat and Urry, 1982). Similarly, Sayer defines structures as 'sets of internally related objects or practices' (Sayer, 1984). Sayer uses the example of the relationship between landlords and tenants to illustrate a structure in society. The existence of a landlord depends upon the existence of tenants, and 'The landlord tenant relation itself presupposes the existence of private property, rent, the production of an economic surplus and so on; together they form a structure.'

Structures impose limitations or constraints upon what happens, but mechanisms and the variables that affect them determine the actual course of events. For example, the structure of relationships between landlords and tenants does not determine which individual occupies the property being rented, but it does determine that the tenant pays rent and the landlord does not. Structures are often unobservable, but a natural or social scientist can work out that they are there by observing their effects. Social classes cannot be seen, nor can the infrastructure and superstructure of society, but to a Marxist they are real.

Science and sociology

According to the realist view of science, much of sociology is scientific. To realist sociologists such as Keat and Urry (1982), Marxist sociology is scientific because it develops models of the underlying structures and processes in society, which are evaluated and modified in the light of empirical evidence. Unlike positivists, realists do not automatically reject interpretive sociology as unscientific, because they believe that studying unobservable meanings and motives is perfectly compatible with a scientific subject.

From this point of view there is relatively little difference between social and natural sciences. Some branches of natural science which have the luxury of studying 'closed' systems can be more precise than sociology, but others face the same difficulty as sociology in trying to deal with highly complex open systems. Both natural sciences and sociology have common aims: they try to develop models and theories that explain the world as objectively as possible on the basis of the available evidence.

Whether sociology can be completely objective is the subject of the final section.

Sociology, methodology and values

One of the reasons that sociologists have been so concerned with the question of whether sociology is a science is the widespread assumption that science is objective, or value-free. Robert Bierstedt has stated:

> Objectivity *means that the conclusions arrived at as the result of inquiry and investigation are independent of the race, colour, creed, occupation, nationality, religion, moral preference, and political predisposition of the investigator. If his research is truly objective, it is independent of any subjective elements, any personal desires, that he may have.*
>
> Bierstedt, 1963

However, even Bierstedt's own definition of objectivity may reveal his values. By assuming that the investigator is male, Bierstedt could be accused of having a patriarchal bias in his work. The quest for objectivity may not be as straightforward as it first appears.

Many of the founders of sociology believed that sociology could and should be value-free. Early positivists such as Comte and Durkheim argued that objectivity was attainable by adopting a 'scientific' methodology. Marx also believed that his sociology was objective and 'scientific', although he saw society very differently. Weber did not think complete value-freedom was possible, but he did believe that, once a topic for research had been chosen, the researcher could be objective. He argued that sociologists should not make value judgements, that is, they should not state what aspects of society they found desirable or undesirable.

Despite the claims of these important sociologists, it is doubtful whether their own work met the criteria necessary for complete value-freedom. The concluding sections of Chapters 2–13 have shown that the values of sociologists have influenced their work, whatever area of social life they have studied.

Functionalists in general have been accused of holding politically conservative views in assuming that existing social institutions serve a useful purpose. This implies that anything other than slow evolutionary change is harmful to society.

Durkheim accepted the need for certain changes in society, but his personal values are evident in his belief that the inheritance of wealth should be abolished and professional associations should be established (see pp. 691–3).

Few would claim that Marx's sociology was free from his political and moral beliefs. Marx's desire for proletarian revolution influenced most aspects of his work.

Weber's work often appears more value-free than that of functionalists or Marxists, but there is little doubt that his personal values influenced his research. Weber's writings on bureaucracy (see Chapter 15) are strongly influenced by his fear that bureaucratic organizations would stifle human freedom. In his words, 'What can we oppose to this machinery in order to keep a portion of mankind free from this parcelling-out of the soul, from this supreme mastery of the bureaucratic way of life' (quoted in Nisbet, 1967).

Even if it is true that such eminent sociologists allowed their values to influence their research, it does not necessarily follow that it is impossible to achieve value-freedom in sociology. To many contemporary sociologists, there is, however, no prospect of a completely value-free sociology. According to this view, total objectivity is impossible because values inevitably enter every stage of the production of sociological knowledge.

Weber recognized that values would influence the choice of topics for study. He argued that the sociologist had to have some way of choosing from the almost infinite number of possible areas of social life that could be studied. Weber believed that 'value relevance' would influence the choice. Researchers would choose to research topics which they thought were important, and, more significantly, which they thought were of central importance to society. Weber himself chose to study the advent of capitalism and the nature of bureaucracy, because he saw them as the most important developments in Western societies.

The values of other sociologists have also been evident in their choice of topics for research. Peter Townsend demonstrated his belief that poverty is a serious problem by devoting years of his life to its study (see pp. 296–300). Marxists have shown the importance they attach to inequality in their studies of wealth, income and stratification. Feminists have revealed their values by deciding that it is important to study such aspects of social life as domestic violence, rape and housework. Simply by selecting an issue to study, sociologists reveal what aspects of society they believe are significant.

Having selected a topic, sociologists then choose what aspects of that topic to study, and what approach they are going to adopt. According to Alvin Gouldner this involves making 'domain assumptions' (Gouldner, 1971). These are the basic assumptions that sociologists make about the nature of social life and human behaviour. Gouldner says:

Domain assumptions about man and society might include, for example, dispositions to believe that men are rational or irrational; that society is precarious or fundamentally stable; that social problems will correct themselves without planned intervention; that human behaviour is unpredictable; that man's true humanity resides in his feelings and sentiments.

Gouldner, 1971

Gouldner believes that in practice all sociologists tend to commit themselves to a particular set of domain assumptions, and these direct the way that research is conducted and conclusions are reached. Without some starting point, research cannot proceed and sociological knowledge cannot be created. Domain assumptions about human behaviour – such as whether it is governed by external or internal stimuli and whether it is rational or irrational – will tend to determine whether quantitative or qualitative methods are adopted.

In designing and carrying out research all researchers have to be selective. When producing a questionnaire or planning an interview some questions have to be chosen and others excluded. The choice will be influenced by the theories and hypotheses to which a particular researcher attaches credibility. Once the data have been collected, researchers need to interpret the results, and very often the results do not speak for themselves.

For example, in the debate about secularization, the development of sects, cults and new religious movements has been variously interpreted both as evidence for and as evidence against the theory of secularization, depending on the standpoint of the researchers (see pp. 485–6).

Similarly, the proletarianization thesis has guided much of the research into routine non-manual workers, and Marxists and non-Marxists have tended to produce different types of data, which they have interpreted in different ways, and which have led them to very different conclusions (see pp. 66–9).

Interpretive sociologists have tended to be very critical of those using quantitative methods. They have argued that many sociologists simply impose their own views of reality on the social world. As a result they distort and misrepresent the very reality they seek to understand. Research techniques such as interviews, questionnaires and social surveys are a part of this process of distortion. They come between the sociologist and the social world and so remove any opportunity he or she might have of discovering social reality.

From this point of view, direct observation of everyday activity provides the most likely, if not the only, means of obtaining valid knowledge of the social world. This at least allows researchers to come face to face with the reality they seek to understand. Since the social world is seen to be a construction of its members, that world can only be understood in terms of members' categories and constructs. Thus Jack Douglas argues that sociologists must 'study the phenomena of everyday life on their own terms', they must 'preserve the integrity of that phenomena' (Douglas, 1971).

While phenomenologists might be looking in the right direction, the problem of validity remains unsolved. Though face-to-face with social reality, the observer can only see the social world through his or her own eyes. No two sociologists will see that world in exactly the same way. A participant observer cannot note and record everything that happens in their presence and, like the sociologist devising a questionnaire, has to be selective. In these circumstances the researcher's values will influence what events they believe to be important.

Critical researchers believe it is important to understand how the social world is seen from the viewpoint of those being studied. However, they do not accept that this alone will produce objective knowledge. To them it is also important to look beyond the commonsense knowledge of people to uncover the structures of oppression which lie behind everyday life (see pp. 982–6). However, critics believe that the oppressive structures they discover simply reflect their own prejudices: feminists will always find patriarchal oppression, Marxists will find class exploitation, critical gay sociologists will find homophobia, and anti-racists will find racism.

Because of these sorts of considerations, Derek Phillips argues that 'An investigator's values influence not only the problems he selects for study but also his methods for studying them and the sources of data he uses' (Phillips, 1973). In 'Anti-Minotaur: the myth of a value free sociology' (1975), Gouldner makes a similar point. He argues that, just as the bull and the man in the mythical Minotaur cannot be separated, so facts and values cannot be separated in sociological research.

Weber argued that sociologists' values should be kept out of their research, and that they should not make value judgements – judgements about right or wrong. Gouldner regards this as dishonest. Since sociologists must have values, they should be open about them so that others can decide for themselves to what degree values have influenced the research. Gouldner says:

If sociologists ought not to express their personal values in the academic setting, how then are students to be safeguarded against the unwitting influence of these values which shape the sociologist's selection of problems, his preferences for certain hypotheses or conceptual schemes, and his neglect of others. For these are unavoidable and, in this sense, there is and can be no value-free sociology. The only choice is between an expression of one's values, as open and honest as it can be ... and a vain ritual of moral neutrality which, because it invites men to ignore the vulnerability of reason to bias, leaves it at the mercy of irrationality.

Gouldner, 1975

Some postmodernists such as Lyotard (1984) reject altogether the possibility of producing any objective knowledge. To Lyotard the creation of knowledge is just a language game which can only be judged in terms of its saleability. There is no way of distinguishing between true and untrue knowledge, no way of being objective. For many postmodern writers, knowledge simply reflects the viewpoint and the values of different social groups. No one viewpoint and set of values can be seen as superior to any other. As Martyn Hammersley says, postmodernism involves 'a sustained scepticism and distrust of all claims to knowledge' (Hammersley, 1995).

Given these problems, sociology might appear to consist of little more than personal opinions. If this were the case there would seem little point in the subject existing. However, some sociologists believe that it is positively desirable for sociologists to be committed to certain values. For example, Phil Carspecken, along with other critical social scientists, believes that sociologists should be committed to changing the world.

Nevertheless, this does not prevent sociologists from trying to avoid bias in their research. Although humans might view the world differently, there is an objective world which 'resists' human action. For example, a person cannot walk through a brick wall whether they think it exists or not. The way the material world resists our actions provides some basis for reaching agreement about objective statements. Truth claims – claims that you have made an objective statement – are based upon reaching such

agreements about what does and does not exist. These agreements in turn can be used to evaluate the claims of different theories. A critical researcher cannot therefore find whatever they want to find.

Empirical investigations, which are more than the subjective interpretations of individuals, mean that sociology can be more than just value-laden opinions. Truth claims, even if accepted now, may be rejected at some point in the future. A consensus about what is and is not true may break down. However, because they are based upon reaching agreements about what is true, they have a more solid foundation than individual interpretations.

Carspecken even argues that, up to a point, values can be evaluated as well. He uses the example of somebody arguing that poverty is not bad because 'there has always been poverty and always will be; it is natural' (Carspecken 1996). In this case the value claim that poverty is not bad can be critically examined by using examples of societies which have no poverty, and by trying to show that some things which are natural are not necessarily good. Carspecken says, 'We might point to many things in nature that are morally repugnant to human beings and claim that humans must alter nature and establish morality through their own efforts.'

Such arguments can only proceed by finding some sort of common ground – something which all those discussing the issue can agree is good or bad. Such common ground may not always be attainable, but often it is, and some rational evaluation of values becomes possible.

If Carspecken's views are correct, then values are integral to sociology and indeed to all disciplines, but that does not prevent rational debate and the empirical testing of theories. Sociology can make claims about the truth and hope to gain acceptance for them. From this viewpoint, sociologists should also accept and welcome a commitment to using the production of sociological knowledge to try to improve society.

Sociological theory

Sociological theory

Introduction

A theory is a set of ideas that provides an explanation for something. A sociological theory is a set of ideas that provides an explanation for human society. Critics of sociology sometimes object to the emphasis that sociologists place on theory, and suggest it might be better to let 'the facts' speak for themselves. But there are no facts without theory. For example, in Western society, the generally accepted facts that the world is round and that it orbits the sun are inseparable from theories that explain the nature and movement of heavenly bodies. However, in some non-Western societies whose members employ different theories, the view that the world is flat and the solar system revolves around it is accepted as a statement of fact. Clearly the facts do not speak for themselves.

Like all theory, sociological theory is selective. No amount of theory can hope to explain everything, or account for the infinite amount of data that exist, or encompass the endless ways of viewing reality. Theories are therefore selective in terms of their priorities and perspectives and the data they define as significant. As a result, they provide a particular and partial view of reality.

There are a wide variety of sociological theories, and they can be grouped together according to various criteria. One of the most important of these is the distinction between structural perspectives and social action perspectives. This distinction will form the framework for the early parts of this chapter. However, there is also an important distinction between modern and postmodern perspectives in sociology. This distinction will be discussed in detail later in the chapter.

Structural versus social action theories

Structural perspectives and social action perspectives differ in the way they approach the analysis of society. Structural, or macro, perspectives analyse the way society as a whole fits together. Thus, despite their differences, both functionalism and Marxism use a model of how society as a whole works. Many functionalists base their model of society around the assumption of functional prerequisites or basic needs, and go on to explain how different parts of society help to meet those needs. Marxists, on the other hand, see society as resting upon an economic base or infrastructure, with a superstructure rising above it. They see society as divided into social classes which have the potential to be in conflict with each other.

The main differences between functionalist and Marxist perspectives, then, concern the ways in which they characterize the social structure. Functionalists stress the extent to which the different elements of the social structure fit together harmoniously. Marxists stress the lack of fit between the different parts, particularly social classes, and so emphasize the potential for social conflict.

Marxism is one example of a conflict perspective. There are a variety of interpretations and adaptations of Marx's work, and some neo-Marxists question some of the concepts used by Marx, while accepting his overall approach. Other conflict theorists agree with Marx and neo-Marxists that there is conflict in society, but disagree about the causes and types of conflict. They draw upon the work of Max Weber, who argued that many groups, apart from classes, can be in conflict for the scarce resources in society (see pp. 36–9).

Not all sociological perspectives base their analysis upon an examination of the structure of society as a whole. Rather than seeing human behaviour as being largely determined by society, they see society as being the product of human activity. They stress the meaningfulness of human behaviour, denying that it is primarily determined by the structure of society.

These approaches are variously called social action approaches, interpretive sociology, or micro sociology. Max Weber was the first sociologist to advocate a social action approach (although he also uses elements of a structural approach in parts of his work). In contemporary sociology there are two main varieties of this type of sociology.

Symbolic interactionists try to explain human behaviour and human society by examining the ways in which people interpret the actions of others, develop a self-concept or self-image, and act in terms of meanings. They do not deny the existence of some elements of a social structure: for example, they acknowledge the presence of social roles, and some interactionists also use the concept of social class. However, they believe that the social structure is fluid and constantly changing in response to interaction.

Ethnomethodology moves even further from a structural approach by denying the existence of a social structure as such. To ethnomethodologists, the social world consists of the definitions and categorizations of members of society. These subjective meanings are social reality. The job of the sociologist, in their view, is to interpret, describe and above all to understand this subjective reality.

It is not possible to provide clear dividing lines between sociological perspectives. There are many approaches that do not fit neatly even into such broad categories as structural or social action perspectives. For example, the description of Marx's social theories later in this section will show that elements of a social action approach can be found within his work; and Weber's work also uses elements of both types of perspective. Nevertheless, it is reasonable to divide much sociology into these two categories, because the emphasis within perspectives like functionalism and Marxism is so different from that found within interactionism and ethnomethodology.

Some sociologists have made a conscious attempt to bridge the apparent gulf between social action and structural perspectives. Max Weber was arguably the first sociologist to try to combine an analysis of the structures of society with analysis of individual social actions; more recently, the sociologist Paul Willis has tried to combine Marxist analysis with an interactionist approach to social action; and Anthony Giddens, another sociologist, has also tried to bridge the gap that seems to separate structural and social action approaches.

Some of the most recent approaches within sociology have not been particularly concerned with issues to do with the difference between structural and social action perspectives. Postmodernism in particular defies categorization in these terms. Much of the inspiration for postmodernism comes from the post-structuralist perspectives discussed in Chapter 12 (see pp. 913–16). Post-structuralism takes the analysis of language as its starting point, rather than the analysis of social structures or social action. However, most postmodernists tend to be hostile to structural perspectives that claim to be able to explain how society works. Postmodernists generally reject the claim that any single theory is able to explain the social world.

This brief summary cannot do justice to the subtleties and complexities of sociological theory. Some of these complexities will be examined later in this chapter, but it is important to note that the chapter is far from comprehensive. There are a number of other perspectives that have not been included. Furthermore, sociology is a developing discipline and sociological perspectives are continually being refined and developed in the light of theoretical debate and empirical investigation. Nevertheless, it is possible to outline the central features of the most influential perspectives in the discipline.

Functionalism

Functionalist analysis has a long history in sociology. It is prominent in the work of Auguste Comte (1798–1857) and Herbert Spencer (1820–1903), two of the founding fathers of the discipline. It was developed by Emile Durkheim (1858–1917) and refined by Talcott Parsons (1902–79). During the 1940s and 1950s functionalism was the dominant social theory in American sociology. Since that time it has steadily dropped from favour, partly because of damaging criticism, partly because other approaches are seen to answer certain questions more successfully, and partly because it simply went out of fashion.

Society as a system

Functionalism views society as a system: that is, as a set of interconnected parts which together form a whole. The basic unit of analysis is society, and its various parts are understood primarily in terms of their relationship to the whole. The early functionalists often drew an analogy between society and an organism such as the human body. They argued that an understanding of any organ in the body, such as the heart or lungs, involves an understanding of its relationship to other organs and, in particular, its contribution towards the maintenance of the organism. In the same way, an understanding of any part of society requires an analysis of its relationship to other parts and, most importantly, its contribution to the maintenance of society. Continuing this analogy, functionalists argued that, just as an organism has certain basic needs that must be satisfied if it is to survive, so society has basic needs that must be met if it is to continue to exist. Thus social institutions such as the family and religion are analysed as a part of the social system rather than as isolated units. In particular, they are understood with reference to the contribution they make to the system as a whole.

Functional prerequisites

These basic needs or necessary conditions of existence are sometimes known as the functional prerequisites of society. Various approaches have been used to identify functional prerequisites. Some sociologists have examined a range of societies in an attempt to discover what factors they have in common. For example, Davis and Moore (1967) claimed that all societies have some form of social stratification, and George Peter Murdock (1949) maintained that the family exists in every known human society. From these observations it is assumed that institutional arrangements, such as social stratification and the family, meet needs that are common to all societies. Thus, from the universal presence of social stratification, it is argued that all societies require some mechanism to ensure that social positions are adequately filled by motivated persons. From the universality of the family, it is assumed that some mechanism for the reproduction and socialization of new members is a functional prerequisite of society.

However, the problem with this approach is its assumption that the presence of the same institution in every society indicates that it meets the same need. Simply because a form of stratification exists in all societies does not necessarily mean that it reflects 'the universal necessity which calls forth stratification in any social system', as Davis and Moore claim. Put another way, it cannot be assumed that stratification systems perform the same function in all societies. (Davis and Moore's theory of stratification is outlined in Chapter 2, pp. 27–8.)

An alternative approach to the identification of functional prerequisites involves an analysis of those factors that would lead to the breakdown or termination of society. Thus Marion J. Levy (1952) argued that a society would cease to exist if its members became extinct, if they became totally apathetic, if they were involved in a war of all against all, or if they were absorbed into another society. Therefore, in order for a society to survive, it must have some means of preventing these events from occurring. These means are the functional prerequisites of society.

For example, to ensure that members of society do not become extinct, a system for reproducing new members and maintaining the health of existing members is essential. This involves role differentiation and role assignment. Individuals must be assigned to produce food and to reproduce and care for new members of society. In order for these essential services to be maintained, individuals must be sufficiently motivated to perform their roles. If

they were totally apathetic, the social system would collapse through lack of effort. A system of goals and rewards is necessary to motivate members of society to want to do what they have to do in order to maintain the system. By specifying the factors that would lead to the termination of society, Levy claimed to have identified the basic requirements that must be met if society is to survive.

The problem with this approach to the specification of functional prerequisites is its reliance on common sense and ingenuity. In the case of a biological organism it is possible to identify basic needs, since it can be shown that if these needs are not met, the organism dies. However, societies change rather than die. As a result, it is not possible to identify unequivocally those aspects of a social system that are indispensable to its existence. Functionalists using Levy's approach have drawn up lists of functional prerequisites that are often similar in content but never quite the same.

A related approach involves the deduction of functional prerequisites from an abstract model of the social system. For example, if society is viewed as a system, certain survival needs can be deduced from an abstract model of the system. Any system is made up of interconnected parts. If a system is to survive, there must be a minimum amount of integration between its parts. There must be some degree of fit, which requires an element of mutual compatibility of the parts. From this type of analysis, the functional prerequisites of society may be inferred. Thus any social system requires a minimum amount of integration between its parts.

From this assumption, functional analysis turns to an examination of the parts of society, to investigate how they contribute to the integration of the social system. In this respect, religion has often been seen as a powerful mechanism for social integration. Religion is seen to reinforce the basic values of society. Social norms, which derive from these values, structure and direct behaviour in the various institutions of society. The parts of the social system are integrated in that they are largely infused with the same basic values. Were the various institutions founded on conflicting values, the system would tend to disintegrate. Since religion promotes and reinforces social values, it can be seen as an integrating mechanism. But the problem with deducing functional prerequisites such as integration from an abstract model of the social system is that they are inferred rather than unequivocally identified.

The concept of function

The concept of 'function' in functionalist analysis refers to the contribution of the part to the whole. More specifically, the function of any part of society is the contribution it makes to meeting the functional prerequisites of the social system. Parts of society are functional in so far as they maintain the system and contribute to its survival. Thus a function of the family is to ensure the continuity of society by reproducing and socializing new members. A function of religion is to integrate the social system by reinforcing common values.

Functionalists also employ the concept of 'dysfunction' to refer to the effects of any social institution which detract from the maintenance of society. However, in practice, they have been primarily concerned with the search for functions, and relatively little use has been made of the concept of dysfunction.

The ideology of functionalism

Functionalist analysis has focused on the question of how social systems are maintained. This focus has tended to result in a positive evaluation of the parts of society. With their concern for investigating how functional prerequisites are met, functionalists have concentrated on functions rather than dysfunctions. This emphasis has resulted in many institutions being seen as beneficial and useful to society. Indeed some institutions, such as the family, religion and social stratification, have been seen as not only beneficial but indispensable. This view has led critics to argue that functionalism has a built-in conservative bias which supports the status quo. The argument that certain social arrangements are beneficial or indispensable provides support for their retention, and a reason to reject proposals for radical change. Responses to this criticism will be examined in a later section (see pp. 1039–40). (For various views on the ideological basis of functionalism, see the concluding sections of Chapters 2 to 12.)

This section has presented a brief outline of some of the main features of functionalist analysis. The sections that follow will consider the views of some of the major functionalist theorists.

Emile Durkheim

Social facts as constraints

Critics of functionalism have often argued that it pictures the individual as having little or no control over his or her own actions. Rather than constructing their own social world, members of society appear to be directed by the system. For example, they are organized into families and systems of stratification because society requires these social arrangements in order to survive. Many have questioned the logic of treating society as if it were something separate from its members, as if it shaped their actions rather than being constructed by them.

Durkheim (1938, first published 1894) rejected such views. He argued that society has a reality of its own over and above the individuals who comprise it. Members of society are constrained by 'social facts', by 'ways of acting, thinking and feeling, external to the individual, and endowed with a power of coercion, by reason of which they control him'. Beliefs and moral codes are passed on from one generation to the next and shared by the individuals who make up a society. From this point of view it is not the consciousness of the individual that directs behaviour, but common beliefs and sentiments that transcend the individual and shape his or her consciousness. Having established to his own satisfaction that social facts can, at least for purposes of analysis, be treated separately from social actors, Durkheim is free to treat society as a system which obeys its own laws. He is now in a position to 'seek the explanation of social life in the nature of society itself'.

The causes and functions of social facts

Durkheim argues that there are two ways of explaining social facts. In both cases the explanation lies in society. The first method involves determining the cause of a social fact, seeking to explain its origin. In Durkheim's view, 'The determining cause of a social fact should be sought among the social facts preceding it and not among the states of individual consciousness.' As was discussed in Chapter 14 (see pp. 974–81), the causes of variations in suicide rates are to be found in social facts, in society rather than in the individual (Durkheim, 1970, first published 1897). However, the explanation of a social fact also involves an analysis of its function in society, of its contribution to 'the general needs of the social organism', of its 'function in the establishment of social order'. Durkheim assumes that the explanation for the continuing existence of a social fact lies in its function, that is, in its usefulness for society.

Durkheim is at pains to point out the distinction between cause and function. Thus the cause of the Christian religion lies in the specific circumstances of its origin among a group of Jews under Roman rule. Yet its functions – the reasons for its retention over a period of nearly 2,000 years – require a different form of explanation. Durkheim argues that 'if the usefulness of a fact is not the cause of its existence, it is generally necessary that it be useful in order that it might maintain itself'. Social facts therefore continue in existence because they contribute in some way to the maintenance of society, because they serve 'some social end'.

Social order and human nature

Much of Durkheim's work is concerned with functional analysis, with seeking to understand the functions of social facts. He assumes that society has certain functional prerequisites, the most important of which is the need for social order. This is necessary because of human nature. Durkheim has a 'homo duplex' model of human nature: that is, he believes that humans have two sides to their nature. One side is selfish or egotistical. Humans are partly driven by selfish biological needs, such as the need to satisfy hunger. Inevitably this means that they tend to look after their own interests, which makes it difficult for individuals to be integrated into society. However, there is another side to human nature: the ability to believe in moral values. Society has to make use of this side of human nature if social life is to be possible. But how is social life to be achieved? This question still needs to be answered.

The collective conscience and social stability

Durkheim sees the answer in consensus, in a 'collective conscience' consisting of common beliefs and sentiments. Without this consensus or agreement on fundamental moral issues, social solidarity would be impossible and individuals could not be bound together to form an integrated social unit. Without social obligations backed by moral force, the cooperation and reciprocity that social life requires would be absent. If narrow self-interest rather than mutual obligation were the guiding force, conflict and disorder would result. In Durkheim's words, 'For where interest is the only ruling force each individual finds himself in a state of war with every other.' The collective conscience constrains individuals to act in terms of the requirements of society. Since the collective conscience is a social fact and therefore external to the individual, it is essential that it be impressed upon him or her. Thus Durkheim argues that, 'society has to be present in the individual'.

Durkheim's functionalism is set in the framework of the above argument. It may be illustrated by his analysis of the functions of religion (Durkheim, 1961, first published 1912).

Threats to social solidarity

Durkheim was aware of the possibility that societies might not function smoothly. This is evident in his work on the division of labour (Durkheim, 1947, first published 1893) (see pp. 691–3), which suggests that industrial societies based on organic solidarity might break down. They could be undermined if egoism or anomie started to reduce the control that society had over the individual. Although Durkheim saw the possibility of conflict within industrial society, he believed that it could be kept within manageable limits through the existence of professional associations, the teaching of moral values in the education system, and

through society functioning in a way that treated all its members fairly.

Talcott Parsons

The problem of social order

The name of Talcott Parsons is synonymous with functionalism. Over a period of some 50 years, Parsons published numerous articles and books, and during the 1940s and 1950s he became the dominant theorist in American sociology. This section will briefly examine aspects of his work.

Like Durkheim, Parsons (1951) began with the question of how social order is possible. He observed that social life is characterized by 'mutual advantage and peaceful cooperation rather than mutual hostility and destruction'. A large part of Parsons's sociology is concerned with explaining how this state of affairs is accomplished. He started with a consideration of the views of the seventeenth-century English philosopher Thomas Hobbes, who claimed to have discovered the basis of social order.

According to Hobbes, humanity is directed by passion and reason. Its passions are the primary driving force, reason being employed to devise ways and means of providing for their satisfaction. If people's passions were allowed free rein, they would use any means at their disposal, including force and fraud, to satisfy them. The net result would be 'the war of all against all'. However, fear of this outcome is generated by the most basic of human passions, that of self-preservation. Guided by the desire for self-preservation, people agree to restrain their passions, give up their liberty and enter into a social contract with their fellows. They submit to the authority of a ruler or governing body in return for protection against the aggression, force and fraud of others. Only because of this sovereign power is the war of all against all prevented, and security and order established in society.

Hobbes presented a picture of humans as rational, self-interested and calculating. They form an ordered society with their fellows through fear of the consequences if they do not. This is very different from Durkheim's view of people acting in response to moral commitments and obeying social rules because they believe them to be right.

Parsons shared Durkheim's views. He argued that Hobbes's picture of people pursuing personal ends, restrained only by sovereign power, fails to provide an adequate explanation for social order. Parsons believed that only a commitment to common values provides a basis for order in society.

Parsons illustrated this point by reference to social relationships, which at first sight would appear to exemplify Hobbes's view of people as self-interested and calculating. He examined transactions in the market place. In a business transaction, the parties concerned form a contract. In order for the conduct of business to be orderly, it is essential that contracts be bound by a 'system of regulatory, normative rules'. In Parsons's view, fear of the consequences is insufficient to motivate people to obey the rules. A moral commitment is essential. Thus, rules governing business transactions must ultimately derive from shared values which state what is just, right and proper. Order in the economic system is therefore based on a general agreement concerning business morality. From this agreement stem rules which define a contract as valid or invalid. For example, a contract obtained by force or fraud is not binding. Parsons argued that the world of business, like any other part of society, is, by necessity, a moral world.

Value consensus

Value consensus forms the fundamental integrating principle in society. If members of society are committed to the same values, they will tend to share a common identity, which provides a basis for unity and cooperation. From shared values derive common goals. Values provide a general conception of what is desirable and worthwhile. Goals provide direction in specific situations. For example, in Western society, members of a particular workforce will share the goal of efficient production in their factory – a goal which stems from the general view of economic productivity. A common goal provides an incentive for cooperation.

Roles provide the means whereby values and goals are translated into action. A social institution consists of a combination of roles. For instance, a business firm is made up of a number of specialized roles that combine to further the goals of the organization. The content of roles is structured in terms of norms, which define the rights and obligations applicable to each particular role. Norms can be seen as specific expressions of values. Thus the norms that structure the roles of manager, accountant, engineer and shop-floor worker owe their content partly to the value of economic productivity. Norms tend to ensure that role behaviour is standardized, predictable and therefore orderly. This means that from the most general level – the central value system – to the most specific – normative conduct – the social system is infused with common values. This provides the basis for social order.

Social equilibrium

The importance Parsons placed on value consensus led him to state that the main task of sociology is to analyse the 'institutionalization of patterns of value orientation in the social system'. When values are institutionalized and behaviour is structured in terms of them, the result is a stable system. A state of 'social equilibrium' is attained, the various parts of the system being in a state of balance. There are two main ways in which social equilibrium is maintained. The first involves socialization, by means of which society's values are transmitted from one generation to the next and internalized to form an integral part of individual personalities. In Western society, the family and the education system are the major institutions concerned with this function. (See Chapter 11, pp. 779–80, for Parsons's views on the functions of education, and Chapter 8, pp. 509–10, for his views on the functions of the family.)

Social equilibrium is also maintained by the various mechanisms of social control which discourage deviance and so maintain order in the system. The processes of socialization and social control are fundamental to the equilibrium of the social system and therefore to order in society.

Functional prerequisites

Parsons viewed society as a system. He argued that any social system has four basic functional prerequisites – adaptation, goal attainment, integration and pattern maintenance. These can be seen as problems that society must solve if it is to survive. The function of any part of the social system is understood as its contribution to meeting the functional prerequisites. Solutions to the four survival problems must be institutionalized if society is to continue in existence. In other words, solutions must be organized in the form of ordered, stable social institutions which persist through time.

The first functional prerequisite, adaptation, refers to the relationship between the system and its environment. In order to survive, social systems must have some degree of control over their environment. At a minimum, food and shelter must be provided to meet the physical needs of members. The economy is the institution primarily concerned with this function.

Goal attainment refers to the need for all societies to set goals towards which social activity is directed. Procedures for establishing goals and deciding on priorities between goals are institutionalized in the form of political systems. Governments not only set goals but allocate resources to achieve them. Even in a so-called free enterprise system, the economy is regulated and directed by laws passed by governments.

Integration refers primarily to the 'adjustment of conflict'. It is concerned with the coordination and mutual adjustment of the parts of the social system. The law is the main institution that meets this need. Legal norms define and standardize relations between individuals and between institutions, and so reduce the potential for conflict. When conflict does arise, it is settled by the judicial system and does not therefore lead to the disintegration of the social system.

Pattern maintenance refers to 'the maintenance of the basic pattern of values, institutionalized in the society'. Institutions that perform this function include the family, the educational system and religion. In Parsons's view, 'the values of society are rooted in religion'. Religious beliefs provide the ultimate justification for the values of the social system. (See Chapter 7, pp. 434–5, for Parsons's analysis of the functions of religion.)

Parsons maintained that any social system can be analysed in terms of the functional prerequisites he identified. Thus, all parts of society can be understood with reference to the functions they perform in the adaptation, goal attainment, integration and pattern maintenance systems.

Social change

Functionalism has often been criticized for failing to provide an adequate explanation for social change. If the system is in equilibrium, with its various parts contributing towards order and stability, it is difficult to see how it changes. Parsons approached this problem by arguing that, in practice, no social system is in a perfect state of equilibrium, although a certain degree of equilibrium is essential for the survival of societies. The process of social change can therefore be pictured as a 'moving equilibrium'.

This may be illustrated in the following way. The adaptation, goal attainment, integration and pattern maintenance systems are inter-related; a change in one will therefore produce responses in the others. For example, a change in the adaptation system will result in a disturbance in the social system as a whole. The other parts of the system will operate to return it to a state of equilibrium. In Parsons's words, 'Once a disturbance has been introduced into an equilibrated system there will tend to be a reaction to this disturbance, which tends to restore the system to equilibrium.' This reaction will lead to some degree of change, however small, in the system as a whole. Although social systems never attain complete equilibrium, they tend towards this state. Social change can therefore be seen as a 'moving equilibrium'.

Social evolution and pattern variables

Parsons viewed social change as a process of 'social evolution' from simple to more complex forms of society. He regarded changes in adaptation as a major driving force of social evolution. The history of human society from the simple hunting and gathering band to the complex nation-state represents an increase in the 'general adaptive capacity' of society. As societies evolve into more complex forms, control over the environment increases. While economic changes might provide an initial stimulus, Parsons believed that, in the long run, cultural changes – that is, changes in values – determine the '*broadest patterns of change*'. For example, he argued that the structure of modern societies owes much to values inherited from ancient Israel and classical Greece.

Parsons identified two sets of cultural values, which he called pattern variables A and B. These pattern variables consist of the ways that society answers basic questions such as: 'How should rewards be allocated to individuals?' and 'Should members of society look after their own interests or those of the social groups to which they belong?'

The two sets of pattern variables are summarized in Table 15.1.

Table 15.1 Talcott Parsons's concept of pattern variables

Pattern variables A	Pattern variables B
Ascription Status is ascribed; it is determined by the type of family into which a person is born.	**Achievement** Status is achieved through a person's own efforts: for example, through hard work.
Diffuseness People enter into relationships with others to satisfy a large range of needs: for example, the relationship between mother and child.	**Specificity** People enter into relationships with others to satisfy particular needs: for example, the relationship between a customer and shopkeeper.
Particularism Individuals act differently towards particular people: for example, they are loyal to their family but not to strangers.	**Universalism** Individuals act according to universal principles: for example, everyone is equal before the law, so a policewoman would arrest her husband if necessary.
Affectivity Gratification is immediate. People act to gratify their desires as soon as possible.	**Effective neutrality** Gratification is deferred: for example, saving money to put a deposit on a house in the future.
Collective orientation People put the interests of the social groups to which they belong before their own interests.	**Self-orientation** People pursue their own interests first, rather than those of the social group to which they belong.

might be seen as institutions that closely control and direct human behaviour or social actions. Although Weber was aware of, and indeed concerned about, the power of bureaucracies in restricting human freedom, he nevertheless saw them as composed of individuals carrying out social actions. Thus he believed that bureaucracies consisted of individuals carrying out rational social actions designed to achieve the goals of bureaucracies.

Significantly, Weber saw the whole development of modern societies in terms of a move towards rational social action. Thus, to Weber, modern societies were undergoing a process of rationalization, as affective or emotional action and action directed by custom and tradition (traditional action) became less important. Weber's views on bureaucracy will now be examined in detail.

Bureaucracy and rationalization

Weber believed that bureaucratic organizations were the dominant institutions of industrial society (Weber, 1964). We will examine Weber's definition of bureaucracy in detail shortly but, briefly, he saw it as an organization with a hierarchy of paid, full-time officials who formed a chain of command. A bureaucracy is concerned with the business of administration: with controlling, managing and coordinating a complex series of tasks. Bureaucratic organizations are increasingly dominating the institutional landscape: departments of state, political parties, business enterprises, the military, education and churches are all organized on bureaucratic lines.

To appreciate the nature of modern society, Weber maintained that an understanding of the process of bureaucratization is essential. Marxists see fundamental differences between capitalist and socialist industrial societies. To Weber their differences are minimal compared to the essential similarity of bureaucratic organization. This is the defining characteristic of modern industrial society.

Bureaucracy and rational action

Weber's view of bureaucracy must be seen in the context of his general theory of social action. He argued that all human action is directed by meanings. Thus, in order to understand and explain an action, the meanings and motives that lie behind it must be appreciated. Weber identified various types of action that are distinguished by the meanings on which they are based. These include 'affective' or 'emotional action', 'traditional action' and 'rational action':

1 Affective or emotional action stems from an individual's emotional state at a particular time. A loss of temper which results in verbal abuse or physical violence is an example of affective action.

2 Traditional action is based on established custom. Individuals act in a certain way because of ingrained habit: because things have always been done that way. They have no real awareness of why they do something; their actions are simply second nature.

3 By comparison, rational action involves a clear awareness of a goal: it is the action of a manager who wishes to increase productivity or of a builder contracted to erect a block of flats. In both cases the goal is clearly defined. Rational action also involves a systematic assessment of the various means of attaining a goal and the selection of the most appropriate means to do so. Thus, if a capitalist in the building trade aimed to maximize profit, she or he would carefully evaluate factors such as alternative sites, raw materials, building techniques, labour costs and the potential market, in order to realize her or his goal. This would entail a precise calculation of costs and the careful weighing up of the advantages and disadvantages of the various factors involved. The action is rational since, in Weber's words, rational action is 'the methodical attainment of a definitely given and practical end by means of an increasingly precise calculation of means'.

Weber believed that rational action had become the dominant mode of action in modern industrial society. He saw it expressed in a wide variety of areas: in state administration, business, education, science, and even in Western classical music. He referred to the increasing dominance of rational action as the 'process of rationalization'.

Bureaucratization is a prime example of this process. A bureaucratic organization has a clearly defined goal. It involves the precise calculation of the means to attain this goal and systematically eliminating those factors that stand in the way of the achievement of its objectives. Bureaucracy is therefore rational action in an institutional form.

Bureaucracy and control

Bureaucracy is also a system of control. It involves a hierarchical organization in which superiors strictly control and discipline the activities of subordinates. Weber argued that, in any large-scale task, some people must coordinate and control the activities of others. He stated that 'the imperative coordination of the action of a considerable number of men requires control of a staff of persons'. In order for this control to be effective, it must be regarded as legitimate. There must be a 'minimum of voluntary submission' to higher authority.

Legitimacy can be based on various types of meanings. For example, it can result from traditional or rational meanings, and therefore can take the form of traditional authority or rational authority. The *form* of the organizational structure derives from identified aspects of the social structure such as class, parties, status groups and bureaucracies, all of these groupings were made up of individuals carrying out social actions. Furthermore, it was social actions which, according to Weber, should be the focus of study in sociology.

Social action

In one of his most important works, *Economy and Society* (1978, first published in the 1920s), Weber said, 'Sociology (in the sense in which this highly ambiguous word is used here) is a science concerning itself with the interpretive understanding of social action and thereby with a causal explanation of its course and consequences.' By making this statement Weber was trying to spell out the precise limits of what could and could not be explained in sociological terms.

To Weber, a social action was an action carried out by an individual to which a person attached a meaning; an action which, in his words, 'takes account of the behaviour of others and is thereby oriented in its course'. Thus, an action that a person does not think about cannot be a social action. For example, an accidental collision of bicycles or an involuntary cry of pain are not social actions because they are not the result of any conscious thought process. Furthermore, if an action does not take account of the existence and possible reactions of others, it is not social. If a person prays in private, in secrecy, it cannot be a social action – nobody knows about it and the actor could not be taking account of the possible actions of others.

Social action and *Verstehen*

Having identified the subject matter of sociology, Weber went on to suggest how social action could be explained. Before the cause of a social action could be found, it was necessary to understand the meaning attached to it by the actor. He distinguished two types of understanding.

First, he referred to *aktuelles Verstehen*, which can roughly be translated as direct observational understanding. For example, it is possible to understand that someone is angry by observing their facial expression. Similarly, it is possible to understand what is happening when a woodcutter hits a piece of wood with an axe – that is, the woodcutter is chopping wood. However, this is not, to Weber, a sufficient level of understanding to begin to explain social action.

The second type of understanding is *erklärendes Verstehen*, or explanatory understanding. In this case the sociologist must try to understand the meaning of an act in terms of the motives that have given rise to it. Thus *erklärendes Verstehen*

would require an understanding of why the woodcutter was chopping wood. Was it in order to earn a wage, to make a fire, or to work off anger? To achieve this type of understanding it is necessary to put yourself in the shoes of the person whose behaviour you are explaining. You should imagine yourself in their situation to try to get at the motives behind their actions.

Causal explanations

Even this level of understanding is not sufficient to explain a series of actions or events. For a full causal explanation it is necessary to determine what has given rise to the motives that led to the actions. Here Weber advocated the use of methods closer to a positivist approach. He attempted to discover connections between events and to establish causal relationships. This can be seen from his study, *The Protestant Ethic and the Spirit of Capitalism* (1958) (see pp. 447–51).

Weber tried to show that there was a relationship between ascetic Protestantism and capitalism. He claimed that ascetic Protestantism preceded capitalism and was found almost exclusively in those countries that became capitalist. Nevertheless, this was not sufficient to convince Weber that there was a causal connection between the two, because it did not establish how or why ascetic Protestantism contributed to the rise of capitalism. In order to establish this link, Weber tried to understand the motives of ascetic Protestants for adopting capitalist behaviour. He believed that their main motive was to convince themselves that they were predestined to go to heaven.

Weber's work on the rise of capitalism illustrates his belief that social actions, particularly those involving large numbers of people behaving in similar ways, could lead to large-scale social changes such as the advent of capitalism. Furthermore, even when Weber sounds rather like a structuralist sociologist, he usually insists that he is really describing a type of social action. Thus, while society might contain institutions and social groups, these institutions and social groups are composed of individuals engaged in social action. Weber said:

> when reference is made in a sociological context to a state, a nation, a corporation, a family or an army corps, or to similar collectivities, what is meant is ... only a certain kind of development of actual or possible social actions of individual persons.
>
> Weber, 1958

Social action and bureaucracy

Weber's general views on the relationship between institutions and social action can be illustrated by his important work on bureaucracies. Bureaucracies class and the subject class that Marx identified as the basis for conflict in society.

As a consequence, there are many different 'quasi-groups' or potential groups that could be in conflict with each other. Some of these quasi-groups will join together and act to pursue their common interests. Individuals may belong to a whole variety of different groups, and they are not necessarily confined in all areas of social life to subordinate or dominant groups. Dahrendorf said, 'Since domination in industry does not necessarily involve domination in the state, or a church, or other associations, total societies can present the picture of a plurality of competing dominant (and, conversely, subjected) aggregates.' Thus, a person who is a manager and has a position of authority in a company will tend to act to maintain that authority; but if, for example, the same person has a subordinate position in a religious organization, they may try to change the organization to increase their own authority.

Dahrendorf and conflict theory – a critique

Not surprisingly, Marxists do not accept Dahrendorf's view that Marx's theory is no longer applicable to contemporary societies. For example, the British Marxist John Westergaard (1997) believes that Britain is still fundamentally divided between two classes, and he denies that inequality between rich and poor has been decreasing in recent decades.

More importantly, though, some sociologists question whether Dahrendorf's approach can actually explain conflict. Ian Craib (1984) points out that Dahrendorf admits that subordinate groups may defer to the authority of dominant groups as well as challenging it. Thus members of a workforce may work conscientiously or they may strike, but Dahrendorf fails to explain adequately why they will follow one course rather than another. Craib suggests that Dahrendorf's only answer is to suggest that it is a matter of individual choice, but this does not actually explain why on some occasions there is conflict – for example, a strike – and on others there is none.

More generally, conflict theory, whether Dahrendorf's or that of other writers, produces a rather confused picture of the social structure. Society is portrayed as consisting of so many different groups, all of which may be in conflict with each other, that it is difficult to get a clear picture of how society works. It is not clear what the end result of the conflict will be: who will win and who will lose. Nor does conflict theory provide an adequate explanation of why one group will be successful and another will not. Marxism and neo-Marxism give more coherent answers to these types of question. On the other hand, conflict theory is able to encompass conflict between such groups as men and women, which does not fit neatly into a Marxist framework for understanding society.

Conflict theory represented an important break from Marxism and helped to provide the basis for the development of some later theories. In particular, post-structuralists and postmodernists have gone much further in arguing that there are numerous types of social division and sources of inequality. Indeed, post-structuralists and postmodernists think more in terms of *difference* than division and inequality (see pp. 1068–75 for a discussion of postmodernism).

Social action and interpretive perspectives

Sociologists who adopt social action or interpretive perspectives usually reject the view that society has a clear structure that directs individuals to behave in certain ways. Some social action theorists do not deny the existence of a social structure, but see this structure as rising out of the action of individuals. Thus Weber, who to some extent spans the gap between structural and social action perspectives, acknowledges the existence of classes, status groups and parties, but he challenges the view of Durkheim that society exists independently of the individuals who make up society. Symbolic interactionists accept the existence of social roles, but deny that these roles are fixed and inflexible, or determined by the supposed 'needs' of the social system. Phenomenology and ethnomethodology represent a much more radical rejection of structural perspectives. They deny the existence of any sort of social structure.

All of these perspectives argue that sociologists need to understand and interpret human behaviour and discover the meanings that lie behind it. Phenomenology and ethnomethodology claim that sociology can go no further than reaching an understanding of the meanings that individuals attach to the world around them.

These perspectives will now be examined in detail.

Max Weber

The German sociologist Max Weber (1864–1920) is widely regarded as one of the three great founders of sociology, with Marx and Durkheim. Although Weber

Conflict theory

Conflict theory has its origins in the work of Max Weber. As Chapter 2 indicated (see pp. 36–8), Weber rejected the view that the division between the owners and non-owners of property was the only significant division between groups in society. He argued that there could be numerous divisions within the two basic classes, depending upon the 'market situation' of individuals (Weber, 1978).

Furthermore, he suggested that people could be divided by their status situation and political interests as well as by their economic position. 'Parties' could be formed on the basis of status groupings or classes, but it was also possible for them to cut across class or status groups.

Weber's views on classes, status groups and parties reflect the main themes of conflict theory. Conflict theorists argue that the social structure is much more complex than Marx's work suggests. It consists of many different groups, not just two classes. Furthermore, although conflict theorists accept that these groups have different interests, these interests are not just economic. For example, a particular group might strive for greater prestige or status rather than greater economic power.

In a neat summary of conflict theory, Ian Craib describes it in the following way: 'Society is like a more or less confused battle ground. If we watch from on high, we can see a variety of groups fighting each other, constantly forming and reforming, making and breaking alliances' (Craib, 1984).

Conflict theory has strongly influenced the work of John Goldthorpe on stratification (see pp. 114–17). However, in order to illustrate and evaluate conflict theory, the work of another sociologist, Ralph Dahrendorf, will now be examined.

Ralf Dahrendorf – authority and conflict

Post-capitalism

Dahrendorf's conflict theory arose out of a critical evaluation of the work of Karl Marx (Dahrendorf, 1959). Dahrendorf accepted that Marx's description of capitalism was generally accurate in the nineteenth century when Marx was writing, but he argued that in the twentieth century it had become outdated as a basis for explaining conflict. Dahrendorf argued that important changes had taken place in countries such as Britain and the USA. They were now 'post-capitalist' societies.

Dahrendorf claimed that, far from the two main classes becoming polarized, as Marx had predicted, the opposite had happened. The proportion of skilled and semi-skilled workers had grown, as had the size of the 'new middle class' of white-collar workers, such as clerks, nurses and teachers. Inequalities in income and wealth had been reduced, partly because of changes in the social structure, and partly because of measures taken by the state. Social mobility had become more common, and, crucially, the link between ownership and control in industry had been broken. Managers, rather than owners, exercised day-to-day control over the means of production.

In these circumstances, Marx's claim that conflict was based upon the ownership or non-ownership of wealth was no longer valid. This was because there was no longer a close association between wealth and power. Shareholders, for example, might own the wealth of a company, but in practice they did not exercise close control over the management.

In view of these changes, Dahrendorf argued that conflicts were no longer based upon the existence of the two classes identified by Marx, nor were they based upon economic divisions. Instead, Dahrendorf saw conflict as being concerned with authority.

Authority

To Dahrendorf, authority is legitimate power attached to the occupation of a particular social role within an organization. Thus, for example, a manager in a company, or a teacher in a classroom, has the right to take certain decisions regardless of the wishes of the workforce or pupils. A manager has the authority to instruct workers to arrive on time, and a teacher has the authority to instruct pupils to do homework. All organizations – or associations, as Dahrendorf calls them – have positions of domination and subjection. Some are able to take decisions legitimately and issue commands, and others are not. It is this situation which Dahrendorf saw as the basis for conflict in 'post-capitalist' societies.

Authority and quasi-groups

Dahrendorf believed that the existence of dominant and subordinate positions produces a situation in which individuals have different interests. Those occupying dominant positions have an interest in maintaining a social structure that gives them more authority than others. Those in subordinate positions, on the other hand, have an interest in changing a social structure that deprives them of authority. This conflict of interests is present in a much wider range of social relationships than the economic conflict of interests between the ruling